APIC Text
of Infection Control
and Epidemiology

4th Edition

Volume III

Printed in the United States of America
Fourth edition, June 2014
ISBN: 1-933013-61-3

Inquiries about this book or other APIC products and services may be directed to:

APIC
1275 K Street NW, Suite 1000
Washington, DC 20005
Phone: 202-789-1890
Fax: 202-789-1899
Email: info@apic.org
Web: www.apic.org

TABLE OF CONTENTS

CHAPTER 69

Xenotransplantation

David K.C. Cooper, MD, PhD, FRCS
Thomas E. Starzl Transplantation Institute
University of Pittsburgh Medical Center
Pittsburgh, PA

ABSTRACT

Xenotransplantation is the transplantation of organs, tissues, or cells between different species (e.g., pig to human). It offers great potential in resolving the inadequate number of available human organs and cells for clinical transplantation. For a number of physiologic and logistic reasons, the pig is being investigated as a source of organs and cells for this purpose. There are several immunologic barriers that need to be overcome; these are in part related to the presence of natural antipig antibodies in humans that develop during infancy. These include hyperacute and acute humoral rejection, as well as the development of a thrombotic microangiopathy in the graft that may be associated with a consumptive coagulopathy in the recipient.

The most successful approach to overcoming these barriers is by genetically engineering the pig to provide it with resistance to the human humoral and cellular immune responses. Organs and cells from pigs that (1) do not express the important antigen Galα1,3Gal (the major target for human antipig antibodies) and/or (2) express a human complement-regulatory protein (e.g., CD46, CD55) do not exhibit hyperacute rejection. Pigs that express a human antithrombotic gene (e.g., thrombomodulin, endothelial protein C receptor, or CD39) are also now available. It is hoped that a combination of these genetic modifications will offer protection against the development of thrombotic microangiopathy. Most progress has been made with pig islet transplantation in immunosuppressed, diabetic nonhuman primates, where normoglycemia has been maintained for periods in excess of 1 year without the need for exogenous insulin.

The physiologic, safety, and regulatory aspects of xenotransplantation are briefly reviewed. As the potential benefits of xenotransplantation are so considerable, extending to many conditions for which transplantation is not currently undertaken, it is well worth persisting in attempts to overcome the immunologic barriers that remain.

KEY WORDS

- Antibody, anti-gal
- Infection
- Physiology
- Pig
- Rejection
- Xenotransplantation

ABBREVIATIONS

- AHXR, acute humoral xenograft rejection
- Gal, galactose-1,3-galactose
- GTKO, 1,3-galactosyltransferase gene-knockout
- NeuGc, N-glycolylneuraminic acid
- TM, thrombotic microangiopathy

KEY CONCEPTS

- The increasing shortage of human organs for transplantation has created renewed interest in the potential use of animal organs for this purpose.[1]

- Cross-species transplantation is known as "xenotransplantation."

- The pig has been identified as the most likely source of organs and cells for transplantation into humans. Although there are many good logistic reasons for this choice (Table 69-1), there are a number of immunologic, and possibly physiologic, barriers that need to be overcome for xenotransplantation to become clinically successful.

- The potential risk of transfer of an infectious organism from the pig organ to the human recipient and, perhaps more importantly, from the recipient to other members of the community has to be considered.

Table 69-1. The Advantages and Disadvantages of the Pig as a Potential Source of Organs and Cells for Humans, in Comparison with Those of the Baboon in this Role

	Pig	Baboon
Availability	Unlimited	Limited
Breeding potential	Good	Poor
Period to reproductive maturity	4–8 months	3–5 years
Length of pregnancy	114 ± 2 days	173–193 days
Number of offspring	5–12	1–2
Growth	Rapid (adult human size within 6 months)*	Slow (9 years to reach maximum size)
Size of adult organs	Adequate	Inadequate**
Cost of maintenance	Significantly lower	High
Anatomical similarity to humans	Moderately close	Close
Physiological similarity to humans	Moderately close	Close
Relationship of immune system to humans	Distant	Close
Knowledge of tissue typing	Considerable (in selected herds)	Limited
Necessity for blood type compatibility with humans	Probably important	Important
Experience with genetic engineering	Considerable	None
Risk of transfer of infection (xenozoonosis)	Low	High
Availability of specific pathogen-free animals	Yes	No
Public opinion	More in favor	Mixed

*Breeds of miniature swine are approximately 50 percent of the weight of domestic pigs at birth and sexual maturity and reach a maximum weight of approximately 30 percent of standard breeds.
**The size of certain organs (e.g., the heart) would be inadequate for transplantation into adult humans.
From Cooper DKC. A brief history of cross-species organ transplantation. *Proc (Bayl Univ Med Cent)* 2012 January;25(1):49–57.

BACKGROUND

In the United States alone, more than 100,000 patients waited for an organ transplant in 2013, yet the number of organs that are likely to become available in the current year is approximately 30,000.[53] Therefore, patients awaiting a kidney transplant will have to continue with dialysis for a longer period of time, during which their physical condition may deteriorate, making them less likely to survive or benefit from the transplant. Patients awaiting organs for which there is no life-support system, such as the liver, may die if an organ does not become available. Even though there are systems, such as left ventricular assist devices, that may provide support for a patient with end-stage cardiac failure for months or even years, these can still be associated with major complications and are less than ideal.

In addition, there are many patients who might benefit from the transplantation of pig cells that could cure a medical condition. A good example of this is diabetes, in which pig pancreatic islets would provide insulin to control the glycemic state of the patient.[2] There are an estimated 1.5 million individuals with type 1 diabetes (and 20 million with type 2 diabetes) in the United States alone, and therefore the number of patients who might benefit from porcine cellular transplants is considerable.

Although there have been encouraging results with the allotransplantation of islets from deceased human donors,[3] this source will never be sufficient to provide therapy for the millions of patients with this disease. Porcine insulin, which differs in structure by only one amino acid from human insulin, was used clinically for many years, and therefore its efficacy is proven. If porcine islets could be transplanted successfully without the need for excessive immunosuppressive therapy, this might provide a successful means of maintaining normoglycemia in diabetic patients.

Xenotransplantation is not a new phenomenon. During the past 100 years, there have been several attempts at xenotransplantation in human patients, usually with organs from nonhuman primates, none of which were considered successful.[4] The most notable was a series of chimpanzee kidney transplants in patients with renal failure carried out by Keith Reemtsma at Tulane University in the early 1960s. Although the majority of his patients lived for only a matter of weeks, one led an active life for 9 months until she died suddenly from what was believed to be an electrolyte disturbance—but not from rejection.

A number of pig organ transplants have been carried out in humans, but these have been uniformly unsuccessful.[4] In recent years, however, the ability to genetically modify pigs to provide their organs and tissues with some protection from the human immune response has resulted in a steady improvement in the experimental results; however, further research and experimentation is needed before undertaking clinical trials.[2,5,6]

IMMUNOLOGIC RESPONSES TO PIG ORGAN AND CELL TRANSPLANTS

Organ Xenotransplantation

When a pig organ is transplanted into a human or nonhuman primate, there is an immediate immune response, known as "hyperacute rejection" (Figure 69-1A).[7] This takes place within

Hyperacute Rejection (HAR) (Figure 1A)

Complement-mediated injury associated with the immediate binding of preformed anti-pig antibodies to antigens expressed on the vascular endothelium of the pig organ (e.g., Galα1,3Gal). Defined as occurring within the first 24 hours.

↓

Acute Humoral Xenograft Rejection (AHXR)

A delayed antibody-mediated response often, but not always, associated with the production of elicited antibodies, that leads to vascular endothelial activation and injury caused by complement and cellular components of the immune system (e.g., NK cells and macrophages). Histopathology similar to that of HAR. May take days or weeks to develop and cause graft failure.

↓

Acute Cellular Rejection (ACR)

A cellular response, including T cells, that is similar, but not identical, to that seen after allotransplantation. Perhaps surprisingly, it has rarely been described after pig-to-primate organ xenotransplantation, and has not proved a common problem. This is possibly because T cell activation leads to a more rapid antibody response that results in AHXR before significant T cell infiltration occurs in the graft.

↓

Thrombotic Microangiopathy (TM) (Figure 1B)

Fibrin deposition and platelet aggregation result in thrombosis within the vessels of the graft, even in the absence of an elicited antibody response. Endothelial cell activation (e.g., by antibodies), may result in a change from the normal anticoagulant state of the vascular endothelium to a procoagulant state, resulting in fibrin and platelet deposition. This is probably associated with the numerous molecular incompatibilities between the pig and primate coagulation systems that prevent maintenance of an anticoagulant state after xenotransplantation.

↓

Chronic Rejection (Figure 1C)

Has been documented in pig cardiac grafts that survive for >3 months in baboons. Similar histopathological appearance to that seen after allotransplantation. Pathogenesis is poorly understood.

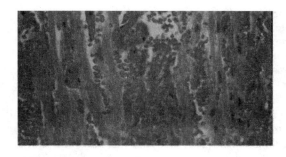

Figure 1A: Hyperacute Rejection

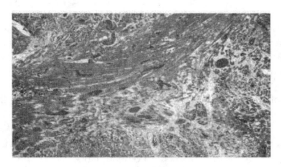

Figure 1B: Thrombotic Microangiopathy

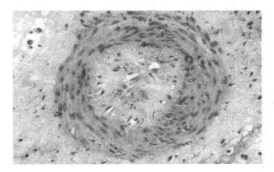

Figure 1C: Chronic Rejection

Figure 69-1. Summary of the known immunologic barriers to pig-to-primate organ transplantation. (From Zhu X, Dor FJMF, Cooper DKC. Pig-to-non-human primate heart transplantation: immunologic progress over 20 years. *J Heart Lung Transplant* 2007;26:210–218, with permission).

minutes or hours of the transplant and is related to binding of primate natural (preexisting) antipig antibodies to the graft vascular endothelial cells. Antibody deposition initiates complement-mediated injury of the endothelial lining, resulting in thrombosis, interstitial hemorrhage, and edema that disrupts graft function.

The most important antibodies directed against pig tissues bind to galactose-α1,3-galactose (Gal).[8,9] Gal is found on the surface of all pig vascular endothelial cells and some other tissues,[10] and is also present in all other mammals, with the exception of humans and Old World nonhuman primates (e.g., great apes, baboons, Old World monkeys).[11] These primate species lost expression of Gal several million years ago, and the absence of Gal resulted in primates making antibodies against this now "foreign" antigen. These antibodies develop during neonatal life and are almost certainly a response to Gal-expressing viruses and microorganisms that colonize the primate's gastrointestinal tract.[12] Antibodies that develop in this way are known as natural or preformed antibodies (and are believed to be T-cell-independent), as opposed to elicited antibodies (T-cell-dependent) that develop after direct exposure to an antigen (e.g., antibodies that develop after an organ transplant).

Genetic engineering techniques allow for the insertion of a gene (a transgene) or for the knockout of a gene. Knockout of the gene for the enzyme α1,3-galactosyltransferase, which adds the Gal sugar to oligosaccharide chains, results in so-called α1,3-galactosyltransferase gene-knockout (GTKO) pigs.[13-15] These pigs no longer express the Gal antigen and are relatively protected from hyperacute rejection.

Additional genetic modifications of pigs have helped further. The cells of humans are to some extent protected from complement-mediated injury by the presence of complement-regulatory proteins on their surfaces (e.g., decay accelerating factor [DAF, CD55],[16] membrane cofactor protein [MCP, CD46][17]). Although pig cells have equivalent complement-regulatory proteins, these are less able to provide protection from the effects of human complement. The expression of high levels of a human complement-regulatory protein in the pig vascular endothelium provides considerable protection from hyperacute rejection. The combination of GTKO and complement-regulatory protein is even more successful[18] and prevents hyperacute rejection from occurring.

If hyperacute rejection is prevented, a similar form of rejection can occur but generally takes a few days to develop. This is known as "acute humoral xenograft rejection" (AHXR) (Figure 69-1) and is probably also related to the deposition of antibody and complement, which activate the endothelium,[19] and the effect of graft infiltration by innate immune cells (e.g., polymorphonuclear leukocytes, macrophages, natural killer [NK] cells) that together destroy the graft. When a GTKO pig organ has been transplanted, the antibodies involved are natural antibodies directed against non-Gal antigens, the exact nature of which remains uncertain.[5,20]

Humans are known to have natural antibodies to at least one other antigen on pig cells, namely N-glycolylneuraminic acid (NeuGc).[21] However, as all nonhuman mammals express this oligosaccharide, including Old World nonhuman primates such as chimpanzees, it is impossible to investigate its effect in in vivo experimental models (e.g., pig-to-baboon organ transplantation). All information, therefore, has to be obtained from staining of pig tissues for expression of NeuGc and laboratory assays such as antibody binding assays (flow cytometry) and serum cytotoxicity assays using human sera. In some cases, these indicate that NeuGc may be at least an equal of, or an even greater barrier to, clinical xenotransplantation than Gal. There is increasing evidence, therefore, that this antibody-antigen interaction will need to be prevented if a pig organ or cells are transplanted into a human patient; the recent production of pigs in which the gene for NeuGc has been deleted (as well as that for Gal) is a major step toward this goal.[22]

In addition, if the recipient's T-cells are not suppressed by pharmacologic immunosuppressive therapy, elicited anti-nonGal antibodies develop and contribute to destruction of the graft.[5,6] The histopathologic picture of AHXR is similar to that of hyperacute rejection, but cellular infiltration is more prominent.

Pure acute cellular rejection, caused largely by infiltrating T and B cells (Figure 69-1), as seen in allografts, has to date been seen rarely in xenotransplantation. It would appear that AHXR develops before acute cellular rejection or that the immunosuppressive regimens that have been used experimentally are largely efficient in preventing T-cell activation and T- and B-cell infiltration of the graft.

Here again, genetic engineering of the organ-source pigs may prove beneficial. Pigs transgenic for the T-cell costimulation blockade agent, CTLA4-Ig, have been produced successfully.[23] In vitro assays demonstrated the immunosuppressive effect of human T-cell activation. Blood levels of soluble CTLA4-Ig in these pigs were between 10- and 100-fold higher than the therapeutic level aimed for in patients receiving the agent after organ allotransplantation. Although these data indicated the great success of the genetic engineering, the high levels of CTLA4-Ig rendered the pigs immunocompromised, prohibiting their long-term survival. Subsequent efforts have been directed toward expressing CTLA4-Ig in only selected tissues (e.g., the islets). With such local expression, the pigs are healthy; yet when the islets are isolated and transplanted into a recipient nonhuman primate, they provide a local immunosuppressive effect.

A second approach has been to express a mutant human major histocompatibility complex (MHC) class II transactivator gene in the pig. This results in downregulation of swine leukocyte class II expression and reduces upregulation of expression after activation of the pig endothelial cells, thus reducing the human T-cell response.[24] In vitro studies have confirmed the beneficial effect of this approach, and in vivo studies are presently under way.

If both hyperacute and AHXR can be prevented, then the grafts have to date failed from the development of a thrombotic microangiopathy (TM) (Figure 69-1B).[25-27] Small vessels in the graft become occluded by fibrin and platelet aggregation. When this becomes advanced, the loss of platelets and clotting factors in the graft may result in the development of a consumptive coagulopathy in the recipient primate.[28] The initiating cause of the TM is almost certainly immune-related and probably results from activation of the vascular endothelial cells by antibody and complement, changing the phenotype of the cells from an anticoagulant state to a procoagulant state. However, there are several known incompatibilities in the coagulation/anticoagulation factors between pig and primate that almost certainly contribute to coagulation dysregulation between graft and host.[5,6,29] Furthermore, the mechanism is complicated in that not only do the activated porcine endothelial cells express high levels of tissue factor (a procoagulant molecule) and increased tissue factor activity, but exposure of primate platelets and monocytes to the porcine endothelial cells results in increased tissue factor activity on these primate structures also.[28,30]

This problem may be surmountable by further genetic manipulation of the organ source pig (e.g., by the insertion of an "anticoagulant" or "antithrombotic" gene, such as thrombomodulin, endothelial protein C receptor, tissue factor pathway inhibitor [TFPI], or CD39).[31] By suppressing tissue factor activity on the porcine endothelial cells, TFPI may prevent the change to a procoagulant phenotype and may also prevent activation of the recipient cells and platelets. CD39 is another critical thromboregulatory molecule on endothelial cells that may limit platelet activation. The expression of several of these genes may overcome this problem, but additional drug therapy to maintain an antithrombotic state may be required. This may, however, be as simple as administration of aspirin or other oral antiplatelet agent.

Chronic rejection (graft atherosclerosis) has been documented in pig cardiac xenografts that have functioned for more than 3 months in baboons and has a similar histopathological appearance to that seen after allotransplantation (Figure 69-1C).[25] Its pathogenesis remains poorly understood but is almost certainly associated with a prolonged low-grade immune response.

Cell Xenotransplantation

Considerable attention has been paid to the transplantation of porcine islets of Langerhans as a means of providing a source of insulin in patients with type 1 diabetes.[2]

Islets from adult wild-type (unmodified) pigs, if carefully isolated, do not express the Gal epitope, and therefore the problem of anti-Gal antibodies is negated. Although adult porcine islets do not express Gal, fetal and neonatal islets (that may prove preferable sources of islets for clinical transplantation) do express Gal, and therefore GTKO pigs would be essential, or at least preferable, in these cases. Similarly, NeuGc will require deletion. Cell xenotransplants, such as those of carefully isolated islets, contain few or no vascular endothelial cells and are therefore to some extent protected from the early humoral response and are rejected largely by a cellular mechanism, as are allografts.

This can be inhibited by currently available immunosuppressive agents, particularly those that result in blockade of T-cell costimulation. Currently, genetically engineered adult porcine islets have been demonstrated to maintain normoglycemia in diabetic monkeys for periods in excess of 1 year,[32] and wild-type (unmodified) adult and neonatal pig islets for periods in excess of 6 months.[33,34] However, the immunosuppressive regimens utilized in these studies would not be clinically applicable; therefore, current studies are aimed toward reducing the intensity of the immunosuppressive regimen and ensuring that all agents administered are approved for use in human patients.

The current site of transplantation of both alloislets and xenoislets is the portal vein, where the islets lodge in the liver. Direct contact between islets and blood leads to an immediate inflammatory response that destroys a large percentage of the islets infused; this is known as the instant blood-mediated inflammatory reaction (IBMIR).[35] It is a response to cells that are not normally present in the blood—in this case, the islets. Until recently, it was thought to be primarily a nonspecific inflammatory response that involved activation of the coagulation and complement systems. Recent evidence strongly suggests that the antipig immune response is playing a significantly greater role and that IBMIR may even be a form of hyperacute rejection.[36] It can be reduced, though not completely prevented, by treatment of the recipient with anticoagulant and anticomplement agents, but genetic engineering of the pig will probably prove more beneficial.

To date, genetically engineered pigs that express the complement regulatory protein CD46 have proved to be the most successful sources of porcine islets, achieving maintenance of normoglycemia in diabetic monkeys for periods extending for more than 12 months.[32] The expression of CD46 probably reduces IBMIR but also is beneficial in protecting the islets long term. More recently, the availability of pigs that express not only CD46 in the islets but also an anticoagulant/antithrombotic gene, such as TFPI and/or CD39, have also shown encouraging results, with maintenance of insulin-independent normoglycemia for more than 1 year. Techniques are available (e.g., by the use of an insulin-specific promoter) that enable the desired gene to be expressed in the islets alone, thus negating any potential detrimental effects (e.g., systemic anticoagulation) that might result from widespread expression in the pig. However, success has not yet been consistent, and further study is required.

An alternative approach that is being explored by some groups is encapsulation of the islets before transplantation into various sites in the recipient (e.g., peritoneal cavity, muscle, subcutaneous fat). The capsule is designed to prevent harmful antibodies or cells from gaining contact with the islets, thus theoretically preventing rejection or other injury and yet allowing insulin to be released from the islets and eventually enter the circulation. The great advantage of this approach would be that immunosuppressive drug therapy, with its associated long-term complications, would be unnecessary. Some encouraging results have been reported, with islet graft survival extending to 6 months in nonimmunosuppressed baboons.[37] A well-regulated clinical trial is being undertaken in New Zealand, though no results have yet been published. It appears, however, that graft survival has not been reported for longer than 6 months, and it is not known whether this is associated with eventual damage from an immune response or from loss of viability of the encapsulated islets as nutrients are no longer able to reach and sustain them.

Similar studies are progressing with encapsulation of hepatocytes, aimed as a means of treating acute hepatic failure.

Pig Neuronal Cell Xenotransplantation

Several degenerative neurological conditions (e.g., Parkinson disease) might be cured or improved by the transplantation of embryonic pig neuronal precursor cells that would produce the hormone that is deficient (e.g., dopamine). The transplantation of pig neuronal cells expressing an immunosuppressive agent, LEA29Y (belatacept), has resulted in remarkable improvement in movement of monkeys with a Parkinson-like condition, though systemic immunosuppressive therapy was also administered.[38] Some of these monkeys developed a neoplastic complication, posttransplantation lymphoproliferative disease, suggesting that the immunosuppressive therapy was excessive. However, these results were encouraging and indicate the potential of xenotransplantation in diseases that affect millions of humans.

Pig Corneal Xenotransplantation

Worldwide, particularly in Asia and the developing world, there is a critical shortage of deceased human corneas for transplantation into the millions of patients with corneal blindness.[39] Genetically engineered pigs offer a solution to this shortage. In vitro studies by Hara[18] and his colleagues indicate that corneal endothelial cells from pigs with specific genetic modifications are no more immunogenic than human corneal endotheloial cells. As corneas can be obtained from young healthy pigs rather than older deceased humans, there are other advantages, such as a greater number of viable cells in the cornea at the time of transplantation.[18]

Furthermore, because the cornea is very poorly vascularized, it has some degree of "immune privilege," making it less susceptible to rejection than other organ transplants. Corneal transplantation from wild-type (unmodified) pigs has resulted in graft survival for several weeks or months in nonhuman primates that received only local immunosuppressive therapy (i.e., injection of a corticosteroid into the cornea). The pig cornea can also be decellularized ex vivo, leaving only a "scaffold" of collagen matrix and, after transplantation into a nonhuman primate recipient, is recellularized by host T-cells. This procedure reduces the immunogenicity of the graft further.

Pig Red Blood Cell Transfusion

In many parts of the world, there is an extreme shortage of blood for transfusion, and this shortage has become exacer-

bated by the high incidence of human immunodeficiency virus (HIV) in several countries, limiting the availability of acceptable blood donors. Initial in vitro studies of red blood cells from GTKO pigs indicate that, though not yet comparable to human ABO-compatible red blood cells (RBCs), they are equivalent to ABO-incompatible RBCs.[40] Further genetic manipulation (e.g., deletion of NeuGc) may enable them to become a successful alternative to human RBC transfusion.

Induction of Tolerance to Pig Organs and Cells

The ideal goal in both allotransplantation and xenotransplantation is the induction of immunological "tolerance," in which the immune system of the recipient is manipulated so that the transplanted organ or cells are accepted as "self'" with no effort made to reject them. The identification and availability of the "donor" prior to the transplant allows the procedure to be "timed" and may facilitate the induction of tolerance to the transplanted organs of cells. Efforts in this respect have been made through inducing hematopoietic cell chimerism,[41] or by pig thymic transplantation,[42] but without complete success to date.

PHYSIOLOGIC DIFFERENCES

The physiological aspects of xenotransplantation have been reviewed.[43] Evidence from pig organ transplantation in nonhuman primates indicates that the function of a life-supporting pig kidney is adequate for periods of up to 3 months before thrombotic microangiopathy (TM) and/or AHXR intervene. However, albuminuria is problematic, and it is not yet known whether this is the result of an ongoing low-grade immune response or a physiological incompatibility. Phosphate metabolism has also been reported to be abnormal. Heterotopic heart transplants have functioned for periods of up to 8 months, though life-supporting orthotopic heart transplants have been documented for less than 2 months. These studies suggest that, from a physiological perspective, these pig organs will function satisfactorily if transplanted into humans.

The liver produces approximately 2,000 different proteins and is much less likely to be physiologically compatible after xenotransplantation. Many of the porcine proteins may not function adequately in a primate host. The liver may, however, function adequately for sufficiently long to allow it to be used as a bridge to allotransplantation in patients with acute liver failure who would otherwise die within days. If one or more pig proteins (e.g., albumin) do not function satisfactorily in a human host, it will be possible to express the human gene for the specific protein in the pig by genetic engineering techniques.

As mentioned, there is clearly significant dysregulation between the coagulation systems of pig and primate, which are problematic but steadily becoming resolved. As the liver is the major source of complement in the body, after porcine liver transplantation the liver will produce pig complement, rather than primate complement, and it is known that this is less destructive to porcine cells than primate complement. This may, therefore, prove an immunologic advantage after liver xenotransplantation.

POTENTIAL INFECTION RISKS

Immunosuppressed patients undergoing allotransplantation are at risk from the healthcare-associated or opportunistic infections that may develop in any subject with a depressed immune system. Patients with xenografts will be at the same risk. However, concern has been raised about the potential for the transfer of a porcine microorganism or virus with the transplanted organ into the recipient and, perhaps more importantly, of the potential risk of the transfer of that infectious agent to those who come into contact with the recipient.[44] These would include not only relatives and friends but also members of the medical and nursing staff.

It will, however, be possible to monitor the organ-source herd at frequent intervals (before their organs are used) to ensure the absence of significant microorganisms. The housing of pigs under isolation conditions will prevent contact with other animals or insects and also minimize the risk of the transfer of an infection from a human handler to the pigs. All feed and supplies coming into the pig facility will be sterilized. The herd should, therefore, be free of all significant infectious agents.

The existence of porcine endogenous retroviruses (PERVs), which are present in the genome of every pig cell, will clearly ensure that these are transplanted with the organ. Although PERVs do not appear to provide problems in pigs—and though their equivalent, human endogenous retroviruses, do not appear problematic in humans—concern has been raised that PERVs might be problematic in a human host, particularly if that host is immunosuppressed. Although PERVs can transfer from a pig cell to a human cell under specific in vitro co-culture laboratory conditions, there has to date been no evidence of transfer of PERVs to a human or nonhuman primate in vivo.[45,46] The risk, therefore, appears to be small. Furthermore, techniques such as RNA interference (RNAi) are currently available that could suppress activation of PERVs and prevent proliferation after transplantation.[47,48] PERVs would also appear to be susceptible to treatment by certain pharmacologic agents. This potential problem, therefore, does not appear to be one that would prevent clinical trials of xenotransplantation if the benefits of those trials are likely to be considerable to the patients.[49]

With respect to certain infectious agents, there are significant advantages of xenotransplantation. For example, in most allotransplants, one or more potentially infectious viruses, such as cytomegalovirus (CMV) and Epstein-Barr virus (EBV), are transplanted with the organ. The organ-source pig will be free of these viruses. Furthermore, certain herpes viruses (e.g., CMV), hepatitis viruses (e.g., Hepatitis B and Hepatitis C), and HIV are thought incapable of infecting porcine cells. This would prove a significant advantage if a pig liver was transplanted into a patient with, for example, Hepatitis B, as the liver may not become re-infected, which is the norm when an allotransplant is carried out.

REGULATION

Xenotransplantation will be regulated by authorities such as the U.S. Food and Drug Administration (FDA) and equivalent national organizations elsewhere. Regulatory oversight of xenotransplantation will be more rigorous than that of allotransplantation. The xenograft will be a "biological product," and the transfer of microorganisms, such as CMV or EBV, will almost certainly not be permissible. Most regulatory concerns are therefore concentrated on the potential transfer of an infectious organism to the recipient and particularly to the public at large. Guidelines have been drawn up by several national committees or regulatory authorities that indicate the circumstances under which a clinical trial of xenotransplantation would be permissible. In most cases, monitoring of the organ-source pig herd before the transplant and monitoring of the recipient after the transplant receive priority.[50]

In the initial clinical trials of xenotransplantation, both the human recipient and his or her close relatives and friends may require monitoring for signs of infection for many years. It will therefore be important that recipients and their families provide fully informed consent for this experimental form of therapy. Furthermore, once the xenotransplant has been undertaken, even if it proves unsuccessful and the graft is destroyed or removed, the patient will continue to need to be monitored, possibly for his or her lifetime. In contrast to most clinical trials, therefore, it will be difficult for the patient to withdraw completely from the trial.

Discussion of such ethical aspects of xenotransplantation continue,[51] and the regulations that will be required have not yet been finalized. However, it is not thought that they will prohibit initiation of clinical trials. Unfortunately, recent clinical trials that have been undertaken in countries where that lack a national regulatory authority has caused some concern among professionals in this field.[52] However, the most recent known trial is being closely regulated by the New Zealand Department of Health.

SUMMARY AND CONCLUSIONS

Xenotransplantation offers the potential to resolve the current shortage of organs and cells for transplantation in patients with end-stage organ failure or other serious and debilitating diseases. Although organ xenotransplantation is not yet ready to be introduced as a standard practice, clinical trials of porcine islet xenotransplantation are currently under way and clinical trials of corneal xenotransplantation are being planned. There is every reason to believe that, with the currently available genetically engineered pigs and pharmacologic agents, normoglycemia could be maintained on a long-term basis in patients with diabetes. Pig corneas could provide sight for blind patients for prolonged periods of time, if not permanently. It should always be remembered that, with the ready availability of organ- or cell-source pigs, retransplantation would always be available, which is not always the case with allotransplantation. Further advances are required in the genetic engineering of pigs before organ xenotransplantation is likely to be sufficiently successful to warrant clinical trials. However, the potential benefits of xenotransplantation would be considerable and would extend to many conditions for which transplantation is not currently undertaken. Therefore, it is worth persisting in attempts to overcome the immunologic barriers that remain.

REFERENCES

1. Cooper DK, Lanza RP. *Xeno - The Promise of Transplanting Animal Organs into Humans.* New York: Oxford University Press, 2000:1–274.
2. van der Windt DJ, Bottino R, Kumar G, et al. Clinical islet xenotransplantation – how close are we? *Diabetes* 2012 Dec;61(12):3046–3055.
3. Shapiro AM. State of the art of clinical islet transplantation and novel protocols of immunosuppression. *Curr Diab Rep* 2011 Oct;11(5):345–354.
4. Cooper DK. A brief history of cross-species organ transplantation. *Proc (Bayl Univ Med Cent)* 2012 Jan;25(1):49–57.
5. Ekser B, Ezzelarab M, Hara H, et al. Clinical xenotransplantation – the next medical revolution? *Lancet* 2012 Feb 18;379(9816):672–683.
6. Cooper DK, Ayares D. The immense potential of xenotransplantation in surgery. *Int J Surg* 2011;9(2):122–129.
7. Rose AG, Cooper DK, Human PA, et al. Histopathology of hyperacute rejection of the heart - experimental and clinical observations in allografts and xenografts. *J Heart Lung Transplant* 1991 Mar-Apr;10(2):223–234.
8. Good AH, Cooper DK, Malcolm AJ, et al. Identification of carbohydrate structures that bind human antiporcine antibodies: implications for discordant xenografting in man. *Transplant Proc* 1992 Apr;24(2):559–562.
9. Cooper DK, Good AH, Koren E, et al. Identification of α-galactosyl and other carbohydrate epitopes that are bound by human anti-pig antibodies: relevance to discordant xenografting in man. *Transpl Immunol* 1993;1(3):198–205.
10. Oriol R, Ye Y, Koren E, et al. Carbohydrate antigens of pig tissues reacting with human natural antibodies as potential targets for hyperacute vascular rejection in pig-to-man organ xenotransplantation. *Transplantation* 1993 Dec;56(6):1433–1442.
11. Galili U, Shohet SB, Kobrin E, et al. Man, apes, and Old World monkeys differ from other mammals in the expression of alpha-galactosyl epitopes on nucleated cells. *J Biol Chem* 1988 Nov 25;263(33):17755–17762.
12. Galili U, Mandrell RE, Hamadeh RM, et al. Interaction between human natural anti- -galactosyl immunoglobulin G and bacteria of the human flora. *Infect Immun* 1988 Jul;56(7):1730–1737.
13. Cooper DK, Koren E, Oriol R. Genetically engineered pigs. *Lancet* 1993 Sep 11;342(8872):682–683.
14. Phelps CJ, Koike C, Vaught TD, et al. Production of 1,3-galactosyltransferase-deficient pigs. *Science* 2003 Jan 17;299(5605):411–414.
15. Kolber-Simonds D, Lai L, Watt SR, et al. Production of alpha-1,3-galactosyltransferase null pigs by means of nuclear transfer with fibroblasts bearing loss of heterozygosity mutations. *Proc Natl Acad Sci U S A* 2004 May 11;101(19):7335–7340.
16. Cozzi E, White DJG. The generation of transgenic pigs as potential organ donors for humans. *Nat Med* 1995 Sep;1(9):964–966.
17. Loveland BE, Milland J, Kyriakou P, et al. Characterization of a CD46 transgenic pig and protection of transgenic kidneys against hyperacute rejection in non-immunosuppressed baboons. *Xenotransplantation* 2004 Mar;11(2):171–183.
18. Hara H, Long C, Lin YJ, et al. In vitro investigation of pig cells for resistance to human antibody-mediated rejection. *Transplant Int* 2008 Dec;21(12):1163–1174.
19. Gollackner B, Goh S-K, Qawi I, et al. Acute vascular rejection of xenografts: roles of natural and elicited xenoreactive antibodies in activation of vascular endothelial cells and induction of procoagulant activity. *Transplantation* 2004 Jun 15;77(11):1735–1741.
20. Ezzelarab M, Ayares D, Cooper DK. Carbohydrates in xenotransplantation. *Immunol Cell Biol* 2005 Aug;83(4):396–404.
21. Padler-Karavani V, Varki A. Potential impact of the non-human sialic acid N-glycolylneuraminic acid on transplant rejection risk. *Xenotransplantation* 2011 Jan-Feb;18(1):1–5.
22. Lutz AJ, Li P, Estrada JL, et al. Double knockout pigs deficient in N-glycolylneuraminic acid and galactose1,3-galactose reduce the humoral barrier to xenotransplantation. *Xenotransplantation* 2013 Jan-Feb;20(1):27–35.
23. Phelps C, Ball S, Vaught T, et al. Production and characterization of transgenic pigs expressing porcine CTLA4-Ig. *Xenotransplantation* 2009 Nov-Dec;16(6):477–485.
24. Hara H, Witt W, Crossley T, et al. Human dominant-negative class ii transactivator transgenic pigs - effect on the human anti-pig T-cell immune response and immune status. *Immunology* 2013 Sep;140(1):39–46.
25. Kuwaki K, Knosalla C, Dor FJMF, et al. Suppression of natural and elicited antibodies in pig-to-baboon heart transplantation using a human anti-CD154 monoclonal antibody-based regimen. *Am J Transplant* 2004;4:363–372.
26. Houser SL, Kuwaki K, Knosalla C, et al. Thrombotic microangiopathy and graft arteriopathy in pig hearts following transplantation into baboons. *Xenotransplantation* 2004 Sep;11(5):416–425.
27. Kuwaki K, Tseng Y-L, Dor FJMF, et al. Heart transplantation in baboons using α1,3-galactosyltransferase gene-knockout pigs as donors: initial experience. *Nat Med* 2005 Jan;11(1):29–31.
28. Ezzelarab M, Garcia B, Azimzadeh A, et al. Rejection of 1,3-galactosyltransferase gene-knockout pig organ grafts in baboons is predominantly associated with the innate immune system. *Transplantation* 2009 Mar 27;87(6):805–812.
29. Cowan PJ, Robson SC, d'Apice AJF. Controlling coagulation dysregulation in xenotransplantation. *Curr Opin Organ Transplant* 2011 Apr;16(2):214–221
30. Lin CC, Chen D, McVey JH, et al. Expression of tissue factor and initiation of clotting by human platelets and monocytes after incubation with porcine endothelial cells. *Transplantation* 2008 Sep 15;86(5):702–709.
31. Cooper DK, Ekser B, Burlak C, et al. Clinical lung xenotransplantation – what genetic modifications to the pig may be necessary? *Xenotransplantation* 2012 May-Jun;19(3):144–158.
32. van der Windt DJ, Bottino R, Casu A, et al. Long-term controlled normoglycemia in diabetic non-human primates after transplantation with hCD46 transgenic porcine islets. *Am J Transplant* 2009 Dec;9(12):2716–2726.
33. Hering BJ, Wijkstrom M, Graham ML, et al. Prolonged diabetes reversal after intraportal xenotransplantation of wild-type porcine islets in immunosuppressed nonhuman primates. *Nat Med* 2006 Mar;12(3):301–303.
34. Cardona K, Korbutt GS, Milas Z, et al. Long-term survival of neonatal porcine islets in nonhuman primates by targeting costimulation pathways. *Nat Med* 2006 Mar;12(3):304–306.
35. van der Windt DJ, Bottino R, Casu A, et al. Rapid loss of intraportally-transplanted islets: an overview of pathophysiology and preventive strategies. *Xenotransplantation* 2007 Jul;14(4):288–297.
36. van der Windt DJ, Marigliano M, He J, et al. Early islet damage after direct exposure of pig islets to blood: has humoral immunity been underestimated? *Cell Transplant* 2012;21(8):1791–1802.
37. Dufrane D, Goebbels RM, Gianello P. Alginate macroencapsulation of pig islets allows correction of streptozotocin-induced diabetes in primates up to 6 months without immunosuppression. *Transplantation* 2010 Nov 27;90(10):1054–1062.
38. Lévêque X, Cozzi E, Naveilhan P, et al. Intracerebral xenotransplantation: recent findings and perspectives for local immunosuppression. *Curr Opin Organ Transplant* 2011 Apr;16(2):190–194.
39. Hara H, Cooper DK. Xenotransplantation – the future of corneal transplantation? *Cornea* 2011 Apr;30(4):371–378.
40. Cooper DK, Hara H, Yazer M. Genetically-engineered pigs as a source for clinical red blood cell transfusion. *Clin Lab Med* 2010 Jun;30(2):365–380.
41. Tseng Y-L, Sachs DH, Cooper DK. Porcine hematopoietic progenitor cell transplantation in nonhuman primates: a review of progress. *Transplantation* 2005 Jan 15;79(1):1–9.
42. Yamada K, Yazawa K, Shimizu A, et al. Marked prolongation of porcine renal xenograft survival in baboons through the use of 1,3-galactosyltransferase gene-knockout donors and the cotransplantation of vascularized thymic tissue. *Nat Med* 2005 Jan;11(1):32–34.
43. Ibrahim Z, Busch J, Awwad M, et al. Selected physiologic compatibilities and incompatibilities between human and porcine organ systems. *Xenotransplantation* 2006 Nov;13(6):488–499.
44. Onions D, Cooper DK, Alexander TJL, et al. An assessment of the risk of xenozoonotic disease in pig-to-human xenotransplantation. *Xenotransplantation* 2000 May;7(2):143–155.
45. Patience C, Patton GS, Takeuchi Y, et al. No evidence of pig DNA or retroviral infection in patients with short-term extracorporeal connection to pig kidneys. *Lancet* 1998 Aug 29;352(9129):699–701.
46. Paradis K, Langford G, Long Z, et al. Search for cross-species transmission of porcine endogenous retrovirus in patients with living pig tissue. The XEN 111 Study Group. *Science* 1999 Aug 20;285(5431):1236–1241.
47. Dieckhoff B, Petersen B, Kues WA, et al. Knockdown of porcine endogenous retrovirus (PERV) expression by PERV-specific shRNA in transgenic pigs. *Xenotransplantation* 2008 Feb;15(1):36–45.
48. Ramsoondar J, Vaught T, Ball S, et al. Production of transgenic pigs that express porcine endogenous retrovirus small interfering RNAs. *Xenotransplantation* 2009 May-Jun;16(3):164–180.
49. Fishman JA. Xenosis and xenotransplantation: current concepts and challenges (Abstract PL5:2). *Xenotransplantation* 2005;12:370.

50. Schuurman H-J. Regulatory aspects of pig-to-human islet transplantation. *Xenotransplantation* 2008 Mar-Apr;15(2):116–120.

51. Smetanka C, Cooper DK. The ethics debate in relation to xenotransplantation. *Rev Sci Tech* 2005 Apr;24(1):335–342.

52. Sgroi A, Buhler LH, Morel P, et al. International human xenotransplantation inventory. *Transplantation* 2010 Sep 27;90(6):597–603.

53. United Network for Organ Sharing, 2013. http://www.unos.org

CHAPTER 70

Biofilms

Randall D. Wolcott, MD
Founder and President
Southwest Regional Wound Care Center
Lubbock, TX

ABSTRACT

Microorganisms have the ability to live in two forms: planktonic (free-floating) and biofilm (attached or sessile). Most medical information from the hospital laboratory deals with planktonic organisms and relates to Koch's postulates and the corresponding germ theory: one organism, one disease. However, the preferred method of microbial life, based on survival and community diversity, is the multispecies biofilm or sessile community of organisms. In fact, studies now indicate that organism survival 3.4 billion years ago was based on biofilm architecture. Historically, diseases recognized as being associated with biofilms are consistent with chronic infections such as: (1) otitis media, (2) periodontitis, (3) native valve endocarditis, (4) cystic fibrosis, (5) indwelling medical device infections, and (6) prostatitis. Today, that list has expanded considerably, emphasizing the oral-systemic link and chronic wounds. Each of the diverse niches and tissues of the human body can suffer a biofilm infection which manifests as a chronic infection clinically. Enhanced pathogenicity related to biofilms and their recalcitrant nature is associated with their chemophysical properties, acting as hydrated polymers and demonstrating properties of both liquids and solids. Biofilms also possess well-defined molecular mechanisms to produce and maintain chronic infections. Individual species are selected for in specific host environments yet any microorganism alone and/or in synergy with other microbes (even commensals) growing as a biofilm can produce infection. Biofilm infection occurs when a microbe attaches to a host surface, up-regulates up to 800 new genes producing a distinct new biofilm phenotype of the microbe and then self-secretes a polymer matrix while also incorporating fibrin and other host proteins in its protective cover. The way biofilm feeds itself is to inflame the tissues to which it is attached and extract nutrients from the plasma that percolates through its substance.

When microorganisms are up-regulated to the biofilm phenotype, there is significant negative impact on the laboratory capacity to recover the organisms, predict antibiotic susceptibility, and even provide meaningful clinical information for management of patient infection. Further, the majority of inhabitants of a biofilm are viable but nonculturable, necessitating nonculture DNA-based techniques such as polymerase chain reaction, sequencing, and other molecular methods.

Cohabitants of a biofilm have at least 100- to 1,000-fold increase in the ability to resist antibiotic treatment and are not cleared by normal host defenses. Biofilms exchange genetic factors more efficiently and possess multiple colony defenses. Biofilms may be monospecies or multispecies, composed of eukaryote (fungus and yeast), and/or prokaryote organisms with multiple mechanisms to encourage genetic diversity, a key survival strategy. A biofilm infection when combined into one disease entity is more costly and deadly than all cancers combined. For example ventilator acquired pneumonia (67,000), chronic obstructive pulmonary disease (50,000), wounds (50,000), and all other chronic infections kill approximately 500,000 people per year. Most biofilm disease is managed by removing or replacing body parts (legs, heart valves, lungs, etc.), which should stop once we can truly understand and manage biofilm disease.

KEY CONCEPTS

- Biofilms are attached (sessile) and may be monospecies or mixed species, prokaryote, or eukaryote.

- Biofilms contain cohabiting microorganisms living in an architecturally defined, three-dimensional environment.

- Cohabitants in biofilms are often part of the host normal flora, which, because of environmental selective pressures, overgrow or replace commensal organisms (ecological hypothesis). The majority of biofilm cohabitants are viable but nonculturable, necessitating newer nonculture lab techniques.

- Biofilms attach to surfaces, which facilitates "cross-talk" between cells of divergent phenotypes and origin.

- The complexity and robustness of a biofilm is defined by its genetic and phenotypic diversity.

- Biofilms allow synergies among all the cohabitants, making each biofilm unique.

- Clinical consequences of the biofilm are:

  - Planned staging for release (metastasis) of the attached microorganism to distal sites.

- Fragments of the biofilm with intact biofilm defenses can spread the infection.
- Increased resistance (1,000 times or more) to physiological antibiotic concentrations.
- Neutralization of host defense mechanisms, including phagocytosis.
- Enhanced exchange of genetic material, with potentially more virulent phenotypes, and multidrug resistance.
- Increased number of organisms per unit of tissue or indwelling medical device.
- Increased occlusion and reduced flow of catheter lumens.
- Include physical disruption and multiple concurrent strategies to suppress the reaccumulation of the biofilm.
- Prevention is preferable.

BACKGROUND

This chapter describes and summarizes the growing knowledge about medical biofilms: their structure, the consequence to medical practice and infection prevention, and emerging strategies for management of biofilm. We now understand that microorganisms have the potential to live free-floating (planktonic) or attached (biofilm), and that the latter is the preferred method of growth because it is the introductory pathway for survival. These are not mutually exclusive; organisms can and do exist simultaneously in both phenotypes. Also the surface of attachment, biotic versus abiotic (nonliving), are much more important than originally recognized.

BASIC PRINCIPLES

Biofilms appeared in early fossil records dating to 3.4 billion years ago. Planktonic organisms are specialized bacteria that spend an enormous amount of cellular energy on chemotaxis and methods of pathogenicity. They are associated with disease transmission and symptoms, reflecting Koch's postulates (1864), and are exogenous, often vector-associated disease unmasked in the 19th century.

Attached organisms grow in a three-dimensional architecture that is well-defined and enables diversity and cohabitation to the survivor that benefit all members of the community. They are associated with chronic infections.

There is a growing list of diseases associated with biofilms. The original diseases studied were often tissue-associated infections and included otitis media, periodontitis, native valve endocarditis, cystic fibrosis, prostatitis, and infections related to tissue/indwelling medical device (IMD) interfaces. The list also now includes sinusitis, necrotizing fasciitis, osteomyelitis, infectious kidney stones, and biliary infections. Hence, the increased role of biofilms in disease reflects the increased use of IMDs and abiotic (nonliving) surfaces to which organisms can attach.

Germ Theory (Planktonic vs. Biofilm)

Historically, clinical microbiology has evolved by following: (1) Louis Pasteur and the germ theory of disease, which in essence says that one organism causes one disease; and (2) Robert Koch's postulates (one organism must always be found in those with the disease, must be isolated in culture from someone with disease, the isolated organism causes disease when introduced into a healthy host, and the organism must be re-isolated from the inoculated diseased host). Based on this knowledge, it was expected that efforts to eradicate the microorganisms would result in clinical improvements to the patient. The focus was on acquisition of disease from an external (exogenous) source. Progress in disease prevention and control were historical measurements of the civilization's ability to understand transmissibility.

How things have changed! In the 1960s and 1970s, nosocomial (now referred to as healthcare-associated) infections were thought to be associated primarily with normal flora, often defined as the patient's own, endogenous free-floating or planktonic microbiota. When discussing biofilms, planktonic refers to organisms that float or drift in the environment and sessile refers to organisms that are attached or established in a particular location or on a particular site. These infections were clearly associated with microbial reservoirs within the normal hosts, and the four major microbial reservoirs include the gastrointestinal tract, gynecological/urinary tract, skin, and mouth. These infections were still associated predominantly with a planktonic paradigm and its recognized mechanisms of pathogenicity.

During the 1980s and 1990s, the use of medical devices with abiotic surfaces became more common. Here, attached microorganisms existed in an attached ecosystem made up of a number of communities, composed of eukaryotic (microorganism with distinct membrane-bound nucleus) and/or prokaryotic (microorganism without a distinct, membrane-bound nucleus or membrane-bound organelles, and with DNA not organized into chromosomes) cells living in a defined, three-dimensional biofilm community. The biofilm community is characterized by diversity both genetic (shared supragenome or polymicrobial) and phenotypic which better ensures survival of at least a portion of the biofilm which can then reconstitute the whole. Interestingly, this concept was postulated by Eli Metchnikoff as early as the 1850s.

Microorganisms, together in a nested environment, are supportive of one another and positioned in such a way as to define nutritional benefit to each other (synergies) in order to cohabit effectively. The use of antibiotics may select against planktonic phenotype of a particular species yet at the same time not affect that same microorganism growing in biofilm phenotype, thereby allowing for more individual calls to accumulate (Figure 70-1). A major feature of antibiotic selective pressure is that the biofilm phenotype loses susceptibility and grows to a higher bioburden level than its singular planktonic members. "Persister cells" in biofilms maintain consistency of cohabitants even during antibiotic therapy, being metabolically inert.

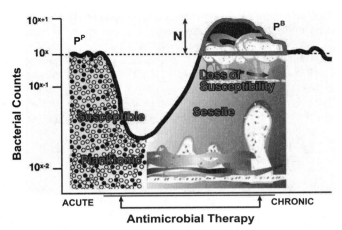

Figure 70-1. Transition of microbial phenotypes and relationships to disease; planktonic (P^P) to biofilm (P^B).

Table 70-2. Biofilms: Structure and Function where "Form = Function"

Microbially derived *sessile* communities characterized by:

- Cells attached to a *stratum*, or *interface* or to *each other*,
- Embedded in a *matrix* of extracellular polymeric substance *they* produced or incorporate from the environment, and
- Exhibits an altered *phenotype* with respect to *growth* rate and *gene* transcription
- Complex communities where competition is replaced by cooperation
- Advantages of cooperation include:
  - Collective action
  - Diffusion sensing
  - Group selection
  - Economic use of resources

Synergies:
Passive resistance
Metabolic cooperation
By-product influence
Quorum sensing systems
An enlarged gene pool with more efficient DNA sharing

It has been postulated that biofilms may, in fact, be a better explanation for a number of emerging diseases and for understanding the disease process of resistance. Additional diseases potentially associated with biofilms include legionnaires' disease, strep throat, *Helicobacter pylori* peptic ulcer, certain chronic bowel diseases, chronic wounds, and the oral-systemic link, in which oral plaque acts as a microbial reservoir. Also of importance to the practitioner, however, is the potential for infections associated with medical devices and IMDs. Table 70-1 lists devices used in both inpatient and outpatient populations that have potential for biofilm-associated disease.

BIOFILMS: FORM = FUNCTION

Donlan and Costerton gave a clinical and realistic definition of medical biofilms: "The new definition of a biofilm is a microbially derived sessile community characterized by cells that are irreversibly attached to a substratum or interface or to each other, are embedded in a matrix of extracellular polymeric substances that they have produced, and exhibit an altered phenotype with respect to growth rate and gene transcription."[1] Historically, this has been a somewhat controversial definition, which has changed as more knowledge has been gained and more information analyzed. An updated version of this definition is shown in Table 70-2.

The biofilm is a primitive type of developmental biology in which spatial organization of the cells within the matrix optimizes utilization of available nutritional resources.[2] Additionally, there is a mobilized enzyme system in which the milieu and the enzyme activities are constantly changing and evolving to appropriate steady states relevant to the composition and cohabitation of the members. This is a dynamic environment in which microbial cells do reach homeostasis and in which organisms optimally organize to make use of metabolic by-products.[3] This steady state can be radically altered by applying physical factors, two of the most important being the application of high sheer and nutritional availability.

There is a great phenotypic heterogeneity within the biofilm community, with numerous microenvironments (Table 70-3). In a poetic sense, a biofilm is an ecological consortium

Table 70-1. Inpatient and Outpatient Use of Indwelling Medical Devices

IMDs Associated with Inpatient Use	IMDs Associated with Outpatient Use
Sutures	Sutures
Orthopedic devices (fixators, nails, screws)	Orthopedic devices (fixators, nails, screws)
Intravenous catheters*	Contact lenses
Endotracheal tubes*	Mechanical heart valve
Urinary catheters*	Voice prosthesis
Central venous catheters*	Penile implants
	Pacemakers/automated intracardiac devices
	Prosthetic joints
	Breast implants
	Dental implants
	Peritoneal dialysis catheters

*Indicates that use of the device has shifted from primarily inpatient use to increased use in an outpatient environment.

Table 70-3. Characteristics of Biofilms—Biofilm Communities

- "Cross-talk," "quorum sensing" methods of communication between multiple prokaryotic and/or eukaryotic species
- Multispecies microbial composition reflecting site-specific microbes
- Dynamic environment, influenced by peripheral stress
- Microbial cells reach homeostasis, "persister cells" are metabolically inert
- Optimally organized to make use of available nutrients
- Show great microbial heterogeneity
- Numerous microenvironments, with pH diverse microcommunities
- Wide range of enzymatic activities

of (usually) mixed bacterial species evolved for its survival by biodiversity. The principle is through diversity—as long as one member survives it can rebuild the biofilm. Production of a matrix or glycocalyx containing polymeric sugars, proteins, DNA, and environmental substances enhances attachment and acts as a superficial glue and potential barrier to penetration by antimicrobials. There is an incredible metabolic cooperation. The differences in pH, oxygen tension, and electronic potential in the developing biofilm microenvironment contribute to significant changes in organism form and function after attachment.

Biofilm is an engineering term that arose from the study of matrix properties and based on defining the impact of bacterial slime on heat exchanges, river beds, ion-exchange columns, and the interface of two distinct mediums (e.g., oil/water, air/soil). Hence, the physical parameters are best defined and quantified by engineering measurements, two of which are particularly significant to dentistry and medicine. Viscoelastic (referring to materials that are viscous and elastic) and rheological (referring to materials that flow) properties define an extremely hydrated polymer, which has both elastic (solid) and viscous (liquid-like) properties.

A key component in the maturity and evolution of biofilms is capacity for cell-to-cell communication, which can be restricted to same species or global, such as autoinducer 2. Interspecies communication is necessary for cohabitation and biodiversity within the polymicrobial biofilm. Quorum sensing is a universal feature of biofilm formation, although a number of systems have been defined that show recognizable differences within Gram-negative and -positive bacteria. *Quorum sensing* is the phenomenon that allows organisms in a biofilm to sense the cell density of its environment within the biofilm via the accumulation of present signaling molecules.

Figure 70-2 summarizes the cyclic nature and consequences in stages of biofilm growth (stages I–IV). A number of key additional features should be emphasized. The biofilm thickness on the luminal surface of an IMD is not universal, nor is the staging or activity (I–IV). In fact, it appears that often there is a quiescence behavior to the biofilm. Only "hot zones" are associated with active cyclic production of the community, which in turn is potentially associated with mechanisms of pathogenicity. The biofilm is not stiff, but rather flexible. It is often described as more like a kelp bed in the ocean, moving

4 Stages of Plaque Biofilm Growth: I Attachment (Lag), II Growth (Log), III Maturity (Stationary), IV Dispersal (Death)

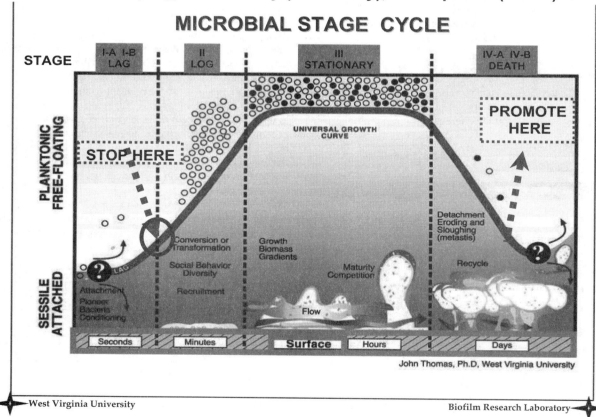

Figure 70-2. The four stages of biofilm growth.

back and forth with the ocean current, rather than a stiff, rigid building as in a city; more recently, authors have described it as "lava-like."

EPIDEMIOLOGY

There are 100 to 1,000 times more prokaryotic than eukaryotic cells living in, on, and with *Homo sapiens*, and they are predominantly anaerobic. Any microorganism colonizing the host has the potential to become a planktonic pathogen, and certain aerobic isolates have over time become marker disease organisms, associated with IMDs, as shown in Table 70-4. These are often initial or primary colonizers on the device and over time will develop a multispecies biofilm (Gram-positive and -negative organisms). IMDs of a given body site become associated with the normal flora and/or pathogens that are "native" to that anatomical location, promoting the theme that normal biofilm ecosystems are established as site specific. Biofilm development most often reflects normal flora closest to the IMD. The four reservoirs are, in order of microbial burden from highest to lowest: gastrointestinal, genitourinary (male and female), oral cavity/respiratory, and skin. Recently, the oral cavity reservoir has been expanded to include organisms causing sinusitis.

Candida species and *Candida albicans* are very frequent colonizers,[4] but are often overlooked clinically as contaminants. To put this in its proper perspective, it is necessary to understand that *Candida albicans* forms a very resistant biofilm,[5,6] utilizing its biphasic nature (yeast and hyphae), and is a reversibly adherent complex.[4] As such, it can act as an essential network for other secondary colonizers, forming a multispecies ecosystem.[7-9]

Although biofilms occur naturally, today's increased association between biofilms and disease reflects changes in medical practices. As noted, biofilms are the preferred method used by microorganisms for survival, especially when environmental selective pressures are present. Naturally occurring biofilms are found in drinking water lines, urban water systems, oil recovery equipment, food processing areas, ship hulls, and at any interface between a solid and nonsolid surface. The increased impact of biofilms in medicine is a result of the explosive growth in the past decade or so in the use of IMDs, including both simple and complex devices (Table 70-5).[10] Simple devices include catheters and stents. In the United States, approximately millions of catheters of all types are used annually. Coronary stents (percutaneous coronary intervention procedures) increased threefold in the 1990s. Literally hundreds of thousands of dental implant procedures (also simple IMDs) occur each year in the United States. In the complex arena, the use of automatic, implantable cardioverter defibrillators (ICD) has increased more than 100-fold since first approved in the early 1990s. Further, hundreds of thousands of knee replacements are performed in the United States annually, a number that will continue to grow. The growth in medical circulatory support is estimated to have been between 20 and 30 percent per annum between 1999 and 2004.

Table 70-4. Planktonic Organisms Associated with Indwelling Medical Devices

INDWELLING MEDICAL DEVICES	Staphylococcus epidermidis	Staphylococcus aureus	Coagulase-negative Staphylococci	Streptococcus spp.	Candida spp.	Enterococcus spp.	Enteric Gram spp.	Escherichia coli	Pseudomonas aeruginosa
	Gram-positive Organisms						Gram-negative Organisms		
Central venous catheter	X	X	X*		X				
Joint prostheses		X	X	X		X		X	X
Cardiovascular devices (i.e., prosthetic heart valves)	X	X	X	X	X	X			
Urinary catheters	X		X		X	X		X	
Intrauterine devices	X	X		X	X	X			
Artificial voice prosthesis	X			X	X				
Endotracheal tubes		X		X	X	X	X		
Dialysis catheters		X			X				X
Central nervous system devices	X	X				X			
Penile implants						X		X	
Cochlear devices					X				X
Surgical site devices	X	X							
Contact lenses	X	X		X					

*Underline (X) denotes principal organisms.

Table 70-5. Anti-infectives Commonly Used on Indwelling Medical Devices

Anti-infective Coating/Material	Indwelling Medical Device
Metals	
Silver	Endotracheal tubes, urinary catheters, intravascular catheters
Antibiotics	
Minocycline-rifampin	Impregnated catheters
Vancomycin (with or without heparin)	Catheter locks
Dicloxacillin	Intravascular catheter
Clindamycin	Intravascular catheter
Cefazolin with benzalkonium chloride	Catheter
Triclosan	Sutures
Anti-infective Biomaterials/Polymers	
Polypeptides	
Chlorhexidine	Sponge dressings
Chlorhexidine-silver-sulfadiazine	Impregnated catheters
Iodinated alcohol	Catheter hubs
Fusidic acid	Intravascular catheter
Hydrophilic-coated polyurethane with glycopeptides teicoplanin	Central venous catheter
Irgasan (disinfectant)	Catheter
Hydrophilic hydromer-coating	Central nervous system shunts
Other	
Polypeptides	Various experimental biomaterials

As early as 2001, preventing and controlling disease related to biofilms figured in two of the seven healthcare challenges identified by the U.S. Centers for Disease Control and Prevention (CDC): reducing hospital-associated catheter-associated adverse events by 50 percent and reducing hospitalizations and mortality from respiratory tract infections among long-term care patients by 50 percent. Biofilms are common to each of these infection types, which is not surprising since the National Institutes of Health (NIH) estimated that 80 percent of healthcare-associated infections (HAIs) are biofilm associated.[11]

More recently, campaigns including the Institute for Healthcare Improvement (IHI) 100,000 Lives and Protecting 5 Million Lives have focused on measures related to central line-, surgical-, and ventilator-associated infections. The 2008 Centers for Medicare & Medicaid Services (CMS) pay-for-performance reimbursement measures included "no pay" for HAIs, catheter-associated urinary tract infections, and central line (vascular catheter)-associated infections.

The growing impact of intravascular catheter-related infections in healthcare has been quantified. The Healthcare Infection Control Practices Advisory Committee's 2002 *Guidelines for the Prevention of Intravascular Catheter-Related Infections* cites references that estimate 250,000 cases of intravascular catheter-related infections annually, with an approximate mortality of around 12 to 25 percent for each infection, with a cost of around $25,000.

Ventilator-associated pneumonia (VAP) and endotracheal tube lumen biofilms occur at a rate of 7.5/1,000 vent days in medical intensive care units (ICUs) and 13.6/1,000 vent days in surgical ICUs. VAP is associated with attributable costs in excess of $11,000 per episode and case fatality rates are about 20 percent. There are also associated increases in multidrug-resistant isolates, particularly Gram-negative isolates, after 7 days of ventilation.

Lastly, it is very important to note the two genetic studies of the NIH. "Roadmaps" are designed to unmask the resident flora of humans and the complete genotyping of these isolates, complementing the human genetic and metabolic landscape. The two studies are entitled *The Human Microbiome Project* and the *Human Oral Microbiome Database*, and complement the human metagenomics strategies employed to unmask the genetic makeup of *Homo sapiens*. Together they hope to connect normal genealogy and predisposition to disease.

BIOFILM-ASSOCIATED INFECTIONS

A biofilm infection begins when a single planktonic bacteria attaches to a host environment. If host defenses do not clear the bacterium within a short period of time, the microbe quickly changes to a biofilm phenotype. Attachment is a strong signal to start up-regulating operons which control as many as 800 genes whose products are specific for biofilm phenotype. The microbe undergoes a tremendous metamorphosis, much like a caterpillar to a butterfly. The bacteria, although genetically identical, phenotypically are quite different. The new biofilm phenotype microbe produces senescence of the surrounding host cells, secretes a protective matrix, and begins quorum sensing to dictate the different phenotypes throughout the biofilm community.

Once biofilm has reached a stable community (climax community), it has a problem with nutrient source. If the bacterium were to secrete virulence factors and kill its host's tissue, it would lose its stable substrate to which it is attached. Biofilm takes a different strategy in that it inflames the host tissue to which it is attached so that plasma will escape from the surrounding capillaries and percolate through the biofilm. This provides a constant and regulated source of nutrition to the biofilm community.

For biofilm to be successful in producing a host chronic infection it must be able to induce senescence in host cells. One mechanism that microbes use to produce senescence is to eject effector proteins through a type 3 secretory system. These effector proteins work directly on specific host pathways to block apoptosis, migration, and to usurp the cytoskeleton of the cell. This prevents host cells from shedding and the biofilm from losing its attachment to the host.[12]

The most common nutrient depletion with biofilms is development of an anoxic region within the core of the biofilm. In vitro biofilm models have been developed to exploit this property of biofilm to allow propagation of anaerobic bacteria in what is viewed as an oxygen environment like the surface of a chronic wound.[13] Also in vivo polymicrobial biofilm models now allow evaluation of hypoxia, pH, and species interactions. The ability of biofilms to provide an environment for anaerobic growth through oxygen depletion may be an important factor for the increase in the virulence of biofilm infections.[14,15]

Waste products, molecules that bacteria produce which are end products and are of no benefit to the metabolizing member, are released into the local biofilm environment. Many of these metabolites such as ammonia, lactic acid, and carbon dioxide can have significant influence on the surrounding microorganisms.[16] Studies have demonstrated that *Fusobacterium nucleatum* and *Prevotella intermedia* generate ammonia which raises the pH suitable for *Porphyromonas gingivalis* and that *Fusobacterium nucleatum* also provides an increased carbon dioxide environment which increases the pathogenicity of *Porphyromonas gingivalis*.[17] Also it has been shown that waste products from *Pseudomonas aeruginosa* may protect *Staphylococcus aureus* from aminoglycosides.[18,19]

Passive resistance is when one of the members in the biofilm possesses a resistance factor that can protect other members of the biofilm that do not have the factor. There are numerous biofilm defenses that limit the effectiveness of antibiotics. However, the easy sharing of mobile genetic elements, such as *mec*A cassettes and genes encoding extended-spectrum beta-lactamases, raises concern for increasing passive resistance in polymicrobial infections. For example, a beta-lactamase-producing strain of *Haemophilus influenzae* was cocultured with *Streptococcus pneumoniae* deficient in any resistance

factors. *H. influenzae* increased the minimum inhibitory concentration (MIC)/minimal bactericidal concentration (MBC) of *S. pneumoniae* by amoxicillin.[20]

The clinical concern relative to the synergies of polymicrobial biofilm is that the infection will be more severe and recalcitrant to treatment. There are many examples that show that this is indeed the case. Low levels of *Pseudomonas aeruginosa* mixed with *S. aureus* increased infection rates in a rat model. In the mouse model *Prevotella* increases the pathogenicity of *S. aureus*.[21] *Escherichia coli* produced marked increase in the size of abscess formation with *Bacteroides fragilis* in a diabetic mouse model.[22] There is also clinical evidence to suggest that polymicrobial infections are more severe.[23]

As described, diseases that were historically associated with biofilms included periodontal diseases, otitis media, native valve endocarditis, cystic fibrosis, IMD infections, and prostatitis. Following is a brief description of these diseases and their associations with sessile, cohabitating communities most associated with infection prevention. This is an overview with primary emphasis on those diseases important to infection preventionists.[24,25]

Traditional: Biotic Surfaces

Periodontal Diseases/Subgingival Plaque

Three of the oral flora particularly associated with biofilms and the destructive process associated with periodontal disease are: *Porphyromonas gingivalis, Bacteroides forsythus*, and *Treponema denticola*.

Biofilm formation is greatly influenced by the sheer forces of supragingival versus subgingival processes. Organism population, its density, and its individual composition are influenced by the features described earlier, but particularly by sheer forces. Interestingly, there are three biofilms within the subgingival plaque: (1) the biofilm associated with abiotic surface or enamel; (2) the biofilm associated with the living tissue on the outer aspect of the periodontal pocket; and (3) the biofilm of a "flox" that is mixed species and free-floating.

The consequences of oral biofilm diseases are associated not only with tooth loss. Among women, poor oral hygiene is now known to be associated with low birth weight babies and premature ruptured membranes. Recently, its importance in VAP, arteriosclerosis, diabetes, and others have gained national and international attention.[26]

Otitis Media

Otitis media has dumbfounded physicians and practitioners for some time, given the multitude of studies with significantly different results. We now better understand the diseases associated with biofilms and the fact that organisms grown in the laboratory in a planktonic state/environment may not predict the actual success or failure of organisms attached in the biofilm-associated disease.

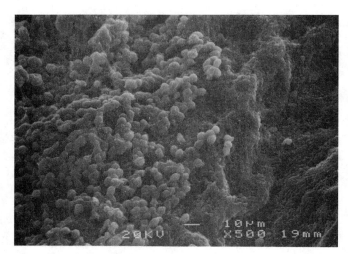

SEM 70-1. Biofilms in chronic rhinosinusitis.

Sinusitis

Rhinosinusitis infections have always been considered recalcitrant to clinical management, including "washout" techniques, which have implied biofilm resilience. Now sinus infections in general, and rhinosinusitis in particular, have been added to the list of biofilm diseases with traditional three-dimensional architecture definition (SEM 70-1). Further, the four reservoirs of *Homo sapiens* have been modified to link the sinus and mouth area as one of the reservoirs.

Native Valve/Vascular Implant Endocarditis

Streptococci are the etiological agents in more than half of infective endocarditis cases, with staphylococci accounting for another one-fourth of cases. Many strains are common commensals of the skin and oral cavity. Endocarditis is associated with congenital heart defects, prosthetic heart valves, and vascular grafts, and is most likely caused by clots of platelet and fibrin that amass where turbulent flow is aggravated by abnormal tissue, pre-existing heart disease, or an indwelling vascular catheter. Damaged endothelium exposes the underlying basement membrane, which consists of collagens, laminin, vitronectin, and fibronectin, thereby providing a substratum for bacterial adherence. Bacterial endocarditis might also illustrate how turbulent flow contributes to the formation of vegetations. Although turbulence has been traditionally thought to induce clot formation and tissue damage, it is conceivable that clumps of biofilm-associated cells respond to the turbulent flow of the cardiac environment by producing more adhesion factors called extracellular polymeric substances (EPS). Large vegetations are particularly friable and amplify the risk of embolization (detachment through clumping dispersal), which might cause infarcts and septic abscesses in other tissues.

Importantly, aggressive antibiotic therapy in the treatment of endocarditis is consistent with the role of biofilms in these infections. In vivo studies in a rabbit model with *E. coli* as the infectious agent required sustained antibiotic treatment concentrations that were 220 times the serum MBCs.

Cystic Fibrosis/Cystic Fibrosis Pneumonia

Cystic fibrosis (CF) is an autosomal recessive disease that is caused by mutations in the cystic fibrosis transmembrane conductance regulator (*CFTR*) gene, which results in dysfunctional electrolyte secretion and absorption and results in thick, sticky mucous in respiratory and gastrointestinal tracts. Although multiple, complex physiological dysfunctions are present, the primary site of morbidity is the respiratory system. Pulmonary colonization of the lower respiratory tract of CF patients begins in infancy or early childhood, most commonly by *S. aureus* and *H. influenzae*. However, by adolescence and early adulthood, most CF patients have become colonized with *P. aeruginosa*.

There are two salient features regarding colonization of the CF lung with *P. aeruginosa*. First, *P. aeruginosa* grows in biofilms within the CF lung. Microscopic analysis of sputum from CF patients showed that *P. aeruginosa* forms biofilm-like structures consisting of clusters of bacteria surrounded by a dense matrix. The second salient feature of *P. aeruginosa* colonization of the CF lung is the selection of mucoid variants of *P. aeruginosa*, which are characterized by overproduction of the exopolysaccharide alginate and a resistance to antibiotic therapy.

P. aeruginosa has several adhesins and binds to a broad range of receptors and cell types in the respiratory tract. Yoon et al. have also shown that anaerobic growth might be an important feature of *P. aeruginosa* growing in biofilms in CF patients. *P. aeruginosa* formed vigorous biofilms under anaerobic conditions, leading to the buildup of toxic nitrogen metabolites. Interestingly, *P. aeruginosa* antibiotic resistance and biofilm formation seem to be induced at the same time. It was speculated that antibiotic-resistant phenotypic variants of *P. aeruginosa* observed in CF infections were either selected within biofilms by sublethal antibiotic treatment or by the specific environment of the CF lung (characterized by osmotic and oxidative stress).[27]

Traditional: Abiotic Surfaces

Indwelling Medical Devices

There are significant numbers and types of IMDs. Device composition is very important to the formation of biofilms. One feature in defining a biofilm's integrity, cohesiveness, and three-dimensional architecture is the substratum to which the biofilm was formed and which, for an IMD, is the material that makes up the device. Obviously, in recent years, there have been a wide variety of device materials developed. Some device materials are hydrophobic (water hating) and others are hydrophilic (water loving). Material-related factors can have an impact on the ability of an organism population to adhere.

There is one universal feature among IMDs: the potential for microorganisms to access them (they are "indwelling" in the body by definition). In the common example of a catheter introduced into the body, bacteria can access the catheter either extraluminally (outside the catheter) or intraluminally (inside the lumen of the catheter). Initially, it was felt that colonization occurred on the extraluminal or outside surface of the catheter, but recent data clearly suggest that intraluminal growth is a significant way in which biofilms maintain and survive—and potentially promote infection. The turbulent shear dynamics of fluid movement within the lumen enhances the progression and architecture of the intraluminal biofilm.

Both urinary catheters and central venous catheters have the potential for biofilm-related infectious complications via both extraluminal and intraluminal colonization. Urinary tract infections (UTIs) related to catheter use are common and, although they do not contribute as significantly to cost or mortality as central line-associated infections do, are a considerable problem in healthcare. Infections associated with central venous catheters are the most commonly described of the healthcare-associated bloodstream infections. These infections prolong the average length of stay significantly in the ICU with a concomitant significant excess cost per each afflicted ICU patient. The attributable mortality is also significant, with risk of death dependent in part on infecting organism. Staphylococci are often the infecting organism associated with a central venous catheter biofilm. However, the list of possible pathogens also includes *Candida* species, enterococci, enteric Gram-negative bacteria, and/or environmental Gram-negatives.[28,29]

Unmasking New Biofilm-associated Infections

Oral

The oral cavity is now recognized as the most diverse ecosystem in *Homo sapiens*, with over 1,000 phylotypes or generally distinct microorganisms. Biofilm-associated diseases have migrated from traditional (e.g., periodontitis and gingivitis) to infections associated with dentures,[17] to systemic diseases linked to oral microbial imbalance (focusing most recently on dental plaque/biofilms) (Figure 70-3).[30-32] The three-dimensional structures of endotracheal biofilms also confirm the uniqueness of an oral flora signature, by emphasizing diversity (SEM 70-2). Research (NASCENT trial)[33] related to the antimicrobial activity of silver

when incorporated as a component of endotracheal tubes has been promising and has resulted in the recent U.S. Food and Drug Administration (FDA) approval of a silver-coated endotracheal tube for use in patients ventilated for longer than 24 hours.

Oral Systemic Link: Oral Care

There is an accumulating body of data that implicates dental plaque as a reservoir for pulmonary infection in critical care and institutionalized elderly patients, and that instituting a program of dental hygiene can reduce episodes of healthcare-associated pneumonia (HAP).

There is historical evidence that in healthcare settings, oral hygiene undertaken on patients has been poorly performed, with inconsistent adherence to evidence-based practice. This had been especially true in the ICU, where oral care interventions focused on comfort measures rather than as a means of removing plaque and pathogens. The British Dental Society for Disability and Oral Health guidelines (2000) recommend tooth brushing to maintain oral hygiene in intubated critically ill adults. Tooth brushing is considered the most effective mechanical tool for removing plaque. The inability of foam swabs to adequately remove plaque compared with a toothbrush is well documented in normal individuals. However, in the United States, the majority of critical care nurses prefer foam swabs, as they fear dislodging the endotracheal tube. A more recent survey of oral hygiene practices among European nurses found that the majority used oral antiseptics in preference to mechanical methods of cleaning. Strategies to reduce the risk of biofilm-associated VAP infections were published in the 2008 Society for Healthcare Epidemiology of America/Infectious Diseases Society of America hospital-associated infection compendium.[34] This guide includes recommendations to perform regular oral care with an antiseptic solution and specific strategies to minimize contamination of respiratory therapy equipment.

Chronic Wounds

Chronic wounds encompass several divergent diseases all quite possibly linked to biofilms and the transition from predominantly planktonic microbial ecosystems to a complex biofilm dominated ecosystem (Figure 70-4). The factors during the transition are still to be defined, but it is increasingly clear that biofilms reduce microorganism recovery and stop planktonic cell proliferation (see Figure 70-1).

An essential transition component is critical colonization. This involves presence of bacteria on the surface of the wound and not yet into the deeper tissues, but to such an extent that the buildup of secreted toxins, as well as host cell cytokines and proteases, impairs the healing progress. Because critical colonization does not involve the invasion of bacteria into viable tissues, local clinical signs of redness, pain, heat, and swelling are usually not manifest. However, other more subtle clinical signs may indicate that superficial bacterial levels are delaying healing. The critically colonized wound can appear healthy, with an absence of nonviable tissue. However, the granulation tissue may have

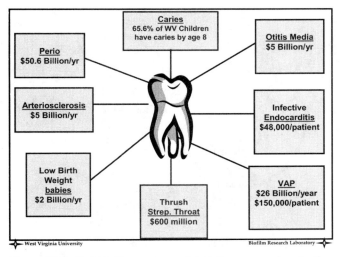

Figure 70-3. Oral biofilms and associated diseases: oral systemic.

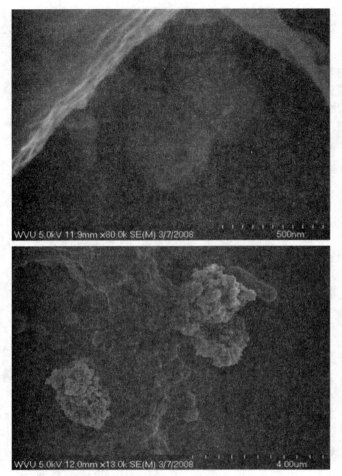

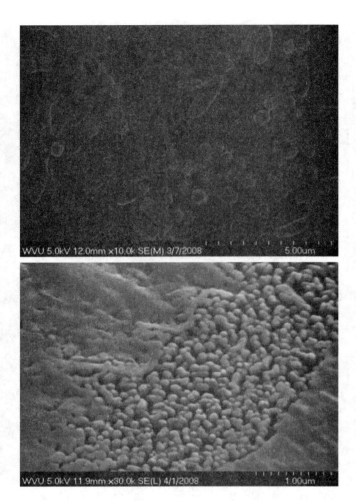

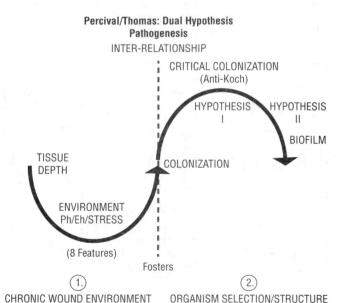

SEM 70-2. Biofilms in lumen of an endotracheal tube (ETT).

a characteristic color and texture, in which healthy granulation tissue is often described as beefy red; the granulation tissue in a critically colonized wound may appear bright red in color, foamy in appearance, and may bleed quite easily. Critically colonized wounds also may exhibit new areas of tissue breakdown, bridging of epithelium, and sudden odor and increased exudate production. Yet, in many cases, the only sign of critical colonization of the wound surface may be a plateau in healing progress.[35,36]

The progression to wound healing may become compromised by the biofilm community—that is, the microbial-to-host balance is weighted in favor of the microorganisms—and the term *critically colonized* has been used to describe this state. At this stage, the microorganisms, while interfering with the wound healing process, may not necessarily induce any clinical signs of infection, although there may be subtle signs that indicate bacterial imbalance (e.g., change in wound color or odor together with the presence of revitalized tissue and ischemia).[37]

A consequence of new biofilm information is that both sutures and dressings are now recognized as potential devices that can provide an abiotic surface for growth. Scanning electron

Percival/Thomas: Dual Hypothesis Pathogenesis

INTER-RELATIONSHIP

CRITICAL COLONIZATION
(Anti-Koch)

HYPOTHESIS I   HYPOTHESIS II

BIOFILM

TISSUE DEPTH

COLONIZATION

ENVIRONMENT
Ph/Eh/STRESS

(8 Features)

Fosters

①
CHRONIC WOUND ENVIRONMENT

②
ORGANISM SELECTION/STRUCTURE

Figure 70-4. Transition of planktonic to biofilm phenotypes.

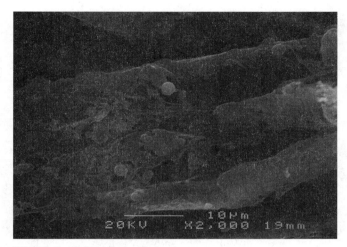

SEM 70-3. Biofilms in braided sutures.

micrograph images show a braided suture filling the spaces between the braids (SEM 70-3); several investigators recognize that gauze may act as a "biofilm reactor," providing a rebound surface for biofilm structures in a protected environment. Hence, it is not surprising that a number of gauze incorporate silver, CHG, PHMB, iodine, and other anti-infectives, whose benefit still needs clarification.

LABORATORY DIAGNOSIS

Diseases associated with biofilms offer very unique and perplexing problems for the diagnostic laboratory. Since the evolution of the germ theory and the preponderance of one organism, one disease concepts, microbiology laboratories have used both broth and solid mediums that focus on isolation of planktonic micro-organisms.[38-40] Hospital laboratory testing does not specifically detect biofilms. For central line catheters, catheter tip cultures can be misleading. The traditional method of the Maki roll technique requires concomitant blood samples within 24 hours.[40]

Advances in non-culture-based laboratory techniques have been used to circumvent the issue of multispecies biofilms containing nonviable and/or viable but nonculturable cells. A variety of molecular methods, including polymerase chain reaction (PCR) coupled with density gradient gel electrophoresis (DGGE), have been applied to laboratory work on biofilms.[41] In addition, quantitative scanning microscopy techniques have been employed to unmask the magnificent heterogeneity and complex biofilm ecosystem, particularly in wounds. These techniques are not used in the routine hospital laboratory, but are instrumental in biofilm research and investigational laboratories.

Diagnosing Polymicrobial Communities

The clinical significance of shared genetic information, metabolic synergies, and coaggregation/colocalization symbiosis is that new diagnostic and therapeutic methods will be required. Since, as discussed above, minor bacterial constituents can provide a multitude of different advantages to their neighbors, including increased virulence, then it becomes important to identify all the species present and their relative contribution to the infection. Clinical diagnostic methodologies are focused on identifying the most abundant organisms producing an infection, but for biofilms this will have to give way to methods that can identify and quantitate each individual member of the polymicrobial community. Molecular methods have demonstrated the ability to precisely define the identity and quantity of each species of a polymicrobial biofilm infection.[42,43]

The 16S ribosomal DNA (rDNA) has been called the genomic fingerprint, and molecular methods (PCR and sequencing) evaluating the 16S rDNA region are usually capable of reading this genomic fingerprint.[44] PCR methods are more suited to looking at unique genetic targets within a particular species but are also used to evaluate the 16S rDNA. However, the specificity of PCR is a limitation in that microorganisms can only be identified if a specific primer is developed and validated. Because there are thousands of different species present in biofilm infections this is currently impractical. To avoid the necessity of developing an almost infinite number of primers, innovators have integrated PCR of the bacterial 16S ribosomal DNA gene with rapid evaluation of this gene utilizing mass spectroscopy. The Plex ID (Abbott Molecular, Des Plaines, IL) utilizes multiple general primer sets to cover the different variable regions of the 16S rDNA as well as other chromosomal and plasmid regions so that the vast majority of the currently reported bacterial species can be identified. By utilizing advanced mathematical algorithms, segments of the 16S rDNA can be correlated with specific species with a very high level of confidence. This allows rapid same-day identification and some quantitation of the more prevalent organisms within a polymicrobial infection.

Sequencing technology such as pyrosequencing based on a light signal accurately determine the sequence of long segments of specific regions of bacterial DNA, such as the 16S ribosomal gene. These technologies can give a 99 percent accurate code for the 16S gene that is then compared against accessible databases to identify the microorganism with a high degree of certainty. The copy number for each specific organism can be compared to the total number of copies for all organisms providing good relative quantification for each microbial species present.

An issue is whether the bacterial DNA identified is from bacteria that are alive. Post et al. reported "These findings indicate that purified DNA and DNA from intact but nonviable bacteria do not persist in the middle ear cleft in the presence of an effusion."[45] So it seems likely that the majority of organisms identified by their DNA are indeed viable organisms.

Molecular methods, even at this early stage, can handle the challenges of correctly diagnosing polymicrobial infection. Once good DNA is obtained, most molecular platforms are extremely capable of accomplishing their analysis. Yet cleaning up the data post analysis such as chimera checking, noise suppression, and data housekeeping after the run is critical. Reporting the identification and amounts of the organisms present requires complex bioinformatics to reduce the massive data down to reliable, clinically useful results. Yet, with all these technical hurdles, molecular methods have demonstrated the unique ability to reliably evaluate biofilm infection.[46]

Another avenue of biofilm research is in the arena of susceptibility testing of antimicrobials. The use of a poloxamer in this type of investigation has gained international recognition. A poloxamer is a reverse gel. It is liquid at 4°C and is a solid at 37°C. Because of its chemical composition, the poloxamer induces the biofilm's phenotype and allows for standard disk susceptibility methods (although the drug concentrations need to reflect the recalcitrant nature of biofilms and the site of the IMD).

TREATMENT AND PREVENTION

Treatment and management of biofilm-associated diseases is complicated by the same difficulties described for laboratory detection; namely, that biofilm diseases are difficult to treat, often hard to detect in their chronic association, and not manageable with the traditional antimicrobial schemes based on planktonic free-floating germ theory life forms. Given that organisms have the potential to be biphasic (or two life forms, planktonic or sessile), antimicrobial therapies must address both the sessile and planktonic forms of an individual or mixed species consortia (see Table 70-6).

Several features are often considered when designing and implementing new antimicrobial strategies directed toward biofilm diseases. It is important that an antimicrobial's molecular weight, size, configuration, pH activity, and antiquorum sensing are appropriate for the biofilm environment. Clearly, the antimicrobial's half-life, serum binding, and concentration-dependent (CD) or time-dependent (CI) properties are applicable to the nonbiofilm form, but may have little or altered impact on biofilm-associated central line-associated infections

and VAP. These are areas in which significant improvement in antimicrobial treatment and management should be made.

Catheter removal could be the most effective treatment and is often the treatment of choice. For urinary catheters, this can be the best option. However, this may be impractical or impossible for central venous catheters, especially if it means loss of the only available access site, or if it may lead to a difficult procedure based on the patient's clinical situation.

Prevention is better than cure. New prevention strategies are being developed. One of these incorporates a beneficial biofilm mediated by use of probiotics (providing supplements of "good" bacteria). Names imply approach: replacement therapy, biotherapy, competitive exclusion bacteriotherapy, and therapeutic microbiology. The probiotic organisms need to have a stable, selected competitive advantage and be able to establish biofilm "residency." A preparation containing *Lactobacillus* species has been used in Japan since 1995 and in the United Kingdom since 2008 (introduced in the United States in January 2009), and has been effective in reversing periodontal and gingival diseases. Over-the-counter probiotics, which most typically contain *Lactobacillus*, *Bifidobacterium*, or yeast such as *Saccharomyces*, have been used with varying degrees of effectiveness in clinical and nonclinical settings.

An effective and sometimes underutilized approach in the management and treatment of biofilm-associated infections related to central venous catheters is the catheter care team. The team is developed around standardized, best practice patient care, including sterile insertion practice and appropriate dressing and wound care. The team can be expected to have a high level of expertise and provide good case monitoring. When a catheter care team is in place they will play an essential role in good infection prevention related to central line-associated infections. These teams bring standardization and best practices

Table 70-6. Medical Biofilm Diseases

	Probable	Possible		Generally Accepted
Nasal polyps	Epididymitis	Atherosclerosis	Otis externus	Periodontal disease
Conjunctivitis	Urinary stones	Diabetes (pancreatic beta amyloid formation)	Otitis medius	Osteonecrosis of the jaw (bisphosphonate therapy)
Iritis	Chronic pancreatitis	Alzheimer disease (beta amyloid formation)	Cholesteatoma	Mastitis
Chronic bronchitis	Ascending cholangitis	Multiple sclerosis	Mastoiditis	Ventilator acquired pneumonia
Asthma	Atopic dermatitis	Chronic inflammation induced cancers	Chronic tonsillitis	Cystic fibrosis
Duodenal ulcer	Psoriasis	Autoimmune diseases	Chronic rhinosinusitis	Gastric ulcers (*Helicobacter pylori*)
Crohn disease	Burns	Altered commensals (autism, mood, obesity)	Osteomyelitis	Chronic obstructive pulmonary disease
Ulcerative colitis	Surgical site infections		Chronic meningitis	Peritoneal dialysis catheters
Diverticulitis	Folliculitis		Ventricular shunt infections	Urinary catheters
Proctitis	Abscess		Amniotic fluid sludge	Intravenous catheters
Pelvic inflammatory disease	Chronic vaginosis		Bacterial endocarditis	Infected medical devices
Chronic prostatitis	Postoperative endophthalmitis		Wounds	Gallstones
Interstitial cystitis				

to site preparation and procedural techniques, and can determine appropriateness of antimicrobial bonded catheters and prophylactic locks. The best practice "bundled" approach for prevention of catheter-associated infections (often used by catheter teams) has received much interest in recent years and is reviewed in the HAI compendium on central line-associated bloodstream infections (also see Supplemental Resources and Chapter 34 Intravascular Device Infections).

CONCLUSIONS

The biofilm phenotype is the preferred method of microorganism growth; given the option of existing as free-floating, planktonic form or within a biofilm, organisms preferentially attach and adhere. Clinically, biofilm phenotypes are associated with survival and planktonic with symptoms. Attachment can occur on abiotic (IMDs) or biotic (sloughing) surfaces and require unique adaptations and cross-talk among cells and across species (as well as across prokaryote or eukaryote types). Recently, biofilms have been recognized as being associated with chronic infections, particularly chronic wounds. In the oral cavity, plaque biofilms have been identified as a reservoir for oral-systemic infections, particularly VAP. Therefore, interventions to reduce the risk of VAP require reassessment of and compliance with good oral care in the ICU setting.

Biofilms confer unique characteristics to normal flora isolates that are up-regulated to a biofilm phenotype. These include development of higher organism concentrations, loss of antibiotic susceptibility, enhanced virulence, and altered cellular expression. Biofilms offer very unique and partially unrecognized challenges to detection and recovery by the microbiology laboratory. The biofilm characteristics are best defined by engineering criteria, especially viscoelastic and rheology. Normal, traditional strategies for biofilm elimination and control do not work well in medical practice, where the number of biofilm-associated diseases is increasing.

FUTURE TRENDS

It is becoming quite apparent that biofilms are an integrated part of *Homo sapiens*, and may be one of the best defenses against introduction of foreign or unbalanced microbial ecosystems. Hence, a new strategy might employ a two-pronged approach: (1) abiotic surfaces (IMDs) coated with anti-infectives against selected "marker" organisms, essential for biofilm three-dimensional integrity and structures ("smart devices"); and (2) biotic surfaces colonized with replacement therapy organisms, or probiotics, that reinforce the beneficial normal flora of the sites at risk ("smart probiotics") or site specific.

Both of these options are incumbent upon markedly improved laboratory detection utilizing culture independent methods (molecular) and new susceptibility testing of mixed species in a biofilm phenotype (poloxamer). The new important species will be recognized by the ongoing studies at the NIH, dealing with the Human Microbiome Project and the Human Oral Microbiome International Database.

REFERENCES

1. Donlan RM, Costerton JW. Biofilms: survival mechanisms of clinically relevant microorganisms. *Clin Microbiol Rev* 2002;15:167–193.
2. Fux CA, Costerton JW, Stewart PS. Survival strategies of infectious biofilms. *Trends Microbiol* 2005;13:34–40.
3. Habash M, Reid G. Microbial biofilms: their development and significance for medical device-related infections. *J Clin Pharmacol* 1999;39:887–898.
4. Douglas LJ. Candida biofilms and their role in infection. *Trends Microbiol* 2003;11:30–36.
5. Ramage G, Martinez JP, Lopez-Ribot JL. Candida biofilms on implanted biomaterials: a clinically significant problem. *FEMS Yeast Res* 2006;6: 979–986.
6. Ramage G, Wickes BL, Lopez-Ribot JL. Biofilms of Candida albicans and their associated resistance to antifungal agents. *Am Clin Lab* 2001;20:42–44.
7. Lundstrom T, Sobel J. Nosocomial candiduria: a review. *Clin Infect Dis* 2001;32:1602–1607.
8. Kuhn DM, Chandra J, Mukherjee PK, et al. Comparison of biofilms formed by Candida albicans and Candida parapsilosis on bioprosthetic surfaces. *Infect Immun* 2002;70:878–888.
9. Dasgupta MK. Biofilms and infection in dialysis patients. *Semin Dial* 2002; 15:338–346.
10. Donlan RM. Biofilms and device-associated infections. *Emerg Infect Dis* 2001;7:277–281.
11. National Institutes of Health (NIH). Research on microbial biofilms (PA-03-047). NIH website. 2002. Available at: http://grants.nih.gov/grants/guide/pa-files /PA-03-047.html.
12. Raymond B, Young JC, Pallett M, et al. Subversion of trafficking, apoptosis, and innate immunity by type III secretion system effectors. *Trends Microbiol* 2013;21:430–441.
13. Sun Y, Smith E, Wolcott R, et al. Propagation of anaerobic bacteria within an aerobic multi-species chronic wound biofilm model. *J Wound Care* 2009;18:426–431.
14. Borriello G, Werner E, Roe F, et al. Oxygen limitation contributes to antibiotic tolerance of Pseudomonas aeruginosa in biofilms. *Antimicrob Agents Chemother* 2004;48:2659–2664.
15. Nguyen D, Joshi-Datar A, Lepine F, et al. Active starvation responses mediate antibiotic tolerance in biofilms and nutrient-limited bacteria. *Science* 2011;334:982–986.
16. Elias S, Banin E. Multi-species biofilms: living with friendly neighbors. *FEMS Microbiol Rev* 2012 Jan 9 [Epub ahead of print].
17. Diaz PI, Zilm PS, Rogers AH. Fusobacterium nucleatum supports the growth of Porphyromonas gingivalis in oxygenated and carbon-dioxide-depleted environments. *Microbiology* 2002;148:467–472.
18. Hoffman LR, Deziel E, D'Argenio DA, et al. Selection for Staphylococcus aureus small-colony variants due to growth in the presence of Pseudomonas aeruginosa. *Proc Natl Acad Sci U S A* 2006;103:19890–19895.
19. Hendricks KJ, Burd TA, Anglen JO, et al. Synergy between Staphylococcus aureus and Pseudomonas aeruginosa in a rat model of complex orthopaedic wounds. *J Bone Joint Surg Am* 2001;83-A:855–861.
20. Weimer KE, Juneau RA, Murrah KA, et al. Divergent mechanisms for passive pneumococcal resistance to beta-lactam antibiotics in the presence of Haemophilus influenzae. *J Infect Dis* 2011;203:549–555.
21. Mikamo H, Kawazoe K, Izumi K, et al. Studies on the pathogenicity of anaerobes, especially Prevotella bivia, in a rat pyometra model. *Infect Dis Obstet Gynecol* 1998;6:61–65.
22. Mastropaolo MD, Evans NP, Byrnes MK, et al. Synergy in polymicrobial infections in a mouse model of type 2 diabetes. *Infect Immun* 2005;73: 6055–6063.
23. Tuttle MS, Mostow E, Mukherjee P, et al. Characterization of bacterial communities in venous insufficiency wounds by use of conventional culture and molecular diagnostic methods. *J Clin Microbiol* 2011;49:3812–3819.
24. Hall-Stoodley L, Costerton JW, Stoodley P. Bacterial biofilms: from the natural environment to infectious diseases. *Nat Rev Microbiol* 2004;2:95–108.
25. Hall-Stoodley L, Stoodley P. Biofilm formation and dispersal and the transmission of human pathogens. *Trends Microbiol* 2005;13:7–10.
26. Heo SM, Haase EM, Lesse AJ, et al. Genetic relationships between respiratory pathogens isolated from dental plaque and bronchoalveolar lavage fluid from patients in the intensive care unit undergoing mechanical ventilation. *Clin Infect Dis* 2008;47:1562–1570.
27. Yoon SS, Hennigan RF, Hilliard GM, et al. Pseudomonas aeruginosa anaerobic respiration in biofilms: relationships to cystic fibrosis pathogenesis. *Dev Cell* 2002;3:593–603.
28. Donlan RM, Murga R, Bell M, Toscano CM, et al. Protocol for detection of biofilms on needleless connectors attached to central venous catheters. *J Clin Microbiol* 2001;39:750–753.
29. Murga R, Miller JM, Donlan RM. Biofilm formation by gram-negative bacteria on central venous catheter connectors: effect of conditioning films in a laboratory model. *J Clin Microbiol* 2001;39:2294–2297.

30. Feldman C, Kassel M, Cantrell J, et al. The presence and sequence of endotracheal tube colonization in patients undergoing mechanical ventilation. *Eur Respir J* 1999;13:546–551.
31. Foglia E, Meier MD, Elward A. Ventilator-associated pneumonia in neonatal and pediatric intensive care unit patients. *Clin Microbiol Rev* 2007;20: 409–425, table.
32. Grap MJ, Munro CL. Preventing ventilator-associated pneumonia: evidence-based care. *Crit Care Nurs Clin North Am* 2004;16:349–358, viii.
33. Kollef MH, Afessa B, Anzueto A, et al. Silver-coated endotracheal tubes and incidence of ventilator-associated pneumonia: the NASCENT randomized trial. *JAMA* 2008;300:805–813.
34. Coffin SE, Klompas M, Classen D, et al. Strategies to prevent ventilator-associated pneumonia in acute care hospitals. *Infect Control Hosp Epidemiol* 2008;29 Suppl 1:S31–S40.
35. Cutting KF, White RJ. Criteria for identifying wound infection—revisited. *Ostomy Wound Manage* 2005;51:28–34.
36. White RJ, Cutting KF. Critical colonization—the concept under scrutiny. *Ostomy Wound Manage* 2006;52:50–56.
37. Wolcott RD, Ehrlich GD. Biofilms and chronic infections. *JAMA* 2008;299: 2682–2684.
38. Kite P, Dobbins BM, Wilcox MH, et al. Evaluation of a novel endoluminal brush method for in situ diagnosis of catheter related sepsis. *J Clin Pathol* 1997;50:278–282.
39. Kite P, Dobbins BM, Wilcox MH, et al. Rapid diagnosis of central-venous-catheter-related bloodstream infection without catheter removal. *Lancet* 1999;354:1504–1507.
40. Levin PD, Hersch M, Rudensky B, et al. The use of the arterial line as a source for blood cultures. *Intensive Care Med* 2000;26:1350–1354.
41. Dowd SE, Sun Y, Secor PR, et al. Survey of bacterial diversity in chronic wounds using Pyrosequencing, DGGE, and full ribosome shotgun sequencing. *BMC Microbiol* 2008;8:43.
42. Dowd SE, Delton HJ, Rees E, et al. Survey of fungi and yeast in polymicrobial infections in chronic wounds. *J Wound Care* 2011;20:40–47.
43. Dowd SE, Wolcott RD, Sun Y, et al. Polymicrobial nature of chronic diabetic foot ulcer biofilm infections determined using bacterial tag encoded FLX amplicon pyrosequencing (bTEFAP). *PLoS One* 2008;3:e3326.
44. Sontakke S, Cadenas MB, Maggi RG, et al. Use of broad range16S rDNA PCR in clinical microbiology. *J Microbiol Methods* 2009;76:217–225.
45. Post JC, Aul JJ, White GJ, et al. PCR-based detection of bacterial DNA after antimicrobial treatment is indicative of persistent, viable bacteria in the chinchilla model of otitis media. *Am J Otolaryngol* 1996;17:106–111.
46. Rhoads DD, Cox SB, Rees EJ, et al. Clinical identification of bacteria in human chronic wound infections: culturing vs. 16S ribosomal DNA sequencing. *BMC Infect Dis* 2012;12:321.

SUPPLEMENTAL RESOURCES

Advanced Reading

Adair CG, Gorman SP, Feron BM, et al. Implications of endotracheal tube biofilm for ventilator-associated pneumonia. *Int Care Med* 1999;2(10):1072–1076.

Atela I, Coll P, Rello J, et al. Serial cultures of skin and catheter hub specimens from critically ill patients with central venous catheters: molecular epidemiology of infection and implications for clinical management. *J Clin Microbiol* 1997;35: 784–790.

Bahrani-Mougeot FK, Paster BJ, Coleman S, et al. Molecular analysis of oral and respiratory bacterial species associated with ventilator-associated pneumonia. *J Clin Microbiol* 2007;45:1588–1593.

Bibashi E, Memmos D, Kokolina E, et al. Fungal peritonitis complicating peritoneal dialysis during an 11-year period: Report of 46 cases. *Clin Infect Dis* 2003;36:927–931.

Blot F, Nitenber G, Chachaty E, et al. Diagnosis of catheter-related bacteremia: a prospective comparison of the time to positivity of hub-blood verses peripheral-blood cultures. *Lancet* 1999;354:1071–1077.

Ceri H, Olson ME, Stremick C, et al. The Calgary biofilmdevice: New technology for rapid determination of antibiotic susceptibilities of bacterial biofilms. *J Clin Microbiol* 1999;37(6):1771–1776.

Chandra J, Mukherjee PK, Leidich SD, et al. Antifungal resistance of candidal biofilms formed on denture acrylic in vitro. *J Dent Res* 2001;80:903–908.

Costerton JW. Biofilm theory can guide the treatment of device-related orthopaedic infections. *Clin Orthop Relat Res* 2005;437:7–11.

Costerton JW, Stewart PS, Greenberg EP. Bacterial biofilms: A common cause of persistent infections. *Science* 1999;284:1318–1322.

Crinch CJ, Maki DG. The promise of novel technology for the prevention of intravascular device-related bloodstream infection. I. Pathogenesis and short term devices, clinical infectious diseases. *Healthcare Epidemiol* 2002;34:1232–1242.

Crump JA, Collignon PJ. Intravascular catheter-associated infections. *Eur J Clin Microbiol Infect Dis* 2000;19:1–8.

Darouiche RO, Radd II. Aseptic approaches and novel antimicrobial catheters for prevention of infection of vascular catheters. In: Sawan SP, Manivannan G, eds. *Anti-microbial/Anti-infective Materials: Principles, Applications, Devices, and Regulatory Issues*. Lancaster, PA: Technomic Publishing, 1999.

Foxman B. Epidemiology of urinary tract infections: Incidence, morbidity, and economic costs. *Dis Mon* 2003;49(2):53–70.

Giamarellou H. Nosocomial cardiac infections. *J Hosp Infect* 2002;50:91–105.

Hanna HA, Radd II, Hackett B, et al. Antibiotic-impregnated catheters associated with significant decrease in nosocomial and multidrug-resistant bacteremias in critically ill patients. *Chest* 2003;124:1030–1038.

Kaandorp CJ, Dinant HJ, van de Larr MA, et al. Incidence and sources of native prosthetic joint infection: A community based prospective survey. *Ann Rheum Dis* 1997;56:470–475.

Mermel LA, Farr BM, Sherertz RJ, et al. Guidelines for the management of intravascular catheter-related infections. *Clin Infect Dis* 2001;32: 1249–1272.

Montero AJ, Romero JA, Vargas CA, et al. *Candida* infection of cerebrospinal fluid shunt devices: Report of two cases and review of the literature. *Acta Neurochir (Wien)* 2000;142(1):67–74.

Phelan DM, Osmon DR, Keating MR, et al. Delayed reimplantation arthroplasty for candidal prosthetic joint infection: A report of 4 cases and review of the literature. *Clin Infect Dis* 2002;34:930–938.

Raad I. Management of intravascular catheter-related infections. *J Antimicrob Chemother* 2000;45:267–270.

Radford DR, Challacombe SJ, Walter JD. Denture plaque and adherence of *Candida albicans* to denture-base materials in vivo and in vitro. *Crit Rev Oral Biol Med* 1999;10:99–116.

Raghavendran K, Mylotte JM, Scannapieco FA. Nursing home-associated pneumonia, hospital-acquired pneumonia and ventilator-associated pneumonia: The contribution of dental biofilms and periodontal inflammation. *Periodontol* 2007;44:164–177.

Scannapieco FA. Pneumonia in nonambulatory patients: The role of oral bacteria and oral hygiene. *JAMA* 2006;137(suppl 10):21S–25S.

Senpuku H, Sogame A, Inoshita E, et al. Systemic diseases in association with microbial species in oral biofilm from elderly requiring care. *Gerontology* 2003;49:301–309.

Websites

Biofilm Research Laboratory. Available at: http://www.hsc.wvu.edu/som /pathology/Thomas (detailed biofilm lab protocols for blood, urine, LRI, fungus, and dental isolates).

Center for Biofilm Engineering. Available at: http://www.erc.montana.edu.

Centers for Disease Control and Prevention Link to Infection Control Guidelines. Available at: http://www.cdc.gov/ncidod/dhqp/index.html.

HAI Compendium. Available at: http://www.shea-online.org/about /compendium.cfm.

Human Microbiome Project. Available at: http://nihroadmap.nih.gov/hmp.

Human Oral Microbiome Database. Available at: http://homd.org.

Wound Care: Southwest Regional Wound Care Center. Available at: http://www.woundcarecenter.net.

CHAPTER 71

Bordetella pertussis

Amanda M. Valyko, MPH, CIC
Infection Control Practitioner
University of Michigan Health System
Ann Arbor, MI

ABSTRACT

Bordetella pertussis *is a highly communicable, acute, infectious respiratory disease that remains a cause of high morbidity and mortality among children worldwide. Reinfection is common in both previously vaccinated and nonvaccinated individuals. Asymptomatic and subclinical infections occur frequently among adolescents and adults. Macrolide agents are the drugs of choice for treatment and prophylaxis of pertussis. Acellular vaccine is available for infants, adolescents, and adults, including pregnant and postpartum women in the United States. Specific interventions are required to prevent the transmission of disease.*

KEY CONCEPTS

- Pertussis epidemics occur in cycles of 2 to 5 years.

- Vaccination immunity for pertussis wanes over time.

- Pertussis is highly contagious and has an impact on both the community and healthcare facilities.

- The diagnosis of pertussis can be made through direct culture, direct fluorescent antibody testing, or polymerase chain reaction assay.

- Clinical manifestations of pertussis are broken down into two stages: the catarrhal stage and the paroxysmal stage.

- Vaccines are available.

- Both community outbreaks and healthcare setting outbreaks have been reported.

BACKGROUND

Pertussis (whooping cough) is a highly communicable, acute, infectious respiratory disease caused by *Bordetella pertussis*. *B. pertussis* is a small, aerobic, Gram-negative pleomorphic bacillus (0.2 to 0.5 μm in diameter). The bacteria are fastidious and difficult to culture and have an incubation period of 10 to

14 days. *B. pertussis* produces multiple antigenic and biologically active products, including pertussis toxin (PT), filamentous hemagglutinin (FHA), agglutinogens, adenylate cyclase (AC) toxin, pertactin, fimbriae, tracheal colonization factor, and tracheal cytotoxin (TCT), which are responsible for the clinical features of pertussis disease.[1,2] Two closely related organisms are *Bordetella parapertussis*, which causes a pertussis-like syndrome in humans, and *Bordetella bronchiseptica*, which produces respiratory tract illness in animals, although it has been occasionally reported in humans, including several case reports of *B. bronchiseptica* infection in HIV-infected patients as well as a single case report of an immunocompetent infant with recurrent pneumonia due to *B. bronchiseptica*.[3,4]

BASIC PRINCIPLES

- Pertussis remains a cause of high morbidity and mortality among children worldwide.

- Widespread use of pertussis vaccine in the United States since the late 1940s has reduced the number of reported pertussis cases and deaths by 98 percent. The estimate of children vaccinated with three or more doses of pertussis vaccine has exceeded 90 percent since 1994.[5] However, despite steady coverage levels of vaccine among preschool children[6] and mandatory vaccination among school-age children, pertussis remains endemic in the United States. In 2012, 32,680 cases of pertussis were reported to the Centers for Disease Control and Prevention (CDC).[7]

- Although cyclic, pertussis is increasing with the highest rates occurring among young infants and adolescents. Waning immunity approximately 5 to 10 years after booster vaccination increases susceptibility among adolescents and adults.[8] Improvement in laboratory testing and increased reporting may be contributing to the increased numbers of cases reported in adolescents and adults.[8,9]

HISTORY OF THE DISEASE

Pertussis was first recognized in the 16th century.[10] The name accurately describes the disease (*per*, meaning intensive or pernicious, and *tussis*, meaning cough).[11] Cherry,[10] in a comprehensive historical review, noted that a disease consistent with pertussis (although given another name) was first mentioned in England in 1540. An outbreak with symptoms also consistent with pertussis occurred in 1578 in Paris. It was Sydenham who first gave the illness the name "pertussis" in 1679. Not until 1900 did Bordet and Gengou observe the causative organism (obtained from sputum) under a microscope. Because of the difficulties encountered while attempting to grow the organism, it would take another 6 years to actually isolate it.

EPIDEMIOLOGY AND TRANSMISSION

Pertussis outbreaks among adolescents and adults, including healthcare personnel, are increasingly reported. A pertussis outbreak occurred among adults at an oil refinery in Illinois in August to October 2002.[12] A countywide pertussis outbreak occurred in 2003 that was associated with users of a high school weight room.[13] In 2004, a tertiary care center reported two pertussis outbreaks, one community based, and one associated with infected healthcare personnel.[14] An outbreak among newborns in 2004 was determined to be the result of direct exposure to a healthcare provider with pertussis.[15] In 2005, an outbreak of pertussis occurred among adolescents at a military community.[16] All of these outbreaks reinforce the need for healthcare providers to recognize that asymptomatic and subclinical infections are common in adolescents and adults.[17,18] Even when a cough is present, pertussis is often overlooked in the differential diagnosis in adolescent and adult patients. Other etiologic agents of cough illness that should be ruled out include adenoviruses, *Mycoplasma pneumoniae*, *Chlamydia pneumoniae*, and respiratory syncytial virus.[19] Incidence rates of pertussis are reported to have increased 400 percent during the period 1990 to 2001, with approximately 50 percent of cases found in adolescents (aged 10 to 19 years) and adults (aged ≥20 years).[12] Exposure to unrecognized cases of pertussis in adolescents and adults may provide an explanation as to the increase of pertussis seen in susceptible children.[20,21] Infants, particularly those younger than 6 months of age, are at highest risk for pertussis and its complications (pneumonia, seizures, encephalopathy, and death).[22,23]

Historically, epidemics of pertussis have been found to be cyclic, occurring every 2 to 5 years. Studies of pertussis in adults suggest that immunity following *B. pertussis* vaccination is not lifelong and that reinfection is common in both previously vaccinated and nonvaccinated persons.[20] As a result, the increased incidence among adolescents and adults that has been reported[9,12,24,25] may play an important role in the transmission of pertussis to susceptible infants.[26] Immunity from childhood vaccination wanes 5 to 10 years after the last whole-cell vaccine dose (usually given at 4 to 6 years of age). Twelve years after the last dose of vaccine, there was almost no residual protection. The efficacy of the whole-cell diphtheria-tetanus-pertussis (DTP) vaccine, no longer used in the United States, was estimated to be between 70 and 90 percent.[27]

Because pertussis is so highly contagious, secondary attack rates may exceed 80 percent among susceptible household contacts.[28] Transmission occurs by direct contact with respiratory secretions or large aerosol droplets from the respiratory tract of infected persons. The period of communicability starts with the onset of the catarrhal stage and extends into the paroxysmal stage[19] (Figure 71-1).

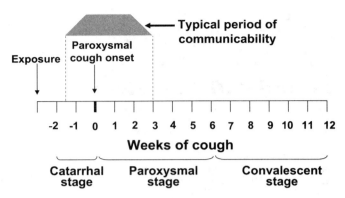

Figure 71-1. Period of communicability of pertussis. (From Bisgard K. Background. In: *Guidelines for the Control of Pertussis Outbreaks*. Atlanta, GA: Centers for Disease Control and Prevention; 2000. Used with permission.)

It is important to recognize that pertussis is truly a worldwide disease that has no boundaries. Even with a global vaccination level of approximately 80 percent in 1999, an estimated 48.5 million pertussis cases occurred in children worldwide.[29] There were an estimated 295,000 deaths that year, occurring mostly in Africa. This is not surprising because incidence and mortality rates are closely tied to the presence of immunization programs, good nutrition, and the availability of quality medical care. Countries in which documented immunization rates have fallen have experienced an increase in incidence rates (Japan, Sweden, and United Kingdom).[30] Decreased immunization rates may also pose a potential problem during a disaster if the disease occurred in crowded refugee camps.[29]

DIAGNOSIS

The gold standard methodology for the laboratory diagnosis of pertussis is culture, utilizing either fresh Bordet-Gengou or Regan-Lowe media. The specimen of choice is a nasopharyngeal aspirate or swab (calcium alginate or polyethylene terephthalate). If direct inoculation of the medium is not possible, specimens must be placed in Regan-Lowe transport medium (one-half strength charcoal agar supplemented with horse blood and cephalexin) and stored at 4°C until processed.[3,31,32] The sensitivity of culture has been reported to range from 15 to 80 percent, with lower performance if the patient has begun a regimen of effective antibiotic therapy (erythromycin, trimethoprim-sulfamethoxazole, azithromycin, or clarithromycin) or if the specimen is obtained more than 3 weeks after onset of cough.[33]

Direct fluorescent antibody (DFA) testing may be also used to diagnose pertussis infection. The test is highly specific at 98 percent. The sensitivity has been reported at 52 percent. Due to this low sensitivity, culture confirmation should be attempted if DFA testing is performed.[33,34]

Polymerase chain reaction (PCR) tests for identification of *B. pertussis* are now rapid and specific, with a higher sensitivity than either culture or DFA.[33-37] It is important that calcium alginate swabs should not be used for nasopharyngeal collection if PCR testing will be performed because they have been shown to be inhibitory.[31] PCR, despite being labor intensive,[38] has been used as a rapid method to document healthcare-associated cases of pertussis.[39] Enzyme-linked immunosorbent assay (ELISA) techniques to identify serum antibodies to pertussis are another option for diagnosis if acute and convalescent sera are available.[19,28,31]

Cases may be classified as "probable" or "confirmed" based on laboratory findings. The pertussis case definition developed and adopted by the Council of State and Territorial Epidemiologists (CSTE) and the Centers for Disease Control and Prevention (CDC) defines a clinical case of pertussis as a cough illness lasting 2 weeks or more with paroxysms of coughing, inspiratory "whoop," or posttussive vomiting without other apparent cause. (In outbreak settings, a case may be defined as a cough illness lasting ≥2 weeks.) The laboratory criteria for diagnosis are isolation of *B. pertussis* from clinical specimen or positive PCR for *B. pertussis*. Cases are further classed as "probable," in which the case meets the clinical case definition but is not laboratory confirmed and is not epidemiologically linked to a laboratory-confirmed case, or, "confirmed," in which the case is laboratory confirmed or one that meets the clinical case definition and is epidemiologically linked to a laboratory-confirmed case.[9,40]

CLINICAL MANIFESTATION

The incubation period of pertussis in nonimmunocompromised patients is usually 7 to 10 days, with a range of 6 to 21 days. Rarely, the incubation period may be as long as 42 days. Classically, the onset, known as the catarrhal stage, is insidious with symptoms similar to that of the common cold: coryza (runny nose), sneezing, low-grade fever, and a mild, occasional cough that gradually becomes more severe. This stage lasts 1 to 2 weeks. The cough that began during the catarrhal stage progresses steadily, becoming paroxysmal (numerous, rapid coughing). It is during this second paroxysmal stage that the diagnosis of pertussis is usually suspected. The patient appears well between bouts of coughing, and if no paroxysm of coughing occurs during the physical examination, the diagnosis may be missed. The classic symptoms of pertussis include whoop, vomiting, apnea, and cyanosis immediately after a paroxysm of coughing. Infants younger than 6 months may have an atypical presentation with a short catarrhal stage, gagging and gasping, or apnea as prominent early manifestations. The "whoop" may be absent.[31] Paroxysmal attacks occur more frequently at night, with an average of 15 attacks per 24 hours.[41] The paroxysmal stage lasts 1 to 6 weeks but may persist for as long as 10 weeks. During the convalescent stage, the cough becomes less paroxysmal and gradually disappears. This stage may persist for many months, particularly during subsequent viral upper respiratory tract infections that may cause paroxysms. Symptoms of pertussis are milder in vaccinated persons, and the diagnosis

Table 71-1. Signs and Symptoms of Pertussis

Signs and Symptoms	Adults**	Children ≤24 Months†
Paroxysmal cough	15 (94 percent)	118 (65 percent)
Sputum production	12 (75 percent)	
Awakened by cough	14 (88 percent)	
Cough-induced vomiting	5 (31 percent)	116 (64 percent)
Whoop		18 (10 percent)
Cyanosis with cough		108 (59 percent)
Convulsion*		9 (5 percent)
Fever		61 (34 percent)
Apnea		45 (25 percent)
Cyanosis		108 (59 percent)

*A total of 11 patients (6 percent) had one or more convulsions.

**Wright SW, Edwards KM, Decker MD, Zeldin MH. Pertussis infection in adults with persistent cough. *JAMA* 1995;273(13):1044–1046.

†Gan VN, Murphy T. Pertussis in hospitalized children. *Am J Dis Child* 1990;144(10):1130–1134.

may be missed in adolescents and adults, who often have less characteristic symptoms (Table 71-1).

PATHOGENESIS

The pathogenesis of pertussis is complex. The organism attaches to ciliated epithelial cells in the respiratory tract. As mentioned, *B. pertussis* produces a number of biologically active substances that are thought to play a role in attachment to respiratory epithelium (pertussis toxin, filamentous hemagglutinin, pertactin, agglutinogens), cell toxicity (pertussis toxin, tracheal cytotoxin), and disruption of the host immune response (pertussis toxin and adenylate cyclase). These antigens evade the host defenses; thus, one sees lymphocytosis and impaired chemotaxis.[2] Of these, pertussis toxin is thought to be of major importance. Pertussis toxin prevents migration of lymphocytes to areas of infection and adversely affects phagocytosis and intracellular killing. It also affects glucose metabolism, resulting in a mild, compensated hyperinsulinemia.[42] Antibodies to pertussis toxin are usually found after natural disease and vaccination; however, no serologic correlate of clinical protection has been identified.

TREATMENT AND POSTEXPOSURE PROPHYLAXIS

In 2005, the CDC issued guidelines for recommended antimicrobial agents for the treatment and postexposure prophylaxis of pertussis (Table 71-2).[43] The macrolide agents erythromycin, clarithromycin, and azithromycin are preferred for the treatment of pertussis in persons 1 month of age and older. For infants younger than 1 month, azithromycin is preferred; erythromycin and clarithromycin are not recommended. For treatment of persons aged 3 months of age and older, an alternative agent to macrolides is trimethoprim-sulfamethoxazole (TMP-SMZ).

Table 71-2. CDC Recommendations for Treatment/Prophylaxis of Pertussis

		Primary Agents		Alternate Agent*
Age Group	Azithromycin	Erythromycin	Clarithromycin	TPM-SMZ
<1 month	Recommended agent. 10 mg/kg per day in a single dose for 5 days (only limited safety data available)	Not preferred. Erythromycin is associated with infantile hypertrophic pyloric stenosis. Use if azithromycin is unavailable; 40–50 mg/kg per day in four divided doses for 14 days	Not recommended (safety data unavailable)	Contraindicated for infants aged <2 months (risk for kernicterus)
1–5 months	10 mg/kg per day in a single dose for 5 days	40–50 mg/kg per day in four divided doses for 14 days	15 mg/kg per day in two divided doses for 7 days	Contraindicated at age <2 months. For infants aged ≥2 months, TMP 8 mg/kg per day, SMZ 40 mg/kg per day in two divided doses for 14 days
Infants (aged ≥6 months) and children	10 mg/kg in a single dose on day 1 then 5 mg/kg per day (maximum: 500 mg) on days 2–5	40–50 mg/kg per day (maximum: 2 g per day) in four divided doses for 14 days	15 mg/kg per day in two divided doses (maximum: 1 g per day) for 7 days	TMP 8 mg/kg per day, SMZ 40 mg/kg per day in two divided doses for 14 days
Adults	500 mg in a single dose on day 1 then 250 mg per day on days 2–5	2 g per day in four divided doses for 14 days	1 g per day in two divided doses for 7 days	TMP 320 mg per day, SMZ 1600 mg per day in two divided doses for 14 days

*Trimethoprim-sulfamethoxazole (TMP-SMZ) can be used as an alternative agent to macrolides in patients aged ≥2 months who are allergic to macrolides, who cannot tolerate macrolides, or who are infected with a rare macrolide-resistant strain of *Bordetella pertussis*.

For postexposure prophylaxis, a macrolide can be administered if the person has no contraindication to its use.

Pertussis symptoms may be greatly diminished when effective antimicrobial therapy is started during either the catarrhal stage or within 2 weeks of cough onset.[31] However, once the paroxysmal stage has begun, antimicrobial therapy has little effect on the course of illness and is indicated primarily to limit the spread of the organism to others. Patients are no longer infectious after 5 days of effective therapy.

OUTBREAKS

Transmission of pertussis in hospital settings has been documented in numerous reports (Table 71-3). Recent outbreaks cost estimates vary from just over $80,000 to more than $200,000. Cost estimates typically include testing, prophylaxis, and labor costs. At a tertiary healthcare facility with adult and pediatric beds, 17 symptomatic cases of pertussis were identified among healthcare personnel (HCP) resulting from a 1-day exposure. The total measured cost of that outbreak to the hospital was $81,382, including costs incurred by the HCP of $6,512.[44] Another tertiary facility experienced two outbreaks. The first was community based, but the second involved many HCP. There was documentation of transmission of pertussis from patients to HCP, but no documentation of transmission from HCP to patients. Costs associated with the second outbreak were $236,284.

Hospital outbreaks have resulted from failure to recognize and isolate infected infants and children, failure to recognize and treat disease in staff members, and failure to rapidly institute control measures.[45] Either HCP or a patient may introduce B. pertussis into the hospital or clinic, and subsequent transmission to patients or HCP (or both) may occur. The risk of developing pertussis for patients or staff during these outbreaks is often difficult to quantify because the definition of what constitutes exposure continues to be refined.

Transmission of pertussis to susceptible contacts living in the same household is a common occurrence. A case of pertussis should be immediately reported to local health department authorities to facilitate identification and antibiotic treatment or prophylaxis of household contacts.[31]

PREVENTION

Current Advisory Committee on Immunization Practices Recommendations

Infants and Children

The Advisory Committee on Immunization Practices (ACIP) recommends a licensed acellular pertussis vaccine (DTaP), containing diphtheria, tetanus toxoids, and acellular pertussis vaccines for all five doses of the routine diphtheria, tetanus, and pertussis vaccination series and for the remaining doses in the series for children who have started the vaccination series with whole-cell DTP vaccine (no longer available in the United States). The primary series of DTaP consists of four doses of vaccine. The first three doses are given at 4- to 8-week intervals (with a minimum of 4 weeks between) beginning at 6 weeks to 2 months of age. The fourth dose is given 6 to 12 months after the third. If the child received all four primary doses before turning 4 years old, a fifth (booster) dose should be given before the child enters

Table 71-3. Outbreaks of Pertussis in Hospital Settings Indicating Number of Patients and Staff With Clinical Disease and Impact of Outbreak

Author	Setting	Clinical Pertussis		No. Screened	Interventions	Cost
		No. of Patients	No. of Staff			
Calugar et al.[44]	Tertiary care with adult and pediatric beds		17	307 close contacts of those staff	184 lab tests; 324 treatment and prophylaxis; 725 labor hours; 808 letters distributed; 560 administrative leave hours	$6512 for healthcare personnel $81,382 total costs
Zivna et al.[25] Shefer et al. (1995)	Tertiary care medical center/affiliated ambulatory care settings 800-bed hospital	189	210	353 staff	287 employees received treatment/prophylaxis; erythromycin for 350 patients and 40 staff; 630 staff vaccinated	Total cost $85,066–$98,456 Not noted
Baggett et al. (2007) Wiblin et al.[54]	(A) 500-bed tertiary care hospital	3	7	738 (388 staff, 256 patients, 85 visitors)	187 laboratory tests; 516 treated	$263,357
	(B) 250-bed pediatric hospital (C) 640-bed hospital		513	737 (417 staff, 120 patients, 200 visitors)	120 laboratory tests; 413 treated; 298 employees and 60 patients had face-to-face exposure; erythromycin for all high-risk persons	$121,130 $4357 for prophylaxis alone
Leekha, Thompson, & Sampathkumr[14a] Zivna et al.[25]	2,036-bed tertiary care center with two outbreaks Tertiary care medical center/ affiliated ambulatory care settings	97 first outbreak 58 second outbreak 18	12 first outbreak 64 second outbreak 2	2,337 first outbreak 1,976 second outbreak 353 staff	287 employees received treatment/prophylaxis	Not measured in first outbreak $236,284 second outbreak Total cost $85,066–$98,456
Baggett et al. (2007)	(A) 500-bed tertiary care		7	738 (388 staff, 256 patients, 85 visitors)	187 laboratory tests; 516 treated	$263,357
	(B) 250-bed pediatric hospital		5	737 (417 staff, 120 patients, 200 visitors)	120 laboratory tests; 413 treated	$121,130
Leekha, Thompson, & Sampathkumr[14a]	2,036-bed tertiary care center with two outbreaks	97 first outbreak 58 second outbreak	12 first outbreak 64 second outbreak	2,337 first outbreak 1,976 second outbreak		Not measured in first outbreak $236,284 second outbreak

school. ACIP also notes that interruption of the recommended schedule, or delayed doses, does not lead to a reduction in the level of immunity reached on completion of the primary series. There is no need to restart a series regardless of the time that has elapsed between doses.[31]

Recommendations for vaccination of adolescents have also been issued. Adolescents 11 to 18 years of age should receive a single dose of Tdap (containing tetanus toxoids, reduced diphtheria toxoids, and acellular pertussis).[46]

Children age 7 to 10 years that are not fully vaccinated against pertussis should receive a single dose of Tdap.[47]

Pregnant Women

The current ACIP recommendation is to vaccinate pregnant women with Tdap during every pregnancy, regardless of the patient's prior Tdap vaccination history, to provide the highest concentration of maternal antibodies to the infant. If Tdap is not administered during pregnancy, it should be administered immediately postpartum.[48]

In 2007, Dylag and Shah[49] conducted a study combining several of these recommendations. Within their level III neonatal intensive care unit (NICU), eligible parents were offered the Tdap vaccine. Of the 495 parents offered the vaccine (82.8 percent of the 598 eligible parents), 86.9 percent (430 parents) received the vaccine. The remaining 11.1 percent of the parents who refused the vaccine either thought pertussis was not a significant health threat or did not believe in vaccination. Based on the results of this study, the NICU appears to be an excellent place to immunize parents and perhaps other close contacts of neonates who are at high risk.

All Other Adults

ACIP recommends that all adults aged 19 years and older that have not received a dose of Tdap should receive a single dose, regardless of the interval since their last tetanus or diphtheria toxoid-containing vaccine.[47,50]

At this time, other than in pregnant women, ACIP is not making recommendations regarding revaccination of adults with Tdap. This is still being evaluated and is expected to be addressed in the future.

RISK REDUCTION

The CDC and prevention and infectious disease experts recommend the following guidelines for managing pertussis exposures.[50-53]

- Implement Droplet Precautions in addition to Standard Precautions for suspected or known infected patients.

- Cohort exposed patients.

- Provide postexposure prophylaxis for all asymptomatic exposed employees, patients, and visitors regardless of immunization history.

- Evaluate all symptomatic employees for pertussis and provide appropriate antimicrobial therapy.

- Furlough symptomatic employees during the first 5 days of their therapy.

More expansive measures are indicated when extensive outbreaks extend from the community into the healthcare institution.[43] These include:

- Educate continuously with in-services on high-risk units and via hospital newsletters, and educational fact sheets, fax network to community physicians, and the news media.

- Distribute standardized checklists, forms, and guidelines developed by the infection preventionist (IP).

- Engage IPs to assist with management of the exposures.

- Evaluate employees for respiratory symptoms and illness.

- Institute Isolation Precautions for patients admitted with suspected pertussis.

- Cohort patients displaying classic symptoms of coughing, etc.

- Consider requiring all visitors to wear surgical masks while in the affected facility.

- Restrict inpatients to the assigned unit. Consider masking inpatients if they leave the unit.

- Limit or restrict facilitywide visitors and consider placing security officers at elevators.

- Provide inpatient sibling and employee day care but do not allow symptomatic children.

- Consider providing acellular pertussis vaccination for exposed staff.

It should be noted that the use of vaccines for HCP, even during outbreak situations, remains a matter of controversy, and is not currently recommended by the ACIP. Early diagnosis of pertussis before secondary transmission occurs is difficult because pertussis is highly communicable in the catarrhal stage, when symptoms are still nonspecific. Pertussis should be one of the differential diagnoses for any patient with an acute cough illness lasting 7 days or more without an apparent cause, particularly if accompanied by paroxysms of coughing or vomiting after coughing, whoop, or apnea. Nasopharyngeal cultures or PCR should be obtained whenever possible.

Patients admitted to the inpatient facility or undergoing outpatient evaluation with suspected or confirmed pertussis should be placed on Droplet Precautions to prevent spread of infection (private room, mask for personnel entering the room, mask on patient when traveling in the hospital). Droplet Precautions should continue until the condition is clinically improved and the patient has received at least 5 days of appropriate antimicrobial therapy.

Relieve symptomatic HCP (e.g., unexplained rhinitis or acute cough) with known pertussis exposure from work activities within healthcare settings. A nasopharyngeal specimen should be obtained for *B. pertussis* culture or PCR and appropriate antimicrobial therapy initiated. Return to work is permitted after completing at least 5 days of antimicrobial therapy. HCP with known pertussis exposure who are asymptomatic need not be excluded from duty but should receive antimicrobial prophylaxis as soon as possible.

The approach to postexposure prophylaxis for HCP (shown in Table 71-2) is the same as for treatment of pertussis. Because the nature and duration of exposure sufficient for transmission of pertussis are unknown, the following guidelines may be used by IPs to determine eligibility for prophylaxis with a minimum amount of confusion. Of primary importance is that for transmission to occur, the source case must truly have pertussis, and the nature and duration of contact must be evaluated. The source case should be documented to have pertussis in one of the following ways: (1) proven by culture; (2) an acute cough illness for 14 days or longer with at least one associated symptom (paroxysmal cough, posttussive vomiting, or whoop) and supportive laboratory evidence of pertussis infection (DFA testing, positive serologic findings, or PCR); or (3) clinically consistent illness as described immediately preceding and an epidemiologic link to a culture-positive case.

Transmission requires close contact with respiratory secretions without having worn respiratory protection devices. Close contact includes unprotected face-to-face contact with a patient who is symptomatic (e.g., in the catarrhal or paroxysmal period of illness); sharing a confined space in close proximity for a prolonged period of time (e.g., 1 hour or more) with a symptomatic patient; or direct contact with respiratory, oral, or nasal secretions from a symptomatic patient (e.g., an explosive cough or sneeze on the face, sharing food, sharing eating utensils during a meal, kissing, mouth-to-mouth resuscitation, suctioning, intubation, bronchoscopy, or performing a full medical examination of the nose and throat).[54] Because neonates and young infants are at highest risk of severe disease and complications from pertussis, a more conservative definition of contact may be used for such patients (e.g., being in an enclosed room with a documented case for 1 hour or longer or shorter if the infant is being held).

CONCLUSIONS

Despite widespread use of pertussis vaccines in the United States since the late 1940s, pertussis remains endemic in the

United States. It is also possible that the accuracy of diagnosis and reporting of illness to public health authorities, along with the cyclic nature of the disease, may be contributing to the apparent increase in the number of cases in recent years. Healthcare providers must recognize that asymptomatic and subclinical infections are common in adolescents and adults and that pertussis is often overlooked in adult patients. Exposure to unrecognized cases of pertussis in adolescents and adults may provide an explanation as to the increase of pertussis seen in susceptible children. Infants, particularly those younger than 6 months, are at highest risk for pertussis and its complications (pneumonia, seizures, encephalopathy, and death).

Reinfection is common in previously vaccinated and nonvaccinated individuals. Immunity from childhood vaccination wanes 5 to 10 years after the last vaccine dose (usually given at 4 to 6 years of age), and by 12 years after the last dose of vaccine there is almost no residual protection. Currently, the ACIP recommends a licensed DTaP (combination diphtheria, tetanus toxoids, and acellular pertussis vaccines) for all five doses of the routine diphtheria, tetanus, and pertussis vaccination series and for the remaining doses in the series for children who have started the vaccination series with whole-cell DTP vaccine.

FUTURE TRENDS

As vaccine recommendations are updated and target groups are expanded, it will be important to assess the effectiveness. As more data become available regarding waning vaccine protection as well as data supporting the safety of multiple vaccines, additional boosters in adults may be able to address this issue. In the meantime, early detection remains a key factor in prevention. Educating providers not only to consider pertussis, but also to employ Droplet Precautions early in a patient encounter will mitigate exposures. For the most current information on pertussis access the CDC website on pertussis at http://www.cdc.gov/pertussis/.

INTERNATIONAL PERSPECTIVE

Pertussis represents a global health issue with a significant impact on the health of children in developed and undeveloped countries. With struggling public health infrastructures and inconsistent or absent immunization programs, continued epidemics of this and other vaccine-preventable diseases can be expected. Global travel also aids in the transmission of pertussis to susceptible populations.

REFERENCES

1. Hewlett EL. A commentary on the pathogenesis of pertussis. *Clin Infect Dis* 1999;28(Suppl 2):94–98.
2. Forbes B, Sahm D, Weissfeld AS. Pertussis. In: Forbes B, Sahm D, Weissfeld AS, eds. *Bailey and Scott's Diagnostic Microbiology*, 12th ed. St. Louis, MO: Mosby, 2007:435–438.
3. Dworkin MS, Sullivan PS, Buskin SE, et al. Bordetella bronchiseptica infection in human immunodeficiency virus-infected patients. *Clin Infect Dis* 1999;28(5):1095–1099.
4. Rath BA, Register KB, Wall J, et al. Persistent *Bordetella bronchiseptica* pneumonia in an immunocompetent infant and genetic comparison of clinical isolates with kennel cough vaccine strains. *Clin Infect Dis* 2008;46:905–908.
5. Centers for Disease Control and Prevention (CDC). Pertussis—United States, 2001–2003. *MMWR Morb Mortal Wkly Rep* 2005;54(50):1283–1286.
6. Centers for Disease Control and Prevention (CDC). National, state, and urban vaccination coverage levels among children aged 19–35 months, United States, 2002. *MMWR Morb Mortal Wkly Rep* 2003;52(31):728–732.
7. Centers for Disease Control and Prevention (CDC). Notifiable diseases and mortality tables. *MMWR Morb Mortal Wkly Rep* 2013;62(34):466–479.
8. Centers for Disease Control and Prevention (CDC). Pertussis outbreak in an Amish community—Kent County, Delaware, September 2004–February 2005. *MMWR Morb Mortal Wkly Rep* 2006;55(30):817–821.
9. Guris D, Strebel PM, Bardenheier B, et al. Changing epidemiology of pertussis in the United States: increasing reported incidence among adolescents and adults, 1990–1996. *Clin Infect Dis* 1999;28(6):1230–1237.
10. Cherry JD. Pertussis in the preantibiotic and prevaccine era, with emphasis on adult pertussis. *Clin Infect Dis* 1999;28(Suppl 2):107–111.
11. Robbins JB. Pertussis in adults: introduction. *Clin Infect Dis* 1999;28(Suppl 2):91–93.
12. Centers for Disease Control and Prevention (CDC). Pertussis outbreak among adults at an oil refinery, Illinois, August–October 2002. *MMWR Morb Mortal Wkly Rep* 2003;52(1):1–4.
13. Sotir MJ, Cappozzo DL, Warshauer DM, et al. A countywide outbreak of pertussis. *Arch Pediatr Adolesc Med* 2008;162(1):79–85.
14. Leekha S, Thompson RL, Sampathkumar P. Epidemiology and control of pertussis outbreaks in a tertiary care center and the resource consumption associated with these outbreaks. *Infect Control Hosp Epidemiol* 2009;30(5):467–473.
15. Centers for Disease Control and Prevention (CDC). Hospital-acquired pertussis among newborns—Texas, 2004. *MMWR Morb Mortal Wkly Rep* 2008;57(22):600–603.
16. Mancuso JD, Snyder A, Stigers J, et al. Pertussis outbreak in a US military community: Kaiserslautern, Germany, April–June 2005. *Clin Infect Dis* 2007;45:1476–1478.
17. Cromer BA, Goydos J, Hackell J, et al. Unrecognized pertussis infection in adolescents. *Am J Dis Child* 1993;147(5):575–577.
18. Long SS, Welkon CJ, Clark JL. Widespread silent transmission of pertussis in families: antibody correlates of infection and symptomatology. *J Infect Dis* 1990;161(3):480–486.
19. Bisgard K. Background. In: *Guidelines for the Control of Pertussis Outbreaks*. Atlanta, GA: Centers for Disease Control and Prevention, 2000:4.
20. Cherry JD. Pertussis in adults. *Ann Intern Med* 1998;128(1):64–65.
21. Birkebaek NH, Kristiansen M, Seefeldt T, et al. Bordetella pertussis and chronic cough in adults. *Clin Infect Dis* 1999;29(5):1239–1242.
22. Vitek CR, Pascual FB, Baughman AL, et al. Increase in deaths from pertussis among young infants in the United States in the 1990s. *Pediatr Infect Dis J* 2003;22(7):628–634.
23. Mikelova LK, Halperin SA, Scheifele D, et al. Predictors of death in infants hospitalized with pertussis: a case-control study of 16 pertussis deaths in Canada. *J Pediatr* 2003;143(5):576–581.
24. Yih WK, Lett SM, des Vignes FN, et al. The increasing incidence of pertussis in Massachusetts adolescents and adults, 1989–1998. *J Infect Dis* 2000;182(5):1409–1416.
25. Zivna I, Bergin D, Casavant J, et al. Impact of *Bordetella pertussis* exposures on a Massachusetts tertiary care medical system. *Infect Control Hosp Epidemiol* 2007;28(6):708–712.
26. Izurieta HS, Kenyon TA, Strebel PM, et al. Risk factors for pertussis in young infants during an outbreak in Chicago in 1993. *Clin Infect Dis* 1996;22(3):503–507.
27. Zimmerman RK, Wald ER, Ahwesh ER. Pertussis, pertussis vaccine, and care of exposed persons. *J Am Board Fam Pract* 1996;9(6):422–434.
28. Edwards KM, Decker MD. Pertussis vaccine. In: Plotkin SA, Orenstein WA, Offit PA, eds. *Vaccines*, 4th ed. Philadelphia: Saunders, 2003:471–528.
29. American Public Health Association. Pertussis. In: Heymann DL, ed. *Control of Communicable Diseases Manual*, 19th ed. Washington, DC: American Public Health Association, 2008:399–404.
30. Gangarosa EJ, Galazka AM, Wolfe CR, et al. Impact of anti-vaccine movements on pertussis control: the untold story. *Lancet* 1998;351(9099):356–361.
31. American Academy of Pediatrics. Pertussis. In: Pickering L, Baker CJ, Long SS, et al., eds. *Red Book: 2006 Report of the Committee on Infectious Diseases*, 29th ed. Elk Grove Village, IL: American Academy of Pediatrics, 2012:498–520.
32. Hallander HO. Microbiological and serological diagnosis of pertussis. *Clin Infect Dis* 1999;28(Suppl 2):99–106.
33. Gregory DS. Pertussis: a disease affecting all ages. *Am Fam Physician* 2006;74(3):420–426.
34. Qin X, Galanakis E, Martin ET, et al. Multitarget PCR for diagnosis of pertussis and its clinical implications. *J Clin Microbiol* 2007;45(2):506–511.

35. Reizenstein E, Lindberg L, Mollby R, et al. Validation of nested *Bordetella* PCR in pertussis vaccine trial. *J Clin Microbiol* 1996;34(4):810–815.

36. Reizenstein E. Diagnostic polymerase chain reaction. *Dev Biol Stand* 1997;89:247–254.

37. Sotir MJ, Cappozzo DL, Warshauer DM, et al. Evaluation of polymerase chain reaction and culture for diagnosis of pertussis in the control of a county-wide outbreak focused among adolescents and adults. *Clin Infect Dis* 2007;44(9):1216–1219.

38. Erlandsson A, Backman A, Tornqvist E, et al. PCR assay or culture for diagnosis of *Bordetella pertussis* in the routine diagnostic laboratory? *J Infect* 1997;35(3):221–224. [published erratum appears in *J Infect* 1998;36(3):357].

39. Matlow AG, Nelson S, Wray R, et al. Nosocomial acquisition of pertussis diagnosed by polymerase chain reaction. *Infect Control Hosp Epidemiol* 1997;18(10):715–716.

40. Centers for Disease Control and Prevention (CDC). Case definitions for infectious conditions under public health surveillance. *MMWR Morb Mortal Wkly Rep* 1997;46(RR-10):25.

41. Centers for Disease Control and Prevention (CDC). Pertussis. In: Atkinson W, Wolfe C, Hamborsky J, eds. *Epidemiology and Prevention of Vaccine-Preventable Diseases,* 12th ed. 2nd printing. Washington, DC: Public Health Foundation, 2012:215–232.

42. Cherry JD, Heininger U. Pertussis and other *Bordetella* infections. In: Feigin RD, Cherry JD, Demmler GJ, et al., eds. *Textbook of Pediatric Infectious Diseases*, Vol 1, 6th ed. Philadelphia: Saunders, 2009:1683-1706.

43. Centers for Disease Control and Prevention (CDC). Recommended antimicrobial agents for the treatment and postexposure prophylaxis of pertussis. *MMWR Morb Mortal Wkly Rep* 2005;54(RR-14):1–16.

44. Calugar A, Ortega-Sanchez IR, Tiwari T, et al. Nosocomial pertussis: costs of an outbreak and benefits of vaccinating health care workers. *Clin Infect Dis* 2006;42(7):981–988.

45. Weber DJ, Rutala WA. Pertussis: An underappreciated risk for nosocomial outbreaks [editorial; comment]. *Infect Control Hosp Epidemiol* 1998;19(11):825–828.

46. Centers for Disease Control and Prevention (CDC). Prevention of pertussis among adolescents: recommendations for use of tetanus toxoids, reduced diphtheria toxoids, and acellular pertussis (Tdap) vaccine: recommendations from the Advisory Committee on Immunization Practices (ACIP), and the Healthcare Infection Practices Advisory Committee. *Pediatrics* 2006;117(3):965–978.

47. Centers for Disease Control and Prevention (CDC). Updated recommendations for use of tetanus toxoid, reduced diphtheria toxoid and acellular pertussis (Tdap) vaccine from the Advisory Committee on Immunization Practices, 2010. *MMWR Morb Mortal Wkly Rep* 2011;60(41):1424–1426.

48. Centers for Disease Control and Prevention (CDC). Updated recommendations for use of tetanus toxoid, reduced diphtheria toxoid, and acellular pertussis vaccine (Tdap) in pregnant women — Advisory Committee on Immunization Practices (ACIP), 2012. *MMWR Morb Mortal Wkly Rep* 2013;62(07):131–135.

49. Dylag AM, Shah SI. Administration of tetanus, diphtheria, and acellular pertussis vaccine to parents of high-risk infants in the neonatal intensive care unit. *Pediatrics* 2008;122(3):e550–e555.

50. Centers for Disease Control and Prevention (CDC). Updated recommendations for use of tetanus toxoid, reduced diphtheria toxoid, and acellular pertussis (Tdap) vaccine in adults aged 65 years and older — Advisory Committee on Immunization Practices (ACIP), 2012. *MMWR Morb Mortal Wkly Rep* 2012;61(25):468–470.

51. Bolyard EA, Tablan OC, Williams WW, et al. Guideline for infection control in healthcare personnel, 1998, Hospital Infection Control Practices Advisory Committee. *Infect Control Hosp Epidemiol* 1998;19(6):407–463 [published erratum appears in *Infect Control Hosp Epidemiol* 1998;19(7):493].

52. Weber DJ, Rutala WA. Management of healthcare workers exposed to pertussis. *Infect Control Hosp Epidemiol* 1994;15(6):411–415.

53. Haiduven DJ, Hench CP, Simpkins SM, et al. Standardized management of patients and employees exposed to pertussis [see comments]. *Infect Control Hosp Epidemiol* 1998;19(11):861–864.

54. Wiblin RT, Pottinger J, Carter C, et al. *Control of pertussis exposures at a university hospital during a community-based outbreak*. Poster presented at The Society for Healthcare Epidemiology of America (SHEA), Orlando, FL, April 5–7, 1998.

CHAPTER 72

Clostridium difficile Infection and Pseudomembranous Colitis

Jason E. Bowling, MD
Assistant Professor
Department of Medicine/Division of Infectious Diseases
Director of Hospital Epidemiology, University Health System
The University of Texas Health Science Center at San Antonio
San Antonio, TX

ABSTRACT

Clostridium difficile *is a Gram-positive, spore-forming anaer-obic bacillus that produces two large toxins, A and B, which cause diarrhea and colitis in susceptible patients whose normal colonic bacterial flora has been previously disrupted by prior antimicrobial treatment. Rates of* C. difficile *infection in the United States have tripled since the year 2000, mortality has increased, and a toxin variant strain of* C. difficile *known as BI/NAP1/027 has become widespread in North America and Europe. Pseudomembranous colitis is seen in about half the patients with symptomatic* C. difficile *infection and is characterized by formation of punctate pseudomembranes that can cover the entire colonic surface in severe cases. High-risk environments include acute care hospitals and long-term care facilities in which the use of antimicrobials is high (increasing the size of the susceptible population) and the environment is heavily contaminated by the spores of* C. difficile *(increasing the risk of patient contact with the organism). Good personnel hand hygiene, gloving, barrier precautions, and thorough environmental cleaning to prevent transmission of the spores to the patient can accomplish prevention and control.* C. difficile *infection also can be prevented by reducing overall antimicrobial usage and by avoiding use of certain specific antimicrobials, such as clindamycin, third-generation cephalosporins, and fluoro-quinolones. Treatment is with another antimicrobial agent, either metronidazole (first choice for mild to moderately severe disease) or oral vancomycin (first choice for severe* C. difficile *infection).*

KEY CONCEPTS

- Patient susceptibility to *Clostridium difficile* infection requires prior antimicrobial treatment.

- Healthcare personnel transmit *C. difficile* on their hands.

- *C. difficile* spores may contaminate the healthcare environment.

- Patients asymptomatically colonized with *C. difficile* are at reduced risk of infection.

- Barrier precautions can be used to prevent *C. difficile* from reaching the patient.

- Thorough environmental cleaning reduces spore contamination and *C. difficile* infection incidence.

- Effective antimicrobial stewardship can effectively reduce *C. difficile* infection rates.

BACKGROUND

Clostridium difficile infection (CDI) is an infectious bacterial diarrhea that occurs almost invariably in patients who have taken antibiotics recently (usually within 2 months). It was previously believed that the responsible organism, *C. difficile*, is part of the normal flora and proliferates to cause disease when antibiotics are given. Several studies suggest that this is an incorrect hypothesis and that patients who are colonized asymptomatically with *C. difficile* are at decreased, not increased, risk of CDI compared with patients in the same hospital environment who are not previously colonized with *C. difficile*.[1]

Pseudomembranous colitis (PMC) is a more severe form of CDI in which patients exhibit a colitis characterized by the presence of pseudomembranes on the colon surface. The colonic mucosa shows punctate-to-confluent, yellow, white, or gray plaques that are readily visualized at endoscopy, but are observed in only about half of all patients with symptomatic CDI. Biopsy specimens show a neutrophilic mucosal infiltrate beneath the necrotic plaques or pseudomembranes.

It has been shown that *C. difficile*, a Gram-positive, spore-forming anaerobic organism, causes disease by producing two large toxins, toxin A (an enterotoxin and cytotoxin) and toxin B (a cytotoxin). A third toxin, known as binary toxin, has been found in about 5 percent of *C. difficile* isolates and in 100 percent of the BI/NAP1/027 epidemic strain. The ability of the organism to produce spores enables *C. difficile* to survive for months in the environment of healthcare institutions, from which it is spread by transfer of spores directly from the contaminated environment to the patient or by transfer on the hands of healthcare personnel (HCP) who fail to follow good hand hygiene and gloving practices. It is generally accepted that any hospitalized patient can acquire the *C. difficile* organism, but for CDI to occur, it is necessary for the patient to have received antimicrobials (that disrupt the normal bacterial flora). Certain cancer chemotherapeutic agents (which also have antibiotic activity) also place patients at risk.[2–6]

BASIC PRINCIPLES

CDI is one of the most common and costly healthcare-associated infections (HAIs). Understanding its unique epidemiological association with prior antimicrobial treatment is key to learning the best methods of prevention, control, and treatment. The difficulty of eliminating *C. difficile* spore contamination of the hospital environment can be best understood by considering the extreme measures that federal agencies have taken in decontaminating buildings after the anthrax spore contamination of mail centers and office buildings.

TRENDS

Several trends are evident with regard to CDI. The rate of disease has been increasing in hospitals in the United States, Canada, and Europe. Third-generation cephalosporins have supplanted clindamycin as the highest risk antimicrobials associated with CDI.[7] Association with the use of fluoroquinolone antimicrobials is an emerging trend. A cohort study found fluoroquinolone use to be the most important risk factor for CDI during an epidemic.[8] An epidemic strain of *C. difficile* designated BI/NAP1/027 that produces high levels of toxins A and B, possesses a third toxin— binary toxin, which is highly resistant to fluoroquinolone antibiotics–and has spread widely throughout North America and Europe with associated high mortality and morbidity.[9,10]

EPIDEMIOLOGY

CDI attack rates vary widely from hospital to hospital and within hospitals over time. Rates ranging from less than 1 per 1,000 discharges to more than 25 per 1,000 discharges have been observed. Because the at-risk population is limited essentially only to patients who receive antimicrobials, the actual rates per at-risk patient are more than twice as high, as only about half of hospitalized patients receive antimicrobials.

Employee hands and a variety of environmental sites have been found to be contaminated with *C. difficile* spores, the latter in proportion to the status of the patient in the room; environmental rates of contamination are highest if the patient in the room has active CDI with diarrhea, intermediate if the patient is asymptomatically carrying *C. difficile*, and low if the patient does not have *C. difficile* in the stool. Commodes, baby baths, and electronic thermometer handles are among the environmental sites implicated in the transmission of *C. difficile*.[2,4]

Through the use of many genetic typing methods, *C. difficile* outbreaks have been shown to be caused predominantly by single strains, supporting the hypothesis that the majority of CDI

is transmitted within the healthcare facility.[2,3,9,11] Some hospitals also have documented a wide variety of strains causing disease simultaneously and have shown the presence of *C. difficile* in the stools of some patients at the time of admission, particularly if the patient was recently hospitalized. Uncolonized patients have been shown to acquire *C. difficile* at a linear rate of about 8 percent per week in high-incidence hospitals, but most patients remain asymptomatic even if they acquire a toxigenic strain.[12] It has been shown that patients who become asymptomatically colonized with *C. difficile* are at decreased risk of CDI.[1] About 40 percent of *C. difficile* strains in hospitals lack the genes to produce toxins A and B and are considered nontoxigenic and harmless to patients. If a patient acquires one of these strains, he or she is not at risk for developing CDI. A patient who acquires a toxigenic strain of *C. difficile* is protected from getting CDI if he or she is able to develop a rapid anamnestic serum immunoglobulin G (IgG) antibody response to toxin A.[13] Patients who fail to develop an anamnestic antibody response develop CDI and are at increased risk of a recurrence of CDI if they fail to develop antibody during the course of their illness.[14]

Some hospitals may observe a predominant single strain of *C. difficile*, whereas others have a wide diversity of strains causing CDI.[3,13–15] Data on asymptomatic carriage and rates of acquisition of *C. difficile* in hospitals with low rates of CDI are not known. Based on rectal swab culture data, most healthcare-associated CDI is the result of acquisition and infection with *C. difficile* organisms acquired in the hospital, rather than from organisms that colonized the patient before hospitalization. Other risk factors include prolonged hospital stay, advanced age, and intestinal tube feedings.[6,16,17] Normal humans in most studies have only a 1 to 3 percent rate of asymptomatic stool colonization with *C. difficile*, whereas patients with colonoscopy-proven PMC generally have a 90 percent or greater rate of presence of *C. difficile* or its toxin. There is an important exception, however: 50 percent of infants through about 1 year of age harbor the organism and its toxin without any gastrointestinal tract symptoms. In addition, it is well known that 20 percent of hospitalized patients of all ages asymptomatically carry toxigenic and nontoxigenic strains of *C. difficile* in their stool.[2,3]

CLINICAL FEATURES

Diarrhea is the most common clinical symptom of CDI. It is almost never grossly bloody and ranges in consistency from soft unformed stools to watery or mucoid and in frequency from 3 to 20 or more bowel movements per day.[6] Some HCP who are experienced in caring for these patients are able to distinguish a characteristic fecal odor. Clinical symptoms include abdominal pain and cramping (22 percent of patients) and fever (28 percent of patients).[6] Laboratory findings include leukocytosis (>10,000 white blood cells/mm^3) in 50 percent of patients, at times greater than 40,000 white blood cells/mm^3, and occult fecal blood in 26 percent of patients.[6]

Patients who develop an ileus are at especially high risk of fulminant CDI and complications of *C. difficile*, particularly toxic megacolon and perforation of the colon. Toxic megacolon complicating *C. difficile* diarrhea occurred in 3.1 percent of patients in one hospital and resulted in 64 percent mortality. Overall mortality in the past was usually low in patients with CDI because of the excellent response to treatment. Mortality ranged from 0.6 to 3.5 percent of patients seen at two hospitals in a 10-year period; however, in hospitals experiencing outbreaks with the BI/NAP1/027 strain of *C. difficile*, 30-day attributable mortality was 6.9 percent. Elderly patients are at highest risk for mortality and the older the patient the higher the risk of death with CDI.

Extracolonic manifestations of *C. difficile* infection are rare. Reactive arthritis, usually involving large joints, has been described, as has ascites. *C. difficile* has been isolated from body sites other than stool, including joint fluid, blood, peritoneal fluid, splenic abscess, and ascites, but these are rare events.

Recurrence of *C. difficile* diarrhea after treatment occurs in 15 to 25 percent of patients. The term recurrence rather than relapse is preferred because about 40 percent of patients have recurrences that are not caused by the original organism and are not relapses, but rather are reinfections with a new strain of *C. difficile*. Recurrence does not correlate with continued isolation of the organism from stool after treatment, which occurs commonly. The risk factors for recurrence are increased age, decreasing quality-of-life score, continued hospitalization, and failure to develop an anamnestic or recall serum antibody response to toxin A.[12]

DIAGNOSIS

Diagnostic studies for CDI should be performed only on patients who are symptomatic. The usual symptom is diarrhea. The presence of three or more unformed or watery stools in a 24-hour period in a hospitalized patient is sufficient indication to submit a specimen for *C. difficile* testing. Studies on asymptomatic patients should be conducted only for epidemiological purposes, not as a "test of cure" after treatment or to identify carriers for treatment because it has been shown that carrier treatment is usually futile, and the presence of toxin or the organism in stool after successful treatment does not predict which patients will have recurrence of CDI.[18,19] There are many diagnostic tests for CDI available, each with different advantages and disadvantages.

Stool Culture

C. difficile is readily recovered from stool using cycloserine-cefoxitin-fructose agar selective medium. Placing the plates in an anaerobic environment for at least 4 hours to reduce (remove oxygen from) them before inoculation markedly enhances the culture yield. Culture is the most sensitive test of stool available, but has some false-positive results due to the presence of non-toxigenic *C. difficile* isolates; confirmation of toxin production in vitro is recommended to be certain the isolate is toxigenic.[18] It is generally considered the "gold standard" for CDI diagnostic tests because of its sensitivity but the turnaround time of 7 days prevents it from being employed in the clinical setting.[20]

Cell Cytotoxicity Assay

C. difficile toxin may be detected by adding stool extract with and without neutralizing antitoxin to cell culture monolayers. The toxin is presumed to be present if a cytotoxic effect is produced by stool extract but is prevented by the addition of specific neutralizing antitoxin. This is the most specific test for CDI but is not as sensitive as stool culture for toxigenic *C. difficile*.[18] This assay is labor intensive, requires a skilled reader, and has a turnaround time of up to 72 hours from sample receipt.[20]

Enzyme Immunoassay for Toxins A and B

Enzyme immunoassays are commercially available that use monoclonal antibodies to detect toxin A and usually polyclonal antibodies to detect toxin B. They are generally rapid and specific and conserve technical time, but are less sensitive than the cell cytotoxicity assay. More recent studies indicate that these assays do not have appropriate sensitivity to be used as an independent diagnostic test for CDI.[20]

Latex Test or Enzyme Immunoassay for *C. difficile* Antigen

The latex test initially was developed to detect *C. difficile* toxin A but actually detects another antigen, glutamate dehydrogenase (GDH). The latex test is less sensitive and less specific than other tests and does not give information about the presence of toxin.[18] Use of this test as the sole test for diagnosis of CDI should be discouraged. When testing for GDH is done by enzyme immunoassay, the sensitivity is improved, although specificity is poor because GDH is found in both toxigenic as well as nontoxigenic *C. difficile*, as well as in other organisms. The GDH enzyme immunoassay has been used as the first step in a two-step testing algorithm, suggesting that negative GDH specimens can be eliminated from further testing; however, this observation may not be valid if the sensitivity of the GDH assay is not sufficiently high.[21,22]

Colon Endoscopy

Flexible sigmoidoscopy, proctoscopy, and colonoscopy all can be used to detect PMC and are the only means to detect PMC other than surgery or autopsy. These modalities are insensitive in the detection of CDI, however, because results of endoscopy (visualization of PMC) are positive in only about 50 to 55 percent of patients who have diarrhea and whose stools are positive in the cell cytotoxin test and positive for *C. difficile* by culture.[6] Also, endoscopic procedures entail certain potential risks to the patient and are expensive. The American College of Gastroenterology provides specific recommendations for use of endoscopy in CDI diagnosis to include the need for a rapid diagnosis with an expected delay in laboratory testing or the inability to obtain stool specimen because of ileus.[20]

Nucleic Acid Amplification Tests

Nucleic acid amplification tests using two different methods, polymerase chain reaction (PCR) and loop mediated isothermal amplification of DNA, to detect toxin genes of *C. difficile* in stool have been approved by the U.S. Food and Drug Administration (FDA). These assays have high sensitivity and specificity and possess a short turnaround time of several hours.[20] Several studies have evaluated these assays in comparison to other available diagnostic tests because of its promise as a rapid, sensitive, and specific method to diagnose CDI when applied to appropriate patient populations who meet the criteria for diarrhea (three or more loose or unformed stools in 24 hours).[22,23] One study comparing 11 different available rapid assays for diagnosis of CDI on the same 600 stool sample set found PCR testing for toxin B gene to be the most useful single test.[24] Disadvantages of these tests include cost and the risk of false-positive results in asymptomatic patients. It is important to utilize these assays only in appropriate patients to minimize both of these potential drawbacks.[20] Overall, clinical laboratories are more frequently adopting and using this type of diagnostic testing for CDI.

TREATMENT

The first line of treatment is to discontinue the provoking antimicrobials if they are still in use. Symptoms resolve within 48 to 72 hours in 20 to 25 percent of patients by simply stopping the offending antimicrobials.[25] Oral metronidazole and oral vancomycin for 10 days are highly effective at stopping diarrhea in patients with mild to moderately severe CDI, but metronidazole is far less expensive, and there is widespread reluctance to use oral vancomycin in hospitals because of concern about selecting vancomycin-resistant enterococci (VRE). However, randomized blinded clinical trials indicate that vancomycin is superior to metronidazole for the treatment of severe CDI and it is currently the recommended drug for treatment of severely ill patients with CDI.[26,27] Average time to resolution of diarrhea with treatment is about 3 days, but diarrhea may not resolve for 6 to 7 days.[25] Recurrences of diarrhea occur in 15 to 25 percent of patients treated with either agent.[19] For first recurrences, treatment with metronidazole should be repeated if disease is mild to moderate, but if severe, vancomycin should be given. For subsequent recurrences, there is no standardized treatment, but the use of a tapering dose of vancomycin over multiple weeks followed by pulse doses of a single dose every other to every third day has shown efficacy in uncontrolled trials.

Fidaxomicin received approval in the United States for the treatment of CDI in 2011. A randomized blinded clinical trial comparing fidaxomicin to vancomycin showed similar cure rates. There was a lower rate of recurrence seen in patients treated with fidaxomicin if the infection was due to a non-BI/NAP1/027 strain of C. difficile.[28]

Increasing morbidity and increasing numbers of patients with recurrent disease have accompanied the increasing rate of CDI. Patients with recurrent CDI can develop prolonged, chronic disease which can last for years. Because of the lack of efficacy of the standard antibiotics for CDI treatment in recurrent disease, alternative therapies are being investigated. Fecal microbiota transplantation (FMT), also described in the literature as fecal transplantation and fecal bacteriotherapy, demonstrates

significant potential benefit as an alternative treatment option in this context. The concept behind FMT is that recurrent CDI persists because of the altered balance of normal colonic flora in the bowel due to prior receipt of antibiotics. This provides a favorable environment for C. difficile to flourish. FMT addresses this problem by reestablishing the normal flora by infusion of healthy donor feces. A recent review of the literature determined a success rate of 96 percent in the approximately 200 cases of FMT reported.[29] In a recently published clinical trial designed to prospectively evaluate the benefit of FMT, patients with recurrent CDI were randomized to therapy with vancomycin alone or a brief course of vancomycin followed by duodenal infusion of healthy donor feces. The investigators stopped this trial early when an interim safety analysis revealed significantly better treatment outcomes in the study group receiving FMT.[30] Currently, timing and application of FMT has not been standardized and remains an area of controversy as discussed later in this chapter.

Early recurrences within 30 days of treatment are usually relapses with the same organism, but later recurrences are likely to be due to infection with a new C. difficile strain, particularly if the patient remains hospitalized. Asymptomatic persistence of C. difficile and its toxins in stools after treatment is relatively common and should not be looked for by repeated stool testing or be treated with additional metronidazole or vancomycin unless diarrhea recurs. The organism is most likely to disappear if the patient is left untreated. Only symptomatic patients should be treated.[19] More extensive recommendations for treatment of CDI have been published and outlined in clinical practice guidelines.[31,32]

INFECTION PREVENTION

Control measures can be divided into two general approaches: (1) interrupting horizontal transmission of C. difficile, and (2) minimizing the possibility of clinical illness if C. difficile is acquired. Many control measures have been employed, but few have shown clear evidence of effectiveness when applied in clinical situations. Recommendations for control of CDI have been reviewed by Gerding and colleagues and published in clinical practice guidelines.[32,33] Definitions for surveillance of healthcare-associated and community-associated CDI have been recommended.[34] These metrics were used as the basis for public reporting of CDI. All acute care hospitals participating in Centers for Medicare & Medicaid Services (CMS) publically report their surveillance data for CDI via the National Healthcare Safety Network (NHSN) managed by the Centers for Disease Control and Prevention (CDC). All facilities reporting to NHSN use CDC surveillance definitions and reporting instructions.[35] CMS required participating acute care hospitals to start CDI reporting in January 2013.

Measures directed at interruption of horizontal transmission include barrier precautions (hand hygiene/hand washing, gloving, isolation, and cohorting), and environmental cleaning and disinfection. Of the preceding measures, only the use of disposable gloves by personnel when handling body substances and the replacement of electronic thermometers with disposables have been shown in practice to reduce CDI rates.[36,37] It would seem to be prudent and to make sense intuitively to isolate and cohort patients and to clean the environment with sporicidal agents, but when 1:10 hypochlorite solution was used in the rooms of patients with CDI, the rate of CDI decreased significantly only on the bone marrow transplant unit, where the CDI rate was the highest. There was no effect when the solution was used on the neurosurgical intensive care unit or general medical unit where rates were already low.[38] Given that use of hypochlorite solution is a respiratory and skin irritant, and may be caustic to environmental surfaces, it may be prudent to reserve this agent for areas of the hospital where CDI rates are high.

Major questions remain about how long patients with CDI should remain in contact isolation. It is clear that there is greater risk of HCP hand contamination in the room of a patient with symptomatic CDI than in the room of a patient who is asymptomatic. Current recommendations indicate that isolation can be stopped when diarrhea has ceased, usually for several days; however, the environment of the patient room may remain highly contaminated until it can be terminally cleaned. In outbreak situations, isolation of CDI patients has been extended for the duration of hospitalization; however, there are no controlled data to support such a measure. Widespread environmental disinfection with hypochlorite solutions has not been evaluated sufficiently for efficacy and has potential major drawbacks because of the odor, respiratory and skin irritation, and damage to surfaces. Asymptomatic carriers of *C. difficile* are difficult to identify, and may be the source of transmission to other patients; however, it is not known what should be done about them if they are detected. The best approach at this time is to recommend hand hygiene following all patient contacts. Because alcohol-based hand rubs are ineffective against *C. difficile* spores, but are highly effective against other hospital pathogens and have high usage compliance rates, they should be continued in use unless it can be shown that CDI rates are high, in which case hand washing (which is effective at spore removal) should be implemented.

Because measures to interrupt horizontal transmission of *C. difficile* have proved difficult, efforts to minimize the possibility of clinical illness if transmission occurs have been attempted. These include minimizing or preventing antimicrobial use in patients and, for patients who receive antimicrobials, various methods of prophylaxis to prevent CDI. Antimicrobial restriction of clindamycin and control of use of extended-spectrum cephalosporins have been effective at reducing CDI rates in several outbreaks.[16,39] The prophylactic use of a yeast, *Saccharomyces boulardii*, has been shown to reduce antibiotic-associated diarrhea but not CDI in humans. Lactobacilli did not prevent antibiotic-associated diarrhea in adults, and prefeeding of live yogurt cultures does not prevent *C. difficile* diarrhea in hamsters. *C. difficile* antibodies derived from cow milk and chicken eggs prevent disease in hamsters, as does precolonization with nontoxigenic *C. difficile*, but results of studies in humans are not available. Careful risk analysis of

specific antimicrobial use associated with CDI is likely to identify antimicrobials that can be controlled or restricted as part of a successful CDI prevention effort. Finally, a "bundle" approach to dealing with CDI outbreaks has also been employed with good success.[33,40]

AREAS OF CONTROVERSY

The most controversial areas of CDI are those involving treatment management and diagnosis. The role of FMT in the treatment of patients with recurrent CDI is still being established. The FDA is currently developing policies for the use of FMT and emphasizes the need for informed consent that includes the caveat that this treatment modality is investigational and has potential risks.[41] The management of patients with fulminant CDI is also controversial because these patients frequently have an ileus that prevents oral treatment from reaching the colonic site of infection. The selection of the best laboratory test for detection of *C. difficile* or its toxins is also a major area of controversy. More clinical laboratories are adopting and using stool PCR testing for CDI because of its sensitivity, specificity, and rapid turnaround time. A prospective cohort study showed that using stool PCR testing instead of enzyme immunoassay or cell cytotoxicity assay lead to a 50 percent increase in CDI incidence rate.[42] Current CDI surveillance reporting does not account for different diagnostic tests which confounds the ability to compare hospitals. This is a particular concern and area of controversy in the current era of mandatory public reporting of CDI. An additional area of controversy is whether community CDI rates are increasing and whether the number of patients with CDI who have no antimicrobial exposure is increasing.

IMPLICATIONS FOR MULTIPLE PRACTICE SETTINGS

CDI rates in the ambulatory care setting are much lower than in the acute care hospital or long-term care setting, but some areas of the country are reporting increased incidence of community-associated CDI, and some of these patients have no identified antimicrobial exposure.[43] Within acute care and long-term care environments, CDI rates can be expected generally to parallel the rate of antimicrobial use in the patient population. Reports from the state of Ohio suggest that the incidence of CDI in long-term care facilities may be higher than previously observed.[44] CDI rates vary widely from institution to institution, however, and over time in a single institution.

FINANCIAL AND COST BENEFITS

The monetary cost of a case of CDI in a hospitalized patient in one U.S. hospital has been found to be $3,669, which projects to a national cost for U.S. hospitals of $1.1 billion each year.[45] A more recent study based on CDI experience in Massachusetts' hospitals indicates that the projected national annual hospital costs of CDI infection management are $3.2 billion.[46] Prevention of CDI has obvious financial benefit for the healthcare system, especially for the hospitalized acute care population.

CONCLUSIONS

CDI is one of the most common and costly HAIs. The risk is linked closely to the use of antimicrobials in these patients. Herein lies the problem and the opportunity for prevention. Avoidance of unnecessary antimicrobial use provides a nearly 100 percent guarantee of avoidance of CDI. Even if the best efforts to prevent transmission of *C. difficile* in the hospital are not always successful, CDI still can be prevented if the number of susceptible patients can be minimized by the practice of good antimicrobial stewardship as part of the infection prevention effort.

FUTURE TRENDS

There are major needs for the following:

1. Better methods to prevent disease in hospitals and long-term care facilities, including restoration of the disrupted flora in the gut and development of vaccines.

2. Improved treatment regimens that achieve high levels of initial response and reduce the current high rate of recurrence, potentially avoiding the use of antimicrobial treatment altogether.

3. More effective therapies for patients with fulminant disease to reduce mortality and morbidity.

4. Strategy for addressing the different diagnostic assays for CDI used to improve comparisons of CDI rates among different healthcare facilities.

INTERNATIONAL PERSPECTIVE

CDI occurs worldwide in hospitals and long-term care facilities and is likely to be underdiagnosed because of a lack of clinical suspicion or unavailability of laboratory testing. Rates in countries such as the United Kingdom and Australia appear to be at least as high as in U.S. hospitals, but specific comparison data are limited. The BI/NAP1/027 strain of *C. difficile* has caused outbreaks in hospitals in Canada, the United Kingdom, and Western Europe.

REFERENCES

1. Shim JK, Johnson S, Samore MH, et al. Primary symptomless colonization by *Clostridium difficile* and decreased risk of subsequent diarrhoea. *Lancet* 1998;351:633–636.
2. McFarland LV, Mulligan M, Kwok RYY, et al. Nosocomial acquisition of *Clostridium difficile* infection. *N Engl J Med* 1989;320:204–210.
3. Johnson S, Clabots CR, Linn FV, et al. Nosocomial *Clostridium difficile* colonization and disease. *Lancet* 1990;336:97–100.
4. Fekety R, Kim KH, Brown D, et al. Epidemiology of antibiotic-associated colitis: isolation of *Clostridium difficile* from the hospital environment. *Am J Med* 1981;70:906–908.
5. Kelly CP, Pothoulakis C, LaMont JT. *Clostridium difficile* colitis. *N Engl J Med* 1994;330:257–262.
6. Gerding DN, Olson MM, Peterson LR, et al. *Clostridium difficile*-associated diarrhea and colitis in adults: a prospective case-controlled epidemiologic study. *Arch Intern Med* 1986;146:95–100.
7. Bignardi GE. Risk factors for *Clostridium difficile* infection. *J Hosp Infect* 1998;40:1–15.
8. Pepin J, Saheb N, Coulombe M, et al. Emergence of fluoroquinolones as the predominant risk factor for *Clostridium difficile*-associated diarrhea: a cohort study during an epidemic in Quebec. *Clin Infect Dis* 2005 Nov 1; 41(9):1254–1260.

9. Loo VG, Poirier L, Miller MA, et al. A predominantly clonal multi-institutional outbreak of *Clostridium difficile*-associated diarrhea with high morbidity and mortality. *N Engl J Med* 2005;353:2442–2449.
10. McDonald LC, Killgore GE, Thompson A, et al. An epidemic, toxin gene-variant strain of *Clostridium difficile*. *N Engl J Med* 2005;353: 2433–2441.
11. Samore M, Killgore G, Johnson S, et al. Multicenter typing comparison of sporadic and outbreak *Clostridium difficile* isolates from geographically diverse hospitals. *J Infect Dis* 1997;176:1233–1238.
12. Clabots CR, Johnson S, Olson MM, et al. Acquisition of *Clostridium difficile* by hospitalized patients: evidence for colonized new admissions as a source of infection. *J Infect Dis* 1992;166:561–567.
13. Kyne L, Warny M, Qamar A, et al. Asymptomatic carriage of *Clostridium difficile* and serum levels of IgG antibody against toxin A. *N Engl J Med* 2000;342:390–397.
14. Kyne L, Warny M, Qamar A, et al. Association between antibody response to toxin A and protection against recurrent *Clostridium difficile* diarrhoea. *Lancet* 2001;357:189–193.
15. Samore MH. Wide diversity of *Clostridium difficile* types at a tertiary referral hospital. *J Infect Dis* 1994;170:615–621.
16. Simor AE, Yake SL, Tsimidis K. Infection due to *Clostridium difficile* among elderly residents of a long-term care facility. *Clin Infect Dis* 1993;17:672–678.
17. Bliss DZ, Johnson S, Savik K, et al. Acquisition of *Clostridium difficile* and associated diarrhea in hospitalized patients receiving tube feeding. *Ann Intern Med* 1998;129:1012–1019.
18. Kelly PJ, Peterson LR. The role of the clinical microbiology laboratory in the management of *Clostridium difficile*-associated diarrhea. *Infect Dis Clin North Am* 1993;7:277–293.
19. Johnson S, Homann SR, Bettin KM, et al. Treatment of asymptomatic *Clostridium difficile* carriers (fecal excretors) with vancomycin or metronidazole. *Ann Intern Med* 1992;117:297–302.
20. Kufelnicka AM, Kirn TJ. Effective utilization of evolving methods for the laboratory diagnosis of *Clostridium difficile* infection. *Clin Infect Dis* 2011 June 15;52(12):1451–1457.
21. Reller ME, Lema CA, Perl TM, et al. Yield of stool culture with isolate toxin testing versus a two-step algorithm including stool toxin testing for detection of toxigenic *Clostridium difficile*. *J Clin Microbiol* 2007;45(11): 3601–3605.
22. Sloan LM, Duresko BJ, Gustafson DR, et al. Comparison of real-time PCR for detection of the tcdC gene with four toxin immunoassays and culture in diagnosis of *Clostridium difficile* infection. *J Clin Microbiol* 2008;46(6):1996–2001.
23. Peterson LR, Manson RU, Paule SM, et al Detection of toxigenic *Clostridium difficile* in stool samples by real-time polymerase chain reaction for the diagnosis of C. difficile-associated diarrhea. *Clin Infect Dis* 2007;45(9):1152–1160.
24. Eastwood K, Else P, Charlett A, et al. Comparison of nine commercially available *Clostridium difficile* toxin detection assays, a real-time PCR assay for C. difficile tcdB, and a glutamate dehydrogenase detection assay to cytotoxin testing and cytotoxigenic culture methods. *J Clin Microbiol* 2009 Oct;47(10):3211–3217.
25. Teasley DG, Gerding DN, Olson MM, et al. Prospective randomized trial of metronidazole versus vancomycin for *Clostridium difficile*-associated diarrhea and colitis. *Lancet* 1983;2:1043–1046.
26. Zar FA, Bakkanagari SR, Moorthi KM, et al. A comparison of vancomycin and metronidazole for the treatment of *Clostridium difficile*-associated diarrhea, stratified by disease severity. *Clin Infect Dis* 2007;45:302–307.
27. Louie T, Gerson M, Grimard D, et al. *Results of a phase III trial comparing tolevamer, vancomycin and metronidazole in patients with Clostridium difficile-associated diarrhea (CDAD)*. The 47th Annual Interscience Conference on Antimicrobial Agents and Chemotherapy. Volume Abstract K-425a. Chicago, 2007.
28. Louie TJ, Miller MA, Mullane KM, et al. Fidaxomicin versus vancomycin for *Clostridium difficile* infection. *N Engl J Med* 2011 Feb 3;364(5): 422–431.
29. Bakken JS, Borody T, Brandt LJ, et al. Treating *Clostridium difficile* infection with fecal microbiota transplantation. *Clin Gastroenterol Hepatol* 2011;9(12):1044–1049.
30. Nood E, Vrieze A, Nieuwdorp M, et al. Duodenal infusion of donor feces for recurrent *Clostridium difficile*. *N Engl J Med* 2013 Jan 31;368(5): 407–415.
31. Gerding DN, Muto CA, Owens RC Jr. Treatment of *Clostridium difficile* infection. *Clin Infect Dis* 2008;46(Suppl 1):S32–S42.
32. Cohen SH, Gerding DN, Johnson S, et al. Clinical practice guidelines for *Clostridium difficile* infection in adults: 2010 update by the Society for Healthcare Epidemiology of America (SHEA) and the Infectious Diseases Society of America (IDSA). *Infect Control Hosp Epidemiol* 2010;31(5): 431–455.

33. Gerding DN, Muto CA, Owens RC Jr. Measures to control and prevent *Clostridium difficile* infection. *Clin Infect Dis* 2008;46(Suppl 1):S43–S49.
34. McDonald LC, Coignard B, Dubberke E, et al. Recommendations for surveillance of *Clostridium difficile*-associated disease. *Infect Control Hosp Epidemiol* 2007;28(2):140–145.
35. Centers for Disease Control and Prevention (CDC). *Multidrug-Resistant Organism & Clostridium difficile Infection (MDRO/CDI) Module*. CDC website. 2013. Available at: http://www.cdc.gov/nhsn/PDFs/pscManual/12pscMDRO_CDADcurrent.pdf.
36. Johnson S, Gerding DN, Olson MM, et al. Prospective, controlled study of vinyl glove use to interrupt *Clostridium difficile* nosocomial transmission. *Am J Med* 1990;88:137–140.
37. Brooks SE, Veal RO, Kramer M, et al. Reduction in the incidence of *Clostridium difficile*-associated diarrhea in an acute care hospital and a skilled nursing facility following replacement of electronic thermometers with single-use disposables. *Infect Control Hosp Epidemiol* 1992;13:98–103.
38. Mayfield JL, Leet T, Miller J, et al. Environmental control to reduce transmission of *Clostridium difficile*. *Clin Infect Dis* 2000;31:995–1000.
39. Settle CD, Wilcox MH, Fawley WN, et al. Prospective study of the risk of *Clostridium difficile* diarrhoea in elderly patients following treatment with cefotaxime or piperacillin-tazobactam. *Aliment Pharmacol Ther* 1998;12:1217–1223.
40. Muto CA, Blank MK, Marsh JW, et al. Control of an outbreak of infection with the hypervirulent *Clostridium difficile* BI strain in a university hospital using a comprehensive "bundle" approach. *Clin Infect Dis* 2007;45:1266–1273.
41. U.S. Food and Drug Administration (FDA). *Guidance for Industry Enforcement Policy Regarding Investigational New Drug Requirements for Use of Fecal Microbiota for Transplantation to Treat* Clostridium difficile *Infection Not Responsive to Standard Therapies*. FDA website. 2013. Available at: http://www.fda.gov/downloads/BiologicsBloodVaccines/GuidanceComplianceRegulatoryInformation/Guidances/Vaccines/UCM361393.pdf.
42. Longtin Y, Trottier S, Brochu G, et al. Impact of the type of diagnostic assay of *Clostridium difficile* infection and complication rates in a mandatory reporting program. *Clin Infect Dis* 2013 Jan 1;56(1):67–73.
43. Kutty PK, Benoit SR, Woods CW, et al. Assessment of *Clostridium difficile*-associated disease surveillance definitions, North Carolina, 2005. *Infect Control Hosp Epidemiol* 2008;29(3):197–202.
44. Ohio Department of Health. Available at: http://www.odh.ohio.gov/~/media/ODH/ASSETS/Files/health%20statistics%20-%20disease%20-%20selected%20notifiable%20diseases/cdiffreport.ashx.
45. Kyne L, Hamel MB, Polavaram R, et al. Health care costs and mortality associated with nosocomial diarrhea due to *Clostridium difficile*. *Clin Infect Dis* 2002;34:346–353.
46. O'Brien JA, Lahue BJ, Caro JJ, et al. The emerging infectious challenge of *Clostridium difficile*-associated disease in Massachusetts's hospitals: clinical and economic consequences. *Infect Control Hosp Epidemiol* 2007;28(11):1219–1227.

SUPPLEMENTAL RESOURCES

Carrico R. et al. *Guide to Elimination of Clostridium difficile Transmission in Healthcare Settings*. Washington, DC: APIC, 2013.

SHEA, APIC, IDSA Hand Hygiene Task Force. Guideline for hand hygiene in healthcare settings. *MMWR Recomm Rep* 2002;51(RR-16):1–44.

Centers for Disease Control and Prevention (CDC). *Healthcare-associated infections (HAIs),* Clostridium difficile *infection*. CDC website. 2013. Available at: http://www.cdc.gov/HAI/organisms/cdiff/Cdiff_infect.html.

Cohen SH, Gerding DN, Johnson S, et al. Clinical practice guidelines for *Clostridium difficile* infection in adults: 2010 update by the Society for Healthcare Epidemiology of America (SHEA) and the Infectious Diseases Society of America (IDSA). *Infect Control Hosp Epidemiol* 2010;31(5):431–455.

Creutzfeldt-Jakob Disease and Other Prion Diseases

Beth Ann Kavanagh, MT(ASCP), MS, MBA, CIC
Director, Infection Control and Prevention
University Health System
San Antonio, TX

ABSTRACT

Creutzfeldt-Jakob disease is one of several neurologically degenerative diseases caused by a group of protein particles that are infectious by nature of their ability to replicate in the central nervous system and interrupt crucial neuron functioning. Creutzfeldt-Jakob disease and other prion diseases were originally called slow virus diseases because of their prolonged incubation period and initial designation as a viral condition. In the 1980s, it was proposed that the etiology of these neurodegenerative diseases was not viral in nature but due to an "infectious" protein particle that was transmissible through infected tissue and could be distinguished from any other infectious agent by a crucial lack of nucleic acid material. Creutzfeldt-Jakob disease and other prion diseases with demonstrated transmissibility remain a concern for the healthcare community because of their inherent resistance to traditional disinfection/sterilization methods and devastating clinical outcomes. Prevention measures in hospitals include Standard Precautions for general patient care and adherence to extensive chemical or increased temperature sterilization in the confines of the operating room. Prion diseases represent the frontier for infectious disease research.

KEY CONCEPTS

- Prion proteins are synthesized normally in brain tissue.

- Prion diseases occur sporadically in nature, by familial transmission (gene mutation), iatrogenically, and by ingestion of abnormal prions, as in the case of the bovine encephalopathies.

- Prions are highly resistant to routine sterilization/disinfection methods.

- Prion eradication involves chemical or increased temperature/extended cycle sterilization or a combination of both.

- Healthcare providers should be educated on prion diseases to recognize risk factors in patients and take appropriate precautions, protect the health of staff, and prevent unsuspected exposures to patients.

BACKGROUND

Creutzfeldt-Jakob disease (CJD), originally known as a *slow virus* disease, was first described by Creutzfeldt in 1920 and later in 1921 by Jakob.[1] In their descriptions of the disease, the physicians noted cases of unusual neurological degeneration leading to rapid central nervous system collapse and certain death. At autopsy, the patients described were noted to have little tissue inflammation, yet they had extensive loss of normal brain tissue and replacement by glial cells, giving the brain a starlike or "spongy" (spongiform) appearance.

During the next four decades, few cases of what would come to be known as CJD were recorded in the medical literature. In 1957, CJD became associated with another slow virus disease known as *kuru*. This condition was described in the investigational work of epidemiologists studying a neurodegenerative fatal condition occurring among the Fore natives of New Guinea.[2] The distinguishing epidemiological characteristic of kuru was the practice of cannibalism among the Fore women and children. The natives freely admitted to using family members as a source of protein to feed their nutritionally depleted children while maintaining an element of ritual honoring of deceased tribal members. Cannibalism of family members dying of "shivering disease" (kuru) led directly to the transmission of this disease to women and children.

A third neurodegenerative disease, Gerstmann-Sträussler-Scheinker (GSS) syndrome, first described in 1928, was found to be similar to CJD by virtue of onset of dementia and rapid neurological degeneration leading to death.[3] Other human diseases (e.g., fatal familial insomnia) and animal encephalopathies (including scrapie in sheep and goats, transmissible mink encephalopathy, chronic wasting disease of elk and deer, exotic ungulate encephalopathy, and feline and bovine spongiform encephalopathy [BSE]) have all been grouped together into a category of neurological disorders referred to as the *transmissible neurodegenerative diseases* or *transmissible spongiform encephalopathies* (TSE). The diseases were linked by their neurological manifestations (primarily in the central nervous system), sometimes long incubation periods (as in the case of kuru and CJD), progressive and ultimately fatal outcomes, and, characteristically, the spongiform transformations in brain tissue in the absence of an inflammatory response.

In 1982, Prusiner proposed the name *prion* (proteinaceous infectious particles) for the agents that caused the transmissible neurodegenerative diseases of humans and animals. It took more than 10 years for the prion theory of disease to be accepted by the scientific community. In 1997, Prusiner won the Nobel Prize in medicine for his work on prion diseases. Prion diseases of humans are known to occur sporadically, by gene mutation (familial disease), iatrogenically, and by ingestion of contaminated meat products (e.g., beef, bone meal).

MOLECULAR PROPERTIES OF PRIONS

Most research into prion diseases was done using animal models infected with the prion disease of sheep called *scrapie*. Animals with scrapie have large lesions surrounded by exfoliated areas of sheepskin caused by rubbing or scraping of the skin on fence posts. Brain tissue studied in scrapie-infected animals contained two forms of prion protein (PrP); one form was sensitive to protease digestion, and the other form was a protease-resistant isoform designated *PrPsc* (scrapie). The normal isoform (protein configuration) of PrP, designated *PrPc*, is predominantly present on cell surfaces of uninfected animals and is rapidly synthesized and degraded in vitro. The secondary protein structure of PrPc contains only 3 percent sheeting. The abnormal form, PrPsc, in contrast, is primarily found in infected vesicles, contains 43 percent sheeting in its secondary protein structure and is slowly synthesized and degraded in vitro.[4] The secondary protein structure is important in understanding mechanisms to inactivate or denature the protein.

Purification of PrPsc from the brains of scrapie-infected animals allowed the amino acid sequence of the protein to be determined and subsequently the mapping of the *PrP* gene.[5] The *PrP* gene has been located on the short arm of human chromosome 20 and a homologous region of the mouse chromosome 2.[6] The *PrP* gene is closely linked to genes that control the incubation time to onset of disease in scrapie-infected mice and confirms that PrP plays a crucial role in prion disease development.

PrPsc accumulates in the cells primarily in cytoplasmic vacuoles and lysosomes. It arises from a posttranslational conversion of normal PrPc to the abnormal isoform after an infectious dose of PrPsc has been introduced into the brain.[7] Studies indicate that when PrPsc is introduced into the brain, it disseminates by slowly spreading within the axons of nerve cells and accumulating within cells.[8] PrPc and PrPsc molecules bind together to convert the normal PrPc to the abnormal PrPsc isoform. When introduced into the brain, PrPsc replicates; many models of prion replication have been put forward.[9] As PrPsc interacts with PrPc and causes an unfolding and refolding of the protein conformation, an exponential conversion of PrPc to PrPsc occurs. The cascade of accumulations of the replicated abnormal PrPsc results in neuronal dysfunction by a process not yet clearly defined.

Mutations in the *PrP* gene are responsible for inherited human prion diseases, including familial CJD, GSS syndrome, and fatal familial insomnia.[10] More than 20 different mutations have been identified, including a common mutation on a lysine-for-glutamic acid substitution in codon 200. Recently, it was discovered that a polymorphism of methionine/valine on codon

129 created distinctive histopathological lesion profiles that determined the clinical course of those affected with variant forms of CJD (vCJD).[11]

CHARACTERISTICS OF CREUTZFELDT-JAKOB DISEASE

CJD occurs naturally in either of two forms: the sporadic type (occurring at a rate of 1 case per 1 million population) and the familial type due to a genetic mutation that can be passed from generation to generation and has been documented in geographical clusters in various parts of the world.[61] Most recorded cases are of the sporadic type (85 to 95 percent), but the bulk of available knowledge of the pathogenesis of CJD and the role of the *PrP* gene has come from studies done on the familial cases. Iatrogenic CJD also has occurred, caused by introduction of prion-laden tissue (transplanted or extracted from diseased individuals) into the brain or body of an otherwise healthy patient or by the use of contaminated medical (neurosurgical) equipment during an invasive procedure or surgery. This condition has occurred when tissue transplants (dura mater, pericardium, and cornea) have been taken from patients with unsuspected CJD at the time of death and used as donor organs/tissue in transplantation procedures. Pooled pituitary hormone preparations (growth hormone and gonadotropin) harvested from cadavers have also contributed to many iatrogenic CJD cases.[12] Contaminated surgical equipment or implantation of electrodes deep in the brain can also transmit infectious prions from one patient to another.

Sporadic CJD has no gender restrictions and occurs at a mean onset of 50 to 70 years of age. Earlier onset of symptoms is more characteristic of new, variant forms of CJD (vCJD), which have been associated with consuming contaminated meat products or iatrogenic sources of infection in which large inoculum size may influence onset of symptoms. The classic disease occurs as a rapid and progressive dementia with several distinctive clinical manifestations, including ataxia, myoclonic seizures, visual or sensory deficits, abnormal psychiatric behavior, and coordination deficits. Mental deterioration of the patient occurs rapidly. The average time frame from onset of symptoms to time of death is 7 to 9 months. Patients with CJD may show abnormalities on electroencephalogram. A characteristic pattern consisting of a slow background of waves with generalized bilateral synchronized biphasic or triphasic periodic sharp wave complexes is present in 67 to 95 percent of patients.[13]

Definitive diagnosis of CJD is made by direct examination of the brain tissue. The observation of neuronal loss, reactive gliosis, and neuronal vacuolation (spongiform appearance) with an absence of inflammatory cells is consistent with the diagnosis of CJD.[14] Routine diagnostic tests are rarely of value in making a diagnosis of CJD. Cerebrospinal fluid (CSF) from patients with suspected CJD is usually found to be acellular with normal glucose levels and protein that may be slightly elevated. Some patients have been found to have elevated serum protein levels of S100 protein.[15] Proteins that are found specifically in the

CSF may be more useful in diagnosing CJD, however. One such specific protein is called the *14–3-3 protein*, for which Western blot assays have been developed. The 14–3-3 protein has been reported in 95 percent of patients with sporadic CJD and less frequently with familial CJD.[16] Elevations of this protein also can be seen in patients with herpes encephalitis, metabolic encephalopathy, intracerebral metastatic cancer, and hypoxic encephalopathy, resulting in some degree of false positivity when the test is used. Computed tomography (CT) scans and magnetic resonance imaging (MRI) also have been used to detect abnormalities in patients with rapidly progressive dementia, but the exact sensitivity and specificity of these tests have not been well established for CJD. A CT scan shows cerebral atrophy in CJD as opposed to cerebellar atrophy. MRI utilizing diffusion weight (DWI) and fluid attenuated inversion recovery (FLAIR) images have been shown to have a sensitivity of >90 percent in detecting characteristic changes in the basal ganglia thalamus and cortex. Radiologists who are not familiar with changes noted in CJD may miss subtle changes that are primarily seen within the cortex or perceive lesions as artifact.[17] Immunological tests (monoclonal and polyclonal antibodies) for PrPsc have proved to be sensitive and specific in brain tissue that is obtained at autopsy or by brain biopsy.[62]

In 1997, the National Prion Disease Pathology Surveillance Center was established at Case Western Reserve University to provide a variety of diagnostic tests to aid in the confirmation of CJD and to perform surveillance activity for prion disease in the United States. The center performs Western blot assays on brain tissue, immunohistochemical tests for PrP on fixed tissue, analysis of DNA extracted from blood or brain, and analysis of CSF for 14–3-3 protein.

OTHER PRION DISEASES

Gerstmann-Sträussler-Scheinker Syndrome

GSS syndrome is a genetically transmitted prion disease due to an autosomal dominant type of inheritance. The disease occurs at a rate of 1 to 10 cases per 100 million population per year, making it an extremely rare disease. The mean onset of the disease is 43 to 48 years with an average of 5 years' duration of clinical illness. The most striking feature of the disease is progressive spinocerebellar degeneration and accompanying dementia.[18] Impairment of the individual affects intelligence, memory, attention, and cognitive thinking skills. Clinical findings include ataxia, tremors, spasticity, nystagmus, and dysarthria. Laboratory tests for GSS syndrome generally are not helpful. Definitive diagnosis of the disease requires visual examination of the brain tissue and findings of amyloid plaques detected primarily in the cerebellum.

Fatal Familial Insomnia

Fatal familial insomnia (FFI) is one of the newer prion entities to be described. This disease also is transmitted genetically through autosomal dominance. The characteristic feature of the disease is the presentation of insomnia with dysautonomia, tachycardia, hypertension, and motor deficits and changes that include spasticity,

hyperreflexia, and dysarthria. Patients can have hallucinations, memory problems, and confusion.[14] The mean onset of the disease is in middle age (35 to 61 years old) with duration of the course of disease approximately 13 months until death.

New Variant Creutzfeldt-Jakob Disease

In 1995, it was recognized that patients significantly younger than 50 years of age were diagnosed with symptoms similar to CJD. Thirty-nine cases of vCJD were described in British medical journals in 1997 and 1998.[19,20] The patients had a mean age of onset of 29 years (range, 16 to 48 years), and the duration of illness was approximately 14 months (longer than sporadic CJD). In contrast with classic CJD cases, these patients had sensory and psychiatric deficits and disturbances. Their symptoms included pain, dysesthesias, and paresthesias of the face, hands, feet, and legs. Psychiatric manifestations included depression, psychosis, and anxiety and resultant weight loss, withdrawal, apathy, and personality change. Auditory hallucinations were noted in several cases. Definitive diagnosis of vCJD can be made only from direct examination of the brain tissue. Patients with CJD may have PrPsc detectable in lymphoid tissue. The pathological characteristics of the disease are different from sporadic or classic CJD. The vCJD cases sampled at autopsy showed spongiform changes and amyloid plaques distributed throughout the cerebellum. The plaques had dense eosinophilic centers and pale peripheries upon being stained for PrPsc.[19]

When subjected to electrophoresis, PrPsc from vCJD cases has mobility patterns distinct from sporadic CJD and more similar to the PrPsc from BSE cases.[21] It has been proposed that vCJD is the result of bovine-to-human transmission of BSE. This suggestion is based on the observation that cases of vCJD were described after large outbreaks of BSE in the United Kingdom when infected cattle may have been introduced into the marketplace. It is speculative how many individuals will develop vCJD in the United Kingdom and in other countries where epidemics of BSE have occurred. The incidence of CJD cases in the United Kingdom increased from 3 in 1995 to 28 in 2000 with many deaths.[22]

In 2002, the first case of vCJD was reported in the United States by the Florida State Health Department.[23] The patient had lived in the United Kingdom from 1980 to 1992 and was likely exposed to BSE during that time. Since that time, two additional cases have been reported in the United States; one patient was born and raised in the United Kingdom, and the other case had been exposed to BSE-contaminated cattle products in Saudi Arabia. Since 1996 (current to June 28, 2012), 227 vCJD cases have been reported within 12 countries. Of the 227 cases, 182 cases had resided in either the United Kingdom or alternatively in France (27 cases). Information on the vCJD cases can be found at http://www.cdc.gov/ncidod/dvrd/vcjd/factsheet_nvcjd.htm.

Blood and Organ Donation

As global travel expands, it is increasingly likely that European citizens with BSE will seek medical treatment in the United States. Travel history and time spent living in countries where

BSE has been diagnosed have become part of screening tools used to determine if a patient is considered a high-risk candidate for surgery or blood and organ donation. Persons who resided in or traveled to the United Kingdom for 6 months or more between 1980 and 1996 are not permitted to donate blood or plasma in the United States.[24] Information about blood eligibility in the United States is found on the website of the American Red Cross: Giving Blood: Blood Eligibility Guidelines (http://www.redcrossblood.org/donating-blood/eligibility -requirements/eligibility-criteria-alphabetical-listing#arc3).

TRANSMISSION OF PRION DISEASES

Prion diseases are not spread person to person, and in general patients with prion diseases can be cared for by healthcare personnel and family members without risk of transmission of infectious particles. Iatrogenic cases of prion disease have occurred as the result of direct inoculation of prion particles into the brain or spinal cord of patients undergoing procedures in the hospital. Contaminated surgical equipment or electrodes in the brain also have transmitted infectious prions from one patient to another. In these instances, standard sterilization/ disinfection methods have been inadequate.

It is very important that patients who are known or suspected to have prion disease are identified before any surgical procedure involving tissues that may be infectious. Instruments used in these cases will require special processing; environmental cleaning and disinfecting in surgery and laboratory settings will require procedures that will inactivate prions; and disposal of contaminated waste will require special handling. Specifics can be found in the CJD in Patient-Care Areas section of the Healthcare Infection Control Practices Advisory Committee's 2003 guidelines for environmental infection control in health-care facilities[25] (http://www.cdc.gov/mmwr/preview/mmwrhtml /rr5210a1.htm).

Outside of the hospital, prion transmission can occur by an oral route or by ingestion of infectious particles. This route of transmission is not an efficient one but may be effective if repeated doses of prion particles are introduced through multiple feedings. Ingestion is the characteristic route of transmission for kuru, and the implied route for vCJD, and is most likely responsible for other spongiform encephalopathies common among animal species. Transmission of prion particles in animals may be limited by a species barrier that depends on the homology of the prions and the ability of the PrPsc to interact with the PrPc.[22] Humans seem to be susceptible to animal encephalopathies, however, as in the case of hunters ingesting infected organs and meat from wild animals (squirrels or elk) during hunting season and developing disease.[26]

In the healthcare setting, risk of transmission to patients has been associated with direct contact with infectious tissues. A hierarchy of infectivity of various tissues in the healthcare setting has been suggested by Rutala.[26] Table 73-1 provides a comparison of the World Health Organization (WHO) infectivity categories to those suggested by Rutala and Weber.[27]

Tissues known to be highly infectious include brain, dura mater, pituitary tissue, spinal cord, and eye; tissues of low infectivity include lung, liver, kidney, spleen, lymph nodes, and CSF. No known risk of transmission is associated with contact with blood. No known infectivity has been detected in heart, skeletal muscle, peripheral nerves, adipose tissue, gingival tissue, intestine, adrenal gland, thyroid, prostate, or testes, or in bodily secretions or excretions such as sweat, tears, saliva, phlegm (sputum), stool, urine, semen, and breast milk. Risk assessment and prevention of exposure through the use of personal protective equipment and disposable equipment are the best means to reduce any risk of transmission in the healthcare setting.

Iatrogenic transmission within the healthcare setting can occur when patients are exposed directly to infectious prion materials via inadequately sterilized neurosurgical equipment, contaminated lyophilized dura mater, corneal transplants, cortical electroencephalogram electrodes, and injections of cadaveric pituitary-derived growth hormone.[22] A 2003 Centers for Disease Control and Prevention (CDC) report summarized 97 cases of iatrogenic transmission of CJD in Japan related to receipt of dura mater grafts from cadavers. The vehicle of transmission was a single brand of dural graft (Lyodura; B. Braun Melsungen AG, Melsungen, Germany) produced in Germany before May 1987.[28] A recent update of the related cases of CJD identified through surveillance by the Japanese Ministry of Health and Welfare that were associated with use of this graft material has brought the total number of cases to 132.[29] All the patients had received dura mater grafts between 1978 and 1993 for tumors, brain hemorrhage, trigeminal neuralgia treatment, intracranial aneurysm, hematoma from trauma, unspecified anomalies, and ossification of the spinal posterior longitudinal ligament. Illness onset occurred from 1985 to 2006, with the incubation period ranging from 1.2 to 24.8 years with a median and mean incubation of 12.4 and 11.8 years, respectfully. The first case of CJD associated with a Lyodura graft was reported in the United States, and the company actively worked with authorities to revise collection and processing of the graft material to reduce the risk of prion transmission.

No known transmission of sporadic CJD by blood has been documented. However, since December 2003, four transfusion-related cases of vCJD have been described.[30,31] In some countries affected by BSE outbreaks, blood products are leukodepleted because of the potential transmissibility of vCJD through lymphoreticular tissues.[32] The risk of acquiring CJD after any surgery has also been studied, and the risk for acquisition of sporadic CJD is actually noted to be slightly higher after general surgical procedures than neurological surgery.[33]

Healthcare personnel are hypothetically at risk for work-related exposures when they may have been exposed to high-risk tissues. There are reported incidences of a pathologist, two neurosurgeons, an orthopedic research physician, nurses, and histology technicians who have been diagnosed with CJD, but these have occurred at the same incidence as in the general population.[34,35] Among healthcare personnel, an incidence of disease of 1 to 1.8 per 1 million healthcare personnel is considered to be

Table 73-1. Transmissible Spongiform Encephalopathy and Tissue Infectivity: A Comparison of World Health Organization Infectivity Categories* to Rutala and Weber Recommendations**

WHO Categories[†]	Rutala and Weber Categories[‡]	WHO Tissues, Secretions, Excretions by Infectivity Category	Rutala and Weber Tissues, Organs, Body Fluids by Risk Category
High infectivity	High risk—from a high-risk patient[§]	Brain, spinal cord, retina, optic nerve, spinal ganglia, trigeminal ganglia, pituitary gland, dura mater	Posterior eye, brain (including dura mater), spinal cord, pituitary tissue
Low infectivity	Low risk—from high-risk patient	Peripheral nerves, spleen, lymph node, tonsil, rectum, placenta, ovary, uterus, lung, liver, kidney, cornea, blood, CSF	CSF, kidney, liver, lung, lymph nodes, spleen, placenta, olfactory epithelium
No detectable infectivity	No risk tissues—from a high-risk patient	Adipose tissue Bile Bone/bone marrow Colostrum Cord blood Dental pulp Embryos Feces Fetus Gingival tissue Heart muscle Intestine Milk Nasal mucous Placenta fluids Prostate Saliva Semen Serous exudates Skeletal muscle Sweat Tears Tendon Testis Thyroid gland Trachea Urine	Adipose tissue Adrenal gland Blood (whole) Bone marrow Feces Gingival tissue Heart Intestine Leukocytes Breast Milk Peripheral nerve Placenta Prostate Saliva Semen Serum Skeletal muscle Sputum Sweat Tears Testis Thyroid gland Urine Vaginal secretions

Courtesy of Georgia P. Dash, RN, MS, CIC.

*World Health Organization (WHO). *WHO Tables on Tissue Infectivity in Transmissible Spongiform Encephalopathies*. WHO website. 2010. Available at: http://www.who.int/bloodproducts /tablestissueinfectivity.pdf?ua=1.

**Rutala WA, Weber DJ. SHEA guideline: Guideline for disinfection and sterilization of prion-contaminated medical instruments. *Infect Control Hosp Epidemiol* 2010;31(2):107–117.

[†]World Health Organization (WHO). WHO Guidelines on Tissue Infectivity in Transmissible Spongiform Encephalopathies. WHO website. 2006. Available at: http://www.who.int/bloodproducts/cs /TSEPUBLISHEDREPORT.pdf. Paragraph 4, page 117: "It is also important to understand that categories of infectivity are not the same as categories of risk, which require consideration not only of the level of infectivity in tissue, but also of the amount of tissue to which a person or animal is exposed, and the route by which infection is transmitted. For example, although the level of tissue infectivity (concentration of infectivity in tissue as reflected by titre) is the most important factor in estimating the risk of transmission by instrument cross-contamination during surgical procedures (e.g., neurosurgery versus general surgery), it is only one determinant of the risk of transmission by blood transfusions, in which a large amount of low-infectivity material is administered directly into the circulation, or the risk of transmission by food that, irrespective of high or low infectivity, involves the comparatively inefficient oral route of infection."

[‡]Rutala WA, Weber DJ. SHEA guideline: Guideline for disinfection and sterilization of prion-contaminated medical instruments. *Infect Control Hosp Epidemiol* 2010;31(2):108, Table 1. Comparative frequency of infectivity in organs, tissue and body fluids of humans with transmissible spongiform encephalopathies (Creutzfeldt-Jakob Disease). "Footnote a: high risk indicates a rate of transmission to inoculated animals of ≥50%; low risk indicates a rate of transmission to inoculated animals ≥10%–20% (except for lung tissue, for which transmission is 50%); no risk indicates a rate of transmission to inoculated animals of 0% (several tissues in this category had few tested specimens)."

[§]Rutala WA, Weber DJ. Creutzfeldt-Jakob disease: recommendations for disinfection and sterilization. *Clin Infect Dis* 2001;32:1352. "High risk patient-patient with suspected or known CJD."

expected. Even a hypothetical risk necessitates that an awareness of potential for transmission and use of precautions and barriers is appropriate. Standard Precautions should be used when handling items contaminated with high-risk tissues from patients with confirmed or suspected disease, and those items should be labeled "biohazardous" or "Prion Precautions." Attention should be focused on avoiding needlestick exposures, splashes into mucous membranes, and scalpel injuries when high-risk tissues are being handled or encountered. Disposable equipment should be used for invasive procedures, such as lumbar punctures and CSF specimen collection, whenever possible.[36]

Because bovine and other animal products may be involved in the manufacture of biological and pharmaceutical products, such as animal feeds, vaccines, and bacterial and eukaryotic cell lines, care must be taken in the removal, processing, and handling of all tissues that could potentially be contaminated with spongiform encephalopathies, primarily vCJD, that could be transmitted to humans.[30]

METHODS FOR INACTIVATION OF THE CREUTZFELDT-JAKOB DISEASE AGENT

Prion diseases such as CJD represent a unique infection prevention problem because prions exhibit an unusual resistance to conventional chemical and physical decontamination methods. Because CJD is not readily inactivated by conventional disinfection and sterilization procedures, and because of the invariably fatal outcome of CJD, the procedures for disinfection and sterilization of the CJD prion have been conservative and controversial. Recommendations to prevent transmission of infectious prions from contaminated medical devices have been based primarily on prion inactivation studies.

Disinfection and Sterilization

Recommendations for the cleaning and sterilization of instruments used on patients with suspected or confirmed CJD have been provided by the WHO.[36] The recommendations from the WHO are based on exposure to highly infectious material (brain, spinal cord, and eyes) versus low-infectivity tissues (CSF, kidneys, liver, lungs, lymph nodes, spleen, and placenta). The final recommendations on sterilization and disinfection came from studies that intentionally contaminated equipment with brain tissue or tissue homogenates from patients with CJD and tested tissue for prion log decrease. In contrast with routine hospital protocol, no precleaning procedures (enzymatic or detergent/decontamination treatment) were done. Precleaning normally reduces microbial contamination by 4 logs.[26] The major intent of sterilization is the further log reduction of prion particles to a negligible number because prions are resistant to conventional sterilization processes. Variables in the disinfection studies done included the prion strain, prion concentration, test tissue, test animal, duration of follow-up, method of calculating the log decrease of the prion with disinfection, and exposure conditions. All studies have shown, however, that the TSE agents are difficult to inactivate.[37] No studies reflect reprocessing procedures in a clinical setting.

Another component that must be integrated into the disinfection and sterilization process is the risk of infection associated with the use of the medical device. Medical devices are categorized as *critical, semicritical,* or *noncritical.* All critical and semicritical instruments/equipment can be exposed to potentially infectious material (high-risk and low-risk tissue). Critical items are items that enter sterile tissue or the vascular system and include surgical instruments and implants. Semicritical items have contact with mucous membranes or nonintact skin (e.g., endoscopes and respiratory therapy equipment). Noncritical items (e.g., floors, walls, blood pressure cuffs, and furniture) come in contact with intact skin but not with mucous membranes. Intact skin should act as an effective barrier to microorganisms and prions.

Conventional sterilization methods are not acceptable for critical and semicritical items that have contact with high-risk tissue (e.g., brain) from a high-risk patient (e.g., with suspected or known CJD), and they must be reprocessed in a manner to ensure the elimination of prions or be disposable. The combined contribution of cleaning and use of an effective physical or chemical reprocessing procedure should eliminate the risk of CJD transmission. Critical or semicritical instruments or medical devices that have contact with low-risk or no-risk tissue can be treated by means of conventional methods because the devices have not resulted in transmission of CJD.

Effectiveness of Disinfection or Sterilization Procedures

The reduction of infectious units, defined in the literature as the $\log_{10}$ lethal dose $(LD)_{50}/g$ of infectious material, occurring during the disinfection or sterilization process is referred to as the *inactivation* or *removal factor*.[38-40] The probability of an instrument remaining capable of transmitting disease depends on the initial degree of contamination and the effectiveness of decontamination procedures. An instrument contaminated with 50 mg of brain tissue from a person infected with CJD and with a titer of 1×10^5 (50 percent LD intracerebral units/g) would have 5×10^3 infectious units of prion.[41] It has been suggested that a titer loss of 10^4 prions should be regarded as an indication of appropriate disinfection of CJD.[40] The effectiveness of a disinfection or sterilization procedure should be considered, however, in conjunction with the effectiveness of cleaning. Studies done with microbial agents show that cleaning according to the conventional methods used in current healthcare practice results in a reduction of 10^4 infectious units. Cleaning followed by disinfection would result in a reduction of 10^7 infectious units (4-log reduction with cleaning plus a >3-log reduction due to effective sterilization). If tissues with high prion infectivity (e.g., brain) are contaminated with 10^5 prions/g, cleaning followed by use of a sterilization procedure should eliminate infectivity and provide a significant margin of safety.

Disinfection

Prions exhibit an unusual resistance to conventional chemical and physical decontamination methods. Most disinfectants are inadequate for the elimination of prion infectivity. Antimicrobial agents that have been shown to be ineffective (<3 log reduction in 1 hour) against CJD or other TSEs are listed in Table 73-2.[38-40,42-47] A formic acid soaking is required for inactivation of prion infectivity in tissue specimens obtained from patients with CJD.[48] Formic acid causes the prion proteins to unfold and inactivate.

There are four chemicals that reduce the titer of infectious units by greater than 4 logs: chlorine, phenol, guanidine thiocyanate, and sodium hydroxide.[38-40,42,43,49-52] Of these chemical compounds, the disinfectant that is readily available and that provides the most consistent prion inactivation results is chlorine.[42] The corrosive nature of chlorine makes it unsuitable, however, for semicritical devices, such as endoscopes. Flexible and rigid endoscopes have been used in brain surgery.[53,54] If these endoscopes come into contact with high-risk tissue in a patient with known or suspected CJD, either the scopes should undergo sterilization (if possible) or single-use devices should be used. Endoscopes that come into contact with other tissues (e.g., from the gastrointestinal tract, respiratory tract, joints, and abdomen) can be disinfected by conventional methods. Table 73-3 provides a comparison of recommendations for disinfection and sterilization of instruments/equipment used for patients with suspected/known TSE noting the WHO guidelines and those outlined by Rutala and Weber. This table provides its own citations for convenience of the reader in evaluating the comparisons.

Table 73-2. Ineffective or Unreliable Methods of Eliminating Infectivity

Acetone
Ethanol
Glutaraldehyde
Ortho-phthalaldehyde
Peroxidate
Ammonia
Hydrochloric acid
Phenolics
Chlorine dioxide
Ethylene oxide
Hydrogen peroxide
Potassium permanganate
Detergents (unless specific formulation)
Formaldehyde
Iodophor
Radiation dry heat
Freezing
Peracetic acid
Routine steam sterilization
Microwave
UV light
Tego (dodecyl-di[aminoethyl]-glycine)
Sodium deoxycholate
Sodium dodecyl sulfate

Sterilization

Although there is some disagreement about the ideal time and temperature cycle,[55] the recommendations of 121°C to 132°C for 60 minutes (gravity) and of 134°C for 18 minutes or more (prevacuum) are reasonable on the basis of the scientific literature. These methods should result in a decrease of greater than 5 logs, and adequate cleaning should result in an additional 4-log reduction, which provides a significant margin of safety (brain tissue concentration 10^5 prions/g).[41] Other steam sterilization cycles, such as 132°C for 15 minutes (gravity), have been shown to be only partially effective.[42]

Unacceptable sterilization processes for adequate prion log reduction include gaseous (i.e., ethylene oxide) and physical (e.g., dry heat, boiling, and autoclaving at conventional exposure conditions at 121°C for 15 minutes) processes.[39,42,43,56] Standard gravity displacement steam sterilization at 121°C has been studied with different strains of CJD, BSE, and scrapie and has been shown to be only partially effective, even after exposure times of 120 minutes. As the temperature and exposure time was increased, greater inactivation of the prion agents was achieved.

Several investigators have found that combining sodium hydroxide (0.09 N for 2 hours) with steam sterilization at 121°C

for 1 hour results in complete inactivation of infectivity (>7.4 logs).[52,56] However, the use of this mechanism of sterilization in healthcare facilities is problematic because the combination of sodium hydroxide and steam sterilization may be deleterious to surgical instruments and is potentially dangerous to employees exposed to noxious fumes.

Guidelines for Reprocessing Medical Devices Potentially Contaminated with Creutzfeldt-Jakob Disease[22,55,57,58]

High-risk Tissues from High-risk Patients (with Known or Suspected Creutzfeldt-Jakob Disease) and Critical or Semicritical Items

1. Devices that are constructed so that cleaning procedures result in effective tissue removal (e.g., surgical instruments) can be cleaned and sterilized by autoclaving either at 134°C for 18 minutes or longer in a prevacuum sterilizer or at 132°C for 1 hour in a gravity displacement sterilizer.

2. Devices that can be cleaned should be reprocessed by standard published protocols. Place the contaminated items in a container filled with a liquid (e.g., saline, water, or phenolic solution) to retard adherence of organic material to the medical device. Remove any liquids before continuing to the next step, which is an initial decontamination done in an autoclave using 134°C for 18 minutes in a prevacuum sterilizer or 132°C for 1 hour in a gravity displacement sterilizer, or by soaking in 1 N sodium hydroxide for 1 hour. Terminal cleaning, wrapping, and sterilization can be done by conventional means. Devices that cannot be cleaned or that are too difficult to clean should be discarded.

3. To minimize drying of tissues and body fluids on the object, instruments should be kept moist until cleaned and decontaminated.

4. Flash sterilization should not be used for reprocessing.

5. Items that permit only low-temperature sterilization (e.g., ethylene oxide or hydrogen peroxide gas plasma) should be discarded.

6. Contaminated items that are not processed according to these recommendations (e.g., medical devices used for brain biopsy before diagnosis) should be recalled and appropriately reprocessed. To minimize patient exposure to neurosurgical instruments from a patient who is later given a diagnosis of CJD, hospitals should consider using the aforementioned sterilization guidelines for neurosurgical instruments used on all patients undergoing brain biopsy. Alternatively, neurosurgical instruments used in such cases could be disposable.

7. Environmental surfaces (noncritical) contaminated with high-risk tissues (e.g., laboratory surface in contact with brain tissue of a person infected with CJD) should be cleaned and then spot-decontaminated with a 1:10 dilution of sodium hypochlorite (i.e., bleach) for a contact time of 15 minutes. To minimize environmental contamination, disposable cover sheets could be used on work surfaces.

Table 73-3. WHO Infection Control Guidelines for Transmissible Spongiform Encephalopathies versus Rutala and Weber Creutzfeldt-Jakob Disease: Recommendations for Disinfection and Sterilization

Patient Category	Tissue Risk Category	Medical Device Category[1]	Options for Instrument Disinfection/Sterilization		Concurrence of WHO Guidelines with Rutala/Weber Recommendations
			WHO Heat-resistant Instrument Options[3]	Rutala/Weber Heat-resistant Instrument Recommendations[4]	
Confirmed or Suspected Cases of TSE	High Risk/Infectivity	Critical & Semicritical	**NB. WHO states:** "Although CSF is classified as a low infectivity tissue and is less infectious than high infectivity tissues instruments contaminated by CSF should be handled in the same manner as those contacting high infectivity tissues."[2] Incineration is the preferred method for all instruments exposed to high infectivity tissues.	No recommendation for incineration of reusable instruments. Instruments that cannot be cleaned may be discarded or subjected to alternate methods of decontamination/sterilization.	No
				Mechanically clean devices that are constructed so that cleaning procedures result in effective tissue removal. Instruments should be kept moist until cleaned and decontaminated. Cleaning of instruments in a washer-disinfector is acceptable. Decontamination should occur as soon as possible. After the device is clean, it should be sterilized by either autoclaving (i.e. steam sterilization) or using a combination of sodium hydroxide and autoclaving.	Partial
			Surgical instruments that are going to be reused may be mechanically cleaned in advance of subjecting to decontamination/sterilization. Instruments should be kept moist to prevent tissue adherence. Instruments to be cleaned in automated mechanical processors must be decontaminated before processing through these machines and the washers (or other equipment) should be run through an empty cycle before any further routine use.		
	Rutala/Weber Considers CSF as low risk and originally did not recommend handling instruments contaminated with CSF in the same manner that instruments contaminated with high-risk tissues were handled. Now more consistent with WHO and other entities.		WHO Option # 6 (see below) agrees with Rutala/Weber Option # 1 with regard to cleaning instruments and sterilizing by autoclaving at 134°C for ≥18 min in a prevacuum sterilizer; no mention is made of cleaning alone followed by gravity displacement sterilizer at 121° to 132°C.	**Rutala/Weber Option # 1:** Devices that are constructed so that cleaning procedures result in effective tissue removal (e.g., surgical instruments) can be cleaned and then sterilized by autoclaving at 134°C for ≥18 min in a prevacuum sterilizer or at 121° to 132°C for 1 hour in a gravity displacement sterilizer.	Partial
			WHO Option # 1: Immerse in sodium hydroxide (1 N NAOH which is 40 g of NAOH in 1 liter of water) and heat in a gravity displacement autoclave at 121°C for 30 min; clean, rinse in water, and subject to routine sterilization.	No recommendation for immersing in NAOH and simultaneously heating in a gravity displacement autoclave.	No
			WHO Option # 2: Immerse in sodium hydroxide (1N NAOH) or sodium hypochlorite (20,000 ppm available chlorine; common commercial formulation of bleach is 5.25 percent sodium hypochlorite to attain 20,000 ppm and 1 part bleach plus 1.5 parts water should be used) for 1 hour; transfer instruments to water; heat in a gravity displacement autoclave at 121°C for 1 hour; clean and subject to routine sterilization.	No recommendation for first immersing in 1N NAOH or sodium hypochlorite (20,000 ppm) followed by higher sterilization temperatures for extended times. No recommendations for the use of sodium hypochlorite.	No
			WHO Option # 3: Immerse in 1N NAOH or sodium hypochlorite (20,000 ppm) for 1 hour; remove and rinse in water; then transfer to open pan and heat in a gravity displacement autoclave at 121°C or a porous load (prevacuum) autoclave at 134°C for 1 hour; clean and subject to routine sterilization.	No recommendation for first immersing in 1N NAOH or sodium hypochlorite (20,000 ppm) followed by higher sterilization temperatures for extended times. No recommendations for the use of sodium hypochlorite. No recommendation for prevacuum autoclave for 1 hour, recommended time is ≥18 min.	No
			WHO Option # 4: Immerse in 1N NAOH and boil for 10 min at atmospheric pressure; clean, rinse in water, and subject to routine sterilization.	No recommendation for immersing in 1N NAOH and boiling.	No

		WHO Heat Sensitive Instruments Options[6]	Rutala/Weber Heat Sensitive Instrument Recommendations[7]	Concurrence of WHO Guidelines with Rutala/Weber Recommendations
		WHO Option # 5: Immerse in sodium hypochlorite (20,000 ppm available chlorine) (preferred) or 1N NAOH (alternative) at ambient temperature for 1 hour; clean; rinse in water, and subject to routine sterilization. Alternative of immersion in 1N NAOH for 1 hour followed by routine sterilization is congruent with Rutala/Weber Option # 2.	**Rutala/Weber Option # 2:** Devices that are impossible or difficult to clean should be discarded. No recommendation for immersion in sodium hypochlorite.	Partial
		WHO Option # 6: Autoclave at 134°C for 18 min (in worse case scenarios; e.g., brain tissue bake-dried onto surfaces) infectivity will be largely but not completely removed.[5]	Only those instruments that are constructed so that cleaning procedures result in effective tissue removal are recommended for cleaning followed by prevacuum autoclaving at 134°C for >18 min. Instruments that are impossible or difficult to clean should be discarded.	No
Confirmed or Suspected Cases of TSE	**High Risk/Infectivity** Eye, brain, spinal cord NB: WHO includes CSF, Rutala/Weber do not include CSF	**Critical & Semicritical** **WHO Recommendation:** Complex and expensive instruments that cannot be subjected to the recommendations for heat-resistant instruments should, to the extent possible, be protected from surface contamination. Those parts of the instrument that come into contact with internal tissues of patients should be subjected to the most effective decontaminating procedure that can be tolerated by the instrument. All adherent material must be removed and, if possible, the exposed surfaces cleaned using a decontamination method recommended in Annex III of the WHO recommendations. WHO recommendations in Annex III entitled, Chemical methods for surfaces and heat sensitive instruments state: flood with 2N NAOH or undiluted sodium hypochlorite; let stand for 1 hour; mop up and rinse with water. Where surfaces cannot tolerate NAOH or hypochlorite, thorough cleaning will remove most infectivity by dilution and some additional benefit may be derived from the use of one or another of the partially effective methods listed in Section 5.1. (Section 5.1 refers the reader to options 1-6 listed above.) No mention is made of utilization of low temperature sterilization methods (e.g., ethylene oxide or hydrogen peroxide gas plasma) after disinfection to sterilize critical or semicritical instruments.[8]	Items that permit only low–temperature sterilization (e.g., ethylene oxide or hydrogen peroxide gas plasma) should be discarded.	No

continued

Table 73-3. WHO Infection Control Guidelines for Transmissible Spongiform Encephalopathies versus Rutala and Weber Creutzfeldt-Jakob Disease: Recommendations for Disinfection and Sterilization (cont'd)

Patient Category	Tissue Risk Category	Medical Device Category	Options for Instrument Disinfection/Sterilization — WHO Recommendation Instruments Reused Prior to Appropriate Decontamination/Sterilization	Rutala/Weber Recommendation Instruments Reused Prior to Appropriate Decontamination/Sterilization	Concurrence of WHO Guidelines with Rutala/Weber Recommendations
Confirmed or Suspected Cases of TSE	High Risk/Infectivity Eye, brain, spinal cord NB: WHO includes CSF for decontamination purposes, Rutala/Weber do not include CSF AND Low Risk/Infectivity WHO: Kidney, liver, lung, lymph nodes, placenta, spleen Rutala/Weber: CSF, kidney, liver, lung, lymph nodes, spleen	Critical & Semicritical	"Decontamination and sterilization recommendations should be applied even if the instrument has been re-used before discovery of potential contamination"[9] Note: WHO does not distinguish whether this recommendation applies to only those instruments that came in contact with high-risk/infectivity tissue or low-risk tissue.	"Contaminated items that are not processed according to these recommendations (e.g., medical devices used for brain biopsy before diagnosis) should be recalled and appropriately reprocessed. Hospitals should consider using the aforementioned guidelines for neurosurgical instruments (heat resistant and heat sensitive) on patients undergoing brain biopsy when a specific lesion has not been demonstrated. Alternatively, neurosurgical instruments used in such cases could be disposable."[10] Note: This recommendation appears only in the recommendation section for critical and semicritical items used on high-risk tissue from patients with confirmed or suspected of CJD.	Partial
Confirmed or Suspected Cases of TSE	Low Risk/Infectivity WHO: Kidney, liver, lung, lymph nodes, placenta, spleen Rutala/Weber: CSF, kidney, liver, lung, lymph nodes, spleen	Critical & Semicritical	Options 1–6 listed above (found in WHO Infection Control Guidelines for Transmissible Spongiform Encephalopathies, Annex III) apply.[11]	These instruments/devices can be cleaned and either disinfected or sterilized by use of conventional protocols of heat or chemical sterilization or high level disinfection.[12]	No
Confirmed or Suspected Cases of TSE	No Risk/Infectivity See Table 1 for WHO and Rutala/Weber listing of No Risk/Infectivity tissues and body fluids	Critical & Semicritical	Routine cleaning and disinfection procedures.[13]	These devices/instruments can be cleaned and either disinfected or sterilized by means of conventional protocols of heat or chemical sterilization, or by means of high-level disinfection. Endoscopes (except neurosurgical endoscopes) would be contaminated only with no-risk materials, and thus, standard cleaning and high-level disinfection protocols would be adequate reprocessing.[14]	Yes
Confirmed or Suspected Cases of CJD	All tissue categories	Critical & Semicritical	Options 1–6 listed above (found in WHO Infection Control Guidelines for Transmissible Spongiform Encephalopathies, Annex III) apply.[15]	No distinction is made between vCJD and other TSEs with regard to cleaning/disinfection/sterilization recommendations.	No
Persons with known prior exposure to human pituitary derived hormones, cornea, or dura mater grafts	High Risk/Infectivity Eye, brain, spinal cord; WHO includes CSF Low Risk/Infectivity WHO: Kidney, liver, lung, lymph nodes, placenta, spleen No Risk/Infectivity	Critical & Semicritical	WHO Recommendations for High Risk/Infectivity: Options 1–6 listed above (found in WHO Infection Control Guidelines for Transmissible Spongiform Encephalopathies, Annex III) apply.[16] WHO Recommendations for Low Risk/Infectivity: routine cleaning and disinfection procedures.[17] WHO Recommendations for No Risk/Infectivity: routine cleaning and disinfection procedures.[18]	Address persons with suspected or confirmed TSEs, but do not address persons with known prior exposure to human pituitary derived hormones, cornea, or dura mater grafts who are not suspected or confirmed to have TSE.	Not addressed in Rutala/Weber recommendations
Members of families with heritable forms of TSE	High Risk/Infectivity Eye, brain, spinal cord WHO includes CSF Low Risk/Infectivity WHO: Kidney, liver, lung, lymph nodes, placenta, spleen No Risk/Infectivity	Critical & Semicritical	WHO Recommendations for High Risk/Infectivity: No consensus reached. The majority felt that the TSE decontamination Options 1–6 listed above (found in WHO Infection Control Guidelines for Transmissible Spongiform Encephalopathies, Annex III) should be used but a minority of WHO guidelines' authors felt this was unwarranted.[19] WHO Recommendations for Low Risk/Infectivity: routine cleaning and disinfection procedures.[20]	Address persons with suspected or confirmed TSEs, but do not address family members with heritable forms of TSE who are not suspected or confirmed to have TSE.	Not addressed in Rutala/Weber recommendations

WHO Recommendations for No Risk/Infectivity: routine cleaning and disinfection procedures.[21]

			WHO Recommendations for No Risk/Infectivity: routine cleaning and disinfection procedures.[21]		
Confirmed or Suspected Cases of TSE	High Risk/Infectivity Eye, brain, spinal cord WHO includes CSF	Noncritical equipment	WHO Recommendations: It is important to mechanically clean and disinfect equipment and surfaces that are subject to potential contamination. Surfaces that are contaminated by TSE agents can be disinfected by flooding for 1 hour, with NAOH or sodium hypochlorite, followed by water rinses (see Annex III), WHO recommendations in Annex III entitled, Chemical methods for surfaces and heat sensitive instruments state: "flood with 2N NAOH or undiluted sodium hypochlorite; let stand for 1 hour; mop up and rinse with water."[22] Note change in concentration of these agents.	Noncritical equipment contaminated with high-risk tissue (from confirmed or suspect case of TSE) should be cleaned then disinfected with a 1:10 dilution of sodium hypochlorite or 1N NAOH depending on material compatibility. All contaminated surfaces must be exposed to the disinfectant. Immersion time is not stated in recommendations section; however, studies cited in Rutala/Weber Recommendations, Table 3 (p. 1351) indicate 1-hour immersion in sodium hypochlorite (studies list variable ppm of available chlorine ranging from, 000–10,000 ppm) show a ≥3 log reduction of prions.[23]	No
Confirmed or Suspected Cases of TSE	High Risk/Infectivity Eye, brain, spinal cord WHO includes CSF	Noncritical environmental surfaces	WHO Recommendations: It is important to mechanically clean and disinfect equipment and surfaces that are subject to potential contamination. Surfaces that are contaminated by TSE agents can be disinfected by flooding for 1 hour, with NAOH or sodium hypochlorite, followed by water rinses (see Annex III). WHO recommendations in Annex III entitled, Chemical methods for surfaces and heat-sensitive instruments state: "flood with 2N NAOH or undiluted sodium hypochlorite; let stand for 1 hour; mop up and rinse with water." Note change in concentration of these agents.	"Environmental surfaces (noncritical) contaminated with high-risk tissues (e.g., laboratory surface in contact with brain tissue of a person infected with CJD) should be cleaned and then spot-decontaminated with a 1:10 dilution of sodium hypochlorite (i.e., bleach) for a contact time of at least 15 minutes."[24]	No
Confirmed or Suspected Cases of TSE	Low Risk/Infectivity WHO: Kidney, liver, lung, lymph nodes, placenta, spleen Rutala/Weber: CSF, kidney, liver, lung, lymph nodes, spleen	Noncritical environmental surfaces	WHO Recommendations: It is important to mechanically clean and disinfect equipment and surfaces that are subject to potential contamination. Surfaces that are contaminated by TSE agents can be disinfected by flooding for 1 hour, with NAOH or sodium hypochlorite, followed by water rinses (see Annex III). WHO recommendations in Annex III entitled, Chemical methods for surfaces and heat-sensitive instruments state: "flood with 2N NAOH or undiluted sodium hypochlorite; let stand for 1 hour; mop up and rinse with water." Note change in concentration of these agents.	"Environmental surfaces contaminated with low-risk tissues from a high-risk patient require only standard (use disinfectants recommended by OSHA for disinfection of blood contaminated surfaces) disinfection."[25]	No
Confirmed or Suspected Cases of TSE	No Risk/Infectivity	Noncritical environmental surfaces	WHO Recommendations: routine cleaning and disinfection procedures.	Rutala/Weber Recommendations: "Environmental surfaces contaminated with no-risk tissues or fluids require only standard disinfection (use disinfectants recommended by OSHA for decontamination of blood-contaminated surfaces (e.g., 1:10 to 1:100 dilution of 5.25 percent sodium hypochlorite)."[26]	Yes

Courtesy of Georgia P. Dash, RN, MS, CIC.

Medical Device Category: critical (enters sterile tissue or vascular system); semicritical (comes into contact with mucous membranes or skin that is not intact); noncritical (come in contact with intact skin).

1. World Health Organization (WHO). *WHO Infection Control Guidelines for Transmissible Spongiform Encephalopathies.* Report of WHO Consultation. Geneva, Switzerland: WHO, 1999: Section 3.5.1, p. 8.
2. Ibid, Annex III, p. 29.
3. Rutala WA, Weber DJ. Creutzfeldt-Jakob disease: recommendations for disinfection and sterilization. *Clin Infect Dis* 2001;32:1354–1355.
4. Ibid, p. 1352.
5. Op. Cit., WHO, Annex III, p. 14.
6. Op. Cit., Rutala WA, Weber DJ, p. 1354–1355.
7. Op. Cit., WHO, Annex III, p. 30.
8. Op. Cit., WHO, p. 14.
9. Op. Cit., Rutala WA, Weber DJ, p. 1355.
10. Op. Cit., WHO, Table 9, p. 16.
11. Op. Cit., Rutala WA, Weber DJ, p. 1355.
12. Op. Cit., WHO, Table 9, p. 16
13. Op. Cit., Rutala WA, Weber DJ, p. 1355.
14. 15–21. Op. Cit., WHO Table 9, p. 16.
15. 22. Op. Cit., WHO, Annex III, p. 30.
16. 23–26. Op. Cit., Rutala WA, Weber DJ, p. 1351.
17. Rutala WA, Weber DJ. SHEA guideline: Guideline for disinfection and sterilization of prion-contaminated medical instruments. *Infect Control Hosp Epidemiol* 2010;31(2):107–117.

8. Noncritical equipment contaminated with high-risk tissue should be cleaned and disinfected with a 1:10 dilution of sodium hypochlorite or 1 *N* sodium hydroxide, depending on material compatibility. All contaminated surfaces must be exposed to the disinfectant.

9. Equipment that requires special prion reprocessing should be identified after use. Clinicians and reprocessing technicians should be thoroughly trained on how to tag the equipment properly and the special prion reprocessing protocols.

10. For ease of cleaning and to minimize percutaneous injury and generation of aerosols, use nonpowered instruments (e.g., drills or saws) or ensure that disposable protective equipment covers are available for powered instruments.

Low-risk Tissues from a High-risk Patient and Critical or Semicritical Medical Devices

1. These devices can be cleaned and either disinfected or sterilized by use of conventional protocols of heat or chemical sterilization or high-level disinfection.

2. Environmental surfaces contaminated with low-risk tissues require only standard disinfectants recommended for bloodborne pathogens by the Occupational Safety and Health Administration (OSHA) for disinfection of blood-contaminated surfaces.

No-risk Tissues from a High-risk Patient and Critical or Semicritical Medical Devices

1. These devices can be cleaned and either disinfected or sterilized by means of conventional protocols of heat or chemical sterilization or by means of high-level disinfection.

2. Endoscopes (except neurosurgical endoscopes) would be contaminated only with no-risk materials, and standard cleaning and high-level disinfection protocols would be adequate for reprocessing.

3. Environmental surfaces contaminated with no-risk tissues or fluids require only standard disinfection (bloodborne pathogen approved) for decontamination of blood-contaminated surfaces (e.g., 1:10 to 1:100 dilution of 5.25 percent sodium hypochlorite). To minimize environmental contamination, disposable cover sheets could be used on work surfaces.

Unrecognized Potential Prion Exposures—Joint Commission Sentinel Event Alert

In 2001, the Joint Commission on Accreditation of Healthcare Organizations, now known as The Joint Commission, received reports of two separate incidents at accredited hospitals in which a total of 14 patients may have been exposed to CJD through instruments used during brain surgeries on patients with unsuspected cases of CJD and issued a Sentinel Event Alert.[59] Lessons learned from sentinel events include the following:

1. A patient with CJD or prion disease does not always present with symptoms of CJD.

2. The time interval between biopsy and pathology report should be monitored and reviewed to ensure the shortest time from biopsy to results.

3. Instruments used in brain biopsy procedures should not be reused when the patient's diagnosis is uncertain at the time of the procedure.

In 2003 one hospital reported an unsuspected case of CJD in a patient who had undergone a craniectomy in the prior year.[60] Operating room instruments were processed in typical fashion (steam sterilization at 270°F [132°C] for 4 minutes). Eleven months after the surgical procedure, the patient died and an autopsy confirmed CJD. When the diagnosis was confirmed, all operating room instruments underwent immediate prevacuum sterilization at 274°F (134°C) for 18 minutes. In the interim time period, however, the more than 3,600 neurosurgical patients who had undergone surgical procedures were considered to be potentially exposed by the state health department. The incident was fully disclosed to the public, and all patients who were potentially exposed were notified by letter. As a result of this occurrence, this institution mandated that all operating room instruments be routinely processed at 274°F (134°C) for 18 minutes. Potential CJD exposures after an unsuspected case can have an enormous emotional and financial impact. Routine use of extended processing can be implemented to help prevent unintentional CJD exposures. In the future, other large institutions may consider the extended processing in light of cases of prion diseases in the United States and increasing BSEs in Europe.

CONCLUSIONS

CJD and other prion diseases of humans and animals represent a unique form of infectious disease that continues to intrigue medical researchers. The number of cases of prion diseases, exclusive of CJD, may continue to increase as exposures from the past decades become manifest in the diseases of the future. The problems presented by the resistance of the physical properties of prion proteins to normal sterilization processes within the medical setting may be met by expanding the limits of technology and introducing new methods to meet the challenge of prion disease.

FUTURE TRENDS

As the number of cases of prion diseases continues to increase, there is the need for rapid diagnosis, treatment possibilities, and protection of patients through efficacious methods and ease of sterilization and disinfection.

INTERNATIONAL PERSPECTIVE

As past exposures become manifest in diseases of the future, concerns regarding CJD and other prion diseases will remain an international concern. Some of those specific concerns include the dura mater grafts in Japan and resultant cases, increased time and temperature settings in autoclaves manufactured in Europe, anticipated increasing numbers of cases, and unknown exposures in Europe with vCJD in the United Kingdom, in particular. The use of leukodepleted blood in some foreign countries as a CJD prevention activity demonstrates the level of international concern with prion disease.

REFERENCES

1. Rhodes R. *Deadly Feasts*. New York: Simon & Schuster, 1997.
2. Zigas V, Gajdusek DC. Kuru: clinical study of a new syndrome resembling paralysis agitans in natives of the Eastern Highlands of Australian New Guinea. *Med J Aust* 1957;2:745–754.
3. Master CL, Gajdusek DC, Gibbs CJ Jr. Creutzfeldt-Jakob virus isolations from the Gerstmann-Straussler-Scheinker syndrome. *Brain* 1981;108: 559–588.
4. Johnson RT. *Viral Infections of the Nervous System*, 2nd ed. Philadelphia: Lippincott-Raven, 1998.
5. Pruisner SB. Chemistry and biology of prions. *Biochemistry* 1992;31: 12277–12288.
6. Sparkes RS, Simon M, Cohn VH, et al. Assignment of the human and mouse prion protein genes to homologous chromosome. *Proc Natl Acad Sci U S A* 1986;83:7358–7362.
7. Basler K, Oesch B, Scott M, et al. Scrapie and cellular PrP isoforms are encoded by the same chromosomal gene. *Cell* 1986;46:417–428.
8. Kimberlin RH, Walker CA. Pathogenesis of mouse scrapie: evidence for neural spread of infection to the CNS. *J Gen Virol* 1980;51:183–187.
9. Weissmann C. A unified theory of prion propagation. *Nature* 1991;352: 679–683.
10. Hsiao KK, Pruisner SB. Inherited human prion diseases. *Neurology* 1990;40:1820–1827.
11. Edler J, Mollenhaeuer B, Heinemann U, et al. Movement disturbances in the differential diagnosis of Creutzfeldt-Jakob disease. *Mov Disord* 2009;24(3):350–356.
12. Frasier SD, Foley TP. Clinical review: Creutzfeldt-Jakob disease in recipients of pituitary hormones. *J Clin Endocrinol Metab* 1994;78:1277–1279.
13. Levy RS, Chiappa KH, Burke CJ, et al. Early evolution and incidence of electroencephalographic abnormalities in Creutzfeldt Jakob disease. *J Clin Neurophysiol* 1986;3:1–21.
14. Tyler KL. Prions and prion diseases of the central nervous system (transmissible neurodegenerative diseases). In: Mandell GL, Bennett JE, Dolin R, eds. *Principles and Practice of Infectious Diseases*. Philadelphia: Churchill Livingstone, 2000:1971–1985.
15. Otto M, Wiltfang J, Schultz E, et al. Diagnosis of Creutzfeldt-Jakob disease by measurement of S100 protein in serum: prospective case-control study. *BMJ* 1998;316:577–582.
16. Zerr I, Bodemer M, Gefeller O, et al. Detection of 14-3-3 protein in the cerebral spinal fluid supports the diagnosis of Creutzfeldt-Jakob disease. *Ann Neurol* 1998;43:32–40.
17. Carswell C, Thompson A, Lukic A, et al. MRI findings are often missed in the diagnosis of Creutzfeldt-Jakob disease. *BMC Neurol* 2012;153:1–5.
18. Farlow MR, Yee RD, Dlouhy SR, et al. Gerstmann-Straussler-Scheinker disease: extending the clinical spectrum. *Neurology* 1989;39(11):1446–1452.
19. Will RG, Ironside JW, Zeidler M, et al. A new variant of Creutzfeldt-Jakob disease in the UK. *Lancet* 1996;3347:921–925.
20. Zeidler M, Stewart GE, Barrachough C, et al. New variant Creutzfeldt-Jacob disease: neurological features and diagnostic tests. *Lancet* 1997;350:903–907.
21. Collinge J, Sidle KCL, Meads J, et al. Molecular analysis of prion strain variation and the aetiology of "new variant" CJD. *Nature* 1996;383:685–690.
22. Blatter T. Implications of prion diseases for neurosurgery. *Neurosurg Rev* 2002;25:195–203.
23. Probable variant Creutzfeldt-Jakob disease in a US resident—Florida, 2002. *MMWR Morb Mortal Wkly Rep* 2002;51:927–929.
24. Berger JR, Weismann E, Weisman B. Creutzfeldt-Jakob disease and eating squirrel brains. *Lancet* 1997;350:642.
25. Sehulster LM, Chinn RYW. Guidelines for environmental infection control in health-care facilities. Recommendations from CDC and the Healthcare Infection Control Practices Advisory Committee (HICPAC). *MMWR Recomm Rep* 2003;52(RR10):1–42.
26. Rutala W. APIC Guideline for selection and use of disinfectants. *Am J Infect Control* 1996;24:313–342.
27. Rutala WA, Weber DJ. Creutzfeldt-Jakob disease: recommendations for disinfection and sterilization. *Clin Infect Dis* 2001;32:1348–1356.
28. Centers for Disease Control and Prevention. Update: Creutzfeldt-Jakob disease associated with cadaveric dura mater grafts—Japan 1979-2003. *MMWR Morb Mortal Wkly Rep* 2003;52(48):1179–1181.
29. Centers for Disease Control and Prevention. Update: Creutzfeldt-Jakob disease associated with cadaveric dura mater grafts—Japan 1978-2008. *MMWR Morb Mortal Wkly Rep* 2008;5742:1152–1154.
30. World Health Organization (WHO). WHO Guidelines on Tissue Infectivity Distribution in Transmissible Spongiform Encephalopathies. WHO website. 2006. Available at: http://www.who.int/bloodproducts /TSEPUBLISHEDREPORT.pdf?ua=1.
31. Health Protection Agency United Kingdom. New case of transfusion associated cCJD in the United Kingdom. *Dis Rep CDR Wkly* 2006;16 (serial online).
32. Klein MS, Frigg R, Flechsig E, et al. A crucial role for B cells in neuroinvasive scrapie. *Nature* 1997;390:687–690.
33. Collins S, Law MG, Fletcher A, et al. Surgical treatment and risk of sporadic Creutzfeldt-Jakob disease: a case control study. *Lancet* 1999;353: 693–697.
34. Berger JR, David NJ. Creutzfeldt-Jakob disease in a physician: a review of the disorder in healthcare workers. *Neurology* 1993;43:205–206.
35. Mitrova EBG. Creutzfeldt-Jakob disease in health professionals in Slovakia. *Eur J Epidemiol* 2000;16:353–355.
36. World Health Organization (WHO). WHO Guidelines on Transmissible Spongiform Encephalopathies in relation to Biological and Pharmaceutical Products. WHO website. 2003. Available at: http://whqlibdoc.who.int /hq/2003/a85721.pdf.
37. Rohwer RG. Virus-like sensitivity of the scrapie agent to heat inactivation. *Science* 1984;223:600–602.
38. Brown P, Rohwer RG, Green EM, et al. Effect of chemicals, heat, and histopathologic processing on high-infectivity hamster-adapted scrapie virus. *J Infect Dis* 1982;145:683–687.
39. Brown P, Gibbs CJ, Amyx HL, et al. Chemical disinfection of Creutzfeldt-Jakob disease virus. *N Engl J Med* 1982;306:1279–1282.
40. Kimberlin RH, Walker CA, Millson GC, et al. Disinfection studies with two strains of mouse-passaged scrapie agent: guidelines for Creutzfeldt-Jakob and related agents. *J Neurol Sci* 1983;59:355–369.
41. Brown P, Gibbs CJ, Rodgers-Johnson P, et al. Human spongiform encephalopathy: the National Institutes of Health series of 300 cases of experimentally transmitted disease. *Ann Neurol* 1994;35:513–529.
42. Brown P, Rohwer RG, Gadjusek DC. Newer data on the inactivation of scrapie virus or Creutzfeldt-Jakob disease virus in brain tissue. *J Infect Dis* 1986;153:1145–1148.
43. Dickinson AG, Taylor DM. Resistance of scrapie agent to decontamination. *N Engl J Med* 1978;299:1413–1414.
44. Hartley EG. Action of disinfectants on experimental mouse scrapie. *Nature* 1967;213:1135.
45. Zobeley E, Flechsig E, Cozzio A, et al. Infectivity of scrapie prions bound to a stainless steel surface. *Mol Med* 1999;5:240–243.
46. Taylor DM. Resistance of scrapie agent to peracetic acid. *Vet Microbiol* 1991;27:19–24.
47. Tateishi J, Tashima T, Kitamoto T. Practical methods for chemical inactivation of Creutzfeldt-Jakob disease pathogen. *Microbiol Immunol* 1991;35:163–166.
48. Brown P, Wolff A, Gajdusek C. A simple and effective method for inactivating virus infectivity in formalin-fixed tissue samples from patients with Creutzfeldt-Jakob disease. *Neurology* 1990;40:887–890.
49. Taguchi F, Tamai Y, Uchida K, et al. Proposal for a procedure for complete inactivation of the Creutzfeldt-Jakob disease agent. *Arch Virol* 1991;119:297–301.
50. Taylor DM, Fraser H, McConnell I, et al. Decontamination studies with the agents of bovine spongiform encephalopathy and scrapie. *Arch Virol* 1994;139:313–326.
51. Manuelidis L. Decontamination of Creutzfeldt-Jakob disease and other transmissible agents. *J Neurovirol* 1997;3:62–65.
52. Ernst DR, Race RE. Comparative analysis of scrapie agent inactivation methods. *J Virol Methods* 1993;41:193–202.
53. Bauer BL, Hellwig D. Minimally invasive endoscopic neurosurgery: a survey. *Acta Neurochir Suppl (Wien)* 1994;61:1–12.
54. Perneczky A, Fries G. Endoscope-assisted brain surgery: part 1. evolution, basic concept, and current technique. *Neurosurgery* 1998;42:219–225.
55. Geertsma RE, van Asten JAAM. Sterilization of prions: requirements, complications, implication. *Zentralbl Steril* 1995;3:385–394.
56. Steelman VM. Activity of sterilization processes and disinfectants against prions (Creutzfeldt-Jakob disease agent). In: Rutala WA, ed. *Disinfection, Sterilization and Antisepsis in Health Care*. Champlain, NY: Polyscience Publications, 1997:255–271.
57. Rutala WA, Weber DJ. Management of equipment contaminated with the Creutzfeldt-Jakob disease agent. In: Rutala WA, ed. *Disinfection, Sterilization and Antisepsis*. Washington, DC: Association for Professionals in Infection Control and Epidemiology, 2001:167–172.
58. Rutala WA, Weber DJ. Creutzfeldt-Jakob disease: risks and prevention of nosocomial acquisition. *Infect Control Today* 2001;5:47–50.
59. The Joint Commission (TJC). Sentinel Event Alert—exposure to Creutzfeldt-Jakob disease. TJC website. 2001. Available at: http://www .jointcommission.org/sentinel_event_alert_issue_20_exposure_to _creutzfeldt-jakob_disease/.

60. Pokrywka M, Andro R, Bingham P, et al. Creutzfeld Jakob Disease (CJD): impact of an unsuspected case. University of Pittsburgh Medical Center, Pittsburgh, PA. Presented at the 13th Annual Meeting of the Society for Healthcare Epidemiology of America, Washington, DC, 2003.

61. Hsaio KK, Meiner Z, Kahana E, et al. Mutation of the prion protein in Libyan Jews with Creutzfeldt-Jacob disease. *N Engl J Med* 1991;324: 1091–1097.

62. Castellani R, Parchi P, Madoff L, et al. Biopsy diagnosis of Creutzfeldt-Jakob disease by Western blot: a case report. *Brain Pathol* 1997;28:623–626.

SUPPLEMENTAL RESOURCES

American Red Cross. Giving blood: blood eligibility guidelines. Available at: http://www.redcrossblood.org/donating-blood/eligibility-requirements/eligibility-criteria-alphabetical-listing.

Association for Advancement of Medical Instrumentation. Available at: http://www.aami.org.

Association of PeriOperative Registered Nurses. Available at: http://www.aorn.org.

Carrico RM, Furman C, Hyde DC, et al. *Dealing with Creutzfeldt-Jakob Disease: A Comprehensive Guide for Healthcare Personnel.* Chicago: Spectrum, 2005.

Centers for Disease Control and Prevention website on CJD. Available at: http://www.cdc.gov/ncidod/dvrd/cjd/.

Furman C, Carrico RM, Hyde DC. *Dealing with Creutzfeldt-Jakob Disease: Information for Patients, Families, and Caregivers.* Chicago: Spectrum, 2004.

Health Canada. Classic CJD in Canada, infection control guidelines. Health Canada website. 2002. Available at: http://www.collectionscanada.gc.ca/webarchives/20071120090348/http://www.phac-aspc.gc.ca/publicat/ccdr-rmtc/02vol28/28s5/index.html.

World Health Organization. WHO infection control guidelines for transmissible spongiform encephalopathies. Available at: http://www.who.int/csr/resources/publications/bse/WHO_CDS_CSR_APH_2000_3/en/.

CHAPTER 74

Central Nervous System Infection

Belinda Ostrowsky MD, MPH
Director of Antimicrobial Stewardship
Associate Professor of Medicine
Montefiore Medical Center
Bronx, NY

ABSTRACT

Bacterial colonization of the nasopharynx is a common first step in the development of acute bacterial meningitis and many other kinds of infection. The most common etiologic agents of bacterial meningitis are the pneumococci, meningococci, and group B streptococci. Pneumococcal meningitis is age-dependent, with the highest rates occurring at the extremes of age. A primary goal is to determine whether the patient has bacterial meningitis, specifically meningococcus, because there is the need for Transmission-based Precautions, prophylaxis issue for close contacts, and requirements for reporting to public health departments. Most cases of viral aseptic meningitis are benign and self-limited without indications for Transmission-based Precautions. There are evolving issues regarding infections of ventricular shunts, including difficulty in diagnosis, treatment length/route, surveillance, and newer data that antibiotic-impregnated catheters may have some role in reducing infections. Identifying those patients who could have herpes simplex infection is important, because highly effective antiviral treatment is available. Acute encephalitis may reflect infection with bacteria, viruses, rickettsiae, or fungi, or it may be a noninfectious sequel to a prior infection. Arboviruses are important causes of vectorborne encephalitis for which therapy is limited to supportive care. This includes West Nile virus cases, which have recently been reported throughout the United States. Brain abscess is usually the result of direct extension from a bacterial infection such as sinusitis, otitis, mastoiditis, and dental or facial purulent foci. Spinal or cranial epidural abscesses are commonly the result of metastatic spread from regional sites of purulence. Extraordinary infectious particles called prions are the agents responsible for the four spongiform encephalopathies, namely, Creutzfeldt-Jakob disease, kuru, Gerstmann-Sträussler-Scheinker syndrome, and fatal familial insomnia. Most cases of Creutzfeldt-Jakob disease are sporadic, but much attention has focused on the rare occurrence of a new variant form of Creutzfeldt-Jakob disease, which is caused by a transmissible prion that may be spread via organ/tissue transplantation. Although rare, suspected/confirmed Creutzfeldt-Jakob disease cases raise disinfection/sterilization issues for surgical instrumentation.

KEY CONCEPTS

- Epidemiology and therapy of bacterial meningitis
- Cerebrospinal fluid shunt infections
- Aseptic meningitis
- Chronic meningitis
- Encephalitis
- Spongiform encephalopathies
- Mycotic aneurysm
- Brain abscess
- Infection prevention and control implications

BACKGROUND

Central nervous system (CNS) infections may be caused by a variety of agents and manifest with different symptoms and disease processes. Many infections are successfully managed with pharmacological or surgical intervention, some are self-limiting, and a few are untreatable.

BASIC PRINCIPLES

- Meningitis is defined as inflammation of the meninges, the superficial lining tissues of the brain and spinal cord. Common bacteria (e.g., pneumococci, meningococci) or viral pathogens (e.g., herpes simplex virus [HSV], enteroviruses, arboviruses, or mumps) are the usual causes of acute meningitis. Spirochetes (e.g., *Treponema* or *Borrelia*), fungi (*Cryptococcus* or *Candida*), and protozoa (*Naegleria* or *Angiostrongylus*) also may cause acute meningitis. Important diagnostic clues in acute bacterial meningitis are the abrupt or subacute onset of headache, stiff neck, and fever, as well as the presence of inflammatory cells in the cerebrospinal fluid (CSF; especially neutrophils) and positive Gram stain. Distinguish acute bacterial meningitis, especially meningococcus (and to a lesser extent *Haemophilus influenzae*, though this is rare since widespread vaccination), as soon as possible because of the need for isolation, reports to state/local health departments, and prophylaxis to close contacts (a narrowly defined group).

- CSF shunt infections can present a diagnostic dilemma. There are limited data on several aspects regarding these infections, including use of intraventricular instillation, length of treatment, role for surveillance cultures, and routine catheter exchange. Preliminary data support short-course perioperative prophylaxis (preoperatively and first 24 hours) and possible benefits of impregnated intraventricular catheters in preventing infections.

- Encephalitis: Inflammation of the brain may be the result of acute viral infection of brain cells or may reflect a bacterial, fungal, or rickettsial infection, as well as a noninfectious sequel to an earlier systemic infection. Other disease processes, such as malignancy or a rheumatological disorder (e.g., systemic lupus erythematosus), may also produce symptoms of brain inflammation similar to those caused by infectious encephalitis. The defining clinical feature of encephalitis is altered consciousness, but other signs include seizures, abnormal movements, weakness, and, less commonly, sensory deficits. The enteroviruses are the most common causes of encephalitis, and these infections occur mainly in the summer and early fall. Most have no specific treatment. West Nile virus was diagnosed in a patient cluster in the New York City region in 1999, and since then cases have been seen throughout the United States. Herpes encephalitis is important to consider in the differential diagnosis of patients with encephalitis because diagnostic testing and treatment are available.

- Brain abscess: The majority of brain abscesses occur as the result of direct extension from infections, such as frontal sinusitis, mastoiditis, chronic otitis media, and dental or facial purulent foci. A substantial minority are hematogenous (usually from a cardiac or pulmonary source), and these are often multiple and bilateral.

- Spinal epidural abscess is relatively uncommon, but it occurs in hosts with a broad age range and without gender predominance. Spinal epidural abscesses occur most commonly in the lumbar area, less frequently in the thoracic or cervical area, and least frequently in the sacral region. Infection may be introduced by hematogenous spread from a distant site; by direct extension from vertebral osteomyelitis, perinephric, or psoas abscesses; or by penetrating injuries, paraspinal injections, or spinal surgery. Skin and soft tissue infections are the identified or presumed source in nearly half the cases. On average, three to six contiguous spinal segments are involved. *Staphylococcus aureus* is the most commonly isolated etiologic agent.

- Intracranial epidural abscesses account for approximately 10 percent of all epidural abscesses. In the past, intracranial epidural abscesses were often a consequence of sinusitis, mastoiditis, or otitis media, but recently they most often follow a neurosurgical procedure. Patients with abscess in contiguity with implanted foreign material are at the highest risk.

- Bovine spongiform encephalopathy (BSE): The infectious agent responsible for BSE is a prion, a misfolded version of a normal cellular protein called *PrP*. Prions are self-replicating but devoid of nucleic acid. The particular prion responsible for BSE was probably derived from sheep (in which the infection is known as *scrapie*), although this origin is disputed. BSE is transmissible to humans by ingestion or implantation of infected tissue, and clinically it was recognized as a variant form of neurodegeneration known as new variant Creutzfeldt-Jakob disease (nvCJD). This has implications for cleaning and sterilization of equipment used in neurosurgical procedures for suspected/confirmed cases.

- Four recognized prion-related infections of humans are: kuru, Gerstmann-Sträussler-Scheinker syndrome, fatal familial insomnia (FFI), and CJD. All four are neurodegenerative illnesses with an ultimately fatal course, and there are no effective therapies.

  ○ Kuru is manifested by loss of motor coordination followed by dementia. It is apparently related to human cannibalism and has been recognized only in the highlands of Papua, New Guinea, where approximately 2,600 cases have occurred since 1957.

  ○ Gerstmann-Sträussler-Scheinker syndrome is characterized by loss of coordination followed by dementia and death within 2 to 6 years. It is typically familial, and approximately 50 affected families have been identified.

  ○ CJD is characterized by dementia followed within 1 to 2 months by loss of motor coordination, myoclonus, visual disturbances, hypokinesia, and rigidity. CJD does not usually affect the peripheral nervous system. Most cases are sporadic, but there are cases of iatrogenic nvCJD after dural grafts, corneal transplantation, liver transplantation, administration of human growth or gonadotropic hormones, or use of contaminated neurosurgical instruments or stereotactic electrodes.

  ○ FFI is characterized by disturbed functions of the autonomic nervous system, insomnia, and dementia. Nine extended families with the syndrome have been reported. The clinical course leading to death is approximately 1 year. FFI, like other prion diseases, is transmissible to experimental animals, and virtually all reported cases have been associated with an asparagine for aspartic acid substitution in the prion protein.

There are significant implications for infection preventionists (IPs) including confirming the appropriate diagnosis to verify that proper infection precautions are put in place and efficient prophylaxis is offered to close or high-risk contacts as appropriate. In most cases no isolation or prophylaxis is needed and reassurance to contacts, including healthcare personnel (HCP), is essential. Emerging pathogens and the risk of iatrogenic introduction (e.g., contamination of medications) of CNS pathogens have introduced new challenges for IPs.

CENTRAL NERVOUS SYSTEM INFECTION

Meningitis

Meningitis: Etiology and Pathophysiology

Meningitis is defined as inflammation of the meninges, the superficial lining tissues of the brain and spinal cord. Common bacteria such as pneumococci, meningococci, or viral pathogens such as herpes simplex virus (HSV), enteroviruses, arboviruses, or mumps are the usual causes of acute meningitis. Spirochetes (e.g., *Treponema* or *Borrelia*), fungi (*Cryptococcus* or *Candida*), and protozoa (*Naegleria* or *Angiostrongylus*) also may cause acute meningitis.[1] Important diagnostic clues in acute meningitis are the abrupt or subacute onset of headache, stiff neck, and fever, as well as the presence of inflammatory cells in the CSF. Microbial colonization of the nasopharynx is a common first step in the host-parasite relationship that precedes several disparate infections, including acute bacterial meningitis. Many bacterial species express surface receptors that mediate attachment to the host's nasopharyngeal mucosa. After mucosal attachment, pathogens such as meningococci or pneumococci gain access to vacuoles in mucosal epithelial cells and then may enter the blood via regional capillaries. Hematogenous dissemination of microorganisms is followed by invasion of the subarachnoid space and initiation of a diffuse inflammatory reaction of the tissues bathed by the CSF.

Meningitis: Epidemiology

The most common etiologic agents of bacterial meningitis are *Neisseria meningitidis, Streptococcus pneumoniae, Haemophilus influenzae,* group B streptococci, and *Listeria monocytogenes.* Among patients aged more than 50 years and for all immunocompromised patients, the most frequently occurring pathogens are *S. pneumoniae, L. monocytogenes,* and aerobic Gram-negative bacilli. Neonates are especially predisposed to infections with group B streptococci and Gram-negative bacilli (e.g., *Klebsiella pneumoniae* or *H. influenzae*). *N. meningitidis* is the major cause of bacterial meningitis in patients between 2 and 18 years of age.[1,2]

The most significant change in the epidemiology of bacterial meningitis in recent years has been the huge decrease in frequency of *H. influenzae* type b (Hib) meningitis since the introduction of the conjugate *H. influenzae* vaccine in 1987.[1] Before the introduction of effective vaccines, *H. influenzae* was the leading cause of bacterial meningitis in the United States among children younger than 5 years of age. Because of routine use of the Hib conjugate vaccine, the incidence of *H. influenzae* disease in infants and young children has decreased by 99 percent to less than 1 case per 100,000 children aged younger than 5 years. In the United States, *H. influenzae* disease occurs primarily in underimmunized children and among infants too young to have completed the primary immunization series.[3]

Acute Meningitis: Diagnosis, Empiric Antibiotic, and Adjunctive Therapy

The lumbar puncture (LP) is widely recognized as a necessary part of the early diagnostic evaluation of patients with suspected meningitis because the sensitivity of clinical symptoms, including the classic triad of fever, neck stiffness, and altered mental status exam, is low. CSF appearance, opening pressure (taken during this collection by using a simple column manometer; can be used for both for diagnosis and therapeutically), cellularity, biochemical evaluation, and Gram stain provide critically important diagnostic information as well as guidance for therapy.[4] The preliminary CSF findings can provide keys to the diagnosis quickly and guide treatment for the patient and potential need for infection prevention precautions/isolation and prophylaxis for close contacts.[5] Table 74-1 provides some guidelines for the interpretation of the initial CSF findings obtained in acute/subacute meningitis before culture results provide an etiological diagnosis.

Some physicians have adopted a routine policy of performing a computed tomography (CT) scan of the head *before* the diagnostic LP in patients with suspected bacterial meningitis.[6] The rationale for the CT scan is unsuspected, focal, intracranial mass lesions may result in brain stem herniation and even death after an LP because of the creation of a high CSF pressure gradient (lower pressure below the foramen magnum) between the cranial and spinal CSF compartments after removal of lumbar spinal fluid. Unfortunately, the screening CT scan is often associated with a delay of several hours in the performance of an LP, and the administration of empirical antibiotic therapy (a median of 4 hours in one study from arrival in emergency department and the administration of antibiotics). This delay in treatment can be prevented by administration of antibiotics before the CT scan. However, antibiotic treatment before sampling the CSF may lead to a falsely negative CSF culture. It would be extremely unusual, however, that all the initial CSF

Table 74-1. Typical Results of Preliminary Cerebrospinal Fluid Examination in Acute/Subacute Meningitis[2,5]

Causative Organism	Opening Pressure	Glucose (Ratio of CSF to Serum Glucose)	Predominant Inflammatory Cell	WBC Counts	Total Protein	Staining
Bacteria	Elevated	Normal to decreased	Neutrophils (early or partially treated may have lymphocyte predominance)	≥1,000/mm³	Elevated (mild to very)	Gram* stain may show GPC or GNC/GNR
Virus	Usually normal	Usually normal	Lymphocytes	<100 per mm³	Normal to elevated	Gram stain, negative
Fungi	Variable	Low	Lymphocytes	Variable	Elevated	India ink, positive
Tuberculosis	Variable	Low (can be extremely depressed levels)	Lymphocytes	Variable	Elevated	AFB stain, positive

*Positive in 60 to 80 percent of untreated bacterial meningitis/40 to 60 percent of partially treated cases. AFB, acid-fast bacillus (e.g., mycobacterial species); GNC, Gram-negative coccus; GNR, Gram-negative rods (bacillus); GPC, Gram-positive coccus.

studies such as cell count, glucose, protein, and Gram stain would be falsely normal with the administration of this one dose of antibiotics before the LP, even if the antibiotics may inhibit growth on the culture.[2,5]

Clinical studies that help to resolve this dilemma are sparse, but a recently published prospective study of 301 adults with suspected meningitis supports the recommendation that patients with bacterial meningitis should have blood cultures drawn promptly, and if the LP must be delayed, parenteral empirical antibiotic therapy should be initiated immediately.[2,7,8] Experts have suggested that those with new-onset seizure, an immunocompromised state, signs that are suspicious for space occupying lesion, or moderate to severe impaired consciousness should have imaging before LP. An LP may also be harmful in patients with coagulopathy because of the chance of needle-induced subarachnoid hemorrhage or development of a spinal subdural and epidural hematoma.[2]

In these settings the risk and benefit of the LP and delay in treatment will be weighed against the level of suspicion for meningitis and other diagnoses. Although there are scant data on a direct relationship between treatment delay and poor outcome, given the catastrophic potential outcomes from meningitis, empiric treatment in clinically consistent situations is reasonable until additional evaluation and results are obtained. Appropriate antibiotic treatment of most common types of bacterial meningitis should reduce the risk of dying from meningitis to less than 15 percent, although the risk is higher among the elderly.[9]

Empiric (initial) antibiotics for meningitis are based on the most common bacteria causing disease according to the patient's age and clinical setting and on patterns of antimicrobial susceptibility. After the results of culture and susceptibility testing are available, antimicrobial therapy can be modified for optimal treatment. Empiric antibiotic regimens are as follows:[2,10]

- For preterm neonates up to 1 month of age, empiric treatment should have activity against group B streptococcus, most coliforms, and *Listeria*. An acceptable regimen would be ampicillin and cefotaxime.

- For infants 1 month to adults to age 50 years who are immunocompetent, empiric regimen should cover *S. pneumoniae*, meningococcus, and *H. influenzae* (now rare). An acceptable regimen would be cefotaxime or ceftriaxone and vancomycin.

- For adults aged more than 50 years, alcoholics, and those with other debilitating associated disease or impaired cellular immunity, empiric treatment should cover *S. pneumoniae*, *Listeria*, and Gram-negative coverage. An acceptable regimen would be ampicillin and cefotaxime or ceftriaxone and vancomycin.

The issue of whether to use steroids for meningitis or suspected meningitis has been controversial, especially in adults.[2] The value of dexamethasone has been documented in children with *H. influenzae*.[2] A recent prospective randomized multicenter trial of 301 patients with suspected meningitis in combination with cloudy CSF, bacteria in CSF on Gram staining, or a

CSF leukocyte count of more than 1,000/mm^3 showed that adjunctive treatment with dexamethasone before or with the first dose of antimicrobial therapy reduced the risk of unfavorable outcome from 25 to 15 percent. Mortality was reduced from 15 to 7 percent. The benefit was greatest in patients with intermediate disease severity (defined by Glasgow Coma Scale) and those with pneumococcal meningitis, in whom unfavorable outcome declined from 52 to 26 percent. In patients with pneumococcal meningitis mortality was reduced from 34 to 14 percent (based on reduced mortality from systemic causes). The benefits of dexamethasone were not offset by side effects of the dexamethasone treatment.[11]

The practical implications of the study are still in evolution; however, most experts agree to the use of steroids for highly suspected/proven pneumococcal meningitis.[2,11–13] The issue of empiric treatment for meningitis (because the study used the steroids before or with the first doses of antibiotics) and use in proven bacterial meningitis with other organisms is still controversial. Particularly in some adult patients with suspected meningitis, adjunctive steroids can be harmful (those with septic shock with meningitis).[2,12]

Meningitis: Acute Bacterial Meningitis (Common)

Acute Meningitis: Pneumococcal Meningitis

S. pneumoniae is the most common cause (irrespective of age) of bacterial meningitis in the United States (estimated 2,000 cases/year). A major change in the epidemiology of meningitis has been the worldwide emergence of antimicrobial resistance in *S. pneumoniae*. Rates of penicillin resistance as high as 35 percent have been reported in some geographic areas in the United States (especially the Southeast).[10,13] Recently, increasing numbers of pneumococcal isolates have demonstrated resistance to multiple antibiotics; however, pneumococcal resistance to vancomycin has never been described.[13] This explains the rationale for the change in empirical antibiotic choice in the last several years (a combination of ceftriaxone or cefotaxime *and* vancomycin).

After isolation of the causative microorganism and quantitative susceptibility testing, discontinuation of the vancomycin is feasible if the minimum inhibitory concentration of the pneumococcal isolate indicates susceptibility to the chosen third-generation cephalosporin.[13] In addition, the recognition that higher concentration of antibiotics can be achieved in non-CSF sites and by intravenous preparation (vs. oral, particularly for penicillin) has prompted changes in the guidelines that hospital laboratories use for susceptibility testing for pneumococcal isolates ("breakpoint changes").[13] This point is mainly to underscore that the ultimate choices of antibiotics and dosing once an isolate is recovered may be complicated and is often done in consultation with an infectious diseases specialist.

There are currently two types of pneumococcal vaccines: pneumococcal conjugate vaccine (PCV13) and pneumococcal polysaccharide vaccine (PPSV23). The Centers for Disease Control (CDC) Advisory Committee on Immunization Practices

(ACIP) recommends that PCV13 be used for all children younger than 5 years of age as a four-dose series beginning at 2 months of age. Children between ages 2 and 5 years who have underlying medical conditions or were not and/or incompletely vaccinated are eligible for supplemental shots with PCV13.

All adults 65 years or older should receive the PPSV23 vaccine, as well as anyone between ages 2 and 64 with chronic medical problems, those that are immunosuppressed, those that smoke, or those that reside in health facilities. Those adults who have not previously received PPV13 should get a dose of PPV13 first and continue to receive recommended doses of PPSV. The efficacy of Prevnar has been reported as 97.4 percent in preventing invasive pneumococcal disease caused by the seven strains of pneumococcus represented in the vaccine and 93.9 percent efficacy in preventing invasive disease caused by all pneumococcal serotypes. The new vaccine now includes six additional serotypes for added protection.[13]

The risk of pneumococcal meningitis increases at the extremes of age. As with some other meningeal pathogens, pneumococcal infection usually follows recent nasopharyngeal colonization by a virulent strain of pneumococci. Pneumococci have been isolated commonly from the upper respiratory tract of asymptomatic adults. Pneumococcal nasopharyngeal colonization rates are generally higher in children and decline with age. Sickle cell anemia, asplenia, primary or acquired immunodeficiency states, and active or passive exposure to cigarette smoke, as well as cirrhosis, alcoholism, and CSF leak, are risk factors for pneumococcal meningitis.[13]

Acute Meningitis: Meningococcal Meningitis

Each year, an estimated 1,400 to 2,800 cases of meningococcal disease occur in the United States (see Chapter 87 *Neisseria Meningitidis*). *N. meningitidis* causes almost all meningococcal infections and comprises the serogroups A, B, C, Y, and W-135.[9] Serogroup B is the most prevalent in the United States, and this has important implications because of the lack of an effective vaccine against this serogroup.[9,14] The incidence of *Neisseria* infections is greatest in the winter and early spring, and organisms are transmitted from person to person by droplet spread resulting from close contact with a person who is colonized or infected. Asymptomatic nasal carriage of *N. meningitidis* is relatively low in children but may be as high as 25 percent in young adults.[14]

Immunocompromised persons at any age are particularly susceptible to meningococcal infections. Risk factors for meningococcal infection include contact with a carrier, recent viral respiratory infection, and complement deficiency. The mortality rate of isolated meningococcal meningitis is 2 to 5 percent, whereas meningococcal sepsis is a more serious illness with 20 to 40 percent mortality. In addition to meningitis, other complications of meningococcal bacteremia include arthritis, myocarditis, pericarditis, endophthalmitis, and pneumonia.[9,15]

Treatment for meningococcal diseases with high-dose penicillin, ceftriaxone, or cefotaxime is effective against susceptible

and even moderately nonsusceptible strains. However, when penicillin is used for treatment, pharyngeal colonization with the infecting *N. meningitidis* strain may persist. Because eradication of meningococcal colonization in the index case protects contacts, the penicillin-treated index patient may need to take rifampin, fluoroquinolone, or cephalosporin to avoid transmission to others.[15]

In addition to high-dose antibiotic administration, adjunctive corticosteroid therapy with dexamethasone (0.15 mg/kg intravenously [IV] every 6 hours for 4 days) has afforded a reduction of neurologic sequelae in multiple studies in children, and some authors recommend it for high-risk adult patients (e.g., those with a high concentration of bacteria in CSF, impaired mental status, cerebral edema, or significantly elevated intracranial pressure).[15,16]

Because close contact with patients with meningococcal disease increases risk for developing infection, even isolated cases can generate severe anxiety to patients' families, as well as school and healthcare personnel who have had recent contact with a patient infected with *N. meningitidis*. The exposed household, school, or child care contacts must be observed carefully. However, nasal or throat swab cultures are not useful for determining risk (and should not be collected).[9,14,15]

Suspected and confirmed cases of acute meningitis (especially when *N. meningitidis* and *H. influenzae* are of concern) should be placed on Droplet Precautions, and healthcare personnel should use a surgical mask when evaluating these patients until the patient has received a full 24 hours of antibiotics.[15]

Close contacts of all persons with invasive meningococcal infection should receive a prophylactic antibiotic as soon as possible and ideally within hours of the diagnosis of the primary case. The practical issue is to define "close contacts" for both lay persons and healthcare personnel because once even a possible diagnosis of meningitis is entertained it may raise fear and anxiety.

"Close contacts" are defined in Table 74-2 and include household members, child care center contacts, anyone with direct contact with a patient's oral secretions in a personal or professional capacity, or nonhousehold member with shared dwelling

Table 74-2. High-Risk Personal Contacts for which Meningococcal Chemoprophylaxis is Recommended[14,15]

1. Household contacts, especially younger than 2 years of age
2. Child care or preschool contact at any time during 7 days before onset of illness
3. Direct exposure to index patient's secretions through kissing or through sharing toothbrushes or eating utensils, markers of close social contact, at any time during 7 days before onset of illness
4. Mouth-to-mouth resuscitation, unprotected contact during endotracheal intubation during 7 days before onset of illness
5. Frequently slept in same dwelling as index patient during 7 days before onset of illness
6. Passengers seated directly next to the index case during airline flights lasting more than 8 hours

and eating.[9,14,15] Thus, most healthcare personnel associated with patients' care will *not* be close contacts because their level of contact with the patient was more casual. Suspected meningitis cases should be placed on droplet isolation. Healthcare personnel who had exposure to patients with the proper personal protective equipment (surgical mask) would not be considered exposed.

The attack rate for household contacts exposed to patients who have meningococcal disease was estimated as 4 cases/ 100 persons exposed (500 to 800 times the rate for the total population and many times higher than that of healthcare personnel).[14] Because the rate of secondary disease for close contact is highest immediately after onset of diseases in the index patients, antimicrobial prophylaxis should be administered as soon as possible within 24 hours of diagnosis of the primary case but may be given up to 10 to 14 days after contact (chemoprophylaxis administered >14 days after exposure is probably of limited or no value).[14-16] However, it is important to underscore that there is time for at least the initial evaluation of the index patient. Often the clinical presentation, CSF initial testing (including Gram stain), and clinical suspicion of those caring and providing consultation for the patient are key. Not all cases are meningitis, and not all bacterial meningitis cases require mobilizing resources to prophylaxis of close contacts. Discerning likely aseptic viral meningitis is important.

Recommended regimens for antibiotic chemoprophylaxis in adults include rifampin, ciprofloxacin, or ceftriaxone, all of which are 90 to 95 percent effective in reducing nasopharyngeal carriage of *N. meningitidis* (Table 74-2).[15] Ciprofloxacin (500 mg by mouth) is especially a favored regimen in nonpregnant adults, because it is oral and requires only one dose. Azithromycin is an acceptable alternative but not recommended routinely.

A recent *Morbidity and Mortality Weekly Report* described a cluster of three cases of serogroup B, fluoroquinolone-resistant meningococcal disease that occurred among residents of the border area of North Dakota and Minnesota during 2007 and 2008.[17] The first of these cases was epidemiologically linked and closely molecularly related to a 2006 case with the same resistance occurring in the same geographical area. The report recommended a change in chemoprophylaxis for contacts of meningococcal diseases in that limited geographic region and vigilance/surveillance for resistance in other areas. Other case reports have documented rifampin resistance. These isolated cases illustrate the need to perform appropriate susceptibility testing on meningococcal isolates. Thus, there are no other general recommendations to change prophylaxis from the regimens described above.

More than 98 percent of meningococcal disease cases in the United States are sporadic, whereas the other 2 percent are associated with outbreaks.[14] Multiple studies have illustrated a higher risk of meningococcal disease among college students, particularly those who reside in dormitories. Several recent outbreaks have been in this college setting (13 [26 percent] of

50 outbreaks within organized facilities during 1994 to 2002 were in colleges).[14] In 2000, the ACIP recommended that college students/parents be informed of the risk of meningococcal diseases and potential benefit to vaccination (described below).[16]

There are two meningococcal vaccinations currently available.[9,16] The tetravalent meningococcal polysaccharide vaccine, MPV4 (Menomune-A/C/Y/W135; Sanofi Pasteur, Swiftwater, PA) has been available since the 1970s and has been used in mass vaccination among international travelers and the military. Usefulness is now more limited because it does not confer long-lasting immunity and does not cause sustainable reduced nasopharyngeal carriage.

A tetravalent meningococcal conjugate vaccine, MCV4 (Menactra, Sanofi Pasteur, Lyon, France) was licensed in January 2005 for persons aged 11 to 55 years. The vaccination is for those aged 11 to 12 years, before entry to high school, college freshmen living in dorms, and other populations at risk (microbiologist with exposure, military, travelers, those with terminal complement deficiencies and anatomic/ functionally asplenic) and has more recently been used in certain outbreak settings.[16]

The decision to implement mass vaccination to prevent meningococcal disease in college or other settings is complicated and would involve public health officials. Details such as the number of cases, attack rate, serogroup and typing, cost, feasibility, and potential for antimicrobial resistance development would be some of the key factors weighed. Other controls, such as closures, travel restrictions, canceling of congregate events, are also part of the control plans.[14,16]

Cases of suspected and confirmed meningococcal disease are reportable to most state and local public health departments. This allows for proper identification and prophylaxis of close contacts, surveillance for clusters/outbreaks and vaccine failures, laboratory aid including susceptibility testing, sero-grouping and typing, and proper information/communication with public (as previously discussed).[16]

Acute Meningitis: Cerebrospinal Fluid Shunt Infections

CSF shunts are used in the setting of hydrocephalus to divert CSF to another part of the body for absorption. There are several controversies (areas without clear data) in the management of shunt infections.[18]

The rate of CNS shunt infection is approximately 5 to 15 percent.[18] Risk factors include intraventricular hemorrhage, subarachnoid hemorrhage, and cranial fracture with CSF leak.[18-20] Fever, headache, nausea, lethargy, and mental status changes are common, but the acuity of signs and symptoms may vary depending on the microbial cause. Clinical manifestations may be subtle or absent. They may present as manifestations of increased intracranial pressure or with symptoms localized to the distal end of the device.

CT or magnetic resonance imaging (MRI) scans of the head are especially indicated if there are clinical signs of a mass lesion or elevated CSF pressure. Signs of meningitis or ventriculitis are indications for sampling of CSF from the shunt reservoir (preferred over ventricular tap or lumbar puncture when possible), and this should be performed with careful attention to sterile technique. Both blood and CSF bacteriologic cultures should be obtained. Gram stain and culture as well as differential cell count, glucose, and protein determinations should be performed on the CSF. Although interpretation of CSF can be challenging, the white cell differential may be a useful clue.[18-20] In one report of 129 shunt placements, a differential with 0.10 percent neutrophils was 90 percent sensitive in predicting infection and had a negative predictive value of 0.99.[20]

Skin flora account for the majority of infections associated with internalized or externalized CNS shunt devices. Shunt infections may also develop from the distal ends of internalized devices, leading to peritonitis or bacteremia with a variety of pathogens.[18] There are no randomized, prospective trials addressing optimal treatment of CNS shunt infections. Management should include removal of the device, external drainage, parenteral antibiotics, and shunt replacement (when CSF is sterile). Empiric parenteral therapy should cover Gram-positive pathogens (especially coagulase-negative *Staphylococcus*) and healthcare-associated Gram-negative organisms. Regimens such as parenteral vancomycin plus an antipseudomonal cephalosporin or carbapenem would be acceptable. Regimens can be narrowed on the basis of CSF cultures. The duration of antibiotic therapy depends on the implicated pathogen and presence of retained hardware.[18]

There have been limited trials evaluating the clinical efficacy of intraventricular antibiotics. There has been one randomized trial studying the inflammatory markers in the CSF of 21 neonates with Gram-negative bacilli meningitis and ventriculitis which demonstrated increased inflammatory markers in the group that received intraventricular antibiotics compared to the group that received parenteral antibiotic therapy alone. This may suggest a poorer outcome in those who receive intraventricular antibiotics. It may be useful when parenteral antibiotics fail to sterilize the CSF, with antimicrobial resistance (where susceptible antibiotics are those with poor CSF penetration) or where devices cannot be removed. There are no antibiotics that are U.S. Food and Drug Administration approved for intraventricular use and no standardized dose. The most clinical experience has been with vancomycin and gentamicin.[18]

Routine prospective CSF analysis has little value in predicting infection and may increase the risk of iatrogenic infection.[18] Some favor surveillance CSF analysis when the predisposing diagnosis is associated with an increased risk of infection, such as subarachnoid or intraventricular hemorrhage or cranial fracture. Others advocate for CSF analysis only when infection is suspected on clinical grounds.[18]

Another area of controversy is perioperative prophylaxis.[18,20-22] There are no randomized trials, but a recent meta-analysis

of 15 observational studies concluded that use of systemic prophylaxis antibiotics before placement and for the initial 24 hours after device placement decreases rates of shunt infection.[21]

Antibiotic-impregnated catheters have shown some promise in reducing the incidence of CNS shunt infections. In a randomized trial of 288 device placements, patients with antibiotic-impregnated catheters were less likely to develop positive CSF cultures than those who received control catheters.[23] A meta-analysis showed reduction of shunt infections with impregnated catheters.[21] Prophylactic catheter change is not effective for preventing CNS shunt infection and is not recommended.[18]

Acute Meningitis: Aseptic Meningitis

Aseptic meningitis is defined broadly as meningeal inflammation that is *not* due to bacteria or fungi.[24] Viral pathogens are only one of several etiological categories[24] (reviewed in Table 74-3).

From a practical point of view, distinguishing these cases from bacterial meningitis as soon as possible is important. First, from an infection prevention perspective, Transmission-based Precautions are not indicated for cases of aseptic meningitis as they are for bacterial meningitis. In addition, aseptic meningitis is usually less severe than bacterial meningitis and rarely fatal, a fact that can be underscored to the public and the healthcare personnel at risk of exposure. Most cases are self-limited and do not require specific treatment. There is also no special prophylaxis for close contacts.[25]

Acute Meningitis: Viral Meningitis

Viral aseptic meningitis is the most common infectious disease involving the CNS.[25,26] Epidemiologic studies reveal that it is more common in males than females and approximately four times more common in children who are 1 year of age or older. Clinical features occurring in older children include headache, fever, irritability, nuchal rigidity, nausea, and vomiting. However, cases may also occur in infants aged less than 2 to 3 months of age. In neonates (2 weeks), enteroviral meningitis may be a devastating illness. A bulging anterior fontanel and nuchal rigidity may be combined with vomiting, anorexia, rash, and upper respiratory signs and symptoms. Beyond the neonatal period, severe disease and poor outcomes are rare.

Table 74-3. Differential Diagnosis of Aseptic Meningitis[24]

1. Viral infections (enteroviruses, mumps, arboviruses, lymphocytic choriomeningitis virus, herpes simplex, varicella-zoster, adenoviruses, Epstein-Barr virus, parvovirus B19)
2. Nonviral infections (partially treated bacterial meningitis, parameningeal infections, brain abscess, spirochetal or fungal infections, tuberculosis, toxoplasmosis, rickettsial infections, *Mycoplasma pneumoniae*, cat scratch disease, and amebic meningoencephalitis)
3. Noninfectious etiologies include ingestion of nonsteroidal anti-inflammatory drugs, brain tumor, carcinomatous meningitis, intrathecal drugs, radiographic dyes, lead poisoning, and benign intracranial hypertension
4. Unknown etiologies include Kawasaki disease and Mollaret syndrome

Acute Meningitis: Enteroviruses and Human Immunodeficiency Virus

The most common causes of viral aseptic meningitis in the United States are lymphocytic choriomeningitis virus and coxsackie B viruses. Aseptic meningitis is less frequently caused by echoviruses or coxsackie A virus.[26] Particular clinical stigmata are associated with certain enteroviral serotypes. For example, echovirus 9 is associated with maculopapular rashes. Painful vesicles on the posterior pharynx are seen with coxsackievirus A, and the presence of pericarditis or pleurisy suggests coxsackie B virus. The peak occurrence of viral aseptic meningitis is in July, August, and September with a nadir in early spring. Despite significant short-term morbidity, there is little evidence of long-term neurologic or developmental sequelae. Pleconaril, a novel, oral, systemically active, small molecule inhibitor of enteroviruses and rhinoviruses, has been shown to shorten the course of illness compared to placebo, especially early in the disease course.[27–29] A unique clinical situation is seen in children and adults with humoral immune deficiency because of their inability to mount adequate enteroviral immunity. For example, patients with agammaglobulinemia develop a chronic or recurrent enteroviral meningitis and meningoencephalitis that may last several years with a fatal outcome or may even relapse and recur over decades.[24] Other patients may present with typical aseptic meningitis symptoms caused by acute human immunodeficiency virus (HIV) infection. When this occurs, the patients may be unaware of their recently acquired HIV infection. Therefore, elements of the history related to intravenous drug use or possible sexually transmitted infection should be elicited. The most common clinical features are headache, fever, and meningeal signs. The symptomatic illness is self-limited but may be recurrent. When HIV infection is considered in this setting it may be important to request that a viral polymerase chain reaction (PCR) assay be performed on CSF or blood.[24]

Chronic Meningitis

It is often difficult to distinguish chronic meningitis from the more common forms of acute meningitis or encephalitis. A widely accepted but arbitrary definition of chronic meningitis is one in which neurological signs or symptoms persist or progress and the CSF remains abnormal for at least 4 weeks. This category of illness is problematic, and a large fraction of patients with chronic meningitis remain without an etiological diagnosis even after extensive and systematic evaluation. The agents of chronic infections such as tuberculosis, syphilis, histoplasmosis, Lyme disease, cryptococcosis, candidiasis, brucellosis, and other less common infectious and noninfectious etiologies may also cause chronic meningitis. Diagnostic physical findings are rare, and the cause ultimately must be established in the laboratory. Noninfectious causes of chronic meningitis include sarcoidosis, Behçet disease, neoplasms, granulomatous angiitis, uveomeningoencephalitis, and chronic benign lymphocytic meningitis. Serological studies of blood and CSF are very important in evaluating the patient with chronic meningitis. Tests for cryptococcal antigen and for antibodies

to *Brucella, Histoplasma, Toxoplasma, Sporothrix,* and *Treponema* should be performed routinely. Gripshover and Ellner[30] have written an extensive review and discussion of this difficult diagnostic and therapeutic problem.

Encephalitis

Acute Encephalitis

Inflammation of the brain may be the result of acute viral infection of brain cells or may reflect a bacterial, fungal, or rickettsial infection, as well as a noninfectious sequel to an earlier systemic infection. Other disease processes such as malignancy or a rheumatological disorder (e.g., systemic lupus erythematosus) may also produce symptoms of brain inflammation similar to those caused by infectious encephalitis. The defining clinical feature of encephalitis is altered consciousness, but other signs include seizures, abnormal movements, weakness, and, less commonly, sensory deficits. The enteroviruses (Table 74-4) are the most common causes of encephalitis, and these infections occur mainly in the summer and early fall. Some organisms produce symptoms typical of both encephalitis and meningitis, resulting in syndromes termed *meningoencephalitis*.[31]

Diagnostic Studies

It should be a primary goal to determine if the patient with encephalitis could have HSV as the etiologic agent. The reasons for the primacy of HSV in the differential diagnosis are as follows: (1) it is relatively common; (2) treatment usually improves the outcome; and (3) the treatment of choice (acyclovir or its congeners) is effective and well tolerated by

Table 74-4. Human Encephalitis Viruses Occurring in the United States (Modified after Storch[31])

Herpes viruses	Herpes simplex Varicella-zoster Epstein-Barr Cytomegalovirus Human herpesvirus 6 Herpes B virus
Arthropodborne viruses	St. Louis encephalitis Eastern equine encephalitis Western equine encephalitis California encephalitis group West Nile encephalitis
Enteroviruses	Echovirus Coxsackievirus Poliovirus
"Childhood disease" viruses	Mumps Measles Rubella
Respiratory disease viruses	Influenza Parainfluenza Adenovirus
Rabies	
Lymphocytic choriomeningitis virus	
Human immunodeficiency virus (HIV)	
Jamestown Canyon (JC) virus	

most individuals.[32,33] Encephalitis syndromes that are due to most other etiologic agents do not share these encouraging characteristics. An LP with measurement of opening pressure and routine CSF studies (e.g., cell count, routine chemistries, as well as Venereal Disease Reference Laboratory [VDRL], Gram stain, bacterial and fungal cultures, and cryptococcal antigen assay) should be performed on CSF from cases of suspected encephalitis.

CSF also should be submitted for viral culture or PCR assays (e.g., HSV, cytomegalovirus, varicella-zoster virus [VZV], Epstein-Barr virus, and enteroviruses).[34,35] PCR assays are also available to detect HIV, JC virus (John Cunningham virus), and an increasing number of other microbial pathogens. The quality, including the sensitivity and specificity, can vary based on the lab.[34,35]

Epidemiology

Epidemiologic characteristics of the encephalitis syndrome may help to confirm certain etiologies such as rabies (bite wounds or contact with wild animals including bats). A history of patient contact with horses, other animals, or knowledge of local outbreaks of encephalitis (e.g., information from the state or local health departments about the current prevalence of West Nile virus infections) may provide support for consideration of arthropodborne (usually mosquitoes in the United States) or enteroviral encephalitis. Careful questioning of the parents of a child with signs of encephalitis will generally encourage or exclude serious consideration of measles, mumps, rubella, as well as recent respiratory illness compatible with influenza, parainfluenza, or adenovirus, as potential causes of viral encephalitis.

Most states require reporting suspected or confirmed cases of viral encephalitis to state and local health departments. These entities may be able to offer additional CSF testing for specific etiology through referral laboratories. In addition, surveillance or public health action may be needed. For example, for West Nile virus cases, a search for reservoirs for the mosquito vectors that carry the virus is performed in the vicinity of the index patient's home and travel in attempt to prevent transmission to other vulnerable hosts. Public information about other protective measures, such as use of insect repellents and removal of stagnant water, is also shared during the times West Nile virus activity is noted (in the Northeast during later summer/early fall).

Herpes Simplex-1

HSV-1 (the commonly recurrent mouth or "cold sore" virus) is the most common cause of acute, nonepidemic viral encephalitis in the United States. There is no seasonal predilection. Active infection with HSV-1 usually occurs because of endogenous latent viral reactivation. The clinical onset is typically sudden but occasionally it may be subacute. HSV-1 has a tropism for the medial, temporal, and inferior frontal lobes of the brain. The resulting symptoms include headache, fever, gustatory or olfactory hallucinations, and bizarre behavior. Accompanying herpes labialis ("cold sore") is seen in less than 10 percent of

cases. This contrasts with the common but not uniform occurrence of mucocutaneous lesions in HSV-2 meningitis (vagina, perirectal area, or mouth).[32] Head CT scanning or MRI can aid in the diagnosis of HSV-1 encephalitis if typical focal brain lesions are revealed. PCR testing for HSV can be obtained, supporting the diagnosis.[33] Treatment with acyclovir (10 mg/kg IV every 8 hours for 10 to 14 days) can significantly reduce the morbidity and mortality of this infection, unless the patient is comatose at the onset of therapy. Given that this is one of the rare treatable encephalitis diagnoses, empiric treatment may be started while awaiting testing. For patients with CNS symptoms of HSV only (not skin or other manifestations), there are no specific isolation requirements.

Arboviruses

The arboviruses seen in North America include the causative agents of California, St. Louis, West Nile, Venezuelan equine, and Western or Eastern equine encephalitides.[35] Each of these viral infections may produce a clinically indistinguishable syndrome of acute headache, fever, and mental status changes, occurring mainly in the summer. They are vectorborne by mosquitoes or ticks, and the etiological diagnosis is usually made by an increasing antibody titer specific for the etiologic virus in the comparison of acute and convalescent sera from the affected patient. There is no specific treatment for any member of this group.

Japanese Encephalitis

This infection is caused by a flavivirus that is endemic to India and Japan, where it is a major public health problem. Mosquitoes transmit Japanese encephalitis, and it may occur in tourists who spend prolonged periods in rural regions of Southeast Asia. The diagnosis can be confirmed by detection of Japanese encephalitis virus immunoglobulin M antibodies in the CSF. There is no specific treatment, but a safe and effective vaccine is available.[35]

Varicella-zoster Virus

This form of encephalitis usually occurs as a complication of clinically evident chickenpox. CNS involvement develops at the end of the first week of the exanthem. The most frequent manifestation is acute cerebellar ataxia, but the clinical spectrum may range from meningitis to diffuse encephalitis. Encephalitis may also rarely occur during clinically disseminated VZV (with typical rash). In these cases airborne isolation is needed for a hospitalized patient. Treatment with acyclovir has been used in severe cases with some success.

West Nile Virus

West Nile virus, a mosquitoborne flavivirus, was first isolated from a febrile patient in the West Nile Region of Uganda in 1937. It remained sporadic encephalitis in Africa, Europe, and Asia until its surprise detection in the New York City region in 1999. In the last few years, cases have been seen throughout the United States, including the West Coast.[36,37] Nearly all infections result from mosquito bites; however, transmission via breast milk, transmission through transplanted organs and transfused blood, and occupational transmission by means of percutaneous exposure have occurred.[36] West Nile virus may have a wide range of presentations with neuroinvasive syndromes (West Nile encephalitis, West Nile meningitis, or West Nile meningoencephalitis) and West Nile fever (a less severe viral syndrome characterized by fever, headache, tiredness, aches, and sometimes rash), and many patients will be asymptomatic. People aged more than 50 years and the immunosuppressed (transplant recipients) are at higher risk for severe disease. There is no specific treatment for West Nile virus.[34]

Brain Abscess

Pathophysiology

The majority of brain abscesses occur as the result of direct extension from infections, such as frontal sinusitis, mastoiditis, chronic otitis media, and dental or facial purulent foci.[37] See Table 74-5. A substantial minority are hematogenous (usually from a cardiac or pulmonary source), and these are often multiple and bilateral.

Chronic sinusitis-related brain abscesses occur mainly in young to middle-aged adults, and they are typically polymicrobial, yielding anaerobic and aerobic bacterial species. Osteomyelitis of the posterior wall of the frontal sinus may cause simultaneous epidural abscess, frontal lobe brain abscess, or subdural empyema. Temporal lobe abscesses are often a complication of purulent otitis media, and they usually yield multiple organisms, including streptococci, *Bacteroides* spp., and aerobic Gram-negative bacilli. Brain abscess occurring as a complication of facial infection often develops through intervening septic thrombophlebitis. Facial injury may seem trivial; for example, a pencil point or other sharp object may penetrate the orbital wall and be detected only after a long latent period (even several years) with the onset of seizures caused by an encapsulated frontal lobe abscess. Approximately one-third of brain abscesses arise by hematogenous spread from a distant primary focus. These usually have a pulmonary origin (lung abscess, bronchiectasis) or a cardiac origin (*S. aureus* endocarditis of aortic or mitral valves or tricuspid endocarditis with a right-to-left cardiac shunt).[37]

Table 74-5. Microbial Etiologies of Brain Abscess[37]

Organisms	Total (%)
Staphylococcus aureus	92 (13.4)
Gram-negative bacilli (aerobic)	108 (15.7)
Streptococci	220 (32.1)
Anaerobic streptococci	66 (9.6)
Bacteroides spp. Group	74 (10.8)
Other bacteria (*Listeria* spp., *Mycobacteria*, etc.)	80 (11.7)
Fungi, protozoa (*Cryptococcus*, *Candida*, *Toxoplasma*, etc.)	46 (6.7)
Total	686 (100)

Clinical Features

Brain abscesses may occur at any age but are rare in infancy. The peak incidence is usually between 40 and 50 years old and is predominant in males. Almost all patients with brain abscess will give a history of headache and fever, but focal neurological abnormalities are often absent. Occasionally, patients will have a history of progressive obtundation, seizure activity, or focal neurological findings. Somnolence, vomiting, and third or sixth cranial nerve palsies are common. Papilledema is an important and often late sign that should prompt immediate head imaging (MRI or CT scan) and neurosurgical evaluation. The symptom course of a brain abscess may extend over several weeks or even months, but a hematogenous brain abscess caused by virulent organisms (e.g., *S. aureus*) may have a fulminant course with high fever and death in 2 weeks or less. Successful treatment usually requires surgery plus antibiotic therapy. Patients with rapidly progressing symptoms may even present with pyogenic meningitis (headache, high fever, and a stiff neck) from brain abscess rupture into the subarachnoid space.[37]

Epidural and Subdural Abscesses

Epidural Abscess: Anatomy

The epidural space is a true or potential space bounded by the dura and the adjacent cranial or vertebral bones. It surrounds both the brain and the spinal cord. However, the posterior epidural space below the foramen magnum is a true anatomic space containing fat and blood vessels, whereas the entire cranial and the *anterior* spinal epidural spaces are only potential spaces with dura firmly adherent to bone. This anatomic difference results in the much higher frequency of posterior spinal epidural abscesses.

Epidural Abscess: Spinal Epidural Abscess

This condition is relatively uncommon, but it occurs in hosts with a broad age range and without gender predominance. Seventy percent of cases present with abscess formation in the posterior space between the dura and the vertebral bodies. Spinal epidural abscesses occur most commonly in the lumbar area, less frequently in the thoracic or cervical area, and least frequently in the sacral region. Infection may be introduced by hematogenous spread from a distant site, by direct extension from vertebral osteomyelitis, perinephric or psoas abscesses, or by penetrating injuries, paraspinal injections, or spinal surgery. Skin and soft tissue infections are the identified or presumed source in nearly half the cases. On average, three to six contiguous spinal segments are involved. *S. aureus* is the most commonly isolated etiologic agent.[38,39]

Epidural Abscess: Symptom Progression in Spinal Epidural Abscess

The four-stage clinical classification based on the sequential occurrence of signs and symptoms caused by spinal epidural abscess is widely accepted.[38] See Table 74-6.

Table 74-6. Clinical Progression of Signs and Symptoms of Spinal Epidural Abscess[38]

Stage 1. Back pain and tenderness
Stage 2. Nerve root pain, radiculopathy, tendon reflex changes
Stage 3. Motor weakness, sensory deficits
Stage 4. Paralysis

Stages 1 and 2 may be evident for longer periods but usually last only 3 to 4 days and are followed 4 to 5 days later by complete paralysis, which may quickly become irreversible even with adequate surgical drainage and appropriate antimicrobial therapy. Patients whose symptoms/signs progress rapidly through the early stages and all those exhibiting stage 3 to 4 signs should be regarded as neurological emergencies, evaluated radiologically (usually by MRI of the spine), and considered for immediate surgical drainage. A delay in the diagnosis after the development of neurological dysfunction is usually responsible for poor outcomes.[38] Patients with a more acute development of spinal epidural abscess will usually have fever, leukocytosis, and an elevated erythrocyte sedimentation rate (ESR). Blood cultures obtained before antibiotic therapy often will reveal the etiologic bacterium (50 to 70 percent of cases), but intraoperative cultures of the abscess contents have the highest yield and the greatest significance. Lumbar puncture and CSF examination usually are not very helpful.[38]

Published case series have noted that "spinal epidural abscess" was frequently absent from the differential diagnosis on admission of the patient to the hospital. The most common incorrect clinical diagnoses are trauma, degenerative joint disease, musculoskeletal pain, vertebral osteomyelitis, tuberculosis of the spine, or metastatic neoplasia. In addition to surgical drainage and debridement, treatment of spinal epidural abscess should include prolonged parenteral antibiotic therapy (4 to 8 weeks, depending on the adequacy of surgical drainage, clinical response, and the presence or absence of osteomyelitis). When *empirical* antibiotic therapy is elected, it should always include an appropriate antistaphylococcal agent (e.g., ampicillin/sulbactam, oxacillin, nafcillin, or vancomycin especially in areas with high rates of methicillin-resistant S. *aureus*), with additional antimicrobials when there are clinical clues suggesting a particular anatomic site (e.g., cefepime or ceftriaxone if there is evidence of a renal origin of the spinal infection).

Epidural Abscess: Intracranial Epidural Abscess

Intracranial epidural abscesses account for approximately 10 percent of all epidural abscesses.[37] In older published reports, intracranial epidural abscesses were often noted to be a consequence of sinusitis, mastoiditis, or otitis media, but in recent case series they most often follow a neurosurgical procedure. Patients with abscess in contiguity with implanted foreign material are at the highest risk. Above the foramen magnum, the dura comprises the inner lining of the skull, and the epidural space is only a potential space. Consequently, epidural intracranial infections result mainly from extension of contiguous infections, such as sinusitis, orbital cellulitis, and rhinocerebral mucormycosis, or as complications of traumatic skull fracture, neurosurgical procedure, or intracranial fetal monitoring. An intracranial epidural abscess generally expands slowly, dissecting the dura away from the inner table of the skull. The causative organisms are usually those associated with the primary infection. For example, those originating in the paranasal sinuses are generally caused by hemolytic streptococci and anaerobes (*Propionibacterium* and *Peptococcus* spp.), whereas those associated with penetrating trauma are S. *aureus* or coagulase-negative staphylococci. The organisms responsible for mucormycosis are the Zygomycetes (*Mucor, Absidia, Rhizopus* spp.). These fungal infections usually originate in the paranasal sinuses or the retro-orbital space, and the typical host is a diabetic presenting with acidosis and a focal invasive cranial infection. The symptoms of cranial epidural abscess may be nonspecific, such as fever, headache, nausea, vomiting, and lethargy. These may have been present for several weeks or even months and may be misinterpreted as reflecting only the primary process (e.g., sinusitis or even a recent traumatic skull fracture) before head imaging is obtained and a diagnosis of epidural abscess is made. Hyponatremia may occur in 30 percent of patients, serving as a clue to the discovery of an intracranial inflammatory mass. An important complication of cranial epidural abscess is the development of thrombosis of the valveless emissary veins between the skull and the meninges. This may lead to the development of a subdural empyema, meningitis, or brain abscess complicating the epidural abscess.

CT or MRI scanning of the head can establish the diagnosis of cranial epidural abscess. The therapy is fundamentally the same as for spinal epidural abscess, namely, a combination of neurosurgical drainage and the parenteral administration of appropriate antibiotics. If the dura is not destroyed, simple debridement is often satisfactory and can provide the necessary microbiological sampling for culture and susceptibility testing that permits the appropriate choice of antibiotic agents.

Transmissible Spongiform Encephalopathies

Spongiform Encephalopathy: Bovine Spongiform Encephalopathy

A recent epidemic of BSE (see Chapter 73 Creutzfeldt-Jakob Disease and Other Prion Diseases) began in the United Kingdom in 1986 and affected approximately 200,000 cattle.[39] The infectious agent responsible for BSE is a prion, a misfolded version of a normal cellular protein called *PrP*. Prions are self-replicating but devoid of nucleic acid. The particular prion responsible for BSE was probably derived from sheep (in which the infection is known as *scrapie*), although this origin is disputed. BSE is transmissible to humans by ingestion or implantation of infected tissue, and clinically it was recognized as a variant form of neurodegeneration known as new variant Creutzfeldt-Jakob Disease (nvCJD).[40] It was later shown that iatrogenic nvCJD occurred after the transplantation of infected dura mater, pituitary, or eye tissues. Notably, the latent period between graft placement (e.g., dura) and the onset of symptoms of nvCJD may be as long as 22 years.[41]

Human cases of nvCJD have major distinguishing clinical and pathophysiological features (a younger age of onset than classic CJD and the presence of distinctive amyloid as found in all 76 patients with nvCJD who were tested).[42] The link between cattle with BSE and the distinctive molecular and biological features of nvCJD has been convincingly established.[43–46] The source of infection is believed to be ingestion of beef contaminated by nervous system tissue (probably residue of spinal cord or paraspinal ganglia). The first case of nvCJD was recognized in 1994, nearly a decade after BSE was described in cattle. This incubation period of infection is consistent with experimental infections in animals and iatrogenic nvCJD in humans.[42–44] Exposure of medical and surgical instruments to what is possibly infectious human tissue and the transfer of tissue as grafts and transplants has become a matter of great concern, more so than the nearly negligible risk posed by cases of sporadic CJD.[45–47]

Spongiform Encephalopathy: Human Prion Diseases

This topic was reviewed by Prusiner (the discoverer of prions), a leading investigator in the field.[48] There are four recognized prion-related infections of humans: kuru, Gerstmann-Sträussler-Scheinker syndrome, FFI, and CJD. All four are neurodegenerative illnesses with an ultimately fatal course and there are no effective therapies. See also Chapter 73 Creutzfeldt-Jakob Disease and Other Prion Diseases.

Kuru is manifested by loss of motor coordination followed by dementia. It is apparently related to human cannibalism and has been recognized only in the highlands of Papua, New Guinea, where approximately 2,600 cases have occurred since 1957. The duration of overt illness before death is usually 3 to 12 months.[48]

Gerstmann-Sträussler-Scheinker syndrome is characterized by loss of coordination followed by dementia and death within 2 to 6 years. It is typically familial, and approximately 50 affected families have been identified.[48]

CJD is characterized by dementia followed within 1 to 2 months by loss of motor coordination, myoclonus, visual disturbances, hypokinesia, and rigidity. CJD does not usually affect the peripheral nervous system. Most cases are sporadic, but there are cases of iatrogenic nvCJD after dural grafts, corneal transplantation, liver transplantation, the administration of human growth or gonadotropic hormones, or the use of contaminated neurosurgical instruments or stereotactic electrodes.[48] In 10 to 15 percent of cases there is familial inheritance of a mutation of the prion protein gene. Laboratory diagnostic testing is rarely helpful in CJD, but some patients have elevated serum levels of S100 protein or an elevated "14–3–3" protein in the CSF.[49,50] The clinical course leading to death is typically approximately 1 year.

FFI is characterized by disturbed functions of the autonomic nervous system, insomnia, and dementia. Nine extended families with the syndrome have been reported. The clinical course leading to death is approximately 1 year. FFI, like other prion diseases, is transmissible to experimental animals, and virtually all reported cases have been associated with an asparagine for aspartic acid substitution in the prion protein.[48,51]

Spongiform Encephalopathy: Preventing the Spread of New Variant Form of Creutzfeldt-Jakob Disease

Iatrogenic transmission of the CJD agent has been reported in more than 250 patients worldwide.[45] These cases have been linked to use of contaminated human growth hormone, dura mater and corneal grafts, or neurosurgical equipment. Of the six cases linked to the use of contaminated equipment, four were associated with neurosurgical instruments and two were associated with stereotactic electroencephalogram depth electrodes. All these occurred before the routine implementation of sterilization procedures currently used in healthcare facilities. No such cases have been reported since or from surfaces such as floors, walls, or countertops.[45]

Disposable instruments should be used whenever possible on patients with suspected or confirmed CJD. A standard sterilization protocol for reusable instruments should be implemented, which includes the most stringent disinfection possible (e.g., the combined use of 1N sodium hydroxide and autoclaving at 134°C) as recommended in recent World Health Organization guidelines on infection prevention for CJD.[45,46] No effective sterilization procedure exists for instruments that are too delicate to withstand these harsh procedures. Notably, prions may be extraordinarily heat resistant. In experiments with the hamster-adapted scrapie agent, prions remained infectious after heating to ash at 600°C but not when heated to 1,000°C.[52] Surgical instruments should be disinfected to the maximum extent possible, for example, by washing repeatedly with detergent/proteinase solutions and exposing the washed instruments to 6 M urea or 4 M guanidinium thiocyanate, which have shown moderate to good disinfection of BSE in tissue extracts.[46] (See Chapter 73 Creutzfeldt-Jakob Disease and Other Prion Diseases.)

Mycotic Aneurysm

Dr. William Osler coined the term *mycotic aneurysm* in 1885. Mycotic cerebral aneurysms are localized dilatations of intracerebral arteries due to infection of the vessel wall. The term *mycotic* erroneously may imply fungal infection, but almost any microorganism may cause these *infectious aneurysms*. Septic emboli to a cerebral vessel wall may produce focal septic arteritis, which can lead to local vessel dilatation and rupture, with resulting intracerebral hemorrhage. Some believe that hematogenous microbial seeding of a previously damaged atherosclerotic vessel is the most common mechanism, and that this accounts for the 3:1 male predominance.[53] Mycotic aneurysms may be shown to result from septic microembolization to the vasa vasorum of intracranial arteries.[54] However, the small peripheral intracranial arteries that are frequently involved are devoid of vasa vasorum, and direct bacterial penetration of the arterial wall is an alternative mechanism. Intracranial or somatic mycotic aneurysms occur as rare complications of

S. aureus infectious endocarditis, but they may also complicate endocarditis caused by streptococci, other bacteria, or fungi (e.g., *Candida* spp.).

Mycotic aneurysm rupture tends to occur early in the course of a patient's systemic infection. Ruptured mycotic aneurysms comprise only a small percentage of all intracranial aneurysms. Most cerebral mycotic aneurysms present clinically as a sudden, often fatal, subarachnoid or intracerebral hemorrhage. Before rupture, premonitory signs or symptoms include seizures, ischemic deficits (stroke), or cranial nerve abnormalities. Rupture may occur even after the patient has been started on appropriate antibiotics, sometimes even after therapy has been completed. Some aneurysms may leak slowly before rupture, producing symptoms of meningeal irritation. When rupture occurs, it usually causes either subarachnoid or intracranial hemorrhage, but subdural hematomas have been described. Also described, though rarely, are asymptomatic mycotic aneurysms that resolve with antibiotic therapy.

Especially problematic are mycotic aneurysms resulting from prosthetic valve endocarditis in patients receiving full antico-agulation.[55] The diagnosis of mycotic aneurysm has reflected the evolution of angiographic methodology. Magnetic resonance angiography represents a recent advance in detection of cerebral aneurysms. If hemorrhage has occurred, conventional cerebral angiography is still the method of choice.

Optimal management of intracerebral mycotic aneurysms should include medical and surgical collaboration. Appropriate antibiotic therapy should be initiated as soon as possible using the guidelines for treatment of infectious endocarditis.[56] The distal location of most intracerebral mycotic aneurysms associated with infectious endocarditis permits ligation and excision with fewer complications compared with surgery for berry aneurysms in or near the circle of Willis. Serial angiographic studies may be useful because aneurysms may change in size or new lesions may develop. Surgery is indicated for aneurysms that are increasing in size. It has also been recommended that for aneurysms related to infectious endocarditis, the duration of antibiotic therapy be extended to 6 to 8 weeks even if the organism is highly susceptible and the aneurysm has been resected surgically. However, the natural history of an intracerebral mycotic aneurysm is unpredictable, and therapy must be individualized, especially in patients with multiple lesions. Some aneurysms may regress and resolve on antibiotic therapy, whereas others may enlarge.

The American Heart Association has reviewed the topic of mycotic aneurysms secondary to bacterial endocarditis.[57] The mortality rate of recognized mycotic aneurysm may be as high as 80 percent for aneurysms that have ruptured and 30 percent if the aneurysm is intact. However, most published case descriptions do not specify the reasons for choosing a particular therapeutic approach. Differences in outcome may relate to the patient's clinical condition at the time of diagnosis and to the size and location of the mycotic aneurysm.

Infection Prevention and Isolation Implications

For most of the CNS infections described, Standard Precautions effectively limit the transmission of these infections because they are not efficiently spread person to person. However, empiric use of Transmission-based Precautions, specifically Airborne or Droplet Precautions, may be indicated in some situations until diagnosis is confirmed (see Chapter 29 Isolation Precautions [Transmission-based Precautions]). For suspected meningitis cases, it is essential to recognize (and exclude when possible) acute bacterial meningitis, especially meningococcus (and to a lesser extent *H. influenzae*, now a rare condition since the widespread requirements for vaccination), as soon as possible. This is because of the need for providing isolation, reporting to state/local health departments, providing prophylaxis to close contacts (including assessing who fits into this narrow defined group), and allaying fear. Clinician impression and laboratory testing of CSF, including Gram stain and white blood cell count with differential, can provide clues to preliminary diagnosis.

Iatrogenic introduction of CNS infections due to breaches in infection control techniques remains a threat to patients. An article published in January 2010 in the *Morbidity and Mortality Weekly Report* describes two clusters of meningitis among five otherwise healthy women who received spinal anesthesia during labor and subsequently developed clinical meningitis. Four cases were confirmed to be caused by *Streptococcus salivarius*, a bacterium of the normal oral flora which was likely transmitted via the administering anesthesiologist and/or contaminated equipment as it was not necessarily a common practice to wear masks while performing bedside spinal procedures for one of the sites where this epidemic was found.[58]

More recently, the *New England Journal of Medicine* described in December 2012 an outbreak of fungal meningitis in otherwise immunocompetent patients who received epidural or paraspinal glucocorticoid injections contaminated with environmental molds from a single compounding pharmacy in New England. Due to rapid recognition of the outbreak by an astute clinician, and subsequent cooperation by local, state, and federal public health officials, high-risk patients were quickly identified and notified of their exposure. This led to rapid prompt evaluation and initiation of therapy, which were essential in preventing more severe sequelae of the disease.[59]

Both examples underscore the importance of strict infection control practices in the prevention of infection, particularly CNS infections.[58,59] In addition, the cooperation between infection preventionists and the state and local health departments cannot be underestimated. Infection preventionists are often the liaisons to state and local health departments for reporting, follow-up on potential clusters of disease, and other requests (including additional laboratory testing, e.g., viral encephalitis). They are likely to be involved in such activities as setting policy for care of ventricular shunts, postexposure prophylaxis, and sterilization/disinfection issues, such as those for suspected/confirmed CJD cases. Infection preventionists should collaborate with the surgical team to track and monitor any postsurgical infections involving the CSF and to track any progression of infection to the CSF in neonates and other hospitalized patients.

CONCLUSIONS

CNS infection may be caused by a variety of agents and manifest with different symptoms and disease processes. Many infections are successfully managed with pharmacological or surgical intervention, some are self-limiting, and a few are untreatable.

INTERNATIONAL PERSPECTIVE

CNS infections are common throughout the world in industrialized countries and in developing and resource-poor settings. The critical difference is that in the developing and resource-poor countries, access to care, medications, vaccinations, and sanitary conditions is extremely limited at best. The population in these settings often faces unsanitary conditions and poor nutrition, which also contributes to exposure to some agents and a poor response against infection when it does occur.

Berkhout[60] reports on the first worldwide conference, 2008 Infectious Diseases of the Nervous System: Pathogenesis and World Impact on Neuroinfection, which was held at the Pasteur Institute of Paris. The developed world actively studies and researches better management of viral encephalitis and bacterial meningitis. However, there is much less attention focused on the often fatal nervous system infections caused by neurotropic viruses, parasites, and mycobacteria in tropical regions and underdeveloped countries. The gathering promoted worldwide interactions among scientists and presented the latest research results on these neurotropic pathogens. Policymakers, medical teams, scientists, and pharmaceutical companies are challenged to create systems in developing countries for sharing of care with access to vaccines for prevention and drugs for treatment of these life-altering neurotropic pathogens: HIV alone and in combination with other infectious agents, tickborne encephalitis, rabies and rabies-related lyssaviruses, cryptococcal meningitis, *S. pneumoniae*, *H. influenzae*, and *N. meningitides*.[60-64]

REFERENCES

1. Short WR, Tunkel AR. Changing epidemiology of bacterial meningitis in the United States. *Curr Infect Dis Rep* 2000 Aug;2(4):327–331.
2. van de Beek D, de Gans J, Tunkel AR, et al. Community-acquired bacterial meningitis in adults. *N Engl J Med* 2006 Jan 5;354(1):44–53.
3. Iqbal K, Mayer L, Srivastava P, et al. Hemophilus influenzae type b invasive disease. In: *Manual for the Surveillance of Vaccine-Preventable Diseases*, 4th ed. Atlanta: Centers for Disease Control, 2008.
4. Ellenby MS, Tegtmeyer K, Lai S, Braner DA. Videos in clinical medicine. Lumbar puncture. *N Engl J Med* 2006 Sep;355(13):e12.
5. Seehusen DA, Reeves MM, Fomin DA. Cerebrospinal fluid analysis. *Am Fam Physician* 2003 Sep 15;68(6):1103–1108.
6. Hasbun R, Abrahams J, Jekel J, et al. Computed tomography of the head before lumbar puncture in adults with suspected meningitis. *N Engl J Med* 2001 Dec 13;345(24):1727–1733.
7. Arnon SI. Bacterial meningitis: principles and practical aspects of therapy. *Curr Infect Dis Rep* 2000 Aug;2(4):337–344.
8. Arnon SI, Peduzzi P, Quagliarello V. Community acquired bacterial meningitis: risk stratification for adverse clinical outcome and effect of antibiotic timing. *Ann Intern Med* 1998;129:862–869.
9. Centers for Disease Control and Prevention (CDC). Meningococcal disease: frequently asked questions. CDC website. 2012. Available at: http://www.cdc.gov/meningococcal/about/index.html.
10. Whitney CG, Farley MM, Hader J, et al. Increasing prevalence of multidrug-resistant Streptococcus pneumoniae in the United States. *N Engl J Med* 2000 Dec 28;343(26):1917–1924.
11. de Gans J, van de Beek D. Dexamethasone in adults with bacterial meningitis. *N Engl J Med* 2002 Nov 14;347(20):1549–1556.
12. Greenwood BM. Corticosteroids for acute bacterial meningitis. *N Engl J Med* 2007 Dec 13;357(24):2507–2509.
13. Pilishvili T, Noggle B, Moore MR. Pneumococcal disease. In: *Manual for the Surveillance of Vaccine-Preventable Diseases*, 5th ed. Atlanta, GA: Centers for Disease Control, 2012.
14. MacNeil J, Cohn A. Meningococcal disease. In: *Manual for the Surveillance of Vaccine-Preventable Diseases*, 5th ed. Atlanta, GA: Centers for Disease Control, 2011.
15. American Academy of Pediatrics. Meningococcal infections. In: *Red Book 2012*, 29th ed. Elkgrove Village, IL: American Academy of Pediatrics, 2012:500–509.
16. Bilukha OO, Rosenstein N. Prevention and control of meningococcal disease. Recommendations of the Advisory Committee on Immunization Practices (ACIP). *MMWR Recomm Rep* 2005 May 27;54(RR-7):1–21.
17. Centers for Disease Control and Prevention (CDC). Emergence of fluoroquinolone-resistant Neisseria meningitides—Minnesota and North Dakota, 2007–2008. *MMWR Morb Mortal Wkly Rep* 2008 Feb 22;57(7):173–175.
18. Baddour LM, Flynn PM, Fekete T. Infections of central nervous system shunts and other devices. *UpToDate* website. 2008. Available at: http://www.uptodate.com/contents/infections-of-central-nervous-system-shunts-and-other-devices.
19. McClinton D, Carraccio C, Englander R. Predictors of ventriculoperitoneal shunt pathology. *Pediatr Infect Dis J* 2001 Jun;20(6):593–597.
20. Lan CC, Wong TT, Chen SJ, et al. Early diagnosis of ventriculoperitoneal shunt infections and malfunctions in children with hydrocephalus. *J Microbiol Immunol Infect* 2003 Mar;36(1):47–50.
21. Ratilal B, Costa J, Sampaio C. Antibiotic prophylaxis for surgical introduction of intracranial ventricular shunts. *Cochrane Database Syst Rev* 2006 Jul 19;(3):CD005365.
22. Prabbhu VC, Kaufman HH, Voelker JL, et al. Prophylactic antibiotics with intracranial pressure monitors and external ventricular drains: a review of the evidence. *Surg Neurol* 1999 Sep;52(3):226–236.
23. Zabramski JM, Whiting D, Darouiche RO, et al. Efficacy of antimicrobial-impregnated external ventricular drain catheters: a prospective, randomized, controlled trial. *J Neurosurg* 2003 Apr;98(4):725–730.
24. Ramachandran TS. Aseptic meningitis. *MedScape* website. 2013. Available at: http://emedicine.medscape.com/article/1169489-overview.
25. Centers for Disease Control and Prevention (CDC). *Meningitis: Viral Meningitis*. CDC website. 2012. Available at: http://www.cdc.gov/meningitis/viral.html.
26. Nicolosi A, Hauser WA, Beghi E, et al. Epidemiology of central nervous system infections in Olmstead County, Minnesota, 1950–1981. *J Infect Dis* 1986 Sep;154(3):399–408.
27. Pevear DC, Tull TM, Seipel ME, et al. Activity of pleconaril against enteroviruses. *Antimicrob Agents Chemother* 1999 Sep;43(9):2109–2115.
28. Rothbart HA, Webster AD. Treatment of potentially life-threatening enterovirus infections with pleconaril. *Clin Infect Dis* 2001 Jan 15;32(2):228–235.
29. Desmond RA, Accortt NA, Talley L, et al. Enteroviral meningitis: natural history and outcome of pleconaril therapy. *Antimicrob Agents Chemother* 2006 Jul;50(7):2409–2414.
30. Gripshover BM, Ellner JJ. Chronic meningitis. In: Mandell GL, Bennett JE, Dolin R, eds. *Principles and Practice of Infectious Diseases*. Philadelphia: Churchill Livingstone, 2000:997–1009.
31. Storch GA. Essentials of diagnostic virology. In: *Essentials of Diagnostic Virology*. New York: Churchill Livingstone, 2000:37–58.
32. Schlesinger Y, Tebas P, Gaudreault Keener M, et al. Herpes simplex virus type 2 meningitis in the absence of genital lesions: improved recognition with use of the polymerase chain reaction. *Clin Infect Dis* 1995 Apr;20(4):842–848.
33. Lakeman FD, Whitley RJ. Diagnosis of herpes simplex encephalitis: application of polymerase chain reaction to cerebrospinal fluid from brain-biopsied patients and correlation with disease. National Institute of Allergy and Infectious Diseases Collaborative Antiviral Study Group. *J Infect Dis* 1995 Apr;171(4):857–863.
34. Petersen LR, Hayes EB. Westward ho?—The spread of West Nile virus. *N Engl J Med* 2004 Nov 25;351(22):2257–2259.
35. Solomon T. Flavivirus encephalitis. *N Engl J Med* 2004 Jul 22;351(4):370–378.
36. Centers for Disease Control and Prevention (CDC). West Nile virus infection in organ donor and transplant recipients—Georgia and Florida, 2002. *MMWR Morb Mortal Wkly Rep* 2002 Sep 6;51(35):790.
37. Wispelwey B, Dacey RG, Scheld WM. Brain abscess. In: Scheld WM, Whitley RJ, Durack DT, eds. *Infections of the Central Nervous System*, 2nd ed. Philadelphia: Lippincott Raven, 1997:507–522.
38. Maslen DR, Jones SR, Crislip MA, et al. Spinal epidural abscess. Optimizing patient care. *Arch Intern Med* 1993 Jul 26;153(14):1713–1721.

39. Darouiche RO. Spinal epidural abscess. *N Engl J Med* 2006 Nov 9; 355(19):2012–2020.
40. Brown P, Will RG, Bradley R, et al. Bovine spongiform encephalopathy and variant Creutzfeldt-Jakob disease: background, evolution and current concerns. *Emerg Infect Dis* 2001 Jan-Feb;7(1):6–16.
41. Centers for Disease Control and Prevention (CDC). Update: Creutzfeldt-Jakob disease associated with cadaveric dura mater grafts—Japan, 1979–2003. *MMWR Morb Mortal Wkly Rep* 2003 Dec 5;52(48):1179–1181.
42. Collinge J, Sidle KC, Meads J, et al. Molecular analysis of prion strain variation and the aetiology of 'new variant' CJD. *Nature* 1996 Oct 24;383(6602):685–690.
43. Bruce ME, Will RG, Ironside J, et al. Transmissions to mice indicate that 'new variant' CJD is caused by the BSE agent. *Nature* 1997 Oct 2; 389(6650):498–501.
44. Scott MR, Will R, Ironside J, et al. Compelling transgenetic evidence for transmission of bovine spongiform encephalopathy prions to humans. *Proc Natl Acad Sci U S A* 1999 Dec 21;96(26):15137–15142.
45. Centers for Disease Control and Prevention (CDC). *Questions and Answers: Creutzfeldt-Jakob Disease Infection Control Practices.* CDC website. 2010. Available at: http://www.cdc.gov/ncidod/dvrd/cjd/qa_cjd _infection_control.htm.
46. World Health Organization (WHO). WHO infection control guidelines for transmissible spongiform encephalopathies: Report of a WHO Consultation. Geneva: WHO, 1999.
47. Rutala WA, Weber DJ. Creutzfeldt-Jakob disease: recommendations for disinfection and sterilization. *Clin Infect Dis* 2001 May 1;32(9):1348-56.
48. Prusiner SB. Shattuck lecture—neurodegenerative diseases and prions. *N Engl J Med* 2001 May 17;344(20):1516–1526.
49. Otto M, Wiltfang J, Schutz E, et al. Diagnosis of Creutzfeldt-Jakob disease by measurement of S100 protein in serum: prospective case-control study. *BMJ* 1998 Feb 21;316(7131):577–582.
50. Zerr I, Bodemer M, Otto M, et al. Diagnosis of Creutzfeldt-Jakob disease by two-dimensional electrophoresis of cerebrospinal fluid. *Lancet* 1996 Sep;348(9031):846–849.
51. McLean CA, Storey E, Gardner RJ, et al. The D178N (cis-129M) "fatal familial insomnia" mutation associated with diverse clinicopathologic phenotypes in an Australian kindred. *Neurology* 1997 Aug;49(2):552–558.
52. Brown P, Rau EH, Johnson BK, et al. New studies on the heat resistance of hamster-adapted scrapie agent: threshold survival after ashing at 600 degrees C suggests an inorganic template of replication. *Proc Natl Acad Sci U S A* 2000 Mar 28;97(7):3418–3421.
53. Bayer AS, Scheld WM. Endocarditis and intravascular infections. In: Mandell GL, Bennett JE, Dolin R, eds. *Principles and Practice of Infectious Diseases,* 5th ed. Philadelphia: Churchill Livingstone, 2000: 857–902.
54. Molinari GF, Smith L, Goldstein MN, et al. Pathogenesis of cerebral mycotic aneurysms. *Neurology* 1973 Apr;23(4):325–332.
55. Francioli PB. Complications of infective endocarditis. In: Scheld WM, Whitlet RJ, Durack DT, eds. *Infections of the Central Nervous System,* 2nd ed. Philadelphia: Lippincott Raven, 1997:423–553.
56. Wilson WR, Karchmer AW, Dajani AS, et al. Antibiotic treatment of adults with infective endocarditis due to streptococci, enterococci, staphylococci and HACEK microorganisms. *JAMA* 1995;274:1706–1713.
57. Bayer AS, Bolger AF, Taubert KA, et al. Diagnosis and management of infective endocarditis and its complications. *Circulation* 1998 Dec 22-29; 98(25):2936–2948.
58. Centers for Disease Control and Prevention. Bacterial meningitis after intrapartum spinal anesthesia—New York and Ohio, 2008-2009. *MMWR Morb Mortal Wkly Rep* 2010 Jan 29;59(3):65–69.
59. Kainer MA, Reagan DR, Nguyen DB, et al. Fungal infections associated with contaminated methylprednisolone in Tennessee. *N Engl J Med* 2012 Dec 6;367(23):2194–2203.
60. Berkhout B. Infectious diseases of the nervous system: pathogenesis and worldwide impact. *IDrugs* 2008 Nov;11(11):791–795.
61. Sloan D, Dlamini S, Paul N, et al. Treatment of acute cryptococcal meningitis in HIV infected adults, with an emphasis on resource-limited settings. *Cochrane Database Syst Rev* 2008 Oct 8;(4):CD005647.
62. Raising the profile of pneumococcal disease. *Lancet* 2008 Oct 25; 372(9648):1438.
63. Scarborough M, Thwaites GE. The diagnosis and management of acute bacterial meningitis in resource-poor settings. *Lancet Neurol* 2008 Jul;7(7):637–648.
64. Rendi-Wagner P. Advances in vaccination against tick-borne encephalitis. *Expert Rev Vaccines* 2008 Jul;7(5):589–596.

CHAPTER 75

Enterobacteriaceae

Darlene Miller, DHSc, MPH, MA, SM (NRM, ASCP), MT (ASCP), CIC
Research Associate Professor
Department of Ophthalmology
Scientific Director
Abrams Ocular Microbiology Laboratory
Anne Bates Leach Eye Hospital/Bascom Palmer Eye Institute
University of Miami Miller School of Medicine
Miami, FL

ABSTRACT

Enterobacteriaceae are a large, diverse group of facultative Gram-negative rods, recovered as natural inhabitants of the environment and the large intestines of humans and animals. They are important pathogens in healthcare- and community-associated infections in the United States and worldwide. The spectrum of infections includes bacteremias, pneumonias, surgical site infections, and urinary tract infections. Patients at greatest risk include those in medical and surgical intensive care units and residents of short- and long-term acute care hospitals. Infants, the elderly, the immunocompromised, and those with extensive exposure to healthcare are the most vulnerable. In developing countries they are among the leading cause of diarrheal disease and death of children under age 5. Increasing antibiotic resistance to third-generation cephalosporins, fluoroquinolones, and carbapenems results in diminished treatment choices for the prevention and management of both healthcare- and community-associated infections. Several members of this group may also be used to launch biological weapons. Strategies for prevention include healthcare personnel education and training, checklists, surveillance, and zero tolerance for noncompliance with evidence-based best practices. Adoption and monitoring of patient and quality improvement outcomes are essential to reducing infections and developing a culture of patient safety.

KEY CONCEPTS

- Enterobacteriaceae are among the most common, life threatening, and preventable healthcare-associated infections (e.g., bacteremia, pneumonias, and surgical site infections).

- They are important pathogens in common community-associated infections (urinary tract infections, diarrheal diseases, lower respiratory tract infections).

- Members include Gram-negative, short, coccobacillary, or straight, non-spore-forming bacilli that grow well in the presence or absence of oxygen (facultative).

- Members of this group are normal inhabitants of the gastrointestinal tract of humans, cattle, other mammals, reptiles, and fowl. They are also recovered worldwide from soil, plants, sewage, aquatic environments, improperly prepared food, and contaminated water and medical equipment.

- Members of this family are often recovered as transient residents on hands of healthcare personnel and are frequent colonizers of patients with extended hospital stays or treatment with broad-spectrum antibiotics.

- Virulence factors include: toxins, adhesions, hemolysins, plasmids, fimbriae, pili, enzymes, mobile genetic elements, and biofilm production. Members initiate both overt and opportunistic infections in humans.

- All grow well on routine laboratory media. Molecular methods and biochemical profiles (via kits or automated systems) are used to identify members in as early as 2 hours. Serology and, additionally, molecular techniques are used to characterize specific serotypes (e.g., *Escherichia coli* O157:H7) or clones associated with diarrheal diseases and outbreaks.

- Patients at greatest risk for healthcare-associated infections include infants; children; the elderly; debilitated, immunocompromised patients; patients with catheters or other indwelling medical devices; those in intensive care units, on broad-spectrum antibiotics, in long-term care, or on dialysis; or those with extended hospital stay. Populations in crowded areas or areas with poor sanitation are at greater risk for gastrointestinal infections.

- Treatment outcomes with third-generation cephalosporins are no longer predictable.

- Increasing recovery of extended-spectrum beta-lactamase-producing and other multidrug-resistant members dictate in vitro susceptibility testing and knowledge of local antibiograms.

- The emergence of carbapenemase-producing Enterobacteriaceae is a mounting public health concern. Carbapenemase enzymes have broad spectrum hydrolyzing activity, thereby rendering all penicillins, cephalosporins, and carbapenems ineffective. They are often located on mobile genetic elements with other resistant genes which results in multidrug or "pan"-resistant members with limited or no therapeutic options.

- The majority of Enterobacteriaceae species in the United States remain susceptible to the fluoroquinolones, amikacin, and imipenem. New options for multidrug- or pan-resistant isolates include colistin, polymyxins, and tigecycline.

- Strict adherence to evidence-based "best practices" (hand washing, use of alcohol-based hand rub, barrier protection, proper maintenance of equipment and the environment, healthcare personnel and consumer education) are required to prevent and control these infections.

- Several members in this group may be used as biological weapons (*Yersinia pestis, Salmonella* species, *Shigella, and Escherichia coli*).

IMPORTANCE TO INFECTION PREVENTION AND CONTROL

Enterobacteriaceae may account for 80 percent of clinically significant isolates of Gram-negative bacilli and 50 percent of clinically significant bacteria recovered in clinical microbiology laboratories. They are also the etiologic agents in nearly one-third (30 to 35 percent) of all septicemia cases, more than 80 percent of urinary tract infections, and a significant percentage of pneumonia and intestinal infections.[1,2] They are also important agents in myriad other preventable healthcare- and community-associated infections. These include skin and soft tissue, osteomyelitis, septic arthritis, ocular infections, intraabdominal abscesses, and wound and lower respiratory site infections.[1-6] More importantly, healthcare-associated infections (HAIs) associated with the Enterobacteriaceae are among the most life threatening, preventable, and costly infections encountered in healthcare facilities. Implementation and adherence to evidence-based best practices for the prevention, surveillance, and control of these preventable infections across the continuum of care will reduce their contributions to HAIs as well as improve patient safety. The single most important means to effectively reduce the transmission and horizontal spread of Enterobacteriaceae and other microorganisms in all healthcare settings is compliance with proper hand washing. Compliance with hand washing and other basic tenets of infection prevention (aseptic technique, education, and surveillance) is important to reduce the risk of colonization and infection. Surveillance programs should be implemented and maintained to monitor epidemiology, emerging resistance, shifting pathogen trends, and to detect outbreaks, direct therapy, and guide quality improvement and patient outcomes.[7-9]

Implementation of Standard Precautions and aggressive infection control and prevention practices in all healthcare settings is also warranted to reduce transmission of microorganisms from person to person, for both recognized and unrecognized reservoirs. Transmission-based Precautions may be required for patients with infectious diarrhea or other enteric pathogens that are highly transmissible or of epidemiological importance (e.g., bioterrorism agent, carbapenemase-producing [CPE], and other multidrug-resistant isolates).[10]

Adopting the strategies and recommendations in the Compendium of Strategies to Prevent Healthcare-Associated Infections in Acute Care Hospitals provided by the combined Society for Healthcare Epidemiology of America (SHEA) and the Infectious Disease Society of Standards and Practice Guideline Committee taskforce along with the new Centers for Disease Control and Prevention (CDC) guidelines for detection and prevention of carbapenem-resistant Enterobacteriaceae (CRE) should be routinely implemented to detect and protect patients from infections with this group of organisms.[11-14]

BACKGROUND

The purpose of this chapter is to provide a brief overview of the epidemiology and pathogenesis of the family Enterobacteriaceae and to highlight strategies to prevent and reduce infections and other adverse patient outcomes associated with members of this group.

The Enterobacteriaceae are a large, diverse family of small, Gram-negative, coccobacillary, or straight rods. They inhabit a wide variety of niches, including soil, plants, water, and gastrointestinal tracts of humans and animals. Because of their natural affinity for the gastrointestinal tract, members are often referred to as "enterics" or coliforms. The majority of the species is morphologically indistinguishable and shares similar biochemical and physiological features. All are oxidase negative, ferment glucose, reduce nitrate, and grow equally as well in air (aerobic) or without air (anaerobic). All but three genera are motile. Enterics are the most frequent group of Gram-negative rods encountered in the microbiology laboratory and among the most common causing community- and healthcare-associated infections. Currently there are more than 30 genera and 120 species in the family Enterobacteriaceae. Taxonomic and molecular characterizations keep this list is in a constant change of flux and expansion.[1-4,15] However, 95 percent of those associated with human disease or colonization are restricted to as few as 10 genera and 20 to 25 species. The most familiar species recovered from extraintestinal disease are *Escherichia coli, Enterobacter cloacae, Klebsiella pneumoniae, Serratia marcescens,* and *Proteus mirabilis. Salmonella* species, *Shigella* species, and *E. coli* are common agents of gastroenteritis and colitis (see Tables 75-1 and 75-2).[1-4,15]

BASIC PRINCIPLES

Pathogenesis

A variety of specific and nonspecific virulence factors interact to initiate colonization or establish disease. Common to all members is the complex antigenic structure of the cell wall and outer surface appendages. The O or somatic antigen is a heat-stable lipopolysaccharide composed of three components: (1) an antigenic variable O polysaccharide (unique to species), (2) a core polysaccharide (common to all species), and (3) lipid A. Endotoxin activity is coupled with the lipid A portion. Lipid A is released during growth, cell death, or lysis. Many of the adverse systemic manifestations (fever, shock,

Table 75-1. Extraintestinal Infections Associated with Common Enterobacteriaceae

Organisms	Clinical Syndrome(s)	Mechanisms	Risk Factor(s)	Infection Prevention Issues	Laboratory Identification/Tests
Escherichia coli	UTI, most common, pyelonephritis, cystitis	Adherence to urinary tract epithelium cells with Type P, Type 1 fimbriae (uropathogenic strains). Organisms are seeded from the gastrointestinal tract with specific serotypes (e.g., 04, 06, 075 are frequent serotypes).	Community-sexually active females, others (short urethra; colonization of vagina, closeness of anus) Health-care related: catheterization, prolonged institutional stay, underlying disease (diabetes, cancer, etc), obstruction of urinary flow.	Limit catheterization and LOS in healthcare facilities; use silver-impregnated catheters. Perform targeted surveillance in high risk areas. Practice aseptic technique, use gloves, and wash hands between patients. Use closed drainage system. Maintenance of unobstructed urine flow. Education of healthcare providers on the proper care and insertion of catheters.	Culture and quantitation of clean catch or catheterized urine.
	Pneumonia, bronchitis (LRTI)	Colonization of lower respiratory tract. Aspiration of contaminated respiratory secretions	Community-rare, underlying disease-diabetes, COPD, alcoholism Health-care related: immunosuppressed or debilitated, ventilator-dependent patients, presence of gastric intubation, endotracheal tube, supine position, ICU patients at greater risk. Increased fibronectin degrading protease in saliva.	Colonization vs infection. Difficulty in establishing actual infection, quantitative cultures. Reduction of oropharyngeal and gastric colonization and aspiration in ventilator-dependent patients. Reprocessing, staffing issues.	Specimen of choice in descending order: BAL > PSB > PCA > EA > sputum
	Bacteremia	Organisms may enter the bloodstream from a focus of infection of the urinary or the gastrointestinal tracts. Strains with S-fimbrial antigens associated with neonatal sepsis.	Community-age, malnutrition, trauma, underlying disease Health-care related: colonization, admission to ICU comorbidities, UTI, presence of catheter, invasive procedures. Cross contamination (hands of HCP).	As for UTI, maintenance and care of IV or other catheter. Adherence to strict infection prevention protocols, especially hand washing. Establishment of a needless and alcohol-based system for caregivers. Contaminated fomites and solutions.	Adequate number, volume, and timing of blood cultures
	Wound, surgical site infections	Organisms are usually endogenous or acquired from the environment, usually at the time of surgery.	Mainly-Health-care related: Hair removal. Duration and type of surgery. Underlying disease. Trauma including burns, surgery, accidents. Older patients are more susceptible to wound infections (declining immunity)	Cross contamination, duration of surgery, preoperative antibiotics. Use of corticosteroids. Surgeon specific surveillance and feedback.	Use aseptic technique to collect pus, tissue of drainage. Prompt delivery to microbiology. Evaluation for presence of organisms (stains and culture) and resistant isolates (sensitivity)
	Neonatal meningitis	Colonization of the gastrointestinal tract at the time of delivery from colonized birth canal; 75 percent of cases are associated with K1 capsular antigen or strains with S fimbriae	Infants in their first month of life.	Management with antibiotic therapy. Cross contamination (hands of HCP, equipment)	CSF culture and sensitive. Gram stain of CSF may reveal the organisms.
	Central nervous system Infections (adults)	Neurosurgical patients, neonates, and procedures that penetrate the CNS	Hospital patients undergoing surgery of the CNS.	Management with antibiotic therapy.	CSF culture and sensitive. Gram stain of CSF may reveal the organisms.
Klebsiella pneumoniae	Necrotizing lobal pneumonia. "Currant jelly" appearance of sputum (lung necrosis and blood). Bronchitis and bronchopneumonias (less severe presentation)	Presence of capsular aids in adherence to respiratory mucosa. Types 1, 3. *Klebsiella* may be a commensal on skin, in the nasopharynx, and GI tract and infections are endogenous.	Community: alcoholics, individuals with compromised pulmonary function, severe underlying disease.	Management with antibiotic therapy. Cross contamination (hands of HCP, equipment).	Sputum with "currant jelly" appearance. A positive sputum must be supported by clinical signs (fever, presence of WBC on Gram stain and signs of system inflammation). Detection of carbapenemase producing strain may be missed with current automated systems.

(continued)

Table 75-1. Extraintestinal Infections Associated with Common Enterobacteriaceae (cont'd)

Organisms	Clinical Syndrome(s)	Mechanisms	Risk Factor(s)	Infection Prevention Issues	Laboratory Identification/Tests
	Healthcare-associated pneumonia	Colonization of lower respiratory tract. Aspiration of contaminated respiratory secretions.	Health-care related: immunosuppressed or debilitated, ventilator-dependent patients, presence of gastric intubation, endotracheal tube, supine position, ICU patients at greater risk. Increased fibronectin degrading protease in saliva.	Colonization vs Infection. Difficulty in establishing actual infection, quantitative cultures. Reduction of oropharyngeal and gastric colonization and aspiration in ventilator dependent patients. Reprocessing, staffing issues.	Specimen of choice in descending order: BAL > PSB > PCA > EA > sputum
	Neonatal meningitis, meningitidis	Colonization and invasion of bloodstream.	Premature and underweight infants. Presence of medical device.	Colonization of GI tract with GNI. Cross contamination (hands of HCP).	CSF culture and sensitive. Gram stain of CSF may reveal the organisms.
	UTIs	Adherence to urinary tract epithelium cells with Type 1 fimbriae (uropathogenic strains). Organisms are seeded from the gastrointestinal tract with specific serotypes (e.g., O4, O6, O75 are frequent serotypes).	Community-rare Health-care-related: catheterization, prolonged institutional stay, underlying disease (diabetes, cancer, etc), obstruction of urinary flow.	Same as for *E. coli*	Culture and quantitation of clean catch or catheterized urine.
	Wound, surgical site infections	Organisms are usually endogenous or acquired from the environment—usually at the time of surgery.	Mainly-Health-care related: Hair removal. Duration and type of surgery. Underlying disease. Trauma including burns, surgery, accidents. Older patients are more susceptible to wound infections (declining immunity).	Cross contamination, duration of surgery, preoperative antibiotics. Use of corticosteroids. Surgeon-specific surveillance and feedback.	Use aseptic technique to collect pus, tissue of drainage. Prompt delivery to microbiology. Evaluation for presence of organisms (stains and culture) and resistant isolates (sensitivity).
Enterobacter cloacae	Healthcare-associated pneumonia, UTI, sepsis, neonatal meningitis, surgical wound infections	Opportunistic pathogens, colonization and adherence to tissues, transmission on hands of HCP, exposure to contamination of food, solutions, and medical equipment. Reduction of normal or resident flora by exposure to broad-spectrum antibiotics.	Health-care related: immunosuppressed or debilitated, ventilator-dependent patients, presence of gastric intubation, endotracheal tube, supine position, ICU patients at greater risk. Increased fibronectin degrading protease in saliva. Presence of indwelling medical devices, IV, catheters, etc. Cross contamination (hands of HCP). Broad-spectrum antibiotics.	Same as for *E. coli*	Same as for *E. coli*
Serratia marcescens	Surgical wound infections, bacteremias, UTI, LRTI, and bacteremias	Opportunistic pathogens, colonization, transmission, hands of HCP, contamination of food, infusion fluids, and enteral feeds.	Same as for *E. coli*	Same as for *E. coli*	Appropriate specimens from infected organ system or site. May include blood, urine, pus, sputum, tissue, CSF, or other.
Citrobacter species	Neonatal meningitis, UTI, respiratory infections	Opportunistic pathogen	Infants <2 (meningitis), same as for *E. coli*	Same as for *E. coli*	Same as for *E. coli*
Proteus species	UTI, kidney stones, pyelonephritis, renal abscess	Organisms hydrolyze urea, form a type of kidney stone, block the flow of urine, opportunistic pathogen	Indwelling Foley catheter. Prolonged long stay in healthcare facility.	Same as for *E. coli*	Culture
	Pneumonia, surgical, wound infections	Destructive ear infection, septicemia	Same as for *E. coli*	Same as for *E. coli*	Appropriate specimens from infected organ system or site.
Morganella species	UTI, surgical wound infections, and respiratory infections	Opportunistic pathogen	Same as for *E. coli*	Same as for *E. coli*	Appropriate specimens from infected organs system or site
Providencia species	UTI, surgical wound infections	Opportunistic pathogen	Same as for *E. coli*	Same as for *E. coli*	Appropriate specimens from infected organs system or site

BAL, bronchoalveolar lavage; CSF, cerebrospinal fluid; CNS, central nervous system; COPD, chronic obstructive pulmonary disease; GI, gastrointestinal; HCP, healthcare personnel; ICU, intensive care unit; LOS, Length of Stay; PCA, protected catheter aspirate; PSB, protected specimen brush; UTI, urinary tract infection; WBCs, white blood cells.

APIC Text of Infection Control and Epidemiology

Table 75-2. Enteric Infections Associated With Common Enterobacteriaceae

Organisms	Clinical Syndrome	Mechanism(s)	Common Source(s)	Risk Group(s)
Escherichia coli (EHEC) enterohemorrhagic	Hemorrhagic colitis-characterized by severe cramping, watery diarrhea that becomes grossly bloody. Complications: Hemolytic uremic syndrome (HUS), thrombotic thrombocytopenic purpura (TTP)	Production of potent verotoxin, Shiga-like toxins that damage the lining of the intestines. These are similar or identical to the toxin produced by *Shigella* dysenteriae. Disease is associated with certain serotypes. Ex: *E. coli* 0157:H7, 026:H11, 0111:H8, 0103:H2	Uncooked or raw hamburger, milk, apple cider. Person to person in day care and nursing homes.	Children (<5) and the elderly at greatest risk. Young (HUS), elderly (TTP)
Escherichia coli (ETEC) enterotoxigenic	Gastroenteritis, traveler's diarrhea-watery diarrhea, nausea, abdominal cramps, self-limiting	Colonization of the small intestines, proliferation and toxin production, heat stable and/or heat labile enterotoxins-leakage of electrolytes	Food or water contaminated with human sewage or animal feces. Infected food handlers. Poor sanitation.	Travelers to foreign countries
Escherichia coli (EPEC) enteropathogenic	Infantile diarrhea-watery or bloody diarrhea, may be prolonged and lead to dehydration, electrolyte imbalance, and death	Organisms adhere to and damage the small intestines by production of a cell associated verotoxin, which is mediated by a plasmid. Other virulence factors include bundle forming pili and intimin. Serotypes: 018:H7, 044:H3, 020:H2	Contaminated beef, chicken, and infant formula. Contaminated water.	Infants that are bottle fed: reconstitution of formula with contaminated water
Escherichia coli (EIEC) enteroinvasive	Bacillary dysentery-characterized by a mild diarrhea with mucus and blood in the stool. Abdominal cramps, fever, chills, and generalized malaise. Complications: HUS (pediatric cases)	Low infectious dose-organisms possess plasmids which mediated the invasion and destruction of epithelial cells of the colon.	Contaminated beef, chicken, and infant formula. Contaminated water.	Infants and children in emerging nations
Escherichia coli (EAEC) enteroaggressive	Acute and chronic diarrhea—watery diarrhea, vomiting	Enteroaggressive heat stable enterotoxin (EAST1)	Contaminated food or water	All age groups
Escherichia coli (DHEC) diffusely adherent	Infantile diarrhea—watery or bloody diarrhea, may be prolonged and lead to dehydration, electrolyte imbalance, and death	Alpha hemolysin and cytotoxic necrotizing factor 1	Contaminated food or water	Infants in emerging nations
Escherichia coli	Necrotizing enterocolitis	Multifactorial	NICU	Infants with low birth weight, low gestational age, low Apgar score, perinatal complications, hyaline membrane disease, and umbilical catheterization
Salmonella serotype Typhi	Typhoid, enteric revers, febrile illness, intermittent fever with headache, malaise, and anorexia. Bacteremia, asymptomatic carriage (gallbladder).	Infectious dose = HIGH (1,000,000 organisms). 10–14 days incubation: Heat stable and labile enterotoxins similar to those of *Shigella* and *E. coli*. Organisms attach, penetrate, and invade the mucosa of enterocytes in the small intestine. Mucosal infection progresses to hemorrhage and ulceration and sometimes perforation. Vi-capsular antigen is important. Transmission is via fecal-oral route.	Contaminated food or water, duodenal intubation	All age groups, international travelers, laboratory workers, HIV patients
Salmonella serotype Enteritidis	Gastroenteritis, nausea, vomiting, nonbloody diarrhea, fever, abdominal cramps, myalgias, and headache. Spontaneous resolution. Bacteremia.	Infectious dose = HIGH (100,000,000), 6–48 hours after ingestion of contaminated food. Enterotoxins locally invade the epithelial cells of the gut, then migrate to the lamina propria layer where they multiply and stimulate active fluid secretion.	Contaminated food. Luncheon food, precooked roast beef, cold cuts. Dairy products.	Most common isolate in the U.S. All age groups, HIV patients (bacteremia), laboratory workers
Salmonella serotype Typhimurium	Gastroenteritis, bacteremia as above	As above	Contaminated food or water. Eggs, Fiberoptic endoscope, clover sprouts, milk, ice cream, raw ground beef.	Elderly, infants, immunocompromised
Salmonella Serotype, others	Gastroenteritis, bacteremia as above	As above	Contaminated food or water, rectal thermometer, rubber tubing, alfalfa sprouts	All age groups, HIV patients

(continued)

Table 75-2. Enteric Infections Associated With Common Enterobacteriaceae (cont'd)

Organisms	Clinical Syndrome	Mechanism(s)	Common Source(s)	Risk Group(s)
S. dysenteriae (serogroup A)	Bacillary dysentery: characterized by a mild diarrhea with mucus and blood in the stool. Abdominal cramps, fever, chills, and generalized malaise. Complications: HUS (pediatric cases)	Infectious dose is LOW (100 to 200 organisms). Shiga toxin is two-stage disease. First ingestion: noninvasive colonization, production of enterotoxin; watery diarrhea; blocks uptake of glucose and electrolytes. Second: adherence and invasion of large intestines, increased cytotoxic activity; inhibits protein synthesis causing cell death and damage to the large intestines.	Contaminated food and water. Person-to-person (fecal-oral) transmission.	Mainly a pediatric disease, common in emerging nations
S. flexneri (serogroup B)	Bacillary dysentery; most common in emerging nations	As above	Contaminated food and water. Person-to-person (fecal-oral) transmission.	Mainly a pediatric disease; common in emerging nations
S. boydii (serogroup C)	Bacillary dysentery	As above	Contaminated food and water. Person-to-person (fecal-oral) transmission.	
S. sonnei (serogroup D)	Bacillary dysentery; most common cause in the United States	As above	Men who have sex with men, day care and mental institutions, unchlorinated wading pool. Contaminated food or water (person-to-person outbreaks = largest).	Children in child care, institutionalized populations (prisons, mental institutions). Native Americans, orthodox Jews, and international travelers
K. pneumoniae	Enteritis, colitis, necrotizing enterocolitis	Heat stable and heat-labile enterotoxin	NA	Children under 3 in emerging/developing countries
Enterobacter species	Necrotizing enterocolitis	Heat stable and heat-labile enterotoxin	NICU	Children under 3 in emerging/developing countries
Citrobacter freundii	Infantile diarrhea (rare), enteritis, colitis	Verotoxin, antigen 0157	NA	Infants
Yersinia	Bloody diarrhea			
	Enterocolitis	Enterotoxin	Unpasteurized milk, contaminated water, raw, undercooked pork	Young children, males, adults

disseminated intravascular coagulation [DIC]) of Gram-negative infections are due to endotoxin (lipid A). K, or capsular, antigens are made of either proteins or polysaccharides. The capsule or "slime layer" protects encapsulated strains from phagocytosis and serum killing. Capsular antigens on *Salmonella* species are classified as Vi antigens and play an important role in disease. H or flagellar antigens are located on flagella and are constructed of proteins. These appendages confer motility and, along with pili, facilitate attachment[1-5,15] (Table 75-3).

Serological classification is based on the presence and detection of the O, K, and H antigens. Differential combinations of these antigens within and between species allow for great antigenic diversity and gradient of pathogenicity. There are at least 150 O, 100 K, and 50 H serotypes. Specific serotypes are linked with specific disease syndromes (i.e., *Escherichia coli* O157:H7).[1-5,15,16]

The tendency to grow as microcolonies surrounded by a complex organic matrix or *biofilm* on surfaces, medical devices, and within living and dead tissues protects members from the deleterious effects of antibiotics, toxic substances, and serum killing. Inside this matrix of extracellular polymers, organisms are highly resistant to antibiotics, immune clearance, and eradication. This mode of growth may be implicated in up to 60 percent of persistent and chronic HAIs. Documented biofilm-associated enteric infections include biliary tract infection, bacterial prostatitis, intensive care unit (ICU) pneumonia, urinary catheter cystitis, and biliary stent blockage.[17,18]

Epidemiology

Enterobacteriaceae rarely infect patients that are immunocompetent. Host defenses must be breached for disease to occur. The skin or mucous membranes may be breached by trauma, surgery, catheterization, tracheal intubation, or antibiotic therapy. Opportunistic organisms or pathogens may gain entry through third-degree burns, ulcers, intravenous catheters, surgical or instrumental manipulation, or contaminated food and beverages.[1,2,4,5,7,11,16,19,20]

Common vehicles associated with outbreaks include contaminated IVs, enteral feeding and saline solutions, disinfectants, electrocardiogram bulbs, powered infant formulas, urinals, and blood culture equipment. Medical interventions such as corticosteroid administration, radiotherapy, and other immunosuppressive therapy also contribute to the risk of infection. Cancer- or

Table 75-3. Virulent Factors Associated With the Enterobacteriaceae

TYPE	Factor	Mechanisms of Action
Structure	Cell wall (LPS-polysaccharides and lipid A) endotoxin	Common to all aerobic and some anaerobic, Gram-negative bacteria, released upon death. Activates macrophages, white blood cells, releases cytotoxins, causes "septic shock," necrosis, DIC, and death.
	Somatic O antigens	Confirms specific serotype. Serotypes are associated with specific syndromes.
	Flagellar H antigens	Facilitates motility and adherence to gastrointestinal, urinary epithelial cells. Also assists in invasion of mucosa.
	Capsule, K antigens	Prevents phagocytosis, evades immune mechanisms.
	Pili, fimbriae	Facilitates adherence and invasion of mucosa and epithelial cells, first step in colonization.
	"Pathogenic islands"	Provides resistance to antibiotics, production of toxins, hemolysins; may be chromosomal or plasmid mediated.
Toxins	Endotoxins	Cells wall, mainly Lipid A (see structure)
	Exotoxins (Enterotoxins)	Heat-labile elevates cAMP, with altered electrolyte transport and excessive fluid secretion, cell destruction, short range, tissue specificity.
		Heat-stabile elevates cyclic GMP, increases secretion of fluids from small intestines.
		Shiga-like toxin: excessive tissue destruction
	Neurotoxins	Targets central nervous system, inhibits protein synthesis, resulting in headaches, meningeal symptoms and seizures (*S. dysenteriae*).
	Hemolysins (cytotoxins-membrane bound)	Lysis of red and white blood cells, uremic syndrome, long range, targets many cells and tissues.
Plasmids	Colonization factors, hemolysins, antibiotic drug resistance (R), toxins	Assists in adherence to epithelial cells, causes cell destruction, provides protection against antibiotics.

drug-induced neutropenia is also an important predisposing factor in bacteremia.[1,2,4,5,7,11,19]

The normal gastrointestinal flora in small numbers is important in preventing disease through bacterial competition. Disruption of the normal intestinal flora by antibiotic therapy, instrumentation, or surgery compromises this defense mechanism and may allow "enterics" to colonize or overgrow. Increased hospital stays and exposure to broad-spectrum antibiotics increase the chance of colonization with the Enterobacteriaceae. Prolonged antimicrobial therapy may "select" and lead to the emergence of multidrug-resistant organisms that result in longer stay, added medical intervention, and/or death.

Increased production of salivary protease, which leads to degradation of fibronectin and exposed binding sites for Gram-negative rods, is a risk factor for patients in long-term care facilities or with an extended ICU stay. In general, the very young, very old, immunocompromised, or debilitated are at greatest risk for HAIs. Those exposed to contaminated food and water are at greatest risk for common community-associated enteric infections.

Enterobacteriaceae are spread in healthcare settings from person to person via the hands of healthcare personnel or from environmental fomites and reservoirs such as mechanical devices, environmental foci, or contaminated solutions. Community reservoirs usually include contaminated food and water. Establishment of disease is multifaceted and involves a combination and interaction of factors that are host, pathogen, medical intervention, and environment specific.[1-5]

Clinical Syndromes

Although declining, members of the Enterobacteriaceae remain important pathogens in the four most common device- and procedure-related infections in acute care facilities (Figure 75-1). They are among the top 10 pathogens recovered from patients in U.S. ICUs, with infections ranging from 19.6 percent of central line-associated bloodstream infections (CLABSIs) to 47.9 percent of catheter-associated urinary tract infections (CAUTIs), according to results reported in the 2009 to 2010 National Healthcare Safety Network (NHSN) survey (Figures 75-2, and 75-3). Members also ranked in the top 10 pathogens recovered from ventilator-associated pneumonia (VAP; 30.6 percent) and surgical site infections

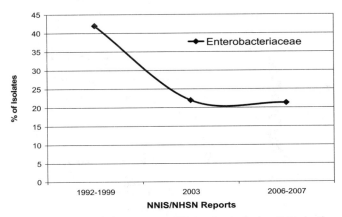

Figure 75-1. Trends in recovery of Enterobacteriaceae HAIs in the United States.

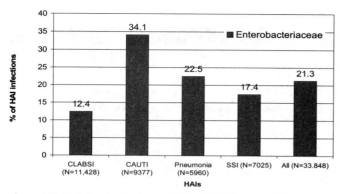

Figure 75-2. Enterobacteriaceae HAIs: NHSN January 2005 to October 2007.

(SSIs; 22.4 percent). *E. coli* (39.9 percent, *n* = 9,351) was the most frequently recovered Enterobacteriaceae, followed by *Klebsiella* species (pneumonia, oxytoca; 27.6 percent, *n* = 6,470), *Enterobacter* species (16.3 percent, *n* = 3,821), *Proteus* species (8.7 percent, *n* = 2,031), and *Serratia* species (7.4 percent, *n* = 1,737) (Figure 75-3).[21,22]

Blood Infections (Bacteremia, Septicemia)

Bloodstream infections (BSIs) or bacteremias caused by the Enterobacteriaceae are usually a result of contiguous spread from the urinary tract, lungs, or gastrointestinal tract. Other portals of entry include surgical sites, decubiti, and central venous lines. These are life-threatening infections due in part to the systemic effects of endotoxins (fever, shock, thrombocytopenia, activation of complement, DIC, and decreased peripheral circulation) and in part to the difficulty of managing frequent multidrug-resistant isolates.[23]

There has been a 69 percent decline in the percentage of Enterobacteriaceae recovered as bloodstream pathogens in National Nosocomial Infections Surveillance (NNIS) hospitals since the early 1980s. In the latest data from NHSN (2009 to 2010), they accounted for 19.6 percent. This was a 58

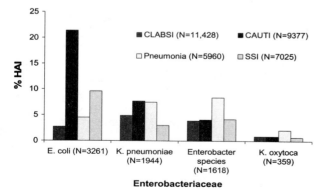

Figure 75-3. Pathogen distribution of Enterobacteriaceae: NHSN January 2005 to October 2007.

percent increase in the percentage of Enterobacteriaceae reported for the NHSN 2006 to 2007 baseline data. Frequent isolates, in descending order, were *Klebsiella* species (7.9 percent, *n* = 2,407), of *Enterobacter* species (4.5 percent, *n* = 1,365), *E. coli* (4.0 percent, *n* = 1,206), *Serratia* species (2.5 percent, *n* = 762), and *Proteus* species (0.8 percent, *n* = 232). The first three members were among the top 10 pathogens recorded from CLBSIs with ranks of 5, 8, and 9, respectively.[21,22,24,25]

Although, patient populations in acute care ICUs are at an increased risk for CLABSIs, recent data document the increasing risks in patient populations outside the ICU. This is associated with the increasing number of central lines in these areas. Frequent independent risk factors are microbial colonization of the catheter hub and insertion site, femoral and/or jugular catheterization, prior extended hospital stay, and prolonged catheterization.[23,26]

Education of personnel in the insertion and care of the central lines, performance of a CLABSI risk assessment, proper maintenance of central lines, and appropriate antibiotic therapy are recommendations that may help reduce healthcare-associated BSIs.[23,26]

Respiratory Tract Infections

Pneumonia is the second most common healthcare-related infection linked with the Enterobacteriaceae (30.6 percent, NHSN 2009 to 2010 survey). For patients with known risk factors (intubation, comorbidities), Enterobacteriaceae are among the top five etiological agents recovered in severe early onset (<5 days of hospitalization) healthcare-related pneumonias (*Enterobacter, Klebsiella,* and *E. coli*) and late onset (>5 days hospitalization) pneumonias (Enterobacter, other Gram-negative rods, *Klebsiella,* and *E. coli*).[21–23]

Klebsiella species (10.1 percent, *n* = 854) were the most frequent Enterobacteriaceae recovered from VAP in the 2009 to 2010 NHSN survey. It was the third most frequent pathogen isolated from healthcare-associated pneumonia. This was followed by *Enterobacter* species (8.6 percent, *n* = 827, ranked no. 4), *E. coli* (5.9 percent, *n* = 504, ranked no. 6), *Serratia* species (4.6 percent, *n* = 386, ranked no. 7), and Proteus species (1.4 percent, *n* = 114, not ranked in the top 10 pathogens).[22]

Patients with healthcare-associated pneumonias in acute care facilities are often debilitated, ventilator-dependent, and have been previously colonized or exposed to aspirated oropharyngeal contents. Other risk factors include prolonged broad-spectrum antibiotic therapy, increased gastric pH, or loss of fibronectin.[1-4] Enteric community-associated pneumonias usually involve patients with underlying disease, alcoholics, or the malnourished. Organisms include *Klebsiella pneumoniae* and *Enterobacter* species and, to a lesser extent, *E. coli*. Gram-negative enterics also play an important role in nursing home pneumonias. Patients with reduced cough reflex or compromised lung capacity are at greater risk in all settings.[1,3-5,22]

Management of "enteric" pneumonia remains important and demanding. These organisms are more likely to be multi-drug resistant and form biofilm. Efforts to delay colonization, avoidance or reduction of time on ventilators, compliance with hand-washing protocols, and proper patient positioning can lessen the incidence of healthcare-associated pneumonias.

Recommendations and strategies to prevent VAP include active surveillance, educating personnel in the care of VAP patients and their equipment, applying a multidisciplinary approach, and increasing accountability.[27]

Urinary Tract Infections

Enterobacteriaceae are important etiologic agents of both community-associated and healthcare-associated urinary tract infections. Infections may range from painful urination to severe systemic illness. Severe infections may progress to sepsis, which may be fatal.

Sexually active women are at highest risk for community-associated infections. The single most important risk factor for HAIs is catheterization or obstructed urinary flow. Frequent risk factors associated with catheterization include duration of urinary catheterization, absence of antibiotic use, female gender, absence of use of a urinometer, microbial colonization of the drainage bag, diabetes mellitus, abnormal serum creatinine, and improper catheter care.[8,28–30]

Enterobacteriaceae were the leading cause of CAUTI (47.9 percent) in the 2009 to 2010 NHSN survey. E. coli (26.8 percent, n = 5,660) was the top pathogen recovered from CAUTIs. This was followed by Klebsiella species (11.2 percent, n = 2,365, ranked no. 3), Proteus species (4.8 percent, n = 1,013, ranked no. 6), Enterobacter species (4.2 percent, n = 880, ranked no. 8), and Serratia species (1.0 percent, n = 204, not in the top 10).[22,24,31]

In two point prevalence surveys (survey 1, July 2010 to January 2011; survey 2, January 2011 to July 2011) in the Chicago area, Lin et al. found a high rate of Klebsiella pneumoniae carbapenemase (KPC) colonization among 24 short-stay and 7 long-term acute care hospitals (LTACHs). Among LTACHs, 30.4 percent (119/391) of patients were colonized with KPC-producing Enterobacteriaceae, compared to 3.3 percent (30 of 910) of short-stay hospital ICU patients. Long-term care facilities may play an important role as reservoirs and in the dissemination of these extremely drug-resistant pathogens.[32]

Prevention and control of healthcare-associated CAUTIs includes education of personnel on the insertion and care of catheters, surveillance, avoidance of catheterization when possible, reduced duration of catheterization, and adherence to Standard Precautions.[29,30]

Surgical Site Infections

In the 1990 to 1996 NNIS, Enterobacteriaceae accounted for approximately one-fourth of incisional SSIs. This was a 25 percent decline since the 1980 to 1982 report.[24,31,33] The frequency of the organism recovered is dependent on the type of surgery and is usually resident flora.[24,31,33] Common pathogens include E. coli, Enterobacter species, Klebsiella species, and Proteus species.

Enteric pathogens constituted 22.4 percent of SSIs in the 2009 to 2010 NHSN survey. E. coli (9.4 percent, n = 1,981) was the most frequent pathogen and ranked number 3 among the top 10 pathogens responsible for SSIs. Other members included Enterobacter species (4.0 percent, n = 849, ranked no. 6), Klebsiella species (4.0 percent, n = 844, ranked no. 7), Proteus species (3.2 percent, n = 667, ranked no. 9), and Serratia species (1.8 percent, n = 385, not in the top 10). Antibiotic prophylaxis or empiric therapy with third-generation cephalosporins may selectively allow overgrowth of resistant isolates. Proper attention to aseptic techniques, appropriate prophylactic antibiotics, minimal organ manipulation, and shorter surgery times may assist in reduction of this type of infection. Other recommendations include education, surveillance, risk assessment, and accountability.[22,34]

Central Nervous System Infections

HAIs of the central nervous system (CNS) occur in neurosurgical patients, neonates, and patients undergoing procedures that penetrate the CNS. Premature or low-birth-weight infants are at particular risk for infections with E. coli, and K. pneumoniae and, less frequently, Citrobacter diversus and Serratia marcescens.[1-4] In the latest NHSN survey (2009 to 2010), Enterobacteriaceae accounted for 2 percent of SSIs. Enterobacter species (7.2 percent, n = 31) was the most frequently recovered Gram-negative rod recovered from neurological surgery. Other members of the Enterobacteriaceae recovered from CNS infections included Klebsiella species (3.5 percent, n = 15), E. coli (2.8 percent, n = 12), Serratia species (2.1 percent, n = 9), and Proteus species (0.9 percent, n = 4).

Gastrointestinal Tract Infections

Acute gastroenteritis and infectious diarrhea are caused by several members of the Enterobacteriaceae. E. coli, Salmonella species, and Shigella sonnei are the most common.[4,35] Enterotoxigenic strains of Klebsiella, Enterobacter, Serratia, Citrobacter, and Proteus have been isolated from infants and children with acute gastroenteritis.[1,3,4,36] Infections are usually the result of contact with infected individuals or consumption of contaminated food, water, milk, or other beverages. Exposure to contaminated fomites or environmental surfaces account for fewer cases. Transmission is via the fecal-oral route.[4]

Globally, annual deaths due to acute diarrheal diseases occur predominantly in young children. Rates in some countries are 1,000-fold higher than rates in the United States. Some populations in the United States, however, have diarrhea rates (and living conditions) that approach those seen in developing countries. Annual diarrheal death rates in the United States range from 500 to 10,000 cases. Patients or populations at greatest risk include infants, children, the elderly, the immunocompromised, and populations in custodial institutions. Laboratory workers, who handle infectious materials, are also at risk for acquiring these infections.[35,37]

Summary data from the Foodborne Disease Active Surveillance Network (FoodNet) revealed 19,089 infections, 4,247 hospitalizations, and 68 deaths. Infections with *Salmonella* species were the most common reported enteric disease (17.6 illnesses per 100,000 persons) and were associated with the largest number of hospitalizations (2,290) and deaths (29). Shiga toxin-producing *E. coli* (STEC) O157 infection caused 0.9 illnesses per 100,000. For the other enteric pathogens, the number of infections and incidence included: *Shigella* (1,780; 3.8 per 100,000), STEC non-O157 (451; 1.0 per 100,000); STEC O157 (442; 0.9 per 100,000), and *Yersinia* (159; 0.3 per 100,000).[35]

Keys to the prevention and control of infectious diarrhea incorporate proper infection control interventions, hand washing compliance, implementation of Standard and Transmission-based Precautions, avoidance of undercooked meat or seafood, avoidance of unpasteurized milk or soft cheeses, and selective use of available typhoid vaccines for travelers to areas where typhoid is endemic.[36]

Common Pathogens—Nongastrointestinal (Table 75-1)

Escherichia coli

E. coli is the most common cause of community- and healthcare-associated urinary tract and bloodstream infections. It is the most common enteric recovered from the aerobic bowel flora. *E. coli* may also be recovered in HAIs such as neonatal meningitis, wound infections, and peritonitis. Colonization of the lower respiratory tract may happen without causing disease. *E. coli* is an uncommon cause of community-associated pneumonias, but is the third leading cause in hospitalized patients. It was the most frequently recovered Enterobacteriaceae (39.9 percent, *n* = 9,351) in the 2009 to 2010 NHSN survey and ranked in the top 10 recovered pathogens for CAUTI (no. 1), CLBSI (no. 9), VAP (no. 6), and SSI (no. 3).[22]

Increasing resistance to the beta lactams in general and the carbapenems specifically is a mounting public health concern.[2,36,38,39]

Enterobacter species

The *Enterobacter* species are increasingly important causes of HAIs due to emergence of highly resistant isolates. Most frequently encountered members include *Enterobacter cloacae, Enterobacter aerogenes,* and *Enterobacter agglomerans.* Although community-associated infections are rare, *Enterobacter* species are "opportunists," causing healthcare-related infections in the compromised or debilitated patient. They may also colonize the respiratory and urinary tracts, wounds, decubitus ulcers, and other sites. Clinical syndromes include lower respiratory tract infections, urinary tract infections, and septicemias and wound infections. Patients on prolonged periods of broad-spectrum antimicrobial therapy or ventilators appear to be at greatest risk for acquiring infection.

Treatment of *Enterobacter* infections is quite challenging. Emergence of multidrug-resistant isolates associated with carbapenemase, and other extended-spectrum beta-lactamase (ESBL) producers, coupled with the selection of resistant mutants during therapy, all contribute to the difficulty of treating *Enterobacter* infections. Consultation with an infectious disease specialist and laboratory evaluation of these isolates are mandatory for effective therapy and management.[2,4,15,40-44]

Klebsiella species

Virulence factors for *Klebsiella* species include a large capsule and LPS (endotoxins). *Klebsiella* species are responsible for community-associated and healthcare-related respiratory infections. The hallmark community infection is primary lobar pneumonia. Patients present with fever, shortness of breath, and purulent sputum with a currant jelly appearance. The currant jelly appearance is due to a mixture of blood and necrotic lung tissue. This type of necrotizing infection is often seen in alcoholics and patients with chronic or debilitating underlying disease. Less frequently encountered community respiratory infections included bronchitis and bronchopneumonia.[15,19,45-47]

Healthcare-related pneumonias are seen in nursing homes, debilitated patients, and ventilator-dependent patients. *Klebsiella* species (*K. pneumoniae, K. oxytoca*) may also asymptomatically colonize the upper respiratory tract of patients in long-term and acute care facilities without causing disease. Bacteremia and urinary tract infections with *Klebsiella pneumoniae* are often recovered from patients with indwelling catheters. Enteropathogenic *K. pneumoniae* strains have been isolated from infants with diarrhea.[15,19,45-47]

Treatment of *Klebsiella* infections have become problematic is several regions of the country due to increasing prevalence of carbapenemase-producing strains. These strains produce broad-spectrum beta lactamases that inactivate all beta lactams including imipenem, meropenem, ertapenem, and aztreonam. They often carry plasmids and transposons that further confer resistance to multiple classes of other antibiotics (e.g., aminoglycosides, fluoroquinolones) and facilitate dispersion and transmission.[15,19,45-47] Carbapenem-resistant *Klebsiella* pneumonia (CRKP) is the most frequently isolated carbapenemase-producing Enterobacteriaceae.

Common Pathogens—Gastrointestinal (Table 75-2)

Escherichia coli Infections

Enteropathogenic or diarrheagenic *E. coli* strains are important sources of morbidity and mortality in emerging and developed nations. Infants and children are the largest at-risk populations. At least seven diarrheagenic *E. coli* strains have been associated with human disease. Only five are well characterized: enterotox-igenic (ETEC), enteroinvasive (EIEC), enteropathogenic (EPEC), enterohemorrhagic (EHEC), and enteroaggressive (EAggEC). Diarrhea-associated hemolytic *E. coli* (DHEC) and cytolethal distending toxin-producing *E. coli* (CDTEC) are newly identified strains, and their role in enteric disease is controversial.[35,36,38,39]

ETEC is a major cause of gastroenteritis worldwide. Infants and children are commonly affected in areas with poor sanitation. ETEC is also the cause of traveler's diarrhea. Most of these cases are due to ingestion of contaminated food or water while traveling in endemic areas. Symptomatic disease develops after a 1- to 2-day incubation and may persist up to 4 days. Patients present with a profuse, watery diarrhea, cramps, nausea, vomiting, and dehydration. Symptoms are due to the actions of two plasmid-mediated enterotoxins, one heat labile (LT) and one heat stable (ST). The heat-labile toxin is similar to that produced by *V. cholera* and stimulates hypersecretion of fluids and electrolytes. Diagnostic tests include EIA for enterotoxins and cell culture for cytotoxicity.[36,38,39]

EIEC produces bacillary dysentery-like illness with invasion and destruction of the colonic epithelium. Attachment and invasion is plasmid mediated. Foreign travel and contaminated food and water are important risk factors. Patients present with fever, cramps, watery diarrhea that progress to dysentery, and blood, mucus, and leukocytes in the scant stools. Confirmation is by observation of cytopathic effect of HeLa cell culture.[36,38,39]

EPEC is a major cause of infantile diarrhea in impoverished nations. Outbreaks of EPEC have occurred in U.S. nurseries. Children >2 years of age are most commonly affected. Disease is caused by a plasmid-mediated adherence and destruction of epithelial cells. Symptoms include watery diarrhea, fever, nausea, vomiting, and mucus in nonbloody stool. Diagnostic tests include adherence to Hep2 cells.[36,38,39]

EAggEC is a significant cause of diarrhea in developing nations and has been associated with a persistent, watery diarrhea with vomiting and dehydration in infants. A type of traveler's diarrhea has also been associated with this species. Pathogenicity has not been established. A toxin and a hemolysin have been detected, but their role in disease is uncertain.[36,38,39]

EHEC, also known as STEC-Shiga-toxin producing *E. coli* (Table 75-2), is further discussed in Chapter 83 Foodborne Illnesses.

Shigella Infections

Infection with species of *Shigella* ranges from asymptomatic to severe bacillary dysentery. Abdominal cramps, diarrhea, fever, and bloody stools characterize bacillary dysentery. Symptoms are mediated by an exotoxin or SHIGA toxin, which is neurotoxic, cytotoxic, and enterotoxic. Organisms invade, multiply, and damage the colonic mucosa. Disease progresses from a watery diarrhea to dysentery with frequent small stools containing blood and mucus, tenesmus, cramps, and fever. As little

as 200 organisms (10^2) can initiate disease. The A subunit of the Shiga toxin adheres to small intestine receptors and blocks absorption of electrolytes, glucose, and amino acids from the intestinal lumen (enterotoxic). The B subunit binds host-cell glycolipid in the large intestines, prohibiting protein synthesis and cell death (cytotoxic).[4,36]

Four species with more than 45 O serotypes have been documented: *Shigella dysenteriae* causes the most severe form of bacillary dysentery, *Shigella flexneri* is the most common cause of shigellosis in developing nations, *Shigella sonnei* is the most common cause of shigellosis in United States and other developed nations. Humans and other higher primates are the only natural reservoirs. *Shigella* species can be recovered in 15 to 20 percent of the pediatric diarrhea in the United States and is a major cause of diarrheal disease in developing nations. Transmission is person to person via the fecal-oral route (primarily by contaminated hands). Secondary transmission frequently occurs.[4,36]

Salmonella Infections

How many, and what name to assign to, species belonging to the genus *Salmonella* can be confusing. Taxonomically, all strains of *Salmonella* belong to two species—*Salmonella enterica*, recovered from humans and warm-blooded animals, and *Salmonella bongori*, recovered from reptiles and the environment. Each species is further divided into subspecies and serovars. All human species would be classified as serovars within subspecies group 1 of *S. enterica*. The new nomenclature would change *Salmonella typhi* to *Salmonella enterica* serovar typhi, written as *S. typhi*.[23] The preceding nomenclature has not caught on, and the genus continues to be recognized by the more familiar names (*S. enteritidis, S. typhi, S. typhimurium, S. choleraesuis,* and *S. paratyphi*), which are based on serologic typing and geographic origin. Only about 200 of the known 2,000 or more serotypes are recovered in the United States each year.[36,48–50]

Salmonella species are ubiquitous in nature and are commensals of many animals, including poultry, birds, reptiles, livestock, rodents, domestic pets, and humans. Humans are the only reservoirs for *S. typhi* and *S. paratyphi*. Human illness is linked to ingestion of foods or water contaminated by feces of an infected animal or person. The required infective dose is very high (10^{6-8} organisms). Multiplication in food is necessary for transmission and symptomatic disease. Common source outbreaks have included raw and undercooked eggs and egg products, dairy products, fruits, vegetables, pet turtles, marijuana, and rarely food handlers. Fecal-oral transmission from person to person is important. Worldwide more than 3 million cases of *Salmonella* are reported each year. In the United States, more than 50,000 cases are reported annually. This is only 10 percent of the actual cases. Populations at greatest risk are children under 5, adults greater than 60 years, and patients with AIDS and sickle cell disease. Men who have sex with other men are also at increased risk. *Salmonella* strains are able to invade and multiply in the gut, invoking an inflammatory response and stimulation of active fluid secretion.[36,48–50]

Four clinical syndromes are associated with *Salmonella* infections: enteritidis, septicemia, enteric fever, and asymptomatic carrier.[36,48–50] **Enteritis:** Symptoms appear 6 to 48 hours after ingestion of contaminated food or water. These may include nausea, vomiting, nonbloody diarrhea, fever, abdominal cramps, and myalgias and may persist from 2 to 7 days. No treatment is required. **Septicemia:** In severe cases, *Salmonella* may invade the bloodstream. Populations at greatest risk are at the extremes of ages and persons who are HIV positive. Complications include osteomyelitis, endocarditis, and arthritis. **Enteric fever:** Onset occurs 10 to 14 days after ingestion. Patients present with nonspecific febrile illness and may complain of headache, myalgias, malaise, and anorexia. The duration may last several weeks with progression to gastrointestinal invasion. Following the initial bacteremic phase, colonization of the gallbladder can occur. **Asymptomatic carrier:** *S. typhi* and *S. paratyphi* strains may be maintained in the carrier state by humans. About 1 to 5 percent of patients will become chronic carriers. The gallbladder is the reservoir in most patients.

Multidrug resistance among the *Salmonella* is increasing. Therapy should be guided by in vitro susceptibility testing and consultation with ID services.[36,48–50]

Yersinia Infections

The genus *Yersinia* is composed of 11 species. Only three are of immediate interest to infectious disease personnel. These are *Y. pestis*, *Y. enterocolitica,* and *Y. pseudotuberculosis*. Yersiniosis is a zoonotic disease and involves both intestinal and extraintestinal sites. *Y. enterocolitica* and *Y. pseudotuberculosis* are largely enteric pathogens responsible for acute bacteria enteritis. Patients infected with *Yersinia* present with an acute, febrile diarrhea, enterocolitis, or an acute mesenteric lymphadenitis, which mimics appendicitis. Natural reservoirs are wild and domestic birds and animals. Humans are accidental hosts.[2,51–54]

Enteric disease is the result of ingestion of contaminated food and water or by contact with infected people or animals. The highest isolation rates occur during the winter season in temperate climates, including northern Europe and North and South America. Common outbreak vehicles have included tofu, raw or undercooked pork, and milk. The incubation period is 3 to 7 days.[12,23,24]

Nonenteric diseases for these strains include septicemia, arthritis, intraabdominal abscess, hepatitis, osteomyelitis, and blood transfusion-related bacteremia and endotoxic shock. *Y. enterocolitica* survives at 4°C or refrigerated temperatures and can multiply to toxic levels in contaminated blood products. There are no reliable detection methods to rule out the presence of this microorganism in the blood supply.[51–53,55–62]

Human plague is normally a zoonotic disease following the bite of an infected flea or rarely by direct inhalation or handling of contaminated animal tissues or fluids. Rodents are the natural reservoir of *Y. pestis*. Reservoirs (infected fleas) are maintained in two epidemiological forms. In urban plague (black plague), the disease is preserved in rat populations and spread among rats or to humans by infected fleas. Control of rat populations can eliminate this natural reservoir.[63,64]

The second, sylvatic plague, is difficult to eliminate, because reservoirs are multiple (prairie dogs, mice, rabbits, rats, and domestic animals) and widespread. Patients become symptomatic 2 to 8 days following the bite of an infected flea. Resultant clinical disease may occur in several forms.[4,54,62,65]

Bubonic Plague

The most common naturally occurring human disease symptoms include fever, chills, weakness, and development of an acutely swollen, tender lymph node or bubo in the groin, axilla, or cervical regions. Buboes are usually very painful. Bubonic plague has a 14 to 75 percent fatality rate. No person-to-person spread has been identified.

Primary Septicemia Plague

A minority of patients will develop sepsis with no discernible bubo. Secondary sepsis may arise from bubonic plague. In advance disease, gangrene of fingers and toes may occur ("black death"). Primary septicemic plague is not spread directly person to person. Case fatality rates range from 22 to 100 percent.

Primary Pneumonic Plague

Inhalation of plague bacilli results in primary pneumonic plague. Incidence is rare in the United States. Ninety percent of the cases are fatal. Patients are highly infectious and spread the disease by respiratory droplet. Symptoms include fever, cough, mucopurulent sputum, hemoptysis, and chest pain. The chest x-ray is usually consistent with bronchopneumonia. Secondary pneumonic plague may develop in a few patients with bubonic or septicemic plague via hematogenous spread to the lungs. Common symptoms are those of severe bronchopneumonia, chest pain, dyspnea, cough, and hemoptysis.[4,54,62,65]

Plague Meningitis

Plague meningitis follows the hematogenous seeding of the organisms into the meninges and is associated with fever and meningitis.

Plague Pharyngitis

Plague pharyngitis follows inhalation or ingestion of plague bacilli and is associated with cervical lymphadenopathy.[4,54,62,65]

Enterobacteriaceae as Biological Weapons

Yersinia pestis is a high-impact biological agent that presents a heightened bioterrorism risk. The epidemiology of plague following its use as a biological weapon would differ significantly from that of naturally occurring disease. Exposure would be more likely to be in the form of an aerosol. Outbreaks of pneumonic plague would result with symptoms initially resembling the flu or other severe respiratory infections. Healthcare facilities could be overwhelmed. There are no rapid diagnostics for detection of the organism. Current infection control interventions to prevent person-to-person spread of pneumonic plague are limited with little data available to make specific recommendations regarding appropriate measures. Available evidence indicates that person-to-person transmission occurs via respiratory droplets.[26] Recommendations in the APIC and CDC Bioterrorism Readiness Plan include the use of Standard Precautions plus Droplet Precautions. Consult the APIC and CDC Bioterrorism Readiness Plan for details on patient placement, transport, cohorting, and postexposure management.[2,4,54,62,63,65,66]

Other Enterobacteriaceae as Biological Weapons

Biological warfare is a serious and continuing threat. Healthcare providers must remain vigilant and alert to illness patterns and diagnostic clues that might indicate an unusual infectious disease outbreak associated with intentional release of a biological agent.[28,29] We must think outside the box to detect nontraditional disease presentation and possible agents. Several members of the Enterobacteriaceae have potential for use as biological weapons (Table 75-4). Two species, Y. pestis[26] and

Table 75-4. Common ESBLS and Carbapenemases Associated With Enterobacteriaceae

Beta-lactamases TYPE	Class	Description	Common Enterobacteriaceae species	Possible Alternative Therapy*
Extended-spectrum beta-lactamases				
TEM ESBLs	A	ESBLs (serine-dependent) derived from mutations in the *TEM-1, TEM-2* genes. They have varying hydrolysis profiles which include penicillins, broad- and extended-spectrum cephalosporins, and monobactams. These enzymes are inhibited by clavulanic acid. Most are carried on plasmids or transposons. TEM is name after a Greek patient (TEMoniera) from which it was first isolated.	*Klebsiella* species *Escherichia coli* *Proteus mirabilis* *Citrobacter freundii* *Serratia marcescens* (they can share among the family)	Imipenem Imipenem/cilastin Meropenem Aminoglycosides Fluoroquinolones Tigecycline
SHV ESBLs	A	ESBLs derived from mutations in the *SHV-1*. SHV (**s**ul**phy**dryl **v**ariable) enzymes are mainly cephalosporinases and are inhibited by clavulanic acid. These confer resistance to cefotaxime and ceftazidime by hydrolyzing cefotaxime and to a lesser degree ceftazidime.	*Enterobacter* species *Citrobacter* species *Klebsiella pneumoniae*	Imipenem Imipenem/cilastin Meropenem Aminoglycosides Fluoroquinolones Tigecycline
AmpC ESBLs	C	Mainly chromosomally-mediated ESBLs that are inducible and capable of hydrolyzing broad- and extended-spectrum cephalosporins. They may also have some low level activity against the carbapenems. They are not inhibited by the clavulanic acid or other beta-lactamases inhibitors.	Enterobacter cloacae Serratia marcescens Citrobacter freundii Morganella morganii	Imipenem Meropenem Aminoglycosides Fluoroquinolones
CTX-M ESBLs	A	ESBLs that hydrolyze cefotaxime and to a lesser degree ceftazidime and aztreonam. They also have high affinity for cefepime. These are the most rapidly spreading ESBLs nationally and internationally and appearing with increasing frequency in the community. They are more readily inactivated by tazobactam than clavulanic acid and sulbactam.	*Escherichia coli* *Klebsiella pneumoniae* *Salmonella* species *Shigella* species *Citrobacter freundii* *Serratia marcescens*	Imipenem Imipenem/cilastin Meropenem Aminoglycosides Fluoroquinolones Tigecycline
Carbapenemases				
KPC 1-4	A	ESBLs that confer resistance to extended-spectrum cephalosporins and **carbapenems**. Enzymes are inhibited by clavulanic acid. *Klebsiella pneumoniae* carbapenemases are mostly plasmid mediated. KPC-1 (North Carolina), KPC-2 (Baltimore), and KPC-3 (most frequent, New York), KPC-4 (Scotland). High potential for spread. Mainly isolated on the U.S. East Coast. The most common carbapenemases.	*Klebsiella pneumoniae* *Klebsiella oxytoca* *Salmonella enterica* *Enterobacter* species	Aminoglycosides Fluoroquinolones Polymyxins Tigecycline Colistin
SMC1-3		Chromosomally mediated carbapenemases.	*Serratia marcescens*	As above
IMI-1		Chromosomally mediated carbapenemases.	*Enterobacter cloacae*	As above
MBL	B	ESBLs-metallo-beta-lactamase with a zinc rather than a serine core. Have broad-spectrum activity. Capable of hydrolyzing all penicillins, cephalosporins, monobactams (except aztreonam), and **carbapenems**. Affinity for imipenem and other carbapenems varies. These are inhibited by EDTA, but not clavulanic acid.	*Serratia marcescens* *Klebsiella pneumoniae*	Aminoglycosides Fluoroquinolones Aztreonam
	NDM	New Delhi, novel MBL, emerged in 2009 from Swedish patient after medical care in India. Confers "pan-resistance" with 50 percent mortality; hydrolyzes all penicillins, cephalosporins, and carbapenems.	*Klebsiella pneumoniae* *Escherichia coli* *Enterobacter cloacae*	Very limited options (combination therapy is warranted), colistin, tigecycline
OXA-48, OXA-181	D	Carbapenemase enzymes that preferentially hydrolyze oxacillin. Those with activity against Enterobacter are mainly OXA-48. Have a peculiar profile, weakly hydrolyzes carbapenems, with low level activity against cefotaxime, no activity against ceftazidime or other third-generation cephalosporin. They are not inhibited by clavulanic acid.	*Enterobacter* species *Klebsiella pneumoniae* *Escherichia coli*	Ceftazidime Colistin Aminoglycosides Fluoroquinolones Polymyxin

Salmonella[30] species, already have been dispersed with harmful intent. At least one, again *Y. pestis,* has been listed as a Category A agent in the CDC assessment of potential biological terrorism agents.[29] Agents in Category A present the greatest threat to the public in terms of illness and deaths. They require focused and determined efforts to improve surveillance and laboratory diagnosis.

Enteric pathogens such as *Salmonella, Shigella,* and enterotoxigenic *E. coli* may be used to threaten or compromise our food supply. These organisms are one tier down in Category B. These organisms have the potential to cause widespread disease, but less serious illness and deaths. Category C is reserved for those biological agents that are currently not believed to present a high bioterrorism risk but might emerge in the future.[67,68]

Laboratory Identification

No special requirements, except those in place for routine collection and transport of specimens, are needed to recover the Enterobacteriaceae from sources outside the gastrointestinal tract. Pus, sputum, blood, tissue, and other sterile specimens should be collected and processed according to routine microbiological protocol. Specimens (stools, rectal swabs) to rule out enteric pathogens should be collected fresh and delivered to the microbiology laboratory within 2 hours. Samples should be placed in an adequate transport media (Stuart's, Cary-Blair) and refrigerated, if they cannot be delivered within the 2-hour time limit. Rectal swabs are a less desirable sample except in outbreak investigations.[1,3,4,15]

On Gram stain, the Enterobacteriaceae all appear as Gram-negative coccobacilli or rods with no distinguishing characteristics. Special stains such as methylene blue or Wayson may highlight identifying characteristics (i.e., safety pin or bipolar staining characteristic of *Y. pestis*). Most Enterobacteriaceae grow readily on simple microbiological plating media and on media used for biochemical characterization. All members grow on routine laboratory media such as blood or MacConkey agar. Selective and differential agars such as HE (Hekton enteric), XLD (xylose-lysine-deochocolate), and SS (*Salmonella-Shigella*) agars are commonly used to isolate enteric pathogens from feces and other gastrointestinal sites. Enhanced recovery of enteropathogenic *E. coli* or *Yersinia* species may be aided by Sorbitol MacConkey (SMAC) agar or Cefsulodin-Irgasan-Novobiocin (CIN) agars, respectively.[1,3,4,15]

Microbiologists use commercial kits, automated systems, simple screening tests, and conventional biochemical tube tests for identification. With some automated systems and kits, the common pathogens may be identified in as little as 2 hours. Strains that have been exposed to prolonged antimicrobial therapy may no longer react typically in these systems and present identification problems for the laboratory. Because of the expanding number of Enterobacteriaceae, current automated and commercial kits may have problems identifying emerging pathogens (i.e., *Hafnia alvei* [gastroenteritis], *Rahnella aquatilis* [HAIs in immunocompromised patients]).[1–4,15]

Molecular probes and nucleic acid amplification techniques are also increasingly used to rapidly identify enteric and emerging pathogens. A variety of phenotypic (biotyping, serotyping, antibiograms, bacteriocin. and phage typing) and genotypic (plasmid analysis, restriction fragment length polymorphism, ribotyping, polymerase chain reaction [PCR], pulse-field gel electrophoresis, DNA probes, and DNA sequencing) methods are used for epidemiological investigations. New technologies such as the mass spectrometer are being used to more efficiently identify new and older species. This technology affords a more rapid and accurate identification.[69,70]

Treatment

Empirical therapy for the Enterobacteriaceae is no longer predictable. Selection of antibiotic therapy for infections with Enterobacteriaceae must be guided by in vitro susceptibility test results, local antibiotic pressures, and clinical experience. Knowledge of the local resistant trends is important for management and appropriate selection of empirical therapy. Patterns will vary dependent on the patient population, prescribing formulary, usage, testing system, and clinical practice.[71,72]

Intrinsic resistance to first-generation cephalosporins and ampicillin is a genetic property of several Enterobacteriaceae. Resistance to additional or multiple antimicrobials may be acquired by acquisition of extrachromosomal genes (plasmids, transposons, etc.) or through chromosomal modification or mutation. Common resistant mechanisms include production of antibiotic modifying enzymes (i.e., beta lactamases, ESBLs), decreased penetration into the cell (aminoglycosides), modification of the cell wall precursor (vancomycin), alteration of the ribosomal or enzyme target (macrolides, quinolones), efflux mechanism (tetracyclines), and overproduction of targeted enzymes (sulfonamides). Mechanisms may be chromosomal or plasmid regulated.[73–75]

Although most members remain susceptible to the most frequently prescribed antimicrobials (i.e., fluoroquinolones, third-generation cephalosporins), others, especially *Enterobacter, Klebsiella,* and *Serratia* species, have emerged with resistance to multiple antibiotics.

The increasing prevalence of multidrug-resistant Enterobacteriaceae, especially those producing extended-spectrum beta-lactamases (ESBLs) capable of inactivating all beta-lactam antibiotics severely restricts therapy and threatens patient safety. More than 200 ESBLs have emerged among the Enterobacteriaceae associated with HAIs. The most common ESBL-producing pathogens included *Klebsiella* species and *E. coli.* The ESBL-resistant genes are carried on plasmids or other mobile genetic elements, along with resistance to the fluoroquinolones and aminoglycosides. They can readily be transmitted to other members of the family. Other beta-lactamases, AmpC, and carbapenem-producing Enterobacteriaceae (CPE) (Table 75-4) are capable of hydrolyzing most beta-lactam antibiotics. Multidrug resistance among the Enterobacteriaceae varies by ICU organisms, geographic regions, and country and is an increasing concern for all healthcare providers.[76–83]

In the 2009 to 2010 NHSN summary report comparing resistant rates, the highest multidrug resistance (16.8 percent) was documented for CLABSIs. Resistance to carbapenems (12.8 percent) was four times that for *E. coli* and *Enterobacter* species (both 3.7 percent). Broad-spectrum resistance to the cephalosporins was widespread and highest for *Enterobacter* isolates (Figure 75-3).[22,84]

Carbapenem-producing and Carbapenem-resistant Enterobacteriaceae

Among the most challenging and troublesome trends in the treatment of Enterobacteriaceae-associated HAIs is the emergence of resistance to the carbapenems. This is a worrisome trend because these drugs are usually the last option for the treatment of multidrug-resistant infections among our sickest patients. Even more daunting is that these carbapenem-resistant Enterobacteriaceae (CRE) may become members of the normal enteric flora and serve as reservoirs for community spread.

Carbapenemases are hydrolyzing enzymes that confer resistance to the expanded spectrum cephalosporins, monobactams, and the carbapenems (imipenem, meropenem, and ertapenem) (Table 75-4). The mechanism is due to the presence of genes (bla_{kpc}, bla_{sme}, bla_{vim}) that are carried on conjugative plasmids or due to porin changes in cell membrane. The presence of a plasmid is often flanked by transposons that carry additional resistant mechanisms to fluoroquinolones and aminoglycosides.[85]

The carbapenemase family of enzymes include the *Klebsiella pneumoniae* carbapenemases (KPC-1, KPC-2, KPC-3), *Serratia marcescens* enzyme (SME-1, *Serratia* species), and Verona integron-encoded metallo-beta-lactamase (VIM-1). They are predominantly of the KPC, VIM, IMP, NDM and OXA-48 types (Table 75-4).[6,83,86–88]

In the United States, most cases of have been reported from the East Coast and recovered mainly from *K. pneumoniae* with sporadic isolation from other Enterobacteriaceae including *Klebsiella oxytoca*, *Citrobacter freundii*, *Salmonella* ssp., *Enterobacter* spp., and *E. coli*.

KPC producing *K. pneumoniae* have become endemic in the Northeast but have been reported from at least 42 states.[13,14]

Surveillance (NHSN) data collected during the first months of 2012 estimated that at least one CRE HAI was documented in 4.6 percent of acute care hospitals, 3.9 percent of short-stay hospitals, and 17.8 percent of long-term acute care hospitals in patients with a CAUTI or CLABSI. Data from NNIS/NHSN (2001, 2011) and the Surveillance Network-USA (TSN) for 2001 and 2010 documented an increase in the percentages of NHSN CRE from 1.2 percent in 2001 to 4.2 percent. The rate for the TSN went from 0 percent in 2001 to 1.4 percent in 2010. This increase was fueled by a sixfold increase in carbapenem-producing *K. pneumoniae*.[89]

Laboratory Detection

The true incidence and prevalence of carbapenemase-producing or -resistant Enterobacteriaceae is not known. This is due in part to the lack of routine screening by most microbiology laboratories and the inadequacy of routine in vitro susceptibility tests (automated systems, disk diffusion, or E tests) to detect low-level resistance in carbapenemase-producing strains of Enterobacteriaceae.

In 2008, the Clinical and Laboratory Institute (CLSI) recommended using the modified Hodge test (MHT) to screen Enterobacteriaceae strains with elevated minimal inhibitory concentrations (2 to 4 μg/mL) to the carbapenems or reduced disk diffusion zones for the presence of carbapenemases.[90]

Anderson and colleagues evaluated the sensitivity of meropenem, imipenem, and ertapenem using disk diffusion, E tests, microbroth (reference method), and automated systems versus the modified Hodge test for documenting the presence of CPE, documenting greater than 90 percent sensitivity and specificity with only the reference microbroth dilution method (BMD) and the modified Hodge test. Ertapenem was the most sensitive for detecting low level resistance. The modified Hodge test was 100 percent sensitive and specific for the presence of carbapenemases. It is a phenotypic test and is not specific for the KPC enzymes. PCR techniques are currently the most reliable method for confirming the presence of KPC enzymes.[91]

In 2010, CLSI revised carbapenem susceptible breakpoints for ertapenem (S $\leq$0.25 μg/mL), imipenem (S $\leq$1 μg/mL), and meropenem (S $\leq$1 μg/mL) and established a new breakpoint for doripenem (S $\leq$1 μg/mL). MICs outside these ranges are considered nonsusceptible and additional screening is required. The new breakpoints were established to eliminate the need for the MHT, which is time consuming, and to more accurately predict carbapenemases' outcomes.[92]

No change has been observed in the U.S. Food and Drug Administration breakpoints and many laboratories rely on the older, higher breakpoints and phenotypic tests to document the presence of carbapenemase-producing strains. This may result in missed opportunities isolated with low level production.[83]

Prevention measures for containment and identification of colonized patients in low, endemic, or during outbreaks should include implementation of the tier 2 recommendations for multidrug-resistant organisms, and the collection of rectal swabs for screening asymptomatic and high risk patients. Updated recommendations for the detection, monitoring, and control of CRE are outlined in the 2009 CDC *Guidelines for Control of CRE in Acute Care and Long-term Care Facilities* and the 2010 CRE toolkit.[13,14,93]

Fluoroquinolones

Fluoroquinolone resistance among Enterobacteriaceae may result in clinical failure and compromise outcomes. The majority of resistance to fluoroquinolones among the Enterobacteriaceae is chromosomally mediated. Recently, plasmid-mediated resistance has emergence to both third-generation cephalosporins and quinolones. This coresistance further reduces the selection and use of antibiotics to treat these HAIs in the hospital and the community.[74,80,94–96]

New Therapeutic Options for the Enterobacteriaceae

Colistin and polymyxins are alternative antibiotics for the treatment of CPE and other multidrug-resistant strains and may be included singularly or in combination with other antibiotics. However, heteroresistance and declining resistance for *Enterobacter* species have been documented.[97,98]

In a retrospective study of patients from Barnes Jewish hospital (June 1, 2006 to February 1, 2008) with clinical and microbiological KPC bacteremia, in vitro testing revealed high susceptibility rates for tigecycline (28/29 [97 percent]), minocycline (22/29 [76 percent]), and fosfomycin (25/29 [86 percent]) against the KPC-positive isolates.

van Duin and colleagues also identified aminoglycosides, tigecycline, and temocillin as additional drugs used in the treatment of CREs. Issues include limited efficacy, increasing resistance, and multiple toxicities.[88]

Few therapeutic options remain for treating multidrug-resistant Enterobacteriaceae. Current approaches include use of drug combinations and older drugs. In addition, there are new drugs in the pipeline for management.[35,87,99,100]

Strategies required to manage and reduce antibiotic resistance include ongoing surveillance, molecular epidemiological techniques, hand hygiene, antimicrobial controls, and administration support.[21,35,88]

APPLICABLE GUIDELINES

Guidelines for the prevention and control of HAIs have been published by the CDC and several professional societies. The global *Compendium of Strategies to Prevent Healthcare-associated Infections in Acute Care Hospitals* is important in reestablishing a culture of prevention and patient safety across the continuum of care. These can be downloaded from the CDC and/or the APIC Web page.

Recent and relevant guidelines released by the CDC are available at www.cdc.gov or www.cdc.gov/hicpac/pubs.html and include the 2012 CRE Toolkit - Guidance for Control of Carbapenem-resistant Enterobacteriaceae (CRE) guideline for the prevention of intravascular catheter-related infections and guidelines for prevention of catheter-associated urinary tract infections.

Guidance for control of infections with carbapenem-resistance or carbapenemase-producing Enterobacteriaceae in acute care facilities provides new guidance for CRE infection prevention and control in an effort to limit the further emergence of these organisms.

The 2008 guidelines for *Disinfection and Sterilization in Healthcare Facilities* provide evidence-based recommendations for the cleaning, disinfection, and sterilizing of patient care medical devices and equipment as well as cleaning and disinfecting the healthcare environment in healthcare facilities. These are also available on the APIC website and/or as a download from the CDC.[101]

Other applicable guidelines include Guidelines for Isolation Precautions in Hospitals,[102] Guideline for Environmental Infection Control in Healthcare Facilities,[103] Hand Hygiene,[104] and Management of Multidrug-resistant Organisms in Healthcare Settings,[105] as well as:

APIC Elimination Guides for Prevention of Mediastinitis Surgical Site Infections (2008)

Guide to the Elimination of Catheter-Related Bloodstream Infections (2009)

Guide to the Elimination of Catheter-Associated Urinary Tract Infections (CAUTI) (2008)

Guide to the Elimination of Ventilator-Associated Pneumonia (2009)

The APIC elimination guidelines are available for download or purchase (www.apic.org) and provide the infection preventionist with evidence-based information for monitoring and reducing HAIs across the continuum of care.

CONCLUSIONS

Although incidence and prevalence of HAIs due to the Enterobacteriaceae may be declining, they remain important pathogens in all healthcare facilities. Enterobacteriaceae are among the top 10 pathogens recovered from the top four device-associated infections (CLABSI, CAUTI, VAP, and SSI). Non-*E. coli* enteropathogenic strains are emerging pathogens and increasingly implicated in healthcare- and community-associated diarrheal diseases.

Immediate challenges facing the infection prevention professionals in the 21st century include older and sicker patients, multidrug- and pan-resistant organisms, reduced staff, limited reimbursement, and diversity of healthcare settings. Infection preventionists must develop plans to focus surveillance on the high-risk patient populations while expanding and applying the principles of healthcare epidemiology to all settings.[71,106]

Reduction of HAIs as part of a larger "patient safety" campaign must be the focus of healthcare providers in all settings worldwide. Currently in the United States, hospital infections contribute to an estimated 90,000 deaths each year, with a staggering economic cost of $4.5 to $5.7 billion annually.[11,107] Occurrences of high incidences of preventable adverse events in international hospitals have also been reported.[11,107–109]

Research and evidence-based medicine algorithms to prevent infections and/or more quickly detect patients who are at risk are also on the agenda. More prudent use of antibiotics, increased barrier precautions, patient positioning, selective disinfection, use of silver alloy urinary catheters, and increased compliance to hand hygiene guidelines are practices and research initiatives targeted for reducing and preventing HAIs.[110–113] Implementing patient safety practices such as root cause analysis and continuous quality improvement are tools the infection preventionist can use to enhance their infection prevention and control practice.[114] It is a matter of patient safety and survival.

FUTURE TRENDS

There has been a steady decline in the percentage of Enterobacteriaceae recovered from NNIS/NHSN hospitals in the last two decades.

Nevertheless, they remain leading causes of community- and healthcare-associated infections. In addition, increasing reports of resistance to the expanded spectrum cephalosporins, fluoroquinolones, and carbapenems severely compromise therapeutic options and patient outcomes in the United States and worldwide.

There is mounting public health concern about the emergence and spread of multidrug- and pan-resistant CPE and the dwindling arsenal of antibiotics for their management. Although, initially found only in acute care hospitals, they have been found as colonizers and in the feces and urine of nonsymptomatic patients in long-term care facilities that might serve as a reservoir. Infection preventionists and other healthcare providers must refocus their efforts to detect and protect patients from infections with these and other members of the Enterobacteriaceae.

INTERNATIONAL PERSPECTIVES

HAIs are patient safety issues worldwide.[36,39] The Enterobacteriaceae are among the top five causes of infections in both developed and developing countries with prevalence ranging from 4 to 32 percent.[41–43] The most frequently involved infections in descending occurrence were SSIs, UITs, lower respiratory infections, and bloodstream infections.[109,115,116]

Increasing antibiotic resistance among healthcare-associated pathogens worldwide is emerging as one of the leading global public health issues. Worldwide resistance of the Enterobacteriaceae to third-generation cephalosporins and now the fluoroquinolones further reduces available therapeutic options and increases the risk for adverse patient outcomes.[73,75,79,117,118] CRE isolates due to KPC enzymes have been recovered in Europe, Asia, and South America. The class B metallo-beta-lactamases (MBLs), first identified in Japan, have disseminated globally with reports of isolates documented in the United States, Canada, England, Italy Australia, Korea, Malaysia, Brazil, Columbia, Singapore, Taiwan, and mainland China.

The New Delhi MBL (NDM-1) was first isolated from a Swedish patient hospitalized in India and since has spread and caused outbreaks in the United States, Europe, Asia, and Australia. Between January 2009 and February 2011, eight Enterobacteriaceae isolates with NDM-1 type production were reported to the CDC. All isolates were recovered from patients who had traveled to India or Pakistan for medical procedures.[83,119]

A second outbreak involving the *Klebsiella pneumoniae* and the NDM-l were reported to the CDC in 2012 from the Colorado Department of Public Health and Environment. Strains from the eight patients were molecularly linked. Reservoir or how the carbapenemase-producing *K. pneumoniae* strain entered the facility remains unclear.[120]

The first isolate of *K. pneumoniae* with OXA-48 was identified in Turkey since then Enterobacteriaceae with OXA-48-type enzymes have been recovered in Europe, the Middle East, and Northern Africa.[83,87,119,121,122]

Increased public surveillance, systematic approaches, and global collaboration are all necessary to help reduce the burden of preventable HAIs and improve patient safety worldwide.

REFERENCES

1. Black SB, Weinstein RA. *Enterobacteriaceae*. In: Mayhall C, ed. *Hospital Epidemiology and Infection Control*. Philadelphia: Lippincott Williams & Wilkins, 2004:545–574.
2. Donnenberg MS. *Enterobacteriaceae*. In: Mandell DAB, ed. *Principle and Practice of Infectious Disease*. Philadelphia: Churchill Livingstone Elsevier, 2010.
3. Church L. *Enterobacteriaceae*. In: Schlossberg D, ed. *Clinical Infectious Disease*. New York: Cambridge University Press, 2008:945–951.
4. Farmer JB, Janda M. Enterobacteriaceae: Introduction and identification. In: Murray P, ed. *Manual of Clinical Microbiology*. Washington, DC: ASM, 2007:649–669.
5. Kallen AJ, Srinivasan A. Current epidemiology of multidrug-resistant gram-negative bacilli in the United States. *Infect Control Hosp Epidemiol* 2010;31 Suppl 1:S51–4.
6. Le Hello S, Falcot V, Lacassin F, et al. Molecular epidemiology of carbapenem-resistant Acinetobacter baumannii in New Caledonia. *Clin Microbiol Infect* 2008;14(10):977–981.
7. Bearman GM, Munro C, Sessler CN, et al. Infection control and the prevention of nosocomial infections in the intensive care unit. *Semin Respir Crit Care Med* 2006;27(3):310–324.
8. Gaynes R, Edwards JR. Overview of nosocomial infections caused by gram-negative bacilli. *Clin Infect Dis* 2005;41(6):848–854.
9. Richards MJ, Edwards JR, Culver DH, et al. Nosocomial infections in medical intensive care units in the United States. National Nosocomial Infections Surveillance System. *Crit Care Med* 1999;27(5):887–892.
10. Siegel JD, Rhinehart E, Jackson M, et al. Guideline for isolation precautions in hospitals. *Am J Infect Control* 2007;35:S65–S164.
11. Klevens RM, Edwards JR, Richards CL Jr, et al. Estimating health care-associated infections and deaths in U.S. hospitals, 2002. *Public Health Rep* 2007;122(2):60–66.
12. Yokoe DS, Mermel LA, Anderson DJ, et al. A compendium of strategies to prevent healthcare-associated infections in acute care hospitals. *Infect Control Hosp Epidemiol* 2008;29 Suppl 1:S12–21.
13. Centers for Disease Control and Prevention. Guidance for control of infections with carbapenem-resistant or carbapenemase-producing Enterobacteriaceae in acute care facilities. *MMWR Morb Mortal Wkly Rep* 2009;58(10):256–260.
14. Centers for Disease Control and Prevention (CDC). *2012 CRE Toolkit: Guidance for Control of Carbapenem-resistant Enterobacteriaceae (CRE)*. CDC website. 2010. Available at: http://www.cdc.gov/hai/pdfs/cre/cre-guidance-508.pdf.
15. Abbott S. *Klebsiella, Enterobacter, Citrobacter, Serratia, Plesiomonas and other Enterobacteriaceae*. In: Murray P, ed. *Manual of Clinical Microbiology*. Washington, DC: ASM, 2007:698–715.
16. Boning RA, Ocampo-Sosa AA, Poirel L, et al. Biochemical and genetic characterization of carbapenem-hydrolyzing beta-lactamase OXA-229 from Acinetobacter bereziniae. *Antimicrob Agents Chemother* 2012;56(7): 3923–3927.

17. Costerton JW, Stewart PS, Greenberg EP. Bacterial biofilms: a common cause of persistent infections. *Science* 1999;284(5418):1318–1322.
18. Vertes A, Hitchins V, Phillips KS. Analytical challenges of microbial biofilms on medical devices. *Anal Chem* 2012;84(9):3858–3866.
19. Gastmeier P, Geffers C, Sohr D, et al. [Surveillance of nosocomial infections in intensive care units. Current data and interpretations]. *Wien Klin Wochenschr* 2003;115(3–4):99–103.
20. Edwards JR, Peterson KD, Mu Y, et al. National Healthcare Safety Network (NHSN) report: data summary for 2006 through 2008, issued December 2009. *Am J Infect Control* 2009;37(10):783–805.
21. Hidron AI, Edwards JR, Patel J, et al. NHSN annual update: antimicrobial-resistant pathogens associated with healthcare-associated infections: annual summary of data reported to the National Healthcare Safety Network at the Centers for Disease Control and Prevention, 2006–2007. *Infect Control Hosp Epidemiol* 2008;29(11):996–1011.
22. Sievert DM, Ricks P, Edwards JR, et al. Antimicrobial-resistant pathogens associated with healthcare-associated infections: summary of data reported to the National Healthcare Safety Network at the Centers for Disease Control and Prevention, 2009–2010. *Infect Control Hosp Epidemiol* 2013;34(1):1–14.
23. O'Grady NP, Alexander M, Burns LA, et al. Guidelines for the prevention of intravascular catheter-related infections. *Am J Infect Control* 2011;39 (4 Suppl 1):S1–34.
24. NNIS System. National Nosocomial Infections Surveillance (NNIS) System report, data summary from January 1990-May 1999, issued June 1999. *Am J Infect Control* 1999;27(6):520–532.
25. NNIS System. National Nosocomial Infections Surveillance (NNIS) System report, data summary from October 1986-April 1998, issued June 1998. *Am J Infect Control* 1998;26(5):522–533.
26. Marschall J, Mermel LA, Classen D, et al. Strategies to prevent central line-associated bloodstream infections in acute care hospitals. *Infect Control Hosp Epidemiol* 2008;29 Suppl 1:S22–30.
27. Coffin SE, Klompas M, Classen D, et al. Strategies to prevent ventilator-associated pneumonia in acute care hospitals. *Infect Control Hosp Epidemiol* 2008 Oct;29 Suppl 1:S31–40.
28. Cornia PB, Takahashi TA, Lipsky BA. The microbiology of bacteriuria in men: a 5-year study at a Veterans' Affairs hospital. *Diagn Microbiol Infect Dis* 2006;56(1):25–30.
29. Lo E, Nicolle L, Classen D, et al. Strategies to prevent catheter-associated urinary tract infections in acute care hospitals. *Infect Control Hosp Epidemiol* 2008;29 Suppl 1:S41–50.
30. Gould CV, Umscheid CA, Agarwal RK, et al. Guideline for prevention of catheter-associated urinary tract infections 2009. *Infect Control Hosp Epidemiol* 2010;31(4):319–326.
31. NNIS System. National Nosocomial Infections Surveillance (NNIS) system report, data summary from January 1992-April 2000, issued June 2000. *Am J Infect Control* 2000;28(6):429–448.
32. Lin MY, Lyles-Banks RD, Lolans K, et al. The importance of long-term acute care hospitals in the regional epidemiology of *Klebsiella pneumoniae* carbapenemase-producing Enterobacteriaceae. *Clin Infect Dis* 2013 Nov;57(9):1246–1252.
33. NNIS System. National Nosocomial Infections Surveillance (NNIS) report, data summary from October 1986-April 1996, issued May 1996. A report from the National Nosocomial Infections Surveillance (NNIS) System. *Am J Infect Control* 1996;24(5):380–388.
34. Anderson DJ, Kaye KS, Classen D, et al. Strategies to prevent surgical site infections in acute care hospitals. *Infect Control Hosp Epidemiol* 2008;29 Suppl 1:S51–61.
35. Centers for Disease Control and Prevention. Vital signs: incidence and trends of infection with pathogens transmitted commonly through food—foodborne diseases active surveillance network, 10 U.S. sites, 1996–2010. *MMWR Morb Mortal Wkly Rep* 2011;60:749–755.
36. Nataro JP, Bopp CA, Fields PI, et al. *Escherichia, Shigella, and Salmonella*. In: Murray P, ed. *Manual of Clinical Microbiology*. Washington, DC: ASM, 2007:670–687.
37. Miller MA, Sentz J, Rabaa MA, et al. Global epidemiology of infections due to *Shigella, Salmonella* serotype *Typhi*, and enterotoxigenic *Escherichia coli*. *Epidemiol Infect* 2008;136(4):433–435.
38. Clarke SC. Diarrhoeagenic *Escherichia coli*—an emerging problem? *Diagn Microbiol Infect Dis* 2001;41(3):93–98.
39. Clarke SC, Haigh RD, Freestone PP, et al. Enteropathogenic *Escherichia coli* infection: history and clinical aspects. *Br J Biomed Sci* 2002;59(2):123–127.
40. Dalben M, Varkulja G, Basso M, et al. Investigation of an outbreak of Enterobacter cloacae in a neonatal unit and review of the literature. *J Hosp Infect* 2008;70(1):7–14.
41. Hoffmann H, Schmoldt S, Trülzsch K, et al. Nosocomial urosepsis caused by Enterobacter kobei with aberrant phenotype. *Diagn Microbiol Infect Dis* 2005;53(2):143–147.
42. Hoffmann H, Stindl S, Ludwig W, et al. Reassignment of enterobacter dissolvens to *Enterobacter cloacae* as *E. cloacae* subspecies dissolvens comb. nov. and emended description of *Enterobacter asburiae* and *Enterobacter kobei*. *Syst Appl Microbiol* 2005;28(3):196–205.
43. Hoffmann H, Stindl S, Ludwig W, et al. *Enterobacter hormaechei subsp. oharae* subsp. nov., *E. hormaechei subsp. hormaechei* comb. nov., and *E. hormaechei subsp. steigerwaltii* subsp. nov., three new subspecies of clinical importance. *J Clin Microbiol* 2005;43(7):3297–3303.
44. Hoffmann H, Stindl S, Stumpf A, et al. Description of *Enterobacter ludwigii sp. nov.*, a novel *Enterobacter* species of clinical relevance. *Syst Appl Microbiol* 2005;28(3):206–212.
45. Ananthan, Raju S, Alavandi S. Enterotoxigenicity of *Klebsiella pneumoniae* associated with childhood gastroenteritis in Madras, India. *Jpn J Infect Dis* 1999;52(1):16–17.
46. Erbay A, Kanyilmaz D, Us E, et al. A cluster of *Klebsiella pneumoniae* bacteremia in a radiation oncology ward. *Am J Infect Control* 2008;36(9):678–680.
47. Wisplinghoff H, Bischoff T, Tallent SM, et al. Nosocomial bloodstream infections in US hospitals: analysis of 24,179 cases from a prospective nationwide surveillance study. *Clin Infect Dis* 2004;39(3):309–317.
48. Gordon MA, Graham SM, Walsh AL, et al. Epidemics of invasive *Salmonella enterica serovar enteritidis* and *S. enterica Serovar typhimurium* infection associated with multidrug resistance among adults and children in Malawi. *Clin Infect Dis* 2008;46(7):963–969.
49. Lazinska B, Rokosz A, Sawicka-Grzelak A, et al. [Strains of genus *Salmonella* isolated from extraintestinal infections]. *Med Dosw Mikrobiol* 2005;57(3):287–294.
50. Sengupta S, Jagadishchandra K, Murty R, et al. An unusual post-operative wound infection with *Salmonella typhi*: case report. *Indian J Med Sci* 2000;54(4):149–150.
51. Abdel-Haq NM, Asmar BI, Abuhammour WM, et al. *Yersinia enterocolitica* infection in children. *Pediatr Infect Dis J* 2000;19(10):954–958.
52. Constantiniu S. Isolation of *Yersinia* group in human infections, animals and environment factors. *Arch Roum Pathol Exp Microbiol* 1990;49(2):131–137.
53. Kapperud G. [*Yersinia enterocolitica* infection. Epidemiology, risk factors and preventive measures]. *Tidsskr Nor Laegeforen* 1994;114(14):1606–1608.
54. Inglesby TV, Dennis DT, Henderson DA, et al. Plague as a biological weapon: medical and public health management. Working Group on Civilian Biodefense. *JAMA* 2000;283(17):2281–2290.
55. Dallal MM, Khorramizadeh MR, MoezArdalan K. Occurrence of enteropathogenic bacteria in children under 5 years with diarrhoea in south Tehran. *East Mediterr Health J* 2006;12(6):792–797.
56. el-Sherbini M, al-Agili S, el-Jali H, et al. Isolation of *Yersinia* enterocolitica from cases of acute appendicitis and ice-cream. *East Mediterr Health J* 1999;5(1):130–135.
57. Ethelberg S, Olsen KE, Gerner-Smidt P, et al. Household outbreaks among culture-confirmed cases of bacterial gastrointestinal disease. *Am J Epidemiol* 2004;159(4):406–412.
58. Fitzgerald SD, Visser J, Mosser T, et al. Clinical challenge. Acute necrotizing enteritis with microabscesses due to *Yersinia pseudotuberculosis*. *J Zoo Wildl Med* 2000;31(1):129–130.
59. Foligne B, Dessein R, Marceau M, et al. Therapeutic potential of *Yersinia* anti-inflammatory components. *Adv Exp Med Biol* 2007;603:361–366.
60. Frick JS, Fink K, Kahl F, et al. Identification of commensal bacterial strains that modulate *Yersinia enterocolitica* and dextran sodium sulfate-induced inflammatory responses: implications for the development of probiotics. *Infect Immun* 2007;75(7):3490–3497.
61. Fruhmorgen P. [Rare infectious colitis: diagnosis and therapy]. *Bildgebung* 1995;62 Suppl 1:47–49.
62. Fuchizaki U, Machi T, Kaneko S. Clinical challenges and images in GI. *Yersinia enterocolitica* mesenteric adenitis and terminal ileitis. *Gastroenterology* 2006;131(5):1379, 1659.
63. Ligon BL. Plague: a review of its history and potential as a biological weapon. *Semin Pediatr Infect Dis* 2006;17(3):161–170.
64. Stenseth NC, Atshabar BB, Begon M, et al. Plague: past, present, and future. *PLoS Med* 2008;5(1):e3.
65. Inoue N. [Germs and toxins in bioterrorism]. *Nippon Rinsho* 2003;61 Suppl 2:81–91.
66. O'Toole T, Inglesby TV. Facing the biological weapons threat. *Lancet* 2000;356(9236):1128–1229.
67. Rotz LD, Khan AS, Lillibridge SR, et al. Public health assessment of potential biological terrorism agents. *Emerg Infect Dis* 2002;8(2):225–230.
68. Rotz LD, Koo D, O'Carroll PW, et al. Bioterrorism preparedness: planning for the future. *J Public Health Manag Pract* 2000;6(4):45–49.
69. Emonet S, Shah HN, Cherkaoui A, et al. Application and use of various mass spectrometry methods in clinical microbiology. *Clin Microbiol Infect* 2010;16(11):1604–1613.

70. Fournier PE, Drancourt M, Colson P, et al. Modern clinical microbiology: new challenges and solutions. *Nat Rev Microbiol* 2013;11(8):574–585.

71. Goyanes MJ, Cercenado E, Insa R, et al. High rates of antimicrobial co-resistance among *Enterobacteriaceae*: comparative analysis between clinical isolates resistant and susceptible to third-generation cephalosporins. *Rev Esp Quimioter* 2007;20(2):216–221.

72. Jarvis WR. Controlling healthcare-associated infections: the role of infection control and antimicrobial use practices. *Semin Pediatr Infect Dis* 2004;15(1):30–40.

73. Gould CV, Rothenberg R, Steinberg JP. Antibiotic resistance in long-term acute care hospitals: the perfect storm. *Infect Control Hosp Epidemiol* 2006;27(9):920–925.

74. Neuhauser MM, Weinstein RA, Rydman R, et al. Antibiotic resistance among gram-negative bacilli in US intensive care units: implications for fluoroquinolone use. *JAMA* 2003;289(7):885–888.

75. Slama TG. Gram-negative antibiotic resistance: there is a price to pay. *Crit Care* 2008;12 Suppl 4:S4.

76. Bell JM, Chitsaz M, Turnidge JD, et al. Prevalence and significance of a negative extended-spectrum beta-lactamase (ESBL) confirmation test result after a positive ESBL screening test result for isolates of *Escherichia coli* and *Klebsiella pneumoniae*: results from the SENTRY Asia-Pacific Surveillance Program. *J Clin Microbiol* 2007;45(5):1478–1482.

77. Bradford PA. Extended-spectrum beta-lactamases in the 21st century: characterization, epidemiology, and detection of this important resistance threat. *Clin Microbiol Rev* 2001;14(4):933–951.

78. Cagnacci S, Gualco L, Roveta S, et al. Bloodstream infections caused by multidrug-resistant *Klebsiella pneumoniae* producing the carbapenem-hydrolysing VIM-1 metallo-beta-lactamase: first Italian outbreak. *J Antimicrob Chemother* 2008;61(2):296–300.

79. Chaudhary U, Aggarwal R. Extended spectrum-lactamases (ESBL) - An emerging threat to clinical therapeutics. *Indian J Med Microbiol* 2004;22(2):75–80.

80. Colodner R. Extended-spectrum beta-lactamases: a challenge for clinical microbiologists and infection control specialists. Am J Infect Control 2005;33(2):104–107.

81. Subha A, Devi VR, Ananthan S. AmpC beta-lactamase producing multi-drug resistant strains of *Klebsiella spp.* & *Escherichia coli* isolated from children under five in Chennai. *Indian J Med Res* 2003;117:13–18.

82. Brink A, Coetzee J, Clay C, et al. The spread of carbapenem-resistant *Enterobacteriaceae* in South Africa: risk factors for acquisition and prevention. *S Afr Med J* 2012;102(7):599–601.

83. Gupta N, Limbago BM, Patel JB, et al. Carbapenem-resistant *Enterobacteriaceae*: epidemiology and prevention. *Clin Infect Dis* 2011;53(1):60–67.

84. NNIS System. National Nosocomial Infections Surveillance (NNIS) System Report, data summary from January 1992 through June 2004, issued October 2004. *Am J Infect Control* 2004;32(8):470–485.

85. Srinivasan A, Patel JB. *Klebsiella pneumoniae* carbapenemase-producing organisms: an ounce of prevention really is worth a pound of cure. *Infect Control Hosp Epidemiol* 2008;29(12):1107–1109.

86. Lahlaoui H, Poirel L, Barguellil F, et al. Carbapenem-hydrolyzing class D beta-lactamase OXA-48 in *Klebsiella pneumoniae* isolates from Tunisia. *Eur J Clin Microbiol Infect Dis* 2012;31(6):937–939.

87. Nordmann P, Dortet L, Poirel L. Carbapenem resistance in *Enterobacteriaceae*: here is the storm! *Trends Mol Med* 2012;18(5):263–272.

88. van Duin D, Kaye KS, Neuner EA, et al. Carbapenem-resistant *Enterobacteriaceae*: a review of treatment and outcomes. *Diagn Microbiol Infect Dis* 2013;75(2):115–120.

89. Jacob JT. Vital Signs: Carbapenem-resistant *Enterobacteriaceae*. *Morb Mortal Wkly Rep* 2013;62(9):165–170.

90. Clinical and Laboratory Standards Institute (CLSI). *Performance standards for antimicrobial susceptibility testing; 18th informational supplement. CLSI document M100-S18*. Wayne, PA: CLSI, 2008.

91. Anderson KF, Lonsway DR, Rasheed JK, et al. Evaluation of methods to identify the *Klebsiella pneumoniae* carbapenemase in *Enterobacteriaceae*. *J Clin Microbiol* 2007;45(8):2723–2725.

92. Clinical and Laboratory Standards Institute (CLSI). *Performance standards for antimicrobial susceptibility testing; twentieth informational supplement (June 2010 update). CLSI document M100-S20-U*. Wayne, PA: CLSI, 2010.

93. Calfee D, Jenkins SG. Use of active surveillance cultures to detect asymptomatic colonization with carbapenem-resistant *Klebsiella pneumoniae* in intensive care unit patients. *Infect Control Hosp Epidemiol* 2008;29(10):966–968.

94. Cohen AE, Lautenbach E, Morales KH, et al. Fluoroquinolone-resistant *Escherichia coli* in the long-term care setting. *Am J Med* 2006;119(11):958–963.

95. Kim JY, Lautenbach E, Chu J, et al. Fluoroquinolone resistance in pediatric bloodstream infections because of *Escherichia coli* and *Klebsiella* species. *Am J Infect Control* 2008;36(1):70–73.

96. Han JH, Nachamkin I, Tolomeo P, et al. Temporal changes in resistance mechanisms in colonizing *Escherichia coli* isolates with reduced susceptibility to fluoroquinolones. *Diagn Microbiol Infect Dis* 2013;76(4):491–496.

97. Pintado V, San Miguel LG, Grill F, et al. Intravenous colistin sulphomethate sodium for therapy of infections due to multidrug-resistant gram-negative bacteria. *J Infect* 2008;56(3):185–190.

98. Walkty A, DeCorby M, Nichol K, et al. In vitro activity of colistin (polymyxin E) against 3,480 isolates of gram-negative bacilli obtained from patients in Canadian hospitals in the CANWARD study, 2007–2008. *Antimicrob Agents Chemother* 2009;53(11):4924–4926.

99. Gupta S, Govil D, Kakar PN, et al. Colistin and polymyxin B: a re-emergence. *Indian J Crit Care Med* 2009;13(2):49–53.

100. Livermore DM, Warner M, Mushtaq S, et al. What remains against carbapenem-resistant *Enterobacteriaceae*? Evaluation of chloramphenicol, ciprofloxacin, colistin, fosfomycin, minocycline, nitrofurantoin, temocillin and tigecycline. *Int J Antimicrob Agents* 2011;37(5):415–419.

101. Rutala WA, Weber DJ, and Healthcare Infection Control Professional Advisory Committee (HICPAC). *Guideline for Disinfection and Sterilization in Healthcare Facilities, 2008*. CDC website. 2008. Available at: http://www.cdc.gov/hicpac/pdf/guidelines/Disinfection_Nov_2008.pdf.

102. Siegel JD, Rhinehart E, Jackson M, et al. 2007 Guideline for Isolation Precautions: Preventing Transmission of Infectious Agents in Health Care Settings. *Am J Infect Control* 2007;35(10 Suppl 2): S65–164.

103. Sehulster L, Chinn RY. Guidelines for environmental infection control in health-care facilities. Recommendations of CDC and the Healthcare Infection Control Practices Advisory Committee (HICPAC). *MMWR Recomm Rep* 2003;52(RR-10):1–42.

104. Boyce JM, Pittet D. Guideline for Hand Hygiene in Health-Care Settings: recommendations of the Healthcare Infection Control Practices Advisory Committee and the HICPAC/SHEA/APIC/IDSA Hand Hygiene Task Force. *Infect Control Hosp Epidemiol* 2002;23(12 Suppl):S3–40.

105. Siegel JD, Rhinehart E, Jackson M, et al. Management of multidrug-resistant organisms in health care settings, 2006. *Am J Infect Control* 2007;35(10 Suppl 2):S165–193.

106. Shah AA, Hasan F, Ahmed S, et al. Extended-spectrum beta-lactamases (ESbLs): characterization, epidemiology and detection. *Crit Rev Microbiol* 2004;30(1):25–32.

107. Jarvis WR. The state of the science of health care epidemiology, infection control, and patient safety, 2004. *Am J Infect Control* 2004;32(8):496–503.

108. Bouza E, San Juan R, Muñoz P, et al. A European perspective on nosocomial urinary tract infections I. Report on the microbiology workload, etiology and antimicrobial susceptibility (ESGNI-003 study). European Study Group on Nosocomial Infections. *Clin Microbiol Infect* 2001;7(10):523–531.

109. Harbarth S, Ruef C, Francioli P, et al. Nosocomial infections in Swiss university hospitals: a multi-centre survey and review of the published experience. *Swiss-Noso Network. Schweiz Med Wochenschr* 1999;129(42):1521–1528.

110. Zhanel GG, DeCorby M, Nichol KA, et al. Antimicrobial susceptibility of 3931 organisms isolated from intensive care units in Canada: Canadian National Intensive Care Unit Study, 2005/2006. *Diagn Microbiol Infect Dis* 2008;62(1):67–80.

111. Lazzari S, Allegranzi B, Concia E. Making hospitals safer: the need for a global strategy for infection control in health care settings. *World Hosp Health Serv* 2004;40(2):32,34,36–42.

112. Thomas EJ, et al. A comparison of iatrogenic injury studies in Australia and the USA. I: Context, methods, casemix, population, patient and hospital characteristics. *Int J Qual Health Care* 2000;12(5):371–378.

113. Vincent CG, Neale G, Woloshynowych M, Adverse events in British hospitals: preliminary retrospective record review. *BMJ* 2001;322(7285):517–519.

114. Gerberding JL. Hospital-onset infections: a patient safety issue. *Ann Intern Med* 2002;137(8):665–670.

115. Rosenthal VD, Maki DG, Mehta A, et al. International Nosocomial Infection Control Consortium report, data summary for 2002–2007, issued January 2008. *Am J Infect Control* 2008;36(9):627–637.

116. Jones ME, Draghi DC, Thornsberry C, et al. Emerging resistance among bacterial pathogens in the intensive care unit—a European and North American Surveillance study (2000–2002). *Ann Clin Microbiol Antimicrob* 2004;3:14.

117. Macgowan AP. Clinical implications of antimicrobial resistance for therapy. *J Antimicrob Chemother* 2008;62 Suppl 2:ii105–114.

118. Paterson DL. Resistance in gram-negative bacteria: Enterobacteriaceae. *Am J Infect Control* 2006;34(5 Suppl 1):S20–28; discussion S64–73.

119. Grundmann H, Livermore DM, Giske CG, et al. Carbapenem-non-susceptible Enterobacteriaceae in Europe: conclusions from a meeting of national experts. *Euro Surveill* 2010;15(46):pii 19711.

120. Centers for Disease Control and Prevention. Notes from the field: hospital outbreak of carbapenem-resistant Klebsiella pneumoniae producing New Delhi metallo-beta-lactamase—Denver, Colorado, 2012. *MMWR Morb Mortal Wkly Rep* 2013;62(6):108.

121. Drew RJ, Turton JF, Hill RL, et al. Emergence of carbapenem-resistant Enterobacteriaceae in a UK paediatric hospital. *J Hosp Infect* 2013; 84(4):300–304.
122. Patel G, Perez F, Bonomo RA. Carbapenem-resistant Enterobacteriaceae and Acinetobacter baumannii: assessing their impact on organ transplantation. *Curr Opin Organ Transplant* 2010 Oct 7 [Epub ahead of print].

SUPPLEMENTAL RESOURCES

Heyman D, ed. Control of Communicable Disease, 19th ed. Washington, DC: American Public Health Association, 2008.

Mandell GL. Mandell, Douglas, and Bennett's Principles and Practice of Infectious Diseases. Philadelphia: Churchill, Livingstone Elsevier, 2010.

Mayhall CG, ed. Hospital Epidemiology and Infection Control, 4th ed. Philadelphia: Lippincott Williams & Wilkins, 2011.

Pickering LK, ed. *Red Book 2012: Report of the Committee on Infectious Disease*, 29th ed. New York: American Academy of Pediatrics, 2012.

Websites

American Society for Microbiology. Available at: www.asm.org.

Association for Professionals in Infection Control and Epidemiology. Available at: www.apic.org.

Centers for Disease Control and Prevention. Available at: www.cdc.gov.

CHAPTER 76

Enterococci

Lennox K. Archibald, MD, PhD, FRCP, DTM&H
Hospital Epidemiologist
Malcom Randall VA Medical Center
Gainesville, FL

ABSTRACT

Enterococcus is an important organism because it is one of eight classes of pathogens that account for approximately 70 percent of healthcare-associated infections in the United States. This chapter reviews the bacteriology, epidemiology, and infection prevention elements of this organism, as well as diagnosis and treatment of the clinical diseases it produces. The use of active surveillance is discussed as an effective strategy for the reduction of vancomycin-resistant enterococci.

KEY CONCEPTS

- Enterococci are Gram-positive, catalase-negative, nonspore-forming cocci that can exist singly, in pairs, or in chains. They grow under facultative anaerobic conditions, with optimum growth occurring at 35°C to 37°C.

- Enterococci typically colonize the human gastrointestinal and biliary tracts; less commonly, they colonize the female genital tract and male urethra, the perineum, the oral cavity, and the skin.

- Of the approximately 38 species, *Enterococcus faecalis* and *Enterococcus faecium* are the most common isolates encountered in the clinical setting; the former is associated with approximately 90 percent of human enterococcal infections, whereas the latter is associated with as many as 15 percent of such infections.

- *Enterococcus* is one of eight classes of pathogens that account for approximately 70 percent of healthcare-associated infections in U.S. hospitals.

- After vancomycin-resistant enterococci have been introduced into a healthcare setting, transmission is determined by selective pressure due to antimicrobial use, the proportion of colonized patients within the facility or unit, the number of susceptible patients within the setting, and adherence to prevention efforts by healthcare personnel.

- Active surveillance cultures for resistant pathogens in intensive care units with isolation of colonized persons appears to be an effective strategy for vancomycin-resistant enterococci control in some institutions; isolation purely on the basis of history of previous vancomycin-resistant enterococci detection appears to be of little benefit.

- Standard Precautions and isolation of the occasional patient recognized to be colonized through routine clinical cultures have not proved effective in reducing rates of vancomycin-resistant enterococci infections.

BACTERIOLOGY

Enterococcus species are Gram-positive, catalase-negative, nonspore-forming cocci that can exist singly, in pairs, or in chains. They grow under facultative anaerobic conditions with optimum growth occurring at 35°C to 37°C. Growth colonies are morphologically larger than those of streptococci and usually are nonhemolytic or α-hemolytic, though some enterococci strains may exhibit β-hemolysis. The name "enterococcus" reflects their tendency to reside in the human gastrointestinal tract, where their intrinsic properties give them the ability to survive in that environment. These properties include the ability of the majority of strains to grow at a wide range of temperature (10°C to 45°C) and pH (4.5 to 9.6) and the ability to maintain growth in the presence of high concentrations (6.5 percent) of sodium chloride and bile salts.[1] Other biochemical properties include the ability to hydrolyze esculin in the presence of 40 percent bile (bile-esculin [BE] test); the ability to hydrolyze leucine-β-naphthylamide to produce leucine aminopeptidase (LAP); and production of pyrrolidonyl arylamidase by hydrolyisis of pyrrolidonyl-β-naphthylamide (PYR). Presumptive identification of a Gram-positive coccus as an *Enterococcus* species in the medical microbiology laboratory can be made by demonstrating that the isolate grows in the presence of 6.5 percent sodium chloride at 45°C, is catalase-negative, and is positive for the BE, LAP, and PYR tests.[2]

Enterococcus species previously were classified with the *Streptococcus* genus that possesses the Lancefield group D antigen (lipoteichoic acid) in their cell walls.[1-3] During the mid to late 1980s, the application of DNA molecular techniques to group D streptococci taxonomy resulted in the reclassification of these streptococci into two genera—a distinct *Enterococcus* genus separate from group D streptococci.[3] The current criteria for belonging to the genus *Enterococcus* includes phenotypic testing as well as DNA typing and 16S rRNA gene sequencing.[2] Based on the analysis of 16S rRNA sequences, at least 38 species of *Enterococcus* have now been identified.[2]

EPIDEMIOLOGY

Enterococci are now considered the most abundant Gram-positive cocci that colonize the human gastrointestinal and biliary tracts. Less commonly, they colonize the female genital tract, the male urethra, the perineum, the oral cavity, and the skin. Certain *Enterococcus* species can be found in soil, water, food, plants, animals, birds, insects, and reptiles.[2] Most enterococcal infections occur in hospitalized patients, especially in the ICU setting. Of the approximately 38 species now identified, *Enterococcus faecalis* and *Enterococcus faecium* are the most common isolates encountered in the clinical setting; the former is associated with approximately 90 percent of human enterococcal infections and the latter is associated with up to 15 percent of such infections.[4–6] Other enterococcal species have been infrequently associated with human infections, especially in the hospitalized compromised patient (Table 76-1). Although *E. faecalis* and *E. faecium* are microorganisms of low virulence, they are rendered pathogenic in debilitated and immunocompromised patients and those with comorbidities such as diabetes, chronic congestive heart failure, or chronic obstructive pulmonary disease, especially those receiving broad-spectrum antimicrobial therapy or having one or more in situ invasive medical devices (e.g., intravascular catheters, mechanical ventilators, urinary catheters).[7–12]

Although the major mode of spread of *Enterococcus* in healthcare settings in the United States is via direct or indirect contact transmission mediated by transient carriage on the hands of healthcare personnel (HCP), the actual chain of transmission of enterococci in healthcare settings remains a complex interplay of (1) the host (i.e., the patient) who might or might not be colonized; (2) the organism itself—generally innocuous in the normal healthy individual but rendered opportunistic in a susceptible host; and (3) the environment as defined above.[9,13] It is well documented that enterococci may remain viable for days to weeks on dry, inert, environmental surfaces (fomites), including clothing and laboratory coats. Such contaminated surfaces may act as a source or intermediary for direct or indirect contact transmission via the hands of HCP. Other sites of environmental contamination in healthcare facilities include thermometers, sphygmomanometers, stethoscopes, upholstery, bedrails, computer keyboards, white coats, ties, medicine preparation areas, patients' hospital clothing, linen, doorknobs, electrocardiogram monitors, intravenous fluid pumps, and commodes.[3,12,14–28]

Table 76-1. *Enterococcus* Species

Known cause of infection	Potential for infection
E. avium	E. caccae
E. casseliflavus	E. cecorum
E. dispar	E. columbae
E. durans	E. flavescens
E. faecalis	E. gilvus
E. faecium	E. hawaiiensis
E. gallinarum	E. italicus
E. hirae	E. pallens
E. malodoratus	E. saccharolyticus
E. mundtii	E. sanguinicola
E. pseudoavium	E. seriolicida
E. raffinosus	E. sulfureus
E. solitaries	

After vancomycin-resistant enterococci (VRE) have been introduced into a healthcare setting, transmission is determined by selective pressure due to antimicrobial use, the proportion of colonized patients, the availability of susceptible patients, and adherence to prevention efforts.[29] Complicating the mechanism of transmission even further are various other risk factors, including the proportion of colonized patients already resident in the pertinent inpatient unit, the availability of susceptible patients, the degree of adherence to infection prevention efforts in the facility, staffing levels, severity of illness of susceptible patients, and the cellular factors that determine the virulence and pathogenicity of enterococci. Virulence factors, though not fully understood, include:

- Cytolysin, a hemolysin that causes β-hemolysis of human, rabbit, and equine but not sheep erythrocytes[14,30–32];

- Aggregation substance, a surface-bound, plasma-encoded protein that mediates adhesion to a variety of eukaryotic cell surfaces[33];

- Extracellular superoxide production[34];

- Enterococcal surface protein;

- Pheromones, small peptides that promote conjugative transfer of plasmid DNA[35];

- Bacteriocin, a plasmid-coded enzyme that lyses Gram-positive and Gram-negative bacteria; gelatinase; and hyaluronidase.

Most of these virulence factors have been identified in *E. faecalis* but have rarely been detected in other enterococcal species.[31]

Data from the National Healthcare Safety Network (NHSN) and the Centers for Disease Control and Prevention (CDC) indicate that among the eight pathogen groups that account for approximately 70 percent of healthcare-associated infections (HAIs) in U.S. hospitals, the three most commonly reported pathogens are *Staphylococcus aureus* (15.6 percent), *Enterococcus* spp. (13.9 percent), and *Escherichia coli*. Of the microorganisms that predominate among the four major infection sites (i.e., bloodstream, surgical wounds, respiratory tract, and urinary tract), *Enterococcus* spp. are the third most common cause of surgical site infections (SSIs) (12 percent) and the second most common cause of bloodstream infections (BSIs).[36]

The incidence and prevalence of VRE have been increasing significantly over the past two decades; these rate increases are clearly more marked in the intensive care unit (ICU) versus the non-ICU inpatient setting.[37,38] From 1989 to 2004, the proportion of ICU *Enterococcus* spp. infections that were caused by VRE and reported to the National Nosocomial Infections Surveillance (NNIS) system increased from 0.4 percent to more than 33 percent. This rate increase, in particular, is of enormous clinical importance because documentation during the 1990s showed that at least 83 percent of VRE isolates were resistant to most of the available antimicrobials.[39,40] Although newer agents like daptomycin and linezolid have proven effective against VRE, treatment options for patients with VRE HAIs remain limited, often to unproven combinations of other antimicrobials or experimental compounds.

Unfortunately, current data suggest that the number of hospitalizations with infection due to vancomycin-resistant pathogens is still increasing in the United States.[41] Other data from the Surveillance and Control of Pathogens of Epidemiological Importance (SCOPE) study, a multicenter surveillance system for bloodstream infections in the United States, have established that *Enterococcus* spp. are the third most common (9 percent) cause of healthcare-associated BSIs after coagulase-negative staphylococcus (31 percent) and *S. aureus* (20 percent)—consistent with CDC data.[42]

ANTIMICROBIAL RESISTANCE AND SUSCEPTIBILITY TESTING ISSUES

Antimicrobial resistance among enterococci to a growing number of agents is increasing across the United States and can be a manifestation of their pathogenicity. Enterococci are inhibited by β-lactam agents (e.g., ampicillin) but generally are not killed by them. Such resistance may be intrinsic or acquired and can manifest at low or high levels to the agent of concern (Table 76-2).

Intrinsic resistance: Intrinsic resistance in enterococci is basically inherent resistance resulting from natural characteristics that are chromosomally encoded in the genome of the organism. Enterococci are inherently resistant to β-lactam agents (cephalosporins, penicillinase-resistant penicillins, and monobactams), aminoglycosides, and trimethoprim/sulfamethoxazole. The majority of strains express this intrinsic resistance in chromosomal resistance genes. Such strains may manifest intrinsic low-level resistance to various aminoglycosides or intermediate susceptibility or resistance to fluoroquinolones and are generally less susceptible than streptococci (10- to 1,000-fold) to penicillin or ampicillin.

Table 76-2. Agents Associated with Intrinsic and Acquired Antimicrobial Drug Resistance in Enterococci

Intrinsic Resistance
β-Lactams (particularly cephalosporins and penicillinase-resistant penicillins)
Aminoglycosides (low concentrations)
Clindamycin
Fluoroquinolones
Trimethoprim-sulfamethoxazole

Acquired Resistance
High concentrations of β-lactams, through alteration of penicillin binding proteins (PBPs) or production of β-lactamase
Aminoglycosides (high concentrations)
Glycopeptides (vancomycin, teicoplanin)
Tetracycline
Erythromycin
Fluoroquinolones
Rifampin
Chloramphenicol
Fusidic acid
Nitrofurantoin

Gold HS, Moellering RC Jr. Antimicrobial drug resistance. *N Engl J Med* 1996;335:1445–1453.

Acquired resistance: Acquired antimicrobial resistance among enterococci has been described for a number of agents including penicillins (includes organisms with and without β-lactamase), macrolides, tetracyclines, lincosamides, chloramphenicol, vancomycin, quinolones, quinupristin/dalfopristin, linezolid, and daptomycin. Aminoglycoside, β-lactam, and glycopeptide antimicrobials will be the focus of the following review of acquired resistance. All enterococci express some level of resistance (i.e., inherent resistance) to aminoglycosides based on failure of this class of agent to be actively transported into the cell. Notwithstanding, combinations of low concentration of penicillin and aminoglycosides are bactericidal for various strains of enterococci. The action of the penicillin on the cell wall renders entry of the aminoglycoside into the cell and allows it to act at the ribosomal site. Aminoglycosides fail to provide synergy with cell wall active agents for bactericidal activity if high-level resistance (minimum inhibitory concentration [MIC] greater than 2,000 μg/mL) is detected. High-level resistance among enterococcal strains renders aminoglycoside use futile, as these strains are not amenable to the synergistic effects of the aminoglycoside with penicillin.[1,43,44]

Although enterococci may appear susceptible to sulphonamides in vitro, they are able to circumvent the block in folate synthesis caused by sulphonamides, resulting in resistance to this class of antimicrobial agent in vivo. Most strains of enterococci have relatively high MICs for β-lactam agents, such as penicillins and cephalosporins.

Until the 1980s, ampicillin, a β-lactam agent, was a commonly used and effective antimicrobial for enterococcal infections. Since then, resistance to ampicillin has been increasing among *E. faecalis* and *E. faecium*. Ampicillin resistance can occur by either one of two mechanisms. The more prevalent mechanism, occurring most often in *E. faecium* isolates, is a decreased affinity of the penicillin-binding proteins for the β-lactam agent, resulting in high-level ampicillin resistance.[45] Alternatively, ampicillin resistance can occur from β-lactamase production from genes located in the chromosome or transferable plasmids.[46–48] Susceptibility testing with ampicillin is often used to predict susceptibility to amoxicillin, amoxicillin-clavulanic acid, ampicillin-sulbactam, piperacillin, and piperacillin-tazobactam among non-β-lactamase-producing enterococci.[2] In addition, susceptibility to ampicillin can be used to predict the susceptibility of *E. faecalis* to imipenem.[49,50] Of note, however, is the fact that susceptibility of enterococci to penicillin cannot be predicted by the susceptibility to ampicillin.

VRE epidemiology: Vancomycin and teicoplanin are glycopeptides with similar properties. They work by inhibiting cell wall synthesis in Gram-positive bacteria by binding with two D-alanine substrates. The cross-linking enzyme responsible for cell wall synthesis cannot then work properly, preventing cell wall synthesis. In resistant isolates, one of the two D-alanine substrates is replaced with D-lactate. This does not allow for vancomycin to bind properly, enabling cross-linking to progress. As of this writing, teicoplanin is available for patients in Europe only, not in the United States. Current MIC benchmarks for

Table 76-3. Glycopeptide Resistance Genes Among *Enterococcus* Species

Gene	Location of *van* genes	Type of expression	Characteristics
*van*A	Plasmid; chromosome genes carried on conjugative transposon (Tn1546)	Inducible	High-level resistance to both vancomycin (MIC, 64 to 1,000 μg/mL) and teicoplanin (MIC, 16 to 512 μg/mL) Identified in *E. faecium, E. faecalis, E. avium, E. casseliflavus, E. durans, E. gallinarum, E. hirae, E. mundtii, E. raffinosus, E. sanguinicola*
*van*B	Plasmid; chromosome transferred by conjugation	Inducible	Acquired inducible resistance to various concentrations of vancomycin (MIC, 4 to 1,000 μg/mL) but remains susceptible to teicoplanin (MIC, 0.5 to 1 μg/mL) Identified in *E. faecium* and *E. faecalis, E. durans, E gallinarum*
*van*C	Chromosome	Constitutive	Intrinsic, constitutive, low-level resistance to vancomycin (MIC, 2 to 32 μg/mL) but remains susceptible to teicoplanin (MIC, 0.5 to 1 μg/mL). Identified in *E. gallinarum* and *E. casseliflavus, E. flavescens*
*van*D	Chromosome	Constitutive	Constitutive resistance to vancomycin and low levels of teicoplanin Identified in *E. faecium, E. faecalis, E. avium, E. gallinarum, E. raffinosus*
*van*E	Chromosome	Inducible	Identified in *E. faecalis*
*van*G	Chromosome transferred by conjugation	Inducible	Identified in *E. faecalis*
VanL	Unknown	Unknown	Low-level resistance to vancomycin; susceptible to teicoplanin Identified in *E. faecalis*

susceptibility and resistance to vancomycin among enterococci isolates have been set by the Clinical and Laboratory Standards Institute as follows: vancomycin-susceptible, MIC less than 4 μg/mL; intermediate resistance, MIC of 8 to 16 μg/mL; and vancomycin-resistant, MIC of at least 32 μg/mL.[51]

In 1988, the first isolates of vancomycin-resistant *E. faecalis* and *E. faecium* were reported in the United Kingdom and France.[52,53] Shortly thereafter, in 1989, similar resistant strains emerged in the United States.[18,39,54] Subsequently, VRE spread rapidly throughout healthcare facilities across Europe and the United States.[55,56] In Europe, VRE isolates were also identified in animal and community reservoirs.[15–17,26,52] The first report of VRE outside the healthcare setting was from sewage treatment plants.[15,57] VRE have also been recovered from livestock feces, uncooked chicken meat, and persons who work at farms or processing plants.[15–17,26,52,58,59] Epidemiological studies in Europe have shown an association between subtherapeutic doses of avoparcin, a growth-promoting glycopeptide antibiotic used in animal husbandry, and VRE recovery from animals reared for food.[26,59–61] In contrast, avoparcin use in animal husbandry in the U.S. is prohibited.[17] A little over a decade ago, the CDC established that a large proportion of chickens sold in U.S. supermarkets were contaminated by quinupristin-dalfopristin-resistant *E. faecium*.[62] However, the low prevalence and low level of resistance of the strains of *E. faecium* isolated from human stool specimens suggested that the use of virginiamycin in animals had not yet had a substantial influence in the United States.[62]

There are three key mechanisms of vancomycin resistance among *E. faecalis* and *E. faecium*: transferability of resistance through chromosomal exchange; expression of latent resistant genes leading to intrinsic resistance; and resistance acquired through the mobility of resistance genes on plasmids and/or transposons via conjugation, transduction, or transformation. At least seven reported phenotypes (*van*A through *van*L) of vancomycin resistance have been ascertained or characterized; subtypes exist within each major group

as well: *van*B1-3, *van*C1-4, *van*D1-5, and *van*G1-2.[2] The characteristics of the most common phenotypes are outlined in Table 76-3. Enterococci that acquire the *van*A phenotype are highly resistant to vancomycin and teicoplanin. Antimicrobial drug resistance does not necessarily imply greater virulence among enterococcal isolates. Some studies have shown that crude mortality rates among patients with *E. faecium* bacteremia were not significantly different for patients with vancomycin-susceptible isolates versus and vancomycin-resistant isolates when adjustments were made for severity of illness.[10,11]

DIAGNOSTIC MICROBIOLOGY

Detection and identification of enterococci is generally straightforward in the clinical microbiology laboratory. Once presumptive phenotypic characterization (catalase-negative, PYR-positive, LAP-positive, Gram-positive cocci that grow in 6.5 percent sodium chloride at 45°C) has been carried out, the species can be differentiated based on acid formation in mannitol and sorbose broths and hydrolysis of arginine.[63] Selective media, such as colistin-nalidixic acid agar (CNA), are available and assist in isolation (hemolysis can be read directly from the CNA plates). There are several commercial, automated systems now available for the identification of *Enterococcus* species.[2] Most of these systems are reliable for the identification of *E. faecalis* and *E. faecium*. A variety of molecular methods (e.g., DNA-DNA hybridization, 16S rRNA gene sequencing, and polymerase chain reactin [PCR]) are now available in reference and various medical microbiology laboratories, enabling rapid identification and typing of isolates. However, there are no convincing data that availability of these techniques for the rapid identification of enterococci in routine clinical specimens (e.g., blood, wound, or urine cultures) results in more favorable patient outcomes. That said, molecular typing will, of course, continue to play an important, albeit adjunct, role in the characterization of outbreaks, epidemiologic and microbiologic research, taxonomy, and surveillance of HAIs and antimicrobial resistance associated with *Enterococcus* species.

In screening clinical specimens for VRE, one validated method is rapid phenotypic characterization, which can be achieved by growth on bile esculin azide agar (BEAA agar) with vancomycin 6 μg/mL (Remel, KS) followed by a subculture with a 30-μg vancomycin disk for phenotypic analysis. This method distinguishes vanA and VanB strains from vanC strains within 24 hours based on the vancomycin growth-inhibition zone. Specifically, vanA and vanB fail to produce inhibition zones of more than 6 mm, whereas vanC isolates tend to produce inhibition zones 15 mm or more. Results falling within the 6- to 15-mm zone require further analysis. This differentiation is significant because vanC isolates have low-level resistance and do not present the treatment problems of vanA and vanB strains.[64] Other methods used to identify vancomycin resistance in enterococci include automated systems, such as Vitek and conventional MicroScan systems.[65–67] Further characterization of isolates involves the identification of resistance genes by PCR, repetitive PCR, or characterization by pulse field gel electrophoresis (PFGE).[68,69] Molecular strain typing by these methods is useful in identifying horizontal transmission as well as assisting in the conduct and control of HAI outbreaks.

INFECTION & DISEASE VERSUS COLONIZATION

Colonization is the presence of a microorganism in or on a host, with growth and multiplication, but without any overt clinical expression or detected immune reaction in the host at the time the microorganism is isolated. In a colonized patient, VRE may establish itself as part of a patient's flora in multiple or specific anatomic sites. For example, VRE colonize the gastrointestinal tract and can be found on the skin due to fecal shedding or in decubitus ulcers. Colonization with VRE generally precedes infection, but not all patients with colonization become infected. Persons either colonized or infected with VRE can serve as sources for secondary transmission. Enteric VRE colonization is typically asymptomatic and not associated with either diarrhea or constipation. Various risk factors have been associated with VRE colonization or infection (Table 76-4).

Risk factors for VRE colonization or infection include prolonged length of hospital stay, use of broad-spectrum antibiotics, having an indwelling invasive device, or close proximity to another patient colonized or infected by VRE.[18,70,71] The associated rise in environmental colonization pressure is now considered the major reservoir for infection and transmission.[12,72,73] Colonization pressure has been defined as the proportion of other patients colonized within a defined population or geographical unit.[12,19] Although acquisition of VRE is affected by colonization pressure, antimicrobial use, or enteral feeding, the effects of the latter two risk factors are more significant when colonization pressure is less than 50 percent; when the colonization pressure is greater than 50 percent, antimicrobial use and enteral feeding appear to have no effect on VRE acquisition.[12] Distinguishing between enterococcal contamination, colonization, and infection can be difficult but is very important if judicious use of antimicrobials is to be instituted in healthcare facilities.

Table 76-4. Risk Factors Associated with *Enterococcus* Species Infections

Risk Category	Specific Risk
Host	Age
	Immunocompromised
	Higher severity of illness
	Enteral feedings
	Burns
	Chronic renal failure
	Malignancy
	Neutropenia
Specific exposures	Inpatient in the intensive care unit (ICU)
	Prior exposure to vancomycin, third-generation cephalosporins, or antianaerobic agents
	Invasive procedures
	Surgical re-exploration
	Enteral tube feedings
	Contaminated medical equipment
	Prolonged hospital or ICU stay
	Prolonged antimicrobial therapy or preceding therapy
	Proximity to a previously known patient with VRE colonization or infection
	Exposure to a healthcare personnel assigned to another VRE patient
	Intrahospital transfer
	Colonization pressure
	Sucralfate
	Hemodialysis
	Transfer from long-term care facility

Thus, careful clinical assessment and interpretation of cultures that yield growth of enterococci is essential to avoid unnecessary and potentially harmful antimicrobial therapy.

CLINICAL DISEASE MANAGEMENT AND THERAPY

Enterococci are more likely to cause disease in immunocompromised or debilitated patients in the ICU setting or surgical ward. Affected patients are more likely to have comorbidities such as chronic heart or renal failure, liver cirrhosis, or diabetes; have one or more in situ invasive devices; or be undergoing treatment with broad-spectrum antimicrobials. That enterococci can colonize or infect patients who receive antimicrobial therapy for unrelated nonenterococcal infections adds to the complexity of enterococcal infection pathogenesis and treatment. The majority of patients with serious VRE infections also have enteric colonization with VRE. The fact that no single agent is entirely bactericidal against enterococci, compounded by the emergence of multidrug resistance to several classes of agents among VRE isolates, underlie the reality that enterococcal infections can be extremely difficult to treat and is one of the reasons that management of deep or systemic enterococcal infections in susceptible hosts often requires combination antimicrobial therapy.[18,43]

Enterococci are important causes of BSIs, endocarditis, urinary tract infections, meningitis, and SSIs. Urinary tract infections, generally, do not require bactericidal therapy; monotherapy is sufficient. For invasive infections such as BSIs, endocarditis, meningitis, or intra-abdominal sepsis, a therapeutic regimen with bactericidal activity is indicated. For patients with enterococcal infections, treatment options are contingent on the susceptibility profile of the clinical isolate and whether the infection is superficial, deep, or systemic. Determining the therapeutic regimen and duration of treatment may require the expertise of an infectious diseases consultant. Because of the inherent properties that reduce the affinity of their penicillin-binding proteins for β-lactams, all enterococci require 4 to 16 μg/mL of penicillin for inhibition. This inherent penicillin resistance is enhanced with β-lactamase-producing strains of enterococci, especially *E. faecalis*. However, for infections caused by susceptible isolates, ampicillin or penicillin are the indicated cell wall agents. *Enterococcus* species are resistant to all cephalosporins and most are resistant to oxacillin, nafcillin, streptomycin, and erythromycin. Isolates should be tested routinely for susceptibility to penicillin, ampicillin, vancomycin, quinupristin/dalfopristin, and linezolid.

Agents with Activity Against VRE

Quinupristin/dalfopristin (a mixture of streptogramin agents) was developed in the late 1980s and has been approved by the U.S. Food and Drug Administration (FDA) for the intravenous treatment of *E. faecium* infections.[74] The FDA has not approved quinupristin/dalfopristin for *E. faecalis* infections because resistance to this agent has been detected consistently in *E. faecalis* isolates.[75-77] A growing body of literature has documented treatment success against VRE infections.[78,79] However, quinupristin/dalfopristin is limited by its lack of activity against vancomycin-resistant *E. faecalis* and its musculoskeletal side effects (myalgia and arthralgia).[79]

Linezolid is a synthetic oxazolidinone agent that binds to the 50S ribosome and inhibits the initiation of protein synthesis.[80] It is available in intravenous and oral preparations and has bacteriostatic activity against VRE isolates. Side effects include thrombocytopenia, leucopenia, peripheral neuropathy, lactic acidosis, and raised hepatic enzyme levels. Some studies have documented efficacy in the treatment of VRE infections, though there are reports of acquired resistance in some VRE isolates.[81-83]

Daptomycin is a large cyclic lipopeptide that binds to bacterial membranes and causes rapid depolarization of membrane potential.[84] Although its action is bactericidal against VRE, it has been approved by the FDA for treatment of complicated skin and soft tissue infections caused by susceptible strains, not for treating VRE infections. Side effects include myalgias, weakness, raised creatine phosphokinase, neuropathy, and significant myopathy. Thus, creatine kinase levels should therefore be checked before commencing therapy with this agent. Daptomycin should be discontinued in patients who are symptomatic and have creatine kinase levels greater than five times the upper limit of normal or, in asymptomatic patients, an increase of greater than 10 times the upper limit of normal. Daptomycin resistance among *E. faecalis* isolates has been reported.[85]

Tigecycline is a glycylcycline agent derived from minocycline.[86,87] It is bacteriostatic and has a broad spectrum of activity against growth of resistant Gram-positive and Gram-negative pathogens. Currently, it is approved only for complicated skin and skin structure infections and intra-abdominal infections, including those caused by vancomycin-susceptible *E. faecalis*. At present, tigecycline does not have FDA approval for infections caused by *E. faecium* and VRE.[86]

Chloramphenicol inhibits bacterial protein synthesis and is bacteriostatic for most bacterial pathogens. Use in the United States has been limited due to unavailability of an oral preparation and its potential for bone marrow toxicity. Although it has demonstrated activity against some strains of enterococci, no significant effect of its use on mortality could be demonstrated.[88] Chloramphenicol resistance among European and U.S. enterococcal isolates is increasing.[5,89]

Telavancin is a lipoglycopeptide that has bactericidal activity against various Gram-positive microorganisms, including *Enterococcus* spp. It has been approved by the FDA for treatment of complicated skin infections caused by vancomycin-susceptible *E. faecalis*; however, it has not been approved by the FDA for the treatment of VRE infections. Although the in vitro activity of telavancin against *Enterococcus* is very good, there is a paucity of published outcome data regarding the utility of using this agent for enterococcal infections.

Enterococcal Bloodstream Infections

Risk factors associated with enterococcal BSIs include intrinsic factors linked to the patient (host) and extrinsic factors linked to the environment, practices, and procedures, therapies, and device use (Table 76-4). Enterococcal BSIs are either primary (direct entry into the bloodstream from the gastrointestinal tract or an intravascular device) or secondary to concomitant infection at another anatomic site (e.g., urinary tract or burn sites, respiratory tract).[90-93] More recent data indicate that among patients colonized with VRE, approximately 4 percent develop VRE BSIs due to a related strain.[71] Independent risk factors for BSIs among colonized patients include admission from a long-term care facility, infection of an additional body site, or exposure to vancomycin.[71]

The diagnosis of a BSI (nonendocarditis) is based mainly on at least two sets of blood cultures positive for enterococcal growth but, not uncommonly, is made on the basis of a single positive blood culture. The subsequent decision to initiate therapy should be made within the context of symptoms and clinical signs, the presence of at least one indwelling intravascular devices, culture results from other anatomic sites, and deciding whether the infection is primary or secondary. Most patients would be expected to be started on empiric antimicrobial therapy, which can be tailored after results of antimicrobial susceptibility testing become available or discontinued after 1 to 2 weeks of therapy. For bacteremia in the absence of native-valve endocarditis, a prosthetic valve, or history of intravenous drug abuse, it remains unclear whether monotherapy with a single β-lactam agent is better than combination therapy by the addition of gentamicin.[94-97] The agent of choice for monotherapy is ampicillin if the enterococcal strain is susceptible, vancomycin if there is β-lactam resistance or allergy, and ampicillin/sulbactam (or amoxicillin/clavulanate) if strain is a β-lactamase producer. For nonendocarditis VRE BSIs in the absence of β-lactam resistance, combination therapy with ampicillin and gentamicin should be considered. When strains exhibit both vancomycin and β-lactam resistance, newer agents such as linezolid or quinupristin/dalfopristin (E. faecium only) have to be considered. In summary, traditional antimicrobial treatment for ampicillin- and glycopeptide-susceptible enterococcal infection remains a penicillin-, ampicillin-, semisynthetic penicillin-based regimen, or vancomycin in a penicillin-intolerant individual. The need for a bactericidal combination with a cell wall-active agent combined with an aminoglycoside is most supported for native or prosthetic valve endocarditis but is unproven for the majority of infections caused by enterococci.[29,83]

Endocarditis: Enterococcal endocarditis is no longer a unimicrobial, community-acquired disease of Caucasian men.[98] Other data suggest that the presence of a prosthetic valve and infection by E. faecalis are associated with an increased risk for endocarditis.[98] At the same time, however, most cases of enterococcal BSIs are not associated with endocarditis.[42,98,99,100] For patients with enterococcal endocarditis, treatment options are contingent on the susceptibility profile of the isolate. Specific antimicrobial therapy must be aggressive, using bactericidal rather than bacteriostatic agents. Antimicrobial susceptibility studies should be carried out for penicillin, ampicillin, vancomycin, quinupristin/dalfopristin, and linezolid. The isolate must be tested for β-lactamase production and for high-level resistance to gentamicin and streptomycin. If high-level resistance is ascertained for the latter two agents, aminoglycosides should not be administered singly or in combination therapy. Treatment may involve a single agent if the isolate is highly susceptible in vitro; combination therapy is suggested if synergism is possible. Treatment is prolonged, usually 4 to 6 weeks. Drug selection and duration of treatment should involve the expertise of an infectious diseases consultant.

For native or prosthetic valve endocarditis caused by Enterococcus species that are susceptible to penicillin, gentamicin, and vancomycin, choices of therapeutic regimens include ampicillin plus gentamicin for 4 to 6 weeks or penicillin plus gentamicin for 4 to 6 weeks. If the patient is penicillin intolerant, vancomycin plus gentamicin is an alternative therapeutic regimen. For intrinsic penicillin resistance, vancomycin plus gentamicin is the combination of choice. For endocarditis caused by β-lactamase-producing, vancomycin-susceptible enterococci, ampicillin-sulbactam plus gentamicin or vancomycin plus gentamicin are indicated. Finally, for endocarditis caused by enterococci that are resistant to penicillin, gentamicin, and vancomycin, an infectious disease consultation is recommended; choices of antimicrobials for this scenario include linezolid, quinupristin/dalfopristin, and imipenem. For more information, refer to the Infectious Diseases Society of America (IDSA) guidelines for the treatment of infective endocarditis.[101]

Enterococcal Urinary Tract Infection

Enterococci are a common cause of urinary tract infections (UTIs); most of these infections are healthcare-associated. Among healthy ambulatory patients, less than 5 percent of UTIs are caused by enterococci, compared to significantly higher rates among hospitalized patients. Risk factors for enterococcal UTI include urinary tract instrumentation, indwelling catheterization, genitourinary tract disease associated with obstruction, and prior antimicrobial exposures.[102,103] There are no clinical manifestations of enterococcal UTI that distinguish this etiologic agent from other urinary pathogens.

It is important to remember that the susceptibility profiles reported for urinary pathogens are breakpoint MICs related to blood concentrations of antimicrobial agents. The achievable concentrations of such agents in the urine are usually many-fold higher than serum concentrations. Hence, "drug-resistant" enterococcal infections of the lower urinary tract often can be treated with conventional dosing of nitrofurantoin, ampicillin, amoxicillin, or fosfomycin.[104,105] Complicated UTIs may be associated with a greater severity of illness and risk of kidney damage; such infections require intravenous ampicillin or vancomycin therapy.

Enterococcal Closed-Space Infections

Enterococci can cause intra-abdominal and pelvic abscesses, usually as part of a mixed (i.e., polymicrobial) infection following abdominal surgery or trauma.[106] More than a decade ago, the presence of enterococcus was recognized as an independent predictor of treatment failure in complicated intra-abdominal infections.[107] It was also recognized that antimicrobials that lack activity against Enterococcus can often be employed successfully in intra-abdominal infections, even when enterococci are present as part of the polymicrobial flora.[108] Although secondary enterococcal BSIs are not usual in patients with enterococcal intra-abdominal sepsis, breakthrough enterococcal septicemia may occur in an immunocompromised host and is associated with high mortality.[108] Intra-abdominal sepsis caused by enterococcal species have been quite problematic in liver transplant patients.[109,110]

For orthotopic liver transplant recipients, the source of VRE infection is often the gastrointestinal tract; in this patient population, VRE infection is an independent predictor of morbidity and mortality.[111]

VRE is now recognized as an emerging healthcare-associated pathogen that causes potentially fatal intra-abdominal infections in the postsurgical setting.[112] Enterococcal surgical site infections may be the source of secondary enterococcal BSIs. In uncomplicated intra-abdominal infection, the infectious process might involve just a single organ, and no anatomical disruption is present.[113] Generally, such infections can be treated with surgical resection alone with no antimicrobial therapy apart from perioperative prophylaxis.[113] In the majority of cases, wound healing will occur with routine wound management strategies. Management of complicated intra-abdominal sepsis includes standardized antimicrobial monotherapy or combination therapy.[113] For intra-abdominal infections, routine coverage against enterococci is not recommended but might be indicated for specific clinical conditions, such as the presence of septic shock in patients previously receiving prolonged treatment with cephalosporins, immunosuppressed patients at risk for bacteremia, patients with prosthetic heart valves, or a history of recurrent intra-abdominal infection complicated by severe sepsis.[113]

Wound and Joint Infections

Enterococcus species are the third most common cause of SSIs in U.S. healthcare facilities.[36] In addition, *Enterococcus* is often implicated in cases of osteomyelitis and joint sepsis, including prosthetic joint infections. Treatment of these infections is contingent on the susceptibility of the implicated isolate. Osteomyelitis and joint infections require at least 4 to 6 weeks of parenteral therapy, which is often adjunct to surgical management. For patients with prosthetic joint infections who have actually completed a prolonged course of antimicrobial therapy, and in whom the original prosthesis remains in situ, long-term suppressive therapy might have to be considered.

Enterococcal Pneumonia and Meningitis

Enterococcal respiratory tract infections are rare events; in one occasional report, it was described as a complication of topical antimicrobial prophylaxis.[114] Enterococci are a rare cause of meningitis, occurring primarily in patients who have undergone neurosurgical procedures and persons with in situ intraventricular or intrathecal devices or ventriculoperitoneal shunts, a history of head trauma, and existing anatomic defects or congenital anomalies of the central nervous system.[115–117] Combination antimicrobial therapy is recommended for enterococcal meningitis.

Stool Colonization with *Enterococcus*

Over the past decade, several studies have been published to elucidate the natural history and risk factors associated with enteric VRE colonization and to establish the utility of eradication. Two uncontrolled, short-term clinical studies suggested efficacy of oral bacitracin in the eradication of enteric VRE colonization.[118,119] However, two other studies using oral bacitracin therapy showed no significant difference in VRE eradication rates after a longer follow-up period.[120,121] Other studies using different antimicrobial interventions have also drawn different conclusions: 5 days of oral doxycycline and rifampin was successful in eradicating enterococcal carriage[122]; in contrast, oral bacitracin plus gentamicin did not reduce VRE colonization or bacteremia.[123] Of note, a substantial number (37 to 66 percent) of nontreated patients in these studies had spontaneous eradication of enteric VRE.

CONTROL AND PREVENTION OF VRE INFECTIONS

That endemic and epidemic HAIs are preventable has periodically been reaffirmed by milestone reports dating from as far back to Semmelweis, to the myriad studies published over the past two decades dealing with the unequivocal effect of hand washing with soap and water; proper care of urinary catheters, respirators, intravascular catheters, and surgical wounds; numerous evidence-based infection control guidelines published by the CDC; and position papers issued by the SHEA, the Association of Practitioners of Infection Control, and the IDSA.

The Hospital Infection Control Practices Advisory Committee (HICPAC) guidelines, aimed at preventing and controlling VRE transmission in healthcare settings, were published initially in 1995[124] and updated in 2007.[125] Although implementation of these guidelines following VRE outbreak investigations played no small part in the resolution of these outbreaks, there are still no published outcome studies to show how implementation of the HICPAC guidelines might have resulted in reducing rates of VRE infections in facilities across the nation.[126,127] Eradicating VRE from ICUs or other high-risk areas may be extremely difficult. However, the current HICPAC recommendations require resource-intensive efforts, including behavior modification and costly financial allocations.

The HICPAC guidelines stress that the prevention and control of vancomycin resistance will require a coordinated, concerted effort from various departments of a hospital and administrative support.[125] HICPAC strongly encourages hospitals to develop their own institution-specific plans that address the following elements: (1) prudent, judicious vancomycin use by clinicians; (2) facility-wide, unit-targeted, and informal education of hospital personnel regarding vancomycin resistance, and hand hygiene in conjunction with other control measures; (3) early detection and prompt reporting of vancomycin resistance in enterococci and other Gram-positive microorganisms by the hospital microbiology laboratory to monitor trends and effectiveness of interventions; and (4) immediate implementation of appropriate infection control measures to prevent person-to-person transmission of VRE.[124,125] The use or modification of these recommendations, as outlined for acute care settings, remains a challenge for extended care facilities, small hospitals, and home care settings.[128]

Numerous reports presented at the SHEA annual meetings over the past decade have repeatedly shown control of endemic or epidemic VRE infections through implementation of the SHEA guidelines with more emphasis on Contact Precautions and less on Standard Precautions. In fact, the CDC has not provided any evidence-based data showing that Standard Precautions and passive surveillance have actually started to control the spread and transmission of VRE.[129] The SHEA guidelines are based on identification and containment of spread through (1) active surveillance cultures to identify the reservoir for spread; (2) routine hand hygiene; (3) barrier precautions for patients known or suspected to be colonized or infected with VRE; (4) implementation of an antimicrobial stewardship program aimed particularly at reducing the overprescribing of vancomycin and cephalosporins; and (5) decolonization of colonized patients.[130] There is now growing evidence that active surveillance cultures reduce the incidence of VRE infections and that programs described in the SHEA guidelines are effective and cost effective.[129,131,132]

The SHEA and HICPAC guidelines are similar in that they both aim to improve patient outcomes through improvement of hand hygiene measures and enhancement of prescribing practices through an antimicrobial stewardship program. The key difference is the role of active surveillance cultures in each guideline: the SHEA guideline recommends more aggressive use of active surveillance cultures, whereas the HICPAC isolation guideline calls for individual facilities to assess their own needs and risks and to implement routine clinical cultures when a problem is ascertained.[133] The CDC has recommended Contact Precautions for preventing intrahospital transmission of important antimicrobial-resistant pathogens, including VRE. Various studies confirm that this approach works only when sufficient active-surveillance cultures are obtained to detect the reservoir for spread.[134,135] Active VRE surveillance involves prospective evaluation of patients to determine colonization pressure and transmission rates. Although abundant resources are required for active surveillance, it facilitates early detection and potential containment of VRE. In contrast, passive surveillance involves screening culture specimens obtained for other clinical reasons.

The role of scheduled rotation of antimicrobial agents in the prevention and control of VRE has been evaluated.[136] Sequential cycling of antimicrobials presumably reduces the selection pressure for the emergence of particular antimicrobial resistance genes for at least some infections.[137,138] However, the rotation of Gram-negative antimicrobial agents among ICU patients has not shown any reduction in rates of VRE acquisition. Currently, there are no data that have conclusively demonstrated reductions in rates of VRE infections through scheduled antimicrobial cycling.[138-141]

Finally, the issue of when to discontinue Contact Precautions remains a perennial issue and concern in acute care facilities. In fact, as stated in the HICPAC guidelines, there is a paucity of published data on when to discontinue Contact Precautions for patients colonized with VRE. According to these guidelines, in the context of an outbreak caused by VRE, Contact Precautions should be used indefinitely for all previously infected and known colonized patients.[125] The HICPAC guidelines go on to say that if active surveillance cultures are used to detect and isolate patients colonized with VRE, and there is no decolonization of these patients, it would be prudent to use Contact Precautions for the duration of the stay in the setting where they were first implemented.[125] The HICPAC guidelines conclude that it is reasonable to discontinue Contact Precautions when three or more VRE surveillance cultures are repeatedly negative over the course of a week or two in a patient who has not received antimicrobial therapy for several weeks, especially in the absence of a draining wound, profuse respiratory secretions,

or evidence implicating the specific patient in ongoing VRE transmission within the facility.[125] Likewise, HICPAC states that if active surveillance cultures are used to detect and isolate patients colonized with VRE, and there is no decolonization of these patients, it is logical to assume that Contact Precautions would be used for the duration of stay in the setting where they were first implemented.

SUMMARY AND CONCLUSIONS

Enterococcus species are members of normal human and animal gastrointestinal flora. They are extremely hardy and have been recovered from a variety of environmental surfaces and equipment in healthcare facilities; transmission via hands of HCP is common. Because of their intrinsic and acquired resistance to many antimicrobial agents, they remain an infection control concern and present significant therapeutic challenges. Active surveillance cultures for VRE in ICUs followed by isolation of colonized persons appears to be an effective strategy for VRE control in some institutions. Isolation purely on the basis of history of previous VRE detection, at least for VRE, appears to be of little benefit. Standard Precautions and isolation of the occasional patient recognized to be colonized through routine clinical cultures have not proved effective in reducing rates of VRE infections.

FUTURE TRENDS & RESEARCH

Enormous challenges remain for controlling transmission of healthcare-associated pathogens in acute care facilities and conducting similar evaluations and strategies in long-term care facilities and the home care setting. These challenges include development of uniform surveillance definitions and protocols and a nonpunitive reporting system for HAIs in long-term care facilities and home care; identification of high-risk infections (e.g., bloodstream, pneumonia, or wounds) that need to be focused on in these settings; and determination of relevant numerators and denominators for calculating device-specific rates for infections in these settings. These challenges are likely to be tempered by the fact that by focusing on specific, albeit high-risk, infections, the true magnitude and epidemiology of VRE transmission in the home and long-term care facilities will likely remain unknown or uncharacterized for some time to come. The onus is now on healthcare professionals and healthcare administrators to invest intelligently in infection prevention and control programs, to enhance existing surveillance activities in targeted areas, and to avoid regarding death and morbidity as inevitable. Hospital epidemiologists and the CDC also have a responsibility to evaluate the effectiveness and cost benefit of the programs described in the SHEA guidelines for the control of VRE transmission in the acute care facilities.

REFERENCES

1. Murray BE. The life and times of the *Enterococcus. Clin Microbiol Rev* 1990 Jan;3(1):46–65.
2. Teixeira LM, Carvalho MGS, Shewmaker PL, et al. *Enterococcus.* In: Versalovic J, Carroll GF, Jorgensen JH, Landry ML, et al., eds. *Manual of Clinical Microbiology.* Washington, DC: ASM Press, 2011:350–364.

3. Schleifer K, Kilpper-Balz R. Transfer of *Streptococcus faecalis* and *Streptococcus faecium* to the genus *Enterococcus* nom. rev. as *Enterococcus faecalis* comb. nov. and Enterococcus *faecium* comb. nov. *Int J Syst Bacteriol* 1984;34:31–34.

4. Ruoff KL, de la Maza L, Murtagh MJ, et al. Species identities of enterococci isolated from clinical specimens. *J Clin Microbiol* 1990 Mar;28(3): 435–437.

5. Low DE, Keller N, Barth A, et al. Clinical prevalence, antimicrobial susceptibility, and geographic resistance patterns of enterococci: results from the SENTRY Antimicrobial Surveillance Program, 1997–1999. *Clin Infect Dis* 2001 May 15;32 Suppl 2:S133–S145.

6. Moellering RC, Jr. Emergence of *Enterococcus* as a significant pathogen. *Clin Infect Dis* 1992 Jun;14(6):1173–1176.

7. Loeb M, Salama S, Armstrong-Evans M, et al. A case-control study to detect modifiable risk factors for colonization with vancomycin-resistant enterococci. *Infect Control Hosp Epidemiol* 1999 Nov;20(11):760–763.

8. Edmond MB, Ober JF, Dawson JD, et al. Vancomycin-resistant enterococcal bacteremia: natural history and attributable mortality. *Clin Infect Dis* 1996 Dec;23(6):1234–1239.

9. Edmond MB, Ober JF, Weinbaum DL, et al. Vancomycin-resistant *Enterococcus faecium* bacteremia: risk factors for infection. *Clin Infect Dis* 1995 May;20(5):1126–1133.

10. Lautenbach E, Bilker WB, Brennan PJ. Enterococcal bacteremia: risk factors for vancomycin resistance and predictors of mortality. *Infect Control Hosp Epidemiol* 1999 May;20(5):318–323.

11. Garbutt JM, Ventrapragada M, Littenberg B, et al. Association between resistance to vancomycin and death in cases of *Enterococcus faecium* bacteremia. *Clin Infect Dis* 2000 Mar;30(3):466–472.

12. Bonten MJ, Slaughter S, Ambergen AW, et al. The role of "colonization pressure" in the spread of vancomycin-resistant enterococci: an important infection control variable. *Arch Intern Med* 1998 May 25;158(10): 1127–1132.

13. Morris JG Jr, Shay DK, Hebden JN, et al. Enterococci resistant to multiple antimicrobial agents, including vancomycin. Establishment of endemicity in a university medical center. *Ann Intern Med* 1995 Aug 15;123(4): 250–259.

14. Jett BD, Huycke MM, Gilmore MS. Virulence of enterococci. *Clin Microbiol Rev* 1994 Oct;7(4):462–478.

15. Bates J, Jordens Z, Selkon JB. Evidence for an animal origin of vancomycin-resistant enterococci. *Lancet* 1993 Aug 21;342(8869): 490–491.

16. Torres C, Reguera JA, Sanmartin MJ, et al. vanA-mediated vancomycin-resistant *Enterococcus* spp. in sewage. *J Antimicrob Chemother* 1994 Mar;33(3):553–561.

17. McDonald LC, Kuehnert MJ, Tenover FC, et al. Vancomycin-resistant enterococci outside the health-care setting: prevalence, sources, and public health implications. *Emerg Infect Dis* 1997 Jul-Sep;3(3):311–317.

18. Cetinkaya Y, Falk P, Mayhall CG. Vancomycin-resistant enterococci. *Clin Microbiol Rev* 2000 Oct;13(4):686–707.

19. Bonten MJ, Weinstein RA. The role of colonization in the pathogenesis of nosocomial infections. *Infect Control Hosp Epidemiol* 1996 Mar;17(3):193–200.

20. Shay DK, Maloney SA, Montecalvo M, et al. Epidemiology and mortality risk of vancomycin-resistant enterococcal bloodstream infections. *J Infect Dis* 1995 Oct;172(4):993–1000.

21. Noskin GA, Bednarz P, Suriano T, et al. Persistent contamination of fabric-covered furniture by vancomycin-resistant enterococci: implications for upholstery selection in hospitals. *Am J Infect Control* 2000 Aug;28(4): 311–313.

22. Livornese LL Jr, Dias S, Samel C, et al. Hospital-acquired infection with vancomycin-resistant *Enterococcus faecium* transmitted by electronic thermometers. *Ann Intern Med* 1992 Jul 15;117(2):112–116.

23. Boyce JM. Environmental contamination makes an important contribution to hospital infection. *J Hosp Infect* 2007 Jun;65 Suppl 2:50–54.

24. Boyce JM, Opal SM, Chow JW, et al. Outbreak of multidrug-resistant *Enterococcus faecium* with transferable vanB class vancomycin resistance. *J Clin Microbiol* 1994 May;32(5):1148–1153.

25. Karanfil LV, Murphy M, Josephson A, et al. A cluster of vancomycin-resistant *Enterococcus faecium* in an intensive care unit. *Infect Control Hosp Epidemiol* 1992 Apr;13(4):195–200.

26. Bates J, Jordens JZ, Griffiths DT. Farm animals as a putative reservoir for vancomycin-resistant enterococcal infection in man. *J Antimicrob Chemother* 1994 Oct;34(4):507–514.

27. Bonten MJ, Hayden MK, Nathan C, et al. Epidemiology of colonisation of patients and environment with vancomycin-resistant enterococci. *Lancet* 1996 Dec 14;348(9042):1615–1619.

28. Tacconelli E, Cataldo MA. Vancomycin-resistant enterococci (VRE): transmission and control. *Int J Antimicrob Agents* 2008 Feb;31(2): 99–106.

29. Linden PK, Miller CB. Vancomycin-resistant enterococci: the clinical effect of a common nosocomial pathogen. *Diagn Microbiol Infect Dis* 1999 Feb;33(2):113–120.

30. Gilmore MS, Segarra RA, Booth MC, et al. Genetic structure of the *Enterococcus faecalis* plasmid pAD1-encoded cytolytic toxin system and its relationship to lantibiotic determinants. *J Bacteriol* 1994 Dec;176(23):7335–7344.

31. Mundy LM, Sahm DF, Gilmore M. Relationships between enterococcal virulence and antimicrobial resistance. *Clin Microbiol Rev* 2000 Oct;13(4):513–522.

32. Coburn PS, Hancock LE, Booth MC, et al. A novel means of self-protection, unrelated to toxin activation, confers immunity to the bactericidal effects of the *Enterococcus faecalis* cytolysin. *Infect Immun* 1999 Jul;67(7):3339–3347.

33. Kreft B, Marre R, Schramm U, et al. Aggregation substance of *Enterococcus faecalis* mediates adhesion to cultured renal tubular cells. *Infect Immun* 1992 Jan;60(1):25–30.

34. Huycke MM, Joyce W, Wack MF. Augmented production of extracellular superoxide by blood isolates of *Enterococcus faecalis*. *J Infect Dis* 1996 Mar;173(3):743–746.

35. Clewell DB. Bacterial sex pheromone-induced plasmid transfer. *Cell* 1993 Apr 9;73(1):9–12.

36. Sievert DM, Ricks P, Edwards JR, et al. Antimicrobial-resistant pathogens associated with healthcare-associated infections: summary of data reported to the National Healthcare Safety Network at the Centers for Disease Control and Prevention, 2009-2010. *Infect Control Hosp Epidemiol* 2013 Jan;34(1):1–14.

37. Fridkin SK, Gaynes RP. Antimicrobial resistance in intensive care units. *Clin Chest Med* 1999 Jun;20(2):303–316, viii.

38. Archibald L, Phillips L, Monnet D, et al. Antimicrobial resistance in isolates from inpatients and outpatients in the United States: increasing importance of the intensive care unit. *Clin Infect Dis* 1997 Feb;24(2):211–215.

39. Frieden TR, Munsiff SS, Low DE, et al. Emergence of vancomycin-resistant enterococci in New York City. *Lancet* 1993 Jul 10;342(8863):76–79.

40. Centers for Disease Control and Prevention (CDC). Nosocomial enterococci resistant to vancomycin –United States, 1989-1993. *MMWR Morb Mortal Wkly Rep* 1993 Aug 6;42(30):597–599.

41. Ramsey AM, Zilberberg MD. Secular trends of hospitalization with vancomycin-resistant *Enterococcus* infection in the United States, 2000-2006. *Infect Control Hosp Epidemiol* 2009 Feb;30(2):184–186.

42. Wisplinghoff H, Bischoff T, Tallent SM, et al. Nosocomial bloodstream infections in US hospitals: analysis of 24,179 cases from a prospective nationwide surveillance study. *Clin Infect Dis* 2004 Aug 1;39(3):309–317.

43. Moellering RC, Jr. The Garrod Lecture. The *Enterococcus*: a classic example of the impact of antimicrobial resistance on therapeutic options. *J Antimicrob Chemother* 1991 Jul;28(1):1–12.

44. Leclercq R. Enterococci acquire new kinds of resistance. *Clin Infect Dis* 1997 Jan;24 Suppl 1:S80–S84.

45. Rybkine T, Mainardi JL, Sougakoff W, et al. Penicillin-binding protein 5 sequence alterations in clinical isolates of *Enterococcus faecium* with different levels of beta-lactam resistance. *J Infect Dis* 1998 Jul;178(1):159–163.

46. Murray BE. Beta-lactamase-producing enterococci. *Antimicrob Agents Chemother* 1992 Nov;36(11):2355–2359.

47. Boyce JM, Opal SM, Potter-Bynoe G, et al. Emergence and nosocomial transmission of ampicillin-resistant enterococci. *Antimicrob Agents Chemother* 1992 May;36(5):1032–1039.

48. Patterson JE, Masecar BL, Zervos MJ. Characterization and comparison of two penicillinase-producing strains of *Streptococcus* (*Enterococcus*) *faecalis*. *Antimicrob Agents Chemother* 1988 Jan;32(1):122–124.

49. CLSI. *Performance Standards for Antimicrobial Susceptibility Testing: Twenty-Fourth Informational Supplement.* CLSI document M100-S24. Wayne, PA: Clinical and Laboratory Standards Institute, 2014.

50. Weinstein MP. Comparative evaluation of penicillin, ampicillin, and imipenem MICs and susceptibility breakpoints for vancomycin-susceptible and vancomycin-resistant *Enterococcus faecalis* and *Enterococcus faecium*. *J Clin Microbiol* 2001 Jul;39(7):2729–2731.

51. CLSI. *Performance Standards for Antimicrobial Susceptibility Testing: Sixteenth Informational Supplement. M100-S16 Methods for dilution antimicrobial susceptibility tests for bacteria that grow aerobically.* Approved Standard. 2006;26.

52. Uttley AH, Collins CH, Naidoo J, et al. Vancomycin-resistant enterococci. *Lancet* 1988 Jan 2–9;1(8575–6):57–58.

53. Leclercq R, Derlot E, Duval J, et al. Plasmid-mediated resistance to vancomycin and teicoplanin in *Enterococcus faecium*. *N Engl J Med* 1988 Jul 21;319(3):157–161.

54. Sahm DF, Kissinger J, Gilmore MS, et al. In vitro susceptibility studies of vancomycin-resistant *Enterococcus faecalis*. *Antimicrob Agents Chemother* 1989 Sep;33(9):1588–1591.

55. Woodford N, Johnson AP, Morrison D, et al. Current perspectives on glycopeptide resistance. *Clin Microbiol Rev* 1995 Oct;8(4):585–615.
56. Woodford N, Morrison D, Johnson AP, et al. Plasmid-mediated vanB glyco-peptide resistance in enterococci. *Microb Drug Resist* 1995 Fall;1(3):235–240.
57. Klare I, Heier H, Claus H, Witte W. Environmental strains of *Enterococcus faecium* with inducible high-level resistance to glycopeptides. *FEMS Micro-biol Lett* 1993 Jan 1;106(1):23–29.
58. Klare I, Heier H, Claus H, et al. *Enterococcus faecium* strains with vanA-mediated high-level glycopeptide resistance isolated from animal foodstuffs and fecal samples of humans in the community. *Microb Drug Resist* 1995 Fall;1(3):265–272.
59. Klare I, Heier H, Claus H, et al. vanA-mediated high-level glycopeptide resistance in *Enterococcus faecium* from animal husbandry. *FEMS Micro-biol Lett* 1995 Jan 15;125(2-3):165–171.
60. Aarestrup FM. Occurrence of glycopeptide resistance among *Enterococcus faecium* isolates from conventional and ecological poultry farms. *Microb Drug Resist* 1995 Fall;1(3):255–257.
61. Aarestrup FM, Ahrens P, Madsen M, et al. Glycopeptide susceptibility among Danish *Enterococcus faecium and Enterococcus faecalis* isolates of animal and human origin and PCR identification of genes within the VanA cluster. *Antimicrob Agents Chemother* 1996 Aug;40(8):1938–1940.
62. McDonald LC, Rossiter S, Mackinson C, et al. Quinupristin-dalfopristin-resistant *Enterococcus faecium* on chicken and in human stool specimens. *N Engl J Med* 2001 Oct 18;345(16):1155–1160.
63. Murray PR, ed. *Manual of Clinical Microbiology,* 9th ed. Washington, DC: ASM Pres, 2007.
64. Sahm DF, Free L, Smith C, et al. Rapid characterization schemes for surveillance isolates of vancomycin-resistant enterococci. *J Clin Microbiol* 1997 Aug;35(8):2026–2030.
65. Kohner PC, Patel R, Uhl JR, et al. Comparison of agar dilution, broth microdilution, E-test, disk diffusion, and automated Vitek methods for test-ing susceptibilities of *Enterococcus* spp. to vancomycin. *J Clin Microbiol* 1997 Dec;35(12):3258–3263.
66. Willey BM, Kreiswirth BN, Simor AE, et al. Detection of vancomycin resis-tance in *Enterococcus* species. *J Clin Microbiol* 1992 Jul;30(7):1621–1624.
67. Tenover FC, Swenson JM, O'Hara CM, et al. Ability of commercial and reference antimicrobial susceptibility testing methods to detect vancomycin resistance in enterococci. *J Clin Microbiol* 1995 Jun;33(6):1524–1527.
68. Tenover FC, Arbeit RD, Goering RV, et al. Interpreting chromosomal DNA restriction patterns produced by pulsed-field gel electrophoresis: criteria for bacterial strain typing. *J Clin Microbiol* 1995 Sep;33(9):2233–2239.
69. Tenover FC, Arbeit RD, Goering RV. How to select and interpret molecular strain typing methods for epidemiological studies of bacterial infections: a review for healthcare epidemiologists. Molecular Typing Working Group of the Society for Healthcare Epidemiology of America. *Infect Control Hosp Epidemiol* 1997 Jun;18(6):426–439.
70. Salgado CD. The risk of developing a vancomycin-resistant *Enterococcus* bloodstream infection for colonized patients. *Am J Infect Control* 2008 Dec;36(10):S175.e5–8.
71. Olivier CN, Blake RK, Steed LL, et al. Risk of vancomycin-resistant *Enterococcus* (VRE) bloodstream infection among patients colonized with VRE. *Infect Control Hosp Epidemiol* 2008 May;29(5):404–409.
72. Drees M, Snydman DR, Schmid CH, et al. Antibiotic exposure and room contamination among patients colonized with vancomycin-resistant enterococci. *Infect Control Hosp Epidemiol* 2008 Aug;29(8):709–715.
73. Drees M, Snydman DR, Schmid CH, et al. Prior environmental contami-nation increases the risk of acquisition of vancomycin-resistant enterococci. *Clin Infect Dis* 2008 Mar 1;46(5):678–685.
74. Batts DH, Lavin BS, Eliopoulos GM. Quinupristin/dalfopristin and linezolid: spectrum of activity and potential roles in therapy—a status report. *Curr Clin Top Infect Dis* 2001;21:227–251.
75. Collins LA, Malanoski GJ, Eliopoulos GM, et al. In vitro activity of RP59500, an injectable streptogramin antibiotic, against vancomycin-resistant gram-positive organisms. *Antimicrob Agents Chemother* 1993 Mar;37(3):598–601.
76. Singh KV, Murray BE. Differences in the *Enterococcus faecalis* lsa locus that influence susceptibility to quinupristin-dalfopristin and clindamycin. *Antimicrob Agents Chemother* 2005 Jan;49(1):32–39.
77. Singh KV, Weinstock GM, Murray BE. An *Enterococcus faecalis* ABC homologue (Lsa) is required for the resistance of this species to clindamy-cin and quinupristin-dalfopristin. *Antimicrob Agents Chemother* 2002 Jun;46(6):1845–1850.
78. Winston DJ, Emmanouilides C, Kroeber A, et al. Quinupristin/Dalfopristin therapy for infections due to vancomycin-resistant *Enterococcus faecium.* *Clin Infect Dis* 2000 May;30(5):790–797.
79. Raad I, Hachem R, Hanna H, et al. Treatment of vancomycin-resistant enterococcal infections in the immunocompromised host: quinupristin-dalfopristin in combination with minocycline. *Antimicrob Agents Chemother* 2001 Nov;45(11):3202–3204.
80. Perry CM, Jarvis B. Linezolid: a review of its use in the management of serious gram-positive infections. *Drugs* 2001;61(4):525–551.
81. Birmingham MC, Rayner CR, Meagher AK, et al. Linezolid for the treat-ment of multidrug-resistant, gram-positive infections: experience from a compassionate-use program. *Clin Infect Dis* 2003 Jan 15;36(2):159–168.
82. Rayner CR, Baddour LM, Birmingham MC, et al. Linezolid in the treat-ment of osteomyelitis: results of compassionate use experience. *Infection* 2004 Feb;32(1):8–14.
83. Linden PK. Optimizing therapy for vancomycin-resistant enterococci (VRE). *Semin Respir Crit Care Med* 2007 Dec;28(6):632–645.
84. Boucher HW, Sakoulas G. Perspectives on Daptomycin resistance, with emphasis on resistance in Staphylococcus aureus. *Clin Infect Dis* 2007 Sep 1;45(5):601–608.
85. Hidron AI, Schuetz AN, Nolte FS, et al. Daptomycin resistance in *Enterococcus faecalis* prosthetic valve endocarditis. *J Antimicrob Chemother* 2008 Jun;61(6):1394–1396.
86. Waites KB, Duffy LB, Dowzicky MJ. Antimicrobial susceptibility among pathogens collected from hospitalized patients in the United States and in vitro activity of tigecycline, a new glycylcycline antimicrobial. *Antimicrob Agents Chemother* 2006 Oct;50(10):3479–3484.
87. Rossi F, Andreazzi D. Overview of tigecycline and its role in the era of antibiotic resistance. *Braz J Infect Dis* 2006 Jun;10(3):203–216.
88. Lautenbach E, Schuster MG, Bilker WB, et al. The role of chlorampheni-col in the treatment of bloodstream infection due to vancomycin-resistant *Enterococcus.* *Clin Infect Dis* 1998 Nov;27(5):1259–1265.
89. Lautenbach E, Gould CV, LaRosa LA, et al. Emergence of resistance to chloramphenicol among vancomycin-resistant enterococcal (VRE) blood-stream isolates. *Int J Antimicrob Agents* 2004 Feb;23(2):200–203.
90. Gray J, Marsh PJ, Stewart D, et al. Enterococcal bacteraemia: a prospec-tive study of 125 episodes. *J Hosp Infect* 1994 Jul;27(3):179–186.
91. Patterson JE, Sweeney AH, Simms M, et al. An analysis of 110 serious enterococcal infections. Epidemiology, antibiotic susceptibility, and outcome. *Medicine (Baltimore)* 1995 Jul;74(4):191–200.
92. Maki DG. Through a glass darkly. Nosocomial pseudoepidemics and pseudobacteremias. *Arch Intern Med* 1980 Jan;140(1):26–28.
93. Maki DG, Agger WA. Enterococcal bacteremia: clinical features, the risk of endocarditis, and management. *Medicine (Baltimore)* 1988 Jul;67(4):248–269.
94. Graninger W, Ragette R. Nosocomial bacteremia due to *Enterococcus faecalis* without endocarditis. *Clin Infect Dis* 1992 Jul;15(1):49–57.
95. Gullberg RM, Homann SR, Phair JP. Enterococcal bacteremia: analysis of 75 episodes. *Rev Infect Dis* 1989 Jan-Feb;11(1):74–85.
96. Watanakunakorn C, Patel R. Comparison of patients with enterococcal bacteremia due to strains with and without high-level resistance to gentamicin. *Clin Infect Dis* 1993 Jul;17(1):74–78.
97. Hoge CW, Adams J, Buchanan B, et al. Enterococcal bacteremia: to treat or not to treat, a reappraisal. *Rev Infect Dis* 1991 Jul-Aug;13(4):600–605.
98. Anderson DJ, Murdoch DR, Sexton DJ, et al. Risk factors for infective endocarditis in patients with enterococcal bacteremia: a case-control study. *Infection* 2004 Apr;32(2):72–77.
99. Weinstein MP, Towns ML, Quartey SM, et al. The clinical significance of positive blood cultures in the 1990s: a prospective comprehensive evalua-tion of the microbiology, epidemiology, and outcome of bacteremia and fungemia in adults. *Clin Infect Dis* 1997 Apr;24(4):584–602.
100. Edmond MB, Wallace SE, McClish DK, et al. Nosocomial bloodstream infections in United States hospitals: a three-year analysis. *Clin Infect Dis* 1999 Aug;29(2):239–244.
101. Baddour LM, Wilson WR, Bayer AS, et al. Infective endocarditis: diagnosis, antimicrobial therapy, and management of complications: a statement for healthcare professionals from the Committee on Rheuma-tic Fever, Endocarditis, and Kawasaki Disease, Council on Cardiovascular Disease in the Young, and the Councils on Clinical Cardiology, Stroke, and Cardiovascular Surgery and Anesthesia, American Heart Association: endorsed by the Infectious Diseases Society of America. *Circulation* 2005 Jun 14;111(23):e394–434.
102. Krieger JN, Kaiser DL, Wenzel RP. Urinary tract etiology of bloodstream infections in hospitalized patients. *J Infect Dis* 1983 Jul;148(1):57–62.
103. Morrison AJ, Jr., Wenzel RP. Nosocomial urinary tract infections due to *Enterococcus.* Ten years' experience at a university hospital. *Arch Intern Med* 1986 Aug;146(8):1549–1551.
104. Zhanel GG, Hoban DJ, Karlowsky JA. Nitrofurantoin is active against vancomycin-resistant enterococci. *Antimicrob Agents Chemother* 2001 Jan;45(1):324–326.

105. Minassian MA, Lewis DA, Chattopadhyay D, et al. A comparison between single-dose fosfomycin trometamol (Monuril) and a 5-day course of trimethoprim in the treatment of uncomplicated lower urinary tract infection in women. *Int J Antimicrob Agents* 1998 Apr;10(1):39–47.

106. Bartlett JG. Intra-abdominal sepsis. *Med Clin North Am* 1995 May;79(3):599–617.

107. Burnett RJ, Haverstock DC, Dellinger EP, et al. Definition of the role of *Enterococcus* in intraabdominal infection: analysis of a prospective randomized trial. *Surgery* 1995 Oct;118(4):716–721; discussion 721–723.

108. Dougherty SH. Role of *Enterococcus* in intraabdominal sepsis. *Am J Surg* 1984 Sep;148(3):308–312.

109. Wade JJ, Rolando N, Williams R, et al. Serious infections caused by multiply-resistant *Enterococcus faecium*. *Microb Drug Resist* 1995 Fall;1(3):241–243.

110. Linden PK, Pasculle AW, Manez R, et al. Differences in outcomes for patients with bacteremia due to vancomycin-resistant *Enterococcus faecium* or vancomycin-susceptible *E. faecium*. *Clin Infect Dis* 1996 Apr;22(4):663–670.

111. Papanicolaou GA, Meyers BR, Meyers J, et al. Nosocomial infections with vancomycin-resistant *Enterococcus faecium* in liver transplant recipients: risk factors for acquisition and mortality. *Clin Infect Dis* 1996 Oct;23(4):760–766.

112. Poduval RD, Kamath RP, Corpuz M, et al. Intraabdominal vancomycin-resistant *Enterococcus* infections: the new threat. *J Clin Gastroenterol* 2001 Apr;32(4):333–335.

113. Blot S, De Waele JJ. Critical issues in the clinical management of complicated intra-abdominal infections. *Drugs* 2005;65(12):1611–1620.

114. Bonten MJ, van Tiel FH, van der Geest S, et al. *Enterococcus faecalis* pneumonia complicating topical antimicrobial prophylaxis. *N Engl J Med* 1993 Jan 21;328(3):209–210.

115. Shaikh ZH, Peloquin CA, Ericsson CD. Successful treatment of vancomycin-resistant *Enterococcus faecium* meningitis with linezolid: case report and literature review. *Scand J Infect Dis* 2001;33(5):375–379.

116. Stevenson KB, Murray EW, Sarubbi FA. Enterococcal meningitis: report of four cases and review. *Clin Infect Dis* 1994 Feb;18(2):233–239.

117. Webster DP, Griffiths S, Bowler IC. Failure of linezolid therapy for post-neurosurgical meningitis due to *Enterococcus faecium*. *J Antimicrob Chemother* 2009 Mar;63(3):622–623.

118. Chia JK, Nakata MM, Park SS, et al. Use of bacitracin therapy for infection due to vancomycin-resistant *Enterococcus faecium*. *Clin Infect Dis* 1995 Dec;21(6):1520.

119. O'Donovan CA, Fan-Havard P, Tecson-Tumang FT, et al. Enteric eradication of vancomycin-resistant *Enterococcus faecium* with oral bacitracin. *Diagn Microbiol Infect Dis* 1994 Feb;18(2):105–109.

120. Weinstein JW, Roe M, Towns M, et al. Resistant enterococci: a prospective study of prevalence, incidence, and factors associated with colonization in a university hospital. *Infect Control Hosp Epidemiol* 1996 Jan;17(1):36–41.

121. Mondy KE, Shannon W, Mundy LM. Evaluation of zinc bacitracin capsules versus placebo for enteric eradication of vancomycin-resistant *Enterococcus faecium*. *Clin Infect Dis* 2001 Aug 15;33(4):473–476.

122. Dembry LM, Uzokwe K, Zervos MJ. Control of endemic glycopeptide-resistant enterococci. *Infect Control Hosp Epidemiol* 1996 May;17(5):286–292.

123. Hachem R, Raad I. Failure of oral antimicrobial agents in eradicating gastrointestinal colonization with vancomycin-resistant enterococci. *Infect Control Hosp Epidemiol* 2002 Jan;23(1):43–44.

124. Recommendations for preventing the spread of vancomycin resistance: recommendations of the Hospital Infection Control Practices Advisory Committee (HICPAC). *Am J Infect Control* 1995 Apr;23(2):87–94.

125. Siegel JD, Rhinehart E, Jackson M, et al. Management of multidrug-resistant organisms in health care settings, 2006. *Am J Infect Control* 2007 Dec;35(10 Suppl 2):S165–S193.

126. Jochimsen EM, Fish L, Manning K, et al. Control of vancomycin-resistant enterococci at a community hospital: efficacy of patient and staff cohorting. *Infect Control Hosp Epidemiol* 1999 Feb;20(2):106–109.

127. Shay DK, Goldmann DA, Jarvis WR. Reducing the spread of antimicrobial-resistant microorganisms. Control of vancomycin-resistant enterococci. *Pediatr Clin North Am* 1995 Jun;42(3):703–716.

128. Herwaldt LA, Smith SD, Carter CD. Infection control in the outpatient setting. *Infect Control Hosp Epidemiol* 1998 Jan;19(1):41–74.

129. McGeer AJ. News in antimicrobial resistance: documenting the progress of pathogens. *Infect Control Hosp Epidemiol* 2004 Feb;25(2):97–98.

130. Muto CA, Jernigan JA, Ostrowsky BE, et al. SHEA guideline for preventing nosocomial transmission of multidrug-resistant strains of Staphylococcus aureus and *Enterococcus*. *Infect Control Hosp Epidemiol* 2003 May;24(5):362–386.

131. Ostrowsky BE, Trick WE, Sohn AH, et al. Control of vancomycin-resistant *Enterococcus* in health care facilities in a region. *N Engl J Med* 2001 May 10;344(19):1427–1433.

132. Perencevich EN, Fisman DN, Lipsitch M, et al. Projected benefits of active surveillance for vancomycin-resistant enterococci in intensive care units. *Clin Infect Dis* 2004 Apr 15;38(8):1108–1115.

133. Jackson M, Jarvis WR, Scheckler WE. HICPAC/SHEA—conflicting guidelines: what is the standard of care? *Am J Infect Control* 2004 Dec;32(8):504–511.

134. Farr BM, Jarvis WR. Would active surveillance cultures help control healthcare-related methicillin-resistant Staphylococcus aureus infections? *Infect Control Hosp Epidemiol* 2002 Feb;23(2):65–68.

135. Farr BM, Salgado CD, Karchmer TB, et al. Can antibiotic-resistant nosocomial infections be controlled? *Lancet Infect Dis* 2001 Aug;1(1):38–45.

136. Puzniak LA, Mayfield J, Leet T, et al. Acquisition of vancomycin-resistant enterococci during scheduled antimicrobial rotation in an intensive care unit. *Clin Infect Dis* 2001 Jul 15;33(2):151–157.

137. McGowan JE, Jr. Strategies for study of the role of cycling on antimicrobial use and resistance. *Infect Control Hosp Epidemiol* 2000 Jan;21(1 Suppl):S36–S43.

138. Gerding DN. Antimicrobial cycling: lessons learned from the aminoglycoside experience. *Infect Control Hosp Epidemiol* 2000 Jan;21(1 Suppl):S12–S17.

139. Cadena J, Taboada CA, Burgess DS, et al. Antibiotic cycling to decrease bacterial antibiotic resistance: a 5-year experience on a bone marrow transplant unit. *Bone Marrow Transplant* 2007 Jul;40(2):151–155.

140. Bruno-Murtha LA, Brusch J, Bor D, et al. A pilot study of antibiotic cycling in the community hospital setting. *Infect Control Hosp Epidemiol* 2005 Jan;26(1):81–87.

141. Dominguez EA, Smith TL, Reed E, et al. A pilot study of antibiotic cycling in a hematology-oncology unit. *Infect Control Hosp Epidemiol* 2000 Jan;21(1 Suppl):S4–S8.

CHAPTER 77

Environmental Gram-negative Bacilli

Marguerite Gribogiannis, BS, MPA, CIC
Infection Control Practitioner
Advocate Lutheran General Hospital
Park Ridge, IL

ABSTRACT

Pseudomonas spp., Acinetobacter spp., and other glucose nonfermentative bacilli are common causes of healthcare-associated infections. These ubiquitous pathogens contribute to a wide variety of clinical syndromes and are particularly notable for their intrinsic antimicrobial resistance. Pseudomonas spp. originally gained notoriety under the outdated terms "nosocomial" or "hospital-acquired" pathogens over a 40-year time frame; they continue to afflict patients in a variety of healthcare settings. Acinetobacter infections have played an increasingly prominent role, mainly in hospital outbreaks and in endemic infections. A host of other nonfermentative bacilli also can result in outbreaks when infection prevention measures are not followed.

KEY CONCEPTS

- Microbiologic characterization of important glucose nonfermentative Gram-negative bacilli.

- Review of major clinical syndromes.

- Treatment and management of infections associated with nonfermentative bacilli.

- Principles used to prevent and control healthcare-associated nonfermentative bacilli and their reservoirs.

BACKGROUND

Arising primarily from an aquatic background, the ubiquitous nonfermentative Gram-negative bacilli have minimal growth requirements and cause a wide array of opportunistic infections. These organisms have many reservoirs within hospitals and other healthcare settings and are frequently resistant to commonly used antibiotics. *Pseudomonas aeruginosa* gained notoriety as a threat in the 1960s as streptococcal and staphylococcal infections were eclipsed by aerobic Gram-negative bacilli as causes of bacteremia.[1] *Acinetobacter* spp. are now recognized as important pathogens that cause difficult-to-treat

infections, particularly in compromised hosts and military personnel, due to the organism's inherent properties of antimicrobial resistance. Strains of *Acinetobacter baumannii* completely resistant to usual antimicrobial agents have been reported.[2,3] *Acinetobacter* spp. cause a significant percentage of endemic infections and several reported epidemics each year.[4] Some of these reports reflect an interest in improving typing methods for use in epidemic investigations, but other reports emphasize epidemics in specialized settings, such as *Acinetobacter* infections in neonatology units or military field hospitals.[4-10]

BASIC PRINCIPLES

A basic principle in the prevention of infection with any of these organisms is to minimize endogenous and exogenous sources of acquisition. Careful studies have suggested that 2.6 to 24 percent of patients admitted to the hospital carry *P. aeruginosa* in their stool, and infection with these strains has been documented.[11-13] These cases usually are "secondarily endogenous" (colonization occurs while in the hospital but prior to infection) or related to cross-transmission.[14] One study estimated the incidence of *P. aeruginosa* infections as high as 60 percent, but this varies with the presence of environmental reservoirs and healthcare personnel infection prevention practices.[15] Less clear is the role of the architectural environment.[16]

Ongoing Trends

The incidence of Gram-negative bacteremia continued to increase into the 1970s, although subsequently Gram-positive pathogens and *Candida* spp. played an increasingly important role.[17] *P. aeruginosa* continues to be an important cause of healthcare-associated bacteremia, although its percentage of contribution to all bacteremias varies widely from hospital to hospital.[17] Non-*aeruginosa* pseudomonads and *Acinetobacter* spp. have also become increasingly important as causes of bacteremia, causing as many as 13 percent of bloodstream infections at some institutions.[17] Intravenous catheter-associated infections are caused by *P. aeruginosa* in 3 to 6 percent and *Acinetobacter* spp. in 1 to 2 percent of cases.[18] Enterobacteriaceae are the most common pathogens resulting in urinary tract infections in hospitalized patients, but *P. aeruginosa* is the third most common cause overall.[11] Other NFB are important causes, particularly with prolonged catheterization. *P. aeruginosa* is second only to *Staphylococcus aureus* as a cause of burn infections. Generally, *P. aeruginosa* causes less than 10 percent of surgical site infections.[19] Aerobic Gram-negative bacilli generally cause more than 60 percent of healthcare-associated pneumonias.[20,21]

Practice-specific Trends

Although this chapter focuses primarily on intensive care unit (ICU) and general ward-related infections, nonfermentative bacilli (NFB) are important pathogens in other settings, such as nursing homes. *P. aeruginosa* is an important pathogen in severe pneumonias in institutionalized older people.[22] Microbiologic surveillance of nursing home residents has identified *P. aeruginosa* as a primary isolate in a patient population that is frequently treated with antimicrobial agents.[23] Recommendations for controlling antimicrobial resistance in long-term care facilities have been proposed by a task force of the Society for Healthcare Epidemiology of America (SHEA).[24]

International Trends

NFB have been widely reported as hospital pathogens around the globe. An outbreak in a neonatal ICU in India resulted in 68 strains of *A. baumannii* from the blood and cerebrospinal fluid of neonates during a 6-month period.[25] NFB have been reported as important hospital pathogens in Brazil, the United Kingdom, Spain, Turkey, Israel, and many other countries. Disaster-related NFB infections were reported after the 2004 Southeast Asian tsunami.[26]

Epidemiology and Infectious Agents

Members of the genus *Pseudomonas* are aerobic, motile, Gram-negative bacilli commonly found in moist environments.[27] They constitute the most common healthcare-associated pathogens among the NFBs. This grouping has undergone changes in nomenclature, and several organisms once characterized within the *Pseudomonas* genus have been reclassified. These include *Acinetobacter, Alcaligenes, Stenotrophomonas, Flavobacterium, Sphingomonas, Flavimonas, Chryseobacterium, Comamonas, Burkholderia*, and others.[28] *Pseudomonas* spp. are catalase-positive, use oxidative rather than fermentative pathways to obtain energy from carbohydrates, and are usually oxidase-positive. *P. aeruginosa* is the most important and frequently isolated pathogen within this genus.[27]

Members of the genus *Acinetobacter* are generally encapsulated, nonmotile, aerobic Gram-negative bacilli that may appear coccoid in their stationary growth phase.[29] They are oxidase-negative, nonnitrate reducing, unable to ferment glucose, and lack color.[30] In fact, this paucity of distinctive characteristics previously resulted in frequent misidentification and subsequently has contributed to a number of taxonomic revisions.[29] The taxonomy of *Acinetobacter* spp. is complex, with 25 DNA homology groups and multiple named species.[31] The most clinically important are sometimes grouped together as *A. calcoaceticus-A. baumannii* complex.[4]

Stenotrophomonas maltophilia (formerly classified as *Xanthomonas maltophilia*) is a motile Gram-negative aerobic bacillus that differs from *P. aeruginosa* by generally being oxidase-negative, although a few strains are weakly oxidase-positive.[28] Occasionally, *S. maltophilia* can be confused with *Burkholderia cepacia*.[32] A variety of other glucose nonfermenters can be clinically significant, including *Alcaligenes, Chryseomonas, Comamonas, Flavimonas,* Gilardi rod group 1, *Myroides, Ochrobactrum, Oligella, Ralstonia, Rhizobium, Shewanella,* and *Weeksella*.[30,31,33,34]

Occurrence and Reservoirs

The vast majority of the organisms discussed in this chapter are well adapted to proliferating in relatively pure water.[11,28,35] This is particularly true for the pseudomonads, *Flavobacterium,* and *Acinetobacter*. This accounts for the slang term "waterbugs" that is often used in referring to these organisms.

ENVIRONMENTAL GRAM-NEGATIVE BACILLI

Acinetobacter

Most epidemics have involved respiratory tract infections. Because these organisms are widely distributed in water sources, it is not surprising that many outbreaks have been associated with pressure transducers, humidifiers, ventilators, and other respiratory therapy equipment, including a manual weaning criteria machine.[9,35,36] More than one outbreak has been linked to contaminated mattresses.[37,38] *Acinetobacter* is notable for its ability to persist in the environment with survival on dry inanimate surfaces for about a month.[39] Infected and colonized patients may distribute the organism widely. In one report, environmental cultures following a patient's discharge documented the organism on side room walls, floors, and at least 13 other different types of horizontal surfaces in and near his room. Curtains have been culture positive for as long as 13 days after patient discharge.[40]

Outbreaks have implicated the role of hydrotherapy of burn patients, hand transmission in the surgical ICU, contaminated irrigation tubing in a burn unit, and contaminated endoscopes for biliary or upper gastrointestinal tract procedures.[10,41–46] These supplement the other commonly reported sources of sinks, respiratory therapy equipment, disinfectants, and distilled and other water supplies.[12,15,47,48] Food is a potential source of a number of Gram-negative bacilli.[11,48] Tomatoes are a classic source of *P. aeruginosa. Acinetobacter* spp. can be isolated from a host of foods and as a contaminant of human milk.[47,48] For this reason, special diets have been advocated for granulocytopenic patients.

Enteral feedings and oral solutions can become contaminated with a variety of organisms, including *Pseudomonas* spp., *Acinetobacter* spp., and other NFB.[49,50] *Acinetobacter* spp. are one of only a few Gram-negative organisms that can routinely reside on healthy, dry human skin.[29] One survey in New York identified *A. baumannii* on the hands of 10 percent of community residents.[51]

Pseudomonas

P. aeruginosa, the most virulent member of this group of organisms, is a classic healthcare-associated pathogen and the most frequently isolated of all the organisms discussed in this chapter. It is particularly dreaded as a cause of sepsis and ecthyma gangrenosum in the neutropenic host and as the cause of malignant external otitis in patients with diabetes mellitus. Burn infections, endocarditis, meningitis, gastrointestinal tract, eye, and musculoskeletal infections are also well described.[11] Its numerous virulence factors, ability to survive in moist environments, growth with minimal nutritional requirements, tolerance for a variety of temperatures, and innate antibiotic resistance all contribute to its success in causing healthcare-associated infections (HAIs).[11]

Essentially, whenever a moist environment is present with a patient having absent or circumvented host defenses, the possibility of pseudomonal infection is real. Outbreaks in the past have identified other reservoirs, including orthopedic plaster, transvenous pacemakers, operating room suction apparatus, and mattresses.[11] Cockroaches have also been suggested as possible vectors.[52] Bowel colonization of patients is important for *P. aeruginosa*.[11-13,15] Stool cultures are generally more sensitive than are rectal swabs in detecting colonization.[13] Infected patients are an important reservoir for essentially all Gram-negative pathogens. Respiratory tract infection or colonization, wound infections, and infected urine are all important sources of bacteria and may result in substantial environmental contamination, in addition to seeding the hands of healthcare personnel.[15,30,41] A reported *P. aeruginosa* meningitis outbreak was associated with the rinsing of spinal needles with contaminated saline.[53] Nontransient carriage of Gram-negative bacilli on the hands of healthcare personnel has been noted.[54] Disinfectants and various germicides may become contaminated with numerous types of NFB, including *Pseudomonas* spp., *S. maltophilia*, *Flavobacterium meningosepticum*, *Alcaligenes faecalis*, and *Alcaligenes xylosoxidans*.[55]

Essentially, any wet healthcare environment, including ice machines, multidose vials, and tap water, can serve as a reservoir once contaminated. Flowers frequently harbor indigenous, multiresistant Gram-negative bacilli, including NFB.[56]

Stenotrophomonas maltophilia and *Burkholderia cepacia*

S. maltophilia and *B. cepacia* can be found in water, soil, plants, animal sources, and decaying organic materials. Both organisms have been widely identified from many sources within the hospital setting, including tap and distilled water, thermometers, contaminated disinfectants, dialysis fluids, catheters, and ventilator temperature sensors.[32]

Mechanisms of Transmission

Convincing demonstration of the transmission of Gram-negative bacilli through the air has been extremely rare. *P. aeru-* *ginosa* and other Gram-negative bacilli were linked to healthcare-associated bacteremias that occurred after the introduction of a novel chute-hydropulping waste disposal system in a 16-story hospital.[57] One report has implicated airborne transmission of *A. baumannii* on the basis of settle plate cultures and contamination of adjacent bedding, but other routes of transmission were not able to be excluded.[40,58]

Contamination may occur during the manufacture, distribution, or administration of many products used in healthcare delivery. Generally, the offending organism must be able to proliferate in the contaminated product to reach levels that result in clinical symptoms. For *P. aeruginosa* this has included a variety of solutions and antiseptics. For *P. putida* and *P. fluorescens* this also includes blood and blood by-products. *Alcaligenes xylosoxidans* has been associated with contaminated dialysate, chlorhexidine, and respiratory equipment. *Chryseobacterium meningosepticum* has been associated with contaminated ice, water, and humidifiers.[59] Endoscopes, which are difficult to disinfect, and automated endoscope reprocessors can serve as reservoirs for NFB.[7,60] *Comamonas* spp. infections have been associated with exposure to tropical fish tanks and endogenous infection from the gastrointestinal tract such as appendicitis.

Incubation

The concept of an incubation period is not as useful in evaluating HAI outbreaks or epidemics for NFB as for many other pathogens because infection may result from colonization that happened either recently or remotely.

Clinical Features

The NFBs produce a large variety of clinical syndromes in both normal and compromised hosts because of their virulence factors. The most common clinical scenarios are urinary tract infections; respiratory tract infections, particularly in ICU patients; primary and secondary bloodstream infections; and wound infections.[34] *Acinetobacter* spp. have been reported to cause suppuration in any organ system but particularly as a pathogen in ventilator-associated pneumonia, meningitis, urinary tract infection, peritonitis, endocarditis, and soft tissue infections.[7,29,30,61] Some reports regarding these organisms demonstrate seasonal variation with a peak in the summer.[4] Thus, endogenous infections and seasonal variation may obscure the onset of an outbreak.

Burkholderia cepacia (formerly *Pseudomonas cepacia*) is most frequently noted as a cause of respiratory tract infections in patients with cystic fibrosis.[62,63] Persistent infection has been associated with worsening pulmonary function and increased mortality.[64] Three distinct clinical patterns exist: (1) chronic asymptomatic carriage, (2) progressive deterioration, and (3) rapid, often fatal deterioration in previously mildly affected patients with necrotizing pneumonia and bacteremia.[32] *B. cepacia* pneumonia may cause cavitation in nearly 30 percent of patients.[65]

In patients without cystic fibrosis B. cepacia, infections are almost all healthcare-associated or related to intravenous drug abuse. Outbreaks have been related to intra-aortic balloon pumps, contaminated water sources, respiratory therapy equipment such as reusable electronic ventilator temperature probes, or contaminated disinfectants (classically from "topping" off bottles of the disinfectant).[66-68] Even a single significant HAI with B. cepacia may warrant investigation, but this organism may also cause pseudoepidemics.[69,70]

Ralstonia pickettii (formerly Pseudomonas pickettii and Burkholderia pickettii) has been responsible for epidemics of bloodstream infections associated with contaminated distilled or "sterile" water. Contamination may occur by manufacturers or less commonly be related to narcotic tampering.[71,72] Indwelling intravenous catheter infections have also been reported.[73]

Stenotrophomonas maltophilia has been reported to cause abscesses, meningitis, endocarditis, conjunctivitis, wound infections, urinary tract infections, and pneumonia.[74] The resistance of S. maltophilia to aminoglycosides, imipenem, and many cephalosporins is more notable than the production of any unique clinical syndrome. Outbreak investigations have implicated respiratory therapy or monitoring equipment, contaminated disinfectants, and ice machines.[17,55,75]

Agrobacterium tumefaciens has been implicated in HAIs, including urinary tract infections, peritonitis, wound infections, prosthetic valve endocarditis, and sepsis.[75]

Pseudomonas fluorescens, P. putida, P. alcaligenes, P. stutzeri, Comamonas acidovorans (formerly P. acidovorans), and Comamonas spp. have all been reported as pathogens.[74]

Alcaligenes xylosoxidans subspecies xylosoxidans can cause a wide array of clinical syndromes typical of other Gram-negative bacilli. Outbreaks have been linked to contaminated deionized water used for hemodialysis, a contaminated diagnostic tracer, and the reuse of disposable pressure monitoring equipment.[17,76-78] A. xylosoxidans and A. faecalis have been reported as present in contaminated chlorhexidine, a phenolic germicide, and aqueous eosin.[55,77,79,80]

Chryseobacterium meningosepticum (formerly Flavobacterium meningosepticum) has been isolated from contaminated chlorhexidine and may grow in water with minimal nutritional requirements. Recent outbreaks have been related to a faulty pasteurizer tank and contaminated pressure transducers.[81,82] Weeksella zoohelcum and Weeksella virosa were formerly considered part of the Flavobacterium genus. All these organisms have been reported to cause a spectrum of HAIs.[74]

Populations at Risk

These pathogens are generally considered low-virulence pathogens but are important throughout the world. They function as opportunists in hospitalized or institutionalized patients compromised by age, surgery, chemotherapy, or device use.

Laboratory Diagnosis and Procedures

In the bacteriology laboratory, simple media permit the growth of NFB, but selective media, such as MacConkey agar,[27,28,31] are generally chosen. Commercial systems are available for identification by genus and species.[83] Biochemical test patterns, colonial morphologic appearance, and antibiograms are useful strain markers for some Gram-negative bacilli, but antibiograms have less utility for organisms that are typically multiply resistant, such as Acinetobacter, Stenotrophomonas, and other NFB.[5] Although widely available and easy to perform, these methods frequently show only a modest capability to discriminate between strains that are often present in the environment or as normal flora.[83]

Historically, serologic typing and pyocin typing were the most widely used methods for studying the epidemiology of P. aeruginosa.[84] However, like phage typing and bacteriocin typing, serotyping has largely been replaced by molecular methods that are less variable and less cumbersome.[83]

DNA-based typing methods are somewhat limited by technical aspects of their performance, occasionally having complex banding patterns and a lack of a standard methodology used by all laboratories. However, they have gained acceptance as the best available methods for precise epidemiological typing of strains.[83,85,86] Typing by pulsed-field gel electrophoresis of genomic DNA can be reproducibly done. Initial studies using repetitive element sequence polymerase chain reaction demonstrated that these methods are useful and quite rapid.[87,88] These tests have gained popularity because they require less effort and expense. Analysis of plasmid or chromosomal DNA has been important in numerous epidemiological investigations.[83-85,89] Protein-based typing has been accomplished by a number of approaches, including immunoblot fingerprinting, polyacrylamide gel electrophoresis of cellular proteins, and multilocus enzyme electrophoresis, and have been used to aid epidemiological investigations.[83] Pyrolysis mass spectrometry has been described as a rapid method for strain identification of S. maltophilia.[75] Whole-genome sequencing, a process determining the complete DNA sequence of a microbe's genome, has been useful to resolve subtle differences between closely related isolates of multidrug-resistant A. baumannii in a military hospital setting.[90]

Susceptibility Patterns and Treatment Strategies

Antibiotic therapy is directed by in vitro susceptibility testing. Clinicians frequently must rely on combination therapy when treating these organisms empirically because antimicrobial resistance is common. Information regarding local patterns of antimicrobial resistance is vital. For P. aeruginosa bacteremia, combination therapy with an aminoglycoside and a beta-lactam with antipseudomonal activity is frequently continued because of a suggestion of improved survival with this approach.[11] Acinetobacter spp. and S. maltophilia in particular are prone to resistance to both aminoglycosides and cephalosporins.[48] In both of these cases, resistance to all commonly tested antimicrobial agents has been observed.[91] S. maltophilia is most reliably susceptible to trimethoprim-sulfamethoxazole and usually resistant to imipenem.[74] Controlled trials have supported the use of monotherapy in nongranulocytic patients with mild to moderate pseudomonal infections.[59] The primary concern about this approach has been the emergence of antibiotic resistance.

Prevention and Control Measures

Despite the rare naysayer who may criticize routine hand washing, the overwhelming opinion in the infection prevention community is that hand washing remains a primary means of preventing HAI.[4,92–94] It remains rare to find reports that raise the possibility of hand washing contributing to the spread of disease but commonplace to find epidemics linked to noncompliance with the practice of routine hand washing.[41] In a classic review of healthcare-associate bacteremia, Maki[95] cited more than 100 studies implicating hand carriage in the spread of Gram-negative organisms. Although Gram-negative organisms generally do not persist on intact skin for more than a few hours, it often is more difficult to prove transmission via the hands of healthcare personnel. Published literature supports the idea that greater availability of sinks for hand washing increases hand-washing behavior.[96] A variety of approaches, including strict segregation of patients with cystic fibrosis, based on carriage of this organism have been tried in order to reduce transmission of *B. cepacia*.[97] Both hospital outbreaks and social contacts outside the hospital have been implicated in transmission.[97,98] Contact Precautions also may play a role in the interruption of *A. baumannii* transmission.[99]

Areas of Controversy

A number of areas remain controversial in the prevention, diagnosis, and treatment of infections from NFB even for a single clinical condition such as ventilator-associated pneumonia. *Pseudomonas* spp. and *Acinetobacter* spp. are important causes of healthcare-associated pneumonia, and the role of selective decontamination of the digestive tract remains debated.[100] Similarly, the appropriate use of monotherapy versus combination therapy in the treatment of these infections remains contested.[101] Clinicians are also examining new ways to shorten the duration of antimicrobial therapy for these important and common infections.[102] The appropriate role for invasive diagnostic testing for confirming ventilator-associated pneumonia remains controversial in part because of the lack of a gold standard for establishing the diagnosis.[103]

Financial and Cost-Benefit Issues

Most of the costs for preventing and managing these infections are not unique to the NFB. Environmental controls, hand hygiene programs, institutional surveillance, and the rapid response to evidence of epidemic or endemic infections result in benefit to patients in the form of reduced Gram-positive and Gram-negative infections.[104]

CONCLUSIONS

The prevention and control of HAIs from NFB remains an important challenge because of the frequent pathogenic role of these organisms in modern healthcare facilities worldwide. The continued frequent reports of outbreaks of these organisms highlight the multifactorial and multidisciplinary approaches needed for their control. Careful attention to safe device use, rapid diagnosis, and appropriate treatment will minimize their negative impact on patients.

FUTURE TRENDS

There is still much to be learned regarding the prevention of infections secondary to NFB. No doubt, the taxonomy of these bacteria will continue to evolve, as will typing methods to rapidly identify epidemic strains coupled with information technology programs and computer systems to track and assess strain-specific information. Additional research is needed to help resolve a number of lingering questions. For example, most Category II recommendations from the *Guidelines for Environmental Infection Control in Health-Care Facilities* would benefit from the availability of additional relevant data, and many of these recommendations relate to the control of Gram-negative infections.[105]

INTERNATIONAL PERSPECTIVE

Concerns and challenges regarding infection prevention and control programs globally have been recently reviewed.[106] Although the epidemiology of infections with NFB is less well defined in the third world, it is clear that limited resources challenge most hospitals in lesser developed countries. Fortunately, infection prevention appears to be gaining increased attention even where resources are restricted.

REFERENCES

1. Eickhoff TC. Hospital infections. In: Dowling HF, ed. *Disease-a-Month*. Chicago, IL: Year Book Medical, 1972:3–40.
2. Mahgoub S, Ahmed J, Glatt AE. Completely resistant *Acinetobacter baumannii* strains. *Infect Control Hosp Epidemiol* 2002 Aug;23(8):477–479.
3. Landman D, Quale JM, Mayorga D, et al. Citywide clonal outbreak of multiresistant *Acinetobacter baumannii* and *Pseudomonas aeruginosa* in Brooklyn, NY: the preantibiotic era has returned. *Arch Intern Med* 2002 Jul 8;162(13):1515–1520.
4. Munoz-Price LS, Weinstein RA. *Acinetobacter* infection. *N Engl J Med* 2008 Mar 20;358(12):1271–1281.
5. Dijkshoorn L, Aucken HM, Gerner-Smidt P, et al. Correlation of typing methods of *Acinetobacter* isolates from hospital outbreaks. *J Clin Microbiol* 1993 Mar;31(3):702–705.
6. Chang HL, Tang CH, Hsu YM, et al. Nosocomial outbreak of infection with multidrug-resistant *Acinetobacter baumanii* in a medical center in Taiwan. *Infect Control Hosp Epidemiol* 2009;30(1):34–38.
7. Struelens MJ, Carlier E, Maes N, et al. Nosocomial colonization and infection with multiresistant *Acinetobacter baumannii*: outbreak delineation using DNA macrorestriction analysis and PCR-fingerprinting. *J Hosp Infect* 1993 Sep;25(1):15–32.
8. Shete VB, Ghadage DP, Muley VA, et al. *Acinetobacter* septicemia in neonates admitted to intensive care units *J Lab Physicians* 2009 Jul;1(2):73–76.
9. Thurm V, Ritter E. Genetic diversity and clonal relationships of *Acinetobacter baumannii* strains isolated in a neonatal ward: epidemiological investigations by allozyme, whole-cell protein and antibiotic resistance analysis. *Epidemiol Infect* 1993 Dec;111(3):491–498.
10. Sunenshine RH, Wright MO, Maragakis LL, et al. Multidrug-resistant *Acinetobacter* infection mortality rate and length of hospitalization. *Emerging Infect Dis* 2007 Jan;13(1):97–103.
11. Pollack M. *Pseudomonas aeruginosa*. In: Mandell GL, Douglas RG, Bennett JE, eds. *Principles and Practice of Infectious Diseases*. New York: Churchill Livingstone, 2000:2310–2335.

12. Kropec A, Huebner J, Riffell M, et al. Exogenous or endogenous reservoirs of nosocomial *Pseudomonas aeruginosa* and *Staphylococcus aureus* infections in a surgical intensive care unit. *Intensive Care Med* 1993;19(3):161–165.

13. Allen KD, Bartzokas CA, Graham R, et al. Acquisition of endemic *Pseudomonas aeruginosa* on an intensive therapy unit. *J Hosp Infect* 1987 Sep;10(2):156–164.

14. Orsi GB, Mansi A, Tomao P, et al. Lack of association between clinical and environmental isolates of *Pseudomonas aeruginosa* in hospital wards. *J Hosp Infect* 1994 May;27(1):49–60.

15. Döring G, Hörz M, Ortelt J, et al. Molecular epidemiology of *Pseudomonas aeruginosa* in an intensive care unit. *Epidemiol Infect* 1993;110(3):427–436.

16. Hota S, Hirji Z, Stockton K, et al. Outbreak of multidrug-resistant *Pseudomonas aeruginosa* colonization and infection secondary to imperfect intensive care unit room design. *Infect Control Hosp Epidemiol* 2009 Jan;30(1):25–33.

17. Pittet D. Nosocomial bloodstream infections. In: Wenzel RP, ed. *Prevention and Control of Nosocomial Infections*. Baltimore: Williams & Wilkins, 1993:512–555.

18. Widmer AF. IV-related infections. In: Wenzel RP, ed. *Prevention and Control of Nosocomial Infections*. Baltimore: Williams & Wilkins, 1993:556–579.

19. Mayhall CG. Surgical infections including burns. In: Wenzel RP, ed. *Prevention and Control of Nosocomial Infections*. Baltimore: Williams & Wilkins, 1993:614–664.

20. Craven DE, Steger KA, Duncan RA. Prevention and control of nosocomial pneumonia. In: Wenzel RP, ed. *Prevention and Control of Nosocomial Infections*. Baltimore: Williams & Wilkins, 1993:580–599.

21. George DL. Epidemiology of nosocomial ventilator-associated pneumonia. *Infect Control Hosp Epidemiol* 1993 Mar;14(3):163–169.

22. El-Sohl AA, Aquilina AT, Dhillon RS, et al. Impact of invasive strategy on the management of antimicrobial treatment failure in institutionalized older people with severe pneumonia. *Am J Respir Crit Care Med* 2002 Oct 15;166(8):1038–1043.

23. Smith PW, Bennett G, Bradley S, et al. SHEA/APIC guideline: infection prevention and control in the long-term care facility, July 2008. *Infect Control Hosp Epidemiol* 2008 Sep;29(9):785–814.

24. Rosenbaum P, Aureden K, Cloughessy M, et al. APIC *Guide to the Elimination of Multidrug-resistant Acinetobacter baumannii Transmission in Healthcare Settings*. Association of Professionals in Infection Control website. 2010. Available at: http://apic.org/Professional-Practice/Implementation-guides.

25. Mittal N, Nair D, Gupta N, et al. Outbreak of *Acinetobacter* spp septicemia in a neonatal ICU. *Southeast Asian J Trop Med Public Health* 2003 Jun;34(2):365–366.

26. Maegele M, Gregor S, Steinhausen E, et al. The long-distance tertiary air transfer and care of tsunami victims: injury pattern and microbiological and psychological aspects. *Crit Care Med* 2005 May;33(5):1136–1140.

27. Kiska D, Gilligan P. *Pseudomonas*. In: Murray P, Baron E, Jorgensen J, et al., eds. *Manual of Clinical Microbiology*, 8th ed. Washington, DC: ASM Press, 2003:719–728.

28. Sewell DL. Bacteriology. In: McClatchey KD, ed. *Clinical Laboratory Medicine*. Baltimore: Williams & Wilkins, 1994:1144–1149.

29. Allen DM, Hartman BJ. *Acinetobacter* species. In: Mandell GL, Douglas RG, Bennett JE, eds. *Principles and Practice of Infectious Diseases*. New York: Churchill Livingstone, 2000:2339–2344.

30. Seifert H, Baginski R, Schulze A, et al. The distribution of *Acinetobacter* species in clinical culture materials. *Zentralbl Bakteriol* 1993 Nov;279(4):544–552.

31. Schreckenberger P, Daneshvar M, Weyant R, et al. *Acinetobacter, Achromobacter, Chryseobacterium, Moraxella,* and other nonfermentative Gram-negative rods. In: Murray P, Baron E, Jorgensen J, et al., eds. *Manual of Clinical Microbiology*, 8th ed. Washington, DC: ASM Press, 2003:749–779.

32. Maschmeyer G, Gobel U. *Stenotrophomonas maltophilia* and *Burkholderia cepacia* complex. In: Mandell GL, Douglas RG, Bennett J, Dolin R, eds. *Principles and Practice of Infectious Diseases*, 7th ed. Philadelphia: Churchill Livingstone, 2010:2861–2868.

33. Gilardi GL. *Pseudomonas*. In: Lennette EH, Balows A, Hausler WJ, et al., eds. *Manual of Clinical Microbiology*, 4th ed. Washington, DC: American Society for Microbiology, 1985:350–372.

34. Murray PR. *Pseudomonas* and related nonfermenters. In: Murray PR, Kobayashi GS, Pfaller MA, et al., eds. *Medical Microbiology*. St Louis, MO: Mosby. 1990:253–259.

35. Roberts LA, Collignon PJ, Cramp VB, et al. An Australia-wide epidemic of *Pseudomonas* pickettii bacteraemia due to contaminated "sterile" water for injection. *Med J Aust* 1990 Jun 18;152(12):652–655.

36. Ahmed J, Haddad J, Kay ME, et al. Acinetobacter anitratus pneumonia outbreak in the intensive care unit (ICU) traced to a manual weaning criteria machine. *Am J Infect Control* 1993 Jan;21(2):85.

37. Habib J, Shurtleff S, Fish J, et al. Nosocomial transmission of aminoglycoside resistant Acinetobacter anitratus in a burn unit linked to mattresses. *Am J Infect Control* 1993;21:100.

38. Sherertz RJ, Sullivan ML. An outbreak of infections with Acinetobacter calcoaceticus in burn patients: contamination of patients' mattresses. *J Infect Dis* 1985 Feb;151(2):252–258.

39. Karageorgopoulos DE, Falagas ME. Current control and treatment of multidrug-resistant Acinetobacter baumannii infections. *Lancet Infect Dis* 2008 Dec;8(12):751–762.

40. Peleg AY, Seifert H, Paterson DL. Acinetobacter baumannii: emergence of a successful pathogen. *Clin Microbiol Rev* 2008 Jul;21(3):538–582.

41. Widmer AF, Wenzel RP, Trilla A, et al. Outbreak of Pseudomonas aeruginosa infections in a surgical intensive care unit: probable transmission via hands of a health care worker. *Clin Infect Dis* 1993 Mar;16(3):372–376.

42. Tredget EE, Shankowsky HA, Joffe AM, et al. Epidemiology of infections with Pseudomonas aeruginosa in burn patients: the role of hydrotherapy. *Clin Infect Dis* 1992 Dec;15(6):941–949.

43. Kolmos HJ, Thuesen B, Nielsen SV, et al. Outbreak of infection in a burns unit due to Pseudomonas aeruginosa originating from contaminated tubing used for irrigation of patients. *J Hosp Infect* 1993 May;24(1):11–21.

44. Centers for Disease Control (CDC). Nosocomial infection and pseudoinfection from contaminated endoscopes and bronchoscopes—Wisconsin and Missouri. *MMWR Morb Mortal Wkly Rep* 1991 Oct 4;40(39):675–678.

45. Struelens MJ, Rost F, Deplano A, et al. Pseudomonas aeruginosa and Enterobacteriaceae bacteremia after biliary endoscopy: an outbreak investigation using DNA macrorestriction analysis. *Am J Med* 1993 Nov;95(5):489–498.

46. Sader HS, Pignatari AC, Leme IL, et al. Epidemiologic typing of multiply drug-resistant Pseudomonas aeruginosa isolated from an outbreak in an intensive care unit. *Diagn Microbiol Infect Dis* 1993 Jul;17(1):13–18.

47. Grundmann H, Kropec A, Hartung D, et al. Pseudomonas aeruginosa in a neonatal intensive care unit: reservoirs and ecology of the nosocomial pathogen. *J Infect Dis* 1993 Oct;168(4):943–947.

48. Gennari M, Lombardi P. Comparative characterization of Acinetobacter strains isolated from different foods and clinical sources. *Zentralbl Bakteriol* 1993 Nov;279(4):553–564.

49. Oie S, Kamiya A, Hironaga K, et al. Microbial contamination of enteral feeding solution and its prevention. *Am J Infect Control* 1993 Feb;21(1):34–38.

50. Millership SE, Patel N, Chattopadhyay B. The colonization of patients in an intensive treatment unit with gram-negative flora: the significance of the oral route. *J Hosp Infect* 1986 May;7(3):226–235.

51. Zeana C, Larson E, Sahni J, et al. The epidemiology of multidrug-resistant Acinetobacter baumannii: does the community represent a reservoir? *Infect Control Hosp Epidemiol* 2003 Apr;24(4):275–279.

52. Fotedar R, Banerjee U, Shriniwas. Vector potential of the German cockroach in dissemination of Pseudomonas aeruginosa. *J Hosp Infect* 1993 Jan;23(1):55–59.

53. Corbett JJ, Rosenstein BJ. Pseudomonas meningitis related to spinal anesthesia. *Neurology* 1971 Sep;21(9):946–950.

54. Guenthner SH, Hendley JO, Wenzel RP. Gram-negative bacilli as nontransient flora on the hands of hospital personnel. *J Clin Microbiol* 1987 Mar;25(3):488–490.

55. Weber DJ, Rutala WA. The environment as a source of nosocomial infections. In: Wenzel RP, ed. *Prevention and Control of Nosocomial Infections*. Philadelphia: Lippincott Williams & Wilkins, 2003:575–597.

56. Kates SG, McGinley KJ, Larson EL, et al. Indigenous multiresistant bacteria from flowers in hospital and nonhospital environments. *Am J Infect Control* 1991 Jun;19(3):156–161.

57. Grieble HG, Bird TJ, Nidea HM, et al. Chute-hydropulping waste disposal system: a reservoir of enteric bacilli and Pseudomonas in a modern hospital. *J Infect Dis* 1974 Dec;130(6):602–607.

58. Daschner FD, Habel H. Hospital outbreak of multi-resistant Acinetobacter anitratus: an airborne mode of spread? *J Hosp Infect* 1987 Sep;10(2):211–212.

59. Bergogne-Berezin E. Pseudomonads and miscellaneous gram-negative bacilli. In: Cohen J, Powderly WG, eds. *Infectious Diseases*. Edinburgh: Mosby, 2004:2203–2226.

60. Alvarado CJ, Reichelderfer M. APIC guideline for infection prevention and control in flexible endoscopy. Association for Professionals in Infection Control. *Am J Infect Control* 2000 Apr;28(2):138–155.

61. Siegman-Igra Y, Bar-Yosef S, Gorea A, et al. Nosocomial Acinetobacter meningitis secondary to invasive procedures: report of 25 cases and review. *Clin Infect Dis* 1993 Nov;17(5):843–849.

62. Gladman G, Connor PJ, Williams RF, et al. Controlled study of Pseudomonas cepacia and Pseudomonas maltophilia in cystic fibrosis. *Arch Dis Child* 1992 Feb;67(2):192–195.

63. Burdge DR, Nakielna EM, Noble MA. Case-control and vector studies of nosocomial acquisition of Pseudomonas cepacia in adult patients with cystic fibrosis. *Infect Control Hosp Epidemiol* 1993 Mar;14(3):127–130.

64. Isles A, Maclusky I, Corey M, et al. Pseudomonas cepacia infection in cystic fibrosis: an emerging problem. *J Pediatr* 1984 Feb;104(2):206–210.

65. Yamagishi Y, Fujita J, Takigawa K, et al. Clinical features of Pseudomonas cepacia pneumonia in an epidemic among immunocompromised patients. *Chest* 1993 Jun;103(6):1706–1709.

66. Panlilio AL, Beck-Sague CM, Siegel JD, et al. Infections and pseudoinfections due to povidone-iodine solution contaminated with Pseudomonas cepacia. *Clin Infect Dis* 1992 May;14(5):1078–1083.

67. Weems JJ Jr. Nosocomial outbreak of Pseudomonas cepacia associated with contamination of reusable electronic ventilator temperature probes. *Infect Control Hosp Epidemiol* 1993 Oct;14(10):583–586.

68. Rutala WA, Weber DJ, Thomann CA. An outbreak of Pseudomonas cepacia bacteremia associated with a contaminated intra-aortic balloon pump. *J Thorac Cardiovasc Surg* 1988 Jul;96(1):157–161.

69. Heard S, Lawrence S, Holmes B, et al. A pseudo-outbreak of Pseudomonas on a special care baby unit. *J Hosp Infect* 1990 Jul;16(1):59–65.

70. Weinstein RA, Stamm WE. Pseudoepidemics in hospital. *Lancet* 1977 Oct;2(8043):862–864.

71. Lacey S, Want SV. Pseudomonas pickettii infections in a paediatric oncology unit. *J Hosp Infect* 1991 Jan;17(1):45–51.

72. Maki DG, Klein BS, McCormick RD, et al. Nosocomial Pseudomonas pickettii bacteremias traced to narcotic tampering. A case for selective drug screening of health care personnel. *JAMA* 1991 Feb;265(8):981–986.

73. Raveh D, Simhon A, Gimmon Z, et al. Infections caused by Pseudomonas pickettii in association with permanent indwelling intravenous devices: four cases and a review. *Clin Infect Dis* 1993 Nov;17(5):877–880.

74. Sanford JP. *Pseudomonas* species (including Melioidosis and Glanders). In: Mandell GL, Douglas RG, Bennett JE, eds. *Principles and Practice of Infectious Diseases.* New York: Churchill Livingstone, 1995:1980–2003.

75. McGowan JE, Del Rio C. Other gram-negative bacilli. In: Mandell GL, Douglas RG, Bennett JE, eds. *Principles and Practice of Infectious Diseases.* New York: Churchill Livingstone, 1995:2106–2117.

76. McGuckin MB, Thorpe RJ, Koch KM, et al. An outbreak of Achromobacter xylosoxidans related to diagnostic tracer procedures. *Am J Epidemiol* 1982 May;115(5):785–793.

77. Martin MA. Nosocomial infections related to patient care support services: dietetic services, central services department, laundry, respiratory care, dialysis, and endoscopy. In: Wenzel RP, ed. *Prevention and Control of Nosocomial Infections.* Baltimore: Williams & Wilkins, 1993:93–138.

78. Reverdy ME, Freney J, Fleurette J, et al. Nosocomial colonization and infection by Achromobacter xylosoxidans. *J Clin Microbiol* 1984 Feb;19(2):140–143.

79. Shigeta S, Yasunaga Y, Honsumi K, et al. Cerebral ventriculitis associated with Achromobacter xylosoxidans. *J Clin Pathol* 1978 Feb;31(2):156–161.

80. Boukadida J, Monastiri K, Snoussi N, et al. Nosocomial neonatal meningitis by Alcaligenes xylosoxidans transmitted by aqueous eosin. *Pediatr Infect Dis J* 1993 Aug;12(8):696–697.

81. Pokrywka M, Viazanko K, Medvick J, et al. A Flavobacterium meningosepticum outbreak among intensive care patients. *Am J Infect Control* 1993 Jun;21(3):139–145.

82. Hekker TA. van Overhagen W, Schneider AJ. Pressure transducers: an overlooked source of sepsis in the intensive care unit. *Intensive Care Med* 1990;16(8):511–512.

83. Pfaller MA. Microbiology: the role of the clinical laboratory in hospital epidemiology and infection control. In: Wenzel RP, ed. *Prevention and Control of Nosocomial Infections.* Baltimore: Williams & Wilkins, 1993:385–405.

84. Poh CL, Yeo CC. Recent advances in typing of Pseudomonas aeruginosa. *J Hosp Infect* 1993 Jul;24(3):175–181.

85. Barg NL. An introduction to molecular hospital epidemiology. *Infect Control Hosp Epidemiol* 1993 Jul;14(7):395–396.

86. Goering RV. Molecular epidemiology of nosocomial infection: analysis of chromosomal restriction fragment patterns by pulsed-field gel electrophoresis. *Infect Control Hosp Epidemiol* 1993 Oct;14(10):595–600.

87. Woods CR, Versalovic J, Koeuth T, et al. Whole-cell repetitive element sequence-based polymerase chain reaction allows rapid assessment of clonal relationships of bacteria isolates. *J Clin Microbiol* 1993 Jul;31(7):1927–1931.

88. Gräser Y, Klare I, Halle E, et al. Epidemiological study of an Acinetobacter baumannii outbreak by using polymerase chain reaction fingerprinting. *J Clin Microbiol* 1993 Sep;31(9):2417–2420.

89. Goering RV. Molecular epidemiology of nosocomial infection: analysis of chromosomal restriction fragment patterns by pulsed-field gel electrophoresis. *Infect Control Hosp Epidemiol* 1993 Oct;14(10):595–600.

90. Lewis T, Loman NJ, Bingle L, et al. High-throughput whole-genome sequencing to dissect the epidemiology of Acinetobacter baumanii isolates from a hospital outbreak. *J Hosp Infect* 2010 May;75(1):37–41.

91. Ang SW, Lee ST. Emergence of a multiply-resistant strain of Acinetobacter in a burns unit. *Ann Acad Med Singapore* 1992 Sep;21(5):660–663.

92. Doebbeling BN, Stanley GL, Sheetz CT, et al. Comparative efficacy of alternative hand-washing agents in reducing nosocomial infections in intensive care units. *N Engl J Med* 1992 Jul 9;327(2):88–93.

93. Daschner FD. Useful and useless hygienic techniques in intensive care units. *Intensive Care Med* 1985;11(6):280–283.

94. Boyce JM, Pittet D. Guideline for Hand Hygiene in Health-Care Settings: Recommendations of the Healthcare Infection Control Practices Advisory Committee and the HICPAC/SHEA/APIC/IDSA Hand Hygiene Task Force. Society for Healthcare Epidemiology of America/Association for Professionals in Infection Control/Infectious Diseases Society of America. *MMWR Recomm Rep* 2002 Oct 25;51(RR-16):1–45.

95. Maki DG. Epidemic nosocomial bacteremias. In: Wenzel RP, ed. *Handbook of Hospital Acquired Infection.* Boca Raton, FL: CRC, 1981:371–512.

96. Kaplan LM, McGuckin M. Increasing handwashing compliance with more accessible sinks. *Infect Control* 1986 Aug;7(8):408–410.

97. Smith DL, Gumery LB, Smith EG, et al. Epidemic of Pseudomonas cepacia in an adult cystic fibrosis unit: evidence of person-to-person transmission. *J Clin Microbiol* 1993 Nov;31(11):3017–3022.

98. Anderson DJ, Kuhns JS, Vasil ML, et al. DNA fingerprinting by pulsed field gel electrophoresis and ribotyping to distinguish Pseudomonas cepacia isolates from a nosocomial outbreak. *J Clin Microbiol* 1991 Mar;29(3):648–649.

99. Gbaguidi-Haore H, Legast S, Thouverez M, et al. Ecological study of the effectiveness of isolation precautions in the management of hospitalized patients colonized or infected with Acinetobacter baumannii. *Infect Control Hosp Epidemiol* 2008 Dec;29(12):1118–1123.

100. Nafziger DA, Wiblin T. Nosocomial pneumonia. In: Wenzel RP, ed. *Prevention and Control of Nosocomial Infections.* Philadelphia: Lippincott Williams & Wilkins, 2003:312–330.

101. Chinn R. Antimicrobial therapy of nosocomial pneumonia. In: Jarvis WR, ed. *Nosocomial Pneumonia.* New York: Marcel Dekker, 2000:93–124.

102. Aarts MA, Brun-Buisson C, Cook DJ, et al. Antibiotic management of suspected nosocomial ICU-acquired infection: does prolonged empiric therapy improve outcome? *Intensive Care Med* 2007 Aug;33(8):1369–1378.

103. Greene LR, Sposato K. *Guide to the Elimination of Ventilator-Associated Pneumonia.* Association of Professionals in Infection Control and Epidemiology website. 2009. Available at: http://apic.org/Professional-Practice/Implementation-guides.

104. Nettleman MD. Cost and cost benefit of infection control. In: Wenzel RP, ed. *Prevention and Control of Nosocomial Infections.* Philadelphia: Lippincott Williams & Wilkins, 2003:33–41.

105. Sehulster L, Chinn RY. Guidelines for environmental infection control in health-care facilities. Recommendations of CDC and the Healthcare Infection Control Practices Advisory Committee (HICPAC). *MMWR Recomm Rep* 2003 Jun 6;52(RR-10):1–42.

106. Lynch P, Rosenthal V, Borg M, et al. Infection control: a global view. In: Jarvis WR, ed. *Bennett & Brachman's Hospital Infections.* Philadelphia: Lippincott Williams & Wilkins, 2007:255–271.

CHAPTER 78

Fungi

Jose Cadena, MD
Assistant Professor of Medicine
Department of Medicine/Infectious Diseases
University of Texas Health Science Center at San Antonio
Assistant Chief of Infectious Diseases
Medical Director Infection Control
South Texas Veterans Healthcare System
San Antonio, TX

George R. Thompson, MD
Assistant Professor of Medicine
Department of Medicine, Division of Infectious Diseases
Co-director, Coccidioidomycosis Serology Laboratory
Department of Medical Microbiology and Immunology
University of California - Davis
Davis, CA

Thomas F. Patterson, MD, FACP, FIDSA
Professor of Medicine
Chief, Division of Infectious Diseases
The University of Texas Health Science Center at San Antonio
Staff Physician, South Texas Veterans Healthcare System
San Antonio, TX

ABSTRACT

The face of healthcare-associated fungal infection is changing. Candida *spp. continue to play a significant role, with high associated morbidity and mortality; however, non-*albicans Candida *spp. are increasing in incidence, as are opportunistic molds and other unusual fungal pathogens.*

The diagnosis of fungal pathogens has also undergone a major shift. New antigen and antibody tests, as well as rapid diagnostic polymerase chain reaction tests, are increasingly used.

Finally, the options for antifungal therapy are much broader. Newer azoles and echinocandins have proven as efficacious as traditional agents like amphotericin B, but with improved side effect profiles.

KEY CONCEPTS

- Fungi are increasingly being identified as healthcare-associated pathogens.

- Immunocompromised patients are at increased risk for fungal infections.

- *Candida* spp. are common endogenous flora.

- Exposure to antibiotics may predispose patients to *Candida* spp. infections.

- Most molds are ubiquitous in nature, making exposure unavoidable.

- Environmental controls may help reduce the risk of infection with certain fungi.

- Resistance to antifungal agents is well documented and now serves as a genuine clinical problem.

BACKGROUND

This chapter reviews the epidemiology, clinical presentation, diagnosis, and treatment of fungal pathogens, with an emphasis on new developments. Endemic mycoses are briefly mentioned, but, as they do not generally cause healthcare-associated infections (HAIs), the remarks only highlight a few unusual aspects of these infections.

BASIC PRINCIPLES

- Patients at high risk for healthcare-associated fungal infections include patients with leukemia, patients with solid tumors and leukopenia, bone marrow transplant patients, injection drug users, patients who have undergone intra-abdominal or cardiothoracic surgery, burn patients, and premature or low-birth-weight infants.

- *Candida* spp. are the fourth most common cause of HAIs, but the epidemiology of *Candida* has been incompletely defined. Further prospective studies utilizing molecular typing techniques are needed to clarify the role of fomites and healthcare personnel (HCP) hands in the healthcare-associated transmission of fungi. Additional infection prevention strategies are needed, as mortality, morbidity, and cost from these infections remain high.

- A comprehensive guideline for the treatment of *Candida* infection has recently been published and should help to determine the best treatment for each patient circumstance.[1]

- Prevention of healthcare-associated *Candida* infections can be addressed by considering each risk factor for infection.

- *Aspergillus* spp. are ubiquitous molds found in decaying organic matter. The risk factors for development of invasive aspergillosis (IA) include steroids, prolonged neutropenia, and acquired immunodeficiency syndrome (AIDS). Multiple outbreaks have been reported in conjunction with intrahospital or surrounding construction.

- As in the treatment of *Candida* infection, newer azole agents and echinocandins offer new modalities of therapy to patients with IA. Similarly, comprehensive guidelines for the treatment for aspergillosis have been published.[2]

- Strategies to decrease the incidence of IA fall into three broad categories: (1) decreasing the duration of neutropenia/corticosteroid use, (2) decreasing exposure of patients to conidia, and (3) prophylaxis in high-risk patients. Emphasis should be placed on prevention, as infection carries a high mortality.

FUNGI TYPES

Candida and Related Pathogenic Yeasts

Identification

Fungi are eukaryotic organisms with cell walls containing chitin, cellulose, or both. Yeasts are unicellular organisms that reproduce by budding and typically, but not always, produce circular, mucoid colonies upon culture.

Clinically, the most frequently isolated yeasts are *Candida*, of which there are more than 80 species. *Candida* reproduces asexually by mitosis to produce blastoconidia. *Candida* appears Gram-positive. The cell walls also stain with Gomori methenamine silver stain and periodic-acid Schiff reagent.

In tissues, *Candida* may transform from blastoconidia (budding yeast cells) to pseudohyphae (elongated chains secondary to incomplete division), and finally into an extensive network of hyphae.[3]

Candida is a normal commensal of the human gastrointestinal and female genital tract. Phenotypically, it is identified by morphology of colonies on cornmeal agar plates, Gram stains, germ-tube formation (distinguishes *Candida albicans* from other *Candida* spp.), and carbohydrate assimilation (API systems).

Molecular biologic techniques that are helpful in epidemiologic investigations include restriction enzyme analysis (REA), electrophoretic karyotyping (EK), and DNA fingerprinting using polymerase chain reaction (PCR). Restriction enzyme analysis involves extracting DNA, cutting the DNA into large fragments with enzymes (infrequent cutters), and comparing the resulting DNA fragment sizes. Small differences in banding patterns may be missed as large fragments of DNA are compared.[4] EK involves the extraction and comparison of smaller fragments of DNA than can be achieved with REA. EK not only delineates species but can also delineate strain types that cannot be separated on the basis of phenotypic typing. DNA fingerprinting using PCR is rapid and simple and more sensitive in separating strain types than is EK.[5]

Epidemiology/Transmission

Fungi are increasingly identified as healthcare-associated pathogens. From 1980 to 1990, National Nosocomial Infections Surveillance Systems (NNIS, currently National Healthcare Safety Network) found that in participating hospitals, fungi comprised 7.9 percent of 344,610 healthcare-associated pathogens. Of these fungal infections, 79 percent were due to *Candida* spp.[6] Between 1991 and 2000, *Candida* was the fifth most common blood isolate and the fourth most common isolate from all sites in intensive care units (ICUs).[7] Most recently, among 2,039 hospitals reporting to the National Healthcare Safety Network (NHSN) between 2009 and 2010, *Candida* spp. accounted for about 9.5 percent of the 81,139 pathogens reported as etiological agents for 69,475 HAIs, becoming the fifth most common pathogen in HAIs. Furthermore, *C. albicans* was the seventh most common cause of catheter-related bloodstream infections (BSIs) and the fourth most common cause of catheter-associated urinary tract infections (UTIs).[8]

Healthcare-associated candidemia accounts for 1.0 percent to 1.5 percent of hospital-acquired BSIs.[9] Increases in healthcare-associated fungal infections have occurred at all hospitals, regardless of size or teaching affiliation.[10] In a study of 306 episodes of fungal BSIs in 34 participating centers, Pfaller et al. demonstrated that 80 percent were healthcare-associated. Fifty percent occurred in patients housed in ICUs.[9] In participating centers in the United States, 46 percent of the fungal BSIs were due to non-*albicans* species, most commonly *Candida glabrata*.[11] A recent multicentric study (PATH Alliance® registry), including 23 medical centers in the United States and two in Canada, confirmed these findings. This registry records invasive fungal infections (IFI) and reported 3,548 cases of infections by *Candida* spp, encompassing 53 percent of the IFI in the registry from 2004 to 2008. Most infections were caused by *C. albicans* (42.1 percent), followed by *C. glabrata* (26.7 percent), *C. parapsilosis* (15.9 percent), *C. tropicalis* (8.7 percent), and *C. krusei* (3.4 percent). *C. albicans* infections were more common among neonatal ICU (NICU) patients and patients in surgical units. *C. glabrata* was more common in older patients, patients with bone marrow transplants (BMTs) and solid organ transplants, and patients that had received previous antifungal therapy. *C. parapsilosis* infection has been associated with the presence of intravenous catheters and recent surgery and was commonly described in NICU patients. *C. tropicalis* was observed among BMT patients. *C. krusei* occurred most commonly among neutropenic, leukemic, or BMT patients.[12]

Patients at high risk for healthcare-associated fungal infections include patients with solid tumors, leukemia, and leukopenia; BMT patients; injection drug users; patients who have undergone intra-abdominal or cardiothoracic surgery; burn patients; and premature or low-birth-weight infants.[13]

General risk factors for *Candida* infection include receipt of broad-spectrum antibiotics, central venous catheterization, immunosuppression, neutropenia, urinary catheterization, prosthesis (e.g., vascular grafts), and total parenteral nutrition.[13] Risk factors specific to candidemia in postcardiac surgery patients include ongoing mechanical ventilation for 10 or more days, cardiopulmonary bypass for more than 120 minutes, and diabetes mellitus. APACHE (acute physiology and chronic health evaluation) II score of 30 or greater at onset of candidemia was an independent predictor of candidemia-related death in this population.[14]

In a prospective, multicentric observational study performed by the International Pediatric Fungal Network between 2007 and 2011, the authors enrolled 196 pediatric and 26 neonatal patients with candidemia. The most common predisposing factors in this cohort included hematological malignancies (19 percent), solid organ tumors (9 percent), gastrointestinal abnormalities (16 percent, the most common was short bowel), and surgery/trauma (15 percent—with the most common being abdominal surgery). Species other than *Candida albicans* accounted for the greatest number of cases of invasive candidemia (56 percent of pediatric cases, 52 percent of neonatal cases). However, among the individual *Candida* spp., *C. albicans* was the leading pathogen. Outcomes were best for *C. parapsilosis* and worst for *C. glabrata*.[15]

Compared with neonatal patients with coagulase-negative staphylococcal infections, neonates with candidemia had greater exposure to systemic steroids, antibiotics, and catecholamines, as well as a sevenfold higher mortality rate. Candidemic neonates were also more likely to have required mechanical ventilation and less likely to be tolerant of enteral feeding.[16] Prolonged use of third-generation cephalosporins increased risk for candidemia.

A prospective cohort study of six geographically scattered NICUs from 1993 to 1995 resulted in 2,847 neonates enrolled. Of these, 1.2 percent developed candidemia, for a rate of 0.63 per 1,000 catheter days. Multivariate analysis, controlled for birth weight and abdominal surgery, revealed the following risk factors: gestational age under 32 weeks, 5-minute Apgar less than 5, shock, disseminated intravascular coagulation (DIC), prior use of intralipids, parenteral nutrition, presence of central venous catheter, H2 blockers, mechanical ventilation, or length of ICU stay greater than 7 days. Colonization of the gastrointestinal tract (GI) tract preceded candidemia in 43 percent of patients.[17] Postnatal steroids and necrotizing enterocolitis also increase fungal risk.[18]

C. parapsilosis is particularly common among neonates. Most neonates are colonized prior to developing infection, but colonization tends to occur later after birth, thus *C. parapsilosis* does not tend to cause early neonatal sepsis. Potential factors associated with *C. parapsilosis* in neonates include the use of cephalosporins, the presence of a central venous catheter, and use of total parenteral nutrition.[19]

A recent study based on population-based surveillance found that the incidence of candidemia among residents of Baltimore and Atlanta showed that the crude incidence of candidemia increased. The authors compared the rate of candidemia between 1992 and 1993 in Atlanta and 1998 and 2000 in Baltimore, with the rate of candidemia between 2008 and 2011 at each location. The rates of candidemia were highest among individuals over 65 years of age. However, the rate of candidemia was lower among infants less than 1 year of age, suggesting a change in the epidemiology of the disease.[20]

Patients with human immunodeficiency virus (HIV) are at risk to develop oropharyngeal candidiasis. This occurs when they have very low CD4 cell counts. The most common etiologic agent is *C. albicans*, but other species like *C. glabrata* and *C. dubliniensis* have been implicated. Patients receiving antiretroviral therapy have a lower risk of developing oropharyngeal candidiasis, whereas those with a history of esophageal candidiasis or wearing dentures are at risk of colonization with fluconazole-resistant organisms. Most patients respond to therapy with fluconazole, but the dose may need to be increased when clinical response is not achieved.[21]

In solid organ transplants, the incidence of fungal infections has increased, with recent prospective data showing an incidence of 3.1 percent for any invasive fungal infection.[22] *Candida* spp. were responsible for the majority of disease, with mortality seen in 66 percent of those with invasive candidiasis.

Previously, it was felt that most episodes of *Candida* infection have resulted from the patient's own endogenous flora.[23] Recently, however, patient-to-patient transmission has been implicated. The precise role fomites play in the epidemiology of hospital-associated *Candida* infection is still being investigated.

HCP hands have been shown to harbor *Candida* spp., and molecular studies have suggested that transmission through the hands of HCP may contribute to outbreaks.[24] In a prospective study of 25 patients with third-degree burns and receipt of 10 to 14 days of broad-spectrum antibiotics, 75 percent of the patients diagnosed with invasive yeast by skin biopsy were previously colonized with the same organisms. In addition, multiple surfaces in the burn unit were heavily contaminated with yeast. However, no biotyping was done to show whether strains were related.[25]

Yeasts have been detected on 80 percent of HCP hands, and *Candida* spp. have been recovered from 63 percent of nurses studied. The best method for recovery of yeasts from HCP hands appears to be a bag wash in brain/heart infusion broth supplemented with gentamicin and vancomycin.[26] During a recent outbreak of neonatal infection with *C. parapsilosis*, the hands of one of the NICU physicians was found to have the same molecular pattern (using random polymorphism DNA analysis) as two of the three patients involved, and a strain on the hands of a nurse was found to be consistent with the third case.[27]

In an attempt to document healthcare-associated transmission, Taylor et al. performed DNA fingerprinting of 91 *C. albicans* isolates from 32 patients in an ICU. The isolates from individual patients were distinct, revealing no cross-transmission.[28]

An outbreak of *C. parapsilosis* has been traced to a contaminated vacuum transfer pump used to prepare parenteral nutrition solutions.[29] Similarly, an outbreak caused by a single strain of *C. glabrata* was responsible for nine infections in a pediatric population in Turkey. The source was thought to be bottles used for milk feeding that had been improperly handled.[30]

C. parapsilosis has also been shown to be healthcare-acquired in BMT patients, with REA analysis showing one strain common to four patients, three staff members, and two environmental surfaces.[31]

Congenital or perinatal infection with *C. glabrata* has been described in neonates.[32] Patients with newly acquired *C. glabrata* colonization or infection had longer durations of hospitalization and more frequent prior antimicrobial use than patients from whom *Candida* species were not recovered.[32] Also, patients generally carried the same strain type of *C. glabrata* longitudinally. Hands of HCP did not appear to be a factor in transmission. In a BMT population, 71 percent of patients that cultured positive for *C. glabrata* also carried other *Candida* species.[33]

In a retrospective case control study of patients with and without candidemia from July 1, 1997, to June 30, 2001, the crude mortality for candidemia was 61 percent. Attributable mortality was 49 percent, highlighting the seriousness of these infections. The cost of candidemia is estimated to increase hospital costs by $6,000 to $29,000 per episode and the length of hospital stay by 3 to 13 days.[34,35] Similar results were reported in a group of patients by Dodds Ashley et al., including data from 119 patients with candidiasis. The attributable costs, adjusted for sex, age, race-ethnicity, and number of comorbid illness was $38,734 in 2004 dollars.[36]

The epidemiology of *Candida* is in its infancy. Further prospective studies utilizing molecular typing techniques are needed to clarify the role of fomites and HCP hands in the healthcare-associated transmission of fungi. Additional prevention strategies are needed, because mortality, morbidity, and cost from these infections remain high.

Diagnosis

Candida can be isolated from mouth washings of 50 percent of healthy persons and in the stool of 90 to 100 percent of halthy adults. For this reason, isolation of *Candida* spp. from mucosal surfaces and nonsterile body sites (mouth, rectum, vagina, skin) is not diagnostic of disease.

Mucosal (vaginal or mucocutaneous) candidiasis is typically diagnosed by appearance of the mucosal plaques, symptoms, and 10 percent potassium hydroxide preparation of fresh scrapings to look for budding yeast cells and pseudohyphae, with positive follow-up culture.

The diagnosis of UTI can be difficult, especially in patients with indwelling bladder catheters. Typically the urine will contain more than 5 white blood cells (WBCs) per high-power field, as

well as being positive for leukocyte esterase and/or nitrites, with culture growing greater than or equal to 10^5 colony forming units (cfu)/mL of *Candida*. Even 10^5 cfu/mL titers of candiduria may fail to differentiate colonization from infection in the catheterized patient. Upper tract disease should be suspected if candidal casts (hyphal casts) are present in a fresh urine sample,[37] or fungal balls are seen in the kidneys on ultrasonography.

Fungal organisms isolated from a normally sterile body site concurrent with signs and symptoms of infection are diagnostic of deep tissue or disseminated infection. Tissue samples show the presence of yeast cells plus hyphal forms on appropriate staining.

Disseminated candidiasis can be diagnosed by positive blood cultures, but unfortunately current blood culture systems may miss up to 50 percent of invasive candidiasis.[38] Accordingly, a negative blood culture does not exclude invasive candidiasis.

1,3-beta-D-glucan detection is emerging as a useful method of diagnosis of invasive candidiasis. Results can be obtained within 72 to 96 hours, as the test is usually a "send-out" to a specialized laboratory. Sensitivity ranges from 70 to 80 percent and increases if multiple sequential surveillance specimens are available. Also important is the negative predictive value (NPV) of two negative beta-D-glucan tests in ruling out invasive candidiasis, especially in a high-risk febrile patient with NPV greater than 98 percent.[39]

Real-time PCR has also been examined and compared to conventional blood cultures and 1,3-B-D-glucan (BDG) testing in the diagnosis of candidiasis. PCR using plasma or sera was more sensitive than BDG testing for diagnosing invasive candidiasis with similar specificity, and PCR was more sensitive for deep-seated candidiasis. PCR and BDG testing were both more sensitive than blood cultures for deep-seated candidiasis.[40]

Following isolation of *Candida* spp. in blood fluid or tissue samples, it is essential to identify the causative organism to the species level allowing for more rapid determination of antifungal drug susceptibility. All laboratories should ensure rapid species identification even for urinary and mucosal isolates. For blood isolates, rapid *Candida* identification within 3 to 4 hours is possible using multiple different methodologies that are currently available (PNA FISH, MALDI-TOF, or chromogenic agar—though the later requires identification of colony phenotype).[41,43]

It is hoped that in the near future, these newer diagnostic modalities will allow early detection and therefore earlier treatment of fungal infections.

Clinical Manifestations

Clinical manifestations of *Candida* infection vary with the organ system involved. Oral and mucosal candidiasis often presents with alteration of taste and dryness of the mouth as well as tongue soreness and pain. Esophageal candidiasis presents as dysphagia with odynophagia.

Vaginal candidiasis commonly presents with "cheesy" white vaginal discharge and vulvovaginal burning or itching, as well as burning on urination because of periurethral irritation.

Urinary tract signs and symptoms depend on whether cystitis or upper tract disease is present. Cystitis presents with dysuria, frequency, urgency, and nocturia, as well as suprapubic pain. Fortunately, an ascending infection is rare. Upper tract disease presents with fever, flank pain/tenderness, and rarely second-ary candidemia. It is more common in patients with diabetes, especially in association with obstruction, and is further compli-cated by papillary necrosis or fungal balls in the urinary tract as demonstrated by ultrasound.[37]

Disseminated candidiasis should be suspected in high-risk pa-tients with unexplained fever (especially in the immunocompro-mised host on broad-spectrum antibiotics), unexplained central nervous system signs and symptoms, or clinical deterioration in a compromised host.

Complications of candidemia/disseminated candidiasis include endophthalmitis, endocarditis, or purulent pericarditis; menin-gitis; suppurative thrombophlebitis; and vertebral osteomyelitis. Hepatosplenic candidiasis is typically seen in severely immuno-suppressed patients and presents as fever, hepatosplenomegaly, and elevated alkaline phosphatase with a typical appearance on computed tomography (CT) scan of multiple small hypodense lesions in the liver and spleen.[1]

Pathogenesis

Colonization of the oropharynx and GI tract has been shown to increase with hospitalization, with more *C. albicans* species in the mouth, and more non-*albicans* species in the rectum and urinary tract.[44]

Antibiotics predispose to *Candida* infection by reducing the normal bacterial flora and allowing *Candida* to proliferate. The most important defenses against *Candida* are intact integument and mucosal barriers. *Candida* can enter the vascular system via peripheral or central catheters or injection drug use. Urinary catheters provide an irritative focus and mucosal ulcerations allowing the fungi to traverse bladder mucosa, in the same way that chemotherapeutic agents, irradiation, and GI surgery disrupt oral and gut mucosa, allowing *Candida* a portal of entry into the vascular system.

Neutrophils are the main line of defense against fungi, as they ingest and kill blastoconidia. However, hyphae in tissues are more resistant to phagocytosis.[45] *Candida* are killed in pha-gosomes by myeloperoxidase, hydrogen peroxide, superoxide anion, and chymotrypsin-like cationic proteins.[46]

Lymphocytes and cell-mediated immunity play a role in the host defense against superficial candidiasis, as evidenced by the fact

that AIDS patients are more prone to develop mucocutaneous candidiasis. Once candidemia occurs, the potential exists for microabscess formation in a variety of tissues.[47]

Treatment

Mucocutaneous candidiasis is best treated with oral or topical azoles (the later reserved solely for vulvovaginal candidiasis), unless the infection becomes recurrent or refractory.

Lower UTIs, if asymptomatic (especially in patients with indwell-ing urinary catheters), do not require treatment. Symptomatic UTIs, especially upper tract disease, require systemic antifun-gals.

The mortality of candidemia is high, typically 50 to 75 per-cent.[13,22,48] Mortality is virtually 100 percent if the patient remains persistently neutropenic.[9] Delay in diagnosis invariably translates into delay in initiation of appropriate antifungal therapy and higher mortality.[49] The gold standard for ther-apy of fungemia or disseminated candidemia previously was intravenous amphotericin B (AmB); however, recent studies have shown that parenteral azoles (fluconazole, voriconazole) or the echinocandin drug class are as effective and less toxic with echinocandins use associated with lower mortality in a recent meta-analysis.[50]

The characteristics of an ideal antifungal would be broad spectrum of activity, fungicidal activity, lack of development of resistance during therapy, availability of both oral and intra-venous (IV) forms, good penetration into body fluids, and lack of toxicity.[51] To date, no agent is available that meets all these criteria, but some of the newer azole agents and echinocandins come close and have replaced AmB as first-line therapy for systemic candidiasis.[1]

A comprehensive guideline for the treatment of *Candida* infec-tion has recently been published and should help to determine the best treatment for each patient's circumstances.[1]

Development and Impact of Resistance to Antimicrobial Agents

The recent standardization of methods of performing mini-mum inhibitory concentration (MICs) in fungi has facilitated the detection of resistant strains.[52] Correlation between in vitro MIC data and in vivo response to therapy remains incomplete; however, use of in vitro susceptibility is increasingly available and facilitates treatment.

In general, *C. lusitaniae* is less susceptible to AmB and can develop resistance to AmB while on therapy.[53] *C. glabrata* isolates are also intrinsically less susceptible to AmB, as well as all available azole agents, but are highly susceptible to the echinocandin class of antifungals.[54]

Primary resistance to fluconazole is present in *C. krusei*, which fortunately remains an infrequent cause of invasive disease.[55]

Studies by Pfaller et al. suggest that drug-resistant isolates of *Candida* spp. may emerge from among endemic strains.[56]

AmB resistance is felt to be secondary to changes in ergosterol content of fungal cell membranes. One study has shown BSIs in immunocompromised patients caused by yeast isolates with MICs greater than 0.8 µg/mL to be 100 percent fatal, versus 47 percent mortality if MICs are 0.8 µg/mL or less.[57] Of considerable concern were the numerous reports of *C. albicans* resistance to fluconazole in patients with advanced AIDS, resulting in azole-resistant mucosal candidiasis; however, with the availability of active antiretroviral therapy (ART), refractory oral and esophageal candidiasis due to azole-resistant *Candida* spp. has decreased considerably.

In a global susceptibility study from 1997 to 2007, yeast isolates from 41 countries were collected.[58] From the beginning of the study period to December 2007, the proportion of isolates that were *C. albicans* decreased, whereas *C. glabrata*, *C. tropicalis,* and *C. parapsilosis* isolates increased in frequency. Although resistance to fluconazole varied by country, the overall rate of susceptibility to fluconazole remained stable and infrequent. Voriconazole had a 10- to 100-fold greater in vitro activity against most yeast species than fluconazole, but this has not turned out to be an advantage in treatment of candidiasis syndromes with rare exceptions.

C. albicans can be separated into five clades or groups: I, II, III, SA, and E. The predominant clade varies geographically. Flucytosine resistance is found almost exclusively in clade I organisms.[59]

C. glabrata vaginitis refractory to azoles has been successfully treated with topical boric acid or topical flucytosine cream.[60]

Accordingly, *C. glabrata* emerged as the Achilles heel of the entire azole drug class, including voriconazole and posaconazole. Fortunately, echinocandin agents are broad-spectrum fungicidal agents against *Candida*, and in vitro and clinical resistance is uncommon though increasingly reported.[61] Although *C. parapsilosis* isolates have higher MICs to echinocandins, this has not translated into clinical resistance, yet caution is still recommended during treatment of *C. parapsilosis* with this class.[1]

Prevention and Risk Reduction

Prevention of healthcare-associated *Candida* infections can be addressed by considering each risk factor for infection.

Judicious use of antibiotics will decrease *Candida* overgrowth in oral, vaginal, and gut mucosa. Central venous catheters should also be used only when indicated, and aseptic technique should be followed when the catheter is inserted and accessed.

Oral nutritional solutions should be used whenever possible. When parenteral nutrition becomes necessary, total parenteral nutrition solutions should be mixed in the pharmacy in laminar flow hoods using aseptic technique; bags should not be re-spiked; and solutions containing lipids should have a hang time of no more than 12 hours.[29]

The prophylactic or empirical use of oral fluconazole is widely practiced and has been shown to decrease the incidence of fungal infections in neutropenic patients, but unfortunately no effect on mortality was seen.[62] A similar trial in the ICU showed no improvement in the composite outcome when prophylactic fluconazole was prescribed compared to placebo.[63] Additionally, as more institutions used prophylactic azoles, problems with azole-resistant fungi such as *C. glabrata* increased.[64] Patients receiving chemotherapy, those at risk for neutropenia, those in ICUs with high rates of candidemia, and those with high risk solid or BMT should receive antifungal prophylaxis, usually with an azole.[65]

Antifungal prophylaxis in neonates has been shown to decrease rates of candidiasis among neonates, and in units where rates of candidiasis are elevated, fluconazole prophylaxis is recommended particularly among neonates born before 27 weeks' gestation or those weighing less than 1,000 grams.[66]

Among patients with HIV and recurrent mucocutanous candidiasis, fluconazole has been shown to decrease the number of recurrences.[1]

Aspergillus

Identification

Aspergillus spp. are ubiquitous molds found in decaying organic matter. Conidia (spores) are inhaled, followed by germination and appearance of 2- to 5-µm wide hyphae that are frequently septate and branch at 45-degree angles. Histologic appearance in tissue can be confused with *Fusarium, Scedosporium*, and other hyaline molds; therefore, culture confirmation is necessary.

Epidemiology/Transmission

The route of acquisition of *Aspergillus* is typically via inhalation of conidia (spores), which are ubiquitous in nature and within the hospital environment (potted plants, flowers etc).[67]

The risk factors for development of IA include leukemia, lymphoma, receiving high-dose or prolonged corticosteroids, prolonged neutropenia, solid organ transplant, and AIDS.[68] Patients at risk include those with aspergillosis, which was the second most common invasive fungal infection on the Path Alliance registry. It encompassed 1,001 isolates, of 7,525 isolates included. The most common species causing disease were *A. fumigatus* (543; 54 percent of total *Aspergillus* infections), *A. flavus* (74 cases; 7.4 percent), *A. niger* (65 cases; 6.5 percent), *A. terreus* (32 cases; 3.2 percent), and other species (34; 3.4 percent).[69]

In a subset of the Path Alliance Registry, among patients with hematopoietic stem cell transplant, IA was the most common cause of IFI (59 percent), followed by invasive candidiasis and other mold infections. Invasive fungal infection in this population occurs more frequently among allogeneic BMTs (68.8 percent) than among autologous BMTs (31.2 percent). *A. fumigatus* was the most common isolate. Among *Candida* IFI, most cases included non-*albicans Candida*, including *C. glabrata*. Researchers observed a trend toward fewer *Aspergillus* infections and more Mucorales (zygomycoses) infections, perhaps due to the common utilization of voriconazole for IFI prophylaxis.[70]

Another study based on autopsies over a 20-year period at a reference cancer center (1989–2008) observed a lower rate of IFI as patients age, with only Mucorales showing a significant increase over time. Among *Aspergillus* spp. isolated in this study, *A. fumigatus* was the most common. This study was limited by the fact that many *Aspergillus* spp. infections were identified based on histopathology, but cultures were frequently negative.[71]

One pseudo-epidemic occurred in a pediatric BMT unit due to faulty storage of culture plates. Stored plates on a shelf in a laboratory responsible for culturing clinical samples with resultant increased number of airborne conidia was the source of the pseudo-outbreak.[72]

Multiple outbreaks have been reported in conjunction with intrahospital or surrounding construction.[69] An outbreak in a renal transplant unit involving 10 patients was associated with window air conditioners heavily colonized with *A. flavus* and *A. fumigatus* at a time when there was construction adjacent to the hospital.[73]

The importance of airborne transmission was evidenced by an outbreak of *Aspergillus* infection among heart transplant patients. During this outbreak, there were seven cases of IA among heart transplant patients (compared to no cases in the pre-intervention period). The cases included six cases of invasive pulmonary aspergillosis (one with mediastinitis), and one case of mediastinitis. All cases except one had *A. fumigatus* isolated. The hospital performed routine air samplings with fungal cultures at least monthly. They found that the air in the operating rooms did not contain detectable conidial counts; however, the spore levels in the major heart surgery ICU were between 20 and 400 cfu. Furthermore, the strains isolated from the environment were genotypically similar to those of the patients in three of the six isolates that underwent genotyping testing. Despite the strong correlation with the presence of *Aspergillus* conidia on the air and this outbreak, there is not a clear threshold in the conidial count beyond which intervention is recommended, although greater than 16.7 cfu/mm^3 has been proposed.[74]

Environmental sources of *Aspergillus* outbreaks in hospitals have been associated with open windows,[75] contamination of particle board frames surrounding air filters,[76] backflow of contaminated air from exhaust ducts (with contamination of filters),[77] gaps in filters and support frames permitting entry of unfiltered outside air,[78] and contamination of humidified cell culture incubators in a laboratory culturing lymphokine-activated killer cells for reinfusion into patients.[79]

An outbreak of 10 cases in 26 BMT patients in New York was associated with hospital construction in a BMT unit with 10 percent efficiency of filtration and less than five air exchanges per hour. This was the first report of a higher incidence of aspergillosis associated with chronic myelogenous leukemia and aplastic anemia.[80]

A prospective study of 23 U.S. transplant centers found that *Aspergillus* spp. were responsible for 19 percent of all IFIs in solid organ transplant recipients.[22] In hematopoietic stem cell transplant recipients, however, aspergillosis was the most common IFI (43 percent), exceeding even that of invasive candidiasis (28 percent).[48] Aspergillosis generally occurs within the first 120 days after stem cell transplant.

In one university hospital, the proportion of invasive *Aspergillus* infections caused by *A. terreus* has been increasing relative to other *Aspergillus* spp. Molecular typing showed strain diversity among isolates, so no common source is suspected. The etiology for the increase is unknown.[81]

Many difficulties arise in determining whether a case of IA is healthcare- or community-associated. The first of these is that many patients are discharged and readmitted or allowed out on passes. Second, surveillance culture results alone do not accurately reflect the true number of IA cases, as they are often not diagnosed antemortem; therefore, autopsy records must also be reviewed. Even with the inclusion of autopsy cases, deceased patients with IA who do not undergo autopsy will be missed. Third, reactivation of endogenous organisms may produce infection, as evidenced by the fact that 50 percent of patients with acute myelogenous leukemia developed IA, whereas those suffering neutropenia developed a second episode of IA during subsequent chemotherapy-induced granulocytopenia. Fourth, *Aspergillus* strains in the hospital environment may be genetically diverse.[82]

Diagnosis

As discussed, *Aspergillus* in histologic sections can be confused with other pathogenic molds. For this reason, confirmatory culture data are essential. The combination of histology and positive culture is the gold standard for diagnosis.[83]

The poor candidacy of many patients with suspected IA for surgical or other diagnostic procedures has increased interest in noninvasive testing. The galactomannan enzyme immunoassay (EIA) has been proven reliable in patients with hematologic malignancy; however, the reported sensitivity varies greatly (44 to 90 percent).[84,85] False-positive results have been reported in patients receiving semisynthetic penicillins (piperacillin-tazobactam and amoxicillin-clavulanate) and in those infected with the dimorphic fungi *Histoplasma capsulatum* or *Blastomyces dermatididis* due to the presence of galactomannan in these species as well.[86] Serial EIA testing of high-risk patients is recommended, though the testing frequency remains unclear and murine models have demonstrated the utility of daily screening given the rapid tissue destruction of invasive pulmonary aspergillosis (IPA) in neutropenic hosts.[87] Serum galactomannan determination also provides prognostic information with declining values associated with improvements in patient outcomes.[88]

Serum BDG (a component of the fungal cell wall) determination also may be helpful, though this marker is not specific for *Aspergillus* and its presence may indicate a number of invasive fungal infections.[89] The negative predictive value of BDG has generated interest in its use as a screening test in high-risk patients.[90]

PCR-based methods have also been evaluated and appear promising, but testing is not yet cleared by the U.S. Food and Drug Administration for the diagnosis of *Aspergillus*.[91] The use of multiple concurrent modalities has not been prospectively evaluated but may be a significant advance in noninvasive diagnostic testing for *Aspergillus* spp.[92] Caution must be exercised in the interpretation of radiographic imaging, as chest radiographs may be unremarkable in patients with pulmonary symptoms, whereas CT scans or magnetic resonance imaging (MRI) show extensive pulmonary involvement. CT scan of the chest can be diagnostic if the halo sign (a zone of intermediate attenuation surrounding a higher-attenuation mass and separating it from the surrounding parenchyma) is seen.[93]

MRI has yet to be studied extensively in IPA. The diagnosis of IPA with use of MRI may be rather problematic, because MRI findings are not as characteristic as the CT findings during the early course of IPA.[94]

Clinical Manifestations

Sinus involvement by *Aspergillus* can present as allergic fungal sinusitis with rhinorrhea and nasal obstruction or invasive sinusitis with vascular invasion.[95]

Several forms of pulmonary *Aspergillus* disease are described. Allergic bronchopulmonary aspergillosis is seen in patients with preexisting asthma in association with eosinophilia, elevated immunoglobulin E (IgE), and fleeting pulmonary infiltrates. Patients often cough up hyphal plugs, and the treatment of choice is itraconazole in an attempt to avoid corticosteroids.[96]

Aspergillomas are fungal balls that may form their own cavity or develop in a preexisting lung cavity (e.g., bullous emphysema or sarcoidosis). Patients often present with hemoptysis, and the treatment of choice is surgical because of poor penetration of antifungals into cysts or cavities. Patients with chronic granulomatous disease are more prone to IPA with pneumonia and insidious onset of fever.[97]

IPA is associated with immunosuppression, steroids, and neutropenia. Patients develop fever, dense pulmonary infiltrates, hemoptysis, and/or pleuritic chest pain; however, the lack of an immunologic response due to underlying-host defects mandates a high level of clinical suspicion for infection. The disease is rapidly fatal if untreated. As neutropenia resolves, lesions tend to cavitate.[98] IPA mortality ranges from 65 to 100 percent but is invariably fatal if neutropenia persists.[99,100]

Disseminated disease involves multiple organ systems, but concurrent lung involvement is almost always observed.

A major patient group recently recognized as being high risk for IPA includes those with chronic obstructive pulmonary diseases (COPD) or those with a prolonged course in the ICU.[101]

Pathogenesis

Aspergillus conidia are ubiquitous, and thus environmental exposure is largely unavoidable. In allergic bronchopulmonary aspergillosis, the fungus does not invade lung tissue but remains in paranasal sinuses and ectatic bronchi, eliciting an IgE antibody-dependent reaction with prominent sputum eosinophils.

In immunosuppressed patients, germination occurs, followed by vascular invasion and tissue infarction, necrosis, and hemorrhage. In autopsy studies of patients with IA, the majority ultimately succumb to pulmonary hemorrhage.[102]

Neutrophils and macrophages are of paramount importance in host defenses against aspergillosis. Granulocytes damage hyphae by phagocytosis and oxidative killing.[103]

Cell-mediated immunity probably plays a role, albeit a lesser one, as evidenced by the fact that AIDS patients are more prone to IA owing to leukocyte and macrophage dysfunction secondary to abnormalities of T-cell function and increasing use of corticosteroids.[104]

Also, the use of OKT3, which decreases T-cell immunity, predisposes patients who undergo liver transplantation to IA independent of steroid use.[105]

Treatment

The gold standard of therapy previously was high-dose (1.0 to 1.5 mg/kg/d) intravenous AmB deoxycholate; however, a major factor contributing to the lack of success with AmB deoxycholate was dose-limiting toxicity, especially nephrotoxicity.

Voriconazole, available both orally and intravenously, is now considered the drug of first choice for IA. A prospective randomized study showed superiority when compared with AmB deoxycholate and significantly reduced mortality at 12 weeks.[106] Duration of therapy depends on the immune status of the patient involved and often continues for several weeks or months.[68] Blood levels of voriconazole must be obtained frequently to both ensure that adequate levels have been achieved (greater than 2 µg/mL) and attempt to avoid toxicity (which occurs more frequently with levels greater than 5 µg/mL).[107] There are multiple potential drug interactions with concomitant-administered drugs, and potentially interactions should be reviewed before prescribing.

Posaconazole is another broad-spectrum triazole related to itraconazole. It has similar in vitro activity as voriconazole and enjoys a safer toxicity profile; however, posaconazole is not available parenterally. Although used as treatment for IA in some cases, posaconazole is typically used for antifungal prophylaxis in patients with acute myelogenous leukemia or with graft-versus-host disease.[108,109]

Itraconazole, an orally available azole considered second-line therapy for IA,[110] has good in vitro activity against *Aspergillus*. Side effects include edema, nausea and vomiting, rash, hypokalemia, and elevated liver function tests. Side effects are more commonly seen with doses exceeding 400 mg/day. Failure rates with itraconazole are in the 30 percent range. Itraconazole, now only available as an oral preparation, is not a first-line therapy but occasionally is used as maintenance after initial induction therapy.

Experience with echinocandins for aspergillosis is limited to retrospective series; however, a combination therapy trial evaluating voriconazole plus anidulafungin versus voriconazole alone has recently been completed, though the results have not yet been published.

Lipid formulations of AmB (liposomal AmB and lipid complex AmB) at higher doses of 5 mg/kg/d have largely replaced AmB deoxycholate, demonstrating considerably less but not absent nephrotoxicity.[68]

Prevention and Risk Reduction

Strategies to decrease the incidence of IA fall into three broad categories: (1) decreasing the duration of neutropenia/corticosteroid use, (2) decreasing exposure of patients to conidia, and (3) prophylaxis in high-risk patients. Emphasis should be placed on prevention, because infection carries a high mortality.

Strategies for prevention of aspergillosis in healthcare settings include education of the staff to suspect the disease in patients with predisposing conditions. Susceptible patients should be protected against exposure. Exposures include conidia, which may be found in the air and water. Management of the air delivered to patients with BMT is particularly important. BMT patients should be placed in rooms with at least 12 air exchanges per hour, with high-efficiency particulate air (HEPA) filtration, ideally with positive pressure when compared to the corridor, and well-sealed windows. Doors should remain closed whenever possible. In centers that provide BMT, construction should be thoroughly monitored, and an infection control risk assessment is strongly recommended for all construction projects. Construction projects require solid barriers and negative pressure ventilation. It is important to note that even projects outside the building may increase the air contamination if located close to the air intake, so the air intake may need to be sealed. Planning for construction should be performed by a multidisciplinary team, including infection control. BMT patients should avoid construction sites, and supplies should not be transferred through construction sites to avoid contamination. Spore control activities should be enhanced, with particular emphasis on proper ventilation (usually negative and ventilating outside) on indoor construction sites. Carpeting should be avoided in BMT areas, and dust-generating activities should be precluded. Water leaks should be promptly repaired to avoid mold growth.[111]

Hand hygiene, avoidance of crowded areas of the hospital, proper cleaning, and disinfection of equipment are also important. Flowers and potted plants should not be allowed in areas where immunosuppressed patients are admitted, as they may harbor *Aspergillus* spp. and other fungi.[111,112]

Decreased risk of IA has also been shown in liver transplant patients with the use of tacrolimus for posttransplant immunosuppression, probably by decreasing the need for steroids.[113]

Decreased incidence of pulmonary IA has also been shown with nebulized AmB as well as low-dose IV AmB.[114] Randomized control studies have shown efficacy in preventing invasive fungal infection, especially aspergillosis, with daily oral posaconazole, which was superior to fluconazole and itraconazole in both patients with prolonged neutropenia or graft-versus-host disease receiving steroid therapy.[108,109]

Patients who suffered IA while undergoing chemotherapy should be given prophylaxis during subsequent treatments until resolution of neutropenia.[68]

Endemic Mycoses

Because endemic mycoses are generally not passed person to person in the healthcare setting, a full discussion of *blastomycosis, histoplasmosis, cryptococcosis,* and *coccidioidomycosis* is beyond the scope of this chapter. However, several interesting cases are presented in brief.

Cases of disseminated, fatal *coccidioidomycosis* have occurred in organ transplant recipients from unrecognized donor infection at the time of transplant; in fact, isogenicity has been proven by whole-genome sequencing.[115] Transplant patients have also been reported to develop invasive cryptococcosis from asymptomatic organ donors.[116] These cases typically present very early after transplantation, with disease that appears to occur preferentially in liver transplant recipients and involves unusual sites, such as the transplanted organ or the surgical site. These patients may have unrecognized pretransplant or donor-derived cryptococcosis.

Past reports have also observed outbreaks of histoplasmosis in an inpatient facility. Fifty-seven pediatric patients, the majority undergoing treatment for acute leukemia, were diagnosed with histoplasmosis. In this population, histopathologic examination of localized lung tissue and *Histoplasma* urine antigen testing were helpful in making the diagnosis. Patients were treated with AmB followed by a prolonged course of azole drugs with a 100 percent success rate.[117]

These cases illustrate the varied presentation of endemic mycosis in today's hospitalized patients.

Miscellaneous Fungi Associated with Healthcare-associated Outbreaks

For diseases that occur sporadically, like invasive fungal infections caused by an unusual fungal agent, when two or more cases of an infection are detected, an outbreak should be suspected. A recent review of the literature was able to characterize 36 such outbreaks reported between 1990 and 2011 (excluding *Candida* and *Aspergillus*). Duration of the outbreaks was variable, and among the 18 outbreaks where the source was identified, 16 were due to contaminated devices or solutions, and two occurred through transmission from a nurse's hands. Most outbreaks occurred in ICUs, and the time between cases was a median of 30 days (this emphasizes the importance of maintaining a high level of suspicion). In surgical patients, infections are most likely due to inoculation or contact with contaminated substances; in immunocompromised patients, infection occurs through inhalation, injection, or ingestion of contaminated substances. Mortality is elevated and duration of the epidemic tends to be shorter when the source of the infection is detected.[118]

Invasive fungal infections by non-*candida*, non *Aspergillus* yeast and molds include Mucormycetes (in particular *Lichtheimia, Rhizomucor,* and *Rhizopus*), endemic mycosis and other molds (such as *Acremonium, Alternaria, Bipolaris, Fusarium, Scedosporum*), and some yeast (*Cryptococcus, Malassezia, Pneumocystis, Rhodotorula, Saccharomyces, Trichosporon*), among others.[69]

Exserohilum rostratum

E. rostratum was implicated in a large national outbreak of fungal meningitis occurring among patients receiving methylprednisolone spinal injections. The median time from injection to disease was variable (range 12 to 121 days). Fever, headache, worsening back pain, cauda equina syndrome, and posterior circulation stroke were reported among the first cohort of cases reported from a Tennessee clinic. Most patients had granulocytic pleocytosis on the cerebrospinal fluid, with high total protein and low glucose. Risk for infection was associated with the use of contaminated lots of methylprednisolone, female gender, translaminar epidural glucocorticoid injection, and multiple procedures.[119] The U.S. Centers for Disease Control and Prevention (CDC) reports that there were 741 cases reported in 20 states and that only 32 percent of the cases had laboratory-confirmed disease. The source of the infection was the New England Compounding Center in Framingham, Massachusetts, which compounded three lots of contaminated methylprednisolone for injections.[120]

Microsporum canis (Ringworm)

M. canis causes infections of keratinized areas of the body (skin, hair, nails) and fluoresces yellow-green under a Wood's lamp. An outbreak of six cases in a preterm level II nursery were traced to an asymptomatic nurse. All six patients had breaks in skin integrity at the site of infection.[115] An additional outbreak was reported from another NICU. The source was a nurse whose cat was sick with *M. canis;* the outbreak involved six patients, each of whom developed cutaneous involvement. The outbreak was controlled with contact isolation of affected cases, removal of the nurse from service, and treatment of her and her cat.[121] Several outbreaks in schools have been reported. In a recent report, six cats, four dogs, and four veterinarian students developed cutaneous involvement after contact with stray cats. The possibility of cutaneous infection transmission may be an important consideration when allowing animals in healthcare settings.[122]

Scedosporium spp.

Scedosporium is a fungus that most commonly causes mycetoma. Inhaled spores can lead to disseminated disease, which is rapidly fatal in immunocompromised patients. A case is described of healthcare-associated acquisition in a post liver transplant patient. The organism is a ubiquitous soil fungus that is resistant to AmB but sensitive to itraconazole, posaconazole, and voriconazole.[84] Healthcare-associated clusters of disease secondary to *Scedosporium* spp. have been reported. The case involved six patients with acute nonlymphocytic leukemia who developed disease after inhalation of the organism. Environmental air sample isolates were similar to those from affected patients.[123]

Saksenaea vasiformis

S. vasiformis is an agent in the order Mucorales that is isolated from soil. A case is described of a motorcycle accident patient who was on corticosteroids for closed head trauma who developed extensive necrosis on the 12th hospital day with *S. vasiformis* at a right wrist arterial line site.[124]

Other Mucorales have been associated with a wide array of HAIs and traumatic injuries, including those associated with tornadoes, other natural disasters, and shrapnel injuries, which have been increasingly reported. In a recent review that included cases of HAIs from 1970 to 2010, the most commonly reported organs involved included skin (57 percent), the GI tract (15 percent), and the lungs (8 percent). Outbreaks have been linked to adhesive bandages, ostomy bags and other adhesive devices, wooden tongue depressors, environmental contamination during construction, nasal packing, infected donor organs, central venous catheters, urinary catheters, insulin injections, peritoneal dialysis, and steroid injections, among others.[125]

R. oryzae and R. rhizopodoformis have been described to cause cutaneous disease outbreaks related to the use of elastoplast dressings.[126] Pulmonary or sinus disease related to Rhizopus is more common in patients with diabetic ketoacidosis, leukemia, and lymphoma.[127]

Early clinical signs of rhinocerebral mucormycosis include perinasal cellulitis/paraesthesia, periorbital edema, mucopurulent rhinorrhea, and nasal crusting.[128]

Several studies have reported an increased occurrence of sinocerebral and pulmonary mucormycosis. Of note, there are several reports of breakthrough infections in patients receiving maintenance voriconazole therapy.[129] The treatment of choice remains ablative radical surgery and high-dose IV lipid formulation AmB (5 mg/kg/d), in some cases with adjunctive therapy with an echinocandin. A delay in therapy results in considerable mortality. Monotherapy with posaconazole has shown encouraging results in salvage studies and in combination therapy with AmB; however, this medication is typically used only after control and stabilization of the initial disease process.[130]

Trichosporon spp.

Trichosporon spp. are yeasts that may cause fever and positive blood cultures; they are resistant to echinocandin antifungal agents. Fifteen patients are described with Trichosporon isolated over a 6-year period. Five patients were infected, five possibly infected, and five colonized. All 15 patients had malignancies; 100 percent of infected patients died. No environmental cultures were positive for Trichosporon.[131]

Recently, an outbreak of Trichosporon asahii was reported in India. It involved eight neonates that developed fungemia, six of which died. The authors hypothesized that the source of the outbreak was the laminar flow unit used for preparation of IV fluids.[132]

Fusarium spp.

Fusarium is a soil and water organism that can cause skin or pulmonary lesions in immunocompromised patients. It is one of the few molds identified on standard blood culture media that is most often not a contaminant and is variably susceptible to antifungals. Risk factors for infection include tissue damage, severe immunosuppression, and receipt of a graft from a human leukocyte antigen–mismatched or unrelated donor. A common clinical presentation includes persistent fever, skin lesions, and pulmonary infection. Blood cultures are positive in 40 percent of cases, and mortality remains high at 50 to 80 percent. In immunocompetent patients, infection is often preceded by penetrating trauma, though hospital water systems have been implicated.[133] Voriconazole and posaconazole show improved susceptibility; however, resistance remains a problem.[134]

Fusarium spp. also not uncommonly cause corneal and eye infections, generally initiated by some type of trauma or contaminated ocular solutions.[135] Other frequent fungal causes of corneal infection include Aspergillus, Curvularia, and Candida spp. Topical AmB is the treatment of choice for Candida spp., but topical natamycin (5 percent) is used for infections with filamentous fungi.[136]

A recent multistate outbreak of endophalmitis caused by Fusarium incarnatum-equiseti species complex and Bipolaris hawaiiensis has been reported, involving 32 patients in seven states who underwent vitrectomy with epiretinal membrane peeling using Brilliant Blue G (BBG) dye, or triamcinolone injection from Franck's Compounding Lab in Florida.[137]

Malassezia spp.

An outbreak of M. furfur involving three cases within 72 hours in a NICU has also been described. Risk factors included central venous catheter, low birth weight, and lipid emulsions. Person-to-person transmission was theorized, as two HCP were colonized. However, no typing was done.[138]

M. pachydermatis was responsible for a cluster of eight cases of infection and colonization in a NICU over a 6-month period. Molecular typing showed that the isolates were distinct. No etiology was determined; however, risk factors for infection included indwelling catheters and parenteral lipid formulations.[139]

Phaeohyphomycosis (Darkly Pigmented Organisms)

From 1996 to 2001, 101 cases of culture-proven central nervous system infections with phaeohyphomycosis were reviewed. Cladophialophora bantiana was the most frequently isolated pathogen, followed by Ramichloridium mackenziei. Fifty percent of cases occurred in immunocompetent hosts. A recent review of phaeohyphomycosis at the M.D. Anderson Cancer Center revealed that 11 percent of isolates were responsible for invasive, often disseminated disease in severely immunocompromised hosts.[140] An aggressive medical and surgical approach is warranted, though mortality still remains high. Voriconazole has good in vitro activity and may prove to be the drug of choice for these infections.[141]

Exophilia spp. have also been implicated in contaminated corticosteroid injections, as described above. Improper autoclaving techniques were utilized by the compounding pharmacy.[142] Olecranon bursitis caused by Exophilia oligospermia has been successfully treated with aspiration and intrabursal administration of AmB.[143]

An outbreak of eight cases of Exophilia jeanselmei infections occurred from December 1996 through September 1997 at a hospital in Brazil. Cases were associated with neutropenia, longer duration of hospitalization, and use of corticosteroids. The patient strains genetically matched a strain recovered from deionized water used in the pharmacy to prepare solutions.[144] Finally, infection with Alternaria and Phialophora spp. has also occurred in renal transplant patients, where infection presented with dark-colored subcutaneous nodules that subsequently ulcerated.[145] In all these infections, histopathologic staining of melanin in the cell wall with the Masson-Fontana stain can be useful to establish a diagnosis.

Bipolaris spp.

As outlined above, *Bipolaris hawaiiensis* was reported as the etiological agent in an outbreak of endopthalmitis. In a cluster from an ophthalmology practice in New York, eight patients developed endopthalmitis, three of which were secondary to *Bipolaris hawaiiensis* after intraocular injection of bevanzisumab and triamcinolone.[146]

Hyalohyphomycoses: *Acremonium, Penicillium* (Opportunistic Lightly Pigmented Molds)

Acremonium has been reported to cause fungemia in immunocompromised patients, and clusters of catheter-related BSIs in a hematopoietic stem cell transplant unit have been described.[147] There is a documented cluster of four cases of eye infection after laser surgery. The cases were performed in the same operating room by different surgeons, though unfortunately no definitive source was identified.[148]

Trichophyton rubrum

Outbreaks of cutaneous disease have occurred in a geriatric hospital,[149] though invasive disease in immunocompromised patients has been reported.[150]

Rhodotorula

Rhodotorula spp. cause BSI in immunocompromised patients with catheters. Ten bloodstream isolates were examined for susceptibility to various antifungal agents. MICs for AmB and posaconazole were lower than those for other triazoles or echinocandins, suggesting that they may be favored agents in treatment of these unusual infections.[151]

Blastoschizomyces capitatus

Twenty-six cases of infection with this unusual pathogen from a Spanish tertiary care hematology unit were reviewed. The majority of the patients had acute leukemia and developed infection during prolonged periods of neutropenia. The majority had fungemia. Outcome was improved with prompt removal of the central venous catheter, good performance status, and early therapy. Mortality remained high at 52 percent.[152]

CONCLUSIONS

The field of mycology has recently seen major advances in therapeutic options, diagnostic tools, and strategies for the prevention and treatment of IFIs. Despite these developments, mortality remains high—especially in severely immunosuppressed patients. The number of patients at risk continues to increase with the greater number of solid organ and BMT patients, the use of corticosteroids and other immune-modulating drugs, patients with advanced AIDS, and trauma. Infections caused by *Candida* spp. are more commonly seen in the healthcare setting and are of increased epidemiologic concern. Infections and/or outbreaks caused by some of the more unusual fungi have been well documented and should heighten our awareness of the role of the environment in organism transmission.

REFERENCES:

1. Pappas PG, Kauffman CA, Andes D, et al. Clinical practice guidelines for the management of candidiasis: 2009 update by the Infectious Diseases Society of America. *Clin Infect Dis* 2009 Mar 1;48(5):503–535.
2. Walsh TJ, Anaissie EJ, Denning DW, et al. Treatment of aspergillosis: clinical practice guidelines of the Infectious Diseases Society of America. *Clin Infect Dis* 2008 Feb 1;46(3):327–360.
3. Sudbery PE. Growth of Candida albicans hyphae. *Nat Rev Microbiol* 2011 Aug 16;9(10):737–748.
4. Sanchez V, Vazquez JA, Barth-Jones D, et al. Epidemiology of nosocomial acquisition of Candida lusitaniae. *J Clin Microbiol* 1992 Nov;30(11):3005–3008.
5. Saghrouni F, Ben Abdeljelil J, Boukadida J, et al. Molecular methods for strain typing of Candida albicans: a review. *J Appl Microbiol* 2013 Jun;114(6):1559–1574.
6. Banerjee SN, Emori TG, Culver DH, et al. Secular trends in nosocomial primary bloodstream infections in the United States, 1980-1989. National Nosocomial Infections Surveillance System. *Am J Med* 1991 Sep 16;91(3B):86S–89S.
7. Safdar N, Maki DG. The commonality of risk factors for nosocomial colonization and infection with antimicrobial-resistant Staphylococcus aureus, enterococcus, gram-negative bacilli, Clostridium difficile, and Candida. *Ann Intern Med* 2002 Jun 4;136(11):834–844.
8. Sievert DM, Ricks P, Edwards JR, et al. Antimicrobial-resistant pathogens associated with healthcare-associated infections: summary of data reported to the National Healthcare Safety Network at the Centers for Disease Control and Prevention, 2009-2010. *Infect Control Hosp Epidemiol* 2013 Jan;34(1):1–14.
9. Pfaller M, Wenzel R. Impact of the changing epidemiology of fungal infections in the 1990s. *Eur J Clin Microbiol Infect Dis* 1992 Apr;11(4):287–291.
10. Beck-Sagué C, Jarvis WR. Secular trends in the epidemiology of nosocomial fungal infections in the United States, 1980-1990. National Nosocomial Infections Surveillance System. *J Infect Dis* 1993 May;167(5):1247–1251.
11. Wisplinghoff H, Bischoff T, Tallent SM, et al. Nosocomial bloodstream infections in US hospitals: analysis of 24,179 cases from a prospective nationwide surveillance study. *Clin Infect Dis* 2004 Aug 1;39(3):309–317.
12. Pfaller M, Neofytos D, Diekema D, et al. Epidemiology and outcomes of candidemia in 3648 patients: data from the Prospective Antifungal Therapy (PATH Alliance®) registry, 2004-2008. *Diagn Microbiol Infect Dis* 2012 Dec;74(4):323–331.
13. Marchetti O, Bille J, Fluckiger U, et al. Epidemiology of candidemia in Swiss tertiary care hospitals: secular trends, 1991-2000. *Clin Infect Dis* 2004 Feb 1;38(3):311–320.
14. Michalopoulos AS, Geroulanos S, Mentzelopoulos SD. Determinants of candidemia and candidemia-related death in cardiothoracic ICU patients. *Chest* 2003 Dec;124(6):2244–2255.
15. Steinbach WJ, Roilides E, Berman D, et al. Results from a prospective, international, epidemiologic study of invasive candidiasis in children and neonates. *Pediatr Infect Dis J* 2012 Dec;31(12):1252–1257.
16. Benjamin DK Jr, Ross K, McKinney RE Jr, et al. When to suspect fungal infection in neonates: A clinical comparison of Candida albicans and Candida parapsilosis fungemia with coagulase-negative staphylococcal bacteremia. *Pediatrics* 2000 Oct;106(4):712–718.
17. Saiman L, Ludington E, Pfaller M, et al. Risk factors for candidemia in Neonatal Intensive Care Unit patients. The National Epidemiology of Mycosis Survey study group. *Pediatr Infect Dis J* 2000 Apr;19(4):319–324.
18. Leibovitz E. Strategies for the prevention of neonatal candidiasis. *Pediatr Neonatol* 2012 Apr;53(2):83–89.
19. Chow BD, Linden JR, Bliss JM. Candida parapsilosis and the neonate: epidemiology, virulence and host defense in a unique patient setting. *Expert Rev Anti Infect Ther* 2012 Aug;10(8):935–946.

20. Cleveland AA, Farley MM, Harrison LH, et al. Changes in incidence and antifungal drug resistance in candidemia: results from population-based laboratory surveillance in Atlanta and Baltimore, 2008-2011. *Clin Infect Dis* 2012 Nov 15;55(10):1352–1361.
21. Patel PK, Erlandsen JE, Kirkpatrick WR, et al. The Changing Epidemiology of Oropharyngeal Candidiasis in Patients with HIV/AIDS in the Era of Antiretroviral Therapy. *AIDS Res Treat* 2012;2012:262471.
22. Pappas PG, Alexander BD, Andes DR, et al. Invasive fungal infections among organ transplant recipients: results of the Transplant-Associated Infection Surveillance Network (TRANSNET). *Clin Infect Dis* 2010 Apr 15;50(8):1101–1111.
23. Hota B. Contamination, disinfection, and cross-colonization: are hospital surfaces reservoirs for nosocomial infection? *Clin Infect Dis* 2004 Oct 15;39(8):1182–1189.
24. van Asbeck EC, Huang YC, Markham AN, et al. Candida parapsilosis fungemia in neonates: genotyping results suggest healthcare workers hands as source, and review of published studies. *Mycopathologia* 2007 Dec;164(6):287–293.
25. Schonian G, Meusel O, Tietz HJ, et al. Identification of clinical strains of Candida albicans by DNA fingerprinting with the polymerase chain reaction. *Mycoses* 1993 May-Jun;36(5-6):171–179.
26. Strausbaugh LJ, Sewell DL, Tjoelker RC, et al. Comparison of three methods for recovery of yeasts from hands of health-care workers. *J Clin Microbiol* 1996 Feb;34(2):471–473.
27. Hernández-Castro R, Arroyo-Escalante S, Carrillo-Casas EM, et al. Outbreak of Candida parapsilosis in a neonatal intensive care unit: a health care workers source. *Eur J Pediatr* 2010 Jul;169(7):783–787.
28. Taylor BN, Harrer T, Pscheidl E, et al. Surveillance of nosocomial transmission of Candida albicans in an intensive care unit by DNA fingerprinting. *J Hosp Infect* 2003 Dec;55(4):283–289.
29. Thompson B, Robinson LA. Infection control of parenteral nutrition solutions. *Nutr Clin Pract* 1991 Apr;6(2):49–54.
30. Nedret Koç A, Kocagöz S, Erdem F, et al. Outbreak of nosocomial fungemia caused by Candida glabrata. *Mycoses* 2002 Dec;45(11-12):470–475.
31. Sanchez V, Vazquez JA, Barth-Jones D, et al. Nosocomial acquisition of Candida parapsilosis: an epidemiologic study. *Am J Med* 1993 Jun;94(6):577–582.
32. Quirke P, Hwang WS, Validen CC. Congenital Torulopsis glabrata infection in man. *Am J Clin Pathol* 1980 Jan;73(1):137–140.
33. Vazquez JA, Dembry LM, Sanchez V, et al. Nosocomial Candida glabrata colonization: an epidemiologic study. *J Clin Microbiol* 1998 Feb;36(2):421–426.
34. Gudlaugsson O, Gillespie S, Lee K, et al. Attributable mortality of nosocomial candidemia, revisited. *Clin Infect Dis* 2003 Nov 1;37(9):1172–1177.
35. Morgan J, Meltzer MI, Plikaytis BD, et al. Excess mortality, hospital stay, and cost due to candidemia: a case-control study using data from population-based candidemia surveillance. *Infect Control Hosp Epidemiol* 2005 Jun;26(6):540–547.
36. Dodds Ashley E, Drew R, Johnson M, et al. Cost of invasive fungal infections in the era of new diagnostics and expanded treatment options. *Pharmacotherapy* 2012 Oct;32(10):890–901.
37. Kauffman CA, Fisher JF, Sobel JD, et al. Candida urinary tract infections--diagnosis. *Clin Infect Dis* 2011 May;52 Suppl 6:S452–S456.
38. Clancy CJ, Nguyen MH. Finding the "missing 50%" of invasive candidiasis: how nonculture diagnostics will improve understanding of disease spectrum and transform patient care. *Clin Infect Dis* 2013 May;56(9):1284–1292.
39. Ostrosky-Zeichner L, Alexander BD, Kett DH, et al. Multicenter clinical evaluation of the (1-->3) beta-D-glucan assay as an aid to diagnosis of fungal infections in humans. *Clin Infect Dis* 2005 Sep 1;41(5):654–659.
40. Nguyen MH, Wissel MC, Shields RK, et al. Performance of Candida real-time polymerase chain reaction, beta-D-glucan assay, and blood cultures in the diagnosis of invasive candidiasis. *Clin Infect Dis* 2012 May;54(9):1240–1248.
41. Gherna M, Merz WG. Identification of Candida albicans and Candida glabrata within 1.5 hours directly from positive blood culture bottles with a shortened peptide nucleic acid fluorescence in situ hybridization protocol. *J Clin Microbiol* 2009 Jan;47(1):247–248.
42. Kirkpatrick WR, Zimmerman JD, Haikal FP, et al. Screening for drug-resistant Candida yeasts with chromogenic agar. *Med Mycol* 2010 Sep;48(6):807–816.
43. Spanu T, Posteraro B, Fiori B, et al. Direct maldi-tof mass spectrometry assay of blood culture broths for rapid identification of Candida species causing bloodstream infections: an observational study in two large microbiology laboratories. *J Clin Microbiol* 2012 Jan;50(1):176–179.
44. Odds FC, Evans EG. Distribution of pathogenic yeasts and humoral antibodies to candida among hospital inpatients. *J Clin Pathol* 1980 Aug;33(8):750–756.
45. Lewis LE, Bain JM, Lowes C, et al. Stage specific assessment of Candida albicans phagocytosis by macrophages identifies cell wall composition and morphogenesis as key determinants. *PLoS Pathog* 2012;8(3):e1002578.
46. Wellington M, Dolan K, Krysan DJ. Live Candida albicans suppresses production of reactive oxygen species in phagocytes. *Infect Immun* 2009 Jan;77(1):405–413.
47. Lionakis MS, Netea MG. Candida and host determinants of susceptibility to invasive candidiasis. *PLoS Pathog* 2013 Jan;9(1):e1003079.
48. Kontoyiannis DP, Marr KA, Park BJ, et al. Prospective surveillance for invasive fungal infections in hematopoietic stem cell transplant recipients, 2001-2006: overview of the Transplant-Associated Infection Surveillance Network (TRANSNET) Database. *Clin Infect Dis* 2010 Apr 15;50(8):1091–1100.
49. Garey KW, Rege M, Pai MP, et al. Time to initiation of fluconazole therapy impacts mortality in patients with candidemia: a multi-institutional study. *Clin Infect Dis* 2006 Jul 1;43(1):25–31.
50. Andes DR, Safdar N, Baddley JW, et al. Impact of treatment strategy on outcomes in patients with candidemia and other forms of invasive candidiasis: a patient-level quantitative review of randomized trials. *Clin Infect Dis* 2012 Apr;54(8):1110–1122.
51. Thompson GR 3rd, Cadena J, Patterson TF. Overview of antifungal agents. *Clin Chest Med* 2009 Jun;30(2):203–215, v.
52. Pfaller MA. Antifungal drug resistance: mechanisms, epidemiology, and consequences for treatment. *Am J Med* 2012 Jan;125(1 Suppl):S3–S13.
53. Young LY, Hull CM, Heitman J. Disruption of ergosterol biosynthesis confers resistance to amphotericin B in Candida lusitaniae. *Antimicrob Agents Chemother* 2003 Sep;47(9):2717–2724.
54. Pfaller MA, Messer SA, Woosley LN, et al. Echinocandin and triazole antifungal susceptibility profiles for clinical opportunistic yeast and mold isolates collected from 2010 to 2011: application of new CLSI clinical breakpoints and epidemiological cutoff values for characterization of geographic and temporal trends of antifungal resistance. *J Clin Microbiol* 2013 Aug;51(8):2571–2581.
55. Orozco AS, Higginbotham LM, Hitchcock CA, et al. Mechanism of fluconazole resistance in Candida krusei. *Antimicrob Agents Chemother* 1998 Oct;42(10):2645–2649.
56. Pfaller MA, Lockhart SR, Pujol C, et al. Hospital specificity, region specificity, and fluconazole resistance of Candida albicans bloodstream isolates. *J Clin Microbiol* 1998 Jun;36(6):1518–1529.
57. Powderly WG, Kobayashi GS, Herzig GP, et al. Amphotericin B-resistant yeast infection in severely immunocompromised patients. *Am J Med* 1988 May;84(5):826–832.
58. Pfaller MA, Diekema DJ, Gibbs DL, et al. Results from the ARTEMIS DISK Global Antifungal Surveillance Study, 1997 to 2007: a 10.5-year analysis of susceptibilities of Candida Species to fluconazole and voriconazole as determined by CLSI standardized disk diffusion. *J Clin Microbiol* 2010 Apr;48(4):1366–1377.
59. Odds FC. In Candida albicans, resistance to flucytosine and terbinafine is linked to MAT locus homozygosity and multilocus sequence typing clade 1. *FEMS Yeast Res* 2009 Oct;9(7):1091–1101.
60. Sobel JD, Chaim W, Nagappan V, et al. Treatment of vaginitis caused by Candida glabrata: use of topical boric acid and flucytosine. *Am J Obstet Gynecol* 2003 Nov;189(5):1297–1300.
61. Thompson GR 3rd, Wiederhold NP, Vallor AC, et al. Development of caspofungin resistance following prolonged therapy for invasive candidiasis secondary to Candida glabrata infection. *Antimicrob Agents Chemother* 2008 Oct;52(10):3783–3785.
62. Goodman JL, Winston DJ, Greenfield RA, et al. A controlled trial of fluconazole to prevent fungal infections in patients undergoing bone marrow transplantation. *N Engl J Med* 1992 Mar 26;326(13):845–851.
63. Schuster MG, Edwards JE Jr, Sobel JD, et al. Empirical fluconazole versus placebo for intensive care unit patients: a randomized trial. *Ann Intern Med* 2008 Jul 15;149(2):83–90.
64. Wingard JR, Merz WG, Rinaldi MG, et al. Association of Torulopsis glabrata infections with fluconazole prophylaxis in neutropenic bone marrow transplant patients. *Antimicrob Agents Chemother* 1993 Sep;37(9):1847–1849.
65. Freifeld AG, Bow EJ, Sepkowitz KA, et al. Clinical practice guideline for the use of antimicrobial agents in neutropenic patients with cancer: 2010 update by the infectious diseases society of america. *Clin Infect Dis* 2011 Feb 15;52(4):e56–e93.
66. Clerihew L, Austin N, McGuire W. Prophylactic systemic antifungal agents to prevent mortality and morbidity in very low birth weight infants. *Cochrane Database Syst Rev* 2007 Oct 17;(4):CD003850.
67. Dykewicz CA. Summary of the guidelines for preventing opportunistic infections among hematopoietic stem cell transplant recipients. *Clin Infect Dis* 2001 Jul 15;33(2):139–144.
68. Walsh TJ, Anaissie EJ, Denning DW, et al. Treatment of aspergillosis: clinical practice guidelines of the Infectious Diseases Society of America. *Clin Infect Dis* 2008 Feb 1;46(3):327–360.

69. Azie N, Neofytos D, Pfaller M, et al. The PATH (Prospective Antifungal Therapy) Alliance® registry and invasive fungal infections: update 2012. *Diagn Microbiol Infect Dis* 2012 Aug;73(4):293–300.

70. Neofytos D, Horn D, Anaissie E, et al. Epidemiology and outcome of invasive fungal infection in adult hematopoietic stem cell transplant recipients: analysis of Multicenter Prospective Antifungal Therapy (PATH) Alliance registry. *Clin Infect Dis* 2009 Feb 1;48(3):265–273.

71. Lewis RE, Cahyame-Zuniga L, Leventakos K, et al. Epidemiology and sites of involvement of invasive fungal infections in patients with haematological malignancies: a 20-year autopsy study. *Mycoses* 2013 Nov;56(6):638–645.

72. Weems JJ Jr, Andremont A, Davis BJ, et al. Pseudoepidemic of aspergillosis after development of pulmonary infiltrates in a group of bone marrow transplant patients. *J Clin Microbiol* 1987 Aug;25(8):1459–1462.

73. Lentino JR, Rosenkranz MA, Michaels JA, et al. Nosocomial aspergillosis: a retrospective review of airborne disease secondary to road construction and contaminated air conditioners. *Am J Epidemiol* 1982 Sep;116(3):430–437.

74. Pelaez T, Muñoz P, Guinea J, et al. Outbreak of invasive aspergillosis after major heart surgery caused by spores in the air of the intensive care unit. *Clin Infect Dis* 2012 Feb 1;54(3):e24–e31.

75. Weems JJ, Jr., Davis BJ, Tablan OC, et al. Construction activity: an independent risk factor for invasive aspergillosis and zygomycosis in patients with hematologic malignancy. *Infect Control* 1987 Feb;8(2):71–75.

76. Arnow PM, Sadigh M, Costas C, et al. Endemic and epidemic aspergillosis associated with in-hospital replication of Aspergillus organisms. *J Infect Dis* 1991 Nov;164(5):998–1002.

77. Sarubbi FA Jr, Kopf HB, Wilson MB, et al. Increased recovery of Aspergillus flavus from respiratory specimens during hospital construction. *Am Rev Respir Dis* 1982 Jan;125(1):33–38.

78. Mahoney DH Jr, Steuber CP, Starling KA, et al. An outbreak of aspergillosis in children with acute leukemia. *J Pediatr* 1979 Jul;95(1):70–72.

79. Arnow PM, Houchins SG, Richards JM, et al. Aspergillus fumigatus contamination of lymphokine-activated killer cells infused into cancer patients. *J Clin Microbiol* 1991 May;29(5):1038–1041.

80. Rotstein C, Cummings KM, Tidings J, et al. An outbreak of invasive aspergillosis among allogeneic bone marrow transplants: a case-control study. *Infect Control* 1985 Sep;6(9):347–355.

81. Baddley JW, Pappas PG, Smith AC, et al. Epidemiology of Aspergillus terreus at a university hospital. *J Clin Microbiol* 2003 Dec;41(12):5525–5529.

82. Panackal AA, Li H, Kontoyiannis DP, et al. Geoclimatic influences on invasive aspergillosis after hematopoietic stem cell transplantation. *Clin Infect Dis* 2010 Jun 15;50(12):1588–1597.

83. De Pauw B, Walsh TJ, Donnelly JP, et al. Revised definitions of invasive fungal disease from the European Organization for Research and Treatment of Cancer/Invasive Fungal Infections Cooperative Group and the National Institute of Allergy and Infectious Diseases Mycoses Study Group (EORTC/MSG) Consensus Group. *Clin Infect Dis* 2008 Jun 15;46(12):1813–1821.

84. Herbrecht R, Letscher-Bru V, Oprea C, et al. Aspergillus galactomannan detection in the diagnosis of invasive aspergillosis in cancer patients. *J Clin Oncol* 2002 Apr 1;20(7):1898–1906.

85. Maertens J, Verhaegen J, Lagrou K, et al. Screening for circulating galactomannan as a noninvasive diagnostic tool for invasive aspergillosis in prolonged neutropenic patients and stem cell transplantation recipients: a prospective validation. *Blood* 2001 Mar 15;97(6):1604–1610.

86. Verweij PE, Mennink-Kersten MA. Issues with galactomannan testing. *Med Mycol* 2006 Sep;44 Suppl:179–183.

87. Hope WW, Petraitis V, Petraitiene R, et al. The initial 96 hours of invasive pulmonary aspergillosis: histopathology, comparative kinetics of galactomannan and (1->3) beta-d-glucan and consequences of delayed antifungal therapy. *Antimicrob Agents Chemother* 2010 Nov;54(11):4879–4886.

88. Koo S, Bryar JM, Baden LR, et al. Prognostic features of galactomannan antigenemia in galactomannan-positive invasive aspergillosis. *J Clin Microbiol* 2010 Apr;48(4):1255–1260.

89. Odabasi Z, Mattiuzzi G, Estey E, et al. Beta-D-glucan as a diagnostic adjunct for invasive fungal infections: validation, cutoff development, and performance in patients with acute myelogenous leukemia and myelodysplastic syndrome. *Clin Infect Dis* 2004 Jul 15;39(2):199–205.

90. Obayashi T, Yoshida M, Mori T, et al. Plasma (1-->3)-beta-D-glucan measurement in diagnosis of invasive deep mycosis and fungal febrile episodes. *Lancet* 1995 Jan 7;345(8941):17–20.

91. Donnelly JP. Polymerase chain reaction for diagnosing invasive aspergillosis: getting closer but still a ways to go. *Clin Infect Dis* 2006 Feb 15;42(4):487–489.

92. Thompson GR 3rd, Patterson TF. Pulmonary aspergillosis: recent advances. *Semin Respir Crit Care Med* 2011 Dec;32(6):673–681.

93. Georgiadou SP, Sipsas NV, Marom EM, et al. The diagnostic value of halo and reversed halo signs for invasive mold infections in compromised hosts. *Clin Infect Dis* 2011 May;52(9):1144–1155.

94. Blum U, Windfuhr M, Buitrago-Tellez C, et al. Invasive pulmonary aspergillosis. MRI, CT, and plain radiographic findings and their contribution for early diagnosis. *Chest* 1994 Oct;106(4):1156–1161.

95. Thompson GR 3rd, Patterson TF. Fungal disease of the nose and paranasal sinuses. *J Allergy Clin Immunol* 2012 Feb;129(2):321–326.

96. Stevens DA, Schwartz HJ, Lee JY, et al. A randomized trial of itraconazole in allergic bronchopulmonary aspergillosis. *N Engl J Med* 2000 Mar 16;342(11):756–762.

97. Segal BH, DeCarlo ES, Kwon-Chung KJ, et al. Aspergillus nidulans infection in chronic granulomatous disease. *Medicine (Baltimore)* 1998 Sep;77(5):345–354.

98. Caillot D, Couaillier JF, Bernard A, et al. Increasing volume and changing characteristics of invasive pulmonary aspergillosis on sequential thoracic computed tomography scans in patients with neutropenia. *J Clin Oncol* 2001 Jan 1;19(1):253–259.

99. Fukuda T, Boeckh M, Carter RA, et al. Risks and outcomes of invasive fungal infections in recipients of allogeneic hematopoietic stem cell transplants after nonmyeloablative conditioning. *Blood* 2003 Aug 1;102(3):827–833.

100. Marr KA, Carter RA, Boeckh M, et al. Invasive aspergillosis in allogeneic stem cell transplant recipients: changes in epidemiology and risk factors. *Blood* 2002 Dec 15;100(13):4358–4366.

101. Meersseman W, Lagrou K, Maertens J, et al. Invasive aspergillosis in the intensive care unit. *Clin Infect Dis* 2007 Jul 15;45(2):205–216.

102. Weinberger M, Elattar I, Marshall D, et al. Patterns of infection in patients with aplastic anemia and the emergence of Aspergillus as a major cause of death. *Medicine (Baltimore)* 1992 Jan;71(1):24–43.

103. Segal BH. Role of macrophages in host defense against aspergillosis and strategies for immune augmentation. *Oncologist* 2007;12 Suppl 2:7–13.

104. Mylonakis E, Barlam TF, Flanigan T, et al. Pulmonary aspergillosis and invasive disease in AIDS: review of 342 cases. *Chest* 1998 Jul;114(1):251–262.

105. Kusne S, Torre-Cisneros J, Mañez R, et al. Factors associated with invasive lung aspergillosis and the significance of positive Aspergillus culture after liver transplantation. *J Infect Dis* 1992 Dec;166(6):1379–1383.

106. Herbrecht R, Denning DW, Patterson TF, et al. Voriconazole versus amphotericin B for primary therapy of invasive aspergillosis. *N Engl J Med* 2002 Aug 8;347(6):408–415.

107. Lat A, Thompson GR 3rd. Update on the optimal use of voriconazole for invasive fungal infections. *Infect Drug Resist* 2011;4:43–53.

108. Cornely OA, Maertens J, Winston DJ, et al. Posaconazole vs. fluconazole or itraconazole prophylaxis in patients with neutropenia. *N Engl J Med* 2007 Jan 25;356(4):348–359.

109. Ullmann AJ, Lipton JH, Vesole DH, et al. Posaconazole or fluconazole for prophylaxis in severe graft-versus-host disease. *N Engl J Med* 2007 Jan 25;356(4):335–347.

110. Denning DW, Lee JY, Hostetler JS, et al. NIAID Mycoses Study Group Multicenter Trial of Oral Itraconazole Therapy for Invasive Aspergillosis. *Am J Med* 1994 Aug;97(2):135–144.

111. Tomblyn M, Chiller T, Einsele H, et al. Guidelines for preventing infectious complications among hematopoietic cell transplantation recipients: a global perspective. *Biol Blood Marrow Transplant* 2009 Oct;15(10):1143–1238.

112. Tablan OC, Anderson LJ, Besser R, et al. Guidelines for preventing health-care–associated pneumonia, 2003: recommendations of CDC and the Healthcare Infection Control Practices Advisory Committee. *MMWR Recomm Rep* 2004 Mar 26;53(RR-3):1–36.

113. Torre-Cisneros J, Mañez R, Kusne S, et al. The spectrum of aspergillosis in liver transplant patients: comparison of FK 506 and cyclosporine immunosuppression. *Transplant Proc* 1991 Dec;23(6):3040–3041.

114. Monforte V, Ussetti P, Gavalda J, et al. Feasibility, tolerability, and outcomes of nebulized liposomal amphotericin B for Aspergillus infection prevention in lung transplantation. *J Heart Lung Transplant* 2010 May;29(5):523–530.

115. Engelthaler DM, Chiller T, Schupp JA, et al. Next-generation sequencing of Coccidioides immitis isolated during cluster investigation. *Emerg Infect Dis* 2011 Feb;17(2):227–232.

116. Sun HY, Alexander BD, Lortholary O, et al. Unrecognized pretransplant and donor-derived cryptococcal disease in organ transplant recipients. *Clin Infect Dis* 2010 Nov 1;51(9):1062–1069.

117. Adderson EE. Histoplasmosis in a pediatric oncology center. *J Pediatr* 2004 Jan;144(1):100–106.

118. Repetto EC, Giacomazzi CG, Castelli F. Hospital-related outbreaks due to

rare fungal pathogens: a review of the literature from 1990 to June 2011. *Eur J Clin Microbiol Infect Dis* 2012 Nov;31(11):2897–2904.

119. Kainer MA, Reagan DR, Nguyen DB, et al. Fungal infections associated with contaminated methylprednisolone in Tennessee. *N Engl J Med* 2012 Dec 6;367(23):2194–2203.

120. Centers for Disease Control and Prevention (CDC). Spinal and paraspinal infections associated with contaminated methylprednisolone acetate injections - Michigan, 2012-2013. *MMWR Morb Mortal Wkly Rep* 2013 May 17;62(19):377–381.

121. Drusin LM, Ross BG, Rhodes KH, et al. Nosocomial ringworm in a neonatal intensive care unit: a nurse and her cat. *Infect Control Hosp Epidemiol* 2000 Sep;21(9):605–607.

122. Hermoso de Mendoza M, Hermoso de Mendoza J, Alonso JM, et al. A zoonotic ringworm outbreak caused by a dysgonic strain of Microsporum canis from stray cats. *Rev Iberoam Micol* 2010 Jun 30;27(2):62–65.

123. Guerrero A, Torres P, Duran MT, et al. Airborne outbreak of nosocomial Scedosporium prolificans infection. *Lancet* 2001 Apr 21;357(9264):1267–1268.

124. Oberle AD, Penn RL. Nosocomial invasive Saksenaea vasiformis infection. *Am J Clin Pathol* 1983 Dec;80(6):885–888.

125. Rammaert B, Lanternier F, Zahar JR, et al. Healthcare-associated mucormycosis. *Clin Infect Dis* 2012 Feb;54 Suppl 1:S44–S54.

126. Bottone EJ, Weitzman I, Hanna BA. Rhizopus rhizopodiformis: emerging etiological agent of mucormycosis. *J Clin Microbiol* 1979 Apr;9(4):530–537.

127. Passamonte PM, Dix JD. Nosocomial pulmonary mucormycosis with fatal massive hemoptysis. *Am J Med Sci* 1985 Feb;289(2):65–67.

128. Chang C, Gershwin ME, Thompson GR 3rd. Fungal disease of the nose and sinuses: an updated overview. *Curr Allergy Asthma Rep* 2013 Apr;13(2):152–161.

129. Marty FM, Cosimi LA, Baden LR. Breakthrough zygomycosis after voriconazole treatment in recipients of hematopoietic stem-cell transplants. *N Engl J Med* 2004 Feb 26;350(9):950–952.

130. van Burik JA, Hare RS, Solomon HF, et al. Posaconazole is effective as salvage therapy in zygomycosis: a retrospective summary of 91 cases. *Clin Infect Dis* 2006 Apr 1;42(7):e61–e65.

131. Walsh TJ, Newman KR, Moody M, et al. Trichosporonosis in patients with neoplastic disease. *Medicine (Baltimore)* 1986 Jul;65(4):268–279.

132. Vashishtha VM, Mittal A, Garg A. A fatal outbreak of Trichosporon asahii sepsis in a neonatal intensive care Unit. *Indian Pediatr* 2012 Sep;49(9):745–747.

133. Anaissie EJ, Kuchar RT, Rex JH, et al. Fusariosis associated with pathogenic fusarium species colonization of a hospital water system: a new paradigm for the epidemiology of opportunistic mold infections. *Clin Infect Dis* 2001 Dec 1;33(11):1871–1878.

134. Thompson GR 3rd, Wiederhold NP. Isavuconazole: a comprehensive review of spectrum of activity of a new triazole. *Mycopathologia* 2010 Nov;170(5):291–313.

135. Grant GB, Fridkin S, Chang DC, et al. Postrecall surveillance following a multistate fusarium keratitis outbreak, 2004 through 2006. *JAMA* 2007 Dec 26;298(24):2867–2868.

136. Thomas PA, Kaliamurthy J. Mycotic keratitis: epidemiology, diagnosis and management. *Clin Microbiol Infect* 2013 Mar;19(3):210–220.

137. Centers for Disease Control and Prevention (CDC). Notes from the field: Multistate outbreak of postprocedural fungal endophthalmitis associated with a single compounding pharmacy - United States, March-April 2012. *MMWR Morb Mortal Wkly Rep* 2012 May 4;61(17):310–311.

138. Richet HM, McNeil MM, Edwards MC, et al. Cluster of Malassezia furfur pulmonary infections in infants in a neonatal intensive-care unit. *J Clin Microbiol* 1989 Jun;27(6):1197–1200.

139. Chryssanthou E, Broberger U, Petrini B. Malassezia pachydermatis fungaemia in a neonatal intensive care unit. *Acta Paediatr* 2001 Mar;90(3):323–327.

140. Ben-Ami R, Lewis RE, Raad II, et al. Phaeohyphomycosis in a tertiary care cancer center. *Clin Infect Dis* 2009 Apr 15;48(8):1033–1041.

141. Revankar SG. Phaeohyphomycosis. *Infect Dis Clin North Am* 2006 Sep;20(3):609–620.

142. Centers for Disease Control and Prevention (CDC). Exophiala infection from contaminated injectable steroids prepared by a compounding pharmacy--United States, November 2002. *MMWR Morb Mortal Wkly Rep* 2002 Dec 13;51(49):1109–1112.

143. Bossler AD, Richter SS, Chavez AJ, et al. Exophiala oligosperma causing olecranon bursitis. *J Clin Microbiol* 2003 Oct;41(10):4779–4782.

144. Nucci M, Akiti T, Barreiros G, et al. Nosocomial outbreak of Exophiala jeanselmei fungemia associated with contamination of hospital water. *Clin Infect Dis* 2002 Jun 1;34(11):1475–1480.

145. Yehia M, Thomas M, Pilmore H, et al. Subcutaneous black fungus (phaeohyphomycosis) infection in renal transplant recipients:three cases. *Transplantation* 2004 Jan 15;77(1):140–142.

146. Sheyman AT, Cohen BZ, Friedman AH, et al. An outbreak of fungal endophthalmitis after intravitreal injection of compounded combined bevacizumab and triamcinolone. *JAMA Ophthalmol* 2013 Jul 1;131(7):864–869.

147. Ioakimidou A, Vyzantiadis TA, Sakellari I, et al. An unusual cluster of Acremonium kiliense fungaemias in a haematopoietic cell transplantation unit. *Diagn Microbiol Infect Dis* 2013 Mar;75(3):313–316.

148. Alfonso JF, Baamonde MB, Santos MJ, et al. Acremonium fungal infection in 4 patients after laser in situ keratomileusis. *J Cataract Refract Surg* 2004 Jan;30(1):262–267.

149. Peachey RD, English MP. An outbreak of Trichophyton rubrum infection in a geriatric hospital. *Br J Dermatol* 1974 Oct;91(4):389–397.

150. Nir-Paz R, Elinav H, Pierard GE, et al. Deep infection by Trichophyton rubrum in an immunocompromised patient. *J Clin Microbiol* 2003 Nov;41(11):5298–5301.

151. Zaas AK, Boyce M, Schell W, et al. Risk of fungemia due to Rhodotorula and antifungal susceptibility testing of Rhodotorula isolates. *J Clin Microbiol* 2003 Nov;41(11):5233–5235.

152. Martino R, Salavert M, Parody R, et al. Blastoschizomyces capitatus infection in patients with leukemia: report of 26 cases. *Clin Infect Dis* 2004 Feb 1;38(3):335–341.

Diarrheal Diseases: Viral

Anil Mangla, MD
Chief Epidemiologist
San Antonio Metropolitan Health District
San Antonio, TX

ABSTRACT

It is estimated that 10 percent of the population will have at least one episode of infectious diarrhea each year. Although many diarrheal diseases are self-limiting, some may be chronic and require ongoing treatment. Disease manifestations range from almost asymptomatic to severe and—in some cases—deadly. Viruses, parasites, or bacteria may be the infectious agents causing these episodes. Primary modes of transmission for most gastroenteritis agents are fecal-oral and foodborne; however, some agents may be spread from person to person. Because these agents are so different, viral agents, bacterial agents, and parasitic agents are examined in separate chapters.

KEY CONCEPTS

- Viruses are recognized as a leading cause of diarrheal disease in children.

- Rotavirus is the most common cause of severe diarrhea in children.

- Noroviruses cause the majority of viral gastroenteritis worldwide.

- Fecal-oral spread is the most common mode of transmission of viral gastroenteritis agents.

- Secondary transmission may occur with viral gastroenteritis agents.

- Acute gastroenteritis is one of the most common diseases in humans worldwide.

- Most cases of gastroenteritis resolve in 5 to 10 days.

BACKGROUND

Acute gastroenteritis is one of the most common diseases in humans worldwide. Viruses are recognized as a leading cause of this disease, particularly in children.[1] Viral gastroenteritis, which can vary from asymptomatic to severe disease leading to dehydration and death, affects people of all ages, but the severity is seen in those at the extremes of age, such as children and elderly persons.[1-3] Viral gastroenteritis occurs in two distinct epidemiologic patterns: endemic childhood diarrhea and epidemic disease.[4] Rotavirus is the most common cause of severe diarrhea in children. However, enteric adenoviruses, astroviruses, and Sapporo-like virus exhibit a similar pattern of disease.[4] Epidemic disease is best exemplified by the norovirus; there have been outbreaks associated with astroviruses and group B rotavirus.[2,5] Other viruses that have been identified as causative agents of diarrhea include toroviruses, coronaviruses, and picobirnaviruses.

BASIC PRINCIPLES

Calicivirus

Etiologic Agent

Human caliciviruses, members of the *Caliciviridae* family, have emerged as a major cause of viral gastroenteritis.[1,3] The two human genera, noroviruses (previously known as Norwalk-like viruses) and Sapporo-like viruses (SLVs), have been separated based on differences in genome organization, morphology, and genetic and antigenic properties.[3] These genera can be further divided into genetic clusters: the noroviruses, including the Norwalk virus (the prototype of the genus), Southampton virus, Snow Mountain agent, Hawaii virus, Toronto virus, Bristol virus, and Jena virus, and the SLVs (including the Sapporo virus [the prototype of the genus]), Parkville virus, and London virus.[1,6] The first norovirus, Norwalk virus, was named after the location of a "winter vomiting" outbreak in 1968 at an elementary school in Norwalk, Ohio.[7] The agent was finally identified in 1972 by the use of electron microscopy (EM).[8]

Noroviruses can be grouped into five genogroups (GI through GV), which are further divided into at least 34 genotypes. Human disease primarily is caused by GI and GII noroviruses, with most outbreaks caused by GII.4 strains. During the past decade, new GII.4 strains have emerged every 2 to 3 years, replacing previously predominant GII.4 strains. Emergence of these new norovirus strains has often, but not always, led to increased outbreak activity.[9]

Epidemiology

Noroviruses cause the majority of acute viral gastroenteritis disease worldwide.[10] This increased recognition of noroviruses is the result of recent availability of improved techniques to diagnose noroviruses. Human calicivirus cannot be grown in culture, and adequate viral detection methods are not always widely available; therefore, it has been difficult to establish the true burden of the disease.[2,11,12] In addition, the epidemiology of foodborne and waterborne diseases is changing rapidly with changes in human behavior, shifts toward a global economy, industry, and microbial adaptations.[13] The recent recognition of noroviruses as a major cause of outbreaks and sporadic disease has been the result of newer norovirus-specific diagnostic techniques.[14]

Noroviruses are now recognized as the most common cause of sporadic cases of diarrhea in the community.[3,15] Outbreaks have been associated with nursing homes, schools, cruise ships, camps, restaurants, military installations, and airplane travel.[14,15] According to the Centers for Disease Control and Prevention (CDC), 348 outbreaks were reported between January 1996 and November 2000.[14] During 2006, the CDC reported 114 confirmed norovirus outbreaks. This increase is associated with the emergence of two new cocirculating strains of GII.4. Seventy percent of these outbreaks were associated with norovirus variants (Minerva and Laurens).[16] A large proportion of these outbreaks in 2006 occurred in long-term care facilities.[16] Although outbreaks of calicivirus can occur year-round, marked seasonal patterns of outbreaks have been observed. In the northern hemisphere, norovirus-causing gastroenteritis—"winter vomiting disease"—is most common in the winter and early spring. In the southern hemisphere, outbreaks are seen most frequently in the spring/summer.[17]

CaliciNet is the outbreak surveillance network for noroviruses in the United States, launched in March 2009. From its inception to May 2010, 552 outbreaks were submitted to CaliciNet. Foodborne and person-to-person transmission were reported for 78 (14 percent) and 340 (62 percent) of the outbreaks, respectively, whereas the transmission route for the 134 remaining outbreaks was not reported. A total of 395 (72 percent) outbreaks were typed as GII.4, of which 298 (75 percent) belonged to a new variant, GII.4 New Orleans, which first emerged in October 2009.[18] More than half of all norovirus outbreaks reported in the United States occur in long-term care facilities.[19] Emergence of a new GII.4 strain, GII.4 Sydney, caused most (53 percent) of the norovirus outbreaks reported through CaliciNet during September to December 2012.[9]

Transmission

Fecal-oral spread, or aerosol formation after projectile vomiting, is the probable primary mode of viral transmission.[20-22] Norovirus is found in the stool and vomitus of infected persons. Primary infection results from exposure to or ingestion of a fecally contaminated vehicle, such as contaminated food or water,[11,20] whereas secondary infection results via person-to-person contact, aerosolized vomitus, fomites, and infected food handlers.[23] According to the CDC, of 348 outbreaks of norovirus from

January 1996 through November 2000, the sources of outbreaks were food (39 percent), person-to-person contact (12 percent), and contaminated water (3 percent). No direct mode of transmission could be identified in 18 percent of cases.[14]

Certain characteristics of noroviruses may facilitate the spread of the virus during epidemics: low infectious dose, prolonged asymptomatic shedding, environmental stability, substantial strain diversity, and lack of lasting immunity.[20] The virus is highly infectious, and a small inoculum—as few as 10 to 100 virions—is sufficient to cause infection.[16] Infected persons can remain contagious after recovery because asymptomatic viral shedding can continue for as long as 3 weeks.[3] In addition, the virus is relatively stable in the environment. It survives freezing, heating to 60°C, and chlorine.[20]

Disease Manifestations

Typically, the average incubation period of the virus is 12 to 48 hours,[24] with gradual or abrupt development of symptoms. Patients present with abdominal cramps with or without nausea, vomiting, and diarrhea (together or alone).[12] Vomiting is often a predominant feature. Clinical symptoms for norovirus infection last a median of 5 days, and those for SLV-related symptoms a median of 6 days.[3] The duration of shedding of SLV appears shorter than that of norovirus, with SLV shedding subsiding after 14 days and norovirus subsiding 3 weeks after the onset of illness.[3]

Most patients are resistant to reinfection for 4 to 6 months; however, there is no development of long-term immunity.[12,25] Serologic studies have shown that antibodies against norovirus are obtained early in life and reach prevalence close to 100 percent at the age of 9 to 10 years.[3,26,27] It appears that the antibodies do not correlate with protective immunity in adults because symptomatic norovirus infection occurs in adults.[3] There appears to be a fraction of individuals in clinical outbreaks and volunteer studies that are unaffected by norovirus exposure. Recent serological studies indicate that individuals who are nonsecretors of blood group A and B antigens have significantly lower antibody titers to norovirus (genogroup II) than do secretors, suggesting that nonsecretors are less prone to infection or resistant to norovirus infection.[12,28]

Infections are self-limiting, and most patients recover uneventfully without sequelae. Those who are unable to maintain hydration, typically very young and elderly persons, are at risk for dehydration, resulting in electrolyte disturbances that may require hospitalization.

Diagnosis

Human calicivirus cannot be grown in culture, nor are routine laboratory tests helpful in diagnosing infection. Advances in the diagnosis of noroviruses have progressed from EM, requiring the presence of 106 virus/mL or more of stool, to the ability to detect illness using nucleic acid detection by reverse transcriptase (RT)-polymerase chain reaction (PCR).[25]

EM is most beneficial in detecting the virus from its morphological characteristics but can only be successfully used in the very early part of the illness.[6] Immunoelectron microscopy (IEM) can improve the sensitivity of EM by 10- to 100-fold.[20] In this technique, immune serum is used to enhance the detection of the virus. However, the technique is only useful for specimens collected during the early stages of disease (first 24 to 48 hours).[12,20]

The immune adherence hemagglutination assay (IAHA) was developed to allow the evaluation of Norwalk antibody levels in greater numbers of sera.[6] This test uses purified norovirus as the antigen, and antigen/antibody complement interactions are detected by agglutination of sensitized human O erythrocytes.[6] This assay was replaced by radioimmunoassay (RIA). RIA has helped identify norovirus and related viruses as a common cause of nonbacterial gastroenteritis.

Noroviruses can be detected by enzyme immunoassay (ELISA).[20,25] This type of test can also be used to detect the presence of antibody in the infected patient by detecting a four-fold increase in immunoglobulin G (IgG) antibody titer between acute (within 5 days of onset) clinical illness and convalescence (3 to 6 weeks after acute illness). The disadvantage of the serologic assays currently available is that all antigenic types of noroviruses cannot be detected.[20]

RT-PCR assays to detect calicivirus have provided a sensitive and specific tool for noroviruses and SLV investigations. RT-PCR is the most sensitive diagnostic assay for the detection of human caliciviruses.[6] The advantage of the sequencing assays is that they can detect the viral particles from the stools of infected patients in numbers as low as 100 particles/mL, even after the acute clinical infection has resolved. Noroviruses can be detected in stool samples stored at 4°C for several months and at −70°C for many years.[6] The major disadvantages are (1) the assays require exquisite care to prevent contamination in the laboratory and (2) few laboratories are equipped to perform these analyses.[14] In addition, the available primers for RT-PCR assays detect multiple strains of calicivirus, and other strains can escape detection.[6] Thus, this technique is used primarily for epidemic outbreak investigations. RT-PCR and EIA have been used together to identify and quantify noroviruses with some success.[29]

Treatment

Treatment of human calicivirus infection is symptomatic, and its aim is to prevent or treat the dehydration secondary to the disease.[25] It is important to start liquid intake early to correct the water deficit that is often associated with vomiting and diarrhea. Rarely, parenteral intravenous therapy may be required. Currently, there are no vaccines for calicivirus.

Infection Prevention and Public Health Concerns

Noroviruses are highly contagious, with a low infectious inoculum of less than 100 viral particles[20]; therefore, interruption of transmission is extremely important. Direct spread from person to person from handling contaminated secretions or objects becomes important in outbreaks involving a closed environment, such as day care centers, nursing homes, and cruise ships.[5] Even inhalation of aerosolized infectious secretions has been implicated for person-to-person spread, especially in closed environments when an obvious common source of water or food cannot be readily implicated.[23]

To implement infection prevention measures, it is important to identify the etiologic agents involved in a viral infection outbreak. Noroviruses are able to survive in water and are relatively resistant to chlorination.[20] Thus, fecal contamination of large bodies of water used for drinking or recreational activities, such as swimming pools, may serve as the prime source of an outbreak. Shellfish, which are filter feeders, are efficient in concentrating the microbes from contaminated water.[12,20,25] The virus does not replicate in food as many bacteria do and is destroyed by thorough cooking. Ingestion of inadequately cleaned and cooked shellfish or fresh salads washed in contaminated water is often implicated in large foodborne outbreaks, as are food handlers with symptomatic or asymptomatic norovirus infection.[12]

Noroviruses have a very short incubation period and are highly infectious; therefore, any patient with undiagnosed acute gastroenteritis is best placed in appropriate precautions. It is essential that strict attention be paid to hand hygiene with use of soap and water before and after contact with the patient and/or inanimate objects that can be contaminated. It is also necessary to clean all surfaces with suitable disinfectants.[1,20,25]

Secondary transmissions are a concern.[30] For example, prevention of food contamination during preparation requires that food handlers maintain strict personal hygiene at all times. Ill workers should be excluded from food handling, and food preparers should minimize direct contact with ready-to-eat foods.[31] Keeping the spread of virus from being introduced into healthcare settings is difficult, and some advocate closing affected units to new patient admissions, excluding affected staff from work for 48 hours after recovery, and rigorous disinfection as key features of control.[32]

Outbreaks of norovirus have been traced to contaminated municipal drinking water, well water, lakes, swimming pools, and commercial ice.[20] In one recent study, it was estimated that 12 to 16 percent of norovirus gastroenteritis was introduced by contaminated food or water.[33] Methods that prevent sewage/fecal contamination of large bodies of water are less effective due to the inability to assay water for the presence of noroviruses and because of the relative resistance of the noroviruses to chlorination.[34] It is important to implement safeguards, including changes in tracing, screening, and recall of contaminated food products; closing of contaminated oyster beds; restricting elapsed time before previously infected people can return to work; and timely prevention and control measures in healthcare settings.[35]

When it is not possible to get laboratory confirmation of norovirus, the CDC recommends that health departments use Kaplan criteria to determine if an outbreak was possibly caused by the norovirus. There are four components of the Kaplan criteria: (1) a mean (or median) illness duration of 12 to 60 hours, (2) a mean (or median) incubation period of 24 to 48 hours, (3) more than 50 percent of people with vomiting, and (4) no bacterial agent found in stool culture. When all four are present, it is very likely that the outbreak was caused by norovirus. However, about 30 percent of norovirus outbreaks do not meet these criteria. If the criteria are not met, it does not mean that outbreak was not caused by norovirus.[36]

Rotavirus

Etiologic Agent

Rotavirus is a member of the *Reoviridae* family that causes gastroenteritis in infants and young children. Intact virus particles resemble a wheel with spokes and a rim when viewed by EM.[37] Rotaviruses exhibit great diversity. They exist in seven distinct serogroups, A through G, that differ antigenically, though human pathogens belong to groups A, B, and C.[38] Among the human pathogenic rotaviruses, at least 42 different serotype combinations have been identified; however, four serotype combinations (G1-G4) are predominant worldwide, representing more than 90 percent of infections.[39]

Epidemiology

In both developed and developing countries, almost all children are infected with rotavirus by 2 to 3 years of age.[37] It is the most common cause of severe dehydration among children worldwide, with a death rate of approximately 527,000 annually among children under 5 years of age with diarrhea as of 2004.[40] Each year in the world, approximately 111 million episodes are the cause of 25 million clinic visits and 2 million hospitalizations in children under 5 years of age as of 2000.[41] In the United States, during the prerotavirus vaccine era, four of five children were symptomatic for rotavirus gastroenteritis, one in seven required a clinic or emergency department visit, one in 70 was hospitalized, and one in 200,000 died from rotavirus infection, within the first 5 years of life.[42] The maximum incidence occurs in infants from the ages of 6 to 24 months, which correlates with the time that maternal antibody titers decline.[37] Whether or not breast-feeding protects infants from rotavirus diarrheas is unclear.[37]

Asymptomatic infection can also occur. Adults can be afflicted with symptomatic rotavirus infection, but the disease course is usually mild.[43] It is occasionally reported as the cause of traveler's diarrhea[44] and diarrhea caused among healthcare personnel.[45] Rotavirus has been detected as a cause of gastroenteritis among adults residing in aged-care facilities in 13 percent of outbreaks.[46] However, the highest incidence in adults is in parents of infected children.[47]

In temperate climate zones, seasonal pandemics are observed of repeatable onset and duration with a peak of cases in the cooler months of each year.[37] In tropical climates, seasonality is less pronounced, yet infection remains most common in the cooler and drier times of the year.[37] Dry weather may promote transmission, as the rotavirus particle is inactivated more quickly in conditions of relatively high humidity.[37]

Transmission

Virus transmission occurs primarily through the fecal-oral route but can also occur through close person-to-person contact[48,49] and through fomites.[49,50] Although rotavirus has been shown to reside in other locations, such as the urine and upper respiratory specimens, transmission has not been associated with its presence in these locations.[51] The reservoir for rotavirus is not fully understood; however, infected infants shed virus for a period of 4 to 10 days.[37] Community-wide outbreaks of rotavirus attributed to fecally contaminated water and perpetuated by person-to-person transmission have been reported but are uncommon.[52,53]

Disease Manifestations

Rotavirus infects and replicates in the villous epithelial cells lining the small intestine.[54,55] The mechanism by which rotavirus causes diarrhea is not well understood, though studies have suggested a variety of mechanisms, including reduction in absorptive surface, stimulation of intestinal secretion of fluids, impaired absorption, and endotoxic effects from the NSP4 protein, which is secreted by rotavirus.[37] The most common presentation among children begins with fever and vomiting for 2 to 3 days, followed by a nonbloody diarrhea.[56] Vomiting is more common and prolonged with rotaviral gastroenteritis than most other causes of pediatric gastroenteritis.[56] Diarrhea is usually profuse, with as many as 20 bowel movements per day, which causes an isotonic dehydration. Patients with syndromes that include profuse vomiting are at risk for the most severe dehydration. Repeat bouts of rotavirus gastroenteritis are usually less severe than initial disease.[57] Gastrointestinal symptoms are often preceded by cough and coryza, though the presence of the virus within cells of the respiratory system has not been shown to affect the spread of the virus.[56] Rotavirus is not usually associated with fecal leukocytes, but fecal leucoycytosis has been reported.[37]

In adults, rotavirus causes a wider spectrum of manifestations, making it difficult to describe a typical clinical presentation. Studies in normal, healthy adult volunteers subjected to rotavirus ingestion have yielded an onset of illness that is typically 2 to 6 days, with a duration of 1 to 5 days.[58,59] Symptoms in these adult studies most frequently consisted of diarrhea, headache, fever, nausea, malaise, and abdominal cramping.[58,59]

Children with immunodeficiencies may have rotavirus-induced chronic diarrhea.[37] Immunocompromised patients are at risk for sustained symptoms and dissemination of rotavirus.[37] Rotavirus infections in patients with human immunodeficiency virus (HIV) cause a chronic diarrhea and can be associated with recurrence in this patient population.[60]

Rotavirus-specific immunoglobulin M (IgM) is evident in serum and duodenal fluid.[61] Stool immunoglobulin A (IgA) titers peak at 14 to 17 days after initiation of disease but remain detectable for greater than 1 year.[62] Although the antibodies produced will cross-react with subsequent rotavirus infections, initial antibody responses are serotype specific and do not confer lifelong immunity.[63]

Diagnosis

There is no identifying symptomatology associated with rotavirus-induced acute gastroenteritis. Diagnosis requires identification of the etiologic agent from fecal matter or rectal swabs. A commercially available enzyme-linked immunosorbent assay (ELISA) is commonly used to test specimens for rotavirus antigen.[64] Latex agglutinin kits are also available but are somewhat less sensitive than other methods.[64] Commercial assays are directed at group A rotaviruses and do not detect nongroup A rotavirus types.[58,64] Because bacterial pathogen detection in stool specimens yields a low sensitivity, it has been postulated that testing stool for rotavirus antigen could be a very cost-effective practice.[58] However, the fact that adults do not shed as much virus as children when infected could influence this practice in older patient populations. More sensitive methods have been developed, including PCR, which is up to 1,000 times more sensitive than detection with ELISA.[65] PCR is currently used in epidemiologic studies and allows determination of P and G types and permits more definition of strain differences.[37]

Treatment

Fluid and electrolyte replacement with early nutritional support are the main focuses of treatment for self-limiting diarrheal conditions, in addition to providing symptomatic relief to infected patients. Two phases of treatment are recommended by the CDC: rehydration and maintenance.[66] Oral rehydration solutions of reduced osmolarity are indicated in the treatment of mild to moderate dehydration. An initial rapid rehydration should occur, over 3 to 4 hours.[66]

Infants should continue breast-feeding on demand even during acute rehydration. Older children should resume age-appropriate unrestricted diets, including complex carbohydrates, meats, yogurt, fruits, and vegetables; foods high in simple sugars should be avoided.[66] Early feeding decreases changes in intestinal permeability caused by infection,[67] reduces illness duration, and improves nutritional outcomes.[68]

Antibiotics and antisecretory agents are not indicated; however, antidiarrheals such as loperamide and diphenoxylate can be used to help control diarrhea, but these agents are rarely used in children.[66] Oral hydration solutions are effective in treating dehydration related to rotavirus gastroenteritis, even in the presence of moderate vomiting, and are preferred over intravenous rehydration.[37,66]

If oral rehydration is not successful and symptoms of dehydration persist, intravenous fluids and hospital admission may be needed. Oral doses of human serum immunoglobulin are not indicated for routine use but may have a role in treating chronic rotavirus diarrhea.[37] Oral immunoglobulin has been shown to be successful in decreasing the duration of illness in several patient groups, including immunocompetent and immunocompromised children, as well as adults undergoing bone marrow transplantation.[69,70]

Prevention by immunization is a critical approach to decreasing the impact of rotavirus infection. Currently there are two licensed vaccines available in the United States: RotaTeq and Rotarix.[37] RotaTeq is a pentavalent human-bovine (WC3) reassortant live-attenuated, oral vaccine developed by Merck Research Company.[38] RotaTeq contains four live reassortant rotaviruses (G1, G2, G3, and G4) and an attachment protein (P7).[38] In two phase III trials, the efficacy of RotaTeq against rotavirus gastroenteritis of any severity after completion of a three-dose regimen was 74 percent and against severe rotavirus gastroenteritis was 98 percent.[38] RotaTeq was licensed in February 2006 by the U.S. Food and Drug Administration (FDA) for use among infants in the United States and is routinely recommended as a three-dose schedule at 2, 4, and 6 months of age.[61] Rotarix, a live-attenuated human rotavirus vaccine, is an oral vaccine developed by Avant Immunotherapeutics and licensed to GlaxoSmith Kline Biochemicals, who further modified the strain.[38] Rotarix has been tested in 11 Latin American countries and Finland in phase III trials on more than 63,000 children. In a subset efficacy trial, the vaccine demonstrated a protection rate of 85 percent against severe rotaviral gastroenteritis and 100 percent protection against the most severe dehydrating rotaviral disease.[38] Rotarix was licensed in April 2008 by the FDA for use among infants in the United States and is routinely recommended as a two-dose schedule at 2 and 4 months of age.[71]

A CDC report indicates that there was delayed onset and diminished magnitude of rotavirus activity during the 2007 to 2008 and 2008 to 2009 seasons in the United States when compared with the median during 2000 to 2006. This appears to coincide with increasing use of rotavirus vaccine (RotaTeq) among infants during that time period.[72]

Although the CDC reported that the 2008 to 2009 season had 15 percent more positive rotavirus test results than the 2007 to 2008 season, the number of positive test results during each season remained substantially lower (60 to 64 percent lower) than the median observed during 2000 to 2006.[72] Figure 79A-1 depicts this decrease as well as the delayed onset of the 2007 to 2008 season, by 11 weeks, and the 2008 to 2009 season, by 6 weeks.[72]

The 2009 to 2010 season had a decline in positive rotavirus tests. The 2010 to 2011 season was eight weeks shorter than the prevaccine baseline. During the 2011 to 2012 season, the starting threshold was never achieved nationally.[73] During these last two seasons, there was a 74 to 90 percent reduction nationwide in the number of positive rotavirus tests compared to the prevaccine baseline. In addition, the number of tests performed declined annually 28 to 36 percent in the same period.[73] During the five postvaccine seasons from 2007 to 2012, a biennial pattern of increases in rotavirus activity occurred, still remaining substantially below prevaccine levels.[73]

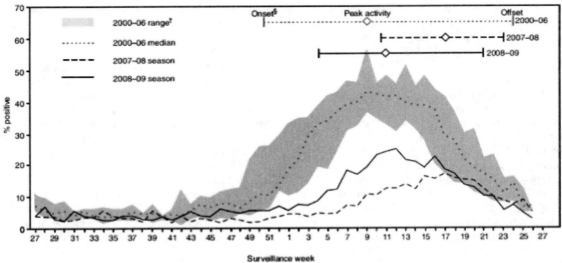

* A median of 67 laboratories (range: 62 to 72) contributed rotavirus testing data to NREVSS during July 2000 to June 2009.

† Range created using the maximum or minimum percentage of rotavirus-positive tests for each surveillance week during 2000–2006. Maximums and minimums for each week might have occurred during any of the six rotavirus seasons during 2000–2006.

§ The onset of rotavirus season was defined as the first of two consecutive weeks during which the percentage of stool specimens testing positive for rotavirus was ≥10 percent; offset was defined as the last of two consecutive weeks during which the percentage of stool specimens testing positive for rotavirus was ≥10 percent.

Figure 79A-1. Percentage of rotavirus tests with positive results, by surveillance week from participating laboratories, National Respiratory and Enteric Virus Surveillance System (NREVSS), United States, July 2000–June 2009.*[72]

Preliminary data presented by the CDC at the Association for Professionals in Infection Control and Epidemiology (APIC) meeting in June 2013 demonstrate a 73 percent mean annual reduction in number of rotavirus-positive tests compared to the prevaccine levels in the United States, as seen in Figure 79A-2.[74]

Some postmarketing studies have demonstrated a small risk of intussusception for infants from the two rotavirus vaccines.[75] The CDC's Vaccine Information Statement summarizes these and indicates that the risk of intussusception from rotavirus vaccination ranges from about 1 in 20,000 U.S. infants to 1 in 100,000 U.S. infants after vaccination. This risk is highest within a week after the first or second vaccine dose.[62] This small increased risk of intussusception is outweighed by the benefits of rotavirus vaccination.[75]

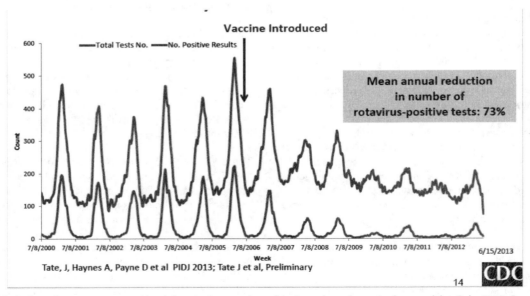

Figure 79A-2. Rotavirus tests at reporting laboratories, number of tests and number rotavirus-positive July 2000–June 2013.[74]

Infection Prevention and Public Health Concerns

Rotavirus transmission can be avoided by limiting exposure by the fecal-oral route. Contact with contaminated food and water should be avoided. Rotavirus survives in the environment on hard surfaces, in water supplies, and on the hands of humans.[76] Because a large proportion of virions survive on human hands for more than 60 minutes, hand washing is essential to the prevention of spread. Patients identified as infected should be placed in Contact Isolation during inpatient visits because of continuous fecal shedding. Infants infected with rotavirus shed the virus in high concentrations in the feces for as long as 7 days after onset of gastroenteritis.[37] Particular attention should be given to ensure handling of diapers in a proper manner.

Common hand-washing agents and disinfectants do not affect rotavirus, but 70 percent ethanol and chlorine-containing solutions are effective.[76] A human challenge study found the following compounds effective in interrupting transfer of rotavirus from stainless steel to a finger: a disinfectant spray (0.1 percent orthophenylphenol and 79 percent ethanol), sodium hypochlorite (800 ppm free chlorine), and a phenol-based product (14.7 percent phenol diluted 1:256 in tapwater). Quaternary ammonium product (7.05 percent quaternary ammonium compound diluted 1:128 in tap water) and tap water did not stop the spread of rotavirus.[77]

Well water can become contaminated with rotavirus. Killing or inactivating the virus requires boiling the water at a rolling boil for 1 minute; a point-of-use filter will not remove it.[78]

For infection control at the population level, routine infant rotavirus immunization is making a significant public health impact in infants.[75] In response to an outbreak of rotavirus gastroenteritis, postexposure vaccine prophylaxis is not a recommended strategy.[42]

Astroviruses

Etiologic Agent

Astroviruses are members of the family *Astroviridae* and are recognized as an important cause of gastroenteritis in adults and especially children.[79] Under EM, astroviruses have a characteristic five- or six-pointed star visible on some particles.[79] There are eight established genotypes corresponding with eight serotypes, with serotype 1 being the predominant serotype in most studies.[79]

Epidemiology

Astroviruses are found worldwide[80,81] and have been detected in diarrheal stools of children brought to medical attention in a variety of settings, including schools, daycare settings, and pediatric wards.[1,81] In hospital-based studies, rates of 2 to 16 percent were detected and in community-based studies rates of 5 to 17 percent were detected.[66] The viruses have also been found to cause illness in adults and immunocompromised patients, such as transplant patients and HIV-infected individuals.[82,83] Seroprevalence studies in the United States and elsewhere have demonstrated the presence of astrovirus antibodies in more than 90 percent of children by 9 years of age,[84] suggesting that infection, largely asymptomatic, is common.[79]

Transmission

Transmission of astrovirus is presumably by the fecal-oral route, and there have been associations with consumption of sewage-polluted shellfish and ingestion of water from contaminated sources.[79,85,86] The virus has been demonstrated to survive on inert surfaces long enough to suggest that fomites could play a role in secondary transmission.[85]

Disease Manifestations

The predominant symptom of astrovirus gastroenteritis is watery diarrhea; however, nausea, headache, malaise, and low-grade fever may occur; vomiting occurs less commonly.[79] In general, the symptoms are similar to those seen in rotavirus-infected children, but they are milder. The incubation period is approximately 3 to 4 days.[79] Disease manifestations usually last 5 days or less when coexisting pathogens are not present.[79] The duration of virus shedding, as assessed by PCR, may be a long as 35 days.[79] The pathogenesis of the disease induced by astrovirus has not yet been established.[1] Symptomatic disease occurs mainly in small children and elderly persons, which suggests a reduction in antibodies throughout the process of aging, but the determinants of immunity are not well known.[1] The fact that astrovirus has been associated with outbreaks of disease in older children and adults suggests that immunity to disease may be overcome by larger-than-normal inocula of infectious spread by atypical vehicles of infection.[4]

Diagnosis

Unlike other viral agents of gastroenteritis, astroviruses are often shed in large amounts in stool and can be readily detected by EM.[79] Detection of astrovirus in cell culture has been carried out by IEM or immunofluorescence.[79] An ELISA was developed in the 1990s and was found to have comparable sensitivity (91 percent) and specificity (98 percent) to IEM.[87] Reverse-transcriptase PCR is even more sensitive in detecting astrovirus.[79] Genotyping of the virus is also available.[4]

Treatment

Treatment of viral gastroenteritis caused by astroviruses is supportive, if needed. Treatment is similar to that of other viral gastroenteritis: prevent or treat the dehydration secondary to disease.[79] Fluid and electrolyte replacement with early nutritional support are the main focuses of treatment for self-limiting diarrheal conditions.[66] Illness is generally self-limited.

Infection Prevention and Public Health Concerns

Interruption of transmission of the infection is important, especially in hospitals and centers that care for small children. Therefore, it is essential to reinforce hygiene measures and clean all surfaces with suitable disinfectants.[1] Viruses from the gastrointestinal tract, including astrovirus, persist for approximately 2 months on surfaces. This can be a continuous source of transmission; reinforcing the importance of regular preventive surface disinfection.[88]

Enteric Adenoviruses

Etiologic Agent

Human adenoviruses were first isolated from adenoid tissues in 1953 and named for the tissue of its origin.[89] It is a nonenveloped icosahedral virus containing a 36-kb, double-stranded DNA genome. The *Adenoviridae* family is divided into five genera; those causing disease in humans are categorized into the *Mastadenovirus* genus.[90] The human mastadenoviruses are further divided into six subgenera (A through G) and 53 serotypes on the basis of antigenicity.[91] The serotypes 40 and 41 of subgenus F account for most cases of gastroenteritis in children. Serotypes 31, 12, and 18 of subgenus A and serotypes 1, 2, 5, and 6 of subgenus C have been identified as causative agents for gastroenteritis.[1,92]

Epidemiology

Enteric adenovirus infection occurs worldwide and has been associated with as many as 15 percent of cases of gastroenteritis in children.[93,94] It is considered to be the second most common cause of viral gastroenteritis, next to rotavirus.[94] Enteric adenovirus primarily affects children younger than 4 years, with very little seasonal variation.[95] Enteric adenovirus has been recognized as a causative agent of gastroenteritis in transplant recipients (both stem cell and solid organ)[96] as well as patients with AIDS.[97]

Transmission

Adenovirus is spread through droplet or fecal-oral transmission from individuals with acute infection or asymptomatic viral shedding postinfection.[92] Adenoviruses 40 and 41 are shed in feces in large numbers. They are frequently found in fecally polluted waters and have been detected in shellfish but have not been apparently associated with foodborne illness.[98] Fecal-oral transmission does account for sporadic diarrheal illness in children.[99] Convincing evidence of donor organ-associated transmission of adenovirus is supported by observations noting that infection often occurs early after transplantation and often involves the donor organ (e.g., lung or intestine).[96]

Disease Manifestation

A distinctive feature of enteric adenovirus infection is protracted diarrhea. The incubation period of 8 to 10 days is longer than that for other viral gastroenteritis,[73] as is the duration of diarrhea. Diarrhea may be associated with fever or vomiting and may last as long as 2 weeks.[92] The illness is generally mild and self-limited; however, it can be severe and persistent in immunocompromised hosts.[93,100] Adenoviruses are highly immunogenic and confer type-specific immune responses that result in lifelong protection.[101]

Diagnosis

Enteric adenoviruses (serotypes 40 and 41) cannot be cultured on standard human tissue culture cells. They require the culture cells transformed by adenovirus.[92] Diagnosis is usually made by ELISA, especially for serotypes 40 and 41 in stool samples. Serotypes can be identified by neutralization and hemagglutination inhibition assays or PCR.[93] PCR has become widespread due to greater sensitivity, specificity, and rapid turnaround.[92]

Treatment

Enteric adenovirus infection usually resolves without specific therapy. Treatment is supportive, as with other viral gastroenteritis.

Infection Prevention and Public Health Concerns

Contact and Droplet Precautions in addition to Standard Precautions should be practiced. Infected workers should not work until symptoms have resolved.[99] There is no vaccine available for the general public, nor any targeting of the types most likely to cause gastrointestinal disease. But as of 2011 a new live, oral vaccine against adenovirus types 4 and 7 is available to U.S. military personnel who are 17 to 50 years of age. It is administered to military recruits entering basic training in order to prevent acute respiratory disease.[102]

Toroviruses

Although toroviruses are among the established agents of gastroenteritis in animals, the role in diarrheal illness in humans remains to be elucidated.[103] The few controlled studies have shown that toroviruses have a more consistent association with illness than enteric coronaviruses.[104]

Their associations with neonatal necrotizing enterocolitis, healthcare-associated gastroenteritis, and acute and persistent diarrhea in children have been reported.[103,105–107] A 2012 study using direct EM reported finding toroviruses as the most commonly identified cause of healthcare-associated infection at the Hospital for Sick Children in Toronto, Canada.[107]

Coronaviruses

Enteric coronaviruses have been most frequently associated with gastroenteritis in neonates, infants, and patients with AIDS.[104] However, their significance as causative agents of gastroenteritis was unclear until 2002, when the severe acute respiratory syndrome (SARS) outbreak occurred in China. SARS-coronavirus caused significant gastrointestinal disease. In one Hong Kong outbreak, a total of 38.4 percent of patients with SARS-coronavirus developed diarrhea, and some presented with fever and gastrointestinal symptoms only.[93,108] The diarrhea was usually mild, and no deaths were attributed to the gastroenteritis.[108] In the Toronto outbreak, 23.6 percent of the 144 patients had diarrhea on presentation.[109] Rigorous application of hospital infection control procedures, particularly Contact and Droplet Precautions, provided a strong beneficial effect on the spread of the SARS coronavirus.[110]

Picobirnaviruses

Picobirnaviruses have been implicated as a cause of gastroenteritis in immunocompromised hosts.[111] Their role as causative agents in normal hosts is unclear because the prevalence of the viruses in fecal specimens of individuals with or without diarrhea was similar.[79] Evidence for genetic relatedness between human and animal viral strains has been found; suggesting extant crossing points in the ecology and evolution of heterologous viral strains.[112]

REFERENCES

1. Wilhelmi I, Roman E, Sánchez-Fauquier A. Viruses causing gastroenteritis. *Clin Microbial Infect* 2003 Apr;9(4):247–262.
2. Glass RI, Noel J, Ando T, et al. The epidemiology of enteric caliciviruses from humans: a reassessment using new diagnostics. *J Infect Dis* 2000 May;181 Suppl 2:S254–S261.
3. Rockx B, De Wit M, Vennema H, et al. Natural history of human calicivirus infection: a prospective cohort study. *Clin Infect Dis* 2002 Aug 1;35(3):246–253.
4. Glass RI, Bresee J, Jiang B, et al. Gastroenteritis viruses: an overview. *Novartis Found Symp* 2001;238:5–19; discussion 19–25.
5. Fankhauser RL, Noel JS, Monroe SS, et al. Molecular epidemiology of "Norwalk-like viruses" in outbreaks of gastroenteritis in the United States. *J Infect Dis* 1998 Dec;178(6):1571–1578.
6. Atmar RL, Estes MK. Diagnosis of noncultivatable gastroenteritis viruses, the human caliciviruses. *Clin Microbiol Rev* 2001 Jan;14(1):15–37.
7. Adler JL, Zickl R. Winter vomiting disease. *J Infect Dis* 1969;119(6):668–673.
8. Kapikian AZ, Wyatt RG, Dolin R, et al. Visualization by immune electron microscopy of a 27-nm particle associated with acute infectious nonbacterial gastroenteritis. *J Virol* 1972 Nov;10(5):1075–1081.
9. Centers for Disease Control and Prevention (CDC). Emergence of new norovirus strain GII.4 Sydney — United States, 2012. *MMWR Morb Mortal Wkly Rep* 2013 Jan 25;62(3):55.
10. Hutson AM, Estes MK, Atmar RL. Re: Nosocomial outbreak of norovirus gastroenteritis and investigation of ABO histo-blood group type in infected staff and patients. *J Hosp Infect* 2004 Oct;58(2):163–164.
11. Estes MK, Ball JM, Guerrero RA, et al. Norwalk virus vaccines: challenges and progress. *J Infect Dis* 2000 May;181 Suppl 2:S367–S373.
12. Dolin R, Treanor JJ. Noroviruses and Other Caliciviruses. In: Mandell GL, Bennett JE, Dolin R, eds. *Principles and Practice of Infectious Diseases.* Vol 2, 7th ed. Philadelphia, PA: Elsevier Churchill Livingstone, 2010:2399–2405.
13. Altekruse SF, Cohen ML, Swerdlow DL. Emerging foodborne diseases. *Emerg Infect Dis* 1997 Jul-Sep;3(3):285–293.
14. Centers for Disease Control and Prevention (CDC). Norovirus activity—United States, 2002. *MMWR Morb Mortal Wkly Rep* 2003 Jan 24;52(3):41–45.
15. Widdowson MA, Glass R, Monroe S, et al. Probable transmission of norovirus on an airplane. *JAMA* 2005 Apr 20;293(15):1859–1860.
16. Centers for Disease Control and Prevention (CDC). Norovirus activity—United States, 2006–2007. *MMWR Morb Mortal Wkly Rep* 2007 Aug;56(33):842–846.
17. Marshall JA, Hellard ME, Sinclair MI, et al. Incidence and characteristics of endemic Norwalk-like virus-associated gastroenteritis. *J Med Viro* 2003 Apr;69(4):568–578.
18. Vega E, Barclay L, Gregoricus N, et al. Novel surveillance network for norovirus gastroenteritis outbreaks, United States. *Emerg Infect Dis* 2011 Aug;17(8):1389–95
19. Centers for Disease Control and Prevention (CDC). *Norovirus Trends and Outbreaks.* CDC website. 2013. Available at: http://www.cdc.gov/norovirus/trends-outbreaks.html.
20. Parashar U, Quiroz ES, Mounts AW, et al. "Norwalk-like viruses." Public health consequences and outbreak management. *MMWR Morb Mortal Wkly Rep* 2001 Jun 1;50(RR-9):1–17.
21. Lopman BA, Adak GK, Reacher MH, et al. Two epidemiologic patterns of norovirus outbreaks: surveillance in England and wales, 1992–2000. *Emerg Infect Dis* 2003 Jan;9(1):71–77.
22. Mounts AW, Ando T, Koopmans M, et al. Cold weather seasonality of gastroenteritis associated with Norwalk-like viruses. *J Infect Dis* 2000 May;181 Suppl 2:S284–S287.
23. Fankhauser RL, Monroe SS, Noel JS, et al. Epidemiologic and molecular trends of "Norwalk-like viruses" associated with outbreaks of gastroenteritis in the United States. *J Infect Dis* 2002 Jul 1;186(1):1–7.
24. LeBaron CW, Furutan NP, Lew JF, et al. Viral agents of gastroenteritis. Public health importance and outbreak management. *MMWR Recomm Rep* 1990 Apr 27;39(RR-5):1–24.
25. Dolin R. Noroviruses—challenges to control. *N Engl J Med* 2007 Sep 13;357(11):1072–1073.
26. Jingo Y, Qian Y, Huo Y, et al. Seroprevalence against Norwalk-like human caliciviruses in Beijing, China. *J Med Virol* 2000 Jan;60(1):97–101.
27. Smit TK, Steele AD, Peenze I, et al. Study of Norwalk virus and Mexico virus infections at Ga-Rankuwa Hospital, Ga-Rankuwa, South Africa. *J Clin Microbiol* 1997 Sep;35(9):2381–2385.
28. Larsson MM, Rydell GE, Grahn A, et al. Antibody prevalence and titer to norovirus (genogroup II) correlate with secretor (FUT2) but not with ABO phenotype or Lewis (FUT3) genotype. *J Infect Dis* 2006 Nov 15;194(10):1422–1427.
29. Tatsumi M, Nakata S, Sakai Y, et al. Detection and differentiation of Norwalk virus by reverse transcription-polymerase chain reaction and enzyme-linked immunosorbent assay. *J Med Virol* 2002 Oct;68(2):285–290.
30. Jaykus LA. Epidemiology and detection as options for control of viral and parasitic foodborne disease. *Emerg Infect Dis* 1997 Oct-Dec;3(4):529–539.
31. Centers for Disease Control and Prevention (CDC). Outbreaks of Norwalk-like viral gastroenteritis—Alaska and Wisconsin, 1999. *MMWR Morb Mortal Wkly Rep* 2000 Mar 17;49(10):207–211.
32. Lopman BA, Reacher MH, Vipond IB, et al. Epidemiology and cost of nosocomial gastroenteritis, Avon, England, 2002–2003. *Emerg Infect Dis* 2004 Oct;10(10):1827–1834.
33. de Wit MA, Koopmans MP, van Duynhoven YT. Risk factors for norovirus, Sapporo-like virus, and group A rotavirus gastroenteritis. *Emerg Infect Dis* 2003 Dec;9(12):1563–1570.
34. Schaub SA, Oshiro RK. Public health concerns about caliciviruses as waterborne contaminants. *J Infect Dis* 2000 May;181 Suppl 2:S374–S380.
35. Thornton AC, Jennings-Conklin KS, McCormick MI. Noroviruses: agents in outbreaks of acute gastroenteritis. *Disaster Manag Response* 2004 Jan-Mar;2(1):4–9.
36. Centers for Disease Control and Prevention (CDC). *Responding to Norovirus Outbreaks.* CDC website. 2013. Available at: http://www.cdc.gov/norovirus/php/responding.html.
37. Dormitzer PR. Rotaviruses. In: Mandell GL, Bennett JE, Dolin R, eds. *Principles and Practice of Infectious Diseases.* Vol 2, 7th ed. Philadelphia: Elsevier Churchill Livingstone, 2010;2105–2115.
38. Dennehy PH. Rotavirus vaccines: an overview. *Clin Microbiol Rev* 2008 Jan;21(1):198–208.
39. Gentsch JR, Laird AR, Bielfelt B, et al. Serotype diversity and reassortment between human and animal rotavirus strains: implications for rotavirus vaccine programs. *J Infect Dis* 2005 Sep 1;192 Suppl 1:S146–59.
40. Parashar UD, Burton A, Lanata C, et al. Global mortality associated with rotavirus disease among children in 2004. *J Infect Dis* 2009 Nov 1;200 Suppl 1:S9–S15.
41. Parashar UD, Hummelman EG, Bresee JS, et al. Global illness and deaths caused by rotavirus disease in children. *Emerg Infect Dis* 2003 May;9(5):565–572.
42. Payne DC, Wikswo M, Parashar UD. Rotavirus. In: Roush SW, McIntyre L, Baldy LM, eds. *Manual for the surveillance of vaccine-preventable diseases, 5th ed.* Atlanta, GA: Centers for Disease Control and Prevention, 2011;13-1–13-11.
43. Hrdy DB. Epidemiology of rotaviral infection in adults. *Rev Infect Dis* 1987 May-Jun;9(3):461–469.
44. Shah N, DuPont HL, Ramsey DJ. Global etiology of travelers' diarrhea: systematic review from 1973 to the present. *Am J Trop Med Hyg* 2009 Apr;80(4):609–614.
45. Trop Skaza A, Beskovnik L, Zohar Cretnik T. Outbreak of rotavirus gastroenteritis in a nursing home, Slovenia, December 2010. *Euro Surveill* 2011 Apr 7;16(14).
46. Marshall J, Botes J, Gorrie G, et al. Rotavirus detection and characterization in outbreaks of gastroenteritis in aged-care facilities. *J Clin Virol* 2003 Dec;28(3):331–340.
47. Brandt CD, Kim HW, Yolken RH, et al. Comparative epidemiology of two rotavirus serotypes and other viral agents associated with pediatric gastroenteritis. *Am J Epidemiol* 1979 Sep;110(3):243–254.
48. Wikswo ME, Hall AJ. Outbreaks of acute gastroenteritis transmitted by person-to-person contact—United States, 2009-2010. *MMWR Surveill Summ* 2012 Dec 14;61(9):1–12.
49. Centers for Disease Control and Prevention (CDC). Notes from the field: outbreaks of rotavirus gastroenteritis among elderly adults in two retirement communities—Illinois, 2011. *MMWR Morb Mortal Wkly Rep* 2011 Oct 28;60(42):1456.
50. Julian TR, Canales RA, Leckie JO, et al. A model of exposure to rotavirus from nondietary ingestion iterated by simulated intermittent contacts. *Risk Anal* 2009 May;29(5):617–632.

51. Vollet JJ 3rd, DuPont HL, Pickering LK. Nonenteric sources of rotavirus in acute diarrhea. *J Infect Dis* 1981 Nov;144(5):495.

52. Koroglu M, Yakupogullari Y, Otlu B, et al. A waterborne outbreak of epidemic diarrhea due to group A rotavirus in Malatya, Turkey. *New Microbiol* 2011 Jan;34(1):17–24.

53. Karmakar S, Rathore AS, Kadri SM, et al. Post-earthquake outbreak of rotavirus gastroenteritis in Kashmir (India): an epidemiological analysis. *Public Health* 2008 Oct;122(10):981–989.

54. Davidson GP, Goller I, Bishop RF, et al. Immunofluorescence in duodenal mucosa of children with acute enteritis due to a new virus. *J Clin Pathol* 1975 Apr;28(4):263–266.

55. Bishop RF, Davidson GP, Holmes IH, et al. Virus particles in epithelial cells of duodenal mucosa from children with acute non-bacterial gastroenteritis. *Lancet* 1973 Dec;2(7841):1281–1283.

56. Tallett S, MacKenzie C, Middleton P, et al. Clinical, laboratory, and epidemiologic features of a viral gastroenteritis in infants and children. *Pediatrics* 1977 Aug;60(2):217–222.

57. Velázquez FR, Matson DO, Calva JJ, et al. Rotavirus infections in infants as protection against subsequent infections. *N Engl J Med* 1996 Oct 3; 335(14):1022–1028.

58. Anderson EJ, Weber SG. Rotavirus infection in adults. *Lancet Infect Dis* 2004 Feb;4(2):91–99.

59. Kapikian AZ, Wyatt RG, Levine MM, et al. Oral administration of human rotavirus to volunteers: induction of illness and correlates of resistance. *J Infect Dis* 1983 Jan;147(1):95–106.

60. Albrecht H, Stellbrink HJ, Fenske S, et al. Rotavirus antigen detection in patients with HIV infection and diarrhea. *Scand J Gastroenterol* 1993 Apr;28(4):307–310.

61. Davidson GP, Hogg RJ, Kirubakaran CP. Serum and intestinal immune response to rotavirus enteritis in children. *Infect Immun* 1983 May;40(2): 447–452.

62. Bernstein DI, McNeal MM, Schiff GM, et al. Induction and persistence of local rotavirus antibodies in relation to serum antibodies. *J Med Virol* 1989 Jun;28(2):90–95.

63. Jiang B, Gentsch JR, Glass RI. The role of serum antibodies in the protection against rotavirus disease: an overview. *Clin Infect Dis* 2002 May 15;34(10):1351–1361.

64. Parashar UD, Alexander JP, Glass RI. Prevention of rotavirus gastroenteritis among infants and children. Recommendations of the Advisory Committee on Immunization Practices (ACIP). *MMWR Recomm Rep* 2006 Aug 11;55(RR-12):1–13.

65. Wilde J, Yolken R, Willoughby R, et al. Improved detection of rotavirus shedding by polymerase chain reaction. *Lancet* 1991 Feb 1;337(8737):323–326.

66. King CK, Glass R, Bresee JS, et al. Managing acute gastroenteritis among children: oral rehydration, maintenance, and nutritional therapy. *MMWR Recomm Rep* 2003 Nov 21;52(RR-16):1–16.

67. Isolauri E, Juntunen M, Wiren S, et al. Intestinal permeability changes in acute gastroenteritis: effects of clinical factors and nutritional management. *J Pediatr Gastroenterol Nutr* 1989 May;8(4):466–473.

68. Sandhu BK. Rationale for early feeding in childhood gastroenteritis. *J Pediatr Gastroenterol Nutr* 2001 Oct;33 Suppl 2:S13–S16.

69. Guarino A, Canani RB, Russo S, et al. Oral immunoglobulins for treatment of acute rotaviral gastroenteritis. *Pediatrics* 1994 Jan;93(1):12–16.

70. Losonsky GA, Johnson JP, Winkelstein JA, et al. Oral administration of human serum immunoglobulin in immunodeficient patients with viral gastroenteritis. A pharmacokinetic and functional analysis. *J Clin Invest* 1985 Dec;76(6):2362–2367.

71. Cortese MM, Parashar UD. Prevention of rotavirus gastroenteritis among infants and children: recommendations of the Advisory Committee on Immunization Practices (ACIP). *MMWR Recomm Rep* 2009 Feb 6; 58(RR-2):1–25.

72. Centers for Disease Control and Prevention (CDC). Reduction in rotavirus after vaccine introduction — United States, 2000-2009. *MMWR Morb Mortal Wkly Rep* 2009 Oct 23;58(41):1146–1149.

73. Tate JE, Haynes A, Payne DC, et al. Trends in national rotavirus activity before and after introduction of rotavirus vaccine into the national immunization program in the United States, 2000 to 2012. *Pediatr Infect Dis J* 2013 Jul;32(7):741–744.

74. Cortese MM. *Summary of Intussusception Risk and Benefits of Rotavirus Vaccination in the United States.* Centers for Disease Control and Prevention website, ACIP Presentation Slides. 2013. Available at: http://www.cdc.gov/vaccines/acip/meetings/slides-jun-2013.html.

75. Centers for Disease Control and Prevention (CDC). *Provider Information: Rotavirus Vaccine Information Statements.* CDC website. 2013. Available at: http://www.cdc.gov/vaccines/hcp/vis/vis-statements /rotavirus-hcp-info.html.

76. Ansari SA, Springthorpe VS, Sattar SA. Survival and vehicular spread of human rotaviruses: possible relation to seasonality of outbreaks. *Rev Infect Dis* 1991 May-Jun;13(3):448–461.

77. Sattar SA, Jacobsen H, Rahman H, et al. Interruption of rotavirus spread through chemical disinfection. *Infect Control Hosp Epidemiol* 1994 Dec;15(12):751–756.

78. Centers for Disease Control and Prevention (CDC). *Rotavirus and Drinking Water from Private Wells.* CDC website. 2009. Available at: http://www.cdc.gov/healthywater/drinking/private/wells/disease/rotavirus .html#how_remove_from_water.

79. Dolin R, Treanor JJ. Astroviruses and Picobirnaviruses. In: Mandell GL, Bennett JE, Dolin R, eds. *Principles and Practice of Infectious Diseases.* Vol 2, 7th ed. Philadelphia: Elsevier Churchill Livingstone, 2010: 2407–2409.

80. Méndez-Toss M, Griffin DD, Calva J, et al. Prevalence and genetic diversity of human astroviruses in Mexican children with symptomatic and asymptomatic infections. *J Clin Microbiol* 2004 Jan;42(1):151–157.

81. Walter JE, Mitchell DK. Role of astroviruses in childhood diarrhea. *Curr Opin Pediatr* 2000 Jun;12(3):275–279.

82. Espul C, Martinez N, Noel JS, et al. Prevalence and characterization of astroviruses in Argentinean children with acute gastroenteritis. *J Med Virol* 2004 Jan;72(1):75–82.

83. Grohmann GS, Glass RI, Pereira HG, et al. Enteric viruses and diarrhea in HIV-infected patients. Enteric Opportunistic Infections Working Group. *N Engl J Med* 1993 Jul 1;329(1):14–20.

84. Yamashita T, Kobayashi S, Sakae K, et al. Isolation of cytopathic small round viruses with BS-C-1 cells from patients with gastroenteritis. *J Infect Dis* 1991 Nov;164(5):954–957.

85. Abad FX, Villena C, Guix S, et al. Potential role of fomites in the vehicular transmission of human astroviruses. *Appl Environ Microbiol* 2001 Sep; 67(9):3904–3907.

86. Riou P, Le Saux JC, Dumas F, et al. Microbial impact of small tributaries on water and shellfish quality in shallow coastal areas. *Water Res* 2007 Jun;41(12):2774–2786.

87. Herrmann JE, Nowak NA, Perron-Henry DM, et al. Diagnosis of astrovirus gastroenteritis by antigen detection with monoclonal antibodies. *J Infect Dis* 1990 Feb;161(12):226–229.

88. Kramer A, Schwebke I, Kampf G. How long do nosocomial pathogens persist on inanimate surfaces? A systematic review. *BMC Infect Dis* 2006 Aug 16;6:130.

89. Rowe WP, Huebner RJ, Gilmore LK, et al. Isolation of a cytopathogenic agent from human adenoids undergoing spontaneous degeneration in tissue culture. *Proc Soc Exp Biol Med* 1953 Dec;84(3):570–573.

90. Harrach B, Benkö M, Both GW, et al. Family Adenoviridae. In: King AMQ, Adams MJ, Carstens EB, et al. (eds.) *Virus Taxonomy: Classification and Nomenclature of Viruses. Ninth Report of the International Committee on Taxonomy of Viruses.* San Diego: Elsevier Academic Press, 2011:125–141.

91. Harrach B, Benkö M, Both GW, et al. Family Adenoviridae. In: King AMQ, Adams MJ, Carstens EB, et al. (eds.) *Virus Taxonomy: Classification and Nomenclature of Viruses. Ninth Report of the International Committee on Taxonomy of Viruses.* 2012. Available at: http://www.ictvonline.org/.

92. Rhee EG, Barouch DH. Adenovirus. In: Mandell GL, Bennett JE, Dolin R, eds. *Principles and Practice of Infectious Diseases.* Vol 2, 7th ed. Philadelphia: Elsevier Churchill Livingstone, 2010:2027–2033.

93. Clark B, McKendrick M. A review of viral gastroenteritis. *Curr Opin Infect Dis* 2004 Oct;17(5):461–469.

94. Lennon G, Cashman O, Lane K, et al. Prevalence and characterization of enteric adenoviruses in the South of Ireland. *J Med Virol* 2007 Oct;79(10):1518–1526.

95. Dennehy PH. Viral Gastroenteritis in children. *Pediatr Infect Dis J* 2011 Jan;30(1):63–64.

96. Ison MG. Adenovirus infections in transplant recipients. *Clin Infect Dis* 2006 Aug 1;43(3):331–339.

97. Thomas PD, Pollok RC, Gazzard BG. Enteric viral infections as a cause of diarrhoea in the acquired immunodeficiency syndrome. *HIV Med* 1999 Oct;1(1):19–24.

98. Carter MJ. Enterically infecting viruses: pathogenicity, transmission and significance for food and waterborne infection. *J Appl Microbiol* 2005;98(6):1354–1380.

99. Aitken C, Jeffries DJ. Nosocomial spread of viral disease. *Clin Microbiol Rev* 2001 Jul;14(3):528–546.

100. Kojaoghlanian T, Flomenberg P, Horwitz MS. The impact of adenovirus infection on the immunocompromised host. *Rev Med Virol* 2003 May-Jun;13(3):155–171.

101. Lenaerts L, De Clercq E, Naesens L. Clinical features and treatment of adenovirus infections. *Rev Med Virol* 2008 Nov-Dec;18(6): 357–374.

102. Centers for Disease Control and Prevention (CDC). *Adenoviruses: Prevention & Treatment.* CDC website. 2013. Available at: http://www.cdc .gov/adenovirus/hcp/prevention-treatment.html.

103. Lodha A, de Silva N, Petric M, et al. Human torovirus: a new virus associated with neonatal necrotizing enterocolitis. *Acta Paediatr* 2005;94(8): 1085–1088.

104. McIntosh K, Perlman S. Coronaviruses, Including Severe Acute Respiratory Syndrome (SARS)-associated Cornoavirus. In: Mandell GL, Bennett JE, Dolin R, eds. *Principles and Practice of Infectious Diseases*. Vol 2, 7th ed. Philadelphia: Elsevier Churchill Livingstone, 2010:2187–2194.

105. Jamieson FB, Wang EE, Bain C, et al. Human torovirus: a new nosocomial gastrointestinal pathogen. *J Infect Dis* 1998 Nov;178(5):1263–1269.

106. Koopmans MP, Goosen ES, Lima AA, et al. Association of torovirus with acute and persistent diarrhea in children. *Pediatr Infect Dis J* 1997 May;16(5):504–507.

107. Gubbay J, Al-Rezqi A, Hawkes M, et al. The role of torovirus in nosocomial viral gastroenteritis at a large tertiary pediatric centre. *Can J Infect Dis Med Microbiol* 2012 Summer;23(2):78–81.

108. Leung WK, To KF, Chan PK, et al. Enteric involvement of severe acute respiratory syndrome-associated coronavirus infection. *Gastroenterology* 2003 Oct;125(4):1011–1017.

109. Booth CM, Matukas LM, Tomlinson GA, et al. Clinical features and short-term outcomes of 144 patients with SARS in the greater Toronto area. *JAMA* 2003 Jun 4;289(21):2801–2809.

110. Seto WH, Tsang D, Yung RW, et al. Effectiveness of precautions against droplets and contact in prevention of nosocomial transmission of severe acute respiratory syndrome (SARS). *Lancet* 2003 May 3;361(9368): 1519–1520.

111. Giordano MO, Martinez LC, Rinaldi D, et al. Diarrhea and enteric emerging viruses in HIV-infected patients. *AIDS Res Hum Retroviruses* 1999 Nov 1;15(16):1427–1432.

112. Ganesh B, Bányai K, Martella V, et al. Picobirnavirus infections: viral persistence and zoonotic potential. *Rev Med Virol* 2012 Jul;22(4):245–256.

Diarrheal Diseases: Bacterial

Mary C. Thomas, MB, BS, DTM&H, MPH
Senior Epidemiologist
San Antonio Metropolitan Health District
San Antonio, TX

ABSTRACT

It is estimated that 10 percent of the population will have at least one episode of infectious diarrhea each year. Although many diarrheal diseases are self-limiting, some may be chronic and require ongoing treatment. Disease manifestations range from almost asymptomatic to severe and—in some cases—deadly. Viruses, parasites, or bacteria may be the infectious agents causing these episodes. Primary modes of transmission for most gastroenteritis agents are fecal–oral and foodborne; however, some agents may be spread from person to person. Because these agents are so different, viral agents, bacterial agents, and parasitic agents are examined in separate chapters.

KEY CONCEPTS

* Outbreaks of severe gastroenteritis have been associated with multiple strains of enteropathogenic *Escherichia coli*.

* Other common bacterial causes of diarrhea include *Salmonella*, *Shigella*, and *Campylobacter* species.

* Bacterial agents of diarrhea are often linked to food sources that have become contaminated with human or animal fecal waste.

BASIC PRINCIPLES

Escherichia coli Bacterial Gastroenteritis

Background

Escherichia coli a Gram-negative motile bacillus belonging to the family *Enterobacteriaceae*. Although many strains of *E. coli* are harmless, certain types can cause foodborne illnesses. More than 30 serotypes of *E. coli* produce cytotoxic *Shigella*-like toxins; *E. coli* O157:H7 is the best known of these in the United States and will be the primary focus of this section.

E. coli is divided into categories based on virulence traits, epidemiologic profiles, and the clinical symptoms it produces. The five categories are as follows: enteroaggregative *E. coli* (EAEC), enterohemorrhagic *E. coli* (EHEC), enteropathogenic *E. coli* (EPEC), enterotoxigenic *E. coli* (ETEC), and enteroinvasive *E. coli* (EIEC). The combination of letters and numbers in the name of the bacterium (e.g., *E. coli* serotype O157:H7) refers to the specific markers found on the organism's surface. Several different strains of *E. coli* can cause bloody diarrhea and have led to kidney failure in children and immunocompromised adults through a condition called hemolytic-uremic syndrome (HUS).

E. coli O157:H7, an EHEC-expressing somatic (O) antigen 157 and flagellar (H) antigen 7, was first described in 1982 in two separate case reports. At the Hospital for Sick Children in Toronto, Karmali et al. identified cytotoxin-producing *E. coli* of various serotypes, including *E. coli* O157:H7, in the stools of children with HUS.[1] A week later, Riley et al. at the Centers for Disease Control and Prevention (CDC) reported their findings in an investigation of an outbreak of bloody diarrhea that was associated with the consumption of hamburger meat in a fast food restaurant.[2] Stool cultures demonstrated a previously unknown pathogen, *E. coli* O157:H7.

Since then, various epidemiologic studies from different parts of the world have established other serotypes of *Shigella*-toxin–producing *E. coli* as a major cause of bloody diarrhea (hemorrhagic colitis) and HUS in temperate climates and as an important cause of uncomplicated watery diarrhea in other geographic areas.[3]

Epidemiology

It has been known for more than 20 years that intestinal infection and colonization of cattle with EHEC can lead to EHEC-contaminated food. EHEC is excreted by as many as 10 percent of healthy cattle, and about 1 percent of retail ground beef samples in the United States culture positive for *E. coli* O157:H7. Infection has been reported to occur after the ingestion of as few as 10 to 100 organisms, usually acquired after eating inadequately cooked ground beef. EHEC has been described with multiple episodes of hemorrhagic colitis associated with outbreaks from fast food restaurants, nursing homes, and cafeterias.

EHEC causes an estimated 75,000 illnesses per year in the United States, with 3000 hospitalizations and 60 deaths.[4] Outbreaks not directly involving beef include municipal water supplies, milk, uncooked vegetables, cheese curd, apple cider, lettuce, alfalfa sprouts, and other products fecally contaminated by cattle.[4] Other animals, including pigs, sheep, and deer, can also carry EHEC.

Because low numbers of these organisms can cause illness, person-to-person spread within families and in day care centers has resulted in further propagation of disease. Even brief visits to dairy farms and petting zoos have been incriminated as potential risk factors for children. One recent outbreak was described after exposure to calves at a petting farm[5] and another to exposure from a building contaminated with *E. coli* O157 months earlier during a county fair.[6] The low-level exposure associated with swimming in contaminated water can also lead to serious infection. Prevalence has been reported to be higher during summer months and in northern states than in southern states of the United States.

Between 1982 and 2002, the CDC reported that in 350 U.S. outbreaks, foodborne transmission accounted for 52 percent of the cases. No cause was identified in 21 percent of the cases, 14 percent were person-to-person, 9 percent were waterborne, 3 percent were from animal contact such as petting zoos, and 0.3 percent were laboratory related.[7]

Although *E. coli* O157:H7 can affect a person at any age, children younger than 10 years and elderly persons have the highest incidence of extraintestinal symptoms and the highest mortality. Studies have shown the age-specific incidence of O157:H7 infections declines gradually in the first several decades of life, with the incidence of HUS falling dramatically between the first and second decades. The reasons for this attack pattern are largely unknown.[8-10]

EAEC has been implicated in sporadic diarrhea in children and adults in both developing and developed countries and have been identified as the cause of several outbreaks worldwide. Although EAEC has been associated with acute diarrhea in some studies, it is most commonly linked to a persistent diarrhea in children.[11,12] However, in adults, it is a common source of traveler's diarrhea. The nature of the diarrhea from EAEC, its epidemiology, and recovery rate closely parallel those of ETEC. Some have suggested that traveler's diarrhea from EAEC could approach 25 percent of the cases in which no causative agent is found.[13]

Typical or non-Shiga-toxin–producing EPEC has been associated with outbreaks of diarrhea in newborn nurseries and childhood diarrhea in developing countries. In these cases, it has been found to pass from person to person. Atypical or Shiga-toxin–producing EPEC is a more common cause of diarrhea in industrialized countries. The sole reservoir for typical EPEC is humans, whereas atypical EPEC is also found in animals.[3] EPEC is associated with a persistent diarrhea lasting 2 or more weeks, though no real connection has been established between atypical EPEC and endemic diarrhea. The predilection of EPEC for young children and the increased resistance seen in older children and adults may be related to the development of immunity or the loss of intestinal receptors for the organism's specific adhesions.[14]

Infections attributed to ETEC are often acquired by ingesting fecally contaminated water (including ice cubes) or food by travelers to the developing world. Most studies agree that ETEC is the most common cause of traveler's diarrhea. The organism has been identified in 16 to 70 percent of cases, with the lower incidence seen in Asia and higher incidence in Latin America. A higher incidence is also seen in warmer months than in colder months. It has been reported that ETEC causes more than 650 million cases of diarrhea worldwide and 380,000 deaths in children younger than 5 years.

ETEC is emerging as a significant diarrheal pathogen in the United States. Most reported cases in the United States are from travelers who have left the country, but the CDC reported 16 outbreaks of ETEC in the United States from 1996 through 2003. Outbreaks on cruise ships account for many of the cases. Raw vegetables and herbs are increasingly implicated in the outbreaks.[15] People living in developing countries are most likely immune as a result of prior exposure.[16]

EIEC strains produce a syndrome identical to that seen in acute shigellosis. Although developing countries have reported outbreaks of EIEC, this organism does not appear to be a frequent cause of sporadic diarrhea in the United States, but it may be underdiagnosed.[17]

Clinical Manifestations

Enterohemorrhagic *E. coli* has an incubation period of 1 to 9 days (mean, 3 to 4 days). Initially, abdominal pain and tenderness, fatigue, myalgias, and headache may be present. Vomiting can occur at any time. After initial symptoms, the organism can cause a characteristic hemorrhagic colitis, with visible blood and leukocytes in the feces. Diarrhea symptoms may last from 3 to 7 days (mean, 5 days). Hemorrhagic colitis is most prominent in persons older than 65 years, with lethality in this age group ranging between 15 and 23 percent.[18,19] Complications such as ischemic colitis and perforation have been reported. Fever has been reported in about one-third of patients but has often defervesced once the diarrhea becomes bloody. This pattern and the absence of fever at presentation help to differentiate *E. coli* O157:H7 from other bacterial diarrheal pathogens.[20]

After about 7 days, just as the diarrhea is subsiding, other systemic symptoms may occur. Systemic complications include HUS in 6 to 9 percent of infected children with evidence of microangiopathic hemolytic anemia, acute renal failure, and thrombocytopenia. One estimate is that EHEC causes at least 70 percent of postdiarrheal HUS in the United States, with 80 percent of these caused by *E. coli* O157:H7 and the other 20 percent by different serotypes of EHEC. This is the reverse of the pattern seen in other parts of the world. HUS is the most common cause of acute renal failure in U.S. children. The risk of developing HUS is higher at the extremes of age. Overall, statistics show that approximately 5 percent of patients die with HUS, and 10 percent are left with long-term sequela, such as hypertension or chronic renal failure.[21,22]

Previous infection with *E. coli* O157:H7 does not necessarily protect against subsequent infections. In fact, children who have had *E. coli* O157:H7-associated HUS appear to have an increased risk of having a second episode of diarrhea-associated HUS as compared with children in the general population.[10,23,24]

EPEC may cause severe diarrhea (including epidemic diarrhea) in neonates but milder, generally self-limited diarrhea in older children and adults. Polymorphonuclear neutrophils are not seen in the stool. Typically, there is a more insidious onset over 3 to 6 days. Stools may be watery to yellow-green without blood, mucus, or pus. Severe dehydration and shock may progress to death.

ETEC symptoms usually begin 3 to 14 days after ingestion of the organism. Infections with the organism are a common cause of watery diarrhea, abdominal cramps, and, occasionally, nausea and vomiting in travelers. Stool does not demonstrate leukocytes. The incubation period for EIEC is shorter, usually 2 to 3 days after ingestion. The sequelae of EPEC, ETEC, and EIEC infections are not well described. As mentioned, EAEC infection may be a source of chronic diarrhea.

Laboratory Diagnosis

E. coli can be identified on selective media such as MacConkey agar as pink colonies, indicating that the organism ferments lactose. However, *E. coli* O157:H7 does not ferment lactose and is more readily identified with MacConkey agar containing sorbitol (SMAC medium).[25] Some labs screen all stools for *E. coli* O157:H7, whereas others screen only bloody stools (95 percent of cultures positive for O157:H7 come from patients with visibly bloody stools or a history of bloody diarrhea). The rate of successful stool isolation is highest in the first 6 days after onset of EHEC diarrhea. Culture on SMAC is not effective for identifying Shiga toxin–producing *E. coli* other than O157:H7. SMAC has been improved by the addition of cefixime and potassium tellurite to the agar, which largely inhibits the physiologic flora.[26] In addition, enzyme-linked immunosorbent assay (ELISA) kits, Vero cell cytotoxicity assays, and polymerase chain reaction (PCR) techniques have been developed for rapid detection of the O157 antigen and Shiga-like toxins in stool.[27]

E. coli O157:H7 can be further identified by using slide agglutination with specific antiserum or anti-O157 latex reagents.[28] Because of the geographic, temporal, and age-affected variability in infection rates of O157 and because of the wide dispersion that may occur during a foodborne diarrhea outbreak, cases can be difficult to link epidemiologically. DNA fingerprinting techniques of the bacterial isolates of cases are also used to determine the potential source of an outbreak.[29] If culture confirmation of *E. coli* O157:H7 is not possible in a patient with HUS, serology can be helpful. Patients with *E. coli* O157:H7-associated HUS have an early antibody response to the O157 lipopolysaccharide antigen.[30,31] Serum should be obtained within the first 10 days of diarrhea in a patient in

whom HUS is suspected. *E. coli* O157:H7 infection without HUS is not as well understood.[32]

ETEC is currently diagnosed by using DNA probes that identify genes for the heat-labile (LT) and heat-stable (ST) enterotoxin.[33]

EPEC contains specific virulence factors that are associated with serotypes of *E. coli*. Serotyping may be useful for presumptive identification of EPEC strains in stool. The fluorescent actin staining test detects aggregated actin filaments beneath EPEC that have attached to intestinal epithelial cells, thus allowing the identification of strains that produce attaching and effacing lesions.[34] Detection of EPEC adherence factor (EAF) by DNA probe or PCR is currently available only in research or reference laboratories.

EIEC appears to be limited to a few serotypes and, because they are antigenically similar to *Shigella*, the two may often be mistaken for each other.[35-37] To verify the identity of EIEC, the invasive potential of the organism should be demonstrated by the Sereny test (guinea pig conjunctivitis), in HeLa cells, or the plasmid associated with invasiveness in *Shigella* or EIEC should be identified.[28,38-40]

Unless EAEC are recovered repeatedly and there are no other identified pathogens, the isolation of EAEC from diarrhea does not guarantee that it is the causative agent. The Hep-2 adherence test remains the standard for EAEC identification. Still, other bacteria demonstrate adherence phenotypes, and further speciation is necessary.[41,42] Certain EAEC-specific probes have been developed to aid in the identification of the organism, but probe-negative EAEC diarrhea outbreaks have been described in Eastern Europe and Japan.[28,40,43,44] Thus, no current DNA probe routinely identifies EAEC strains.

Treatment

Supportive care of the symptoms associated with HUS is currently the only treatment for EHEC diarrheal infection (i.e., transfusion for anemia, dialysis and/or electrolyte management for renal failure, monitoring for bleeding sequela and neurological compromise). Antiperistaltic agents increase the risk of systemic complications after infections with EHEC and should be avoided.

Antibiotic therapy has not been shown to lessen disease morbidity or reduce systemic complications. In fact, animal models have shown an increase in the production of Shiga toxins after the administration of antibiotics. Several clinical studies have also related the use of antibiotics with an increased incidence of HUS in children. A study in 2000 in the United States showed an increased risk of HUS following *E. coli* O157:H7 infection in children younger than 10 years who received antibiotic therapy with trimethoprim/sulfamethoxazole (TMP-SMX) or a beta-lactam, compared with no antibiotic.[20] However, a randomized, prospective, controlled trial in children and a meta-analysis of several studies found no association between HUS and antibiotic administration.[45,46]

The use of systemic antisera and oral toxin-binding agents also has been supported by results from human trials.[47,48] A study in 1998 showed benefit in the prevention of HUS when orally administered antitoxin was given,[49] but a prospective multicenter trial found no difference in morbidity or mortality when comparing an oral binding agent to placebo.[50]

Illness associated with ETEC infection is generally self-limited, lasting 1 to 5 days. However, the duration of the illness can be reduced by antimicrobial therapy at the onset of symptoms. Worldwide, there has been reported increasing resistance of the organism to ampicillin, TMP-SMX, and tetracycline.[51,52] A fluoroquinolone for 3 days is generally recommended for adult U.S. travelers, whereas TMP-SMX is still recommended for children. Although, to date, there is not a significant problem with fluoroquinolone resistance, ETEC infections are increasingly resistant to available antimicrobials. Continued use of fluoroquinolones in livestock feed and the over-the-counter availability in other countries make the possibility of resistance more likely. The same is probably true for EPEC, EAEC, and EIEC strains.[53-55] With concerns about quinolone resistance, the use of rifaximin as an effective nonabsorbed treatment against ETEC and other noninvasive strains of E. coli is increasing.

Because of the potential in some patients for persistent diarrhea and the risk of malnutrition and growth impairment, treatment may be sought in some patients with EAEC infection.[56] Because of the prevalence of multidrug-resistant strains, susceptibility testing is recommended. In fact, a study in 1993 reported that travelers who had prophylaxis with co-trimoxazole not only became infected with EAEC strains but also had a higher risk of being infected with antibiotic-resistant EAEC strains.[57] Still, the majority of strains are usually susceptible to ciprofloxacin. Azithromycin and rifaximin have been shown to shorten the course of EAEC diarrhea in adults. Some have suggested such a regimen for children with severe or persistent illness.[58]

Because of its antimicrobial and antisecretory properties, bismuth subsalicylate has been used for prevention of diarrhea in travelers (especially from ETEC), but it provides only modest protection and must be taken daily at high doses.

A skin patch for vaccination against the LT enterotoxin from ETEC has shown some protection against moderate to severe diarrhea in phase II trials and decreased duration of illness.[59] Additional trials are ongoing.

Infection Prevention and Public Health Concerns

Contact Precautions are required in any patient presenting with diarrhea. All human excrement should be treated as a biohazard subject to infection prevention measures, whether or not an infectious etiology is suspected.[21,32]

Although E. coli O157:H7 is a popular target for physicians and patients to credit for acute diarrhea beginning a few hours after ingestion of a high-profile food (i.e., hamburger meat, apple juice, milk, fresh produce, or water), it is important to remember that the typical incubation period for the organism is 3 to 5 days. The minimal incubation period is almost always greater than 24 hours, and illness related to the organism is not caused by the ingestion of a preformed toxin, as is seen with diarrhea caused from Staphylococcus aureus or Bacillus cereus.[32] However, a significant delay in obtaining cultures from patients with a high index of suspicion of E. coli O157:H7 infection may help proliferate person-to-person transmission from the index case. If two or more family members have become ill with O157:H7 and ate the same food item, other contacts in the household should be instructed not to consume the item, and it should be saved for diagnostic testing. Culturing asymptomatic contacts is not recommended because specific therapy is recommended for those individuals.[32]

Because of the risk of person-to-person transmission of E. coli O157:H7, children who have had documented infection with the organism should not return to day care or school until they have had multiple negative cultures. These same recommendations should be applied to food handlers and healthcare providers, even though transmission is most likely during the diarrheal phase.[60] The physician should ensure that cases of suspected or documented E. coli O157:HUS infection are reported to the local health department, as with any reportable disease.

Salmonella Bacterial Gastroenteritis

Etiologic agent

Salmonella, a genus of the Enterobacteriaceae family, is a common cause of bacterial gastroenteritis. There are two species in the genus Salmonella: S. enterica, which contains six subspecies, and S. bongori. Salmonella subspecies are further divided into more than 2,400 serotypes based on the somatic (O), surface (Vi), and flagellar (H) antigens. The majority of these serotypes belong to S. enterica subspecies enterica (I). The usual habitat of S. enterica subspecies enterica (I) is warm-blooded animals, contrary to the other six Salmonella subspecies, which have cold-blooded animals as their usual habitats.[61] Clinically, Salmonella infections are classified into typhoid fever and Salmonella gastroenteritis.

Typhoid fever

Epidemiology

Typhoid fever, also referred to as enteric fever, is most often caused by S. enterica subspecies enterica serotype Typhi, referred to as S. typhi for simplification. S. paratyphi A and B also cause similar, but less severe, clinical syndromes. Contrary to other Salmonella serotypes that are considered zoonotic in nature, S. typhi and S. paratyphi only colonize humans. Improvements in food handling processes and water treatment have resulted in substantial reduction in the incidence rate of typhoid fever in the United States in the last century. The current incidence rate of typhoid fever in the Unites States is estimated to be 0.2/100,000 person-years.[62] Most cases of typhoid and paratyphoid fever in the United States nowadays are associated with international travel to the Indian subcontinent, Southeast Asia, or South and Central America, where the disease is endemic.[63]

Transmission

Typhoid fever is transmitted by the fecal-oral route through food and water contaminated by infected individuals or chronic carriers. The incubation period ranges between 5 and 21 days, depending on the inoculum dose of the ingested bacteria.[64]

Disease Manifestations

Symptoms of typhoid fever usually start with diarrhea and other nonspecific symptoms that usually resolve before the onset of fever. These symptoms include headache, anorexia, myalgia, and generalized weakness. Confusion and psychosis have been rarely reported.[65] Fever usually starts as low grade in the first week of illness, but rises in the second week to 39°C or 40°C. Relative bradycardia is not a sensitive or specific sign for typhoid fever. Almost half the patients with typhoid fever have hepatosplenomegaly. Rose spots are a faint salmon-colored maculopapular rash that transiently appears on the trunk in a small proportion of patients with typhoid fever. Cervical lymphadenopathy is another uncommon physical finding.[66] Untreated typhoid fever may be complicated by intestinal perforation, which is associated with high mortality.[67] Other less common complications include necrotizing cholecystitis, endocarditis, pericarditis, and orchitis.[64]

Diagnosis

Blood cultures are positive in only 50 to 70 percent of patients with typhoid fever. Bone marrow culture has a higher yield, as great as 90 percent.[68] The diagnosis of typhoid fever may be also made by isolation of S. typhi or S. paratyphi from stool, duodenal aspirate, or rose spots. Other nonspecific laboratory findings in patients with typhoid fever include leukopenia, anemia, thrombocytopenia, and elevation in liver and muscle enzymes.[69]

Treatment

Because of the increasing resistance rates to ampicillin, chloramphenicol, and TMP-SMX among S. typhi isolates worldwide, fluoroquinolones have become the treatment of choice for typhoid fever.[66] Nonetheless, emerging S. typhi isolates with resistance to nalidixic acid and decreased susceptibility to ciprofloxacin have been described.[70] It is estimated that resistance to nalidixic acid among S. typhi isolates in the United States increased from 19.2 percent in 1999 to 48.4 percent in 2005.[71] Because nalidixic acid resistance is associated with reduced susceptibility to ciprofloxacin, high doses of fluoroquinolones are usually recommended. Isolates that are resistant to ciprofloxacin may be treated with third-generation cephalosporins or azithromycin.[72,73]

Infection Prevention and Public Health Concerns

Two vaccinations are currently available in the United States for prevention of typhoid fever in travelers to endemic countries: an oral vaccine and an injectable vaccine.

Nontyphoidal Salmonella

Epidemiology

The incidence rate of culture-confirmed salmonellosis in the United States was estimated to be 14.9/100,000 person-years in 2007. The incidence rate of salmonellosis has declined by only 8 percent in the last decade, which is the smallest decline among all other bacterial causes of acute gastroenteritis in the United States.[74] As with other enteric pathogens, Salmonella infections demonstrate seasonal variation, with a peak in incidence rate during the summer and early fall.[75-77] Infants have the highest incidence rate of sporadic Salmonella gastroenteritis.[77] Individuals with human immunodeficiency virus (HIV) infection are at much higher risk of salmonellosis than is the general population.[78]

Transmission

S. enteritidis is the most common cause of outbreak-related acute gastroenteritis in the United States.[79] The infective dose is thought to be less than 1,000 organisms.[80] The infection is usually acquired through ingestion of undercooked meat, poultry, unpasteurized eggs, and dairy products.[81-84] Recent outbreaks have been associated with exposure to tomatoes, unpasteurized orange and apple juice, peanut butter, fruit salad, and dried dog and cat food, possibly due to cross-contamination.[85-89] Salmonellosis also has been associated with exposure to exotic pets, including reptiles, turtles, iguanas, snakes, rodents, and rarely dogs and cats.[90,91] Acid-suppressing medications were associated with increased risk of salmonellosis in long-term care facility residents.[92]

Disease Manifestations

Nontyphoidal Salmonella infection is usually a self-limited illness. The incubation period ranges from 6 to 48 hours. Symptoms are similar to other bacterial causes of acute gastroenteritis and mostly consist of diarrhea lasting as long as 7 days with or without fever. Diarrhea may be watery, but occasionally patients may have mucus or blood in the stool. Although patients may vomit once or twice, vomiting is not a persistent feature of this illness. Other symptoms include crampy abdominal pain that improves with defecation. Patients usually have abdominal tenderness on examination.[93]

Salmonella bacteremia is more likely in infants, elderly persons, immunocompromised hosts, and patients with diseases associated with hemolysis, such as sickle cell disease.[94,95] S. choleraesuis and S. dublin are the most likely non-Typhi serotypes to be associated with bacteremia. High-grade or persistent bacteremia, especially in older individuals, raises the suspicion for an endovascular infection, resulting in seeding atherosclerotic plaques or aneurysms in the aorta.[96] Extraintestinal Salmonella infections have been reported in the urinary tract, genital tract, bones, and joints.[64] Bone involvement appears to be common in patients with sickle cell disease. Healthcare-associated Salmonella infections have been reported in burn units.[97] Patients with HIV infection have higher mortality and higher recurrence rates of salmonellosis compared with the general population.[78]

Diagnosis

The diagnosis is made by isolation of *Salmonella* from stool culture. *Salmonella* is a Gram-negative, nonspore-forming, facultative anaerobic bacillus. Similar to other *Enterobacteriaceae*, *Salmonella* is an oxidase-negative glucose fermenter. Several culture media are used to screen for *Salmonella* species from stool specimens, including low selective media, such as MacConkey and deoxycholate agar, or intermediate-selective media, such as *Salmonella-Shigella*, xylose-lysine-deoxycholate, or Hektoen agar.[98] Occasionally, blood cultures might be positive in patients with nontyphoidal *Salmonella* infections.

Treatment

Antibiotic treatment for *Salmonella* gastroenteritis is not routinely recommended for most individuals because it is mostly a self-limited disease. Antibiotics should be considered for neonates, patients older than 50 years, immunocompromised hosts, and those with heart valvular or endovascular abnormalities. *Salmonella* bacteremia should always be treated with antibiotics based on *in vitro* antimicrobial susceptibility results.[64]

Nontyphoidal *Salmonella* isolates continue to demonstrate increasing resistance to several antibiotics. A strain of multidrug-resistant *S. typhimurium* (DT 104) has spread worldwide. This strain acquired plasmid-mediated resistance from isolates to ampicillin, chloramphenicol, streptomycin, sulfonamide, and tetracycline (ACSSuT resistance pattern).[99,100] The prevalence of multidrug-resistant *S. typhimurium* in the United States increased from less than 1 percent in 1980 to 33.7 percent in 1996.[101] Fortunately, the prevalence of *S. typhimurium* isolates with ACSSuT resistance pattern decreased to 22.2 percent in 2005.[71] Infection with antimicrobial-resistant nontyphoidal *Salmonella*, especially *S. typhimurium*, is associated with increased risk of bacteremia and hospitalization.[102]

Currently, fluoroquinolones and third-generation cephalosporins are the preferred antimicrobial agents for empirical treatment of salmonellosis. Resistance rates to fluoroquinolones have increased since the licensing of these antimicrobials for veterinary use in 1995.[103] Plasmid-mediated fluoroquinolone resistance has been reported recently.[104] Resistance to nalidixic acid among *Salmonella* non-Typhi isolates in the United States increased from 0.4 percent in 1996 to 2.9 percent in 2005. Resistance to third-generation cephalosporins also increased from 0.2 to 2.9 percent during the same time period. *S. newport* is the most common third-generation cephalosporin-resistant non-Typhi serotype.[71] Concurrent resistance to fluoroquinolones and third-generation cephalosporins occurs in 0.19 percent of *Salmonella* isolates in the United States.[105]

Infection Prevention and Public Health Concerns

Healthcare-associated transmission of salmonellosis to other hospitalized patients or healthcare personnel is rare. The use of Standard Precautions, including barrier precautions such as gloves, is recommended upon direct contact with patients with salmonellosis. In addition, hand washing should always be emphasized. Routine screening of asymptomatic food handlers for stool carriage of *Salmonella* is not justified.[64]

A variety of public health measures have been undertaken to decrease the incidence rate of salmonellosis, including improvements in food processing, pasteurization of juice and dairy products, and other precautions to decrease cross-contamination. Because children younger than 5 years have the highest incidence rate of salmonellosis, education of food handling precautions to individuals caring for children should be encouraged. Breast-feeding decreases the risk of salmonellosis.

Shigella Bacterial Gastroenteritis

Etiologic Agent

Shigella is a genus of Gram-negative facultative anaerobic bacilli that cause bacillary dysentery by invoking a strong immune response after invading the epithelium of the large intestine. It belongs to the family *Enterobacteriaceae* and is closely related to *E. coli*; however, a key difference is the high level of virulence found with *Shigella* spp. Certain strains of invasive *E. coli* cause bacillary dysentery that is indistinguishable from shigellosis and share many of the same somatic antigens. The four species able to cause human disease are *S. dysenteriae*, *S. flexneri*, *S. boydii*, and *S. sonnei*, or serogroups A through D, respectively. The differences between them are based upon the O antigen component of the lipopolysaccharide component of the cell wall. *S. dysenteriae* serotype 1 has been recognized as the major epidemic strain of this group of organisms. This serotype is associated with high fatality rates due to its ability to produce a virulence protein known as Shiga toxin.[106] Because of the wide range of serotypes that cause disease worldwide, development of a multivalent vaccine is needed, and research to this end is ongoing.[107] Vaccine development is a priority due to the possibility that shigellosis could re-emerge due to its high infectious potential and its ability to develop multidrug resistance.[108]

Epidemiology

Shigellosis is an important public health problem, especially in developing countries. Humans are the only hosts of *Shigella*. The peak incidence on a worldwide basis is among children 1 to 4 years of age; however, outbreaks of *S. dysenteriae* type 1 affect all age groups equally. This prevalence is linked to poor hygiene and contaminated water supplies. In the United States and Europe, groups at risk for infection include children in day care centers, migrant workers, individuals traveling to developing countries, habitants of custodial institutions, and men who have sex with men. HIV infection is associated with a more severe clinical presentation of shigellosis that can include recurrence of intestinal involvement and even bacteremia.[109,110]

A literature review published in 1999 estimated that the annual number of *Shigella* episodes is approximately 164.7 million throughout the world, with almost all (163.2 million) occurring in developing countries and causing 1.1 million deaths.[111] According to this review, 69 percent of all cases and 61 percent of all deaths occurred in children younger than 5 years. In addition, the median percentages of isolates of *S. dysenteriae*, *S. flexneri*, *S. boydii*, and *S. sonnei* were 6 percent, 60 percent, 6 percent, and 15 percent, respectively, in developing countries, with 30 percent of *S. dysenteriae* being type 1. In developed nations, 77 percent of isolates were *S. sonnei*, with only 1 percent of cases caused by *S. dysenteriae*.[111] However, a more recent population-based study in Thailand showed an estimated incidence that was 10 to 100 times greater, suggesting that incidence rates of shigellosis are generally underestimated.[112] In addition, a landmark prospective epidemiologic study was conducted across six Asian countries.[113] The authors found that the incidence of *Shigella* among other enteric diseases was similar to past reports, with approximately 5 percent of all reported cases of diarrhea being caused by *Shigella* spp.[111] This study also found, by using a PCR technique, that 33 percent of culture-negative samples had detectable *Shigella* antigen, highlighting the need for improved diagnostic tools. Finally, a trend toward less severe clinical disease was observed in this study.[113]

Although Shiga dysentery is caused primarily by epidemic outbreaks, most shigellosis is a manifestation of endemic strains. These are responsible for as many as 10 percent of all episodes of diarrhea in children younger than 5 years in developing countries.[114] *S. sonnei* generally causes disease that is less severe and is associated with common-source outbreaks in the United States, often involving contaminated water and uncooked food.[115] *S. boydii* was first identified from an outbreak in India and is uncommonly the causative agent of disease other than in that region.[116]

Shigella infection leads to the development of protective immunity. Endemic infections lead to an incidence peak during the first 5 years and then decline, suggesting that immunoprotection diminishes repeated infection rates.[117] This response is serotype specific and directed toward the lipopolysaccharide O antigen of the organism. Antibody responses have been shown to be mounted against antigenic determinants of *Shigella*, which typically decline after 1 to 2 years. A longitudinal study in children revealed a 76 percent protection efficiency to re-infection with the same serotype.[114] In other studies that focus on adults, volunteers infected with *S. sonnei* were protected from disease manifestations, including fever and diarrhea, following rechallenge with the same strain.[118]

Transmission

Shigella is highly contagious, as it has been shown that an extremely low inoculum (as few as 10 organisms) is able to cause disease.[119] This low dose of organisms is responsible for the high transmissibility and also for the high recurrence rates present in developing areas. It is not clear why such a low-dose response occurs, though studies suggest that infection with

Shigella does not require reduced gastric acidity.[120] One study demonstrates that *Shigella* can survive at a pH as low as 2.5 for at least 2 hours.[121] In comparison, *Shigella* and invasive *E. coli* share the same virulence determinants, but invasive *E. coli* requires a dose 1,000 times higher for infectivity.[38] The predominant route of transmission is fecal-oral contact. Although the organism can also be transmitted by contaminated water, food, and other objects, it displays relatively poor survival outside of human hosts. Flies and other insects can also serve as a vector for spread in situations in which fecal material is exposed.[122]

Although most spread is through person-to-person contact, epidemics have occurred through the contamination of water supplies and food stores. Water wells are often identified as sources of outbreaks. In addition, hand transmission has been demonstrated to be a common means for *Shigella* spread, especially in custodial institutions.[123] Long-term carriage of *Shigella* has been documented to occur in a small percentage of infected persons, which can contribute to the spread of the disease.[124]

Disease Manifestations

Shigella spp. cause dysentery by invading the mucosa of the intestine, where the bacteria multiply within colonic epithelial cells. They then cause cell death and spread laterally to infect adjacent cells, leading to the development of mucosal inflammation, ulceration, and bleeding.[125] The host then develops diarrhea and possibly dysentery with severe abdominal cramping, frequent bloody stools, and tenesmus. This initial invasion of the colonic epithelium and lamina propria initiates the inflammatory process in the colon, causing a cytokine-mediated inflammation followed by necrosis of the epithelium, resulting in colitis and ulceration that manifests a bloody, mucoid type of diarrhea. This acute inflammatory response of the host contributes to the pathophysiology of the process of this disease.

Shigella invades epithelial cells by reorganizing the cytoskeleton through a process of macropinocytosis.[126] *Shigella* species produce three different enterotoxins: chromosome-encoded *Shigella* enterotoxin 1 (almost exclusively produced by *S. flexneri*),[127] plasmid-mediated *Shigella* enterotoxin 2 (found in many serotypes),[128] and the phage-borne Shiga toxin (produced by *S. dysenteriae*). Shiga toxin produces enterotoxic, cytotoxic, and neurotoxic effects. It binds to receptors in the small bowel, thereby blocking the absorption of many electrolytes and proteins, and it causes fever and abdominal cramping.

Manifestations depend upon the infecting species and its virulence factors, the age of the host, and the immune status. The incubation phase usually is 1 to 4 days but may be as long as 8 days in some cases.[129] Severity can range from a short-term, watery diarrhea to inflammatory bowel disease. Constitutional symptoms usually arise within 1 to 2 days of ingestion of the organism and include fever, malaise, and cramping. However, watery diarrhea can often be the only clinical manifestation in cases of mild infection.[117] Physical examination findings may include high fever, abdominal tenderness, and hyperactive bowel sounds. Progression to dysentery can occur within hours to days and can cause more the 20 dysenteric stools per day, which can lead to the loss of serum proteins and nitrogen stores that can increase malnutrition, especially in patients in developing countries.[130] Although anorexia can persist and lead to deterioration of nutritional status, extensive fluid loss is rare with shigellosis, so rates of severe dehydration are low.[131]

Extraintestinal manifestations that have been described to occur include seizures,[132,133] hemolytic anemia leading to hemolytic uremic syndrome,[134] and Reiter's syndrome.[135] However, most infections are self-limiting and resolve within 5 to 7 days. Life-threatening complications are most often observed in infants and children living in developing countries and include dehydration, hyponatremia, toxic megacolon, and intestinal perforation.[132]

Diagnosis

Clinicians should include shigellosis in their differential diagnosis in patients presenting with watery diarrhea and fever. Bloody, mucoid stools can indicate Shigella infection, but other species cannot be excluded (i.e., E. coli, Salmonella enteritidis, Entamoeba histolytica, and Yersinia enterocolitica). Sigmoidoscopy reveals diffuse erythema of the colonic mucosa accompanied by small ulcers. However, diagnosis is dependent upon identification of the bacteria from the feces. Shigella can be cultured, and it is best to collect samples early in the course of the disease and before beginning antimicrobial treatment because colony counts decline, and having negative stool cultures at the midpoint of a patient's course can be common.[122,136] Isolation is performed by streaking selective agar media and aerobic incubation, which disallow the growth of anaerobic normal gut flora. In addition, because strains of S. dysenteriae and S. sonnei do not grow well on selection agars, a liquid enrichment medium can be inoculated with stool and subcultured onto selective agar after a short growth period. Following overnight incubation, colonies are inoculated into triple sugar iron agar slants. Shigella will produce an alkaline slant with no gas bubbles in the agar; this reaction provides a presumptive identification.[115] Antimicrobial susceptibility testing should be performed on all isolated Shigella cultures.

Although total white blood cell counts are not consistent in patients with shigellosis, leukopenia and leukocytosis can both be observed. In addition, a "left shift" in a patient with diarrhea can be indicative of bacillary dysentery. Direct microscopic examination of stool samples will exhibit the presence of high numbers of polymorphonuclear leukocytes; however, this is also a feature of other bacterial infections of the colon, including salmonellosis, E. coli colitis, and Campylobacter enteritis.[137] Serologic examination of individual patients is not helpful in directing therapy, because antibody responses do not develop until after the disease has resolved. However, this serology can help in the epidemiologic evaluation of outbreaks caused by a known serotype.[136] More sensitive and rapid techniques have been developed to identify Shigella, utilizing gene probes and PCR technology. However, these techniques require specialized equipment and are not yet widely used. Recently, PCR techniques have been developed to identify particular Shigella and E. coli O serotypes, but mostly these can identify only one pathogen type at a time.[138,139] A DNA microarray technique that targets O serotype-specific genes so that robust subtyping is possible with these organisms recently has been described and could be utilized in the future.[140]

Treatment

The cornerstone of therapy for shigellosis is rehydration. Although severe dehydration is rare, adequate hydration can decrease other sequelae and relegate infection with Shigella to a self-limiting disease. Effective antimicrobial therapy can cause dramatic symptomatic improvement within 48 hours and can limit the duration of the illness to 3 days.[141] Without appropriate antimicrobial therapy, the risk of complication is significantly increased, such that if Shigella is suspected patients should be treated with an antimicrobial agent based upon local susceptibility patterns, according to the World Health Organization (WHO). If improvement in symptoms is observed within 2 days, treatment should be continued for 5 days.

Shigella resistance to sulfonamides, tetracyclines, and ampicillin is widespread, so these agents should not be used empirically.[142] The drugs of choice currently include the fluoroquinolones and azithromycin. Quinolones, including ciprofloxacin, levofloxacin, and norfloxacin, are effective in one or two doses for mild forms of the disease and should be continued for 3 to 5 days for more severe infections.[143,144] Fluoroquinolone resistance and the potential for cartilage damage in children have spurred the investigation of alternative therapies. Azithromycin has been shown in randomized trials to be an effective treatment option for shigellosis.[145] In addition, recent studies have shown that both cefixime and ceftriaxone have adequate cure rates in children with Shigella infection.[146,147] Although empiric therapy is important in the treatment of these patients, inadequate antimicrobial therapy has the potential to exacerbate the disease due to the effect of antimicrobial agents on normal host flora that compete with Shigella. Therefore, it is imperative to consult local resistance patterns when making therapeutic decisions in these cases. The use of antimotility agents is generally not recommended because of their potential to increase the mucosal invasion of the bacteria. The use of diphenoxylate has been associated with the worsening of bacillary dysentery and could increase the incidence of development of toxic megacolon.[148] Diarrhea in this case is thought to be a protective mechanism for limiting the infectibility of the organism.

Currently, no protective vaccine exists against Shigella, but several vaccines using antigenic determinants or live or attenuated bacteria are under development.[125] Studies that show homologous immunity after infection with a particular strain demonstrate the potential for the development of a protective vaccine.[149] Immunization experiments have demonstrated that protective immunity from vaccination can approximate that which is imparted from recovery from the disease itself.[150]

Infection Prevention and Public Health Concerns

The most effective method of controlling spread of the disease is through the preservation of clean water and adequate fecal waste disposal. To establish safe water supplies, general sanitation and effective sewage systems are of critical importance in limiting shigellosis, as well as all enteric bacterial infections. Chlorination of the water supply also diminishes the threat of *Shigella* outbreaks. Insecticides have also been shown to decrease the incidence of shigellosis by impacting insects as vectors for spread.[151] These are the long-term strategies for developing countries and regions to use controlling the incidence and spread of shigellosis.

Other intervention strategies include individual educational programs to inform the public of various measures, including the avoidance of fecal contamination of food. Personal food hygiene and refrigeration are among the strategies for improvement. The degree of contact between patients with the disease and susceptible individuals is a major determinant of transmission. Through education, this can be minimized along with other aspects, including hand washing and thorough cooking of foods. In addition, breast-feeding of infants plays a large role in limiting the incidence of infection in infants in developing countries. This is thought to be due to a combination of decreased exposure to contaminated water supplies, earlier development of intestinal flora, and maternal transfer of protective antibodies.[152]

Although the severity of illness caused by *Shigella* has seemingly declined during the past decades, a major concern is that because of the potential for epidemic outbreaks and the increasing development of antimicrobial resistance, the profile of shigellosis could be easily altered on a local or worldwide stage, causing the infection to become an even greater public health concern.[108] This underscores the need for vaccine development, as well as the investigation of alternative antimicrobial therapies that could provide efficacy in multidrug-resistant infections.

Yersinia Bacterial Gastroenteritis

Background

Yersinia enterocolitica is a Gram-negative coccobacillus that causes the disease yersiniosis in humans. *Yersinia pseudotuberculosis* can cause a similar disease state in humans but is not as well described. Both are fairly infrequent causes of diarrhea and abdominal pain in the United States but are relatively common in northern Europe.

Epidemiology

Y. enterocolitica colonizes the lymphoid tissue of the oropharynx of pigs and other animals. Although this does not cause disease in the animal, biotype 4 serogroup O:3 and O:9 are the strains most commonly isolated from pigs and are the strains most associated with human yersiniosis.[153,154] A few cases from other strains have been described in relation to consumption of milk, chocolate milk, powdered milk, tofu, spring water, and bean sprouts. Serotype O:3-related gastrointestinal illnesses are most commonly seen in the fall and winter in the United States and have been associated with contamination of infant formula and/or bottles during the family's preparation of raw pork intestines (chitterlings) or consumption of chitterlings during holiday meals.[155,156] The organism may be excreted for several weeks after infection and fecal-oral transmission has been reported.[157] The organism's ability to grow at 4°C means that refrigerated meats can be sources of infection.

In addition to infants, other groups appear to be at higher risk of developing yersiniosis. Race appears to be an important risk factor, with 54 percent of cases of yersiniosis occurring in African Americans.[158] Iron-overloaded patients being treated with deferoxamine have shown a strong association to developing sepsis secondary to *Yersinia* infection, as the iron chelator enhances the growth of the organism and inhibits leukocyte responses.[159] Separate studies have evaluated the risk of yersiniosis in patients with beta-thalassemia even when deferoxamine was not being used.[160] Refrigerated stored blood has been identified as a source of sepsis from *Y. enterocolitica*.[161]

Clinical Manifestations

Yersiniosis is most commonly associated with enterocolitis, mesenteric adenitis, terminal ileitis, septicemia, and various immunoreactive conditions, especially reactive arthritis. After an incubation period of 4 to 7 days of an inoculum of ~109 organisms, mucosal ulcerations in the colon, necrotic lesions in Peyer patches, and enlargement of mesenteric lymph nodes may occur.[162]

Acute gastroenteritis symptoms of fever, nausea and vomiting, diarrhea, and abdominal pain may occur with *Y. enterocolitica* infection but cannot be differentiated from other causes. Symptoms may last 1 to 3 weeks. When pain localizes in the right lower quadrant and is associated with peripheral leukocytosis and fecal leukocytes and blood, appendicitis must be excluded but may be a clue for the regional mesenteric lymphadenitis or terminal ileitis associated with yersiniosis.

Approximately 10 to 30 percent of adults develop a reactive polyarthritis involving the knees, ankles, toes, wrists, and/or fingers beginning a few days to months after the onset of acute symptoms. These symptoms may persist more than 1 month in two-thirds of cases and more than 4 months in one-third of cases. Persistent pain consistent with sacroiliitis has been associated in patients with HLA-B27.[163] Other conditions such as erythema nodosum, exudative pharyngitis, pneumonia, empyema, osteomyelitis, endocarditis, and lung abscesses have also been reported.

Laboratory Diagnosis

Routine laboratory results during yersiniosis include nonspecific findings of leukocytosis or elevated sedimentation rate. Most laboratories in the United States do not routinely screen for *Yersinia* species. The organism may be isolated from stool, lymph nodes, oral pharynx, blood, or any abscess site. Its isolation from stool samples is made more difficult by its relatively slow growth at 37°C and overgrowth of coliforms. Selective growth medium (cefsulodin-irgasin-novobiocin) is available and enables a distinct morphology when the organism is incubated at 28°C or lower. Serology and documentation of a fourfold increase in convalescent titers may be useful.

Treatment

Y. enterocolitica typically demonstrates *in vitro* susceptibility to aminoglycosides, chloramphenicol, tetracycline, TMP-SMX, piperacillin, ciprofloxacin, and the third-generation cephalosporins. Yersinieae are typically resistant to macrolides, and resistance to fluoroquinolones has been reported.[164] There are no data to indicate that all cases of *Yersinia* enterocolitis require antibiotic therapy. However, caution should be observed in the underlying immune status of the patient. More severe cases such as sepsis do require antibiotic management. Patients with long-term sequela of yersiniosis (i.e., reactive arthritis) may be treated with nonsteroidal anti-inflammatory agents.

Infection Prevention and Public Health Concerns

Yersiniosis is a fairly uncommon cause of gastroenteritis in the United States. Still, safe food processing and preparation and hand hygiene, especially during the preparation of pork or handling of pigs, are necessary to prevent its transmission. Waterborne transmission can be prevented through routine water treatment procedures, and transfusion-associated transmission may be prevented through routine testing of blood transfusion products and limiting their storage time.

Campylobacter Bacterial Gastroenteritis

Etiologic Agent

Campylobacter species are microaerophilic, motile, non-spore-forming, curved Gram-negative rods. They are a member of the *Campylobacteraceae* family. Among the several *Campylobacter* species associated with human disease, *C. jejuni* and *C. coli* are the most common causes of acute gastroenteritis.[165] On the other hand, *C. fetus* is more likely to cause extraintestinal infections, including bloodstream and endovascular infections, especially in immunocompromised hosts.[166]

Epidemiology

Campylobacter is a leading cause of acute bacterial gastroenteritis in developed countries. The incidence rate of culture-confirmed *Campylobacter* infection was estimated to be 21.9/100,000 person-years between 1996 and 1999 in the United States. It appears that the incidence rate of *Campylobacter* infection in the United States declined by 31 percent in 2007 to 12.8/100,000 person-years.[74,75,167] This compares with an incidence rate of 30.2 and 39.1 per 100,000 person-years in Canada and the Netherlands, respectively, as recently reported.[168,169] Similar to other enteric pathogens, there is a seasonal variation in *Campylobacter* infection, with a peak in the incidence rate during the summer and early fall.[75-77,167,170] Children younger than 5 years and young adults between 15 and 29 years of age appear to be at higher risk of infection than do individuals in other age groups. Similarly, the incidence rate of *Campylobacter* infection is higher in men than in women.[75,167,171] Patients with HIV infection also are at increased risk of *Campylobacter* infection.[172]

Transmission

Campylobacter is commonly found in the gastrointestinal tract of cattle, poultry, and other animals. Therefore, consumption of poorly cooked meat or poultry products is the major source of sporadic *Campylobacter* infections. Other reported sources of infection include unpasteurized milk and cheeses, unchlorinated water that is potentially contaminated with animal feces, contact with pets with diarrhea, and fecal-oral person-to-person transmission.[170,173-175]

Ingestion of as little as 500 organisms has been associated with infection in humans. Fatty media such as milk, for example, decrease inhibition by gastric acid and facilitate passage into the small intestine.[176,177]

Disease Manifestations

The incubation period is from 1 to 7 days. Higher organism load is associated with a shorter incubation period. The symptoms of *Campylobacter* infection usually start with a prodrome of fever, headache, malaise, and myalgia. Gastrointestinal symptoms start 1 to 2 days later with diarrhea and abdominal pain. Various forms of diarrhea have been reported, ranging from severe watery diarrhea with more than 10 bowel movements a day to bloody diarrhea. Abdominal pain is often colicky and relieved by defecation. Right lower quadrant abdominal pain sometimes mimics acute appendicitis. Tenesmus is another relatively common gastrointestinal symptom. Symptoms usually last from 1 day to 1 week and may be shortened with appropriate antimicrobial therapy.[178-180]

Campylobacter infection is usually a self-limited illness in patients with normal immunity. Fatality has been reported, especially in patients at the extremes of age.[134] Recurrence has been described in untreated patients. Reactive arthritis has been reported in 1.9 to 9.6 percent of patients following *Campylobacter* infection.[181,182] Guillain-Barré syndrome is the most severe complication of *Campylobacter* infection. It is estimated to occur in 1 in every 2,000 people with *Campylobacter* infection. Forty percent of patients with Guillain-Barré syndrome have culture or serologic evidence of *Campylobacter* infection at the time of presentation with neurological symptoms.[183]

Diagnosis

Because the symptoms of bacterial gastroenteritis overlap, microbiologic testing is usually required for the diagnosis of *Campylobacter* infection. *C. jejuni* grows best at 42°C and requires filtration techniques and selective cephalosporin-containing media for isolation in stool cultures. Blood-free media, such as charcoal cefoperazone deoxycholate agar and charcoal-based selective medium, and blood-containing media, such as Campy-CVA and Skirrow medium, have been used for isolation of *Campylobacter* species from stool specimens.[165] Blood cultures are positive in only 1 percent of patients with *Campylobacter* gastroenteritis.[177]

Treatment

Erythromycin and other macrolides remain the treatment of choice for *Campylobacter* gastroenteritis.[184] Trends of increasing resistance to fluoroquinolones have been reported from different geographic locations in the world.[185] It appears that there is a temporal association between increasing fluoroquinolone resistance among *Campylobacter* isolates in the United States and the licensing of these antibiotics for veterinary use in 1995.[103,185,186] It was estimated that 21.7 percent of *Campylobacter* isolates in the United States were resistant to ciprofloxacin in 2005, compared with only 12.9 percent of isolates in 1997.[71] Moreover, returning travelers with *Campylobacter* infections are more likely to have a fluoroquinolone-resistant isolate.[187] Longer duration of symptoms has been described in patients with fluoroquinolone-resistant *Campylobacter* infections. Therefore, the empirical use of fluoroquinolones for *Campylobacter* infections has been discouraged. *C. jejuni* is usually resistant to penicillins and cephalosporins. Susceptibility to TMP-SMX is unreliable.[188]

Infection Prevention and Public Health Concerns

Healthcare-associated transmission of *Campylobacter* infection to other hospitalized patients or healthcare personnel is rare. Standard Precautions, including Barrier Precautions, such as gloves, should be applied upon direct contact with patients with *Campylobacter* infections. Efforts to improve food-processing techniques, especially in poultry products, are essential to reducing the incidence rate of *Campylobacter* infections. Breast-feeding appears to decrease the risk of *Campylobacter* infection in infants.[175]

Edwardsiella tarda

Etiologic Agent

Edwardsiella tarda is a *Bacillus* of the family *Enterobacteriaceae*. It was first described as a new genus in 1965 by Ewing et al.[189] The organism is a Gram-negative rod that is oxidase negative, reduces nitrate to nitrite, and utilizes glucose fermentatively. It is characterized as a nonlactose-fermentative organism that, similar to the *Salmonella* species, is hydrogen-sulfide positive, citrate positive, phenylalanine-deaminase negative, and lysine and ornithine decarboxylating. To distinguish this organism from *Salmonella*, *Arizona*, and *Citrobacter* species, *E. tarda* is indol positive, arginine-dihydrolase negative, and fails to utilize mannitol. The organism is assacharolytic except for glucose.[189]

Epidemiology

E. tarda has been found in freshwater sources (lakes, rivers, and well water), sewage, and a variety of animals, including freshwater fish (catfish, eels, turbot, mullet, Chinook salmon, flounder, carp, tilapia, trout, and striped bass), saltwater fish (grouper), reptiles (snakes, tortoises, turtles), amphibians (frogs), crustaceans, birds, and mammals (including cows and humans).[189,190] Seventy-five percent of catfish pond water samples and 64 percent of mud samples also contained the organism. *E. tarda* was universally culturable from frogs, turtles, and crayfish living in these catfish ponds.[190-193] It is thought that the consumption of water and fish infected with this organism might underlie some of the outbreaks seen.[194,195] Transmission of infection to humans has been seen as wound infections in patients who keep and maintain freshwater aquariums in their homes[196,197] and in individuals sustaining traumatic wounds associated with freshwater fishing or other freshwater exposures.[198-200]

Disease Manifestations

E. tarda is the only species of this genus known to cause disease in humans.[201-203] *E. tarda* has been cultured primarily from the stool of patients with diarrhea as the causative agent of the diarrheal syndrome.[204] Although most patients with *E. tarda*–related diarrhea are immunocompetent, gastroenteritis may also occur in the setting of immunocompromise.[205] It may also be found colonizing the stool of healthy individuals without diarrhea. Most patients with diarrheal disease caused by *E. tarda* demonstrate mild secretory illness that is self-limited, but occasionally patients may have a more severe dysenteric and protracted disease course.[204]

E. tarda has also been shown to cause extraintestinal disease.[196,206] In contrast to the diarrheal disease, invasive disease with *E. tarda* is often seen in patients with underlying immunocompromise. Underlying disease conditions that predispose patients to infection with *E. tarda* include liver disease,[203] malignancy, pancytopenia, autoimmune disorders, sickle cell disease, and neonatal age.[207,208] Sepsis, salpingitis,[209] subfrenic and pelvic abscesses, tubo-ovarian abscess,[209] posttraumatic wound infection,[209,210] posttraumatic bacterial peritonitis, pleural infection, hepatic abscesses,[211] and urinary tract infection[212] have all been reported with this agent.

Edwardsiella species are best known as fish pathogens and likely infect humans coming in contact with infected water or food (fish) sources.[192,211]

The pathogenic features of *Edwardsiella* species have been partially uncovered. *E. tarda* strains have been found to invade HEP-2 cells, demonstrate chemotaxis, and produce hemolysin[213] and lysosome inhibitor.[214]

Diagnosis

E. tarda is easily grown on both selective and nonselective bacterial support media. Colonies are smooth and pearly, similar to other *Enterobacteriaceae*. On MacConkey and EMB agar, the organism is nonlactose fermentative.[189] The organism is not enriched by growth in selenite broth. On Hektoen enteric and XLD agars, it produces clear colonies with black centers. The organism is present in the databases for all of the major automated instruments. The key biochemicals used for screening this organism include positive indol and hydrogen sulfide reaction and negative lactose, mannitol, and oxidase reactions.[189]

In fish, where *E. tarda* is a particularly important pathogen, PCR techniques have been developed for rapid detection of this organism.[193,198]

Treatment

From several clinical case reports of isolates from cases of diarrhea, it is known that most cases of diarrhea are self-limiting and will resolve in a few days without any specific treatment. For cases of invasive disease, antibiotic therapy is warranted.[201]

Isolates of *E. tarda* from fish, human, and other animal sources have been shown to have more than 90 percent susceptibility to antibiotic treatment to the antibiotics tested. Norfloxacin, nalidixic acid, tetracycline, chloramphenicol, ampicillin trimethoprim, sulfamethoxazole, ciprofloxacin, and enrofloxacin were found to be the most effective on a weight basis.[212] In the United States, most isolates lack this added resistance, probably due to lower antibiotic pressure on the animal (fish) sources.

Infection Prevention and Public Health Concerns

E. tarda is not a common human pathogen. Efforts to control human disease should focus on managing outbreaks in fish and limiting the handling and consumption of infected fish or using and coming in contact with water that has infected fish.[215]

Aeromonas species

Etiologic Agent

The genus *Aeromonas* is made up of several species of water-loving bacteria. Most infections with these agents are caused by three species, *A. hydrophilia, A. caviae,* and *A. sobria,* though more than a dozen species are recognized within this family, several having been shown to cause human disease.[216] *Aeromonas* is in the family *Aeromonadaceae*, and the aeromonads fall into the group of oxidase-positive fermenters.[217]

Epidemiology

The aeromonads are found naturally in many environmental sites, most notably in water sources[218] and in soil. They are commensals and pathogens in many cold-blooded animals, including reptiles, fish, and amphibians.[219] They are found as required symbiotic commensal flora in leeches that require *Aeromonas* to provide proteolytic enzymes needed to digest blood.[219] They cause furunculosis and ulcerative disease in fish.[217] Contact with fish is a potential mode of transmission.[220,221]

Disease Manifestations

Diarrhea attributed to *Aeromonas* occurs most often in young children[222] and in individuals with recent foreign travel.[221] The clinical presentation most commonly associated with this organism includes watery diarrhea, abdominal pain, and vomiting.[223] Fever is variably present. There are usually no fecal leukocytes detected. The diarrhea is usually nonbloody. Most cases are self-limited, though occasional cases may be chronic in nature.[224] Associated morbidities included Gram-negative bacteremia and tissue and muscle infections.[216,225] The species most commonly associated with diarrheal syndromes are *A. hydrophilia, A. sobria,* and *A. caviae*.[221,226] The association of the *Aeromonas* species with diarrhea is not completely resolved, however. There are several studies in the literature that clearly point to the role of these organisms in causing human diarrheal disease.[222] Several of the more commonly seen species produce identifiable enterotoxins.[216] There have been reported outbreaks of diarrheal disease in long-term care facilities that have been linked to *Aeromonas* as the only pathogen isolated from the stool.[226] One of these outbreaks demonstrated the same strain of bacterium cultured from six children and one sink in a hospital ward in India.[226] One researcher found that *Aeromonas* species were more likely to be isolated from soft stool than from blood or watery stool, again suggesting they are not associated with diarrhea.[223]

The *Aeromonas* species have been definitively associated with a variety of invasive infections besides diarrhea.[227] These infections include cellulitis, wound infections,[228] septicemia, pneumonia[229] endocarditis, urinary tract infections,[230] meningitis, peritonitis,[231] hepatobiliary infections, and ear infections.[224,225,228,230,232] Iatrogenic infections with *Aeromonas* have been linked to the use of medicinal leeches, which are known to harbor *Aeromonas* species in their intestinal tract as part of their flora.[219,233]

Diagnosis

Aeromonas species should be routinely screened for as part of the routine stool culture. Most laboratories will use the overnight growth from stool on the sheep blood agar plate to perform a sweep oxidase screen. This should detect all oxidase-positive organisms, including *Aeromonas, Plesiomonas,* and *Vibrio* species. Most isolates are expected to be oxidase-positive glucose fermenters with DNAse positivity. Most species are beta-hemolytic on sheep blood agar and are motile.[217]

Treatment

Antibiotic therapy for acute diarrhea attributed to *Aeromonas* species is rarely required because of the self-limited nature of this syndrome. However, in cases of diarrhea, chronic diarrhea may be seen in approximately 50 percent of patients, so treatment may be required.[234] Most isolates originating from stool specimens would not have antibiotic susceptibility performed or reported. Information on antibiotic susceptibility patterns therefore comes from cases with invasive disease where therapy is suggested. A study looking at the susceptibility pattern of clinical isolates demonstrated universal susceptibility to gentamycin, amikacin, ciprofloxacin, and trimethoprim-sulfamethoxazole.[234] Aeromonas species may contain inducible broad-spectrum beta-lactamase enzymes, so penicillins, cephalosporins, and carbapenems should be avoided; the fluoroquinolones, such as ciprofloxacin, should represent first-line therapy.[234]

Infection Prevention and Public Health Concerns

Aeromonas species are rarely seen in epidemic situations. When seen causing outbreaks of diarrhea, common-source contaminated food or water is implicated in Aeromonas transmission.[226] Most of the significant iatrogenic spread of Aeromonas occurs in the setting of leech therapy and is therefore unavoidable. External decontamination of the leeches with a bleach solution prior to use may help to limit this type of infection.[233]

Plesiomonas shigelloides

Etiologic Agent

Similar to Aeromonas species, Plesiomonas shigelloides is in the process of being reclassified based on genetic relatedness. Originally part of the family Vibrionaceae, it is now thought that P. shigelloides is more closely related to the genus Proteus. However, phenotypically it behaves more like a Vibrionaceae in that it is oxidase positive,[235] glucose fermentative, and is found in many water environments and in cold-blooded animals.[236] P. shigelloides is the only species in the genus.

Epidemiology

P. shigelloides is present in groundwater worldwide. Similar to Aeromonas species, it infects various cold-blooded animals, such as turtles, lizards, snakes, fish, shellfish, and frogs[237] as well as warm-blooded animals, such as pigs, dogs, cats, goats, and monkeys.[237] Human infection generally occurs through the consumption of infected water or food. Human cases of diarrhea have been associated with consumption of contaminated water,[238] food washed in contaminated water,[236,238] or raw shellfish.[235,239] Infections are more common during the summer in tropical regions when the bacterial counts in the groundwater are generally high.

Disease Manifestations

P. shigelloides causes gastroenteritis in adults and children.[239,240] This usually presents as a mild watery diarrhea without blood or mucus. Symptoms tend to be self-limiting,[241] resolving in about 3 days, though a longer disease course may be seen in some.[241] Associated symptoms include vomiting,

fever, and abdominal pain in a significant number of patients. P. shigelloides is often identified along with other enteropathogens.[241] Extraintestinal infections with this organism are known to occur and include sepsis,[242] cellulitis, meningitis,[243] acute cholecystitis,[244] pneumonia,[245] and septic arthritis. Although asymptomatic carriage may be seen in some patients, these appear to be the minority of cases.[240]

Diagnosis

P. shigelloides can be readily cultured from stool on both sheep blood agar and MacConkey plates. It can be detected on the blood agar plate by performing a sweep oxidase, which is positive with this organism. It is lactose nonfermentative on the MacConkey agar. It can be differentiated from the species of Aeromonas by its lack of hemolysis on the blood agar plate, negative DNAse activity, and decarboxylation of lysine, ornithine, and arginine. It is mannitol negative and inositol positive.

Treatment

Diarrhea with P. shigelloides is predominantly self-limited and should require only supportive care but no antibiotics. Only invasive or persistent disease should be treated.[240] Most strains are susceptible to the quinolones, trimethoprim-sulfamethoxazole, tetracycline, chloramphenicol, and aminoglycosides.[236]

Infection Prevention and Public Health Concerns

Because most infections are linked to the consumption of contaminated food or water, the public health focus should be to ensure the safety of the water supply and clean food and observing hand hygiene of food handlers.[246] Contaminated ground water needs to be adequately chlorinated, filtered, or boiled before consumption or use in any food preparation activities.[238] WHO recommends that people avoid bathing in contaminated water due to the risk of inoculation of water into the mouth.[236]

Bacillus cereus

Etiologic Agent

Bacillus cereus is a Gram-positive, spore-forming Bacillus belonging to the B. cereus group within the genus Bacillus. There are six species recognized within this genus: B. anthracis, B. mycoides, B. pseudomycoides, B. weihenstephanensis, B. thuringiensis, and B. cereus sensu stricto. The taxonomic classifications of the various genera are very problematic, in that B. anthracis, B thuringiensis, and B. cereus are very closely related, sharing their 16s rRNA sequences.[247] Analysis of chromosomal markers similarly demonstrates significant homology, suggesting that B. cereus, B. anthracis, and B. thuringiensis should be considered in the same species.[247] A more complete discussion of the taxonomy of this organism is presented by Arnesen et al.[248]

B. cereus grows aerobically but also is capable of tolerating anaerobic growth conditions. The production of endospores allows this organism to survive under stressful situations (heating, acidic pH, and desiccating conditions) encountered in nature and food manufacturing.[249]

Epidemiology

B. cereus has been isolated from many food sources, including meats and meat products; milk and other dairy products; vegetables; fruit; baby food; pasta; rice; bread; spices; soups; starch; probiotics; and dietary supplements.[250] Its presence in a variety of food items likely reflects the highly adherent quality of the endospores, resulting in their inclusion in many food products. Nonfood sources include dirt, tobacco, environmental sources, and manure.[250] In a study of ready-to-eat foods in a Danish market, more than 98 percent of food items tested contained some *B. cereus*-like organisms, with 0.5 percent of samples containing bacterial counts above 10^4 cfu/g of food. The highest levels of bacterial growth of *B. cereus*-like organisms were found in fresh vegetables (tomatoes and cucumbers), heat-treated rice cakes, and desserts with milk, rice, and cake custard.[251] Studies looking at the incidence of *B. cereus* in human stool have identified this organism both in healthy controls (1.8 percent of individuals) and in patients with diarrhea (9.5 percent). A nonsignificant distribution depending upon age was also seen, with children younger than 1 year being less likely than children older than 1 year or adults to harbor this organism. Those strains seen in asymptomatic individuals were more likely to lack all genes coding for hemolytic and nonhemolytic toxins.[252] The incidence of human diarrheal or vomiting disease caused by *B. cereus* has not been well documented because no countries require reporting of cases, and there is probably also underreporting due to the short, self-limiting disease course seen with this organism. From CDC data collected on foodborne illness surveillance in the United States, *B. cereus* was the confirmed pathogen identified in 0.5 to 1.1 percent of outbreaks seen yearly.[253]

The pathogenic potential of *B. cereus* is linked to the production of one or more toxins. The toxins involved in diarrheal disease are the hemolysin BL complex (HBL), nonhemolytic enterotoxin complex (NHE), and cytotoxin, whereas a single toxin (cereulide) is responsible for emetic disease.[254,255] In the study by Al-Khatib et al., 48 percent of isolates contain the genes coding for all three of the hemolytic enterotoxin genes HBL, whereas 58 percent carried two, and 68 percent carried three genes in this complex. Similarly, the nonhemolytic enterotoxin genes demonstrated 100 percent distribution within the diarrhea-associated strains, with 71 percent of isolates containing all three genes within that complex.[252]

Disease Manifestations

There are two forms of gastrointestinal disease caused by *B. cereus*, emetic disease and diarrheal disease. The disease is due to several toxins, which includes four hemolysins, emesis-inducing toxin, and proteases.[256,257] Emetic disease results from the ingestion of a preformed cyclic heat-stable dodecadepsipep-

tide, cereulide, and is present in food in which sporulation and bacterial growth has occurred.[258] The foods most commonly implicated in the poisoning are fried or boiled rice, cooked noodles, and pastries. In the United States, fried rice is the single most common food source implicated in cases of emetic disease, and most of these outbreaks can be traced to improper holding times or temperature of storage of the food products.[259,260] Diarrheal diseases are caused by several toxins that are produced during vegetative growth of the organism once they have germinated within the small intestine.[255,261] Symptoms include abdominal pain, nausea, and watery diarrhea, with onset of symptoms seen 8 to 16 hours after ingestion. Duration of symptoms is generally short, 12 to 24 hours, but occasional cases may persist for days. In contrast to emetic disease, meats, dairy products, and vegetables are the most commonly implicated food sources associated with diarrheal disease.[261,262]

In addition to gastrointestinal disease, *B. cereus* occasionally causes nonintestinal manifestations.[257] Infections with this organism include periodontitis, wound and other skin infections, keratitis, endophthalmitis, posttraumatic ophthalmitis, necrotizing meningitis and meningoencephalitis, brain abscess, endocarditis, and sepsis, especially in patients with underlying immunocompromise in whom there has been a preceding gastrointestinal syndrome.[256]

Diagnosis

B. cereus colonies grow rapidly on blood agar, producing flat and spreading colonies with undulating edges. The colonies are gray with a ground-glass appearance. Beta-hemolysis is generally very pronounced. Bacterial cells are large, measuring 1.0 to 1.2 μm by 3.0 to 5.0 μm. Spores are produced after several days of aerobic growth, are oval in shape, and do not distend the cell. *B. cereus* is motile, does not ferment mannitol, and is lecithinase positive on egg yolk agar.[263] Specialty media have been specifically designed to detect *B. cereus* present in food.[264] The MIDI cell wall fatty acid analyzer can also be used to speciate the *Bacillus* species. It is important to note that many clinical laboratories do not routinely identify *Bacillus* species from stool specimens unless it is specifically to rule out *B. anthracis*.

For toxin detection assays Ped-2E9 assay could be used as a rapid method for sensitive detection of enterotoxins. This is more reliable than the two commercial diarrheal toxin assay kits (BDE-VIA and BCET-RPLA).[265] Because pathogenic and nonpathogenic strains of *B. cereus* differ in the amounts of the various enterotoxins produced, quantitative assays to detect both HBL and NHE are necessary to differentiate fecal flora from truly pathogenic strains of this organism.[266] PCR assays have been designed to identify genes specific to the emetic toxin cereulide,[267] to the two enterotoxic protein complexes HBL and NHE, and enterotoxin T (bc-D-ENT).[266]

Strain typing may provide additional important information regarding outbreak situations.[265] The enterotoxin genes of 49 strains belong to different phylogenetic branches of the *B. cereus* group assessed using a panel of *B. cereus* strains with known toxin profiles and were successfully applied to characterize strains from food and clinical diagnostic labs as well as for the toxin gene profiling of *B. cereus*.[253]

Treatment

Most studies do not address treatment because the vomiting and diarrheal diseases stimulated by *B. cereus* are generally short and self-limiting, requiring no therapeutic interventions. In studies looking at the susceptibility pattern for diarrheal strains of *B. cereus*, all strains are expected to be susceptible to chloramphenicol, clindamycin, and gentamicin but resistant to ampicillin, cephalothin, and oxacillin.[251] Most strains of *B. cereus* produce beta-lactamases, rendering them resistant to all penicillins and cephalosporins. The use of β-lactams as single agents appears to be a limited option for the future, but the discovery of novel β-lactamase inhibitors or inhibitor combinations will allow use of β-lactams against multidrug-resistant bacteria.[268]

Infection Prevention and Public Health Concerns

Outbreaks caused by *B. cereus* are likely underreported due to the short time course of illness. Many patients likely do not present for either treatment or diagnosis. The single most important way to prevent outbreaks with *B. cereus* is to store at-risk food items under the appropriate storage conditions, particularly with regard to temperature and length of storage.[260]

REFERENCES

1. Karmali MA, Steele BT, Petric M, et al. Sporadic cases of haemolytic-uraemic syndrome associated with faecal cytotoxin and cytotoxin-producing *Escherichia coli* in stools. *Lancet* 1983 Mar 19;1(8325):619–620.
2. Riley LW, Remis RS, Helgerson SD, et al. Hemorrhagic colitis associated with a rare *Escherichia coli* serotype. *N Engl J Med* 1983 Mar 24;308(12):681–685.
3. Trabulsi LR, Keller R, Tardelli Gomes TA. Typical and atypical enteropathogenic *Escherichia coli*. *Emerg Infect Dis* 2002 May;8(5):508–513.
4. Ewing WH. Studies on the occurrence of *Escherichia coli* serotypes associated with diarrheal disease. Atlanta: U.S. Communicable Disease Center, Laboratory Branch, 1963.
5. Centers for Disease Control and Prevention (CDC). Outbreaks of *Escherichia coli* O157:H7 infections among children associated with farm visits—Pennsylvania and Washington, 2000. *MMWR Morb Mortal Wkly Rep* 2001 Apr 20;50(15):293–297.
6. Centers for Disease Control and Prevention. Outbreak of *Escherichia coli* O157:H7 and *Campylobacter* among attendees of the Washington County Fair—New York, 1999. *MMWR Morb Mortal Wkly Rep* 1999 Sep 17;48(36):803–805.
7. Rangel J, Sparling P, Crowe C, et al. Epidemiology of *Escherichia coli* O157:H7 outbreaks, United States, 1982–2002. *Emerg Infect Dis* 2005 Apr;11(4):603–609.
8. Rogers MF, Rutherford GW, Alexander SR, et al. A population-based study of hemolytic-uremic syndrome in Oregon, 1979–1982. *Am J Epidemiol* 1986 Jan;123(1):137–142.
9. Tarr PI, Hickman RO. Hemolytic uremic syndrome epidemiology: a population-based study in King County, Washington, 1971 to 1980. *Pediatrics* 1987 Jul;80(1):41–45.
10. Tarr PI, Tran NT, Wilson RA. *Escherichia coli* O157:H7 in retail ground beef in Seattle: results of a one-year prospective study. *J Food Prot* 1999 Feb;62(2):133–139.
11. Bhan MK, Bhandari N, Sazawal S, et al. Descriptive epidemiology of persistent diarrhoea among young children in rural northern India. *Bull World Health Organ* 1989;67(3):281–288.
12. Bhan MK, Raj P, Levine MM, et al. Enteroaggregative *Escherichia coli* associated with persistent diarrhea in a cohort of rural children in India. *J Infect Dis* 1989 Jun;159(6):1061–1064.
13. Adachi JA, Jiang ZD, Mathewson JJ, et al. Enteroaggregative *Escherichia coli* as a major etiologic agent in traveler's diarrhea in 3 regions of the world. *Clin Infect Dis* 2001 Jun 15;32(12):1706–1709.
14. Nataro JP, Kaper JB. Diarrheagenic *Escherichia coli*. *Clin Microbiol Rev* 1998 Jan;11(1):142–201.
15. Beatty M, Bopp C, Wells J, et al. Enterotoxin producing *Escherichia coli* O169:H41,United States. *Emerg Infect Dis* 2004 Mar;10(3):518–521.
16. Oldfield EC 3rd, Wallace MR. The role of antibiotics in the treatment of infectious diarrhea. *Gastroenterol Clin North Am* 2001 Sep;30(3):817–836.
17. Mandell GL, Bennett JE, Raphael D. Mandell, Douglas, and Bennett's *Principles and Practice of Infectious Diseases,* 5th ed. Philadelphia: Churchill Livingstone, 2000.
18. Jackson MP, Newland JW, Holmes RK, et al. Nucleotide sequence analysis of the structural genes for Shiga-like toxin I encoded by bacteriophage 933J from *Escherichia coli*. *Microb Pathol* 1987 Feb;2(2):147–153.
19. Karmali MA, Arbus GS, Petric M, et al. Hospital-acquired *Escherichia coli* O157:H7 associated haemolytic uraemic syndrome in a nurse. *Lancet* 1988 Mar 5;1(8584):526.
20. Wong CS, Jelacic S, Habeeb RL, et al. The risk of the hemolytic-uremic syndrome after antibiotic treatment of *Escherichia coli* O157:H7 infections. *N Engl J Med* 2000 Jun 29;342(26):1930–1936.
21. Mead PS, Griffin PM. *Escherichia coli* O157:H7. *Lancet* 1998 Oct 10;352(9135):1207–1212.
22. Ochoa TJ, Cleary TG. Epidemiology and spectrum of disease of *Escherichia coli* O157. *Curr Opin Infect Dis* 2003 Jun;16(3):259–263.
23. Robson WL, Leung AK, Miller-Hughes DJ. Recurrent hemorrhagic colitis caused by *Escherichia coli* O157:H7. *Pediatr Infect Dis J* 1993 Aug;12(8):699–701.
24. Siegler RL, Griffin PM, Barrett TJ, et al. Recurrent hemolytic uremic syndrome secondary to *Escherichia coli* O157:H7 infection. *Pediatrics* 1993 Mar;91(3):666–668.
25. March S, Ratnam S. Sorbitol-MacConkey medium for detection of *Escherichia coli* O157:H7 associated with hemorrhagic colitis. *J Clin Microbiol* 1986 May;23(5):869–872.
26. Karch H, Bielaszewska M, Bitzan M, et al. Epidemiology and diagnosis of Shiga toxin-producing *Escherichia coli* infections. *Diagn Microbiol Infect Dis* 1999 Jul;34(3):229–243.
27. Lopez-Saucedo C, Cerna JF, Villegas-Sepulveda N, et al. Single multiplex polymerase chain reaction to detect diverse loci associated with diarrheagenic *Escherichia coli*. *Emerg Infect Dis* 2003 Jan;9(1):127–131.
28. Silva RM, Toledo MR, Trabulsi LR. Correlation of invasiveness with plasmid in enteroinvasive strains of *Escherichia coli*. *J Infect Dis* 1982 Nov;146(5):706.
29. Bender JB, Hedberg CW, Besser JM, et al. Surveillance by molecular subtype for *Escherichia coli* O157:H7 infections in Minnesota by molecular subtyping. *N Engl J Med* 1997 Aug 7;337(6):388–394.
30. Chart H, Smith HR, Scotland SM, et al. Serological identification of *Escherichia coli* O157:H7 infection in haemolytic uraemic syndrome. *Lancet* 1991 Jan 19;337(8734):138–140.
31. Greatorex JS, Thorne GM. Humoral immune responses to Shiga-like toxins and *Escherichia coli* O157 lipopolysaccharide in hemolytic-uremic syndrome patients and healthy subjects. *J Clin Microbiol* 1994 May;32(5):1172–1178.
32. Tarr P, Neill M. *Escherichia coli* O157:H7. *Gastroenterol Clin North Am* 2001 Sep;30(3):735–751.
33. Moseley S, Echeverria P, Seriwatana J, et al. Identification of enterotoxigenic *Escherichia coli* by colony hybridization using three enterotoxin gene probes. *J Infect Dis* 1982 Jun;145(6):863–869.
34. Knutton S, Baldwin T, Williams PH, et al. Actin accumulation at sites of bacterial adhesion to tissue culture cells: basis of a new diagnostic test for enteropathogenic and enterohemorrhagic *Escherichia coli*. *Infect Immun* 1989 Apr;57(4):1290–1298.
35. Levine MM. *Escherichia coli* that cause diarrhea: enterotoxigenic, enteropathogenic, enteroinvasive, enterohemorrhagic, and enteroadherent. *J Infect Dis* 1987 Mar;155(3):377–389.
36. Orskov F. Virulence factors of the bacterial cell surface. *J Infect Dis* 1978 May;137(5):630–633.
37. Tulloch EF Jr, Ryan KJ, Formal SB, et al. Invasive enteropathic *Escherichia coli* dysentery. An outbreak in 28 adults. *Ann Intern Med* 1973 Jul;79(1):13–17.
38. DuPont HL, Formal SB, Hornick RB, et al. Pathogenesis of *Escherichia coli* diarrhea. *N Engl J Med* 1971 Jul 1;285(1):1–9.
39. Harris JR, Wachsmuth IK, Davis BR, et al. High-molecular-weight plasmid correlates with *Escherichia coli* enteroinvasiveness. *Infect Immun* 1982 Sep;37(3):1295–1298.

40. Sansonetti PJ, d'Hauteville H, Ecobichon C, et al. Molecular comparison of virulence plasmids in *Shigella* and enteroinvasive *Escherichia coli*. *Ann Microbiol* (Paris) 1983 May-Jun;134A(3):295–318.

41. Radsel-Medvescek A, Zargi R, Acko M, et al. Colonic involvement in salmonellosis. *Lancet* 1977 Mar 12;1(8011):601.

42. Rowland HA. The complications of typhoid fever. *J Trop Med Hyg* 1961 Jun;64:143–152.

43. Marier R, Wells JG, Swanson RC, et al. An outbreak of enteropathogenic *Escherichia coli* foodborne disease traced to imported French cheese. *Lancet* 1973;2:1376–1378.

44. Sonnenwirth AC, Weaver RE. *Yersinia enterocolitica*. *N Engl J Med* 1970 Dec 24;283(26):1468.

45. Safdar N, Said A, Gangnon R, et al. Risk of hemolytic uremic syndrome after antibiotic treatment of *Escherichia coli* O157:H7 enteritis: a meta-analysis. *JAMA* 2002 Aug 28;8(8):996–1001.

46. Proulx F, Turgeon J, Delage G, et al. Randomized, controlled trial of antibiotic therapy for *Escherichia coli* O157:H7 enteritis. *J Pediatr* 1992 Aug;121(2):299–303.

47. Kitov PI, Sadowska JM, Mulvey G, et al. Shiga-like toxins are neutralized by tailored multivalent carbohydrate ligands. *Nature* 2000 Feb 10;403(6770):669–672.

48. Paton AW, Morona R, Paton JC. A new biological agent for treatment of Shiga toxigenic *Escherichia coli* infections and dysentery in humans. *Nat Med* 2000 Mar;6(3):265–270.

49. Rowe P. Shiga Toxin-producing *Escherichia coli* Infections: Challenges and Opportunities. In: Kaper J, O'Brien A, eds. *Escherichia coli O157:H7 and Other Shiga Toxin-Producing E coli.* Washington, DC: ASM Press, 1998.

50. Trachtman H, Cnaan A, Christen E, et al. Effect of an oral Shiga toxin-binding agent on diarrhea-associated hemolytic uremic syndrome in children: a randomized controlled trial. *JAMA* 2003 Sep 10;290(10):1337–1344.

51. Murray BE, Mathewson JJ, DuPont HL, et al. Emergence of resistant fecal *Escherichia coli* in travelers not taking prophylactic antimicrobial agents. *Antimicrob Agents Chemother* 1990 Apr;34(4):515–518.

52. Thornton SA, Wignall SF, Kilpatrick ME, et al. Norfloxacin compared to trimethoprim/sulfamethoxazole for the treatment of travelers' diarrhea among U.S. military personnel deployed to South America and West Africa. *Mil Med* 1992 Feb;157(2):55–58.

53. Acar JF, Goldstein FW. Trends in bacterial resistance to fluoroquinolones. *Clin Infect Dis* 1997 Jan;24(Suppl 1):S67–S73.

54. Martinez-Martinez L, Pascual A, Jacoby GA. Quinolone resistance from a transferable plasmid. *Lancet* 1998 Mar 14;351(9105):797–799.

55. Molbak K, Baggesen DL, Aarestrup FM, et al. An outbreak of multidrug-resistant, quinolone-resistant *Salmonella* enterica serotype typhimurium DT104. *N Engl J Med* 1999 Nov 4;341(19):1420–1425.

56. Steiner TS, Lima AA, Nataro JP, et al. Enteroaggregative *Escherichia coli* produce intestinal inflammation and growth impairment and cause interleukin-8 release from intestinal epithelial cells. *J Infect Dis* 1998 Jan;177(1):88–96.

57. Cohen MB, Hawkins JA, Weckbach LS, et al. Colonization by Enteroaggregative *Escherichia coli* in travelers with and without diarrhea. *J Clin Microbiol* 1993 Feb;31(2):351–353.

58. Huang DB, Dupont HL. Enteroaggregative *Escherichia coli*: an emerging pathogen in children. *Semin Pediatr Infect Dis* 2004 Oct;15(4):266–271.

59. Frech S, Dupont H, Bourgeois A, et al. Use of a patch containing heat-labile toxin from *Escherichia coli* against travellers' diarrhoea: a phase II, randomized, double-blind, placebo-controlled field trial. *Lancet* 2008 Jun 14;371(9629):2019–2025.

60. Belongia EA, Osterholm MT, Soler JT, et al. Transmission of *Escherichia coli* O157:H7 infection in Minnesota child day-care facilities. *JAMA* 1993 Feb 17;269(7):883–888.

61. Brenner FW, Villar RG, Angulo FJ, et al. *Salmonella* nomenclature. *J Clin Microbiol* 2000 Jul;38(7):2465–2467.

62. Mermin JH, Townes JM, Gerber M, et al. Typhoid fever in the United States, 1985–1994: changing risks of international travel and increasing antimicrobial resistance. *Arch Intern Med* 1998 Mar 23;158(6):633–638.

63. Gupta SK, Medalla F, Omondi MW, et al. Laboratory-based surveillance of paratyphoid fever in the United States: travel and antimicrobial resistance. *Clin Infect Dis* 2008 Jun 1;46(11):1656–1663.

64. Pegues DA, Ohl ME, Miller SI. *Salmonella* Species, Including *Salmonella* typhi. In: Mandell GL, Bennett JE, Dolin R, eds. *Principles and Practice of Infectious Diseases,* 6th ed. Philadelphia: Elsevier Churchill Livingstone, 2005;2636–2654.

65. Verghese A. The "typhoid state" revisited. *Am J Med* 1985 Sep;79(3):370–372.

66. Parry CM, Hien TT, Dougan G, et al. Typhoid fever. *N Engl J Med* 2002 Nov 28;347(22):1770–1782.

67. van Basten JP, Stockenbrugger R. Typhoid perforation. A review of the literature since 1960. *Trop Geogr Med* 1994;46(6):336–339.

68. Farooqui BJ, Khurshid M, Ashfaq MK, et al. Comparative yield of *Salmonella* typhi from blood and bone marrow cultures in patients with fever of unknown origin. *J Clin Pathol* 1991 Mar;44(3):258–259.

69. Khan M, Coovadia YM, Connoly C, et al. The early diagnosis of typhoid fever prior to the Widal test and bacteriological culture results. *Acta Trop* 1998 May;69(2):165–173.

70. Threlfall EJ, Ward LR. Decreased susceptibility to ciprofloxacin in *Salmonella* enterica serotype typhi, United Kingdom. *Emerg Infect Dis* 2001 May-Jun;7(3):448–450.

71. Centers for Disease Control and Prevention (CDC). *National Antimicrobial Resistance Monitoring System—Enteric Bacteria 2005 Annual Report.* 2005. CDC website. Available at: http://www.cdc.gov/narms/.

72. Threlfall EJ, Ward LR, Skinner JA, et al. Ciprofloxacin-resistant *Salmonella* typhi and treatment failure. *Lancet* 1999 May 8;353(9164):1590–1591.

73. Crump JA, Kretsinger K, Gay K, et al. Clinical response and outcome of infection with *Salmonella* enterica serotype typhi with decreased susceptibility to fluoroquinolones: a United States FoodNet Multicenter Retrospective Cohort Study. *Antimicrob Agents Chemother* 2008 Apr;52(4):1278–1284.

74. Preliminary FoodNet data on the incidence of infection with pathogens transmitted commonly through food—10 states, 2007. *MMWR Morb Mortal Wkly Rep* 2008 Apr 11;57(14):366–370.

75. Samuel MC, Vugia DJ, Shallow S, et al. Epidemiology of sporadic *Campylobacter* infection in the United States and declining trend in incidence, FoodNet 1996–1999. *Clin Infect Dis* 2004 Apr 15;38(Suppl 3):S165–S174.

76. Al-Hasan MN, Lahr BD, Eckel-Passow JE, et al. Seasonal Variation in Enterobacteriaceae Bloodstream Infection: A Population-based Study. In: *48th Interscience Conference on Antimicrobial Agents and Chemotherapy.* Washington, DC: American Society for Microbiology/Infectious Diseases Society of America, 2008.

77. Olsen SJ, Bishop R, Brenner FW, et al. The changing epidemiology of *Salmonella*: trends in serotypes isolated from humans in the United States, 1987–1997. *J Infect Dis* 2001 Mar 1;183(5):753–761.

78. Celum CL, Chaisson RE, Rutherford GW, et al. Incidence of salmonellosis in patients with AIDS. *J Infect Dis* 1987 Dec;156(6):998–1002.

79. Lynch M, Painter J, Woodruff R, et al. Surveillance for foodborne-disease outbreaks—United States, 1998–2002. *MMWR Surveill Summ* 2006 Nov 10;55(10):1–42.

80. Blaser MJ, Newman LS. A review of human salmonellosis: I. Infective dose. *Rev Infect Dis* 1982 Nov-Dec;4(6):1096–1106.

81. Multistate outbreak of *Salmonella* typhimurium infections associated with eating ground beef—United States, 2004. *MMWR Morb Mortal Wkly Rep* 2006 Feb 24;55(7):180–182.

82. Three outbreaks of salmonellosis associated with baby poultry from three hatcheries—United States, 2006. *MMWR Morb Mortal Wkly Rep* 2007 Mar 30;56(12):273–276.

83. Braden CR. *Salmonella* enterica serotype enteritidis and eggs: a national epidemic in the United States. *Clin Infect Dis* 2006 Aug 15;43(4):512–517.

84. De Valk H, Delarocque-Astagneau E, Colomb G, et al. A community-wide outbreak of *Salmonella* enterica serotype typhimurium infection associated with eating a raw milk soft cheese in France. *Epidemiol Infect* 2000 Feb;124(1):1–7.

85. Centers for Disease Control and Prevention (CDC). Multistate outbreaks of Salmonella infections associated with raw tomatoes eaten in restaurants—United States, 2005–2006. *MMWR Morb Mortal Wkly Rep* 2007 Sep 7;56(35):909–911.

86. Vojdani JD, Beuchat LR, Tauxe RV. Juice-associated outbreaks of human illness in the United States, 1995 through 2005. *J Food Prot* 2008 Feb;71(2):356–364.

87. Multistate outbreak of *Salmonella* serotype Tennessee infections associated with peanut butter—United States, 2006–2007. *MMWR Morb Mortal Wkly Rep* 2007 Jun 1;56(21):521–524.

88. Centers for Disease Control and Prevention (CDC). Salmonella oranienburg infections associated with fruit salad served in health-care facilities—northeastern United States and Canada, 2006. *MMWR Morb Mortal Wkly Rep* 2007 Oct 5;56(39):1025–1028.

89. Centers for Disease Control and Prevention (CDC). Update: recall of dry dog and cat food products associated with human *Salmonella* schwarzengrund infections—United States, 2008. *MMWR Morb Mortal Wkly Rep* 2008 Nov 7;57(44):1200–1202.

90. Mermin J, Hutwagner L, Vugia D, et al. Reptiles, amphibians, and human *Salmonella* infection: a population-based, case-control study. *Clin Infect Dis* 2004 Apr 15;38(Suppl 3):S253–S261.

91. Centers for Disease Control and Prevention (CDC). Multistate outbreak of human *Salmonella* infections associated with exposure to turtles—United States, 2007–2008. *MMWR Morb Mortal Wkly Rep* 2008 Jan 25;57(3):69–72.

92. Bowen A, Newman A, Estivariz C, et al. Role of acid-suppressing medications during a sustained outbreak of *Salmonella* enteritidis infection in a long-term care facility. *Infect Control Hosp Epidemiol* 2007 Oct;28(10):1202–1205.

93. Saphra I, Winter JW. Clinical manifestations of salmonellosis in man; an evaluation of 7779 human infections identified at the New York *Salmonella* Center. *N Engl J Med* 1957 Jun 13;256(24):1128–1134.

94. Han T, Sokal JE, Neter E. Salmonellosis in disseminated malignant diseases. A seven-year review (1959–1965). *N Engl J Med* 1967 May 11;276(19):1045–1052.

95. Mussche MM, Lameire NH, Ringoir SM. *Salmonella* typhimurium infections in renal transplant patients. Report of five cases. *Nephron* 1975;15(2):143–150.

96. Parsons R, Gregory J, Palmer DL. *Salmonella* infections of the abdominal aorta. *Rev Infect Dis* 1983 Mar-Apr;5(2):227–231.

97. Nair D, Gupta N, Kabra S, et al. *Salmonella* senftenberg: a new pathogen in the burns ward. *Burns* 1999 Dec;25(8):723–727.

98. Nataro JP, Bopp CA, Fields PI, et al. *Escherichia, Shigella*, and *Salmonella*. In: Murray PR, Baron EJ, Pfaller M, eds. *Manual of Clinical Microbiology*, 9th ed. Washington, DC: American Society for Microbiology, 2007;679–683.

99. Casin I, Breuil J, Brisabois A, et al. Multidrug-resistant human and animal *Salmonella* typhimurium isolates in France belong predominantly to a DT104 clone with the chromosome- and integron-encoded beta-lactamase PSE-1. *J Infect Dis* 1999 May;179(5):1173–1182.

100. Allen CA, Fedorka-Cray PJ, Vazquez-Torres A, et al. In vitro and in vivo assessment of *Salmonella* enterica serovar Typhimurium DT104 virulence. *Infect Immun* 2001 Jul;69(7):4673–4677.

101. Glynn MK, Bopp C, Dewitt W, et al. Emergence of multidrug-resistant *Salmonella* enterica serotype typhimurium DT104 infections in the United States. *N Engl J Med* 1998 May 7;338(19):1333–1338.

102. Varma JK, Molbak K, Barrett TJ, et al. Antimicrobial-resistant nontyphoidal *Salmonella* is associated with excess bloodstream infections and hospitalizations. *J Infect Dis* 2005 Feb 15;191(4):554–561.

103. Angulo FJ, Nargund VN, Chiller TC. Evidence of an association between use of anti-microbial agents in food animals and anti-microbial resistance among bacteria isolated from humans and the human health consequences of such resistance. *J Vet Med B Infect Dis Vet Public Health* 2004 Oct-Nov;51(8-9):374–379.

104. Gay K, Robicsek A, Strahilevitz J, et al. Plasmid-mediated quinolone resistance in non-Typhi serotypes of *Salmonella* enterica. *Clin Infect Dis* 2006 Aug 1;43(3):297–304.

105. Whichard JM, Gay K, Stevenson JE, et al. Human *Salmonella* and concurrent decreased susceptibility to quinolones and extended-spectrum cephalosporins. *Emerg Infect Dis* 2007 Nov;13(11):1681–1688.

106. Thorpe CM, Smith WE, Hurley BP, et al. Shiga toxins induce, superinduce, and stabilize a variety of C-X-C chemokine mRNAs in intestinal epithelial cells, resulting in increased chemokine expression. *Infect Immun* 2001 Oct;69(10):6140–6147.

107. Kweon MN. Shigellosis: the current status of vaccine development. *Curr Opin Infect Dis* 2008 Jun;21(3):313–318.

108. Sansonetti PJ. The bacterial weaponry: lessons from *Shigella*. *Ann N Y Acad Sci* 2006 Aug;1072:307–312.

109. Kristjansson M, Viner B, Maslow JN. Polymicrobial and recurrent bacteremia with *Shigella* in a patient with AIDS. *Scand J Infect Dis* 1994;26(4):411–416.

110. Angulo FJ, Swerdlow DL. Bacterial enteric infections in persons infected with human immunodeficiency virus. *Clin Infect Dis* 1995 Aug;21(Suppl 1):S84–S93.

111. Kotloff KL, Winickoff JP, Ivanoff B, et al. Global burden of *Shigella* infections: implications for vaccine development and implementation of control strategies. *Bull World Health Organ* 1999;77(8):651–666.

112. Chompook P, Samosornsuk S, von Seidlein L, et al. Estimating the burden of shigellosis in Thailand: 36-month population-based surveillance study. *Bull World Health Organ* 2005 Oct;83(10):739–746.

113. von Seidlein L, Kim DR, Ali M, et al. A multicentre study of *Shigella* diarrhoea in six Asian countries: disease burden, clinical manifestations, and microbiology. *PLoS Med* 2006 Sep;3(9):e353.

114. Ferreccio C, Prado V, Ojeda A, et al. Epidemiologic patterns of acute diarrhea and endemic *Shigella* infections in children in a poor peri-urban setting in Santiago, Chile. *Am J Epidemiol* 1991 Sep 15;134(6):614–627.

115. Niyogi SK. Shigellosis. *J Microbiol* 2005 Apr;43(2):133–143.

116. Pazhani GP, Niyogi SK, Singh AK, et al. Molecular characterization of multidrug-resistant *Shigella* species isolated from epidemic and endemic cases of shigellosis in India. *J Med Microbiol* 2008 Jul;57(Pt 7):856–863.

117. Taylor DN, Echeverria P, Pal T, et al. The role of *Shigella* spp., enteroinvasive *Escherichia coli*, and other enteropathogens as causes of childhood dysentery in Thailand. *J Infect Dis* 1986 Jun;153(6):1132–1138.

118. Herrington DA, Van de Verg L, Formal SB, et al. Studies in volunteers to evaluate candidate Shigella vaccines: further experience with a bivalent Salmonella typhi-Shigella sonnei vaccine and protection conferred by previous Shigella sonnei disease. *Vaccine* 1990 Aug;8(4):353–357.

119. DuPont HL, Levine MM, Hornick RB, et al. Inoculum size in shigellosis and implications for expected mode of transmission. *J Infect Dis* 1989 Jun;159(6):1126–1128.

120. Evans CA, Gilman RH, Rabbani GH, et al. Gastric acid secretion and enteric infection in Bangladesh. *Trans R Soc Trop Med Hyg* 1997 Nov-Dec;91(6):681–685.

121. Gorden J, Small PL. Acid resistance in enteric bacteria. *Infect Immun* 1993 Jan;61(1):364–367.

122. Levine OS, Levine MM. Houseflies (Musca domestica) as mechanical vectors of shigellosis. *Rev Infect Dis* 1991 Jul-Aug;13(4):688–696.

123. Hardy AV, Watt J. Studies of the acute diarrheal diseases; epidemiology. *Public Health Rep* 1948 Mar 19;63(12):363–378.

124. Levine MM, DuPont HL, Khodabandelou M, et al. Long-term *Shigella*-carrier state. *N Engl J Med* 1973 May 31;288(22):1169–1171.

125. Schroeder GN, Hilbi H. Molecular pathogenesis of *Shigella* spp.: controlling host cell signaling, invasion, and death by type III secretion. *Clin Microbiol Rev* 2008 Jan;21(1):134–156.

126. Sansonetti PJ, Egile C. Molecular bases of epithelial cell invasion by *Shigella* flexneri. *Antonie Van Leeuwenhoek* 1998 Nov;74(4):191–197.

127. Venkatesan M, Fernandez-Prada C, Buysse JM, et al. Virulence phenotype and genetic characteristics of the T32-ISTRATI *Shigella* flexneri 2a vaccine strain. *Vaccine* 1991 May;9(5):358–363.

128. Nataro JP, Seriwatana J, Fasano A, et al. Identification and cloning of a novel plasmid-encoded enterotoxin of enteroinvasive *Escherichia coli* and *Shigella* strains. *Infect Immun* 1995 Dec;63(12):4721–4728.

129. Levine MM, DuPont HL, Formal SB, et al. Pathogenesis of *Shigella* dysenteriae 1 (Shiga) dysentery. *J Infect Dis* 1973 Mar;127(3):261–270.

130. Mathan VI, Mathan MM. Intestinal manifestations of invasive diarrheas and their diagnosis. *Rev Infect Dis* 1991;13(Suppl 4):S311–S313.

131. Butler T, Speelman P, Kabir I, et al. Colonic dysfunction during shigellosis. *J Infect Dis* 1986 Mar-Apr;154 Suppl 4:817–824.

132. Bennish ML. Potentially lethal complications of shigellosis. *Rev Infect Dis* 1991;13(Suppl 4):S319–S324.

133. Galanakis E, Tzoufi M, Charisi M, et al. Rate of seizures in children with shigellosis. *Acta Paediatr* 2002;91(1):101–102.

134. Gradel KO, Schonheyder HC, Dethlefsen C, et al. Morbidity and mortality of elderly patients with zoonotic *Salmonella* and *Campylobacter*: a population-based study. *J Infect* 2008 Sep;57(3):214–222.

135. Finch M, Rodey G, Lawrence D, et al. Epidemic Reiter's syndrome following an outbreak of shigellosis. *Eur J Epidemiol* 1986 Mar;2(1):26–30.

136. DuPont HL, Hornick RB, Dawkins AT, et al. The response of man to virulent *Shigella* flexneri 2a. *J Infect Dis* 1969 Mar;119(3):296–299.

137. Harris JC, Dupont HL, Hornick RB. Fecal leukocytes in diarrheal illness. *Ann Intern Med* 1972 May;76(5):697–703.

138. DebRoy C, Fratamico PM, Roberts E, et al. Development of PCR assays targeting genes in O-antigen gene clusters for detection and identification of *Escherichia coli* O45 and O55 serogroups. *Appl Environ Microbiol* 2005 Aug;71(8):4919–4924.

139. Feng L, Tao J, Guo H, et al. Structure of the *Shigella* dysenteriae 7 O antigen gene cluster and identification of its antigen specific genes. *Microb Pathog* 2004 Feb;36(2):109–115.

140. Li Y, Cao B, Liu B, et al. Molecular detection of all 34 distinct O-antigen forms of *Shigella*. *J Med Microbiol* 2009 Jan;58(Pt 1):69–81.

141. Salam MA, Bennish ML. Antimicrobial therapy for shigellosis. *Rev Infect Dis* 1991 Mar-Apr;13(Suppl 4):S332–S341.

142. Levine MM. Antimicrobial therapy for infectious diarrhea. *Rev Infect Dis* 1986 May-Jun;8(Suppl 2):S207–S216.

143. Bennish ML, Salam MA, Haider R, et al. Therapy for shigellosis. II. Randomized, double-blind comparison of ciprofloxacin and ampicillin. *J Infect Dis* 1990 Sep;162(3):711–716.

144. Bennish ML, Salam MA, Khan WA, et al. Treatment of shigellosis: III. Comparison of one- or two-dose ciprofloxacin with standard 5-day therapy. A randomized, blinded trial. *Ann Intern Med* 1992 Nov 1;117(9):727–734.

145. Khan WA, Seas C, Dhar U, et al. Treatment of shigellosis: V. Comparison of azithromycin and ciprofloxacin. A double-blind, randomized, controlled trial. *Ann Intern Med* 1997 May 1;126(9):697–703.

146. Varsano I, Eidlitz-Marcus T, Nussinovitch M, et al. Comparative efficacy of ceftriaxone and ampicillin for treatment of severe shigellosis in children. *J Pediatr* 1991 Apr;118(4 Pt 1):627–632.

147. Ashkenazi S, Amir J, Waisman Y, et al. A randomized, double-blind study comparing cefixime and trimethoprim-sulfamethoxazole in the treatment of childhood shigellosis. *J Pediatr* 1993 Nov;123(5):817–821.

148. DuPont HL, Hornick RB. Adverse effect of Lomotil therapy in shigellosis. *JAMA* 1973 Dec 24;226(13):1525–1528.

149. Hardy AV, Watt J. Newer procedures in laboratory diagnosis and therapy in the control of bacillary dysentery. *Am J Public Health Nations Health* 1944 May;34(5):503–509.

150. DuPont HL, Hornick RB, Snyder MJ, et al. Immunity in shigellosis. II. Protection induced by oral live vaccine or primary infection. *J Infect Dis* 1972 Jan;125(1):12–16.

151. Watt J, Lindsay DR. Diarrheal disease control studies; effect of fly control in a high morbidity area. *Public Health Rep* 1948 Oct 8;63(41):1319–1333.

152. Mata LJ, Urrutia JJ, Garcia B, et al. *Shigella* infection in breast-fed Guatemalan Indian neonates. *Am J Dis Child* 1969 Feb;117(2):142–146.

153. Kapperud G. *Yersinia enterocolitica* in food hygiene. *Int J Food Microbiol* 1991 Jan;12(1):53–65.

154. Funk J, Troutt H, Isaacson R, et al. Prevalence of pathogenic *Yersinia enterocolitica* in groups of swine at slaughter. *J Food Prot* 1998 Jun;61(6):977–982.

155. Bottone E. *Yersinia enterocolitica*: The charisma continues. *Clin Microbiol Rev* 1997 Apr;10(2):257–276.

156. Lee L, Gerber A, Lonsway D, et al. *Yersinia enterocolitica* O:3 infections in infants and children, associated with the household preparation of chitterlings. *N Engl J Med* 1990 Apr 5;322(14):984–987.

157. Abdel-Haq N, Asmar B, Abuhammour W, et al. *Yersinia enterocolitica* infection in children. *Pediatr Infect Dis J* 2000 Oct;19(10):945–948.

158. Centers for Disease Control and Prevention. 1996 Final FoodNet Surveillance Report. Atlanta, GA: Centers for Disease Control and Prevention, 1998 October.

159. Robins-Browne R, Prpic JK. Desferrioxamine and systemic yersiniosis. *Lancet* 1983 Dec 10;2(8363):1372.

160. Adamkiewicz T, Berkovitch M, Krishnan C, et al. Infection due to *Yersinia enterocolitica* in a series of patients with beta-thalassemia: incidence and predisposing factors. *Clin Infect Dis* 1998 Dec;27(6):1362–1366.

161. Red Blood Cell Transfusions Contaminated With *Yersinia enterocolitica*—United States, 1991–1996, and Initiation of a National Study to Detect Bacteria-Associated Transfusion Reactions. Atlanta, GA: Centers for Disease Control and Prevention, 1997.

162. Bradford W, Noce P, Gutman L. Pathologic features of enteric infection with *Yersinia enterocolitica*. *Arch Pathol* 1974 Jul;98(1):17–22.

163. van der Heijden I, Res P, Wilbrink B, et al. *Yersinia enterocolitica*: a cause of chronic polyarthritis. *Clin Infect Dis* 1997 Oct;25(4):831–837.

164. Capilla S, Ruiz J, Gon iP, et al. Characterization of the molecular mechanisms of quinolone resistance in *Yersinia enterocolitica* O:3 clinical isolates. *J Antimicrob Chemother* 2004 Jun;53(6):1068–1071.

165. Fitzgerald C, Nachamkin I. *Campylobacter* and *Arcobacter*. In: Murray PR, Jorgensen JH, Pfaller M, Baron EJ, et al, eds. *Manual of Clinical Microbiology*, 9th ed. Washington, DC: American Society for Microbiology, 2007;933–942.

166. Pacanowski J, Lalande V, Lacombe K, et al. *Campylobacter* bacteremia: clinical features and factors associated with fatal outcome. *Clin Infect Dis* 2008 Sep 15;47(6):790–796.

167. Ailes E, Demma L, Hurd S, et al. Continued decline in the incidence of *Campylobacter* infections, FoodNet 1996–2006. *Foodborne Pathog Dis* 2008 Jun;5(3):329–337.

168. Galanis E. *Campylobacter* and bacterial gastroenteritis. *CMAJ* 2007 Sep 11;177(6):570–571.

169. van Hees BC, Veldman-Ariesen MJ, de Jongh BM, et al. Regional and seasonal differences in incidence and antibiotic resistance of *Campylobacter* from a nationwide surveillance study in The Netherlands: an overview of 2000–2004. *Clin Microbiol Infect* 2007 Mar;13(3):305–310.

170. Altekruse SF, Stern NJ, Fields PI, et al. *Campylobacter jejuni*—an emerging foodborne pathogen. *Emerg Infect Dis* 1999 Jan-Feb;5(1):28–35.

171. Michaud S, Menard S, Arbeit RD. Campylobacteriosis, Eastern Townships, Quebec. *Emerg Infect Dis* 2004 Oct;10(10):1844–1847.

172. Sorvillo FJ, Lieb LE, Waterman SH. Incidence of Campylobacteriosis among patients with AIDS in Los Angeles County. *J Acquir Immune Defic Syndr* 1991;4(6):598–602.

173. Blaser MJ, Taylor DN, Feldman RA. Epidemiology of *Campylobacter jejuni* infections. *Epidemiol Rev* 1983;5:157–176.

174. Friedman CR, Hoekstra RM, Samuel M, et al. Risk factors for sporadic *Campylobacter* infection in the United States: a case-control study in FoodNet sites. *Clin Infect Dis* 2004 Apr 15;38(Suppl 3):S285–S296.

175. Fullerton KE, Ingram LA, Jones TF, et al. Sporadic *Campylobacter* infection in infants: a population-based surveillance case-control study. *Pediatr Infect Dis J* 2007 Jan;26(1):19–24.

176. Black RE, Levine MM, Clements ML, et al. Experimental *Campylobacter jejuni* infection in humans. *J Infect Dis* 1988 Mar;157(3):472–479.

177. Blaser MJ, Allos BM. *Campylobacter jejuni* and Related Species. In: Mandell GL, Bennett JE, Dolin R, eds. *Principles and Practice of Infectious Diseases*, 6th ed. Philadelphia: Elsevier Churchill Livingstone, 2005;2548–2557.

178. Skirrow MB. *Campylobacter* enteritis: a "new" disease. *Br Med J* 1977 Jul 2;2(6078):9–11.

179. Skirrow MB. *Campylobacter*. *Lancet* 1990 Oct 13;336(8720):921–923.

180. Blaser MJ, Berkowitz ID, LaForce FM, et al. *Campylobacter* enteritis: clinical and epidemiologic features. *Ann Intern Med* 1979 Aug;91(2):179–185.

181. Pope JE, Krizova A, Garg AX, et al. *Campylobacter* reactive arthritis: a systematic review. *Semin Arthritis Rheum* 2007 Aug;37(1):48–55.

182. Townes JM, Deodhar AA, Laine ES, et al. Reactive arthritis following culture-confirmed infections with bacterial enteric pathogens in Minnesota and Oregon: a population-based study. *Ann Rheum Dis* 2008 Dec;67(12):1689–1696.

183. Allos BM, Lippy FT, Carlsen A, et al. *Campylobacter jejuni* strains from patients with Guillain-Barré syndrome. *Emerg Infect Dis* 1998 Apr-Jun;4(2):263–268.

184. Engberg J, Aarestrup FM, Taylor DE, et al. Quinolone and macrolide resistance in *Campylobacter jejuni* and *C. coli*: resistance mechanisms and trends in human isolates. *Emerg Infect Dis* 2001 Jan-Feb;7(1):24–34.

185. Smith KE, Besser JM, Hedberg CW, et al. Quinolone-resistant *Campylobacter jejuni* infections in Minnesota, 1992–1998. Investigation team. *N Engl J Med* 1999 May 20;340(20):1525–1532.

186. Wegener HC. The consequences for food safety of the use of fluoroquinolones in food animals. *N Engl J Med* 1999 May 20;340(20):1581–1582.

187. Kassenborg HD, Smith KE, Vugia DJ, et al. Fluoroquinolone-resistant *Campylobacter* infections: eating poultry outside of the home and foreign travel are risk factors. *Clin Infect Dis* 2004 Apr 15;38(Suppl 3):S279–S284.

188. Lachance N, Gaudreau C, Lamothe F, et al. Susceptibilities of beta-lactamase-positive and -negative strains of *Campylobacter coli* to beta-lactam agents. *Antimicrob Agents Chemother* 1993 May;37(5):1174–1176.

189. Ewing WH, McHorter AC, Escobar MR, et al. Edwardsiella, a new genus of Enterobacteraceae based on a new species E. tarda. *Int Bull Bacteriol Nomen Tax* 1965;15:33–38.

190. Park SB, Aoki T, Jung TS. Pathogenesis of and strategies for preventing Edwardsiella tarda infection in fish. *Vet Res* 2012 Oct 4;43:67.

191. Salgado-Mirando P, Palomares E, Jurado M, et al. Isolation and distribution of bacterial flora in farmed rainbow trout from Mexico. *J Aquat Anim Health* 2010 Dec; 22(4):244–247.

192. Mohanty BR, Sahoo PK. Edwardsiellosis in fish: a brief review. *J Biosci* 2007 Dec;32(7):1331–1344.

193. Lan J, Zhang XH, Wang Y, et al. Isolation of an unusual strain of Edwardsiella tarda from turbot and establish a PCR detection technique with the gyrB gene. *J Appl Microbiol* 2008 Sep;105(3):644–651.

194. Schlenker C, Surawicz CM. Emerging infections of the gastrointestinal tract. *Best Pract Res Clin Gastroenterol* 2009;23(1):89–99.

195. Herrera FC, Santos JA, Otero A, et al. Occurrence of foodborne pathogenic bacteria in retail prepackaged portions of marine fish in Spain. *J Appl Microbiol* 2006 Mar;100(3):527–536.

196. Wang IK, Kuo HL, Chen YM, et al. Extraintestinal manifestations of Edwardsiella tarda infection. *Int J Clin Pract* 2005 Aug;59(8):917–921.

197. John AM, Prakash JA, Simon EG, et al. Edwardsiella tarda sepsis with multiple liver abscesses in a patient with Cushing's syndrome. *Indian J Med Microbiol* 2012 Jul-Sep;30(3):352–354.

198. LeHane L, Rawlin GT. Topically acquired bacterial zoonoses from fish: a review. *Med J Aust* 2000 Mar;173(5) 256–259.

199. Ota T, Nakano Y, Nishi M, et al. A case of liver abscess caused by Edwardsiella tarda. *Intern Med* 2011;50(13):1439–1442.

200. Yousuf RM, How SH, Amran M, et al. Edwardsiella tarda septicemia with underlying multiple liver abscesses. *Malays J Pathol* 2006 Jun;28(1):49–53.

201. Tsuji A, Hirasawa K, Arakuma T, et al. A 12-year-old boy with acute gastroenteritis caused by Edwardsiella tarda O4:H4. *J Infect Chemother* 2008 Dec;14(6):433–435.

202. Leung KY, Siame BA, Tenkink BJ, et al. Edwardsiella tarda - virulence mechanisms of an emerging gastroenteritis pathogen. *Microbes Infect* 2012 Jan;14(1):26–34.

203. Ohara Y, Kikuchi M, Goto T, et al. Successful treatment of a patient with sepsis and liver abscess caused by Edwardsiella tarda. *Intern Med* 2012;51(19):2813–2817.

204. Engel JJ, Martin TL. Edwardsiella tarda as a cause of postdysenteric ulcerative colitis. *Int J Colorectal Dis* 2006 Mar;21(2):184–185.

205. Spencer JD, Hastings MC, Rye AK, et al. Gastroenteritis caused by Edwardsiella tarda in a pediatric renal transplant recipient. *Pediatr Transplant* 2008 Mar;12(2):238–241.

206. Nelson JJ, Nelson CA, Carter JE. Extraintestinal manifestations of Edwardsiella tarda infection: a 10-year retrospective review. *J La State Med Soc* 2009 Mar-Apr;161(2):103–106.

207. Mowbray EE, Buck G, Humbaugh KE, et al. Maternal colonization and neonatal sepsis caused by Edwardsiella tarda. *Pediatrics* 2003 Mar;111(3):e296–e298.

208. Hashavya S, Averbuch D, Berger I, et al. Neonatal sepsis following maternal amnionitis by Edwardsiella tarda: a case report and a review of the literature. Eur J Pediatr 2011 Jan;170(1):111–113.
209. Golub V, Kim AC, Krol V. Surgical wound infection, tuboovarian abscess, and sepsis caused by Edwardsiella tarda: case reports and literature review. Infection 2010 Dec;38(6):487–499.
210. Crosby SN, Snoddy MC, Atkinson CT, et al. Upper extremity myonecrosis caused by Edwardsiella tarda resulting in transhumeral amputation: case report. J Hand Surg Am 2013 Jan;38(1):129–132.
211. Manchanda V, Singh NP, Eideh HK, et al. Liver abscess caused by Edwardsiella tarda biogroup 1 and identification of its epidemiological triad by ribotyping. Indian J Med Microbiol 2006 Apr;24(2):135–137.
212. Sharma I, Paul D. Prevalence of community acquired urinary tract infections in silchar medical college, Assam, India and its antimicrobial susceptibility profile. Indian J Med Sci 2012 Nov-Dec;66(11-12):273–279.
213. Dong X, Fan X, Wang B, et al. Invasin of Edwardsiella tarda is essential for its haemolytic activity, biofilm formation and virulence towards fish. J Appl Microbiol 2013 Jul;115(1):12–19.
214. Wang C, Hu YH, Sun BG, et al. Edwardsiella tarda Ivy: a lysozyme inhibitor that blocks the lytic effect of lysozyme and facilitates host infection in a manner that is dependent on the conserved cysteine residue. Infect Immun 2013 Oct;81(10):3527–3533.
215. Griffin MJ, Quiniou SM, Cody T, et al. Comparative analysis of Edwardsiella isolates from fish in the eastern United States identifies two distinct genetic taxa amongst organisms phenotypically classified as E. tarda. Vet Microbiol 2013 Aug 30;165(3-4):358–372.
216. Igbinosa IH, Igumbor EU, Aghdasi F, et al. Emerging Aeromonas species infections and their significance in public health. ScientificWorldJournal 2012;2012:625023.
217. Andělová A, Porazilová I, Krejcí E. Aeromonas agar is a useful selective medium for isolating aeromonads from faecal samples. J Med Microbiol 2006 Nov;55(Pt 11):1605–1606.
218. Borchardt MA, Stemper ME, Standridge JH. Aeromonas isolates from human diarrheic stool and groundwater compared by pulsed-field gel electrophoresis. Emerg Infect Dis 2003 Feb;9(2):224–228.
219. Sartor C, Limonzin-Perotti F, Legré R, et al. Nosocomial infections with Aeromonas hydrophila from Leeches. Clin Infect Dis 2002 Jul 1;35(1):E1–E5.
220. Subashkumar R, Vivekanandhan G, Raja SS, et al. Typing of Aeromonas hydrophila of fish and human diarrhoeal origin by outer membrane proteins and lipopolysaccharides. Indian J Microbiol 2007 Mar;47(1):46–50.
221. Morinaga Y, Yanagihara K, Araki N, et al. Clinical characteristics of seven patients with Aeromonas septicemia in a Japanese hospital. Tohoku J Exp Med 2011;225(2):81–84.
222. Subashkumar R, Thayumanavan T, Vivekanandhan G, et al. Occurrence of Aeromonas hydrophila in acute gastroenteritis among children. Indian J Med Res 2006 Jan;123(1):61–66.
223. Chu YW, Wong CH, Tsang GKL, et al. Lack of association between presentation of diarrhoeal symptoms and faecal isolation of Aeromonas spp. amongst outpatients in Hong Kong. J Med Microbiol 2006 Mar;55(Pt 3):349–351.
224. Danaher PJ, Mueller WP. Aeromonas hydrophila septic arthritis. Mil Med 2011 Dec;176(12):1444–1446.
225. Chao CM, Lai CC, Tang HJ, et al. Skin and soft-tissue infections caused by Aeromonas species. Eur J Clin Microbiol Infect Dis 2013 Apr;32(4):543–547.
226. Taneja N, Khurana S, Trehan A, et al. An outbreak of hospital acquired diarrhea due to Aeromonas sobria. India Pediatr 2004 Sep;41(9):912–916.
227. Cabrera R LE, Castro E G, Ramírez A MM, et al. [Isolation and identification of species from the genera Aeromonas, Vibrio, and Plesiomonas from extraintestinal samples in Cuba]. Rev Chilena Infectol 2007 Jun;24(3):204–208.
228. Azzopardi EA, Azzopardi SM, Boyce DE, et al. Emerging gram-negative infections in burn wounds. J Burn Care Res 2011 Sep-Oct;32(5):570–576.
229. Nagata M, Takeshima Y, Tomii K, et al. Fulminant fatal bacteremic pneumonia due to Aeromonas hydrophila in a non-immunocompromised woman. Intern Med 2011;50(1):63–65.
230. Mandal J, Dhodapkar R, Acharya NS, et al. Urinary tract infection due to Aeromonas spp., a lesser known causative bacterium. J Infect Dev Ctries 2010 Oct 28;4(10):679–681.
231. Liakopoulos V, Arampatzis S, Kourti P, et al. Aeromonas hydrophila as a causative organism in peritoneal dialysis-related peritonitis: case report and review of the literature. Clin Nephrol 2011 Feb;75 Suppl 1:65–68.
232. Morinaga Y, Yanagihara K, Araki N, et al. Clinical characteristics of seven patients with Aeromonas septicemia in a Japanese hospital. Tohoku J Exp Med 2011;225(2):81–84.
233. Sha J, Kozlova EV, Chopra AK. Role of various enterotoxins in Aeromonas hydrophila-induced gastroenteritis: generation of enterotoxin gene-deficient mutants and evaluation of their enterotoxic activity. Infect Immun 2002 Apr;70(4):1924–1935.
234. Wang JH, Wang CY, Chi CY, et al. Clinical presentations, prognostic factors, and mortality in patients with Aeromonas sobria complex bacteremia in a teaching hospital: a 5-year experience. J Microbiol Immunol Infect 2009 Dec;42(6):510–515.
235. Kain KC, Kelly MT. Clinical features, epidemiology, and treatment of Plesiomonas shigelloides diarrhea. J Clin Microbiol 1989 May;27(5):998–1001.
236. Noonburg GE. Management of extremity trauma and related infections occurring in the aquatic environment. J Am Acad Orthop Surg 2005 Jul-Aug;13(4):243–253.
237. Gonzáles-Rey C, Svenson SB, Bravo L, et al. Serotypes and antimicrobial susceptibility of Plesiomonas shigelloides isolated from humans, animals, and aquatic environments in different countries. Comp Immunol Microbiol Infect Dis 2004 Mar;27(2):129–139.
238. Wouafo M, Pouillot R, Kwetche PF, et al. An acute foodborne outbreak due to Plesiomonas shigelloides in Yaounde, Cameroon. Foodborne Pathog Dis 2006 Summer;3(2):209–211.
239. Bai Y, Dai YC, Li JD, et al. Acute diarrhea during army field exercise in southern China. World J Gastroenterol 2004 Jan;10(1):127–131.
240. Holmberg SD, Watchsmuth IK, Hickman-Brenner FW, et al. Plesiomonas enteric infections in the United States. Ann Intern Med 1986 Nov;105(5):690–694.
241. Phavichitr N, Catto-Smith A. Acute gastroenteritis in children: what role for antibacterials? Paediatr Drugs 2003;5(5):279–290.
242. Auxiliadora-Martins M, Bellissimo-Rodrigues F, Viana JM, et al. Septic shock caused by Plesiomonas shigelloides in a patient with sickle beta-zero thalassemia. Heart Lung 2010 Jul-Aug;39(4):335–339.
243. Ozdemir O, Sari S, Terzioglu S, et al. Plesiomonas shigelloides sepsis and meningoencephalitis in a surviving neonate. J Microbiol Immunol Infect 2010 Aug;43(4):344–346.
244. Woo PC, Lau SK, Yuen KY. Biliary tract disease as a risk factor for Plesiomonas shigelloides bacteraemia: a nine-year experience in a Hong Kong hospital and review of the literature. New Microbiol 2005 Jan;28(1):45–55.
245. Schneider F, Lang N, Reibke R, et al. Plesiomonas shigelloides pneumonia. Med Mal Infect 2009 Jun;39(6):397–400.
246. Danchaivijitr S, Rongrungruang Y, Kachintorn U, et al. Prevalence and effectiveness of an education program on intestinal pathogens in food handlers. J Med Assoc Thai 2005 Dec;88 Suppl 10:S31–S35.
247. Punina NV, Zotov VS, Parkhomenko AL, et al. Genetic diversity of Bacillus thuringiensis from different geo-ecological regions of Ukraine by analyzing the 16S rRNA and gyrB Genes and by AP-PCR and saAFLP. Acta Naturae 2013 Jan;5(1):90–100.
248. Arnesen LP, Fagerlund A, Granum PE. From soil to gut: Bacillus cereus and its food poisoning toxins. FEMS Microbiol Rev 2008 Jul;32(4):579–606.
249. van der Voort M, Abee T. Sporulation environment of emetic toxin-producing Bacillus cereus strains determines spore size, heat resistance and germination capacity. J Appl Microbiol 2013 Apr;114(4):1201–1210.
250. Moravek M, Dietrich R, Buerk C, et al. Determination of the toxic potential of Bacillus cereus isolates by quantitative enterotoxin analyses. FEMS Microbiol Lett 2006 Apr;257(2):293–298.
251. Rosenquist H, Smidt L, Andersen SR, et al. Occurrence and significance of Bacillus cereus and Bacillus thuringiensis in ready-to-eat food. FEMS Microbiol Lett 2005 Sep;250(1):129–136.
252. Al-Khatib MS, Khyami-Horani H, Badran E, et al. Incidence and characterization of diarrheal enterotoxins of fecal Bacillus cereus isolates associated with diarrhea. Diagn Microbiol Infect Dis 2007 Dec;59(4):383–387.
253. Lynch M, Painter J, Woodruff R, et al. Surveillance for foodborne-disease outbreaks—United States, 1998–2002. MMWR Surveill Summ 2006 Nov 10;55(10):1–42.
254. Ehling-Schulz M, Fricker M, Scherer S. Bacillus cereus, the causative agent of an emetic type of food-borne illness. Mol Nutr Food Res 2004 Dec;48(7):479–487.
255. Ceuppens S, Boon N, Uyttendaele M. Diversity of Bacillus cereus group strains is reflected in their broad range of pathogenicity and diverse ecological lifestyles. FEMS Microbiol Ecol 2013 Jun;84(3):433–450.
256. Ramarao N, Sanchis V. The pore-forming haemolysins of bacillus cereus: a review. Toxins (Basel) 2013 Jun 7;5(6):1119–1139.
257. Bottone EJ. Bacillus cereus, a volatile human pathogen. Clin Microbiol Rev 2010 Apr;23(2):382–398.
258. Ehling-Schulz M, Fricker M, Scherer S. Identification of emetic toxin producing Bacillus cereus strains by a novel molecular assay. FEMS Microbiol Lett 2004 Mar;232(2):189–195.
259. Dierick K, Van Coillie E, Swiecicka I, et al. Fatal family outbreak of Bacillus cereus-associated food poisoning. J Clin Microbiol 2005 Aug;43(8):4277–4279.

260. Hedberg CW, Palazzi-Churas KL, Radke VJ, et al. The use of clinical profiles in the investigation of foodborne outbreaks in restaurants: United States, 1982-1997. *Epidemiol Infect* 2008 Jan;136(1):65–72.

261. Ding T, Wang J, Park MS, et al. A probability model for enterotoxin production of Bacillus cereus as a function of pH and temperature. *J Food Prot* 2013 Feb;76(2):343–347.

262. Doménech-Sánchez A, Laso E, Pérez MJ, et al. Emetic disease caused by Bacillus cereus after consumption of tuna fish in a beach club. *Foodborne Pathog Dis* 2011 Jul;8(7):835–837.

263. Jenson I. Bacillus: Detection by Classical Culture Techniques. In: *Encyclopedia of Food Microbiology*. San Diego: Academic Press, 2004;149–158.

264. Fricker M, Reissbrodt R, Ehling-Schulz M. Evaluation of standard and new chromogenic selective plating media for isolation and identification of Bacillus cereus. *Int J Food Microbiol* 2008 Jan 15;121(1):27–34.

265. Gray KM, Banada PP, O'Neal E, et al. Rapid Ped-2E9 cell-based cytotoxicity analysis and genotyping of Bacillus species. *J Clin Microbiol* 2005 Dec;43(12):5865–5872.

266. Moravek M, Dietrich R, Buerk C, et al. Determination of the toxic potential of Bacillus cereus isolates by quantitative enterotoxin analyses. *FEMS Microbiol Lett* 2006 Apr;257(2):293–298.

267. Ehling-Schulz M, Fricker M, Scherer S. Identification of emetic toxin producing Becillus cereus strains by a novel molecular essay. *FEMS Molucular Lett* 2004 Mar 19;232(2):189–195.

268. Bush K, Macielag MJ. New β-lactam antibiotics and β-lactamase inhibitors. *Expert Opin Ther Pat* 2010 Oct;20(10):1277–1293.

Diarrheal Diseases: Parasitic

Julie A. Ribes, MD, PhD
Professor of Pathology and Laboratory Medicine
University of Kentucky Chandler Medical Center
Lexington, KY

ABSTRACT

It is estimated that 10 percent of the population will have at least one episode of infectious diarrhea each year. While many diarrheal diseases are self-limiting, some may be chronic and require ongoing treatment. Disease manifestations range from almost asymptomatic to severe, and, in some cases, deadly. Viruses, parasites, or bacteria may be the infectious agents causing these episodes. Primary modes of transmission for most gastroenteritis agents are fecal-oral and foodborne; however, some agents may be spread from person to person. Because these agents are so different, viral agents, bacterial agents, and parasitic agents are examined in separate chapters.

KEY CONCEPTS

- Although many of the parasitic agents of diarrhea are tropical in distribution, some, such as *Giardia* and *Cryptosporidium*, are prevalent worldwide.

- Fecal-oral is the most common route of transmission for parasitic agents causing gastroenteritis.

BACKGROUND

It is estimated that 10 percent of the population each year will have at least one episode of infectious diarrhea. Although most of these episodes will resolve within 5 to 10 days (reflecting either bacterial or viral syndromes), parasitic infections are generally considered in the differential for patients with chronic symptoms and those with appropriate travel histories or other risk factors. Many clinicians underestimate the significance of these parasitic agents in causing diarrheal disease. In the correct patient setting of immunocompromise, recent foreign travel, participation in certain recreational activities, association with a community outbreak, occupational/animal exposures, or consumption of high-risk foods or beverages, parasitic agents should enter into the differential for chronic diarrheal disease.[1] Parasitic diarrhea is not a hospital-associated disease process but a community-associated one. Patients developing diarrhea more than 3 days after admission should not be routinely testing for ova and parasite (O&P) or for routine bacterial cultures[2,3] but should be investigated for the presence of *Clostridium difficile* colitis.[4] Table 79C-1 summarizes the significant parasitic pathogens causing enteritis.

However, even routine O&P, with its wet preparations and trichrome stains, does not adequately detect all parasites. Studies looking at the number of stools required to detect a parasitic infection indicate that even three specimens submitted for examination over a 1-week period will detect only 58 percent of the significant pathogens present in the patient. Six or more specimens may be required to reach a level of more than 80 percent detection.[5] The coccidian organisms may not be detected at all using the routine O&P exam. In addition, morphologic identification of the coccidian organisms requires the use of special staining techniques.[6,7] The modified acid-fast stain may be used to detect the oocysts of all three of these coccidian organisms.[7-9] The size distribution of the modified acid-fast staining oocysts together with their overall morphology allow these organisms to be differentiated from one another.[6] Additional assays such as direct fluorescence antibody staining, antigen detection, enzyme immunoassays, polymerase chain reaction (PCR), and serology are also available to detect or speciate some of the more important pathogens (see Table 79C-1).

BASIC PRINCIPLES

The following sections delineate the epidemiology, disease presentation, diagnostic testing characteristics, treatment options, infection prevention, and public health issues for the most common diarrheal parasites.

Entamoeba histolytica

Etiologic Agent

Entamoeba histolytica is the amoebic protozoan that causes amebiasis,[10] presenting with a range of symptoms from the asymptomatic carrier state to amoebic dysentery and extraintestinal invasive disease in humans.[11] The cyst form of *E. histolytica* is the infective form of this organism. Cysts are shed in the stool of infected patients and remain stable in damp environments, on foods, and in water sources. The trophozoite is the reproductive form and is the stage that causes invasive disease in humans. Two other morphologically similar but nonpathogenic species of *Entamoeba* are also known to infect humans, *Entamoeba dispar* and *Entamoeba moshkovskii*.[11-14]

Table 79C-1. Parasites Causing Diarrhea Syndromes and the Appropriate Testing Required for Their Detection

Organism	Testing Available
Entamoeba histolytica/dispar	Routine O&P with trichrome and concentrate Speciate with PCR Antigen detection by EIA (some will speciate)
Entamoeba polecki	Routine O&P with trichrome and concentrate
Blastocystis hominis	Routine O&P with trichrome and concentrate
Dientamoeba fragilis	Routine O&P with trichrome and concentrate
Giardia lamblia	Antigen detection EIA Direct fluorescence-antibody staining Routine O&P with trichrome and concentrate
Balantidium coli	Routine O&P with trichrome and concentrate
Cryptosporidium parvum	Antigen detection EIA Direct fluorescence-antibody staining Modified acid-fast staining Direct fluorescence-antibody staining
Cyclospora cayetanensis	Modified acid-fast staining Epifluorescence microscopy Routine O&P with trichrome and concentrate may not detect this organism
Isospora belli	Modified acid-fast staining Epifluorescence microscopy Routine O&P may not detect this organism in the formalin concentrate

From Centers for Disease Control and Prevention (CDC).

EIA, enzyme immunoassay; O&P, ova and parasite examination; PCA, polymerase chain reaction.

Epidemiology

E. histolytica infections are seen worldwide. It is estimated that there are 450 to 480 million people infected with E. histolytica. Of these, 35 to 50 million develop symptomatic disease, and approximately 40,000 to 100,000 die each year of infections with this organism.[15–17] The greatest burden of disease is seen in Central and South America, Africa, and India.[16] Disease with E. histolytica is rarely seen in Europe or in North America. Cases seen in industrialized countries are seen predominantly in foreign travelers and immigrants,[1,18] institutionalized patients,[18,19] nursing home patients,[20] and homosexual males (particularly those with human immunodeficiency virus [HIV] infections having CD4 lymphocyte counts of less than 100 cells/μL).[21–24] Transmission generally occurs through fecal-oral routes. Most cases of infection with this agent are acquired through ingestion of food or water contaminated with human fecal wastes originating from chronic asymptomatic carriers.[25] E. histolytica is one of the more common protozoa detected in human sewage.[26]

The three species, E. histolytica, E. dispar, and E. moshkovskii, are indistinguishable from one another morphologically but appear to differ according to pathogenicity. E. histolytica is considered a true, potentially invasive pathogen, whereas both E. dispar and E. moshkovskii are considered nonpathogenic, asymptomatic colonizers of the colon.[11–14] It is estimated that E. dispar causes 90 percent of the asymptomatic colonization seen in patients in E. histolytica-endemic regions of the world.[27] Much of the colonization previously thought to be due to E. histolytica is now considered to be due to E. dispar.

E. dispar is also responsible for much of the intestinal colonization seen in men who have sex with men.[22,28] Although seen worldwide, there are very few cases of E. moshkovskii in humans, and these cases mostly represent asymptomatic colonization.[12] Recent publications from India, however, have suggested potential pathogenicity for this species.[13,29]

Disease Manifestations

Infection with E. histolytica may present in several ways. In as many as 90 percent of all infections with E. histolytica, patients are asymptomatically colonized or have minimal symptoms.[15,17,30] In a longitudinal study of asymptomatic cases of amebiasis, conversion to active disease was seen in about 10 percent of cases within several weeks to 1 year of initial infection.[30] Spontaneous resolution of colonization was seen in the remaining patients within 1 year of initial evaluation. In another longitudinal study, clearance of intestinal colonization occurred much more slowly with an estimated half-life of about 13 months.[31]

In approximately 10 percent of patients, E. histolytica will cause bloody diarrhea.[15] Patients may have 10 or more diarrheal movements each day during active dysentery with this parasite. Fever, dehydration, and weight loss are commonly seen.[32] Entamoeba histolytica in its most severe enteral form produces an invasive disease with colonic ulcers.

E. histolytica also produces invasive disease outside of the colon, leading to the formation of abscesses in the affected tissues. Symptoms of hepatic abscess formation include right upper quadrant pain, fever, and hepatomegaly. Jaundice, if present, is a bad prognostic indicator. Extraintestinal disease arises from hematogenous spread of the trophozoites after they have invaded the colonic wall and penetrated into the portal vein. The majority of abscesses occur in the right hepatic lobe, which receives most of the blood drained from the colon.[33] Abscesses may rarely be found in other tissues also, including lung, brain, and genitourinary tract.[33] Despite the luminal origin of the infection, at the time of diagnosis of amoebic abscess, most patients will have neither intestinal symptoms nor evidence of colonization with E. histolytica.[34] Diagnosis of extraintestinal amebiasis may be made years after initial infection, so intestinal colonization is generally cleared. In one study in Brazil, only 2 percent of patients with hepatic abscesses had concurrent diarrhea.[33]

Diagnosis

Diagnosis of amoebic infection may be made based on morphologic detection using wet preparations, formalin-ethyl acetate concentrate, and polyvinyl alcohol (PVA)-fixed stool specimen.[6,25] Trophozoites measure 10 to 60 μm in diameter, with the invasive forms measuring greater than 20 μm. Trophozoites have a single nucleus that measures 3 to 5 μm in diameter. The nucleus has a discrete, centrally placed karyosome and even peripheralization of the chromatin. Cysts measure 10 to 20 μm in diameter and have as many as four nuclei. The nuclei have a morphology similar to that of the trophozoites. Chromatoidal bodies, if present, are cigar-shaped with rounded ends.[6] The sensitivity of the routine O&P is suboptimal and requires the examination of at least three specimens submitted on separate days to detect 60 to 80 percent of infected patients because of the intermittent shedding of the cysts and trophozoites.[15] A single specimen is expected to detect infection in less than half of patients, whereas five or more specimens may be required to detect infection in more than 90 percent of patients with the organism.[5] E. histolytica, E. dispar, and E. moshkovskii are morphologically identical in both the cyst and trophozoites forms, so if speciation is not performed using a species-specific assay, the report should reflect detection of E. histolytica/dispar/moshkovskii. The presence of intracellular red blood cell (RBC) fragments within trophozoites, generally considered to indicate pathogenicity, has been used as a marker for E. histolytica infection, but E. dispar has also been reported to ingest RBC, making this identification unreliable.[35] Because the World Health Organization (WHO) recommends treating only those patients with confirmed E. histolytica,[10] patients should be evaluated using E. histolytica-specific testing modalities, such as serology or antigen detection.[16] Although culture techniques have been developed to detect intestinal amoebae, they are not widely available and have a level of sensitivity less than that of direct examination by routine O&P.[34] Serologic testing is useful in making a definitive diagnosis, particularly in cases of amebic liver abscess.[33] A number of antibody detection assays are commercially available that detect E. histolytica-specific antibody production. Detection of immunoglobulin (Ig) G and IgM antibody responses using indirect immunofluorescence assay may be used to differentiate acute infection with remote exposure. These assays may be particularly helpful in confirming a diagnosis of extraintestinal disease, with a reported sensitivity of 93.6 percent and specificity of 96.7 percent.[36] Antigen testing of stool and abscess fluid may be performed using several commercially available kits that have in large replaced zymodeme testing.[14,34,35] Because the antigens detected by these assays are denatured in formalin, fresh stool is required for testing. Although some assays have been designed to detect antigens specific for E. histolytica, other assays detect antigens present in both E. histolytica and E. dispar and thus are not useful in differentiating disease by these organisms. The sensitivity of these antigen assays is more than 95 percent for the detection of amebiasis and is therefore much preferable to routine microscopy for the detection of disease.[14,35] PCR assays and microarray testing have been developed and have the potential to distinguish the three species discussed, but none are yet commercially available for use in most clinical laboratories. Larger reference laboratories, including the Centers for Disease Control and Prevention (CDC), may offer this testing to confirm speciation, but again, fresh stool specimens are required for most of these PCR assays.[34]

Treatment

The World Health Organization (WHO) recommends treatment for all confirmed cases of E. histolytica infection or colonization regardless of symptoms due to the potential development of active disease seen in patients with asymptomatic colonization.[10] The choice of drugs for treatment will depend on the disease presentation in the patient. Luminal E. histolytica infections (symptomatic and asymptomatic) may be treated with luminal amebicides, such as iodoquinol, paromomycin, or diloxanide furoate, whereas tissue invasive infections require treatment with tissue amebicides that are readily absorbed into the bloodstream, such as metronidazole, tinidazole, dehydroemetine, or chloroquine.[16,37,38] Because little of these agents remain in the colon, treatment with a tissue amebicide should be followed by treatment with a luminal agent to eliminate any possible intestinal reservoir still remaining. Prophylaxis for amebiasis is not recommended.[10] Infections proven to be E. dispar or E. moshkovskii do not require treatment.[11,27]

Infection Prevention and Public Health Concerns

In portions of the world where E. histolytica is endemic, contamination of the food and water supply with human fecal matter creates a potential reservoir for disease spread. Human fecal waste should never be used as fertilizer on crops that are for human or animal consumption. Water supplies that have been contaminated with human fecal waste should not be consumed or used in food preparation unless boiled for 10 minutes.[37] Amoebic cysts may also be destroyed using iodination or treatment with 5 to 10 percent acetic acid. Fresh fruits and vegetables contaminated with human fecal waste must be washed in soap and water and then soaked for 15 minutes in vinegar solution.[39] The cysts are not killed by the amount of chlorine used in routine water purification.[37] Patients with E. histolytica are potentially infectious and serve as important reservoirs for infection. Person-to-person transmission via the fecal-oral route has been reported in hospitals for the intellectually disabled, probably based on fecal play in this patient population.[19] E. histolytica/dispar is a well-known sexually transmitted infection (STI), again based on fecal-oral transfer during high-risk sexual acts.[22,28] Good hand-washing technique following toileting should always be practiced. For caregivers, hand washing between patients is also required to prevent iatrogenic spread. There is currently no vaccine available for the prevention of amebiasis.

Blastocystis hominis

Etiologic Agent

Blastocystis hominis is an intestinal protozoon of unresolved classification. Originally thought to be a yeast, it is now considered a protozoa, perhaps belonging to the phylum Sarcomastigophora.[6] The organism has been demonstrated to have both an amoeboid trophozoite stage and a cyst-like stage. It appears to reproduce by binary fission.

Epidemiology

B. hominis has a worldwide distribution and is one of the more commonly identified parasites seen in human stool specimens in the United States[40-42] and in individuals traveling to developing nations, such as Peace Corps volunteers.[40] It has been identified in diverse patient populations, including immunocompromised hosts, elderly individuals, patients institutionalized in mental hospitals, immigrants, and individuals with recent foreign travel.[43] In mental institutions, colonization rates of 31.9 to 40.8 percent have been described.[43,44] *B. hominis* has been identified in the stool of animals, including monkeys, cattle, pigs, rodents, and fowl.[45,46] Humans and animals share some of the same strains.[45] Its mode of transmission is not completely known but is probably via the fecal-oral route. One study has suggested that consumption of contaminated water is responsible for human infestations,[47] whereas contact with infected animals has also been suggested as a risk for transmission.[48] It has been suggested that *B. hominis* is possibly becoming a more significant agent transmitted person-to-person in the day care setting.[41,49,50] It is frequently seen causing infections with other enteric parasites.[42,43,51]

Disease Manifestations

Previously thought to be a nonpathogen, *B. hominis* is now considered by some to have pathogenic potential, particularly in immunocompromised hosts. In cases where pathogenicity has been hypothesized, the most common complaints include diarrhea, stomach pain, anorexia, and flatus.[41,50,52,53] Vomiting and constipation are reported less often.[50] Invasive disease leading to death has reportedly been seen in one patient.[54] Individuals infected with this parasite may also be asymptomatically colonized.[40] Yakoob et al. have suggested that *B. hominis* may play a role in causing irritable bowel syndrome (IBS). In a study of 95 subjects with IBS, 46 percent were positive for *B. hominis* by culture, whereas only 7 percent of healthy controls were positive for this organism.[55] The pathogenicity of this parasite is still hotly disputed in some infectious disease and parasitology circles, with some researchers still maintaining that this organism is nonpathogenic.[56,57]

Diagnosis

Diagnosis of colonization and infection with *B. hominis* is made by routine O&P examination of the stool.[6] The cyst-like stage is the diagnostic stage for this organism and is easily identified on both wet preparation and on PVA smears. *B. hominis* ranges in size from 6 to 40 μm in diameter, but more often falls into the 5 to 15 μm size range. It is characterized by the presence of a large central vacuole that displaces the nuclei to the organism's periphery. Amoeboid forms may also be seen in some specimens. Compared to the direct exam, both xenic culture and PCR have been shown to be more sensitive in detecting *B. hominis* in clinical specimens.[58] Because of this organism's potential pathogenicity, the College of American Pathologists requires the semiquantitative reporting of *B. hominis* when it is present in proficiency testing and patient specimens to allow for clinical correlation if the patient has symptoms.

Treatment

The clinical significance of this organism is questionable, so there is some dispute as to the need for treatment of individuals infected with *B. hominis*.[57,58] Trimethoprim-sulfamethoxazole 320/1,600 mg daily for adults and 6/30 mg/kg daily for children has been shown to be effective in eradicating *B. hominis* and in diminishing or eliminating symptoms in most, but not all, patients.[59] *The Medical Letter*[38] cites additional references supporting the use of trimethoprim-sulfamethoxazole and a reference supporting the use of nitazoxanide in children but warns of metronidazole resistance.

Infection Prevention and Public Health Concerns

The presence of *B. hominis* in clinical specimens serves as a marker of contamination of the food or water supply with human fecal waste. It can also indicate sexual activities leading to fecal-oral exchange. In patients in whom *B. hominis* is found as the only intestinal parasite (particularly in small numbers), additional effort should be made to look for other diarrhea-producing parasites in subsequent specimens.[58] Healthcare providers should practice good hand-washing techniques between patients so as not to transfer the organism from patient to patient. No iatrogenic outbreaks have been identified with this organism.

Dientamoeba fragilis

Etiologic Agent

Dientamoeba fragilis is a flagellate whose pathogenic potential is debated widely.[6] This organism has only been shown to have a trophozoite stage, and apparently has no cystic form. The trophozoite is both the infective and replicative phase, reproducing by binary fission.

Epidemiology

D. fragilis is seen in a worldwide distribution and is one of the most commonly encountered parasites seen. A study of more than 43,000 individuals in Canada demonstrated that 4.2 percent were infected with this protozoa.[60] Similarly, a study of more than 14,000 patients in New York state demonstrated a prevalence of 2.4 percent, with both pure infections and coinfections with other parasites seen.[61] Focal clusters of higher incidence of infection have been seen in African Americans in Philadelphia and in Native Americans on a South Dakota reservation, with rates of 24.5 and 37.8 percent, respectively, seen in these populations.[62,63]

The mode of transmission for this organism is somewhat cryptic. Having no cyst stage, it is unknown how the organism survives outside the colon or how it survives the acid environment of the stomach to establish infection, assuming fecal-oral transmission. Several researchers have suggested that *D. fragilis* becomes enclosed within helminth eggs, particularly *Enterobius vermicularis*, which protects the organism from the deleterious effects of the stomach's acid.[64–66] Simultaneous infections with both *D. fragilis* and *E. vermicularis* occur 9 to 20 times more frequently than would be expected for random occurrence, supporting this linkage for transmission.[60,65]

Disease Manifestations

The pathogenicity of this organism has been widely disputed. The organism was first identified as a nonpathogen,[64] but according to some researchers, it may cause diarrhea, flatus, perianal itching, nausea, vomiting, anorexia, fatigue, and abdominal discomfort.[60,61,67–69]

Diagnosis

Detection of this parasite in fecal specimens is somewhat problematic because it may be difficult to visualize in routine O&P preparations.[6] The organism measures 5 to 15 μm in diameter, with most falling into the 9 to 12 μm size range. Most have two nuclei, although 30 to 40 percent have only one. The nuclei have a central karyosome surrounded by smaller fragments, making the nuclei appear somewhat indistinct in stained preparations. Indirect fluorescent antibody staining of trophozoites using an antibody preparation has shown promise as a technique for improving detection of *D. fragilis* in patient specimens.[70] However, these antibodies are not yet commercially available. Other clues to infection with *D. fragilis* include the presence of eosinophilia, an uncommon finding for most protozoal infections but a routine finding in patients with helminth infections.[6,60,67]

Treatment

There is relatively little information about appropriate therapy for dientamoebiasis. Eradication of *D. fragilis* infection in children may be accomplished using diiodohydroxyquin (30 to 40 mg/kg/day for 21 days) or metronidazole (250 mg three times a week for 1 week).[67] *The Medical Letter*[38] provides dosing recommendations for iodoquinol in both adults and children, as well as for a number of second-line therapies, including paromomycin, tetracycline, and metronidazole. Erythromycin, paromomycin, and secnidazole have also been reported to be effective in eradicating intestinal carriage and symptoms.[68]

Infection Prevention and Public Health Concerns

Unlike most of the other parasites that cause diarrhea, *D. fragilis* is not spread directly but most likely is spread with *E. vermicularis* infections. Fecal-oral spread is still a concern because this is the manner in which *E. vermicularis* is spread. In the day care setting, encouraging children and caregivers to wash their hands frequently may lead to decreased incidence of diarrhea in this setting.[71] This would affect the transmission of *D. fragilis* and *E. vermicularis*. Implementing prompt therapy and separating individuals with symptoms from the rest of the population in an outbreak situation can also limit spread to additional employees and children.[72]

Giardia (lamblia) duodenalis

Etiologic Agent

Giardia duodenalis is the etiologic agent of giardiasis. The taxonomy of this organism is in debate. Although it is most widely known by *Giardia lamblia*, the rules of taxonomy indicate that *Giardia duodenalis* is the preferred designation. *Giardia* is a flagellated protozoa in the phylum Sarcomastigophora.[6] It has both a trophozoite stage (the replicative stage) and a cyst stage (the infective stage of the organism). The cysts are extremely stable in wet locations in the environment and serve as the reservoir for infection.

Epidemiology

This organism is seen in a worldwide distribution and is one of the most commonly seen parasites in the United States.[1] It is seen as both an organism contracted during foreign travels and from exposures here in the United States. Transmission is seen most commonly via ingestion of cysts in contaminated water sources (well water, fresh recreational water exposures, wilderness water recreation, etc.).[73] Animal exposures are also very important in transmission.[6] Acquisition of infection is often linked to the consumption of freshwater, presumably contaminated with beaver fecal matter (giving the human disease the name "beaver fever"). Dogs and cats have also been implicated as the reservoir for human cases.[74] *G. lamblia* is one of the most common parasites to be isolated from human sewage.[26] As a fecal-oral pathogen, *G. lamblia* may be spread from person to person if good hand-washing technique is not practiced following toileting or diaper changes. This is a classic "day care agent."[41] Transmission has also been seen within institutionalized patients in mental hospitals and in nursing homes.[20] Person-to-person spread is also seen in the setting of homosexual male sexual practices.[21,23]

Disease Manifestations

Infections with *G. lamblia* range from totally asymptomatic to chronic diarrhea syndromes. Asymptomatic carriage is the most common manifestation. The most common symptomatic manifestation seen with guardianships is a syndrome of profuse, watery diarrhea, profound foul-smelling flatulence, and fever. Although guardianship is usually self-limiting, the syndrome also may be very long lived, persisting for weeks or months, particularly in the immunocompromised hosts. Children appear to be most susceptible to infection, and in developing countries, the prevalence rate of infection can run 20 to 40 percent. Chronic or repeat infections may contribute to retardation of growth and development in children.[37,75] Extraintestinal disease with *Giardia* has not been described.

Diagnosis

Because giardiasis is one of the more frequently seen parasitic infections, there have been several diagnostic tests developed for the evaluation of patients. On wet preparations, *G. lamblia* may be appreciated by its tumbling or "falling leaf" motility.[6] Giardiasis is easily detected on both the formalin-ethyl-acetate concentrated stool and on PVA and other permanent preparations. The cysts are small, oval, and refractile on wet mounts. Cysts measure 8 to 19 μm with most cysts falling within the 11 to 14 μm length. Intracytoplasmic fibrils and a clustering of four nuclei at one end of the cyst are detectible in both wet and permanently stained smears. Trophozoites are teardrop shaped and measure 10 to 20 μm in length. Trophozoites have two nuclei that give this organism the typical "owl eye" appearance. Although the trophozoites have eight flagella, these are not usually visualized on the trichrome stain used in the clinical laboratory. *Giardia* antigens may be reliably detected using one of a number of commercially available enzyme immunoassays (EIAs) or direct immunofluorescence assays (IFAs).[76–79] Direct antigen assays come in 96-well EIA formats for batch testing large numbers of specimens or single-use cartridge formats that may be used for small volume of testing or rapid test turnaround times. In laboratories lacking expertise in microscopic parasitology, an EIA can be used as a sensitive and specific testing modality for the detection of this parasite. Testing may be performed on stool that has been fixed in formalin using both IFA and EIA formats. Diagnosis by serologic detection of antibody production in patients is not recommended at this time.[80]

Treatment

Metronidazole or tinidazole are the first-line drugs of choice for treating G. lamblia infections.[37,38,81,82] There is some concern about the development of drug resistance for this parasite.[83]

Infection Prevention and Public Health Concerns

G. lamblia is spread quite readily from person to person via sexual and casual means. Transmission within the day care setting is well known.[41] A decrease in frequency of enteric pathogen transmission has been found if children and caregivers are encouraged to wash their hands frequently, particularly following high-risk activities such as toileting or diaper changing.[71] Very few cysts are required for infection (possibly as few as 10), making this a significant pathogen in food and water supplies.[83] Giardial cysts are stable in the environment in water sources for weeks or months and are known to contaminate fresh-surface water sources worldwide.[37,83] Giardial cysts are not killed by the routine chlorination used for the water supply[37] and have been identified in untreated sewage.[26] Water treatments that are effective against G. lamblia cysts include boiling water for at least 1 minute. Some filtration systems have been demonstrated to be effective in removing giardial cysts.[73] Protective immunity develops in humans only after repeated challenge with the organism. Although vaccines have been developed from trophozoite antigens for use in dogs and cats, no human vaccine is yet available.[84]

Cryptosporidium parvum

Etiologic Agent

Cryptosporidium parvum is a protozoon of the phylum Apicomplexa and a member of the coccidian family. It reproduces in the lining cells of the mammalian small bowel and, less often, in other epithelial cells.[6] Oocysts shed in the stool of the host are infective when ingested in food or drink. No intermediate host is required to carry out the life cycle, and humans represent an accidental host.

Epidemiology

C. parvum is a zoonotic pathogen whose primary reservoir is cattle.[37] The mechanism of transmission is thought to be contamination of the water supply by fecal material from cattle or other animals. The oocysts of C. parvum are stable in the environment and require high levels of chlorine for killing to occur in water sources. Thus, in pools or drinking water supplies that

are not adequately chlorinated, oocysts may survive and infect human and other mammalian hosts. In addition, their very small size makes their filtration from water sources difficult.[83] As a result of its transmission pattern, disease with this organism is seen primarily as source-contact related outbreaks. The most widely recognized outbreak occurred in 1993 in association with the contamination of the municipal water source in Milwaukee, Wisconsin, with cryptosporidial oocysts originating from cattle.[85] An estimated 403,000 immunocompromised and immunocompetent people were infected with this organism. Outbreaks have since been linked to drinking and recreational water contaminated with fecal materials containing cryptosporidial oocysts.[86-89] Cryptosporidial cysts are widely distributed in nearly all raw water samples tested.[83] Disease transmission has also been described through consumption of unpasteurized apple cider made with ground-fall apples[90] and through person-to-person contact secondary to poor hand washing following toileting (fecal-oral contamination).[91] Person-to-person transmission is seen through sexual behaviors leading to fecal-oral contact or inoculation, particularly in the gay community.[21] Transmission in mental institutions and in nursing homes has also been observed.[20,44]

Disease Manifestations

The infective dose of cryptosporidial cysts that can cause disease in a competent host is estimated to be from more than 100 down to a single cyst.[83] After an incubation period of 5 to 28 days, C. parvum produces a profuse watery diarrheal syndrome with associated abdominal pain, nausea, fever, and fatigue.[92] The disease course can be quite variable, ranging from a self-limited diarrhea to a more severe and protracted syndrome most commonly seen in immunocompromised patient populations. In these compromised patients, it can produce extreme weight loss and wasting.[93,94] Even in the competent host, diarrhea stimulated by this pathogen may last for several weeks. Asymptomatic intestinal carriage may also be seen with this organism.[37]

Diagnosis

It is noteworthy that cryptosporidial infections may not be detected using the routine O&P unless there are large numbers of oocysts found in the stool. Although they may be picked up in the formalin-ethyl-acetate wet preparation if in significant numbers, cases often present with a low parasite burden. To improve detection rates, some laboratories use a modified acid-fast stain (the modified Kenyon stain) similar to that used for detecting nocardia. In the modified Kenyon stain, oocysts stain from bright pink to pale pink or may even remain unstained.[42] They are round and measure about 5 μm in diameter and may easily be mistaken for yeast cells in clinical specimens.[6] More efficient methods for detecting oocysts in patients with cryptosporidiosis include the highly sensitive and specific direct fluorescent-antibody stain or any of a number of commercially available EIAs. Both direct fluorescent-antibody assay (DFA) and EIAs have been shown to be more sensitive than the modified acid-fast stain, particularly in the setting of low organism burden.[76,77,95,96]

Treatment

Most infections with *C. parvum* resolve spontaneously and require no treatment. If infection persists, the choice of therapy is relatively limited and particularly problematic, especially in the setting of HIV infection. *The Medical Letter*[38] lists nitazoxanide as the treatment of choice for both children and adults but cites concerns about the efficacy of the drug in the setting of HIV infection. Trials looking at individuals coinfected with cryptosporidium and HIV infection have shown mixed results, some finding utility with nitazoxanide and others not.[37,97–100] Capparelli and Syed[97] suggest that efficacy in the setting of HIV infection might require higher doses than called for by the U.S. Food and Drug Administration (FDA)-approved dosing. Paromomycin has been shown to have only modest efficacy, whereas nitazoxanide has been used in otherwise healthy children younger than 4 years.[37] Clarithromycin and rifabutin have been effectively used in the setting of HIV infection as a prophylactic agent.[101]

Infection Prevention and Public Health Concerns

Infection prevention issues focus on water quality and prevention of fecal-oral spread. The oocysts of *C. parvum* are notoriously difficult to kill. They are extremely resistant to the halogens (both iodine and chlorine) used to kill coliform bacteria by wilderness travelers.[73] Even iodine resins have no proven effect on these cysts. The size of the oocysts (4 to 6 μm) makes them very difficult to remove using water filtration systems. Only reverse osmosis filters capable of removing particles of less than 1 μm can reliably remove *C. parvum* cysts.[83]

Cyclospora cayetanensis

Etiologic Agent

Cyclospora cayetanensis is a coccidian organism of the phylum Apicomplexa that is closely related to the bird pathogens, the eimerias. The agent is also known as "crypto grande" or "large crypto" due to its larger size and staining characteristics similar to those of the cryptosporidia seen with the modified acid-fast stain.[6] Similar to *Cryptosporidium parvum*, *C. cayetanensis* is round and stains with the modified acid-fast stain. The cysts of *C. cayetanensis* are roughly double the size of its cryptosporidial counterpart, thus its name "crypto grande."

Epidemiology

C. cayetanensis has been known to cause disease in humans since 1977. Although the disease occurs predominantly in tropical and subtropical regions, it is seen worldwide, usually associated with importation of contaminated food products or contaminated water sources.[100] Outbreaks of diarrheal disease in humans have been linked to consumption of Guatemalan raspberries,[101–106] basil,[107] a variety of green leafy vegetables,[108,109] snow peas,[110] and Asian freshwater clams.[111]

Disease Manifestations

Similar to *Cryptosporidium parvum*, *C. cayetanensis* stimulates a profuse watery diarrhea. The incubation period is usually short (1 to 7 days). Associated symptoms include nausea, vomiting, abdominal cramping and pain, loss of appetite, and constitutional symptoms. Although most people experience a self-limited illness, some patients continue to have symptoms for weeks or months and sustain significant weight loss.[37,112] Although most cases reported in the literature represent normal hosts, illness with the organism may also be seen in immunocompromised populations.[112]

Diagnosis

While a number of staining procedures have been reported to detect *Cyclospora* spp.,[113] the modified acid-fast stain is the only stain capable of reliably detecting all three of the coccidians in clinical specimens.[114] Epifluorescence is also used by some diagnostic laboratories, taking advantage of the organism's ability to fluoresce under ultraviolet light.[6] Similar to *Cryptosporidium*, *Cyclospora* is round, but approximately double the size at about 10 μm in diameter.[6] Adequate evaluation of each specimen requires review of at least 200 fields under oil before calling a specimen negative. In contrast to *C. parvum*, there are no other commercially available EIA or DFA tests that can detect cyclosporiasis. Although there are PCR assays that are being developed to detect this pathogen, none are currently available for diagnostic testing.

Treatment

Trimethoprim/sulfamethoxazole (TMP/SMX) (TMP 160 mg plus SMX 800 mg twice daily for 7 days) has been shown in placebo-controlled studies to effectively treat adults with intestinal cyclosporiasis.[37,115] In some individuals with refractory disease, longer duration of treatment may be required for complete eradication. Pediatric dosing is also available.[38] Ciprofloxacin has been found to be less effective but may be used for patients who cannot tolerate TMP/SMX.[37]

Infection Prevention and Public Health Concerns

Because most cases of cyclosporiasis that are not acquired overseas are linked to foodborne outbreaks, clinicians should remain alert to clusters of disease so that appropriate outbreak investigations can be initiated through the local department of health and the CDC.[110] Although the reporting of cases is not mandatory in all states and territories, the CDC tracks all cases on a nationwide basis, so reporting is encouraged. Cyclosporiasis is a foodborne and waterborne illness, so taking proper precautions to sterilize the drinking water by boiling and avoiding consumption of uncooked fruits and vegetables when traveling to endemic regions of the world are prudent measures to take to limit exposures. Travelers should avoid contact with nonpotable water sources for bathing and recreational activities.

Isospora belli

Etiologic Agent

Isospora belli is a coccidian organism of the phylum Apicomplexa that is primarily a pathogen of cats.[6] Most instances in which humans contract illness are associated with close contact of the human with an infected cat, primarily handling of contaminated feces. Humans are an accidental host.

Epidemiology

I. belli is an uncommon human pathogen, linked most commonly to the handling of contaminated cat feces.[6] Unsporulated oocysts are passed in the feces of infected animals and humans. These undergo sporulation in the environment, developing into the infective stage within 5 to 6 days. Infection is acquired by ingestion (fecal-oral contamination). This organism is capable of carrying out its entire life cycle in a single host and does not require any intermediate host.[6] It has emerged as a significant cause of protracted diarrhea in patients with acquired immunodeficiency syndrome (AIDS) in Haiti and, to a lesser extent, in the United States.[116,117]

Disease Manifestations

I. belli produces a diarrheal illness that in most cases resolves spontaneously.[118] This organism may cause disease in both immunocompetent and immunocompromised hosts, often producing prolonged, profuse watery diarrhea, anorexia, weight loss, and fever.[119,120] The typical disease course presents with fever, diarrhea, and abdominal pain. The patients usually recover within several days to several weeks. The longer time course generally leads to significant weight loss. Infection may lead to malabsorption and steatorrhea.[118,121]

Diagnosis

In contrast to the other coccidian, I. belli may be definitively identified on Formalin wet preps of stool due to their large size (22 to 33 μm × 10 to 19 μm) and refractile shell.[6] However, they are generally shed in small numbers and may be intermittently passed, thus making the diagnosis inconsistent. The oocysts are also detected using the modified Kenyon acid-fast stain. Although they may show variation in staining intensity similar to that of the other coccidian, their large size and characteristic morphology make these less likely to be missed on either the routine O&P or the modified acid-fast stain. Again, at least 200 fields must be reviewed under oil before a specimen can be considered negative. Due to the intermittent shedding, review of multiple diarrheal stools is required to rule out this infective agent. Histopathology may be diagnostic but is usually less sensitive than O&P. Peripheral eosinophilia is commonly seen with this infection.[118,122] Charcot-Leiden crystals in the stool may also be associated with infection by this pathogen.

Treatment

Most cases of infection in immunocompetent hosts are self-limiting and require no treatment. However, in the setting of HIV/AIDS, disease may go on for weeks or months. Treatment with trimethoprim/sulfamethoxazole 160 mg/800 mg four times daily for 10 days will usually clear infection in adults, but higher doses or longer treatment regimens may be required in the setting of HIV.[38] If relapse occurs, it will generally happen within weeks to months of initial treatment, and retreatment is required for cure.[37]

Infection Prevention and Public Health Concerns

Isosporiasis is a relatively uncommon human pathogen. Because the oocysts are passed in an unsporulated form, there is no human-to-human transmission. Management of human and animal wastes that decrease the contact with sporulated oocysts decreases the risk of acquiring infection. Thus, changing cat litter and decontaminating the litter box every 3 to 4 days (before sporulation occurs) is expected to control transmission.

Balantidium coli

Etiologic Agent

Balantidiasis is caused by the ciliate Balantidium coli.[6] B. coli is the only ciliate with known pathogenicity in humans. It has a cyst form, which is shed in the stool of the host and is stable in the environment. The cyst is the infective stage of the organism. Once ingested, the organism excysts to become the replicative trophozoite form.

Epidemiology

B. coli are distributed worldwide. Although most cases are seen in tropical/subtropical regions of the world, including Central and South America, the Philippines, Southeast Asia, and the Middle East, cases have also been identified in Canada, the United States, and Europe.[123] Pigs are the usual hosts for B. coli. In pigs, there are few or no symptoms because most are asymptomatically colonized. In studies looking at the rate of colonization of pigs, more than 50 percent carry this organism in their gut.[124] Handling pigs,[125] slaughtering pigs,[125,126] and using pig manure to fertilize crops have all been associated with transmission to humans.[125] A study of indigenous peoples in the Amazon demonstrated the acquisition of B. coli intestinal carriage was linked to the initiation of pig keeping by these tribes.[127] However, only about 25 percent of the cases of human disease seen worldwide have a known pig link.[125] This suggests that other reservoirs exist for this organism. Additional animal reservoirs include sheep, horses, cows, guinea pigs, fowl, turtles, cockroaches, and a variety of primates.[123] Exposure to contaminated water sources has been implicated in some cases where pig exposure was not present.[128,129] Coinfection with other parasites is frequently seen, again indicating probable contamination of a food or water source with fecal materials.[123,125,128] Disease has been identified in at least two patients in whom immunocompromise was likely an underlying risk factor for infection.[128,129] Interestingly, neither patient was exposure to pigs, so some other form of exposure was probable in these cases. Patients in mental hospitals are also a particular at-risk population.[130,131] Although there is no known pig exposure in this population, there are a number of other risk factors for being infected with intestinal parasites, including pica, geophagia, coprophagia, coprophilia, and fecal play, that explain the high rate of infection of these patients with both pathogenic and non-pathogenic intestinal parasites. Infections in infants have been linked to advancing the diet from breast milk to fruits and cereals and thus are likely linked to contaminated food or water.[132]

Disease Manifestations

Three main gastrointestinal syndromes have been identified in association with *B. coli*: colonization, chronic diarrhea, and dysenteric diarrheal syndrome.[125] Asymptomatic colonization is the most common presentation with this organism.[124,125] In a study of indigent populations of children in Bolivia, 1.2 percent of children were found to be colonized with *B. coli*.[124] In those with formed stools, the children shed on the cyst forms in their stool. In those with soft stool, cysts and/or trophozoites were detected. Their families nearly universally kept pigs as their potential exposure and more than 50 percent of the pigs tested were positive for *B. coli* in their stools. If symptomatic for disease, most individuals present with chronic, nonbloody diarrheal syndrome.[125,128] Patients often complain of nausea, vomiting, and explosive, watery diarrhea. Occasional, alternating periods of constipation may be seen.[126,132] The time course for chronic disease ranges from weeks to years.[125] One patient reportedly had intermittent symptoms for two decades. Dysenteric disease is also seen. Patients usually present with bloody, mucousy diarrhea with 5 to 25 bowel movements each day. Cases of chronic diarrhea may escalate into dysentery. Diarrheal movements are often described as having a "pig pen" odor, and the breath of these patients is also described as fetid.[125,129] Appendiceal involvement has been seen in a number of patients.[123,125] Ulcer formation may be superficial or can progress to the full thickness of the intestinal wall,[131] leading to peroration and peritonitis.[126]

Extraintestinal disease with *B. coli* has been seen on rare occasion. Cavitary lung disease with hemoptysis due to *B. coli* was seen in one patient with no associated gastrointestinal disease.[133] Pulmonary infection without cavitation and without intestinal *Balantidiasis* has also been described.[134] An additional case was identified in which chronic diarrhea with this agent progressed to also involve the lung.[135] Although many of the original publications are in Spanish, Esteban et al. summarized the disease presentation from these additional published reports to include ileitis, vaginitis, pleural infection, and liver abscesses.[124]

Diagnosis

Most cases of balantidiasis are diagnosed by direct detection of the trophozoites or cysts in clinical specimen. Sigmoidoscopy has been used to aid in diagnosis. Ulcers seen in *B. coli* infections are similar to those seen in amebiasis.[123,125] Lesions start out as small and punctate and have a "flask-shaped" wall associated with the lesions when viewed in cross-section.[123] Ulcers may be superficial or may penetrate through the entire bowel wall. A fibrous cap is often seen covering the ulcer's surface. The large ciliates are readily visible in hematoxylin-and-eosin stained sections of the ulcers.

B. coli trophozoites are large, measuring 30 to 150 μm by 40 to 55 μm.[123] In invasive disease, forms as large as 300 μm

may be seen. The organism is oval to slightly pyriform in shape. At the tapered end, there is a groove called a peristome that serves both to ingest and excrete materials. Cilia cover the entire pellicle, and these can be detected in both wet and stained preparations. If viewed in freshly collected stool, the organisms can be seen to produce a gliding motility using these cilia. The trophozoite has a kidney-bean-shaped macronucleus and a round micronucleus. Large vacuoles may be seen within the trophozoite forms.[6] The cyst form is somewhat smaller than the trophozoites, measuring 40 to 65 μm. They are round to slightly oval and lack the peristome and the pellicle with cilia but are surrounded by a cyst capsule instead. Although *B. coli* may be cultured in xenic and monoxenic culture, this is not routinely done for diagnosis because of the lack of routine availability of these culture methods in clinical labs and because of the length of time required for growth.[136]

Treatment

The drug of choice is tetracycline 500 mg four times a day for 10 days for adults and 40 mg/kg/day for a maximum of 2 g in 4 doses daily for 10 days in children. *The Medical Letter* also provides alternative therapies using metronidazole and iodoquinol. None of these treatments are FDA-approved indications.[38]

Infection Prevention and Public Health Concerns

B. coli infections are not tremendously prevalent, even in populations that live in close proximity to pigs, the major reservoir. Infection prevention practices that would help to limit infections with this organism would be directed at appropriate hand washing following handling of pigs, their meat, or their manure. In situations in which people live in close proximity to pigs, efforts should be made to prevent contamination of the drinking water with pig fecal matter.

REFERENCES

1. Rosenblatt JE. Laboratory diagnosis of parasitic infections. *Mayo Clin Proc* 1994;69:779–780.
2. Seigel DL, Edelstein PH, Nachamkin I. Inappropriate testing for diarrheal diseases in the hospital. *JAMA* 1990;263:1012–1019.
3. Fan K, Morris AJ, Reller LB. Application of rejection criteria for stool cultures for bacterial enteric pathogens. *J Clin Microbiol* 1993;31:2233–2235.
4. Bauer TM, Lalvani A, Frehrenbach J, et al. Derivation and validation of guidelines for stool cultures for *enteropathogenic bacteria* other than Clostridium difficile in hospitalized adults *JAMA* 2001;285:313–319.
5. Mathur TN, Kaur J. The frequency of excretion of cysts of *Entamoeba histolytica* in known cases of non-dysenteric amoebic colitis based on 21 stool examinations. *Indian J Med Res* 1973;61:330–333.
6. Ash L, Orihel T. Protozoa. In: *Atlas of Human Parasitology*, 4th ed. Chicago: ASCP Press, 1997:45–132.
7. Garcia LS, Bruckner DA, Brewer TC, et al. Techniques for recovery and identification of Cryptosporidium oocysts from stool specimens. *J Clin Microbiol* 1983;18:185–190.
8. Mank TG, Zaat JOM, Deelder AM, et al. Sensitivity of microscopy versus enzyme immunoassay in the laboratory diagnosis of giardiasis. *Eur J Clin Microbiol Infect Dis* 1997;16:615–619.
9. Clarke SC, McIntyre M. Acid-fast bodies in fecal smears stained by the modified Ziehl-Neelsen technique. *Br J Biochem Sci* 2001;58:7–10.
10. WHO/PAHO/UNESCO Report: A consultation with experts on amoebiasis Mexico City, Mexico 28–29 January, 1997. *Epidemiol Bull Pan Am Health Org* 1997;18:13–14.
11. Pritt BS, Clark CG. Amebiasis. *Mayo Clin Proc* 2008;83:1154–1160.
12. Clark CG, Diamond LS. The Laredo strain and other 'Entamoeba histolytica-like' amoebae are Entamoeba moshkovskii. *Mol Biochem Parasitol* 1991;46:11–18.

13. Parija SC, Khairnar K. *Entamoeba moshkovskii* and Entamoeba dispar-associated infections in Pondicherry, India. *J Health Popul Nutr* 2005;23:292–295.
14. Solaymani-Mohammadi S, Rezaian M, Babaei Z, et al. Comparison of a stool antigen detection kit and PCR for diagnosis of *Entamoeba histolytica* and Entamoeba dispar infections in asymptomatic cyst passers in Iran. *J Clin Microbiol* 2006;44:2258–2261.
15. Walsh JA. Problems in recognition and diagnosis of amebiasis: estimation of the global magnitude of morbidity and mortality. *Rev Infect Dis* 1986; 8:228–238.
16. World Health Organization (WHO). Amoebiasis. *Weekly Epidemiol Record* 1997;72(14):97–100.
17. Guerrant RL. Amebiasis: introduction, current status, and research questions. *Rev Infect Dis* 1986;8:218–227.
18. Krogstad DJ, Spencer HC, Healy GR, et al. Amebiasis: epidemiologic studies in the United States, 1971–1974. *Ann Intern Med* 1978;88:89–97.
19. Nagakura K, Tachibana H, Kaneda Y, et al. Amebiasis in institutions for the mentally retarded in Kanagawa prefecture, Japan. *Jpn J Med Sci Biol* 1990;43:123–131.
20. Strausbaugh LJ, Sukmar SR, Joseph CL. Infectious disease outbreaks in nursing homes: an unappreciated hazard for frail elderly persons. *Clin Infect Dis* 2003;36:870–876.
21. Peters CS, Sable R, Janda WM, et al. Prevalence of enteric parasites in homosexual patients attending an outpatient clinic. *J Clin Microbiol* 1986;24:684–685.
22. Allason-Jones E, Mindel A, Sargeaunt P, et al. *Entamoeba histolytica* as a commensal intestinal parasite in homosexual men. *N Engl J Med* 1986;315:353–356.
23. Phillips SC, Mildvan D, William DC, et al. Sexual transmission of enteric protozoa and helminths in a venereal-disease-clinic population. *N Engl J Med* 1981;305:603–606.
24. Lowther SA, Dworkin MS, Hanson DL, et al. *Entamoeba histolytica/ Entamoeba dispar* infections in human immunodeficiency virus-infected patients in the United States. *Clin Infect Dis* 2000;30:955–959.
25. Tanyuksel M, Petri WA. Laboratory diagnosis of amebiasis. *Clin Microbiol Rev* 2003;16:713–729.
26. Santamaria J, Toranzos GA. Enteric pathogens and soil: a short review. *Int Microbiol* 2003;6:5–9.
27. Huston CD, Petri WA Amebiasis: clinical implications of the recognition of Entamoeba dispar. *Curr Infect Dis Rep* 1999;1:441–447.
28. Weinke T, Friedrich-Janicke B, Hopp P, et al. Prevalence and clinical importance of *Entamoeba histolytica* in two high-risk groups: travelers returning from the tropics and male homosexuals. *J Infect Dis* 1990;161: 1029–1031.
29. Haque R, Ali IK, Clark CG. A case report of *E. moshkovskii* infection in a Bangladeshi child. *Parasitol Int* 1999;47:201–202.
30. Gathiram V, Jackson TFHG. A longitudinal study of asymptomatic carriers of pathogenic zymodemes of *Entamoeba histolytica*. *S Afr Med J* 1987;72:669–672.
31. Blessman J, Ali IKM, Nu PAT, et al. Longitudinal study of intestinal *Entamoeba histolytica* infections in asymptomatic adult carriers. *J Clin Microbiol* 2003;41:4745–4750.
32. Adams EB, MacLeod IN. Invasive amebiasis: I. Amebic dysentery and its complications. *Medicine* 1977;56:315–323.
33. Salles JM, Moraes LA, Salles MC. Hepatic amebiasis. *Brazil J Infect Dis* 2002;7:96–110.
34. Fotedar R, Stark D, Beebe N, et al. Laboratory diagnostic techniques for Entamoeba species. *Clin Micro Rev* 2007;20:511–532.
35. Haque R, Neville LM, Hahn P, et al. Rapid diagnosis of Entamoeba infection by using Entamoeba and *Entamoeba histolytica* stool antigen detection kits. *J Clin Microbiol* 1995;33:2558–2561.
36. Shamsuzzaman SM, Haque MR, Hasin SK, et al. Evaluation of indirect fluorescent antibody test and enzyme-linked immunosorbent assay for diagnosis of hepatic amebiasis in Bangladesh. *J Parasitol* 2000;86:611–615.
37. Farthing MJG, Cevellos AM, Kelly P. Intestinal protozoa. In: Cook GC, Zumla AI, eds. *Manson's Tropical Diseases*, 21st ed. London, England: WB Saunders, 2003:1373–1410.
38. Medical Letter. Drugs for parasitic infections. *Med Lett* 2004;1–12.
39. Petri WA, Singh U. Diagnosis and management of amebiasis. *Clin Infect Dis* 1999;29:1117–1125.
40. Hewaldt BL, de Arroyave KR, Wahlquist SP, et al. Multiyear prospective study of intestinal parasitism in a cohort of Peace Core volunteers in Guatemala. *J Clin Microbiol* 2001;39:34–42.
41. Miller SA, Rosario CL, Rojas CL, et al. Intestinal infection and associated symptoms in children attending day care centers in Trujillo, Venezuela. *Trop Med Int Health* 2003;8:342–347.
42. Ribes JA, Seabolt JP, Overman SB. Point prevalence of Cryptosporidium, Cyclospora, and Isospora infections in patients being evaluated for diarrhea. *Am J Clin Pathol* 2004;122:28–32.
43. Cirioni O, Giacometti A, Drenaggi D, et al. Prevalence and clinical relevance of Blastocystis hominis in diverse patient populations. *Eur J Epidemiol* 1999;15:389–393.
44. Giacometti A, Cirioni O, Balducci M, et al. Epidemiologic features of intestinal parasitic infections in Italian mental institutions. *Eur J Epidemiol* 1997;13:825–830.
45. Abe N. Molecular and phylogenetic analysis of Blastocystis isolates from various hosts. *Vet Parasitol* 2004;120:235–242.
46. Yoshikawa H, Abe N, Wu Z. PCR-based identification of zoonotic isolates of Blastocystis from mammals and birds. *Microbiology* 2004;150: 1147–1151.
47. Leelayooua S, Rangsin R, Taamasri P, et al. Evidence of waterborne transmission of Blastocystis hominis. *Am J Trop Med Hyg* 2004;70:658–662.
48. Rajan-Salim H, Suresh-Kumar G, Vellayan S, et al. Blastocystis in animal handlers. *Parasitol Res* 1999;85:1032–1033.
49. Koutsavlis AT, Valiquette L, Allard R, et al. Blastocystis hominis: a new pathogen in day-care centers? *Can Commun Dis Rep* 2001;27:76–84.
50. Quadri SM, Al-Okaili GA, Al-Dayel F. Clinical significance of Blastocystis hominis. *J Clin Microbiol* 1989;27:2407–2409.
51. Garcia LS, Bruckner DA, Clancy MN. Clinical relevance of Blastocystis hominis. *Lancet* 1984;1:1233–1234.
52. Sheehan DJ, Raucher BG, McKitrick JC. Association of Blastocystis hominis with signs and symptoms of human disease. *J Clin Microbiol* 1986;24:548–550.
53. Doyle PW, Helgason MA, Mathias RG, et al. Epidemiology and pathogenicity of Blastocystis hominis. *J Clin Microbiol* 1990;28:116–121.
54. Vannatta JB, Adamson D, Mullican K. Blastocystis hominis infection presenting as recurrent diarrhea. *Ann Intern Med* 1985;102:495–496.
55. Yakoob J, Jafri W, Jafri N, et al. Irritable bowel syndrome: in search of an etiologic agent: the role of Blastocystis hominis. *Am J Trop Med Hyg* 2004;70:384–385.
56. Miller RA, Minshew BH. Blastocystis hominis: an organism in search of a disease. *Rev Infect Dis* 1088;10:930–938.
57. Markell EK, Udkow MP. Blastocystis hominis: pathogen or fellow traveler? *Am J Trop Med Hyg* 1986;35:1023–1026.
58. Stensvold CR, Arendrup MC, Jespersgaard C, et al. Detecting Blastocystis using parasitologic and DNA-based methods: a comparative study. *Diagn Microbiol Infect Dis* 2007;59:303–307.
59. Ok UZ, GirginKardesler N, Balcioglu I, et al. Effect of trimethoprim-sulfamethoxazole in Blastocystis hominis infection. *Am J Gastroenterol* 1999;94:3245–3247.
60. Yang J, Scheolten TH. Dientamoeba fragilis: a review with notes on its epidemiology, pathogenicity, mode of transmission, and diagnosis. *Am J Trop Med Hyg* 1977;26:16–22.
61. Kean BH, Malloch CL. The neglected ameba: Dientamoeba fragilis. A report of 100 "pure" infections. *Am J Digest Dis* 1966;2:735–746.
62. Weiner D, Brooke MM, Witkow A. Investigation of parasitic infections in the central area of Philadelphia. *Am J Trop Med* 1959;8:625–629.
63. Melvin DM, Brooke MM. Parasitologic surveys on Indian reservations in Montana, South Dakota, New Mexico, Arizona, and Wisconsin. *Am J Trop Med* 1962;11:765–772.
64. Dobell C. Researches on the intestinal protozoa of monkeys and man: the life-history of Dientamoeba fragilis: observations, experiments, and speculations. *Parasitology* 1940;32:417–461.
65. Burrows RB, Swerdlow MA. Enterobius vermicularis as a probable vector of Dientamoeba fragilis. *Am J Trop Med Hyg* 1956;5:258–265.
66. Ockert G. Symptomatology, pathology, epidemiology, and diagnosis of Dientamoeba fragilis. In: Honigberg BM, ed. *Trichomonads Parasitic in Humans*. Berlin: Springer-Verlag, 1990:364–410.
67. Spencer MJ, Garcia LS, Chapin MR. Dientamoeba fragilis. An intestinal pathogen in children? *Am J Dis Child* 1979;133:390–393.
68. Johnson EH, Windsor JJ, Clark CG. Emerging from obscurity: biological, clinical, and diagnostic aspects of Dientamoeba fragilis. *Clin Microbiol Rev* 2004;17:553–570.
69. Yoeli M. A report on intestinal disorders accompanied by large numbers of Dientamoeba fragilis. *Trop Med Hyg* 1955;58:38–41.
70. Chan FTH, Guan MX, Mackenzie AMR. Application of indirect immunofluorescence to detection of Dientamoeba fragilis trophozoites in fecal specimens. *J Clin Microbiol* 1993;31:1710–1714.
71. Black RE, Dykes A, Anderson KE, et al. Handwashing to prevent diarrhea in daycare centers. *Am J Epidemiol* 1981;113:445–451.
72. Keystone JS, Yang J, Grisdale D, et al. Intestinal parasites in metropolitan Toronto day-care centers. *Can Med Assoc J* 1984;131:733–735.
73. Backer H. Water disinfection for intentional and wilderness travelers. *Clin Infect Dis* 2002;34:355–364.
74. Adam RD. Biology of Giardia lamblia. *Clin Microbiol Rev* 2001;14:447–475.
75. Yardley JH. Giardiasis. In: Binford CH, Connor DH, eds. *Pathology of Tropical and Extraordinary Diseases, an Atlas*. Washington, DC: Armed Forces Institute of Pathology, 1976:328–331.

76. Garcia LS, Shimizu RY. Evaluation of nine immunoassay kits (enzyme immunoassay and direct fluorescence) for detection of *Giardia lamblia* and *Cryptosporidium parvum* in human fecal specimens. *J Clin Microbiol* 1997;35:1526–1529.
77. Garcia LS, Shimizu RY, Novak S, et al. Commercial assay for detection of *Giardia lamblia* and *Cryptosporidium parvum* antigens in human fecal specimens by rapid solid-phase qualitative immunochromatography. *J Clin Microbiol* 2003;41:209–212.
78. Garcia LS, Garcia PJ. Detection of *Giardia lamblia* antigens in human fecal specimens by a solid-phase qualitative immunochromatographic assay. *J Clin Microbiol* 2006;44:4587–4588.
79. Fedorko DP, Williams EC, Nelson NA, et al. Performance of three enzyme immunoassays and two direct fluorescence assays for detection of *Giardia lamblia* in stool specimens preserved in ECOFIX. *J Clin Microbiol* 2000;38:2781–2783.
80. Faubert G. Immune response to Giardia duodenalis. *Clin Microbiol Rev* 2000;13:35–54.
81. Vesy CJ, Peterson WL. Review article: the management of Giardiasis. *Aliment Pharmacol Ther* 1999;13:843–850.
82. Harris JC, Plummer S, Lloyd D. Antigiardial drugs. *Appl Microbiol Biotechnol* 2001;57:614–619.
83. Steiner TS, Theilman NM, Guerrant RL. Protozoal agents: what are the dangers for the public water supply? *Ann Rev Med* 1997;48:329–340.
84. Olson ME, Ceri H, Morck DW. Giardia vaccination. *Parasitol Today* 2000;16:213–217.
85. Mac Kinzie WR, Hoxie NJ, Proctor ME, et al. A massive outbreak in Milwaukee of Cryptosporidium infection transmitted through the public water supply. *N Engl J Med* 1994;331:161–167.
86. McNulty JM, Fleming DW, Gonzalez AH. A community-wide outbreak of cryptosporidiosis associated with swimming at a wave pool. *JAMA* 1994;272:1597–1600.
87. Wright MS, Collins PA. Waterborne transmission of *Cryptosporidium, Cyclospora,* and *Giardia. Clin Lab Sci* 1997;10:287–290.
88. Centers for Disease Control and Prevention (CDC). Protracted outbreaks of cryptosporidiosis associated with swimming pool use—Ohio and Nebraska, 2000. *MMWR Morb Mortal Wkly Rep* 2001;50:406–410.
89. Centers for Disease Control and Prevention (CDC). Cryptosporidiosis outbreaks associated with recreational water use—5 states, 2006. *MMWR Morb Mortal Wkly Rep* 2007;56:729–732.
90. Millard PS, Gensheimer KF, Addiss DG, et al. An outbreak of Cryptosporidiosis from fresh-pressed apple cider. *JAMA* 1994;272:1592–1596.
91. Bruce BB, Blass MA, Blumberg HM, et al. Risk of *Cryptosporidium parvum* transmission between hospital roommates. *Clin Infect Dis* 2000; 31:947–950.
92. Marshall MM, Naumovitz D, Ortega Y, et al. Waterborne protozoan pathogens. *Clin Microbiol Rev* 1997;10:67–85.
93. Chen XM, Keithley JS, Playa CV, et al. Cryptosporidiosis. *N Engl J Med* 2002;346:1723–1731.
94. Hunter PR, Nichols G. Epidemiology and clinical features of Cryptosporidium infections in immunocompromised patients. *Clin Microbiol Rev* 2002;15:145–154.
95. Harrington BJ, Kassa H. A comparison of an immunoassay with acid–fast staining to detect Cryptosporidium. *Lab Med* 2002;6:451–454.
96. Johnson SP, Ballard MM, Beach J, et al. Evaluation of three commercial assays for detection of Giardia and Cryptosporidium organisms in fecal specimens. *J Clin Microbiol* 2003;41:623–626.
97. Capparelli EV, Syed SS. Nitazoxanide treatment of *Cryptosporidium parvum* in human immunodeficiency virus-infected children. *Pediatr Infect Dis J* 2008;27:1041.
98. Doumbo O, Rossignol F, Pichard E, et al. Nitazoxanide in the treatment of cryptosporidial diarrhea and other intestinal parasitic infections associated with acquired immunodeficiency syndrome in tropical Africa. *Am J Trop Med Hyg* 1997;56:637–639.
99. Rossignol JFA, Ayoub A, Ayers MS. Treatment of diarrhea caused by *Cryptosporidium parvum:* a prospective randomized, double-blind, placebo-controlled study of nitazoxanide. *J Infect Dis* 2001;184:103–106.
100. Amadi B, Mwiya M, Musuku J, et al. Effect of nitazoxanide on morbidity and mortality in Zambian children with cryptosporidiosis: a randomized controlled trial. *Lancet* 2002;360:1375–1380.
101. Holmberg SD, Moorman AC, von Bargen JC, et al. Possible effectiveness of clarithromycin and rifabutin for cryptosporidiosis chemoprophylaxis in HIV disease. *JAMA* 1998;279:384–386.
102. Herwaldt BL. *Cyclospora cayetanensis:* a review, focusing on the outbreaks of cyclosporiasis in the 1990s. *Clin Infect Dis* 2000;31:1040–1057.
103. Centers for Disease Control and Prevention (CDC). Outbreaks of *Cyclospora cayetanensis* infections—United States, 1996. *MMWR Morb Mortal Wkly Rep* 1996;45:549–551.
104. Centers for Disease Control and Prevention (CDC). Outbreaks of Cyclosporiasis —1997. *MMWR Morb Mortal Wkly Rep* 1997;278:521–523.
105. Herwaldt BL, Ackers ML, the Cyclospora work group. An outbreak in 1996 of cyclosporiasis associated with imported raspberries. *N Engl J Med* 1997;336:1548–1556.
106. Fleming CA, Caron D, Gunn JE, et al. A foodborne outbreak of *Cyclospora cayetanensis* at a wedding. *Arch Intern Med* 1998;158:1121–1125.
107. Herwaldt BL, Beach MJ, and the Cyclospora working group. The return of Cyclospora in 1997: another outbreak of cyclosporiasis in North America associated with imported raspberries. *Ann Intern Med* 1999;130:210–220.
108. Ho AY, Lopez AS, Eberhart MG, et al. Outbreak of cyclosporiasis associated with imported raspberries, Philadelphia, Pennsylvania, 2000. *Emerg Infect Dis* 2000;8:783–788.
109. Centers for Disease Control and Prevention (CDC). Outbreaks of cyclosporiasis—Northern Virginia–Washington, D.C.–Baltimore, Maryland, metropolitan area, 1997. *MMWR Morb Mortal Wkly Rep* 1997;46:689–691.
110. Sherchand JB, Cross JH, Jimba M, et al. Study of *Cyclospora cayetanensis* in health care facilities, sewage water and green leafy vegetables in Nepal. *Southeast Asian J Trop Med Public Health* 1999;30:58–63.
111. Doller PC, Dietrich K, Filipp N, et al. Cyclosporiasis outbreak in Germany associated with the consumption of salad. *Emerg Infect Dis* 2002;8:992–994.
112. Centers for Disease Control and Prevention (CDC). Outbreak of cyclosporiasis associated with snow peas—Pennsylvania, 2004. *MMWR Morb Mortal Wkly Rep* 2004;53:1–3.
113. Graczyk TK, Ortega YR, Conn DB. Recovery of waterborne oocysts of *Cyclospora cayetanensis* by Asian Freshwater calms (Corbicula fluminea). *Am J Trop Med Hyg* 1998;59:928–932.
114. Pape JW, Verdier RI, Boncy M, et al. Cyclospora infection in adults infected with HIV: clinical manifestations, treatment and prophylaxis. *Ann Intern Med* 1998;121:654–657.
115. Visvesvara GS, Moura H, Kovacs-Nace E, et al. Uniform staining of Cyclospora oocysts in fecal smears by a modified safranin technique with microwave heating. *J Clin Microbiol* 1997;35:730–797.
116. Eberhard ML, Pieniazek NJ, Arrowood MJ. Laboratory diagnosis of Cyclospora infections. *Arch Pathol Lab Med* 1997;121:792–797.
117. Hoge CW, Shlim DR, Ghimire M, et al. Placebo-controlled trial of cotrimoxazole for Cyclospora infections among travelers and foreign residents in Nepal. *Lancet* 1995;345:691–693.
118. DeHovitz JA, Pape JW, Boncy M, et al. Clinical manifestations and therapy of Isospora belli infection in patients with the acquired immunodeficiency syndrome. *N Engl J Med* 1986;315:87–90.
119. Soave R, Johnson WD. Cryptosporidium and Isospora belli infections. *J Infect Dis* 1988;157:225–229.
120. Dammin GJ, Dooley JR. Coccidiosis. In: Binford CH, Connor DH, eds. *Pathology of Tropical and Extraordinary Diseases, an Atlas.* Washington, DC: Armed Forces Institute of Pathology, 1976:332–333.
121. Brandborg LL, Goldberg SB, Breidenbach WC. Human coccidiosis—a possible cause of malabsorption: the life cycle in small-bowel mucosal biopsies as a diagnostic feature. *N Engl J Med* 1970;283:1306–1313.
122. Ackers JP. Gut coccidian–Isospora, *Cryptosporidium, Cyclospora* and *Sarcocystis. Semin Gastrointest Dis* 1997;8:33–44.
123. Arean VM, Koppisch E. Balantidiasis. *Am J Pathol* 1956;32:1089–1115.
124. Esteban JG, Aguirre C, Angles R, et al. Balantidiasis in Aymara children from the northern Bolivia. *Am J Trop Med Hyg* 1998;59:922–927.
125. Swartzwelder JC. Balantidiasis. *Am J Dig Dis* 1950;17:173–179.
126. Ferry T, Bouhour D, De Monbrison F, et al. Severe peritonitis due to *Balantidium coli* acquired in France. *Eur J Clin Microbiol Infect Dis* 2004;23:393–395.
127. Lawrence DN, Neel JV, Abadie SH, et al. Epidemiologic studies among Amerindian populations of Amazonia. *Am J Trop Med* 1980;29:530–537.
128. Lerman RH, Hall WT, Barrett O. *Balantidium coli* infection in a Vietnam returnee. *CA Med* 1970;112:17–18.
129. Yazar S, Altuntas F, Sahin I, et al. Dysentery caused by *Balantidium coli* in a patient with non-Hodgkin's lymphoma from Turkey. *World J Gastroenterol* 2004;10:458–459.
130. Giacometti A, Cireoni O, Balducci M, et al. Epidemiologic features of intestinal parasitic infections in Italian mental institutions. *Eur J Epidemiol* 1997;13:825–830.
131. Baskerville L, Ahmed Y, Ramchand S. *Balantidium colitis. Dig Dis* 1970;15:727–731.
132. Vijaya D, Anand Kumar BH, Joseph M. Balantidiasis in an infant. *Indian J Pediatr* 2000;67:781.
133. Sharma S, Harding G. Necrotizing lung infection caused by the protozoan *Balantidium coli. Can J Infect Dis* 2003;14:163–166.
134. Anargyrou K, Petrikkos GL, Suller MTE, et al. Pulmonary *Balantidium coli* infection in a leukemic patient. *Am J Hematol* 2003;73:180–183.
135. Landas SD, Savva S, Frydas A, et al. Invasive balantidiasis presented as chronic colitis and lung involvement. *Dig Dis Sci* 1989;34:1621–1623.
136. Clark CG, Diamond LS. Methods for cultivation of luminal parasitic protists of clinical importance. *Clin Microbiol Rev* 2002;15:329–341.

CHAPTER 80

Herpes Virus

John Anthony Zaia, MD
Professor and Chair, Department of Virology
Beckman Research Institute, City of Hope Medical Center
Duarte, CA

ABSTRACT

The Herpesviridae family is large and found among all vertebrates. The viruses share a common structure and a common biology consisting of a chronic intermittent infection fluctuating between low-level activity (latency) and high-level replication (reactivation). There are eight known herpesviruses of humans, and these form three subfamilies (the alpha-, beta-, and gamma-herpesviruses) that have laboratory and clinical features in common. These characteristics range from rashes to malignancies. The methods for prevention and treatment of these infections are discussed in this chapter.

KEY CONCEPTS

- The herpesviruses are among the 1.7 million healthcare-associated infections that occur annually in hospitals in the United States. Breaches in infection prevention protocols and lack of pathogen-specific education on transmission, disease presentation, and prevention matters are major contributing factors. Immunocompromised and young individuals are at greatest risk. Implementing and adhering to Standard, Contact, and Droplet Precautions can reduce these numbers.

- The herpesviruses are a family of eight DNA viruses that initiate acute, chronic, and latent infections of the skin, epithelial cells, lymphocytes, and neurons. These include herpes simplex type 1, herpes simplex type 2, varicella-zoster virus, Epstein-Barr virus, cytomegalovirus, human herpesvirus 6, human herpesvirus 7, and human herpesvirus 8.

- Herpesviruses are transmitted by close intimate contact or exposure to virus-containing body fluids (saliva, urine, blood, breast milk, and contaminated respiratory or genital secretions). Exposure and first infections are acquired in childhood.

- Each herpesvirus has a preferred tissue target, but infections usually present as generalized or local infections of neonates, young children, healthy adults, and immunocompromised patients.

- After initial infections, latency may be established in tissues or neurons and reactivate in response to stress, infections, medications, sunlight, or surgery.

- Most infections are asymptomatic. Active disease may present as virus-filled blisters on the face or genitals, fever, malaise, sore throat, rash, or tumors.

BACKGROUND

Viruses are named and organized into groups, or families, based on their physical properties and their growth patterns relative to specific hosts or organ tissues. The family of viruses called Herpesviridae has more than 100 members, is represented across the wide range of vertebrate animals, and is even found in some mollusks. There are few genetic similarities between herpesviruses of lower vertebrates compared with those of higher animals, but because they look alike by electron microscopy, these widely differing viruses are all members of the same family. The appearance that makes each of them a herpesvirus is the presence of a double-stranded DNA core, an icosahedral capsid, a tegument layer between the capsid and the envelope, and a bilipid membrane envelope (see Figure 80-1). For the vertebrate species that are more closely related, their herpesviruses are also somewhat similar and can share cross-reacting antigens. Yet, with some exceptions, the herpesviruses are very species-specific and do not replicate or produce disease outside a limited host range. For example, the herpesviruses of catfish do not infect humans. However, as species become closer, there is not only the similarity of virus genes but also the potential for cross-species infection and disease. Thus, herpesvirus simiae of Cercopithecine monkeys shares proteins with human herpesviruses and is a serious pathogen in man.

The primary infection may or may not produce a serious disease, but during this initial infection, there can be an "escape" from normal immune surveillance, with certain viruses more effective at this than others. The result is the ability of the virus to survive for the lifetime of the animal. When virus infection subsides, which is associated with a limitation of the gene expression ("latency"), there is cessation of virus replication or a profound reduction in virus growth. Herpesvirus latency is the state of virus infection in which there is no significant virus replication. In practical terms, latency appears to be due to a functional absence of sufficient cellular transcription factors for permissive replication. Because cells vary in states of transcriptional activation, the ability of the virus to replicate and be detected alternates between latency and reactivation. Herpesvirus reactivation is the renewal of virus replication in cells that

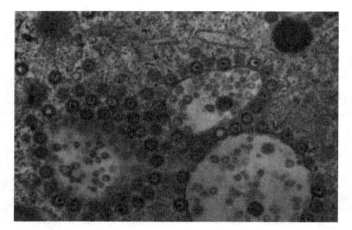

Figure 80-1. Structure of a herpesvirus.

previously have been infected with that specific herpesvirus. Thus, herpesviruses have the ability to remain in selected tissues of the host, for example, in nerve, breast, or salivary tissue or in lymphoid organs. When reactivation occurs, disease syndromes can occur that are different from the primary infection. Thus, reactivation of herpes simplex type 1 (HSV-1) causes a fever blister; varicella-zoster virus (VZV) can cause shingles; cytomeg-alovirus (CMV) can cause retinitis; and Epstein-Barr virus (EBV) can cause lymphoid proliferation and malignancy.

Despite the relative lack of serious disease in the healthy individual, it has become recognized that the immune system works overtime to control these latent infections. For example, for CMV and EBV, it is not unusual to find asymptomatic adults

with 10 percent or more of total T lymphocytes committed to control of these infections.

When the immune system is immature, fails, or is purposely altered during cancer or other therapies, there can be serious infections with these viruses. For example, there can be dis-semination of HSV-1 and CMV in the newborn, CMV retinitis in patients with acquired immunodeficiency syndrome (AIDS), EBV lymphoproliferative syndromes after organ transplan-tation, and other serious manifestations of these herpesvirus infections that are not seen in persons with an intact immune system. These viruses may vary in infection patterns and in dis-ease presentation, but the seriousness of the resultant diseases is such that it is important to be familiar with the spectrum of human herpesvirus infection and pathogenesis.

This chapter reviews the important aspects relating to the understanding of the herpesviruses of humans and focuses on the relative differences among these viruses, their diagnoses and treatment, and the current methods for their control.

BASIC PRINCIPLES

Classification

There are eight herpesviruses that have been isolated from humans; each has a numerical designation and a common name, which will be the preferred terminology in this chapter. This terminology and certain of the distinguishing clini-cal characteristics of these eight viruses are shown in Table 80-1.

Table 80-1. The Human Herpesviruses

Virus		Population Frequency[a]	Age at Infection	Clinical Disease	Antiviral Therapy	Prevention
HSV-1	HHV1	50%–60%	Infancy Childhood	Gingivostomatitis Keratitis CNS (rare)	Yes	Contact Control
HSV-2	HHV2	15%–25%	Adolescence Young Adults	Genital infection Meningitis	Yes	Contact Control
VZV	HHV3	95%	Childhood	Skin vesicles Zoster	Yes	Vaccine & Contact Control
EBV	HHV4	75%	Childhood Adolescence	Mononucleosis B-cell lymphoma Hodgkin lymphoma NP carcinoma Hairy leucoplakia	No	Contact Control
CMV	HHV5	60%	Fetus/infants Children Young Adults	Birth defects CNS/eye Pneumonia Enteritis	Yes	Contact Control
HHV-6	HHV6	90%	Infancy	Roseola Encephalitis	Yes	Unknown
HHV-7	HHV7	90%	Infancy	Roseola	No	Unknown
KSHV	HHV8	1%–5%	Variable	Kaposi's sarcoma Primary effusion lymphoma Multicentric Castleman disease	No	Contact Control

[a]The frequencies are shown for a Western country and will vary with living conditions (i.e., social crowding and poverty). HSV, herpes simplex virus; VZV, varicella zoster virus; EBV, Epstein-Barr virus; CMV, cytomegalovirus; HHV, human herpesvirus; KSHV, Kaposi's sarcoma herpes virus; CNS, central nervous system; NP, nasopharyngeal.

Similarities and Differences among the Herpesviruses

Although the herpesviruses look alike, they demonstrate a wide range of biologic and clinical differences, and these differences are used to further divide them into subfamilies. The further classification of the herpesviruses is based primarily on the biologic behavior of the virus in tissue culture, and this permits a division into three subfamilies, called Alphaherpesvirinae, Betaherpesvirinae, and Gammaherpesvirinae. The alpha-herpesviruses—HSV-1, HSV-2, and VZV—have a wider range of infection than do other herpesviruses, including a more rapid and lytic infection and lack of persistence of infection in vitro. CMV, HHV-6, and HHV-7 are beta-herpesviruses that grow more slowly in culture, are cell associated but still lytic, and share common protein sequences. EBV and Kaposi's sarcoma-associated herpesvirus (KSHV) are gamma-herpesviruses that, though lytic at times, can grow productively in vitro and in vivo by immortalizing the infected cells and by supporting cellular proliferation. These gamma-herpesviruses contribute to genetic instability and multistep tumorigenicity.

Epidemiologic Principles of the Herpesviruses

These viruses are generally acquired in childhood and, except for the alpha-herpesviruses, there is often no significant disease associated with primary infection. From time to time, the virus can reactivate and become infectious, usually in specific body fluids. These viruses can exist in an immune population and be transmitted after reactivation to nonimmune persons. Reactivation allows release of infectious virus days, months, or years after initial infection and even at times when the host shows no sign of disease.

Although disease is usually mild in immunologically healthy persons, each of these viruses can produce life-threatening infection in immunosuppressed persons. Much of the prevention and treatment of these viruses is directed to the control of herpesviruses in this population. Hematopoietic stem cell transplantation (HSCT) and solid organ transplantation (SOT) are continually expanding fields of medicine with increasingly novel methods for limiting the natural host community. As a consequence, new and unusual presentations for herpesvirus infections have occurred. In the earliest HSCT experiences, CMV was the significant pathogen producing a previously unrecognized syndrome of fever and interstitial pneumonia. With T-cell-depleted HSCT and SOT, EBV was observed to produce a posttransplant lymphoproliferative disease. The viral etiology of Kaposi's sarcoma (KS) in AIDS has been shown to be due to KSHV, and this virus is also a problem in transplantation medicine.

SPECIFIC HERPESVIRUSES

Herpes Simplex Viruses Type 1 and Type 2

Nature of HSV-1 and HSV-2

The alpha-herpesviruses, HSV-1 and HSV-2, are distinct viruses based on antigenic and genetic composition, but they are considered together here because of the similarity of disease presentation and epidemiology. They were first noted to be different in subtle tissue culture growth patterns and were separated by serologic means into a type of virus usually isolated from oral specimens (HSV-1) and a type usually isolated from genital specimens (HSV-2). HSV-1 and HSV-2 share about 50 percent of their genetic sequences, and both can infect and replicate in cutaneous tissues such as skin and mucous membranes, enter into the adjacent sensory nerve fibers, and move up the nerve to the cell nucleus, where they can become latent in cell bodies or ganglia of the central nervous system (CNS). Upon reactivation, the virus can return to the cutaneous distribution area of the infected nerve to appear as "recurrent herpes."

Epidemiology of HSV-1 and HSV-2

Humans are the only natural reservoir for HSV-1 and HSV-2, and spread is solely via human-to-human contact with infected material, usually from mucous membranes or skin. The virus does not spread by aerosol, and it is unlikely to be spread by fomites due to its lability. The differing epidemiologic patterns of these two viruses are due to the sites of infection from which they are transmitted. HSV-1 is usually an oral infection, known as herpes labialis or herpes gingivostomatitis, and spreads in early childhood via infected saliva and skin. This also accounts for high endemic levels of HSV-1 infection in areas of close contact and crowding, such as socioeconomically depressed areas, and for high rates of new infection in situations associated with close contact, for example, college dormitories. HSV-2 is usually a genital infection, known as herpes genitalis, and spreads by sexual contact. Because HSV-1 infection usually precedes HSV-2 infection and because there is some protection afforded by HSV-1 immunity, the primary infection with HSV-2 can be asymptomatic. Only 10 percent of HSV-2-seropositive individuals report a history of herpes genitalis. More importantly for virus spread, asymptomatic virus reactivation and shedding occurs, and observations in seropositive persons have detected virus on approximately 3 percent of days studied.[1] The risks for HSV-2 seropositivity include female gender, age at first sexual intercourse, years of sexual activity, ethnic background (African American and Hispanic more so than white or Asian), drug use, and lower socioeconomic status. HSV-1 is now the cause of approximately half of all new cases of herpes genitalis in the United States.[2]

Clinical Disease with HSV-1 and HSV-2

HSV-1 Disease

Primary HSV-1 infection most often presents as herpes gingivostomatitis in youngsters between the ages of 6 months and 5 years or as herpes pharyngitis in adolescents and young adults.[3] In children, this is a serious disease with high fever, listlessness, sore throat, and lymphadenopathy. In young adults, the disease presents as severe sore throat and tonsillitis. Recurrence of HSV-1 is called herpes labialis (frequently called cold sores or fever blisters) and presents with a prodromal tingling or burning followed within 6 to 24 hours by a cluster of vesicles or red papules at the vermilion border of the lips or adjacent skin on the face. Lesions evolve rapidly to a crusted ulcer in 2 days and heal in 6 to 10 days.

HSV-2 Disease

For HSV-2, the incubation period after sexual contact can range from 3 to 14 days but usually appears as vesicular lesions and denuded areas of genital mucous membranes within 1 week. Disease is more severe in women than in men, and symptoms include local pain, burning, tenderness of the involved areas, urethritis, constitutional symptoms of fever, headache, and malaise, and even meningeal symptoms. On moist areas, the initial vesicle ruptures quickly and a yellow-gray denuded ulcer surrounded by a red rim is seen; on dry skin, the vesicles progress to pustules and then dry and crust during a period of several days. The symptoms peak after 3 to 4 days, and viral shedding lasts for 12 to 14 days. Pain and local symptoms remit after 2 weeks, and complete healing occurs by 4 weeks. Recurrence of HSV-2 infection can appear as asymptomatic infection or as a painful cluster of vesicles in a localized area innervated by the pudendal nerves. The clinical syndrome after HSV-1 herpes genitalis is similar to that of HSV-2 but with less recurrence.

Other Manifestations of HSV-1 or HSV-2 Diseases

HSV-1 can spread to other sites of the body or can produce immune-mediated syndromes, which are described here.

Herpes Simplex Virus Keratitis and Other Ocular Disease

HSV-1 can be autoinoculated to the cornea during primary or recurrent infection. Lesions can be recurrent and result in scarring of the cornea. Stromal keratitis and iritis can occur after HSV infection.

Herpes Simplex Virus Encephalitis and Meningitis

HSV-1 encephalitis is the leading cause of sporadic acute necrotizing encephalitis in the United States; there are approximately 1,000 cases per year. This can occur either as a primary infection or as recurrent infection.[4] Primary HSV-2 infection is often associated with cerebrospinal pleocytosis and symptomatic meningitis.[5]

Herpes Whitlow and Herpes Gladiatorum (Scrumpox)

HSV-1 and HSV-2 can infect remote or adjacent cutaneous sites after direct contact. Medical personnel and patients with oral or genital infection can autoinoculate by touching infected areas during herpes labialis or herpes genitalis. The infected paronychia is called herpetic whitlow. When infection occurs on the back, following contact with infected saliva during such interactions as wrestling or rugby, the condition is called herpes gladiatorum or "scrumpox."

Esophagitis, Hepatitis, and Enteritis

In the immunocompromised host, HSV-1 reactivation occurs in as many as 70 percent of patients, depending on the degree of immunosuppression. Oral infection can spread to the esophagus, small bowel, and liver. Perianal infection can spread to adjacent skin on the buttocks, producing painful skin ulcers.

Neonatal Herpes

Neonatal HSV infection occurs in 1 in 3,000 to 5,000 live births in the United States, with two-thirds of cases due to HSV-2 and one-third due to HSV-1.[6,7] The risk of infection is higher after primary maternal infection but can occur after recurrent herpes genitalis. Disease is usually of three types: disseminated infection involving multiple organs; portal-of-entry infection involving the skin, eyes, and mouth; and encephalitis with or without infection of skin, eyes, or mouth.

Eczema Herpeticum

Disorders of the skin, such as eczema, pemphigus, burns, or other dermatoses, can be infected with HSV and lead to widely disseminated and life-threatening infection. The generalized vesicular rash in this situation has been called Kaposi's varicelliform eruption. In burn units, this is a particular problem because HSV-1 reactivation can occur during stress, and autoinoculations of skin lesions can occur.[8]

Diagnosis of HSV-1 and HSV-2

Although viral culture has been a frequently used and reliable method of virus diagnosis, the most rapid method is indirect immunofluorescent staining of a lesion (swabbed specimen) examined on a slide.[4] This does not distinguish between HSV-1 and HSV-2, but type-specific antibody assays are commercially available. Polymerase chain reaction (PCR) assay can be effective at detecting HSV infection in body fluids or biopsy material.[4,9]

Treatment and Prevention of HSV-1 and HSV-2 Infection

HSV-1 and HSV-2 can be treated or prevented using antiviral agents. In addition to antiviral prophylaxis, the use of sunscreen for prevention of herpes labialis and condoms for preventing genital contact with viruses is recommended. Used daily, valacyclovir and acyclovir are highly effective in suppressing recurrences of genital herpes.[10,11]

Varicella-Zoster Virus

Nature of Varicella-Zoster Virus

VZV is the third of the alpha-herpesviruses; it can grow relatively rapidly with lytic infection but cannot maintain prolonged infection in tissue culture. The virus is distinct from HSV in both genetic sequence and clinical syndromes. The viruses of chicken pox and herpes zoster have been shown to be identical by physical and chemical analyses.

Epidemiology of Varicella-Zoster Virus Infection

VZV has no animal reservoir and spreads only from humans to humans. The primary infection with VZV causes a disseminated infection called chicken pox. Prior to the availability of the VZV vaccine, approximately 3.7 million cases of chicken pox occurred each year in the United States, 83 percent in children younger than 9 years.[12] Infection spreads via airborne mechanisms, with an infection rate of more than 90 percent in households with susceptible children. VZV infection occurred in as much as 95 percent of the population and was one of the most common infections of mankind. Immunity would quickly occur in an isolated population, so chicken pox spread from older immune generations to susceptible children by exposure to herpes zoster, the reactivation form of the viral life cycle. When a case of herpes zoster is the source of contact for a new case of chicken pox, it is likely that the virus spreads by direct contact with skin or skin squames. In households with a zoster exposure, the susceptible children have an infection rate of 25 percent.[13] There are approximately 1,000,000 cases of herpes zoster in the United States per year,[14] with the incidence constant for each age group through midadulthood. Herpes zoster incidence increases with increasing age, especially after age 50, is more common among immunocompromised persons.[15]

Clinical Aspects of Varicella-Zoster Virus Infection

Chicken Pox

In healthy children, VZV infection manifests as a vesicular rash often associated with prodromal malaise, pharyngitis, rhinitis, and abdominal pain. The rash appears 15 days after VZV exposure, with a range of 10 to 21 days. The vesicular eruption on skin emerges in successive crops during the first 3 to 4 days of illness, usually with an accompanying rash or spots on the mucous membranes. The skin vesicles begin on the head and quickly progress to the trunk, arms, and finally the legs (this may be termed a descending appearance), with rapid development of inflammatory changes and crusting in successive crops. A pathognomonic appearance is all stages of the rash, macules, vesicles, papules, and crusts, seen in the same region of the skin. The severity of disease is linked to the extent that the infection invades the mucosal surfaces of respiratory, alimentary, and genitourinary systems. The patient with chicken pox can have severe laryngitis, laryngotracheobronchitis, vaginitis, urethritis, pancreatitis, and enteritis. The immunocompromised host also may have severe abdominal pain or back pain, a hallmark of such progressive VZV infection.[16]

Herpes Zoster

Herpes zoster (also called "shingles" or "zona") occurs when VZV infection reactivates in cranial or spinal nerve ganglia, spreads to the cutaneous nerves, and infects the skin in the exact distribution of the nerve.[17] The most common area of involvement is the trunk, presumably because this is the area of greatest primary VZV infection, followed by cranial dermatomes, and then by cervical and lumbar dermatomes. Zoster is a syndrome of pain and vesicular eruption in a unilateral cutaneous distribution. If pain alone is present, without rash, the syndrome is called zoster sine herpete. The pain of herpes zoster that persists after the healing of skin lesions is termed postherpetic neuralgia and can last for

months. Virus reactivation in the spinal or cranial nerve ganglia, with the resultant intense inflammation and hemorrhagic necrosis of nerve cells, can result in nerve dysfunction manifested clinically by meningitis and myelitis, with or without paresis at sites of involved nerves. In addition, intense inflammation of the cutaneous site of infection results in scarring of the involved epidermis. This is of particular concern when the cornea or other ophthalmic structures are involved.

Diagnosis of Varicella-Zoster Virus Infection

The history and physical examination remain the primary methods for diagnosing chicken pox and shingles. In chicken pox, lesions are seen in all stages of development, including macules, vesicles, pustules, and crusted lesions, often with a history of recent exposure to a VZV infection. In certain individuals, especially those at high risk for complications of VZV infection, specific diagnosis can be pursued by laboratory methods. The most rapid and accurate method is the direct immunofluorescent stain of a skin scraping for VZV antigen using a commercially available kit. Conventional methods of culture of VZV or serology for VZV antibody also can be used to confirm the diagnosis, but these are rarely necessary in routine clinical practice.

Treatment and Prevention of Varicella-Zoster Virus Infection

Chicken pox and herpes zoster can be treated using antiviral agents. Because chicken pox is rarely seen in the vaccine era, it is important to be aware of management options necessary to minimize complications. Skin and subcutaneous infections are the leading bacterial cause of morbidity in patients with chicken pox, and attention to skin hygiene and early treatment of bacterial infections is important. Antiviral medication is not recommended in the otherwise healthy child but should be used in children with medical problems and in adults in whom there could be a predisposition to disseminated VZV infection.[18]

For the management of herpes zoster, the major concern should be for the control of pain and the prevention of inflammation that could alter organ function, for example, eyesight. Antiviral treatment has been shown to be effective using acyclovir, valacyclovir, famciclovir, and brivudine. The reader is referred to specialized text for the management of pain in these patients.[19]

The most important method for preventing chicken pox is use of the VZV vaccine. This vaccine is recommended for all healthy children and is also recommended for eligible healthcare personnel and day care workers, college students, prisoners, military recruits, nonpregnant women of child-bearing age, and international travelers who have not previously had VZV infection as indicated by negative antibody assay. For persons older than 60 years, there is a vaccine for prevention of herpes zoster.[17,20]

Varicella vaccine is recommended for postexposure administration for unvaccinated healthy people aged 12 months and older who are without other evidence of immunity to prevent or modify the disease. The vaccine should be administered as soon as possible within 5 days after exposure to rash, if there are no contraindications to use. The varicella-zoster immune globulin (VZIG) product used in the United States is currently available under an investigational new drug protocol. VZIG provides maximum benefit when administered as soon as possible after exposure but may be effective if administered as late as 10 days after exposure. If VZIG is not available, the U.S. Centers for Disease Control and Prevention (CDC) recommends that administration of intravenous immune globulin be considered as an alternative (also within 10 days of exposure).[21]

Although there are limited published data on the benefit of acyclovir as postexposure prophylaxis, if VZIG is not available some experts recommend prophylaxis with acyclovir beginning 7 to 10 days after exposure for people without evidence of immunity and with contraindications for varicella vaccination.

The use of acyclovir and valacyclovir after organ transplantation lessens the incidence of VZV infection.[22-25] In addition, acyclovir can also be used to supplement VZIG to prevent chicken pox in high-risk newborns and children.[26,27]

Cytomegalovirus

Nature of Human Cytomegalovirus

Human CMV is a beta-herpesvirus and is one of the most ubiquitous of the herpesviruses. Its growth in tissue culture is lytic but slower than the alpha-herpesviruses, and it was named for the cytopathic effect produced after infection. CMV is the largest of the human herpesviruses in size of genome, with approximately 240 kilobase pairs of DNA encoding nearly 200 proteins.[28] There are many strains of CMV, which probably accounts for the ability to be reinfected with multiple CMV infections. PCR assays that amplify the hypervariable regions encoding two surface glycoproteins, gB and gH, have been used to differentiate CMV strains by group.[29]

Epidemiology of Human Cytomegalovirus

With more than 60 percent of CMV-seropositive pregnant women excreting CMV in cervical sites and in breast milk, this virus is one of the first infections encountered by the newborn.[30] In addition, 1 percent of mothers who are seropositive at preconception transmit the virus to their child in utero.[31] If not infected during the neonatal period, the young child may receive additional exposure in day care centers, which have a 50 to 60 percent CMV excretion rate. Once infected, the child will excrete virus in saliva and urine for many months. Thus, CMV is spread by contact with infected persons in childhood. After puberty, sexual transmission of the virus occurs in 1 to 2 percent of the adult population seroconverts per year. CMV is also transmitted in blood products and organs.[32]

Clinical Syndromes of Cytomegalovirus Infection

Congenital Infection

Cytomegalic inclusion disease is the most severe manifestation of congenital CMV infection and results from intrauterine infection in the first and second trimesters of pregnancy, occurring in 3,000 to 4,000 infants annually in the United States.[31] Hepatosplenomegaly is universal, and cutaneous hematopoietic elements create a "blueberry muffin" appearance to the skin. Infection of the brain occurs, with resultant microcephaly, intrauterine growth retardation, and postnatal mental and motor retardation. CMV is the leading infectious cause of mental retardation in the United States.

Subclinical congenital CMV infection occurs when congenital infection is in the late second and third trimester and presents late with sensorineural hearing loss, school failure, and motor impairment. Preterm infants can be infected with CMV through blood transfusions, and this can result in pallor and hypotension ("gray baby syndrome") and respiratory distress.

Cytomegalovirus Mononucleosis and Hepatitis

The vast majority of primary CMV infections in healthy persons are asymptomatic, but infection can be associated with nonspecific symptoms of fever, malaise, mononucleosis with or without hepatitis, leukopenia, and atypical lymphocytosis, particularly in otherwise healthy young adults. This heterophile-negative mononucleosis can occur after heart-lung bypass, where it is termed "postperfusion syndrome," and in patients in intensive care and burn units.[33,34] Chronic fatigue syndrome has been anecdotally associated with CMV infection, but it is not clear whether this is due to the CMV itself or whether CMV is associated because of its ubiquitous nature.

Transplantation and AIDS-related Cytomegalovirus Infection

Overview

Formerly, human CMV was considered a pathogen only for the fetus. But it is recognized to be a more serious pathogen in the organ transplant recipient, in whom it produces a range of syndromes from fever, leukopenia, and thrombocytopenia to more serious organ-specific dysfunction, with or without bacterial and fungal superinfections. It was first noted to produce significant disease in the SOT population. During the first decade of marrow transplantation, CMV was the leading infectious cause of death.[35] In addition, in the pre-antiretroviral therapy era of AIDS, CMV was a significant cause of morbidity and mortality. It is observed that there is increased disease and mortality in SOT of CMV seropositive donors to seronegative organ recipients. However, in HSCT, when the transplant donor is CMV seropositive and the recipient seronegative, protection from CMV infection is conveyed through the transfer of memory T cells.[36] A significant reduction in CMV disease has occurred in patients with AIDS, who receive human immunodeficiency virus (HIV) treatment and have at least partial recovery of CD4 lymphocytes to more than 200 cells/μL. This attests to the importance of immunologic control of CMV in disease pathogenesis. Thus, among the risk factors for CMV disease, immunosuppression or immunodeficiency is of primary importance. The absence of CMV-specific, CD4-positive, T-cell function is a marker for risk of CMV disease.[37,38] In addition, patients with detectable cytotoxic T-lymphocyte (CTL) activity targeted to CMV have much less disease than do those without CTL.[39,40]

Interstitial Pneumonia

Cytomegalovirus-interstitial pneumonia (CMV-IP) presents with dyspnea (air hunger) and oxygen desaturation in blood and progresses to respiratory failure.[35] This is a particular problem in organ transplantation, and in the absence of preemptive antiviral therapy, the usual onset of CMV-IP is during the 2 months after the transplantation. With preemptive therapy, the onset of disease is 150 to 180 days after transplant. Treatment requires respiratory support and control of the virus infection. The use of immunosuppressive drugs should be decreased as much as possible. Antiviral therapy uses either ganciclovir or foscarnet, with the addition of intravenous immunoglobulin. Although this use of intravenous immunoglobulin has not been established with controlled trials, it has become conventional therapy in the marrow transplant patient on the basis of case reports.[41]

Cytomegalovirus Enteritis

CMV infection can involve any location in the gastrointestinal system, from esophagus to rectum, with or without hepatitis. The classical presentation is with fever, loss of appetite, and abdominal pain. In severe infection, diarrhea and abdominal bleeding, with or without perforation of the bowel, can occur.

Cytomegalovirus Retinitis

In the pre-antiretroviral therapy era in AIDS, the most frequently seen form of CMV disease was retinitis. With improved treatment of AIDS, the incidence of retinitis has decreased significantly.[42] Currently, CMV retinitis is seen primarily in patients with AIDS and antiretroviral failure and in SOT recipients on long-term immunosuppression.[43] The disease presents with variable degrees of monocular visual impairment and funduscopic findings of yellow-white exudates with or without hemorrhage. In advanced disease, both eyes become involved, and there is eventual retinal detachment and blindness. In some newly treated patients with AIDS who have recovering CD4+ counts, there is a syndrome of vitreous inflammation and macular edema, which is called "immune reconstitution disorder" due to a restored immune response to occult CMV infection of the eye.[44]

Diagnosis of Cytomegalovirus Infection

Active infection with CMV can be diagnosed by PCR or viral culture of CMV from urine, saliva, throat swab specimens, or other body tissues. Serologic tests that detect CMV antibodies (IgM and IgG antibody to CMV) are widely available from commercial laboratories. Tissue culture isolation of CMV is rarely used, but methods for detection of CMV by histology or of CMV antigens by immunohistochemistry are frequently used methods for diagnosis. The enzyme-linked immunosorbent assay (ELISA) is the most commonly available serologic test for measuring antibody to CMV. Various fluorescence assays and

indirect hemagglutination and latex agglutination tests are also available.[45]

There are two general categories of CMV diagnostic assays, those that depend on virus infection in tissue culture for a positive end point and those that require molecular methods for detection of virus protein, RNA, or DNA. Detection of CMV pp65 in granulocytic nuclei, utilizing monoclonal antibody staining of peripheral blood leukocytes, can be used to document early CMV dissemination in immunocompromised patients.[46] This CMV antigenemia assay correlates with CMV blood infection, and the onset of antigenemia precedes the detection of "infectious" CMV using the culture-based assays.[47] Thus, the antigenemia assay is a surrogate marker for CMV blood infection and, as such, has become a valuable tool for determining the preemptive use of antiviral agents.[48]

Among the molecular methods of CMV detection are the PCR assay, the DNA hybrid capture assay, and the nucleic acid sequence-based amplification.[49] The PCR assay is a versatile method for diagnosing CMV and can be used for quantitative characterization of CMV infection. PCR assay improves the early detection and treatment of CMV infection after transplantation.[50] Quantitative PCR is particularly useful for monitoring the response to treatment.[51]

The hybrid capture systems use a synthetic strand of RNA to "find" a strand of homologous DNA from a clinical specimen. This "hybrid" RNA/DNA is captured in a tube coated with antibody to RNA/DNA complexes and then detected using an antibody-based assay.[49] The specificity of the CMV hybrid capture assay is similar to that of the antigenemia assay[52] and compares well with PCR-based methods in the care of transplant patients.[53] The nucleic acid sequence-based amplification assay (NASBA) detects CMV using an RNA amplification technique in which a CMV-specific RNA molecule can be made into DNA and then serve as a template for amplification of RNA copies, which are then detected.[49] A potential advantage of the RNA amplification system is that a positive result indicates the presence of actively replicating virus. The NASBA compares well with PCR and blood culture when used to manage antiviral therapy in transplant patients.[54] The ultimate choice of assay to use should be based on clinical need, and the most important needs are detection of CMV infection early enough to prevent disease and confirmation of treatment response or failure. It is clear that the PCR, hybrid capture, and NASBA assays report the earliest detection times of CMV reactivation. However, the antigenemia assay has the advantage of low-technology requirements and ease of performance. But the choice of assay must be made based on the resources at each medical center and the type of patients treated.[49]

Treatment of Cytomegalovirus Infection

Antiviral Agents for Cytomegalovirus Prevention

Ganciclovir, foscarnet, and cidofovir are antiviral drugs approved for the treatment of CMV infection. Valganciclovir is an oral agent with high bioavailability and is the drug of choice for prevention of CMV in SOT patients. Foscarnet is especially useful when there is concern about the marrow toxicity of ganciclovir. Because foscarnet is associated with nephrotoxicity, hypocalcemia, and hypophosphatemia, attention must be given to adequate hydration and electrolyte balance. Foscarnet is usually administered intravenously with concomitant administration of saline. Attention must be given to Mg++ and Ca++ levels, and this can be supplemented with an infusion of magnesium sulfate and potassium phosphate with calcium supplementation if hypocalcemia occurs.

Risk-Adapted Prophylactic Antiviral Management

There are two methods of CMV prevention: preemptive use of antiviral agent and risk-adapted prophylaxis. The preemptive strategy for prevention of CMV disease aims at early treatment of reactivated infection prior to the onset of disease. This method relies critically on an efficient method for surveillance and reporting of CMV reactivation following HSCT. CMV infection in blood or in the lungs of patients with asymptomatic disease is the significant risk factor for subsequent disease. In the preemptive strategy, ganciclovir is given to asymptomatic transplant recipients at the time of laboratory-positive active CMV infection of blood.[55,56] The goal of preemptive ganciclovir use is to limit exposure of this marrow-toxic agent to persons who have demonstrated reactivation of CMV infection.

Control of Iatrogenic Cytomegalovirus Transmission

The risk of CMV infection in the low-birth-weight neonate and in the CMV-seronegative transplant recipient, for whom the donor is also CMV seronegative, is determined by exposure to blood product support. When blood components are filtered, nearly all primary CMV infection can be prevented, and no preventive antiviral treatment is necessary in this population.[57–59]

Epstein-Barr Virus

Nature of the Epstein-Barr Virus

EBV is a gamma-herpesvirus, meaning that the virus can cause both lytic and nonlytic infection and, more importantly, can maintain itself in long-term chronic active infection. Its ability to induce cell replication contributes to its oncogenicity. The EBV genome contains 172 kilobase pairs of double-stranded DNA. There are two types of EBV, type 1 and type 2 (sometimes called type A and type B), which differ primarily in the nuclear antigens expressed during latency. In Western countries, type 1 predominates, but in Africa the types are equally prevalent.[60] The biologic aspects of EBV replication, which contribute to lymphoproliferation and malignancy, are described later in this chapter.

Epidemiology of Epstein-Barr Virus

The EBV virus grows in the epithelium of the oropharynx, and shedding into saliva explains the transmission of infection from such activities as kissing and sharing glassware. Among lower socioeconomic groups, EBV spreads in childhood; in industrialized societies, infection occurs in adolescents and young adults. The virus spreads systemically and infects B lymphocytes, which become a primary site of infection and in which the virus persists indefinitely.[61] Transfusion of blood and tissue transplantation can spread EBV to susceptible recipients.[62,63]

Clinical Diseases of Epstein-Barr Virus

EBV is most important as the cause of infectious mononucleosis and is associated with neoplastic diseases such as nasopharyngeal carcinoma,[64] Burkitt lymphoma,[65,66] non-Hodgkin lymphoma in AIDS,[67,68] and Hodgkin disease.[68] The pathogenesis of EBV-associated disease is in part directly related to the immune status of the infected person. A healthy immune response to initial infection induces a T-cell response that produces an atypical lymphocytosis and the enlarged lymph nodes (colloquially called "glands") seen in mononucleosis (previously called "glandular fever"). Any state of chronic immunosuppression, such as occurs after SOT, or inborn immunodeficiency, such as the X-linked lymphoproliferative syndrome, can result in prolonged EBV infection, providing the molecular environment for potential neoplastic changes in lymphoid cells. Posttransplant lymphoproliferative disease (PTLD) is defined as a spectrum of abnormal proliferation of lymphoid cells in response to EBV with or without malignant neoplastic change. The pathogenesis of PTLD is based on the interaction between EBV and B cells and the treatment-related modification of immune factors necessary to control this interaction.[69]

Infectious Mononucleosis

Infectious mononucleosis (IM) is a syndrome characterized by sore throat, exudative pharyngitis, fever, lymphadenopathy with or without malaise, anorexia, headache, myalgia, and hepatosplenomegaly. In the immunosuppressed patient, unlike the immunologically healthy person in whom the T-lymphocyte response contributes the "mononuclear" element to the hematologic findings, there is not a true hematologic mononucleosis. Similarly, the serologic findings important in the diagnosis of EBV infection are not reliable in the immunosuppressed population, and a direct EBV DNA detection method (PCR assay) should be used for assessing infection.[70–72]

Posttransplant Lymphoproliferative Disease

The same nonspecific signs of fever and malaise can occur at the start of PTLD, and the syndrome eventually presents as a focal or multifocal occurrence of lymphoid proliferation.[73] Focal proliferations of lymphoid cells can occur nearly anywhere, but the most common areas involved are the central nervous system, the gastrointestinal tract, and the lymphoid system.[74–76] Aggressive immunoblastic lymphoma can be seen early after transplantation.[77] (For a complete review of this disorder, see the online resource of Transplantation Pathology Internet Services.)

Hairy Leukoplakia

Although more rare in the transplant patient than in the patient with untreated AIDS, chronic EBV infection can cause hairy leukoplakia. Oral hairy leukoplakia presents as a white lesion on the tongue or oral mucosa due to epithelial hyperplasia. When EBV is present, it can be detected in the epithelial cells in these lesions, and it is known to replicate using viral polymerase to produce high amounts of infectious virus.[78] Replication by viral polymerase distinguishes the lytic form of infection from a latent form, which replicates using cellular enzymes. The lytic form is susceptible to antiviral agents.

Epstein-Barr Virus-induced Neoplasms

EBV has been associated with several neoplasms; the most common are nasopharyngeal carcinoma and lymphoma. The EBV-induced proliferation of cells leading to malignancy occurs in two stages: the first is the actual induction of proliferation, and the second stage is the development of a fixed genetic change by means of chromosomal or other mutational alteration.[66,69] After transplantation surgery, non-Hodgkin lymphomas are associated with EBV in 90 percent of instances of this complication.[68] Prior to the availability of rituximab, the association of EBV with non-Hodgkin lymphoma occurred in more than 70 percent of cases associated with prior PTLD.[79,80] In addition to B-cell neoplasms, EBV has been found in association with approximately 25 percent of T-cell lymphomas occurring in transplant recipients.[81]

Diagnosis of Epstein-Barr Virus

IM is characterized by a relative and absolute lymphocytosis, with atypical lymphocytes often more than 10 percent of the total white blood cell count. A heterophile antibody response is made following acute infection, and the diagnosis is usually confirmed when patients present with the triad of fever and pharyngitis, atypical lymphocytosis, and positive heterophile antibody. EBV infection can be confirmed with a panel of antibody tests to the EBV early and late proteins. Chronic active EBV is a poorly understood syndrome consisting of persistent mononucleosis symptoms, an unusual pattern of EBV antibodies, and increased EBV genomes in tissues. In the management of immunosuppressed patients, a quantitative PCR assay can be used to diagnose and assess reactivation of EBV infection.[82,83]

Treatment of Epstein-Barr Virus Infection

General Approach

EBV is inhibited in vitro by several antiviral agents, including acyclovir, ganciclovir, foscarnet, penciclovir, and interferon. However, only oral hairy leukoplakia responds effectively to acyclovir. There is little clinical benefit from antiviral agents during IM, chronic mononucleosis,[84] and even fulminant infection associated with X-linked immunoproliferative syndrome.[85] These agents inhibit only the replication of linear EBV DNA that occurs during lytic infection when EBV-encoded DNA polymerase is active. Such is the case with acyclovir in hairy leukoplakia. But these agents have no influence on the episomal form of virus found in latently infected cells that replicate using cellular enzymes. This explains why EBV-seropositive persons treated with acyclovir continue to have cultivatable EBV in circulating lymphocytes.[86] Nevertheless, acyclovir and ganciclovir have been used in PTLD with occasional reports of success.[87] Ganciclovir is more active than acyclovir against EBV in vitro and can effectively reduce the nasopharyngeal excretion of EBV after transplantation.[88]

Management of Epstein-Barr Virus in Immunosuppressed Patients

PTLD is a life-threatening complication of all transplantation groups. It is associated with a mortality of more than 50 percent if untreated. For PTLD, reduction in immunosuppression is the first aspect of patient care. Local control of disease is important, particularly if associated with gastrointestinal bleeding, so surgical intervention should be considered based on the disease presentation. Monitoring of EBV PCR in at-risk patients and preemptive treatment has been shown to be useful in the prevention of PTLD.[86,89] Treatment consists of administration of a monoclonal antibody, called rituximab, with specificity for B-cell surface proteins that has been approved for the treatment of B-cell lymphomas.[90] Antiviral therapy is helpful only if the virus remains in the early lytic phase of infection, and there are anecdotal experiences with improvement in PTLD. In addition, an important interventional treatment-influencing outcome of PTLD is adoptive humoral and cellular immunotherapy.[91,92]

Human Herpesvirus-6 and Human Herpesvirus-7

Nature of HHV-6 and HHV-7

HHV-6 and HHV-7 are both classified in the genus *Roseolovirus*, both are beta-herpesviruses, and both are distinct viruses based on their genetic composition. These two viruses are considered together here because of the similarity of disease presentation and epidemiology. HHV-6 was first isolated from patients with B-cell lymphoproliferative diseases, but the virus replicates primarily in T lymphocytes with a preference for CD4 cells. HHV-6 is related genetically and antigenically to CMV with two serologic strains: HHV-6A and HHV-6B. HHV-6A is associated with infection in immunosuppressed adults, especially patients with AIDS and transplant recipients. HHV-6B is associated with infection in infancy, especially febrile syndromes, febrile convulsions, and rash.

HHV-7 is a T-lymphotropic virus, and infection can occur in persons with high HHV-6 antibody, indicating that the two viruses do not result in cross-protection. Less is known about HHV-7, and except for anecdotal associations with syndromes similar to HHV-6 and an unconfirmed association with pityriasis rosea, there is no clear understanding of HHV-7-induced disease.

Epidemiology of HHV-6 and HHV-7

HHV-6 is present in vaginal secretions and saliva; seroconversion occurs in most infants between 6 months and 2 years of age. The peak infection begins late in the first year as the maternal antibody declines, and by 3 years of age approximately 95 percent of children have been infected with this virus. This widespread occurrence of infection early in life suggests that the virus has an efficient mechanism for spread. HHV-6 is present in saliva and can be detected in 85 percent of healthy adults.[93] Thus, it appears that virus is spread by contact with oral secretions. Maternal and child isolates are identical, suggesting the source of virus is within the household. HHV-7 infection occurs slightly later in infancy and early childhood and is also present in oral secretions, suggesting a route of spread that is similar to that of HHV-6.

Clinical Features of Infection

Primary Infection

HHV-6B is associated with roseola (also called "infantum subitum" or "sixth disease") and febrile seizures in infants. Primary HHV-6 infection usually occurs before 2 years of age, producing 3 to 4 days of high fever, followed by sudden loss of fever and the appearance of generalized macular-erythematous rash, thus the name "exanthem subitum." The virus appears to have an affinity for the CNS and has been associated with up to a third of febrile convulsions in infancy[94] and with encephalitis.[95] In adults, there have been case reports of mononucleosis with or without rash and of demyelinating CNS disease associated with HHV-6. As noted, the clinical spectrum of HHV-7 is not known, but it has been associated with roseola-like syndrome in children.

Reactivation Disease

The seroprevalence for HHV-6 and HHV-7 after childhood approaches 100 percent, so virtually all organ donors and recipients can be assumed to be HHV-6 and HHV-7 antibody positive. Following bone marrow transplantation, HHV-6 reactivates in 36 to 46 percent of recipients, and this occurs during the first 1 to 2 months after transplant.[96-99] The generally high seroprevalence of HHV-6 has made clear separation of virus causality difficult in the HSCT population, in which several herpesviruses, especially CMV and EBV, can reactivate at the same time. A retrospective analysis of HHV-6 infection in children undergoing allogeneic HSCT with and without ganciclovir prophylaxis suggests that ganciclovir prevented HHV-6 reactivation, and in those with reactivation, the clinical syndromes included skin rash, interstitial pneumonitis, persistent thrombocytopenia, enterocolitis, and thrombotic microangiopathy. In addition, cases of graft failure have been noted in association with rising HHV-6 DNA levels.[100] Analysis of clinical syndromes associated with high levels of HHV-6 DNA in allogeneic recipients of HSCT showed encephalitis and poor platelet engraftment.[98]

Because of the preference of HHV-6 for neurologic tissue, an evaluation of encephalitis after allogeneic bone marrow transplantation was made, and results suggested a correlation with HHV-6 infection.[1] HHV-6 DNA has been observed in cerebrospinal fluid specimens from as many as 25 percent of marrow transplant patients with CNS symptoms.[101,102] HHV-6 encephalitis is associated with seizures and abnormal electroencephalogram findings but not with cerebrospinal fluid pleocytosis or pathognomonic findings from imaging studies. Microangiopathic syndromes have been associated with HHV-6 after autologous HSCT.[103] In addition, HHV-6 has long been thought to be a cause of interstitial pneumonitis, and it appears to be a minor cause of the disease in this population, with CMV being the major cause. Of note, mixed infection with HHV-6A and HHV-6B has been found in autopsy studies, suggesting that multiple infections with strains of HHV-6 occur in the HSCT population.

Laboratory Diagnosis

The diagnosis of HHV-6 infection can be made by virus isolation from blood, PCR assay in clinical specimens, and serologic tests for antibody. Acute and convalescent antibody assays, using an ELISA or indirect immunofluorescent-antibody (IFA) method, can be used for diagnosis of primary infection. PCR is most useful when evaluating tissue specimens related to organ-specific syndromes, but because HHV-6 DNA could be derived from cells infected at remote times, an RNA-based assay should be used to confirm active infection.[104]

Treatment of HHV-6

HHV-6 is susceptible to ganciclovir and foscarnet and only relatively susceptible to acyclovir. Foscarnet or ganciclovir are recommended as first-line agents for treatment of this infection.

Human Herpesvirus Type 8

Nature of HHV-8

Human herpesvirus type 8 (also called KSHV) is a gamma-herpesvirus that was first discovered in KS of patients with AIDS. As a gamma-herpesvirus, HHV-8 induces cell proliferation and has been linked to three hematopoietic neoplasms: KS, multicentric Castleman disease, and primary effusion lymphoma (PEL).[5] KSHV is classified as a gamma-2 herpesvirus, or rhadinovirus, and it differs from EBV in the manner by which it alters cell cycle. KSHV incorporates certain cellular gene homologs, thereby modifying the cellular control of proliferation and survival.

Epidemiology of HHV-8

The epidemiology of KSHV is complex, with global distribution of virus but with low endemicity, except in pockets of high prevalence in Africa, in certain South American tribes, and in males who have sex with males (MSM). The virus is present in saliva and, based on intrafamily spread of infection in Africa, it is likely that the virus spreads via contact with oral secretions. Among MSM populations, the spread of KSHV was initially thought to be via semen, but the titers of virus are highest in saliva, and it is now thought that oral contact is the main route of spread, although oral-genital routes cannot be excluded. It is not known why, if the virus is present in saliva in high titers, the seroprevalence of KSHV is so low in most populations. KSHV could be a newly emergent infection that is only now spreading globally. In developed countries, the virus has become a problem in medically challenged patients with spread via blood and body organs. Thus, KSHV infection is an increasing problem in transplant populations.

In the transplant setting, treatment-related KS is seen primarily in SOT and predominantly in renal allograft recipients with only rare occurrences in HSCT. In renal transplant recipients, the incidence of KS varies and can be as high as 23 percent in recipients with antibody to KSHV.[105,106] There is suggestive evidence that the virus infection is transferred from donor to recipient by the allograft. Detection of KSHV DNA in the donor organ or of antibody in the recipient has been found prior to the onset of KS, suggesting that the risk of infection could be defined with these tests. The occurrence of KS appears to be associated with the degree of immunosuppression, and the reports have indicated that use of mycophenolate mofetil after renal allografting has increased the incidence of KS.[107]

Disease Associated with Kaposi's Sarcoma-associated Herpesvirus

KS is a complex lesion with vascular, spindle-shaped cells derived from endothelium and inflammatory cells derived from monocytes and macrophages. PEL is a tumor of B lymphocytes that proliferates in body cavities such as the pleural space and peritoneum. The lymphocytes contain KSHV genomes in nearly all PEL tumors, and 70 percent also have latent EBV. Multicentric Castleman disease is a reactive proliferation of B lymphocytes, producing a plasmablastoid accumulation of cells in enlarged lymph nodes. The disease is not a malignancy per se but appears to be a reaction to the viral interleukin-6 (IL-6) and cellular IL-6 that is induced by the KSHV infection. Other syndromes associated with KSHV and seen in transplant patients are aplastic anemia, fever, cutaneous rash, hepatitis, lymphoid proliferation that mimics primary effusion lymphoma, and EBV-related PTLD.

Diagnosis of Kaposi's Sarcoma-associated Herpesvirus

Serologic assays for antibody to KSHV are generally research tools because of the various latent and lytic antigens used for the antibody detection. As with EBV, the antibody assays that are becoming useful clinically use protein antigens that represent either the latent or the lytic phase of infection. The diagnosis of KSHV is usually generated from a pathology specimen indicating one of the neoplasms known to be associated with this virus; PCR assays are available to confirm virus infection.

Treatment of Kaposi's Sarcoma-associated Herpesvirus

There is no antiviral treatment for KSHV. The treatment of neoplastic syndromes associated with KSHV in immunodefi-

cient populations includes chemotherapy and radiotherapy. In populations that receive treatment-related immunosuppression (e.g., SOT patients), the recommendation is to reduce or withdraw immunosuppressive medication to permit the immune system to recover and suppress the KSHV.[108]

CONCLUSIONS

The Herpesviridae is a large family of viruses found among all vertebrates, with eight known to infect humans within three subfamilies: alpha-, beta-, and gamma-herpesviruses. Each of the eight has certain laboratory and clinical features in common. The viruses may present as a chronic intermittent infection fluctuating between low-level activity or "latency" and high-level replication or "reactivation." Infections vary from rashes to malignancies. The eight human strains were highlighted in this chapter, including methods for prevention and treatment.

FUTURE TRENDS

Vaccines for Herpesviruses

The only approved vaccine for a human herpesvirus is the VZV vaccine, but with several vaccines for animal herpesviruses, it is suggested that there eventually will be vaccines for other human herpesviruses. Among the most widely tested experimental vaccines are those for HSV and EBV.[109,110] EBV vaccines have been used in the experimental treatment of EBV-associated Hodgkin disease and may yield a vaccine that is useful in the general public. A critical need identified by the National Institutes of Health in the United States is the development of vaccine to prevent the morbidity and expense associated with congenital CMV infection. At present, several vaccines are in trials, and it is likely that a CMV vaccine will be available in the near future.

Understanding Immunity to the Herpesviruses

Recently reagents have become available for quantitation of virus-specific CD4- and CD8-positive T cells after natural infection and in immunosuppressed populations. These studies have demonstrated that for EBV and CMV, and likely for the other beta- and gamma-herpesviruses, there is a major commitment by the immune system to the control of these infections. It is not unusual to see 10 to 12 percent of total CD8 cells committed to a single peptide epitope of CMV or EBV, and because there are potentially hundreds of immunological targeted epitopes of these herpesviruses, it is possible that the majority of our T cells are directed toward these viruses. This burden of immune surveillance over time has even been suggested to result in eventual immune fatigue and lead to pathology in elderly persons.

With regard to HSCT populations, quantitative tests of cellular immunity have shown that donor immunity contributes substantially to the CMV-specific cellular immune status of the recipient. In the future, such quantitative immunologic assessment methods may prove useful for defining risks for other herpesviruses and for deciding which patients need antiviral therapy.

Cell-Based Gene Therapy for Herpesviruses

In EBV and in CMV, improved methods for scale-up of EBV-specific cytotoxic T lymphocytes (CTLs) from normal marrow donors have been developed. This type of approach illustrates the potential for cellular therapy to eliminate EBV complications after transplantation. Gene transfer approaches are also being considered for prevention of PTLD by prophylactic infusion of EBV-specific CTLs.[111] The use of such immunotherapy is being studied for prevention of CMV disease in HSCT. The major complication of such treatment would be graft-versus-host disease, and other genetic manipulations have been suggested to protect the recipient from potential T-cell reactivity.[61]

INTERNATIONAL PERSPECTIVE

The herpesviruses are global in the human population. Areas with endemic diseases that affect the immune systems, such as HIV causing AIDS, can have higher rates of infection in these populations.

REFERENCES

1. Wald A, Zeh J, Selke S, et al. Reactivation of genital herpes simplex virus type 2 infection in asymptomatic seropositive persons. *N Engl J Med* 2000 Mar 23;342(12):844–850.
2. Lafferty WE, Downey L, Celum C, et al. Herpes simplex virus type 1 as a cause of genital herpes: impact on surveillance and prevention. *J Infect Dis* 2000 Apr;181(4):1454–1457.
3. Buddingh GJ, Schrum DI, Lanier JC, et al. Studies of the natural history of herpes simplex infections. *Pediatrics* 1953 Jun;11(6):595–610.
4. Whitley RJ, Lakeman F. Herpes simplex virus infections of the central nervous system: therapeutic and diagnostic considerations. *Clin Infect Dis* 1995 Feb;20(2):414–420.
5. Skoldenberg B, Jeansson S, Wolontis S. Herpes simplex virus type 2 and acute aseptic meningitis. Clinical features of cases with isolation of herpes simplex virus from cerebrospinal fluids. *Scand J Infect Dis* 1975;7(4):227–232.
6. Kimberlin DW, Lin CY, Jacobs RF, et al. Natural history of neonatal herpes simplex virus infections in the acyclovir era. *Pediatrics* 2001 Aug;108(2):223–229.
7. Whitley R, Davis EA, Suppapanya N. Incidence of neonatal herpes simplex virus infections in a managed-care population. *Sex Transm Dis* 2007 Sep;34(9):704–708.
8. Foley FD, Greenawald KA, Nash G, et al. Herpesvirus infection in burned patients. *N Engl J Med* 1970 Mar 19;282(12):652–656.
9. Wald A, Huang ML, Carrell D, et al. Polymerase chain reaction for detection of herpes simplex virus (HSV) DNA on mucosal surfaces: comparison with HSV isolation in cell culture. *J Infect Dis* 2003 Nov 1;188(9):1345–1351.
10. Gupta R, Wald A, Krantz E, et al. Valacyclovir and acyclovir for suppression of shedding of herpes simplex virus in the genital tract. *J Infect Dis* 2004 Oct 15;190(8):1374–1381.
11. Kimberlin DW, Whitley RJ. Chapter 64 Antiviral Therapy of HSV-1 and -2. In: Arvin A, Campadelli-Fiume G, Mocarski E, et al., eds. *Human Herpesviruses: Biology, Therapy, and Immunoprophylaxis.* Cambridge: Cambridge University Press, 2007.
12. Preblud SR. Varicella: complications and costs. *Pediatrics* 1986 Oct;78(4 Pt 2):728–735.
13. Seiler HE. A study of herpes zoster particularly in its relationship to chickenpox. *J Hygiene* 1949 Sep;47(3):253–262.
14. Centers for Disease Control and Prevention (CDC), National Center for Immunization and Respiratory Diseases (NCIRD), Division of Viral Diseases. *Shingles (Herpes Zoster)*. CDC website. November 8, 2013. Available at: http://www.cdc.gov/shingles/.
15. Lopez A, Schmid S, Bialek S. Varicella. In: *Manual for the Surveillance of Vaccine-Preventable Diseases*, 5th ed., 2011. Available at: http://www.cdc.gov/vaccines/pubs/surv-manual/chpt17-varicella.html.
16. David DS, Tegtmeier BR, O'Donnell MR, et al. Visceral varicella-zoster after *bone marrow transplant*ation: report of a case series and review of the literature. *Am J Gastroenterol* 1998 May;93(5):810–813.
17. Harpaz R, Ortega-Sanchez IR, Seward JF. Prevention of herpes zoster: recommendations of the Advisory Committee on Immunization Practices (ACIP). *MMWR Recomm Rep* 2008 Jun;57(RR-5):1–30; quiz CE2-4.
18. Zaia JA. Clinical Infectious Disease. In: Schlossberg D, ed. *Clinical Infectious Disease*. New York: Cambridge University Press, 2008:1311–1318.
19. Dworkin RH, Johnson RW, Breuer J, et al. Recommendations for the management of herpes zoster. *Clin Infect Dis* 2007 Jan 1;44(Suppl 1):S1–S26.
20. Oxman MN, Levin MJ, Johnson GR, et al. A vaccine to prevent herpes zoster and postherpetic neuralgia in older adults. *N Engl J Med* 2005 Jun 2;352(22):2271–2284.
21. Marin M, Bialek SR. *Varicella (Chickenpox)*. Centers for Disease Control and Prevention (CDC) website. August 1, 2013. Available at: http://wwwnc.cdc.gov/travel/yellowbook/2014/chapter-3-infectious-diseases-related-to-travel/varicella-chickenpox
22. Lundgren G, Wilczek H, Lönnqvist B, et al. Acyclovir prophylaxis in *bone marrow transplant* recipients. *Scand J Infect Dis* Suppl 1985;47:137–144.
23. Steer CB, Szer J, Sasadeusz J, et al. Varicella-zoster infection after allogeneic *bone marrow transplant*ation: incidence, risk factors and prevention with low-dose aciclovir and ganciclovir. *Bone Marrow Transplant* 2000 Mar;25(6):657–664.
24. Fiddian P, Sabin CA, Griffiths PD. Valacyclovir provides optimum acyclovir exposure for prevention of cytomegalovirus and related outcomes after organ transplantation. *J Infect Dis* 2002 Oct 15;186(Suppl 1):S110–S115.
25. Weinstock DM, Boeckh M, Sepkowitz KA. Postexposure prophylaxis against varicella zoster virus infection among hematopoietic stem cell transplant recipients. *Biol Blood Marrow Transplant* 2006 Oct;12(10):1096–1097.
26. Goldstein SL, Somers MJ, Lande MB, et al. Acyclovir prophylaxis of varicella in children with renal disease receiving steroids. *Pediatr Nephrol* 2000 Apr;14(4):305–308.
27. Huang YC, Lin TY, Lin YJ, et al. Prophylaxis of intravenous immunoglobulin and acyclovir in perinatal varicella. *Eur J Pediatr* 2001 Feb;160(2):91–94.
28. DeMarchi JM, Blankenship ML, Brown GD, et al. Size and complexity of human cytomegalovirus DNA. *Virology* 1978 Sep;89(2):643–646.
29. Chou SW. Differentiation of cytomegalovirus strains by restriction analysis of DNA sequences amplified from clinical specimens. *J Infect Dis* 1990 Sep;162(3):738–742.
30. Stern H, Tucker SM. Prospective study of cytomegalovirus infection in pregnancy. *Br Med J* 1973 May 5;2(5861):268–270.
31. Stagno S, Pass RF, Cloud G, et al. Primary cytomegalovirus infection in pregnancy. Incidence, transmission to fetus, and clinical outcome. *JAMA* 1986 Oct 10;256(14):1904–1908.
32. Zaia JA. Viral infections associated with *bone marrow transplant*ation. *Hematol Oncol Clin North Am* 1990 Jun;4(3):603–623.
33. Deepe GS Jr, MacMillan BF, Linnemann CC Jr. Unexplained fever in burn patients due to cytomegalovirus infection. *JAMA* 1982 Nov 12;248(18):2299–2301.
34. Limaye AP, Kirby KA, Rubenfeld GD, et al. Cytomegalovirus reactivation in critically ill immunocompetent patients. *JAMA* 2008 Jul 23;300(4):413–422.
35. Applebaum FR, Meyers JD, Fefer A, et al. Nonbacterial nonfungal pneumonia following marrow transplantation in 100 identical twins. *Transplantation* 1982 Mar;33(3):265–258.
36. Boland GJ, Vlieger AM, Ververs C, et al. Evidence for transfer of cellular and humoral immunity to cytomegalovirus from donor to recipient in allogeneic *bone marrow transplant*ation. *Clin Exp Immunol* 1992 Jun;88(3):506–511.
37. Krause H, Hebart H, Jahn G, et al. Screening for CMV-specific T cell proliferation to identify patients at risk of developing late onset CMV disease. *Bone Marrow Transplant* 1997 Jun;19(11):1111–1116.
38. Ehrnst A, Barkholt L, Brattström C, et al. Detection of CMV-matrix pp65 antigen in leucocytes by immunofluorescence as a marker of CMV disease. *J Med Virol* 1993 Feb;39(2):118–124.
39. Quinnan GV Jr, Kirmani N, Rook AH, et al. Cytotoxic t cells in cytomegalovirus infection: HLA-restricted T-lymphocyte and non-T-lymphocyte cytotoxic responses correlate with recovery from cytomegalovirus infection in bone-marrow-transplant recipients. *N Engl J Med* 1982 Jul 1;307(1):7–13.
40. Reusser P, Riddell SR, Meyers JD, et al. Cytotoxic T-lymphocyte response to cytomegalovirus after human allogeneic *Bone Marrow Transplant*ation: pattern of recovery and correlation with cytomegalovirus infection and disease. *Blood* 1991 Sep 1;78(5):1373–1380.
41. Schmidt GM, Kovacs A, Zaia JA, et al. Ganciclovir/immunoglobulin combination therapy for the treatment of human cytomegalovirus-associated interstitial pneumonia in bone marrow allograft recipients. *Transplantation* 1988 Dec;46(6):905–907.

42. Jabs DA, Van Natta ML, Kempen JH, et al. Characteristics of patients with cytomegalovirus retinitis in the era of highly active antiretroviral therapy. *Am J Ophthalmol* 2002 Jan;133(1):48–61.

43. Piper H, Ciulla TA, Danis RP, et al. Changing therapeutic paradigms in CMV retinitis in AIDS. *Expert Opin Pharmacother* 2000 Dec;1(7):1343–1352.

44. French MA. HIV/AIDS: immune reconstitution inflammatory syndrome: a reappraisal. *Clin Infect Dis* 2009 Jan 1;48(1):101–107.

45. Centers for Disease Control and Prevention (CDC), National Center for Immunization and Respiratory Diseases, Division of Viral Diseases. *Cytomegalovirus (CMV) and congenital CMV infection. Interpretation of laboratorty tests.* CDC website. December 6, 2010. Available at: http://www.cdc.gov/cmv/clinical/lab-tests.html.

46. van der Bij W, Torensma R, van Son WJ. Rapid immunodiagnosis of active cytomegalovirus infection by monoclonal antibody staining of blood leukocytes. *J Med Virol* 1988 Jun;25(2):179–188.

47. Boeckh M, Bowden RA, Goodrich JM, et al. Cytomegalovirus antigen detection in peripheral blood leukocytes after allogeneic marrow transplantation. *Blood* 1992 Sep 1;80(5):1358–1364.

48. Boeckh M, Gooley TA, Myerson D, et al. Cytomegalovirus pp65 antigenemia-guided early treatment with ganciclovir versus ganciclovir at engraftment after allogeneic marrow transplantation: a randomized double-blind study. *Blood* 1996 Nov 15;88(10):4063–4071.

49. Zaia JA, Molinder KM. Advances in CMV Diagnostic Testing and Their Implications for the Management of CMV Infection in Transplant Recipients. In: Singh N, Aguado JM, eds. *Infectious Complications in Transplant Patients.* Boston: Kluwer Academic Publishers, 2000:75–92.

50. Einsele H, Ehninger G, Hebart H, et al. Polymerase chain reaction monitoring reduces the incidence of cytomegalovirus disease and the duration and side effects of antiviral therapy after *bone marrow transplant*ation. *Blood* 1995 Oct 1;86(7):2815–2820.

51. Emery VC, Sabin CA, Cope AV, et al. Application of viral-load kinetics to identify patients who develop cytomegalovirus disease after transplantation. *Lancet* 2000 Jun 10;355(9220):2032–2036.

52. Mazzulli T, Drew LW, Yen-Lieberman B, et al. Multicenter comparison of the digene hybrid capture CMV DNA assay (version 2.0), the pp65 antigenemia assay, and cell culture for detection of cytomegalovirus viremia. *J Clin Microbiol* 1999 Apr;37(4):958–963.

53. Hebart H, Gamer D, Loeffler J, et al. Evaluation of Murex CMV DNA hybrid capture assay for detection and quantitation of cytomegalovirus infection in patients following allogeneic stem cell transplantation. *J Clin Microbiol* 1998 May;6(5):1333–1337.

54. Hebart H, Rudolph T, Loeffler J, et al. Evaluation of the NucliSens CMV pp67 assay for detection and monitoring of human cytomegalovirus infection after allogeneic stem cell transplantation. *Bone Marrow Transplant* 2002 Aug;30(3):181–187.

55. Ljungman P, Aschan J, Lewensohn-Fuchs I, et al. Results of different strategies for reducing cytomegalovirus-associated mortality in allogeneic stem cell transplant recipients. *Transplantation* 1998 Nov 27;66(10):1330–1334.

56. Zaia JA. Prevention of cytomegalovirus disease in hematopoietic stem cell transplantation. *Clin Infect Dis* 2002 Oct 15;35(8):999–1004.

57. Miller WJ, McCullough J, Balfour HH Jr, et al. Prevention of cytomegalovirus infection following *bone marrow transplant*ation: a randomized trial of blood product screening. *Bone Marrow Transplant* 1991 Mar;7(3):227–234.

58. Sullivan KM, Kopecky KJ, Jocom J, et al. Immunomodulatory and antimicrobial efficacy of intravenous immunoglobulin in *bone marrow transplant*ation. *N Engl J Med* 1990 Sep 13;323(11):705–712.

59. Bowden RA, Slichter SJ, Sayers MH, et al. Use of leukocyte-depleted platelets and cytomegalovirus-seronegative red blood cells for prevention of primary cytomegalovirus infection after marrow transplant. *Blood* 1991 Jul 1;78(1):246–250.

60. Rowe M, Young LS, Cadwallader K, et al. Distinction between Epstein-Barr virus type A (EBNA 2A) and type B (EBNA 2B) isolates extends to the EBNA 3 family of nuclear proteins. *J Virol* 1989 Mar;63(3):1031–1039.

61. Babcock GJ, Decker LL, Volk M, et al. EBV persistence in memory B cells in vivo. *Immunity* 1998 Sep;9(3):395–404.

62. Gerber P, Walsh JH, Rosenblum EN, et al. Association of EB-virus infection with the post-perfusion syndrome. *Lancet* 1969 Mar 22;1(7595):593–595.

63. Haque T, Thomas JA, Falk KI, et al. Transmission of donor Epstein-Barr virus (EBV) in transplanted organs causes lymphoproliferative disease in EBV-seronegative recipients. *J Gen Virol* 1996;77(Pt 6):1169–1172.

64. Raab-Traub N, Flynn K, Pearson G, et al. The differentiated form of nasopharyngeal carcinoma contains Epstein-Barr virus DNA. *Int J Cancer* 1987 Jan 15;39(1):25–29.

65. Henle G, Henle W, Diehl V. Relation of Burkitt's tumor-associated herpes-type virus to infectious mononucleosis. *Proc Natl Acad Sci U S A* 1968 Jan;59(1):94–101.

66. Klein G. Lymphoma development in mice and humans: diversity of initiation is followed by convergent cytogenetic evolution. *Proc Natl Acad Sci U S A* 1979 May;76(5):2442–2446.

67. Cohen JI. Epstein-Barr virus lymphoproliferative disease associated with acquired immunodeficiency. *Medicine* (Baltimore) 1991;70(2):137–160.

68. Weiss LM, Chang KL. Molecular biologic studies of Hodgkin's disease. *Semin Diagn Pathol* 1992 Nov;9(4):272–278.

69. Klein G. Epstein-Barr virus strategy in normal and neoplastic B cells. *Cell* 1994 Jun 17;77(6):791–793.

70. Ambinder RF, Mann RB. Detection and characterization of Epstein-Barr virus in clinical specimens. *Am J Pathol* 1994 Aug;145(2):239–252.

71. Rooney CM, Loftin SK, Holladay MS, et al. Early identification of Epstein-Barr virus-associated post-transplant lymphoproliferative disease. *Br J Haematol* 1995 Jan;89(1):98–103.

72. Stevens SJ, Verschuuren EA, Pronk I, et al. Frequent monitoring of Epstein-Barr virus DNA load in unfractionated whole blood is essential for early detection of posttransplant lymphoproliferative disease in high-risk patients. *Blood* 2001 Mar 1;97(5):1165–1171.

73. Hanto DW, Gajl-Peczalska KJ, Frizzera G, et al. Epstein-Barr virus (EBV) induced polyclonal and monoclonal B-cell lymphoproliferative diseases occurring after renal transplantation. Clinical, pathologic, and virologic findings and implications for therapy. *Ann Surg* 1983 Sep;198(3):356–369.

74. Sullivan JL, Medveczky P, Forman SJ, et al. Epstein-Barr virus-induced lymphoproliferation: implications for anti-viral chemotherapy. *N Engl J Med* 1984 Nov 1;311(18):1163–1167.

75. Caldas C, Ambinder R. Epstein-Barr virus and *bone marrow transplant*ation. *Curr Opin Oncol* 1995 Mar;7(2):102–106.

76. Verschuur A, Brousse N, Raynal B, et al. Donor B cell lymphoma of the brain after allogeneic marrow transplantation for acute myeloid leukemia. *Bone Marrow Transplant* 1994 Sep;14(13):467–470.

77. Jones C, Bleau B, Buskard N, et al. Simultaneous development of diffuse immunoblastic lymphoma in recipients of renal transplants from a single cadaver donor: transmission of Epstein-Barr virus and triggering by OKT3. *Am J Kidney Dis* 1994 Jan;23(1):130–134.

78. Sixbey JW, Nedrud JG, Raab-Traub N. Epstein-Barr virus replication in oropharyngeal epithelial cells. *N Engl J Med* 1984 May 10;310(19):1225.

79. Knowles DM, Cesarman E, Chadburn A, et al. Correlative morphologic and molecular genetic analysis demonstrates three distinct categories of posttransplantation lymphoproliferative disorders. *Blood* 1995 Jan 15;85(2):552–565.

80. Oudejans JJ, Jiwa M, van den Brule AJ, et al. Detection of heterogeneous Epstein-Barr virus gene expression patterns within individual post-transplantation lymphoproliferative disorders. *Am J Pathol* 1995 Oct;147:923–933.

81. Van Gorp J, Doornewaard H, Verdonck LF, et al. Post-transplant T-cell lymphoma. Report of three cases and a review of the literature. *Cancer* 1994 Jun 15;73(12):3064–3072.

82. Paya CV, Fung JJ, Nalesnik MA, et al. Epstein-Barr virus-induced post-transplant lymphoproliferative disorders. ASTS/ASTP EBV-PTLD Task Force and The Mayo Clinic Organized International Consensus Development Meeting. *Transplantation* 1999 Nov 27;68(10):1517–1525.

83. Wagner HJ, Cheng YC, Huls MH, et al. Prompt versus preemptive intervention for EBV lymphoproliferative disease. *Blood* 2004 May 15;103(10):3979–3981.

84. Sullivan JL, Byron KS, Brewster FE, et al. Treatment of life-threatening Epstein-Barr virus infection with acyclovir. *Am J Med* 1982 Jul 20;73(1A):262–266.

85. Okano M, Thiele GM, Kobayashi RH, et al. Interferon-gamma in a family with X-linked lymphoproliferative syndrome with acute Epstein-Barr virus infection. *J Clin Immunol* 1989 Jan;9(1):48–54.

86. Yao QY, Ogan P, Rowe M, et al. Epstein-Barr virus-infected B cells persist in the circulation of acyclovir-treated virus carriers. *Int J Cancer* 1989 Jan 15;43(1):67–71.

87. Pirsch JD, Stratta RJ, Sollinger HW. Treatment of severe Epstein-Barr virus-induced lymphoproliferative syndrome with ganciclovir: two cases after solid organ transplantation. *Am J Med* 1989 Feb;86(2):241–244.

88. Preiksaitis J, Diaz-Mitoma F, Mirzayans F, et al. Quantitative oropharyngeal Epstein-Barr virus shedding in renal and cardiac transplant recipients: relationship to immunosuppressive therapy, serological responses and the risk of post-transplant lymphoproliferative disorder. *J Infect Dis* 1992 Nov;166(5):986–994.

89. Meijer E, Cornelissen JJ. Epstein-Barr virus-associated lymphoproliferative disease after allogeneic haematopoietic stem cell transplantation: molecular monitoring and early treatment of high-risk patients. *Curr Opin Hematol* 2008 Nov;15(6):576–585.

90. Leget GA, Czuczman MS. Use of rituximab, the new FDA-approved antibody. *Curr Opin Oncol* 1998 Nov;10(6):548–551.

91. Papadopoulos EB, Ladanyi M, Emanuel D, et al. Infusions of donor leukocytes to treat Epstein-Barr virus-associated lymphoproliferative disorders

after allogeneic bone marrow transplantation. *N Engl J Med* 1994 Apr 28;330(17):1185–1191.

92. Barker J, Doubrovina E, Sauter C, et al. Successful treatment of EBV-associated posttransplantation lymphoma after cord blood transplantation using third-party EBV-specific cytotoxic T lymphocytes. *Blood* 2010 Dec 2;116(23):5045–5049.

93. Cone RW, Huang ML, Ashley R, et al. Human herpesvirus 6 DNA in peripheral blood cells and saliva from immunocompetent individuals. *J Clin Microbiol* 1993 May;31(5):1262–1267.

94. Kondo K, Nagafuji H, Hata A, et al. Association of human herpesvirus 6 infection of the central nervous system with recurrence of febrile convulsions. *J Infect Dis* 1993 May;167(5):1197–1200.

95. Yamanishi K, Kondo K, Mukai T, et al. Human herpesvirus 6 (HHV-6) infection in the central nervous system. *Acta Paediatr Jpn* 1992 Jun;34(3):337–343.

96. Drobyski WR, Eberle M, Majewski D, et al. Prevalence of human herpesvirus 6 variant A and B infections in bone marrow transplant recipients as determined by polymerase chain reaction and sequence-specific oligonucleotide probe hybridization. *J Clin Microbiol* 1993 Jun;31(6):1515–1520.

97. Kadakia MP, Rybka WB, Stewart JA, et al. Human herpesvirus 6: infection and disease following autologous and allogeneic bone marrow transplantation. *Blood* 1996 Jun 15;87(12):5341–5354.

98. Ljungman P, Wang FZ, Clark DA, et al. High levels of human herpesvirus 6 DNA in peripheral blood leucocytes are correlated to platelet engraftment and disease in allogeneic stem cell transplant patients. *Br J Haematol* 2000 Dec;111(3):774–781.

99. Miyoshi H, Tanaka-Taya K, Hara J, et al. Inverse relationship between human herpesvirus-6 and -7 detection after allogeneic and autologous stem cell transplantation. *Bone Marrow Transplant* 2001 May;27(10):1065–1070.

100. Drobyski WR, Dunne WM, Burd EM, et al. Human herpesvirus-6 (HHV-6) infection in allogeneic *Bone Marrow Transplant* recipients: evidence of a marrow-suppressive role for HHV-6 in vivo. *J Infect Dis* 1993 Mar;167(3):735–739.

101. Zerr DM, Gooley TA, Yeung L, et al. Human herpesvirus 6 reactivation and encephalitis in allogeneic *bone marrow transplant* recipients. *Clin Infect Dis* 2001 Sep 15;33(6):763–771.

102. Wang FZ, Linde A, Hägglund H, et al. Human herpesvirus 6 DNA in cerebrospinal fluid specimens from allogeneic bone marrow transplant patients: does it have clinical significance? *Clin Infect Dis* 1999 Mar;28(3):562–568.

103. Matsuda Y, Hara J, Miyoshi H, et al. Thrombotic microangiopathy associated with reactivation of human herpesvirus-6 following high-dose chemotherapy with autologous bone marrow transplantation in young children. *Bone Marrow Transplant* 1999 Oct;24(8):919–923.

104. Van den Bosch G, Locatelli G, Geerts L, et al. Development of reverse transcriptase PCR assays for detection of active human herpesvirus 6 infection. *J Clin Microbiol* 2001 Jun;39(6):2308–2310.

105. Regamey N, Tamm M, Binet I, et al. Transplantation-associated Kaposi's sarcoma: herpesvirus 8 transmission through renal allografts. *Transplant Proc* 1999 Feb-Mar;31(1-2):922–923.

106. Cattani P, Capuano M, Graffeo R, et al. Kaposi's sarcoma associated with previous human herpesvirus 8 infection in kidney transplant recipients. *J Clin Microbiol* 2001 Feb;39(2):506–508.

107. Eberhard OK, Kliem V, Brunkhorst R. Five cases of Kaposi's sarcoma in kidney graft recipients: possible influence of the immunosuppressive therapy. *Transplantation* 1999 Jan 15;67(1):180–184.

108. Moosa MR, Treurnicht FK, van Rensburg EJ, et al. Detection and sub-typing of human herpesvirus-8 in renal transplant patients before and after remission of Kaposi's sarcoma. *Transplantation* 1998 Jul 27;66(2):214–218.

109. Koelle DM, Corey C. Recent progress in herpes simplex virus immunobiology and vaccine research. *Clin Microbiol Rev* 2003 Jan;16(1):96–113.

110. Duraiswamy J, Sherritt M, Thomson S, et al. Therapeutic LMP1 polyepitope vaccine for EBV-associated Hodgkin disease and nasopharyngeal carcinoma. *Blood* 2003 Apr 15;101(8):3150–3156.

111. Heslop HE, Perez M, Benaim E, et al. Transfer of EBV-specific CTL to prevent EBV lymphoma post bone marrow transplant. *J Clin Apher* 1999;14(3):154–156.

SUPPLEMENTAL RESOURCES

Centers for Disease Control and Prevention (CDC). Available at: http://www.cdc.gov.

International Herpesviruses Management Forum. Available at: http://www.ihmf.org.

Jarvis WR, ed. *Bennett and Brachman's Hospital Infections*, 5th ed. Philadelphia: Lippincott Williams & Wilkins, 2007.

Mandel GL, Bennett JE, Dolin R. *Principles and Practice of Infectious Disease*, 6th ed. St. Louis: Churchill Livingstone, 2005.

Mayhall CG. *Hospital Epidemiology and Infection Control*, 3rd ed. Philadelphia: Lippincott Williams & Wilkins, 2004.

Transplantation Pathology Internet Services. Available at: http://tpis.upmc.edu.

White DE, Fenner FJ. *Medical Virology*, 4th ed. San Diego: Academic Press, 1994.

APPLICABLE GUIDELINES

Centers for Disease Control and Prevention (CDC). Recommended adult immunization schedule—United States, 2009. *MMWR Morb Wkly Rep* 2008;57(53). Available at: http://www.cdc.gov/mmwr/preview/mmwrhtml/mm5753a6.htm.

Centers for Disease Control and Prevention (CDC). Recommended immunization schedules for persons aged 0 through 18 years—United States, 2009. *MMWR* 2008;57(51&52). Available at: http://www.cdc.gov/mmwr/preview/mmwrhtml/mm5751a5.htm.

Centers for Disease Control and Prevention (CDC). Updated recommendations for use of VariZIG — United States, 2013. *MMWR Morb Mortal Wkly Rep* [serial online]. 2013 Jul 19;62(28):574–576. Available at: http://www.immunize.org/acip/acipvax_varic.asp.

Harpaz R, Ortega-Sanchez IR, Seward JF, et al. Prevention of herpes zoster: recommendations of the Advisory Committee on Immunization Practices (ACIP). *MMWR Recomm Rep* 2008 Jun 6;57(RR-5):1–30.

Kimberlin DW, Whitley RJ. Chapter 64 Antiviral Therapy of HSV-1 and -2. In: Arvin A, Campadelli-Fiume G, Mocarski E, et al., eds. *Human Herpesviruses: Biology, Therapy, and Immunoprophylaxis*. Cambridge: Cambridge University Press, 2007. Avalilable at: http://www.ncbi.nlm.nih.gov/books/NBK47444/?report=printable.

Marin M, Broder KR, Temte JL, et al. Use of combination measles, mumps, rubella, and varicella vaccine: recommendations of the Advisory Committee on Immunization Practices (ACIP). *MMWR Recomm Rep* [serial online]. 2010 May 7;59(RR-3):1–12. Available at: http://www.immunize.org/acip/acipvax_varic.asp.

Marin M, Güris D, Chaves SS, Schmid S, et al. Prevention of varicella: recommendations of the Advisory Committee on Immunization Practices (ACIP). *MMWR Recomm Rep* 2007 Jun 22;56(RR-4):1–40.

Workowski KA, Berman SM, Centers for Disease Control and Prevention. Sexually transmitted diseases treatment guidelines, 2010. *MMWR Recomm Rep* 2010 Dec 17;59(RR-12):1–110.

CHAPTER 81

HIV/AIDS

Patti Grota, PhD, RN, CNS-M-S, CIC
Assistant Professor
Schreiner University
Kerrville, TX

ABSTRACT

The human immunodeficiency virus and its resultant acquired immunodeficiency syndrome has transitioned from an acute to a chronic disease. Therefore, there are significant challenges to both care of the patient and care of the community through transmission prevention. For healthcare personnel, there is a need to understand the transmission, social, legal, and treatment issues. This chapter presents an overview of the background, transmission, prevention, and treatment of human immunodeficiency virus infection and acquired immunodeficiency syndrome, as well as information on legal and confidentiality issues relating to human immunodeficiency virus/acquired immunodeficiency syndrome.

KEY CONCEPTS

- Although studies show that human immunodeficiency virus may have jumped from chimpanzees to humans as far back as the 1800s, it was first recognized in man in the United States as recently as the late 1970s.

- Human immunodeficiency virus affects specific cells of the immune system called CD4 cells, or T cells, subsequently compromising the natural immune system's ability to fight off infection.

- Acquired immunodeficiency syndrome is the stage of human immunodeficiency virus when the immune system is so badly damaged that the person develops opportunistic infections and cancers. Without treatment, people who develop acquired immunodeficiency syndrome typically survive about 3 years.

- Only certain body fluids (blood, semen ["cum"], preseminal fluid, rectal fluids, vaginal fluids, and breast milk) from a human immunodeficiency virus-infected person can transmit human immunodeficiency virus to another person.

- Three-fourths of all cases are sexually transmitted through having unprotected sex.

- Globally, more than 34 million people are living with human immunodeficiency virus.

- As newer human immunodeficiency virus diagnostic methods are developed, the ability to identify human immunodeficiency virus infection in the early stages of transmission also improves.

- Although there is no cure, treatment with antiretroviral medications has improved survival.

- The use of drug-resistant testing has become an important part of human immunodeficiency virus clinical care.

- Although historically vaccines have been the best weapon against the world's most deadly diseases, there is unfortunately no effective human immunodeficiency virus vaccine available.

- Key components of a human immunodeficiency virus prevention program center on the use of Standard Precautions in healthcare settings, risk reduction through behavioral modification programs, and medication adherence programs.

BACKGROUND[1]

The human immunodeficiency virus (HIV) originated in Africa. Retrospective studies of sera indicate that the virus was present in sub-Saharan Africa in the 1950s. All studies of sera collected during the 1960s in many parts of the world indicate a very low prevalence of HIV antibodies. The epidemic transmission of the virus began in the 1970s and early 1980s. A timeline of some of the most historically important aspects of this includes the following:

- 1959: First documented case of acquired immunodeficiency syndrome (AIDS) in the world. The patient was a sailor from England who died of *Pneumocystis carinii* pneumonia (PCP) and cytomegalovirus infection. (Note that this organism has been renamed *Pneumocystis jirovecii*.) Studies of stored tissue from the patient proved that the patient was infected with HIV.

- 1968: The first documented case of AIDS in the United States. Retrospective studies indicated the presence of HIV infection in a young patient who was found to have Kaposi's sarcoma at autopsy.

- 1981: Previously healthy homosexual men with biopsy-confirmed PCP and Kaposi's sarcoma were reported from California and New York. Common to these cases was an underlying severe cellular immunodeficiency marked by a dramatic reduction in CD4 lymphocytes. These were the first reported cases of AIDS, a disease that at that time was of unknown etiology.

- 1984: Recognition of the human immunodeficiency virus type 1 (HIV-1) as the etiologic agent of AIDS.

- 1985: A serologic test to detect HIV antibodies was developed. With implementation of the test in blood banks, the risk of acquiring HIV after a blood transfusion decreased significantly.

- 1986: A second type of HIV virus is identified in patients with AIDS from West Africa. HIV-2 produces the same clinical manifestations as HIV-1 but causes disease almost exclusively in Africa.

- 1987: The U.S. Food and Drug Administration (FDA) approved AZT (zidovudine), the first anti-HIV drug.

- 1995: A new class of very potent anti-HIV drugs, the protease inhibitors, is available for clinical use. After an initial hope that combination therapy using these potent new drugs may cure the infection, clinical studies indicate that eradication of HIV infection cannot be achieved with our current therapy.

- 2000: The United Nations estimated that as of December 2000, 58 million people had been infected with HIV.

- 2011: At the International AIDS Society's Conference on HIV Pathogenesis, Treatment, and Prevention, scientists announce that two studies have confirmed that individuals taking daily antiretroviral drugs experienced infection rates more than 60 percent lower than those on a placebo.[2]

BASIC PRINCIPLES

Epidemiology

A national surveillance system has been in place in the United States since the first reported cases in 1981. All 50 states require reporting of AIDS cases to the local health authorities, which then report to the Centers for Disease Control and Prevention (CDC). The first 100,000 cases of AIDS were reported to the CDC over an 8-year period. The second 100,000 cases were reported over a 2-year period. As of June 2011, approximately 1,148,200 cases of HIV have been reported to the CDC.[3]

Minorities are overrepresented in the U.S. AIDS epidemic, particularly African Americans (approximately 60 percent of cases) and Hispanic Americans (approximately 20 percent of cases). Male-to-male sexual contact is the most prevalent mode of transmission.[4] AIDS is the sixth leading cause of death among people 25 to 44 years of age in the United States, down from number one in 1995.[5] In the United States, 1,148,200 people are living with HIV, with an additional estimated 207,600 of those undiagnosed. There were about 47,500 new infections in the United States in 2010, with the number of new HIV infections highest among individuals 25 to 34 years of age (31 percent), followed by individuals 13 to 24 years of age (26 percent).[4]

The World Health Organization (WHO) estimated that 34 million people were living with HIV at the end of 2011.[6] The number of those newly infected has fallen, particularly in the Caribbean and sub-Saharan Africa. However, the number of newly infected persons in the Middle East and North Africa has increased. The incidence of newly infected persons in the United States has remained stable.[6]

Transmission

The HIV virus is relatively fastidious and cannot survive for long periods outside the human body.[7] The virus can be transmitted as free virus in secretions or as cell-associated virus by transmission of live cells (e.g., blood products, breast milk, semen). Transmission requires parenteral, broken skin, or mucous membrane contact with contaminated blood or body fluids or both. Fluids such as saliva, tears, urine, and sweat should not be considered a transmission risk unless blood is present.[7]

The epidemic was first described in men having sex with men, but other risk groups were rapidly identified, including injection drug users (IDUs) and recipients of blood products.[1] Approximately 70 percent of U.S. cases are in those practicing male-to-male sex or in IDUs. Heterosexual transmission accounts for approximately 30 percent of U.S. HIV transmission.[8] Worldwide, however, most of the cases are heterosexually acquired. In the United States, females outnumber males in the heterosexual risk category. Part of the explanation for the growing number of females in the heterosexual risk category may be that male-to-female transmission is approximately twice as efficient as female-to-male transmission. HIV can also be transmitted from pregnant women to their unborn babies during the birthing process.

Fluids (blood, semen, vaginal secretions, and breast milk) from an HIV-infected person can transmit HIV. These fluids must come in contact with a mucous membrane or damaged tissue or be directly injected into the bloodstream (from a needle or syringe) for transmission to occur. In the United States, HIV is most commonly transmitted through sexual behaviors (anal or vaginal sex) or sharing needles with an infected person. It is less common for HIV to be transmitted through oral sex or for an HIV-infected woman to pass the virus to her baby before or during childbirth. It is also possible to acquire HIV through exposure to infected blood, transfusions of infected blood, blood products, or organ transplantation, though this risk is extremely remote due to rigorous testing of the U.S. blood supply and donated organs.[7]

The first test to detect antibodies to HIV was licensed in March 1985. Since that time, all blood and tissue donors have been tested. However, because screening tests measure antibodies to the virus, which may take up to 6 months after exposure to appear, the probablility of transmission via blood products, though extremely low, still exists. All blood donors are also questioned regarding behavioral risk factors for HIV and recent flulike symptoms. The risk for acquiring HIV infection through blood transfusion today is estimated conservatively to be one in 1.5 million, based on 2007–2008 data.[9]

Prevention

The most important step in prevention is education.[10] The public needs to be made aware of risk behaviors that transmit HIV. Furthermore, the HIV/AIDS Strategy for the United States, supported by CDC, recommends using a combination of scientifically proven, cost-effective, and scalable interventions and prevention strategies directed toward the most vulnerable populations in the United States who are most affected by, or at greatest risk for, HIV infection.[11] There are over 75 evidence-based risk-reduction strategies identified as successful, including Centering Pregnancy Plus (CPP), Becoming a Responsible Teen (BART), Brief Group Counseling, Communal Effectance: AIDS Prevention (CE-AP), and Female Condom Skills Training.[11]

Testing is an important tool in the nation's efforts to curtail the spread of HIV. A person does not know that he or she has HIV unless he or she has been tested. Almost one in six people in the United States who have HIV do not know they are infected.[12] The CDC recommends that healthcare providers test everyone between the ages of 13 and 64 at least once as part of routine healthcare. A person who continues to have unsafe sex or unprotected sex, or who continues to share injection drug equipment, should get tested at least once a year. Sexually active gay and bisexual men may benefit from more frequent testing. Pregnant women should be routinely counseled and voluntarily tested for HIV. Early diagnosis allows a pregnant woman to receive effective antiretroviral therapies for her own health, as well as preventive drugs to improve the chances that her infant will be born free of infection.[13]

Counseling, which should be provided before and after testing, provides a unique opportunity to educate individuals about HIV, how to avoid infection, how to protect others if they are HIV-positive, and options for treatment and follow-up. It also plays a vital role in reducing the transmission of HIV from mother to infant.

Pathogenesis and Clinical Presentation of HIV Infection

Pathogenesis of HIV Infection[14,15]

HIV is a double-stranded ribonucleic acid (RNA) virus that uses host cells, particularly CD4 cells, to replicate. HIV is a retrovirus. Normally, DNA produces RNA that is used in protein synthesis in the cell's ribosomes. The infecting virus is able to create viral DNA from the viral RNA using the viral enzyme reverse transcriptase and integrate this viral DNA into the cell's DNA using the viral enzyme integrase.[16] A new virion is produced, which is composed of a nucleoprotein core surrounded by a lipid layer containing viral surface (gp120) and transmembrane (gp41) envelope proteins. The nucleoprotein core contains two copies of viral genomic RNA, viral proteases, and reverse transcriptase (Figure 81-1).

The critical step in the pathogenesis of HIV disease occurs when the virus envelope protein (gp120) binds to cells carrying the CD4 receptors. The viral RNA can then enter the

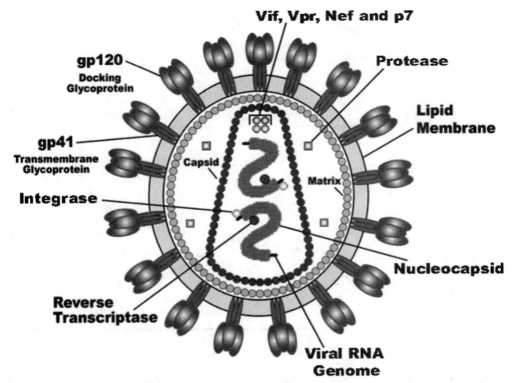

Figure 81-1. Structure of HIV (National Institutes of Health).

CD4 cell. The CD4 cells are depleted by a possibly indirect mechanism not yet fully understood.[17,18] As CD4 cell counts decline, the production of critical lymphokines that support the entire immune system declines. Over time, interleukin-2 (IL-2) production falls. Because IL-2 is critical to the growth and replication of CD4 cells, this results in the collapse of the entire immune system. In patients with HIV infection, the deterioration of the immune system progresses over years. Patients die with advanced disease because of an opportunistic infection or malignancy. The average time from viral transmission to death in patients without treatment is approximately 10 to 12 years. However, there is a widespread variation for individual patients in relation to progression of disease and the time from infection to development of AIDS or death. The two most important predictors of disease progression in patients with HIV are the CD4 cell count and viral load. However, HIV-infected individuals on antiretroviral therapy with a recent undetectable viral load who have maintained or had recovery of CD4 (+) cell counts to at least 500 cells/µL showed no evidence for an increased risk of death compared with the general population.[19]

CD4 Cell Count

The normal values for CD4 cell count range from 500 to 1,400 cells/mm³. The value of CD4 cells is the product of three variables: total white blood cell count, percentage of lymphocytes, and percentage of lymphocytes that bear the CD4 receptor. The CD4 count can vary greatly (up to 25 percent); therefore, single measurements are less helpful than trends.

The variation is greater as the CD4 count becomes lower. The CD4 percentage is less variable than the absolute CD4 count. Figure 81-2 depicts the progression of CD4 count in the average patient without treatment.

At the moment of transmission the patient starts with a normal CD4 count. This value drops significantly during the first 6 weeks at the time of uncontrolled viral replication. After 3 months of infection, when the patient develops the cellular and humoral response against HIV, there is an improvement in the CD4 count value, but it does not return to preinfection levels. During the following years, the progressive reduction in the CD4 cells is due to the HIV virus killing CD4 cells, as well as a reduced production of CD4 cells. Approximately 3 years after infection, the value of CD4 cells reaches the lower normal level of 500 cells/mm³. With progression of the disease, the value of CD4 reaches the level of 200 cells/mm³. Below this value, a patient is considered to have AIDS. The time to development of AIDS or death decreases with a steeper decline in the CD4 cell count. When the CD4 count reaches 50 cells/mm³, the patient has severe immune suppression. It is not uncommon to see patients with very advanced disease with CD4 values less than 10 cells/mm³.

Viral Load

A higher viral burden is associated with a more rapid progression of disease. Quantitative determination of the HIV RNA in plasma is used to measure the viral load, or viral burden.

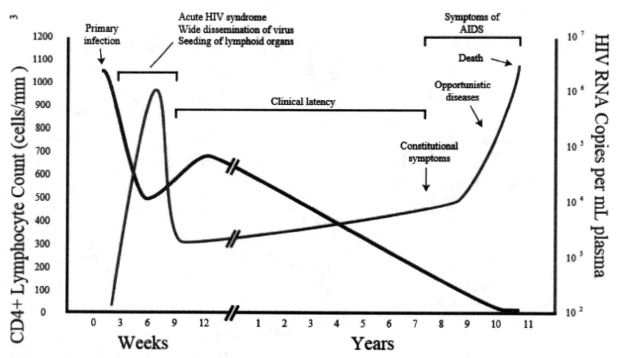

Figure 81-2. Typical course of HIV infection that shows the relationship between the levels of HIV (viral load) and CD4+ T-cell counts over the average course of untreated HIV infection (Author: Sigve, Used under Creative Commons CC0 1.0 Universal).

Determination of the plasma HIV RNA can be performed in the laboratory using techniques such as HIV RNA PCR, or branched-chain DNA. The tests have a minimal threshold for detection of HIV. The standard tests detect a minimum of 400 copies/mL. New generation tests detect as low as 50 copies/mL. The viral load in HIV patients may range from a value of less than 50 copies/mL, or undetectable, to a value of greater than 750,000 copies/mL.

Figure 81-2 depicts the changes in viral load in an average patient without treatment. At the time of HIV transmission, the host has an undetectable viral load. During the first weeks of infection there is uncontrolled viral replication and the viral load reaches values of 105 copies/mL of plasma. Once the patient develops an immune response to the infection, there is a 2- to 3-log decrease in plasma HIV RNA levels. The viral load stabilizes at a new level, called the "set point." This viral load level dictates the future rate of infection progression. The higher the set point, the more rapidly the patient progresses to AIDS. Even in the absence of antiretroviral therapy (ART), the viral load remains relatively stable over a period of several years. After several years of viral load stability, there is a rapid increase of viral load that is followed by a decrease in CD4 cell counts. During the last stages of the disease, there is uncontrolled viral replication, with viral load levels reaching 106 HIV RNA copies/mL.

Stages of HIV Infection

The natural history of a patient with HIV infection from the time of transmission to death can be divided into the following six stages: (1) incubation period, (2) acute retroviral syndrome, (3) asymptomatic HIV infection, (4) symptomatic HIV infection, (5) AIDS, and (6) advanced HIV infection. The rate of progression from the incubation period to advanced HIV infection in a patient without treatment and the correlation with the CD4 count and viral load is depicted in Figure 81-2. The rate of progression for an individual patient may change significantly from this standard model. A particular patient may rapidly progress to AIDS after 2 to 3 years of infection. On the other hand, some patients may remain asymptomatic with CD counts in the normal range even after 10 years of infection without ART. These patients are called long-term nonprogressors.

Clinical Progression of HIV

1. *Incubation period*: Figure 81-2 depicts the natural history of HIV infection in patients without treatment. The first stage of infection is the incubation period. This period starts with acquisition of HIV and finishes when the patient develops the first clinical manifestations of HIV infection. In the majority of patients, the incubation period lasts 2 to 4 weeks but in some patients may last for several months. After entering the body, the virus travels to the regional lymph nodes and then enters the systemic circulation. During the incubation period, though the patient is clinically asymptomatic, the virus disseminates primarily to the brain and the lymphatic system, the viral load increases, and the CD4 count decreases.

2. *Acute retroviral syndrome*: After an incubation period of 2 to 4 weeks, the patient develops a complex of symptoms that is called the acute retroviral syndrome. This syndrome is also called acute HIV infection, primary HIV infection, or acute seroconversion syndrome. After viral transmission, the acute retroviral syndrome manifests in approximately 80 to 90 percent of patients. Although the syndrome is commonly severe enough for the patient to seek medical attention, the presence of acute retroviral syndrome may not be recognized by primary care physicians. Patients with the acute retroviral syndrome may present signs and symptoms primarily related to viral multiplication in the lymphatic system (e.g., infectious mononucleosis-like syndrome) or viral multiplication in the central nervous system (e.g., aseptic meningitis syndrome). The duration of the acute retroviral syndrome is less than 2 weeks for most patients. The clinical recovery is associated with development of an immune response to HIV that is associated with a decrease in viral load and increase in CD4 cell count. As part of this immune response, the patient develops antibody titers with positive HIV serology. Determination of the HIV serology test is of no help in the diagnosis of acute retroviral syndrome because at the time the patient is symptomatic the antibody titers are undetectable and HIV serology is negative. During the acute retroviral syndrome there is a high level of HIV viremia with plasma HIV RNA titers of 105 copies/mL. Therefore, when a patient presents with signs and symptoms compatible with acute retroviral syndrome, the laboratory diagnosis is based on the determination of HIV RNA titers or viral load, not determination of HIV serology.

3. *Asymptomatic HIV infection*: During this stage of the disease the patient is clinically asymptomatic. The physical examination of most patients is unremarkable, but some patients may present with persistent generalized lymphadenopathy. During this period, though the patient is asymptomatic, every day there is a significant replication of HIV with destruction of CD4 cells that is partially compensated with an increased production of new CD4 cells. During this asymptomatic stage, there is a persistent decrease in CD4 cells of approximately 30 to 90 cells/mm³ every year.

4. *Symptomatic HIV infection*: After years of asymptomatic infection, the patient starts to develop early symptoms that are related to HIV infection but are not AIDS indicators. Some of these are very unspecific, such as fever or weight loss. This stage was called AIDS-related complex or ARC in the past. In most patients, during this stage the CD4 cell count is in the range of 500 cells/mm³ to 200 cells/mm³. Table 81-1 defines the conditions used to class HIV infections and AIDS.

5. *AIDS*: A patient with HIV infection is considered to have AIDS when the CD4 cell count is less than 200 cells/mm³ or the patient presents with a condition associated with severe immune deficiency. In 1993, the CDC revised the classification system for HIV infection to emphasize the clinical importance of the CD4+ T-lymphocyte count in the categorization of HIV-related clinical conditions. This classification system replaced the system published by the CDC in 1986. Consistent with the

1993 revised classification system, the CDC also expanded the AIDS surveillance case definition to include all HIV-infected persons who have less than 200 CD4+ T-lymphocytes/uL, or a CD4+ T-lymphocyte percentage of total lymphocytes of less than 14. This expansion included the addition of three clinical conditions: pulmonary tuberculosis, recurrent pneumonia, and invasive cervical cancer—and retained the 23 clinical conditions in the AIDS surveillance case definition published in 1987 used by all states for AIDS case reporting effective January 1, 1993 (Table 81-1).

6. *Advanced HIV infection*: This stage of the disease, also defined as advanced AIDS, applies to patients with CD4 cell counts less than 50 cells/mm^3. At this stage, patients have limited life expectancy even with optimal therapy of HIV infection and opportunistic infections.

Approximately one-third of new reported cases of AIDS in the United States are based on the finding of a CD4 count less than 200 cells/mm^3, and two-thirds of the reported cases are based on the diagnosis of an AIDS-defining condition. The AIDS-defining conditions reported to the CDC in 1997 and 2008 are listed in Table 81-2.

In 1994–1997, 1998–2002, and 2003–2007, rates of opportunistic infections (per 1,000 person-years) were 89.0, 25.2,

Table 81-1. HIV Infection and AIDS: Defining Conditions[20]

Bacterial infections, multiple or recurrent*
Candidiasis of bronchi, trachea, or lungs
Candidiasis of esophagus[†]
Cervical cancer, invasive[§]
Coccidioidomycosis, disseminated or extrapulmonary
Cryptococcosis, extrapulmonary
Cryptosporidiosis, chronic intestinal (>1 month's duration)
Cytomegalovirus disease (other than liver, spleen, or nodes), onset at age >1 month
Cytomegalovirus retinitis (with loss of vision)[†]
Encephalopathy, HIV related
Herpes simplex: chronic ulcers (>1 month's duration) or bronchitis, pneumonitis, or esophagitis (onset at age >1 month)
Histoplasmosis, disseminated or extrapulmonary
Isosporiasis, chronic intestinal (>1 month's duration)
Kaposi sarcoma[†]
Lymphoid interstitial pneumonia or pulmonary lymphoid hyperplasia complex[*†]
Lymphoma, Burkitt (or equivalent term)
Lymphoma, immunoblastic (or equivalent term)
Lymphoma, primary, of brain
Mycobacterium avium complex or *Mycobacterium kansasii,* disseminated or extrapulmonary[†]
Mycobacterium tuberculosis of any site, pulmonary,[†§] disseminated,[†] or extrapulmonary[†]
Mycobacterium, other species or unidentified species, disseminated[†] or extrapulmonary[†]
Pneumocystis jirovecii pneumonia[†]
Pneumonia, recurrent[†§]
Progressive multifocal leukoencephalopathy
Salmonella septicemia, recurrent
Toxoplasmosis of brain, onset at age >1 month[†]
Wasting syndrome attributed to HIV

*Only among children aged <13 years. (CDC. 1994 Revised classification system for human immunodeficiency virus infection in children less than 13 years of age. *MMWR* 1994;43[No. RR-12].)

[†]Condition that might be diagnosed presumptively.

[§]Only among adults and adolescents aged ≥13 years. (CDC. 1993 Revised classification system for HIV infection and expanded surveillance case definition for AIDS among adolescents and adults. *MMWR* 1992;41[No. RR-17].)

Table 81-2. AIDS-Defining Conditions As Reported to CDC in 1997 (2003–2007)

• *Pneumocystis jiroveci*	24% (3.9%)
• Wasting syndrome	18%
• Tuberculosis	9%
• Kaposi's sarcoma	7%
• Disseminated *M. avium*	5% (2.5%)
• Chronic herpes simplex	5%
• HIV-associated dementia	5%
• Recurrent bacterial pneumonia	5%
• Toxoplasmosis	4%
• CMV disease	3% (1.8%)

and 13.3, respectively, and rates of opportunistic malignancies were 23.4, 5.8, and 3.0. Following the advent of highly active ART (HAART), the opportunistic illness rates declined precipitously and stabilized at low levels in 2003–2007. During that time, there were no significant changes in annual rates of opportunistic infections or opportunistic malignancies; the leading opportunistic illnesses (rate per 1,000 person-years) were esophageal candidiasis (5.2), *Pneumocystis* pneumonia (3.9), cervical cancer (3.5), *Mycobacterium avium* complex infection (2.5), and cytomegalovirus disease (1.8). Thirty-six percent of opportunistic illness events occurred at CD4 cell counts of at least 200 cells/µL.[21]

Diagnostic Test for HIV Infection

The original HIV diagnostic testing algorithm was developed by the CDC in 1989.[22] Recently, alterations to the original testing algorithm have been proposed that incorporate advancements made in HIV diagnostic testing, thereby increasing the sensitivity while reducing the turnaround time and cost. In particular, the highly infectious phase of HIV infection (the interval between the appearance of HIV RNA in plasma and the detection of HIV-1 antibodies) contributes disproportionately to HIV transmission. To address this problem, the CDC has been evaluating a new HIV diagnostic algorithm soon to be released that will reduce the risk of interpreting results erroneously as negative.[22]

1. *Standard serologic tests:* The most commonly used laboratory test for diagnosis of HIV infection is the serologic detection of antibodies to the virus. The standard serologic test consists of a screening enzyme immunoabsorbent assay (EIA) followed by a confirmatory Western blot (WB). In a patient with a positive EIA test, the test should be repeated. In a patient with a repeatedly positive EIA test, a confirmatory WB is performed. These serologic assays show sensitivity and specificity rates of 99.9 percent.

There is always a delay from the time of infection until the patient develops positive serology. After transmission of the virus, most patients develop antibodies at the time that there is clinical resolution of the acute retroviral syndrome. This time delay, called the window period, averages 21 days but in some patients may extend for several months. If serologic testing is performed during the window period, the test will be negative in a patient who is infected with HIV. Serologic testing during the window period produces a false-negative result.

2. *Viral load*: When a physician considers that a patient may have an acute retroviral syndrome, the HIV serology is of no diagnostic value, as the patient is still in the window period. In this clinical scenario, the diagnosis of acute HIV infection is performed by determination of quantitative HIV RNA (viral load). During the incubation period of HIV infection and during the acute retroviral syndrome, the antibody tests are negative but the patient has high levels of HIV RNA in plasma. RNA tests detect the virus directly (instead of the antibodies to HIV) and thus can detect HIV at about 10 days after infection—as soon as it appears in the bloodstream and before antibodies develop. These tests cost more than antibody tests and are generally not used as a screening test.[22]

3. *Rapid HIV tests*: The FDA approved a rapid test for diagnosis of HIV infection that can offer a result in 15 minutes. A negative rapid test is reported as a definitive negative HIV test. A reactive test result needs to be confirmed with standard serologic tests. The rapid test has been used for determining the serologic status of the source in healthcare personnel (HCP) exposures and for pregnant women who present in labor and have not been previously tested. The use of rapid HIV testing for counseling purposes is increasing.[23]

Follow-up diagnostic testing is performed if the first immunoassay result is positive. Follow-up tests include an antibody differentiation test, which distinguishes HIV-1 from HIV-2; an HIV-1 nucleic acid test, which looks for virus directly; or the WB or indirect immunofluorescence assay, which detect antibodies.

Immunoassays are generally very accurate, but follow-up testing allows the patient and his or her healthcare provider to be sure the diagnosis is right. If the first test is a rapid test, and it is positive, the patient is directed to a medical setting to get follow-up testing. If the first test is a lab test, and it is positive, the lab will conduct follow-up testing, usually on the same blood specimen as the first test.

False-positive tests are rare. If tests are conducted during the window period, they can give a false-negative result.

In-home tests: Currently there are only two home HIV tests: OraQuick In-home HIV test and the Home Access HIV-1 Test System. The HIV test should be FDA-approved.[24]

Treatment of HIV Infection

Goals of Antiretroviral Therapy

The primary goals for initiating ARV therapy are to:

- Reduce viral load as much as possible for as long as possible.
- Reduce HIV-associated morbidity and prolong the duration and quality of survival.

- Restore and preserve immunologic function.
- Maximally and durably suppress plasma HIV viral load.
- Prevent HIV transmission.

The viral suppression allows immune reconstitution that translates to increased number of CD4 cells and a better pathogen-specific immune response. Then, with appropriate therapy, the patient will have a decreased viral load, increased CD4 count, and decreased risk for opportunistic infections. This will translate to improved quality of life and prolongation of life.

Although ARV therapy has clear benefits, there are some drawbacks. All drugs have side effects; therapy usually involves taking several drugs multiple times a day, and compliance with the regimen must be strict to prevent development of viral resistance. Because viral resistance to a drug may produce cross-resistance to other drugs, development of resistance to a current regimen may render future antiretroviral therapy ineffective. Thus, HIV drug-resistance testing is recommended in persons with HIV infection at entry into care regardless of whether ART will be immediately initiated or deferred.[24]

Medications

In 1987, a drug called AZT became the first approved treatment for HIV disease. Since then, over 30 drugs categorized in six different classes have been approved to treat people living with HIV/AIDS, and more are under development. Antiretroviral drugs used in the treatment of HIV infection are listed on the FDA website (http://www.fda.gov/).

These drugs may be called by many different names, including:

- "The cocktail"
- Antiretrovirals (ARVs)
- Highly active antiretroviral therapy (HAART or ART)

Taking three different HIV medications is more effective than taking one medication because each class of drug attacks the virus at a different point in its life cycle. Taking more than one drug also helps protect against HIV drug resistance.[25]

HIV Life Cycle and Antiretroviral Targets

Using the gp120 surface glycoproteins, HIV attaches to the CD4 cellular receptors and coreceptors and penetrates the cells. Drugs that block the attachment of the virus are known as entry inhibitors or fusion inhibitors. Once inside the cell, the viral RNA is transformed to viral DNA by the viral enzyme reverse transcriptase. This represents an important target site during the HIV life cycle. There are currently two classes of ARV drugs that act at this level, the nucleoside and nucleotide reverse transcriptase inhibitors and the non-nucleoside reverse transcriptase inhibitors. Following the transcription from RNA to DNA, the viral DNA moves to the nucleus of the cell and integrates to the host cell DNA in the chromosomes, producing a lifelong infection. Using host cell enzymes and ribosomes, the transcription and translation of proviral DNA produces new HIV proteins. These newly produced HIV proteins are made as polyproteins. One essential step during the last stage of assembly and release of the new virus is the modification of viral polyproteins by specific enzymes such as HIV proteases. This represents another target for ART. Drugs that act at this level are known as protease inhibitors.

Specifically, the six classes of ARV are described as:

- *Nucleoside/nucleotide reverse transcriptase inhibitors (NRTIs)* act as faulty building blocks in production of viral DNA production. This blocks HIV's ability to use reverse transcriptase to correctly build new DNA that the virus needs to make copies of itself.

- *Non-nucleoside reverse transcriptase inhibitors (NNRTIs)* act directly on reverse transcriptase to prevent it from functioning correctly.

- *Protease inhibitors (PIs)* block the protease that cuts long strands of genetic material created by the virus and prevent those long strands of genetic material from being cut up into functional pieces.

- *Fusion inhibitors* block HIV from entering the cells. Fusion inhibitors can target the sites on either HIV or CD4 cells and prevent HIV from "docking" into healthy cells.

- *Entry inhibitors-CCR5 co-receptor antagonist* inhibits or blocks HIV from cell entry using the CCR5 receptor.

- *HIV integrase strand transfer inhibitors (INSTI)* block the process of reverse transcription (by blocking the HIV enzyme integrase) and prevent the virus from adding its DNA into the DNA in the CD4 cells. Preventing this process prevents the virus from replicating and making new viruses.

What Drugs to Start

Guidelines for the use of ARV agents in HIV-infected adult, adolescent, pediatric, and perinatal cases are under constant review and scrutiny as new evidence is released. Because the practice of ART is very specialized and complex, providing specifics on therapy is beyond the scope of this chapter. Most up-to-date guidelines for the use of ARV agents in adults, adolescents, and special populations are published by the National Institute of Health (NIH).[26]

When to Start Therapy

Considering the risk and benefits of ART, the decision to start therapy must be individualized. Factors that must be considered in the decision are the patient's willingness and readiness to initiate therapy, the availability of resources, and any comorbid conditions. Although controversy still exists among experts regarding when to start therapy in a patient who is asymptomatic, the NIH recommends initiating treatment in all HIV-infected individuals as soon as diagnosed as long as the patient is committed to therapy for an indefinite period of time. Initiating ART early in disease progression inhibits HIV replication so

that plasma HIV RNA levels (viral load) remain low. In addition, durable viral suppression improves immune function and lowers the risk of both AIDS-defining and non-AIDS defining complications, prolonging life.[25]

Treatment During Pregnancy

If mothers have HIV, infants can become infected during pregnancy, during labor and delivery, and to a lesser degree during breast-feeding. If the pregnant woman who has HIV is treated with ARV agents during pregnancy and labor, the risk of passing HIV to the infant is reduced drastically.[27] Thus, all pregnant women should be offered HIV testing. If an HIV-infected pregnant woman has already been on ART, therapy should be continued. Because of concerns about teratogenicity, efavirenz should not be used in women who are planning pregnancy or during the first trimester of pregnancy.

Trends in AIDS incidence among children continue to demonstrate the dramatic success of efforts to reduce perinatal (mother-to-child) transmission. Clinical trials showed that HIV-infected women could reduce the risk of transmitting the virus to their babies by as much as two-thirds through administration of zidovudine (AZT), which is known to cross the placenta. AZT is given to HIV-infected mothers during their last two trimesters of pregnancy, through labor, and then to their babies for 6 weeks after birth. Infected mothers do not always seek prenatal care, so it is not always possible to provide the full course of treatment. Even if only given after birth, AZT appears to substantially reduce the chances of vertical transmission of HIV to newborns. For the purpose of preventing perinatal transmission of HIV, ART is indicated in all pregnant women regardless of viral load, CD4 count, or clinical status.

Prevention of Opportunistic Infections

The prevention of opportunistic infections is an important aspect of the clinical management of patients with HIV. The use of HAART has led to decreased morbidity and improved survival in patients with AIDS. The CDC, the NIH, and the HIV Medicine Association of the Infectious Diseases Society of America have published guidelines for the prevention and treatment of opportunistic infections in HIV-infected adults and adolescents.[28]

Risk for HIV Transmission in the Healthcare Setting

Risk for HIV Transmission to Patients

Although there is the possibility of transmission from patient to patient or from HCP to patient, it is extremely rare. In 1990, the CDC described the first case of HIV transmission from HCP to a patient (dentist to patient). In total, five cases of HIV transmission were suggested.[29] All cases had strains that were genetically similar to the dentist's strain. This case generated much anxiety on the part of patients. However, even with numerous look-back studies involving thousands of patients cared for by HIV-positive HCP, only three additional cases have been reported: (1) probable transmission from an orthopedic surgeon to a patient in France; (2) probable transmission from a nurse to a patient, also in France; and (3) probable transmission from a gynecologist to a patient during a cesarean delivery in Spain. Currently, the CDC recommends that HCP use Standard Precautions to prevent HCP-to-patient as well as patient-to-HCP transmission.

In the healthcare setting, there is the possibility of transmission from patient to patient, though the risk is extremely limited. The greatest risk for patient-to-patient transmission is during invasive procedures when instruments or syringes are reused without effective cleaning and sterilization between uses. Infection preventionists must ensure that FDA guidelines are strictly enforced to prevent this occurrence (see www.fda.gov for guidelines on reprocessing of single- use devices; also see Chapter 32 Reprocessing Single Use-Devices).

Risk for HIV Transmission from Patients to Healthcare Personnel

As of December 2010, the CDC is aware of 57 HCP in the United States who have been documented as having seroconverted to HIV after occupational exposures. Of these, 26 developed AIDS. When the very high number of caregivers with a high rate of exposure is considered, this number, though regrettable, represents an extremely low occurrence of the disease. These individuals who seroconverted included 24 nurses, 19 laboratory workers (16 of whom were clinical laboratory workers), 6 physicians, 2 surgical technicians, 1 dialysis technician, respiratory therapist, 1 health aide, 2 housekeeper/maintenance workers, and 1 embalmer/morgue technician.[30] It is interesting to note that this number has not increased since reported in 2002.

The risk for HIV transmission from a single percutaneous exposure to HIV-positive blood is estimated to be 0.3 percent to 0.4 percent. The risk after mucous membrane exposure is on the order of 0.09 percent.[31]

Recommendations to Prevent Transmission

In 1985 and 1986, the CDC published recommendations to prevent the transmission of HIV in the workplace. In 1987 and again in 1998, more comprehensive documents were published in response to increasing concern from HCP about occupational exposure to HIV. In September 2013, the CDC again published recommendations, entitled Updated U.S. Public Health Service Guidelines for the Management of Occupational Exposures to Human Immunodeficiency Virus and Recommendations for Post-exposure Prophylaxis.[32]

All of these documents continue to stress the importance of applying blood and body fluid precautions to all patients and designated this policy Standard Precautions (see Chapter 28 Standard Precautions and Chapter 105 Minimizing Exposure to Blood and Body Fluids).

Management of Occupational Exposures

The most current recommendations for management of occupational exposures to HIV are included in Updated U.S. Public Health Service Guidelines for the Management of Occupational Exposures to Human Immunodeficiency Virus and Recommendations for Post-exposure Prophylaxis.[32] Infection preventionists and occupational health professionals are referred to this document for recommendations for post-exposure prophylaxis (PEP).

Healthcare organizations should have a policy and readily accessible protocol for postexposure management. A method for providing evaluation of an exposure event as well as a rapid response process must be addressed in the facility plan. Occupational exposures should be considered urgent medical events to ensure timely postexposure management.

The first action after exposure involves an immediate first aid to the exposed site, including cleaning of the exposed/injured site. A soap-and-water hand wash should be performed to remove visible proteinaceous material. Alcohol is virucidal, so an alcohol-based hand hygiene agent can be used after soap-and-water hand wash has been performed. Caustic chemicals such as bleach should not be used in an attempt to disinfect or cleanse the skin. Squeezing or "milking" the injured site is not necessary. Once the area has been washed, evaluation by a skilled professional should be sought. Chapter 101 Occupational Exposure to Bloodborne Pathogens addresses postexposure management in detail.

Consultation with local experts and/or the National Clinicians' Postexposure Prophylaxis Hotline (PEPline, 1-888-448-4911) is advised when the source person's virus is known or suspected to be resistant to one or more of the drugs considered for the PEP regimen. Other indications for consultation with experts include delayed exposure report, unknown source person, or pregnancy in the exposed person.

Ethical and Legal Issues for Healthcare Personnel Caring for Patients with HIV

HIV Testing

The CDC recommends that healthcare providers test everyone between the ages of 13 and 64 at least once as part of routine healthcare. Almost one in five people in the United States who have HIV do not know they are infected.[13] After the transmission of HIV by the Florida dentist and Australian and French surgeons, the general public has voiced concern regarding the risk of transmission of infection from HCP. The Society of Hospital Epidemiologists of America (SHEA) recommends restrictions in practice for HIV-positive HCP who have greater than 5×10^2 genome equivalents.[33]

Every patient is considered a potential risk. By using Standard Precautions, protection is provided and there is no need to know the patient's HIV status as it pertains to treatment, except to protect the possibly immunocompromised patient.

Caring for Patients with HIV

Working with patients who are facing an illness with a long unpredictable course and fatal outcome, caregivers have the opportunity to facilitate the patient's role as an active participant in his or her health, work, family, and community. Caring for patients with HIV can be exceptionally rewarding and, at the same time, frustrating and stressful. Stressors arise from specific issues directly related to HIV and from more general concerns of a chronic illness in an environment of limited resources. By recognizing positive and difficult aspects of HIV care, HCP can be more effective in caring for the needs of both patients and themselves.

Attitude and behavior adjustments need to be made through education concerning prevention, transmission, and treatment of HIV. Courses and training programs have had remarkable success in AIDS/HIV education and for dispelling myths and misconceptions concerning HIV.

HCP who work for hospitals, home health agencies, or walk-in clinics, along with their employers, generally lack legal backing to deny care to a patient with HIV/AIDS or any "infectious" disease. Refusing to care for a patient could result in dismissal. Requests for different assignments may be made, but an employer is not obligated to honor the request. In certain circumstances, policy may permit temporary reassignment for an immunosuppressed HCP to decline care of infected clients. Any policy must be applied consistently and fairly.

Public policy in the area of HIV/AIDS issues continues to progress. HCP are counseled to keep current with laws and court rulings in the state, as well as employment policies and procedures.

Discrimination Against Patients with HIV Infection

The Americans with Disabilities Act (ADA) of 1995 identifies HIV as a disability. This affords patients infected with HIV special protection under federal law. This assists with discrimination in the workplace, when dealing with housing issues, and in social and medical services.[34]

Signed into law on July 26, 1990, the ADA is wide-ranging legislation intended to make U.S. society more accessible to people with disabilities. The ADA's protection applies primarily, but not exclusively, to disabled individuals. One is considered disabled if he or she meets at least any one of the following criteria: he or she has a physical or mental impairment that substantially limits one or more of his or her major life activities; he or she has a record of such an impairment; he or she is regarded as having such impairment. The ADA protects patients with infectious diseases from discrimination in access to services and employment. The duty to treat in regard to healthcare facilities that receive Medicare and other federal funds also applies.

It was reported in June 25, 1998, that HIV-infected people are protected by the federal ban on discrimination against disabled persons even if they have no symptoms of AIDS.[34,35] The ruling went against a Maine dentist who told an HIV-infected patient that he would fill her cavity in a hospital but not in his office. The woman sued under the ADA, a federal civil rights law that bars disability discrimination.

This landmark decision was a victory not just for people with disabilities, but also for the Justice Department, which included people with HIV under the scope of this law. This federal law also protects those with disabilities in regard to employment issues, public accommodations including hospitals and clinics, and access to medical treatment. Title III, which is the most far-reaching ADA title in a healthcare context, prohibits discrimination by enterprises that are considered places of public accommodation. Title III classifies private healthcare services as a public accommodation without regard to whether service providers are considered recipients of federal financing.

Knowledge Regarding a Patient's HIV/AIDS Status[36]

Employers, healthcare providers, and other individuals have expressed much doubt and uncertainty about whether they have a right or obligation to disclose the status of an individual known to them to be HIV infected to others with whom the individual may come into contact. This issue must be examined critically as current law reflects rational, thoughtful consideration of the need to know in certain circumstances. It is forbidden to disclose this information except in limited circumstances.

Most people with HIV face, at least briefly, some issue regarding public knowledge of their status. They deal with discrimination in obtaining employment and insurance. Knowledge of their status may touch other parts of their lives, such as custody of children or maintaining personal relationships. In the long run, only adequate public education will help solve these problems.

Laws that govern who should have knowledge of a patient's HIV/AIDS status are obscure at times. One thing is clear: anyone who reveals information about a patient's HIV status could face both civil liability and disciplinary action for unauthorized disclosure of confidential information under the Health Insurance Portability and Accountability Act (HIPAA). The Office of Civil Rights (OCR), in the Department of Justice, enforces the HIPAA Privacy and Security Rules, a set of federal standards to protect the privacy and security of patients' medical records and other health information maintained by covered entities: health plans; most doctors, hospitals, and many other healthcare providers; and healthcare clearinghouses. These standards provide patients with access to their medical records and exert significant control over how their personal health information is used and disclosed. Persons with HIV/AIDS who believe that their health information privacy rights have been violated may file a complaint with OCR.

There are legal statutes that determine who can be forced to take an HIV test, have tests taken without their knowledge, or results revealed against their will. Similarly, statutes exist that offer general control over medical records, which may directly or indirectly reveal a person's HIV status, and federal and state constitutional protection of privacy in the face of government intrusion.

Unless they have given explicit permission, a patient's health status should not be discussed with anyone other than direct caregivers, doctors, or the patient. HCP should check with the facility's risk manager or a supervisor to ascertain who is authorized to inform those who need to know.

When consent is needed to disclose health information, it should be made in writing. It must specifically indicate what information will be released, to whom, and for how long the consent is valid. In releasing HIV-related data, a statement should be included that prohibits the receiving party from further disclosing the information without the patient's evidence of consent.

HCP should not discuss health issues in public areas where others may overhear. When giving HIV-related instructions to a patient, HCP should take that patient to a private room. Any incident in which it is suspected that health information has been disclosed improperly or without authorization should be reported.

Reporting to the Public Health System

Physicians, hospitals, and laboratories must promptly report both HIV-positive patients and confirmed cases of AIDS to the public health service in accordance with their state reportable diseases laws. Unless tested anonymously, patients must be identified by name and other information provided for statistical purposes; however, cases of asymptomatic HIV infection may be reported by initials or code numbers in lieu of a name. It is essential to know local law and policies that impact HIV care delivery and to establish a relationship with the individuals responsible for this reporting.

Human Services Available for HIV Patients

A number of social services are available to individuals with HIV. This is a chronic disease. The ability of the individual to maintain an optimal level of health is dependent upon the ability to continue medical care as well as have basic needs met. It is important that infection preventionists be aware of the care coordination and that other human, social, and faith-based services be available for individuals with HIV/AIDS so this information can be readily available for those in need.

CONCLUSION

Although infection with HIV has no cure, key components of a HIV prevention program center on the use of Standard Precautions in healthcare settings, risk reduction through behavioral modification programs, and medication adherence programs. Progress has been made in diagnostic testing during the highly infectious period, the window state, and testing for

HIV-resistant patterns. Even though an HIV vaccine has not yet been successful, there has been advancements in the study of PEP for people who are at high risk of getting HIV.[37] Education is the most effective method to promote risk reduction; it should include information about the infection, modes of spread, and prevention. The application of a bloodborne pathogen prevention plan including Standard Precautions is still the most important infection prevention strategy to prevent workplace transmission. Reporting requirements for HIV infection and AIDS vary based on locality and applicable laws.

REFERENCES

1. Sharp PM, Hahn BH. Origins of HIV and the AIDS Pandemic. *Cold Spring Harb Perspect Med* [serial online]. 2011 Sep;1(1): a006841. Available at: http://www.ncbi.nlm.nih.gov/pmc/articles/PMC3234451/.
2. AIDS.gov. *A timeline of AIDS.* Available at: http://aids.gov/hiv-aids-basics/hiv-aids-101/aids-timeline/.
3. Division of HIV/AIDS Prevention, National Center for HIV/AIDS, Viral Hepatitis, Sexual Transmitted Diseases and Tuberculosis Prevention, Centers for Disease Control and Prevention (CDC). *HIV/AIDS Basic Statistics.* CDC website. February 12, 2014. Available at: http://www.cdc.gov/hiv/basics/statistics.html.
4. Division of HIV/AIDS Prevention, National Center for HIV/AIDS, Viral Hepatitis, Sexual Transmitted Diseases and Tuberculosis Prevention, Centers for Disease Control and Prevention (CDC). *CDC HIV Surveillance Report 2011.* CDC website. Available at: http://www.cdc.gov/hiv/pdf/statistics_2011_HIV_Surveillance_Report_vol_23.pdf#Page=17
5. National Library of Medicine (NLM). *HIV/AIDS.* NLM website. May 19, 2013. Available at: http://www.ncbi.nlm.nih.gov/pubmedhealth/PMH0001620/.
6. UNAIDS. *Global AIDS Response Progress Reporting 2014.* UNAIDS website. Available at: http://www.unaids.org/en/dataanalysis/knowyourepidemic/.
7. Division of HIV/AIDS Prevention, National Center for HIV/AIDS, Viral Hepatitis, Sexual Transmitted Diseases and Tuberculosis Prevention, Centers for Disease Control and Prevention (CDC). *HIV/AIDS.* CDC website. January 7, 2014. Available at: http://www.cdc.gov/hiv/resources/qa/transmission.htm.
8. Division of HIV/AIDS Prevention, National Center for HIV/AIDS, Viral Hepatitis, Sexual Transmitted Diseases and Tuberculosis Prevention, Centers for Disease Control and Prevention (CDC). *Epidemiology of HIV Infection through 2011.* CDC website. Available at: http://www.cdc.gov/hiv/pdf/statistics_surveillance_Epi-HIV-infection.pdf.
9. Centers for Disease Control and Prevention (CDC). HIV transmission through transfusion – Missouri and Colorado, 2008. *MMWR Morb Mortal Wkly Rep* [serial online]. 2010 Oct 22;59(41):1335–1339. Available at: http://www.cdc.gov/mmwr/preview/mmwrhtml/mm5941a3.htm.
10. Office of National AIDS Policy. The White House. *Implementing the National HIV/AIDS Strategy, Overview of Agency Operational Plans.* February 2011. Available at: http://aids.gov/federal-resources/national-hiv-aids-strategy/nhas-operational-plan-overview.pdf.
11. Division of HIV/AIDS Prevention, National Center for HIV/AIDS, Viral Hepatitis, Sexual Transmitted Diseases and Tuberculosis Prevention, Centers for Disease Control and Prevention (CDC). *High-Impact HIV Prevention: CDC's Approach to Reducing HIV Infections in the United States.* CDC website. April 17, 2013. Available at http://www.cdc.gov/hiv/policies/hip.html.
12. Division of HIV/AIDS Prevention, National Center for HIV/AIDS, Viral Hepatitis, Sexual Transmitted Diseases and Tuberculosis Prevention, Centers for Disease Control and Prevention (CDC). *HIV/AIDS Testing.* CDC website. February 12, 2014. Available at: http://www.cdc.gov/hiv/basics/testing.html.
13. Branson BM, Handsfield HH, Lampe MA, et al. Revised recommendations for HIV testing of adults, adolescents, and pregnant women in health-care settings. *MMWR Recomm Rep* [serial online]. 2006 Sep 22;55(RR-14); 1–17. Available at: http://www.cdc.gov/mmwr/preview/mmwrhtml/rr5514a1.htm.
14. Weber J. The pathogenesis of HIV-1 infection. *Br Med Bull* 2001;58(1): 61–72.
15. Lane HC. Pathogenesis of HIV infection: total CD4+ T-cell pool, immune activation, and inflammation. *Top HIV Med* [serial online]. 2010 Feb-Mar;18(1):2–6. Available at: http://www.iasusa.org/sites/default/files/tam/18-1-2.pdf.
16. Zheng YH, Lovsin N, Peterlin BM. Newly identified host factors modulate HIV replication. *Immunol Lett* 2005 Mar 15;97(2):225–234.

17. Cloyd MW, Chen JJ, Adeqboyega P, et al. How does HIV cause depletion of CD4 lymphocytes? A mechanism involving virus signaling through its cellular receptors. *Curr Mol Med* 2001 Nov;1(5):545–550.

18. Doitsh G, Cavrois M, Lassen KG, et al. Abortive HIV infection mediates CD4 T cell depletion and inflammation in human lymphoid tissue. *Cell* 2010 Nov 24;143(5):789–801.

19. Rodger AJ, Lodwick R, Schechter M, et al. Mortality in well controlled HIV in the continuous antiretroviral therapy arms of the SMART and ESPRIT trials compared with the general population. *AIDS* 2013 Mar 27;27(6): 973–979.

20. Schneider E, Whitmore S, Glynn KM, et al. Revised surveillance case definitions for HIV infection among adults, adolescents, and children aged <18 months and for HIV infection and AIDS among children aged 18 months to <13 years—United States, 2008. *MMWR Recomm Rep* [serial online]. 2008 Dec 5;57(RR-10):1–12. Available at: http://www.cdc .gov/mmwr/pdf/rr/rr5710.pdf.

21. Buchacz K, Baker RK, Palella FJ Jr, et al. AIDS-defining opportunistic illnesses in US patients, 1994–2007: a cohort study. *AIDS* 2010 June; 24(10):1549–1559.

22. Centers for Disease Control and Prevention (CDC). Detection of acute HIV infection in two evaluations of a new HIV diagnostic testing algorithm-United States, 2011-2013. *MMWR Morb Mortal Wkly Rep* 2013 June 21;62(24):489–494.

23. Kallenborn JC, Price TG, Carrico R, et al. Emergency department management of occupational exposures: cost analysis of rapid HIV test. *Infect Control Hosp Epidemiol* 2001;22:289–293.

24. Division of HIV/AIDS Prevention, National Center for HIV/AIDS, Viral Hepatitis, Sexual Transmitted Diseases and Tuberculosis Prevention, Centers for Disease Control and Prevention (CDC). *What Kinds of Tests are Available and How Do They work?* CDC website. February 12, 2014. Available at: http://www.cdc.gov/hiv/basics/testing.html.

25. AIDSMEDS. *Treatment for HIV & AIDS*. November 18, 2013. Available at: http://www.aidsmeds.com/list.shtml.

26. Department of Health and Human Services, Panel on Antiretroviral Guidelines for Adults and Adolescents. *Guidelines for the Use of Antiretroviral agents in HIV-1-Infected Adults and Adolescents.* Available at: http://aidsinfo.nih.gov/ContentFiles/AdultandAdolescentGL.pdf.

27. Branson BM, Handsfield HH, Lampe MA, et al. Revised recommendations for HIV testing of adults, adolescents, and pregnant women in health-care settings. MMWR Recomm Rep [serial online]. 2006 Sep 22;55(RR-14); 1–17. Available at: http://www.cdc.gov/mmwr/preview/mmwrhtml /rr5514a1.htm.

28. Panel on Opportunistic Infections in HIV-Infected Adults and Adolescents. Guidelines for the prevention and treatment of opportunistic infections in HIV-infected adults and adolescents: recommendations from the Centers for Disease Control and Prevention, the National Institutes of Health, and the HIV Medicine Association of the Infectious Diseases Society of America. Available at http://aidsinfo.nih.gov/contentfiles/lvguidelines /adult_oi.pdf. Accessed January 17, 2014.

29. Recommendations for preventing transmission of human immunodeficiency virus and hepatitis B virus to patients during exposure-prone invasive procedures. *MMWR Recomm Rep* [serial online].1991 Jul 12;40(RR-8): 1–9. Available at: http://www.cdc.gov/mmwr/preview/mmwrhtml /00014845.htm.

30. Centers for Disease Control and Prevention, National Center for Emerging and Zoonotic Infectious Diseases (NCEZID), Division of Healthcare Quality Promotion (DHQP). *Surveillance of Healthcare Personnel with HIV/ AIDS, as of December 2010.* CDC website. May 23, 2011. Available at: http://www.cdc.gov/HAI/organisms/hiv/Surveillance-Occupationally -Acquired-HIV-AIDS.html.

31. Beltrami EM, Williams IT, Shapiro CN, et al. Risk and management of blood-borne infections in health care workers. *Clin Microbiol Rev* 2000 July; 13(3): 385–407.

32. Kuhar DT, Henderson DK, Struble KA, et al. Updated US Public Health Service guidelines for the management of occupational exposures to human immunodeficiency virus and recommendations for postexposure prophylaxis. *Infect Control Hosp Epidemiol* 2013 Sep;34(9):875–892.

33. Henderson DK, Dembry L, Fishman NO, et al. SHEA Guideline for management of healthcare workers who are infected with hepatitis B virus, hepatitis C virus, and/or human immunodeficiency virus. *Infect Control Hosp Epidemiol* 2010 Mar;31(3):203–232.

34. Washingtonpost.com. *Supreme Court, Key Cases 1997–1998. Americans with Disabilities Act: Bragdon v. Abbott.* Available at: http:// www.washingtonpost.com/wp-srv/national/longterm/supcourt/1997-98 /bragdon.htm.

35. Asseo L. *Court votes for HIV rights.* CBS News website. June 25, 1998. Available at: http://www.cbsnews.com/2100-204_162-12584.html.

36. U.S. Department of Health & Huuman Services (HHS). *Protecting the Civil Rights and Health Information Privacy Rights of People Living with HIV/AIDS.* HHS website. Available at: http://www.hhs.gov/ocr /civilrights/resources/specialtopics/hiv/index.html.

37. Division of HIV/AIDS Prevention, National Center for HIV/AIDS, Viral Hepatitis, Sexual Transmitted Diseases and Tuberculosis Prevention, Centers for Disease Control and Prevention (CDC). *HIV/AIDS: PrEP 101.* CDC website. February 12, 2014. Available at: http://www.cdc.gov/hiv /basics/prep.html.

SUPPLEMENTAL RESOURCES

Centers for Disease Control and Prevention (CDC). *HIV Testing Implementation Guidance for Correctional Settings.* CDC website. January 2009.

Chapman LE, Sullivent EE, Grohskopf LA, et al. Recommendations for postexposure interventions to prevent infection with hepatitis B virus, hepatitis C virus, or human immunodeficiency virus, and tetanus in persons wounded during bombings and other mass-casualty events—United States, 2008: recommendations of the Centers for Disease Control and Prevention (CDC). *MMWR Recomm Rep* [serial online]. 2008 Aug 1;57(RR-6): 1–21. Available at: http://www.cdc.gov/mmwr/preview/mmwrhtml /rr5706a1.htm.

Smith DK, Grohskopf LA, Black RJ, et al. Antiretroviral postexposure prophylaxis after sexual, injection-drug use, or other nonoccupational exposure to HIV in the United States: recommendations from the U.S. Department of Health and Human Services. *MMWR Recomm Rep* [serial online]. 2005 Jan 21; 54(RR-2):1–20. Available at: http://www.cdc.gov/mmwr/preview/mmwrhtm l/rr5402a1.htm.

CHAPTER 82

Influenza

Hilary Babcock, MD, MPH
Instructor, Infectious Diseases
Washington University School of Medicine
St. Louis, MO

ABSTRACT

Influenza viruses are responsible for acute respiratory illnesses during winter seasons in temperate climates. Epidemic influenza occurs due to small changes in surface glycoproteins, a process known as antigenic drift. Large changes in those proteins, known as antigenic shift, are responsible for larger pandemic influenza outbreaks. Seasonal influenza is expected annually, but the threat of pandemic influenza due to a large change in seasonal strains or introduction of a novel strain requires infection prevention and control programs to have surveillance, interventions, and emergency preparedness plans in place. Influenza can cause a spectrum of disease in humans, ranging from a self-limited respiratory infection to a more fulminant illness. The very young and very old are more susceptible to severe disease, as are individuals with certain underlying medical conditions. Several antiviral drugs are available for treatment of influenza, but vaccination and respiratory etiquette are the primary control strategies. Each year, vaccines are modified to reflect the strains most likely to be circulating.

KEY CONCEPTS

- Influenza is a contagious respiratory disease transmitted from person to person primarily via virus-laden droplets.

- Outbreaks of healthcare-associated influenza can occur and affect both patients and healthcare personnel.

- Vaccination is the primary method for preventing influenza and its complications.

- Healthcare personnel compliance with annual influenza vaccination is an expected behavior to protect patients, staff, and families.

- Standard Precautions including respiratory hygiene and cough etiquette and Droplet Precautions are effective infection prevention methods used to prevent influenza transmission in healthcare facilities.

- Influenza prevention plans include education, vaccination, isolation, and surveillance, as well as restricting visitors and healthcare personnel who are ill and enhancing infection prevention measures during outbreaks.

BACKGROUND

Influenza epidemics in the United States result in an average of 3,300 to 48,000 deaths[1] and more than 200,000 hospitalizations annually. Infection rates are highest among children, but serious illness and death occur predominantly among individuals 65 years old and older and individuals who have certain medical conditions, such as chronic pulmonary or heart diseases.[2-5] Influenza pandemics occur episodically, the most recent in 2009 when a novel 2009 influenza A (H1N1) was identified as causing illness in at least 191 countries.[6] Vaccination is the primary method for preventing influenza and its complications, and recommendations for vaccine and antiviral drug use are published regularly by the Advisory Committee on Immunization Practices (ACIP).[7] Information regarding influenza surveillance and control is available on the Centers for Disease Control and Prevention (CDC) website, through the CDC Voice and Fax Information systems, and on the CDC website Influenza.gov. (See Supplemental Resources.)

BASIC PRINCIPLES

Epidemiology

Influenza is primarily spread between individuals via respiratory secretions (droplet spread). Viral shedding can start 24 to 48 hours after infection, and typically 24 hours before the onset of symptoms.[8] Shedding normally persists 5 to 7 days but can be 10 days or longer in children and the immunocompromised.[8,9] Thus, most adults are considered infectious from the day before symptoms begin until approximately 7 days after the onset of illness.

Clinical Manifestations

Influenza can manifest in a variety of ways, ranging from asymptomatic infection to prostration in more severe cases. Upper respiratory symptoms tend to occur most frequently, along with systemic symptoms of fever, headache, and myalgia, most often with acute onset. Although these symptoms are common in influenza, they are not specific for influenza since they are also common in other viral respiratory illnesses.[10-12] Establishing the diagnosis of influenza, as opposed to a respiratory illness due to another virus, remains an important clinical challenge.

In addition to the typical manifestations described, the illness may present differently in young children, the elderly, and immunocompromised individuals. Children may present with otitis media and young children may exhibit initial symptoms reminiscent of bacterial sepsis with high fevers and febrile seizures.

In elderly patients with influenza, fever and cough remain frequent findings although the temperature elevation might be blunted compared with younger patients.[13] Underlying illnesses and medications may mask symptoms in hospitalized patients. Therefore, absence of influenza-like symptoms does not effectively rule out influenza, and high clinical suspicion must be maintained during the appropriate season.[12]

Complications of Influenza

The patients at highest risk of developing complications and requiring hospitalization from influenza include children younger than 5 years, patients 65 years or older, pregnant women, obese patients, and those with chronic underlying medical conditions. The most significant medical condition associated with development of complications is asthma, but other pulmonary, cardiac, hematologic, metabolic, and neurologic conditions also increase the risk of complications.[14-16] During the influenza A 2009 (H1N1) pandemic, previously healthy younger adults had an increased incidence of complications.

Viral Pneumonia

Influenza pneumonia is usually bilateral and unassociated with isolation of typical bacterial pathogens, although influenza virus may be isolated from sputum. The mortality can be high, and treatment with antiviral medications (discussed later in this chapter) is appropriate. Pneumonia is more common in older adults with comorbidities. Patients with pneumonia are symptomatic longer than patients without pneumonia.[17] Influenza pneumonia can also occur in younger patients, especially during pandemics as seen with influenza A 2009 (H1N1) when a mean age as low as 32 years was observed in one center.[18] Up to 70 percent of critically ill patients can have hypoxia with diffuse patchy opacities seen in a chest roentgenogram.[19,20]

Bacterial Coinfection

During the influenza epidemic of 1918 to 1919, secondary bacterial pneumonia was the most common cause of death.[21] During the 2009 pandemic influenza A (H1N1), up to 30 percent of patients managed in intensive care units (ICUs) had documented bacterial coinfection, defined as bacterial pneumonia or bacteremia.[22] The number increased up to 55 percent of patients in autopsy series when reviewing fatal cases.[23] Bacterial pneumonia usually complicates influenza infection 4 to 14 days after improvement in initial symptoms and presents with fever and productive cough. In severely ill patients bacterial coinfection can develop as early as 5 days after the onset of influenza symptoms.[22]

Staphylococcus aureus is the most common cause of bacterial coinfection, in particular pneumonia, closely followed by Strep-

tococcus pneumoniae and Streptococcus pyogenes. Other healthcare-associated pathogens have also been implicated in severely ill patients. Community-associated methicillin-resistant S. aureus has been reported as the causative agent of severe necrotizing community-associated pneumonia associated with influenza, even in patients without underlying comorbid medical conditions. On January 30, 2008, the CDC issued a health alert on influenza-associated pediatric mortality and S. aureus coinfection. It was recommended that healthcare providers be alert to the possibility of bacterial coinfection among children with influenza and request bacterial cultures if children are severely ill or if community-associated pneumonia is suspected.[24] The CDC conducts annual surveillance for pediatric deaths associated with influenza.

Rare Syndromic Complications

Influenza infection has been associated with encephalitis, transverse myelitis, Reye's syndrome, myositis, myocarditis, pericarditis, and renal failure.[25-27]

Virus Identification and Characterization

Influenza viruses are divided into three categories, designated A, B, and C. All three contain negative-sense, segmented, single-strand RNA molecules. The influenza A viruses are the most common clinical isolates, and they are further subdivided by differences in two surface proteins: hemagglutinin (H) and neuraminidase (N). Three H and two N antigenic subtypes account for virtually all human infections. The most prevalent influenza A strains in humans in the last 30 years have been H3N2 and H1N1. In recent years, influenza A and B strains also have been named according to the city or state and year of their initial isolation, for example, A/Texas/36/91 (H1N1) or B/Hong Kong/330/2001. Influenza A strains are the predominant cause of pandemics. Influenza B strains can also cause annual epidemic disease, but the clinical illnesses tend to be milder than illnesses caused by influenza A. Influenza C strains can be identified in up to 13 percent of influenza infections, but they either produce mild illness (usually a "common cold") or are detected with another respiratory virus which makes it difficult to asses its clinical role.[28] Influenza C strains have not been associated with large epidemics.[29]

Non-human Reservoirs

Influenza A viruses infect many different animals, most notably swine and poultry, who serve as reservoirs and can occasionally be transmitted between human and animal species. The H5, H7, and H9 strains preferentially infect birds but can spread to humans.

An H5N1 avian influenza strain was recovered during an outbreak in Hong Kong in 1997 that killed six people. It was contained with aggressive control measures but recurred in humans in 2003. Now labeled highly pathogenic avian influenza A (HPAI H5N1), it has been circulating in Asia, Africa, the Pacific, Europe and the Near East with more than 600 human cases reported to the World Health Organization (WHO). The HPAI H5N1 strain is transmitted readily between birds and from birds to humans and only rarely transmitted between humans. It causes significant mortality in affected individuals.[30,31] A new avian influenza A (H7N9) causing human infections was reported in China on April 1, 2013. It caused severe respiratory disease in humans, with high rates of admission and death.[32] The outbreak was contained and no human-to-human transmission was reported.

Swine influenza A strains are usually H1N1, H3N2, and H1N2. They cause outbreaks of influenza in pigs, and sporadically human infection. They are often referred to as "variant viruses" when this happens. Influenza H3N2v are strains that normally circulate in pigs, but occasionally cause infection in humans, most commonly associated with exposure to pigs at agricultural fairs during summer months in the United States.[33]

The new virus that caused the 2009 pandemic, now labeled "2009 H1N1 influenza," was carried by genetic elements closely related to swine H1N1, but never found among U.S. pig herds. It also contained avian elements. This strain is now one of the annual circulating influenza strains.

Diagnosis

Influenza can be diagnosed in a variety of ways. Clinical diagnosis relies on symptoms suggestive of influenza, including upper respiratory symptoms with fever and myalgia. However, in influenza season, a high degree of suspicion should be maintained as not all patients have classic influenza-like illness (ILI) symptoms.[12]

Commercially available rapid influenza diagnostic tests (RIDTs) are designed for antigen detection directly from nasopharyngeal swabs. They have modest sensitivity (40 to 70 percent) but are highly specific (90 to 95 percent).[34] The performance of RIDTs varies based on seasonality when influenza viruses are circulating in the community. Immunofluorescence antibody testing may increase the sensitivity of the assay. However, neither a negative fluorescent antibody test nor RIDT provide sufficient evidence to rule out the clinical diagnosis of influenza.

Influenza A and B viruses propagate well in tissue culture (e.g., Madin Darby canine kidney, a continuous cell culture line also known as MDCK cells, and primary monkey kidney cells). Many (but not all) influenza isolates produce cytopathic effect in tissue culture, which may be detected microscopically. Reverse transcription-polymerase chain reaction (RT-PCR) is increasingly used where available for its high sensitivity and rapid turnaround time. RT-PCR has become the gold standard for the diagnosis of influenza. It has higher sensitivity than culture and can also be used to differentiate between influenza types and subtypes.[35]

If there is clinical suspicion of influenza infection in a hospitalized patient, then empiric treatment should be initiated. Only culture and PCR are sensitive enough to rely on for ruling out influenza infection, and thus for removing suspected influenza patients from Droplet Precautions.

A good review of laboratory diagnostics for influenza, including rapid influenza tests, can be found on the CDC's "Seasonal Flu" website under "Guidance for Clinicians on the Use of Rapid Influenza Diagnostic Tests," which is available online at: http://www.cdc.gov/flu/professionals/diagnosis/clinician_guidance_ridt.htm.

Treatment

The treatment of influenza includes supportive measures for all cases and antiviral therapy in certain cases. There are four antiviral agents for the treatment and prevention of influenza. Amantadine and rimantadine work by blocking the viral M2 protein ion channel.[36] However, these older agents are not currently recommended in the United States due to increased resistance. The neuraminidase blockers oseltamivir and zanamivir are the preferred antivirals and work by inhibiting viral release after replication in infected cells. They have activity against both influenza A and B, and resistance among circulating viruses is currently low but does vary by strain. Currently, neuraminidase inhibitor can be used for treatment and prophylaxis of influenza. Resistance can emerge rapidly, however, and clinicians should review annual recommendations on antiviral treatment to ensure appropriate use.

Most healthy outpatients with influenza will recover with supportive measures alone and do not require antiviral treatment. However, antiviral treatment should be initiated promptly in a patient who meets any of the following criteria:

1. Hospitalized
2. Severe, complicated, or progressive disease
3. High risk for influenza complications
   - Age <2 or >65
   - Immunosuppressed
   - Pregnant
   - Morbid obesity
   - Chronic care facility resident
   - American Indians/Alaska Natives
   - <19 years on chronic aspirin
   - Other chronic medical problems as mentioned before.

Treatment with oseltamivir and zanamivir should be started as early as possible, when indicated. Early treatment has been shown to shorten the duration of illness and hospitalization and may also reduce the risk of complications and death. The benefit is greater the earlier therapy is initiated. Most data suggest that starting therapy within 48 hours of initiation of symptoms reduces the duration of illness. However, in multiple studies performed during and after the influenza A 2009 (H1N1) pandemic, there appeared to be benefit from treatment even beyond the 48 hours after symptom onset. These studies found benefits such as reducing the duration of symptoms, duration of hospitalization, complications, respiratory failure, and death even when antiviral therapy was initiated up to 5 days after symptom onset.[37-40] The impact of antiviral treatment in severely ill patients is not entirely clear, but treatment is usually recommended in that setting.

Prevention and Control: Annual Influenza Vaccination

The severity of most influenza epidemics is influenced by the degree of immunity in the population. Clinical studies have shown that protection from influenza infection is primarily strain specific (i.e., antigen specific). Influenza vaccination is the preferred method for preventing influenza and its complications in individuals. A more subtle benefit that accrues from individual vaccination is herd immunity, which occurs when enough people in a community are immunized, then it is more difficult for the infection to reach people who are not immunized, or do not respond to the vaccine. The immunized population protects the nonimmune by lowering the prevalence of infection in the community.

Starting in 2010, the ACIP recommend that all persons aged 6 months and older should receive routine annual influenza vaccine. Vaccinating individuals before the seasonal increase in influenza virus circulation is the most effective means of reducing the incidence and complications of influenza. Vaccination is far more cost effective than chemoprophylaxis with antiviral agents after exposure.[41,42] Vaccination coverage can be increased by administering the vaccine during hospitalizations or during routine healthcare visits before the influenza season. Vaccination of healthcare personnel (HCP) and others in close contact with individuals at high risk for severe influenza illness and its complications can reduce transmission of influenza. When vaccine supply is limited, vaccination efforts should focus on persons at high risk for medical complications due to influenza and their close contacts, described as follows:

1. All children 6 months to 18 years of age, and all adults 50 years of age and older.

2. Adults and children with underlying medical conditions, including cardiovascular, renal, pulmonary, metabolic (including diabetes), hematologic, and neurologic disorders; morbid obesity; and children receiving long-term aspirin therapy who might be at risk for Reye's syndrome if infected with influenza.

3. Adults and children who are immunosuppressed.

4. Pregnant women and breastfeeding mothers.

5. Residents of long-term care facilities.

6. Household contacts of anyone meeting the above criteria, and contacts of infants younger than 6 months.

7. Healthcare personnel.

There are three formulations of influenza vaccine available: inactivated influenza vaccine (IIV), live-attenuated influenza vaccine (LAIV), and recombinant influenza vaccine (RIV).[43] The vaccines differ in the number of antigens that they contain, the route of administration, and antigen presentation. Traditionally, influenza vaccines, both inactivated and live attenuated, have contained three influenza strains, two influenza A and one influenza B strain. The 2013 to 2014 influenza season will be the first time a quadrivalent vaccine will be available. The quadrivalent influenza vaccines contain an additional influenza B virus strain.

The IIV can be trivalent or quadrivalent, and all are injectable. Most formulations are administered intramuscularly except for one that is given as an intradermal injection. The IIV is contraindicated in patients with a severe, anaphylactic allergic reaction to eggs or any vaccine components. A new cell culture-based IIV is available but still contains some egg protein and the same precautions should be taken. In patients with a mild reaction to egg products, for which hives is the only symptom, IIV can be administered by a healthcare provider familiar with egg allergy if the recipient is observed for at least 30 minutes after vaccination. There is also a high dose IIV that is available for people over the age of 65. This vaccine is also a trivalent, inactivated, injectable vaccine that appears to promote a more robust immune response in older adults; the clinical impact is unclear.

The LAIV is an alternative for healthy, nonpregnant patients aged 2 to 49 years. In 2013, the only available LAIV is quadrivalent. It contains live virus that has been altered so that it survives only at the cooler temperatures in the nasal mucosa. It is not licensed for use during pregnancy, but postpartum women are eligible to receive the LAIV. It should be avoided in patients 2 to 4 years of age with a history of reactive airway disease, although the risk the LAIV poses in such patients is unclear. Patients receiving chronic aspirin therapy should not be given the LAIV because to the risk of Reye's syndrome with wild-type virus. Viral shedding of the attenuated virus may occur, at very low levels, for up to 7 days after receipt of the LAIV. Out of an abundance of caution, LAIV is not recommended for care providers, including HCP or family members, who will have close contact with severely immunosuppressed persons (defined as those patients such as stem cell transplant recipients who are so immunosuppressed that they currently require a protective environment) in the 7 days after vaccination.[44,45] LAIV should be avoided in patients with history of any kind of allergic reaction to egg products because of limited available data, even when hives is the only reaction.

The RIV, released in 2013, is a trivalent, intramuscular, alternative for persons aged 18 to 49 years. It differs from IIV and LAIV in that it is composed of three recombinant hemagglutinin (HA) proteins for influenza A and B, rather than live attenuated or inactivated virus. Its recombinant production uses an insect virus expression system and so does not depend upon the use of eggs. It is an alternative for patients with any type of reaction to egg products, in the appropriate age group.

Vaccination with all forms is contraindicated in patients with an anaphylactic allergic reaction to any component of the vaccine.

Caution is urged in individuals with a history of Guillain-Barré syndrome (GBS) within 6 weeks following a previous influenza immunization. There is conflicting evidence regarding the risk of GBS following vaccine administration, although most reports have shown no such association.[46]

Because it is impossible to predict when an influenza epidemic will occur in a community, influenza vaccination should be offered in the community as soon as the vaccine becomes available. Vaccine should be offered to everyone >6 months of age, at every encounter during influenza season to increase the chance of immunization. Persons with moderate to severe acute febrile illness usually should not be vaccinated until their symptoms have subsided. However, individuals with minor illnesses (with or without fever) can receive influenza vaccine. In general, inactivated vaccines do not interfere with the immune response to other inactivated vaccines or to live vaccines and can be coadministered.[7] However, it is prudent to check the annual ACIP influenza vaccination recommendations for any changes or caveats for that year's vaccine options. Standing orders and reminder systems can increase the rate of immunization in residents of nursing homes and patients who are hospitalized. Programs can also increase the rate of immunization of HCP.[47] See "Healthcare Personnel with Influenza Illness" section in this chapter.

Vaccine Side Effects and Complications

Before vaccination, patients should be informed of the following:

1. The vaccine is formulated annually to protect against influenza strains likely to circulate in the United States in the upcoming winter.

2. IIV contains noninfectious viral components and cannot cause influenza. LAIV can cause nasal congestion, sore throat, and headache for a few days.

3. Respiratory diseases unrelated to influenza vaccination can occur after vaccination.

4. Fever, malaise, myalgia, and other systemic symptoms can occur after vaccination, especially in persons with no prior exposure to influenza vaccine (e.g., young children). However, in placebo-controlled studies, rates were similar between vaccine and placebo recipients.

5. Influenza vaccine should not be administered to persons known to have anaphylactic hypersensitivity to eggs or other components of the vaccine without first consulting a physician.

In the United States, some formulations of IIV might contain small amounts of thimerosal (a mercury containing compound) as a preservative. Some people have raised concerns about mercury toxicity chiefly among infants and pregnant women. Improvements in the vaccine manufacturing processes have resulted in vaccine batches with no detectable or only very low levels of thimerosal. No evidence of harm caused by thimerosal in vaccines has been reported. Preservative-free influenza vaccine is available. The LAIV contains no thimerosal.

Prevention and Control: Antiviral Chemoprophylaxis

Annual influenza vaccination is the best way to prevent influenza, but antivirals medication are approximately 70 to 90 percent effective in preventing influenza and can be useful adjuncts to vaccination. Routine chemoprophylaxis is not recommended to avoid development of resistance, but there are specific situations and patients that would benefit from chemoprophylaxis.[35] Chemoprophylaxis with antivirals is recommended when there is a respiratory outbreak of influenza among high-risk persons in institutional settings (e.g., nursing homes). All exposed or at-risk residents, as well as unvaccinated personnel, should receive at least 2 weeks of antiviral therapy. Antivirals should be continued for at least 1 week after the last known case was identified with a minimum of 2 weeks of total treatment. Unvaccinated HCP only require 2 weeks of treatment after receiving the vaccine. Other scenarios in which antivirals can be considered include postexposure prophylaxis in patients or HCP at high risk of complications from influenza who are not able to receive the vaccine.

Healthcare Personnel with Influenza Illness

All HCP who develop signs and symptoms of an upper respiratory infection should be restricted from patient care activities until they have recovered. HCP who develop lab-confirmed influenza should be instructed to immediately stop patient care activities, don a facemask until they are away from patient care areas and other personnel, and notify their supervisors and infection prevention personnel. They should be excluded from work for 5 days or for at least 24 hours after they no longer have a fever, whichever is longer. If cough and sneezing are still present upon return to work, then adherence to respiratory hygiene, cough etiquette, and frequent hand hygiene should be reinforced. If the HCP cares for patients in a protective environment (e.g., hematopoietic stem cell transplant patients), temporary reassignment or exclusion from work should be considered until completely asymptomatic to avoid exposing high-risk patients.

Influenza Vaccination Considerations: Healthcare Personnel

The CDC has recommended influenza vaccination of HCP since 1984. Despite the known benefits of vaccination, rates show that only 72 percent of HCP were vaccinated during the 2012 to 2013 influenza season.[48] Recent data confirm that HCP vaccination can result in decreased mortality among nursing home residents. Regulatory agencies are increasing requirements that healthcare facilities offer free vaccinations, with education and incentives to increase compliance rates, as well as encouraging public reporting of facility HCP influenza vaccination rates. The CDC's Healthy People 2020 campaign has set an HCP vaccination rate of 90 percent as the target.

A comprehensive influenza infection prevention plan includes early identification and isolation of patients, annual education about influenza and the benefits of vaccination for HCP and patients, restricting ill patients and HCP, and hand hygiene as well as vaccination of HCP. Healthcare facilities must evaluate HCP influenza vaccination rates annually and use the data to implement improvement plans and tools aimed at increasing vaccination rates every year.[49] Voluntary vaccination program strategies with requirements for nonimmune HCP (e.g., wearing a mask, area reassignment) have successfully increased vaccination rates, but programs making influenza vaccination a condition for employment have shown the greatest success.[47,50,51]

Influenza Infection Prevention Measures in Healthcare Settings

Influenza is spread from person to person primarily by deposition of large droplets, droplet nuclei, or aerosols onto the mucosal surfaces of the upper or lower respiratory tract of a susceptible person during close contact with an infected person. The primary mode of transmission appears to be through large droplets. The extent of transmission by hands or fomites is unknown, but it is not considered to be a primary mode of transmission. During the 2009 H1N1 influenza pandemic, there were multiple reports of healthcare-associated outbreaks.[52,53] There have also been reports of healthcare-associated transmission of influenza from previously vaccinated inpatients,[54] and of healthcare-associated transmission of influenza in nonepidemic time periods.[55] The fundamental elements to prevent influenza transmission as defined by the CDC are presented in Table 82-1.

Droplet Precautions

Patients with influenza infection should be in private rooms on Droplet Precautions for 7 days after diagnosis or 24 hours after the resolution of fever and respiratory symptoms, whichever is longer.[56] Droplet Precautions may be maintained for longer duration in children and immunocompromised patients who may shed virus longer. Everyone entering the patient's room should wear an isolation or surgical mask. HCP and visitors should discard the mask when exiting the patient's room, and practice good hand hygiene after removing personal protective equipment (PPE).

If the patient must leave his or her room for testing, he or she should wear a barrier mask. If the patient cannot tolerate a mask, the HCP transporting the patient must assist the patient

Table 82-1. Fundamental Elements to Prevent Influenza Transmission[56]

- Administration of influenza vaccine
- Implementation of respiratory hygiene and cough etiquette
- Appropriate management of ill healthcare personnel
- Adherence to infection control precautions for all patient care activities and aerosol-generating procedures
- Implementing environmental and engineering infection control measures

in complying with good respiratory etiquette (see Chapters 28 Standard Precautions, and 29 Isolation Precautions). If sufficient private rooms are unavailable, room sharing with high-risk patients should be avoided and adequate spatial separation between patients should be maintained. It may be wise to postpone elective surgery in affected patients.

Airborne Precautions

Although there are limited data available on influenza transmission related to aerosols, some authorities recommend implementing Airborne Precautions, including the use of N95 mask or respirators during activities with a high likelihood of producing respiratory aerosols, including:

- Aerosol-generating procedures (e.g., endotracheal intubation, nebulizer treatment, and bronchoscopy) performed on patients with confirmed or suspected pandemic influenza.

- Emergency intubation or cardiac pulmonary resuscitation of patient with confirmed or suspected pandemic influenza.

The recommendations state that negative pressure rooms are not routinely required for patients with influenza illness. However, airborne infection isolation rooms should be used when performing high-risk aerosol-generating procedures. If workflow, timing, resources, availability, or other factors prevent the use of airborne infection isolation rooms, these activities should be done in a private room (with the door closed) or other enclosed area. Staff in the room should be limited to the minimum number of essential personnel and all should wear respirators.

Control of Influenza Outbreaks in Healthcare Settings

For suspected influenza outbreaks in institutions, testing of respiratory specimens from patients with suspected influenza should be performed as early as possible.[56] If RIDTs are used in this setting, negative results should be confirmed by RT-PCR testing. An investigation should be prompted when two or more persons inside a closed setting (e.g., school, nursing facility, hospital) develop clinical signs and symptoms compatible with influenza virus infection within 2 to 3 days of each other. If individuals at high risk of influenza complications reside in that setting, then empiric control measures should be considered.

During an influenza outbreak in a healthcare setting, the following measures should be taken to protect patients and HCP and to reduce the risk of healthcare-associated influenza transmission:

- Perform rapid influenza virus or PCR testing of patients and personnel with recent onset of symptoms suggestive of influenza. While rapid antigen testing is helpful for confirming influenza infection, it should not be relied upon to exclude the diagnosis.

- If possible, obtain viral cultures or RT-PCR from a subset of patients so that the virus type and subtype can be determined (may need to arrange this with local or state public health laboratories).

- Implement Droplet Precautions for all patients with suspected or confirmed influenza.
- Separate suspected and confirmed influenza patients from asymptomatic patients.
- Restrict personnel movement from areas of the facility having outbreaks.
- Immunize unvaccinated patients and HCP with currently recommended influenza vaccine.
- Administer influenza antiviral chemoprophylaxis and treatment to nonimmune patients and health HCP according to current recommendations.
- Consider antiviral chemoprophylaxis for all HCP, regardless of their vaccination status, if the health department determines the outbreak is caused by a variant of influenza virus that is a suboptimal match with the vaccine.
- Limit or stop elective medical and surgical admissions.
- Restrict cardiovascular and pulmonary surgery to emergency cases during influenza outbreaks, especially those characterized by high attack rates and severe illness, in the community or acute care facility.

Special Considerations: Pregnant Women and Infants

Pregnant women and small infants are at increased risk of hospitalization from influenza complications. Pregnant women with confirmed or suspected influenza are recommended to receive antiviral treatment with oseltamivir or zanamivir. Pregnancy should not be considered a contraindication for treatment. Neuraminidase inhibitors are "Pregnancy Category C" medications, and although a few adverse events have been reported in animal studies, no causal relation has been established. On the other hand, benefit from treatment has been demonstrated and treatment should start early. Oseltamivir is the preferred choice of treatment in pregnancy. See Table 82-2 for recommendations for preventing influenza transmission between hospitalized infected mothers and their infants.[57]

INFLUENZA SURVEILLANCE IN HEALTHCARE FACILITIES

The annual infection prevention and control risk assessment must include the assessment of influenza risk and a plan for influenza surveillance. Infection prevention surveillance must be able to detect annual seasonal influenza epidemics and will therefore include both laboratory and syndromic surveillance components. The syndromic surveillance component is based on the ability to detect ILI. (For information on the clinical signs and diagnosis of influenza, visit the CDC website. See Supplemental Resources.)

ILI surveillance in a healthcare facility can be linked to emergency department visits, influenza antiviral usage, and ab-

Table 82-2. Guidance for Prevention and Control of Influenza in the Peri- and Postpartum Settings

Pregnant women have been shown to be at increased risk of hospitalization from complications secondary to influenza infection. Infection prevention measures for hospitalized pregnant and recently delivered women and their infants are detailed here. These guidelines were developed for clinicians and public health officials.

Before Delivery
- Prior to delivery, hospitalized influenza-infected pregnant women should be placed on Droplet Precautions.
- Droplet Precautions should continue for 7 days after illness onset or until 24 hours after the resolution of fever and respiratory symptoms, whichever is longer.

During Delivery
- Pregnant women with influenza in the labor and delivery suite should be placed on Droplet Precautions. The pregnant woman does not need to wear a mask during labor and delivery, but all healthcare personnel and family in the room should wear a mask.
- All persons in the delivery room should practice hand hygiene before and after handling the baby.

After Delivery
- Due to the high risk of complications from influenza infection in a neonate, facilities should consider separating the baby from the mother who is ill with suspected or confirmed influenza during the hospital stay.
- A healthy caregiver should perform feedings if possible. Mothers can express their milk if they intend to breastfeed.
- Optimal length of separation has not been established, and will need to be assessed on a case-by-case basis. During the influenza A 2009 (H1N1) pandemic, guidance recommended to continue separation until the mother:
  o Received antiviral treatment >48 hours,
  o Remained afebrile without antipyretics for >24 hours, and
  o Was able to control cough and respiratory secretions.
- If separation is not possible then the following measures should be taken:
  o Place physical barriers between mother and newborn (e.g., curtain).
  o Keep the baby ≥6 feet away for the ill mother.
  o Ensure a healthy adult is present to care for the newborn.
- If no other adult is present, then the mother should wear a surgical/isolation facemask and practice hand hygiene before each contact with the newborn.

Nursery
- Infants without symptoms, born to mothers with suspected or confirmed influenza, can be cared for in the nursery using Standard Precautions and observed closely for symptoms.
- Symptomatic mothers, other family members, and visitors should not enter the nursery.
- A newborn that develops symptoms should be placed on Droplet Precautions.

Visitors
- Visitors that were in contact with the mother prior to hospitalization should be screened for symptoms before being allowed entry to the unit.
- Visitors of influenza-infected mothers and their infants should receive infection prevention education on Droplet Precautions and hand hygiene and should be asked to practice these measures during their hospital visit.

senteeism in HCP. In addition, many state and local health departments collaborate with healthcare facilities, schools and childcare facilities, pharmacies, long-term care facilities, and medical clinics to collect ILI surveillance data. This then becomes another source of ILI surveillance information that can be utilized in the infection prevention influenza surveillance plan. The annual influenza surveillance serves as a test of the ability to detect pandemic influenza in hospitalized patients and staff.[58] Some healthcare facilities may link to a public health syndromic surveillance database and receive real-time notifications that alert the infection preventionist (IP) to an increase in ILI in the community (e.g., Department of Defense Electronic Surveillance System for the Early Notification of Community-Based Epidemics [ESSENCE][59] or the University of Pittsburgh's open source Real-time Outbreak Surveillance [RODS]).

During influenza season, the influenza surveillance for the facility should also include healthcare-associated transmission of seasonal influenza among patients and HCP in the facility. This information can be used to implement interventions to prevent ongoing transmission within the healthcare facility.[60,61]

The CDC provides a checklist for pandemic influenza preparedness, including surveillance.[62]

FUTURE TRENDS

Future research activities include vaccine development and vaccine acceptance among general and healthcare populations. In addition, improvements in surveillance and tracking will enable a more rapid response to increasing case rates.

INTERNATIONAL PERSPECTIVE

When considering the international impact of influenza, one of the first areas of concern is a pandemic, as most recently experienced in 2009 to 2010. Much work has been done to prepare for pandemics both in the United States and worldwide. Preparedness planning includes elements such as rapid diagnosis, treatment, prophylaxis, rapid vaccine development and distribution, use and availability of appropriate PPE, safety of HCP, as well as social and political implications. International cooperation has been critical to the development of preparedness programs, as influenza does not respect international borders.

REFERENCES

1. Centers for Disease Control and Prevention (CDC). Estimates of deaths associated with seasonal influenza --- United States, 1976-2007. *MMWR Morb Mortal Wkly Rep* 2010 Aug;59(33):1057–1062.
2. Nguyen AM, Noymer A. Influenza mortality in the United States, 2009 pandemic: burden, timing and age distribution. *PLoS One* 2013 May 22;8(5):e64198.
3. Cox CM, D'Mello T, Perez A, et al. Increase in rates of hospitalization due to laboratory-confirmed influenza among children and adults during the 2009-10 influenza pandemic. *J Infect Dis* 2012 Nov;206(9):1350–1358.
4. Thompson WW, Shay DK, Weintraub E, et al. Influenza-associated hospitalizations in the United States. *JAMA* 2004 Sep 15;292(11):1333–1340.
5. Glezen WP, Greenberg SB, Atmar RL, et al. Impact of respiratory virus infections on persons with chronic underlying conditions. *JAMA* 2000 Jan;283(4):499–505.
6. Jain S, Kamimoto L, Bramley AM, et al. Hospitalized patients with 2009 H1N1 influenza in the United States, April-June 2009. *N Engl J Med* 2009 Nov 12;361(20):1935–1944.
7. Centers for Disease Control and Prevention (CDC). Prevention and control of seasonal influenza with vaccines. Recommendations of the Advisory Committee on Immunization Practices -- United States, 2013-2014. *MMWR Morb Mortal Wkly Rep* 2013 Sep 20;62(RR-07):1–43.
8. Carrat F, Vergu E, Ferguson NM, et al. Time lines of infection and disease in human influenza: a review of volunteer challenge studies. *Am J Epidemiol* 2008 Apr 1;167(7):775–785.
9. Weinstock DM, Gubareva LV, Zuccotti G. Prolonged shedding of multi-drug-resistant influenza A virus in an immunocompromised patient. *N Engl J Med* 2003 Feb 27;348(9):867–868.
10. Monto AS, Gravenstein S, Elliott M, et al. Clinical signs and symptoms predicting influenza infection. *Arch Intern Med* 2000 Nov;160(21):3243–3247.
11. Babcock HM, Merz LR, Fraser VJ. Is influenza an influenza-like illness? Clinical presentation of influenza in hospitalized patients. *Infect Control Hosp Epidemiol* 2006 Mar;27(3):266–270.
12. Babcock HM, Merz LR, Dubberke ER, et al. Case-control study of clinical features of influenza in hospitalized patients. *Infect Control Hosp Epidemiol* 2008 Oct;29(10):921–926.
13. Treanor J. Influenza viruses, including avian influenza and swine influenza. In: Mandell GL, Douglas RG, Bennett J, Dolin R, eds. *Principles and Practice of Infectious Diseases*, 7th ed. Philadelphia: Churchill Livingstone, 2010:2265–2288.
14. Centers for Disease Control and Prevention (CDC). Hospitalized patients with novel influenza A (H1N1) virus infection - California, April-May, 2009. *MMWR Morb Mortal Wkly Rep* 2009 May 22;58(19):536–541.
15. Centers for Disease Control and Prevention (CDC). Intensive-care patients with severe novel influenza A (H1N1) virus infection - Michigan, June 2009. *MMWR Morb Mortal Wkly Rep* 2009 Jul 17;58(27):749–752.
16. Hanshaoworakul W, Simmerman JM, Narueponjiradul U, et al. Severe human influenza infections in Thailand: oseltamivir treatment and risk factors for fatal outcome. *PLoS One* 2009 Jun 25;4(6):e6051.
17. Murata Y, Walsh EE, Falsey AR. Pulmonary complications of interpandemic influenza A in hospitalized adults. *J Infect Dis* 2007 Apr;195(7):1029–1037.
18. Kumar A, Zarychanski R, Pinto R, et al. Critically ill patients with 2009 influenza A (H1N1) infection in Canada. *JAMA* 2009 Nov 4;302(17):1872–1879.
19. Rello J, Pop-Vicas A. Clinical review: primary influenza viral pneumonia. *Crit Care* 2009;13(6):235.
20. Rello J, Rodríguez A, Ibañez P, et al. Intensive care adult patients with severe respiratory failure caused by Influenza A (H1N1)v in Spain. *Crit Care* 2009;13(5):R148.
21. Morens DM, Taubenberger JK, Fauci AS. Predominant role of bacterial pneumonia as a cause of death in pandemic influenza: implications for pandemic influenza preparedness. *J Infect Dis* 2008 Oct 1;198(7):962–970.
22. Rice TW, Rubinson L, Uyeki TM, et al. Critical illness from 2009 pandemic influenza A virus and bacterial coinfection in the United States. *Crit Care Med* 2012 May;40(5):1487–1498.
23. Gill JR, Sheng ZM, Ely SF, et al. Pulmonary pathologic findings of fatal 2009 pandemic influenza A/H1N1 viral infections. *Arch Pathol Lab Med* 2010 Feb;134(2):235–243.
24. Centers for Disease Control and Prevention (CDC). Seasonal Flu and Staph Infections. CDC website. 2011. Available at: http://www.cdc.gov/flu/professionals/flustaph.htm.
25. Watanabe T. Renal complications of seasonal and pandemic influenza A virus infections. *Eur J Pediatr* 2013 Jan;172(1):15–22.
26. Dawood FS, Chaves SS, Perez A, et al. Complications and Associated Bacterial Coinfections Among Children Hospitalized With Seasonal or Pandemic Influenza, United States, 2003-2010. *J Infect Dis* 2013 Sep 26.
27. Ekstrand JJ. Neurologic complications of influenza. *Semin Pediatr Neurol* 2012 Sep;19(3):96–100.
28. Calvo C, García-García ML, Borrell B, et al. Prospective study of influenza C in hospitalized children. *Pediatr Infect Dis J* 2013 Aug;32(8):916–919.
29. Hirsilä M, Kauppila J, Tuomaala K, et al. Detection by reverse transcription-polymerase chain reaction of influenza C in nasopharyngeal secretions of adults with a common cold. *J Infect Dis* 2001 Apr 15;183(8):1269–1272.
30. Tran TH, Nguyen TL, Nguyen TD, et al. Avian influenza A (H5N1) in 10 patients in Vietnam. *N Engl J Med* 2004 Mar 18;350(12):1179–1188.
31. Wang H, Feng Z, Shu Y, et al. Probable limited person-to-person transmission of highly pathogenic avian influenza A (H5N1) virus in China. *Lancet* 2008 Apr 26;371(9622):1427–1434.
32. Gao HN, Lu HZ, Cao B, et al. Clinical findings in 111 cases of influenza A (H7N9) virus infection. *N Engl J Med* 2013 Jun 13;368(24):2277–2285.
33. Centers for Disease Control and Prevention (CDC). Influenza A (H3N2) variant virus-related hospitalizations: Ohio, 2012. *MMWR Morb Mortal Wkly Rep* 2012 Sep 28;61:764–767.
34. Centers for Disease Control and Prevention (CDC). *Guidance for Clinicians on the Use of Rapid Influenza Diagnostic Tests*. CDC website. 2013. Available at: http://www.cdc.gov/flu/professionals/diagnosis/clinician_guidance_ridt.htm.
35. Harper SA, Bradley JS, Englund JA, et al. Seasonal influenza in adults and children--diagnosis, treatment, chemoprophylaxis, and institutional outbreak management: clinical practice guidelines of the Infectious Diseases Society of America. *Clin Infect Dis* 2009 Apr;48(8):1003–1032.
36. Bright RA, Shay DK, Shu B, et al. Adamantane resistance among influenza A viruses isolated early during the 2005-2006 influenza season in the United States. *JAMA* 2006 Feb 26;295(8):891–894.
37. Hsu J, Santesso N, Mustafa R, et al. Antivirals for treatment of influenza: a systematic review and meta-analysis of observational studies. *Ann Intern Med* 2012 Apr 3;156(7):512–524.
38. Louie JK, Yang S, Acosta M, et al. Treatment with neuraminidase inhibitors for critically ill patients with influenza A (H1N1)pdm09. *Clin Infect Dis* 2012 Nov;55(9):1198–1204.
39. Siston AM, Rasmussen SA, Honein MA, et al. Pandemic 2009 influenza A(H1N1) virus illness among pregnant women in the United States. *JAMA* 2010 Apr 21;303(15):1517–1525.

40. Yu H, Feng Z, Uyeki TM, et al. Risk factors for severe illness with 2009 pandemic influenza A (H1N1) virus infection in China. *Clin Infect Dis* 2011 Feb 15;52(4):457–465.

41. Gravenstein S, Davidson HE. Current strategies for management of influenza in the elderly population. *Clin Infect Dis* 2002 Sep 15;35(6):729–737.

42. Lee PY, Matchar DB, Clements DA, et al. Economic analysis of influenza vaccination and antiviral treatment for healthy working adults. *Ann Intern Med* 2002 Aug 20;137(4):225–231.

43. Centers for Disease Control and Prevention (CDC). Prevention and control of seasonal influenza with vaccines. Recommendations of the Advisory Committee in Immunization Practices - United States, 2013-2014. *MMWR Recomm Rep* 2013 Sep 20;62(RR-07):1–43.

44. Block SL, Yogev R, Hayden FG, et al. Shedding and immunogenicity of live attenuated influenza vaccine virus in subjects 5-49 years of age. *Vaccine* 2008 Sep 8;26(38):4940–4946.

45. Talbot TR, Babcock H, Cotton D, et al. The use of live attenuated influenza vaccine (LAIV) in healthcare personnel (HCP): guidance from the Society for Healthcare Epidemiology of America (SHEA). *Infect Control Hosp Epidemiol* 2012 Oct;33(10):981–983.

46. Stowe J, Andrews N, Wise L, et al. Investigation of the temporal association of Guillain-Barre syndrome with influenza vaccine and influenzalike illness using the United Kingdom General Practice Research Database. *Am J Epidemiol* 2009 Feb 1;169(3):382–388.

47. Zimmerman RK, Lin CJ, Raymund M, et al. Hospital policies, state laws, and healthcare worker influenza vaccination rates. *Infect Control Hosp Epidemiol* 2013 Aug;34(8):854–857.

48. Centers for Disease Control and Prevention (CDC). Influenza vaccination coverage among health-care personnel--United States, 2012–13 influenza season. *MMWR Morb Mortal Wkly Rep* 2013 Sep 27;62(38):781–786.

49. Talbot TR, Babcock H, Caplan AL, et al. Revised SHEA position paper: influenza vaccination of healthcare personnel. *Infect Control Hosp Epidemiol* 2010 Oct;31(10):987–995.

50. Babcock HM, Gemeinhart N, Jones M, et al. Mandatory influenza vaccination of health care workers: translating policy to practice. *Clin Infect Dis* 2010 Feb 15;50(4):459–464.

51. Rakita RM, Hagar BA, Crome P, et al. Mandatory influenza vaccination of healthcare workers: a 5-year study. *Infect Control Hosp Epidemiol* 2010 Sep;31(9):881–888.

52. Veenith T, Sanfilippo F, Ercole A, et al. Nosocomial H1N1 infection during 2010-2011 pandemic: a retrospective cohort study from a tertiary referral hospital. *J Hosp Infect* 2012 Jul;81(3):202–205.

53. Ostovar GA, Kohn N, Yu KO, et al. Nosocomial influenza in a pediatric hospital: comparison of rates of seasonal and pandemic 2009 influenza A/H1N1 infection. *Infect Control Hosp Epidemiol* 2012 Mar;33(3):292–294.

54. Berg HF, Van Gendt J, Rimmelzwaan GR, et al. Nosocomial influenza infection among post-influenza-vaccinated patients with severe pulmonary diseases. *J Infect* 2003 Feb;46(2):129–132.

55. Horcajada JP, Pumarola T, Martínez JA, et al. A nosocomial outbreak of influenza during a period without influenza epidemic activity. *Eur Respir J* 2003 Feb;21(2):303–307.

56. Centers for Disease Control and Prevention (CDC). *Prevention Strategies for Seasonal Influenza in Healthcare Settings*. CDC website. 2013. Available at: http://www.cdc.gov/flu/professionals/infectioncontrol/healthcaresettings.htm.

57. Centers for Disease Control and Prevention (CDC). *Guidance for the Prevention and Control of Influenza in the Peri- and Postpartum Settings*. CDC website. 2011. Available at: http://www.cdc.gov/flu/professionals/infectioncontrol/peri-post-settings.htm.

58. Occupational Safety and Health Administration (OSHA). *Pandemic Influenza Preparedness and Response Guidance for Healthcare Workers and Healthcare Employers*. OSHA website. 2009. Available at: https://www.osha.gov/Publications/OSHA_pandemic_health.pdf.

59. Marsden-Haug N, Foster VB, Gould PL, et al. Code-based syndromic surveillance for influenzalike illness by International Classification of Diseases, Ninth Revision. *Emerg Infect Dis* 2007 Feb;13(2):207–216.

60. Siegel JD, Rhinehart E, Jackson M, Chiarello L. 2007 Guideline for Isolation Precautions: Preventing Transmission of Infectious Agents in Health Care Settings. *Am J Infect Control* 2007 Dec;35(10 Suppl 2):S65–164.

61. Lee TB, Montgomery OG, Marx J, et al. Recommended practices for surveillance: Association for Professionals in Infection Control and Epidemiology (APIC), Inc. *Am J Infect Control* 2007 Sep;35(7):427–440.

62. Centers for Disease Control and Prevention (CDC). Hospital Pandemic Influenza Planning Checklist. CDC website. 2007. Available at: http://www.flu.gov/planning-preparedness/hospital/hospitalchecklist.pdf.

SUPPLEMENTAL RESOURCES

Centers for Disease Control and Prevention (CDC). Available at: http://www.cdc.gov/flu/

Centers for Disease Control and Prevention (CDC). Information on the clinical signs and diagnosis of influenza. CDC website. 2013. Available at: http://www.cdc.gov/flu/professionals/diagnosis/.

Centers for Disease Control and Prevention/National Center for Infectious Diseases (CDC/NCID). Seasonal influenza (flu). CDC website. 2014. Available at: http://www.cdc.gov/ncidod/diseases/flu/fluvirus.htm.

University of Pittsburgh. Open Source Real-time Outbreak Surveillance (RODS). RODS website. 2013. Available at: http://openrods.sourceforge.net/.

The Society for Healthcare Epidemiology of America (SHEA). SHEA Resources and Statements. SHEA website. 2013. Available at: http://www.shea-online.org/HAITopics/Influenza.aspx.

CHAPTER 83

Foodborne Illnesses

Ynes Ortega, PhD, MPH
Associate Professor
Center for Food Safety
University of Georgia
Griffin, GA

ABSTRACT

According to the U.S. Centers for Disease Control and Prevention, each year foodborne diseases cause an estimated 48 million illnesses every year in the United States. This includes 9.4 million caused by known pathogens.[1] It is estimated that 55,961 hospitalizations and 1,351 deaths occur annually in the United States from foodborne illnesses, and that 31 major pathogens are primarily responsible.[2] Those most affected are very young, elderly, immunocompromised, and underserved (as it relates to racial and ethnic populations) populations. New foodborne diseases are emerging, and increased global travel and trade broaden the opportunities and deepen the risks of contracting and spreading foodborne illness.

KEY CONCEPTS

- Physicians and other healthcare professionals should[2]:

  - Recognize the potential for a foodborne etiology in a patient's illness.

  - Realize that many cases of foodborne illness have gastrointestinal tract symptoms.

  - Obtain stool cultures in appropriate settings and recognize that testing for some specific pathogens (e.g., *Escherichia coli* O157:H7, *Vibrio* species) must be requested.

  - Report suspected cases to appropriate public health officials

  - Talk with patients about ways to prevent foodborne diseases. Preventing foodborne diseases through food safety education is effective when the healthcare professional increases the patient's understanding of the relationship between a specific behavior that may have caused the foodborne illness. The five major control factors for pathogens are personal hygiene, adequate cooking, avoiding cross-contamination, keeping food at safe temperatures, and avoiding foods from unsafe sources.

  - Appreciate that any patient with foodborne illness may represent the sentinel case of a more widespread outbreak.

BACKGROUND

To provide practical and concise information on the diagnosis, treatment, and reporting of foodborne illnesses, several government agencies and professional associations collaboratively developed *Diagnosis and Management of Foodborne Illnesses: A Primer for Physicians and Other Health Care Professionals.*[2] This primer was developed by the American Medical Association, the American Nurses Association–American Nurse Foundation, the U.S. Centers for Disease Control and Prevention (CDC), the U.S. Food and Drug Administration's Center for Food Safety and Nutrition, and the U.S. Department of Agriculture's Food Safety and Inspection Service. Copies can be downloaded from the website of the CDC (www.cdc.gov/mmwr/preview/mmwrhtml/rr5304a1.htm). Updated information on foodborne pathogen surveillance and studies aimed at estimating the number of episodes, hospitalizations, and deaths caused by foodborne etiologies assist with the analysis of food safety policy and interventions.

The primary focus of this chapter is the four summary tables that can be found in the primer. These tables, which are reproduced here, succinctly present the etiology, incubation period, signs, symptoms, and other essential information about bacterial, viral, parasitic, and noninfectious foodborne illnesses.

New information on food safety is constantly emerging. Recommendations and precautions for people and those at high risk are updated whenever new data about preventing foodborne illnesses become available. Physicians and other healthcare professionals need to be aware of and follow the most current information on food safety.

BASIC PRINCIPLES

- Foodborne illness is related to food ingestion. Gastrointestinal (GI) tract symptoms are the most common clinical manifestations of foodborne illness.

- Foodborne illnesses can be caused by microorganisms, marine organisms, fungi (and their related toxins), and chemical contaminants.

- The bacterial agents most often associated with foodborne illness in the United States include *Salmonella* spp. (11 percent), *Clostridium perfringens* (10 percent), and *Campylobacter* spp. (9 percent).

- Viruses are the most common cause of foodborne illness (58 percent), though testing for viral etiologies of diarrheal disease is rare.

- Leading causes of hospitalizations are nontyphoidal *Salmonella* spp. (35 percent), norovirus (26 percent), *Campylobacter* spp. (15 percent), and *Toxoplasma gondii* (8 percent).[3]

- Leading causes of death are nontyphoidal *Salmonella* spp. (28 percent), *T. gondii* (24 percent), *Listeria monocytogenes* (19 percent), and norovirus (11 percent).[3]

- Requirements for reporting diseases and conditions are mandated by state and territorial laws and/or regulations, but physicians and infection preventionists are encouraged to report all foodborne illness they encounter in an effort to recognize and promote an early response to an outbreak. Some factors to explore to determine the etiology of potential foodborne illness include the incubation period, duration of the resultant illness, predominant clinical symptoms, and the population involved in the outbreak.

FOODBORNE ILLNESS

Bacterial Agents

See Table 83-1.

Viral Agents

See Table 83-2.

Parasitic Agents

See Table 83-3.

Noninfectious Agents

See Table 83-4.

Table 83-1. Foodborne Illnesses (Bacterial)

Etiology	Incubation Period	Signs and Symptoms	Duration of Illness	Associated Foods	Laboratory Testing	Treatment
Bacillus anthracis	2 d to weeks	Nausea, vomiting, malaise, bloody diarrhea, acute abdominal pain	Weeks	Insufficiently cooked contaminated meat	Blood	Penicillin is first choice for naturally acquired gastrointestinal anthrax. Ciprofloxacin is second option.
Bacillus cereus (diarrheal toxin)	8–16 hr	Abdominal cramps, watery diarrhea, nausea	24–48 hr	Meats, stews, gravies, vanilla sauce, vegetables, milk products	Testing not necessary, self-limiting (consider testing food and stool for toxin in outbreaks).	Supportive care
Bacillus cereus (preformed enterotoxin)	1–6 hr	Sudden onset of severe nausea and vomiting; diarrhea may be present	24 hr	Improperly refrigerated cooked and fried rice, meats, pasta, pastry, noodles	Normally a clinical diagnosis. Clinical laboratories do not routinely identify this organism. If indicated, send stool and food specimens to reference laboratory for culture and toxin identification.	Supportive care
Brucella abortus, B. melitensis, and *B. suis*	7–21 d	Fever, chills, sweating, weakness, headache, muscle and joint pain, diarrhea, bloody stools during acute phase	Weeks	Raw milk, goat cheese made from unpasteurized milk, contaminated meats	Blood culture and positive serology	Acute: rifampin and doxycycline daily for 6 weeks. Infections with complications require combination therapy with rifampin, tetracycline, and an aminoglycoside.
Campylobacter jejuni	2–5 d	Diarrhea, cramps, fever and vomiting; diarrhea may be bloody	2–10 d	Raw and undercooked poultry, unpasteurized milk, contaminated water	Routine stool culture; Campylobacter requires special media and incubation at 42°C to grow.	Supportive care. For severe cases, antibiotics such as erythromycin and quinolones may be indicated early in the diarrheal disease. Guillian-Barré syndrome can be a sequela.
Clostridium botulinum— children and adults (preformed toxin)	12–72 hr	Vomiting, diarrhea, blurred vision, diplopia, dysphagia, and descending muscle weakness	Variable (from days to months). Can be complicated by respiratory failure and death.	Home-canned foods with a low acid content, improperly canned commercial foods, home-canned or fermented fish, herb-infused oils, baked potatoes in aluminum foil, cheese sauce, bottled garlic, foods held warm for extended periods of time (e.g., in a warm oven)	Stool, serum, and food can be tested for toxin. Stool and food can also be cultured for the organism. The tests can be performed at some state health department laboratories and the CDC.	Supportive care. *Botulinum* antitoxin is helpful if given early in the course of the illness. Contact the state health department. The 24-hour number for professionals and general public is 770-488-7100 (CDC/Agency for Toxic Substances Disease Registry).

Table 83-1. Foodborne Illnesses (Bacterial) *(continued)*

Etiology	Incubation Period	Signs and Symptoms	Duration of Illness	Associated Foods	Laboratory Testing	Treatment
Clostridium botulinum—infants	3–30 d	In infants younger than 12 months, lethargy, weakness, poor feeding, constipation, hypotonia, poor head control, poor gag and sucking reflex	Variable	Honey, home-canned vegetables and fruits, corn syrup	Stool, serum, and food can be tested for toxin. Stool and food can also be cultured for the organism. The tests can be performed at some state health department laboratories and the CDC.	Supportive care. Botulism immune globulin can be obtained from the Infant Botulism Prevention Program, Health and Human Services, California at 510-540-2646. *Botulinum* antitoxin is generally not recommended for infants.
Clostridium perfringens toxin	8–16 hr	Watery diarrhea, nausea, abdominal cramps; fever is rare	24–48 hr	Meats, poultry, gravy, dried or precooked foods, time- and/or temperature-abused food	Stools can be tested for enterotoxin and cultured for organism. Because *Clostridium perfringens* can normally be found in stool, quantitative cultures can be done.	Supportive care. Antibiotics not indicated.
Enterohemorrhagic *Escherichia coli* (EHEC), including *E. coli* O157:H7 and other Shiga toxin-producing *E. coli* (STEC)	1–8 d	Severe diarrhea that is often bloody, abdominal pain, and vomiting. Usually, little or no fever is present. More common in children younger than 4 years.	5–10 d	Undercooked beef, especially hamburger, unpasteurized milk and juice, raw fruits and vegetables (e.g., sprouts), salami (rarely), and contaminated water	Stool culture; *E. coli* O157:H7 requires special media to grow. If *E. coli* O157:H7 is suspected, specific testing must be requested. Shiga toxin testing may be done using commercial kits; positive isolates should be forwarded to public health laboratories for confirmation and serotyping.	Supportive care, monitor renal function, hemoglobin, and platelets closely. *E. coli* O157:H7 infection is also associated with hemolytic uremic syndrome (HUS), which can cause lifelong complications. Studies indicate that antibiotics may promote the development of HUS.
Enterotoxigenic *E. coli* (ETEC)	1–3 d	Watery diarrhea, abdominal cramps, some vomiting	3–7 d	Water or food contaminated with human feces	Stool culture. ETEC requires special laboratory techniques for identification. If suspected, must request specific testing.	Supportive care. Antibiotics are rarely needed except in severe cases. Recommended antibiotics include trimethoprim/sulfamethoxazole (TMP-SMX) and quinolones.
Cronobacter sakazakii	Infants within a few days	In premature babies and babies younger than 1 year old: Fever, poor feeding, irritability, jaundice, seizures. Some babies develop meningitis, necrotizing enterocolitis, sepsis. Death rate is 10 to 80 percent in infants younger than 2 months old. Can be serious in the elderly or immunocompromised	Among survivors 2–8 weeks	Powdered baby formula, powdered milk, herbal teas, starches. Person to person	Laboratory culture	Ampicillin and gentamicin
Listeria monocytogenes	9–48 hr for gastrointestinal symptoms, 2–6 wk for invasive disease. At birth and infancy	Fever, muscle aches, and nausea or diarrhea. Pregnant women may have mild flulike illness, and infection can lead to premature delivery or stillbirth. Elderly or immunocompromised patients may have bacteremia or meningitis. Infants infected from a mother at risk for sepsis or meningitis.	Variable	Fresh soft cheeses, unpasteurized or inadequately pasteurized milk, ready-to-eat deli meats, hot dogs	Blood or cerebrospinal fluid (CSF) cultures. Asymptomatic fecal carriage occurs; therefore, stool culture usually not helpful. Antibody to listeriolysin may be helpful to identify outbreak retrospectively.	Supportive care and antibiotics; intravenous ampicillin, penicillin, or TMP-SMX are recommended for invasive disease.

(continued)

Table 83-1. Foodborne Illnesses (Bacterial) *(continued)*

Etiology	Incubation Period	Signs and Symptoms	Duration of Illness	Associated Foods	Laboratory Testing	Treatment
Salmonella spp.	1–3 d	Diarrhea, fever, abdominal cramps, vomiting. *S. typhi* and *S. paratyphi* produce typhoid with insidious onset characterized by fever, headache, constipation, malaise, chills, and myalgia; diarrhea is uncommon, and vomiting is usually not severe.	4–7 d	Contaminated eggs, poultry, unpasteurized milk or juice, cheese, contaminated raw fruits and vegetables (alfalfa sprouts, melons). *S. typhi* epidemics are often related to fecal contamination of water supplies or street-vended foods.	Routine stool cultures	Supportive care. Other than for *S. typhi* and *S. paratyphi*, antibiotics are not indicated unless there is extra-intestinal spread of infection or the risk of such spread. Consider ampicillin, gentamicin, TMP-SMX, or quinolones if indicated. A vaccine exists for *S. typhi*.
Shigella spp.	24–48 hr	Uncommon cause of foodborne illness and vomiting is usually not severe. Abdominal cramps, fever, and diarrhea. Stools may contain blood and mucus.	4–7 d	Food or water contaminated with human fecal material. Usually person-to-person spread, fecal-oral transmission. Ready-to-eat foods (e.g., raw vegetables, salads, sandwiches) touched by infected food workers.	Routine stool cultures	Supportive care. TMP-SMX recommended in the United States if organism is susceptible; nalidixic acid or other quinolones may be indicated if organism is resistant, especially in developing countries.
Staphylococcus aureus (performed enterotoxin)	1–6 hr	Sudden onset of severe nausea and vomiting. Abdominal cramps. Diarrhea and fever may be present.	24–48 hr	Unrefrigerated or improperly refrigerated meats, potato and egg salads, cream pastries.	Normally a clinical diagnosis. Stool, vomitus, and food can be tested for toxin and cultured if indicated.	Supportive care
Vibrio cholerae (toxin)	24–72 hr	Profuse watery diarrhea and vomiting, which can lead to severe dehydration and death within hours.	3–7 d, causes life-threatening dehydration.	Contaminated water, fish, shellfish, street-vendor food; typically from Latin America or Asia.	Stool culture; *V. cholerae* requires special media to grow. If *V. cholerae* is suspected, specific testing must be requested.	Supportive care with aggressive oral and intravenous rehydration. In cases of confirmed cholera, tetracycline or doxycycline is recommended for adults, and TMP-SMX for children (younger than 8 y).
Vibrio parahaemolyticus	2–48 hr	Watery diarrhea, abdominal cramps, nausea, vomiting	2–5 d	Undercooked or raw seafood, such as fish, shellfish	Stool cultures. *V. parahaemolyticus* requires special media to grow. If *V. vulnificus* is suspected, specific testing must be requested.	Supportive care and antibiotics; tetracycline, doxycycline, and ceftazidime are recommended.
Vibrio vulnificus	1–7 d	Vomiting, diarrhea, abdominal pain, bacteremia, and wound infections. Most common in immunocompromised persons or in patients with chronic liver disease (presenting with bullous skin lesions). Can be fatal in patients with liver disease and immunocompromised persons.	2–8 d	Undercooked or raw shellfish, especially oysters; other contaminated seafood, and open wounds exposed to seawater.	Stool, wound, or blood cultures. *V. vulnificus* requires special media to grow. If *V. vulnificus* is suspected, specific testing must be requested.	Supportive care and antibiotics; tetracycline, doxycycline, and ceftazidime are recommended.
Yersinia enterocolitica and *Y. pseudo-tuberculosis*	24–48 hr	Appendicitis-like symptoms (diarrhea and vomiting, fever, and abdominal pain) occur primarily in older children and young adults. May develop erythema nodosum with *Y. pseudotuberculosis*.	1–3 wk, usually self-limiting	Undercooked pork, unpasteurized milk, tofu, contaminated water. Infection has occurred in infants whose caregivers handled chitterlings.	Stool, vomitus, or blood culture. *Yersinia* requires special media to grow. If *Yersinia* is suspected, specific testing must be requested. Serology is available in research and reference laboratories.	Supportive care. If septicemia or other invasive disease occurs, antibiotic therapy with gentamicin or cefotaxime. Doxycycline and ciprofloxacin also effective.

Table 83-2. Foodborne Illnesses (Viral)

Etiology	Incubation Period	Signs and Symptoms	Duration of Illness	Associated Foods	Laboratory Testing	Treatment
Hepatitis A	28 d average (15–50 d)	Diarrhea, dark urine, jaundice, and flulike symptoms (i.e., fever, headache, nausea, and abdominal pain).	Variable, 2 wk–3 mo	Shellfish harvested from contaminated waters, raw produce, contaminated drinking water, undercooked foods, and cooked foods that are not reheated after contact with infected food handler.	Increase in alanine transaminase (ALT), bilirubin. Positive immunoglobulin M (IgM) and antihepatitis A antibodies.	Supportive care. Prevention with immunization.
Hepatitis E	15–60 days	Fever, fatigue, loss of appetite, nausea, vomiting, abdominal pain, jaundice, dark urine, clay-colored stools, joint pain.	Infectious up to 14 days after onset of jaundice.	Contaminated water or foods. Uncooked/ undercooked pork or deer meat. Shellfish.	Testing for Hepatitis E virus (HEV) or HEV RNA. Considered in persons returning from HEV-endemic regions and seronegative for Hepatitis A, B, C, or other hepatotropic viruses.	Supportive care. No FDA-approved vaccine available in the United States.
Noroviruses (and other caliciviruses)	12–48 hr	Nausea, vomiting, abdominal cramping, diarrhea, fever, myalgia, and some headache. Diarrhea is more prevalent in adults, and vomiting is more prevalent in children.	12–60 hr	Shellfish, fecally contaminated foods, ready-to-eat foods (salads, sandwiches, ice, cookies, fruit) touched by infected food workers.	Routine reverse transcriptase polymerase chain reaction (RT-PCR) and electron microscopy (EM) on fresh unpreserved stool samples. Clinical diagnosis, negative bacterial cultures. Stool is negative for white blood cells (WBCs).	Supportive care such as rehydration. Good hygiene.
Rotavirus	1–3 d	Vomiting, watery diarrhea, low-grade fever. Temporary lactose intolerance may occur. Infants, children, and elderly and immunocompromised persons are especially vulnerable.	4–8 d	Foods contaminated with feces. Ready-to-eat foods (salads, fruit) touched by infected food workers.	Identification of virus in stool via immunoassay.	Supportive care. Severe diarrhea may require fluid and electrolyte replacement. Vaccine currently available for infants
Other viral agents (astroviruses, adenoviruses, parvoviruses)	10–70 hr	Nausea, vomiting, diarrhea, malaise, abdominal pain, headache, fever.	2–9 d	Foods contaminated with feces. Ready-to-eat foods touched by infected food workers. Some shellfish.	Identification of the virus in early acute stool samples. Serology. Commercial enzyme-linked immunosorbent assay (ELISA) kits are now available for adenoviruses and astroviruses.	Supportive care, usually mild, self-limiting. Good hygiene.

Table 83-3. Foodborne Illnesses (Parasitic)

Etiology	Incubation Period	Signs and Symptoms	Duration of Illness	Associated Foods	Laboratory Testing	Treatment
Angiostrongylus cantonensis	1 wk–1 mo	Severe headaches, nausea, vomiting, neck stiffness, paresthesias, hyperesthesias, seizures, and other neurologic abnormalities.	Several weeks to several months.	Raw or undercooked intermediate hosts (e.g., snails or slugs), infected paratenic (transport) hosts (e.g., crabs, freshwater shrimp), fresh produce contaminated with intermediate or transport hosts.	Examination of CSF for elevated pressure, proteins, leukocytes, and eosinophils; serologic testing using ELISA to detect antibodies to *A. cantonensis*.	Supportive care. Repeat lumbar punctures and corticosteroid therapy may be used for more severely ill patients.
Anisakis simplex	24h–2wk	Invasive anisakiasis: severe stomach and abdominal pain, nausea, vomiting, diarrhea. Some develop a strong allergic reaction	Weeks to months	Ocean fish and cephalopods. Cod, haddock, fluke, Pacific salmon, herring, flounder, monkfish, squid	History of consumption of raw ocean fish, endoscopy, radiography, surgery	Removal of worm from body by endoscopy or surgery
Cryptosporidium spp.	2–10 d	Diarrhea (usually watery), stomach cramps, upset stomach, slight fever.	May be remitting and relapsing over weeks to months.	Any undercooked food or food contaminated by an ill food handler after cooking; drinking water.	Request specific examination of the stool for *Cryptosporidium*. May need to examine water or food.	Supportive care, self-limited. If severe, consider paromomycin for 7 days. For children aged 1 to 11 years, consider nitazoxanide for 3 days.
Cyclospora cayetanensis	1–14 d, usually at least 1 wk	Diarrhea (usually watery), loss of appetite, substantial loss of weight, stomach cramps, nausea, vomiting, fatigue.	May be remitting and relapsing over weeks to months.	Various types of fresh produce (imported berries, lettuce, herbs), water.	Request specific examination of the stool for *Cyclospora*. May need to examine water or food.	TMP-SMX for 7 d
Giardia lamblia	1–2 weeks	Malodorous diarrhea, malaise, abdominal pain, flatulence, weight loss. Prolonged infections in children may result in stunted growth and development.	2–6 weeks. May persist for months.	Contaminated water or fresh food. Person to person.	Ova and parasite examination. Commercial direct fluorescence antibody test kits, ELISA.	Metronidazole
Entamoeba histolytica	2–3 d to 1–4 wk	Diarrhea (often bloody), frequent bowel movements, lower abdominal pain.	May be protracted (several weeks to several months).	Any uncooked food or food contaminated by an ill food handler after cooking; drinking water.	Examination of stool for cysts and parasites; may need at least three samples.	Metronidazole
Tenia solium (teniasis)	2–4 months	Usually asymptomatic, nausea, diarrhea, abdominal pain, general malaise. Complications may result in autoinfection and development of cysticercosis.	Years	Insufficiently cooked pork.	Ova and parasite examination. Fecal ELISA test. Examination of expelled proglotids and/or scolex.	Antihelminthic drugs praziquantel or niclosamide
Tenia solium (cysticercosis)	2 months to years	Can be asymptomatic, depends on localization of cyst. Neurocysticercosis presents with seizures, headache, altered mental status, increased intracranial pressure.	Months–years	Contaminated water, foods, or hands during food preparation.	If in eye by ophthalmoscope, if in brain, computed tomography (CT) or serology.	Antiinflamatory and antihelminthic drugs. Treatment should be carefully monitored by experts on matter. Surgery may be needed.

Table 83-3. Foodborne Illnesses (Parasitic) *(continued)*

Etiology	Incubation Period	Signs and Symptoms	Duration of Illness	Associated Foods	Laboratory Testing	Treatment
Toxoplasma gondii	5–23 d	Generally asymptomatic; 20 percent may develop cervical lymphadenopathy and/or a flulike illness. In immunocompromised patients, central nervous system (CNS) disease, myocarditis, or pneumonitis is often seen.	Months	Accidental ingestion of contaminated substances (e.g., soil contaminated with cat feces on fruit and vegetables), raw or partly cooked meat (especially pork, lamb, or venison). Passed from mother (who acquired acute infection during pregnancy) to child.	Isolation of parasites from blood or other body fluids; observation of parasites in patient specimens via microscopy or histology. Detection of organisms is rare; serology (reference laboratory needed) can be a useful adjunct in diagnosing toxoplasmosis. However, IgM antibodies may persist for 6 to 18 months and thus may not necessarily indicate recent infection. PCR of bodily fluids. For congenital infection, isolation of *T. gondii* from the placenta, umbilical cord, or infant blood. PCR of white blood cells, CSF, or amniotic fluid, or IgM and IgA serology performed by a reference laboratory.	Asymptomatic healthy, but infected, persons do not require treatment. Spiramycin or pyrimethamine plus sulfadiazine may be used for pregnant women. Pyrimethamine plus sulfadiazine (with or without steroids) may be given for ocular disease when indicated. Folic acid is given with pyrimethamine plus sulfadiazine therapy to counteract bone marrow suppression.
Toxoplasma gondii (congenital infection)	In infants at birth	Treatment of the mother may reduce severity and/or incidence of congenital infection. Most infected infants have few symptoms at birth. Later, they generally develop signs of congenital toxoplasmosis (mental retardation, severely impaired eyesight, cerebral palsy, seizures) unless the infection is treated.				
Trichinella spiralis	1–2 d for initial symptoms, others begin 2–8 wk after infection.	Acute: nausea, diarrhea vomiting, fatigue, fever, abdominal discomfort followed by muscle soreness, weakness, and occasional cardiac and neurologic complications.	Months	Raw or undercooked contaminated meat, usually pork or wild game meat (e.g., bear or moose).	Positive serology or demonstration of larvae via muscle biopsy. Increase in eosinophils.	Supportive care plus mebendazole or albendazole.

Table 83-4. Foodborne Illnesses (Noninfectious)

Etiology	Incubation Period	Signs and Symptoms	Duration of Illness	Associated Foods	Laboratory Testing	Treatment
Aflatoxins	Cumulative effect	Hemorrhage, jaundice, premature cell death, tissue necrosis of the liver. Edema of lower extremities, abdominal pain, vomiting. Chronic exposure may lead to hepatocellular carcinoma.	Not described	Corn, sorghum, rice, cottonseed, peanuts, tree nuts, cocoa beans, nutmeg.	Presence of aflatoxins in blood, milk, urine.	Supportive care
Antimony	5 min–8 hr usually <1 hr	Vomiting, metallic taste	Usually self-limited	Metallic container	Identification of metal in beverage or food	Supportive care
Arsenic	Few hours	Vomiting, colic, diarrhea	Several days	Contaminated foods	Urine; may cause eosinophilia	Gastric lavage, broncheoalveolar lavage
Cadmium	5 min–8 hr usually less than 1 hr	Nausea, vomiting, myalgia, increase in salivation, stomach pain	Usually self-limited	Seafood, oysters, clams, lobster, grains, peanuts	Identification of metal in food	Supportive care
Ciguatera fish poisoning (ciguatera toxin)	2–6 hr 3 hr 2–5 d	*GI*: abdominal pain, nausea, vomiting, diarrhea *Neurological*: paresthesias, reversal of hot or cold, pain, weakness *Cardiovascular*: bradycardia, hypotension, increase in T-wave abnormalities.	Days to weeks to months	A variety of large reef fish; grouper, red snapper, amberjack, and barracuda (most common).	Radioassay for toxin in fish or a constant history.	Supportive care, IV mannitol. Children more vulnerable.

(continued)

Table 83-4. Foodborne Illnesses (Noninfectious) *(continued)*

Etiology	Incubation Period	Signs and Symptoms	Duration of Illness	Associated Foods	Laboratory Testing	Treatment
Copper	5 min–8 hr usually less than 1 hr	Nausea, vomiting, blue or green vomitus	Usually self-limited	Metallic container	Identification of metal in beverage or food	Supportive care
Mercury	1 wk or longer	Numbness, weakness of legs, spastic paralysis, impaired vision, blindness, coma. Pregnant women and the developing fetus are especially vulnerable.	May be protracted	Fish exposed to organic mercury, grain treated with mercury fungicides.	Analysis of blood, hair	Supportive care
Mushroom toxins, short-acting (museinol, muscarine, psilocybin, coprius artemetaris, ibotenic acid)	<2 hr	Vomiting, diarrhea, confusion, visual disturbance, salivation, diaphoresis, hallucinations, disulfiram-like reaction, confusion, visual disturbance.	Self-limited	Wild mushrooms (cooking may not destroy these toxins)	Typical syndrome and mushroom identified or demonstration of the toxin.	Supportive care
Mushroom toxin, long-acting (amanitin)	4–8 hr diarrhea; 24–48 hr liver failure	Diarrhea, abdominal cramps, leading to hepatic and renal failure.	Often fatal	Mushrooms	Typical syndrome and mushroom identified and/or demonstration of the toxin.	Supportive care; life-threatening, may need life support.
Nitrite poisoning	1–2 hr	Nausea, vomiting, cyanosis, headache, dizziness, weakness, loss of consciousness, chocolate-brown colored blood.	Usually self-limiting	Cured meats, any contaminated foods, spinach exposed to excessive nitrification.	Analysis of the food, blood	Supportive care, methylene blue
Pesticides (organophosphates or carbamates)	Few minutes to few hours	Nausea, vomiting, abdominal cramps, diarrhea, headache, nervousness, blurred vision, twitching, convulsions, salivation, can progress to paralysis and respiratory arrest.	Usually self-limited	Any contaminated foods	Analysis of the food, blood	Atropine; 2-PAM (Pralidoxime) is used when atropine is not able to control symptoms and is rarely necessary in carbamate poisoning.
Puffer fish (tetrodotoxin)	Less than 30 min	Paresthesias, vomiting, diarrhea, abdominal pain, ascending paralysis, respiratory failure.	Death usually in 4–6 hr.	Puffer fish	Detection of tetrodotoxin in fish.	Life-threatening, may need respiratory support.
Scombroid (histamine)	1 min–3 hr	Flushing, rash, burning sensation of skin, mouth and throat, dizziness, urticaria, paresthesias.	3–6 hr	Fish: bluefin tuna, skipjack, mackerel, martin, escolar, and mahi-mahi.	Demonstration of histamine in food or clinical diagnosis.	Supportive care
Shellfish toxins (diarrheic, neurotoxic, amnesic)	Diarrhea shellfish poisoning (DSP), 30 min–2 hr Neurotoxic shellfish poisoning (NSP), few minutes to hours Amnesic shellfish poisoning (ASP), 24–48 hr	Nausea, vomiting, diarrhea, and abdominal pain accompanied by chills, headache, and fever. Tingling and numbness of lips, tongue, and throat; muscular aches; dizziness; reversal of the sensations of hot and cold; diarrhea; and vomiting. Vomiting, diarrhea, abdominal pain, and neurological problems, such as confusion, memory loss, disorientation, seizure, coma.	Hours to 2–3 d	A variety of shellfish, primarily mussels, oysters, scallops, and shellfish from the Florida coast and the Gulf of Mexico. Toxins are produced by microscopic algae (dinoflagelates, algae), and cyanobacteria and accumulated by shellfish.	Detection of the toxin in shellfish; high-pressure liquid chromatography.	Supportive care, generally self-limiting. Elderly persons are especially sensitive to ASP.

Table 83-4. Foodborne Illnesses (Noninfectious) *(continued)*

Etiology	Incubation Period	Signs and Symptoms	Duration of Illness	Associated Foods	Laboratory Testing	Treatment
Shellfish toxins (paralytic shellfish poisoning)	30 min–3 hr	Diarrhea, nausea, vomiting leading to paresthesias of mouth, lips; weakness, dysphasia, dysphonia, respiratory paralysis.	Days	Scallops, mussels, clams, cockles. Toxins are produced by microscopic algae (dinoflagelates, algae), and cyanobacteria and accumulated by shellfish.	Detection of toxin in food or water where fish are located; high-pressure liquid chromatography.	Life-threatening, may need respiratory support.
Sodium fluoride	Few minutes–2 hr	Salty or soapy taste, numbness of mouth, vomiting, diarrhea, dilated pupils, spasms, pallor, shock, collapse.	Usually self-limited	Dry foods (such as dry milk, flour, baking powder, cake mixes) contaminated with sodium fluoride-containing insecticides and rodenticides.	Testing of vomitus or gastric washings; analysis of the food.	Supportive care
Thallium	Few hours	Nausea, vomiting, diarrhea, painful paresthesias, motor polyneuropathy, hair loss.	Several days	Contaminated food	Urine, hair	Supportive care
Tin	5 min–8 hr. usually less than 1 hr	Nausea, vomiting, diarrhea	Usually self-limited	Metallic container	Analysis of the food	Supportive care
Vomitoxin	Few minutes to 3 hr	Nausea, headache, abdominal pain, vomiting	Usually self-limited	Grains such as wheat, corn, barley	Analysis of the food	Supportive care
Zinc	Few hours	Stomach cramps, nausea, vomiting, diarrhea, myalgia.	Usually self-limited	Metallic container	Analysis of the food, blood and feces, saliva or urine.	Supportive care

Prions and Transmissible Spongiform Encephalopathies

Prions are proteins that under normal physiologic conditions are found on a variety of cells, particularly in the nervous tissue. The disease develops when normal prions come into contact with disease-causing prions. These proteins are misfolded and can induce other normally folded proteins to misfold and cause variant Creutzfeldt-Jakob disease (vCJD). It can be acquired by ingestion of diseased cattle meat. Symptoms appear after about 10 years and include depression, psychiatric problems, and neurologic symptoms that can lead to death. Disease can last from months to years. Diagnosis of vCJD is based on patient history and clinical symptoms. Supportive therapy is recommended.

CONCLUSIONS

The relationship between the safety of our food supply and the development of illness has become an increasingly important concern for both consumers and healthcare providers. Food that is contaminated with a disease-causing pathogen often looks, smells, and tastes like a safe food product, so connecting the illness with a food is very difficult unless other patients present with the same symptoms. Travel to areas where sanitation is not ideal and consumption of foods prepared without proper cooking practices that may be risk factor for acquiring emerging and exotic diseases not endemic to the place of residence.

In a healthcare setting, the infection preventionist should be actively involved in monitoring and evaluating the operational aspects of food service in an effort to prevent foodborne illness in patients, families, visitors, medical staff, and healthcare facility staff. In addition to this internal monitoring and evaluation, the infection preventionist is responsible for reporting cases of potential foodborne illnesses to the appropriate public health entities. It is therefore important for infection preventionists to report noticeable increases in unusual illnesses, symptom complexes, or disease patterns (even without definitive diagnosis) to public health authorities. Prompt reporting of unusual patterns of diarrheal/GI tract illness, for example, can allow public health officials to initiate an epidemiologic investigation earlier than would be possible if the report was delayed until a definitive etiologic diagnosis was made.

FUTURE TRENDS

In addition to the information presented in this chapter, emerging infections are becoming increasingly recognized as important aspects of food safety. Examples of avian influenza and its impact on poultry, bovine spongiform encephalopathy and its impact on the beef industry, and the emergence of severe acute respiratory syndrome (SARS) and its epidemiologic links to the open-air markets in some Asian countries demonstrate the relationships among cultures, environments, and food safety. New information on food safety is constantly emerging and should be part of the continuous education process of the infection preventionist. Recommendations and additional information can be obtained through public health information networks such as the CDC and local health departments. Healthcare professionals need to be aware of and follow the most current information on food safety.

INTERNATIONAL PERSPECTIVE

Increased opportunities for travel and trade bring increased risks of contracting and spreading a foodborne illness locally, regionally, and even globally. In many parts of the world, the incidence of traditional foodborne illnesses and the emergence of new diseases are the result of shifts in human demographics and food preferences, changes in food production and distribution systems, globalization, microbial adaptation, and strained or inadequate public health systems.

REFERENCES

1. Gould LH, Walsh KA, Vieira AR, et al. Surveillance for Foodborne disease outbreaks – United States, 1998-2008. *MMWR Surveill Summ* [serial online]. 2013 Jun 28;62(2):1–34. Available at: http://www.cdc.gov/mmwr/preview/mmwrhtml/ss6202a1.htm?s_cid=ss6202a1_w.
2. American Medical Association, American Nurses Association–American Nurses Foundation, Centers for Disease Control and Prevention, et al. Diagnosis and management of foodborne illnesses: a primer for physicians and other health care professionals. *MMWR Morb Mortal Wkly Rep* [serial online]. 2004 Apr 16;53(RR-04):1–33. Available at: www.cdc.gov/mmwr/preview/mmwrhtml/rr5304a1.htm.
3. Scallan E, Hoekstra RM, Angulo FJ, et al. Foodborne illness acquired in the United States—major pathogens. *Emerg Infect Dis* 2011 Jan;17(1):7–15.

SUPPLEMENTAL RESOURCES

American Medical Association (AMA). Available at: http://search0.ama-assn.org/main/jsp/templates/primaryJSP/fullview.jsp?keyword=foodborne&FilterList=&advancedSearch=&sort=&pagination=.

Batz MB, Hoffmann S, and Morris JG. Ranking the disease burden of 14 pathogens in food sources in the United States using attribution data from outbreak investigations and expert elicitation. *J Food Prot* 2012 Jul;75(7):1278–1291.

Center for Food Safety and Applied Nutrition, Food and Drug Administration. Available at: http://www.cfsan.fda.gov.

Centers for Disease Control and Prevention (CDC). Available at: http://www.cdc.gov/foodsafety/cme.htm.

Council of State and Territorial Epidemiologists (CSTE). Details on specific state requirements available at: www.cste.org/nndss/reportingrequirements.htm. CSTE, Suite 303–2872 Woodcock Boulevard, Atlanta, GA 30341; telephone: 770 458–3811.

Fan X, Sokorai KJ, Engemann J, et al. Inactivation of *Listeria innocua*, *Salmonella typhimurium*, and *Escherichia coli* O157:H7 on surface and stem scar areas of tomatoes using in-package ozonation. *J Food Prot* 2012 Sep;75(9):1611–1618.

FDA Bad Bug Book. Available at: http://www.fda.gov/downloads/food/foodborneillnesscontaminants/ucm297627.pdf.

Food Safety and Inspection Service, U.S. Department of Agriculture. Available at: http://www.fsis.usda.gov.

Lund BM, O'Brien SJ. The occurrence and prevention of foodborne disease in vulnerable people. *Foodborne Pathog Dis* 2011 Sep;8(9):961–973.

Scallan E, Griffin PM, Angulo FJ, et al. Foodborne illness acquired in the United States—unspecified agents. *Emerg Infect Dis* 2011 Jan;17(1):16–22.

Sofos JN, Geornaras I. Overview of current meat hygiene and safety risks and summary of recent studies on biofilms, and control of *Escherichia coli* O157:H7 in non-intact, and *Listeria monocytogenes* in ready-to-eat, meat products. *Meat Sci* 2010 Sep;86(1):2–14.

Thayer DW. Irradiation of food—helping to ensure food safety. *N Engl J Med* 2004 Apr 29;350(18):1811–1812.

Todd EC, Michaels BS, Greig JD, et al. Outbreaks where food workers have been implicated in the spread of foodborne disease. Part 7. Barriers to reduce contamination of food by workers. *J Food Prot* [serial online]. 2010 Aug;73(8):1552–6155. Available at: http://www.ncbi.nlm.nih.gov/pubmed?term=Smith%20D%5BAuthor%5D&cauthor=true&cauthor_uid=20819372.

CHAPTER 84

Legionella pneumophila

Janet E. Stout, PhD
Special Pathogens Laboratory
Department of Civil and Environmental Engineering
University of Pittsburgh, Swanson School of Engineering
Pittsburgh, PA

Angella M. Goetz, RN, MNEd, CIC
Senior Consultant
Special Pathogens Laboratory
Pittsburgh, PA

ABSTRACT

Legionella pneumophila *is a common cause of both community-acquired and healthcare-associated pneumonia. Clinical manifestations are nonspecific, but high fever, diarrhea, and hyponatremia are often distinctive. Diagnostic modalities include culture on selective media and urinary antigen detection. Quinolone and macrolide antibiotics are highly effective when initiated early in the course. Endemic hospital-acquired Legionnaires' disease is often underdiagnosed and overlooked. Infection has been linked to drinking water distribution systems of acute care and extended care facilities, with warm water systems typically implicated. Health departments and public agencies have issued infection prevention guidelines aimed at preventing outbreaks in facilities in which Legionnaires' disease has been overlooked. These guidelines include diagnostic testing for* Legionella *infection and culturing of the drinking water distribution system. Superheating and flushing or hyperchlorination of the water distribution are short-term approaches to terminate an outbreak. Long-term systemic water treatment with copper-silver ionization, chlorine dioxide, and monochloramine has also been shown to be effective in controlling* Legionella. *Proactive culturing for* Legionella *of the water distribution system when cases of hospital-associated Legionnaires' disease have not been discovered is an evidence-based method of prevention.*

KEY CONCEPTS

- Diagnosis and treatment of Legionnaires' disease

- Proactive surveillance of the environment to assess risk and justify preventive interventions

- Disinfection of water distribution systems

BACKGROUND

Legionella pneumophila was first identified as the infectious agent causing pneumonia among attendees at the 1976 American Legion Convention held at a Philadelphia, Pennsylvania hotel.[1] The first known outbreak of healthcare-associated Legionnaires' disease was retrospectively identified at St. Elizabeth's Hospital, Washington, DC, in 1965. Although epidemics dominated the earlier reports, L. pneumophila is now known to be a common cause of sporadic and healthcare-associated pneumonia. The Centers for Disease Control and Prevention (CDC) estimates that less than 5 percent of cases are diagnosed and reported to the CDC.[2]

Based on the National Notifiable Disease Surveillance System (NNDSS) and the Supplemental Legionnaires' Disease Surveillance System, CDC found that confirmed cases from 2000 to 2009 increased 217 percent from 1,110 in 2000 to 3,522 in 2009. The crude national incidence rate increased 192 percent (0.39 to 1.15 per 1,000). In 2009, the NNDSS received over 3,500 case reports, the most since legionellosis became reportable in 1976.

For a case to be considered confirmed by NNDSS, it must be clinically compatible with legionellosis and meet at least one of the confirmatory laboratory criteria: (1) recovery of Legionella sp. in culture, (2) detection of L. pneumophila serogroup 1 antigen in urine, or (3) a fourfold or greater rise in L. pneumophila serogroup 1 antibodies.[3]

MICROBIOLOGY

The family Legionellaceae contains more than 50 species. Legionella organisms are aerobic Gram-negative fastidious bacteria that do not grow on standard bacteriologic media; thus, specialized laboratory methods and culture media are necessary for diagnosis. The lack of in-hospital availability of these methods leads to underdiagnosis. Legionella species can cause pneumonia (Legionnaires' disease) and Pontiac fever, a flulike illness. Approximately 25 species of Legionella have been demonstrated to cause human infection, with the remainder having been isolated from the environment and not linked to human infection.[4] The species most commonly associated with disease is L. pneumophila. Although numerous serogroups exist, most infections in healthcare facilities are caused by L. pneumophila serogroups 1, 4, and 6. Other species implicated in infections include L. micdadei, L. bozemanii, and L. dumoffii. These species are also notably underdiagnosed because diagnosis requires the use of respiratory cultures since commonly used urinary antigen test fails to identify these species.

Reservoir

The natural habitat for *Legionella* is water; thermally polluted rivers and streams are more likely to harbor *Legionella*. Because the organism is chlorine tolerant, it survives the water treatment processes and passes into the drinking water distribution systems in small numbers. Water distribution systems provide favorable water temperatures (105°F to 120°F [41°C to 49°C]), physical protection within biofilms, and nutrients to promote growth.

PATHOGENESIS

Pathogenic microorganisms cause pneumonia by entering the lung via aspiration or direct inhalation. Both mechanisms are operative for *Legionella*. Although aerosolization with direct inhalation originally was thought to be the primary mode of transmission, epidemiologic studies now show that aspiration is more common, especially in healthcare-associated cases. This is supported by the consistent association of increased risk of Legionnaires' disease in cigarette smokers, patients with chronic pulmonary disease, and persons who abuse alcohol— conditions predisposing to pneumonias caused by aspiration.[5]

L. pneumophila causes more severe pneumonia than most bacterial pathogens, and patients with Legionnaires' disease are more likely to be admitted to intensive care units than are patients with pneumonia caused by other microbial etiologies.[5] Cell-mediated immunity is the primary host defense mechanism.[6-9] It has been suggested that the ability of *Legionella* to replicate within protozoa has provided *Legionella* with the capacity to replicate in human alveolar macrophages and monocytes.[10] Once *Legionella* has been internalized into the host cell, a bacterial vacuole associates with mitochondria and the endoplasmic reticulum. The bacteria subverts host cell processes that would normally eliminate an intracellular threat. The type IV secretion and Dot/Icm systems appear to be required for intracellular replication and establishment of the *Legionella*-containing vacuole. *L. pneumophila* also possesses other virulence factors such as lipopolysaccharide, flagella, pili, and outer membrane proteins, exoproteases, and cytotoxins.

EPIDEMIOLOGY

Risk Factors

Risk factors for Legionnaires' disease have consistently been found to include advanced age, male gender, cigarette smoking, alcohol abuse, and chronic pulmonary disease. Immunosuppressed hosts are most frequently involved in healthcare acquisition. Solid organ transplant recipients appear to be at highest risk. Other risk factors include corticosteroid usage and renal failure. Infections in patients with acquired immunodeficiency syndrome (AIDS) are relatively uncommon, but when they occur, clinical manifestations may be unusually severe.

Healthcare-associated *Legionella* infection has been reported in immunosuppressed children and in children with underlying pulmonary disease.[11-13] A review of the literature for *Legionella* cases in children found that 51 percent were under 2 years of age and 54 percent were healthcare-associated.[13] An outbreak of 11 cases of Legionnaires' disease was reported in newborn babies in a Cyprus neonatal unit. The mortality rate in this outbreak was 27 percent and the source of *Legionella* bacteria was the water system of the neonatal unit.[14] Legionellosis has also been reported in infants delivered by water birth; aspiration of contaminated water is the presumed mechanism.[15,16]

Legionella ranked as the third most common etiologic agent among all outbreaks associated with drinking water, with two-thirds of the legionellosis outbreaks occurring in healthcare settings.[17] Flooding and increased rainfall have been suggested as contributing factors.[18-20] Seasonality with increased incidence during the summer months has also been reported.[21,22]

Community-acquired Pneumonia

Based on a large-scale Ohio study of community-acquired pneumonia, fewer than 10 percent of sporadic community-acquired legionellosis cases are diagnosed.[2] Prospective studies of community-acquired pneumonia (CAP) have shown that *Legionella* ranks in the top four causes of pneumonia. Outbreaks of community-acquired legionellosis infections continue to be linked to hotels, decorative fountains, spa displays, and cruise ships.[1,2,23-25] Sporadic community-acquired cases have been linked to dental offices,[3] apartment buildings (especially if residents are elderly),[26,27] and home and workplace water systems.[28,29]

Community-acquired Legionnaires' disease in Europe has increased 12 percent from 2009 to 2010. The German Competence Network of Community-Acquired Pneumonia study group estimated 56,000 to 118,000 cases annually based on the incidence ratio of 180 to 360 cases per one million people.[30] In this CAPNETZ study, *Legionella* pneumonia in ambulatory patients was shown to differ in clinical characteristics and outcome compared to patients requiring hospitalization. Ambulatory patients with *Legionella* pneumonia were younger and had fewer comorbidities and a milder clinical course without fatalities.

The number of reported cases and clinical presentation of Legionnaires' disease varies with age. In the United States between 2000 and 2009, 74 percent of cases were in persons 50 years of age and older.[3] Patients ages 65 and older with CAP caused by *Legionella* have a higher frequency of comorbidity and presented less frequently with fever and laboratory abnormalities of Legionnaires' disease than do younger patients. Consequently, a high index of suspicion and the routine application of urinary antigen detection is critical for diagnosing *Legionella* pneumonia in elderly patients.[31]

Healthcare-associated Pneumonia

Since the late 1970s, numerous hospitals and long-term care facilities have reported outbreaks of healthcare-associated

Legionnaires' disease.[12,32-35] Transmission has been consistently linked to the drinking water distribution systems. The incidence of healthcare-associated infection depends on the degree of contamination of the drinking water system with the Legionella and the susceptibility of the patient population to infection. The proportion of water distribution system outlets that are positive for Legionella (percent distal site positivity) correlates with occurrence of disease, but the density (reported as colony forming units per milliliter [cfu/mL]) of Legionella in the water obtained from these distal sites does not.[36-40] Decorative water fountains in healthcare facilities have also been linked to clusters of Legionnaires' disease in patients.[41,42] Unrecognized endemic disease may exist over a prolonged period of time in the absence of active surveillance for cases. Case fatality can be as high as 33 percent for healthcare-acquired Legionnaires' disease compared to 13 percent for community-acquired cases.[43]

There is a growing number of cases of healthcare-associated Legionnaires' disease among the elderly patients and patients in assisted living and long-term care facilities.[27,44,45] Sporadic and outbreak-related cases occur in this population due to comorbidities, impaired immunity, and propensity for aspiration. Increased incidence of legionellosis in patients in long-term care facilities has followed the increased use of Legionella diagnostic testing in this patient population.

Mode of Transmission

Aspiration is a major route of transmission, especially in healthcare-associated pneumonia.[46] Intubation, surgery requiring general anesthesia, and nasogastric tubes have been associated with healthcare-associated legionellosis via aspiration.[33,47] Person-to-person transmission does not occur; thus, isolation of these patients is not required. Aerosolization by use of respiratory tract devices (such as humidifiers and nebulizers), aspiration, and instillation directly into the lung during respiratory tract manipulation have all been linked to healthcare-associated infections.[47,48] In addition to drinking water distribution systems of healthcare facilities, Legionella may be transmitted from a variety of man-made aquatic devices including evaporative condensers, whirlpool spas, industrial equipment, and decorative fountains.[25]

Despite widespread belief, air conditioners have not been implicated in Legionnaires' disease. The role of cooling towers has also been overestimated.[49] Healthcare-associated Legionnaires' disease attributed to cooling towers has dramatically decreased following the discovery that the organism can colonize the drinking water of hospitals.[32] Although the first environmental isolate was from a showerhead,[50] an epidemiological link between showering and disease has not been convincingly demonstrated.[33,47] One study showed an inverse relationship between showering and healthcare-associated Legionnaires' disease—patients that got Legionnaires' disease were too sick to have showered and aspiration was the presumed mode of transmission.[47] However, a British study reported that Legionnaires' disease was higher among older adults who showered when compared to those who took tub baths.[27] The relative risk (RR) was 7.02 (0.45 to 128.21) for showering versus 0.13 (0.02 to 1.09) for any tub baths.[27]

CLINICAL PRESENTATION

Legionella infection can manifest in the following ways: as asymptomatic seroconversion, as a flulike illness without pneumonia (Pontiac fever), as Legionnaires' disease (pneumonia), or on very rare occasions as extrapulmonary infection.

Legionella pneumonia (Legionnaires' Disease)

Pneumonia is the most common clinical infection. Laboratory abnormalities are common but nonspecific and include renal and hepatic dysfunction, thrombocytopenia, leukocytosis, and hypophosphatemia. Hyponatremia (serum sodium less than 130 mEq/L) occurs significantly more frequently in Legionnaires' disease than in pneumonias of other etiologies. Hematuria and proteinuria are also common. Serum ferritin levels have also been noted to be elevated in Legionnaires' disease.[5] Elevated procalcitonin levels are a marker for severity of illness.[5]

The incubation period from time of exposure to onset of Legionnaires' disease is typically 2 to 10 days. The infection produces a broad spectrum of symptoms, from mild cough and low-grade fever to rapidly progressive pneumonia, stupor, and multiorgan failure. Chest radiographs usually show a new infiltrate, which increases in size and density and may progress to multiple lobes. The cough is slightly productive and may be blood-tinged and nonpurulent; pleuritic chest pain is common. Lung abscesses can occur in immunosuppressed hosts. Fever is almost always present, with temperatures often exceeding 40°C (104°F). Nonspecific complaints including malaise, myalgias, anorexia, headache, and confusion are often present. Gastrointestinal tract symptoms are occasionally prominent and include nausea, vomiting, and abdominal pain. Watery diarrhea is seen in 25 to 50 percent of patients.

Legionella can disseminate via the blood to extrapulmonary sites. Endocarditis and pericarditis are the most common extrapulmonary infections.[51,52] Two cases of osteomyelitis have been reported.[53] Myocardial involvement has been reported.[54] Wound infections can occur from contamination of the wound by water colonized with Legionella organisms. L. pneumophila cellulitis without pneumonia was reported in a 65-year old immunocompromised patient.[55] Unfortunately, extrapulmonary sites are infrequently cultured for Legionella (which needs specialized culture media), thus cases may be underreported.

Neurologic symptomatology is common in patients with severe Legionnaires' disease, especially confusion. Problems range from myositis to acute disseminated encephalomyelitis. Hyperintense lesions of the splenium of the corpus callosum were noted in a patient with human immunodeficiency virus (HIV) infection and a diagnosis of Legionella pneumonia.[56]

Pontiac Fever

Legionella infection may also present as an acute self-limiting entity known as Pontiac fever. Onset is usually 24 to 48 hours after exposure and occurs in persons without underlying disease.

Pneumonia is not present. Common symptoms include high fever, chills, myalgias, and headache. Recovery occurs within 2 to 5 days without treatment. Healthcare-associated cases have not been reported previously. However, in a survey of 19 retirement homes, 11 Pontiac fever-like episodes occurred over a 4-month period in the nurses, but no cases of *Legionella* were found in patients. Of the cases affecting the nurses, eight complied with the definition of Pontiac fever. Water concentrations of *Legionella* organisms were more than 10,000 cfu/L.[57] Thus far, fatality cases have not been linked to Pontiac fever. Whirlpool spas have also been the source of some outbreaks.[58,59] In one family, four members who used their own private whirlpool spa became ill; one with *Legionella* pneumonia and three with Pontiac fever. The whirlpool spa, garden shower, and garden hose of this household were all positive for *L. pneumophila* serogroup 1.[60] An outbreak of Pontiac fever caused by *L. longbeachae* was linked to aerosolized potting mix.[61] The attack rate reported in Pontiac fever outbreaks has been high (95 percent) compared with the attack rates seen in Legionnaires' disease outbreaks (0.1 percent to 5 percent).[2]

DIAGNOSIS

Clinical awareness is critical for rapid diagnosis and treatment of Legionnaires' disease. Due to nonspecific clinical presentation, it is not possible to predict the presence of *Legionella* infection, and underdiagnosis of Legionnaires' disease is common. This was demonstrated by Hollenback et al., who determined that even when following the Infectious Disease Society of America (IDSA) guidelines for testing for *Legionella* species, 41 percent of *Legionella* cases were missed.[62] The practice guidelines for the management of community-acquired pneumonia have been criticized for recommending testing for *Legionella* only for patients with "enigmatic" pneumonia.[63]

Testing for *Legionella* species is recommended for all patients with community-acquired pneumonia and requires specialized diagnostic laboratory tests. The definitive test for the diagnosis of Legionnaires' disease is isolation of the organism by culture. The sensitivity in reference laboratories is at least 80 percent. Unlike routine sputum cultures, special conditions are required to recover this slow-growing and fastidious bacteria. In addition, to achieve a high yield from sputa, the specimen must be plated on multiple specialized media that contain antibiotics to suppress normal flora, which may interfere with the organism's growth.[64,65] Other clinical specimens for diagnosis may include lung tissue, pleural fluid, tracheal aspirate, and bronchial washings; concentration of specimens (e.g., by centrifugation) prior to inoculation of media is recommended.[64] Culture specimens are invaluable if an epidemiological link to an environmental source is to be made. Molecular subtyping methods include monoclonal antibody subtyping and pulsed-field gel electrophoresis (PFGE) of bacterial DNA. Sequence-based typing methods are also used, but are available only in reference laboratories.

Unlike many common pneumonia-causing bacteria, *Legionella* organisms are not easily visualized with Gram stain. However, the organism may be detected with the direct fluorescent-antibody

(DFA) stain examined under an ultraviolet microscopic for same-day results. There are limited species and serogroups detected with DFA staining, and the sensitivity (range, 25 to 75 percent) is lower than isolation by culture.[64]

The urinary antigen is now the most commonly used test for (Figure 84-1). In a review of Legionnaires' disease cases reported to the CDC from 2005 to 2009, the urine antigen test was used to confirm 97 percent of U.S. resident cases.[3] The urine antigen test also constitutes 73 percent of diagnostic tests for *Legionella* pneumonia in Europe.[30] Although its use has undoubtedly increased the number of cases identified, a disadvantage of this test is the inability to detect serogroups and species other than *L. pneumophila* serogroup 1. The sensitivity of the test is approximately 80 to 90 percent with a specificity of 90 to 100 percent. It should be noted that in some hospitals, the urine antigen test has failed to be positive when the infecting organism is a subtype of *L. pneumophila* serogroup 1 such as Bellingham or OLDA—strains more common in hospitalized patients.[66] The test can remain positive for days even during the administration of antibiotic therapy and for prolonged periods in immunocompromised patients. The urinary antigen testing methods include both enzyme immunoassay (EIA) and immunochromatographic membrane (ICT) assay.[64] The Binax NOW test was the first ICT test, but at least seven other manufacturers now offer a version of this test. It is important to note that the sensitivity and specificity has been variable with some of these tests and both false-positive and false-negative test results have

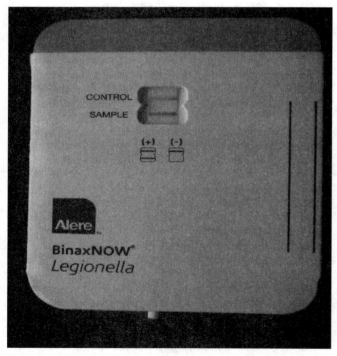

Figure 84-1. *Legionella* urinary antigen immunochromatographic (ICT) test showing positive result after insertion of urine-soaked swab and 15-minute incubation. Pink "Sample" line indicates a positive result.

been reported.[67,68] Therefore, a positive antigen test result may rule in *L. pneumophila* serogroup 1, but the rate of false-negative findings should cause the clinician to be cautious about withdrawing anti-*Legionella* therapy.

Serology has become less important with the advent of rapid diagnostic tests and now accounts for less than 1 percent of diagnosed cases. Fourfold seroconversion is required for definitive diagnosis, so both an acute serology and convalescent serology are required 4 to 12 weeks after onset of illness. Maximal sensitivity requires both immunoglobulin G and immunoglobulin M antibody determination. Polymerase chain reaction (PCR)-based assays for *Legionella* are highly specific but not more sensitive than culture.[69] Use of PCR on respiratory specimens increased the diagnosis of community-acquired Legionnaires' disease due to *L. longbeachae* in New Zealand—an area where *L. longbeachae* is endemic.[70]

In an epidemiologic investigation, both phenotypic and genotypic methods alone, or in combination, can be used. This may be useful to link patient isolates and environmental reservoirs. Pulsed-field gel electrophoresis (PFGE) and methods have been used including serotyping, monoclonal antibody subtyping, isoenzyme analysis, restriction fragment length polymorphism of rRNA (ribotyping) or chromosomal DNA, amplified fragment length polymorphism, repetitive-element PCR, restriction endonuclease (analysis of whole-cell DNA), arbitrarily primed PCR, and 16S-23S spacer analysis. Results linking patient isolates with an environmental source should be interpreted with caution and considered along with epidemiological information.[64] Coordination with local, state, regional, or national health departments is recommended in a suspected outbreak. (See Chapter 12 Outbreak Investigations.)

TREATMENT

Antibiotic therapy is highly effective if initiated early. Quinolones (levofloxacin, ciprofloxacin) and macrolides (azithromycin, clarithromycin) are the drugs of choice for treatment.[33] Azithromycin or levofloxacin can be considered as first-line treatment. Other antibiotics used successfully include tetracycline, tigecycline, and clarithromycin.[71] Doxycycline has been successfully used, and rifampin has been used in combination with other antibiotics for severe cases, though data is lacking for increased efficacy. Erythromycin is no longer the antibiotic of choice due to side effects. Defervescence usually occurs within 3 to 5 days. Duration of therapy is usually 10 to 14 days; however, longer duration (21 days) may be appropriate for some immunosuppressed patients. The mortality rate for healthcare-associated *Legionella* pneumonia has decreased from 46 percent in 1982 to less than 10 percent with the advent of quinolone therapy.[72]

PREVENTION AND CONTROL OF HEALTHCARE-ASSOCIATED LEGIONNAIRES' DISEASE

The knowledge that Legionnaires' disease is linked to exposure to the bacteria from the water distribution system of hospitals and other buildings has prompted numerous guidance documents for disease prevention. The first such document was published in 1993 by the Allegheny County Health Department in Pittsburgh, Pennsylvania.[73] This guidance differed from the CDC's in that environmental testing for *Legionella* was to be performed annually without the precondition of identified cases of healthcare-associated cases. The premise of this recommendation was the common misdiagnosis or missed diagnosis of Legionnaires' disease due to the lack of diagnostic testing. Although numerous studies have demonstrated the utility of this approach as a prevention strategy, the role for routine testing of water systems continues to be debated.

In studies in the United States, Italy, France, Taiwan, Spain, Greece, and most European countries, routine culturing of the hospital drinking water for *Legionella* is recommended.[74] Approximately 60 percent of private hospitals and 93 percent of public hospitals in Southeastern Italy were positive for *Legionella* spp. *L. pneumophila* serogroup 1 was the most frequently isolated species. Risk assessment evaluation proved useful in predicting *Legionella* spp. contamination in water systems.[75]

Culturing the Water Distribution System of Healthcare Facilities

The water distribution system in healthcare facilities has been the source of *Legionella* outbreaks in both acute and chronic care facilities. Consequently, a primary objective of a healthcare facility should be to monitor and maintain the potable water distribution system in such a manner so that *Legionella* will be controlled. When a patient receives a diagnosis of healthcare-associated Legionnaires' disease, culturing of the water sites to which the patient was exposed is indicated.[76] Distal sites include water faucets, ice machines, water used in respiratory tract devices, and any other water source to which the patient is exposed.[76,77] Sites might include water in other units where the patient may have been, such as the radiology department or the physical therapy department. If a link is found between an environmental site and the patient with Legionnaires' disease, expanded surveillance for other cases of healthcare-associated *Legionella* pneumonia should then be undertaken. Particular attention should be focused on areas housing high-risk patients, such as transplant units and intensive care units. If additional cases are found, a system-wide culturing of the water distribution system should be undertaken. Routine environmental culturing should continue; however, the time interval can be expanded if the cultures remain negative and cases cease to be diagnosed. The knowledge that the medical facility's water supply is colonized with *Legionella* should be shared with clinicians. This knowledge will increase an index of suspicion in clinicians to order the appropriate testing. Positivity of water culture sites should also be shared with administration to justify in-house availability of *Legionella* laboratory tests for patients with suspected pneumonia.[78,79] Additional information on performing environmental surveillance is available from informational websites such as www.legionella.org.

Culturing the Potable Water Distribution System in the Absence of Disease

The most important risk factor for healthcare-associated legionellosis is the presence of Legionella in the hospital drinking water.[80] The 2004 recommendations—the latest guidelines published by the CDC—do not offer recommendations for routine culturing of a healthcare facility's water distribution system that does not have a high-risk population, such as transplant units.[81] Given that many hospital water systems harbor Legionella and cases often go undiagnosed, this approach has not been successful in preventing outbreaks. Alternatively, when prospective surveillance of hospital drinking water has been performed, it has led to the discovery and prevention of healthcare-associated Legionnaires' disease.[39,40] For this reason, the states of Maryland and New York and the city of Pittsburgh (Allegheny County, Pennsylvania) and surrounding areas have adopted proactive guidelines for culturing hospital drinking water as a preventive measure even in the absence of known cases of healthcare-associated Legionnaires' disease.[82] Outside the United States, Germany, Italy, Spain, France, the Netherlands, and Denmark have also enacted proactive guidelines. Following the publication of guidelines to prevent Legionella in Italy in 2005, 129 healthcare facilities and 533 other buildings had their water systems cultured. Of these, 79 percent of the healthcare facilities and 45 percent of the other buildings had sites that were positive. During this time 97 cases of legionellosis were reported. Their findings confirmed the need to do routine environmental surveillance to control disease.[75] Evaluation of the effects of the Allegheny County (Pittsburgh, Pennsylvania) Health Department proactive guidelines on Legionella infections showed a significant decrease in healthcare-associated Legionella pneumonia. Cases decreased dramatically in the Pittsburgh area, from 33 to 9 percent ($p \leq .0001$).[73] Two unexpected benefits that arose from proactive surveillance were (1) in long-term care facilities, community-acquired Legionella pneumonia cases were found, as well as healthcare-associated cases; (2) unfavorable publicity and litigation involving Allegheny County medical facilities ceased.[73] If diligent monitoring and maintenance does not occur, outbreaks can easily be missed and become a legal nightmare. After a Taiwan investigator linked healthcare-associated Legionnaires' disease to the hospital's water supply, several hospitals initiated routine environmental surveillance and also found Legionella colonization.[83]

According to the World Health Organization (WHO), testing for Legionella is recommended as part of a risk management approach referred to as a water safety plan and would be performed under the following circumstances: (1) when water systems are treated with biocides and temperatures are lower than necessary for control; (2) in systems not achieving control through treatment programs; and (3) in hospital wards with high-risk patients. The WHO has published guidance on developing a water safety plan.[84] The typical elements of a water safety plan are to (1) describe the water system in sufficient detail that areas where water quality can be impacted are readily identifiable; (2) assess the risks for Legionella colonization

and disease; (3) implement control measures to reduce the identified risks; and (4) perform annual reviews to verify that control measures are in fact controlling Legionella (see Figure 84-2). Legionella testing can provide evidence that the water safety plan is effective and that control measures are operating properly. It must be noted that while surrogate markers for the presence of Legionella have been sought (e.g., total bacterial counts and physicochemical parameters), none have been shown to reliably predict the presence/absence of Legionella. ATP testing of water is also not correlated to the presence/absence of Legionella and should not be used for this purpose. Knowledge of Legionella positivity in hospital drinking water is the only factor known with certainty to be predictive of risk for Legionnaires' disease.[85]

Interpretation of any testing results should take into account the risk profile of exposed patients and the proportion of positive sampling sites. Concentration-based targets (cfu/mL) have been used as an indicator of risk for legionellosis in many guidelines. In controlled studies specifically designed to assess the utility of cfu/mL targets, this parameter was found to fail to correlate with risk of disease. Numerous studies have found that the extent of colonization in a building is predictive of risk. When the distal site positivity of water fixtures exceeds 30 percent, the risk of hospital-associated legionellosis increases correspondingly. Although distal site positivity is not a foolproof cut point, a considerable amount of evidence supports it as a pragmatic cut point. This was noted by Rivera et al. in a study in Spanish healthcare facilities. They asserted that the number of Legionella-disseminating points and the number of potentially exposed patients is a more important determinant of transmission risk than the dose (concentration).[86] Allen et al. published an article in which the authors purported to evaluate the accuracy of the 30 percent cut point for assessing the risk of Legionnaires' disease.[87] Unfortunately, no meaningful conclusions could be drawn because the study retrospectively applied the 30 percent criteria to studies where clinical surveillance was not conducted in parallel with environmental surveillance. Because concurrent surveillance was not performed for many of the studies that Allen et al. reviewed, it would be inaccurate to retroactively conclude that no cases of Legionnaires' disease occurred during the study period.

The sampling plan for environmental surveillance should include a minimum of 10 outlets plus the hot water tanks. Locations for sampling should roughly represent the water distribution system (i.e., sites on multiple floors and wings; high-risk areas such as hematology/oncology, transplant units, medical surgical units, and intensive care units). The complexity of the system will need to be taken into account in determining the appropriate number of samples to take. Swab and first draw hot water samples are typically collected. The sensitivity of each type of sample varies and the ability to concentrate water sometimes provides greater sensitivity. According to the CDC, volumes of water less than a liter are acceptable, and many laboratories use sample collection volumes of 250 mL.[88] Culture on selective media and use of pretreatment methods such as acid or heat treatment remains the recommended method

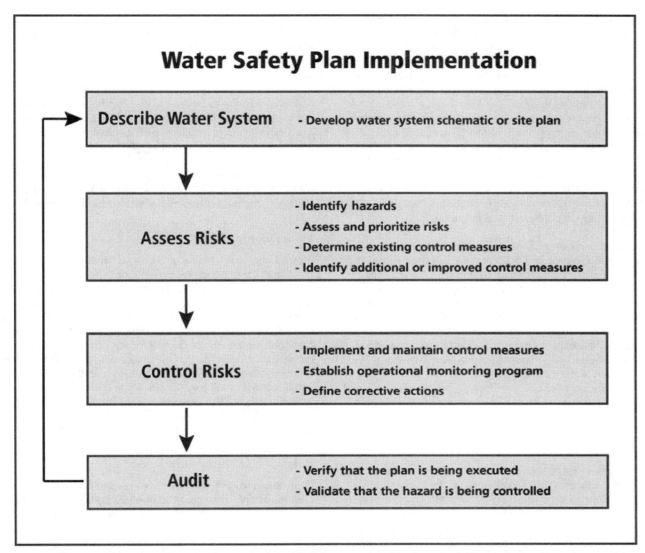

Water Safety Plan Implementation

Describe Water System — Develop water system schematic or site plan

Assess Risks
- Identify hazards
- Assess and prioritize risks
- Determine existing control measures
- Identify additional or improved control measures

Control Risks
- Implement and maintain control measures
- Establish operational monitoring program
- Define corrective actions

Audit
- Verify that the plan is being executed
- Validate that the hazard is being controlled

Figure 84-2. Elements of a water safety plan for prevention of building-associated Legionnaires' disease. *Legionella* environmental testing aids in risk assessment and verifying controls are effective.

for *Legionella* testing. According to the CDC, detection of *Legionella* species by direct fluorescent antibody staining is not suitable for environmental samples. PCR for identification of *Legionella* species is also not recommended.

Standardized culture methods include ISO 11731: Detection and Enumeration of *Legionella* and CDC: Procedures for the Recovery of *Legionella* from the Environment.[88,89] Laboratory results should include specific reporting of *Legionella* species and serogroups in addition to *L. pneumophila* serogroup 1. Laboratories may perform the testing with the requirements that they meet proficiency and quality performance standards through an approved accrediting body. Laboratories chosen for processing of water samples for *Legionella* should be experienced in *Legionella* isolation and specifically certified for proficiency in the CDC ELITE program, Public Health

of England's (PHE) *Legionella* External Quality Assessment (EQA) scheme, or an equivalent program.

Disinfection of Hospital Drinking Water Distribution Systems

There continue to be references in articles and guidelines to control measures that can be taken to minimize *Legionella* colonization of hospital water systems. These include maintenance of hot water tanks, removal and cleaning of aerators or showerheads, and removal of dead leg pipe. Unfortunately, these measures alone have not been shown to effectively reduce or control *Legionella* for any length of time.[90,91] Maintaining hot water temperature at 60°C (140°F) will minimize growth of *Legionella*. It should be emphasized that this approach alone will not be effective unless systemwide disinfection has already been initiated.

When considering systemic disinfection, an evidence-based approach should be applied. The basis for decision-making for many hospitals in determining which type of system to implement and which commercial product to purchase includes anecdotal reports of success and unsubstantiated testimonials from commercial vendors. Any new disinfection method that is being considered for purchase should undergo a standardized evaluation with the following steps: (1) demonstrated efficacy in vitro against Legionella organisms, (2) anecdotal experience of efficacy in controlling Legionella contamination in individual hospitals, (3) controlled studies of prolonged duration (years, not months) of the efficacy of minimizing Legionella growth and preventing cases of Legionnaires' disease in individual hospitals, and (4) confirmatory reports from multiple hospitals with prolonged duration of follow-up or validation.[92]

Complete elimination of Legionella from a hospital water supply is not a realistic end point and has not been shown to be necessary to reduce or eliminate hospital-associated Legionnaires' disease.[92] There are now a number of options for short-term and long-term disinfection of water systems and these have been demonstrated to be effective in vitro and in the field.[93] Hospitals that install disinfection systems should monitor the disinfectant on a regular basis as well as perform periodic Legionella cultures to demonstrate effectiveness.[94] The selection of the disinfection system should be made in consultation with the infection preventionist, facility engineers, and the water safety team. Use of U.S. Environmental Protection Agency-registered and labeled disinfectants is recommended.

Superheat and Flush

If eradication is urgent, such as during an outbreak, superheating and flushing warrant primary consideration. Hot water temperatures are elevated to greater than 70°C (158°F) for 3 to 5 days with flushing of each hot-water faucet and showerhead for 30 minutes.[90] A 5- to 10-minute flush was erroneously recommended by the CDC,[76] and such shorter flush times have been shown to be ineffective.[90,95] The advantage of this method is that disinfection of the water distribution system can be instituted rapidly. Superheat and flush may be combined with shock hyperchlorination. This method is logistically tedious and the benefits are short-term; re-establishment of colonization invariably occurs. Superheating for treatment presents a challenge at distal taps where mixing valves are installed. These valves need to be bypassed in order to achieve the desired temperature. Caution is advised when superheating water due to risk of scald injury.

Copper-Silver Ionization Systems

Copper-silver ionization continuously releases copper and silver ions into the hot water system. The flow cell houses the metal electrodes and is typically installed on the hot water recirculation system. The positively charged copper and silver ions form bonds with the negatively charged ions on the bacterial cell wall, resulting in lysis and bacterial cell death. Monitoring ion concentrations and maintenance of equipment to reduce scale formation on the electrodes is necessary. Follow-up of 16 U.S.

hospitals with copper-silver ionization systems in place for 5 to 11 years has showed success where other methods such as chlorination had failed.[92]

Chlorine Dioxide

Chlorine dioxide can be used to disinfect both the cold and hot water systems. Unlike chlorine, chlorine dioxide does not form carcinogenic byproducts such as trihalomethanes.[96,97] It is odorless and tasteless and inhibits biofilm development. Chlorine dioxide has been shown to control Legionella, but more information is needed to ascertain long-term efficacy.[98,99] Methods for producing chlorine dioxide include controlled mixing of chemical precursors or electrochemical generation.

Monochloramine

Monochloramine is stable, prevents bacterial regrowth, and has the ability to penetrate biofilm more effectively than chlorine.[100,101] In one study, Legionella was not detected with sampling in medical facilities that received water from a municipality that treated water with monochloramine rather than free chlorine. Until recently the ability to generate and apply monochloramine on-site for disinfection of hospital water systems was not available. A monochloramine generation system is now available in the United States from an Italian company, and it has been evaluated for efficacy in controlling Legionella in two healthcare facilities—one Italian hospital and one hospital in Pittsburgh—over a 2-year period.[102,103] Both studies demonstrated effective control over prolonged duration.

Point-of-Use Water Filters

Point-of-use water filters have been used to effectively remove Legionella and other bacteria from water filtered through these devices.[104,105] The period of approved use of these devices has continually increased from the original 14-day use period to 61 days of use for the faucet filters. In addition to use for prevention of exposure to Legionella, they have also been used to prevent exposure to Pseudomonas aeruginosa.[106] In-line filters for ice machines are also available and can be used in high-risk units.

Hyperchlorination

Sustained hyperchlorination is not recommended because of marginal efficacy, corrosion to the plumbing system, and release of carcinogenic byproducts into the drinking water.

Other Infection Prevention Measures

Hands-free electronic sensor faucets have been an engineering intervention for infection prevention to limit hand contamination and to reduce water usage. However, since 2001 there have been reports of increased recovery of Legionella and Pseudomonas aeruginosa from these water fixtures.[107-110] The combination of mixing valves to reduce temperature and flow restriction to reduce water use produce an environment that may be more conducive to bacterial growth compared to manual-type faucets with separate hot and cold controls. Recommendations to restrict their use in high-risk areas have been made.

Other infection prevention measures include prohibiting the use of portable room humidifiers, rinsing respiratory equipment such as the ventilator bag apparatus with sterile water, using only sterile water to fill nebulizer reservoirs, prohibiting bathing of surgical wounds with tap water, and using sterile water to flush nasogastric tubes.[48,76,111] In an outbreak situation, sterile or bottled water should be considered for drinking when caring for immunosuppressed patients. Many measures applied for prevention of healthcare-associated legionellosis are tedious, logistically difficult, and ineffective. Measures that are not evidence-based include prohibition of showering,[112] removal of dead legs in the plumbing system,[90] removal and cleaning of showerheads and faucet aerators,[90,95] routine maintenance, and periodic flushing of distal fixtures with hot water.

Standard Precautions are used with patients with *Legionella* infection; Isolation Precautions are not required because person-to-person spread does not occur. (See Chapter 29 Isolation Precautions [Transmission-based Precautions].)

Education

Although identification of *Legionella* species occurred more than 30 years ago, there continues to be fear and misunderstanding when Legionnaires' disease is diagnosed. Thus, it is imperative that both the medical facility's epidemiologist and infection preventionists institute educational measures if healthcare-associated legionellosis is occurring in a facility or during community outbreaks. Education should include healthcare personnel at all levels, including administrative staff, nursing staff, pharmacy, engineering, and housekeeping. Brochures and other handouts are useful tools for the education of patients and visitors if concerns are high in the community (e.g., documented or suspected outbreaks). A team approach is an excellent method for handling problems related to outbreaks of Legionnaires' disease or a contaminated water distribution system. In addition to the hospital epidemiologist (or chairman of the infection prevention committee) and the infection prevention staff, the team should include representation from administration, nursing, engineering, and other individuals in the medical facility who would be considered an asset to the program.

CONCLUSIONS

Legionnaires' disease is underdiagnosed because of a lack of availability of in-hospital diagnostic tests, especially *Legionella* culture on selective media. Proactive surveillance of hospital drinking water can confirm the presence of *Legionella*, help to assess the risk of healthcare-associated legionellosis, prompt a higher index of suspicion among clinicians, and provide evidence to justify the cost of implementing a potable water disinfection system. Disinfection systems for hospitals are being aggressively marketed; evidence-based criteria and documented hospital experience should be used as selection criteria of

vendors. Cost is often a concern when administrators are faced with decisions regarding installation of new water disinfection systems and the maintenance and monitoring of any system. However, the increased morbidity and mortality and legal problems associated with healthcare-associated infections should negate any administrator's hesitancy.[113] Each healthcare facility should extend the activities of the environment-of-care team to include water safety to prevent and control exposures to waterborne pathogens such as *Legionella*.

FUTURE TRENDS

Improved laboratory tests for diagnosis and environment surveillance need to be developed. PCR and other point-of-care testing for clinical specimens need to be validated.

INTERNATIONAL PERSPECTIVE

Although *Legionella* infections have been reported from all inhabitable continents, most community-acquired outbreaks and clusters of healthcare-associated Legionnaires' disease have been reported from North America and Europe. Regional differences in disease incidence exist, but it is likely that cases from the rest of the world are significantly underreported. More cases of illness due to non-*pneumophila* species, such as *Legionella longbeachae,* have been reported in Europe.

REFERENCES

1. Fraser DW, Tsai T, Orenstein W, et al. Legionnaires' disease: description of an epidemic of pneumonia. *N Engl J Med* 1977 Dec 1;297(22):1189–1197.
2. Benin AL, Benson RF, Besser RE. Trends in Legionnaires' disease, 1980–1998: declining mortality and new patterns of diagnosis. *Clin Infect Dis* 2002 Nov 1;35(9):1039–1046.
3. Centers for Disease Control and Prevention (CDC). Legionellosis-United States, 2000-2009. *MMWR Morb Mortal Wkly Rep* 2011 Aug 19;60(32):1083–1086.
4. Gobin I, Newton PR, Hartland EL, et al. Infections caused by nonpneumophila species of Legionella. *Rev Med Microbiol* 2009;20:1–11.
5. Pedro-Botet ML, Stout, JE, Yu VL. Clinical manifestations and diagnosis of *Legionella* infection. 2013. Available at: http://www.uptodate.com.
6. Molmeret M, Bitar DM, Han L, et al. Cell biology of the intracellular infection by *Legionella pneumophila*. *Microbes Infect* 2004 Jan;6(1):129–139.
7. Molofsky AB, Swanson MS. Differentiate to thrive: lessons from the *Legionella pneumophila* life cycle. *Mol Microbiol* 2004 Jul;53(1):29–40.
8. Steinert M, Heuner K, Buchrieser C, et al. Legionella pathogenicity: genome structure, regulatory networks and the host cell response. *Int J Med Microbiol* 2007 Nov;297(7–8):577–587.
9. Neild AL, Roy CR. Immunity to vacuolar pathogens: what can we learn from *Legionella*? *Cell Microbiol* 2004 Nov;6(11):1011–1018.
10. Newton HJ, Ang DKY, van Driel IR, et al. Molecular pathogenesis of infections caused by Legionella pneumophila. *Clin Microbiol Rev* 2010 Apr;23(2):274–298.
11. Yu VL, Lee TC. Neonatal legionellosis: the tip of the iceberg for pediatric hosptial-acquired pneumonia? *Ped Infect Dis J* 2010 Mar;29(3):282–284.
12. Shachor-Meyouhas Y, Bamberger E, Nativ T, et al. Fatal hospital-acquired *Legionella* pneumonia in a neonate. *Pediatr Infect Dis J* 2010 Mar; 29(3):280–281.
13. Greenberg D, Chiou CC, Famigilleti R, et al. Problem pathogens: paediatric legionellosis - implications for improved diagnosis. *Lancet Infect Dis* 2006 Aug;6(8):529–535.
14. Unit for Surveillance and Control of Communicable Diseases. Legionnaires' disease in a neonatal unit of a private hospital, Cyprus, December 2008: preliminary outbreak report. *Euro Surveill* 2009 Jan 15;14(2). pii: 19090.
15. Franzin L, Scolfaro C, Cabodi D, et al. Legionella pneumophila pneumonia in a newborn after water birth: a new mode of transmission. *Clin Infect Dis* 2001 Nov 1;33(9):e103–e104.
16. Franzin L, Cabodi D, Scolfaro C, et al. Microbiological investigation of a nosocomial case of Legionella pneumophila pneumonia associated with water birth and review of neonatal cases. *Infez Med* 2004 Mar;12(1):69–75.

17. Craun GF, Brunkard JM, Yoder JS, et al. Causes of outbreaks associated with drinking water in the United States from 1971 to 2006. *Clin Microbiol Rev* 2010 Jul;23(3):507–528.
18. Rivera JM, Granizo JJ, Aguilar L, et al. Is there a relationship between monthly rainfall and the isolation of Legionella in potable water systems in Spanich healthcare facilities? *Infect Control Hosp Epidemiol* 2009 Mar; 30(3):306–308.
19. Apisarnthanarak A, Warren DK, Mayhall CG. Healthcare-associated infections and their prevention after extensive flooding. *Currt Opin Infect Dis* 2013 Aug;26(4):359–365.
20. Garcia-Vidal C, Labori M, Viasus D, et al. Rainfall as a risk factor for sporadic cases of *Legionella pneumophila* pneumonia. *PLoS One* 2013 Apr 16;8(4):e61036.
21. Herra-Lara S, Fernandez-Fabrella E, Cerevera-Jaun A, et al. Do seasonal changes and climate influence the etiology of community-acquired pneumonia? *Arch Bronconeummol* 2013 Apr;49(4):140–145.
22. Beaute J, Zucs P, DeJong B. European Legionnaires' disease Surveillance Network. Legionnaires' disease in Europe, 2009-2010. *Euro Surveill* 2013 Mar 7;18(10):20417.
23. Den Boer JW, Yzerman EP, Schellekens JFP, et al. A large outbreak of Legionnaires' disease at a Dutch flower show. *Emerg Infect Dis* 2002 Jan; 8(1):37–43.
24. Erdogan H, Arslan H. Evaluation of a Legionella outbreak emerged in a recently opening hotel. *Mikrobiyol Bul* 2013 Apr;47(2):240–249.
25. Coetzee N, Duggal H, Hawker J, et al. An outbreak of Legionnaires' disease associated with a display spa pool in retail premises, Stoke-on-Trent, United Kingdom. *Euro Surveill* 2012 Sep 13;17(37). pii: 20271.
26. Ricci ML, Fontana S, Pinci F, et al. Pneumonia associated with a dental unit waterline. *Lancet* 2012 Feb 18;379(9816):684.
27. Silk BJ, Foltz JL, Ngamsnga K, et al. Legionnaires' disease case-finding algorithm, attack rates, and risk factors during a residential outbreak among older adults: an environmental and cohort study. *BMC Infect Dis* 2013 Jun 27;13(1):291.
28. Stout JE, Muder RR. *Legionella* in residential water systems. *ASHRAE Journal* 2004:52–54.
29. Pedro-Botet ML, Stout JE, Yu VL. Legionnaires' disease contracted from patient homes: the coming of the third plague? *Eur J Clin Microbiol Infect Dis* 2002 Oct;21(10):699–705.
30. von Braun H, Eweg S, Marre R, et al. Competence network for Community-Acquired Pneumonia Study Group. Community-acquired pneumonia: new insight from the german competence network for community-acquired pneumonia. *Clin Infect Dis* 2008 May 1;46(9):1356–1364.
31. Sopena N, Pedro-Botet L, Mateu L, et al. Community-acquired Legionella pneumonia in elderly patients: characterisitics and outcome. *J Am Geriatr Soc* 2007 Jan;55(1):114–119.
32. Joseph CA, Watson JM, Harrison TG, et al. Nosocomial Legionnaires' disease in England and Wales. *Epidemiol Infect* 1994 Apr;112(2):329–345.
33. Sabria M, Yu VL. Hospital-acquired legionellosis: solutions for a preventable disease. *Lancet Infect Dis* 2002 Jun;2(6):368–373.
34. Moore T. *Legionella bacteria found at four more Queensland hospitals.* Brisbane Times website. June 29, 2013. Available at: http://www.brisbanetimes.com.au/queensland/legionella-bacteria-found-at-four-more-queensland-hospitals-20130623-2oqdf.html.
35. Lecointe D, Faqundez E, Pierron P, et al. Management of the Legionella-line risk in a multicentre area's hospital: Lessons learned of a six-year experience. *Pathol Biol (Paris)* 2010 Apr;58(2):131–136.
36. Kohler JR, Maiwald M, Luck PC, et al. Detecting legionellosis by unselected culture of respiratory tract secretions and developing links to hospital water strains. *J Hosp Infect* 1999 Apr;41(4):301–311.
37. Boccia S, Laurenti P, Borella P, et al. Prospective three year surveillance for nosocomial and environmental *Legionella*: implications for infection control. *Infect Control Hosp Epidemiol* 2006 May;27(5):459–465.
38. Best M, Yu VL, Stout J, et al. Legionellacae in the hospital water supply—epidemiological link with disease and evaluation of a method of control of nosocomial Legionnaires' disease and Pittsburgh pneumonia. *Lancet* 1983 Aug 6;2(8345):307–310.
39. Stout JR, Muder RR, Mietzner S, et al. Role of environmental surveillance in determining the risk of hospital-acquired legionellosis: a national surveillance study with clinical correlations. *Infect Control Hosp Epidemiol* 2007 Jul;28(7):818–824.
40. Sabria M, Modol JM, Garcia-Nuñez M, et al. Environmental cultures and hospital-acquired Legionnaires' disease: a 5-year prospective study in 20 hospitals in Catalonia, Spain. *Infect Control Hosp Epidemiol* 2004 Dec;25(12):1072–1076.
41. Palmore TN, Stock F, White M, et al. A cluster of nosocomial Legionnaires' disease linked to a contaminated hospital decorative water fountain. *Infect Control Hosp Epidemiol* 2009 Aug;30(8):764–768.
42. Haupt TE, Heffernan RT, Kazmierczak JJ, et al. An outbreak of Legionnaires' disease associated with a decorative water wall fountain in a hospital. *Infect Control Hosp Epidemiol* 2012 Feb;33(2):185–191.

43. Jesperson S SOS, Schonheyder HC, Fine MJ, et al. Clinical features fo mortality in admitted patients with community-and hospital-acquired Legionellosis: A Danish historical cohort study. *BMC Infect Dis* 2010 May 21;10:124.
44. Seenivasan MH, Yu VL, Muder RR. Legionnaires' disease in long-term care facilities: overview and proposed solutions. *J Am Geriatr Soc* 2005 May; 53(5):875–880.
45. Sugihara E, Dambara T, Aiba M, et al. Clinical characteristics of 8 sporadic cases of community-acquired Legionella pneumonia in advanced age. *Intern Med* 2007;46(8):461–465.
46. Yu VL. Could aspiration be the major mode of transmission of *L. pneumophila*: a critical review. *Am J Med* 1993 Jul;95(1):13–15.
47. Blatt SP, Parkinson MD, Pace E, et al. Nosocomial Legionnaires' disease: aspiration as a primary mode of transmission. *Am J Med* 1993 Jul;95(1):16–22.
48. Woo AH, Goetz A, Yu VL. Transmission of *Legionella* by respiratory equipment aerosol generating devices. *Chest* 1992 Nov;102(5):1586–1590.
49. Yu VL. Cooling towers and legionellosis: a conundrum with proposed solutions. *Int J Hyg Environ Health* 2008 Jul;211(3–4):229–234.
50. Tobin JO, Beare J, Dunnell M, et al. Legionnaires' disease in a transplant unit: isolation of the causative agent from shower baths. *Lancet* 1980 Jul 19;2(8186):118–121.
51. Lowry PW, Tomkins LS. Nosocomial legionellosis: a review of pulmonary and extrapulmonary syndromes. *Am J Infect Control* 1993 Feb;21(1):21–27.
52. Leggieri N, Gouriet F, Thuny F, et al. Legionella longbeachae and endocarditis. *Emerg Infect Dis* 2012 Jan;18(1):95–97.
53. Sanchez MC, Sebti R, Hassoun P, et al. Osteomyelitis of the patella caused by Legionella aniza. *J Clin Microbiol* 2013 Aug;51(8):2791–2793.
54. Burke PT, Shah R, Thabolingam R, et al. Suspected *Legionella* - induced perimyocarditis in an adult in the absence of pneumonia. *Tex Heart Inst J* 2009;36(6):601–603.
55. Han JH, Nguyen JC, Harada S, et al. Relapsing Legionella pneumophila cellulitis: a case report and review of the literature. *J Infect Chemother* 2010 Dec;16(6):439–442.
56. Robbins NM, Kumar A, Blair BM. Legionella pneumophila infection presenting as headache, confusion and dysarthria in a human immunodeficiency virus-1 (HIV-1) positive patient: case report. *BMC Infect Dis* 2012 Sep 22;12:225.
57. Remen T, Mathieu L, Hautemaniere A, et al. Pontiac fever among retirement home nurse associated with airborne *Legionella*. *J Hosp Infect* 2011 Aug;78(4):269–273.
58. Huhn GD, Adam B, Ruden R, et al. Outbreak of travel-related Pontiac fever amont hotel guests illustrating the need for better diagnostic tests. *J Trav Med* 2005 Jul-Aug;12(4):173–179.
59. Hahn GD, Adam B, Ruden R, et al. Outbreak of travel-related Pontiac fever among hotel guests illustrating the need for better diagnostic tests. *J Trav Med* 2005; 12: 173–179.
60. Euser SM, Pelgrim M, den Boer JW. Legionnaires' disease and Pontiac fever after using a private outdoor whirlpool spa. *Scan J Infect Dis* 2010 Dec;42(11–12):910–916.
61. Cramp GJ, Harte D, Douglas NM, et al. An outbreak of Pontiac fever due to *Legionella longbeachae* serogroup 2 found in potting mix in a horticultural nursery in New Zealand. *Epidemiol Infect* 2010 Jan;138(1):15–20.
62. Hollenback B, Dupont I, Mermel LA. How often is a work-up for Legionella pursued in patients with pneumonia? A retrospective study. *BMC Infect Dis* 2011 Sep 7;11:237.
63. Yu VL, Ramirez J, Roig J, et al. Legionnaires' disease and the updated IDSA guidelines for community-acquired pneumonia. *Clin Infect Dis* 2004 Dec 1;39(11):1734–1737.
64. Stout JE, Rihs JD, Yu VL. Legionella. In: Murray PR BE, Jorgensen JH, et al., eds. *Manual of Clinical Microbiology,* 8th ed. Washington, D.C.: ASM Press, 2003.
65. Murdoch DR. Diagnosis of *Legionella* infection. *Clin Infect Dis* 2003 Jan 1;36(1):64–69.
66. Shimada T, Noguchi Y, Jackson JL, et al. Systematic review and metaanalysis urinary antigen tests for Legionellosis. *Chest* 2009 Dec;136(6):1576–1585.
67. Bruin JP, Diederen BMW. Evaluation of Meridian TRU Legionella, a new rapid test for detection of Legionella pneumonphila serogroup 1 antigen in urine samples. *Euro J Clin Microbiol Infect Dis* 2013 Mar;32(3):333–334.
68. Rihs JD, Jarraud S, Luck PC, et al. Lack of comparable sensitivity and specificity among seven Legionella urinary antigen test kits. *Interscience Conference on Antimicrobial Agents and Chemotherapy Annual Meeting, Boston, MA* 2010; Abstract No. 2473.
69. Diederen BM, Kluytmans JA, Vandenbroucke-Grauls CM, et al. Utility of real-time PCR for diagnosis of Legionnaires' disease in routine clinical practice. *J Clin Micro* 2008 Feb;46(2):671–677.
70. Murdoch DR, Podmore RG, Anderson TP, et al. Impact of routine systematic polymerase chain reaction testing on case finding for Legionnaires' disease: a pre-post comparison study. *Clin Infect Dis* 2013 Nov;57(9):1275–1281.

71. Pedro-Botet ML, Yu VL. Treatment strategies for *Legionella* infection. *Expert Opin Pharmacother* 2009 May;10(7):1109–1121.

72. Yu VL, Greenberg RN, Zadeikis N, et al. Levofloxacin efficacy in the treatment of community-acquired Legionellosis. *Chest* 2004 Jun;125(6):2135–2139.

73. Squier CL, Stout JE, Krsytofiak S, et al. A proactive approach to prevention of healthcare-acquired Legionnaires' disease: the Allegheny County (Pittsburgh) experience. *Am J Infect Control* 2005 Aug;33(6):360–367.

74. Lin YE, Stout JE, Yu VL. Prevention of hospital-acquired legionellosis. *Current Opinion Infect Dis* 2011 Aug;24(4):350–356.

75. Napoli C, Fasano F, Iotta R, et al. *Legionella* spp. and Legionellosis in southern Italy: disease epidemiology and environmental surveillance in community and health-care facilities. *BMC Public Health* 2010 Nov 2;10:660.

76. Sehulster L, Chinn RY, Centers for Disease Control and Prevention (CDC), et al. Guidelines for environmental infection control in health-care facilities: recommendations of CDC and the Healthcare Infection Control Practices Advisory Committee (HICPAC). *MMWR Recomm Rep* 2003 Jun 6;52(RR-10):1–42.

77. Bencini MA, Yzerman EPF, Koornstra RHT, et al. A case of Legionnaires' disease caused by aspiration of ice water. *Archs Environ Occup Health* 2005 Nov-Dec;60(6):302–306.

78. Goetz A, Yu VL. Screening for nosocomial legionellosis by culture of the water supply and targeting of high-risk patients for specialized laboratory testing. *Am J Infect Control* 1991 Apr;19(2):63–66.

79. Lin YE, Stout JE, Yu VL. Prevention of hospital-acquired Legionellosis. *Curr Opin Infects Dis* 2011 Aug;24(4):350–356.

80. Yu VL. Resolving the controversy on environmental cultures for *Legionella*. *Infect Control Hosp Epidemiol* 1998 Dec;19(12):893–897.

81. Centers for Disease Control and the Healthcare Infection Control Practices Advisory Committee. Guidelines for preventing health-care-associated pneumonia, 2003. *MMWR* 2004 Mar 26;53(RR-3):1–36.

82. Maryland Department of Health and Mental Hygiene (DHMH). *Report of the Maryland Scientific Working Group to Study Legionella in Water Systems in Healthcare Institutions.* DHMH website. June 14, 2000. Available at: http://phpa.dhmh.maryland.gov/IDEHASharedDocuments /Legionella-Scientific-Working-Group-Guidance.pdf.

83. Chien ST, Hsueh JC, Lin HH, et al. Epidemiological investigation of a case of nosocomial Legionnaires' disease in Taiwan: Implications for routine environmental surveillance. *Clin Microbiol Infect* 2010 Jun;16(6):761–763.

84. World Health Organization (WHO). *Legionella and the Prevention of Legionellosis.* WHO website. 2007. Available at: http://www.who.int /water_sanitation_health/emerging/legionella.pdf.

85. Stout JE, Yu VL. Environmental culturing for Legionella: can we build a better mouse trap? *Am J Infect Control* 2010 Jun;38(5):341–343.

86. Rivera JM, Aguilar L, Granizo JJ, et al. Isolation of Legionella species/ serogroups from water cooling systems compared with potable water systems in Spainish healthcare facilities. *J Hosp Infect* 2007 Dec;67(4):360–366.

87. Allen JG, Myatt TA, Macintosh DL, et al. Assessing risk of health care-acquired Legionnaires' disease from environmental sampling: the limits of using a strict percent positivity approach. *Am J Infect Control* 2012 Dec;40(10):917–921.

88. Centers for Disease Control and Prevention (CDC). *Procedures for the Recovery of Legionella from the Environment.* U.S. Department of Health and Human Services, Atlanta. 1992.

89. International Organization for Standardization (ISO). *Water Quality - Detection and Enumeration of Legionella.* ISO 11731. International Organization for Standardization, Geneva, Switzerland 1–16. 1998.

90. Stout JE. Preventing legionellosis. *ASHRAE Jl* 2007;49:58–61.

91. Yu VL, Stout JE. Legionellosis in nursing homes and long-term care facilities: what the Slovenian experience can teach us. *Scan J Infect Dis* 2012 Sep;44(9):716–719.

92. Stout JE, Yu VL. Experiences of the first 16 hospitals using copper-silver ionization for *Legionella* control: implications for the evaluation and other disinfection modalities. *Infect Control Hosp Epidemiol* 2003 Aug;24(8):563–568.

93. Lin YE, Stout JE, Yu VL. Controlling Legionella in hospital drinking water: an evidence-based review of disinfection methods. *Infect Control Hosp Epidemiol* 2011 Feb;32(2):166–173.

94. Decker BK, Palmore TN. The role of water in healthcare-associated infections. *Current Opinion in Infectious Diseases* 2013 Aug;26(4):345–351.

95. Chen YS, Liu YC, Lee SS, et al. Abbreviated duration of superheat-and-flush and disinfection of taps for *Legionella* disinfection: lessons learned from failure. *Am J Infect Control* 2005 Dec;33(10):606–610.

96. Cedergren MI, Selbing AJ, Lofman O, et al. Chlorination byproducts and nitrate in drinking water and risk for congenital cardiac defects. *Environ Res* 2002 Jun;89(2):124–130.

97. Hosein IK, Hill DW, Tan TY, et al. Point-of-care controls for nosocomial legionellosis combined with chlorine dioxide potable water decontamination: a two-year survey at a Welsh teaching hospital. *J Hosp Infect* 2005 Oct;61(2):100–106.

98. Zhang Z, McCann C, Stout JE, et al. Safety and efficacy of chlorine dioxide for *Legionella* control in a hospital water system. *Infect Control Hosp Epidemiol* 2007 Aug;28(8):1009–1012.

99. Srinivasan A, Bova G, Ross T, et al. A 17-month evaluation of a chlorine dioxide water treatment system to control *Legionella* species in a hospital water supply. *Infect Control Hosp Epidemiol* 2003 Aug;24(8):575–579.

100. Kool JL, Carpenter JC, Fields BS. Effect of monochloramine disinfection of municipal drinking water on risk of nosocomial Legionnaires' disease. *Lancet* 1999 Jan 23;353(9149):272–277.

101. Flannery B, Gelling LB, Vugia DJ, et al. Reducing *Legionella* colonization in water systems with monochloramine. *Emerg Infect Dis* 2006 Apr;12(4):588–596.

102. Marchesi I, Marchegiano P, Bargellini A, et al. Control of Legionella contamination in a hospital water distribution system by monochloramine. *Amer J Infect Control* 2012 Apr;40(3):279–281.

103. Kandiah S, Yassin MH, Stout JE. Monochloramine use for prevention of Legionella in hospital water systems. *Infect Disord Drug Targets* 2013 Jun;13(3):184–190.

104. Sheffer PJ, Stout J.E, Wagener MM, et al. Efficacy of new point-of-use water filter for preventing exposure to *Legionella* and waterborne pathogens. *Am J Infect Control* 2005 Jun;33(5 Suppl 1):S20–S25.

105. Von Berg RP, Eckmanns T, Bruderek J, et al. Use of terminal tap water filter systems for prevention of nosocomial legionellosis. *J Hosp Infect* 2005 Jun;60(2):159–162.

106. Holmes C, Cervia JS, Ortolano GA, et al. Preventive efficacy and cost-effectiveness of point-of-use water filtration in a subacute care unit. *Am J Infect Control* 2010 Feb;38(1):69–71.

107. Hargreaves J, Shireley L, Hansen S, et al. Bacterial contamination associated with electronic faucets: a new risk for healthcare facilities. *Infect Control Hosp Epidemiol* 2001 Apr;22(4):202–205.

108. Merrer J, Girou E, Ducellier D, et al. Should electronic faucets be used in intensive care and hematology units? *Intensive Care Medicine* 2005 Dec;31(12):1715–1718.

109. Yapicioglu H, Gokmen TG, Yildizdas D, et al. Pseudomonas aeruginosa infections due to electronic faucets in a neonatal intensive care unit. *J of Paediatr Child Health* 2012 May;48(5):430–434.

110. Snydor ERM, Bova G, Gimburg A, et al. Electronic-eye faucets: Legionella species contamination in healthcare settings. *Infect Control Hosp Epidemiol* 2012 Mar;33(3):235–240.

111. Lowry PW, Blankenship RJ, Gridley W, et al. A cluster of *Legionella* sternal wound infections due to postoperative exposure of contaminated tap water. *N Engl J Med* 1991 Jan 10;324(2):109–113.

112. Singh N, Stout JE, Yu VL. Prevention of Legionnaires' disease in transplant recipients: recommendations for a standardized approach. *Transplant Infect Dis* 2004 Jun;6(2):58–62.

113. Stout JE, Yu VL. Hospital-acquired Legionnaires' disease: new developments. *Curr Opin Infect Dis* 2003 Aug;16(4):337–341.

SUPPLEMENTAL RESOURCES

American Society of Heating, Refrigerating and Air-Conditioning Engineers. Available at: http://www.ashrae.org.

American Society of Heating, Refrigeration, and Air-conditioning Engineers (ASHRAE). Minimizing the risk of legionellosis from building water systems (GPC-12). Available at: http://www.ashrae.org or http://www.baltimoreaircoil.com.

Bassetti S, Widmer AF. *Legionella* resources on the World Wide Web. *Clin Infect Dis* 2002 Jun 15;34(12):1633–1640.

The Legionella Experts. Available at: http://www.legionella.org.

Legionnaires' Disease. Available at: http://www.q-net.net.au/~legion.

Maryland Department of Health and Mental Hygiene. Available at: http://www.dhmh.state.md.us/html/legionella.htm.

Sehulster L, Chinn RY, Centers for Disease Control and Prevention (CDC), et al. Guidelines for environmental infection control in health-care facilities. Recommendations of CDC and the Healthcare Infection Control Practices Advisory Committee (HICPAC). *MMWR Recomm Rep* 2003;52(RR-10):1–42.

Tablan OC, Anderson LJ, Besser R, et al. Centers for Disease Control and Prevention. Guidelines for preventing health-care–associated pneumonia, 2003: recommendations of CDC and the Healthcare Infection Control Practices Advisory Committee. *MMWR Recomm Rep* 2004;53(RR-3):1–36.

CHAPTER 85

Lyme Disease (*Borrelia burgdorferi*)

Kathleen Roye-Horn, RN, CIC
Consultant
Horn IP Consulting
Fleming, NJ

ABSTRACT

Lyme disease is a multisystem disease that occurs in North America, Europe, and Asia; it is the most common tickborne disease in the United States and is endemic in several areas. The number of reported cases has increased steadily since 1982, when systematic national surveillance was initiated; the actual number of patients diagnosed with Lyme disease is thought to be much higher than the reported number. Most individuals diagnosed early with the characteristic rash, erythema migrans, respond well to short courses of oral antibiotics. In patients who present with later stages of illness, the diagnosis is based on clinical and epidemiological evidence of disease and is supported by serologic testing. Accurate diagnosis is possible through use of a two-tiered antibody test. The stage and organ system involved guide the selection of an antibiotic regimen. Untreated infection can spread to joints, the heart, and the nervous system. Personal protective measures are important for prevention of infection. Lyme disease is a national notifiable disease (voluntary); however, many states require mandatory surveillance and reporting.

KEY CONCEPTS

- Lyme disease is the most common tickborne disease in the United States.

- Black-legged ticks (deer ticks) act as vectors to transmit *Borrelia burgdorferi*, the causative agent of Lyme disease.

- Lyme disease is associated with a variety of symptoms.

- Lyme disease can be reliably diagnosed.

- Effective antimicrobial therapy is available to treat Lyme disease.

- Patients with Lyme disease may be co-infected with other tickborne diseases.

- Methods exist to reduce the risk of exposure to infected ticks.

- Lyme disease is reportable in the United States.

BACKGROUND

Lyme disease, a systemic illness caused by the spirochete *Borrelia burgdorferi,* is the most common tickborne disease in the United States. In 2011, 47 states reported 33,097 cases of Lyme disease that fulfilled the Centers for Disease Control and Prevention (CDC) surveillance case definition; it was the sixth most common notifiable disease.[1] Lyme disease primarily affects the skin, heart, joints, and nervous system and is often divided into early and late stages.[2] The earliest manifestation is the skin lesion erythema migrans, which appears as an expanding erythematous skin lesion at the site of a deer tick bite.[3]

BASIC PRINCIPLES

Lyme disease is caused by a coiled spirochete, *B. burgdorferi,* named for its discoverer, Willy Burgdorfer, PhD.[4,5] Allen Steere, MD, clinically described the disease as an infectious illness in 1977, suggesting that its epidemiology indicated involvement of an arthropod vector due to its seasonality and clustering in rural areas. Burgdorfer subsequently observed the spirochetes in midgut tissue taken from ticks collected in a Lyme-endemic area and produced the characteristic skin rash in injected rabbits. The organism has since been cultured from the blood, skin, synovial fluid, and cerebrospinal fluid (CSF) of infected patients.[6-8] With the exception of skin biopsy specimens, it is difficult to culture *B. burgdorferi* from sites of infection.

B. burgdorferi displays phenotypic and genotypic diversity and has been classified into separate genospecies. The three principal species associated with human disease are *B. burgdorferi sensu stricto*, which includes all strains studied thus far from the United States and some European and Asian strains, and *B. garinii* and *B. afzelii,* both of which include strains from Europe and Asia.[9,10] The three *Borrelia* species are collectively referred to as *B. burgdorferi sensu lato.* Disease expression is thought to be related to differences in genospecies.[10]

B. burgdorferi is transmitted through the skin of the host via a tick bite. After an incubation period of several days to weeks, the organism migrates outward in the skin, producing the characteristic skin rash, erythema migrans. In some patients, the organism spreads in lymph nodes (regional lymphadenopathy) or hematologically disseminates to other organs (liver, heart, brain, joints) or skin sites (secondary skin lesions).[11]

The presence of *B. burgdorferi* elicits strong host immune responses, with the subsequent release of inflammatory mediators. Histopathologic studies have indicated that mixed, predominantly mononuclear cellular infiltrates with monocytes/macrophages, but also T and B lymphocytes, are present in infected tissues.[12] It is believed that a combined effect of local spirochetal infection with an intense immunologic reaction to the organism is responsible for disease expression.

Anti-*Borrelia* antibodies are produced in response to infection. In serum, specific immunoglobulin M (IgM) antibody titers against *B. burgdorferi* usually reach a peak between the third and sixth week after the onset of disease; specific immunoglobin G (IgG) antibody titers rise more slowly and are generally highest months later, when arthritis may be present. Antibodies are typically detected with two-tier serologic testing using an enzyme-linked immunosorbent assay (ELISA) or immunofluorescence assay, followed by a Western blot for confirmation when the ELISA is positive or equivocal.[13,14] Antibody titers may persist for months to years after successful disease therapy.[15,16]

Epidemiology

Lyme disease is distributed worldwide. The majority of cases occur in temperate regions and coincide with the presence of principal tick vectors such as *Ixodes ricinus* in Europe and *Ixodes persulcatus* in Eastern Europe and Asia.[17] In the United States, Lyme disease has been reported in all 50 states but occurs most commonly in three principal areas: New England and the Mid-Atlantic states, the upper Midwest with concentration in the Great Lakes region, and several counties in northern California; 96 percent of all reported cases are from 13 states.[1] These areas correspond to the distribution of the predominant tick vectors of Lyme disease in the United States—*Ixodes scapularis* (eastern black-legged tick) in the East and Midwest, and

Reported Cases of Lyme Disease – United States, 2011

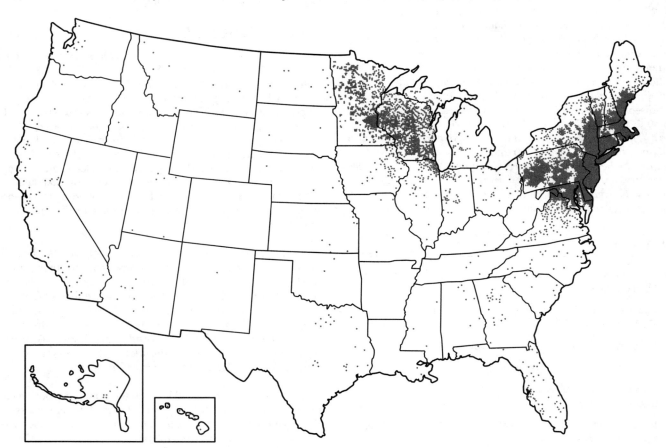

1 dot placed randomly within county of residence for each confirmed case

Figure 85-1. Lyme disease map 2011. Though Lyme disease cases have been reported in nearly every state, cases are reported from the infected person's county of residence, not the place where they were infected. (Source: www.cdc.gov/lyme/stats/maps/map2011.html)

APIC Text of Infection Control and Epidemiology

Black-legged Tick (*Ixodes scapularis*)

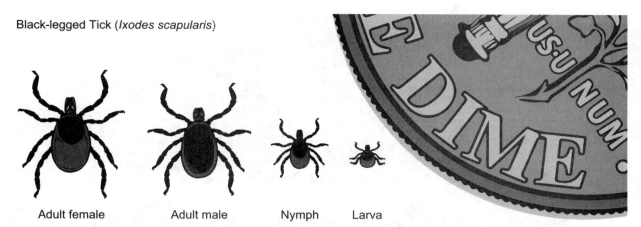

| Adult female | Adult male | Nymph | Larva |

Figure 85-2. Black-legged tick. Relative sizes of several ticks at different life stages. In general, adult ticks are approximately the size of a sesame seed and nymphal ticks are approximately the size of a poppy seed. (Source: www.cdc.gov/lyme/transmission/index.html)

Ixodes pacificus (western black-legged tick) in the West. *Ixodes* ticks typically become infected with spirochetes during the larval and nymphal stages by feeding on a spirochetemic host, which serves as a reservoir.[18] The CDC, using medical insurance claims plus clinical laboratory data and self-reported cases from a survey of the general public, estimates that the number of diagnosed Lyme disease cases in the United States each year is around 300,000; this is a tenfold difference from the number of cases reported through the national surveillance system.[19]

Ixodes scapularis has a three-stage, 2-year life cycle. *I. scapularis* feeds from spring through fall but may be active on warm winter days. The preferred host is the white-footed mouse in the larval and nymphal stages and white-tailed deer in the adult stage. In highly endemic areas, from 10 to more than 50 percent of *I. scapularis* ticks carry *B. burgdorferi*.[20] *Ixodes pacificus* completes its life cycle in 3 years, feeding on black-tailed deer and other large mammals as an adult and small mammals, birds, and lizards in its larval and nymphal stages. Early stages feed spring through fall, but adults are most active in winter.[21]

The Lyme disease spirochete is maintained naturally in enzootic cycles requiring vector ticks, reservoir animals, and maintenance hosts. Humans are only an incidental host of the tick, with contact typically made in areas of underbrush, leaf litter, or high grasses. Rarely, tick exposure may occur in well-mown lawns in endemic areas, especially if those lawns are moist and shady. Ticks are found around the edges of cut lawns that are within 10 feet of tick habitats. Lyme disease affects all age groups, though the greatest number of cases occurs in children 5 to 9 years of age and adults aged 55 to 59 years of age.[1] The incidence of exposure (early manifestation) peaks from June to August, coinciding with periods when nymphal ticks are feeding, and tapers off in the early fall. Adult ticks, abundant during the early and late fall in the East and in winter in the West, are less likely to transmit the disease to humans because they prefer deer as hosts and are more readily detected and removed from humans. Animal models have demonstrated that transmission is unlikely to occur before a minimum of 36 hours of

tick attachment and feeding.[22,23] This is not the case for other tickborne diseases, however, in which transmission can occur after a brief period of attachment.[21]

Only 25 percent of patients with erythema migrans recall the tick bite that transmitted disease.[14,24] This likely reflects the small size of the tick and the lack of pain or pruritus generally associated with the bite. In addition, the tick often attaches at a site that may not be easily visualized by the host. Individuals who have multiple tick exposures may develop an allergic response to the bite, which alerts them to the presence of the tick. Whether due to early tick removal or the immune response at the site, these individuals are less likely to develop Lyme disease.[25]

Clinical Manifestations

Lyme disease is typically divided into three clinical stages, which are termed early localized, early disseminated, and late disseminated infection. Overlap of these stages may occur, and most patients do not exhibit all stages; in fact, seroconversion can occur in asymptomatic individuals.[26] In highly endemic areas of the United States, seropositivity rates of greater than 4 percent have been documented, with even higher rates occurring in Europe.[10]

Early Localized Lyme Disease

Erythema migrans, the most distinct clinical marker for Lyme disease, begins at the site of the tick bite 7 to 14 days (range, 3 to 30 days) after tick detachment. It appears as an expanding erythematous skin lesion, usually round or oval, which may eventually develop central clearing over days to weeks if untreated.[27,28] The CDC recommends using a 5-cm minimum for erythema migrans lesions to help distinguish it from other types of reactions. Lesions can range widely in size, with size being a function of duration, but size is unrelated to prognosis.[24] The thigh, groin, popliteal fossa, back, abdomen, and axilla are common sites of erythema migrans; these sites

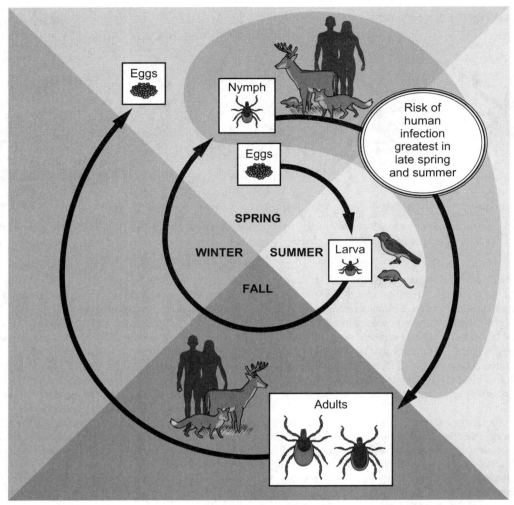

Figure 85-3. Life cycle of black-legged tick. This diagram shows the lifecycle of black-legged ticks that can transmit Lyme disease. (Source: www.cdc.gov/lyme/transmission/black-legged.html)

would be unusual for community-acquired cellulitis. The lesion may be warm to the touch but is generally asymptomatic and easily missed if not seen. Occasionally these lesions may develop blistering or scabbing in the center; remain an even, intense red without clearing; or develop a bluish discoloration.[29,30] Although spirochetes can be readily cultured from the expanding edge of erythema migrans lesions, visualization of the characteristic rash by an experienced practitioner is sufficient for diagnosis.[14,31] Untreated erythema migrans resolves after several weeks, and treated lesions usually clear within several days.

An erythematous reaction that develops while the tick is still attached or within the first 48 hours after detachment is likely to be a noninfectious hypersensitivity reaction to the tick bite. A lesion smaller than 5 cm that begins to disappear within 24 to 48 hours may be a transient inflammatory reaction to an arthropod bite.[14,28]

A rash that has been mistaken for Lyme's erythema migrans occurs after the bite of the *Amblyomma americanum,* or lone star, tick. Found mainly in the southeast and south central United States, the lone star tick cannot transmit Lyme disease but is the vector of other tickborne diseases.[32]

Early Disseminated Lyme Disease

Secondary skin lesions may develop within days of onset of erythema migrans; spread is thought to be via hematogenous dissemination from the site of primary infection.[33] The lesions are similar in appearance to erythema migrans but are generally smaller and uniformly erythematous. Skin involvement is often accompanied by flulike symptoms (malaise, fatigue, headache, fever, chills, myalgia, and arthralgia). Mild hepatitis, splenomegaly, sore throat, nonproductive cough, testicular swelling, conjunctivitis, and regional and generalized lymphadenopathy may also occur during early stages.[30]

Peripheral or central nervous system (CNS) involvement can occur early or late in disease and affects 15 to 20 percent of untreated patients. Unilateral or bilateral seventh-nerve (facial) palsies are the most common neurologic abnormalities. Less frequent involvement includes meningitis or meningoencephalitis, cranial neuritis, and peripheral neuritis or radiculitis. Analysis of CSF typically reveals a lymphocytic pleocytosis, protein elevation, and specific antibodies against *B. burgdorferi*. Lyme encephalitis is extremely rare. Neurologic abnormalities usually resolve completely but may persist for months.[8]

Cardiac involvement is estimated to occur in 4 to 10 percent of untreated patients. It is typically seen from June through December, 4 days to 7 months after the tick bite or erythema migrans. Transient and varying degrees of atrioventricular block are the most common manifestations. Rarely pericarditis, myocarditis, ventricular tachycardia, or cardiomegaly is seen. Acute carditis is typically self-limited, though some patients require the insertion of a temporary pacemaker for high-degree atrioventricular block. Long-term sequelae or late complications are rare.[3,34]

Because other *Borrelia* species cause disease in Europe, manifestations of disease there differ. A rare cutaneous manifestation of Lyme disease seen in 3 percent of patients in Europe is *Borrelia* lymphocytoma. This presents as a solitary bluish-red swollen lesion typically on the earlobe in children and on the breast, nipple, or scrotum in adults. It generally appears later and lasts longer than the original erythema migrans.[35,36]

Late Disseminated Lyme Disease

If left untreated, late disseminated Lyme infection causes pain and joint swelling in 60 percent of cases. This sequence is seen much less frequently today than 20 years ago, probably due to earlier recognition and treatment. The initial pattern of joint involvement consists of migratory arthralgias followed by intermittent attacks of arthritis lasting from days to months. Large joints are most commonly involved, particularly knees and hips; however, other large joints or the temporomandibular joint may be involved. Knee swelling is often prominent, with the development of large effusions and Baker cysts.[21,37]

Response to antibiotics is typically excellent, though effusions may take months to completely resolve. Persistent pain and swelling in the same joint for a period longer than a year is unusual for Lyme disease and would suggest another diagnosis.[14,33]

A subgroup of patients with Lyme arthritis develops a chronic, potentially erosive arthritis that persists after resolution of infection. The risk of this chronic, noninfectious arthritis is high in patients with the alloantigen HLA-DR4, whereas patients with HLA-B27 are not at risk.[38] Synovectomy has been successful in treating patients who experience failed treatment for inflammatory arthritis.[39,40]

Late neurologic Lyme disease is now a rare occurrence because most patients with Lyme disease are diagnosed and treated early. A small number of patients will, if left untreated, progress to have encephalomyelitis, peripheral neuropathy, or encephalopathy. Standard antibiotic therapy is generally successful in resolution of CNS disease.[14] In patients with symptoms suggestive of late neurologic Lyme disease, it is important to rule out other possible causes, such as multiple sclerosis.[8,41]

Before the availability of confirmatory diagnostic tests, ocular problems, particularly optic neuritis occurring in seropositive patients in Lyme disease-endemic areas, were often thought to be attributable to Lyme disease. Since confirmation of positive antibody tests with immunoblotting has become the standard, eye disease is recognized as a rare complication. The most common manifestation is in children with early disseminated disease involving a meningitis, papilledema, and increased intracranial pressure. When optic neuritis does occur, it generally presents as a unilateral or bilateral papillitis during the early disseminated stage.[42,43]

Pregnancy

Prenatal exposure to Lyme disease has not been found to be associated with an increased risk of adverse pregnancy outcome.[44] Lyme disease acquired during pregnancy and left untreated may lead to infection of the placenta and possible stillbirth; however, no negative effects on the fetus have been found when the mother receives appropriate antibiotic therapy. Maternal-to-fetal transmission has been documented in only three cases; in each of these cases, treatment was lacking or inadequate. Chronic congenital Lyme disease has never been documented. There are no reports of Lyme disease transmission from breast milk.[45,46]

Persistent Symptoms

Leonard Sigal, MD, was quoted in the *New York Times* in 2001 as saying, "Lyme disease, although a problem, is not nearly as big a problem as most people think. The bigger problem is Lyme anxiety."[46] Although this anxiety can be attributed in part to misinformation in the lay press and on the Internet, another factor may be that a small subset of treated patients experience persistent symptoms, such as fatigue, myalgias, arthralgias, dysesthesias, and/or mood and memory disturbances. These symptoms continue after the prescribed antibiotic regimen is finished, lasting for weeks or months. This discord between antibiotic therapy ending and symptoms continuing leads patients to worry that infection is still present and further treatment is warranted. Although the etiology of such symptoms is unclear, studies have repeatedly shown that prolonged or repeated courses of antibiotics are not necessary, can cause harm, and do not hasten resolution of these symptoms.[41,48,49] One tool to offer patients in this situation is use of a personal diary in which they note symptoms daily; they can then look back in the diary and see that they are making slow progress, which might not otherwise be apparent to them.

The symptoms mentioned are generally mild and self-limiting, lasting less than 6 months, and have been referred to as "post-Lyme disease symptoms," reflecting that symptoms persist after the infection is no longer present. When symptoms are reported to be more severe and last more than 6 months after diagnosis, terms such as "post-Lyme disease syndrome," "posttreatment chronic Lyme disease," and "chronic Lyme disease" have been applied. Studies of patients with post-Lyme disease complaints have used varied case definitions, enrollment criteria, and patient populations. In some cases, the term has been applied to patients who have not been diagnosed using standard methods or who have not been adequately treated. Some patients in this group may have coinfection, with another tickborne disease causing their symptomatology. Patients with joint complaints may have a degree of joint erosion causing their pain. Neither laboratory studies nor treatment trials done with scientific rigor support the persistence of *B. burgdorferi* infection in patients who have received adequate therapy.[41,48,49]

Reinfection

Reinfection with Lyme disease has been well documented in Lyme-endemic areas. This occurs in patients who are treated with antibiotics in early-stage disease, generally with erythema migrans only, before a protective immune response can develop. Reinfection in patients with more advanced Lyme disease, with late manifestations such as Lyme arthritis or neurological disease, is rare or does not occur.[10,50]

Diagnosis

One step in evaluating the potential for Lyme disease is to determine if the patient had a bite from a tick capable of transmitting Lyme disease. Healthcare providers in endemic areas should learn to identify these *Ixodes* ticks and to estimate the degree of engorgement as a marker of feeding time.[21] Testing ticks removed from patients for *Borrelia* is not recommended.[14,21,23]

Figure 85-4. Black-legged tick engorged. Male, female, and engorged female with straight pin. (Source: www.ct.gov/caes/lib/caes/documents/special_features/tickhandbook.pdf)

Early Disease

Erythema migrans, present in about 90 percent of cases, is diagnostic of Lyme disease.[11,26] *B. burgdorferi* can be cultured from skin lesions, but the test is not readily available and is unnecessary for routine patient care. A history of a tick bite and residence or travel in an endemic area should be sought in patients complaining of a summer flulike illness with fever, chills, myalgias, fatigue, headache, and malaise. Serologic tests typically are negative during this stage because a measurable antibody response takes weeks to develop. If serologic tests are done at this stage, convalescent testing should be repeated in 2 to 6 weeks.[10]

Specific IgM antibody responses against *B. burgdorferi* develop 2 to 4 weeks after the onset of erythema migrans. This reflects the normal humoral antibody lag time between infection onset and detectable serum antibody levels.[41] IgG antibody levels appear approximately 6 weeks after disease onset but may not peak until months or even years later. Patients receiving antibiotics for erythema migrans may never have measurable antibody responses.

Established Disease

Specific antibody testing is helpful in establishing the diagnosis in patients with cardiac, neurologic, or arthritic manifestations. In almost all such patients, specific IgG antibody responses will be positive. Laboratory diagnosis is limited by false-positive results related to mononucleosis, syphilis, or certain autoimmune diseases; interlaboratory variability; seropositive test results among asymptomatic persons residing in endemic areas; receipt of the Lyme vaccine prior to 2002; and difficulty distinguishing past from current infections.[11,49,51]

Guidelines have been published for laboratory evaluation and interpretation in the diagnosis of Lyme disease.[13,51,52] Recommendations include testing only patients with clear clinical symptoms of Lyme disease; using a two-test protocol in which either positive or indeterminant ELISA or immunofluorescence assays are followed by Western blot confirmatory testing; withholding Lyme disease antibiotic therapy from patients with only vague symptoms, such as malaise, when the probability of Lyme disease is low; and providing empirical antibiotic therapy for patients who present with a rash resembling erythema migrans if they live in or have visited a high-risk area.

In patients with suspected Lyme arthritis or neurologic Lyme disease, the Infectious Disease Society of America recommends testing CSF for intrathecal antibodies. Polymerase chain reaction testing is also an option in these patients.[14]

Alternative Methods of Detection

Various assays have been proposed for use in confirming the diagnosis of Lyme disease. These include reverse Western blots, lymphocyte transformation tests, borreliacidal antibody assay, immune complex disruption, and T-cell proliferative responses.

Two-Tiered Testing for Lyme Disease

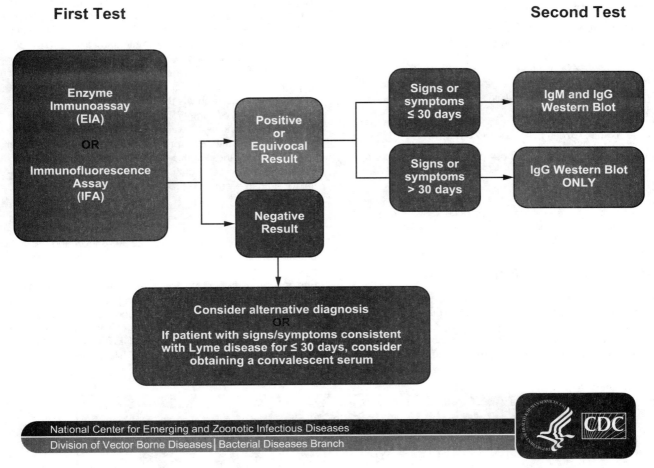

Figure 85-5. Two tier testing. The Two-tier Testing Decision Tree describes the steps required to properly test for Lyme disease. (Source: www.cdc.gov/lyme/healthcare/clinician_twotier.html)

These tests have not been sufficiently studied to become a standard part of routine clinical diagnostic testing of Lyme disease. The C6 antibody test is a relatively new form of ELISA that identifies a specific region of *Borrelia* protein; it has improved specificity with similar sensitivity to that of the IgM ELISA when used in early disease.[26] The Lyme urine antigen test is not approved for use by the U.S. Food and Drug Administration (FDA) and is not recommended by the CDC or the American Lyme Disease Foundation for patient diagnosis or care; it has a high false-positive rate.[2,11]

Treatment

Lyme *Borrelia* is very sensitive to treatment with the tetracyclines, most penicillins, second- and third-generation cephalosporins and, to a lesser degree, macrolides. Resistance has been shown to first-generation cephalosporins, certain fluoroquinolones, and rifampin.[10]

Erythema Migrans and Early Disease

Doxycycline 100 mg by mouth twice daily or amoxicillin 500 mg three times a day for 10 to 21 days are agents of choice. Doxycycline is not recommended for children younger than 8 years or pregnant or lactating women. Cefuroxime axetil 500 mg twice daily for 14 to 21 days and azithromycin 500 mg daily for 7 to 10 days are appropriate for patients who are allergic to penicillin and who cannot take tetracyclines.

Neurologic Manifestations

1. Facial palsy alone may be treated with oral antibiotics as recommended for early disease.

2. Other manifestations: ceftriaxone 2 g/day intravenously (IV) for 14 to 28 days with cefotaxime 2 g every 8 hours IV or penicillin G 20 million units IV daily for 14 to 28 days as an alternative

Lyme Carditis

1. Mild (first-degree atrial-ventricular [AV] block): doxycycline 100 mg twice daily for 14 to 21 days or amoxicillin 500 mg three times daily for 14 to 21 days

2. Moderate to severe: ceftriaxone 2 g/day for 14 to 21 days or cefotaxime 2 g every 8 hours IV daily for 14 to 28 days

Lyme Arthritis

1. Doxycycline 100 mg twice daily or amoxicillin 500 mg three times a day for 28 days

2. Ceftriaxone 2 g/day IV for 14 to 28 days

Pediatric dosages differ from those provided here.[14,35]

Pregnancy

Treatment during pregnancy is as described above, except doxycycline should not be used due to potential side effects to both the mother and fetus.[10]

PREVENTION AND PROTECTION

Prevention of Lyme disease is best accomplished by preventing tick bites. Although prevention of Lyme disease is itself an important goal, successful strategies can be expected to have the additional benefit of preventing other tickborne diseases. Methods for reducing the risk of Lyme disease include vector control and personal protection, including antibiotic prophylaxis in select cases.

Tick habitat alteration can work in limited areas, such as backyards and residential areas. Removing leaf litter and mowing in areas of human activity are effective in destroying tick habitat and reducing tick numbers; one study found a 73 to 100 percent reduction in tick density when leaf litter removal was done in March and June.[53,54] Targeted application of acaricides such as permethrin, deltamethrin, carbaryl, diazinon, chlorpyrifos, or cyfluthrin to tick habitats that are shared/used by humans is also effective, reducing tick populations by as much as 100 percent for as long as 12 weeks.[53,55] These are most effective when applied in the early spring and fall. There are a number of drawbacks to these applications: these products kill more than the intended ticks; timing is critical; they hold the potential for human harm; and there is early evidence of resistance developing.[53,56–58]

Public health prevention efforts have focused on enhancing general knowledge of Lyme disease, tick avoidance, and promoting precautionary behavior, such as repellent use and daily tick checks for individuals living or vacationing in endemic areas. Personal protection includes wearing light-colored clothing in order to find ticks more easily, tucking pant cuffs into socks to keep ticks from gaining access to exposed skin, using tick or insect repellents, and performing tick checks.[21] Repellents containing N,N-Diethyl-meta-toluamide (DEET) are very effective against ticks when applied to the skin, significantly reducing

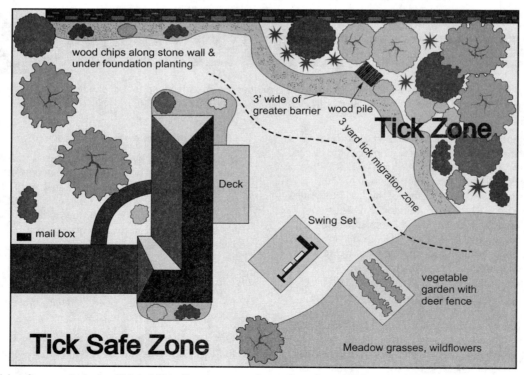

Figure 85-6. Tick safe zone. Reducing tick habitat. (Source: www.cdc.gov/lyme/prev/in_the_yard.html)

both the number and frequency of tick bites. They are available in 5 to 100 percent formulations, with a formulation up to 30 percent recommended for adults and children over 2 years old. Higher concentrations produce a more long-lasting effect but are not recommended for children. DEET is safe when used according to the manufacturers' directions. Adults should apply DEET to children so the product is less likely to get into their eyes and mouth. Combination products of DEET and sunscreen are not recommended, as DEET is not water-soluble and could reach problematic levels if re-applied for sun protection.

Picaridin is another effective skin product; it requires more frequent application but has the advantage of being safe to use on plastics, such as eyeglasses, which can be damaged by DEET-containing products. Other repellents commonly marketed as being tick repellents are not as effective as DEET and picaridin; these include garlic, eucalyptus oil, and citronella, all of which do repel mosquitoes.

According to the American Academy of Pediatrics, insect repellents should not be used on children under 2 months of age.

Permethrin-based repellents can be used on clothing and fabric of outdoor equipment such as tents and mosquito netting. An insecticide, it kills ticks and mosquitoes on contact. It is applied by spray or immersion and retains its acaricidal properties through multiple launderings.[21,53] Clothing should be treated before it is put on and allowed to dry for 2 to 4 hours. Permethrin should not be applied to skin.[21]

Showering within 2 hours of tick exposure and performing daily tick checks after being outdoors in tick habitats are thought to have some benefit in preventing Lyme disease. Because movement of B. burgdorferi from the feeding tick's midgut to its salivary glands then into the host takes at least 36 hours, finding and removing the tick prior to that may provide some protection.[53] Ticks can be very difficult to find, however, and adherence to daily checks can be difficult.[26] In a study published in Emerging Infectious Diseases in February 2008, wearing long clothing that decreases the area of exposed skin and using repellents on skin or clothing were shown to be more effective prevention methods than doing tick checks or using acaricides on property.[59]

Antibiotic prophylaxis to prevent Lyme disease after a known tick bite is not routinely warranted. The risk of infection from a deer tick bite in a Lyme disease-endemic area is low. A cost-benefit analysis of antibiotic prophylaxis for Lyme disease following tick attachment found that prophylaxis is warranted if the incidence of Lyme disease following tick bite is at least 3.6 percent.[60] One randomized, double-blind trial of patients residing in an endemic area from whom I. scapularis ticks had been removed within 72 hours found that a single dose of 200 mg of doxycycline was effective in preventing Lyme disease when compared with placebo.[61] Therefore, in an area endemic for Lyme disease (greater than 20 percent of ticks infected with Borrelia), single-dose antibiotic prophylaxis can be considered for individuals with an Ixodes tick attached for more

than 36 hours when prophylaxis can begin within 72 hours of tick removal.[53]

Individuals who received the recombinant OspA Lyme disease vaccine when it was available from 1998 to 2002 are unlikely to have current protection because its protective effect was not long lasting.[62,63] Since the vaccine was withdrawn from the market in 2002 due to poor sales and fear of side effects, research has continued on development of a Lyme disease vaccine. Lyme disease vaccines have been available for dogs since 1990 and continue in use.[26] New human vaccines are being studied using different Borrelia antigens and new, innovative technologies are being considered, such as vaccinating against the tick itself or vaccinating a major reservoir, the Peromyscus mouse, to reduce carriage of the organism.[53,64]

CO-INFECTION

I. scapularis ticks serve as vectors not only of B. burgdorferi but also of Anaplasma phagocytophilum and Babesia microti, agents of human granulocytic anaplasmosis (formerly called human granulocytic ehrlichiosis) and babesiosis. Transmission of these organisms can result in single infections following a tick bite, or infections can occur in combination, resulting in co-infection.[14,21,32] When symptoms inconsistent with Lyme disease, such a high fever, occur in a patient diagnosed with Lyme disease, co-infection must be considered so that appropriate diagnostic and treatment decisions can be made. In areas with significant risk of these diseases, or when tick studies have indicated the presence of these organisms in the environment, consideration should be given to routine testing for co-infection with multiple tickborne pathogens.[10,21,26,32]

LYME DISEASE AS A REPORTABLE DISEASE

Lyme disease is a nationally notifiable disease. Although national reporting is voluntary, many states have made Lyme disease reportable by regulation. The surveillance case definition was developed for national reporting of Lyme disease and is not intended for use in clinical diagnosis; it was revised in 2011. Confirmed and probable cases are reportable, using the case definition that can be found on the CDC website. (See Supplemental Resource.)

CONCLUSIONS

Lyme disease is the most common tickborne disease in the United States. Most individuals diagnosed early with erythema migrans are cured following short courses of oral antibiotics. The stage and organ system involved guide the selection of an antibiotic regimen in disseminated disease. Although there can be chronic sequelae following infection, cure rates are high for all stages. Prolonged or repeated courses of antibiotic show no benefit when symptoms remain. Personal protective measures are important for prevention of infection. Prevention methods include vector control and personal protection. Public health prevention efforts have focused on enhancing general knowledge of Lyme disease, tick avoidance, and promoting precautionary behavior, such as use of repellents and daily tick checks. Antibiotic prophylaxis to prevent Lyme disease after a known tick bite is warranted in select cases. Currently there are no Lyme disease vaccines commercially available for use in humans.

REFERENCES

1. Adams DA, Gallagher KM, Jajosky RA, et al. Summary of Notifiable Diseases, United States, 2011. *Morb Mortal Wkly Rep* 2013 Jul 5;60(53): 1–117.
2. Wright WF, Riedel DJ, Talwani R, et al. Diagnosis and management of Lyme disease. *Am Fam Physician* 2012 Jun 1;85(11):1086–1093.
3. Bhate C, Schwartz RA. Lyme disease Part 1.Advances and perspectives. *J Am Acad Dermatol* 2011 Apr;64(4):619–636.
4. Burgdorfer W, Barbour AG, Hayes SF, et al. Lyme disease: tickborne spirochetosis? *Science* 1982 Jun 18;216(4552):1317–1319.
5. Steere AC, Grodzicki RL, Kornblatt AN, et al. The spirochetal etiology of Lyme disease. *N Engl J Med* 1983 Mar 31;308(13):733–740.
6. Benach JL, Bosler EM, Hanrahan JP. Spirochetes isolated from the blood of two patients with Lyme disease. *N Engl J Med* 1983 Mar 31;308(13):740–742.
7. Snydman DR, Schenkein DP, Berardi VP, et al. *Borrelia burgdorferi* in joint fluid in chronic Lyme arthritis. *Ann Intern Med* 1986 Jun;104(6): 798–800.
8. Halperin J. Nervous system Lyme disease. *Infect Dis Clin North Am* 2008 Jun;22(2):261–274.
9. Dressler F, Ackermann R, Steere AC. Antibody responses to the three genomic groups of *Borrelia burgdorferi* in European Lyme borreliosis. *J Infect Diseases* 1994 Feb;169(2):313–318.
10. Stanek G, Wormser GP, Gray J, et al. Lyme borreliosis seminar. *The Lancet* 2012 Feb 4;379(9814):461–473.
11. Bratton RL, Whiteside JW, Hovan MJ, et al. Diagnosis and treatment of Lyme disease. *Mayo Clin Proc* 2008 May;83(5):566–571.
12. Baranton, G, Postic D, Saint Girons I, et al. Delineation of *Borrelia burgdorferi* sensu stricto, *Borrelia garinii* sp. nov., and group VS461 associated with Lyme borreliosis. *Int J Syst Bacteriol* 1992 Jul;42(3):378–383.
13. Centers for Disease Control and Prevention (CDC). Recommendations for test performance and interpretation from the Second National Conference on Serologic Diagnosis of Lyme Disease. *MMWR Morb Mortal Wkly Rep* 1995 Aug 11;44(31):590–591.
14. Wormser GP, Dattwyler RJ, Shapiro ED, et al. The clinical assessment, treatment and prevention of Lyme disease, human granulocytic anaplasmosis, and babesiosis: clinical practice guidelines by the Infectious Diseases Society of America. *Clin Infect Dis* 2006 Nov 1;43(9):1089–1134.
15. Wormser GP. Early Lyme disease. *N Engl J Med* 2006 Jun 29;354(26): 2794–2801.
16. Feder HM, Abeles M, Bernstein M, et al. Diagnosis, treatment, and prognosis of erythema migrans and Lyme arthritis. *Clin Dermatol* 2006 Nov-Dec;24(6):509–520.
17. Stanek G, Strle F, Gray J, et al. History and Characteristics of Lyme Borreliosis. In: Gray JS, Kahl O, Lane RS, et al., eds. *Lyme Borreliosis Biology, Epidemiology and Control.* New York: CABI Publishing, 2002;1–28.
18. Tilly K, Rosa P, Stewart PE. Biology of infection with *Borrelia burgdorferi*. *Infect Dis Clin North Am* 2008 Jun;22(2):217–234.
19. Centers for Disease Control and Prevention (CDC). *Press release: CDC provides estimate of Americans diagnosed with Lyme disease each year.* CDC website. Aug 19, 2013. Available at: http://www.cdc.gov/media/releases/2013/p0819-lyme-disease.html.
20. Anderson JF, Magnarelli LA. Biology of ticks. *Infect Dis Clin North Am* 2008 Jun;22(2):195–215.
21. Stafford KC III. *Tick Management Handbook.* Connecticut Agricultural Experiment Station website. 2004. Available at: http://www.ct.gov/caes/lib/caes/documents/special_features/tickhandbook.pdf.
22. Piesman J, Dolan MC. Protection against Lyme disease spirochete transmission provided by prompt removal of nymphal *Ixodes scapularis* (Acari: Ixodidae). *J Med Entomology* 2002 May;39(3):509–512.
23. Falco RC, McKenna D, Nowakowski J, et al. Evaluation of patient assessment of tick bite duration and eligibility for Lyme disease prophylaxis in a clinical setting [Abstract, p 203]. In: Programs and Abstracts of the 10th International Conference on Lyme Borreliosis and Other Tick-borne Diseases (Vienna, Austria), Austrian Society for Hygiene, Microbiology, and Preventive Medicine, 2005:120.
24. Nadelman RB, Nowakowski J, Forseter G, et al. The clinical spectrum of early Lyme borreliosis in patients with culture-confirmed erythema migrans. *Am J Med* 1996 May;100(5):502–508.
25. Burke G, Wikel SK, Spielman A, et al. Tick-borne Infection Study Group. Hypersensitiovity to ticks and Lyme disease risk. *Emerg Infect Dis* 2005 Jan;11(1):36–41.
26. Hu LT. In the clinic. Lyme disease. *Ann Intern Med* 2012 Aug 7;157(3): ITC2-2–ITC2-16.
27. Rahn DW. Natural History of Lyme Disease. In: Evans J, Rahn DW, eds. *Lyme Disease.* Philadelphia: American College of Physicians, 1997: 35–48.
28. Dandache P, Nadelman RB. Erythema migrans. *Infect Dis Clin North Am* 2008 Jun;22(2):235–260.
29. Nadelman RB, Wormser GP. Erythema migrans and early Lyme disease. *Am J Med* 1995 Apr 24;98(4A):15S–23S.
30. Nadelman RB, Nowakowski J, Forseter G, et al. The clinical spectrum of early Lyme borreliosis in patients with culture-confirmed erythema migrans. *Am J Med* 1996 May;100(5):502–508.
31. Berger BW, Johnson RC, Kodner C, et al. Cultivation of *Borrelia burgdorferi* from erythema migrans lesions and perilesional skin. *J Clin Microbiol* 1992 Feb;30(2):359–361.
32. Centers for Disease Control and Prevention (CDC). *Tickborne diseases of the United States, a reference manual for health care providers.* CDC website. 2013. Available at: http://www.cdc.gov/lyme/resources/TickborneDiseases.pdf.
33. Wormser GP, McKenna D, Carlin J, et al. Brief communication: hematogenous dissemination in early Lyme disease. *Ann Intern Med* 2005 May 3; 142(9):751–755.
34. Fish AE, Pride YB, Pinto DS. Lyme carditis. *Infect Dis Clin North Am* 2008 Jun;22(2):275–288.
35. Treatment of Lyme disease. *Med Letter Drugs Ther* 2007 Jun 18; 49(1263):49–51.
36. Vanousová D, Hercogová J. Lyme borreliosis treatment. *Dermatol Ther* 2008 Mar-Apr;21(2):101–109.
37. Steere AC, Schoen RT, Taylor E. The clinical evolution of Lyme arthritis. *Ann Intern Med* 1987 Nov;107(5):725–731.
38. Kalish RA, Leong JM, Steere AC. Association of treatment-resistant chronic Lyme arthritis with HLA-DR4 and antibody reactivity to OspA and OspB of *Borrelia burgdorferi*. *Infect Immun* 1993 Jul;61(7):2774–2779.
39. Puius Y, Kalish R. Lyme arthritis: pathogenesis, clinical presentation, and management. *Infect Dis Clin North Am* 2008 Jun;22(2):289–300.
40. Smith BG, Cruz AI, Milewski MD, et al. Lyme disease and the orthopaedic implications of Lyme arthritis. *J Am Acad Orthop Surg* 2011 Feb;19(2): 91–100.
41. Halperin JJ, Baker P, Wormser G. Common misconceptions about Lyme disease. *Am J Med* 2013 Mar;126(3):264.e1–7.
42. Jacobson D. Lyme disease and optic neuritis: long-term follow-up of seropositive patients. *Neurology* 2003 Mar 11;60(5):881–882.
43. Sibony P, Halperin J, Coyle P, et al. Reactive Lyme serology in optic neuritis. *J Neuroophthalmol* 2005 Jun;25(2):71–82.
44. Strobino BA, Williams CL, Abid S, et al. Lyme disease and pregnancy outcome: a prospective study of two thousand prenatal patients. *Am J Obstet Gynecol* 1993 Aug;169(2 Pt 1):367–374.
45. Feder HM Jr. Lyme disease in children. *Infect Dis Clin North Am* 2008 Jun;22(2):315–326.
46. American Academy of Pediatrics, Committee on Infectious Diseases. Lyme Disease. In: Pickering LK, ed. *Red Book*, 29th ed. Elk Grove Village, IL: American Academy of Pediatrics, 2012.
47. Kolata G. Lyme disease is hard to catch and easy to halt, study finds. *The New York Times.* June 13, 2001:A1
48. Klempner MS, Baker PJ, Shapiro ED, et al. Treatment trials for post-Lyme disease symptoms revisited. *Am J Med* 2013 Aug;126(8):665–669.
49. Marques A. Chronic Lyme disease: a review. *Infect Dis Clin North Am* 2008 Jun;22(2):341–360.
50. Nadelman RB, Wormser GP. Reinfection in patients with Lyme disease. *Clin Inf Dis* 2007 Oct 15;45(8):1032–1038.
51. Depietropaolo DL, Power JH, Gill JM, et al. Diagnosis of Lyme disease, *Am Fam Phsy* 2005 Jul 15;72(2):297–304.
52. Centers for Disease Control and Prevention (CDC). *Lyme disease, Two step laboratory testing.* CDC website. 2011. Available at: http://www.cdc.gov/lyme/diagnosistesting/LabTest/TwoStep.
53. Clark RP, Hu LT. Prevention of Lyme disease and other tick-borne infections. *Infect Dis Clin North Am* 2008 Sep;22(3):381–396.
54. Schulze TL, Jordan RA, Hung RW. Suppression of adult *Ixodes scapularis* (Acari Ixodidae) following removal of leaf litter. *J Med Entomol* 1995 Sep; 32(5):730–733.
55. Schulze TL, Jordan RA, Krivenko AJ. Effects of barrier application of granular deltamethrin on subadult *Ixodes scapularis* (Acari Ixodidae) and nontarget forest floor arthropods. *J Econ Entomol* 2005 Jun;98(3):976–981.
56. Schulze TL, Jordan RA, Hung RW, et al. Effects of an application of granular carbaryl on nontarget forest floor arthropods. *J Econ Entomol* 2001 Feb;94(1):123–128.

57. Llewellyn DM, Brazier A, Brown R, et al. Occupational exposure to permethrin during its use as a public hygiene insecticide. *Ann Occup Hyg* 1996 Oct;40(5):499–509.

58. Miller RJ, Davey RB, George JE. First report of permethrin-resistant Boophilus microplus (Acari Ixodidae) collected within the United States. *J Med Entomol* 2007 Mar;44(2):308–315.

59. Vázquez M, Muehlenbein C, Cartter M, et al. Effectiveness of personal protective measures to prevent Lyme disease. *Emerg Infect Dis* 2008 Feb; 14(2):210–216.

60. Magid D, Schwartz B, Craft J, et al. Prevention of Lyme disease after tick bites, a cost-effectiveness analysis. *N Engl J Med* 1992 Aug 20;327(8): 534–541.

61. Nadelman RB, Nowakowski J, Fish D, et al. Prophylaxis with single-dose doxycycline for the prevention of Lyme disease after an *Ixodes scapularis* tick bite. *N Engl J Med* 2001 Jul 12;345(2):79–84.

62. Steere AC, Sikand VK, Maurice F, et al. Vaccination against Lyme disease with recombinant *Borrelia Burgdorferi* outer-surface lipoprotein A with adjuvant. *N Engl J Med* 1998 Jul 23;339(4):209–215.

63. Sigal LH, Zahradnik JM, Lavin P, et al. A vaccine consisting of recombinant *Borrelia burgdorferi* outer-surface protein A to prevent Lyme disease. *N Engl J Med* 1998 Jul 23;339(4):216–222.

64. Earnhart C, Marconi R. An octavalent Lyme disease vaccine induces antibodies that recognize all incorporated OspC type-specific sequences. *Hum Vaccin* 2007 Nov-Dec;3(6):281–289.

SUPPLEMENTAL RESOURCES

Centers for Disease Control and Prevention (CDC). *Lyme Disease (Borrelia burgdorferi): 2008 Case Definition.* Available at: http://www.cdc.gov/lyme/healthcare/clinicians.html#case-definition.

CHAPTER 86

Measles, Mumps, Rubella

Michael Anne Preas RN, BSN, CIC
Director, Infection Prevention
University of Maryland Medical Center
Baltimore, MD

CHAPTER OVERVIEW

This chapter covers three distinct viral diseases that are prevented with a combined and effective vaccine. For convenience, the chapter is separated into three sections to more suitably discuss the uniqueness of each disease entity—measles, mumps, and rubella.

ABSTRACT—MEASLES

Measles is a highly contagious febrile exanthem. In most immunocompetent individuals, measles is a self-limited condition with a distinct clinical prodrome of cough, coryza, and conjunctivitis followed by a morbilliform skin eruption. Measles is more severe in young, malnourished, and immunocompromised individuals. Even healthy individuals may experience complications, such as otitis media, bronchopneumonia, encephalitis, and laryngotracheobronchitis. A live virus vaccine to prevent measles has been available since 1963 and has resulted in substantial reduction (approaching 99 percent) of measles in countries with active measles vaccine programs. Despite the availability of this effective vaccine, measles still causes significant morbidity and mortality worldwide, especially in nonindustrialized nations. Measles occurs only in humans (no animal reservoir), and the current vaccine is highly effective. For these reasons, the World Health Organization (WHO) has targeted measles for global elimination. Because measles is so highly contagious, healthcare facilities need to be prepared to safely care for measles patients. Measles immunity (natural or vaccinated) among healthcare personnel and use of proper isolation guidelines and postexposure protocols need to be established to minimize the potential for healthcare-associated transmission of measles.

KEY CONCEPTS—MEASLES

- Measles is a highly contagious febrile exanthema.

- The live vaccine significantly reduced measles in nations with high vaccine coverage and resulted in a 71 percent decrease in measles deaths between 2000 and 2011 worldwide, as well as a decrease of approximately 90 percent in the eastern Mediterranean and Africa regions.

- Morbidity and mortality are still high in nonindustrialized nations.

- Complications can occur in malnourished, pregnant, immunocompromised, and young patients.

BACKGROUND—MEASLES

Measles (rubeola, 7-day measles) is a distinct clinical syndrome with a characteristic prodrome of respiratory tract symptoms (cough, coryza, and conjunctivitis), followed by a febrile exanthem and a recovery period that includes a persistent cough for many weeks. Measles occurs throughout the world. It is one of the most highly contagious infectious diseases in humans. In parts of the world where measles vaccination has been instituted, the incidence of measles has decreased substantially. In much of the nonindustrialized world, measles is still responsible for significant morbidity and mortality. It remains a leading cause of death among young children globally, despite the availability of a safe and effective vaccine. An estimated 159,000 people died of measles in 2011; mostly children under 5 years of age.[a]

BASIC PRINCIPLES—MEASLES

The measles virus is a ribonucleic acid (RNA)-containing paramyxovirus with one serotype, classified in the genus *Morbillivirus* in the family Paramyxoviridae.[1-4] It is an enveloped, nonsegmented, single-stranded, negative-sense RNA virus. Measles is antigenically distinct from, but related closely to, canine distemper virus and rinderpest virus.[1] Humans are the only natural host for wild measles virus.[5] Measles virus, in contrast with other paramyxoviruses, does not contain specific neuraminidase activity, and it does not adsorb to neuraminic acid–containing cellular receptors.[1] Measles virus hemagglutinates red blood cells, but other *Morbillivirus* spp. do not.

EPIDEMIOLOGY—MEASLES

Measles has been recognized as a disease for approximately 2,000 years. In the ninth century, Rhazes, a Persian physician from Baghdad, provided the first written account of measles.[6] The first account of measles in North America was described in Boston in 1657 by John Hall.[7] It was not until 1955, however, when Enders and Peebles[8] successfully propagated wild measles virus in primary human renal tissue culture cells that a significant understanding of measles was possible. The isolation and propagation of wild measles virus allowed the development of a vaccine, which was licensed for the first time in the United States in 1963. Humans are the only source of measles infection; there is no animal reservoir. Measles is one of the more highly contagious of all infectious diseases and is seen in every country of the world. Before the availability of live measles vaccine, epidemics of measles in temperate climates occurred periodically every 2 to 6 years and lasted approximately 3 to 4 months in late winter and early spring. In a remote region or on isolated islands, epidemics have longer interepidemic periods of 10 years or more. Epidemics of measles are less marked in equatorial regions. In countries where the live measles vaccine has been used in most of the population, the incidence of measles has decreased by approximately 99 percent.[9,10] In 1993, endemic transmission of measles in the United States was interrupted.[11,12] Subsequent cases in the United States represent imported cases or secondary transmission from imported cases.

The childhood immunization program in the United States has resulted in a greater than 99 percent reduction in reported cases of measles.[4] Since 1965, after widespread use of the measles vaccine (first licensed in 1963), the incidence of the disease has declined in all age groups. A relatively recent (1988 to 1991) recrudescence of measles has been documented; however, the adverse consequences can be associated with suboptimal immunization rates in preschool children, especially in urban areas. Although the major contributing factor to this recurrence of measles was a low immunization rate in preschool-aged children, vaccine failure also played a role (primary vaccine failure occurs in 5 percent of children immunized at 12 months of age). Waning immunity (secondary vaccine failure) may occur, but this did not seem to be a major contributor to the resurgence that began in the late 1980s. Many underdeveloped countries with low immunization rates still have major problems with endemic and epidemic measles.

In 1978, the Department of Health, Education, and Welfare established the elimination of sustained (indigenous) transmission of measles virus in the United States and Canada by 1982 as a formal goal.[4] Although this goal was not achieved, considerable progress was made toward measles elimination from the United States. Before licensure of the measles vaccine in 1963, there was an average of 400,000 measles cases reported each year in the United States. Because nearly all children acquired measles, however, the number was more likely 3.5 million cases per year (i.e., an entire birth cohort).[13] Since the new two-dose measles, mumps, and rubella (MMR) vaccine recommendations were implemented in the United States, imported cases increased from 59 percent of all reported cases in 1997 to 85 percent in 2004.[14-16]

From January to July 2008, 131 measles cases were reported to the Centers for Disease Control and Prevention (CDC), whereas from 2000 to 2007, the country averaged 63 cases per year. Although 89 percent were imported from or associated with other countries, particularly Europe, 91 percent of

cases were in those who were unvaccinated or of unknown vaccination status.[17] During 2011, 222 cases of measles were reported to the CDC from 30 states—the highest number of reported measles since 1996.[2] The majority (approximately 85 percent) of cases were in people who were unimmunized or had unknown immunization status.[2]

By 1980, the National Childhood Immunization Initiative succeeded in establishing immunization laws requiring administration of many specific vaccines, including measles vaccine, preferably as MMR, before enrollment into public school in most states.[13] Most states have laws requiring the second dose of measles vaccine before enrollment in elementary school or middle school.

Global eradication of measles is feasible, and an eradication program is in progress.[18] The World Health Organization (WHO) and partners in the Measles and Rubella Initiative have developed a Global Measles & Rubella Strategic Plan 2012–2020. The plan presents a five-pronged strategy to cut global measles deaths by at least 95 percent by 2015 compared with 2000 levels and to achieve measles and rubella elimination in at least five WHO regions by 2020. The strategies include high vaccination coverage; monitoring spread of disease using laboratory-backed surveillance; outbreak preparedness and response and case management; communication and community engagement; and research and development. Between 2000 and 2011, new cases of measles dropped 58 percent from 853,500 in 2000 to 355,000 in 2011.[19] Estimated global coverage with a first dose of vaccine increased from 72 percent in 2000 to 84 percent in 2011. The number of countries providing the second dose through routine services increased from 97 in 2000 to 141 in 2011. Since 2000, with support from the Measles & Rubella Initiative, more than 1 billion children have been reached through mass vaccination campaigns— about 225 million of them in 2011.[20]

Measles virus grows in the cells that line the back of the throat and lungs.[1] Respiratory secretions are the source of virus leading to transmission. Individuals are most contagious during the respiratory (catarrhal) prodromal phase, corresponding to the period from 1 to 2 days before the onset of symptoms (3 to 5 days before the onset of rash) to 4 days after the first appearance of the rash. Measles is transmitted person to person by direct contact with infectious droplets, principally by airborne spread but also by contact. Immunocompromised persons have prolonged excretion of virus from respiratory secretions, and transmission may occur throughout the duration of the symptoms and possibly longer.[4] Asymptomatic contagious carriers do not seem to exist.

Transmission in hospitals and healthcare facility waiting rooms demonstrates a continued need for healthcare facilities to be vigilant and involved with prevention. Healthcare personnel (HCP) should be immune (natural infection or appropriately immunized) and therefore at a decreased risk for acquisition of the disease while working in the healthcare facility.[19] Because some populations may not have access to primary care providers or adhere to appropriate immunization schedules, all patient encounters at healthcare facilities should be used as an opportunity to update immunizations for measles and all other appropriate immunizations for children and adults.

CLINICAL MANIFESTATIONS—MEASLES

Measles has a distinct clinical presentation that allows clinical diagnosis and differentiation from other viral exanthems. Illness usually begins 8 to 12 days after exposure. Respiratory tract symptoms (cough, coryza, and conjunctivitis), fever, and malaise are noted first; these are followed in 2 to 4 days by the characteristic rash. The exanthem begins as an erythematous, macular, or maculopapular eruption. It is usually noted first on the scalp, face, and neck as discrete lesions. These initial lesions enlarge and coalesce as lesions progress to involve the chest, back, and upper extremities. The rash continues to progress with coalescence of lesions on the chest, back, and arms. New discrete lesions may be noted on the abdomen and buttocks. This pattern continues downward on the body with clearing of the initial skin lesions on the face by the time the lower extremities are affected. As the lesions clear, the rash color changes from pink-red to a brawny color, then finally to fine desquamation. Fever is also a prominent sign of measles. The magnitude of the fever parallels the extent of the rash. Koplik spots (enanthem) are present at the end of the prodrome and beginning of the rash. These whitish spots present on the buccal mucosa, typically opposite the molars, are present in 50 to 90 percent of cases, and are pathognomonic for measles. Cough is also present in all cases of measles. When evaluating patients with an erythematous rash, measles should be considered only if the patient has fever, significant cough, and a prodrome including coryza and conjunctivitis.

Of the common childhood exanthems, measles produces the greatest morbidity and mortality. Complications include acute otitis media (superinfection with usual bacterial pathogens), bronchopneumonia (measles giant cell pneumonia and secondary bacterial pneumonia), laryngotracheobronchitis (croup), generalized adenopathy, splenomegaly, and encephalitis.[21] Severe measles and complications (except encephalitis) are more likely to occur in young children (under 2 years of age); individuals who are immunocompromised through malnutrition or have a primary immunodeficiency, particularly cellular immunodeficiencies; and pregnant women.[22-24] In immunocompromised populations, the rash may be atypical or not present at all. Encephalitis occurs more commonly in school-aged children.[25,26] Less common complications of measles include keratitis/corneal ulceration, pericarditis, myocarditis, hepatitis, stomatitis, mesenteric lymphadenitis (pseudoappendicitis syndrome), diarrhea, and appendicitis.[27,28] Although the incidence of measles is the same for males and females, complications such as otitis media, laryngitis, and pneumonia are more common in males.[26] Mortality, predominantly due to respiratory tract or neurologic complications, is seen primarily in immunocompromised or malnourished children. Overcrowding and intensive exposure (e.g., household contact or multiple simultaneous contacts) to measles may predispose individuals to more severe complications including death.

Acute measles encephalitis occurs in approximately 1 of every 1,000 cases and can result in permanent brain damage.[4] Subacute sclerosing panencephalitis (SSPE) is a rare degenerative central nervous system complication characterized by behavioral and intellectual deterioration and seizures. It may occur years after measles infection because of the persistence of the measles virus within the central nervous system.

Infection during pregnancy has been associated with more severe illness and an increased risk of miscarriage or preterm delivery. There is no convincing evidence that measles occurring during pregnancy is responsible for congenital malformations.

Milder forms of measles ("modified measles") occur in individuals with some degree of immunity (e.g., children under 6 months of age born to mothers who have had measles or individuals who have received blood products containing measles immunoglobulin [Ig]G antibodies). This illness includes similar clinical findings as typical measles except that the rash and fever are significantly reduced in intensity and duration.

Between 1963 and 1967, a killed measles vaccine was in use in the United States, and the resultant humoral immunity to the vaccine waned within a few years. However, the cell-mediated immunity to measles persisted. After exposure to wild measles, recipients of this killed vaccine developed *atypical* measles, a severe form of measles with a characteristic fever, rash (purpuric rash that may be more prominent on distal extremities), pneumonitis, and hepatitis. The syndrome is hypothesized to result from a hypersensitivity to the measles virus in a partially immune host. The role of humoral or cellular immunity in the pathogenesis of this syndrome is still not elucidated.

The differential diagnoses for patients with a febrile, morbilliform (measles-like rash) presentation include the following:

1. Other viral exanthems (e.g., rubella, roseola, parvovirus B19), differentiated by respiratory tract prodrome, high fever, Koplik spots, and characteristic appearance and progression of the rash

2. Epstein-Barr virus (EBV, mononucleosis), particularly with morbilliform antibiotic drug eruption (e.g., amoxicillin or ampicillin)

3. *Mycoplasma pneumoniae* infection with rash

4. Drug eruption (e.g., phenobarbital, phenytoin, sulfonamides)

5. Kawasaki disease

6. Toxic shock syndrome

CLINICAL/LABORATORY DIAGNOSIS—MEASLES

A specific diagnosis of measles can usually be made on the basis of clinical presentation alone because of the characteristic prodrome (cough, coryza, and conjunctivitis with or without Koplik spots) and febrile exanthem. As cases of measles become less frequent, however, physicians and other healthcare providers will have less experience with measles infections. These circumstances may diminish the reliability of clinical diagnosis.

Detection of measles virus or antigens in clinical specimens or tissue can establish a recent infection with the measles virus. Viral isolation is possible from respiratory secretions, blood, urine, and, in special circumstances, skin biopsy. Specimens should be collected early in the acute phase of infection to have the greatest likelihood of isolating the measles virus. Specimens should be transported as quickly as possible to the viral laboratory because measles virus is very labile. Transport and storage of specimens is best at 4°C because freezing causes considerable loss of recoverable virus. Virus isolation in cases of measles can be valuable because genotyping assists in the determination of whether the case is endemic or imported. Measles antigen detection in exfoliated cells and tissue can be accomplished using immunofluorescence or polymerase chain reaction (PCR).

Serologic testing may be used to confirm the clinical diagnosis of measles or to assess immunity. The presence of measles IgM antibody by enzyme immunoassay (EIA) confirms a diagnosis of recent measles. Measles-specific IgM antibodies may not be present until 72 hours after the onset of the rash, however. Seroconversion or a fourfold increase in measles IgG antibody titer by EIA, hemagglutination inhibition (HAI), or neutralizing antibodies can also be used to confirm a recent measles infection.

TREATMENT—MEASLES

Because measles is generally a self-limited condition in well-nourished, immunocompetent individuals, treatment is usually limited to supportive care that includes the following:

1. Discourage activity during time of fever

2. Encourage adequate hydration

3. Administer agents for fever control (acetaminophen or ibuprofen)

4. Keep room humidified

5. Use antitussives judiciously

Vitamin A has been shown to be valuable for children with vitamin A deficiency. It is recommended for all children with measles who live in communities where vitamin A deficiency is endemic and in geographical locations where the measles case-fatality rate is 1 percent or greater. Although vitamin A deficiency is not a common problem in the United States and other industrialized nations, low serum vitamin A levels have been seen in children with severe measles from these areas. Vitamin A supplementation should be considered in the following individuals:[2]

1. Children 6 months to 2 years old who require hospitalization (e.g., croup, pneumonia, diarrhea)

2. All individuals 6 months old and older with an immunodeficiency or definite or possible vitamin A deficiency (e.g., ophthalmologic evidence of vitamin A deficiency, impaired

intestinal absorption, moderate-to-severe malnutrition, or recent immigrant from areas where high mortality rates due to measles have been observed)

The dose of vitamin A is 100,000 international units (IU) orally in infants 6 to 12 months of age and 200,000 IU orally in children 1 year of age and older. Data are limited on safety and need for vitamin A supplementation for infants younger than 6 months. The dose should be repeated 24 hours and 4 weeks after the first dose for children with vitamin A deficiency.

No specific antiviral therapy is available for measles. Ribavirin (aerosol or intravenous) has been given to treat severely affected or immunocompromised children with measles. Efficacy of ribavirin in measles has not been established by clinical trials, however, and it has not been approved for this indication by the U.S. Food and Drug Administration.

PREVENTION AND INFECTION CONTROL MEASURES—MEASLES

The current measles vaccine used in the United States is a live attenuated measles strain prepared in a chick embryo fibroblast cell culture. This vaccine strain, licensed in 1968, is a further attenuated preparation of the Enders-Edmonston strain formerly called Moraten. This strain causes fewer adverse events than the Edmonston B Strain (original live attenuated measles vaccine available in 1963). Measles vaccine is available in a monovalent (measles-only) formulation, combined with rubella vaccine as the MR vaccine, and combined with mumps and rubella vaccines as the MMR vaccine. Measles vaccination of susceptible individuals with the current live-attenuated vaccine causes a mild or clinically inapparent, noncommunicable measles infection. Measles antibodies develop in at least 95 percent of susceptible children vaccinated at age 12 months of age or older.[2] Vaccination of immune individuals is not deleterious. Immunization of individuals whose measles immune status is unknown may be prudent and cost-efficient. Combined MMR vaccine should be given when measles vaccination is indicated if recipients also are likely to be susceptible to mumps or rubella or both.

Serious adverse events after measles vaccine administration are rare. Fever of 39.4°C (103°F) or higher may occur in 5 to 15 percent of susceptible vaccines. The fever is noted 7 to 12 days after receipt of the MMR vaccination and usually lasts 1 to 2 days. Transient rash occurring with the fever occurs in a smaller number of susceptible vaccine recipients (5 percent). Transient thrombocytopenia has rarely occurred temporally associated with administration of measles-containing vaccines. It is more common in individuals with prior thrombocytopenia. Encephalitis and encephalopathy are extremely rare (fewer than 1 per 1 million doses administered) as vaccine-induced neurologic diseases. When seizures occur after measles vaccine, they usually are associated with fever (simple febrile convulsions).

Children with minor illnesses, including those with fever, may be vaccinated with the measles vaccine. The measles vaccine should not be administered during febrile illnesses when there

Table 86-1. Interval Between Administration of Human-Derived Blood or Immunoglobulin Products and Vaccines Containing Live Rubella or Measles Virus

Indication	Product	Dose (mg IgG/kg)	Route	Interval Between Immune Globulin and Vaccine (mo)
Tetanus prophylaxis	TIG	10	IM	3
Hepatitis A prophylaxis, contact prophylaxis, international travel	IG	3.3 (0.02 mL/kg), 10 (0.06 mL/kg)	IM	3
Hepatitis B prophylaxis	HBIG	10	IM	3
Rabies prophylaxis	HRIG	22 (20 IU/kg)	IM	4
Varicella prophylaxis	VZIG	20–40 (125 U/10 kg) (maximum = 625 U)	IM	5
Measles prophylaxis, nonimmunocompromised contact and immunocompromised contact	IG	40 (0.25 mL/kg) (nonimmunocompromised contact), 80 (0.5 mL/kg) (immunocompromised contact)	IM	5 (nonimmunocompromised contact), 6 (immunocompromised contact)
Blood transfusion				
Washed RBCs		10 mL/kg = negligible IgG	IV	0
RBCs, adenine-saline added		10 mL/kg = 10 mg IgG/kg	IV	3
Packed RBCs		10 mL/kg = 60 mg IgG/kg	IV	6
Whole blood		10 mL/kg = 80–100 mg IgG/kg	IV	6
Platelets		10 mL/kg = 160 mg IgG/kg	IV	7
Plasma products		10 mL/kg = 160 mg IgG/kg	IV	7

RBCs, red blood cells.

Modified from Measles. In: *2012 Red Book: Report of the Committee on Infectious Diseases*, 29th ed. Evanston, IL: American Academy of Pediatrics, 2012; 38.

are other manifestations that suggest a serious illness. Children whose measles vaccine is deferred because they have more severe illnesses or other manifestations that suggest a serious illness may be vaccinated shortly after recovery.

Measles vaccine is produced in chick embryo cell culture and does not contain significant amounts of egg cross-reacting proteins. Although there is an extremely low risk for an anaphylactic reaction to measles-containing vaccines, persons with severe reactions after egg ingestion should be vaccinated with extreme caution. Skin testing for egg hypersensitivity is not predictive of reactions to the measles vaccine.

Live measles containing vaccines should not be administered to the following individuals:

1. Pregnant women

2. Individuals with significantly altered immunity (primary or secondary immunodeficiency); measles-containing vaccines may be given to human immunodeficiency virus-infected individuals as long as they do not have evidence of current severe immunosuppression at the time of immunization. Severe immunosuppression is defined as CD4+ T-lymphocyte percentages less than 15 percent at any age or a CD4 count less than 200 lymphocytes/mm for persons older than 5 years of age.

3. Individuals who recently received human immunoglobulin or immunoglobulin-containing blood products; individuals who

have recently received human blood products need to defer live measles virus vaccine for a time period based on the dose and route of the blood product (Table 86-1).

Certain situations can reduce the protective efficacy of the measles vaccine. Inactivated (killed) measles vaccine is not considered to provide adequate protection and can place recipients at risk for atypical measles. The current measles vaccine in use in the United States is a live vaccine. Improper handling of this live vaccine could result in inactivation of the vaccine with a loss of potency and reduction in immune response. Passively acquired maternal antibodies reduce replication of the measles vaccine virus. Partial immunity to measles at the time of measles vaccine administration causes reduction in antigen production, which results in inadequate levels of measles immune response. In the setting of a measles outbreak, particularly among preschool-aged children, the measles vaccine (monovalent vaccine preferred, but MMR can be given) may be administered to children at risk. Children immunized before their first birthday should be reimmunized at age 12 to 15 months and again before entering school (ages 4 to 6 years).[2]

In addition to maternal measles antibodies, therapeutic administration of blood products that contain measles antibody reduces measles vaccine virus replication and results in suboptimal immune response.[4,29] Table 86-2 describes the interval between human blood product administration and the timing for appropriate administration of measles vaccine.[2]

Table 86-2. Interval Between Administration of Human-Derived Blood or Immunoglobulin Products and Vaccines Containing Live Rubella or Measles Virus

Indication	Product	Dose (mg IgG/kg)	Route	Globulin and Vaccine (mo)
Replacement for humoral immunodeficiencies	IGIV	300–400	IV	8
RSV prophylaxis	RSV-IGIV, palivizumab	750 (RSV-IGIV)	IV, IM	9
Immune thrombocytopenic purpura	IGIV	400, 1000, 1600–2000	IV	8, 10, 11
Kawasaki disease	IGIV	2000	IV	11

RSV, respiratory syncytial virus.

Modified from Watson JC, Hadler SC, Dykewicz CA, et al. Measles, mumps and rubella—vaccine use and strategies for elimination of measles, rubella and congenital rubella syndrome and control of mumps: recommendations of the Advisory Committee on Immunization Practices (ACIP) *MMWR Morb Mortal Wkly Rep.* 1998 May 22;47(RR-8):1–57.

Two doses of the measles vaccine are recommended to ensure universal protection. Primary vaccine failure occurs in 5 percent of measles vaccine recipients. The second dose is given to increase the likelihood that this 5 percent who initially did not develop protective antibody levels will subsequently develop immunity.

Healthcare facilities should establish vaccination programs to ensure that all HCP who may be in contact with patients with measles are immune to measles.[4] HCP are at a unique risk for acquiring measles because patients who are ill with measles frequently present for medical care. A lack of familiarity with clinical manifestations of measles enhances the likelihood that HCP will be inadvertently exposed to patients with measles who are not properly isolated.

Measles vaccination during the 72 hours after measles exposure may be protective. Susceptible (nonimmune) HCP, patients, or others who are exposed to a case of measles should be vaccinated as soon as possible, preferably within 72 hours after exposure. Exposure to measles is not a contraindication to immunization with the measles vaccine. If time since exposure has been greater than 72 hours or in certain immunocompromised individuals, however, immunoglobulin may be the preferred method of prophylaxis.

Immunoglobulins[2] (immune serum globulin [ISG] or intravenous immunoglobulin [IVIG]) may prevent or modify measles in susceptible persons if given within 6 days of exposure. Susceptible household contacts of patients with measles, particularly infants under 1 year or age, immunocompromised persons, and pregnant women, are candidates for immunoglobulin. The usual recommended dose of ISG is 0.5 mL/kg body weight given intramuscularly. Immunocompromised children should receive 0.5 mL/kg body weight. The maximal dose of ISG is 15 mL. ISG is less expensive and can be given more easily than IVIG. If ISG is in short supply or there is a contraindication to intramuscular injections (e.g., bleeding disorders), IVIG can be administered at a dose of 100 to 400 mg/kg. For patients routinely receiving IVIG (e.g., patients with hypogammaglobulinemia, autoimmune disease), the usual dose of 400 mg/kg should be sufficient for measles prophylaxis for exposures occurring 3 weeks after the most recent IVIG infusion.

Relevant Information for Measles Exposure Episode Management

Measles is a reportable disease in the United States and, depending on the extent of the exposure, the local health department may play a key role in exposure management. Because of the infrequency with which measles is seen at most healthcare facilities, management of measles cases or potential exposure episodes requires an understanding of its clinical presentation, transmission characteristics, populations at risk, and incubation period. Typically, measles has an onset of symptoms 8 to 12 days after exposure (fever, cough, coryza, and conjunctivitis are the initial manifestations—prodrome to rash).[2] The rash usually appears on average 14 days after exposure. The period of contagion begins 1 to 2 days before the onset of overt symptoms (respiratory symptoms, not rash) and continues until 4 days after development of the rash. The duration of viral excretion (transmissibility) is prolonged for at least the duration of illness in immunocompromised individuals. Measles does not occur in individuals with prior immunity to measles. Criteria that may be used to determine immune status of individuals include the following:

- Lab evidence of immunity

- Documention of age appropriate vaccination with a live measles virus containing vaccine

- Lab confirmation of disease. Physician diagnosed history of measles is no longer considered an acceptable criterion of evidence of immunity.[29]

Documentation of adequate vaccination requires written verification of the receipt of two doses of measles vaccine on or after the first birthday because vaccine given before the first birthday cannot be considered to satisfy the two-dose requirement. Reliability of a physician-diagnosed history of measles depends on epidemiologic factors and the experience of the physician. In addition, most persons born before 1957 were infected naturally and should be considered immune.[30] Individuals born before 1957 without a history of measles should be screened serologically for immunity.

Measles is highly contagious and is spread by large and small droplets. Susceptible patients who have been exposed to an individual with measles (contagious) should be placed in an airborne infection isolation room from the fifth to the twenty-first day after exposure (regardless of whether they received measles vaccine or immunoglobulin for this specific exposure) or from the onset of symptoms until 4 days after the onset of the rash if the patient becomes ill.[2,27] Susceptible HCP who have been exposed to an individual with measles should be furloughed (relieved from healthcare activities) from the fifth to the twenty-first day after exposure, regardless of whether they received measles vaccine or immunoglobulin after exposure or until 4 days after development of their rash. HCP who develop measles should be furloughed until they have had their rash for 4 days. Susceptible patients and personnel may be given a live attenuated measles-containing vaccine within 72 hours of exposure to modify disease. This vaccine does not modify the need for isolation precautions or furlough. Susceptible patients and HCP who are immunocompromised should be given immunoglobulin to modify their disease (as described previously). Immunoglobulin does not modify the need for isolation or furlough.

Airborne infection isolation requires a single (private) room with negative pressure ventilation, adequate air exchanges per hour, and direct exhaust to the outside environment or recirculated through a high-efficiency particulate air filter before returning to circulation; susceptible persons should not enter the isolation room.[2,31] Mask, gowns, and gloves are not essential, but HCP should follow Standard Precautions.[31] For patients with proven or suspected measles, airborne infection isolation should start with the onset of symptoms (respiratory tract or rash) and be maintained until 4 days after the appearance of the rash. Patients with documented or suspected SSPE, atypical measles, and measles vaccine–induced fever or rash do not require any form of isolation.[2]

CONCLUSIONS—MEASLES

Measles remains an important infection worldwide, and the availability of an effective vaccine has significantly reduced cases. Endemic measles essentially has been eliminated in the United States, but the ease of global travel still allows imported measles cases. Until global elimination of measles is a reality, healthcare providers should be aware of the clinical manifestations of measles, means of diagnosis, and methods to limit transmission. Healthcare facilities should ensure adequate immunity of HCP, such as through use of the live measles vaccination, appropriate environmental controls, (negative airflow isolation rooms), and exposure management guidelines and policies.

FUTURE TRENDS—MEASLES

The goal is to maintain measles elimination efforts in the United States through rapid and efficient public health response resulting in limited outbreak size, especially in communities with subpopulations who choose not to vaccinate their children.[32]

INTERNATIONAL PERSPECTIVE—MEASLES

Despite an effective vaccine, measles still results in considerable morbidity and mortality in many areas of the world. The impact of measles is greatest in children, especially those who are malnourished or have immunodeficiency conditions (primary or acquired). The Measles and Rubella Initiative's goal is now to reduce measles deaths worldwide by 95 percent by 2015 and to eliminate measles and rubella in at least five of six WHO regions by 2020.[20]

ABSTRACT—MUMPS

Mumps is a systemic, commonly self-limited, viral infection caused by an enveloped ribonucleic acid virus belonging to the genus Rubulavirus, which is a member of the Paramyxoviridae family. Clinical infection is characterized by swollen salivary glands (parotitis), high fever, and fatigue. Parotitis, when present, is usually bilateral and is observed in 30 to 40 percent of those infected. Humans are the only natural host. Transmission occurs through droplets of respiratory secretions. Communicability is comparable to influenza and rubella, less than that of varicella or measles, and is maximal from 2 days before onset of parotitis to 9 days after. The average incubation period for mumps is 18 days, with a range of 12 to 25 days. After licensure of a vaccine against this virus, the incidence has decreased dramatically. For example, in 1989 there were more than 5,700 cases reported compared with 231 cases in 2001. Most cases occur in children aged between 5 and 14 years; however, outbreaks can still be seen even when immunization levels are high. In 2006, the United States experienced the largest mumps outbreak in two decades, affecting primarily college students aged 18 to 24 years.

KEY CONCEPTS—MUMPS

- Since 1989, there has been a steady decline in reported mumps cases, most likely as a result of implementation of the second-dose recommendation for measles vaccine (as MMR vaccine).

- The most important intervention to keep incidence low is to ensure that susceptible persons, including healthcare personnel, receive two doses of MMR.

- Outbreaks have been common whenever large groups of individuals are in close contact or a significant number of susceptible persons are gathered, such as in schools, military settings, prisons, ships, and remote islands.

- Humans are the only known natural host of mumps virus.

- Transmission is by droplet spread of respiratory secretions, through direct contact with infected fluids (primarily saliva or urine), and occasionally via fomites.

- Supportive measures and use of analgesic-antipyretics for pain and fever are typical measures for those with disease, with attention to adequate hydration.

- Droplet Precautions are recommended for people with acute mumps infection for 9 days after onset of parotid swelling. Susceptible healthcare personnel should not care for such patients; use immune personnel instead.[31]

BACKGROUND—MUMPS

The mumps virus, included in the genus *Rubulavirus* and within the family Paramyxoviridae (includes parainfluenza and Newcastle disease virus), causes mumps. The name "mumps" likely came from an old English verb for "grimace, grin, or mumble."[33] This single-stranded ribonucleic acid (RNA), lipid-enveloped virus was established as the etiologic agent of mumps in 1934,[34] and subsequently a vaccine incorporating an attenuated form was prepared by Buynak and Hilleman in 1966.[35] Mumps infection, though systemic, is usually self-limited with symptoms of unilateral or bilateral parotitis, high fever, and fatigue. Most cases are seen in children and adolescents between the ages of 5 and 19 years.

Historically, outbreaks of mumps were common among military personnel, and the incidence of this disease was third behind influenza and gonorrhea as a cause of hospitalization among soldiers during World War I. An estimated 212,000 cases occurred in the United States in 1964, and starting in 1968, mumps became a nationally reportable disease. With the development and implementation of an effective vaccine, incidence decreased rapidly to approximately 3,000 cases per year. However, beginning in 1986, there was a resurgence of mumps with a peak in 1987 of 12,848 reported cases, primarily among adolescents and college-age adults who were born before consistent requirement for mumps vaccine in children. Outbreaks have occurred in healthcare facilities as well, primarily a reflection of birth cohort-related susceptibility.

Since 1989, there has been a steady decline in reported mumps cases, from 5,712 cases to a provisional total of 231 cases in 2001, the lowest annual total ever reported. The decrease in mumps in recent years is most likely the result of implementation of the second dose recommendation for measles vaccine (as MMR vaccine). Primary prevention by ensuring susceptible persons receive two doses of MMR is the most important intervention to keep incidence of this viral disease as low as possible.

More recently, in 2006, an outbreak of mumps resulted in reports of 2,597 cases of mumps in 11 states in the United States. From 2009 through 2010, mumps outbreaks occurred in a religious community in the Northeastern United States, with approximately 3,500 cases.[36] In 2011, a university campus in California reported 29 cases of mumps, of which 22 (76 percent) occurred among persons previously vaccinated with the recommended two doses of MMR vaccine.[36] The age group most affected was young adults aged 18 to 24 years; most were college students, but the disease spread to all age groups. Subsequently, the Advisory Committee on Immunization Practices (ACIP) updated the recommendations for mumps vaccination.

BASIC PRINCIPLES—MUMPS

Virology

The surface proteins on the mumps virion (virus) perform two functions: hemagglutination-neuraminidase activity and cell fusion. During the 18-day incubation period, the virus multiplies in the upper respiratory tract tissue after infection of T lymphocytes. Lymph nodes are the focal point for viral replication, and viremia allows dissemination throughout the body.[37] (Also refer to Chapter 22 Microbial Pathogenicity and Host Response, for more information on T lymphocytes and immunity.)

Pathogenesis

The virus is acquired by respiratory droplets and subsequently replicates in the nasopharynx and regional lymph nodes. After 12 to 25 days, a viremia occurs that lasts from 3 to 5 days. During the viremia, the virus spreads to multiple tissues, including the meninges, and glands such as the salivary, pancreas, testes, and ovaries. Inflammation in infected tissues leads to characteristic symptoms of parotitis and, in up to 10 percent of cases, aseptic meningitis.

Immune Response and Primary Prevention

After infection, both cell-mediated and humoral-mediated immune responses develop. The latter produces virus-specific antibody, which appears to be key to resolution of initial infection. The stimulation of immune response through use of mumps virus vaccine has resulted in a notable decline in the incidence of mumps and its associated complications. Primary prevention (i.e., use of live-attenuated vaccine) is very effective as evidenced by dramatic declines in wild virus infections. The vaccine used in the United States is composed of the Jeryl Lynn B strain of mumps that is attenuated through a series of passages via cell cultures. Another strain, the Urabe Am[9] used in Japan, Europe, Canada, and other countries since 1979 to the early 1990s, was withdrawn because of an observed adverse event involving vaccine-virus meningitis that appeared within 4 weeks after receipt.[38-40] A third vaccine formulation using the Rubini strain used in some countries does not appear to be as effective in eliciting immune response.[41]

Neutralizing antibody is evident by approximately 2 weeks after immunization, with more than 97 percent of recipients developing evidence of immune response after a single dose. Mumps-specific neutralizing antibody persists for more than 25 years, and immunity probably is lifelong. Clinical efficacy of the vaccine in preventing disease ranges from 90 to 97 percent.

EPIDEMIOLOGY—MUMPS

Disease Trends

Before licensing of the mumps vaccine in the 1960s, more than 200,000 cases of mumps occurred each year, often in epidemic levels every 2 to 5 years, predominantly among young children.[42] In 1977, the U.S. Public Health Service

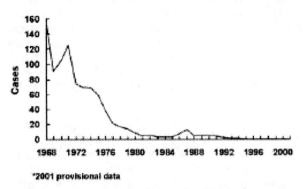

Figure 86-1. Number of reported cases (in 1000s) of mumps, U.S., 1968–2011. Source: CDC. http://www.cdc.gov/mmwr/preview/mmwrhtml/rr6204a1.htm#Tab1

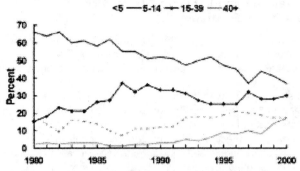

Figure 86-2. Age distribution of reported cases of mumps, United States, 1980–2000. Source: CDC.

recommended universal vaccination against mumps for children 12 months of age and older.[43] Revised recommendations released in 1980 to include susceptible children, adolescents, and adults have, in combination with laws requiring mumps vaccination for school entry, resulted in a steady decline in incidence (e.g., 2 per 100,000 population in 1988 to 0.7 per 100,000 population in 1993).[43] Figure 86-1 illustrates this declining incidence since provision of mumps vaccine on a national basis. Comprehensive school immunization laws, routine vaccination of young children, and policies targeting older populations of susceptible persons have all contributed to the decline in incidence of mumps. For example, reported incidence rate of mumps in states with legal requirements for vaccination before entry to school were 1.3 cases per 100,000 population versus 2.9 cases per 100,000 population for states without such requirements.[43] States in which vaccination laws were less comprehensive reported intermediate mumps incidence, with the highest incidence reported in states without such laws.[44]

Administration of the mumps vaccine has resulted in a 99 percent decline in the incidence of mumps in the United States.[43] Before vaccine licensure in 1967 and during the early years of vaccine use, most reported cases occurred in the 5- to 9-year age group; 90 percent of cases occurred among children under 15 years of age. As illustrated in Figure 86-2, in the late 1980s there was a shift in greater incidence of disease among older children. The peak number of cases in the United States in 1987 (12,848) primarily affected those aged 10 to 19 years, who were born before implementation of routine vaccination and school entry immunization requirements. Since 1990, persons aged 15 years and older have accounted for 30 to 40 percent of cases per year. Males and females are affected equally. Seroepidemiologic studies in other countries have identified a low incidence of mumps where vaccine coverage is high; low vaccine use results in susceptible populations, especially among adolescents and young adults.[45]

Outbreaks have been common whenever large groups of individuals are in close contact or a significant number of susceptible persons are gathered, such as in schools, military settings, prisons, ships, and remote islands.[43,46-48] A report by Kaplan et al.[49] on an outbreak of mumps among employees at three Chicago futures exchanges reflects the change in populations at risk. A total of 119 cases were observed among employees and their contacts, and 77 percent of these were in persons younger than 30 years (median 5 to 25 years). Cost of control for this outbreak was approximately $1,500 per case (compared with the cost of mumps vaccine of $4 to $9 in 1988 dollars), and almost none of the cases could produce written documentation of receipt of mumps vaccine.

Mode of Transmission, Infectivity, and Incubation Period

Humans are the only known natural host of mumps virus. Transmission is by droplet spread of respiratory secretions, via direct contact with infected fluids (primarily saliva or urine), and occasionally via fomites. The virus attaches to epithelial cells of the respiratory tract and replicates. The period of communicability begins 1 to 2 days (but can be up to 7 days) before onset of symptoms (e.g., parotid swelling) through 9 days thereafter.[50] Risk of transmission to a susceptible person is highest over the 7-day period beginning 2 days before parotitis. Those with relatively few or no symptoms can transmit the disease, and 30 to 40 percent of infections are subclinical. The incubation period ranges from 12 to 25 days (usually 16 to 18 days). Infectivity is greatest just before parotid swelling.

TREATMENT—MUMPS

Supportive measures and use of analgesic-antipyretics for pain and fever are typical measures for those with disease. Attention to adequate hydration is important.

PREVENTION AND INFECTION CONTROL MEASURES—MUMPS

Prevention and Control of Mumps within Healthcare Facilities

Transmission of mumps within hospitals and long-term care facilities housing adolescents and young adults has been reported.[51-55] Although Droplet Precautions are recommended for people with acute mumps infection, use of Isolation Precautions for persons with infection has not been shown to be very effective.[56,57] This probably reflects the fact that the virus is shed before onset of clinical disease, and asymptomatic cases can also transmit infection. Transmission in hospitals in Tennessee has been studied by Wharton et al.[54] Most cases examined were community acquired; however, six healthcare personnel (HCP) in three different institutions and nine patients in a long-term care setting for adolescents and adults were infected after exposure in the healthcare setting.

Fischer et al.,[55] while acknowledging that mumps vaccine has not been demonstrated to be effective in preventing infection postexposure, suggests that it may prevent tertiary cases when administered soon after diagnosis of the index case.[55] Two of 149 exposed employees (one with an inaccurate history of mumps in childhood) and 1 of 29 exposed patients developed an infection from a 12-year-old foreign-born girl in this report.[55] Total expenditures for control of this outbreak were $3,140, which reinforces the value of ensuring that two doses of MMR are given to susceptible HCP regardless of birth year; one case in this report occurred in an individual born before 1957.

Exposed HCP may be infectious for 12 to 25 days after their exposure. Recommendations for control and prevention of mumps in healthcare settings include (1) administering vaccine (preferably MMR) to all who are not immune, unless otherwise contraindicated; (2) restricting susceptible HCP from care of patients with acute mumps, and, when feasible, using immune personnel instead; and (3) excluding susceptible personnel after exposure from duty from the twelfth day after the first exposure to the twenty-sixth day after the last exposure or, if symptoms develop, until 9 days after the onset of parotitis.[58] Passive antibody administered after exposure is not effective in preventing disease. Transmission of mumps from HCP to patients has not been a major problem in hospitals in the United States, reflecting high levels of natural and vaccine-induced immunity in the general population. Droplet Precautions (i.e., placement in a private room if possible and use of a mask by HCP when working within 6 feet of the patient infected with mumps until 9 days after onset of parotid swelling) are recommended.[31,56]

Primary Prevention Using Mumps Vaccine

The principal strategy to prevent mumps is to achieve and maintain high immunization levels, primarily in infants and young children through vaccination programs with two doses of MMR vaccine.[59] In addition, all others thought to be susceptible should be vaccinated unless otherwise contraindicated.[59] The mumps vaccine virus cannot be transmitted to other persons.

Two doses of mumps vaccine, as combination MMR vaccine, separated by at least 4 weeks, are routinely recommended for all children. The first dose should be given on or after the first birthday. The second dose should be given between the ages of 4 and 6 years, preferably before entering kindergarten or first grade. If not, the second dose should be given during a subsequent health visit between the ages of 11 and 12 years. All persons born in or after 1957 should have documentation of at least one dose of MMR.

Although birth before 1957 is generally acceptable evidence of immunity against MMR, healthcare facilities should consider recommending a dose of MMR vaccine to unvaccinated workers born before 1957 who do not have a history of physician-diagnosed or laboratory evidence of immunity.[58,60] Recommendations for use of mumps vaccine for preschool-aged children through adolescents, women of childbearing age, those with underlying human immunodeficiency virus (HIV) infection, and those in colleges/post–high school educational institutions are available elsewhere.[50,61] Recipients of a killed mumps vaccine or one of unknown type, available between 1950 and 1978, should be revaccinated with MMR if at high risk for mumps infection (e.g., HCP). Immunity from this killed vaccine was transient, and the vaccine was administered rarely after licensure of the live-attenuated vaccine in 1967.

During a mumps outbreak, a second dose of mumps vaccine should be considered for children aged 1 to 4 years and adults who have received one dose. In healthcare settings, an effective routine MMR vaccination program for HCP is the best approach to prevent nosocomial transmission. It is recommended that healthcare facilities strongly consider administering two doses of a live mumps virus vaccine to unvaccinated HCP born before 1957 who do not have evidence of mumps immunity.

Because immunoglobulin may interfere with response to MMR vaccine, it should not be given for 5 to 6 months or more after administration of vaccine. The type of antibody-containing immunoglobulin product and clinical circumstances may preclude this spacing interval. Primary vaccination failures among populations with high vaccination use have been reported.[62-65] Current recommendations for a second dose of MMR vaccine between ages 4 and 6 years can reduce vaccine failures. Efficacy has also been diminished because of an alteration in the specific strain of virus used in vaccine preparation, resulting in outbreaks of disease.[65] Information on adverse reactions after MMR vaccination, precautions, and contraindications has been published.[33,66] MMR vaccine may interfere with response to a tuberculin skin test (TST). Therefore, TST can be performed either on the same day MMR vaccine is given or 4 to 6 weeks later.

In the United States, each state and territory has regulations or laws governing the reporting of diseases and conditions of public health importance. Probable or confirmed cases should be reported immediately to the local and state health departments and contacts identified; follow-up serologic testing, when indicated, should be accomplished.

Steps involved in control of outbreaks of mumps in healthcare settings include:

1. Definition of target population

2. Identification of susceptible persons needing vaccination

3. Exclusion of susceptible HCP who are exempt from vaccination (e.g., medical or religious reasons) from the affected institution or setting until the outbreak is terminated

4. Active surveillance for mumps until two incubation periods (i.e., 5 to 6 weeks) have elapsed since onset of the last case.[50,60]

Mumps is less transmissible than measles and other microorganisms spread via the airborne or droplet routes. A high level of immunity among HCP through provision of vaccine is the most effective method for preventing spread in healthcare settings. Risk for transmission in a healthcare facility is low because it generally reflects incidence within the surrounding community or population served.

Although mumps vaccination has not been shown to be effective in preventing mumps in persons already infected, it will prevent infection in persons who are not infected. If susceptible persons can be vaccinated early in the course of an outbreak, they can be protected. However, cases are expected to continue to occur among newly vaccinated persons who are already infected for at least 3 weeks after vaccination because of the long incubation period. As with all vaccines, there are some individuals who will not gain immunity after receipt of mumps vaccine. Because vaccine effectiveness is not 100 percent, a second dose of mumps-containing vaccine is recommended during outbreak situations for individuals who have received only one dose previously. Studies have shown a trend toward a lower attack rate among children who have received two doses of mumps vaccine as opposed to those who have received one dose.[33] Furthermore, birth before 1957 does not guarantee mumps immunity, and in outbreak settings vaccination with a mumps-containing vaccine should be considered for those born before 1957 who may be exposed to mumps and may be susceptible.[62-65]

The MMR vaccine is very safe, and the most common adverse events associated with vaccination include pain at the site of vaccination and induration. The frequency of more severe events, such as anaphylaxis or allergic reaction, is 1.6 per 100,000 doses.[66-68] Concerns about association between MMR and autism have prompted scrutiny of this possible link by several consumer advocacy groups. An extensive study of 537,303 children found strong evidence against any causal link between MMR vaccine and autism. In addition, 10 of 12 authors of a study of a small number of patients that stated a possible association between MMR and autism have retracted this interpretation. Periodic resurgence of such concerns may undermine confidence or create lingering doubt about the safety of vaccines; however, these misconceptions need to be countered with scientific evidence and strategies to reinforce the lifesaving benefits of immunization.[69] The alternative to decreased immunity among populations will be a resurgence of disease and greater burden of associated morbidity, mortality, and costs on society as a whole.

Financial and Cost-Effectiveness Analysis

Primary prevention against mumps for HCP mitigates disease-associated morbidity, expenditure of time and effort for control measures, and disruption of healthcare delivery associated with transmission in healthcare settings and the community. Immunization of susceptible persons has been shown to be cost-effective, with a ratio of $1 in vaccine cost to between $7 and $14 in disease-associated expense.[70,71]

CONCLUSIONS—MUMPS

Mumps is an infrequent cause of infection in both the community and within healthcare facilities in the United States. When infection does occur, it is most often a self-limited viral illness characterized by parotitis. Prior experience has demonstrated that transmission of infection can occur even in populations with a relatively high proportion of immunized persons. The mumps vaccine has been a notable success in preventing infection, as evidenced by a decrease of more than 200,000 cases per year before its implementation to a low of just more than 200 cases in 2001 in the United States. To sustain this success, continual attention to ensuring that vaccine is provided to susceptible persons as part of an organized immunization program is critical.

Infection prevention failures resulting in healthcare-associated transmission have occurred in outbreaks involving healthcare facilities that admitted adolescents and young adults. Review of isolation procedures, HCP immune status, and provision of appropriate vaccination should be considered.

FUTURE TRENDS—MUMPS

Compromised confidence in efficacy of vaccines is a constant threat to resurgence of diseases that are preventable. HCP must keep current with ongoing research involving vaccines and advocate for their use as one of the most cost-effective interventions to improve health. Surveys of HCP, however, have found unfamiliarity with national immunization schedules for susceptible populations (i.e., ensuring two doses of MMR) and incorrect association between vaccine and adverse events.[72,73] Such weaknesses pose a threat to resurgence of vaccine-preventable diseases. Despite ample scientific investigation of adverse events and improvement in the delivery of vaccine, in 2001, only 77.2 percent of U.S. toddlers aged 19 to 35 months had received recommended immunizations.[74] Healthcare providers at all levels, therefore, will need to be advocates for and facilitate provision of vaccines at all healthcare encounters.

INTERNATIONAL PERSPECTIVE—MUMPS

The World Health Organization (WHO) reports an average annual incidence of mumps in many parts of the world of between 100 and 1,000 per 100,000 population with epidemic peaks noted every 2 to 5 years—especially when no national vaccination initiative is present (e.g., Southeast Asia and select countries in Africa).[75] Approximately 120 countries have incorporated mumps vaccine into their national immunization programs, and after widespread immunization, incidence of disease decreases dramatically. The WHO recommends use of mumps vaccine in countries with efficient national vaccination programs and sufficient resources to sustain such a program.

A seroprevalence survey in Japan revealed that 15.9 percent of more than 270 newly hired HCP lacked evidence of antibody against mumps virus, and a subsequent vaccination program was determined as cost effective.[76] Another survey among hospitals in New South Wales, Australia, found that only 14 percent of hospitals provide MMR immunization and that susceptibility to measles and other viral infections ranges between 14 and 28 percent.[77] To prevent transmission of mumps in the general population and healthcare facilities, greater attention must be paid to assessment and provision of vaccine.

ABSTRACT—RUBELLA (GERMAN MEASLES)

Rubella was first described in the German literature in the early part of the nineteenth century. Since that time, rubella has been clearly defined as a mild, self-limited viral exanthem with a potential to cause serious disease in the fetus. Isolation of the virus in 1962 was the first step in the development of a live-attenuated vaccine. The timing of the first isolation was remarkable because it shortly predated one of the most devastating worldwide pandemics of rubella in 1964 and 1965. In the United States alone, there were more than 12 million cases of rubella with greater than 20,000 cases of the congenital rubella syndrome (2,100 neonatal deaths). The licensure of the first rubella vaccine in 1969, with subsequent improvements in the vaccine (RA 27/3 licensed in 1979), has resulted in dramatic reductions in rubella cases and congenital rubella syndrome in the United States (23 cases of rubella and two cases of congenital rubella syndrome in 2001) and in other countries with successful rubella immunization programs. Unfortunately, many developing nations have yet to benefit from the rubella vaccine, where resources are not available to allow universal routine rubella immunizations. In 2003, only seven confirmed cases of rubella were reported in six states in the United States. The majority of these cases occurred in those aged more than 20 years.

KEY CONCEPTS—RUBELLA

- There is mild acute exanthematous infection of children and adults.

- Greatest health risk is associated with fetal infection (acute clinical manifestations, birth defects, and long-term sequelae) acquired after maternal infection in the first trimester of pregnancy.

- Live-virus vaccine has markedly reduced rubella infections and perinatal consequences in countries with successful rubella immunization programs.

BACKGROUND—RUBELLA

Rubella virus, first isolated in 1962 by Parkman and Weller, is in the genus *Rubivirus* in the Togaviridae family. It has a single positive-stranded ribonucleic acid (RNA) genome, an icosahedral capsid, and a lipoprotein envelope. The name "rubella" comes from the Latin for "little red." It was previously called "third disease" and was thought to be a mild variant of measles or scarlet fever. Humans are the only natural hosts for rubella. However, under experimental conditions, a wide range of vertebrate species may be infected with the rubella virus. Rubella virus is labile and readily inactivated by several chemical agents (e.g., chlorine, formalin, trypsin, deoxycholate), lipid solvents, heat (greater than 56°C), cold (less than −10°C to −20°C), ultraviolet light, and extremes of pH (less than 6.8 and greater than 8.1).[78–80]

BASIC PRINCIPLES—RUBELLA

There are two distinct genotypes of rubella virus differentiated by nucleotide sequences that code for structural proteins.[78,79] However, only minor immunologic differences exist between the two genotypes, and immunity to one rubella virus provides protection against all other rubella viruses (one antigenic type).[80] Humans are the only natural hosts of the rubella virus.

Rubella infection of nonpregnant individuals results in a benign, self-limited illness. Although there is a characteristic presentation for acquired rubella (an exanthem and lymphadenopathy), many infections with rubella are asymptomatic. Of greater consequence is *in utero* infection, which results in the congenital rubella syndrome (intrauterine growth retardation, mental retardation, congenital heart disease, deafness, and numerous ocular abnormalities).

Infection with the rubella virus commences in the respiratory epithelium of the nasopharynx. The virus spreads rapidly from the nasopharynx to regional lymphatics. Viremia follows lymphatic involvement (approximately 5 to 7 days after exposure), occurs 1 to 2 days before the onset of rash, and peaks just before the onset of the rash. Viremia is not detectable soon after the onset of rash. However, rubella virus replication continues in the nasopharynx for up to 6 to 14 days after the appearance of the rash. Transplacental passage of the virus may occur as a result of viremia or after placental infection.

EPIDEMIOLOGY—RUBELLA

The availability of a safe, live-virus rubella vaccine has resulted in dramatic declines in both acquired rubella infections and the congenital rubella syndrome in populations with effective rubella vaccine programs. Occasional rubella outbreaks in unvaccinated populations continue to occur in the United States. However, these are becoming less common and do not appear to spread even in under-vaccinated populations, likely because of effective herd immunity.[80-86]

Humans are the only known vertebrate host and only source of rubella. Postnatally acquired rubella is transmitted chiefly through direct or droplet contact. The virus is shed primarily in respiratory secretions (nasopharyngeal and to a lesser degree oropharyngeal), allowing transmission via direct contact and to a lesser degree via droplet transmission.[81] Efficient transmission to susceptible persons requires prolonged and intimate contact. Individuals infected with rubella are contagious from a few days before the onset of symptoms (7 days before rash) to 7 to 14 days after the rash. Children with congenital rubella shed virus from both respiratory secretions and urine. Children with congenital rubella should be considered to be contagious until 1 year or more of age, unless they have had repeated negative virus cultures of the nasopharynx and urine.

Before the widespread use of rubella vaccine, rubella was an epidemic disease occurring in 6- to 9-year cycles. Most clinically identified cases occurred in school-aged and preschool-aged children. The peak incidence of rubella infection in the prevaccine era was in the late winter and early spring. However, in areas with low levels of vaccine use, an endemic level of rubella transmission occurs year-round. Immunity after infection is usually lifelong and durable. However, reinfection has been documented on rare occasions and has even resulted in transmission of rubella virus to the fetus with a resulting congenital rubella syndrome.[87,88]

Since the availability of a rubella vaccine in 1969, widespread rubella outbreaks have been prevented. This reduction in rubella transmission occurred despite high proportions of selected populations remaining susceptible (no natural infection and no vaccine). Most persons born after 1969, and many born between 1964, the year of the last major worldwide rubella epidemic, and 1969, who were not vaccinated (i.e., approximately 20 percent of the population) are not rubella immune. Therefore, this reduction in rubella transmission presumably reflects the influence of "herd immunity."

The National Childhood Immunization Initiative succeeded in establishing laws requiring rubella vaccination before entering public school in most states in the United States by 1980. Consequently, the majority of unprotected individuals in the United States were born between 1964 and 1975. Some of these susceptible individuals may have been reached after the new two-dose schedule recommendation for measles (many received MMR vaccine) and when secondary and undergraduate/graduate schools began requesting/requiring proof of rubella immunity for enrollment.

Surveillance data for rubella and congenital rubella continue to show a steady decline in reported cases to record low levels. Reported cases of postnatal rubella declined to a low of

23 cases in 2001.[89] In 1995 and 1996, there were only four and two confirmed cases, respectively, of congenital rubella syndrome reported in the United States.[85] In 2001, there were two cases of congenital rubella syndrome among 11 women with rubella infection during their pregnancy; of these, 10 mothers were foreign-born Hispanics.[89]

During the 1970s, the age spectrum of reported rubella shifted gradually toward older individuals. In 1979, 36 percent of rubella cases were among persons older than 20 years of age. The first shift toward cases in older patients presumably reflected the initial emphasis on vaccinating infants and schoolchildren. However, by 1981, the age spectrum once again shifted sharply toward younger cases. In 1981, only 24 percent of cases were among persons older than 20 years of age.[85] The second shift toward cases in younger patients represented a decrease in susceptible adults, because those vaccinated as schoolchildren were entering adulthood, plus an increase in efforts to identify the remaining susceptible adolescents and young adults, particularly during prenatal care. These more recent cases of rubella were occurring in unvaccinated children (as was the case for measles during the measles resurgence in 1988 to 1991). More recently from 1992 to 2000, there has been another shift with an increase in the proportion of cases in older individuals, primarily between the ages of 15 and 39 years. However, the significance of this shift is not clear because of the relatively small number of total cases of reported rubella. In 2000, 87 percent of rubella cases occurred in persons 15 to 39 years of age. In 2003, seven confirmed cases were reported in six states, the lowest number of rubella cases ever reported in the United States.

Because there is no animal reservoir for rubella, elimination of indigenous transmission of rubella in the United States (and possibly the world) is feasible.[84] Because rubella is transmitted less readily than measles, sustained (indigenous) transmission should be easy to eliminate. On the other hand, rubella is less clinically distinctive, so imported cases are harder to recognize and control. In 2010, on the basis of surveillance data, the Pan American Health Organization indicated that the World Health Organization (WHO) Region of the Americas had achieved the rubella and congenital rubella syndrome elimination goals set in 2003.[84] Verification of maintenance of rubella elimination in the region is ongoing. However, an expert panel reviewed available data and unanimously agreed in December 2011 that rubella elimination has been maintained in the United States.[59,90]

CLINICAL MANIFESTATIONS—RUBELLA

Postnatal rubella or German measles is generally a mild, viral exanthem with little risk for morbidity or mortality. After an incubation period of 14 days (range 12 to 23 days), postnatal illness begins with a prodrome consisting of malaise, headache, low-grade fever, mild conjunctivitis, and lymphadenopathy. This prodrome may be so mild as to go unnoticed. The rash follows the prodrome or at times it may be the first symptom noted in children and adults. Respiratory tract symptoms, constitutional symptoms, and rash are quite variable in presentation (25 to

50 percent of individuals infected with rubella are asymptomatic). Not all ill patients with an acute rubella infection have a discernible rash. Rubella should be suspected in susceptible individuals who develop a fine maculopapular rash and lymphadenopathy after a possible rubella exposure. Compared with the rash of measles, the rash in patients with rubella is usually less intense in color, more variable in its presentation, and of shorter duration (3 days for rubella; 5–7 days for measles). It has both scarlatiniform and morbilliform characteristics. Arthritis or arthralgia or both occur in up to one-third of adolescent and adult women infected with rubella. Thrombocytopenia, encephalitis, neuritis, and orchitis rarely occur.

Rubella virus may be transmitted to the fetus after viremia or placental infection during the entire gestation period. However, the risk for fetal damage and sequelae is primarily seen after transmission occurring in early gestation. The risk for the congenital rubella syndrome by gestational age is as follows: first month, 45 percent; second month, 25 percent; third month, 15 percent; fourth month, 10 percent; and minimal risk during all later months. Rubella infection in a susceptible mother after the twelfth week of gestation is not likely to cause adverse consequences to either the fetus or the mother. Children who are born with congenital rubella syndrome may exhibit some or many of the following conditions: intrauterine growth retardation, petechiae/purpura, mental retardation, anemia, hepatosplenomegaly, congenital heart defects (particularly patent ductus arteriosus and peripheral pulmonary stenosis), radiolucent bone disease, cataracts, glaucoma, retinitis, failure to thrive, and occasionally postnatal death. In addition to the congenital rubella syndrome, early gestation infection rubella has been associated with an increased rate of miscarriages and stillbirths.

CLINICAL/LABORATORY DIAGNOSIS—RUBELLA

Because most rubella infections are asymptomatic or associated with mild nonspecific symptoms, diagnosis of rubella based on clinical findings alone is difficult, particularly in nonepidemic periods or locations. The rash has characteristics of both scarlet fever (scarlatiniform) and measles (morbilliform) and may be confused with mild cases of either of these infections. In addition to measles and scarlet fever, other infections with presentations that at times may be similar to rubella include infectious mononucleosis due to the Epstein-Barr virus (EBV), cytomegalovirus (CMV) or toxoplasma maternal infections, roseola infantum (human herpesvirus 6 [HHV-6] and human herpesvirus 7 [HHV-7]), erythema infectiosum (parvovirus B-19), and many of the enteroviral infections. (Also see Chapter 41 Neonates, Chapter 42 Pediatrics, Chapter 43 Perinatal Care, Chapter 80 Herpes Virus, and Chapter 88 Parvovirus.)

Infants with congenital rubella may present with clinical manifestations that may be indistinguishable from perinatally acquired CMV and toxoplasmosis. Thrombocytopenia, petechiae/purpura, anemia, hepatomegaly, splenomegaly, retinopathies, bone abnormalities, eighth nerve deafness,

and intrauterine growth retardation may be seen with congenital infections with rubella, CMV, or toxoplasmosis. Congenital heart defects, particularly patent ductus arteriosus and pulmonary branch stenosis, cataracts, and congenital glaucoma would be unlikely in congenital infections other than congenital rubella.

Nonspecific laboratory testing is usually not helpful in the diagnosis of rubella postnatal infection of infants, children, and adults. Occasionally, mild leukopenia and atypical lymphocytes may be noted on the complete blood count (CBC). Otherwise, nonspecific screening laboratory test results are normal and unremarkable. Therefore, a laboratory diagnosis of rubella depends on specific viral diagnostic studies.

Rubella virus can be grown in a variety of primary and continuous cell lines. In many primary cell culture lines, rubella virus produces a persistent infection without obvious cytopathic effect.[79] Rubella does produce a cytopathic effect in some continuous cell lines (rabbit kidney cell line RK-13, Vevo cells, and SIRC cells) and in primary African green monkey cells.[79,81]

Virus isolation from a number of body sites (throat swab, urine, synovial fluid, amniotic fluid, cerebrospinal fluid) confirms the diagnosis of rubella infection. Virus excretion by individuals with postnatal rubella is transient and occurs from up to 10 days before the onset of symptoms (usually when the rash is noted) to 15 days after the onset of rash. Individuals with congenital rubella infection may excrete virus for many months and even years. Prolonged virus excretion (greater than 4 weeks) would be most consistent with congenital infection. A prenatal diagnosis of congenital rubella infection may be accomplished by isolation of rubella virus from amniotic fluid.[91]

Virus isolation of rubella is time-consuming and expensive. In addition, the paucity of rubella cases has markedly reduced the experience of viral diagnostic laboratories for identifying rubella in cell culture. Virus isolation of rubella is usually reserved for specific clinical situations (e.g., investigation of atypical arthritis, diagnosis of congenital rubella, prenatal investigation of congenital infection, and certain complications of postnatal rubella). If rubella infection is being considered, the viral diagnostic laboratory should be notified to enhance the likelihood that appropriate steps are taken to identify the rubella virus in cell culture. Consultation with a state laboratory or the Centers for Disease Control and Prevention (CDC) might be considered.

Serology has now become the most convenient and available method for establishing the diagnosis of both postnatal and congenital rubella infections. Currently, there are a number of serological assays (e.g., enzyme-linked immunosorbent assay, latex agglutination, immunofluorescent antibody, and radial hemolysis test) that can detect either rubella-specific immunoglobulin (Ig)G or rubella-specific IgM antibodies. Acute postnatal rubella infection can be presumed by the demonstration of a rubella-specific IgM antibody on a single acute serum. A fourfold increase or seroconversion in rubella antibody (either IgG or IgM) in paired acute and convalescent specimens (minimum of

7 days apart; optimally 14 to 21 days after acute sera) assayed by the same test would also establish a diagnosis of acute rubella infection. A single positive rubella-specific IgG antibody merely verifies infection with rubella, either from a past or recent infection. Rubella-specific IgM antibody results may be confounded by the fact that a false positive occurs as a result of problems with the assay (poor specificity) or associated with other clinical conditions, such as recent infections with parvovirus or heterophile-positive EBV or persons with a positive rheumatoid factor.[92] Reinfection with rubella can also result in a positive rubella-specific IgM antibody.

Serologic diagnosis of congenital infection with rubella may be established by a positive rubella-specific IgM antibody in the affected newborn (not from cord blood) or persistence of rubella-specific IgG antibodies beyond 9 months in an infant with a compatible clinical syndrome who has not received the rubella vaccine and who is not from an endemic area. Intrauterine infection with rubella may be detected by the presence of rubella-specific IgM in fetal blood.[93,94] However, this antibody may not be detectable until 22 weeks of gestation.[93,94]

Placental biopsy, detection of rubella antigen with monoclonal antibody, cordocentesis with detection of rubella RNA by *in situ* hybridization, and PCR have also been used to establish a diagnosis of congenital rubella infection.[78,95,96]

TREATMENT—RUBELLA

Rubella is a mild and self-limited infection. Treatment is supportive and usually only indicated for the uncommon occurrence of fever and joint symptoms (arthralgia or arthritis). Immunoglobulin had been advocated for the prevention or modification of rubella in exposed, susceptible pregnant women.[78] Immune serum globulin (ISG) was found to reduce symptoms but not consistently prevent viremia.[97] Whether intravenous immunoglobulin (IVIG) could prevent viremia needs to be established. However, immunoglobulin might still be considered in the management of an exposed, susceptible pregnant woman for whom an abortion is not an option.[78]

PREVENTION/INFECTION CONTROL MEASURES—RUBELLA

The currently licensed rubella vaccine is a live-attenuated rubella strain (RA 27/3) prepared in human diploid cell cultures.[82,85] This vaccine was licensed in the United States in 1979 and replaced previous live-attenuated vaccine strains (e.g., HPV-77 and Cendehill). The RA 27/3 induces an increased and more durable antibody response with fever side effects than prior rubella vaccines.

Ninety-five percent of individuals under 12 months of age receiving a single dose of the rubella vaccine develop serologic evidence of rubella immunity. Many of those who fail to have seroconversion after vaccination are seropositive by specialized, highly sensitive tests. Thus, rubella vaccination provides presumptive evidence of immunity. Rubella vaccine results in more than 90 percent protective efficacy after either natural exposure or artificial challenge studies. Rubella vaccine provides similar protection from reinfection and prevention of viremia as natural rubella. Available data suggest that one dose of rubella vaccine provides long-term and probably lifelong immunity. Currently, two doses of rubella vaccine are recommended in conjunction with the recommendation for two doses of the measles vaccine.

Vaccinated persons can shed vaccine virus for up to 28 days after vaccination, but there is no evidence that person-to-person vaccine virus transmission occurs. Vaccinated persons can develop subclinical rubella infection as manifested by an increase in antibody titer, but they usually do not become viremic. Thus, if a previously immunized pregnant woman is exposed to natural rubella or a live rubella vaccine, the fetus is presumed to be protected. Congenital rubella syndrome has occurred only rarely in women with prior evidence of immunity (naturally acquired or vaccine-induced) before pregnancy.

Adverse reactions after administration of the rubella vaccine occur primarily in susceptible vaccinees. These adverse events are similar to, although less severe than, those of natural rubella. They appear less frequently with the current RA 27/3 vaccine strain. Fever, rash, and lymphadenopathy occur in 5 to 15 percent of susceptible individuals who receive the MMR vaccine approximately 5 to 12 days after vaccination. The actual role of each component of the vaccine on the development of fever is unknown. Transient joint pains (arthralgia or even transient arthritis) may occur 7 to 21 days after vaccination and are more common in adult women (approximately 25 percent of susceptible adult women). Chronic or persistent arthritis is reported in less than 1 percent of rubella vaccinees. The occurrence of moderate or severe arthropathy after administration of rubella vaccine is rare and not different from that which occurred in placebo recipients in a controlled trial.[85,98–100]

Transient central or peripheral nervous system manifestations have also been reported after receipt of rubella vaccine. A causal relationship between the rubella vaccine (RA 27/3) and recurrent/persistent joint symptoms, neuropathy, or collagen vacuolar disease has not been established and is unlikely.

Rubella vaccine should not be given to pregnant women. Pregnancy should be avoided for 4 weeks after rubella or MMR vaccination. From 1971 to 1989, the CDC monitored 321 known rubella-susceptible pregnant women who had inadvertently been vaccinated with rubella vaccine within 3 months before or up to 3 months after conception (94 received HPV-77 or Cendehill vaccine, 226 received RA 27/3 vaccine, and one was unknown). None of the 324 offspring had malformations compatible with congenital rubella. However, five infants (three exposed to HPV-77 or Cendehill and two exposed to RA 27/3) had persistent serologic evidence consistent with subclinical infection. Thus, the current vaccine poses a negligible risk of vaccine-associated malformations (estimated risk is 0 to 1.6 percent).[85] Vaccination during or just before pregnancy is normally not an indication for elective abortion. Nevertheless, the vaccine should not be given to women who are known or suspected to be pregnant; vaccinated women should not become pregnant for 3 months after vaccination.

Minor illnesses, with or without fever, are not a contraindication for administering the rubella vaccine. However, individuals with moderate to severe acute illness should not be vaccinated until the illness has resolved.

Individuals with altered immunity (primary or secondary immunodeficiency) may be at increased risk for complications after receipt of live-virus vaccines. Rubella vaccine is contraindicated in individuals with B-lymphocyte (humoral), T-lymphocyte (cell-mediated), and combined (cell-mediated and humoral) immunodeficiencies. Children with complement deficiencies or phagocytic function deficiencies and human immunodeficiency virus–infected children who are not severely immunocompromised (Immunologic Categories 1 or 2) may receive the live rubella vaccine.[82]

Rubella vaccine response can be diminished if immunoglobulin has been administered recently. The interval between immunoglobulin administration and rubella vaccine administration that will ensure an adequate immune response to the rubella vaccine will vary by dose, route, and type of immunoglobulin preparation given. Rubella vaccine should not be given to an individual in a time period from 2 weeks before up to 3 months after the administration of a blood transfusion or immunoglobulin products (e.g., IVIG, IG, TIG). However, when the rubella vaccine is given with the measles vaccine or when high doses of immunoglobulin are given (e.g., IVIG for Kawasaki disease), longer intervals between administration of the immunoglobulin product and vaccination with the live-virus vaccine (rubella or MMR) may be required to ensure optimal immune response (see Table 86-1).

The need to prescreen potential vaccinees for rubella antibodies is uncertain.[82,86] Prescreening is cost effective when the cost of serologic testing is low. When prescreening is not available or cost effective, rubella immunization of susceptible healthcare personnel (HCP) or other at-risk adults without a history of clinical rubella infection should be performed. Rubella immunization of a rubella-immune individual should have no adverse consequences.

Rubella represents a hazard to both pregnant HCP and pregnant patients. This provides two distinct goals for rubella control within healthcare settings: (1) protecting pregnant HCP and (2) protecting susceptible pregnant patients. The ethical basis for asserting that healthcare facilities should take special measures to protect their personnel is the potential heightened risk of rubella exposure and possible acquisition that results from a healthcare-related occupation. Individuals who have rubella may present to healthcare facilities for care. Children who have the congenital rubella syndrome would undoubtedly need medical services. These children excrete high titers of virus for prolonged periods of time (usually considered contagious until 1 year of age). Immunization programs aimed at protecting HCP should be (1) voluntary and (2) directed at postpubertal females.

Healthcare facilities have an absolute responsibility to ensure that all reasonable measures are taken to prevent exposure of susceptible pregnant patients to HCP or other patients with rubella. Consequently, HCP immunization programs can be justified because they serve to protect pregnant patients. These programs should (1) include all HCP, including males and infertile females; (2) be mandatory; and (3) be provided without cost to HCP. In practice, an appropriate rubella screening and immunization program for HCP should serve both purposes.

All HCP capable of becoming pregnant should be encouraged to verify their immunity to rubella by serologic testing and/or receiving the rubella vaccine.[85] Documentation of the presence of rubella antibody and receipt of the rubella vaccine are the only acceptable means to document rubella immunity. The clinical manifestations of rubella are not distinct enough to permit clinical diagnosis to serve as documentation of immunity.

Maternal rubella immunity may not provide absolute protection to the fetus.[87,88] Rubella transmission to the fetus of rubella-immune mothers has been reported on a few occasions. It seems prudent, therefore, that pregnant HCP, even if they are known to be rubella immune, not care for patients known to have rubella.

Healthcare settings with a relatively high risk of rubella exposure include the emergency department, nurseries, neonatal-care units, pediatric inpatient units, and outpatient clinics. Susceptible pregnant HCP should be aware of these high-risk areas.

The presence of rubella-susceptible HCP has led to sporadic outbreaks of rubella in hospitals.[82,84] Some rubella outbreaks have resulted in exposure of pregnant patients to rubella, although most of the transmission occurring in these outbreaks has been from patients to HCP and between HCP. The Advisory Committee on Immunization Practices and American Academy of Pediatrics recommend rubella vaccination for "persons (both male and female) working in hospitals and clinics who might contract rubella from infected patients or who, if infected, might transmit rubella to pregnant patients … unless there are contraindications."[82–84]

The American Hospital Association Advisory Committee on Infections Within Hospitals has recommended that "susceptible personnel, that is, men and women in all age-groups, who have contact with female patients in the childbearing years should be immunized" and that this immunization should be obligatory.[101]

Precautions and Isolation Techniques for Patients with Rubella

For rubella, Droplet Precautions in addition to Standard Precautions are required for 7 days after the onset of the rash; a single room is preferred. Special air handling and ventilation are not necessary, and the door may remain open. No recommendation is made on wearing a mask for immune HCP. Gowns, facial protection, and gloves should be worn for patient contacts based on anticipated exposure per Standard Precautions.[31]

Contact Precautions are required for infants with or suspected of having congenital rubella until 1 year of age. Repeated negative cultures of the nasopharynx and urine of a congenitally infected infant after 3 months of age would suggest that the infant has a low likelihood for transmission. Accordingly, Standard Precautions should be followed.[31]

Postexposure rubella immunization has not been shown to prevent illness but is not associated with any harmful side effects. Theoretically, rubella vaccine given within 3 days of exposure might prevent illness.[81,82] Therefore, exposed nonpregnant susceptible women should receive rubella vaccination to prevent future infection if the identified exposure does not result in natural disease.

The routine use of serum immunoglobulin for postexposure prophylaxis of rubella in early pregnancy cannot be recommended because there are no efficacy data available.[101,102] However, if exposure occurs early in pregnancy (first 20 weeks) and termination of pregnancy is not an option, ISG administration can be considered within 72 hours of exposure. ISG (0.55 mL/kg) may prevent or modify infection in an exposed susceptible person. However, protection of the fetus has not been established, and there have been anecdotal reports of infants with congenital rubella after ISG administration to their mothers.[82]

CONCLUSIONS—RUBELLA

Rubella is a mild, self-limited disease that has its greatest health impact when maternal infection results in viremia and transmission to the fetus in early gestation. Maternal antibodies provide immunity and prevent viremia. Rubella antibodies are produced after natural infection and vaccination with a live-virus vaccine. In industrialized nations such as the United States, successful rubella vaccine programs have nearly eliminated indigenous cases of rubella and the congenital rubella syndrome. Until rubella immunization is universal in the developing world, there will still be significant numbers of children affected by the congenital rubella syndrome and a risk for importation of cases into nations with highly immunized populations.

FUTURE TRENDS—RUBELLA

Ultimately, universal rubella immunization of young children and screening susceptible women of childbearing age would be optimal, but targeted approaches may be necessary until adequate resources are available.

INTERNATIONAL PERSPECTIVE— RUBELLA

Although postnatal rubella is typically a mild self-limited disease, congenital rubella syndrome can be a devastating disease affecting more than 100,000 children from developing countries. Successful immunization programs have markedly reduced rubella and the congenital rubella syndrome in the industrialized world, but most countries in Africa and Asia do not include rubella as part of their routine immunizations. In addition, many developing countries with rubella vaccine as part of the routine immunization schedule do not have adequate vaccine coverage (less than 80 percent) to result in decreases in the congenital rubella syndrome to levels occurring in industrialized nations.

In resource-poor countries, different approaches to rubella vaccine distribution have been undertaken. Immunization of adolescent girls or women of childbearing age does not significantly reduce the occurrence of rubella infections because most rubella infections occur in younger children unaffected by the vaccine administration. However, this approach can result in significant reductions in the congenital rubella syndrome.

REFERENCES

a World Health Organization (WHO). *Measles fact sheet*. WHO website. February 2013. Available at: http://www.who.int/mediacentre /factsheets/fs286/en/.
1. Cherry JD. Measles. In: Feigin RD, Cherry JD, eds. *Textbook of Pediatric Infectious Diseases*, 4th ed. Philadelphia: WB Saunders; 1998:2054–2074.
2. Measles. In: *2012 Red Book: Report of the Committee on Infectious Diseases*, 29th ed. Evanston, IL: American Academy of Pediatrics, 2012;489–492.
3. American Academy of Pediatrics Committee on Infectious Diseases. Measles: reassessment of the current immunization policy. *Pediatrics* 1989 Dec;84(6):1110–1113.
4. Watson JC, Hadler SC, Dykewicz CA, et al. Measles, mumps and rubella—vaccine use and strategies for elimination of measles, rubella and congenital rubella syndrome and control of mumps: recommendations of the Advisory Committee on Immunization Practices (ACIP). *MMWR Recomm Rep* 1998 May 22;47(RR-8):1–57.
5. Kempe CH, Fulginiti VA. The pathogenesis of measles virus infection. *Arch Ges Virusforsch* 1965;16:103–128.
6. Griffin DE, Bellini WJ. Measles Virus. In: Fields BN, Knipe DM, Howley PM, eds. *Fields Virology* Vol I, 3rd ed. New York: Raven Press, 1996;1267–1312.
7. Caulfield E. Early measles epidemics in America. *Yale J Biol Med* 1943 Mar;15(4):531–536.
8. Enders JF, Peebles TC. Propagation in tissue cultures of cytopathogenic agents from patients with measles. *Proc Soc Exp Biol Med* 1954 Jun;86(2):277–286.
9. Krugman S. Present status of measles and rubella immunization in the United States: a medical progress report. *J Pediatr* 1977 Jan;90(1):1–12.
10. Atkinson WL, Hadler SC, Redd SB, et al. Measles surveillance—United States, 1991. *MMWR CDC Surveill Summ* 1992 Nov 20,41(6):1–12.
11. Bellini WJ, Rota PA. Genetic diversity of wild-type measles viruses: implications for global measles elimination programs. *Emerg Infect Dis* 1998 Jan-Mar;4(1):1–7.
12. Rota JS, Heath JL, Rota PA, et al. Molecular epidemiology of measles virus: identification of pathways of transmission and implications for measles elimination. *J Infect Dis* 1996 Jan;173(1):32–37.
13. Centers for Disease Control and Prevention (CDC). *Measles Surveillance: Report No. 11, 1977–1981*. Atlanta, GA: CDC, 1982;6–89.
14. Papania MJ, Seward JF, Redd SB, et al. Epidemiology of measles in the United States, 1997–2001. *J Infect Dis* 2004 May 1;189 Suppl 1: S61–S68.
15. Centers for Disease Control and Prevention (CDC). Epidemiology of measles—United States, 2001–2003. *MMWR Morb Mortal Wkly Rep* 2004 Aug 13;53(31):713–716.
16. Centers for Disease Control and Prevention (CDC). Measles—United States, 2004. *MMWR Morb Mortal Wkly Rep* 2005 Dec 9;54(48):1229–1231.
17. Centers for Disease Control and Prevention (CDC). Update: measles—United States, January-July 2008. *MMWR Morb Mortal Wkly Rep* 2008 Aug 22;57(33):893–896.
18. Hopkins DR, Hinman AR, Koplan JP, et al. The case for global measles eradication. *Lancet* 1982 Jun 19;1(8286):1396–1398.
19. Atkinson WL, Markowitz LE, Adams NC, et al. Transmission of measles in medical settings: United States, 1985–1989. *Am J Med* 1991 Sep 16;91(3B):320S–324S.
20. Measles and Rubella Initiative. *Measles deaths decline, but elimination progress stalls in some regions*. January 17, 2013. Available at: http://www.measlesrubellainitiative.org/measles-news/measles-deaths-decline-elimination-progress-stalls-regions/.

21. Progress towards interrupting indigenous measles transmission—region of the Americas, January-November, 2001. *MMWR* 2001;50:1133–1137.
22. Gershon AA. Measles Virus (Rubeola). In: Mandell GL, Bennett JE, Dolin R, eds. *Mandell, Douglas and Bennett's Principles and Practice of Infectious Diseases.* New York: Churchill Livingstone, 1995;1519.
23. Christensen PE, Schmidt H, Bang HO, et al. An epidemic of measles in Southern Greenland, 1951. *Acta Med Scand* 1953;144:431.
24. Kaplan LJ, Daum RS, Smaron M, et al. Severe measles in immunocompromised patients. *JAMA* 1992 Mar 4;267(9):1237–1241.
25. Barkin RM. Measles mortality: a retrospective look at the vaccine era. *Am J Epidemiol* 1975 Oct;102(4):341–349.
26. Barkin RM. Measles mortality: analysis of the primary cause of death. *Am J Dis Child* 1975 Mar;129(3):307–309.
27. Cherry JD. Measles Virus. In: Feigin RD, Cherry JD, eds. *Textbook of Pediatric Infectious Diseases.* Philadelphia: WB Saunders, 1998;2054.
28. Griffin DE, Bellini WJ. Measles Virus. In: Fields BN, Knipe DM, Howley PM, eds. *Fields' Virology.* Philadelphia: Lippincott-Raven, 1996;1267.
29. American Academy of Pediatrics Committee on Infectious Diseases. Recommended timing of routine measles immunization for children who have recently received immune globulin preparations. *Pediatrics* 1994 Apr;93(4):682–685.
30. Schwarcz S, McCaw B, Fukushima P. Prevalence of measles susceptibility in hospital staff: evidence to support expanding the recommendations of the Immunization Practices Advisory Committee. *Arch Intern Med* 1992 Jul;152(7):1481–1483.
31. Siegel JD, Rhinehart E, Jackson M, et al., 2007 Guideline for Isolation Precautions: Preventing Transmission of Infectious Agents in Healthcare Settings. *Am J Infect Control* 2007;35:S65–S164.
32. Centers for Disease Control and Prevention (CDC), National Center for Immunization and Respiratory Diseases, Division of Viral Diseases. *Documentation and Verification of Measles, Rubella and Congenital Rubella Syndrome Elimination in the Region of the Americas. United States National Report March 28, 2012.* CDC website. Available at: http://www.cdc.gov/measles/downloads/Report-elimination-measles-rubella-crs.pdf.
33. Plotkin SA, Wharton M. Mumps Vaccine. In: Plotkin SA, Mortimer EA Jr, eds. *Vaccines,* 3rd ed. Philadelphia: WB Saunders, 1999;267–292.
34. Johnson CD, Goodpasture EW. An investigation of the etiology of mumps. *J Exp Med* 1934 Jan 1;59(1):1–19.
35. Buynak EB, Hilleman MR. Live attenuated mumps virus vaccine. I. Vaccine development. *Proc Soc Exp Biol Med* 1966 Dec;123(3):768–775.
36. McLean HQ, Fiebelkorn AP, Temte JL, et al. Prevention of measles, rubella, congenital rubella syndrome, and mumps, 2013: summary recommendations of the Advisory Committee on Immunization Practices (ACIP) *MMWR Recomm Rep* 2013 Jun 14;62(RR-04):1–34.
37. Carbone KM, Wolinsky JS. Mumps virus. In: Knipe DM, Howley PM, eds. *Fields Virology,* 4th ed. Philadelphia: Lippincott Williams & Wilkins, 2001;1381–1400.
38. McDonald JC, Moore DL, Quennec P. Clinical and epidemiologic features of mumps meningoencephalitis and possible vaccine-related disease. *Pediatr Infect Dis J* 1989 Nov;8(11):751–755.
39. Sugiura A, Yamada A. Aseptic meningitis as a complication of mumps vaccination. *Pediatr Infect Dis J* 1991 Mar;10(3):209–213.
40. Miller E, Goldacre M, Pugh S, et al. Risk of aseptic meningitis after measles, mumps, and rubella vaccine in UK children. *Lancet* 1993 Apr 17;341(8851):979–982.
41. Amela C, Pachon I, de Ory F. Evaluation of the measles, mumps and rubella immunization programme in Spain by using sero-epidemiological survey. *Eur J Epidemiol* 2003;18(1):71–79.
42. Centers for Disease Control and Prevention (CDC). Mumps surveillance: 1973. *MMWR* 1973;23:431.
43. van Loon FPL, Holmes SJ, Sirotkin BI, et al. Mumps surveillance: United States:1988–1993. CDC Surveillance Summaries. *MMWR CDC Surveill Summ* 1995 Aug 11;44(3):1–14.
44. Chaiken BP, Williams NM, Preblud SR, et al. The effect of school entry law on mumps activity in a school district. *JAMA* 1987 May 8;257(18):2455–2458.
45. Nardone A, Pebody RG, van den Hof S, et al. Sero-epidemiology of mumps in western Europe. *Epidemiol Infect* 2003 Aug;131(1):691–701.
46. Philip RN, Reinhard KR, Lockman DB. Observations on a mumps epidemic in a "virgin" population. *Am J Hyg* 1959 Mar;69(2):91–111.
47. Meyer MB. An epidemiological study of mumps: its spread in schools and families. *Am J Hyg* 1962;75:259–281.
48. Pugh RN, Akinosi B, Pooransingh S, et al. An outbreak of mumps in the metropolitan area of Walsall, UK. *Int J Infect Dis* 2002 Mar;6:283–287.
49. Kaplan KM, Marder DC, Cochi SL, et al. Mumps in the workplace: further evidence of the changing epidemiology of a childhood vaccine-preventable disease. *JAMA* 1988 Sep 9;260(10):1434–1438.
50. American Academy of Pediatrics (AAP). Summaries of infectious diseases: mumps. In: Pickering LK, ed. *2003 Red Book: Report of the Committee on Infectious Diseases.* 26th ed. Elk Grove Village, IL: AAP, 2003;439–443.
51. Sparling D. Transmission of mumps. *N Engl J Med* 1969 Jan 30;280(5):276.
52. Glick D. An isolated case of mumps in a geriatric population. *J Am Geriatr Soc* 1970 Aug;18(8):642–644.
53. Faoagali JL. An assessment of the need for vaccination amongst junior medical staff. *N Z Med J* 1976 Aug 25;84(570):147–150.
54. Wharton M, Cochi SL, Hutcheson RH, et al. Mumps transmission in hospitals. *Arch Intern Med* 1990 Jan;150(1):47–49.
55. Fischer PR, Brunetti C, Welch V, et al. Nosocomial mumps: report of an outbreak and its control. *Am J Infect Control* 1996 Feb;24(1):13–18.
56. Guideline for isolation precautions in hospitals. Part II. Recommendations for isolation precautions in hospitals. Hospital Infection Control Practices Advisory Committee. *Am J Infect Control* 1996;24(1):32–52.
57. Brunell PA, Brickman A, O'Hare D, et al. Ineffectiveness of isolation of patients as a method of preventing the spread of mumps: failure of the mumps skin-test antigen to predict immune status. *N Engl J Med* 1968 Dec 19;279(25):1357–1361.
58. Krause PJ, Gross PA, Barrett TL, et al. Quality standard for assurance of measles immunity among health care workers. *Infect Control Hosp Epidemiol* 1994 Mar;15(3):193–199.
59. Watson JC, Hadler SC, Dykewicz CA, et al. Measles, mumps, and rubella—vaccine use and strategies for elimination of measles, rubella, and congenital rubella syndrome and control of mumps: recommendations of the Advisory Committee on Immunization Practices (ACIP). *MMWR Recomm Rep* 1988 May 22;47(RR-8):1–57.
60. Bolyard EA, Tablan OC, Williams WW, et al. Guideline for infection control in health care personnel, 1998. *Am J Infect Control* 1998;26:289–354.
61. Atkinson WL, Pickering LK, Schwartz B, et al. General recommendations on immunization. Recommendations of the Advisory Committee on Immunization Practices (ACIP) and the American Academy of Family Physicians (AAFP). *MMWR Recomm Rep* 2002 Feb 8;51(RR-2):1–36.
62. Hersh BS, Fine PEM, Kent WK, et al. Mumps outbreak in a highly vaccinated population. *J Pediatr* 1991 Aug;119(2):187–193.
63. Briss PA, Fehrs LJ, Parker RA, et al. Sustained transmission of mumps in a highly vaccinated population: assessment of primary vaccine failure and waning vaccine-induced immunity. *J Infect Dis* 1994 Jan;169(1):77–82.
64. Cheek JE, Baron R, Atlas H, et al. Mumps outbreak in a highly vaccinated school population. *Arch Pediatr Adolesc Med* 1995 Jul;149(7):774–778.
65. Goncalves G, de Araujo A, Cardoso MLM. Outbreak of mumps associated with poor vaccine efficacy—Oporto, Portugal, 1996. *Euro Ssurveill* 1998 Dec;3(12):119–121.
66. D'Souza RM, Campbell-Lloyd S, Isaacs D, et al. Adverse events following immunization associated with 1998 Australian Measles Control Campaign. *Commun Dis Intell* 2000 Feb 17;24(2):27–33.
67. Madsen KM, Hviid A, Vestergaard M, et al. A population-based study of measles, mumps, and rubella vaccination and autism. *N Engl J Med* 2002 Nov 7;347(19):1477–1482.
68. Murch SH, Anthony A, Casson DH, et al. Retraction of an interpretation. *Lancet* 2004 Mar 6;363(9411):750.
69. Offit PA, Coffin SE. Communicating science to the public: MMR vaccine and autism. *Vaccine* 2003 Dec 8;22(1):1–6.
70. Koplan JP, Preblud SR. A benefit-cost analysis of mumps vaccine. *Am J Dis Child* 1982 Apr;136(4):362–364.
71. White CC, Koplan JP, Orenstein WA. Benefits, risks, and costs of immunization for measles, mumps, and rubella. *Am J Public Health* 1985;75(7):739–744.
72. Petrovic M, Roberts R, Ramsay M. Second dose of measles, mumps, rubella vaccine: questionnaire survey of health professionals. *BMJ* 2001 Jan 13;322(7278):82–85.
73. Smith A, McCann R, McKinlay I. Second dose of MMR vaccine: health professionals' level of confidence in the vaccine and attitudes towards the second dose. *Commun Dis Public Health* 2001 Dec;4(4):273–277.
74. Wood DL. Increasing immunization coverage. *Pediatrics* 2003;112:978–981.
75. World Health Organization (WHO). Mumps virus vaccines. February 2003. WHO website. Available at: http://www.who.int/immunization/topics/mumps/en/index.html.
76. Asari S, Deguchi M, Tahara K, et al. Seroprevalence survey of measles, rubella, varicella, and mumps antibodies in health care workers and evaluation of a vaccination program in a tertiary care hospital in Japan. *Am J Infect Control* 2003 May;31(3):157–162.
77. Brotherton JML, Bartlett MJ, Muscatello DJ, et al. Do we practice what we preach? Health care worker screening and vaccination. *Am J Infect Control* 2003 May;31(3):144–150.
78. Gershon AA. Rubella Virus (German measles). In: Mandell GL, Bennett JE, Dolin R, eds. *Mandell, Douglas and Bennett's Principles and Practice of Infectious Diseases,* 5th ed. Philadelphia: Churchill Livingstone, 2000;1708–1712.

79. Maldonado YA. In: Long SS, Pickering LK, Prober CG, eds. *Principles and Practice of Pediatric Infectious Diseases*, 2nd ed. Philadelphia: Churchill Livingstone, 2003;1123–1129.

80. Bellini WJ, Icenogle JP. Measles and Rubella Viruses. In: Murray PR, Baron EJ, Jorgensen JH, et al., eds. *Manual of Clinical Microbiology*. Vol. 2, 8th ed. Washington DC: ASM Press, 2003;1389–1403.

81. Cherry JD. Rubella. In: Feigin RD, Cherry JD, et al., eds. *Textbook of Pediatric Infectious Diseases,* 4th ed. Philadelphia: WB Saunders, 1998;1922–1949.

82. American Academy of Pediatrics (AAP). Rubella. In: Pickering LK, ed. *2003 Red Book: Report of the Committee on Infectious Diseases,* 26th ed. Elk Grove Village, IL: AAP, 2003;536–541.

83. Cooper LZ, Alford CA. Rubella. In: Remington JS, Klein JO, eds. *Infectious Diseases of the Fetus and Newborn Infant,* 5th ed. Philadelphia: WB Saunders; 2001:347–388.

84. Centers for Disease Control and Prevention (CDC). Rubella and congenital rubella syndrome—United States, 1985–1988. *MMWR Morb Mortal Wkly Rep* 1989 Mar 24;38(11):173–178.

85. Watson JC, Hadler SC, Dykewicz CA, et al. Measles, mumps, and rubella–vaccine use and strategies for elimination of measles, rubella, and congenital rubella syndrome and control of mumps: recommendation of the immunization practices advisory committee (ACIP). *MMWR Recomm Rep* 1991 May 22;47(RR-8):1–57.

86. Subharao EK, Amin S, Kumar ML. Prevaccination serologic screening for measles in health care workers. *J Infect Dis* 1991 Apr;163(4): 876–878.

87. Das BD, Lakhani P, Kurtz JB, et al. Congenital rubella after previous maternal immunity. *Arch Dis Child* 1990 May;65(5):545–546.

88. Levine JB, Berkowitz CD, St Geme JW Jr. Rubella virus reinfection during pregnancy leading to late-onset congenital rubella syndrome. *J Pediatr* 1982 Apr;100(4):589–591.

89. Centers for Disease Control and Prevention (CDC). Summary of notifiable disease: United States, 2001. *MMWR* 2001;50(No. 53):1–136.

90. Siegel M, Fuerst HT, Peress NS. Comparative fetal mortality in maternal virus diseases: a prospective study on rubella, measles, mumps, chickenpox, and hepatitis. *N Engl J Med* 1966 Apr 7;274(14):768–771.

91. Levin MJ, Oxman MN, Moore MG, et al. Diagnosis of congenital rubella in utero. *N Engl J Med* 1974 May 23;290(21):1187–1188.

92. Thomas HI, Barrett E, Hesketh LM, et al. Simultaneous IgM reactivity by EIA against more than one virus in measles, parvovirus B19 and rubella infection. *J Clin Virol* 1999 Oct;14(2):107–118.

93. Daffos F, Forestier F, Grangeot-Keros L, et al. Prenatal diagnosis of con-genital rubella. *Lancet* 1984 Jul 7;2(8393):1–3.

94. Grose C, Itani O, Weiner C. Prenatal diagnosis of fetal infection: advances from amniocentesis to cordocentesis–congenital toxoplasmosis, rubella, cytomegalovirus, varicella virus, parvovirus and human immunodeficiency virus. *Pediatr Infect Dis J* 1989 Jul;8(7):459–468.

95. Terry GM, Ho TL, Warren RC, et al. First trimester prenatal diagnosis of congenital rubella: a laboratory investigation. *Br Med J (Clin Res Ed)* 1986 Apr 5;292(6525):930–933.

96. Bosma TJ, Corbett KM, Eckstein MB, et al. Use of PCR for prenatal and postnatal diagnosis of congenital rubella. *J Clin Microbiol* 1995 Nov;33(11):2881–2887.

97. Schiff GM. Titered lots of immune globulin. Efficacy in prevention of rubella. *Am J Dis Child* 1969 Aug;118(2):322–327.

98. Preblud SR, Serdula MK, Frank JA Jr, et al. Rubella vaccination in the United States: a ten year review. *Epidemiol Rev* 1980;2:171–194.

99. Plotkin SA. Rubella Vaccine. In: Plotkin SA, Mortimer EA Jr, eds. *Vaccines*, 2nd ed. Philadelphia: WB Saunders, 1994;303.

100. Tingle AS, Mitchell LA, Grace M, et al. Randomized double-blind placebo-controlled study on adverse effects of rubella immunization in seronegative women. *Lancet* 1997 May 3;349(9061):1277–1281.

101. Eickhoff TC, Axnick KJ, Cole WR, et al. Recommendations for the control of rubella within hospitals. *Infect Control* 1981 Sep-Oct;2(5):410–411, 424.

102. McCallin PF, Fuccillo DA, Ley AC, et al. Gammaglobulin as prophylaxis against rubella-induced congenital anomalies. *Obstet Gynecol* 1972 Feb;39(2):185–189.

SUPPLEMENTAL RESOURCES

Centers for Disease Control and Prevention (CDC). *Immunization schedules.* CDC website. January 31, 2014. Available at: http://www.cdc.gov/vaccines /schedules/index.html.

Centers for Disease Control and Prevention (CDC). *Infectious diseases related to travel.* CDC website. December 13, 2013. Available at: http://wwwnc.cdc .gov/travel/yellowbook/2014/chapter-3-infectious-diseases-related-to-travel /measles-rubeola.

Centers for Disease Control and Prevention (CDC). *Measles (Rubeola).* CDC website. November 8, 2013. Available at: http://www.cdc.gov/measles /index.html.

Centers for Disease Control and Prevention (CDC). *Rubella (German Measles, Three-Day Measles).* CDC website. April 29, 2011. Available at: http://www .cdc.gov/rubella/.

Centers for Disease Control and Prevention (CDC). *Vaccines and preventable diseases:* Immunization Action Coalition. Available at: http://www.immunize.org.

McLean HQ, Fiebelkorn AP, Temte JL, et al. Prevention of measles, rubella, congenital rubella syndrome, and mumps, 2013: Summary recommendations of the Advisory Committee on Immunization Practices (ACIP). *MMWR Recomm Rep* [serial online]. 2013;62(RR-4);1-34. Available at: http://www.cdc.gov /mmwr/preview/mmwrhtml/rr6204a1.htm.

Centers for Disease Control and Prevention (CDC). *Vaccines and preventable diseases: mumps vaccination.* CDC website. February 7, 2013. Available at: http://www.cdc.gov/vaccines/vpd-vac/mumps/default.htm.

Roush S, McIntyre L, Baldy LM. Mumps. In: *Manual for the Surveillance of Vaccine-Preventable Diseases,* 5th edition. Available at: http://www.cdc.gov /vaccines/pubs/surv-manual/index.html.

World Health Organization (WHO). *Health topics: measles.* WHO website. Available at: http://www.who.int/topics/measles/en/.

World Health Organization (WHO). *Rubella.* WHO website. Available at: http://www.who.int/immunization/topics/rubella/en/index.html.

CHAPTER 87

Neisseria meningitidis

Gio Baracco, MD, FACP
Associate Professor of Clinical Medicine
Division of Infectious Diseases
University of Miami Miller School of Medicine
Veterans Affairs Healthcare System
Miami, FL

ABSTRACT

Neisseria meningitidis *is an aerobic, Gram-negative diplococcus that colonizes the nasopharynx of many healthy individuals. Microbial and host factors combine to allow this organism to invade the bloodstream and get into the central nervous system, causing severe sepsis and meningitis. Hypervirulent strains may be transmitted from person to person through respiratory secretions, causing outbreaks of meningococcal disease. Several areas of the world, especially sub-Saharan Africa, have hyperendemic meningococcal disease. In the United States, most cases are sporadic; only approximately 2 percent of cases occur as outbreaks. However, outbreak-related cases have greater morbidity and mortality than sporadic cases. Patients with meningococcal disease should be promptly identified, and Droplet Precautions should be started when the diagnosis is initially suspected. Household contacts and individuals with direct exposure to patients' respiratory secretions require the administration of chemoprophylaxis. Five meningococcal serogroups cause the majority of cases: A, B, C, Y, and W-135; quadrivalent (A, C, Y, and W-135) polysaccharide and conjugate vaccines are available and recommended for populations at highest clinical or epidemiological risk of developing invasive meningococcal disease.*

KEY CONCEPTS

- Meningococcal disease is a severe, potentially lethal, transmissible infection. Appropriate infection prevention and other public health interventions are effective in preventing the spread of this disease within the hospital and the community.

- *Neisseria meningitidis* is transmitted via respiratory droplets from colonized or infected individuals to susceptible ones.

- Persons at high risk of infection (epidemiological or medical) should be vaccinated ahead of the exposure.

- Patients with confirmed or suspected meningococcal disease should be placed on Droplet Precautions to prevent nosocomial transmission of the disease.

- Post-exposure chemoprophylaxis is an effective way to prevent disease in exposed individuals.

BACKGROUND

Neisseria meningitidis, also known as meningococcus, is the bacterium responsible for thousands of cases of severe sepsis and meningitis around the world. Meningococcal disease causes significant morbidity and mortality, especially surrounding epidemic outbreaks, and thus prevention of meningococcal transmission and disease is an important public health goal. Effective strategies for the prevention and management of meningococcal disease are available and based on a deep understanding of meningococcal pathogenesis and virulence, combined with widespread use of antibiotics and effective vaccines. These interventions have effectively diminished the impact of meningococcal disease and are discussed in detail in this chapter.

BASIC PRINCIPLES

Epidemiology

Vieusseux[1] published the first description of meningococcal disease in 1805, when he described an outbreak of severe sepsis and meningitis in Geneva, Switzerland. Meningococcal disease is still hyperendemic in many areas of the world. The highest burden of meningococcal disease occurs in the so-called meningitis belt in sub-Saharan Africa, an area comprising 22 countries from Senegal in the West to Ethiopia in the East, with an estimated total population of more than 400 million people.[2] Epidemic and endemic diseases are caused primarily by six meningococcal serogroups: A, B, C, X, Y, and W-135. The incidence of meningococcal disease tends to be cyclical, with peaks and troughs occurring every 5 to 8 years. However, the incidence and pattern in each geographical area shows great variability. Serogroup A causes large outbreaks of meningococcal disease in the meningitis belt every 8 to 10 years since at least 1905, with attack rates as high as 1,000 per 100,000 people reported in affected communities.[3] Large outbreaks are rare outside of Africa, though in 2000 and 2001 several hundred pilgrims attending the Hajj in Saudi Arabia were infected with *N. meningitidis* serotype W-135.[4,5] Acquisition of this meningococcal serotype continues to be a problem for pilgrims to the Hajj,[6] despite aggressive measures taken by the Saudi government to prevent it.[7]

The Centers for Disease Control and Prevention (CDC) estimates that between 800 and 1,200 cases of invasive meningococcal disease occur annually in the United States. This corresponds to a case rate of 0.3 per 100,000 persons. This number has been declining steadily since the late 1990s.[8] A large population-based surveillance program has shown that in 2011, serogroups Y, B, and C accounted for 36 percent, 28 percent, and 25 percent of U.S. isolates, respectively.[9]

The age distribution of invasive meningococcal disease in the United States follows a multimodal distribution, with peaks in infants aged less than 5 years (especially between 0 and 6 months), adolescents and young adults aged 16 to 21 years, and adults older than 65 years.[8]

Nasopharyngeal colonization is a prerequisite for the development of invasive meningococcal disease. Transmission occurs when nasopharyngeal secretions from a colonized person reach the upper respiratory tract of a susceptible individual via respiratory droplets or direct handling of respiratory secretions.[10] Because humans are the only host of N. meningitidis, all transmission is human to human. No animal or environmental reservoirs have been identified, and the disease is not transmitted through arthropod vectors. Surveys performed in the absence of an outbreak demonstrate that approximately 10 percent of healthy persons will carry this organism at any one point in time. Crowded living conditions (e.g., military barracks or college dormitories),[11] active and passive smoking, and viral respiratory illnesses increase the likelihood of transmission by increasing the aerosolization of bacteria and by decreasing the local immunologic barriers to infection, leading to up to 50 percent carriage rates.[12] However, only a small minority of those colonized will develop invasive meningococcal disease. The rate of carriage per se is not necessarily a predictor of meningococcal outbreaks but seems to be a marker indicating that conditions for enhanced transmission are present. Development of invasive disease seems to be more a factor of being colonized with the right strain. Genetic recombination and mutations of the bacterium in the population contribute to the development of more virulent strains, increasing the risk of serious disease. For instance, the risk of meningococcal disease in household contacts of infected patients is approximately 3 per 1,000 persons,[13] which is approximately 500 to 800 times greater than the risk of the general population.[14] In addition, some host factors will also make it more likely that a colonized person develops invasive disease, though patients with these conditions account for only a minority of cases with invasive meningococcal disease. These host factors include functional or anatomic asplenia, a deficiency of properdin, and a deficiency of terminal complement components.

In the United States, meningococcal disease occurs most often during the winter and early spring.[14] Most cases are sporadic, and much less often (approximately 2 percent) they occur as outbreaks or case clusters. A total of 69 outbreaks of meningococcal disease, representing 229 cases, were reported between 1994 and 2002. Forty-three (62 percent) of these outbreaks

involved N. meningitidis serogroup C, 17 (25 percent) involved serogroup B, and 9 (13 percent) involved serogroup Y. No outbreaks of N. meningitidis infection involving serogroups A or W-135 were detected.[15] Recently, several clusters of group C invasive meningococcal disease have been reported in men who have sex with men in the United States, Canada, and several European countries.[16,17] However infrequent, outbreaks remain an important public health issue. Patients with outbreak-associated illness are more likely to die than patients with sporadic disease. The High case fatality rate associated with outbreaks of meningococcal disease may be related to the strains involved, the host, or the environment.[15]

Healthcare-associated transmission of N. meningitidis and secondary cases of meningococcal disease can occur. The index case for healthcare-associated spread may have pneumonia or tracheobronchitis. Aerosolization of respiratory secretions is a risk factor for disease. In one study of a patient with N. meningitidis pneumonia, 8 of 92 hospital personnel who had cared for the patient became carriers. In another case of serogroup B meningococcal meningitis, a nurse who assisted with intubation of the case patient developed serogroup B meningococcal meningitis.[18]

Transmission to laboratory workers is also a concern and reinforces the importance of masks, gowns, and gloves when manipulating secretions or potential aerosols, biosafety cabinet (BS-2) precautions for working with cultures of N. meningitidis, and immunization of microbiology laboratory personnel. In 2002, the CDC reported two cases of fatal laboratory-associated meningococcal disease that occurred in microbiologists who had handled clinical specimens of N. meningitidis serogroup C. This study identified an additional 14 cases of laboratory-acquired meningococcal disease occurring in the preceding 15 years through a Listserv survey. The overall fatality rate in this series was 50 percent.[19]

Clinical Presentation

The clinical manifestations and the degree of severity of meningococcal disease vary widely. Patients with meningococcal infection present with or without involvement of the central nervous system in about equal proportions. One of the classic features of meningococcal disease is the presence of a petechial or purpuric rash that appears concomitantly with fever, malaise, and headache.

The most common forms of invasive meningococcal disease can be summarized as follows:[20]

1. Bacteremia without sepsis. Meningococcal disease may present as a nonspecific febrile illness. Patients are often diagnosed as having a viral upper respiratory infection or viral exanthem and are frequently discharged from the hospital without specific antibiotic therapy. The diagnosis is made when blood cultures return with N. meningitidis. Many patients recover spontaneously.

2. Meningococcemia without meningitis (27 percent of cases). Patients with this syndrome present with fever, malaise, and a petechial or purpuric rash that may progress to purpura fulminans, a condition characterized by cutaneous hemorrhage and necrosis. This syndrome is accompanied by the rapid development of hypotension, acute adrenal insufficiency (Waterhouse-Friedrickson syndrome), multiorgan failure, and severe coagulopathy from disseminated intravascular coagulation, and may result in the patient's death within a few hours from the onset of symptoms.

3. Meningitis with or without meningococcemia (70 percent of cases). The classic triad of clinical manifestations suggesting meningitis—headache, fever, and meningeal signs—occurs in only about one quarter of the patients with meningococcal meningitis. The patient's mental status varies from normal to comatose. Deep tendon reflexes are usually normal, and no pathologic reflexes are present. The cerebrospinal fluid of patients with untreated meningococcal meningitis is usually cloudy and has pleocytosis with a predominance of neutrophils, low glucose, and high protein levels. In most of the cases, the organisms are seen on Gram stain or can be identified using latex agglutination assays. The culture is almost invariably positive as long as the sample was obtained before the administration of antibiotics.

4. Meningococcal meningoencephalitis. Patients present with a profoundly altered mental status, meningeal signs, and an abnormal cerebrospinal fluid. The deep tendon and superficial reflexes are altered (either absent or rarely hyperactive). Pathologic reflexes are frequently present.

5. Meningococcal pneumonia. Patients present with fever, cough, and chest pain. A history of a recent upper respiratory infection is present in about half of the patients, and viral infections such as influenza may predispose frail colonized patients to develop meningococcal pneumonia. Establishing the specific etiologic diagnosis in these patients is challenging, because nasopharyngeal carriage of N. meningitidis is common and blood cultures have low yield. However, the prognosis seems to be good, with no fatalities reported in a cohort of 68 Air Force recruits with group Y meningococcal pneumonia treated with penicillin.[21]

Variations of these manifestations can occur, and patients can progress from one form to the other during the course of their disease. Less common syndromes, including urethritis, supraglottitis, and a chronic bacteremic syndrome with rash and arthritis similar to chronic gonococcal disease have also been described. Small children and elderly patients also tend to present with atypical and protean clinical manifestations.

Diagnosis

The diagnosis of meningococcal disease is made by identification of N. meningitidis from blood, cerebrospinal fluid, or other sterile fluids from patients with compatible signs and symptoms. Colonization can be ascertained by isolating the microorganism from nasopharyngeal secretions.

Neisseria species are Gram-negative cocci usually seen in pairs with the adjacent sides flattened. N. meningitidis grows best in a moist environment at 35°C to 37°C with 5 to 10 percent carbon dioxide. It grows well on blood agar base, supplemented chocolate agar, trypticase soy agar, Mueller-Hinton agar (for sterile body sites), and selective media such as Thayer-Martin agar (to detect nasopharyngeal colonization). Samples need to be transported and plates should be set up promptly, because the microorganism does not tolerate desiccation well. Growth of oxidase-positive colonies and Gram-negative diplococci with the right clinical context provides a presumptive identification of N. meningitidis. Fermentation of glucose and maltose, but not sucrose, lactose, or fructose, may be used for species confirmation. Molecular methods, such as polymerase chain reaction (PCR) techniques, may supplement culture for the detection of meningococcus, especially in patients previously treated with antibiotics.[20]

N. meningitidis, unlike the other human pathogenic Neisseria (N. gonorrhea), has a polysaccharide capsule that serves as an antiphagocytic virulence factor. The capsule is antigenically and chemically unique and allows for the classification of meningococcal strains into at least 13 serogroups. However, almost the entire disease burden occurring worldwide is caused by only six serogroups: A, B, C, W-135, X, and Y. The serologic group may be determined by a slide agglutination test, using first polyvalent and then monovalent antisera.[3] Meningococci may be further classified on the basis of their outer membrane proteins (protein serotype), and lipo-oligosaccharides (immunotype).[20]

Meningococcal populations are diverse and dynamic, and epidemiological investigations require high-resolution techniques. Molecular subtyping with the use of multilocus enzyme electrophoresis, pulsed-field gel electrophoresis, or DNA sequence analysis can be helpful in identifying closely related strains with the potential to cause outbreaks and in understanding the genetic characteristics of N. meningitidis.[22]

Management

Prompt administration of effective antibiotics dramatically improves the outcome of patients with invasive meningococcal disease. With adequate treatment, patients with meningococcal meningitis have a mortality rate of less than 5 percent.

Sulfonamides were the first antibiotic class used effectively to treat invasive meningococcal disease. However, the emergence of resistance in a significant proportion of pathogenic strains has resulted in the discontinuation of the use of this class of antibiotics.[23]

Penicillin G and third-generation cephalosporins such as ceftriaxone are consistently active against N. meningitidis, have potent bactericidal activity, and have acceptable penetration into the central nervous system.[20] Although rare, penicillin-insensitive strains of N. meningitidis have been reported in Europe and the United States. These organisms usually retain susceptibility to ceftriaxone and cefotaxime. It is for these reasons that ceftriaxone at doses of 1 to 2 g every 12 hours is considered the antibiotic of choice for the treatment of invasive meningococcal disease. Penicillin G 300,000 U/kg/d up to a maximum of 24 million units per day administered every 2 hours or by continuous infusion is a perfectly reasonable alternative. Chloramphenicol, at doses of 25 mg/kg intravenously every 6 hours up to a maximum dose of 1 g every 6 hours, can be used in patients intolerant to beta-lactam antibiotics.

Prevention

Prevention of meningococcal disease must occur at several levels. Public health interventions to decrease the incidence of meningococcal disease in the community include immunization of high-risk individuals, advice to travelers, and chemoprophylaxis of household contacts of patients with meningococcal disease. At the hospital level, rapid identification and institution of Droplet Precautions based on suspicion of meningococcal disease, appropriate antibiotic therapy of the patient, and chemoprophylaxis of healthcare personnel who were in direct contact with the patient's nasopharyngeal secretions are the most important interventions to take. In addition to observing appropriate biosafety practices, laboratory technicians working in the microbiology laboratory should be immunized against N. meningitidis.

Immunization

There are currently four licensed meningococcal vaccines in the United States. A quadrivalent (A, C, Y, W-135) polysaccharide meningococcal vaccine (MPSV4) was licensed in the United States in 1978. The polysaccharide vaccine's main limitation is that its immunogenicity and duration of protection is limited. In addition, it has little effect on nasopharyngeal carriage rates and therefore does not provide herd immunity. In January 2005, the U.S. Food and Drug Administration licensed a new meningococcal conjugate vaccine (MenACWY-D), in which the antigens are conjugated to diphtheria toxoid. This conjugate vaccine provides an enhanced primary response among infants and a strong anamnestic response at re-exposure. It is currently licensed as a one-dose vaccine for individuals aged 2 to 55 years and as a two-dose vaccine for children 9 to 23 months old. In 2010, a second tetravalent conjugate vaccine was licensed (MenACWY-CRM). In this vaccine, the meningococcal antigens are bound to CRM_{197}, a nontoxic form of diphtheria toxin. It is approved as a single-dose vaccine for people ages 2 to 55 years. A third meningococcal conjugate vaccine was approved in 2012 (Hib-MenCY-TT). This is a combined vaccine with antigens to Haemophilus influenzae type B and serotypes C and Y of N. meningitidis bound to tetanus toxoid. It is approved in a four-dose regimen for infants aged 6 to 18 months. All four vaccines are safe and effective. Efficacy was established for MPSV4 by direct clinical trials of monovalent serogroups A and C and combined A/C vaccines and by inferring immunity based on equivalent serum bactericidal antibody (SBA) levels for serotypes Y and W-135. Efficacy of all three conjugate vaccines has been inferred by using SBA levels against each of the antigens in the vaccines. All currently available vaccines have the limitation of not protecting against infection caused by N. meningitidis serogroup B.[8]

The CDC's Advisory Committee on Immunization Practices (ACIP)[8] recommends that the following groups of individuals receive meningococcal immunization:

- All children at age 11 or 12 years or at age 13 to 18 years, if not previously vaccinated, should receive a single dose of a MenACWY vaccine. A booster dose should be administered at age 16 to 18 if the first dose was received prior to the 16th birthday.

- Persons at increased risk for meningococcal disease:

  ○ Persons with persistent terminal complement component deficiency, anatomic or functional asplenia

  ○ Travelers or residents of countries where meningococcal disease is hyperendemic or epidemic

  ○ First-year college students age 21 or under living in residential housing.

  ○ Microbiologists who are routinely exposed to isolates of N. meningitidis.

  ○ Persons at risk during a community outbreak attributable to a vaccine serogroup

Hib-MenCY-TT is indicated for children 2 to 18 months old. A MenACWY vaccine is preferred for children aged 9 months and older, as well as for adults with any of the preceding indications who are aged 55 years or under. MPSV4 is the only vaccine indicated for adults older than 55 years of age, though persons older than 55 years who were vaccinated previously with MenACWY and are recommended for revaccination should continue to receive a MenACWY vaccine.

Human immunodeficiency virus (HIV) infection is not an indication for routine MenACWY vaccination. However, if an HIV-positive patient has another indication for vaccination, he or she should receive a two-dose primary series, administered 8 to 12 weeks apart, because patients with HIV do not respond optimally to a single dose.[8]

The CDC has recommended thresholds for initiating vaccination campaigns in the setting of an outbreak.[8] A vaccination campaign should be started when at least three cases of meningococcal disease caused by the same serogroup have been identified in a community or organization in less than 3 months, with a resulting primary attack rate greater than 10 cases/100,000 population. In organizational settings, the occurrence of even two cases in such a short period may warrant consideration of a vaccination campaign. These recommendations contrast with those of the World Health Organization, which recommends a threshold of five cases in 1 week for populations of less than 30,000 people, or 15 cases per 100,000 population per week in populations of 30,000 to 100,000 people.[24]

Chemoprophylaxis

An important intervention for the prevention of sporadic meningococcal disease is antimicrobial chemoprophylaxis of close contacts of a patient with invasive meningococcal disease.[8]

Close contacts are individuals who are exposed within 7 days of the onset of symptoms and who belong to one of the following groups:

- Household members
- Child-care center contacts
- Anyone directly exposed to the patient's oral secretions (e.g., through kissing, mouth-to-mouth resuscitation, endotracheal intubation, or endotracheal tube management)
- For travelers, antimicrobial chemoprophylaxis should be considered for any passenger who had direct contact with respiratory secretions from an index patient or for anyone seated directly next to an index patient on a prolonged flight (i.e., more than 8 hours).

Antimicrobial chemoprophylaxis is not indicated for contacts of patients with *N. meningitidis* isolated only from nonsterile sites (oropharyngeal, conjunctival, or respiratory specimens). Antibiotics are also not indicated for asymptomatic nasopharyngeal carriers of *N. meningitidis*.

Chemoprophylaxis should be initiated as soon as possible, ideally within 24 hours of initial exposure. Conversely, chemoprophylaxis administered more than 14 days after onset of illness in the index patient is probably of limited or no value. Oropharyngeal or nasopharyngeal cultures are not helpful in determining the need for chemoprophylaxis and might unnecessarily delay institution of this preventive measure.[8]

Rifampin, ciprofloxacin, and ceftriaxone have comparable efficacy and are good alternatives. The patient's age and presence of contraindications, and clinician and patient preference, determine the selection of antibiotic.

Recommended regimens[8] are as follows:

- For children under 1 month of age: rifampin 5 mg/kg every 12 hours for 2 days
- For children over 1 month of age: rifampin 10 mg/kg (maximum 600 mg) every 12 hours for 2 days, or (for children aged <15 years) ceftriaxone 125 mg as a single intramuscular dose
- For adults: ciprofloxacin 500 mg by mouth as a single dose, rifampin 600 mg by mouth every 12 hours for 2 days, or ceftriaxone 250 mg as a single intramuscular dose

Azithromycin is not recommended as first-line chemoprophylaxis, but one study showed that a single 500-mg dose was effective in eradicating nasopharyngeal carriage and may be considered for prophylaxis if there is sustained ciprofloxacin resistance in a local community.[8]

Ciprofloxacin should not be used for children unless there are no other viable alternatives. Both rifampin and ciprofloxacin should not be used in pregnant or lactating women because of their teratogenic potential. Rifampin may impair the efficacy of oral contraceptives, so alternative contraceptive methods should be advised while a patient is taking this drug.

Systemic antibiotics other than third-generation cephalosporins used to treat meningococcal disease are ineffective in eradicating meningococcal nasopharyngeal carriage, so patients with meningococcal disease treated with any regimen other than ceftriaxone or other third-generation cephalosporins should also be given chemoprophylaxis.[8]

FUTURE TRENDS

Improving the use of existing vaccines across populations, performing research and development of more broadly effective vaccines, ensuring vaccine availability, and having the ability to perform rapid diagnosis are major areas for future work.

INTERNATIONAL PERSPECTIVE

Although relatively few cases are diagnosed in the United States, meningococcal disease is highly endemic in many areas of the world. *N. meningitidis* is responsible for large epidemics (causing thousands of deaths) in many West and Central African countries (the so-called meningitis belt). Prevention efforts in developing countries include routine vaccination of the entire population (i.e., Saudi Arabia) or school children (i.e., Sudan). The World Health Organization promotes a three-pronged approach to the public health response of epidemic meningococcal disease in developing countries, involving epidemic preparedness (surveillance, case detection and investigation, and laboratory confirmation), prevention (vaccinating all individuals 1 to 29 years of age in the African meningitis belt with meningococcal A conjugate vaccine), and epidemic response through appropriate case management and reactive mass vaccination campaigns.[25]

Travelers to the meningitis belt in sub-Saharan Africa during the dry season (December to June) or to areas affected by meningococcal outbreaks are advised to be vaccinated. It is recommended that travelers be vaccinated at least 10 days before travel to allow immunity to build. However, vaccination still should be provided for travelers leaving in fewer than 10 days.[26] The government of Saudi Arabia requires that visitors traveling to Mecca during the annual Hajj and Umrah pilgrimages obtain a tetravalent vaccine at least 10 days before their arrival in the country, and that the vaccination has occurred in the previous 3 years. Updated information regarding ongoing epidemics and vaccination requirements for travelers can be found on the CDC's Web site (http://www.cdc.gov).

REFERENCES

1. Vieusseux M. Memoire sur la maladie qui a regne a Geneve au printemps de 1805. *J Med Chir Pharmacol* 1805;11:163.
2. World Health Organization. Meningococcal disease in countries of the African meningitis belt, 2012 – emerging needs and future perspectives. *Wkly Epidemiol Rec* 2013 Mar 22;88(12):129–136.
3. Chang Q, Tzeng YL, Stephens DS. Meningococcal disease: changes in epidemiology and prevention. *Clin Epidemiol* 2012;4:237–245.
4. Centers for Disease Control and Prevention (CDC). Serogroup W-135 meningococcal disease among travelers returning from Saudi Arabia—United States, 2000. *MMWR Morb Mortal Wkly Rep* 2000 Apr;49(16):345–346.
5. Dull PM, Abdelwahab J, Sacchi CT, et al. *Neisseria meningitidis* serogroup W-135 carriage among US travelers to the 2001 Hajj. *J Infect Dis* 2005 Jan 1;191(1):33–39.

6. Ceyhan M, Celik M, Demir ET, et al. Acquisition of meningococcal serogroup W-135 carriage in Turkish Hajj pilgrims who had received the quadrivalent meningococcal polysaccharide vaccine. *Clin Vaccine Immunol* 2013 Jan;20(1):66–68.

7. Al-Tawfiq JA, Memish ZA. The Hajj: updated health hazards and current recommendations for 2012. *Euro Surveill* 2012 Oct 11;17(41):20295.

8. Cohn AC, MacNeil JR, Clark TA, et al. Prevention and control of meningococcal disease: recommendations of the Advisory Committee on Immunization Practices (ACIP). *MMWR Recomm Rep* 2013 Mar 22;62(RR-2):1–28.

9. Centers for Disease Control and Prevention (CDC). *Active bacterial core surveillance (ABCs) report emerging infections program network Neisseria meningitidis, 2011.* 2013. Available at: http://www.cdc.gov/abcs/reports-findings/survreports/mening11.pdf.

10. Gasparini R, Amicizia D, Lai PL, et al. Neisseria meningitides, pathogenetic mechanisms to overcome the human immune defences. *J Prev Med Hyg* 2012 Jun;53(2):50–55.

11. Stephens DS, Zimmer SM. Pathogenesis, Therapy, and prevention of meningococcal sepsis. *Curr Infect Dis Rep* 2002 Oct;4(5):377–386.

12. Memish ZA. Meningococcal disease and travel. *Clin Infect Dis* 2002 Jan;34(1):84–90.

13. Meningococcal Disease Surveillance Group. Meningococcal disease: secondary attack rate and chemoprophylaxis in the United States, 1974. *JAMA* 1976 Jan 19;235(3):261–265.

14. Rosenstein NE, Perkins BA, Stephens DS, et al. Meningococcal disease. *N Engl J Med* 2001 May 3;344(18):1378–1388.

15. Brooks R, Woods CW, Benjamin DK Jr, et al. Increased case-fatality rate associated with outbreaks of *Neisseria meningitidis* infection, compared with sporadic meningococcal disease, in the United States, 1994-2002. *Clin Infect Dis* 2006 Jul 1;43(1):49–54.

16. Weiss D, Varma JK. Control of recent community-based outbreaks of invasive meningococcal disease in men who have sex with men in Europe and the United States. *Euro Surveill* 2013 Jul 11;18(28).

17. Simon MS, Weiss D, Gulick RM. Invasive meningococcal disease in men who have sex with men. *Ann Intern Med* 2013 Aug 20;159(4):300–301.

18. Centers for Disease Control and Prevention (CDC). Nosocomial meningococcemia—Wisconsin. *MMWR* 1978;27:358–363.

19. Centers for Disease Control and Prevention (CDC). Laboratory acquired meningococcal disease—United States, 2000. *MMWR Morb Mortal Wkly Rep* 2002 Feb 22;51(7):141–144.

20. Apicella M. *Neisseria meningitidis.* In: Mandell G, Bennet J, Dolin R, eds. *Mandell, Douglas, and Bennett's Principles and Practice of Infectious Diseases,* 7th ed. Philadelphia: Elsevier, 2010:2737–2752.

21. Koppes GM, Ellenbogen C, Gebhart RJ. Group Y meningococcal disease in United States Air Force recruits. *Am J Med* 1977 May;62(5):661–666.

22. Jolley KA, Brehony C, Maiden MC. Molecular typing of meningococci: recommendations for target choice and nomenclature. *FEMS Microbiol Rev* 2007 Jan;31(1):89–96.

23. Oppenheim BA. Antibiotic resistance in *Neisseria meningitidis. Clin Infect Dis* 1997 Jan;24 Suppl 1:S98–101.

24. World Health Organization (WHO). *Managing meningitis epidemics in Africa: A quick reference guide for health authorities and health-care workers.* 2010. WHO website. Available at: www.who.int/csr/resources/publications/HSE_GAR_ERI_2010_4/en/index.html.

25. World Health Organization (WHO). *Meningococcal Meningitis. Fact Sheet No 141.* Geneva, World Health Organization, November 2012. WHO website. Available at: http://www.who.int/mediacentre/factsheets/fs141/en/index.html.

26. Cohn A, MacNeil JR. *Meningococcal Disease.* Centers for Disease Control and Prevention website. 2013. Available at: http://wwwnc.cdc.gov/travel/yellowbook/2014/chapter-3-infectious-diseases-related-to-travel/meningococcal-disease.

GUIDELINES

Cohn AC, MacNeil JR, Clark TA, et al. Prevention and control of meningococcal disease. Recommendations of the Advisory Committee on Immunization Practices (ACIP). *MMWR Recomm Rep* 2013 Mar 22;62(RR-2):1–28.

SUPPLEMENTAL RESOURCES

Key Web Links

Centers for Disease Control and Prevention (CDC), National Center for Immunization and Respiratory Diseases. *Meningococcal disease.* CDC website. December 31, 2013. Available at: http://www.cdc.gov/meningococcal/index.html.

World Health Organization (WHO). *Global alert and response (GAR). Meningococcal disease.* WHO website. Available at: http://www.who.int/csr/disease/meningococcal/en/.

CHAPTER 88

Parvovirus

Jeanette Lepinski, MSN, RN, CIC
Director of Infection Prevention & Control
Sinai Health System
Chicago, IL

ABSTRACT

Human parvovirus B19 is an enterovirus and the causative agent of erythema infectiosum. This illness, with its characteristic rash, commonly occurs during childhood and produces long-lasting immunity. Often, outbreaks are cyclical, lasting 1 or more years, with 3 or more years of low-level activity. Transmission likely occurs by the droplet mode. Additionally, vertical and parenteral transmission have been reported. The illness is generally mild and self-limited. The typical "slapped cheek" rash develops when the virus can no longer be isolated from respiratory secretions. The risk for transmission is minimized with appropriate infection prevention practices, such as hand hygiene, respiratory etiquette, and Droplet Precautions.

KEY CONCEPTS

- Human parvovirus B19 causes erythema infectiosum, also called fifth disease, slapped cheek rash, or gloves and socks syndrome.

- Human parvovirus B19 enters through and infects the respiratory tract, then seeds the bone marrow.

- Human parvovirus B19 can be transmitted parenterally through blood and blood product transfusion.

- Outbreaks are often cyclical.

- Approximately half of adults have evidence of antibodies to human parvovirus B19.

- Infection during pregnancy may cause variable effects in the fetus depending on gestational age.

- Human parvovirus B19 has been implicated in other disease processes.

- Human parvovirus B19 has been identified as the primary causative agent of transient aplastic crisis.

- Treatment for infection with the virus includes supportive care.

- Severely immunocompromised individuals may benefit from intravenous immunoglobulin therapy.

- Infection prevention in healthcare settings includes Droplet Precautions in addition to Standard Precautions.

BACKGROUND

Human parvovirus B19 (PVB19) was first identified in 1974 and was subsequently recognized as the causative agent of a globally endemic mild or asymptomatic human infection. The illness is common in children and manifests with cold-like symptoms followed by a "slapped cheek" rash with lace-like pupura on the trunk, arms, and legs. It may also manifest in a glove and socks pattern. Illness in adults is not uncommon and may manifest with flulike symptoms, with severe persistent arthralgias. Approximately half of the population is immune due to previous infection. Outbreaks often occur in school settings and may be cyclic over several years. The virus is spread via the respiratory tract through droplets and secretions, but infection can occur from blood and blood products or from mother to fetus via vertical transmission.

BASIC PRINCIPLES

PVB19 is in the *Parvoviridae* family of DNA viruses. Although most of the viruses in this family infect a variety of animals, PVB19 has been limited to humans. Because there are other disease processes associated with this virus, or the illness may be similar to others, a definitive confirmation or differential diagnosis may be required. The infection may be prolonged or more severe in immunocompromised individuals. Confirmation of infection may be verified in the laboratory through a variety of tests. Infection prevention includes Transmission-based Droplet Precautions in addition to Standard Precautions.[1]

Parvovirus Information

Identification of Infectious Agent

Taxonomy

The *Parvoviridae* family consists of a large group of small, single-stranded DNA viruses approximately 20 to 25 nm in size. The family includes 41 known viruses recognized as individual species and is divided into two subfamilies: *Densovirinae* and *Parvovirinae*. The *Densovirinae* subfamily includes viruses infecting insects, whereas the *Parvovirinae* infect animal species.

The subfamily of *Parvovirinae* may be further separated into three genera: *Parvovirus*, *Dependovirus*, and *Erythrovirus*.[2,3]

Parvovirus is found in many animal species, and some are of veterinary interest. *Erythrovirus* comprises PVB19, V9, and parvoviruses. *Dependovirus* includes adeno-associated virus (AAV) serotypes 1 to 6. This group of viruses is generally species specific.[2-6] For example, PVB19 has been shown to cause disease only in humans.[7,8]

Human Parvovirus B19

In 1975, PVB19 was first isolated from serum specimens of healthy blood donors and named as such for the position occupied on the laboratory testing plate. The virus was originally thought to have a single genotype. However, three discrete serotypes have been identified. Virus serotypes 2 and 3 have been found to have higher prevalence in the North and South America and Western Europe. Strain type 3 has been found to be endemic in certain parts of Africa. The prevalence and clinical significance of these serotypes is not presently known.

This virus is nonenveloped and resistant to detergents/solvents and remains stable in the environment for prolonged periods. PVB19 is also thermostable and can survive at 60°C (140°F) for up to 12 hours.[5,7-10] In one study, PVB19 was inactivated after being suspended in 5 percent or 25 percent human serum albumin solution, phosphate-buffered saline, or complete medium at 60°C. However, the virus was resistant to heat inactivation in liquid 60 percent sucrose.[10] Another study found intravenous immunoglobulin (IVIG) treated with heat and polyethelene glycol was rapidly inactivated to below detectable levels. Other studies have shown that PVB19 could be sensitive to a 5-minute contact time with accelerated hydrogen peroxide (5,000 ppm) or sodium hypochlorite (3,000 to 5,000 ppm) at room temperature.[11,12] Formaldehyde and β-propriolactone have been shown to destroy the virus' antigenicity.[13] Due to the size of the virus, filters with a pore size of 35 nm do not effectively filter out the virus.[14]

Epidemiology and Transmission

Occurrence

The virus is generally asymptomatic but may be manifested as a papular purpuric rash resembling slapped cheeks. This condition is also known as gloves and socks syndrome, erythema infectiosum, or fifth disease.[15] (The designation fifth disease was given because it was listed as the fifth of six common rash-producing diseases of childhood, which included measles, scarlet fever, rubella, Dukes disease, and roseola.)

PVB19 is more commonly acquired during childhood in late winter or early spring. Approximately half of all adults have long-lasting immunity as a result of previous infection.[16] Approximately 90 percent of elderly persons are thought to be seropositive for PVB19, as are 40 to 60 percent of young adults, 30 to 40 percent of adolescents, and 2 to 15 percent of children aged 1 to 5 years.[14]

Outbreaks

Outbreaks of PVB19 are often cyclical, lasting 1 to 2 years, followed by 3 or more years of low-level activity. Epidemics among school-aged children in the United States usually begin in midwinter and end at summer recess. During school outbreaks, approximately 20 to 30 percent of susceptible teachers may become infected. Additionally, approximately 50 percent of susceptible household members become infected when exposed.[15,16]

Infectious Process

PVB19 enters through and infects the respiratory tract, then seeds the bone marrow, where immature red blood cells (RBCs) and lymphocytes (B and T cells) are infected. The virus is lytic, shutting off RBC production and causing a reticulocytopenic anemia.

The incubation period is usually 4 to 14 days after exposure. However, the infection may present up to 20 days later. The viremic phase occurs approximately 6 days after infection and usually persists for up to a week.[15-18] Viral DNA may be detected in the blood, respiratory secretions, urine, tears, synovial cells, liver, and endothelium of the myocardium during the viremic stage.[19] Mild symptoms may be present before the antibody response is detected and at the peak of viremia. Ten to 13 days after infection, an immunoglobulin M (IgM) antibody response is mounted, viremia begins to clear, and reticulocytosis develops in an attempt to correct the anemia. Because the rash of erythema infectiosum develops after the antibody response has begun, it is presumably caused in part by the immune response.

Thus, the illness can be biphasic, with some systemic symptoms associated with joint pain, viremia, and rash and others associated with an immune response to the infection. Additionally, immune complexes identified in PVB19 infection may contribute to the disease process. In individuals with normal RBC production, a significant anemia usually does not develop. However, persons with sickle cell disease, systemic lupus erythematosis, or hereditary spherocytosis who require increased RBC production may rapidly develop severe anemia.[17,19,20]

Primary Mode of Transmission

The mode of PVB19 transmission occurs by the respiratory route through respiratory secretions and droplets of saliva.[1,15] During the viremic period, coldlike symptoms may be present. Person-to-person spread is through direct contact with the respiratory secretions of infected individuals, especially with close contact for prolonged periods of time. The slow rate of spread in schools suggests transmission involves environmental fomites. Sharing eating or drinking utensils facilitates viral spread. By the time the characteristic slapped cheek rash has developed, the virus is no longer found in respiratory secretions and the host is no longer considered contagious. If PVB19 advances to transient aplastic crisis (TAC), viremia generally persists and the virus can still be transmitted to others.[15,18]

Parenteral Transmission

PVB19 can be transmitted parenterally through blood and blood product transfusion. It can be transmitted to persons with hemophilia who receive coagulation factor concentrates treated by standard blood-bank methods.[21] This virus can also be transmitted to individuals receiving plasma-derived coagulation factor concentrate treated by the solvent/detergent method for inactivating viruses. More recently, Kooistra and colleagues[22] demonstrated that during epidemic seasons, blood donations with high levels of parvovirus viremia that are devoid of concurrent antibodies may play a role in infecting immunocompromised and parvovirus-naïve recipients.[22]

Vertical Transmission

Of childbearing women, 50 to 60 percent are already immune to PVB19. However, when pregnant women become infected, vertical transmission occurs in approximately one-third of fetuses.[21,23,24] The infection is thought to occur in approximately 1 in 400 pregnancies. Spontaneous abortion occurs in less than 10 percent of pregnant females who contract the virus within the first trimester.[23–25] The highest risk for fetal death seems to occur when PVB19 is contracted within the first 20 weeks of gestation.[13,26,27]

Transmission in the Healthcare Setting

PVB19 transmission has been documented to healthcare personnel in the healthcare setting. Transmission may occur with unprotected respiratory exposure to persons with the virus via the droplet route. Percutaneous exposure to contaminated blood or blood products has been documented. In addition, transmission from individuals with aplastic crisis to other susceptible individuals has been reported.[28,29]

Infectivity and Incubation Periods

Incubation Period

The incubation period for PVB19 varies depending on the clinical manifestation of the disease. A range of 4 to 14 days is most common, but it may be as long as 21 days. With natural infections, such as those that occur in households, the incubation period extends from 13 to 18 days. Two to 3 weeks after infection, rash and joint symptoms may develop.[22]

Infectivity

Viremia peaks during the first 2 days of the illness, during which time the symptoms are similar to the common cold. Generally the illness is contagious for 4 to 5 days before the rash appears. Children with fifth disease caused by PVB19 are generally considered noncontagious by the time the slapped cheek rash appears. This is different from other illnesses that manifest rashes, such as measles, in which the person is contagious during the rash stage.

In individuals who develop PVB19 infection with TAC, viremia generally persists and the infectious period lasts for the duration of the illness, usually approximately 7 days after the onset of symptoms. Peak viremia generally occurs 7 to 12 days after exposure and may last for 3 to 7 days. However, those who develop chronic infections may remain infectious for years until viremia resolves.[1,22,30]

Clinical Manifestations

Erythema Infectiosum

PVB19, the causative agent of erythema infectiosum, generally produces a mild, self-limited illness most often seen in school-aged children. Because the illness is typically mild, it generally resolves without medical treatment in otherwise healthy individuals. This form of PVB19 typically begins with low-grade fever, malaise, or coldlike symptoms. Several days later, an erythematous facial rash and a reticulated red rash on the trunk and extremities appear. This rash may occasionally cause itching and usually resolves within 7 to 10 days. However, it may come and go over a period of weeks and occasionally months. This virus has been associated with various other rashes, including vesicular, petechial, purpuric, morbilliform, and papular rashes.[30,33] Of note, meningoencephalitis also may be associated with PVB19 infection. The symptoms may mimic those of bacterial meningitis. PVB19 DNA has been found in the CSF of this population but not in the brain tissue.[33–36]

Polyarthralgia and Polyarthritis

PVB19 has been associated with various forms of autoimmune diseases that affect the large and small blood vessels, joints, and connective tissue. Although the molecular basis of the autoimmune phenomena is unclear, it is possibly related to apoptotic damage and an increased production of cytokine.[3] Additionally, the pathogenesis involving arthralgias may be related to immune complexes deposited in synovial fluids.[13,37,38]

PVB19 is generally manifested as polyarthropathy in adults. Arthralgias and arthritis have been reported in all joints, but most frequently occur in the distal joints. Most frequently, the hands, wrists, and knees are affected with pain and swelling, generally resolving within 1 to 2 weeks. Bilateral joint pain is a common complaint and occurs more often in adults with PVB19 infection. Arthritic conditions usually resolve over several weeks without prolonged disability. However, symptoms can persist for months and even years.[39,40]

An association between PVB19 and rheumatoid arthritis appears to exist. One study found that 62 percent of controls without arthralgic conditions had positive immunoglobulin G (IgG) titers, indicating past infection, whereas only 9 percent were positive for viral DNA and had no evidence of rheumatological disease.[41] Rheumatoid factor may routinely be found in PVB19-infected persons who have a history of rheumatoid conditions. In addition to arthralgias, inflammatory arthritis occurs in almost 50 percent of adult patients, with 15 percent of cases resulting as an aftermath of infections with PVB19.[42] There is evidence to suggest an association of PVB19 infection and juvenile rheumatic diseases. In one study, 35 percent of children with rheumatic disease were found to have detectable amounts of PVB19 DNA in their serum or synovial fluid. PVB19 infection should be considered in the differential diagnosis of children and adults initially presenting with polyarthralgias/polyarthritis.[41] A relationship has been suggested between chronic PVB19 infection, and the following: fibromyalgia syndrome, chronic fatigue syndrome, and systemic lupus erythromatosis.[36,42] However, one investigation reported that none of the fibromyalgia syndrome cases had evidence of PVB19 viremia as detected by polymerase chain reaction (PCR) analysis.[42]

Infections in the Immunocompromised Host

PVB19 infection in immunocompromised individuals, including individuals infected with human immunodeficiency virus (HIV), and those with congenital immunodeficiencies receiving immunosuppressive therapy for cancer, leukemia, lymphoma, renal transplant, or other solid organ transplants, can result in pure RBC aplasia, chronic infection, and chronic severe anemia. Chronic bone marrow suppression has been described in this population.[30,42–49] This severe anemia is caused by the lysis of erythroid precursor cells. Making the diagnosis is particularly important, because these patients often respond to treatment with IVIG. Therefore, this infection should be considered in the differential diagnosis in the presence of reticulocytopenic anemia in immunosuppressed patients.[2,5] IVIG therapy induces reticulocytosis and generally resolves the anemia.[2,44,45]

Patients with Renal Disease and Renal Transplant Recipients

PVB19 has been epidemiologically linked as the causative agent of acute glomerulopathy and is associated with the anemia present in individuals with end-stage renal disease or postrenal transplantation. Some case reports have also implicated the virus as the potential cause of glomerulonephritis and collapsing glomerulopathy; however, a causal relationship was not been established.[46] The typical onset of anemia after PVB19 infection in renal transplant recipients occurs within 2 to 34 months. In one study the virus was detected in 23 percent (11 patients) of renal transplant recipients who presented with anemia. Another study by Porignaux and colleagues found that 10 percent of the patients being followed developed PVB19 viremia in the first year posttransplant.[48] Another study found the median time to onset of PVB19 disease after transplant was 7 weeks. Anemia was present in 98.8 percent of patients, followed by leukopenia in 37.5 percent and thrombocytopenia in 21 percent of patients. The following were also reported in association with PVB19 infection: hepatitis, myocarditis, and pneumonitis. Finally, 10 percent of patients experienced allograft tissue loss or dysfunction related to PVB19 disease. PVB19 infection should, therefore, be considered in the differential diagnosis in the presence of anemia in post-renal transplant patients. Not all patients who have undergone transplant are able to mount an antibody response to PVB19 infection; thus, PCR testing may be necessary to make an accurate diagnosis in immunocompromised individuals.[47]

Fetal and Neonatal Infection

Approximately 50 percent of women of childbearing age are susceptible to PVB19 infection. The highest risk for contracting the virus during pregnancy occurs during outbreaks in the community. During such epidemics, nonimmune pregnant women who have more frequent contact with children are at the greatest risk for contracting the illness. The risk for infection varies by the type of exposure. Approximately one-third of fetuses with B19 infection may be adversely affected. Outcomes are related to gestational age at which infection occurs, with the worst outcomes between 4 and 20 weeks' gestation. Prior to 4 weeks, there is no intrauterine transmission and after 20 weeks there is no risk of hydrops.[23–25]

The fetus has an immature immune system and does not have the ability to mount an adequate response to the infection. Severe anemia with hemoglobin counts as low as 2 g/dL have been reported. When anemia is severe, congestive heart failure and nonimmune fetal hydrops may develop. Nonimmune hydrops secondary to PVB19 infection occurs in less than 3 percent of pregnancies at approximately 2 to 4 weeks after maternal infection. Because myocardial cells in the fetus can also be infected, there may be direct damage to the heart itself.[4–7,12,15,25,30,32]

When PVB19 is contracted within the first trimester, there is an increased risk for anencephaly, polymicrogyria, and spontaneous abortion. Infections occurring in the second and third trimesters are more often associated with fetal ascites, severe anemia, and nonimmune hydrops.[32,56,57] Kudielka et al.[58] reported a case of PVB19 infection acquired during the second trimester of a mother with congenital spherocytosis. The infection resulted in severe hemolysis and failure of the reticulocytic response, resulting in anemia and aplastic crisis. High doses of IgG were administered to the primigravida, with laboratory test results returning to normal within 5 days of treatment. Ultimately, a healthy term infant was born.[59] The risk for fetal death from a household exposure to erythema infectiosum is between 0.4 and 1.5 percent, whereas the risk from a school exposure is between 0.2 and 0.75 percent. During community outbreaks, the risk ranges between 0.03 and 0.12 percent. Finally, the risk is between 0.01 and 0.03 percent with no known exposure. Pregnant women potentially exposed to PVB19 should be advised of the risks. Often, intrauterine PVB19 infection has no long-term effect on the fetus; however, abnormalities in neurodevelopmental status can be present in up to 30 percent of surviving fetuses with the growth and general health status remaining normal.[57,59] The risk for fetal death is approximately 2 to 9 percent. The risk for fetal death is probably greatest when infection occurs during the first half of pregnancy.[12,23,24]

Transient Aplastic Crisis

PVB19 has been identified as the primary causative agent of TAC. Community and household outbreaks have been associated with this syndrome.[12,15] Persons with hemoglobinopathies manifested by altered RBC production or turnover (e.g., sickle cell disease or thalassemia) may develop TAC with a reticulocytopenic anemia.[15,17] Initially, an acute exanthema characterized by symmetrical purpuric rashes or painful edema and erythema of the hands and feet develop. Other areas of the body are less affected. The exanthema may progress to purpuric papules and petechia that are sharply marginated on the wrists and ankles. PVB19 was the first virus discovered to be associated with the condition known as gloves and socks syndrome.[5]

Chronic Infection

Chronic infection has been demonstrated in immunocompromised persons, which may result in persistent anemia.[63] However, the pathogenesis of disease other than anemia is not clear. For example, rash and joint pains occur after the viremia has been cleared and may result from immune complex or other immune-mediated complications of infection. Chronic PVB19 infection has been demonstrated in patients with no known immune deficiency, without anemia, and with either no disease or various diseases including neuropathy, recurrent rash, and systemic vasculitis. The PVB19 virus persists in nonerythroid cells of some persons, but it is not known if this persistence causes disease. Viremia may be present for months to years after acute infection occurs.[13,17,60–63] Secondary infections have also been shown to occur in health adults, despite prior positive antibody tests.[64]

Association with Other Disease Entities

Radioactive in situ hybridization has confirmed the presence of PVB19 in endothelial cells of the myocardium within the veins, arteries, and arterioles in the presence of acute inflammatory cardiomyopathy.[65–68] The infection has also been reported in association with a variety of other diseases, including systemic vasculitis, idiopathic thrombocytopenia purpura, hepatitis, and hemophagocytic syndrome.[68] Although PVB19 replicates most efficiently in erythroid precursor cells, it is possible that abortive or low-efficiency infections occur in other cells and contribute to some of the disease.[69,70] However, a causative relationship between this viral infection and the previously mentioned diseases has not yet been demonstrated.[67,70–73]

Diagnosis

PVB19 Immunoglobulin M

PVB19 IgM antibodies targeting viral VP2 proteins develop after infection occurs in a nonimmune host. Serological tests for these antibodies are most commonly used to detect PVB19 infection in individuals with normal immune systems. When TAC occurs, IgM is present at the onset of symptoms. IgM titers begin to fall during the second month after the onset of illness and usually become negative within 4 to 6 months. A variety of assays for identifying IgM exist.[74,75]

Table 88-1. Immunity Status Based on Antibody Testing

Immunity Status	Immunoglobulin G	Immunoglobulin M
Susceptible host	Negative	Negative
Recent infection (past 7–10 days)	Negative	Positive
Recent infection (past 7–120 days)	Positive	Positive
Past infection	Positive	Negative

PVB19 Immunoglobulin G

Initially, IgM antibodies develop, followed by IgG antibodies a few days later. IgG antibodies are generally present within 2 to 3 weeks after infection and by the onset of rash in persons with erythema infectiosum. These antibodies (IgG) tend to persist long term and are thought to indicate the presence of protective immunity. Therefore, past infection is best detected by the presence of PVB19 IgG antibodies. A variety of assays have been developed for this purpose. Unlike IgM antibody assays, many of these have acceptable sensitivity and specificity.[74,75] Refer to Table 88-1 for interpretation of IgM and IgG antibodies.

PVB19 Antigen Detection

Antibody assays are often not helpful in detecting infection in immunosuppressed individuals or chronic infection in those who are immunologically normal. In these populations, it may be necessary to perform tests for viral detection; however, PVB19 is difficult to cultivate in vitro.[17] The most sensitive way to detect PVB19 virus is by isolating its DNA by direct hybridization or PCR amplification. Nucleic acid hybridization and PCR assays are the most sensitive methods and may be required in some individuals. However, these tests are less sensitive in individuals with low levels of viremia.[2,3,40]

Histological Identification

The presence of the PVB19 virus can also be suggested by histological changes, the most characteristic of which are large normoblasts (erythroid precursor cells) with marginated chromatin and eosinophilic nuclear inclusions. Parvovirus-like particles can be detected by electron microscopy in a variety of specimens. In situ hybridization or immunohistological studies can be used to confirm the presence of PVB19 in tissue or cells. These types of studies have been essential to the current understanding of the pathogenesis of PVB19 disease.

Management

Supportive

Approximately 20 percent of individuals who become infected with PVB19 do not develop symptoms. In some, a nonspecific illness may occur without the characteristic rash. The majority of cases require no treatment. For those who develop symptoms, supportive treatment may be offered, including antipyretics, analgesics, and antihistamines to help to control symptoms.

Additionally, activity restriction and rest may be indicated.[30] In cases of myocarditis, while supportive measures may be used, these are often of a more critical nature, including pressors and possibly long-term use of a ventricular assist device to allow for recovery of the myocardium over time.[76–78]

Immunoglobulin G Intravenous Therapy

Prolonged illness or more severe illness may occur in immunocompromised individuals. Therefore, PVB19 should be considered in the differential diagnosis in the presence of reticulocytopenic anemia in persons receiving immunosuppressive therapy for cancer, leukemia, lymphoma, or tissue transplantation and those with HIV infection. Those with severe viremia may require IVIG therapy. This treatment usually results with reticulocytosis, an increase in hematocrit, and control of the viremia. However, the infection may not always be cured by IVIG, and additional courses may be required when anemia recurs.[19,43] However, IgG therapy is not without risk. There have been reports of myocardial infarction, acute renal failure, and less frequently, thrombotic events.[79]

Blood Transfusions

Individuals with TAC can rapidly develop severe anemia and may require supportive therapy, including blood transfusions.[2,15,17,45]

Infection Prevention and Control Measures

Hand Hygiene and Standard Precautions

Appropriate hygienic practices including adequate handwashing practices, use of alcohol-based hand washes, and not sharing food and eating and drinking utensils should diminish the risk for acquiring PVB19 infection.[1,80] For all cases, Standard Precautions (respiratory hygiene and cough etiquette, hand hygiene, environmental cleaning) will minimize the transmission of respiratory pathogens in healthcare settings. The components of respiratory hygiene and cough etiquette include the following: covering the mouth and nose during coughing and sneezing, using tissues to contain respiratory secretions with prompt disposal into a nontouch receptacle, offering a surgical mask to persons who are coughing to decrease contamination of the surrounding environment, and turning the head away from others while maintaining spatial separation of at least 3 feet when coughing.[1] Therefore, all individuals should be instructed to cover their mouths and noses when coughing or sneezing and immediately discard soiled tissue followed by hand disinfection.[1,30]

Transmission-Based Precautions for Erythema Infectiosum

The virus cannot be isolated in the secretions of otherwise healthy individuals after the onset of erythema infectiosum rash, arthralgias, and arthritis. It is acceptable to use Standard Precautions after these symptoms develop. However, Droplet Precautions are indicated for certain hospitalized patients with PVB19 infection. Patients with transient aplastic or erythrocyte crisis should remain isolated for a full 7 days after admission. Viremic patients with an aplastic crisis, immunosuppression with chronic infection, and anemia should be isolated for the duration of the illness or hospitalization. These patients should not share rooms with pregnant women, those who may be pregnant, or immunocompromised individuals. Neonates with PVB19 infection should be placed in droplet isolation. Current guidelines for Isolation Precautions should be consulted for additional information regarding infection prevention practices for patients with PVB19 infection. In addition, the Centers for Disease Control and Prevention and Healthcare Infection Control Practices Advisory Committee's Guidelines for Infection Control in Healthcare Personnel (published in 1998) has a section on parvovirus considerations for healthcare personnel.[1,80]

CONCLUSIONS

PVB19, the agent of a human infection from the *Parvoviridae* family, is globally endemic, and infection is often asymptomatic. The disease process is most often acquired in childhood and may manifest with mild symptoms followed by a rash (erythema infectiosum). Transmission is frequently via the respiratory tract, but the virus may also be found in blood and blood products. Vertical transmission from mother to fetus can be devastating depending on gestational age at time of maternal infection. The PVB19 infection may be confused with other illnesses, and the agent has been implicated in other disease processes. Infection prevention measures include applying Standard Precautions coupled with Droplet Precautions to prevent transmission in healthcare settings.

FUTURE TRENDS

Detection of PVB19 in Donated Blood Products

Real-Time Nucleic Acid Testing

A study was performed in Germany and Austria by Schmidt et al.[81] in which 2.8 million blood donations were screened for PVB19 using the nucleic acid testing (NAT) method. Blood containing neutralizing antibodies known as VP2 were found in donations containing less than 105 international units/mL. These units were thought to be safe, and they were released for use. These blood recipients are involved in a follow-up study of infectivity.[81] However, another study using the NAT method, cited at the U.S. Food and Drug Administration Nucleic Acid Testing Workshop in December 2001, found a high rate of false-positive results.[80]

Receptor-Mediated Hemagglutination

Wakamatsu et al.[82] screened blood donors using the receptor-mediated hemagglutination (RHA) method. This test is based on an interaction between PVB19 and the P antigen located on human erythrocytes. They concluded that large-scale screening of donated blood for PVB19 using a combination of RHA and RHA inhibition testing has high specificity and may be useful in screening donor units for PVB19.[82]

Health Council of the Netherlands

A committee of the Health Council of the Netherlands recommends a risk group approach for the administration of "big-virus safe" cellular blood products to patients with underlying hematological disease, pregnant women, and those with immunodeficiency. Big-virus safe blood products are those derived from a blood donor in whom IgG antibodies against PVB19 have been detected in two separate blood samples taken at least 6 months apart. Patients within a risk group may experience serious complications if infected with PVB19. Those patients not within a risk group may continue to receive cellular blood products pursuant to current safety criteria.[83]

Additional studies are needed to identify reliable testing methods for potentially infectious PVB19 in blood products.

Ultraviolet C Radiation

An effective method of increasing the safety of potentially PVB19 contaminated factor VIII concentrates, without losing coagulation activity, may include ultraviolet C radiation in the presence of catechins (including epigallocatechin gallate).[84]

Vaccine Development

There is currently no approved human vaccine for PVB19. A 2006 clinical randomized, placebo-controlled, double-blind clinical trial of the immunogenicity and safety of two dose levels of a recombinant human parvovirus B19 vaccine is evaluating the safety of study vaccine healthy parvovirus B19 seronegative adults and will verify that the vaccine produces immunity. The evaluation of the study may lead to development of commercially available PVB19 vaccine. However, currently a double-blind trial has been discontinued due to unexplained cutaneous events in 3 of 43 enrolled subjects.[83,85]

REFERENCES

1. Siegel JD, Rhinehart E, Jackson M, et al. 2007 Guideline for Isolation Precautions: Preventing Transmission of Infectious Agents in Healthcare Settings, June 2007. CDC website. Available at: http://www.cdc.gov /ncidod/dhqp/gl_isolation.html.
2. Brown KE. The expanded range of parvoviruses which infect humans. Rev Med Virol 2010 Jul;20(4):231–244.
3. Durigon EL, Erdman DD, Gary GW, et al. Multiple primer pairs for polymerase chain reaction (PCR) amplification of human parvovirus B19 DNA. J Virol Methods 1993 Oct;44(2–3):155–165.
4. Rubio M, Guerra S, Almendral JM. Genome Replication and postencapsidation functions mapping to the nonstructural gene restrict the host range of a murine parvovirus in human cells. J Virol 2001 Dec;75(23):11573–11582.
5. Nelson B, Seabury-Stone M. Update on selected viral exanthems. Curr Opin Pediatr 2000 Aug;12(4):359–364.
6. Lukashov V, Goudsmit J. Evolutionary relationships among parvoviruses: virus-host coevolution among autonomous primate parvoviruses and links between adeno-associated and avian parvoviruses. J Virol 2001 Mar;75(6): 2729–2740.
7. Pattison JR. The Discovery of Human Parvoviruses. In: Pattison JR, ed. Parvoviruses and Human Disease. Boca Raton, FL: CRC Press, 1998:1–4.
8. Berns KI, Bergion M, Bloom M, et al. Parvoviridae. In: Murphy FA, Fauquet CM, Bishop DHL, et al., eds. Viral Taxonomy: Classification and Nomenclature of Viruses. Sixth Report of the International Committee on Taxonomy of Viruses. New York: Springer-Verlag, 1995:169–178.
9. Astell CR, Luo W, Brunstein J, et al. B19 Parvovirus: Biochemical and Molecular Features. In: Anderson LJ, Young NS, eds. Monographs in Virology: Human parvovirus B19. New York: Karger, 1997:16–41.
10. Yunoki M, Tsujikawa M, Urayama T, et al. Heat sensitivity of human parvovirus B19. Vox Sang 2003 Apr;84(3):164–169.
11. Omidbakhsh N, Sattar SA. Broad-spectrum microbial activity, toxicologic assessment and materials compatibility of a new generation of accelerated hydrogen peroxide-based environmental surface disinfectant. Am J Infect Control 2006 Jun;34(5):251–257.
12. Favero MS, Arduino MJ. Decontamination and Disinfection. In: Fleming DO, Hunt DL, eds, Biological Safety, Principles and Practices, 4th ed. Washington D.C.: ASM Press, 2000:373–438.
13. Cohen BJ, Brown KE. Laboratory infection with human Parvovirus B19. J Infection 1992 Jan;24(1):113–114.
14. Yunoki M, Urayama T, Tsujikawa M, et al. Inactivation of parvovirus B19 by liquid heating incorporated in the manufacturing process of human intravenous immunoglobulin preparations. Br J Haematol 2005 Feb;128(3):401–404.
15. Heymann DL. In American Public Health Association (Ed.) Control of Communicable Diseases Manual, 18th ed. Washington D.C: American Public Health Association, 2004:196–199.
16. von Landenberg P, Lehmann HW, Modrow S. Human parvovirus B19 infection and antiphospholipid antibodies. Autoimmunity Rev 2007 Apr;6(5):278–285.
17. Zerbini M, Musiani M. Human Parvoviruses. In: Murray PR, ed. Manual of Clinical Microbiology, 8th ed. Washington, DC: ASM Press, 2003: 1534–1543.
18. Servey JT, Reamy BV, Hodge J. Clinical presentation of parvovirus B19 infection. Am Fam Physician 2007 Feb 1;75(3):373–376.
19. Bultmann BD, Klingel K, Soltar K, et al. Parvovirus B19: a pathogen responsible for more than hematologic disorders. Vichows Arch 2003: Jan;442(1):8–17.
20. Servant A, Laperche, S, Lallemand, F, et al. Genertic diversity within human erythromiriuses: Identification of three genotypes. J.Virol 2002 Sep;76(18):9124–9134.
21. Yaegashi N, Niinuma T, Chisaka H, et al. The incidence of, and factors leading to parvovirus B19-related hydrops fetalis following maternal infection: report of 10 cases and meta analysis. J Infect 1998 Jul;37(1):28–35.
22. Kooistra K, Mesman HJ, De Waal M, et al. Epidemiology of high level parvovirus B19 viraemia among Dutch blood donors, 2003–2009. Vox Sang 2011 Apr;100(3):261–266.
23. Riipinen A, Väisänen E, Nuutila M, et al. Parvovirus b19 infection in fetal deaths. Clin Infect Dis 2008 Dec 15;47(12):1519–1525.
24. American College of Obstetrics and Gynecologists. Perinatal viral and parasitic infections. ACOG Practice Bulletin No. 20, September 2000. Intl J Gynaecol Obstet 2002 Jan;76(1):95–107.
25. Goff M. Parvovirus B19 in pregnancy. J Midwifery Womens Health 2005 Nov-Dec;50(6):536–538.
26. White DG, Woolf AD, Mortimer PP, et al. Human parvovirus arthropathy. Lancet 1985 Feb 23;1(8426):419–421.
27. Bell LM, Naides SJ, Stoffman P, et al. Human parvovirus B19 infection among hospital staff members after contact with infected patients. N Engl J Med 1989 Aug 24;321(8):485–491.
28. Ray SM, Erdman DD, Berschling JD, et al. Nosocomial exposure to parvovirus B19: low risk of transmission to healthcare workers. Infect Control Hosp Epidemiol 1997 Feb;18(2):109–114.
29. Dowell SF, Torok TJ, Thorp JA, et al. Parvovirus B19 infection in hospital workers: community or hospital acquisition? J Infect Dis 1995 Oct;172(4): 1076–1079.
30. Ramiriz MM, Mastrobattista JM. Diagnosis and management of human parvovirus B19 infection. Clin Perinatol 2005 Sep;32(3):697–704.
31. Bilenchi R, De Paola M, Poggiali S, et al. Papular-pupuric "gloves and socks" syndrome. G. Ital Dermatol Venereol 2012 Feb;147(1):119–121.
32. Centers for Disease Control and Prevention (CDC). Update: rashes among schoolchildren—27 states, October 4, 2001–June 3, 2002. MMWR Morb Mortal Wkly Rep 2002 Jun 21;51(24):524–527.
33. Aronin SI, Quagliarello V. Bacterial meningitis. Infect Med 2003;20: 142–153.
34. Florea AV, Ionescu DN, Melem MF. Parvovirus B19 infection in the immunocompromised host. Arch Pathol Lab Med 2007 May;131(5):799–804.
35. Lehmann W, von Landenberg P, Modrow S. Parvovirus B19 infection and autoimmune disease. Autoimmun Review 2003 Jun;2(4):218–223.
36. Douvoyinnis M, Litman N, Goldman DL. Neurologic manifestations associated with parvovirus B19 infection. Clin Infect Dis 2009 Jun 15;48(12): 1713–1723.
37. Chen, DY, Chen YM, Lan JL, et al. Significant association of past parvovoirs B19 infection with cytopenia in both adult-onset Still/'s dieases and systemic lupus erythematosus patients. Clin Chim Acta 2012 May 18; 413(9–10):855–860.
38. Kerr JR, Bracewell J, Laing I, et al. Chronic fatigue syndrome and arthralgia following parvovirus B19 infection. J Rheumatol 2002 Mar;29(3): 595–602.

39. Takehashi Y, Murai C, Shibata S, et al. Human parvovirus B19 as a causative agent for rheuhmatoid arthritis. *Proc Natl Acad Sci USA* 1998 Jul 7; 95(14):8227–8232.
40. Brown, KE. Detection and quantitation of parvovirus B19. *J Clin Virol* 2004 Sep;31(1):1–4.
41. Lehman HW, Knoll A, Kuster KA, et al. Frequent infection with a viral pathogen, parvovirus B19, in rheumatic diseases of childhood. *Arthritis Rheum* 2003 Jun;48(6):1631–1638.
42. Young NS, Brown KE. Parvovirus B19. *N. Engl J Med* 2004 Feb 5; 350(6):586–597.
43. Koch WC, Massey G, Russell CE, et al. Manifestations and treatment of human parvovirus B19 infection in immunocompromised patients. *J Pediatr* 1990 Mar;116(3):355–359.
44. Eid A, Brown RA, Patel R, et al. Parvovirus B19 infections after transplantation: A review of 98 cases. *Clin Inf Dis* 2006 Jul 1;43(1):40–48.
45. Kurtzman GJ, Cohen B, Meyers P, et al. Persistent B19 parvovirus infection as a cause of severe chronic anaemia in children with acute lymphocytic leukaemia. *Lancet* 1988 Nov 19;2(8621):1159–1162.
46. Waldman M, Kopp JB. Parvovirus B19 and the kidney. *Clin J Am Soc Nephrol* 2007 Jul;2 Suppl 1:S47–S56.
47. Cavallo R, Merlino C, Re D, et al. B19 virus infection in renal transplant recipients. *J Clin Virol* 2003 Apr;26(3):361–368.
48. Porignaux R, Vuiblet V, Barbe C, et.al. Frequent occurrence of parvovirus B19 DNAnemia in the first year after kidney transplantation. *J Med Virol* 2013 Jun;85(6):1115–1121.
49. Gosset C, Vigletti D, Hue K, et al. How many times can parvovirus B19-related anemia recur in solid organ transplant recipients? *Transpl Infect Dis* 2012 Oct;14(5):E64–E70.
50. Centers for Disease Control and Prevention (CDC). Parvovirus: excerpt from Guidelines for Infection Control in Healthcare Personnel. *Am J Infect Control* 1998;26:289–354.
51. Carter ML, Farley TA, Rosengren S, et al. Occupational risk factors for infection with parvovirus B19 among pregnant women. *J Infect Dis* 1991 Feb;163(2):282–285.
52. Koch WC, Adler SP. Human parvovirus B19 infections in women of childbearing age and within families. *Pediatr Infect Dis J* 1989 Feb;8(2):83–87.
53. De jong EP, De haan TR, Kroes AC, et al Parvovirus B19 infection in pregnancy. *J Clin Virol* 2006 May;36(1):1–7.
54. Courtier G, Schauer GM, Parer JT, et al. Polymicrogyria in a fetus with human oarvovirus B19 infection: a case with radiologic-pathologic correlation. *Ultrasound Obstet Gynecol* 2012 Nov;40(5):604–606.
55. Nunoue T, Kusuhara K, Hara T. Human fetal infection with parvovirus B19: maternal infection in gestation, viral persistence, and fetal prognosis. *Pediatr Infect Dis J* 2002 Dec;21(12):1133–1136.
56. Young NS, Brown KE. Parvovirus B19. *N Engl J Med* 2004 Feb 5;350(6): 586–597.
57. Nagel HT, De Haan TR, Vandenbussche FP, et al. Long term outcome after transfusion for hydops associated with parvovirus B19 infection. *Obstet Gynecol* 2007 Jan;109(1):42–47.
58. Kudielka I, Nagele F, Chalubinski K, et al. B19 parvovirus infection in a primipara with congenital spherocytosis. *Acta Obstet Gynecol Scand* 1998 Aug;77(7):785–786.
59. DeJong EP, Lindenburg IT, van Klink JM, et al. Intrauterine transfusion for parvovirus B19 infection: Long term neurodevelopmental outcome. *Am J Obstet Gynecol* [serial online]. 2012 Mar;206(3):204.e1–5. Available at: http://www.ajog.org/article/S0002-9378(11)02475-6/abstract.
60. Myloankis E, Dickinson BP, Mileno MD, et al. Persistent parvovirus B19 related anemia of seven years' duration in an HIV infected patient: Complete remission associated with highly active antiretroviral therapy. *Am J Hemat* 1999 Feb;60(2):164–166.
61. Faden H, Gary GW Jr, Anderson LJ. Chronic parvovirus infection in a presumably immunologically normal woman. *Clin Infect Dis* 1992 Oct;15(4):595–597.
62. Finkel TH, Torok TJ, Ferguson PJ, et al. Chronic parvovirus B19 infection and systemic necrotizing vasculitis: opportunistic infection or aetiological agent? *Lancet* 1994 May 21;343(8908):1255–1258.

63. Soderlund M, von Essen R, Haapasarri J, et al. Persistence of parvovirus B19 DNA in synovial membranes of young patients with and without chronic arthropathy (see comments). *Lancet* 1997 Apr 12;349(9058): 1063–1065.
64. Bock CT, Klingel K, Aberle S, et al. Human parvovirus B19: a new emerging pathogen of inflammatory cardiomyopathy. *J Vet Med B Infect Dis Vet Public Health* 2005 Sep-Oct;52(7–8):340–343.
65. Kaufmann J, Buccola JM, Stead W, et al. Secondary symptomatic parvovius B19 infection in a healthy adult. *J Gen Intern Med* 2007 Jun;22(6): 877–878.
66. Bultman BD, Klingel K, Solter K, et al. Fatal parvovirus B19-associated myocarditis clinically mimicking ischemic heart disease: an endothelial cell-mediated disease. *Hum Pathol* 2003 Jan;34(1):92–95.
67. Kandolf R. Virus etiology of inflammatory cardiomyopathy. *Dtsch Med Wochenschr* 2004 Oct 8;129(41):2187–2192.
68. Klingel K, Sauter M, Bock CT, et al. Molecular pathology of inflammatory cardiomyopathy. *Med Microbiol Immunol* 2004 May;193(2–3): 101–107.
69. Bowles NE, Vallejo J. Viral causes of cardiac inflammation. *Curr Opin Cardiol* 2003 May;18(3):182–188.
70. Brown KE, Anderson SM, Young NS. Erythrocyte P antigen: cellular receptor for B19 parvovirus. *Science* 1993 Oct 1;262(5130):114–117.
71. Brown KE, Hibbs JR, Gallinella G, et al. Resistance to parvovirus B19 infection due to lack of virus receptor (erythrocyte P antigen). *N Engl J Med* 1994 Apr 28;330(17):1192–1196.
72. Torok TJ. Unusual Clinical Manifestations Reported in Patients with Parvovirus B19 Infection. In: Anderson LJ, Young NS, ed. *Monographys in Virology: Human Parvovirus B19.* New York: Karger, 1997;61.
73. Sokol EM, Melchior M, Cornu C, et al. Acute parvovirus B19 infection associated with fulminant hepatitis of favourable prognosis in young children. *Lancet* 1998 Nov 28;352(9142):1739–1741.
74. Anderson LJ, Tsou C, Parker RA, et al. Detection of antibodies and antigens of human parvovirus B19 by enzyme-linked immunosorbent assay. *J Clin Microbiol* 1986 Oct;24(4):522–526.
75. Cohen BJ, Mortimer PP, Pereira MS. Diagnostic assays with monoclonal antibodies for the human serum parvovirus-like virus (SPLV). *J Hygiene (Lond.)* 1983 Aug;91(1):113–130.
76. Seng C, Watkins P, Morse D, et al. Parvovirus B19 outbreak on an adult ward. *Epidemiol Infect* 1994 Oct;113(2):345–353.
77. Shauer A, Gotsman I, Keren A, et.al. Acute viral myocarditis: Current concepts in diagnosis and treatment. *IMAJ* 2013 Mar;15(3):180–185.
78. George,CLS, Ameduri RK, Reed RC, et al. Long-term use of ventricular assist device as a bridge to recovery in acute fulminant myocarditis. *Ann Thorac Surg* 2013 Mar;95(3):e59–e60.
79. Bassols A. Parvovirus B19 and the new century. *Clin Infect Dis* 2008 Feb 15;46(4):537–539.
80. Stramer SL, Kane KL, Byers ML, et al. *Parvovirus B19 and HAV screening of whole blood donations.* Presented at the Food and Drug Administration Nucleic Acid Testing Workshop, December 2001 and modified for Blood Products Advisory Committee, National Institutes for Health, Washington DC, December 12, 2002.
81. Schmidt M, Thermann, A, Drexler E, et al. Blood donor screening for parvovirus B19 in Germany and Austria. *Transfusion* 2007 Oct;47(10): 1775–1782.
82. Wakamatsu C, Takakura F, Kojima E, et al. Screening of blood donors for human parvovirus B19 and characterization of the results. *Vox Sang* 1999;76(1):14–21.
83. ClinicalTrials.gov. B-19 Parvovirus Vaccine Study. Available at: http: //clinicaltrials.gov/ct2/show/NCT00379938.
84. Sugawara H, Motokawa R, Abe H, et al. Inactivation of parvovirus B19 in coagulation factor concentrates by UVC radiation: assessment by an in vitro infectivity assay using CFU-E derived from peripheral blood CD34+ cells. *Transfusion* 2001 Apr;41(4):456–461.
85. Bernstein DI, El Sahly HM, Keitel WA, et al. Safety and immunogenicity of a candidate parvovirus B19 vaccine. *Vaccine* 2011 Oct 6;29(43): 7357–7363.

CHAPTER 89

Rabies

David M. Brewer, DVM, DACVIM (Neurology)
Neurologist/Neurosurgeon
Bush Veterinary Neurology Service
Leesburg, VA

Casey P. Neary, DVM
Veterinary Neurology/Neurosurgery
Bush Veterinary Neurology Service
Leesburg, VA

ABSTRACT

Rabies is a zoonotic disease that is usually transmitted via virus-containing saliva from the bite of an infected animal. The virus infects the central nervous system, resulting in an acute, progressive, fatal encephalomyelitis. Although rabies in domestic animals has significantly decreased in the United States since the mid-20th century, rabies in terrestrial wildlife and bats in the United States and other developed countries, as well as canine rabies in developing countries, continues to present risk for human infections. Human infections can be prevented through avoiding exposure to rabid animals, pre-exposure rabies vaccination of individuals in high-risk occupations, and postexposure prophylaxis (vaccination and rabies immunoglobulin administration) for individuals with exposure with high risk for rabies virus transmission.

KEY CONCEPTS

- Rabies is a fatal viral infection transmitted primarily by bites of infected animals.

- Rabies infections in humans can be prevented by avoiding exposure and by using pre-exposure (vaccination) or postexposure (vaccination and rabies immunoglobulin) prophylaxis.

- Animal rabies control programs are effective in reducing the risk of human and animal infections.

- Rabies is a nationally notifiable disease.

BACKGROUND

Rabies is a fatal viral disease of the central nervous system (CNS), causing acute, progressive encephalomyelitis that affects mammals, including humans. There are several variants of the virus, each of which has adapted to specific hosts—primarily bats and carnivorous mammals. In the United States, the main reservoirs of the virus are wildlife, including raccoons, skunks, foxes, and bats, which account for more than 90 percent of rabid animals reported.[1] With the advent of vigorous canine rabies control programs beginning in the 1940s, domestic dogs have been eliminated as a reservoir of rabies in the United States. This, combined with the development of effective biologics (vaccine and rabies immunoglobulin), has reduced the number of U.S. human deaths attributable to rabies to an annual average of one to two.[2]

Despite the successes seen in canine rabies control, rabies continues to be a disease of clinical and public health importance in the United States and abroad. Globally, there are 55,000 human rabies deaths each year, and dogs are the major infective host.[2] In the United States alone, approximately 20,000 to 40,000 persons receive postexposure prophylaxis (PEP) annually.[3] A variety of factors contribute to high levels of PEP administration in the United States: the significant epizootic of raccoon-variant rabies in raccoons and other terrestrial animals in the Eastern and Southeastern United States; the persistence of unvaccinated domestic animals; and the continued recognition of bats as a reservoir of rabies virus. The goal of this chapter is to provide a basic understanding of the clinical and epidemiological characteristics of rabies in order to aid the reader in making informed decisions during risk assessments for animal exposures and in the care of patients for whom rabies is in the differential diagnosis.

BASIC PRINCIPLES

Definitions related to rabies transmission are provided here.

Bite contact: any penetration of the skin by the teeth of an animal.

Domestic animal: a species of mammal that is accustomed to living in or about the habitation of man and is dependent on man for food or shelter, including but not limited to dogs, cats, ferrets, and livestock.

Fluorescent antibody testing: laboratory method used to assess animal tissue for evidence of rabies virus infection.

Isolation: confinement of an animal in a double-door, escape-proof enclosure; the animal is not removed from the enclosure at any time except for transport.

Nonbite contact: contamination of an abrasion, open wound, or mucous membrane with saliva or other potentially infectious material from an animal.

Oral rabies vaccine (ORV): used for the oral vaccination of wild animals against rabies; it consists of a vaccine-filled plastic pouch that is enclosed in fishmeal or directly coated with flavoring for use with raccoons, foxes, and coyotes. ORV is a live vaccinia virus-rabies glycoprotein vaccine, and its use is restricted to state- or federal-approved programs.

Postexposure prophylaxis (PEP): the administration of rabies vaccine and rabies immunoglobulin to individuals following an exposure with a high risk for transmission of rabies virus.

Pre-exposure prophylaxis: an abbreviated rabies vaccination schedule for individuals working in occupations associated with a high risk of exposure to rabies virus.

Quarantine: confinement of an animal by leash, an escape-proof enclosure, or another manner that ensures protection of the public's health. Note: The situations in which isolation or quarantine is applied vary from state to state and country to country.

Rabies immunoglobulin (RIG): in the United States, this is purified plasma from hyperimmune donors. RIG is usually administered at the site of exposure and quickly provides a short duration of passive immunity (21-day half-life).

Rabies titer testing: testing of serum from individuals who previously received rabies vaccine for the presence of rabies virus-neutralizing antibodies. Testing is generally limited to assess the requirement of booster vaccination for individuals in high-risk occupations.

Rabies vaccine for humans: in the United States, it is an inactivated virus vaccine that is administered intramuscularly (IM). By 7 to 9 days after vaccination, an active immune response is induced, resulting in the production of rabies virus-neutralizing antibodies that usually persists for at least 2 years.

CHARACTERISTICS, DIAGNOSIS, AND CONTROL

Rabies Virus and Transmission

Rabies virus is a bullet-shaped, single-stranded RNA virus of the family Rhabdoviridae and the genus *Lyssavirus*; it is relatively labile because it is inactivated by desiccation and ultraviolet irradiation. Pathogenesis of the disease involves travel of the virus via the peripheral nerves to the CNS, causing encephalomyelitis. The disease is almost always fatal once symptoms appear. The most common mode of transmission of rabies virus is through the bite of an infected animal. The virus may be shed in the saliva of an infected animal for several days prior to the onset of symptoms and continues to shed throughout the

course of illness. The incubation period in the victim may depend on the location of the bite, virus variant, infectious dose, and immune status. The incubation period can vary from days (e.g., from high viral load exposures to the head), to months or even years in rare cases (e.g., from low viral load exposures extremely distal to the head, i.e., feet or hands).

Nonbite exposures from terrestrial animals have rarely caused rabies. These exposures include contamination of an abrasion, open wound, or mucous membrane with saliva or other potentially infectious material, such as neural tissue from an infected animal. Other nonbite routes of transmission have been documented and include concentrated aerosol transmission and corneal and solid organ transplantation.[2-4] Petting a rabid animal or contact with blood, urine, or feces of a rabid animal are not considered exposures. Additionally, ingestion of raw meat of an infected animal is not considered exposure.

Clinical Signs in Humans and Animals

Clinical signs of rabies vary by species—the most reliable signs in animals are behavioral changes and unexplained paralysis. There are two classic forms of rabies in animals: the furious form, in which aggression is pronounced and the animal may attack humans, other animals, or inanimate objects, and the dumb form, in which there is minimal or no behavior change and partial paralysis predominates. A classic example of the dumb form of rabies is the dog with an inability to swallow or keep its mouth closed, mimicking the appearance of "something caught in its throat."

In humans, the first signs of rabies are usually nonspecific and may include fever, chills, sore throat, malaise, headache, and weakness; often there is paresthesia at or near the exposure site. The neurological phase follows with hyperactivity; behavior changes such as agitation, anxiety, or fear; and sometimes seizures. Hydrophobia is a classic sign of rabies in humans with fear exhibited at the sight of water or while drinking it; this is caused by severe spasms of the muscles involved in swallowing. Early paralysis associated with rabies in humans affects the bitten extremity or may be symmetric or diffuse. As the disease progresses, there is generalized paralysis, a deterioration of mental status, and finally coma. Rabies is a rapidly fatal disease with death occurring a few days after the onset of symptoms. Supportive therapy may prolong a patient's life, but death is almost always inevitable. Reports of humans or animals recovering from rabies are rare, and these individuals usually have severe neurologic sequelae.

Bats and Rabies

Bats are increasingly implicated as important wildlife reservoirs for rabies variants transmitted to humans. There was a 21.7 percent increase in the number of rabid bats reported from 2011 to 2012. Currently, vaccination of bats is not considered feasible; therefore, emphasis is placed on public education and prevention.[1] From 1990 to 2007, a total of 34 naturally acquired bat-associated human cases of rabies were reported in the United States.[5] If a bat bites a person, it should be captured and tested for rabies. If the bat is not available for testing, PEP is recommended for all persons who have sustained bite, scratch, or mucous membrane exposures. Further, because bat bites can inflict limited injury and may be undetected, PEP is appropriate if there is reasonable probability that such contact occurred (e.g., a sleeping person awakens to find a bat in close proximity or an adult witnesses a bat in the room with a previously unattended child or a mentally disabled or intoxicated person).[6-8] The importance of capturing and testing any bat that has known or suspected human contact cannot be overemphasized.

Other Wild Animals and Rabies

Raccoons, skunks, and foxes are the most common reservoirs for rabies in the United States. Geographic ranges show that the raccoon is most prevalent along the East Coast, and the skunk and fox are more prevalent in the West and Midwest. Growing numbers of rabid mongooses have been reported in Puerto Rico. The canine rabies virus variant has been eliminated from the United States.[1] If a wild animal has bite or nonbite exposure contact with a human and the animal is available, it should be tested for rabies. If the animal tests positive or is not available for testing, PEP should be administered. Rodents (such as squirrels, hamsters, guinea pigs, gerbils, chipmunks, rats, and mice) and lagomorphs (rabbits and hares) are almost never found to be rabid, and exposures to them rarely require PEP. Groundhogs (woodchucks) account for the majority of rabies cases in rodents. Although rabies in these rodents is rare, risk assessment of human exposures to these species, and decisions regarding PEP administration, should include an evaluation of the prevalence of rabies in other terrestrial species (i.e., raccoons, skunks, foxes) in the geographic area of exposure. This information is available from local or state public health agencies.

Management of Rabies in Animals

Animal vaccination programs are essential for the control and prevention of rabies. Dogs, cats, and ferrets should be vaccinated according to state laws and regulations. Other domestic animals at risk in rabies-endemic areas should be vaccinated if an approved vaccine is available. Following an exposure of an animal or human to a suspected rabid animal, the local health department should perform a risk assessment. This includes the epidemiology of rabies in the area (endemic reservoir hosts present; species of the exposing animal), a determination of type of exposure (i.e., bite versus nonbite exposure), circumstances of the exposure (i.e., provoked versus unprovoked), availability of the animal for quarantine or testing, and health and vaccination status of the animal.

The following guidelines are adapted from the *Compendium of Animal Rabies Prevention and Control, 2011*.[9] Dogs, cats, and ferrets currently vaccinated and exposed to a rabid animal should be revaccinated immediately, kept under the owner's control, and observed for 45 days. If not currently vaccinated,

exposed domestic animals should be euthanized and tested. If the owner refuses to agree to euthanasia of the animal, it must be placed in strict isolation for 6 months and vaccinated immediately or 1 month prior to release from isolation to assure that the animal is vaccinated at the end of quarantine if it does not develop rabies. Healthy dogs, cats, and ferrets that bite humans should be quarantined for 10 days after the exposure. If the animal does not exhibit signs and symptoms consistent with rabies during the quarantine period, the animal can be released, and the bite victim is considered at no risk for exposure to rabies. If the animal exhibits signs and symptoms consistent with rabies during the 10-day quarantine, dies during the quarantine, or is a stray, it should be euthanized and tested. Animals unwanted by their owners may be held for the 10-day quarantine or euthanized and tested immediately. Unvaccinated livestock should be euthanized immediately if exposed to a rabid animal. Vaccinated livestock should be revaccinated with a USDA-approved vaccine. Direct transmission from one animal to another in a herd is unlikely; therefore, restrictions on the remainder of the herd are typically unnecessary. Consultation with local health department personnel is recommended for potential rabies exposure situations involving animals not discussed here.

Rabies Testing of Animals

In the United States, rabies in both humans and animals has been a nationally notifiable condition since 1944.[10] Because rabies testing requires intact brain/brainstem, care should be taken in using appropriate methods of euthanasia if testing of suspect animals is warranted. Nevertheless, animals whose heads have been damaged (through trauma, decay, etc.) may still be appropriate for testing. The appropriate health department laboratory should be contacted before deciding to discard a damaged animal so that an accurate assessment can be made of the utility of testing.

Laboratories performing rabies testing generally receive animal heads, as the testing requires the removal of the brain from the cranium. In addition to receiving pre-exposure vaccinations, laboratory workers processing these tissues use personal protective equipment and appropriate engineering controls and follow enhanced safety practices to reduce their risk of exposure to rabies from the bone fragments, tissue, and fluid encountered during this process. A direct fluorescence antibody assay is the gold standard in the diagnosis of rabies.[9] Once the brain is removed, touch impression smears are made from several parts of the brain (brainstem, cerebellum, and hippocampus). These smears are stained with fluorescent-labeled antirabies antibodies and examined for intracytoplasmic inclusions. The standardized protocol (available at http://www.cdc.gov/rabies/pdf/RabiesD-FASPv2.pdf) should be performed by a qualified laboratory that has been designated by the state or local health department.[9] Histopathologic examination of tissues for Negri bodies has been performed historically, but this method lacks the sensitivity and specificity of fluorescent antibody testing of tissue and is no longer routinely used. There are enhanced laboratory techniques available to determine the reservoir host from which the virus originated.

Management of Rabies in Humans

Rabies in humans is a preventable disease if treatment is begun prior to the manifestation of symptoms. The current recommended treatment regimen is given in *Use of a Reduced (4-Dose) Vaccine Schedule for Postexposure Prophylaxis to Prevent Human Rabies: Recommendations of the Advisory Committee on Immunization Practices*[11] (summarized in Table 89-1). Treatment initially requires appropriate cleansing of the bite wound (if present), followed by intramuscular administration of human rabies vaccine on days 0 (the first day of vaccination), 3, 7, and 14. Immunosuppressed individuals require an additional dose of vaccine on day 28 and a postvaccination virus-neutralizing antibody titer to ensure acceptable antibody response.[11] Rabies immunoglobulin is also administered on day 0 at a dosage of 20 IU/kg body weight, with the full dose being infiltrated at the site of the bite if anatomically feasible. RIG should not be administered with the same needle or at the same site as the vaccine. The Advisory Committee on Immunization Practices (ACIP) also gives recommendations for pre-exposure vaccinations of individuals among high-risk groups, such as veterinarians, animal handlers, veterinary technicians, certain laboratory workers, and persons visiting foreign countries where canine rabies is endemic and access to adequate medical care might be limited. The pre-exposure vaccination regimen (Table 89-2)[5,11] requires administration of vaccine on days 0, 7, and 21 or 28 (RIG is not administered as part of this regimen). Pre-exposure vaccinations may protect persons with unapparent exposures to rabies and persons whose PEP may be delayed; it eliminates the need for RIG, and it decreases the number of doses of PEP vaccine needed to two (days 0 and 3). Both pre-exposure vaccination and PEP can be administered during pregnancy if indicated.

If an animal cannot be found, but there is a potential that it will be, PEP may be postponed for a few days. Alternatively (if indicated by the risk assessment), PEP can be started and then discontinued when the animal is found to be healthy after 10 days from the exposure or tested and found negative for rabies. Initiation of PEP for suspected high-risk rabid animal exposures should not be delayed for the full 10 days with the expectation of finding the exposing animal.

In the event that an individual misses a treatment, rabies vaccine should be given as soon as possible and the regular treatment schedule resumed. People who began treatment for rabies overseas should be evaluated on a case-by-case basis. If the vaccine given in a foreign country is an unfamiliar one, discuss the issue with the state or local health department or the Centers for Disease Control and Prevention (CDC).

Serious adverse reactions to a rabies vaccine should be reported to the Vaccine Adverse Event Reporting System (see Supplemental Resources). Most reactions to modern vaccines are less serious than with previously available vaccines, and the vaccination regimen can be continued with management of the adverse reaction. For very serious reactions, consult with the local or state health department or the CDC to determine if vaccination should be continued.

Table 89-1. Rabies Postexposure Prophylaxis Schedule—United States, 2008

Vaccination Status	Treatment	Regimen[a]
Not previously vaccinated	Wound cleansing	All postexposure prophylaxis should begin with immediate thorough cleansing of all wounds with soap and water. If available, a virucidal agent such as povidone-iodine solution should be used to irrigate the wounds.
	Rabies immunoglobulin (RIG)	Administer 20 IU/kg body weight. If anatomically feasible, the full dose globulin (RIG) should be infiltrated around the wound(s), and any remaining volume should be administered intramuscularly (IM) at an anatomical site distant from vaccine administration. Also, RIG should not be administered in the same syringe as vaccine. Because RIG might partially suppress active production of antibody, no more than the recommended dose should be given.
	Vaccine	Human diploid cell vaccine (HDCV) or purified chick embryo cell vaccine (PCECV) 1.0 mL, IM (deltoid area[c]), one each on days 0[d], 3, 7, 14, and 28.
Previously vaccinated[b]	Wound cleansing	All postexposure prophylaxis should begin with immediate thorough cleansing of all wounds with soap and water. If available, a virucidal agent such as povidone-iodine solution should be used to irrigate the wounds.
	RIG	RIG should not be administered.
	Vaccine	HDCV or PCECV 1.0 mL, IM (deltoid area[c]), one each on days 0[d] and 3.

[a]These regimens are applicable for all age groups, including children.
[b]Any person with a history of a complete pre-exposure or postexposure vaccination regimen with HDCV, PCECV, or rabies vaccine adsorbed, or previous vaccination with any other type of rabies vaccine and a documented history of antibody response to the prior vaccination.
[c]The deltoid area is the only acceptable site of vaccination for adults and older children. For younger children, the outer aspect of the thigh can be used. Vaccine should never be administered in the gluteal area.
[d]Day 0 is the day the first dose of vaccine is administered.
From Manning SE, Rupprecht CE, Fishbein D, et al. Human rabies prevention—United States, 2008: recommendations of the Advisory Committee on Immunization Practices. *MMWR Recomm Rep* 2008;57(RR-3):1–28. Available at: http://www.cdc.gov/mmwr/preview/mmwrhtml/rr5703a1.htm..

Following pre-exposure vaccination, an individual at frequent risk of exposure should be tested for presence of rabies-neutralizing antibodies every 2 years. Booster vaccinations should be administered if the antibody level falls below acceptable levels—complete virus neutralization at a 1:5 serum dilution by the rapid fluorescent focus inhibition test (RFFIT). High-risk individuals working with live rabies virus in research facilities or vaccine production facilities should have a rabies antibody titer performed every 6 months. State or local health departments have information regarding laboratories available for rabies antibody titer determination.

Table 89-2. Rabies Pre-exposure Prophylaxis Schedule—United States, 2008

Type of Vaccination	Route	Regimen
Primary	Intramuscular	Human diploid cell vaccine (HDCV) or purified chick embryo cell vaccine (PCECV); 1.0 mL (deltoid area), one each on days 0,[a] 7, and 21 or 28
Booster[b]	Intramuscular	HDCV or PCECV; 1.0 mL (deltoid area), day 0 only

[a]Day 0 is the day the first dose of vaccine is administered.
[b]Persons in the continuous-risk category should have a serum sample tested for rabies virus-neutralizing antibody every 6 months, and persons in the frequent-risk category should be tested every 2 years. An intramuscular booster dose of vaccine should be administered if the serum titer falls to maintain a value of at least complete neutralization at a 1:5 serum dilution by rapid fluorescent focus inhibition test.
From Manning SE, Rupprecht CE, Fishbein D, et al. Human rabies prevention—United States, 2008: recommendations of the Advisory Committee on Immunization Practices. *MMWR Recomm Rep* 2008;57(RR-3):1–28. Available at: http://www.cdc.gov/mmwr/preview/mmwrhtml/rr5703a1.htm.

For suspected cases of human rabies, public health authorities should be contacted immediately to assist in obtaining the most current testing and treatment protocols. CDC infection prevention recommendations for the care of patients with known or suspected rabies do not supersede the utilization of Standard Precautions.[5] Although confirmed person-to-person transmission of rabies has not been documented, it is a theoretical possibility. Several authors have recommended that healthcare personnel use Contact Precautions including wearing mouth and eye protection while caring for patients to protect mucous membranes from exposure to contaminated saliva.[12,13] In addition, PEP has been recommended for healthcare personnel with nonintact skin or mucous membrane exposure to potentially infective saliva.[13,14] Submission of specimens from patients suspected of being infected with rabies virus should be coordinated with the local or state health department and the CDC. Instructions for specimen collection and handling, and the forms required for submission, are available from the CDC rabies website (see Supplemental Resources).

Prevention and Control of Rabies

Prevention and control of rabies involves the efforts of state and local officials as well as the entire community. Vaccination programs, leash laws, licensing, stray animal control, bite reporting, prompt treatment, pre-exposure vaccination, and proper risk assessments are essential to the prevention and control of rabies. Education of the public is also essential and should include the following recommendations: limit exposure to wild or stray animals, do not keep wild animals as pets, and maintain up-to-date vaccinations for pets.[5] The use of oral bait containing rabies vaccine to immunize wildlife animal reservoirs, such as foxes, raccoons, and coyotes, has proven successful in rabies control in certain communities. Because currently used oral rabies vaccine is a live, recombinant vaccinia-rabies glycoprotein virus, human exposure to the vaccine can result in vaccinia infection, as has been recently documented in one individual with no serious sequelae.[15]

CONCLUSIONS

Despite success seen in rabies control in domestic animals in developed countries, rabies continues to be an issue of significant clinical and public health importance. The annual number of human cases observed in the United States is low, no doubt due to the diligence of clinical and public health practitioners investigating and providing appropriate follow-up for potential high-risk exposures. Although not a medical emergency, rabies exposure is a medical urgency, requiring prompt attention but allowing for ample time to investigate the exposure situation and determine the most appropriate management course to take.

FUTURE TRENDS

Human rabies is fatal in almost all cases; there have been countless failed attempts to treat human rabies cases. In 2004, a 15-year-old girl survived rabies infection without the use of any rabies vaccine or immunoglobulin by induction of a coma, a brain-sparing procedure that allowed for natural immune responses to overcome the infection.[16] This protocol (Milwaukee Protocol) has been attempted in other patients without success but is constantly being refined and may have potential in patients in whom rabies infection is suspected early on in the clinical diagnostic process.

Currently in the United States, RIG is a product of human hyperimmune serum; it is expensive and available in limited quantities. To eliminate the need for human donors, researchers have developed monoclonal antibody cocktails to replace the use of RIG. At least one commercial company has completed initial safety studies in humans of its product.[17] Human testing is ongoing and may soon yield a product that can be produced in unlimited amounts without the disadvantages associated with a human hyperimmune serum product. An initial safety and tolerability study appears promising.[18]

The CDC has developed a direct rabies immunohistochemical test (dRIT) that has been used for active rabies surveillance studies by the U.S. Department of Agriculture, Wildlife Services, and in other field studies in Africa. It has acceptable sensitivity and specificity for rabies screening tests and high concordance with the currently accepted direct fluorescent antibody test.[19] The advantages of this test are that it can be used on preserved tissue samples, does not require a fluorescence microscope (only a light microscope is required), can be performed under less-than-ideal laboratory conditions, and can be performed by personnel with only dRIT-specific laboratory training.

There are ongoing efforts to contain the spread and control potential "point-source" outbreaks of raccoon-variant rabies from the currently delineated endemic zone in the United States. The U.S. Department of Agriculture, Animal Plant and Health Inspection Service, Wildlife Services is the lead agency in this prevention and control activity.[20] Aerial dropping of ORV has been used in an attempt to establish an immune barrier on the western edge of this zone, at the expenditure of significant federal, state, and local resources. A variety of studies have evaluated factors, including the area to cover with bait, the density of bait dropped in an area, and the number of times to perform the drops. Investigations continue to determine the most effective strategies (financially and scientifically) to maintain this immune barrier, as well as how aerial ORV drops can be used in point-source outbreak control.

INTERNATIONAL PERSPECTIVE

Special circumstances to consider internationally center on two areas. First, the level of endemic canine rabies is high in many developing countries. This results in increased risk of human infections not only for citizens of those countries but also for travelers to these countries (consult the CDC rabies website; see Supplemental Resources). If warranted for travelers to developing countries, pre-exposure vaccination should be initiated far enough in advance of travel to allow for completion of the series. Second, the formulation of rabies vaccine and RIG varies in different parts of the world.[2,3] Because these differences can affect the dosing, route of administration, and occurrence of side effects, consultation with appropriate public health officials should occur in situations where biologics from alternative or multiple sources may have to be utilized.

REFERENCES

1. Dyer J, Wallace R, Orciari L, et al. Rabies surveillance in the United States during 2012. *J Am Vet Med Assoc.* 2013 Sep 15;243(6):805-815.
2. Centers for Disease Control and Prevention. *Rabies.* National Center for Emerging and Zoonotic Infectious Diseases (NCEZID) Division of High-Consequence Pathogens and Pathology (DHCPP) rabies website. Available at: http://www.cdc.gov/rabies/.
3. Centers for Disease Control and Prevention (CDC). Investigation of rabies infections in organ donor and transplant recipients—Alabama, Arkansas, Oklahoma, and Texas, 2004. *MMWR* [serial online]. 2004;53(26):586–589. Available at: http://www.cdc.gov/mmwr/preview/mmwrhtml/mm5326a6.htm.
4. World Health Organization (WHO). *Rabies.* WHO website. July 2013. Available at: http://www.who.int/mediacentre/factsheets/fs099/en/.
5. Manning SE, Rupprecht CE, Fishbein D, et al. Human rabies prevention—United States, 2008: recommendations of the Advisory Committee on Immunization Practices. *MMWR Recomm Rep* [serial online]. 2008;57(RR-3):1–28. Available at: http://www.cdc.gov/mmwr/preview/mmwrhtml/rr5703a1.htm.
6. Centers for Disease Control and Prevention (CDC). Human rabies—California, Georgia, Minnesota, New York, and Wisconsin, 2000. *MMWR Morb Mortal Wkly Rep* [serial online]. 2000;49(49):1111–1115. Available at: http://www.cdc.gov/mmwr/preview/mmwrhtml/mm4949a3.htm.
7. Centers for Disease Control and Prevention (CDC). Public health dispatch: human rabies—Quebec, Canada, 2000. *MMWR Morb Mortal Wkly Rep* [serial online]. 2000;49(49):1115–1116. Available at: http://www.cdc.gov/mmwr/preview/mmwrhtml/mm4949a4.htm.
8. Centers for Disease Control and Prevention (CDC). Human rabies—California, 2002. *MMWR Morb Mortal Wkly Rep* [serial online]. 2002;51(31):686–688. Available at: http://www.cdc.gov/mmwr/preview/mmwrhtml/mm5131a4.htm.
9. National Association of State Public Health Veterinarians, Inc., Centers for Disease Control and Prevention (CDC). Compendium of animal rabies prevention and control, 2011: National Association of State Public Health Veterinarians, Inc. (NASPHV). *MMWR Recomm Rep* [serial online]. 2011 Nov 4;60(RR-6):1-17. Available at: http://www.cdc.gov/mmwr/pdf/rr/rr6006.pdf.
10. Centers for Disease Control and Prevention (U.S.), Office of Surveillance, Epidemiology and Laboratory Services, Division of Notifiable Diseases and Healthcare Information. *2012 Nationally Notifiable Diseases and Conditions and Current Case Definitions.* CDC website. 2012. Available at: http://stacks.cdc.gov/view/cdc/12088.
11. Rupprecht SE, Briggs D, Brown CM, et al. Use of a reduced (4-dose) vaccine schedule for postexposure prophylaxis to prevent human rabies: recommendcation of the Advisory Committee on Immunization Practices. *MMWR Recomm Rep* [serial online]. 2010L59(RR-2):1-9. Available at: http://www.cdc.gov/mmwr/preview/mmwrhtml/rr5902a1.htm.
12. Jackson AC, Warrell MJ, Rupprecht CE, et al. Management of rabies in humans. *Clin Infect Dis* 2003;36:60–63.
13. Weber DJ, Rutala WA. Risks and prevention of nosocomial transmission of rare zoonotic diseases. *Clin Infect Dis* 2001;32:446–456.
14. American Academy of Pediatrics. Rabies. In: Pickering LK, ed. *Red Book: 2003 Report of the Committee on Infectious Diseases,* 26th ed. Elk Grove Village, IL: American Academy of Pediatrics; 2003:514–521.
15. Rupprecht CE, Blass L, Smith K, et al. Human infection due to recombinant vaccinia-rabies glycoprotein virus. *N Engl J Med* 2001;345(8):582–586.
16. Centers for Disease Control and Prevention (CDC). Recovery of a patient from clinical rabies—Wisconsin, 2004. *MMWR Morb Mortal Wkly Rep* [serial online]. 2004;53(50):1171–1173. Available at: http://www.cdc.gov/mmwr/preview/mmwrhtml/mm5350a1.htm.
17. Python C, Quiambao B, Marissen W, et al. *Development of CL184 human monoclonal antibody cocktail for rabies postexposure prophylaxis: update on clinical evaluation.* XIX International Conference on Rabies in the Americas. Atlanta, GA, October 1, 2008.
18. Bakker AB, Python C, Kissling CJ, et al. First administration to humans of a monoclonal antibody cocktail against rabies virus: safety, tolerability, and neutralizing activity. *Vaccine* 2008 Nov 5;26(47):5922-5927.
19. Lembo T, Niezgoda M, Velasco-Villa A, et al. Evaluation of a direct, rapid immunohistochemical test for rabies diagnosis. *Emerg Infect Dis* [serial online]. 2006;12(2):310–313. Available at: http://www.cdc.gov/ncidod/EID/vol12no02/05-0812.htm.
20. United States Department of Agriculture, Animal Plant and Health Inspection Service- Wildlife Services. Cooperative Rabies Management Program, National Report 2009. Available at: http://www.aphis.usda.gov/wildlife_damage/oral_rabies/downloads/NationalReport_2009.pdf.

SUPPLEMENTAL RESOURCES

Baer GM, ed. *The Natural History of Rabies.* 2nd ed. Boca Raton, FL: CRC Press; 1991.

Centers for Disease Control and Prevention, National Center for Infectious Diseases. Rabies website. Available at: http://www.cdc.gov/rabies. The section titled "Professional Resources" has information regarding specimen collection and submission.

Jackson AC, Wunner WH, eds. *Rabies.* Orlando, FL: Academic Press; 2002.

Heymann DL, Rabies. In: *Control of Communicable Diseases Manual,* 18th ed. Washington, DC: American Public Health Association; 2004:438–447.

Vaccine Adverse Event Reporting System. https://vaers.hhs.gov/index.

Vaccine and immune globulin availability. Available at: www.cdc.gov/rabies/resources/availability.html

Bringing dogs into the United States. Available at http://www.cdc.gov/animalimportation/dogs.html; http://www.cdc.gov/animalimportation/pdf/dog-import.pdf

Standard rabies vaccination certificate: Available at: http://www.cdc.gov/rabies/pdf/nasphv_form51.pdf

CHAPTER 90

Respiratory Syncytial Virus

Joan Godich, BSN, RN
Nurse Consultant
Walter Reed National Military Medical Center
Bethesda, MD

ABSTRACT

Respiratory syncytial virus is one of the most important causes of respiratory tract infection in infants and the elderly worldwide. Transmitted by direct and indirect contact, respiratory syncytial virus spreads as readily in the hospital as it does in the community, making healthcare-associated infection common. Respiratory syncytial virus is a major preventable healthcare-associated infection with frequent outbreaks that can lead to high mortality rates in healthcare facilities. Proper infection prevention measures, including hand hygiene, standard and contact precautions, cohorting, and rapid diagnostic techniques, are critical in controlling the spread of respiratory syncytial virus in healthcare facilities and establishing a culture of patient and employee safety. Timely implementation of standard infection control measures will minimize its medical and economic impact.

KEY CONCEPTS

- Respiratory syncytial virus is an RNA virus and a member of the Paramyxovirus family. Currently there are two serotypes: A and B.

- Respiratory syncytial virus is one of the leading causes of respiratory illness in infants, young children, and the elderly.

- Infections with respiratory syncytial virus are seasonal with predictable community outbreaks occurring in the winter and spring. In temperate climates, infections may appear year-round.

- Immunity to respiratory syncytial virus is short lived, and repeat (but milder) infections are common.

- Clinical syndromes in infants and children include upper respiratory infection, bronchiolitis, pneumonia, croup (rare), otitis media, and sudden infant death syndrome. Lower respiratory infections are also seen in adults.

- Respiratory syncytial virus is spread by respiratory secretions, and transmission is through direct or indirect contact with nasal droplets from infected individuals or by indirect contact with contaminated hands or fomites.

- Meticulous hand hygiene, contact precautions, and rapid detection are paramount to reducing morbidity and mortality associated with these common viral infections.

BACKGROUND

Respiratory syncytial virus (RSV) causes lower respiratory infections in infants and young children worldwide.[1] The Centers for Disease Control and Prevention (CDC) reports that during the period 1997 to 2006, approximately 132,000 to 172,000 children under the age of 5 years were hospitalized for RSV infection annually in the United States. First isolated from chimpanzees in 1956,[2] RSV quickly became recognized as an important cause of lower respiratory tract infections in infants.[3] Despite reports in the 1960s of RSV infection in adults with pneumonia, the seriousness of RSV infection in adults and the elderly was not appreciated for nearly three decades.[4]

Across ages and global divides, the attack rate of RSV infection is very high. Although it is a seasonal pathogen, it infects up to 50 percent of children in the first year of life and 90 percent by 2 years of age. Natural infection does not confer full immunity, and reinfection throughout life is common and is usually associated with milder disease.

RSV infection is generally benign in the immunocompetent child or adult; however, factors that increase the risk of severe RSV lower respiratory tract illness include patients at the extremes of age, such as premature neonates or the elderly, as well as patients with other risk factors such as chronic lung disease (CLD), congenital heart disease (CHD), or compromised immunity.

The purpose of this chapter is to review the role of RSV as a healthcare-associated infection (HAI). The focus will include new developments in understanding of seasonal and geographic parameters in RSV transmission, review the effectiveness of various methods aimed at preventing transmission, and highlight new and emerging diagnostic, therapeutic, and preventive measures for RSV.

BASIC PRINCIPLES

RSV is a member of the family Paramyxoviridae, genus *Pneumovirus*.[5] The genome is composed of a single-stranded, nonsegmented genome that encodes 11 viral proteins. The envelope contains a fusion (F) protein and an attachment (G) protein but no hemagglutinin or neuraminidase. Two subgroups of RSV, A and B, have been recognized based on antigenic variations in structural proteins. Heterogeneity among both group A and B viruses has also been noted based on immunologic reactivity with monoclonal antibodies and nucleotide sequence determinations. Both subgroups of RSV are commonly isolated; however, group A viruses predominate.[6]

RSV is an infectious agent that is transmitted by direct and indirect contact. The spread of RSV occurs as readily in the hospital as it does in the community, making it an HAI.[7] Proper infection prevention measures, including hand hygiene, contact precautions, cohorting, and rapid diagnostic techniques, are critical in controlling the spread of RSV in hospitals and curtailing its medical and economic impact.

RESPIRATORY SYNCYTIAL VIRUS

Epidemiology

In temperate climates, annual community outbreaks of RSV infections usually occur during late fall, winter, and early spring. The timing and severity of outbreaks in a community vary somewhat from year to year. In tropical climates, the pattern of RSV infection is different. In countries near the equator, the virus is detected year-round. As one moves away from the equator, there is a seasonal association with decrease in temperature both north and south of the equator. Rainfall, however, seems to have a positive association with RSV outbreaks north of the equator and a negative association south of the equator. Epidemics start in coastal areas and move inland with similar strains of RSV appearing in disparate geographic loci. This phenomenon has led some researchers to hypothesize that RSV is present year-round, causing epidemics when the appropriate environmental and host factors are present.

Environmental Factors

RSV is quickly inactivated by ether, chloroform, detergents, freezing at -20°C, heating at 55°C, and low pH conditions. On hands, RSV remains infective for less than 1 hour. On environmental surfaces, RSV may survive up to 30 hours depending on humidity.[7] Other environmental settings implicated in RSV transmission include crowding, day care attendance, exposure to environmental air pollutants such as smoke, and large family size.[8] These environmental aspects are risk factors for RSV infection and are considered in decisions to administer immunoprophylaxis.[9] Some of these conditions, such as crowding, are also climate dependent and may play a role in the epidemiology and seasonal patterns of RSV infection.

Host Factors

Host factors increase the risk of acquiring RSV infection and affect the severity the infection has on the exposed individual. Immunocompromised children and adults, as well as patients with chronic heart disease and lung disease, suffer higher mortality rates from RSV.[10] Immunocompromised persons include premature neonates, the elderly, patients with primary and secondary immunodeficiency, transplant recipients, and cancer patients receiving chemotherapy. Patients with chronic heart and lung conditions include those with bronchopulmonary dysplasia, cystic fibrosis, and CHD. Compromise of the immune system as well as the organ systems contribute to the pathogenesis of RSV disease.

Mode of Transmission

Transmission of RSV is by direct contact with infected patients via large-particle droplets that generally do not traverse more than 3 feet. Indirect transmission can occur from hands or fomites that are contaminated with RSV. In a classic study on RSV transmission, Hall and Douglas demonstrated that direct contact plays a critical role.[11] Volunteers were assigned to one of three categories in handling infants with RSV: (1) routine care where contact was not limited, (2) limited contact where exposure to the environment was not restricted, and (3) no contact where there was no direct contact and the caregiver sat next to the crib. Five out of seven (71 percent) of the full contact, four of the 10 (40 percent) with limited contact, and none of the 14 (0 percent) no-contact caregivers became infected with RSV.[11] Transmission is also related to the amount of virus secreted by the infectious host. Infants and immunocompromised persons shed more virus than do immunocompetent persons, and they commonly serve as reservoirs for RSV infections.

Pathogenesis

Inoculation of RSV occurs most often through the eyes, nose, or mouth. Once exposed, the incubation period ranges from 2 to 8 days. The exact mechanism of virus spread down the respiratory tract is not known. Spread may be from cell to cell or by microaspiration of secretions. The virus is contained in the respiratory tract, however, and cannot be cultured from the blood of immunocompetent individuals.[12] In the respiratory tract, the fusion protein binds to the respiratory epithelium. Direct cytopathic changes result in hyperplasia and squamous metaplasia with desquamation. An infiltrate of mononuclear cells and polymorphonuclear cells is seen. The clinical picture of bronchiolitis results from obstruction of small airways, mucous secretion, and syncytium formation. Pneumonia, hyperinflation, consolidation, bronchoconstriction, and hemorrhage can occur.

Clinical Features

The initial and most common presentation of RSV is an upper respiratory tract infection including sneezing, rhinorrhea, nasal congestion, cough, and often fever. Progression to lower-tract disease may result in bronchiolitis, tracheobronchitis, and pneumonia. Exacerbation of underlying reactive airway disease, chronic lung disease, and other conditions that cause cardiopulmonary compromise is common. Chest radiographs may reveal hyperinflation, peribronchial cuffing, consolidation, or atelectasis. Hypoxemia and apnea are often seen in infants with RSV and are a common reason for hospitalization and monitoring. Although most patients recover from RSV in 1 to 2 weeks, respiratory failure and death can occur, especially in the immunocompromised and patients with underlying cardiopulmonary disease.

Diagnosis

Laboratory diagnostic tests for RSV infection include antigen detection, culture, and amplified nucleic acid methods. Each has strengths and weaknesses that must be recognized in deciding which test methods to use in a particular clinical setting.

Accurate test results for each of these methods depend on the quality of patient specimen submitted to the laboratory. Common methods of collecting upper respiratory specimens include nasopharyngeal swabs, washes, and aspirates. Comparative studies have generally shown nasopharyngeal aspirates to be superior to swabs.[13] More cellular elements in a specimen maximize the chance of rapidly detecting respiratory viruses no matter which test method is used. Serologic diagnosis of RSV is rarely clinically useful.

The most rapid test methods are usually solid-phase immunoassays for detecting RSV antigens in respiratory tract secretions. An expanding selection of these commercial U.S. Food and Drug Administration (FDA)–approved tests has become available because of the clinical and economic importance of rapid diagnosis of RSV for infection control purposes. These tests are relatively simple and inexpensive, and they can be completed in approximately 30 minutes with minimal personnel training and expertise. Virus particles need not be viable to be detected. The disadvantage of the immunoassays is relatively poor analytic performance, particularly low sensitivity. In some comparisons, RSV enzyme immunoassay has been found to be less than 60 percent sensitive, in contrast to claims in package inserts.

In April 2012, the FDA approved labeling changes (Warnings and Precautions) for Synagis (palivizumab) injection regarding RSV diagnostic test interferences:

> Palivizumab may interfere with immunological-based RSV diagnostic tests such as some antigen detection-based assays. In addition, palivizumab inhibits virus replication in cell culture and therefore may also interfere with viral culture assays. Palivizumab does not interfere with reverse transcriptase-polymerase chain reaction based assays. Assay I interference could lead to false-negative RSV diagnostic test results. Therefore, diagnostic test results, when obtained, should be used in conjunction with clinical findings to guide medical decisions.[14]

RSV antigens can also be detected by staining respiratory epithelial cells with fluorescein isothiocyanate (FITC)–conjugated anti-RSV antibodies (direct fluorescent antibody test, or DFA) and examining with fluorescent microscopy. Analyte-specific reagents are commercially available and relatively inexpensive. This test requires approximately 1 hour, and interpretation is best performed by highly skilled and experienced personnel.

RSV DFA can be slightly more sensitive than isolation in culture, and viral viability is not required. This is the only method that allows direct evaluation of specimen quality (cellularity).

Isolation in culture is considered the gold standard of laboratory RSV diagnosis, even though the virus is relatively labile and sensitive to transport conditions. Culture of RSV from respiratory specimens can be performed in shell vials with results available after 48 hours of incubation. Shell vial cultures may be backed up with traditional culture in a variety of cell types, which can detect other respiratory viruses in addition to RSV. Detection of RSV in traditional cell cultures can be problematic because typical cytopathic effect may not be evident. Experienced laboratory personnel are required to interpret cytopathic effect, and time to results may be as long as 10 days.

At least one reverse transcription polymerase chain reaction (RT-PCR) kit is available for RSV and additional respiratory viruses.[15] In comparative studies, sensitivity of RT-PCR for RSV is greater than culture and/or DFA, though at present it has limited availability and tends to be more expensive. Specificity of RT-PCR is difficult to determine because there is not an equally sensitive standard for comparison, except perhaps serology combined with DFA and culture.

Once RSV is identified in the patient population, presumptive diagnosis of RSV infection cases is sometimes used for infection prevention purposes in subsequent similar cases. This saves the cost of laboratory testing unless it is needed to determine cessation of viral shedding.

Treatment

The mainstay treatment of RSV is supportive care; hydration, oxygenation, and mechanical ventilation may be required. Ribavirin, an antiviral agent with activity against RSV, is approved for treatment of severe RSV infections in hospitalized infants and young children. However, its use is controversial due to the requirement for aerosol administration, the potential for toxicity among exposed healthcare personnel, and questionable efficacy.[16]

Prevention

To date, no vaccine is available for active immunoprophylaxis of RSV infection. Only one product is available for passive immunoprophylaxis: palivizumab (marketed under the name Synagis). Palivizumab, a humanized mouse monoclonal antibody, is the only agent approved by the FDA for prevention of RSV disease in high-risk children (i.e., younger than 24 months with CLD requiring medical therapy (e.g., diuretics, supplemental oxygen, bronchodilators, or steroids), as well as children under 24 months with a history of premature birth. Premature birth is strictly defined as less than 35 weeks' gestation; however, children less than 32 weeks' gestation receive priority in the cost-benefit equation of immunoprophylaxis. Children between 32 weeks' and 35 weeks' gestation should be considered for prophylaxis if two or more environmental and clinical risk factors are present: childcare attendance, school-aged siblings, exposure to environmental pollutants, congenital abnormalities of the airways, or severe neuromuscular disease.

Every month during the RSV season, palivizumab is given at a dose of 15 mg/kg intramuscularly. The American Academy of Pediatrics' recommendations include considering the use of immunoprophylaxis with palivizumab in patients with CHD if they are under 24 months of age and receiving medication to control congestive heart failure, have moderate to severe pulmonary hypertension, or have cyanotic heart disease. It is worth noting, however, that monoclonal antibody of palivizumab only binds the fusion protein of RSV and does nothing to prevent infection with other viruses.

Respiratory syncytial virus immune globulin intravenous (RSV-IGIV), previously used for prophylaxis, is no longer available.

Despite passive immunity, breakthrough RSV infections occur. To prevent these and all RSV infections, infection control measures cannot be overemphasized. These include proper hand hygiene techniques (using soap and water or alcohol-based hand sanitizer agents), contact precautions including gloves and gowns when having contact with the patient, and cohorting of patients; these are critical infection control practices to control the spread of RSV. Because the consequences of RSV infection can be devastating in immunocompromised patients, particularly neonates and stem cell transplant recipients, additional infection control measures have been advocated for these patient populations: wearing a surgical mask when in the room, droplet precautions (wearing a surgical mask when within 3 feet of the patient), prohibiting symptomatic visitor as well as healthcare worker contact with patients, and prohibiting children under 12 years of age from visiting. Methods involving the use of masks and respiratory precautions likely have more to do with the awareness of RSV and subsequent care with contact precautions rather than prevention of spread via the respiratory route.

Financial and Cost-Benefit Issues

Each clinical setting must determine its lowest cost-benefit management program for RSV infection. Important parameters include (1) risk factors and demographics of patient population, (2) cost of preventive measures, (3) cost of testing/screening methods, (4) cost of treatment measures, and (5) cost of disease (hospital stay, days off work or school, cost of secondary complications) to index patient and secondary cases, including healthcare personnel.

When effective vaccines become available, dollars spent on prevention by vaccine will probably provide the most benefit. The current method of prevention by passive immunoprophylaxis for high-risk patients remains costly and is offered only during the period when patients are most likely to be exposed.

Cost-benefit of laboratory testing/screening methods depends partly on the cost of providing the tests and partly on the costs averted by testing/screening. In many clinical inpatient settings,

testing is used for cohorting to avoid nosocomial transmission because specific antiviral treatment is rarely administered. Some settings have opted to minimize laboratory testing and instead cohort by risk factors and symptoms. If a "test of cure" is used to release RSV-infected patients from isolation, the laboratory test chosen must be sufficiently sensitive to determine that viral shedding has ceased (thus excluding immunoassays) and sufficiently specific to avoid keeping patients in isolation needlessly. Immunosuppressed patients may shed viable RSV for months after initial infection. Traditional culture methodology for detection would add 10 additional days of isolation before results were available, but shell vial testing adds only 2 days. There are insufficient data to know whether antigen detection tests or RT-PCR remain positive after viable virus shedding has ceased, complicating the decision process.

CONCLUSIONS

RSV is an important respiratory pathogen worldwide, especially among the very young, immunocompromised persons, and the elderly. The mode of transmission and high-attack rate make RSV an important nosocomial pathogen, necessitating rapid diagnosis and timely implementation of infection prevention measures. Antiviral treatment has not been of marked value, whereas passive immunization with palivizumab has had a significant impact on RSV morbidity and mortality. Prevention strategies are critical for disease management, whereas supportive and symptomatic management remain the mainstay of treatment. Research continues on the development of several different types of vaccines and an enhanced-potency humanized RSV monoclonal antibody. Active immunization is in development and shows promise for curtailing the impact of RSV disease in the future.

FUTURE TRENDS

Early studies with RSV vaccines were disappointing in that an increase in the severity of disease was observed in vaccine recipients.[17, 18] This phenomenon, and the fact that attack and case morbidity rates are high in infants under 6 months of age (when maternal antibody is still present), has led to the concern that the humoral immune response may be involved in disease progression rather than protection. However, subsequent studies have found that higher maternal antibody levels are protective against RSV disease[16,19] and that passive immunity with palivizumab is efficacious. These findings have renewed interest and hope in the development of an RSV vaccine.

For more than 50 years, researchers have been working on developing a vaccine for RSV. Current RSV vaccine strategies include the following vaccine development approaches: (1) attenuating the virus or (2) using recombinant technology to present viral antigens, often in the context of a replication-competent or replication-incompetent vector.

A number of attenuated RSV vaccines have now been tested clinically. The development of live-attenuated vaccines presents significant challenges. A concern is that viruses with compensatory mutations in the live-attenuated vaccines may associate with reversion to pathogenic phenotypes and lead to increased frequencies of adverse reactions *in vivo*. Manufacturing and distribution present difficulties due to the fact that the virus is sensitive to temperature changes. Also, attenuated strains are difficult to propagate to high titers.

At this time, there is greater flexibility in recombinant technology. This is true for the RSV antigen(s) and in the ways in which the antigen is expressed. Because each is capable of eliciting neutralizing antibodies and T-cell responses, the major target antigens of recombinant vaccine technology are RSV G and F. Additionally, reverse genetics can serve as delivery systems for RSV antigens. The RSV vaccine field today has a variety of new concepts and vectors, and there are currently a number of recombinant vaccines in preclinical testing stages.[20]

INTERNATIONAL PERSPECTIVE

The international impact of RSV is significant. RSV is the most frequent reason that children in developed countries are hospitalized during the winter months. In 2005, 33 million new cases of RSV infection occurred in children under age 5, including more than 3 million severe cases that required hospitalization. Each year in developing countries, RSV infection contributes to the mortality of an estimated 66,000 to 199,000 children. In the United States, an estimated 10,000 RSV-associated deaths occur annually among adults over 65. There is no worldwide estimate of RSV in the elderly.[21]

Discrepancy exists among developed and developing countries, as well as between the developed and developing world. For undetermined reasons, hospitalization rates even among industrialized nations vary. In 2004, the World Health Organization (WHO) published results of a study that assessed the burden of RSV-associated lower respiratory infection in four developing countries: Indonesia, Mozambique, Nigeria, and South Africa. Study findings demonstrated that RSV contributed to a substantial but variable burden of lower respiratory infection in children under 5 years of age.[22]

Mortality rates of RSV are low in both the developed and developing world but vary significantly among studies; case fatality rates range from 0 to 12 percent with an overall trend to higher mortality in developing countries.[23] The impact of RSV globally was so significant that in 1995 WHO declared RSV vaccine development one of the top priorities of the Global Programme of Vaccines.[24]

REFERENCES

1. Centers for Disease Control and Prevention (CDC). Respiratory syncytial virus activity—United States, July 2011-January 2013. *MMWR Morb Mortal Wkly Rep* 2013 Mar 1;62(8):141–144.
2. Morris JA, Blount RE, Savage RE. Recovery of cytopathic agent from chimpanzee with coryza. *Proc Soc Exp Biol Med* 1956;92:544–594.
3. Chanock RM, Roizman G, Myers R. Recovery from infants with respiratory illness of a virus related to chimpanzee coryza agent: isolation, properties and characterization. *Am J Hyg* 1957; 66:281–290.
4. Falsey AR, Walsh EE. Respiratory syncytial virus infection in adults. *Clin Microbiol Rev* 2000;13(3):371–384.
5. Collins PL, Chanock RM, Murphy BR. Respiratory syncytial virus. In: Knipe DM, Howley PM, eds. *Fields virology*. 4th ed. Baltimore: Lippincott Williams & Wilkins; 2001:1443–1485.
6. Sullender WM. Respiratory syncytial virus genetic and antigenic diversity. *Clin Microbiol Rev* 2000 Jan;13(1):1–15.
7. Goldman DA. Epidemiology and prevention of pediatric viral respiratory infections in healthcare institutions. *Emerg Infect Dis*. 2001 Mar-Apr;7(2):249–253.
8. Bulkow LR, Singleton RJ, Karron RA, et al. Risk factors for severe respiratory syncytial virus infection among Alaska Native children. *Pediatrics* 2002 Feb;109(2):210–216.
9. American Academy of Pediatrics Committee on Infectious Diseases and Committee on Fetus and Newborn. Revised indications for the use of palivizumab and respiratory syncytial virus immune globulin intravenous for the prevention of respiratory syncytial virus infections. *Pediatrics* 2003 Dec;112(6 Pt 1):1442–1446.
10. Meissner HC. Selected populations at increased risk from respiratory syncytial virus infection. *Pediatr Infect Dis J* 2003 Feb;22(2 Suppl):S40–S45.
11. Hall CB, Douglas RG Jr. Modes of transmission of respiratory syncytial virus. *J Pediatr* 1981 Jul;99(1):100–103.
12. Brandenburg AH, Neijens HJ, Osterhaus ADME. Pathogenesis of RSV lower respiratory tract infection: implications for vaccine development. *Vaccine* 2001 Apr 6;19(20–22):2769–2782.
13. Ahluwalia G, Embree J, McNicol P, et al. Comparison of nasopharyngeal aspirate and nasopharyngeal swab specimens for respiratory syncytial virus diagnosis by cell-culture, indirect immunofluorescence assay, and enzyme-linked-immunosorbent-assay. *J Clin Microbiol* 1987 May; 25(5):763–767.
14. U.S. Food and Drug Administration (FDA). MedWatch The FDA Safety Information and Adverse Event Reporting Program. Synagis Prescribing information April 2012. Available at: http://www.fda.gov/Safety/MedWatch/SafetyInformation/ucm302524.htm.
15. Hindiyeh M, Hillyard DR, Carroll KC. Evaluation of the Prodesse Hexaplex multiplex PCR assay for direct detection of seven respiratory viruses in clinical specimens. *Am J Clin Pathol* 2001 Aug;116(2):218–224.
16. Glezen WP, Paredes A, Allison JE, et al. Risk of respiratory syncytial virus infection of infants from low-income families in relationship to sex, ethnic group, and maternal antibody level. *J Pediatr* 1981 May;98(5):708–715.
17. Fulginiti VA, Eller JJ, Sieber OF, et al. Respiratory virus immunization. I. A field trial of two inactivated respiratory virus vaccines, an aqueous univalent parainfluenza vaccine and an alum-precipitated respiratory syncytial virus vaccine. *Am J Epidemiol* 1969 Apr;89(4):435–448.
18. Kim HW, Canchola JG, Brandt CD, et al. Respiratory syncytial virus disease in infants despite prior administration of antigenic inactivated vaccine. *Am J Epidemiol* 1969 Apr;89(4):422–434.
19. Rudraraju R, Jones BG, Sealy R, et al. Respiratory syncytial virus: current progress in vaccine development. *Viruses* 2013 Feb 5;5(2):577–594.
20. Prince GA, Horshwood RL, Chanock RM. Quantitative aspects of passive immunity in respiratory syncytial virus infection in infant cotton rats. *J Virol* 1985 Sep;55(3):517–520.
21. Schluger NW. *Respiratory syncytial virus*. Acute Respiratory Illness Atlas Website. Available at: http://www.ariatlas.org/understanding_aris/respiratory_syncytial_virus.
22. Robertson SE, Roca A, Alonso P, et al. Respiratory syncytial virus infection: denominator-based studies in Indonesia, Mozambique, Nigeria and South Africa. *Bull World Health Organ* 2004 Dec; 82(12):914–922.
23. Collins PL, Chanock RM, Murphy BR. Respiratory Syncytial Virus. In: Knipe DM, Howley PM, eds. *Fields Virology*, 4th ed. Baltimore: Lippincott Williams & Wilkins; 2001:1443–1485.
24. Crowe JE Jr. Current approaches to the development of vaccines against disease caused by respiratory syncytial virus (RSV) and parainfluenza virus (PIV)—a meeting report of the WHO program for vaccine development. *Vaccine* 1995 Mar;13(4):415–421.

SUPPLEMENTAL RESOURCES

American Academy of Pediatrics Respiratory Syncytial Virus Policy. Available at: http://www.aap.org/policy/rsvpolicy.pdf.

Association for Professionals in Infection Control and Epidemiology. Available at: http://www.apic.org.

Centers for Disease Control and Prevention Guidelines for Preventing Healthcare associated pneumonia. Available at: http://www.cdc.gov/mmwr/Preview/Mmwrhtml/rr5303a1.htm.

Centers for Disease Control and Prevention Respiratory Syncytial Virus Information. Available at: http://www.cdc.gov/rsv/index.html Infection Control Today Web site. Available at: http://www.infectioncontroltoday.com/.

National Institute of Allergy and Infectious Diseases, http://www.niaid.nih.gov/topics/rsv/research/, Accessed July 2013.

World Health Organization (WHO). Available at: http://www.who.int

APPLICABLE GUIDELINES

Boyce JM, Pittet D, Healthcare Infection Control Practices Advisory Committee, et al. Guideline for Hand Hygiene in Health-Care Settings. Recommendations of the Healthcare Infection Control Practices Advisory Committee and the HICPAC/SHEA/APIC/IDSA Hand Hygiene Task Force. Society for Healthcare Epidemiology of America/Association for Professionals in Infection Control/Infectious Diseases Society of America. *MMWR Recomm Rep* 2002;51(RR-16):1–45.

Respiratory Syncytial Virus. In: Pickering LK, Baker CJ, Kinberlin DW, Kimberlin DW, Long SS, eds. *Red Book: 2012 report of the Committee on Infectious Diseases,* 29th ed. Elk Grove Village IL: American Academy of Pediatrics; 2012: 609–617.

Rutala WA, Weber DJ, Healthcare Infection Control Practices Advisory Committee. Guideline for Disinfection and Sterilization in Healthcare Facilities, 2008. Available at: http://www.cdc.gov/ncidod/dhqp/pdf/guidelines/Disinfection_Nov_2008.pdf. Accessed March 25, 2009.

Siegel JD, Rhinehart E, Jackson M, et al. 2007 Guideline for Isolation Precautions: Preventing Transmission of Infectious Agents in Health Care Settings, *Am J Infect Control* 2007;35:S65–S164.

CHAPTER 91

Sexually Transmitted Diseases

Sindy M. Paul, MD, MPH, FACPM
Medical Director
Division of HIV, STD, and TB Services
New Jersey Department of Health
Trenton, NJ

ABSTRACT

The first part of this chapter covers sexually transmitted diseases. The second part of the chapter is devoted to gynecology. Many changes to the recommendations for prevention, diagnosis, and treatment of sexually transmitted diseases have recently been published. Education and counseling previously were recommended for patients with human papillomavirus and herpes simplex virus. The recommendations for human papillomavirus have been updated. Chlamydia screening recommendations have been updated. New tests are now available specifically for diagnosing human papillomavirus. Two vaccines for preventing the reduction of the sequelae of human papillomavirus infection are now available. Guidelines for the treatment of herpes simplex virus, scabies, pubic lice, and bacterial vaginosis have been revised. Cephalosporin and quinolone-resistant Neisseria gonorrhoeae *have become more prevalent in the United States, prompting new treatment recommendations. The diagnosis of gonococcal and chlamydial infections has improved with new analytical procedures. The gynecology section of this chapter emphasizes the impact of vaginal flora on postoperative infections and procedure-specific risks.*

KEY CONCEPTS

Sexually Transmitted Diseases

- More cases of genital *Chlamydia trachomatis* infections are being reported, likely reflecting more screening and improved tests. Perinatal infections may result in conjunctivitis and pneumonia in newborns. The most serious sequelae of *C. trachomatis* in women include pelvic inflammatory disease, ectopic pregnancy, infertility, and pelvic pain syndrome. In men, sequelae include epididymitis, prostatitis, proctitis, proctocolitis, and Reiter syndrome. Sexually active adolescent women should be screened at least annually, even if symptoms are not present. Annual screening of all sexually active women 20 to 25 years of age is also recommended, as is screening of older women with risk factors (i.e., those with new or multiple sex partners).

- Overall, rates of gonorrhea decreased in the United States from the 1970s to 1997 but have since increased. As with chlamydia, rates of gonorrhea are particularly high in the 15-to-24-year-old group. In men, rates are highest in the 20-to-29-year-old group. The incidence among men who have sex with men has increased dramatically. The dominant risk factor for acquiring gonorrhea is sexual intercourse with an infected partner. Pregnant women should be screened and treated for gonorrhea before delivery.

- Patients infected with *N. gonorrhoeae* are often coinfected with *C. trachomatis*. This has led to the recommendation that patients treated for gonococcal infections also be treated routinely with a regimen effective against uncomplicated *C. trachomatis* infection.

- Cephalosporin and quinolone-resistant *N. gonorrhoeae* have increased in prevalence and have become more common throughout the United States. As a result, quinolones are no longer recommended for the treatment of *N. gonorrhoeae* infections.

- Certain types of human papillomavirus are causing genital and anal warts. Other human papillomavirus types in the anogenital region have been strongly associated with cervical tumors. This is the most common sexually transmitted viral disease in the United States. Most human papillomavirus infections are asymptomatic, subclinical, or unrecognized. Treatment may reduce, but does not eliminate, the risk of transmission. Two human papillomavirus vaccines are available. Cervarix is a bivalent vaccine and Gardasil is a quadrivalent vaccine. Gardasil and Cervarix are recommended for use in females between 9 and 26 years of age and are recommended as a routine vaccination for girls 11 to 12 years of age. Gardasil can also be used to vaccinate males in this age range. Receipt of the vaccine or the presence of genital warts is not an indication for a change in the frequency of Papanicolaou tests or for cervical colposcopy.

- *Herpesvirus hominis* is an alternative name for herpes simplex virus. Herpes simplex virus type 1 (HSV-1) is transmitted primarily by contact with oral secretions and herpes simplex virus type 2 (HSV-2) by contact with genital secretions. Most people infected with HSV-2 have not had the diagnosis. The primary infection has a mean duration of 12 days and may be associated with a fever, malaise, anorexia, and tender bilateral inguinal adenopathy. Approximately two thirds of the patients have subsequent, usually milder recurrences. The diagnosis of genital herpes should be confirmed by laboratory testing. Complications and sequelae of genital herpes can include neuralgia, meningitis, ascending myelitis, urethral stricture, urinary retention, and secondary bacterial infection. The virus from an active genital infection may be transmitted during vaginal delivery, causing neonatal herpes infection, which can range from a mild localized presentation to a fatal disseminated infection. There is no known cure for genital herpes, though systemic antiviral drugs partially control the symptoms and signs of herpes episodes.

- Chancroid is worldwide in distribution and caused by the bacterium *Haemophilus ducreyi*. In the United States, chancroid usually occurs in outbreaks but is endemic in some areas. The prevalence of chancroid is decreasing worldwide and in the United States. An estimated 10 percent of people who acquire chancroid in the United States are coinfected with HSV or *Treponema pallidum*. That percentage is higher among those outside the United States. Chancroid is most frequently found in uncircumcised non-Caucasian men. Women account for only 10 percent of reported cases. Men frequently present with one ulcer, whereas women frequently have multiple lesions. The lesions are generally confined to the genital area and perineum. There is no asymptomatic carrier state. All patients should be tested for human immunodeficiency virus at the time of diagnosis, given that chancroid has been associated with an increased risk of heterosexual HIV transmission.

- Donovanosis, caused by *Klebsiella* (formerly *Calymmatobacterium*) *granulomatis*, is a genital ulcerative disease seen more commonly in tropical and developing areas than in the United States. Wounds caused by donovanosis can be complicated by secondary infection and may lead to lymphedema.

- *Phthirus pubis* (pubic or crab louse) often afflicts persons with poor hygiene, communal lifestyles, and multiple sex partners. Transmission occurs primarily through intimate physical or sexual contact. Symptoms range from slight discomfort to severe itching. Pubic lice can also infest the eyelashes, eyebrows, axilla, scalp, or other body hairs. Secondary bacterial infection can occur from excoriations, with ensuing regional lymphadenitis. Patients with *Phthirus pubis* should be evaluated for other sexually transmitted diseases.

- Scabies is caused by *Sarcoptes scabiei*. The female mite burrows under the skin to deposit eggs. The disorder is worldwide in distribution, and recently there have been increases in the number of cases in the United States and Europe. Scabies most commonly affects families, sexual partners, school-aged children, chronically ill patients, and people in communal living situations. Immunocompromised patients are prone to develop crusted or Norwegian scabies, which often leads to debilitating pain and skin breakdown. The mode of transmission of all forms is person-to-person contact or contact with clothing, towels, or linens. Epidemics within healthcare facilities have occurred in the United States.

- Syphilis is a complex systemic illness caused by the spirochete *Treponema pallidum*. Syphilis is acquired by sexual contact; passage through the placenta (congenital syphilis); kissing or other close contact with an active lesion; transfusion of human blood; or accidental direct inoculation. The rate of primary and secondary syphilis reported in the United States show that gay and bisexual men and young people are at the greatest risk. In 2011, men who have sex with men accounted for 72 percent of the primary and secondary syphilis cases in the United States. Clinically, syphilis is categorized as primary, secondary, early latent, late latent, latency of unknown duration, and tertiary. Patients may seek treatment for signs and symptoms of primary syphilis, such as a papule or chancre at the site of infection. Secondary syphilis demonstrates manifestations that include, but are not limited to, skin rash, patchy hair loss (alopecia areata), mucocutaneous lesions, and lymphadenopathy. Latent infections typically are those that lack clinical manifestations and are detected by serologic testing. Tertiary infection can encompass cardiac (aortic root aneurysm/aortic insufficiency), ophthalmic, and auditory sequelae; central nervous system complications (neurosyphilis); aseptic meningitis; generalized paresis; and tabes dorsalis. Gummatous lesions of the soft tissue and bone may be observed. Untreated, early syphilis in pregnant women results in perinatal death in as many as 40 percent of cases, and if acquired during the 4 years preceding pregnancy, may lead to infection of the fetus in more than 70 percent of cases. All patients with syphilis should be tested for human immunodeficiency syndrome.

- Three main clinical entities cause vaginitis: trichomoniasis, vulvovaginal candidiasis, and bacterial vaginosis. Trichomoniasis is sexually transmitted, whereas candidiasis usually is not. The role of sexual transmission is unknown in bacterial vaginosis. Vaginitis is characterized by a vaginal discharge or vulva itching and irritation; a fishy odor may be present.

- Lymphogranuloma venereum is caused by *C. trachomatis* serovars L1, L2, or L3. These strains are distinct from those that cause nongonococcal urethritis. Lymphogranuloma venereum is endemic in many parts of the world, including Asia, Africa, and South America. It is rare in the United States, where it is seen predominantly among homosexual males. Lymphogranuloma venereum is the only *C. trachomatis* infection that causes constitutional symptoms. In the first phase, a small, painless herpetiform vesicle, nonindurated papule, or ulcer may develop locally. This lesion may heal quickly and is followed by inguinal or perirectal lymphadenopathy or bubo, fever, and other constitutional symptoms. The third phase of illness is characterized by lymph node suppuration, abscess, lymphedema, or fistula formation, or a combination of these. A presumptive diagnosis is made by excluding other causes of genital ulcers or inguinal lymphadenopathy and is supported by the detection of *C. trachomatis*.

- Hysterectomies are the second most common surgical procedure for women of reproductive age (behind cesarean section) in the United States. Posthysterectomy infections usually arise from contamination of the surgical site by endogenous flora. The length of hospital stay for all types of hysterectomies has decreased, and many patients are discharged before manifestation of a postoperative wound infection is recognized. Postdischarge surveillance is necessary to identify these infections. Perioperative antibiotic prophylaxis is recommended for hysterectomies to decrease the risk of postoperative wound infection.

- Procedures that do not result in operative site exposure to flora in the lower genital tract include laparoscopy, ovarian cystectomy, and hysterosalpingography; therefore, antibiotic prophylaxis is not recommended for these procedures.

- Pelvic gynecologic surgeries, like other pelvic procedures, pose an increased risk of occupational exposure of healthcare personnel to bloodborne pathogens.

BACKGROUND

The Centers for Disease Control and Prevention (CDC) estimates that 20 million sexually transmitted diseases (STDs) occur annually in the United States, and almost half are among young people between the ages of 15 and 24 years.[1] Many STDs are undiagnosed; others are not reported, including common viral infections, such as human papillomavirus (HPV) and genital herpes. These diseases represent a significant public health threat.

Efforts to prevent, detect, and treat STDs have had some success. For example, new vaccines promise to decrease the morbidity and mortality associated with HPV and its complications. Several challenges, including increasing rates of several STDs and establishment of antimicrobial resistance, have emerged. In addition, disparities in STD prevalence by gender, socioeconomic class, race, and sexual orientation persist.

BASIC PRINCIPLES

Patients suffering from one STD may also have one or more other STDs. Patients and their sex partners should be screened and treated accordingly. The presence of STDs increases the likelihood of both transmitting and acquiring human immunodeficiency virus (HIV). Individuals with STDs are three to five times more likely to acquire HIV if exposed to the virus through sexual contact than are noninfected individuals. Conversely, if an HIV-infected individual is coinfected with an STD, he or she is three to five times more likely than other HIV-infected persons to transmit HIV through sexual contact. The lower part of the reproductive tract is heavily colonized with bacteria. Anaerobes are 10 times more common in the vagina than aerobes. Normal vaginal flora includes lactobacilli, various species of streptococci, *Gardnerella vaginalis*, strains of Enterobacteriaceae, and anaerobes. A number of naturally occurring events can alter the vaginal flora, including pregnancy, delivery, menopause, abdominal or vaginal hysterectomy, and hospitalization.

Either the vaginal or the abdominal routes are used to perform gynecologic procedures. The vaginal route is a clean, nonsterile approach, thereby increasing the risk of infection through contamination by vaginal flora. The abdominal route is a sterile approach that carries postoperative wound infection risks similar to those for other abdominal clean surgical procedures.

SEXUALLY TRANSMITTED DISEASES AND GYNECOLOGY

Sexually Transmitted Diseases

Chlamydia Infections

In the United States alone during 2011, 1,412,791 cases of genital *Chlamydia trachomatis* infections were reported to the CDC. This case count corresponds to a rate of 457.6 cases per 100,000 and represents an increase of 8 percent compared with the previous year. The increase most likely represents increased screening for chlamydia, more complete reporting, and more sensitive testing methods.[1]

Chlamydiae are obligate intracellular bacteria with a biphasic life cycle. The extracellular "elementary body" is the infectious form of the organism, whereas the "reticulate body" is the replicative form. The incubation period has not been clearly defined, but it is probably 7 to 14 days or longer.[2] Genital infection with *C. trachomatis* may result in urethritis, epididymitis, cervicitis, acute salpingitis, or other pelvic symptoms. Patients may present with dysuria and urethral discharge. The discharge tends to be gray, white, and sometimes clear, and may be either slight or copious in amount. However, the infection is often asymptomatic in men and women. Perinatal infections may result in inclusion conjunctivitis and pneumonia in newborns. The *C. trachomatis* infection may result in premature rupture of membranes, premature birth, and stillbirth. *C. trachomatis* is also the etiologic agent of lymphogranuloma venereum and trachoma.[3]

The most serious sequelae of *C. trachomatis* in women include pelvic inflammatory disease (PID), ectopic pregnancy, and infertility.[4] In men, sequelae include epididymitis, prostatitis, proctitis, proctocolitis, and Reiter syndrome.[5]

The CDC recommends that sexually active women <25 years of age should be screened at least annually, even if symptoms are not present. Screening of older women with risk factors (i.e., those with new or multiple sex partners) is also recommended. Sexually active men in high-prevalence settings such as STD clinics and correctional facilities should also be tested.[4] However, the United States Preventive Services Task Force (USPTF) recommends screening for persons less than 24 years of age.[6]

Classic trachoma is the only *C. trachomatis* infection that can be diagnosed on clinical grounds alone in the proper epidemiologic setting. Trachoma is an eye infection that is not sexually transmitted. Other chlamydial infections require laboratory confirmation for a definitive diagnosis. In females, *C. trachomatis* infection can be diagnosed by testing urine or endocervical or vaginal specimen swabs. In males, a specimen obtained from urine or urethral swab can be used. Rectal infection can be diagnosed from a rectal swab specimen. Nucleic acid amplification tests (NAATs) are the most sensitive tests for detecting chlamydiae and are approved by the United States. Culture, direct immunofluorescence, demonstration of chlamydial antigen by enzyme-linked immunosorbent assay (ELISA), and nucleic acid hybridization tests are also used.[2] Self-collected vaginal swabs perform as well as those collected by providers and are an acceptable specimen collection method by women.[4]

An average of five or more polymorphonuclear leukocytes per oil immersion field in a Gram stain from an endourethral swab or the presence of 10 leukocytes per high-power field in first-catch urine strongly suggests urethritis. The absence of organisms suggesting *N. gonorrhoeae* establishes the diagnosis of nongonococcal urethritis (NGU) in the proper clinical setting. In men, *C. trachomatis* has become slightly less prevalent but still accounts for 15 to 55 percent of NGU infections. The etiology of the majority of cases of nonchlamydial NGU is unknown. Possible etiologic agents of NGU include *Mycoplasma genitalium*, *Ureaplasma urealyticum*, herpes simplex virus (HSV), adenovirus, and *Trichomonas vaginalis*.[2] Enteric bacteria have been identified as an uncommon cause of NGU and may be associated with insertive anal sex. Diagnostic and treatment procedures for these organisms should be done only when these infections are suspected (e.g., contact with trichomoniasis and genital lesions or severe dysuria and meatitis, which may suggest genital herpes) or when NGU is not responsive to therapy. Although *C. trachomatis* and *N. gonorrhoeae* may be implicated as etiologic agents of mucopurulent cervicitis (MPC), in most cases the organisms cannot be isolated.[3] Mucopurulent cervicitis may be diagnosed if a purulent or mucopurulent endocervical exudate is seen or a friable endocervical mucosa is evident. Empiric treatment should be considered for a patient who is suspected of having gonorrhea or chlamydia if the prevalence of these infections is high in the patient population and if follow-up cannot be assured.[4]

The recommended treatment regimens for *C. trachomatis* infection include azithromycin (1 g by mouth [PO] in a single dose) or doxycycline (100 mg PO twice daily [bid] for 7 days). Alternative regimens include erythromycin base (500 mg PO bid for 7 days); erythromycin ethylsuccinate (800 mg bid for 7 days); ofloxacin (300 mg PO bid for 7 days); or levofloxacin (500 mg daily for 7 days). HIV-infected patients should receive the same treatment as those not infected with HIV. In cervicitis, consideration for treating *Neisseria gonorrhoeae* should be entertained if the local prevalence of gonococcal infections is greater than 5 percent.[4]

Patients should be instructed to abstain from sexual intercourse for 7 days after the one-dose treatment of azithromycin or until completion of a 7-day regimen. In general, patients do not need to be retested after completing treatment with doxycycline or azithromycin unless symptoms persist, reinfection is suspected, or the patient is pregnant.[4]

Treating infected patients prevents transmission to sex partners. Treatment of sex partners helps prevent reinfection of the index patient and transmission to other partners. Patients should be instructed to refer their sex partners for evaluation, testing, and treatment if they had sexual contact with the patient during the 60 days preceding onset of the patient's symptoms or chlamydia diagnosis. The most recent sex partner should be evaluated and treated, even if the last sexual contact has been longer than 60 days since the onset of symptoms or diagnosis. If local medical laws and regulations permit and concerns exist that heterosexual sex partners who are referred for evaluation and treatment will not seek these services, patient delivery of antibiotic therapy through a prescription or the medication itself to their partners can be considered.[4]

Recommended regimens for the treatment of pregnant women are azithromycin (1 g in a single dose) or amoxicillin (500 mg bid for 7 days). Tetracyclines and fluoroquinolones are contraindicated in pregnancy. Unlike the general population, pregnant women should routinely have repeat testing for chlamydia by NAAT 3 weeks after the completion of treatment.[4]

Neonatal *C. trachomatis* infection results from perinatal exposure to the mother's infected cervix. Prenatal screening and treatment of pregnant women can prevent neonatal chlamydial infections. Neonatal ocular prophylaxis with silver nitrate solution or antibiotic ointments does not prevent perinatal transmission of *C. trachomatis* from mother to infant, but it should be done because ocular prophylaxis with these agents prevents gonococcal ophthalmia. Chalmydia should be considered for all infants aged ≤30 days with conjunctivitis, especially if the mother has a history of untreated chlamydia infection. However, neonatal *C. trachomatis* infection is most frequently recognized by conjunctivitis that develops 5 to 12 days after birth. *C. trachomatis* also can cause a subacute, afebrile pneumonia with onset at ages 1 to 3 months. Although *C. trachomatis* has been the most frequent identifiable infectious cause of ophthalmia neonatorum, perinatal chlamydial infections (including ophthalmia and pneumonia) have occurred less frequently because of the institution of widespread prenatal screening and treatment of pregnant women.[4]

Ophthalmia neonatorum in the neonate can be diagnosed using both tissue culture and nonculture tests (e.g., direct fluorescence antibody [DFA] tests, enzyme immunoassay, and NAAT). Most nonculture tests are not cleared by the FDA for the detection of chlamydia from conjunctival swabs, and clinical laboratories must verify the procedure according to Clinical Laboratory Improvement Amendments (CLIA) regulations. Specimens for culture isolation and nonculture tests should be obtained from the everted eyelid using a dacron-tipped swab or the swab specified by the manufacturer's test kit, and they must contain conjunctival cells, not exudate alone. Specific diagnosis of *C. trachomatis* infection confirms the need for treatment not only for the neonate but also for the mother and her sex partner(s). Ocular specimens from infants being evaluated for chlamydial conjunctivitis also should be tested for *N. gonorrhoeae*.[4]

The recommended treatment of neonatal *C. trachomatis* is erythromycin base or ethylsuccinate 50 mg/kg/day PO divided into four doses daily for 14 days. Because the efficacy of erythromycin treatment is only approximately 80 percent, a second course of therapy might be necessary. Note that an association between oral erythromycin and infantile hypertrophic pyloric stenosis (IHPS) has been reported in infants aged <6 weeks who were treated with this drug. Infants treated with erythromycin should be followed for signs and symptoms of IHPS. Topical antibiotic therapy alone is inadequate for treatment of chlamydial infection and is unnecessary when systemic treatment is administered. Infant follow-up is recommended to determine whether initial treatment was effective.[4]

The possibility of concomitant chlamydial pneumonia should be considered. The characteristic signs of chlamydial pneumonia in infants include (1) a repetitive staccato cough with tachypnea and (2) hyperinflation and bilateral diffuse infiltrates on a chest radiograph. In addition, peripheral eosinophilia ($\geq$400 cells/mm^3) occurs frequently. Wheezing is rare, and infants are typically afebrile. Because clinical presentations differ, initial treatment and diagnostic tests should include *C. trachomatis* for all infants aged 1 to 3 months who are suspected of having pneumonia (especially those whose mothers have untreated chlamydial infection). The recommended treatment is erythromycin base or ethylsuccinate PO divided into four doses daily for 14 days. Because the efficacy of erythromycin treatment is only approximately 80 percent, a second course of therapy might be necessary. Infant follow-up is recommended to determine if the pneumonia has resolved, though some infants with chlamydial pneumonia continue to have abnormal pulmonary function tests later in childhood.[4]

The recommended infection prevention measures include Standard Precautions.[7]

Neisseria gonorrhoeae Infection

Gonorrhea is the second most common notifiable disease reported in the United States.[8] Following a 73.8 percent decline in the reported rate of gonorrhea from 1975 to 1997, overall rates increased 4 percent between 2010 and 2011 to 104.2 per 100,000 population, or 321,849 reported cases, in 2011. The prevalence of *N. gonorrhoeae* infection varies widely by geographical region. *N. gonorrhoeae* infection also highlights some striking disparities among race; the gonorrhea rate among blacks was 17 times that of whites in 2011. The gonorrhea rate of African-American women is 14 times that of white women. As with chlamydia, rates of gonorrhea in women are particularly high in the 15-to-24-year-old group. In men, rates are highest in the 20-to-29-year-old group.[1]

N. gonorrhoeae is a nonmotile, nonspore forming, Gram-negative diplococcus that can be observed within neutrophils during microscopic examination of a Gram-stained specimen. Aside from perinatal transmission, the dominant risk factor for acquiring gonorrhea is sexual intercourse with an infected partner. Transmission by fomites (including linens and towels) has been a rare cause of epidemic spread of gonococcal vaginitis.[4]

The incubation period is generally 2 to 5 days but ranges from 1 to 10 days or longer. More than 90 percent of men have no symptoms with urethritis as the predominant manifestation.

Urethral discharge and dysuria are the major symptoms. As opposed to NGU, the discharge generally is more profuse and purulent. In women, the primary locus of disease is the endocervix. As with *C. trachomatis*, many women have no or only minor symptoms. The predominant symptoms are those of cervicitis, occasional urethritis, increased vaginal discharge, and intermenstrual bleeding. Abdominal or pelvic pain is suggestive of salpingitis.[9] Anorectal and pharyngeal infections are common. Approximately 40 percent of women with gonococcal cervicitis have positive rectal cultures and 20 percent display symptoms of gonococcal pharyngitis.[6]

Because the prevalence of gonorrhea is variable, healthcare providers should consider local gonorrhea epidemiology when making screening decisions. Widespread screening is not recommended because gonococcal infections among women are frequently asymptomatic; targeted screening of young women (i.e., those aged <25 years) at increased risk for infection is a primary component of gonorrhea control in the United States. The U.S. Preventive Services Task Force (USPSTF) does not recommend screening for gonorrhea in men and women who are at low risk for infection. The USPSTF recommends screening sexually active women, including those who are pregnant. Clinicians should also provide gonorrhea screening to patients at increased risk for infection, such as women with previous gonorrhea infection, other STDs, and those with new or multiple sex partners especially if there is a history of inconsistent condom use. Also included are those who use drugs illegally or engage in commercial sex work, and those living in communities with a high prevalence of disease. All persons found to have gonorrhea also should be tested for other STDs, including chlamydia, syphilis, and HIV.[4]

For men with symptoms, a Gram stain of a male urethral specimen that demonstrates polymorphonuclear leukocytes with intracellular Gram-negative diplococci can be considered diagnostic because of high specificity (>99 percent) and sensitivity (>95 percent). However, because of lower sensitivity, a negative Gram stain should not be considered sufficient to rule out infection in men who have no symptoms. Gram stain of endocervical specimens, pharyngeal, or rectal specimens also is insufficient to detect infection and thus is not recommended. With the increased utility and availability of highly sensitive and specific testing methods, and because a specific diagnosis may enhance partner notification, specific laboratory testing for *N. gonorrhoeae* is recommended.[4]

Laboratory diagnosis of gonorrhea relies on the identification of *N. gonorrhoeae* at the infected site. Culture, nucleic acid hybridization, or NAATs can be used for the diagnosis of genital infection. NAATs offer the widest range of testing specimen types because they are FDA cleared for use with endocervical swabs, vaginal swabs, male urethral swabs, and female and male urine. However, product inserts for each NAAT vendor must be carefully examined to assess current indications because FDA-cleared specimen types may vary. NAATs are highly sensitive and specific. DNA amplification by either polymerase chain reaction (PCR) or ligase chain reaction offers sensitivity and specificity comparable, or even superior, to culture. The convenience of these latter tests makes screening much more practical. In nongenital sites (i.e., rectum and pharynx), the culture should be used. Some NAATs may cross-react with nongonococcal *Neisseria* and related organisms that are commonly found in the throat. Note that some noncommercial laboratories have initiated the NAAT of rectal and pharyngeal swab specimens after establishing the performance of the test to meet the CLIA requirements.[4]

Because nonculture tests cannot provide antimicrobial susceptibility results, in cases of persistent gonococcal infection after treatment, clinicians should perform both culture and antimicrobial susceptibility testing. For legal purposes, a confirmed culture is the only definitive test.[9] When obtaining a culture is not practical or possible, a presumptive diagnosis can be based on microscopic identification of Gram-negative intracellular diplococci on a smear of urethral or endocervical exudates.[5] All patients tested for gonorrhea should also be tested for other STDs, including Chlamydia, syphilis, and HIV.[4]

Until recently, treatment was empiric and susceptibility testing was not routinely done. The CDC started a surveillance system to monitor resistant strains of *N. gonorrhoeae* in 1986. The Gonococcal Isolate Surveillance System (GISP) is a CDC-supported sentinel surveillance system to monitor *N. gonorrhoeae* susceptibility among urethral isolates obtained from men at participating STD clinics. Data from GISP are used to develop treatment recommendations before widespread treatment failures can adversely impact individual patients and become a major public health problem. Effective treatment of *N. gonorrhoeae* remains the central component of prevention and control of this organism.[10]

When discussing treatment options, several principles must be considered. Patients infected with *N. gonorrhoeae* are often coinfected with *C. trachomatis*. This has led to the recommendation that patients treated for gonococcal infections also receive treatment with a regimen effective against uncomplicated *C. trachomatis* infection. This can be cost effective, and some specialists believe the practice has resulted in substantial decreases in the prevalence of chlamydial infections.[4]

Using GISP, the CDC tracked the emergence of fluoroquinolone-resistant *N. gonorrhoeae* (QRNG) in the United States. QRNG initially emerged in Asia during the early 1990s. It was sporadically seen in the United States until the early 2000s when it initially emerged in Hawaii and California. Men who have sex with men (MSM) were disproportionately infected. By 2007, the prevalence of QRNG in the United States exceeded 5 percent of GISP isolates. The cephalosporins remained the treatment of choice for *N. gonorrhoeae* in the 2010 CDC STD treatment guidelines.[10]

Cephalosporin resistance was initially noted in Asia during the 2000s and later in Europe. Through GISP, the CDC documented cephalosporin resistance in the United States, specifically an increase in the minimum inhibitory concentrations

(MIC) of cefixime. The increases were most pronounced in isolates from MSM in the same regions where QRNG emerged in the United States.[10]

Treatment of *N. gonorrhoeae* is complicated by cephalosporin resistance, and particularly by resistance to ceftriaxone. Because previously recommended treatment regimens may no longer be effective, the CDC published a major change in its treatment guidelines on February 15, 2013. The preferred regimen is ceftriaxone (IM) for one dose plus azithromycin PO for one dose or doxycycline for 7 days. The alternative regimen for urogenital or rectal *N. gonorrhoeae* is as follows: (1) if ceftriaxone is not available, cefixime PO for one dose plus azithromycin PO for one dose or doxycycline PO bid for 7 days; (2) if the patient has a severe cephalosporin allergy, azithromycin PO for one dose. Laboratories that detect cephalosporin isolates with an MIC >0.25 μg/mL for cefixime or an MIC >0.125 μg/mL for ceftriaxone should promptly notify the ordering clinician and the local STD control program.[10]

Patients with gonococcal infection who are coinfected with HIV should receive the same treatment regimen as those who do not have HIV.[4]

For pharyngeal gonorrhea, the CDC recommends a single intramuscular dose of ceftriaxone plus azithromycin PO for one dose or doxycycline PO daily for 7 days.[4]

In the pregnant patient, the use of a cephalosporin-based regimen is recommended. Because spectinomycin is no longer available in the United States, azithromycin PO can be considered for women who cannot tolerate a cephalosporin. Either azithromycin or amoxicillin is recommended for treatment of presumptive or diagnosed *C. trachomatis* infection during pregnancy.[4]

In patients with gonococcal conjunctivitis, a single dose of ceftriaxone is recommended. A one-time saline lavage of the infected eye should be considered. Patients treated for gonococcal conjunctivitis should also be treated presumptively for concurrent *C. trachomatis* infection.[4]

In patients with evidence of disseminated gonococcal infections, petechial or pustular acral lesions, asymmetrical arthralgia, tenosynovitis, or septic arthritis, the recommended regimen is ceftriaxone (1 g intravenous [IV] daily). Alternative regimens include cefotaxime and ceftizoxime. If unable to use cephalosporins, spectinomycin would be acceptable. All of the preceding regimens should be continued for 24 to 48 hours after improvement is observed, at which time the patient may be switched to cefixime to complete a full 7 days of antibiotic therapy. In patients with gonococcal endocarditis, treatment with ceftriaxone (IV every 12 hours for at least 4 weeks) is recommended, and in patients with meningitis, treatment for 10 to 14 days is advised.[4]

Infected mothers may transmit *N. gonorrhoeae* to the newborn in utero, perinatally, or in the postpartum period. Gonococcal conjunctivitis of the newborn (ophthalmia neonatorum) is the most commonly recognized manifestation. The most important preventative measure is routine screening and treatment of pregnant women for gonorrhea before delivery. Ocular prophylaxis using erythromycin opthalmic ointment 0.5 percent in each eye is recommended for all neonates because it can prevent sight-threatening gonococcal ophthalmia and because it is safe, easy to administer, and inexpensive. Erythromycin is the only antibiotic ointment currently recommended for use in neonates. Although used in the past, silver nitrate and tetracycline ophthalmic ointment are no longer available in the United States. Bacitracin is not effective and povidone iodine has not been studied adequately. If erythromycin ointment is not available, infants at risk for exposure to N. gonorrhoeae (especially those born to a mother with untreated gonococcal infection or who have received no prenatal care) can be administered ceftriaxone. Nongonococcal causes of neonatal ophthalmia include Moraxella catarrhalis, and other Neisseria species that are indistinguishable from N. gonorrhoeae on a Gram stain. The treatment of choice is ceftriaxone. Topical antibiotic treatment alone is not adequate to treat established infections and is unnecessary if systemic treatment is instituted.[4]

Patients with uncomplicated N. gonorrhoeae who are treated with one of the recommended or alternative regimens do not need to routinely return for a test or cure. Patients with symptoms that persist after treatment or whose symptoms recur shortly after treatment with a recommended or alternative regimen should have a culture for N. gonorrhoeae, and any gonococci that are isolated should be tested for antimicrobial susceptibility. The clinicians and laboratories should report treatment failures or resistant gonococcal isolates to the CDC through the state and local public health authorities.[8]

Because the majority of infections identified after treatment with one of the recommended regimens result from reinfection, rather than treatment failure, clinicians should consider advising all patients with N. gonorrhoeae to be retested 3 months after treatment. If patients do not return for retesting in 3 months, providers are encouraged to test these patients whenever they next seek medical care within the following 12 months, regardless of whether the patient believes his or her sex partners were treated. Retesting is different from test of cure to detect therapeutic failure, which is not recommended.[4]

There is a need for patient education and referral and treatment of sex partners. Persistent urethritis, cervicitis, or proctitis may be caused by C. trachomatis and other organisms.[4]

All sex partners of a patient with diagnosed N. gonorrhoeae or C. trachomatis should be evaluated and treated if their last sexual encounter was within 60 days before the onset of symptoms or diagnosis of the index patient. If a patient's last sexual intercourse was more than 60 days before diagnosis or the onset of symptoms, the patient's most recent sex partner should be treated. Expedited partner therapy is a potential mechanism for treating heterosexual partners of patients infected with N. gonorrhoeae in certain jurisdictions.[5] If this strategy is employed, educational materials should also be provided to the partner in addition to a prescription or the actual antimicrobial. Partner-delivered therapy currently is not recommended for homosexual males. The patients and their sex partners should be instructed to avoid sexual intercourse until the therapy is completed and they no longer have symptoms.[4]

The recommended infection prevention measures include Standard Precautions.[7]

Genital and Anal Warts (Condyloma Acuminatum): Human Papillomavirus

Human papillomavirus (HPV) is the most common sexually transmitted viral disease in the United States.[11] It is estimated that more than 50 percent of sexually active persons become infected at least once in their lifetime. More than 100 types of HPV exist, of which, more than 40 types can infect the genital area. The majority of HPV infections are asymptomatic, unrecognized, or subclinical. HPV usually is self-limited and occurs more frequently than visible genital warts among both men and women and cervical cell changes among women.[5] A recently developed vaccine should decrease the sequelae of infection with HPV.[4]

Certain types of HPV (e.g., types 6 and 11) cause genital and anal warts. Other HPV types in the anogenital region (e.g., types 16, 18, 31, 33, and 35) have been strongly associated with cervical tumors.[4]

Typical genital warts are single or multiple soft, fleshy, papillary or sessile, painless growths around the anus, vulva-vaginal area, penis, urethra, or perineum. Most HPV infections are asymptomatic, subclinical, or unrecognized.[4] In circumcised men, the penile shaft is the most common site of lesions, and the preputial cavity is involved in 85 to 90 percent of the cases. Most lesions in women are found over the posterior introitus and, less frequently, on the labia and the clitoris, as well as the perineum, vagina, anus, cervix, and urethra.[9] In addition, to the external genitalia (i.e., penis, vulva, scrotum, perineum, and perianal skin), genital warts can occur on the uterine cervix and in the vagina, urethra, anus, and mouth. Intra-anal warts are observed predominantly in patients who have had receptive anal intercourse. These warts are distinct from perianal warts, which can occur in men and women who do not have a history of anal sex. HPV types 6 and 11 have also been associated with conjunctival, nasal, oral, and laryngeal warts. Genital warts are usually asymptomatic, but depending on the size and anatomic location, genital warts can be painful, friable, or pruritic.[4]

Complications and sequelae of HPV infection include tissue destruction from enlarging lesions. During pregnancy, the warts are extremely vascular and can enlarge and possibly cause obstruction of the birth canal, necessitating cesarean section. Malignant transformation of anal condylomata may occur.[11]

A presumptive diagnosis is based on clinical appearance. Condyloma latum (secondary syphilis) can be excluded by obtaining dark-field examination or serologic tests for syphilis or both. Some providers with experience and expertise treating genital warts find it useful to apply 3 to 5 percent acetic acid. This usually turns HPV-infected genital mucosal tissue to a whitish color. Acetic acid application is not a specific test for HPV infection, and the specificity and sensitivity of this procedure for screening have not been defined. Therefore, the routine use of this procedure for screening to detect HPV infection is not recommended.[4]

HPV tests that detect viral nucleic acid (i.e., DNA or RNA) or capsid protein are available for women over 30 years of age undergoing cervical cancer screening. The four tests approved by the FDA for use in the United States are the HC II High-Risk HPV test (Qiagen), HC II Low-Risk HPV test (Qiagen), Cervista HPV 16/18 test, and Cervista HPV High-Risk test (Hologics). These tests should not be used for men, for women under 20 years of age, or as a general test for STDs.[4] The use of HPV DNA testing should supplement, not replace, Pap testing.[12]

Women with HPV infection on such testing should be counseled that HPV infection is common, infection is frequently transmitted between partners, and that infection usually goes away on its own. If any Pap test or biopsy abnormalities have been observed, further evaluation is recommended. Screening women or men with the HPV test, outside of the above recommendations for use of the test with cervical cancer screening, is not recommended.[4]

Vaginal or cervical warts are often found only by culdoscopy or Pap test. Subclinical infection often is diagnosed indirectly on the cervix by Pap test, colposcopy, or biopsy results, and on the penis, vulva, and other genital skin by the appearance of white areas after application of acetic acid. Histologic changes suggestive of HPV infection can be demonstrated with Pap smear testing.[4]

The diagnosis can be confirmed by biopsy, but this is rarely needed. A biopsy should be obtained if the diagnosis is uncertain; the lesions do not respond to standard therapy; the disease worsens during standard therapy; the patient is immunocompromised; or the warts are pigmented, indurated, fixed, or ulcerated.[4]

The primary goal of treatment is to remove visible warts. Treatment can result in wart-free periods for many patients. The treatment selected is based on patient preference, available resources, and provider experience. There is no ideal treatment for all patients and no evidence to suggest that any one treatment is superior to the others. Treatment does not completely eliminate the risk of transmission but can lessen it. Untreated warts may remain unchanged, resolve spontaneously, or increase in size or number.[4]

The recommended treatments for external genital warts are either patient-applied or provider-administered. For patient-applied treatments, the patient must be able to identify and reach the warts to be treated. Recommended patient-applied treatments include podofilox (0.5 percent solution or gel bid for 3 days followed by 4 days of no therapy if the total wart area does not exceed 10 cm^2 and the total volume of podofilox is limited to 0.5 mL/day [treatment may be repeated for a total of four cycles; safety during pregnancy has not been established]); or imiquimod (5 percent cream at bedtime 3 times a week for as long as 16 weeks [safety during pregnancy has not been established]). The recommended provider-administered regimens include cryotherapy with liquid nitrogen or cryoprobe (application can be repeated every 1 to 2 weeks) or podophyllin (10 to 25 percent in a compound tincture of benzoin, repeated weekly if necessary if the total wart area does not exceed 10 cm^2 and the total volume of podophyllin is limited to 0.5 mL/day [safety during pregnancy has not been established]); trichloroacetic acid (TCA) or bichloracetic acid (BCA) (80 to 90 percent); or surgical removal via tangential scissor excision, tangential shave excision, curettage, or electrosurgery. Alternative treatments for external genital warts include intralesional interferon or laser surgery. For women with cervical warts, high-grade squamous intraepithelial lesions must be ruled out by colposcopy and a biopsy before treatment. A specialist with expertise in squamous intraepithelial lesions should provide care for these patients.[4]

Options for the treatment of vaginal warts include cryotherapy with liquid nitrogen (the use of a cryoprobe is not recommended in the vagina because of the risk of vaginal perforation or fistula formation), or TCA or BCA (80 to 90 percent) applied to the warts (can be repeated weekly).[4]

The recommended treatment for accessible meatal warts is cryotherapy with liquid nitrogen or podophyllin (10 to 25 percent in compound tincture of benzoin), which can be repeated weekly if necessary (safety during pregnancy has not been established). Although data are limited, some specialists also recommend using podofilox and imiquimod to treat distal meatal warts. Anal warts that are accessible by anoscope may be treated with cryotherapy with liquid nitrogen or with TCA or BCA (80 to 90 percent), which can be repeated weekly if necessary, or by surgical removal. Patients with warts on the rectal mucosa should be provided care in consultation with a specialist.[4]

Immunocompromised or HIV-infected patients may not have good response to HPV therapy and may experience more frequent recurrences. Squamous cell carcinomas occur more frequently among immunosuppressed persons and may arise in or resemble genital warts; therefore, a biopsy is recommended to confirm the diagnosis.[4]

The treatment of genital warts in pregnant women needs to take into consideration the potential adverse effects of some of the medications on the fetus, the risk of perinatal transmission, and potential mechanical obstruction of the vagina. The treatment options for pregnant women are more limited than for other patients. Imiquimod, podophyllin, and podofilox should not be used during pregnancy. Because genital warts can proliferate and become friable during pregnancy, many specialists advocate their removal during pregnancy. HPV types 6 and 11 have been documented to cause respiratory papillomatosis in infants and children via an incompletely understood mechanism. The value of a cesarean section in preventing respiratory papillomatosis is unknown; thus, a cesarean section should not be performed solely to prevent transmission of HPV infection to the newborn. However, a cesarean section may be indicated for women with genital warts if the wart(s) obstruct the pelvic outlet or if vaginal delivery would result in excessive bleeding.[4]

Posttreatment follow-up after visible genital warts have cleared is not mandatory but may be helpful. Patients should be advised to watch for recurrences, which occur most frequently during the first 3 months. Because the sensitivity and specificity of self-diagnosis of genital warts are unknown, patients concerned about recurrences should be offered a follow-up evaluation 3 months after treatment. Earlier follow-up visits also may be useful for some patients to document the absence of warts, monitor for or treat complications of therapy, and provide an additional opportunity for patient education and counseling. Women should be counseled to undergo regular Pap screening as recommended for women without genital warts. The presence of genital warts is not an indication for a change in the frequency of Pap tests or for cervical colposcopy.[4]

Two HPV vaccines are licensed in the United States. Cervarix is a bivalent vaccine containing HPV types 16 and 18. Gardasil is a quadrivalent vaccine that includes HPV types 6, 11, 16, and 18. Both vaccines offer protection against the HPV types that cause 70 percent of cervical cancers (i.e., types 16 and 18). Gardasil also protects against the types that cause 90 percent of genital warts (i.e., types 6 and 11). Either vaccine can be administered to girls aged 11 to 12 years and can be administered to those as young as 9 years of age. Girls and women aged 13 to 26 years who have not started or completed the vaccine series also should receive the vaccine. HPV vaccine is indicated for girls in this age group because benefit is greatest if it is administered before the onset of sexual activity. Gardasil can also be used in males aged 9 to 26 years to prevent genital warts. Administering the vaccine to boys before the onset of sexual activity is optimal. Both HPV vaccines are administered as a three-dose series of IM injections over a 6-month period with the second and third doses given 1 to 2 and then 6 months after the first dose. Ideally, the same vaccine product should be used for the entire three-dose series.[4] HPV vaccination is not recommended for pregnant women but can be safely administered to breastfeeding mothers. Because it contains no infectious particles, the vaccine is safe in immunocompromised persons.[12] HPV vaccination is available for eligible children and adolescents under 19 years of age through the Vaccines for Children (VFC) program (available by calling CDC INFO [800-232-4636]). Women who received an HPV vaccine should continue routine cervical cancer screening because 30 percent of cervical cancers are caused by HPV types other than 16 or 18.[4]

A positive HPV DNA test result might cause partner concerns, worry about disclosure, and feelings of guilt, anger, and stigmatization. Counseling patients is important. Resources available to patients include pamphlets, hotlines (such as the CDC National STD/HIV Hotline 800-227-8922), and websites.[5] (See Supplemental Resources.) The information should be provided in a neutral, nonstigmatizing context and emphasize that HPV is common, asymptomatic, and transient. Specific counseling messages should include the following:

- Genital HPV infection is caused by a virus that is common among sexually active adults.[4]

- Infection is usually sexually transmitted. Because the incubation period is variable, it is often difficult to determine the source of infection.[4]

- Within ongoing relationships, the sexual partner is usually infected by the time a patient is diagnosed, though there may be no symptoms or signs of infection.

- Because genital HPV is common among persons who have been sexually active, and because the duration of infectivity is unknown, the value of disclosing a past diagnosis of genital HPV infection to future partners is unclear.

- Candid discussions about other STDs should be encouraged and attempted whenever possible.

- The likelihood of transmission to future partners and the duration of infectivity after treatment are unknown. The use of latex condoms has been associated with a lower rate of cervical cancer, an HPV-associated disease.[4]

- The types of HPV that usually cause external genital warts are not associated with cancer.[4]

- Recurrence of genital warts within the first several months after treatment is common and usually indicates recurrence rather than reinfection.[4]

Women with high-risk HPV infections should be counseled about partner notification and provided with information that is individualized based on the patient's circumstances. Some women might benefit from having their partners included in an informed discussion about their diagnosis. Although there is no evidence that supports partner notification or partner clinical evaluation, referral for partners of patients with high-risk HPV might be appropriate and can include the following information:

- The immune system clears HPV infection most of the time.[4]

- In some persons, HPV infection does not resolve.[4]

- HPV is very common and usually has no symptoms.[4]

- It can infect the genital areas of both men and women.[4]

- Most sexually active persons get HPV at some time in their lives, though most will never know it.[4]

- Even persons with only one lifetime sex partner can get HPV if their partner was infected.[4]

- The most common manifestation of HPV infection in men is genital warts.[4]

- Partners who are in a long-term relationship tend to share HPV. Sexual partners of HPV-infected patients also likely have HPV, though they might have no signs or symptoms of infection.[4]

- Detection of high-risk HPV infection in a woman does not mean that the woman or her partner is engaging in sexual activity outside of a relationship.[4]

Prevention measures for current and subsequent sex partners and risk reduction should also be discussed. This includes counseling women about condom use if appropriate depending on their current circumstances. Consistent male condom use by partners of sexually active women can reduce the risk for cervical and vulvovaginal HPV infection. Condom use by couples in long-term partnerships may decrease the time required to clear the woman's HPV infection. Skin not covered by a condom remains vulnerable to HPV infection. HPV vaccines are available and recommended for girls and young women aged 9 to 26 years, even in those who have been diagnosed with HPV infection. Male partners can be vaccinated with Gardasil to prevent genital warts.[4]

Routine screening and treatment of sex partners is not indicated. However, partners may benefit from recommending assessment for genital warts and other STDs and from counseling about HIV infection. The female sexual partners of a person with genital warts should be reminded that cytological screening for cervical cancer is recommended for all sexually active women.[4]

The recommended infection prevention measures include Standard Precautions.[7]

Herpes Genitalis

Genital herpes or herpes simplex is a chronic, lifelong viral infection caused by *Herpesvirus hominis*. This virus, known as HSV, is a DNA virus for which humans appear to be the only natural reservoir. Two types of HSV have been identified: HSV-1 and HSV-2. The majority of cases of recurrent genital herpes are caused by HSV-2, though HSV-1 may become more common as a cause of first-episode genital herpes. At least 50 million people in the United States have genital HSV infection.[4,13] The increase in the number of office visits for genital HSV suggests a growing incidence of genital herpes.[1] The principal mode of transmission is direct mucous membrane contact with infected secretions. (HSV-1 is transmitted primarily by contact with oral secretions and HSV-2 by contact with genital secretions.) Persons unaware that they have the infection or who have no symptoms when transmission occurs transmit the majority of genital herpes infections. The majority of people infected with HSV-2 have not had a diagnosis of genital herpes. Many such persons have mild or unrecognized infections but shed virus intermittently in the genital tract.[4,13] Counseling regarding the natural history of genital herpes, sexual and perinatal transmission, and methods to reduce transmission is integral to clinical management.[4]

The incubation period is 2 to 12 days.[11] Single or multiple vesicles appear anywhere on the genitalia. Typically, patients have bilateral lesions of the external genitalia. Vesicles may appear on an erythematous base and spontaneously rupture to form shallow ulcers. The lesions resolve spontaneously without scarring. The first occurrence is termed "primary infection." Primary infection has a mean duration of 12 days and may be associated with fever, malaise, anorexia, and tender bilateral inguinal adenopathy. Lesions of primary genital herpes can persist for several weeks in some patients. Approximately two-thirds of patients have subsequent, usually milder, recurrences. Recurrent infection is often preceded by prodromal symptoms such as pain, burning, tingling, or itching; the mean duration of recurrence is 4 to 5 days. The 1-year recurrence rate for the first episode of HSV-2 is 90 percent, whereas that for HSV-1 is 55 percent.[13]

Complications and sequelae of genital herpes can be due to local extension or spread beyond the genital region. Neuralgia, meningitis, ascending myelitis, urethral stricture, urinary retention, and secondary bacterial infection can occur. In neonates, virus from an active genital infection may be transmitted during vaginal delivery, causing neonatal herpes infection. Neonatal herpes infection can range from a mild localized infection to a fatal disseminated infection.[13] The evaluation of all patients who have genital ulcers should include serologic testing for syphilis and a diagnostic evaluation for HSV. *Haemophilus ducreyi* should be searched for in areas with high prevalence of chancroid. The specific tests utilized in the evaluation of genital ulcers include dark-field microscopy or a direct immunofluorescence test for *Treponema pallidum*, culture or antigen tests for HSV, and *H. ducreyi* culture. If the *T. pallidum* studies are initially negative, some experts would recommend three consecutive monthly serologic syphilis tests. All patients should be tested for HIV at the time of diagnosis because patients with genital ulcerations are at increased risk for HIV infection.[4]

The diagnosis of genital herpes should be confirmed by laboratory testing because the clinical diagnosis of genital herpes is both insensitive and nonspecific. The classic painful multiple vesicular or ulcerative lesions are absent in many infected persons. Therefore, the diagnosis of genital herpes should be confirmed by laboratory testing and also because both type-specific and nontype specific antibodies to HSV develop during the first several weeks after infection and persist indefinitely; virologic tests and type-specific antibody tests should be done. Both laboratory-based and point-of-care tests for HSV-2 antibodies are available from capillary blood or serum during a clinic visit. The sensitivities of these tests vary from 80 to 98 percent and the specificities are at least 96 percent. False-negative results might be more frequent at early stages of infection. False-positive results can occur, especially in patients with a low likelihood of HSV infection. Repeat or confirmatory testing may be indicated in some settings, especially if recent genital herpes infection is suspected. Immunoglobulin M (IgM) testing for HSV is not useful because the IgM tests are not type specific and might be positive during recurrent episodes of herpes.[4]

Cell culture and PCR is the preferred HSV test. PCR assays for HSV DNA are the preferred test, as it is more sensitive than viral culture. Viral culture has a low sensitivity, especially if the lesions are recurrent, and the sensitivity decreases rapidly as the lesions heal. PCR is the test of choice for detecting HSV in spinal fluid to diagnose central nervous system (CNS) HSV infection. Viral culture isolates should be typed to determine which type of HSV is causing the infection. It should be noted that because the virus sheds intermittently, not detecting HSV by culture or PCR does not indicate an absence of HSV infection. Cytologic detection of cellular changes of HSV infection should not be used because it is an insensitive and nonspecific method of diagnosis. This is true both for genital lesions (i.e., Tzanck preparation) and for cervical Pap smears.[4]

Type-specific HSV serologic assays might be useful in the following scenarios: (1) recurrent genital symptoms or atypical symptoms with negative HSV cultures; (2) a clinical diagnosis of genital herpes without laboratory confirmation; or (3) a partner with genital herpes. HSV serologic testing should be considered for persons presenting for an STD evaluation (especially for persons with multiple sex partners), persons with HIV infection, and MSM with behaviors or conditions that increase risk for HIV acquisition. Screening for HSV-1 and HSV-2 in the general population is not indicated. Because nearly all HSV-2 infections are sexually acquired, the presence of type-specific HSV-2 antibody implies anogenital infection. These patients should be given education and counseling appropriate for persons with genital herpes. The presence of HSV-1 antibody alone is more difficult to interpret. Most persons with HSV-1 antibody have oral HSV infection acquired during childhood, which might be asymptomatic. Lack of symptoms in an HSV-1 seropositive person does not differentiate between anogenital, orolabial, or cutaneous infection. However, persons infected with HSV-1 are at increased risk for acquiring HSV-2.[4]

Although there is no known cure for genital herpes, antiviral chemotherapy provides clinical benefits to the majority of patients with symptoms and is the mainstay of management. Systemic antiviral drugs partially control the symptoms and signs of herpes episodes when used to treat first clinical episodes and recurrent episodes or when used as a daily suppressive therapy. Three antiviral medications have been shown to provide clinical benefit for genital herpes: acyclovir, valacyclovir, and famciclovir. Topical therapy with antiviral drugs gives minimal clinical benefit and is not recommended.[4]

The treatment recommendations for primary infection begin with a careful history that should be obtained to establish that this is the patient's first episode of genital herpes. The recommended regimens include acyclovir (400 mg PO bid for 7 to 10 days); acyclovir (200 mg PO five times a day for 7 to 10 days); famciclovir (250 mg PO bid for 7 to 10 days); or valacyclovir (1 g PO bid for 7 to 10 days). Allergic and other adverse reactions to acyclovir, valacyclovir, and famciclovir are uncommon. Acyclovir desensitization has been described. If healing is incomplete after 10 days of treatment, therapy can be extended.[4]

Most patients with an asymptomatic first episode of genital HSV-2 infection will have recurrent episodes of genital lesions. Because many patients with mild or infrequent outbreaks may benefit from antiviral therapy, treatment options should be discussed with all patients. Episodic antiviral therapy can shorten the duration of lesions. Effective treatment for recurrent genital herpes requires that treatment start during the prodrome or within 1 day after the onset of lesions. The patient should be provided with a supply of medication or a prescription for the medication with instructions on how to start treatment at the first sign of prodrome or genital lesions. The recommended regimens for episodic recurrent infection include acyclovir; famciclovir; or valacyclovir.[4]

Continuous suppressive therapy should be discussed with all patients with HSV-2 infection because recurrence is very common. Suppressive therapy decreases the rate of recurrence and reduces, but does not eliminate, subclinical viral shedding. The recommended regimens for daily suppressive therapy use the same drugs as in the treatment of episodic recurrent infections. Valacyclovir may be less effective than other valacyclovir- or acyclovir-dosing regimens for patients who have 10 or more recurrent episodes per year.[4]

IV therapy should be provided for patients with severe disease or complications requiring hospitalization (e.g., disseminated infection, pneumonitis, hepatitis, or encephalitis). The recommended regimen is acyclovir (IV every 8 hours for 2 to 7 days or until clinical improvement is attained), followed by oral antiviral agents to complete a proscribed course of therapy. The dose of acyclovir may need to be adjusted for patients with renal impairment.[4]

HSV lesions are common among persons infected with HIV. The lesions may be painful, severe, and atypical. Episodic or suppressive therapy with oral agents is often beneficial. The recommended regimens for episodic infection include acyclovir; famciclovir; or valacyclovir. The recommended regimens for daily suppressive therapy include acyclovir; famciclovir; or valacyclovir. For severe cases, treatment may need to be initiated with perinatal acyclovir. If lesions persist or recur during treatment, HSV resistance should be suspected. A viral isolate should then be obtained for sensitivity testing, and the patient should be treated in consultation with a specialist. All acyclovir-resistant strains are resistant to valacyclovir, and most are resistant to famciclovir. Foscarnet is often effective for the treatment of acyclovir-resistant genital herpes. Topical cidofovir gel also may be effective. This preparation is not commercially available and must be compounded at a pharmacy.[4]

Counseling of infected patients and their sex partners is important to help patients cope with infection and to prevent sexual and perinatal transmission. Initial counseling is provided at the first visit. However, patients need to learn about the chronic aspects of genital herpes after the initial episode subsides. Patients can be referred to many resources, including the

CDC National STD/HIV hotline.[4] Specific counseling messages should include the following components:

- The natural history of genital herpes infection should be explained with emphasis on the potential for recurrent episodes, asymptomatic viral shedding, and sexual transmission.[4]

- During the first episode, patients should be advised that effective suppressive and episodic treatments are available for preventing or shortening the duration of recurrent episodes.[4]

- Asymptomatic persons diagnosed with HSV-2 infection by type-specific serologic testing should receive the same counseling messages as persons with symptomatic infection. In addition, they should be taught about the clinical manifestations of genital herpes.[4]

- Patients should be advised to abstain from sexual contact with uninfected partners while lesions or prodromal symptoms are present.[4]

- Latex condoms used consistently and properly may offer some protection if the infected areas are covered and protected by the condom. Condoms have been effective in preventing male-to-female transmission.[4]

- All patients with HSV infection should be encouraged to tell their current sex partners that they have genital herpes and to inform future sex partners before starting a sexual relationship.[4]

- Patients need to be advised that transmission of HSV can also occur during the asymptomatic periods. Asymptomatic shedding is more common for HSV-2 than HSV-1. Viral shedding is most frequent during the first 12 months of infection with HSV-2.[4]

- The risk of HSV-2 sexual transmission can be decreased by the daily use of valacyclovir by the infected person.[4]

- Sex partners, even those with no symptoms, should be advised that they may be infected. They should be offered type-specific testing.[4]

The risk for neonatal infection should be explained to all patients, including men. Pregnant women and women of childbearing age who have genital herpes should inform their obstetrical providers and those who will care for their newborn infant. Pregnant women who are not infected with HSV-2 should be advised to avoid intercourse during the third trimester with men who have genital herpes. Similarly, pregnant women who are not infected with HSV-1 should be counseled to avoid genital exposure to HSV-1 during the third trimester (e.g., oral sex with a partner with oral herpes and vaginal intercourse with a partner with genital HSV-1 infection).[4]

Sexual partners with asymptomatic HSV-2, as diagnosed by type-specific testing, should also receive these counseling messages. They should also be taught about the clinical manifestations of genital herpes.[4]

Sex partners are likely to benefit from evaluation and counseling. Symptomatic sex partners should be evaluated and treated the same way as patients with genital lesions. Sex partners with no symptoms should be questioned about genital lesions, encouraged to recognize symptoms, and offered type-specific serologic testing for HSV infection.[4]

HIV-infected persons may have prolonged or severe episodes of genital, perianal, or oral herpes. These patients may have severe, painful, and atypical lesions. HSV shedding is increased in HIV-infected persons. Although antiretroviral therapy reduces the severity and frequency of symptomatic genital herpes, frequent subclinical shedding still occurs. Clinical manifestations of genital herpes might worsen during immune reconstitution after initiation of antiretroviral therapy.[4]

Suppressive or episodic therapy with oral antiviral agents is effective in decreasing the clinical manifestations of HSV among HIV-positive persons. The extent to which suppressive antiviral therapy will decrease HSV transmission from this population is unknown. HSV type-specific serologies can be offered to HIV-positive persons during their initial evaluation if infection status is unknown, and suppressive antiviral therapy can be considered in those who have HSV-2 infection. The daily recommended suppressive therapy for HIV-infected persons is acyclovir, famciclovir, or valacyclovir. The recommended episodic therapy is acyclovir for 5 to 10 days, famciclovir for 5 to 10 days, or valacyclovir 5 to 10 days.[4]

If lesions persist or recur in an HIV-infected patient receiving antiviral treatment, HSV resistance should be suspected. A viral isolate should be obtained for sensitivity testing. These patients should be managed in consultation with an HIV specialist, and alternate therapy should be administered. All acyclovir-resistant strains are resistant to valacyclovir, and the majority are also resistant to famciclovir. Foscarnet, every 8 hours until clinical resolution is attained, is frequently effective to treat acyclovir-resistant genital herpes. Intravenous cidofovir once weekly might also be effective. Imiquimod is a topical alternative, as is topical cidofovir gel 1 percent, which is not commercially available and must be compounded at a pharmacy. These topical preparations should be applied to the lesions once daily for 5 consecutive days.[4]

Most babies who acquire neonatal herpes are born to mothers who lack histories of clinically evident genital herpes. The risk for perinatal transmission is high (30 to 50 percent) among women who acquire genital herpes near the time of delivery. The risk of perinatal transmission is low (≤ 1 percent) among women with histories of recurrent herpes at term or those who acquire genital HSV during the first half of pregnancy. Prevention of neonatal herpes depends on preventing acquisition of genital HSV infection during late pregnancy and avoiding exposure of the infant to herpetic lesions during delivery.[4]

Pregnant women in the third trimester without known genital herpes should be counseled to avoid intercourse with partners known or suspected of having genital herpes and to avoid cunnilingus with partners known or suspected to have orolabial herpes. Some specialists believe that type-specific serologic tests may be used to identify pregnant women at risk for HSV infection and to guide counseling with regard to the risk of acquiring genital herpes during pregnancy. Such testing and counseling may be especially important when a woman's sexual partner has HSV infection.[4]

All pregnant women should be asked whether they have a history of genital herpes. At the onset of labor, all women should be questioned carefully about symptoms of genital herpes, including prodrome, and should be examined carefully for herpetic lesions. Women without symptoms or signs of genital herpes or its prodrome can deliver vaginally. Most specialists recommend that women with recurrent genital herpetic lesions at the onset of labor should be delivered by cesarean section to prevent neonatal herpes. However, such delivery does not eliminate the risk for HSV transmission to the infant completely. Routine viral cultures of pregnant women with recurrent genital herpes are not recommended for those with or without visible herpetic lesions because they do not predict viral shedding at the time of delivery.[4]

The safety of systemic acyclovir, valacyclovir, and famciclovir therapy in pregnant women has not been established. Acyclovir may be administered orally to pregnant women with a first episode of genital herpes or severe recurrent herpes and should be administered intravenously to pregnant women with severe HSV infection. Preliminary data suggest that acyclovir treatment late in pregnancy may reduce the frequency of cesarean sections among women who have recurrent genital herpes by diminishing the frequency of recurrences at term. Some specialists recommend this treatment. Because the risk for herpes is high for infants of women who acquire genital HSV in late pregnancy, these women should be treated in consultation with an HSV specialist. Some specialists recommend acyclovir therapy in this circumstance; some recommend routine cesarean section to reduce the risk for neonatal herpes; and others recommend both.[4]

Infants exposed to HSV during birth, as documented by virologic testing or presumed by observation of lesions, should be followed up carefully in consultation with a specialist. Some specialists recommend that these infants have surveillance cultures of mucosal surfaces to detect HSV infection before clinical signs of neonatal herpes develop. Some specialists also recommend the use of acyclovir for infants born to women who acquired HSV near term because the risk for neonatal herpes is high for these infants.[4]

All infants who have evidence of neonatal herpes should be promptly evaluated and treated with systemic acyclovir. The recommended regimen for infants treated for known or suspected neonatal herpes is acyclovir (20 mg/kg body weight IV every 8 hours for 21 days for disseminated and CNS disease or 14 days for disease limited to the skin and mucous membranes).[4]

The recommended infection prevention measures include Standard Precautions and in some instances Standard Precautions plus Contact Precautions. The Standard Precautions plus Contact Precautions are recommended for persons with disseminated HSV and severe primary HSV or neonatal HSV until the lesions are dry and crusted. Standard Precautions are recommended for patients with mucocutaneous recurrent (skin, oral, genital) lesions.[7]

Chancroid

Chancroid is a sexually transmitted genital ulcerative disease with worldwide distribution. It is caused by *Haemophilus ducreyi*. The prevalence of chancroid is decreasing worldwide and in the United States. Chancroid usually occurs in outbreaks but is endemic in some areas. An estimated 10 percent of people who acquire chancroid in the United States are coinfected with HSV or *T. pallidum*. An even higher percentage of persons infected outside the United States are coinfected with HSV or *T. pallidum*.[4] Chancroid is most frequently found in uncircumcised non-Caucasian men. Women account for only 10 percent of reported cases.[14]

The incubation period is usually 5 to 7 days but may vary from 1 to several weeks. Men frequently present with one ulcer, whereas women frequently have multiple lesions. The lesions are generally confined to the genital area and perineum. A typical lesion begins as a tender papule with surrounding erythema. This papule soon becomes pustular and evolves to form a painful, sharply demarcated, nonindurated ulcer. The ulcer may be necrotic or may be surrounded by an erythematous halo. Accompanying adenopathy is usually unilateral. A characteristic inguinal bubo occurs in 50 to 60 percent of cases. The most common clinical manifestation among heterosexual men is tender unilateral inguinal or femoral lymphadenopathy. Women and homosexually active men may have proctocolitis or inflammatory involvement of perirectal or perianal lymphatic tissues that can result in fistulas and strictures. There is no asymptomatic carrier state. Chancroid has been associated with an increased risk of heterosexual HIV transmission.[14] Patients should be tested for HIV infection at the time chancroid is diagnosed.[4]

A probable diagnosis of chancroid can be made for clinical and surveillance purposes and is based on meeting all of the following criteria: (1) the patient has one or more painful genital ulcers; (2) the patient has no evidence of *T. pallidum* infection by dark-field examination of ulcer exudate or serologic test for syphilis performed at least 7 days after the onset of ulcers; (3) typical clinical presentation of genital ulcers, if present, and regional lymphadenopathy are typical for chancroid; and (4) a test for HSV performed on the ulcer exudate is negative. The combination of a painful ulcer and tender inguinal adenopathy, with supportive inguinal adenopathy, is almost pathognomonic. A definitive diagnosis requires identification of *H. ducreyi* by smear and culture of the lesion or bubo aspirate; Gram stain preparations may show Gram-negative coccobacilli in chains ("school of fish"). The special culture media for *H. ducreyi* is not widely available commercially and has a sensitivity of less than 80 percent. There is no FDA-approved PCR test for *H. ducreyi*. However, some commercial laboratories have developed their own PCR tests.[4]

The recommended treatment for chancroid is azithromycin; ceftriaxone; ciprofloxacin (contraindicated in pregnant and lactating women); or erythromycin base. The advantage of azithromycin and ceftriaxone is single-dose therapy. Patients who are circumcised respond better to treatment than do uncircumcised patients. Worldwide, some isolates with intermediate resistance to ciprofloxacin or erythromycin have been reported. Antimicrobial susceptibility testing should be performed on *H. ducreyi* that is isolated from patients who do not experience response to recommended therapies.[4]

HIV-infected patients with chancroid are more likely to have more slowly healing ulcers. They may require a longer course of treatment, and treatment failure can occur with any of the recommended regimens. Some specialists recommend a 7-day course of erythromycin for HIV-infected persons. There are limited data on the efficacy of ceftriaxone and erythromycin, so these regimens should be used for HIV-infected persons only if follow-up can be assured. Patients should be re-examined 3 to 7 days after initiation of therapy. If the ulcers have not improved within 7 days, resistance may be present. Chancroid may have been misdiagnosed, a coinfecting STD may be present, the patient may have HIV, or treatment was not taken as instructed. Male patients who are uncircumcised and patients with HIV infection have worse response to treatment than do those who are circumcised or HIV negative.[4]

HIV-infected patients who have chancroid need to be monitored closely because, in general, these patients are more likely to experience treatment failure and to have ulcers that heal more slowly. HIV-infected patients may also require longer courses of therapy than those recommended for HIV-negative patients, and treatment failures can occur with any regimen. Because evidence is limited concerning the therapeutic efficacy of the recommended ceftriaxone and azithromycin regimens in HIV-infected patients, these regimens should be used for such patients only if follow-up can be ensured. Some specialists prefer the erythromycin 7-day regimen for treating HIV infection.[4]

The amount of time it takes for the ulcers to heal completely depends on the size of the ulcer. Large ulcers may require more than 2 weeks for healing. Healing is slower for some uncircumcised men who have ulcers under the foreskin. Adenopathy resolves more slowly than ulcers. Needle aspiration or incision and drainage may be required. Although needle aspiration is an easier procedure, incision and drainage may be preferable because it avoids the need for subsequent drainage procedures.[4]

Patients should be retested 3 months after diagnosis of chancroid if the initial test results for syphilis and HIV were negative.[5]

Sexual partners encountered by the patient during the 10 days preceding the onset of symptoms should be examined and treated with a recommended regimen, regardless of the presence or absence of symptoms.[4]

Although systemic spread does not occur, chancroid may be complicated; the lesions may become secondarily infected and necrotic. Buboes may rupture, suppurate, and result in fistulas. Ulcers increase the chance of acquiring HIV infection and may cause paraphimosis or phimosis. Superinfection of ulcers may also occur and lead to destruction of the external genitalia.[14]

No adverse effects of chancroid on pregnancy outcome have been reported. However, ciprofloxacin is contraindicated during pregnancy and lactation.[4]

The recommended infection prevention measures include Standard Precautions.[7]

Pediculosis

Phthirus pubis (pubic or crab louse) is a grayish ectoparasite, measuring 1 to 4 mm. It has a segmented thorax, pointed head, and claws that help to cling to hairs. Lice often afflict those with poor hygiene, communal lifestyles, and multiple sex partners. Transmission occurs primarily through intimate physical or sexual contact.[15]

Symptoms range from slight discomfort to severe itching. Erythematous papules, nits, or adult lice (or a combination of these) clinging to pubic, perineal, or perianal hairs are present and often are noticed by patients. Pubic lice can also infest the eyelashes, eyebrows, axilla, scalp, or other body hairs. Secondary bacterial infection can occur resulting from excoriations with ensuing regional lymphadenitis.[4,16]

Patients usually seek medical care due to the pruritus because they see the lice or nits. A presumptive diagnosis is made when a patient has a recent history of exposure and has pruritic, erythematous macules, papules, or secondary excoriations in the genital region. A diagnosis is confirmed by finding lice or nits attached to genital hairs. Patients with pediculosis pubis should be evaluated for other STDs.[4,16]

Recommended treatment regimens include permethrin (1 percent cream rinse applied to the affected areas and washed off after 10 minutes) or pyrethrins with piperonyl butoxide (nonprescription) (applied to the infested and adjacent hairy area and washed off after 10 minutes). Alternative regimens include malathion or ivermectin. Reported resistance to pediculicides has been increasing and is widespread. Malathion can be used when treatment failure is believed to have resulted from drug resistance. The odor and long duration of application for malathion make it a less attractive alternative than the recommended pediculcides. Ivermectin has been successfully used to treat lice, but it has only been evaluated in studies involving a limited number of participants. The preceding regimens should not be applied to the eyes. If the eyelashes are infected, occlusive ophthalmic ointment (i.e., petroleum jelly) should be applied to the eyelid margins (bid for 10 days). Pregnant and lactating women should be treated with either permethrin or pyrethrins with piperonyl butoxide. HIV-infected patients who have pediculosis pubis should receive the same treatment regimen as those who do not have HIV.[4,17]

Sexual partners encountered within the prior month should be treated. Patients should avoid sexual contact with their partner(s) until all have been treated and re-evaluated to rule out persistent pediculosis pubis.[4]

Clothing or bed linen may have been contaminated and should be washed and dried by machine (hot cycle), dry cleaned, or removed from body contact for at least 72 hours. Fumigation of living areas is not necessary.[4]

Infection prevention measures include Standard Precautions plus Contact Precautions until 24 hours after treatment.[7] Healthcare personnel with pediculosis pubis should be restricted from patient contact until they have been treated and observed to be free of adult and immature lice.[15]

Scabies

The causative organism, *Sarcoptes scabiei*, is 0.3 to 0.4 mm in size. The female mite burrows under the skin to deposit eggs. The disorder is worldwide in distribution, and the United States and Europe have recently seen an increase in the number of scabies cases. This recent wave of infestations has affected people of all socioeconomic levels without regard to race, gender, age, or standards of personal hygiene. Scabies most commonly affects families, sexual partners, school-aged children, chronically ill patients, and people in communal living situations. The mode of transmission is direct skin-to-skin contact (e.g., shaking hands, wrestling, dancing), sexual contact, or from undergarments, towels, or linens. Outbreaks of scabies in a variety of healthcare settings have been increasing since 1970 in the United States.[15,17]

Symptoms include intense nocturnal itching, the presence of a pleomorphic rash that most commonly involves the hands (including interdigital areas and palms), flexor aspects of the wrists, extensor surfaces of the elbow, anterior axillary folds, extensor areas of the knees, lateral borders of the feet, ankles, toes, breasts, genitals (especially the penis and scrotum), buttocks, and abdomen (specifically the periumbilical area). Secondary bacterial infections can occur.[16]

The diagnosis is often made on clinical grounds alone. A history of exposure to a person with scabies within the preceding 2 months supports the diagnosis. Symptoms do not develop for 2 to 6 weeks in people with no prior exposure but occur rapidly for those with prior exposure. Definitive diagnosis is made by microscopic identification of the mite and its eggs, larvae, or feces from a lesion scraping.[4,16]

The recommended treatment regimens are 5 percent permethrin cream (applied to all areas of the body from the neck down and washed off after 8 to 14 hours) or ivermectin (should not be used by pregnant or lactating patients; safety in treatment of children weighing less than 15 kg has not been determined). Alternative regimens include 1 percent lindane (1 oz lotion or 30 g cream applied thinly to all body areas from the neck down and washed off thoroughly after 8 hours

(not recommended for pregnant or lactating women, children younger than 2 years, or persons with extensive dermatitis; should not be used immediately after a bath or shower). Lindane is not recommended as first-line therapy because of toxicity; it should be used as an alternative only if the patient cannot tolerate other therapies or if other therapies have failed. HIV-infected patients with uncomplicated scabies should receive the same treatment regimen as patients without HIV.[4,16]

In Norwegian or crusted scabies, millions of mites inhabit the skin producing widespread disease that resembles psoriasis. Norwegian scabies are a particular risk for institutionalized patients with neurologic defects and for immunocompromised or HIV-infected patients. Other high-risk patients include those who are malnourished, those on systemic or potent topical glucocorticoids, organ transplant recipients, those who are physically disabled, and those with various hematologic malignancies. The appropriate treatment of crusted scabies remains unclear. Substantial treatment failure may occur with single topical scabicide or ivermectin treatment. Therefore, some specialists recommend combining topical treatment with ivermectin or repeated treatments with ivermectin. In high-risk patients, special attention must be paid to the fingernails, which should be closely trimmed to reduce injury from excessive scratching. Due to the risk of neurotoxicity, lindane is not recommended for use in high-risk patients. HIV-infected and other immunosuppressed patients with crusted scabies should be treated in consultation with a specialist.[4,15-17]

Patients need to be warned that the rash and pruritus can persist for as long as 2 weeks after adequate therapy. Signs or symptoms occurring more than 2 weeks after treatment may be due to treatment failure, reinfection from persons or fomites, poor penetration into the skin of patients with crusted scabies, or cross-reactivity of antigens from household mites. Some specialists recommend retreatment after 1 to 2 weeks for patients who continue to have symptoms, whereas other specialists recommend retreatment only if live mites are observed. Patients with no response to the recommended treatment should be re-treated with an alternative regimen.[4]

Sexual partners, close household contacts, and close personal contacts within the preceding month should be examined and treated. Clothing or bed linens should be washed and dried by machine (hot cycle), dry cleaned, or removed from body contact for at least 72 hours. Fumigation of living areas is not necessary.[4] Routine cleaning of the environment, especially upholstered furniture, will aid in eliminating mites. Additional environmental cleaning procedures may be warranted for crusted scabies.[5,15]

Scabies epidemics frequently occur in nursing homes, hospitals, residential facilities, and communities. Control of an epidemic can be achieved only if everyone is treated in the same 24-to-48-hour period. This approach prevents "ping-pong" infestation. An epidemic should be managed in consultation with a specialist and public health professionals.[5]

Infection prevention measures include Standard Precautions plus Contact Precautions until 24 hours after treatment is started.[7] Gloves should be worn when touching the clothing or bed linens of the infested patient. It is important for people with direct patient contact to wear long-sleeved gowns and cover the wrist area between the gloves and the gown.[15] Infected healthcare personnel should be restricted from patient contact until cleared by medical evaluation.[17]

Syphilis

Syphilis is a complex systemic illness caused by the spirochete *T. pallidum*. The organisms are slender, tightly coiled, unicellular, helical cells that are 5 to 15 μm long. Syphilis can be acquired by sexual contact, passage through the placenta (congenital syphilis), kissing or other close contact with an active lesion, transfusion of human blood, or accidental direct inoculation.[18]

In 2011, 13,970 cases of primary and secondary syphilis were reported (4.5 cases per 100,000 population). Increased incidences have mostly occurred in males, particularly in the MSM population, whereas infections have been declining in women.[1,7]

The median incubation period before clinical manifestations is 21 days with a range of 3 to 90 days. Clinically, syphilis can be divided into the following stages: incubating, primary, secondary, early latent/latency of unknown duration/late latent, and tertiary.[18]

Patients may seek treatment for signs and symptoms of primary syphilis, an ulcer or chancre at the site of infection. The chancre is characteristically a solitary, painless, indurated lesion at the site of inoculation. It may last 1 to 5 weeks and heal spontaneously. Secondary syphilis can affect nearly every organ system. Manifestations include, but are not limited to, skin rash, patchy hair loss (alopecia areata), mucocutaneous lesions, and lymphadenopathy. Condyloma latum is a flat, moist plaque found in the genital or perirectal area that is usually asymptomatic but highly infectious. Latent syphilis lacks overt clinical manifestations and can be detected by serologic testing.[4] Latent syphilis can be divided into early and late stages and also includes latency of unknown duration. For treatment purposes, the early latent period encompasses the time of infection to about 1 year after infection. During this time, the patient remains infectious, and relapses may occur. The late latent period encompasses approximately 1 year after infection, until the onset of tertiary disease.[5] Tertiary infection can encompass cardiac (aortic root aneurysm/aortic insufficiency), ophthalmic, and auditory sequelae; CNS complications (neurosyphilis); aseptic meningitis; generalized paresis; and tabes dorsalis. Gummatous lesions of the soft tissue and bone may be observed.[4]

Untreated, early syphilis in pregnant women results in perinatal death in as many as 40 percent of cases, and if acquired during the 4 years preceding pregnancy, may lead to infection of the fetus in more than 70 percent of cases.[1] Congenital syphilis—infection of the neonate acquired from an infected mother—deserves special consideration. An inflammation of the umbilical cord (necrotizing funisitis) is a characteristic finding. The clinical pattern varies, but rhinitis ("snuffles") may be present in the early infantile form, followed by a diffuse maculopapular desquamative rash. There may be generalized steochondritis and perichondritis with prominent involvement of the nose (saddle nose) and lower extremities (saber shins).[5]

Dark-field examinations and direct fluorescent antibody tests of lesion exudates or tissue are the definitive methods for diagnosis of early syphilis. A presumptive diagnosis is possible with nontreponemal tests (venereal disease research laboratory [VDRL], rapid plasma reagin [RPR]) and treponemal tests (fluorescent treponemal antibody-absorbed [FTA-ABS] or *T. pallidum* particle agglutination [TP-PA]).[4] It is important to keep in mind that one-third of patients with primary and late stage syphilis may have negative serologic findings.[5] The use of only one type of serologic test is insufficient for the diagnosis because false-positive nontreponemal test results can occur as secondary to various unrelated medical conditions, such as autoimmune conditions, older age, and injection-drug use. Nontreponemal antibody titers usually correlate with disease activity, and results should be reported quantitatively. Nontreponemal tests usually become nonreactive with time after treatment; however, in some patients, nontreponemal antibodies can persist at a low titer for a long period. Most patients who have a reactive treponemal test will remain reactive for the remainder of their lives, regardless of treatment or disease activity. Treponemal titers correlate poorly with disease activity and should not be used to assess treatment response.[4]

All patients with syphilis should be tested for HIV. Serologic tests are accurate and reliable for the diagnosis of syphilis and for following an HIV-infected patient's response to treatment. However, atypical syphilis serologic test results—whether unusually high, unusually low, or showing fluctuating titers—can occur in HIV-infected persons. When serologic tests do not correspond with clinical findings suggestive of early syphilis, use of other tests such as a biopsy and dark-field microscopy should be considered.[4]

Patients with intact immune systems should have nontreponemal titers repeated at 6 and 12 months after treatment. If titers increase fourfold, the serologic titers fail to decrease fourfold within 12 to 24 months of therapy, or signs and symptoms attributable to syphilis develop, the patient should be treated for late latent syphilis. All patients with latent syphilis should be clinically evaluated for tertiary disease or signs of neurological sequelae. Clinical signs of neurosyphilis include cranial nerve dysfunction, meningitis, stroke, acute or chronic altered mental status, loss of vibration sense, and auditory and ophthalmic abnormalities. These symptoms require further investigation and treatment for neurosyphilis.[4]

The diagnosis of neurosyphilis usually depends on various combinations of reactive serologic test results, abnormalities of the cerebral spinal fluid (CSF) cell count or protein, or a reactive VDRL-CSF, with or without clinical manifestations.[4]

Parenteral penicillin G is the preferred drug treatment for all stages of syphilis and is the only therapy with documented efficacy for syphilis during pregnancy. Pregnant women who report a penicillin allergy should be desensitized. During the treatment of syphilis, the Jarisch-Herxheimer reaction may be observed, which is an acute febrile reaction accompanied by headache, myalgia, and other symptoms that usually occur in the first 24 hours. It is generally unresponsive to antipyretic therapy and may induce early labor or cause fetal distress. This concern should not prevent or delay therapy.[4]

For primary or secondary syphilis, a single dose of 2.4 million units of benzathine penicillin G intramuscularly is recommended. For children, 50,000 units/kg up to the adult dose of 2.4 million units in a single dose is advised. Treatment failures can occur with any regimen.[4]

Although clinical experience supports the effectiveness of penicillin for latent syphilis, limited evidence is available for guidance in choosing a specific regimen. For early latent syphilis, a single dose of 2.4 million units of benzathine penicillin G is recommended. For late latent syphilis or latent syphilis of unknown duration, three doses of 2.4 million units of benzathine penicillin in weekly doses, totaling 7.2 million units, are recommended. In children who are not allergic to penicillin, early latent syphilis is treated with benzathine penicillin G (50,000 units/kg to 2.4 million units) and should be administered as three doses at weekly intervals. In patients allergic to penicillin, the only acceptable alternatives for latent syphilis are doxycycline (100 mg bid) or tetracycline (500 mg four times per day [qid] for 28 days). The efficacy of these regimens in HIV-infected patients has not been studied. Pregnant women who are allergic should be desensitized and treated with penicillin. Tetracycline is contraindicated for pregnant women. Following treatment for latent syphilis, follow-up serologies should be obtained at 6, 12, and 24 months. If signs of treatment failure are present, the patient should be receiving three weekly doses of benzathine penicillin G.[4]

Patients with latent syphilis should be evaluated clinically for evidence of tertiary disease (e.g., aortitis and gumma) and syphilitic ocular disease (e.g., iritis and uveitis). Patients who have syphilis and who demonstrate any of the following criteria should have a prompt CSF examination:

- Neurologic or ophthalmic signs or symptoms.

- Evidence of active tertiary syphilis (e.g., aortitis and gumma)

- Treatment failure

- HIV infection with late latent syphilis or syphilis of unknown duration.[4]

The treatment for tertiary syphilis in patients who have no evidence of neurosyphilis is benzathine penicillin G (2.4 million units IM weekly for 3 weeks). Patients who are pregnant or allergic to penicillin should be treated according to the treatment regimens recommended for latent syphilis.[4] Neurosyphilis is treated with aqueous crystalline penicillin G

(18 to 24 million units per day; 3 to 4 million units IV every 4 hours or by continuous infusion) for 10 to 14 days. Some specialists recommend that after completion of treatment, patients receive benzathine penicillin G (2.4 million units weekly for an additional 3 weeks). An alternative regimen of procaine penicillin (2.4 million units IM daily) plus probenecid (500 mg PO bid), both for 10 to 14 days, can be employed if compliance is ensured.[4] If CSF pleocytosis was present initially, a CSF examination should be repeated every 6 months until the cell count is normal. Patients who have neurosyphilis should be tested for HIV.

Many specialists recommend treating patients who have evidence of auditory disease caused by syphilis in the same manner as patients who have neurosyphilis, regardless of CSF examination results. Although systemic steroids are used frequently as adjunctive therapy for otologic syphilis, they have not been proven beneficial.[4] HIV-positive patients who have syphilis may be at increased risk for neurologic complications. The magnitude of these risks is not well defined. Patients with late latent syphilis or syphilis should have a CSF examination to evaluate for neurosyphilis. Some experts also recommend that HIV-infected patients with an RPR titer of at least 1:32 or a CD4 count of up to 350 should have a CSF examination. The treatment of all stages of syphilis is the same for patients with and those without HIV. HIV-infected patients who are treated for primary or secondary syphilis should be followed up clinically and serologically for treatment failure at 3, 6, 9, 12, and 24 months. HIV-infected patients who are treated for latent syphilis should be followed up clinically and with serology at 6, 12, 18, and 24 months. The appearance of any clinical symptoms or the failure of the RPR titer to decline fourfold by 12 to 24 months should prompt a repeat CSF exam to guide further treatment. The efficacy of alternative regimens has been studied only in small trials. Ceftriaxone may be effective for the treatment of syphilis in HIV-infected persons if close follow-up is assured. The dose and duration of ceftriaxone therapy is unclear.[4,19]

Between 2008 and 2011, the rate of congenital syphilis decreased by almost 20 percent. In 2011, 360 or 8.5 cases of congenital syphilis were reported per 100,000 live births in the United States.

STD Trends

Infants with congenital syphilis should be treated with aqueous crystalline penicillin G (50,000 units/kg/dose IV every 12 hours for the first 7 days of life and every 8 hours thereafter for a total of 10 days).[5] Infants and children who require treatment for syphilis but who have a history of penicillin allergy or develop an allergic reaction presumed secondary to penicillin should be desensitized, if necessary, and then treated with penicillin.[4]

For identification of at-risk sexual partners, the periods before treatment are (1) 3 months plus duration of symptoms for primary syphilis; (2) 6 months plus duration of symptoms for secondary syphilis; and (3) 1 year for early latent syphilis. Sexual transmission of *T. pallidum* occurs only when mucocutaneous syphilitic lesions are present. The presence of these lesions is uncommon after the first year of infection. However, persons exposed sexually to a patient who has syphilis in any stage should be evaluated clinically and serologically and treated with a recommended regimen, according to the recommendations provided below:[4]

- Persons who were exposed within the 90 days preceding the diagnosis of primary, secondary, or early latent syphilis in a sex partner may be infected even if seronegative and should be treated presumptively.[4]

- Persons who were exposed more than 90 days before the diagnosis of primary, secondary, or early latent syphilis in a sex partner should be treated presumptively if the serologic test results are not available immediately and the opportunity for follow-up is uncertain.[4]

- For purposes of partner notification, and presumptive treatment of exposed sex partners, patients with syphilis of unknown duration who have high nontreponemal serologic test titers (i.e., 1:32), can be assumed to have early syphilis. However, serologic titers should not be used to differentiate early from late latent syphilis for the purpose of determining treatment.[4]

- Long-term sex partners of patients who have latent syphilis should be evaluated clinically and serologically for syphilis and treated on the basis of the evaluation findings.[4]

The recommended infection prevention measures include Standard Precautions.[7]

Vaginitis

Vaginitis is usually characterized by a vaginal discharge or vulvar itching and irritation. A vaginal odor may be present. Three main clinical entities cause vaginitis: trichomoniasis, vulvovaginal candidiasis, and bacterial vaginosis. Trichomoniasis is sexually transmitted, whereas candidiasis usually is not. The role of sexual transmission is unknown in bacterial vaginosis.[4]

Trichomoniasis

Trichomoniasis is caused by *T. vaginalis*, a motile, flagellated protozoan that can infect the urogenital tract in both women and men. An estimated 7.4 million cases of trichomoniasis occur in men and women each year.[20]

The clinical presentation in females includes diffuse, malodorous, yellow-green vaginal discharge, pruritus, vulvar irritation, and lower abdominal discomfort. The symptoms may become worse with menstruation, and the patient may also complain about dysuria. In males, urethritis may occur. However, some women and many men have no symptoms.[20] Some men with *T. vaginalis* have NGU.[4]

Diagnosis is made by microscopic examination of a wet preparation of vaginal secretions; a drop of secretion is placed on a slide (a drop of saline may be added if the secretion is thick) and quickly examined for the motile trichomonads. The sensitivity of the wet prep is approximately 60 to 70 percent. Two point-of-care tests have recently been approved by the FDA: The OSOM *Trichomonas* rapid test is an immunochromatographic capillary flow dipstick test that can be performed on vaginal secretions, and the Affirm VP III is a nucleic acid probe that detects *T. vaginalis*, *Gardnerella vaginalis*, and *Candida albicans*. The culture remains the most sensitive commercially available diagnostic test for trichomoniasis. The culture should be employed if trichomoniasis is suspected but not confirmed by microscopy. In men, wet preparation is insensitive, and culture testing of urethral swab, urine, and semen is required for optimal sensitivity.[4]

Patients with *T. vaginalis* should be screened for other STDs such as *N. gonorrhoeae*, *C. trachomatis*, and HIV. The inflammatory response to trichomoniasis may increase the risk of HIV transmission.[20]

Trichomoniasis increases the incidence of premature rupture of membranes, preterm delivery, and low-birth weight. Pregnant women should be treated to relieve the symptoms; however, data have not shown that treating pregnant women with no symptoms reduces the risk of adverse pregnancy outcomes related to *T. vaginalis*.[4] Approximately 2 to 17 percent of the female offspring of infected women acquire trichomoniasis, probably through transmission as the neonate passes through the infected birth canal.[20]

The recommended treatment regimens are metronidazole (2 g PO in a single dose) or tinidazole (2 g PO in a single dose). Metronidazole 500 mg given orally bid for 7 days is an alternative regimen, but intravaginal metronidazole gel is not recommended. Pregnant women may be treated with a single 2-g oral dose of metronidazole (pregnancy category B). Tinidazole is pregnancy category C, and its safety in pregnancy has not been well evaluated. A consistent association between the use of metronidazole during pregnancy and fetal harm or birth defects has not been demonstrated. Exposure of nursing infants to metronidazole and tinidazole can be reduced by not nursing for 12 to 24 hours after the last dose of metronidazole or for 72 hours after the last dose of tinidazole. Patients with HIV and trichomoniasis should receive the same treatment regimen as patients who do not have HIV. Because metronidazole has a disulfiram (Antabuse) effect, alcohol should not be consumed during administration or until 24 hours after treatment is completed. Patients should not consume alcohol while on tinidazole and should continue to abstain for 72 hours after treatment is completed.[4]

The incidence, persistence, and recurrence of trichomoniasis in HIV-infected women are not correlated with immune status.[4] Follow-up visits are unnecessary if symptoms resolve. If treatment failure occurs after a single dose of metronidazole, the patient should be re-treated with metronidazole (500 mg bid for 7 days) or tinidazole (2 g PO in a single dose). If treatment fails repeatedly, the patient can be treated with metronidazole (2 g PO daily for 5 days) or tinidazole (2 g PO daily for 5 days). Patients with laboratory-documented *T. vaginalis* infections who have no response to 5 days of treatment and have not been reinfected should be treated in consultation with an expert, and evaluation of the susceptibility of *T. vaginalis* to metronidazole and tinidazole should be done. Consultation is available from the CDC.[4]

Contacts must receive treatment or the disease may recur. Patients should be instructed to avoid sexual contact until they and their partners are cured. A cure is defined as the absence of symptoms after completion of treatment; this can also be verified by a microbiologic test.[4]

The recommended infection prevention measures include Standard Precautions.[7]

Vulvovaginal Candidiasis

Vulvovaginal candidiasis (VVC) is most frequently caused by the yeast *C. albicans*. Other *Candida* or *Torulopsis* species may occasionally be present. Antibiotic use can precipitate VVC in women who have vaginal *Candida* colonization.[4] VVC is also frequently seen during pregnancy and in patients with diabetes mellitus.[21] However, the majority of healthy women with uncomplicated VVC have no identifiable precipitating factors. VVC can occur concomitantly with STDs.[4]

An estimated 75 percent of women will have at least one episode of VVC, 40 to 45 percent will have two or more episodes, and 5 percent will have four or more episodes per year. Although the incidence of VVC in HIV-infected women remains unknown, vaginal *Candida* colonization rates among HIV-infected women are higher than those among uninfected women with similar demographic characteristics and high-risk behaviors. The colonization rate for HIV-infected women correlates with increasing severity of immunosuppression. Symptomatic VVC is more common in HIV-infected women and similarly correlates with severity of the immunodeficiency. The typical clinical presentation of marked pruritus, dyspareunia, external dysuria, vaginal soreness, and "cottage cheese-like" vaginal discharge is not specific for VVC. The VVC is classified as uncomplicated or complicated based on the clinical presentation, microbiology, and host factors. Uncomplicated VVC is sporadic or infrequent, mild to moderate, likely to be due to *C. albicans*, and in an immunocompetent host. Approximately 10 percent of women will have complicated VVC. Complicated VVC is defined as recurrent, severe, or non-*albicans* candidiasis and occurs in women with uncontrolled diabetes, debilitation, immunosuppression, or during pregnancy.[4]

The diagnosis of uncomplicated VVC is suggested clinically by external dysuria and vulvar pruritus, pain, swelling, and redness and erythema in the vulvovaginal area.[4]

Signs include a white, thick, curdy vaginal discharge, vulvar edema, fissures, or excoriations. The diagnosis can be made by placing a sample of vaginal secretions on a slide and adding a drop of 10 percent potassium hydroxide (KOH). The KOH dissolves other cell material and debris and allows the yeast forms to be seen easily during microscopic examination. A Gram stain of the vaginal discharge can also be done to see the yeast or pseudohyphae. For a woman with negative wet mounts, vaginal cultures for *Candida* should be considered if she has any signs or multiple symptoms. If *Candida* cultures cannot be done, empiric treatment can be considered for women with symptoms and any sign of VVC on examination when the wet mount is negative. Because 10 to 20 percent of women are colonized with vaginal *Candida* species and other yeasts, a positive culture without signs or symptoms is not an indication for treatment.[4]

Uncomplicated VVC is effectively treated locally with short-course topical formulations (i.e., single dose and regimens of 1 to 3 days). The topically applied azole drugs are more effective than nystatin. Treatment with azoles results in relief of symptoms and negative cultures in 80 to 90 percent of patients who complete therapy. VVC frequently occurs during pregnancy. Only topical azole therapies, applied for 7 days, are recommended for use among pregnant women. Among HIV-infected women, systemic azole exposure is associated with the isolation of non-*albicans Candida* species from the vagina.[4]

The CDC lists 14 different topical regimens that may be used. It is important to note that the creams and suppositories recommended are oil-based and may weaken latex condoms and diaphragms. Fluconazole (150 mg PO given in a single dose), an oral agent, is also a recommended therapy. Only topical azole therapies, applied for 7 days, are recommended for use in pregnant women. Intravaginal preparations of butoconazole, clotrimazole, miconazole, and tioconazole are available over-the-counter (OTC), whereas fluconazole requires a prescription. However, unnecessary or inappropriate use of OTC preparations is common and may cause a delayed treatment of other causative agents for vulvovaginitis, which could result in adverse clinical outcomes.[4]

Treatment of HIV-infected women with VVC is the same as that for HIV-seronegative women. Women with underlying debilitating medical conditions (e.g., uncontrolled diabetes or those undergoing corticosteroid treatment) do not have good response to short-term therapies. Efforts should be made to correct modifiable conditions, and prolonged (e.g., 7 to 14 days) conventional antimycotic therapy is necessary.[4]

Topical agents do not usually cause systemic side effects, though they may cause local burning or irritation. Oral agents may cause nausea, abdominal pain, and headache. Oral azoles have been rarely associated with abnormal elevations of liver enzymes. Clinically important interactions may occur when these oral agents are administered with other drugs, including astemizole, calcium channel antagonists, cisapride, coumadin, cyclosporin A, oral hypoglycemic agents, phenytoin, protease inhibitors, tacrolimus, terfenadine, theophylline, trimetrexate, and rifampin. Follow-up is unnecessary unless symptoms persist or recur within 2 months of the initial onset of symptoms.[4]

VVC is not usually acquired through sexual intercourse, so treatment of partners is not recommended. However, a minority of male sexual partners may have balanitis and may benefit from treatment with topical antifungal agents to relieve symptoms.[4]

Recurrent VVC, defined as four or more episodes of symptomatic VVC in 1 year, affects less than 5 percent of women and is defined as more than four episodes of symptomatic VVC each year. C. glabrata and other non-albicans Candida species are found in 10 to 20 percent of these patients. Vaginal cultures are needed so that unusual species such as C. glabrata can be identified. Compared with C. albicans, C. glabrata does not form hyphae or pseudohyphae and is not easily distinguished on microscopy. The treatment of recurrent VVC involves an extended course of therapy (e.g., 7 to 14 days of topical therapy or a 150-mg dose of fluconazole repeated 3 days later) to achieve mycologic remission before starting maintenance antifungal treatment. The first-line maintenance antifungal regimen is fluconazole (100 mg, 150 mg, or 200 mg PO weekly for 6 months). Topical clotrimazole (200-mg vaginal suppositories twice weekly or 500-mg vaginal suppositories once weekly for 6 months) or other intermittently dosed topical therapies also can be used.[4]

Based on available data, VVC treatment in HIV-infected women should not differ from that for uninfected women. Although long-term prophylactic therapy with fluconazole, at a dose of 200 mg weekly, has been effective in reducing C. albicans colonization and symptomatic VVC, this regimen is not recommended for routine primary prophylaxis in HIV-infected women without recurrent VVC. Given the frequency at which recurrent VVC occurs in the immunocompetent healthy population, the occurrence of recurrent VVC should not be considered an indication for HIV testing.[4]

Severe VVC presents as extensive vulvar erythema, edema, excoriation, and fissure formation. The recommended treatment is 7 to 14 days of topical azole or oral fluconazole in two sequential doses with the second dose given 72 hours after the initial dose.[4]

Treatment of non-albicans VVC is not as clear-cut. The optimal treatment regimen remains unknown. Options include longer duration of therapy (7 to 14 days) with a nonfluconazole azole drug (oral or topical) as first-line therapy. If recurrence occurs, 600 mg of boric acid in a gelatin capsule is recommended, administered vaginally once daily for 2 weeks. This regimen has clinical and mycologic eradication rates of approximately 70 percent. If symptoms recur, referral to a specialist is advised.[4]

The recommended infection prevention measures include Standard Precautions.[7]

Bacterial Vaginosis

Bacterial vaginosis (BV), formerly called nonspecific vaginitis, is a clinical syndrome characterized by replacement of the normal H_2O_2-producing vaginal Lactobacillus species with high concentrations of anaerobic bacteria (Prevotella species and Mobiluncus species), G. vaginalis, and M. hominis. BV is the most common cause of vaginal discharge and malodor; however, as many as 50 percent of women with BV may report no symptoms.[4]

BV is associated with having multiple sex partners, a new sex partner, douching, and lack of vaginal lactobacilli. It remains uncertain if BV results from acquisition of a sexually transmitted pathogen. Women who have never been sexually active are rarely affected. Treatment of male sex partners has not been beneficial in preventing the recurrence of BV.[4]

The clinical presentation includes a complaint of mild to moderate vaginal discharge. The discharge is usually thin and homogenous. The inflammation and irritation are much less severe than in VVC or trichomoniasis.[22] The following criteria are used to make the diagnosis: (1) vaginal pH greater than 4.5; (2) unpleasant, fishy odor is present either before or after 10 percent KOH is added to vaginal secretions (the whiff test); (3) a wet mount of vaginal secretions shows epithelial cells covered with bacteria ("clue cells"); and (4) homogeneous, white, noninflammatory discharge that smoothly coats the vaginal walls. The gold standard diagnostic test is a Gram stain for examination of the bacterial flora showing paucity of lactobacilli and predominance of Gram-negative organisms. Culture for G. vaginalis is not recommended. However, a DNA probe (Affirm VP III) test for high concentrations of G. vaginalis may have utility. The cervical Pap tests have limited sensitivity in diagnosing BV. Other commercially available tests that may be useful to diagnose BV include card testing to detect elevated pH and trimethylamine or proline aminopeptidase. However, card testing has low sensitivity and specificity and therefore is not recommended. PCR also has been used in research settings, but its clinical utility is uncertain.[4]

BV during pregnancy is associated with adverse outcomes, including premature rupture of membranes, preterm labor, preterm birth, amnionitis, late-term miscarriage, and postpartum endometriosis. There is an increased risk of endometritis, salpingitis, and posthysterectomy vaginal cuff infection.[22]

Diagnosis of BV is based on clinical criteria or a Gram stain. To make the diagnosis using clinical criteria, three of the following symptoms or signs must be present:

- Homogeneous, thin, white discharge that smoothly coats the vaginal walls

- Presence of clue cells on microscopic examination

- pH of vaginal fluid greater than 4.5

- A fishy odor of vaginal discharge before or after addition of 10 percent KOH (i.e., the whiff test)[4]

The gold standard when using a Gram stain is to determine the relative concentration of lactobacilli (long Gram-positive rods), Gram-negative and Gram-variable rods and cocci (i.e., G. vaginalis, Prevotella, Porphyromonas, and peptostreptococci), and curved Gram-negative rods (*Mobiluncus*) characteristic of BV. Other commercially available tests that may be useful for the diagnosis of BV include a card test for the detection of elevated pH and trimethylamine and proline aminopeptidase.[4]

The goal of treatment is to relieve the signs and symptoms and to reduce the risk for infectious complications after an abortion or hysterectomy. All women with symptomatic disease require treatment, regardless of pregnancy status. More information is needed before recommending treatment for all pregnant women with asymptomatic disease.[4]

Recommended regimens include metronidazole; 2 percent clindamycin cream; or metronidazole gel 0.75 percent. Note: Patients should be advised to avoid consuming alcohol during treatment with metronidazole and for 24 hours thereafter. Clindamycin cream is oil based and may weaken latex condoms and diaphragms for 5 days after use. In addition, topical clindamycin preparations should not be used in the second half of pregnancy.[4]

Alternative regimens include clindamycin, clindamycin ovules intravaginally once at bedtime for 3 days, tinidazol, or tinidazol PO daily for 5 days. Additional alternative regimens include metronidazole, or a single dose of clindamycin intravaginal cream, though data on the performance of these alternative regimens are limited.[4]

In pregnant women, systemic therapy may be preferable to treat possible subclinical upper-tract infections (metronidazole or clindamycin).[4] Due to an increased risk of preterm birth, clindamycin cream is not recommended for pregnant patients.[22] HIV-infected patients with BV should receive the same treatment regimen as patients without HIV. BV appears to be more persistent in HIV-positive women.[4,5]

Consideration should be given to screening and treating symptomatic or asymptomatic BV before surgical abortion or hysterectomy procedures are performed.[4]

The use of lactobacillus intravaginal suppositories to restore normal flora and treat BV has been evaluated in several studies. The clinical and microbiologic efficacy of using these suppositories was assessed. However, no currently available lactobacillus suppository was determined to be better than placebo 1 month after therapy for either clinical or microbiologic cure. No data support the use of douching for treatment or relief of symptoms.[4]

BV has been associated with adverse pregnancy outcomes (e.g., premature rupture of the membranes, chorioamnionitis, preterm labor, preterm birth, intra-amniotic infection, postpartum endometritis, and postcesarean wound infection). Therefore, all pregnant women who have symptomatic disease should be treated. Some specialists prefer using systemic therapy to treat possible subclinical upper genital tract infections.[4]

Treatment of BV in asymptomatic pregnant women at high risk for preterm delivery (i.e., those who have previously delivered a premature infant) with a recommended oral regimen has reduced preterm delivery in three of four randomized controlled trials. Some specialists recommend screening and oral treatment of these women. However, the optimal treatment regimens have not been established. If screening is conducted, screening and treatment should be performed during the first prenatal visit.[4]

The recommended regimens for pregnant women are metronidazole or clindamycin. Note that intravaginal clindamycin cream should be used during only the first half of pregnancy.[4]

The follow-up visits are unnecessary if symptoms resolve. However, evaluation of pregnant women 1 month after completion of the therapy should be considered to make sure that treatment was effective. Routine treatment of sexual partners is not recommended.[4]

The recommended infection prevention measures include Standard Precautions.[7]

Lymphogranuloma venereum

Lymphogranuloma venereum (LGV) is caused by *C. trachomatis* serovars L1, L2, or L3. These strains are distinct from those that cause NGU. In many parts of the world, including Asia, Africa, and South America, LGV is endemic; it occurs sporadically elsewhere. However, LGV is rare in the United States where it occurs predominantly among MSM. Lack of universal screening and reporting means that reliable incidence and prevalence data for the United States are unavailable.[4,5]

LGV is the only *C. trachomatis* infection that causes constitutional symptoms. In the first phase, a small, painless, herpetiform vesicle, nonindurated papule, or ulcer may develop locally. However, the lesions may have disappeared by the time the patient presents for evaluation. This lesion is followed by inguinal or perirectal lymphadenopathy or bubo, fever, and other constitutional symptoms. The third phase of illness is characterized by lymph node suppuration, abscess, lymphedema, ulceration, or fistula formation, or a combination of these. The most common clinical manifestation among heterosexual men is tender, usually unilateral, inguinal or femoral unilateral lymphadenopathy. Sexually active women and MSM may have proctocolitis (including mucoid or hemorrhagic rectal discharge, anal pain, constipation, fever, or tenesmus) or inflammatory involvement of perirectal or perianal lymphatic tissues that can result in fistulas and strictures.[4,5] LGV is an invasive, systemic infection. If LGV proctocolitis is not treated early, it may lead to chronic, colorectal fistulas and strictures. Genital and colorectal LGV lesions may also develop secondary bacterial infection or be coinfected with other sexually and nonsexually transmitted pathogens.[4]

Diagnosing LGV is a challenge. The differential diagnosis includes syphilis, genital herpes, donovanosis, and chancroid.

Excluding other causes of genital ulcers or inguinal lymphade-nopathy usually makes the diagnosis. The clinical suspicion can be supported by identification of C. trachomatis from infected tissue (genital and lymph node lesion swab or bubo aspirate) specimens by culture, direct immunofluorescence, or NAAT. Chlamydia serologies of 1:64 or higher also support the diagnosis in the appropriate clinical scenario. The NAATs for C. trachomatis are not FDA cleared for testing rectal specimens. The methods for differentiating LGV-associated C. trachomatis strains from non-LGV strains exist but are not often used. Molecular procedures (such as PCR-based genotyping) can be used to differentiate LGV from non-LGV C. trachomatis. However, these tests are not widely available.[4]

In the absence of specific LGV diagnostic testing, patients with a clinical syndrome consistent with LGV, including proctocol-itis or genital ulcer disease with lymphadenopathy, should be treated for LGV.[4]

The treatment cures LGV and prevents ongoing tissue damage. Fluctuant buboes should be aspirated through normal skin or incision and drainage to prevent the formation of inguinal/femoral ulcerations. The recommended antimicrobial regimen for LGV is doxycycline (100 mg PO bid for at least 21 days; contraindicated for pregnant women). Alternative regimens include erythromycin base (500 mg PO qid for 21 days). Some specialists believe that azithromycin (1 g PO once weekly for 3 weeks) is likely to be effective, but clinical data are lacking. Doxycycline is contraindicated in pregnant women. Pregnant and lactating women should be treated with erythromycin. Azithromycin may be useful in this instance, but no published safety or efficacy data are available. Patients should be followed up clinically until signs and symptoms resolve. Anecdotal evidence suggests that HIV-infected patients may require prolonged therapy, and resolution may be delayed.[4]

HIV-positive patients with LGV should be treated with the same regimens as those who are HIV negative. However, a longer duration of therapy may be necessary, and delay in resolution of symptoms might occur.[4]

Sexual partners should be examined, tested for urethral or cer-vical chlamydial infection, and treated if sexual contact occurred during the 30 days preceding onset of the patient's symptoms.[4]

The recommended infection prevention measures include Standard Precautions.[7]

Granuloma Inguinale (Donovanosis)

Donovanosis is a genital ulcer disease caused by *Klebsiella granulomatis* (formerly *Calymmatobacterium granulomatis*). Although rare in the United States, it is endemic in many trop-ical and developing regions, including India, southern Africa, central Australia, and Papua New Guinea.[4]

Donovanosis is characterized by progressive painless ulcers with-out adenopathy. The ulcers have rolled edges, look "beefy red,"

are very vascular, and tend to bleed easily. The clinical presenta-tion also can include hypertrophic, necrotic, or sclerotic variants. Adenopathy and pain may be present if the ulcers become secondarily infected. Visualizing "Donovan bodies" on biopsy or tissue crush preparation makes diagnosis. K. granulomatis is dif-ficult to culture. No PCR tests are FDA approved for diagnosis.[4]

Treatment is effective and stops disease progression. Healing typ-ically proceeds inward from the ulcer margins. Prolonged therapy is usually needed to allow granulation and re-epithelialization of the ulcers. Relapses may occur for as long as 18 months.[4]

The recommended regimen is doxycycline (100 mg PO bid for 3 weeks or until lesions heal). Several alternative regimens exist, including azithromycin (1 g PO weekly for 3 weeks), ciproflox-acin (750 mg PO bid for 3 weeks), erythromycin base (500 mg PO bid for 3 weeks), and trimethoprim/sulfamethoxazole DS (1 tablet PO bid for 3 weeks). All regimens should be contin-ued until the lesions have healed. If healing does not start after several days of treatment, some experts recommend adding an aminoglycoside (i.e., gentamicin 1 mg/kg IM/IV every 8 hours). Doxycycline is contraindicated in pregnancy, so erythromycin base (500 mg PO qid) should be used in pregnant patients and an aminoglycoside should be strongly considered.[4]

HIV-infected patients with donovanosis should receive the same regimens as those who do not have HIV. Consideration should be given to the addition of a parenteral aminoglycoside (e.g., gentamicin).[4]

It is important to note that pregnancy is a relative contrain-dication to the use of sulfonamides and that doxycycline and ciprofloxacin are contraindicated in pregnant women. Pregnant and lactating women should be treated with the erythromycin regimen, and consideration should be given to the addition of a parenteral aminoglycoside (e.g., gentamicin). Azithromycin may prove useful for treating granuloma inguinale during pregnancy, but published data are lacking.[4]

Sexual contacts within the previous 60 days should be exam-ined and offered treatment. Therapy in the absence of symp-toms is of unproven benefit.[4]

The recommended infection prevention measures include Standard Precautions.[7]

Epididymitis

Epididymitis can be caused by a variety of organisms. C. trachomatis or N. gonorrhoeae are common etiologic agents for acute epididymitis among sexually active men younger than 35 years. Acute epididymitis caused by sexually transmitted enteric organisms (e.g., Escherichia coli) also occurs among men who are the insertive partner during anal intercourse. Fungi and mycobacteria are more likely to cause acute epididymitis in immunosuppressed patients than in immunocompetent patients.[4]

Urethritis is usually seen with sexually transmitted acute epididymitis. In these patients, the urethritis is frequently asymptomatic and is rarely, if ever, accompanied by bacteriuria.[4]

Sexually transmitted epididymitis is uncommon among men older than 35 years. However, bacteriuria secondary to obstructive urinary disease is relatively common with nonsexually transmitted epididymitis in this age group associated with urinary tract instrumentation or surgery, systemic disease, or immunosuppression.[4]

Acute epididymitis is a clinical syndrome consisting of pain, swelling, and inflammation of the epididymis of less than 6 weeks' duration. The acute epididymitis typically includes unilateral testicular pain and tenderness. Hydrocele and palpable swelling of the epididymis usually are present. Although the inflammation and swelling usually begin in the tail of the epididymis, they can spread to involve the rest of the epididymis and testicle. The spermatic cord is usually tender and swollen.[4]

Chronic epididymitis is characterized by a 3-month or longer history of symptoms of discomfort or pain in the scrotum, testicle, or epididymis that is localized on clinical examination. Chronic epididymitis has been subcategorized into inflammatory chronic epididymitis, obstructive chronic epididymitis, and chronic epididymalgia.[4]

Testicular torsion is a surgical emergency that should be considered in all cases of acute epididymitis. However, testicular torsion occurs more frequently among adolescents and in men without evidence of inflammation or infection. Emergency testing for torsion may be indicated when the onset of pain is sudden, pain is severe, or the test results available during the initial examination do not support a diagnosis of urethritis or urinary tract infection. If the diagnosis is questionable, a specialist should be consulted immediately because testicular viability may be compromised. Radionuclide scanning of the scrotum is the most accurate radiologic method of diagnosis, though it is not routinely available. The color duplex Doppler ultrasonography has a sensitivity of 70 percent and a specificity of 88 percent in diagnosing acute epididymitis.[4]

The evaluation of epididymitis should include either of the following:

- Gram stain of urethral secretions demonstrating at least five white blood cells (WBCs) per oil-immersion field. The Gram stain is the preferred rapid diagnostic test for evaluating urethritis. It is highly sensitive and specific for documenting both urethritis and the presence or absence of gonococcal infection. The gonococcal infection is established by documenting the presence of WBC-containing intracellular Gram-negative diplococci on urethral Gram stain.[4]

- Positive leukocyte esterase test on first-void urine or microscopic examination of first-void urine sediment demonstrating at least 10 WBCs per high-power field.[4]

Culture, nucleic acid hybridization tests, and nucleic acid amplification tests are available for the detection of both

N. gonorrhoeae and C. trachomatis. The culture and nucleic acid hybridization tests require urethral swab specimens, whereas amplification tests can be performed on urine specimens. Because of their higher sensitivity, amplification tests are preferred for the detection of C. trachomatis. Depending on the risk, patients whose conditions have been diagnosed as a new STD should receive testing for other STDs.[4]

The majority of patients can be treated on an outpatient basis. Hospitalization should be considered when severe pain suggests other diagnoses, such as testicular torsion, testicular infarction, or abscess. Hospitalization should also be considered when patients are febrile or may not adhere to an antimicrobial regimen.[4]

Empiric therapy is indicated before laboratory test results are available. The goals of treatment of acute epididymitis caused by C. trachomatis or N. gonorrhoeae are (1) microbiologic cure of infection, (2) improvement of signs and symptoms, (3) prevention of transmission to others, and (4) a decrease in potential complications, such as infertility or chronic pain. As an adjunct to therapy, bed rest, scrotal elevation, and analgesics are recommended until fever and local inflammation have subsided.[4]

The recommended regimen for acute epididymitis that is most likely caused by C. trachomatis or N. gonorrhoeae is ceftriaxone IM in a single dose plus doxycycline orally for 10 days. The recommended regimen for acute epididymitis that is most likely caused by enteric organisms, or for patients' allergic to cephalosporins or tetracyclines, is ofloxacin orally for 10 days or levofloxacin orally once daily for 10 days. Patients who have uncomplicated acute epididymitis and also have HIV should receive the same treatment regimen as patients who do not have HIV.[4]

Patients who do not experience improvement within 3 days of the initiation of treatment require re-evaluation of both the diagnosis and therapy. The swelling and tenderness that persist after completion of antimicrobial therapy should be evaluated comprehensively. The differential diagnosis includes tumor, abscess, infarction, testicular cancer, tuberculosis, and fungal epididymitis.[4]

Patients with acute epididymitis that is confirmed or suspected to be caused by N. gonorrhoeae or C. trachomatis should be instructed to refer sex partners for evaluation and treatment if their contact with the index patient was within the 60 days preceding onset of the patient's symptoms. Patients should be instructed to avoid sexual intercourse until they and their sex partners are cured, which is defined as the completion of therapy with the patient and partners no longer having symptoms.[4]

The recommended infection prevention measures include Standard Precautions.[7]

STDs and HIV

STDs increase the likelihood of both transmitting and acquiring HIV. Individuals with STDs are three to five times more likely to acquire HIV if exposed to the virus through sexual contact than are noninfected individuals. In addition, if an HIV-infected individual also has an STD, he or she is three to five times more likely than other HIV-infected persons to transmit HIV through sexual contact.[23,24]

STDs facilitate the transmission of HIV, the contraction of HIV, or both. Studies show that *C. trachomatis* and *T. pallidum* lipoproteins increase HIV replication. The STD pathogens may disrupt the mucosal tissue, increase the number of cells receptive to HIV, or increase the number of receptors expressed per cell. Elevated levels of HIV-1 RNA in semen have been found in patients with gonorrhea, trichomoniasis, and genital ulcers. Elevated levels of HIV-1 DNA have been found in cervicovaginal specimens from patients with gonorrhea, chlamydia, cervicovaginal ulcer, or cervical mucus.[24] Men who have gonorrhea and HIV are more than twice as likely to have HIV in their genital secretions, and the median concentration of HIV in their semen is as much as 10 times greater than that for coinfected men. The higher the concentration of HIV in semen or genital fluids, the more likely it is that HIV will be transmitted to a sex partner.

STDs also appear to increase susceptibility through breaks in the skin. Genital ulcers such as those present in syphilis, herpes, and chancroid create a portal of entry for HIV. In addition, inflammation resulting from genital ulcers or nonulcerative STDs, such as chlamydia, gonorrhea, and trichomoniasis, increase the concentration of cells in genital secretions that can serve as targets for HIV (e.g., CD_4+ cells).[25]

Detecting and treating STDs can substantially reduce HIV transmission. Treating STDs in HIV-infected individuals decreases both the amount of HIV in genital secretions and how frequently HIV is found in those secretions, thereby decreasing the risk of transmission.[26] Early detection and treatment of curable STDs should become a major, explicit part of a comprehensive HIV prevention program.[25]

Gynecology

Gynecologic Flora

To understand the etiology of gynecologic infections, it is important to know the normal flora of the female reproductive tract. The lower part of the reproductive tract is heavily colonized by bacteria. Anaerobes are 10 times more common in the vagina than aerobes.[27] Normal vaginal flora commonly includes lactobacilli, various species of streptococci, *G. vaginalis*, strains of Enterobacteriaceae, and anaerobes. A number of naturally occurring events can alter the vaginal flora. During pregnancy, lactobacilli and yeasts increase in the vagina while other bacteria, especially anaerobes, decrease. At the time of delivery, the anaerobic population is increasing, and by 6 weeks after delivery, the vaginal flora returns to the prepartum distribution.[27]

The vaginal flora is also affected by menopause. Women who receive estrogen treatment have increased numbers of lactobacilli and diphtheroids. Women who are not receiving estrogen treatment have a higher ratio of anaerobes. Postmenopausal women have a lower risk of infection after vaginal procedures, such as hysterectomy, than do women of reproductive age.[27]

Other factors also affect vaginal flora. For example, *Bacteroides fragilis* and aerobes (especially *E. coli*, *Klebsiella*, *Enterobacter*, and enterococci) increase within 5 days after abdominal or vaginal hysterectomy.[28,29] Hospitalization can result in more virulent vaginal organisms, including enterococci, *B. fragilis*, and resistant Enterobacteriaceae. Antimicrobial therapy reduces the normal flora, thus allowing amplification of yeast growth. An increased number of *E. coli* are seen in patients with invasive cancer. Douching monthly or more frequently is associated with an increase in bacterial vaginosis because it disrupts the normal flora. An increase in *G. vaginalis* and *M. hominis* has been found, as well as a lack of hydrogen peroxide–producing lactobacilli.[30] The alterations of the female reproductive system that increase the risk of infection are presented in Table 91-1.

Table 91-1. Alterations of the Female Reproductive System That Increase Risk of Infection

Alterations	Example	Mechanism
Obstruction	Congenital anomalies such as imperforate hymen; neoplasms; foreign bodies, such as tampons, diaphragms or pessaries.	Interrupts normal flow of fluids (e.g., blood); stagnation of fluids provides media for microbial growth; tampon use may be associated with toxic shock syndrome.
Trauma	Surgery, abortions, sexual abuse.	Mucosal surfaces may be disrupted, enhancing microbial attachment and penetration, alters or impedes blood supply, devitalized tissue provides bacterial growth medium; skin defenses (such as acidity) are destroyed. Recommendations on management of possible sexual exposure to HIV have been published.
Impaired host defenses	Antimicrobial therapy; presence of bacterial vaginosis may increase risk of infection following hysterectomy.	Change in vaginal flora or pH may allow pathogens to proliferate and alter ability of mucosa to resist microbial penetration; consider screening and treatment for bacterial vaginosis before elective hysterectomy.

From Rein MF. Volvovaginitis and Cervicitis. In: Mandell GL, Bennett JE, Dolin R, eds. *Principles and Practice of Infectious Disease*, 6th ed. New York: Churchill Livingstone, 2005:1357–1371.

APIC Text of Infection Control and Epidemiology

Gynecologic Surgical Site Infections

Gynecologic procedures are performed by either the vaginal or the abdominal routes. The risk of infection depends in part on the approach. The vaginal route is a nonsterile approach, thereby increasing the risk of infection through contamination by vaginal flora. For example, vaginal flora may cause a cervical cuff infection after a vaginal hysterectomy. The abdominal route is a sterile approach that carries minimal postoperative wound infection risks similar to those for other clean abdominal surgical procedures. Another potential source of gynecologic healthcare-associated infections (HAIs) are devices that are introduced into the reproductive system. These devices may permit entry of microorganisms by direct contamination (from nonsterile equipment or the hands of healthcare personnel) or through indirect contamination via reservoirs associated with equipment, such as the dye used for a hysterosalpingogram.[27]

Approximately, 600,000 hysterectomies are performed annually in the United States, making the surgery the second most frequently performed surgical procedure for women of reproductive age (behind cesarean section) in the country. The rate of hysterectomy in the United States has decreased slightly from 5.4 per 1000 in 2000 to 5.1 per 1000 in 2004. Overall rates were highest among women 40 to 44 years of age and lowest among women 15 to 24 years of age. Geographically, the overall rate from 2000 through 2004 was highest for women living in the South (6.3 per 1000) and lowest for those in the Northeast (4.3 per 1000).[31]

Postoperative fever is observed in 15 to 33 percent of women undergoing a vaginal or abdominal hysterectomy. Two episodes of unexplained fever (less than 38°C, at least 4 hours apart, and more than 24 hours after surgery) may be due to pelvic or cuff cellulitis, pelvic abscess, or an infection that is remote from the operative site.[27]

Posthysterectomy infections usually arise from endogenous flora contaminating the surgical site or field. The National Nosocomial Infections Surveillance (NNIS) system defines postoperative wound infections as superficial, deep incisional, and organ/space.[32,33] The CDC includes statistics for hysterectomies in the NNIS system. The data for January 1992 through June 2002 indicates an infection incidence for abdominal hysterectomies of 1.4 per 100 operations with a risk index of 0; 2.34 per 100 operations with a risk index of 1; and 5.39 per 100 operations with a risk index of 2 or 3. The infection incidence for vaginal hysterectomies is 1.23 per 100 operations with a risk index of 0. The NNIS data for vaginal hysterectomies with a risk index greater than 0 are not available. Comparisons of hospitals' to NNIS rates must be done employing the same surveillance methodology.[33,34]

The length of hospital stay for all types of hysterectomies has decreased.[35] Therefore, many patients are discharged before manifestation of a postoperative wound infection, and postdischarge surveillance is necessary to identify these infections.

Perioperative antibiotic prophylaxis is recommended for hysterectomies to decrease the risk of postoperative wound infection. If a facility's surveillance data show that hysterectomy wound infections are of concern, compliance with antibiotic prophylaxis usage should be examined as a risk factor. The literature indicates that more than 70 percent of the patients studied received no antibiotic prophylaxis.[27] Mention must also be made of other gynecologic procedures. Some procedures do not result in operative site exposure to flora in the lower genital tract. These include laparoscopy, ovarian cystectomy, and hysterosalpingography. Antibiotic prophylaxis is not recommended for laparoscopy or ovarian cystectomy. Data are not available on the benefit of antibiotic prophylaxis for ovarian cystectomy.[27]

The risks and prevention of procedure-specific infections are presented in Table 91-2. In addition to the risk of postoperative wound infections, it must be mentioned that pelvic gynecologic surgery, like other pelvic procedures, poses an increased risk of occupational exposure to bloodborne pathogens for healthcare personnel. Use of the new safety devices by operative personnel has been shown to prevent sharps injuries.[27]

Gynecologic Procedures: Colposcopy

Colposcopy allows the cervix, vagina, and vulva to be examined through a binocular microscope. A 3 to 5 percent acetic acid solution is applied during colposcopy, and biopsies are obtained of all lesions that are suspected of being neoplastic. A colposcopy is considered satisfactory when the entire squamocolumnar junction and the margin of all visible lesions are visualized. Potential indications for colposcopy include the care of women with atypical squamous cells of undetermined significance, atypical squamous cells that cannot exclude high-grade SIL, atypical glandular cells, low-grade squamous intraepithelial lesions, or high-grade squamous intraepithelial lesions.[37]

As with other reusable medical devices, cleaning and disinfection of colposcopes is important to reduce the risk of HAIs. The manufacturer of the equipment used in colposcopy is responsible, under federal regulation, to provide the user with cleaning and sterilization/high-level disinfection recommendations. The user is responsible for developing work practices based on the manufacturers' recommendations.

CONCLUSIONS

STDs carry serious health consequences for the public health and for those directly affected by these diseases. Some population groups in the United States are more vulnerable to STDs and the associated health and economic costs, including women and infants, adolescents and young adults, minorities, MSM, and people in corrections facilities.[1] Targeted STD prevention and treatment services can help identify infections among these populations, prevent complications, and reduce further transmission into the broader community.

Table 91-2. Procedure-Specific Infections: Risks and Prevention

Procedure	Risk(s)	Intervention(s) to Decrease Risk
Transabdominal procedures: performed by needle aspiration or incision through the abdominal wall (e.g., laparoscopy, hysterectomy, tubal and ovarian procedures).	Introduction of microorganisms into the wound or abdominal cavity with resultant peritonitis or incisional infection; laparoscopy has low risk of incisional infection; pelvic infection may occur in 0.1% to 0.3% of patients.	Use careful preoperative skin preparation; use prophylactic antibiotics as appropriate; sterilize laparoscopes before each use; if not feasible, use high-level disinfection.
Transvaginal procedures Dilation and curettage (D&C) **Intrauterine devices (IUDs)**	D&C has a risk of perforation of the uterus, endometritis, and tubal infections. An IUD acts as a foreign body; perforation of the uterus is possible; PID, tubal infections, and possibly peritonitis may occur.	Teach patient appropriate hygiene practices and to avoid tampon use for 2 to 6 weeks. Consider other (noninvasive) forms of birth control and avoid use in nulliparous females.
Vaginal hysterectomy	Vaginal hysterectomy associated with the risk of "cuff" infection; vaginal or intestinal microorganisms are most common.	Use general surgical interventions and use prophylactic antimicrobial agents as appropriate.
Diaphragm fitting	Transmission of STDs (e.g., HIV, HSV, HBV).	One study supported cleaning with soap and water followed by 15-minute soak in 70% alcohol; no data are available on efficacy of disinfectants against human papillomavirus because of inability to grow virus in vitro.
Cryosurgical procedure	Transmission of STDs and other organisms from contaminated probes.	Use cleaning followed by high-level disinfection of probes between patient use.
Transvaginal ultrasound	Transmission of STDs and other organisms from contaminated probes.	Cover probe with condom because condom may fail; most recommend cleaning and then using high-level disinfection of probe between each use. Ultrasound gel has been associated with cluster of infections; minimize potential for contamination of gel by keeping it in original container. Others have indicated alternative biocides that could be used for surface disinfection of the probe.
Abortion (includes removal or expulsion of products of conception before end of normal gestation period).	Use of poor aseptic technique or unsterilized instruments results in microbial contamination of endometrium; retained tissue can be a medium for bacterial growth.	Use aseptic technique; remove retained tissue promptly; instruct patient in hygiene practices.
Laser-assisted gynecologic procedure	The plume generated may contain viral DNA; may present a risk of exposure for the patient and operative personnel.	Evacuate plume through filter device; maintain good ventilation; consider use of high-filtration laser mask when laser is in use. SurePath should be considered superior to conventional tests used to detect low-grade and high-grade squamous intraepithelial lesions.[35,36]

From Rein MF. Volvovaginitis and Cervicitis. In: Mandell GL, Bennett JE, Dolin R, eds. *Principles and Practice of Infectious Disease,* 6th ed. New York: Churchill Livingstone, 2005:1357–1371.

Vaginal flora and medical devices are potential sources for HAIs linked with gynecological procedures. The risk of infections after gynecological procedures can be reduced through good infection prevention and proper cleaning and disinfection/sterilization of medical devices/instruments.

FUTURE TRENDS

Future trends and research regarding STDs involve early and rapid identification, improved and more rapid contact investigations as shown through social network modeling, addressing increasing drug resistance, and enabling individuals across all socioeconomic groups to access the necessary healthcare and health education.

INTERNATIONAL PERSPECTIVE

The impact of STDs and their resultant health consequences represent a global challenge. The effects upon populations and the social and cultural differences demonstrate the need for enhanced medical and social programs.

REFERENCES

1. Centers for Disease Control and Prevention (CDC). *Trends in Reportable Sexually Transmitted Diseases in the United States, 2011 National Data for Chlamydia, Neisseria gonorrhea, and Syphilis.* U.S. Department of Health and Human Services website. Available at: http://www.cdc.gov/std/stats.
2. Stamm WE, Jones RB, Batteiger BE. Chlamydia trachomatis (Trachoma, Perinatal Infections, Lymphogranuloma Venereum, And Other Genital Infections). In: Mandell GL, Bennett JE, Dolin R, eds. *Principles and Practice of Infectious Disease,* 6th ed. New York: Churchill Livingstone; 2005:2239–2255.
3. Centers for Disease Control and Prevention (CDC). Chlamydia trachomatis, *genital infections—1996 case definition.* CDC National Notifiable Diseases Surveillance System website. December 13, 2013. Available at: http://www.cdc.gov/nndss/script/casedef.aspx?CondYrID=634&Date Pub=1/1/1996%2012:00:00%20AM.
4. Workowski KA, Berman SM, Centers for Disease Control and Prevention. Sexually transmitted diseases treatment guidelines, 2010. *MMWR Recomm Rep* 2010 Dec 17;59(RR-12):1–110.
5. Paul SM. Chapter 101. Sexually Transmitted Diseases. In: *APIC Text of Infection Control and Epidemiology.* Washington, DC; APIC; 2000.
6. U.S. Preventive Services Task Force (USPSTF). *Recommendations for Adults.* USPSTF website. November 2013. Available at: http://www.uspreventiveservicestaskforce.org/adultrec.htm.
7. Siegel JD, Rhinehart E, Jackson M, et al. *2007 Guidelines for Isolation Precautions: Preventing Transmission of Infectious Agents in Healthcare Settings.* CDC website. Available at: http://www.cdc.gov/hicpac/2007ip/2007isolationprecautions.html

8. Centers for Disease Control and Prevention (CDC). Update to CDC's sexually transmitted diseases treatment guidelines, 2006: fluoroquinolones no longer recommended for treatment of gonococcal infections. *MMWR Morb Mortal Wkly Rep* 2007 Apr 13;56(14):332–336.
9. Handsfield HH, Sparling PF. Neisseria gonorrhoeae. In: Mandell GL, Bennett JE, Dolin R, eds. *Principles and Practice of Infectious Disease,* 6th ed. New York: Churchill Livingstone, 2005:2514–2529.
10. Bonnez W, Reichman RC. Papillomaviruses. In: Mandell GL, Bennett JE, Dolin R, eds. *Principles and Practice of Infectious Disease*, 6th ed. New York: Churchill Livingstone, 2005:1841–1856.
11. Centers for Disease Control and Prevention (CDC). CDC Grand Rounds: the growing threat of multidrug-resistant gonorrhea. *MMWR Morb Mortal Wkly Rep* 2013 Feb 15;62(6):103–106.
12. Centers for Disease Control and Prevention (CDC). Advisory Committee on Immunization Practices (ACIP) recommended immunization schedules for persons 0-18 years of age and adults aged 19 and over–United States, 2013. *MMWR Surveill Summ* 2013 Feb 1;62 Suppl 1:1.
13. Corey L. Herpes Simplex Virus. In: Mandell GL, Bennett JE, Dolin R, eds. *Principles and Practice of Infectious Disease,* 6th ed. New York: Churchill Livingstone, 2005:1762–1780.
14. Murphy TL. Haemophilus Species (Including Chancroid). In: Mandell GL, Bennett JE, Dolin R, eds. *Principles and Practice of Infectious Disease*, 6th ed. New York: Churchill Livingstone, 2005:2661–2669.
15. Bolyard EA, Tablan OC, Williams WW, et al. Guidelines for infection control in healthcare personnel, 1998. *Infect Control Hosp Epidemiol* 1998 Jun;19(6):407–463.
16. Paul S. *Infection Control in Long Term Care Facilities.* Trenton, NJ: New Jersey Department of Health and Senior Services; October 1992.
17. Leone PA. Scabies and pediculosis pubis: an update of treatment regimens and general review. *Clin Infect Dis* 2007 Apr 1;44 Suppl 3:S153–S159.
18. Tramont EC. Treponema pallidum (Syphilis). In: Mandell GL, Bennett JE, Dolin R, eds. *Principles and Practice of Infectious Disease*, 6th ed. New York: Churchill Livingstone, 2005:2768–2785.
19. Zetola NM, Klausner JD. Syphilis and HIV infection: an update. *Clin Infect Dis* 2007;44:1222–1228.
20. Rein MF. Trichomonas vaginalis. In: Mandell GL, Bennett JE, Dolin R, eds. *Principles and Practice of Infectious Disease*, 6th ed. New York: Churchill Livingstone, 2005:2768–2784.
21. Edwards JE Jr. Candida species. In: Mandell GL, Bennett JE, Dolin R, eds. *Principles and Practice of Infectious Disease*, 6th ed. New York: Churchill Livingstone, 2005:2938–2957.
22. Rein MF. Volvovaginitis and Cervicitis. In: Mandell GL, Bennett JE, Dolin R, eds. *Principles and Practice of Infectious Disease*, 6th ed. New York: Churchill Livingstone, 2005:1357–1371.
23. Cohen M. Sexually transmitted diseases enhance HIV transmission: no longer a hypothesis. *Lancet* 1998;351(Suppl 3):5–7.
24. Wasserheit JN. Epidemiologic synergy: interrelationships between human immunodeficiency virus infection and other sexually transmitted diseases. *Sex Transm Dis* 1992 Mar-Apr;19(2):61–77.
25. Ohm MJ, Galask RP. The effect of antibiotic prophylaxis on patients undergoing total abdominal hysterectomy. *Am J Obstet Gynecol* 1976 Jun 15;125(4):448–454.
26. Centers for Disease Control and Prevention (CDC). *The Role of STD Detection and Treatment in HIV Prevention: CDC Fact Sheet.* Available at: http://www.cdc.gov/std/hiv/stds-and-hiv-fact-sheet-press.pdf.
27. Ness RB, Hilier SL, Richter HE, et al. Douching in relation to bacterial vaginosis, lactobacilli, and facultative bacteria in the vagina. *Obstet Gynecol* 2002 Oct;100(4):765.
28. Smith DK, Grohskopf LA, Black RJ, et al. Antiretroviral postexposure prophylaxis after sexual, injection-drug use, or other nonoccupational exposure to HIV in the United States: recommendations from the U.S. Department of Health and Human Services. *MMWR Recomm Rep* 2005 Jan 21;54(RR-2):1–20.
29. Keshavarz H, Hillis SD, Kieke MA, et al. (CDC). Hysterectomy surveillance—United States, 1994–1999. *MMWR* 2002;51(SS05):1–8.
30. Emori TG, Culver DH, Horan TC, et al. National Nosocomial Infections Surveillance (NNIS) systems: description of surveillance methodology. *Am J Infect Control* 1991 Feb;19(1):19–35.
31. Centers for Disease Control and Prevention (CDC). Hysterectomy in the United States, 2000–2004. CDC website. Available at: http://www.cdc.gov/reproductivehealth/WomensRH/00-04-FS _Hysterectomy.htm.
32. Emori TG, Culver DH, Horan TC, et al. National Nosocomial Infections Surveillance (NNIS) systems: description of surveillance methodology. *Am J Infect Control* 1991;19(1):19–35.
33. Gaynes RP, Horan TC. Surveillance of Nosocomial Infections. In: Mayhall CG, ed. *Hospital Epidemiology and Infection Control,* 2nd ed. Philadelphia: Lippincott Williams & Wilkins; 1999:1285–1317.
34. National Nosocomial Infections Surveillance (NNIS) System. National Nosocomial Infections Surveillance (NNIS) Report, data summary from January 1992 to June 2002, issued August 2002. *Am J Infect Control* 2002 Dec;30(8):458–475.
35. Farquhar CM, Steiner CA. Hysterectomy rates in the United States 1990–1997. *Obstet Gynecol* 2002 Feb;99(2):229–234.
36. American College of Obstetrics and Gynecology. ACOG Technology Assessment in Obstetrics and Gynecology No. 2: Cervical Cytology Screening. *Obstet Gynecol* 2002 Dec;100(6):1423–1427.
37. American Society for Colposcopy and Cervical Pathology (ASCCP). Consensus Guidelines for Colposcopy, 2002. ASCCP website. Available at: http://www.asccp.org/pdfs/consensus/algorithms.pdf.

SUPPLEMENTAL RESOURCES

American Social Health Association. Available at: http://www.ashastd.org/.

Centers for Disease Control and Prevention (CDC) Division of STD Prevention. Sexually transmitted diseases (STDs). Available at: http://www.cdc.gov/std /default.htm.

Centers for Disease Control and Prevention (CDC) National STD/HIV hotline. Telephone: 1-800–227–8922.

National Network of STD/HIV Prevention Training Centers (PTCs). Available at: http://depts.washington.edu/nnptc/.

CHAPTER 92

Skin and Soft Tissue Infections

Anucha Apisarnthanarak, MD
Associate Professor
Division of Infectious Diseases
Thammasat University Hospital
Pratumthani, Thailand

Linda M. Mundy, MD, PhD
Director, Worldwide Epidemiology
Research and Development, GlaxoSmithKline
Collegeville, PA

ABSTRACT

Skin and soft tissue infections are common clinical problems that vary in type and severity. Breach of the skin from trauma, surgery, or primary skin disease is often a precursor to microbial penetration through the epidermis with a consequent range in progression from a superficial, self-limited infection to a life-threatening infection. If purulence at the site of infection is accessible for culture, procurement of a diagnostic test specimen will often provide clinically relevant, diagnostic information regarding microbial etiology, drug susceptibility, and potentially effective antibiotic therapy.

KEY CONCEPTS

- Anatomy of skin and subcutaneous tissues

- Pathophysiology of skin and soft tissue infections

- Microbiology of human skin and emergence of skin and soft tissue infections

- Clinical approach to the diagnosis of skin and soft tissue infections

- Common skin and soft tissue infections

- Infections associated with underlying conditions

- Cutaneous manifestations of systemic infections

- Necrotizing soft tissue infections

- Immunocompromised hosts: skin and soft tissue infections

- Management of skin and soft tissue infections due to drug-susceptible and multidrug-resistant pathogens

BACKGROUND

Skin and soft tissue infections (SSTIs) comprise a wide variety of common clinical entities that range from mild abrasions to rapidly progressive, life-threatening necrotizing infections. Most skin infections are readily recognized and easily treated, but the more severe cases may initially appear benign, prompting a delay in diagnosis and treatment that may result in subsequent deep tissue infection with associated risks of morbidity and mortality. The purpose of this chapter is to provide a systematic classification of diagnoses and treatments of SSTIs, inclusive of surgical site infections (SSIs), for hospital epidemiologists and infection prevention specialists. SSIs are a major source of excess clinical and economic burden and several initiatives have targeted improvements in case identification, standardized reporting, and optimized quality of care for postsurgical patients at risk for infection.[1-6] Approaches to diagnosis and treatment of SSTIs should be guided by understanding of the type of infection and severity of the clinical presentation. Empiric treatment should include coverage of drug-resistant *Staphylococcus aureus* and drug-resistant Gram-negative bacilli, if such pathogens are suspected on the basis of local epidemiology, risk factors, or clinical features of the case presentation.[7,8]

BASIC PRINCIPLES

Anatomy of the Skin and Underlying Soft Tissues

Epidermis. Beginning at the skin surface, each successive layer of integument provides different mechanisms of immune protection. The outermost layer of the skin is the epidermis, a continually renewing stratified squamous epithelium and the major physical barrier of the skin. This protective layer can be invaded or bypassed by microbes through hair follicles and sebaceous glands. The basal layer of cells is the keratinocytes, which divide, differentiate, and eventually are sloughed from the skin surface.

Dermis. The dermis is separated from the epidermis by a basement membrane and from the deep fascia by an adipose-rich subcutaneous region. Collagen is a major dermal constituent that provides the pliability, elasticity, and tensile strength of the skin. Dermal collagen and elastin are embedded in a glycoprotein matrix, which provides a strong supportive skin structure. The interruption of dermal blood flow can restrict humoral and cellular host defenses against invading microorganisms and predispose to infection.

Subcutaneous tissue and deep fascia. The subcutaneous tissue layer is composed of fat cells, which serve as heat insulators, shock absorbers, and depots of caloric reserves. The superficial fascia separates the skin from underlying muscles and a deep fascial layer.

SKIN AND SOFT TISSUE INFECTIONS

Pathophysiology of Skin and Soft Tissue Infections

Skin integrity, bacterial colonization of the skin and the invasive potential of microbial pathogens, and the host's systemic defense mechanisms each contribute to host-microbe interactions associated with skin and soft tissue infection.

Skin integrity and barrier functions of the skin. SSTIs often arise from defects in the integrity of the epidermis associated with trauma, postoperative wounds, burns, or an underlying dermatosis. In certain circumstances, the portal of entry can be remote from the site of clinical infection, as evident in bacterial cellulitis of the lower extremity associated with tinea pedis and toe web intertrigo.[9] In some cases of cutaneous infection, the portal of entry cannot be identified. Focal skin infection may be the result of hematogenous seeding of the skin, as occurs in bacterial endocarditis or sepsis. Isolation of the etiological microorganism is often unsuccessful because of lack of purulence for diagnostic test specimen procurement, specimen transport and processing, or laboratory detection methods.

Bacterial factors associated with normal skin flora and bacterial invasion of skin. Normal skin flora is often colonized with *Corynebacterium* spp., *Propionibacterium acnes*, and coagulase-negative staphylococci. Commensal and pathogenic bacteria detected on the skin express proteases that influence host risks for SSTIs.[10] Proteases secreted by commensal bacteria contribute to homeostatic bacterial coexistence on skin, whereas proteases from pathogenic bacteria are used as virulence factors associated with breach of skin integrity.[10] Infection is initiated by microbial penetration of the epidermis to deeper tissue and cleavage planes where bacterial hyaluronidases break down host polysaccharides, fibrinolysins digest fibrin barriers, and lecithinases and lipases destroy skin cell membranes and adipocytes.[10,11] In addition, the local production of bacterial exotoxins by organisms such as *S. aureus* or group A streptococci may result in generalized inflammation such as staphylococcal scalded skin syndrome, toxic shock syndrome (TSS), or scarlet fever.[11] Some commensal and pathogenic bacteria are able to adhere to and colonize skin with altered integrity and within wounds. Initial bacterial adherence is due to hydrophobicity, ion exchange, and specific binding of bacterial adhesion molecules to cellular receptors. Staphylococci secrete polysaccharides that can form a biofilm together with multilayer cell clusters.[12] The highly structured communities within a biofilm are resistant to distinct immune effectors and have a decreased susceptibility to antibiotics in vivo.[12–14] Treatment that targets biofilm formation may improve wound healing and reduce wound infections.[14,15]

Host systemic defense mechanisms. Local blood circulation and host immune defenses are the primary determinants of the host response to invasive pathogens. The systemic clinical findings associated with SSTIs are often mediated by host cytokines. Lymphedema, chronic venous insufficiency, prior cellulitis, nephrotic syndrome, and diabetes mellitus are some of the recognized local and systemic predisposing factors to SSTIs. Infecting microbes may enter the lymphatic system, resulting in lymphangitis and regional lymphadenitis, or they may enter the circulatory system and cause bacteremia.

Microbiological Diagnosis

Historically, the etiological agents associated with SSTIs have been clinically predicted from the host presentation; diagnostic tests for the microbial etiology have had a relatively minor role in evaluation and management. The recent increase in prevalence of multidrug-resistant (MDR) bacterial pathogens in community and healthcare settings has augmented the benefit of specimen procurement for Gram stain and culture of purulent drainage, fluctuance, or tissue necrosis in SSTI cases.[16] The isolation of a single pathogen is highly significant and can guide de-escalation of treatment after initial broad empiric antimicrobial coverage. Moreover, isolation of the causative organism may have epidemiological importance for surveillance and for infection prevention and control interventions recommended for patients with methicillin-resistant *S. aureus* (MRSA), vancomycin-resistant enterococci (VRE), and MDR Gram-negative bacilli.

Emergence of Drug-resistant Pathogens in Skin and Soft Tissue Infections

Staphylococcal infections of skin and soft tissues are frequently encountered in community and healthcare settings. In recent years, community-acquired MRSA (CA-MRSA) infections have been reported in uncomplicated skin infections such as impetigo, secondarily infected open wounds, and more complicated SSTI such as cellulitis.[17–23] The most common microorganism isolated from hospitalized patients with SSTIs has been *S. aureus*, with a range in MRSA prevalence from as high as 23 percent in Western Europe to 47 percent in the United States.[18–20] Risk factors for MRSA infection among patients in healthcare settings include prior exposure to antimicrobial agents, prolonged hospital stay, stay in an intensive care or burn unit, proximity to patients colonized or infected with MRSA, use of invasive devices, surgical procedures, and underlying illness.[24] Methicillin resistance is defined as an oxacillin minimum inhibitory concentration (MIC) of at least 4 μg/mL, and such isolates are also resistant to other beta-lactams such as dicloxacillin and cefazolin.[19] Transmission dynamics for MRSA have been observed among healthy individuals, postpartum women, inmates within the criminal justice systems, and members of sports teams.[24–27] Modeling frameworks to further inform on the evolution and spread of MRSA suggest within-host and population-level competition between MSSA and MRSA strains.[28–30] Strains of *S. aureus* with reduced susceptibility to vancomycin (VRSA) have been identified in France, Japan, and the United States.[31–34] Among seven cases of VRSA infection identified between 2002 and 2005 in the United States, all had a history of underlying chronic skin ulcers and either colonization or infection with MRSA and enterococci.[34] Although SSTIs due to VRSA remain rare, SSTIs due to CA-MRSA may be responsible for up to 50 visits per 1,000patients, with more severe clinical presentations and higher SSTI recurrence rates among persons with CA-MRSA than persons with community-associated MSSA (CA-MSSA) SSTI.[35,36]

Colonization and infection with CA-MRSA can occur in individuals with no prior healthcare exposures, as well as in distinct patient groups whose common characteristic appears to be close person-to-person contact.[37–40] Thus, clinical and epidemiological risk factors in persons hospitalized for *S. aureus* infection cannot reliably distinguish between CA-MSSA and CA-MRSA. Treatment of complicated, purulent, and fluctuant SSIs involves incision and drainage in addition to oral or parenteral antibiotic therapy. Trimethoprim-sulfamethoxazole, clindamycin, doxycycline, and linezolid are often feasible treatment options.[41,42] With the increasing report of CA-MRSA SSTI, healthcare practitioners in outpatient and inpatient settings need to be familiar with prevention and treatment strategies for CA-MRSA.[41,42]

Enterococci are normal inhabitants of the gastrointestinal tract that are associated with SSTIs and invasive infections. In recent years, surveillance data suggest that both the percentage of *Enterococcus faecium* among enterococcal isolates and the proportion of vancomycin-resistant *E. faecium* (VREF) have significantly increased.[43] Judicious use of vancomycin is recommended to minimize the emergence of vancomycin-resistant enterococcal (VRE) infections in both the community and in healthcare facilities. Results from randomized clinical trials of VRE in SSTIs report treatment response to quinupristin-dalfopristin, linezolid, and daptomycin.[44–46]

MDR Gram-negative microorganisms now account for a significant portion of complicated SSTIs.[47–49] Risk factors for MDR Gram-negative infections include previous exposure to antimicrobial agents and recent healthcare encounters. The clinical presentations of MDR Gram-negative infections vary from benign to severe life-threatening infections such as necrotizing fasciitis. A high index of clinical suspicion is necessary for prompt case identification, isolation of the patient, and selection of appropriate antimicrobial therapy.

Clinical Approach

The patient's medical history and physical examination are key factors in the evaluation and management of SSTIs. The medical history should include a thorough review of comorbidities, recent trauma, environmental exposures, and recent antimicrobial exposure. One of the important early steps in evaluating patients with SSTIs is to determine if the lesion is discrete or diffuse, and if it is localized or spreading. There are four general clinical categories of SSTI: (1) discrete or localized skin lesions without toxicity; (2) discrete or localized skin lesions with toxicity; (3) diffuse or spreading infections in a normal host; and (4) diffuse or spreading lesions in an abnormal host. For patients with localized lesions, the absence of systemic toxicity (fever, chills, or malaise) implies that the infection has been restricted to the clinically evident site by effective host defenses. Such infections include impetigo, folliculitis, furuncles, carbuncles, and whitlow. In contrast, patients with discrete skin lesions associated with systemic toxicity must be considered to have disseminated SSTIs such as disseminated gonococcal infection, ecthyma gangrenosum, or other bacteremia, viremia, or fungemia. Spreading of erythematous skin lesions to involve the deeper structures of the dermis and the subcutaneous fat is typically referred to as cellulitis. When the infection extends even deeper into the adjacent fascia, it is usually classified as a necrotizing fasciitis. In a normal host with no recent epidemiologically significant exposures, the differential diagnosis includes erysipelas, streptococcal or staphylococcal cellulitis, streptococcal gangrene, and necrotizing fasciitis. If there is a history of recent relevant exposures, certain other infectious etiologies should be considered. Patients with evidence of SSTI with either fluctuance or necrotic tissue should have an expedited assessment for incision and drainage, surgical debridement, specimen procurement, and initial broad empiric therapy. Some host abnormalities are associated with a predisposition to particular types of SSTI that include polymicrobial foot infections in patients with diabetes mellitus and *Vibrio* spp. infections in patients with cirrhosis. Patients with conditions that lead to chronic edema are predisposed to cellulitis caused by streptococci and patients with iron overload are susceptible to *Listeria* spp., *Yersinia* spp., and *Vibrio vulnificus* infections.

Common Skin Infections

Impetigo. Impetigo is a superficial skin infection occurring predominantly in children and persons of advanced age.[50–52] The skin lesion, or group of lesions, is typically characterized by erythema, or blisters, without crusts that later progress to lesions that ooze and form yellow or honey-colored crusts surrounded by an erythematous margin. Bullous impetigo is generally associated with *S. aureus* infection, whereas nonbullous impetigo is usually associated with group A streptococcal infection. Bacteria isolated from bullous skin lesions have been shown in some subjects to contain the same strain of *S. aureus* as identified for nasal colonization, though the predictive value of screening for colonization in the outpatient setting remains inconclusive. Impetigo caused by group A streptococci is rarely associated with systemic signs or symptoms, though glomerulonephritis is a recognized complication.[53] Untreated impetigo may slowly enlarge and involve new skin sites over several weeks. Epidemics of impetigo have been reported, most often in summer months.[54]

Folliculitis. Folliculitis is a circumscribed infectious process originating in hair follicles that can be classified as superficial or deep and by microbial etiology. Classically, this infection is caused by *S. aureus*. Less commonly, *Pseudomonas aeruginosa* folliculitis has been associated with water exposures. The initial lesions appear papulo-urticarial, usually within 48 hours of exposure, with evolution to pustular folliculitis. Treatment of superficial infections may be warm saline compresses and topical antimicrobial therapy, but infections that are more extensive often require oral or parenteral antimicrobial therapy.

Furuncles and carbuncles. A furuncle or boil is a focal erythematous skin infection complicating an antecedent folliculitis or developing as a deep nodule near a hair follicle. It almost never occurs on the palms or soles. A relatively thick dermis prevents spontaneous drainage to the surface and contributes to the hard, nodular, painful character of the lesion. Eventually, abscess formation occurs. The most common pathogen causing this type of skin infection is *S. aureus,* and treatment usually includes incision and drainage; warm moist compresses may be effective for smaller lesions. A carbuncle is larger than a furuncle, with infection spreading under and between fibrous septa in deep skin tissues, forming a series of interconnected small abscesses. Carbuncles usually occur at the nape of the neck or on the back or thighs, with drainage through clustered skin sites. *S. aureus* is the most common pathogen, and treatment is the same as for furuncles. The major problems associated with furuncles and carbuncles are the spread of infection and the risk for recurrence.

Erysipelas. Erysipelas is a painful, bright red, edematous, indurated skin plaque with an advancing raised border, sharply demarcated from the surrounding normal skin.[55-57] The most common sites of infection are the legs and face, often with previous cutaneous injury or congenital lymphatic disorders (e.g., lymphangiectasia). Group A streptococci is the most common microbial etiology, and the initial lesion spreads locally, and often rapidly, via the lymphatic system. Other less common pathogens are *Streptococcus* groups B, C, and G. Drainage is usually scant, and the organisms are not easily visualized via Gram stain or recovered in cultures. Two historical trials of erysipelas from the 1930s reported a nonantimicrobial treatment response to subjects randomized to receive ultraviolet light.[58,59] Today, mild erysipelas can usually be treated with oral antistreptococcal agents such as penicillin or clindamycin. For moderate to severe infections, parenteral therapy with penicillin is warranted. An enhanced response to therapy may be achieved by the addition of clindamycin to inhibit bacterial exotoxin production.[55] The duration of therapy is variable, but parenteral therapy may be required until resolution of the inflammation and fever, followed by a switch to oral therapy to complete a 2-week treatment course.

Cellulitis. Cellulitis has many of the features of erysipelas, but it often extends into subcutaneous tissues.[55-57] Cellulitis can be differentiated from erysipelas because it is not raised and is indistinctly demarcated from adjacent uninvolved skin. It is usually quite painful and tender, occurring most often on the legs, usually below the knee. In some cases, the overlying epidermis undergoes bullous formation or even focal necrosis resulting in epidermal sloughing and erosion; dermal and subcutaneous abscess formation rarely occurs. Red linear streaking and tender regional lymphadenopathy reflect efferent infection and lymphangitis. The most common microbial etiologies of cellulitis are *S. aureus* and *S. pyogenes,* though lymphangitis is typically associated with group A streptococcal infection.[60] Initial empiric and subsequent treatment is usually by host factors, etiological agents, proximity of vital organs, and the need for hospitalization.[61-66]

Paronychia. Paronychia is infection of the proximal or lateral fingernail or toenail folds. The development of paronychia has been associated with repeated trauma or chronic moisture (e.g., dishwashing) to the hands or feet. Acute paronychia is most often due to *S. aureus* or group A streptococci via breach of skin integrity. In contrast, chronic paronychia is often caused by *Candida albicans*, and these chronic infections are common among individuals who have hands or feet in water for extended periods of time. Hence, minimizing water exposure is an important component of the treatment plan.

Infections Related to Underlying Conditions

Secondary infections may develop in areas of preexisting damage, such as postoperative wounds, accidental trauma, bites, pressure ulcers, and neuropathic foot ulcers. The microbial etiology often reflects a preexisting condition and the resident microbial flora. These infections are usually localized, but they can sometimes result in deep tissue invasion with consequent risk for bacteremia and osteomyelitis.

Surgical site infections. The Centers for Disease Control and Prevention (CDC) has developed standardized definitions and surveillance criteria for SSI, and subsequent evaluations of such guidelines have been published.[67] In 2004–2005, a CDC initiative was undertaken to combine three national healthcare surveillance systems that focused on different populations and events to a single National Healthcare Safety Network (NHSN).[68] The SSI definitions were categorized into three nominal groups: superficial incisional SSI, deep incisional SSI, and organ/space infections. The superficial incisional SSI occurs within 30 days of the operative procedure and involves only skin and subcutaneous tissue in a patient with purulent drainage, a clinical isolate with organisms from an aseptically obtained culture, signs or symptoms of infection, or diagnosis by a surgeon or attending physician. Superficial incisional SSIs are further stratified as either superficial incisional primary (SIP) SSI in the primary incision of a patient who had an operation with one or more incisions or superficial incisional secondary (SIS) SSI in the secondary incision of a patient who had an operation with more than one incision.[68] Deep incisional SSIs occur within 30 or 90 days of the operative procedure, depending on the operative procedure as defined by NHSN, and involve deep soft tissues of the incision, and the patient has at least one specific sign or symptom of an SSI or a diagnosis of a deep SSI by a surgeon or attending physician.[69] These deep incisional SSI are also further stratified as deep incisional primary (DIP) SSI or deep incisional secondary (DIS) SSI.

An organ/space SSI involves any part of the body, excluding the skin fascia or muscle layers, that is opened or manipulated during the operative procedure, occurs within 30 days of the operative procedure as defined by NHSN, and occurs in a patient with purulent drainage, aseptically recovered organisms, an abscess, or diagnosis of organ/space SSI by a surgeon or attending physician.[69] For decades, the most common bacterial pathogens isolated from SSI have been *S. aureus*, coagulase-negative staphylococci, *Enterococcus* spp., and *Escherichia coli*, followed by several less commonly occurring bacteria and *C. albicans*. More recently, empiric SSI treatment has become more challenging given the emergence of MDR pathogens, and the categorization of such makes geographic comparisons difficult.[70]

Recurrent postsurgical cellulitis. Recurrent cellulitis is commonly associated with postsurgical procedures such as venectomy for coronary artery bypass grafting, varicose vein stripping, radical mastectomy, and postradiation therapy with altered integrity of lymphatic drainage. Patients may experience acute onset of pain, fever, and erythema at the site of a healed surgical scar. In healed donor vein site infections of the legs, tinea pedis may provide a portal of entry for infecting bacteria.[9] Although fungal pathogens are not usually isolated in this form of cellulitis, it is postulated that an underlying anatomic abnormality (e.g., impaired local lymphatic or venous drainage) predisposes to invasion with *Streptococcus* spp., *Staphylococcus* spp., or less commonly, other organisms. Cellulitis of this type often recurs with the same or similar anatomic distribution over several months or years. Acute episodes generally respond to standard empirical antimicrobial therapy for lower extremity cellulitis. Treatment of the predisposing tinea pedis, if present, should be part of the therapeutic strategy.

Postbite wound infections. Postbite infections occur after human, animal, and insect exposures.[71-73] Human bites are more prone to serious infectious complications than bites from animals. Clenched-fist injuries require that a physician experienced in hand surgery evaluates the wound to determine if the fascia is intact or if there has been deeper tissue penetration.[74] Bacterial infections after clenched-fist trauma are often polymicrobial, and the bacteriology includes *S. aureus*, *Moraxella* spp., β-lactamase-producing oral anaerobes such as *Prevotella* spp., and *Eikenella corrodens*.[74] Human bites are also a transmission source for bloodborne pathogens such as human immunodeficiency virus, Hepatitis B virus, and even syphilis.

Postbite infections from cats are more common (28 to 80 percent) than from dog bites (3 to 18 percent), with high risk for infection with *Pasteurella multocida* or *Pasteurella* species, often within 24 hours of the exposure.[71-73] Infection from aerobes (streptococci, staphylococci, *Moraxella* spp., *Corynebacterium* spp., and *Neisseria* spp.) and anaerobes (*Fusobacterium*, *Bacteroides*, *Porphyromonas*, and *Prevotella* spp.) has often been identified after cat and dog bites; *E. corrodens* has rarely been reported. Routine prophylactic antibiotics remain controversial, though empiric antibiotic therapy is most often recommended after human and animal bites with

a combination regimen of β-lactam–β-lactamase inhibitor or ceftaroline.[73] Antibiotic prophylaxis has been recommended for bite wounds with full-thickness punctures, severe crush injuries, hand or foot sites, and sites with bone, joint, ligament, or tendon involvement. Prophylaxis is usually administered for a minimum of 3 to 5 days. Surgical management dictates that bite wounds be treated and left open, though facial lesions are often closed for cosmetic reasons. Complications of bite wounds to the hand include septic arthritis, tenosynovitis, and osteomyelitis. Healthy appearing dogs and cats should be quarantined for 10 days and sacrificed only if signs of rabies appear in the biting animal. Rabies prophylaxis regimens should be carefully considered.[75,76]

Of relevance, CA-MRSA has been identified in necrotizing fasciitis, which may initially mimic the appearance of a spider bite.[77] Some MRSA SSTI have been antecedent to spider bites, though in a study of more than 100 common household spiders, none were culture-positive for *S. aureus* or MRSA.[78]

Infections associated with trauma. The extent of the traumatic injury, environmental contamination (e.g., soil, standing water, sea water), and location of the injury are relevant in predicting the number and types of pathogens in the wound.[79] Infecting microorganisms can be derived from an exogenous source or the endogenous microflora (e.g., when intestinal perforation has been a consequence of the trauma). Most infections resulting from traumatic injury are associated with *S. aureus* or *Streptococcus* spp. Recent exposures may play a role in certain types of infection. For example, *Erysipelothrix rhusiopathiae* may cause cutaneous infections in anglers, butchers, and abattoir workers.[56] Puncture wounds of the foot, from penetration of a nail or other sharp object through the sole of a shoe, require careful assessment, especially in diabetic patients.[80,81] Subsequent wounds are often infected with *P. aeruginosa*. *Vibrio vulnificus*, *Aeromonas hydrophilia*, *Plesiomonas shigelloides*, and *Chromobacterium* spp., especially after injuries associated with water immersion. Traumatic wounds contaminated with soil may be infected with *Clostridium* spp., *Pseudomonas* spp., or fungi.[79,82]

Pressure ulcers. Pressure ulcer infections are most commonly associated with immobility, advanced age, and inadequate nutrition, yet they can sometimes be associated with severe morbidity and sepsis. The most frequent anatomic areas are the sacrum, coccyx, greater trochanters, feet, elbows, and other pressure sites in bedbound individuals. Pressure ulcers in the sacrum, hip, and foot are particularly prone to colonization and secondary polymicrobial infection with fecal flora. In most cases these infections require combined medical and surgical care, with challenges related to chronic cutaneous wounds that are refractory to available advanced therapies.[83]

Diabetic foot infections. Foot infections are a significant cause of chronic osteomyelitis, limb loss, and sepsis in diabetic patients.[84] Neuropathy and angiopathy are the major pathophysiological factors contributing to infection in this group of patients. Although *S. aureus* or β-hemolytic streptococci usually cause initial diabetic foot infections, a mix of aerobic and anaerobic flora often causes secondarily infected foot wounds.[85] Superinfection has been attributed to Enterobacteriaceae, anaerobes (particular *Bacteroides fragilis* group), enterococci, and *P. aeruginosa*. Therapy is often complicated by physical factors such as patient immobility, diminished cutaneous sensation (neuropathy), and loss of subcutaneous soft tissue mass (padding over bony protuberances). Secondary bone infections (chronic osteomyelitis) are common, and, when present, require consideration of surgical debridement and long-term (6 or more weeks) antimicrobial therapy. Chronic foot ulcers are common problems in diabetic patients with neuropathy, and optimal glucose control is an important component of treatment response. Successful treatment may require debridement of devitalized tissue or callus, the design of physical padding or prostheses to prevent continued tissue trauma, or hyperbaric oxygen therapy.[86] Cooperative management between the internist and the orthopedic surgeon is highly desirable.

Cutaneous Manifestations of Systemic Infections

Skin lesions such as ecthyma gangrenosa, generalized erythroderma, purpura fulminans, and the characteristic appearance of cutaneous gangrene provide important clues to the diagnosis of life-threatening, tissue-destructive infections. Skin lesions often result from a preceding bacteremia (*Neisseria meningococcus, Staphylococcus,* or *Pseudomonas*), fungemia (*Candida* or *Cryptococcus*), systemic viral infection (varicella or measles), recurrent focal viral infection (herpes simplex or varicella zoster), or the rickettsioses (Rocky Mountain spotted fever and epidemic or endemic typhus). In many circumstances, the appearance of the skin lesions provides an important clue to the etiology of the systemic illness. Another cutaneous manifestation of a systemic infection is the rash caused by a bacterial exotoxin. Two microorganisms in this category are streptococci that elaborate the erythrogenic exotoxin responsible for scarlet fever and staphylococci that produce toxins associated with scalded skin syndrome and TSS.

Necrotizing Soft Tissue Infections

This group of life-threatening infections may cause massive tissue damage, gangrene, profound systemic toxemia, and death. Rapid progressive destruction of cutaneous fat and subcutaneous fascia are the hallmarks of these infections, and the skin is often, but not uniformly, involved. A high index of suspicion is necessary to make an early diagnosis of group A streptococcal necrotizing fasciitis, clostridial myonecrosis, Ludwig angina (face-neck), and Fournier gangrene (scrotum-perineum).[87,88] *P. aeruginosa* infection with sepsis and resultant ecthyma gangrenosum, and *Vibrio* infections may result in focal necrotic skin and soft tissue lesions.

Necrotizing fasciitis and necrotizing soft tissue infections. These infections are aggressive and involve fascia and adjacent soft tissues with a characteristic undermining of tissue planes. Patients with necrotizing fasciitis often have concurrent

morbidities, such as diabetes mellitus, peripheral vascular disease, obesity, and malnutrition.[87,88] Prompt surgical exploration and debridement should be sought in all cases of rapidly evolving focal soft tissue inflammation and necrosis, and includes the opportunity to obtain tissue for Gram stain and culture.

Type 1 necrotizing fasciitis is a mixed infection caused by common aerobic and anaerobic bacteria.[87] Gas in the soft tissues is a classic feature of these infections and is particularly common in postoperative cases or patients with diabetes mellitus or peripheral vascular disease. Specimens commonly yield polymicrobial flora with pathogens such as *S. aureus, E. coli, Peptostreptococcus* spp., *Prevotella* spp., *Bacteroides* spp., microaerophilic streptococci, and *Clostridium* spp. Type 1 necrotizing fasciitis usually occurs at or near a surgical site (e.g., radical neck surgery) and has subacute onset within 4 days of surgery or a traumatic event. Some of these soft tissue infections may be referred to as "Meleney's synergistic gangrene" or, when the perineum and genitalia are involved, as "Fournier gangrene."[87]

Type 2 necrotizing fasciitis is caused by group A streptococci (*S. pyogenes*).[87] Gas is absent from soft tissues in type 2 necrotizing fasciitis, yet there is rapid clinical progression often associated with systemic signs suggestive of TSS. Streptococcal exotoxins (hemolysins, streptolysins O and S, and leukocidins) function as superantigens in the host and are thought to be responsible for many of the systemic features of this syndrome (hypotension, renal impairment, coagulopathy, and acute respiratory distress syndrome). Gangrene results after thrombosis of cutaneous and deep blood vessels and is often associated with focal intense pain. It may occur in otherwise healthy individuals and is characterized by sudden onset and widespread necrosis of fascia and deep subcutaneous tissues, sometimes with initial sparing of the skin and muscle.

Necrotizing fasciitis: Fournier gangrene. This is a distinctive form of type 1 necrotizing fasciitis typically affecting the male perineum and scrotum, with occasional extension to the abdominal wall or buttocks. In women, it can occur between the perineum and vagina. Predisposing factors include diabetes mellitus, alcohol abuse, local trauma, paraphimosis, periurethral extravasation of urine, perirectal or perianal infection, and pelvic surgery.[78] These infections begin abruptly with severe pain, and they may spread rapidly to the anterior abdominal wall or to the gluteal tissues. Cellulitis occurs near the portal of entry, and the involved area usually becomes progressively indurated and tender. As gangrene of the perineum develops, swelling and crepitation increase. Prompt surgical debridement and broad-spectrum, parenteral antibiotic therapy for polymicrobial infections with Gram-positive, Gram-negative, and anaerobic bacteria are indicated.

Necrotizing fasciitis: gas gangrene. Gas gangrene is usually induced by deep, penetrating trauma (e.g., gunshot or stab wound, crush injury). The wound causes compromise of the local blood supply and creates a relatively anaerobic tissue environment promoting the proliferation of *Clostridium perfringens* or related clostridial species. Clostridial soft tissue infection is usually heralded by intense and progressive pain at the affected site. Signs of systemic toxicity (e.g., fever, chills, tachycardia, shock) often follow.[89] Gas in soft tissues (crepitus) may be detected by physical examination or imaging studies via computed tomography or magnetic resonance imaging. Radiographic imaging is less specific or sensitive than the detection of crepitus on physical examination, but imaging may be particularly helpful in identifying gas in deeper tissues.[89] Clostridial exotoxins are thought to play a major role in the development of systemic symptoms and local tissue necrosis. In clostridial cellulitis, gas is invariably found in the skin, but deep tissues may be spared. Initially, the overlying skin appears pale but eventually develops an orange discoloration followed by development of hemorrhagic or clear bullae. In addition, thin brown serosanguinous drainage may develop. Microscopic examination of the drainage reveals few, if any, white blood cells and many Gram-positive or Gram-variable boxcar-shaped bacilli (*C. perfringens*). Even in cellulitis, clostridial infections require both early surgical intervention and empirical antibiotic therapy.

Skin/Soft Tissue Infections in Immunocompromised Hosts

A wide variety of SSTI may occur in immunocompromised hosts and the pathogens identified in normal hosts are uncommon or occur with different clinical manifestations.[90–92] These organisms include mycobacteria, herpesviruses, *Nocardia* spp., *Cryptococcus neoformans*, *Histoplasma capsulatum*, *Coccidioides immitis*, *Toxoplasma gondii*, *Candida* spp., *Aspergillus* spp., *Pseudallescheria boydii*, *Sporothrix schenckii*, *Mucoromycotina* spp., and the enteroviruses. Despite the differential list of microbial etiologies, the clinical appearances of infected cutaneous lesions are often similar to those characterized in normal hosts. Many are the result of hematogenous spread occurring over several days, resulting in erythematous nodules or papules that are usually widely distributed and are minimally to moderately tender. Biopsy and culture of suspicious lesions are often necessary to make an etiologic diagnosis, because routine blood cultures are often negative (though lysis after centrifugation blood cultures are more sensitive and should be obtained). However, one should remember that the pathogens seen in normal hosts also occur in immunocompromised patients, and the degree of tissue inflammation and/or discomfort can be minimal.

Treatment of Skin and Soft Tissue Infections

Four management principles are key to successful SSTI treatment outcomes.[93] These principles include (1) early diagnosis and differentiation of necrotizing versus nonnecrotizing SSTI, (2) early initiation of appropriate empiric broad-spectrum antimicrobial therapy with consideration of risk factors for specific pathogens and mandatory coverage for MRSA and MDR Gram-negative bacteria, (3) source control (i.e., early aggressive surgical intervention for drainage of abscesses and debridement

of necrotizing soft tissue infections), and (4) pathogen identification followed by appropriate de-escalation of antimicrobial therapy. Initial management of complicated SSTIs should include collection of specimens for Gram stain, culture, and antimicrobial susceptibility testing from all patients who have abscesses or purulent lesions. Culture and susceptibility findings are useful for individual patient management and in regional surveillance for antimicrobial resistance. It has been documented that physicians and other healthcare personnel cannot accurately predict the pathogen associated with an SSTI.[93]

Empiric antibiotic therapy should be reviewed if and when susceptibility data are available. For MSSA, antistaphylococcal penicillin or a first-generation cephalosporin may be suitable. For CA-MRSA infections, trimethoprim and sulfamethoxazole (TMP-SMX), clindamycin, or tetracycline may be suitable. For healthcare-associated MRSA, vancomycin, linezolid, daptomycin, or rifampin plus fusidic acid may be suitable.[94,95] For CA-MRSA culture-positive wounds, in vitro susceptibility to TMP-SMX, tetracycline, erythromycin, clindamycin, and vancomycin should be assessed. If the isolate is resistant to erythromycin but susceptible to clindamycin, the clindamycin D-zone test should be performed if clindamycin therapy is being considered. For HA-MRSA culture-positive wounds, an MDR phenotype and in vitro susceptibility to vancomycin, rifampin, and linezolid should be assessed.[94,95] Given the increasing prevalence of MDR pathogens reported for complicated SSTI, pathogen identification is of paramount importance.[70,93] All patients who have complicated SSTIs should have blood cultures obtained on admission and, if possible, before initiation of empiric antimicrobial therapy. In addition, cultures should be obtained directly from the incision and drainage of an abscess or intraoperative tissue when surgical debridement is performed.

Future Antimicrobial Drug Research and Development for SSTI

Future research and development programs that target antimicrobial treatment of SSTI will potentially enroll more severely ill subjects than in prior decades. In 2010, the U.S. Food and Drug Administration recommended that for randomized clinical trials of acute bacterial skin and skin structure infection, subjects with cellulitis, erysipelas, and wounds have a minimum surface area of 75 cm^2 (measured as a multiple of length by width), accompanied by lymph node enlargement or systemic symptoms such as fever greater than or equal to 38°C.[96]

Infection Control for Skin and Soft Tissue Infections Caused by MDR Pathogens

Contact Precautions are recommended by the CDC for hospitalized patients with SSI and SSTI caused by MRSA and MDR Gram-negative bacilli.[97] This guidance includes the use of a private room, wearing gloves on entering the room, wearing a gown if contact with the patient or items in the room is anticipated, and hand washing on removal of the gloves.[97] Despite the guideline, adherence to the guidelines has been suboptimal, and hand washing in particular is inadequate.[98]

Topical mupirocin is effective in reducing nasal colonization of *S. aureus*, but the use of topical mupirocin to reduce the risk of surgical or nonsurgical infections caused by *S. aureus* has not been consistently high.[99,100] It also is not clear that topical mupirocin reduces MRSA colonization.[101] Attempts at combining topical mupirocin with antibacterial baths (e.g., in chlorhexidine or systemic agents) deserve further study.[102,103]

For SSI, recent evidence suggests that implementing surgical checklists, as created by the World Health Organization, was associated with reduction in mortality and morbidity.[104] Notably, the rates of SSIs were reduced in several medical centers from resource adequate and resource-limited settings.[103] Studies of silver-coated antimicrobial dressings, which help promote wound healing and inhibit biofilm formation, have been tested in various populations (e.g., burn wound, trauma wound, and to prevent SSI) and reveal promising outcomes.[105-107] Lastly, surveillance of SSI, especially after transfer from acute care to long-term care facilities is an important factor for accurate post-discharge SSI surveillance.

CONCLUSIONS

Healthcare professionals caring for patients with SSTI should practice strict compliance with the infection prevention practices and policies of the institution in which they practice. Hand hygiene, while easier to endorse than to enforce, is an essential component of patient and healthcare personnel safety. A high index of suspicion for the emergence of antimicrobial-resistant pathogens should be considered, and contact isolation is a recommended component of the care of patients with drug-resistant pathogens. Antimicrobial stewardship is complicated by the limited specimen procurement and diagnostic armamentarium available for SSTI and infection prevention practitioners have a key role in the ongoing education of providers and patients.

REFERENCES

1. Herwaldt L, Cullen J, Scholz D, et al. A prospective study of outcomes, healthcare resource utilization, and costs associated with postoperative nosocomial infections. *Infect Control Hosp Epidemiol* 2006 Dec;27(12):1291–1298.
2. Steinberg SM, Popa MR, Michalek JA, et al. Comparison of risk adjustment methodologies in surgical quality improvement. *Surgery* 2008 Oct;114(4):662–667.
3. Khuri SF, Henderson WG, Daley J, et al. Successful implementation of the Department of Veterans Affairs' National Surgical Quality Improvement Program in the private sector: the Patient Safety in Surgery Study. *Ann Surg* 2008 Aug;248(2):329–336.
4. Rowell KS, Turrentine FE, Hutter MM, et al. Use of national surgical quality improvement program data as a catalyst for quality improvement. *J Am Coll Surg* 2007 Jun;204(6):1293–1300.
5. Petherick ES, Dalton JE, Moore PJ, et al. Methods for identifying surgical wound infection after discharge form hospital: a systematic review. *BMC Infect Dis* 2006 Nov;6:170.
6. Bratzler DW, Hunt DR. The surgical infection prevention and surgical care improvement projects: national initiatives to improve outcomes for patients having Surgery. *Clin Infect Dis* 2006 Aug;43(3):322–330.
7. Charlebois ED, Perdreau-Remington F, Kreisworth B, et al. Origins of community strains of methicillin-resistant *Staphylococcus aureus*. *Clin Infect Dis* 2004 Jul;39(1):47–54.
8. Miller LG, Perdreau-Remington F, Bayer AS, et al. Clinical and epidemiologic characteristics cannot distinguish community-associated methicillin-resistant *Staphylococcus aureus* infection from methicillin-susceptible S. aureus infection: a prospective investigation. *Clin Infect Dis* 2007 Feb;44(4):471–482.
9. Björnsdóttir S, Gottfredsson M, Thórisdóttir AS, et al. Risk factors for acute cellulitis of the lower limb: a prospective case-control study. *Clin Infect Dis* 2005 Nov 15;41(10):1416–1422.
10. Koziel J, Potempa J. Protease-armed bacteria in the skin. *Cell Tissue Res* 2013 Feb;351(2):325–337.
11. Burlak C, Hammer CH, Robinson MA, et al. Global analysis of community-associated methicillin-resistant *Staphylococcus aureus* exoproteins reveals molecules produced in vitro and during infection. *Cell Microbiol* 2007 May;9(5):1172–1190.
12. Babra C, Tiwari J, Costantino P, et al. Human methicillin-sensitive Staphylococcus aureus biofilms: potential associations with antibiotic resistance persistence and surface polysaccharide antigens. *J Basic Microbiol* 2013 May 17 [Epub ahead of print].
13. Koyama N, Inokoshi J, Tomoda H. Anti-infectious agents against MRSA. *Molecules* 2012 Dec 24;18(1):204–224.
14. Smith K, Gemmell CG, Lang S. Telavancin shows superior activity to vancomycin with multidrug-resistant Staphylococcus aureus in a range of in vitro biofilm models. *Eur J Clin Microbiol Infect Dis* 2013 Oct;32(10):1327–1332.
15. Chuangsuwanich A, Charnsanti O, Lohsiriwat V, et al. The efficacy of silver mesh dressing compared with silver sulfadiazine cream for the treatment of pressure ulcers. *J Med Assoc Thai* 2011 May;94(5):559–565.
16. Stevens DL, Bisno AL, Chambers HF, et al. Practice guidelines for the diagnosis and management of skin and soft tissue infections. *Clin Infect Dis* 2005 Nov 15;41(10):1373–1406.
17. Eckmann C, Dryden M. Treatment of complicated skin and soft-tissue infections caused by resistant bacteria: value of linezolid, tigecycline, daptomycin and vancomycin. *Eur J Med Res* 2010 Nov 30;15(12):554–563.
18. Gagliotti C, Balode A, Baquero F, et al. Escherichia coli and Staphylococcus aureus: bad news and good news from the European Antimicrobial Resistance Surveillance Network (EARS-Net, formerly EARSS), 2002 to 2009. *Euro Surveill* 2011 Mar 17;16(11).
19. Rennie RP, Jones RN, Mutnick AH. Occurrence of antimicrobial susceptibility patterns of pathogens isolated from skin and soft tissue infections; report from the SENTRY Antimicrobial Surveillance Program (United States and Canada, 2000). *Diagn Microbiol Infect Dis* 2003 Apr;45(4):287–293.
20. Moet GJ, Jones RN, Biedenbach DJ, et al. Contemporary causes of skin and soft tissue infections in North America, Latin America, and Europe: report from the SENTRY Antimicrobial Surveillance Program (1998–2004). *Diagn Microbiol Infect Dis* 2007 Jan;57(1):7–13.
21. Salgado CD, Farr BM, Calfee DP. Community-acquired methicillin-resistant *Staphylococcus aureus*: a meta-analysis of prevalence and risk factors. *Clin Infect Dis* 2003 Jan 15;36(2):131–139.
22. Farley JE. Epidemiology, clinical manifestations, and treatment options for skin and soft tissue infection caused by community-acquired methicillin-resistant *Staphylococcus aureus*. *J Am Acad Nurse Pract* 2008 Feb;20(2):85–92.
23. Cookson BD. Methicillin resistant *Staphylococcus aureus* in the community: new battlefronts, or are the battles lost? *Infect Control Hosp Epidemiol* 2000 Jun;21(6):398–403.
24. Farley JE, Ross T, Stamper P, et al. Prevalence, risk factors, and molecular epidemiology of methicillin-resistant *Staphylococcus aureus* among newly arrested men in Baltimore, Maryland. *Am J Infect Control* 2008 Nov;36(9):644–650.
25. Kazakova SV, Hageman JC, Matava M, et al. A clone of methicillin-resistant *Staphylococcus aureus* among professional football players. *N Engl J Med* 2005 Feb;352(5):468–475.
26. Bratu S, Eramo A, Kopec R, et al. Community-associated methicillin-resistant *Staphylococcus aureus* in hospital nursery and maternity units. *Emerg Infect Dis* 2005 Jun;11(6):808–813.
27. Saiman L, O'Keefe M, Graham PL, et al. Hospital transmission of community-acquired methicillin-resistant *Staphylococcus aureus* among postpartum women. *Clin Infect Dis* 2003 Nov;37(10):1313–1319.
28. Spicknall IH, Foxman B, Marrs CF, et al. A modeling framework for the evolution and spread of antibiotic resistance: literature review and model categorization. *Am J Epidemiol* 2013 Aug 15;178(4):508–520.
29. Bratu S, Landman D, Gupta J, et al. A population-based study examining the emergence of community-associated methicillin-resistant *Staphylococcus aureus* USA300 in New York City. *Ann Clin Microbiol Antimicrob* 2006 Nov 30;5:29.
30. Salgado CD, Farr BM, Calfee DP. Community-acquired methicillin-resistant *Staphylococcus aureus*: a meta-analysis of prevalence and risk factors. *Clin Infect Dis* 2003 Jan 15;36(2):131–139.
31. Hiramatsu K. The emergence of *Staphylococcus aureus* with reduced susceptibility to vancomycin in Japan. *Am J Med* 1998 May 29;104(5A):7S–10S.
32. Ploy MC, Grélaud C, Martin C, et al. First clinical isolate of vancomycin-intermediate *Staphylococcus aureus* in a French hospital. *Lancet* 1998 Apr 18;351(9110):1212.

33. Cheng S, Sievert DM, Hageman JC, et al. Infection with vancomycin-resistant *Staphylococcus aureus* containing the vanA resistance gene. *N Engl J Med* 2003 Apr 3;348(14):1342–1347.
34. Sievert DM, Rudrik JT, Patel JB, et al. Vancomycin-resistant *Staphylococcus aureus* in the United States, 2002–2006. *Clin Infect Dis* 2008 Mar 1;46(5):668–674.
35. Weber JT. Community-associated methicillin-resistant *Staphylococcus aureus*. *Clin Infect Dis* 2005 Aug;41 Suppl 4:S269–S272.
36. Miller LG, Quan C, Shay A, et al. A prospective investigation of outcomes after hospital discharge for endemic, community-acquired methicillin-resistant and -susceptible *Staphylococcus aureus* skin infection. *Clin Infect Dis* 2007 Feb;44(4):483–492.
37. Hidron AI, Kourbatova EV, Halvosa JS, et al. Risk factors for colonization with methicillin-resistant *Staphylococcus aureus* (MRSA) in patients admitted to an urban hospital: emergence of community-associated MRSA nasal carriage. *Clin Infect Dis* 2005 Jul 15;41(2):159–166.
38. Ellis MW, Hospenthal DR, Dooley DP, et al. Natural history of community-acquired methicillin-resistant *Staphylococcus aureus* colonization and infection in soldiers. *Clin Infect Dis* 2004 Oct 1;39(7):971–979.
39. Rim JY, Bacon AE 3rd. Prevalence of community-acquired methicillin-resistant *Staphylococcus aureus* colonization in a random sample of healthy individuals. *Infect Control Hosp Epidemiol* 2007 Sep;28(9):1044–1046.
40. Zafar U, Johnson LB, Hanna M, et al. Prevalence of nasal colonization among patients with community-associated methicillin-resistant *Staphylococcus aureus* infection and their household contacts. *Infect Control Hosp Epidemiol* 2007 Aug;28(8):966–969.
41. Popovich KJ, Hota B. Treatment and prevention of community-associated methicillin-resistant *Staphylococcus aureus* skin and soft tissue infections. *Dermatol Ther* 2008 May-Jun;21(3):167–179.
42. Avdic E, Cosgrove SE. Management and control strategies for community-associated methicillin-resistant *Staphylococcus aureus*. *Expert Opin Pharmacother* 2008 Jun;9(9):1463–1479.
43. Treitman AN, Yarnold PR, Warren J, et al. Emerging incidence of Enterococcus faecium among hospital isolates (1993 to 2002). *J Clin Microbiol* 2005 Jan;43(1):462–463.
44. Ploufe JF. Emerging therapies for serious gram-positive bacterial infections: a focus on linezolid. *Clin Infect Dis* 2000 Sep;31 Suppl 4:S144–S149.
45. Péchère JC. Current and future management of infections due to methicillin-resistant staphylococci infections: the role of quinupristin/dalfopristin. *J Antimicrob Chemother* 1999 Sep;44 Suppl A:11–18.
46. Garau J. Management of cSSTIs: the role of daptomycin. *Curr Med Res Opin* 2006 Nov;22(11):2079–2087.
47. Vayalumkal JV, Jadavji T. Children hospitalized with skin and soft tissue infections: a guide to antibacterial selection and treatment. *Paediatr Drug* 2006;8(2):99–111.
48. Lee SY, Kuti JL, Nicolau DP. Antimicrobial management of complicated skin and skin structure infections in the era of emerging resistance. *Surg Infect (Larchmt)* 2005;6(3):283–295.
49. Bernard P. Management of common bacterial infections of the skin. *Curr Opin Infect Dis* 2008 Apr;21(2):122–128.
50. Bangert S, Levy M, Hebert AA. Bacterial resistance and impetigo treatment trends: a review. *Pediatr Dermatol.* 2012 May-Jun;29(3):243–248.
51. Koning S, van der Sande R, Verhagen AP, et al. Interventions for impetigo. *Cochrane Database Syst Rev* 2012 Jan 18;1:CD003261.
52. Geria AN, Schwartz RA. Impetigo update: new challenges in the era of methicillin resistance. *Cutis.* 2010 Feb;85(2):65–70.
53. Ilyas M, Tolaymat A. Changing epidemiology of acute post-streptococcal glomerulonephritis in Northeast Florida: a comparative study. *Pediatr Nephrol* 2008 Jul;23(7):1101–1106.
54. Loffeld A, Davies P, Lewis A, et al. Seasonal occurrence of impetigo: a retrospective 8-year review (1996–2003). *Clin Exp Dermatol* 2005 Sep;30(5):512–514.
55. Lazzarini L, Conti E, Tositti G, et al. Erysipelas and cellulitis: clinical and microbiological spectrum in an Italian tertiary care hospital. *J Infect* 2005 Dec;51(5):383–389.
56. Veraldi S, Girgenti V, Dassoni F, et al. Erysipeloid: a review. *Clin Exp Dermatol* 2009 Dec;34(8):859–862.
57. Kilburn SA, Featherstone P, Higgins B, et al. Interventions for cellulitis and erysipelas. *Cochrane Database Syst Rev* 2010 Jun 16;(6):CD004299.
58. Snodgrass WR, Anderson T. Sulphanilamide in the treatment of erysipelas: a controlled series of 270 cases. *Brit Med Journal* 1937;1156–1159.
59. Snodgrass WR, Anderson T. Prontosil in the treatment of erysipelas: a controlled series of 312 cases. *BMJ* 1937;101–104.
60. O'Loughlin RE, Roberson A, Cieslak PR, et al. The epidemiology of invasive group A streptococcal infection and potential vaccine implications: United States, 2000–2004. *Clin Infect Dis* 2007 Oct 1;45(7):853–862.
61. Peralta G, Padrón E, Roiz MP, et al. Risk factors for bacteremia in patients with limb cellulitis. *Eur J Clin Microbiol Infect Dis* 2006 Oct;25(10):619–626.
62. Pallin DJ, Binder WD, Allen MB, et al. Clinical trial: comparative effectiveness of cephalexin plus trimethoprim-sulfamethoxazole versus cephalexin alone for treatment of uncomplicated cellulitis: a randomized controlled trial. *Clin Infect Dis* 2013 Jun;56(12):1754–1762.
63. Griffith ME, Ellis MW. Antimicrobial activity against CA-MRSA and treatment of uncomplicated nonpurulent cellulitis. *Expert Rev AntiInfect Ther* 2013 Aug;11(8):777–780.
64. Friedland HD, O'Neal T, Biek D, et al. CANVAS 1 and 2: analysis of clinical response at day 3 in two phase 3 trials of ceftaroline fosamil versus vancomycin plus aztreonam in treatment of acute bacterial skin and skin structure infections. *Antimicrob Agents Chemother* 2012 May;56(5):2231–2236.
65. Craft JC, Moriarty SR, Clark K, et al. A randomized, double-blind phase 2 study comparing the efficacy and safety of an oral fusidic acid loading-dose regimen to oral linezolid for the treatment of acute bacterial skin and skin structure infections. *Clin Infect Dis* 2011 Jun;52 Suppl 7:S520–S526.
66. Pan A, Cauda R, Concia E, et al. Consensus document on controversial issues in the treatment of complicated skin and skin-structure infections. *Int J Infect Dis* 2010 Oct;14 Suppl 4:S39–S53.
67. Henriksen NA, Meyhoff CS, Wetterslev J, et al. Clinical relevance of surgical site infection as defined by the criteria of the Centers for Disease Control and Prevention. *J Hosp Infect* 2010 Jul;75(3):173–177.
68. Horan TC, Andrus M, Dudeck MA. CDC/NHSN surveillance definition of health care-associated infection and criteria for specific types of infections in the acute care setting. *Am J Infect Control* 2008 Jun;36(5):309–332.
69. Centers for Disease Control and Prevention (CDC). *CDC/NHSN surveillance definitions for specific types of infections.* CDC website. January 2014. Available at: http://www.cdc.gov/nhsn/pdfs/pscmanual/17pscnosinfdef_current.pdf.
70. Magiorakos AP, Srinivasan A, Carey RB, et al. Multidrug-resistant, extensively drug-resistant and pandrug-resistant bacteria: an international expert proposal for interim standard definitions for acquired resistance. *Clin Microbiol Infect* 2012 Mar;18(3):268–281.
71. Jaindl M, Grünauer J, Platzer P, et al. The management of bite wounds in children—a retrospective analysis at a level I trauma centre. *Injury* 2012 Dec;43(12):2117–2121.
72. Cheah AE, Chong AK. Bites to the hand: are they more than we can chew? *Singapore Med J* 2011 Oct;52(10):715–718.
73. Goldstein EJ, Citron DM, Merriam CV, et al. Ceftaroline versus isolates from animal bite wounds: comparative in vitro activities against 243 isolates, including 156 Pasteurella species isolates. *Antimicrob Agents Chemother* 2012 Dec;56(12):6319–6323.
74. Talan DA, Abrahamian FM, Moran GJ, et al. Clinical presentation and bacteriologic analysis of infected human bites in patients presenting to emergency departments. *Clin Infect Dis* 2003 Dec 1;37(11):1481–1489.
75. Gautret P, Le Roux S, Faucher B, et al. Epidemiology of urban dog-related injuries requiring rabies post-exposure prophylaxis in Marseille, France. *Int J Infect Dis* 2013 Mar;17(3):e164–e167.
76. Manning SE, Rupprecht CE, Fishbein D, et al. Human rabies prevention—United States, 2008: recommendations of the Advisory Committee on Immunization Practices. *MMWR Recomm Rep* 2008 May 23;57(RR-3):1–28.
77. Young LM, Price CS. Community-acquired methicillin-resistant *Staphylococcus aureus* emerging as an important cause of necrotizing fasciitis. *Surg Infect (Larchmt)* 2008 Aug;9(4):469–474.
78. Baxtram C, Mongkolpradit T, Kasimos JN, et al. Common house spiders are not likely vectors of community-acquired methicillin-resistant *Staphylococcus aureus* infections. *J Med Entomol* 2006 Sep;43(5):962–965.
79. Eliya MC, Banda GW. Primary closure versus delayed closure for non-bite traumatic wounds within 24 hours post injury. *Cochrane Database Syst Rev* 2011 Sep 7;(9):CD008574.
80. Belin R, Carrington S. Management of pedal puncture wounds. *Clin Podiatr Med Surg* 2012 Jul;29(3):451–458.
81. East JM, Yeates CB, Robinson HP. The natural history of pedal puncture wounds in diabetics: a cross-sectional survey. *BMC Surg* 2011 Oct 17;11:27.
82. Ibnoulkhatib A, Lacroix J, Moine A, et al. Post-traumatic bone and/or joint limb infections due to Clostridium spp. *Orthop Traumatol Surg Res* 2012 Oct;98(6):696–705.
83. Maderal AD, Vivas AC, Eaglstein WH, et al. The FDA and designing clinical trials for chronic cutaneous ulcers. *Semin Cell Dev Biol* 2012 Dec;23(9):993–999.
84. Moura LIF, Dias AM, Carvalho E, et al. Recent advances on the development of wound dressings for diabetic foot ulcer treatment—a review. *Acta Biomater* 2013 Jul;9(7):7093–7114.

85. Demetriou M, Papanas N, Panopoulou M, et al. Tissue and swab culture in diabetic foot infections: neuropathic versus neuroischemic ulcers. *Int J Low Extrem Wounds* 2013 Jun;12(2):87–93.

86. Cimşit M, Uzun G, Yildiz S. Hyperbaric oxygen therapy as an ant-infective agent. *Expert Rev Anti Infect Ther* 2009 Oct;7(8):1015–1026.

87. Morgan MS. Recent advances in the treatment of necrotizing fasciitis. *Curr Infect Dis Rep* 2011 Oct;13(5):461–469.

88. Schuster L, Nunez DR. Using clinical pathways to aid in the diagnosis of necrotizing soft tissue infections synthesis of evidence. *World Evid Based Nurs* 2012 Apr;9(2):88–99.

89. Stevens DL, Aldape MJ, Bryant AE. Life-threatening clostridial infections. *Anaerobe* 2012 Apr;18(2):254–259.

90. Valeriano-Marcet J, Carter JD, Vasey FB. Soft tissue disease. *Rheum Dis Clin North Am* 2003 Feb;29(1):77–88.

91. Spampinato C, Leonardi D. Candida infections, causes, targets, and resistance mechanisms: traditional and alternative antifungal agents. *Biomed Res Int* 2013;2013:204237.

92. Skiada A, Rigopoulos D, Larios G, et al. Global epidemiology of cutaneous zygomycosis. *Clin Dermatol* 2012 Nov-Dec;30(6):628–632.

93. Napolitona LM. Severe soft tissue infection. *Infect Dis Clin North Am* 2009 Sep;23(3):571–591.

94. Hsueh PR, Chen WH, Teng LJ, et al. Nosocomial infections due to methicillin-resistant Staphylococcus aureus and vancomycin-resistant enterococci at a university hospital in Taiwan from 1991 to 2003: resistance trends, antibiotic usage and in vitro activities of newer antimicrobial agents. *Int J Antimicrob Agents* 2005 Jul;26(1):43–49.

95. Morgan M. Treatment of MRSA soft tissue infections: an overview. *Injury* 2011 Dec;42 Suppl 5:S11–S17.

96. U.S. Department of Health and Human Services, Food and Drug Administration (FDA), Center for Drug Evaluation and Research (CDER). *Guidance for industry acute bacterial skin and skin structure infections: developing drugs for treatment.* FDA website. October 2013. Available at: http://www.fda.gov/downloads/drugs/guidancecomplianceregulatory information/guidances/ucm071185.pdf.

97. Siegel JD, Rhinehart E, Jackson M, et al. 2007 Guideline for Isolation Precautions: Preventing Transmission of Infectious Agents in Health Care Settings. *Am J Infect Control* 2007 Dec;35 (10 Suppl 2): S65–S164.

98. Krein SL, Kowalski CP, Hofer TP, et al. Preventing hospital-acquired infections: a national survey of practices reported by U.S. hospitals in 2005 and 2009. *J Gen Intern Med* 2012 Jul;27(7):773–779.

99. Schweizer ML, Herwaldt LA. Surgical site infections and their prevention. *Curr Opin Infect Dis* 2012 Aug;25(4):378–384.

100. Hebert C, Robicsek A. Decolonization therapy in infection control. *Curr Opin Infect Dis* 2010 Aug;23(4):340–345.

101. Bradley SF. Eradication or decolonization of methicillin-resistant Staphylococcus aureus carriage: what are we doing and why are we doing it? *Clin Infect Dis* 2007 Jan 15;44(2):186–189.

102. Camins BC, Richmond AM, Dyer KL, et al. A crossover intervention trial evaluating the efficacy of a chlorhexidine-impregnated sponge in reducing catheter-related bloodstream infections among patients undergoing hemodialysis. *Infect Control Hosp Epidemiol* 2010 Nov;31(11): 1118–1123.

103. Buehlmann M, Frei R, Fenner L, et al. Highly effective regimen for decolonization of methicillin-resistant Staphylococcus aureus carriers. *Infect Control Hosp Epidemiol* 2008 Jun;29(6):510–516.

104. de Vries EN, Prins HA, Crolla RM, et al. Effect of a comprehensive surgical safety system on patient outcomes. *N Engl J Med* 2010 Nov 11;363(20):1928–1937.

105. Powers JG, Morton LM, Phillips TJ. Dressings for chronic wounds. *Dermatol Ther* 2013 May-Jun;26(3):197–206.

106. Lund-Nielsen B, Adamsen L, Kolmos HJ, et al. The effect of honey-coated bandages compared with silver-coated bandages on treatment of malignant wounds-a randomized study. *Wound Repair Regen* 2011 Nov;19(6): 664–670.

107. Storm-Versloot MN, Vos CG, Ubbink DT, et al. Topical silver for preventing wound infection. *Cochrane Database Syst Rev* 2010 Mar 17;(3): CD006478.

CHAPTER 93

Staphylococci

Karsten Becker, MD
Professor of Medical Microbiology
Institute of Medical Microbiology
University Hospital of Münster
Westfalian Wilhelms-University of Münster
Münster, Germany

Robin Köck, MD
Institute of Hygiene
University Hospital of Münster
Westfalian Wilhelms-University of Münster
Münster, Germany

ABSTRACT

The genus Staphylococcus *comprises more than 40 validly described species, with the coagulase-positive species* Staphylococcus aureus *and the coagulase-negative species* S. epidermidis *and* S. haemolyticus *as the most common causes of healthcare-associated infections caused by staphylococci. Many staphylococcal species are both commensal microorganisms and pathogens. In particular,* S. aureus *is still one of the most feared pathogens, becoming increasingly virulent and resistant to antibiotic agents. This versatile pathogen harbors a wide array of virulence factors to enable colonization, invasion, aggression, and persistence processes. The study of slow-growing variant forms of* S. aureus *(i.e., the small-colony variants) has helped in the understanding of the persistent and recurrent infections. In the last decades, methicillin-resistant* S. aureus *strains have become endemic in hospitals worldwide, rendering almost all β-lactam antibiotics (penicillins, cephalosporins, and carbapenems) ineffective. Additionally, community-associated methicillin-resistant* S. aureus *in persons without previous healthcare exposures as well as livestock-associated methicillin-resistant* S. aureus *have been increasingly reported. The majority of community-associated methicillin-resistant* S. aureus *strains have acquired Panton-Valentine leukocidin encoding genes, thereby greatly increasing their virulence. All these new strains and variants represent challenges for clinical microbiologists, infection preventionists, and epidemiologists.*

KEY CONCEPTS

- *Staphylococcus* species are generally divided into two groups: coagulase-positive staphylococci (*S. aureus* and some other of primarily veterinarian concern) and coagulase-negative staphylococci.

- *Staphylococcus* species are often part of the normal bacterial flora (microbiota).

- *Staphylococcus* species are common causes of healthcare-associated infections, including bacteremia, endocarditis, pneumonia, osteomyelitis, surgical site infections, skin and soft tissue infections, and device-associated infections. In addition, *S. aureus* can cause toxin-mediated diseases.

- Methicillin-resistant *S. aureus* is a frequent pathogen in healthcare-associated infections and has been shown to be associated with increased mortality in *S. aureus* bacteremia. Additionally, community-acquired and livestock-associated methicillin-resistant *S. aureus* have emerged.

- Resistance in staphylococcal species toward antibiotics of certain groups appears to be increasing.

- Hand hygiene and other precautions have been used successfully to prevent transmission and control outbreaks of *S. aureus* including methicillin-resistant *S. aureus*.

BACKGROUND

The roots of modern infection prevention can be traced to the response to hospital outbreaks of staphylococcal infection in the 1950s and 1960s.[1] In the 1970s and early 1980s, attention focused on Gram-negative organisms as the most important healthcare-associated pathogens after Gram-positive infections were controlled. This, in turn, led to the development of many new antibacterial agents with potent activity against Gram-negative organisms (e.g., third-generation cephalosporins). In the 1990s, however, staphylococci again emerged as important healthcare-associated pathogens because of resistance to β-lactam antibiotics.[2] A most frightening development has been the spread of methicillin-resistance among *S. aureus* in the community, as these strains are attacking previously healthy young people (mean age, 14 years) with a devastating mortality rate (37 percent) in patients with necrotizing pneumonia.[3] Development of resistance in Gram-negative rods is an emerging threat; however, some progress in combating methicillin-resistant *S. aureus* (MRSA) has been achieved.

BASIC PRINCIPLES

The genus *Staphylococcus,* currently comprising 45 species and 21 subspecies, belongs to the family Staphylococcaceae of the order Bacillales (phylum Firmicutes) (Figure 93-1). They are Gram-positive, nonmotile, non-spore-forming cocci measuring 0.5 to 1.5 μm in diameter. They tend to form "clusters" in

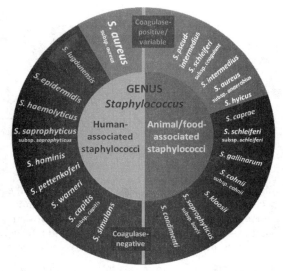

Figure 93-1. The genus *Staphylococcus*. A selection of human- (left) and animal/food-associated (right). Coagulase-positive species are in the light grey area of the wheel. Coagulase-negative (sub-) species are in the dark grey area. Five species listed in the top left (*S. aureus* to *S. saprophyticus*) are the most medically important. *S. lugdunensis* holds a hybrid position as coagulase-negative species due to some clinical resemblances to *S. aureus*.

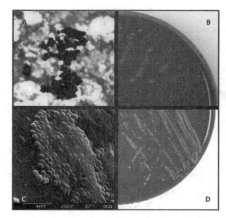

Figure 93-2. Cellular and colonial morphology of staphylococci. (A) *S. aureus* grown in blood culture occurring as Gram-positive cocci in clusters in light microscopy; (B) colonial morphology of *S. aureus* showing large, yellow-grayish pigmented colonies surrounded from a zone of hemolysis on Columbia blood agar; (C) electron microscopy of *S. epidermidis* cells on a foreign body surface imbedded in biofilm matrix (courtesy of G. Peters, Münster); (D) colonial morphology of *S. epidermidis* showing unpigmented and unhemolytic colonies on Columbia blood agar.

Gram stains of clinical specimens or cultures. This "clustering" helps to distinguish them from streptococci, which tend to form chains of cocci (Figure 93-2).

Growth Characteristics

Staphylococci are normally catalase-positive. *S. aureus* grows rapidly under both aerobic (with oxygen) and anaerobic (without oxygen) conditions on blood agar and many other media.

S. aureus often grows as off-white or light-yellow to dark orange-yellow colonies, whereas the colonies of clinically relevant coagulase-negative staphylococci (CoNS) are mostly bright white. However, definitively differentiating between CoNS and *S. aureus* is only possible through the use of biochemical, immunological, and/or molecular methods. Individual colonies tend to be well defined, smooth, and hemolytic. Although the species name comes from the tendency of *S. aureus* to have a yellow pigmentation, this only occurs under certain growth conditions. For example, anaerobically grown or small colony variant (SCV) *S. aureus* fails to form pigment or hemolysins.

The Coagulase Test

It is critical to be able to distinguish between *S. aureus* and CoNS.[4] Within the CoNS, the *S. epidermidis* group (*S. epidermidis S. haemolyticus, S. hominis,* and some other species) causes most CoNS infections in humans. It is therefore important to differentiate *S. lugdunensis* (resembling in some aspects *S. aureus*) and *S. saprophyticus* subsp. *saprophyticus* (causes urinary tract infections). The most commonly used test is

the coagulase tube test. *S. aureus* strains are coagulase-positive, whereas the other *Staphylococcus* spp. causing infections in humans are coagulase-negative. The coagulase-negative species *S. saprophyticus* is distinguished from other CoNS by its ability to ferment mannitol and by resistance to novobiocin. In contrast to many other CoNS, *S. lugdunensis* is clumping factor positive, as is *S. aureus*, and may cause severe infections.

STAPHYLOCOCCUS AUREUS

Antibiotic Resistance

In the early 1940s, the first member of the β-lactam antibiotic family, penicillin, became available, and almost all staphylococci were highly susceptible. One decade later, 65 percent to 80 percent of healthcare-associated *S. aureus* isolates were reported to be resistant to penicillin. At present, many community and more than 90 percent of hospital-associated *S. aureus* isolates are resistant to penicillin. The mechanism causing this resistance in *S. aureus* and other staphylococcal species is the production of an enzyme, staphylococcal β-lactamase (penicillinase). This enzyme destroys the β-lactam ring of β-lactamase-sensitive narrow-spectrum penicillins (penicillin G and V) and susceptible broad-spectrum penicillins (e.g., ampicillin, amoxicillin, mezlocillin, and piperacillin).

Understanding the mechanism of this resistance led to the development of β-lactamase-resistant penicillins (methicillin, oxacillin, cloxacillin, dicloxacillin, flucloxacillin, and nafcillin) and first-generation cephalosporins (e.g., cephalothin and cefazolin). Penicillin-resistant *S. aureus* (PRSA) isolates that are methicillin-susceptible *S. aureus* (MSSA) are resistant to penicillinase-labile penicillins but remain susceptible to the penicillinase-stable penicillins (so-called antistaphylococcal penicillins), the β-lactam/β-lactamase inhibitor combinations, and the first- and second-generation cephalosporins and carbapenems. The members of the large family of β-lactam antibiotics kill *S. aureus* cells by binding specifically to enzymes (transpeptidases) located in the staphylococcal cell wall. These transpeptidases are involved in the synthesis of cell wall peptidoglycan and are referred to as penicillin-binding proteins (PBPs).

Molecular Basis of Methicillin-resistant Staphylococcus aureus

MRSA, which can also be referred to as oxacillin-resistant *S. aureus* (ORSA), and strains of other methicillin-resistant staphylococcal species have acquired the *mecA* gene encoding an additional PBP, designated PBP2a (PBP2')[5]. PBP2a is characterized by low β-lactam affinity toward methicillin and penicillinase-labile penicillins. The *mecA* gene and its recently described homolog (*mecC*, originally described as *mecA*$_{LGA251}$) are acquired on a mobile, foreign DNA element, the staphylococcal cassette chromosome *mec* (SCC*mec*) element. The SCC*mec* element occurs in several main types (10/2013: I–XI) and many subtypes[6,7]. The SCC*mec* types I and V encode exclusively for resistance to β-lactam antibiotics. Types II, III, and others determine multiresistance, as these cassettes contain additional drug resistance genes on transposons and integrated plasmids. Type XI contains a *mecA* homolog designated *mecC*[8,9].

Borderline-resistant Staphylococcus aureus

Some penicillinase hyperproducers, the so-called borderline-resistant *S. aureus* (BORSA), mimic low-level resistance to methicillin even though they do not possess the *mecA* gene. For treatment purposes, this distinction can be important (see Chapter 25 Laboratory Testing and Diagnostics).

Global Spread and Importance of Methicillin-resistant Staphylococcus Aureus

Methicillin became available in October 1960 for treating infections caused by β-lactamase-producing, penicillin-resistant *S. aureus*. However, within 6 months, strains resistant to methicillin were identified, first in England, then in other European countries[10]. Even though methicillin is no longer the agent of choice for treatment and susceptibility testing, the acronym MRSA continues to be used to describe *S. aureus* strains resistant to almost all β-lactam antibiotics (penicillins, cephalosporins, carbapenems) with the exception of the recently introduced anti-MRSA cephalosporins.

Starting at the end of the 1960s in Europe and Australia, epidemic multidrug-resistant MRSA clones (SCC*mec* types I–III, type IV subtypes) became a significant problem, which was followed closely by increased rates in the United States (recent U.S. MRSA rates ranging from approximately 30 percent to more than 50 percent) (Figure 93-3)[11,12]. Except for some

	HA-MRSA	CA-MRSA	LA-MRSA
Common risk factors	• Stays in hospitals, homes for the elderly, care homes • Chronic wounds • Catheters • Antibiotic treatment	• Close physical contacts with increased risk of abrasive skin injury (*e.g.*, team sports, recruit training) • Low socioeconomic conditions	• Direct contact with agricultural livestock (*e.g.*, farmers, veterinarians, abattoir employees)
Prevalent genotypes (U.S.)	• **ST 5** (*USA100, USA800*; t001, t002) • ST8 (*USA500*; t064) • **ST36** (*USA200*; t018) • ST45 (*USA600*; t004) • ST72 (*USA700*; t126)	• **ST 1** (*USA400*; t128, t558) • **ST 8** (*USA300*; t008) • ST30 (*USA1100*; t019) • ST59 (*USA1000*; t216, t316) • ST80 („European"; t044, t416)	• ST398 (t011, t034)
SCC*mec* types	• I, II, III, IV, VI, and VIII	• IVa, V, and VII	• IX, X, and XI (*mecC*)
PVL genes possession	• Rare	• Common	• Single cases
Antimicrobial susceptibility pattern	• Multiresistant	• Mostly no or only single additional resistances	• Tetracycline-resistant, seldom other resistances

Figure 93-3. Epidemiological MRSA types. Most common U.S. clonal lineages are given in bold; PFGE types (U.S. nomenclature) are given in italic; for *spa* types, the nomenclature according to the RidomSpaServer is used (http://spa.ridom.de, which is curated by SeqNet.org).

European countries with very stringent MRSA control precautions, MRSA rates have rapidly increased worldwide over the recent decades.[13–16] However, there are also signs of stabilization or even decrease in the incidence of MRSA infections in some regions (United States and several European countries such as France, Germany, and the United Kingdom).[17,18] MRSA has been found to be associated with increased morbidity, mortality, and hospital length of stay in *S. aureus* bacteremia and other entities.[19–21]

For *S. pseudintermedius*, an animal-associated (e.g., dogs, cats, horses) coagulase-positive staphylococcal species occasionally found in respective bite wounds, the acquisition of the *mecA*-encoded methicillin resistance has been also increasingly reported.[22]

Healthcare-associated Methicillin-resistant Staphylococcus aureus (HA-MRSA) Strains

Healthcare-associated MRSA (also designated as hospital-associated, or epidemic MRSA) strains are frequently resistant to many other classes of antibiotics, including macrolides (e.g., erythromycin), ketolides, lincosamides (e.g., clindamycin), tetracyclines, quinolones, and aminoglycosides (e.g., gentamicin), thus fulfilling the term "multidrug-resistant" (Figure 93-3). There is variable susceptibility to rifampin, fusidic acid, fosfomycin, trimethoprim-sulfamethoxazole, and other antibiotic compounds and disinfectants.

Community-associated Methicillin-resistant Staphylococcus aureus (CA-MRSA) Strains: Emerging Issues in Patients without Risk for HA-MRSA

An ongoing problem is the emergence of MRSA infections in patients with no apparent risk factors, including recent hospitalization. MRSA with unique genetic elements, designated CA-MRSA, are increasing in the United States and worldwide.[23] In the United States, the predominant clone is USA300 (ST-8), replacing the USA 400 (ST-1) clone most prominent before 2001 (Figure 93-3).[24–27] Meanwhile, the USA300 clone has emerged as the predominant cause of staphylococcal skin and soft tissue infections.[24] Outside of North America, a broader array of different CA-MRSA clones (besides ST-8, e.g., ST-5, ST-30 [Southwest Pacific clone], ST 59, ST-80 [European clone] ST-88, ST772 [Bengal Bay clone], and ST1797) is found.[26,28–31]

Most CA-MRSA strains carry genes encoding for the Panton-Valentine leukocidin (PVL), which is a bicomponent, pore-forming exotoxin with potent cytolytic and inflammatory activities.[32] PVL targets cells of the immune system, in particular human polymorphonuclear neutrophils.[3,33]

CA-MRSAs are associated with smaller SCC*mec* types (mostly subtype IVa, rarely types V and VII). Of interest, these types do not carry several typical resistance markers found in HA-MRSA, namely resistance to quinolone, clindamycin, and macrolides. However, multidrug-resistant CA-MRSA strains that have acquired multiresistant conjugative plasmids were also reported.[34]

Livestock-associated Methicillin-resistant Staphylococcus aureus (LA-MRSA) Strains: Emerging Issue in Farming

MRSA colonization and, less frequently, MRSA infections have been increasingly reported for many animal species.[35] MRSA clones found among companion animals such as dogs, cats, and small mammals are often show human molecular lineages indicating a transmission from human to pets. However, strains of MRSA that colonize livestock—in particular, pigs, cattle, and poultry—are caused by one specific clonal complex of MRSA (CC/ST398) that is distinct from human-derived strains (Figure 93-3).[36] LA-MRSA is regularly transmitted from colonized animals to farmers and other persons with close contact to agricultural livestock or their products. These individuals are the major source for the introduction of LA-MRSA into the healthcare setting.[37,38] Compared to what is found in Europe, the presence of LA-MRSA in pigs (4.6 percent) and swine farm workers (20.9 percent) in the United States is lower.[39]

Vancomycin Resistance in Staphylococci

Since 1996, vancomycin-intermediate *S. aureus* (VISA) isolates have been identified first in Japan (Mu50 strain from a surgical wound infection that was refractory to vancomycin therapy) followed by further detections in the United States, Europe, and other regions.[40–42] Also in 1996, a Japanese group identified the first heterogeneous VISA (hVISA) strain (Mu3) with reduced susceptibility to vancomycin from a patient with MRSA pneumonia.[43] The hVISAs are interpreted as precursors to VISA. In 2002, a complete vancomycin-resistant *S. aureus* (VRSA) was identified from a temporary dialysis catheter-associated exit site infection of a Michigan resident. This was followed by several additional cases elsewherein the United States and in other parts of the world.[44–46]

The mechanism of VISA generation is thought to be caused in general by complex cell wall alterations resulting in cell wall reorganization and thickening in addition to reduced autolytic activity.[47–49] Because most VISAs are also resistant to the glycopeptide called teicoplanin, which is widely used outside of the United States, some authors prefer the acronym GISA (glycopeptide-intermediate *S. aureus*). Cases of true VRSA are still rare and are characterized by the acquisition of a glycopeptide resistance-encoding gene (*vanA*) originating from enterococci.

In the past decade, a phenomenon called "vancomycin MIC creep" was reported from some medical centers describing an overall population drift in clinical *S. aureus* isolates toward reduced vancomycin susceptibility but below the susceptibility breakpoint.[50,51] However, other studies noted no changes or even reductions in vancomycin MIC values.[52,53]

Clindamycin-inducible Resistance and the D Test

Erythromycin resistance in *S. aureus* is caused by the *erm* gene (erythromycin ribosome methylase), which confers resistance to the complete macrolide-lincosamide-streptogramin B antibiotic class, or by *msrA* causing macrolide and streptogramin (MLS$_B$) resistance.[54] In some erythromycin-resistant strains, inducible resistance to clindamycin may manifest when production of a methylase allows clindamycin resistance to be expressed. Standard susceptibility test methods do not recognize inducible MLS$_B$ resistance. Failure to identify inducible MLS$_B$ resistance may lead to clinical failure of clindamycin therapy. Conversely, labeling all erythromycin-resistant staphylococci as clindamycin resistant prevents the use of clindamycin (which is a useful therapeutic choice for skin and soft tissue infections, especially in penicillin-allergic patients) for infections caused by staphylococci in infections that are truly clindamycin-susceptible.[55]

There is a disk diffusion test called the D test, or D zone test, for detection of clindamycin-inducible resistance. In this test, the D-shaped zone of inhibition adjacent to a standard 15-μg erythromycin disk can identify *S. aureus* or CoNS strains with inducible resistance to clindamycin.[56] Clinical laboratories should have the capability to test staphylococci strains for clindamycin-inducible resistance in erythromycin-resistant isolates (Figure 93-4).

Other Antimicrobial Resistance in Staphylococci

Although still a rare phenomenon, some strains of *S. aureus* have developed resistance to more recently introduced alternative antibiotics with anti–*S. aureus* activity (including

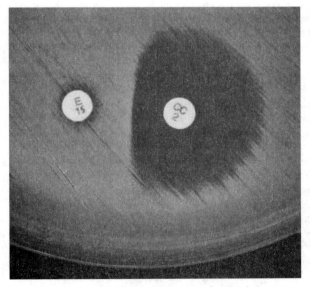

Figure 93-4. Clindamycin disk induction test for *Staphylococcus*. Clindamycin-inducible resistance: "D" shape of the clindamycin zone adjacent to a standard 15-μg erythromycin disk in conventional disk diffusion test. (From http://wwwn.cdc.gov/nltn/pdf/2004/2_hindler_d-test.pdf.)

activity to MRSA). Although linezolid, the first oxazolidinone on the market, shows sustained potency and spectrum (less than 1.0 percent resistant strains),[57-59] resistance due to rRNA mutations has been detected in vitro and in the clinical setting.[60,61] The first linezolid-resistant MRSA was reported in 2001 from a patient treated with this agent for dialysis-associated peritonitis.[62] More alarming, a mobile, plasmid-borne linezolid resistance mechanism based on an RNA methyltransferase resistance gene (*cfr*) has emerged recently, but its incidence has remained low.[58,63]

Also, reports of treatment failures resulting from MRSA strains with reduced susceptibility or resistance to daptomycin, have been documented in the United States and Taiwan.[64-67] However, daptomycin still has excellent activity against MRSA.[68,69] The mechanism of resistance to daptomycin appears to be diverse, involving both cell membrane and cell wall events; the incidence of the development of spontaneous resistance appears to be very low.[70,71]

Tigecycline is the first drug approved in the class of glycylcyclines. Only a very few isolates (less than 0.5 percent) have so far been reported showing in vitro minimum inhibitory concentration (MIC) values around or above its threshold; however, this agent is still highly active against MRSA.[59,72,73] The mechanism of tigecycline resistance remains to be elucidated for staphylococci.

Currently, there are two available cephalosporins with MRSA activity—ceftaroline and ceftobiprole. Ceftaroline has been shown to be active against MRSA.[74,75] The same was reported for ceftobiprole, although this antimicrobial is under re-evaluation.[76,77]

Laboratory Identification and Susceptibility Testing of *Staphylococcus aureus*

Direct Examination by Gram Stain

Gram stain is an important testing technique but does not distinguish *S. aureus* from CoNS or other cocci occurring in clusters (e.g., "micrococci"). When testing sterile fluids (e.g., cerebrospinal fluid [CSF] and joint aspirates), Gram staining followed by direct microscopic examination may be helpful. For normally nonsterile fluids (e.g., respiratory secretions and swabs from wound surfaces), Gram staining is less appropriate for presumptive determination of *S. aureus*; however, the presence of inflammatory cells might support the impact of the microscopic findings.

Isolation, Identification, and Susceptibility Testing of *Staphylococcus aureus*

Columbia blood agar containing 5 percent defibrinated blood is the primary culture plate used for isolating *S. aureus* and CoNS from clinical specimens.[4] The recovery rate of *S. aureus* and other staphylococci can be significantly enhanced by the simultaneous use of an enrichment broth, which will be streaked after

24 and 48 hours of incubation on Columbia blood agar. For heavily contaminated sources such as feces, the use of selective agars for *S. aureus* such as mannitol salt agar might be helpful, but they have shown limited sensitivity and specificity. Current improvements in laboratory testing include the development of chromogenic solid agar media for *S. aureus* and/or MRSA detection. These media allow for more rapid presumptive determination. For all these agars, it is mandatory to confirm putative *S. aureus* isolates by biochemical, molecular, and/or spectroscopic approaches. Classical methods include testing coagulase production, advanced third-generation latex agglutination assays for simultaneous detecting of protein A, clumping factor A, and the clinically most prevalent capsular polysaccharide serotypes 5 and 8, as well as biochemical procedures that are part of commercial manual and automated biochemical test systems. Targeting *S. aureus*-specific and universal genes followed by sequencing, respectively, allow highly specific identification of *S. aureus* by DNA amplification methods such as PCR. Most recently, matrix-assisted laser desorption ionization time-of-flight (MALDI-TOF) mass spectrometry (MS) has been introduced as an alternative high-throughput approach for very rapid and specific identification of staphylococcal colonial material.[78] Of note, despite the molecular and MS developments for *S. aureus* detection and identification, cultivation of the pathogen is mandatory for subsequent further characterization of a given isolate for resistance testing and, if necessary, for determination of virulence factors or for genotyping purposes.

Antimicrobial susceptibility testing of *S. aureus* should be performed according to Clinical and Laboratory Standards Institute (CLSI) (www.clsi.org) or European Committee on Antimicrobial Susceptibility Testing (EUCAST) (http://www.eucast.org) reference methods.[79,80] Cefoxitin, a cephamycin antibiotic, which is a stronger inducer of the *mecA* regulatory system, has replaced oxacillin as a surrogate marker for testing methicillin resistance (*S. aureus* and *S. lugdunensis*, MIC ≥ 8 μg/mL). Of utmost importance is to distinguish MRSA from MSSA, which might be challenging due to the heteroresistance phenomenon of MRSA isolates (i.e., only a few bacterial cells of a suspension express β-lactam resistance in vitro). An alternative phenotypic method for fast and reliable verification of pure colonies suspicious for MRSA is the use of anti-PBP2a monoclonal antibodies supplied as a simple latex agglutination assay.[81,82] If the latex test is used for SCVs, then the number of colonies must be increased 100-fold.[83] The slow growth of MRSA SCVs makes disk diffusion and automated methods invalid.[84]

Since heterogeneous MRSA, SCV phenotype MRSA, and BORSA strains might be misdiagnosed by phenotypic methods for the detection and identification of MRSA, it has been strongly suggested to use a second method of identifying MRSA to verify the result for a given suspicious isolate.[83,85–87]

Screening for MRSA

Screening for MRSA has the specific purpose of detecting colonization in patients and, in outbreak situations, in medical personnel who have direct contact with colonized or infected patients. Thus, high-throughput approaches may be applied as chromogenic agars and/or bouillon media for cultivation and preliminary identification of MRSA, as well as polymerase chain reaction (PCR)-based techniques (see next section) for more rapid direct identification of MRSA carriers. Both approaches need a valid verification of species and oxacillin resistance in presumed MRSA isolates.

Molecular Genetic Methods of Identification

Molecular genetic methods that detect the presence of species-specific markers and resistance-indicating sequences were introduced starting in the early 1990s and have become important to ensure correct identification of a given isolate as MRSA.[88,89] For the molecular identification of the species, in-house and commercial procedures have been described targeting either *S. aureus*-specific variable regions of universal genes (e.g., 16 and 23 rRNA genes, *rpoB*, *tuf*) or genes and gene fragments unique for *S. aureus* (e.g., *nuc*, *coa*, *clfA*, *femA* and *B*).[87,88,90–93] The presence of the *mecA* gene or of its homologs (*mecC*) indicates the organism as methicillin-resistant, regardless of the strain or species of staphylococci. Of note, many currently available commercial tests do not target *mecC*.[94] In the case of discrepant results (phenotypic tests indicating MRSA versus negative molecular assay), the putative presence of a *mecA* homolog should be addressed (e.g., by applying respective in-house PCR strategies as published).[8,9,95] Molecular methods are particularly important for characterizing MRSA of phenotypic variants (e.g., SCVs) and low-level heterogeneous MRSA.[83,87]

For molecular MRSA diagnostics, the sample (pure bacterial culture versus clinical specimens) as well as the intended purpose (MRSA screening versus detection of MRSA infection) has to be taken into consideration. Some available assays detect MRSA directly in certain clinical specimens (e.g., nasal specimen), whereas others require bacterial isolates from culture.

There are two general approaches to using rapid PCR-based MRSA screening from nasal swabs (and/or from other predilection sites, if approved), each with advantages and disadvantages. In the case of the so-called multiple-loci approach, the *mecA* gene plus an *S. aureus*-specific DNA sequence is targeted. In the presence of "contaminating" co-occurring methicillin-resistant CoNS from the physiological flora in parallel to MSSA, false-positive PCR results may occur.[96] The other approach, designated "single-locus amplification," overcomes this limitation by amplifying both a taxonomic and resistance marker in one step.[97] Here, the use of a surrogate marker (SCC*mec* region instead of *mecA*) may lead to false-positive or false-negative results (e.g., due to the exchange of the *mecA* gene by other genes, partial excision of the cassette ["drop out" isolates], and variability of the cassette primer binding sites).[98,99] Overall, all commercially available molecular amplification-based rapid MRSA screening assays are characterized by very good negative predictive values (approximately 97 to 99 percent) and hampered by moderate positive predictive values (approximately 65 to 95 percent).[100,101]

Given the limitations of both molecular strategies, *cultures remain essential* for confirming molecular results, for epidemiological purposes (genotyping), determination of the complete resistance profile (susceptibility testing), and, if necessary, the identification of further features (e.g., toxins). To achieve both rapidity and high predictive values, it is advantageous to use both PCR and cultures for MRSA screening.

Identification of Vancomycin (Glycopeptide)-intermediate Staphylococcus aureus *(VISA, GISA) and Vancomycin (Glycopeptide)-resistant* Staphylococcus aureus *(VRSA/GRSA)*

The detection of reduced susceptibility to vancomycin may be unreliable, and vancomycin nonsusceptibility is most likely underreported.[102,103] According to the CLSI recommendations, isolates with MICs between 4 and 8 μg/mL are classified as VISA, whereas hVISA strains appear to be susceptible to vancomycin. VRSA strains (MICs of at least 16 μg/mL) can be reliably detected by the broth microdilution reference method.[104] To avoid reporting VISA isolates as "intermediate," the vancomycin MIC breakpoint has been refixed by the European Committee on Antimicrobial Susceptibility Testing (EUCAST) with more than 2 μg/mL as "resistant" for *S. aureus* (http://www.srga.org/eucastwt/MICTAB/MICglycopeptides_v2.html). Heteroresistance to daptomycin is rarely reported for hVISA/VISA isolates.[105]

Brain heart infusion (BHI) vancomycin (6 μg/mL) agar screen plate can be used to enhance the sensitivity of detecting VISA and VRSA isolates.[104] All isolates determined to have an elevated MIC for vancomycin (at least 4 μg/mL) using a MIC method that has not been validated for VISA/VRSA testing should be sent to a reference laboratory.[104] In particular, screening for hVISA requires labor-intensive additional testing (population analysis) to reveal its heterovariant phenotype.[106] The Centers for Disease Control and Prevention (CDC) website provides helpful information on VISA/VRSA (http://www.cdc.gov).

Diagnosis of Toxin-mediated Syndromes

In addition to clinical signs, the diagnosis of the staphylococcal toxic shock syndrome (TSS), caused mainly by the toxic shock syndrome toxin-1 (TSST-1), and the staphylococcal scalded skin syndrome (SSSS), caused by exfoliative toxins, is supported by the absence of protective antibody titers. Detection of isolates tested positive for the possession of genes encoding TSST-1 (or seldom staphylococcal enterotoxins [SEs] A and C) in TSS or for the possession of genes encoding exfoliative toxins (ETs) (classically ETA and ETB, newly described ETD) in SSSS may corroborate the diagnosis. Several PCR methods for classical toxin-encoding genes have been published and a few assays are commercially available.[107–109] PCR methods have been also reported to detect the genes of the more recently described nonclassical enterotoxins and enterotoxin-like pyrogenic toxin superantigens (PTSAgs), starting with SEG and reaching the letter U; however, their clinical impact is unclear.[110,111]

In cases of staphylococcal food poisoning, the staphylococcal enterotoxins (classically SEA–SEE) may be detected directly in food, vomit, or stool samples, which often harbor only the preformed heat-stable toxin. These antigen tests may not be readily available as a test of isolates in most hospital laboratories. Ultrasensitive immuno-PCR methods for toxin antigen detection may be available in research or reference laboratories.[112]

The detection of the CA-MRSA/MSSA associated PVL-encoding genes (*lukS/F-PV*) can be performed by in-house PCR or commercially available assays.[113]

Typing Methods to Identify Different Methicillin-resistant *Staphylococcus aureus* Strains

During an MRSA outbreak situation, epidemiological investigations play an important role when used to differentiate clones of *S. aureus* (Figure 93-2). Identifying isolates with the same patterns from different patients suggests that the organisms originated from a single clone. Finding a unique clone in different patients who have a temporal or geographic relationship suggests transmission of the organism from patient to patient from a common source or mechanism.

Biotyping (chemical reactions) and antimicrobial susceptibility patterns can sometimes provide useful initial clues to strain identity. However, *S. aureus* may demonstrate very little variability in biotyping or susceptibility patterns, which makes these approaches less useful to differentiate among strains. As a result, other methods have been developed to distinguish one staphylococcal strain from another.[114–116] In the past, phage typing of *S. aureus* isolates was used to distinguish among strains in outbreak investigations. However, this technique is available only from reference laboratories because of expense, poor discriminating power, poor reproducibility, and complexity. Due to these limitations and difficulty in typing some MRSA strains, this method has been replaced by molecular typing approaches. Genotyping has now become an indispensable part of the hospital epidemiologist's armamentarium in investigating clusters of infections and outbreaks. If available, a molecular typing method should be used to investigate a cluster or an epidemic of *S. aureus* (particularly MRSA) infection. Molecular typing of chromosomal structures could also be supplemented by typing of the SCC*mec* element.

Pulsed-field Gel Electrophoresis

Analysis of chromosomal DNA restriction patterns by pulsed-field gel electrophoresis (PFGE) was a gold standard for years and the primary technique used for MRSA typing. PFGE is still used in many laboratories.[117] For PFGE, the isolates are cultured and embedded in agarose and lysed, then the isolate's DNA is digested with restriction endonucleases. Slices of the agarose containing the resultant "restricted DNA" are placed in wells of an agarose gel, where it is separated into individual fragment patterns under the influence of electric current. Usually, more than 14 fragments of DNA are resolved by this method and visible after ethidium bromide staining.

The fragment patterns of the tested isolates are compared to determine their relatedness. Depending on the fragment patterns, the isolates can be identified as follows:

- *Genetically indistinguishable* (the same fragment patterns)

- *Closely related* (two to three band differences resulting from a single genetic event such as point mutation, deletion, or insertion)

- *Possibly related* (four to six band differences resulting from two genetic events such as deletion, insertion, gain, or loss of restriction sites)

- *Unrelated* to the outbreak strain (seven or more differences resulting from three or more genetic events)[117]

This "fingerprint" method has the advantage of reproducibility and resolving power as a standard technique for epidemiologically typing of *S. aureus*. For the United States, a national database of PFGE patterns defining originally eight lineages (USA100 through USA800) of pulsed-field types.[118] However, interlaboratory reproducibility and interpretation remain critical issues leading to replacement of time-consuming and expensive PFGE by sequence-based methods.[119] An example of a PFGE pattern from a LTC facility investigation is shown in Figure 93-5.[120]

Sequencing Methods

There are a couple of advantages to using sequence-based methods. One advantage is that sequencing data can be readily compared between different laboratories because of their portability. Another advantage is that these data are stored in expanding web-based databases, thereby producing a powerful resource for global epidemiology.[121] For *S. aureus*, the two main sequencing methods used are multilocus sequence typing (MLST) and typing of the polymorphic region X of protein A

(*spa* typing) consisting of several numbers of variable 24 bp-repeats.[122-124] MLST sequences internal fragments of seven housekeeping gene loci, which are then used to characterize isolates resulting in allelic profiles or sequence types (STs). MLST may be less suitable for routine infection control due to high cost and labor intensity. Single-locus typing, particularly *spa* typing, is commonly used instead. This method has the advantage that only a single gene has to be sequenced and that its discriminatory power is comparable to PFGE and MLST typing analysis. Two nomenclatures (Harmsen [Ridom] and Koreen/Kreiswirth) for *spa* typing are in use.[123,125] An algorithm has been established that allows analysis of clonal relatedness of strains based on *spa* repeat regions.[126] Related STs and *spa* types, respectively, are grouped together as clonal complexes (CCs). The multiple-locus variable-number tandem-repeat assay (MLVA) is an alternative approach that has been shown to differentiate among strains that are indistinguishable by PFGE.[127]

Pathogenesis

S. aureus is an extraordinarily versatile organism that is able to produce a variety of proteins (enzymes, exotoxins, and adhesins) that are important virulence factors and are important for the pathogenesis of the different infections and toxin-mediated syndromes caused by this pathogen.

Virulence factors enable *S. aureus* and CoNS to colonize or invade human or animal hosts by adhering to host cells, tissues, and inserted devices.[128-131] Protein A, a bacterial surface protein adhesin of *S. aureus,* is able to bind to the tumor-necrosis factor α-receptor (TNF-R1), which has been shown to be abundant on airway epithelial cells. Binding of protein A to the TNF-α receptor elicits a TNF-α-like response, which leads to recruitment of neutrophils to the lung. Protein A also induces shedding of the receptor, which leads to binding of protein A and of TNF-α, thereby regulating protein A-induced recruitment of neutrophils.[132,133] Further details on adhesive mechanisms of staphylococci are given below (see the Coagulase-Negative Staphylococci section in this chapter).

Peptidoglycan, a polysaccharide polymer making up 50 percent of the bacterial cell wall, maintains cell wall integrity. Purified peptidoglycan can elicit many of the responses observed with endotoxin administration. Thus, it may be an important factor in producing the sepsis picture that is associated with severe *S. aureus* infection. Within the cell envelope, complex teichoic acid (TA) polymers are incorporated, which are either covalently linked to peptidoglycan (wall teichoic acid, WTA) or to the cytoplasmic membrane (lipoteichoic acid, LTA).[134] TAs are part of a group of phosphate-containing polymers that make up 40 percent of the cell wall by weight. Teichoic acids may be immunosuppressive and involved with adherence of *S. aureus* to mucosal surfaces and damaged tissues. Teichoic acids with higher amounts of D-alanine esters were associated with greater resistance to cationic antibiotics.[135]

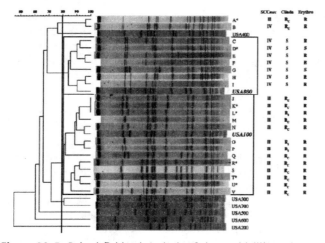

Figure 93-5. Pulsed-field gel analysis of the methicillin-resistant strains. (From Lesse AJ, Mylotte JM. Clinical and molecular epidemiology of nursing home–associated *Staphylococcus aureus* bacteremia. *Am J Infect Control* 2006 Dec;34(10):642–650.)

APIC Text of Infection Control and Epidemiology

S. aureus can produce extracellular polysaccharides (capsules) that enhance microbial virulence caused by interference with phagocytosis.[136] Most clinical strains belong to capsule group 5 or 8.[137] Capsule expression supports persistence of the bacteria in the bloodstream of the host and can promote abscess formation.[138]

S. aureus produces many enzymes, some of which have been implicated in the pathogenesis of infection. Catalase converts hydrogen peroxide to water and oxygen and may inhibit polymorphonuclear leukocytes (PMNs) from killing the ingested organism after phagocytosis. Coagulase (an enzyme used to distinguish between S. aureus and other staphylococci in laboratory testing) may contribute to pathogenesis. Hyaluronidase may be involved in the formulation of abscesses by enhancing the organism's ability to spread through tissues.

The pan-genome of S. aureus contains a huge variety of toxins, including pyrogenic toxin superantigens (PTSAgs), exfoliative toxins, and pore-forming toxins.[139] The staphylococcal PTSAgs comprise the toxic shock syndrome (TSS) toxin (TSST-1) and the staphylococcal enterotoxins and enterotoxin-like toxins, respectively (SEs/SEls). Staphylococcal enterotoxins A through E are the classical enterotoxins proven for superantigenicity and emetic capacity. Exfoliative toxins that circulate in blood during infection are responsible for the skin findings in staphylococcal scalded skin syndrome, which occurs in children. A pore-forming toxin called α-hemolysin (or α-toxin) lyses a broad range of host cells, including bacteria-destroying phagocytes, and it has been shown to play a significant role in S. aureus pneumonia.[140,141] S. aureus also produces β- and γ-hemolysins, which may add to the pathogenicity of S. aureus, but they seem to be less potent virulence factors.

Clinical isolates of S. aureus are able to produce up to four bicomponent pore-forming toxins with the capacity to lyse cells of the immune system.[142,143] The pore-forming PVL kills human neutrophils by creating pores in the cell membrane.[33] PVL is carried by a phage and is carried by few of S. aureus strains (less than 5 percent). There is a strong association between this toxin and skin and soft tissue infections, but PVL has also been associated with severe necrotizing pneumonia.[3,113,144] This pneumonia is characterized by a sudden onset followed by rapid worsening of symptoms. Severe respiratory failure, and airway hemorrhages lead to high mortality.[145] Recently, clones of CA-MRSA strains that carry PVL have emerged worldwide.[146] The spread of these strains suggests that the combination, methicillin resistance plus PVL, confers a selective advantage to the strains. The arginine catabolic mobile element (ACME) carried by CA-MRSA strains (especially by USA300 strains) may be associated with virulence also. Elimination of ACME significantly reduced bacterial infectivity of target organs in a rabbit infection model and increased competitive fitness of the parent strain.[147]

S. aureus can sometimes act as an intracellular pathogen. Following internalization, S. aureus may adapt its metabolism to an intracellular lifestyle allowing long-term persistence within host cells.[148-152] These processes may lead to the generation of a special phenotype, SCV, which is of smaller size and has less pigmentation and less hemolysis, and can persist within the protected environment of the host cell.[84,153,154] SCVs are associated with persistent and recurrent infection, particularly from patients with chronic osteomyelitis, patients with device-related infections, patients with abscesses, and patients with both cystic fibrosis and chronic airway infection.[84,153,155-157] SCV strains are able to produce large quantities of proteases, which cause tissue damage to joints, and adhesins, which facilitate tissue attachment and uptake by host cells.[158,159] Of note, S. aureus SCVs retain the ability to revert to more rapidly growing organisms that produce larger quantities of toxins. In addition, the slow growth of S. aureus SCVs make them less responsive to cell wall-active antibiotics, and their decreased electron transport results in little aminoglycoside uptake because of reduced transmembrane potential, which is required for aminoglycoside uptake.[160] By persisting within the host cells, they are able to phenotypically resist antibiotics and escape host immune response.[161]

Clinical Manifestations

S. aureus can cause suppurative infections of bone (osteomyelitis), soft tissue (abscesses and cellulitis), closed spaces (empyema), and heart valves (endocarditis). It also can release extracellular toxins that result in toxin-mediated syndromes. S. aureus infections may lead to overwhelming sepsis and shock in elderly persons (the most common cause of bacteremic death in people over 65 years of age). Any localized S. aureus infection can become invasive and lead to bacteremia. S. aureus is pre-eminent among bacteria in its ability to cause metastatic foci of infection once the bloodstream is invaded. Because of this characteristic, S. aureus infections may require a prolonged course of intravenous antibiotics. Duration of treatment is determined by the site(s) of infection.

Skin and Soft Tissue Infections

Localized skin infections without a rash are common and are characterized by local abscess formation. These infections include folliculitis, furuncles, carbuncles, and impetigo. Many of the strains causing skin and soft tissue infections will carry PVL, and they may be resistant to methicillin. They are predominantly community-associated infections. S. aureus is the second-most common cause of cellulitis, whereas Streptococcus pyogenes is the most common. Both organisms must be considered when treating cellulitis, as organisms are difficult to recover by aspiration of the skin.

Disseminated Infections

S. aureus can also cause disseminated infection. After bloodstream invasion by S. aureus, various body sites are at risk for secondary infection. Examples of these secondary infections are vertebral osteomyelitis and septic arthritis. In both examples, S. aureus is the most common organism causing these types of infections. S. aureus is one of the most common organisms causing all types of healthcare-associated infections (HAIs).[162] A complication of bacteremia is the development of endocarditis. Although incidence of endocarditis related to *S. aureus* bacteremia declined over the years because of vigorous antibiotic intervention, it has re-emerged as the population has aged, as more intravascular devices are used, and as the organism has developed more resistant to antibiotic therapy.[163]

Toxin-mediated Complications

S. aureus is also the causative agent for classical toxin-mediated diseases. The PTSAgs (TSST-1 and SEs/SEls) are the most potent activators of T lymphocytes, resulting in a massive release of proinflammatory cytokines and eventuating in shock, multiorgan failure, and death.[164,165] In addition, they have, for example, mitogenic activity and they are able to induce high fevers and stimulate neutrophil recruitment to a site of infection, resulting in local inflammation.

TSS caused mainly by TSST-1 (seldom by SEB or SEC) is characterized by fever, desquamative skin rash, low blood pressure, and multiple organ failure. It occurs in patients who are harboring toxin-producing *S. aureus*. TSS was originally described in menstruating women who were using hyperabsorbable tampons.[166] TSS has been subsequently observed in many other types of *S. aureus* infections, including postoperative wound infection.[167]

SEs cause the symptoms of foodborne illness.[165] When an enterotoxin-forming *S. aureus* strain contaminates food, and the food is inadequately refrigerated or undercooked, the organism proliferates and produces toxins. The toxins are relatively heat stable; therefore, incompletely reheated food can also cause food poisoning. The toxins are tasteless. Ingestion of food contaminated with toxin produces a sudden onset of nausea, vomiting, abdominal cramps, and diarrhea 2 to 6 hours after food ingestion, which typically subsides within 8 to 12 hours.

The phage-encoded exfoliative toxins (ETs)—also known as epidermolytic toxins—cause SSSS, also known as pemphigus neonatorum or Ritter disease. SSSS is typically found in infants.[168] This syndrome becomes evident with skin changes that look as if the child has suffered a burn with large blisters and reddened or sunburned skin.

Epidemiology and Transmission

Epidemiology

S. aureus is often carried by humans as part of their physiological microbial flora. Forty to 50 percent of newborns are colonized shortly after birth (40 to 50 percent), but colonization can decrease with age depending on maternal carriage of *S. aureus*, breastfeeding, and number of siblings.[169] Persistent carriers (10 to 35 percent) may have one strain over prolonged time. Other carriers may harbor *S. aureus* intermittently.[170] *S. aureus* generally colonizes the anterior nares and the pharynx. From there, *S. aureus* can be transferred to skin and other body areas. The vaginal carriage rate in

adult premenopausal women is about 10 percent, and bacterial counts increase at the time of menses (studies of vaginal carriage of *S. aureus* were initiated because of the occurrence of TSS in menstruating women in the late 1970s).[171]

Patients with diabetes who are receiving insulin, patients receiving long-term hemodialysis, and users of illicit intravenous drugs also have a higher carriage rate than the general population.[172-174] The higher carriage rate coupled with PMN deficiencies that interfere with killing of *S. aureus* leads to a higher incidence of *S. aureus* infection in these groups.

The CDC estimated that 65,269 cases of invasive MRSA infections (bloodstream infections, pneumonia, osteomyelitis, endocarditis, wounds, and cellulitis) occurred in the United States in 2011.[175] Of these, 16,560 cases (25 percent; 5.31/100,000 population year) were community-associated and 47,340 were healthcare-associated (75 percent; 20.06/100,000 population year). However, of all healthcare-associated cases, 34,876 (74 percent) were defined as infections with a community onset because the infection was detected from cultures taken in an outpatient setting or before the fourth calendar day of hospitalization. These patients also had risk factors such as history of hospitalization in the previous year. These data underscore the importance of MRSA as a source of community-acquired infections in the United States. A recent meta-analysis suggested that CA-MRSA infections began to appear in the United States in the early or middle 1980s, increased slowly through the 1990s, and began to rapidly emerge beginning in 2000. In the late 2000s a plateau was observed on a high incidence rate ranging between 84/100,000 people under Tricare-insured persons and 566 cases/100,000 people among Maryland veterans.[176]

Data from national U.S. surveillance systems on HAIs show that pathogen-specific pooled mean central line-associated bloodstream infection (CLABSI) incidence per 1,000 central line days decreased between 2002 and 2010 in intensive care units (ICUs) in the United States.[177] During this period, the CLABSI incidence density rate of *S. aureus* had fallen below those of *Candida* spp., *Enterococcus* spp., and Gram-negative rods—at least in adult ICUs. However, *S. aureus* is still a predominant cause of ventilator-associated events (VAE) in the United States, which is underpinned by data from 31 U.S. community hospitals, where the top three causative pathogens were MRSA (24.5 percent), *Pseudomonas* spp. (14.0 percent), and *Klebsiella* spp. (11.9 percent).[178] Pooled data of 69,475 HAIs (CLABSI, catheter-associated urinary tract infections, VAE, and surgical site infections [SSIs]) that occurred from 2009 to 2010 show that staphylococci were the predominant pathogens detected, with *S. aureus* accounting for 16 percent and CoNS for 11 percent of all HAIs.[162] In this dataset, *S. aureus* was ranked as the most important bacterium to cause VAE and SSI, and CoNS were predominant among CLABSI. Of all *S. aureus* infections, 44 to 59 percent were MRSA, which reflects how endemic MRSA has become in the United States. This stands in contrast to European countries where, according to 2011 data from the European

Antimicrobial Resistance Surveillance Network (EARS-Net), MRSA accounted for less than 5 percent of all *S. aureus* bloodstream infections in 8 of 30 countries, for less than 20 percent in 16 of 30 countries, and more than 40 percent in only 4 of 30 countries (http://www.ecdc.europa.eu/en/activities/surveillance/EARS-Net).

Transmission

Patients infected with MRSA or colonized asymptomatically are thought to represent the major sources for the introduction of MRSA in healthcare institutions.[179–181] MRSA is transmitted from patient to patient primarily via hand contacts of staff and care providers.[182,183] This mechanism of transmission emphasizes the need of rigorous hand hygiene; two studies have demonstrated that an increase of hand hygiene compliance (from 48 to 66 percent compliance and from 19 to 48 percent) resulted in a decrease of MRSA by 50 to 60 percent, respectively.[184,185]

Additionally, MRSA can be spread throughout the hospital environment, where it is able to survive on inanimate surfaces for at least 7 days and up to 7 months.[186,187] Hence, inanimate surfaces may also represent vectors for the transmission of MRSA in healthcare facilities, which underscores the importance of surface disinfection and cleaning.[188]

Colonized or infected healthcare personnel may also serve as a source or reservoir of MRSA, especially in outbreak situations.[189] Risk factors for acquiring MRSA during hospitalization vary and depend on the population studied and circumstances (endemic or epidemic). Important patient risk factors include prolonged hospitalization, antimicrobial therapy, stay in an ICU or burn unit, and exposure to a colonized or infected patient.[20,183]

The overall infection dose for MRSA is unknown. However, from in vitro data it can be presumed that less than 100 bacteria are sufficient, if inoculated in a wound.[190] In addition, many authors have estimated the "reproduction rate" for MRSA in healthcare settings (i.e., the number of secondary cases per index case due to transmission of the pathogen) ranging between 0.06 and 0.93.[191,192] Recently, a systematic review found that the daily transmission rate of MRSA was 1.37 to 140/1,000 patient-days, if Contact Precautions were not applied, and 0.81 to 9.0/1,000 patient-days if Contact Precautions were applied.[193]

Until recently, most MRSA infections were acquired in hospitals. But as early as 1993, the MRSA strains from healthy people who had not previously been exposed to the healthcare system were identified.[194] These CA-MRSAs have been predominantly isolated from children in day care centers, athletes, students, military recruits, man who have sex with men, jailed inmates, and homeless people.[34,195–197]

Hence, transmission of these strains occurs mainly where there is close physical contact between people.[198] The occurrence of CA-MRSA has also caused efforts to investigate the transmissibility of MRSA in households. It was found that, in case of an index case, MRSA transmission affected 47 percent of all household contacts.[199] Another study revealed that each MRSA index patient transmitted MRSA to one to four household members.[200]

Effective transmission of MRSA is also observed between animals and humans. This has been investigated predominantly on livestock farms. On European pig farms where MRSA CC398 is endemic, it was found that 77 to 86 percent of all farmers carry the same MRSA molecular strain as their animals.[201,202] Even after short-term exposure, intermittent MRSA CC398 carriage was detected. For the transmission of MRSA between companion animals and pet owners, there is limited data elucidating the frequency of transmission. In one study, it was found that, when sampling pets living in households of patients (n = 49) with MRSA infection, in 8 percent of the cases MRSA was detected in at least one companion animal.[203]

Treatment

Decolonization of Staphylococcus aureus *Carriage*

In the past two decades, there has been an emphasis on trying to eradicate MRSA colonization from the anterior nares and various other body sites to control epidemics. The impact of a nasal decolonization from *S. aureus*, whether the *S.aureus* is methicillin resistant or not, is a matter of recent debate. It has been assumed that colonizing strains may serve as endogenous reservoirs for overt clinical infections or may spread to other patients.[204–206]

Prospective studies showed that nasal carriage is a source of and risk for subsequent bacteremia and other infections caused by this pathogen.[204,207–209] Data suggest a benefit to the decolonized patient, especially if the patient has underlying diseases that may lead to hospitalization. This reasonable rationale is consistent with many studies showing reduced infections when nasal colonization is reduced prior to surgery and in hemodialysis patients.[210–218] The reason for debate is that recolonization and relapse occur frequently—mostly after discharge from a hospital. The success of mupirocin-based decolonization therapy was shown to be 94 percent 1 week after treatment and 65 percent 2 weeks thereafter.[209,219] However, a Cochrane database review demonstrated that the use of mupirocin ointment, though not necessarily leading to long-term eradication but enabling short-term decolonization in many cases, results in a statistically significant reduction in *S. aureus* infections in patients nasally colonized with this pathogen.[220] Of note, strains can become resistant to mupirocin used for eradication.[221]

Therapy for Staphylococcus aureus *Infection*

In general, for annually updated and further information regarding the therapy of *S. aureus* infections, the current edition of *The Sanford Guide to Antimicrobial Therapy*[222] or other guidelines should be consulted. For skin and soft tissue infection, incision and drainage is the first treatment consideration. This is a prerequisite for the ultimate success of any antimicrobial regimen for cutaneous and subcutaneous abscesses or empyema.

The most active compounds for the therapy of staphylococcal infections in general are the members of the β-lactam class, with penicillin G as "number one" in activity followed by penicillinase-resistant penicillins and cephalosporins of the first and second generation. However, development of resistances (1) by β-lactamase leading to resistance to non-penicillinase-resistant β-lactams and (2) by acquisition of the SCCmec element leading to resistance to all β-lactams (with the exception of the novel cephalosporins with MRSA activity) limit their use currently.

Thus, the increasing threat caused by multidrug-resistant pathogens including MRSA has led to the development of several novel antibiotic (sub)classes, as well as compounds with substantial enhancements in the established antibiotic classes. Some compounds of these classes with anti-MRSA activity have already been introduced on the market (e.g., linezolid, dapto-mycin, tigecycline, ceftobiprole, ceftaroline).[223] Indications for these agents are based on noninferiority studies demonstrating that the novel compounds are as efficacious as the standard in the treatment of respective patients.[66,224-226] Although all these novel agents and those that are in the pipeline are welcome additions to the therapeutic armamentarium, further studies are highly warranted to investigate their complete clinical impact, their safety, and the development of resistance. In addition to novel compounds, a renewed interest in older agents with anti-staphylococcal activity (e.g., fosfomycin, fusidic acid, rifampicin) is noted.

In the rare case of penicillin-susceptible S. aureus infection, penicillin G can be used effectively. However, since most S. aureus infections are caused by strains resistant to penicillin, the use of free or fixed combination with a β-lactamase inhibitor (clavulanic acid or tazobactam) or other β-lactamase-resistant agents is necessary. For MSSA that is penicillin-resistant, penicillinase-resistant penicillins such as nafcillin, oxacillin, cloxacillin, flucloxacillin, and dicloxacillin remain the most effective antibiotics, in particular for serious infections such as endocarditis or bone and joint infections. First-generation (e.g., cefalotin, cefazolin) cephalosporins are equally effective and potentially less toxic for the treatment of minor staphylococcal infections, such as skin and soft tissue infections.[227] In addition, they might be useful alternatives in patients with penicillin hypersensitivity or intolerance. Second-generation cephalosporins or cephamycins (e.g., cefuroxime, cefoxitin) are considered somewhat less effective than the first generations in covering S. aureus; however, they are sufficiently active against staphylococci. Cefepime, a fourth-generation cephalosporin, may also have sufficient activity against staphylococci. Carbapenems (e.g., imipenem, meropenem), as extremely broad-spectrum agents exhibiting also good activity against MSSA, should be held in reserve. For patients with penicillin allergy or chronic renal failure, clindamycin or vancomycin is commonly prescribed. The use of vancomycin for severe MSSA

infections is not advised, as it is inferior to the use of β-lactams in terms of mortality, bacteriological outcome, or relapsed infection.[228] For all antibiotic treatments of S. aureus infections that are intended to be performed by oral administration, it should be kept in mind that these antibiotics may have a low oral bioavailability (e.g., cefuroximaxetil and flucloxacillin). There is no evidence that S. aureus infections can be reliably treated with an antimicrobial drug against which resistance is expressed in vitro.[229]

MRSA represent a major therapeutic challenge due to the limited antimicrobial treatment options, in particular for severe, invasive infections, because appropriate substances are either less active than β-lactams against staphylococci or have problems in terms of toxicity and/or pharmacokinetic and pharmacodynamic parameters.[230] Traditionally, all β-lactam antibiotics are inadequate for therapy of MRSA. However, novel investigational anti-PBP2a β-lactams of the cephalosporin and carbapenem classes with increased PBP2a affinities and low MICs are being investigated.[231] The so-called anti-MRSA cephalosporins (ceftobiprole [recently withdrawn from the market] and ceftaroline) may be suitable options for empiric therapy of MRSA infections.[232-235] However, further clinical studies are needed to define their definite role in patient care.

Because healthcare-associated MRSA strains (and some reported community-associated MRSA strains) are multidrug-resistant, they are also frequently resistant to other antibiotic classes, such as macrolides, lincosamides, tetracyclines, and aminoglycosides. Therefore, glycopeptides (vancomycin preferentially over teicoplanin) and recently introduced novel antibiotics such as linezolid, daptomycin, and tigecycline, are the drugs of choice for MRSA infections.[66,236,237]

For severe MRSA infections except bacteremic pneumonia, vancomycin is still widely regarded as the drug of choice.[238] In an attempt to improve the bactericidal capacity in patients treated with vancomycin for severe staphylococcal infections (in particular, endocarditis), several combinations (aminoglycosides, rifampin, co-trimoxazole, fosfomycin, and fusidic acid) have been advocated.[239] However, they are still a matter of debate, and contradictory opinions are reported.[240] It has been suggested that using rifampicin with vancomycin improves outcome in uncomplicated bacteremia. Fusidic acid, fosfomycin, or aminoglycosides in combination with vancomycin may be relevant as an alternative to rifampicin. Unfortunately, there are only a few, partly uncorroborated studies available supporting combination therapy.[241] In the case of rifampicin, fusidic acid, and fosfomycin, resistance occurs rapidly; therefore, these compounds must always be administered in combination with another antibiotic.

Daptomycin, a cyclic lipopeptide, has an in vitro spectrum of activity exhibiting a concentration-dependent bactericidal activity for most clinically relevant Gram-positive bacteria, including MRSA.[242] Although daptomycin is not indicated for the treatment of pneumonia (because the drug is inactivated by surfactant), this agent is indicated for the treatment of complicated skin and soft tissue infections caused by MSSA or MRSA.[243,244] The U.S. Food and Drug Administration (FDA) also approved the use of daptomycin for bacteremia caused by MRSA and right-sided endocarditis.[245]

Trimethoprim-sulfamethoxazole (SXT), a folate antagonist, may occasionally be useful in combination with rifampin.[239] When using SXT, one should keep in mind that S. aureus produces a very potent DNase that releases thymidine from DNA found in damaged host tissues and pus. As thymidine is known to reduce the activity of SXT, this agent should be used with caution.[246]

Quinolones (e.g., ciprofloxacin) are known to be become ineffective during treatment.[247] The newer quinolones (e.g., gatifloxacin, levofloxacin, moxifloxacin) have activity against Gram-positive organisms. Particularly due to the phenomenon of "collateral damage," a term that stands for the selection of drug-resistant organisms and the unwanted development of colonization or infection with multidrug-resistant organisms (MDROs), quinolones should not be used to treat staphylococcal infections.[248]

Tetracylines should be avoided for the therapy of S. aureus infections because their activity might be weak or not safe enough. Almost all LA-MRSA isolates exhibit resistance to tetracyclines.[38] The minocycline derivate tigecycline, the first available glycylcycline, is a bacteriostatic agent with activity against a wide range of aerobic and anaerobic Gram-positive and Gram-negative microorganisms. This antibiotic is indicated for complicated skin and soft tissue infections (MSSA and MRSA) and complicated intra-abdominal infections (only MSSA).[243]

Clindamycin, a lincosamide, is widely used against S. aureus, particularly for skin and soft tissue infections based on the good tissue penetration. However, the inducible macrolide-lincosamide group B streptogramin (MLS$_B$) resistance may limit its use and clinical treatment failure has been observed.[249]

The first oxazolidinone available on the market, linezolid, is a narrow-spectrum anti-Gram-positive compound that is rather bacteriostatic (concentration-dependent) against staphylococci and shows very long postantibiotic effect against S. aureus.[250] It is approved in the United States for the treatment of health-care-associated pneumonia and complicated skin and skin tissue infections, including diabetic foot infections caused by MSSA or MRSA. For MSSA, it is also indicated in the treatment of community-associated pneumonia and uncomplicated skin and soft tissue infections. For the treatment of MRSA pneumonia, vancomycin was the only available drug for many years. Unfortunately, the cure rates for S. aureus were disappointing, with mortality rates of almost 50 percent compared with 5 percent rates if the patients were treated with β-lactams.[251,252] An alternative therapeutic option for the treatment of MRSA pneumonia is linezolid, which has in contrast to vancomycin favorable lung pharmacokinetics and concentrations in the alveolar lining fluid that exceed the linezolid MIC for MRSA during the entire dose-to-dose interval.[253] Some studies reported clinical outcomes of study patients treated with linezolid to

be significantly better than those treated with vancomycin therapy.[254,255] However, this superiority has not been fully confirmed by other clinical studies including randomized clinical trials especially when considering mortality as the outcome parameter.[256,257]

Prevention and Risk Reduction

Ten to 35 percent of healthy adults are permanently colonized with S. aureus (primarily in the nose) and the others are at least intermittently colonized.[170] Therefore, S. aureus may be recovered from numerous body sites in both patients and medical personnel.[258,259] S. aureus is endemic to the healthcare environment and serves as a potential source for outbreaks. Because of the high incidence of endemic (background) S. aureus colonization and infection, outbreak identification is sometimes difficult. An outbreak is indicated by temporal and geographic clusters of S. aureus infection that exceed the baseline, especially in a special-care unit (e.g., ICUs and burn units) or in patients who rarely become infected (e.g., patients undergoing arthroscopy). Hence, outbreak control depends on careful epidemiological investigation to define what factors are important in causing infection among a population at risk. Standard epidemiological investigative techniques should be used, including defining a case, the population at risk, and the temporal sequence of the outbreak. Investigations are hampered if it is impossible to distinguish rapidly among strains. Consequently, molecular typing techniques are essential in the verification and characterization of an outbreak situation.

The management of MRSA could be perceived as a paradigm for preventing healthcare-associated transmission of multidrug-resistant microorganisms. Evidence-based guidelines to control and prevent MRSA colonization and infection have been established in many countries.[260] Examples of guidelines in the United States include those from the CDC and the Society for Healthcare Epidemiology of America (SHEA), and they are graded according to the evidence available from the literature.[261,262] Guidelines reflect the specific national epidemiological situation. For example, Dutch or Scandinavian guidelines reflect the low prevalence of MRSA in these countries. Given the low prevalence, it is possible for these countries to follow extensive eradication policies to contain MRSA—including case-tracing for single cases of MRSA colonization in the population, screening, strict single-room isolation in the healthcare setting, and decolonization of carriers after discharge from hospitals. In countries where MRSA is more disseminated (such as the United States) or where there are financial constraints, prevention of MRSA is usually restricted to more general principles, such as early MRSA detection (screening), the use of isolation precautions when caring for MRSA patients (gloves and gowns), and active decolonization. These measures are recommended by the majority of national guidelines. Recently, some investigators found that "shotgun" methods (i.e., performing decolonization therapies for all patients instead of only those identified by targeted screening) could be more effective in reducing the occurrence of HA MRSA.[263] Although this could represent an alternative in settings with "spillover" MRSA incidence, the various flaws identified for this specific study should be kept in mind.[264] Particularly, such an approach can facilitate the emergence of resistance against mupirocin beyond what has been observed already when this agent was widely used.[265] These effects could hamper MRSA prevention and control in the long run.

To ensure the proper implementation and consistent adherence to the prevention guidelines, educational programs for healthcare personnel should be conducted, assessed, and repeated as necessary.[266]

Since interinstitutional patient transfers play an important role transmission of healthcare-associated pathogens, hospitals are epidemiologically linked. Coordinated citywide or regional infection prevention and control policies and established healthcare networks can address this challenge and maintain patient safety throughout the continuum of care.[267,268]

Of note, some authors have recently described the effectiveness of several "bundles" that combine a series of preventive measures.[268,269] The evaluation of such bundles including their effectiveness, feasibility, and applicability to different healthcare settings and patients could guide future preventive efforts and tailor MRSA prevention measures to meet setting-specific needs. Overall, the major components (i.e., bundles) for *S. aureus*/MRSA prevention include the following: hand hygiene, Contact Precautions, surveillance, environmental cleaning, decolonization therapies, and antibiotic stewardship (see below).

Hand Hygiene

Failure to perform appropriate hand hygiene is generally considered to be the leading cause of MRSA spread. Consistent compliance with proper hand hygiene procedures is therefore a chief recommendation for the prevention of MRSA transmission.[261,270] The *Five Moments for Hand Hygiene* initiative developed by the World Health Organization recommends that staff disinfect their hands appropriately before and after all patient contacts, after contact with the patient's environment, after contact with potentially contaminated specimens, and before aseptic procedures. (http://www.who.int/gpsc/tools/Five_moments/en/). In addition, there needs to be adequate staff-to-patient ratios (especially in high-risk settings for transmissions, such as ICUs) that enable compliance with hand hygiene.

Contact Precautions

The use of Contact Precautions (such as gloves and gowns) is a tier one recommendation of the CDC/Healthcare Infection Control Practices Advisory Committee (HICPAC) MDRO guideline published in 2006.[262] See Chapter 29 Isolation Precautions (Transmission-based Precautions) for more information about this important infection prevention aspect of MRSA prevention and risk reduction.

Surveillance

Surveillance for targeted MDROs is a hallmark of infection prevention and is a tier one recommendation of the CDC/HICPAC

Tier 1. General Recommendations for Routine Prevention and Control of MDROs in Healthcare Settings

Surveillance
- Use standardized laboratory methods follow published guidelines for determining antimicrobial susceptibilities of targeted and emerging MDROs.
- Establish systems to ensure that clinical micro labs (in-house and outsourced) promptly notify infection control or a medical director/designee when a novel resistance pattern for that facility is detected. (IB)
- In hospitals and LTCFs:
- ...develop and implement laboratory protocols for storing isolates of selected MDROs for molecular typing when needed to confirm transmission or delineate epidemiology of MDRO in facility. (IB)
- ...establish laboratory-based systems to detect and communicate evidence of MDROs in clinical isolates (IB)
- ...prepare facility-specific antimicrobial susceptibility reports as recommended by CLSI; monitor reports for evidence of changing resistance that may indicate emergence or transmission of MDROs (IA/IC)
- ...develop and monitor special-care unit-specific antimicrobial susceptibility reports (e.g., ventilator dependent
- units, ICUs, oncology units). (IB)
- ...monitor trends in incidence of target MDROs in the facility over time to determine if MDRO rates are decreasing or if additional interventions are needed. (IA)

Tier 2. Recommendations for Intensified MDRO Control Efforts

Surveillance
- Calculate and analyze incidence rates of target MDROs (single isolates/patient; location-, service specific) (IB)
- Increase frequency of compiling, monitoring antimicrobial susceptibility summary reports (II)
- Implement laboratory protocols for storing isolates of selected MDROs for molecular typing; perform typing if
- needed (IB)
- Develop and implement protocols to obtain active surveillance cultures from patients in populations at risk. (IB) (See recommendations for appropriate body sites and culturing methods.)
- Conduct culture surveys to assess efficacy of intensified MDRO control interventions.
- Conduct serial (e.g., weekly) unit specific point prevalence culture surveys of the target MDRO to determine if transmission has decreased or ceased. (IB)
- Repeat point-prevalence culture surveys at routine intervals and at time of patient discharge or transfer until transmission has ceased. (IB)
- If indicated by assessment of the MDRO problem, collect cultures to assess the colonization status of roommates and other patients with substantial exposure to patients with
- known MDRO infection or colonization. (IB)
- Obtain cultures from HCP for target MDROs when there is epidemiologic evidence implicating the staff member as a source of ongoing transmission. (IB)]

Figure 93-6. Recommendations for MDRO Surveillance from HICPAC Management of MDRO in Healthcare Settings, 2006.[262]

MDRO guideline published in 2006. Active surveillance for MRSA is a tier two recommendation of the CDC/HICPAC MDRO guideline published in 2006.[262] See Figure 93-6 and Chapter 11 Surveillance for more information about this important aspect of MRSA prevention and risk reduction.

Environmental Cleaning

Cleaning and disinfection protocols can be instrumental in the control of possible environmental contamination with MRSA (see Chapter 107 Environmental Services).

Decolonization Therapies

The evidence for performing therapies to decolonize patients with MRSA carriage is summarized above. The majority of studies have evaluated approaches using mupirocin nasal ointment alone or in combination with topical treatment of the skin and the pharynx.

Antibiotic Stewardship

Various studies have documented that the previous use of antibiotics is a risk factor for MRSA isolation among inpatients.[271,272] A recent meta-analysis has calculated that the relative risk of acquiring MRSA was 3-fold, 2.9-fold, 2.2-fold, and 1.9-fold increased for patients who had taken quinolones, glycopeptides, cephalosporins, and other β-lactam antibiotics, respectively.[273] Moreover, interventions targeted on prudent antibiotic prescribing have been shown to be associated with a reduction of antimicrobial resistance among healthcare-associated bacterial pathogens.[274]

COAGULASE-NEGATIVE STAPHYLOCOCCI

Currently, there are more than 30 identified species and subspecies of CoNS (Figure 93-1). The most important human pathogens, in terms of frequency and/or severity of illness, include *S. epidermidis, S. haemolyticus, S. saprophyticus* subsp. *saprophyticus,* and *S. lugdunensis,* followed by *S. capitis, S. hominis,* and *S. warneri.* Rare pathogens in human infections include *S. caprae, S. cohnii, S. pasteuri, S. pettenkoferi, S. schleiferi, S. xylosus,* and other species. Nowadays, laboratories should differentiate CoNS, because several approaches are available for this purpose, and automated identification systems often provide speciation with an accuracy of 70 to 90 percent.

Antibiotic Resistance

CoNS isolates tend to be more resistant to antimicrobials than *S. aureus* isolates, though this gap is unfortunately closing. Similar to *S. aureus,* more than 90 percent of all *S. epidermidis* and *S. haemolyticus* isolates (community- or healthcare-associated) are resistant to penicillin because of production of β-lactamase.[275] The mechanism and expression of methicillin resistance in CoNS are similar to those in *S. aureus.* More than 80 percent of hospital-associated isolates are methicillin-resistant and, in addition, are also often multidrug-resistant.[73,276,277] In contrast to *S. aureus,* reduced or nonsusceptibility to glycopeptides is more common, usually heterogeneous, and (particularly for teicoplanin) is an emerging phenomenon.[278–280] In a recent UK study, 20.8 percent of all CoNS tested ($n = 1214$) were not susceptible to teicoplanin, but only one vancomycin-intermediate CoNS isolate was found.[281] In particular, *S. haemolyticus* shows unique predisposition among CoNS to acquire resistance to glycopeptides, often combined with methicillin resistance.[280,282] However, the vast majority of CoNS isolates are still susceptible to vancomycin, as reported from many studies.[68,73,277,283] Although the exact mechanism of staphylococcal glycopeptide resistance remains unknown, the basic mechanisms leading to reduced susceptibility to glycopeptides might be similar in both CoNS and *S. aureus.* Also for CoNS, cell wall thickening was reported.[284] Although rare to date, CoNS strains resistant to the recently introduced antimicrobials, including linezolid, daptomycin, and tigecycline, have been reported.[277,285,286]

A special form of CoNS "phenotypic" resistance has been demonstrated within biofilms produced by many different CoNS strains. The species- and strain-specific mechanisms of biofilm-associated CoNS antimicrobial resistance are likely multifactorial.[287,288] There have been mixed results from efforts to incorporate antimicrobial agents in medical devices to prevent CoNS colonization and biofilm formation; however, some of the newer agents offer some promise of penetration of biofilm

to inhibit or kill adherent staphylococci[289,290] (see Chapter 70 Biofilm and Associated Pathogens).

Epidemiology

The capability of CoNS to cause infections is divergent. Medium-pathogenic staphylococci—including *S. epidermidis* group species, *S. lugdunensis,* and *S. saprophyticus* as typical members—could be separated from nonpathogenic staphylococci represented by species associated with (mostly fermented) food of plant and animal origin. CoNS species that are specific to animal species may occasionally colonize humans, although their isolation from various human clinical specimens has been described. Under defined conditions (immunodeficiency, implanted foreign bodies), these opportunistic pathogens may be found in human infections.

About a dozen CoNS species are well recognized as opportunistic pathogens and are able to cause clinically significant and rarely severe infections.[291] They are natural inhabitants of human skin and mucous membranes. *S. epidermidis* is the most prevalent species on human skin (65 to 90 percent of all staphylococci recovered), followed by *S. haemolyticus* and *S. hominis.* In addition, *S. saprophyticus* subsp. *saprophyticus* is a common cause of urinary tract infection in young women and is characterized by its capacity to adhere to uroepithelial cells.[292] *S. saprophyticus* urinary tract infections are almost all community acquired and peak in the spring.

Foreign body-related (FBR) infections (FBRIs), also called device-associated healthcare-associated infections (DA-HAIs), represent the most important clinical entity caused by CoNS. CoNS account for the majority of FBRIs, both of temporarily and permanently implanted devices.[293,294] The most common infection is associated with intravenous catheters; thus, they are a very common and increasing cause of healthcare-associated bacteremia.[162] From the U.S. nationwide SCOPE database, at the end of a 7-year period, the most common isolates recovered from healthcare-associated BSIs were CoNS (31 percent) followed by *S. aureus* (20 percent).[295] Patients with FBR-BSIs had significantly longer ICU and/or hospital lengths of stay, with higher mortality rate and hospital costs compared with uninfected patients.[296,297] In addition, CoNS infections are related to peritoneal dialysis catheters, CSF shunts, prosthetic valves, temporarily and permanently implanted devices, and vascular grafts.[298–301]

Almost all *S. epidermidis* infections are healthcare associated except for prosthetic valve infections, right-sided endocarditis of intravenous drug users, and some cases of peritoneal dialysis-associated catheter-associated peritonitis. Reservoirs of CoNS in the hospital setting have been difficult to identify. Until recently, it was believed that CoNS that cause infection come from the patient's indigenous flora. However, recent publications showed substantial evidence for strain transmission of CoNS among hospitalized patients. Applying molecular genotyping methods, defined CoNS strains causing bacteremia were shown to persist in a neonatal ICU for one decade and could be recovered from the hands of personnel at the end of that period.[302] Also for non-neonatal ICUs and wards, clonal spread of endemic, multi-drug-resistant CoNS lineages has been shown.[303,304] In addition, outbreaks that are caused by cross-transmission have been reported.[305,306]

Diagnosis

Gram stain of clinical specimens does not discriminate between *S. aureus* and CoNS. CoNS grow readily on many different media, but most commonly sheep blood agar is used (Figure 93-1).[4] Routine identification of CoNS is classically performed in many laboratories using commercial test systems based on biochemical procedures that can differentiate between *S. aureus* and CoNS species mainly involved in human infections. Recently, CoNS identification by nucleic acid-based and mass spectroscopic methods supplements or replaces the classical diagnostic approaches.[4] Antimicrobial susceptibility testing of CoNS should be performed in general as noted for *S. aureus*; however, partially different breakpoints should be considered.[79,80]

Because CoNS colonize the mucosa and skin, a decision must be made for any given CoNS isolate from a clinical specimen about whether it represents a true infection, colonization, or a contamination at the time cultures were obtained. This is especially true when evaluating cultures related to skin and soft tissue infections, surgical site infections, and positive blood cultures.[307] Precisely, because CoNS are an important cause of healthcare-associated BSIs, interpretation of cultures growing CoNS should be done based on knowledge of the usual types of infections caused by this organism, clinical and microbiological findings, and their pathogenesis.[308]

Although CoNS are the most common organisms isolated in blood cultures, a large proportion of these isolates represent events of contamination rather than true bacteremia.[309] The difficulty, however, is trying to make the correct categorization, especially when CoNS are detected in blood cultures from patients in ICUs, who are often febrile and have one or more intravascular catheters or other devices in place. Several indicators can be used to identify true CoNS bacteremia, including occurrence of multiple positive blood culture sets, growth in both aerobic and anaerobic bottles, detection of positive blood cultures less than 48 hours after cultures are obtained, and presence of foreign bodies in the patient, which predispose to CoNS infection (especially intravascular catheters that are left in place for more than 3 days).[310,311] However, in the presence of signs of sepsis, a single blood culture positive for CoNS may be significant.[312] For isolates of non–*S. epidermidis* CoNS, the finding of methicillin resistance may be associated with true bacteremia. Conversely, hints that CoNS isolated from blood cultures may be contaminants include the finding that only the aerobic bottle of a set is positive; having two or more sets of blood cultures with only one or a minority of bottles being positive; the finding in a patient who does not have a foreign body in place (especially useful in patients who have blood cultures done on admission to the hospital); delayed growth

(more than 48 hours) of a positive blood culture, indicating small numbers of organisms in the initial specimen (i.e., skin contamination); and more than one strain (usually detected by differences in antibiograms or colony morphologic appearance) of CoNS isolated in positive cultures.[310] Clinical and laboratory models have been developed to rapidly classify blood cultures in terms of contaminants or true-positive cultures using both clinical and laboratory data.[313,314] However, no generally accepted gold standard exists for differentiating pathogenic CoNS from contaminants.

Clinical Manifestations

Unlike *S. aureus*, which causes acute, pyogenic infections, infections caused by CoNS tend to be more gradual in onset and less severe overall. The exception is *S. lugdunensis* (discussed later in the chapter). The increasing use of indwelling or implanted foreign bodies has become essential in modern clinical practice but is associated with the possibility of infectious complications. Signs and symptoms that suggest catheter-associated infection, such as purulent drainage from the exit site or skin erythema, are usually absent despite a positive semi-quantitative catheter culture that implicates the catheter as the source of the bacteremia. CoNS, in particular *S. epidermidis*, are the most common organisms that cause infections in CSF shunts.[301,315] Infections usually occur close in time to placement, revision, or other manipulation of the shunt. Additionally, *S. epidermidis* (followed by *S. haemolyticus*) is the most common organism isolated from patients with peritonitis associated with peritoneal dialysis.[316] Peritonitis is usually manifested by abdominal pain and development of cloudy peritoneal fluid. Furthermore, chronic, polymer-associated clinical syndromes may also be at least in part associated with *S. epidermidis*. These syndromes include the aseptic loosening of joint prostheses due to infections of prosthetic joints, postoperative late-onset endophthalmitis after implantation of artificial intraocular lenses, and fibrous and capsular contracture syndrome after mammary augmentation with silicone prostheses.[317–319] A characteristic of these infections is that they develop slowly and may have only minimal signs and symptoms.

Although increasingly reported, CoNS are still a rather uncommon cause of native valve endocarditis. However, they are the most common cause of prosthetic valve endocarditis (approximately 40 percent of all cases) and of vascular graft infections.[320–323] Many of the cases of *S. epidermidis* prosthetic valve endocarditis that occur within the first year postoperatively are caused by inoculation of the organism at the time of surgery, especially cases that become clinically apparent within the first 2 months after surgery. Although clinical courses of CoNS-caused prosthetic valve endocarditis, they have been traditionally described as subacute or chronic without fulminant signs of infection. More aggressive presentations have recently been acknowledged.[324–326]

In contrast to healthy, term infants where CoNS habitually represent commensals, preterm newborns are specifically predisposed to invasive CoNS infections because of they are immunologically immature and have impaired skin and mucosal barriers. Thus, CoNS septicemia of preterm infants has been recognized as one of the major types of late-onset neonatal infection.[327–330] S. lugdunensis, a skin commensal preferentially of the lower parts of the human body, has a specific position among CoNS rather resembling S. aureus in many aspects. This species is an emerging pathogen that is being more frequently recovered from patients; however, it is infrequently detected compared with S. aureus and S. epidermidis. S. lugdunensis is known to cause aggressive and destructive courses of endocarditis with high mortality unusually fulminant for a CoNS species.[331,332] S. lugdunensis bacteremia is associated with endocarditis at an extremely high percentage (up to 50 percent).[333] It has been implicated also in other invasive diseases, such as soft tissue abscesses, septic arthritis, peritonitis, meningitis, and foreign body-associated infections.[334–336] Although virulence factors remain largely unknown, some studies suggest that the organism has the ability to form biofilms on host tissues or prosthetic surfaces and interact with host cells. The formation of small-colony and other phenotypic variants was described in a case of recurrent pacemaker-associated BSI.[337]

Pathogenesis

In the case of foreign body-associated infections, the host defense mechanisms often seem to be unable to handle the infection and, in particular, to eliminate the microorganisms from the infected polymer device. In addition, antibiotic therapy is frequently unable to interrupt this kind of infection despite the appropriate application of antibiotics with proved in vitro activity. The pathogenesis of foreign body-associated infections caused by S. epidermidis is characterized by colonization of the polymer surface through the formation of a thick, multilayered biofilm (Figure 93-1).[338] Biofilm formation proceeds in two stages, comprising (1) a rapid attachment of the staphylococci to the surface of the implanted device followed by (2) a more prolonged accumulation phase that involves cell proliferation and intercellular adhesion.[289] Finally, staphylococcal cells may disaggregate from the macrocolony on the polymer surface and drift into the bloodstream, resulting in metastatic and embolic complications.

To initiate invasive infections, staphylococcal cells must adhere to the extracellular matrix (ECM) or cells of the host tissue. This multifactorial process is very complex and essentially mediated by adhesins, which are staphylococcal proteins undergoing strong interactions with host structures. The group of proteinaceous surface-associated adhesins can be divided into two groups. The first group comprises proteins that are covalently bound to the bacterial cell wall (microbial surface components recognizing adhesive matrix molecules, MSCRAMMs). The second group comprises noncovalently linked proteins that are secreted but rebind to the bacterial cell surface—these include the secretable expanded repertoire adhesive molecules (SERAMs; so far only in S. aureus), bifunctional autolysin/adhesins, and membrane-spanning proteins (e.g., Embp in S. epidermidis).[339] MSCRAMMS of CoNS comprise the

accumulation-associated protein Aap, the biofilm-associated protein (Bap)-homologous protein (Bhp), and the clumping factor (Clf).[340] Bifunctional autolysins have been demonstrated for S. epidermidis (AtlE), S. saprophyticus (Aas), S. lugdunensis, and some other CoNS species.[341–343] Of the group of nonproteinaceous staphylococcal adhesins, a specific polysaccharide antigen termed "polysaccharide intercellular adhesin" (PIA) encoded by the icaADBC operon has been shown to be involved in intercellular adhesion and biofilm accumulation.[344–346] Also, other factors such as the accumulation-associated protein (AAP) seem to be involved in accumulation and biofilm formation, as well.[340] Furthermore, the cell wall teichoic acid covalently linked to the peptidoglycan is implicated in adherence processes of S. epidermidis.[347]

S. lugdunensis and the subspecies of S. schleiferi resemble S. aureus in that these species may express a clumping factor and/or produce a thermostable DNase and coagulase, respectively. Clinical isolates of S. lugdunensis may produce extracellular slime or glycocalyx, which has a role in bacterial colonization and interferes with the phagocytosis-associated activities of neutrophils.[348] Esterases, proteases, lipases, and other enzymes that may act as invasion factors have also been detected in this species.[287] A few reports are available on the interaction of S. lugdunensis with components of the ECM and host tissues and the presence of MSCRAMMs.[349]

S. saprophyticus subsp. saprophyticus shows a greater capacity to adhere specifically to uroepithelial cells compared with other CoNS. A surface-exposed 160-kDa protein with hemagglutinin/adhesin properties mediates the specific binding to uroepithelial cells.[350] Further proteins, such as the S. saprophyticus surface-associated protein (Ssp) and a serine-aspartate repeat protein (Sdrl), also may be involved in the interaction with the uroepithelium.[351,352]

Treatment

Since the majority of clinical CoNS strains are methicillin resistant, most infections by CoNS require treatment with glycopeptides (e.g., vancomycin). In addition, teicoplanin has potential for use as an alternative in the treatment of infections caused by CoNS. However, in general, it exhibits higher MICs than vancomycin in CoNS. It must be pointed out that glycopeptides are poorly bactericidal against staphylococci. The newly marketed agents, including linezolid, tigecycline, daptomycin, and ceftaroline, show excellent activity against CoNS.[58,74,277,353] If an isolate is methicillin susceptible, replacement of vancomycin by β-lactamase-resistant penicillins is advisable. Simultaneous use of antibiotics of the cell-wall active class (including vancomycin) and rifampin act synergistically to treat infections with CoNS. However, combination of antibiotics is not generally recommended for catheter-associated BSIs caused by CoNS.[354]

As the use of devices and biofilm formation are critical determinants of CoNS, a general decision has to be addressed: whether to remove the foreign body and/or whether to initiate calculated antimicrobial treatment.[289,355] This also holds true for implant infections caused by CoNS, which remain a therapeutic challenge as they frequently result in failure of conservative antibiotic therapy and require withdrawal of the foreign device.[356] Therefore, for easy-to-change devices, the optimal treatment of a foreign body infection by CoNS is the removal of the device when possible and its replacement is still needed.[357-360] Regardless of the type of device, removal of implanted devices is recommended when the patient shows signs of severe sepsis, septic phlebitis, and septic shock. In some circumstances, salvage of the device is the preferred option. Foreign body infections associated with long-term or permanent catheters (e.g., Port-a-cath or Hickman-type catheter) may be treated successfully "through the line."[361] However, persistent or relapsing fever and other signs of treatment failure are clear indications for removal of a medical device.[354] In the case of uncomplicated CoNS and foreign body infections—and provided that the device is removed—duration of parenteral therapy may be short (about 5 to 7 days).[356] If an intraluminal infection is suspected and the implanted device is retained, systemic antibiotic therapy for at least 10 to 14 days are recommended.[354]

Endocarditis that is caused by CoNS—depending on its resistance profile—is often treated with a combination of β-lactamase–resistant penicillin or vancomycin plus an aminoglycoside and/or rifampin.[355,362] In cases of prosthetic valve endocarditis, surgical removal of the infected prosthesis may be necessary to effect a cure.

FUTURE TRENDS

Worldwide, CA-MRSA strains are a significant threat to healthy people of all ages and are of particular concern in young children. To make matters worse, these strains also spread rapidly from person to person. Two trends make the CA-MRSA strains even more challenging: their entry into the hospitals where they may establish as hospital "flora" and the potential for acquisition of further mobile elements (e.g., plasmids) carrying additional resistances and/or virulence factors.[34,363-365] Because prior viral infection may increase the patient's susceptibility to necrotizing pneumonia,[3] the next influenza pandemic could be devastating because of the severe course of MRSA pneumonia.

S. aureus strains predominantly associated with domestic animals, in particular with pigs, cattle, and poultry, are emerging rapidly in particular in areas with high prevalence of farming. In several Europe and Asian countries (e.g., The Netherlands, Germany, France, Singapore) and Canada, an unusual S. aureus lineage (MLST CC398; corresponding spa-types t011, t034, t108, and relatives; nontypeable applying usual PFGE protocols) was found, which was shared by animals, the farmers and veterinarians.[366] Recent findings suggest that this livestock-associated clonal lineage, which belongs to a separate biotype and comprises methicillin-susceptible as well as methicillin-resistant isolates, is quite virulent. LA-MRSA strains have been regularly cultured from patients with invasive infections caused by this pathogen.[36,37] Outbreaks with CC398 LA-MRSA were reported and some CC398 isolates have now been associated with the PVL toxin.[367,368]

The import of MRSA CC398 from animal reservoirs into hospitals results in the spread of MRSA.[37,369,370] Thus, livestock has become an important source of MRSA. Increasingly, also patients without reporting contact to animals were found to be colonized or infected, with LA-MRSA reaching 15 percent or more in some European countries.[371,372] Matters of further concern include the observation of a cfr plasmid conferring transferable resistance against oxazolidinones that was found in MRSA CC398 background.[373]

The recent detection of a mecA homolog in livestock and clinical isolates of S. aureus—designated mecC—raises questions regarding the prevalence, burden, and impact of MRSA not detectable with available nucleic acid-based detection approaches.[8,9,94,95] One could speculate that further mecA homologs may remain undetected and may circulate hidden in animal or patient populations.

Concerning non-S. aureus staphylococcal species, S. lugdunensis has been recognized as an emerging pathogen that is being more frequently recovered from patients. In addition to its generally accepted role as an aggressive cause of infectious native and prosthetic valve endocarditis and of various kinds of foreign body-related infections, there is increasing evidence that this CoNS species is also a usual cause of skin and soft tissue infections.[336,374,375] Recently, a case of necrotizing fasciitis has been reported.[376] Of utmost importance, optimized identification methods have to be applied to enhance S. lugdunensis detection.[336] Thus, often showing a more fulminant course, infections with S. lugdunensis tend to bear a resemblance to S. aureus infections rather than those caused by CoNS.[377] Besides SCVs, S. lugdunensis may show further colonial variation that delays identification by the clinical laboratory personnel.[337,378] Thus, S. lugdunensis may pose a serious challenge for the future.

Emergence of methicillin resistance in the coagulase-positive species S. pseudintermedius isolates recovered from animals in veterinary clinics around the world has been reported.[22] Probably underreported due to likely misidentification as S. aureus, the real importance of this species for human infections is unknown. However, human clinical cases, also with methicillin-resistant strains, have been reported.[379,380] The clinical impact of the recently described human-associated CoNS species, S. pettenkoferi, is currently not fully assessable.[381] However, several BSIs and other infectious entities have been increasingly described in the past years.[382,383] Finally, the emergence of CoNS strains with decreased susceptibility to glycopeptides will further narrow the spectrum of our therapeutic armamentarium.[281,384]

One of the most important questions is how safe our therapeutic options for the treatment of MRSA infections are in future. The certainly underdiagnosed hVISA status and the putative vancomycin creep phenomenon may further limit the therapeutic applicability of the glycopeptides. The therapeutic significance of the recently available MRSA-active cephalosporins has not yet been fully evaluated. All antibiotic agents introduced in the past decade on the market are restricted in their approval and feature meanwhile resistant isolates. Though the pipeline for antibiotics with Gram-positive activity might be not as empty as reported for compounds against Gram-negative microorganisms, the situation has to be considered as limited. Agents developed could include lipoglycopeptides such as dalbavancin, oritavancin, and telavancin or β-lactam combinations with "second-generation" β-lactamase inhibitors such as avibactam. Agents that ameliorate the effect of biofilm in medical devices are also an area of important research. All this demands a more careful, rationale usage of the antibiotic armamentarium active against staphylococci.

REFERENCES

1. Wise RI, Ossman EA, Littlefield DR. Personal reflections on nosocomial staphylococcal infections and the development of hospital surveillance. Rev Infect Dis 1989 Nov-Dec;11(6):1005–1019.
2. Grosserode MH, Wenzel RP. The continuing importance of staphylococci as major hospital pathogens. J Hosp Infect 1991 Sep;19 Suppl B:3–17.
3. Gillet Y, Issartel B, Vanhems P, et al. Association between Staphylococcus aureus strains carrying gene for Panton-Valentine leukocidin and highly lethal necrotising pneumonia in young immunocompetent patients. Lancet 2002 Mar;359(9308):753–759.
4. Becker K, von Eiff C. Staphylococcus, Micrococcus, and Other Catalase-positive Cocci. In: Versalovic J, Carroll KC, Funke G, Jorgensen JH, Landry ML, Warnock DW, editors. Manual of Clinical Microbiology, 10th ed. Washington, D.C.: ASM Press, 2011.
5. Berger-Bächi B. Genetic basis of methicillin resistance in Staphylococcus aureus. Cell Mol Life Sci 1999 Nov;56(9-10):764–770.
6. Ito T, Katayama Y, Asada K, et al. Structural comparison of three types of staphylococcal cassette chromosome mec integrated in the chromosome in methicillin-resistant Staphylococcus aureus. Antimicrob Agents Chemother 2001 May;45(5):1323–1336.
7. Shore AC, Coleman DC. Staphylococcal cassette chromosome mec: Recent advances and new insights. Int J Med Microbiol 2013 Aug;303 (6-7):350–359.
8. García-Álvarez M, Holden MT, Lindsay H, et al. Meticillin-resistant Staphylococcus aureus with a novel mecA homologue in human and bovine populations in the UK and Denmark: a descriptive study. Lancet Infect Dis 2011 Aug;11(8):595–603.
9. Shore AC, Deasy EC, Slickers P, et al. Detection of staphylococcal cassette chromosome mec type XI encoding highly divergent mecA, mecI, mecR1, blaZ and ccr genes in human clinical clonal complex 130 methicillin-resistant Staphylococcus aureus. Antimicrob Agents Chemother 2011 Aug;55(8):3765–3773.
10. Jevons MP. "Celbenin"-resistant Staphylococci. Br Med J 1961;1(5219):124–125.
11. Diekema DJ, BootsMiller BJ, Vaughn TE, et al. Antimicrobial resistance trends and outbreak frequency in United States hospitals. Clin Infect Dis 2004 Jan 1;38(1):78–85.
12. Klevens RM, Morrison MA, Nadle J, et al. Invasive methicillin-resistant Staphylococcus aureus infections in the United States. JAMA 2007 Oct 17;298(15):1763–1771.
13. Stefani S, Varaldo PE. Epidemiology of methicillin-resistant staphylococci in Europe. Clin Microbiol Infect 2003 Dec;9(12):1179–1186.
14. Zinn CS, Westh H, Rosdahl VT. An international multicenter study of antimicrobial resistance and typing of hospital Staphylococcus aureus isolates from 21 laboratories in 19 countries or states. Microb Drug Resist 2004 Summer;10(2):160–168.
15. Shittu AO, Lin J. Antimicrobial susceptibility patterns and characterization of clinical isolates of Staphylococcus aureus in KwaZulu-Natal province, South Africa. BMC Infect Dis 2006 Jul;6:125.
16. Rosenthal VD, Maki DG, Mehta A, et al. International Nosocomial Infection Control Consortium report, data summary for 2002-2007, issued January 2008. Am J Infect Control 2008 Nov;36(9):627–637.
17. Kallen AJ, Mu Y, Bulens S, et al. Health care-associated invasive MRSA infections, 2005-2008. JAMA 2010 Aug 11;304(6):641–648.
18. European Centre for Disease Prevention and Control. Antimicrobial resistance surveillance in Europe 2011. Annual Report of the European Antimicrobial Resistance Surveillance Network (EARS-Net). Stockholm: ECDC, 2012.
19. Cosgrove SE, Sakoulas G, Perencevich EN, et al. Comparison of mortality associated with methicillin-resistant and methicillin-susceptible Staphylococcus aureus bacteremia: a meta-analysis. Clin Infect Dis 2003 Jan 1;36(1):53–59.
20. Shorr AF. Epidemiology of staphylococcal resistance. Clin Infect Dis 2007 Sep 15;45 Suppl 3:S171–S176.
21. Köck R, Becker K, Cookson B, et al. Methicillin-resistant Staphylococcus aureus (MRSA): burden of disease and control challenges in Europe. Euro Surveill 2010 Oct 14;15(41):19688.
22. Perreten V, Kadlec K, Schwarz S, et al. Clonal spread of methicillin-resistant Staphylococcus pseudintermedius in Europe and North America: an international multicentre study. J Antimicrob Chemother 2010 Jun;65(6):1145–1154.
23. Udo EE, Pearman JW, Grubb WB. Genetic analysis of community isolates of methicillin-resistant Staphylococcus aureus in Western Australia. J Hosp Infect 1993 Oct;25(2):97–108.
24. King MD, Humphrey BJ, Wang YF, et al. Emergence of community-acquired methicillin-resistant Staphylococcus aureus USA 300 clone as the predominant cause of skin and soft-tissue infections. Ann Intern Med 2006 Mar 7;144(5):309–317.
25. Deurenberg RH, Stobberingh EE. The molecular evolution of hospital- and community-associated methicillin-resistant Staphylococcus aureus. Curr Mol Med 2009 Mar;9(2):100–115.
26. DeLeo FR, Otto M, Kreiswirth BN, et al. Community-associated meticillin-resistant Staphylococcus aureus. Lancet 2010 May 1;375(9725):1557–1568.
27. David MZ, Daum RS. Community-associated methicillin-resistant Staphylococcus aureus: epidemiology and clinical consequences of an emerging epidemic. Clin Microbiol Rev 2010 Jul;23(3):616–687.
28. Schaumburg F, Köck R, Mellmann A, et al. Population dynamics among methicillin resistant Staphylococcus aureus in Germany during a 6-year period. J Clin Microbiol 2012 Oct;50(10):3186–3192.
29. Williamson DA, Roberts SA, Ritchie SR, et al. Clinical and molecular epidemiology of methicillin-resistant Staphylococcus aureus in New Zealand: rapid emergence of sequence type 5 (ST5)-SCCmec-IV as the dominant community-associated MRSA clone. PLoS One 2013 Apr 25;8(4):e62020.
30. Shambat S, Nadig S, Prabhakara S, et al. Clonal complexes and virulence factors of Staphylococcus aureus from several cities in India. BMC Microbiol 2012 May 1;12:64.
31. Moremi N, Mshana SE, Kamugisha E, et al. Predominance of methicillin resistant Staphylococcus aureus -ST88 and new ST1797 causing wound infection and abscesses. J Infect Dev Ctries 2012 Aug 21;6(8):620–625.
32. Panton PN, Valentine FCO. Staphylococcal toxin. Lancet 1932; 219(5662):506–508.
33. Löffler B, Hussain M, Grundmeier M, et al. Staphylococcus aureus panton-valentine leukocidin is a very potent cytotoxic factor for human neutrophils. PLoS Pathog 2010 Jan 8;6(1):e1000715.
34. Diep BA, Chambers HF, Graber CJ, et al. Emergence of multidrug-resistant, community-associated, methicillin-resistant Staphylococcus aureus clone USA300 in men who have sex with men. Ann Intern Med 2008 Feb 19;148(4):249–257.
35. Fluit AC. Livestock-associated Staphylococcus aureus. Clin Microbiol Infect 2012 Aug;18(8):735–744.
36. van Belkum A, Melles DC, Peeters JK, et al. Methicillin-resistant and -susceptible Staphylococcus aureus sequence type 398 in pigs and humans. Emerg Infect Dis 2008 Mar;14(3):479–483.
37. Köck R, Schaumburg F, Mellmann A, al. Livestock-associated methicillin-resistant Staphylococcus aureus (MRSA) as causes of human infection and colonization in Germany. PLoS One 2013;8(2):e55040.
38. Köck R, Siam K, Al-Malat S, et al. Characteristics of hospital patients colonized with livestock-associated meticillin-resistant Staphylococcus aureus (MRSA) CC398 versus other MRSA clones. J Hosp Infect 2011 Dec;79(4):292–296.
39. Smith TC, Gebreyes WA, Abley MJ, et al. Methicillin-resistant Staphylococcus aureus in pigs and farm workers on conventional and antibiotic-free swine farms in the USA. PLoS ONE 2013 May 7;8(5):e63704.
40. Hiramatsu K, Hanaki H, Ino T, et al. Methicillin-resistant Staphylococcus aureus clinical strain with reduced vancomycin susceptibility. J Antimicrob Chemother 1997 Jul;40(1):135–136.
41. Centers for Disease Control and Prevention. Staphylococcus aureus with reduced susceptibility to vancomycin—United States, 1997. MMWR Morb Mortal Wkly Rep 1997 Aug 22;46(33):765–766.
42. Robert J, Bismuth R, Jarlier V. Decreased susceptibility to glycopeptides in methicillin-resistant Staphylococcus aureus: a 20 year study in a large French teaching hospital, 1983-2002. J Antimicrob Chemother 2006 Mar;57(3):506–510.
43. Hiramatsu K, Aritaka N, Hanaki H, et al. Dissemination in Japanese hospitals of strains of Staphylococcus aureus heterogeneously resistant to vancomycin. Lancet 1997 Dec 6;350(9092):1670–1673.
44. Centers for Disease Control and Prevention (CDC). Staphylococcus aureus resistant to vancomycin—United States, 2002. MMWR Morb Mortal Wkly Rep 2002 Jul 5;51(26):565–567.

45. Saha B, Singh AK, Ghosh A, et al. Identification and characterization of a vancomycin-resistant *Staphylococcus aureus* isolated from Kolkata (South Asia). *J Med Microbiol* 2008 Jan;57(Pt 1):72–79.

46. Chang S, Sievert DM, Hageman JC, et al. Infection with vancomycin-resistant *Staphylococcus aureus* containing the *vanA* resistance gene. *N Engl J Med* 2003 Apr 3;348(14):1342–1347.

47. Cui L, Ma X, Sato K, et al. Cell wall thickening is a common feature of vancomycin resistance in *Staphylococcus aureus*. *J Clin Microbiol* 2003 Jan;41(1):5–14.

48. Boyle-Vavra S, Labischinski H, Ebert CC, et al. A spectrum of changes occurs in peptidoglycan composition of glycopeptide-intermediate clinical *Staphylococcus aureus* isolates. *Antimicrob Agents Chemother* 2001 Jan;45(1):280–287.

49. Howden BP, Davies JK, Johnson PD, et al. Reduced vancomycin susceptibility in *Staphylococcus aureus*, including vancomycin-intermediate and heterogeneous vancomycin-intermediate strains: resistance mechanisms, laboratory detection, and clinical implications. *Clin Microbiol Rev* 2010 Jan;23(1):99–139.

50. Steinkraus G, White R, Friedrich L. Vancomycin MIC creep in non-vancomycin-intermediate *Staphylococcus aureus* (VISA), vancomycin-susceptible clinical methicillin-resistant *S. aureus* (MRSA) blood isolates from 2001-05. *J Antimicrob Chemother* 2007 Oct;60(4):788–794.

51. Wang G, Hindler JF, Ward KW, et al. Increased vancomycin MICs for *Staphylococcus aureus* clinical isolates from a university hospital during a 5-year period. *J Clin Microbiol* 2006 Nov;44(11):3883–3886.

52. Holmes RL, Jorgensen JH. Inhibitory activities of 11 antimicrobial agents and bactericidal activities of vancomycin and daptomycin against invasive methicillin-resistant *Staphylococcus aureus* isolates obtained from 1999 through 2006. *Antimicrob Agents Chemother* 2008 Feb;52(2):757–760.

53. Musta AC, Riederer K, Shemes S, et al. Vancomycin MIC plus heteroresistance and outcome of methicillin-resistant *Staphylococcus aureus* bacteremia: trends over 11 years. *J Clin Microbiol* 2009 Jun;47(6):1640–1644.

54. Leclercq R. Mechanisms of resistance to macrolides and lincosamides: nature of the resistance elements and their clinical implications. *Clin Infect Dis* 2002 Feb 15;34(4):482–492.

55. Frank AL, Marcinak JF, Mangat PD, et al. Clindamycin treatment of methicillin-resistant Staphylococcus aureus infections in children. *Pediatr Infect Dis J* 2002 Jun;21(6):530–534.

56. Fiebelkorn KR, Crawford SA, McElmeel ML, et al. Practical disk diffusion method for detection of inducible clindamycin resistance in *Staphylococcus aureus* and coagulase-negative staphylococci. *J Clin Microbiol* 2003 Oct;41(10):4740–4744.

57. Flamm RK, Farrell DJ, Mendes RE, et al. LEADER surveillance program results for 2010: an activity and spectrum analysis of linezolid using 6801 clinical isolates from the United States (61 medical centers). *Diagn Microbiol Infect Dis* 2012 Sep;74(1):54–61.

58. Flamm RK, Mendes RE, Ross JE, et al. An international activity and spectrum analysis of linezolid: ZAAPS Program results for 2011. *Diagn Microbiol Infect Dis* 2013 Jun;76(2):206–213.

59. Dowzicky MJ. Susceptibility to tigecycline and linezolid among gram-positive isolates collected in the United States as part of the tigecycline evaluation and surveillance trial (TEST) between 2004 and 2009. *Clin Ther* 2011 Dec;33(12):1964–1973.

60. Gales AC, Sader HS, Andrade SS, et al. Emergence of linezolid-resistant *Staphylococcus aureus* during treatment of pulmonary infection in a patient with cystic fibrosis. *Int J Antimicrob Agents* 2006 Apr;27(4):300–302.

61. Wilson P, Andrews JA, Charlesworth R, et al. Linezolid resistance in clinical isolates of *Staphylococcus aureus*. *J Antimicrob Chemother* 2003 Jan;51(1):186–188.

62. Tsiodras S, Gold HS, Sakoulas G, et al. Linezolid resistance in a clinical isolate of *Staphylococcus aureus*. *Lancet* 2001 Jul 21;358(9277):207–208.

63. Long KS, Poehlsgaard J, Kehrenberg C, et al. The Cfr rRNA methyltransferase confers resistance to phenicols, lincosamides, oxazolidinones, pleuromutilins, and streptogramin A antibiotics. *Antimicrob Agents Chemother* 2006 Jul;50(7):2500–2505.

64. Skiest DJ. Treatment failure resulting from resistance of *Staphylococcus aureus* to daptomycin. *J Clin Microbiol* 2006 Feb;44(2):655–656.

65. Huang YT, Hsiao CH, Liao CH, et al. Bacteremia and infective endocarditis caused by a non-daptomycin-susceptible, vancomycin-intermediate, and methicillin-resistant *Staphylococcus aureus* strain in Taiwan. *J Clin Microbiol* 2008 Mar;46(3):1132–1136.

66. Fowler VG, Jr., Boucher HW, Corey GR, et al. Daptomycin versus standard therapy for bacteremia and endocarditis caused by *Staphylococcus aureus*. *N Engl J Med* 2006 Aug 17;355(7):653–665.

67. Jones RN, Fritsche TR, Sader HS, et al. LEADER surveillance program results for 2006: an activity and spectrum analysis of linezolid using clinical isolates from the United States (50 medical centers). *Diagn Microbiol Infect Dis* 2007 Nov;59(3):309–317.

68. Zhanel GG, Adam HJ, Baxter MR, et al. Antimicrobial susceptibility of 22746 pathogens from Canadian hospitals: results of the CANWARD 2007-11 study. *J Antimicrob Chemother* 2013 May;68 Suppl 1:i7–22.

69. Sader HS, Flamm RK, Jones RN. Antimicrobial activity of daptomycin tested against Gram-positive pathogens collected in Europe, Latin America, and selected countries in the Asia-Pacific Region (2011). *Diagn Microbiol Infect Dis* 2013 Apr;75(4):417–422.

70. Silverman JA, Oliver N, Andrew T, et al. Resistance studies with daptomycin. *Antimicrob Agents Chemother* 2001 Jun;45(6):1799–1802.

71. Bayer AS, Schneider T, Sahl HG. Mechanisms of daptomycin resistance in *Staphylococcus aureus*: role of the cell membrane and cell wall. *Ann N Y Acad Sci* 2013 Jan;1277:139–158.

72. Brandon M, Dowzicky MJ. Antimicrobial susceptibility among gram-positive organisms collected from pediatric patients globally between 2004 and 2011: Results from the Tigecycline Evaluation and Surveillance Trial. *J Clin Microbiol* 2013 Jul;51(7):2371–2378.

73. Kresken M, Becker K, Seifert H, et al. Resistance trends and in vitro activity of tigecycline and 17 other antimicrobial agents against Gram-positive and Gram-negative organisms, including multidrug-resistant pathogens, in Germany. *Eur J Clin Microbiol Infect Dis* 2011 Sep;30(9):1095–1103.

74. Sader HS, Flamm RK, Jones RN. Antimicrobial activity of ceftaroline tested against staphylococci with reduced susceptibility to linezolid, daptomycin or vancomycin from USA Hospitals (2008-2011). *Antimicrob Agents Chemother* 2013 Jul;57(7):3178–3181.

75. Karlowsky JA, Adam HJ, Decorby MR, et al. In vitro activity of ceftaroline against gram-positive and gram-negative pathogens isolated from patients in Canadian hospitals in 2009. *Antimicrob Agents Chemother* 2011 Jun;55(6):2837–2846.

76. Walkty A, Adam HJ, Laverdière M, et al. In vitro activity of ceftobiprole against frequently encountered aerobic and facultative Gram-positive and Gram-negative bacterial pathogens: results of the CANWARD 2007-2009 study. *Diagn Microbiol Infect Dis* 2011 Mar;69(3):348–355.

77. von Eiff C, Friedrich AW, Becker K, et al. Comparative in vitro activity of ceftobiprole against staphylococci displaying normal and small-colony variant phenotypes. *Antimicrob Agents Chemother* 2005 Oct;49(10):4372–4374.

78. Clark AE, Kaleta EJ, Arora A, et al. Matrix-assisted laser desorption ionization-time of flight mass spectrometry: a fundamental shift in the routine practice of clinical microbiology. *Clin Microbiol Rev* 2013 Jul;26(3):547–603.

79. European Committee on Antimicrobial Susceptibility Testing. *Breakpoint tables for interpretation of MICs and zone diameters. Version 3.1.* February 11, 2013. Available at: http://www.eucast.org/fileadmin/src/media/PDFs/EUCAST_files/Breakpoint_tables/Breakpoint_table_v_3.1.pdf.

80. Clinical and Laboratory Standards Institute (CLSI). Performance Standards for Antimicrobial Susceptibility Testing; Twenty-Third Informational Supplement (M100-S23). Wayne: CLSI, 2013.

81. Nakatomi Y, Sugiyama J. A rapid latex agglutination assay for the detection of penicillin- binding protein 2'. *Microbiol Immunol* 1998;42(11):739–743.

82. Yamazumi T, Marshall SA, Wilke WW, et al. Comparison of the Vitek Gram-Positive Susceptibility 106 card and the MRSA-screen latex agglutination test for determining oxacillin resistance in clinical bloodstream isolates of *Staphylococcus aureus*. *J Clin Microbiol* 2001 Jan;39(1):53–56.

83. Kipp F, Becker K, Peters G, et al. Evaluation of different methods to detect methicillin resistance in small-colony variants of *Staphylococcus aureus*. *J Clin Microbiol* 2004 Mar;42(3):1277–1279.

84. Proctor RA, von Eiff C, Kahl BC, et al. Small colony variants: a pathogenic form of bacteria that facilitates persistent and recurrent infections. *Nat Rev Microbiol* 2006 Apr;4(4):295–305.

85. Felten A, Grandry B, Lagrange PH, et al. Evaluation of three techniques for detection of low-level methicillin-resistant *Staphylococcus aureus* (MRSA): a disk diffusion method with Cefoxitin and Moxalactam, the Vitek 2 system, and the MRSA-screen latex agglutination test. *J Clin Microbiol* 2002 Aug;40(8):2766–2771.

86. Kipp F, Kahl BC, Becker K, et al. Evaluation of two chromogenic agar media for recovery and identification of *Staphylococcus aureus* small-colony variants. *J Clin Microbiol* 2005 Apr;43(4):1956–1959.

87. Becker K, Harmsen D, Mellmann A, et al. Development and evaluation of a quality-controlled ribosomal sequence database for 16S ribosomal DNA-based identification of *Staphylococcus* species. *J Clin Microbiol* 2004 Nov;42(11):4988–4995.

88. Brakstad OG, Aasbakk K, Maeland JA. Detection of *Staphylococcus aureus* by polymerase chain reaction amplification of the *nuc* gene. *J Clin Microbiol* 1992 Jul;30(7):1654–1660.

89. Murakami K, Minamide W, Wada K, et al. Identification of methicillin-resistant strains of staphylococci by polymerase chain reaction. *J Clin Microbiol* 1991 Oct;29(10):2240–2244.

90. Mellmann A, Becker K, von Eiff C, et al. Sequencing and staphylococci identification. *Emerg Infect Dis* 2006 Feb;12(2):333–336.

91. Straub JA, Hertel C, Hammes WP. A 23S rDNA-targeted polymerase chain reaction-based system for detection of *Staphylococcus aureus* in meat starter cultures and dairy products. *J Food Prot* 1999 Oct;62(10): 1150–1156.

92. Martineau F, Picard FJ, Ke D, et al. Development of a PCR assay for identification of staphylococci at genus and species levels. *J Clin Microbiol* 2001 Jul;39(7):2541–2547.

93. Mason WJ, Blevins JS, Beenken K, et al. Multiplex PCR protocol for the diagnosis of staphylococcal infection. *J Clin Microbiol* 2001 Sep;39(9): 3332–3338.

94. Becker K, Larsen AR, Skov RL, et al. Evaluation of a modular multiplex-PCR methicillin-resistant *Staphylococcus aureus* (MRSA) detection assay adapted for mecC detection. *J Clin Microbiol* 2013 Jun;51(6):1917–1919.

95. Kriegeskorte A, Ballhausen B, Idelevich EA, et al. Human MRSA isolates with novel genetic homolog, Germany. *Emerg Infect Dis* 2012 Jun;18(6): 1016–1018.

96. Becker K, Pagnier I, Schuhen B, et al. Does nasal cocolonization by methicillin-resistant coagulase-negative staphylococci and methicillin-susceptible *Staphylococcus aureus* strains occur frequently enough to represent a risk of false-positive methicillin-resistant *S. aureus* determinations by molecular methods? *J Clin Microbiol* 2006 Jan;44(1):229–231.

97. Huletsky A, Giroux R, Rossbach V, et al. New real-time PCR assay for rapid detection of methicillin-resistant *Staphylococcus aureus* directly from specimens containing a mixture of staphylococci. *J Clin Microbiol* 2004 May;42(5):1875–1884.

98. Donnio PY, Oliveira DC, Faria NA, et al. Partial excision of the chromosomal cassette containing the methicillin resistance determinant results in methicillin-susceptible *Staphylococcus aureus*. *J Clin Microbiol* 2005 Aug;43(8):4191–4193.

99. Ito T, Okuma K, Ma XX, et al. Insights on antibiotic resistance of *Staphylococcus aureus* from its whole genome: genomic island SCC. *Drug Resist Updat* 2003 Feb;6(1):41–52.

100. Desjardins M, Guibord C, Lalonde B, et al. Evaluation of the IDI-MRSA assay for detection of methicillin-resistant *Staphylococcus aureus* from nasal and rectal specimens pooled in a selective broth. *J Clin Microbiol* 2006 Apr;44(4):1219–1223.

101. Warren DK, Liao RS, Merz LR, et al. Detection of methicillin-resistant *Staphylococcus aureus* directly from nasal swab specimens by a real-time PCR assay. *J Clin Microbiol* 2004 Dec;42(12):5578–5581.

102. Appelbaum PC. Reduced glycopeptide susceptibility in methicillin-resistant *Staphylococcus aureus* (MRSA). *Int J Antimicrob Agents* 2007 Nov;30(5):398–408.

103. Appelbaum PC. The emergence of vancomycin-intermediate and vancomycin-resistant *Staphylococcus aureus*. *Clin Microbiol Infect* 2006 Mar;12 Suppl 1:16–23.

104. Wikler MA, Bush K, Cockerill FR, III, et al. Supplement CLSI document M100-S18. Performance Standards for Antimicrobial Susceptibility Testing; Eigthteenth Informational Supplement. Clinical and Laboratory Standards Institute document ed. Wayne: Clinical and Laboratory Standards Institute, 2008.

105. Kelley PG, Gao W, Ward PB, et al. Daptomycin non-susceptibility in vancomycin-intermediate *Staphylococcus aureus* (VISA) and heterogeneous-VISA (hVISA): implications for therapy after vancomycin treatment failure. *J Antimicrob Chemother* 2011 May;66(5):1057–1060.

106. Rybak MJ, Leonard SN, Rossi KL, et al. Characterization of vancomycin-heteroresistant *Staphylococcus aureus* from the metropolitan area of Detroit, Michigan, over a 22-year period (1986 to 2007). *J Clin Microbiol* 2008 Sep;46(9):2950–2954.

107. Becker K, Roth R, Peters G. Rapid and specific detection of toxigenic *Staphylococcus aureus*: use of two multiplex PCR enzyme immunoassays for amplification and hybridization of staphylococcal enterotoxin genes, exfoliative toxin genes, and toxic shock syndrome toxin 1 gene. *J Clin Microbiol* 1998 Sep;36(9):2548–2553.

108. Johnson WM, Tyler SD, Ewan EP, et al. Detection of genes for enterotoxins, exfoliative toxins, and toxic shock syndrome toxin 1 in *Staphylococcus aureus* by the polymerase chain reaction. *J Clin Microbiol* 1991 Mar;29(3):426–430.

109. Sakurai S, Suzuki H, Machida K. Rapid identification by polymerase chain reaction of staphylococcal exfoliative toxin serotype A and B genes. *Microbiol Immunol* 1995;39(6):379–386.

110. Becker K, Friedrich AW, Lubritz G, et al. Prevalence of genes encoding pyrogenic toxin superantigens and exfoliative toxins among strains of *Staphylococcus aureus* isolated from blood and nasal specimens. *J Clin Microbiol* 2003 Apr;41(4):1434–1439.

111. Blaiotta G, Ercolini D, Pennacchia C, et al. PCR detection of staphylococcal enterotoxin genes in *Staphylococcus* spp. strains isolated from meat and dairy products. Evidence for new variants of seG and seI in *S. aureus* AB-8802. *J Appl Microbiol* 2004;97(4):719–730.

112. Fischer A, von Eiff C, Kuczius T, et al. A quantitative real-time immuno-PCR approach for detection of staphylococcal enterotoxins. *J Mol Med* 2007 May;85(5):461–469.

113. Lina G, Piémont Y, Godail-Gamot F, et al. Involvement of Panton-Valentine leukocidin-producing *Staphylococcus aureus* in primary skin infections and pneumonia. *Clin Infect Dis* 1999 Nov;29(5):1128–1132.

114. Deurenberg RH, Vink C, Kalenic S, et al. The molecular evolution of methicillin-resistant *Staphylococcus aureus*. *Clin Microbiol Infect* 2007 Mar;13(3):222–235.

115. Weller TM. Methicillin-resistant *Staphylococcus aureus* typing methods: which should be the international standard? *J Hosp Infect* 2000 Mar; 44(3):160–172.

116. Tenover FC, Arbeit R, Archer G, et al. Comparison of traditional and molecular methods of typing isolates of *Staphylococcus aureus*. *J Clin Microbiol* 1994 Feb;32(2):407–415.

117. Tenover FC, Arbeit RD, Goering RV, et al. Interpreting chromosomal DNA restriction patterns produced by pulsed-field gel electrophoresis: criteria for bacterial strain typing. *J Clin Microbiol* 1995 Sep;33(9): 2233–2239.

118. McDougal LK, Steward CD, Killgore GE, et al. Pulsed-field gel electrophoresis typing of oxacillin-resistant *Staphylococcus aureus* isolates from the United States: establishing a national database. *J Clin Microbiol* 2003 Nov;41(11):5113–5120.

119. van Belkum A, van Leeuwen W, Kaufmann ME, et al. Assessment of resolution and intercenter reproducibility of results of genotyping *Staphylococcus aureus* by pulsed-field gel electrophoresis of SmaI macrorestriction fragments: a multicenter study. *J Clin Microbiol* 1998 Jun;36(6):1653–1659.

120. Lesse AJ, Mylotte JM. Clinical and molecular epidemiology of nursing home-associated *Staphylococcus aureus* bacteremia. *Am J Infect Control* 2006 Dec;34(10):642–650.

121. Maiden MC, Bygraves JA, Feil E, et al. Multilocus sequence typing: a portable approach to the identification of clones within populations of pathogenic microorganisms. *Proc Natl Acad Sci U S A* 1998 Mar 17;95(6): 3140–3145.

122. Shopsin B, Gomez M, Montgomery SO, et al. Evaluation of protein A gene polymorphic region DNA sequencing for typing of *Staphylococcus aureus* strains. *J Clin Microbiol* 1999 Nov;37(11):3556–3563.

123. Harmsen D, Claus H, Witte W, et al. Typing of methicillin-resistant *Staphylococcus aureus* in a university hospital setting by using novel software for spa repeat determination and database management. *J Clin Microbiol* 2003 Dec;41(12):5442–5448.

124. Enright MC, Day NP, Davies CE, et al. Multilocus sequence typing for characterization of methicillin-resistant and methicillin-susceptible clones of *Staphylococcus aureus*. *J Clin Microbiol* 2000 Mar;38(3):1008–1015.

125. Koreen L, Ramaswamy SV, Graviss EA, et al. spa typing method for discriminating among *Staphylococcus aureus* isolates: implications for use of a single marker to detect genetic micro- and macrovariation. *J Clin Microbiol* 2004 Feb;42(2):792–799.

126. Mellmann A, Weniger T, Berssenbrugge C, et al. Based Upon Repeat Pattern (BURP): an algorithm to characterize the long-term evolution of *Staphylococcus aureus* populations based on spa polymorphisms. *BMC Microbiol* 2007 Oct 29;7:98.

127. Tenover FC, Vaughn RR, McDougal LK, et al. Multiple-locus variable-number tandem-repeat assay analysis of methicillin-resistant *Staphylococcus aureus* strains. *J Clin Microbiol* 2007 Jul;45(7):2215–2219.

128. Foster TJ. Colonization and infection of the human host by staphylococci: adhesion, survival and immune evasion. *Vet Dermatol* 2009 Oct;20(5-6): 456–470.

129. Chavakis T, Wiechmann K, Preissner KT, et al. *Staphylococcus aureus* interactions with the endothelium: the role of bacterial "secretable expanded repertoire adhesive molecules" (SERAM) in disturbing host defense systems. *Thromb Haemost* 2005 Aug;94(2):278–285.

130. Speziale P, Pietrocola G, Rindi S, et al. Structural and functional role of *Staphylococcus aureus* surface components recognizing adhesive matrix molecules of the host. *Future Microbiol* 2009 Dec;4(10):1337–1352.

131. Johannessen M, Sollid JE, Hanssen AM. Host- and microbe determinants that may influence the success of *S. aureus* colonization. *Front Cell Infect Microbiol* 2012 May 4;2:56.

132. Clarke SR, Foster SJ. Surface adhesins of *Staphylococcus aureus*. *Adv Microb Physiol* 2006;51:187–224.

133. Gomez MI, Lee A, Reddy B, et al. *Staphylococcus aureus* protein A induces airway epithelial inflammatory responses by activating TNFR1. *Nat Med* 2004 Aug;10(8):842–848.

134. Xia G, Kohler T, Peschel A. The wall teichoic acid and lipoteichoic acid polymers of Staphylococcus aureus. *Int J Med Microbiol* 2010 Feb;300(2-3):148–154.

135. Peschel A, Otto M, Jack RW, et al. Inactivation of the dlt operon in *Staphylococcus aureus* confers sensitivity to defensins, protegrins, and other antimicrobial peptides. *J Biol Chem* 1999 Mar 26;274(13):8405–8410.

136. O'Riordan K, Lee JC. *Staphylococcus aureus* capsular polysaccharides. *Clin Microbiol Rev* 2004 Jan;17(1):218–234.

137. von Eiff C, Taylor KL, Mellmann A, et al. Distribution of capsular and surface polysaccharide serotypes of *Staphylococcus aureus*. *Diagn Microbiol Infect Dis* 2007 Jul;58(3):297–302.

138. Tzianabos AO, Wang JY, Lee JC. Structural rationale for the modulation of abscess formation by *Staphylococcus aureus* capsular polysaccharides. *Proc Natl Acad Sci U S A* 2001 Jul 31;98(16):9365–9370.

139. Grumann D, Nübel U, Bröker BM. *Staphylococcus aureus* toxins - Their functions and genetics. *Infect Genet Evol* 2013 Mar 26. pii: S1567-1348 (13)00086-5. [Epub ahead of print].

140. Berube BJ, Bubeck Wardenburg J. *Staphylococcus aureus* α-toxin: nearly a century of intrigue. *Toxins (Basel)* 2013 Jun;5(6):1140–1166.

141. Bubeck Wardenburg J, Bae T, et al. Poring over pores: α-hemolysin and Panton-Valentine leukocidin in *Staphylococcus aureus* pneumonia. *Nat Med* 2007 Dec;13(12):1405–1406.

142. Yoong P, Torres VJ. The effects of *Staphylococcus aureus* leukotoxins on the host: cell lysis and beyond. *Curr Opin Microbiol* 2013 Feb;16(1): 63–69.

143. von Eiff C, Friedrich AW, Peters G, et al. Prevalence of genes encoding for members of the staphylococcal leukotoxin family among clinical isolates of *Staphylococcus aureus*. *Diagn Microbiol Infect Dis* 2004 Jul;49(3): 157–162.

144. Diep BA, Sensabaugh GF, Somboona NS, et al. Widespread skin and soft-tissue infections due to two methicillin-resistant Staphylococcus aureus strains harboring the genes for Panton-Valentine leucocidin. *J Clin Microbiol* 2004 May;42(5):2080–2084.

145. Löffler B, Niemann S, Ehrhardt C, et al. Pathogenesis of Staphylococcus aureus necrotizing pneumonia: the role of PVL and an influenza coinfection. *Expert Rev Anti Infect Ther* 2013 Oct;11(10):1041–1051.

146. Vandenesch F, Naimi T, Enright MC, et al. Community-acquired methicillin-resistant *Staphylococcus aureus* carrying Panton-Valentine leukocidin genes: worldwide emergence. *Emerg Infect Dis* 2003 Aug;9(8):978–984.

147. Diep BA, Stone GG, Basuino L, et al. The arginine catabolic mobile element and staphylococcal chromosomal cassette mec linkage: convergence of virulence and resistance in the USA300 clone of methicillin-resistant Staphylococcus aureus. *J Infect Dis* 2008 Jun 1;197(11):1523–1530.

148. Sachse F, Becker K, von Eiff C, et al. *Staphylococcus aureus* invades the epithelium in nasal polyposis and induces IL-6 in nasal epithelial cells in vitro. *Allergy* 2010 Nov;65(11):1430–1437.

149. von Eiff C, Becker K, Metze D, et al. Intracellular persistence of *Staphylococcus aureus* small-colony variants within keratinocytes: A cause for antibiotic treatment failure in a patient with Darier's disease. *Clin Infect Dis* 2001 Jun 1;32(11):1643–1647.

150. Tuchscherr L, Heitmann V, Hussain M, et al. *Staphylococcus aureus* small-colony variants are adapted phenotypes for intracellular persistence. *J Infect Dis* 2010 Oct 1;202(7):1031–1040.

151. Kriegeskorte A, König S, Sander G, et al. Small colony variants of *Staphylococcus aureus* reveal distinct protein profiles. *Proteomics* 2011 Jun;11(12):2476–2490.

152. Seggewiß J, Becker K, Kotte O, et al. Reporter metabolite analysis of transcriptional profiles of a *Staphylococcus aureus* strain with normal phenotype and its isogenic *hemB* mutant displaying the small-colony-variant phenotype. *J Bacteriol* 2006 Nov;188(22):7765–7777.

153. Kahl B, Herrmann M, Everding AS, et al. Persistent infection with small colony variant strains of *Staphylococcus aureus* in patients with cystic fibrosis. *J Infect Dis* 1998 Apr;177(4):1023–1029.

154. von Eiff C, Peters G, Becker K. The small colony variant (SCV) concept - the role of staphylococcal SCVs in persistent infections. *Injury* 2006 May;37 Suppl 2:S26–S33.

155. von Eiff C, Becker K. Small-colony variants (SCVs) of staphylococci: A role in foreign body-associated infections. *Int J Artif Organs* 2007 Sep;30(9):778–785.

156. von Eiff C, Bettin D, Proctor RA, et al. Recovery of small colony variants of *Staphylococcus aureus* following gentamicin bead placement for osteomyelitis. *Clin Infect Dis* 1997 Nov;25(5):1250–1251.

157. Kipp F, Ziebuhr W, Becker K, et al. Detection of *Staphylococcus aureus* by 16S rRNA directed in situ hybridisation in a patient with a brain abscess caused by small colony variants. *J Neurol Neurosurg Psychiatry* 2003 Jul;74(7):1000–1002.

158. Jonsson IM, von Eiff C, Proctor RA, et al. Virulence of a *hemB* mutant displaying the phenotype of a *Staphylococcus aureus* small colony variant in a murine model of septic arthritis. *Microb Pathog* 2003 Feb;34(2): 73–79.

159. Vaudaux P, Francois P, Bisognano C, et al. Increased expression of clumping factor and fibronectin-binding proteins by *hemB* mutants of *Staphylococcus aureus* expressing small colony variant phenotypes. *Infect Immun* 2002 Oct;70(10):5428–5437.

160. Baumert N, von Eiff C, Schaaff F, et al. Physiology and antibiotic susceptibility of *Staphylococcus aureus* small colony variants. *Microb Drug Resist* 2002 Winter;8(4):253–260.

161. Tuchscherr L, Medina E, Hussain M, et al. *Staphylococcus aureus* phenotype switching: an effective bacterial strategy to escape host immune response and establish a chronic infection. *EMBO Mol Med* 2011 Mar;3(3):129–141.

162. Sievert DM, Ricks P, Edwards JR, et al. Antimicrobial-resistant pathogens associated with healthcare-associated infections: summary of data reported to the National Healthcare Safety Network at the Centers for Disease Control and Prevention, 2009-2010. *Infect Control Hosp Epidemiol* 2013 Jan;34(1):1–14.

163. Baddour LM, Wilson WR, Bayer AS, et al. Infective endocarditis: diagnosis, antimicrobial therapy, and management of complications: a statement for healthcare professionals from the Committee on Rheumatic Fever, Endocarditis, and Kawasaki Disease, Council on Cardiovascular Disease in the Young, and the Councils on Clinical Cardiology, Stroke, and Cardiovascular Surgery and Anesthesia, American Heart Association. *Circulation* 2005 Jun 14;111(23):e394–e434.

164. Dinges MM, Orwin PM, Schlievert PM. Exotoxins of *Staphylococcus aureus*. *Clin Microbiol Rev* 2000 Jan;13(1):16–34.

165. Llewelyn M, Cohen J. Superantigens: microbial agents that corrupt immunity. *Lancet Infect Dis* 2002 Mar;2(3):156–162.

166. Schuchat A, Broome CV. Toxic shock syndrome and tampons. *Epidemiol Rev* 1991;13:99–112.

167. Strausbaugh LJ. Toxic shock syndrome. Are you recognizing its changing presentations? *Postgrad Med* 1993 Nov 1;94(6):107–117.

168. Stanley JR, Amagai M. Pemphigus, bullous impetigo, and the staphylococcal scalded-skin syndrome. *N Engl J Med* 2006 Oct 26;355(17):1800–1810.

169. Peacock SJ, Justice A, Griffiths D, et al. Determinants of acquisition and carriage of *Staphylococcus aureus* in infancy. *J Clin Microbiol* 2003 Dec;41(12):5718–5725.

170. van Belkum A, Verkaik NJ, de Vogel CP, et al. Reclassification of *Staphylococcus aureus* nasal carriage types. *J Infect Dis* 2009 Jun 15;199(12):1820–1826.

171. Martin RR, Buttram V, Besch P, et al. Nasal and vaginal *Staphylococcus aureus* in young women: quantitative studies. *Ann Intern Med* 1982 Jun;96(6 Pt 2):951–953.

172. Kirmani N, Tuazon CU, Murray HW, et al. *Staphylococcus aureus* carriage rate of patients receiving long-term hemodialysis. *Arch Intern Med* 1978 Nov;138(11):1657–1659.

173. Tuazon CU, Perez A, Kishaba T, et al. *Staphylococcus aureus* among insulin-injecting diabetic patients. An increased carrier rate. *JAMA* 1975 Mar 24;231(12):1272.

174. Tuazon CU, Sheagren JN. Increased rate of carriage of *Staphylococcus aureus* among narcotic addicts. *J Infect Dis* 1974 Jun;129(6):725–727.

175. Centers for Disease Control and Prevention (CDC). *Active Bacterial Core Surveillance Report, Emerging Infections Program Network, Methicillin-Resistant Staphylococcus aureus, 2011*. CDC website. Available at: http://www.cdc.gov/abcs/reports-findings/survreports/mrsa11.pdf

176. Dukic VM, Lauderdale DS, Wilder J, et al. Epidemics of community-associated methicillin-resistant *Staphylococcus aureus* in the United States: a meta-analysis. *PLoS One* 2013;8(1):e52722.

177. Fagan RP, Edwards JR, Park BJ, et al. Incidence trends in pathogen-specific central line-associated bloodstream infections in US intensive care units, 1990-2010. *Infect Control Hosp Epidemiol* 2013 Sep;34(9):893–899.

178. Suk Lee M, Walker V, Chen LF, et al. The epidemiology of ventilator-associated pneumonia in a network of community hospitals: a prospective multicenter study. *Infect Control Hosp Epidemiol* 2013 Jul;34(7):657–662.

179. Wagenvoort JH, De Brauwer EI, Sijstermans ML, et al. Risk of re-introduction of methicillin-resistant *Staphylococcus aureus* into the hospital by intrafamilial spread from and to healthcare workers. *J Hosp Infect* 2005 Jan;59(1):67–68.

180. Siegel JD, Rhinehart E, Jackson M, et al. 2007 guideline for isolation precautions: preventing transmission of infectious agents in health care settings. *Am J Infect Control* 2007 Dec;35(10 Suppl 2):S65–164.

181. Gurieva TV, Bootsma MC, Bonten MJ. Decolonization of patients and health care workers to control nosocomial spread of methicillin-resistant *Staphylococcus aureus*: a simulation study. *BMC Infect Dis* 2012 Nov 14;12:302.

182. Mulligan ME, Murray LK, Ribner BS, et al. Methicillin-resistant *Staphylococcus aureus*: a consensus review of the microbiology, pathogenesis, and epidemiology with implications for prevention and management. *Am J Med* 1993 Mar;94(3):313–328.

183. Boyce JM. Methicillin-resistant *Staphylococcus aureus* in hospitals and long-term care facilities: microbiology, epidemiology, and preventive measures. *Infect Control Hosp Epidemiol* 1992 Dec;13(12):725–737.

184. Pittet D, Hugonnet S, Harbarth S, et al. Effectiveness of a hospital-wide programme to improve compliance with hand hygiene. Infection Control Programme. *Lancet* 2000 Oct 14;356(9238):1307–1312.

185. Lai KK, Fontecchio S, Melvin Z, et al. Impact of alcohol-based, waterless hand antiseptic on the incidence of infection and colonization with methicillin-resistant

Staphylococcus aureus and vancomycin-resistant enterococci. *Infect Control Hosp Epidemiol* 2006 Oct;27(10):1018–1024.

186. Sexton T, Clarke P, O'Neill E, et al. Environmental reservoirs of methicillin-resistant *Staphylococcus aureus* in isolation rooms: correlation with patient isolates and implications for hospital hygiene. *J Hosp Infect* 2006 Feb;62(2):187–194.

187. Kramer A, Schwebke I, Kampf G. How long do nosocomial pathogens persist on inanimate surfaces? A systematic review. *BMC Infect Dis* 2006 Aug 16;6:130.

188. Dancer SJ, White LF, Lamb J, et al. Measuring the effect of enhanced cleaning in a UK hospital: a prospective cross-over study. *BMC Med* 2009 Jun 8;7:28.

189. Albrich WC, Harbarth S. Health-care workers: source, vector, or victim of MRSA? *Lancet Infect Dis* 2008 May;8(5):289–301.

190. Dancer SJ. Importance of the environment in meticillin-resistant *Staphylococcus aureus* acquisition: the case for hospital cleaning. *Lancet Infect Dis* 2008 Feb;8(2):101–113.

191. Cooper BS, Medley GF, Stone SP, et al. Methicillin-resistant *Staphylococcus aureus* in hospitals and the community: stealth dynamics and control catastrophes. *Proc Natl Acad Sci U S A* 2004 Jul 6;101(27):10223–10228.

192. Esveld MI, de Boer AS, Notenboom AJ, et al. Secundaire besmetting met meticillineresistente *Staphylococcus aureus* in Nederlandse ziekenhuizen (juli 1994-juni 1996). *Ned Tijdschr Geneeskd* 1999 Jan 23;143(4):205–208.

193. Tübbicke A, Hübner C, Hübner NO, et al. Cost comparison of MRSA screening and management - a decision tree analysis. *BMC Health Serv Res* 2012 Dec 1;12:438.

194. Udo EE, Pearman JW, Grubb WB. Genetic analysis of community isolates of methicillin-resistant *Staphylococcus aureus* in Western Australia. *J Hosp Infect* 1993 Oct;25(2):97–108.

195. Pan ES, Diep BA, Carleton HA, et al. Increasing prevalence of methicillin-resistant *Staphylococcus aureus* infection in California jails. *Clin Infect Dis* 2003 Nov 15;37(10):1384–1388.

196. Shahin R, Johnson IL, Jamieson F, et al. Methicillin-resistant Staphylococcus aureus carriage in a child care center following a case of disease. Toronto Child Care Center Study Group. *Arch Pediatr Adolesc Med* 1999 Aug;153(8):864–868.

197. Zinderman CE, Conner B, Malakooti MA, et al. Community-acquired methicillin-resistant *Staphylococcus aureus* among military recruits. *Emerg Infect Dis* 2004 May;10(5):941–944.

198. Kazakova SV, Hageman JC, Matava M, et al. A clone of methicillin-resistant *Staphylococcus aureus* among professional football players. *N Engl J Med* 2005 Feb 3;352(5):468–475.

199. Mollema FP, Richardus JH, Behrendt M, et al. Transmission of methicillin-resistant Staphylococcus aureus to household contacts. *J Clin Microbiol* 2010 Jan;48(1):202–207.

200. Johansson PJ, Gustafsson EB, Ringberg H. High prevalence of MRSA in household contacts. *Scand J Infect Dis* 2007;39(9):764–768.

201. Cuny C, Nathaus R, Layer F, et al. Nasal colonization of humans with methicillin-resistant *Staphylococcus aureus* (MRSA) CC398 with and without exposure to pigs. *PLoS ONE* 2009 Aug 27;4(8):e6800.

202. Köck R, Loth B, Köksal M, et al. Persistence of nasal colonization with livestock-associated methicillin-resistant *Staphylococcus aureus* in pig farmers after holidays from pig exposure. *Appl Environ Microbiol* 2012 Jun;78(11):4046–4047.

203. Ferreira JP, Anderson KL, Correa MT, et al. Transmission of MRSA between companion animals and infected human patients presenting to outpatient medical care facilities. *PLoS One* 2011;6(11):e26978.

204. von Eiff C, Becker K, Machka K, et al. Nasal carriage as a source of *Staphylococcus aureus* bacteremia. *N Engl J Med* 2001 Jan 4;344(1):11–16.

205. Solberg CO. Spread of Staphylococcus aureus in hospitals: causes and prevention. *Scand J Infect Dis* 2000;32(6):587–595.

206. Herwaldt LA. *Staphylococcus aureus* nasal carriage and surgical-site infections. *Surgery* 2003 Nov;134(5 Suppl):S2–S9.

207. Pujol M, Peña C, Pallares R, et al. Nosocomial *Staphylococcus aureus* bacteremia among nasal carriers of methicillin-resistant and methicillin-susceptible strains. *Am J Med* 1996 May;100(5):509–516.

208. Kluytmans JA, Mouton JW, VandenBergh MF, et al. Reduction of surgical-site infections in cardiothoracic surgery by elimination of nasal carriage of *Staphylococcus aureus*. *Infect Control Hosp Epidemiol* 1996 Dec;17(12):780–785.

209. Ammerlaan HS, Kluytmans JA, Wertheim HF, et al. Eradication of methicillin-resistant Staphylococcus aureus carriage: a systematic review. *Clin Infect Dis* 2009 Apr 1;48(7):922-930.

210. Kluytmans J. Reduction of surgical site infections in major surgery by elimination of nasal carriage of Staphylococcus aureus. *J Hosp Infect* 1998 Sep;40 Suppl B:S25–S29.

211. Wenzel RP, Perl TM. The significance of nasal carriage of *Staphylococcus aureus* and the incidence of postoperative wound infection. *J Hosp Infect* 1995 Sep;31(1):13–24.

212. Nicholson MR, Huesman LA. Controlling the usage of intranasal mupirocin does impact the rate of *Staphylococcus aureus* deep sternal wound infections in cardiac surgery patients. *Am J Infect Control* 2006 Feb;34(1):44–48.

213. Cimochowski GE, Harostock MD, Brown R, et al. Intranasal mupirocin reduces sternal wound infection after open heart surgery in diabetics and nondiabetics. *Ann Thorac Surg* 2001 May;71(5):1572–1578.

214. Walsh EE, Greene L, Kirshner R. Sustained reduction in methicillin-resistant *Staphylococcus aureus* wound infections after cardiothoracic surgery. *Arch Intern Med* 2011 Jan 10;171(1):68–73.

215. Sankar B, Hopgood P, Bell KM. The role of MRSA screening in joint-replacement surgery. *Int Orthop* 2005 Jun;29(3):160–163.

216. Gernaat-van der Sluis AJ, Hoogenboom-Verdegaal AM, Edixhoven PJ, et al. Prophylactic mupirocin could reduce orthopedic wound infections. 1,044 patients treated with mupirocin compared with 1,260 historical controls. *Acta Orthop Scand* 1998 Aug;69(4):412–414.

217. Kim DH, Spencer M, Davidson SM, et al. Institutional prescreening for detection and eradication of methicillin-resistant *Staphylococcus aureus* in patients undergoing elective orthopaedic surgery. *J Bone Joint Surg Am* 2010 Aug 4;92(9):1820–1826.

218. Wilcox MH, Hall J, Pike H, et al. Use of perioperative mupirocin to prevent methicillin-resistant Staphylococcus aureus (MRSA) orthopaedic surgical site infections. *J Hosp Infect* 2003 Jul;54(3):196–201.

219. McConeghy KW, Mikolich DJ, LaPlante KL. Agents for the decolonization of methicillin-resistant *Staphylococcus aureus*. *Pharmacotherapy* 2009 Mar;29(3):263–280.

220. van Rijen M, Bonten M, Wenzel R, et al. Mupirocin ointment for preventing *Staphylococcus aureus* infections in nasal carriers. *Cochrane Database Syst Rev* 2008 Oct 8;(4):CD006216.

221. Walker ES, Vasquez JE, Dula R, et al. Mupirocin-resistant, methicillin-resistant Staphylococcus aureus: does mupirocin remain effective? *Infect Control Hosp Epidemiol* 2003 May;24(5):342–346.

222. Gilbert DN, Moellering RC, Jr., Eliopoulos GM, et al. *The Sanford Guide to Antimicrobial Therapy*, 43rd ed. Sperryville, VA: Antimicrobial Therapy, Inc., 2013.

223. Johnson MD, Decker CF. Antimicrobial agents in treatment of MRSA infections. *Dis Mon* 2008 Dec;54(12):793–800.

224. Oliva ME, Rekha A, Yellin A, et al. A multicenter trial of the efficacy and safety of tigecycline versus imipenem/cilastatin in patients with complicated intra-abdominal infections [Study ID Numbers: 3074A1-301-WW; Clinical Trials.gov Identifier: NCT00081744]. *BMC Infect Dis* 2005 Oct 19;5:88.

225. Rubinstein E, Cammarata S, Oliphant T, et al. Linezolid (PNU-100766) versus vancomycin in the treatment of hospitalized patients with nosocomial pneumonia: a randomized, double-blind, multicenter study. *Clin Infect Dis* 2001 Feb 1;32(3):402–412.

226. Sacchidanand S, Penn RL, Embil JM, et al. Efficacy and safety of tigecycline monotherapy compared with vancomycin plus aztreonam in patients with complicated skin and skin structure infections: Results from a phase 3, randomized, double-blind trial. *Int J Infect Dis* 2005 Sep;9(5):251–261.

227. Rayner C, Munckhof WJ. Antibiotics currently used in the treatment of infections caused by *Staphylococcus aureus*. *Intern Med J* 2005 Dec; 35 Suppl 2:S3–16.

228. MacGowan AP. Clinical implications of antimicrobial resistance for therapy. *J Antimicrob Chemother* 2008 Nov;62 Suppl 2:ii105–ii114.

229. Uekötter A, Peters G, Becker K. Is there any rationale for treatment of *Staphylococcus aureus* infections with antimicrobials that are determined to be ineffective in vitro? *Clin Microbiol Infect* 2011 Aug;17(8):1142–1147.

230. Wood CA, Wisniewski RM. β-lactams versus glycopeptides in treatment of subcutaneous abscesses infected with *Staphylococcus aureus*. *Antimicrob Agents Chemother* 1994 May;38(5):1023–1026.

231. Guignard B, Entenza JM, Moreillon P. Beta-lactams against methicillin-resistant *Staphylococcus aureus*. *Curr Opin Pharmacol* 2005 Oct;5(5):479–489.

232. Nicholson SC, Welte T, File TM, Jr., et al. A randomised, double-blind trial comparing ceftobiprole medocaril with ceftriaxone with or without linezolid for the treatment of patients with community-acquired pneumonia requiring hospitalisation. *Int J Antimicrob Agents* 2012 Mar;39(3):240–246.

233. Noel GJ, Strauss RS, Amsler K, et al. Results of a double-blind, randomized trial of ceftobiprole treatment of complicated skin and skin structure infections caused by gram-positive bacteria. *Antimicrob Agents Chemother* 2008 Jan;52(1):37–44.

234. Friedland HD, O'Neal T, Biek D, et al. CANVAS 1 and 2: analysis of clinical response at day 3 in two phase 3 trials of ceftaroline fosamil versus vancomycin plus aztreonam in treatment of acute bacterial skin and skin structure infections. *Antimicrob Agents Chemother* 2012 May;56(5):2231–2236.

235. Farrell DJ, Flamm RK, Sader HS, et al. Spectrum and potency of ceftaroline tested against leading pathogens causing skin and soft-tissue infections in Europe (2010). *Int J Antimicrob Agents* 2013 Apr;41(4):337–342.

236. Itani KM, Dryden MS, Bhattacharyya H, et al. Efficacy and safety of linezolid versus vancomycin for the treatment of complicated skin and soft-tissue infections proven to be caused by methicillin-resistant *Staphylococcus aureus*. *Am J Surg* 2010 Jun;199(6):804–816.

237. Florescu I, Beuran M, Dimov R, et al. Efficacy and safety of tigecycline compared with vancomycin or linezolid for treatment of serious infections with methicillin-resistant *Staphylococcus aureus* or vancomycin-resistant enterococci: a Phase 3, multicentre, double-blind, randomized study. *J Antimicrob Chemother* 2008 Sep;62 Suppl 1:i17–i28.

238. Stevens DL. The role of vancomycin in the treatment paradigm. *Clin Infect Dis* 2006 Jan 1;42 Suppl 1:S51–S57.

239. Markowitz N, Quinn EL, Saravolatz LD. Trimethoprim-sulfamethoxazole compared with vancomycin for the treatment of *Staphylococcus aureus* infection. *Ann Intern Med* 1992 Sep 1;117(5):390–398.

240. Deresinski S. Vancomycin in combination with other antibiotics for the treatment of serious methicillin-resistant Staphylococcus aureus infections. *Clin Infect Dis* 2009 Oct 1;49(7):1072–1079.

241. Forrest GN, Tamura K. Rifampin combination therapy for nonmycobacterial infections. *Clin Microbiol Rev* 2010 Jan;23(1):14–34.

242. Fenton C, Keating GM, Curran MP. Daptomycin. *Drugs* 2004;64(4): 445–455.

243. Eckmann C, Dryden M. Treatment of complicated skin and soft-tissue infections caused by resistant bacteria: value of linezolid, tigecycline, daptomycin and vancomycin. *Eur J Med Res* 2010 Nov 30;15(12):554–563.

244. Seaton RA. Daptomycin: rationale and role in the management of skin and soft tissue infections. *J Antimicrob Chemother* 2008 Nov;62 Suppl 3:iii15–iii23.

245. Levine DP. Clinical experience with daptomycin: bacteraemia and endocarditis. *J Antimicrob Chemother* 2008 Nov;62 Suppl 3:iii35–iii39.

246. Proctor RA. Role of folate antagonists in the treatment of methicillin-resistant *Staphylococcus aureus* infection. *Clin Infect Dis* 2008 Feb 15;46(4):584–593.

247. Trucksis M, Hooper DC, Wolfson JS. Emerging resistance to fluoroquinolones in staphylococci: an alert. *Ann Intern Med* 1991 Mar 1;114(5): 424–426.

248. Paterson DL. "Collateral damage" from cephalosporin or quinolone antibiotic therapy. *Clin Infect Dis* 2004 May 15;38 Suppl 4:S341–S345.

249. Siberry GK, Tekle T, Carroll K, et al. Failure of clindamycin treatment of methicillin-resistant *Staphylococcus aureus* expressing inducible clindamycin resistance in vitro. *Clin Infect Dis* 2003 Nov 1;37(9):1257–1260.

250. Moellering RC. Linezolid: the first oxazolidinone antimicrobial. *Ann Intern Med* 2003 Jan 21;138(2):135–142.

251. González C, Rubio M, Romero-Vivas J, et al. Bacteremic pneumonia due to Staphylococcus aureus: A comparison of disease caused by methicillin-resistant and methicillin-susceptible organisms. *Clin Infect Dis* 1999 Nov;29(5):1171–1177.

252. Rubinstein E, Kollef MH, Nathwani D. Pneumonia caused by methicillin-resistant *Staphylococcus aureus*. *Clin Infect Dis* 2008 Jun 1;46 Suppl 5:S378–S385.

253. Conte JE, Jr., Golden JA, Kipps J, et al. Intrapulmonary pharmacokinetics of linezolid. *Antimicrob Agents Chemother* 2002 May;46(5):1475–1480.

254. Wunderink RG, Cammarata SK, Oliphant TH, et al. Continuation of a randomized, double-blind, multicenter study of linezolid versus vancomycin in the treatment of patients with nosocomial pneumonia. *Clin Ther* 2003 Mar;25(3):980–992.

255. Wunderink RG, Rello J, Cammarata SK, et al. Linezolid vs vancomycin: analysis of two double-blind studies of patients with methicillin-resistant *Staphylococcus aureus* nosocomial pneumonia. *Chest* 2003 Nov;124(5):1789–1797.

256. Wunderink RG, Niederman MS, Kollef MH, et al. Linezolid in methicillin-resistant *Staphylococcus aureus* nosocomial pneumonia: a randomized, controlled study. *Clin Infect Dis* 2012 Mar 1;54(5):621–629.

257. Kalil AC, Murthy MH, Hermsen ED, et al. Linezolid versus vancomycin or teicoplanin for nosocomial pneumonia: a systematic review and meta-analysis. *Crit Care Med* 2010 Sep;38(9):1802–1808.

258. Kluytmans JA, Mouton JW, Ijzerman EP, et al. Nasal carriage of *Staphylococcus aureus* as a major risk factor for wound infections after cardiac surgery. *J Infect Dis* 1995 Jan;171(1):216–219.

259. Williams RE. Healthy carriage of *Staphylococcus aureus*: its prevalence and importance. *Bacteriol Rev* 1963 Mar;27:56–71.

260. Humphreys H. National guidelines for the control and prevention of methicillin-resistant *Staphylococcus aureus*—what do they tell us? *Clin Microbiol Infect* 2007 Sep;13(9):846–853.

261. Muto CA, Jernigan JA, Ostrowsky BE, et al. SHEA guideline for preventing nosocomial transmission of multidrug-resistant strains of *Staphylococcus aureus* and *Enterococcus*. *Infect Control Hosp Epidemiol* 2003 May;24(5):362–386.

262. Siegel JD, Rhinehart E, Jackson M, et al. Management of Multidrug-Resistant Organisms In Healthcare Settings, 2006. *Am J Infect Control* 2007 Dec;35(10 Suppl 2):S165–93.

263. Huang SS, Septimus E, Kleinman K, et al. Targeted versus universal decolonization to prevent ICU infection. *N Engl J Med* 2013 Jun 13;368(24):2255–2265.

264. Schwaber MJ, Rubinovitch B, Carmeli Y. Targeted decolonization to prevent ICU infections. *N Engl J Med* 2013 Oct 10;369(15):1470.

265. Patel JB, Gorwitz RJ, Jernigan JA. Mupirocin resistance. *Clin Infect Dis* 2009 Sep 15;49(6):935–941.

266. Harbarth S. Control of endemic methicillin-resistant *Staphylococcus aureus*-recent advances and future challenges. *Clin Microbiol Infect* 2006 Dec;12(12):1154–1162.

267. Ciccolini M, Donker T, Köck R, et al. Infection prevention in a connected world: The case for a regional approach. *Int J Med Microbiol* 2013 Aug;303(6-7):380–387.

268. Welsh CA, Flanagan ME, Kiess C, et al. Implementing the MRSA bundle in ICUs: one citywide collaborative's key lessons learned. *Infect Control Hosp Epidemiol* 2011 Sep;32(9):918–921.

269. Jain R, Kralovic SM, Evans ME, et al. Veterans Affairs initiative to prevent methicillin-resistant *Staphylococcus aureus* infections. *N Engl J Med* 2011 Apr 14;364(15):1419–1430.

270. Henderson DK. Managing methicillin-resistant staphylococci: a paradigm for preventing nosocomial transmission of resistant organisms. *Am J Med* 2006 Jun;119(6 Suppl 1):S45–S52.

271. Weber SG, Gold HS, Hooper DC, et al. Fluoroquinolones and the risk for methicillin-resistant Staphylococcus aureus in hospitalized patients. *Emerg Infect Dis* 2003 Nov;9(11):1415–1422.

272. Monnet DL. Methicillin-resistant *Staphylococcus aureus* and its relationship to antimicrobial use: possible implications for control. *Infect Control Hosp Epidemiol* 1998 Aug;19(8):552–559.

273. Tacconelli E, De Angelis G, Cataldo MA, et al. Does antibiotic exposure increase the risk of methicillin-resistant Staphylococcus aureus (MRSA) isolation? A systematic review and meta-analysis. *J Antimicrob Chemother* 2008 Jan;61(1):26–38.

274. Davey P, Brown E, Charani E, et al. Interventions to improve antibiotic prescribing practices for hospital inpatients. *Cochrane Database Syst Rev* 2013 Apr 30;4:CD003543.

275. John JF, Harvin AM. History and evolution of antibiotic resistance in coagulase-negative staphylococci: Susceptibility profiles of new anti-staphylococcal agents. *Ther Clin Risk Manag* 2007 Dec;3(6): 1143–1152.

276. Gordon RJ, Miragaia M, Weinberg AD, et al. *Staphylococcus epidermidis* colonization is highly clonal across US cardiac centers. *J Infect Dis* 2012 May 1;205(9):1391–1398.

277. Sader HS, Jones RN. Antimicrobial activity of daptomycin in comparison to glycopeptides and other antimicrobials when tested against numerous species of coagulase-negative Staphylococcus. *Diagn Microbiol Infect Dis* 2012 Jun;73(2):212–214.

278. Natoli S, Fontana C, Favaro M, et al. Characterization of coagulase-negative staphylococcal isolates from blood with reduced susceptibility to glycopeptides and therapeutic options. *BMC Infect Dis* 2009 Jun 4;9:83.

279. Falcone M, Giannella M, Raponi G, et al. Teicoplanin use and emergence of *Staphylococcus haemolyticus*: is there a link? *Clin Microbiol Infect* 2006 Jan;12(1):96–97.

280. Biavasco F, Vignaroli C, Varaldo PE. Glycopeptide resistance in coagulase-negative staphylococci. *Eur J Clin Microbiol Infect Dis* 2000 Jun;19(6):403–417.

281. Hope R, Livermore DM, Brick G, et al. Non-susceptibility trends among staphylococci from bacteraemias in the UK and Ireland, 2001-06. *J Antimicrob Chemother* 2008 Nov;62 Suppl 2:ii65–ii74.

282. Biavasco F, Vignaroli C, Lazzarini A, et al. Glycopeptide susceptibility profiles of *Staphylococcus haemolyticus* bloodstream isolates. *Antimicrob Agents Chemother* 2000 Nov;44(11):3122–3126.

283. Mendes RE, Deshpande LM, Costello AJ, et al. Molecular epidemiology of *Staphylococcus epidermidis* clinical isolates from U.S. hospitals. *Antimicrob Agents Chemother* 2012 Sep;56(9):4656–4661.

284. Sanyal D, Greenwood D. An electronmicroscope study of glycopeptide antibiotic-resistant strains of *Staphylococcus epidermidis*. *J Med Microbiol* 1993 Sep;39(3):204–210.

285. Gu B, Kelesidis T, Tsiodras S, et al. The emerging problem of linezolid-resistant Staphylococcus. *J Antimicrob Chemother* 2013 Jan;68(1):4–11.

286. Kresken M, Leitner E, Seifert H, et al. Susceptibility of clinical isolates of frequently encountered bacterial species to tigecycline one year after the introduction of this new class of antibiotics: results of the second multicentre surveillance trial in Germany (G-TEST II, 2007). *Eur J Clin Microbiol Infect Dis* 2009 Aug;28(8):1007–1011.

287. von Eiff C, Peters G, Heilmann C. Pathogenesis of infections due to coagulase-negative staphylococci. *Lancet Infect Dis* 2002 Nov;2(11): 677–685.

288. Otto M. Molecular basis of Staphylococcus epidermidis infections. *Semin Immunopathol* 2012 Mar;34(2):201–214.
289. von Eiff C, Jansen B, Kohnen W, et al. Infections associated with medical devices: pathogenesis, management and prophylaxis. *Drugs* 2005;65(2):179–214.
290. Uçkay I, Pittet D, Vaudaux P, et al. Foreign body infections due to *Staphylococcus epidermidis*. *Ann Med* 2009;41(2):109–119.
291. von Eiff C, Arciola CR, Montanaro L, et al. Emerging *Staphylococcus* species as new pathogens in implant infections. *Int J Artif Organs* 2006 Apr;29(4):360–367.
292. Raz R, Colodner R, Kunin CM. Who are you—*Staphylococcus saprophyticus*? *Clin Infect Dis* 2005 Mar 15;40(6):896–898.
293. Donlan RM. Biofilms and device-associated infections. *Emerg Infect Dis* 2001 Mar-Apr;7(2):277–281.
294. Hugonnet S, Sax H, Eggimann P, et al. Nosocomial bloodstream infection and clinical sepsis. *Emerg Infect Dis* 2004 Jan;10(1):76–81.
295. Wisplinghoff H, Bischoff T, Tallent SM, et al. Nosocomial bloodstream infections in US hospitals: analysis of 24,179 cases from a prospective nationwide surveillance study. *Clin Infect Dis* 2004 Aug 1;39(3):309–317.
296. Warren DK, Quadir WW, Hollenbeak CS, et al. Attributable cost of catheter-associated bloodstream infections among intensive care patients in a nonteaching hospital. *Crit Care Med* 2006 Aug;34(8):2084–2089.
297. Dimick JB, Pelz RK, Consunji R, et al. Increased resource use associated with catheter-related bloodstream infection in the surgical intensive care unit. *Arch Surg* 2001 Feb;136(2):229–234.
298. Elieson M, Mixon T, Carpenter J. Coronary stent infections: a case report and literature review. *Tex Heart Inst J* 2012;39(6):884–889.
299. Herrmann M, Weyand M, Greshake B, et al. Left ventricular assist device infection is associated with increased mortality but is not a contraindication to transplantation. *Circulation* 1997 Feb 18;95(4):814–817.
300. Szeto CC, Kwan BC, Chow KM, et al. Coagulase negative staphylococcal peritonitis in peritoneal dialysis patients: review of 232 consecutive cases. *Clin J Am Soc Nephrol* 2008 Jan;3(1):91–97.
301. Scheithauer S, Bürgel U, Ryang YM, et al. Prospective surveillance of drain associated meningitis/ventriculitis in a neurosurgery and neurological intensive care unit. *J Neurol Neurosurg Psychiatry* 2009 Dec;80(12):1381–1385.
302. Huebner J, Pier GB, Maslow JN, et al. Endemic nosocomial transmission of *Staphylococcus epidermidis* bacteremia isolates in a neonatal intensive care unit over 10 years. *J Infect Dis* 1994 Mar;169(3):526–531.
303. Widerström M, Monsen T, Karlsson C, et al. Molecular epidemiology of meticillin-resistant coagulase-negative staphylococci in a Swedish county hospital: evidence of intra- and interhospital clonal spread. *J Hosp Infect* 2006 Oct;64(2):177–183.
304. Liakopoulos V, Petinaki E, Efthimiadi G, et al. Clonal relatedness of methicillin-resistant coagulase-negative staphylococci in the haemodialysis unit of a single university centre in Greece. *Nephrol Dial Transplant* 2008 Aug;23(8):2599–2603.
305. Kelly S, Collins J, Maguire M, et al. An outbreak of colonization with linezolid-resistant *Staphylococcus epidermidis* in an intensive therapy unit. *J Antimicrob Chemother* 2008 Apr;61(4):901–907.
306. Milisavljevic V, Wu F, Cimmotti J, et al. Genetic relatedness of *Staphylococcus epidermidis* from infected infants and staff in the neonatal intensive care unit. *Am J Infect Control* 2005 Aug;33(6):341–347.
307. Costa SF, Miceli MH, Anaissie EJ. Mucosa or skin as source of coagulase-negative staphylococcal bacteraemia? *Lancet Infect Dis* 2004 May;4(5):278–286.
308. Thylefors JD, Harbarth S, Pittet D. Increasing bacteremia due to coagulase-negative staphylococci: fiction or reality? *Infect Control Hosp Epidemiol* 1998 Aug;19(8):581–589.
309. Bates DW, Cook EF, Goldman L, et al. Predicting bacteremia in hospitalized patients. A prospectively validated model. *Ann Intern Med* 1990 Oct 1;113(7):495–500.
310. Kirchhoff LV, Sheagren JN. Epidemiology and clinical significance of blood cultures positive for coagulase-negative staphylococcus. *Infect Control* 1985 Dec;6(12):479–486.
311. Ruhe J, Menon A, Mushatt D, et al. Non-*epidermidis* coagulase-negative staphylococcal bacteremia: clinical predictors of true bacteremia. *Eur J Clin Microbiol Infect Dis* 2004 Jun;23(6):495–498.
312. Favre B, Hugonnet S, Correa L, et al. Nosocomial bacteremia: clinical significance of a single blood culture positive for coagulase-negative staphylococci. *Infect Control Hosp Epidemiol* 2005 Aug;26(8):697–702.
313. Beekmann SE, Diekema DJ, Doern GV. Determining the clinical significance of coagulase-negative staphylococci isolated from blood cultures. *Infect Control Hosp Epidemiol* 2005 Jun;26(6):559–566.
314. Elzi L, Babouee B, Vögeli N, et al. How to discriminate contamination from bloodstream infection due to coagulase-negative staphylococci: a prospective study with 654 patients. *Clin Microbiol Infect* 2012 Sep;18(9):E355–E361.
315. Conen A, Walti LN, Merlo A, et al. Characteristics and treatment outcome of cerebrospinal fluid shunt-associated infections in adults: a retrospective analysis over an 11-year period. *Clin Infect Dis* 2008 Jul 1;47(1):73–82.
316. Shin JH, Kim SH, Jeong HS, et al. Identification of coagulase-negative staphylococci isolated from continuous ambulatory peritoneal dialysis fluid using 16S ribosomal RNA, tuf, and SodA gene sequencing. *Perit Dial Int* 2011 May-Jun;31(3):340–346.
317. Peel TN, Cheng AC, Buising KL, et al. Microbiological aetiology, epidemiology, and clinical profile of prosthetic joint infections: are current antibiotic prophylaxis guidelines effective? *Antimicrob Agents Chemother* 2012 May;56(5):2386–2391.
318. Pittet B, Montandon D, Pittet D. Infection in breast implants. *Lancet Infect Dis* 2005 Feb;5(2):94–106.
319. Recchia FM, Busbee BG, Pearlman RB, et al. Changing trends in the microbiologic aspects of postcataract endophthalmitis. *Arch Ophthalmol* 2005 Mar;123(3):341–346.
320. Hill EE, Herijgers P, Herregods MC, et al. Evolving trends in infective endocarditis. *Clin Microbiol Infect* 2006 Jan;12(1):5–12.
321. Moreillon P, Que YA. Infective endocarditis. *Lancet* 2004 Jan 10;363(9403):139–149.
322. Alonso-Valle H, Fariñas-Alvarez C, García-Palomo JD, et al. Clinical course and predictors of death in prosthetic valve endocarditis over a 20-year period. *J Thorac Cardiovasc Surg* 2010 Apr;139(4):887–893.
323. Leroy O, Meybeck A, Sarraz-Bournet B, et al. Vascular graft infections. *Curr Opin Infect Dis* 2012 Apr;25(2):154–158.
324. Karchmer AW, Archer GL, Dismukes WE. *Staphylococcus epidermidis* causing prosthetic valve endocarditis: microbiologic and clinical observations as guides to therapy. *Ann Intern Med* 1983 Apr;98(4):447–455.
325. Lalani T, Kanafani ZA, Chu VH, et al. Prosthetic valve endocarditis due to coagulase-negative staphylococci: findings from the International Collaboration on Endocarditis Merged Database. *Eur J Clin Microbiol Infect Dis* 2006 Jun;25(6):365–368.
326. Ortega JR, Garcia A, Medina A, et al. Endocarditis protésica precoz de gran agresividad por *S. epidermidis* [Highly aggressive early prosthetic endocarditis by *S. epidermidis*]. *Rev Esp Cardiol* 2002 Mar;55(3):315–318.
327. Didier C, Streicher MP, Chognot D, et al. Late-onset neonatal infections: incidences and pathogens in the era of antenatal antibiotics. *Eur J Pediatr* 2012 Apr;171(4):681–687.
328. Yalaz M, Altun-Köroglu O, Ulusoy B, et al. Evaluation of device-associated infections in a neonatal intensive care unit. *Turk J Pediatr* 2012 Mar-Apr;54(2):128–135.
329. Dimitriou G, Fouzas S, Giormezis N, et al. Clinical and microbiological profile of persistent coagulase-negative staphylococcal bacteraemia in neonates. *Clin Microbiol Infect* 2011;17(11):1684–1690.
330. Linder N, Hernandez A, Amit L, et al. Persistent coagulase-negative staphylococci bacteremia in very-low-birth-weight infants. *Eur J Pediatr* 2011 Aug;170(8):989–995.
331. Anguera I, Del Río A, Miró JM, et al. *Staphylococcus lugdunensis* infective endocarditis: description of 10 cases and analysis of native valve, prosthetic valve, and pacemaker lead endocarditis clinical profiles. *Heart* 2005 Feb;91(2):e10.
332. Liang M, Mansell C, Wade C, et al. Unusually virulent coagulase-negative *Staphylococcus lugdunensis* is frequently associated with infective endocarditis: a Waikato series of patients. *N Z Med J* 2012 May 11;125(1354):51–59.
333. Zinkernagel AS, Zinkernagel MS, Elzi MV, et al. Significance of *Staphylococcus lugdunensis* bacteremia: report of 28 cases and review of the literature. *Infection* 2008 Aug;36(4):314–321.
334. Li YM, Blaskiewicz DJ, Hall WA. Shunt-related intracranial abscess caused by *Staphylococcus lugdunensis* in a hydranencephalic patient. *World Neurosurg* 2013 Dec;80(6):e387–9.
335. Sampathkumar P, Osmon DR, Cockerill FR, III. Prosthetic joint infection due to *Staphylococcus lugdunensis*. *Mayo Clin Proc* 2000 May;75(5):511–512.
336. Böcher S, Tønning B, Skov RL, et al. *Staphylococcus lugdunensis*, a common cause of skin and soft tissue infections in the community. *J Clin Microbiol* 2009 Apr;47(4):946–950.
337. Seifert H, Oltmanns D, Becker K, et al. *Staphylococcus lugdunensis* pacemaker-related infection. *Emerg Infect Dis* 2005 Aug;11(8):1283–1286.
338. Peters G, Locci R, Pulverer G. Microbial colonization of prosthetic devices. II. Scanning electron microscopy of naturally infected intravenous catheters. *Zentralbl Bakteriol Mikrobiol Hyg [B]* 1981;173(5):293–299.
339. Heilmann C. Adhesion Mechanisms of Staphylococci. In: Linke D, Goldman A, eds. *Bacterial Adhesion. Chemistry, Biology and Physics*. Springer Science+Business Media. 2011; 105–123.
340. Hussain M, Herrmann M, von Eiff C, et al. A 140-kilodalton extracellular protein is essential for the accumulation of *Staphylococcus epidermidis* strains on surfaces. *Infect Immun* 1997 Feb;65(2):519–524.
341. Bourgeois I, Camiade E, Biswas R, et al. Characterization of AtlL, a bifunctional autolysin of *Staphylococcus lugdunensis* with

N-acetylglucosaminidase and N-acetylmuramoyl-l-alanine amidase activities. *FEMS Microbiol Lett* 2009 Jan;290(1):105–113.

342. Heilmann C, Hussain M, Peters G, et al. Evidence for autolysin-mediated primary attachment of *Staphylococcus epidermidis* to a polystyrene surface. *Mol Microbiol* 1997 Jun;24(5):1013–1024.

343. Hell W, Meyer HG, Gatermann SG. Cloning of *aas*, a gene encoding a *Staphylococcus saprophyticus* surface protein with adhesive and autolytic properties. *Mol Microbiol* 1998 Aug;29(3):871–881.

344. Mack D, Fischer W, Krokotsch A, et al. The intercellular adhesin involved in biofilm accumulation of *Staphylococcus epidermidis* is a linear beta-1,6-linked glucosaminoglycan: purification and structural analysis. *J Bacteriol* 1996 Jan;178(1):175–183.

345. Heilmann C, Schweitzer O, Gerke C, et al. Molecular basis of intercellular adhesion in the biofilm-forming *Staphylococcus epidermidis*. *Mol Microbiol* 1996 Jun;20(5):1083–1091.

346. Gerke C, Kraft A, Süßmuth R, et al. Characterization of the N-acetylglu-cosaminyltransferase activity involved in the biosynthesis of the *Staphylococcus epidermidis* polysaccharide intercellular adhesin. *J Biol Chem* 1998 Jul 17;273(29):18586–18593.

347. Hussain M, Heilmann C, Peters G, et al. Teichoic acid enhances adhesion of *Staphylococcus epidermidis* to immobilized fibronectin. *Microb Pathog* 2001 Dec;31(6):261–270.

348. Stout RD, Li Y, Miller AR, et al. Staphylococcal glycocalyx activates macrophage prostaglandin E2 and interleukin 1 production and modulates tumor necrosis factor alpha and nitric oxide production. *Infect Immun* 1994 Oct;62(10):4160–4166.

349. Mitchell J, Tristan A, Foster TJ. Characterization of the fibrinogen-binding surface protein Fbl of *Staphylococcus lugdunensis*. *Microbiology* 2004 Nov;150(Pt 11):3831–3841.

350. Meyer HG, Wengler-Becker U, Gatermann SG. The hemagglutinin of *Staphylococcus saprophyticus* is a major adhesin for uroepithelial cells. *Infect Immun* 1996 Sep;64(9):3893–3896.

351. Gatermann S, Kreft B, Marre R, et al. Identification and characterization of a surface-associated protein (Ssp) of *Staphylococcus saprophyticus*. *Infect Immun* 1992 Mar;60(3):1055–1060.

352. Sakinc T, Kleine B, Gatermann SG. SdrI, a serine-aspartate repeat protein identified in *Staphylococcus saprophyticus* strain 7108, is a collagen-binding protein. *Infect Immun* 2006 Aug;74(8):4615–4623.

353. Kratzer C, Rabitsch W, Hirschl AM, et al. In vitro activity of daptomycin and ti-gecycline against coagulase-negative staphylococcus blood isolates from bone marrow transplant recipients. *Eur J Haematol* 2007 Nov;79(5):405–409.

354. Mermel LA, Farr BM, Sherertz RJ, et al. Guidelines for the management of intravascular catheter-related infections. *Clin Infect Dis* 2001 May 1;32(9):1249–1272.

355. Bouza E, Burillo A, Munoz P. Empiric therapy for intravenous central line infections and nosocomially-acquired acute bacterial endocarditis. *Crit Care Clin* 2008 Apr;24(2):293–2ix.

356. Sabatier C, Ferrer R, Valles J. Treatment strategies for central venous catheter infections. *Expert Opin Pharmacother* 2009 Oct;10(14):2231–2243.

357. O'Grady NP, Alexander M, Burns LA, et al. Guidelines for the prevention of intravascular catheter-related infections. *Clin Infect Dis* 2011 May;52(9):e162–e193.

358. Mermel LA, Allon M, Bouza E, et al. Clinical practice guidelines for the diagnosis and management of intravascular catheter-related infection: 2009 Update by the Infectious Diseases Society of America. *Clin Infect Dis* 2009 Jul 1;49(1):1–45.

359. Chittick P, Sherertz RJ. Recognition and prevention of nosocomial vascular device and related bloodstream infections in the intensive care unit. *Crit Care Med* 2010 Aug;38(8 Suppl):S363–S372.

360. Raad I, Hanna H, Maki D. Intravascular catheter-related infections: advances in diagnosis, prevention, and management. *Lancet Infect Dis* 2007 Oct;7(10):645–657.

361. Samore MH, Burke JP. Infections of long intravenous lines: new developments and controversies. *Curr Clin Top Infect Dis* 2000;20:256–270.

362. Pierce D, Calkins BC, Thornton K. Infectious endocarditis: diagnosis and treatment. *Am Fam Physician* 2012 May 15;85(10):981–986.

363. Seybold U, Kourbatova EV, Johnson JG, et al. Emergence of communi-ty-associated methicillin-resistant *Staphylococcus aureus* USA300 geno-type as a major cause of health care-associated blood stream infections. *Clin Infect Dis* 2006 Mar 1;42(5):647–656.

364. Popovich KJ, Weinstein RA, Hota B. Are community-associated methicillin-resistant *Staphylococcus aureus* (MRSA) strains replacing traditional nosocomial MRSA strains? *Clin Infect Dis* 2008 Mar 15;46(6):787–794.

365. Boyle-Vavra S, Ereshefsky B, Wang CC, et al. Successful multiresistant community-associated methicillin-resistant *Staphylococcus aureus* lineage from Taipei, Taiwan, that carries either the novel Staphylococcal chromosome cassette *mec* (SCC*mec*) type V$_T$ or SCC*mec* type IV. *J Clin Microbiol* 2005 Sep;43(9):4719–4730.

366. Armand-Lefevre L, Ruimy R, Andremont A. Clonal comparison of *Staphylococcus aureus* isolates from healthy pig farmers, human controls, and pigs. *Emerg Infect Dis* 2005 May;11(5):711–714.

367. Wulf MW, Markestein A, van der Linden FT, et al. First outbreak of methicillin-resistant Staphylococcus aureus ST398 in a Dutch hospital, June 2007. *Euro Surveill* 2008 Feb 28;13(9).

368. Welinder-Olsson C, Florén-Johansson K, Larsson L, et al. Infection with Panton-Valentine leukocidin-positive methicillin-resistant *Staphylococcus aureus* t034. *Emerg Infect Dis* 2008 Aug;14(8):1271–1272.

369. Bartels MD, Boye K, Rhod LA, et al. Rapid increase of genetically diverse methicillin-resistant *Staphylococcus aureus*, Copenhagen, Denmark. *Emerg Infect Dis* 2007 Oct;13(10):1533–1540.

370. Wulf M, Voss A. MRSA in livestock animals-an epidemic waiting to happen? *Clin Microbiol Infect* 2008 Jun;14(6):519–521.

371. Wulf MW, Verduin CM, van Nes A, et al. Infection and colonization with methicillin resistant *Staphylococcus aureus* ST398 versus other MRSA in an area with a high density of pig farms. *Eur J Clin Microbiol Infect Dis* 2012 Jan;31(1):61–65.

372. Lekkerkerk WS, Sande-Bruinsma N, van der Sande MA, et al. Emergence of MRSA of unknown origin in the Netherlands. *Clin Microbiol Infect* 2012 Jul;18(7):656–661.

373. Kehrenberg C, Cuny C, Strommenger B, et al. Methicillin-resistant and -susceptible *Staphylococcus aureus* strains of clonal lineages ST398 and ST9 from swine carry the multidrug resistance gene *cfr*. *Antimicrob Agents Chemother* 2009 Feb;53(2):779–781.

374. Arias M, Tena D, Apellaniz M, et al. Skin and soft tissue infections caused by *Staphylococcus lugdunensis*: Report of 20 cases. *Scand J Infect Dis* 2010 Dec;42(11-12):879–884.

375. Papapetropoulos N, Papapetropoulou M, Vantarakis A. Abscesses and wound infections due to Staphylococcus lugdunensis: report of 16 cases. *Infection* 2013 Apr;41(2):525–528.

376. Hung T, Zaghi S, Yousefzadeh J, et al. Necrotizing fasciitis associated with *Staphylococcus lugdunensis*. *Case Rep Infect Dis* 2012;2012:453685.

377. Seenivasan MH, Yu VL. *Staphylococcus lugdunensis* endocarditis—the hidden peril of coagulase-negative staphylococcus in blood cultures. *Eur J Clin Microbiol Infect Dis* 2003 Aug;22(8):489–491.

378. Leung MJ, Nuttall N, Pryce TM, et al. Colony variation in *Staphylococcus lugdunensis*. *J Clin Microbiol* 1998 Oct;36(10):3096–3098.

379. Savini V, Barbarini D, Polakowska K, et al. Methicillin-resistant *Staphylococcus pseudintermedius* infection in a bone marrow transplant recipient. *J Clin Microbiol* 2013 May;51(5):1636–1638.

380. Riegel P, Jesel-Morel L, Laventie B, et al. Coagulase-positive *Staphylococcus pseudintermedius* from animals causing human endocarditis. *Int J Med Microbiol* 2011 Mar;301(3):237–239.

381. Trülzsch K, Grabein B, Schumann P, et al. *Staphylococcus pettenkoferi* sp. nov., a novel coagulase-negative staphylococcal species isolated from human clinical specimens. *Int J Syst Evol Microbiol* 2007 Jul;57(Pt 7):1543–1548.

382. Loïez C, Wallet F, Pischedda P, et al. First case of osteomyelitis caused by "*Staphylococcus pettenkoferi*". *J Clin Microbiol* 2007 Mar;45(3):1069–1071.

383. Mihaila L, Defrance G, Levesque E, et al. A dual outbreak of bloodstream infections with linezolid-resistant *Staphylococcus epidermidis* and *Staphylococcus pettenkoferi* in a liver Intensive Care Unit. *Int J Antimicrob Agents* 2012 Nov;40(5):472–474.

384. Tacconelli E, Tumbarello M, Donati KG, et al. Glycopeptide resistance among coagulase-negative staphylococci that cause bacteremia: epidemiological and clinical findings from a case-control study. *Clin Infect Dis* 2001 Nov 15;33(10):1628–1635.

SUPPLEMENTAL RESOURCES

Additional Resources Available from the Centers for Disease Control and Prevention

Centers for Disease Control and Prevention (CDC), National Center for Emerging and Zoonotic Infectious Diseases (NCEZID), Division of Healthcare Quality Promotion (DHQP). *Healthcare Infection Control Practices Advisory Committee (HICPAC)*. CDC website. November 25, 2013. Available at: http://www.cdc.gov/hicpac/.

Centers for Disease Control and Prevention (CDC), National Center for Emerging and Zoonotic Infectious Diseases (NCEZID), Division of Healthcare Quality Promotion (DHQP). *2007 Guideline for Isolation Precautions: Preventing Transmission of Infectious Agents in Healthcare Settings*. CDC website. December 9, 2010. Available at: http://www.cdc.gov/hicpac/2007IP/2007isolationPrecautions.html.

Centers for Disease Control and Prevention (CDC), National Center for Emerging and Zoonotic Infectious Diseases (NCEZID), Division of Healthcare Quality Promotion (DHQP). National Healthcare Safety Network (NHSN). CDC website. September 24, 2013. Available at: http://www.cdc.gov/nhsn/.

Centers for Disease Control and Prevention (CDC), National Center for Emerging and Zoonotic Infectious Diseases (NCEZID), Division of Healthcare Quality Promotion (DHQP). *State-based HAI prevention.* CDC website. September 27, 2012. Available at: http://www.cdc.gov/hai/state-based/prevention-projects.html.

National Center for Immunization and Respiratory Diseases, Division of Bacterial Diseases. *Active Bacterial Core surveillance (ABCs). Surveillance reports.* CDC website. October 21, 2013. Available at: http://www.cdc.gov/abcs /reports-findings/surv-reports.html.

Centers for Disease Control and Prevention (CDC), National Center for Emerging and Zoonotic Infectious Diseases (NCEZID), Division of Healthcare Quality Promotion (DHQP). *Methicillin-resistant* Staphylococcus aureus *(MRSA) infections.* CDC website. September 16, 2013. Available at: http://www.cdc.gov/mrsa/.

Centers for Disease Control and Prevention (CDC), National Center for Emerging and Zoonotic Infectious Diseases (NCEZID), Division of Healthcare Quality Promotion (DHQP). *Methicillin-resistant* Staphylococcus aureus *(MRSA) infections. MRSA tracking.* CDC website. September 16, 2013. Available at: http://www.cdc.gov/mrsa/tracking/index.html.

Centers for Disease Control and Prevention (CDC), National Center for Emerging and Zoonotic Infectious Diseases (NCEZID), Division of Healthcare Quality Promotion (DHQP). *Methicillin-resistant* Staphylococcus aureus *(MRSA) infections. General information about MRSA in the community.* CDC website. September 10, 2013. Available at: http://www.cdc.gov/mrsa /community/index.html.

Centers for Disease Control and Prevention (CDC), National Center for Emerging and Zoonotic Infectious Diseases (NCEZID), Division of Healthcare Quality Promotion (DHQP). *Healthcare-associated infections (HAIs).* Staphylococcus aureus *in healthcare settings.* CDC website. January 17, 2013. Available at: http://www.cdc.gov/HAI/organisms/staph.html.

Centers for Disease Control and Prevention (CDC), National Center for Emerging and Zoonotic Infectious Diseases (NCEZID), Division of Healthcare Quality Promotion (DHQP). *Healthcare-associated infections (HAIs). General information about VISA/VRSA.* CDC website. August 23, 2013. Available at: http://www.cdc.gov/HAI/organisms/visa_vrsa/visa_vrsa.html.

Centers for Disease Control and Prevention (CDC), National Center for Emerging and Zoonotic Infectious Diseases (NCEZID), Division of Healthcare Quality Promotion (DHQP). *Methicillin-resistant* Staphylococcus aureus *(MRSA) infections. Environmental cleaning & disinfecting for MRSA.* CDC website. September 10, 2013. Available at: http://www.cdc.gov/mrsa/community /enviroment/index.html.

Centers for Disease Control and Prevention (CDC). *Safe healthcare. Selected category: MRSA.* CDC website. Available at: http://blogs.cdc.gov /safehealthcare/category/mrsa/.

Additional Resources from Association for Professionals in Infection Control and Epidemiology (APIC)

Guide to the Elimination of MRSA Transmission

Guide to the Elimination of MRSA in Long-Term Care

The Infection Preventionist's Guide to the Lab

Ready Reference for Microbes, 3rd edition

Additional Resources from Other Professional Organizations

Society for Healthcare Epidemiology of America (SHEA). *Guidelines & resources.* SHEA website. Available at: http://www.shea-online.org /GuidelinesResources.aspx.

Infectious Diseases Society of America (IDSA). *Guidelines/patient care.* IDSA website. Available at: http://www.idsociety.org/Guidelines_Patient_Care/.

Infectious Diseases Society of America (IDSA). *Management of Patients with Infections Caused by Methicillin-Resistant Staphylococcus Aureus: Clinical Practice Guidelines by the Infectious Diseases Society of America (IDSA).* IDSA website. Available at: http://www.idsociety.org/IDSA/Site_Map /Guidelines/Patient_Care/IDSA_Practice_Guidelines/Infections_by_Organism /Bacteria/MRSA.aspx.

Calfee DP, Salgado CD, Classen D, et al. *Strategies to prevent transmission of methicillin-Resistant Staphylococcus aureus in acute care hospitals.* JSTOR website. Available at: http://www.jstor.org/stable/10.1086/591061.

European Centre for Disease Prevention and Control (ECDC). *Healthcare-associated infections.* ECDC website. Available at: http://www.ecdc.europa .eu/en/healthtopics/Healthcare-associated_infections/Pages/index.aspx.

European Centre for Disease Prevention and Control (ECDC). *Antimicrobial resistance.* ECDC website. Available at: http://www.ecdc.europa.eu/en /healthtopics/antimicrobial_resistance/Pages/index.aspx/.

European Centre for Disease Prevention and Control (ECDC). *European Antimicrobial Resistance Surveillance Network (EARS-Net).* ECDC website. Available at: http://www.ecdc.europa.eu/en/activities/surveillance/EARS-Net /Pages/index.aspx.

Additional Resources for Laboratory Methods

Multi Locus Sequence Typing (MLST). Available at: http://saureus.mlst.net/.

Ridom Spa Server. Available at: http://spaserver.ridom.de/.

CHAPTER 94

Streptococci

Carol E. Chenoweth, MD
Professor, Department of Internal Medicine, Division of Infectious Diseases
Clinical Professor, Department of Epidemiology
University of Michigan Health System
Ann Arbor, MI

ABSTRACT

The genus Streptococcus encompasses a broad range of colonizing and pathogenic organisms. Streptococci inhabit animals as well as humans and can cause infection in both. They are found most abundantly as commensals in the mouth, gastrointestinal tract, and genitourinary tract. When pathogenic, they are important causes of skin and soft tissue infection, pharyngitis, pneumonia, and bacteremia. This chapter describes the microbiologic and clinical characteristics of the streptococci typically seen in human infection and emphasizes features of transmission and prevention.

KEY CONCEPTS

- Streptococci are common commensal organisms.

- Streptococci are Gram-positive cocci growing in pairs or chains.

- More than 30 species of streptococci have been identified; classification is based primarily on patterns of hemolysis.

- Streptococci can be spread by both direct and indirect routes.

- Streptococcus species cause a variety of infections ranging from mild pharyngitis to severe necrotizing fasciitis.

- Resistance to antimicrobial agents is being reported with increasing frequency in some Streptococcus species (e.g., Streptococcus pneumoniae).

BACKGROUND

Streptococci are Gram-positive, non–spore-forming spherical or ovoid bacteria (cocci) that grow in pairs or chains and can be distinguished from staphylococci by their inability to produce catalase.[1] Most streptococci are facultative anaerobes, though some may require strict anaerobic conditions for growth. There are more than 30 identified species of the genus Streptococcus; classification of streptococcal organisms depends on patterns of hemolysis, growth characteristics, biochemical reactions, and antigenic composition.[1,2] Streptococci cause a variety of diseases and conditions that depend on the species of organism present, the body site involved, and host factors. Basic principles of the major groups of streptococci are discussed next.

BASIC PRINCIPLES

Group A *Streptococcus*

Group A *Streptococcus* (GAS) is among the most frequent and important pathogens found in humans. Spread of GAS occurs by direct person-to-person contact. Healthcare-associated outbreaks of streptococcal pyoderma, a purulent streptococcal infection of the skin, have declined substantially but still occur. Aggressive group A streptococcal infections associated with shock, bacteremia, and multiorgan failure are being reported with increasing frequency.[3]

Identification

GAS are Gram-positive cocci occurring in pairs or short chains (resembling a short string of beads). A negative catalase test result distinguishes streptococci from staphylococci.[1] Although facultatively anaerobic, most are oxygen tolerant and grow readily in air. When cultivated on blood agar plates, GAS appear as white-to-gray colonies, 1 to 2 mm in diameter, and are surrounded by clear, colorless zones within which the red blood cells in the medium have been completely lysed (β-hemolysis). GAS are presumptively distinguished from other β-hemolytic streptococci by their susceptibility to bacitracin.

Epidemiology and Transmission

Streptococcal pharyngitis is most common among children 5 to 15 years of age; however, all age groups are susceptible. GAS cause approximately 15 percent of all sore throats in children.[4,5] Spread of GAS occurs by direct person-to-person contact, probably by infected droplets of saliva or nasal secretions and perhaps by hand-to-hand-to-mouth contact.[4,5] Crowding (such as occurs in schools and military barracks) facilitates transmission and may account for the increased incidence of GAS infections in the colder months of the year. Fomites (contaminated clothing, blankets, dust) do not appear to play a significant role in disease transmission.[6]

Asymptomatic nasopharyngeal carriage of GAS occurs at a rate of 15 to 20 percent in school-age children and has been associated with transmission of infection. Adults are asymptomatically colonized with GAS at much lower rates. Those who carry the organism are more effective transmitters of disease if they have only recently become colonized and have a large number of streptococci recoverable from the throat. Foodborne and waterborne outbreaks of GAS infection are well documented.[7] Foodborne outbreaks have been associated with contamination of food by a streptococcal carrier and allowing the food to stand at room temperature.[7]

Streptococcal pyoderma is a purulent streptococcal infection of the skin. This infection typically occurs among economically disadvantaged children (aged 2–5 years) dwelling in tropical or subtropical climates; skin infections also are prevalent in northern climates during the summer months. Poor hygiene is a risk factor for the development of streptococcal pyoderma because GAS can initially colonize unbroken skin.[3,8] The mode of transmission of GAS pyoderma is poorly understood but likely includes skin-to-skin contact as well as transmission by fomites such as towels, shed skin scales, contaminated dust, and arthropod vectors.[8]

Erysipelas and cellulitis are also acute inflammatory GAS skin infections. Erysipelas often affects infants and persons older than 30 years, and GAS cellulitis may occur after trauma, including surgery.[8,9]

Healthcare-associated outbreaks of GAS skin infection have declined substantially with improved attention to infection prevention, but such outbreaks continue to be reported.[10] Outbreaks of GAS in nurseries,[11] among postpartum women,[12,13] or in surgical site infections[14] have been traced to healthcare personnel (HCP) who are nasopharyngeal, anal, or vaginal streptococcal carriers. Such infections constitute infection prevention emergencies because identification and treatment of the carrier can curtail the outbreak.[15] In addition to asymptomatic carriage, HCP with active streptococcal skin infections have been implicated in healthcare-associated transmission of GAS skin infections.[13] In addition to carriers, severe outbreaks of GAS have been linked to nonadherence to standard infection control practice in long-term and long-term acute care facilities.[16-19]

Aggressive GAS infections associated with shock, bacteremia, and multiorgan failure are being reported with increasing frequency [3,20] and occur at a rate of 3.5 cases per 100,000 persons in the United States.[21] Although risk factors for invasive GAS infections include the presence of surgical wounds, diabetes mellitus, and other underlying medical problems, there appears to be an increased incidence of cases in otherwise healthy young adults with minor, even trivial trauma.[3] Age and residence in long-term care facilities have been recently identified as risk factors for invasive infection.[10,19] Recent clonal outbreaks of GAS disease have also been described in communities, in long-term care facilities, and among family members.[10,22,23]

Diagnosis

Throat culture remains the gold standard for diagnosis of streptococcal pharyngitis.[22] However, a positive culture does not dif-

ferentiate between acute infection and the asymptomatic carrier state. Rapid tests that identify group A carbohydrate antigen by latex agglutination or enzyme immunoassay are an alternative method of diagnosis.[24] In a patient with suggestive symptoms, a positive rapid antigen detection test (RADT) establishes the diagnosis of GAS pharyngitis, because this test is highly specific. Given the 80 to 90 percent sensitivity of this test, however, consideration should be given to performing a throat culture in a patient with pharyngitis who has a negative RADT for GAS.[4] Newer RADTs may have a sensitivity approaching that of throat culture, thus obviating the need for backup throat culture if the RADT is negative[4,25,26]

Serodiagnosis of a recent streptococcal infection can be made by detecting antibodies to streptococcal extracellular products. Three serologic tests in common use include assays for antistreptolysin O (ASO), anti-DNase B, and antihyaluronidase. These tests may be used in the diagnosis of acute rheumatic fever, a nonsuppurative complication of untreated streptococcal pharyngitis.[27]

Streptococcal skin infections are often diagnosed by sight. If an open wound is present, obtaining a culture may be appropriate. Diagnosis of invasive GAS infection is made by isolating the organism from blood or other normally sterile body fluid (spinal, synovial, peritoneal, or pleural) or by obtaining a tissue biopsy specimen in the setting of suggestive clinical signs and symptoms.

Clinical Infections

Manifestations of streptococcal pharyngitis include abrupt onset of sore throat accompanied by malaise, fever, and headache. Nausea, vomiting, and abdominal pain are common in children. Physical examination reveals an erythematous posterior pharynx with enlarged, hyperemic tonsils containing gray-white exudates. Tender, swollen submandibular lymph nodes are present, as well as a fever of 101°F (38.3°C) or higher. In the absence of complications, the pharyngitis is self-limited, and fever abates in 3 to 5 days. Patients with streptococcal pharyngitis who do not receive antibiotic therapy are at risk for developing late nonsuppurative complications, including acute rheumatic fever and poststreptococcal glomerulonephritis.[2-5]

Scarlet fever results from infection with a streptococcal strain that elaborates erythrogenic toxin.[2,3] When scarlet fever occurs, it is usually the result of pharyngeal infection, but it can occur in the setting of GAS skin infection or sepsis. It is characterized by a diffuse red rash that typically appears on the second day of illness, lends a sandpaper texture to the skin, and fades over the course of a week. It is followed by desquamation of the skin. Severe forms of scarlet fever with systemic toxicity and sepsis are rare in the antibiotic era.

Erysipelas is an acute inflammation of the skin and cutaneous lymphatic vessels. It manifests as well-demarcated areas of erythema and swelling that may advance rapidly.[8,9] Erysipelas commonly affects the face and in such cases may be preceded by GAS pharyngitis. It may occur on the trunk or extremities at a surgical site or wound and is often accompanied by chills, fever, and toxicity. Blebs and bullae may form on the affected areas of skin and leave raw, weeping wounds with rupture.

Streptococcal pyoderma, or impetigo, is a purulent skin infection that begins as papules and evolves to form vesicles and then pustules. The pustules enlarge and rupture over 4 to 6 days to form thick, "stuck-on," amber-colored crusts. Ulcerated lesions are known as ecthyma. Impetigo often occurs on multiple areas of exposed body sites, including the lower extremities, and remains well localized. Systemic symptoms are usually absent.[8]

Streptococcal cellulitis manifests as a warm, erythematous, edematous, and painful spreading inflammation of the skin and subcutaneous tissues.[8,9] Margins may advance rapidly but are not well demarcated or raised as in erysipelas. Cellulitis usually results from infection of an antecedent incidental or larger break in skin integrity (trauma, burns, surgery), and the organism may invade the lymphatics and bloodstream. Lymphangitis can accompany cellulitis and is characterized by red, tender streaks leading to tender, enlarged lymph nodes.

Necrotizing fasciitis (NF) is a severe invasive GAS infection involving the subcutaneous tissue extending to the fascia and fat, most commonly affecting the extremities.[3,8] NF typically begins at a site of often trivial trauma. Pain at the site of minor trauma may be the initial symptom. Within 24 hours the area becomes erythematous, swollen, warm, and tender. The infection and symptoms spread to involve adjacent tissues. Patients frequently report deep muscle pain or arthralgia in the area that appears out of proportion to the physical findings. Over the subsequent 24 to 48 hours, the affected areas take on a purple then blue coloration and blisters containing clear yellow fluid develop. Gangrene occurs after 4 to 5 days and is characterized by a well-demarcated area covered by a necrotic eschar and surrounding erythema. NF is often a fulminant illness with shock and multiorgan failure. It is a life-threatening illness with very high mortality in the absence of early and aggressive surgical debridement and antibiotic therapy.[9,28]

Although other bacteria are known to cause toxic shock syndrome (TSS), some cases can be related to streptococcal infections. Skin or mucous membranes are the portal of entry for streptococci in 60 percent of patients with TSS, with no definite portal of entry in the remaining 40 percent of patients. In the latter group, it is presumed that the source of infection is streptococci in the pharynx or intestine with transient bacteremia.[3,8] Suction lipectomy, hysterectomy, vaginal delivery, bunionectomy, and bone pinning have preceded streptococcal TSS in unpublished reports.[3,8] Soft tissue infection is evident in approximately 80 percent of patients and evolves to NF or myositis in 70 percent.[29] The early symptoms of streptococcal TSS include myalgias, malaise, chills, fever, nausea, vomiting, and diarrhea. This is followed by tachycardia, fever, tachypnea, and marked pain, which progresses out of proportion to the physical findings.[3,8] Confusion is present in half of the patients at presentation. Hypotension and shock frequently develop and are associated with multisystem organ dysfunction (particularly renal impairment and acute respiratory distress syndrome). Mortality is high (30 percent) despite aggressive treatment.[3,29]

Pathogenesis

Streptococci have surface molecules (M proteins, hyaluronic acid, and C5a peptidase) that allow evasion of phagocytosis and proliferation in tissues. Extracellular products released by GAS (DNases, hyaluronidase, streptokinase) facilitate liquefaction of pus and spread of streptococci through tissues.[3,28] Dysregulation of the coagulation and anticoagulation pathways may occur in GAS infection, leading to a decrease in tissue perfusion, hypoxia, and subsequent tissue necrosis and organ failure. TSS is thought to be the result of "superantigen" production by GAS, the elaboration of extracellular toxins that cause widespread nonspecific activation of the immune system with subsequent marked inflammatory response.[30]

Treatment

Penicillin is the drug of choice in the treatment of streptococcal infections.[4] Penicillin resistance has not yet been identified in GAS infections. Failures of penicillin treatment for GAS pharyngitis are not uncommon despite the lack of resistance to penicillin, and some authors recommend cephalosporins as first-line agents for treatment of GAS pharyngitis.[4,31] Erythromycin is recommended for penicillin-allergic patients, but there have been reports of GAS resistant to erythromycin.[32,33] In addition, there have been recent reports of high-level fluoroquinolone resistance among GAS.[34]

In severe skin infections such as NF and myositis, early and aggressive surgical intervention is mandatory with drainage of the site, debridement, or, in some cases, fasciotomy or amputation. Penicillin appears to be less efficacious in the setting of fulminant streptococcal infection, and this may be the result of large inoculum size with slowed growth of the organisms; in such a situation there is lower expression of penicillin-binding targets.[3,8,9,28] In experimental models of myositis, antibiotics such as clindamycin and erythromycin appear to be more effective than penicillin, possibly related to the inhibition of toxin production by the former two drugs.[8,9] Rare cases of clindamycin resistance have been reported. Therefore, the combination of both penicillin and clindamycin is recommended to treat serious GAS infections, such as NF and TSS.[8,9]

Intravenous immunoglobulin (IVIG) may be a beneficial adjunctive therapy for TSS, because it is postulated to neutralize GAS toxin.[35,36] A recent randomized, placebo-controlled trial demonstrated a decrease in mortality with the use of IVIG, but because of the small number of patients enrolled, the difference in mortality between IVIG and placebo groups was not statistically significant.[35] The usefulness of this therapy requires further study.[36]

Prevention and Control

Infection prevention measures, including strict compliance with Standard Precautions including respiratory etiquette and hand hygiene between patients, appropriate precautions for infected

Table 94-1. Transmission-based Precautions for *Streptococcus* Species

Organism/Disease	Type of Precaution	Duration of Precautions	Comments
Pneumonia			
Streptococcus, Group A			
Adults	D	U 24 h	See Streptococcal Disease (group A *Streptococcus*) in next entry. Contact Precautions if skin lesions present.
Infants and young children	D	U 24 h	Contact Precautions if skin lesions present.
Pneumococcal pneumonia	S		Use Droplet Precautions if evidence of transmission within a patient care unit or facility.
Streptococcal Disease (Group A *Streptococcus*)			
Skin, wound, or burn			
Major	C, D	U 24 h	No dressing or dressing does not contain drainage adequately.
Minor or limited	S		Dressing covers and contains drainage adequately.
Endometritis (puerperal sepsis)	S		
Pharyngitis in infants and young children	D	U 24 h	
Pneumonia	D	U 24 h	
Scarlet fever in infants and young children	D	U 24 h	
Serious invasive disease	D	U 24 h	Outbreaks of serious invasive disease have occurred secondary to transmission among patients and HCP. Contact Precautions for draining wound as above; follow recommendations for antimicrobial prophylaxis in selected conditions.
Streptococcal Disease (Group B *Streptococcus*), Neonatal	S		
Streptococcal Disease (not Group A or B) unless covered elsewhere	S		

Precaution types: A, airborne ; C, contact; D, droplet; S, standard; when A, C, and D are specified, also use S. Duration of precautions: CN, until off antimicrobial treatment and culture-negative; DI, duration of illness (with wound lesions, DI means until wounds stop draining); DE, until environment completely decontaminated; U, until time specified in hours (h) after initiation of effective therapy; Unknown: criteria for establishing eradication of pathogen has not been determined.

Adapted from Siegel JD, Rhinehart E, Jackson M, et al. *2007 Guideline for Isolation Precautions: Preventing Transmission of Infectious Agents in Healthcare Settings.* Available at: http://www.cdc.gov/hicpac/pdf/isolation/isolation2007.pdf.

patients, and aseptic technique, are useful in the prevention of healthcare-associated streptococcal infections.[37] See Table 94-1 for information on Transmission-based Precautions. During outbreaks of GAS infection, transmission prevention and control measures may also include cohorting of cases and treatment of carriers. Some authors have advocated the use of prophylactic antibiotics for household contacts of serious GAS infections,[22] though the Centers for Disease Control and Prevention (CDC) does not recommend routine screening and prophylaxis in such situations.[38]

To prevent additional healthcare-associated GAS infections, enhanced surveillance and limited epidemiologic investigation are warranted following one episode of healthcare-associated GAS infection on a surgical or obstetric ward. After identification of a patient with postoperative or postpartum GAS, medical and laboratory records should be reviewed to identify other infections, and isolates from infected patients should be stored and surveillance heightened to identify additional episodes. Limited HCP screening should be undertaken. Most healthcare-associated transmission is traced to carriers involved in direct patient care; screening should include all HCPs who were present at the delivery, who performed vaginal examinations before deliv-

ery, who were present in the operating room during a procedure, and who changed dressings on open wounds.

Screening of HCPs should include culture of the nares, throat, vagina, rectum, and skin. HCPs may return to work pending culture results. Any HCP whose culture is positive for GAS should refrain from patient care for the first 24 hours of antimicrobial treatment. The regimen should be tailored to the carriage site; previous reports have indicated anal carriage may be difficult to eradicate. Appropriate treatment for a positive rectal culture may be vancomycin 250 mg orally four times a day and rifampin 600 mg orally twice a day for 10 days. For a positive throat, vaginal, or skin culture, appropriate treatment may be penicillin 500 mg four times a day for 10 days with rifampin 600 mg orally twice a day for the last 4 days of the 10-day course.[10,15]

Group B *Streptococcus*

Group B *Streptococcus* (GBS) is a common inhabitant of the lower gastrointestinal (GI) and genital tracts. Nonpregnant adults with underlying medical conditions are at increased risk for GBS infection. GBS can be transmitted vertically to newborns during labor and delivery, and apparently via breast milk. The use of intrapartum prophylaxis with antibiotics has led to a decline in the incidence of GBS neonatal infection. Early neonatal GBS infection occurs within the first 6 days of life and arises from GBS acquired from colonized mothers during delivery. Late neonatal infection occurs between 7 and 89 days and results from intestinal colonization.

Identification

Streptococcus agalactiae is the species comprising the Lancefield GBS. GBS exhibits β-hemolysis and grows facultatively. Colonies of GBS are gray-white and flat, and Gram stain reveals Gram-positive diplococci. Latex agglutination or other immunologic methods are used to detect group B-specific cell wall antigen for identification of the organism. GBS are also characterized by resistance to bacitracin and trimethoprim-sulfamethoxazole and can be distinguished from group D streptococci by an inability to hydrolyze esculin.[39]

Epidemiology and Transmission

GBS are common inhabitants of the lower GI and genital tracts, and studies have demonstrated a genital/lower GI tract colonization rate of more than 20 percent in women.[39] A recent prevalence study of GBS in male and nonpregnant female college students demonstrated that 34 percent of women and 31 percent of males were colonized, with tampon use in women being a risk factor for colonization.[40] Pregnancy alone does not affect the prevalence of GBS colonization, but diabetes mellitus has been associated with higher colonization rates in pregnant women.[41] Sexual activity is a risk factor for GBS colonization,[42] and multiparous women and those over 20 years of age have lower genital colonization rates.[39] Nonpregnant adults with diabetes mellitus, human immunodeficiency virus (HIV) infection, malignancy, and chronic liver disease are at increased risk for GBS infection.

GBS can be transmitted vertically to newborns during labor and delivery,[42] and there has been apparent transmission via breast milk.[43] In nonpregnant adults, transmission can occur through direct contact, including via sexual contact.[40] GBS has been transmitted from person to person in hospitals, particularly under conditions of crowding and poor hand washing.[39]

Diagnosis

The diagnosis of invasive GBS infection is made by isolating the organism from blood, cerebrospinal fluid (CSF), or other normally sterile body sites. Recovery of the organism from mucous membranes is typically indicative of colonization rather than infection. Screening of pregnant women for the presence of GBS colonization requires both vaginal and rectal cultures.[24] Tests that detect GBS antigen are available but are not sensitive enough to reliably identify maternal GBS colonization[24] and, in general, are not thought to be of sufficient sensitivity and specificity to establish a diagnosis of GBS infection.[40] Polymerase chain reaction detection of GBS nucleic acids is being investigated as a more rapid and sensitive alternative to culture.[44]

Clinical Infections

GBS neonatal infections are associated with increased morbidity and mortality. GBS invasive infection typically occurs within the first week of life (early-onset disease), and initial case series reported mortality rates as high as 50 percent, which has declined to 4 percent in recent years.[45-47] Manifestations can include pneumonia, sepsis, meningitis, and bone/joint infection. Meningitis is more common in late-onset GBS infection, which occurs from 1 week to 3 months after birth.[45-47] Risk factors for GBS neonatal infection in infants born to colonized mothers include preterm delivery, prolonged membrane rupture during labor, maternal fever during labor, and maternal history of prior infant with GBS sepsis. Rates of neonatal GBS diseases decreased 33 percent from 2003 to 2005, but incidence among black infants increased 70 percent, suggesting racial disparity in prenatal care.[42]

GBS infections during pregnancy are not uncommon.[48] Urinary tract infection due to GBS occurs in 2 to 4 percent of pregnancies.[24] Amnionitis, endometritis, sepsis, or meningitis can also occur in pregnant women, and GBS infection may account for 15 to 25 percent of cases of peripartum fever.[39]

Primary bacteremia without a focal site of infection occurs with GBS infection and carries a high mortality.[39] GBS endocarditis usually occurs in the setting of valvular heart disease and predominantly affects adults over 50 years of age; more than half of patients have an underlying medical condition such as diabetes mellitus, HIV, cirrhosis, neoplasia, or immunologic disease.[39,49] GBS endocarditis is characterized by rapid destruction of the affected valve(s), large vegetations, frequent embolization, and a 50 percent mortality rate.[39,49]

Soft tissue infection is the most common site of focal GBS disease and manifests as cellulitis, foot or decubitus ulceration, and skin abscess, especially in patients with underlying diabetes. More severe disease can occur in the form of pyomyositis or NF, particularly in patients with underlying medical illnesses such as diabetes mellitus.[39,50]

GBS is a significant cause of pyogenic arthritis in nonpregnant adults, typically occurring in middle-aged persons with coexisting illnesses such as diabetes mellitus, malignancy, or liver disease.[51] A high case-fatality rate is associated with these infections. Meningitis is also seen in patients with underlying comorbid conditions and has a mortality rate of 34 percent.[39]

Pathogenesis

In GBS neonatal infections, heavy maternal colonization is associated with an increased risk for preterm labor, which in turn is a significant risk factor for neonatal infection.[39] Intrauterine infection of the fetus therefore likely occurs via ascending spread of GBS from the vagina of a pregnant, asymptomatically colonized woman and subsequent rupture of membranes before 37 weeks' gestation.[24,39] Infants can also become infected during passage through the vaginal canal during childbirth. Neonates with invasive GBS infection display lower titers of maternal antibodies to GBS than healthy neonates whose mothers are colonized with GBS.[39]

The source of GBS infection in the nonpregnant adult and in late neonatal sepsis appears in most cases to be endogenous respiratory, genitourinary, or GI colonization.[39] Virulence factors include capsular polysaccharide, β-hemolysis, C5a peptidase, adhesions, and immunogenic surface proteins.[52]

Treatment

Penicillin is the drug of choice for treatment of GBS infection. Cardiac surgery is usually required for treatment of GBS endocarditis.[49] Antimicrobial resistance of GBS to penicillin has not been described to date.[24] There is increasing resistance to erythromycin and clindamycin, however.[45,53]

Prevention

The use of intrapartum prophylaxis with antibiotics has led to a 70 percent decline in the incidence of GBS neonatal infection since the early 1990s, and a 33 percent decline since 2000 and 2001,[42,54] though GBS disease continues to cause illness and death among newborns.[24] A recent study showed that the risk of neonatal GBS disease decreased by half by culturing all women for GBS at 35 to 37 weeks' gestation and giving intrapartum prophylaxis to carriers, compared with using prophylaxis only if women present in labor with fever, prolonged rupture of membranes, or preterm delivery.[54] These findings led to a recent revision of the original 1996 guidelines on prevention of perinatal GBS infection issued by the CDC.[24] The 2010 guidelines still recommend universal prenatal screening of all pregnant women at 35 to 37 weeks' gestation for vaginal and rectal GBS colonization and intrapartum prophylaxis of colonized women using penicillin. Women with GBS bacteriuria during pregnancy or those who have previously given birth to an infant with GBS disease should also receive intrapartum prophylaxis.[24] Although these recommendations have resulted in decreased neonatal infections, there remains concern that the increased use of antibiotic prophylaxis for GBS could ultimately lead to an increase in prevalence of GBS or non-GBS neonatal infections due to organisms resistant to penicillin.[24,55] The cost-benefit ratio of this strategy has also been questioned.[56] Vaccines for use in pregnant women that would prevent GBS neonatal infection are under study.[57,58]

Standard Precautions are recommended for prevention of healthcare-associated transmission of GBS; proper hand hygiene will decrease the risk of cross-contamination (see Table 94-1).

Streptococcus pneumoniae

S. pneumoniae is the most common cause of community-acquired pneumonia, the most common cause of bacterial meningitis in adults, and the second most common cause of bacterial meningitis in children.[59] It is also the most commonly isolated pathogen in otitis media and acute sinusitis. Two vaccine formulations are available. One is a 23-polyvalent vaccine recommended for all persons aged 65 years and older and anyone aged 2 to 64 years with medical conditions putting them at risk of pneumococcal infection; the other vaccine is a conjugated vaccine and is recommended for all persons aged 2 years and older who have medical conditions that place them at risk for pneumococcal disease. (See following section on Prevention.)

Identification

On Gram stain, pneumococci appear as lancet-shaped Gram-positive diplococci. Colonies of pneumococci have a mucoid or smooth appearance on blood agar as a result of their polysaccharide capsule and are surrounded by a zone of partial hemolysis with a greenish discoloration, known as α-hemolysis. Identification is confirmed by the presence of bile solubility and susceptibility to optochin.[59]

Epidemiology and Transmission

Serious pneumococcal infection is most prevalent in the very young and very old. Patients with bronchopulmonary disease or underlying conditions that compromise immunity are predisposed to pneumococcal infections. Pneumococci are transmitted from person to person through close contact, and infection results from the microaspiration of organisms colonizing the nasopharynx; 5 to 10 percent of healthy adults and 20 to 40 percent of healthy children are colonized with pneumococci,[59] so hospitalized patients do not require isolation. Epidemics of pneumococcal pneumonia occur especially under conditions of crowding and poor ventilation.[60,61] Healthcare-associated pneumococcal infection, particularly pneumonia, can occur, particularly in the elderly or persons with comorbid illnesses.[62] Pneumococcal infection in this setting may arise from the patient's own flora acquired before admission or through horizontal spread after admission.

Diagnosis

A presumptive diagnosis of pneumococcal pneumonia in a patient with compatible signs and symptoms is strongly suggested by the presence of polymorphonuclear leukocytes and Gram-positive diplococci in sputum specimens along with isolation of *S. pneumoniae* in sputum culture.[59] Definitive diagnosis requires isolation of *S. pneumoniae* from blood cultures in the presence of a new pulmonary infiltrate. Approximately 25 percent of patients with pneumococcal pneumonia will have positive blood cultures, though these data are from the preantibiotic era.[59] A urine test that detects pneumococcal polysaccharide can allow rapid diagnosis of pneumococcal pneumonia, and polymerase chain reaction on respiratory secretions is under investigation.[63]

The diagnosis of pneumococcal meningitis may be made by CSF Gram stain and culture or detection of capsular polysaccharide antigen in the CSF via latex agglutination. The latter test may have some use in patients who have received antibiotics before lumbar puncture and have negative CSF Gram stain and culture.[59]

Clinical Infections

Pneumococcal pneumonia is characterized by an often abrupt onset of fever, chills, pleuritic chest pain, and cough productive of rust-colored sputum. Patients usually appear ill with fever to 102°F to 103°F (38.9°C–39.4°C). Subsegmental lobar consolidation is seen on chest radiography in a majority of cases. Empyema (infection of the pleural space) is the most common complication of pneumococcal pneumonia and occurs in 2 percent of cases.[59]

The clinical signs and symptoms of pneumococcal meningitis are similar to those seen in cases of bacterial meningitis caused by other organisms. The greatest mortality occurs in patients at extremes of ages and is estimated at 20 to 60 percent.[59] The rates of pneumococcal meningitis in children and nonimmunized adults have decreased substantially since introduction of the pediatric 7-valent conjugated pneumococcal vaccine.[64,65]

Otitis media and sinusitis are other common manifestations of pneumococcal infection. Less-common clinical syndromes include conjunctivitis, endocarditis, purulent pericarditis, septic arthritis, and soft tissue infection.[59]

Pathogenesis

Pneumococcal colonization of the nasopharynx is common and can be found in up to 60 percent of young children in day care.[59] Once colonization is present, infection can occur when pneumococci move into other areas of the body. Pneumococcal pneumonia, for example, is thought to result from the microaspiration or inhalation of organisms colonizing the nasopharynx. Ciliary clearance mechanisms can remove organisms that enter the sinuses, lungs, or eustachian tubes. Clearance mechanisms can be impaired through smoking, chronic obstructive pulmonary disease, or acute viral infection (e.g., influenza), leading to an increased risk for pneumococcal infection.[59]

Anticapsular antibody is protective against pneumococcal infection, and thus persons with diminished antibody responses to pneumococcus are also at increased risk for infection. Such risk groups include persons with multiple myeloma, HIV infection, and lymphoma. Persons with diabetes mellitus, malnutrition, alcoholism, chronic liver or kidney disease, and sickle cell disease also have a higher incidence of pneumococcal infection than the general population because of a variety of defects in immunity to pneumococcus. Pneumococcal meningitis arises from bacteremic spread to the meninges from another site of colonization or infection.[64]

Treatment

Penicillin G has traditionally been the antimicrobial agent of choice in patients with pneumococcal infection. Recently, however, strains have emerged that are resistant to penicillin and to other antibiotics.[66,67] As discussed below, the trends in antibiotic resistance in pneumococci have reversed since introduction of the conjugated pneumococcal vaccine.[68] Despite resistance, β-lactam antibiotics have been effective for invasive nonmeningeal infections caused by penicillin-resistant pneumococci.[69] Empiric regimens for pneumococcal infection should be based on the prevalence and patterns of drug resistance among pneumococcal isolates in the community.[70] Empiric combination therapy with vancomycin and an extended-spectrum cephalosporin (ceftriaxone or cefotaxime) is recommended for treatment of life-threatening pneumococcal infection (e.g., meningitis) until results of culture and susceptibility testing are known.[71]

Development and Impact of Resistance to Antimicrobial Agents

Penicillin-resistant strains of *S. pneumoniae* are being reported with increasing frequency. Resistance to penicillin is often accompanied by resistance to other antimicrobial agents,[66] including newer-generation fluoroquinolones,[67] though the overall prevalence of newer-generation fluoroquinolone-resistant pneumococci remains low in the United States. Most strains are resistant to older fluoroquinolones, such as ciprofloxacin.[67,72] Resistant strains exhibit altered penicillin-binding proteins that have reduced affinity for penicillin.[59] These strains appear to have emerged by human-to-human spread of a few clonal groups of multiresistant pneumococci. Infection with penicillin-resistant pneumococcal strains occurs with increased frequency in children (particularly those in day care); persons who are elderly, alcoholic, or immunosuppressed; and those previously receiving antimicrobial therapy.[59] The prevalence of these resistance strains has decreased since wide use of conjugated pneumococcal vaccination in children.[68]

Prevention

A vaccine containing polysaccharide from 23 serotypes of *S. pneumoniae* is available and covers 85 to 90 percent of serotypes causing bacteremic pneumococcal disease in the United States.[73,74] The vaccine has been proven effective in preventing pneumococcal bacteremia, but not pneumococcal pneumonia, in older adults.[75] The polysaccharide vaccine is recommended for all persons aged 65 years and older. It is also recommended for all persons aged 2 years and older with medical conditions placing them at risk for pneumococcal disease, including sickle cell disease, asplenia or splenic dysfunction, chronic renal or liver disease, chronic pulmonary or cardiovascular disease, organ transplantation, HIV infection, immunosuppressive drug therapy, alcoholism, or nasopharyngeal CSF leak. Revaccination after 5 years should be performed if there is ongoing risk for pneumococcal infection.[73,74]

The polysaccharide 23-valent vaccine is not effective in children under 2 years of age. A heptavalent conjugate vaccine was recently introduced for use in this population, and it can significantly reduce the incidence of otitis media, meningitis, pneumonia, and invasive pneumococcal disease in children,[64,76-78] and epidemiologic data suggest there may be a secondary decline in invasive pneumococcal disease among nonvaccinated adults.[77] Conjugate vaccines reduce nasopharyngeal carriage of vaccine-type strains, though they increase the frequency of carriage of nonvaccine-type strains.[76] Infections due to nonvaccine strains have increased in prevalence since introduction of the conjugated vaccine; this will have implications for future vaccine development.[68,79]

Patients with pneumococcal pneumonia may be cared for using Standard Precautions, though Droplet Precautions are recommended if there is evidence that transmission has occurred within a facility[37] (see Table 94-1).

Viridans *Streptococcus*

The α-hemolytic and nonhemolytic streptococci other than pneumococci or enterococci are often referred to collectively as the viridans group of streptococci. The term "viridans" refers to the green-colored α-hemolysis that occurs when these organisms are cultured on blood agar. Some of the clinically significant species of viridans streptococci include *S. sanguis, S. salivarius, S. mitis*, and the *S. mutans* group.

Identification

Antigenic analysis of many strains has led to the recognition of a number of immunologic varieties, but only a few are classified into the Lancefield groups (A to O). Viridans streptococci can be distinguished from pneumococci by their bile insolubility and resistance to optochin and from enterococci by their inability to grow in 6.5 percent sodium chloride.[80] Viridans streptococci are fastidious with respect to their nutritional growth requirements, though most strains grow well in blood culture media.[80] The clinically significant species of viridans streptococci can be distinguished by a variety of biochemical tests,[80] though more recently they have been defined on the basis of genetic relatedness through molecular techniques.[81]

Epidemiology and Transmission

Viridans streptococci comprise a large percentage of the flora of the oral cavity and, for example, make up 28 percent of the flora of dental plaque and 45 percent of the flora from the tongue.[80] In addition, they colonize the GI tract and female genital tract and can be part of the skin flora.[80]

The incidence of viridans streptococcal bacteremia is increasing in patients with neutropenia secondary to cancer or bone marrow transplantation (BMT), and viridans streptococcal bacteremias have occurred in 12 to 18 percent of neutropenic transplant recipients.[81] BMT recipients are at particularly high risk, especially patients under 18 years of age, patients undergoing autologous BMT, and patients with a primary diagnosis of acute lymphocytic leukemia.[81-85] Although the recent trend toward use of autologous peripheral blood stem cell transplantation in combination with growth factors significantly reduces the duration of neutropenia, this technique, even with the use

of prophylactic ampicillin, has not reduced the incidence of viridans streptococcal infection.[84] In patients with neutropenic cancer, the presence of mucositis, treatment with high-dose cytosine arabinoside, and prophylaxis with a fluoroquinolone or trimethoprim-sulfamethoxazole all have been identified as risk factors for the development of viridans streptococcal bacteremia.[81,83]

Diagnosis

Although a single positive blood culture for viridans species may be associated with either insignificant transient bacteremia or contamination, persistently positive blood cultures suggest the possibility of endocarditis.[80] In the absence of recent antibiotics, the sensitivity of blood cultures in identifying viridans streptococci causing endocarditis is 96 percent for the first set and 98 percent after two sets of blood cultures.[80]

Clinical Infections

Dental caries is one of the most common manifestations of disease due to viridans streptococci. In the preantibiotic era, viridans streptococci caused 75 percent of cases of endocarditis but currently account for 30 to 40 percent of cases.[80] The clinical course of viridans streptococcal endocarditis is typically subacute and occurs most often in patients with underlying valvular heart disease.

In patients with bacteremia, fever is usually present, and the majority of patients have concomitant oral inflammation/mucositis.[80,81,84] Up to 25 percent of patients with viridans streptococcal bacteremia after BMT can develop a toxic shock-like syndrome with hypotension, rash, and acute respiratory distress syndrome.[81,85] The mortality rate of viridans streptococcal bacteremia in immunocompromised persons has been as high as 12 percent despite adequate antibiotic therapy.[80]

Pathogenesis

Viridans streptococci are organisms of low virulence and do not have endotoxin or produce toxins.[80] Extracellular dextran allows the organisms to adhere to cardiac valves, leading to endocarditis, and viridans streptococci can use sucrose to produce polysaccharides known as glucans that allow adhesion to dental surfaces.[80] The *S. mutans* genome was recently sequenced and found to contain additional virulence genes, including adhesins, proteases, and genes for acid tolerance.[86]

Treatment

Penicillin G has been the drug of choice for viridans streptococcal infections. The combination of penicillin G and gentamicin is synergistic in the treatment of endocarditis and can shorten the course of therapy.[80] Alternatives for penicillin-allergic patients include cephalosporins and vancomycin.

Resistance of viridans streptococci to a number of antibiotics has been increasing, and susceptibility to penicillin can no longer be assumed.[84] A study of 352 isolates of α-hemolytic streptococci revealed that 13 percent demonstrated high-level penicillin resistance, and 43 percent had intermediate resistance to penicillin.[87] Furthermore, a significant percentage of these isolates were also resistant to cephalosporins and erythromycin. Resistance to penicillin and other antibiotics varies among different species of viridans streptococci; therefore, antimicrobial susceptibility testing is important in determining the optimal treatment of viridans streptococcal infections.[80] Speciation and antimicrobial susceptibilities in some laboratories may require special request by managing physicians.

Prevention

Antibiotic prophylaxis against viridans streptococcal infection in patients with neutropenic cancer is controversial because not all studies have shown efficacy,[82] and the routine use of prophylaxis for patients with neutropenia is not recommended.[81] Furthermore, the use of prophylactic antibiotics in this setting has resulted in the emergence of resistance.[81] For example, bacteremia due to viridans streptococci with diminished susceptibility to fluoroquinolones has occurred in stem cell transplant recipients during levofloxacin prophylaxis for neutropenia.[88]

Other Large-Colony β-Hemolytic Streptococcus

Group C streptococci (e.g., *S. equi*, *S. equisimilis*, and *S. zooepidemicus*) are common inhabitants of many animals, including horses, cows, dogs, and birds and can cause significant infections in these animals. Human infections may result from contact with infected animals or animal products. Certain species of group C streptococci can be part of the normal human nasopharyngeal and genital tract flora.[80]

Identification

On blood agar, these organisms grow in large colonies surrounded by a zone of β-hemolysis. Most of these organisms are classified within the Lancefield groups C or G and are less likely to be susceptible to bacitracin than are GAS.[80]

Epidemiology and Transmission

Group G streptococci can colonize the human nasopharynx, skin, and intestinal tract. Infections due to group G streptococci appear to be increasing in frequency and are often seen in the elderly or in patients with underlying malignancy.[80,89] Outbreaks of group G pharyngitis have been reported and in some cases have been thought to be foodborne.[80] Outbreaks, including those of healthcare-associated origin, of cellulitis, and from wound infections due to group C and G streptococci have been reported, with infections resembling those caused by GAS.[90]

Diagnosis

The diagnosis of group C or G streptococcal infection is typically made by recovery of the organisms on culture. Infection due to certain species of group C and G streptococci may result in an elevated ASO antibody titer.[80]

Clinical Infections

Clinical infections are often severe and resemble those caused by group A and B streptococci. Manifestations of clinical disease include pharyngitis, skin and soft tissue infection, septic arthritis, osteomyelitis, bacteremia and endocarditis, and meningitis. In addition, both group C and G streptococci have been associated with puerperal sepsis and endometritis as sporadic cases or epidemic outbreaks.[80]

Pathogenesis

Groups C and G streptococci appear to produce exotoxins and superantigens similar to those of GAS, perhaps explaining some of the likeness to GAS in disease manifestations.[80]

Treatment

Infections due to groups C and G streptococci usually respond well to penicillin G. Other antimicrobial agents active against these organisms include cephalosporins, erythromycin, and vancomycin.

Minute-Colony *Streptococcus*

Minute-colony streptococci form colonies that are very tiny (< 0.5 mm) and may have any of the three hemolytic patterns on blood agar.[91] This genetically heterogeneous group of organisms is often referred to as the *S. anginosus-milleri* group or the *S. intermedius* group and includes *S. intermedius*, *S. constellatus*, and *S. anginosis*. Unlike large-colony streptococci, these organisms are microaerophilic or anaerobic and usually occur in mixed infections with other organisms. A characteristic caramel-like odor on agar cultures is helpful in confirming the presence of the organisms.[92]

Epidemiology and Transmission

These organisms may be found among the normal oral and pharyngeal flora, as well as the GI tract. Minute-colony streptococci tend to cause pyogenic infections with abscess formation, differentiating them from other viridans streptococci.

Diagnosis

Organisms with typical colony morphology and microaerophilic/anaerobic growth can be cultured from sites of infection. Differentiation from other streptococci is based on biochemical testing.

Clinical Infections

Minute-colony streptococci tend to cause pyogenic infections with abscess formation, differentiating them from other viridans streptococci. The most common infections associated with the minute-colony streptococci are liver, abdominal/pelvic, lung, and brain abscesses.[91,93] Bacteremias are often the result of a concurrent suppurative focus of infection, such as a visceral abscess.[91] Cancer and alcoholism have been shown to be risk factors for bacteremia, and pulmonary infections and dental procedures may predispose to head and neck infections due to minute-colony streptococci. Central nervous system infections have been associated with congenital heart disease, sinusitis, and otitis media.[92]

Pathogenesis

The portal of entry for the organisms often involves trauma to a mucosal barrier, as in GI bleeding,[93] or, in the case of lung abscess, can be the result of aspiration.[92] Minute-colony streptococci can grow well in acidic environments, such as those found in abscesses, and produce hydrolytic enzymes that may facilitate spread of infection and production of pus.[92] In vitro studies have shown synergistic growth between minute-colony streptococci and oral anaerobes.[92]

Treatment

The mainstay of treatment for these organisms is penicillin G. Vancomycin, clindamycin, and cephalosporins are also active. Resistance among minute-colony streptococci to penicillin is uncommon but has been described, particularly among *S. anginosus* and *S. intermedius*.[92] Reduced susceptibility to third-generation cephalosporins has also been noted among some strains.[94] In addition to antimicrobial therapy, drainage of abscesses is an important aspect of treatment.

Nonenterococcal Group D *Streptococcus*

The nonenterococcal group D streptococci, for the most part, exhibit α-hemolysis or no hemolysis. They can be distinguished from group D enterococcus by their inability to grow in high salt concentrations. The most common nonenterococcal group D *Streptococcus* to cause human infection is *S. bovis*.

Epidemiology and Transmission

Bacteremias due to *S. bovis* are frequently associated with GI malignancy and chronic liver disease. Fecal carriage of *S. bovis* is more common in patients with malignant colon lesions compared with healthy persons, in whom *S. bovis* colonization is rare.[95] Chronic liver disease appears to be another predisposing factor for *S. bovis* bacteremia.[95]

Clinical Infections

The most important clinical infections caused by *S. bovis* are bacteremias and endocarditis. Evaluation of the GI tract is recommended for persons with *S. bovis* bacteremia to exclude the presence of malignancy.[96]

Pathogenesis

The GI tract is the usual portal of entry for *S. bovis*, though the biliary and urinary tracts and dental procedures may be sources of entry in some cases.[96] Endocarditis typically occurs in the setting of abnormal or prosthetic heart valves.

Treatment

Penicillin is the treatment of choice. Cephalosporins or vancomycin may be used in penicillin-allergic patients.

CONCLUSIONS

The *Streptococcus* genus encompasses a variety of organisms causing mild to severe clinical infections. *Streptococcus* species are often found as commensals in humans and animals and therefore are difficult if not impossible to avoid. Several control measures can be used to prevent the spread of organisms from person to person, the most important of which is hand washing. Vaccines are used for prevention of infection from several *Streptococcus* species but are not available for most organisms. Resistance to antimicrobial agents has been reported in some species and is of increasing concern. As patient populations age and the number of immunocompromised patients increase, infections with *Streptococcus* species will become increasingly important from an epidemiological standpoint. Penicillin remains the drug of choice in the treatment of most streptococcal infections, though there is increasing evidence of antimicrobial resistance in some strains.

FUTURE TRENDS

Current research on streptococcal infections focuses primarily on prevention of infection through vaccine use and development. A vaccine for use in pregnant women that would prevent GBS neonatal infection is currently under study. Several vaccine candidates for the prevention of GAS infections are in various stages of development.[97]

In addition, a new conjugate vaccine appears to be decreasing the incidence of invasive pneumococcal disease in children. Some evidence suggests that there may be a secondary decline in invasive pneumococcal disease among nonvaccinated adults. The emergence of infections caused by nonvaccine strains of pneumococci deserves further study.

INTERNATIONAL PERSPECTIVE

Streptococcus infections are seen worldwide and are epidemiologically important in most countries. The international community should continue to share information about resistance trends, prevention strategies, and outbreaks.[97]

REFERENCES

1. Ruoff KL, Bisno AL. Classification of Streptococci. In: Mandell G, Bennett J, Dolin R, eds. *Principles and Practice of Infectious Diseases*, 7th ed. Philadelphia: Elsevier Churchill Livingstone; 2010:2591–2592.
2. Elsayed S, Laupland KB. Emerging gram-positive bacterial infections. *Clin Lab Med* 2004 Sep;24(3):587–603, v.
3. Wong CJ, Stevens DL. Serious group a streptococcal infections. *Med Clin North Am* 2013 Jul;97(4):721–736, xi-xii.
4. Shulman ST, Bisno AL, Clegg HW, et al. Clinical practice guideline for the diagnosis and management of group A streptococcal pharyngitis:2012 update by the Infectious Diseases Society of America. *Clin Infect Dis* 2012 Nov 15;55(10):1279–1282.
5. Wessels MR. Clinical practice: Streptococcal pharyngitis. *N Engl J Med* 2011 Feb 17;364(7):648–655.

6. Musher DM. How contagious are common respiratory tract infections? *N Engl J Med* 2003 Mar 27;348(13):1256–1266.
7. Farley TA, Wilson SA, Mahoney F, et al. Direct inoculation of food as the cause of an outbreak of group A streptococcal pharyngitis. *J Infect Dis* 1993 May;167(5):1232–1235.
8. Bisno AL, Stevens DL. Streptococcal infections of skin and soft tissues. *N Engl J Med* 1996 Jan 25;334(4):240–245.
9. Stevens DL, Bisno AL, Chambers HR, et al. Practice guidelines for the diagnosis and management of skin and soft-tissue infections. *Clin Infect Dis* 2005 Nov 15;41(10):1373–1406.
10. Jordan HT, Richards CL Jr, Burton DC, et al. Group A streptococcal disease in long-term care facilities: descriptive epidemiology and potential control measures. *Clin Infect Dis* 2007 Sep 15;45(6):742–752.
11. Campbell JR, Arango CA, Garcia Prats JA, et al. An outbreak of M serotype 1 group A Streptococcus in a neonatal intensive care unit. *J Pediatr* 1996 Sep;129(3):396–402.
12. Raymond J, Schlegel L, Garnier F, et al. Molecular characterization of *Streptococcus pyogenes* isolates to investigate an outbreak of puerperal sepsis. *Infect Control Hosp Epidemiol* 2005 May;26(5):455–461.
13. Ejlertsen T, Prag J, Pettersson E, et al. A 7 month outbreak of relapsing postpartum group A streptococcal infections linked to a nurse with atopic dermatitis. *Scand J Infect Dis* 2001;33(10):734–737.
14. Kolmos HJ, Svendsen RN, Nielsen SV. The surgical team as a source of postoperative wound infections caused by *Streptococcus pyogenes*. *J Hosp Infect* 1997 Mar;35(3):207–214.
15. Centers for Disease Control and Prevention (CDC). Nosocomial group A streptococcal infections associated with asymptomatic health care workers—Maryland and California, 1997. *MMWR Morb Mortal Wkly Rep* 1999 Mar 5;48(8):163–166.
16. Arnold KE, Schweitzer JL, Wallace B, Salter M, et al. Tightly clustered outbreak of group A streptococcal disease at a long-term care facility. *Infect Control Hosp Epidemiol* 2006 Dec;27(12):1377–1384.
17. Deutscher M, Schillie S, Gould C, Baumbach J, et al. Investigation of a group A streptococcal outbreak among residents of a long-term acute care hospital. *Clin Infect Dis* 2011 Apr 15;52(8):988–994.
18. Bisno AL, Baracco GJ. Lethal streptococcal outbreak in a long-term acute care hospital: What went wrong and why? *Clin Infect Dis* 2011 Apr 15;52(8):995–996.
19. Thigpen MC, Richards CL Jr, Lynfield R, et al. Invasive group A streptococcal infection in older adults in long-term care facilities and the community, United States, 1998-2003. *Emerg Infect Dis* 2007 Dec;13(12):1852–1859.
20. Hoge CW, Schwartz B, Talkington DF, et al. The changing epidemiology of invasive group A streptococcal infections and the emergence of streptococcal toxic shock like syndrome. A retrospective population based study. *JAMA* 1993 Jan 20;269(3):384–389.
21. O'Brien KL, Beall B, Barrett NL, et al. Epidemiology of invasive group A streptococcus disease in the United States, 1995–1999. *Clin Infect Dis* 2002 Aug 1;35(3):268–276.
22. Laustrup HK, Justesen US, Pedersen C. Household transmission of invasive group A streptococcus with necrotizing fasciitis. *Scand J Infect Dis* 2003;35(6–7):414–415.
23. Gamba MA, Martinelli M, Schaad HJ, et al. Familial transmission of a serious disease producing group A streptococcus clone: case reports and review. *Clin Infect Dis* 1997 Jun;24(6):1118–1121.
24. Verani JR, McGee L, Schrag SJ. Prevention of perinatal group B streptococcal disease: Revised guidelines for the CDC 2010. *MMWR Morb Mortal Wkly Rep* 2010 Nov 19;59(RR-10):1–36.
25. Neuner JM, Hamel MB, Phillips RS, et al. Diagnosis and management of adults with pharyngitis: a cost-effectiveness analysis. *Ann Intern Med* 2003 Jul 15;139(2):113–122.
26. Bisno AL. Diagnosing strep throat in the adult patient: do clinical criteria really suffice? *Ann Intern Med* 2003 Jul 15;139(2):150–151.
27. Bisno AL. Nonsuppurative poststreptococcal sequelae: rheumatic fever and glomerulonephritis. In: Mandell G, Bennett J, Dolin R, eds. *Principles and Practice of Infectious Diseases, 7th ed.* Philadelphia: Elsevier Churchill Livingstone; 2010:2611–2622.
28. Young MH, Aronoff DM, Engleberg NC. Necrotizing fasciitis: pathogenesis and treatment. *Expert Rev Anti Infect Ther* 2005 Apr;3(2):279–294.
29. Stevens DL. Streptococcal toxic-shock syndrome: spectrum of disease, pathogenesis, and new concepts in treatment. *Emerg Infect Dis* 1995 Jul-Sep;1(3):69–78.
30. Cunningham MW. Pathogenesis of group A streptococcal infections. *Clin Microbiol Rev* 2000 Jul;13(3):470–511.
31. Pichichero ME. Penicillin failures?! *Pediatrics* 2002 Jun;109(6):1189–1190; discussion 1190–1192.
32. Martin JM, Green M, Barbadora KA, et al. Erythromycin resistant group A streptococci in schoolchildren in Pittsburgh. *N Engl J Med* 2002 Apr 18;346(16):1200–1206.
33. Katz KC, McGeer AJ, Duncan CL, et al. Emergence of macrolide resistance in throat culture isolates of group A streptococci in Ontario, Canada, in 2001. *Antimicrob Agents Chemother* 2003 Jul;47(7):2370–2372.
34. Richter SS, Diekema DJ, Heilmann KP, et al. Fluoroquinolone resistance in Streptococcus pyogenes. *Clin Infect Dis* 2003 Feb 1;36(3):380–383.
35. Darenberg J, Ihendyane N, Sjolin J, et al. Intravenous immunoglobulin G therapy in streptococcal toxic shock syndrome: a European randomized, double blind, placebo controlled trial. *Clin Infect Dis* 2003 Aug 1;37(3):333–340.
36. Stevens DL. Dilemmas in the treatment of invasive Streptococcus pyogenes infections. *Clin Infect Dis* 2003 Aug 1;37(3):341–343.
37. Siegel JD, Rhinehart E, Jackson M, et al. 2007 Guideline for Isolation Precautions: Preventing Transmission of Infectious Agents in Healthcare Settings. Available at: http://www.cdc.gov/ncidod/dhqp/pdf/isolation2007.pdf.
38. Prevention of Invasive Group A Streptococcal Infections Workshop Participants. Prevention of invasive group A streptococcal disease among household contacts of case patients and among postpartum and postsurgical patients: recommendations from the Centers for Disease Control and Prevention. *Clin Infect Dis* 2002 Oct 15;35(8):950–959.
39. Edwards MS, Baker CJ. Streptococcus agalactiae (Group B Streptococcus). In: Mandell G, Bennett J, Dolin R, eds. *Principles and Practice of Infectious Diseases, 7th ed.* Philadelphia: Elsevier Churchill Livingstone; 2010:2655–2666.
40. Bliss SJ, Manning SD, Tallman P, et al. Group B Streptococcus colonization in male and nonpregnant female university students: a cross sectional prevalence study. *Clin Infect Dis* 2002 Jan 15;34(2):184–190.
41. Meyn LA, Moore DM, Hillier SL, et al. Association of sexual activity with colonization and vaginal acquisition of group B Streptococcus in nonpregnant women. *Am J Epidemiol* 2002 May 15;155(10):949–957.
42. Centers for Disease Control and Prevention (CDC): Trends in perinatal group B streptococcal disease—United States, 2000–2006. *MMWR Morb Mortal Wkly Rep* 2009 Feb 13;58(05):109–112.
43. Dinger J, Muller D, Pargac N, et al. Breast milk transmission of group B streptococcal infection. *Pediatr Infect Dis J* 2002 Jun;21(6):567–568.
44. Haberland CA, Benitz WE, Sanders GD, et al. Perinatal screening for group B streptococci: cost benefit analysis of rapid polymerase chain reaction. *Pediatrics* 2002 Sep;110(3):471–480.
45. Phares CR, Lynfield R, Farley MM, et al. Epidemiology of invasive group B streptococcal disease in the United States, 1999–2005. *JAMA* 2008 May 7;299(17):2056–2065.
46. Lukas SL, Schrag SJ. Clinical sepsis in neonates and young infants, United States, 1988-2006. *J Pediatr* 2012 Jun;160(6):960–965.
47. Edmond KM, Kortsalioudaki C, Scott S, et al. Group B streptococcal disease in infants aged younger than 3 months: systematic review and meta-analysis. *Lancet* 2012 Feb 11;379(9815):547–556.
48. Deutscher M, Lewis M, Zell ER, et al. Incidence and severity of invasive Streptococcus pneumonia, group A Streptococcus, and group B Streptococcus infections among pregnant and postpartum women. *Clin Infect Dis* 2011 Jul 15;53(2):114–223.
49. Sambola A, Miro JM, Tornos MP, et al. Streptococcus agalactiae infective endocarditis: analysis of 30 cases and review of the literature, 1962-1998. *Clin Infect Dis* 2002 Jun 15;34(12):1576–1584.
50. Sendi P, Johansson L, Norrby-Teglund A. Invasive group B streptococcal disease in non-pregnant adults: a review with emphasis on skin and soft-tissue infections. *Infection* 2008 Mar;36(2):100–111.
51. Nolla JM, Gomez Vaquero C, Corbella X, et al. Group B streptococcus (Streptococcus agalactiae) pyogenic arthritis in nonpregnant adults. *Medicine* 2003 Mar;82(2):119–128.
52. Herbert MA, Beveridge CJ, Saunders NJ. Bacterial virulence factors in neonatal sepsis: group B streptococcus. *Curr Opin Infect Dis* 2004 Jun;17(3):225–229.
53. Castor ML, Whitney CG, Como-Sabetti K, et al. Antibiotic resistance patterns in invasive group B streptococcal isolates. *Infect Dis Obstet Gynecol* 2008 (2008), Article ID 727505.
54. Schrag SJ, Zell ER, Lynfield R, et al. A population based comparison of strategies to prevent early onset group B streptococcal disease in neonates. *N Engl J Med* 2002 Jul 25;347(4):233–239.
55. Van Dyke MK, Phares CR, Lynfield R, et al. Evaluation of universal antenatal screening for group B streptococcus. *N Engl J Med* 2009 Jun 18;360(25):2626–2636.
56. Khandelwal M, Harmanli OH. Prevention of early onset group B streptococcal disease in neonates. *N Engl J Med* 2002 Nov 28;347(22):1798–1799; author reply 1798–1799.
57. Baker CJ, Rench MA, Fernandez M, et al. Safety and immunogenicity of a bivalent group B streptococcal conjugate vaccine for serotypes II and III. *J Infect Dis* 2003 Jul 1;188(1):66–73.
58. Edwards MS. Group B streptococcal conjugate vaccine: a timely concept for which the time has come. *Hum Vaccin* 2008 Nov-Dec;4(6):444–448.

59. Musher DM. Streptococcus pneumoniae. In: Mandell G, Bennett J, Dolin R, eds. *Principles and Practice of Infectious Diseases, 7th ed.* Philadelphia: Elsevier Churchill Livingstone; 2010:2623–2642.

60. Hoge CW, Reichler MR, Dominguez EA, et al. An epidemic of pneumococcal disease in an overcrowded, inadequately ventilated jail. *N Engl J Med* 1994 Sep 8;331(10):643–648.

61. Nuorti JP, Butler JC, Crutcher JM, et al. An outbreak of multidrug resistant pneumococcal pneumonia and bacteremia among unvaccinated nursing home residents. *N Engl J Med* 1998 Jun 25;338(26):1861–1868.

62. Paradisi F, Corti G, Cinelli R. Streptococcus pneumoniae as an agent of nosocomial infection: treatment in the era of penicillin resistant strains. *Clin Microbiol Infect* 2001;7(Suppl 4):34–42.

63. Klugman KP, Madhi SA, Albrich WC. Novel approaches to the identification of Streptococcus pneumoniae as the cause of community-acquired pneumonia. *Clin Infect Dis* 2008 Dec 1;47(Suppl 3):S202–S206.

64. Hsu HE, Shutt KA, Moore MR, et al. Effect of pneumococcal conjugate vaccine on pneumococcal meningitis. *N Engl J Med* 2009 Jan 15;360(3):244–256.

65. Thigpen MC, Whitney CG, Messonnier NE, et al. Bacterial meningitis in the United States, 1998-2007. *N Engl J Med* 2011 May 26;364(21):2016–2025.

66. Whitney CG, Farley MM, Hadler J, et al. Increasing prevalence of multidrug resistant Streptococcus pneumoniae in the United States. *N Engl J Med* 2000 Dec 28;343(26):1917–1924.

67. Chen DK, McGeer A, de Azavedo JC, et al. Decreased susceptibility of Streptococcus pneumoniae to fluoroquinolones in Canada. Canadian Bacterial Surveillance Network. *N Engl J Med* 1999 Jul 22;341(4):233–239.

68. Richter SS, Heilmann KP, Dohrn CL, et al. Changing epidemiology of antimicrobial-resistant Streptococcus pneumoniae in the United States, 2004-2005. *Clin Infect Dis* 2009 Feb 1;48(3):e23–e33.

69. Yu VL, Chiou CC, Feldman C, et al. An international prospective study of pneumococcal bacteremia: correlation with in vitro resistance, antibiotics administered, and clinical outcome. *Clin Infect Dis* 2003 Jul 15;37(2):230–237.

70. Mandell LA, Wunderink RG, Anzueto A, et al. Infectious Diseases Society of America/American Thoracic Society Consensus Guidelines on the management of community-acquired pneumonia in adults. *Clin Infect Dis* 2007 Mar 1;44 Suppl 2:S27–S72.

71. Tunkel AR, Hartman BJ, Kaplan SL, et al. Practice guidelines for the management of bacterial meningitis. *Clin Infect Dis* 2004 Nov 1;39(9):1267–1284.

72. Karlowsky JA, Thornsberry C, Jones ME, et al. Factors associated with relative rates of antimicrobial resistance among Streptococcus pneumoniae in the United States: results from the TRUST Surveillance Program (1998-2002). *Clin Infect Dis* 2003 Apr 15;36(8):963–970.

73. Nuorti JP, Whitney CG, Centers for Disease Control and Prevention (CDC). Prevention of pneumococcal disease among infants and children-use of the 13 valent pneumococcal conjugate vaccine and 23-valent pneumococcal polysaccharide vaccine—recommendations of the Advisory Committee on Immunization Practices (ACIP). *MMWR Recomm Rep* 2010 Dec 10;59(RR-11):1–18.

74. Centers for Disease Control and Prevention (CDC); Advisory Committee on Immunization Practices. Updated recommendations for prevention of invasive pneumococcal disease among adults using the 23-valent pneumococcal polysaccharide vaccine (PPSV23). *MMWR Morb Mortal Wkly Rep* 2010 Sep 3;59(34):1102–1106.

75. Jackson LA, Thom E, Simpson JL, et al. Effectiveness of pneumococcal polysaccharide vaccine in older adults. *N Engl J Med* 2003 May 1;348(18):1747–1755.

76. Whitney CG, Farley MM, Hadler J, et al. Decline in invasive pneumococcal disease after the introduction of protein polysaccharide conjugate vaccine. *N Engl J Med* 2003 May 1;348(18):1737–1746.

77. Centers for Disease Control and Prevention (CDC). Pneumonia hospitalizations among children before and after introduction of pneumococcal conjugate vaccine—United States, 1997–2006. *MMWR Morb Mortal Wkly Rep* 2009 Jan 16;58(1):1–4.

78. Hicks, LA, Harrison LH, Flannery B, et al. Incidence of pneumococcal disease due to non-pneumococcal conjugate vaccine (PCV7) serotypes in the United States during the era of widespread PCV7 vaccination, 1998–2004. *J Infect Dis* 2007 Nov 1;196(9):1346–1354.

79. Moore MR, Gertz JE Jr, Woodbury RL, et al. Population snapshot of emergent Streptococcus pneumoniae serotype 19A in the United States. *J Infect Dis* 2005 Apr 1;197(7):1016–1027.

80. Sinner SW, Tunkel AR. Viridans Streptococci, Groups C and G Streptococci, and Gemella morbillorum. In: Mandell G, Bennett J, Dolin R, eds. *Principles and Practice of Infectious Diseases, 7th ed.* Philadelphia: Elsevier Churchill Livingstone; 2010:2667–2680.

81. Tunkel AR, Sepkowitz KA. Infections caused by viridans streptococci in patients with neutropenia. *Clin Infect Dis* 2002 Jun 1;34(11):1524–1529.

82. Bilgrami S, Feingold JM, Dorsky D, et al. Streptococcus viridans bacteremia following autologous peripheral blood stem cell transplantation. *Bone Marrow Transplant* 1998 Mar;21(6):591–595.

83. Bochud PY, Eggiman P, Calandra T, et al. Bacteremia due to viridans streptococcus in neutropenic patients with cancer: clinical spectrum and risk factors. *Clin Infect Dis* 1994 Jan;18(1):25–31.

84. Bruckner L, Gigliotti F. Viridans group streptococcal infections among children with cancer and the importance of emerging antibiotic resistance. *Semin Pediatr Infect Dis* 2006 Jul;17(13):153–160.

85. Reilly AF, Lange BJ. Infections with viridans group streptococci in children with cancer. *Pediatr Blood Cancer* 2007 Nov;49(6):774–780.

86. Ajdić D, McShan WM, McLaughlin RE, et al. Genome sequence of Streptococcus mutans UA159, a cariogenic dental pathogen. *Proc Natl Acad Sci U S A* 2002 Oct 29;99(22):14434–14439.

87. Doern GV, Ferraro MJ, Brueggemann AB, et al. Emergence of high rates of antimicrobial resistance among viridans group streptococci in the United States. *Antimicrob Agents Chemother* 1996 Apr;40(4):891–894.

88. Razonable RR, Burak KW, van Cruijsen H, et al. Bacteremia due to viridans group Streptococci with diminished susceptibility to levofloxacin among neutropenic patients receiving levofloxacin prophylaxis. *Clin Infect Dis* 2002 Jun 1;34(11):1469–1474.

89. Sylvetsky N, Raveh D, Schlesinger Y, et al. Bacteremia due to beta hemolytic Streptococcus group G: increasing incidence and clinical characteristics of patients. *Am J Med* 2002 Jun 1;112(8):622–626.

90. Efstratiou A. Outbreaks of human infection caused by pyogenic streptococci of Lancefield groups C and G. *J Med Microbiol* 1989 Jul;29(3):207–219.

91. Shlaes DM, Lerner PI, Wolinsky E, et al. Infections due to Lancefield group F and related Streptococci (S. milleri, S. anginosus). *Medicine* 1981 May;60(3):197–207.

92. Petti CA, Stratton CW. Streptococcus anginosus Group. In: Mandell G, Bennett J, Dolin R, eds. *Principles and Practice of Infectious Diseases, 7th ed.* Philadelphia: Elsevier Churchill Livingstone; 2010:2681–2685.

93. Bert F, Bariou Lancelin M, Lambert Zechovsky N. Clinical significance of bacteremia involving the "Streptococcus milleri" group: 51 cases and review. *Clin Infect Dis* 1998 Aug;27(2):385–387.

94. Belko J, Goldmann DA, Macone A, et al. Clinically significant infections with organisms of the Streptococcus milleri group. *Pediatr Infect Dis J* 2002 Aug;21(8):715–723.

95. Gonzlez Quintela A, Martinez Rey C, Castroagudin JF, et al. Prevalence of liver disease in patients with Streptococcus bovis bacteraemia. *J Infect* 2001 Feb;42(2):116–119.

96. Arias CA, Murray BE. Enterococcus species, Streptococcus bovis, and Leuconostoc species. In: Mandell G, Bennett J, Dolin R, eds. *Principles and Practice of Infectious Diseases, 7th ed.* Philadelphia: Elsevier Churchill Livingstone; 2010:2643–2653.

97. Dale JB. Current status of group A streptococcal vaccine development. *Adv Exp Med Biol* 2008;609:53–63.

CHAPTER 95

Tuberculosis and Other Mycobacteria

José A Cadena, MD
Assistant Professor of Medicine
Division of Infectious Diseases
University of Texas Health Science Center at San Antonio
Medical Director, Infection Control
South Texas Veterans and Valley Coastal Bend Veterans
    Health Care Systems
San Antonio, TX

ABSTRACT

Tuberculosis remains a significant infection in the United States and around the world. Patients infected with Mycobacterium tuberculosis *can have an asymptomatic infection that can be persistent (latent tuberculosis infection), progressive primary disease, or—years (even decades) later—a reactivation leading to active disease. In most cases, tuberculosis is transmitted from patients with pulmonary or laryngeal disease through airborne droplet nuclei. Prevention of tuberculosis is based on detection of cases, airborne isolation in appropriate negative pressure rooms, respiratory etiquette, use of N95 respirators, and early and complete treatment of tuberculosis cases based on susceptibility testing. Patients with active tuberculosis must be treated for long periods. Many persons infected with* M. tuberculosis *have no signs and symptoms and are said to have latent tuberculosis infection. The tuberculin skin test and the interferon gamma release assays can be used to diagnose latent tuberculosis infection. Persons with latent tuberculosis infection may warrant treatment to prevent the development of active disease.*

KEY CONCEPTS

- Tuberculosis is present worldwide. It is estimated that about one-third of the world's population is infected with tuberculosis.

- The rise of tuberculosis in the United States in the late 1980s and early 1990s, with several documented hospital outbreaks of active tuberculosis and tuberculin skin test conversions, led to a renewed appreciation for the need for aggressive measures to control tuberculoisis in healthcare institutions.

- *M. tuberculosis*, the causative agent of tuberculoisis, is an aerobic, acid-fast bacillus. People are infected with *M. tuberculosis* primarily via inhalation.

- Novel and highly specific molecular testing based on nucleic acid analysis to facilitate early detection of tuberculosis infection are available and validated in high prevalence countries. It also allows for detection of rifampin resistance.

- Patients diagnosed with latent tuberculosis infection should receive therapy to prevent future tuberculosis reactivation. A course of therapy with isoniazid alone for 9 months or the combination of weekly rifapentin and isoniazid for 12 weeks are recommended alternatives.

- Multidrug-resistant tuberculosis and extensively drug-resistant tuberculosis strains have emerged in recent years and are more difficult to treat.

- Nontuberculous mycobacteria can cause a variety of diseases, including pulmonary, skin, and soft tissue infections, especially in immunocompromised individuals.

BACKGROUND

The highest incidence rates of active tuberculosis (TB) occur in Africa (363 cases per 100,000 people) and Southeast Asia (180 cases per 100,000 people in 2006).[1] Because of aggressive control efforts and implementation of the World Health Organization's (WHO's) Stop TB global initiative, the incidence per capita of TB has declined globally, but this has been offset by an increase in the number of cases resulting from population growth.

Case rates for TB in the United States declined from the 1930s through the early 1980s, with the near eradication of TB in the country predicted by the turn of the century.[2] However, rates of TB actually rose in the United States from 9.3 cases per 100,000 people in 1985 to 10.5 cases per 100,000 in 1992.[3-6] The rise in TB during the 1980s and early 1990s correlated with the human immunodeficiency virus (HIV) epidemic.[7]

In New York City, cases of TB declined to historic low levels in 1978 but then began to increase and peaked in 1992.[8] Fires in the Bronx decreased the number of available rental homes and increased overcrowding. Shelters were markedly overcrowded and drug abuse increased, and New York City had one of the highest rates of acquired immunodeficiency syndrome (AIDS) in the country.[8] The rate of drug-resistant TB increased from 6 to 7 percent to 25 percent of infections in 1992.[8] Furthermore, even among those with previous positive tuberculin skin testing (TST), reinfection with drug-resistant organisms was thought to be an important contributor to transmission. By 1994, 20 healthcare personnel had acquired multidrug-resistant TB (MDR-TB); 45 percent of them died. The high incidence of disease was finally curbed and controlled by implementation of expanded treatment regimens, increasing coverage of direct observed therapy (DOT, including involuntary detention and administration of therapy when needed), and implementation of Centers for Disease Control and Prevention (CDC) recommended infection control interventions.[8]

The increase in TB led to renewed vigor in diagnosing and treating patients with TB. This intervention led to a progressive decline in the rate of TB in the United States. By 2011 the rate of TB was 3.4 per 100,000, a decline of 5.8 percent from 2010. TB cases among foreign-born persons comprised 62 percent of the cases in the United States, with a rate of 17.2 per 100,000 in foreign-born versus 1.5 per 100,000 in U.S.-born individuals. The number of TB cases in the United States has decreased by 62 percent since 1992. However, the percentage of TB cases in foreign-born persons has continued to increase since 1993. Six extensively drug-resistant TB (XDR-TB, defined as TB resistant to INH, rifampin, any fluoroquiolone, and at least one of the injectable second line drugs [amikacin, kanamycin, or capreomycin]) cases were reported in 2011.[9]

The proportion of cases that received at least INH, rifampin, and pyrazinamide increased from 72 percent in 1993 to 88 percent in 2011, with the proportion of patients completing therapy increasing from 64 percent to 88 percent in 2009.[9]

Implementation of the CDC's TB infection prevention recommendations may have led to fewer reports of healthcare-associated outbreaks of TB.[8,10]

MYCOBACTERIUM TUBERCULOSIS

TB is produced by the *Mycobacterium tuberculosis* (MTB) complex, which includes *M. tuberculosis, M. bovis, M. canetti, M. africanum, M. microti, M. caprae, M. pinnipedii,* and *M. mungi.* MTB is the most common causative agent of TB in the United States. MTB is an aerobic, poorly staining Gram-positive bacillus. Like other mycobacteria, it is acid-fast, meaning that certain stains, such as Kinyoun or Ziehl-Neelsen, will not decolorize with acid-alcohol. Mycobacteria are not unique in this property. Other organisms, such as *Nocardia* spp., *Rhodococcus* spp., and *Legionella micdadei* may also stain with acid-fast stains under some conditions. Nevertheless, the abbreviation AFB, for acid-fast bacilli, is frequently considered to be synonymous with mycobacteria.[11]

Pathophysiology

TB is usually transmitted through airborne particles, usually 1 to 5 μm in size, that are generated by individuals with pulmonary and laryngeal TB.[10,12] When produced indoors (i.e., hospital room), these particles may be suspended in the air for prolonged periods of time and travel through the ventilation system of the building to infect susceptible individuals located in other areas.[12,13] The infectious droplet can go to the alveoli, be phagocyted by macrophages (where MTB can survive), produce local infection, and, in some cases, disseminate. The mycobacteria first spread to the regional lymph nodes and subsequently disseminate throughout the body. Although the person may have some mild symptoms, the initial infection usually goes unrecognized. During this stage of initial infection, the individual is not contagious unless active disease develops. Specific immunity develops in about 10 to 12 weeks, and further spread of the organism is prevented. Within 2 to 12 weeks the purified protein derivative (PPD) skin test/interferon-γ release assays becomes positive, but infection may remain asymptomatic for several years (latent TB infection or LTBI) or progress to active TB.

Within 2 years of the initial infection approximately 5 percent of persons develop active TB because of a failure of the immune system to control the mycobacteria. If no disease develops within this 2-year period, the patient continues to have a low annual risk of reactivation. In general, the remaining risk is about 5 to 10 percent (for a total lifetime risk of about 10 to 15 percent).[11]

Persons at risk of TB infection include those who have close contact with pulmonary or laryngeal TB cases (in contact for days or weeks), foreign-born persons (within 5 years of arrival to the United States), residents and employees in crowded settings, healthcare personnel (HCP), some underserved/low-income populations, and infants exposed to high-risk adults. [10]

Persons with LTBI at increased risk of progressing to active TB include persons with HIV; persons with PPD conversion within the past 2 years; individuals with silicosis, diabetes mellitus, chronic renal failure/end stage renal disease, hematological malignancies, cancer, or those with 10 percent below ideal body weight; persons receiving immunosuppressive treatments or organ transplant; patients with a history of intestinal bypass or gastrectomy; people with chest radiograph (CXR) consistent with prior TB; and individuals with history of crack cocaine, alcohol, tobacco, and injection-drug use.[10] Diabetes mellitus may be of particular concern given its increasing prevalence in the U.S. population.[14]

Source patients at increased risk of TB transmission include those with cough, cavitations on CXR, positive smears, laryngeal or pulmonary TB involvement, failure to cover mouth when coughing, inappropriate use of TB medications, and those that undergo aerosol-generating procedures such as bronchoscopy (see Table 95-1).[12,13,15,16] In addition, environmental factors such as TB exposures in closed spaces, inadequate ventilation, air recirculation, poor management of specimens, and inadequate cleaning of reusable medical equipment may contribute to transmission.[10,13,17]

Clinical Features

Clinical features of TB are variable. Before the beginning of the HIV epidemic, about 85 percent of TB cases were limited to the lungs and 15 percent had either extrapulmonary or both

Table 95-1. Clinical and Environmental Factors Associated with Increased Risk of TB Transmission

Increased Risk of TB Transmission[8]	
Characteristics of patients with TB that increase risk of transmission	
Sputum/aerosol-producing activities	Studies in the 1960s showed that contacts of individuals that higher cough frequency (greater than 48 times per night) were more likely to have TST conversion. It was also noted that speaking loudly for 5 minutes produced a similar number of infectious particles as a cough. Singing and coughing may be similarly infectious.[13]
Positive AFB smear results	Smear positivity correlates with transmission. Studies performed between 1930 and 1971 showed that close contacts have a 29 to 79 percent chance of having a positive PPD. Household contacts of smear-positive TB cases have a 30 to 50 percent higher rate compared to individuals in their community. Reactivity among smear-negative contacts is 0 to 8 percent.[13,16]
Laryngeal or pulmonary TB cavitation on chest x-rays	Laryngeal TB is highly infectious. Transmission has been documented after very short periods of exposure. This was initially reported in guinea pigs and later in human outbreaks.[12] Patients with cavitary TB are more likely to have persistently positive AFB in the sputum after induction therapy.[18,19]
Inappropriate cough etiquette, respiratory hygiene	Although solid data are lacking, covering the mouth when coughing may lead to decreased aerosolization of infectious particles.
Inappropriate anti-TB treatment	Drug-resistant TB can lead to delays in diagnosis and institution of appropriate therapy, prolonged infectivity, and transmission. This has been well documented among patients with MDR-TB and HIV coinfection. XDR-TB has been associated with very high mortality among HIV patients in developing countries.[15]
Cough-inducing or aerosol-generating procedures	Duration of exposure correlates with infection, and use of cough-generating procedures has been found to further contribute to this. In an outbreak of TB, exposure to patients undergoing respiratory manipulation through mechanical ventilation in an emergency department resulted in TST conversion among 14 percent (16/112) of exposed HCP after only 4 hours of exposure. In addition, a high rate of TST conversion has been reported when respiratory procedures were performed in areas with inappropriate ventilation.[13,17]
M. tuberculosis strain	Some strains have been associated with increased infectiousness. For example, one single strain caused 10 percent of TB infections from 1991 to 1994 in New York City[13]
Environmental factors that facilitate TB transmission	
TB exposure in enclosed/small spaces, inadequate ventilation, recirculation of air	Several outbreaks have been associated with recirculated air. These included not only healthcare settings, but also naval ships, school buses, classrooms, and bars.[13,17,20] Equally important is duration of exposure. Previous studies in patients exposed to a school bus driver described this correlation: the longer the child was on the bus, the more likely he or she was to have positive TST.[13]
Inadequate disinfection of medical equipment	Transmission of TB has been associated with inadequate disinfection of bronchoscopes. Bronchoscopy has also been associated with transmission of TB through aerosolization.[17]
Improper handling of specimens	TB has been transmitted through punctures (i.e., prosector's warts).[13]

pulmonary and extrapulmonary involvement (this can vary depending on the race, ethnicity, age, comorbidities, genotype of MTB strain, and patient immune status).[21,22] Patients with HIV tend to have more atypical presentations, with extrapulmonary compromise occurring in 62 percent of cases. Clinical presentation is variable in HIV-positive patients; patients with CD4 T-cell count of less than 75 may present with disseminated disease, with absent pulmonary symptoms, and a clinical course characterized by chronic fevers, widespread organ involvement, and early mortality.[21] The presence of cough, fevers, night sweats, or weight loss has a sensitivity of 80 percent to detect cases where additional testing to rule out active TB is indicated.[23]

Primary TB infection is usually asymptomatic, with a few patients developing fevers, cough, or erythema nodosum. Patients with advanced HIV disease can develop progressive dissemination during primary infection. Radiological presentation can be variable, but the classic Ghon complex (includes a primary focus of infection, or infiltrate and lymphadenopathy on draining lymph nodes) or, in progressive cases, a miliary pattern can be reported. Dissemination during this primary TB infection can be controlled by the immune system, but multiple nonpulmonary sites of controlled infection can be established and can lead to extrapulmonary disease during postprimary TB reactivation.[21,22,24]

Postprimary TB usually manifests with productive cough, fevers (37 to 80 percent), and night sweats. It is characterized by infiltrates located on the upper lobes or the superior segments of the lower lobes, and is frequently associated with cavitation on chest x-rays. Respiratory symptoms usually last more than 2 to 3 weeks (this is particularly useful to help differentiate from other respiratory illnesses like influenza), and cough may initially be nonproductive but subsequently followed by sputum production as tissue necrosis progresses. Pulmonary TB can be associated with hemoptysis (may be small amounts if secondary to superficial erosion of airway, or massive amounts if it is the result of rupture of a dilated vessel on the pulmonary cavity, known as a Rasmussen aneurysm), weight loss, chest pain, anorexia, malaise, and debilitation.[25,26] Patients with HIV and higher CD4 T-cell counts may have the typical apical infiltrates of postprimary TB. In patients with HIV and low CD4 cell counts, the presentation of pulmonary TB may be atypical with a military pattern, lower lobe infiltrates, or even normal chest x-rays.

Extrapulmonary TB may be associated with different symptoms based on the organ of involvement. TB lymphadenitis usually presents with painless cervical or supraclavicular lymphadenopathy. Disease can progress, developing overlying erythema and eventually sinus tracts. Pleural involvement is characterized by pleuritic chest pain, sometimes without apparent lung parenchymal involvement. Pleural TB may be paucibacillary but occasionally can manifest as empyema. TB meningitis is usually caused by reactivation of MTB or dissemination. It usually involves the base of the brain, and cranial nerve involvement, headaches, and decreased level of consciousness of variable duration (days to weeks) are characteristic. Diagnosis is usually made through lumbar puncture, where a lymphocytic pleocytosis with low glucose and high protein is observed. AFB stain of the cerebrospinal fluid (CSF) requires a large volume sample (usually > 6 mL), but yield is modest. Culture is required for confirmation. Less commonly, TB may present with a focal lesion (tuberculoma) and focal neurological deficits.[22]

TB can involve the spine (Pott disease, usually involving the thoracic spine but possibly involving any level of the spine), it is slowly progressive over weeks to months or even years, and can lead to spinal deformity and, eventually, spinal instability. Involvement of other bones and joints is possible, and the most common manifestation is swelling and pain. Biopsy is required to confirm the diagnosis.[22]

Genitourinary (GU) TB has been associated with sterile pyuria. All levels of the GU tract can be involved, and in males TB can manifest as prostatitis, orchitis, or epididymitis. Clinical features may be subtle and sometimes extensive damage to the GU tract is present before diagnosis is confirmed. In females involvement of the genital tract is more common, with menstrual irregularities, pelvic pain, and infertility being common complaints. Diagnosis is usually obtained through AFB cultures of the urine or tissue biopsy. Pulmonary involvement in patients with GU TB is not uncommon.[22]

Peritoneal involvement in TB may present as ascites, abdominal pain, and weight loss (usually with lymphocytic pleocytosis) and requires peritoneal biopsy and AFB stain for confirmation. Yield of AFB stains in peritoneal fluid is low. If adenosine aminhydrolase is elevated in the peritoneal fluid it may be helpful. Involvement of the gastrointestinal (GI) tract usually occurs proximal to the terminal ileus, but involvement of any area of the GI tract from mouth to anus has been reported. Terminal ileum and cecum are most common sites of GI/abdominal involvement in TB, and clinical manifestations such as pain and obstruction (with or without a mass), ulcerations, and fistulas/fissures are not uncommon.[22]

Pericardial TB may present with fevers, weight loss, and pain, and later with hemodynamic compromise. Dyspnea, orthopnea, and lower extremity edema occur later in the disease course. Pain usually changes with position. Diagnosis usually requires aspiration of pericardial fluid and pericardial biopsy.[22]

Laboratory Diagnosis/Procedures

Active Tuberculosis

Microbiological Diagnosis

The definitive diagnosis of active TB depends on the identification of MTB in specimens from the patient. Patients with suspected TB who are admitted to the hospital should be placed in appropriate airborne infectious isolation (AII), as discussed under Infection Prevention Measures.

Because pulmonary disease is the most common form of TB, patients with suspected TB should have a CXR. If the radiograph is abnormal, or if the patient has respiratory complaints, sputum specimens should be collected for AFB staining and culture or other direct tests. AFB staining and culture of sputum should be obtained three times, at least 8 hours apart, and cultures should be performed on liquid media.[10,21] Having three negative sputum smears is recommended in order to discontinue respiratory isolation.[27] Automatic liquid media systems can help decrease time to positivity (i.e., microbacteria growth indicator tube). In resource limited settings, solid culture media are frequently employed.[21]

If the patient is not producing sputum, respiratory therapists who have been appropriately trained can use nebulized hypertonic saline to induce sputum for laboratory testing. Gastric washings can be used in pediatric patients, as small children often swallow their secretions rather than expectorate.

If sputum specimens are negative for AFB on staining and the diagnosis is uncertain, the patient may need to undergo bronchoscopy with bronchoalveolar lavage (BAL) and perhaps biopsy to obtain additional specimens.

If extrapulmonary disease is suspected, the involved tissue biopsy or fluid should be submitted to the laboratory for testing. In this case, the tissue should be submitted for mycobacterial culture and/or other testing with a portion sent for histopathological preparation with special stains for AFB.

MTB can be cultured in special broth media or on solid media. Although traditionally considered to be slow growing, use of modern broth culture methods allows the organism to be recovered in as little as a few days. Likewise, species identification, which has traditionally required slow biochemical tests, has been improved with the introduction of molecular biological techniques. Deoxyribonucleic acid (DNA) probe and polymerase chain reaction (PCR)-based technologies can often provide definitive species identification on the same day that growth of the organism has been confirmed. Two nucleic acid amplification tests (NAA test) have been approved by the U.S. Food and Drug Administration (FDA) to identify MTB in respiratory specimens even before a specimen smear is AFB positive.[28] These tests allow rapid identification of MTB, but an AFB culture is still required for definitive diagnosis. Additionally, an isolated positive NAA test in a patient with a low clinical suspicion for TB cannot be used to confirm diagnosis.[28]

WHO recommends a first-line molecular diagnostic test that simultaneously detects TB in sputum and evaluates for rifampin resistance. It is a self-contained, automatic cartridge-based nucleic analysis system that can identify targeted nucleic acid sequences. The rifampin resistance is amenable to testing because 95 percent of resistant isolates have mutations on the *rpoB* gene, which encodes the active site of the bacterial

RNA polymerase. The sensitivity of the assay is two orders of magnitude better than sputum microscopy—as good as solid culture media but slightly lower than liquid culture media. This test has been validated in large clinical trials performed in resource-limited settings. The sensitivity of the test is around 90.4 percent and the specificity is 98.4 percent. The sensitivity of the assay is slightly lower for HIV-positive patients with pulmonary TB. The test has been mostly studied for the diagnosis of pulmonary TB; in the future, as more data become available, use in extrapulmonary sites may be possible.[29]

Susceptibility

Although DNA technologies are extremely helpful in speeding the diagnosis of TB, cultures will still be required for the foreseeable future because identification of antimicrobial sensitivities requires growth of the organism. Susceptibility testing should be done on an initial isolate from every patient with newly diagnosed TB. Likewise, susceptibility testing should be done if the patient remains culture positive after 3 months of treatment.[23] Globally, MDR-TB has increasingly become a problem.[1] About 310,000 cases of MDR-TB were reported in 2011. Most of these cases were reported from China, India, Russian, Pakistan, and South Africa. Furthermore, XDR-TB was identified in the United States in 1993. The annual number of cases has decreased from 18 in 1993 to two in 1997.[30] In 2008, there were five cases; in 2009, zero cases; in 2010, one case; and in 2011, six cases.[9] Patients with XDR-TB have a high mortality rate. In a study from Africa, mean time to death after diagnosis was 16 days.[31]

There are several possible techniques that may be used for TB susceptibility testing. The most widespread is the agar proportion method on Löwenstein-Jensen agar and Middlebrook 7H11 agar. However, the accuracy of this method to evaluate resistance to second line drugs is less well established. Rifampin resistance can be detected within 2 hours. The microscopic observation drug susceptibility assay (MODS) uses a liquid culture media to observe microscopic growth of MTB and evaluate drug resistance.[31]

Clinical Diagnosis

Although actual growth of MTB from patient specimens is required for the definitive diagnosis of TB, a presumptive diagnosis may be made on clinical grounds. Patients who present with an appropriate clinical history and characteristic CXR findings (e.g., upper lobe infiltrates) may be started on appropriate therapy (see section on therapy of active disease) while sputum specimens are being obtained.

If a patient is thought to have TB, even if the sputum or tissue specimens are AFB smear-negative, anti-TB drug therapy should be continued empirically. Even if the organism fails to grow, a clinical response to anti-TB therapy is sufficient to make a presumptive diagnosis of TB and finish a full course of treatment. Likewise, the presence of caseating granulomas on tissue biopsy or the presence of lymphocytic pleocytosis and

hypoglycorrhachia in the spinal fluid may be sufficient, along with the patient's clinical presentation, to commit the patient to a full course of anti-TB therapy, even if the organism does not grow.[32]

Latent Tuberculosis Infection

Screening and treatment of LTBI is recommended for groups with high prevalence of LTBI and/or those at risk for TB exposure/disease. Two methods of screening are currently recommended: TST or interferon gamma release assays (IGRA).[33]

Tuberculin Skin Test

TST involves injection of purified protein derived from the mycobacterial cell wall. The test relies on the fact that persons who have been infected with TB will have a delayed-type hypersensitivity reaction to this reagent. The TST is a screening tool to detect people with LTBI; it cannot be used for ruling in or ruling out active TB. This is because a positive TST merely indicates a history of LTBI at some time in the past—it conveys no information regarding the current status of the person's infection (which may even have been cured previously). Likewise, a negative test does not rule out active TB because people with active TB may well have a negative TST even in the presence of positive controls. (It is for this reason that control testing is no longer recommended—it adds no clinically useful information.[33]) In fact, up to 20 percent of persons with active TB will have negative TST results.

Candidates for Screening

TST should be done for those at risk for acquiring TB so that treatment of LTBI can be instituted to prevent the development of active disease. HCP, employees and inmates of prisons, nursing home residents and employees, foreign-born persons from areas with high endemic rates of TB, intravenous (IV) drug users, homeless persons, residents of inner city neighborhoods, and patients with HIV, end-stage renal disease, diabetes, or other immunosuppressing diseases should be tested. People exposed to a patient with active TB should also be tested. Pregnancy is not a contraindication for TST.[10]

Mantoux Test

The preferred way to perform TST is by the Mantoux method.[8,10] A tuberculin syringe is used to inject 5 tuberculin units (5 TU—usually 0.1 mL) of PPD intradermally. The test is generally placed on the volar (palmar) surface of the forearm, but it may be placed on the dorsal surface if necessary. A properly placed test raises a small wheal at the site of injection.

The TST is read 48 to 72 hours after placement. A positive test is determined by the number of millimeters of induration (not erythema) caused by the reaction to the tuberculin. Different cut points are used depending on the likelihood of the individual having a TB infection and on the likelihood of progressing to active TB if infection is present. Criteria for TST interpretation

Table 95-2. Criteria for Positive Mantoux Tuberculin Test Reactions[34]

Induration Size (mm) For Positive Test	Group
≥5 mm	HIV-positive persons Recent contacts of TB case Fibrotic changes on CXR consistent with old TB Patients with organ transplants and other immunosuppressed patients (≥ 15 mg/day prednisone for 1 month)
10mm	Recent arrivals (< 5 years) from high-prevalence countries Injection drug users (HIV-negative) Residents and employees of high-risk congregate settings: healthcare facilities, prisons, shelters, etc. Mycobacteriology lab personnel Persons with high-risk clinical conditions (e.g., chronic renal failure, silicosis, gastrectomy, malnutrition) Medically underserved high-risk minorities Children < 4 years of age or infants and children exposed to adults in high-risk categories
≥15 mm	Persons with no risk factors for TB

developed by the CDC and the American Thoracic Society (ATS)[10,34,35] are listed in Table 95-2. It is important to note the actual number of millimeters of induration when recording a TST result, and not just negative or positive, because new information about the patient may change the interpretation of the test. In addition, for persons receiving serial TSTs the exact size is important in interpretation of subsequent tests. A test is considered a conversion (i.e., a change from negative to positive) if there is an increase in the amount of induration by 10 mm compared with the previous test.[34]

Interferon Gamma Release Assays

In 2001 the FDA approved the first IGRA, but it was less specific than the TST. More recently, new IGRAs that are more specific have been developed. They evaluate the release of interferon gamma from the host cell when exposed to TB proteins such as the early secretory antigenic target 6 (ESAT-6) and the culture filtrate protein 10 (CFP-10). These proteins are present on MTB organisms but absent from BCG strains, and most nontuberculous mycobacterium, increasing the specificity of the test (these antigens are present on *M. marinum*, *M. kansasii*, and *M. szulgai*). In 2007 a test was approved allowed for the antigens to be in contact with blood in special tubes. After an incubation period of about 12 to 16 hours, the plasma is separated and interferon gamma can be measured. Specificity of this test is high, around 99 percent.[33]

Finally, in July 2008, a test was approved by the FDA that used an enzyme-linked immunospot assay is used to measure the number of cells that secrete interferon gamma (spots at each test well). Specificity is around 88 percent.[33]

TST and IGRAs can both be used to diagnose latent TB infection. Both groups of tests have limitations. TST may be better to detect remote exposures, but IGRAs can be more specific. There is some individual variations on interferon gamma release in individuals, so occasional reversion or conversion of IGRAs

have been reported on serially tested individual patients.[36] TST is preferred in children under 5 years of age, as more data are available for TST than for IGRAs in this population. IGRAs may be preferred in patients with a history of bacillus Calmette–Guérin (BCG) therapy for bladder cancer or vaccination and on those unlikely to return for reading if TST is administered.[33]

Whereas the sensitivity of QFT-G for detecting MTB infection in persons with untreated, culture-confirmed TB is approximately 80 percent in published studies,[37,38] its sensitivity for particular groups of TB patients (e.g., young children and immunocompromised patients) has not been determined. The agreement between QFT-G and TST results in persons at increased risk for LTBI facilitated approval and acceptance of TST.[33]

QFT-G can be used in all circumstances in which the TST is used, including contact investigations, evaluation of recent immigrants who have had BCG vaccination, and TB screening of HCP and others undergoing serial evaluation for MTB infection. QFT-G usually can be used in place of (and not in addition to) the TST.[33,39,40]

Treatment

Therapy of Active Disease

Initial therapy for active TB will always need to be started before antimicrobial sensitivities are known and, frequently, even before the organism itself has been cultured. Appropriate treatment of TB should include at least two drugs to which the organism is sensitive to prevent the development of resistance. Comprehensive treatment recommendations for TB have been provided by the ATS, CDC, and the Infectious Diseases Society of America.[41]

To ensure that at least two effective drugs are being given, patients are typically started on four-drug therapy with INH, rifampin (RIF), pyrazinamide (PZA), and ethambutol (EMB). If there is a high likelihood that the patient has TB that is resistant to more than one drug, more than four drugs may need to be given initially. This should be done in consultation with someone experienced in treating MDR-TB. If XDR-TB is suspected, specialist care is essential. In some circumstances (e.g., pregnancy or severe liver disease), the typical initial regimen must be altered; this, too, should be done by someone experienced in treating TB. The final drug regimen can be determined once sensitivities are known.

Directly observed therapy (DOT) should be considered the standard of care for all patients, regardless of the individual's clinical or social status.[42] TB treatment regimens require taking multiple drugs consistently for a long period of time. Failure to take the drugs appropriately may lead to the development of MDR-TB and almost certainly to treatment failure. Compliance with multiple self-administered drugs (prescribed for any reason) is very poor, and HCP cannot reliably predict who will or will not be compliant. With DOT, HCP deliver the medication and watch the patient take the pills. DOT allows for the option of doses being given less frequently than daily. Patient self-administered therapy should be taken daily to minimize the impact of the occasional missed dose.

Typically, after a 2-month initial phase, a continuation phase using fewer drugs can be used once sensitivities are known. The total duration of therapy is typically 6 months but may be longer, depending on circumstances. Patients with extrapulmonary TB are generally treated the same as patients with pulmonary disease, though MTB meningitis and bone and joint disease are often treated for 9 to 12 months. Patients with pulmonary cavities that remain culture positive after 2 months of appropriate therapy usually require extension of the maintenance phase with INH and RIF from 4 to 7 months (total of 9 months of therapy) due to the high failure rate (around 22 percent) with a 6-month course of therapy.[41]

All patients should have at least monthly sputum samples collected for stain and culture to document clearing of the infection. Patients who do not respond appropriately should be referred to someone experienced in the treatment of TB. Two or more drugs should be added to a failing regimen (never one agent alone given risk of developing resistance).[41]

Patients started on therapy should have a baseline aspartate aminotransferase (AST), visual acuity, and color vision check. While on therapy, patients should be monitored clinically for drug toxicity; hepatotoxicity (liver) is the most common adverse reaction. Although most often caused by INH, hepatotoxicity may also be caused by RIF and PZA. EMB has ocular (eye) toxicity. Pyridoxine (vitamin B6) supplements should be considered in patients on INH to reduce the risk of peripheral neuropathy (see section on INH in the treatment of LTBI).

Treatment of Latent Tuberculosis Infection

All persons found to have a positive TST or IGRA (as discussed) should be evaluated for the presence of active TB. This evaluation should include questions about possible exposures to TB, a review of symptoms that might be suggestive of TB (e.g., fever, night sweats, weight loss, or cough lasting more than 2 weeks), a lung exam, and CXR. Patients with a suggestive CXR (e.g., an upper lobe or cavitary infiltrate) or suggestive symptoms should have three sputum specimens collected for AFB stain and culture. Treatment of LTBI should be withheld in such patients until cultures are negative to prevent the possibility of treating active TB with only a single drug. If there is a strong suspicion of active TB, four-drug therapy should be started (see Therapy of Active Disease).

Because of the relatively high risk of developing TB within 2 years of the initial exposure, all persons who have had a negative skin test within the previous 2 years and who now have a positive test (recent converters) should be treated for LTBI, regardless of age. Likewise, in patients who are at risk for TB (including, but not limited to, patients with HIV, patients on steroids or other immunosuppressive drugs, recent contacts of patients with active TB, patients with diabetes mellitus, patients with end-stage renal disease, and immigrants from areas with

high endemic rates of TB who have been in the United States less than 5 years), a positive TST is generally considered an indication for treatment even if the TST is not a recent conversion.[34]

In general, any patient with LTBI should be considered for preventive therapy.

Isoniazid

INH, 5 mg/kg (up to 300 mg) as a daily oral dose, is the drug of choice for treatment of LTBI. The most recent recommendations are for 9 months of therapy with INH for children and adults, including adults with HIV.[34,43]

Drug-induced hepatitis is the most concerning potential side effect of INH. The incidence increases with age, from essentially 0 percent in those under 20 years of age to 2 to 3 percent in those over 50. Excessive ethanol ingestion increases the risk of hepatic toxicity. Nonalcoholic liver disease may also increase the risk, though this is less clear. Patients taking INH should be monitored for symptoms of hepatitis (malaise, nausea/vomiting, abdominal pain, jaundice, and scleral icterus) at least monthly. If monthly follow-up is not possible, INH should not be prescribed. Monthly screening of serum transaminases (liver enzyme tests, including AST and alanine aminotransferase [ALT]) can be considered but is expensive, compliance can be difficult, and it is not recommended as a routine measure. AST or ALT should be checked in any patient who reports symptoms that may be attributable to drug-induced hepatitis; the INH doses should be held pending results of the test. INH therapy should be stopped in any symptomatic patient with a transaminase level more than three times the upper limit of normal and in any asymptomatic patient with a transaminase level more than five times the upper limit of normal. Patients with a less-significant elevation should be followed closely with serial enzyme evaluations. Hepatic toxicity is usually completely reversible if the drug is stopped promptly, but fatal cases of INH-induced hepatitis have been reported.

Pyridoxine (vitamin B6) clearance is increased in patients taking INH. Pyridoxine deficiency can lead to peripheral neuropathy, with initial manifestations of numbness and tingling in the hands and feet. Pyridoxine should be given to all patients with poor nutrition or at increased risk for developing peripheral neuropathy (e.g., alcoholics, diabetic patients, pregnant women) at a dose of 50 mg taken orally every day. Consideration should be given to giving pyridoxine to all patients on INH.

Rifampin for the Treatment of LTBI

In patients with a positive TST who warrant treatment of LTBI but who cannot take INH, and in those whose positive skin test has a high likelihood of being caused by INH-resistant MTB (e.g., recent converters after an exposure to a patient with INH-resistant TB), RIF 10 mg/kg (max 600 mg) in a daily oral dose can be given for 4 months. If the patient is taking other medications that may interact with RIF, or if the patient wears soft contact lenses that will be stained by RIF in the tears and is not at very high risk for the development of active TB, then withholding therapy and monitoring for signs or symptoms of active TB is an acceptable alternative. Recent studies suggest that overall adverse drug events are less common with a 4-month RIF regimen.[44] This, combined with the significantly shorter duration of therapy, may lead to higher overall rates of compliance. This is an area of active investigation.

Rifapentine and INH for Treatment of LTBI

Therapy for LTBI with 9 months of INH is difficult given prolonged duration of therapy. The rate of completion of INH therapy may be as low as 60 percent. More recently, the combination of rifapentine and INH weekly for 12 weeks has been proposed as an alternative to INH. Benefits observed are a higher rate of completion of therapy and shorter duration of therapy with a minimal increase in adverse events.[45] Disadvantages include the recommendation to administer as DOT and the slightly higher rate of adverse events in the combination group.

The INH/rifapentine combination is recommended in individuals who are at least 12 years of age and are at risk for developing active TB (such as exposure to active TB, recent TST or IGRA conversion, or radiological findings of healed TB). The choice between the combination regimen and the INH monotherapy should be based also on the feasibility of DOT implementation and the individual social and medical situation of the patient.[46]

Other Regimens to Avoid and Management of LTBI in Contacts with MDR-TB

At one time a 2-month regimen of RIF plus PZA was considered an acceptable alternative therapy for LTBI when INH could not be used. However, this regimen is no longer recommended because of high rates of drug-induced hepatitis (sometimes fatal) and should only be considered under unusual circumstances.[47]

For persons who have converted their skin tests after exposure to patients with MDR-TB, consideration can be given to using multiple drugs to which the organism was sensitive or forgoing treatment of LTBI and monitoring the patient for evidence of active TB. This decision should involve both the patient and a physician experienced in dealing with MDR-TB.

Bacille Calmette-Guérin Vaccination

BCG is an attenuated strain of *M. bovis* that is given as a live bacterial vaccine to prevent the development of active TB. Studies of BCG have shown a wide range of effectiveness, from 0 to 80 percent.[48-51] Part of the difficulty in interpreting any of these studies is that there is no standard preparation of BCG. Nevertheless, in areas where TB is highly endemic, BCG vaccination is probably an effective strategy in reducing severe cases of TB, especially in children.

BCG vaccination may induce an induration on a TST, the degree to which it does wanes with time. Current recommendations in the United States are to interpret TST results without considering BCG vaccination status, because a positive test is much more likely to represent latent TB than to represent an unusually strong BCG reaction.[52]

BCG is not recommended in most HCP in the United States given its unproven efficacy to prevent TB in adults.[53] BCG is recommended for those who are continuously exposed to patients with active MDR-TB in settings where transmission to HCP is likely and comprehensive control measures have not been successful. Because it is a live vaccine, BCG should not be given to HIV-infected or otherwise severely immunocompromised persons.

Infection Prevention Measures

Tuberculosis Prevention in Healthcare Settings

TB remains a safety challenge for healthcare systems in the United States. In the recent past, there were multiple reports of patients who acquired the infection while receiving medical care.[54-56] This is partly due to the complexity of the diagnosis, atypical presentations, and, perhaps, the perception that TB is a problem of the past—as the disease became less prevalent over the past 15 years.[55,57-60] In addition, it is difficult to trace unsuspected exposures in healthcare settings, and screening methods like TST may not always be useful.[10,18] Many clinicians may not have frequently treated TB given its declining prevalence, and some specialties are less likely to make an early diagnosis of TB, leading to delays in airborne isolation.[55,59] Furthermore, it seems like TB transmission in healthcare settings frequently goes undetected. In some low prevalence countries, TB is only suspected by epidemiological links in about 25 percent of the cases.[18] HCP tend to be frequently affected. Also, patients that are part of clusters tend to have more pulmonary disease and cavitary disease, which have been shown to be associated with increased risk of transmission.[10,18]

Early detection and diagnosis of TB and LTBI may be challenging when testing foreign-born HCP due to misperceptions regarding TST interpretation in the setting of remote BCG vaccination and perceived low risk of active TB.[61] Failure to detect or prevent active TB has led to extensive contact investigations and transmission to patients. Availability of more specific tests to diagnose LTBI, like interferon release assays, may help reduce the concerns about false-positive PPD tests in HCP with prior BCG vaccination.[61,62]

Although interferon gamma release assays are more specific, they tend to be more expensive and can still have occasional false-positive results. as some organisms like *M. kansasii*, *M. szulgai,* and *M. marinum* can have ESAT-6 and CFP-10, which induce release of interferon measured by these assays.[61] Currently, they can be used in the same settings as TST, but they share limitations, including the fact that they measure an immunological response, which may lead to false negatives among immunosuppressed patients.[62]

The dynamics of TB transmission in hospital settings are complex. Although pulmonary TB is most commonly implicated in outbreaks, extrapulmonary and disseminated TB have been shown to lead to potential clusters of transmission. D'Agata et al. reported a case of disseminated TB that manifested as fever and testicular pain and was found to have an associated prostatic abscess, requiring orchiectomy and packing of the wound and twice a day irrigation. The patient's radiographs were originally normal and, as his condition deteriorated, showed only interstitial infiltrates that improved with diuresis. The patient underwent BAL, and cultures were negative for AFB (no biopsies were taken). The patient died, and disseminated TB with caseating granulomas was noted in several tissues, including the lungs. At that facility, the rate of PPD conversion was 0.2 percent. Among the providers in contact with the patient after the surgery (nurses, students, and pathology personnel), 12/95 (13 percent) had a PPD conversion to more than 10 mm. The major risk factor for PPD conversion was packing of the wound.[56]

Failure to isolate patients with active TB is not uncommon in North America. In Canada, Greenaway et al. evaluated the management of TB patients including 429 patients admitted to 17 hospitals over a 3-year period. They found that TB diagnoses were initially missed in 45 percent of cases, and even after 1 week, 30 percent of the patients were still not properly treated.[60] They found that atypical manifestations and absence of cough were associated with delayed diagnosis. They further classified hospitals among those with low, moderate, and high admission rates of TB patients; the ones with higher rate of admission were less likely to delay isolation. Hospitals with lower rate of TB patient admission were also most likely to get TST conversion, even after adjusting for other factors.[60]

Several interventions to prevent and control the spread of TB have been proposed.[63] Since 1889 the New York City Department of Health recommended a comprehensive management program including surveillance, public education, isolation of infectious patients, and free laboratory testing of patients. This program expanded and eventually suffered from its own success. In 1988, only eight of the original 24 TB clinics remained. The diminished public health efforts to control TB and the HIV epidemic resulted in a cure rate of more than 50 percent of patients with TB by 1989, higher proportions of resistance, and high rates of relapse. Outbreaks of TB became common in hospitals.[63] However, in 1992 several interventions were implemented, including reinstitution of DOT (proportion of completion of therapy increased to 90 percent), intense case management, and (in only about 1 percent of cases) involuntary detention. Individual housing was provided to homeless persons (instead of large communal dormitories), and practices to screen, isolate, and follow up with incarcerated individuals with TB were implemented. Treatment regimens were expanded to include four medications in about 89 percent of cases.[63] This led to a significant decrease in the incidence of TB as early as 1994.[63]

In 2005, the CDC recommended a multilevel intervention strategy to prevent healthcare-associated TB transmission, and in 2009 the WHO published similar recommendations (see Table 95-3).[10,76] The intervention strategies included implementation of administrative, environmental, and respiratory protection controls.[10,76] The effectiveness of these protective intervention strategies is dependent on HCP recognizing and isolating patients with pulmonary TB. A deviation from the CDC protocols due to the delay in identifying and diagnosing TB or placing patients with suspected TB under appropriate isolation precautions has been associated with an increased

Table 95-3. CDC and WHO Recommendations for Preventing TB Transmission in Healthcare Settings

	CDC[10]	WHO[76]
Administrative controls	• Assign responsibility for TB infection control • Conducting TB risk assessment • Disseminate written TB infection control plan to detect, isolate (airborne), and treat suspected or confirmed TB cases • Timely availability, testing, and reporting of testing to infection control and ordering provider • Effective practices for management of suspected or confirmed TB cases • Proper cleaning and disinfection of contaminated equipment • Train HCP on TB prevention, transmission, and symptoms • Screening and management program of HCP at risk for, with, or exposed to TB • Use epidemiology-based prevention principles such as using setting related infection data • Use signs advising proper infection control practices (i.e., respiratory hygiene and cough etiquette) • Coordinate with local or state health department efforts to control TB	• Develop facility plan for TB control, promote local coordinating bodies for TB prevention/control • Optimize use of available spaces and consider renovation or additional construction to optimize implementation of controls • On-site surveillance of TB among HCP; assess the facility • Advocacy, communication, and social mobilization for patients, HCP, and visitors • Evaluate and monitor TB control measures • Participate in research • Triage, separation of TB patients, infection control strategies (cough etiquette/respiratory hygiene), and decrease time in healthcare facility • Prevention of HIV for HCP, ART for those who are positive, and LTBI and TB treatment • Rapid testing, shorter turnaround time of testing, parallel rather than sequential investigation of cases and use of algorithms
Environmental controls/ personal protective equipment	• Develop and implement a respiratory protection program • Train HCP on respiratory protection and patients on respiratory hygiene and cough etiquette • Use and availability of negative-pressure rooms based on risk assessment (ongoing monitoring of negative-pressure ventilation rooms) • UV light may be used in addition to appropriate ventilation	• Use of respirators • Ventilator systems: ideally 12 air exchanges per hour • UV light irradiation when appropriate/ventilation not available
Additional comments	Infection prevention interventions are based on predefined risk assessments, which place settings in one of three categories: low risk, medium risk, or ongoing transmission. Need for HCP PPD screening is defined based on these categories.	Includes elements of TB prevention not only in the healthcare setting but also at the national and subnational levels.

rate of TST conversion (marker of TB infection).[64] This has been described in multiple healthcare-associated outbreak investigations.[65-70] Failure to follow isolation precaution guidelines places not only other patients but also HCP at high risk of developing active TB.[66] Furthermore, TB-infected HCP can lead to TB transmission to coworkers, patients, and visitors,[61] which has serious implications for patient safety. This has been described in outpatient and inpatient settings, adult and children populations, and hemodialysis centers.[71-75] TB exposure investigation and postexposure follow-up can be difficult. In Atlanta, an extensive investigation of healthcare-associated transmission of TB identified eight HCP who developed active pulmonary TB and subsequently exposed 586 patients. Facility and county health department personnel were able to contact 34 percent of those exposed to complete an appropriate evaluation. Approximately 72 percent of the patients were lost to follow-up, many of whom were homeless and HIV positive and were at high risk of developing active TB.[75] Possible infection prevention and control measures that could have prevented the outbreak include timely detection of TB in both patients and HCP, prompt initiation of Airborne Precautions for suspected TB cases (i.e., placement of patients in negative pressure rooms and use of N95 respirators by HCP), initiation of appropriate anti-TB therapy, adherence to guidelines for discontinuing isolation, and annual training and TB testing for HCP.[10]

Despite the widespread implementation of effective and evidence-based interventions (like the CDC and WHO guidelines to prevent TB), TB exposure continues to occur in U.S. healthcare settings, and additional research has been initiated to evaluate the causes of the failure of the proposed controls, in particular in regions where TB continue to be more prevalent.[10,76]

Tuberculosis Control Plan

The rise of TB in the United States in the late 1980s and early 1990s, with several documented hospital outbreaks of active TB and TST conversions, led to a renewed appreciation for the need for aggressive measures to control TB in healthcare institutions. In 1994, the CDC published extensive guidelines on what should be considered when developing a TB control plan.[77] The CDC revised the guidelines in 2005 to include recommendations for laboratories and additional outpatient and nontraditional healthcare settings. These guidelines include expanded measures aimed at reducing incidence of TB and eliminating TB transmission from undiagnosed patients to HCP.[10]

Control measures should be undertaken for patients who are likely to be contagious. Patients with pulmonary or laryngeal disease (or suspected disease) are considered contagious. Most patients with extrapulmonary TB are not contagious because the organism is not aerosolized. Exceptions occur when a mechanism for aerosolizing the MTB organisms is provided. For instance, HCP have been infected by irrigating cutaneous wounds caused by MTB, as well as during the performance of autopsies on patients with extrapulmonary TB.[78-80]

Risk Assessment

The first step in developing a TB control plan is to assess the institution's TB risk. This depends on both the prevalence of recognized and unrecognized TB patients in the healthcare facility and in the surrounding community, as well as on patterns of TST conversions or positive blood assay for *M. tuberculosis* (BAMT) results in employees. Risk categories, now simplified in the 2005 CDC guidelines (low risk, medium risk, and potential ongoing transmission), can be assigned to individual areas of the facility using criteria listed in Table 95-4. A low-risk assignment can be applied to settings in which persons with TB are not expected to be encountered or to areas in which patients are not seen (e.g., administrative areas). In addition, a medium-risk category can be assigned to persons in settings who will be exposed to persons with TB or clinical specimens that might contain MTB. The new classification of potential ongoing transmission should be applied to any setting (or group of HCP) if evidence of person-to-person transmission of MTB has occurred during the preceding year. These risk categories also define what screening procedures should apply to HCP in each setting.[10] If there is difficulty in classifying a setting as low or medium risk, the setting should be classified as medium risk.

Administrative Controls

Administrative controls consist of the policies and procedures used to identify patients with potential TB as rapidly as possible so that they may be appropriately isolated and other controls initiated. Administrative controls are the most important part of a TB control plan, because other controls rely on appropriate identification of pulmonary TB patients.

In healthcare facilities at low risk that do not admit patients with TB, plans should include methods for identifying patients who may potentially have TB, mechanisms for appropriately isolating the patient while arrangements for transfer are being made, and applying a surgical mask to the patient.

In healthcare facilities that do admit patients with TB, administrative plans should include methods for identifying patients with possible TB. This may include the radiology department notifying the infection preventionist of all suspicious CXR and the microbiology lab providing notification of patients on whom an AFB stain and culture have been ordered. Some institutions automatically isolate all patients with HIV (and other high-risk patients) who have any pulmonary infiltrate and/or signs or symptoms of pulmonary disease until MTB can be ruled out.

The emergency room and clinic areas should have plans for appropriately isolating patients being seen as outpatients. These plans should include details on placing the patient in a separate area from other patients and placing a surgical mask on him or her until appropriate isolation can be arranged. The admissions office should know where appropriate airborne infection isolation (AII) rooms are within the facility.[81] HCP should be educated on appropriate isolation techniques (also see Chapters 29 Isolation Precautions (Transmission-based Precautions), and 114 Heating, Ventilation, and Air Conditioning).

Table 95-4. Risk Classifications for Healthcare Settings That Serve Communities with High Incidence of TB and Recommended Frequency of Screening for MTB Infection among Healthcare Personnel*[10]

| Setting | Risk Classification[†] | | Potential Ongoing Transmission[‡] |
	Low Risk	Medium Risk	
Inpatient <200 beds	<3 TB patients/year	≥3 TB patients/year	Evidence of ongoing MTB transmission, regardless of setting
Inpatient ≥200 beds	<6 TB patients/year	≥6 TB patients/year	Evidence of ongoing MTB transmission, regardless of setting
Outpatient and nontraditional facility-based	<3 TB patients/year	≥3 TB patients/year	Evidence of ongoing MTB transmission, regardless of setting
TB treatment facilities	Setting in which • Persons who will be treated have been demonstrated to have LTBI and not TB • A system is in place to promptly detect and triage persons who have signs or symptoms of TB to a setting in which persons with TB are treated • No cough-inducing or aerosol-generating procedures are performed	Settings in which • Persons with TB are encountered • Criteria for low risk is not otherwise met	Evidence of ongoing MTB transmission, regardless of setting
Laboratories	Laboratories in which clinical specimens that might contain MTB are not manipulated	Laboratories in which clinical specimens that might contain MTB are manipulated	Evidence of ongoing MTB transmission, regardless of setting
Recommendations for Screening Frequency			
Baseline two-step TST or one IGRA[§]	Yes, for all HCP upon hire	Yes, for all HCP upon hire	Yes, for all HCP upon hire
Serial TST or IGRA screening of HCP	No**	Every 12 months[††]	As needed in the investigation of potential ongoing transmission[§§]
TST or IGRA for HCP upon unprotected exposure to *MTB*	Perform a contact investigation (i.e., administer one TST as soon as possible at the time of exposure, and, if the TST result is negative, place another TST 8–10 weeks after the end of exposure to *MTB*)[¶¶]		

*HCP refers to all paid and unpaid persons working in healthcare settings who have the potential for exposure to MTB through air space shared with persons with TB.

[†]Settings that serve communities with a high incidence of TB or that treat populations at high risk (e.g., those with HIV infection or other immunocompromising conditions) or that treat patients with drug-resistant TB might need to be classified as medium risk, even if they meet the low-risk criteria.

[‡]A classification of potential ongoing transmission should be applied to a specific group of HCP or to a specific area of the healthcare setting in which evidence of ongoing transmission is apparent, if such a group or area can be identified. Otherwise, a classification of potential ongoing transmission should be applied to the entire setting. This classification should be temporary and warrants immediate investigation and corrective steps after a determination has been made that ongoing transmission has ceased. The setting should be reclassified as medium risk, and the recommended time frame for this medium risk classification is at least 1 year.

[§]All HCP should have a baseline two-step TST or one IGRA result at each new healthcare setting, even if the setting is determined to be low risk. In certain settings, a choice might be made to not perform baseline TB screening or serial TB screening for HCP who (1) will never be in contact with or have shared air space with patients who have TB (e.g., telephone operators who work in a separate building from patients) or (2) will never be in contact with clinical specimens that might contain MTB. Establishment of a reliable baseline result can be beneficial if subsequent screening is needed after an unexpected exposure to MTB.

**HCP whose duties do not include contact with patients or TB specimens do not need to be included in the serial TB screening program.

[††]The frequency of testing for infection with MTB will be determined by the risk assessment for the setting.

[§§]During an investigation of potential ongoing transmission of MTB, testing for MTB infection should be performed every 8 to 10 weeks until lapses in infection controls have been corrected and no further evidence of ongoing transmission is apparent.

[¶¶]Procedures for contact investigations should not be confused with two-step TST, which is used for newly hired HCP.

Once the decision to place the patient in AII has been made, patient and family education is important. The patient should understand why isolation measures are required. Even if the patient is in an appropriate isolation room, he or she should be instructed to cover the mouth with a tissue when coughing to minimize the number of organisms released into the air. Patient transport should be limited. If the patient must leave the room, he or she should be instructed to wear a surgical mask. Surgical masks were designed to prevent the spread of particles from the wearer into the air, and so they are appropriate for use in this situation.

Patients with suspected TB may be released from AII once TB has been adequately excluded as a possible diagnosis. The decision depends in part on the clinical suspicion for TB. If there is low clinical suspicion (but still enough to do an evaluation), the patient may be moved from AII once three sputum samples are negative for AFB on smear. If, however, there is a high clinical

suspicion for TB, the patient must remain in isolation even if three sputum samples are AFB smear negative. The patient may have AII discontinued if an alternative diagnosis is found and TB ruled out.

Isolation for hospitalized patients with pulmonary TB may be discontinued when the patient has been on the appropriate treatment for at least 2 weeks, has had a good clinical response (e.g., resolution of fevers and cough), and has had three consecutive negative AFB smears. Some institutions require longer than 2 weeks of therapy.

Environmental Controls

Preventing the flow of infectious airborne particles from the patient's room by the use of negative-pressure ventilation and reducing the concentration of airborne particles by means of frequent air exchanges are cornerstones of TB engineering control. AII rooms for TB patients should be at negative pressure relative to the hallway, so that air flows from the hall into the room. A minimum of 6 to 12 air exchanges an hour is recommended to reduce the concentration of infectious airborne particles; new facilities should provide at least 12 air exchanges per hour. The air from an AII room should be directly vented outside in a location that prevents it from re-entering the facility's ventilation system. If recirculation of the air is unavoidable, then the air must be filtered through a high-efficiency particulate air (HEPA) filter to remove droplet nuclei before the air re-enters the main ventilation system. The door to the patient's room should be kept closed at all times to maintain proper negative pressure and airflow. The AII room should have an automatic door closer installed and a permanent visual monitoring system to ensure that negative pressure is maintained.[81] (Also see Chapter 114 Heating, Ventilation, and Air Conditioning.)

The TB control plan should provide for daily monitoring for room(s) used for AII in patients with known or suspected TB. Regular (monthly) inspection and testing of all AII rooms to verify and document proper negative pressure, so the rooms are always ready to receive TB patients. The admissions office and infection prevention should be notified of rooms that fail testing so that they will not be used until repairs are made. Changes in the facility's ventilation system should be made in consultation with the infection preventionist to ensure that the need for AII rooms is met.[81]

Ultraviolet germicidal irradiation (UVGI) may be used as an adjunct to negative-pressure ventilation and high airflows. UVGI is bactericidal for MTB, but proper placement is critical for its effectiveness.[81–83] Concerns over the use of UV lights include the possibility for sunburn, skin cancers, and cataracts in HCP with frequent exposure to the lights. If UV lights are in place, they must be monitored and maintained appropriately to ensure the safety of the patient and HCP. UV lighting alone is not acceptable to control airborne spread of MTB[10] (also see Chapter 114 Heating, Ventilation, and Air Conditioning).

Personal Respiratory Protection

Personal respiratory protection consists of wearing a respirator or other protective device to prevent the inhalation of infectious droplet nuclei. Currently the U.S. Occupational Safety and Health Administration (OSHA) has mandated that HCP who may be exposed to TB must wear respiratory protection that meets at a minimum the N95 rating. In some settings with a higher than usual risk of inhaling infectious particles, a more protective respirator may be used. HCP should don the respirator. Fit testing should be performed to ensure a tight facial seal before entering the AII room. HCP should not remove the respiratory protection until they are outside of the AII room.

HCP must be trained in proper use, handling, and storage of the respirator and fit tested to ensure that the respirator provides an adequate face seal so that inhaled air comes through the filter rather than around the sides. Annual fit testing is mandatory under OSHA regulations[84] and recommended in current CDC guidelines for preventing transmission of TB.[10] Annual fit testing can also serve as an effective training tool when included in infection prevention training for HCP. The healthcare facility should purchase several types and sizes of N95 respirators so that a seal can be achieved for a variety of face types.

If an employee cannot be properly fit tested with an N95 respirator, he or she may use alternative respiratory protection such as a powered air purifying respirator with an appropriate particulate filter.

Intrafacility Movement of Tuberculosis Patients

Operating Room

Elective procedures on patients with known or suspected TB should be deferred until the patient can be removed from AII, either because TB was ruled out or because the patient has been treated and otherwise meets criteria established by the healthcare facility.

If a procedure cannot be delayed, an effort must be made to minimize the risk of transmission to HCP in the operating room (OR).[85] The surgical procedure should be the last of the day, if possible, to minimize the number of HCP in the area. If possible, the patient should be intubated in an AII room and brought directly to the OR—not permitted to linger in a preoperative holding area. An antibacterial filter should be placed on the endotracheal tube or at the expiratory side of the ventilator circuit. OR personnel should wear N95 respirators. (Note: Respirators with an exhalation valve or under positive pressure do not protect the sterile field; special N95 surgical masks are commercially available.) Ideally, the patient should be taken to an AII room before being extubated. If this is not possible, the patient may recover in the OR. A portable HEPA filter may be used in the OR during intubation and extubation to supplement air cleaning but should not be used during surgery.[85.] If the patient is intubated or extubated in the OR, the doors may not be opened until the amount of time required to remove 99 percent of airborne contaminants is reached.[10] To promote airflow through the in-room air exhausts, some facilities may place damp towels along the bottoms of the room doors to minimize airflow outside the OR. (Also refer to Chapter 114 Heating, Ventilation, and Air Conditioning for discussion of an alternative method reported for managing TB patients in the OR setting.)

Other Areas

Patients with known or suspected TB should be confined to AII rooms to the extent possible. In the event that some test or procedure must be done, the patient should wear a surgical mask when outside the room. An N95 respirator is acceptable, but masks with exhaust valves must not be used as alternatives. Because surgical masks are intended as exhalation filters, they can prevent aerosolizing infectious particles into the air. If the patient is continuously wearing a surgical mask, HCP in the area may not need to wear N95 respirators. However, because the patient's proper use of the mask cannot be guaranteed, respirators should be considered for HCP in the procedure and test areas.

Routine Employee TB Skin Testing

Initial Testing on Employment

It is important that all HCP have a TST or IGRA on employment to establish a baseline with which subsequent tests can be compared. This will prevent mislabeling a positive test after a TB exposure as a skin test conversion. A baseline TST (or IGRA) should be completed regardless of history of BCG vaccination because the interpretation of the test and subsequent management are not affected.

Newly hired HCP who have a history of a positive TST or IGRA should provide written proof of their result for appropriate documentation and follow-up. If an employee has had a positive test, the occupational health record should note whether he or she been appropriately screened for active TB, what the CXR results were, and whether treatment of LTBI was completed. Additionally, the test-positive HCP should be educated regarding symptoms of active disease and how, when, and where to report symptoms if they develop.

The TST should administered and read by properly trained personnel. HCP should not be allowed to read their own TST. Errors in collecting and transporting blood specimens or in running and interpreting the assay can decrease the accuracy of BAMT.[10]

HCP with a negative initial TST and who do not have documentation of a previous negative within the prior 12 months should receive a second TST (two-step) at least 1 week later to assess for the booster phenomenon. The booster phenomenon occurs because a person's reaction to tuberculin PPD can wane with time, and therefore the initial TST may be negative. The tuberculin, however, serves as a stimulus for the person's immune response, in a sense reminding it that it has seen TB antigens before. When a second TST is placed, it is subsequently positive because of the earlier reminder to the immune system. Note that serial tests with PPD alone will not induce a positive response to subsequent tests if the recipient has not been infected with TB. Unlike TST, IGRA requires a single visit for a test, as no booster phenomenon is needed for an accurate result.

Recurrent Healthcare Personnel Testing

The need for and frequency of routine recurrent TST or IGRA depend on the risk to the HCP in a given area at a given healthcare facility. Low-risk settings may perform TST or IGRA only at the time of hire and may choose not to do recurrent testing. Medium-risk settings may perform annual testing of all HCP who work in certain areas of the facility. HCP in settings classified as potential ongoing transmission, need to be tested for infection every 8 to 10 weeks with either IGRA or TST,

until lapses in infection prevention have been corrected and no additional evidence of ongoing transmission is apparent.[10] Once it is determined that ongoing transmission has ceased, the setting should be reclassified as medium risk. The latest CDC guidelines, as well as federal, state, and local regulations, should be incorporated into the healthcare facility's policy; some settings or locales may still require annual or more frequent testing of HCP, regardless of risk classification.

Management of Healthcare Personnel with Positive Skin Tests or Blood Assay for *Mycobacterium tuberculosis*

All HCP who have a positive TST or IGRA should be evaluated the same as anyone with a positive test, as outlined in the section on LTBI. Ideally, an occupational health professional (physician or experienced nurse) should make this evaluation. The healthcare facility should provide INH to HCP if treatment of LTBI is indicated. This will promote compliance and reduce the risk of active TB in the future, thus reducing the risk of TB for patients and other HCP. The healthcare facility may be able to obtain a supply of INH from the local health department to use in such situations. If the facility's occupational health clinic has started the employee on INH or other treatment of LTBI, adequate follow-up should be provided.

HCP who have had a positive TST or IGRA do not need further testing, as these do not provide any useful additional information. Instead, at the time of annual testing, all HCP with a history of a positive test (whether or not treatment of LTBI was completed) should complete a questionnaire to ensure that they are not experiencing common symptoms of TB (e.g., persistent cough, weight loss, fevers, night sweats). A positive answer to any question should prompt further evaluation. The HCP should also be reminded to notify occupational health and their private physicians if any of these symptoms occur in the future.

Management of Healthcare Exposures

Identification of Those Exposed

Occasionally TB is diagnosed in a patient in whom it was not initially suspected, and thus the patient was not placed into AII. When this occurs, patients, HCP, and visitors may have been exposed to TB, so an epidemiological investigation should take place. Consultation with the local health jurisdiction is prudent at this point.

The first step in an exposure investigation is to establish the infectious period. A patient with evidence of lung or laryngeal disease should be assumed to be potentially infectious, even if expectorated sputum samples were AFB smear negative.[10] If TB was diagnosed from a nonrespiratory site, the patient should have a CXR, symptom review, and sputum analysis for AFB stains to determine if he or she also has pulmonary TB. If the patient has no evidence of pulmonary disease by radiograph and symptom review, and the sputum samples show no AFB, the patient is not likely to spread disease by the airborne route and AII need not be continued. No investigation of others will be needed. The exception will be for patients who have had procedures that may aerosolize TB from extrapulmonary sources (e.g., irrigation and debridement of a TB soft tissue infection, performance of an autopsy).

A concentric circle approach may be used to identify close contacts of the patient while hospitalized or in other healthcare settings. If the patient is thought to be infectious, a list should be developed of all close contacts (people with prolonged exposure time) such as roommates, direct care providers, and visitors who might have been exposed to the source patient. This may be difficult for individuals not documented in the medical record (patient chart), such as student nurses, medical students, volunteers, and others (some of whom may not be employees). Developing a list of other patients who may have been exposed in common areas, such as radiology waiting rooms, may also be problematic or even impossible. The positivity rate of skin test or IGRA results among close contacts will determine the need to expand the investigation to those contacts with less exposure. The effort that should be put into such an undertaking will depend in part on how infectious the patient is determined to be.

Tuberculin Skin Test or Blood Assay for MTB of Tuberculosis Contacts

Testing of all persons potentially exposed to the source patient is usually unnecessary. Patients who shared a room with the source patient and HCP who had the most frequent or extensive contact (e.g., nurses, physicians, others who spent more than brief moments in the room) should have a TST or BAMT as soon as possible, ideally within 2 weeks of exposure, to establish baseline results (i.e., to ensure that these persons do not already have a positive TST or BAMT assay for any reason). Visitors and patients who have already been discharged from the healthcare facility should be referred to the local health department for testing.

After initial testing, exposed patients and HCP should be retested in 8 to 10 weeks.[10] If the patients and HCP with the greatest degree of exposure have any skin test conversions or positive BAMT results, then patients, visitors, and HCP with lesser degrees of exposure should be tested (potentially in groups based on degree of exposure). Once a group shows no positive results, groups of patients, HCP, and visitors with lesser degrees of exposure need not be tested.

Assessment of Tuberculosis Control Plan

If a facility discovers that a patient with TB was not initially placed in AII, it should review the patient's chart immediately and assess the healthcare facility's administrative controls to determine how the lapse could have been prevented.

If the patient met criteria but was not isolated, the reasons should be determined and appropriate corrective measures should be documented and implemented. Measures may include additional education and training for HCP.

Part of the assessment may examine why the patient did not meet the healthcare facility's established criteria for AII.

Tuberculosis Control in Long-term Care Facilities

TB occurs with higher than expected frequency in the elderly and may be disproportionately represented in long-term care facilities (LTCFs).[86,87] This may be a result of reactivation of latent infection or to new infection acquired from other residents with active TB. Like other healthcare settings, LTCFs should have TB control plans and AII capabilities if they accept patients with suspected or confirmed infectious TB. These plans should take into account the level of TB in their local community. At a minimum, residents and HCPs should receive two-step TST or BAMT on admission or at hire. Induration of 10 mm or more is considered a positive test for LTCF residents (unless they meet criteria for ≥5 mm).[34] The decision to treat should be based on established guidelines. Although there are concerns about development of INH hepatitis in the elderly, the 1999 ATS guidelines does not include any age limits on treatment of LTBI of unknown duration.[34] The Society for Healthcare Epidemiology of America published comprehensive guidelines for TB control in LTCFs in 2004.[87]

State Tuberculosis Control

All states have laws requiring certain HCP and healthcare entities to report proven and suspected cases of TB (active disease and possibly latent infection) to state or local health departments. Responsibility for reporting, the time frame for reporting, and the information that must be included in the report varies by state. Hospitals and other healthcare facilities should ensure that appropriate personnel are designated for reporting suspect and confirmed TB to the appropriate authorities in a timely manner.

Areas of Controversy and Rapid Change

Some healthcare facilities have negative-pressure operating rooms (or rooms that can be converted to negative pressure) for use with patients with active TB or other airborne-spread infections. Although such rooms may reduce the risk of MTB transmission to others, the individual patient may be put at some increased risk for a surgical site infection. There are currently no data on the extent of this risk or the extent of the risk of spread of airborne pathogens from the OR if currently recommended precautions are followed. This issue is not addressed in the CDC environmental guidelines[85]; thus, no general guidance can be given. On theoretical grounds, the benefit to both the individual patient and others would be derived from an OR that had an anteroom. The anteroom could be negative pressure to both the OR and the outside corridor, thus providing the patient the benefit of a positive pressure OR while providing the appropriate pressure relationship to the corridor to protect HCP and other patients. (See Chapter 114 Heating, Ventilation and Air Conditioning for discussion about an alternative method for management of a TB patient in the OR.)

NONTUBERCULOUS MYCOBACTERIA

Epidemiology

Nontuberculous mycobacteria (NTM) are widely distributed through the world and can be found on soil and water. There is no evidence of human-to-human NTM transmission. Infection usually occurs from environmental sources, though sources are difficult to characterize. Asymptomatic infection is common, and skin testing studies in areas of low TB prevalence have shown that exposure starts at a young age and peaks around age 12. The rate of infection by NTM is between 1 and 1.8 per 100,000 in industrialized nations. In the United States, the most common NTM is *M. avium* complex (MAC). The most common site of isolation is the lungs, but skin and soft tissue infection, lymph node involvement, and bloodstream infection have been reported. Disseminated disease has also been reported in immunosuppressed patients. Disseminated disease tend to occur in patients with AIDS and CD4 counts <50 cells/mm^3, and in patients with interferon-γ deficiency.[88]

NTM are found readily in the environment. They may transiently colonize the airway or skin when acquired from an environmental source and only rarely cause disease. The exception may be leprosy, but skin-to-skin contact is not thought to be the major infectious pathway, contrary to centuries of belief.[89]

Microbiology of Nontuberculous Mycobacteria

The taxonomy of NTM is an expanding field. The 1997 ATS guidelines reported 50 species; the 2007 IDSA/ATS guidelines describe 125 species. This was in part due to the availability and adoption of DNA sequencing (in particular, sequencing the gene for the 16S ribosomal RNA [16S rRBA], which is highly conserved, and a difference in less than 1 percent in its sequence is compatible with a new species). This expansion is due to the improved identification of new species, not due to the surge in new clinical entities orspecies.[88]

Like all mycobacteria, NTM are acid-fast, aerobic, Gram-positive rods (though they may not stain well with the Gram stain). The Runyon classification system is a method that classifies NTM into one of four groups on the basis of growth rates, pigmentation, and colony morphology. With newer broth culture techniques, however, even mycobacteria traditionally considered slow growers, like MTB or *M. avium*, can be grown relatively quickly. Fluorochrome stain is the preferred method of staining of samples to detect NTM, although the Ziehl–Neelsen or Kinyoun stain are less sensitive alternatives.

To enhance diagnosis and detection of NTM, current guidelines recommend performing cultures on both liquid media and solid media. They also recommend using supplemental culture media and lower temperatures for the culture of synovial fluid, bone, and soft tissue (to aid in diagnosis of more fastidious NTM, such as *M. haemophilum* and *M. marinum*; *M. haemophilum* also requires iron supplementation).

Clinical Features

MAC is the leading cause of NTM disease in the United States and many other countries. NTM disease is most easily classified by site.

Pulmonary Disease

Pulmonary disease is the most common clinical presentation of NTM infection. MAC, *M. kansasii, M. abscessus,* and *M. fortuitum* are the most common etiological agents in NTM pulmonary disease in the United States; less frequent are *M. xenopi, M. malmoense, M. szulgai, M. simiae,* and others. MAC is the leading NTM causing pulmonary disease. The second most common organism varies by country and region.[88]

NTM pulmonary disease presents with cough, with or without fever, weight loss, hemoptysis, and progressive dyspnea. Usually symptoms are nonspecific, and imaging can show fibrocavitary of showing nodules and bronchiectasis. Because the infection occurs primarily in patients with prior pulmonary pathology (i.e., chronic obstructive pulmonary disease, bronchiectasis), it is sometimes difficult to make a clinical diagnosis of pulmonary NTM disease.[88]

A hypersensitivity syndrome associated with exposure to indoor hot water reservoirs (tub lung) has also been described. This is characterized by a hypersensitivity reaction to aerosols, usually from warm/hot water sources colonized with MAC. Patients affected are usually younger and present with dyspnea, cough, and fever. Sometimes the hypersensitivity pneumonitis may be severe, leading to respiratory failure. *M. immunogenum* has been identified as a possible cause of this clinical syndrome in machinists with occupational exposure to metalgrinding fluids. Therapy usually involves steroids and possibly antimycobacterial medications for a short period of time and avoidance of exposures.[88]

Disseminated Disease

Disseminated disease usually occurs in patients with AIDS, and most cases are due to MAC. Other NTM like *M. kansasii* and, less frequently *M. fortuitum, M. scrofulaceum, M. gordonae, M. haemophilum, M. genavense, M. marinum, M. xenopi, M. malmoense, M. celatum,* and *M. simiae* can cause disease in AIDS patients. Dissemination is extremely rare in nonHIV infected patients, but it has been reported in patients with renal disease or leukemia, patients who have received cardiac transplants and patients receiving therapy with high-dose corticosteroids.[88]

Clinical presentation of disseminated NTM may be nonspecific, and symptoms include fever, night sweats, weight loss, abdominal pain, and occasionally diarrhea. Patients may have hepatosplenomegaly and lymphadenopathy. Anemia is common, as is elevated alkaline phosphatase and lactate dehydrogenase. In AIDS patients, disseminated MAC presents as fever of unknown origin, and disseminated *M. kansasii, M. chelonae, M. abscessus,* and *M. haemophilum* present with multiple subcutaneous nodules or abscesses.[88]

Skin and Soft Tissue Infection

Although virtually all the NTM have been described to cause cutaneous infections, *M. fortuitum*, *M. marinum*, *M. chelonea*, *M. abscessus*, and *M. ulcerans* are the most common. There may be a history of a puncture (e.g., stepping on a nail) or other traumatic injury.

M. marinum causes cutaneous lesions after exposure to swimming pools, fish tanks, or other water sources. The organisms may enter through previously unappreciated superficial nicks and abrasions. The lesions first appear as papules that later ulcerate. Because special culture conditions must be used to isolate the organism, the microbiology lab should be alerted if this is a diagnostic consideration.

M. leprae is the cause of leprosy (Hansen disease). This is a chronic skin infection with prominent neurological involvement. Much of the damage is a result of the peripheral neuropathy, so patients are unaware of harm being done to their tissues. *M. leprae* is not highly contagious, and only standard precautions are needed when dealing with a patient who has leprosy.

In addition to cutaneous disease, deeper abscesses, tenosynovitis, septic arthritis, bursitis, and osteomyelitis have all been described in patients with NTM.

Lymphadenitis

Lymphadenitis occurs primarily in young children. The cervical, submandibular, maxillary, and supraclavicular nodes are the most common sites of presentation. The nodes may enlarge to the point that they drain spontaneously, but systemic symptoms are usually absent. MAC is the most common cause. The second most common cause varies by country. In adults, disease occurs almost exclusively in persons with HIV.

Laboratory Diagnosis and Procedures

Diagnosis of Pulmonary Disease

Because atypical mycobacteria may colonize the airway transiently in an immunocompetent host, the growth of such an organism is not necessarily indicative of infection. The IDSA/ATS guidelines require the presence of clinical criteria (symptoms compatible with NTM pulmonary disease, radiological changes, AND exclusion of other diagnosis) and microbiological criteria (isolation of NTM in multiple sputum cultures, or at least one BAL or biopsy). Even following these criteria, when unusual low virulence organisms like *M. gordonae* are isolated, expert consultation is recommended.[88]

Diagnosis at Other Sites

The growth of a mycobacterium from a skin biopsy or a normally sterile body site can establish the diagnosis of NTM infection. Because some species (e.g., *M. marinum*) require special culture conditions for optimal growth, the microbiology lab should be notified if an NTM infection is suspected so that the appropriate cultures will be done.

Common Confirmatory Tests

Phenotypic testing based on growth rate, pigmentation, and biochemical tests has been employed for identification of NTM in the past. Rapid-growing NTM develop within 7 days of culture (usually *M. fortuitum*, *M. abscessus*, *M. chelonae*), and can be further identified based on their pigmentation on culture media. Alternatively, high-performance liquid chromatography can be a rapid and efficient way to identify NTM. However, this test has some limitations (i.e., it has problems identifying species in the *M. simiae* complex). DNA probes have been developed and can be very useful to speciate NTM when they grow in cultures (available for several mycobacterium such as MAC, *M. kansasii*, and *M. gordonae*). Finally DNA sequence analysis of the 16S rRNA gene can be used for an accurate identification to the species level.[88]

Treatment Strategies

The therapy of NTM can be difficult because not all anti-TB drugs are effective. As with TB, multiple drug regimens are used to treat NTM. The specific drugs used depend on the species of mycobacterium and are best chosen in consultation with someone experienced in treating such infections. Most NTM infections respond well to treatment but may require prolonged therapy.

Infection Prevention and Control Measures

Healthcare-associated infections (HAIs) caused by NTM are being increasingly identified. Outbreaks and sporadic reports of infections caused by NTM in the United States have a strong geographic relationship to the Gulf Coast and southeastern states. NTM are ubiquitous, and the physiopathology of infection is not entirely clear, making infection prevention challenging. Reservoirs in the environment, host susceptibility and characteristics, and mechanisms of infection have not been entirely characterized. However, there are two instances where there is a clear link with healthcare-associated transmission: skin and soft tissue infections and hypersensitivity lung disease from indoor water sources.[88]

Tap water has been a common source for many outbreaks, and some NTM are almost exclusively isolated from municipal water sources (*M. kansasii*, *M. xenopi*, and *M. simiae*). Several NTM like MAC can survive at high water temperatures in hospital water systems. While colonizing water systems, NTM produce biofilms that allow them to survive despite high water flow rates, which makes elimination challenging.[88]

Surgical Site Infections

NTM surgical site infections (SSIs) have been described after cardiothoracic surgery,[90,91] augmentation mammoplasty,[92,93] rhinoplasty,[94] and other surgeries. In most cases the source of the infection was exposure to tap water or a contaminated fluid.[88] In one outbreak, contaminated gentian violet used to mark the patient was identified as the source.[93] In an outbreak of NTM abdominal wound SSIs, the lubricant used for the laparoscopes proved to be the reservoir.[95]

Postinjection Abscesses

A number of sporadic cases, as well as outbreaks of localized cutaneous abscesses, have been reported that were traced to injections with contaminated needles. Unlike other health-care-associated diseases, epidemic postinjection abscesses are most often caused by *M. chelonae*,[96,97] though outbreaks involving *M. fortuitum* and *M. abscessus* have also been reported.[98,99]

Dialysis-associated Infections

Several hemodialysis outbreaks have been reported due to contamination of the water used in dialysis.[95,100,101] Mycobacteria have been reported to cause peritonitis in patients on peritoneal dialysis.[102] NTM accounts for less than 3 percent of these reported infections; however, NTM may be a more common cause and are simply underdiagnosed.

Catheter-associated Infections

Catheter-associated infections are currently the most common HAI caused by NTM.[88,95,103] Optimal treatment requires removal of the catheter (intravascular or urinary) and administration of antibiotic therapy.

Infections Related to Implanted Devices

NTM infections have occurred with prosthetic hips, prosthetic knees, pacemakers, defibrillators, and myringotomy tubes.[95] Most cases have been sporadic.

Pseudoinfection and Pseudo-outbreaks

Numerous pseudoinfections and pseudo-outbreaks with NTM have been reported. This has often been linked to inappropriately cleaned bronchoscopes and endoscopes or contaminated endoscope washers.[104–107] Contaminated hospital water supplies and ice machines have also led to direct culture contamination or patient colonization with NTM.[106,108–110] Contaminated laboratory equipment and culture cross-contamination have also been reported.[111–113]

Prevention and Control of Nontuberculous Mycobacteria Infections

Surveillance plays an important role in early recognition and identification of outbreaks and pseudo-outbreaks caused by NTM. Because NTM infections may be difficult to diagnose, the recovery of a single NTM isolate from a surgical patient, dialysis patient, or sterile site should prompt further investigation to ensure that additional cases have not gone unrecognized. NTM obtained from a bronchoscopy specimen is less likely to represent an HAI but may still warrant at least a chart review. Because NTM are not typically spread person-to-person, there is no need to follow anything other than Standard Precautions.

If an NTM is identified, a review of the patient's medical records should be performed to determine whether the patient is truly infected and to obtain demographic and medical information.

If the occurrence appears to be an HAI, a case definition should be made and microbiology and pathology records reviewed to find additional cases. A case-control investigation may be useful. The laboratory should be notified to save all isolates so that case and environmental isolates may be compared using molecular typing. Investigations should focus on essential issues that have already been described, including the relationship of NTM to tap and distilled water, ice, and improperly or inadequately disinfected or sterilized instruments. Policies and procedures for obtaining and processing specimens and disinfecting implicated equipment should be reviewed. Written policies and procedures may be adequate; however, witnessing the actual performance of the procedure may show the execution was not adequate. Selected environmental cultures may be useful to delineate the source of the contamination (also see Chapter 12 Outbreak Investigations).

HCPs who work in areas that have immunosuppressed, high-risk patients or who perform diagnostic or therapeutic procedures requiring high-level disinfection of instruments should receive education about the relationship between NTM and water, the role of NTM as potential pathogens, and appropriate disinfection procedures. Personnel using glutaraldehyde or other high-level disinfectants must monitor disinfectant concentrations, the duration of disinfectant activity after activation, and the immersion time required (also see Chapter 31 Cleaning, Disinfection, and Sterilization). Active surveillance, periodic review of cleansing and disinfection of equipment, and use of only sterile water to rinse critical and semicritical items are recommended measures to prevent pseudo-outbreaks from NTM. Use of tap water for processing bronchoscopes should be avoided. This may led to pseudo-outbreaks.[88] Use of in-line filters may help reduce water contamination. Ice should be considered potentially contaminated, and its use should be limited in operating rooms (also see Chapter 115 Water Systems Issues and Prevention of Waterborne Infections in Healthcare Facilities).

Patients who have been exposed to contaminated bronchoscopes or other critical or semicritical instruments should be monitored closely for the development of disease. Use of ethylene oxide to sterilize endoscopes or other instruments between patients should eliminate contamination resulting from NTM. However, processing with ethylene oxide may be cost prohibitive and require extended time for sterilization and aeration after sterilization. Emphasis on adequate cleaning and disinfection, as opposed to routine sterilization, may be sufficient if errors are identified and corrected[83] (also see Chapter 55 Endoscopy). In addition, when collecting sputum specimens, it is important that patients not rinse with or drink tap water before an expectorated specimen is collected.[88]

HCP in dialysis units should be aware of the relationship between water and NTM.[70] It is important to be meticulous when disinfecting and reusing dialyzers, and HCP must perform careful surveillance for infections. NTM are relatively resistant to chlorine and glutaraldehyde, and decontamination of dialyzers and dialysis machines may be difficult. Facilities should routinely collect and evaluate water cultures as a quality assurance measure in dialysis units to monitor possible contamination or colonization. Routine culturing can protect patients from potential infection by eliminating excessive water colonization. In addition, Renalin may be a less effective disinfectant than formaldehyde or glutaraldehyde, so its use must be monitored closely as well. Dialysis centers that reuse dialyzers or perform high-flux dialysis should be particularly meticulous in their disinfection practices and their surveillance (also see Chapter 39 Dialysis).

During surgery, it is important to avoid use of tap water or ice from tap water, especially during cardiac or augmentation mammoplasty. Contact of surgical wounds with tap water should also be avoided. Patients with central lines should properly cover their central lines when taking a shower and should avoid contact of the line with tap water.[88]

Quaternary ammonia does not eliminate some NTM like *M. abscessus* and *M. chelonae*.[114] When patients receive injections, use of benzalkonium chloride to disinfect the skin should be avoided. Multidose vial use should be discouraged. Patients should be educated to avoid injection of alternative medicine or unapproved substances, given risk of contamination with NTM.[88]

CONCLUSIONS

TB infection and disease remain a global concern. Although rates of TB in the United States have decreased in recent years, it is estimated that about one-third of the world's population is infected. Diagnosis and treatment of TB are important to prevent adverse outcomes and prevent spread in healthcare settings and communities. An effective TB control plan must include infection prevention and control measures to decrease the risk of transmission in healthcare settings. MDR-TB and XDR-TB strains have emerged and are more difficult to treat. NTM can cause infections, especially in immunocompromised individuals.

FUTURE TRENDS

Although aggressive control measures have resulted in decreased incidence across the globe, population growth has offset gains. Increasing antimicrobial resistance with MDR-TB and XDR-TB strains is an emerging, worldwide concern. Technology advancement and techniques may be applied to help identify outbreaks and linkage to common sources.

REFERENCES

1. World Health Organization (WHO). Global tuberculosis control: surveillance, planning, financing, *WHO Report 2008*. Geneva: WHO/CDS/TB, 2008.
2. Corbett EL, Watt CJ, Walker N, et al. The growing burden of tuberculosis global trends and interactions with the HIV epidemic. *Arch Intern Med* 2003 May 12;163(9):1009–1021.
3. Centers for Disease Control and Prevention. Update: tuberculosis elimination—United States. *MMWR Morb Mortal Wkly Rep* 1990 Mar 16;39(10):153–156.
4. Brudney K, Dobkin J. Resurgent tuberculosis in New York City. Human immunodeficiency virus, homelessness, and the decline of tuberculosis control programs. *Am Rev Respir Dis* 1991 Oct;144(4):745–749.
5. Reichman LB. The U-shaped curve of concern [editorial]. *Am Rev Respir Dis* 1991 Oct;144(4):741–742.
6. Blumberg HM. Tuberculosis and infection control: What now? *Infect Control Hosp Epidemiol* 1997 Aug;18(8):538–541.
7. Hopewell PC. Impact of human immunodeficiency virus infection on the epidemiology, clinical features, management, and control of tuberculosis. *Clin Infect Dis* 1992 Sep;15(3):540–547.
8. Paolo WF Jr, Nosanchuk JD. Tuberculosis in New York city: recent lessons and a look ahead. *Lancet Infect Dis* 2004 May;4(5):287–293.
9. Centers for Disease Control and Prevention (CDC). *Reported Tuberculosis in the United States, 2011.* CDC website. October 2012. Available at: http://www.cdc.gov/tb/statistics/reports/2011/pdf/report2011.pdf.
10. Jensen PA, Lambert LA, Iademarco MF, et al. Guidelines for preventing the transmission of Mycobacterium tuberculosis in health-care settings, 2005. *MMWR Recomm Rep* 2005 Dec 30;54(RR-17):1–141.
11. Centers for Disease Control and Prevention (CDC). *Core Curriculum on Tuberculosis: What the Clinician Should Know*, 6th ed. Atlanta: Centers for Diasease Control and Prevention; 2013. Available at: http://www.cdc.gov/tb/education/corecurr/pdf/corecurr_all.pdf.
12. Braden CR. Infectiousness of a university student with laryngeal and cavitary tuberculosis. Investigative team. *Clin Infect Dis* 1995 Sep;21(3):565–570.
13. Sepkowitz KA. How contagious is tuberculosis? *Clin Infect Dis* 1996 Nov;23(5):954–962.
14. Restrepo BI, Camerlin AJ, Rahbar MH, et al. Cross-sectional assessment reveals high diabetes prevalence among newly-diagnosed tuberculosis cases. *Bull World Health Organ* 2011 May 1;89(5):352–359.
15. Wells CD, Cegielski JP, Nelson LJ, et al. HIV infection and multidrug-resistant tuberculosis: the perfect storm. *J Infect Dis* 2007 Aug 15;196 Suppl 1:S86–S107.
16. Wang JY, Lee LN, Yu CJ, et al. Factors influencing time to smear conversion in patients with smear-positive pulmonary tuberculosis. *Respirology* 2009 Sep;14(7):1012–1019.
17. Fennelly KP. Transmission of tuberculosis during medical procedures. *Clin Infect Dis* 1997 Nov;25(5):1273–1275.
18. Diel R, Seidler A, Nienhaus A, et al. Occupational risk of tuberculosis transmission in a low incidence area. *Respir Res* 2005 Apr 14;6:35.
19. Millership SE, Anderson C, Cummins AJ, et al. The risk to infants from nosocomial exposure to tuberculosis. *Pediatr Infect Dis J* 2009 Oct;28(10):915–916.
20. Menzies D, Fanning A, Yuan L, et al. Hospital ventilation and risk for tuberculous infection in canadian health care workers. Canadian Collaborative Group in Nosocomial Transmission of TB. *Ann Intern Med* 2000 Nov 21;133(10):779–789.
21. Zumla A, Raviglione M, Hafner R, et al. Tuberculosis. *N Engl J Med* 2013 Feb 21;368(8):745–755.
22. Diagnostic standards and classification of tuberculosis in adults and children. *Am J Respir Crit Care Med* 2000 Apr;161(4 Pt 1):1376–1395.
23. Getahun H, Kittikraisak W, Heilig CM, et al. Development of a standardized screening rule for tuberculosis in people living with HIV in resource-constrained settings: individual participant data metaanalysis of observational studies. *PLoS Med* 2011 Jan 18;8(1):e1000391.
24. Slavin RE, Walsh TJ, Pollack AD. Late generalized tuberculosis: a clinical pathologic analysis and comparison of 100 cases in the preantibiotic and antibiotic eras. *Medicine (Baltimore).* 1980 Sep;59(5):352–366.
25. Schlossberg D. Acute tuberculosis. *Infect Dis Clin N Am* 2010 Mar;24(1):139–146.
26. Banner AS. Tuberculosis: Clinical aspects and diagnosis. *Arch Intern Med* 1979 Dec;139(12):1387–1390.
27. Siddiqui AH, Perl TM, Conlon M, et al. Preventing nosocomial transmission of pulmonary tuberculosis: when may isolation be discontinued for patients with suspected tuberculosis? *Infect Control Hosp Epidemiol* 2002 Mar;23(3):141–144.
28. Centers for Disease Control and Prevention (CDC). *Report of an Expert Consultation on the Uses of Nucleic Acid Amplification Tests for the Diagnosis of Tuberculosis.* CDC website. September 2012. Available at: http://www.cdc.gov/tb/publications/guidelines/amplification_tests/default.htm.
29. Lawn SD, Mwaba P, Bates M, et al. Advances in tuberculosis diagnostics: the Xpert MTB/RIF assay and future prospects for a point-of-care test. *Lancet Infect Dis* 2013 Apr;13(4):349–361.
30. Shah SN, Pratt R, Armstrong L, et al. Extensively drug resistant tuberculosis in the United States 1993–2007. *JAMA* 2008 Nov 12;300(18):2153–2160.
31. Jassal M, Bishai WR. Extensively drug-resistant tuberculosis. *Lancet Infect Dis* 2009 Jan;9(1):19–30.
32. Bass JB Jr, Farer LS, Hopewell PC, et al. Treatment of tuberculosis and tuberculosis infection in adults and children, American Thoracic Society and The Centers for Disease Control and Prevention. *Am J Respir Crit Care Med* 1994 May;149(5):1359–1374.

33. Mazurek GH, Jereb J, Vernon A, et al. Updated Guidelines for Using Interferon Gamma Release Assays to Detect Mycobacterium tuberculosis Infection—United States, 2010. *MMWR Recomm Rep* 2010 Jun 25; 59(RR-5):1–25.
34. Targeted tuberculin testing and treatment of latent tuberculosis infection. *MMWR Recomm Rep.* 2000 Jun 9;49(RR-6):1–51.
35. Diagnostic standards and classification of tuberculosis. *Am Rev Respir Dis* 1990 Sep;142(3):725–735.
36. van Zyl-Smit RN, Zwerling A, Dheda K, et al. Within-subject variability of interferon-g assay results for tuberculosis and boosting effect of tuberculin skin testing: a systematic review. *PLoS One* 2009 Dec 30;4(12):e8517.
37. Mori T, Sakatani M, Yamagashi F, et al. Specific detection of tuberculosis infection: An interferon-γ-based assay using new antigens. *Am J Respir Critical Care Med* 2004 Jul 1;170(1):59–64.
38. Kang YA, Lee HW, Yoon HI, et al. Discrepancy between the tuberculin skin test and the whole blood interferon γ assay for the diagnosis of latent tuberculosis infection in an intermediate tuberculosis burden country. *JAMA* 2005 Jun 8;293(22):2756–2761.
39. Mori T, Sakatani M, Yamagashi F, et al. Specific detection of tuberculosis infection: An interferon-γ-based assay using new antigens. *Am J Respir Critical Care Med* 2004 Jul 1;170(1):59–64.
40. Kang YA, Lee HW, Yoon HI, et al. Discrepancy between the tuberculin skin test and the whole blood interferon γ assay for the diagnosis of latent tuberculosis infection in an intermediate tuberculosis burden country. *JAMA* 2005 Jun 8;293(22):2756–2761.
41. American Thoracic Society; CDC; Infectious Diseases Society of America. Treatment of tuberculosis. *MMWR Recomm Rep* 2003 Jun 20; 52(RR-11):1–77.
42. Chaulk CP, Kazandjian VA. Directly observed therapy for treatment completion of pulmonary tuberculosis: Consensus Statement of the Public Health Tuberculosis Guidelines Panel. *JAMA* 1998 Mar 25;279(12): 943–948.
43. Prevention and treatment of tuberculosis among patients infected with human immunodeficiency virus: principles of therapy and revised recommendations. Centers for Disease Control and Prevention. *MMWR Recomm Rep* 1998 Oct 30;47(RR-20):1–58.
44. Menzies D, Long R, Trajman A, et al. Adverse events with 4 months of rifampin therapy or 9 months of isoniazid therapy for latent tuberculosis infection. A randomized trial. *Ann Intern Med* 2008 Nov 18;149(10):689–697.
45. Sterling TR, Villarino ME, Borisov AS, et al. TB Trials Consortium PREVENT TB Study Team. Three months of rifapentine and isoniazid for latent tuberculosis infection. *N Engl J Med* 2011 Dec 8;365(23):2155–2166.
46. Centers for Disease Control and Prevention (CDC). Recommendations for use of an isoniazid-rifapentine regimen with direct observation to treat latent Mycobacterium tuberculosis infection. *MMWR Morb Mortal Wkly Rep* 2011 Dec 9;60(48):1650–1653.
47. Centers for Disease Control and Prevention (CDC); American Thoracic Society. Update: Adverse event data and revised American Thoracic Society/CDC Recommendations against the use of rifampin and pyrazinamide for treatment of latent tuberculosis infection—United States, 2003. *MMWR Morb Mortal Wkly Rep* 2003 Aug 8;52(31):735–739.
48. Fine PE. Bacille Calmette-Guérin vaccines: A rough guide. *Clin Infect Dis* 1995 Jan;20(1):11–14.
49. Brewer TF, Colditz GA. Relationship between Bacille Calmette-Guerin (BCG) strains and the efficacy of BCG vaccine in the prevention of tuberculosis. *Clin Infect Dis* 1995 Jan;20(1):126–135.
50. Wilson ME, Fineberg HV, Colditz GA. Geographic latitude and the efficacy of Bacillus Calmette-Guerin vaccine. *Clin Infect Dis* 1995 Apr;20(4): 982–991.
51. Colditz GA, Brewer TF, Berkey CS, et al. Efficacy of BCG vaccine in the prevention of tuberculosis. *JAMA* 1994 Mar 2;271(9):698–702.
52. American Thoracic Society. Diagnostic standards and classification of tuberculosis. *Am Rev Respir Dis* 1990 Sep;142(3):725–735.
53. The role of BCG vaccine in the prevention and control of tuberculosis in the United States. A joint statement by the Advisory Council for the Elimination of Tuberculosis and the Advisory Committee on Immunization Practices. *MMWR Recomm Rep* 1996 Apr 26;45(RR-4):1–18.
54. Dooley SW, Villarino ME, Lawrence M, et al. Nosocomial transmission of tuberculosis in a hospital unit for HIV-infected patients. *JAMA* 1992 May 20;267(19):2632–2634.
55. Harris TG, Sullivan Meissner J, Proops D. Delay in diagnosis leading to nosocomial transmission of tuberculosis at a New York City health care facility. *Am J Infect Control* 2013 Feb;41(2):155–160.
56. D'Agata EM, Wise S, Stewart A, et al. Nosocomial transmission of Mycobacterium tuberculosis from an extrapulmonary site. *Infect Control Hosp Epidemiol* 2001 Jan;22(1):10–12.
57. Centers for Disease Control and Prevention (CDC). *Reported Tuberculosis in the United States, 2010.* CDC website. 2011. Available at: http://www.cdc.gov/features/dstb2010data/.
58. Jones SG. Evaluation of a human immunodeficiency virus rule out tuberculosis critical pathway as an intervention to decrease nosocomial transmission of tuberculosis in the inpatient setting. *AIDS Patient Care STDS* 2002 Aug;16(8):389–394.
59. Chen TC, Lu PL, Lin WR, et al. Diagnosis and treatment of pulmonary tuberculosis in hospitalized patients are affected by physician specialty and experience. *Am J Med Sci* 2010 Nov;340(5):367–372.
60. Greenaway C, Menzies D, Fanning A, et al. Delay in diagnosis among hospitalized patients with active tuberculosis—predictors and outcomes. *Am J Respir Crit Care Med* 2002 Apr 1;165(7):927–933.
61. Sterling TR, Haas DW. Transmission of Mycobacterium tuberculosis from health care workers. *N Engl J Med* 2006 Jul 13;355(2):118–121.
62. Mazurek GH, Jereb J, Vernon A, et al. Updated guidelines for using Interferon Gamma Release Assays to detect Mycobacterium tuberculosis infection - United States, 2010. *MMWR Recomm Rep* 2010 Jun 25; 59(RR-5):1–25.
63. Frieden TR, Fujiwara PI, Washko RM, et al. Tuberculosis in New York City—turning the tide. *N Engl J Med* 1995 Jul 27;333(4):229–233.
64. Ramirez JA, Anderson P, Herp S, et al. Increased rate of tuberculin skin test conversion among workers at a university hospital. *Infect Control Hosp Epidemiol* 1992 Oct;13(10):579–581.
65. Sepkowitz KA, Raffalli J, Riley L, et al. Tuberculosis in the AIDS era. *Clin Microbiol Rev* 1995 Apr;8(2):180–199.
66. Griffith DE, Hardeman JL, Zhang Y, et al. Tuberculosis outbreak among healthcare workers in a community hospital. *Am J Respir Crit Care Med* 1995 Aug;152(2):808–811.
67. Ehrenkranz NJ, Kicklighter JL. Tuberculosis outbreak in a general hospital: evidence for airborne spread of infection. *Ann Intern Med* 1972 Sep;77(3):377–382.
68. Malone JL, Ijaz K, Lambert L, et al. Investigation of healthcare-associated transmission of Mycobacterium tuberculosis among patients with malignancies at three hospitals and at a residential facility. *Cancer* 2004 Dec 15;101(12):2713–2721.
69. Sprinson JE, Flood J, Fan CS, et al. Evaluation of tuberculosis contact investigations in California. *Int J Tuberc Lung Dis* 2003 Dec;7(12 Suppl 3): S363–S368.
70. Haas DW, Milton S, Kreiswirth BN, et al. Nosocomial transmission of a drug-sensitive W-variant Mycobacterium tuberculosis strain among patients with acquired immunodeficiency syndrome in Tennessee. *Infect Control Hosp Epidemiol* 1998 Sep;19(9):635–639.
71. Bock NN, Sotir MJ, Parrott PL, et al. Nosocomial tuberculosis exposure in an outpatient setting: evaluation of patients exposed to healthcare providers with tuberculosis. *Infect Control Hosp Epidemiol* 1999 Jun;20(6): 421–425.
72. Centers for Disease Control and Prevention (CDC). Mycobacterium tuberculosis transmission in a newborn nursery and maternity ward—New York City, 2003. *MMWR Morb Mortal Wkly Rep* 2005 Dec 23;54(50): 1280–1283.
73. Askew GL, Finelli L, Hutton M, et al. Mycobacterium tuberculosis transmission from a pediatrician to patients. *Pediatrics* 1997 Jul;100(1):19–23.
74. Centers for Disease Control and Prevention (CDC). Tuberculosis transmission in a renal dialysis center—Nevada, 2003. *MMWR Morb Mortal Wkly Rep* 2004 Sep 24;53(37):873–875.
75. Zaza S, Beck-Sagué CM, Jarvis WR. Tracing patients exposed to health care workers with tuberculosis. *Public Health Rep* 1997 Mar-Apr;112(2):153–157.
76. Scano F. *WHO policy on TB infection control in health-care facilities, congregate settings and households.* Geneva, Switzerland: WHO Press, World Health Organization, Geneva, Switzerland, 2009.
77. Guidelines for preventing the transmission of Mycobacterium tuberculosis in health-care facilities, 1994. Centers for Disease Control and Prevention. *MMWR Recomm Rep* 1994 Oct 28;43(RR-13):1–132.
78. Templeton GL, Illing LA, Young L, et al. The risk for transmission of Mycobacterium tuberculosis at the bedside and during autopsy [see comments]. *Ann Intern Med* 1995 Jun 15;122(12):922–925.
79. Hutton MD, Stead WW, Cauthen GM, et al. Nosocomial transmission of tuberculosis associated with a draining abscess. *J Infect Dis* 1990 Feb;161(2):286–295.
80. Frampton MW. An outbreak of tuberculosis among hospital personnel caring for a patient with a skin ulcer. *Ann Intern Med* 1992 Aug 15; 117(4):312–313.
81. Sehulster LM, Chinn RY, Arduino MJ, et al. Guidelines for environmental infection control in healthcare facilities: recommendations of CDC and the Healthcare Infection Control Practices Advisory Committee (HICPAC). CDC website. 2003. Available at: http://www.cdc.gov/hicpac/pdf/guidelines/eic_in_hcf_03.pdf.
82. Nardell EA. Interrupting transmission from patients with unsuspected tuberculosis: A unique role for upper-room ultraviolet air disinfection. *Am J Infect Control* 1995 Apr;23(2):156–164.

83. Stead WW, Yeung C, Hartnett C. Probable role of ultraviolet irradiation in preventing transmission of tuberculosis: A case study. *Infect Control Hosp Epidemiol* 1996 Jan;17(1):11–13.

84. U.S. Department of Labor, Occupational Health and Safety Administration (OSHA). OSHA website. Standard 29 CFR 1910.134(f)(2); Standard Interpretation: Tuberculosis and Respiratory Protection Enforcement. Available at: http://www.osha.gov/pls/oshaweb/owadisp.show_document?p_table=INTERPRETATIONS&p_id=26013.

85. Sehulster L, Chinn RY, CDC, et al. Guidelines for environmental infection control in health-care facilities. Recommendations of CDC and the Health-care Infection Control Practices Advisory Committee (HICPAC). *MMWR Recomm Rep* 2003 Jun 6;52(RR-10):1–42.

86. Bently DW. Tuberculosis in long-term care facilities. *Infect Control Hosp Epidemiol* 1990 Jan;11(1):42–46.

87. Thrupp L, Bradley S, Smith P, et al. SHEA Position Paper: Tuberculosis prevention and control in long-term-care facilities for older adults. *Infect Control Hosp Epidemiol* 2004 Dec;25(12):1097–1108.

88. Griffith DE, Aksamit T, Brown-Elliott BA, at al. An Official ATS/IDSA Statement: Diagnosis, Treatment, and Prevention of Nontuberculous Mycobacterial Diseases. *Am J Respir Crit Care Med* 2007 Feb 15; 175(4):367–416.

89. Gelber RH, Rea TH. Mycobacterium leprae (Leprosy, Hansen's disease). In: Mandell GL, Bennett JE, Dolin R, eds. *Principles and Practice of Infectious Disease,* 5th ed. New York: Churchill Livingstone, 2000:2608.

90. Yew WW, Wong PC, Woo HS, et al. Characterization of *Mycobacterium fortuitum* isolates from sternotomy wounds by antimicrobial suscepti-bilities, plasmid profiles, and ribosomal ribonucleic acid gene restriction patterns. *Diagn Microbiol Infect Dis* 1993 Aug-Sep;17(2):111–117.

91. Wallace RJ Jr, Musser JM, Hull SI, et al. Diversity and sources of rapidly growing mycobacteria associated with infections following cardiac surgery. *J Infect Dis* 1989 Apr;159(4):708–716.

92. Clegg HW, Foster MT, Sander WEJ, et al. Infection due to organisms of the *Mycobacterium fortuitum* complex after augmentation mammoplasty: clinical and epidemiological features. *J Infect Dis* 1983 Mar;147(3): 427–433.

93. Safranek TJ, Jarvis WR, Carson CA, et al. *Mycobacterium chelonae* wound infections after plastic surgery employing contaminated gentian violet marking solution. *N Engl J Med* 1987 Jul 23;317(4):197–201.

94. Soto LE, Bobadilla M, Villalobos Y, et al. Post-surgical nasal cellulitis outbreak due to *Mycobacterium chelonae. J Hosp Infect* 1991 Oct; 19(2):99–106.

95. Rao VK, Fraser V, Wallace RJ Jr. Nontuberculous Mycobacteria. In: Mayhall CG, ed. *Hospital Epidemiology and Infection Control,* 4th ed. Baltimore: Williams & Wilkins, 2000.

96. Gremillion DH, Mursch SB, Lerner RJ. Injection site abscesses caused by *Mycobacterium chelonae. Infect Control* 1983 Jan-Feb;4(1):25–28.

97. Petrini B, Hellstrand P, Eriksson M. Infection with *Mycobacterium chelonae* following injections. Scand *J Infect Dis* 1980;12(3):237–238.

98. Nolan CM, Hashisaki PA, Dundas DF. An outbreak of soft-tissue infections due to *Mycobacterium fortuitum* associated with electromyography. *J Infect Dis* 1991 May;163(5):1150–1153.

99. Centers for Disease Control and Prevention (CDC). Infection with *Myco-bacterium abscessus* associated with intramuscular injection of adrenal cortex extract—Colorado and Wyoming, 1995–1996. *MMWR Morb Mortal Wkly Rep* 1996 Aug 23;45(33):713–715.

100. Bolan G, Reingold AL, Carson LA. Infections with *Mycobacterium chelonae* in patients receiving dialysis and using processed hemodialyzers. *J Infect Dis* 1985 Nov;152(5):1013–1019.

101. Carson LA, Bland LA, Cusick LB. Prevalence of nontuberculous myco-bacteria in water supplies of hemodialysis centers. *Applied Env Microbiol* 1988 Dec;54(12):3122–3125.

102. Hakim A, Hisam N, Reuman PD. Environmental mycobacterial peritonitis complicating peritoneal dialysis: three cases and review. *Clin Infect Dis* 1993 Mar;16(3):426–431.

103. Raad VS II, Khan A, Bodey GP. Catheter-associated infections caused by *Mycobacterium fortuitum* complex: 15 cases and review. *Rev Infect Dis* 1991 Nov-Dec;13(6):1120–1125.

104. Fraser VJ, Jones M, Murray PR, et al. Contamination of flexible fiberoptic bronchoscopes with *Mycobacterium chelonae* linked to an automated bronchoscope disinfection machine. *Am Rev Respir Dis* 1992 Apr; 145(4 Pt 1):853–855.

105. Pappas SA, Schaaff DM, DiCostanzo MB, et al. Contamination of flexible fiberoptic bronchoscopes. *Am Rev Respir Dis* 1983 Mar;127(3): 391–392.

106. Laussucq S, Baltch AL, Smith RP, et al. Nosocomial *Mycobacterium fortuitum* colonization from a contaminated ice machine. *Am Rev Respir Dis* 1988 Oct;138(4):891–894.

107. Uttley AH, Simpson RA. Audit of bronchoscope disinfection: A survey of procedures in England and Wales and incidents of mycobacterial contami-nation. *J Hosp Infect* 1994 Apr;26(4):301–308.

108. Panwalker AP, Fuhse E. Nosocomial Mycobacterium gordonae pseudoinfection from contaminated ice machines. *Infect Control* 1986 Feb;7(2):67–70.

109. Sniadack DH, Ostroff SM, Karlix MA, et al. A nosocomial pseudo-outbreak of *Mycobacterium xenopi* due to a contaminated potable water supply: Lessons in prevention. *Infect Control Hosp Epidemiol* 1993 Nov;14(11):636–641.

110. Stine TM, Harris AA, Levin S, et al. A pseudoepidemic due to atypical mycobacteria in a hospital water supply. *JAMA* 1987 Aug 14;258(6): 809–811.

111. Tokars JI, McNeil TM, Tablan OC. Mycobacterium gordonae pseudoin-fection associated with a contaminated antimicrobial solution. *J Clin Microbiol* 1990 Dec;28(12):2765–2769.

112. Vannier AM, Tarrand JJ, Murray PR. Mycobacterial cross contamination during radiometric culturing. *J Clin Microbiol* 1988 Sep;26(9): 1867–1868.

113. Mehta JB, Kefri M, Soike DR. Pseudoepidemic of nontuberculous mycobacteria in a community hospital. *Infect Control Hosp Epidemiol* 1995 Nov;16(11):633–634.

114. Fraser VJ, Zuckerman G, Clouse RE. A prospective randomized trial comparing manual and automated endoscope disinfection methods. *Infect Control Hosp Epidemiol* 1993 Jul;14(7):383–389.

SUPPLEMENTAL RESOURCES

American Society of Microbiology. Available at: www.asm.org.

Centers for Disease Control and Prevention (CDC). Plan to combat extensively drug-resistant tuberculosis: Recommendations of the Federal Tuberculosis Task Force. *MMWR Recomm Rep* 2009 Feb 13;58(RR-3):1-43.

Centers for Disease Control and Prevention (CDC). *National Center for HIV/ AIDS, Viral Hepatitis, STD, and TB Prevention.* Available at: http://www .cdc.gov/nchstp/tb/default.htm.

Centers for Disease Control and Prevention (CDC). Updated guidelines for the use of nucleic acid amplification tests in the diagnosis of tuberculosis. *MMWR Morb Mortal Wkly Rep* 2009 Jan 16;58(1):7–10.

Centers for Disease Control and Prevention (CDC). *Core Curriculum on Tuber-culosis: What the Clinician Should Know.* Available at: http://www.cdc.gov/ TB/education/corecurr/default.htm.

Targeted tuberculin testing and treatment of latent tuberculosis infection. American Thoracic Society. MMWR Recomm Rep [serial online]. 2000 Jun 9; 49(RR-6):1-51. Available at: http://www.cdc.gov/MMWR/preview/ MMWRhtml/rr4906a1.htm.

Members of the Ad Hoc Committee for the Guidelines for Preventing the Transmission of Tuberculosis in Canadian Health Care Facilities and Other Institutional Settings. Guidelines for preventing the transmission of tuberculosis in Canadian Health Care Facilities and other institutional settings. *Can Commun Dis Rep* 1996 Apr;22 Suppl 1:i–iv, 1–50, i–iv, 1–55.

World Health Organization. *Tuberculosis (TB).* Available at: http://www.who .int/gtb/index.htm.

Viral Hemorrhagic Fevers

Jill E. Holdsworth, MS, CIC
Infection Control Practitioner
Inova Mount Vernon Hospital
Alexandria, VA

ABSTRACT

Viral hemorrhagic fever describes a spectrum of illness ranging from fever with minor evidence of coagulopathy to a syndrome of hemorrhagic diathesis, multiorgan system failure with severe shock, and death. It is typical to see overall vascular system damage, hemorrhage, and overall impairment of the body's ability to regulate. The etiologic agents of viral hemorrhagic fever constitute four distinct families: (1) Flaviviridae (yellow fever virus, dengue fever); (2) Bunyaviridae (Crimean-Congo hemorrhagic fever, hantavirus including Sin Nombre, Rift Valley fever); (3) Filoviridae (Marburg, Ebola); and (4) Arenaviridae (Lassa, New World arenaviruses). Combined, these viruses have both a significant and varied geographic distribution and are often zoonotic. Residence in or travel to endemic areas, healthcare-associated transmission, and bioterrorist attacks are all potential risks of these diseases. Once suspicion of an index case is raised, appropriate isolation, reporting, and preemptive treatment should be initiated. Confirmation is established in Biosafety Level 4 laboratories. Many agents of viral hemorrhagic fever lack effective prevention or treatment. Infection prevention measures are imperative for containment and the protection of healthcare personnel and others. Development of effective treatments and vaccines remain the subject of intensive study.

KEY CONCEPTS

- Hemorrhagic fever viruses have broad geographic distributions.

- Animal reservoirs are important zoonotic sources that vary in each group of viruses; insects often serve as vectors.

- Viremic human hosts can serve as reservoirs for some viral hemorrhagic fevers.

- Incubation periods are 2 to 21 days.

- In severe cases, patients present with fever, nausea, vomiting, myalgia, petechiae, bleeding, and shock.

- Medical care, infection prevention implementation, and public health measures are all critical in managing patients with suspected viral hemorrhagic fever.

- Yellow fever virus is the only hemorrhagic fever virus with a licensed vaccine.

- Treatment is generally supportive.

- Patients should be placed in contact and droplet isolation with mask and eye protection; airborne isolation is recommended in certain instances.

- Bioterrorism should be considered in patients with viral hemorrhagic fever who do not have a history of contact with an infected patient.

BACKGROUND

Hemorrhagic fever has been documented throughout ancient and modern history. The earliest description of symptoms now thought to be dengue was in a Chinese encyclopedia from the Chin Dynasty (221–207 BC). The first reported pandemic of denguelike illness occurred in the late 18th century in three continents.[1] The worst outbreak of viral hemorrhagic fever (VHF) in U.S. history occurred in Philadelphia in 1793 when yellow fever virus (YFV) devastated the city, killing more than 5,000 people—10 percent of the city's population—in just a few months. The nation's capital was shut down, and President Washington moved the government out of the city to escape the epidemic. Public panic was rampant, people walked in the middle of the streets to avoid infected houses, and friends avoided speaking to each other out of fear of disease transmission.[2] YFV continued to plague the United States intermittently until the development of a vaccine in 1930.

Most recently, an outbreak of Ebola hemorrhagic fever occurred in the Luwero District of Uganda. As of December 2, 2012, seven cases were reported (probable and confirmed) of Ebola virus infection, including four deaths. As of November 29, 2012, 15 confirmed and eight probable cases of Marburg hemorrhagic fever were reported in the Kabale, Ibanda, Mbarara, and Kampala districts of Uganda.

Hantavirus pulmonary syndrome (HPS) was first recognized in 1993 in the Four Corners region of the southwestern United States when a cluster of cases of influenza-like illness showed up that progressed quickly to a severe respiratory disease. An unprecedented investigation by the Special Pathogens Branch of the Centers for Disease Control and Prevention (CDC) identified a new virus, Muerto Canyon virus, subsequently named Sin Nombre virus (SNV), as the etiologic agent. Retrospective analysis revealed that earlier cases of respiratory distress syndromes dating to 1959 were caused by HPS.[3] In 2012, 10 cases of hantavirus were confirmed in California. All 10 cases were linked to recent visitors to Yosemite National Park.

VHF is caused by a diverse group of small RNA viruses from four major viral families that are found in different geographic areas as shown in Table 96-1. The viruses naturally reside in an animal reservoir host or arthropod vector. Person-to-person spread can occur from body fluid contact.[4] Many have potential for weaponization, and worldwide health systems take part in ongoing preparation for any case of intentional release of these agents.[5]

BASIC PRINCIPLES

VHF can range from asymptomatic to a mild febrile illness to the hemorrhagic syndrome, including fever with severe shock, multiorgan system failure, and death. Although bleeding is a dramatic finding in these diseases, it is rarely life threatening. The impaired function of multiple organ systems is the primary marker of morbidity and mortality. Etiological viral agents of VHF are taxonomically identifiable by four groups[4]:

1. Flaviviridae: YFV, dengue fever, dengue hemorrhagic fever (DHF), Omsk hemorrhagic fever (OHF), and Kyasanur Forest disease (KFD)

2. Bunyaviridae: Congo-Crimean hemorrhagic fever (CCHF), HPS, hemorrhagic fever with renal syndrome (HFRS), and Rift Valley fever (RVF)

3. Filoviridae: Marburg and Ebola

4. Arenaviridae: Lassa fever and New World arenaviruses, including Guanarito, Sabia, Junin, and Machupo

VIRAL HEMORRHAGIC FEVERS: CAUSE AND EFFECT

Etiologic Agents and Vectors

Table 96-1 details the most important etiologic agents, geographical distribution, and other features of VHF viruses. The agents are RNA viruses covered, or enveloped, in a fatty (lipid) coating. Virus survival is dependent on an animal or insect host: their natural reservoir. Humans may become infected when they come into contact with infected hosts or excreta and may subsequently transmit the virus to one another. Human cases of VHFs occur sporadically and irregularly, and outbreaks cannot be easily predicted.[4]

Initial outbreak in 1967 was associated with exposure to tissue cultures or kidneys of infected African green monkeys imported

Table 96-1. Characteristics of Viruses Causing Viral Hemorrhagic Fever

Virus	Family	Geography	Vector	Host	Epidemiologic Features
Yellow fever virus	Flaviviridae	Central and South America, Africa	*Aedes* and *Haemagogus* mosquito	Monkeys, humans	Three cycles of transmission by vector: urban (human to human), intermediate, (savannah) and sylvatic (jungle, monkey to human)
Omsk hemorrhagic fever	Flaviviridae	Western Siberia	*Dermacentor* ticks	Small mammals	Direct contact with ticks; contact with blood, feces, or urine of an infected or dead rodent; milk of infected goat or sheep
Kyasanur Forest disease	Flaviviridae	India	*Haemaphysalis* ticks	Small mammals, monkeys, birds, bats, cattle	Direct contact with infected ticks, deforestation for cattle grazing increases tick population
Dengue	Flaviviridae	Tropical America, Africa, Asia	*Aedes* mosquito	Humans	Transmitted as is urban yellow fever
Crimean-Congo hemorrhagic fever	Bunyaviridae	Russia, Middle East, Sub-Saharan Africa, Asia, Balkans	*Hyalomma* ticks	Cattle, sheep, goats, hares	Agricultural/cattle workers at risk; has caused healthcare-associated outbreaks
Hantavirus	Bunyaviridae	Worldwide	None	Rodents	Occurs through contact with infected rodents, rodent excreta, often aerosolized material; unlikely spread from person to person
Rift Valley fever	Bunyaviridae	Sub-Saharan Africa, Madagascar, Middle East	*Aedes* mosquito	Cattle, sheep, small mammals	Epizootic outbreaks occur in times of elevated rainfalls and persistent flooding
Marburg	Filoviridae	Sub-Saharan Africa	Not known	Not known	Humans only known source of infections; body fluids are highly infectious
Ebola	Filoviridae	Sub-Saharan Africa	Not known	Not known	As with Marburg
Lassa	Arenaviridae	West and Central Africa	None	Rodents	Occurs through contact with infected rodents, rodent excreta, often aerosolized material; may spread person to person, healthcare-associated outbreak
Guanario	Arenaviridae	Venezuela	None	Rodents	Transmitted as in Lassa
Sabia	Arenaviridae	Brazil	Not known	Not known	May spread person to person
Junin	Arenaviridae	Argentina	None	Rodents	Transmitted as in Lassa
Machupo	Arenaviridae	Bolivia	None	Rodents	Transmitted as in Lassa

for vaccine preparation, but subsequent work does not suggest that these animals are natural virus reservoirs.

Flaviviridae

YFV is an arthropod-borne virus with three known transmission cycles. In sylvatic YFV, transmission occurs between nonhuman primates and mosquito species, usually via mosquitos, and from monkeys to humans during occupational or recreational activities in the jungle. Intermediate transmission cycle occurs from tree hole-breeding *Aedes* species to humans. This cycle usually transmits from monkeys to humans or from human to human via mosquito. Urban YFV is passed between humans and urban mosquitos.

The vector for dengue fever is the female *Aedes* mosquito found predominately in tropical and subtropical areas. Specifically, this group B arbovirus is transmitted by *Aedes aegypti* and *Aedes albopictus*. There are four dengue virus serotypes: DEN-1, DEN2, DEN-3, and DEN-4.[6]

OHF is transmitted by *Dermacentor* ticks, water voles (*Arvicola terrestris*), and non-native muskrats (*Ondatra zibethica*).

KFD is transmitted primarily by the *Haemaphysalis spinigera* tick.

Bunyaviridae

CCHF, caused by the tickborne virus *Nairovirus*, is primarily transmitted to people from ticks and infected livestock animals. Human-to-human transmission is possible when close contact with blood and body fluids occur.

Hantavirus is transmitted from virus shed in rodent excreta by breathing in the virus when stirred up in the air or touching a mucous membrane after contact with rodent excreta or nesting materials. Each hantavirus has a unique rodent host. In the United States, rodents including the deer mouse (*Peromyscus maniculatus*), cotton rat (*Sigmodon hispidus*), rice rat (*Oryzomys palustris*), and white-footed mouse (*P. leucopus*) have been found to carry the agent responsible for HPS, and several other rodent reservoirs are linked to HFRS. *Aedes* mosquitoes spread RVF.

HPS is very rare, but cases have been reported in all areas of the United States except Alaska and Hawaii.

RVF affects domestic animals (cattle, buffalo, sheep, goats, and camels) and humans. RVF is most common during times of heavy rainfall and is a mosquito-borne virus. The excess rainfall allows mosquito eggs to hatch, which are naturally infected with the RVF virus, which then transfer for the virus to livestock.

Filoviridae

A vector for Marburg and Ebola has not been confirmed. Recent studies indicate that fruit bats in Africa and Uganda are a reservoir.[7]

Five subtypes of Ebola virus exist, four of which have caused disease in humans: Ebola-Zaire, Ebola-Sudan, Ebola-Ivory Coast, Ebola-Bundibugyo, and Ebola-Reston.

Arenaviridae

Arenaviridae are transmitted through close contact with food or household items contaminated with rodent excreta. The reservoir for Lassa virus is the "multimammate rat" of the genus *Mastomys*. Some, including Lassa and Machupo, may be spread by person-to-person contact and laboratory transmission via contact with blood or other body fluids. Airborne transmission has been described.[4]

Epidemiology

Because the VHF viruses have a substantial geographic distribution, widespread travel has increased the probability that healthcare personnel will care for patients infected with these diseases. Between 1996 and 2006, the World Health Organization (WHO) reported outbreaks of CCHF in 6 of 10 years in locations in South Africa, South Asia, and Eastern Europe. Ebola epidemics have been noted with a high frequency in several countries in Africa, most recently in the Democratic Republic of Congo in December 2008.[5] The closely related Marburg virus has been the cause of imported disease cased from Uganda to The Netherlands and United States in 2008.[8] An estimated 200,000 cases of yellow fever (YF) occur each year in South America and Africa.[6] This epidemiologic frequency, coupled with the threat of bioterrorism, makes it imperative for the clinician to understand the nature and course of these diseases. The WHO currently tracks outbreaks of Ebola, CCHF, Lassa fever, YF, RVF, and dengue fever.[5] Hantaviruses have a worldwide distribution and originally were known to cause HFRS. By 2007, 465 cases of HPS had been reported in the United States since its initial description.[3]

Pathogenesis and Clinical Features

The precise pathogenesis for VHF varies according to the specific etiologic agent; immunologic and inflammatory mediators are thought to play an important role. In DHF, an immune-mediated pathogenesis is thought to play a role when an individual previously infected with dengue is exposed to a heterologous serotype. In other VHFs, potential pathophysiologic mechanisms include disseminated intravascular coagulation (DIC), consumptive coagulopathy, and hepatic dysfunction.[9] All VHFs can produce thrombocytopenia. Although the major target organ is the vascular endothelium, some VHFs may induce platelet dysfunction.

VHFs are caused by agents that have pronounced aerosol stability and high infectivity.[10] Fortunately, they are not highly transmissible among humans without direct physical contact with infected fluids, presumably because virus-containing aerosols are not easily generated by those infected. Still, they retain a potential for use as biological agents. Programs that have developed weaponized forms of VHF have existed for many years, some in production until recently. For example, the former Soviet Union produced large quantities of Marburg, Ebola, Lassa, Junin, and Machupo viruses until 1992, and the United States weaponized RVF and YFV as part of a biological weapons program that was ended in 1969.[11]

Most VHF viruses cause disease during the period of viremia. When the viremia clears, the patient recovers. The exceptions are the dengue and hantaviruses, which have an immunopathologic basis.[1,3,4] In VHF, hematologic manifestations may be different from those found in sepsis. A vascular syndrome marked by endothelial dysfunction or damage appears to be the primary mechanism of hemorrhage. Bleeding can occur in the absence of DIC. VHF viruses share a similar syndrome of diffuse capillary damage and coagulation dysregulation. Proinflammatory cytokine production, especially tumor necrosis factor (TNF)-α, has also been a consistent finding.[10,12] Cytopathic effects from VHF viruses vary among agents, some causing a marked cytopathic effect, whereas others show little evidence of cell destruction. The major organs involved include the kidney, brain, and liver.

Flaviviruses have an unidentified pathogenesis, but Kupffer cells in the liver appear to be the first cells targeted. Replication and subsequent cellular damage take place in the hepatocytes and myocytes.[13] There is hepatocellular necrosis with sparing of the central vein and portal areas. The eosinophilic degeneration of hepatocytes leads to the formation of Councilman bodies. Bradycardia and arrhythmias are related to myocyte infection. Albuminuria and renal insufficiency reflect prerenal processes and parenchymal invasion. Renal tubular necrosis can develop in advanced illness.

Bunyaviruses exhibit varied effects dependent on the viral agent. CCHF causes massive hemorrhage and DIC but is not as cytotoxic as RVF. There is necrosis seen in hepatocytes expressing viral antigen, but the overall mechanism of disease remains poorly understood.

In HPS, the heart and lung are the target organs of infection with extensive viral replication occurring in endothelial tissues, particularly the pulmonary vascular bed. Subsequent damage to the capillary endothelium produces severe pulmonary edema and hypotensive shock. Typical laboratory findings include left shift in white blood cells, hemoconcentration, neutrophilic leukocytosis, thrombocytopenia, and circulating immunoblasts.

The RVF virus is very cytotoxic, and rapid cell death occurs in all mammalian cells tested, including human endothelial cell cultures.[14] In studies with monkeys, a reliable predictor of outcome was the secretion of interferon (IFN)-α. If levels were detectable within 12 hours of infection, the course was mild. With a later onset of secretion, severe disease and DIC were seen.[15] Delay in the INF response might allow for more extensive infection and cell death, triggering the severe form of the disease.

Filoviruses have a combined cytokine effect and cytotoxic effect. Cytokine release by macrophages, notably TNF-α, plays a role in the alterations in endothelial permeability.[6] Cytokines are suspected in the severe apoptosis of lymphoid organs seen in Ebola infections.[16] Cytotoxic effects are seen in parenchymal cells in multiple organs, including the endothelium. DIC is associated with filovirus infection. Animal studies have demonstrated a slight increase in survival from Ebola with the use of activated protein C as a successful adjuvant treatment for sepsis in humans, supporting the hypothesis that Ebola and sepsis share some common pathways.[17]

Arenaviruses are not highly cytopathic. They have been shown to disrupt cellular function without damaging the cell.[6] The degree of cellular dysfunction exceeds the pattern of cellular damage, suggesting an underlying mechanism. This pattern of dysfunction may also explain the finding of cardiac depression that can accompany arenavirus infections. Thrombocytopenia and platelet dysfunction are associated with bleeding episodes. There is no evidence of major coagulation pathway defects or DIC in arenavirus infections.[11] Thrombocytopenia and platelet dysfunction are associated with bleeding episodes.

Clinical Manifestations

Infections with viruses causing VHF are frequently asymptomatic, but when the infections are symptomatic, there is typically abrupt onset of fever, chills, headache, myalgia, and malaise. A minority of patients progress to a hemorrhagic syndrome. Travel history, incubation period, and the distinguishing clinical features outlined here can help to suggest the viral etiology.

Flaviviridae

YFV is distributed in tropical South America and Africa. It has an incubation period of 3 to 6 days. Bradycardia despite fever (Faget sign) is characteristic. Disease course includes three periods: infection, remission, and intoxication. The period of infection may be asymptomatic or present with influenza-like illness symptoms, fever, myalgia, headache, appetite loss, nausea, or vomiting. The symptoms of the primary infection remit on days 3 to 4 and are termed the period of remission; this is marked by an improvement in fever, nausea, and headache. Most patients will recover at this point without any further sequelae. Some patients, however, will continue into the period of intoxication after a remission that lasts for several hours up to 2 days before the fever recurs. The intoxication occurs in approximately 15 percent of patients[18] and includes a fever (> 40°C), severe headache and myalgia, hemorrhagic diathesis, myocardial invasion, and hepatitis. Deep jaundice and elevation of transaminases continues for several days, with aspartate aminotransferase (AST) elevated more than the level of alanine aminotransferase. Albuminuria is an important feature that differentiates YFV from other causes of viral hepatitis, and it can cause kidney failure.[13,18,19] Approximately 15 percent of patients develop severe disease, and approximately half of these will die. Death usually occurs within 7 to 10 days after the onset of symptoms.[13] Delirium, coma, and hypotension secondary to heart failure may occur before death.[20]

Dengue fever is distributed worldwide, especially in the tropics and subtropics. There is variation in the incubation period, but when the infection remains uncomplicated, the range can be from 3 to 14 days after the infective bite. However, if dengue fever progresses to DHF or dengue shock syndrome (DSS), the incubation period is unknown.[19,21] For 3 to 5 days, the patient is acutely febrile. Clinical manifestations widely vary and initially resemble flu-like symptoms including severe frontal headaches, myalgia, chills, rash, and retro-orbital pain. If the patient is young, anorexia, nausea, and vomiting differentiates dengue fever from other childhood febrile diseases. After the incubation period, the disease progresses to hemorrhagic manifestations, prostration, lumbar back pain, and abdominal tenderness. Localized clusters of petechiae might replace the preceding, fading rash. Shock can last 1 to 2 days, and DSS can result in an acute vascular leak.[19,21] Seventy-five percent of patients develop palpable hepatomegaly. Laboratory findings include elevated amylase levels, hypoalbuminemia, and elevated hematocrit.[19] Other laboratory examinations might show leukopenia, neutropenia, thrombocytopenia, and mildly elevated AST levels. With supportive treatment, patients experience remission within 2 to 3 days, with 1 percent mortality in well-provided centers. In underserved populations, however, mortality rates have reached 50 percent.[19]

OHF and KFD are found in Western Siberia and India, respectively. After a short incubation period of 3 to 8 days, patients exhibit a sudden-onset fever (> 40°C), headache, severe muscle pain, cough, dehydration, GI problems, and papulovesicular lesions of the soft palate. Severe cases show nasal, enteric, or pulmonary hemorrhage.[13] Laboratory studies show leukopenia, thrombocytopenia, and albuminuria. A remission phase of 1 to 2 weeks is seen in some patients, and a subsequent severe illness is marked by meningoencephalitis. Fatality is 0.5 to 3 percent in OHF and 5 to 10 percent in KFD.[13] OHF frequently causes hearing loss, hair loss, and behavioral/phsychological difficulties associated with neutological conditions.

Bunyaviridae

CCHF is endemic in Africa, the Balkans, the Middle East, and Asian countries south of the 50th parallel north.[13,22,23] The incubation range following a tick bite is 1 to 3 days, with a maximum of 9 days, and the incubation period following contact with infected blood or tissues is usually 5 to 6 days, with a maximum of 13 days. Symptoms include sudden onset of fever, myalgia, dizziness, neck pain and stiffness, sore eyes and photophobia, nausea, and vomiting.[22] Sharp mood swings and mental status changes begin after a few days, with confusion and aggression progressing into lethargy, sleepiness, and depression after 2 to 4 more days. Abdominal pain is usually present and may localize to the right upper quadrant, and hepatomegaly is often present. Hemorrhagic symptoms present with major coagulation dysfunction and thrombocytopenia; DIC may manifest on days 3 to 6 of illness. Mild cases are marked by generalized petechial rash on the skin and mucosa, whereas severe cases are marked by ecchymoses, epistaxis, gastrointestinal bleeding, hematuria, and uterine bleeding. Patients might

require multiple transfusions.[10,13,22,23] Liver function test results become elevated, and death can occur from liver failure and hepatorenal syndrome. Mortality approaches 30 percent and results from multiple organ system failure, blood loss, cerebral hemorrhage, pulmonary failure, or dehydration.[22] Patients who recover will typcially begin to show improvement on the ninth or tenth day after the onset of illness. Oral and intravenous forms of ribavirin have been shown to have some benefit for treatment in CCHF cases.

Hantavirus infection with the SNV typically has two main phases of clinical illness: initial and late phase. The initial phase is marked by a febrile prodrome that is nonspecific and nearly impossible to distinguish as a hantavirus infection. It is thought that the initial symptoms may begin to appear between 1 and 5 weeks after exposure to fresh urine, droppings, or saliva of infected rodents. The most frequently reported symptoms include fever, chills, fatigue, and muscle aches, especially in the large muscle groups, such as hips, thighs, back, and sometimes shoulders. In addition, patients may have headache, cough, nausea, abdominal pain, dizziness, and diarrhea. Physical examination may reveal tachypnea, tachycardia, wet rales, and abdominal tenderness. The late phase begins 4 to 10 days after the initial phase of illness. Progression of disease occurs precipitously and is characterized by coughing, shortness of breath, hypotensive shock, noncardiogenic pulmonary edema, and severe lactic acidosis. The clinical picture closely resembles adult respiratory distress syndrome but may also be easily confused with acute myocardial infarction or infections such as plague, leptospirosis, Legionnaires' disease, tularemia, coccidioidomycosis, histoplasmosis, or even severe acute respiratory syndrome. Patients become hypoxemic despite mechanical ventilation with 100 percent oxygen, and fatal pulmonary deterioration may ensue within days. The mortality rate in patients who progress to the second phase of HPS is approximately 38 percent.[24]

RVF has a geographic distribution in sub-Saharan Africa, Madagascar, and the Middle East.[23,25] The incubation period is 2 to 6 days, with most patients experiencing no symptoms or a mild febrile illness with liver abnormalities. Others display an influenza-like illness with sudden onset of fever, headache, backache, and myalgia; in some cases, development of neck stiffness, photophobia, and vomiting may occur. The symptoms of RVF usually last from 4 to 7 days, at which time the immune response becomes detectable with the appearance of immunoglobulin (IgM) and IgG antibodies. Less than 3 percent of patients develop severe disease, and complications include eye disease, meningoencephalitis, and hemorrhagic fever. The proportion of patients developing these complications is approximately 0.5 to 2 percent for eye disease and less than 1 percent for meningoencephalitis and hemorrhagic fever syndrome.[25] Eye diseases, including macular retinitis and vasculitis, can occur in up to 2 percent of patients and usually appear 1 to 3 weeks after the first symptoms, and patients may be afebrile. When the lesions are in the macula, some degree of permanent visual loss will result. Death in patients with only ocular disease is uncommon. Up to 1 percent of patients can also present with meningoencephalitis, beginning 1 to 3 weeks after the first symptoms. Mortality in patients with meningoencephalitis alone is rare.[25] Hemorrhagic symptoms caused by RVF occur 2 to 4 days after the onset of fever. Patients have severe liver disease, jaundice, and hemorrhagic phenomena, such as gingival and gastrointestinal bleeding and purpuric rash. Those infected may remain viremic for up to 10 days. The case-fatality rate for patients developing hemorrhagic disease is high, approximately 50 percent.[13,23,25] Most fatalities occur in the severe hemorrhagic form of the disease. However, the overall fatality rate is less than 1 percent.[13,25]

Filoviridae

Marburg and Ebola are found in sub-Saharan Africa.[26,27] The incubation period is usually from 5 to 10 days, with a range of 2 to 21 days. Patients may present with a sudden onset of high fever, severe headache, backache, joint and muscle aches, sore throat, weakness, conjunctivitis, diarrhea, vomiting, and stomach pain, and a fine, maculopapular rash may develop several days into the illness. Marked mental status changes are often evident by day 5. Bleeding from body orifices occurs in approximately one-third of patients and is associated with high mortality.[28] Hemorrhagic manifestations develop within 5 to 7 days of the onset of symptoms, but the bilirubin level usually remains normal. Laboratory testing may show leukopenia and thrombocytopenia, as well as elevated prothrombin time, liver enzymes, and amylase. Abnormal electrocardiograms and reduced renal function occur in some patients.[13,25] Mortality ranges from 50 to 90 percent. Deaths usually occur during the second week of illness.[10,22]

Arenaviridae

Lassa fever has an incubation period of 3 to 16 days with a gradual onset of fever, chills, headache, myalgias, and sore throat.[23,29] Progression is more insidious than with Marburg or Ebola, and a purulent pharyngitis with white tonsillar patches is a distinguishing characteristic.[30] Retrosternal pain, relative bradycardia, albuminuria with casts, and an axillary petechial rash are seen.[13] Severe cases display shock, hemorrhage, pleural effusion, seizures, encephalopathy, and swelling of the face and neck. The hemorrhagic manifestations and the volume of blood loss are not enough to account for shock in these patients.[29] Eighth nerve deafness (unilateral or bilateral) is seen in 25 percent of those who recover. Only 50 percent will regain function over the next 1 to 3 months.[29] In severe cases, hair loss, ataxia, and loss of coordination may occur during convalescence.[13,29] The mortality rate is 15 to 20 percent in those hospitalized with severe disease.[29] Ribavarin has been used in Lassa fever cases with success, most often when given early in the illness.

New World arenaviruses have an incubation period ranging from 7 to 14 days.[13,21,29] The course is similar to Lassa fever with the notable absence of pharyngitis. Progression to hemorrhage with thrombocytopenia is common.[13,20] Half of patients

with Machupo have intention tremor of tongue and hands, and 25 percent of patients will go on to delirium and convulsions.[13] Mortality is 10 to 20 percent, usually as a result of shock and renal failure.

Laboratory Diagnosis

Suspect VHF in patients with the constellation of symptoms described earlier and an appropriate travel or exposure history within 3 weeks of the onset of symptoms. Diagnostic testing can only be done in Biosafety Level 4 laboratories. Because of the inherent risk of handling specimens, the CDC requires notification before receiving specimens suspected of VHF. Consultation on preparation of specimens and shipping protocols is available 24 hours per day through the Special Pathogens Branch of the CDC.[4,31]

Confirmation of diagnosis requires virus isolation from blood or other body fluids, presence of specific IgM antibody, or demonstration of a fourfold increase in IgG titer between acute and convalescent serum specimens. YF antibodies can cross-react with other flaviviruses, including West Nile virus, dengue fever, and St. Louis encephalitis. Antibodies to the virus may take up to 2 weeks to become detectable; testing for specific antibodies is available through the CDC.

Antigen detection test by enzyme-linked immunosorbent assay is available, but it has limited value in early diagnosis. More rapid diagnostic modalities, such as antigen detection, virus genome detection using reverse transcriptase-polymerase chain reaction assay, and immunohistochemical staining, are also available. The WHO has instituted mobile field laboratories in some African nations, enabling workers to diagnose Ebola within 24 hours.[28] Rapid testing ability decreases healthcare-associated infection rates by correctly identifying suspected cases early.

Implementation Strategies for Diagnosis and Treatment

Strategies include identification of the suspect cases, which should be considered in patients (1) with a temperature 101°F or higher with abnormal bleeding and shock; (2) with a history of travel to an endemic area; (3) who come in contact with a person with unexplained febrile illness with bleeding, or a person who died after an unexplained febrile illness; (4) who work in a laboratory or animal facility that handles hemorrhagic fever viruses; or (5) who are victims of bioterrorism. Initiate supportive treatment for all cases of VHF and include monitoring of electrolytes, replacement of fluid and blood, and correction of coagulopathy. Consultation on preparation of laboratory specimens and shipping protocols is available 24 hours per day through the Special Pathogens Branch of the CDC.[31] The possibility of bioterrorism must be considered in the event of a suspected VHF case without a known exposure.[11,31,32] Patients should be managed per the infection prevention guidelines discussed later in this chapter.

Antiviral Therapy

Currently, there is no U.S. Food and Drug Administration-approved antiviral therapy for the treatment of VHF. However, ribavirin can reduce mortality after infection with Lassa fever and other arenaviruses and bunyaviruses.[33,34] Oral and intravenous (IV) ribavirin has been used with apparent benefit in the treatment of CCHF; Table 96-2 lists the recommended doses.[11,23] Ribavirin is not helpful in cases of VHF caused by flaviviruses or filoviruses. It is important to administer ribavirin immediately pending diagnostic confirmation. If infection with arenaviruses or bunyaviruses is confirmed, a 10-day course of ribavirin should be completed. If infection with filoviruses or flaviviruses is confirmed or VHF is excluded, ribavirin should be discontinued.

The efficacy of passive immunization is controversial. It has been shown to enhance viral replication in experimentally infected animals and has been used with good results in Argentine hemorrhagic fever.[11] Monoclonal antibodies and human-derived products are currently under development. For Ebola, pre-exposure and postexposure prophylaxes have been achieved in animal models by passive transfer of neutralizing human monoclonal antibody, KZ52.[35]

Postexposure prophylaxis is hampered by the lack of effective vaccines and antiviral medications. The Working Group on Civilian Biodefense does **not** recommend prophylactic ribavirin in the absence of the described signs and symptoms of VHF. Persons potentially exposed to VHF agents should be placed under medical surveillance for 21 days. If there are any signs or symptoms of infection, preemptive treatment should be initiated promptly while pending confirmation and viral identification.[11]

Travel Vaccination

A live attenuated 17D vaccine exists for YFV and is the only licensed vaccine for any VHF. It is not useful for postexposure prophylaxis, because YFV has a short incubation period. Travelers over 9 months of age should receive the vaccine at least 10 days before arrival in endemic areas. Immunization is required before travel to some countries. Boosters are

recommended every 10 years. There is an increased risk of postvaccination encephalitis in patients under 6 months of age. Because information regarding the effects in the fetus is limited, an individual risk assessment should be performed on the pregnant woman if travel to endemic areas cannot be avoided.[36] Mothers should avoid nursing after vaccination. The vaccine should be avoided in persons with egg allergies or those with immunodeficiencies.[13] Two serious adverse reaction syndromes have been described: Yellow fever vaccine-associated viscerotropic disease (YEL-AVD) and Yellow fever vaccine-associated neurologic disease (YEL-AND). YEL-AVD is marked by multiple organ failure and disease patterns that mimic naturally acquired YF. Ten cases have been reported in the literature to date.[36] YEL-AND includes clinical syndromes such as meningoencephalitis, Guillain-Barré syndrome, acute disseminated encephalomyelitis, and some rare cases of bulbar and Bell palsies.

Vaccines in Development

Glycoprotein vaccines for Lassa fever have shown effectiveness in protecting primates, but human results are not available.[37] The Candid 1 vaccine is a live attenuated vaccine in development that has been shown to be efficacious in prevention of Argentine hemorrhagic fever (Junin) in humans.[38] A formalin-inactivated RVF vaccine in development has been given to laboratory personnel with subsequent increase in antibody titers. Three doses of inactivated vaccine were required to achieve a fourfold increase in antibody production.[39] A vaccine against dengue-2 virus involves the experimental inoculation of infectious DNA in rhesus macaques. Human trials of this technique and others are in progress with prospects for a recombinant human vaccine at least 5 to 10 years in the future.[40-43] An Ebola virus-like particle produced in insect cells using recombinant technology is being evaluated as possible effective Ebola vaccine.[44] A live attenuated recombinant vaccine against Marburg virus has shown encouraging results in animal studies with the potential of cross-protection across strains.[45]

Infection Prevention

Because of the lack of effective and licensed vaccines and drug therapy, preventing transmission of VHF relies on meticulous adherence to infection prevention measures. Immediately isolate (standard, contact, and droplet)[46] the suspected patient and notify (1) local and state health department, (2) infection prevention personnel, (3) laboratory personnel, and (4) an infectious disease specialist for consultation. In rural areas, placing already-infected patients under mosquito netting to prevent secondary spread will help to control outbreaks.

In the absence of a biologic attack, VHF is unlikely in patients who have traveled only to urban areas or who have onset of symptoms more than 3 weeks after travel. Patients with travel-related fever are more likely to have other infections, such as malaria, hepatitis, and typhoid.

Table 96-2. Recommendations for Ribavirin Therapy in Patients with Clinical Evidence of Viral Hemorrhagic Fever Pending Workup or Confirmed Viral Hemorrhagic Fever Due to Arenaviruses or Bunyaviruses

Patients	Contained casualty setting	Mass casualty setting
Adults	30 mg/kg IV loading (max 2 g/dose), then 16 mg/kg (max 1 g/dose) IV every 6 h for 4 d, then 8 mg/kg IV every 8 h for 6 d	2,000 mg PO loading, then 1,200 mg/d (if > 75 kg) or 1,000 mg (if ≤ 75 kg) PO for 10 d
Children	Same dose as adult	30 mg/kg PO loading, then 15 mg/kg/d (in 2 divided doses) for 10 d

In pregnant patients, although ribavirin is contraindicated, in this setting benefits outweigh risks.

IV, intravenously; PO, orally.

Prehospital Procedures

Standard Precautions for bloodborne pathogens must be applied to patients with suspected VHF undergoing prehospital evaluation. If a patient has respiratory symptoms, the caregivers should use surgical masks with eye protection or face shields. If blood, emesis, urine, or feces are present, the patient should be managed as outlined in the hospitalized patient section.

Hospitalized Patients

The majority of person-to-person and healthcare-associated transmissions occur through direct contact with infected blood and body fluids.[11,32,46–50] However, there is the possibility of spread by airborne means from aerosolized contaminated body fluids of the individual. The CDC recommends standard and droplet isolation for most patient care. For patients with suspected VHF who have prominent cough, vomiting, diarrhea, or hemorrhage, additional precautions must be taken.[46,49] A summary of isolation precautions is noted here:

- Patients should be placed on standard, contact, and droplet isolation precautions for the duration of illness. A single-patient room is preferred. Patients should wear a mask until placed in a room and during transport to contain respiratory droplets.

- All persons entering the room should wear barrier protection: single gloves and fluid-resistant or impermeable gown. All persons coming within 3 feet of the patient should also wear a surgical mask plus face shields, goggles, or another form of eye protection.

- Additional barriers such as aprons, double gloves, and shoe and leg covers should be worn in situations in which contact with copious volumes of blood, feces, or vomit is anticipated. In the final stages of illness, hemorrhage is likely to occur and the viral load is greatest and additional personal protective equipment (PPE) should always be worn.

- Nonessential staff and visitors should be kept to a minimum and should be required to wear appropriate PPE when entering the room. A log of visitors and staff should be maintained.

- PPE should be carefully removed and disposed of in the patient room or anteroom, and soiled shoes should be disinfected.

- Standard Precautions for needle and sharp disposal should be followed to minimize the risk of percutaneous exposure.

- Surgical and obstetric procedures should be kept to a minimum. In cases where such a procedure is required, the state health department and the CDC should be consulted for proper precautions.

- Hospitals may choose to institute Airborne Precautions for patients with VHF who exhibit respiratory symptoms or in procedures with the production of aerosols (nebulized medication administration, endotracheal suctioning, bronchoscopy, positive pressure ventilation, or oscillatory ventilation). N95 respirators will be required for these procedures.

Suitable solutions for disinfecting environmental surfaces include 0.5 percent sodium hypochlorite (1:100 daily dilution of household bleach) or an Environmental Protection Agency (EPA)-registered hospital disinfectant. Soaps and detergents can inactivate the viruses but should not be depended on for disinfection.[49,50] Clothing and linens must be placed in labeled leakproof bags and directly transported to the cleaning area. Linens can be autoclaved or washed in hot water with bleach and must be placed directly into the machine without sorting to avoid any potential exposures.[49] Disposable items used in patient care, such as suction containers and catheters, may be incinerated, decontaminated by autoclave, or immersed in an EPA-registered disinfectant and then handled according to state and local regulations. There is no evidence for transmission of HFVs to humans or animals through exposure to contaminated sewage; the risk of such transmission would be expected to be extremely low with sewage treatment procedures in use in the United States. As an added precaution, however, measures should be taken to eliminate or reduce the infectivity of bulk blood, suctioned fluids, secretions, and excretions before disposal by treatment with a decontaminating agent or autoclaving before disposal.[49]

Laboratory

Laboratory personnel exposure is a significant risk, and tests should be limited to those absolutely necessary for patient care. Phlebotomists and laboratory staff should use protective equipment in accordance with Standard Precautions and the recommendations mentioned earlier. Specimens should be placed in sealed plastic bags and then transported directly to the specimen-handling area of the laboratory in clearly labeled, durable, and leakproof containers. The specimen should remain in the custody of the designated person until testing is done. All specimens, including centrifugation and aliquots of serum, should be handled in at least a class 2 biological safety cabinet following Biosafety Level Three practices. Virus isolation should be done only in a BSL4 laboratory. Serum used in laboratory tests should be inactivated using 1 μg polyethylene glycol p-tert-octylphenyl ether per milliliter of serum.[49] This substance decreases viral titers but may not be 100 percent effective in inactivating virus. Automated systems should be used only if specimens have been inactivated first. The automated system should also be disinfected after use, as recommended by the manufacturer.

Exposure

Any personnel with mucocutaneous or percutaneous exposures to blood, body fluids, secretions, or excretions, including sweat and tears, should immediately wash the affected skin area with soap and water. An antiseptic solution or hand-washing product can be used, but the efficacy has not been documented. Irrigate mucous membranes with large amounts of water or eyewash solution. Exposed persons should be evaluated as a contact and followed up.[49]

A contact is defined as any person exposed to the infected patient or their secretions, excretions, or tissue in the 3 weeks

before the patient's onset of illness.[49] Contacts can be stratified into the level of risk: (1) casual contact, such as staying
in the same hotel or flying on the same plane, does not
constitute a significant exposure—special precautions are not
needed; (2) close contacts, such as household contacts, patient
caregivers, or personnel who have handled laboratory specimens
without protective gear, will need to be placed under surveillance
for 21 days—notify local health authorities; (3) high-risk contacts
are those with mucous membrane, blood, or other body fluid exposure through kissing, sexual intercourse, needlestick, or other
means; these individuals are placed under close surveillance
and monitored for symptoms. If exposure is known to be to an
arenavirus or bunyavirus, prophylactic ribavirin may be given.

Contacts under surveillance should have body temperature
measured twice daily. If temperature of 38.3°C (101°F) or
higher develops, or any symptoms of illness occur, the contact
under surveillance is placed in isolation and given treatment for
presumed VHF until proven otherwise.

Autopsy and Handling of the Human Remains[49]

Handling bodies should be minimized, and the benefit versus
the risk of autopsy must be carefully considered. The CDC
should be contacted about further recommendations regarding
autopsy and appropriate procedures for special circumstances.
Aerosol formation should be avoided. Unnecessary handling
of the body, such as embalming, should be avoided. The
body should be placed in a sealed bag and cremated or buried
promptly in a sealed casket.

CONCLUSIONS

Understanding and proper recognition of VHF are of vital importance because of its high morbidity, mortality, and risk of hospital
spread, as well as its potential use as a bioterrorism agent. Early
treatment with ribavirin can improve survival with some forms
of VHF, and, in these cases, treatment should be initiated while
awaiting virus confirmation. International travel has led to an
increased risk of these diseases spreading from endemic areas,
and recent cases have been imported to Europe and the United
States from endemic countries. Knowledge of pathogenesis and
clinical presentations should help clinicians identify suspected
cases. Appropriate isolation, reporting, preemptive treatment,
and confirmation of diagnosis must be initiated for the suspected
index cases. The exact pathogenesis and modes of transmission are currently under investigation. Vaccinations, antiviral
treatments, and prophylactic therapies are all in development.

FUTURE TRENDS

Mechanisms of disease transmission of many of these agents
remain incompletely understood. The increase in travel and
potential bioterrorism threat make developing new diagnostic
techniques, vaccines, and drug therapies urgent. Vaccines
to Junin (Argentine hemorrhagic fever) and RVF are available as investigational new drugs. A vaccine to KFD is under
development. Development of new antiviral therapies for VHF

is being pursued, as well as development of treatment protocols
for pediatric cases.

There are several candidate vaccines in trial phases for dengue/
severe dengue.

INTERNATIONAL PERSPECTIVE

Globalization makes the spread of VHF out of endemic areas
inevitable, and an understanding of the evolving endemic zones
allows for a better risk assessment for patients planning on
traveling. For YFV, immunization is required before entering
some countries. Information regarding diseases and outbreaks, as
well as the recommended and required vaccinations, is available
at the CDC home page for traveler's health. A guideline from
the CDC on infection control for VHF in the African healthcare
setting is available for infection preventionists working in African
settings. See Supplemental Resources at the end of this chapter.

Hemorrhagic fever viruses pose a valid threat as biological
weapons. The high morbidity and mortality, low inoculum
needed for environmental stability, and feasibility of large-scale
production all serve to make VHFs possible bioterrorism
weapons. Some countries are suspected of having these agents,
and other countries have used these agents in the past.[11]

It is vitally important to understand the perceptions of the
public. A single case will promptly draw public attention and increase fear and anxiety. In the era of borderless communication,
a local outbreak can transform the national audiences into
"armchair victims." This phenomenon is called "vicarious
rehearsal." It may produce multiple negative behaviors, such as
demand for unneeded treatment, multiple unexplained physical symptoms, unreasonable travel restrictions, self-destructive
behavior, and reliance on media rumors. Healthcare personnel
and authorities should avoid over-reassurance, but should repeatedly state concern and keep the public factually up to date.
Physicians and public health officials need to keep the options
of response open and prepare the public for death and grief as
well as unexpected occurrences.

REFERENCES

1. Gubler DJ. Dengue and dengue hemorrhagic fever. *Clin Microbiol Rev*
   1998 Jul;11(3):480–496.
2. Weigley RF. *Philadelphia: A 300-Year History.* New York: William Norton
   and Co., 1982:185.
3. Centers for Disease Prevention and Control (CDC), National Center for
   Emerging and Zoonotic Infectious Diseases (NCEZID). *Hantaviruses.* CDC
   website. November 1, 2012. Available at: http://www.cdc.gov/ncidod
   /diseases/hanta/hps/noframes/outbreak.htm.
4. Centers for Disease Prevention and Control (CDC), National Center for
   Infectious Diseases, Special Pathogens Branch. *Viral hemorrhagic fevers.*
   CDC website. June 19, 2013. Available at: http://www.cdc.gov/ncidod
   /dvrd/spb/mnpages/dispages/vhf.htm.
5. World Health Organization (WHO). *Global alert and response (GAR).
   Alert & response operations.* WHO website. 2013. Available at:
   http://www.who.int/csr/alertresponse/en/.
6. Peters CJ, Zaki SR. Role of endothelium in viral hemorrhagic fevers. *Crit
   Care Med* 2002 May;30(5 Suppl):S268–S273.
7. Leory EM, Kumulungui B, Pourrut X, et al. Fruit bat as a reservoir of Ebola
   virus. *Nature* 2005 Dec 1;438(7068):575–576.
8. Centers for Disease Control and Prevention (CDC), National Center
   for Emerging and Zoonotic Infectious Diseases (NCEZID), Division of

High-Consequence Pathogens and Pathology (DHCPP), Viral Special Pathogens Branch. *Outbreaks.* CDC website. August 29, 2013. Available at: http://www.cdc.gov/ncezid/dhcpp/vspb/outbreaks.html.

9. Dembek ZF, ed. Medical Management of Biological Casualties Handbook, 7th ed. September 2011. Available at: http://www.usamriid.army.mil/education/bluebookpdf/USAMRIID%20BlueBook%207th%20Edition%20-%20Sep%202011.pdf.

10. Peters CJ, Jahrling PB, Khan AS. Patient infected with high-hazard viruses: scientific basis for infection control. *Arch Virol* 1996;11:S141–S168.

11. Borio TL, Inglesby CJP, Schmaljohn AL, et al. Hemorrhagic fever viruses as biological weapons: medical and public health management. *JAMA* 2002 May 8;287(18):2391–2405.

12. Zaki SR, Goldsmith CS. Pathologic features of filovirus infections in humans. *Curr Top Microbiol Immunol* 1999;235:97–116.

13. Shope RE. Introduction to Hemorrhagic Fever Viruses. In: Goldman L, Bennett JC, eds. *Cecil Textbook of Medicine.* Philadelphia: WB Saunders Co., 2000:1841–1848.

14. Peters CJ. Pathogenesis of Viral Hemorrhagic Fevers. In: Nathanson N, Ahmed R, Gonzalez-Scarano F et al., eds. *Viral Pathogenesis.* Philadelphia: Lippincott-Raven, 1997:779–799.

15. Morrill JC, Jennings GB, Johnson AJ, et al. Pathogenesis of Rift Valley fever in rhesus monkeys: role of interferon response. *Arch Virol* 1990;110(3–4):195–212.

16. Zaki SR, Goldsmith CS. Pathologic features of filovirus infections in humans. *Curr Top Microbiol Immunol* 1999;235:97–116.

17. Hensley LE, Stevens EL, Yan SB, et al. Recombinant human activated protein C for the postexposure treatment of Ebola hemorrhagic fever. *J Infect Dis* 2007 Nov 15;196 Suppl 2:S390–S399.

18. World Health Organization (WHO). *Yellow fever. Fact Sheet 100.* WHO website. May 2013. Available at: http://www.who.int/mediacentre/factsheets/fs100/en/.

19. Tsai TF. Flaviviruses Yellow Fever, Dengue Hemorrhagic Fever, Japanese Encephalitis, St. Louise Encephalitis, Tick Borne Encephalitis. In: Mandell GL, Bennett JE, Dolin R, eds. *Mandell, Douglas, and Bennett's Principles and Practice of Infectious Diseases.* New York: Churchill Livingstone, Inc., 2000:1714–1735.

20. Enria DA, Pinheiro F. Emerging and re-emerging diseases in Latin America. Rodent-borne emerging viral zoonosis. Hemorrhagic fevers and Hantavirus infections in South America. *Infect Dis Clin North Am* 2000 Mar;14(1):167–184, x.

21. Zaki SR, Peters CJ. Viral Hemorrhagic Fevers. In: DH Connor, ed. *Pathology of Infectious Diseases.* Stamford, CT: Appleton and Lange, 1997:347–363.

22. World Health Organization (WHO). *Crimean Congo hemorrhagic fever. Fact sheet 208.* January 2013. Available at: http://www.who.int/mediacentre/factsheets/fs208/en/.

23. Peters CJ. California encephalitis, hantavirus pulmonary syndrome, and Bunyaviridae hemorrhagic fevers. In: Mandell GL, Bennett JE, Dolin R, eds. *Mandell, Douglas, and Bennett's Principles and Practice of Infectious Diseases.* Philadelphia: Churchill Livingstone, Inc., 2000:1849–1854.

24. Zaki SR. Hantavirus-associated Diseases. In: Connor DH, ed. *Pathology of Infectious Diseases.* Stamford, CT: Appleton and Lange, 1997:125–136.

25. World Health Organization (WHO). *Marburg haemorrhagic fever—fact sheet.* WHO website. March 31, 2005. Available at: http://www.who.int/csr/disease/marburg/factsheet/en/index.html.

26. World Health Organization (WHO). *Ebola hemorrhagic fever.* WHO website. Available at: http://www.who.int/csr/disease/ebola/en/.

27. Peters CJ. Marburg and Ebola Virus Hemorrhagic Fevers. In: Mandell GL, Bennett JE, Dolin R, eds. *Mandell, Douglas, and Bennett's Principles and Practice of Infectious Diseases.* Philadelphia: Churchill Livingstone, Inc., 2000:1821–1822.

28. Okware SI, Omaswa FG, Zaramba S, et al. An outbreak of Ebola in Uganda. *Trop Med Int Health* 2002 Dec;7(12):1068–1075.

29. Peters CJ. Lymphocytic Choriomeningitis, Lassa Virus, And The South American Hemorrhagic Fevers. In: Mandell GL, Bennett JE, Dolin R, eds. *Mandell, Douglas, and Bennett's Principles and Practice of Infectious Diseases.* Philadelphia: Churchill Livingstone, Inc., 2000:1855–1861.

30. World Health Organization (WHO). *Global alert and response (GAR). Lassa fever.* WHO website. Available at: http://www.who.int/csr/disease/lassafever/en/.

31. Centers for Disease Control and Prevention (CDC), National Center for Emerging and Zoonotic Infectious Diseases (NCEZID), Division of High-Consequence Pathogens and Pathology (DHCPP), Viral Special Pathogens Branch (VSPB). *Specimen submission information.* CDC website. July 1, 2013. Available at http://www.cdc.gov/ncezid/dhcpp/vspb/specimens.html

32. World Heath Organization (WHO). *Global alert and response (GAR). Acute hemorrhagic fever syndrome.* WHO website. Available at: http://www.who.int/csr/don/archive/disease/acute_haemorrhagic_fever_syndrome/en/.

33. Kilgore PE, Ksiazek TG, Rollin PE, et al. Treatment of Bolivian hemorrhagic fever with intravenous ribavirin. *Clin Infect Dis* 1997 Apr;24(4):718–722.

34. Huggins JW. Prospects for treatment of viral hemorrhagic fever with ribavirin, a broad-spectrum antiviral drug. *Rev Infect Dis* 1989 May-Jun;11 Suppl 4:S750–S761.

35. Parren PW, Geisbert TW, Maruyama T, et al. Pre- and postexposure prophylaxis of Ebola virus infection in an animal model by passive transfer of a neutralizing human antibody. *J Virol* 2002 Jun;76(12):6408–6412.

36. Staples JE, Gershman M, Fischer M. Yellow fever vaccine: Recommendations of the Advisory Committee on Immunization Practices (ACIP). *MMWR Recomm Rep* [serial online] 2010 July 30;59(RR-7):1–27. Available at: http://www.cdc.gov/mmwr/pdf/rr/rr5907.pdf.

37. Fisher-Hoch SP, McCormick JB. Towards a human Lassa fever vaccine. *Rev Med Virol* 2001 Sep-Oct;11(5):331–341.

38. Maiztegui JI, McKee KT Jr, Barrera Oro JG, et al. Protective efficacy of a live attenuated vaccine against Argentine hemorrhagic fever. AHF Study Group. *J Infect Dis* 1998 Feb;177(2):277–283.

39. Frank-Peterside N. Response of laboratory staff to vaccination with an inactivated Rift Valley fever vaccine—TSI-GSD 200. *Afr J Med Med Sci* 2000 Jun;29(2):89–92.

40. Putnak R, Fuller J, VanderZanden L, et al. Vaccination of rhesus macaques against dengue-2 virus with a plasmid DNA vaccine encoding the viral pre-membrane and envelope genes. *Am J Trop Med Hyg* 2003 Apr;68(4):469–476.

41. Pugachev KV, Guirakhoo F, Trent DW, et al. Traditional and novel approaches to flavivirus vaccines. *Int J Parasitology* 2003 May;33(5-6):567–582.

42. Pang T. Vaccines for the prevention of neglected diseases: dengue fever. *Curr Opin Biotechnol* 2003 Jun;14(3):332–336.

43. Centers for Disease Control Division (CDC). *Dengue homepage.* CDC website. September 27, 2012. Available at: http://www.cdc.gov/Dengue/faqFacts/fact.html.

44. Sun Y, Carrion R Jr, Ye L, et al. Protection against lethal challenge by Ebola virus-like particles produced in insect cells. *Virology* 2009 Jan 5;383(1):12–21.

45. Daddario-DiCaprio KM, Geisbert TW, Geisbert JB, et al. Cross-protection against Marburg virus strains by using a live, attenuated recombinant vaccine. *J Virol* 2006 Oct;80(19):9659–9666.

46. Centers for Disease Control and Prevention (CDC), National Center for Emerging and Zoonotic Infectious Diseases (NCEZID), Division of Healthcare Quality Promotion (DHQP). *Healthcare-associated infections (HAI).* CDC website. September 16, 2013. Available at: http://www.cdc.gov/ncidod/dhqp/gl_isolation.html.

47. Kortepter M, Christopher G, Cieslak T, et al, eds. *USAMRIID's Medical Management of Biological Casualties Handbook,* 4th ed. Frederick, MD: U.S. Army Medical Research Institute of Infectious Diseases, 2001:1–135.

48. Centers for Disease Control and Prevention (CDC) Office of Safety, Health, and Environment. *Biosafety.* CDC website. November 8, 2013. Available at: http://www.cdc.gov/biosafety/.

49. Centers for Disease Control and Prevention (CDC). *Interim Guidance for Managing Patients with Suspected Viral Hemorrhagic Fever in U.S. Hospitals.* CDC website. May 19, 2005. Available at: http://www.cdc.gov/ncidod/dvrd/spb/pdf/vhf-interim-guidance.pdf.

50. Chin JE. *Control of Communicable Diseases Manual.* Washington, DC: American Public Health Association Publication, 2000:1–624.

SUPPLEMENTAL RESOURCES

Centers for Disease Control and Prevention (CDC). Available at: http://www.cdc.gov.

CDC Hospital Infections Program of Bioterrorism Working Group—Links to CDC bioterror infection control programs. Available at: http://www.bt.cdc.gov.

CDC. Infection control for viral hemorrhagic fevers in the African health care setting. Available at: http://www.cdc.gov/ncidod/dvrd/spb/mnpages/vhfmanual.htm.

A number of education materials on viral hemorrhagic fevers are available on the CDC's Special Pathogens Branch Web site at http://www.cdc.gov/ncezid/dhcpp/vspb/index.html.

Heller MV, Marta RF, Sturk A, et al. Early markers of blood coagulation and fibrinolysis activation in Argentine hemorrhagic fever. *Thromb Haemost* 1995 Mar;73(3):368–373.

Monath TP. Yellow fever. In: Plotkin SA, Orenstein WA, eds. *Vaccines.* Philadelphia: WB Saunders, 1999:815–879.

Travel Health. Available at: http://www.cdc.gov/travel/.

The U.S. Army Medical Research Institute of Infectious Diseases. Available at: http://www.usamriid.army.mil/.

World Health Organization (WHO). Available at: http://www.who.int.

CHAPTER 97

Viral Hepatitis

Tyler E. Warkentien, MD, FACP
Infectious Disease Department
Walter Reed National Military Medical Center
Bethesda, MD

Karen Cromwell, RN, MSM, CIC
Deputy Chief, Infection Prevention and Control Service
Walter Reed National Military Medical Center
Bethesda, MD

ABSTRACT

The purpose of this chapter is to review the epidemiology, description, pathogenesis, clinical features, diagnosis, treatment, and prevention of viral Hepatitis A–E. Viral Hepatitis A and E are non-bloodborne, fecal-oral transmitted viruses with no chronic state. Viral Hepatitis B–D are bloodborne viruses with chronic carrier states. Serological markers have been developed for Hepatitis A–E. Vaccinations are very effective for Hepatitis A and B but not for the other viruses. Postexposure passive prophylaxis with immunoglobulin is effective in both Hepatitis A and B but not in Hepatitis C–E. Standard bloodborne infectious disease precautions should be used in active Hepatitis B–D.

KEY CONCEPTS

- Currently, five hepatotropic viruses, A, B, C, D, and E are responsible for viral hepatitis in the United States. Hepatitis A, Hepatitis B, and Hepatitis C are the most common.

- All five can cause acute inflammation of the liver. Infections with Hepatitis A and Hepatitis E are usually self-limited. Infections with Hepatitis B, Hepatitis C, and Hepatitis D can lead to chronic lifelong infections.

- Chronic Hepatitis B, Hepatitis C, and Hepatitis D can lead to cirrhosis, liver failure, and hepatocellular carcinoma.

- Hepatitis A and Hepatitis E are transmitted via contaminated food and water. Hepatitis B, Hepatitis C, and Hepatitis D are transmitted by blood, sexual contact, exposure to contaminated equipment, and from mother to infant during childbirth.

- Breaches in infection prevention practices may lead to increased risk and exposure to the hepatitis viruses.

- Vaccines are available for Hepatitis A and Hepatitis B. No vaccines are available for Hepatitis C, Hepatitis D, or Hepatitis E, and prevention is the key.

BACKGROUND

This chapter includes a review of viral hepatitides with special mention of new advances in these viruses since the last edition of this textbook. Five hepatotropic viruses known to cause hepatitis have been described and have been named Hepatitis A, B, C, D, and E in historical order of their recognition. Worldwide, cases of hepatitis presumably caused by viruses other than these five also occur. Hepatitis A virus (HAV) and Hepatitis E virus (HEV) are transmitted principally by the fecal-oral route and are occasionally a healthcare infection prevention issue. Hepatitis B virus (HBV), Hepatitis C virus (HCV), and Hepatitis D virus (HDV) are bloodborne pathogens and pose a risk of healthcare-associated transmission or occupational exposure for healthcare personnel (HCP). Critical features of these types of viral hepatitis are summarized in Table 97-1. Standard Precautions, which encompass both universal precautions and body substance isolation, are appropriate for prevention and spread of all types of viral hepatitis in the healthcare environment.[1–3]

Patients and employees in U.S. healthcare facilities are at risk for transmission of hepatitis because of breaches in infection prevention procedures and exposures to asymptomatic carriers, contaminated needles and equipment, and unsafe needle practices. Understanding the epidemiology and pathogenesis of viral hepatitis can help in the development of prevention strategies to protect patients, employees, and the public. Transmission knowledge of hepatitis is also important for compliance with Occupational Safety & Health Administration (OSHA) bloodborne pathogens regulations, communicable disease reporting, and clinical practice review. The recent outbreaks of HCV in U.S. ambulatory centers highlight the need for infection prevention strategies and focus across the continuum of care.[4,5]

BASIC PRINCIPLES

Viruses that infect hepatocytes are considered hepatotropic viruses. These viruses may also infect other cells, but the clinical disease associated with these viruses is characterized by a clinical syndrome consisting of malaise, elevated transaminases, inflammatory infiltrate within the liver, hepatocyte injury, and death.

Table 97-1. Epidemiological and Clinical Features of Viral Hepatitis

Virus	HAV	HBV	HCV	HDV	HEV
Incubation (days)	15–50	60–150	14–168	30–180	14–60
Transmission	Fecal-oral	Blood-body fluid	Blood-body fluid	Blood-body fluid	Fecal-oral
Clinical illness	Children 10% Adults 75%	10%–15%	20%–30%	10%	Variable
Jaundice	Children 5% Adult 30%	5%–20%	5%–10%		Variable
Fulminant	1%	1%	Rare	2%–7.5%	<3% Pregnancy 15%–25%
Chronic	No	Children 90% Adults 5%	75%–85%	Superinfection 80% Coinfection 5%	No
Risk to HCP	+	†††	††	†††	?
Diagnosis					
Acute	IgM anti-HAV	HBsAg IgM anti-HBc (HBeAG) (HBV DNA)	anti-HCV HCV RNA	HbsAg HDV PCR	IgM anti-HEV
Chronic	—	HBsAg IgG anti-HBc (HBeAG) (HBV DNA)	Anti-HCV RIBA HCV RNA	HBsAg IgG anti-HDV	—
Immunity	IgG-anti-HAV	Anti-HBs	No	—	—
Prevention	HH	SP	SP Needle exchange	SP	Sanitation
	HAV vaccine IG	HBV vaccine HBIG		HBV vaccine	

†††, common source of transmission or high exposure risk; ††, moderate source of transmission or moderate risk exposure; +, rare source of transmission or low risk of exposure; —, no known transmission or risk exposure; ?, unknown transmission or risk exposure.
HAV, Hepatitis A virus; HBeAg, Hepatitis B e antigen; HBsAg, Hepatitis B surface antigen; HBV, Hepatitis B virus; HCV, Hepatitis C virus; HCP, healthcare personnel; HDV, Hepatitis D virus; HEV, Hepatitis E virus; HH, hand hygiene; HBIG, Hepatitis B immune globulin; IgM, immunoglobulin M; RIBA, recombinant immunoblot assay; SP, standard precautions.

The clinical syndrome is similar among Hepatitis A–E, but the epidemiology, treatment, and prevention are different. The infection prevention of each of the viral hepatitides contains specific recommendations.

HEPATITIS A

Epidemiology

Description

HAV is assigned its own genus, *Hepatovirus,* in the family Picornaviridae. HAV is a nonenveloped, 27-nm single-stranded RNA virus that can be found by electron microscopy in the feces of persons with this infection. Humans and primates are the only known natural hosts for HAV. Replication of HAV occurs in the hepatocytes, but the virus is not directly cytopathic.[1,3]

Incidence

HAV is highly contagious but rates in the United States have declined by 95 percent since HAV vaccine first became available in 1995. In 2010, 1,670 acute symptomatic cases of Hepatitis A were reported; the incidence was 0.6/100,000, the lowest rate ever recorded. The estimated number of new infections was 17,000 when adjusted for asymptomatic infection and underreporting.[6]

The incidence of HAV in the United States used to vary dramatically by ethnicity and geography, but this has largely disappeared in the HAV vaccine era. Rates have dropped 99 percent in American Indians and Alaskan Natives to rates now below the U.S. rate. Rates in Hispanics have decreased substantially as well, but are still twice as high as non-Hispanics. HAV rates before 1997 were much higher in the western and southwestern regions, but this regional variation no longer exists.[7]

The incidence of HAV varies considerably worldwide, with annual rates depending on the endemicity level of the country. Children from countries where HAV is highly endemic have a high seroprevalence (90 percent) and, because symptoms are limited in young children and adolescents and adults retain lifelong immunity, epidemics are uncommon. In transitional economies of the developing world where sanitation and public infrastructure are improving, fewer children are exposed to Hepatitis A, which in turn actually leads to larger outbreaks due to lower population level immunity in adolescents and adults.[8]

Transmission

HAV is transmitted principally by the fecal-oral route, with the highest level of virus in the feces found in the 2 weeks prior to onset of jaundice or liver enzyme increase.[9] This is also the period of highest infectivity.[10] Transmission is facilitated by intimate personal contact (household, sexual, etc.), poor hygiene, unsanitary conditions, or contaminated water, milk, or food, especially raw shellfish. Additional risk factors include childcare exposure (children, parents, or attendants), intravenous (IV) drug use, travel to an endemic area, chronic institutionalization, men who have sex with men (MSM), and occupation (e.g., sewage worker, pediatric nurse). HAV is rarely transmitted by blood or blood products (e.g., clotting factor concentrates) as a consequence of transient viremia in asymptomatic donors.

Pathogenesis

Infection with HAV occurs in the gastrointestinal tract. HAV is transiently detectable in blood as early as 4 weeks before symptoms. HAV is detectable in feces 2 to 4 weeks before and 1 to 3 weeks following the onset of jaundice. Infected neonates may shed HAV in feces for months. There is no chronic HAV carrier state. HAV replicates in cytoplasm of hepatocytes, and then is shed in bile, which results in high titer of infectious HAV in feces. Disease occurs as a result of host immune response, which causes hepatocyte injury. Development of antibodies to HAV confers lifelong immunity.[1,3]

Clinical Features

Infection is unapparent in 70 percent of young children under 6 years of age. In older children or adults, infection is typically symptomatic, with jaundice occurring in more than 70 percent of patients. Incubation period averages 4 weeks (range, 15–50 days) and may depend on inoculum size. Prodromal (preicteric) symptoms are nonspecific, including malaise, fatigue, anorexia, nausea, vomiting, abdominal discomfort, arthralgia, myalgia, and fever. This phase lasts 1 to 2 weeks. The icteric phase is notable for jaundice, dark urine, pale colored stools, pruritus, and anorexia, but

resolution of prodromal symptoms lasts 1 to 4 weeks. Alanine aminotransferase (ALT) and other hepatocellular enzymes and bilirubin levels rise and then generally recover completely over 2 weeks to 6 months.[1,3,11,12]

Laboratory Diagnosis

Clinical features of acute hepatitis are not specific for HAV infection, so serological diagnosis is necessary (Figure 97-1). Immunoglobulin M antibodies to HAV (IgM anti-HAV) are used to detect acute HAV infection, are detectable within 3 weeks of exposure, and are present at the onset of jaundice. Titer declines over 4 to 6 weeks and is usually not detectable after 6 to 12 months. Immunoglobulin G anti-HAV (IgG anti-HAV) is also detectable at onset of jaundice and remains positive lifelong, indicating immunity to HAV.[1,3]

Treatment

Supportive care (e.g., fluids and nutrition) is the only known management for acute Hepatitis A. Liver transplantation should be considered in the course of fulminant hepatic failure.[1,3]

Prevention

Public health and personal hygiene measures, including hand washing or hand sanitizer, may effectively interrupt further transmission. Risk of transmission of HAV is transient and occurs during the prodrome. Standard Precautions are appropriate to prevent healthcare-associated transmission in most instances. With diapered or incontinent patients, the addition of Contact Precautions is recommended. Postexposure prophylaxis should be considered in instances such as household or sexual contacts or in outbreak situations such as common source exposure in an infected food handler or a case

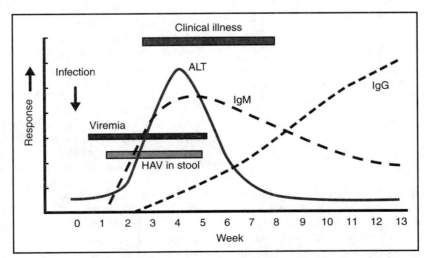

Figure 97-1. Clinical course of Hepatitis A. (From American Medical Association; Centers for Disease Control and Prevention; Center for Food Safety and Applied Nutrition, Food and Drug Administration; Food Safety and Inspection Service, U.S. Department of Agriculture. Diagnosis and management of foodborne illness. A primer for physicians and other health care professionals. *MMWR Recomm Rep* 2004 Apr 16;53(RR-04):1–33.)

of HAV in a childcare center. HAV vaccine is recommended for unvaccinated adults aged 40 or younger with recent (within 2 weeks) exposure to HAV. For persons over 40 with recent (within 2 weeks) exposure to HAV, immune globulin (Ig) is preferred over vaccine.[13] A dose of 0.02 mL/kg intramuscular (IM) protects for up to 3 months. The local health department should be notified immediately about a case of Hepatitis A so that tracing and prophylaxis of contacts can be initiated promptly. For international travelers going to endemic regions, HAV vaccine should be given prior to departure. For those over 40, a higher dose (0.06 mL/kg IM) of Ig can be considered as an alternative to HAV vaccine prior to travel,[13] though this is not routinely practiced.

Active immunization with either licensed single antigen HAV vaccine (HAVRIX, manufactured by GlaxoSmithKline; VAQTA, manufactured by Merck & Co., Whitehouse Station, NJ) or combination TWINRIX (manufactured by GlaxoSmithKline, Rixensart, Belgium), which contains both HAV (in a lower dosage) and HBV antigens, is generally safe and effective. More than 95 percent of adults generate protective antibodies within a month of HAV vaccination. A booster is recommended at 6 to 12 months. There are different formulations for children and adults. In addition to the instances of postexposure prophylaxis and international travel, immunization should be offered to select adult populations that are either at high risk of acquiring HAV or at risk for fulminant presentation once disease is acquired. These groups include patients with chronic liver disease, IV drug users, MSM, persons who receive clotting factor concentrates, persons who work with HAV in experimental lab settings (not routine medical laboratories), and food handlers when health authorities or private employers determine vaccination to be appropriate. HAV vaccine is recommended for all children at age 1 year (12–23 months) with a second dose spaced 6 months apart and all previously unvaccinated children and adolescents age 2 years and older who live in a state, county, or community with a routine vaccination program already in place for children aged 2 years and older.[13]

Solvent-detergent treatment of clotting factor concentrates has failed to prevent transmission of HAV by these products. Heat screening of plasma-derived clotting factors inactivates HAV and other viruses.[1–3,11,12,14–17]

HEPATITIS B

Epidemiology

Description

HBV is a small DNA virus in the family Hepadnaviridae. HBV utilizes its own reverse transcriptase for replication. HBV virus overproduces envelope proteins (e.g., Hepatitis B surface antigen [HBsAg]), which can be detected by testing of serum. Nucleocapsid core antigen (HBcAg) and the e antigen (HBeAg, a marker for viral replication and infectivity) are also generated. Detection of these components or host antibodies to HBsAg, HbeAg, or HBcAg are used to diagnose and monitor acute and chronic HBV.

Historically, HBV was the most common bloodborne pathogen with risk for HCP. The incidence of HBV among HCP dramatically fell in the 1990s because of preventive measures mandated by the OSHA Bloodborne Pathogen Rule of 1991.[1–3,14,16,18–28]

Incidence

In 2009, an estimated 38,000 persons in the United States were newly infected with HBV. This is a decline of approximately 82 percent since 1991, when the United States instituted a national strategy to eliminate HBV infection with the routine vaccination of children was first recommended.[29] The rates of HBV in HCP was at one time higher than that of the general population due to bloodborne exposure risk.[30] However, there was a 95 percent decline from 1983 to 1995 among HCP as a result of behavioral changes and widespread HBV immunization.[31]

In the United States in 2006, a total of 4,713 acute, symptomatic cases of HBV were reported nationwide; 40 percent were hospitalized and 0.8 percent died. The proportion of persons hospitalized for HBV increased with age, from 12 percent among children under age 15 to 51 percent among persons over 60.[32] It is estimated that chronic HBV leads to 4,000 deaths per year from cirrhosis and 800 from hepatocellular carcinoma.[21,28]

Prevalence

Worldwide, 240 million people are chronic HBV carriers. Of carriers, many develop serious liver disease resulting in 600,000 deaths per year. The highest prevalence is in sub-Saharan Africa and East Asia, where 5 to 10 percent of the population are HBsAg positive. High rates of chronic infections are also found in the Amazon and the southern parts of eastern and central Europe. In the Middle East and Indian subcontinent, an estimated 2 to 5 percent of the general population is chronically infected. Less than 1 percent of the population in Western Europe and North America is chronically infected.[33]

The estimated prevalence of chronic Hepatitis B in the United States, according to analysis based on results of the NHANES survey, was 730,000.[34] This estimate is felt to be low, as high-risk groups such as foreign-born individuals and prison populations are underrepresented in the survey. A recent study that used modeling based on prevalence rates of chronic Hepatitis B in 98 countries multiplied by immigration data from those countries estimated the prevalence of foreign-born individuals with chronic Hepatitis B in the United States at 1.3 million in 2009.[35] The risk for chronic infection varies according to the age at infection and is greatest among young children. Approximately 90 percent of infants and 25 to 50 percent of children aged 1 to 5 years will remain chronically infected with HBV. By contrast, approximately 95 percent of adults recover completely from HBV infection and do not become chronically infected.

Transmission

HBV is parenterally transmitted through blood or blood products, sexual contact, or perinatal exposure of an infant. HBeAg positivity is associated with increasing infectivity. In low-prevalence areas such as the United States, HBV is principally transmitted by sexual contact or IV drug use and is less efficiently transmitted by contact with saliva or mucosal surfaces. From 20 to 30 percent of cases in the United States have no known risk factors or route of infection. In nations where HBV is more prevalent, vertical perinatal transmission from HBsAg-positive mother to child or horizontal transmission among young children is more common. HBV is detectable in various body fluids that may be infectious, including blood, semen, vaginal secretions, saliva, tears, cerebrospinal fluid (CSF), ascites, and other serous fluids. Infectivity is enhanced by high virus titer or HBeAg positivity in serum of source patient. No arthropod-borne, waterborne, or airborne transmission is known.

Pathogenesis

Host immune response is more important than HBV cytopathic effects on hepatocytes. During acute HBV, cytotoxic T-lymphocytes initiate liver injury, followed by antibody-mediated immunity. Mutant HBV strains may escape otherwise protective immunity or cause more severe or chronic infection. Immaturity of T-cell immune system (e.g., children, immunosuppressed hosts) may permit chronic HBV infection. Development of surface antibody (anti-HBs) and clearance of HBsAg denote resolution of HBV disease, leading to durable protection from reinfection.[1,3,23,26] The HBV circular DNA does not need to integrate into host DNA to complete the viral life cycle, but when it does, it may act as a mutagen that drives the development of hepatocellular carcinoma.

Clinical Features

The incubation period ranges from 30 to 180 days (mean, 75 days). Prodromal urticarial rash, arthritis, and fever occur in 5 to 10 percent of adults. Neonates or young children are usually asymptomatic. Acute HBV is more insidious and prolonged than HAV. Fulminant hepatic failure is rare but can be fatal without liver transplantation. Symptoms resemble HAV. In acute HBV (Figure 97-2), HBsAg, HBeAg, and HBV DNA are detectable in serum 2 to 7 weeks before onset of symptoms. When symptoms occur, immunoglobulin M anti-HBV core

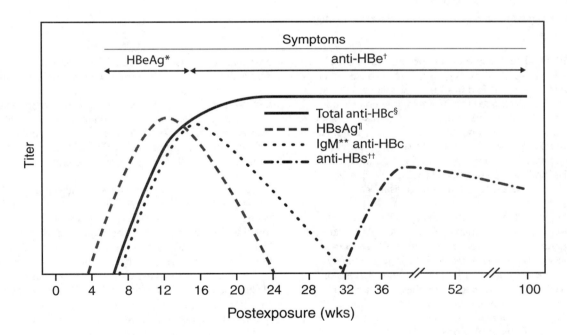

* Hepatitis B e antigen.
† Antibody to HBeAg.
§ Antibody to Hepatitis B core antigen.
¶ Hepatitis B surface antigen.
** Immunoglobulin M.
†† Antibody to HBsAg.

Figure 97-2. Serological course of acute Hepatitis B virus infection with recovery. (From Weinbaum CM, Williams I, Mast EE, et al. Recommendations for identification and public health management of persons with chronic hepatitis B virus infection. *MMWR Recomm Rep* 2008 Sep 19;57(RR-8):1–20.)

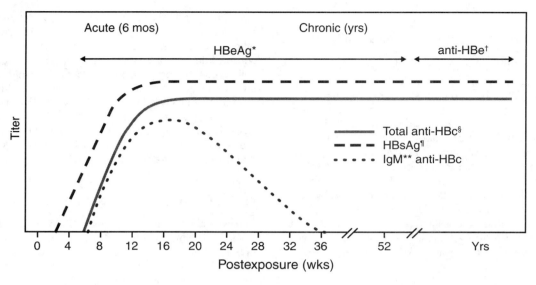

* Hepatitis B e antigen.
† Antibody to HBeAg.
§ Antibody to Hepatitis B core antigen.
¶ Hepatitis B surface antigen.
** Immunoglobulin M.

Figure 97-3. Progress to chronic Hepatitis B infection: serological course.

(IgM anti-HBc) and ALT, aspartate aminotransferase (AST), and bilirubin levels all rise. ALT levels generally exceed AST and are usually elevated 10- to 20-fold from normal. Bilirubin elevations vary with severity. Prolonged prothrombin time (international normalized ratio [INR] ≥ 1.5) or hypoalbuminemia imply severe hepatic injury and may portend fulminant hepatic failure. Acute HBV resolves slowly (weeks to months) following detection of immunoglobulin G anti-HBc (IgG anti-HBc), anti-HBe, and anti-HBs, and disappearance of HBeAg and HBsAg. IgM anti-HBc may persist for months then disappear.

In chronic hepatitis (Figure 97-3), HBsAg, HBeAg, and HBV DNA are detected for more than 6 months, and ALT and AST levels fall but do not always return to normal. These persons remain infectious for others; those with HBeAg are highly infectious and are at greatest risk of developing cirrhosis or hepatocellular carcinoma. Persons who have human immuno-deficiency virus (HIV) or other forms of immunosuppression (e.g., dialysis patients) and who acquire HBV infection are more likely to develop chronic HBV and associated liver complications than are those without these comorbid conditions.[1,3,23,36]

Laboratory Diagnosis

In prodromal or preicteric HBV disease, HBsAg, HBeAg, and HBV DNA are detectable in serum (see Figure 97-2), with HBsAg becoming positive 1 to 10 weeks after an exposure and before the onset of symptoms. Finding HBeAg and high concen-tration of HBV DNA signify high rates of HBV replication and heightened infectivity. With onset of symptoms, rise in levels of

aminotransferases and bilirubin, IgM anti-HBc becomes positive. This is the ideal test to determine whether an acute hepatitis is due to Hepatitis B, since the titer rises with onset of symptoms and falls below detectable levels after several months, so it is not positive in those with chronic Hepatitis B. As acute illness wanes over a period of weeks, aminotransferases and other biochem-ical monitors improve. HBeAg, HBV DNA, and HBsAg may disappear. IgG anti-HBc, anti-HBe, and anti-HBs are detectable.

In chronic HBV, biochemical abnormalities may persist, and a positive serum test for HBsAg for more than 6 months is diag-nostic of chronic Hepatitis B (see Figure 97-3). IgG anti-HBc remains detectable, but IgM anti-HBc declines. Eventually HBV DNA and HBeAg may disappear, and this signifies an asymptomatic carrier. In active chronic infection, transaminases and HBV DNA remain elevated. These patients can either be HBeAg positive or HBeAg negative. HBeAg positive patients can spontaneously convert to anti-HBe, typically with an acute rise in transaminases, then return to normal, along with a fall in HBV DNA and improved liver inflammation level. IgG anti-HBc persists for life in both chronic active HBV and in persons who have cleared an acute infection. Persons with chronic HBV (particularly HBeAg positive and HBV DNA positive) remain infectious for others.[1,3,23]

Treatment

For acute HBV, only supportive care is indicated, and hepato-toxins such as acetominaphen should be avoided. In fulmi-nant HBV, liver transplantation is often required. In chronic

HBV, treatment options include pegylated interferon alfa-2a, lamivudine, adefovir, entecavir, telbivudine, and tenofovir. Pegylated interferon is a subcutaneous injection and efficacy is dependant on host immune response. The side effects of pegylated interferon include flulike symptoms, marrow suppression, depression, and autoimmune thyroiditis; close medical supervision and laboratory monitoring are required. The other therapies are all oral agents that generally have an acceptable side effect profile even after extended use, but because adefovir and tenofovir may cause nephrotoxic effects, periodic monitoring of renal function during therapy is advisable.[37] Other agents, such as lamivudine, can cause viral resistance when used as monotherapy. Entecavir also inhibits HIV replication and can cause HIV resistance, so it should not be used in HIV/HBV co-infected patients who are not on HIV antiretroviral therapy.

Liver transplantation is considered for end-stage chronic HBV complications. Hepatitis B immune globulin (HBIG) with lamivudine prophylaxis improves liver transplant outcome, with reinfection rates as low as 10 percent.[38] Patients with chronic HBV who are susceptible to HAV benefit from HAV vaccine.[1-3,23,25,26,39]

Prevention

Standard Precautions should be used to prevent exposure of HCP to blood or body fluids of HBsAg-positive patients. Counseling should be provided to prevent exposure of sexual or household contacts while the patient has detectable HBsAg. The risk to nonimmune HCP of acquiring HBV after a sharps injury exposure to an HBsAg-positive patient is 6 to 30 percent (the highest risk is if the source patient is HBeAg-positive), so postexposure prophylaxis of HCP with HBIG and vaccine is recommended.[1-3,14-17,20-25,36]

Active Immunization

Routine vaccinations are recommended for HCP prior to starting employment.

Hepatitis B Vaccine

HBV vaccine is available as a single-antigen formulation and also in fixed combination with other vaccines. Two single-antigen recombinant, thimerisol-free vaccines are available in the United States: Recombivax HB (Merck & Co.) and Engerix-B (GlaxoSmithKline Biologicals). Of the three licensed combination vaccines, one (Twinrix [GlaxoSmithKline Biologicals]) is used for vaccination of adults and two (Comvax [Merck & Co.] and Pediarix [GlaxoSmithKline Biologicals]) are used for vaccination of infants and young children. Twinrix contains recombinant HBsAg and inactivated Hepatitis A virus. Comvax contains recombinant HBsAg and *Haemophilus influenzae* type b (Hib) polyribosylribitol phosphate conjugated to *Neisseria meningitidis* outer membrane protein complex. Pediarix contains recombinant HBsAg, diphtheria, and tetanus toxoids and acellular pertussis adsorbed (DTaP), and inactivated poliovirus (IPV).[40]

Seroconversion with detection of protective anti-HBs (>10 mIU/mL) occurs in more than 95 percent of healthy recipients. Risk factors for poor responses to HBV vaccination include age over 40 years, hemodialysis, HIV infection, tobacco smoking, improper vaccine storage, subcutaneous vaccine delivery, and an accelerated vaccine schedule. Persons who are HBsAg positive will also not respond to HBV vaccine. Thus, it could be reasonable to test a nonresponder for HBsAg carriage. Dialysis patients and immunocompromised hosts respond less predictably and should receive a higher dose (40 µg) at each interval. Serum levels of anti-HBs decline slowly over several years after a successful vaccine series. However, routine testing for anti-HBs and routine booster immunization are not recommended except in persons at risk for a poor antibody response (e.g., neonates or immunosuppressed hosts) and at high risk of ongoing exposure.

Pre-immunization testing for HBV markers is not cost effective except in certain populations. If, however, testing for any marker is positive, HBV vaccine is not useful. HBV vaccine is recommended as a routine childhood immunization series beginning in infancy. Despite immunization programs targeted at high-risk groups, as well as recommendations for universal childhood immunization, compliance with HBV vaccination in the general population has been disappointing in the United States and unaffordable in the developing world. HBV vaccination is recommended for persons in certain high-risk groups, including people with multiple sexual partners, sexual partners or household contacts of HBsAg-positive people, MSM, IV drug users, long-term travelers to regions with endemic HBV (see Chapter 118 Travel Health), persons with risk of exposure to blood or body fluids as a result of their occupation, clients and staff at institutions for the developmentally disabled, patients with chronic renal failure and dialysis, patients receiving clotting factor therapy, and inmates at long-term correctional facilities.[40]

Pregnancy is not a contraindication for HBV immunization. HCP with risk of ongoing exposure to body fluids should be tested 1 to 2 months after their third dose of HBV vaccine to determine serological response (anti-HBs). This result is useful in planning for possible future prophylaxis. HCP who do not respond to the primary vaccine series (anti-HBs ≥10 mIU/mL) should complete a second full series and be tested for HBsAg.[41] HBsAg-negative HCP who do not respond to a second vaccine series should subsequently receive HBIG for any known or probable parenteral or mucosal exposure to HBsAg-positive blood or body fluids. Vaccinated HCP whose anti-HBs level has never been tested should be tested for anti-HBs immediately after an occupational exposure to HBV. If the anti-HBs level is adequate, no HBV prophylaxis is necessary. If the anti-HBs level is less than 10 mIU/mL, a single dose of HBIG and a booster dose of HBV vaccine are given. HBIG is not recommended when the HBsAg serostatus of the source patient is unknown or not tested, unless the source patient is high risk for HBV.[41]

HCP who are HBsAg positive require close follow-up. Recent guidelines from the U.S. Centers for Disease Control and Prevention (CDC) provide updated guidance for the management of HBV chronically infected healthcare providers.[42] It is recommended that HBV viral load be monitored and that those with viral levels more than 1,000 IU/mL should not perform exposure-prone procedures such as certain surgeries. The U.S. incidence of HBV infection in hemodialysis units has declined by 95 percent since the 1980s as a result of the use of Universal Precautions and HBV vaccination of patients and HCP in these units.[54] Besides these measures, hemodialysis-specific recommendations include (1) patients should be tested annually for anti-HBs and revaccinated if they are no longer immune (dialysis dose is 40 μg); (2) instruments, medications, and supplies for these patients should not be shared; (3) routine cleaning and disinfection procedures should be followed, with separate clean and contaminated areas; and (4) blood and body fluid specimens should be handled with gloved hands and kept away from areas used for medications or supplies.

Passive Immunization

HBIG is indicated as postexposure prophylaxis for persons not already immune to HBV when they have percutaneous or mucosal exposure to blood or body fluids of a source person testing positively for HBsAg. The dose is 0.06 mL/kg IM as soon as possible after exposure but not delayed more than 7 days. This should be repeated at 30 days if the HBV vaccine series was not begun. HBIG is also recommended for recent sexual contacts of all HBV-infected persons who are not HBV immunized[43] and infants born to mothers who are HBsAg positive.[58] Universal HBsAg testing of pregnant women is recommended to detect all candidate infants for HBIG programs. In each circumstance in which HBIG is used, HBV vaccine is also simultaneously indicated. Combined HBV vaccination and HBIG immunotherapy of newborns at risk can prevent more than 90 percent of prenatally transmitted HBV.[44] The dose of HBIG for neonates is 0.06 mL/kg IM within 12 hours of birth.

HEPATITIS C

Trends

HCV was initially known as non-A, non-B viral hepatitis, which was often seen in the posttransfusion setting. After discovery of the viral antigens, the virus was named Hepatitis C. Like HBV, HCV is a common cause of cirrhosis and hepatocellular carcinoma. Unlike HAV and HBV, though, no vaccine exists. Treatment for HCV is entering a new era with the burgeoning availability of direct antiviral agents.

Epidemiology

Description

HCV is a single-stranded RNA virus in its own genus in the family Flaviviridae. Following detection of its RNA in serum in 1989, the genome of HCV has been cloned, but the virus has not been propagated in vitro. HCV is found as multiple genotypes and genetic subtypes that differ in their geographic distribution. In the United States, genotype 1 is most common,

followed by genotypes 2, 3, and 4. This genetic variation is a major obstacle to development of a vaccine to prevent HCV infection.[1,3,16,21,25,27,45-53]

Incidence

The third National Health and Nutrition Examination Survey (NHANES III), spanning 1988 to 1994, estimated that 1.8 percent (3.9 million) of the U.S. population has been infected with HCV. The annual incidence of acute HCV infections decreased from 180,000 in the mid-1980s to an estimated 19,000 cases in 2005. HCV causes approximately 20 percent of community-acquired acute viral hepatitis, with incidence declining since the late 1980s. Of these HCV infections, 85 percent become chronic. Cirrhosis occurs in 20 percent of patients with chronic HCV, usually occurring after 20 years, whereas hepatocellular carcinoma (HCC) occurs in only 5 percent, usually after 30 years. HCC results in 8,000 to 10,000 deaths per year. HCV is the most common infectious cause of chronic hepatitis, cirrhosis, and HCC in the United States and is the most common indication for liver transplantation.[41,45,52-56]

Prevalence

The World Health Organization estimates that the global prevalence of HCV infection is 3 percent (approximately 170 million HCV-infected persons) worldwide. The highest prevalence is in the Middle East and North Africa, where 7 to 26 percent of some populations are HCV carriers. In the United States, approximately 3.2 million people have HCV infection.

Infection is most prevalent among those born during 1945 to 1965, the majority of whom were likely infected during the 1970s and 1980s when rates were highest. As a result of the high prevalence in this age group, the CDC now recommends that all adults born between 1945 and 1965 be screened at least once for HCV, regardless of other risk factors.[57] In the United States, groups with a high prevalence of HCV infection include IV drug users (60 percent of new cases), persons with multiple sexual partners, HIV patients, hemophiliacs receiving clotting factors prior to 1987, and recipients of blood product transfusions or organ transplants prior to 1992. Other groups at risk are hemodialysis patients, HCP (1 percent prevalence), infants born to HCV-infected mothers, nasal cocaine users, and persons with tattoos and multiple body piercings. In one U.S. inner city hospital emergency department that served a population of drug users, 18 percent of patients were HCV positive. Surveys suggest that approximately one-third of U.S. prison inmates carry HCV. In about 5 percent of all HCV infections, no risk factor can be identified.[45,53,54] As a result of screening for risk factors, only 0.6 percent of blood donors are HCV positive; these are detected by serological testing and excluded from donation.

Transmission

HCV is efficiently transmitted parenterally by blood injection (injecting drug users), organ transplantation, or transfusion of HCV-infected blood or blood products (including clotting factors and intravenous immunoglobulin). Prior to testing blood and blood products in the early 1990s, risk of HCV transmission was 0.19 percent per unit transfused. Since screening was implemented, the risk is only 0.001 percent per unit. Since 1994, no transfusion-associated HCV transmission has been detected. Nonetheless, 5 to 10 percent of HCV cases are transfusion associated. Risk of transmission of HCV from an infected patient to HCP as a result of a needlestick is 1.8 percent. There is a high prevalence of HCV among hemodialysis patients.[58] HCV has been transmitted from surgeon to patient and when safe medical injection equipment or solution protocols have not been followed.[59]

HCV is inefficiently transmitted by sexual intercourse (prevalence ranging from 1.3 percent in North America to 27 percent in Asia in long-term partners), although MSM, persons with multiple sexual partners, and HIV patients have higher rates of seroprevalence for HCV than do monogamous heterosexuals. The average risk for vertical transmission is 6 percent overall and 17 percent in mothers with HIV, which appears to be related to viral titer. No difference in transmission is noted whether the child is breast- or bottle-fed.

HCV is detected in serum, saliva, urine, semen, and ascitic fluid. There is no demonstrated fecal-oral or arthropod-borne transmission.

Pathogenesis

The pathogenesis is poorly understood, but HCV is not integrated into host genome like HBV. HCV has been difficult to culture but can be detected in serum hepatocytes within days of inoculation in experimental animals. The hypervariable region on genome allows for mutants (quasispecies) to emerge soon after infection is established. This quasispecies variability provides escape from effective host immune responses. Cell-mediated immune response causes the manifestations of HCV disease. Vigorous T-cell-mediated immune response is associated with resolution of acute HCV infection, whereas predominantly B-cell (antibody-mediated) response is associated with chronic HCV infection.[1,3,25,46,49,50,52]

Clinical Features

The incubation period ranges between 15 and 160 days (2–26 weeks [mean, 36–49 days]). Shorter incubation (mean, 4 weeks) is seen after transmission through transfused blood products. The patient is usually asymptomatic; only 25 percent of patients with acute HCV develop jaundice. Fulminant hepatitis occurs in less than 1 percent. Fatigue, abdominal pain, and hepatomegaly are the most common clinical presentations. The course may resemble HBV but generally is more indolent.

Chronic HCV infection occurs in up to 85 percent of cases (Figure 97-4). Of these, 20 percent develop cirrhosis (average 21 years following infection), 50 percent have asymptomatic persistent elevations of transaminases, and 30 percent remain HCV carriers without evidence of disease. First symptoms may be liver failure or portal hypertension as a result of the cirrhosis. Also, 25 percent of patients with HCV-associated cirrhosis develop HCC (average 29 years following infection).

Consumption of alcohol aggravates liver damage from HCV and is a significant risk factor for progression from chronic HCV to end-stage liver disease. Other risk factors for complications of HCV infection include male gender, under 40 years of age at exposure, HIV co-infection, abnormal ALT, and

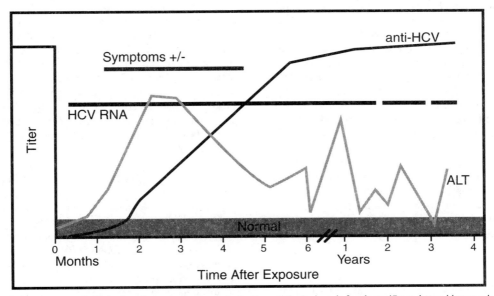

Figure 97-4. Typical time course of clinical and serological events in Hepatitis C virus infections (From http://www.cdc.gov/ncidod /diseases/hepatitis/slideset/index.htm).

fibrosis on biopsy. Nonhepatic complications occur, such as type II cryoglobulinemia, membranoproliferative glomerulonephritis, and porphyria cutanea tarda.[1,3,11,25,45,46,48–50,52,53,60]

Laboratory Diagnosis

Detection of antibodies to HCV (anti-HCV) by enzyme immunoassay (EIA) has evolved as more HCV protein fragments are incorporated into the test (see Figure 97-4). Current assays detect more than 90 percent of HCV infections as early as 6 to 8 weeks after exposure, though seroconversion may be delayed up to 20 weeks in 10 to 20 percent of patients. Sensitivity of testing is approximately 95 percent, but false-positive results may occur. In low-risk populations such as blood donors, 40 percent of all samples positive for HCV by EIA were found to be falsely positive.[61] In the past, a positive EIA test required a second-generation recombinant immunoblot assay as confirmation. However, this test is no longer available in the United States, so confirmation is by HCV polymerase chain reaction (HCV-PCR). The reverse-transcription PRC (RT-PCR) test can detect acute HCV infection as early as 1 to 2 weeks after exposure. The HCV-PCR is also used to monitor HCV viral load and its response to antiviral therapies. HCV RNA assays do not distinguish acute and chronic Hepatitis C.[1,3,25,48,49,52,62–64] Determining the level of viremia is important in gauging clinical response to treatment, so getting a quantitative RNA test is essential.[65]

Once the diagnosis of HCV is made, determining the genotype and extent of liver inflammation is important. Several genotype assays are commercially available, and knowing the genotype will guide treatment decisions (see below). Traditionally, the liver biopsy has been the standard tool to grade liver fibrosis. Based on the extent of fibrosis expansion, presence of bridging fibrosis, and presence/absence of cirrhosis, the extent of disease can be quantified through one of several scoring systems (histologic activity index, METAVIR, or Knodell).[66–68] Noninvasive techniques to estimate extent of liver fibrosis are also available. One such "multitest" uses an algorithm based on values of several laboratory markers to arrive at a screening tool that can detect severe liver fibrosis with a high negative and positive predictive value.[69] The assay is commercially available in the United States (FibroSURE, LabCorp, Burlington, NC). Another noninvasive method involves the use of transient elastography. This test is based on the concept that significant fibrosis can be detected by measuring liver stiffness through an ultrasound technique. It can discriminate between mild and more severe fibrosis[70] and was approved by the U.S. Food and Drug Administration (FDA) in 2013. The most recent version of the American Association of Study of Liver Disease (AASLD) guidelines from 2009 suggest the use of noninvasive testing to determine the presence of advanced fibrosis in chronic HCV but state that these tests should not replace liver biopsy in routine clinical practice.[71]

Treatment

For several years the treatment for HCV, regardless of genotype, was pegylated interferon plus ribavirin (PR). The standard way to assess treatment response is a sustained viral response (SVR), defined as undetectable viral load 24 weeks after the end of therapy.[72] PR has an adequate SVR for genotypes 2 and 3 (70 to 80 percent) but not as good for others, including genotype 1 (45 to 70 percent SVR).[71] Additionally, PR is poorly tolerated, as the pegylated interferon causes flulike symptoms, fatigue, and headaches, and it is an injectable agent. For patients who did not respond to PR or were unable to tolerate it due to side effects, no real second-line options existed. Because of these concerns, substantial effort has been put forth in recent years by the scientific community to better understand the HCV viral genome and replication, with the goal of bringing to market agents that can better control viral replication with better tolerability.

The first target site for drug development is the NS3/NS4a protease. Blockage of this protease terminates the ability of the virus to spread to other cells. The first generation of HCV protease inhibitors were FDA approved in 2012 (bocepravir and telaprevir). Both of these agents were shown to be effective against genotype 1 when used in addition to PR, with SVRs of 63 to 75 percent.[73,74] Additionally, in genotype 1 patients who did not respond to PR previously, many responded to the new three-drug regimen of PR plus a protease inhibitor (59 to 66 percent SVR versus 17 to 21 percent SVR with PR alone).[75,76] These results led the AASLD to revise its guidelines and recommend triple therapy for both treatment-naïve and treatment-experienced genotype 1 patients.[77] However, many drawbacks remain. In this regimen, the side effects of PR are still present, with additional side effects from bocepravir and telapravir (severe rash). Both these agents also have multiple drug interactions and multiple daily dosage requirements, and they are ineffective against most non-genotype 1 viruses. Additionally, as these are direct antiviral agents (DAAs), they carry the risk of drug resistance.[72]

Over the next several years, additional DAAs will become available to overcome these existing drawbacks. For instance, the next protease inhibitor, simepravir, is dosed once daily and has fewer side effects. In a phase III study, the combination of simepravir + PR was shown to be effective against genotype 1, with SVR of 75 to 86 percent, even with a shorter treatment course. There are at least 10 additional protease inhibitors currently in various phases of development, including second-generation agents that have a high barrier to resistance and are potentially active against all four major HCV genotypes.[78]

In addition to protease inhibitors, several other classes of agents are in development. One such class is the NS5b polymerase inhibitors. The polymerase inhibitor in the most advanced stage of development is sofosbuvir. This agent has been shown in phase III studies to achieve SVRs of more than 90 percent when used in combination with PR against genotypes 1 and 4, as well as an SVR of 97 percent against genotype 2 when used with ribavirin alone (it only achieved an SVR of 56 percent against genotype 3, however).[79] A third class of new DAAs includes medications such as daclatesvir, which appear to be effective against multiple genotypes.[78]

There are in fact over 40 DAAs currently in development, signaling a new era for HCV treatment.[72,78] The goal of having all oral regimens effective against all genotypes with good tolerability and easy dosing seems to be within reach. The development of drug resistance is a concern, but this will likely be overcome by using combinations of DAAs from different classes, a strategy similar to the highly active antiretroviral therapy (HAART) that has been so effective for HIV. One such all-oral regimen has been shown to be effective.[80]

Prevention

The risk of posttransfusion HCV has been dramatically reduced since the late 1980s with the institution of policies calling for the screening of blood donors for risk factors and testing them for anti-HCV. Similar rigorous testing is applied to donors of organs and tissues. Solvent-detergent or heat treatment of acellular blood products such as clotting factors and immune globulins inactivates many viruses, including HCV. Avoidance of exposure is the cornerstone of prevention of HCV infection. Uniform application of Standard Precautions in healthcare settings should effectively interrupt healthcare-associated transmission.

Individuals can avoid HCV infection by modifying behaviors that place them at risk. HCV carriers should be counseled to avoid transmitting the virus to others by not sharing razors or toothbrushes and by using condoms for sexual intercourse for those with multiple partners. HCV carriers should not attempt to donate blood, organs, tissues, or semen.[81]

Postexposure prophylaxis using immune globulin is ineffective in preventing HCV and is no longer recommended. Development of a vaccine to prevent HCV infection has been problematic because of viral antigenic diversity and mutation. Therefore, no HCV vaccine is yet available. Pregnancy is not contraindicated for HCV-infected women, as the risk of perinatal transmission to the child averages 5 to 6 percent. Breastfeeding has not been implicated in transmission of HCV and is encouraged.[82]

Needle exchange programs have proven effective in preventing the spread of HCV among injection drug users. Immunization against HAV and HBV is recommended in patients with HCV infections; Twinrix (combined HBV and HAV vaccine, manufactured by GlaxoSmithKline) may be used.[1-3,21,27,48,52]

HEPATITIS D

Trends

Hepatitis D is also known as Hepatitis delta agent and was discovered in 1977.

Epidemiology

Description

HDV is an RNA virus with the smallest genome of all known animal viruses. This genome encodes a single antigen, which is expressed in two forms. HDV resembles plant satellite viruses but not other animal viruses. HDV has some genetic heterogeneity that varies geographically. It depends on simultaneous infection with HBV for its hepatotropism and transmission and is thus considered a parasite of HBV.[1,3,18,51,83-87]

Incidence

Approximately 5,000 to 7,500 new HDV infections occur per year in the United States, principally among IV drug users. The incidence of HDV among patients with hemophilia has declined since the 1980s as a result not only of screening blood and plasma donors for HBV infection but also of solvent-detergent or heat inactivation of viruses in clotting factors and the development of recombinant factors VIII and IX.[2,22,26,39]

Prevalence

Approximately 10 percent of HBV-infected individuals worldwide are co-infected with Hepatitis D. HDV is endemic in Italy and other countries in the Mediterranean basin, western Asia, northern South America, and certain Pacific islands. In western Europe and North America, the seroprevalence of HDV in blood donor populations ranges from 1.4 to 8 percent. The highest prevalence in the United States is among injection drug users (20 to 67 percent of HBV-infected persons). In Taiwan, 91 percent of HBsAg-positive injection drug users are also seropositive for HDV. Historically, 48 to 80 percent of U.S. patients with hemophilia were seropositive for HDV markers, but this rate is declining. Groups at intermediate risk of HDV infection include hemodialysis patients and institutionalized persons. HCP are at risk of acquiring HDV infection via sharps injuries.[1,12,18,83,85]

Transmission

HDV is transmitted principally by percutaneous exposure, but unlike HBV infection, HDV is inefficiently transmitted by sexual intercourse. Perinatal transmission is very rare, and no cases have been documented in the United States. It is not transmitted by the fecal-oral route or casual contact, though routes of transmission in countries in which HDV infection is endemic are not always clear.

Pathogenesis

HDV infection and hepatotropism depend on simultaneous infection with HBV, as the viral envelope for Hepatitis delta virus is the Hepatitis B surface antigen. HDV replicates only in hepatocytes and may be cytopathic. HDV and HBV may co-infect a susceptible host; a person who is already a chronic HBsAg carrier can be superinfected with HDV.[1,3]

Clinical Features

The incubation period of HDV ranges from 30 to 180 days. Simultaneous co-infection with HBV and HDV usually manifests much like acute HBV alone, though there may be a biphasic elevation of ALT with HDV infection. In 90 to 95 percent of cases of acute co-infection, the hepatitis is self-limited, and HBV and HDV are eliminated.

However, fulminant hepatic failure occurs more frequently than is seen with HBV alone. Approximately 5 percent of co-infections result in chronic HBV and HDV infection, a rate that is similar to that of HBV infection alone. Superinfection with HDV in a patient who is a chronic HBsAg carrier often causes more severe acute hepatitis than is seen with HBV/HDV co-infection. Moreover, HDV superinfection results in chronic HDV in greater than 90 percent of survivors of the acute infection. In 10 to 15 percent of these, especially among IV drug users, hepatic damage may progress to cirrhosis and liver failure within 1 to 2 years. Most of the others with chronic HDV have more slowly progressive liver disease resembling chronic HBV. HCC is less common in patients with chronic HDV infection than it is with chronic HBV or HCV. The reasons for this are not clear.[1,3]

Laboratory Diagnosis

A diagnosis of HDV is not tenable unless the patient tests positive for HBsAg. HDV should be suspected when there is a history of percutaneous or sexual exposure in a patient with chronic HDV infection, especially an IV drug user. It should also be suspected in a patient with acute HBV who has a second rise in ALT level or a patient with chronic HBV who develops an acute exacerbation of hepatitis.

The diagnosis of HDV can be made by PCR, IgG anti-HDV, or IgM anti-HDV. The first test should be anti-HDV IgG.[88] Co-infection of HBV and HDV is suggested by the simultaneous finding of a positive test for IgM anti-HBc. The anti-HDV IgG is short-lived in co-infection and is not protective. It may remain elevated as a "serologic scar" in superinfection patients who clear their HDV infection. A positive anti-HDV IgG should be followed up with HDV PCR to evaluate for evidence of active infection.[88]

Treatment

In acute HDV, supportive care is given. For chronic HDV, high-dose interferon alfa (IFN-a) may induce remission of disease in 40 to 50 percent of selected patients with histologic and biochemical response as well as viral suppression. However, relapse viremia is common and effects are unlikely to last once therapy is stopped.[89] The side effects of interferon therapy may be a severe limitation to its use. Regarding antiviral medications, lamivudine has been shown to be ineffective,[90] but tenofovir has been shown in a small study to decrease HDV viral loads, particularly when used with interferon.[91] In acute fulminant HDV or end-stage hepatic failure or cirrhosis, liver transplantation is often necessary.[7,18,19,51,83,85–87]

Prevention

General preventive measures for HDV, as for HBV, include modification of high-risk behaviors by individuals. Standard Precautions are used in healthcare settings. Postexposure passive immunization with HBIG with HBV vaccine can prevent infection with HBV. By eliminating HBV, co-infection with HDV will not occur. Preexposure active immunization with HBV vaccine will prevent co-infection with HDV. No vaccine to prevent HDV superinfection is yet available. Patients with chronic HDV infection should be candidates for HAV vaccine. Needle exchange programs may be effective in preventing the spread of HDV among injection drug users.[1–3]

HEPATITIS E

Trends

Hepatitis E is unique among the hepatic viruses in that it carries a particularly high mortality rate among pregnant women.

Epidemiology

Description

HEV is a small RNA virus in the Hepeviridae family. Its genome was cloned and sequenced in 1990 and 1991. The HEV genome encodes the synthesis of several proteins, and there is substantial worldwide geographic divergence among genotypes. However, only one common serotype has been found, which has been useful in developing serological tests for HEV. HEV is detected in serum during prodromal infection and in feces as infection progresses.[1,3,17,87,92,93]

Incidence

HEV is thought to cause at least 50 percent of sporadic acute viral hepatitis in developing countries, where it is also the most common cause of epidemics of enterically transmitted viral hepatitis. Epidemics of HEV seem to occur cyclically related to heavy rainfall and flooding in endemic areas. The peak incidence age is 15 to 40 years old. Attack rate is 1 to 10 percent, and secondary cases occur in 3 percent of contacts. HEV is endemic in the former Soviet Union and equatorial developing areas, especially south Asia, Africa, Mexico, and Central America. In these areas, HEV occurs sporadically as well as in periodic epidemics. Large epidemics occurred in India in 1955 to 1956 (30,000 cases) and China in 1986 to 1988 (120,000 cases). In Thailand, 3.6 percent of adolescents and 15.7 percent of adult blood donors have serological evidence of previous HEV. The reservoir for HEV in endemic areas may be zoonotic infection in swine, chickens, and rats. Contamination of water sources by feces from these animals may result in sporadic cases, as well as epidemics during floods and widespread disruption of sanitation. In the United States, clinically recognized HEV is generally seen as isolated sporadic cases in persons who have recently traveled to an endemic area. No secondary cases in household contacts have occurred in the United States.[1,3,12,16,17,26,86,92,93]

Transmission

Transmission is fecal-oral generally via ingestion of contaminated water, and there is a strong association of epidemics with floods, poor sanitation, and poor hygiene. Rare transfusion-associated cases have occurred; sexual transmission has not been documented. Infection during pregnancy results in a high frequency of fetal loss, and vertical transmission can occur in up to 50 percent of cases.[94]

Pathogenesis

Animal studies show replication of HEV in liver, blood cells, and other organs. Early liver damage may result from direct cytopathic effect of HEV, but later pathologic effects are immune mediated. HEV is transiently present in serum during prodrome, and at the onset of clinical disease it is found in feces. Fecal shedding of HEV persists for 1 week to 2 months. Appearance of anti-HEV roughly correlates with cessation of viral replication and beginning resolution of disease.[1,3,17]

Clinical Features

The incubation period of HEV is between 2 and 9 weeks (mean, 45 days), and it is generally a self-limiting disease that is relatively severe compared with HAV. There is a prodromal (pre-icteric) phase of nonspecific constitutional symptoms followed by an icteric phase that lasts several weeks. Fulminant HEV is rare (0.5 to 4 percent) except in pregnant women, in whom HEV occurring in the third trimester carriers a 20 percent maternal fatality rate and a 50 percent rate of fetal loss. Mortality rate of those infected during the third trimester was 100 percent in one study.[94] There is no chronic hepatitis or carrier state in humans with HEV.[26,60,86]

Diagnosis

Usually, clinical syndrome plus travel history are the first clues to suggest HEV. Exclusion of other causes of hepatitis heightens suspicion for HEV. Previously, the only available HEV-specific serologic tests used recombinant antigens and had a high rate of false positives in low-prevalence settings such as the United States (false-positive rate of 3 percent of U.S. blood donors). However, two recently developed tests (includes the HEV IgM ELISA 3.0 and the Rapid Point of Care test) have been shown to be highly sensitive and specific.[95,96] These are now diagnostic tests of choice, and the Rapid Point of Care test is particularly useful in endemic regions, as it is highly specific (98.6 to 99.7 percent specificity)[95,96] and does not require advanced laboratory equipment.

Treatment

Supportive care should be provided, as for any acute hepatitis. With fulminant HEV, liver transplantation is indicated.[1,3]

Prevention

In endemic areas, prevention is primarily achieved on an environmental level by ensuring separation of the water supply from sewage. During outbreaks when sanitation has eroded, efforts such as water chlorination may be inadequate.[97] Boiling or other disinfection of the water supply should still be attempted, and avoidance of uncooked fruits, vegetables, and shellfish in these settings is also prudent. Pregnant women should be cautious about travel to endemic regions due to elevated mortality risk. Unlike with HAV, passive immunization with IG has not been shown to protect against HEV transmission or disease. Several potentially effective prototype HEV vaccines are being studied but none is yet available.[98] Standard Precautions are adequate to prevent HEV transmission in healthcare settings. The finding of asymptomatic carriage of HEV in swine raises concern of xenotransplantation from pigs to humans.[1-3,15,17,26,99]

CONCLUSIONS

In summary, HAV is an enteric transmitted virus that has an acute viral syndrome with no chronic disease state that is diagnosed by HAV IgM serological marker and has an effective vaccine and passive immunoprophylaxis with IG, which is very effective if given before or within 2 weeks after exposure. HBV is a bloodborne virus with both an acute viral syndrome and a chronic disease state and is diagnosed by anti-HBcIgM and/or HBsAg serological markers. It has an effective vaccine and passive immunoprophylaxis with IG that is very effective if given within 7 days of exposure. HCV is a bloodborne virus whose transmission is very high among injection drug users, is characterized by a chronic disease state, is diagnosed by anti-HCV and HCV-PCR, and has no effective vaccine. HDV is a bloodborne virus that is principally transmitted like HBV by percutaneous exposure, but not efficiently by sexual intercourse, and is characterized by both an acute syndrome and a chronic disease state (that persists in patients with chronic HBV). HEV is an enteric transmitted virus that has an acute viral syndrome with no chronic disease state that is diagnosed by HEV IgM serological marker or PCR. It has no effective vaccines, and the best prophylaxis is improvement of sanitary conditions.

FUTURE TRENDS

With regard to HAV and HEV, the proportion of adult patients affected by foodborne HAV may continue to expand following the elimination of person-to-person epidemics among children. In recent reports, 11 percent of the population over 60 years of age in specific developed countries were susceptible to HAV infection. With regard to HBV, there is a decrease in transmission among HCP because of Standard Precautions, OSHA-mandated immunization, and the use of HBV HBIG. Liver transplantation will continue to be a viable treatment for liver failure secondary to HBV. With regard to HCV, the epidemic is peaking. A new era in treatment of HCV has arrived with the availability of directly acting antiviral therapy. Interferon-free therapy, especially for genotype 2 or 3 infection, will likely soon be standard practice.

INTERNATIONAL PERSPECTIVE

Complications of cirrhosis and HCC from chronic HBV and HCV remain the leading causes of liver-related death worldwide. The incidence of HBV and HCV in the populous areas of Asia and Africa remains the critical underlying problem. Perinatal prophylaxis in patients with active HBV remains critical in controlling the worldwide epidemic. HAV continues to be prevalent in nonindustrialized countries among children. HDV and HEV have very high prevalences in specific areas of the world. Control of the bloodborne viruses will depend on precautionary measures with blood supply and intravenous drugs, whereas control of the enteric viruses will depend on the increasing sanitation systems and food-handling practices.

REFERENCES

1. Baker DA. Viral hepatitis. In: Olmsted RN, ed. *Infection Control and Applied Epidemiology*. St. Louis: Mosby, 1996.
2. Guideline for isolation precautions in hospitals. Part II. Recommendations for isolation precautions in hospitals. Hospital Infection Control Practices Advisory Committee. *Am J Infect Control* 1996 Feb;24(1):32–52.
3. Berenguer M, Wright TL. Viral hepatitis A through G. In: Feldman M, Sleisenger MH, Scharschmidt BF, eds. *Gastrointestinal and Liver Disease*, 7th ed. Philadelphia: WB Saunders; 1998, 1278–1334.
4. Centers for Disease Control and Prevention (CDC), Division of Viral Hepatitis and National Center for HIV/AIDS, Viral Hepatitis, STD, and TB Prevention. *Healthcare-associated hepatitis B and C outbreaks reported to the Centers for Disease Control and Prevention (CDC) in 2008–2012*. CDC website. May 21, 2013. Available at: http://www.cdc.gov/hepatitis/outbreaks/healthcarehepoutbreaktable.htm
5. Rao AK, Luckman E, Wise ME, et al. Outbreak of hepatitis C virus infections at an outpatient hemodialysis facility: the importance of infection control competencies. *Nephrol Nurs J* 2013 Mar-Apr;40(2):101–110, 164.
6. Centers for Disease Control and Prevention (CDC), Division of Viral Hepatitis and National Center for HIV/AIDS, Viral Hepatitis, STD, and TB Prevention. *Hepatitis A FAQs for health professionals*. CDC website. June 6, 2013. Available at: http://www.cdc.gov/hepatitis/HAV/HAVfaq.htm#general
7. Advisory Committee on Immunization Practices (ACIP), Fiore AE, Wasley A. Prevention of hepatitis A through active or passive immunization: recommendations of the Advisory Committee on Immunization Practices (ACIP). *MMWR Recomm Rep* 2006 May 19;55(RR-7):1–23.
8. World Health Organization (WHO). *Hepatitis A fact sheet*. WHO website. July 2013. Available at: http://www.who.int/mediacentre/factsheets/fs328/en/.
9. Skinhoj P, Mathiesen LR, Kryger P. Faecal excretion of hepatitis A virus in patients with symptomatic hepatitis A infection. *Scand J Gastroenterol* 1981; 16:1057–1059..
10. Krugman S, Ward R, Giles JP. Infectious hepatitis: detection of virus during the incubation period and in clinically inapparent infection. *N Engl J Med* 1959 Oct 8;261:729–734.
11. Vento S, Garofano T, Renzini C, et al. Fulminant hepatitis associated with hepatitis A virus superinfection in patients with chronic hepatitis C. *N Engl J Med* 1998 Jan 29;338(5):286–290.
12. Willner IR, Uhl MD, Howard SC, et al. Serious hepatitis A: an analysis of patients hospitalized during an urban epidemic in the United States. *Ann Intern Med* 1998 Jan 15;128(2):111–114.
13. Advisory Committee on Immunization Practices (ACIP) Centers for Disease Control and Prevention (CDC). Update: Prevention of hepatitis A after exposure to hepatitis A virus and in international travelers. Updated recommendations of the Advisory Committee on Immunization Practices (ACIP). *MMWR Morb Mortal Wkly Rep* 2007 Oct 19;56(41):1080–1084.
14. Immunization of health-care workers: recommendations of the Advisory Committee on Immunization Practices (ACIP) and the Hospital Infection Control Practices Advisory Committee (HICPAC). *MMWR Recomm Rep* 1997 Dec 26;46(RR-18):1–42.
15. Lemon SM, Thomas DL. Vaccines to prevent viral hepatitis. *N Engl J Med* 1997 Jan 16;336(3):196–204.
16. McCloy E. Occupational aspects of hepatitis viruses. *Curr Opin Infect Dis* 1997 Oct;10(5):385–389.
17. Yarbrough PO. Advances in hepatitis E. *Curr Opin Infect Dis* 1997 Oct;10(5):398–401.
18. Hadler SC, Alcala de Monzon M, Bensabath G, et al. Epidemiology of hepatitis delta virus infection in less developed countries. *Prog Clinic Biol Res* 1991;364:21–31.
19. Incident Investigation Teams and Others. Transmission of hepatitis B to patients from four infected surgeons without hepatitis B e antigen. *N Engl J Med* 1997 Jan 16;336(3):178–84.
20. Centers for Disease Control and Prevention (CDC). Outbreaks of hepatitis B virus infection among hemodialysis patients—California, Nebraska, Texas, 1994. *MMWR Morb Mortal Wkly Rep* 1996 Apr 12;45(14):285–289.
21. Gerberding JL. Management of occupational exposures to bloodborne pathogens. *N Engl J Med* 1995 Feb 16;332(7):444–451.
22. Harpaz R, Von Seidlein L, Averhoff FM, et al. Transmission of hepatitis B virus to multiple patients from a surgeon without evidence of inadequate infection control. *N Engl J Med* 1996 Feb 29;334(9):549–554.
23. Lee WM. Hepatitis B virus infection. *N Engl J Med* 1997 Dec 11; 337(24):1733–1745.
24. Mahoney FJ, Stewart K, Hu H, et al. Progress toward the elimination of hepatitis B virus transmission among health care workers in the United States. *Arch Intern Med* 1997 Dec 8–22;157(22):2601–2605.
25. Mamiya N, Worman HJ. Epidemiology, prevention, clinical features and therapy of hepatitis B, C, and G. *Curr Opin Infect Dis* 1997 Oct;10(5):390–397.
26. McCarron B, Main J, Thomas HC. Viral hepatitis, new viruses and therapies. *Curr Opin Infect Dis* 1996 Oct;9(5):359.
27. Schreiber GB, Busch MP, Kleinman SH, et al. The risk of transfusion-transmitted viral infections. *N Engl J Med* 1996 Jun 27;334(26):1685–1690.
28. Befeler AS, Di Bisceglie AM. Hepatitis B. *Infect Dis Clin North Amer* 2000 Sep;14(3):617–632.
29. Centers for Disease Control and Prevention (CDC), Division of Viral Hepatitis and National Center for HIV/AIDS, Viral Hepatitis, STD, and TB Prevention. *Hepatitis B FAQs for health professionals*. CDC website. January 31, 2012. Available at: http://www.cdc.gov/hepatitis/HBV/HBVfaq.htm#overview.
30. Dienstag JL, Ryan DM. Occupational exposure to hepatitis B virus in hospital personnel: infection or immunization? *Am J Epidemiol* 1982 Jan;115(1):26–39.
31. Mahoney FJ, Stewart K, Hu H, et al. Progress toward the elimination of hepatitis B virus transmission among health care workers in the United States. *Arch Intern Med* 1997 Dec 8–22;157(22):2601–2605.
32. Wasley A, Grytdal S, Gallagher K, et al. Surveillance for acute viral hepatitis—United States, 2006. Surveillance Summaries. *MMWR Surveill Summ* 2008 Mar 21;57(2):1–24.
33. World Health Organization (WHO). *Hepatitis B fact sheet*. WHO website. July 2013. Available at: http://www.who.int/mediacentre/factsheets/fs204/en/.
34. Wasley A, Kruszon-Moran D, Kuhnert W, et al. The prevalence of hepatitis B virus infection in the United States in the era of vaccination. *J Infect Dis* 2010 Jul 15;202(2):192–201.
35. Kowdley KV, Wang CC, Welch S, et al. Prevalence of chronic hepatitis B among foreign-born persons living in the United States by country of origin. *Hepatology* 2012 Aug;56(2):422–433.
36. Chin J. *Control of Communicable Disease Manual. An Official Report of the American Public Health Association*, 17th ed. Washington, DC: American Public Health Association, 2000.
37. Dienstag JL. Hepatitis B virus infection. *N Engl J Med* 2008 Oct 2;359(14):1486–1500.
38. Lok AS. Prevention of recurrent hepatitis B post-liver transplantation. *Liver Transpl* 2002 Oct;8(10 Suppl 1):S67–S73.
39. Dienstag JL, Schiff ER, Wright TL, et al. Lamivudine as initial treatment for chronic hepatitis B in the United States. *N Engl J Med* 1999 Oct 21; 341(17):1256–1263.
40. Mast EE, Weinbaum CM, Fiore AE, et al. A comprehensive immunization strategy to eliminate transmission of hepatitis B virus infection in the United States: recommendations of the Advisory Committee on Immunization Practices (ACIP) Part II: immunization of adults. *MMWR Recomm Rep* 2006 Dec 8;55(RR-16):1–33.
41. U.S. Public Health Service. Updated U.S. Public Health Service guidelines for the management of occupational exposure to HBV, HCV and HIV and recommendations for postexposure prophylaxis. *MMWR Recomm Rep* 2001 Jun 29;50(RR-11):1–52.
42. Centers for Disease Control and Prevention (CDC). Updated CDC Recommendations for the Management of Hepatitis B Virus–Infected Health-Care Providers and Students. *MMWR Recomm Rep* 2012 Jul 6;61(RR-3):1–12.
43. Mast EE, Weinbaum CM, Fiore AE, et al. A comprehensive immunization strategy to eliminate transmission of hepatitis B virus infection in the United States: recommendations of the Advisory Committee on Immunization Practices (ACIP) Part II: immunization of adults. *MMWR Recomm Rep* 2006 Dec 8;55(RR-16):1–33.
44. Stevens CE, Taylor PE, Tong MJ, et al. Yeast-recombinant hepatitis B vaccine: efficacy with hepatitis B immune globulin in prevention of perinatal hepatitis B virus transmission. *JAMA* 1987 May 15;257(19):2612–2616.
45. Alter MJ, Mast EE. The epidemiology of viral hepatitis in the United States. *Gastroenterol Clin North Am* 1994 Sep;23(3):437–455.
46. Conry-Cantilena C, VanRaden M, Gibble J, et al. Routes of infection, viremia, and liver disease in blood donors found to have hepatitis C virus infection. *N Engl J Med* 1996 Jun 27;334(26):1691–1696.
47. Esteban JI, Gomez J, Martell M, et al. Transmission of hepatitis C virus by a cardiac surgeon. *N Engl J Med* 1996 Feb 29;334(9):555–560.
48. Gross JB Jr. Clinician's guide to hepatitis C. *Mayo Clin Proc* 1998 Apr;73(4):355–360.
49. Jenny-Avital ER. Hepatitis C. *Curr Opin Infect Dis* 1998 Jun;11(3):293–299.
50. McDonnell WM, Lucey MR. Hepatitis C infection. *Curr Opin Infect Dis* 1995 Oct;8(5):384.
51. Shapiro CN, Margolis HS. Worldwide epidemiology of hepatitis A virus infection. *J Hepatol* 1993;18(Suppl 2):S11–S14.
52. Sharara AI, Hunt CM, Hamilton JD. Hepatitis C. *Ann Intern Med* 1996 Oct 15;125(8):658–668.

53. Wasley A, Alter MJ. Epidemiology of hepatitis C: geographic differences and temporal trends. *Semin Liver Dis* 2000;20(1):1–16.
54. Global surveillance and control of hepatitis C. Reports of a WHO consultation organized in collaboration with the Viral Hepatitis Prevention Board, Antwerp Belgium. *J Viral Hepat* 1999 Jan;6(1):35–47.
55. Yen T, Keeffe EB, Ahmed A. The epidemiology of hepatitis C virus infection. *J Clin Gastro* 2003 Jan;36(1):47–53.
56. Kim WR. The burden of hepatitis C in the United States. *Hepatology* 2002 Nov;36(5 Suppl 1):S30–S34.
57. Smith BD, Morgan RL, Beckett GA. Recommendations for the Identification of Chronic Hepatitis C Virus Infection Among Persons Born During 1945–1965. *MMWR Recomm Rep* 2012 Aug 17;61(RR-4):1–32.
58. de Jesus Rodrigues de Freitas M, Fecury AA, de Almeida MK, et al. Prevalence of hepatitis C virus infection and genotypes in patient with chronic kidney disease undergoing hemodialysis. *J Med Virol* 2013 Oct;85(10):1741–1745.
59. Duckworth GJ, Heptonstall J, Aitken C. Transmission of hepatitis C virus from a surgeon to a patient. The Incident Control Team. *Commun Dis Public Health* 1999 Sep;2(3):188–192.
60. Pradat P, Alberti A, Poynard T, et al. Predictive value of ALT levels for histologic findings in chronic hepatitis C: a European collaborative study. *Hepatology* 2002 Oct;36(4 Pt 1):973–977.
61. Damen M, Zaaijer HL, Cuypers HTM, et al. Reliability of the third-generation recombinant immunoblot assay for hepatitis C virus. *Transfusion* 1995 Sep;35(9):745–749.
62. Centers for Disease Control and Prevention (CDC). Recommendations for follow up of health-care workers after occupational exposure to hepatitis C virus. *MMWR Morb Mortal Wkly Rep* 1997 Jul 4;46(26):603–606.
63. Gretch DR, dela Rosa C, Carithers RL Jr, et al. Assessment of hepatitis C viremia using molecular amplification technologies: correlations and clinical implications. *Ann Intern Med* 1995 Sep 1;123(5):321–329.
64. Gross JB, Persing DH. Hepatitis C: advances in diagnosis. *Mayo Clin Proc* 1995 Mar;70(3):296–297.
65. Pawlotsky JM. Use and interpretation of virological tests for hepatitis C. Hepatology 2002 Nov;36(5 Suppl 1):S65–S73.
66. Knodell RG, Ishak KG, Black WC, et al. Formulation and application of a numerical scoring system for assessing histological activity in asymptomatic chronic active hepatitis. *Hepatology* 1981 Sep-Oct;1(5):431–435.
67. Bedossa P, Poynard T: An algorithm for the grading of activity in chronic hepatitis C. *Hepatology* 1996 Aug;24(2):289–293.
68. Ishak K, Baptista A, Bianchi L, et al: Histological grading and staging of chronic hepatitis. *J Hepatol* 1995 Jun;22(6):696–699.
69. Imbert-Bismut F, Ratziu V, Pieroni L, et al. Biochemical markers of liver fibrosis in patients with hepatitis C virus infection: a prospective study. *Lancet* 2001 Apr 7;357(9262):1069–1075.
70. Foucher J, Chanteloup E, Vergniol J, et al. Diagnosis of cirrhosis by transient elastography (FibroScan): a prospective study. *Gut* 2006 Mar;55(3):403–408.
71. Ghany MG, Strader DB, Thomas DL. Diagnosis, management, and treatment of hepatitis C: an update. *Hepatology* 2009 Apr;49(4):1335–1374.
72. Liang TJ, Ghany MG. Current and future therapies for hepatitis C virus infection. *N Engl J Med* 2013 May;368(20):1907–1917.
73. Poordad F, McCone J Jr, Bacon BR, et al. Boceprevir for untreated chronic HCV genotype 1 infection. *N Engl J Med* 2011 Mar 31;364(13):1195–206.
74. Jacobson IM, McHutchison JG, Dusheiko G, et al. Telaprevir for previously untreated chronic hepatitis C virus infection. *N Engl J Med* 2011 Jun 23;364(25):2405–2416.
75. Bacon BR, Gordon SC, Lawitz E, et al. Boceprevir for previously treated chronic HCV genotype 1 infection. *N Engl J Med* 2011 Mar 31;364(13):1207–1217.
76. Zeuzem S, Andreone P, Pol S, et al. Telaprevir for retreatment of HCV infection. *N Engl J Med* 2011 Jun 23;364(25):2417–2428.
77. Ghany MG, Nelson DR, Strader DB, et al. An update on treatment of genotype 1 chronic hepatitis C virus infection: 2011 practice guideline by the American Association for the Study of Liver Diseases. *Hepatology* 2011 Oct;54(4):1433–1444.
78. Aghemo A, De Francesco R. New horizons in hepatitis C antiviral therapy with direct-acting antivirals. *Hepatology* 2013 Jul;58(1):428–438.
79. Lawitz E, Mangia A, Wyles D, et al. Sofosbuvir for previously untreated chronic hepatitis C infection. *N Engl J Med* 2013 May 16;368(20):1878–1887.
80. Gane EJ, Stedman CA, Hyland RH et al. Nucleotide polymerase inhibitor sofosbuvir plus ribavirin for hepatitis C. *N Engl J Med* 2013 Jan 3;368(1):34–44.
81. Workowski KA, Berman S, Centers for Disease Control and Prevention (CDC). Sexually Transmitted Diseases Treatment Guidelines, 2010. *MMWR Recomm Rep* 2010 Dec 17;59(RR-12):1–110.
82. Center for Disease Control (CDC), Division of Viral Hepatitis and National Center for HIV/AIDS, Viral Hepatitis, STD, and TB Prevention. *Hepatitis C information for health professionals.* CDC website. May 7, 2013. Available at: http://www.cdc.gov/hepatitis/HCV/index.htm.
83. Di Bisceglie A, Negro F. Diagnosis in hepatitis delta virus infections. *Hepatology* 1989 Dec;10(6):1014–1016.
84. Farci P, Chessa L, Balestrieri C, et al. Treatment of chronic hepatitis D. *J Viral Hepat* 2007 Nov;14 Suppl 1:58-63.
85. Farci P, Mandas A, Coiana A, et al. Treatment of chronic hepatitis D with interferon α-2A. *N Engl J Med* 1994 Jan 13;330(2):88–94.
86. Mast EE, Purdy MA, Krawczynski K. Hepatitis E. *Baillieres Clin Gastroenterol.* 1996 Jul;10(2):227–242.
87. Alter MJ, Kruszon-Moran D, Nainan DV. The prevalence of hepatitis C virus infection in the United States, 1988 through 1994. *N Engl J Med* 1999 Aug 19;341(8):556–562.
88. Olivero A, Smedile A. Hepatitis delta virus diagnosis. *Semin Liver Dis* 2012 Aug;32(3):220–227.
89. Farci P, Mandas A, Coiana A, et al. Treatment of chronic hepatitis D with interferon alfa-2a. *N Engl J Med* 1994 Jan 13;330(2):88–94.
90. Lau DT, Doo E, Park Y, et al. Lamivudine for chronic delta hepatitis. *Hepatology* 1999 Aug;30(2):546–549.
91. Boyd A, Miailhes P, Brichler S, et al. Effect of tenofovir with and without interferon on HDV replication in HIV-HBV-HDV infected patients. *AIDS Res Hum Retroviruses* 2013 Dec;29(12):1535–1540.
92. Kwo PY, Schlauder GG, Carpenter HA, et al. Acute hepatitis E by a new isolate acquired in the United States. *Mayo Clin Proc* 1997 Dec;72(12):1133–1136.
93. Purdy MA, Krawczynski K. Hepatitis E. *Gastroenterol Clin North Am* 1994 Sep;23(3):537–546.
94. Singh S, Mohanty A, Joshi YK, et al. Mother-to-child transmission of hepatitis E virus infection. *Indian J Pediatr* 2003 Jan;70(1):37–39.
95. Chen HY, Lu Y, Howard T, et al. Comparison of a new immunochromatographic test to enzyme-linked immunosorbent assay for rapid detection of immunoglobulin m antibodies to hepatitis e virus in human sera. *Clin Diagn Lab Immunol* 2005 May;12(5):593–598.
96. Myint KS, Guan M, Chen HY, et al. Evaluation of a new rapid immunochromatographic assay for serodiagnosis of acute hepatitis E infection. *Am J Trop Med Hyg.* 2005 Nov;73(5):942–946.
97. Guthmann JP, Klovstad H, Boccia D, et al. A large outbreak of hepatitis E among a displaced population in Darfur, Sudan, 2004: the role of water treatment methods. *Clin Infect Dis* 2006 Jun 15;42(12):1685–1691.
98. Shrestha MP, Scott RM, Joshi DM, et al. Safety and efficacy of a recombinant hepatitis E vaccine. *N Engl J Med* 2007 Mar 1;356(9):895–903.
99. Zuckerman J. Vaccination against viral hepatitis. *Curr Opin Infect Dis* 1997 Oct;10(5):379–384.

SUPPLEMENTAL RESOURCES

Alter MJ. Epidemiology and prevention of hepatitis B. *Semin Liver Dis* 2003 Feb;23(1):39–46.

Averhoff FM, Moyer LA, Woodruff BA, et al. Occupational exposures and risk of hepatitis B virus infection among public safety workers. *J Occup Environ Med* 2002 Jun;44(6):591–596.

Centers for Disease Control and Prevention CDC). *Hepatitis Surveillance Report Number 56.* Atlanta: CDC; 1996.

Hadler SC. Global Impact of Hepatitis A Virus Infection: Changing Patterns. In: Hollinger FB, Lemon SM, Margolis HS, eds. *Viral Hepatitis and Liver Disease.* Baltimore: Williams & Wilkins, 1991;14–19.

Hoofnagle JH, Carithers RL Jr, Shapiro C, et al. Fulminant hepatic failure: summary of a workshop. *Hepatology* 1995 Jan;21(1):240–252.

McHutchison JG, Manns M, Patel K, et al. Adherence to combination therapy enhances sustained response in genotype-1-infected patients with chronic hepatitis C. *Gastroenterology* 2002 Oct;123(4):1061–1069.

Recommendations for prevention and control of hepatitis C virus (HCV) infection and HCV-related chronic disease. Centers for Disease Control and Prevention. *MMWR Recomm Rep* 1998 Oct 16;47(RR-19):1–39.

Recommendations for preventing transmission of infections among chronic hemodialysis patients. *MMWR Recomm Rep* 2001 Apr 27;50(RR-5):1–43.

Rizzetto M, Hadziyannis S, Hansson BG, et al. Hepatitis delta virus infection in the world. Epidemiological patterns and clinical expression. *Gastroenterol Int* 1992;5:18.

Seeff LB, Hoofnagle JH. The National Institutes of Health Consensus Development Conference Management of Hepatitis C 2002. Consensus Development Conference, NIH. *Clin Liver Dis* 2003 Feb;7(1):261–287.

Wong JB, McQuillan GM, McHutchison PT. Estimating future hepatitis C morbidity, mortality and costs in the United States. *Am J Public Health* 2000 Oct;90(10):1562–1569.

WEB LINKS

Centers for Disease Control and Prevention (CDC). *Guidelines for viral hepatitis surveillance and case management.* CDC website. June 2, 2009. Available at: http://www.cdc.gov/hepatitis/Statistics/SurveillanceGuidelines.htm.

Centers for Disease Control and Prevention (CDC), National Center for Injury Prevention and Control (NCIPC), Office of Noncommunicable Diseases, Injury and Environmental Health. *Emergency preparedness and response: blast and bombing injuries.* CDC website. March 2, 2012. Available at: http://www.bt.cdc.gov/masscasualties/blastinjuryfacts.asp.

Centers for Disease Control and Prevention (CDC), National Center for HIV/AIDS, Viral Hepatitis, STD, and TB Prevention. *Viral hepatitis.* CDC website. March 12, 2013. Available at: http://www.cdc.gov/hepatitis/index.htm.

Centers for Disease Control and Prevention (CDC), National Center for Emerging and Zoonotic Infectious Diseases (NCEZID), Division of Healthcare Quality Promotion (DHQP). *Injection safety.* CDC website. June 6, 2013. Available at: http://www.cdc.gov/injectionsafety/.

American Liver Foundation
75 Maiden Lane, Suite 603
New York, NY 10038-4810
Phone: 1-800-GO-LIVER (465-4837), 1-888-4HEP-USA (443-7872), or 212-668-1000
Fax: 212-483-8179
Email: info@liverfoundation.org
Internet: www.liverfoundation.org

Centers for Disease Control and Prevention
Division of Viral Hepatitis
1600 Clifton Road

Mail Stop C-14
Atlanta, GA 30333
Phone: 1-800-CDC-INFO (232-4636)
Fax: 404-371-5488
Email: cdcinfo@cdc.gov
Internet: www.cdc.gov/hepatitis

Hepatitis Foundation International
504 Blick Drive
Silver Spring, MD 20904-2901
Phone: 1-800-891-0707 or 301-622-4200
Fax: 301-622-4702
Email: hfi@comcast.net
Internet: www.hepatitisfoundation.org

APPLICABLE GUIDELINES

Advisory Committee on Immunization Practices (ACIP) Centers for Disease Control and Prevention (CDC). Update: Prevention of hepatitis A after exposure to hepatitis A virus and in international travelers. Updated recommendations of the Advisory Committee on Immunization Practices (ACIP). *MMWR Morb Mortal Wkly Rep* 2007 Oct 19;56(41):1080–1084.

Mast EE, Weinbaum CM, Fiore AE, et al. A comprehensive immunization strategy to eliminate transmission of hepatitis B virus infection in the United States: recommendations of the Advisory Committee on Immunization Practices (ACIP) Part II: immunization of adults. *MMWR Recomm Rep* 2006 Dec 8;55 (RR-16):1–33.

Siegel JD, Rhinehart E, Jackson M, et al. 2007 guideline for isolation precautions: preventing transmission of infectious agents in healthcare settings. Available at: http://www.cdc.gov/ncidod/dhqp/gl_isolation.html.

Strader D, Wright,T, Thomas DL, et al. AASLD Practice guideline. Diagnosis, management, and treatment of Hepatitis C. *Hepatology* 2004 Apr;39(4):1147–1171.

U.S. Department of Labor, Occupational Safety & Health Administration (OSHA). *Bloodborne pathogens and needlestick prevention.* OSHA website. Available at: http://www.osha.gov/SLTC/bloodbornepathogens/standards.html.

CHAPTER 98

West Nile Virus

Michael A. Pentella, PhD, CIC, D (ABMM)
Director, Bureau of Laboratory Sciences
William A. Hinton State Laboratory Institute
Jamaica Plain, MA

ABSTRACT

Since introduction into the Western Hemisphere, West Nile virus (Flaviviridae: Flavivirus) has established enzootic transmission in nearly every part of the United States and southern Canada and has become an important public health concern. Although approximately 80 percent of individuals infected with West Nile virus are asymptomatic, others have clinical manifestations ranging from febrile illness to neurologic syndromes and possibly death. West Nile virus has a broad host and vector range with competent mosquito and bird vectors, which has led to the establishment of the virus throughout the Western Hemisphere. Although it is primarily transmitted through the bite of an infected mosquito, other modes of West Nile virus transmission have been identified and include infection through transplants of infected organs, transfusion of blood or blood products, intrauterine fetal infection, neonatal infection through breast-feeding, occupational exposure in the field, and laboratory-acquired infections from needlestick or sharps injuries. Controlling the spread of West Nile virus, as well as other emerging vectorborne viral disease, requires laboratory diagnostic testing in conjunction with epidemiologic surveillance, vector control programs, and a variety of personal precautions. No human vaccine is currently available; however, there is an equine vaccine.

KEY CONCEPTS

- West Nile virus is an arthropodborne virus (arbovirus) primarily transmitted through the bite of infected mosquitoes.

- Approximately 80 percent of people infected with West Nile virus are asymptomatic; those with symptoms usually experience a mild febrile illness.

- A very few (less than 1 percent) go on to develop neurologic manifestations of encephalitis or flaccid paralysis.

- West Nile virus is a seasonal disease; a variety of personal precautions to protect against mosquitoes and reduce mosquito populations can be performed to prevent infections from West Nile virus and other arboviruses effectively.

BACKGROUND

West Nile virus (WNV) was first identified as a pathogen from a woman with a febrile illness in the West Nile District of Uganda in the 1937.[1] Prior to its appearance in the United States, it was considered to be of low virulence. Before WNV appeared in New York in 1999, it had never been seen in the Western Hemisphere. The resulting epizootic (large disease outbreak in animals) developed into an ongoing epidemic of a mosquito-transmitted viral disease in the United States and the largest recorded outbreak of WNV in the world. At the peak of the WNV outbreak in 2003, there were 9,862 cases reported, with 2,866 cases of neuroinvasive disease and 264 fatalities in the United States. Since then the incidence has waned, and in 2008 there were 1,370 cases reported with 640 neuroinvasive disease and 37 fatalities in the United States.[2] In 2012, an increase in infections was detected with the highest number of cases reported since 2004.

It is thought that the strain of WNV that is being transmitted in the Western Hemisphere is more virulent than strains seen prior to 1999 outside of the United States.[3] WNV is now established in North America and can be considered a seasonal disease that strikes every summer and into the fall.

DEFINITIONS AND BASIC PRINCIPLES

Definitions

Arthropods: insects that include mosquitoes, ticks, and biting midges

Arbovirus: a contraction of the words *arthropod-borne virus*; these are viruses that are transmitted by arthropods; arthropods serve as a vector for transmission

Amplifying host: vertebrate host that serves as a reservoir for an arbovirus; infection with the arbovirus results in high titers of virus in the circulation

West Nile fever: uncomplicated febrile illness resulting from WNV infection

West Nile neuroinvasive disease (meningoencephalitis): clinical syndrome used to describe encephalitis, meningitis, myelitis, or overlapping syndromes of each resulting from WNV infection

Basic Principles

WNV is a flavivirus and member of the Japanese encephalitis virus complex; this includes WNV, Japanese encephalitis, St. Louis encephalitis, and Murray Valley encephalitis viruses. They also are closely related to other well-known flaviviruses, dengue and yellow fever viruses. The relative amount of an arbovirus present in the environment is the result of a complex interaction between the virus, its arthropod vector, and the specific amplifying host. Each arbovirus has specific amplifying hosts (e.g., birds, small vertebrate mammals, or rodents) that serve as the primary reservoir in the environment. For WNV, birds are the primary amplifying host because when they become infected they develop high levels of viremia that allow for ease of transmission. Mosquitoes, the arthropod vector for WNV, become infected during the blood meal and serve to transmit the virus and maintain the bird-mosquito-bird cycle. *Culex* spp. mosquitoes are the primary vectors transmitting WNV. *Culex* spp. permit the virus to winter over in temperate climates, because they hibernate as infected adult mosquitoes. In the spring, the mosquitoes emerge and infect birds. This is a self-perpetuating cycle because there are ample numbers of mosquitoes to serve as vectors and birds to serve as susceptible hosts. Humans and horses are not integral to this amplification cycle and are considered incidental, or dead-end, hosts. When humans and large mammals are infected, the level of viremia is low enough and presents for a short enough duration that the mosquito vector taking a blood meal is unlikely to acquire the infecting arbovirus.

VIROLOGY, EPIDEMIOLOGY, AND CLINICAL MANAGEMENT

Characteristics of West Nile Virus

WNV is a small, enveloped virus with a single-stranded RNA genome of approximately 11,000 nucleotides. There are two phylogenetic lineages of WNV that are separated based on genome homology: Lineage 1 is distributed worldwide (West Africa, the Middle East, Eastern Europe, North America, and Australia), whereas lineage 2 is limited to Africa. The virus introduced into New York in 1999 is most closely related to a lineage 1 virus isolated from a goose in Israel in 1998, though the exact mechanism of the introduction is unknown.[4]

Epidemiology Surveillance Activities

West Nile Virus Transmission

WNV is primarily transmitted by the bite of infected mosquitoes. Birds serve as the primary reservoir host and mosquitoes are the arthropod vector. For example, *C. pipiens* (the northern house mosquito) is a major arthropod vector within the WNV transmission cycle. *C. pipiens* prefers to feed on birds and lays its eggs in standing, "dirty" water commonly found in urban areas (i.e., catch basins, pool covers, birdbaths, discarded tires). WNV has been shown to infect hundreds of bird species; most survive the infection. The resulting infection causes a high-titer viremia for many species, which aids in acquisition of the virus

by mosquitoes taking a blood meal. WNV spread rapidly across the United States and Canada from 2001 through 2004 by means of migratory birds that fly south to Central and South America in the fall and back north in the spring to the United State and Canada along specific flyways. Major outbreaks were observed 1 year after introduction via migratory birds, probably through distribution in resident birds.[5] Humans are incidental hosts for WNV, as are other mammals, including horses.

Novel Modes of West Nile Virus Transmission

Healthcare-associated transmission of WNV through contaminated blood, blood products and organs, and from mother to child through breast milk has been identified. In the fall of 2002, healthcare-associated infection with WNV occurred in four recipients of organ donations shortly after transplantation. Because each patient had received organs from a single donor, the transplanted organs were identified as the route of acquisition.[6,7] Further investigation of this case determined that the organ donor became infected after transfusion with WNV-contaminated blood products. Additional investigations determined that donation of blood and blood products by WNV-infected individuals before the development of symptoms has the potential to transmit the virus to the recipients of the products.[8] As a result, in July 2003, the U.S. Food and Drug Administration (FDA) mandated WNV screening of blood products.

Workers at risk for occupational exposure include (1) those who work outdoors such as farmers, foresters, landscapers, etc. and (2) laboratory,[9] field, and clinical workers who have contact with infected animals and blood, perform necropsies of infected birds, or handle WNV-infected tissues or fluids.[10] Heathcare personnel should be educated regarding the risk of transmission of WNV through blood and body fluids and educated that Standard Precautions are appropriate.[11] WNV also has been shown to be transmitted from mother to child vertically[12] and through breast-feeding.[13]

Clinical Manifestations of West Nile Virus Infection

Being bitten by an infected mosquito does not necessarily cause symptomatic illness. After a mosquito bite, the incubation period may be as short as 2 days or as long as 14 days. The virus enters the lymph nodes and multiplies before entering the bloodstream. An infected person is infectious for 6 to 7 days before the onset of clinical illness, but infectiousness ends shortly after symptoms appear. Approximately 80 percent of people who are infected with WNV are asymptomatic, but approximately 20 percent of infected individuals experience a mild febrile illness, which can be severe but is usually self-limiting; besides a fever, symptoms include fatigue, headache, muscle weakness, neck pain or stiffness, eye pain, malaise, anorexia, nausea, vomiting, and rash. This febrile illness is known as West Nile fever. In less than 1 percent of individuals, WNV can cause encephalitis, meningitis, or a polio-like flaccid paralysis[3] that can lead to permanent neurological sequelae and death. The risk for serious disease increases with age and in immunocompromised patients. Symptoms of West Nile encephalitis include the rapid onset of severe headache, high fever, stiff neck, confusion, loss of consciousness, and muscle weakness. Symptoms of mild WNV disease usually last for only 3 to 6 days; however, WNV fever can be a serious illness requiring several months or longer to resolve.[14]

Laboratory Diagnostic Testing

Testing should only be performed on patients who have symptoms suggestive of WNV, such as headache, fever, stiff neck, and muscular weakness, and a diagnosis of encephalitis and/or meningitis. The preliminary diagnosis of WNV infection can be based on the patient's signs and symptoms, risk of exposure such as activities that would expose them to mosquito bites, travel history, or the incidence of WNV from surveillance data of the location where the infection is thought to have occurred.

WNV infection can be detected with acute or convalescent phase serum by serological assays, which utilize enzyme immunoassay (EIA) immunoglobulin M (IgM) antibody capture method. Cerebrospinal fluid (CSF) can also be tested for IgM antibodies by EIA. There are several FDA-approved tests available in the United States.[15] It is important to note that the degree of proficiency may vary between laboratories.[16] The positive results obtained with a commercially available product need to be confirmed by testing at a state public health laboratory or the U.S. Centers for Disease Control and Prevention (CDC). Although antibody may be absent when symptoms first develop, greater than 90 percent of WNV-infected individuals have detectable antibodies by day 8 postinfection. If the IgM WNV antibody is positive in blood or CSF and confirmed by another method, it is likely that the person has a current WNV infection or that they had one in the recent past. If the IgM antibody is detected in the CSF, it suggests that the WNV infection is present in the central nervous system. If IgM WNV and immunoglobulin G (IgG) WNV antibodies are detected in the initial sample, it is likely that the person contracted the WNV infection at least 3 weeks prior to the test. If the IgG WNV antibody is positive and the IgM WNV antibody level is low or not detectable, it is most likely that the person was previously exposed to WNV but is not currently infected. If WNV IgG antibody titers in convalescent samples continue to rise, this change would indicate a more recent infection. If the WNV IgG antibody levels have not changed or have decreased, this would indicate a past but not recent infection.

The presence of WNV antibodies may indicate an infection, but they cannot be used to predict the severity of an individual's symptoms or their prognosis. Testing of single serum specimens from "worried well" or mildly symptomatic patients is typically not indicated because the clinical impact of a positive result in these cases is minimal.

A nucleic acid amplification test (NAAT) for WNV is available. This test amplifies and measures WNV genetic material to detect the presence of the virus. This test can detect a current infection with the virus often before antibodies to the virus are detectable. Although it can specifically identify the presence of

WNV, there must be a sufficient amount of viral particles present in the sample to detect it. Because humans are secondary hosts of WNV, virus levels in humans are usually relatively low and do not persist for very long. A NAAT may detect WNV as long as the virus is actively replicating in the person. Therefore, when a patient becomes symptomatic, NAAT for WNV is not useful. Nucleic acid testing is most useful as a screen for WNV in donated units of blood, tissue, or organs; for detecting WNV; and for testing birds and mosquito pools to detect the presence and spread of WNV in the community. It is possible to determine that WNV has spread to a particular area and is in the mosquito population before any human cases are identified. NAAT also may be used to test the blood or tissues postmortem to determine whether WNV may have caused or contributed to death. A negative test cannot be used to definitively rule out the presence of WNV.

Culture for WNV is rarely performed and requires use of Biosafety Level 3 (BSL-3) laboratory precautions, which necessitates special engineering controls for the laboratory and additional procedural precautions and protective equipment for the staff (see *Biosafety in Microbiologic and Clinical Laboratories* in Supplemental Resources at the end of this chapter for additional information on laboratory biosafety). As such, performance of plaque reduction neutralization test (PRNT) and other arboviral culture methods are mostly available only at some state public health laboratories and the CDC.

NAAT and viral cultures are used in research settings to identify the strain of virus causing the infection and to study its attributes. Different strains of WNV have been isolated and associated with different epidemics around the world.

Because the likelihood of virus being present in any clinical specimen from suspect cases is low, Standard Precautions for specimen collection and handling are appropriate.

Testing of Blood, Blood Products, and Organs Prior to Transfusion or Transplantation

In May 2003 prior to the mosquito season, the FDA implemented "Guidance to Industry" recommendations for assessing donor suitability and product safety for donors with proven WNV infections or with illnesses potentially caused by WNV.[17] The guidance originally recommended deferral of donors who reported fever with headache in the week before donation. It also recommended that blood-bank facilities encourage donors to self-report post donation illnesses that could be WNV. Subsequently, data indicated that self-reporting of fever with headache did not predict WNV-contaminated product, and it was eliminated. In December 2005, the FDA approved the first test to screen for WNV in donors of blood organs, cells, and tissues. Thus a screening test, NAAT, is used for blood donor screening in the United States. Donors are deferred for 120 days after WNV disease or a positive test.[18] The policy has been successful at preventing healthcare-associated transmission of WNV through the screening of donor's blood, blood products, and organs for transplantation.

Treatment of West Nile Virus Infections

Treatment for severe WNV illness is supportive care; this can involve hospitalization, intravenous fluids and nutrition, respiratory support, and prevention of secondary infections. There is no specific antiviral therapy. There are three equine WNV vaccines licensed for use in the United States, and the human vaccine is in clinical trials.

Practices to Reduce the Risk of West Nile Virus Infection

Education of the public regarding protection and avoidance is an important mechanism for WNV prevention. The public should be informed of the modes of transmission and the importance of preventing mosquito bites throughout the entire mosquito season. This activity provides protection not only against WNV infection, but also against other diseases transmitted by mosquitoes. Individuals should be advised to take personal protective measures to reduce the risk of exposure to mosquitoes, particularly around dusk and dawn, when mosquito feeding is most active. Applying insect repellent to skin, wearing protective clothing, and minimizing outdoor activities during peak mosquito-feeding times are effect prevention strategies.[2] Because mosquitoes lay their eggs in standing water, risk reduction activities should also focus on eliminating these potential breeding sites and preventing access of adult mosquitoes to dwellings by ensuring that window and door screens are intact and fit tightly. Examples of risk reduction activities and descriptions of biological and chemical agents for mosquito control are detailed elsewhere.[2]

CONCLUSIONS

Since WNV first appeared in the United States in 1999, it has caused a significant number of cases of acute morbidity and mortality. The future dimensions of the WNV epidemic remain unknown. WNV is transmitted to humans primarily through a bite of an infected mosquito. The vast majority of those infected are asymptomatic. Of those who do have signs and symptoms, the vast majority have a mild febrile illness; a fraction of those will have neurologic syndromes and possibly death. The risk of severe illness increases with age and in immunocompromised hosts. There is no antiviral therapy or vaccine. This continuing epidemic of WNV serves as an example of the threat an emerging agent poses to a vulnerable population.

FUTURE TRENDS AND RESEARCH

Clinical

A great deal has been learned of the short-term morbidity and mortality of WNV infection, but there remains much to be studied about the long-term clinical, neurological, and functional sequelae that result from West Nile neuroinvasive disease. The long-term aspects of WNV pose a significant source of morbidity to patients well past the acute illness.

Ecological

The ongoing WNV epidemic serves as a model for other potential emerging vectorborne viral diseases such as Rift Valley fever and has refocused our attention on arboviral diseases. Reinvestment of resources has allowed for studies in a variety of areas of the WNV environmental cycle that may have implications for related arboviruses, such as St. Louis encephalitis. Results from these studies not only will answer basic questions about WNV but also should assist in managing future outbreaks.

INTERNATIONAL PERSPECTIVE

WNV is one of the most widely distributed flaviviruses worldwide. Besides North America, WNV has a geographic range that includes Africa, Europe, the Middle East, west and central Asia, and Oceania during the past decade. It is expected to continue to spread into Central America and eventually South America as well. However, to date, the incidence of illness in the Caribbean, Central America, and Mexico is low—this is in spite of serologic evidence of substantial WNV activity. The reason for the decrease in morbidity needs to be further studied but may be due to a number of reasons such as the presence of other flaviviruses in the area.

REFERENCES

1. Smithburn KC, Hughes, TP, Burke AW, et al. a neurotropic virus isolated from the blood of a native of Uganda. *Am J Trop Med Hyg* 1940;20:471–492.
2. Centers for Disease Control and Prevention (CDC), National Center for Emerging and Zoonotic Infectious Diseases (NCEZID), Division of Vector-Borne Diseases (DVBD). *West Nile Virus*. CDC website. Jaunuary 7, 2014. Available at: http://www.cdc.gov/ncidod/dvbid/westnile/index.htm.
3. Brault AC, Langevin SA, Bowen RA, etal. Differential virulence of West Nile strains for American crows. *Emerg Infect Dis* 2004 Dec;10(12):2161–2168.
4. Lanciotti RS, Roherig JT, Deubel V, et al. Origin of the West Nile virus responsible for an outbreak of encephalitis in the northeastern United States, *Science* 1999 Dec 17;286(5448):2333–2337.
5. Gubler DJ. The continuing spread of West Nile Virus in the western Hemisphere. *Clin Infect Dis* 2007 Oct 15;45(8):1039–1046.
6. Centers for Disease Control and Prevention (CDC). Public health dispatch: West Nile virus infection in organ donor and transplant recipients—Georgia and Florida, 2002, *MMWR Morb Mortal Wkly Rep* [serial online]. 2002 Sep 6;51(35):790. Available at: http://www.cdc.gov/mmwr/preview/mmwrhtml/mm5135a5.htm.
7. Iwamoto M, et al: Transmission of West Nile virus from an organ donor to four transplant recipients, *N Engl J Med* 2003 May 29;348(22):2196–2203.
8. Centers for Disease Control and Prevention (CDC). Public health dispatch: Investigation of blood transfusion recipients with West Nile virus infections. *MMWR Morb Mortal Wkly Rep* [serial online]. 2002 Sep 13;51(36):823. Available at: http://www.cdc.gov/mmwr/preview/mmwrhtml/mm5136a5.htm.
9. Centers for Disease Control and Prevention (CDC). Laboratory-acquired West Nile virus infections—United States, 2002. *MMWR Morb Mortal Wkly Rep* [serial online]. 2002 Dec 20;51(50):1133–1135. Available at: http://www.cdc.gov/mmwr/preview/mmwrhtml/mm5150a2.htm.
10. Centers for Disease Control and Prevention (CDC), National Institute for Occupational Safety and Health Education and Information Division. *NIOSH Safety and Health, West Nile Virus*. CDC website. August 27, 2012. Available at: http://www.cdc.gov/niosh/topics/westnile/.
11. Goetz AM, Goldrick BA. West Nile virus: a primer for infection control professionals. *Am J Infect Control* 2004 Apr;32(2):101–105.
12. Centers for Disease Control and Prevention (CDC). Intrauterine West Nile virus infection—New York, 2002. *MMWR Morb Mortal Wkly Rep* [serial online]. 2002 Dec 20;51(50):1135–1136. Available at: http://www.cdc.gov/mmwr/preview/mmwrhtml/mm5150a3.htm.
13. Centers for Disease Control and Prevention: Possible West Nile virus transmission to an infant through breast-feeding—Michigan, 2002. *MMWR Morb Mortal Wkly Rep* [serial online]. 2002 Oct 4;51(39):877–878. Available at: http://www.cdc.gov/mmwr/preview/mmwrhtml/mm5139a1.htm.

14. Watson JT, Pertel PF, Jones RC, et al. Clinical characteristics and functional outcomes of West Nile fever. *Ann Internal Med* 2004 Sep 7;141(5): 360–365.

15. U.S. Food and Drug Administration (FDA). Center for Devices and Radiological Health. *CLIA - Clinical Laboratory Improvement Amendments.* FDA website. March 3, 2014. Available at: http://www.accessdata.fda.gov /scripts/cdrh/cfdocs/cfCLIA/Results.cfm.

16. Niedrig M, Mantke OD, Altmann D, et al. First international diagnostic accuracy study for the serological detection of West Nile virus Infection. *BMC Infect Dis* 2007 Jul 3;7:72.

17. Food and Drug Adminstration (FDA). *Recommendations for the assessment of donor suitability and blood and blood product safety in cases of known or suspected West Nile virus infection. U.S. Department of Health and Human Services Food and Drug Administration, Center for Biologics Evaluation and Research (CBER) June 2005.* FDA website. Available at http://www.fda.gov/ForConsumers/ConsumerUpdates /ucm074111.htm.

18. Alter HG, Stramer SL, Dodd RY. Emerging infectious diseases that threaten the blood supply. *Semin Hematol* 2007 Jan;44(1):32–41.

SUPPLEMENTAL RESOURCES

Centers for Disease Control and Prevention (CDC). *Epidemic/epizootic West Nile virus in the United States: revised guidelines for surveillance, prevention, and control.* CDC website. Available at: http://www.cdc.gov/westnile /resources/pdfs/wnvFactsheet_508.pdf.

Mackenzie JS, Barrett AD, Buebel V, eds: *Current topics in microbiology and immunology: Japanese encephalitis and West Nile virus infections,* Berlin: Springer-Verlag, 2002.

National Atlas of the United States. West Nile Virus Maps. Available at: http://nationalatlas.gov/virusmap.html.

U.S. Department of Health and Human Services, Centers for Disease Control and Prevention (CDC), National Institutes of Health. *Biosafety in microbiological and biomedical laboratories,* ed5. Washington, 2007; U.S. Government Printing Office. CDC website. Available at: http://www.cdc.gov/biosafety/publications/bmbl5/.

Petersen LR. West Nile Virus. In: Scheld WM, Hooper DC, Hughes JM, eds: *Emerging Infections 7.* Washington, DC: ASM Press, 2005.

CHAPTER 99

Parasites

Jan Lienau, BSN, RN, CIC
Infection Preventionist II
Greer Medical Campus
Greenville Health System
Greer, SC

ABSTRACT

A parasite is defined as any organism living within or on an-other living creature and deriving advantage from doing so while causing disadvantage to the host. Parasites may spend part or all of their life cycle with the host. The epidemiology and transmission of most parasites is well defined. Parasites are rarely spread by direct person-to-person contact; therefore, they usually require little attention from infection preventionists. However, infestations with ectoparasites or epidermal parasites are fairly common among the community and healthcare facilities and can be responsible for infections of the epidermis or external layer of the skin. Healthcare-associated transmission has been reported with scabies, lice, and maggots. This chapter focuses on parasites (primarily ectoparasites) that may directly affect the health-care setting but also briefly covers those that may be seen in individual patients.

KEY CONCEPTS

- Scabies and lice are transmitted through direct contact with infested persons.

- Outbreaks of scabies have been well described in hospitals, long-term care facilities, and other healthcare institutions.

- Humans are the only natural reservoir of scabies and body, head, and pubic lice.

- Treatment exists for both scabies and lice, although cases of resistance have been reported.

- Protozoa are single-celled amoebae, flagellates, ciliates, and tissue-dwelling organisms; however, most are not human parasites.

- Helminthes, including a variety of nematodes, cestodes, and trematodes, can cause human disease.

BASIC PRINCIPLES

Scabies

Skin infestations by the mite *Sarcoptes scabiei* var. *hominis* (Figure 99-1) are commonly known as scabies. The adult mite has a round body and four pairs of legs; the female is larger than the male and measures less than 0.5 mm long.

The adult female is attracted to human skin predominantly by human odor and burrows in the upper layer of the epidermis, where she lays two to three eggs each day. The eggs require 10 days to progress through larval and nymph stages to form adult mites, which have a life span of approximately 1 to 2 months.[1-4]

Epidemiology

Humans are the natural reservoir of *S. scabiei* var. *hominis*. This parasite is not a vector of infectious agents. Mites are transmitted through direct contact with infested persons; less frequently, transmission may occur through contact with clothing or bedding (fomites). Spread of the mite to a different part of the body can occur by manual transfer or scratching. A slightly different mite causes scabies in dogs (*S. scabiei* var. *canis*) and may be transmitted to humans through direct contact with an infested animal. Infestation with *S. scabiei* var. *canis* is self-limited in humans.[1-4]

The female mite is capable of moving at speeds up to 2.5 cm per minute and can penetrate skin rapidly in 2.5 to 45 minutes. Mites can survive as long as 3 days on stuffed chairs, sofas, and tile floors, whereas nymphs can survive 2 to 5 days at 25°C and 45 to 75 percent humidity.

Approximately 300 million annual cases of scabies occur worldwide. Persons infested with scabies are usually children, sexually active young adults, or persons who exist in close physical contact with large numbers of people. Outbreaks of scabies have been well described in hospitals, including nurs-eries and intensive care units, principally because of delayed recognition and lack of patient isolation. Reports indicate that scabies occurs in approximately 5 to 25 percent of long-term facilities annually and can also be spread in homeless shelters.[5-9] Outbreaks probably occur owing to large numbers of mites that reside under a person's fingernails while scratching. In a recent

Figure 99-1. Scabies (*Sarcoptes scabiei*).

Ventral view

review, the mean number of infested patients per hospital outbreak was 18 (attack rate of 13 percent), and the mean number of infested healthcare personnel (HCP) was 39 (35 percent attack rate). Although control involves extensive treatment of patients, employees, and visitors, education to prevent mass hysteria and "psychogenic scabies" is often required.

Clinical Presentation

The incubation period (exposure to onset of symptoms) for primary infestation occurs as early as 10 days but is typically 4 to 6 weeks. Because of previous sensitization, symptoms in patients with reinfestation usually appear in 1 to 3 days. Approximately two-thirds of cases have burrow-type pruritic lesions on hands, webs of fingers, wrists, and extensor surfaces of elbows and knees, as well as outer surfaces of feet, armpits, buttocks, and waist. Spread can also occur to arms, trunk, legs, penis, scrotum, and nipples. In geriatric patients, scabies often appears as excoriations and tends to present on the back. Variation in lesion appearance often leads to misdiagnosis. Dermatological manifestations include burrows, papules, scales, vesicles, bullae, crusts, pustules, nodules, and excoriations. The burrows often appear as grayish, threadlike elevations in the outer layer of the skin. Burrows occur less frequently in infants and children. However, there may be eczematous involvement of the head, neck, palms, and soles. This type of dermatological involvement is also seen frequently in immigrants and homeless individuals because of poor nutrition and sanitary conditions. In bedridden patients, scabies may be limited to sites in constant contact with sheets or nursing care, including the warm, moist skin environments of the buttocks and back.

The typical presenting symptom in most patients with scabies is intense pruritus, which is usually more severe at night. Scratching often produces bleeding and scab formation, thus leading to secondary bacterial infection, typically caused by group A streptococci and/or *Staphylococcus aureus*.

Nodular scabies is caused by hypersensitivity to mites; however, mites are seldom found in nodules present for more than 30 days. Characteristic lesions appear as reddish brown pruritic nodules on the male genitalia, groin, and axillae. Although nodular scabies often clears spontaneously, skin lesions may

persist for more than 1 year despite treatment. Nodular scabies is found in about 7 to 10 percent of patients with scabies, particularly small children.

Crusted (Norwegian) scabies presents as a crusty, scaly dermatitis usually of the hands and feet, including dystrophic nails. Some affected individuals may have a generalized erythematous eruption. Norwegian scabies is highly contagious owing to the large numbers of mites present (ranging from thousands to millions compared with 3 to 50 for common scabies). Despite the large number of mites, itching is remarkably minimal. There appears to be a predilection for mentally challenged, chronically debilitated, homeless, or immunologically deficient persons (e.g., long-term corticosteroid use, immunosuppressive therapy, hematological malignancies, or acquired immunodeficiency syndrome [AIDS]).

Special Considerations in Persons with Human Immunodeficiency Virus

There is a special predisposition of human immunodeficiency virus (HIV) patients to acquire "ordinary" scabies[10–12] that converts to crusted scabies as their CD4 cell counts fall. HIV-associated scabies can rapidly spread to other patients and HCP.[6,7] In some cases, crusted scabies may be the signifying condition in patients with previously undiagnosed HIV infection. About 20 percent of HIV patients with scabies have been reported to develop secondary bacteremia with *Staphylococcus epidermidis*, *S. aureus*, and Gram-negative rods.[12] Although a theoretical possibility, there has been no evidence that the scabies mite transmits HIV.

Diagnostic Tests

Definitive diagnosis of scabies infestation is by microscopic examination of mites extracted by a needle or a scalpel. Using a hand lens, recent burrows should be identified and used to obtain skin scrapings. The skin scrapings are mounted on a slide with mineral oil and microscopically examined for eggs, mature and immature mites, and fecal pellets. Burrows can be more readily visualized by swabbing the suspected infestation area with India ink. After several minutes the excess ink should be wiped away, leaving the burrows darkly stained. Skin scrapings may be nondiagnostic in up to one-third of cases; therefore, repeated sampling is often necessary to confirm the diagnosis. Skin biopsies can also be performed, especially for atypical lesions or cases that cannot be diagnosed by skin scraping. Infection can also be detected by amplification of *Sarcoptes* DNA using polymerase chain reaction assay. Some patients with scabies may experience elevated immunoglobulin E titers.

Treatment

Treatment for scabies is usually a topical scabicide applied to the neck, trunk, and all extremities, including beneath fingernails. In infants, treatment may also require application to the scalp. Elderly patients frequently require facial and scalp application to eliminate the infestation. The drug of choice is one to two applications of 5 percent permethrin cream, which is left on the skin for 8 to 14 hours before thoroughly washing off. Treatment may be repeated in 5 days, especially in severe cases. Permethrin kills mites, lice, and other arthropods by disrupting sodium transport in their nerve cell membranes. This compound is poorly absorbed in mammals but may cause skin irritation.[1-4,8,9,11-13]

An alternative topical scabicide is 1 percent gamma benzene hexachloride (lindane) lotion. Unfortunately, excessive application of lindane and skin absorption has been associated with neurotoxicity and seizures, especially in young children. Sporadic drug resistance has also been reported. Other alternative topical treatments include 10 percent crotamiton (which requires several applications and is associated with a high treatment failure rate) as well as sulfur creams, malathion, and benzyl benzoate.[14]

The antihelmintic drug ivermectin, given as a single oral dose of 200 μg/kg (with an additional dose repeated 2 weeks later), can be considered to be an effective first-line systemic therapeutic option for scabies in otherwise healthy patients and many patients with HIV.[15-17] Unfortunately, ivermectin resistance has developed both in vitro and in vivo.[18] Furthermore, this drug can cause rare serious side effects.[19]

The hyperkeratotic lesions of crusted scabies may necessitate use of 6 percent salicylic acid or manual débridement before a scabicide can be applied. Systemic therapy with oral ivermectin may be advisable. Concomitant bacterial infection should be treated with appropriate antimicrobial agents.

Patients should be examined at 2 and 4 weeks following treatment, which allows the original lesions to heal and any remaining eggs to hatch.

Itching can be relieved by the use of over-the-counter oral antihistamines such as diphenhydramine hydrochloride or prescription hydroxyzine hydrochloride.

Prevention and Control Measures

Because of the high risk of transmission, the diagnosis of scabies should be considered in any patient with a pruritic cutaneous eruption, especially involving hands, wrists, and elbows. Patients in a hospital or other healthcare facility should be placed in Contact Precautions until 24 hours after treatment. In persons with crusted scabies, the duration of isolation time is often longer, with some authorities recommending that precautions remain in place for at least 4 days after treatment.[4]

Environmental fomites have been well documented as a source of transmission in many scabies outbreaks. Live mites have been recovered from bed linens, chairs, and the floor surrounding the infested patient's bed. Shared walking belts, skin creams, and lotions have also been shown to be a means of transmission. Clothing and linens should be washed by machine in the hot cycle for at least 10 minutes (50°C or 122°F), then tumbled in a hot dryer for 20 minutes or bagged for 10 days. Placing inanimate objects in a freezer for several days can also kill mites. It is usually not necessary to clean outerwear or furniture because they do not typically come into prolonged direct contact with infested areas. Small disposable items such as creams and lotions should be discarded because of the risk of transmission.

Because scabies transmission can occur during the lengthy egg incubation period, household members and intimate contacts should be treated preemptively. It may also be prudent to treat asymptomatic HCP who have had close contact with infested patients during such activities as bathing and applying topical lotions or massages.

Implications for Institutional Spread

Scabies is becoming increasingly more common, particularly among immunocompromised patients and residents of long-term care facilities. High attack rates among HCP may occur when caring for patients with undiagnosed scabies, especially those with crusted lesions. Typical distribution of lesions in HCP includes the forearms, abdomen, and thighs. Infested HCP may spread scabies to other patients or coworkers. Thus, control of a scabies outbreak is typically achieved by treatment of the entire population at risk over the same 24- to 48-hour period, whether or not symptoms are present. All recently used clothing, bed linens, and towels should be washed in the hot cycle or, if necessary, dry cleaned 24 hours after treatment.[14]

PEDICULOSIS

Pediculosis is defined as any type of louse infestation.[1-4,20-22] Lice are visible (2 to 3 mm long) wingless parasites with three pairs of lateral legs ending in "claws." Three species of lice infest humans: *Pediculus humanus capitis* (head louse), *P. humanus corporis* (body louse), and *Phthirus pubis* (crab or pubic louse); however, there are more than 3000 species of lice (Figure 99-2).

Eggs are laid by the fertilized adult and appear as oval "nits" on hairs or fibers of clothing.

After 7 to 10 days, small nymphs emerge from the eggs and must feed on blood within 24 hours. Nymphs molt three times during the maturation process.

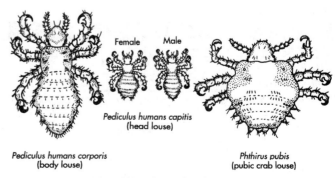

Figure 99-2. Species of lice that infest humans.

Epidemiology

Humans are the only natural reservoirs of body, head, and pubic lice. Epidemics of pediculosis still occur and may be associated with poor hygiene, overcrowding, and inadequate facilities for keeping people and clothing clean. There appears to be increasing number of cases among persons of all socio-economic levels. Likely contributing factors include communal living, and widespread travel (Table 99-1).[1-4,20-22]

Among school-age children, the closeness of individuals and proximity of their clothing in storage contribute to the spread of head lice. In the United States during 1998, an estimated 12 to 24 million school days were lost because of "no-nit" policies, which exclude children who had any residual nits (egg cases). This exclusion is now considered unnecessary if the child has had proper treatment. Head lice are rare in children of African American descent.[21]

In the past, body lice have been important in the transmission of epidemic typhus (*Rickettsia prowazekii*), relapsing fever (*Borrelia recurrentis*), and trench fever (*Bartonella quintana*)[20]; head lice and pubic lice do not transmit disease.

Transmission

Head lice are transmitted through direct contact with the louse or contact with personal items such as hats, helmets, headset earphones, brushes, combs, or bedding. Head lice die within 24 to 48 hours after leaving a host.

Body lice are transmitted through direct contact with the louse or through contact with clothing or bedding. The lice cling to clothing, especially seams. With heavy infestation, eggs (nits) may attach to hairs.

Pubic lice are transmitted by direct contact with the louse through close physical contact, especially sexual intercourse. Transmission may also occur via clothing or bedding. Transmission through other inanimate objects (e.g., toilet seats) is extremely rare because of the short life span of lice apart from a human host.

Clinical Manifestations

Lice bites cause intense itching and occasionally fever. Bites can be hemorrhagic because of an anticoagulant that is introduced. Excoriated bite sites often become secondarily infected by bacteria, causing impetigo or pyoderma. With head lice, secondary bacterial infection may produce scarring, matted hair, and scalp ulcerations.

Diagnosis

Pediculosis capitis

Few adult lice are typically seen with head lice infestation, but often numerous nits are firmly attached to hair shafts. Nits are initially attached close to skin because eggs cannot hatch at temperatures less than 22°C (71.6°F). Thus nits that are more than 12 mm (0.5 inches) from skin have probably hatched, depending on temperature and humidity conditions. Given that scalp hair grows about 0.5 mm daily, the presence of nits 10 cm or longer away from the scalp indicates the infestation is at least 6 months old. Nits can be differentiated from dandruff or hair casts because they do not slide along hair and can only be removed from the hair shaft using a fine-tooth comb. Infested hair also demonstrates fluorescence under ultraviolet light (Wood's lamp).

Phthirus pubis

Infestation with pubic lice is usually identified by the presence of nits attached to pubic hair. The duration of infestation can be estimated by the distance of the nit from the skin, as hair grows approximately 0.5 inches per month.

Pediculosis corporis

Because body lice are rarely found on the body except when feeding, they are usually identified on clothing.

Treatment[1-4,22-26]

There are four main pediculicide options for treating head lice and pupic lice: pyrethroids, pyrethrins, malathion, and lindane. Pyrethroids, such as permethrin 1 percent cream, are often considered to be the drug of choice because a single dose provides a residual effect lasting several days. This residual protection confers an advantage over lindane; however, pyrethroids may be associated with increased pruritus. Pyrethrins, such as piperonyl butoxide, have few major side effects such as rare cases of corneal damage. Malathion lotion uses an irreversible cholinesterase inhibitor that is a superior ovicide to lindane or pyrethrins. Furthermore, malathion is less toxic than lindane and possesses greater residual activity than lindane shampoo; however, this compound is flammable and has an unpleasant smell. Lindane (1 percent gamma benzene hexachloride) remains widely used, but resistance has been reported, and excessive or prolonged use can lead to convulsions or neurological toxicity. Regardless of which specific topical agent is used, application should be repeated in 1 week to eliminate

Table 99-1. Characteristics of Lice That Infest Humans

Characteristic	Body and Head Lice	Pubic Lice
Time for incubation of ova	8–9 days	8–9 days
Time from egg to adult	10 days	15 days
Life span of female	30–35 days	35 days
Common site of infection	Head: Especially, back of head, neck, ears axillae, and scalp Body: Shoulders, waist, and areas of clothing contact	Genital region; rarely in eyelashes
Time of survival off host	Head: 2 days Body: 4–7 days	1 day

newly hatched nymphs unless all nits have been removed with a nit comb or hair removal. Eyelid involvement can be treated with 1 percent yellow oxide of mercury ophthalmic ointment or petrolatum ophthalmic ointment. Although ivermectin is active against most types of resistant lice, it is not ovicidal. Thus, ivermectin is primarily used for cases that did not respond to topical therapy and is administered using two oral doses (200 μg/kg) given 10 days apart. Trimethoprim-sulfamethoxazole has been demonstrated to be 80 percent effective against head lice and can be used to treat staphylococcal superinfection.[23-25]

Application of pediculicides to patients with body lice is usually not necessary. Patients should be bathed and clothes treated as detailed below.

Prevention and Control

Family members and contacts of patients with pediculosis should be examined methodically for lice and nits. Treatment is only indicated if infestation is detected. The only exception is sexual contacts of patients with pubic lice; these individuals may be treated simultaneously without examination.

Head lice and eggs may be transmitted by fomites (e.g., hair brushes, caps, scarves, and coats); however, eggs cannot hatch in inanimate environments or at room temperature. Potential for fomite spread is greatest for body lice because lice and eggs can survive apart from human hosts longer compared with other lice.

There are several methods for fomite disinfection. The simplest method for clothing or bedding disinfection is washing and drying at relatively high temperature (60°C or 140°F for 5–10 minutes). Heating by ironing or dry cleaning is also an option.

For items that cannot be heated, placing them in a freezer for 12 to 24 hours may be effective. Nonwashable items can also be sealed in a leakproof plastic bag. Items that harbor pubic lice should remain sealed for 7 days, whereas items with head lice should be sealed for 10 to 14 days. Articles with body lice require even longer storage because eggs may survive for up to 30 days.

Isolation of patients can be discontinued after initial treatment and proper disinfection or removal of clothing, bedding, and other contaminated personal items. HCP do not require prophylactic or preemptive treatment unless they demonstrate evidence of infestation. Except for vacuuming and standard cleaning protocols, special cleaning of rooms inhabited by infested patients (e.g., fumigation or use of insecticidal sprays) is not recommended.

MYIASIS

Myiasis is defined as human infestation by larvae (maggots) of a large variety of dipterous flies.[1,27-35] Eggs are laid by mature female flies on skin, wounds, mouth, nose, and ears. Fly larvae hatch from the eggs and do not multiply before developing into adult flies. Human infestation by larvae varies depending on the fly species. Involvement ranges from superficial, where the larvae are confined to necrotic tissue (e.g., *Musca domestica*, housefly, or blowfly) to burrowing within normal skin (e.g., *Dermatobia hominis*, bot fly, or African tumbu fly).

Epidemiology

Myiasis is more common in warmer tropical climates where cattle and other animals serve as reservoirs for various fly species. In the case of *D. hominis*, mosquitoes act as the reservoir (eggs are laid on the abdomen of mosquitoes) and fly larvae enter at the site of a mosquito bite.

In healthcare, maggots have been used therapeutically to consume devitalized tissue and débride necrotic wounds.[31,32]

Healthcare-associated myiasis often occurs in debilitated patients with necrotic wounds or fecal discharge who are subject to neglected nursing care, especially during summertime. One Midwestern U.S. intensive care unit outbreak of nasal green blowfly (*Phaenicia sericata*) myiasis was related to a mouse infestation within the hospital.[33]

Ophthalmomyiasis most commonly occurs in North America by infestation of the nasal bot fly larvae (*Oestrus ovis*), especially in the southern United States, including California, Texas, and Hawaii.[34,35]

Clinical Manifestations

Parasitic (furuncular) myiasis results from larval invasion of unbroken skin or periorificial tissue, producing an abscess-type lesion that may drain purulent material. Larvae burrow into skin, causing dermatitis, and may also migrate to other organs (e.g., ear, nose, eye, brain), causing serious illness or death.

Diagnosis

The diagnosis of myiasis is often recognized when visually inspected by an experienced clinician. However, burrowed lesions may require tissue biopsy. If speciation of fly larvae is desired, formal consultation with an accredited entomologist, the local public health department, or tertiary pathology referral center (e.g., U.S. Armed Forces Institute of Pathology, Washington, DC) is strongly recommended. Fly larvae can be collected and kept alive in a bottle containing moist sand and raw meat until they develop into mature flies. Maggots can also survive on a blood agar culture medium.

Treatment

Treatment involves removal of fly larvae. This is often accomplished by covering the wound, which contains the breathing orifice of the insect, with a thick impermeable layer of petrolatum ointment. Liquid paraffin, beeswax, pork fat, or chewing gum has also been used for this purpose. Suffocation will cause the larvae to migrate to the skin surface in search of air. Topical anesthetics (e.g., ethyl chloride spray or lidocaine injection) may be helpful, especially if surgical excision is performed. Application of 10 percent chloroform in vegetable oil can be used for aural myiasis.

Prevention

Preventive measures include the use of simple physical barriers to prevent fly entry into the environment (e.g., window screens). Appropriate waste disposal and location of waste receptacles are also important to prevent flying insects from entering patient care areas. Adequate insect control programs using pyrethrin aerosol, other insecticide repellents, or insect extermination lamps may be required in summer months.

BED BUGS (*CIMEX LECTULARIUS*)[36-39]

Bed bugs are small, reddish brown, flattened, wingless insects (Figure 99-3) that feed solely on the blood of humans and other warm-blooded animals, usually at night. Their saliva causes intense pruritus, which can lead to secondary bacterial infection. Bed bugs grow up to 7 mm in length with a life span ranging from 4 months to 1 year. A female bed bug can lay a total of 200 eggs during its lifetime, usually at a rate of three to four per day after a blood meal. Bed bug eggs are white, measure 0.1 cm in size, and have an adherent coating. The eggs incubate 6 to 17 days before hatching and nymphs undergo five molts before maturing into adults. Each nymphal stage requires a full blood meal. Although *Cimex* spp. bed bugs have been experimentally infected with several viruses under laboratory conditions, disease transmission to humans has not been clinically demonstrated, as opposed to the *Reduviidae* spp. bed bugs, which transmit Chagas disease in South America.

Epidemiology

Bed bugs became uncommon after World War II as a result of the use of dichlorodiphenyltrichloroethane pesticide in developed countries but have recently reemerged, likely because of increased travel and international trade. They form nests in cracks, furniture seams, bed frames, and mattresses. These insects can survive for several months without feeding and can hide within crevices and other small recessed spaces. These locations include walls, headboards, baseboards, mattress seams, areas of clutter, and undersides of furniture, especially in adjoining apartments, homeless shelters, and hotels. A characteristic finding is small drops of blood on bed sheets or pillows caused by engorged bed bugs that were crushed. Bed bug infestations also emit an odor caused by dark oily excrement.

Clinical Presentation

Bed bug bites cause pruritic macules in previously unexposed patients. In patients with repeated bites, there may be papules, urticaria, or bullae resulting from a hypersensitivity reaction.

Treatment

Treatment of patients is primarily symptomatic, consisting of anti-inflammatory topical corticosteroid preparations, oral antihistamines, and antibacterial agents for secondary infection. The major intervention is environmental control, with recognition of infestation and use of pesticides such as malathion or pyrethrins. Approved lightly sprayed pesticides should be administered by a licensed exterminator to all places of harbor.

Hospital Response

Most patients from bed bug-infested dwellings do not carry bed bugs on their body or clothing. Because these insects have not been proven to transmit serious disease and are not easily spread, they are mainly an environmental pest control issue rather than an infection prevention problem. If decontamination of infested articles is desired, bagging and heating them to 120°F for at least 10 to 20 minutes is more effective than attempting to freeze items, which requires several days to be successful.

IMPORTANT PATHOGENIC PROTOZOA[40]

The reader is encouraged to access information on these parasites from the Centers for Disease Control and Prevention or public health websites (see Supplemental Resources).

Protozoa are single-celled amoebae, flagellates, ciliates, and tissue-dwelling organisms. A large variety of protozoa exists, but most are not pathogenic to humans.[41] Infections with parasitic protozoa are typically not related to infection prevention activities in hospitals. However, some of them have important public health considerations in terms of both the organism and of vectors or sources.

Epidemiology

Protozoa are typically divided into groups depending on their method of transmission.

Figure 99-3. Bed bug (*Cimex lectularius*). (Provided with permission by Dr. Michael F. Potter of the University of Kentucky, Lexington, KY.)

Water- or foodborne:

- *Entamoeba histolytica*: amoebiasis (intestinal or disseminated); worldwide; higher prevalence in areas with poor sanitation
- *Blastocystis hominis*: intestinal infection; worldwide distribution
- *Dientamoeba fragilis*: intestinal parasite, often asymptomatic but may cause disease; worldwide
- *Cryptosporidium parvum*: cryptosporidiosis causing intestinal, biliary, or respiratory tract disease; worldwide; reservoir is human and cattle and contaminated water sources are often implicated in outbreaks
- *Cyclospora cayetanensis*: cyclosporiasis intestinal infection; worldwide
- *Giardia lamblia*: giardiasis intestinal infection; worldwide; reservoir is human and many animal species
- *Isospora belli (also Cystoisospora)*: intestinal infection; worldwide (mainly tropical and subtropical locales)
- *Acanthamoeba* spp.: may cause serious infections of the eye (*Acanthamoeba keratitis*), brain, and spinal cord in immunocompromised people (granulomatous amebic encephalitis), and disseminated infection in persons with a compromised immune system; worldwide; contaminated water sources, including pools or hot tubs, soil, air (in association with cooling towers, heating, ventilation and air conditioner systems), sewage systems, and drinking water systems (shower heads, taps)
- *Naegleria fowleri*: causes very rare but severe brain infection; worldwide; reservoir is warm freshwater and soil

Insectborne:

- *Plasmodium* spp.: causes malaria in tropical and subtropical locales; transmitted to humans via bite of *Anopheles* mosquito; reservoir is humans, possibly other primates
- *Trypanosoma* spp.: causes African sleeping sickness (tropical Africa) transmitted by *Glossina* (tsetse) fly and Chagas disease (Central and South America) transmitted by blood-sucking species of Reduviidae (e.g., kissing bug, cone-nose bug); reservoir is mainly humans, and possibly domestic and wild animals
- *Babesia* spp.: causes babesiosis worldwide; transmitted by *Ixodes* ticks; reservoir is deer mice or other small mammals
- *Leishmania* spp.: causes leishmaniasis or kala azar worldwide; transmitted by sandflies; reservoir is humans and many animal species, including wild and domestic Canidae (foxes, dogs); some marsupials

Animalborne:

- *Toxoplasma gondii*: toxoplasmosis foodborne illness; worldwide; generally not serious except when infection occurs during pregnancy (maternal to fetal transmission) or in immunocompromised people; cats are an important reservoir (become infected after eating small animals and birds)

Sexually transmitted:

- *Trichomonas vaginalis*: trichomoniasis sexually transmitted infection; worldwide

IMPORTANT PATHOGENIC WORMS: CLASSIFICATION[41]

Intestinal roundworms (nematodes):

- *Ascaris lumbricoides*: ascariasis; tropic and subtropical locales; reservoir is humans, pigs (different species)
- *Enterobius vermicularis*: pinworm; worldwide
- *Trichuris trichiura*: whipworm; worldwide
- *Necator americanus*: hookworm; worldwide
- *Ancylostoma duodenale*: hookworm; worldwide
- *Strongyloides stercoralis*: mainly tropical and subtropical locales
- *Capillaria philippinensis*: capillariasis; endemic in the Philippines, also occurs in Thailand. Rare cases reported from other countries.

Tissue roundworms:

- *Wucheria bancrofti*: a cause of elephantiasis (lymphatic filariasis); tropics and subtropics; vector is various mosquito species
- *Brugia* spp.: a cause of elephantiasis (lymphatic filariasis); tropics and subtropics; vector is various mosquito species
- *Onchocerca* spp.: cause of river blindness; transmitted by black fly
- *Dirofilaria immitis*: dog heartworm
- *Loa loa*: African eye roundworm
- *Trichinella spiralis*: trichinosis or trichinellosis; worldwide; ingestion of infected meat, including domestic pig and wild animals
- *Angiostrongylus cantonensis*

Intestinal tapeworms (cestodes):

- *Taenia* spp.: worldwide; raw or undercooked meat
- *Diphyllobothrium latum*: worldwide; fish tapeworm
- *Hymenolepis nana*: dwarf and rat tapeworm; worldwide; rodent, and humans

Tissue tapeworms:

- *Echinococcus* spp.: worldwide; hydatid cysts in tissues

Intestinal flukes (trematodes):

- *Clonorchis sinensis:* liver fluke
- *Fasciola hepatica:* common liver or sheep liver fluke
- *Fasciolopsis buski:* giant fluke of Southeast Asia
- *Paragonimus westermani:* lung fluke, worldwide

Tissue flukes:

- *Schistosoma* spp.: blood or snail fluke, tropical regions, snail is intermediate host

Information sheets on some of the most significant parasites are located on the CDC website at http://www.cdc.gov/parasites/az/.

CONCLUSIONS

Although a variety of human parasites exist, relatively few have direct impact on infection preventionists. Ectoparasites may be spread through direct or indirect contact with infested persons or fomites. Outbreaks of ectoparasites have been well documented in a variety of healthcare and institutional settings.

FUTURE TRENDS

As the number of immunocompromised patients increases, the risk of serious parasitic or ectoparasitic disease often rises. Although effective treatments exist, resistance has been documented. Additionally, many treatments are associated with side effects and can cause additional problems. Efforts should be directed toward improving available treatments and reducing risk of transmission.

INTERNATIONAL PERSPECTIVE

Ectoparasites are seen around the world. This is in contrast to most parasitic protozoa and parasitic worms (nematodes, trematodes, and cestodes), which are mostly seen outside the United States and other developed countries. In resource-constrained countries, many human parasites are transmitted through contaminated water sources or food products. However, given the increasing modern global travel, more patients with parasitic diseases have been seen in healthcare systems worldwide.

REFERENCES

1. Schlossberg D. Arthropods and Leeches. In: Goldman L, Ausiello D, eds. *Cecil Textbook of Medicine*, 22nd ed. Philadelphia: WB Saunders, 2004;2123–2129.
2. Chosidow O. Scabies and pediculosis: Neglected diseases to highlight. *Clin Microbiol Infect* 2012 Apr;18(4):311–312.
3. Cestari TF, Martignago BF. Scabies, pediculosis, bed bugs, and stinkbugs: Uncommon presentations. *Clin Dermatol* 2005 Nov-Dec;23(6):545–554.
4. Leone PA. Scabies and pediculosis pubis: an update of treatment regimens and general review. *Clin Infect Dis* 2007 Apr 1;44 Suppl 3:S153–S159.
5. Degelau J. Scabies in long-term care facilities. *Infect Control Hosp Epidemiol* 1992 Jul;13(7):421–425.
6. Vorou R, Remoudaki HD, Maltezou HC. Nosocomial scabies. *J Hosp Infect* 2007 Jan;65(1):9–14.
7. Mathieu ME, Wilson BB. Scabies. In: Mandell GL, Bennett JE, Dolin R, eds. *Principles and Practice of Infectious Diseases,* 6th ed. Philadelphia: Elsevier, 2005:3302–3307.
8. Zafar AB, Beidas SO, Sylvester LK. Control of transmission of Norwegian scabies. *Infect Control Hosp Epidemiol* 2002 May;23(5):278–279.
9. Cordoro K, *Dermatologic Manifestations of Scabies*. Medscape Reference 2009 Dec.
10. Portu JJ, Santamaria JM, Zubero Z, et al. Atypical scabies in HIV-positive patients. *J Am Acad Dermatol* 1996 May;34(5 Pt 2):915–917.
11. Corbett EL, Crossley I, Holton J, et al. Crusted ("Norwegian") scabies in a specialist HIV unit: successful use of ivermectin and failure to prevent nosocomial transmission. *Genitourin Med* 1996 Apr;72(2):115–117.
12. Lam S, Brennessel D. Norwegian scabies and HIV infection-case report and literature review. *Infectious Diseases in Clinical Practice* 1993;2(3):169–173.
13. Obasanjo OO, Wu P, Conlon M, et al. An outbreak of scabies in a teaching hospital: lessons learned. *Infect Control Hosp Epidemiol* 2001 Jan;22(1):13–18.
14. Roos TC, Alam M, Roos S, et al. Pharmacotherapy of ectoparasitic infections. *Drugs* 2001;61(8):1067–1088.
15. Meinking TL, Taplin D, Hermida JL, et al. The treatment of scabies with ivermectin. *N Engl J Med* 1995 Jul 6;333(1):26–30.
16. Sule HM, Thacher TD. Comparison of ivermectin and benzyl benzoate lotion for scabies in Nigerian patients. *Am J Trop Med Hyg* 2007 Feb;76(2):392–395.
17. Garcia D, Iglesias D, Terashima A, et al. Use of ivermectin to treat an institutional outbreak of scabies in a low-resource setting. *Infect Control Hosp Epidemiol* 2007 Dec;28(12):1337–1338.
18. Currie BJ, Harumal P, McKinnon M, et al. First documentation of in vivo and in vitro ivermectin resistance in Sarcoptes scabiei. *Clin Infect Dis* 2004 Jul 1;39(1):e8–e12.
19. Veit O, Beck B, Steuerwald M, et al. First case of ivermectin—induced severe hepatitis. *Trans R Soc Trop Med Hyg* 2006 Aug;100(8):795–797.
20. Badiaga, S, Brouqui P. Human louse-transmitted infectious diseases. *Clin Microbiol Infect* 2012 Apr;18(4):332-337.
21. Roberts RJ. Clinical practice. Head lice. *N Engl J Med* 2002 May 23;346(21):1645–1650.
22. Mathieu ME, Wilson BB. Lice. In: Mandell GL, Bennett JE, Dolin R, eds. *Principles and Practice of Infectious Diseases*, 6th ed. Philadelphia: Elsevier; 2005;3202–3204.
23. Drugs for head lice. *Med Lett Drugs Ther* 2005Aug 15–29;47(1215–1216):68–70.
24. Jones KN, English JC III. Review of common therapeutic options in the United States for the treatment of pediculosis capitis. *Clin Infect Dis* 2003 Jun 1;36(11):1355–1361.
25. Burkhart CG. Relationship of treatment-resistant head lice to the safety and efficacy of pediculosis. *Mayo Clin Proc* 2004 May;79(5):661–666.
26. Foucault C, Ranque S, Badiaga S, et al. Oral ivermectin in the treatment of body lice. *J Infect Dis* 2006 Feb 1;193(3):474–476.
27. Mathieu ME, Wilson BB. Myiasis and tungiasis. In: Mandell GL, Bennett JE, Dolin R, eds. *Principles and Practice of Infectious Diseases*, 6th ed. Philadelphia: Elsevier, 2005;3307–3310.
28. Diaz JH. The epidemiology, diagnosis, management, and prevention of ectoparasitic diseases in travelers. *J Travel Med* 2006 Mar-Apr;13(2):100–111.
29. Feldmeier H, Eisele M, Saboia-Moura RC, et al. Severe tungiasis in underprivileged communities: case series form Brazil. *Emerg Infect Dis* 2003 Aug;9(8):949–955.
30. Chan JCM, Lee JS, Dai DL, et al. Unusual cases of human myiasis due to old worm screwworm fly acquired indoors in Hong Kong. *Trans R Soc Trop Med Hyg* 2005 Dec;99(12):914–918.
31. Beckendorf R, Klotz SA, Hinkle N, et al. Nasal myiasis in an intensive care unit linked to hospital-wide mouse infestation. *Arch Intern Med* 2002 Mar 25;162(6):638–640.
32. Sherman RA, Shimoda KJ. Presurgical maggot debridement of soft tissue wounds is associated with decreased rates of postoperative infection. *Clin Infect Dis* 2004 Oct 1;39(7):1067–1070.
33. Sherman RA. Wound myiasis in urban and suburban United States. *Arch Intern Med* 2000 Jul 10;160(13):2004–2014.
34. Kajioka EH, Hagao CF, Karas S, et al. Ophthalmomyiasis in Hawaii. *Hawaii Med J* 2004 Mar;63(3):78–79.
35. Sigauke E, Beebe WE, Gander RM, et al. Case report: ophthalmomyiasis externa in Dallas County, Texas. *Am J Trop Med Hyg* 2003 Jan;68(1):46–47.
36. Paul J, Bates J. Is infestation with the common bed bug increasing? *BMJ* 2000 Apr 22;320(7242):1141.
37. Hwang SW, Svoboda TJ, De Jong IJ, et al. Bed bug infestations in an urban environment. *Emerg Infect Dis* 2005Apr;11(4):533–538.
38. Elston DM, Stockwell S. What's eating you? Bed bugs. *Cutis* 2000 May;65(5):262–264.

39. Goddard J. Bed bugs bounce back—but do they transmit disease? *Infections in Medicine* 2003;20(10):473–474.
40. Heymann DL, ed. *Control of Communicable Diseases Manual,* 18th ed. Washington, DC: American Public Health Association, 2004.
41. Cook GC, Zumla AI, Weir J. *Manson's Tropical Diseases.* Philadelphia: WB Saunders, 2003.

SUPPLEMENTAL RESOURCES

Centers for Disease Control and Prevention (CDC), National Center for Emerging and Zoonotic Infectious Diseases (NCEZID), Division of Foodborne, Waterborne, and Environmental Diseases (DFWED). *Cryptosporidium (also known as "Crypto").* CDC website. January 16, 2013. Available at: http://www.cdc.gov/crypto/index.html.

Centers for Disease Control and Prevention (CDC), National Center for Emerging and Zoonotic Infectious Diseases (NCEZID), Division of Foodborne, Waterborne, and Environmental Diseases (DFWED). Parasites - Giardia. CDC website. March 8, 2011. CDC website. Available at: http://www.cdc.gov/parasites/giardia/.

Centers for Disease Control and Prevention (CDC), National Center for Emerging and Zoonotic Infectious Diseases (NCEZID), Division of Foodborne, Waterborne, and Environmental Diseases (DFWED). *Parasites - taeniasis.* CDC website. January 10, 2013. Available at: http://www.cdc.gov/parasites/taeniasis/.

Centers for Disease Control and Prevention (CDC), National Center for Emerging and Zoonotic Infectious Diseases (NCEZID), Division of Foodborne, Waterborne, and Environmental Diseases (DFWED). *Parasites - enterobiasis (also known as pinworm infection).* CDC website. January 10, 2013. Available at: http://www.cdc.gov/parasites/pinworm/.

Centers for Disease Control and Prevention (CDC), National Center for Emerging and Zoonotic Infectious Diseases (NCEZID), Division of Foodborne, Waterborne, and Environmental Diseases (DFWED). *Parasites - amebiasis (also known as* Entamoeba histolytica *infection).* CDC website. November 2, 2010. Available at: http://www.cdc.gov/parasites/amebiasis/

Centers for Disease Control and Prevention (CDC), National Center for Emerging and Zoonotic Infectious Diseases (NCEZID), Division of Foodborne, Waterborne, and Environmental Diseases (DFWED). *Sexually transmitted diseases (STDs) - trichomoniasis.* CDC website. September 5, 2013. Available at: http://www.cdc.gov/std/trichomonas/default.htm.

Centers for Disease Control and Prevention (CDC), National Center for Emerging and Zoonotic Infectious Diseases (NCEZID), Division of Foodborne, Waterborne, and Environmental Diseases (DFWED). *Parasites - toxoplasmosis (*Toxoplasma *infection).* CDC website. January 10, 2013. Available at: http://www.cdc.gov/toxoplasmosis/.

Centers for Disease Control and Prevention (CDC), National Center for Emerging and Zoonotic Infectious Diseases (NCEZID), Division of Foodborne, Waterborne, and Environmental Diseases (DFWED). Acanthamoeba - *granulomatous amebic encephalitis (GAE); keratitis.* CDC website. October 22, 2013. Available at: http://www.cdc.gov/parasites/acanthamoeba/.

Centers for Disease Control and Prevention (CDC), National Center for Emerging and Zoonotic Infectious Diseases (NCEZID), Division of Foodborne, Waterborne, and Environmental Diseases (DFWED). *Malaria.* CDC website. August 9, 2012. Available at: http://www.cdc.gov/malaria/

Centers for Disease Control and Prevention (CDC), National Center for Emerging and Zoonotic Infectious Diseases (NCEZID), Division of Foodborne, Waterborne, and Environmental Diseases (DFWED). Naegleria fowleri - *primary amebic meningoencephalitis (PAM).* CDC website. November 14, 2013. Available at: http://www.cdc.gov/parasites/naegleria/.

Centers for Disease Control and Prevention (CDC), National Center for Emerging and Zoonotic Infectious Diseases (NCEZID), Division of Foodborne, Waterborne, and Environmental Diseases (DFWED). *Parasites - leishmaniasis.* CDC website. January 10, 2013. Available at: http://www.cdc.gov/parasites/leishmaniasis/index.html.

Centers for Disease Control and Prevention (CDC), National Center for Emerging and Zoonotic Infectious Diseases (NCEZID), Division of Foodborne, Waterborne, and Environmental Diseases (DFWED). *Parasites - Schistosomiasis.* CDC website. November 7, 2012. Available at: http://www.cdc.gov/parasites/schistosomiasis/.

CHAPTER 100

Occupational Health

Sue Sebazco, RN, MBA, CIC
Director of IC & Employee Health & Education
Texas Health
Arlington, TX

ABSTRACT

This chapter outlines the infection prevention considerations when designing and implementing an occupational health program for a healthcare facility. The content includes objectives for an occupational health program along with the major components. The risk for transmission of infections between healthcare personnel and patients is discussed. Guidelines for work restrictions for healthcare personnel with infectious diseases and exposure management are provided. There are suggestions for measuring improvement in the prevention of occupational injuries and exposures. The chapter also includes a description of workers' compensation.

KEY CONCEPTS

- An occupational health program is an essential and cornerstone element in efforts to provide a safe environment for patients and healthcare personnel.

- Elements of an occupational health program include surveillance, education, immunization, and injury prevention and response.

- Transmission of infection to and from healthcare personnel is a recognized risk and the infection preventionist must work collaboratively with the occupational health provider.

- The occupational health program and infection preventionist work collaboratively to implement pre-exposure vaccination programs, particularly those that are required annually, postexposure intervention responses, and other program activities to prevent exposure to infection diseases.

- Because there are a number of common infectious processes with no indications for postexposure intervention, an occupational health program must be structured so patients and healthcare personnel are actively protected.

- Work restrictions in the healthcare facility related to communicable diseases must be clearly outlined in policy and enforcement/accountability methods built in to the process.

- Performance measurements must be developed so that exposure opportunities are limited for patients, visitors, and healthcare personnel.

- The infection preventionist should be familiar with workers' compensation law and application in the occupational health program.

BACKGROUND

Healthcare organizations need to provide a safe environment for both patients and healthcare personnel (HCP). During the past four decades there has been an increased awareness of occupational hazards to HCP. Regulatory and licensing agencies are also aware of the need to address the prevention of hazards in the healthcare workplace. An infection preventionist (IP) has a vital role within the organization in identifying risk of communicable diseases to the patient and HCP, assessing the potential adverse outcomes, implementing pre-exposure and postexposure policies and procedures, and evaluating the effectiveness of measures taken. To carry out this function effectively, the IP needs an occupational health policy (OHP) that is based on valid, evidence-based strategies. Recommended practices need to be based on the epidemiology of infectious disease transmission in the healthcare facility, targeting the HCP as a potential source or host. The organization needs to analyze what elements should be included in its facility's OHP by recognizing the characteristics of the patient, client, or resident population served, as well as those of the HCP. The type of facility, the services provided, the geographical location, and the diseases that are endemic in the community populations served also influence the elements that need to be included.

An organizational structure may not formally include the IP as a member of the OHP. However, the IP of a healthcare organization is often called on to participate when infection prevention issues for HCP need to be addressed. Often the IP is asked to provide credible references to support the policies and practices that are in place.

The OHP uses a process improvement approach directed by a risk assessment to develop appropriate policies and procedures. Working collaboratively with the OHP staff, the IP provides input to the risk assessment by providing feedback on infection prevention practices. Results of infection prevention compliance observations reported by the IPs often identify trends that affect HCP safety and provide opportunities for improvement.

BASIC PRINCIPLES

Infection prevention policies, procedures, and practices in an OHP are designed to interrupt the transmission of infection between the HCP and patients. Some infectious processes that present a possible threat to HCP may be prevented with administration of pre-exposure immunizations. Other infectious processes caused by communicable diseases may have specific indications for postexposure interventions. Yet, some infectious processes may be prevented primarily by prevention strategies.

The Centers for Disease Control and Prevention (CDC) defines the term *HCP* as all paid and unpaid persons working in healthcare settings who have the potential for exposure to infectious materials, including body substances, contaminated medical supplies and equipment, contaminated environmental surfaces, or contaminated air.[1] Health Canada's Centre for Infectious Disease Prevention refers to *healthcare worker* as any individual who has the potential to acquire or transmit infectious agents during the course of his or her work in healthcare.[2] These terms include nurses, nursing assistants, physicians, technicians, therapists, pharmacists, students and trainees, contractual staff not employed by the healthcare facility, emergency medical service personnel, dental personnel, laboratory personnel, autopsy personnel, researchers, and volunteers who have direct patient care. Persons not directly involved in patient care but potentially exposed to infectious agents (e.g., clerical, dietary, housekeeping, maintenance, and volunteers) are also to be included as HCP or healthcare workers.

Healthcare is delivered not only in acute care hospitals and long-term care facilities, but also in freestanding surgical and outpatient centers, emergency care clinics, persons' homes, and during prehospital emergency care. HCP in any setting may acquire infections from or transmit infections to persons to whom they provide care, other personnel, household members, or other community contacts.

The healthcare organization's administration, medical staff, and other HCP need to support the infection prevention objectives of an OHP. These objectives are to (1) educate HCP about the principles of infection prevention and their individual responsibility for infection prevention, (2) collaborate with the infection prevention and control department in monitoring and investigating potentially harmful infectious exposures and outbreaks, (3) provide care to personnel for work-related illnesses or exposures, (4) identify work-related infection risks and institute appropriate preventive measures, and (5) contain costs by preventing infectious diseases that result in absenteeism and disability.[1]

There are elements that should be included when designing an occupational health service for HCP.[1] The IP may be involved in many of these functions. These include the following.

- Collaboration or oversight by a licensed healthcare provider responsible for the medical orders for pre-exposure vaccination, medical health screening, and postexposure treatment.

- Coordination with other departments that support the infection prevention objectives can ensure surveillance for infection in personnel and assist with exposure investigation and implementation of preventive measures.

- Medical evaluations performed before placement can ensure that personnel will not pose a risk for infection transmission. Additionally, information gathered through this evaluation may lead to identifying personnel who may be at increased risk for infection and whose placement may need to be considered carefully. It has not been demonstrated that a physical examination is cost effective for infection prevention purposes. Periodic evaluations may need to be performed for job assignments or work-related problems.

- Personnel health and safety education can contribute to the workers' compliance with infection prevention practices through understanding of the rationale. Federal, state, and local regulations may exist in regard to requirements for employee education and training. Items to be considered are risks for a job category, preventive measures, and educational materials that are appropriate in content, vocabulary, and language.

- Immunization programs provide protection from vaccine-preventable diseases for both HCP and those under their care. Vaccine preventable infectious diseases include Hepatitis A and B, influenza, measles, mumps, rubella, tetanus, pertussis, and varicella-zoster (chickenpox). The U.S. Public Health Service's Advisory Committee on Immunization Practices (ACIP) addresses recommended immunization practices. For vaccinations recommended for HCP see Table 100-1. Immunizations are discussed further in Chapter 103 Immunization of Healthcare Personnel.

- Management of job-related illnesses and exposures should also be provided for the HCP. Postexposure follow-up, medical surveillance, and reporting are mandated by regulatory agencies.

- Work restrictions may be indicated for workers who present with illnesses that may be transmitted in the workplace. See Table 100-2 for a summary of suggested work restrictions.[1] The facility should have a policy in place that identifies who has the authority to remove personnel from duty.

- Health counseling to provide targeted information about the risk for and prevention of occupationally acquired infections should be available to personnel. Personnel may need to be reassured regarding an exposure and educated on the risks for acquiring an infection and benefits of postexposure prophylaxis regimens. Personnel also must be educated to report a community exposure to a communicable infectious disease.

- Maintenance of records, data management, and confidentiality are major requirements by federal, state, and local standards of the OHP. A computerized personnel database is preferred. Copies of individual records are to be made available to personnel on request.

Table 100-1. Immunization Schedule for Healthcare Personnel

Vaccine	Indication	Schedule
Hepatitis A	Laboratory and primate worker	1 mL intramuscularly at 0, 6 months
Hepatitis B	Occupational exposure to blood, blood products, or bodily secretions	Three doses of 1 mL intramuscularly at 0, 1, and 6 to 12 months
Hepatitis A and B	As for Hepatitis A and Hepatitis B	1 mL intramuscularly at 0, 1, and 6 months
Influenza	Persons attending high-risk patients (e.g., elderly, other) Inactivated vaccine FluMist	One dose of 0.5 mL intramuscularly annually Intranasal dose of 0.2 mL annually (split between both nostrils)
MMR Measles	Adults born after 1957 without a history of physician-diagnosed measles, serological immunity, or documentation of having received two doses of vaccine	0.5 mL subcutaneously at 0, and at least 1 month later
Mumps	Adults born after 1957 without a history of physician-diagnosed measles, serological immunity, or documentation of having received two doses of vaccine	0.5 mL subcutaneously once
Rubella	Unimmunized women of childbearing age and healthcare personnel	0.5 mL subcutaneously once
Polio	Laboratory and other healthcare personnel who come in contact with the live virus	Three doses of 0.5 mL subcutaneously. First two doses separated by 4 to 8 weeks, and a third dose 6 to 12 months after the second dose.
Td	Persons without a history, or an unknown history of Td immunization or >10 years since last dose	Unimmunized: 3 doses of 0.5 mL intramuscularly at 0, 1 to 2, 6 months Booster: 1 dose every 10 years
Tdap	Healthcare personnel with direct patient contact, healthy adults 19 to 64; close contacts of those (<1 year Td dose)	0.5 mL intramuscularly one-time dose (can be substituted for any)
Varicella	Adults nonimmune to varicella	0.5 mL subcutaneously at time 0 weeks and 4 to 8 weeks later

From Shefer A, Atkinson W, Friedman C, et al. Immunization of health-care personnel: Recommendations of the Advisory Committee on Immunization Practices (ACIP). *MMRW Recomm Rep* 2011;60(RR07):1–45.

Occupational Health Hazards

Postexposure Interventions

Some infectious processes present a possible threat to HCP and have specific indications for postexposure intervention. Figure 100-1 provides an algorithm for assessment of occupational exposure and when to implement an intervention.

Tuberculosis

The CDC publishes recommendations on controlling the spread of tuberculosis (TB) in healthcare facilities.[4] The Occupational Health and Safety Administration (OSHA) has a compliance directive addressing occupational exposure to TB in healthcare facilities, where the CDC has identified TB transmission to be at high risk.[5] This was written as a directive to their field offices to clarify the application of the General Duty Clause when inspecting facilities identified as belonging in these high-hazard groups. OSHA's General Duty Clause requires each employer to provide its employees a place of employment free from recognized hazards.[6]

An unidentified case of pulmonary or laryngeal TB can be a source of unprotected exposure to HCP. Personnel should be educated about TB, how it is spread, its signs and symptoms, and preventive measures.

The facility's annual TB risk assessment will determine the types of administrative, environmental, and respiratory controls that are appropriate to the setting. The three TB screening risk classifications are low risk, medium risk, and potential ongoing transmission. The TB screening risk classification, along with the facility's state regulations, directs how often tuberculin skin testing (TST) is required and for which HCP. See Chapter 95 Tuberculosis and Other Mycobacteria, for additional information on TB risk assessments. A TB screening program should include part-time, temporary, contract, and full-time HCP. HCP who have duties that involve face-to-face contact with patients with suspected or confirmed TB disease, as well as those involved in the following, should also be included:[4]

1. Entering patient rooms or treatment rooms, whether or not a patient is present.

2. Participating in aerosol-generating or aerosol-producing procedures.

3. Participating in suspected or confirmed *Mycobacterium tuberculosis* specimen processing.

4. Installing, maintaining, or replacing environmental control in areas in which persons with TB are encountered.

Latent TB infection (LTBI) refers to a condition that occurs after initial infection with *Mycobacterium tuberculosis (M. tuberculosis)*. Within 2 to 12 weeks after the initial infection, the immune response limits additional multiplication of the tubercle bacilli and test results for *M. tuberculosis* infection become positive. Certain bacilli remain in the body and viable for multiple years. These persons are asymptomatic and not infectious.[4]

Table 100-2. Summary of Suggested Work Restrictions for HCP Exposed to or Infected With Infectious Diseases of Importance in Healthcare Settings, in the Absence of State and Local Regulations (Modified from ACIP Recommendations)

Disease/Problem	Work Restriction	Duration	Category
Conjunctivitis	Restrict from patient contact and contact with the patient's environment	Until discharge ceases	II
Cytomegalovirus infections	No restriction		II
Diarrheal diseases			
Acute stage (diarrhea with other symptoms)	Restrict from patient contact, contact with the patient's environment, or food handling	Until symptoms resolve	IB
Convalescent stage, *Salmonella* spp.	Restrict from care of high-risk patients	Until symptoms resolve; consult with local and state health authorities regarding need for negative stool cultures	IB
Diphtheria	Exclude from duty	Until antimicrobial therapy completed and two cultures obtained 24 hours apart are negative	IB
Enteroviral infections	Restrict from care of infants, neonates, and immunocompromised patients and their environments	Until symptoms resolve	II
Hepatitis A	Restrict from patient contact, contact with patient's environment, and food handling	Until 7 days after onset of jaundice	IB
Hepatitis B			
Personnel with acute or chronic Hepatitis B surface antigenemia who do not perform exposure-prone procedures	No restriction*; refer to state regulations; Standard Precautions should always be observed	Until Hepatitis B e antigen is negative	II
Personnel with acute or chronic Hepatitis B e antigenemia who perform exposure-prone procedures	Do not perform exposure-prone invasive procedures until counsel from an expert review panel has been sought; panel should review and recommend procedures the worker can perform, taking into account specific procedure as well as skill and technique of worker; refer to state regulations		II
Hepatitis C	No recommendation	Until lesions heal	Unresolved issue
Herpes simplex			
Genital	No restriction		II
Hands (herpetic whitlow)	Restrict from patient contact and contact with the patient's environment		IA
Orofacial	Evaluate for need to restrict from care of high-risk patients		II
Human immunodeficiency virus	Do not perform exposure-prone invasive procedures until counsel from an expert review panel has been sought; panel should review and recommend procedures the worker can perform, taking into account specific procedure as well as skill and technique of the worker; Standard Precautions should always be observed; refer to state regulations		II
Measles			
Active	Exclude from duty	Until 7 days after the rash appears	IA
Postexposure (susceptible personnel)	Exclude from duty	From 5th day after first exposure through 21st day after last exposure and/or 4 days after rash appears	IB
Meningococcal infections	Exclude from duty	Until 24 hours after start of effective therapy	IA
Mumps			
Active	Exclude from duty	Until 9 days after onset of parotitis	IB
Postexposure (susceptible personnel)	Exclude from duty	From 9th day after first exposure through 26th day after last exposure or until 9 days after onset of parotitis	II
Pediculosis	Restrict from patient contact	Until treated and observed to be free of adult and immature lice	IB
Pertussis			
Active	Exclude from duty	From beginning of catarrhal stage through third week after onset of paroxysms or until 5 days after start of effective antimicrobial therapy	IB
Postexposure (asymptomatic personnel)	No restriction, prophylaxis recommended		II
Postexposure (symptomatic personnel)	Exclude from duty	Until 5 days after start of effective antimicrobial therapy	IB
Rubella			
Active	Exclude from duty	Until 5 days after rash appears	IA
Postexposure (susceptible personnel)	Exclude from duty	From 7th day after first exposure through 21st day after last exposure	IB

Table 100-2. Summary of Suggested Work Restrictions for HCP Exposed to or Infected With Infectious Diseases of Importance in Healthcare Settings, in the Absence of State and Local Regulations (Modified from ACIP Recommendations) (cont'd)

Disease/Problem	Work Restriction	Duration	Category
Scabies	Restrict from patient contact	Until cleared by medical evaluation	IB
Staphylococcus aureus infection			
Active, draining skin lesions	Restrict from contact with patients and patients' environment or food handling	Until lesions have resolved	IB
Carrier state	No restriction, unless personnel are epidemiologically linked to transmission of the organism		IB
Streptococcal infection, group A	Restrict from patient care, contact with patient's environment, or food handling	Until 24 hours after adequate treatment started	IB
Tuberculosis			
Active disease	Exclude from duty	Until proved noninfectious	IA
PPD converter	No restriction		IA
Varicella			
Active	Exclude from duty	Until all lesions dry and crust	IA
Postexposure (susceptible personnel)	Exclude from duty	From 10th day after first exposure through 21st day (28th day if VZIG given) after last exposure	IA
Zoster			
Localized, in healthy person	Cover lesions; restrict from care of high-risk patient†	Until all lesions dry and crust	II
Generalized or localized in immunosuppressed person	Restrict from patient contact	Until all lesions dry and crust	IB
Postexposure (susceptible personnel)	Restrict from patient contact	From 10th day after first exposure through 21st day (28th day if VZIG given) after last exposure or, if varicella occurs, until all lesions dry and crust	IA
Viral respiratory infections, acute febrile	Consider excluding from the care of high-risk patients‡ or contact with their environment during community outbreak of RSV and influenza	Until acute symptoms resolve	IB

*Unless epidemiologically linked to transmission of infection.

†Those susceptible to varicella and who are at increased risk of complications of varicella, such as neonates and immunocompromised persons of any age.

‡High-risk patients as defined by the ACIP for complications of influenza.

From Centers for Disease Control and Prevention. Guidelines for infection control in the healthcare worker, 1998. *Am J Infect Control* 1998;26:289–354.

The purified protein derivative (PPD)-based TST has been used in the United States to diagnose LTBI. There are *in vitro* cytokine-based immunoassays for the detection of *M. tuberculosis* infection. These tests measure cell-mediated immune responses to peptides from two *M. tuberculosis* proteins that are not present in any bacille Calmette-Guérin (BCG) vaccine strain and are absent from the majority of nontuberculosis *Mycobacteria*. One such blood assay for *M. tuberculosis* (BAMT) is the QuantiFERON-TB Gold test (QFT-G). Additional cytokine-based immunoassays are under development. Specific guidelines regarding use of QFT-G as part of an OHP are provided by the CDC.[7]

A TB control program should be developed according to the most current CDC recommendations. The program should be designed according to the results of the risk assessment that includes the TB experience in the facility and whether or not the facility will be or has the capability of providing care to persons with TB.

A TST should be administered, read, and interpreted by trained personnel. Use the intradermal (Mantoux) method to administer the PPD-based TST. Tine tests should not be used. Baseline screening should be conducted at the time of hire. Those individuals who have a history of having received the BCG vaccination should be included unless they have documentation of a previous positive reaction. A two-step TST should be performed when the initial TST is negative and there is no documented negative TST during the preceding 12 months. Interpretation of the TST depends on measured TST induration in millimeters, the person's risk for being infected with *M. tuberculosis*, and risk for progression to active TB if infected. Interpret the TST test according to the CDC guidelines. See Table 100-3 for information regarding results of TST and QFT tests. The frequency of periodic follow-up TST tests is based on the facility's risk assessment. Exempt those employees who have a positive baseline TST or have had adequate treatment for TB.

If personnel have a positive TST, a chest radiograph should be done promptly to check for active disease. A history of exposure should be obtained to determine if infection is occupational or community-associated. The person should be instructed to report symptoms that are suggestive of TB. Chest radiographs do not need to be repeated unless the person is symptomatic. However, there may be some state or local regulations that require periodic chest radiographs for personnel with a documented positive TST. If a person is a recent converter, the person should be referred to a healthcare provider for consideration of preventive therapy.

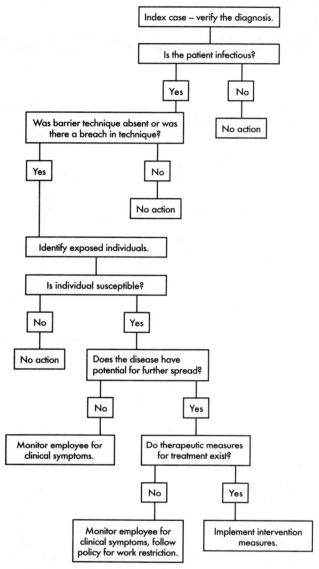

Figure 100-1. Algorithm for management of healthcare worker exposure.

Anergy is a condition in which a person has diminished ability to exhibit delayed T-cell hypersensitivity to antigens because of a condition or situation resulting in altered immune function. An inability to react to a skin test is called cutaneous anergy. In the past, skin tests for anergy were used in conjunction with TSTs for screening programs for *M. tuberculosis* among the immune-compromised and human immunodeficiency virus (HIV)-infected persons. Anergy testing is no longer recommended because it has been found to have poor predictive value.[3]

If there has been unprotected exposure of workers to TB, TSTs should be administered at the time of the exposure and repeated at 12 weeks postexposure to look for possible converters. Chest radiographs are performed only on those with prior positive TST and who are currently symptomatic. Consider retesting immunocompromised personnel at least every 6 months.[4]

Personnel who have laryngeal or pulmonary TB are excluded from work until they are receiving adequate therapy, the cough has resolved, and there have been three consecutive sputum smears negative for acid-fast bacilli. The occupational health department should obtain periodic documentation from the healthcare provider. If treatment is discontinued, the person needs to be promptly evaluated for infectiousness.

Immunocompromised personnel should be counseled regarding potential risks associated with caring for persons with TB. It may be necessary to offer reasonable accommodations for the work setting.

The *M. tuberculosis* infection conversion rate should be a component of the facility's risk assessment. A TST conversion is a 10-mm or greater increase in the size of the TST induration during a 2-year period in a person with a documented negative (<10 mm) baseline two-step TST result or a person who is not an HCP with a negative (<10 mm) TST result within 2 years. The conversion rate is the percentage of persons whose test result for *M. tuberculosis* infection has converted within a specified period. To calculate a conversion rate, divide the number of conversions among personnel in the setting in a specified period (numerator) by the number of personnel who received tests in the setting over the same period and multiply by 100.

Table 100-3. Interpretations of Tuberculin Skin Test and QuantiFERON-TB Test Results According to the Purpose of Testing for *Mycobacterium tuberculosis* Infection in Healthcare Setting

Purpose of Testing	Tuberculin Skin Test	QuantiFERON-TB Test
Baseline	≥10 mm is considered a positive result (either first or second step)	Positive (only one-step)
Serial testing without known exposure	Increase of ≥10 mm is considered a positive result (TST conversion)	Change from negative to positive (QFT conversion)
Known exposure (close contact)	≥5 mm is considered a positive result in persons who have a baseline TST result of 0 mm; an increase of ≥10 mm is considered a positive result in persons with a negative baseline TST result or previous follow-up screening TST result of ≥0 mm	Change to positive

From Centers for Disease Control and Prevention. Guidelines for preventing the transmission of *Mycobacterium tuberculosis* in health-care settings, 2005. *MMWR Recomm Rep* 2005;54(RR-17):1–144.

Respiratory Protection Program

The generally accepted respiratory protection that is used to protect personnel from a person with suspected or confirmed TB is a particulate N95 respirator, a requirement identified in OSHA's respiratory protection standard. The standard requires the employer to designate a program administrator who is qualified by appropriate training or experience that is commensurate with the complexity of the program to administer or oversee the respiratory protection program and conduct the required evaluations of program effectiveness. The employer also needs to provide respirators, training, and medical evaluations at no cost to the employee. Furthermore, the employer is required to have a sufficient number of respirator models and sizes so that the respirator is acceptable to, and correctly fits, the user.[8,9] OSHA's standard requires that each person assigned to wear a respirator must receive a fit test before the person is required to wear the respirator in the workplace. After fit testing, the HCP must perform a seal check with each use. A user seal check is an action conducted by the respirator user to determine if the respirator is properly seated to the face. The fit test needs to be repeated annually or whenever respirator design or facial changes, such as in extreme weight loss or gain, occur that could affect the proper fit of the respirator.

A qualitative fit test (QLFT) is one that results in a pass or fail fit test and one that assesses the adequacy of respirator fit that relies on the individual's response to the test agent.

A quantitative fit test (QNFT) is an assessment of the adequacy of respirator fit by numerically measuring the amount of leakage into the respirator. A user seal check is an action conducted by the respirator user to determine if the respirator is properly seated to the face.

A powered air-purifying respirator (PAPR) is an air-purifying respirator that uses a blower to force the ambient air through air-purifying elements to the inlet covering. A fit test is not required.[9]

OSHA requires an employer to establish and implement a written respiratory protection program with worksite-specific procedures. The program is to be updated as necessary and should include procedures for selecting respirators for use in the workplace; medical evaluations of employees required to use respirators; fit testing procedures; and procedures for proper use, storing, and discarding of respirators. The plan should outline training that includes the respiratory hazards to which the employees are potentially exposed during routine and emergency situations. The proper use of respirators, including putting on and removing them, any limitations on their use, and their maintenance, should also be covered. There should be procedures for regularly evaluating the effectiveness of the program.[9]

In situations in which respirator use is not required and employees request a respirator, employers may provide respirators or permit employees to use their own. However, in such cases, the employer should determine if wearing a respirator would in itself create a hazard. The employer needs to provide the required information for employees using respirators when not required under the standard. In addition, the employer must establish and implement those elements of a written respiratory protection program necessary to ensure that any employee using a respirator voluntarily is medically able to use that respirator, and that the respirator is cleaned, stored, and maintained so that its use does not present a health hazard to the user.

Bloodborne Pathogens

The very nature of a healthcare setting will require contact between HCP and the persons they serve. One of the areas of concern for personnel is bloodborne pathogens (BBP) exposures. There are many ways to prevent transmission. These include promoting the Hepatitis B vaccination for personnel who have contact with blood, considering all patients as a potential source of infection, using appropriate barriers when performing tasks that require contact with blood, and preventing percutaneous injuries. Despite the evolution of a safer work environment in the past few decades, occupational exposures do occur. Management of occupational exposures to Hepatitis B virus (HBV), Hepatitis C virus (HCV), and HIV are outlined in the updated U.S. Public Health Service guidelines[9] and covered in Chapter 101 Occupational Exposure to Bloodborne Pathogens.

An OHP in a healthcare setting should include the following elements of an effective postexposure management program: clearly stated policies and procedures that address confidentiality of exposed and source persons and how to manage the exposure; education and training of workers to alleviate misconceptions and fears; and resources for rapid access to clinical care, postexposure prophylaxis (PEP), and testing of the source person and worker. An assessment of the injury may identify ways to prevent future injuries.

OSHA's BBP standard provides directives for employers to develop an exposure plan that includes providing the Hepatitis B vaccine to employees within 10 days of employment. The standard also requires the employer to provide training on potential hazards, personal protective equipment (PPE), engineering controls, and work practices before the employee's initial assignment. An element of the revision to OSHA's BBP rule in 2001 was the need to maintain a sharps injury log.[10-12] The log needs to protect the privacy of the injured worker and include the identification of the device, location of the incident, circumstances surrounding the incident, the procedure being performed, the body part affected, and the objects or substances involved. Another 2001 revision to the standard was the requirement of the documentation of annual consideration and implementation of appropriate engineering controls and solicitation of non-managerial HCP in evaluating and choosing safe medical devices. The exposure control plan should also be reviewed and updated annually.

Hepatitis B Virus

The Hepatitis B vaccination has contributed to the significant decrease of HBV among HCP.[13] At the time of hire, HCP's potential for exposure should be determined and their vaccine status assessed. Post-vaccine screening is advised for personnel at ongoing risk for blood exposure to determine whether response to the vaccine has occurred and to determine the need for revaccination. Revaccinate nonresponders with an additional three-dose series and retest. If the worker is still a nonresponder, then test for Hepatitis B surface antigen (HBSAg) to make sure the worker does not have chronic antigemia. Nonresponders in chronic dialysis centers who do not respond for HBSAg and Hepatitis B surface antibody (anti-HBs) should be tested every 6 months. Risk factors for nonresponse include age, smoking, obesity, immunosuppression, renal failure, and a family history of nonresponse. [14]

An exposure to HBV is defined as the source person being HBSAg positive or the person's status being unknown. If the exposed person is vaccinated, but the vaccine response is unknown, then perform a baseline test for anti-HBs. Baseline testing is not necessary if the exposed person has not been vaccinated or the vaccine response is known. If the exposed person has not been vaccinated, begin the vaccine series at the time of the exposure and administer Hepatitis B immune globulin (HBIG) as soon as possible after the exposure, preferably within 24 hours.

One of the frequently asked questions is whether or not booster doses of the Hepatitis B vaccine are necessary. The current response is no. Maintenance of anti-HBs above 10 mIU/mL is not necessary. It is believed that the majority of responders will show an anamnestic response to vaccine challenge.

Hepatitis C Virus

The average risk for transmission of HCV following a percutaneous exposure is 1.8 percent. Transmission rarely occurs from mucosal contact with HCV-infected blood. There has been no transmission reported to personnel from intact or nonintact skin exposures to blood. [14] Recommendations for follow-up of occupational HCV exposures are discussed in Chapter 101 Occupational Exposure to Bloodborne Pathogens.

A worker who has been exposed to HCV should refrain from donating blood, plasma, organs, tissue, or semen. There is no need for modification of sexual practices, refraining from becoming pregnant, or special precautions to prevent secondary transmission. There are no existing recommendations regarding restricting the professional activities of HCP with HCV infection. However, discussion following a report of surgeon-to-patient transmission suggested that limitations, if any, should be determined on a case-by-case basis after consideration of factors that influence transmission. These considerations should include the provider's inability or unwillingness to comply with infection control standards. [14]

Human Immunodeficiency Virus

The CDC followed HCP who sustained an exposure incident from an HIV-positive source through June 2001. There were 57 HCP who had documented occupationally acquired immune deficiency syndrome (AIDS)/HIV. A case-control study identified

risks for transmission. [10] The risk factors identified were: (1) a deep injury from a device with visible blood, (2) the device was from the source person's vein or artery, and (3) the source person died of AIDS within 60 days after the exposure incident.

The average risk for transmission of HIV by the exposure type is 0.3 percent for percutaneous, 0.1 percent for mucous membrane contact, and less than 0.1 percent for nonintact skin contact. [14]

Immediately following the exposure, the HCP and source person should be tested to establish HIV-AB status. HIV testing of needles or other sharps is not recommended. See Chapter 101 Occupational Exposure to Bloodborne Pathogens, for information regarding postexposure management.

Varicella

Transmission of varicella has been documented from sources from healthcare-associated exposures that have included patients, HCP, and visitors. In adults, a history of varicella is highly predictive of serologic immunity, and most adults who have negative or uncertain histories of varicella are also seropositive. HCP are considered to have immunity if they have laboratory evidence of immunity, a history of clinical diagnosed or verified varicella or zoster, or documentation of age-appropriate vaccination. It is recommended that the varicella vaccine be administered to all HCP without evidence of immunity. [15] Prevaccination serological screening is often cost effective. Postvaccination testing is not necessary or recommended because assays for vaccine immunity are not adequately sensitive. A small percentage of vaccinated individuals will develop a vaccine rash following the varicella vaccine. The risk for disease transmission from this rash is extremely low. In fact, to date, there have been no documented cases of disease transmission after HCP varicella vaccination.

If an unvaccinated susceptible personnel is exposed to varicella, then exclude the person from duty from the 10th day after exposure through the 21st day after exposure, or until all lesions are dry and crusted if varicella occurs. Serotest vaccinated personnel who are exposed to varicella immediately after exposure to assess the presence of antibody. If seronegative, exclude the person from duty from day 10 through day 21 postexposure. If fever, upper respiratory tract symptoms, or rash develop, then exclude the person from duty.

Consider administering the vaccination for exposed unvaccinated personnel without documented immunity. The efficacy of postexposure vaccination is unknown. Therefore, personnel vaccinated after exposure should be managed as previously recommended for unvaccinated persons.

Varicella-zoster immune globulin (VZIG) has not been recommended for immune-competent personnel. However, its use may be considered for immunocompromised or pregnant workers postexposure. If used, extend the time that the worker is excluded from duty from 21 days to 28 days postexposure.

Meningococcal Disease

Meningococcal disease is caused by a variety of serogroups of *Neisseria meningitides (N. meningitides)*. Healthcare-associated transmission is uncommon. When proper infection prevention precautions are not used, transmission of the pathogen from patient to personnel may occur. This occurs through contact with respiratory secretions of patients who have meningococcemia, meningococcal meningitis, or a lower respiratory tract infection with *N. meningitidis* or through handling laboratory specimens.

Postexposure prophylaxis is advised for persons who have had intensive, unprotected contact with infected patients.[1] Unprotected means without wearing a mask and intensive contact would be mouth-to-mouth resuscitation, endotracheal intubation, endotracheal tube management, or close examination of the oropharynx. Prophylactic therapy should be administered immediately after the unprotected exposure. Current recommended regimens to eradicate carriage are rifampin 600 mg orally every 12 hours for 2 days, a single dose of ciprofloxacin 500 mg orally, or a single dose of ceftriaxone 250 mg intramuscularly. Rifampin and ciprofloxacin are not recommended for pregnant women.

It is currently recommended to offer pre-exposure vaccination to laboratory personnel who handle soluble preparations of *N. meningitidis*.[16]

Measles, Mumps, Rubella

The measles, mumps, rubella (MMR) vaccination should not be administered to pregnant HCP or HCP who might become pregnant within the next 28 days.

Rubella

Because healthcare-associated transmission of rubella has occurred from both male and female personnel to susceptible personnel and patients, ensuring immunity among all HCP is the most effective way to eliminate transmission.[1] Personnel should have documentation of one dose of live rubella vaccine on or after their first birthdays or laboratory evidence of immunity to rubella. A dose of MMR is recommended for those HCP who were born before 1957 and who do not have laboratory evidence of immunity.[17] Exposed personnel not immune to rubella need to be excluded from duty from the 7th day after the first exposure through the 21st day after the last exposure.

Measles

Measles transmission has occurred in healthcare facilities. Data suggest that HCP have a risk for measles 19 times greater than that of the general population.[1] The measles virus is transmitted 3 to 4 days before as well as after the rash appears. In 2005, a measles outbreak of 34 cases was the result from one case imported from Europe. Therefore, it is essential that all personnel have presumptive evidence of immunity to measles. Presumptive evidence of immunity is written documentation of vaccination with two doses of MMR vaccine administered at least 28 days apart, laboratory evidence of immunity, laboratory confirmation of disease, or birth before 1957. The MMR vaccination should be administered to those who cannot provide documentation of these conditions. The measles vaccine should be administered to susceptible HCP who have had contact with a measles patient within 72 hours of the exposure. Personnel who are not immune to measles need to be excluded from duty 5 days after the first exposure to 21 days after the last exposure.[1]

Mumps

Mumps can be spread in a healthcare facility. According to the CDC there are usually 250 to 300 cases of mumps reported in the United States each year. In 2006, more than 5,700 cases were reported as the result of an outbreak that began in Iowa and spread to 11 states. In 2006, the ACIP changed its recommendation for just one dose to two doses, because of the improved efficacy of two doses. Most mumps cases in HCP have been community-associated.[1] Personnel have presumptive evidence of immunity if they have written documentation of vaccination with two doses of MMR vaccine administered at least 28 days apart, laboratory evidence of immunity, laboratory confirmation of disease, or birth before 1957. Two doses of MMR vaccine should be administered to those who lack this documentation. Susceptible personnel who are exposed to mumps need to be excluded from duty the 9th day after the first exposure to the 26th day after the last exposure.[18]

Scabies and Pediculosis

Healthcare-associated transmission of conventional and "Norwegian," or crusted, scabies has occurred in various healthcare settings. It is spread by prolonged skin-to-skin contact with an infested individual. Contact Precautions can reduce spread from patient to personnel. Exposed personnel should be evaluated for signs and symptoms of mite infestation. Appropriate therapy should be provided for confirmed or suspected scabies.

Pediculosis is caused by infestation with any of three species of lice: human head louse, human body louse, and pubic, or crab, louse. Healthcare-associated transmission of head and body lice is unlikely, and healthcare-associated transmission of pubic lice is very unlikely. Pediculosis treatment should be provided for exposed personnel if they have evidence of infestation. Do not routinely offer prophylactic scabicides or pediculicides unless transmission has occurred.

Personnel with either scabies or pediculosis should be excluded from duty until they receive appropriate initial treatment and it is found to be effective.[1]

Pertussis

Pertussis was previously thought to be exclusively a childhood disease. However, this highly contagious disease has resulted in healthcare-associated transmission in both patients and personnel. Seventeen healthcare providers were infected with pertussis from one infected infant. In another case, one healthcare provider was related to 87 cases. Immunity to pertussis is essential for HCP. The ACIP now recommends that those who provide direct patient care should receive a dose of tetanus, diphtheria, and pertussis (Tdap) vaccine.[19]

Postexposure prophylaxis is indicated for personnel exposed to pertussis. The regimen used is a 14-day course of either erythromycin 500 mg four times daily or one tablet of trimethoprim-sulfamethoxazole twice daily.[1]

Exposed personnel do not need to be excluded from duty. Personnel in whom symptoms develop (e.g., cough lasting 7 days or more, particularly if accompanied by paroxysms of coughing, inspiratory whoop, or post-tussive vomiting) should be excluded until 5 days after the start of appropriate therapy.

Influenza

Influenza is a contagious viral respiratory illness. The CDC reports that every year an average of 5 to 20 percent of the population in the United States gets seasonal influenza, resulting in more than 200,000 hospitalizations and about 3,000 to 49,000 deaths annually in the United States. Influenza causes mild to severe disease. Those at high risk for complications from influenza are seniors, infants and young children, persons with chronic medical conditions, and pregnant women.[20]

Symptoms of influenza include fever (usually high), headache, extreme tiredness, dry cough, sore throat, runny or stuffy nose, and muscle aches. Stomach symptoms, such as nausea, vomiting, and diarrhea, also can occur but are more common in children than adults. Complications of influenza include bacterial pneumonia, ear infections, sinus infections, dehydration, and worsening of chronic medical conditions, such as congestive heart failure, asthma, or diabetes.

Influenza viruses may be shed 1 day before the onset of symptoms and up to 5 days after the individual becomes ill. Spread of influenza mainly occurs when those with the illness cough or sneeze. Fomites contaminated with influenza viruses may also serve as a reservoir when individuals touch them and then touch their nose or mouth.

Each year influenza vaccination is recommended for HCP. The CDC[15] as well as a number of professional organizations, including APIC and the Society for Healthcare Epidemiology of America (SHEA),[21] have endorsed vaccination against influenza for all HCP. Many professional organizations, including SHEA, view influenza vaccination of HCP as a core patient safety practice and one in which noncompliance should not be tolerated.[21] One goal for HCP immunization should be to administer the influenza vaccine to as many HCP as possible and preferably before influenza activity begins in the community. Therefore, an effective OHP in a healthcare organization must include an annual influenza prevention campaign that includes vaccination of HCP, especially those who provide direct care, as its primary focus. Education efforts that dispel the myths regarding

influenza vaccine and relay the many benefits of receiving the vaccine yearly for individual HCP and HCP's coworkers and family members are other components that support this primary endeavor. Accrediting and regulatory agencies are increasingly adding components of a prevention and control program to their standards and requirements.

One example of a program is a modified mandatory program. HCP must receive the vaccine or sign a declination after reading the benefits of receiving vaccine versus risks to self and patients and others by not receiving the vaccine. In some healthcare facilities, if HCP refuses the influenza vaccine, it is mandatory that that HCP wear a barrier mask during influenza season when providing direct patient care. Another method that has been used successfully in increasing vaccination rates is providing a monetary incentive to receive the vaccine. Providing the vaccine at convenient times and locations has also increased compliance. There is a high compliance rate associated with mandatory programs that require receiving the vaccine as a condition of employment.

There are two types of the influenza vaccination. The former abbreviation TIV (trivalent inactivated influenza vaccine, previously used for inactivated influenza vaccines) has been replaced with the new abbreviation IIV (inactivated influenza vaccine). One is an inactive vaccine injection that is approved for use in people 6 months of age and older, including healthy people and people with chronic medical conditions. The nasal-spray flu vaccine is a vaccine made with live, weakened influenza viruses that do not cause influenza (live attenuated influenza vaccine [LAIV]). LAIV is approved for use in healthy people 2 to 49 years of age who are not pregnant.[19] An inactivated trivalent vaccine (TIV) containing 60 mcg of hemagglutinin antigen per influenza vaccine virus strain is an alternative inactivated vaccine for persons ≥65 years. The majority of TIV preparations are administered intramuscularly. An intradermally administered TIV was licensed in May 2011 and is an alternative for persons 18 to 64 years. RIV refers to recombinant hemagglutinin influenza vaccine and is egg-free and may be used for persons aged 18 to 49 years who have no other contraindications.

Initially there was concern that LAIV transmission from a recently vaccinated person could cause a clinically important illness in an immunocompromised contact. However, this has not been reported. There is a theoretical risk that a live, attenuated vaccine virus could be transmitted to the severely immune-suppressed person. Therefore, there is rationale for avoiding use of LAIV among HCP or other close contacts of severely immunocompromised persons. As a precautionary measure, HCP who receive LAIV should not provide care for severely immune-suppressed patients in protective environments for 7 days after vaccination. Hospital visitors who have received LAIV should also avoid contact with these designated patients. Some healthcare facilities expand this group, but this is outside of the CDC guidelines.

It takes about 2 weeks after vaccination for antibodies to develop that protect against influenza virus infection. Vaccines can be offered as early as September and continue throughout the influenza season often as late as March in the following year.

Another component of an influenza prevention and control program is providing chemoprophylaxis to patients, residents, and HCP when warranted, such as during an outbreak. Additional outbreak control measures include initiating Droplet Precautions and establishing cohorts of patients with confirmed or suspected influenza. The unvaccinated staff should be re-offered influenza vaccinations. LAIV should be avoided because the antiviral medication will prevent viral replication needed to stimulate a vaccine response. Contact between ill staff or visitors and patients should be restricted. Adamantanes and neuraminidase inhibitors have been successfully used to control outbreaks caused by antiviral susceptible strains when antivirals are combined with other infection prevention measures. The CDC conducts enhanced surveillance in collaboration with local and state health departments. IPs should monitor information available on the incidence and resistance patterns identified in their communities. If an outbreak is caused by a strain of influenza virus that is not well matched by the vaccine for that season, chemoprophylaxis should be considered for all employees, regardless of their vaccination status.[20]

Infectious Processes with No Postexposure Interventions Indicated

There are common infectious processes for which there are no indications for postexposure intervention.

Herpes Simplex Virus

Personnel with primary or recurrent orofacial herpes simplex infections should be evaluated on a case-by-case basis to assess the potential for transmission to high-risk patients. High-risk patients include neonates, intensive care unit patients, patients with severe burns or eczema, and severely immunocompromised patients. Personnel with orofacial herpes simplex should be instructed to cover and not touch infected lesions. Observing hand hygiene policies is mandatory. Precautions need to be taken to prevent secretions from the lesions from having contact with patients with dermatitis. Herpetic whitlow is a herpes simplex infection of the fingers or hands. Personnel with herpetic whitlow need to be excluded from contact with patients until their lesions heal.[1]

Herpes Zoster Virus (Shingles)

Reactivation of latent varicella-zoster virus can occur decades after the initial infection known as chickenpox. This reactivation is known as zoster or shingles. It is a localized, generally painful cutaneous eruption that occurs most frequently among older adults and immunocompromised persons.

Transmission has been documented in healthcare settings between patients or from patients to HCP. However, transmission from HCP to patients has not been documented. Persons with localized zoster are less likely to transmit the virus to susceptible persons in household or occupational settings if their lesions are covered. Zoster lesions contain high concentrations of the zoster virus that can be spread, presumably by the airborne route, and cause primary varicella in exposed susceptible persons. Therefore, susceptible personnel should not provide direct patient care when other immune HCP are available. HCP can know when they are immune when their VZV antibodies are reactive. Localized zoster is only contagious after the rash erupts and until the lesions crust. Zoster is less contagious than varicella.[22]

Healthcare organizations may consider excluding personnel with zoster from work until their lesions dry and form a crust. Those with localized zoster should avoid contact with susceptible persons at high risk for severe varicella in household and occupational settings until lesions are crusted. Persons at high risk include pregnant women, all premature infants born to susceptible mothers, infants born at less than 28 weeks' gestation or who weigh 1,000 grams or less regardless of maternal immune status, and immunocompromised persons of all ages.[22]

In May 2006, the U.S. Food and Drug Administration (FDA) licensed a live attenuated vaccine for the prevention of herpes zoster and its sequelae. In June 2008, the ACIP released its recommendation for routine vaccination of all persons aged 60 years or older with one dose of zoster vaccine.

Cytomegalovirus

The two principle reservoirs of cytomegalovirus in healthcare facilities are infants and young children and immunocompromised patients. The consistent use of Standard Precautions when caring for all persons should interrupt spread from the person shedding the virus to personnel. There is no need to reassign pregnant HCP from caring for these patients. Pregnant personnel need to be counseled on how transmission occurs and the importance of infection prevention procedures to prevent transmission.[1]

Parvovirus

Human parvovirus B19 (B19) is the cause of erythema infectiosum (Fifth disease). This is a common rash illness, usually acquired in childhood. Although rare, transmission to HCP has been reported. B19 may be transmitted through contact with infected persons, fomites, or large droplets. Infected individuals are infectious before the appearance of the rash; those with infection and aplastic crisis for up to 7 days after onset of illness; and persons with chronic infection for years. Personnel should be educated about risks and infection prevention procedures. Pregnant personnel are at no greater risk for infection. However, if acquired during the first half of pregnancy, the risk for fetal death is increased. Therefore, girls and women of childbearing age should be instructed in risk for transmission and infection prevention procedures.[1]

Respiratory Syncytial Virus

Respiratory syncytial virus (RSV) can be transmitted directly through large droplets during close contact with infected individuals. Although RSV is most common in infants and children, outbreaks have been reported in bone marrow transplant units, intensive care units, and long-term care facilities. Transmission is greatest during the early winter months. RSV can occur simultaneously with other respiratory viruses and may go unrecognized. It may not be possible to restrict personnel with viral respiratory illness during the winter. Personnel with acute respiratory infections should be excluded from caring for high-risk patients.[1]

Staphylococcal Infection or Carriage

Personnel with a draining lesion suspected to be caused by *Staphylococcus aureus (S. aureaus)* need to be excluded from patient care or food handling until appropriate culture results have ruled out infection or adequate therapy has resulted in resolution of their infection. Only those workers who are epidemiologically linked to disseminating the organism should be cultured. Culture surveys of personnel can detect carriers, but do not indicate when carriers are likely to disseminate organisms.[1]

Multidrug-resistant Organisms and Healthcare Personnel

There are no recommendations for restrictions of HCP who are colonized with multidrug-resistant organisms, such as methicillin-resistant *S. aureus* (MRSA), unless a person is epidemiologically linked to transmission within the facility. As with any active infection, HCP who have draining skin lesions should be removed from patient care activities or food handling until the person receives appropriate therapy and the infection has resolved.

Pregnant Healthcare Personnel

Pregnant HCP often express concern that they may be at increased risk for acquisition of infections because of their pregnancy. There are few instances when work restrictions are recommended for the pregnant HCP. See Chapter 104 Pregnant Healthcare Personnel.

Emerging Pathogens

Vaccinia (Smallpox)

In 1980, smallpox was eradicated as a naturally occurring disease. It is feared that this disease may be brought back as a biological weapon. Supplemental recommendations from the ACIP published in 2003 asked communities and acute care hospitals to form smallpox preparedness teams who would be vaccinated and ready to care for infected patients if there was a smallpox attack. State and local health departments have since requested that the CDC provide guidance regarding appropriate interval for revaccination of individuals who participate in the civilian smallpox responder vaccination program. The CDC has released the following recommendation.

After consideration of available scientific evidence and the practical issues relevant to pre-event vaccination, CDC recommends revaccination of volunteer responders from the pre-event smallpox program on an as-needed, "out-the-door" basis. "Out-the-door" basis is defined as receiving revaccination only after there is determination of a credible smallpox threat to public health and prior to engaging in activities involving a risk of exposure to smallpox virus. "Out-the-door" revaccination would only apply to first

responders who had been vaccinated as part of the U.S. Civilian Smallpox Preparedness and Response and had a documented vaccine "take." A "take" typically appears as a vesicle surrounded by a red areola, which becomes umbilicated and then pustular by days 7 to 11 after vaccination. Skin reactions after revaccination are typically less pronounced with more rapid progression and healing than those after primary vaccinations. The "out-the-door" recommendation would be activated only after a smallpox outbreak is confirmed or highly suspected, or there is credible evidence of a release or imminent release of smallpox virus.[23]

The vaccinia virus is similar to smallpox virus, but is less harmful and will protect against smallpox. There is a usual progression of the vaccination site and special precautions that need to be followed so as not to self-inoculate or spread to close household contacts or persons to whom they provide care.[24] The CDC has begun distribution of a new-generation smallpox vaccine, to civilian laboratory personnel, the military, and state public health preparedness programs. This is a live, vaccinia virus smallpox vaccine derived from plague purification cloning. The FDA licensed this vaccine for use in the United States in August 2007.

Severe Acute Respiratory Syndrome

There are viruses that cause respiratory infections that are well known whereas others are newly discovered, such as human metapneumovirus and Middle East respiratory syndrome coronavirus (MERS-CoV). HCP need to recognize the importance of consistently applying Standard Precautions when caring for all patients. Severe acute respiratory syndrome (SARS) serves as an example of how an emergent virus can be present in a population and go undetected as an emerging pathogen exposing unsuspecting HCP.

SARS has been transmitted within a healthcare facility, and most often the source of transmission has been an unidentified case or failure to don and remove PPE appropriately. Occupational acquisition of SARS has been documented. Therefore, the OHP in a healthcare facility that could possibly care for a patient with SARS has to include elements that address personnel issues associated with SARS.[25]

HCP should be informed that they are expected to comply with all infection prevention and public health recommendations. They should also be made aware that those recommendations may change as a SARS outbreak progresses.

An exposure reporting process needs to be established. This process should include methods for identifying exposed personnel (e.g., self-reporting by employees and logs of personnel entering the rooms of patients with SARS). Measures should be developed for symptom monitoring in accordance with public health recommendations. Systems need to be developed for HCP follow-up and possible work restrictions after unprotected exposures to patients with SARS. Personnel need to be instructed to notify each facility at which they work if any one of those facilities is providing care to SARS patients. Quarantine may be used as an exposure management tool, and appropriate measures need to be developed to help personnel comply with restriction.

HCP will need to have access to mental health professionals to help them cope with the emotional strain of managing a SARS outbreak.

Avian Influenza

Avian influenza is commonly called bird flu. Infections with avian influenza viruses in domestic poultry cause two main forms of disease. They are distinguished by low and high extremes of virulence. The low pathogenic form may go undetected and usually causes only mild symptoms. The highly pathogenic form spreads more rapidly through flocks of poultry, may cause disease that affects multiple internal organs, and has a mortality rate of 90 to 100 percent, often within 48 hours. Type A influenza viruses have many different subtypes. The subtypes differ because of changes in certain proteins on the surface of the influenza A virus (hemagglutinin [HA] and neuraminidase [NA] proteins). There are 16 known HA subtypes and nine known NA subtypes of influenza A viruses and many different combinations of HA and NA proteins are possible. Each combination represents a different subtype. All known subtypes of influenza A viruses can be found in birds. Infections with these avian influenza viruses can occur in humans. Most of the infections occurring in humans are the result of contact with infected poultry or surfaces contaminated with the secretions and/or the excretions from infected birds. Spread from one ill person to another has been reported rarely, and these reports have been limited and unsustained. It is likely that the three known A subtypes of the human influenza viruses that currently circulate among humans originally came from birds. These are H1N1, H1N2, and H3N2. The influenza A viruses are constantly changing. They may adapt over time to infect and spread among humans.[26]

Avian influenza in humans may present with typical human influenza symptoms such as fever, cough, sore throat, and muscle aches. The infection can also present as eye infections, pneumonia, severe respiratory diseases (e.g., acute respiratory distress), and other severe and life-threatening complications. The symptoms may depend on which virus caused the infection. Prescription medicines approved in the United States for human influenza viruses should work in treating avian influenza infection in humans. However, resistance to these drugs may develop, so these medications may not always be effective. Additional studies are needed to demonstrate the effectiveness of these medicines.

The avian influenza virus H5N1 has caused the largest number of detected cases of severe disease and death in humans. More than half of the people reported infected with the virus have died. However, H5N1 remains a very rare disease in humans. The virus does not infect humans easily, and person-to-person spread is difficult. Most severely ill people are more likely to be diagnosed and reported, and milder cases may go unreported. For current information about avian influenza and cumulative case numbers, see the World Health Organization (WHO) avian influenza website.

Workers' Compensation

The IP may be asked to help assess a situation to determine if a worker has experienced occupational acquisition of an infectious agent or disease. The IP should be familiar with the workers' compensation system in place within their facility.

The workers' compensation system is a wage-replacement system of disability insurance for the individual who sustains an illness or injury in the course of employment. Most expenses related to the illness or injury, including medical and other costs associated with the rehabilitation, is covered. These programs vary from state to state and country to country. The laws are designed to relieve employers of liability from common-law suits involving negligence and are based on employer-employee relationship instead of theory of negligence. The laws hold that the employers insure costs of occupational disabilities without regard to any fault involved. Most jurisdictions require employers to obtain insurance or prove financial ability to carry their own risk (e.g., self-insured). In some states the employees may choose between accepting compensation provided by law or instituting a lawsuit against the employer.[27-31]

The components of a workers' compensation program may include medical benefits, weekly compensation benefits, safety and rehabilitation programs charged to study the cause of accidents and promote prevention, and retraining of workers who are unable to return to their pre-injury status.

All states in the United States recognize responsibility for specific provisions for occupational diseases. Disease that results from occupational exposure usually is eligible for compensation if the occupational exposure is the sole cause of disease; the occupational exposure is one of several causes of the disease; the occupational exposure aggravates a pre-existing disease (e.g., asthma); or the occupational exposure hastens the onset of disability. The burden of proving that disease was occupationally acquired lies with the workers. Most states do not provide compensation for a disease that is an ordinary disease of life (e.g., stroke, heart attack).

Measuring Improvement in Preventing Occupational Exposure

When applied to occupational health and safety, surveillance involves collection, analysis, and dissemination of data on hazards that have endangered or may endanger HCP. The current emphasis is on protecting HCP from occupational acquisition of disease. There is a need to evaluate interventions and practices for effectiveness.

An epidemiological approach can be taken to manage occupational exposures.[21] Reductions or increases in injuries and exposures are monitored over time. The causes of the injuries and exposures are then identified. Variations that occur are analyzed. Prevention strategies are designed and implemented. The effectiveness of prevention strategies is tracked by comparing injury and exposure rates to previous rates. Feedback is then provided to the HCP involved in the effectiveness of the prevention strategies.

The rates of reported injuries and exposures for measuring performance improvement are calculated in the following ways:[32]

1. The average daily census of occupied beds in the institution for the same year can be used as the denominator that can be compared with other institutions. For example,

   - Total number of needlesticks reported in 1 year divided by

   - Total number of occupied beds/average daily census

   - Equals the number of needlesticks per bed per year

2. The rates can be identified per occupational category. For example,

   - Total number of needlesticks reported by nurses in 1 year divided by

   - Number of full-time equivalent nurses employed in that year

   - Equals the rate of needlesticks per full-time equivalent nurse per year

3. A device-based rate can be used to compare needlestick risk from different devices and to evaluate the effectiveness of the product design. The type of needle must be identified when each needlestick is reported. For example:

   - Number of needlesticks from device type in 1 year divided by

   - Number of that device type used or purchased in same year

   - Equals the number of needlesticks per device type in 1 year

CONCLUSIONS

The role of the IP in an OHP in a healthcare facility is to provide reassurance to personnel concerned with issues relating to infectious agents that may be encountered in the workplace. The IP may also participate in designing plans that address emerging pathogens and possible bioterrorism agents. The IP's knowledge of the principles of how infectious agents are spread and proven control measures can be invaluable when an organization is faced with the need to address an emergent situation.

As a review of the information provided in this chapter, the reader should review the two scenarios that follow and ensure understanding of actions taken.

Scenario 1: Meningococcal Exposure

A 17-year-old female Caucasian patient presented to the emergency department on a Saturday afternoon with fever, headache, nausea and vomiting, stiff neck, and a petechial rash. A spinal tap was performed, and the spinal fluid Gram stain demonstrated Gram-negative diplococci. At the time of the patient's admission, bacterial antigen panels were still performed and the one performed on her spinal fluid was positive for *Neisseria meningitidis*.

The IP noted the laboratory results on Monday morning and called the employee health department to see if the staff were aware of the situation. The employee health nurse replied that she had been receiving calls from emergency department staff that were on duty on Saturday evening. The IP and employee health nurse referred to the organization's protocol approved by the medical director to determine who should receive postexposure prophylaxis (PEP). Staff members who did not have a procedure mask in place and actually examined the oropharynx, intubated or assisted with intubation, or gave mouth-to-mouth resuscitation (for which there was no need in this case) would be offered PEP. Because the appropriate precautions recommended for meningococcal disease are Droplet Precautions, they determined that they may offer PEP to those staff members who were unprotected and assisted in the spinal tap or were within 3 feet of the patient's oropharynx.

The staff members who provided care to this patient were screened to determine potential exposure. If they met the established criteria to receive PEP, they were offered a one-time dose of ciprofloxacin 500 mg by mouth. If there was a pregnant staff member, she would have been offered a one-time dose of ceftriaxone 250 mg intramuscularly. Azithromycin in a single dose has also been effective.

Five staff members received PEP. The emergency department staff admitted they did not wear a procedure mask during the initial assessment of the patient or when performing the spinal tap. There were no secondary cases identified. Ideally, antimicrobial chemoprophylaxis should be administered less than 24 hours after identification of the index patient. Chemoprophylaxis administered more than 14 days after onset of illness in the index patient is probably of limited or no value.[33]

Scenario 2: Disseminated Herpes Zoster and Susceptible Healthcare Personnel

A 24-year-old female RN who works in a community acute care hospital provided a history of never having chickenpox during her post-hire assessment. This history was confirmed when the results of her varicella zoster antibody indicated she was susceptible. She received two doses of the varicella vaccine and was instructed to report any exposures to varicella in the community or in the hospital. One evening she admitted a patient to the medical unit who had a generalized rash. The following day the physician diagnosed the patient's vesicular rash as disseminated shingles (herpes zoster), and the patient was placed in Airborne Isolation as well as Contact Precautions.

The RN reported her unprotected exposure to the employee health service. She was monitored daily during days 10 to 21 after her exposure. The process was for her to report to employee health service each day she was on duty during this time period to determine whether any of the following symptoms were present: fever, skin lesions, or systemic symptoms. On the days that she was not on duty she was to call the employee health service if any symptoms occurred.

She did not exhibit any evidence of acquiring varicella from this exposure.

If this RN had been pregnant, she would have been referred to her obstetrician to consider whether she should receive VZIG because of the exposure. If she had received VZIG, her monitoring would have been extended from 21 to 28 days after her exposure because VZIG may delay the onset of disease.

FUTURE TRENDS

The potential of emerging pathogens yet to be identified is real. The IP plays a vital role in ongoing education of the worker population and as an advisor to administration when planning for an event. HCP need to recognize the importance of hand hygiene practices, Standard Precautions, respiratory hygiene, and Transmission-based Precautions to reduce the risk for transmission within the healthcare facility and into the community.

INTERNATIONAL PERSPECTIVE

The SARS outbreak of 2003 began in one country and spread to other continents by way of international travel. This epidemic demonstrated the need for all countries to be vigilant about the incidence of infectious diseases worldwide. In April 2012 another viral respiratory illness caused by a coronavirus was first reported in Saudi Arabia and has been linked to four countries on the Arabian Peninsula. Referred to as MERS-CoV, concern worldwide exists regarding the potential for spread to additional countries.[34] The literature has reported the spread of vaccine-preventable diseases introduced into a previously vaccinated but waning population from individuals who traveled from areas where vaccinations were not as prevalent or readily available.

When planning an OHP for a healthcare facility, consideration needs to be made for the incidence of infectious diseases identified in the community that may be introduced into the HCP pool. The infectious diseases may differ from country to country and from areas within a country.

REFERENCES

1. Centers for Disease Control and Prevention. Guidelines for infection control in the healthcare worker, 1998. *Am J Infect Control* 1998;26:289–354.
2. Division of Nosocomial and Occupational Infections, Bureau of Infectious Diseases, Centre for Infectious Disease Prevention and Control. *Prevention and Control of Occupational Infections in Health Care: Infection Control Guidelines.* Ottawa, Ontario, Canada: Health Canada, 2002:28S1.
3. Shefer A, Atkinson W, Friedman C, et al. Immunization of health-care personnel: Recommendations of the Advisory Committee on Immunization Practices (ACIP). *MMRW Recomm Rep* 2011;60(RR07):1–45.
4. Centers for Disease Control and Prevention. Guidelines for preventing the transmission of Mycobacterium tuberculosis in health-care settings, 2005. *MMWR Recomm Rep* 2005;54:1–144.
5. U.S. Department of Labor. *Enforcement policy and procedures for occupational exposure to tuberculosis, OSHA instruction.* Washington, DC: Occupational Safety and Health Administration, U.S. Department of Labor, 1993.
6. Occupational Safety and Health Administration (OSHA). General Duty Clause. OSHA website. 2013. Available at: https://www.osha.gov/pls/oshaweb/owadisp.show_document?p_id=3359&p_table=oshact.
7. Centers for Disease Control and Prevention (CDC). Division of Tuberculosis Elimination. *Interferon-Gamma Release Assays (IGRAs) – Blood Tests for TB Infection.* Fact Sheets. CDC website. 2011. Available at: http://www.cdc.gov/tb/publications/factsheets/.
8. Layne RD. The OSHA interpretation of respiratory protection requirements with regards to tuberculosis (TB) exposure. OSHA website. 2004. Available at: http://www.osha.gov/pls/oshaweb/owadisp.show_document?p_table=INTERPRETATIONS&p_id=24895.
9. Shalouh DG. The OSHA interpretation of tuberculosis and respiratory protection enforcement. OSHA website. 2008. Available at: http://www.osha.gov/pls/oshaweb/owadisp.show_document?p_table=Interpretations&p_id=26013.
10. Centers for Disease Control and Prevention. Updated U.S. Public Health Service guidelines for the management of occupational exposures to HIV and recommendations for post-exposure prophylaxis. *MMWR Recomm Rep* 2005;54:1–18.
11. U.S. Department of Labor. 29 CFR Part 1910.1030. Occupational exposure to bloodborne pathogens: final rule. *Fed Regist* 1991;56:64174–64182.
12. U.S. Department of Labor. 29 CFR Part 1910.1030. Occupational exposure to bloodborne pathogens; needle-stick and other sharps injuries: final rule. *Fed Regist* 2001;55:5317–5325.
13. Centers for Disease Control and Prevention. A comprehensive immunization strategy to eliminate transmission of hepatitis B virus infection in the United States: recommendations of the Advisory Committee on Immunization Practices (ACIP). *MMWR Recomm Rep* 2006;54:1–23.
14. Centers for Disease Control and Prevention. Updated U.S. Public Health Service guidelines for the management of occupational exposures to HBV, HCV, and HIV and recommendations for post-exposure prophylaxis. *MMWR Recomm Rep* 2001;50:1–52.
15. Centers for Disease Control and Prevention. Prevention of varicella: recommendations of the Advisory Committee on Immunization Practices (ACIP). *MMWR Recomm Rep* 2007;56:1–40.
16. Centers for Disease Control and Prevention. Recommended adult immunization schedule: United States, 2013. *J Midwifery Womens Health* 2013;58(2):215–220.
17. Advisory Committee for Immunization Practices. Notice to readers: revised ACIP recommendations for avoiding pregnancy after receiving a rubella-containing vaccine. *MMWR Morb Mortal Wkly Rep* 2001;50:1117.
18. Centers for Disease Control and Prevention. Updated recommendations for isolation of persons with mumps. *MMWR Morb Mortal Wkly Rep* 2008;57:1103–1105.
19. Shefer A, Atkinson W, Friedman C, et al. Immunization of health-care personnel, Recommendations of the Advisory Committee on Immunization Practices. *MMWR* 2011;60(RR07):1–45.
20. Centers for Disease Control and Prevention. Prevention and control of influenza: recommendations of the Advisory Committee on Immunization Practices (ACIP). *MMWR Recomm Rep* 2013;62(RR07):1–43.
21. Talbot TR, Babcock H, Caplan AL, et al. Revised SHEA Position Paper: Influenza Vaccination of Healthcare Personnel. Vanderbilt website. 2010. Available at: http://www.mc.vanderbilt.edu/documents/infectioncontrol/files/2010%20Revised%20SHEA%20PP%20HCW%20Fluvax%20FINAL.pdf.
22. Centers for Disease Control and Prevention. Prevention of herpes zoster: recommendations of the Advisory Committee on Immunization Practices (ACIP). *MMWR Recomm Rep* 2008;57:1–30.
23. Centers for Disease Control and Prevention (CDC). Information for people selected for smallpox response teams. CDC website. 2009. Available at: http://emergency.cdc.gov/agent/smallpox/responseteams.asp.
24. Centers for Disease Control and Prevention. Smallpox vaccination and adverse reactions: guidance for clinicians. *MMWR Recomm Rep* 2003;52:1–28.
25. Centers for Disease Control and Prevention (CDC). Severe acute respiratory syndrome (SARS). CDC website. 2013. Available at: http://www.cdc.gov/sars/index.html.
26. Centers for Disease Control and Prevention (CDC). Information on Avian Influenza. CDC website. 2014. Available at: http://www.cdc.gov/flu/avianflu/.
27. U.S. Chamber of Commerce. *Analysis of Workers' Compensation Laws.* Washington, DC: US Government Printing Office, 1993.
28. Felton JS. The injured worker and learned helplessness. *Occup Environ Med Rep* 1994;8:45–48.
29. Martin JM. Stress-related workers' compensation claims. *Am Assoc Occup Health News J* 1992;40(suppl B):370–375.
30. Boden LI. Workers' compensation. In: Levy BS, Wegeman A, eds. *Occupational Health: Recognizing and Preventing Work-Related Diseases.* Boston: Little, Brown, 1995.
31. Pozgar GDS. Labor relations. In: *Legal Aspects of Healthcare Administration*, 5th ed. Gaithersburg, MD: Aspen, 1993:449–476.
32. Jagger J. Calculating needle-stick rates. In: *BD Safety Compliance Initiative Exposure Prevention Information Network.* Franklin Lakes, NJ: Becton Dickinson, 1992.

33. Centers for Disease Control and Prevention (CDC). Pink Book. Chapter 13 Meningococcal Disease. CDC website. 2012. Available at: http://www.cdc.gov/vaccines/pubs/pinkbook/mening.html.
34. Centers for Disease Control and Prevention (CDC). Middle East Respiratory Syndrome: Interim guidelines for healthcare providers. CDC website. 2013. Available at http://www.cdc.gov/coronavirus/mers/interim-guidance.html.

SUPPLEMENTAL RESOURCES

U.S. Department of Health and Human Services. *TB Respiratory Protection Program in Health Care Facilities: Administrator's Guide.* Publication No. 99-143. Washington, DC: Department of Health and Human Services, 1999.

Websites

Association for Professionals in Infection Control and Epidemiology, Inc. Available at: http://www.apic.org.

Centers for Disease Control and Prevention. Available at: http://www.cdc.gov.

International Federation of Infection Control. Available at: http://www.ific.narod.ru/manual/occup.htm.

Occupational Safety and Health Administration. Available at: http://www.osha.gov.

Public Health Agency of Canada. Infectious Diseases. Available at: http://www.phac-aspc.gc.ca/id-mi/index-eng.php.

Society of Healthcare Epidemiologists of America. Available at: http://www.shea-online.org/.

Occupational Exposure to Bloodborne Pathogens

Sonia Miller, RN, BSN, MSN, CIC
Chief, Infection Prevention & Control
Fort Belvoir Community Hospital
Fort Belvoir, VA

ABSTRACT

Preventing transmission of bloodborne viruses in healthcare settings requires a multifaceted approach, including promoting Hepatitis B vaccination of all healthcare personnel who may have contact with blood or body fluids, considering all patients as potentially infectious, using appropriate barriers to prevent blood and body fluid contact, preventing percutaneous injuries by eliminating unnecessary needle use, implementing devices with safety features, using safe work practices when handling needles and other sharp devices, and safely disposing of sharps and blood-contaminated materials. Postexposure management is also an integral component of a complete program to prevent infection following bloodborne pathogen exposure and an important element of workplace safety. This chapter focuses on the risk and management of occupational blood exposures.

KEY CONCEPTS

- Prevention of occupational blood exposures is the primary way to reduce transmission of Hepatitis B virus, Hepatitis C virus, and human immunodeficiency virus among healthcare personnel.

- Healthcare personnel who may come into contact with blood and body fluids should be vaccinated against Hepatitis B.

- The risk of Hepatitis B virus seroconversion after a percutaneous injury ranges from 23 to 62 percent depending on the Hepatitis B e antigen status of the source person.

- The average risk of seroconversion after a percutaneous injury involving blood infected with Hepatitis C virus is approximately 1.8 percent.

- The average risk of seroconversion after a percutaneous injury involving blood infected with human immunodeficiency virus is approximately 0.3 percent.

- All healthcare personnel taking human immunodeficiency virus postexposure prophylaxis should be evaluated within 48 to 72 hours after exposure and monitored for drug toxicity for at least 2 weeks.

- Healthcare organizations and facilities should set up programs to prevent exposure to bloodborne viruses and to manage cases of exposure if they occur.

BACKGROUND

Exposure to bloodborne pathogens poses a serious risk to healthcare personnel (HCP). Avoiding occupational blood exposures through adherence to Standard Precautions and other safe work practices is essential. The most effective means to prevent transmission of Hepatitis B virus (HBV), Hepatitis C virus (HCV), and human immunodeficiency virus (HIV) in healthcare settings include Hepatitis B vaccination, the use of appropriate barriers to prevent blood and body fluid contact, and preventing percutaneous injuries by eliminating unnecessary needle use, implementing devices with safety features, using safe work practices when handling needles and other sharp devices, and safely disposing of sharps and blood-contaminated materials. Despite improved methods of preventing exposure, occupational exposures continue to occur. In this chapter, we provide information about HBV, HCV, and HIV infection and review the risk and management of occupational blood exposure, including recommendations for postexposure prophylaxis (PEP).

BASIC PRINCIPLES

Definition of Healthcare Personnel and Exposure

In this context, healthcare personnel (HCP) is defined as all persons (e.g., employees, students, contractors, attending clinicians, public safety workers, or volunteers) whose activities involve contact with patients or with blood or other body fluids from patients in a healthcare, laboratory, or public safety setting.[1,2]

An exposure that might place HCP at risk for HBV, HCV, or HIV infection is defined as a percutaneous injury (e.g., a needlestick or cut with a sharp object) or contact of mucous membrane or nonintact skin (e.g., exposed skin that is chapped, abraded, or afflicted with dermatitis) with blood, tissue, or other body fluids that are potentially infectious.[1-3] The probability of infection after exposure of a susceptible person depends on the route of exposure, the concentration of infectious virions in the implicated body fluid, the volume of infective material transferred, and, for HBV, the susceptibility of the exposed person.

In addition to blood and body fluids containing visible blood, semen and vaginal secretions are also considered potentially infectious. Although semen and vaginal secretions have been implicated in the sexual transmission of HBV, HCV, and HIV, they have not been implicated in occupational transmission from patients to HCP. The following fluids also are considered potentially infectious: cerebrospinal fluid, synovial fluid, pleural fluid, peritoneal fluid, pericardial fluid, and amniotic fluid. The risk for transmission of HBV, HCV, and HIV infection from these fluids is unknown; the potential risk to the HCP from occupational exposures to these fluids has not been assessed by epidemiologic studies in healthcare settings. Feces, nasal secretions, saliva, sputum, sweat, tears, urine, and vomitus are not considered potentially infectious unless they contain blood. The risk for transmission of HBV, HCV, and HIV infection from these fluids and materials is extremely low.

Any direct contact (i.e., contact without barrier protection) to concentrated virus in a research laboratory or production facility is considered an exposure that requires clinical evaluation. For human bites, the clinical evaluation must include the possibility that both the person bitten and the person who inflicted the bite were exposed to bloodborne pathogens. Transmission of HBV or HIV infection by this route has rarely been reported.[4-6]

BLOODBORNE PATHOGENS AND OCCUPATIONAL EXPOSURE

Hepatitis B Virus

Epidemiology

HBV is transmitted by percutaneous or mucosal exposure to infectious blood or body fluids. HBV is comparatively stable in the environment; it is resistant to drying, simple detergents, and alcohol; and it has been found to remain viable at room temperatures for 7 days or longer.[7,8] Infectious levels of HBV DNA can be detected on environmental surfaces in the absence of visible blood.[7]

For adults, the two primary sources of HBV infection are sexual contact and percutaneous exposure to blood.[7] Among susceptible HCP, in the absence of PEP, the risk of HBV infection after a needlestick injury is 37 to 62 percent if the source patient is Hepatitis B e antigen (HBeAg) positive and 23 to 37 percent if the patient is HBeAg negative.[2] Because infected patients can have high concentrations of HBV in blood or body fluids and HBV is stable at ambient temperatures, transmission of HBV also can occur in healthcare settings through less apparent modes, such as exposure to contaminated environmental surfaces or equipment that has been inadequately disinfected or through exposures of nonintact skin. Many of the infections that occurred before widespread vaccination of HCP likely resulted from such exposures (e.g., inoculation into cutaneous scratches, lesions, or mucosal surfaces).[2,8,9] The estimated number of HBV infections among HCP in the United States has decreased from more than 10,000 in 1983 to fewer than 400 in 2002.[8]

Clinical Features

HBV infection can produce either asymptomatic or symptomatic infection. The average incubation period is 90 days (range: 60 to 150 days) from exposure to onset of jaundice and 60 days (range: 40 to 90 days) from exposure to onset of abnormal serum alanine aminotransferase (ALT) levels. HBV infection results in clinically apparent hepatitis in about one-third of acutely infected adults. Jaundice, dark urine, and scleral icterus usually are present by the time patients seek medical attention. The most striking laboratory findings are extreme elevations in the serum aminotransferase levels. ALT and aspartate aminotransferase (AST) levels may be elevated to more than 10 times the normal levels, whereas the alkaline phosphatase levels are increased to a much lesser extent. The fatality rate among persons with reported cases of acute Hepatitis B is 0.5 to 1.0 percent, with the highest rates in adults older than 60 years.[7] Among adults with acute HBV infection, less than 5 percent progress to chronic HBV infection and are at risk for chronic hepatitis, cirrhosis, and primary hepatocellular carcinoma.

Laboratory Diagnosis

Hepatitis B is differentiated from other causes of hepatitis by serologic assays (Table 101-1).[7,9] Several well-defined antigen-antibody systems are associated with HBV infection, including Hepatitis B surface antigen (HBsAg) and antibody to Hepatitis B surface antigen (anti-HBs); Hepatitis B core antigen (HBcAg) and anti-HBc; and HBeAg and antibody to HBeAg (anti-HBe). Serologic assays are commercially available for all of these except HBcAg because no free HBcAg circulates in blood. These markers of HBV infection change over time, with different patterns seen in patients with acute infection that resolves and patients with chronic infection (Table 101-1).

Transient HBsAg positivity has been reported for as long as 18 days after Hepatitis B vaccination and is clinically insignificant.[7] Otherwise, the presence of HBsAg is indicative of ongoing HBV infection and potential infectiousness. In newly infected persons, HBsAg is present in serum 6 to 60 days (mean, 30 days) after exposure to HBV and persists for variable periods. Anti-HBc develops in all HBV infections, appearing at onset of symptoms or liver test abnormalities in acute HBV infection, rising rapidly to high levels, and persisting for life. Acute or recently acquired infection can be distinguished by the presence of the immunoglobulin M (IgM) class of anti-HBc, which persists for approximately 6 months.

In persons who recover from HBV infection, HBsAg is eliminated from the blood and anti-HBs develop, typically within 3 to 4 months. The presence of anti-HBs indicates immunity from HBV infection. After recovery from natural infection, most persons will be positive for both anti-HBs and anti-HBc, whereas only anti-HBs develop in persons who are successfully vaccinated against Hepatitis B. The persistence of HBsAg for 6 months after the diagnosis of acute HBV is indicative of progression to chronic HBV infection. Persons who do not recover from HBV infection and become chronically infected remain

Table 101-1. Interpretation of Patterns of Hepatitis B Virus Serologic Markers

Serologic Markers				
HBsAg	**Total Anti-HBc**	**IgM Anti-HBc**	**Anti-HBs**	**Interpretation**
–	–	–	–	Susceptible, never infected
+	–	–	–	Acute infection, early incubation**
+	+	+	–	Acute resolving infection
+	–	–	–	Acute resolving infection
–	+	–	+	Past infection, recovered and immune
+	+	–	–	Chronic infection
–	+	–	–	False positive (i.e., susceptible), past infection, or "low-level" chronic infection
–	–	–	+	Immune if titer is ≥10 mIU/mL

Abbreviations: HBsAg, Hepatitis B surface antigen; Anti-HBc, antibody to Hepatitis B core antigen. The total anti-HBc assay detects both IgM and IgG antibody; IgM, immunoglobulin M; Anti-HBs, antibody to Hepatitis B surface antigen; +, positive; –, negative.

**Transient HBsAg positivity (lasting 18 days or less) might be detected in some patients during vaccination.

Adapted from Table 1, Recommendations for preventing transmission of infections among chronic hemodialysis patients. *MMWR Recomm Rep* 2001 Apr 26;50(No. RR-05):1–43.

positive for HBsAg (and anti-HBc), though a small proportion (0.5 to 2 percent per year) clear HBsAg and develop anti-HBs.[7]

HBeAg can be detected in the serum of persons with acute or chronic HBV infection. The presence of HBeAg correlates with viral replication and high levels of virus (i.e., high infectivity). Anti-HBe correlates with the loss of replicating virus and with lower levels of virus. However, all HBsAg-positive persons should be considered potentially infectious, regardless of their HBeAg or anti-HBe status. HBV infection can also be detected using qualitative or quantitative tests for HBV DNA. These tests are most commonly used for patients being managed with antiviral therapy.

Treatment, Prevention, and Control

No specific treatment exists for acute Hepatitis B; supportive care is the mainstay of therapy. Persons who have chronic HBV infection require medical evaluation and regular monitoring. The initial evaluation of patients with chronic HBV infection includes history, physical examination, and laboratory testing to assess the following: liver disease, HBV replication (e.g., HBeAg, anti-HBe, and HBV DNA), and viral coinfections.[10] Therapeutic agents approved by the U.S. Food and Drug Administration (FDA) for treatment of chronic Hepatitis B can achieve sustained suppression of HBV replication and remission of liver disease in certain persons. At present, seven drugs are licensed in the United States for the treatment of HBV infection: interferon alfa, pegylated interferon alfa-2a, lamivudine, adefovir, entecavir, telbivudine, and tenofovir.[10,11] Persons with chronic HBV infection can benefit from counseling regarding ways to prevent transmitting HBV infection to others.[7,12,13] Vaccination of sexual and household contacts is recommended to prevent transmission.[7,12]

Hepatitis B vaccination is the most effective measure to prevent HBV infection and its consequences.[7] Hepatitis B vaccine provides both pre- and postexposure protection against HBV infection. The currently available vaccines in the United States are produced by recombinant DNA technology. Three intramuscular doses of Hepatitis B vaccine induce a protective antibody response in more than 90 percent of healthy recipients. Adults who develop a protective antibody response are protected from clinical disease and chronic infection. The duration of vaccine protection is under investigation, but available evidence indicates that nearly all vaccinated persons remain protected against HBV infection.[7] HCP at ongoing risk for percutaneous injuries should be tested 1 to 2 months after completion of the three-dose vaccination series for anti-HBs.[2] Factors associated with a lack of response include improper vaccination (e.g., improperly stored vaccine, gluteal inoculation, subcutaneous injection, improperly timed dosing), obesity, older age, and smoking. Persons who do not experience response to the primary vaccine series should receive a second three-dose series or be evaluated for HBsAg positivity. Booster doses of Hepatitis B vaccine are not necessary, and periodic serologic testing to monitor antibody concentrations after completion of the vaccine series is not recommended.

Since 1982, substantial progress has been made toward reducing the risk for HBV infection in adults.[7,14] The Occupational Safety and Health Administration's (OSHA's) Bloodborne Pathogen Standard mandates provision of Hepatitis B vaccine at no cost to all HCP and others at occupational risk for blood exposure.[15] The substantial declines in the incidence of acute Hepatitis B that have occurred among HCP have been attributed to implementation of Standard Precautions in healthcare settings, use of sharps with safety features, increasing levels of Hepatitis B vaccination coverage among HCP, and use of PEP.[8]

Postexposure Prophylaxis

The need for prophylaxis for persons sustaining accidental percutaneous or mucosal exposures to blood should be based on several factors, including the HBsAg status of the source and the Hepatitis B vaccination and vaccine-response status of

Table 101-2. Recommended Postexposure Prophylaxis for Exposure to Hepatitis B Virus

Vaccination and Antibody Response Status of Exposed HCP*	Treatment		
	Source HBsAg[†] Positive	Source HBsAg[†] Negative	Source Unknown or Not Available for Testing
Unvaccinated	HBIG§ × 1 and initiate Hepatitis B vaccine series	Initiate Hepatitis B vaccine series	Initiate Hepatitis B vaccine series
Previously vaccinated			
Known responder[¶]	No treatment	No treatment	No treatment
Known nonresponder**	HBIG × 1 and initiate revaccination or HBIG × 2[††]	No treatment	If known high-risk source, treat as if source were HBsAg positive
Antibody response unknown	Test exposed person for anti-HBs§§ 1. If adequate,[¶] no treatment is necessary 2. If inadequate,** HBIG × 1 and vaccine booster	No treatment	Test exposed person for anti-HBs: 1. If adequate, no treatment is necessary 2. If inadequate, administer vaccine booster and recheck titer in 1–2 months

*Persons who have previously been infected with HBV are immune to reinfection and do not require postexposure prophylaxis.

[†]Hepatitis B surface antigen.

§Hepatitis B immune globulin; dose is 0.06 mL/kg intramuscularly.

[¶]A responder is a person with adequate levels of serum antibody to HBsAg (i.e., anti-HBs ≥10 mIU/mL).

**A nonresponder is a person with inadequate response to vaccination (i.e., serum anti-HBs <10 mIU/mL).

[††]The option of giving one dose of HBIG and reinitiating the vaccine series is preferred for nonresponders who have not completed a second three-dose vaccine series. For persons who previously completed a second vaccine series but did not respond, two doses of HBIG are preferred.

§§Antibody to HBsAg.

Source: CDC. http://www.cdc.gov/mmwr/preview/mmwrhtml/rr5011a1.htm

the exposed person. Such exposures usually involve persons for whom Hepatitis B vaccination is recommended. Any blood or body fluid exposure to unvaccinated HCP should lead to initiation of the Hepatitis B vaccine series. Table 101-2 summarizes recommendations for prophylaxis after percutaneous or mucosal exposure to blood according to the HBsAg status of the exposure source and the vaccination and vaccine-response status of the exposed person.[2]

When Hepatitis B immune globulin (HBIG) is indicated, it should be administered as soon as possible after exposure (preferably within 24 hours). The effectiveness of HBIG when administered later than 7 days after exposure is unknown. When Hepatitis B vaccine is indicated, it should also be administered as soon as possible (preferably within 24 hours) and can be administered simultaneously with HBIG at a separate site (vaccine should always be administered in the deltoid muscle).[2]

For exposed persons who are in the process of being vaccinated but have not completed the vaccination series, vaccination should be completed as scheduled, and HBIG should be added as indicated (Table 101-2). Persons exposed to HBsAg-positive blood or body fluids that are known not to have a response to a primary vaccine series should receive a single dose of HBIG and should reinitiate the Hepatitis B vaccine series with the first dose of the Hepatitis B vaccine as soon as possible after exposure. Alternatively, they should receive two doses of HBIG, one dose as soon as possible after exposure, and the second dose 1 month later. The option of administering one dose of HBIG and reinitiating the vaccine series is preferred for nonresponders who did not complete a second three-dose vaccine series. For persons who previously completed a second vaccine series but did not develop a response, two doses of HBIG are preferred.[2]

Hepatitis C Virus

Epidemiology

HCV infection is the most common chronic bloodborne infection in the United States, affecting an estimated 3.2 million persons.[16] HCV-associated end-stage liver disease is the most frequent indication for liver transplantation among U.S. adults.[17]

The incubation period for acute HCV infection ranges from 2 to 24 weeks (averaging 6 to 7 weeks).[17] HCV transmission occurs primarily through exposure to infected blood. Injection drug use remains the most commonly identified risk factor for transmission, but other transmission modes include transfusion and solid organ transplantation from infected donors, unsafe medical practices, occupational exposure to infected blood, birth to an infected mother, and sex with an infected partner.

HCP exposed to infected blood through needlestick injuries may acquire HCV infection; the transmission risk per exposure is approximately 1.8 percent.[2] Injuries resulting in deep punctures or wounds with bleeding and procedures involving a needle placed in a patient's artery or vein increase the risk of HCV transmission.[18] Transmission rarely occurs from mucous membrane exposures to blood, and, more rarely, has been documented from nonintact skin exposures to blood.[19]

Data are limited on survival of HCV in the environment. Degradation of HCV occurs when serum containing HCV is left at room temperature. Specific animal infectivity studies have shown survival as long as 16 hours but not longer than 4 days.[20] The potential for environmental survival of HCV suggests that environmental contamination with blood containing HCV could pose a risk for transmission in the healthcare setting. The risk for transmission from exposure to fluids or tissues other than HCV-infected blood has not been quantified but is expected to be low. HCV is not known to be transmissible through the airborne route or through casual contact in the workplace.

Clinical Features

HCV infection produces a spectrum of clinical illness similar to that of HBV infection and is indistinguishable from other forms of viral hepatitis based on clinical symptoms alone. Serologic tests are necessary to establish a specific diagnosis of Hepatitis C. Most adults acutely infected with HCV are asymptomatic. After acute infection, 15 to 25 percent of persons appear to resolve their infection without sequelae, as defined by sustained absence of HCV RNA in serum and normalization of ALT levels.[17] Chronic HCV infection develops in most people (75 to 85 percent); 60 to 70 percent of these chronically infected people have persistent or fluctuating ALT elevations, indicating active liver disease. Thus, a single ALT determination cannot be used to exclude ongoing hepatic injury, and long-term follow-up of patients with HCV infection is required to determine their clinical outcome or prognosis.

The course of chronic liver disease is usually insidious, progressing slowly without symptoms or physical signs in the majority of patients during the first two or more decades after infection.[17] Chronic Hepatitis C frequently is not recognized until asymptomatic persons are identified as HCV-positive during blood-donor screening or elevated ALT levels are detected during routine physical examinations. Most studies have reported that cirrhosis develops in 10 to 20 percent of persons with chronic Hepatitis C over a period of 20 to 30 years, and hepatocellular carcinoma in 1 to 5 percent, with striking geographic variations in rates of this disease. However, when cirrhosis is established, the rate of development of hepatocellular carcinoma might be as high as 1 to 4 percent per year.

Laboratory Diagnosis

Laboratory testing is necessary to establish a specific diagnosis of Hepatitis C.[9,17,21] The two major types of tests available for the laboratory diagnosis of HCV infections are serologic assays for antibodies to HCV (anti-HCV) and nucleic acid tests to detect HCV RNA. Testing for anti-HCV is recommended for initially identifying persons with HCV infection and includes initial screening with an immunoassay, and, if positive, confirmation by an additional, more specific, assay.[21] Anti-HCV may be detected within 5 to 6 weeks after the onset of infection, but it is not possible to determine if someone has acute, chronic, or past infection with an anti-HCV test. HCV RNA may be detected within 1 to 2 weeks of exposure to the virus and several weeks before elevations of ALT and detection of anti-HCV.

Treatment, Prevention, and Control

HCV-positive persons benefit from evaluation for the presence and severity of chronic liver disease.[17] Antiviral therapy is recommended for persons with persistently elevated ALT levels, detectable HCV RNA, and a liver biopsy that indicates either portal or bridging fibrosis or moderate degrees of inflammation and necrosis. No clear consensus exists on whether to treat patients with persistently normal serum transaminases. Successful treatment eliminates viremia and the potential for HCV transmission and further chronic liver disease.[22,23] In randomized clinical trials, the highest response rates have been achieved with the combination of weekly subcutaneous injections of long-acting peginterferon alfa and oral ribavirin. This combination of drugs has resulted in virus elimination (sustained virologic response) in 40 to 50 percent of treated persons infected with genotypes 1 or 4 and in 75 to 85 percent of those infected with genotypes 2 or 3.[22,23]

No vaccine against HCV infection exists. National recommendations for prevention and control of HCV infection, issued in 1998, emphasize primary prevention activities to reduce the risk for HCV transmission.[17] These activities include screening and testing of blood donors, viral inactivation of plasma-derived products, risk-reduction counseling and screening of persons at risk for HCV infection, and adherence to Standard Precautions and safe work practices in healthcare settings.

Postexposure Management

PEP with immunoglobulin antiviral agents or immunomodulators is not recommended after exposure to HCV-positive blood.[2,24] There is currently no PEP for HCV; the intent of current U.S. recommendations for postexposure management is to achieve early identification of chronic infection and, if present, referral to a specialist knowledgeable in this area for additional follow-up and medical management.[2]

According to U.S. Public Health Service guidelines, HCP who have been exposed to an HCV-positive source should have baseline testing for anti-HCV and ALT activity performed, followed by testing for anti-HCV and ALT activity at 4 to 6 months after the exposure to detect infection. These guidelines also indicate that testing for HCV RNA may be performed 4 to 6 weeks after exposure if earlier detection of infection is desired.[2]

Early detection strategies, which call for more frequent and aggressive testing to monitor the exposed individual, have been advocated for several reasons.[24,25] First, this approach might help alleviate some of the worker's stress and anxiety associated with the exposure or reduce loss to follow-up.[25] Second, limited data indicate that antiviral therapy might be most effective when started early in the course of HCV infection.[2,22,24,25] Although the optimal timing for initiating treatment has not been determined, current practice guidelines support a delay of 2 to 4 months after acute onset to allow for spontaneous clearance.[22] This issue is further complicated by additional questions regarding optimal treatment regimens and duration of treatment.[22] The need for experienced providers to evaluate and discuss treatment options underscores the importance of appropriate medical referrals and counseling as part of HCV postexposure management.[2,24]

Human Immunodeficiency Virus

Epidemiology

In the United States, approximately 1.1 million adults and adolescents were living with HIV by the end of 2006.[26] The primary means of acquiring infection among adults involves the exchange of body fluids through unprotected sexual intercourse with an infected partner and injection drug use using shared needles and syringes. The virus also can be perinatally transmitted to children born to infected mothers. Since 1985, all donated blood in the United States is screened for HIV. The risk of HIV infection due to transfusion of screened blood products is estimated to be 2 per 1 million units transfused.[27] Screening does not eliminate the potential for a seronegative but infected unit from a recently infected donor to escape detection.

HIV is not transmitted by the airborne route, household or workplace contact with infected persons, exposure to contaminated environmental surfaces, or insect vectors. The virus is easily inactivated by most common disinfectants; including household bleach (diluted 1:10 to 1:100).[1]

Groups of workers at risk for acquiring HIV infection occupationally are HCP and other workers in contact with blood or other body fluids who sustain accidental percutaneous or mucosal inoculations with HIV-infected material. The magnitude of risk depends on the severity of exposure, but, on the average, is about 0.3 percent after percutaneous injury. The risk for infection following mucosal exposures is estimated to be lower, at approximately 0.09 percent. In the absence of direct exposure, HCP are not at occupational risk for HIV infection. In the United States, through December 2006, 57 HCP have been documented as having seroconverted to HIV following occupational exposures.[28] In addition, 140 other cases of HIV infection or AIDS have occurred among HCP who have not reported other risk factors for HIV infection and who report a history of occupational exposure to blood, body fluids, or HIV-infected laboratory material, but for whom seroconversion after exposure was not documented. The number of these workers who acquired their infection through occupational exposures is unknown.

Clinical Features and Laboratory Diagnosis

The clinical course of HIV infection is variable and changing with the advent of antiretroviral therapy and treatment and prophylaxis for infectious complications. Early after infection, within a few weeks to months, an acute flu-like febrile illness characterized by malaise, pharyngitis, lymphadenopathy, maculopapular rash, and headache may occur. At initial presentation of such patients, HIV antibody screening tests (EIA) may be negative, but viral antigen (p24 antigen) and nucleic acid amplification testing (e.g., polymerase chain reaction) allow the diagnosis to be established at this stage.

Following initial infection, most persons have generalized asymptomatic lymphadenopathy and appear well. However, laboratory tests document a gradual decline in the number of circulating T-helper lymphocytes (CD4 cells) beginning soon after infection and continuing over the next several years. T-helper cells are essential components of the immune system and mediate aspects of both cellular and humoral immunity.

In the absence of therapy, symptoms, signs, and illness suggestive of mild to moderate immunodeficiency appear after about

5 years, when CD4 cells decrease by about 50 percent, to less than 500 cells/mm³. Intermittent fever, oral thrush, bacterial pneumonia, enteric infections, and reactivated tuberculosis (TB) are typically diagnosed at this time. When CD4 cell counts fall below 200 cells/mm³, serious opportunistic infections can occur. Pneumocystis pneumonia (PCP) was the most common index diagnosis in the first 5 years of the epidemic, but the advent of effective prophylaxis and highly active combination antiretroviral therapy has decreased the incidence of PCP. The incidence of other opportunistic infections and malignancies, including Kaposi's sarcoma, lymphoma, disseminated TB, toxoplasmosis, and cryptococcal meningitis, also has decreased.

With the exception of TB, the infectious complications of HIV infection generally are not transmissible to healthy persons and pose no risk in the workplace. Indeed, the causative organisms of these complications (e.g., Candida and Toxoplasma) are ubiquitous, and most adults have already been exposed. Opportunistic infections in HIV-infected patients usually represent reactivation of dormant organisms when the immune system can no longer keep them inactive.

Treatment, Prevention, and Control

Treatment should be offered to all patients with symptoms ascribed to HIV infection and all patients with CD4 cell counts below 350 cells/mm³.[29] Recommendations for offering antiretroviral therapy in asymptomatic patients requires analysis of many real and potential risks and benefits. Information from clinical trials regarding the treatment of acute HIV infection is very limited. Ongoing clinical trials are addressing the question of the long-term clinical benefit of potent treatment regimens for primary infection. Antiretroviral therapy should also be initiated in pregnant women, patients with HIV-associated nephropathy, and patients coinfected with HBV when treatment is indicated, regardless of CD4 T-cell count. Prior to initiating antiretroviral therapy, all patients should undergo HIV drug-resistance testing (preferably genotype testing in antiretroviral-naive patients) and be screened for HLA-B*5701 before an abacavir-containing regimen is used. If antiretroviral therapy is initiated, the goals of therapy should include maximal and durable suppression of viral load, restoration and/or preservation of immunologic function, improvement of quality of life, and reduction of HIV-related morbidity and mortality.[29]

People at risk for direct contact with blood and other potentially infected materials should receive specific instruction in Standard Precautions, as recommended by the Centers for Disease Control and Prevention (CDC)[1,3,30] and mandated by OSHA.[15] For most environments outside of healthcare settings, common sense and attention to personal hygiene are adequate to protect workers. Gloves should be worn to clean up sites of visible blood contamination. Environmental surfaces can then be decontaminated with disinfectant solutions or household bleach (diluted 1:10 to 1:100).[1]

Postexposure Prophylaxis

Workers sustaining accidental parenteral exposures to HIV should be counseled to undergo baseline and follow-up testing for 6 months after exposure (e.g., 6 weeks, 3 months, and

Table 101-3. Recommended HIV Postexposure Prophylaxis for Percutaneous Injuries

| Exposure Type | Infection Status of Source | | | | |
	HIV Positive, Class 1*	HIV Positive, Class 2*	Known Source, Unknown HIV Status†	Unknown Source§	HIV Negative
Less severe¶	Recommend basic two-drug PEP	Recommend expanded three-drug PEP	Generally, no PEP warranted; however, consider basic two-drug PEP** for source with HIV risk factors†	Generally, no PEP warranted; however, consider basic two-drug PEP** in settings where exposure to HIV-infected persons is likely	No PEP warranted
More severe§§	Recommend expanded three-drug PEP	Recommend expanded three-drug PEP	Generally, no PEP warranted; however, consider basic two-drug PEP** for source with HIV risk factors†	Generally, no PEP warranted; however, consider basic two-drug PEP** in settings where exposure to HIV-infected persons is likely	No PEP warranted

*HIV positive, Class 1—asymptomatic HIV infection or known low viral load (e.g., <1,500 RNA copies/mL). HIV positive, Class 2—symptomatic HIV infection, AIDS, acute seroconversion, or known high viral load. If drug resistance is a concern, obtain expert consultation. Initiation of postexposure prophylaxis (PEP) should not be delayed pending expert consultation, and, because expert consultation alone cannot substitute for face-to-face counseling, resources should be available to provide immediate evaluation and follow-up care for all exposures.

†Source of unknown HIV status (e.g., deceased source person with no samples available for HIV testing).

§Unknown source (e.g., a needle from a sharps disposal container).

¶Less severe (e.g., solid needle and superficial injury).

**The designation "consider PEP" indicates that PEP is optional and should be based on an individualized decision between the exposed person and the treating clinician.

‡If PEP is offered and taken, and the source is later determined to be HIV negative, PEP should be discontinued.

§§More severe (e.g., large-bore hollow needle, deep puncture, visible blood on device, or needle used in patient's artery or vein).

6 months) to diagnose infection. Since 1996, the U.S. Public Health Service (PHS) has recommended postexposure chemoprophylaxis with antiretroviral agents after certain needlestick, mucous membrane, and nonintact skin exposures to HIV-infected sources that pose a risk of infection transmission (Tables 101-3 and 101-4).[2,31] Most HIV exposures warrant a two-drug regimen using two nucleoside reverse transcriptase inhibitors (NRTIs) or one NRTI and one nucleotide reverse transcriptase inhibitor (NtRTI). Combinations that can be considered for PEP includes zidovudine (ZDV) and lamivudine (3TC) or emtricitabine (FTC); stavudine [d4T] and 3TC or FTC; and tenofovir (TDF) and 3TC or FTC. The addition of a third (or even fourth) drug should be considered for exposures that pose an increased risk for transmission or that involve a source in whom antiretroviral drug resistance is likely. The PHS recommends that expanded PEP regimens be protease inhibitor (PI)-based. The PI preferred for use in expanded PEP regimens is lopinavir/ritonavir (LPV/RTV). Other PIs acceptable for use in expanded PEP regimens include atazanavir, fosamprenavir, RTV-boosted indinavir, RTV-boosted saquinavir, or nelfinavir.

Table 101-4. Recommended HIV Postexposure Prophylaxis for Mucous Membrane Exposures and Nonintact Skin* Exposures

| Exposure Type | Infection Status of Source | | | | |
	HIV Positive, Class 1†	HIV Positive, Class 2†	Known Source, Unknown HIV Status§	Unknown Source¶	HIV Negative
Small volume**	Consider basic two-drug PEP†	Recommend basic two-drug PEP	Generally, no PEP warranted; however, consider basic two-drug PEP‡ for source with HIV risk factors§§	Generally, no PEP warranted; however, consider basic two-drug PEP‡ in settings where exposure to HIV-infected persons is likely	No PEP warranted
Large volume¶¶	Recommend basic two-drug PEP	Recommend expanded three-drug PEP	Generally, no PEP warranted; however, consider basic two-drug PEP† for source with HIV risk factors§§	Generally, no PEP warranted; however, consider basic two-drug PEP‡ in settings where exposure to HIV-infected persons is likely	No PEP warranted

*For skin exposures, follow-up is indicated only if there is evidence of compromised skin integrity (e.g., dermatitis, abrasion, or open wound).

†HIV Positive, Class 1—asymptomatic HIV infection or known low viral load (e.g., <1,500 RNA copies/mL). HIV Positive, Class 2—symptomatic HIV infection, AIDS, acute seroconversion, or known high viral load. If drug resistance is a concern, obtain expert consultation. Initiation of postexposure prophylaxis (PEP) should not be delayed pending expert consultation, and, because expert consultation alone cannot substitute for face-to-face counseling, resources should be available to provide immediate evaluation and follow-up care for all exposures.

§Source of unknown HIV status (e.g., deceased source person with no samples available for HIV testing).

¶Unknown source (e.g., splash from inappropriately disposed blood).

**Small volume (i.e., a few drops).

†The designation, "consider PEP," indicates that PEP is optional and should be based on an individualized decision between the exposed person and the treating clinician.

§§If PEP is offered and taken, and the source is later determined to be HIV negative, PEP should be discontinued.

¶¶Large volume (i.e., major blood splash).

Selection of the PEP regimen should consider the comparative risk of infection represented by the exposure; information about the exposure source, including history of and response to antiretroviral therapy based on clinical response, CD4+ T-cell counts, viral load measurements, and current disease stage; and tolerability of PEP, including the potential toxicity of the regimen. Data from animal models of prophylaxis with these agents suggest that antiviral activity is diminished when treatment is delayed for more than 24 hours. For this reason, immediate reporting and access to chemoprophylaxis is recommended. Testing to determine the HIV infection status of an exposure source should be performed as soon as possible. Use of an FDA-approved rapid HIV-antibody test kit should be considered, particularly if testing by EIA cannot be completed within 24 to 48 hours.[31]

In addition to follow-up serologic testing, monitoring for PEP toxicity is needed if PEP is taken. A complete blood count and renal and hepatic profiles should be done at baseline and 2 weeks after initiation of PEP. If the PEP regimen includes a PI, the exposed person also should be monitored for hypoglycemia, crystalluria, hematuria, hemolytic anemia, and hepatitis. The PEP regimen should be discontinued or modified and expert consultation obtained if PEP toxicity develops.[31]

Occupational exposure to HIV can be a frightening experience. Consultation with clinicians knowledgeable about HIV transmission risks who can provide supportive counseling to the worker is essential during the follow-up interval. The CDC recommends that occupationally exposed personnel practice safer sex by using condoms correctly and consistently and avoid pregnancy, breastfeeding, and blood and organ donation for 6 months after exposure.[31]

CONCLUSIONS

Exposure to bloodborne viruses is a serious concern to HCP. Prevention of transmission of HBV, HCV, and HIV infection in healthcare settings requires a multifaceted approach, including promoting Hepatitis B vaccination of all HCP who may have contact with blood or body fluids, practicing Standard Precautions, and preventing percutaneous injuries. Postexposure management also is an integral component of a complete program to prevent bloodborne virus transmission. Healthcare organizations should make available to their personnel a system that includes written protocols for prompt reporting, evaluation, counseling, treatment, and follow-up of occupational exposures.[2,31]

Recommendations for HBV postexposure management include initiation of the Hepatitis B vaccine series to any susceptible, unvaccinated person who sustains an occupational blood or body fluid exposure. PEP with HBIG and/or Hepatitis B vaccine series should be considered for occupational exposures after evaluation of the HBsAg status of the source and the vaccination and vaccine-response status of the exposed person. Table 101-2 provides guidance for selecting the appropriate HBV PEP.

Immunoglobulin and antiviral agents (e.g., interferon with or without ribavirin) are not recommended for PEP of HCV exposure. For HCV postexposure management, the HCV status of the source and exposed person should be determined, and for HCP exposed to an HCV-positive source, follow-up HCV testing should be performed to determine if infection develops.

Recommendations for HIV PEP include a basic 4-week regimen of two drugs (ZDV plus 3TC or FTC; d4T plus 3TC or FTC; or TDF plus 3TC or FTC) for most HIV exposures and an expanded regimen that includes the addition of a third drug for HIV exposures that pose an increased risk for transmission (Tables 101-3 and 101-4). When the source person's virus is known or suspected to be resistant to one or more of the drugs considered for the PEP regimen, the selection of drugs to which the source person's virus is unlikely to be resistant is recommended.

Occupational exposures should be considered urgent medical concerns to ensure timely postexposure management and administration of HBIG, Hepatitis B vaccine, and/or HIV PEP.

FUTURE TRENDS

Future directions in the area of management of occupational blood exposures include more systematic (e.g., Internet-based) surveillance of occupationally acquired HBV, HCV, and HIV infection through systems such as the CDC's National Healthcare Safety Network; better definition of the epidemiology of blood contact and the efficacy of preventive measures; development and evaluation of new safety devices and protective barriers; modification/improvement of HIV PEP regimens; and development and evaluation of vaccines for HIV and HCV.

INTERNATIONAL PERSPECTIVE

In the international arena, the same risk factors and prevention strategies apply to occupational blood exposures and bloodborne virus transmission. However, countries with the highest prevalence of HBV, HCV, and HIV infection often have limited resources for infection prevention, sterile supplies, personal protective equipment, occupational exposure management, and PEP.[32] This may result in greater opportunity for occupational exposures and infection transmission.

Preventive strategies for international HCP are important because the likelihood that these workers will interact with patients with HBV, HCV, and HIV infection is high. As in the United States, strategies for prevention of occupational bloodborne virus infection include (1) Hepatitis B vaccination; (2) routine use of barriers such as gloves, gowns, and eye protection; (3) careful handling of sharp instruments and use of devices with safety features; and (4) provision of exposure management, including PEP, as appropriate.[31]

A number of special challenges exist in international settings. Scarce resources influence which prevention strategies will be adopted in healthcare settings. Strategies for changing behaviors of HCP to handle and dispose of sharps safely and use barrier precautions need to be culturally appropriate. Finally, the stigma of bloodborne virus infection, particularly HIV infection, influences the willingness of HCP to be tested after occupational exposure and complete follow-up for occupational exposure management.

REFERENCES

1. Panlilio AL, Cardo DM, Grohskopf LA, et al. Updated U.S. Public Health Service guidelines for the management of occupational exposures to HIV and recommendations for postexposure prophylaxis. *MMWR Recomm Rep* 2005 Sep 30;54(RR-9):1–17.
2. U.S Public Health Service. Updated U.S. Public Health Service guidelines for the Management of Occupational Exposures to HBV, HCV, and HIV and Recommendations for Postexposure Prophylaxis. *MMWR Recomm Rep* 2001 Jun 29;50(RR-11):1–52.
3. Centers for Disease Control and Prevention (CDC). Update: universal precautions for prevention of transmission of human immunodeficiency virus, Hepatitis B virus, and other bloodborne pathogens in health-care settings. *MMWR Morb Mortal Wkly Rep* 1988 Jun 24;37(24):377–382, 387–388.
4. Shapiro CN, McCaig LF, Gensheimer KF, et al. Hepatitis B virus transmission between children in day care. *Pediatr Infect Dis J* 1989 Dec;8(12):870–875.
5. Richman KM, Rickman LS. The potential for transmission of human immunodeficiency virus through human bites. *J Acquir Immune Defic Syndr* 1993 Apr;6(4):402–406.
6. Vidmar L, Poljak M, Tomazic J, et al. Transmission of HIV-1 by human bite. *Lancet* 1996 Jun 22;347(9017):1762.
7. Mast EE, Weinbaum CM, Fiore AE, et al. A comprehensive immunization strategy to eliminate transmission of Hepatitis B virus infection in the United States: recommendations of the Advisory Committee on Immunization Practices (ACIP) Part II: Immunization of adults. *MMWR Recomm Rep* 2006 Dec 8;55(RR-16):1–33.
8. Williams IT, Perz JF, Bell BP. Viral hepatitis transmission in ambulatory health care settings. *Clin Infect Dis* 2004 Jun 1;38(11):1592–1598.
9. Beltrami EM, Williams IT, Shapiro CN, et al. Risk and management of blood-borne infections in health care workers. *Clin Micro Rev* 2000 Jul;13(3):385–407.
10. Lok AS, McMahon BJ. Chronic Hepatitis B. *Hepatology* 2007 Feb; 45(2): 507–539.
11. Dienstag JL. Hepatitis B virus infection. *N Engl J Med* 2008 Oct 2;359(14): 1486–1500.
12. Weinbaum CM, Williams I, Mast EE, et al. Recommendations for identification and public health management of persons with chronic Hepatitis B virus infection. *MMWR Recomm Rep* 2008 Sep 19;57(RR-8):1–20.
13. Sorrell MF, Belongia EA, Costa J, et al. National Institutes of Health Consensus Development Conference statement: management of Hepatitis B. *Ann Intern Med* 2009 Jan 20;150(2):104–110.
14. Centers for Disease Control and Prevention (CDC). Hepatitis B vaccination—United States, 1982–2002. *MMWR Morb Mort Wkly Rep* 2002 Jun 28;51(25):549–552, 563.
15. Occupational Safety and Health Administration, Department of Labor. Occupational exposure to bloodborne pathogens. Final rule. *Fed Regist* 1991 Dec 6;56(235):64004–64182.
16. Armstrong GL, Wasley A, Simard EP, et al. The prevalence of Hepatitis C virus infection in the United States, 1999 through 2002. *Ann Intern Med* 2006 May 16;144(10):705–714.
17. Centers for Disease Control and Prevention (CDC). Recommendations for prevention and control of Hepatitis C virus (HCV) infection and HCV-related chronic disease. *MMWR Recomm Rep* 1998 Oct 16; 47(RR-19):1–39.
18. Yazdanpanah Y, De Carli G, Migueres B, et al. Risk factors for Hepatitis C virus transmission to health care workers after occupational exposure: a European case-control study. *Clin Infect Dis* 2005 Nov; 41(10):1423–1430.
19. Beltrami EM, Kozak A, Williams IT, et al. Transmission of HIV and Hepatitis C virus from a nursing home patient to a health care worker. *Am J Infect Control* 2003 May;31(3):168–175.
20. Kamili S, Krawczynski K, McCaustland K, et al. Infectivity of Hepatitis C virus in plasma after drying and storing at room temperature. *Infect Control Hosp Epidemiol* 2007 May; 28(5):519–524.
21. Alter MJ, Kuhnert WL, Finelli L, et al. Guidelines for laboratory testing and result reporting of antibody to Hepatitis C virus. Centers for Disease Control and Prevention. *MMWR Recomm Rep* 2003 Feb; 52(RR-3):1–13,15.
22. Strader DB, Wright T, Thomas DL, et al. American Association for the Study of Liver Diseases (AASLD) diagnosis, management, and treatment of Hepatitis C. *Hepatology* 2004 Apr;39(4):1147–1171.
23. Heathcote J, Main J. Treatment of Hepatitis C. *J Viral Hepat* 2005 May;12(3):223–235.
24. Henderson DK. Managing occupational risks for Hepatitis C transmission in the health care setting. *Clin Microbiol Rev* 2003 Jul;16(3):546–568.
25. Puro V, De Carli G, Cicalini S, et al. European recommendations for the management of healthcare workers occupationally exposed to Hepatitis B virus and Hepatitis C virus. *Euro Surveill* 2005 Oct; 10(10):260–264.
26. Centers for Disease Control and Prevention (CDC). HIV prevalence estimates–United States, 2006. *MMWR Morb Mort Wkly Rep* 2008 Oct 3; 57(39):1073–1076.
27. Schreiber GB, Busch MP, Kleinman SH, et al. The risk of transfusion-transmitted viral infections. *N Engl J Med* 1996 Jun 27;334(26): 1685–1690.
28. Centers for Disease Control and Prevention (CDC). Surveillance of occupationally acquired HIV/AIDS in healthcare personnel, as of December 2010. Fact sheet. Available at: http://www.cdc.gov/HAI/organisms/hiv/Surveillance-Occupationally-Acquired-HIV-AIDS.html.
29. Panel on Antiretroviral Guidelines for Adults and Adolescents. Guidelines for the use of antiretroviral agents in HIV-1-infected adults and adolescents. Department of Health and Human Services. Last updated February 12, 2013. Available at: http://aidsinfo.nih.gov/contentfiles/lvguidelines /adultandadolescentgl.pdf.
30. Siegel JD, Rhinehart E, Jackson M, et al. 2007 Guideline for Isolation Precautions: Preventing Transmission of Infectious Agents in Healthcare Settings. June 2007. Available at: http://www.cdc.gov/hicpac/pdf/iso lation/isolation2007.pdf.
31. Kuhar DT, Henderson DK, Struble KA, et al. Updated US public health service guidelines for the management of occupational exposures to human immunodeficiency virus and recommendations for postexposure prophylaxis. *Infection Control Hosp Epidemio,* 2013 Sep;34 (9):875-892.
32. Prüss-Ustün A, Rapiti E, Hutin Y. Estimation of the global burden of disease attributable to contaminated sharps injuries among health-care workers. *Am J Ind Med* 2005 Dec;48(6):482–490.

SUPPLEMENTAL RESOURCES

Centers for Disease Control and Prevention (CDC), Division of Surveillance, Hazard Evaluations, and Field Studies. *Bloodborne infectious diseases: HIV/ AIDS, Hepatitis B, Hepatitis C.* CDC website. January 21, 2012. Available at: http://www.cdc.gov/niosh/topics/bbp/.

Division of Healthcare Quality Promotion, Centers for Disease Control and Prevention. Telephone: 800–893–0485. Available at: http://www.cdc.gov/ ncidod/dhqp/index.html.

Division of Viral Hepatitis, Centers for Disease Control and Prevention. Telephone: 888–443–7232. Available at: http://www.cdc.gov/hepatitis/index.htm.

National Healthcare Safety Network. Available at: http://www.cdc.gov/ncidod /dhqp/nhsn.html.

Occupational Safety and Health Administration (OSHA). *Bloodborne pathogens and needlestick prevention.* OSHA website. Available at: http://www.osha.gov /SLTC/bloodbornepathogens/index.html.

PEPline (National HIV/AIDS Clinicians' Consultation Center). Telephone 888–448–4911 (24 hours/7 days a week). Available at: http://www.nccc.ucsf .edu//PEPline.html.

CHAPTER 102

Volunteers, Contract Workers, and Other Nonemployees Who Interact with Patients

Sue Sebazco, RN, MBA, CIC
Director of Infection Control and Employee Health & Education
Texas Health
Arlington, TX

ABSTRACT

Many individuals who are not employees of the healthcare facility may come into contact with patients. For the purpose of this chapter, these nonemployees are individuals who do not receive compensation from the healthcare facility or appointment recognition or have direct care student status in the hospital environment but do have a relationship with the organization to perform specific services.

As with the volunteer or contract worker, a nonemployed individual will provide services at the request and with the approval of the healthcare facility. This designation indicates that the facility is aware of and has approved their activities. Therefore, the healthcare facility has the responsibility to establish safe practice policies and procedures for these groups. This difference is in contrast to others such as a patient's own spiritual leader or a friend who stays with a patient and assists the patient or provides support at the patient's request or invitation. Thus, family members and friends of the patient are not included in the status of nonemployed individuals.

Healthcare industry representatives, contracted sitters, contract construction workers, volunteer community clergy, pet therapists, and volunteers are examples of nonemployee individuals who may interact directly or indirectly with patients during their inpatient stay. These individuals provide a variety of necessary services, such as delivering mail, flowers, or personal care items to the patients' bedsides; transporting patients within the facility; providing spiritual support or comfort; providing education or observation; and staffing the gift shop and visitor waiting areas.

All nonemployee individuals permitted to function at the facility who have direct contact with patients and visitors must understand the transmission and prevention of disease within the framework of their duties to reduce the risk for exposure to potential pathogens. Each facility should establish a plan for protecting approved nonemployee individuals that includes a list of allowed and prohibited duties; evidence of an initial two-step tuberculosis skin test and annual tuberculin skin test guided by the facility's annual tuberculosis risk assessment and individual state laws; a health history that includes immunization status; education about Standard Precautions, infection prevention practices in specific areas such as the operating room, tuberculosis, and bloodborne pathogens; and the risks of exposure to communicable diseases and prevention.

KEY CONCEPTS

- Nonemployee individuals must understand the transmission and prevention of disease within the framework of their duties to reduce the risk for occupational exposure to potential pathogens.

- Nonemployee individuals must be compliant to requests for prescreening health records including immunizations and tuberculosis screening.

- Nonemployee individuals who have more sustained contact with patients may require more intensive training in exposure prevention specific for their function.

- The types of individual tasks, environments, or patient contacts should be carefully evaluated along with the associated expected risk.

- It is critical to ensure the competency of volunteers, contracted personnel, and other nonemployee staff as they perform their assigned duties with patients.

BACKGROUND

Declining financial resources, population aging, and increasing public expectations mark today's healthcare environment. Hospitals have historically used volunteers and other nonemployees to provide a variety of cost-effective and sometimes unique services to improve the quality of patient care. Some of the services that these individuals may provide range from casual contact to more direct patient contact in high-risk areas.[1] Casual contact occurs when delivering items to the patients, providing direction, and working in the gift shop.[2] Direct patient contact happens when transporting patients within the facility and visiting with patients to provide spiritual or emotional comfort. Technical and sales personnel may work in the operating room or specifically with a patient to provide a service such as fitting an adaptive device or a wheelchair. Those volunteers and nonemployees of the hospital providing services to patients and visitors must understand the transmission and prevention of disease within the framework of their duties to reduce the risk for occupational exposure to potential pathogens. The types of services or patient contact should be carefully evaluated, along with the associated expected disease transmission risk.

BASIC PRINCIPLES

There are few published guidelines that address the protection of nonemployee individuals in the healthcare setting. This literature most often is related specifically to those individuals referred to as volunteers. After literature review, there were no documented cases of infection in volunteers or other nonemployee individuals from an exposure to communicable disease in the healthcare setting but the possibility does exist as these individuals provide more services and interact more with patients and the healthcare facilities.

In December 1991, the Occupational Safety and Health Administration (OSHA) published a safety and health standard on managing bloodborne pathogens in the workplace. The standard was designed to reduce the possibility of healthcare personnel (HCP) exposure to blood or other potentially infectious fluids, but the standard leaves unspecified whether unpaid personnel are included in the regulation.[3,4]

In the original and 2005 updated Centers for Disease Control and Prevention (CDC) *Guidelines for Preventing the Transmission of Mycobacterium Tuberculosis in Health-Care Settings*, recommendations apply to all paid and unpaid employees.[4,5] Both publications state, "The term HCWs refers to all paid and unpaid persons working in health-care settings who have the potential for exposure to *M. tuberculosis*."[4,5] The purpose of these documents is to provide recommendations that will reduce the transmission of tuberculosis (TB) in health-care facilities.[4] The CDC's November 4, 2005, publication *Controlling Tuberculosis in the United States* advises that education and TB prevention activities are based on the level of TB risk identified for the facility's area.[6] TB screening should be included for those HCP who enter patient rooms or treatment rooms regardless if the patient is present.[5] Additionally, in the *Infection Control Guidelines for Home Health Care*, volunteers are specifically referred to in relationship to TB exposure control. These guidelines may provide the base for a volunteer service plan for the prevention of exposure to all communicable diseases.[2]

Nonemployee individuals who have more sustained or specialized contact with patients may require more intensive training in exposure prevention. Therefore, understanding the tasks of these individuals is essential to establishing a plan for the protection of both nonemployee HCP and the patients during their services.

The Plan for Nonemployee Healthcare Personnel Services

Each facility should establish a plan for the protection of non-employee HCP and for the protection of the patient and other staff consisting of the following:

- A listing of duties that nonemployee HCP are permitted to perform and not permitted to perform. Nonemployee HCP must know that he or she has the right to refuse to perform activities that may cause undue risk for communicable disease exposure, whether they have or have not been trained in that activity.

- Transporting specimens and used procedure trays. In some facilities, nonemployee HCP may be responsible for transporting specimens and used procedure trays. Non-employee HCP must be instructed to transfer specimens and procedure trays according to healthcare setting policy. Nonemployee HCP should not transport specimens that are not appropriately contained in a closed bag or container.

- Contact with blood or body fluid. Nonemployee HCP are not to engage in tasks that necessitate contact with items or surfaces visibly soiled with blood or other body fluids, but should be instructed to notify appropriate personnel for cleanup.

- Special precautions. Nonemployee HCP should not enter rooms with infection prevention Transmission-based Precautions signs or with a special sign (e.g., "check with nurse before entering room") without consulting with the nurse caring for that patient or another designated authority.

- Nonemployed HCP must be included in the facility's TB control plan. If the individual is associated with an industry or contract service such as construction, the contract should include the requirement for TB screening. If the individual is a volunteer, the healthcare facility should provide that testing or at least require the volunteer to provide appropriate documentation from his or her primary care provider, health department, or other designated healthcare professional. Regardless of who actually does the testing, before assignment, a two-step tuberculin skin test (TST) or a single blood assay for *Mycobacterium tuberculosis* (BAMT) test should be completed on all HCP independent of setting or risk to provide a baseline.[5] Annual serial TB testing is based on the healthcare setting's risk assessment classification and individual state laws.[5,6] HCP in low-risk settings should have follow-up testing only if an unprotected exposure occurs with an infectious TB patient unless otherwise stated in state health law.[5] This test should be completed by the employee/occupational health department, by the facility designee, or by the company or contract service of record for the individual. Nonemployee HCP with a previously positive TST or with a history of treated TB should not have a skin test but should provide documentation of an assessment for reactivation as well as continue with a follow-up process similar to that required for employed HCP. Documentation of reactive TST from a healthcare provider should be kept on file. "HCWs who work in a health-care setting but do not receive payment from that setting should receive baseline training TB infection prevention policies and procedures, the TB screening program, and procedures for reporting an *M. tuberculosis* infection test conversion or diagnosis of TB disease."[5]

- Nonemployee HCP should be given initial and annual education about Standard Precautions and Transmission-based Precautions, including hand hygiene[7] and respiratory hygiene/cough etiquette,[8] tuberculosis,[5] bloodborne pathogens,[3] risk for exposure to communicable diseases, and prevention and infection prevention policies and procedures related to the scope of their assignment.

- Consideration should be given to requiring all nonemployee HCP to provide documentation of a preplacement assessment containing health history, immunizations, and prior exposure to communicable diseases.

Exposure Prevention

In addition to the tremendous emotional burden that is carried by an individual exposed to another's blood or body fluid, exposure follow-up consumes considerable time, money, and resources for the healthcare facility. It is more useful to prevent the exposure from occurring. The following measures may be taken to reduce the risk for exposure:

- Adopt policies that decrease exposures, including engineering controls.

- Teach nonemployee HCP to follow the standard and transmission-based isolation guidelines as established by the facility, including appropriate use of personal protective equipment (PPE).

- Educate nonemployee HCP on the signs and symptoms that would indicate the need to stay home to prevent the spread of infectious conditions.[5]

Any nonemployee HCP exposed to blood or body fluids must immediately report the exposure. Based on contract or service agreement, the exposed individual should report to his or her supervisor in the facility or the HCP's home company completes an incident report and follows the process as established by the healthcare facility. During orientation, and annually thereafter, the nonemployee should be taught the appropriate reporting mechanism to facilitate postexposure workup. Postexposure follow-up should follow the guidelines established by employee/occupational health services.

Health Requirements

Health requirements should reflect the policies of the facility for all employees. As part of the plan, the following health requirements should be reviewed with all nonemployee HCP during orientation:

1. Any nonemployee HCP with a draining skin lesion, including fever blisters, should not have contact with patients and should not handle patient care equipment.

2. Nonemployee HCP are to exclude themselves from the hospital if they experience symptoms of respiratory or gastrointestinal infection or other infectious diseases until the condition resolves.

3. Any questions regarding illness and the performance of services should be directed to the director of the department where services are rendered or the director's designee, infection prevention representative, or to employee health services.

4. Nonemployee HCP should be educated on vaccines available for their protection.

5. Nonemployee HCP who have a risk for exposure to blood or body fluids should be eligible to receive the Hepatitis B vaccine provided by the facility or via their employer's occupational health program as detailed in the Bloodborne Pathogen Standard.[3]

6. Influenza vaccine is strongly recommended for individuals in close contact with persons in high-risk groups, HCP, and those older than 65 years of age. Therefore, nonemployee HCP should be encouraged to receive the vaccine.[9]

7. Nonemployee HCP older than 65 years of age and those who meet the other high-risk criteria for illness should receive a pneumococcal vaccine following current vaccine recommendations.[10,11]

8. Nonemployee HCP should be immune to measles, mumps, and rubella. Laboratory evidence or physician documentation of measles, mumps, and rubella immunity should be obtained.[11-13]

9. Varicella vaccine is recommended for the nonimmune and those who have contact with high-risk individuals. This would include HCP and nonemployee HCP who have contact with at-risk patients.[12,14]

10. One-time administration of one dose of tetanus, diphtheria, and acellular pertussis vaccination is recommended for all HCP with direct patient contact.[12,15] Nonemployee HCP should also be considered for this vaccine if their job duties would involve direct patient contact.

Other vaccines may be desirable depending on the volunteer's role in the facility and federal or state regulations.

Healthcare Industry Representatives

The Health Industry Representative Association defines a healthcare industry representative (HCIR) as "an individual who sells, promotes, and gives training and advice concerning medical devices, systems and procedures."[16] These individuals have seen their roles greatly expand as technology advances. These representatives may typically be present in the operating room but should not scrub, be allowed in the sterile field, or be involved in direct patient care. Therefore, the function of the HCIR requires additional scrutiny related to duties. These individuals are subject to the same standards as other nonemployee HCP but require additional education in the following areas:

1. Concepts of a sterile field
2. Aseptic principles
3. Biohazardous waste
4. Fire, laser, and electrical safety
5. Facility-specific emergency codes and evacuation procedures
6. Operating room traffic patterns and general practices[17,18]
7. Dress code and other hygiene recommendations
8. Operating room policies for bringing in instrumentation and devices

Some medical companies provide training courses for their employee HCIRs; however, the program should be evaluated by the facility to ensure that education is adequate for the hospital setting. Additionally, the Association of preOperative Registered Nurses (AORN) does endorse an online training course that these individuals can complete for needed education.[16] The hospital may also use one of the commercial or self-developed tracking systems for HCIRs, which allows the representatives to log in officially as an HCIR, receive identification tags for each day they are in a facility, and perform required system education and verification of passing scores before working in the facility and specialty areas.

Education for Nonemployee Healthcare Personnel

Education is extremely important to eliminate the risk for exposure to communicable diseases. Following the guidelines for education and training, found in another section of this text, effective educational programs should be developed and provided. Orientation should be conducted before assignment. This education should be developed and prepared by the infection prevention department and should include the following:

- Infection prevention policies and procedures
- Modes of infection transmission
- Bloodborne pathogen exposure prevention
- TB information
- Hand hygiene
- Other state or local regulatory requirements
- Processes for reporting of unsafe situations, including recognized breaches in infection prevention processes

An initial and annual infection prevention education program for all active nonemployee HCP must be done. The healthcare setting should have a method to determine that those employed by outside agencies are compliant with current education and training requirements or are responsible for training them through the facility's current infection prevention and control education program.[9] Education must include facility-specific policies and practices to ensure the safety of both the individual and the patient. Competency training and checklists for specific procedures may be helpful in ensuring the standard of care.

CONCLUSIONS

Volunteers and other nonemployee HCP are an important part of many healthcare organizations. With the increasing demands on the healthcare environment, the skills of the nonemployee HCP are valuable resources that can often improve the quality and delivery of the patient care. Education in infection prevention and support is needed to protect both the nonemployee HCP and their contacts. Evaluation of the nonemployee HCP duties and risks can assist in developing an education plan to maintain a safe work environment.

REFERENCES

1. Handy F, Srinivasan N. Valuing volunteers: An economic evaluation of the net benefits of hospital volunteers. *Nonprofit and Voluntary Sector Quarterly* 2004;33:28–54.
2. Abrytyn E, Goldmann DA, Scheckler WE, eds. *Saunders Infection Control Reference Service*. Philadelphia: W. B. Saunders, 1998:96–97, 417–418.
3. Occupational Safety and Health Administration (OSHA). *Bloodborne pathogens*. OSHA website. 2013. Available at: http://www.osha.gov/pls /oshaweb/owadisp.show_document?p_table=STANDARDS&p_id=10051.
4. Centers for Disease Control and Prevention (CDC). Guidelines for preventing the transmission of Mycobacterium tuberculosis in health-care facilities,1994—CDC. Notice of final revisions to the "Guidelines for Preventing the Transmission of Mycobacterium Tuberculosis in health-care facilities, 1994". *Fed Regist* 1994 Oct 28;59(208):54242–54303.
5. Jensen PA, Lambert LA, Iademarco MF, et al. Guidelines for preventing the transmission of Mycobacterium tuberculosis in health-care settings, 2005. *MMWR Recomm Rep* 2005 Dec 30;54(RR-17):1–141.
6. Centers for Disease Control and Prevention (CDC). Controlling tuberculosis in the United States: recommendations from the American Thoracic Society, CDC, and the Infectious Diseases Society of America. *MMWR Recomm Rep* 2005;54:1–81.
7. Boyce JM, Pittet D. Guideline for Hand Hygiene in Health-Care Settings. Recommendations of the Healthcare Infection Control Practices Advisory Committee and the HICPAC/SHEA/APIC/IDSA Hand Hygiene Task Force. Society for Healthcare Epidemiology of America/Association for Professionals in Infection Control/Infectious Diseases Society of America. *MMWR Recomm Rep* 2002 Oct 25;51(RR-16):1–45.
8. Noonan D. The health care volunteer. *Hosp Health Netw* 1998 Jul 5;72(13):124.
9. Siegel JD, Rhinehart E, Jackson M, Chiarello L. *2007 Guideline for Isolation Precautions: Preventing Transmission of Infectious Agents in Healthcare Settings*. Centers for Disease Control and Prevention website. 2007. Available at: http://www.cdc.gov/hicpac/pdf/isolation /Isolation2007.pdf.
10. Fiore AE, Shay DK, Broder K, et al. Prevention and control of influenza: recommendations of the Advisory Committee on Immunization Practices (ACIP), 2008. *MMWR Recomm Rep* 2008 Aug 8;57(RR-7):1–60.
11. Centers for Disease Control and Prevention (CDC). Prevention of pneumococcal disease: recommendations of the Advisory Committee on Immunization Practices (ACIP). *MMWR* 1997 Apr 4;46(No. RR-8):1–24.
12. Advisory Committee on Immunization Practices. Recommended adult immunization schedule: United States, 2009. *Ann Intern Med* 2009 Jan 6;150(1):40–44.
13. Centers for Disease Control and Prevention (CDC). Notice to readers: updated Recommendations of the Advisory Committee on Immunization Practices (ACIP) for the control and elimination of mumps. *MMWR Morb Mortal Wkly Rep* 2006 Jun 9:55(22):629–630.
14. Marin M, Güris D, Chaves SS, et al. Prevention of varicella: recommendations of the Advisory Committee on Immunization Practices (ACIP). *MMWR Recomm Rep* 2007 Jun 22;56(RR-4):1–40.
15. Murphy TV, Slade BA, Broder KR, et al. Prevention of pertussis, tetanus, and diphtheria among pregnant and postpartum women and their infants recommendations of the Advisory Committee on Immunization Practices (ACIP). *MMWR Recomm Rep* 2008 May 30;57(RR-4):1–51.
16. Health Industry Representatives Association (HIRA). HIRA website. 2013. Available at: http://www.hira.org.
17. American College of Surgeons (ACS). [ST-33] Statement on Health Care Industry Representatives in the Operating Room. ACS website. 2000. Available online at: http://www.facs.org/fellows_info/statements/st-33.html.
18. Reichert M, Schultz JK. Do you know about the rep in your OR? *OR Manager* 2004 Feb;20(2):22–24.

CHAPTER 103

Immunization of Healthcare Personnel

Valerie Sparks, BSN, CIC
Infection Control Coordinator
Midland Memorial Hospital
Midland, TX

ABSTRACT

Immunization is the most effective means of preventing Hepatitis A and B; influenza; measles, mumps, and rubella; polio; pertussis, tetanus, and diphtheria; varicella; and other vaccine-preventable diseases. In medical institutions, susceptibility among healthcare personnel to vaccine-preventable diseases can have devastating consequences. Any medical facility or organization that provides direct patient care is encouraged to formulate a comprehensive immunization policy for all healthcare personnel, as indicated by the Centers for Disease Control and Prevention (found at http://www.cdc.gov/vaccines/adults/rec-vac/hcw.html) and by the Advisory Committee on Immunization Practices (found at http://www.cdc.gov/vaccines/acip/).

KEY CONCEPTS

- An overview of the guidelines for immunization of healthcare personnel.

- A brief review of the basic principles of immunization and misconceptions regarding immunizations.

- Review of specific vaccines pertinent to healthcare personnel.

- Basic information necessary to establish a healthcare personnel immunization program.

- A listing of general resource material and additional information on these issues.

BACKGROUND

Immunization is the most effective means of preventing Hepatitis A and B; influenza; measles, mumps, and rubella; polio; pertussis; tetanus-diphtheria; varicella; and other vaccine-preventable diseases. Unfortunately, adults who escape immunization at the recommended time in childhood often fail to attain adequate protection later in life. In medical institutions, susceptibility among healthcare personnel (HCP) to vaccine-preventable diseases can have devastating consequences. HCP who acquire vaccine-preventable disease not only suffer morbidity and mortality as a result of infection, but also serve as vectors for transmitting disease to other staff members and patients. Outbreaks of vaccine-preventable diseases have been well documented in medical institutions.[1-4] In these situations, if high-risk patients are exposed and become infected, substantial morbidity and mortality may occur. Once an outbreak is under way, the cost of emergency measures to control vaccine-preventable outbreaks within institutions can be enormous and disruption of vital hospital routines burdensome. Current trends in healthcare cause concern that similar transmission of vaccine-preventable diseases can occur in home health and long-term care settings and community settings (health clinics, etc.). The fact that these outbreaks can be prevented by immunizing HCP against vaccine-preventable diseases should serve as strong motivation for an effective immunization program.

The purpose of this chapter is to provide an overview of the guidelines for immunization of HCP. The chapter starts with a brief review of the basic principles of immunization and misconceptions regarding immunizations. Specific vaccines pertinent to HCP are outlined and the basic information necessary to establish an HCP immunization program is presented. A listing of general resource material and additional information on these issues can be obtained from the resources identified at the end of the chapter.

The Centers for Disease Control and Prevention (CDC) has published guidelines for the immunization of HCP.[5] In this document it states, "Any medical facility or organization that provides direct patient care is encouraged to formulate a comprehensive immunization policy for all HCP."[5]

The CDC further defines HCP as "all paid and unpaid persons working in health-care settings who have the potential for exposure to patients and/or to infectious materials, including body substances, contaminated medical supplies and equipment, contaminated environmental surfaces, or contaminated air. HCP might include (but are not limited to) physicians, nurses, nursing assistants, therapists, technicians, emergency medical service personnel, dental personnel, pharmacists, laboratory personnel, autopsy personnel, students and trainees, contractual staff not employed by the health-care facility, and persons (e.g., clerical, dietary, housekeeping, laundry, security, maintenance, administrative, billing, and volunteers) not directly involved in patient care but potentially exposed to infectious agents that can be transmitted to and from HCP and patients."

BASIC PRINCIPLES

Definitions

Definitions of key terms used in this chapter can be found in Table 103-1. These definitions are derived from the 2011 update published by the Advisory Committee on Immunization Practices (ACIP).[5] The terms vaccination and immunization are often used interchangeably. "Vaccine" is derived from vaccinia, a virus that was used in smallpox vaccines. Thus, "vaccination" actually refers to the prevention of smallpox, whereas "immunization" is a broader term that encompasses the use of any immunobiologic to prevent infectious diseases by inducing immunity. An "immunobiologic" is the antigenic substance or antibody-containing preparation used to induce or produce immunity.

- Immunity may be induced by either active or passive methods. Active immunization involves the development of antibodies or cellular immune response following administration of a vaccine or toxoid.

- Vaccines consist of live (usually attenuated, i.e., "weakened") or inactivated microorganisms or fractions thereof. Toxoids are modified bacterial toxins. Inactivated or killed immunobiologics may consist of the whole microorganism (whole cell pertussis), detoxified exotoxins (diphtheria and tetanus toxoids), soluble capsular material (pneumococcal polysaccharide), surface antigen (Hepatitis B), or components of the organism (subunit influenza).

- For some diseases such as influenza, measles, and polio, both live and inactivated vaccines have been or currently are available. Live, attenuated vaccination involves the use of very small doses of living organisms, which have been

weakened to produce a subclinical infection. Consequently, this approach more closely approximates the immunological response that follows natural infection and may confer more long-lasting immunity than the use of killed organisms. Thus, a single dose of measles, mumps, and rubella (MMR) vaccine is thought to confirm lifelong immunity (even though two doses are now recommended), whereas repeated vaccination and boosters are required for other immunobiologics such as diphtheria and tetanus.

- Passive immunization, on the other hand, refers to the temporary immunity that follows exogenous antibody administration. Sources of antibodies include:

  ○ Human immunoglobulin (IG)

  ○ Specific immunoglobulin preparations (e.g., Hepatitis B immune globulin [HBIG])

  ○ Antitoxins (e.g., diphtheria or botulinum antitoxin). These antibody preparations are harvested from pooled human blood plasma or occasionally derived from the serum of immunized animals.

Types of Immunobiologics

Table 103-2 lists the routine vaccines applicable for use in HCP. Items to note include:

- Immunobiologics produced by different manufacturers contain unique active and inert ingredients.

- Suspending fluids may consist of sterile water, saline, or complex fluids plus small amounts of protein or other constituents from the biological system in which the vaccine was produced.

- Preservatives, antibiotics, and stabilizers are used to inhibit bacterial growth or stabilize the active component of the immunobiologic.

- Adjuvants such as aluminum phosphate enhance the antigenicity of immunobiologics such as toxoids and Hepatitis B vaccine, which, if administered alone, would not elicit a sufficient immunological response.

- The clinical relevance of these components is addressed in subsequent portions of this chapter.

Efficacy and Cost-Benefit Analyses

When used appropriately, immunobiologics prevent infection in the majority of otherwise healthy adults (see Table 103-3 for vaccine efficacy and cost analysis). Using these efficacy rates, Williams and colleagues concluded that widespread immunization programs for adults are cost effective because the cost of immunization is usually much less than the cost of treating a preventable disease.[6]

Immunobiologics are also highly cost effective for HCP, who may be at increased risk of disease themselves and/or of transmitting disease to high-risk patients.

Table 103-1. Glossary of Terms[5]

Immunobiologic	Antigenic substance or antibody containing preparation used to induce immunity and prevent infectious disease.
Active immunization	Use of an antigenic substance to induce immunity by stimulating an immune response. Vaccine: A suspension of live (usually attenuated) or inactivated microorganisms, or fractions thereof. Toxoid: A modified (nontoxic) bacterial toxin that is capable of stimulating antitoxin formation.
Passive immunization	Use of an antibody-containing preparation to enhance or restore immunity. Immunoglobulin (Ig): A sterile solution containing antibodies from human blood. Antitoxin: A solution of antibodies derived from the serum of animals immunized with specific antigens.
Vaccine Monovalent	A vaccine consisting of a single strain or type of organism.
Trivalent	A vaccine consisting of three types or strains of a single organism (e.g., influenza vaccine), or three different organisms (e.g., diphtheria-pertussis-tetanus vaccine).
Quadrivalent	An influenza vaccine consisting of four influenza strains (e.g., two A virus strains, two B virus strains).
Polyvalent	Multiple strains or types of organisms in the vaccine (e.g., 23-valent pneumococcal vaccine).

Table 103-2. Currently Available Vaccines Used in HCP*[5]

Vaccines	Recommendations in brief
Hepatitis B	If HCP do not have documented evidence of a complete Hepatitis B vaccine series, or if HCP do not have an up-to-date blood test indicating immunity to Hepatitis B (i.e., no serologic evidence of immunity or prior vaccination) then: • Offer the three-dose series (the first dose now, the second dose in 1 month, the third dose approximately 5 months after the second dose). • Offer anti-HBs serologic tested 1 to 2 months after the third dose.
Influenza	One dose of influenza vaccine annually.
Measles, Mumps, and Rubella (MMR)	HCP born in 1957 or later and have not had the MMR vaccine, or HCP without an up-to-date blood test indicating immunity to measles, mumps, and rubella (i.e., no serologic evidence of immunity or prior vaccination), should receive two doses of MMR, 4 weeks apart. Documentation of provider-diagnosed disease is not considered acceptable evidence of immunity for measles, mumps, or rubella. The CDC has added laboratory confirmation of disease as acceptable presumptive evidence of immunity for all HCP. Adults born before 1957 generally are considered immune to measles and mumps.
Varicella (chickenpox)	HCP without written documentation confirming two doses of vaccine, laboratory evidence of immunity, or laboratory confirmation of disease; or diagnosis of history of varicella disease by healthcare provider; or diagnosis of history of herpes zoster by healthcare provider are considered nonimmune and should receive two doses of varicella vaccine administered 4 to 8 weeks apart.
Tetanus, Diphtheria, Pertussis (Tdap)	HCP, regardless of age, should receive a single dose of Tdap as soon as feasible if they have not previously received Tdap. HCP should receive Td boosters every 10 years. Tdap is recommended for pregnant HCP during each pregnancy.
Meningococcal	Microbiologists who are routinely exposed to isolates of *N. meningitidis* should get one dose and boost every 5 years if risk continues.

*HCP include physicians, nurses, emergency medical personnel, dental professionals and students, medical and nursing students, laboratory technicians, pharmacists, hospital volunteers, and administrative staff.

Table 103-3. Vaccine Efficacy and Cost Analysis[6]

Vaccine	Efficacy*	Cost Savings
Hepatitis A	~95 to 100 percent	No data available, but disease is very prevalent
Hepatitis B	85 to 95 percent	Yes, in HCP, due to preventable infections (4,411 episodes/100,000 workers over 5 years) and deaths
Influenza	90 percent	Yes, in patients >65 years of age, due to virus-preventable deaths (20,000/year) and hospitalizations (80,000/year)
Pneumococcus	60 to 95 percent	Yes, in high-risk persons, benefit: cost ratio is 2.32:1
Polio	~100 percent	Yes
Measles and rubella	95 to 98 percent	Yes, in all persons, average benefit: cost ratio for immunization programs is 10:1
Tetanus-diphtheria	95 to 100 percent	No data, but immunization costs very low
Varicella	70 to 90 percent	Yes*

*Defined as the ability to prevent disease in young, healthy adults.

For influenza vaccine, enormous cost savings have been projected for elderly adults (>65 years), with 50 to 75 percent effectiveness in reducing deaths of institutionalized high-risk adults. A significant reduction in the number of respiratory illnesses, sick leave, and medical expenditures in healthy working adults who received flu vaccine has been demonstrated,[7] as well as the cost effectiveness in elderly community-dwelling adults.[8] A recent cost-benefit analysis among HCP in the United Kingdom was conducted to determine if it was worth vaccinating HCP against influenza for protection of high-risk patients. Conclusions were: (1) vaccination was highly effective in HCP, with minimal adverse effects; (2) patient mortality was reduced after vaccinating HCP; and (3) vaccinating was cost saving.

Cost-benefit analyses of pneumococcal vaccine demonstrate that the vaccine is clearly cost effective in high-risk groups. Assuming 60 percent efficacy and 60 percent coverage in high-risk groups, 12,000 deaths could be prevented annually. Patrick and Woolley calculated a benefit-cost ratio of 2.32:1

for high-risk groups consisting of patients aged 50 years or older; patients with chronic diseases of the heart, liver, lungs, or kidneys; and those with diabetes mellitus.[9]

The average benefit-cost ratio for widespread measles and rubella immunization programs, including children, exceeds 10:1. Savings are only slightly reduced by the use of the trivalent vaccine MMR in place of the single-virus vaccine.[10] The savings may be even greater for medical staff and hospital personnel, if they are frequently exposed to these diseases.[3]

Cost-benefit analyses are not available for tetanus and diphtheria toxoid use in adults, but immunization is likely to be cost effective because of the low acquisition cost of this immunobiologic.

More recently, the cost effectiveness of various interventions commonly used in older persons has been published, and both influenza and pneumococcal immunization were found to be among the most cost-effective interventions performed.

Missed Opportunities for Disease Prevention

A recurring theme in outbreaks occurring in medical institutions is the failure of physicians, nurses, medical students, interns, and residents as well as nursing, dental, pharmacy, and other allied health students to obtain recommended immunizations. Even when medical institutions require immunization and make immunobiologics available to physicians and staff members, compliance is often poor. Therefore, special efforts must be made if high HCP immunization rates are to be achieved. The CDC has published comprehensive guidelines on immunization of HCP.[5] More recently, multiple professional societies have called for mandatory immunization of HCP with influenza vaccine.[7–17]

Misconceptions and Misperceptions Regarding Immunization

Like most adults, HCP can cite a number of excuses for not obtaining adequate immunization. HCP may view immunizations as "kid stuff," or an imposition on their busy schedules, or unnecessary. For this reason, strong immunization programs and requirements are necessary.

Contraindications

As a result of their exposure to medical information, HCP may have exaggerated fears regarding known adverse reactions or potential complications that have not yet been described. Some may be incorrectly concerned about getting the disease from the vaccine (e.g., influenza, measles). In addition, HCP are concerned about hypersensitivity reactions, viral replication, and efficacy and cost-benefit issues. Although there are some legitimate contraindications to immunization, there remains substantial confusion regarding appropriate indications and exclusions for various vaccines. ACIP compiled a list of common misconceptions concerning contraindications, many of which may apply to HCP (Table 103-4). Finally, there are "anti-vaccine" groups that publish and distribute erroneous or misguided information. Sometimes estimates regarding side effects are exaggerated, yet have some basis in fact, so that even HCP can be influenced by this information.

Adverse Reactions

Unpleasant childhood and young adulthood memories of redness, soreness, and/or fever may prevent adults from seeking re-immunization. Local reactions and low-grade temperatures are associated with bacterial vaccines, such as tetanus-diphtheria (Td) vaccine. These are usually transient and should not preclude further use, providing recommended dosing guidelines are followed. Urticarial or anaphylactic reactions are very rare complications of vaccines and warrant skin testing to confirm the presence of hypersensitivity.

MMR is generally well tolerated. Data from immunization programs reveal that, even though up to one-half of susceptible HCP experience reactions following rubella or MMR vaccination, these reactions are mild and transient. MMR vaccines may cause fever after vaccination, with the measles component most often associated with this adverse event.[18] Occasional and transient rashes also occur.

Table 103-4. Misconceptions Concerning Contraindications to Immunization

Previous local reaction or fever after tetanus-diphtheria (Td) vaccination
Egg intolerance or allergy to feathers
Penicillin or other, nonspecific allergy
Mild acute illness with low-grade fever
Recent exposure to infectious disease
Breastfeeding

Hepatitis B vaccine is also well tolerated. Adverse effects consist primarily of soreness at the injection site and, to a lesser extent, mild systemic symptoms (e.g., fever, headache, fatigue, and nausea). In one vaccination program involving the administration of Hepatitis B vaccine to >100 HCP, local reactions occurred within an hour after injection in >50 percent of recipients and systemic reactions in <10 percent. Adverse reactions were generally mild in severity, and no vaccine recipients missed work because of adverse reactions.[5]

HCP may be reluctant to obtain influenza vaccination because of misgivings about adverse effects. Vaccine candidates may recall the association of Guillain-Barré syndrome (GBS) with the swine influenza immunization program in 1976. Whether this was a temporal relationship or a true cause-and-effect association is hard to know. One report suggested a temporal relationship between influenza vaccine and GBS for vaccines used in 1992 to 1993 and 1993 to 1994 in persons <65 years of age.[19] The risk was on the order of one GBS case per million doses delivered.

Current formulations are well tolerated and are associated with a 3 to 5 percent incidence of local tenderness or low-grade fever. One study in persons >65 years old found that the only side effect in influenza versus placebo vaccine recipients was a transiently sore arm. There was no increased incidence of side effects such as fever, cough, coryza, fatigue, myalgia, headache, nausea, or disability in vaccine recipients compared with placebo recipients.[19]

Pneumococcal vaccine is well tolerated. Minor local side effects such as tenderness and redness are common and reversible within 48 hours. Low-grade fever may occur within the first 24 hours after injection. Other reactions are rare with a systemic reaction rate <1 percent.

Varicella vaccine is also well tolerated, although up to 5 percent of susceptibles may develop a rash and 10 percent a low-grade fever.

Hepatitis A vaccine is very well tolerated with a benign side effect profile.

Lack of a sore arm does not imply that a good antibody response has not resulted. Sore or red arms should be treated symptomatically with ice packs, elevation, and anti-inflammatory medication as needed. Very large or severe local reactions could imply an allergic or Arthrous-type reaction and is best assessed by an allergist or experienced vaccinologist.

Hypersensitivity Reactions

True hypersensitivity reactions are unusual. Potential vaccine allergens include animal proteins, antibiotics, preservatives, and stabilizers. Of these, the most common potential allergen is residual egg protein found in vaccines grown in chick embryo cell cultures (e.g., mumps, measles, or influenza vaccines). Thus, MMR and influenza virus vaccines are contraindicated in persons with histories of anaphylaxis or immediate reactions (e.g., hives, swelling of the mouth and throat, difficulty breathing, hypotension, or shock) following egg ingestion. ACIP points out that there is no evidence that persons with other types of reactions associated with egg ingestion or allergy to chickens or their feathers are at increased risk of reaction following vaccination.

Antibiotics used to prevent bacterial growth in vaccines may also serve as allergens. For example, MMR has trace amounts of neomycin and is contraindicated in patients with histories of anaphylaxis. It should be noted, however, that the usual type of neomycin hypersensitivity is contact dermatitis—a type of delayed or cell-mediated immune response that does not predict anaphylaxis and is not a contraindication to immunization. Fortunately, commercially available immunobiologics do not contain penicillin or its derivatives, the most common cause of antibiotic allergy.

Thimerosal, a mercury-derived preservative, is rarely implicated as a cause of allergic reactions. Persons with histories of hypersensitivity to mercury derivatives are at increased risk for this reaction. The American Academy of Family Physicians, American Academy of Pediatrics, ACIP, and the Public Health Service issued a joint statement in 1999 with the goal of removing or greatly reducing the amount of thimerosal in vaccines. These groups recommend continuation of the current policy of moving rapidly to vaccines that are free of thimerosal as a preservative. Great progress has been made in this regard. Until an adequate supply of each vaccine is available, use of vaccines that do contain thimerosal as a preservative is acceptable.[20] Thimerosal is currently found in several adult vaccines, most in trace amounts (Table 103-5). Employees can be screened for allergy to thimerosal by history (i.e., a previous reaction to a thimerosal-containing vaccine or thimerosal-containing eye drops).

Precautions

A precaution is a condition in a potential vaccine recipient that might increase the risk for either a serious adverse event or that might compromise the ability of the vaccine to produce immunity in the recipient. The 2011 ACIP General Recommendations on Immunization include precautions as a category in their table entitled "Contraindications and Precautions to Commonly Used Vaccines." Examples of precautions include moderate or severe acute illness with or without fever, pregnancy, previous history of GBS, receipt of an antibody-containing product within a certain time period of vaccination, and immunosuppression. ACIP includes "moderate or severe acute illness with or without fever" as a precaution for all vaccines. The decision to delay or administer a vaccination because of moderate or severe illness should be made after assessing the severity of symptoms and etiology of the disease. When a precaution is listed, the vaccination may be deferred until the condition is resolved (e.g., moderate or severe illness is present) unless the benefit of protection from the vaccination outweighs the risk of an adverse reaction.[18]

Viral Replication

It is theoretically possible for live virus vaccines to replicate in an uncontrolled manner in humans; however, this complication is highly unlikely except in persons with altered immune competence. Thus, live vaccines should be avoided in adults with malignancy, symptomatic human immunodeficiency virus (HIV) infection, treatment-induced immune suppression, and similar conditions whenever possible. An exception to this general rule, however, is that according to ACIP guidelines, MMR is recommended for patients with asymptomatic HIV infection who do not have evidence of severe immune suppression (see MMR section) and should be considered for those with symptoms because of the morbidity and mortality of measles infections. Inactivated vaccines (e.g., diphtheria and tetanus toxoids) are not problematic for persons with altered immune competence. Importantly, mild acute illness with low-grade fever and recent exposure to infectious disease are not contraindications for immunization in an otherwise healthy individual.

Breastfeeding and Pregnancy

Female HCP may have concerns regarding immunization during breastfeeding and pregnancy. Breastfeeding should not interfere with routine immunization. According to ACIP, the only vaccine virus that has been isolated from breast milk is rubella, but there is no evidence that such breast milk is harmful to infants or leads to transmission of disease.

On the other hand, pregnancy and the likelihood of pregnancy within 28 days are contraindications to the use of live, attenuated viral vaccines when indicated. Pregnancy is also a contraindication to the use of MMR and varicella vaccines; however, there is no evidence of congenital rubella syndrome in infants born to susceptible mothers who were inadvertently immunized.[21]

Inactivated vaccines do not appear to pose a risk to the fetus and may be safely administered where indicated in the second or third trimester. Inactivated influenza vaccine is recommended for all pregnant women during any trimester.

SPECIFIC IMMUNIZATION GUIDELINES FOR HEALTHCARE PERSONNEL

Hepatitis A

Vaccine Type

There are currently three vaccines containing Hepatitis A virus (HAV) antigen currently licensed in the United States for adults. There are two single-antigen vaccines: HAVRIX (GlaxoSmith-Kline [SKB], Brentford, UK) and VAQTA (Merck, Whitehouse Station, NJ); and a combination vaccine TWINRIX (containing both HAV and Hepatitis B virus [HBV] antigens; GlaxoSmith-Kline). All are inactivated vaccines.[22]

Indications

HCP have not been demonstrated to be at increased risk for HAV infection because of occupational exposure,

Table 103-5. Thimerosal and Expanded List of Vaccines (updated June 20, 2012): Thimerosal Content in Currently Manufactured U.S. Licensed Vaccines[20]

Vaccine	Trade Name	Manufacturer	Thimerosal Concentration*	Mercury
Anthrax	BioThrax	Emergent BioDefense Operations Lansing, LLC	0	0
DTaP	Tripedia†	Sanofi Pasteur, Inc.	≤0.00012 percent	≤0.3 μg/0.5 mL dose
	Infanrix	GlaxoSmithKline Biologicals	0	0
	Daptacel	Sanofi Pasteur, Ltd.	0	0
DTaP-HepB-IPV	Pediarix	GlaxoSmithKline Biologicals	0	0
DT	No trade name	Sanofi Pasteur, Inc.	<0.00012 percent (single dose)	<0.3 μg/0.5mL dose
		Sanofi Pasteur, Ltd.‡	0.01 percent	25 μg/0.5 mL dose
Td	No trade name	MassBiologics	≤0.00012 percent	≤0.3 μg mercury/0.5 mL dose
	Decavac	Sanofi Pasteur, Inc.	≤0.00012 percent	≤0.3 μg mercury/0.5 mL dose
	No trade name	Sanofi Pasteur, Ltd.	0	0
Tdap	Adacel	Sanofi Pasteur, Ltd.	0	0
	Boostrix	GlaxoSmithKline Biologicals	0	0
TT	No trade name	Sanofi Pasteur, Inc.	0.01 percent	25 μg/0.5 mL dose
Hib	ActHIB	Sanofi Pasteur, SA	0	0
	Hiberix	GlaxoSmithKline Biologicals	0	0
	PedvaxHIB liquid	Merck & Co, Inc.	0	0
Hib/HepB	COMVAX§	Merck & Co, Inc.	0	0
Hepatitis B	Engerix-B Pediatric/adolescent	GlaxoSmithKline Biologicals	0	0
	Adult		0	0
	Recombivax HB	Merck & Co, Inc.	0	0
	Pediatric/adolescent		0	0
	Adult (adolescent)		0	0
	Dialysis		0	0
Hepatitis A	Havrix	GlaxoSmithKline Biologicals	0	0
	Vaqta	Merck & Co, Inc.	0	0
HepA/HepB	Twinrix	GlaxoSmithKline Biologicals	0	0
IPV	IPOL	Sanofi Pasteur, SA	0	0
	Poliovax	Sanofi Pasteur, Ltd.	0	0
Influenza	Afluria	CSL Limited	0 (single dose)	0 (0.5mL single dose)
			0.01 percent (multidose)	24.5 μg (0.5 mL multidose)
	Agriflu	Novartis Vaccines and Diagnostics Ltd.	0	0
	Fluzone‖ (multidose presentation)	Sanofi Pasteur, Inc.	0.01 percent	25 μg/0.5 mL dose
	Fluvirin (multidose vial)	Novartis Vaccines and Diagnostics Ltd.	0.01 percent	25 μg/0.5 mL dose
	Fluzone (single-dose presentations)	Sanofi Pasteur, Inc.	0	0
	Fluvirin (single-dose prefilled syringe)	Novartis Vaccines and Diagnostics Ltd.	0	0
	Fluarix	GlaxoSmithKline Biologicals	0	0
	FluMist and FluMist Quadrivalent	MedImmune Vaccines, Inc.	0	0
	FluLaval	ID Biomedical Corporation of Quebec	0.01 percent	25 μg/0.5 mL dose
Japanese encephalitis	IXIARO	Intercell AG	0	0
MMR	MMR-II	Merck & Co, Inc.	0	0
Meningococcal	Menomune A, C, AC and A/C/Y/W-135	Sanofi Pasteur, Inc.	0.01 percent (multidose)	25 μg/0.5 mL dose
			0 (single dose)	0
	Menactra A, C, Y and W-135	Sanofi Pasteur, Inc.	0	0
	Menveo	Novartis Vaccines and Diagnostics Inc.	0	0
Pneumococcal	Prevnar 13 (Pneumo Conjugate)	Wyeth Pharmaceuticals Inc.	0	0
	Pneumovax 23	Merck & Co, Inc.	0	0
Rabies	IMOVAX	Sanofi Pasteur, SA	0	0
	Rabavert	Novartis Vaccines and Diagnostics	0	0
Smallpox (vaccinia), live	ACAM2000	Acambis, Inc.	0	0
Typhoid fever	Typhim Vi	Sanofi Pasteur, SA	0	0
	Vivotif	Berna Biotech, Ltd.	0	0
Varicella	Varivax	Merck & Co, Inc.	0	0
Yellow fever	Y-F-Vax	Sanofi Pasteur, Inc.	0	0
Zoster vaccine live	Zostavax	Merck & Co., Inc.	0	0

*Thimerosal is approximately 50 percent mercury (Hg) by weight. A 0.01 percent solution (1 part per 10,000) of thimerosal contains 50 μg of Hg per 1-mL dose or 25 μg of Hg per 0.5-mL dose.

†Sanofi Pasteur's Tripedia may be used to reconstitute ActHib to form TriHIBit. TriHIBit is indicated for use in children 15 to 18 months of age.

‡This vaccine is not marketed in the United States.

§COMVAX is not licensed for use in infants younger than 6 weeks of age because of decreased response to the Hib component.

‖Children under 3 years of age receive a half-dose of vaccine, i.e., 0.25 mL (12.5 μg mercury/dose.)

including persons exposed to sewage. Hepatitis A vaccine is recommended for persons with chronic liver disease, international travelers, and certain other groups at increased risk for exposure to Hepatitis A. For adults, the most recent guidelines from ACIP recommend the Hepatitis A vaccine for pre-exposure prophylaxis against HAV in those individuals at increased risk for infection and for anyone wishing to obtain immunity against this infection.[22] HCP should receive the Hepatitis A vaccine if they fall into a group at increased risk of infection, work in an area with occupational risk of infection, or if they wish to be immune to HAV infection. The two situations with occupational risk are persons who work with HAV-infected primates or those who work with HAV in a research laboratory setting. HCP at increased risk or who wish to be immune to this infection should inquire about receiving this vaccine from their private healthcare provider (if their place of employment does not provide this vaccine).

Individuals/groups that are or will be at increased risk for HAV infection, and for whom Hepatitis A vaccine is recommended, include:

- Travelers to or persons working in countries with intermediate to high endemicity of HAV infection (including military personnel)

- Men who have sex with men

- Users of injection and noninjection illicit drugs

- HCP who work with HAV-infected primates or with HAV in a research laboratory setting (or other persons with occupational risk of infection)

- Persons who are administered clotting factor concentrates (especially solvent-detergent treated preparations) for clotting factor disorders

- Persons with chronic liver disease, persons waiting or having received liver transplants (not persons with chronic HBV or Hepatitis C virus [HCV] infections without evidence of liver disease)

ACIP's updated statement does not include routine indications for prisoners, staff, and residents of facilities for the developmentally disabled, employees in child day care centers, food handlers, or sewage workers. Hepatitis A vaccination of food handlers might be considered for those who work in areas determined by state and local health authorities or private employers to be appropriate.[21]

Side Effects

All studies to date indicate the exceptional safety profile of the Hepatitis A vaccines. In studies to date, side effects reported in up to 50 percent of recipients included pain and tenderness at the injection site, headache, diarrhea, and other nonspecific symptoms of approximately equal frequency to placebo.[23] In a study of 151 HCP, the most frequent reported side effect was transient soreness at the site of injection in 27 percent of recipients, with no major

symptoms reported.[24] There is a single case report of encephalopathy temporally associated with the third dose of the SKB vaccine in a single individual, with uneventful recovery after 48 hours.[25]

Slight, transient liver function abnormalities have occurred in some vaccine recipients. In one summary report of 104 studies utilizing the SKB vaccine involving >50,000 subjects and >120,000 doses of vaccine, a sero-conversion rate of 100 percent was observed with no serious adverse events considered related to vaccination. The most common adverse events reported to the Vaccine Adverse Events Reporting system from 1995 to 2005 included fever, injection site reactions, rash, and headache.[22]

Strategies for Administration

Mechanisms to ensure that two doses of vaccine are administered with appropriate spacing between doses are necessary. Computerized tracking databases are optimal, especially when used in conjunction with other HCP immunizations and health screening programs.

Spacing With Other Immunobiologics

The ability to initiate the Hepatitis A vaccine series while simultaneously providing immediate protection against infection for travelers by administering immunoglobulin (IG) is desirable. Studies to date generally indicate that IG can safely be administered simultaneously (different anatomical sites, separate injections) with the Hepatitis A vaccine, although the height of the antibody response may be slightly reduced.

Currently, it is recommended that IG continue to be given at the same time as the first dose of Hepatitis A vaccine for individuals who need immediate protection and who are expected to require the longer term protection necessary for pre-exposure prophylaxis, such as travelers to endemic areas. Future research may well indicate the efficacy of a single dose of vaccine as pre-exposure prophylaxis in adult travelers.

Use in Controlling Healthcare-Associated Transmission

Hepatitis A vaccine is not currently licensed for use as postexposure prophylaxis (PEP). There are limited data regarding its efficacy when used during community-wide outbreaks of Hepatitis A, outbreaks in child day care centers, or in foodborne illness outbreaks.[22]

However, IG both prevents and modifies HAV infection and hence is appropriate for prophylaxis in travelers and as PEP in those exposed by close, personal household or sexual contact with a case, or in association with a known outbreak of HAV. IG is a sterile preparation of concentrated antibodies (immunoglobulin) made from pooled human plasma by a process called cold ethanol fractionation. IG provides protection against HAV through passive transfer of antibody.

For PEP and short-term travel (less than 3 months) a single dose of IG (0.02 mL/kg, up to 2 mL) should be given intramuscularly (IM) as soon as possible after exposure or prior to travel. Administration more than 14 days after an exposure is unlikely to be beneficial and hence is not indicated. IG is not recommended for casual contacts of persons with HAV.

For long-term travel, the dose of IG used is 0.06 mL/kg, up to 5 mL IM. The dose should be repeated every 4 to 6 months for the duration of the period at risk.

Contraindications

The currently licensed Hepatitis A vaccine is an inactivated vaccine and cannot cause Hepatitis A. Hepatitis A vaccine should not be administered to persons with a history of a severe allergic reaction to a previous dose of Hepatitis A vaccine or to a vaccine component. There are no other known contraindications other than hypersensitivity.

The safety of Hepatitis A vaccination during pregnancy has not been determined; however, because Hepatitis A vaccine is produced from inactivated HAV, the theoretical risk to the developing fetus is expected to be low. The risk associated with vaccination should be weighed against the risk for Hepatitis A in pregnant women who might be at high risk for exposure to HAV. Because Hepatitis A vaccine is inactivated, no special precautions need to be taken when vaccinating immunocompromised persons.[22]

Administration Schedule

The Hepatitis A vaccine should be administered IM into the deltoid muscle, using a length appropriate for the person's age and size.

The adult formulations of VAQTA and HAVRIX are administered in a two-dose schedule (VAQTA: at time 0, 6 to 18 months later; HAVRIX at time 0, 6 to 12 months later). Primary immunization with TWINRIX consists of three doses, administered on a 0-, 1-, and 6-month schedule, the same schedule as that commonly used for single-antigen Hepatitis B vaccine.[26] See Table 103-6 for dosages.

Table 103-6. Dosage Schedule for Hepatitis A and Hepatitis A and B Vaccines[22]

Age of Vaccinee (years)	Dose	Volume (mL)	Number of Doses	Schedule (months)
HAVRIX				
1–18	720	0.5	2	0, 6 to 12
>18	1,440	1.0	2	0, 6 to 12
VAQTA				
1–18	25	0.5	2	0, 6 to 18
>19	50	1.0	2	0, 6 to 18
TWINRIX				
>18	720	1.0	3	0, 1, 6

For HAVRIX and TWINRIX, the antigen content of the final aqueous preparation is determined by reactivity in a quantitative immunoassay for HAV antigen, and final vaccine potency (per dose) is expressed as enzyme-linked immunosorbent assay (ELISA) units (EL.U.). For VAQTA, the antigen content is expressed as units (U) of HAV antigen.[22]

Post Vaccination Serological Testing

This is not indicated because of the high rate of vaccine response among adults and children.

Effectiveness and Safety

All studies to date indicate that these vaccines are highly immunogenic with excellent safety profiles.[23]

After a single dose of either vaccine, seroconversion rates >90 percent are routinely observed, with HAV antibody (anti-HAV) levels approximating those achieved by a 5-mL dose of IG.[23]

Specifically, after a single 1,440 EL.U. dose of vaccine in adults, 80 to 90 percent have protective levels of antibody after 15 days, and >96 percent seroconvert after 30 days. When a booster dose is given 6 months later, essentially 100 percent of recipients seroconvert. Protective antibody titers develop within 15 to 30 days after vaccination.

After three doses of TWINRIX, antibody responses to both antigens are equivalent to responses seen after the single antigen vaccines are administered separately on standard schedules.

Unresolved Issues

Further studies are needed on the duration of clinical protection after immunization with Hepatitis A vaccine and the need for possible booster doses.

Current data show that protective antibody levels achieved after immunization persist for 5 to 10 years, and preliminary data suggest protective antibody levels may persist for 16 to 25 years;[27] however, the duration of immunologic memory likely may even exceed this time frame.

Recommendations regarding the need for prevaccination serology testing have been evolving. Data from the NHANES III study conducted from 1988 to 1994 showed a prevalence of anti-HAV in a random sample of the general U.S. population of 31 percent.[28] In this study, anti-HAV prevalence increased with age, from 9 percent in children age 6 to 11 years, to 33 percent in adults 40 to 49 years, and to 74 percent in adults more than 50 years. Decisions to perform prevaccination serology testing before administering Hepatitis A vaccine should be based on the expected prevalence of immunity, the cost of vaccination versus testing, and whether such testing will interfere with initiation of vaccination. ACIP has suggested prevaccination testing of persons over the age of 40 before administering Hepatitis A vaccine. Other adults that might be considered for prevaccination serology testing include those born in or living for extensive periods in areas with high or immediate Hepatitis A endemicity, those in certain population groups (Native Americans, Alaska Natives, Hispanics), and those in groups with high prevalence of infection (e.g., injection drug users).[22] Further cost-benefit analyses are needed to determine the role of prevaccination antibody screening in various epidemiologically defined groups.

Although preliminary data suggest that vaccine alone may be useful as PEP and in controlling outbreaks, ACIP recommends studies be completed comparing IG with Hepatitis A vaccine before the vaccine can be recommended for PEP.[22]

Future studies may indicate the efficacy of a single dose of vaccine alone as preexposure prophylaxis for travelers who receive the vaccine at least 14 days prior to travel.

Lastly, accelerated short-term immunization schedules are being investigated.

Commonly Asked Questions

- Can a single dose of the vaccine be used as immediate PEP? The answer to this is unclear, and further studies are needed. Preliminary data suggest that the vaccine alone may be useful as PEP and in controlling outbreaks.[27] However, more data are needed to be conclusive on this issue.

- Can you get hepatitis from the vaccine? Is it a live viral vaccine? You cannot get hepatitis from the vaccine. The vaccine is a whole virus, but an inactivated vaccine. The vaccine-manufacturing process inactivates all known viruses.

- Can you give Hepatitis A vaccine in combination with immunoglobulin? Is it still effective? Yes, both can be given together. Doses of IG of 2 mL or less do not appear to interfere with antibody production. Doses of 5 mL appear to decrease peak antibody titers.

- Should you test for antibody after receiving the vaccine to ensure immunity? There is no current recommendation for post-immunization serological testing. As a practical matter, the vaccine is very highly immunogenic, and in clinical trials essentially all subjects seroconverted after two doses of vaccine.

- Can you receive Hepatitis A and B vaccines at the same time? Absolutely yes! The vaccines should be given with different syringes and at different anatomical sites. Alternatively, there is a combination Hepatitis A and B vaccine available.

- Is a single dose of vaccine sufficient to confer protection? In young healthy adults, 80 to 90 percent have protective levels of antibody 15 days after receiving the first dose of vaccine, and 96 percent seroconvert after 30 days. The booster dose given 6 months later leads to essentially 100 percent seroconversion. Whether this will be true when widely applied to the entire general population is unclear.

Hepatitis B

Vaccine Type

There are currently three Hepatitis B vaccines licensed for adults in the United States: two single-antigen and one combination formulation. The two single-antigen formulations are Recombivax HB (Merck) and Engerix-B (GlaxoSmithKline Biologicals). The combination vaccine is TWINRIX (GlaxoSmithKline).[27,29,30]

The antigen used for Hepatitis B vaccination is Hepatitis B surface antigen (HBsAg), which is either purified from the plasma of persons with chronic HBV infection or produced by recombinant DNA technology. In the United States, recombinant DNA technology is used to express HBsAg in yeast, which then is purified. The two single-antigen vaccines available in the United States are recombinant subunit vaccines. TWINRIX contains recombinant HBsAg and inactivated HAV. The plasma-derived vaccine is no longer available in the United States, but is available in other parts of the world.[27]

Indications

In adults, Hepatitis B vaccine is recommended for pre- and postexposure prophylaxis for all persons at risk for infection by percutaneous or mucosal exposure to blood, sexual exposure, international travel, presence of certain medical conditions, and anyone seeking protection from HBV infection. HCP and public safety workers with reasonably anticipated risk for exposure to blood or blood-contaminated body fluids should receive the vaccine.

The following settings have been identified as those in which Hepatitis B vaccination is recommended for all adults:

- Sexually transmitted infection treatment facilities

- HIV testing and treatment facilities

- Facilities providing drug abuse treatment/prevention services

- Healthcare settings targeting services to injection drug users or men who have sex with men

- Correctional facilities

- End-stage renal disease programs and facilities for chronic hemodialysis patients

- Institutions and nonresidential day care facilities for persons with developmental disabilities[27–29]

Thus, HCP in these settings should be vaccinated.

Serological screening is not necessary prior to immunization unless the institution considers it cost effective or the HCP specifically requests it. There are no known adverse effects to immunizing someone who may already be immune because of previous infection or immunization.

Side Effects

- Mild soreness at the injection site lasting up to 1 to 2 days can occur in up to 29 percent of recipients.

- Occasionally nonspecific constitutional symptoms (low-grade fever [1 to 6 percent], myalgias, malaise, etc.) occur.

- Rare incidence of severe adverse experiences.

Strategies for Administration

Ideally, immunization against HBV should be completed during health professional training because the risk for infection is thought to be highest at this time.[27,29,30] All HCP should be offered vaccine at the time of employment.

Spacing with Other Immunobiologics

Hepatitis B vaccine can be given at any time, in conjunction with any other vaccines, although at different anatomical sites and using separate syringes.

Use in Controlling Healthcare-Associated Transmission

Immunizing HCP against HBV prevents healthcare-associated transmission of the virus from HCP to patient, and from patient to HCP.[27,29,30] PEP after exposure to blood or body fluids is outlined in Table 103-7.

Contraindications

Hepatitis B vaccination is contraindicated for persons with a history of hypersensitivity to yeast or any vaccine component.

Persons with a history of serious adverse events (e.g., anaphylaxis) after receipt of Hepatitis B vaccine should not receive additional doses. As with other vaccines, vaccination of persons with moderate or severe acute illness, with or without fever, should be deferred until illness resolves.

Vaccination is not contraindicated in persons with a history of multiple sclerosis, GBS, autoimmune disease (e.g., systemic lupus erythematosus or rheumatoid arthritis), or other chronic diseases.

Pregnancy is not a contraindication to vaccination. Limited data suggest that developing fetuses are not at risk for adverse events when Hepatitis B vaccine is administered to pregnant women. Available vaccines contain noninfectious HBsAg and should cause no risk of infection to the fetus.[27,29,30]

Administration Schedule

- Immunization against HBV requires three doses, administered IM in the deltoid muscle, regardless of the formulation.

- Adults should receive one 1-mL dose initially, which is repeated at 1 and 6 months.

- The vaccine concentrations as currently formulated are 20 μg/mL for Engerix-B, 10 μg/mL for Recombivax HB, and TWINRIX contains 720 EL.U. of Hepatitis A antigen (50 percent of the HAVRIX adult dose) and 20 μg of recombinant HBsAg protein (the same as the ENGERIX-B adult dose). Higher doses (40 μg/mL) are recommended to provide protection for dialysis and immunocompromised patients.[27,29,30]

Table 103-7. Postexposure Prophylaxis for Hepatitis B in HCP[27]

Vaccination and Antibody Status of Exposed Workers*	Treatment		
	Source HBsAg[†] Positive	Source HBsAg[†] Negative	Source Unknown or Not Available for Testing
Unvaccinated	HBIG§ × 1 and initiate HB vaccine series[¶]	Initiate HB vaccine series	Initiate HB vaccine series
Previously vaccinated			
Known responder**	No treatment	No treatment	No treatment
Known non responder[††]	HBIG × 1 and initiate revaccination or HBIG × 2[§§]	No treatment	If known high risk source, treat as if source were HBsAg positive
Antibody response unknown	Test exposed person for anti-HBs 1. If adequate,** no treatment is necessary 2. If inadequate,[††] administer HBIG × 1 and vaccine booster	No treatment	Test exposed person for anti-HBs 1. If adequate,[¶] no treatment is necessary 2. If inadequate,[¶] administer vaccine booster and recheck titer in 1–2 months

*Persons who have previously been infected with HBV are immune to reinfection and do not require postexposure prophylaxis.

[†]Hepatitis B surface antigen.

§Hepatitis B immunoglobulin; dose is 0.06 mL/kg intramuscularly.

[¶]Hepatitis B vaccine.

**A responder is a person with adequate levels of serum antibody to HBsAg (i.e., anti-HBs ≥10 mIU/mL).

[‡]A non responder is a person with inadequate response to vaccination (i.e., serum anti-HBs <10 mIU/mL).

[§§]The option of giving one dose of HBIG and reinitiating the vaccine series is preferred for nonresponders who have not completed a second three-dose vaccine series. For persons who previously completed a second vaccine series but failed to respond, two doses of HBIG are preferred.

[¶¶]Antibody to HBsAg.

From Centers for Disease Control and Prevention. Updated U.S.P.H.S. guidelines for the management of occupational exposures to HBV, HCV, and HIV and recommendations for post exposure prophylaxis. *MMWR Recomm Rep* 2001;50(RR11):1–42 (Table 3).

- The SKB vaccine is also licensed for use on a 0-, 1-, 2-, and 12-month schedule.
- A 1- or 1.5-inch needle should ensure that the vaccine is given IM, with longer needles necessary in obese persons.

Post Vaccination Serologic Testing

Routine serological testing in all recipients is not necessary after routine vaccination of adults. ACIP does advise serological testing for antibody 1 to 2 months after the last dose of the vaccine in persons whose "subsequent clinical management depends on knowledge of their immune status . . . to determine the need for revaccination and to guide post-exposure prophylaxis."[31] This includes the following groups: certain HCP and public safety workers who are at high risk of continued percutaneous/mucosal blood/body fluid exposure; chronic hemodialysis, HIV-infected, and other immunocompromised individuals; and sex- or needle-sharing partners of HBsAg-positive persons. Examples of HCP and public safety workers at high risk include the following:

- Acupuncturists
- Dentists, dental hygienists
- Emergency medical technicians
- First responders
- Laboratory technologists/technicians
- Nurses, nurse practitioners
- Phlebotomists
- Physicians
- Physician assistants
- Students entering these professions[27,29,30]

Booster doses are not routinely recommended.

An algorithm has been published dealing with the issues on non-response to Hepatitis B vaccine in HCP, with guidelines as to how and when to test for Hepatitis B antibody and what dose(s) of Hepatitis B vaccine to administer, based on risk factors.[32]

Effectiveness and Safety

When properly administered, the three-dose series induces seroconversion in more than 90 percent of otherwise healthy young adults. However, vaccine immunogenicity is related to several factors, such as concomitant medical conditions, gender, age, body weight, and smoking status.

Persons who initially respond to the vaccine with an appropriate antibody response, but who later have waning antibody levels appear to be protected. Hepatitis B surface antibody (anti-HBs) levels decline over time. Regardless, responders continue to be protected, and the majority of responders will show an anamnestic response to vaccine challenge. Declines might be faster among persons vaccinated at a younger age.

Persons who do not have protective levels of anti-HBs 1 to 2 months after revaccination with a second series should be considered nonresponders. Genetic factors may be associated with nonresponses to Hepatitis B vaccination. ACIP does not recommend more than two vaccine series in nonresponders.

Unresolved Issues

- Duration of vaccine-induced protection
- Management of vaccine nonresponders
- Need and frequency for post-vaccination antibody screening and/or routine booster doses of vaccine in the general population

Commonly Asked Questions

- How close does the actual vaccine administration schedule have to be to the recommended schedule for the vaccine to be effective? In general, optimal antibody titers are produced by an interval of at least 1 month between the first two doses and at least 5 months between the second and third doses. The longer the time interval between the second and third doses, the better the antibody response in general, but with the trade off that some individuals will not be protected until receipt of the third dose of vaccine. Thus, the greatest danger comes in trying to decrease the time interval between doses. No matter when previous doses were given, it is safe and effective to simply resume the immunization schedule where it was left off.

- What happens if the vaccine freezes? Freezing destroys the potency of the vaccine, and the vaccine should be discarded. The vaccine should be stored at 2° to 6°C.

- If anti-HBs antibody titers are going to be checked, when is the best time to do so? Anti-HBs titers should be checked no sooner than 30 days after the last dose of vaccine and no later than 6 months after the last dose. The optimal time to determine vaccine response is probably 1 to 2 months after the last dose of vaccine.

- Should we be performing post-immunization antibody testing in HCP? The current recommendations are for post-immunization antibody testing only in persons whose "subsequent clinical management depends on knowledge of their immune status . . . to determine the need for revaccination and to guide post exposure prophylaxis."[27] For the most part, this includes most HCP.

- What options do you have with nonresponders? First it is important to determine if the individual is truly a nonresponder. Negative or low antibody determinations performed more than 6 months after the last dose of vaccine only tell you that the subject could be a normal responder with waning antibody titers, a hyporesponder, or a true nonresponder. An algorithm has been published outlining and detailing the options for trying to correct nonresponse.[32]

  o Nonresponders are defined as those individuals who have received the appropriate vaccine dose in an appropriate dosing interval, in the deltoid muscle, and have no antibody response (<10 mIU/L) where the anti-HBs antibody was determined in the 1- to 6-month window after the third dose of vaccine.

- o Nonresponders can receive another dose of vaccine (with an estimated 20 percent response rate) or another series of three doses (with an estimated 30 to 50 percent response rate). Individuals not responding after a total of six doses of vaccine are unlikely to respond to further vaccine doses.

- o If it is thought that the "nonresponse" is actually a case of waning immunity, a single dose of vaccine is administered with a 1- to 1.5-inch needle to the hub and the anti-HBs determined 1 month later. If this is negative, then another two doses are administered according to the usual schedule, with an anti-HBs determined 1 month after the third dose.

- o If the negative anti-HBs titer is thought to be true nonresponse, then a new series of three doses of vaccine are administered according to the usual schedule, but the 40 mcg "dialysis preparation" dose is used for greater immunogenicity. The vaccine is administered with a 1- to 1.5-inch needle inserted into the deltoid muscle to the hub of the syringe, with the needle held parallel to the ground.[33]

- What should you do for those persons with waning immunity? This refers to those who previously received the Hepatitis B series and were antibody (anti-HBs) positive, but at a later date were found to be antibody negative. Studies show a very low rate of asymptomatic seroconversion among such persons who are subsequently exposed to Hepatitis B, with no evidence of chronic carriage of the virus. This is felt to result from the protective effects of immunological memory. Hence, nothing further needs be done.

- Can the vaccine be administered intradermally (ID)? The vaccine has been used this way in several studies. Although this saves money on vaccine costs, it introduces several concerns. First, the vaccine is not licensed for ID administration. Second, ID administration can result in a lower frequency of protective levels of antibody. Third, post-immunization antibody response should be determined in all recipients of ID administered vaccine, which defeats the purpose of giving the vaccine by this route to lower costs. Lastly, ID administration has been reported to produce pigmented papules, which may be cosmetically undesirable.

- Why can't the vaccine be given by gluteal injection? The vaccine is no longer licensed for gluteal administration because of the high incidence of nonresponse. This is thought to relate to the likelihood that vaccine could be administered into the gluteal fat pad (rather than muscle), thus decreasing vaccine immunogenicity.[34]

- Are regular booster doses of Hepatitis B vaccine advisable? At present, there are no recommendations for booster doses in otherwise healthy individuals. HCP who plan on working in hyperendemic geographic areas (e.g., medical missions in developing world countries) might wish to determine their anti-HBs titer and re-immunize if seronegative. Other than cost, there is no known adverse effect to immunizing an immune individual.

Influenza

Vaccine Type

Several different preparations of influenza vaccine are available. These include inactivated split virus and live attenuated preparations. Every year the specific strains and number of viruses vary and are determined by the World Health Organization in collaboration with other organizations. The U.S. Food and Drug Administration (FDA) then recommends which strains will be used in the Unted States .

Each vaccine normally contains three or four strains of influenza: two type A strains and one or two type B strains. New vaccines are made every year because the strains causing disease change yearly.

Indications

Annual influenza vaccination is recommended for all persons aged >6 months who have no medical contraindications; therefore, vaccination of all HCP who have no contraindications is recommended. HCP are exposed to patients with influenza in the workplace and are thus at risk of occupationally acquired influenza and of transmitting influenza to patients and other HCP.[11]

Live attenuated influenza virus (LAIV) is administered intranasally and is licensed for healthy, nonpregnant persons aged 2 to 49 years. It should not be administered to persons who are immunocompromised or who have serious health conditions. LAIV may cause nasal congestion or runny nose, sore throat, headache, and cough in adults. Fever is not a common side effect of LAIV.[35,36]

Side Effects

The vaccine cannot "cause" the flu. A randomized, double-blind, placebo-controlled, crossover trial showed no difference in side effects between vaccine and placebo recipients.[19]

Side effects of inactivated influenza vaccine (IIV) are generally minimal and minor, rarely lasting up to 24 hours, and include low-grade fever and injection site tenderness occurring in up to 20 percent of individuals.

Strategies for Administration

New polyvalent influenza virus vaccines are prepared every year, based on the anticipated infectious strains. One or more strains may be repeated in subsequent years, but re-immunization every year is recommended to achieve immunity.

Candidates should be vaccinated before the peak season for influenza infection, which usually begins in December. October is the optimal month to begin immunization programs, but vaccination can take place as early as September, provided that the most current vaccine is available, and continue as late as there are influenza outbreaks.

It takes about 14 days after immunization for protective levels of antibody to be produced and circulate in high enough titer to protect against disease.

Employee immunization programs that provide free vaccine in locations and at times that are convenient are likely to increase the number of HCP who receive the vaccine, although high, sustainable rates have not been demonstrated without a mandatory policy. Influenza vaccination rates among HCP within facilities should be regularly measured and reported. Influenza vaccination coverage among HCP should be a measure of quality of care. Such information might be useful to promote compliance with vaccination policies.

One study demonstrated that healthy working adults who received influenza vaccine experienced significantly fewer upper respiratory infections, fewer days of sick leave from work, and less health-related direct costs.[7]

Spacing with Other Immunobiologics

The inactivated vaccine can be given concomitantly with any other vaccine, although at different anatomical sites and using different syringes. The most current ACIP recommendations state that LAIV can be administered simultaneously with inactivated or live vaccines. However, if LAIV and another live vaccine are not given concurrently, at least 4 weeks should elapse before another live vaccine is administered.

Use in Controlling Healthcare-Associated Transmission

Influenza vaccines are effective in preventing healthcare-associated transmission of influenza. For this reason, all HCP caring for hospitalized and other high-risk subjects should receive influenza vaccine on an annual basis.

Centers for Medicare & Medicaid Services (CMS) recommends as part of their conditions of participation that a policy is in effect whereby nursing annually (October 1 to March 30) reviews the indications and contraindications for influenza vaccine for every hospitalized patient. If appropriate, patients are immunized prior to hospital discharge.[37]

Descriptions of programs to immunize high-risk hospitalized patients and outpatients are available.[36]

Strategies to improve influenza vaccination rates have included sending postcards to patients to remind them to get the influenza vaccine and use of a drive-up immunization window for HCP.

Contraindications

Both Inactivated Vaccines and Live, Attenuated Influenza Vaccine

Influenza vaccine is produced using chicken eggs. Hence, persons with anaphylactic reactions to chicken eggs (not feathers!) or other components of the influenza vaccine should not receive this vaccine. Other allergic reactions to chicken egg proteins are also contraindications.

Persons who developed GBS or other neurological syndromes in temporal association (within 6 weeks) with receipt of influenza immunization should not receive further doses of vaccine. No cases of GBS have been reported because of LAIV.[35]

Additional Contraindications to Live, Attenuated Influenza Vaccine

In addition to the preceding contraindications, LAIV should not be administered to adults >49 years old, pregnant women, or persons at high risk for influenza complications with any of the underlying medical conditions that serve as an indication for routine influenza vaccination.

Administration Schedule

The dose of the IIV formulations is 0.5 mL administered IM (deltoid); LAIV is administered as an intranasal spray. Both are administered on an annual basis.

Post Vaccination Serological Testing

Not applicable.

Effectiveness and Safety

Influenza vaccines are safe and do not cause the flu. A randomized, double-blind, placebo-controlled, crossover trial demonstrated that side effects were no different among vaccine versus placebo recipients.[19]

The most common side effect of the inactivated vaccine is minor injection site soreness lasting 1 to 2 days. No known clinically significant changes in concomitantly administered drug pharmacokinetics occur (e.g., warfarin, theophylline, phenytoin). For LAIV, in adults, side effects have included runny nose, headache, sore throat, and cough.

The vaccine is highly effective in preventing clinical illness in young, healthy recipients.

Unresolved Issues

- Improved and more immunogenic/efficacious influenza vaccines are needed, especially for elderly and other high-risk persons.
- Methods to increase the number of HCP who receive annual influenza immunization are needed.
- Whether bias exists in estimating the benefits of vaccination among older adults and the relationship to hospitalizations and death
- Causality of rare events after influenza vaccination, such as GBS
- Expansion of routine influenza vaccination recommendations to reduce/prevent transmission and severe disease burden

Commonly Asked Questions

- Can the vaccine be administered intradermally or in "split" doses to try to reduce side effects? There is an intradermal flu vaccine that is injected into the skin instead of the muscle. The intradermal shot uses a much smaller needle than the regular flu shot, and it requires less antigen to be as effective as the regular flu shot. Antigen is the part of the vaccine that helps your body build up protection against flu viruses. Administering the IM vaccine in two split doses may significantly reduce the protective effect of the vaccine, with no evidence of a decrease in side effect rate or severity. LAIV should only be administered by the intranasal route.

- Can the vaccine be used in immunocompromised persons? Only the inactivated vaccine may be used—not the live, attenuated intranasal vaccine. Inactivated vaccine contains only inactivated virus, so there is no danger of viral replication. Although the vaccine may be less effective (depending on the degree of immune suppression) in such persons, it is particularly indicated in an effort to provide maximal protection against disease.

- Can the vaccine be used in HIV-positive persons? At the current time, the inactivated vaccine only is recommended for use in HIV-positive persons.[29,30,38]

- Can you get the flu from flu shots? This is a commonly expressed concern. Because inactivated vaccine contains only a killed virus, it is impossible to "get the flu" from this vaccine. A recent study showed that flulike symptoms were equally common among flu vaccine and placebo recipients.[28] However, reported side effects from the LAIV have included transient upper airway symptoms such as runny nose, sore throat, and minor systemic symptoms such as myalgias and low-grade fever.[35]

- What about the risk of GBS after getting the flu vaccine? There have been no confirmed cases of GBS caused by inactivated influenza vaccine since the period 1976 to 1977, when the "swine flu" vaccine was used. Little direct evidence exists of any cause-and-effect association of flu vaccine with GBS since then. No cases of GBS have been reported because of LAIV.

- Can patients with a previous history of GBS or other demyelinating disorders safely receive the flu shot? It is prudent to delay immunizing anyone with an active neurological disorder characterized by changing or unstable neurological findings. ACIP and American College of Physicians (ACP) recommendations are that flu vaccine not be given to individuals who have had GBS or other neurological illnesses temporally related (i.e., within 6 weeks) to previously administered vaccine.

- Can I get other vaccines at the same time as the IIV? Among adults aged ≥50 years, the safety and immunogenicity of zoster vaccine and IIV were similar whether administered simultaneously or spaced 4 weeks apart. In the absence of specific data indicating interference, following ACIP's general recommendations for vaccination is prudent.[8] All other adult vaccines can be given at the same time as the inactivated influenza vaccines, but at different anatomical sites. Inactivated vaccines do not interfere with the immune response to other inactivated vaccines or live vaccines.

- Can the nasal spray vaccine (LAIV) be given at the same time as other vaccines? Use of LAIV concurrently with MMR alone, and MMR and varicella vaccine among children aged 12 to 15 months has been studied, and no interference with the immunogenicity to antigens in any of the vaccines was observed. In the absence of specific data indicating interference, following ACIP's general recommendations for vaccination is prudent.[8] Inactivated or live vaccines can be administered simultaneously with LAIV. However, after administration of a live vaccine, at least 4 weeks should pass before another live vaccine is administered.

- Are there any medications that can't be taken at the time of the flu shot? There are no medications that are contraindications to receiving the flu vaccine. However, corticosteroids, chemotherapy agents, and other immune suppressives may decrease the ability of the immune system to respond to the vaccine with protective levels of antibody.

- What are true contraindications to receiving influenza immunization? Anyone with a previous anaphylactic, bronchospastic, or hypotensive reaction to flu vaccine should not receive additional doses of flu vaccine. Additionally, anaphylactic reactions to eggs, egg proteins, or any component of the vaccine or thimerosal (a mercury-derived preservative) are true contraindications. LAIV should not be administered to anyone other than healthy persons aged 2 to 49 years who are not pregnant and who have no chronic or serious medical conditions. It is currently licensed for use only in healthy individuals. Use of LAIV for HCP who care for patients housed in protective environments has been a theoretic concern, but transmission of LAIV in healthcare settings has not been reported.

- Can patients on warfarin or heparin receive flu shots? Taking warfarin or heparin is not a contraindication. It is medically prudent to delay immunizing someone with an uncontrolled bleeding disorder/coagulopathy until the condition is stable.

- Many employees delay the flu vaccine because they are sick. What is the danger of receiving this vaccine when you are under the weather? There is no danger to receiving the flu vaccine during a mild illness. It is prudent to delay receiving the vaccine with a more severe illness/fever simply to avoid labeling a changing clinical course as an adverse reaction to the flu vaccine.

Measles-Mumps-Rubella

Vaccine Type

Measles, mumps, and rubella vaccines are all live, attenuated viral vaccines. The vaccines are available as monovalent, bivalent, and trivalent vaccines. There is also a combination vaccine of MMR with varicella (Pro-Quad [Merck], but that is not indicated in adults). Currently licensed vaccines for adults in the United States are all manufactured by Merck & Co. and include:

- Monovalent (measles only, Attenuvax; mumps only, Mumpsvax; and rubella only, Meruvax)

- Bivalent (measles and mumps, M-M-vax, although currently not available)

- Trivalent (measles, mumps, and rubella, M-M-R II)

Indications

Medical staff and hospital employees are at increased risk of acquiring measles, mumps, and rubella.[2,3,39]

- All persons working in healthcare facilities should be immune to measles, mumps, and rubella.[5] Additionally, it is reasonable to require proof of immunity in the medical setting.

- HCP proof of immunity consists of documented vaccination with two doses of live vaccine administered at least 28 days apart, laboratory evidence of immunity to these diseases, or laboratory confirmation of disease. If such proof is not available, immunization with MMR provides long-lasting protection against all three diseases and is not harmful to persons already immune against one or more of its components. The exception is a medical contraindication to the vaccine.[30]

- Even though persons born before 1957 usually have acquired immunity against measles and rubella as a result of wild virus exposure, healthcare facilities should consider recommending a dose of MMR vaccine to unvaccinated workers born before 1957 who are in either of the following categories: (1) do not have a history of measles disease or laboratory evidence of measles immunity, or (2) lack laboratory evidence of rubella immunity.[30]

- For HCP born in 1957 or later, give two doses of MMR 4 weeks apart if they do not have proof of immunity.[30]

For HCP who have two documented doses of MMR vaccine or other acceptable evidence of immunity to measles, serologic testing for immunity is not recommended. In the event that the HCP has two documented doses of MMR vaccine and tests serologically negative or equivocal in titer results, it is not recommended that the person receive an additional dose of MMR vaccine.

- The dose of MMR or any of the monovalent component vaccines is 0.5 mL administered subcutaneously.

- All HCP at risk of contact with patients with rubella or who are likely to have direct contact with pregnant patients should be immune to rubella.

- Prior to immunization, serological screening is not necessary unless the institution considers it cost effective or the HCP specifically requests it.

- As with measles, mumps, and rubella, immunization is not harmful for persons already immune, and consideration

should be given to the use of trivalent MMR, rather than monovalent vaccine.

Side Effects

- Fever may result after vaccination; the measles component of MMR is most often associated with this adverse event.

- Transient vaccine-associated rashes occur in up to 5 percent of recipients.

- Both parotitis and central nervous involvement have rarely been reported after mumps immunization.

- As many as 25 percent of susceptible women may experience transient arthralgias or arthritis after rubella immunization. When these side effects occur, they generally occur 1 to 3 weeks after immunization and resolve within days to weeks.

- Short-lived peripheral neuritis and paresthesias have been rarely reported in association with rubella immunization of nonimmune individuals.

Strategies for Administration

- MMR is the preferred vaccine formulation. Immunization with MMR is not harmful to a recipient already immune to one or more of these viruses.

- Without proof of immunity, all HCP should ideally receive two doses of MMR, spread apart by a minimum of 1 month between doses.

Spacing with Other Immunobiologics

- Administration of measles vaccine causes temporary mild immune suppression. Under routine use of the licensed vaccine, the only clinical significance of this effect is false-positive tuberculin skin test (TST) after immunization. Measles-containing vaccine can be administered on the same day as TST. If it cannot, then more than 4 weeks should elapse after MMR vaccination to perform TST.[8]

- The vaccine should be given 2 weeks before gammaglobulin or other blood products, or up to 11 months after receipt (depending on the dose of blood product received), for optimal immunogenicity.[18]

- Co-administration with other live viral vaccines (other than oral polio vaccine or varicella) should be avoided and separated by at least 30 days.

Use in Controlling Healthcare-Associated Transmission

- The Redbook recommends measles immunization for those individuals who may not be protected and were exposed to measles within a 72-hour time frame. Nonetheless, these individuals must be relieved of patient duties from days 5 to 21 after exposure.

Contraindications[18]

- Pregnant women or women anticipating conception in the 4 weeks after immunization.

- Previous severe hypersensitivity reaction (including anaphylaxis) to the vaccine or any of its components.

- Known severe immune deficiency (e.g., hematological and solid tumors; receiving chemotherapy; congenital immune deficiency; long-term immune suppressive therapy; or patients with HIV infection who are severely immunocompromised). The one exception is that HIV-positive persons may receive the vaccine if they are: (1) asymptomatic, (2) have an age-specific CD4+ T-lymphocyte percentage of >15 percent, and (3) are one of those persons for whom measles vaccination would otherwise be indicated.

- Precautions include moderate or severe illness with or without fever, history of thrombocytopenia or thrombocytopenic purpura, and recent (<11 month) receipt of antibody-containing blood product (interval depends on specific product).[18]

Administration Schedule

- A second dose of vaccine should be given and documented for all HCP born after 1957 and for those born before 1957 without adequate evidence of immunity.

- Immunization is not necessary for those with documented immunity by serology or by provider-diagnosed illness.

- The vaccine must be used within 8 hours of vaccine reconstitution.

Post Vaccination Serological Testing

Not usually done. Testing for MMR antibody can be done to document immunity in HCP who do not wish to receive a second dose of vaccine.

Effectiveness and Safety

These vaccines are safe and efficacious. Failure rates are in the 5 percent or less range. Seronegative recipients of rubella vaccine, especially adolescent and adult women, appear to have an increased risk of arthralgias and arthritis. The risk appears to be small, and is generally short lived. Occasionally, chronic arthritis has been reported. Rare, isolated cases of polyneuropathy have been reported after immunization with this vaccine or its components.

Rare cases of optic neuritis, viral meningitis, parotitis, and orchitis have been reported following mumps immunization.

Unresolved Issues

- The risk, duration, and pathogenesis of arthritis owing to rubella immunization in seronegative adolescent and adult women need further clarification.

- The impact of waning immunity, especially for measles and mumps, needs additional study.

Commonly Asked Questions

- Should the monovalent measles vaccine be given alone or in combination with the MMR vaccine? Unless there is some other contraindication, it is advisable to receive the protective effect of all three vaccines. There is no harm in immunizing an otherwise immune individual. The known arthralgia and arthritis side effects of rubella vaccine that can occur in seronegative persons do not occur in those who receive the vaccine but are already immune.

- Why is a history of recent receipt of blood products important to know prior to immunizing someone with MMR vaccine? The IG present in these products can interfere with optimal antibody production to the vaccine. Large doses of IG can interfere with vaccine immunogenicity for as long as 9 to 12 months.

- Why don't all HCP receive a dose of measles vaccine, rather than just those born after 1957? Persons born prior to 1957 are statistically more likely to have had wild virus infection, and hence be immune. Nonetheless, several surveys of HCP born prior to 1957 have demonstrated up to a 14 percent seronegative rate. An expert consensus report was published outlining the optimal measles immunization strategy for HCP.[40] In this report the optimal strategy proposed was for all HCP, regardless of date of birth, to demonstrate immunity against measles. As a result, ACIP recommends that facilities consider recommending a dose of MMR to persons born before 1957 if there is no proof of immunity.[29]

- Is it safe to give MMR vaccine to HIV-positive persons? In the small number of persons studied, MMR vaccine has not caused unusual side effects in either symptomatic or asymptomatic individuals. Safety does not appear to be an issue in HIV-positive asymptomatic individuals. It is appropriate to assess the degree of immune suppression and the risk of measles exposure before administering measles vaccine to HIV-positive symptomatic persons. The most recent recommendation from ACIP is that measles vaccine not be administered to those HIV-infected persons who are severely immunocompromised (see Contraindications).[29] This recommendation is related to the death and subsequent finding of measles vaccine virus pneumonitis in an HIV-positive person.

- Because MMR is a live viral vaccine, can vaccinees transmit any of the three vaccine viruses to immunocompromised contacts? There is no evidence for transmission or any adverse effect from administering the vaccine to healthy persons who have contact with immunocompromised persons.

Pneumococcus

Vaccine Type

Pneumococcal polysaccharide vaccine (PPSV) is a polyvalent vaccine that provides protection against the 23 types of pneumococci known to cause bacteremic disease. Pneumococcal conjugate vaccine (called PCV13 or Prevnar 13; Pfizer, New York, NY) is recommended to protect infants and toddlers, and some older children and adults with certain health conditions, from pneumococcal disease.

Indications

Although HCP are not at higher risk than the general adult population for acquiring pneumococcal disease, they may seek immunization because they fall into a high-risk category. The following conditions are indications for pneumococcal vaccine:

- Age 65 years or more.

PPSV is also recommended for persons <65 years with certain underlying medical conditions, including anatomic or functional asplenia; immunocompromise (including HIV infection); chronic lung, heart, or kidney disease; and diabetes.

Side Effects

- Local injection site soreness and erythema may occur in up to 50 percent of recipients, but usually subsides within 24 to 48 hours after administration.

- Anaphylactic reactions have occurred in persons receiving repeat doses of vaccine more often than the current recommendation repeat dosing 6 years after the first dose in high-risk individuals.

- Adverse effects on the fetus after vaccinating pregnant women have not been observed. The product insert advises administration to pregnant women only if clearly needed. It is prudent to wait until after the first trimester of pregnancy before immunizing.

Strategies for Administration

- The ACP's Task Force on Adult Immunization recommends that the 50th birthday be used as a date to review adult immunizations and determine specifically whether pneumococcal vaccine should be given. After age 50, 30 to 40 percent of persons have a high-risk condition for which they should receive the vaccine.[29] The product insert for PPSV recommends routine vaccination of immune competent persons >50 years old.[41]

- Elderly persons with unknown vaccination status should receive one dose of the vaccine.

- There are no routine recommendations for revaccination following a second dose.[41] For revaccination schedule, see "Strategies for Administration."

- It is recommended that the vaccine be administered at least 2 weeks before elective splenectomy if possible and at least 2 weeks prior to the initiation of immune suppressive therapy, as immune response to vaccination may be impaired.[41]

- Persons with asymptomatic or symptomatic HIV infection should be vaccinated as soon as their diagnosis is confirmed.[6]

Spacing with Other Immunobiologics

The vaccine can be administered at any time, concomitantly with other vaccines (including the influenza vaccination), but at different anatomic sites and using separate syringes. Intradermal administration may cause severe local reactions.[41]

Use in Controlling Healthcare-Associated Transmission

Not applicable.

Contraindications

- Hypersensitivity reaction to a previous dose of vaccine or any component of the vaccine.

- Revaccination is contraindicated for persons who had a severe reaction to the initial dose they received.

- Re-immunization more frequently than recommended increases the probability of Arthus-like reactions.

- Although there is no evidence that PPSV is harmful to either a pregnant woman or to her fetus, as a precaution, women with conditions that put them at risk for pneumococcal disease should be vaccinated before becoming pregnant, if possible.

Administration Schedule

The dose of this vaccine is 0.5 mL administered IM or subcutaneously (SQ), preferably in deltoid in adults.

Revaccination

Revaccination of immune competent persons previously vaccinated with one dose of PPSV is not routinely recommended.

ACIP has published guidelines and an algorithm for pneumococcal revaccination.[42]

For all other persons, only the following persons should receive a one-time revaccination:

1. Persons age >65 who received the first dose prior to age 65 and 5 or more years have elapsed since that first dose

2. Persons who are immunocompromised, have functional or anatomical asplenia, or have a condition that leads to rapid antibody loss (nephrotic syndrome, chronic renal failure, renal transplant) and 5 or more years have elapsed since the first dose

Post Vaccination Serological Testing

Not applicable.

Effectiveness and Safety

The vaccine is really 23 vaccines in one, with each serotype vaccine having its own failure rate. Although there has been controversy regarding the efficacy of the vaccine, numerous studies demonstrate that it effectively reduces the incidence of pneumococcal bacteremia among elderly high-risk persons. Recent case-control studies among elderly but otherwise healthy adults have shown efficacy rates of 50 to 70 percent.[41,42]

Studies of younger, healthy adults show excellent protective efficacy against pneumococcal pneumonia and bacteremia. Other than mild local reactions, the vaccine is safe. No neurological disorders have been causally linked to pneumococcal vaccine.

Prevnar 13, a pneumococcal 13-valent conjugate vaccine (which contains 13 different serotypes of the bacterium *Streptococcus pneumoniae*), was approved on December 30, 2011, by the FDA for adults aged 50 years and older to prevent pneumonia and invasive disease caused by the bacterium.

Unresolved Issues

- More immunogenic/efficacious vaccines are needed, and protein-conjugate vaccines are being developed.

- The optimal time for initial and re-immunization remains unclear.[42]

Commonly Asked Questions

- Can the vaccine be administered subcutaneously? The vaccine is licensed for either IM or SQ administration. It can cause severe allergic reactions if the vaccine is administered intradermally.

- Should the vaccine be given to adults younger than age 65 to improve the immunogenicity of the vaccine? ACP's Task Force on Adult Immunization recommends the 50th birthday as a time to assess the need for any immunizations, particularly the pneumococcal vaccine. If there are any indications (see previous discussion) for receiving the vaccine, it should be administered at this time.

- What should you do if you don't know whether pneumococcal vaccine was previously given? If a review of the medical records and inquiry to previous physicians attending the individual are unrewarding, it is reasonable to administer a dose of vaccine. Often a spouse can provide important information in this regard. This is consistent with the guidelines on pneumococcal immunization.[42]

- Can this vaccine be given at the same time as influenza vaccine? Absolutely yes! The vaccines should be given with different syringes at different anatomical sites.

- Who should be revaccinated? ACIP has published guidelines and an algorithm for pneumococcal revaccination.[42] (See also Strategies for Administration in this section.)

Polio

Vaccine Type

In the United States, only an enhanced-potency inactivated, parental whole virus vaccine (IPV) is available. Oral polio vaccine (OPV) has not been used in the United States since 2000 but is still used in many parts of the world. This U.S. policy was implemented to eliminate the risk for vaccine-associated paralytic poliomyelitis, a rare condition that has been associated with the use of the live OPV. The IPV vaccine currently licensed for use and distributed in the United States is IPOL (Sanofi Pasteur, Swiftwater, PA).[43,44]

Indications

Routine primary poliovirus vaccination of adults >18 residing in the United States is not recommended. Most have a minimal risk of poliovirus exposure in the United States and most are immune from childhood immunizations.

In adults, polio vaccine is indicated for those at increased risk of exposure to poliovirus as follows:

- Travelers to regions or countries where poliomyelitis is common

- HCPs in close contact with patients who could have polio

- Laboratory workers handling specimens that may contain polioviruses[43,44]

Side Effects: Enhanced-potency Inactivated Polio

No serious adverse effects have been documented because of this vaccine. However, you need to look for any unusual condition, such as a serious allergic reaction, high fever, or unusual behavior. If a serious allergic reaction occurs, it would happen within a few minutes to a few hours after the shot.

Spacing with Other Immunobiologics

Concomitant administration, of other parenteral vaccines, with separate syringes at separate sites, is not contraindicated. There are no known interactions of IPOL with drugs or foods.

Use in Controlling Nosocomial Transmission

HCP should be immune against polio. It is unlikely that HCP in the United States will come into contact with poliovirus.

Contraindications

- Persons with a history of severe allergic reaction (e.g., anaphylaxis) after a previous dose or to any component of the vaccine including antibiotics neomycin, streptomycin, or polymyxin B.

- Vaccination of persons with acute febrile illness should be deferred until after recovery.

Administration Schedule

- Enhanced-potency polio: four doses (0.5 mL SQ or IM in the deltoid) given at time 2 months, 4 months, 6 to 18 months, and a booster dose at 4 to 6 years.[44]

- For persons with increased risk of exposure who received an incomplete polio vaccine series, a total of four doses with inactivated vaccine is considered a complete series.

- Persons at increased risk of exposure to poliovirus who have previously completed a primary series with one or a combination of polio vaccines can be given additional doses of IPV. Those who have had one or two doses of polio vaccine in the past should get the remaining one or two doses.

- Unvaccinated adults at high risk should receive the primary series of three doses. Two doses separated by 1 to 2 months, and a third dose 6 to 12 months after the second.[44]

Post Vaccination Serological Testing

Not applicable or usually done.

Effectiveness and Safety

- The vaccine is highly effective in preventing polio.

- After two doses of this vaccine, 98 to 100 percent seroconversion occurs.

Unresolved Issues

None.

Commonly Asked Questions

- Are HCP at risk for polio? Yes, although that risk may be low, the potential devastating effects of poliovirus infection are considerable. HCP may care either for patients from other parts of the world where polio is present or individuals who are excreting vaccine virus because of oral vaccine administration in other countries. HCP may travel to countries to work where polio is endemic. Finally, HCP who work in laboratories with poliovirus or polio vaccine viruses may be at risk of exposure.

- Is there a need for any type of booster dose of polio vaccine? Yes, adults who have had three doses of IPV or OPV but are at increased risk (e.g., travelers to endemic areas, HCP indications), can receive another dose of IPV. Otherwise, routine booster doses are neither necessary nor recommended.[43,44]

Tetanus-Diphtheria-Acellular Pertussis

Vaccine Type

In the United States, there is currently one combination tetanus toxoid, reduced diphtheria toxoid, and acellular pertussis vaccine, ADACEL (Sanofi Pasteur), licensed for use in adults. ADACEL contains a tetanus toxoid, a diphtheria toxoid, and acellular pertussis components. The vaccine also contains aluminum phosphate, residual glutaraldehyde, residual formaldehyde, and 2-phenoxyethanol. ADACEL does not contain thimerosal.[45,46]

Indications

HCPs are at risk of acquiring and transmitting pertussis, as evidenced by numerous reports of pertussis outbreaks and exposures in healthcare facilities. ACIP has published routine adult tetanus-diphtheria-acellular pertussis (Tdap) recommendations, as well as specific recommendations for HCP and pregnant/postpartum women.[46,47]

The following are recommendations for a single dose of Tdap. All adults 11 years and older, including those 65 years and older, should get a dose of Tdap vaccine.

- Routine recommendation: Adults should receive a single dose of Tdap to replace a single dose of tetanus-diphtheria (Td) for booster immunization against tetanus, diphtheria, and pertussis if they received the most recent tetanus-containing toxoid 10 or more years previously.

- Vaccination of HCP: Those who have direct contact with patients in hospitals and ambulatory care centers should receive a single dose of Tdap as soon as feasible if they have not previously received Tdap.

- Other HCP: Should receive a single dose of Tdap according to routine adult recommendations.

- For protection of infants aged <12 months: Adults (including parents, grandparents, or HCP) who have or anticipate close contact with an infant <12 months should receive a single dose of Tdap.

- For pregnant women: The Tdap vaccine is now recommended for all women in the third trimester (ideally 27th through 36th week of their pregnancy), even if they have previously received Tdap vaccine.

Side Effects

Pain at the injection site was the most frequently reported local adverse event from the primary adult safety trial conducted in adults who received either a single dose of ADACEL or Td. The most frequently reported systemic adverse events were headache, generalized body aches, and fatigue. Fever was reported with similar low frequency (approximately 1 percent) in both groups. Serious adverse events were reported in 1.9 percent of the vaccinated adults. There were no cases of whole-arm swelling.[45,46]

Strategies for Administration

The objectives of the most recent ACIP Tdap recommendations for adults, HCP, and pregnant or postpartum women are to protect the vaccinated adult against pertussis and reduce the reservoir of pertussis in the population. The strategy is to use Tdap as a one-time alternative to tetanus and diphtheria toxoids adsorbed for adult use (Td) in persons for whom the pertussis component is also indicated.[45,46]

Spacing with Other Immunobiologics

Tdap can be given simultaneously with any other vaccine, using different syringes and injected at different anatomical sites. Some experts recommend administering no more than two injections per muscle, separated by at least 1 inch.[46,47]

Use in Controlling Healthcare-Associated Transmission

There have been reports of using acellular pertussis vaccine during hospital outbreaks of pertussis.[31] Currently, the vaccine is not licensed for use in adults during outbreaks of pertussis in hospitals.

Contraindications

- History of hypersensitivity to vaccine or any of its components
- History of encephalopathy (e.g., coma, prolonged seizures) not attributable to an identifiable cause within 7 days of administration of a pertussis vaccine

Precautions and Reasons to Defer Tdap

- GBS less than 6 weeks after a previous dose of a tetanus-containing toxoid
- Moderate to severe acute illness
- Unstable neurological condition in adult (e.g., cerebrovascular events and acute encephalopathic conditions) until resolved or stabilized
- History of Arthrous hypersensitivity reaction to a tetanus-containing vaccine administered less than 10 years previously
- Tdap is not licensed for adults aged >65 years[45,46]

Administration Schedule

- Tdap is licensed for one-dose administration, not for subsequent every 10-year boosters or wound prophylaxis.
- The one-time dose of Tdap is 0.5 mL administered IM (deltoid).
- Adults should receive a decennial booster (10 years later) after receipt of Tdap.
- Tdap is not licensed for multiple administrations.
- There are no data to support repeat administration of the vaccine.
- Short intervals between Td and Tdap: Tdap can be administered at an interval less than 10 years since receipt of last tetanus-containing toxoid vaccine to protect against pertussis. The dose of Tdap replaces the next scheduled Td booster.
- Special situations in adults:
  - Those with a history of pertussis should receive Tdap according to the routine recommendations.
  - Persons older than age 11 years who require a tetanus-toxoid containing vaccine as part of wound management should receive Tdap instead of Td if they have not previously received Tdap. If Tdap is not available or was administered previously, Td should be administered.
  - Those who have never received tetanus and diphtheria toxoid-containing vaccine should receive a series of three vaccines. The preferred schedule is a single dose of Tdap, a dose of Td 4 or more weeks later, and a second dose of Td 6 to 12 months later. Tdap can substitute for Td for any one of the three doses in the series.[29,45-47]

Post Vaccination Serological Testing

Not routinely done as, currently, no well-accepted serological correlates of protection for pertussis exist.

Effectiveness and Safety

According to ACIP, Tdap vaccines in the United States were licensed on the basis of clinical trials demonstrating immunogenicity not inferior to that of U.S.-licensed Td and the pertussis components of pediatric DTaP manufactured by Sanofi-Pasteur as well as an acceptable safety profile.[47]

Arthrous reaction can occur after a tetanus-toxoid-containing vaccine. ACIP lists Arthrous-like reaction from a previously administered tetanus-toxoid-containing vaccine within the previous 10 years as a precaution for Tdap.

Tdap prelicensure studies in adults support the safety of ADACEL. (However, ACIP points out that the sample sizes were insufficient to detect rare adverse events.) Close monitoring of vaccine safety from the Vaccine Adverse Events Reporting System (VAERS) and post licensure studies of Tdap have been and will continue to be conducted. Such monitoring will enable detection of potential adverse reactions after widespread use of Tdap in adults.[46,47]

Unresolved Issues

As this is a recently licensed vaccine, there are areas of further information needed to assess long-term follow-up issues.

- Need for data on the burden of pertussis among adults and the impact of the Tdap vaccination policy
- Post licensure studies and surveillance to evaluate changes in the incidence of pertussis, the uptake of Tdap, and the duration of effectiveness of Tdap vaccine
- Safety and immunogenicity of Tdap in adults >65 years of age, pregnant women, and their children
- Effectiveness of deferring pertussis prophylaxis among recently vaccinated HCP exposed to pertussis
- Safety, effectiveness, and duration of protection of repeated Tdap doses
- Improved pertussis diagnostic tests
- Determination and evaluation of immunological correlates of protection for pertussis[31]

Commonly Asked Questions

- If HCP receive Tdap and then are exposed to someone with pertussis, is it appropriate to treat the HCP prophylactically or consider the HCP immune? Follow the PEP protocol for pertussis. There have been no new changes in pertussis PEP with the licensure of Tdap.

- Will Tdap replace the Td booster that is routinely recommended every 10 years? At this time Tdap is only approved for one dose except for those during pregnancy.

- If HCP have a history of pertussis infection as a child, is Tdap vaccine recommended for this HCP? HCP with a previous history of pertussis, who have not received Tdap, should receive Tdap according to routine recommendations.

- Should adult HCP get a pertussis booster if their institution is experiencing an outbreak of pertussis? Until studies specify the optimal management of exposed vaccinated HCP or a consensus of experts is reached, healthcare facilities should continue use of PEP for vaccinated HCP with unprotected pertussis exposures.

Vaccinia

Vaccinia vaccine has been included in this chapter for several reasons. First, there are routine, nonemergency indications for use of this vaccine against smallpox and other viruses in the *Orthopoxvirus* genus.[33] Second, smallpox has been designated by the CDC as a Category A agent, and therefore it has a higher potential for use as an agent of bioterrorism, against which the United States needs to protect its citizens.[48] After the anthrax bioterrorism attacks in 2001, a volunteer U.S. Civilian Smallpox Preparedness and Response Program (USCSPRP) resulted in approximately 40,000 civilian personnel from all 50 states (including 17,000 hospital healthcare staff and 13,000 public health response team members) receiving the vaccine. Selected military personnel are administered the smallpox vaccine. Finally, in an emergency smallpox situation, public health officials will likely issue additional recommendations regarding use of smallpox vaccine.

Vaccine

Routine smallpox vaccination among the American public stopped in 1972 after the disease was eradicated in the United States. Until recently, the U.S. government provided the vaccine only to a few hundred scientists and medical professionals working with smallpox and similar viruses in a research setting.

After the events of September and October 2001, however, the U.S. government took further actions to improve its level of preparedness against terrorism. One of many such measures—designed specifically to prepare for an intentional release of the smallpox virus—included updating and releasing a smallpox response plan. In addition, the U.S. government has enough vaccine to vaccinate every person in the United States in the event of a smallpox emergency.[49]

Indications

The categories of indications for use of vaccinia vaccine are divided into routine nonemergency; USCSPRP; and emergency recommendations.

- Routine nonemergency: Vaccinia vaccine is recommended for laboratory workers who directly handle cultures or animals contaminated or infected with non-highly attenuated vaccinia virus, recombinant vaccinia viruses derived from non-highly attenuated vaccine strains, or other orthopoxviruses that infect humans. The vaccine should be considered for HCP who have contact with patients with smallpox or who have received the smallpox vaccine and in situations in which adherence to infection prevention procedures may be compromised.[33]

- USCSPRP: In February 2003, the CDC initiated a call for volunteers to form healthcare response teams to care for the nation's citizens in the event of a smallpox event. Subsequent to 2003, vaccination of response team members has continued, although in much lower numbers. In this program, volunteers need to be carefully screened prior to vaccination and should discuss this decision with their healthcare providers. Extensive guidelines for persons considering vaccination in this program are available.[48] ACIP issued a statement in support of the pre-event program as long as it is carried out within the currently recommended response teams and state and local response plans, as well as according to current vaccination recommendations and protocols. ACIP stated, "At this time, it is unwise to expand beyond its current pre-event smallpox vaccination recommendations because of the new and unanticipated safety concerns, i.e., myo/pericarditis, whose extent and severity, particularly of long-term sequelae, are not yet known."[49]

- In an emergency situation, in which a smallpox agent has been intentionally released or if a susceptible individual has been exposed to a smallpox case, no absolute contraindications regarding vaccination exist. In such cases, any contraindications must be weighed against a potentially fatal smallpox infection[33] and public health officials will likely release additional guidelines for vaccination.

Side Effects

The following are listed as common adverse reactions from the smallpox vaccine:

- Inoculation site signs and symptoms, such as pain, redness, pruritus, or pyogenic infection at vaccination site

- Swelling and tenderness of regional lymph nodes

- Malaise

- Fatigue

- Fever

- Myalgias

- Headache

The preceding adverse events are less frequent in revaccinated persons than first-time vaccine recipients.

More Severe Adverse Events

- Inadvertent inoculation at other sites (most common are face, nose, mouth, lips, genitalia, and rectum)

- Self-limited skin rashes not associated with vaccinia replication in skin, including urticaria and folliculitis

- Encephalitis, encephalomyelitis, and encephalopathy

- Severe disability, permanent neurological sequelae

- Progressive vaccinia (vaccinia necrosum), generalized vaccinia, severe vaccinial skin infections, erythema multiforme major (including Stevens-Johnson syndrome), and eczema vaccinatum

- Myocarditis and/or pericarditis, ischemic heart disease, and nonischemic, dilated cardiomyopathy

- Ocular complications (including but not limited to keratitis and corneal scarring) and blindness

- Transmission of vaccinia virus to contacts[33]

- Death (including death of unvaccinated persons who have contact with vaccinated individuals)

Precise breakdowns of the frequency of serious adverse events by vaccine, and whether first-time or re-vaccinees are available for review.[50,51]

Precautions

ACIP recommends that persons be excluded from receiving smallpox vaccine for either nonemergency indications or to participate in the Smallpox Preparedness and Response Program who have known underlying heart disease, with or without symptoms; or have three or more of the following risk factors for ischemic heart disease: hypertension, high cholesterol, diabetes, heart disease in a first-degree relative (e.g., mother, father, brother, or sister), or smoke cigarettes.[50]

Strategies for Administration

The preferred sites of vaccine administration are into the skin over the insertion of the deltoid muscle in the upper arm. The skin should not be cleaned with alcohol or any other chemical agents prior to vaccination unless grossly contaminated. In such cases, the alcohol must be allowed to dry completely or it may inactivate the vaccine.

Persons who administer the vaccine should receive education on the proper technique. The CDC maintains an extensive and updated website with guidelines, recommendations, training videos, and instructions for HCP. The vaccine is administered via a multipuncture technique with a sterile bifurcated needle (licensed by the FDA for use with and supplied in the vaccine package). The bifurcated needle is dipped into the vaccine vial once and, when removed, contains a droplet with the recommended dosage of the vaccine. Holding the bifurcated needle perpendicular to the skin, 15 punctures are made into the insertion site with strokes vigorous enough to allow a trace of blood to appear within a diameter of approximately 5 mm.

The vaccine site should be kept clean and dry. The CDC website contains detailed information for those who administer the vaccine, which include vaccine preparation, reconstitution, administration, storage, and instructions for interpreting the vaccination response.

Revaccination

ACIP recommends that persons at continued high risk of exposure to smallpox, such as research laboratory workers handling the virus, should receive repeat smallpox vaccination every 3 years.[48,50]

In October 2008, the CDC issued interim guidance for revaccination of persons vaccinated during the USCSPRP:

- Revaccination of persons who received vaccine during the UCSPRP is recommended on an as-needed, and what the CDC has termed, "out-the-door" basis (only after a determination of a credible smallpox threat to public health has been assessed and prior to the volunteers engaging in activities placing them at risk of smallpox virus exposure). This situation would only apply to those initially vaccinated during the implementation of this program and who had evidence of a documented vaccine "take" (successful vaccination).

- In addition, the CDC recommends revaccination of persons who administer smallpox vaccine to others, every 10 years.

Spacing with Other Immunobiologics

If possible, HCP scheduled to receive an annual purified protein derivative TST for tuberculosis screening should not receive the skin test until more than 1 month after smallpox vaccination.[48] There is a possibility that the vaccine may interfere with the tuberculin blood test as well.

Use in Controlling Healthcare-Associated Transmission

In 2003, an outbreak of monkeypox occurred in the United States after importation of exotic rodents, subsequently infected prairie dogs, were sold as pets. As a result of secondary cases of monkeypox in humans, at least 23 persons were vaccinated post exposure with smallpox vaccine, and the CDC issued interim recommendations regarding the use of smallpox vaccine.[51] However, at this time there are no recommendations for use of the vaccine post exposure. For emergency situations, it is likely that the vaccine will be used for those at high risk (see Emergency Indications).

Categories of Contraindications[33,48,52,53]

Emergency indications: There are very few absolute contraindications in the event of an emergency situation, resulting in persons with high risk for smallpox. In addition, it is important to note that those who are at greatest risk of experiencing serious complications after vaccination might also be those at greatest risk for smallpox death. Thus, the risk of serious complications must be weighed against that of experiencing a potentially fatal smallpox infection.[33]

Routine, nonemergency, and/or USCSPRP: Because the vaccinia virus can be spread to others from the site of a recently vaccinated individual, some contraindications apply to both potential vaccinees and their household contacts (including persons with prolonged intimate contact with the potential vaccines). This also includes persons who may have direct contact with the vaccination site, such as sexual contacts. Other contraindications apply only to potential vaccinees.[33,50,51]

Contraindications

Live vaccinia virus can be transmitted to persons in close contact with vaccines; thus, the risks for experiencing the following severe adverse events apply to vaccinees and their close/household contacts.

Risks of severe adverse events are increased in vaccinees with the following conditions:

- Cardiac disease (current or past history).
- Eye disease treated with topical steroids.
- Congenital or acquired immune deficiency disorders, including taking immunosuppressive medications.
- Eczema (or history of eczema), or other acute or chronic exfoliative skin conditions.
- Pregnancy: The vaccine virus caused severe fetal vaccinia and death. If a woman is vaccinated during pregnancy, becomes pregnant within 28 days of vaccination, or if a vaccinee lives in the same household or is a close contact of a pregnant woman, the vaccinee should be counseled regarding the potential harm to the fetus.
- Breastfeeding mothers. It is not known whether the vaccinia virus or its antibodies are excreted in human milk. However, the risk of inadvertent inoculation is increased with the close physical contact involved with breastfeeding.
- Infants <12 months of age (the risk of serious adverse events following vaccination is higher in infants) and live virus can be inadvertently transmitted to an infant from a lactating mother.
- Previous severe reaction to smallpox vaccine or any of its components.
- ACIP advises against nonemergency use of the vaccine in persons <18 years of age.
- ACIP recommends that persons be excluded from the pre-event smallpox vaccination program who have known underlying heart disease, with or without symptoms, or if they have three or more known major cardiac risk factors—hypertension, diabetes, hypercholesterolemia (high cholesterol), heart disease at age 50 in a first-degree relative, and smoking.[50]
- Persons with known or possible latex sensitivity, as the vaccine vial stopper is made of dry natural rubber.

Emergency Indications (Post-release Vaccination)

According to the CDC and ACIP, all contraindications to vaccinia vaccination would be reconsidered during a smallpox emergency, and persons would be advised by public health authorities in such an event. Groups for which such vaccination would be indicated include:

- Persons exposed to the initial release of the virus
- Persons who had face-to-face, household, or close-proximity contact (<6.5 feet or 2 meters) with a confirmed or suspected smallpox case at any time from onset of the case's fever until all scabs have separated
- Personnel involved in the direct medical or public health evaluation, care, or transportation of suspected smallpox cases
- Laboratory personnel who collect or process clinical specimens from confirmed or suspected cases
- Other persons with increased likelihood of contact with infectious materials from a smallpox patient (e.g., personnel responsible for medical waste and/or linen disposal or disinfecting a room that houses smallpox cases)[33]

It is imperative that individuals refer to guidelines from public health officials that would be provided in an emergency smallpox situation.

Post Vaccination Serological Testing

The level of antibody that protects against smallpox is unknown. In addition, the level of antibody required for protection against vaccine virus infection is also unknown. No current recommendations regarding use of serological testing are available.

Effectiveness and Safety

Smallpox vaccine is indicated for active immunization against smallpox disease in persons determined to be at high risk for infection. In an emergency situation, for a person exposed to smallpox, the risk of death from smallpox versus the risk of severe complication from the vaccine must be weighed.

- Generalized rashes are not uncommon following vaccination and are usually self-limiting.
- Ocular and nonocular inadvertent inoculation is the most common side effect, resulting when the virus is transferred from the vaccine site to another site on the vaccinee. This can be prevented by careful hand hygiene and care of the vaccination site.
- Myocarditis/pericarditis occurs at a rate of 5.7 cases/million primary vaccinations.
- The majority of vaccinees have experienced at least one or more adverse event, with 10 percent of primary and 3 percent of re-vaccinees experiencing at least one severe adverse event.
- Vaccinia immunoglobulin (VIG) is available from the CDC for specific severe adverse reactions to the smallpox vaccine.[51]

The data from the CDC smallpox website indicates that VIG was only released once between January 24, 2003, and April 30, 2005, during the USCSPRP.

A recent study conducted among adults vaccinated after 2001 indicated overall and serious adverse event rates of 217 and 26 per 100,000 vaccinees, respectively.[54] Epidemiological studies have supported a causal relationship between myo/pericarditis and smallpox vaccination. No new smallpox vaccine-associated clinical syndromes have been identified.[55]

Varicella

Vaccine Type

Currently one preparation of a live attenuated varicella vaccine, Varivax (Merck) is licensed for use in adults in the United States. Varivax is a lyophilized preparation.

Indications

Varivax vaccine is indicated for protection against varicella and its complications. The most recent ACIP guidelines have expanded the list of indications to all healthy persons >13 years, HIV-infected adolescents, and adults with specific CD4 T-lymphocyte counts, postpartum assessment and vaccination, and approved criteria for evidence of immunity.[56,57] Healthcare institutions should ensure that all HCP have evidence of immunity to varicella.[5] Adults who may be at increased risk of either acquiring or transmitting varicella who do not have evidence of immunity, should receive special consideration for vaccination. This includes susceptible persons older than 13 years in the following high-risk groups.[56,57]

- HCP

- Household contacts of immunocompromised individuals

- Persons who live or work where transmission of varicella zoster virus (VZV) is likely (e.g., teachers of young children, day care employees, and residents and staff members in institutional settings)

- Persons who live or work in environments where transmission can occur (e.g., college students, inmates and staff members of correctional institutions, and military personnel)

- Nonpregnant women of childbearing age (women should be advised to avoid pregnancy for 1 month after each dose of the vaccine)

- Adolescents and adults living in households with children

- International travelers

- Recommended for use in susceptible persons following exposure to varicella, within 3 days and possibly up to 5 days after exposure

- ACIP recommends the use of varicella vaccine for outbreak control for exposed susceptible persons[56]

- Most recently, ACIP has described several special considerations for vaccination, including HIV-infected adults with

CD4T-lymphocyte counts of ≥200 cells/μL (two doses 3 months apart); some situations where mild degrees of immune suppression are present (e.g., those with impaired humoral immunity); and susceptible postpartum nursing mothers.[56]

Evidence of Immunity for HCP

- Written documentation of vaccination with two doses of varicella vaccine.

- Laboratory evidence of immunity or laboratory confirmation of disease.

- Diagnosis or verification of a history of varicella disease by a healthcare provider.

- Diagnosis or verification of a history of herpes zoster by a healthcare provider.

Side Effects

Rash, fever, and injection-site soreness have been the most frequently reported adverse events in the post-licensure period. See Table 103-8 for a summary of adverse events.[58]

Strategies for Administration

Serological screening of personnel with negative or uncertain history of varicella is likely to be cost effective prior to vaccination.[46] Healthcare facilities might consider serological testing of all personnel regardless of history, as a small portion of those with positive disease history might be susceptible.[56]

Vaccine can be offered to susceptible HCP on initial employment or at annual intervals concurrent with other employment-related healthcare activities (i.e., annual TST or annual symptom review for tuberculosis).

Policies for management of vaccinated HCP should be developed for each institution. These policies should be added to those already in place for handling varicella exposures. There are numerous issues to be included in such policies, such as definitions of exposure to varicella; serological testing for immunity to varicella; whether to require or recommend vaccination to nonimmune employees; how to manage vaccinated HCP in the immediate post vaccination period and

Table 103-8. Post-varicella Immunization Side Effects in Adults[58]

Reaction	Percent Post First Dose	Percent Post Second Dose
Fever ≥101°F	10.2 percent	9.5 percent
Injection-site complaints	24.4 percent	32.5 percent
Varicella-like rash (injection site)	3 percent	1 percent
Varicella-like rash (generalized)	5.5 percent	0.9 percent

*Evidence of immunity is defined as either diagnosis of varicella by a healthcare provider or a healthcare provider verification of a history of varicella disease (rather than parental or self-report). U.S. birth before 1980 is not considered evidence of immunity for HCP, pregnant women, and immunocompromised persons.[56]

in future exposures to wild-type varicella; and how to handle patients and HCP who develop vaccine rash. There are many questions to be considered in formulating these policies (see "Further Issues for Consideration").

Spacing with Other Immunobiologics

Varivax can be given at the same time (using separate anatomical sites and syringes) or within 30 days of MMR without increasing adverse reactions. ACIP guidelines state that the simultaneous administration of most widely used live attenuated and inactivated vaccines has not resulted in impaired antibody responses or increased adverse effects with this vaccine.[18,56]

Immunoglobulin, including varicella zoster immunoglobulin (VZIG), should not be given for at least 2 months after vaccination with varicella vaccine. Vaccination with varicella vaccine should be deferred for at least 5 months after administration of blood or plasma infusions, or administration of any immunoglobulin, including VZIG.[56]

Use in Controlling Healthcare-Associated Transmission

To prevent healthcare-associated transmission, healthcare facilities should ensure that all susceptible HCP have been vaccinated with varicella vaccine. Policies must be developed to manage employees who may develop vaccine rash because of the very small risk of vaccine virus transmission.[5,56]

ACIP recommends use of varicella vaccination within 3 to 5 days after exposure for unvaccinated HCP without evidence of immunity to modify the disease. Vaccination more than 5 days after exposure is also indicated, as it protects against subsequent exposures if the current exposure did not result in infection. Persons at increased risk for severe varicella who have contraindications to varicella vaccine should receive VZIG within 96 hours of exposure.

Policies must be developed to manage employees who may develop vaccine rash because of the very small risk of vaccine virus transmission.[5,56] ACIP recommends that if a vaccine-related rash occurs in HCP, the HCP should avoid contact with susceptible persons who are at risk for severe disease/complications. This work restriction should continue until all lesions have crusted or disappeared or no new lesions have occurred within a 24-hour period.[56]

Contraindications (to Single-antigen Vaccine in Adults)[18,56,58]

- Persons with a history of hypersensitivity (e.g., anaphylaxis) after a previous vaccine dose or to any component of the vaccine, including gelatin and neomycin.

- Persons with any malignant condition, including blood dyscrasias, leukemia, lymphomas of any type, or other malignant neoplasms affecting bone marrow or lymphatic systems.

- Pregnant women (and vaccinated women should be counseled to avoid pregnancy for one month after each dose of the vaccine). Women who become pregnant within 1 month of vaccination should be counseled about potential effects to the fetus.

- Persons with substantial suppression of cellular immunity.

- Anyone with a family history of congenital or hereditary immunodeficiency in first-degree relatives unless the immune competence of the potential vaccine has been verified clinically or by a laboratory.

- Persons receiving high-dose systemic immunosuppressive therapy, including those on oral steroids ≥2 mg/kg of body weight or a total of 20 or more mg/day of prednisone or equivalent for persons who weigh >10 kg, when administered for 2 or more weeks. Vaccination can result in a more extensive vaccine-associated rash or disseminated disease in these individuals.[58]

Precautions

- Vaccination of persons who have acute severe illness, including febrile respiratory illness or other infection, including untreated active tuberculosis, should be postponed until the person has recovered. However, TST is not a prerequisite for varicella vaccination. The decision to delay vaccination depends largely on the severity of symptoms and etiology of the disease.

- Varicella vaccines should not be administered for 3 to 11 months after administration of blood, plasma, or immunoglobulin (but not washed red blood cells) because of potential inhibition of immune response by passively transferred antibodies. (The time interval depends on the product.)[18]

- As a precautionary measure, epinephrine injection (1:1,000) should be available for immediate use should an anaphylactic reaction occur.

- The manufacturer recommends vaccine recipients avoid the use of salicylates for 6 weeks after vaccination, as Reye's syndrome has been reported after the use of salicylates during natural varicella infection.[58]

Administration Schedule

All healthy adult HCP without evidence of immunity to varicella should receive two 0.5-mL doses of single-antigen vaccine by subcutaneous administration, 4 to 8 weeks apart. The preferred site of administration is the deltoid muscle.

Additional administration and handling information:[58]

- Not for intravenous injection

- Diluent should be stored separately at room temperature or in a refrigerator

- Vaccine must be stored frozen before reconstitution at an average temperature of about 5°F (–15°C) or colder.

- Once reconstituted, the vaccine should be administered immediately. Discard if reconstituted vaccine is not used within 30 minutes.

- Do not freeze the reconstituted vaccine.

- Duration of protection is unknown at present, and the need for booster doses is not defined; additional studies are needed in this area.

Post Vaccination Serologic Testing

Routine testing for varicella immunity following two doses of vaccine is not recommended for the management of vaccinated HCP. Approximately 99 percent of adults are seropositive after the second dose. However, seroconversion does not always result in full protection against disease.[56] Currently, there are no data available for adults regarding correlates of protection.

Effectiveness and Safety

From prelicensure studies, efficacy of the vaccine in protecting adults from varicella after household exposure was estimated to be 80 percent.[58] Postlicensure studies assessing the effectiveness of the vaccine in preventing moderate to severe varicella have consistently demonstrated high effectiveness.[58] Pre- and postlicensure studies have demonstrated that one dose of the single-antigen vaccine is approximately 85 percent effective in preventing varicella, and 95 percent effective in preventing severe varicella disease. Breakthrough varicella disease that occurs after vaccination is mild.[56]

ACIP defines breakthrough disease as "a case of infection with wild-type VZV occurring > 42 days after vaccination."[56] Breakthrough infection was reported in several postlicensure studies of adolescent and adult vaccine recipients, to occur between 8 and 10 percent, although breakthrough disease was substantially less severe among vaccinated than unvaccinated persons.[59,60]

For the almost 50 million doses distributed in the United States between 1995 and 2005, the overall adverse reporting rate was 52.7 cases/100,000 doses and the serious adverse event reporting rate was 2.6/100,000 doses. Although rare, serious adverse events included pneumonia, hepatitis, severe disseminated varicella infection, and secondary vaccine-virus transmission. It is noteworthy that except for vaccine virus transmission, the other severe events occurred in immunocompromised persons or those with serious medical conditions not known at the time of vaccination. Rash, fever, and injection-site reactions were the most commonly reported adverse events detected during postlicensure safety surveillance.[56]

Vaccinees may potentially be capable of transmitting vaccine virus to close contacts. This has occurred in vaccinees that developed a rash after vaccination. Vaccinated HCP with a vaccine-related rash should therefore avoid close contact with susceptible high-risk individuals, such as newborns, pregnant women, and immunocompromised persons.[56] (See also Strategies for Administration.)

Should inadvertent vaccination to a varicella-immune individual occur, the vaccine has been well tolerated in seropositive individuals, with no serious adverse effects.

Unresolved Issues

- The length of protection from varicella-containing vaccines remains unknown.

- Ongoing surveillance and studies are needed to determine the need for and timing of additional doses in the future.

- The effect of the use of varicella vaccine on the epidemiology of the disease, and the ability of clinicians to recognize breakthrough illness needs to be monitored in the future.

- The long-term effect of varicella vaccine on the incidence of herpes zoster, including those vaccinees exposed to varicella, is not presently known.[58]

Additional Issues

ACIP recommends that healthcare institutions should establish protocols and recommendations for screening and vaccinating HCP and for management of HCP after exposures in the workplace.

Questions that should be addressed and/or considered in formulating healthcare policies for vaccinating HCP and patients include:

- What is the definition of a varicella exposure? Does the definition differ between household versus hospital? Is there a minimal time limit for an exposure (i.e., 2 minutes is not considered an exposure but 10 minutes is)? Is exposure to a person with vaccine rash treated differently from an exposure to wild varicella virus?

- What is accepted as a positive history of varicella? ACIP has recently added criteria for evidence of immunity. For HCP, pregnant women, and immunocompromised persons, there are stricter criteria.[56]

- How many nonimmune employees are employed at the institution? How many varicella exposure incidents occur on average every year? Does the patient population consist of a significant number of high-risk susceptible persons? Do the answers to these questions warrant alternative approaches to managing varicella-exposed nonimmune employees rather than automatic work furloughs?

- What serological test is utilized for determining varicella susceptibility? How are borderline, equivocal, or questionable results handled?

- How will employees be screened for varicella? Will vaccinated employees be considered immune to varicella? Will any serological testing be done in such employees (i.e., after two doses of vaccine, after exposure to wild virus, or not at all)?

- Will vaccinated employees be allowed to work without restrictions in the immediate postvaccination period? If not, what will the restrictions include?

- Will vaccinated employees be considered immune after the first dose, the second dose, or not at all? Will restrictions to HCP only apply if vaccine rash develops? Will restrictions differ if the rash is localized at the injection site or generalized?

- What are the facility's policies regarding precautions for persons in whom a rash develops after vaccination?

Sample strategies for management of vaccinated HCP and patients need to include possibilities of vaccine rash development in the vaccinee, exposure to wild virus, breakthrough disease, and transmission of vaccine virus to unvaccinated persons.

The following strategies may be considered separately or in combination; other strategies may be devised by individual institutions.

- Consider all vaccinees to be immune to varicella—no restrictions regardless of whether vaccine rash develops or if vaccinee is exposed to wild VZV.

- Restrict vaccinated HCP from caring for high-risk susceptible individuals between times of first dose until 1 month after second dose.

- Restrict vaccinated HCP from caring for high-risk susceptible individuals only if vaccine rash develops, whether rash is generalized or localized to the injection site.

- Treat vaccinated HCP as if they are susceptible to varicella. In the immediate postvaccination period, should vaccine rash develop, options to consider for the employee include:

  o Restrict from work until lesions from the rash have completely dried and crusted.

  o Allow employee to work in areas without high-risk susceptible persons until the lesions have completely dried and crusted.

  o Allow employee to work in nonclinical area until all lesions have dried and crusted.

  o Do not restrict the employee in any way.

- Options for treating vaccinated HCP exposed to wild VZV:

  o No restrictions—consider employee immune.

  o Send employee home from day 8 to 21 post exposure for after each exposure to wild VZV.

  o Allow employee to work while face-masked from day 8 to 21 post exposure and to self-screen daily for symptoms; send employee home if disease develops. If disease develops, it would not be considered an exposure if employee complied with masking. This option has been utilized with success for managing hospital employees and patients nonimmune to varicella for numerous years. Algorithm-based policies have been developed for using this same premise for vaccinated employees and patients exposed to varicella.[61]

  o Allow employee to work without restrictions; allow self-screening for symptoms with work furlough if

symptoms develop. However, should disease develop in this case, an exposure may occur because persons who develop varicella can be contagious several days before rash develops.

  o Allow employee to work in an area without high-risk susceptible persons; send home if rash develops.

Note: For any of the preceding options, careful consideration should be given to making such options consistent with current available information on the vaccine as well as existing hospital policies, patient and employee susceptibility in individual institutions, and the incidence of varicella in the institution.

Caution: In this current age of concern regarding biological terrorism, it is imperative that HCP are well informed about the differences between varicella and smallpox rashes. This concern underscores the importance of improving varicella vaccination efforts in both HCP and patients to avoid confusion.

Commonly Asked Questions

- If I am a healthcare provider who is nonimmune to varicella, but I have an immunocompromised child at home, is it safe for me to get the varicella vaccine? This is an important question. The vaccine is particularly indicated for susceptible family members of immunocompromised individuals. Data to date show that there is very limited potential for vaccinees to spread virus to susceptible contacts. The risk of transmission from immunocompromised vaccinees with rash may be higher. In one study of children with leukemia who were vaccinated and developed rash, 15 (17 percent) of their healthy siblings developed varicella vaccine infection, although only 11 developed even a mild rash. The data to date suggest that healthy vaccinated adults have very limited potential to transmit vaccine virus to susceptible contacts. Where this has happened, seroconversion has either been asymptomatic or accompanied by very mild rash.

- Can the vaccine cause herpes zoster? The manufacturer calculated an incidence of 18.5 cases of herpes zoster/100,000 person years, based on follow-up clinical trials in adolescents and adults.[58] Multiple studies and surveillance data have not demonstrated any consistent trends in the incidence of herpes zoster since the vaccine program was initiated in 1995.[56]

- Can the vaccine be used for postexposure prophylaxis? ACIP recommends the vaccine for use in susceptible persons following exposure to varicella.[56] In exposed susceptible persons with contraindications to the vaccine, VZIG can be administered up to 96 hours post exposure.

- What should we do if HCP develop a vaccine-related rash? ACIP advises that HCP who develop a rash after immunization should avoid contact with immunocompromised individuals with a high risk of disease and complications, until all lesions resolve or until no new lesions have appeared within a 24-hour period.[56]

- Where can I get more information on varicella vaccine? ACIP published a revised statement on the use of varicella vaccine.[56]

Table 103-9. Immunization Schedule for HCP[5]

Vaccine	Indication	Schedule
Hepatitis A	Laboratory/primate workers	1 mL IM at 0, 6 months
Hepatitis B	Occupational exposure to blood, blood products, or bodily secretions	Three doses of 1 mL IM at 0, 1, and 6 to 12 months
Hepatitis A & B	As for Hepatitis A and Hepatitis B	1 mL IM at 0, 1, and 6 months
Influenza	Persons attending high-risk patients (e.g., elderly) Inactivated vaccine LAIV	1 dose of 0.5 mL IM annually Intranasal dose of 0.5 mL annually (split between both nostrils)
MMR Measles Mumps Rubella	 Adults born after 1957 without a history of physician-diagnosed measles, serologic immunity, or documentation of having received two doses of vaccine Adults born after 1957 without a history of mumps, serologic immunity, or documentation of having received vaccine Unimmunized women of childbearing age and healthcare personnel	 0.5 mL SQ at 0, and at least 1 month later 0.5 mL SQ once 0.5 mL SQ once
Td	Persons without a history, or an unknown history of Td immunization or >10 years since last dose	Unimmunized: three doses of 0.5 mL IM at 0, 1 to 2, 6 months Booster: one dose every 10 years
Tdap	HCP with direct patient contact, healthy adults 19 to 64; close contacts of those <1 year	0.5 mL IM one-time dose (can be substituted for any Td dose)
Varicella	Adults nonimmune to varicella	0.5 mL SQ at time 0 and 4 to 8 weeks later

IM, intramuscular; SQ, subcutaneous.

General Recommendations for Unimmunized Adult Healthcare Personnel

HCP should be immunized against Hepatitis B, influenza, measles, mumps, rubella, tetanus-diphtheria-pertussis, and varicella. HCP are not at increased risk of acquiring tetanus in comparison with the general population but should nonetheless follow ACIP guidelines (see Table 103-9). Guidelines for primary vaccination of adults not immunized at the recommended time in early infancy are shown in Table 103-10. The guidelines for adults differ from those of children because of age-specific risks of disease and complications.

Some products require more than one dose to ensure a protective adequate antibody response. In addition, some products, such as tetanus toxoid, require periodic booster doses throughout life to maintain satisfactory protection.

The intervals between doses shown in Table 103-10 are considered optimal and are intended to induce immunity as rapidly as possible. Longer intervals do not diminish the antibody response.

Adults who have received some, but not all, of the recommended doses should simply complete the interrupted series without starting over or receiving extra doses.

Conversely, shorter intervals may lessen the antibody response and increase the risk of local or systemic reactions (e.g., tetanus and diphtheria toxoids, Hepatitis B).

Dosing Recommendations

Immunobiologics should be stored, dosed, and administered properly to ensure maximum safety and efficacy (Table 103-11). Additional details are available in the respective manufacturers' prescribing information.

- Storage conditions are important determinants of potency.

- Most immunobiologics should be refrigerated (i.e., 2° to 8°C or 36° to 46°F). Freezing may destroy potency of some vaccines. Exception is varicella vaccine, which is stored frozen.

- MMR should be protected from light and used within 8 hours of reconstitution.

- Varicella vaccine must be used within 30 minutes of reconstitution. Must be kept frozen until ready to use.

- Route of administration impacts on both efficacy and safety:

  o Most vaccines are inactive if administered by mouth.

  o Vaccines containing adjuvants should be administered deep into the muscle mass to avoid local irritation and maximize

Table 103-10. Immunization Schedule for Adults Not Immunized at the Recommended Time in Early Infancy[18]

Vaccine	MMR#1 IPV #1 Td #1	MMR#2 IPV #2 Td #2	IPV #3 Td #3	Td*
Time of administration	First visit	1 to 2 months later	6 to 12 months later	10 years later and every 10 years thereafter

IPV, inactivated polio vaccine; MMR, measles, mumps, and rubella; Td, tetanus and diphtheria toxoids for adults; Tdap, tetanus toxoid, reduced diphtheria toxoid, and acellular pertussis vaccine.

*Tdap should be received once and can be substituted for any Td dose.

Table 103-11. Storage Conditions and Route of Administration for Adult Vaccines[18]

Vaccine	Storage	Route and Dose
Hepatitis A	2° to 8°C (35° to 46°F) (do not freeze)	Intramuscular (1.0 mL)
Hepatitis B	2° to 8°C (35° to 46°F) (do not freeze)	Intramuscular (1.0 mL)
Hepatitis A & B	2° to 8°C (35° to 46°F) (do not freeze)	Intramuscular (1.0 mL)
Influenza virus Inactivated vaccine FluMist	 2° to 8°C (35° to 46°F) (do not freeze) 2° to 8°C (35° to 46°F) (do not freeze)	 Intramuscular (0.5 mL) Intranasal (0.2 mL) split between nostrils
Pneumococcus subcutaneous	2° to 8°C (35° to 46°F) (do not freeze)	Intramuscular or subcutaneous (0.5 mL)
Measles, mumps, and rubella (MMR)	2° to 8°C (35° to 46°F), protect from light Unreconstituted lyophilized (freeze-dried) vaccine can be stored at freezer temperature	Subcutaneous (0.5 mL)
Tetanus and diphtheria (Td)	2° to 8°C (35° to 46°F) (do not freeze)	Subcutaneous (0.5 mL)
Tetanus, diphtheria, pertussis (Tdap)	2° to 8°C (35° to 46°F) (do not freeze)	Intramuscular (0.5 mL)
Vaccinia	Store unreconstituted −15° to −25°C or −5° to −13°F; Reconstituted may be stored in refrigerator 2° to 8°C or 36° to 46°F, then discard after 30 days	Multiple puncture technique onto skin over insertion of deltoid muscle or posterior aspect of arm over triceps muscle. (One drop of vaccine on tip of bifurcated needle.)
Varicella	≤5°F (≤1 to 15°C)*	Subcutaneous (0.5 mL)

*The powdered vaccine should be kept frozen and protected from light before reconstitution. The diluents used to reconstitute the vaccine should be kept at room temperature or in a refrigerator. The reconstituted vaccine must be used within 30 minutes.

immunogenicity. Therefore, an adequate needle length should be used to ensure deep intramuscular injection.[7]

o The site of injection should be chosen carefully to avoid local, neural, vascular, or tissue injury.

o In adults, the deltoid area is the preferred site of administration for both subcutaneous and intramuscular injections.

o The buttock should be avoided because of the risk of injury to the sciatic nerve. Furthermore, administration of Hepatitis B vaccine in the buttocks has been associated with decreased immunogenicity, presumably because of inadvertent injection into the subcutaneous or deep fat tissue.

• Most commercially available vaccines may be given simultaneously on the same day, but not at the same site.

• Simultaneous administration of MMR, poliovirus vaccine, and tetanus and diphtheria toxoids does not diminish efficacy or safety of the individual vaccines in comparison with separate administration.

• Candidates for influenza virus and pneumococcal vaccines often overlap; these two vaccines may be given simultaneously, at separate sites, without increasing the risk of adverse effects. However, it should be noted that influenza virus vaccine is intended for annual use, whereas pneumococcal vaccine is usually given only once.

Doses of immunobiologics have been carefully selected based on theoretical considerations, controlled trials, and clinical experience. Some practitioners use smaller, divided doses in an effort to minimize the risk of adverse reactions, but such practices may result in inadequate protection and increased local reactions.

Conversely, higher doses may increase the risk of local or systemic reactions. ACIP strongly discourages any variation from the recommended volume or number of doses of any vaccine.

Meningococcal Disease

Healthcare facilities should consider including vaccines to prevent meningococcal disease, typhoid, and polio for HCP who have certain conditions or who work in laboratories or regions outside the United States where the risk for work-related exposures exist. Healthcare-associated transmission of *Neisseria meningitis* is rare, but HCP have become infected after direct contact with respiratory secretions of infected persons and in a laboratory setting. HCP can decrease the risk for infection by adhering to precautions to prevent exposure to respiratory droplets and by taking antimicrobial chemoprophylaxis if exposed directly to respiratory secretions.

Vaccine Types

Two quadrivalent conjugate meningococcal vaccines (MCV4 and MPSV4) are licensed for persons aged through 55 years. Both protect against two of the three serogroups that cause the majority of meningococcal disease in the United States and against 75 percent of disease among adults. Both vaccines have similar safety profiles in clinical trials. However, MCV4 is not recommended routinely for all HCP.

Indications

A two-dose vaccine series is recommended for HCP with known asplenia or persistent complement component deficiencies, because these conditions increase the risk for meningococcal disease. HCP traveling to countries in which meningococcal disease is hyperendemic or epidemic also are at risk for infection and should receive vaccine. All other HCP who are at high risk due to their work conditions should receive a single dose of MCV4. Clinical microbiologists and research microbiologists who might be exposed routinely to isolates of *N. meningitides* should receive a single dose of MCV4 and receive booster doses every 5 years if they remain at increased risk. HCP aged >55 years who have any of the above risk factors for meningococcal disease should be vaccinated with MPSV4. HCP with known HIV infection are likely to be at increased risk for meningococcal disease and may elect vaccination. If these HCP are vaccinated, they should receive a two-dose vaccine series.

Postexposure Management of Exposed HCP

PEP is advised for all persons who have had intensive, un-protected contact (i.e., without wearing a mask) with infected patients (e.g., via mouth-to-mouth resuscitation, endotracheal intubation, or endotracheal tube management), including HCP who have been vaccinated with either the conjugate or polysac-charide vaccine.

Antimicrobial prophylaxis can eradicate carriage of *N. menin-gitidis* and prevent infections in persons who have unprotected exposure to patients with meningococcal infections.[62] Rifampin, ciprofloxacin, and ceftriaxone are effective in eradicating nasopharyngeal carriage of *N. meningitidis*. In areas of the United States where ciprofloxacin-resistant strains of *N. meningitidis* have been detected (as of August 30, 2011, only parts of Minnesota and North Dakota), ciprofloxacin should not be used for chemoprophylaxis.[63] Azithromycin can be used as an alternative. Ceftriaxone can be used during pregnancy. PEP should be administered within 24 hours of exposure when feasible; PEP administered >14 days after exposure is of limited or no value.[62] HCP not otherwise indicated for vaccination may be recommended to be vaccinated with meningococcal vaccine in the setting of a community or institutional outbreak of meningococcal disease caused by a serogroup contained in the vaccine.

Establishing a Healthcare Personnel Immunization Program

Rationale for a Healthcare Personnel Immunization Program

It should be a priority for healthcare institutions to provide as safe an environment as possible for both employees and the patients they serve. This includes prevention of disease transmission between HCP and patients, particularly those diseases that are preventable by immunization. HCP are at risk of acquiring several vaccine-preventable diseases in this type of setting. This fact alone should provide motivation for estab-lishment of an effective immunization program for HCP. The rationale for establishing an HCP immunization program has been previously discussed.[5]

The CDC has listed seven elements of a Personnel Health Service for Infection Prevention to assist in effectively attaining infection prevention goals.[5]

1. Coordination with other departments (especially Infection Prevention)

2. Medical evaluations before placement of personnel

3. Personnel health and safety education

4. Immunization programs

5. Protocols for surveillance and management of job-related illnesses and exposures to infectious diseases

6. Counseling services for personnel regarding infection risks related to employment or special conditions (including work restrictions)

7. Maintenance of health records (data management and pro-tection of confidentiality)

It is important to note how the other six elements are related to that of the fourth element, immunization programs. An effective immunization program must be intertwined with these elements, as is illustrated in this section of the chapter.

Goals of a Healthcare Personnel Immunization Program

An effective program should have the following as its goals:

- Achieving high rates of immunization: For those HCP-mandatory vaccines, as chosen by the individual institution, the desirable goal is 100 percent immunization. The only ex-ceptions should be those persons with physician/practitioner-documented medical contraindications or acceptable proof of immunity.

- Devising and implementing specific vaccine policies: The institution must determine which diseases to include and formulate specific policies for immunization of HCP in that institution.

- Providing education about vaccines: This begins with employee/occupational health policies regarding the vaccine-preventable diseases at the specific institution. HCP need to be fully informed regarding the benefits and risks of a vaccine before receiving it. In addition, there must be con-tinuing educational updates as new information on old vac-cines emerges or new vaccines become available. Institution-specific data on HCP immunization rates and disease outbreaks caused by vaccine-preventable diseases at periodic intervals should be communicated to all HCP.

- Justifying the cost: A successful immunization program can justify its cost by demonstrating the cost effectiveness of prevention versus the cost of controlling disease outbreaks among patients and HCP at the institution. ACIP's *Guide for Adult Immunization* states, "The high cost of controlling outbreaks of measles and rubella have been documented repeatedly, suggesting that even in the absence of a formal cost-effectiveness analysis, the benefits of vaccinating adults against these diseases may be substantial."[5]

Current Laws and Medicolegal Issues

- The Occupational Safety and Health Administration (OSHA) regulations: OSHA's Bloodborne Pathogen Standard (a federal standard; state-specific standards also apply) was passed in 1991 and revised in 2001. It requires that employers provide Hepatitis B vaccinations at no charge to HCP designated by each institution to be at risk for exposure. The mandate is for the vaccine to be offered; there is no requirement that it must be accepted. However, HCP who decline the vaccine are required to sign an "informed declination" form.[64,65] In addition, OSHA requirements outline specific employee training programs regarding the frequency, transmission, and illness patterns associated with bloodborne pathogens. This is an ideal time to reinforce the need for coverage against all vaccine-preventable diseases.

- Right-to-know laws: Some states have specific regulations outlining in detail the requirement to inform employees who may be exposed to workplace hazards (e.g., vaccine-preventable diseases), what the risks are, and how to minimize these risks. Every state has laws that entitle persons receiving any kind of medical treatment or medication to be fully informed regarding all indications, possible adverse effects, options, and benefits.

- Codified standards of care: Although not having the specific force of law, agencies and expert groups concerned with the public health or with the health of HCP have published consensus statements regarding HCP immunization. These statements form the "standard of care" that physicians and other practitioners are expected to follow. These standards of care can, in fact, be used to establish fault in legal proceedings. The CDC has proposed specific standards regarding the immunization of HCP against vaccine-preventable diseases.[5] The evidence on which these recommendations are based is categorized as I to III (defined in Table 103-12):

  o Formulate a written comprehensive policy on immunizing HCP (category IB).

  o Administer Hepatitis B vaccine to personnel who perform tasks involving routine and inadvertent contact with blood,

Table 103-12. Categorization Scheme for Recommendations[5]

Category IA—Strongly recommended for implementation and strongly supported by well-designed experimental, clinical, or epidemiological studies

Category IB—Strongly recommended for implementation and supported by certain experimental, clinical, or epidemiological studies and a strong theoretic rationale

Category IC—Required for implementation, as mandated by federal or state regulation or standard

Category II—Suggested for implementation and supported by suggestive clinical or epidemiological studies or a theoretical rationale

No Recommendation—Unresolved issue; practices for which insufficient evidence or no consensus regarding efficacy exist

These categorizations are based on existing data, theoretic rationale, applicability, and economic impact.

other body fluids (including blood-contaminated fluids), and sharps (category IA).

  o Offer influenza vaccine annually to all eligible HCP to protect staff, patients, and family members and to decrease HCP absenteeism. Use of either TIV or LAIV is recommended for eligible HCP. During periods when inactivated vaccine is in short supply, use of LAIV is encouraged for eligible HCP (category IA).[16]

  o Ensure that all personnel have documented immunity to measles and administer measles vaccine to those who do not (category IA [refer to most current ACIP adult immunization schedule to meet this requirement]).

  o Administer mumps vaccine to all personnel without documented evidence of mumps immunity, unless otherwise contraindicated (category IA).

  o Determine whether personnel who may have direct contact with patients who may be excreting polioviruses, or who work in the laboratory handling specimens/cultures that might contain wild poliovirus, have completed a primary vaccination series against polio (category IA).

  o For such personnel listed in the preceding, complete the series with enhanced inactivated polio vaccine (category IB).

  o Vaccinate all personnel without documented immunity to rubella, with an appropriate rubella-containing vaccine (category IA).

  o Administer varicella vaccine to susceptible personnel, especially those that will have contact with patients at high-risk for serious complications (category IA).

- As a further example, some institutions or expert groups have formulated formal statements regarding specific vaccine-preventable diseases. For example, the Infectious Diseases Society of America has published a consensus statement regarding measles immunity in HCP and, more recently, mandatory vaccination against influenza, with a provision for declination of vaccination based on religious or medical reasons.[5] The Joint Commission has long recommended that HCP who have contact with pregnant women should be immune to rubella. In 2007, The Joint Commission approved an infection prevention standard that requires accredited organizations to offer influenza vaccinations to staff, including volunteers and independent contractors, with close patient contact.[17] In 2008, the Association for Professionals in Infection Control and Epidemiology released a position paper on influenza immunization of healthcare personnel in which they recommend "influenza vaccine be required annually for all healthcare personnel with direct patient care."[16]

- Vaccine information statements (VIS): The National Childhood Vaccine Injury Act (NCVIA) of 1986 applies to diphtheria, tetanus, pertussis, measles, mumps, rubella, polio, Hepatitis A, Hepatitis B, *Haemophilus influenzae* type B (Hib), trivalent influenza (inactivated and live), pneumococcal conjugate, meningococcal, rotavirus, human papillomavirus, and varicella vaccines. The NCVIA requires the use of vaccine information statements for these vaccines, that information about the immunization administered is permanently recorded, and that adverse events associated with these vaccines are reported. There are 10 points that must be presented in easily understood terms before immunization with the vaccines can be given.[66]

These include the following:

1. Frequency, severity, and potential long-term effects of the disease to be prevented by the vaccine.

2. Symptoms or reactions to the vaccine that should be brought to the immediate attention of the healthcare provider.

3. Precautionary measures to reduce the risk for any major adverse effects to the vaccine that may occur.

4. Early warning signs or symptoms that may be possible precursors to such major adverse reactions.

5. A description of the manner in which to monitor such major adverse reactions to the vaccine that may occur.

6. A specification of when, how, and to whom any major adverse reaction should be reported.

7. The contraindications to (and basis for delay of) the administration of the vaccine.

8. Identification of the groups, categories, or characteristics of potential recipients of the vaccine who may be at significantly high risk for major adverse reaction to the vaccine compared with the general population.

9. A summary of the relevant federal recommendations for a complete schedule of childhood immunizations and the availability of the National Vaccine Injury Compensation Program.

10. Such other relevant information as may be determined by the secretary of the Department of Health and Human Services.

Barriers to Successful Immunization Programs

In addition to misconceptions regarding immunization, the following can be barriers to successful immunization:

- Institutional and organizational issues: If the institution does not support an immunization program for its employees, the chance for its success is diminished. Institutional support must be in the form of specific immunization requirements for its employees, effective monitoring of compliance, and financial backing for the program.

- Medical issues: Concern over adverse effects of vaccines can serve as a strong deterrent to immunization. This concern may be based on misconceptions regarding vaccines in general. However, it can also be related to specific legitimate medical contraindications present in the recipients.

Institutions that require mandatory immunizations for specific diseases as a condition of employment may be faced with physician-documented contraindications to vaccination in some employees. Those that do not get immunized are then at risk of transmitting or acquiring vaccine-preventable diseases in the future. It is important to counsel such employees about the risks they may face and to provide work restrictions according to the most current infection prevention/occupational health guidelines after exposures.

- HCP issues: In addition to the medical issues listed previously, issues for HCP as a recipient of a vaccine can serve as a barrier to immunization. The fact that this group works in a medical setting can exacerbate some misconceptions about specific vaccines. One example would be that before the recombinant form of Hepatitis B vaccine was developed, there was concern by many HCP of the possibility of acquiring HIV infection from this vaccine. Another example is the fear of getting the swine flu from the influenza vaccine. In both examples, the fears are unwarranted. Nevertheless, they have contributed to poor compliance rates with vaccinations against these two diseases in HCP.

Components of a Successful Healthcare Personnel Immunization Program: The Role of the Infection Preventionist

In today's era of rising costs and shrinking budgets, the infection preventionist (IP) may be asked to wear many hats. It is not unusual to find a practitioner who may be responsible for infection prevention and control, employee health, risk management, performance improvement activities, or some combinations of these roles. Therefore, in delineating the role of the IP in a successful HCP immunization program, it is important to keep in mind that the extent of involvement in the following activities is related to the practitioner's specific job responsibilities.

Administrative

- Defining and articulating an immunization policy; the IP's input into the institution's policies regarding immunization can take several forms, including:

  o Formulating the policies from the infection prevention department

  o Formulating the policies in conjunction with the employee health department

  o Reviewing and giving feedback on policies written by others (e.g. administration, personnel)

  o Incorporating the most recent legislative mandates, guidelines, or standards of practice into policies

Whatever the forum, the IP should have adequate input into these policies.

- Continuously updating specified objectives: The IP must possess current knowledge about immunization as well as institutional events that may be related to the immunization program. It may be necessary to review the objectives of the immunization program at regular intervals to ensure that the information is current.

- Assigning responsibility for the program; possible ways for the IP to be involved in the institution's immunization program include:

  o Responsible for entire program (policy development, monitoring of compliance, administration of the program, record-keeping, education)

  o Responsible to oversee the employee health department's administration of the program

  o Responsible for parts of the program

  o Responsible for the education of employees regarding the program

Implementation

Depending on the specific responsibilities of the IP, the role in implementation of an immunization program may vary. At the same time, it is important to recognize the importance of the IP in contributing to the implementation of such programs.

- Convenience of immunization: HCP are busy individuals. If the procedure for obtaining immunizations is not convenient, it will be difficult to achieve high rates of immunization at the institution. The IP may use formal and informal mechanisms to elicit feedback from HCP to determine reasons for poor compliance if this is a factor.

- Tie-in to other requirements: The immunization program can be tied in to the annual TST or symptom review for tuberculosis or to annual mandated educational programs, when the HCP is already required to be present.

- Subsidize the cost of vaccines: The HCP is more likely to consider immunization if there is no cost on the part of the employee. The IP can present cost analysis data to administration on the benefits of immunization versus working up outbreaks in the medical setting to justify the cost of the program.

- Monitor expectations and concerns: The IP is in an essential position to monitor concerns of HCP regarding the immunization program. Possible strategies for monitoring concerns and expectations include:

  o Providing time for questions and answers on vaccinations at mandated educational programs. Ask HCP about their concerns regarding immunization.

  o Setting up booths to promote the institution's immunization program, for example, during International Infection Prevention Week.

  o Sending out surveys to HCP to elicit information on compliance with the immunization program, including reasons for and against compliance. Feed this information to administration and back to the HCP so that goals for improvement can be targeted.

Education

- The risk of disease, disability, and chronic disease: Annual infection prevention educational programs for HCP are already required according to the OSHA Bloodborne Pathogen Standard.[61,62] Thus, an opportunity to provide information is created for education on the risk of disease and disability that may result from vaccine-preventable diseases at these sessions. The IP is in a critical position to include this information at these sessions.

- Vaccine efficacy and side effects: In addition to the mandated educational sessions for HCP discussed earlier, VIS can be distributed, vaccine updates can be provided, and the IP can include times in the sessions for HCP to ask questions about vaccine efficacy, safety, misconceptions, or other concerns. International Infection Prevention Week is an excellent opportunity each year in October for immunizations to be promoted. The IP can distribute pamphlets, set up displays, conduct educational sessions, or utilize other creative ideas for educating staff about vaccine-preventable diseases. In particular, it is advisable to promote influenza vaccination in HCP at this time.

Documentation

- Standardized recording of vaccine information: As mentioned, the NCVIA has requirements for specific information to be collected during the administration of vaccines. According to ACP, "Health care providers who administer vaccines covered by the NCVIA are required by law to record this information permanently for these vaccines in the recipient's medical record or in an office log or file." The information recorded should include the type of vaccine; dose, site, and route of administration; and name, address, and title of the person who gave the vaccine (required for vaccines covered by NCVIA).[66] Because this information is required for vaccines covered by NCVIA, standardization of the data that need to be recorded can be applied to all vaccines required at the institution. It may also be cost effective and efficient to utilize standardized information forms on vaccines for HCP. These forms may include but are not limited to the following: consent forms, VIS with all applicable information for each vaccine offered, screening forms for eliciting vaccine-preventable disease histories and serology results, exemption forms to be signed by physicians of HCP in instances where there is a medical contraindication to a vaccine that is required by hospital policy, and updates on vaccine information. The CDC has forms available through state and local health departments that meet the NCVIA criteria as information sheets.

- Monitoring compliance with policy: As mentioned, the failure of HCP to obtain recommended immunizations is a recurring problem. Individual institutions are thus faced with not only the responsibility of formulating policies regarding immunization of their employees, but also designing strategies to monitor compliance. This function can also be tied in to an employee database system. Possible strategies for monitoring compliance may include but not be limited to the following:

- o Requiring vaccinations as a condition of employment and not allowing HCP to be hired if they do not comply with the policies.

- o Sending notices to HCP to notify them that they have not received required vaccines.

- o Disciplinary action for HCP who fail to receive required vaccines (unless there are medical contraindications).

- o Periodic follow-up of persons who have declined vaccinations for medical reasons to evaluate whether the exemptions still apply.

- o Relating compliance with performance appraisals and/or credentialing.

- o Taking persons off the schedule if they do not comply with required immunizations within a designated time period.

- o In those cases in which more extreme measures are utilized, it is important to consult with the Labor Relations Department to ensure that existing labor laws are not being violated.

- Developing an appropriate database for storage, accessibility, and review of information: Adequate monitoring and report functions are unlikely to be actively monitored, especially in large institutions, without an appropriate and user-friendly database. Several software programs are available for maintaining immunization records of HCP. The cost of such programs can be justified when weighed against the inefficiency of not computerizing these data. When evaluating which program to purchase, consideration should be given to the amount of data entry required, including personnel time. Programs that have the capability to generate reminder notices, for example, for the second and third Hepatitis B dose or the second varicella vaccine dose, may be more desirable than those without such features.

- The database should be capable of storing the amount of information essential to the institution, be easily accessible, and have different options for review of information. For example, one may want to have information on compliance with Hepatitis B vaccination by job category, unit worked, year, etc.

- The program selected should also be able to accommodate updates in vaccine requirements that may not have been available at the time the system was originally purchased.

CONCLUSIONS

Widespread immunization programs are safe and cost-effective means of reducing the frequency of vaccine-preventable diseases. The absence of such programs in medical institutions can have devastating consequences because of the rapid transmission of vaccine-preventable diseases among HCP and their high-risk patients.

HCP should take advantage of opportunities to work together to ensure universal coverage for themselves and their peers. HCP should be encouraged to become familiar with specific immunization guidelines pertaining to themselves and should obtain and maintain adequate protection against vaccine-preventable diseases.

FUTURE TRENDS

The use of vaccines is a cornerstone to an infection prevention and control program. Mandatory influenza immunization programs and addition of new vaccines into existing programs during economically challenging times are but two important issues that will be part of future planning and discussion.

REFERENCES

1. Maltezou HC, Wicker S. Measles in health-care settings. *Am J Infect Control* 2013 Jul;41(7):661–663.
2. McLean HQ, Fiebelkorn AP, Temte JL, et al. Prevention of measles, rubella, congenital rubella syndrome, and mumps, 2013: summary recommendations of the Advisory Committee on Immunization Practices (ACIP). *MMWR Recomm Rep* 2013 Jun 14;62(RR-04):1–34.
3. Barbadoro P, Marigliano A, Di Tondo E, et al. Measles among health-care workers in a teaching hospital in central Italy. *J Occup Health* 2012;54(4):336–339.
4. Cutts FT, Lessler J, Metcalf CJ. Measles elimination: progress, challenges and implications for rubella control. *Expert Rev Vaccines* 2013 Aug;12(8):917–932.
5. Centers for Disease Control and Prevention (CDC). Immunization of health-care personnel: recommendation of the Advisory Committee on Immunization Practices (ACIP). *MMWR Recomm Rep* 2011 Nov 25;60(RR-7):1–45.
6. Williams WW, Hickson MA, Kane MA, et al. Immunization policies and vaccine coverage among adults. The risk for missed opportunities. *Ann Intern Med* 1988 Apr;108(4):616–625.
7. Real K, Kim S, Conigliaro J. Using a validated health promotion tool to improve patient safety and increase health care personnel influenza vaccination rates. *Am J Infect Control* 2013 Aug;41(8):691–696.
8. Lefebvre JS, Haynes L. Vaccine strategies to enhance immune responses in the aged. *Curr Opin Immunol* 2013 Aug;25(4):523–528.
9. Patrick KM, Woolley FR. A cost-benefit analysis of immunization for pneumococcal pneumonia. *JAMA* 1981 Feb 6;245(5):473–477.
10. Marin M, Broder K, Temte J, Snider D, et al. Use of combination measles, mumps, rubella, and varicella vaccine: recommendations of the Advisory Committee on Immunization Practices (ACIP). *MMWR Recomm Rep* 2010 May 7;59(RR-3):1–12.
11. Centers for Disease Control and Prevention (CDC). Prevention and Control of seasonal influenza with vaccines. Recommendations of the Advisory Committee on Immunization Practices—United States, 2013-14. *MMWR Recomm Rep* 2013 Sep 20;62(RR-07):1–43.
12. Middleton DB, Lin CJ, Smith KJ, et al. Economic evaluation of standing order programs for pneumococcal vaccination of hospitalized elderly patients. *Infect Control Hosp Epidemiol* 2008 May;29(5):385–394.
13. Gardner P, Pickering LK, Orenstein WA, et al. Guidelines for quality standards for immunization. *Clin Infect Dis* 2002 Sep 1;35(5):503–511.
14. Infectious Disease Society of America (IDSA). *Pandemic and Seasonal Influenza.* IDSA website. 2013. Available at: http://www.idsociety.org/InfluenzaPrinciples/.
15. Poland GA, Tosh P, Jacobson RM. Requiring influenza vaccination for healthcare workers: seven truths we must accept. *Vaccine* 2005 Mar 18;23(17-18):2251–2255.
16. Greene L, Cox T, Dolan S, et al. APIC Position Paper: Influenza Vaccination Should Be a Condition of Employment for Healthcare Personnel, Unless Medically Contraindicated. APIC website. 2011. Available at: http://www.apic.org/resource_/tinymcefilemanager/advocacy-pdfs/apic_influenza_immunization_of_hcp_12711.pdf.
17. The Joint Commission (TJC). Standards Information for Hospitals. TJC website. 2014. Available at: http://www.jointcommission.org/accreditation/hap_standards_information.aspx.
18. National Center for Immunization and Respiratory Diseases. General recommendations on immunization – recommendations of the Advisory Committee on Immunization Practices (ACIP). *MMWR Recomm Rep* 2011 Jan 28;60(2):1–64.

19. Margolis KL, Nichol KL, Poland GA, et al. Frequency of adverse reactions to influenza vaccine in the elderly. A randomized, placebo-controlled trial. *JAMA* 1990 Sep;264(9):1139–1141.
20. Centers for Disease Control and Prevention (CDC). Thimerosal in vaccines: a joint statement of the American Academy of Pediatrics and the Public Health Service. *MMWR Morb Mortal Wkly Rep* 1999 Jul 9;48(26):563–565.
21. Centers for Disease Control and Prevention (CDC). Revised ACIP recommendation for avoiding pregnancy after receiving a rubella-containing vaccine. *MMWR Morb Mortal Wkly Rep* 2001 Dec 14;50(49):1117.
22. Fiore AE, Wasley A, Bell BP. Prevention of hepatitis A through active or passive immunization: recommendations of the Advisory Committee on Immunization Practices (ACIP). *MMWR Recomm Rep* 2006 May 19;55 (RR-7):1–23.
23. Matheny SC, Kingery JE. Hepatitis A. *Am Fam Physician* 2012 Dec 1; 86(11):1027–1034.
24. Niu M, Salive M, Krueger C, et al. Two-year review of hepatitis A vaccine safety: data from the Vaccine Adverse Event Reporting System (VAERS). *Clin Infect Dis* 1998 Jun;26(6):1475–1476.
25. Guturu P, Cicalese L, Duchini A. Hepatitis A vaccination in healthcare personnel. *Ann Hepatol* 2012 May-Jun;11(3):326–329.
26. Centers for Disease Control and Prevention (CDC). FDA approval for a combined hepatitis A and B vaccine. *MMWR Morb Mortal Wkly Rep* 2001 Sep 21;50(37):806–807.
27. Mast EE, Weinbaum CM, Fiore AE, et al. A comprehensive immunization strategy to eliminate transmission of hepatitis B virus infection in the United States: recommendations of the Advisory Committee on Immunization Practices (ACIP) Part II: immunization of adults. *MMWR Recomm Rep* 2006 Dec 8;55(RR-16):1–33.
28. Bell BP, Kruszon-Moran D, Shapiro CN, et al. Hepatitis A virus infection in the United States: serologic results from the Third National Health and Nutrition Examination Survey. *Vaccine* 2005 Dec;23(50):5798–5806.
29. Centers for Disease Control and Prevention (CDC). *Adult Immunization Schedules: United States, 2014.* CDC website. 2014. Available at: http://www.cdc.gov/vaccines/schedules/hcp/adult.html.
30. Centers for Disease Control and Prevention. Appendix A: immunization management issues: recommendations of the Immunization Practices Advisory Committee. *MMWR Recomm Rep* 2006 Dec 8;55(RR-16):26–29.
31. Shefer A, Dales A, Nelson M, et al. Use and safety of acellular pertussis vaccine among adult hospital staff during an outbreak of pertussis. *J Infect Dis* 1995 Apr;171(4):1053–1056.
32. Alper C, Kruskall MS, Marcus-Bagley D, et al. Genetic prediction of non-response to hepatitis B vaccine. *N Engl J Med* 1989 Sep 14;321(11): 708–712.
33. Rotz LD, Dotson DA, Damon IK, et al. Vaccinia (smallpox) vaccine: recommendations of the Advisory Committee on Immunization Practices (ACIP), 2001. *MMWR Recomm Rep* 2001 Jun 22;50(RR-10):1–25.
34. Mast EE, Alter MJ. Prevention of Hepatitis B virus infection among healthcare workers. In: Ellis RW, ed. *Hepatitis B Vaccines in Clinical Practice.* New York: Marcel Dekker, 1993:295–308.
35. Clements ML, Murphy BR. Development and persistence of local and systemic antibody responses in adults given live attenuated or inactivated influenza A virus vaccine. *J Clin Microbiol* 1986 Jan;23(1):66–72.
36. Centers for Medicare & Medicaid Services (CMS). Hospital Center. CMS website. 2013. Available at: http://www.cms.gov/Center/Provider-Type/Hospital-Center.html.
37. Centers for Medicare & Medicaid Services (CMS). *Medicare and Medicaid Programs; Reform of Hospital and Critical Access Hospital Conditions of Participation (CMS-3244-F).* CMS website. 2013. Available at: http://www.cms.gov/Regulations-and-Guidance/Legislation/CFCsAndCoPs/Hospitals.html.
38. Executive Summary—Actions to strengthen adult and adolescent immunization coverage in the United States: policy principles of the Infectious Diseases Society of America (IDSA). *Clin Infect Dis* 2007 Jun 15;44(12):1529–1531.
39. Immunization Action Coalition (IAC). *Healthcare Personnel Vaccination Recommendations.* IAC website. 2013. Available at: http://www.immunize.org/catg.d/p2017.pdf.
40. Cohn AC, MacNeil JR, Harrison LH, et al. Changes in Neisseria meningitidis disease epidemiology in the United States, 1998—2007: implications for prevention of meningococcal disease. *Clin Infect Dis* 2010 Jan 15;50(2):184–191.
41. Immunization Action Coalition (IAC). *Package Inserts - Pneumococcal (PPSV).* IAC website. 2012. Available at: http://www.immunize.org/packageinserts/pi_ppsv.asp.
42. Updated recommendations for prevention of invasive pneumococcal disease among adults using the 23-valent pneumococcal polysaccharide vaccine (PPSV23). *MMWR Morb Mortal Wkly Rep* 2010 Sep 3;59(34):1102–1106.
43. Centers for Disease Control and Prevention (CDC). Updated recommendations of the Advisory Committee on Immunization Practices (ACIP) regarding routine poliovirus vaccination. *MMWR Morb Mortal Wkly Rep* 2009 Aug 7;58(30):829–830.
44. Prevots DR, Burr RK, Sutter RW, et al. Poliomyelitis prevention in the United States. Updated recommendations of the Advisory Committee on Immunization Practices (ACIP). *MMWR Recomm Rep* 2000 May 9;49(RR-5):1–22.
45. Immunization Action Coalition (IAC). *Package Inserts –Tdap.* IAC website. 2012. Available at: http://www.immunize.org/packageinserts/pi_tdap.asp.
46. Kretsinger K, Broder KR, Cortese MM, et al. Preventing tetanus, diphtheria, and pertussis among adults: use of tetanus toxoid, reduced diphtheria toxoid, and acellular pertussis vaccine recommendations of the Advisory Committee on Immunization Practices and recommendation of ACIP, supported by the Healthcare Infection Control Practices Advisory Committee (HICPAC), for use of Tdap among healthcare personnel. *MMWR Recomm Rep* 2006 Dec 15;55(RR-17):1–37.
47. Murphy TV, Slade BA, Broder KR, et al. Prevention of pertussis, tetanus and diphtheria among pregnant and post-partum women and their infants. Recommendations of the Advisory Committee on Immunization Practices (ACIP). *MMWR Recomm Rep* 2008 May 30;57(RR-4):1–51.
48. Wharton M, Strikas RA, Harpaz R, et al. Recommendations for using smallpox vaccine in a pre-event vaccination program. Supplemental recommendations of the Advisory Committee on Immunization Practices (ACIP) and the Healthcare Infection Control Practices Advisory Committee (HICPAC). *MMWR Recomm Rep* 2003 Apr 4;52(RR-7):1–16.
49. Centers for Disease Control and Prevention (CDC). *Advisory Committee on Immunization Practices (ACIP) Statement on Smallpox Preparedness and Vaccination.* CDC website. 2003. Available at: http://www.bt.cdc.gov/agent/smallpox/vaccination/acipjun2003.asp.
50. Centers for Disease Control and Prevention (CDC). Supplemental recommendations on adverse events following smallpox vaccine in the pre-event vaccination program: recommendations of the Advisory Committee on Immunization Practices. *MMWR Morb Mortal Wkly Rep* 2003 Apr 4;52(13):282–284.
51. Centers for Disease Control and Prevention (CDC). Update: adverse events following civilian smallpox vaccination—United States, 2003. *MMWR Morb Mortal Wkly Rep* 2003 Aug 29;52(34):819–820.
52. Poland GA, Neff JM. Smallpox vaccine: problems and prospects. *Immunology and Allergy Clinics of North America* 2003 Nov;23(4):731–743.
53. Bonilla-Guerrero R, Poland GA. Smallpox vaccines: current and future. *J Lab Clin Med* 2003 Oct;142(4):252–257.
54. Casey CG, Iskander JK, Roper MH, et al. Adverse events associated with smallpox vaccination in the United States, January-October 2003. *JAMA* 2005 Dec 7;294(21):2734–2743.
55. Neff J, Modlin J, Birkhead GS, et al. Monitoring the safety of a smallpox vaccination program in the United States: report of the joint Smallpox Vaccine Safety Working Group of the advisory committee on immunization practices and the Armed Forces Epidemiological Board. *Clin Infect Dis* 2008 Mar 15;46 Suppl 3:S258–70.
56. Marin M, Güris D, Chaves SS, et al. Prevention of varicella: recommendations of the Advisory Committee on Immunization Practices (ACIP). *MMWR Recomm Rep* 2007 Jun 22;56(RR-4):1–40.
57. Recommendations for the use of live attenuated varicella vaccine. American Academy of Pediatrics Committee on Infectious Diseases. *Pediatrics* 1995 May;95(5):791–796.
58. Varicella Virus Vaccine. Live, VARIVAX®, Package Insert. DrugInserts.com website. 2013. Available at: http://druginserts.com/lib/other/meds/varivax/.
59. Saiman L, LaRussa P, Steinberg SP, et al. Persistence of immunity to varicella-zoster virus after vaccination among healthcare workers. *Infect Control Hosp Epidemiol* 2001 May;22(5):279–283.
60. Ampofo K, Saiman L, LaRussa P, et al. Persistence of immunity to live attenuated varicella vaccine in healthy adults. *Clin Infect Dis* 2002 Mar 15;34(6):774–779.
61. Haiduven DJ, Hench CP, Simpkins SM, et al. Management of varicella-vaccinated patients and employees exposed to varicella in the healthcare setting. *Infect Control Hosp Epidemiol* 2003 Jul;24(7):538–543.
62. Cohn AC, MacNeil JR, Clark TA, et al. Prevention and control of meningococcal disease: recommendations of the Advisory Committee on Immunization Practices (ACIP). *MMWR Recomm Rep* 2013 Mar 22;62(RR-2):1–28.
63. Wu HM, Harcourt BH, Hatcher CP, et al. Emergence of ciprofloxacin-resistant Neisseria meningitidis in North America. *N Engl J Med* 2009 Feb 26;360(9):886–892.
64. Occupational Safety and Health Administration. Occupational exposure to bloodborne pathogens; final rule (29 CFR 1910.1030). *Fed Regist* 1991;56:64175–64182.
65. Occupational Safety and Health Administration. Occupational exposure to bloodborne pathogens. Final rule (29 CFR 1910.1030). *Fed Regist* 2001;66(12):5317–5324.
66. Update: vaccine side effects, adverse reactions, contraindications, and precautions. Recommendations of the Advisory Committee on Immunization Practices (ACIP). *MMWR Recomm Rep* 1996 Sep 6;45(RR-12):1–35.

SUPPLEMENTAL RESOURCES

General References

Grabenstein JD, Grabenstein L. *ImmunoFacts: Vaccines and Immunologics*. St. Louis: Facts and Comparisons, 2002.

Plotkin SA, Orenstein WA, Offit PA, eds. Vaccines, 4th ed. Philadelphia: Saunders, 2003.

U.S. Department of Health and Human Services (HHS). Healthy People 2020, HHS website. 2013. Available at: http://www.healthypeople.gov/2020/default.aspx.

SUGGESTED READINGS

Statements of the Advisory Committee on Immunization Practices. These are statements published periodically in the *MMWR* and available in medical libraries. Statements are published and updated periodically on specific vaccines. The statements are formulated by an expert advisory panel. Available online at: http://www.cdc.gov/vaccines/acip/index.html. Accessed December 3, 2013.

CDC Immunization National Resource Directory. Contact the Centers for Disease Control and Prevention, National Immunization Program for more information at 1-800-CDC-INFO (232-4636)

Epidemiology and Prevention of Vaccine-Preventable Diseases. An excellent review book based on the CDC's course of the same name. This is an outstanding reference for the individual new to the field or who wishes to know more detail.

Healthy People 2020. A comprehensive listing of all the public health-related goals for the nation. Has a specific chapter on immunization goals for the United States.

CDC/ATPM Vaccine Education Modules. The Association of Teachers of Preventive Medicine has produced a series of superb educational modules on each of the vaccine-preventable diseases appropriate for CME/CEU courses. Contact ATPM at 202-842-1980 for more information.

Immunization of Health-Care Workers. Recommendations of the Advisory Committee on Immunization Practices and the Hospital Infection Control Practices Advisory Committee.

Immunizing Health Care Workers: A Practical Approach. Poland G, Schaffner W, Pugliese G, eds. Chicago: ETNA Communications, 2000 (contact at 1-800-552-0076).

INTERNET RESOURCES

Centers for Disease Control and Prevention (CDC). Available at: http://www.cdc.gov.

Food and Drug Administration (FDA). Available at: http://www.fda.gov/cber/vaccines.htm.

Health Canada, LCDC website for the Canadian Immunization Guide. Available at: http://www.phac-aspc.gc.ca/publicat/cig-gci/.

Immunization Action Coalition and the Hepatitis B Coalition. Available at: http://www.immunize.org/.

The Infectious Diseases Society of America and the Vaccine Initiative. Available at: http://www.idsociety.org.

Morbidity and Mortality Weekly Report. Available at: http://www.cdc.gov/mmwr/.

The National Foundation for Infectious Diseases. Available at: http://www.nfid.org.

National Network for Vaccination Information. Available at: http://www.immunizationinfo.org/vaccineInfo/index.cfm.

National Vaccine Program Office. Available at: http://www.hhs.gov/nvpo/index.html.

The Vaccine Page. Available at: http://vaccines.com/.

The WHO Global Programme for Vaccines and Immunization. Available at: http://www.who.int/immunization/gin/en/index.html .

CHAPTER 104

Pregnant Healthcare Personnel

Vicki Allen, MSN, RN, CIC
Infection Control Manager
CaroMont Health
Gastonia, NC

ABSTRACT

Following Standard Precautions (i.e., consider all body fluids except sweat potentially infectious, and use personal protective equipment when exposure to blood or body fluids is anticipated), as recommended by the Centers for Disease Control and Prevention for all healthcare personnel, will protect pregnant healthcare personnel against most infectious agents to which they may be exposed. However, because some infectious agents can cause congenital syndromes in the fetus when primary infection is acquired during pregnancy, there are additional concerns in pregnant or potentially pregnant healthcare personnel. For practical purposes, immunologic function is normal during pregnancy, and an otherwise healthy woman is not considered to be an immunocompromised host. Pregnancy does not increase the risk of acquisition of infections and, for most infectious agents, clinical manifestations of infections are no more severe in pregnant women than in those who are not pregnant. In view of the routes of transmission and ubiquity of some infectious agents (e.g., cytomegalovirus), restricting pregnant women from caring for patients with potentially transmissible infections is considered only for patients infected with parvovirus B19 and for patients with respiratory syncytial virus infections who are receiving ribavirin aerosol. Because patients with vaccine-preventable diseases should be cared for by only immune healthcare personnel, it is especially important for women contemplating pregnancy to obtain the needed vaccines before conception. Similar to nonpregnant healthcare personnel, susceptible pregnant healthcare personnel should be restricted from contact with patients with rubeola, rubella, varicella, and smallpox. Much anxiety among pregnant healthcare personnel results from misinformation concerning epidemiology and transmission of infectious agents. The emphasis must be on education of all healthcare personnel of childbearing age, ideally before pregnancy, or at least as soon as pregnancy is diagnosed. It is important to note that the incidence of cytomegalovirus and parvovirus infection is not increased among healthcare personnel compared with other occupations, especially day care center staff and school teachers.

KEY CONCEPTS

- Consistent adherence of pregnant healthcare personnel to the practices of Standard Precautions, especially hand hygiene, will protect against most exposures to infectious agents of concern during pregnancy.

- Healthcare personnel should be immunized against vaccine-preventable diseases before conception. Once pregnancy occurs, most missed immunizations may still be provided but should occur only after consultation with the healthcare personnel's obstetrician. However, influenza vaccine is recommended for routine administration to pregnant women at any trimester if they will be pregnant during the influenza season, including the first trimester. Although live virus vaccines are not recommended during pregnancy, inadvertent administration of live attenuated virus vaccines (rubella, rubeola, varicella, smallpox) has not been associated with adverse outcomes as tracked in national registries.

- The exposure of nonimmunized pregnant healthcare personnel to varicella zoster virus presents a primary risk to the mother and fetus-neonate.

- Immunization during pregnancy and before conception provides benefit from the disease to the mother during pregnancy and benefit to the neonate by passive antibodies during the first 4 to 6 months of life.

- Reviewing the patient's immunization status before attempts to conceive is prudent.

- There are few healthcare exposures that will be associated with adverse outcomes for pregnant healthcare personnel or her fetus.

BACKGROUND

Consistent adherence to Standard Precautions (i.e., consider all bodily fluids except sweat potentially infectious and use personal protective equipment [PPE] when exposure to blood and body fluid is anticipated), as recommended by the Centers for Disease Control and Prevention (CDC), provides pregnant healthcare personnel (HCP) and all HCP the optimal protection from exposure to infectious agents. Increased adherence to recommended precautions has been demonstrated for pregnant individuals when compared with nonpregnant individuals. Pregnant HCP have the additional concern of coming into contact with an infectious agent that may cause serious illness in the mother and may cause a congenital syndrome or some adverse pregnancy outcome. In general, maternal immune function is normal, but there is some decrease in cell-mediated immunity in the third trimester to viruses and pathogenic fungi.

HCP protection against vaccine-preventable diseases should be achieved by prepregnancy immunization. Immunization of pregnant HCP is indicated either to protect the mother, as is the case with the influenza vaccine, or to ensure the transfer of maternal antibody to the fetus, as with tetanus and influenza. The benefits of preventing disease during pregnancy clearly outweigh concerns about the safety of vaccines or immunoglobulins because no definable risks have been described.

BASIC PRINCIPLES

Patients who may be shedding certain infectious agents for which there is no vaccine may cause the pregnant HCP to be concerned regarding her safety and the safety of her fetus. These may include patients with cytomegalovirus (CMV), parvovirus B19, herpes simplex virus, syphilis, and rubeola, rubella, and varicella if not immune (Table 104-1). Although respiratory syncytial virus (RSV) infection does not have an adverse effect on the pregnant woman, exposure to the ribavirin aerosol used for treatment of RSV is contraindicated during pregnancy based on theoretical, but unproven, adverse effects during pregnancy. It is essential that all HCP practice Standard Precautions to optimize their personal protection when caring for patients. If Standard Precautions are used, restriction of patient care responsibilities for pregnant HCP is rarely indicated. Despite this fact, one cannot underestimate the importance of recognizing the emotional aspects of pregnancy and the real potential for exposures to infectious agents. It may be prudent to consider alterations in patient care activities if fear of safety cannot be adequately

addressed and adequate numbers of staff are available to allow such modifications. Such decisions are best made in collaboration with the healthcare management, the occupational health, and infection prevention and control departments, as well as the individual pregnant HCP. However, it is important to recognize that removing pregnant HCP from caring for the patient known to be infected with an agent of concern may result in re-assignment to a patient in whom an infection may be present but not yet identified, and adherence to Standard Precautions may be less likely. For example, 70 percent of children who attend day care centers may be shedding CMV and may be asymptomatic.

Pregnant HCP should have been immunized according to the schedule for adult immunization. Immunizations should include poliomyelitis; measles, mumps, rubella (MMR); varicella; tetanus; and diphtheria, or there should be a reliable history of having had the disease before becoming pregnant (Table 104-2). Pneumococcal vaccine should be administered preconceptually or during pregnancy in the second or third trimesters, especially if high-risk conditions are present (e.g., metabolic diseases such as diabetes mellitus or thyroid dysfunction; pulmonary, renal, or cardiac diseases; asthma; smoking; or functional or anatomic asplenia). Unfortunately, many adults do not have reliable records or memory of childhood vaccines or illnesses. In addition, HCP generally have access to information about vaccines and vaccine-preventable diseases but may not consider the benefits to themselves during pregnancy or to their newborn infant during the first 6 months of life. Healthcare institutions should mandate that HCP must complete the proper vaccine program as a condition of employment.

No evidence exists for risk from vaccinating pregnant women with inactivated vaccines or toxoids. In addition, pregnancy registries have demonstrated no harmful fetal effects when

Table 104-1. Infectious Agents of Concern to the Pregnant Healthcare Personnel According to Risk of Transmission Associated With Delivery of Healthcare and Available Preventive Measures

Healthcare-associated Acquisition Possible and Prevented by Pre-exposure Vaccine	Healthcare-associated Acquisition Unlikely	Infection Prevention Precautions are the Only Preventive Measures	Postexposure Chemoprophylaxis Effective
Anthrax*	HSV	CMV	HIV
HAVa	Toxoplasmosis	HCV	Neisseria meningitis
HBV		Parvovirus B19	
Influenza		Tuberculosis	Syphilis
N. meningitis†			
Pertussis			
Rubella			
Rubeola			
Varicella			
Tetanus			
Diphtheria			
Smallpox			

*Rare.

†Considered for laboratory workers, for college freshmen living in dormitories, or during a community outbreak.

Table 104-2. Vaccination of Pregnant Women

Vaccine	General Recommendations for Use in Pregnant Women	Contraindicated During Pregnancy
Hepatitis A	Recommended if otherwise indicated	
Hepatitis B	Recommended in some circumstances	
Human papillomavirus (HPV)		Not recommended
Influenza inactivated	Recommended	
Influenza (LAIV)*		Contraindicated
Measles, mumps, rubella (MMR)		Contraindicated
Meningococcal conjugate (MCV4/MenACWY)	May be used if otherwise indicated	
Pneumococcal conjugate (PCV13)	Inadequate data for specific recommendation	
Pneumococcal polysaccharide (PPSV23)	Inadequate data for specific recommendation	
Polio (inactivated poliovirus vaccine [IPV])	May be used if needed	
Tetanus and diphtheria (Td)	Should be used if otherwise indicated	
Tetanus, diphtheria, and pertussis (Tdap)†‡	Recommended	
Varicella		Contraindicated
Zoster (shingles)		Contraindicated
Travel and Other Vaccines		
Anthrax	High risk of exposure: May be used	Low risk of exposure: Not recommended
Bacille Calmette-Guérin (BCG)		Contraindicated
Japanese encephalitis	Inadequate data for specific recommendation	
Meningococcal polysaccharide (MPSV4)	May be used if otherwise indicated	
Rabies	May be used if otherwise indicated	
Typhoid	Inadequate data for specific recommendation	
Vaccinia (smallpox)	Postexposure: recommended	Preexposure: contraindicated
Yellow fever	May be used if benefit outweighs risk	

*LAIV: Do not administer LAIV to pregnant women (Centers for Disease Control and Prevention [CDC]. *Guidelines for Vaccinating Pregnant Women.* CDC website. 2013. Available at: http://www.cdc.gov/vaccines/pubs/preg-guide.htm).

†For women not previously vaccinated with Tdap. If Tdap is not administered during pregnancy, Tdap should be administered immediately postpartum.

‡Wound management: If a Td booster is indicated for a pregnant HCP, healthcare providers should administer Tdap.

From Centers for Disease Control and Prevention. Updated recommendations for use of tetanus toxoid, reduced diphtheria toxoid, and acellular pertussis vaccine (Tdap) in pregnant women – Advisory Committee on Immunization Practices (ACIP), 2012. *MMWR Morb Mortal Wkly Rep* 2013;62 (No. 7):131–135.

polio, rubella, varicella, and smallpox vaccines have been administered inadvertently to women who did not know they were pregnant. Benefits of maternal vaccination include protecting the mother from disease and protecting the neonate from disease for the first 3 to 6 months of life by passively transferred antibody via the umbilical cord.

Disease and Pregnant Healthcare Personnel

There are numerous questions regarding occupational exposures to infectious agents (Table 104-3). This table lists many of the infectious agents pregnant HCP may encounter during employment or in nonoccupational activities.

Counsel pregnant women and women of childbearing age regarding the risk of transmission of infectious diseases (e.g., CMV, hepatitis, HIV, parvovirus, rubella) that, if acquired during pregnancy, may have adverse effects on the fetus, whether the infection is acquired in nonoccupational or occupational environments. Information regarding occupational exposure to infectious agents including preventive measures such as Standard and Transmission-based Precautions is included in Table 104-3 and should be accessible and provided to pregnant HCP. It is not necessary to routinely exclude women strictly on the basis of their pregnancy, or intent to become pregnant, from the care of patients with particular infections that have potential to harm the fetus.

Cytomegalovirus

No vaccine is available for CMV and consistent adherence to Standard Precautions is the only preventive measure. The clinical entity, cytomegalic inclusion disease, was described in 1950. This generalized congenital infection was associated with cytomegalic cells, and typical intranuclear inclusions were found in multiple organs. The virus was grown on cultured human cells in 1956 and is now recognized as the most frequent congenitally and perinatally acquired viral disease known in

Table 104-3. Pregnant Healthcare Worker: Guide to Management of Occupational Exposure

Agent	In-hospital Source	Potential Effect on the Fetus	Rate of Perinatal Transmission	Maternal Screening	Prevention
Anthrax				History of exposure	Pre-pregnancy vaccination; vaccine not licensed for use in pregnancy Postexposure chemoprophylaxis with ciprofloxacin or amoxicillin if source
CMV	Urine, blood, semen, vaginal secretion, immunosuppressed transplant, dialysis, day care	Classic cytomegalic inclusion disease (5 to 10 percent)* Hearing loss (10 to 15 percent)	Primary infection (25 to 50 percent) Recurrent infants (52 percent) Symptomatic (<5 to 15 percent)	Routine screening not recommended; antibody is incompletely protective	Efficacy of CMV immune globulin not established No vaccine available Standard Precautions
HAV	Feces (most common), blood (rare)	No fetal transmission described; transmission may occur at the time of delivery if women still in the infectious phase and cause hepatitis	None	Routine screening not recommended	Vaccine is a killed viral vaccine and can safely be used in pregnancy. Contact Precautions during acute phase. The safety of Hepatitis A vaccination during pregnancy has not been determined; however, because the vaccine is produced from inactivated HAV, the theoretical risk to the developing fetus is expected to be low. The risk associated with vaccination, however, should be weighed against the risk for Hepatitis A in women who might be at high risk for exposure to HAV.
HBV	Blood, bodily fluids, vaginal secretions, semen	Hepatitis, early onset hepatocellular carcinoma	HbsAg + 10 percent HbeAg + 90 percent	Routine HBsAg testing advised	HBV vaccine during pregnancy Neonate: HBIG plus vaccine at birth Standard Precautions
HCV	Blood, sexual	Hepatitis	5 percent (0 to 25 percent)	Routine screening not recommended	No vaccine or immunoglobulin available; postexposure treatment with antiviral agents investigational Standard Precautions
HSV	Vesicular fluid, oropharyngeal and vaginal secretions	Sepsis, encephalitis, meningitis, mucocutaneous lesions, congenital malformation (rare)	Primary genital (33 to 50 percent) Recurrent genital (1 to 2 percent)	Antibody testing minimally useful genital inspection for lesions if in labor	Chemoprophylaxis at 36 weeks decreases shedding Standard Precautions
HIV	Blood, bodily fluids, vaginal secretions, semen	No congenital syndrome. If fetus infected, AIDS in 2 to 4 years.	Depends on HIV viral titer If titer <1,000 virus; rate, 2 percent If titer ≥10,000; rate up to 25 percent	Routine maternal screening advised. If exposed, testing at 3, 6, and 12 months	Antiretroviral chemoprophylaxis available for exposures, postnatal chemoprophylaxis for HIV+ mothers and their infants Standard Precautions
Influenza	Sneezing and coughing, respiratory tract secretions	No congenital syndrome: Influenza in mother could cause hypoxia in fetus	Rare	None	TIV for all pregnant women during influenza season to decrease risk of hospitalization for cardiopulmonary complications in mother Droplet Precautions
Measles (rubeola)	Respiratory secretion coughing	Prematurity spontaneous abortion no congenital syndrome	Rare	Antibody test	Vaccine Airborne Precautions
N. meningitidis	Respiratory secretion of untreated patients or those who have received antimicrobials for <24 hours	Sepsis No congenital syndrome	Unknown	None	Chemoprophylaxis with ceftriaxone or azithromycin Vaccine if indicated for outbreak control Standard Precautions, especially mask, face protection for all intubations
Parvovirus B19	Respiratory secretion, blood, immunocompromised patients	Fetal hydrops, stillbirth, no congenital syndrome	Approximately 25 percent; fetal death <10 percent	No routine screening. B19 DNA can be detected in serum, leukocytes, respiratory secretions, urine, tissue specimens	No vaccine. Defer care of immunocompromised patients with chronic anemia when possible Droplet Precautions

Table 104-3. Pregnant Healthcare Worker: Guide to Management of Occupational Exposure *(continued)*

Agent	In-hospital Source	Potential Effect on the Fetus	Rate of Perinatal Transmission	Maternal Screening	Prevention
Rubella	Respiratory secretions	Congenital syndrome	90 percent in first trimester 40 to 50 percent overall	Routine rubella IgG testing in pregnancy Preconception screening recommended	Vaccine No congenital rubella syndrome described for vaccine Droplet Precautions; Contact Precautions; for points with congenital rubella
Smallpox (vaccinia)	Respiratory secretions, contents of pustular-vesicular lesions	Fetal vaccinia, premature delivery, spontaneous abortion, and perinatal death		History of successful vaccination within previous 5 years	Pre-event contraindicated during pregnancy. Vaccine and vaccinia immunoglobulin after exposure; pre-exposure; pre-exposure vaccine only if smallpox present in the community and exposure to patients with smallpox likely. Airborne infection isolation plus Contact Precautions.
Syphilis	Blood, lesion, fluid, amniotic fluid	Congenital syndrome	Variable 10 to 90 percent depends on stage of maternal disease and trimester of the infection	VDRL RPR FTA ABS	Postexposure prophylaxis with penicillin Standard Precautions gloves until 24 h of effective therapy completed for infants with congenital syphilis and all patients with skin and mucous membrane lesions
Tuberculosis	Sputum, skin lesions	Neonatal tuberculosis; liver most frequently infected	Rare	Tuberculin skin test or BAMT Chest radiograph	Varies with TST reaction size and chest radiograph result Airborne Precautions
Varicella zoster	Droplet or airborne spread of vesicle fluid or secretions of the respiratory tract (scabs are not infective)	Malformations (skin, limb, CNS, eye); chickenpox	Total 25 percent: congenital syndrome (0 to 4 percent)	Antibody	Vaccine; VZIG within 96 hours exposure if susceptible; Airborne and Contact Precautions

TIV, trivalent inactivated.

*Congenital syndrome: varying combinations of jaundice, hepatosplenomegaly, microcephaly, thrombocytopenia, anemia, retinopathy, and skin and bone lesions.

†Live virus vaccine given before or after pregnancy.

humans. It is the single most important infectious cause of mental retardation and congenital deafness in the United States.

CMV infection is restricted to humans. The virus is widespread, and infection is more common than disease. By serology, 80 to 90 percent of individuals are exposed during their lifetime. Seropositivity among women in the reproductive years (15 to 35) is approximately 50 percent in middle and upper socioeconomic groups and 90 percent in the lower socioeconomic groups.

CMV is transmitted most frequently by sexual contact or by direct contact with infected urine, saliva, semen, vaginal secretions, or breast milk. Major risks for primary infections among seronegative women include the following:

1. Age <25 years

2. Multiple sexual partners

3. Exposure to young children (especially those who attend day care) at home and in the work place; for example, day care centers and schools

The rate of seroconversion in seronegative women is 1 to 3 percent per year, but is as high as 10 to 20 percent in women who work in day care centers, and approaches 50 percent when an infected child younger than 2 years of age is present in the home. HCP do not have an increased risk of acquisition of CMV infection.

CMV crosses the placenta with relative ease, and congenital infection occurs in 1 to 2 percent of all pregnancies. Perinatal infections are acquired by exposure to the mother's infected genitourinary tract and by ingestion of breast milk from an infected mother. Organ transplants, blood transfusions, and dialysis centers are other sources of infections. The spread of CMV among the general population is facilitated by asymptomatic primary and recurrent infections, multiple sites of excretion, prolonged and intermittent excretion, and excretion of virus despite the presence of specific immunity. Asymptomatic transmission further supports the need for adherence to Standard Precautions among all HCP when in contact with all patients.

CMV infections are considered congenital if virus excretion or serological evidence (CMV immunoglobulin M [IgM]) is found in the infant within the first 2 weeks of life. Transmission of CMV to the fetus can occur during primary and recurrent infections despite maternal antibody. Although maternal immunity is not completely protective, it plays a major role in reducing the virulence of infection and the severity of the clinical manifestations in the fetus or newborn. The frequency of congenitally infected infants among seropositive women is 2 to 3 percent, whereas primary maternal infections carry an overall risk to the fetus of 25 to 50 percent. Ninety percent of congenitally infected infants will shed virus at birth and do so for 6 years or longer, even in the presence of antibody.

Congenital infections range from asymptomatic and unrecognized (90 percent) to multiple organ system involvement that is sometime incompatible with life in 10 percent or less. Most of the asymptomatic infections do not endanger life, but 10 to 15 percent of these infants are at risk for long-term sequelae, such as progressive sensorineural hearing loss, chorioretinitis, and dental abnormalities.

Approximately 5 to 10 percent of congenitally infected infants will have significant stigmata of infection at birth. Approximately half will have classic cytomegalic inclusion disease, and half will have atypical involvement. All infants will excrete CMV at birth. The rate of mortality infections in infants in this group is 20 to 30 percent. Children are most severely affected as a result of primary maternal infections that occur early in pregnancy.

Acquisition of CMV in the neonatal period is common, but the consequences of perinatally acquired infections are considerably less serious than for congenital infections. Incubation time from exposure to infection (asymptomatic or symptomatic) is 4 to 12 weeks, and greater than 50 percent will be asymptomatic. Blood transfusion was the source of most perinatal CMV infections before there were recommendations for using specially treated blood in low-birth-weight neonates.

Preventing primary infections in seronegative women during pregnancy would be valuable. Because CMV is ubiquitous, there is no treatment available, and the incidence of congenital CMV syndrome with its devastating neurologic effects is rare. Serologic screening is not offered to women routinely. Although transfer to a presumed lower-risk patient care unit is an appealing option, it is difficult to identify such an area in most acute care hospitals or healthcare institutions that care for toddlers.

Hepatitis A Virus

Hepatitis A virus (HAV) infection used to be one of the most frequently reported vaccine-preventable diseases. However, with more widespread use of HAV vaccine in populations defined by higher disease prevalence rates, there has been a 97 percent decrease in the incidence of this infection in the United States. HAV replicates in the liver, is excreted in the bile, and is shed in the stool. Peak infectivity occurs during the 2 weeks before the onset of jaundice or elevation of hepatic transaminases, when the viral concentration in the stool is greatest. Chronic shedding does not occur, and viremia is present only soon after infection and persists through the time of hepatic transaminase elevation.

Transmission is primarily from exposure to contaminated feces, but blood can be a source for a short period of time. Maternal

HAV transmission to the fetus has not been established. HAV infection during pregnancy can cause an increased risk of severe systemic infections, spontaneous abortion, and preterm delivery. Hepatitis A is an inactivated vaccine and, similar to Hepatitis B vaccines, is recommended if another high-risk condition or other indication is present.

Hepatitis B Virus

Hepatitis B virus (HBV) infection during pregnancy can result in severe disease for the mother, fetal loss, or chronic infection of the neonate if born alive. The prolonged HBV viremia may persist from weeks to months and provides adequate time for vertical transmission. Chronic HBV infections occur in 1 to 5 percent of adults with acute HBV infection. However, in neonates, as many as 90 percent will manifest chronic infection; 50 percent of infected infants and 20 percent of infected young children will develop chronic infection. This demonstrates the importance of an effective HBV immunization program in the maternal and child health areas within healthcare facilities.

Pregnancy is not a contraindication to vaccination. Limited data suggest that developing fetuses are not at risk for adverse events when Hepatitis B vaccine is administered to pregnant women. Available vaccines contain noninfectious Hepatitis B surface antigen (HBsAg) and should cause no risk of infection to the fetus.

Postexposure Prophylaxis for HBV During Pregnancy

No apparent risk exists for adverse effects to developing fetuses when Hepatitis B vaccine is administered to pregnant women (CDC, unpublished data, 1990). The vaccine contains noninfectious HBsAg particles and should pose no risk to the fetus. HBV infection during pregnancy might result in severe disease for the mother and chronic infection for the newborn. Therefore, neither pregnancy nor lactation should be considered a contraindication to vaccination of women. Hepatitis B immunoglobulin (HBIG) is not contraindicated for pregnant or lactating women.

HBV vaccine should be administered in pregnancy when a high-risk indication is present. See Chapters 97 Viral Hepatitis, and 103 Immunization of Healthcare Personnel, for all indications for HBV vaccine.

All pregnant women should be screened for HBsAg early in pregnancy and later in pregnancy if indicated by participation in high-risk activities such as multiple sexual partners, illicit drug abuse, and acquisition of another sexually transmitted infection.

Previously unvaccinated women who are HBsAg-negative should receive the HBV vaccine series (0, 1, 6 to 12 months). Infants of HBsAg-negative mothers should receive HBV vaccine at birth, whereas infants of HBsAg-positive women should receive HBIG in addition to the first dose of vaccine as soon as possible and ideally within 12 hours of birth.

Hepatitis C Virus

Hepatitis C virus (HCV) may be transmitted sexually, by exposure to blood via transfusion, sharing needles for intravenous drug use, percutaneous injury, and, rarely, perinatal exposure. Transmission via blood transfusion is prevented by screening blood donors for laboratory evidence of HCV infection. No vaccine and no effective therapy during pregnancy or the postnatal period exist at the current time. In fact, it has not been determined if postexposure prophylaxis (PEP) with antiviral agents is beneficial, because it may inhibit the natural protective immune response. Therefore, preventing occupational exposure is by avoiding percutaneous blood exposures via the use of safety devices and wearing gloves.

The epidemiology of HCV resembles HBV. The prevalence of HCV in the United States is 1.5 percent, but is higher in African Americans and inner city pregnant women. Injectable drug use is the major mode of transmission. Both sexual and maternal-fetal transmission have been described, but with low frequencies. Studies of pregnant women who are HCV seropositive suggest that injectable drug use and sexual contact with injectable drug users are the major risk factors responsible for HCV infection in women. The risk of developing chronic HCV infection without evidence of active liver disease is higher than for HBV infection, approaching 75 percent. The incubation period is 15 to 160 days with a peak at 50 days.

The maternal-fetal transmission risk in an HCV seropositive mother is 10 percent, and infection rates can be correlated with the level of maternal viremia. Studies have shown that acute HCV infection in the first and second trimesters causes fetal hepatic injury, whereas acute HCV infection in the third trimester results in serum transaminase elevations without jaundice or evidence of hepatitis in the neonate.

Herpes Simplex Virus

No vaccine is currently available for herpes simplex virus (HSV), and prevention is by adhering to Standard Precautions. Healthcare-associated HSV infection is most likely to manifest as a herpetic whitlow, is prevented by the use of gloves for contact with mucous membranes, and is unlikely to affect the genital tract or the fetus.

There are two major types of HSV: HSV-1 and HSV-2, with multiple strains of each. HSV-1 and HSV-2 share approximately 50 percent of their DNA sequences. Viral replication occurs in the cell nucleus with production of virus within 10 to 14 hours after infection.

Transmission of HSV occurs by intimate contact, such as oral-oral, oral-genital, and genital-genital contact. Transmission by fomites contaminated by body fluids has been documented. Humans are the sole natural host for HSV, and 55 to 90 percent of the general population has antibodies to HSV-1, HSV-2, or both. In the United States, serologic evidence of infection with HSV-2 ranges from less than 1 percent in those aged 15 years or younger to greater than 25 percent in those aged 30 years. Two-thirds of individuals who are seropositive for HSV-2 report no clinical history or exposure to another infected person.

Human Immunodeficiency Virus

No vaccine is currently available for HIV; however, chemoprophylaxis is available for occupational exposures. Handling PEP is covered in Chapter 101 Occupational Exposure to Blood-borne Pathogens.

HIV infection causes destruction of the immune system, particularly CD4 cells, and can result in the clinical acquired immunodeficiency syndrome (AIDS). The risk factors for women or their sexual partners for acquiring HIV infection are as follows:

- Illicit drug use; especially injectable drug use
- Current or previous multiple sexual partners
- Trading sex for drugs
- Transfusion of blood products before 1985
- Bisexual activity
- Residence in or origin from HIV-endemic areas
- Symptoms of HIV-related illnesses
- History of current sexually transmitted infection

In addition to those listed, risk factors for acquiring HIV are as follows:

- Maternal-fetal transmission
- Transplantation of organs
- Artificial insemination
- Breastfeeding

Maternal-fetal transmission may occur transplacentally in utero or perinatally. The rate of transmission is determined by the viral titer in the mother. Studies in the United States have indicated that the transmission rate in nontreated women is 25 percent, whereas those receiving antiretroviral chemotherapy have a transmission rate of 1 to 8 percent. In Africa, breastfeeding appears to account for 7 to 22 percent of all HIV transmission. When safer forms of nutrition are available, breastfeeding is contraindicated in HIV-infected mothers. Management of the HIV-infected pregnant woman includes antiretroviral therapy during pregnancy, during labor, and after delivery for the neonate. Maternal antiretroviral therapy is continued after delivery.

Despite the increasing use of safety devices, occupational exposures will occur and the seroconversion after percutaneous exposure is 0.3 percent, whereas seroconversion after mucous membrane, nonintact skin exposure is 0.09 percent. Risk of percutaneous transmission is increased with hollow-bore needles and when an increased volume of blood is injected. Consistent adherence to Standard Precautions and use of needleless systems and other safety needles will decrease the risk of exposure.

PEP for Pregnant HCP

If the exposed person is pregnant, the evaluation of risk of infection and need for PEP should be approached as with any other person who has had an HIV exposure. However, the decision to use any antiretroviral drug during pregnancy should involve discussion between the HCP and her healthcare provider(s) regarding the potential benefits and risks to her and her fetus. Certain drugs should be avoided in pregnant women—another reason for involving the pregnant HCP healthcare provider—and, therefore, expert consultation for HIV PEP is advised for known or suspected pregnancy in the exposed person.

Human Papillomavirus

Human papillomavirus (HPV) vaccines are not recommended for use in pregnant women. If a woman is found to be pregnant after initiating the vaccination series, the remainder of the three-dose series should be delayed until completion of pregnancy.

Influenza

Influenza is an acute respiratory illness characterized by myalgias, laryngotracheal bronchitis, fever with a nonproductive cough, and acute and chronic debilitation. In the United States, seasonal epidemics of influenza typically occur during October to March. During 30 seasons from the 1976 to 1977 season through the 2005 to 2006 season, estimated influenza-associated deaths ranged from 3,000 to 49,000 annually. Increased severity of influenza among pregnant women was reported during the pandemics of 1918 to 1919, 1957 to 1958, and 2009 to 2010. Pregnant women are at increased risk for severe illness from influenza because of physiologic changes during pregnancy.

Influenza is transmitted in most instances via respiratory secretions from sneezing and coughing (e.g., droplet transmission). Although airborne transmission via small droplet nuclei has been documented (rarely) under certain conditions, large droplet transmission within 3 feet is the primary means of transmission. Influenza vaccination is the best method of preventing influenza and its complications. The Advisory Committee on Immunization Practices (ACIP) recommends routine annual influenza vaccination for all persons aged ≥6 months that do not have contraindications. Recommendations pertaining to the use of specific vaccines and populations can be found in the annual *Morbidity and Mortality Weekly Report* on prevention and control of seasonal influenza with vaccines.

It is important to note that when there are shortages in vaccine supply, as in the 2004 to 2005 season, vaccine is recommended only for those who are pregnant, those with high-risk conditions, all persons age 65 years or greater (instead of 50 years), HCP with direct face-to-face or hands-on contact with patients, and close household contacts or out-of-home caregivers of infants younger than 6 months of age.

Influenza is a common viral disease, and pregnant HCP can be a vector to patients and become infected with the influenza virus herself. The risk of hospitalization for a pregnant woman with influenza during the second and third trimesters is equivalent to that of nonpregnant individuals with underlying cardiopulmonary disease. All HCP should be immunized with influenza vaccine on a yearly basis to protect themselves, their patients, and their families. Currently, the live attenuated influenza vaccine is not recommended during pregnancy.

Measles, Mumps, and Rubella

A highly effective vaccine exists for measles, and all HCP should have received immunization before having patient contact. The measles-mumps-rubella (MMR) vaccine combines measles, mumps, and rubella vaccines and is highly effective.

The MMR vaccine and its component vaccines should not be administered to women known to be pregnant. Because a risk to the fetus from administration of these live virus vaccines cannot be excluded for theoretical reasons, women should be counseled to avoid becoming pregnant for 28 days after vaccinations with measles or mumps vaccines or MMR or other rubella-containing vaccines.

All women of childbearing age, including those who grew up outside the United States in areas where routine rubella vaccination might not occur, should be vaccinated with one dose of MMR vaccine or have other acceptable evidence of rubella immunity. Nonpregnant women of childbearing age who do not have documentation of rubella vaccination, serologic evidence of rubella immunity, or laboratory confirmation of rubella disease should be vaccinated with MMR vaccine. Birth before 1957 is not acceptable evidence of rubella immunity for women who could become pregnant.

Measles occurs primarily in late winter and spring. Transmission is primarily person-to-person via droplet and airborne routes. Measles is highly contagious, with a secondary household attack rate of 90 percent. Death is usually from pneumonia or acute encephalitis and occurs in 1 to 2 of 1,000 cases, which constitutes the main rationale for universal immunization. MMR is not indicated during pregnancy because it contains three live attenuated vaccines, but it should be given postpartum to the nonimmune woman. This demonstrates the importance of ensuring that an effective postpartum immunization program exists in the maternal and child health areas in healthcare facilities.

Rubella (German measles) is a mild, exanthematous viral infection that primarily affects children. Except for rubella infecting pregnant women, there are practically no complications.

The disease is transmitted by respiratory secretions, and the incubation period is 10 to 14 days. The patient infected with rubella should be placed on Droplet Precautions. The maculopapular rash spreads from the thorax and face to the extremities. A low-grade fever and posterior auricular lymphadenopathy are frequently present. The viremia can persist for as long as 46 days after initial infection. Ensuring immunity of HCP in obstetrical clinics and offices is especially important because transmission of this virus from HCP to pregnant women in these settings has been associated with congenital rubella syndrome.

The presentation of the infection in the newborn may range from no symptoms to the multi-organ system involvement that characterizes the congenital rubella syndrome. The syndrome includes a growth-restricted infant who has a chronic infection with this virus. The gestational age of the infection determines the severity of the syndrome. Maternal infection at less than 8 weeks causes 85 percent fetal infection rate, whereas maternal infection at 20 weeks causes a fetal infection rate of 10 percent. Babies born with congenital rubella should be placed on Contact Precautions.

The signs of infection may be so nonspecific that rubella immunoglobin (Ig) G serology is necessary to confirm infection. All pregnant women should be screened for rubella IgG at a preconception visit or early in pregnancy. If the person is rubella nonimmune, the appropriate time to vaccinate the patient is postpartum with MMR vaccine.

Parvovirus B19

Parvovirus B19 was discovered in 1975 and is the causative agent of erythema infectiosum (also known as fifth disease), a common childhood illness. This agent is of concern to pregnant HCP because B19 can cause infection of fetal red blood cell precursors and lead to severe anemia and high-output cardiac failure in the fetus, hydrops fetalis, and fetal death. Parvovirus B19 infection of patients with hemolytic anemia (e.g., sickle cell disease) can be associated with a transient aplastic crisis and with a prolonged anemia in immunodeficient hosts (e.g., HIV-infected patients, patients receiving chemotherapy).

Respiratory secretions transmit parvovirus B19 during close contact. Patients infected with parvovirus B19 should be placed on Droplet Precautions. However, the period of infectivity is over by the time the rash of fifth disease has occurred; these patients need not be placed on Droplet Precautions. Transmission will occur in 10 to 60 percent of school contacts. The viral infection is characterized by a facial rash that resembles a slapped cheek and a reticular pattern of rash on the arms. The virus may persist for a prolonged period of time in immunocompromised patients, and the duration of infectivity is not known. However, transmission of infection may occur as long as the blood polymerase chain reaction (PCR) remains positive.

B19 infection can be diagnosed by B19 IgM serology after the third day of the rash and is present for 30 to 60 days. B19 IgG is present within 7 days and remains detectable for years. PCR may be used to detect parvovirus B19 in the blood.

The major effect of B19 infection is fetal hydrops and death. The likelihood of fetal death after maternal B19 infection is less than 10 percent. Diagnostic ultrasound is the most widely available test to detect fetal hydrops; this may resolve spontaneously or may be treated via intrauterine digoxin. Thus, fetal infection with parvovirus B19 is not an indication for interruption of pregnancy.

Parvovirus B19 infection in a pregnant woman represents a risk to the unborn child. It therefore makes sense to establish a woman's immunological status early in pregnancy. Five percent of infections in the first 20 weeks of pregnancy will result in fetal death. These are often early miscarriages.

Pertussis

Pertussis is an acute respiratory infection caused by *Bordetella pertussis*. The organism produces multiple toxins that damage respiratory epithelium and can have systemic effects including the promotion of lymphocytosis.

The incubation period for pertussis is 7 to 10 days (range: 5 to 21 days). Classic pertussis is characterized by three phases: catarrhal, paroxysmal, and convalescent. The catarrhal phase lasts 1 to 2 weeks and consists of infection of the conjunctiva, frequent sneezing, a watery nasal discharge, and frequent cough. The cough suggesting tracheal irritation is short, hacking, isolated, and present equally day or night. Fever is uncommon during any phase.

The paroxysmal phase lasts 4 to 6 weeks. During this phase, the patient has intermittent periods of intense coughing (paroxysmal) with periods when the patient lives well. The paroxysms are characterized by severe spasms of coughing, choking, post-tussive, and an inspiratory whoop. Adults with pertussis make repeated visits for medical care and miss work and school.

Pertussis is transmitted from person to person via large respiratory droplets generated by coughing or sneezing. Reports suggest pertussis could be recovered from dry mucus up to 3 days. Persons with pertussis are highly infectious: Attack rates among exposed nonimmune households are as high as 80 to 90 percent. The most infectious periods are the catarrhal and early paroxysmal phases. Patients can remain infectious for 6 weeks or more.

The source of pertussis for infected pregnant women has not been systematically studied. In one study of 111 adults aged 18 to 29 years, the source was a person in the household (25 percent), at work or school (25 percent), a relative (7 percent), a friend (5 percent), and unknown (37 percent). In another study of adults aged 30 to 39 years, the source was a person in the household (44 percent), at school or work (17 percent), a relative (4 percent), a friend (5 percent), and unknown (31 percent).

Although the mortality and morbidity in pregnant women are similar to disease in the nonpregnant woman, the disease in the infant can be severe. Infants aged younger than 12 months and especially age younger than 3 months are most likely to have severe pertussis, require hospitalization, and have respiratory and other complications of pertussis. Most deaths due to pertussis occur in infants less than 2 months of age.

Tetanus toxoid, reduced diphtheria toxoid, and acellular pertussis (Tdap) vaccine is recommended before pregnancy, during pregnancy, or immediately postpartum. The value of antepartum administration is to protect the mother from disease, but also to provide the neonate with passive antibodies for protection from disease until the infant's active immunity occurs. Infant immunization with DTaP (the childhood form of the pertussis vaccine) occurs at 2, 4, and 6 months of life, and the infant is not protected until 6 months of life.

Pertussis is another serious infectious disease that pregnant HCP are susceptible to and can transmit to patients. Only 2 percent of adults in the United States are protected against pertussis so there is a high probability that most HCP are not only susceptible to infection but also can transmit pertussis to their patients, family, or neonate.

In October 2011, in an effort to reduce the burden of pertussis in infants, ACIP recommended that unvaccinated pregnant women receive a dose of Tdap. Vaccination of women with Tdap during pregnancy is expected to provide some protection to infants from pertussis until they are old enough to be vaccinated themselves. Tdap given to pregnant women will stimulate the development of maternal antipertussis antibodies, which will pass through the placenta, likely providing the newborn with protection against pertussis in early life, and will protect the mother from pertussis around the time of delivery, making her less likely to become infected and transmit pertussis to her infant. The 2011 Tdap recommendation did not call for vaccinating pregnant women previously vaccinated with Tdap. On October 24, 2012, ACIP voted to recommend use of Tdap during every pregnancy.

Pregnant Women Due for Tetanus Booster

If a tetanus and diphtheria booster vaccination is indicated during pregnancy (i.e., >10 years since previous Td), then Tdap should be administered. Optimal timing is between 27 and 36 weeks' gestation to maximize the maternal antibody response and passive antibody transfer to the infant.

Wound Management for Pregnant Women

As part of standard wound management to prevent tetanus, a tetanus toxoid-containing vaccine might be recommended for wound management in a pregnant woman if ≥5 years have elapsed since the previous Td booster. If a Td booster is recommended for a pregnant woman, healthcare providers should administer Tdap.

Pregnant Women with Unknown or Incomplete Tetanus Vaccination

To ensure protection against maternal and neonatal tetanus, pregnant women who never have been vaccinated against tetanus should receive three vaccinations containing tetanus and reduced diphtheria toxoids. The recommended schedule is 0, 4 weeks, and 6 through 12 months. Tdap should replace one dose of Td, preferably between 27 and 36 weeks' gestation to maximize the maternal antibody response and passive antibody transfer to the infant.

Smallpox (Vaccinia)

Because of the limited risk but severe consequences of fetal infection, smallpox vaccine should not be administered in a pre-event setting to pregnant women or to women who are trying to become pregnant.

Smallpox is a severe, disseminated viral disease with a characteristic vesicular-pustular rash distributed over the extremities, palms, and soles. It is caused by variola minor and variola major viruses, and was associated with mortality rates as high as 30 percent. The last naturally acquired infection occurred in Somalia in 1977, and global eradication was declared in 1980. Routine vaccination was stopped in the United States in 1972. Smallpox caused excessive mortality in pregnant women: a 33 percent case fatality rate, with 27 percent among vaccinated pregnant women and 61 percent among unvaccinated pregnant women. Excessive rates of premature delivery, spontaneous abortion, and perinatal death were associated with smallpox during pregnancy. Although vaccinia virus used for smallpox vaccination is not teratogenic, fetal vaccinia was a rare complication of vaccination of the pregnant woman, with less than 30 cases reported in the world's literature from 1932 to 1978. Estimated incidence has been 1 of 10,000 exposed, but no cases were observed when approximately 173,000 pregnant women were vaccinated in New York City in 1947.

A targeted smallpox vaccination program (~700,000 military personnel and 40,000 civilians who would serve as members of emergency response teams) was initiated in the United States in December 2002 and January 2003 in response to the perceived threat of smallpox as a bioweapon. Because of potential adverse effects of vaccinia on the fetus, pregnancy was considered a contraindication to receiving the vaccine in this program, and all women in the childbearing age group were screened with a questionnaire and counseled to prevent fetal exposure to vaccinia. As of June 2004, 236 vaccinia-exposed pregnancies were reported to the National Smallpox Vaccine in Pregnancy Registry. Analysis available in June 2004 revealed the following: (1) pregnancy occurred less frequently in vaccinia-exposed women compared with the expected rate of pregnancy in unscreened women of childbearing age; (2) no excess adverse effects were observed in the vaccinia-exposed pregnancy; and (3) 75 percent of the women in the registry were exposed to vaccinia before a pregnancy test could have been positive. Thus, the screening program used was effective in preventing fetal exposure to vaccinia and should be included in all pre-event smallpox vaccination programs. However, if inadvertent vaccination during pregnancy does occur, adverse outcome due to exposure to vaccinia virus is unlikely.

Syphilis

Syphilis is a complex, chronic sexually transmitted infection that can have profound effects on pregnancy. It is characterized by a 3-week incubation stage; a primary stage with a single-cutaneous lesion and regional lymphadenopathy; a secondary stage with mucocutaneous lesions, lymphadenopathy, and spirochetemia; a latent period of variable length; and, finally, a progression to serious systemic manifestations. It is acquired by the fetus transplacentally at any time during pregnancy and can be treated successfully with penicillin.

Syphilis can be acquired by intimate sexual contact and direct, unprotected contact with primary or secondary lesions on mucous membranes or skin. Healthcare-associated acquisition of syphilis is highly unlikely because, according to Standard Precautions, HCP would be wearing gloves for contact with any suspicious lesions or blood of patients with suspected syphilis. If a significant exposure does occur (e.g., percutaneous or mucocutaneous exposure to blood or fluid in lesions before or within the first 24 hours of treatment), PEP should be initiated with penicillin as soon as possible. Fetal risks for infection are directly proportional to the degree of maternal spirochetemia and the duration of the untreated maternal infection. The highest rates of congenital syphilis occur in women with secondary syphilis. Fifty percent of infants born to women with untreated primary or secondary syphilis will have congenital infection at birth. The remainder will be infected at delivery. Only 6 to 14 percent of fetuses of women in the late latent stage will be affected.

Serologic tests for antibody production allow the clinician to make the diagnosis. The nontreponemal test, rapid plasma reagin (RPR) test, or Venereal Disease Research Laboratory (VDRL) test can be used to screen for disease and follow response to therapy. Treponemal tests are used for confirmation if the VDRL or RPR is positive. Common treponemal tests are the microhemagglutination assay for antibodies (MHA-TP) or the fluorescent treponemal antibody-absorption (FTA-ABS).

The efficacy of the currently recommended treatment regimens for adult or antepartum early syphilis is 98 percent; most treatment failures are reinfections. Penicillin is the drug of choice during pregnancy. Treatment failures can occur with penicillin treatment but are more likely to occur if treatment is later in pregnancy, if a drug other than penicillin is used, in the presence of higher treponemal loads characteristic of secondary and early latent syphilis, in the presence of very high VDRL titers at treatment and at delivery, or if delivery occurs within 30 days treatment.

All pregnant women should be screened for syphilis early in pregnancy at the first prenatal visit and at 36 weeks' gestation or at delivery. An additional screening at 28 weeks is recommended for populations with a high prevalence of syphilis or for individuals at high risk.

Tuberculosis

Tuberculosis is a major world health problem, and the World Health Organization (WHO) estimates one-third of the world's population is infected with *Mycobacterium tuberculosis* (*M. tuberculosis*). The prevalence in the United States is 4 to 6 percent. However, many international travelers and immigrants enter the United States each year, so the prevalence may vary.

Transmission of tuberculosis occurs almost exclusively as a result of inhaling infectious particles. These particles are produced when an infected person sneezes and coughs. These particles are 1 to 10 μm in size and remain airborne for prolonged periods of time. Pregnant HCP must be aware of the airborne route of transmission and know that using respiratory protection (e.g., N95 respirator or higher level of respiratory protection) when caring for a patient with suspected or proven tuberculosis will protect her. A pregnant woman is not at increased risk of developing active disease after exposure compared with nonpregnant women.

Currently, the standard screening test for latent tuberculosis infection exposure is the intradermal injection of 0.1 mL of fluid containing five tuberculin units of purified protein derivative (PPD), also known as the tuberculin skin test (TST). Tuberculosis will trigger a delayed hypersensitivity reaction and cause induration. The site is examined 48 to 72 hours after placement. Induration of 5 mm is considered positive in high-risk populations or individuals who have had recent exposure or clinical manifestations highly suggestive of tuberculosis. An induration of 15 mm or more is considered positive in a low-risk population. Induration of 10 mm or more in HCP is considered reactive and requires investigation. An alternative test that would involve serology instead of the intradermal injection is currently under review. The whole-blood interferon gamma release assay is a U.S. Food and Drug Administration (FDA)-approved in vitro cytokine-based assay for cell-mediated immune reactivity to *M. tuberculosis* and might be used instead of TST in tuberculosis screening programs for HCP. This IGRA is an example of a blood assay for *M. tuberculosis* (BAMT). Additional information can be obtained in the chapter that discusses tuberculosis (Chapter 95 Tuberculosis and Other Mycobacteria). Neither pregnancy nor a history of having received bacillus Calmette-Guérin is a contraindication to the use of TST for screening; the frequency of screening is based on the risk assessment for the healthcare institution.

Varicella Zoster Virus

Varicella (chickenpox) and herpes zoster are different manifestations of the same virus. The primary infection is chickenpox when varicella zoster virus (VZV) first infects humans. VZV remains latent for a variable period of time and, when it is reactivated, it presents as shingles or herpes zoster infection.

Because the effects of the varicella virus on the fetus are unknown, pregnant women should not be vaccinated. Nonpregnant women who are vaccinated should avoid becoming pregnant for 1 month after each injection. For persons without evidence of immunity, having a pregnant household member is not a contraindication for vaccination.

Varicella zoster viral particles are transmitted from the respiratory tract via the airborne route, from vesicular lesions by the contact route, or, rarely, by the airborne route with aerosolized vesicular lesions. The infection is highly contagious (90 percent transmission rate to susceptible household contacts) from 1 day before the outbreak of the rash and lasts until the lesions have dried completely. Although this is a disease of children, infection may occur in susceptible adults, and second cases of chickenpox have been documented in the elderly. Apparently 5 cases of varicella per 100,000 pregnancies were expected in the prevaccine era. Incubation period varies from 10 to 21 days for immunocompetent individuals; the average is approximately 14 days after exposure. Fever occurs and is followed by a rash that begins on the face and scalp. It then becomes randomly distributed to the trunk; the palms and soles are spared. New crops continue to appear for 5 days and are present in varying stages.

Chickenpox pneumonia is the most common complication and is expected to occur in 15 to 50 percent of adults when no antiviral treatment is given. Chickenpox pneumonia in pregnancy is more severe than in the nonpregnant adult, with a maternal mortality rate of 41 to 46 percent compared with 11 percent in the nonpregnant adult. Bacterial superinfection of skin lesions, most frequently with group A streptococcus or *Staphylococcus aureus*, may be associated with serious invasive disease, including toxic shock syndrome. Treatment with acyclovir is recommended for the pregnant woman who develops chickenpox.

Fetal death is the result of severe maternal varicella infection, usually accompanied with pneumonia. It has not been shown that the virus causes fetal death or first trimester wastage.

Varicella embryopathy is rare with fewer than 20 cases reported in the literature. The syndrome may include fetal growth restrictions, aplasia of a single limb or chest wall, cicatrization of the skin, and neurologic and ocular abnormalities. In none of the cases has virus been cultured.

HCP without a reliable history of disease should receive the varicella vaccine before pregnancy. Household contacts of pregnant women may receive the varicella vaccine because transmission of the attenuated vaccine virus has not been associated with adverse fetal effects.

A newly released vaccine is now available for prevention of shingles (herpes zoster). It is indicated for persons aged 60 years or greater. It has a 66 percent efficacy in preventing shingles and post hepatic neuropathy. It is contraindicated in immunosuppressed persons.

In December 2012, the FDA approved VariZIG, a varicella zoster immunoglobulin preparation (Cangene Corporation, Winnipeg, Canada) for use in the United States for PEP of varicella for persons at high risk for severe disease who lack

evidence of immunity to varicella* and for whom varicella vaccine is contraindicated. Previously available under an investigational new drug (IND) expanded access protocol, VariZIG, a purified immunoglobulin preparation made from human plasma containing high levels of anti-varicella zoster virus antibodies (immunoglobulin G), is the only varicella zoster immunoglobulin preparation currently available in the United States. VariZIG is now approved for administration as soon as possible following varicella zoster virus exposure, ideally within 96 hours (4 days) for greatest effectiveness. The CDC recommends the use of VariZIG for pregnant women without evidence of immunity.

Zoster (shingles) vaccine is not recommended for use in pregnant women. Women should avoid becoming pregnant for 4 weeks following zoster vaccination.

CONCLUSIONS

Pregnant and nonpregnant HCP are exposed to the same possible infectious agents. For some infectious agents, vaccines are available, and prudent HCP will become immunized before conception. It is important that employee health services departments educate all women of childbearing age on how to protect themselves before considering pregnancy and educate all pregnant HCP on how to protect themselves and their fetuses. Immunized, pregnant HCP will then protect herself and pass antibodies to her neonate to protect the neonate for 3 to 6 months.

For some infectious agents, there is no vaccine available, and pregnant HCP must rely on Standard Precautions, including the appropriate use of hand hygiene, masks, gown, glove and eye protection, and respiratory protection, when exposure to potentially infectious blood and body fluids is likely. Restricting pregnant HCP from caring for patients with certain known infections (e.g., CMV) is not recommended.

FUTURE TRENDS

There are currently a number of vaccines under development that will be of importance to HCP who are pregnant or contemplating pregnancy. These include HSV-2 vaccine, CMV vaccine, RSV vaccine, and group B streptococcus vaccine.

INTERNATIONAL PERSPECTIVE

Globalization will continue to require that immunization against vaccine-preventable diseases be emphasized. It is especially important to recognize the variations in immunization practices

---

* Evidence of immunity to varicella includes (1) documentation of age-appropriate vaccination with varicella vaccine, (2) laboratory evidence of immunity or laboratory confirmation of disease, (3) birth in the United States before 1980 (except for healthcare personnel, pregnant women, and immunocompromised persons), or (4) healthcare provider diagnosis or verification of a history of varicella or herpes zoster. For immunocompromised children aged 12 months to 6 years, two doses of varicella vaccine are considered age-appropriate vaccination.

among all countries. When providing medical care for immigrants and international travelers, it is important to be aware of this potential lack of immunization and, in many cases, presume that the individual is vaccine naïve and proceed with the primary series of indicated vaccines. In addition, increasing international travel can be expected to result in new types of infection that may affect the health and safety of pregnant and nonpregnant HCP. Emphasis on the health and safety of the pregnant woman, as well as the fetus, must include immunization as an effort to reduce illness in the newborn.

REFERENCES

Adler SP. Cytomegalovirus and pregnancy. *Curr Opin Obstet Gynecol* 1992;4:670.

Atmar RI, England JA, Hammill H. Complication of measles during pregnancy. *Clin Infect Dis* 1992;14:217–226.

Boppana SB, Pass RF, Britt WJ. Virus-specific antibody response in mothers and their newborn infants with asymptomatic congenital cytomegalovirus infections. *J Infect Dis* 1993;167:72.

Burk RD, Hevang LY, Ho GYF, et al. Outcome of perinatal hepatitis B exposure is dependent on maternal virus load. *J Infect Dis* 1994;170:14–18.

Centers for Disease Control and Prevention (CDC). STDs and Pregnancy Treatment. CDC website. 2011. Avaiable at: http://www.cdc.gov/std/pregnancy/treatment.htm.

Centers for Disease Control and Prevention (CDC). Advisory Committee on Immunization Practices (ACIP) Recommended Immunization Schedules for Persons Aged 0 Through 18 Years and Adults Aged 19 Years and Older — United States, 2014. Available at: http://www.cdc.gov/vaccines/schedules/hcp/adult.html.

Centers for Disease Control and Prevention (CDC). Guidelines for Vaccinating Pregnant Women. CDC website. 2013. Available at: http://www.cdc.gov/vaccines/pubs/preg-guide.htm.

Centers for Disease Control and Prevention (CDC). Hepatitis A information for Healthcare Professionals. CDC website. 2013. Available at: http://www.cdc.gov/hepatitis/hav/havfaq.htm.

Centers for Disease Control and Prevention (CDC). PRAMs and Flu: Pregnant Women and Influenza Vaccination. CDC website. 2013. Available at: http://www.cdc.gov/prams/flu.html.

Centers for Disease Control and Prevention achievements in public health: elimination of rubella and congenital rubella syndrome United States. 1969-2004. *MMWR Recomm Rep* 2005;4:279–282.

Centers for Disease Control and Prevention. A comprehensive immunization strategy to eliminate transmission of hepatitis B virus infection in the United States: recommendation of the Advisory Committee on Immunization Practices (ACIP). *MMWR Recomm Rep* 2006;55(RR-16):1–33.

Centers for Disease Control and Prevention. General recommendations on immunization. Recommendations of the Advisory Committee on Immunization Practice (ACIP). *MMWR Recomm Rep* 2011;60(2):1–64.

Centers for Disease Control and Prevention. Guideline for infection control in healthcare personnel, 1998. *Am J Infect Control* 1998;26:289–354.

Centers for Disease Control and Prevention. Immunization of Health-Care Personnel. Recommendations of the Advisory Committee on Immunization Practices (ACIP) (HIC-PAC). *MMWR Recomm Rep* 2011;60(No.7):1–46.

Centers for Disease Control and Prevention. Influenza Vaccination of Healthcare personnel. *MMWR Recomm Rep* 2006;55(RR-02):1–16.

Centers for Disease Control and Prevention. Prevention and Control of Seasonal Influenza. Recommendations of the Advisory Committee for Immunization Practices (ACIP) United States, 2013-2014. *MMWR Recomm Rep* 2013;62(RR-07):1–60.

Centers for Disease Control and Prevention. Prevention of hepatitis A through active or passive immunization: recommendations of the Advisory Committee on Immunization Practices (ACIP). *MMWR Recomm Rep* 2006;55(No. RR-7):1–23.

Centers for Disease Control and Prevention. Prevention of Measles, Rubella and Congenital Rubella Syndrome and Mumps. Summary Recommendations of the Advisory Committee for Immunization Practices (ACIP). *MMWR Recomm Rep* 2013;62(RR4):1–38.

Centers for Disease Control and Prevention. Recommendations for preventing transmission Hepatitis B among chronic hemodialysis patients. *MMWR Recomm Rep* 2001;50(RR-5):1–43.

Centers for Disease Control and Prevention. Recommendations for using smallpox vaccine in a pre-event vaccination program. Supplemental recommendations of the Advisory Committee on Immunization Practices (ACIP) and the Healthcare Infection Control Practices Advisory Committee (HICPAC). *MMWR Recomm Rep* 2003;52(RR07):1–16.

Centers for Disease Control and Prevention. Updated Recommendations for Use of VariZIG – United States, 2013. *MMWR Morb Mortal Wkly Rep* 2013;62(28):574–576.

Centers for Disease Control and Prevention. Updated U.S. Public Health Service Guidelines for the Management of Occupational Exposure to HBV, HCV and HIV and Recommendations for Post-exposure Prophylaxis. *MMWR* 2001;50(RR11):1–42.

Cone RW, Hobson AC, Brown Z, et al. Frequent detection of genital herpes simplex virus DNA by polymerase chain reaction among pregnant women. *JAMA* 1994 Sep 14;272(10):792–796.

Dowell SF, Torol TJ, Thorp JA, et al. Parvovirus B19 infection hospital workers: community or hospital acquired. *J Infect Dis* 1995;512:1076–1079.

Gall SA. Maternal immunization. *Obstet Gynecol Clin North Am* 2003;30:626.

Gall SA. Vaccines for pertussis and influenza: recommendations for use in pregnancy. *Clin Obstet Gynecol* 2008;51:486–497.

Harger JH, Adler SP, Voch WC, et al. Prospective evaluation of 618 pregnant women exposed to parvovirus B19: risks and symptoms. *Obstet Gynecol* 1998;91:413–420.

Kulhanjian JA, Soroush V, An DS, et al. Identification of women at unsuspected risk of contracting primary herpes simplex virus type 2 infections during pregnancy. *N Engl J Med* 1992;320:910.

Lemon SM. The natural history of hepatitis A: the potential for transmission by transfusion of blood or blood products. *Vox San* 1994;67(Suppl 4):9–23.

Modrow S, Gartner B. Parvovirus B19 infection in pregnancy. *Dtsh Arztebl* 2006;103(43):2869–2876.

Money DM. Antiviral and antiretroviral use in pregnancy. *Obstet Gynecol Clin North Am* 2003;30:731–749.

Neuzil KM, Reed GW, Mitchel ET, et al. Impact of influenza on acute cardiorespiratory hospitalization in pregnant women. *Am J Epidemiol* 1998;148:1094–1102.

Poland GA, Shefer AM, McCaule M, et al. Standards for adult immunization practices. *Am J Prev Med* 2003;25(2):144–150.

Public Health Service Task Force Recommendations for the Use of Antiretroviral Drugs in Pregnant Women Infected with HIV-1 for Maternal Health and for Reducing Perinatal HIV-1 Transmission in the United States. *MMWR Recomm Rep* 1998;47(RR2):1–30.

Suarez VR, Hankins GDV. Smallpox during pregnancy: from eradicated disease to bioterrorist threat. *Obstet Gynecol* 2002;100:87–93.

Update: Prevention of hepatitis a after exposure to hepatitis a virus and in international travelers. Update/Recommendations of the Advisory Committee on Immunization Practices (ACIP). *MMWR Recomm Rep* 2007;56(41):1080–1084.

Updated Recommendations for Use of Tetanus Toxoid, Reduced Diphtheria Toxoid, and Acellular Pertussis Vaccine (Tdap) in Pregnant Women — Advisory Committee on Immunization Practices (ACIP), 2012. *MMWR Recomm Rep* 2013;62(07):131–135.

Williamson WD, Demmler GI, Percy AK, et al. Progressive hearing loss in infants with asymptomatic congenital cytomegalovirus infection. *Pediatrics* 1992;90:862.

SUPPLEMENTAL RESOURCES

Redbook. Washington, DC: American Academy of Pediatrics (AAP), 2012. AAP website. Available online at: http://aapredbook.aappublications.org/.

CHAPTER 105

Minimizing Exposure to Blood and Body Fluids

Sonia Miller, RN, BSN, MSN, CIC
Chief, Infection Prevention & Control
Fort Belvoir Community Hospital
Fort Belvoir, VA

ABSTRACT

Occupational exposure to contaminated medical devices, specifically percutaneous injuries from contaminated sharps, account for the largest number of healthcare personnel exposures to blood and other potentially infectious materials. To minimize this exposure risk, the most solid base for healthcare personnel safety includes evaluation, selection, and implementation of engineering controls; safe work practices; comprehensive safety programs; and annual review of those elements. This chapter will review device-related causes of sharps injuries, available technologies for reducing injuries, and procedure- and device-specific exposure control measures. A brief discussion will be presented on international healthcare personnel safety and public health relating to exposures to blood and other potentially infectious materials.

KEY CONCEPTS

- Identify trends in percutaneous injuries from contaminated sharps in healthcare settings

- Present information on available and appropriate engineering controls

- Establish strategies for the evaluation, selection, and implementation of engineering controls (e.g., safety-engineered medical devices)

- Provide interventions and implementation practices for incorporating engineering and work practices into patient care

- Provide suggestions, next steps, and international perspectives on the use of safety-engineered medical devices, safe medication delivery, and safe work practices in healthcare

BACKGROUND

Percutaneous injuries among healthcare personnel (HCP) continue to pose a significant public health risk for transmission of human immunodeficiency virus (HIV), Hepatitis B virus (HBV), Hepatitis C virus (HCV), and other bloodborne pathogens.[1]

This is despite a significant decline in the percutaneous injury rates (Figures 105-1 and 105-2),[2] which is attributed to institutional compliance with the Bloodborne Pathogens Standard published by the Occupational Safety and Health Administration (OSHA) in December 1991.[3] Although needlestick injuries among hospital-based HCP in the United States have decreased to 38[4],325 per year in 2000 from an estimated 800,000 to 1 million exposures per year in 1996,[4] every exposure should be regarded as preventable given the potentially disastrous consequence, as illustrated by the following account:

> Near the end of a 12-hour shift in the emergency department, I left the triage area to help a colleague having trouble drawing blood from a patient. It was a moment that changed my life. Seconds later, my gloved index finger was bleeding. I had sustained a deep puncture wound from a needle protruding from an overfilled sharps disposal box. That was 1998. By early 1999, I learned that I had contracted HIV and hepatitis C. The incident signaled the beginning of the end of my 26-year career as a front-line nurse and, for some time, transformed me from caregiver to patient.[5]

Although sharps injuries may be decreasing as a result of implementation of safer devices and new non–needle-based technologies,[6-9] coupled with increased awareness of risk from effective training programs for HCP, it remains difficult to measure the true impact because original surveillance data was acquired through best available sources riddled with misreporting and underreporting of actual exposure incidents. Most data were based on a voluntary reporting system designed by the University of Virginia International Healthcare Worker Safety Center, individual health systems, and state-based reporting systems. Substantial risk for exposure to bloodborne pathogens is burgeoning outside the hospital setting, including nursing homes and residential care facilities, as demonstrated by data from the 1998 to 2000 National Electronic Injury Surveillance System (NEISS), a stratified probability-based sample of U.S. hospital emergency departments.[10]

A comprehensive approach is needed to reduce the risk for exposure to blood and other potentially infectious materials, including the use of Standard Precautions,[11] the implementation of effective disposal systems, worker training and education, and healthcare management safety system buy-in, all of which have contributed to improvements in the safety of the healthcare work environment. Adherence to Standard Precautions

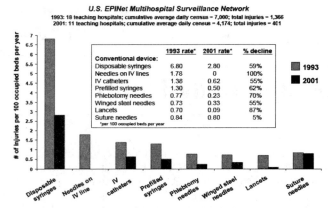

Figure 105-1. Comparison of 1993 and 2001 percutaneous injury rates for nurses, by device (conventional only), 2001 U.S. EPINet Network.

calls for consistent application of infection prevention practices for every patient encounter regardless of a patient's infection status and includes the use of hand hygiene, use of personal protective equipment (e.g., gloves, gown, mask, eye protection, or face shield, depending on the anticipated exposure during direct patient care or contact with potentially contaminated environment), and safe injection practices. Engineering controls target efforts toward using technological strategies to eliminate or minimize exposure to occupational hazards. In the healthcare setting (and with respect to this chapter), this is addressed by the control of occupational exposure to blood and other potentially infectious materials through the use of needleless systems, safer medical devices (such as safety-engineered syringes, intravenous catheters, disposal containers, and adhesive catheter securement devices), and alternative drug delivery systems.

This chapter will focus on only one element of a successful exposure prevention program—the use of engineering controls emphasized by stringent work practice controls.

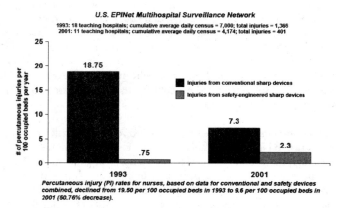

Figure 105-2. Comparison of 1993 and 2001 percutaneous injury rates for nurses, 2001 U.S. EPINet.

BASIC PRINCIPLES

Performance-based regulatory text issued by OSHA is broad-sweeping with regard to exposure control, but its intent is focused and clear. OSHA's Bloodborne Pathogens Standard states that employers are required to use engineering and work practice controls to reduce or eliminate occupational exposure to blood and other potentially infectious materials.[12] With the reduction of exposure to blood and other potentially infectious materials, it is inferred that the risk for exposure to bloodborne pathogens will be reduced to the lowest possible level. With evolving and new technology, employers (e.g., healthcare facilities) must select engineering controls that are effective in reducing injuries from contaminated sharps used for patient care, diagnostic and clinical testing, surgery, and drug and vaccine delivery, to name a few. Safety-engineered devices should be the most appropriate for each specific medical or diagnostic procedure based on a facility's exposure determination and procedures or tasks where exposure to blood or other potentially infectious materials is reasonably anticipated. This will vary from facility to facility depending on the medical and preventive services being performed.

The Needlestick Safety and Prevention Act (NSPA) enacted into law on November 6, 2000, helped clarify OSHA's 1991 standard through the addition of specific examples of engineering controls; additional requirements for device evaluation and employee input to be included in the exposure control plan; and the requirement to maintain a sharps injury log.[13] Injuries from contaminated sharps are not limited to the HCP using them, but often involve other workers coming into contact with contaminated devices, e.g., housekeepers, maintenance personnel, waste haulers. Nearly 40 percent of all injuries occurring from contaminated sharps happen to workers who were not the original user of the sharp device.[14] Hence, it is imperative that a healthcare facility perform a comprehensive review and evaluation of safety-engineered devices to ensure their effectiveness from activation of the safety feature during initial use through disposal.[15]

Thousands of U.S. patents have been issued since 1984 for needles and other medical devices that incorporate injury-prevention features.[16] In 2005, the Food and Drug Administration (FDA) updated its premarket notification process for medical devices with sharps injury-prevention features. All major medical device companies in the United States have marketed devices with safety features as alternatives to conventional devices. The available safety products cover a broad spectrum of sharps devices, including the top device categories identified in the 2011 and 2006 U.S. EPINet reports, and 2002 UK EPINet surveillance systems (Table 105-1),[17-19] which account for the majority of the reported percutaneous injuries. The basic concepts underlying new safety products include the elimination of unnecessary needles and sharps items (e.g., needleless connections in intravenous [IV] lines) and the incorporation of features that shield hands from needles after use, allowing hands to remain behind needles as they are covered.[20] Sheathing, retracting, and blunting needles

Table 105-1. Percutaneous Injury Rates for Top 5 Devices: 2011 and 2006 U.S. EPINet Surveillance Network Data Compared to the 2002 UK EPINet Surveillance Data

Device Type Causing Injury	2011 U.S. EPINet	2006 U.S. EPINet	2002 UK EPINet*
Disposable syringe	37.4%	29.3%	25.7%
Suture needle	18.6%	21.9%	8.8%
Winged steel needle	2.5%	5.6%	6.0%
IV catheter (stylet)	3.9%	2.9%	6.3%
Scalpel, disposable	3.0%	4.6%	4.1%
Lancet	0.4%	1.2%	2.9%

*From Be Sharp, Be Safe campaign by the Royal College of Nursing.

are available safety design approaches. A passive safety device that automatically covers the sharp during use may be more effective at reducing needlestick injuries than one that has to be activated.[21]

This chapter reviews device-related causes of percutaneous injuries and provides a general description of the range of available technology designed to reduce injury risk. Discussion of this technology does not imply endorsement of any specific product. In fact, the availability of such safety technology in the United States may be well in advance of research, particularly randomized trials that would document safety efficacy, user acceptance, and cost effectiveness of specific products. Although reports have been published on the effectiveness and performance of specific safety products, the reports are few compared to the large number of available products, and the findings of these reports are in some cases inconsistent with each other because of different study methods and different circumstances under which the devices were used.[22-28] Therefore, there is a pressing need for research to evaluate the new technology and alternative means of drug and therapeutic delivery for both HCP and patient safety. Guidelines for conducting product evaluation research and cost-effectiveness analysis of products designed to prevent percutaneous injuries have been described in the literature.[29,30] Further research applying consistent and rigorous methods will ultimately assist healthcare institutions in making optimum product decisions that will afford their employees and patients the greatest safety margin at the highest value.

Minimizing Exposure to Blood and Body Fluids

Exposure Prevention Strategies Related to Blood Drawing

Blood-filled, hollow-bore needles, the devices most frequently associated with bloodborne pathogen transmission, primarily include devices that have been used for vascular access or blood drawing.[1] Because of the disproportionate rates of pathogen transmission associated with blood-drawing equipment and IV catheters and the wide array of safety products available, the prevention strategies relevant to these procedures will be presented first.

Equipment used in blood-drawing procedures has been associated with phlebotomy injuries. This equipment includes butterfly-type needles, vacuum-tube phlebotomy needles, disposable syringes, and blood gas syringes. Other devices used to draw blood that have caused injuries resulting in bloodborne-pathogen transmission include fingerstick and heelstick lancets, glass vacuum or specimen tubes, and glass capillary tubes.

Protective designs currently exist for every category of device related to blood drawing, including:

- Shielded or self-blunting needles for vacuum-tube phlebotomy sets
- Plastic vacuum/specimen tubes resistant to breakage
- Retracting, sheathing, or blunting butterfly-type needles
- Blunt cannula blood transfer devices
- Blood gas syringes (used for other purposes as well) with a hinged needle shield that can be put in place over the needle without using the hands
- Automatically retracting fingerstick and heelstick lancets
- Unbreakable plastic capillary tubes for hematocrit determination
- Hemoglobin reader (providing a value that translates into a hematocrit value) that does not use capillary tubes or require centrifugation of the sample

There are relatively few publications on the performance of these devices, though anecdotal reports abound and guidelines for evaluating their safety performance have been published.[29-31] One study reported a 76 percent reduction in injury rates for a safety vacuum-tube phlebotomy set with a self-blunting needle when compared to a conventional phlebotomy needle and a 25 percent reduction in injury rates with a butterfly-type needle that incorporates a protective sliding shield as compared to a conventional butterfly needle.[27] Another study reported an injury reduction of 82 percent with a vacuum-tube phlebotomy device incorporating a needle-shielding tube holder.[22]

Injecting blood into vacuum tubes using conventional syringes is a hazardous practice and should be prohibited. The needle can miss the stopper and stick the opposing hand, the stopper can "blow off" when injecting blood into the tube, or the needle can suddenly disengage as it is being pulled out of the stopper, rebounding and sticking the worker.[20] In a survey of members of a professional phlebotomy association, 63 percent of respondents indicated that they regularly inject blood through stoppers into tubes.[32] This hazardous practice can be avoided by using a device that draws blood directly from the patient (or from a line) into the vacuum tube or other specimen container. When drawing blood with a syringe is absolutely necessary, transfer of blood into a tube should be done with a blunt cannula blood transfer device.

Eliminating the use of unnecessary blood-drawing needles is also important. Needles should not be used on syringes for the purpose of drawing blood samples from venous or arterial lines. Needleless access equipment (blunt cannula, valve systems) should be used instead. For blood culture procedures, needles should not be changed before the inoculation of culture medium because this practice increases the risk for needlestick and has not been shown to reduce contamination of culture specimens.[33]

Removing contaminated needles from blood collection sets is an extremely hazardous practice. When using a blood tube holder with needle attached, the entire unit should be disposed of immediately after use. Using holders with push-button releases or unwinders should be avoided because the increased manipulation required to remove the contaminated needle increases the risk for an injury. A Safety and Health Information Bulletin published by OSHA in 2003 on the hazards of tube holder reuse and needle removal further clarified the organization's position that removal of a contaminated needle is prohibited by the Bloodborne Pathogens Standard unless the removal is required for a medical procedure.[34] Single-use tube holders with safety-engineered needles attached should be evaluated and implemented to reduce injuries occurring from the unprotected back end of the needle when disassembly is performed. Disassembling devices account for nearly 3.2 percent of all injuries from contaminated sharps reported to 2011 EPINet.

Retracting fingerstick and heelstick lancets minimize the risk for sustaining accidental injuries because the lancet automatically retracts after piercing the patient's skin. Retracting lancets also reduce or eliminate (depending on the design), the possibility of cross-contamination between patients because no reusable components come into contact with the puncture site.

Microbore glass capillary tubes are commonly used for measuring hematocrit. They are extremely fragile and can inflict a large laceration when they break during handling or during centrifugation and are extremely hazardous because they contain blood. All injuries from microbore glass capillary tubes are preventable because unbreakable plastic capillary tubes are currently available. Given the seriousness of the injuries they cause and the widespread availability of safe and inexpensive alternatives, the use of microbore glass capillary tubes should be immediately and completely discontinued. Other methods of measuring hematocrit, such as a hemoglobin reader that does not require centrifugation of blood samples, can also provide safer alternatives.

Summary of Safety Recommendations for Blood-Drawing Procedures

The following recommendations should be observed in blood-drawing procedures:

- Blood-drawing devices with integrated safety features designed to prevent percutaneous injuries should be rapidly implemented, including phlebotomy needle/tube holder assemblies, butterfly-type devices, and syringes used for blood drawing. These devices should be closely monitored for user and patient safety and for reliability of laboratory values.

- All unnecessary needles should be eliminated from use, including needles used for drawing blood from intravenous, arterial, and central lines, and replaced by needleless or blunt cannula devices. In addition, the practice of changing needles for blood-culture phlebotomy should be abandoned to avoid the hazard of manually removing a blood-filled needle from the syringe.

- The practice of injecting blood through a stopper into a vacuum tube using an exposed needle should be discontinued. Methods of drawing blood directly into vacuum tubes or other specimen containers or use of a transfer device should be preferentially employed; alternatively, safety syringes with a cylindrical needle shield locked in place over the needle, which allow a vacuum tube to be inserted into the shield during blood injection, will reduce needlestick risk and reduce risk of blood splatter from dislodged tube stoppers.

- Automatically retracting fingerstick and heelstick lancets should be used in place of manual lancets or nonretracting spring-loaded lancets.

- The use of microbore glass capillary tubes for measuring hematocrit should be immediately and completely discontinued. Plastic capillary tubes or alternative methods of measuring hematocrit that do not require capillary tubes should be used.

- Glass blood collection tubes should be replaced by breakage-resistant tubes (e.g., plastic, coated glass).

- Blood-drawing personnel should not remove contaminated needles from blood collection tubes to reuse the tube holder. Following a blood draw, the safety feature should be activated and the needle with the attached tube disposed of as one unit immediately after use.

- Blood-drawing personnel should be advised not to manually recap or remove needles from blood-drawing devices, including blood tube holders.

- Blood-drawing personnel should be explicitly advised not to cut the tip off the index finger (or any other part) of procedure gloves because this increases the risk for blood exposure.

- All facilities should provide puncture-resistant disposal containers within arm's reach of blood-drawing personnel for all phlebotomy procedures.

Engineering Controls for IV Catheters

Preventing injuries from IV catheter stylets is just as critical as preventing injuries from blood-drawing devices because the IV catheter stylets are both large bore and blood filled and therefore can result in a higher probability of infection. Several cases of HIV transmission have been attributed to IV catheter stylets.[35-38] Safety devices are available that provide a protective shield for the stylet before or during its withdrawal from the catheter. A study conducted in three hospitals showed an 83 percent reduction in needlestick rate when a shielded-stylet safety catheter used in the hospitals was compared to a conventional catheter used simultaneously in the same hospitals.[39]

Because of the seriousness of IV catheter stylet injuries and because initial results show device efficacy, it is important for institutions to implement safety IV catheters as quickly as possible and to the full extent that is clinically feasible (barring some clinical applications requiring features that a specific device may not have). The devices should also be monitored in each institution for both user and patient safety. In addition to implementing protective IV catheters, procedure gloves should be worn during the insertion of IV catheters, and a puncture-resistant sharps disposal container should be located within arm's reach of HCP or brought to the bedside for all IV catheter placements.

Other Device Categories

Disposable syringes are the most common cause of reported needlesticks in hospitals, as shown in Table 105-1. The level of risk from a syringe needlestick depends on whether the syringe was used for blood drawing or for injection. The possibility of pathogen transmission, including HIV, HBV, and HCV, should not be dismissed, even under low-risk conditions. It also remains important to prevent needlesticks from syringes because in many cases the original purpose of the device, and/or the source patient on which it was used, cannot be identified, and exposed HCP may have to follow the postexposure protocol for an HIV exposure as a precautionary measure.[1]

The elimination of unnecessary needles from the healthcare workplace is a major safety goal. Needles used to connect IV lines or access IV ports are the primary source of unnecessary needles in U.S. hospitals and account for a high proportion of needlesticks in hospitals where they are used. In one U.S. hospital, 25.8 percent of needlesticks from hollow-bore needles were caused by needles connecting to or accessing IV lines, before the introduction of a needleless IV system.[40] The 1992 FDA safety alert advised hospitals against the use of hypodermic needles with IV systems and noted that in addition to the risk for injury to HCP, patients are at risk as well from needles breaking off inside IV ports and from the unintentional disconnection of IV lines when needles pull out of IV ports, both of which can have potentially serious consequences for patients.[41] Since then, approximately 90 percent of IV catheters and IV access devices, some 80 percent of blood collection devices, and 65 percent of needles and syringes used within U.S. hospitals are safety devices.[42] Needleless access to IV lines with the use of stopcocks and Luer locks has been standard practice for decades in European and most other developed countries.[40]

Hypodermic needles accessing IV ports are less likely than blood-drawing needles to transmit a significant infectious inoculum during a needlestick. Nevertheless, bloodborne pathogens can be transmitted by hypodermic needles used for intermittent IV therapy under specific circumstances. One reported HIV case involved an injury from an intermittent IV needle that was connected to a heparin lock close to the patient, in which blood had backed up into the IV line, filling up the needle.[43] The potential for this high-risk combination of circumstances should be taken into consideration when assessing the hazards of conventional IV equipment.

Because of the wide variety of needleless and protected-needle IV systems currently available,[44] and the relative lack of data on performance, few generalizations can be made that apply to all systems. Some studies have documented substantial declines in injuries related to IV equipment after the introduction of needleless systems.[23,25,45] Other authors emphasize the importance of in-service training and enforcement of use of new equipment for successful implementation of new IV systems.[9,26] In light of the need for performance data on many of the new IV products, all IV systems should be continuously monitored for both patient and HCP safety.

Suture needles ranked second as a cause of reported percutaneous injuries in U.S. hospitals, accounting for 18.6 percent of all percutaneous injuries in 2011 U.S. EPINet data.[17] In the surgical setting, suture needles cause more injuries than any other device. Because underreporting is more prevalent among operating room personnel than workers in other areas of the hospital, the true frequency of suture needle injuries is likely to be much higher,[46] with some data showing an increasing trend.[47] Furthermore, surgeons have been shown to sustain higher rates of percutaneous injuries than other HCP.[48] These high injury rates and the frequency of suture needle injuries, however, do not appear to translate into proportionately high rates of bloodborne pathogen transmission. For example, of the 186 documented and possible cases of occupational HIV transmission in the United States reported by the Centers for Disease Control and Prevention (CDC) as of December 1997, six surgeons were listed in comparison to 34 clinical laboratory technicians (most of them phlebotomists).[32,49,50] Among the factors that may account for this discrepancy is that surgeons, in contrast to phlebotomists, are unlikely to be injured by blood-filled hollow-bore needles, the devices most often associated with bloodborne pathogen transmission.

Suture needles have a much smaller potential for transferring a significant quantity of blood during a needlestick, especially after passing through one or two layers of latex or other glove material.[51] According to U.S. EPINet data from 1995, 86.2 percent of phlebotomists reporting percutaneous injuries were injured by hollow-bore, blood-filled needles. By contrast, only 3.1 percent of physicians reporting injuries in the operating room were injured by blood-filled, hollow-bore needles. It is still important to prevent suture needle injuries, however, to reduce the need for postexposure follow-up and patient testing, minimize interruptions of surgical procedures, and also minimize the potential for patient exposure to blood of the injured surgical personnel. The risk for surgeon-to-patient HIV transmission is small, but it is nevertheless a realistic concern. The French Ministry of Health disclosed the first probable case of surgeon-to-patient HIV transmission in 1997.[52] Suture needles are unique in that the majority of suture needle injuries occur during, rather than after, use of the needles. In 2011 U.S. EPINet data, 18.6 percent of suture needle injuries occurred during suturing and 3.2 percent occurred during passing or disassembly. Therefore, prevention measures that can reduce injuries during, as well as after, suturing will have a much greater potential for injury reduction than measures that target disassembly or disposal only.

Blunt suture needles are available that are not sharp enough, under normal conditions, to cause percutaneous injuries to HCP but are sharp enough to penetrate internal tissues such as muscle and fascia.[53] The potential for injury prevention depends on the proportion of suturing that can be performed with blunt needles. One study reported an 83 percent decline in suture needle injury rates following the introduction of blunt suture needles during gynecological surgery,[54] with blunt suture needles causing no injuries. Another prevention approach is to reduce the use of suture needles and other sharp surgical instruments to a minimum. For example, using stapling devices, adhesive strips, or tissue adhesives for wound closure reduces the use of sharp suture needles.

Injuries from disposable scalpel blades rank fourth as a cause of percutaneous injury, contributing 3 percent of all injuries in 2011 U.S. EPINet (see Table 105-1), with reusable scalpels contributing to an additional 4 percent of the injuries.[17] Scalpel blade injuries most frequently occur in the operating room, with the highest proportion occurring during use, followed by injuries during passing and disassembly. Scalpel blades are more likely than needles to cause deep or otherwise severe injuries resulting in moderate or profuse bleeding. Hence, injuries caused by scalpel blades are associated with a greater likelihood of significant blood contact between patients and surgical personnel. One case of HIV transmission in a surgeon following a scalpel injury has been documented in the Italian SIROH study.[55] Another case of HIV transmission following a scalpel injury that occurred during an autopsy has been documented in a U.S. pathologist.[56]

A variety of prevention alternatives target the different mechanisms of scalpel blade injuries. Options for preventing injuries that occur during cutting include using alternative cutting methods when appropriate, such as blunt electrocautery devices and laser devices, substituting endoscopic surgery for open surgery when possible, using round-tipped scalpel blades instead of sharp-tipped blades, using retractable, disposable scalpels, using alternative materials (e.g., silicone) blades, and avoiding manual tissue retraction by using mechanical retraction devices.

Scalpels with safety features include retracting-blade and shielded-blade scalpels and have the maximum potential to prevent injuries that occur during passing, after use, and during and after disposal. Devices that allow the nonmanual release of scalpel blades from reusable handles provide a method for reducing injury risk during disassembly of scalpels. Such devices include scalpel handles that release scalpel blades and accessory devices that mechanically remove blades. The use of disposable scalpels, which does not require blade removal, also has the potential to prevent disassembly-related injuries.

Possible prevention strategies for injuries that occur during passing of scalpels include a policy of hands-free passing of instruments, which is intended to minimize collisions between hands and sharp instruments by designating a neutral zone where instruments can be placed and picked up. Although there are no randomized, controlled trials showing efficacy of the hands-free technique in reducing injury risk, despite its effectiveness being demonstrated in a prospective study of 3,765 surgi-

cal procedures in a U.S. inner city hospital,[57] its use remains inconsistent.[58]

Although no gloves provide total protection from needlesticks, there are gloves that can be worn under latex, vinyl, or nitrile gloves that resist laceration. These gloves have been made in a variety of materials, such as steel mesh, Kevlar, leather, and a knitted cut-resistant yarn.[59] Laceration-resistant gloves are particularly applicable to the pathology and autopsy settings, where scalpel blades are the most frequent cause of injury and where touch sensitivity is not as critical as in surgery. The gloves can be worn on the nondominant hand, which is where the majority of scalpel injuries occur.[60]

In addition to the specific recommendations for preventing suture needle and scalpel blade injuries, especially in the surgical setting, an evaluation of all surgical instruments should be conducted to eliminate equipment that is unnecessarily sharp. For instance, towel clips have been identified as a cause of injury in the operating room, yet blunt towel clips are available that cannot cause percutaneous injuries and are adequate for securing surgical towels and drapes. Surgical scissors, surgical wire, electrocautery needles, and pick-ups are further examples of devices that do not always need to be sharp.

CONCLUSIONS

Implementation of safety-engineered medical devices is beginning to take shape as a great public and occupational health success story. Through the use of safety disposable syringes, safety blood-collection sets, needleless IV systems, and blunt suture needles, injuries from contaminated sharps have been reduced. Public policy requires the use of engineering and work practice controls, and healthcare systems have recognized not only the need to comply with federal law, but also the need to implement systems that reduce injuries to HCP to best add value to overall safety programs, reduce lost work days, reduce emotional turmoil after an injury, reduce costs associated with postexposure follow-up and prophylaxis, and reduce costs associated with workers' compensation and insurance premiums. Available technologies give healthcare facilities a broad range of options for selection based on clinical needs, worker and patient safety, accuracy of medication delivery, and better patient care.

It is clear that more and better injury data are needed, especially in nonacute care sites. For now, the use of engineering controls has reduced injury rates in nearly all medical specialties in hospitals and other acute care facilities, but the continuation of safety conversion in nursing homes and nontraditional healthcare settings needs to be emphasized further. It is also clear that injuries are still occurring when safety-engineered devices are used because of poor selection, poor work practices, device failure, patient movement, or other reasons; alternative technologies for medication delivery would further reduce sharps injury numbers. For example, newer technologies for drug delivery include the use of medication skin patches, forced air injection systems, and alternative methods for medication absorption, such as oral, nasal, or epidermal.

FUTURE TRENDS

Reductions of injuries from contaminated sharps will continue over time because of the implementation of engineering controls. New non–needle-based technologies will emerge that will further reduce percutaneous injuries in healthcare settings. More surveillance data should be collected from healthcare facilities to assess the success of engineering controls from use of more effective technologies. A root-cause analysis should be conducted to identify departments and specialties with high rates of injuries and to determine reasons these safety-engineered medical devices have not been implemented. As acute care facilities implement safety devices, it will be important to monitor alternative sites or smaller healthcare-providing businesses, such as medical offices, surgical centers, dental offices, and nursing homes to better propagate conversion to safety. Several industries outside typical healthcare that have potential for blatant exposures to blood and other potentially infectious materials should be included for future research, such as funeral homes and mortuaries, piercing and tattoo parlors, and commercial fishing.

Societal issues will emerge as the public becomes more aware of bloodborne pathogens and the importance of preventive measures to reduce the incidence of transmission. Although occupational risk of HBV transmission in our younger generations entering the healthcare workforce systems will decrease in the coming decades as a result of universal childhood immunization, risk for injury will increase for other community workers, including waste haulers, from widespread use of self-injector therapies such as insulin and hormones generating contaminated devices that enter the waste stream. Therefore, it will be important to look toward transitioning all sharps to safety devices to reduce injury rates in and out of the healthcare systems.

INTERNATIONAL PERSPECTIVE

Modeled after the U.S. rules and regulations for the protection of HCP, other countries have begun the process of influencing national policies. Several countries in Europe have introduced safety policies and regulations for HCP safety. Other countries have begun the formation of safety committees and coalitions with visions for HCP safety policy. It is interesting to monitor progress internationally and to see how laws and policies put in place are effectively reducing bloodborne pathogen transmission in healthcare. A global perspective for HCP safety will benefit each country and each system to better compare and contrast measures of success and failure and to implement the most effective programs.

Reuse of contaminated devices from citizen to citizen in Third World countries perpetuates a high rate of disease transmission for HIV, HBV, and HCV. Undoubtedly, mass vaccination programs will serve as valuable public health preventive measures and the benefit of effective engineering controls will remain primary. However, the use of autodisabling syringes will further reduce disease transmission because each syringe is rendered unusable after each injection. Proper sharps disposal will also reduce injuries internationally for these workers and citizens downstream.

REFERENCES

1. U.S. Public Health Service. Updated U.S. Public Health Service guidelines for the management of occupational exposure to HBV, HCV, and HIV and recommendations for postexposure prophylaxis. *MMWR Recomm Rep* 2001 Jun 29;50(RR-11):1–52.
2. Jagger J, Perry J. Comparison of EPINet data for 1993 and 2001 shows marked decline in needlestick injury rates. *Adv Exposure Prev* 2003;6:25–27.
3. Occupational exposure to bloodborne pathogens—OSHA. Final rule. *Fed Regist* 1991 Dec 6;56(235):64004–64182.
4. Panlilio AL, Orelien JG, Srivastava PU, et al. Estimate of the annual number of percutaneous injuries among hospital based healthcare workers in the United States, 1997-1998. *Infect Control Hosp Epidemiol* 2004 Jul;25(7):556–562.
5. Ornstein H, Daley K. Needlestick: adding insult to injury. Interview by Sibyl Shalo. *Am J Nur* 2007 May;107(5):25–26.
6. Whitby M, McLaws ML, Slater K. Needlestick injuries in a major teaching hospital: the worthwhile effect of hospital-wide replacement of conventional hollow-bore needles. *Am J Infect Control* 2008 Apr;36(3):180–186.
7. Lamontagne F, Abiteboul D, Lolom I, et al. Role of safety-engineered devices in preventing needlestick injuries in 32 French hospitals. *Infect Control Hosp Epidemiol* 2007 Jan;28(1):18–23.
8. Clarke SP, Schubert M, Korner T. Sharp-device injuries to hospital staff nurses in 4 countries. *Infect Control Hosp Epidemiol* 2007 Apr;28(4):473–478.
9. Tuma S, Sepkowitz KA. Efficacy of safety-engineered device implementation in the prevention of percutaneous injuries: a review of published studies. *Clin Infectious Dis* 2006 Apr 15;42(8):1159–1170.
10. Chen GX, Jenkins EL. Potential work-related bloodborne pathogen exposures by industry and occupation in the United States part I: an emergency department-based surveillance study. *Am J Ind Med* 2007 Mar;50 (3): 183–190.
11. Siegel JD, Rhinehart E, Jackson M, et al. 2007 Guideline for isolation precautions: preventing transmission of infectious agents in healthcare settings, June 2007. CDC website. Available at: http://www.cdc.gov/hicpac/pdf/ isolation/isolation2007.pdf.
12. Occupational exposure to bloodborne pathogens; needlestick and other sharps injuries; final rule. Occupational Safety and Health Administration (OSHA), Department of Labor. Final rule; request for comment on the Information Collection (Paperwork) Requirements. *Fed Regist* 2001 Jan 18;66(12):5318–5325.
13. Needlestick Safety and Prevention Act of 2000, Pub. L. No. 106-430, 114 Stat. 1901, November 6, 2000.
14. Perry J, Parker G, Jagger J. EPINet Report: 2001 percutaneous injury rates. *Adv Exposure Prev* 2003;6:32–36.
15. Centers for Disease Control and Prevention (CDC). *Sharps Injury Prevention Workbook.* CDC website. Available at: http://www.cdc.gov/sharpssafety /pdf/WorkbookComplete.pdf.
16. Kelly D. Trends in U.S. patents for needlestick prevention technology. *Adv Exposure Prev* 1996;2:7–8.
17. Perry J, Parker G, Jagger J. EPINet Report: 2006 percutaneous injury rates. International Healthcare Worker Safety Center, January, 2009.
18. Perry J, Parker G, Jagger J. EPINet report: 2003 percutaneous injury rates. *Adv Exposure Prev* 2005;7:42–45.
19. Watterson L. Monitoring sharps injuries: EPINet™ surveillance results. *Nurs Stand* 2004 Sep 29-Oct 5;19(3):33–38.
20. Jagger J, Hunt EH, Brand-Elnaggar J, et al. Rates of needle-stick injury caused by various devices in a university hospital. *N Engl J Med* 1988 Aug 4;319(5):284–288.
21. Iinuma Y, Igawa J, Takeshita M, et al. Passive safety devices are more effective at reducing needlestick injuries. *J Hosp Infect* 2005 Dec;61(4):360–361.
22. Billiet LS, Parker CR, Tanley PC, et al. Needlestick injury rate reduction during phlebotomy: a comparative study of two safety devices. *Lab Med* 1999; 22:120–123.
23. Gartner K. Impact of a needleless intravenous system in a university hospital. *Am J Infect Control* 1992 Apr;20(2):75–79.
24. Orenstein R, Reynolds L, Karabaic M, et al. Do protective devices prevent needlestick injuries among health care workers? *Am J Infect Control* 1995 Dec;23(6):344–351.
25. Yassi A, McGill ML, Khokhar JB. Efficacy and cost-effectiveness of a needleless intravenous access system. *Am J Infect Control* 1995 Apr;23(2):57–64.
26. L'Ecuyer PB, Schwab EO, Iademarco E, et al. Randomized prospective study of the impact of three needleless intravenous systems on needlestick injury rates. *Infect Control Hosp Epidemiol* 1996 Dec;17(12):803–808.
27. Centers for Disease Control and Prevention (CDC). Evaluation of safety devices for preventing percutaneous injuries among health-care workers during phlebotomy procedures: Minneapolis-St. Paul, New York City, and San Francisco, 1993–1995. *MMWR Morb Mortal Wkly Rep* 1997 Jan 17;46(2):21–25.

28. Mendelson M, Lin-Chen BY, Solomon R, et al. Evaluation of a safety resheathable winged steel needle for prevention of percutaneous injuries associated with intravascular-access procedures among healthcare workers. *Infect Control Hosp Epidemiol* 2003 Feb;24(2):105–112.
29. Chiarello LA. Selection of needlestick prevention devices: a conceptual framework for approaching product evaluation. *Am J Infect Control* 1995 Dec;23(6):386–395.
30. Laufer F, Chiarello L. Application of cost-effectiveness methodology to the consideration of needlestick prevention technology. *Am J Infect Control* 1994 Apr;22(2):75–82.
31. American Hospital Association. Implementing safer needle devices [briefing]. Chicago: American Hospital Association, 1992.
32. Jagger J. Report on blood drawing: risky procedures, risky devices, risky job. *Adv Exposure Prev* 1994;1:4–9.
33. Leisure MK, Moore DM, Schwartzman JD, et al. Changing the needle when inoculating blood cultures: A no-benefit and high-risk procedure. *JAMA* 1990 Oct 24-31;264(16):2111–2112.
34. Occupational Safety & Health Administration (OSHA). Disposal of contaminated needles and blood tube holders used for phlebotomy. OSHA Safety Health Inform Bull October 15, 2003. OSHA website. Available at: https://www.osha.gov/dts/shib/shib101503.html
35. HIV seroconversion after occupational exposure despite early prophylactic zidovudine therapy. *Lancet* 1993 Apr 24;341(8852):1077–1078.
36. Ippolito G, Salvi A, Sebastiani M, et al. Occupational HIV infection following a stylet injury [letter]. *J Acquir Immune Defic Syndr* 1994 Feb;7(2):208–210.
37. Tait DR, Pudifin DJ, Gathiram V, et al. HIV seroconversions in health care workers. Natal, South Africa, Presented at the 8th International Conference on AIDS, Amsterdam, July 19–24, 1992, Abstract PoC 4141.
38. Metler R, Ciesielski C, Ward J. Occupational exposures resulting in HIV seroconversions, Presented at the 120th Annual Meeting of the American Public Health Association, Washington, DC, November 8–12, 1992, Abstract 2048.
39. Jagger J. Reducing occupational exposures to bloodborne pathogens: where do we stand a decade later? *Infect Control Hosp Epidemiol* 1996 Sep;17(9):573–575.
40. Ippolito G, De Carli G, Puro V, et al. Device-specific risk of needlestick injury in Italian health care workers. *JAMA* 1994 Aug 24-31; 272(8):607–610.
41. Food and Drug Administration (FDA). FDA safety alert: needlestick and other risks from hypodermic needles on secondary I.V. administration sets—piggyback and intermittent I.V. Rockville, MD: U.S. Department of Health and Human Services, Public Health Service, April 16, 1992.
42. Cassak D. *BD's challenge: making everything old new again* (A#2003800092). May 2003. Available at: http://www.bd.com/press/pdfs/BD_Challenge_In_Vivo_01May2003.pdf.
43. AEP interview: Jane Doe, RN. *Adv Exposure Prev* 1995;1:5.
44. ECRI. *Sharps Safety & Needlestick Prevention*, 2nd ed. 2003. ECRI website. Available at: https://www.ecri.org/Documents/Sharps_Safety/SSNP_toc.pdf.
45. Tuma S, Sepkowitz KA. Efficacy of safety-engineered device implementation in the prevention of percutaneous injuries: a review of published studies. *Clin Infect Dis* 2006 Apr 15;42(8):1159–1170.
46. Lynch P, White MC. Perioperative blood contact and exposures: a comparison of incident reports and focused studies. *Am J Infect Control* 1993 Dec;21(6):357–363.
47. Dagi TF, Berguer R, Moore S, et al. Preventable errors in the operating room—part 2: retained foreign objects, sharps injuries, and wrong site surgery. *Curr Probl Surg* 2007 Jun;44(6):352–381.
48. Jagger J, Detmer DE, Blackwell B, et al. Comparative injury risk among operating room, emergency department, and clinical laboratory personnel, abstract. In Bell DM, Rhodes, RS: Special report: conference on prevention of transmission of bloodborne pathogens in surgery and obstetrics. *Infect Control Hosp Epidemiol* 1994;15:345.
49. Harpaz R, Von Seidlein L, Averhoff FM, et al. Transmission of hepatitis B virus to multiple patients from a surgeon without evidence of inadequate infection control. *N Engl J Med* 1996 Feb 29;334(9):549–554.
50. Centers for Disease Control and Prevention (CDC) *Estimated incidence of AIDS and deaths of persons with AIDS, adjusted for delays in reporting, by quarter-year of diagnosis/death, United States, January 1985 through June 1997. HIV/AIDS Surveillance Report.* 1998;9(2):Table 16. Available at: http://www.cdc.gov/hiv/pdf/statistics_hivsur92.pdf.
51. Howard R, Bennet NT. Quantity of blood inoculation in a needlestick injury from suture needles. *J Am Coll Surg* 1994 Feb;178(2):107–110.
52. French National Public Health Network (Reseau National de Sante Publique-RNSP), Ministry of Health and Social Security. HIV transmission from an infected surgeon to one patient in France (press release). January 15, 1997. Paris, France.
53. Montz FJ, Fowler JM, Farias-Eisner R, et al. Blunt needles in fascial closure. *Surg Gynecol Obstet* 1991 Aug;173(2):147–148.
54. Centers for Disease Control and Prevention (CDC). Evaluation of blunt suture needles in preventing percutaneous injuries among health-care workers during gynecologic surgical procedures—New York City, March 1993–June 1994. *MMWR Morb Mortal Wkly Rep* 1997 Jan 17;46(2):25–29.
55. Ippolito G, Studio Italiano Rischio Occupazionale da HIV (SIROH). Scalpel injury and HIV infection in a surgeon [letter]. *Lancet* 1996 Apr 13;347(9007):1042.
56. Johnson M. *Working on a Miracle*. New York: Bantam Books; 1996.
57. Stringer B, Infante-Rivard C, Hanley J. Effectiveness of the hands-free technique in reducing operating theatre injuries. *Occup Environ Med* 2002 Oct;59(10):703–707.
58. Stringer B, Haines T, Goldsmith CH, et al. Perioperative use of the hands-free technique: a semistructured interview study. *AORN J* 2006 Aug;84(2):238–248.
59. Diaz-Buxo JA. Cut resistant glove liner for medical use. *Surg Gynecol Obstet* 1991 Apr;172(4):312–314.
60. Jagger J, Balon M. Suture needle and scalpel blade injuries: frequent but underreported. *Adv Exposure Prev* 1995; 1(3):1–8.

SUPPLEMENTAL RESOURCES

Centers for Disease Control and Prevention (CDC). *Sharps Injury Prevention Workbook*, developed by the CDC to help healthcare facilities prevent needlesticks and other sharps-related injuries to healthcare personnel. Available at: http://www.cdc.gov/sharpssafety/pdf/WorkbookComplete.pdf.

ECRI. Designated as an evidence-based practice center by the Agency for Health Care Policy and Research, ECRI is a nonprofit international health services research organization. Available at: https://www.ecri.org/Products/Pages/Sharps_Safety_Needlestick_Prevention.aspx?sub=Worker and Environmental Safety.

EpiNet. The International Healthcare Worker Safety Center at the University of Virginia Health System is dedicated to the prevention of occupational transmission of bloodborne pathogens. The Center collects data from approximately 70 hospitals using EPINet (referred to as the "EPINet network"). Available at: http://www.healthsystem.virginia.edu/internet/epinet.

Food and Drug Administration (FDA) Safety Alerts: Link page for Safety Alerts and Advisories that warn of the risk of injuries from medical devices. Available at: http://www.fda.gov/MedicalDevices/default.htm; http://www.fda.gov/cdrh/safety.html.

International Health Care Worker Safety Center, University of Virginia. Features a list of safety devices with manufacturers and specific product names. Available at: http://www.healthsystem.virginia.edu/internet/epinet/new/safetydevice.cfm.

National Institute for Occupational Safety and Health (NIOSH) Sharps Disposal Containers: Features information on selecting, evaluating, and using sharps disposal containers. Available at: http://www.cdc.gov/niosh/docs/97-111.

Public Health Agency of Canada. Canada Communicable disease report, Volume: 23S3 - May 1997. Preventing the Transmission of Bloodborne Pathogens in Health Care and Public Service Settings. Available at: http://www.phac-aspc.gc.ca/publicat/ccdr-rmtc/97vol23/23s3/index.html.

Training for Development of Innovative Control Technologies (TDICT) Project. Features "Safety Feature Evaluation Forms" for specific devices. Available at: http://www.tdict.org/evaluation2.html.

U. S. Department of Labor, Occupational Safety and Health Administration. Bloodborne Pathogens and Needlestick Prevention. Available at: http://www.osha.gov/SLTC/bloodbornepathogens/index.html.

CHAPTER 106

Sterile Processing

Julie Jefferson, RN, MPH, CIC
Director, Epidemiology and Infection Control
Rhode Island Hospital
Providence, RI

Martha Young, MS, BS, CSPDT
Consultant
SAVVY Sterilization Solutions
Woodbury, MN

ABSTRACT

Sterile processing is the area most often responsible for reprocessing and sterilizing instrumentation and other reusable medical devices. The process involves handling, collecting, transporting, sorting, disassembling, cleaning, disinfecting, inspecting, packaging, sterilizing, storing, and distributing reprocessed items. The goal is to provide safe, functional, and sterile instruments and medical devices to reduce the transmission of pathogenic organisms from patient to patient and to reduce the risk for surgical site infection. This chapter offers the infection preventionist an introduction to the numerous processes that take place in sterile processing and provides access to resources, published recommended practices, standards and guidelines, and industry standards. The chapter also offers suggested readings to expand the infection preventionist's knowledge of current concepts and practices in sterile processing.

BACKGROUND

The history of sterile processing (SP) has its beginnings associated with the history of sterilization. Sterilization is less than 200 years old. With Louis Pasteur's germ theory, recognized in the mid-1800s, the foundation for sterilization of medical devices was established. This theory proposed that germs were related to illness, which laid the foundation for improving healthcare practices in surgery and clinical units and provided the evidence base for disinfection and sterilization.[1,2] Charles Chamberland, a student of Louis Pasteur, developed the first sterilizer in the mid-nineteenth century. Its design was similar to a pressure cooker, and it allowed for the destruction of microorganisms. The sterilizers were initially placed in the operating rooms, with surgical nurses responsible for the sterilization process.[1,3]

Because of the increase in surgical cases and the increased demand for reprocessing of surgical instruments and equipment, the tasks of handling, collecting, transporting, sorting, disassembling, cleaning, disinfecting, inspecting, packaging, sterilizing, storing, and distributing medical devices were transferred to a dedicated department that was, at the time, referred to as "central services"—but now is more commonly called "sterile processing." In 1924, Misericordia Hospital, now Mercy Catholic Medical Center in Philadelphia, became the first hospital to establish a physically separate and designated area or department for reprocessing instruments and medical devices away from the operating rooms.[1] In the late 1950s and early 1960s, ethylene oxide (EO) sterilizers were developed to address the reprocessing of heat-sensitive devices.

In recent years, new advances and methods of sterilization and a renewed focus on performance improvement have contributed to the ability of SP to improve efficiency, reduce turnaround, and ensure quality and patient safety.

BASIC PRINCIPLES

The SP area is given the responsibility and accountability for reprocessing contaminated instruments and medical devices, especially surgical instruments and equipment. Work activities include handling, collecting, transporting, sorting, disassembling, cleaning, inspecting, disinfecting, packaging, sterilizing, storing, and distributing reprocessed items. During these activities, it is important for the processing staff to be familiar with the principles of cleaning, disinfection, and sterilization, as well as the equipment manufacturers' written instructions for use (IFU) for reprocessing equipment such as mechanical cleaning equipment and sterilizers, and the IFU for chemical solutions, cleaning tools, disinfectants, packaging, cleaning, and sterilization monitors. These instructions provide the information necessary to safely use, monitor the efficacy, and conduct preventive maintenance to ensure quality and process reliability. The chemical solution manufacturers' recommendations provide guidance on the selection, use, mixing, and monitoring of the effectiveness of chemical agents and how to select the type of water (tap, deionized, or distilled) required for product use. The IFU must be followed for the expected outcome of safe, functional, and sterile items that prevent transmission of pathogens and surgical site infections (SSIs) (Chapter 31 Cleaning, Disinfection, and Sterilization and Chapter 32 Reprocessing Single-Use Devices offer additional information.)

Many facilities allow for the cleaning, decontaminating or disinfecting, and reprocessing of reusable items to take place outside SP areas (in the surgical areas or patient care areas). The infection preventionist (IP) needs to be aware of such practices to make certain that all items are reprocessed according to the same standards in all locations within the healthcare system.

The appropriate use of personal protective equipment (PPE) during high-risk cleaning and disinfecting processes reduces the risk for blood and body fluid exposure for processing personnel. Written policies and procedures promote consistent practice among healthcare personnel.

Reprocessing medical devices requires a collaborative association between SP staff and the clinical staff who use the devices, especially in operating rooms. This team must work together to provide safe, efficient, cost-efficient, and high-quality reprocessing.

Consistent implementation of up-to-date published recommended practices and standards of care and up-to-date IFU will facilitate the achievement of positive patient outcomes and quality services.

Orientation and continued educational training on expected practice and regulations are essential for SP staff. Regulatory agencies include federal, state, and local laws, the Occupational Safety and Health Administration (OSHA), the Environmental Protection Agency (EPA), and the Food and Drug Administration (FDA). The Centers for Disease Control and Prevention (CDC) publishes the Healthcare Infection Control Practices Advisory Committee (HICPAC) guidelines and the Association for the Advancement of Medical Instrumentation (AAMI), and the Association of periOperative Registered Nurses (AORN) publishes healthcare recommended practices and standards. In addition, The Joint Commission (TJC) uses these regulations, recommendations, and guidelines, specifically the most up-to-date ANSI/AAMI ST79 *Comprehensive guide to steam sterilization and sterility assurance in healthcare facilities*, as the standards of practice to which healthcare facilities must adhere for accreditation. Lastly, the Facilities Guideline Institute publishes widely accepted guidelines for designing SP areas.

To improve the education, training, and competency of those responsible for processes in SP, states are beginning to establish certification for SP healthcare personnel. In 2004, New Jersey became the first state in the nation to mandate certification for SP professionals and, in 2013, New York became the second state. The Certification Board for Sterile Processing and Distribution (CBSPD, www.sterileprocessing.org) and the International Association for Healthcare Central Service and Materiel Management (IAHCSMM, www.iahcsmm.org) offer certification. Several other states are moving in the same direction.

This chapter offers an introduction to the processes and activities that take place in SP and highlights the measures used to ensure safety and quality. The IP should be familiar with these processes when conducting infection control rounds in SP as recommended by HICPAC and should routinely include results of monitoring activities in the infection prevention and control program reports. The reader will find references and suggested readings containing more detailed information.

Table 106-1 identifies general goals for infection prevention for SP.

The following definitions may be helpful[4-10]:

Aeration: A processing step using warm circulating air to enhance the removal of a chemical sterilization agent residue from processed items and wrapping material. Used with EO sterilization.

Biological indicator (BI): A device used to monitor sterilization processes. The device contains a viable population of highly resistant bacterial spores that are resistant to the type or method of sterilization being monitored.

Chemical indicator (CI): A device used to monitor the presence of one or more predefined process parameters required for a satisfactory sterilization process. The six classes of CIs are defined in ANSI/AAMI ST79[4] and in Table 106-2.

Chemical integrator: A Class 5 integrating indicator designed to react to all critical variables of the sterilization process and used as an internal CI, inside the BI process challenge device (PCD) to monitor implant loads, and in a CI PCD to monitor nonimplant loads.

Decontamination: The use of physical or chemical methods to remove, inactivate, or destroy bloodborne pathogens, rendering them no longer able to transmit infectious particles and rendering the decontaminated item safe for handling.

Disinfection: The destruction of pathogenic (disease-causing) microorganisms, usually by physical or chemical means.

Ethylene oxide (EO): Chemical (gas) that is used to sterilize heat- or moisture-sensitive items; also used as a fumigant.

Event-related sterility: Concept that items are considered sterile unless the integrity of the packaging is compromised (i.e., torn, soiled, wet, or showing evidence of tampering). Shelf life is indefinite.

Hydrogen peroxide (H_2O_2) gas with or without plasma sterilization: A popular low-temperature sterilization method used to process heat- or moisture-sensitive items because of its short cycle and faster turnaround time but with packaging and lumen limitations.

Immediate-use steam sterilization (IUSS) (formerly called flash sterilization): Process designed for the cleaning, steam sterilization, and delivery of patient care items for immediate use.

Parametric release: Declaration by medical device manufacturers that a product is sterile on the basis of physical or chemical process data after validating the cycle using BIs.

Table 106-1. Infection Prevention Goals for Sterile Processing

Point of Use/Transport
At the earliest stage possible, following a procedure, prevent organic matter from drying on instruments and microorganisms from growing on devices.
- Keep instrumentation moist so that bioburden is not dried onto the device.
- Clean devices before biofilm can form.
- Contain contaminated devices to prevent accidental exposure to staff and patients.

Physical Environment of the Sterile Processing Area
Prevent environmental conditions that encourage microbial growth and cross contamination.
- Ensure that the airflow moves from areas of low contamination to areas of higher potential contamination.
- Ensure the proper air exchange frequency to remove possible airborne contaminants.
- Control humidity and temperature levels.
- Prevent the formation of substances that protect microorganisms from further processing steps (biofilm).
- Ensure that the environment provides appropriate lighting for thorough evaluation of instrumentation for debris.
- Ensure staff safety and reduce microbial transport by personnel.
- Ensure that hand hygiene products are available and are used.

Decontamination
Protect workers from contamination with possible infectious materials.
- Ensure that air pressure in the work area is negative (pulls air into the work area) with 10 air exchanges/hour and that all air is exhausted to the outside atmosphere.
- Ensure that gloves, masks, eyewear, and gowns appropriately protect staff from contact with contaminated fluids.
- Ensure that PPE prevents contaminated materials from entering the eyes or mouth.
- Reduce the bioburden and microbes to a level safe for use or further reprocessing.
- Ensure that the instrument manufacturer's written cleaning IFU are followed.
- Ensure that the mechanical cleaning of equipment, including use of cleaning solutions, follow the manufacturer's written IFU.
- Ensure that the cleaning chemicals are appropriate, diluted correctly, and not expired.
- Ensure for manual cleaning that the temperature of the cleaning solution and soaking time is monitored and documented.
- Ensure that tools and equipment used to remove bioburden are in good working order and effective.
- Ensure that the correct size and type of brushes are used for lumens and, if disposable, are discarded after each use and, if reusable, are decontaminated daily.
- Ensure that all disinfection chemicals are appropriate, within effective concentrations by monitoring, and not expired.
- Ensure that manual disinfection processes are physically monitored with a thermometer and timer and that the results are documented.
- Ensure that the decontamination process used for each device is appropriate for that device.
- Ensure that devices are correctly loaded and lumens attached to the correct lumen irrigators of the mechanical cleaning equipment.
- Ensure that the physical monitors of the mechanical cleaning equipment are read after each cycle and documented.
- Ensure that the decontamination process renders the device safe for patient use (if appropriate) or safe for handling for additional processing (enzymatic cleaners alone do not render items safe).
- Ensure that the effectiveness of the cleaning process is being verified by a commercially available monitor.

Preparation and Packaging
Ensure that pack preparation promotes adequate sterilant penetration so that sterilant reaches all surfaces holding microorganisms.
- Ensure that the air in the work area is under positive pressure, there are 10 downward-draft air exchanges per hour, and that the temperature is 20°C to 23°C (68°F to 73°F) and at a relative humidity ranging from 30 to 60 percent.
- Ensure that packaging materials are held at the temperature and humidity listed above for a minimum of 2 hours before use.
- Ensure that instruments are free of debris and in good working order.
- Ensure that the instrument and packaging manufacturer's IFU are followed and that the packaging is not changed unless validated by the instrument manufacturer.
- Ensure that the packaging material is appropriate for the selected sterilization process.
- Ensure that the packaging configuration does not allow microbes to enter through holes, gaps, or tears.
- Disassemble or position instruments for maximum penetration of sterilant.
- Ensure that any packaged accessories are appropriate for use inside instrument trays.
- Ensure that double-peel pouching is done correctly.
- Ensure that each package has a lot control identifier.

Sterilization
Ensure correct loading, sterilization process, cycle selection, and unloading.
- Ensure that the air in the work area is under positive pressure, there are 10 air exchanges per hour, and the temperature is 20°C to 23°C (68°F to 73°F) and at a relative humidity ranging from 30 to 60 percent.
- Ensure that the sterilizer manufacturer's written IFU is followed for operation and that routine and planned maintenance occurs on schedule.
- Ensure that items are loaded correctly according to the sterilizer and packaging manufacturer's written IFU.
- Ensure that the correct sterilization process and cycle parameters are used as directed by the instrument and packaging manufacturer's written IFU.
- Ensure that items are properly cooled before unloading to sterile storage.
- Capture processing errors that prevent sterilization.

Quality Control
Monitor to detect equipment or operator errors or malfunctions that prevent sterilization.
- Ensure that all the chemical and BI manufacturers' written IFU are followed.
- Ensure that the Bowie-Dick test is performed in each dynamic-air-removal steam sterilizer each day in all locations within the healthcare organization.
- Ensure that every package to be sterilized contains CIs on the outside unless the internal CI is visible and on the inside (internal).
- Ensure that the correct BI process challenge device is being used to monitor all the cycles routinely used, that BI process challenge device IFU are being followed, and that BI frequency is correct.
- Ensure that the BI is incubated at the correct temperature, a positive control from the same lot as the test vial is incubated each day a test vial is incubated, that the correct readout time is used, and that the test and control results are documented.
- Ensure that the correct sterilization cycle was used by reading the physical monitor.
- Read all sterility assurance monitoring devices (physical monitors, external chemical and BIs) before release of the load.
- Evaluate each load before release (e.g., visible tears in wrap or moisture).
- Document and report any incidents in which implants were released for use before the result of the BI.
- Ensure that each internal CI is read before the package is placed on the sterile field.

(continued)

Table 106-1. Infection Prevention Goals for Sterile Processing (cont'd)

Recordkeeping
Document the result of the sterilization process.
- Ensure that all sterilization process, sterilizer maintenance, and repair records are documented and that they are maintained in a legible, orderly manner and can be easily retrieved when necessary.
- Ensure that records maintain complete traceability from sterilization through patient use.
- Ensure that implant sterilization and monitoring is traceable to the patient.

Storage
Prevent microbial contamination of sterilized items.
- Ensure that sterilized items are not exposed to extreme temperature differences that result in condensation and contamination.
- Ensure that all storage or transport units do not damage the packaging.
- Ensure that maintenance covers are used when warranted.
- Ensure that the external CI and package integrity are inspected before the item is dispensed.

Adapted with permission from STERIS Corporation (Mentor, OH) training materials.

Pasteurizer: Equipment that uses hot water for a definite period to destroy pathogenic bacteria; often used for respiratory therapy and anesthesia equipment.

Peracetic acid: Liquid oxidizing agent used in automated endoscope reprocessors. Items processed with this agent need to be used immediately because they are wet and cannot be packaged and stored for later use.

Physical monitors (previously called mechanical indicators): A visible monitor (time, temperature, and pressure recorders, digital printouts, and gauges) that enables the operator to determine if sterilizing parameters were met.

Process indicators: Class 1 CIs used as an external CI on the outside of packages or containers to demonstrate that the unit has been exposed to the sterilization process and to distinguish between processed and unprocessed units.

Process challenge device (PCD): Item designed to create a challenge to the sterilization process and used for routine and qualification testing of sterilizers. Previously referred to as a test pack.

Stated value (SV): Part of the CI labeling that provides a value or values of a critical variable at which the indicator is designed to reach its end point as defined by the manufacturer. For example, a Class 5 integrating indicator with a stated value of 2.1 minutes at 135°C should reach its end point when tested at 135°C for 2.1 minutes in a resistometer.

Sterile: State of being free from all living microorganisms.

Sterility assurance level (SAL): Probability of a single viable microorganism occurring on an item after sterilization. SAL is normally expressed as 10^{-6}, which means there is less

than or equal to one chance in a million that a single viable microorganism is present on a sterilized item.

Sterilization: A validated process by which all viable forms of microorganisms (including spores) are destroyed.

Sterilizer: Equipment used to sterilize medical devices, equipment, and supplies by direct exposure to a selected sterilization agent.

Sterilizer, EO: Sterilizer using EO gas under defined gas concentrations and selected temperature, time, and relative humidity to sterilize heat- and moisture-sensitive medical devices.

Sterilizer, steam, gravity-displacement: A sterilizer in which incoming steam displaces residual air through a drain (usually in or near bottom of chamber). There are selected time and temperature parameters needed for correct operation.

Sterilizer, steam, dynamic-air-removal: Types of sterilization cycles in which air is removed from the chamber and the load by means of a series of pressure and vacuum excursions (prevacuum cycle) or by means of a series of steam flushes and pressure pulses above atmospheric pressure (steam-flush pressure-pulse [SFPP] cycle).

Sterilizer, steam: A sterilizer with saturated (greater than 97 percent) steam as a sterilant and pre-established time, temperature, and pressure or vacuum settings.

User verification: Documented procedures performed by SP in a healthcare facility to determine that the specifications for sterilization as defined by the medical device manufacturer have been met.

Table 106-2. Environmental Conditions

Work Area	Air Exchanges/Hour	Airflow	Temperature, °F (°C)	Humidity (%)
Soiled/decontamination	10	Negative (in)	60 and 65 (16 and 18)	30–60
Assembly or prep and pack areas	10, downward draft	Positive (out)	68 and 73 (20 and 23)	30-60 (Ideally 35–50)
Sterilizer loading/unloading	10	Positive (out)	68 and 73 (20 and 23)	30-60
Sterile storage	4, downward draft	Positive (out)	May be as high as 75 (24)	≤70
Sterilizer equipment access rooms	10	Negative (in)	75 and 85 (24 and 29)	30–60

Source: AAMI and FGI guidelines[4,5]

APIC Text of Infection Control and Epidemiology

Validation: Procedures documented by medical device manufacturers to establish that a process will consistently yield products that comply with predetermined specifications when instructions for processing are followed by SP in a healthcare facility.

Table 106-1 lists infection prevention goals for sterile processing that are discussed further. This tool can be used for the SP infection control and prevention rounds or audit.

Sterile Processing

Point of Use

Reprocessing contaminated equipment or instruments for sterilization begins at point of use. The end user is responsible for removing gross soil and debris and for rinsing items at the site of use. Instruments with lumens should be flushed with water (not saline, as salt is corrosive to most instruments). Every attempt should be made to keep instrument or equipment surfaces moist until they can be cleaned to facilitate the removal of soil. Applying enzymatic foam or gel cleaner, using wet towels (water, not saline) placed within the set of used instruments, or presoaking used items in water or cleaning solution are all potential options.[4]

Transportation

Contaminated items should be placed in puncture-resistant leak-proof sealable containers and visibly labeled as biohazardous.[4] The selection of the container (e.g., bins with lids, covered or enclosed carts/containers/totes, impermeable bags, or combinations of each) will depend on the size, presence of sharps (segregated in container), configuration, and volume/numbers of medical devices or instruments being transported. Transporting used instruments submerged in liquids presents additional risk for blood and body fluid exposures, the promotion of biofilm formation, and the possibility of employee injury because of the weight of the container. The liquids should be discarded while wearing PPE.[4] If off-site transportation is required, follow Department of Transportation, state regulations,[4] and OSHA requirements.

Physical Environment

Adequate space in SP is critical to provide for worker safety, good workflow, and efficient and effective work practices to ensure patient safety. The size of the department must be appropriate for the volume of work being performed, the processes being conducted, the types of services provided, and the amount of equipment required to perform the required tasks. Space needs can be affected by the storage and delivery systems employed by the hospital (i.e., case carts, supply carts, special procedure carts, and storage of durable medical supplies [intravenous pumps, portable suction, etc.]). Fans should never be used in the processing area.[4]

Other considerations that are important in SP are the ventilation, temperature, and humidity in the department. These environmental conditions are noted in Table 106-2.

Decontamination Area

Design

The design should include a physical barrier between the decontamination area and the other work areas.[4,5] The floors and walls should consist of nonparticulate/nonfibrous shedding material that can withstand wet vacuuming and washing.[4] The ceiling should have a flush surface with enclosed fixtures and be made from a nonparticulate/nonfibrous material. The work surfaces should be covered with a nonporous material that can withstand frequent cleaning with germicides. The ventilation of the area should have negative air pressure (pulls air into the work area) with 10 air exchanges/hour and all air exhausted to the outside atmosphere.[4] Figure 106-2 summarizes the environmental conditions required for all work areas in SP. Hand hygiene facilities (sinks and waterless alcohol-based hand rubs) should be easily accessible to staff. There should be eyewash stations as identified by OSHA regulation, and safety data sheets (SDSs) for each chemical used within 10 seconds of travel time.[4] Figure 106-1 shows a possible area design for the SP department.

Personal Protective Equipment and Other Safety Measures

Handling of soiled instruments and equipment increases the risk for bloodborne pathogen exposure for the SP worker in addition to other disease-producing organisms. Proper use of PPE is critical to ensure a safe work environment and to meet regulatory requirements. Eye protection, in the forms of safety goggles or full-length face shields, should be worn at all times when cleaning soiled equipment.[4,6,7] All hair should be covered with a surgical cap, and a fluid-resistant face mask should cover the nose and the mouth at all times.[4,6,7] A liquid-resistant covering with sleeves (i.e., backless gown, jumpsuit, or surgical gown) should be worn and should cover the arms and clothing.

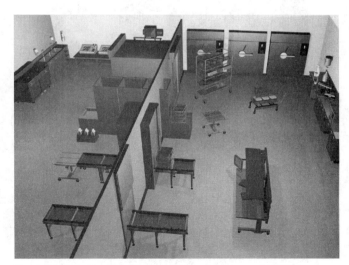

Figure 106-1. Possible SP area design (courtesy of STERIS Corporation).

Gloves should be worn to protect users from contact with blood and body fluids, protect from exposure to chemical cleaning solutions, and offer some protection against sharp objects. General purpose utility gloves that are heavy duty and water-proof should be worn, because they provide more protection than traditional medical examination gloves.[4,6,7] The gloves should be cuffed and long enough to completely cover the exposed hand, arms, and part of the gown. If reusable, heavy duty gloves are used, the manufacturer's recommendations for cleaning, disinfecting, and duration of use should be followed. Liquid-resistant shoe covers should be worn to protect shoes from blood and body fluid exposures that may occur during the decontamination process.[4] SP staff should be trained to manage small and large body fluid spills. Figure 106-2 shows an SP employee wearing PPE for use when working in the decontamination area.

Environmental measures, including engineering controls, should include the use of mechanical devices (e.g., hemostats) to retrieve sharps in containers. No consumption of food or drink and no application of lip balm or contact lenses should be allowed in the work area. Sinks and other hand hygiene facilities, as well as an eyewash station for emergencies, should be readily accessible.[4]

Disinfecting Work Areas

Routine cleaning of the work environment is essential. Work tables, countertops, and other high-touch horizontal surfaces and floors must be cleaned and disinfected at least daily and as needed.[4] Case carts, storage containers, and transportation carts should be decontaminated after each use.[4] Walls,

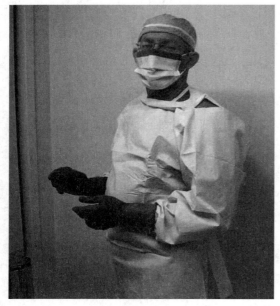

Figure 106-2. Personal protective equipment in decontamination area of sterile processing.

air-intake and -return ducts, storage shelves, and storage areas should be cleaned and disinfected on a regularly scheduled basis and more often if needed.[4]

Cleaning Used Items

The cleaning process is the most critical step in the sterilization process and should follow the written manufacturer's IFU to ensure that the item is effectively cleaned. Blood, body fluids, and other organic and inorganic soil remaining on medical devices interfere with the sterilization process and, if they are not removed, the item(s) cannot be considered sterilized. Instruments with removable parts should be disassembled and cleaned before they are sterilized.

The effectiveness of the cleaning process depends on the quality of the water; the quality, concentration, and type of detergent or enzymatic cleaner; an acceptable washing method (manual, mechanical, or both may be required); proper rinsing and drying; correct preparation of items to be processed by mechanical cleaning equipment; the time and temperature parameters and load capacity of the equipment; and operator performance.[4]

The cleaning process includes selecting the correct cleaning product and using it properly. Manufacturers of the various cleaning agents and instruments can recommend the appropriate cleaning solution. Detergent solutions or the combination of detergent and enzymatic solutions are used to clean medical devices. Detergents work by lowering the surface tension, breaking down fats, oils and grease, and soil into smaller particles and suspending them in solution. Enzymatic solutions work by breaking down proteins, fats, carbohydrates, etc. and may be used to soak instruments with crevices or dried-on proteins or fats. Enough rinsing with water to remove chemical residue from the items should follow manual or mechanical cleaning. Refer to the device manufacturer's written IFU to determine if further decontamination using a microbicidal process is needed.[4] The pH of the chemicals is an important consideration, as certain pH levels may be harmful to the instruments being reprocessed.

Manual Cleaning Method

The manual cleaning method is often recommended for delicate or complex medical devices such as ophthalmology or other microsurgical instruments, lensed instruments, and air-powered drills that cannot be processed through automated or mechanical cleaning equipment or cannot be submerged. Instruments that are difficult to clean can also be disinfected manually if required by the instrument manufacturer. Both outer and inner surfaces must be cleaned, so it is critical at this point to disassemble instruments and equipment before cleaning. When cleaning devices with a sprayer, a brush, or other friction-causing process, immersion under water is used to minimize blood and body fluid aerosolization, decreasing the staff's risk for exposure.[4,5] Brushes of the appropriate type, size (diameter and length), and bristle type and material should be used, and the instrument manufacturer should provide this information in writing.[4] Brushes can be single-use disposable or reusable. If reusable brushes are used, they should be decontaminated at least daily.[4] Single-use brushes should be disposed after each use.

Lumens and channels need to be irrigated or cleaned by suction. The irrigation method should include immersing the item during the procedure. The suction method flushes the cleaning solution through the instrument and returns it to a canister.[4,5] The selection of the proper cleaning product for manual cleaning depends on the type of debris or soil left on items, the length of time between use and cleaning, compatibility with the item being cleaned, and the point at which the product makes items safe for handling.

Follow the manufacturer's IFU for manual cleaning. The temperature of the soaking solution should be monitored and documented to ensure that the temperature of the cleaning solution meets the requirements of the cleaning solution's written IFU.[4] A wireless temperature monitor with a probe that is placed into the solution to transmit data wirelessly via a wifi network to a PC is available. The time the instruments are soaked should also be recorded. The next step is thoroughly rinsing with tap water to remove residue, followed by a final rinse with treated water such as deionized, distilled, or reverse osmosis water. The treated water is necessary to prevent staining of instruments, which prolongs their life and prevents adverse reactions in the patient.[4]

A water-soluble instrument lubricant in a lubricant bath or rinse (e.g., milk bath) may be used on instruments to maintain the function of hinges. The instruments should then be dried with air or a lint-free cloth before packaging.[4]

Endoscopes, powered equipment, or complex items require special attention but still require precleaning before processing. The staff must follow the manufacturer's written IFU for cleaning. The design of some medical devices may not permit steam sterilization and may be candidates for EO or other low-temperature gas sterilization processes, or they can be processed in an automated endoscope reprocessor. Again, the manufacturer's recommendations will stipulate the manner and method for reprocessing equipment.

Mechanical Cleaning Methods

Multiple devices and systems are available to mechanically process contaminated items. The equipment manufacturer's written IFU must be followed to ensure safety for workers and patients, and the instrument manufacturer's written IFU should be followed to ensure effective cleaning of the instruments. Mechanical cleaning equipment removes soil and microorganisms using an automated cleaning and rinsing process and sometimes incorporates a thermal disinfection or chemical disinfectant process. This equipment should be located in the decontamination department.[4]

Ultrasonic Cleaners

Ultrasonic cleaning systems use high-frequency sound waves to remove particles. The sound creates bubbles on the instrument in the water bath; the bubbles then implode and draw out the tiny particles from the crevices, joints, lumens, and other difficult areas of the instrument. Some units may have connectors for lumens. A more detailed explanation of this method can be obtained from the manufacturer. Ultrasonic cleaners are used for fine cleaning and not for final disinfection or sterilization and should be used only after gross soil has been removed.[4] For the ultrasonic cleaner to be effective, the cleaning solution should be changed before it becomes heavily soiled, which also minimizes the risk of cross-contamination.[4] Thorough rinsing follows to dislodge particles. Follow the ultrasonic cleaners' and instrument manufacturers' written IFU to ensure that the instruments are properly cleaned and not damaged. For effective cleaning, the instrument manufacturer may require multiple ultrasonic cycles. Choose the correct cycle and load the instruments properly, especially if using lumen irrigators; this requires the use of the correct connector.

Washer-Disinfectors and Decontaminators

Washer-disinfectors and decontaminators are used for cleaning and intermediate-level disinfection but not final disinfection or sterilization of soiled reusable utensils, trays, bedpans, urinals, rubber and plastic goods, and simple hard-surfaced rigid surgical instruments such as forceps and clamps. Some units may have lumen irrigators. These units usually come with pumps to dispense an enzyme and detergent with a water temperature up to 180°F (82°C) for washing, a lubricant, and a thermal pure-water rinse up to 194°F (90°C) and a drying phase. The cycles (e.g., time at temperature) may vary from manufacturer to manufacturer, so the equipment manufacturer's and instrument manufacturer's written IFU must be followed to ensure that the instruments are properly cleaned. The correct cycle for the load contents must be selected and the items must be loaded as required. Never choose a shorter time (e.g., basin cycle) than suggested for instruments to save time, because the items will not be clean.

Cart and Utensil Washers/Disinfectors

This equipment is used for cleaning and low-level disinfection and drying, not final disinfection or sterilization of carts, containers, utensils, beds, and other miscellaneous reusable items. Some units may have a cycle for cleaning and intermediate-level disinfection of simple hard-surfaced rigid surgical instruments such as forceps and clamps. There is a wash, thermal rinse, and drying phase. The cycles (e.g., time at temperature) may vary from manufacturer to manufacturer, so the equipment manufacturer's and instrument manufacturer's written IFU must be followed to ensure that the instruments are properly cleaned. The correct cycle for the load contents must be selected, and the items must be loaded as required.

Washer/Pasteurizer

Although not a sterilization procedure, pasteurization is an acceptable (and cost-effective) cleaning and high-level disinfection alternative for respiratory therapy and anesthesia equipment. Following a precleaning, the equipment uses hot water (150°F to 170°F or 65°C to 77°C) for at least 30 minutes, killing all pathogenic organisms except bacterial spores. The equipment manufacturer's and instrument manufacturer's written IFU should be followed to ensure that the instruments are processed correctly. The temperature of the final rinse should be monitored with an irreversible thermometer or a remote sensing device.[4]

Automatic Endoscope Reprocessors

This equipment is designed to clean and chemically disinfect the scope. A final rinse is usually part of the process. Not all units have a washing cycle, and it should be determined if manual cleaning is required before use. Again, the operator must know if processed items are safe for handling. If the washer does not have a drying cycle, the scopes should be rinsed with isopropyl alcohol, dried with air under pressure, and hung in a storage cabinet so the tip does not touch the bottom of the cabinet. Scopes should not be stored in their original foam-lined container.

The equipment manufacturer's and scope manufacturer's written IFU must be followed to ensure that the instruments are properly processed. The minimum recommended concentration (MRC) or minimum effective concentration (MEC) of the chemical disinfectant should be tested before each use to ensure that the concentration of the active ingredient is adequate.[7] In addition, the printout should be checked at the beginning and end of the cycle to verify that cycle parameters were met, and the printout should be initialed.[7]

Cleaning Verification of Manual and Mechanical Cleaning Processes

Cleaning verification is the final step in the manual cleaning process and includes visual inspection (see *Inspection of Instruments and Other Items* below) for any visible soil and may include the use of magnification. Because visual inspection alone is not sufficient to assess the efficacy of the cleaning process, a commercially available test that detects the presence of organic residues should be considered to monitor the effectiveness of the cleaning process.[4] In AAMI ST79, Annex D discusses user verification of cleaning processes and Table D.1 lists the in-use tests available to assess efficacy of cleaning of medical devices.[4] AORN recommends that manual cleaning should be evaluated when new types of instruments are reprocessed and periodically at intervals determined by the healthcare facility.[5] Follow the manufacturer's cleaning verification tests as written in the IFU and perform cleaning verification frequently, especially for instruments that are difficult to clean.

Cleaning verification is also important for mechanical cleaning equipment. AAMI ST79 states that mechanical cleaning equipment should be tested upon installation, weekly (preferably daily) during routine use, and after major repairs.[4] All cycles used should be tested when evaluating or changing cleaning chemistry to ensure that the cleaning chemistry and cleaning action is still effective.[4] All cycles used should also be tested after major repairs, which includes replacement of the water pump(s), detergent delivery system, heating system, water delivery system, water treatment system, or computer control, or an upgrade to the software.[4] In AAMI ST79, Annex D discusses user verification of cleaning processes and Table D.2 lists the in-use tests available to assess efficacy of mechanical cleaning equipent.[4] Cleaning verification monitors are available to verify the cleaning efficacy of all the equipment discussed above. This includes the sonic activity of ultrasonic cleaners, the ability of irrigators to clean lumens, the ability of the water in the cart and utensil washers to contact all areas that need to be cleaned, and the overall cleaning efficacy of the equipment.[4] In addition, the water temperature should be monitored because it is a key cleaning parameter. An irreversible thermometer or remote sensing equipment can be used.[4]

Cleaning verification of instruments can occur after manual, ultrasonic, and mechanical cleaning processes to identify failures in the system so corrective action can be taken. The cleaning process must be effective for the disinfection and sterilization process to be effective.[4] AAMI ST79 says that monitoring and documenting the decontamination process parameters is part of a quality system, whether the process is manual or mechanical.[4]

Inspection of Instruments and Other Items

When cleaning and disinfecting have been completed and devices are safe for handling, reprocessed items need to be inspected (see *Cleaning Verification of Manual and Mechanical Cleaning Processes* above). This step may occur in the decontamination area or in the packaging and assembly (clean) area. Some facilities use the decontamination staff for this activity, because any unclean items can quickly be reprocessed. Other facilities prefer the packaging and assembly staff, because the items are inspected for other quality issues before being packaged. A transfer method needs to be established that facilitates the return of unclean items from the clean area to the decontamination area. It is important to note that hand hygiene sinks are not designed to clean and decontaminate reprocessed instruments and should not be used for anything other than hand washing. Next, items need to be inspected for proper function and defects, as well as to ensure that all soil has been removed.[4] The cleaning of orthopedic and neurosurgical instruments pose a significant challenge to SP personnel. Integrity, correct functioning, and the need to replace parts should be addressed at this point. The sharpness of cutting surfaces should be checked. Lighted magnifying glasses should be available at workstations to assist with detailed inspections. Sterilization containers must also be inspected to verify integrity, correct for proper functioning, and replace parts of rigid containers, such as the filters and valves.

Preparation and Packaging

Area Design

The preparation and packaging area should be physically separated from the decontamination area.[4] If it is not possible to achieve separation, as could be the case in clinics or office-based facilities, "the preparation area should be thoroughly cleaned and decontaminated before being used for clean preparation and assembly tasks."[4] Beyond the decontamination area, SP requires positive airflow (pushes air out of the work area into adjacent areas or hallways). Many SP areas receive clean linen, such as surgical towels, to be added to sets and packs. The linen sorting and folding process should be in an enclosed space separate from the remainder of the preparation area(s) to reduce the accumulation of lint. The airflow should be a downdraft type with 10 air exchanges per hour.[4] Housekeeping procedures need to take into account the potential for the presence of lint generated from the surgical linen, because lint can transfer from surgical packs to a surgical wound. Once there, it can act as a foreign body and lead to adverse patient reactions.[8] Housekeeping procedures should be the same as those used to clean operating rooms and delivery rooms.[4]

Packaging of Healthcare Facility Prepared Sets or Trays

The SP staff usually places items into predetermined sets or trays (per the facility's instruction sheets [often called the recipe cards], count sheets, tray lists, or computer-generated sheets). Included on these sets or tray lists may be the presence of implantable items that will require the use of a BI process challenge device (BI PCD) in the load. The arrangement of the items or instruments is critical to the sterilization process to maximize contact with the sterilizing agent. The written IFU from the individual instrument manufacturer, and the instructions for the rigid container, and for the wrap should be followed. Only instruments and other items that require the same sterilization process (e.g., type of sterilizer, cycle time, and temperature) should be placed into a set or tray.[9] Instruments and devices must be opened, unlocked, disassembled, and dry. Other items, such as basins, medicine cups, etc. should be inverted so that moisture does not accumulate during the sterilization process. Peel pouches should not be placed inside of sets or trays because they may interfere with sterilization and drying.[4] Tray liners or other absorbent material may be added, if FDA cleared, for that application and sterilization processs.[4]

When assembling sets or trays, the processor needs to take into consideration the size, weight, design, density of instruments, distribution of mass (density), and composition of the set. Manufacturers of sterilizers, rigid containers, and wraps will note restrictions related to content, weight, and configuration of loads. For ergonomic reasons, instrument sets should not weigh more than 25 pounds.[4] Information and training on packaging and load arrangements should be obtained from manufacturers of sterilizers and packaging, as well as from professional organizations' recommended practices—such as those from AAMI, AORN, and IAHCSMM. It is the responsibility of the staff in SP to follow the IFU, perform product testing, and monitor the sterilization process to determine if the set can be sterilized and dried effectively.[4]

Packaging Materials

Before sterilization, instruments and other items should be packaged to ensure protection during sterilization and to maintain sterility until the device is used. Packaging materials include textile wraps (woven or nonwoven), peel pouches, and rigid containers (metal or plastic). Wrapping products may be single use, disposable (nonwoven), or reusable (woven textile). Peel pouches are preferred when visibility of the item is important or when sterilizing one or more items. Tip guards, holders, or foam sleeves (which must be compatible with the sterilizing agent and validated for that usage by the manufacturer) should be placed over sharp points to prevent damage to the instrument and prevent puncture of the packaging.

The packaging manufacturer's written IFU should be followed. Several performance properties of the packaging materials should be considered, as follows. First, packaging should allow the sterilizing agent to enter and exit the set/pack. The chemical agent needs to be able to penetrate to the interior of the package's content to achieve sterilization. In addition, the packaging material should not retain any residual chemical agent. It is important to follow the sterilizer manufacturer's IFU on type of packaging that can be used for steam and low temperature sterilization processes and labeling of the packaging to ensure that it has been FDA cleared for a specific sterilization process and cycle. It is also important to follow the storage conditions section of the packaging material IFU. "Before use, packaging materials should be held at room temperature (20°C to 23°C [68°F to 73°F]) and at a relative humidity ranging from 30 to 60 percent for minimum of 2 hours."[4] This storage condition is needed to permit adequate steam penetration and superheating, which can result in a steam sterilization process failure. Desiccated packaging material can also result in an EO sterilization process failure.

Second, durability of the packaging is critical, especially when loading and unloading the sterilizing cart. Durability is also important during handling and manipulating during transport and storage. The packaging should be strong enough to withstand normal use in a healthcare setting without tearing or puncturing.

Third, packaging materials should repel moisture and water. Water can allow contamination with microorganisms. Packages should be visually inspected when removed from the sterilizer cart. "If a wet pack is observed, consideration should be given to opening other packs in the questionable load to check for moisture and/or to recalling all items from the load."[4] Refer to Annex P moisture assessment in AAMI ST79 for further assistance in diagnosing and preventing wet packs.[4]

Fourth, the packaging must be made of low-lint material. The presence of lint is troublesome in the SP area because it makes maintaining a clean environment difficult, and, more importantly, lint can collect on surgical instruments and in the surgical incision during surgery. Lint fibers have been associated with postoperative patient complications, such as granulomas, adhesions, and infections.[8]

Finally, ignition resistance is a consideration.[8] Because of the potential hazard for fires in the operating room, materials with low flammability are critical. Manufacturers should provide information on each product's characteristics.

Once the packaging materials have been selected, the SP processor should be shown the proper wrapping and packaging procedures needed to ensure aseptic presentation of sterilized items at the point of use. The correct order and direction of folds and the number of wraps are critical for maintaining sterility and reducing contamination at the site of use. Sterilization indicator tape, not safety pins, paper clips, staples, or other sharp objects, should be used to close woven and nonwoven wraps.[4] The manufacturers of packaging products' IFU should be followed. AAMI ST79 also provides figures showing proper packaging techniques for textile wraps and peel pouches.[4]

Protective packaging should offer impervious protection from environmental contamination. Sterility maintenance covers (dust covers) are used to protect devices from elements in storage and extend their shelf life if they are going to be "subjected to environmental challenges or multiple handling before use."[4] The 2- to 3-mm-thick plastic bags in various sizes are heat-sealed or self-sealing. The sterilized items are placed in dust covers immediately after cooldown or aeration. Minimal handling is recommended when placing items into dust covers.[4] The use of dust covers has diminished with event-related sterility; however, with items that are rarely used, it might be beneficial.

Peel pouches are an invaluable compact and convenient packaging material for single instruments or small, lightweight, low-profile items such as one or two clamps or Army-Navy instruments. Peel pouches are specific for the type of sterilant used. Excess air should be forced out of the pouch before sealing. Sealing can be done with heat or self-sealing adhesives. Pouches should never be stapled or paper-clipped. Labels can be applied to the pouch, or a permanent marker can be used to write on the plastic side. Writing on the paper side can compromise package integrity. Double-peel pouching is not an acceptable practice unless the peel pouching used has been validated for that use.[4] When double-peel pouching, the inner pouch should fit inside the outer pouch without folding and be positioned so the paper faces paper and plastic faces plastic.[4]

Although much more durable than sterilization wrap, rigid sterilization containers can be damaged by poor care or handling techniques. It is important to follow the rigid container manufacturer's written IFU for cleaning with the appropriate chemical solution and for preventive maintenance. Containers need to be disassembled, cleaned, and inspected after each use for dents or cracks that might compromise the integrity of the seal. Used filters should be discarded. The gaskets should be inspected and replaced if torn or cracked, or if they are no longer soft and pliable. Precut filters should be placed and secured in the filter casing according to the manufacturer's IFU. Some manufacturers have replaced the filter design with a valve or reusable filter. In this case, the valve or reusable filter should be assessed for proper functioning and cleaned according to the manufacturer's IFU.

Product Identification and Traceability

Each package should be labeled with a lot control identifier that lists the sterilizer identification number, the date of sterilization, and the cycle number.[4] "Ideally, every reprocessed medical device, especially an implant, should be fully traceable to the patient on whom it is used or in whom it is implanted; such traceability can be accomplished by recording the sterilizer load identifier on the patient chart or the patient name on the load record."[4] The lot control identifier date can be used for stock rotation. Each package should also be labeled with an expiration statement such as "Contents sterile unless package is opened or damaged. Please check before using."[4]

Inventory Tracking

An essential component of the reprocessing is the inventory of medical devices. This involves a manual stock count or a computer-assisted system. Some facilities use manual methods for this tracking, which requires many people. Other facilities use computer systems capable of scanning tagged or labeled instruments; their use has greatly improved the efficiency and efficacy of this task. Either system needs to be in place to track items in sets, track items in stock supply, and track items out for repair.

Sterilization

Area Design

Sterilizers are located along the processing pathway adjacent to where sets are prepared and assembled, on the "clean" side, away from the decontamination area. The number of air exchanges, temperature, and relative humidity ranges are listed in Table 106-2.[4] The sterilizer manufacturer's written IFU for installation should be followed.

Selection of Sterilization Methods

Selecting the method of sterilization to be used is dependent on the sterilization process validated for use by the instrument manufacturer and provided in the written IFU, turnaround needs, the volume of medical devices to be reprocessed, the compatibility of medical devices with the sterilizing method, exclusion of any instruments and materials, space availability, safety, consideration of the advantages and disadvantages of each method, and cost. An overview of advantages and disadvantages of the most common sterilization methods is available in Chapter 31 Cleaning, Disinfection, and Sterilization. The SP staff is responsible for following the healthcare facility's policies and procedures and the instrument, packaging, and sterilizer manufacturers' written IFU. The sterilizer equipment manual for care and maintenance should also be followed to minimize sterilizer downtime and prevent sterilizer malfunctions.[4] When operating a sterilizer, the SP staff is responsible for care and maintenance of the sterilizer, loading the sterilizer, choosing the correct sterilization cycle, monitoring the effectiveness of the process and documenting the results, and unloading the sterilizer. This monitoring includes chemical and BIs.

Loading the Sterilizer

It is important to follow the sterilizer, instrument, and packaging manufacturers' IFU. In general, in a steam sterilizer mixed-load, rigid containers or other containment devices and wrapped instrument sets or trays and basins (tilted on edge and oriented the same way) are placed on the shelf below absorbent items such as textile packs containing towels, drapes, or other absorbent materials to prevent the wetting of the absorbent items by condensate. The rigid containers or other containment devices and wrapped instrument sets or trays should always be placed flat to allow for air removal, sterilant penetration, condensate drainage, drying, and keeping instruments in an orderly arrangement.[4] Containers from different manufacturers should not be stacked because the configurations for air removal and steam penetration may not match.[4] Racks are available to assist in loading peel pouches so they are placed on edge, not flat, with the paper side facing in one direction.[4] The same principles apply to tabletop sterilizers, which are easily overloaded. Ensure that all items in the load have the same recommended sterilization process and cycle parameter.[9]

Selecting the Sterilization Process and Cycle Parameters

It is important to follow the sterilizer, instrument, and container or other packaging manufacturers' written IFU to determine the correct sterilization process and cycle parameters. If there is conflicting information, SP staff should check with the manufacturer of the instrument or other items being sterilized, as it is manufacturer's responsibility to validate the sterilization process recommended in their IFU.[4,6] The same sterilization process and cycle parameters should be used in any location within the facility that is processing a device. This means required, extended steam sterilization cycles should be used in the operating room (OR) if recommended by the IFU. IUSS cycles (no or reduced drying time) should only be used if recommended in the instrument manufacturer's IFU. Sterilization processes and cycle parameters and original packaging (e.g., loaner trays) should not be changed unless validated by the medical device manufacturer.

Unloading of the Sterilizer and Sterile Storage

Time is required to cool down any heat-sterilized items to prevent condensation from forming when the metal equipment or devices come in contact with room air. The load should remain on the cart until items are adequately cooled to prevent contamination of the items from handling.[4] Because cooling time will vary with the load, temperature-sensing devices are available to determine the internal temperature of the package before removing items from the sterilizer rack to storage. EO sterilized items require aeration time in the sterilizer to remove traces of the gas before they are unloaded. The sterilizer manufacturer's IFU should be consulted for more information on unloading the sterilizer.

During removal from the cart, items should be visually inspected for torn or wet packaging and for external CIs that suggest inadequate processing.[4] Items that are dropped or that have compromised packaging or failed external CIs should not be used; they should be returned to the decontamination area for breakdown and reprocessing.[4] Recall of items can be based on the results of the external CI. See the *Recall* section below. Other items are then placed into sterile storage to await distribution. Items should be stored and distributed in a manner to reduce contamination as described in AAMI ST79.[4]

Quality Control

Sterilization process monitoring includes the use of physical monitors, chemical and BIs, and documentation of those results.

Physical Monitors and Bowie-Dick Testing for Equipment Control Monitoring

The sterilization parameters that affect the efficacy of the sterilization process include temperature, exposure times, pressure, vacuum levels, moisture conditions or relative humidity, chemical concentrations, and adequate air removal. Each load's parameters (specific to the type and design of the sterilizer) should be monitored and documented. The SP staff should verify the information provided on the digital printouts, recording charts, displays, or gauges at the end of the cycle by reading and initialing the results.[4] If the physical monitoring results are not correct for the load contents, the load should not be released for use, and the supervisor should be notified to initiate follow-up measures.[4,7,10] Recall of items can be based on the results of the physical monitor. See the *Recall* section below. Do not use sterilizers that do not have recording devices.[4,7,10] Bowie-Dick testing should be done each day, before the first processed load, in each dynamic-air-removal steam sterilizer in all locations in the healthcare facility to detect air leaks, inadequate air removal, inadequate steam penetration, and the presence of noncondensable gases.[4,6] The sterilizer should not be used if the Bowie-Dick test pack does not show a pass. It should be removed from service and repaired.[4] The steam sterilizer and Bowie-Dick test pack IFU should be followed in addition to the information in Section 10 of AAMI ST79.[4]

Chemical Indicators for Exposure, Pack, and Load Control Monitoring

A CI is a device that monitors the presence of one or more of the parameters required for an effective sterilization process or to monitor the sterilizer equipment (e.g., see Bowie-Dick testing under *Physical Monitors and Bowie-Dick Testing for Equipment Control Monitoring*).[4] The device is designed to respond with a characteristic chemical or physical change to one or more of the physical conditions within the sterilizing chamber.[4] CIs are intended to detect potential sterilization process failures that could result from incorrect packaging, incorrect loading of the sterilizer, or malfunctions of the sterilizer. The "pass" response of a CI does not prove that the item accompanied by the indicator is necessarily sterile. AAMI ST79, ST41, and ST58 have defined six classes of CIs: Class 1 (process indicators), Class 2 (Bowie-Dick tests), Class 3 (single-variable indicators), Class 4 (multivariable indicators), Class 5 (integrating indicators), and Class 6 (emulating indicators). A review of the classes of CIs for steam sterilization and their application for monitoring is noted in Table 106-3.

Table 106-3. Classes of Chemical Indicators

Class	Description	Use
Class 1	Process indicators	Process indicators are intended for use with individual units (e.g., packs or containers) to indicate that the unit has been directly exposed to the sterilization process and to distinguish between processed and unprocessed units. They are designed to react to one or more of the critical process variables.[4,7,10] These types of indicators are called external CIs and should be used on the outside of each package unless the internal CI is visible. Examples are sterilization indicator tape, an indicator label, or printed legend as seen on the outside of peel pouches, and load cards.[4,6,10]
Class 2	Indicators for use in specific tests	Class 2 indicators are intended for use in specific test procedures as defined in relevant sterilizer or sterilization standards.[4] An example of this type of indicator would be the Bowie-Dick test that is designed to test for air removal in dynamic-air-removal steam sterilizers.[4]
Class 3	Single-variable indicators	A single-variable indicator is designed to react to one of the critical variables and is intended to indicate exposure to a sterilization process at a stated value (SV) of the chosen variable.[4,7,10] An example of a single-variable indicator is a temperature tube that contains a chemical pellet that melts at a specific temperature. Single-variable indicators may be used as internal CIs for pack control monitoring but would not provide as much information as a Class 4, Class 5, or Class 6.[4,6,7,10]
Class 4	Multivariable indicators	A multivariable indicator is designed to react to two or more of the critical variables and is intended to indicate exposure to a sterilization cycle at SVs of the chosen variables.[4,7,10] These CIs are usually paper strips printed with a color change CI and are used as internal chemicals for pack control monitoring.[4,6,7,10]
Class 5	Integrating indicators	Integrating indicators are designed to react to all critical process variables. The SVs are generated to be equivalent to or to exceed the performance requirements published in the ANSI/AAMI/ISO 11138 series for BIs.[4,7,10] The results of Class 5 integrating indicators are more closely aligned with BI performance and are the most accurate of the internal CIs but do not replace the use of BIs.[5,7] Class 5 integrating indicators may be used as internal CIs for pack control monitoring.[4,6,10] Class 5 CIs may be used as an additional monitoring tool in process challenge packs to monitor nonimplant loads.[4,6] The CI should be in the BI process challenge device used to monitor implant loads.
Class 6	Emulating indicators	Emulating indicators are cycle verification indicators that are designed to react to all critical variables for specified sterilization cycles.[4,7,10] The SVs are generated from the critical variables of the specified sterilization process.[4,7,10] Class 6 CIs may be used as internal CIs for pack control monitoring.[4,6] Class 6 CIs may be used as an additional monitoring tool in process challenge packs to monitor non-implant loads.[4,6] This CI cannot replace the use of a Class 5 CI in the BI process challenge device used to monitor implant loads or the use of a BI.[5,7]

CIs should be used outside of each healthcare-prepared package, tray, or containment device unless the internal CI is visible. These external CIs are used for exposure control to determine if the item has been processed. The external CI should be read when unloading the sterilizer, dispensing or issuing the item for use, and before the item is opened in the OR.[4,6,7] If the external CI suggests inadequate processing, the package should not be used.

CIs should also be used inside of each healthcare-prepared package, tray, or containment device in the area considered the most challenging to sterilant penetration.[4,6,7,10] The containment device manufacturer should be consulted about where to place the internal CIs.[4,7,10] These internal CIs are used for pack control to determine that the sterilant penetrated each package. The internal CI should be read before the package is placed on the sterile field.[11] If the internal CI suggests inadequate processing, the package should not be used and should be returned to SP, and the supervisor should be informed to determine if the load should be recalled (see *Recall* section below).[4,6,10]

Class 5 and Class 6 CIs may also be used inside PCDs as an additional monitor tool for nonimplant loads.[4,6] Class 5 CIs should be used inside of the BI PCDs to monitor implant loads and can be used in defined emergency situations to release implants (see *Biological Indicators for Load Control Monitoring* section below).[4,6]

More details about the use of CIs can be found in Section 10 of AAMI ST79 and ST41 and Section 9 of ST58. Always follow the CI manufacturer's written IFU for proper usage, interpretation of results, and storage conditions.

Biological Indicators for Load Control Monitoring

BIs consist of a standardized, viable population of microorganisms (usually bacterial spores) known to be resistant to the sterilization process being monitored. BIs are the only process indicators that directly monitor the lethality of a given sterilization process and they cannot be replaced by the use of either Class 5 or Class 6 CIs.[4,6] Spores used to monitor a sterilization process have demonstrated resistance to the sterilizing agent and are more resistant than the bioburden found on medical devices or instruments. *Bacillus atrophaeus* spores are used to monitor EO and dry heat sterilization processes, and *Geobacillus stearothermophilus* spores are used to monitor steam sterilization, hydrogen peroxide with or without gas plasma, and ozone sterilization processes.[4,6] BI monitoring is not required for the liquid peracetic acid processor, but a spore strip containing *G. stearothermophilus* spores is available.[6,7] Follow the BI manufacturer's IFU to determine which BI and PCD to use to monitor a specific sterilization process and cycle. Monitoring includes use of the positive control, as well as records of the incubation temperatures and readout time.[4] AAMI ST79 describes the types of BI PCDs and procedures to use for routine and qualification testing for steam sterilizers.[4] AAMI ST41 describes the same information for EO sterilizers.[10] Because there are no standardized BI PCDs for routine and qualification testing for other low-temperature sterilization processes, AAMI ST58 describes the information that should be obtained from the sterilizer and BI manufacturer for preparing and running a BI PCD for routine and qualification testing.[7] All these documents also describe how to run a positive control from the same lot number in each incubator or autoreader each day a test BI is incubated.

Steam sterilizers should be routinely tested at least weekly—preferable daily—with a BI PCD.[4,6] Sterilizer qualification testing is done using a BI PCD after sterilizer installation and relocation, sterilizer malfunctions, and sterilization process failures.[4,6] See Section 10 in AAMI ST79 for more details on how to perform routine sterilizer efficacy and qualification testing of steam sterilizers.[4]

There are two types of BI PCDs for EO testing. One is for routine sterilizer efficacy testing, which should be done in each load and to test the sterilizer after a sterilization process failure, malfunction, or major repair.[10] The second BI PCD is for qualification testing, which is done after sterilizer installation, relocation, or major redesign.[11] See Section 10 of AAMI ST41 for more details on how to perform routine sterilizer efficacy and qualification testing of EO sterilizers.[10]

Hydrogen peroxide with or without plasma and ozone sterilizers should be tested at least daily, but preferably in every sterilization cycle with a BI PCD (as should EO sterilizers).[6,7] A BI PCD should also be used for sterilizer qualification testing during initial installation of the sterilizer and after relocation, major repairs or malfunctions of the sterilizer, and sterilization process failures.[6,7] Because there are no AAMI standardized BI PCDs for these low-temperature gaseous chemical sterilizers for either routine or qualification testing, the sterilizer manufacturer should be consulted for material selection, assembly, and placement.[6,7] Section 9 of AAMI ST58 does provide some basic information about this testing that should also be accessed for more information.[7]

Each load of implants should be monitored with a BI PCD, and the load should be quarantined until the BI results are available.[4,6,7] For steam sterilizers, a Class 5 integrating indicator should also be included in the BI PCD for early release of implants in defined emergency situations.[4,6] "Releasing implants before the BI results are known is unacceptable and should be the exception, not the rule."[4,7] Annex L of AAMI ST79 and Annex M of AAMI ST58 provide an implant log (see Figure 106-3) and exception form to use for documentation of the early release of implants.[4,7] The log and exception form can be used to reduce the frequency of emergency release of implantable items.[4,7] The implant-monitoring documentation should be fully traceable to the patient.[4,6,7]

Monitoring of every load and quarantining loads until the BI result is known is a method to reduce the risk and cost of healthcare-associated infections (HAIs). This method shows the load was effectively sterilized before it was released for use, and it provides a method for identifying a failure in the sterilization process before the sterilized contents are used in patient treatment. This also reduces the cost and impact of a recall and ensures that all implants are monitored.

If a BI is positive, the load should not be released. If the load has already been released, a recall should take place.[4] The cause of the positive result should be investigated. If the positive result is due to the need for major repairs to the sterilizer, sterilizer qualification testing must be performed before the sterilizer is put back into service.[4]

Recalls

AAMI ST79 addresses recalls in Section 10 under "Action to take when BIs, CIs, or physical monitors indicate a failure."[4] In Section 10 of ST79 is Figure 12, which shows a decision tree for conducting investigations of steam sterilization process failures, which indicate when a recall is needed. Table 8 shows a checklist for identifying reasons for steam sterilization process failures. A recall is not needed if the cause of the failure is immediately identifiable, which is usually the result of an operator error and confined only to one load.[4] For example, an operator error that is immediately identifiable is running the wrong sterilization cycle for the load contents. At that point only the error needs to be corrected and the load reprocessed. If the error is not immediately identifiable, which will be the case in the vast majority of sterilization process failures, actions to take include recalling all items that have been processed since the last negative BI. This action would be taken if the BI, CI, or physical monitor identified a problem. The advantage of every-load monitoring with a BI and quarantining until the BI results are known is that only the one load in question is involved, so there is no patient involvement. The decision tree also indicates when qualification testing with BI PCDs is needed.

The Section on Action to take when BIs, CIs, or physical monitors indicate a failure in AAMI ST79 can be used to assist in developing a written policy and procedure to address who, when, and how to recall reprocessed items. In addition, the policy may include compliance components of the Safe Medical Device Act if failure is noted in the reuse of reprocessed items. At a minimum, a log of items within the sterilized load should be reviewed along with the monitoring results, unused items in the load retrieved for reprocessing, a root cause of the sterilization process failure identified, required sterilizer testing completed, and surveillance of involved patients initiated. The recall process is often collaborative and should include the IP, risk manager, surgical services manager, and the surgeon or the attending physician for the involved patients. The same recall process can be used for low-temperature sterilization processes also.[4,10] AAMI ST58 also has in Section 9 information on actions to take if a BI test is positive.[7] The information in AAMI ST79 Figure 12 could also be used for low-temperature sterilization process failures.[4]

Documentation/Recordkeeping

Most regulatory and professional agencies and organizations recommend records be kept of the sterilization cycles. Each item or package should be labeled with a lot control identifier which includes the sterilizer identification number or code, the date of sterilization, and the cycle number.[4,7,10] For each sterilization cycle, the SP staff should document the lot number; date; time; contents of load including quantity, department, and a specific description of the items; exposure time and temperature; operator's name or initials; results of BI testing and Bowie-Dick testing, if applicable; response of the CI placed in the PCD; and any reports of inconclusive or nonresponsive CIs found later in the load.[4,7] Aeration information would be included for EO processed loads.[10] As discussed before, any equipment maintenance, repairs, and calibration must be documented for each sterilizer. This will help assist in determining if a major or minor repair was made to a sterilizer after a sterilization process failure occurred. The SP staff also needs to document when the sterilizers were cleaned or other routine maintenance was performed according to the sterilizer manufacturer's written recommendations for maintenance and cleaning. Digitization of this documentation process will allow quicker access to load information for troubleshooting.[4] Healthcare facilities should follow their facility's policy for the length of time that records must be kept.

Reporting Results of Monitoring

In accordance with TJC standards, the hospital implements infection prevention activities when cleaning, disinfecting, sterilizing, and storing medical equipment, devices, and supplies. The hospital's infection prevention committee or authority should routinely receive reports of the monitoring of the sterilization process. The report should include whether or not testing was conducted according to policy (i.e., daily, every load with implants) as well as the number of positive results and what actions were taken, and how many times implants were released before the BI results were known. This information can be included in infection prevention committee minutes. An example of an implantable device log is shown in Figure 106-3, and an example of a monthly biological monitoring log is shown in Figure 106-4.

Immediate-Use Steam Sterilization

IUSS (formerly called flash sterilization) is a sterilization process designed for the cleaning, steam sterilization, and delivery of patient care items for immediate use.[4] Originally instruments were unwrapped and processed for emergencies when a single instrument was dropped on the floor, but flash sterilization gained wider usage in situations in which the OR schedule did not permit reprocessing in SP. AAMI, the AORN, and TJC do not recommend the use of IUSS because IUSS may be associated with increased risk of infection to patients.[4,11] This is because time constraints to reprocess more quickly lead to pressure on personnel that could result in shortcuts such as eliminating or modifying one or more of the steps in the cleaning, packaging, and sterilization process recommended by the instrument manufacturer's IFU.[6] The result is instruments that are not adequately cleaned or sterilized, and the only time saved is elimination or shortening of the dry cycle. IUSS should not be used as a substitute for sufficient instrument inventory.[6]

To use IUSS instruments, the items to be sterilized need to be decontaminated (cleaned and inspected) in an environment that will minimize the transmission of organisms, just as they would in SP.[4,6] The OR should have the equipment available for manual and/or mechanical cleaning, cleaning solutions, tools such as brushes, water quality, rigid sterilization containers/packaging, and sterilizers and cycles, as does SP and as required in the instrument manufacturer's IFU. The area should be separated from clean areas. To prevent contamination and injury to staff, PPE should be worn when cleaning items. Use the cleaning solutions recommended by the manufacturer; never use antiseptic (hand scrub products or house cleaning products) to clean surgical instruments. Procedures for cleaning soiled instruments should be the same as those used in the SP decontamination area. Cleaning is the most critical step in IUSS and is often the step that is shortened or done incorrectly. The same sterilization process and cycle should be used in the OR as in SP that will include the use of standard

Implantable Devices Load Record

Date	Description of implants	Dept.	Time sterilized (specify AM/PM)	Sterilizer #	Load #	Date/time B1 in incubator	Date/time and B1 result	Early release?	Date/time released to OR	Released by (full name)

Figure 106-3. Example of an implantable device log (AAMI ST79).

Hospital
Biological Monitoring of Sterilizers

Department:_____.   Month/Year:_____.

Sterilizer	# of scheduled BI per policy	# of BI run	BI processed for ≥ 100% of scheduled loads	Positive BI Results	% Positive BI

BI = Biological Indicator
Comments (Action Taken for any Positives):

Fax Monthly Reports to Infection Control @ 444-8154

Figure 106-4. Example of a monthly BI monitoring report.

and extended cycles. IUSS cycles (no or reduced drying time) should only be used if recommended in the instrument manufacturer's IFU.

To prevent contamination of the wet instruments during transfer to the sterile field, rigid sterilization containers or other packaging or wrapping materials that are labeled for IUSS should be used.[4,6] Because the packaging is wet, packages should be immediately opened and the content used.[7] Do not store these items for later use or hold for the next procedure.[6]

The IUSS process should be monitored as described in the *Quality Control* section above. AAMI ST79 in Section 10 describes how to prepare BI PCDs and perform routine and qualification testing of IUSS.[4] AORN states that a Class 5 or Class 6 CI should be used with each sterilization container or tray used for IUSS.[6] Bowie-Dick tests need to be run in dynamic-air-removal steam sterilizers and the cycles need to be documented as described in the *Documentation/Recordkeeping* section with the addition of the reason for IUSS. This information can be used to decrease the use of IUSS for process improvement as required by TJC, AAMI, AORN, and HICPAC. IUSS should not be used for implantable devices except in cases of a defined emergency because of the increased risk of SSIs.[4,6,12] Every implant should be fully traceable to the patient.[4,6]

Loaner Instruments

Written policies and procedures should address the acquisition, responsibility, accountability, and disposition of loaner instruments. IAHCSMM provides on its website *Position Paper on the Management of Loaner Instruments and a Sample Policy & Procedure for Loaner Instrumentation,* which provides information to assist in developing a loaner instrument policy and procedure.[13] These documents discuss the responsibilities of the OR, sales representative, and central sterile supply department or SP area before and after the instruments arrive. This takes planning to ensure that instruments arrive in time for in-servicing of OR and SP staff, processing according to the instrument manufacturer's IFU, quarantining the implants until the BI result is available, and avoiding the use of IUSS.[6,13] IAHCSMM recommends that loaner trays arrive at the healthcare facility at least two business days prior to the scheduled case and that all first-time vendor-loaned sets arrive three business days prior to the scheduled procedure to allow adequate time for training, inspecting, and processing. If a shorter delivery time is accepted, then shortcuts may be taken, implants may be released before the BI results are known, and IUSS may be used with a shorter-than-required cleaning procedure and sterilization process.[6] AORN states that "Late receipt of loaned instruments should not be used to justify IUSS" and also provides some information to assist in developing a loaner instrument policy and procedure.[6]

Managing Items Contaminated With Prions

Transmissible spongiform encephalopathies (TSEs) are degenerative, invariably fatal brain diseases that occur in humans and certain animal species. They are caused by an infectious agent known as a prion (see Chapter 73 Creutzfeldt-Jakob Disease and Other Prion Diseases for additional information on TSEs). The most common TSE (80 to 90 percent) is Creutzfeldt-Jakob disease (CJD).[14] TSEs are not known to be spread by person-to-person contact. Reports indicate that TSEs have been spread by exposure to infectious material from human cadaver tissue and organs, dura and cornea homografts, and contaminated neurosurgical instruments.[14] Prions are resistant to routine disinfection and sterilization methods. In 2000, two separate incidents involving patients resulted in a Joint Commission Sentinel Event Alert (June 2001) and a more recent update in September 2013. Investigations found that the diagnosis of CJD was made following surgical procedures, and the instruments were reprocessed and sterilized by routine methods. The possibility of prion transmission to subsequent surgical patients on whom those instruments were used was a concern.[15]

Because prions are resistant to routine disinfection and sterilization methods, special procedures for TSE and CJD cases are needed. Surgical and SP staff need to be knowledgeable about proper procedures for handling, cleaning, decontaminating, storing, and disposing of used surgical instruments, as well as how to manage the contaminated environment. Determining the best method for handling a suspected or known TSE or CJD case should be based on the infectivity level of the tissue and the items used. Although cerebrospinal fluid is listed as having low infectivity, it is recommended that instruments contaminated with cerebrospinal fluid be treated as highly infectious items.[14]

Detailed information on how to manage and reprocess contaminated items can be found in Chapter 73 Creutzfeldt-Jakob Disease and Other Prion Diseases.

Storage and Shelf Life

Physical storage restrictions are recommended to support an environment that is conducive to maintaining the sterility of reprocessed items. Sterilized items should be stored as follows:

1. 18 inches below the ceiling or the sprinkler head or according to the fire code

2. 8 to 10 inches from the floor

3. At least 2 inches from an outside wall

4. Away from sprinklers and air vents

5. Open rack storage should have a solid bottom to prevent soiling or contamination from the floor during housekeeping

6. Position packages so they are not crushed, bent, compressed, or punctured

7. Store heavy trays/containers on middle shelves but not stacked

8. In areas of limited traffic

9. Clean workroom or clean holding area(s): airflow must be positive pressure with respect to surrounding areas with a minimum of four air exchanges per hour.[16] In an area with controlled temperature and humidity (approximately 24°C [75°F], relative humidity not to exceed 70 percent).

10. Soiled workroom or soiled holding area(s): airflow must be negative pressure with respect to surrounding areas with a minimum of 10 air exchanges per hour.

11. The first item in is the first item out (first in, first out [FIFO]). Items should be rotated. Place newer items in the back part of the area where they are stored.

12. Consideration should be given to storage that will minimize the collection of dust on surfaces.

13. Outside shipping containers and corrugated cartons should not be used as containers.[4]

Items should not be stored under sinks or under exposed water or sewer pipes. Windowsills should be avoided. Closed or covered cabinets are preferred. Open shelving may be used if the area has limited access and monitored ventilation and is frequently cleaned and disinfected.[6]

Event-Related Sterility

Shelf life is event related. With event-related sterility, items are considered sterile unless the integrity of the packaging is compromised (i.e., torn, soiled, wet, or showing evidence of tampering). Conditions that may alter the integrity of the packaging may include the following:

1. Environmental sources of contamination (e.g., moisture, vermin, and air movement associated with traffic)

2. The barrier properties of the packaging material (e.g., the integrity of its seals and its resistance to tearing)

3. Storage and distribution practices (e.g., open versus closed shelving and transport)

4. Inventory control (e.g., realistic standards and stock rotation)

5. Frequency of handling between distribution and the user

Distribution

Care should be taken when handling supplies to avoid dragging, sliding, crushing, bending, compressing, or puncturing the packaging or otherwise compromising the sterility of the contents.[4] The integrity and labeling of each package should be visually inspected, including the external CI, before issuing.

Reprocessed, sterilized items should be transferred in covered or enclosed carts with solid bottoms to prevent or reduce environmental contamination.[4] Items should be arranged to prevent crushing, bending, or compression. Carts and reusable covers should be cleaned, disinfected, and thoroughly dried after each use.[5] Outside shipping containers or corrugated cardboard for distribution or storage are unacceptable.[4]

For transportation of sterile items from an off-site distribution point or commercial reprocessor, sterile supplies should be kept separated from contaminated items.[4] Transporting containers should be designed to prevent compromising sterility; they must offer protection from moisture and condensation, insects, vermin, dust, and dirt. The design of the containers should allow easy loading and unloading without contaminating or damaging the packaging and its contents. The containers need to be secure within the transporting vehicle. High humidity or extreme temperature changes need to be considered to manage condensation on or within the reprocessed trays during transportation.

CONCLUSIONS

SP is most often the department that is responsible for the reprocessing and sterilizing of instrumentation and medical devices. The process involves handling, collection, transporting, sorting, disassembling, cleaning, disinfection, inspecting, packaging, sterilizing, storing, and distributing reprocessed items. If other areas or departments assume the responsibility for reprocessing their own equipment, it is important that they meet the same standards of practice as SP. This chapter has offered an introduction to the processes that are conducted in SP and provides references and resources regarding published recommended practice, standards, and guidelines. These recommended practices, standards, and guidelines should be available and up-to-date for use in writing policies and procedures and answering specific questions. Every infection prevention department and SP area should have an up-to-date copy of AAMI ST79 *Comprehensive Guide to Steam Sterilization and Sterility Assurance in Healthcare Facilities,* AAMI ST58 *Chemical Sterilization and High-level Disinfection in Healthcare Facilities,* AORN *Perioperative Standards and Recommended Practices,* and the CDC *Guideline for Disinfection and Sterilization in Healthcare Facilities.*[4,7,6,12]

It is essential for employee and patient safety to follow the manufacturer's IFU for the operation of cleaning and sterilizing equipment, the reprocessing of instruments and medical devices, the concentration and use of chemical solutions and disinfectants, and the appropriate use of PPE. Any deviation from the instrument or medical device manufacturers' IFU related to cleaning, packaging, loading, and sterilization could result in an ineffective process and an SSI or other adverse outcome. Results of monitoring of processes and outcomes should be reported to the infection prevention committee or authority and ongoing education, competency testing, and certification for staff is critical to achieve desired outcomes. The IP plays a critical role in the successful achievement of these outcomes and can serve as a valuable resource to the SP areas.

REFERENCES

1. Listsky B. Interview in evolution of the central service department. *Infection Control Rounds* 1992;15:10.
2. Lister J. On the antiseptic principle in the practice of surgery. *Br Med J* 1867 Sep 21;2(351):246–248.
3. Perkins J. *Principles and Methods of Sterilization in Health Science.* Springfield, IL: Charles C. Thomas, 1969.
4. Association for the Advancement of Medical Instruments. *ANSI/AAMI ST79:2010 & A1:2010 & A2:2011 & A3:2012 & A4:2013.* Arlington, VA: Association for the Advancement of Medical Instrumentation, 2013.
5. Facilities Guideline Institute. *Guidelines for Design and Construction of Hospitals and Outpatient Facilities.* Dallas: Facilities Guideline Institute, 2010.
6. Association of periOperative Registered Nurses. Recommended practices for sterilization. *Perioperative Standards and Recommended Practices*: Denver: Association of periOperative Registered Nurses, 2013.
7. Association for the Advancement of Medical Instruments. *ANSI/AAMI ST58:2013.* Arlington, VA: Association for the Advancement of Medical Instrumentation, 2013.
8. Kimberly-Clark Health Care. *ESP: Packaging Cycle and Contamination Prevention.* Roswell, GA: Kimberly-Clark Worldwide, Inc., 2003.
9. Association for the Advancement of Medical Instruments. *AAMI TIR31:2008.* Arlington, VA: Association for the Advancement of Medical Instrumentation, 2008.
10. Association for the Advancement of Medical Instruments. *ANSI/AAMI ST41:2008/(R)2012.* Arlington, VA: Association for the Advancement of Medical Instrumentation, 2012.
11. Association of periOperative Registered Nurses. Recommended practices for sterile technique. *Perioperative Standards and Recommended Practices.* Denver, CO: Association of periOperative Registered Nurses, 2013.
12. Rutala WA, Weber DJ, and the Healthcare Infection Control Practices Advisory Committee. *Guideline for disinfection and sterilization in healthcare facilities,* 2008. CDC website. Available at: http://www.cdc.gov/hicpac/pdf/guidelines/disinfection_nov_2008.pdf.
13. International Association of Healthcare Central Service Materiel Management (IAHCSMM). *IAHCSMM Releases Loaner Instrumentation Position Paper, Sample Policy.* IAHCSMM website. Available at: http://iahcsmm.org/CurrentIssues/Loaner_Instrumentation_Position_Paper_Sample_Policy.html.
14. World Health Organization. *WHO Infection Control Guidelines for Transmissible Spongiform Encephalopathies.* Geneva, Switzerland, 1999. Available at: http://whqlibdoc.who.int/hq/2000/WHO_CDS_CSR_APH_2000.3.pdf.
15. Centers for Disease Control and Prevention (CDC). *Questions and answers regarding Creutzfeldt-Jakob Disease Infection Control Practices.* CDC website. August 23, 2010. Available at: http://www.cdc.gov/ncidod/dvrd/cjd/qa_cjd_infection_control.htm.

SUPPLEMENTAL RESOURCES

Block SS. *Disinfection, Sterilization and Preservation,* 5th ed. Philadelphia: Lippincott Williams & Wilkins, 2000.

Hubbard CA. *Building for the Future Construction and Renovation of Sterile Processing Facilities.* Arlington, VA: Association for the Advancement of Medical Instrumentation, 2013.

Seavey R. *Sterile Processing in Healthcare Facilities: Preparing for Accreditation Surveys.* Arlington, VA: Association for the Advancement of Medical Instrumentation, 2013.

ASGE Quality Assurance In Endoscopy Committee, Petersen BT, Chennat J, et al. Multisociety guideline for reprocessing flexible gastrointestinal endoscopes. *Gastrointest Endosc* 2011 Jun;73(6):1075–1084.

Occupational exposure to bloodborne pathogens—OSHA. Final rule. *Fed Regist* 1991 Dec 6;56(235):64004–64182.

Rutala WA. *Disinfection, Sterilization and Antisepsis,* 2010 edition. Washington, DC: Association for Professionals in Infection Control and Epidemiology, 2010.

Petersen BT, Chennat J, Cohen J, et al. Multisociety guideline on reprocessing flexible gi endoscopes: 2011. *Infect Control Hosp Epidemiol* 2011 Jun;32(6):527–537.

One of these texts is a must for any IP who wants to understand central services/sterile processing from the worker's perspective. The first text is the core curriculum for the IAHCSMM Certification test and the second is the core curriculum for the Certification Board test

International Association for Healthcare Central Services and Materiel Management (IAHCSMM). *Central Services Technical Manual,* 7th ed. Chicago: International Association for Healthcare Central Services and Material Management, 2007. www.IAHCSMM.org.

Sterile Processing University, LLC. *The Basics of Sterile Processing and Workbook for The Basics of Sterile Processing,* 5th ed. Lebanon, NJ: Sterile Processing University, LLC, 2013. www.sterileprocessing.org.

CHAPTER 107

Environmental Services

Teresa Chou, MPH, MS, RN, CIC
Manager, Epidemiology and Infection Prevention and Control
Advocate Illinois Masonic Medical Center
Chicago, IL

ABSTRACT

There is increasing evidence that the healthcare environment is an important source of healthcare-associated infections. Every facility must thoroughly clean its environment to prevent it from developing into a reservoir for pathogens. The cleaning needs vary by facility and are assessed by a team of experts. These experts are responsible for providing leadership, establishing effective cleaning protocols, preparing regular cleaning schedules, writing policies and procedures, selecting the appropriate cleaning agents and equipment, and hiring and training staff. They are also prepared to address unexpected situations such as outbreaks, natural disasters, back orders on supplies, unavailability of equipment, and staff shortages. Proper education and training of environmental services personnel are critical components of an effective program. Staff must be educated and trained upon hire, at regular intervals thereafter, and as needed. Programs should be developed to assess the efficacy of the environmental services activities. Even when performance improvement measures are outstanding, there is always room for improvement. Patients, visitors, and personnel expect and deserve a clean environment.

This chapter addresses hand hygiene, disinfection, bloodborne pathogen exposure, laundry and linen, and waste management practices as applicable to environmental services. For more in-depth discussion of these topics, please refer to their respective chapters in this Text.

KEY CONCEPTS

- To properly maintain their environments, healthcare facilities must adhere to federal, state, and local regulations and should follow guidelines established by the Centers for Disease Control and Prevention and professional organizations.

- Each healthcare institution must establish written policies and procedures for cleaning. These policies and procedures must meet regulatory requirements and published standards and recommendations.

- Environmental surfaces are divided into two categories—those with minimal hand contact such as floors and ceilings and those with frequent hand contact (high-touch surfaces).[1]

- High-touch surfaces may be potential reservoirs for microorganisms. These surfaces need to be cleaned more frequently because contact with them may easily lead to cross-transmission of infection.

- Items or surfaces that are less frequently handled may not need to be cleaned as often. Because they experience fewer contacts, they are less likely to be sources of infection.

- To prevent the dispersal of dust, cleaning activities should be conducted with minimal turbulence.

- Individuals responsible for selecting, purchasing, and/or educating others on the use of cleaning products should have a thorough understanding of the terminology and should be knowledgeable about the efficacies and intended uses of different chemical agents.

- Environmental services directors, managers, and supervisors, in conjunction with infection preventionists and other healthcare professionals, determine when personal protective equipment is necessary, write guidelines for its use, and select and purchase appropriate supplies.

- Biohazardous and nonbiohazardous waste must be separated. If both types of waste are inadvertently mixed, the nonbiohazardous waste is considered biohazardous.

- Environmental services address pest control. If there are no experts within the facility, contract licensed professionals should be hired to handle toxic pesticides.

BACKGROUND

Accumulation of dust, soil, and microbial contaminants on environmental surfaces in healthcare facilities is not only aesthetically displeasing, but evidence indicates that it also plays a major role in the spread of healthcare-associated infections (HAIs). Studies have shown that many microorganisms survive on surfaces for long periods of time. For example, *Staphylococcus aureus*, including methicillin-resistant *S. aureus* (MRSA), survives more than 12 months; *Enterococcus*, including vancomycin-resistant enterococci (VRE), lives more than 46 months; *Clostridium difficile* persists more than 5 months; and norovirus resides more than 2 weeks. Among the hardy Gram-negative bacilli, *Acinetobacter* and *Pseudomonas aeruginosa* have been isolated from the environment 11 and

16 months later, respectively, and *Klebsiella* has lasted more than 30 months.[2]

Contact with contaminated surfaces easily leads to cross-transmission of microorganisms between people and the environment.[3] The hands of healthcare personnel (HCP) become contaminated while providing care to a colonized or infected patient. HCP then touch and contaminate the inanimate environment surrounding the patient. Patients also spread their flora on surfaces that they contact. If the surfaces are not properly cleaned, the organisms can live on them for long periods of time. When subsequent HCP, patients, and visitors come into contact with the contaminated surfaces, they can acquire the microbes and pass them on to others, contaminating more surfaces. Susceptible individuals can become colonized and/or infected.

Hand hygiene plays an important role in preventing cross-contamination, and maintaining a clean and healthy environment is equally important.[4] Effective and efficient cleaning methods and schedules are necessary to ensure clean and healthy environments in healthcare facilities.

BASIC PRINCIPLES

Regulatory Requirements and Guidelines

Regulatory requirements for maintaining the environment in healthcare facilities are best summarized by Occupational Safety and Health Administration (OSHA):

> Employers ensure that the worksite is maintained in a clean and sanitary condition. The employer determines and implements appropriate written schedules for cleaning and methods of decontamination based upon the location within the facility and services provided (patient care, food preparation, offices, mechanical rooms), types of surface to be cleaned (metal, impervious, or cloth), and degree and type of soilage (i.e., blood and body fluids or dirt and dust).[5]

It is mandatory to adhere to federal, state, and local regulations about the care of the environment. Healthcare facilities must also follow regulations addressing chemical, physical, and biological safety, as well as ergonomics. Rules vary by state and municipality.

Nonregulatory agencies such as the Centers for Disease Control and Prevention (CDC), Association for Professionals in Infection Control and Epidemiology (APIC), the Association for Healthcare Environment (AHE), and Association of periOperative Registered Nurses (AORN) provide environmental cleaning guidelines. Relevant CDC publications include *Guidelines for Environmental Infection Control in Healthcare Facilities*[1] and *Guideline for Disinfection and Sterilization in Healthcare Facilities.*[6] AHE issued *Practice Guidance for Healthcare Environmental Cleaning.*[7] AORN addresses cleaning recommendations for operating rooms in *Perioperative Standards*

and Recommended Practices.[8] Because these recommendations are often based on existing scientific data, theoretical rationale, applicability, and economics, regulatory surveyors and inspectors often regard them as standards that must be followed.

Cleaning Principles

The key to cleaning and disinfecting environmental surfaces is the use of friction to physically remove visible dirt, organic material, and debris, thereby removing microorganisms.

High-touch and Other Surfaces

The cleaning of environmental surfaces is divided into two categories based on how frequently these items or surfaces are touched and the associated risk of infection transmission. High-touch surfaces or items need to be cleaned frequently because of the high degree of handling and the risk of cross-transmission of infection. Surfaces and items that do not need to be cleaned as frequently are those that are handled less often and are less likely to be sources of infection.[1,6]

High-touch items requiring frequent cleaning include, but are not limited to, medical equipment knobs or handles (e.g., knobs or handles on x-ray machines, cardiac monitors), blood pressure cuffs, bedrails, handheld television controls, nurse call lights, doorknobs, light switches, telephones, and computer keyboards. Many of these surfaces, such as controls on medical equipment, are cleaned after each patient use. The manufacturer's recommended procedures and chemicals for cleaning these surfaces must be followed. Nonadherence with the manufacturer's instructions and using inappropriate cleaning agents may result in damage to the equipment and invalidation of warranties.[9] For example, alcohol is a superb disinfectant but may blur the plastic viewing window of monitors and/or remove labels surrounding knobs. When asked, most manufacturers will provide a list of cleaning agents that will not harm their products.

Alternatively, surfaces such as floors, walls, window curtains, lights, and ventilation grilles usually need less frequent cleaning. Facilities should ensure these surfaces are cleaned routinely by establishing a schedule, creating and following procedures, and using effective cleaning agents. These surfaces must also be cleaned immediately when visibly soiled. It is important to note that cleaning procedures and cleaning agents used for environmental surfaces usually differ from those used for cleaning patient care equipment and instruments.[9] As stated, it is important to adhere to the manufacturer's recommendations.

Patient Zone

There are two zones of care—the patient zone and the healthcare zone.[10] The patient zone consists of the patient and his/her immediate surroundings. Many high-touch surfaces are within the patient zone. For example, in a patient room, the patient zone would be the patient, the patient's bed, and the surrounding high-touch surfaces. The patient zone can quickly become heavily soiled with the patient's flora. If the patient zone is not properly cleaned, the contaminated surfaces can be a reservoir of microorganisms that are subsequently transmitted to the next individual occupying or contacting that zone. At the same time, organisms outside of a patient's zone are foreign and may be potentially harmful if introduced into the zone.

All other areas outside the patient zone fall into the healthcare zone. This includes other surfaces and other patients and their individual patient zones.

Cleaning Procedures

Cleaning schedules and procedures progress from the least soiled areas to the most soiled (patient zone) and from high surfaces to low ones. Routine cleaning is necessary to maintain a basic standard of cleanliness. Procedures must be effective, consistent, and thorough.

Dust contains fungal spores, such as *Aspergillus*, which may cause fatal infections, especially in immunosuppressed individuals.[11] Therefore, it is important to minimize air turbulence and dispersal of dust when cleaning. Environmental services (EVS) personnel should partner with nursing staff to move immuno-suppressed patients away from dust-creating activities. Dust-creating activities include dusting, vacuuming, and waxing and buffing floors. When the duster is dampened, treated with an absorbent chemical, or composed of microfiber, spores adhere to the fabric. High-efficiency particulate air (HEPA) filters in vacuum cleaners collect the dust produced by the machines. If the activity is outside the patient's room, EVS should close the door to the patient's room prior to starting.

Cleaning methods and procedures vary among healthcare settings. Therefore, each institution must establish written policies and procedures. A multidisciplinary approach is recommended because cleaning of the environment involves everyone within the facility. The multidisciplinary team should include EVS, infection prevention and control, nursing, administration, clinical engineering, facilities, materials management, pharmacy, information systems, and food services. Among the team members, EVS and infection preventionists (IPs) will most likely form the strongest partnership. IPs can help educate EVS personnel and other staff, offer advice on cleaning procedures and schedules, provide expertise on cleaning agents, assist in writing policies and procedures, and participate in performance improvement activities. An IP must know the facility's EVS cleaning procedures and schedules, assist in selecting disinfectants used, help review and revise written policies and procedures, and collaborate on quality improvement activities.

Every facility should also develop performance improvement activities to measure the effectiveness of its cleaning program.

Cleaning Agents

EVS, IPs, and other individuals responsible for selecting, purchasing, and/or educating others on the use of cleaning products should have a thorough understanding of the differences

between and the uses of these chemicals. These individuals should also know the relevant terminology (see Appendix) and understand the following issues:

1. Definitions of the terms cleaning, sanitization, disinfection, and sterilization

2. Definitions of soap, antiseptic, disinfectant, sterilant, and sanitizer

3. Differences among the types and uses of antiseptics

4. Differences among the types and uses of disinfectants, including sporicidal disinfectants[12]

5. Differences between disinfectants, disinfectant-detergents, and detergents or cleaning agents containing no antimicrobial properties

6. Manufacturer's specification for use, including dilution and contact time

7. Difference between Environmental Protection Agency (EPA)- and Food and Drug Administration (FDA)-registered products

Disinfectants

Disinfectants are divided into low, intermediate, and high levels.[6] Low-level disinfectants kill most vegetative bacteria, some fungi, and some viruses within the contact time stipulated by the manufacturer. In addition to vegetative bacteria, intermediate-level disinfectants kill hardier organisms such as mycobacteria, most fungi, most viruses, and some spores. High-level disinfectants kill spores as well as all other forms of microorganisms. The action time and spectrum of disinfectants vary. Detergents have no antimicrobial claims. (See Chapter 31 Cleaning, Disinfection, and Sterilization for additional information.)

In general, low- and intermediate-level disinfectants are used for cleaning surfaces and are reviewed and registered with the EPA, whereas high-level disinfectants, sterilants for medical equipment, and antiseptics are evaluated and approved by the FDA.[1] Registration numbers are labeled on the manufacturer's containers of each product. Registered disinfectants are found on the EPA website.[12,13]

There is a debate about whether to use detergents or disinfectants on environmental surfaces. Detergents are more environmentally friendly, not toxic, produce less offensive odors, are unlikely to trigger adverse respiratory reactions, and cost less than disinfectants. Studies show that floors cleaned with a detergent do not increase the risk of HAIs.[6] Unfortunately, detergents do not effectively remove microorganisms from surfaces. Microorganisms on horizontal surfaces may then easily be transmitted to patients and other surfaces via the hands of HCP and visitors. Detergent solutions can also become easily contaminated. Therefore, the CDC recommends using disinfectants for cleaning horizontal surfaces—especially high-touch surfaces—in patient areas, on medical equipment, in isolation rooms, and during outbreaks. Detergents may be used on floors, except in isolation rooms. Using a variety of cleaning agents to clean different surfaces (such as disinfectants for bedside surfaces and detergents for floors) may be inconvenient and create a more complex education process for the EVS department.

Because organic materials such as blood and protein inactivate many disinfectants, organic matter must be removed from surfaces before applying the disinfectant. A large number of disinfectants registered by the EPA are acceptable for routine decontamination of the environment.[1,6,13] EPA-registered quaternary ammonium compounds (quats) are most frequently selected for cleaning environmental surfaces. Occasionally, phenolics have been used when encountering greater contamination, such as in the operating rooms. Bleach (1:10 dilution or 1.5 cups of bleach in a gallon of water) has gained wide acceptance as an effective and inexpensive disinfectant for blood spills, gastrointestinal outbreaks (norovirus), and spore-forming organisms (C. difficile). The EPA also has a list of sporicidal disinfectants effective against C. difficile.[12]

Disinfectants and detergents must be used according to the manufacturer's instructions on the label (e.g., dilution, compatibility, contact time, storage, shelf-life). If the manufacturer's recommendations are not followed, the user assumes the liability for any problems or adverse effects; this disclaimer is stated on the labels of all EPA-registered products. Many disinfectants require a 10-minute contact time, which is not always practical and usually requires more than one application of the chemical because most water-based disinfectants dry within 2 minutes.[14] Multiple studies have shown that a 1-minute contact time is sufficient, and there is no evidence that a 10-minute application results in greater reduction of infections than a 1-minute exposure.[2,6] However, inspectors, surveyors, and other auditors will refer to product label instructions regarding wet contact time when evaluating facility compliance.

Newer 0.5 percent and 1.4 percent hydrogen peroxide solutions for surface cleaning have been found to be highly effective.[2,15] They are bactericidal and virucidal within 30 to 60 seconds, which is the fastest nonbleach contact time.[1] The contact time for mycobacteria is 5 minutes. Hydrogen peroxide falls into the lowest toxicity risk level; it is noncorrosive, compatible with most surfaces, releases a minimally offensive chemical odor, requires only one step to clean and disinfect, and can be purchased as a wipe and liquid. It is more expensive than a quat and bleach.[14]

Detergents and disinfectants that are ready for use or dispensed in premeasured amounts may be preferred over those that require mixing. Disinfectants that are ready for use are sold in individually packaged impregnated wipes, in canisters of multiple impregnated cloths, and as premixed liquids with and without sprays. To ensure their efficacy, premixed solutions should not be further diluted or altered in any way. If it is necessary to prepare a cleaning solution, the manufacturer's instructions for dilution must be closely followed. Machines that dispense premeasured amounts of chemical and water are more

accurate and reliable than manual mixing of solutions. Unless otherwise specified, fresh tap water should be used to dilute the disinfectant or detergent. Containers for the cleaning agents must be labeled in accordance with regulatory requirements (e.g., chemical content, name, expiration date).

Containers with multiple disposable wipes impregnated with disinfectant can make cleaning and disinfection of small spills and surfaces easier and more convenient. These wipes combine cleaning and disinfection into a one-step process at the point of care. Wipes must maintain their wetness until the manufacturer's specified contact time is reached.

It is important to prevent extrinsic contamination of disinfectants and detergents. Dispensing equipment should be well maintained and kept in a clean area to prevent contamination. Disposable containers are generally preferred. Reusable containers should be emptied, cleaned, and dried before they are refilled. The practice of "topping off" nearly empty containers of disinfectants and detergents creates a risk for introducing unwanted microorganisms. All chemicals must be discarded when they have reached their expiration date.

Antiseptics

Antiseptics are approved by the FDA as antimicrobial agents safe for use on skin. They are not to be used for cleaning inanimate objects or environmental surfaces because of their unproven efficacy on nonhuman surfaces. Only 70 to 90 percent isopropyl or ethyl alcohol can be safely used on both skin and environmental surfaces. However, alcohol dries too quickly to be an effective agent for cleaning large surfaces or spills and is expensive.

Special Circumstances

Special considerations must be taken when selecting a disinfectant for use in the following situations or areas:

1. Blood and body fluids
   Many disinfectants are inactivated by blood and other organic matter. If the spill is small, it can be cleaned and disinfected in one step by pouring the disinfectant directly on the spill and cleaning up after the appropriate contact time for the disinfectant has been reached.[3,6] If the spill involves a higher concentration of microorganisms, such as a large body fluid spill or a blood spill in a laboratory, absorbent material can be placed over the spill until all of the fluid is absorbed. The disinfectant solution can be poured over the spill and the absorbent material until both are thoroughly soaked with the disinfectant for the designed contact time. Then the spill site is cleaned. Absorbent powders that solidify liquids are recommended for cleaning large spills.[16]

   OSHA stipulates that blood and body fluid spills be decontaminated with one of the following: an EPA-registered disinfectant effective against Hepatitis B virus (HBV) and the human immunodeficiency virus (HIV), a tuberculocidal disinfectant, or an appropriate dilution of household bleach (5.25 to 6.15 percent sodium hypochlorite solution).[6,13] If the spill occurs on a nonporous surface, a 1:100 dilution of household bleach (one part household bleach plus 99 parts tap water or 0.25 cup of bleach in a gallon of water) is a highly effective disinfectant and is the least expensive.[6] A 1:10 dilution of household bleach (one part household bleach plus nine parts water or 1.5 cups of bleach in a gallon of water) is required for porous surfaces and large spills. Large quantities of blood may inactivate the higher concentration of bleach. Higher concentrations of bleach may also be damaging or corrosive to surfaces.

If a diluted bleach solution is stored in an open container, the chlorine rapidly dissipates and therefore must be prepared daily. When stored in a spray or wash bottle or in a closed, brown opaque container, the bleach solution will remain stable for 30 days and will retain 50 percent of its initial value.[6] For example, a solution with 1,000 parts per million (1:50 dilution) chlorine would contain 500 parts per million (1:100 dilution) chlorine 30 days after initial mixing, if stored in a spray or wash bottle. Any container of bleach solution that has been prepared must be properly labeled with its contents, the dilution, and the expiration date.

Blood and body fluid spills on carpets and upholstery are difficult to clean. Many EPA-registered disinfectants and 1:10 or 1:100 dilution of bleach will stain and/or damage carpets and upholstery. Depending on the type of fabric, these items can be cleaned using an extraction cleaning procedure and standard cleaning products. If the resulting stain is extensive or cannot be removed, the damaged item must be discarded and replaced.

Fortunately, there is no record of anyone having acquired HBV, Hepatitis C virus (HCV), or HIV from environmental surfaces.[1] On the other hand, the surface of medical equipment surfaces may be a reservoir for these pathogens. Multiple outbreaks of HBV have been traced to contaminated items, surfaces of hemodialysis machines, and the environment in clinical laboratories.[17–19] It is imperative that equipment surfaces be routinely cleaned and whenever spills occur.

2. *C. difficile* infections (CDI)
   C. difficile has emerged as a major pathogen of health-care-associated diarrhea and colitis. Multiple outbreaks caused by strains with high mortality rates have been reported.[20–22] The organism produces spores in feces. Surfaces contaminated with feces become a potential reservoir of spores, which can survive in the environment for 5 months.[23] One study found spores in 49 percent of rooms occupied by infected patients and in 29 percent of rooms of asymptomatic carriers. The majority of spores were found in the bathroom and on floors, but they were also found on electronic thermometers, blood pressure cuffs, call lights, television controls, phones, bedrails, linen, intravenous (IV) pumps, tube feedings, light controls, and window sills. Carpeted rooms were more heavily contaminated than uncarpeted ones. *C. difficile* spores were also isolated from surfaces outside of colonized and infected patient rooms, including the workstation of physicians and nurses and in rooms of uninfected patients. Studies have documented that patients acquired CDI from the contaminated hospital environment.[24]

The most frequently used disinfectants (quats and phenolics) are not sporicidal. Some of these agents create harsh conditions that prompt *C. difficile* to transform from the vegetative state to spores.[6] In the past, chlorine-containing compounds were the only sporicidal disinfectants available. Newer EPA-registered sporicidal disinfectants consisting of hydrogen peroxide compounds are also available.[12]

Although bleach is less expensive than other sporicidal agents, its routine use may be problematic. APIC and the CDC recommend a 1:10 dilution of household bleach to clean units with high endemic rates of CDI and during outbreaks of CDI.[6,23,25] Prolonged exposure of metal surfaces and equipment to bleach may lead to pitting and corrosion. Bleach also discolors nonmetal surfaces of hospital furniture. Furthermore, bleach can irritate the respiratory passages of patients, visitors, and HCP. It can cause respiratory distress and induce an asthma attack in susceptible individuals. The odor may also increase nausea in some patients.

Nonbleach-containing sporicidal agents also exude a strong odor that may be unacceptable to some individuals. At present, these newer products are usually more expensive than household bleach.

Ideally, bleach or a sporicidal agent should be used in rooms occupied by patients with CDI, especially for terminal cleaning and during an outbreak. More rigorous use of bleach or other sporicide may be necessary when routine cleaning practices are insufficient to reduce the risks of cross-contamination.[26]

Sporicidal disinfectants alone will not control CDI outbreaks. EVS personnel must follow cleaning procedure according to facility policy and adhere to Contact Precautions by wearing gloves and gowns when cleaning rooms occupied by CDI patients to protect themselves and to prevent the spread of spores.[23–25,27] Researchers have recently shown that use of ultraviolet C (UV-C) light and hydrogen peroxide vapors after physical cleaning will further reduce *C. difficile* from the environment, including from unused supplies.[2,14,28–30]

3. Diarrheal outbreaks: norovirus model
   Meticulous hand hygiene is the key to preventing transmission of microorganisms that cause gastroenteritis. However, when the environment is heavily contaminated, especially during diarrheal outbreaks, hand hygiene alone is not adequate. Extra efforts are needed to thoroughly clean the environment. Because norovirus is the leading cause of gastroenteritis and responsible for multiple outbreaks in healthcare facilities, cleaning methods to control the spread of norovirus serve as a model for controlling diarrheal outbreaks not associated with *C. difficile*.

During outbreaks, the environment, especially high-touch surfaces, are heavily contaminated with microorganisms. High-touch surfaces include commodes, toilets, toilet handles, faucets, bathroom rails, bedrails, telephones, computers, and food preparation areas. The CDC recommends that these surfaces be cleaned and disinfected at least three times per day and that low-touch surfaces be cleaned at least twice a day.[31] Written procedures should emphasize meticulous cleaning moving from the least soiled surface to the most contaminated ones. Gowns and gloves must be worn not only for patient care but also when performing cleaning tasks.

Despite numerous laboratory efforts, routine cell cultures and animal models have failed to satisfactorily replicate Norovirus. This is a major obstacle in the development and testing of exiting and/or new disinfecting products.[32] However, the EPA lists both quats and bleach as being effective against the virus.[13] Regardless of the disinfectant selected, it is important to follow the manufacturer's directions for use and to clean thoroughly. When isolation precautions are discontinued but the patient remains hospitalized, the patient should be moved to a clean room as available, and the previously occupied room terminally cleaned.

Because curtains are touched frequently, CDC and AHE recommend changing privacy curtains when a patient on Contact Precautions is transferred or discharged.[7,31] In addition, upholstered furniture and carpeting must be cleaned and disposable items discarded. CDC recommends that facilities consider steam cleaning furniture and carpets if feasible.[31] If the furniture and carpet are not soiled with feces, using UV-C light or hydrogen peroxide vapors obviates the need for steam cleaning furniture and carpeting.[2,14,28-30] Using these novel methods after physical cleaning helps ensure an environment free of diarrheal pathogens.

4. *Mycobacterium tuberculosis*
Mycobacteria are innately more resistant to disinfectants than most microorganisms. Therefore, it is important to clean surfaces possibly contaminated with mycobacteria, such as *M. tuberculosis,* with an EPA-registered tuberculocidal disinfectant.[1,6,13,33] Disinfectants not tested against the organism are not considered effective. Many tuberculocidal disinfectants require 5- to 10-minute contact time to be effective. Some manufacturers have managed to reduce the contact time. To ensure effective cleaning, the manufacturer's instructions for use must be followed.

5. Nurseries
Bassinets, incubators, scales, and other equipment in nurseries must be cleaned on a routine schedule and when the patient is transferred or discharged. Infants must be removed from their beds before cleaning and disinfecting commences and not returned to them until all surfaces have completely dried.[6] To ensure the longevity of the furniture and equipment, it is important to adhere to the cleaning instructions provided by the manufacturers of the products and to use the disinfectant recommended. Usually a quat

is recommended, as some formulations containing alcohol may cloud the clear plastic on bassinets and incubators.

Because there is an association between the excessive use of a phenolic disinfectant and hyperbilirubinemia in newborns, phenolics are not recommended for use on nursery surfaces (e.g., isolettes, bassinets, scales) with which infants may have contact.[6,34] Surfaces must be thoroughly rinsed and dried after using a phenolic in nurseries.

6. Creutzfeldt-Jakob disease (CJD) and variant CJD (vCJD)
The agents of CJD and vCJD are resistant to commonly used disinfectants. However, there is no evidence that CJD or vCJD has been acquired from environmental surfaces that are routinely cleaned.[6]

The most likely areas where environmental surfaces might become contaminated with CJD or vCJD are in the operating rooms, autopsy areas, and clinical laboratories. Prior to use, surfaces that might become contaminated during a surgical procedure, autopsy, or specimen processing must be lined with impermeable coverings. If unprotected surfaces become contaminated with central nervous system tissues or cerebrospinal fluids containing CJD or vCJD, the body fluids must first be removed using absorbent materials. Then the surface must be flooded with 10,000 to 20,000 parts per million sodium hypochlorite solution (1:5 to 1:3 dilution, respectively, of household bleach). After exposing the surface to the chemical for 30 to 60 minutes, the solution must be removed using additional absorbent material. All materials must then be discarded into a biohazardous waste container. Finally, the surface must be rinsed thoroughly with water.[1]

7. Severe acute respiratory syndrome (SARS)
SARS is caused by the coronavirus. Studies on the virus have shown that it can survive in feces and urine for up to 2 days. EPA-registered virucidal disinfectants and/or a 1:100 dilution of household bleach readily kill the virus.[6] Because the environment of patients with SARS is heavily contaminated, surfaces must be thoroughly cleaned daily and on discharge. Personnel performing cleaning tasks must follow isolation precautions meticulously and wear a gown, gloves, mask, and protective eyewear.[6,25]

8. Multidrug-resistant organisms
Multidrug resistant organisms (MDROs) include MRSA, VRE, multidrug-resistant Gram-negative bacilli, extended-spectrum beta-lactamase producers, carbapenem-resistant Enterobacteriaceae (CRE), and metallo-beta-lactamase CRE. At this time, MDROs have not developed resistance to disinfectants, so no single disinfectant has been specified for use on MDROs.[6] Because these organisms are hardy, removal of MDROs from contaminated surfaces requires meticulous, rigorous cleaning. Contact Precautions must be followed for patient care and cleaning tasks.[25,35] Privacy curtains must be changed after the patient is discharged.[7]

9. Isolation rooms

Except for situations previously discussed, there are no specific disinfectants for use in isolation rooms.[6,25,35] When Isolation Precautions are discontinued but the patient remains hospitalized, the patient should be moved to a clean room as available, and the isolation room should be terminally cleaned and decontaminated using the appropriate disinfectants.

10. Rarely encountered or unusual pathogens

When a rarely seen or unusual organism or an agent of bioterrorism is encountered, it is important to consult the local health department and/or the CDC on methods to clean the environment. According to CDC, most disinfectants are ineffective against *Cryptosporidium*. However, current cleaning and disinfection practices appear satisfactory to prevent healthcare-associated transmission. A 1:10 dilution of household beach is effective against *Escherichia coli* O157:H7.[6] If agents of bioterrorism are encountered and not genetically altered, 1:10 dilution of bleach is used for the initial cleaning, followed by UV irradiation or hydrogen peroxide vapor.[2,6] Genetically altered agents may require more drastic decontamination methods, such as chlorine dioxide gas. In these instances, the facility must consult public health experts at the state or federal (CDC) level.[6]

11. Bed bugs

Bed bugs can be problematic in healthcare facilities, especially those located in major metropolitan areas. Infested patients, visitors, and HCP can bring bed bugs into healthcare facilities on their clothing, in their personal belongings (purses, computers), and in assistive devices such as wheelchairs and walkers. Indications of bed bugs include bites on the individual (some individuals do not react to the bites), egg casings, fecal stains (rusty-colored blood spots due to blood-filled fecal excretions), skin casts in cracks and crevices of belongings, a sweet musty odor, and actually finding the bug. Patients may inform their caretakers that they have bed bugs. If not detected early, the bugs may invade hospital linen, and reside in the cracks and crevices of furniture (mattresses, bed frames, chairs, tables), behind picture frames, under wallpaper, in upholstery and carpeting, and between floor tiles and moldings. Bed bugs can survive for a year without feeding.

If bed bugs are suspected, the patient must be examined and his or her personal belongings should be placed in plastic bags that are tied securely closed or in other sealed containers. Environmental clutter should be removed and the area vacuumed, preferably using a HEPA-filtered vacuum. Reusable equipment such as walkers and wheelchairs should be thoroughly cleaned. For heavy and/or persistent infestations, insecticides may be required.[36] HCP should wear protective gowns and gloves while providing care and when decontaminating infested areas.[25]

When notified about bed bugs, EVS may assist with containment procedures and will contact the facility exterminator. The exterminator will evaluate the furniture and room for infestation, identify items that need to be contained and discarded, apply insecticide, and/or treat the room with high heat (118°F or 48°C for 1 hour).[37] Specially trained dogs may also be used to detect infested sites.

Evaluating Disinfectants

Many types of disinfectants are registered with the EPA. Some are more effective and easier to use than others. When selecting disinfectants or cleaning products, factors to consider include ease of use, efficacy, acceptability, safety, and cost. Resources offered by the manufacturer, such as educational materials and programs, research studies on the product, reliability of the distributor, and availability of the product are important additional considerations.

The IP should have a thorough knowledge of the cleaning agents and disinfectants used by the EVS department. In addition to product names, the IP should know the active ingredient in the product, directions for use, where and how it is used in the facility, how to contact the manufacturer with questions, and where to find the safety data sheet (SDS) (formerly known as material safety data sheet or MSDS). In many facilities, the infection prevention and control committee is required to approve the disinfectants selected for use. (See Chapter 31 Cleaning, Disinfection, and Sterilization for details on types of disinfectants and uses.)

Standard Precautions

The term "Standard Precautions" applies to a synthesis of universal precautions and body substance isolation.[7,25,38] These practices such as wearing appropriate personal protective equipment (PPE) are designed to minimize the risk of transmission of bloodborne pathogens and pathogens from moist body substances. HCP are instructed to handle (1) blood; (2) all body fluids, secretions, and excretions, except sweat; (3) nonintact skin; and (4) mucous membranes as though they might contain infectious agents. EVS personnel must adhere to Standard Precautions when performing cleaning tasks.[7]

Personal Protective Equipment

In accordance with OSHA and CDC, EVS managers and supervisors, in conjunction with IPs and other HCP, determine when PPE is necessary, write usage guidelines, and select and purchase appropriate products. They should educate EVS personnel about PPE, make sure PPE is available, and monitor usage.[5,7,25,39] The PPE training program must include the following:

1. When PPE is worn

2. What PPE to wear

3. How to don, remove, adjust, and wear each type of PPE

4. Limitations of each type of PPE

5. Care, maintenance, useful life, and storage or disposal of PPE

6. Written certification indicating that the employee has received and understood the training

The PPE most commonly used by EVS personnel are gloves, gowns, and protective face wear (mask and eyewear). Gloves must be nonabsorbent. A variety of impervious gloves (latex, latex-free, vinyl, nitrile, rubber) are available. In most situations, disposable gloves are preferred because cleaning, decontaminating, and storing reusable gloves is cumbersome. Heavy-duty gloves are recommended if the task (e.g., handling waste) has a high risk for percutaneous injury. Most heavy-duty gloves are reusable but must be decontaminated after use and stored appropriately. When there is a potential for splashing or splattering, a fluid-resistant or fluidproof gown, apron, mask, and protective eyewear are required.

Disposable apparel must be discarded into the appropriate waste containers after use. Protective apparel that is visibly soiled with blood and other potentially infectious materials must be placed in a biohazardous waste container. Reusable items, especially those that have been contaminated, must be disinfected at the end of each shift or sooner depending on environmental and patient care circumstances. There must be a designated place for soiled reusable aprons, gloves, and other reusable PPE until they can be disinfected. Reusable PPE should not be stored in personnel lockers or removed from the facility.

When cleaning the room of a patient on Isolation Precautions, personnel are required to wear protective apparel, even if the patient is out of the room or has been discharged. For example, when cleaning the room of a patient with suspected or confirmed tuberculosis (TB), EVS personnel must wear a N95 respirator.[25,33] EVS personnel must not remove the PPE until he/she leaves that room. Additionally, the doors to the anteroom (if present) and to the patient room must be kept closed during cleaning.

Cleaning Methods

Policies and Procedures

Every healthcare facility must have written policies and procedures for cleaning. Policies and procedures should be specific to the facility yet meet regulatory requirements and guidelines established by government agencies, accrediting bodies, and professional organizations. Policies and procedures should address departmental concerns, specify cleaning procedures, list the necessary cleaning agents and equipment, provide cleaning schedules, and may include quality control methods. The IP should collaborate with EVS to develop these policies and procedures. At the same time, because these policies and procedures affect the entire facility, a multidisciplinary group consisting of nursing, administration, facilities, pharmacy, clinical engineering, materials management, pharmacy, food services, and information systems should be consulted. AHE's *Practice Guidance for Healthcare Environmental Cleaning* outlines cleaning procedures for a variety of departments in the healthcare facility.[7]

The cleaning process minimizes cross-contamination. Cleaning procedures begin with the least soiled areas and move to the most soiled areas. Cleaning also proceeds from high to low surfaces, allowing dust and debris from high surfaces to fall to lower ones before the lower surfaces are cleaned. To ensure that all surfaces are reached, cleaning should be performed in a systematic manner. After selecting a starting point, such as the door or window, work typically progresses from that point in either a clockwise or counterclockwise direction.

Dusting

Dust contains fungal spores. To capture dust without aerosolizing spores, dusting should be performed using a cloth or dust mop that is chemically treated or made of microfiber. Dusters should never be shaken. All surfaces and fixtures above shoulder height—such as the tops of doors, wall-mounted televisions, overhead lights, pictures, high shelves, and ledges—should be dusted with a specially designed mop or a "high duster," that reaches high surfaces. Dusting should be performed first so particles and dirt that fall to the floor will be captured when the floor is cleaned.

During the dusting procedure, ceilings, ceiling tiles, and walls should be visually inspected for peeling areas and stains, which indicate holes in the roofs and/or leaks from pipes above dropped ceilings or behind walls. Moist false ceiling tiles and drywall provide a growth media for fungi. Leaks and holes should be repaired promptly depending on the extent of the damage and the risks to the environment. Stained tiles should be replaced quickly. Although EVS personnel do not generally repair or replace these items, they are responsible for reporting the problems they encounter to their supervisor or the designated facilities repair person.

Walls, Windows, and Doors

Walls, windows, and doors should be spot-cleaned as needed and completely cleaned on a regular schedule. Door handles and light switches are considered high-touch items. They should be cleaned at least daily, more frequently if an outbreak is occurring, and when a patient is discharged or transferred.[1,7,31] Although designed for floors, microfiber mops can serve as an excellent tool for cleaning walls. However, a clean mop head must be used in these instances.

Horizontal Surfaces

High-touch horizontal surfaces should be wiped at least daily and when visibly soiled with a clean cloth impregnated with an EPA-registered disinfectant. Items that fall in the high-touch category vary by department or area (see Table 107-1). The cleaning cloth can consist of cotton or microfiber, or it can be a disposable synthetic material.

During diarrheal outbreaks in patient areas, the frequency of cleaning for high-touch sites should be increased to at least three times a day, and less frequently touched items should be disinfected at least two times per day.[31]

Table 107-1. Examples of High-touch Surfaces

Patient Room	Bathroom	Operating Room	Kitchen	Office
Bed controls	Bedpan cleaners/flushers	Anesthesia equipment and controls	Cabinet handles	Chair for desk
Bed rails	Call light	Anesthesia supply cart	Countertops	Computer keyboard
Bedside table	Doorknobs	Arm boards	Dishwasher handles and controls	Desk
Bedside commode	Faucet handles	Autoclave door handles	Doorknob	Light switch
Blood pressure cuff	Hand rails	Back table	Drawer handles	Phone
Cabinet knobs	Handheld shower handles	Computer keyboard	Faucets handles	
Call light	Light switch	Door handles	Light switches	
Chair arms/seats	Sinks	IV poles	Phones	
Computer keyboard	Toilet flush	Light switches	Refrigerator handles	
Doorknobs	Toilet seat	Mayo stand	Stove tops and controls	
Glucometer		Medication cart		
Handheld bar- coding devices		Operating bed		
Handheld television control		Operating bed controls		
IV poles		Operating bed straps		
Light switches		Overhead surgical lights		
Monitoring equipment		Patient monitors		
Overbed table		Ring stand		
Privacy curtains		Sponge counter		
Telephone		Storage cabinet door handles		
Thermometer		Telephone		
Ventilator controls		Warmer door handles		

Mattresses and Pillows

Mattress and pillow covers are made of moisture-resistant material and are easy to clean. Fabric covers are not recommended. If used, they must be laundered between patients. Mattresses and pillows with cracks, tears, and permanent stains must be immediately discarded. Mattresses and pillows must be cleaned and disinfected with an EPA-registered disinfectant and according to manufacturer's recommendations between each patient and when visibly soiled.

Many healthcare facilities have contracts with vendors for specialty mattresses and bed frames. The contracts usually stipulate that the vendor deliver, assemble, remove, and decontaminate these mattresses and beds. IPs are responsible for reviewing the company's procedures for cleaning and disinfecting these bed systems. The institution should develop a protocol to ensure that HCP decontaminate the surfaces of these bed systems before they are removed from a patient's room. Bed systems should be placed in a designated area for pickup by the vendor and not left in the hall. If a facility decides to clean and disinfect the specialty bed system, the manufacturer's directions must be closely followed. Because many specialty mattresses and frames are complicated to decontaminate, personnel assigned this task must be appropriately trained and any specific cleaning/disinfecting products or supplies must be available on-site.

Privacy Curtains

The use of privacy curtains varies by patient, and these curtains are often a high-touch item. When patients are not on Isolation Precautions, privacy curtains should be changed and cleaned on a routine schedule and when visibly soiled. The CDC does not suggest more frequent changes if the patient is on Isolation Precautions, but AHE does.[7,35] If the patient is on Contact Precautions, especially for *C. difficile*, MDROs, or norovirus, AHE recommends that the curtains be changed after the patient is discharged, transferred, or taken out of isolation.[7] If the facility

follows these recommendations, it must have an adequate supply of curtains and personnel to remove and hang curtains.

The design of some newer curtains makes hanging and removal easier. In one design, the bottom two thirds of the curtain snaps off while the top third of the curtain remains attached to the curtain track, eliminating the need for tall ladders. The ease of changing these curtains may override their higher cost.

Multiple studies have shown that privacy curtains easily become contaminated with microorganisms and are a source of cross-transmission of pathogens.[40–42] Newer-designed curtains have been impregnated with an antimicrobial coating consisting of one of the following: silver-based compounds, silane quats, triclosan, or zinc pyrithione.[43] When evaluating antimicrobial curtains, the facility should verify that the textile has an EPA registration. This indicates that the manufacturer has shown that the impregnated textile decreases microbial growth, reduces degradation of the fabric over time, and controls odors.[44] The long-term impact of using antimicrobial-impregnated privacy curtains, especially regarding a possible impact on MDROs, is unknown.[77]

If an institution has laundry facilities to wash and dry privacy curtains, the area must meet regulatory requirements for a laundry service. The proper washing and drying temperatures must be reached and the appropriate chemicals must be used. Because these requirements are difficult to achieve and monitor, AHE recommends that healthcare facilities consider using contracted linen and laundry services that meet regulations and are accredited by the Healthcare Laundry Accreditation Council.[7] (Also refer to Chapter 111 Laundry, Patient Linens, Textiles, and Uniforms.)

Window Treatments

Window treatments usually consist of curtains, shades, and blinds. Window curtains are not as frequently touched as bedside curtains and do not need to be changed as often. These curtains should be washable or cleanable. All curtains, shades, and blinds should be cleaned on a regular schedule and when contaminated. Shades are easier to clean than blinds. Cleaning individual slats in blinds is tedious and time-consuming.

Bathrooms

Bathrooms must be cleaned and disinfected at least daily and when visibly soiled. During C. difficile and other diarrheal outbreaks, the frequency should be at least three times per day.[31] The toilet seat and flusher handle, faucet handles, handrails, soap dispenser, nurse call cord, bedpan dispenser, light switch, and doorknobs are high-touch surfaces that require special attention.

The ceramic tile grout around the commode and tub or shower should be checked for mold. If present, the mold must be removed. Countertops that are cracked or moldy must be replaced. If present, mold must be removed using friction and diluted bleach or an appropriate, commercially prepared product.

When a patient has a bedside commode, EVS personnel must clean and disinfect it at least daily and when visibly soiled unless facility policy assigns responsibility for this task to nursing personnel. When no longer needed, the basin must be emptied and the surfaces of the commode decontaminated before it is moved out of the patient's room. This step is particularly important to prevent the spread of enteric pathogens such as norovirus and C. difficile.

Hand Hygiene Agents

In many healthcare facilities, EVS assists in the selection of hand hygiene products and is responsible for maintaining these agents. Because there are multiple product options, EVS personnel should be knowledgeable about the different types of solutions, where each product is used, and how to fill and replace dispensers. EVS personnel should also routinely check expiration dates.

As with disinfectants, the selection of hand hygiene agents is based on use, efficacy, cost, and acceptability by staff. Selection of hand hygiene product should be conducted by a multidisciplinary committee consisting of nurses, physicians, the EVS manager, purchasing agent, and administrator and infection prevention and control department. Hand hygiene products include plain soap (contains no antimicrobial properties), antiseptic (antimicrobial) agents, or alcohol-based waterless agents. Plain soaps are typically placed at sinks for routine hand hygiene in areas where there is minimal potential exposure to blood and body fluids. Examples include public restrooms, administrative departments, offices, and other nonpatient care areas. Antiseptic soaps are recommended in areas where hands have a high risk of acquiring and transmitting HAIs (e.g., patient care areas, laboratories, and decontamination and sterilization).[4]

Soaps are available as a bar, liquid, and tissue or leaflet preparations. Measures must be taken to prevent them from becoming contaminated. Bar soaps are small and should be placed in well-drained containers to minimize contamination. Because maintaining clean dry containers for bar soaps is cumbersome, liquid soaps are often preferred. It is also easier to use disposable pre-packaged containers of liquid soaps, which are discarded when emptied. Emptied reusable containers must be cleaned and dried before they are refilled. The practice of "topping off" often leads to contamination.[4]

Most antiseptics contain one of the following antimicrobial agents: chlorhexidine, triclosan, chloroxylenol (PCMX), iodophor, quat, or alcohol. The antimicrobial activity and degree of persistence of the products vary. Those containing chlorhexidine, triclosan, PCMX, and alcohol are the most popular agents. Chlorhexidine has the broadest spectrum, greatest efficacy, and most sustaining effect.[4] Although recent studies have shown the toxic effects of triclosan, the FDA has not restricted it use.[45] PCMX is more effective against Gram-positive bacteria than Gram-negative bacteria.[4] Iodophors are highly effective against both Gram-negative and Gram-positive bacteria but tend to stain; they are primarily used in the operating rooms or other procedure areas. Antiseptic hand cleaners should be readily available in patient care areas and in areas with routine exposure to blood and body fluids.[4]

When both soaps and antimicrobial agents are used in a facility, competency of personnel on their correct use is crucial. Poor hand hygiene practice has been shown to be a leading cause of HAIs and a significant contributing factor to outbreaks.[4]

Researchers have shown that alcohol-based hand rubs (ABHR) are highly effective hand hygiene agents. The CDC strongly recommends using ABHR except when hands are visibly soiled, before eating, and after using the restroom.[4,46] Initially, the CDC did not recommend that ABHR be used after exposure to spores such as those formed by C. difficile or Bacillus anthracis.[4] It was initially thought that soap and water provided more opportunities for physically removing spores. However, current guidance recommends that ABHR be used if soap and water is not readily available, followed by using soap and water as soon as possible.[46]

Regulatory agencies have established strict guidelines on placement of ABHR in corridors to prevent fires.[47] The regulations for both gel and foam ABHR are identical:

- The corridor must be at least 6 feet wide.

- Dispensers must be at least 4 feet apart.

- Dispenser may not be installed less than 6 inches adjacent to an electrical outlet or switch (measured from the center of the container to the electrical source).

- If mounted over carpeting, the area must have sprinklers and smoke alarms.

Wall-mounted ABHR dispensers may drip, staining walls, floors, and carpets. Stains, especially on carpets, are extremely difficult to remove. Therefore, mounting ABHR dispensers over carpeting is not recommended.

Before they are purchased, dispensers for hand hygiene agents should be closely evaluated for ease of use and delivery of product. Discarding disposable fillers for the dispensers is easier than reprocessing reusable ones. After mounting, the dispensers should be checked regularly to ensure that they are adequately filled, functioning properly, and dispensing the appropriate amount of solution. They should also be cleaned routinely and when visibly soiled.

Some institutions measure hand hygiene compliance based on the amount of hand hygiene products used. If done manually, EVS must save and perhaps count the number of emptied dispensers by the type of agent. Compliance rates are then calculated manually or using a computer program. Newer dispensers automatically count the number of times the agent is dispensed, eliminating the need to save and count the empty containers. These systems are time savers but are expensive and not accurate if a user presses the dispenser more than once.

Waste

Waste is collected from all areas at least daily. If large volumes of waste are generated, more frequent pickups must be scheduled. Filled waste containers must be emptied or replaced before they overflow. Each container should be lined to minimize contamination. In most areas, liners are plastic bags. Lining the container with several layers of bags is optional and helps to reduce contamination of the container if liquids spill. The inside and outside of the receptacles and their covers should be routinely cleaned and disinfected. In patient care areas and departments handling high volumes of blood and body fluids, this should occur at least daily.

There are separate containers for biohazardous and nonbiohazardous waste. Local regulatory agencies may require that biohazardous containers not in continual use (i.e., those in a procedure room or soiled utility room) be kept covered.[48] (Refer to Chapter 113 Waste Management.)

Floors and Carpets

Floors and carpets should be cleaned last to collect any debris that has dropped. Controversy exists about whether a detergent or an EPA-registered disinfectant should be used to clean hard floors. Each healthcare facility needs to decide which to use. A disinfectant must be used to clean floors in critical areas, such as isolation rooms, operating rooms, clean rooms, and other areas designated by the facility. Detergents do not eliminate as much bacteria as disinfectants; however, the microbial load quickly returns to precleaning levels after a disinfectant is used.[6] Studies have not shown floors cleaned with either a detergent or a disinfectant to be associated with an increase in HAIs.[6]

Most floors consist of terrazzo, wood, linoleum, solid or sheet vinyl, vinyl composition tile, rubber, or polylefin.[49] The type of floor determines the cleaning products and cleaning procedures. EVS personnel must be trained to follow the manufacturer's recommendations on the proper cleaning methods and agents to use. Inappropriate cleaning techniques and chemicals may damage the floor.

Floors containing rubber have gained increasing popularity in hospitals. Their cushioning effect reduces serious injuries when a person falls and provides more comfort for HCP when walking and standing. Rubber floors with a finish are easier to maintain than unfinished ones.[49] Finished floors can be cleaned using an autoscrubber. Unfinished rubber floors show more scuff marks, which are difficult to remove and require more manual cleaning time.

Traditionally, the mop-and-bucket technique has been used to clean floors. The cotton string mop and solution in the bucket become increasingly contaminated with use, significantly more so if the solution contains a detergent rather than a disinfectant.[6] The mop and solution must be changed frequently (e.g., every third patient room or hourly) and after being used to clean spills of blood, other potentially infectious materials, an isolation room, or an operating room. These mops must be laundered (by the facility or contracted service) in a manner required by regulatory agencies or discarded.

Use of microfiber mop/pad may be preferred for cleaning floors. They are constructed of densely woven polyester and polyamide (nylon) fibers that have a positive charge, thus they attract negatively charged dust, and are more absorbent than cotton mops.[6,7] Prior to use, the microfiber pads are soaked in a cleaning solution. When cotton and microfiber mops are impregnated with detergent, the microfiber mop significantly reduced the microbial load on the floor compared to the cotton mop. This was not true when both were soaked with a disinfectant.[6,7]

Cotton string mops weigh about 10 pounds, whereas microfiber mops weigh about 2 pounds, making them easier to use. Containers of disinfectants can be attached to some microfiber mop handles and poles, enabling the dispensing of solution during use. These attachments add weight and can be cumbersome for smaller individuals.

After each use, microfiber pads are changed and laundered (or discarded if proper laundering is not an option), thereby minimizing cross-transmission of microorganisms. Prior to first use and after each use, the pads are laundered at less than 140°F (<60°C).[50] The pads are then air dried or machine dried at 100 to 120°F (37.8°–48.9°C). Care is taken not to overdry them, because this results in damage, shrinkage, and shortened life. If used immediately, they may be used damp. The pads should be laundered and dried only with other microfiber products, because they attract lint from other textiles. Bleach and fabric softener are contraindicated in the wash cycle. Fabric softener is also not recommended in the drying cycle.[50] Clean dried pads are stored in clean cabinets or containers.

Microfiber pads have limitations. They may be too large to effectively clean small spaces (behind toilets) or grooved surfaces (grout between tiles), and rough cement surfaces. Nor are they effective on greasy floors in kitchens or high-gloss surfaces such as marble. The pads should not be used to strip and wax floors.

AORN recommends that the operating room floors be wet vacuumed with an EPA-registered disinfectant after all cases have been completed.[7]

Autoscrubbers can be very effective for cleaning floors, leaving them with a clean sheen.[49] These machines apply water and cleaning solution, scrub, extract the liquid, and leave the floor dry in less time than mopping. Scrubbing machines, however, are difficult to use in small spaces. They also need to be properly cleaned and maintained.

Floors also routinely undergo deep scrubbing. During this process, wax and stubborn spots are scrubbed off, then wax is reapplied. This process is lengthy and the floor is often flooded, creating a safety hazard. Therefore, deep scrubbing should be prescheduled during times of low traffic or the area should be closed to traffic when possible.

Carpets collect dust and debris and are more difficult to maintain than floors. Because the dust in carpets contains fungal spores that may induce asthma attacks and cause fatal infections in immunocompromised patients, carpets are not recommended in intensive care units, procedure rooms, high-traffic areas, laboratories, areas where spills frequently occur, and hallways and rooms housing immunosuppressed patients.

Carpets should be maintained with routine vacuuming and deep cleaning, using methods that minimize aerosolization of dust. Vacuums with HEPA filters should be used in critical areas. After a deep scrub, carpets should be thoroughly dried within 72 hours to reduce growth of fungi.[4] During deep scrubbing and drying, carpeted areas should not be used. Carpeting exposed to repeated flooding is likely to contain fungal spores and should be replaced, preferably with nonabsorbent flooring.

Cleaning of floors and carpets should start at the back of the room and move toward the door. Furniture, equipment, and other items should be moved as necessary to enable mopping and vacuuming of areas under them. Floors should be mopped using the "S" stroke, catching dirt and debris on the leading edge of the mop. EVS personnel should pay attention to corners, edges, scuff marks, gum, tar, and other adherent substances. If the area is occupied, EVS personnel should create a dry path (half of the hall or room) to allow people to walk through without falling on the wet floor. Carpets should be vacuumed by moving the machine forward and backward, making a series of "Ns." Each stroke should slightly overlap the previous one. Stains should be removed as soon as possible.

Linen

Clean and soiled linen are stored and handled separately in accordance with state and local health department regulations. Clean linen must be stored in covered carts or enclosed cabinets and kept covered during transport. Personnel must wash their hands before handling clean linen and must wear clean attire.

Personnel must follow Standard Precautions and wear gloves and other PPE (gowns, mask, protective face and eyewear) when handling soiled linen. Linen contaminated with blood and other potentially infectious materials should be labeled or color-coded.[3,25]

Health regulations require that soiled linen be placed in covered containers or bags. Linen containers or bags must be closed securely before being placed into a chute or transported to a temporary holding cart or room. Soiled linen in chutes, carts, or holding rooms should be transported to the laundry facility on a regular schedule (e.g., daily). There is no differentiation in handling linen from isolation and nonisolation patient rooms.

Soiled linen carts should be cleaned and disinfected regularly. If available, a cart washer makes this task easier.

If laundry chutes are available, the chute room and the chute itself should be cleaned on a routine schedule and whenever spills occur. Most likely, the chute room will require daily cleaning. Ideally, laundry chutes should be designed to be at negative pressure to prevent airborne spread of pathogens in the event a bag breaks or opens.[8]

Laundry facilities must adhere to local and state regulations for such entities. There are strict requirements regarding water and drying temperatures, cleaning agents, and work flows. In addition, the Healthcare Laundry Accreditation Council offers voluntary accreditation for commercial laundry facilities. If an institution provides in-house laundry services, IPs are expected to assist in monitoring procedures and compliance with regulatory requirements. If the hospital has a contracted laundry service, the IP should tour the laundry facility, evaluate its compliance with infection prevention and control practices, observe its adherence with regulatory requirements, and become familiar with the contract responsibilities that address infection prevention and control issues. (Also refer to Chapter 111 Laundry, Patient Linens, Textiles, and Uniforms.)

Medical Equipment

If medical equipment is not adequately decontaminated, it may be a source of infection. Some equipment (e.g., IV poles, cardiac monitors, computers, and keyboards) may be easily cleaned by wiping with a disinfectant cloth. Larger more complex equipment requires a two-step process. The surfaces of these items (such as x-ray machines, ventilators, specialty beds) must be carefully disinfected immediately after use and before they are moved out of the room. The equipment should then be taken to a decontamination area, where the necessary internal parts of the machine are removed and disinfected. For example, the outside of the ventilator is wiped with a disinfectant inside the patient's room after use and then taken to the respiratory therapy decontamination room, where the inside components are disinfected. The two-step process is also necessary for any equipment used in high-risk areas such as operating rooms, procedure rooms, and isolation rooms. It is important that each healthcare facility considers cleaning of medical equipment to be a team effort. Facilities need to clearly delineate responsibilities for cleaning medical equipment to specific personnel to avoid lapses in cleaning practice and procedure and to ensure equipment is cleaned by properly trained personnel. Adherence with proper techniques should be monitored as part of a quality/patient safety program. If cleaning is not done correctly, the integrity and warranty of expensive equipment may be compromised.

Equipment Used for Cleaning

Equipment used by EVS (cloths, mops, carts, chemical dispensers, vacuums, autoscrubbers, deep scrubbers, extractors) must be cleaned per facility policy and according to the manufacturer's instructions. More frequent cleaning may be necessary depending on the degree of contamination. Equipment should undergo routine maintenance as specified by the manufacturer and be kept in good repair by a qualified person. Maintenance and repair of mechanical equipment should be documented. Broken equipment that cannot be repaired but is still needed must be replaced.

If a facility has automatic chemical dispensers, the dispensers should be checked and calibrated routinely to ensure accuracy and to control cost. The dispensers should also receive routine maintenance in accordance with the manufacturer's recommendations.

Cleaning items, (e.g., detergent and/or disinfectant solutions, water buckets, cleaning cloths, dusters, toilet brushes, and mops) must be changed routinely and after they are used to clean blood spills or highly contaminated areas such as isolation rooms or operating rooms.[1,8,25] Using contaminated cloths and mops will result in cross-contamination of surfaces, equipment, and hands. CDC recommends changing floor mopping solutions every three rooms and at least every 60 minutes.[6] Used mops and cleaning cloths should never be returned to containers of cleaning solution. They should be laundered or discarded after use. Handles and poles for mops, dusters, and other items should also be wiped with a disinfectant after use.

Reusable cotton cloths and mops should be washed with a detergent and dried at 176°F (80°C) for 2 hours. Reusable clothes may also be disinfected by immersing in hypochlorite (4,000 ppm) for 2 minutes. Cloths and mops exposed to petroleum-based products should be discarded because they are potentially flammable.

EVS staff often use portable carts to transport supplies. Clean items (toilet paper, paper towels, and hand hygiene agents) should be stored above cleaning chemicals. Soiled dusters or mops should be placed in an impervious plastic bag and stored away from clean items; often the bag is hung on the side of the cart for transport. Mop handles/poles and "wet floor" signs

should be wiped with a disinfectant before placing them on the cart. Carts must be cleaned and disinfected per facility policy and whenever visibly soiled. A cart washer may be used if available. Personal items such as purses, lunches, and drinks must not be stored on the carts.

Facilities should keep a log for cleaning equipment (such as vacuum cleaners, floor scrubbers, and carts) to track their location, to ensure that each item receives routine maintenance as recommended by the manufacturer, and to record equipment that is out of service for repairs. It is imperative that cleaning equipment is readily available and functioning properly. Bar coding is helpful in tracking equipment, especially in large institutions.

Innovative Cleaning Methodologies

In the past, the CDC did not recommend using environmental fogging with a quat, phenolic, or formaldehyde as a method of decontaminating air and surfaces.[51] In addition to being a time-consuming and costly procedure, using these chemicals for fogging was not efficacious and possibly toxic. In 2010 the CDC issued a clarification that the previous fogging recommendations do not include newer room decontamination technology (e.g., ozone mists, vaporized hydrogen peroxide). However, CDC does not yet make any recommendation regarding these newer technologies.

Recent studies have shown that ultraviolet (UV) irradiation and hydrogen peroxide vapor are effective in disinfecting the air and surface environments. Because the presence of organic material reduces efficacy, the room must be cleaned prior to using either method.[2,28–30] In addition, the room must be completely unoccupied during these procedures. These methodologies do not replace daily cleaning and, due to their cost, are often used for terminal cleaning or in outbreak situations.

UV light destroys the DNA of microorganisms. It kills vegetative bacteria in 5 to 25 minutes and C. difficile spores in 50 minutes.[2,14] Investigators found that UV treatment further reduced the microbial load of MRSA, VRE, and C. difficile spores significantly, even after the rooms were cleaned.[2,14,28] During UV irradiation, furniture and equipment must be moved away from the walls to allow the rays to reflect off all surfaces. When the walls are painted with nanoscale metal oxides to increase reflection, the effectiveness of UV irradiation is significantly enhanced. The heating, ventilation, and air-conditioning (HVAC) system does not need to be turned off during irradiation.

Similarly, treating a cleaned room with vaporized or aerosolized dry mist hydrogen peroxide significantly reduces HAIs, especially C. difficile and many infections caused by MDROs.[2,14,29] The process evenly distributes hydrogen peroxide throughout the room. This method is useful for cleaning complex equipment and furniture and does not require moving them away from walls. Supplies left in the rooms are also decontaminated and do not need to be discarded.[30]

Hydrogen peroxide vapors can be harmful if inhaled. Prior to decontamination, the room must be unoccupied, the HVAC system switched off, and doors taped. Decontamination takes approximately 2 to 5 hours.[2,14]

The costs of the UV and hydrogen peroxide vapor systems are significant. When evaluating the systems, facilities must weigh expense with the potential cost savings associated with lowering HAI rates.

Cleaning Schedules

Facilities should develop written cleaning schedules to meet the needs of each area being serviced. Cleaning schedules should specify the frequency and timing for cleaning each area of the facility and should be closely followed by EVS staff. Below are recommended cleaning procedures and schedules for specific areas.[1,7,8]

Inpatient Rooms

Cleaning to be performed and when the patient is discharged includes:

- High dusting;
- Spot cleaning of walls, windows, and doors;
- Cleaning of light fixtures, ledges, tables, chairs, beds, and floors;
- Vacuuming of carpets should be performed daily and when the patient is discharged.

Close attention should be paid to cleaning frequently handled medical equipment (e.g., sphygmomanometer, cardiac monitor, IV pump, IV pole, computers).

The same daily cleaning procedures should be followed for isolation and nonisolation rooms. After use in an isolation room, cleaning equipment (water and bucket, cleaning cloths, mop head) should be discarded or disinfected before use in another room. Only clean equipment should be used in rooms of patients who are immunocompromised (such as those who are neutropenic and those who are new transplant recipients).

Operating Rooms

Cleaning operating rooms requires a team approach involving EVS, nursing, and anesthesia personnel.[7,8] Personnel must follow specific cleaning principles in the operating rooms. The operating room suite should have dedicated cleaning tools (e.g., carts, buckets, mop handles, dusting poles, vacuums, floor machines).[7,8] To prevent aerosolization of chemicals, EVS staff should wipe surfaces with disinfectant-saturated wipes or microfiber cloths instead of using spray bottles of disinfectants. Because blood and body fluid spills are common in the OR, EVS staff should use disinfectants that are EPA-registered as effective against HBV and HIV. Sodium hypochlorite is not recommended for routine use

because it can cause pitting of metal and some other surfaces.[6] Alcohol is not recommended for damp dusting large environmental surfaces because it dries too quickly. Reusable cleaning cloths must be freshly laundered and lint-free.

There are three distinct cleaning times for operating rooms: before the first case of the day, between cases, and at the end of the day.[7,8] Before the first case of the day, horizontal surfaces in the operating room should be damp-dusted with a clean lint-free cloth or a wipe dampened with a disinfectant. This task may be performed by nursing personnel. They also clean minor blood and body fluid spills and splatters during a case.

After each case, EVS, nursing, and anesthesia personnel decontaminate horizontal surfaces, equipment, examination tables, anesthesia machines, medication carts, and other items used during a procedure. Personnel should pay particular attention to high-touch surfaces, taking care not to overlook machine controls, the tops of linen hampers, waste containers, computers, and phones. Cleaning of equipment should be delegated to personnel specifically trained to perform each task. Clean, lint-free cloths or disposable wipes should be used for each case. Cleaning cloths or wipes should be changed frequently and after contact with blood and body fluids. The cleaning process should progress from high to low and from clean to dirty. Items that are reprocessed, sharps, and biohazardous and nonbiohazardous waste must be placed in their respective containers and transported to their respective holding areas.

Floors in the operating rooms must be cleaned and disinfected after each case. Reusable string or microfiber mops may be used in between cases and should be changed after each use.[7] If a cotton mop-and-bucket system is used, a clean mop head and fresh disinfectant solution must be used for each case. It is only necessary to clean a 3- to 4-foot perimeter around the operative table after each case unless wider perimeter of contamination is identified.[8] Placing tacky mats on the floor at the entrances to operating rooms is not recommended. There is no evidence that they help prevent infections.[8]

At the conclusion of the operating schedule, blood spills and splatters not wiped up during the case must be cleaned and all items in the operating room decontaminated. Personnel should pay meticulous attention to high-touch surfaces. AORN recommends that floors be cleaned with a wet-vacuum and an EPA-registered disinfectant after the completion of scheduled cases.[8] Ventilation grilles, shelves, and cabinets in the operating rooms should be cleaned routinely and when soiled. If not removed, dust and particles collecting in these areas can become airborne and be a source of contamination or infection. Scrub sinks, work rooms, utility rooms, and corridors should also be thoroughly cleaned and disinfected regularly when OR traffic is low, not in use, and/or whenever visibly contaminated.

Procedure Rooms

Procedure rooms are cleaned and disinfected in a similar manner to operating rooms. After each case, all horizontal surfaces and shields should be cleaned and disinfected.[6,7] Floors may be spot cleaned unless more extensive decontamination is necessary. At the end of each day, all surfaces and the floor should be thoroughly cleaned and disinfected. Walls should be cleaned on a routine schedule and as needed.

Examination Rooms

After each patient, linen or paper on the examination table must be changed or discarded, respectively.[7] Reusable pillows, patient care equipment such as blood pressure cuffs, and horizontal surfaces must be wiped with a disinfectant. Walls and floors should be spot cleaned as needed.

At the end of each day, all horizontal surfaces and the entire floor must be thoroughly cleaned and disinfected. Used suction containers, if present, must be changed, and all waste containers must be emptied or, if disposable and almost full, must be discarded.

Dialysis Unit

Outbreaks of viral hepatitis that have occurred in dialysis units have been linked with contaminated environmental surfaces (dialysis chair or bed, countertops, external surfaces of dialysis machines, scissors, hemostats, clamps, blood pressure cuffs, stethoscopes). Therefore, these surfaces must be routinely disinfected with an EPA-registered disinfectant after each patient. Blood splatters and spills must be cleaned and disinfected immediately using a disinfectant effective against *Mycobacterium tuberculosis* or HBV and HIV or a 1:100 dilution of household bleach.[6] The dialysis machines must be disinfected according to the manufacturer's specifications. Waste containers should be lined with plastic bags; bags must be closed securely and removed after each patient. The waste containers should be disinfected at the end of each day. Floors should be cleaned and disinfected at the end of each day and when visibly soiled. (Refer to Chapter 39 Dialysis.)

Dental Examination Areas

The CDC classifies environmental surfaces in dental offices as clinical contact and environmental surfaces.[6] Clinical contact surfaces are equivalent to high-touch surfaces. Uncovered high-touch surfaces in examination areas (instrument tables, instrument handles, switches, exam lights, sink handles, computer keyboards, x-ray machine controls) must be disinfected with an EPA-registered disinfectant after each patient. The disinfectant must be either tuberculocidal and/or effective against HBV and HIV.

Disposable coverings on clinical contact surfaces such as lights and handles must be removed and discarded after each patient. These surfaces must be disinfected if the disposable coverings are torn or damaged, when the surface is visibly soiled, and at the end of the day.

In contrast to clinical contact surfaces, environmental surfaces (sinks, countertops, waste containers) must be cleaned and

disinfected at least daily and whenever visibly soiled.[6] When the environment is contaminated with blood or body substances, it must be cleaned and disinfected immediately.

Clinical Laboratories

Laboratories require daily cleaning. Countertops must be decontaminated after each shift and whenever spills occur. Most likely, laboratory personnel perform this task. When the laboratory closes, EVS performs a more thorough cleaning of countertops and sinks. EVS personnel do not clean laboratory instruments or equipment. Cleaning schedules for laboratories open 24 hours a day require coordination between EVS and laboratory personnel.

Both biohazardous and nonbiohazardous wastes must be collected at least daily. Laboratories operating 24 hours a day require more frequent waste removal, perhaps at least once a shift. Floors must be cleaned and disinfected daily.

Offices and Conference Rooms

In offices and conference rooms, weekly dusting of horizontal surfaces and cleaning of floors or vacuuming carpets is sufficient, unless they are visibly soiled. Noncritical surfaces, including high-touch surfaces, may be cleaned with a detergent instead of a cleaner/disinfectant.[6,7]

Clean Rooms

In a healthcare facility, a clean room is designed to control airborne contaminants to within predetermined limits. Healthcare providers most frequently use clean rooms for the compounding of sterile pharmaceutical products. A clean room consists of an anteroom and an inner work room with HEPA air filters and closely controlled temperature and humidity levels.

Similar to the operating room, clean rooms have dedicated cleaning equipment. Cleaning equipment must be cleaned and disinfected per an established schedule. Cleaning starts from the innermost work room (location of laminar airflow hood) and moves outward to the anteroom.

Depending on the class of the clean room and local regulatory requirements, the cleaning of surfaces and floors may need to be performed more than once a day and may require documentation in a logbook.[7] Cleaning effectiveness must be performed, evaluated, and documented per facility policy.

Ambulatory Surgery Centers

The number of ambulatory surgery centers (ASCs) in the United States has grown significantly in the last decade, but only recently have regulatory requirements addressing infection control been rigorously enforced. The operating rooms and patient care areas in an ASC must be cleaned and disinfected in the same manner as operating rooms in acute care facilities. However, a survey of 68 ASCs showed that 18.8 percent had environmental cleaning issues. It was found that 12.7 percent of high-touch surfaces in the operating rooms were not appropriately cleaned with an EPA-registered disinfectant, and 18 percent of high-touch surfaces in patient care areas outside of the operating room were not properly cleaned with an approved disinfectant. Blood glucose meters were not cleaned and disinfected after each use in 32.1 percent of the surveyed facilities.[52]

After a serious outbreak occurred in 2009 in Nevada, the U.S. Department of Health and Human Services and The Joint Commission (TJC) initiated more rigorous and focused infection control surveys using criteria consistent with acute care.[53] A 2013 report by TJC stated that two of the top five most challenging standards for ASCs to meet during the first half of 2013 were preventing HAIs associated with medical equipment, devices, and supplies and assessing the risk for acquiring and transmitting infections.[54] Many ASCs need qualified EVS personnel and IPs to guide and implement the appropriate environmental cleaning procedures and infection prevention and control measures. See Chapter 64 Ambulatory Surgery Centers for more information.

Long-term Care Facilities

As the population continues to age and an increasing number of healthcare services are provided outside the hospital, the utilization of long-term care has evolved beyond the traditional concept of residential or custodial care. At the same time, an increasing number of long-term care facility (LTCF) residents are becoming colonized and infected with MDROs and C. difficile, leading to outbreaks associated with these pathogens. As colonized or infected individuals move between various levels of care and/or between care settings, the risk of potential cross contamination and/or transmission of infection increases.[78]

One of the major methods of preventing and controlling the spread of MDROs and CDIs is thorough environmental cleaning. The cleaning requirements in an LTCF must be described and monitored per facility policy. However, compliance can be problematic. A study of high-touch points in an LTCF showed that only 26.9 percent of the surfaces were cleaned and disinfected according to policies. With skilled leadership and persistent training, adherence eventually tripled. This improvement was due to strong leadership in EVS and infection prevention and control and effective training programs.[55]

Outpatient Settings

The CDC's guidelines for cleaning outpatient settings are similar to those for inpatient areas.[56] High-touch surfaces in the patient zone (examination rooms, procedure rooms, and waiting areas) must be cleaned and disinfected with an EPA-registered product. Floors may be cleaned with a detergent instead of a disinfectant unless contaminated with blood and body fluids. Because there are a minimum number of areas at risk for blood and body fluid spills, more carpeting may exist in this setting. Carpets should be vacuumed daily, spot cleaned as needed, and thoroughly cleaned on a routine schedule.

Waste should be collected daily. Because there is significantly less biohazardous waste in this setting, facilities may utilize one large biohazard container in a central location. However, a biohazardous waste container must be available in procedure rooms.

Outpatient facilities must have written cleaning policies and procedures and provide training to staff who perform these functions. Facilities should assign responsibility for overseeing environmental cleaning and disinfecting to a qualified person.

Evaluating Effectiveness of Cleaning

The inanimate environment plays a role in the transmission of HAIs. Studies have shown that only 32 percent of more than 110,000 objects in inpatient and outpatient healthcare facilities are thoroughly cleaned.[2] Reasons for inadequate cleaning may include improper cleaning methods, lack of training, ineffective cleaning agents, and/or malfunctioning equipment. If a room is not thoroughly cleaned and disinfected, transmission of potential pathogens existing on environmental surfaces may occur. Therefore, it is important to evaluate the efficacy of cleaning.[7]

Visual Inspection

EVS personnel and their supervisors should inspect their completed work to ensure that visible evidence verifies that basic cleaning has been done. A written checklist can be helpful in assisting the inspection process. Visual assessments are helpful in determining if a room is aesthetically pleasing and in assessing whether the individual has completed his or her tasks but are not considered a reliable indicator of cleaning efficacy.[2]

ATP Bioluminescence Test

One way to evaluate cleaning efficacy is by using the adenosine triphosphate (ATP) bioluminescence method. In this method, swabs of environmental surfaces are placed in reagent and the amount of light is read by the bioluminometer. Results are indicated as either acceptable or unacceptable. The presence of ATP serves as a surrogate for microbial contamination. It does not identify actual pathogens. Furthermore, the level of ATP detected by bioluminescence has not been conclusively correlated with infection transmission.

Recently, the reliability of the ATP test used in healthcare has been challenged. Because each bioluminometer has its own scale, Whitely et al. questioned the lack of RLU standardization of the readings and the ability to compare results.[58] Rutala also showed that this method was not as accurate as fluorescent markers.[2] Although the test is easy to learn and may be performed quickly, the reagents, bioluminometer, and software to record the readings can be costly.

Fluorescent Markers

Another simple method to evaluate cleanliness is applying an invisible fluorescent mark onto soiled surfaces.[2,27,59] If the fluorescent mark is visible under a UV light after the surface is cleaned, the surface requires recleaning. The fluorescence is simple to apply, easy to remove, and inexpensive, and the results are known immediately after the cleaning has been completed. The mark is applied by dipping a swab in the fluorescent solution and touching the tip of the swab to a surface. A prepackaged fluorescent marking gel containing an applicator sponge is easier to use than a cotton swab and makes uniform circular marks but is only available if a computerized data collection system is also purchased.

When the fluorescence is applied without the knowledge of EVS or patient care providers findings have been extremely educational. Florescent marking can enable the IP or other supervisor to provide immediate feedback to EVS personnel before they leave the area and show them the missed spots that need to be recleaned.

Cultures

Quantitative environmental cultures (swabs, Rodac plates) have been used as markers of thorough cleaning; less than 2.5 cfu/cm^2 is considered acceptable.[13] However, routine culturing of surfaces is not the first choice because it is costly, time-consuming, and results take at least 1 day. Environmental sampling may be performed when recommended by infection prevention and control. Cultures can be helpful in identifying the source of an outbreak.

Comparison of Methods

Rutala et al. compared the accuracy of the different methods for measuring the thoroughness of cleaning.[2] Colony counts on Rodac plates served as the gold standard. In the study, cultures found that 97.7 percent of surfaces studied were adequately clean. In contrast, the ATP bioluminescence indicated that 13.2 to 26.4 percent (depending on the RLU used) were properly cleaned; visual inspection showed that 43.8 percent were properly cleaned; and the fluorescent markers identified that 71.1 percent of surfaces were properly cleaned.

The swab and fluorescent method is the quickest and cheapest test. Most importantly, immediate feedback to personnel leads to more thorough recleaning. Carling et al. demonstrated that use of fluorescent markers and education improved cleaning from 48 percent (9,910 of 20,646 surfaces) to 77 percent (7,287 of 9,646 surfaces).[60]

Waste Management

Every healthcare institution has a solid waste disposal system that involves EVS. There are written policies and procedures for segregating and handling biohazardous waste, nonbiohazardous waste, chemical waste, radioactive waste, regular waste, and recyclable waste. Regardless of type, the institution is responsible for all waste, from creation to final disposal. In this chapter, only biohazardous and nonbiohazardous wastes are discussed. (Refer to Chapter 113 Waste Management.)

Regulations for handling biohazardous waste differ by state. The appropriate state and local regulations governing the institution must be reviewed and followed. IPs must be familiar with these regulations, the institution's waste handling process, and responsibilities of waste haulers contracted to handle biohazardous and nonbiohazardous waste. Infection prevention and control should review documentation indicating that the waste hauler has met regulatory requirements. Because the facility is responsible for its biohazardous waste from creation to disposal, it is imperative that it is properly handled by both the institution and the hauler.

Definition of Biohazardous Waste

Biohazardous waste is also referred to as regulated, infective, infectious, and medical waste. OSHA defines biohazardous waste as[5]:

- Any liquid or semiliquid blood or other potentially infectious materials

- Contaminated items that would release blood or other potentially infectious materials in a liquid or semiliquid state if compressed

- Items that are caked with dried blood or other potentially infectious materials and are capable of releasing these materials during handling

- Sharps (includes needles, scalpel blades, glass, pipettes) contaminated with blood and body fluids

- Pathological and microbiological wastes containing blood or other potentially infectious materials

Definitions of biohazardous waste may differ depending on state and local regulatory agencies. For example, the Illinois Environmental Protection Agency classifies animal waste, isolation waste, and all sharps (used and unused), as biohazardous waste.[48]

Waste from isolation rooms is not considered biohazardous unless visibly contaminated with blood and other potentially infectious materials.[25]

Laboratory waste containing live cultures of microorganisms and agents of bioterrorism must be destroyed before transport out of the laboratory area. Live organisms have a potential for spreading. For example, an outbreak of TB occurred among personnel in a waste disposal facility because cultures of M. tuberculosis were aerosolized.[61]

Handling of Waste

Biohazardous and nonbiohazardous waste must be maintained in separate containers.[1,5,48] If wastes are inadvertently mixed, the nonbiohazardous waste is considered biohazardous.

Most biohazardous waste can be placed in a single leak-resistant red plastic bag or other color bag and labeled with a biohazard symbol. If punctured or contaminated, the bag is placed into a second bag. Bags must be securely closed when filled. Biohazardous waste containers not in continuous use, such as those in the soiled utility room, procedure room, or nursing station, must be kept covered.[1,5,48]

When biohazardous waste is stored, it is placed in a puncture-resistant, leakproof container that is labeled with a biohazard symbol or color-coded red.[5] The storage area must be well ventilated and inaccessible to rodents and other pests.[1]

Waste containers must be noncombustible. Those with a capacity greater than 20 gallons (76 liters) must be covered with lids composed of noncombustible materials.[62]

To prevent percutaneous injuries, personnel should never use their hands or feet to compress waste in containers. Plastic bags should be handled from the top and kept from contacting the body.

Sharps disposal containers must be puncture-resistant, leakproof at the sides and bottom, and closable.[1,5] They must be closed before they are overfilled. HCP must ensure that no sharps protrude from the opening of disposal containers.

Glass is regarded as a sharp and discarded in a puncture-resistant container. Glass containing blood or other potentially infectious materials is treated as biohazardous waste. Some states and some local regulatory agencies consider uncontaminated glass as biohazardous waste.[48]

Broken glass is never handled, even if hands are gloved. Broken pieces should be picked up and discarded by devices such as forceps or by a brush and dustpan or two pieces of cardboard. If contaminated, the device must be decontaminated or discarded.

Waste bags must be secured and closed before transport. Nonbiohazardous waste can be placed in a chute, if available, or kept in a temporary holding room such as a designated "soiled" utility room. Biohazardous waste should never be placed into a chute because of the possibility of rupture or leakage. Biohazardous waste must be transported in securely covered containers to the temporary holding room.

Although there are no guidelines specifying the frequency for cleaning chutes, they should be cleaned on a routine schedule (usually at least daily) and whenever spills occur. The waste holding room should be cleaned at least daily and restricted to EVS employees. The degree of restriction (e.g., locks on doors) varies by local health regulations. Waste should be removed from chute rooms and holding rooms at least daily and sent for final disposal.

Traditionally, biohazardous waste has been either incinerated or steam sterilized. Alternatives to incineration and steam sterilization have been developed and facilities must be carefully evaluate them to determine their acceptability. Incinerators, autoclaves, or other treatment devices must meet all local, state, and federal regulatory agency requirements. Pathologic wastes must be incinerated.

Reusable biohazardous waste containers must be disinfected by the waste hauler with an EPA-registered disinfectant before they are returned to the healthcare institution for use.

Pest Control

The presence of cockroaches, flies, maggots, ants, mosquitoes, mice, rats, bed bugs, and other pests is an indicator of an unhealthy environment in a healthcare facility. Institutions are responsible for minimizing, and if possible eliminating, vermin. The key to minimizing pests is to eliminate food sources, eliminate areas for nests and burrows, install tightly fitting screens on windows and doors, seal off penetrations to the outside, and apply pesticides. Food should not be left out in the open, eating areas should be cleaned frequently, and food waste should be discarded in sealed containers. It takes diligence to control pests, especially bed bugs.

Bed bug control is more costly than other types of pest control.[63] The exterminator needs to make multiple visits and may use a variety of chemicals, expensive high heating devices, and/or a specially trained dog. As of the publication of this book, the heating device for eliminating bed bugs costs approximately $15,000 and a bed bug sniffing dog costs $600 per visit.

EVS is usually responsible for coordinating pest control. Although EVS personnel play a major role in minimizing pests, facilities should consider contracting licensed professionals to handle toxic pesticides. Should the facility decide to have internal employees handle pesticides, these individuals must be licensed and adhere to regulatory requirements (OSHA, state, and local). They must be educated and trained about the chemicals used, the appropriate PPE needed, and when, where, and how to use the pesticides.

Impact of Design on Environmental Contamination

Although institutions have made great strides in creating a warm and welcoming atmosphere by using colorful and patterned fabrics on curtains, furniture, and carpeting; hanging restful pictures; and painting walls various colors, building an environment that minimizes infections is an emerging discipline.[64] Both the EVS manager and IP need to have an understanding of how elements of these new designs impact EVS policies and procedures including associated risks, time requirements, and the need for specialized training or equipment and associated cost.

To help prevent cross-transmission of infections, new healthcare constructions are required to have a full bathroom in each single inpatient rooms.[65] Institutions that provide family-focused care should expect that patients' relatives may stay overnight, and these institutions may consider extending visiting hours. The increased footage for private rooms and bathrooms and presence of overnight guests can create more work for EVS at a time when budgets are forcing reductions in the workforce.

To encourage hand hygiene, sinks must be located so that clinicians can face patients and ABHR dispensers should be placed in line sight of clinicians. With increasing use of hand hygiene agents, EVS personnel need to check and restock dispensers and to clean stains on the walls and floors more frequently.

Many newer textiles (mops, curtains, upholstery, and carpeting) are more durable to bleach and other harsh chemicals. They may also be coated with antimicrobial materials such as metal alloys, quats, and triclosan. Studies have shown that incorporating silver alloys into privacy curtains reduces the microbial contamination of the curtains.[43,44] This may decrease the frequency needed for changing these curtains. Because triclosan and quats are germicides, there is a risk for organisms to develop resistance. *P. aeruginosa* is intrinsically resistant to triclosan.[66]

Silver and copper have been incorporated into some hard environmental surfaces and shown to minimize the growth of microorganisms. The effectiveness of silver on hard surfaces in reducing HAIs has not been adequately studied in health-care.[66] However, Salgado et al. found that copper not only reduced the microbial counts on surfaces but also the HAI rate.[67] Incorporating copper into the bed rails, overbed tables, intravenous poles, and arms of visitor chairs in intensive care units at three hospitals reduced the HAI rate from 0.081 to 0.034 ($p = 0.013$).

Creating a sharklike pattern on high-touch surfaces has also been shown to be antimicrobial. This pattern consists of millions of microscopic diamonds arranged in a pattern that mimics shark skin and prevents bacteria from colonizing and creating a biofilm.[68] Researchers speculate that the pattern requires too much energy for the bacteria to colonize. To date, this technology has not been applied to healthcare.[66]

Operating Budget

The EVS departmental operating budget consists of two major components: (1) salaries and wages and (2) supplies. With the increasing cost of healthcare and reduction in reimbursement for care provided, healthcare administrators are cutting departmental budgets and positions. EVS is often affected and needs strong leaders who can meet these challenges. These leaders can create novel ways to save money while providing the services demanded. At the same time, these directors, managers, and supervisors can offer training, support, and guidance to employees that stem from a wide range of backgrounds.

The number of full-time equivalents (FTEs) assigned to EVS may be based on the square footage of the facility, the responsibilities of the department, and existing conditions. If EVS is responsible for the care of the grounds surrounding the facility, then the square footage of the land requiring care (mowing grass, removing snow, etc.) is included in the calculations. Inside duties vary by assignment. Cleaning an isolation room requires more time than cleaning a regular patient room. Likewise, cleaning the operating room is more demanding than cleaning the corridor. There also needs to be personnel sufficient to handle emergencies, such as an outbreak of gastroenteritis or

C. difficile, and to prepare for special occasions (e.g., surveys by regulatory agencies or TJC, etc.). Assignments for each EVS employee should be carefully planned to maximize productivity with a minimal number of personnel.

Cross-training employees on tasks creates a more versatile EVS department and makes scheduling and assignments easier. For example, personnel may be trained to clean patient rooms and clinics, as well as offices, laboratories, corridors, and operating rooms. Alternatively, they may be cross-trained to wash walls, deep scrub and polish floors, shampoo carpets, and handle waste.

To further maximize efficiency and productivity, supervisors should provide each EVS employee with the daily work flow, establish departmental expectations for the time to complete the tasks, and oversee the work. The goals for turnaround times (between cases in the operating rooms, for cleaning patient rooms) should be realistic. For example, 30 minutes may be the expected turnaround time between cases in the operating rooms and after a patient is discharged or transferred from an inpatient room. If more time is needed, the reasons should be documented and evaluated. EVS supervisors can then make necessary improvements, such as providing re-education programs for staff or allocating more time for similar situations in the future.

Cleaning products and supplies should be evaluated and selected based on effectiveness and cost savings. Items purchased in bulk through a major supplier or through a healthcare consortium are cheaper than when purchased by an individual department or a single facility. EVS may also consider using generic and environmentally friendly products. EVS supervisors should consult with the infection prevention and control team and other personnel outside of the department with expertise about products. If EVS considers saving money by using detergents instead of disinfectants on floors or regular hand-washing soaps rather than antiseptics, EVS should collaborate with the infection prevention and control team prior to implementing the practice.

EVS supervisors must take care to avoid compromising the quality of work to meet budgetary demands. Preventing the environment from being a source of HAIs is crucial for both patient safety and cost savings. The cost of one of the following HAIs is greater than the salary of some EVS employees: catheter-associated bloodstream infection ($45,814), ventilator-associated pneumonia ($40,144), surgical site infection ($20,785), and CDI ($11,285).[69]

EVS Hygiene, Attire, and Behavior

EVS personnel are expected to have good personal hygiene and appearance. They should be educated to bathe daily, contain their hair so it does fall onto their faces and work area, and practice meticulous hand hygiene. Supervisors should make informal or formal inspections on personnel hygiene and appearance. Supervisors can partner with the infection prevention and control department to conduct period observations of hand hygiene compliance (see Table 107-2).

Table 107-2. PROCEDURE FOR MONITORING HAND HYGIENE AND ISOLATION COMPLIANCE

Directions for Hand Hygiene Observations:
1. Observe EVS personnel working in a patient care area.
2. Examples of when EVS personnel should perform hand hygiene:
   a. Before gloving and entering a patient's room to clean.
   b. After cleaning a patient's room and gloves were removed.
   c. Before handling clean lining.
   d. After bagging soiled linen and placing it in the linen cart.
   e. After collecting and bagging trash and placing it in trash cart.
   f. After handling soiled cleaning equipment (mops, cloths, buckets).
   g. After using the bathroom.
   h. Before and after eating or going on a break.
3. Document compliance or noncompliance with hand hygiene. One person can be observed for multiple opportunities to perform hand hygiene.
4. Make at least 20 observations per month per unit (equivalent to 1 observation per day if working an 8-hour shift).
5. Compliance = use of alcohol hand rub or soap and water to wash hands. Length of time hands are washed will not be a factor.
6. At the end of each month, calculate the compliance rate. After obtaining 3 months of data, make a graph. Infection prevention and control may assist with this task.
   a. Denominator = number of observations.
   b. Numerator = number of individuals compliant with hand hygiene.
   c. Compliance rate = number of individuals compliant with hand hygiene / number of observations ×100.
7. Share data with the staff in EVS, infection prevention and control, infection prevention and control committee, and other hospital committees and leadership groups.
8. EVS supervisors should re-educate noncompliant individuals, especially repeat offenders on hand hygiene.

Observing compliance with Isolation Precautions is conducted in the same manner. The need for gowning, gloving, and masking will depend on the isolation category. The individual entering an isolation room can be observed for compliance with both Isolation Precautions and hand hygiene. Again, noncompliant personnel should be educated on the importance of adherence with Isolation Precautions.

Most healthcare facilities issue uniforms to EVS personnel, instruct them on how to launder them, and require them to wear a clean uniform each work day. Uniforms serve to identify EVS personnel for patients, visitors, and other employees.

If EVS personnel work in departments that require scrub attire, they must be educated about regulations regarding how and where scrubs may be worn. Scrubs for the operating rooms and other procedural areas may not be worn home or out of the hospital, and they are laundered by a licensed laundry facility.

Personnel should also be trained in proper behavior when interacting with patients, visitors, and other HCP. They should be instructed to knock on doors before entering, to greet people, and to interact with others courteously. Their behavior can affect patient and HCP satisfaction, an important component of the success of the facility.

Education and Training

All new employees must undergo a documented orientation session. Although most regulatory agencies require only annual education on infection prevention and control, more frequent programs are recommended.

Educational Topics

Orientation programs include at least the following: OSHA's Bloodborne Pathogens Standard, Hazard Communication Standard (revised 2013), TB control, cleaning techniques, cleaning agents, isolation precautions, N95 particulate respirators, personal attire and hygiene, and behavior.[70] Subsequent training programs address and review bloodborne pathogens, hazard communication, TB control, C. difficile, pest control (including cockroaches, rodents, and bed bugs), gastrointestinal outbreaks, EVS problems identified by regulatory agencies, cleaning

methods, new products and equipment, Isolation Precautions, special topics (aspergillosis in immunosuppressed patients and latex allergies), weaknesses identified by continuous quality improvement, and competency testing programs.

Education programs should also cover the health and hygiene of individuals. Personnel with symptoms of highly communicable diseases (fever, fever and flulike symptoms, fever and rash of unknown etiology, diarrhea, conjunctivitis, and exposed open draining lesions) should be instructed to stay home. The importance of complying with screening for TB, obtaining specific vaccinations (influenza, Hepatitis B, tetanus, pertussis, rubella, rubeola, and chickenpox), and adhering with postexposure follow-up should be emphasized.

Educational Levels and Proficiency in English

Educational programs should be appropriate to the personnel. EVS personnel often have the lowest education level among HCP. In 2007, the U.S. Census Bureau showed that 28 percent of "janitors and building cleaners" aged 25 years or over did not have a high school diploma, and 12.3 percent had 9 years or less of education.[71]

The lack of education can be compounded by an increasing number of individuals who are not proficient in English. From 1980 to 2010, there was a 158 percent increase of Americans over age 5 (almost 60 million people) who lived in homes where a language other than English was spoken. In comparison, during this same time period, there was only a 22 percent increase in the proportion of Americans over age 5 living in households where only English was spoken.[72] Among the 166.1 million Americans aged 25 and over who spoke only English at home, 9.6 percent had less than a high school education, but among the 42.7 million people aged 25 and over who spoke a language other than English at home,

APIC Text of Infection Control and Epidemiology

29.2 percent lacked a high school diploma.[73] There has been a significant growth in the number of non-U.S.-born workers in the U.S. civilian labor force.[74,75]

The lack of formal education correlates with low levels of health literacy and understanding the rationale for cleaning policies and procedures, such as for isolation rooms.[76,77] If the reasons for cleaning are not understood, thoroughness of cleaning suffers, and the environment becomes a source of cross-transmission of infections. Subsequent HAIs lead to undesirable patient outcomes and increased healthcare cost.

Educational Methods

To enhance learning, it is important to use multiple educational methods such as visual aids, return demonstrations, repetition, and hands-on training. Interpreters may be provided for individuals not proficient in English but who are able to perform the job. Small groups allow more interaction and are often more effective than large ones.

After an education session, each individual should demonstrate competency, which can be done in a variety of ways. If literacy and/or proficiency in English are not a problem, a written test can be administered. Alternatively, an oral test can be given. Personnel may also be asked to provide a return demonstration. Return demonstrations can be a means of overcoming educational and language barriers. Testing the thoroughness of cleaning is another measure of competency. If an individual is unable to demonstrate competency after an education session, further education and training should be provided.

Education programs should be documented in the following manner:

- Name of employee and his/her identification number
- Name of the presenter
- Qualifications of the presenter, if required (e.g., by OSHA's bloodborne pathogens standard)
- Brief outline of the presentation
- Date and location of the program
- Documentation of the employee's competency.

Frequent re-education programs on the same topics, especially thoroughness of cleaning for high-touch surfaces, may be beneficial.

Performance Improvement Programs

Every EVS department should have ongoing performance improvement programs (also referred to as quality improvement). EVS leadership should develop evaluation tools to study and measure their activities. Thresholds or benchmarks should be established and data collected and analyzed. The findings determine the necessary improvements.

There are numerous topics for performance improvement activities. Determining the thoroughness of cleaning is generally the highest priority. Other studies include meeting turnaround times, appropriate use of PPE, adhering to Isolation Precautions, complying with hand hygiene, and evaluating staff knowledge of cleaning policies and procedures. Personnel may also be evaluated for using cleaning products properly, following procedures after exposure to blood and other potentially infectious materials or hazardous chemicals, and obtaining the influenza vaccination.

Much emphasis has been placed on minimizing turnaround time and maximizing efficiency with fewer EVS personnel and a reduced budget. These performance improvement projects serve as important barometers to ensure the quality of work is not compromised by these reductions.

One of the most effective steps to improving quality is providing feedback on performance improvement findings to staff as soon as possible. For example, one study showed that when results of a fluorescent test were shared with personnel, the thoroughness of cleaning increased from 48 percent to 77 percent.[60]

SUMMARY AND CONCLUSIONS

There is increasing evidence that the environment of a healthcare facility serves as a source of HAIs. An effective EVS program prevents the environment from becoming a reservoir of microorganisms. This is achieved by establishing regular cleaning schedules, outlining thorough and effective cleaning methods, writing policies and procedures, selecting appropriate cleaning agents and equipment, educating and training EVS personnel, and monitoring the thoroughness of cleaning. Infection prevention and control and EVS should partner with each other and other healthcare personnel to achieve these goals.

FUTURE TRENDS

For many centuries, caustic and toxic substances such as carbolic acid and lye were used to clean healthcare institutions. Over the years, equally effective but safer and less harmful disinfectants have been developed. In the 1980s and early 1990s, manufacturers made disinfectants effective against HIV and viral hepatitis. During the next decade, chemists found a way to reduce the long contact times for tuberculocidal disinfectants. Researchers recently created an effective hydrogen peroxide disinfectant that is not highly toxic or corrosive, has minimal odor, and claims the fastest killing time for bacteria and viruses. If effective, its use will increase dramatically in healthcare. As new diseases and microorganisms emerge (SARS, Middle East respiratory syndrome, coronavirus, monkeypox, MDROs, *C. difficile*), testing the efficacy of cleaning against new pathogens and developing new, easier, and more effective disinfectants continues to present a challenge.

Over the years, new products and novel technologies have improved the efficiency and efficacy of cleaning. Some of these inventions include chemical dispensers delivering premixed and premeasured amounts of solutions, microfiber textiles, detachable mop handles with attachments for dispensing cleaning agents, vacuum cleaners with HEPA filters, autoscrubbers, and other floor cleaning machines. Within the past few years, great strides have been made in reducing antimicrobial contamination on high-touch surfaces by impregnating silver into textiles and incorporating copper into hard surfaces. UV light and hydrogen peroxide vapors are novel methods used to ensure maximum cleanliness of the environment after physical cleaning. An increasing number of hospitals are exploring and adopting these new technologies.

In spite of the technological developments, adherence to good, basic environmental cleaning practices remains the biggest challenge. The key to meeting this challenge is education of HCP, strong leadership, and good communication between EVS, infection prevention and control, and other departments.

REFERENCES

1. Sehulster LM, Chinn RY, Arduino MJ, et al. Guidelines for environmental infection control in healthcare facilities: recommendations of CDC and the Healthcare Infection Control Practices Advisory Committee (HICPAC). CDC website. 2003. Available at: http://www.cdc.gov/hicpac/pdf/guidelines/eic_in_hcf_03.pdf.
2. Rutala WA. *New technology in environmental cleaning and evaluation.* Presented at 40th Annual APIC Conference, Fort Lauderdale, FL, June 10, 2013. Available at: http://disinfectionandsterilization.org/slide-presentations/.
3. Weber DJ, Rutala WA. Understanding and preventing transmission of healthcare associated pathogens due to the contaminated hospital environment. *Infect Control Hosp Epidemiol* 2013 May;34(5):449–452.
4. Boyce JM, Pittet D, Healthcare Infection Control Practices Advisory Committee, et al. Guidelines for hand hygiene in health-care settings: recommendations of the Healthcare Infection Control Practices Advisory Committee and the HICPAC/SHEA/APIC/IDSA Hand Hygiene Task Force. *MMWR Recomm Rep* [serial online]. 2002;51(No. RR-16). Available at: http://www.cdc.gov/mmwr/PDF/rr/rr5116.pdf.
5. Occupational Safety and Health Administration (OSHA). *Occupational exposure to bloodborne pathogens, Final rule, 29 CFR Part 1910.1030.* Fed Reg 1991;56:64004–64080. Available at https://www.osha.gov/pls/oshaweb/owadisp.show_document?p_table=standards&p_id=10051.
6. Rutala WA, Weber DJ, Healthcare Infection Control Practices Advisory Committee (HICPAC). *CDC guideline for disinfection and sterilization in healthcare facilities, 2008.* CDC website. Available at: http://www.cdc.gov/hicpac/pdf/guidelines/Disinfection_Nov_2008.pdf.
7. Association for Healthcare Environment (AHE). *Practice guidance for healthcare environmental cleaning,* 2nd ed. Chicago: American Hospital Association, 2012.
8. Association of Operating Room Nurses (AORN). *Perioperative standards and recommended practices, and guidelines, 2013.* Denver: AORN, 2013.
9. Food and Drug Administration (FDA). *Public health notification from FDA, CDC, EPA and OSHA: avoiding hazards with using cleaners and disinfectants on electronic medical equipment.* FDA website. March 21, 2013. Available at http://www.fda.gov/MedicalDevices/Safety/Alertsand Notices/PublicHealthNotifications/ucm062052.htm.
10. Sax H, Allegranzi B, Uçkay I, et al. 'My five moments for hand hygiene': a user-centered design approach to understand, train, monitor and report hand hygiene. *J Hosp Infect* 2007 Sep;67(1):9–21.
11. Arnow P, Sadigh M, Costas C, et al. Endemic and epidemic aspergillosis associated with in-hospital replication of *Aspergillus* organisms. *J Infect Dis* 1991 Nov;164(5):998–1002.
12. Environmental Protection Agency. *Guidance for the efficacy evaluation of products with sporicidal claims against Clostridium difficile.* Available at: http://www.epa.gov/oppad001/cdif-guidance.html.
13. Environmental Protection Agency (EPA). *EPA's registered sterilizers, tuberculocides, and antimicrobial products against certain human public health bacteria and viruses.* EPA website. May 9, 2012. Available at: http://www.epa.gov/oppad001/chemregindex.htm.
14. Rutala WA, Weber DJ. Disinfectants used for environmental disinfection and new room decontamination technology. *Am J Infect Control* 2013 May;41(5 Suppl):S36–S41.
15. Boyce JM, Havill NL. Evaluation of new hydrogen peroxide wipe disinfectant. *Infect Control Hosp Epidemiol* 2013 May;34(5):521–523.
16. Coates D, Wilson M. Powders, composed of chlorine-releasing agent acrylic resin mixtures or based on peroxygen compounds, for spills of body fluids. *J Hosp Infect* 1992 Aug;21(4):241–252.
17. Alter MJ, Ahtone J, Maynard JE. Hepatitis B virus transmission associated with a multiple-dose vial in a hemodialysis unit. *Ann Intern Med* 1983 Sep;99(3):330–333.
18. Syndman DR, Bryan JA, Macon EJ, et al. Hemodialysis-associated hepatitis: report of an epidemic with further evidence on mechanisms of transmission. *Am J Epidemiol* 1976 Nov;104(5):563–570.
19. Lauer JL, VanDrunen NA, Washburn JW, et al. Transmission of hepatitis B virus in clinical laboratory areas. *J Infect Dis* 1979 Oct;140(4):513–516.
20. Muto CA, Pokrywka M, Shutt K, et al. A large outbreak of *Clostridium difficile*-associated disease with an unexpected proportion of deaths and colectomies at a teaching hospital following increased fluoroquinolone use. *Infect Control Hosp Epidemiol* 2005 Mar;26(3):273–280.
21. McDonald LC, Kilgore GE, Thomson A, et al. An epidemic, toxin gene-variant strain of *Clostridium difficile*. *N Engl J Med* 2005 Dec 8; 353(23):2433–2441.
22. McDonald LC, Owings M, Jernigan DB. *Clostridium difficile* infection in patients discharged from U.S. short-stay hospitals, 1996-2003. *Emerg Infect Dis* 2006 Mar;12(3):409–415.
23. Association for Professionals in Infection Control and Epidemiology (APIC). *Guide to preventing Clostridium difficile infections.* Washington, DC: APIC 2013. APIC website. 2013. Available at http://apic.org/Resource_/EliminationGuideForm/59397fc6-3f90-43d1-9325-e8be75d86888/File/2013CDiffFinal.pdf.
24. Kaatz GW, Gitlin SD, Schaberg DR, et al: Acquisition of Clostridium difficile from the hospital environment. *Am J Epidemiol* 1988 Jun;127(6): 1289–1294.
25. Siegel JD, Rhinehart E, Jackson M, et al. *2007 Guideline for isolation precautions: preventing transmission of infectious agents in healthcare settings.* CDC website. Available at: http://www.cdc.gov/hicpac/pdf/isolation/Isolation2007.pdf.
26. Cohen SH, Gerding DN, Johnson S, et al. Clinical practice guidelines for *Clostridium difficile* infection in adults: 2010 update by the Society for Healthcare Epidemiology of America (SHEA) and the Infectious Diseases Society of America (IDSA). *Infect Control Hosp Epidemiol* [serial online]. 2010 May;31(5):431–455. Available at: http://www.jstor.org/stable/10.1086/651706.
27. Muto CA, Blank MK, Marsh JW, et al. Control of an outbreak of infection with hypervirulent *Clostridium difficile* BI strain in a university hospital using a comprehensive bundle approach. *Clin Infect Disease* 2007 Nov 15;45(10):1266–1273.
28. Sitzlar B, Deshpande A, Fertelli D, et al. An environmental disinfection odyssey: evaluation of sequential interventions to improve disinfection of *Clostridium difficile* isolation rooms. *Infect Contol Hosp Epidemiol* 2013 May;34(5):459–465.
29. Barbut F, Yexli S, Otter JA. Activity in vitro of hydrogen peroxide vapour against *Clostridium difficile* spores. *J Hosp Infect* 2012 Jan;80(1):85–87.
30. Otter JA, Nowakowski E, Salkeld JAG, et al. Saving costs through the decontamination of the packaging of unused medical supplies using hydrogen peroxide vapor. *Infect Control Hosp Epidemiol* 2013 May;34(5): 472–478.
31. MacCannell T, Umscheid CA, Agarwal RK, et al. *Guideline for the prevention and control of Norovirus gastroenteritis outbreaks in healthcare settings.* CDC website. Available at: http://www.cdc.gov/hicpac/pdf/norovirus/Norovirus-Guideline-2011.pdf.
32. Duizer E, Schwab KJ, Neill FH, Atmar RL, Koopmans MP, Estes MK. Laboratory efforts to cultivate noroviruses. *J Gen Virol.* 2004 Jan;85(Pt 1): 79–87.
33. Jensen PA, Lambert LA, Iademarco MF, et al. Guidelines for preventing the transmission of Mycobacterium tuberculosis in health-care settings, 2005. *MMWR Recomm Rep* [serial online]. 2005 Dec 30;54(RR-17):1–141. Available at: http://www.cdc.gov/mmwr/pdf/rr/rr5417.pdf.
34. Robertson AF. Reflections on errors in neonatology: II. the "heroic" years, 1950-1970. *J Perinatology* [serial online]. 2003 Mar;23(2):154–61. Available at: http://www.neonatology.org/pdf/7210843a.pdf.
35. Siegel JD, Rhinehart E, Jackson M, et al. *Management of multidrug-resistant organisms in healthcare settings, 2006.* CDC website. Available at: http://www.cdc.gov/hicpac/pdf/MDRO/MDROGuideline2006.pdf.
36. Armed Forces Pest Management Board (AFPMB). Technical Guide No. 44: Bed Bugs - Importance, Biology, and Control Strategies. AFPMB website. 2012. Available at: http://www.afpmb.org/sites/default/files/pubs/techguides/tg44.pdf.
37. Howard J, Hudson N, Calvert G. *Bed Bugs!* CDC website. November 29, 2012. Available at: http://blogs.cdc.gov/niosh-science-blog/2011/09/29/bed-bugs/.

38. Garner JS. Universal Precautions and Isolation Systems. In: Bennett JV, Brachman PS, editors. *Hospital Infections*, 3rd ed. Boston: Little, Brown, 1992;231–244.

39. Occupational Safety and Health Administration (OSHA). *29 CFR Part 1910.132. Personal protective equipment.* OSHA website. June 8, 2011. Available at: https://www.osha.gov/pls/oshaweb/owadisp.show _document?p_table=standards&p_id=9777.

40. Ohl M, Schweizer M, Graham M, Heilmann K, Boyken L, Diekema D. Hospital privacy curtains are frequently and rapidly contaminated with potentially pathogenic bacteria. Am J Infect Control. 2012 Dec;40(10):904–906.

41. Trillis F, Eckstein EC, Budavich R, Pultz MJ, Donskey CJ. Contamination of hospital curtains with healthcare-associated pathogens. Infect Control Hosp Epidemiol. 2008 Nov;29(11):1074-1076.

42. Klakus J, Vaughan NL, Boswell TC. Meticillin-resistant Staphylococcus aureus contamination of hospital curtains. J Hosp Infect. 2008 Feb;68(2): 189–190.

43. Pyrek KM. *Soft-surface contamination in the patient-care environment and antimicrobial textiles.* Infection Control Today website. August 2013. Available at: http://www.infectioncontroltoday.com/~/media/Files /Medical/Ebooks/2013/08/08-13ICT-antimicrobial-textiles-secure.ashx.

44. Luebbert PP, Claffey TM. *Evaluating antimicrobial textiles.* Infection Control Today website. July 3, 2013. Available at: http://www.infection controltoday.com/galleries/2013/06/evaluating-antimicrobial-textiles.aspx.

45. Food and Drug Administration (FDA). *Triclosan: what consumers should know.* FDA website. December 16, 2013. Available at: http://www.fda.gov /ForConsumers/ConsumerUpdates/ucm205999.htm.

46. American Society for Healthcare Engineering (AHSE). *JCAHO announces their official stance of alcohol-based hand rub dispensers in Perspectives.* ASHE Regulatory Advisory, March 10, 2006.

47. Illinois Environmental Protection Agency (EPA). *Potentially infectious medical wastes: a summary of regulatory requirements.* IL EPA website. Available at http://www.epa.state.il.us/land/waste-mgmt/factsheets /general-regs.html.

48. DuBose J, Labrador A. *Sustainable resilient flooring choices for hospitals: perceptions and experiences of users, specifiers and installers.* Health Care Research Collaborative, December 2010. Available at: https://www.premierinc.com/safety/topics/construction/downloads /SustainableResilientFlooring-May2011.pdf.

49. Microfiber Wholesale. *Washing microfiber.* Riverside, CA. Microfiber Wholesale website. Available at: http://www.microfiberwholesale.com /Washing-Microfiber.html.

50. Centers for Disease Control and Prevention (CDC), Healthcare Infection Control Practices Advisory Committee (HICPAC). *Environmental fogging clarification statement.* CDC website. November 25, 2013. Available at: http://www.cdc.gov/hicpac/.

51. Schaefer MK, Jhung M, Dahl M, et al. Infection control assessment of ambulatory surgical centers. JAMA 2010 Jun 9;303(22):2273–2279.

52. U.S. Department of Health and Human Services (HHS). *National action plan to prevent healthcare-associated infections: roadmap to elimination. Ambulatory surgical centers.* HHS website. Available at: http:// www.hhs.gov/ash/initiatives/hai/ambulatory_surgical_centers.html.

53. The Joint Commission (TJC). *Most challenging requirements for the first half of 2013.* TJC website. Available at: http://www.jointcommission.org /assets/1/6/Table_for_jconline_August_28_13.pdf.

54. Applegate D, Simpson K, Wesley K, et al. *Evaluation of environmental cleaning in long term care facilities.* Poster presentation at IDWeek, October 20, 2012. Available at: https://idsa.confex.com/idsa/2012 /webprogram/Paper35775.html.

55. Centers for Disease Control and Prevention (CDC). *Guide to infection prevention in outpatient settings: minimum expectations for safe care.* CDC website. April 2011. Available at: http://www.cdc.gov/hai/pdfs /guidelines/ambulatory-care-04-2011.pdf.

56. Farkas J. *ATP bioluminescence as a rapid microbiological method.* Hygiena website. 2005.Available at: http://www.hygiena.net/tech _library-article-01a.html.

57. Whitely GS, Derry C, Glasbey T. Reliability testing for portable adenosine triphosphate bioluminometers. *Infect Control Hosp Epidemiol* 2013 May; 34(5):538–540.

58. Carling PC, Briggs JL, Perkins J, et al. Improved cleaning of patient rooms using a new targeting method. *Clin Infect Dis* 2006 Feb 1;42(3):385–388.

59. Carling PC, Parry MM, Rupp ME, et al. Improving cleaning of the environment surrounding patients in 36 acute care hospitals. *Infect Control Hosp Epidemiol* 2008 Nov;29(11):1035–1041.

60. Johnson KR, Braden CR, Cairns KL, et al: Transmission of *Mycobacterium tuberculosis* from medical waste, JAMA 2000 Oct 4;284(13):1683–1688.

61. Coté R. *Informational ballot NFPA 101.* June 2011. Available at: http://www.nfpa.org/Assets/files/AboutTheCodes/101/101_A2011 _SAF-FUR_ROP_Supballot.pdf.

62. Centers for Disease Control and Prevention (CDC), U.S. Environmental Protection Agency (EPA). *Joint statement on bed bug control in the United States from the U.S. Centers for Disease Control and Prevention (CDC) and the U.S. Environmental Protection Agency (EPA).* CDC website. May 8, 2013. Available at: http://www.cdc.gov/nceh/ehs /publications/bed_bugs_cdc-epa_statement.htm.

63. Zimring C, Denham ME, Jacob JT, Cowan DZ, Do E, Kamerow D, et al. Evidence-based design of healthcare facilities: opportunities for research and practice in infection prevention. *Infect Control Hosp Epidemiol* 2013 May;34(5):514–516.

64. Facilities Guidelines Institute (FGI). *Guidelines for design and construction of health care facilities.* Dallas, TX: FGI, 2010.

65. Weber DJ, Rutala, WA. Self-disinfecting surfaces: Review of current methodologies and future prospects. *Am J Infect Control* 2013 May;41(5 Suppl): S31–S35.

66. Salgado CD, Sepkowitz KA, John JF, Michels JRHT, Schmidt MG. Copper surfaces reduce the rate of healthcare acquired infections in the intensive care unit. *Infect Control Hosp Epidemiol* 2013 May;34(5):479–486.

67. Sharklet Technologies, Inc. *Inspired by nature.* Corporate website. Available at: http://sharklet.com/technology/.

68. Zimlichman E, Henderson D, Tamir O, et al. Health care-associated infections: a meta analysis of costs and financial impact on the US health care system. *JAMA Intern Med* [serial online]. 2013 Dec 9;173(22):2039–46. Available at: http://archinte.jamanetwork.com/article.aspx?articleid= 1733452.

69. Occupational Safety and Health Administration (OSHA). *29 CFR 1910.1200, Hazard Communication.* OSHA website. June 12, 2013. Available at: https://www.osha.gov/dsg/hazcom/hazcom-faq.html#1.

70. U. S. Bureau of Labor Statistics (BLS). *Table 1.11: Education attainment for workers 25 years and older by detailed occupation, 2009.* BLS website. December 19, 2013. Available at: http://www.bls.gov/emp /ep_table_111.htm.

71. Ryan C. *Language use in the United States 2011: American Community Survey reports.* U.S. Census Bureau website. August 2013. Available at: http://www.census.gov/prod/2013pubs/acs-22.pdf.

72. United States Census Bureau. Table S1603, *Characteristics of people by language spoken at home: 2012 American Community Survey 1-year estimates.* U.S. Census Bureau website. 2012. Available at http://fact finder2.census.gov/faces/tableservices/jsf/pages/productview.xhtml?pid =ACS_12_1YR_S1603&prodType=table.

73. Toossi M. Labor force projections to 2012: The graying of the U.S. workforce. *Monthly Labor Review* 2004 (February):37–57.

74. United States Department of Labor. *Labor Force Characteristics by Race and Ethnicity, 2011. Report 1036.* Bureau of Labor Statistics website. August 2012. Available at: http://www.bls.gov/cps/cpsrace2011.pdf.

75. Koh KH, Berwick DM, Clancy CM, Bauer C, Brach C, Harris LM, Zerhusen EG. New federal policy initiatives to boost health literacy can help the nation move beyond the cycle of costly "crisis care." *Health Aff (Millwood)* 2012 Feb;31(2):434–443.

76. Kutner M, Greenberg E, Jin Y, et al. *The Health Literacy of America's Adults: Results From the 2003 National Assessment of Adult Literacy.* NCES 2006–483. U.S. Department of Education National Center for Education Statistics website. September 2006. Available at: http://nces. ed.gov/pubs2006/2006483.pdf.

77. Schweizer M, Graham M, Ohl M, Heilmann K, Boyken L, Diekema D. Novel hospital curtains with antimicrobial properties: a randomized, controlled trial. *Infect Control Hosp Epidemiol.* 2012 Nov;33(11):1081–1085.

78. Schweon S, Burdsall D. Hanchett M, et al. *Infection Preventionist's Guide to Long-Term Care.* Washington DC: Association for Professionals in Infection Control and Epidemiology, 2013.

APPENDIX

Definitions of Cleaning and Disinfection Terminology

Antimicrobial agent: any agent that kills or suppresses the growth of microorganisms.

Antiseptic: substance that prevents or arrests the growth or action of microorganisms by inhibiting their activity or by destroying them. The term is used especially for preparations applied topically to living tissue.

Bactericide: agent that kills bacteria.

Contact time: time a disinfectant is in direct contact with the surface or item to be disinfected. For surface disinfection, this period is framed by the application to the surface until complete drying has occurred.

Contaminated: state of having actual or potential contact with microorganisms. As used in healthcare, the term generally refers to the presence of microorganisms that could produce disease or infection.

Cleaning: removal, usually with detergent and water or enzyme cleaner and water, of adherent visible soil, blood, protein substances, microorganisms, and other debris from the surfaces, crevices, serrations, joints, and lumens of instruments, devices, and equipment by a manual or mechanical process that prepares the items for safe handling and/or further decontamination.

Culture: growth of microorganisms in or on a nutrient medium; to grow microorganisms in or on such a medium.

Decontamination: according to OSHA, "the use of physical or chemical means to remove, inactivate, or destroy bloodborne pathogens on a surface or item to the point where they are no longer capable of transmitting infectious particles and the surface or item is rendered safe for handling, use, or disposal" [29 CFR 1910.1030]. In healthcare facilities, the term generally refers to all pathogenic organisms.

Detergent: cleaning agent that makes no antimicrobial claims on the label. They comprise a hydrophilic component and a lipophilic component and can be divided into four types: anionic, cationic, amphoteric, and nonionic.

Disinfectant: usually a chemical agent (but sometimes a physical agent) that destroys disease-causing pathogens or other harmful microorganisms but might not kill bacterial spores. It refers to substances applied to inanimate objects. The EPA groups disinfectants by product label claims of "limited," "general," or "hospital" disinfection.

Disinfection: thermal or chemical destruction of pathogenic and other types of microorganisms. Disinfection is less lethal than sterilization because it destroys most recognized pathogenic microorganisms but not necessarily all microbial forms (e.g., bacterial spores).

EPA Registration Number or **EPA Reg. No.**: a hyphenated, two- or three-part number assigned by EPA to identify each germicidal product registered within the United States. The first number is the company identification number, the second is the specific product number, and the third (when present) is the company identification number for a supplemental registrant.

Germicide: agent that destroys microorganisms, especially pathogenic organisms.

Inanimate surface: nonliving surface (e.g., floors, walls, furniture).

Infectious microorganisms: microorganisms capable of producing disease in appropriate hosts.

Intermediate-level disinfectant: agent that destroys all vegetative bacteria, including tubercle bacilli, lipid and some nonlipid viruses, and fungi, but not bacterial spores.

Low-level disinfectant: agent that destroys all vegetative bacteria (except tubercle bacilli), lipid viruses, some nonlipid viruses, and some fungi, but not bacterial spores.

Log reduction in bacteria: Log means logarithm, which is the exponent of 10. A 1-log reduction stands for a 10-fold (one decimal) or 90 percent in numbers of live bacteria. For example 100 bacteria would be reduced to 10. A 3-log reduction on a surface with 1,000,000 microbes would leave 1,000 organisms, which equates to a 99.9 percent reduction.

Microorganisms: animals or plants of microscopic size. As used in healthcare, generally refers to bacteria, fungi, viruses, and bacterial spores.

Mycobacteria: bacteria with a thick, waxy coat that makes them more resistant to chemical germicides than other types of vegetative bacteria.

One-step disinfection process: simultaneous cleaning and disinfection of a noncritical surface or item.

Personal protective equipment (PPE): specialized clothing or equipment worn by an employee for protection against a hazard. General work clothes (e.g., uniforms, pants, shirts) not intended to function as protection against a hazard are not considered to be PPE.

Quat: abbreviation for *quaternary ammonium compound*, a surface-active, water-soluble disinfecting substance that has four carbon atoms linked to a nitrogen atom through covalent bonds.

Safety data sheet (SDS) (formerly known as material safety data sheet or MSDS): information document on substance to ensure that individuals handle and/or use it safely. Information on the sheet includes physical data (melting point, boiling point, flash point), toxicity, health effects, first aid reactivity, storage, disposal, PPE, and procedures for handling spills. Every EPA-registered cleaning agent has an SDS.

Sanitizer: agent that reduces the number of bacterial contaminants to safe levels as judged by public health requirements. Commonly used with substances applied to inanimate objects. According to the protocol for the official sanitizer test, a sanitizer is a chemical that kills 99.999 percent of the specific test bacteria in 30 seconds under the conditions of the test.

Spore: relatively water-poor round or elliptical resting cell consisting of condensed cytoplasm and nucleus surrounded by an impervious cell wall or coat. Spores are relatively resistant to disinfectant and sterilant activity and drying conditions (specifically in the genera *Bacillus* and *Clostridium*).

Sterile or **sterility**: state of being free from all living microorganisms. In practice, usually described as a probability function (e.g., as the probability of a microorganism surviving sterilization being one in one million).

Tuberculocide: an EPA-classified hospital disinfectant that also kills *M. tuberculosis* (tubercle bacilli). EPA has registered approximately 200 tuberculocides. Such agents also are called *mycobactericides*.

Use-life: the length of time a diluted product can remain active and effective. The stability of the chemical and the storage conditions (e.g., temperature and presence of air, light, organic matter, or metals) determine the use-life of antimicrobial products.

Vegetative bacteria: bacteria that are devoid of spores and usually can be readily inactivated by many types of germicides.

Virucide: an agent that kills viruses to make them noninfective.

*Adapted from Rutala WA, Weber DJ, HICPAC. CDC guideline for disinfection and sterilization in healthcare facilities, 2008, Glossary, p. 97-103. http://www.cdc.gov/hicpac/pdf/guidelines/Disinfection_Nov_2008.pdf.

CHAPTER 108

Laboratory Services

Peggy Prinz Luebbert, MS, MT(ASCP), CIC, CHSP
Healthcare Interventions, Inc.
Omaha, NE

ABSTRACT

Infection preventionists should look at the laboratory setting from two perspectives. First, laboratorians are at high risk of occupational infections, and there must be specific policies and procedures in place to protect them from organisms in their unique environment. Second, the laboratory is an essential partner of infection preventionists in assisting in the detection and characterization of pathogens, not only for healthcare-associated infections but also for organisms associated with research, community, or bioterrorism outbreaks.

KEY CONCEPTS

- The laboratory is a unique work environment that may pose infectious disease threats to those who work there.

- Multiple federal, state, and private agencies provide guidelines and regulations to assist in ensuring the safety of the laboratory environment.

- The most common primary accreditation agency for laboratories is the College of American Pathologists.

- Biosafety levels were established to ensure that the laboratory environment is adequately equipped with measures to ensure the safety of those working in them or the surrounding environment.

- Special procedures are used to ensure the safe handling and transport of biohazardous materials.

- Being one of the largest generators of infectious waste in the healthcare setting, specific procedures exist for laboratory infectious waste management.

- The Laboratory Response Network has been established in the United States as a diverse and collaborative system to provide rapid diagnosis and response in the case of a bioterrorism event or related public health emergency.

- The laboratory's role in the infection prevention program is fundamental.

BACKGROUND

Laboratories are special, often unique, work environments that present identifiable infectious disease risks to persons in or near them. Laboratory-acquired infections have been reported since early in the 20th century, but only in the 1970s were accurate data available to try to validate risk.[1-6] In a series of published surveys, Pike and associates reported over 3,000 cases of laboratory-acquired infections (LAIs), including brucellosis, tuberculosis, typhoid, streptococcal infections, and hepatitis.[5,6] These incidents and more current studies suggest that most laboratory-acquired infections occur when the mode of transmission is unknown or as a result of error, accident, or carelessness in the handling of a clinical specimen or known pathogen.[6]

Many federal and state agencies and private organizations in the United States have developed specific guidelines to assist in minimizing the transmission of infectious agents in the laboratory. These include:

- Clinical Laboratory Standards Institute (CLSI), formerly the National Committee for Clinical Laboratory Standards (NCCLS)[7-17]

- Occupational Safety and Health Administration (OSHA)[18]

- Centers for Disease Control and Prevention (CDC)[19,20]

- Food and Drug Administration (FDA)[21]

- American Association of Blood Banks (AABB)[22]

- The College of American Pathologists (CAP)[23]

- Biosafety in Microbiological and Biomedical Laboratories (BMBL)[24]

- American Society for Microbiology (ASM) (refer to Supplemental Resources)

Infection Prevention Team Member

Laboratorians should be an integral part of an infection prevention program. The microbiology laboratory helps to detect and identify microorganisms so that the infection control team can monitor, prevent, and control infection transmission. The laboratorian assists clinicians in diagnosing and determining treatment options. In addition to performing these traditional roles, a laboratory representative should participate as a member of the healthcare organization's infection prevention and control committee. Responsibilities of the laboratorian for the organization and on the infection prevention and control committee may include:

- Explaining basic microbiology principles and practices

- Interpreting culture results and explaining which microbiological approaches could be used to solve specific infection control problems

- Explaining the advantages and limitations, the scope and adequacy, and the costs of microbiological methods used to detect, identify, and assess the antimicrobial susceptibility of the most common pathogens implicated in healthcare-associated infections (HAIs)

- Providing information about changes in methods, reagents, or instrumentation that may substantially affect the laboratory's ability to detect and characterize pathogens that may cause HAIs

- Actively participating in surveillance efforts while planning and executing microbiological and molecular epidemiological investigation of HAIs

- Providing an annual antibiogram of common organisms and the trending associated with resistance patterns of clinical isolates to antibiotics

The laboratory and the infection prevention staff must communicate regularly to be effective. Infection preventionists (IPs) should regularly make rounds in the laboratory to ask questions, review microbiological and molecular epidemiological results, and discuss current issues. Additionally, laboratory staff should become active in infection prevention conferences offered by the Association for Professionals in Infection Control and Epidemiology (APIC) to remain current on issues and concerns that may relate to the laboratory.

BASIC PRINCIPLES

Accreditation

The Centers for Medicare & Medicaid Services (CMS) regulates all laboratory testing (except research) performed on humans in the United States through the Clinical Laboratory Improvement Amendments (CLIA). In most states, CLIA accreditation occurs annually by local state surveyors. CLIA has given deeming authority to a small group of accreditation organizations, including AABB, the American Osteopathic Association (AOA), the American Society for Histocompatibility and Immunogenetics (ASHI), CAP, Commission on Office Laboratory Accreditation (COLA), and the Joint Commission (TJC). A few states with state licensure programs have also received exemption from CLIA program requirements.

Most hospital-based laboratories are accredited by the CAP. These laboratories are typically reviewed every 2 years by a team of peer laboratorians. The CAP inspection process is recognized by TJC, and often TJC will do only a cursory laboratory survey if the laboratory has an up-to-date CAP accreditation. Several months prior to the anticipated inspection, the CAP will send the laboratory a self-scoring checklist to complete

and return. Each question on the checklist is given a phase category that corresponds to a type of deficiency. Phase 0 questions are for information only. Phase I questions represent items that are considered important for the management of an outstanding laboratory service; Phase I deficiencies *should* be corrected. Phase II questions represent items of major importance that are essential to the management of a laboratory. Phase II deficiencies are major defects that *must* be corrected before accreditation can be granted. Examples of Phase I and II questions can be obtained from the CAP.[23]

PRINCIPLES OF LABORATORY TESTING

Biosafety Levels

During the 1970s, in an effort to diminish the risks of LAIs, scientists devised a system for categorizing etiological agents into groups based on their mode of transmission, the type and seriousness of illness resulting from infection, availability of treatment (e.g., antimicrobial drugs), and availability of prevention measures (e.g., vaccination). These etiological agent groupings were the basis for development of guidelines for appropriate facilities, containment equipment, procedures, and work practices to be used by laboratory workers. The BMBL guidelines refer to Biosafety Levels (BL) 1 through 4. The BMBL guidelines are published and regularly reviewed and updated by the U.S. Department of Health & Human Services (HHS), Public Health Services, CDC, and the National Institutes of Health (NIH); they have become the "code of practice for biosafety" in the laboratory setting.[24]

Four Biosafety Levels are also described for activities involving infectious disease research with experimental animals. These four combinations for practices, safety equipment, and facilities are designated Animal Biosafety Levels 1, 2, 3, and 4 and are similar to standard Biosafety Levels.

Biosafety Level 1

Biosafety Level 1 (BL-1) defines conditions suitable for work involving well-characterized microorganisms not known to cause disease in healthy adult humans and of attendant minimal potential hazard to laboratory personnel and the environment. Undergraduate and secondary training/teaching laboratories and some physicians' office laboratories can be categorized as BL-1. These laboratories may not necessarily be separated from the general traffic patterns in the building, and work is generally conducted on open benchtops using standard practices. Special containment equipment or facility design is neither required nor generally used. Laboratory personnel have specific training in the procedures conducted in the laboratory and are supervised by a scientist with general training in microbiology, medical technology, or related sciences. Infection prevention measures for BL-1 include hand hygiene when indicated. *Bacillus subtilis, Naegleria grubri*, and infectious canine hepatitis virus are representative of organisms that may be handled in a BL-1 lab.

Biosafety Level 2

Biosafety Level 2 (BL-2) is similar to BL-1 and is suitable for work involving agents of moderate potential hazard to personnel and the environment. This safety level is appropriate when work is done with any human blood, body fluids, or tissues in which the presence of an infectious agent may be unknown. Unlike Level 1, BL-2 laboratory personnel have specific training in handling pathogenic agents and are directed by competent scientists. Access to the laboratory is limited when work is being conducted, and the laboratory is generally away from general traffic areas. Certain procedures in which infectious aerosols or splashes may be created are conducted in a biologic safety cabinet (BSC) or with other physical containment equipment, and extreme precautions are taken with contaminated sharps. (Also see Chapter 113 Waste Management.)

Except in extraordinary circumstances (e.g., suspected outbreak of hemorrhagic fever), the initial processing of clinical specimens and identification of isolates can be done safely in a BL-2 laboratory. A lab with this designation is equipped to perform the recommended level of testing for bloodborne pathogens such as Hepatitis B virus (HBV) and human immunodeficiency virus (HIV). Containment elements are consistent with OSHA's Bloodborne Pathogen Standard (hand hygiene and appropriate personal protective equipment), as well as those recommended by the NCCLS ruling M29. (Although NCCLS was replaced by the Clinical and Laboratory Standards Institute [CLSI] in 2005, the publication title may still include the NCCLS designation.) HBV, *Salmonella* spp., and *Toxoplasma* spp. are representative of the microorganisms assigned to this containment level.

There is no specification for single-pass directional inward flow of air from a BL-2 laboratory. However, most microbiology laboratories also work with potentially hazardous chemicals. There are published recommendations for preventing buildup of chemical vapors in laboratories. This can be accomplished by using a chemical fume hood and/or having single-pass air when recirculation would increase ambient concentrations of hazardous materials. (Also see Chapter 114 Heating, Ventilation, and Air Conditioning; and Chapter 116 Construction and Renovation.)

Biosafety Level 3

Biosafety Level 3 (BL-3) is applicable to clinical, diagnostic, teaching, research, or production facilities in which work is done with indigenous or exotic agents; such agents may cause serious or potentially lethal disease as a result of exposure by the inhalation route. Often a BL-3-designated laboratory is located within a BL-2 containment laboratory; that is, the microbiology department is inside the general clinical laboratory. Laboratory personnel must have specific training in handling pathogenic, potentially lethal agents, and must be supervised by competent scientists who are experienced in working with such agents. *Mycobacterium tuberculosis*, St. Louis encephalitis virus, and *Coxiella burnetii* are representative of microorganisms transmissible by the aerosol route that are assigned to this level. Primary hazards to personnel working with these agents relate to exposure to infectious aerosols, autoinoculation, and ingestion.

In BL-3 laboratories, greater emphasis is placed on primary and secondary barriers. These barriers protect personnel in

contiguous areas and the wider community from exposure to potentially infectious aerosols and to prevent contamination of the environment. The laboratory has special engineering and design features to provide a controlled environment targeted at managing infectious aerosols. A BL-3 laboratory is separated from other parts of the building by an anteroom with two sets of doors or by access through a BL-2 area. Because of the potential for aerosol transmission, air movement is unidirectional into the laboratory (i.e., from clean areas into the BL-3 area), and all air exhausted from the BL-3 area is directed outside the building without recirculation or is recycled using a high-efficiency particulate air (HEPA) filtration system. All procedures within a BL-3 involving manipulation of infectious materials are conducted within BSCs or other physical containment devices. Personnel must wear appropriate personal protective clothing and equipment while in a BL-3 laboratory and perform hand hygiene when indicated.

BL-3 facilities have solid floors and ceilings and sealed penetrations. They are designed and maintained to allow appropriate decontamination in the event of a significant spill. BL-3 laboratories have single-pass air (nonrecirculating air ventilation systems) to protect personnel. Filtration of exhaust air through HEPA filters is neither required nor recommended in most situations unless the air must be recirculated. Single-pass air that mixes with outside air allows for the rapid dilution of the small numbers of microorganisms that may be released in the laboratory. All waste from a BL-3 laboratory must be rendered noninfectious before final disposal.

Biosafety Level 4

Biosafety Level 4 (BL-4) laboratories are the most sophisticated of laboratories and are required for work with dangerous and exotic agents that pose a high risk of aerosol transmission for life-threatening diseases such as those caused by Marburg and Ebola viruses. Within work areas of the facility, all activities are confined to Class III or II BSCs used by workers wearing one-piece positive-pressure body suits ventilated by a life-support system. Members of the laboratory staff have specific and thorough training in handling extremely hazardous infectious agents. Staff understand the primary and secondary containment functions of standard and special practices, containment equipment, and laboratory design characteristics. The workers are also supervised by competent scientists trained and experienced in handling these agents. All waste is decontaminated before leaving the BL-4 laboratory, and air is exhausted from the BL-4 area through HEPA filters. These types of laboratories are rarely found within a hospital and are typically found in reference and/or research settings.

Biological Risk Assessment

Each clinical laboratory should perform a biological risk assessment on an annual basis or any time a new risk is identified. A biological risk assessment is a process used to identify the hazardous characteristics of a known infectious or potentially infectious agent or material, the activities that can result in a person's exposure to an agent, the likelihood that such exposure will cause an LAI, and the probable consequences of such an infection.

Fundamentally, the primary factors in the risk assessment and selection of precautions fall into two broad categories: agent hazards and laboratory procedure hazards. Although there is no standard approach for conducting a biological risk assessment, the BMBL document suggests a five-step approach to prevent LAIs:

1. *Identify agent hazards and perform an initial assessment of risk.* A review of potential biological agents and their hazardous characteristics should be completed. Hazardous characteristics include their capability to infect and cause disease in a susceptible human host, severity of disease and the availability of preventive measures, and effective treatments. The CDC and the Animal and Plant Health Inspection Service (APHIS) have implemented regulations that govern the possession, use, and transfer of these types of biological agents and toxins that have the potential to pose a severe threat to public health and safety. These agents/toxins are classified as "select agents." Such agents/toxins are registered and updated on a biennial basis by APHIS and a list of these agents, along with the regulations on how to handle them, can be found under the National Select Agent Registry Program; refer to Supplemental Resources in this chapter.

   In the typical clinical/hospital laboratory that is not doing research on these agents/toxins, special procedures must be implemented if one of these agents is identified from a patient culture (i.e., *Francisella tularensis*). For example, all waste and culture supplies, etc., that are contaminated with the select agent must be autoclaved prior to leaving the facility. Additionally, the APHIS/CDC Form 4 "Report of Identification of a Select Agent or Toxin in a Clinical or Diagnostic Laboratory" must be completed and mailed or faxed to APHIS or the CDC within 7 calendar days after identification of a select agent(s) or toxin(s) in a diagnostic specimen. Each laboratory should communicate regularly with their local health departments for the appropriate protocols to follow when identifying a select agent.

   The BMBL also has agent summary statements to help identify known and suspected routes of transmission of an LAI and, when available, information on infective dose, host range, agent stability in the environment, protective immunizations, and attenuated strains of the agent.

   The Control of Communicable Diseases Manual can provide information on various diseases including concise summaries on severity, mode of transmission, and the susceptibility and resistance of humans to disease; refer to Supplemental Resources.

2. *Identify laboratory procedure hazards.* Procedure hazards often found in a clinical lab include agent concentration, suspension volume, equipment and procedures that generate small-particle aerosols and larger airborne particles (droplets), complexity of lab procedures, and use of sharps.

3. *Make a final determination of the appropriate biosafety level and select additional precautions indicated by the*

risk assessment. It is unlikely that a risk assessment would indicate a need to alter the recommended facility safeguards specified for the selected biosafety level. It is important to recognize that staff in the laboratory may differ in their susceptibility to disease. Consultation with an occupational physician knowledgeable in infectious disease is advised.

4. *Evaluate the proficiencies of staff regarding safe practices and the integrity of safety equipment.* An evaluation of the laboratorian's training, experience in handling infectious agents, proficiency in the use of sterile techniques and BSC, ability to respond to emergencies, and willingness to accept responsibility for protecting one's self and others should be assessed.

5. *Review the risk assessment with a biosafety professional, subject matter expert, and the institutional biosafety committee.* Once the risk assessment is completed it should be reviewed by site-specific, and if necessary, local experts in biosafety. This review should include input from the IP, laboratory safety, and infection prevention and control committee, as well as safety committee.

As with any other risk assessment, specific gaps in biosafety should be identified and follow-up actions delineated to procure a safe environment. These actions should be regularly reviewed and updated as necessary.

Laboratory Biosecurity

In response to the anthrax attacks on U.S. citizens in October 2001 and other events, laboratory specialists have recognized that there is a need to consider developing, implementing, and/or improving the security of biological agents and toxins capable of serious or fatal illness to humans. The term "biosecurity" refers to the protection of microbial agents from loss, theft, diversion, or international misuse. Labs should ensure that protective measures are provided and that the costs associated with protection are proportional to the risk. Biosecurity policies and procedures should not seek to protect against every conceivable risk.

For laboratories not handling select agents, the access controls and training requirements specified for BSL-2 and BSL-3 may provide sufficient security for the materials being studied.

A biosecurity risk assessment should be completed for each laboratory using these BMBL recommended steps:

- Identify and prioritize biological materials.
- Identify and prioritize the threat to biological materials.
- Analyze the risk of specific security scenarios.
- Design and develop an overall risk management program.
- Reevaluate the institution's risk posture and protection objectives.

Laboratory Response Network

In 1999, the CDC established the Laboratory Response Network (LRN). The purpose of the LRN is to run a network of laboratories that can respond to biologic and chemical terrorism. This multilevel system is designed to link frontline clinical microbiology laboratories, hospitals, and other institutions to state and local public health laboratories. These, in turn, will support advanced-capacity public health, military, veterinary, agricultural, water, and food testing laboratories at the federal level. LRN labs are designated as either national, reference, or sentinel. Designation depends on the types of tests a laboratory can perform and how it handles infectious agents to protect workers and the public. *National labs* have unique resources to handle highly infectious agents and the ability to identify specific agent strains. *Reference labs*, sometimes referred to as *confirmatory reference*, can perform tests to detect and confirm the presence of a threat agent. These labs ensure a timely local response in the event of a terrorist incident. Rather than having to rely on confirmation from labs at the CDC, reference labs are capable of producing conclusive results. This allows local authorities to respond quickly to emergencies. *Sentinel labs* represent the thousands of hospital-based labs that are on the front lines. Sentinel labs have direct contact with patients. In an unannounced or covert terrorist attack, patients provide specimens during routine patient care. Sentinel labs could be the first facility to spot a suspicious specimen. Standard methods are available on the CDC Website as well as the Website of the American Society for Microbiology (ASM) (see Supplemental Resources). Sentinel labs are required to maintain awareness of bioterrorism agents and their identification. Laboratories should provide appropriate training, know who to call when an agent is suspected, and maintain the appropriate chain-of-custody requirements for specimens. Laboratorians should also be ready to transport specimens and refer testing as needed to the closest state public health laboratory or other approved reference facility.

Work Practices, Safety Equipment, and Facility Safeguards

Clinical laboratories, especially those in healthcare facilities, receive clinical specimens with requests for a variety of diagnostic and clinical support services. Typically, the infectious nature of clinical material is unknown and specimens are often submitted with a broad request for microbiological examination for multiple agents (e.g., sputum submitted for "routine," acid-fast, and fungal cultures). Except in extraordinary circumstances, the initial processing of clinical specimens and serological identification of isolates can be done safely at BSL-2. Primary barriers such as BSC (Class I or II) should be used when performing procedures that might cause splashing, spraying, or splattering of droplets. BSCs should also be used for the initial processing of clinical specimens when the nature of the test requested or other information suggest the likely presence of an agent readily transmitted by infectious aerosol (e.g., *M. tuberculosis*) or when the use of a BSC (Class II) is indicated to protect the integrity of the specimen.

Most of the safe work practices expected in the laboratory as noted by the CDC's BMBL correlate with OSHA's Bloodborne Pathogen Standard and CDC's Standard Precautions. A listing of specific practices for each Biosafety level can be found in the BMBL.

The following standard and special practices, safety equipment, and facility requirements apply to the typical laboratory under BSL-2 criteria:

A. *Standard Microbiological Practices*

1. The laboratory supervisor must enforce the institutional policies that control access to the laboratory.

2. Persons must wash their hands after working with potentially hazardous materials and before leaving the laboratory.

3. Eating, drinking, smoking, handling contact lenses, applying cosmetics, and storing food for human consumption must not be permitted in laboratory areas. Food must be stored outside the laboratory area in cabinets or refrigerators designated and used for this purpose.

4. Mouth pipetting is prohibited; mechanical pipetting devices must be used.

5. Policies for the safe handling of sharps (e.g., needles, scalpels, pipettes, broken glassware) must be developed and implemented. Whenever practical, laboratory supervisors should adopt improved engineering and work practice controls that reduce risk of sharps injuries. Precautions, including those listed in the following, must always be taken with sharp items. These include:

   a. Needles must not be bent, sheared, broken, recapped, removed from disposable syringes, or otherwise manipulated by hand before disposal.

   b. Used disposable needles and syringes must be carefully placed in conveniently located puncture-resistant containers used for sharps disposal.

   c. Nondisposable sharps must be placed in a hard-walled container for transport to a processing area for decontamination, preferably by autoclaving.

   d. Broken glassware must not be handled directly. Instead, it must be removed using a brush and dustpan, tongs, or forceps. Plasticware should be substituted for glassware whenever possible.

6. Perform all procedures to minimize the creation of splashes and/or aerosols.

7. Decontaminate work surfaces after completion of work and after any spill or splash of potentially infectious material with appropriate disinfectant.

8. Decontaminate all cultures, stocks, and other potentially infectious materials before disposal using an effective method. Depending on where the decontamination will be performed, the following methods should be used prior to transport:

   a. Materials to be decontaminated outside of the immediate laboratory must be placed in a durable, leakproof container and secured for transport.

   b. Materials to be removed from the facility for decontamination must be packed in accordance with applicable local, state, and federal regulations.

9. A sign incorporating the universal biohazard symbol must be posted at the entrance to the laboratory when infectious agents are present. Posted information must include the laboratory's biosafety level, the supervisor's name (or other responsible personnel), telephone number, and required procedures for entering and exiting the laboratory. Agent information should be posted in accordance with the institutional policy.

10. An effective integrated pest management program is required. See Appendix G in the BMBL.

11. The laboratory supervisor must ensure that laboratory personnel receive appropriate training regarding their duties, the necessary precautions to prevent exposures, and exposure evaluation procedures. Personnel must receive annual updates or additional training when procedural or policy changes occur. Personal health status may affect an individual's susceptibility to infection and ability to receive immunizations or prophylactic interventions. Therefore, all laboratory personnel and particularly women of childbearing age should be provided with information regarding immune competence and conditions that may predispose them to infection. Individuals having these conditions should be encouraged to self-identify to the institution's healthcare provider for appropriate counseling and guidance.

B. *Special Practices*

1. All persons entering the laboratory must be advised of the potential hazards and meet specific entry/exit requirements.

2. Laboratory personnel must be provided medical surveillance and offered appropriate immunizations for agents handled or potentially present in the laboratory.

3. When appropriate, a baseline serum sample should be stored.

4. A laboratory-specific biosafety manual must be prepared and adopted as policy. The biosafety manual must be available and accessible.

5. The laboratory supervisor must ensure that laboratory personnel demonstrate proficiency in standard and special microbiological practices before working with BSL-2 agents.

6. Potentially infectious materials must be placed in a durable leakproof container during collection, handling, processing, storage, or transport within a facility.

7. Laboratory equipment should be decontaminated routinely, as well as after spills, splashes, or other potential contamination.

   a. Spills involving infectious materials must be contained, decontaminated, and cleaned up by staff properly trained and equipped to work with infectious material.

   b. Equipment must be decontaminated before repair, maintenance, or removal from the laboratory.

8. Incidents that may result in exposure to infectious materials must be immediately evaluated and treated according to procedures described in the laboratory biosafety safety manual. All such incidents must be reported to the laboratory supervisor. Medical evaluation, surveillance, and treatment should be provided and appropriate records maintained.

9. Animals and plants not associated with the work being performed must not be permitted in the laboratory.

10. All procedures involving the manipulation of infectious materials that may generate an aerosol should be conducted within a BSC or other physical containment devices.

C. *Safety Equipment (Primary Barriers and Personal Protective Equipment)*

1. Properly maintained BSCs (preferably Class II), other appropriate personal protective equipment, or other physical containment devices must be used whenever:

   a. Procedures with a potential for creating infectious aerosols or splashes are conducted. These may include pipetting, centrifuging, grinding, blending, shaking, mixing, sonicating, opening containers of infectious materials, inoculating animals intranasally, and harvesting infected tissues from animals or eggs.

   b. High concentrations or large volumes of infectious agents are used. Such materials may be centrifuged in the open laboratory using sealed rotor heads or centrifuge safety cups.

2. Protective laboratory coats, gowns, smocks, or uniforms designated for laboratory use must be worn while working with hazardous materials. Remove protective clothing before leaving for nonlaboratory areas (e.g., cafeteria, library, administrative offices). Dispose of protective clothing appropriately or deposit it for laundering by the institution. It is recommended that laboratory clothing not be taken home.

3. Eye and face protection (goggles, mask, face shield, or other splatter guard) is used for anticipated splashes or sprays of infectious or other hazardous materials when microorganisms must be handled outside the BSC or containment device. Eye and face protection must be disposed of with other contaminated laboratory waste or decontaminated before reuse. Persons who wear contact lenses in laboratories should also wear eye protection.

4. Gloves must be worn to protect hands from exposure to hazardous materials. Glove selection should be based on an appropriate risk assessment. Alternatives to latex gloves should be available. Gloves must not be worn outside the laboratory. In addition, BSL-2 laboratory workers should:

   a. Change gloves when contaminated, integrity has been compromised, or when otherwise necessary. Wear two pairs of gloves when appropriate.

b. Remove gloves and wash hands when work with hazardous materials has been completed and before leaving the laboratory.

c. Do not wash or reuse disposable gloves. Dispose of used gloves with other contaminated laboratory waste. Hand-washing protocols must be rigorously followed.

5. Eye, face, and respiratory protection should be used in rooms containing infected animals as determined by the risk assessment.

D. Laboratory Facilities (Secondary Barriers)

1. Laboratory doors should be self-closing and have locks in accordance with institutional policies.

2. Laboratories must have a sink for hand washing. The sink may be manually, hands-free, or automatically operated. It should be located near the exit door.

3. The laboratory should be designed so that it can be easily cleaned and decontaminated. Carpets and rugs in laboratories are not permitted.

4. Laboratory furniture must be capable of supporting anticipated loads and uses. Spaces between benches, cabinets, and equipment should be accessible for cleaning.

a. Benchtops must be impervious to water and resistant to heat, organic solvents, acids, alkalis, and other chemicals.

b. Chairs used in laboratory work must be covered with a nonporous material that can be easily cleaned and decontaminated with appropriate disinfectant.

5. Laboratory windows that open to the exterior are not recommended. However, if a laboratory does have windows that open to the exterior, they must be fitted with screens.

6. BSCs must be installed so that fluctuations of the room air supply and exhaust do not interfere with proper operations. BSCs should be located away from doors, windows that can be opened, heavily traveled laboratory areas, and other possible airflow disruptions.

7. Vacuum lines should be protected with HEPA filters or their equivalent. Filters must be replaced as needed. Liquid disinfectant traps may be required.

8. An eyewash station must be readily available.

9. Clinical laboratories must maintain proper air handling according to the procedures they are performing. Typically, a clinical lab has negative airflow to the adjacent areas. Specialized areas such as rooms where polymerase chain reaction (PCR) may need positive air pressure to limit potential RNA contamination of the reagents. Facilities should consider mechanical ventilation systems that provide an inward flow of air without recirculation to spaces outside of the laboratory.

10. HEPA-filtered exhaust air from a Class II BSC can be safely recirculated back into the laboratory environment if the cabinet is tested and certified at least annually and operated according to manufacturer's recommendations. BSCs can also be connected to the laboratory exhaust system by either a thimble (canopy) connection or a direct (hard) connection. Provisions to assure proper safety cabinet performance and air system operation must be verified.

11. A method for decontaminating all laboratory wastes should be available in the facility (e.g., autoclave, chemical disinfection, incineration, or other validated decontamination method).

Laboratory Equipment

Biological Safety Cabinets

Various laboratory procedures generate aerosol particles that may spread biohazardous materials to the work area and pose a risk of infection to the worker. BSCs are used to prevent the escape of aerosols or droplets and to protect lab samples from airborne contamination. They are specifically designed to protect the individual and the environment from biological agents and to protect specimens and other materials from biological contamination. These devices are distinct from horizontal or vertical laminar flow hoods, which should never be used for handling biohazardous, toxic, or sensitizing material. Chemical fume hoods also should not be used for biohazards in that they are solely designed to protect the individual from exposure to chemicals and noxious gases. These chemical fume hoods are not equipped with HEPA filters.

There are three general types of BSCs: Classes I, II, and III (Figures 108-1, 108-2, and 108-3).[24] All BSCs must be recertified annually by an independent professional.

There is one type of Class I BSC. This cabinet is similar to a chemical fume hood and has an inward airflow through the front opening. Exhaust air from the BSC is passed through a HEPA filter so that the equipment protects both the worker and the general public. However, the specimens and other materials are potentially subject to contamination.

Class I BSCs are not generally recommended for work that involves biohazardous material.

Class II BSCs are designed to protect the worker, the general public, and the specimen. Airflow velocity at the face of the work opening is at least 75 linear ft/min (lfpm). Both the supply air and the exhaust air are HEPA-filtered. There are four types of Class II BSCs (IIA, IIB1, IIB2, and IIB3). They differ in the amount of recirculation, downflow, and inflow. Usually, all but IIA are considered satisfactory for biohazardous and toxic agents.

Class III BSCs are totally enclosed, ventilated cabinets of gastight construction that offer the highest degree of protection

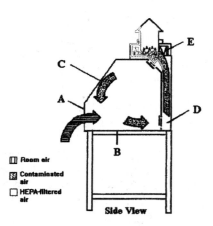

Figure 108-1. Class I biological safety cabinets.

from infectious aerosols. They also protect research materials from biological contamination. Class III BSCs are most suitable for work with hazardous agents that require containment at BL-3 or BL-4. All operations in the work area of the cabinet are performed through attached rubber gloves. The cabinets are operated under negative pressure. Supply air is HEPA-filtered, and the cabinet exhaust air is filtered by two HEPA filters in series or HEPA filtration followed by incineration before discharge outside of the facility. All equipment required by the laboratory activity, such as incubators, refrigerators, and centrifuges, must be an integral part of the cabinet system. The Class III BSC must be connected to double-door autoclaves and chemical dunk tanks to permit sterilization or disinfection of all materials before leaving the cabinet and also to allow supplies to enter the cabinet. Several Class III BSCs are therefore typically set up together as an interconnected system.

Some cabinets contain ultraviolet sterilizers. When required, blowers should be turned on for proper circulation before and after each procedure. Flow alarm systems should be checked each time they are used and should always be readily accessible. Interior surfaces should be decontaminated after each use.

Centrifuges

Centrifuges are commonly used in the clinical laboratory as part of specimen processing. Hazards associated with centrifuging include mechanical failure (e.g., rotor failure, tube or bucket failure) and the creation of aerosols. Aerosols are created by practices such as filling centrifuge tubes, removing plugs or caps from tubes after centrifugation, removing supernatant, suspending sediment pellets, and by the very process of centrifugation itself. The greatest aerosol hazard is created when a tube breaks during centrifugation. Special safety precautions can be used to decrease the risks associated with centrifugation. Examples of these precautions include using sealed tubes and safety buckets that seal with O-rings; filling open centrifuge tubes, rotors, and accessories in a BSC; and always balancing buckets, tubes, and rotors properly before centrifugation.

Phlebotomy

In most hospital settings, the laboratory is responsible for most phlebotomy procedures. Given that it is almost impossible to identify what might be infectious without testing, all patients and their bodily fluids should be handled using Standard Precautions.[8,13,14,16] This is particularly true for a phlebotomist, who may be one of the first contacts a new patient has within a healthcare facility. OSHA's Bloodborne Pathogen Standard requires that gloves be worn when performing venipuncture.

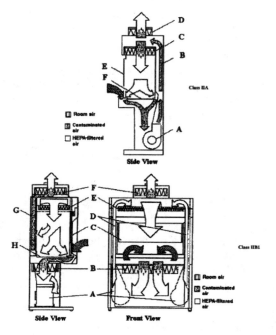

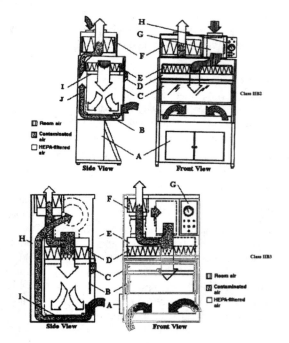

Figure 108-2. Class II biological safety cabinets.

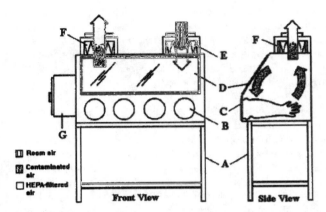

Figure 108-3. Class III biological safety cabinets.

Other protective equipment such as goggles, mask, or lab coat may be required for a procedure based on the risk of exposure (i.e., combative patient, arterial punctures). Safe needles, as defined by OSHA and other agencies, should be used whenever possible. Only single-use disposable tube holders should be used.[25] All phlebotomy needles (even those defined as safe) and lancets should be disposed of promptly in a puncture-resistant container to prevent their reuse or accidental injury to a handler.

Hand hygiene is the single most effective means of preventing transmission of infection. To protect the patient from colonization or infection after phlebotomy, the following measures should be employed: (1) tourniquets should be one-time use or one-patient use only; (2) skin should be antiseptically prepared before phlebotomy with either a 70 percent isopropyl alcohol prep or, in the case of blood cultures, 10 percent povidone iodine solution or chlorhexidine gluconate; and (3) a clean gauze pad, cotton ball, or bandage should be placed over the puncture site to stop bleeding if necessary. To protect the phlebotomist from infection and reduce the risk of infection to others, isolation precautions should be followed closely. Additional procedures may be necessary to avoid contamination of equipment.

Transporting Biohazardous Materials

Laboratories often need to transport biohazardous materials offsite. This transport may be across campus, across town to another laboratory, or across the country to a reference or research laboratory. Personnel who package and ship these specimens must be concerned with their safety and the protection and safety of those who receive the material. They must abide by the complex set of regulations that have been implemented to protect all handlers.[18,26-29] Inasmuch as these regulations are constantly being reviewed and updated, it is recommended that personnel check with each organization on a regular basis for any changes or updates.

Samples transported by local carriers such as cabs, hospital and clinical vehicles, or personal cars must meet packaging standards. In general, the requirements for shipping biohazard materials interstate or intrastate depend on the type and volume of specimen. The regulations define three types of specimens:

biological products, diagnostic (clinical) substances, and infectious (etiological) substances. The respective shipping containers are similar but documentation is different.

Biologic products are finished biological substances for veterinary or human use such as vaccines and reagents. These products must meet public health standards (9 CFR Parts 102–104 and 21 CFR Parts 312 and 600–680). Diagnostic (clinical) material comprises excreta, secretions, blood and its components, as well as tissue and tissue fluids that are being shipped for diagnostic purposes. Infectious substances (etiological) include organisms known to be pathogenic to humans and clinical samples with a high likelihood of being infectious. Infectious substances could include clinical specimens such as an enzyme immunoassay (EIA), HIV-positive serum submitted for Western blot analysis, and sputum samples from patients known to be culture-positive for tuberculosis.

The essential element for protection is the triple-containment packaging, which is required for shipping each of these substances. In all categories and volumes, there must be a primary container accompanied by enough absorbent material to contain the whole sample, a waterproof container, and an outer container. The packaging is expected to be able to withstand rough handling and passage through cancellation machines, sorters, and conveyers throughout transport. The sample identification document must be located outside the secondary containment. Additionally, labels clearly marking the biohazard level must be prominently displayed on the outside container. Depending on the level of biohazard, additional labels and information may need to be displayed as well.

Infectious Waste Management

As one of the principal generators of infectious hazardous waste in healthcare facilities, the clinical laboratory is responsible for the proper handling and disposal of this waste. According to the Environmental Protection Agency's (EPA's) *Guide for Infectious Waste Management*,[7,9] laboratory infectious waste includes cultures and stocks of infectious agents and associated biological matter (includes disposable culture dishes and devices used to transfer, inoculate, and mix cultures), pathological wastes (includes wet tissues, organs, body parts, blood and body fluids removed during surgery, autopsy, and biopsies), human blood and blood products (includes waste blood, serum, plasma, and other blood components), contaminated sharps (including hypodermic needles, syringes, scalpel blades, Pasteur pipettes, broken glass), and isolation wastes (includes blood, excretions, exudates, and secretions from patients with highly communicable diseases).

Many federal agencies have developed guidelines and regulations for handling these wastes. Of primary importance is the CLSI Document GP5—*Clinical Laboratory Waste Management*.[9] In general, waste from the laboratory can be handled just as any other infectious waste in facilities with some awareness of some essential issues that affect laboratories specifically. Also, the Department of Transportation's infectious waste should be segregated in the clinical lab from general laboratory waste and by treatment or disposal methods. Sharps should be placed into appropriate puncture-resistant containers. In most facilities, large quantities of liquid body fluid waste may be safely poured down the sink. Materials of high-water content or density (i.e., anatomical waste) should be incinerated, whereas microbiology laboratory waste may be autoclaved. To the extent feasible, segregation and subsequent treatment should minimize handling and transportation from the generation site to the decontamination mechanism. Containment requirements should be compatible with treatment mechanisms and should not hinder the decontamination process.

In the laboratory, there is a wide variety and a large amount of contaminated sharps. These sharps include phlebotomy needles, vial inoculation needles, scalpel blades, Pasteur pipettes, broken glass, coverslips, glass slides, and capillary tubes. Whenever possible, safer devices should be used to decrease risk of exposure (e.g., cannulas or plastic-tipped pipettes should be used instead of needles or fragile glass or plastic pipettes).

Large quantities of liquid body fluid waste must be disposed of in the laboratory. These include 24-hour urine specimens and vacuumed tubes of blood. If local health codes permit, blood and body fluids may be disposed of by pouring them down a sink into the sanitary sewer. Extreme caution to prevent splashing must be exercised in such disposal of fluids. Water should not be running in the sink while blood or bodily fluids are decanted. Decanting should be followed with copious amounts of water. If there is any risk of splattering, the laboratorian should wear facial protection and a fluidproof apron in addition to the gloves and lab coat. Sinks used for biohazardous waste disposal should not be used for hand washing.

Microbiological cultures should not be discarded directly into sanitary sewers or landfills. These wastes should be autoclaved prior to leaving the facility or incinerated before final disposal either by the laboratory or the biological waste vendor. Most clinical laboratories currently contract incineration to a licensed vendor rather than contend with local and state regulations associated with incinerators. However, laboratories, particularly those involved in anatomical work, may decontaminate and render unrecognizable anatomical wastes by a gravity displacement or prevacuum autoclave.

Steam autoclaves are the method of choice for decontaminating discarded cultures of CDC's select agents and for any material that may be contaminated with these organisms. Examples of these organisms include *Brucella* spp., *Francisella tularensis*, rickettsial agents, and rabies virus. Clinical laboratories are no longer allowed to maintain stock cultures of CDC's select agents.

There is no standard method for autoclaving and monitoring. Time and temperature criteria determined by the manufacturers of the equipment vary with processing times and are usually between 60 and 90 minutes or more at 120°C. Manufacturers' recommended protocols for use

and maintenance should be followed. All autoclaves must be checked at least weekly for proper function using a biological indicator (e.g., *Bacillus stearothermophilus* spores) or its chemical equivalent. The Association for the Advancement of Medical Instrumentation has developed a recommended protocol to use with this monitor.[9]

If laboratory wastes must be stored before disposal, storage should be as brief as possible. The site must be properly identified with a biohazard label, have restricted access, and be located near the site of generation. Long-term storage for waste awaiting offsite disposal should be located near the treatment site or loading dock, have limited access, and meet EPA requirements. The area should be thoroughly cleaned each time it is emptied of waste contents. Direct sewer connections with proper grading from this area are also recommended.

Infection Prevention and Occupational Exposures

From the infection prevention perspective, the goal of occupational health in a clinical lab and in university research laboratories is to promote a safe and healthy workplace. Prospective workers should be educated about the biohazards to which they may be occupationally exposed, the types of exposures that place their health at risk, the nature and significance of such risks, and the appropriate first aid and follow-up for potential exposures. That information should be reinforced annually, at the time of any significant change in job responsibility, and following recognized and suspected exposures.

Workers who may be exposed to highly pathogenic agents—such as in a clinical research lab—should receive a preplacement medical evaluation. Healthcare providers should be cognizant of potential hazards encountered by the worker. A description of the requirements for the position and an understanding of the potential health hazards present in the work environment, provided by the worker's supervisor, should guide the evaluation. The healthcare provider should review the worker's previous and ongoing medical problems, current medications, allergies to medicines, animals, and other environmental proteins, and prior immunizations. With that information, the healthcare provider determines what medical services are indicated to permit the individual to safely assume the duties of the position. Comprehensive physical examinations are rarely indicated. In a research laboratory setting when occupational exposure to human pathogens is a risk, employers should consider collecting and storing a serum specimen prior to the initiation of work with the agent. This is not typically necessary in a clinical laboratory but should be considered for research laboratories in a university setting. It can be used to establish baseline seroreactivity. This will be important should additional blood samples need to be collected for serological testing subsequent to a recognized or suspected exposure.

Commercial vaccines should be made available to workers to provide protection against infectious agents to which they may be occupationally exposed. Investigational vaccines for eastern equine encephalomyelitis virus, Venezuelan equine encephalitis virus, western equine encephalomyelitis virus, and Rift Valley fever viruses may be necessary in some laboratories

Routine, periodic medical evaluations generally are not recommended; however, limited periodic medical evaluations or medical clearances targeted to job requirements may occasionally be warranted (e.g., respirator usage).[3] In special circumstances, it may be appropriate to offer periodic laboratory testing to workers with substantial risk of exposure to infectious agents to detect preclinical or subclinical evidence for an occupationally acquired infection.

Workers should be encouraged to seek medical evaluation for symptoms that they suspect may be related to infectious agents in their work area without fear of reprisal. A high index of suspicion for potential occupational exposures should be maintained during any unexplained illness among workers or visitors to worksites containing biohazards. Modes of transmission, as well as the clinical presentation of infections acquired through occupational exposures, may differ markedly from naturally acquired infections. Fatal occupational infections have resulted from apparently trivial exposures. A close working relationship with the research or clinical program in which the affected employee works is absolutely essential. In the event of injury, consultation between healthcare provider, employee, and the employee's supervisor is required for proper medical management and recordkeeping.

All occupational injuries must be reported to the occupational health department. Laboratory standard operating procedures should include a printed summary of the recommended medical response to specific exposures that can guide immediate response in the workplace and that the injured worker can provide to the treating facility. The medical provider's description of the injury should include:

- The potential infectious agent

- The mechanism and route of exposure (percutaneous, splash to mucous membranes or skin, aerosol, etc.)

- Time and place of the incident

- Personal protective equipment used at the time of the injury

- Prior first aid provided (e.g., nature and duration of cleaning and other aid, time that lapsed from exposure to treatment)

- Aspects of the worker's personal medical history relevant to risk of infection or complications of treatment

- Department supervisor(s), witness (if applicable)

Postexposure serologic testing may be useful, but it is important to determine how information obtained from serologic testing will be interpreted. It is also essential to collect serum specimens at the appropriate interval for a given situation. Assessment of seroreactivity in exposed workers is most helpful when the results of specimens collected over time can be compared. Ideally, specimens collected prior to, at the time of, and several weeks following exposure should be tested simultaneously and results compared to assess changes in the pattern of seroreactivity.

Serum collected too early after exposure may fail to react even when infection has occurred, because antibodies have not yet been produced in detectable quantities. When immediate institution of postexposure prophylaxis may delay seroconversion, or when the agent to which the worker was exposed results in seroconversion, testing of specimens collected late after exposure is particularly important.

Testing of a single serum specimen is generally discouraged and can result in misinterpretation of nonspecific seroreactivity. Evidence of seroconversion or a significant (fourfold) increase in titer associated with a compatible clinical syndrome is highly suggestive of acute infection.

CONCLUSIONS

The laboratory plays an integral role in the clinical setting by providing valuable information to clinicians. Because of its specialized setting, the laboratory and laboratory workers may be at increased risk of contamination/infection. Regulations and recommendations exist to ensure the safety of the laboratory environment and those that work in them.

FUTURE TRENDS

As healthcare resources become more limited, there has been increasing use of reference laboratories. This has signaled a shift from hospital-based laboratories to a more regional approach. In many areas, individual hospitals provide only a small number of laboratory tests on-site. Nonemergent or routine tests are sent to a regional or reference laboratory that supports surrounding healthcare facilities. When changes like this are being considered, it is important to recognize the impact on clinical diagnosis and other ancillary services. For example, if microbiological tests are not conducted in house, will a representative from the referring laboratory be available to sit on the processing laboratory's infection prevention committee?

More and more IPs are working in collaboration with industrial hygienists in maintaining a safe environment in the research and clinical laboratories in large university settings, as well as in research labs in manufacturing and pharmaceutical settings. Concerns of transmission prevention as well as symptom recognitions has stimulated this interesting new area for IPs.

INTERNATIONAL PERSPECTIVE

Given the ease of travel between countries, the world is becoming smaller. Laboratories around the world need to be aware of biologic agents that were once thought to be isolated to specific geographic areas. Additionally, as the global healthcare system grows and changes, we need to recognize that there are no universal laboratory safety regulations.

REFERENCES

1. Centers for Disease Control and Preventon (CDC). Laboratory-acquired vaccinia exposures and infections -- United States, 2005-2007. *MMWR Morb Mortal Wkly Rep* 2008 Apr 18;57(15):401–404.
2. Centers for Disease Control and Prevention (CDC). Laboratory-acquired meningococcal disease -- United States, 2000. *MMWR Morb Mortal Wkly Rep* 2002 Feb 22;51(7):141–144.

3. Jacobson JT, Orlob RB, Clayton JL. Infections acquired in clinical laboratories in Utah. *J Clin Microbiol* 1985 Apr;21(4):486–489.
4. Centers for Disease Control and Prevention (CDC). Laboratory-acquired West Nile virus infections -- United States, 2002. *MMWR Morb Mortal Wkly Rep* 2002 Dec 20:51(50):1133–1135.
5. Pike RM, Sulkin SE, Schulze ML. Continuing importance of laboratory-acquired infections. *Am J Public Health Nations Health* 1965 Feb;55:190–199.
6. Pike RM. Laboratory-associated infections: summary and analysis of 3921 cases. *Health Lab Sci* 1976 Apr;13(2):105–114.
7. Clinical and Laboratory Standards Institute (CLSI). *Protection of Laboratory Workers from Occupationally Acquired Infections; Approved Guideline, Third Edition*. CLSI document M29-A3. Wayne, PA: National Committee for Clinical Laboratory Standards; 2005:25(10).
8. Clinical and Laboratory Standards Institute (CLSI). *Procedures for the Collection of Diagnostic Blood Specimens by Venipuncture; Approved Standard, Fifth Edition*. CLSI document H3-A5. Wayne, PA: National Committee for Clinical Laboratory Standards; 2003:23(32).
9. Clinical and Laboratory Standards Institute (CLSI). *Clinical Laboratory Waste Management; Approved Guideline, Third Edition*. CLSI document GPO5-A3. Wayne, PA: National Committee for Clinical Laboratory Standards; 2011:31(3).
10. Clinical and Laboratory Standards Institute (CLSI). *Urinalysis; Approved Guideline, Third Edition*. CLSI document GP16-A3. Wayne, PA: National Committee for Clinical Laboratory Standards; 2009:29(4).
11. Clinical and Laboratory Standards Institute (CLSI). *Procedures and Devices for the Collection of Diagnostic Capillary Blood Specimens; Approved Standard—Sixth Edition*. CLSI document H04-A6. Wayne, PA: National Committee for Clinical Laboratory Standards; 2008:28(5).
12. Clinical and Laboratory Standards Institute (formerly NCCLS). *Procedures for the Handling and Transport of Diagnostic Specimens and Etiologic Agents (1994), Third Edition; Approved Standard* (Vol.14, No.7) CLSI document H5-A3 (ISSN-0273-3099). Wayne, PA: Clinical and Laboratory Standards Institute; 1994.
13. Clinical and Laboratory Standards Institute (CLSI). *Procedures for the Collection of Arterial Blood Specimens; Approved Standard, Fourth Edition*. CLSI document H11-A4. Wayne, PA: National Committee for Clinical Laboratory Standards; 2004:24(28).
14. Clinical and Laboratory Standards Institute (CLSI). *Planning for Challenges to Clinical Laboratory Operations During a Disaster; A Report*. CLSI document X4-R. Wayne, PA: National Committee for Clinical Laboratory Standards; 2003:23(29).
15. Clinical and Laboratory Standards Institute (CLSI). *Molecular Diagnostic Methods for Infectious Diseases; Approved Guideline, Second Edition*. CLSI document MM3-A2. Wayne, PA: National Committee for Clinical Laboratory Standards; 2006.
16. Clinical and Laboratory Standards Institute (CLSI). *Blood Collection on Filter Paper for Newborn Screening Programs; Approved Standard, Sixth Edition*. CLSI document NB501-A6. Wayne, PA: National Committee for Clinical Laboratory Standards; 2013.
17. Clinical and Laboratory Standards Institute (CLSI). *Clinical Laboratory Safety, Approved Guideline, Third Edition*. CLSI document GP17-A3. Wayne, PA: National Committee for Clinical Laboratory Standards; 2012:32(9).
18. Occupational Safety and Health Administration (OSHA). *Occupational Exposure to Bloodborne Pathogens*; 29 CFR 1910.1030. OSHA Website. Available at: https://www.osha.gov/pls/oshaweb/owadisp.show_document?p_table=standards&p_id=10051.
19. Centers for Disease Control and Prevention (CDC). Guidelines for safe work practices in human and animal medical diagnostic laboratories. Recommendations of a CDC-convened, Biosafety Blue Ribbon Panel. *MMWR Morb Mortal Wkly Rep* 2012 Jan 6: 61(01):1–101.
20. Centers for Disease Control and Prevention (CDC). Tuberculosis infection associated with tissue processing—California. *MMWR Morb Mortal Wkly Rep* 1981 Feb 20:30(6):73–74.
21. U.S. Department of Health and Human Services, Food and Drug Administration (FDA). *Glass Capillary Tubes: Joint Safety Advisory About Potential Risks*. FDA Website. 1999. Available at: http://www.fda.gov/MedicalDevices/Safety/AlertsandNotices/PublicHealthNotifications/ucm062285.htm.
22. Jett BW, Wilkinson SL, Motschman T. Facilities, Work Environment, and Safety. In: Roback JD (ed.), *AABB Technical Manual*, 17th ed. Bethesda, MD: American Association of Blood Banks; 2011.
23. College of American Pathologists. *Laboratory Accreditation Program, Commission on Laboratory Accreditation Inspection Checklist, Laboratory General, Sect. 1*. Northfield, IL: College of American Pathologists; 2012.
24. U.S. Department of Health and Human Services, Public Health Service, Centers for Disease Control and Prevention (CDC), and the National Institutes of Health (NIH). *Biosafety in Microbiological and Biomedical Laboratories*, 5th ed. CDC Website. 2009. Available at: http://www.cdc.gov/biosafety/publications/bmbl5/BMBL.pdf.
25. Dangerous Goods Regulations, 2013. International Air Transport Association (IATA). Montreal: International Air Transport Association; 2013.
26. U.S. Department of Transportation (DOT). *Hazardous Materials Regulations (HMR)*. 49 CFR Part 171–180. 2013. Government Printing Office Website. Available at: http://www.gpo.gov/fdsys/pkg/CFR-2009-title49-vol2/pdf/CFR-2009-title49-vol2-part171.pdf.
27. United States Postal Service (USPS). Domestic Mail Manual. *Nonmailable Matter—Articles and Substances; Special Mailing Rules; Disease, Germs and Biological Products*. U.S. Postal Service Website. 2013 Available at: http://pe.usps.com/archive/pdf/dmmarchive0106/601.pdf.
28. Public Health Service. *42 Code of Federal Regulation (CFT) Part 71: Importation of Etiologic Agents, Hosts and Vectors and Part 72: Interstate Shipment of Etiologic Agents*. Government Printing Office Website. 2008 Available at: http://www.gpo.gov/fdsys/pkg/FR-2008-01-23/html/E8-1050.htm.
29. Occupational Safety and Health Organization (OSHA). *Disposal of contaminated needles and blood tube holders used for phlebotomy*. Safety and Health Bulletin. OSHA Website. October 15, 2003. Available at: https://www.osha.gov/dts/shib/shib101503.html.

SUPPLEMENTAL RESOURCES

American Society for Microbiology: Available at: http://www.asm.org

American Association of Blood Banks: Available at: http://www.aabb.org/content

Animal and Plant Health Inspection Service (APHIS): Available at: http://www.selectagents.gov

Centers for Disease Control and Prevention: Available at: http://www.cdc.gov

College of American Pathologists: Available at: http://www.cap.org/apps/cap.portal

Heymann DL (Ed). Control of Communicable Diseases Manual, 19th ed. Washington, DC: American Public Health Association, 2008.

National Select Agent Registry Program: Available at: http://www.selectagents.gov

Clinical and Laboratory Standards Institute: Available at: http://www.clsi.org

Occupational Safety and Health Administration: Available at: http://www.osha.gov

The Joint Commission: http://www.jointcommission.org

CHAPTER 109

Nutrition Services

Ruby Puckett, MA, RD, FCSI, CFE
President of Foodservice Management Consultants
Program Director for Dietary Manager Training
University of Florida
Gainesville, FL

ABSTRACT

The goal of this chapter is to identify the responsibilities of the food and nutrition services department for infection prevention and to provide methodologies for preventing foodborne illness. This chapter provides insight into the practices and interventions used to prevent foodborne-associated infections and outbreaks. Food Code 2009 and 2013 provide guidance on food safety, sanitation, and other related requirements to protect the food that is prepared and served. Food Code 2009 is still applicable but added supplement to this code is now Food Code 2013. Changes are incorporated in this chapter. Written policies and procedures provide standards for safety and sanitary handling of food and cleaning and maintenance of food service equipment, cleaning supplies, and personnel. The department must also be knowledgeable with the activities that may influence the infection risk of patients, employees, and their customers. Procedures are developed in case of an outbreak. The Hazard Analysis and Critical Control Point guidelines, a national standard for providing safety precautions in food service and assuring safe practices, need to be implemented to verify that the system is working. A disaster preparedness program for the safety of food and water is coordinated with the overall facility plan.

KEY CONCEPTS

- Food and nutrition services provide safe food and beverages and have responsibilities involving prevention strategies.

- Food should be purchased from approved sources that meet the standards developed by regulatory agencies.

- Clean, properly equipped, temperature-controlled storage and working areas must be provided.

- Calibrated measuring instruments should be used to monitor temperatures.

- Food should be received and stored under conditions that maintain nutritional value and minimize the risk of contamination by microorganisms, insects, rodents, and toxic substances.

- Policies and procedures for maintaining staff hygiene, preparing and serving food on a daily basis, separating clean and dirty, and cleaning and sanitizing equipment, utensils, and work areas should be developed.

- Records of food and equipment temperatures must be maintained, and remediation steps when systems are not in control must be developed. Frequent self-inspections should be conducted, and immediate action taken to correct any problem.

- Waste materials should be disposed according to accepted sanitation principles as well as federal and local health department regulations.

- Training programs and employee supervision should be conducted to ensure adherence to approved policies and procedures.

- Schedules should be developed for cleaning, sanitizing, and disinfecting the department and should include use of appropriate agents and, if required, instructions on the use of personal protective equipment.

- Procedures for monitoring time, temperature, and cross-contamination, and also for initiating the hazard analysis critical control principles practices, should be established.

- Correct techniques in handling ice and products in modified atmosphere packing, and also in ultrahigh temperature processing, should be used.

- Policies and procedures should be developed for providing safe food in vending machines.

- Policies and procedures should be developed for collaboration, communication, and participation with infection prevention and public health officials during each step of an investigation of a foodborne outbreak.

- Food and nutrition services should participate on the facility Infection Control Committee.[1]

BACKGROUND

This chapter provides information to assist the infection preventionist (IP) in understanding the food and nutrition services (FNS) department and its unique role in healthcare—providing safe food and beverages to patients, employees, and customers—and its role in reducing the risk of foodborne illness.

FNS is an important component of infection prevention in healthcare facilities. The routine operation of FNS provides nutritious, safe food and beverages for patients, visitors, and healthcare personnel (HCP). During national recalls or local food contamination incidents, the FNS leadership and the IP work together to implement strategies to ensure a safe food supply chain. Appropriate management and control of the delivery of food from the farm to the table is the foundation of safe products. FNS policies and practices follow accepted food management standards as outlined by local, state, federal, and surveying agencies. The Hazard Analysis and Critical Control Point (HACCP) guidelines and other standards related to production, receiving, storage, serving, disaster preparedness, and waste management help to ensure a safe food chain.[1] Adherence to these recommended practices prevents system failures that can lead to foodborne illness. Although breaches in accepted practice may contribute to foodborne illness, there have been multiple outbreaks reported that have been related to food supply chain contamination. The IP, the food service management team, and public health officials must establish open and ongoing communication and work together to identify practices and sources of foodborne illness.

INFECTION RISK

When all personnel work together to provide sanitary and safe care; safe, nutritious food; and medical nutrition therapy, the clientele is best served. When necessary, this also includes investigation of potential foodborne illness. Safe food practice begins with purchasing from approved reputable suppliers and establishing safe storage practices. It also includes holding and serving the food appropriately. The FNS must develop standards for the evaluation of the food served to all customers. Two important standards are time and temperature of the food served and employee hygiene.[1]

FNS leadership must monitor performance against standards for outcomes, record infractions and corrective action taken, and make standard changes, as appropriate, when the standards are poorly designed.

The assistance of state and local health authorities can help enhance the healthcare facility's food safety program and ensure that the food provided to patients, residents, and visitors will be free from infection risk.

FNS has the responsibility to ensure that the facility serves foods and beverages that are safe and free from contamination. Statistics from 2011 show that the major contributing factors for foodborne illness were improper hand washing and bare-hand food contact by a food service employee.[2] Other causes for foodborne illness were the following:

- Improper temperature in storage (dry, refrigerated, freezer and defrosting), production hot-holding, improper cooling, and reheating[3,4]

- Infected person handling food[5]

- Cross-contamination (contaminated prepared food and raw ingredients, contaminated food preparation work area, utensils, and other equipment)[1,6]

- Improper cleaning/sanitizing of utensils, trays, dishes, glasses, equipment, and work areas[6]

- Food from unsafe source, poor utilization of leftovers, adding of unsafe chemicals[1,2]

- Pathogens naturally present in food supply

- Contamination or mishandling during processing, transport, storage, preparation, and/or serving

- Pathogens may grow, when new pathogens are introduced, and other biological, chemical, and physical contaminations may enter food[6]

Hazardous Agents

There have been reported outbreaks of foodborne illness in all areas in the food chain, which affected patients/residents, as well as HCP and visitors. According to the latest information from the Centers for Disease Control and Prevention (CDC), it is estimated that one in six Americans (or 48 million people) get sick, 128,000 are hospitalized, and 3,000 die from foodborne illness annually.[7] Salmonella has been reported as the major cause of illness.[8] There are 250 known foodborne illnesses caused by bacteria, viruses, and parasites. Young children and older adults were most likely to have severe complications or die from these illnesses. Thirteen percent of infections, 24 percent of hospitalizations, and 57 percent of deaths occurred among adults age 65 years or older. Salmonella was the most common infection (1.2 million U.S. illnesses annually) and the most common cause of hospitalization and death that was tracked.[8]

The yearly cost of all foodborne illness is approximately $5 to $6 billion in direct medical expense and loss of productivity. The CDC has estimated that for two major groups of foodborne illness there are 31 known pathogens, including[8]:

- Norovirus (5,461,731 illnesses, 14,663 hospitalizations, 149 deaths)

- Salmonella nontyphoidal (1,027,561 illnesses, 19,336 hospitalizations, 378 death—highest incidence of death)

- Clostridium perfringens (965,958 illnesses; no information available for hospitalization and deaths)

- Campylobacter spp. (845,024 hospitalizations, 76 deaths)

- Staphylococcus aureus (241,148 illnesses)

- Toxoplasma gondii (4,428 hospitalizations, 327 deaths)

- Shiga toxin-producing Escherichia coli (STEC) O157 (2,138 hospitalizations)

- Listeria monocytogenes (255 deaths)[7,8]

Laboratory-confirmed infections with *Campylobacter,* *Cryptosporidium, Salmonella, E. coli* (O157 and non-O157), *Shigella,* and *Yersinia* were the highest among children under 5 years of age. The incidences of *Cyclospora, Listeria,* and *Vibro* infections were the highest among adults 65 years and older.

V. vulnificus is found in raw, improperly cooked, or cooked recontaminated fish, shellfish, or crustaceans, especially oysters harvested along the Gulf of Mexico coast from April to October, when the bacteria thrives in the warm Gulf Coast waters. The Florida Administrative Code states that establishments serving raw oysters are required to display "either on the menu, tabletop, or elsewhere in *plain view of all patrons,* the following notice: There is a risk associated with consuming raw oysters. . .If unsure of your risk, consult a physician."[1]

Foodborne illness can be caused by a variety of organisms. These include bacteria, viruses, parasites, fungi, and helminths (wormlike parasites, hookworms, whipworms, and flukes).[9-11] Illness is caused by ingesting food that contains a pathogenic agent. Common signs and symptoms of illness can range from upset stomach, diarrhea, fever, vomiting, abdominal cramps, and dehydration to a more severe illness and even death.[1,6,10,11] If symptoms are severe or persist, medical help should be sought. This is especially true for pregnant women, newborns, young children, older adults, and people with weakened immune systems.[1,6,10] The local health department should be notified of the foodborne illness.[1,6,10]

Bacterial agents produce foodborne infection after ingestion of a contaminated food product and replication in a susceptible host. They include *Salmonella* spp., *Clostridium botulinum, Clostridium perfringens, Bacillus subtilis, B. cereus, E. coli, Shigella* spp., *Vibrio parahaemolyticus, Streptococcus pyogenes* group A, *Campylobacter* spp., and *Listeria monocytogenes.*[1,10,11]

Food sources for bacteria include protein foods such as milk, raw meat, poultry, shellfish, raw milk, processed meat, soft cheese, ground meat, ham, cold cuts, and fish. Other foods include cereal, rice, starchy foods, cream-filled desserts, raw seed sprouts, and large quantities of food held at room temperature or cooled too slowly, and contaminated water. There have also been outbreaks of ingested strawberries, raspberries, cantaloupe, chopped salad mixes, garlic in oil, peanut butter, and Greek yogurt resulting from improper food handling.[1,10,11,12]

Viruses require living cells to replicate, so—unlike bacteria— they will not replicate in food. Once a virus enters a living cell, it interrupts the cell's life process and uses the cell to produce more viruses. The major source of viral foodborne illness includes contaminated water, iced drinks, water, salads and ready-to-eat foods, food handled by infected employees who failed to follow correct personal hygiene practices, and, if eaten raw, molluscan shellfish (oysters, mussels, and clams harvested from polluted water). Shellfish should be purchased only from a certified source. Potable water is to be used for washing produce, drinking, making cold beverages (noncarbonated), for all preparation of food,

and for cleaning. Viruses include Hepatitis A, Hepatitis E, and norovirus.[1,10,11]

Parasites are organisms that must live in or on a specific host to survive. They do not grow on food. The parasite is transmitted from animals to humans if food is not cooked thoroughly. Parasites are naturally present in many animals such as pigs, cats, rodents, and fish. Pork and fish must be cooked to proper temperature or a foodborne illness caused by parasites could result. Parasites include *Toxoplasma gondii, Entamoeba histolytica, Cryptosporidium parvum,* and *Cyclospora.*[1,10,11] See other chapters in the APIC Text that address these pathogens.

Agents that replicate in food and produce foodborne intoxication when ingested by the host include *Staphylococcus aureus, Bacillus cereus, C. botulinum, Clostridium perfringens, Vibrio cholerae, Shigella* spp., *E. coli, Giardia lamblia, Cryptosporidium parvum, Cyclospora, Trichinella spiralis* (a roundworm found in pork and wild game), and *Anisakis* (a roundworm found in fish). Foods in which they may be found must be cooked thoroughly to destroy potential parasites.[1,6,11]

There are *natural toxins* found in some food sources. They include two fish toxins (scrombroid and ciguatera), shellfish toxins, and mushrooms. Plant food toxins can be found in honey from bees that gathered nectar from mountain laurel and rhododendrons, apricot, kernels, fava beans, Jimson weed, rhubarb, and in milk from cows that have eaten snakeroot, crocus seeds, raw cassava, sunburned green potato skins, raw castor beans, hemlock flowers, and leaves.[1,13]

Monitoring for Contamination

A cluster of similar illnesses that might be attributable to healthcare-prepared food in those who ate at the facility should raise the suspicion of foodborne illness. When such an outbreak is suspected, an investigation that includes epidemiological assessment and appropriate microbiologic monitoring is to be considered. Routine microbiologic sampling of food is not recommended and should be discouraged. Hospital-prepared infant and adult enteral formulas may need to be tested. When the diagnosis of a foodborne illness is verified, food service personnel are to notify their supervisor. Coordination with local public health officials is mandatory in many states. Together the FNS manager, the IP, and public health official should determine which food items are suspect. Samples from the same lot or batch should be saved. When appropriate, food items should be cultured. Comparison samples are not desirable. The actual food from the same batch or lot should be cultured. Routine culturing of food service personnel is not recommended but may be required by some local agencies.[1,6,7,13]

Addressing a Foodborne Outbreak

During a foodborne outbreak, the FNS department should:

- Save suspected foods for culturing by an appropriate laboratory.

- Document departmental conditions at the time of preparation of suspected food.

- Report gastrointestinal symptoms from patients, visitors, or HCP to the IP/employee/occupational health.

- Provide a list of foods served during the suspected interval.

- Implement and supervise control measures to prevent further occurrence of the illness.

- Follow state and local laws/regulations when reporting to local health authorities.[1,13]

Investigating a Foodborne Outbreak

According to the CDC website for foodborne disease, "a foodborne-disease outbreak (FBDO) is defined as an incident in which two or more persons experience a similar illness resulting from the ingestion of a common food."[7] Proving the linkage of the disease to the food requires collecting an optimal specimen for laboratory confirmation.

The CDC has sample questionnaires to assist the IP and FNS manager in collecting data during an outbreak investigation. Details on how to investigate a foodborne illness can also be found in *Foodservice Manual for Health Care Institutions*, 4th ed., Chapter 13, pages 267–276.[1]

The following steps are used in an investigation.

1. Establish that an outbreak exists, as opposed to a pseudo-epidemic or endemic case.

2. Develop case definitions.

3. Verify the diagnosis by appropriate clinical and laboratory tests.

4. Notify appropriate public health authorities.

5. Search for new or additional cases.

6. Characterize the cases in terms of time and place.

   a. Interview those who were sick and those who were not (cases and non-cases) for date of onset, meals/foods eaten (minimally 3 days before onset), and other activities related to the onset.

   b. Calculate food-specific attack rates.

7. Culture implicated food if available (usually not applicable to a standard healthcare facility laboratory).

8. Formulate a hypothesis.

9. Initiate control measures.

10. Prepare and distribute a final report to appropriate personnel, documenting the epidemiological features of the outbreak, mode of transmission of the infectious agent, and control measures implemented.

Please also refer to Chapter 12 Outbreak Investigations and Chapter 83 Foodborne Illnesses.

Surveying Agencies for Healthcare FNS

A healthcare department may be surveyed by The Joint Commission (TJC), the Centers for Medicare & Medicaid Services (CMS), state licensing agencies, the county health department, and the Occupational Safety and Health Administration (OSHA). Surveys are conducted against standards developed by Congress, state legislatures, and by state, county, and municipal agencies. The purpose of the surveys is to protect the health of the public by preventing or correcting unhealthy sanitation practices. Most of the agencies conduct on-site inspections, which may be unannounced. All of the agencies listed have standards/requirements that relate to FNS. The surveyors may ask the FNS director to provide documentation and information pertinent to the survey. Most of the states have adopted U.S. Department of Agriculture (USDA)/Food and Drug Administration (FDA) food code standards. The FNS department should have copies of all applicable standards. It is the responsibility of the FNS director to educate the staff on standards used by the surveyor. Employees need to participate in mock surveys to understand the process used by the surveyors.[1,6]

Environmental Concerns

Plumbing systems are of particular environmental concern for infection prevention in the FNS department. Plumbing systems perform two very important functions: bringing potable water to the operation and removing waste to the sewer system or disposal plant. Plumbing is inspected as a part of the surveying process and local health inspection. The following items are included in a survey or inspection[1,6]:

1. The water supply must be protected from contamination by avoiding *cross-connections* or any physical link through which contaminants from drains, sewers, or waste pipes can enter a potable water supply.[1,5,6]

2. Plumbing fixtures such as hand-washing sinks, toilets, and urinals shall be cleaned as often as necessary to keep them clean.[5] Toilet tissue is provided in each toilet stall, covered waste receptacles are in each restroom, and hand-washing signs are posted in each toilet room used by employees.

3. All poisonous or toxic materials such as insecticides, detergents, disinfectants, or polishes should be clearly labeled and stored separately from food storage or preparation areas.[1,6]

4. Lighting, ventilation, and humidity controls are necessary to prevent the condensation of moisture and growth of molds.[1,6]

5. Heating/ventilation/air condition systems are designed and installed so that air intake and exhaust vents do not cause contamination of food, contact surfaces, equipment, or utensils.[1,6]

Management of Waste and Pest Control

Accumulations of garbage attract and provide refuge for pests (e.g., rodents, roaches, and flies). Leakproof, easily cleaned, pestproof, nonabsorbent garbage containers with tight-fitting lids help to reduce pest infestation. Garbage in containers should be moved as soon as possible from the kitchen area to the facility garbage holding area.[1,6]

Contracts for waste disposal should establish an appropriate pickup and removal schedule to remove garbage and other waste. All containers (cans, compactors, and dumpsites) should be outdoors and on a smooth surface of nonabsorbent material (e.g., concrete and asphalt). These areas need to be separate from food equipment, utensils, and linens.[1,13,14]

Providing prompt waste removal and area cleanliness reduces the risk of insects and vermin at the outside pickup site. Infestations can quickly move into healthcare facilities. Container should be washed in an area with a floor drain connected to a sanitary sewer system.[1,5,15,16]

An integrated pest management (IPM) system uses a variety of techniques to prevent pest infestation. The main objectives of IPM are[1,5,6,13–17]:

- Ensuring that all openings are sealed (e.g., cracks, tears in screens, tight-fitting windows and doors)

- Keeping area in good repair

- Inspecting incoming deliveries for infestation

- Checking produce area for roaches

- Monitoring all dry products in storage area

- Keeping area clean and sanitized

- Hiring a licensed pest control employer/operator—a person trained and licensed in pest management and control—to inspect, identify, evaluate, and report reasons for pests in the facility and report sanitation issues or structural conditions conducive to pest infestation

BASIC PRINCIPLES

The FNS department is responsible for the development of purchasing specifications that meet standards of safety and sanitation for food, equipment, and cleaning supplies. The FNS department should maintain and clean work areas, storage areas, and equipment for the handling of supplies in accordance with state and local health department standards and HACCP guidelines. The department should have written standards for safe preparation, handling, and storage of food to minimize contamination by microorganisms and chemicals.[1] There should be standards for cleaning and sanitizing hoods, grease trays, garbage disposal units, tray liners, and delivery carts.[1] The department needs to have written policies and procedures regarding employee health as outlined in the latest issue of the Food Code.[18] Employee health policies and procedures should be included in the department orientation and handbook, human resources, and employee health and facility infection prevention policies and procedures.[18] To prevent foodborne illnesses, written standards for cleaning and sanitizing trays, utensils, tableware, and other surfaces, and disposal of dietary

waste, are essential. The department is required to comply with the local health department regulations for storage, handling, and disposal of garbage.

Educational programs on food preparation and personal hygiene should be conducted for HCP accompanied by monitoring and feedback of practice compliance.[1,5] Personal hygiene policies and practices are critical to ensuring that food service employees are healthy and provide safe food preparation. Foodborne illness related to S. aureus skin infections and Salmonella has been linked to infected food handlers. Poor personal hygiene by food handlers is the second most common practice associated with foodborne disease.[1]

GUIDELINES FOR FOOD AND NUTRITION RESPONSIBILITES

Purchasing

Purchasing is the first step in the movement of food from the supplier. The purchasing process includes:

- Selecting suppliers to the facility that offer quality products, delivered in safe and sanitary conditions

- Delivery of products in appropriate vehicles (refrigerated, enclosed vehicles)

- Securing products from an approved source. An approved source is one that is inspected based on federal, state, and local laws and has appropriate HACCP procedures in place[1,6,7,19]

- Securing products that have complete, verifiable specifications

- Containment of products in the appropriate packing or containers (avoid products in glass containers due to possible breakage)[1,6,7,18,20]

When food is purchased it may contain intrinsic contamination: microorganisms intrinsically may replicate, causing increased risk of producing food-related illness when ingested. Persons with a compromised immune system, children, pregnant women, and elderly persons are at particular risk from foods with intrinsic microbial contamination. For example, Campylobacter spp., E. coli, and Salmonella spp. have been associated with a variety of products, including beef, pork, poultry, eggs, and most recently peanut butter and its secondary products. Hepatitis A virus has been isolated from shellfish. T. spiralis has been isolated from pork; however, the incidence of related illness has declined in recent years. More recently, enterohemorrhagic E. coli O157:H7 has been associated primarily with undercooked beef. Contaminated fresh produce has caused bacteria, protozoan, and Hepatitis A outbreaks. Listeria monocytogenes has been found in ready-to-eat foods, including luncheon meats and soft cheeses. Imported natural cheeses can also be contaminated with Listeria. Persons with a compromised immune system, children, pregnant women, and elderly persons should avoid these foods and drink only pasteurized juice and cider.[1,6,11]

The purchase of eggs in shells should be limited. Outbreaks of *Salmonella enteritidis* have been traced to the use of clean, whole, uncracked-shell eggs. The FDA classifies whole-shell eggs as potentially hazardous food and recommends limiting the use of eggs in the shell. *Salmonella* infections are a concern in eggs. The intestine of most chickens may contain *Salmonella*. The bacteria from the intestinal tract may be passed on to the hands of the food service personnel and then on to food. Hand washing is vital when handling eggs. Eating raw eggs can be dangerous and is discouraged. The FNS department should use pasteurized eggs as much as possible, and eggs in shells should be limited to preparations requiring them (e.g., boiled, fried, poached and not runny, and catering situations). Potentially hazardous food also should be free of previous extreme alterations in temperature.[1,7,18]

Purchasing food from an approved source is paramount. The CMS recently updated and expanded guidelines regarding food safety in purchasing.[18] The new information states ". . . healthcare facilities the foodservice must purchase and prepare foods from an approved source only. Food from an *unapproved* source includes broad donations, or individual purchases of tomatoes, strawberries, or corn; as well as home-baked goods or home-canned goods from a farm market, roadside stand, or personal home."[20] Generally, food supplies are safe. Products selected should be in commercially filled unopened packages when possible. This would also include tube-feeding formula.[1,6,19-23]

Receiving

Foods received on the loading dock should be inspected immediately. Anything in a damaged container should be rejected. Delivery trucks should be inspected for cleanliness and temperature controls appropriate for fresh and frozen products. A schedule for delivery needs to be followed.

The receiving personnel should check the following items:

- Temperature strips of potentially hazardous foods[1]

- Inspection stamps and labels/tags of meats, eggs, milk, poultry, fish, juice, and pureed foods (eggs should have a grade seal of Grade A or Grade AA and should be clean and have uncracked shells)[7]

- All use-by and expiration dates[1,6,10,23-25]

- Color, texture, odor, and condition of products[1,6,19,23-25]

- Temperature of frozen and refrigerated food, including milk. When the outside temperature reaches 90°F, all refrigerated perishable item need to be refrigerated within 1 hour.[10,26-28]

- Thawed, dripping, and refrozen products[1]

- Open and examine contents of tampered or damaged containers; if appropriate reject product.[1,26,28]

- Inspect for signs of pest infestation and/or spoilage.[1,6,10,23,25]

Storage of Food

Improper storage or poor environmental sanitation may introduce contamination or allow bacteria in the food to increase. To meet food safety requirements, food storage follows a systematic method called FIFO (first in, first out). Food should be protected from cross-contamination by separating raw animal foods during storage, preparation, holding, and display from raw ready-to-eat food, including fruits and vegetables, as well as cooked ready-to-eat foods. 2013 FDA Food Code 3-302.11 changed the above to read, "frozen, commercially processed and packaged raw animal foods stored or displayed with frozen package ready-to-eat food is acceptable."[18] To prevent cross-contamination, no raw foods are to be stored above cooked or ready-to-eat foods.[5,7,23-28]

Key principles of food storage include:

- Store food only in designated areas, never in locker rooms, toilet areas, garbage rooms, mechanical rooms, under sewer lines (that are not adequately shielded), under open stairwells, or near any other source of contamination.[1,26]

- Store in clean wrappers or containers with covers; label contents appropriately with date item received.[1,6,24,26]

- If products are removed from original container that has the lot number, it is important to maintain lot numbers to be able to track and recall in the event of an identified problem.[1,6]

- Store eggs in original container in the refrigerator at 45°F.[7,18,27]

- Remove all corrugated cardboard as soon as possible, because these boxes may deteriorate or damage the product, the product may leak, or water damage may be present; any moisture rots the boxes, and these conditions allow for pest infestation and possible damage to the product.[1,18,26]

- Keep storage areas and vehicles to transport food clean. The area must have variable lighting, ventilation, and air circulation. A temperature range for dry storage is 50°F to 70°F (10°C to 21°C).[1,6,7]

- Low-temperature storage maintenance
  - Fruit and vegetables (except those in dry storage): 40°F to 45°F (4°C to 7°C)
  - Dairy products, eggs, meats, poultry, fish, and shellfish: 32°F to 40°F (0°C to 4°C)
  - Frozen foods: −10°F to 0°F (−23°C to −10°C)[1,6]

- Keep temperature logs of all storage areas; if a problem occurs, correct it and record the methods used to correct it; date, sign, and file.[1,6,8,10]

- Food must be stored 6 inches above the floor on clean racks with slatted shelves or racks that prevent cross-contamination and proper air circulation. Never cover the slats with foil or other materials as this prevents the flow of air.[1,6,26]

- Shelving must allow for cleaning under the bottom shelf or be flush with the floor and away from walls to facilitate cleaning and reduce places for pests to find refuge.[1,6,26]

- Storage shelves should be at least 2 inches from outside walls that may sweat because of differences between inside and outside temperatures. Food storage areas should have an established cleaning schedule to keep the area clean and minimize the risk of insects and rodents.[1,6,24,26]

- Implement cleaning schedules and monitor for cleanliness, temperature, ventilation, and pest infestation.[1,6,10]

- Never store toxic materials used for cleaning and sanitation in food storage area. Label and store in a locked area away from food and paper goods.[1,6,7,26]

- Use the FIFO procedure to rotate stock. Periodically check expiration dates on all food and supplies. It may be necessary to discard foods that are out of date. Food should be stored at the proper temperature, utilizing appropriate thermometers and maintaining temperature log records.[1,6,7,26,29–31]

Food Production System

The food production system must include safe handling of food products. The USDA Food Safety and Inspection Services (FSIS) provides safe handling tips in a program titled FightBac™.[28] It provides four guidelines to keep food safe:

- Clean: wash hands and work surfaces often

- Cook: cook to proper temperature

- Separate: don't cross-contaminate

- Chill: refrigerate promptly

Time and temperature is critical in protecting food in each step in the flow of food. Cooking (preparation and production) is an important step in the flow of food. When food is not properly prepared (e.g., such as not cooking thoroughly), a foodborne illness may occur. Cooking thoroughly destroys most, but not all, biological hazards. Reaching a specific temperature is not adequate to ensure the destruction of all pathogens.[18] Production personnel must hold the end temperature for a specific time. The Food Code states, "a combination of time and temperature to include the end temperature is required."[5] The end temperature is the temperature a food reaches at the end of cooking.[5,7] Check this temperature with a properly calibrated thermometer. Always use an appropriate thermometer to determine the internal temperature.[1,29,31] To measure the internal temperature of meat, place the thermometer in the thickest part of the meat without touching its bones. Insert sideways for thin items. Sanitize thermometer after each use using hot soapy water. Replace in holder and store.[31]

FDA FOOD CODE 2013

Because the highest percentage of foodborne illness results from contaminated lettuce, tomatoes, salads, celery, coleslaw, and fruits such as melons, berries, and papaya, the FDA made the following changes in the 2013 Food Code, effective May 2013[18]:

- Refrigerate cut leafy vegetables because of outbreaks of *Samonella* and enterohemhorragic *E. coli*. These foods are now considered hazardous.

- Although whole tomatoes may still be stored and ripened at room temperature, they must be refrigerated once cut or sliced. Recipes using cut tomatoes must be refrigerated. Processed foods containing cut tomatoes must be refrigerated unless the manufacturer does not require refrigeration.

- Leaves from leafy green vegetables should be removed from the head and cut, shredded, sliced, chopped, or torn. This standard does not include whole heads from which leaves were removed and discarded or fresh herbs such as cilantro or parsley. Handle fresh cut leafy greens with care, including washing. When washing, use running potable water. If soaked or "crisped," potable running water rinse must follow. Keep refrigerated, as cut leafy greens are potentially dangerous foods.

- Chapter 3 NEW §3-401.14 Noncontinuous cooking is a new section providing parameters for cooking raw animal foods using a noncontinuous cooking process.[18]

  - Step 1: Up to 60 minutes initial heating process

  - Step 2: Cooling for 6 hours or less, then hold cold or frozen

  - Step 3: Prior to serving, cook to 165°F for 15 seconds

  - Step 4: Hold hot, cooled, or frozen

A written procedure must be available on-site. Procedures must have prior approval and include:

- Monitoring, corrective actions, and recordkeeping procedures

- System for marking undercooked animal food

- Separate to prevent cross contamination

- Sous-vide often involves a long, slow cooking process in a reduced-oxygen environment, creating a risk of bacterial growth caused to undercooking. Seal the product immediately before cooking. Variance and HACCP plan required for Sous-vide cooking.[18]

- Unattended cooking and hot holding is prohibited, unless monitoring is provided for cooking temperatures or oven temperatures.[18] Monitor for undercooking.

- Comminuted meat cannot be served raw or undercooked from a child's menu. Raw or undercooked meat, eggs, seafood, and raw seed sprouts are currently prohibited on children's menus and in preschools and elder care facilities.[18]

- Four or more eggs may not be pooled unless used in batters or pooled immediately before cooking. Raw eggs must be cooked immediately (within 30 minutes) after breaking. Pasteurized eggs are required if recipe contains four or more eggs and when not cooked within 30 minutes after pooling. New eggs broken for multiple customer orders must be cooked to 155°F (quiche, flan, buffet line scrambled eggs) and must be cooked within 30 minutes after breaking. Consumer advisory is still required if undercooking. Undercooking is still prohibited for establishments serving *only* highly susceptible populations; this includes preschool and elder care. Do not wash eggs.[18]

To Prevent Cross-contamination

Cross-contamination is the transfer of harmful bacteria to a food from other foods, cutting boards, utensils (especially spatulas), surfaces, hands, or poor hygiene. It is prevented by keeping food separate from contaminants by keeping hands, utensils, and food-handling surfaces clean.

- *Always* wash hands and bare arms with warm water (minimum temperature 100°F) before and after handling raw poultry or its juices. Clean and sanitize cutting board, utensils, sinks, and countertops.

- To avoid a buildup of bacteria, marinate in a refrigerator. *Never* use the marinated sauce on cooked meat, fish, or poultry unless it is first boiled (cooked). (Sauce used to marinate contains raw juices that can contain dangerous bacteria.)

- Follow hand-washing and glove-use procedures.[5,7]

- Observe the flow of food during preparation and keep raw foods separate from ready-to-eat foods.[5,7]

Formulas[32-35]

Reduce the risk of contamination when mixing formulas and enteral feedings by designating clean preparation areas. When possible, use commercially reconstituted formulas and feedings. The points below should be used if mixing products:

- Follow a concise procedure for the preparations, including a clean and sanitized work area.

- A foot-activated hand sink, liquid soap (NO bar soap), and one-use disposable towels

- A foot-activated garbage can

- Products should be placed in a clearly visible, labeled container.

- Use correct measurement tools when adding any product.

- After the formula is mixed, label with the name of the product, the date, and the initials of the employee who mixed the formula.

- Monitor compliance to the procedure(s) daily and record results of the cleaning procedures for all equipment, utensils, and work area.

- Train staff who prepare these formulas on safe, sanitary food-handling strategies.

- Consider having staff change from street clothing to department-required uniforms or covering. Hair must be completely covered with a disposable net, and disposable gloves must be worn during food handling.

- Encourage the use of prepared tube-feeding formula to reduce the risk of contamination.

- Never use raw eggs in a formula. If eggs are needed, use only pasteurized liquid or dry eggs.[1,18]

The FNS department is often responsible for delivering the prepared formulas/tube feedings to patient units. Disposable tube feeding equipment (bags, bottles, and tubing) should be used whenever possible, and any reusable bags/bottles must be discarded every 24 hours. The feeding formula that is not pre-packaged should be discarded after hanging in a patient's room for 8 hours. Formulas reconstituted from powder have a 4-hour limit after hanging in a patient's room.[21]

The American Dietetic Association, with the American Academy of Pediatrics' endorsement, has published a book entitled *Infant Feedings: Guidelines for Preparation of Infant Formula and Breast Milk in Health Care Facilities* addressing reconstitution of formula.[35] Nursing personnel are usually responsible for handling and administrating breast milk. Breast milk is a body fluid and is handled accordingly. A procedure should be in place in the event breast milk is administered to the wrong infant. If this occurs, it should be handled as an exposure event and risk management should be notified.[35]

Safe Handling

Food Code 2013 2-103.11(L) Employees are educated in food safety, including major food allergen ingredients and risk. All foods containing allergen must be labeled to include:

1. Name of food

2. Ingredients

3. Name and address of manufacturer or distributor

4. Quantity of contents

A packaging date code for freshness is important in case of a recall, particularly in the case of vending operations.[18]

Handle food with care and thoroughly cook at *every* stage of food preparation. The Food Code recommends that, "meat products should be thawed in a refrigerator at a temperature of 5°C (41°F) or less to 7°C (45°F) or less or submerged under running water to reduce microbial growth."[5,18] Thawing and refreezing of meat products should be avoided. Using commercially filled, unopened packages (e.g., pasteurized milk and milk products, homogenized eggs or homogenized liquid eggs, tube feeding formula) whenever possible will reduce the potential for foodborne illness. "Cooking alone may not destroy all microorganisms or denature all toxins." Some bacteria, such as *Staphylococcus* and several species of *Clostridium,* release toxins that are pathogenic and may not be inactivated at certain temperatures. Using the correct cooking temperatures for meat and poultry products will kill or reduce the number of microorganisms.[1,5,6,28] Some products have established minimum internal temperatures. Examples include those shown in Table 109-1.

Many restaurant menus state that the ingestion of raw beef or seafood is at the risk of the customer. Many commercial food establishments will not serve raw beef and seafood. Undercooked foods can also pose a problem. Rare roast beef and rare beefsteak should be served only to populations that are not highly

Table 109-1 Internal Cooking Temperature Specifications: Minimum Food Temperatures 2009 Food Code Update Bulletin

Temperature	Food
165°F for 15 sec	Poultry (chicken, turkey, duck, goose) Wild game animals Raw eggs not for immediate service Stuffed fish, meats, pork, pasta, ratites (ostrich, rhea, and emu), and poultry Stuffing cooked alone or in the poultry Foods cooked in a microwave Sauces, gravy, and soups Leftovers Casseroles
155°F for 15 sec	Ratites (ostrich, rhea, and emu) Injected meats Chopped or ground meat (veal, beef, pork), fish, or commercially raised game animals Mechanically tenderized meats Eggs on a steam table (yolks and whites are firm, not runny)
145°F for 15 sec	Fish, except as listed above Meat, except as listed in other categories Commercially raised game animals, rabbits Raw eggs cooked for immediate service* All whole cuts of meats such as pork, steaks, roast, and chops

*Regulations require that yolks of fried eggs be cooked. Do not serve raw or uncooked eggs. Follow local and state regulations. (Eggs are refrigerated at 45°F)
From Kitchen Companion Your Safe Food Handbook.[33]

susceptible to foodborne disease. Healthcare facilities should not serve raw beef, seafood, or undercooked eggs to a customer.[18]

The Food Code changed Potentially Hazardous Foods (PHF) to Time/Temperature for Food Safety Foods. These foods that are cooked and refrigerated should be reheated rapidly to 74°C (165°F) or higher for 15 seconds before serving.[18] All reduced-oxygen-packaging methods require controls for growth and/or toxin formation of *Clostridum botulinum* and *Listeria monocytogenes*.[18]

Wash raw fruits, including bananas, melons, and other hard-surface fruits and vegetables, under potable running water before serving or use.[1,7] Food Code 2013 now allows "the use of ozone in washing, treatment, storage, and processing of raw fruits and vegetables."[18] A vegetable brush may be used to wash the outside coating of hard fruits and vegetables.[1]

Only food service workers should be permitted in the food preparation area. All other persons should have limited access and only if thy are conducting food service business. Traffic control of unauthorized individuals through food preparation and service areas will help to keep those areas clean and safe for food preparation.[1,5,18,32]

Microwave Cooking

When preparing food in a microwave oven follow the manufacturer's direction for wattage and time. General principles include:

- Place on a microwave-safe dish.
- Cover with wax paper or paper towel to retain surface moisture.

- Loosen or vent the lid to let steam escape (cooking bags promote safe, even cooking).
- Rotate or stir the food item as directed on package, usually at the midpoint of the cooking. This helps to distribute heat evenly.
- Use a thermometer to check the temperature of at least 165°F in all parts of the food item.
- Allow to stand covered (some directions state in the oven) before serving to obtain a consistent 165°F temperature.
- Partial cooking may be done in a microwave *only* if the food is to be finished cooking immediately, either on stove top, grill, or conventional oven.[1,7,36,37]

Prevention Strategies for Safe Food

Prevention strategies for reducing these risks can significantly reduce microorganism replication. These strategies include[1,5–7,9,10,18,34–37]:

- Labeling all food with the preparation date and time
- Not thawing and refreezing food products; keep product refrigerated or frozen
- Thawing of foods (1) under refrigeration in which food temperature is maintained at or below 41°F; (2) completely submerged under potable running water (at a water temperature of 70°F); (3) place food in a water type bag and submerge in cold water (change the water every 30 minutes); (4) as part of the cooking process; or (5) in a microwave and immediately transferred to conventional cooking equipment with no interruption in the process
- Not precooking and holding meats for final cooking (HACCP procedures must be in place)
- Chilling cooked perishable leftover foods to an internal temperature of 5°C (41°F) or less or to 7°C (45°F) or less within 2 to 4 hours of preparation
- Using shallow containers 2 to 4 inches deep for cooling hot foods to facilitate quick temperature reduction (140°F to 70°F within 2 hours and from 70°F to 40°F within 4 hours)
- Not stacking shallow pans on top of each other (allow air to circulate around foods being chilled)
- Rapidly reheating to 165°F within 2 hours
- Keeping hot foods at 135° or higher
- Stirring food while holding
- Do not pour a batch of new hot foods into a batch of hot food being served
- Not using hot food-holding equipment (such as steam tables) to reheat food
- Not reusing food or condiments that have been previously served to customers (butter, sauces, dressings, chips, or bread)

- Using sanitized, calibrated thermometers to monitor the temperatures, as required

Hold hot foods for serving at above 60°C/140°F (or higher). Hold cold foods for serving at 41°F or lower. The temperature danger zone is 41° F to 135°F, which is the temperature range for rapid multiplication of virtually all bacteria associated with foodborne disease.[1,5-7] Transport meal trays to patient units in temperature-controlled carts to keep food hot or cold. It is important to monitor these temperature-controlled carts and document that food is kept at the appropriate temperature during delivery.[1]

FNS takes every opportunity to reduce the introduction of microorganisms in dining areas, and patient meal service. Protect food from airborne contamination by using sneeze guards at salad bars and serving lines. Food that is purchased to be eaten elsewhere is placed in enclosed containers. Minimally handle patient food when distributing it to the patient. Cover all patient food especially when it is transported in an open cart.[1,6]

The interdisciplinary team in conjunction with FNS coordinates patient mealtimes with their scheduled therapy. Each patient unit has a specific time for meal carts to arrive on the patient unit. Nursing is to have the patient ready to eat when meal carts arrive on the unit. Serving trays may be a joint responsibility of nursing and FNS. The most efficient method is for FNS personnel to promptly serve the patient trays to ensure that foods are served at appropriate temperatures. When a patient is not in his or her room at mealtime, the tray should be replaced on the meal cart or in the unit nourishment room. FNS staff and nursing personnel need to make sure the food is maintained at a safe temperature. When the temperature is not maintained at a safe level, nursing may arrange for a new tray to be delivered to the patient. Soiled trays are to be removed from patient rooms within 1 hour after the meal is complete and returned to the dish room for cleaning, sanitizing, and storage for the next meal. Policies for safe times for food items to be stored in patient care are jointly developed by nursing and FNS. It is important to label contents and date when perishable food was placed in the floor/unit refrigerator. Perishable foods not consumed within 48 to 72 hours of preparation must be discarded, even when placed in appropriate refrigeration. After 24 hours, all open cans of nourishment left in a patient room must be discarded. On a daily basis, nursing or FNS needs to check floor refrigerators and discard any out-of-date items, paying close attention to any time/temperature control for safety foods.[1,6,7,18]

Personnel Policies

Personnel policies and procedures should include a monitoring procedure (e.g., employee health program) to ensure that FNS personnel report current illness. Food Code Chapter 2-2 outlines employee health standards, and the information must be included in department orientation and follow-up inservices. When there are breaches in policies, appropriate action needs to be taken and the outcome results must be documented.

The latest issue of the Food Code states "In a verifiable manner, the employees are required to report information about their health and activities as they relate to diseases transmissible through food."[5,18]

Hand Washing

A procedure demonstrating and monitoring proper hand washing technique is part of every FNS supervisor's responsibility. Correct procedures for hand washing need to be a part of FNS employee orientation and ongoing training.[1,6] Gloves are often required in combination with hand hygiene during food handling and processing, especially when handling foods such as raw fresh fruits and vegetables or ready-to-eat foods. When working with raw foods, employees should minimize bare hand and arm exposure and use suitable utensils, such as deli tissue, spatulas, tongs, single-use gloves, and dispensing equipment.[1,5,6,18]

The Food Code requires that hand sinks are available in or adjacent to restrooms and must be easily accessible to kitchen employees.[5,18] Health departments vary in the number of hand sinks in a kitchen. As a rule of thumb, plan on locating a sink every 15 feet to make it convenient for employees to use frequently. (Each facility will need to comply with local regulations.)

Hand-washing method:

1. Use flowing potable hot water of 110°F to 120°F to wet hands and bare arms (minimum water temperature is 100°F).

2. Apply antibacterial soap on hands, fingers, and bare arms.

3. Rub vigorously for at least 20 seconds.

4. Thoroughly rinse in flowing hot potable water.

5. As necessary, repeat Steps 1 and 2

6. Use a single towel to turn off the water. Use another towel to thoroughly dry hands and arms, as damp hands/arms spread more germs than dry hands/arms. Discard towel in garbage receptacle or keep to open the door. Dispose in garbage can located outside the door.

7. Where approved by state codes, use an electric hand dryer by rubbing hands under the forced warm air for approximately 30 seconds. Food Code 2013 states, "the use of a high-velocity blade non-heated pressurized air for hand drying is allowed."[1,5,6,18]

When to wash hands and arms[1,6,18]:

- After removing contaminated gloves that are dirty/torn[5]

- After removing gloves for any reason

- Before handling food during preparation

- After handling food

- After cleaning a food preparation area
- After handling raw food (including meat, vegetables, or fruit) and preparing ready-to-eat foods
- After busing a table
- After contact with unclean equipment and work surfaces
- After contact with soiled clothing and wash clothes
- After using the restroom
- After using cleaners or chemicals
- After touching hair or face, and any time hands are visibly soiled
- After coughing, sneezing, using a handkerchief or disposable tissue, using tobacco, or eating or drinking
- After engaging in other activities, such as handling chemicals, taking out garbage, and working in dish room

Monitoring hand hygiene compliance is required for accreditation as a component of The Joint Commission National Patient Safety Goal No. 7.[38] In addition, the CDC states, "poor personal hygiene of foodservice employees, in particular improper hand washing, contributes significantly to the risk of foodborne illness. Improving foodservice employees' hand-washing practices is imperative in helping to prevent foodborne illness."[7]

Other important standards found in Food Coode 2009 and 2013 are:

- 2-301.11 Clean conditions
- 2-301.12 Cleaning Procedures
- 2-301.13 Special Hand Wash Procedures
- 2-301.14 When to Wash
- 2.301.15 Where to Wash
- 2.301.16 Hand Antiseptics
- 2 302.11 Maintenance (Fingernail care): Fingernail polish or artificial fingernails may not be worn when working with food unless wearing intact gloves.
- 2.303.11 Jewelry (no jewelry except for a plain ring such as a wedding band may be worn while preparing food).
- 2.304.11 Outer Clothing. Food employees shall wear clean outer clothing to prevent contamination of food, equipment, utensils, linen, and single-service and single use articles.[5,7]

Holding and Serving Prepared Foods

An improper storage or holding temperature is the most common practice associated with a foodborne illness. Organisms that are naturally present in food or introduced during processing or handling can thrive and proliferate under improper conditions. Foodborne bacteria can replicate and may produce food-related infections or toxicity. Key factors leading to foodborne contamination and disease include failure to use food within an appropriate amount of time after preparing it, failure to maintain or store food at an appropriate temperature, or unsanitary methods of displaying and serving food.[1,5,6,36]

Cold foods must be held at 41°F or lower; at this temperature the growth of bacteria is slowed. Do not store packaged products (sandwiches) in direct contact with ice or water if water could enter the packaged product.

Cool food from 135°F to 41°F within a maximum of 6 hours. The first step is to get the food to 70°F within the first 2 hours and then to 41°F in the next 4 hours. To accomplish this reduction, follow these steps[36]:

- Place food in a shallow container (2 inches deep) to increase the surface area and reduce cooling time.
- Divide a large piece of meat or large mass of food into several pieces.
- Stir the food in a container placed in an ice bath.
- Use a blast chiller for rapid cooling.
- Add ice to the ingredients

After properly cooling the food cover, label, date, and refrigerate at 41°F or lower. Food must be discarded if not used by the indicated date.[1,5,6,36]

Ice

Written procedures to prevent ice contamination include[1,6,10,39]:

- Use only potable water to manufacture ice.
- Store ice in a covered ice bin; keep covered when not in use.
- Wash hands before scooping, as freezing temperatures do not destroy all pathogens.
- Use nonbreakable scoop (never glass); store the scoop following local regulations, but never in the ice bin on top of the ice; clean and sanitize daily by running through the dish machine.
- Do not store food or beverages in the ice bins.
- Frequently clean the bin.
- Keep ice bin covered to protect ice from broken glass, china, and chemicals. Do not allow unauthorized personal use.
- Ice used for display of cold foods is not to be used for any other source. Once ice is used, including clean-up, discard it.

Overproduction

Overproduction results in leftovers. FNS will need to develop written policies to address the disposition of over produced food items. To reduce contamination and possible foodborne illness, leftovers need to be properly handled, stored, and dated/labeled (how and when to use, and when to discard).[1] A few examples include:

- Discard foods that have been at room temperature for more than 2 hours.

- Quickly chill (see above) or separate into large protions into smaller portions before refrigerating.

- Label with the date when food should be used or discarded. Use these foods within 7 days when stored at or below 41°F. If the foods are not used within the storage time, discard the foods.

- When using leftovers in their original form, reheat to 165°F for at least 15 seconds.

- Do not heat leftovers more than once. Discard remaining leftovers after first heating.

- When adding leftovers to a new food product, such as soup, do not add until soup is heated; then heat the entire product to165°F.

- When in doubt about the quality of the food, discard it.[1,5,6,36]

Hazard Analysis and Critical Control Point

The National Aeronautics and Space Administration (NASA) and the U.S. Army Natick Research Laboratories developed HACCP in 1960. In 1971, the Pillsbury Company in cooperation with NASA and Natick Research Laboratories improved the process. In 1988, the National Advisory Committee on Microbiological Criteria for Foods took over the HACCP. HACCP is a prevention-based food safety system designed to prevent the occurrence of food safety problems. Like many other quality assurance programs, HACCP provides a common sense approach to identifying and controlling problems that likely exist in an operation.[1]

HACCP is used throughout the food industry and can be useful in the FNS department. HACCP is a system that identifies and monitors specific hazards—biological, chemical, or physical properties—that can adversely affect the safety of the food product. This hazard analysis serves as the basis for establishing critical control points (CCPs). CCPs identify the points in the process that must be controlled to ensure the safety of the food. In addition, critical limits are established that document the appropriate parameters that must be met at each CCP. Monitoring and verification steps are included in the system, again to ensure that potential risks are controlled. The hazard analysis, CCPs and critical limits, and monitoring and verification steps are documented in a HACCP plan.

HACCP comprises seven principles that provide guidelines on the development of an effective HACCP plan.[40-44]

Principle 1: Analyze Hazards

The HACCP team begins by identifying the potentially hazardous food/temperature control for safety (PHF/TCS) foods on each day of the menu cycle. The hazard analysis is performed for five purposes:

- Identify any hazard of significance from growing to plate

- Provide a risk basis for selecting likely hazards

- Identify hazards that can be used to develop preventive measures for a process or product to ensure or improve food safety of the process product

- Identify food allergens

- Identify environmental contaminants (chemicals) and physical hazards

Principle 2: Identify the CCPs

A CCP is a point, step, or procedure in which control is applied and a food safety hazard is prevented, eliminated, or corrected to within acceptable levels. According to the USDA, a specific food system may present an unacceptable health risk where there is a loss of control during critical control points or procedures. Points in food preparation that may be CCPs include:

- Cooking, chilling, receiving, mixing ingredients, and other food handling procedures

- Food procurement, including source of supply and condition of food on receipt

- Food distribution

- Food display

- Employee health, hygiene, and education

- Refrigeration or the adjustment of a food's pH to a level required to prevent hazardous microorganisms from multiplying or toxins from forming

Principle 3: Establish Critical Limits for CCP

The procedures to prevent, reduce, or eliminate hazards are determined at this step, and quality and safety limits are established. A critical limit is a prescribed parameter (e.g., minimum or maximum value) that must be met to ensure that food safety hazards are controlled at each CCP. CCPs include:

- Time and temperatures parameters

- Time humidity

- Water activity (aw), pH

- Preservation, salt concentration

- Available chlorine, viscosity

- Hand washing, illness of personnel

- Storage, preparation, and service
- Temperatures for preparation, holding, and service
- Appropriate use of leftovers and rethermalization

Principle 4: Establish Procedures to Monitor CCPs

Monitoring is a planned sequence of observations of measurements to assess whether a CCP is under control and to produce an accurate record for use in further verification procedures. There are three main purposes for monitoring:

- It tracks the system's operation so that a trend toward a loss of control is recognized and corrective action can be taken to bring the process back to control before a deviation occurs.

- It indicates when a loss of control and a deviation have actually occurred and corrective action is taken.

- It provides written documentation for use in verification of the HACCP plan.

The team decides who will be responsible for monitoring the critical limits, as well as what forms are used to document the activities and the methods to use to inform the staff of the monitoring activities. All information gathered must be objective and measurable. The monitoring procedures track the system or process of operation.

Principle 5: Establish Corrective Actions

Corrective actions are activities taken whenever a critical limit is not met. Corrective actions should determine and correct the cause of noncompliance, determine the disposition of the noncompliant product, and record the corrective actions taken.

Principle 6: Establish a Recordkeeping System

The following are some examples of HACCP plan verification activities used as part of an HACCP program:

- Establishment of appropriate verification inspection schedules

- Review of the HACCP plan

- Review of the operation to check that CCPs are under control and monitoring is effective

- Review of deviations and their resolutions, including disposition of food

- Visual inspections of operations to observe if CCPs are under control

- Random sample collection and analysis

- Self-checking audits

- Check the system when changes are made such as new products, new procedures, new suppliers, and any other changes occur.

Principle 7: Establish Procedures to Verify the System Is Working

This principle requires the preparation and maintenance of a written HACCP plan by the food establishment. The plan must detail the hazards of each individual or categorical product covered by the plan. It must clearly identify the CCPs and the critical limits for each CCP. CCP monitoring and recordkeeping procedures must be included in the establishment's HACCP plan. An implementation strategy is a part of the food establishment's documentation. Follow-up studies and a permanent control program need to be established. Verification and auditing can verify the HACCP system is working correctly and achieving the desired result.

Emergency Management Preparedness

Surveying agencies such as CMS and TJC have established standards for emergency management preparedness. State and local agencies have regulations for the amount of food and potable water to have on hand in case of an emergency (usually, a 72-hour supply); these procedures need to be followed. All personnel need training for their responsibilities during a crisis/emergency. The FNS departments have written plans that are a major part of the facility plan. These plans are included in an all-facility exercise, with emphasis on how food, potable water, and meal trays would be supplied to patients, staff, and others. To augment the facility exercise, FNS uses an exercise called "tabletop planning" in which potential scenarios and planning are discussed by the interdisciplinary team without a simulation exercise.[1,45–47]

Specific steps that FNS will take in anticipation of an emergency include:

1. Monitoring the amount of emergency supplies on hand and comparing that to projected need

2. Following state and local regulations concerning the amount of food and water required per population

3. Checking availability of water purifying materials

4. Checking operation of flashlights and ensuring that a backup supply of batteries is on hand

5. Reviewing employee addresses and phone numbers and updating call backlists

6. Monitoring sanitation for needed supplies and correct storage. Checking supplies for FIFO and rotating supplies as needed.[1]

7. Reviewing emergency response protocols with HCP.

During a disaster, it is a priority to provide drinking water and food to patients and HCP. FNS is often responsible for this critical service of providing potable water and for planning for alternative sources and/or methods to purify water. Potable water is required for drinking, food preparation, and cleaning. FNS's emergency response plan needs to address a plethora of areas, including external and internal departmental communications; adequate staffing for the projected need; procedures for safety, sanitation, and security of food, water, and HCP; management of unauthorized people who enter the department; and management of the clinical role for medical nutrition therapy.[1,45-48]

FNS must work closely work with approved suppliers through procurement contracts for delivery of food and water in an emergency and for establishing stockpile/storage of emergency supplies. Special considerations for food preparation, safety, and delivery must be given when there is an electrical outage, including methods for delivering patient food trays to various floors. Provisions for safely preparing baby formulas and enteral formulas also need to be addressed.[6,35] In addition, strategies to meet refrigeration needs, such as having access to a refrigerated truck, would be important to identify in contracts and services before the incident. If refrigerated trucks are not available, the processes for handling food under those circumstances should be included in written emergency plans. Maintaining a stock of disposable dishes, utensils, and cups will be useful when dishwashing systems are not functioning. Waterless hand sanitizers in compliance with FDA guidelines may be used for hand hygiene during times of emergency. The product should be easy to use with a pleasant or nonirritating smell. The use of bar hand soap is highly discouraged.[1,18,44-46]

Food Safety and Recall

The USDA Food Safety and Inspection notifies the public of a recall. Suppliers may also notify the facility. Items for recall should be separated in the storeroom from products that may be used. Ensure that the product is *not* used. Follow the recall procedure of discarding or returning the product to the supplier.

Cleaning, Sanitizing, and Equipment Maintenance

New standards for the maintenance of equipment, utensils, and linens have been added to Food Code 2013, primarily to align the standards with the EPA terminology and procedures.[49] Table 109-2 identifies changes in chemicals and temperature for sanitation. Another significant change addresses the rinsing of equipment and utensils after being cleaned and sanitized summarized in the steps below.[18]

1. The rinse is applied directly from a potable water supply by a warewashing machine that is maintained and operated as specified in the Food Code.

2. The rinse is applied *only* after the equipment and utensils have been sanitized by application of hot water or by application of a chemical sanitizer solution whose EPA-registered label instructions call for rinsing off the sanitizer after it is applied in a commercial warewashing machine.[22,50]

The selection of products for cleaning and sanitation is important. Select products for specific purposes. Collaborate with the cleaning supply company for recommendations, especially for ware washing and overall cleaning procedures.[50-53]

The use of poorly designed or old equipment that is difficult to clean is more likely to spread microorganisms. Equipment that has cracked and chipped surfaces should not be used. All employees need to be educated and trained for appropriate cleaning and sanitation systems. FNS management should continuously monitor the appropriate use of equipment and cleaning compounds according to manufacturer's recommendations. Scheduled maintenance and cleaning schedules must be followed with routine inspections to ensure that equipment is properly working. A material safety data sheet for all cleaning compounds should be kept on file and accessible as a reference to all HCP.[55] Improper use of cleaning and sanitizing chemicals or equipment may not reduce microorganisms to acceptable levels. Cleaning compounds should be stored separately from food, insecticides, rodenticides, and other poisons.[1,5,6,53-55]

Proper use, cleaning, and sanitizing of cutting boards is essential to prevent cross-contamination. Cutting boards are to be nonabsorbent. The preferred materials for cutting boards include plastic blocks, hard rubber, and nonabsorbent wood. Always use a clean cutting board for food preparation. It is optimal to have separate cutting boards for meat, poultry, and fish; raw fruits and vegetables; and cooked foods. Follow procedures to adequately clean and sanitize each board between uses as a way to help prevent cross-contamination. Replace cutting boards that have become excessively worn or develop hard-to-clean grooves.[1,2,5-7,55]

A clean environment is vital to good sanitation practices. Maintaining a clean environment for food preparation is an important part of a food safety and sanitation program. If FNS fails to use appropriate cleaning and sanitizing techniques, the presence of bacteria and the likelihood of foodborne illness increases. A basic principle to cleaning in FNS is "clean as you go." Clean and sanitize any surface to which food is exposed. This includes dishes, utensils, pots, and pans. Clean all work surfaces, utensils, and equipment thoroughly by rinsing and sanitizing after each use, according to manufacturer's directions. Cleaning schedules should include the time to be cleaned, the procedure for cleaning, and the type of chemical to be used in the cleaning. Cleaning schedules should be posted in a location visible to the HCP. Cleaning consists of removing gross food and other organic matter from working surfaces, utensils, and equipment using potable water. Cloths used for wiping food spills should be used for no other purpose. Wet cloths used for wiping should be stored in a sanitizing solution.[1,7,50-52]

A ready supply of potable hot water (120°F to 140°F [49°C to 60°C]) must always be available. Check the water temperature in dishwashing machines prior to use to ensure that it is sufficient to clean and sanitize. Chemical strips may be used to determine the temperature of the water. Be sure to follow the manufacturer's direction for each phase of the wash and rinse cycle temperature. Keep all parts of the machine clean, including any removable parts.[1] Recommendations for temperatures by wash cycle are:

- Prewash: 110°F to 120°F (use appropriate cleaning agent)

- Wash: 140°F or greater

Table 109-2. Examples of Chemical Sanitizers and Time/Temperature Requirements

Minimum Concentration	Minimum Temperature	Minimum Contact Time *
Chlorine 25 ppm	120°F	10 sec
Chlorine 50–100 ppm	75°F–115°F	30 sec
Chlorine 100 ppm	55°F	10 sec
Iodine 12.5–25 ppm	75°F–120°F minimum 75°F–68°F	30 sec
Quaternary ammonium 180–200 ppm	75°F (minimum)	30 sec

*Contact time shall be consistent with EPA-registered labeling and to harmonize with EPA terminology.[56]

- Rinse: 160°F or greater
- Final rinse: 180°F

The most commonly used sanitizers are chemicals and heat. It is important to select appropriate disinfectants, sanitizers, and detergents as an intervention in preventing foodborne illness. Use a systematic evaluation of products when selecting a sanitizer for use in the FNS department. The FNS leadership needs to know where and how the sanitizer is used, as well as the properties of the water and the equipment, if any, where it will be used. Select products that meet the department's needs. Chemical sanitizers are affected by time of exposure, pH, temperature, and water hardness.[1,6,7]

Examples of commonly used chemical sanitizers and time/temperature requirements are in Table 109-2.

Heat sanitizers, either moist or dry, require a minimum temperature and exposure time. Table 109-3 gives examples of commonly used heat sanitizers and minimum contact time.

The competency of food service workers is essential to ensuring food safety and sanitation. They should be trained in all procedures for cleaning and sanitation, including the proper mixing and use of chemical and heat sanitizers. Procedures should also be available in a hard copy text for quick reference. Training records containing topic, objectives, length of training, name of instructor, and participant should be maintained and filed in the FNS administrative office.[1,5,6,56]

Dishes should be air dried—never dried with a cloth. Air-dried dishes should be stored in a clean dust-free area protected

Table 109-3. Commonly Used Heat Sanitizers

Medium	Temperature	Minimum Contact Time
Steam	200°F	5 min
Water	170°F	5–20 min
Dry heat	180°F	20 min

FDA Code Cleaned food contact surfaces can be sanitized by immersion in water that is 171°F or above for at least 30 seconds.

from splashes, spills, pests, and other forms of contamination.[1,6,7] Avoid stacking utensils within one another until they are completely dry. Cups and glasses are stored in an inverted position.

Vending Machine Guidelines[57,58]

All vending machines must comply with National Automatic Merchandising Association, National Sanitation Foundation (NSF), federal, state, and local codes. Vending machines may be self-operated or sourced out to a vending company. Regardless of who oversees the vending operation, food quality, equipment operation, and maintenance and vending area sanitation, temperature control, safety of food, and out-of-date products are a major concern. If a vending company operates the machines, strict written polices delineating the FNS and company responsibilities must be established. If self-operated, FNS must have written procedures for the operation.

All machines, except those that dispense canned sodas, must have an overheat protection. If not protected from the outside elements, the dispensing compartment of a vending machine must be equipped with a self-closing door.[59]

Vending machines should be located in an area that provides space around and under equipment to facilitate cleaning and maintenance.[1,6,7] Food in the machine should be stored and packaged in clean, protective containers; handled, transported, and vended in a sanitary manner; packaged in single-service containers with expiration dates; and refrigerated or heated and held at correct temperatures (41°F or below for cold foods and 135°F or above for hot foods). The exceptions includes the 30-minute recovery period after loading or servicing and the 120 minutes to heat foods through the 41°F to 135°F temperature zone.[7] Appropriate temperatures are maintained once food is heated and should be maintained until food is served or discarded.[57]

Containers must be kept cleaned and sanitized when used to transfer bulk foods products to machines.

Thermostatic controls should provide adequate refrigeration or heating units or both; ensure the maintenance of applicable temperatures at all times; and prevent the machine from vending the food until serviced by the operator in the event of temperature failure.[7] The thermometers are easily readable and are accurate to ± 3°F. An automatic shutoff should be located in each machine so that the machine shuts off automatically when temperature reaches the danger zone.

PHFs should be held no longer than 24 hours and be labeled with the preparation date and the date when the food is to be consumed, usually no more than 7 days from the date of preparation. Ready-to-eat foods should be discarded within 7 days of preparation when not consumed. All vended PHFs must be in original containers as packaged at the preparation center. Condiments need to be in individual packets. All food must be labeled in accordance with Code of Federal Regulation, Title 21.[58]

Vending equipment must be cleaned and sanitized at least daily. Clean and sanitize all parts of the vending machine that come into direct contact with other PHF by methods approved by the local health authority.[58,60] The exterior construction and surfaces of the equipment should be easy to clean and limit the entrance of insects and rodents. Equipment should be located in such a manner that the space around and under the machine can be easily cleaned and maintained. The interior surfaces and component parts should be made of smooth, nontoxic, corrosion-resistant material, capable of withstanding repeated cleaning and sanitizing, and protected from normal manual contacts, dust, insects, rodents, and other contaminants.[58,60]

The vending machine attendant must conform to hygienic practices while engaged in handling food, food-contact surfaces, utensils, or equipment. Tobacco products in any form are not used while handling food. Personnel with boils, infected wounds, or acute respiratory infections should be restricted from work if there is a likelihood of contaminating food or food-contact surfaces. IPs should be aware of the local or state agencies with authority over vending machines and monitor following established guidelines.[5,18]

CONCLUSIONS

FNS is a key partner in infection prevention, and through its efforts in providing safe food and potable water, it builds a foundation for good nutrition that promotes healing and wellness. Foodborne illness can be significantly reduced and prevented when basic sanitation procedures and local, state, and federal food regulations are followed. The first step in prevention is having policies and procedures in place for safe food handling and personal hygiene and complying with them. Staff education and compliance monitoring are important to ensure consistent and safe practices. FNS department staff should stay abreast of current events related to changes in Food Codes, food contamination, recalls, and outbreaks so they can quickly assess their stock and take appropriate action. Vigilance in following HACCP guidelines strengthens infection prevention efforts. Many FNS departments have the responsibility to feed and nourish patients and staff during times of crisis. It is in the best interests of the customers of FNS for the department to plan for emergencies and test its plans to improve their overall capacity to effectively respond.

INTERNATIONAL PERSPECTIVE

The globalization of the food supply has led to rapid and wide spread international distribution of food pathogens that can inadvertently be introduced into new geographic areas. Travelers, refugees, and immigrants may be exposed to unfamiliar foodborne hazards in new environments. Changes in microorganisms lead to constant evolution of new pathogens, development of antibiotic resistance, and changes in virulence of know pathogens. In many countries as people increasingly consume food prepared outside of the home, growing numbers are potentially exposed to poor hygiene and potentially exposed risk of poor hygiene in community foodservice settings.[61]

The world is a smaller place today because of increased international flights for tourists and expanded international commerce, both of which make the potential for foodborne illness a major public health concern worldwide. An international focus on improving food safety must include these elements to identify and reduce risks: improved surveillance, community education, thorough understanding of the food production chain, use of HACCP strategies, and access to ionizing radiation. The ISO 22000 is a generic food safety management that defines a set of general food safety requirements that apply to all organizations that use HACCP.[62] ISO 22000 uses HACCP to help improve conditions that must be established throughout the entire food chain and the activities and practices that must be performed to establish a hygienic environment.[1] As ISO works with growers, producers, and others in the food chain, it is hopeful that the incidence of foodborne illnesses will decline.[62]

The ISO 22000 will take the collaborative efforts of primary care physicians, FNS, IPs, and public health to establish an effective surveillance and early reporting methodology. These professionals also have a crucial role in educating the public on the importance of basic food safety. The ten most common foods causing foodborne illness, and the most commonly associated organism, in the United States and Canada for the last decade have been listed as[59]:

1. Cantaloupes from Mexico and the United States (*Salmonella*)

2. Ground turkey (*Salmonella*)

3. Eggs (*Salmonella*)

4. Cut celery (*Listeria*)

5. Red peppers from Mexico (*Salmonella*)

6. Peanut butter (*Salmonella*)

7. Spinach (*E. coli*)

8. Tomatoes (*Salmonella*)

9. Roma tomatoes, pre-sliced (*Salmonella*)

10. Deli meat especially sliced turkey (*Listeria*)

In the United States, there have been other major recalls for ground beef (*E. coli*) and chicken (*Salmonella*). Worldwide there are still concerns for typhoid fever, *Listeria*, *E. coli*, and other emerging pathogens. *Salmonella* is the leading cause of foodborne illnesses.[8]

To assist in preventing this global problem, a culture change is necessary. The following suggestions could help in the development of quality improvement program:

• Fully implement the ISO 22000/HACCP program.

• Evaluate farms, slaughterhouses, processing plants, and delivery systems to assess conditions where outbreaks have occurred and, if necessary, shut them down.

- Provide education and training at all steps in the "farm-to-the-table."

- Evaluate temperature maintenance at all steps in the "farm-to-the-table."

- Teach and monitor personal hygiene of employees to include working while ill and above all proper hand-washing procedures.

REFERENCES

1. Puckett RP. *Foodservice Manual for Health Care Institutions,* 4th ed. San Francisco: Jossey-Bass/Wiley, 2013.
2. Vaccaro M. Foodservice employee health inservice. *Nutrition and Foodservice Edge* 2012 May;21(5):11–14.
3. Public Health Madison & Dane County. *Hot and Cold Holding.* Available at: http://www.publichealthmdc.com/environmental/sfc/pdf_files/m09-hotandcoldholding.pdf.
4. Food Service Warehouse (FSW). *Proper cooling and cold-handling methods.* FSW website.
5. U.S. Food and Drug Administration (FDA), Department of Health and Human Services, Public Health Service (PHS). *Food Code 2009.* FDA website. November 8, 2013. Available at: http://www.fda.gov/food/guidanceregulation/retailfoodprotection/foodcode/ucm2019396.htm.
6. Allen SD. *Managing Foodservice and Food Safety.* St. Charles, IL: Association of Nutrition & Foodservice Professionals, 2012.
7. Centers for Disease Control and Prevention (CDC), National Center for Emerging and Zoonotic Infectious Diseases (NCEZID), Division of Foodborne, Waterborne, and Infectious Diseases (DFWED). *Foodborne Diseases Active Surveillance Network (FoodNet).* CDC website. Available at: http://www.cdc.gov/foodnet.
8. Centers for Disease Control and Prevention (CDC). Incidence and Trends of Infection with Pathogens Transmitted Commonly Through Food — Foodborne Diseases Active Surveillance Network, 10 U.S. Sites, 1996–2012. *MMWR Morb Mortal Wkly Rep* [serial online]. 2013 Apr 19;62(15):283–287. Available at http://www.cdc.gov/mmwr/preview/mmwrhtml/mm6215a2.htm.
9. National Restaurant Association. *ServSafe.* Education Foundation of the National Restaurant Association website. Available at: https://www.servsafe.com/home.
10. U.S. Department of Agriculture (USDA), National Agricultural Library (NAL). *Frequently asked questions: pathogens and contaminants.* NAL USDA website. December 26, 2013. Available at: http://fsrio.nal.usda.gov/faq-page/pathogens-and-contaminants.
11. Centers for Disease Control and Prevention (CDC). Parasites. CDC website. Available at: http://www.cdc.gov/parasites/.
12. Puckett RP. e-learning Dietary Manager Training Program, Executive and Professional Education, Division of Continuing Education: University Florida, Gainesville.
13. Seunghee W, Shaklin CW, Lee K-E. A decision tree for selecting the most cost-effective waste disposal strategy in foodservice. *J Am Diet Assoc* 2003 Apr;103(4):475–482.
14. Green Seal, Inc. *GS-46 Green Seal Standard for Restaurants and Food Services, First Edition.* April 20, 2009. Available at: http://www.greenseal.org/Portals/0/Documents/Standards/GS-46/GS-46_Restaurants_and_Food_Services_Standard.pdf.
15. Orkin, LLC. *Assess. Implement. Monitor.* Orkin website. Available at: http://www.orkin.com/commercial/services/integrated-pest-management/.
16. National Restaurant Show Chicago. Rentokil North America Pest Control Booth 5939 *Integrated Pest Control.* Additional information: http://www.Rentokil.com/us/.
17. Food Safety Inspections: Basic Compliance Checklists for GMPs, GAPs, SSOPs and HACCP. Clemson University, College of Agriculture. Available at: http://www.clemson.edu/psapublishing/PAGES/FOODSC/EC708.pdf
18. U.S. Department of Health and Human Services, Public Health Service, Food and Drug Administration (FDA). *Food Code 2013.* FDA website. Available at: http://www.fda.gov/downloads/Food/GuidanceRegulation/RetailFoodProtection/FoodCode/UCM374510.pdf.
19. Donhauser K, Braunback M. Smart purchasing practices for foodservice supplies. *Dietary Manager* [serial online]. 2009;18(10):28–29. Available at: http://www.primeservicesinc.com/Files/PDF/70/DietaryManager.pdf.
20. Puckett RP. Product selection and specifications. *Dietary Manager* [serial online]. 2005 Feb:22–24. Available at: http://www.anfponline.org/Publications/articles/2005_02_038ProductSpecs.pdf.
21. Centers for Medicare & Medicaid Servies (CMS)[0]. ;§483.25(g) Naso-Gastric Tubes. IN: *State Operations Manual (SOM) Appendix PP – Guidance for Long Term Care Facilities.* CMS website. Available at: http://www.cms.gov/Regulations-and-Guidance/Legislation/CFCsAndCoPs/downloads/som107ap_pp_guidelines_ltcf.pdf
22. Reed L. *SPEC: The Comprehensive Foodservice Purchasing and Specification Manual,* 2nd ed. New York: Van Nostrand Reinhold, 2010.
23. Lawn J. Seven mistakes purchasing managers make. *Food Management* 2003;38(3):8.
24. Puckett RP. Effective Foodservice Receiving and Storage Practices. *Dietary Manager* [serial online]. 2007;16(2):12–16. Available at: http://www.anfponline.org/Publications/articles/2007_02_Effective.pdf.
25. Food Receiving. *Food Management* 2009; 2nd Q:57–62.
26. U.S. Department of Agriculture (USDA), National Agricultural Library (NAL). *Food preparation and handling.* NAL USDA website. December 26, 2013. Available at: http://fsrio.nal.usda.gov/food-preparation-and-handling-0.
27. American Egg Board. *A Scientist Speaks about Egg Products.* Park Ridge, IL:American Egg Board, 1981, revised 2010.
28. Partnership for Food Safety Education. *Four Simple Steps to Food Safety.* Fightbac.org website. Available at: http://www.fightbac.org/storage/documents/flyers/fightbac_color_brochure.pdf.
29. U.S. Department of Agriculture (USDA), Food and Safety Inspection Service. *Thermy™ Types of Food Thermometers.* USDA website. Available at: http://www.fsis.usda.gov/wps/portal/fsis/topics/food-safety-education/teach-others/fsis-educational-campaigns/thermy/types-of-food-thermometers/CT_Index.
30. U.S. Department of Agriculture (USDA), Food and Safety Inspection Service. *Is It Done Yet?* USDA website. Available at: http://www.fsis.usda.gov/wps/portal/fsis/topics/food-safety-education/teach-others/fsis-educational-campaigns/is-it-done-yet.
31. U.S. Department of Agriculture (USDA), Food Safety and Inspection Service (FSIS). *Use a food thermometer.* FSIS website. http://www.fsis.usda.gov/wps/wcm/connect/172d856a-e947-4700-915f-69da24c2bf63/iinfographic.pdf?MOD=AJPERES.
32. Critical Elements for Nutrition, Hydration and Tube Feedings CMS Form 20075 (06/07)
33. U.S. Department of Agriculture (USDA), Food Safety and Inspection Service (FSIS).*Kitchen Companion: Your Safe Food Handbook.* FSIS USDA website. Available at: http://www.fsis.usda.gov/wps/wcm/connect/6c55c954-20a8-46fd-b617-ecffb4449062/Kitchen_Companion_Single.pdf?MOD=AJPERES.
34. Puckett RP, Lucas R. *Food and Nutrition through the Life Cycle,* 3rd ed. Dubuque: Kendall/Hunt, 2009;193–199.
35. Pediatric Nutrition Practice group of the American Dietetic Association. *Infant Feeding for Preparation of Formula and Breast Milk in Health Care Facilities,* 2nd ed. Chicago: American Dietetic Association, 2013.
36. National Restaurant Association. *ServSafe Essentials,* 5th ed. Chicago: National Restaurant Association Educational Foundation, 2010.
37. McSwane D, Rue N, Linton R. *Essentials of Food Safety and Sanitation,* 4th ed. Upper Saddle River, NJ: Prentice Hall, 2008.
38. The Joint Commission on Accreditation of Healthcare Organizations (TJC). *2014 National Patient Safety Goals.* TJC website. Available at: http://www.jointcommission.org/standards_information/npsgs.aspx.
39. Food Servise Warehouse (FSW). *Safe ice handling.* FSW website. Accessed Available at: http://www.foodservicewarehouse.com/education/product-safety-public-health/safe-ice-handling-/c28167.aspx.
40. Florida Department of Business and Professional Regulation. *Division of Hotels and Restaurants: Public Food Service Forms and Publications.* Florida Department of Business and Professional Regulation website. Available at: http://www.myfloridalicense.com/dbpr/hr/forms/hr-publications.html.
41. U.S. Department of Health and Human Services, Food and Drug Administration (FDA). *Hazard Analysis & Critical Control Points (HACCP).* FDA website. July 5, 2013. Available at: http://www.fda.gov/Food/Guidance-Regulation/HACCP/.
42. Snyder PO. HACCP in retail industry. *Dairy Food Environmental Sanitation* 1991;11(10):73–81.
43. Puckett RP. Personal and organizational preparedness. The key to surviving a disaster. *Health Care Food Nutr Focus.* 2006 Jan;23(1):1, 3–7.
44. U.S. Department of Health and Human Services, Food and Drug Administration (FDA). *U.S. Food Code 2009Annex 4 Management of Food Safety Practices—Achieving Active Management Control of Foodborne Illness Risk Factors The HACCP System.*
45. Premier, Inc. *Emergency preparedness for healthcare facilities.* Premiere website. Available at: https://www.premierinc.com/safety/topics/disaster_readiness/.
46. Norton LC. Bioterrorism in healthcare foodservice *ASHFA Trends* 2006;8(1):6–7, 13–14.

47. Federal Emergency Management Agency (FEMA). FEMA website. Available at: http://www.fema.gov/.

48. The Joint Commission on Accreditation of Healthcare Organizations (TJC). *Health Care at the Crossroads: Strategies for Creating and Sustaining Community-wide Emergency Preparedness Systems.* 2003. TJC website. Available at: http://www.jointcommission.org/assets/1/18/emergency_preparedness.pdf.

49. U.S. Department of Health and Human Services, Public Health Service, Food and Drug Administration (FDA). *Food Code 2013.* FDA website. Available at: http://www.fda.gov/downloads/Food/GuidanceRegulation/RetailFoodProtection/FoodCode/UCM374510.pdf.

50. Schmidt RH. *Basic elements of equipment cleaning and sanitizing in foodservice operations.* University of Florida IFAS Extension website. Available at: http://edis.ifas.ufl.edu/fs077.

51. North Carolina Department of Health and Human Services. Food Service Orientation Manual, Available at: http://www.ncdhhs.gov/dhsr/acls/pdf/foodsrvman.pdf.

52. Clemson University Department of Food, Nutrition, and Packaging Science. *Define "cleaning" and "sanitizing" and the difference from the two procedures.* FoodSafetySite.com website. Available at: http://www.foodsafetysite.com/educators/competencies/foodservice/cleaning/cas1.html.

53. *Scientific Cleaning Procedures and Sanitation for the Foodservice Industry,* Eco Labs, Inc.

54. Occupational Safety and Health Organization (OSHA), U.S. Department of Labor. *All About OSHA. OSHA 2098.* Washington DC: U.S. Department of Labor, Occupational Safety and Health Administration, 2009.

55. North American Association of Food Equipment Manufacturers (NAFEM). *Industry standards.* NAFEM website. Available at: https://www.nafem.org/information-resources/industrystandards.aspx.

56. Centers for Medicare & Medicaid Servives (CMS). *Health Care Provider Guidance: Emergency Preparedness for Every Emergency.* CMS website. April 9, 2013. Available at: http://www.cms.gov/Medicare/Provider-Enrollment-and-Certification/SurveyCertEmergPrep/HealthCareProviderGuidance.html.

57. Chesapeake Health Department (CHD). *Mobile Food Unit Operation Guide: Guidelines for Foodservice.* Virginia Department of Health website. Available at: http://www.vdh.virginia.gov/lhd/chesapeake/EH%20FORMS/Mobile%20Food%20Unit%20Operation%20Guide%20.pdf.

58. U.S. Department of Health and Human Services, Public Health Service, Food and Drug Administration (FDA). *Food Code 2013.* FDA website. Available at: http://www.fda.gov/downloads/Food/GuidanceRegulation/UCM189448.pdf.

59. World Health Organization (WHO). *Food safety: foodborne disease.* WHO website. Available at: http://www.who.int/foodsafety/foodborne_disease/.

60. Nolan AJ. Vending machine sanitation. Three briefs. *Public Health Rep* [serial online]. 1957 April;72(4):321–324. Available at: http://www.ncbi.nlm.nih.gov/pmc/articles/PMC2031262/.

61. Wilson J. *Unsafe Food Putting Lives at Risk.* Series of articles published in US TODAY September 2011. Available at: http://www.cnn.com/2012/10/24/health/unsafe-food-report/.

62. International Organization for Standardization (ISO). ISO website. Available at: http://www.iso.org/iso/home.html.

CHAPTER 110

Pharmacy Services

Eric S. Kastango, MBA, RPh, FASHP
Principal-CEO
Clinical IQ, LLC
Madison, NJ

Patricia C. Kienle, RPh, MPA, FASHP
Director of Accreditation and Medication Safety
Cardinal Health Phamacy Solutions
Wilkes-Barre, PA

Keith St. John, MS, MT(ASCP), CIC
Director, Clinical Epidemiology
Pharmacy OneSource - Sentri7
Wolters Kluwer Health
Bellevue, WA

ABSTRACT

Since the 1970s, there have been multiple instances of quality problems (e.g., microbial contamination, concentration errors, or pyogenic responses due to endotoxins) associated with compounded sterile and nonsterile pharmacy preparations, many of which resulted in recalls, patient injuries, and deaths. Between January 2000 and before the 2012 nationwide fungal meningitis outbreak, at least 11 outbreaks were identified, involving 207 infected patients and 17 deaths after exposure to contaminated compounded drugs.[1,2] Pharmacists and pharmacy technicians are the professionals primarily responsible for the preparation and storage of compounded sterile and nonsterile preparations. Compounding is the process of combining drug ingredients to prepare medications that are not commercially available (i.e., neonate, pediatric, and geriatric dosage forms or ongoing manufacturer-related drug shortages) or to alter commercially available medications to meet specific patient needs, such as dye-free or liquid formulations.[3] Failure to follow sterile compounding standards[3] and proper aseptic technique has lead to intrinsic (i.e., contamination during the manufacturing process or transport to the healthcare facility) or extrinsic (i.e., contamination during preparation, storage, or administration within the healthcare facility or practitioner's office) contamination, which may result in microbial colonization or infection in the patient.

Pharmacy management personnel should participate in identifying staff who would benefit from education and proficiency evaluation of their aseptic technique and compounding procedures and calculations and, when necessary, to coordinate any medication recalls and traceability to the patients who have received specific products associated with medication errors, endemics, and epidemics. This should include both pharmacy personnel and other clinicians who may compound sterile preparations (including those intended for immediate use), such as anesthesia practitioners, nurses in oncology and other clinics, personnel in allergist offices, dialysis nurses and technicians, etc. A contaminated infusate administered through a central venous catheter is a rare cause of catheter-associated sepsis but one of the most readily identifiable causes of epidemic healthcare-associated bacteremia associated typically with one organism. Because it is not routine to culture infusate specimens in a diagnostic evaluation for a central venous catheter–associated infection unless there is strong evidence, many episodes of infusate-contaminated infections may go undetected unless they are part of a cluster of infections in a discrete patient population (e.g., hospital) or in the early stages of an epidemic.[4]

Pharmacy personnel are responsible for coordinating recalls of pharmaceutical preparations, such as occurs in cases of intrinsic contamination or due to other quality deficiencies (e.g., unacceptable particulate matter or potency). Pharmacists and technicians can be instrumental when they participate in multidisciplinary activities, such as quality assurance and quality improvement teams, infection prevention committees, and antimicrobial stewardship programs, to ensure appropriate preparation and use of pharmaceuticals.

KEY CONCEPTS

- Risks associated with microbial contamination of compounded sterile preparations

- Modes of extrinsic contamination of compounded sterile preparations

- Methods for preventing extrinsic contamination of compounded sterile preparations

- Pharmacy oversight involving antimicrobial stewardship

- Collaboration with infection preventionists

BACKGROUND

Significant patient morbidity and mortality have resulted from both intrinsically and extrinsically contaminated compounded sterile preparations.[2] Most of these events have been related to extrinsically compounded sterile preparations. Pharmacy is primarily responsible for the handling, preparation, and storage of compounded sterile and nonsterile preparations. Respiratory therapists, nuclear medicine technologists, nurses, anesthesia practitioners, dialysis technicians, physician assistants, and physicians also prepare compounded sterile and nonsterile preparations. Pharmacy needs to actively participate in the aseptic training of these persons. Pharmacy personnel need to participate as members of the healthcare team when identifying patients who have received specific compounded sterile preparations associated with outbreaks of endemic and epidemic infusate-associated bloodstream infections (BSIs). Pharmacy personnel are responsible for coordinating recalls of pharmaceutical preparations, such as occurs in cases of intrinsic contamination. Other responsibilities of pharmacists include providing clinical care of patients, distribution of oral solid and liquid dosage forms, managing intravenous (IV) therapy teams, preparing compounded sterile preparations for patients receiving home IV therapy, and oversight of policies and practices for administering medications. The pharmacy department provides oversight of the safe and effective use of medications in other areas of the institution (e.g., therapeutic interchange, medication reconciliation, reviews of medication orders to ensure that they are clinically and therapeutically appropriate, and inspections of patient care areas in the search for outdated medication and to ensure the appropriate storage conditions of medications via monitoring of refrigerated medication storage space). The pharmacy also provides information on pharmaceuticals, including indications, dosage, and route of administration; contraindications; adverse effects; drug interactions; and proper storage. Increasingly, pharmacy is part of the antibiotic/anti-infectives stewardship program designed to ensure proper use of antibiotics (appropriate drug[s], dose, and duration) and safest possible drug(s) and to minimize the risk of precipitating antibiotic-resistant pathogens, collateral damage (e.g., *Clostridium difficile* disease), and costs.

Pharmacy personnel are not at high risk for occupational exposure to infectious diseases unless they are involved in direct patient care, such as during cardiac arrest response. The pharmacy should work with the infection prevention and occupational health departments in managing employee exposure to potentially contagious patients and selecting appropriate postexposure prophylactic agents. Pharmacists may be involved in advocating and administering immunizations (e.g., influenza, diphtheria-tetanus toxoid-acellular pertussis, and pneumococcal vaccines). Pharmacists and technicians working within a healthcare facility should be immune to mumps, measles, rubella, varicella, hepatitis B, and pertussis. Immunity may be demonstrated by physician-diagnosed disease (mumps, measles, varicella), serology (mumps, measles, rubella, varicella, hepatitis B), self-history of disease (varicella), or appropriate immunization (all). All pharmacy personnel should receive annual influenza vaccine unless contraindicated.

There is an important parallel and intersection between pharmacy and infection prevention. First, as it relates to the ongoing management of critical environments where sterile compounding is conducted, pharmacists should work closely with infection preventionists (IPs) to ensure that potential sources of environmental contamination are identified during routine environmental monitoring (i.e., air surface and gloved fingertip sampling) and remediated as needed. Critical compounding environments need to be cleaned and disinfected with appropriate equipment (e.g., microfiber mops and low-linting wipes) and germicidal agents so IPs can provide critical insight and assistance to maintain a state of control in these environments.

Second, the pharmacist conducts surveillance of antimicrobial utilization even as IPs monitor pathogens. The value of collaboration is the ongoing assessment and analyses of the impact of utilization patterns on the emergence (hopefully regression) of multidrug-resistant organisms (MDROs) and microbes of epidemiologic importance. The related activities support and enhance the increasing attention to antimicrobial stewardship programs that demonstrate greatest success when developed as a team effort.

BASIC PRINCIPLES

Contamination of infusates is believed to be an uncommon cause of infections but has resulted in episodes of Gram-negative rod (GNR) bacteremia in individual patients and epidemics.[2,5,6] True incidence of infections related to contaminated infusates is not known. There are two sources of contamination. Intrinsic contamination (that which occurs during the manufacturing process) and extrinsic contamination (that which occurs subsequent to manufacturing, during aseptic manipulations, or while the infusate is in use) of infusates are a less common cause of infection than is cannula-associated contamination but are more likely to result in bacteremia and septic shock.[5] In October 2008, the Society for Healthcare Epidemiology of America and the Infectious Diseases Society of America published a compendium of practice recommendations targeted at the prevention of healthcare-associated infections (HAIs).[7] This publication is in the process of revision and is expected to be released in 2014. This compendium was revised by many healthcare organizations, professional associations, government and accrediting agencies, legislators, regulators, payers, and consumer advocacy groups that have advanced the prevention of HAI as a national imperative. These external pressures have also had an impact on pharmacy practices, as maximizing patient safety remains a critical component of any medication delivery system involved with preparing compounded sterile preparations.[7] In 2004, the United States Pharmacopeial (USP) Convention published the first national and enforceable standards for compounded sterile preparations (i.e., General Chapter 797-Pharmaceutical Compounding-Sterile Preparations).[3] In 2012, both the Centers for Disease Control and Prevention (CDC) and the Centers for Medicare & Medicaid Services acknowledged the importance of the USP chapter in protecting patients against preventable harm from improper use of single-dose/single-use vials.[8,9]

Intrinsic Contamination

Intrinsic and extrinsic contaminations are differentiated based on epidemiologic data. Bacteremia caused by the infusion of contaminated fluids is less common but nevertheless is a potentially serious problem that can affect one patient or dozens depending on the circumstances of contamination (i.e., infusates prepared by nurses versus prepared in the pharmacy).[10] Most healthcare-associated epidemics of infusion-associated septicemia resulting from intrinsic or extrinsic contamination are caused by aerobic Gram-negative bacteria.[11] Pathogens implicated include the Enterobacteriaceae such as *Klebsiella, Enterobacter, Serratia* spp., and *Citrobacter freundii*, and also the nonenterics *Burkholderia cepacia* and *Ralstonia pickettii*.[5,6,11] However, disease can result from intrinsic contamination of medication by endotoxin without the presence of viable bacteria.[12,13]

Intrinsic contamination of infusate has led to epidemics of healthcare-associated sepsis.[5,14,15] Intrinsic contamination of parenteral medications with endotoxin caused an epidemic of clinical sepsis in a newborn nursery.[16] Epidemics of *Candida parapsilosis* and *C. albicans* fungemia have been related to use of contaminated parenteral nutrition (PN).[17-19] Epidemics of septicemia caused by *Staphylococcus saprophyticus* and *Enterobacter cloacae* have resulted from contamination of PN admixtures during compounding or storage.[20]

Extrinsic Contamination

Clusters of postoperative infections have been associated with extrinsic contamination of propofol, an IV hypnotic agent in a 1 percent lipid emulsion; organisms isolated include *S. aureus, C. albicans, Moraxella osloensis, Enterobacter agglomerans*, and *Serratia marcescens*.[21-23] There have been recalls and subsequent shortages of propofol due to the presence of elevated endotoxin levels.[24] An outbreak of severe sepsis (systemic inflammatory response syndrome) occurred in seven postoperative patients in The Netherlands and was related to propofol contaminated with *Klebsiella pneumoniae* and *S. marcescens*.[25]

An outbreak of *E. cloacae* BSIs was associated with contaminated prefilled saline syringes prepared by a home-infusion company distributing to 20 states.[26] Five cases of Hepatitis C were attributed to diversion of fentanyl by healthcare personnel (HCP) infected with Hepatitis C virus (HCV). The diversion of fentanyl resulted in contamination of syringes with HCV, and other HCP subsequently used these syringes to administer fentanyl to patients.[27] Intentional tampering or division must always be considered when an epidemic evaluation of an outbreak implicates extrinsically contaminated narcotics or other controlled substances.

In-use IV fluids have contamination rates of 0.9 to 7.8 percent.[10,28-30] The most common organisms found are coagulase-negative staphylococci. However, GNRs have been found in these infusate solutions. In addition, free endotoxin was found in 2.5 percent.[29] In-use syringes of propofol have shown contamination rates of 5.1 percent (19/376) and 5.6 percent (18/302).[31,32]

Commonly prepared compounded-sterile products are susceptible to microbial contamination. Specific microorganisms have the ability to proliferate in different fluids. *Klebsiella, Serratia*, and *Enterobacter* spp. and *Burkholderia cepacia* can multiply in 5 percent dextrose.[5] *C. albicans* can grow slowly,[5] whereas *Staphylococcus, Proteus, Escherichia coli, Herellea*, and *Pseudomonas aeruginosa* die slowly in dextrose.[33] *Burkholderia cepacia, Pseudomonas aeruginosa, Acinetobacter*, and *Serratia* will grow in distilled water.[5] *P. aeruginosa, Enterobacter*, and *Serratia* can grow in lactated Ringer's solutions.[5] Microbial growth, with the exception of *Candida* species, is possible in 0.9 percent sodium chloride.[34]

Fungi such as *C. albicans* and *C. glabrata* can grow in PN fluids, albeit very slowly; proliferation did not occur when solutions were stored at 4°C for 7 days.[35] The growth of most bacteria is inhibited in PN solutions. The addition of albumin to PN solutions increases the potential for bacterial and fungal growth.[35] *S. aureus, E. coli, E. cloacae, P. aeruginosa*, and *C. albicans* grow in 10 percent fat emulsion solution.[36-38] *Staphylococcus epidermidis, C. albicans*, and *E. coli* survive in total nutrient admixtures (TNAs) in which fat emulsion is combined with dextrose and amino acid mixtures.[39] *P. aeruginosa, S. aureus, S. epidermidis, Enterococcus faecalis*, and group JK (*Corynebacterium jeikeium*), displayed greater growth in TNAs than in PN fluids.[40]

Propofol supported the growth of *S. aureus, E. faecalis, P. aeruginosa*, and *C. albicans*; for *P. aeruginosa* and *E. faecalis*, a bactericidal period was followed, after 48 hours, by increasing growth.[40] Preparations of midazolam HCl, morphine sulfate, fentanyl citrate, bupivacaine HCl, atracurium besylate, vecuronium bromide, epinephrine, dopamine, dobutamine, norepinephrine, and sodium nitroprusside in normal saline and 5 percent dextrose in water were bactericidal for *S. aureus, E. faecalis, P. aeruginosa*, and *E. coli* and did not support growth of *C. albicans* at room temperature in a period of 48 to 72 hours.[40] Propofol and other lipid-based medication can support rapid bacterial growth at room temperature because of their solution pH (between 7 and 8.5) and high lipid content.

Contamination of other pharmaceutical products has led to infections. Intrinsically contaminated albuterol nebulization solutions have led to an outbreak of *B. cepacia*.[41,42] An outbreak of *B. cepacia* caused by contamination of multidose albuterol vials was linked to poor infection prevention practices, including respiratory therapists carrying vials in their pockets for several days. The pH of some solutions tested was not within the recommended range, and the concentration of preservative fell from baseline after 5 days.[42] Intrinsically contaminated saline solution used for respiratory therapy has caused clusters of *R. pickettii* respiratory tract colonization.[43,44]

Bevacizumab is another drug moiety that seems to have an affinity to certain types of pathogenic microorganisms.

The use of contaminated multidose ophthalmic containers has resulted in S. marcescens keratitis[45] and P. aeruginosa corneoscleritis[46]; the organisms were cultured from the container but not from the solution itself.[46,47] Bacteria were cultured from 82 of 638 in-use multidose ophthalmic solutions; on the other hand, 81 opened multidose ophthalmic medications were tested, and no contamination was found.[48] Irrigation with a cardioplegic solution contaminated with E. cloacae led to an outbreak of sepsis.[49] Intrinsic contamination of a product labeled "adrenal cortex extract"—which is not approved by the U.S. Food and Drug Administration (FDA)—caused a series of cases of Mycobacterium abscessus abscesses in patients who received intramuscular injections.[50] Contamination of enteral nutrition has been associated with infections, including septicemia.[51-53] Many microorganisms, including Gram-negative bacteria, Gram-positive bacteria, and fungi, can proliferate in enteral nutrition preparations.[51,53,54] Mineral oil used for bathing infants was contaminated with Listeria monocytogenes, leading to an outbreak of neonatal listeriosis.[55]

A nationwide recall of alcohol prep pads occurred in 2011 as a result of serious acute bacterial infections and patient deaths caused by Bacillus cereus contamination. Although there was suggestive evidence of a temporal association between exposure to the suspect products and the onset of serious bacterial infections, there were no confirmed cases to clearly establish that the products served as the primary source for contamination leading to the clinical infections.[56]

Table 110-1 details the ability of various nutritional and non-nutritional parenteral products to support microbial growth when inoculated. From this information, these solutions are categorized as no antimicrobial activity or inhibit microbial growth for the different organisms for which there are data available. The products that can proliferate certain microbes or show no significant decline in the number of colonies (less than a 20 percent decline from the initial number at 24 hours) will be considered as having no antimicrobial activity. Those that have no increase and show a steady decline in colony-forming units (CFUs) per milliliter (more than a 20 percent decrease from the initial inoculum at 24 hours) will be said to inhibit microbial growth. This 24-hour mark was chosen because many reconstituted/compounded parenteral products are given a 24-hour beyond-use date upon preparation.

The susceptibilities of various non-nutritional parenteral drugs, according to the criteria put forward in the methods section, are shown in Table 110-1. Some particularly noteworthy solutions were 5-fluorouracil, busulfan, gemcitabine, oxaliplatin, paciltaxel, pentostatin, streptozocin, and treosulfan. These drugs were very commonly able to rapidly decrease the presence of many—in some cases, all—of the different microbes with which they were initially inoculated.

Table 110-2 illustrates the vulnerabilities of various nutritional parenteral products to contamination. Most of these solutions showed a wide range of susceptibilities to many bacterial and fungal contaminants. C. albicans demonstrated an ability to either grow very well or sustain prolonged viability in all the nutritional products.

MODES OF CONTAMINATION OF STERILE PHARMACEUTICAL PRODUCTS AND PREPARATIONS

Most IV-associated infections result from microbial contamination of the cannula and the cannula wound.[5,11] Poor aseptic technique has been associated with endemics and epidemics. Failure to employ aseptic technique during preparation and administration of propofol combined with inherent properties of this product contributed to extrinsic contamination and resulted in postoperative infections.[22] When combined with poor compliance with hand hygiene, garbing and poor aseptic technique procedures have led to various BSIs. Batch preparation of propofol syringes outside a laminar airflow workbench was associated with S. aureus BSIs.[68] E. cloacae septicemia resulted from preparation of heparin infusions in an area not specifically designed for such use.[69] An outbreak of B. cepacia sepsis resulted from preparation of heparin infusions for several patients using a single 500-mL bag of dextrose that was stored near a sink.[70]

Preparation of compounded sterile preparations in patient care areas (outside the pharmacy) do not typically use a primary engineering control device (e.g., laminar airflow workbench or biological safety cabinet [BSC]) capable of maintaining International Organization for Standardization (ISO) class 5 (no greater than 100 particles per cubic foot or 3,520 particles per cubic meter) air cleanliness conditions. Individuals mixing compounded sterile preparations (CSPs) outside of pharmacy may not have been trained in the proper technique required for this procedure.

Several epidemics have been traced to use of contaminated single-dose vials (SDVs) and multidose vials (MDVs), including an outbreak of fulminant hepatitis B in a hospital that apparently was caused by contaminated heparin flush solution.[71] Unsafe injection practices, specifically the use of the same syringe but new needles for drawing fluid from a common vial, has led to outbreaks of hepatitis C.[72] Failure to follow proper procedures has also led to an outbreak of hepatitis C from extrinsically contaminated radiopharmaceuticals.[73] Proper technique should always be employed when accessing a common vial. Subcutaneous Mycobacterium chelonei abscesses resulted from contamination of diphtheria-pertussis-tetanus-polio (DPTP) vaccine.[74] Contamination of DPTP vaccine was implicated in two outbreaks of group A streptococcal abscesses.[75] Septic arthritis resulted from intra-articular injections of MDV methylprednisolone contaminated with B. cepacia.[76] Contaminated MDVs were the most likely source of outbreaks of HCV infections.[77] Interestingly, these infection prevention lapses occurred primarily in outpatient settings and not inpatient hospital settings.

Table 110-1. Non-Nutritional Parenteral Solution Microbe Viability

Drug/Solution	Conc. (mg/mL)	S. aureus	E. faecium	P. aeruginosa	C. albicans	B. subtilis	E. coli
5-fluorouracil[57,58]	50.00	IMG		IMG	IMG	IMG	IMG
Alemtuzumab[59]	0.03	NAA	NAA	NAA	NAA		
Bendamustin HCl[60]	0.25	IMG	NAA	NAA	IMG		
Bortezomib[59]	1.00	NAA					
Busulfan[59]	0.50	IMG	IMG	IMG	NAA		
Busulfan[59]	6.00	IMG			IMG		
Cetuximab[59]	2.00	NAA	NAA	NAA	NAA		
Cisplatin[57,58]	1.00	NAA		IMG	NAA	NAA	IMG
Cladribine[60]	0.03	IMG	NAA	NAA	IMG		
Cytarabine[57]					NAA	NAA	
Docetaxel[60]	0.80	NAA	NAA	NAA	NAA		
Doxirubicin (Liposome)[59]	0.15	NAA	NAA	NAA	NAA		
Etoposide phosphate[57,59]	0.09	NAA	NAA	NAA	NAA	IMG	
Fludarabine[60]	0.20	NAA	NAA	NAA	IMG		
Foscarnet sodium[60]	13.00	NAA	NAA	NAA	IMG		
Ganciclovir sodium[60]	0.35	IMG	NAA	NAA	IMG		
Gemcitabine[60]	2.40	IMG	IMG	IMG	NAA		
Idarubicin HCl[60]	0.07	NAA	IMG	NAA	IMG		
Ifosfamide[57]					NAA	NAA	
Irinotecan[59]	0.35	NAA	NAA	NAA	NAA		
Oxaliplatin[60]	0.40	IMG	IMG	IMG	NAA		
Paciltaxel[60]	0.70	IMG	IMG	IMG	NAA		
Pemetrexed[59]	9.00	NAA		NAA			
Pentostatin[60]	0.03	IMG	IMG	NAA	IMG		
Propofol*[61,62]		NAA		NAA	NAA		
Rituximab[59]	1.00	NAA	NAA	NAA	NAA		
Sodium folinate[59]	1.50	NAA	NAA	NAA	NAA		
Streptozocin[59]	3.00	IMG	IMG	IMG	IMG		
Topotecan[59, 60]	1.00	IMG		IMG	NAA		NAA
Topotecan[60]	0.01	NAA	IMG	NAA	NAA		
Trastuzumab[59]	0.40	NAA	NAA	NAA	NAA		
Treosulfan[60]	50.00	IMG	IMG	IMG	IMG		
Vinorelbine[60]	0.10	NAA	IMG	IMG	NAA		

NAA = no antimicrobial activity
IMG = inhibits microbe growth
*Also showed NAA to E. faecalis

In 2002, five cases of *Exophiala dermatitidis* infection associated with injectable methylprednisolone acetate were reported to the CDC.[78] *Exophiala* is a rare fungus that caused the death from meningitis in one patient, sacroiliitis in another, and meningitis in three other patients who had received either epidural or intra-articular injections of methylprednisolone compounded at Pharmacy A. Cases occurred as late as 152 days after an injection. The methylprednisolone had been prepared at an independent compounding pharmacy (nonhospital based) later found to have improperly used an autoclave; the pharmacy also lacked written procedures for autoclave preparation, performed no testing for sterility or appropriate checking of quality indicators, and had inadequate clean room practices as outlined in the American Society of Health-System Pharmacists (ASHP) guidelines for pharmacy-prepared products in effect at that time.[79]

Other clusters of infections associated with products prepared by compounding pharmacies include *S. marcescens* from betamethasone, *E. dermatitidis* from methylprednisolone, *B. cepacia* from heparin-vancomycin flush solution, *S. marcescens*

Table 110-2. Nutritional Solution Microbe Viability

Drug/Solution	S. aureus	S. hemolyticus	E. faecium	P. aeruginosa	C. albicans	B. subtilis	E. coli	T. glabrata	K. pneumoniae	E. cloacae	P. mirabilis	S. epidermidis	S. faecalis	E. aerogenes	Coryne-bacterium
Normal saline[57,60,63]	NAA		NAA	NAA	NAA**	NAA	NAA								
5% Dextrose[57,60,62]	NAA		NAA	NAA	NAA**	NAA	IMG		NAA	NAA					
Lactated Ringers[60]	IMG			NAA	NAA**		NAA								
Amino acid solution*[60]	NAA			IMG	NAA**		NAA								
Casein hydrolysate (in dextrose)*[64]	NAA			IMG	NAA**		NAA	NAA	NAA	NAA	NAA				
Synthetic amino acids (in dextrose)++[64]	IMG			IMG	NAA**		IMG	NAA	IMG	IMG	IMG				
10% Safflower oil[65]	NAA			NAA	NAA**		NAA	NAA	NAA		NAA	NAA		NAA	
10% Soybean oil[65]	NAA			NAA	NAA**		NAA	NAA	NAA		NAA	NAA		NAA	
10% Fat emulsion (Travamulsion 10%)[66]	NAA	IMG		NAA	NAA		NAA	NAA				NAA	IMG		IMG
20% Fat emulsion (Travamulsion 20%)[66]	IMG	IMG		NAA	NAA		NAA	NAA				NAA	IMG		IMG
40% lipid TNA[66]	NAA	NAA		NAA	NAA		NAA	NAA				NAA	NAA		NAA
25% lipid TNA[66]	NAA	NAA		NAA	NAA		NAA	NAA				NAA	NAA		NAA
Albumin 6.25 g (in 0.9% sodium chloride)[67]	NAA			NAA	NAA			NAA					IMG		
TPN (containing albumin)[67]	NAA			NAA	NAA			NAA					IMG		

*Aminofusion®; IMG to *B. fragilis*
**C. albicans* was able to proliferate to almost double its colony size in these solutions.
+ Hyprotigen®
++ Freamine®
# Percent based on caloric content
NAA = no antimicrobial activity
IMG = inhibits microbe growth

from magnesium sulfate, *P. fluorescens* from heparinized sodium chloride flush, *P. aeruginosa* or *B. cepacia* from trypan blue ophthalmic solution, multiple Gram-negative bacilli and endotoxin from cardioplegia solution, *Sphingomonas paucimobilis* from fentanyl, *S. marcescens* from total PN, *Streptococcus mitis* and *Streptococcus oralis* from bevacizumab, *Fusarium incarnatum-equiseti* and *Bipolaris hawaiiensis* from brilliant blue-G and triamcinolone, and *Aspergillus* and *Exserohilum* from methylprednisolone.[2]

The 2012 multistate fungal meningitis outbreak caused by a compounding pharmacy in Massachusetts[80] highlights the impact that poor compliance with federal standard of USP <797> Pharmaceutical Compounding – Sterile Preparations[3] and appropriate attention to aseptic compounding can cause. Some state pharmacy regulations require compliance with USP <797>,[81] so emphasis in those states is more evident. However, many sterile preparations are compounded in areas in health systems outside of pharmacy (such as infusion centers, prescriber offices, and other clinics), where state pharmacy regulations may not apply. USP <797> applies to all persons who prepare CSPs and in all places where CSPs are prepared (e.g., hospitals, nursing units, physicians' offices) and other locations where CSPs are prepared, stored, handled, and transported. The IP can play a key role in championing compliance throughout the health system.

When compounding in large-scale facilities and/or across state boundaries, the U.S. Food and Drug Administration (FDA) may become involved. The ASHP's guide for compounding sterile preparations provides direction concerning traditional compounding, such as that done in a health system for its own patients, and exceeds the general prescriber-pharmacist-single-patient relationship.[82] When the FDA inspects a compounding pharmacy, a public report is available.[83] The inspection report information is valuable to the director of pharmacy, IP, and other health system leaders to evaluate use or potential use of such organizations.

Methods for Preventing Contamination of Compounded Sterile Preparations

The CDC recommends that all parenteral fluids be prepared in the pharmacy using an ISO class 5 primary engineering control (e.g., laminar airflow hood).[84] When preparing hazardous drugs for use in oncology patients in a clinic or outpatient setting, use of a BSC or compounding aseptic containment isolator is required. The Infusion Nurses Society (INS) Standards of Practice recommends that an aseptic compounding program be established and conducted under the direction of the pharmacy.[85]

Since the 1990s, several pharmacy practice documents have been published in hopes of establishing a compounding standard of practice that would be universally adopted and followed when preparing sterile preparations. In 1993, ASHP published a Technical Assistance Bulletin *ASHP Guidelines on Quality Assurance for Pharmacy-Prepared Sterile Products*, with

the goal of accurate and sterile pharmacy-prepared CSPs. This document was revised in 2000, and again in 2013.[86]

The objective of USP <797> is

> to describe conditions and practices that prevent harm, including death, to patients that could result from (1) microbial contamination (nonsterility), (2) excessive bacterial endotoxins, (3) variability in the intended strength of the correct ingredients that exceed either monograph limits for official articles or 10 percent for nonofficial articles, (4) unintended chemical and physical contaminants, (5) ingredients of inappropriate quality in compounded sterile preparations (CSPs).[3]

The current version of USP <797> was published in June 2008 (*USP 31/NF 26*) and provides minimum practice and quality standards for CSPs based on current scientific information and best practices extrapolated from evidence-based practices.

USP Chapter <797> applies to practitioners beyond pharmacists. Drug manufacturers are regulated under the Federal Food, Drug and Cosmetic Act (FFDCA), which requires compliance with USP standards. Practitioners are primarily regulated by state agencies. Although the drugs compounded by practitioners may still be adulterated or misbranded under the FFDCA, all other aspects of their practice are controlled by state law.

The FDA is responsible for the enforcement of the FFDCA. Each general chapter of the USP/NF is assigned a number, which appears in brackets along with the chapter name. General chapters numbered <1> to <999> are requirements and official monographs and standards of the USP/NF. General chapters numbered from <1000> to <1999> are informational, and chapters above <2000> apply to nutritional supplements.

According to USP <797> CSPs are classified by five general categories based on risk of microbial contamination to all compounded sterile preparations.[83] They are:

- *Immediate Use*: CSPs prepared outside of an ISO 5 device, which are intended for immediate use

- *Low-Risk Level With 12-Hour Beyond-Use Dating*: CSPs prepared in ISO class 5 air cleanliness conditions in an unclassified segregated compounding area with ambient air

- *Low-Risk Level*: CSPs prepared in ISO class 5 air cleanliness conditions located within ISO class 7 or 8 buffer areas. The compounding procedure involves simple aseptic manipulations using no more than three commercially available ingredients and not more than two entries into any one final container

- *Medium-Risk Level*: CSPs prepared under batch conditions (multiple individual doses) or CSPs for individual patients using more complex aseptic manipulations (e.g., PN solutions and patient-controlled analgesia) prepared in ISO class 5 air cleanliness conditions in an ISO class 7 or 8 area

- *High-Risk Level*: CSPs prepared from nonsterile ingredients or nonsterile devices or prepared in air quality less than ISO class 5 air cleanliness

Unless CSPs are prepared under the Immediate-Use exclusions detailed in USP Chapter <797>, all CSPs must be (at the minimum) prepared in an ISO class 5 environment, which can be achieved by the use of a primary engineering control (e.g., laminar airflow workbench [LAFW], BSC, or isolators designed for pharmacy compounding). (See Table 110-3).

Personnel preparing CSPs are required to perform appropriate hand hygiene procedures and wear garb (hairnet, beard cover [as needed], shoe covers, gown closed at the collar, and knit cuffs and sterile gloves) that generates low amounts of particles. Makeup and nail polish are prohibited.

The rubber stoppers of containers must be wiped or sprayed and wiped with sterile 70 percent alcohol or another effective sterile disinfecting agent used prior to entry. The vial septum is not sterile under the cap and must be properly disinfected prior to use.[87]

Several factors must be considered in assessing the sterility of single-use containers (ampules, SDVs, IV bags, irrigation bottles, etc.)[8] and MDVs.[88] The aseptic technique of individuals likely to enter specific vials is an important factor in determining sterility. The environment in which the vial will be punctured is important.

The USP describes the procedure for testing the effectiveness of preservatives in MDVs (USP Chapter <51> Antimicrobial Effectiveness Testing).[89] The effectiveness of the preservatives is demonstrated by the inhibition of growth of microorganisms that may be introduced from repeatedly withdrawing individual doses during a 28-day test period. Some drug preparations appear to have sterilizing properties, irrespective of the presence of preservatives.[90]

The effects of refrigeration on the bactericidal activity of preservative in MDV should be considered in setting policy. Solutions containing preservatives (phenol, methylparaben, and benzyl) and inoculated with *S. aureus, P. aeruginosa, E. coli,* and *S. marcescens* show persistence of bacteria longer under refrigeration than at room temperature.[91] The number of entries may affect sterility of MDVs; however, there is no practical way to document this. In addition, frequent use may cause vials to be used up more rapidly, thereby actually reducing the risk of infection.

Expiration dates listed on drug dosage forms are established by the manufacturer and appear in the FDA-approved product labeling. When a dosage form is manipulated, including puncturing an MDV or moving an item from the storage conditions listed in the product labeling to a different temperature, a beyond-use date must be applied if the dosage form will be retained for future use. Setting time limits after first opening SDVs and MDVs can help ensure microbial sterility and chemical stability.[8,88,92]

Table 110-3. Compounded Sterile Preparation Risk Levels[82]

Category of CSP	Device Used	Surrounding Room	Limitations	BUD*
Immediate use	None	Ambient air	Simple mixing of no more than three sterile nonhazardous components	1 hour
Low-risk, 12-hour	ISO 5 hood[†]	Ambient air	Simple mixing of no more than three sterile components	12 hours
Low-risk	ISO 5 hood	ISO 7 clean room[‡]	Simple mixing of no more than three sterile components	48 hours at room temperature, 14 days under refrigeration, 45 days frozen
Medium-risk	ISO 5 hood	ISO 7 clean room	Mixing of all sterile components	30 hours at room temperature, 9 days under refrigeration, 45 days frozen
High-risk	ISO 5 hood	ISO 7 clean room	Includes any nonsterile component or exceeds the BUDs of other categories	24 hours at room temperature, 3 days under refrigeration, 45 days frozen

*The beyond-use date (BUD) is the time that administration of the CSP must begin following mixing of the CSP.
[†]ISO 5 hood is a properly certified laminar air flow workbench, BSC, compounding aseptic isolator, or compounding aseptic containment isolator.
[‡]Some isolators may be certified for use outside a clean room but must meet requirements detailed in USP <797>.

- Manufacturers' expiration dates apply to stability and sterility of unopened vials.

- The CDC recommends that all single-dose and single-use injectable medications and solutions be dedicated for use on a single patient and entered one time. The CDC recommends use of SDVs whenever possible for compounding of parenteral preparations. In times of critical need, contents from unopened single-dose/single-use vials can be repackaged for multiple patients, but only when performed under conditions that are compliant to USP <797> (e.g., qualified personnel, ISO 5 hood in an ISO 7 clean room, beyond-use dates compliant with USP <797> limits, etc.).

- Pharmacy bulk packages (PBPs) are vials containing many single doses. PBPs include large vials of antibiotics, contrast media, and concentrated electrolytes. They are intended for use in an ISO 5 environment for IV additive services. They are not intended for direct patient use or for use outside of appropriate aseptic environments (i.e., an IV hood). SDVs or PBPs (containers of many injectable single-doses) used in ISO class 5 air cleanliness conditions must be discarded after 6 hours unless otherwise specified by the manufacturer.

- The CDC recommends that MDVs should be dedicated to a single patient whenever possible. If MDVs must be used for more than one patient, they should not be kept or accessed in the immediate patient treatment area (e.g., patient rooms or bays, operating room).

- The CDC recommends refrigerating the MDVs after opening if recommended by the manufacturer, cleaning the rubber diaphragm of the vial with alcohol before inserting a device into the vial, using a sterile device each time a vial is accessed, and avoiding touch contamination of the device before penetrating the rubber diaphragm. The MDV should be discarded when empty, when suspected or visible contamination occurs, or when the manufacturer's stated expiration date is reached.[91]

- USP Chapter <797> requires that an MDV after its first opening be discarded within 28 days in accordance with USP Chapter <51>[89] unless otherwise specified by the manufacturer.

- The temperature of refrigerators used to store pharmaceuticals should be checked daily (twice daily if used to store vaccines) and the temperature recorded electronically or on a log that is dated and signed by the person performing the temperature check. Temperatures that are higher or lower than recommended should be immediately addressed and adjusted as defined in the organization's policy. Refrigerators used in pharmacy or other bulk storage areas such as materials management to store medications in general should have their temperature monitored continuously, with alarms set to indicate excessively high or low temperatures.

USP <797> beyond-use dates apply from the time the CSP is compounded up to the point of administration. Once administration begins, CDC recommendations for hang time applies.

The CDC has not made recommendations for the hang time of general IV fluids, though it makes the following comments.[84]

- Manufacturers' recommendations should be followed for specific medications.

- PN (with or without fat) hang time should not exceed 24 hours.

- Fat emulsion hang time should not exceed 24 hours.

  o The INS Standards limit fat emulsion hang time to 12 hours.[85]

- Propofol infusion hang time should not exceed the manufacturer's recommendations (which vary based on manufacturer) and should be changed at the same time as the tubing.

The CDC also lists recommendations for IV tubing changes:[84]

- In patients not receiving blood, blood products or fat emulsions, replace administration sets that are continuously used, including secondary sets and add-on devices, no more frequently than at 96-hour intervals but at least every 7 days.

- Replace tubing used to administer blood, blood products, or fat emulsions within 24 hours of initiating the infusion.

- Replace tubing used to administer propofol infusions every 6 or 12 hours, when the vial is changed, per the manufacturer's recommendations.

Environmental Sampling and Testing

Environmental monitoring is approached differently by the CDC, FDA, and USP. The FDA requires manufacturers to have a comprehensive environmental monitoring plan that involves daily sampling of air, surfaces, and personnel with baseline CFU levels for alert and action levels.[93]

In the 1970s, the CDC began to advocate the discontinuation of environmental monitoring in the hospital because there was no association between infection rates and levels of environmental contamination and because there were no standards for permissible levels of environmental microbial contamination. The issue of routine microbiologic sampling of the environment in healthcare facilities is specifically addressed in the evidence-based document *Guidelines for Environmental Infection Control in Healthcare Facilities—2003*.[94] The CDC environmental guidelines specifically recommend against environmental sampling in all practice settings within the hospital unless part of an investigation, education, or equipment certification.

The USP historical model for environmental monitoring in the clean room is based on a pharmaceutical manufacturing model of routine sampling recommended by the FDA. The emphasis on environmental air quality originates from early studies demonstrating the lack of microbial contamination when sterile drugs, nutrients, and devices were handled and aseptically prepared in controlled environments where the air cleanliness classifications were controlled.[92,95-97]

Based on the CDC and FDA position, the current USP Chapter <797> on pharmaceutical compounding, environmental sampling is recommended as part of a comprehensive quality management program and required under any of the following conditions:

- As part of the commissioning and certification of new facilities and equipment

- Any servicing of facilities and equipment

- As part of the semiannual recertification of facilities and equipment

- In response to identified problems with end products or staff technique

- In response to issues with CSPs, observed compounding personnel work practices, or patient-related infections where the CSP is being considered as a potential source of the infection[3]

The current air, surface, and personnel gloved fingertip sampling requirements in USP Chapter <797> have been broken down into facility-associated environmental sampling and personnel-associated sampling. Environmental sampling is one important quality assurance procedure required of all compounders (pharmacists, technicians, nurses, physicians, and others) and should be tied to activities that pose the greatest risk of contamination to the compounded sterile preparation, such as hand hygiene, garbing and gloving, cleaning, and aseptic compounding procedures.

Each individual who compounds sterile preparations for other than Immediate Use must successfully pass a simulated media fill test (to demonstrate compliance with aseptic compounding practices), a gloved fingertip test (to demonstrate compliance with the ability to aseptically garb), and surface sampling test (to demonstrate the ability to properly clean sterile compounding areas, as well as assure use of effective cleaning solutions and dilutions). The frequency of testing varies depending on the type of CSPs mixed and is detailed in USP <797>.[3] Those individuals (such as nurses and anesthesia personnel) who prepare Immediate-Use CSPs must document competency in aseptic technique and organizational policy.

The frequency of environmental sampling, as well as the methods and materials used to collect the samples, have been harmonized with the recommendations of the American Society of Microbiology.[98] The goal is to ensure that the ISO-classified compounding areas are working properly and are maintaining a state of control relative to the number of airborne nondiscrete particles. The primary engineering controls (laminar airflow workbenches or zones, BSCs, or isolators), which provide unidirectional airflow, are used for all compounding activities, except in emergencies. The buffer area (ISO class 7) and ante area (ISO class 8) must be designed and built to meet the architectural and performance criteria stipulated in USP <797>. Certification procedures such as those outlined in *Certification Guide for Sterile Compounding Facilities* (CAG-003-2006)[99] shall be performed by a qualified individual no less than every 6 months and whenever the device is relocated or altered or a major service occurs.[3]

USP <797> lists recommended action levels for microbial growth.[3] When microbial growth is detected, isolates must be identified to at least the genus level, and appropriate action must be taken.

Aseptic Technique

Based on a review of published literature for the rates of contamination of aseptic media fills in pharmacy settings and two industrial pharmaceutical manufacturer surveys (the first in 1986 and the last in 2001), direct contact (i.e., touch contamination) by compounding personnel poses the highest risk of microbial contaminations of CSPs.[92,95,96,100-106] "It is dangerous to assume that the use of a clean room will independently improve the quality of patient care by eliminating contamina-

tion. Once a baseline environmental quality (ISO class 5 LAFW) is established, admixture quality assurance efforts should focus on other critical factors."[95] Personnel are the greatest source of microbial contamination in industrial aseptic manufacturing, which is attributed to touching and particle shedding.[96]

Recent studies involving medical procedures that require aseptic technique while working in uncontrolled air environments (e.g., patient care units and surgical suites) have demonstrated the incidence of extrinsic contamination and the critical nature of using proper aseptic technique and standard practices to prevent infections.[107-110]

Storage of Pharmaceuticals

The pharmacy should monitor for appropriate storage of pharmaceuticals throughout the institution. Routine inspections should be performed to ensure that expired medications are removed from patient care areas and disposed of properly. Temperatures of refrigerators, freezers, and warmers used to store pharmaceuticals should be closely monitored and recorded daily.

Pharmacist Responsibilities Involving Antimicrobial Stewardship

Concerns about resistance causing increased morbidity, mortality, and healthcare costs have led to recommendations to control antimicrobial use.[111,112] Multidisciplinary groups, including physicians, nurses, pharmacists, laboratory technicians, respiratory therapists, and others, should establish a system for monitoring resistance and antibiotic usage, establish evidence-based practice guidelines and other policies to control the use of antibiotics and respond to data from the monitoring system, and measure outcomes to evaluate the effectiveness of policies. Microbiologists should work with infectious disease clinicians, pharmacists, hospital epidemiologists, IPs, and representatives of clinical departments to choose the drugs that will be tested and routinely reported. Specific responsibilities for pharmacy personnel include promoting optimal use of antimicrobial agents, generation and analysis of data to determine compliance with restriction policies, participation in development of programs for formulary and antimicrobial controls, responsibility for computer medication order entry systems and protocols, and (in collaboration with physicians) patient-specific recommendations for optimal antimicrobial use.[108,113-119]

Pharmacist Participation in Infection Prevention and Control Committee

Pharmacy services should be active participants in the organization's infection prevention and control committee. The committee should review the quality plan elements of pharmacy service's sterile compounding activities, including personnel training and competence, facility issue, and environmental monitoring. Antibiotic stewardship activities should be discussed at the committee.

Infection Preventionist Partnership with the Pharmacy

The IP can provide subject matter expertise to the pharmacy director when it comes to appropriate cleaning and disinfection practices, hand hygiene, environmental sampling, adult education on aseptic technique and other infection control-related topics, proper donning and removal of personal protective equipment, and should participate in regularly scheduled environment of care rounds. The IP can also assist with a gap analysis/risk assessment of various pharmacy practices that ultimately affect patient safety.

The IP should be immediately consulted when a suspected or confirmed contamination event has been identified. Coordination with Department of Health authorities along with State Board of Pharmacy is essential, and it should involve collaboration with the IP and pharmacist, as well as active engagement of the healthcare facility administration to maximize patient safety. The IP is an integral member of the antibiotic stewardship team and has ongoing responsibility for performing surveillance of patients colonized or infected with MDROs. The CDC recently published a monograph on antibiotic resistance threats in the United States that identified certain organisms as threats to human health. The CDC classified these organisms as "urgent," "serious," or "concerning":[120]

Urgent Threats

- *Clostridium difficile*
- Carbapenem-resistant Enterobacteriaceae (CRE)
- Drug-resistant *Neisseria gonorrhoeae*

Serious Threats

- Multidrug-resistant *Acinetobacter*
- Drug-resistant *Campylobacter*
- Fluconazole-resistant *Candida* (a fungus)
- Extended spectrum β-lactamase producing Enterobacteriaceae (ESBLs)
- Vancomycin-resistant *Enterococcus* (VRE)
- Multidrug-resistant *Pseudomonas aeruginosa*
- Drug-resistant non-typhoidal *Salmonella*
- Drug-resistant *Salmonella Typhi*
- Drug-resistant *Shigella*
- Methicillin-resistant *Staphylococcus aureus* (MRSA)
- Drug-resistant *Streptococcus pneumoniae*
- Drug-resistant tuberculosis

Concerning Threats

- Vancomycin-resistant *Staphylococcus aureus* (VRSA)
- Erythromycin-resistant Group A *Streptococcus*
- Clindamycin-resistant Group B *Streptococcus*

CONCLUSIONS

Pharmacy is responsible for preparation and storage of most sterile medications. The pharmacy department should participate in multidisciplinary activities such as quality assurance teams, infection prevention and control committees, and antimicrobial use programs to ensure appropriate preparation and use of pharmaceuticals and sterile products. Recently, Pronovost et al.[108] demonstrated that the application of the five evidence-based procedures recommended by the CDC had the greatest effect on lowering the rate of catheter-associated BSIs. They also demonstrated the lowest barriers to implementation with sustained positive impact on patient outcomes. Such strategies of bundling best practices that are evidence based, observational assessments for compliance, and use of checklists as reminder tools to standardize processes are as relevant to the pharmacy as they are to the clinician caring for the patient at the bedside. The challenge remains to create a culture of patient safety that rewards team building, eliminates hierarchy, and promotes speaking up when potential human error is recognized.

FUTURE TRENDS

Many of the tools that the IP is using to improve patient care at the bedside can be easily adapted to assist the pharmacist in ongoing efforts to ensure enhanced patient safety. The use of observational tools and checklists is just one way the IP can team with the pharmacist to improve the safety of medication preparation and delivery within healthcare facilities. Future opportunities for such collaboration will likely continue and expand across the spectrum of healthcare.

INTERNATIONAL PERSPECTIVE

The profession of pharmacy both in the United States and around the world is experiencing a renaissance regarding the roles of pharmacists in the delivery of healthcare in the 21st century. By moving out of isolation and expanding their traditional roles, which historically have revolved around medication delivery and distribution only, pharmacists are being greeted by teams of healthcare professionals realizing the important role they play in delivering evidence-based, patient-centered care.

IPs are realizing that the pharmacy and the sterile compounding of medications/preparations may be more problem-prone than originally thought and a potential source of HAIs. The opportunity for pharmacists and IPs to work collaboratively is apparent, with the goal of eliminating the ongoing threats to the patient from contaminated medications/preparations while being treated in healthcare facilities.

REFERENCES

1. Meyer C. History of sterile compounding in US hospitals: learning from the tragic lessons of the past. *Am J Health Syst Pharm* 2013 Aug 15;70(16):1414–1427.

2. States C, Jacobs J, Mayer J, et al. Description of outbreaks of health-care-associated infections related to compounding pharmacies, 2000-12. *Am J Health Syst Pharm* 2013 Aug 1;70(15):1301–1312.

3. Pharmaceutical Compounding—Sterile Preparations (general information chapter 797). In: The United States Pharmacopeia, 36th rev., and The National Formulary, 31st ed. Rockville, MD: United States Pharmacopeial Convention, 2013.

4. Macias AE, Huertas M, Ponce de Leon S, et al. Contamination of intra-venous fluids: A continuing cause of hospital bacteremia. *Am J Infect Control* 2010 April;38:217-221.

5. Maki DG, Mermel LA. Infections Due to Infusion Therapy. In: Bennett JV, Brachman PS, eds. *Hospital Infections*, 4th ed. Boston, MA: Little, Brown and Company, 1998;689–724.

6. Muder RR. Frequency of intravenous administration set changes and bacteremia: defining the risk. *Infect Control Hosp Epidemiol* 2001 Mar;22(3):134–135.

7. Yokoe DS, Mermel LA, Anderson DJ, et al. A compendium of strategies to prevent healthcare-associated infections in acute care hospitals. *Infect Control Hosp Epidemiol* 2008 Oct;29 Suppl 1:S12–S21.

8. Centers for Disease Control and Prevention (CDC), National Center for Emerging and Zoonotic Infectious Diseases (NCEZID), Division of Healthcare Quality Promotion (DHQP). *Injection safety: Protect patients against preventable harm from improper use of single-dose/single-use vials.* CDC website. August 30, 2012. Available at: http://www.cdc.gov/injectionsafety/CDCposition-SingleUseVial.html.

9. Department of Health & Human Services, Centers for Medicare & Medicaid Services (CMS). *Safe use of single dose/single use medications to prevent healthcare-associated infections.* S&C:12-35-ALL, June 15, 2012. CME website. Available at: http://www.cms.gov/Medicare/Provider-Enrollment-and-Certification/SurveyCertificationGenInfo/Downloads/Survey-and-Cert-Letter-12-35.pdf.

10. Macias AE, Huertas M, Ponce de Leo S, et al. Endemic infusate contamination and related bacteremias. *Am J Infect Control* 2008 Feb;36(1):48–53.

11. Centers for Disease Control and Prevention. Epidemiologic notes and reports. Nosocomial bacteremias associated with intravenous fluid therapy—USA. 1971. *MMWR Morb Mortal Wkly Rep* 1997 Dec 26;46(51):1227–1233.

12. Kutty PK, Forster TS, Wood-Koob C, et al. Multistate outbreak of toxic anterial segment syndrome, 2005. *J Cataract Refract Surg* 2008 Apr;34(4):585–590.

13. Daufenbach LZ, Alves WA, de Azevedo JB, et al. Pyrogenic reactions and hemorrhage associated with intrinsic exposure to endotoxin-contaminated intravenous solutions. *Infect Control Hosp Epidemiol* 2006 Jul;27(7):735–741.

14. Fernández C, Wilhelmi I, Andradas E. Nosocomial outbreak of Burkholderia pickettii infection due to a manufactured intravenous product used in three hospitals. *Clin Infect Dis* 1996 Jun;22(6):1092–1095.

15. Felts SK, Schaffner W, Melly MA, et al. Sepsis caused by contaminated intravenous fluids. *Ann Intern Med* 1972 Dec;77(6):881–890.

16. Centers for Disease Control and Prevention. Clinical sepsis and death in a newborn nursery associated with contaminated parenteral medications—Brazil, 1996. *MMWR Morb Mortal Wkly Rep* 1998 Jul 31;47(29):610–612.

17. Plouffe JF, Brown DG, Silva J, et al. Nosocomial outbreak of Candida parapsilosis fungemia related to intravenous infusion. *Arch Intern Med* 1977 Dec;137(12):1686–1689.

18. Solomon SL, Khabbaz RF, Parker RH, et al. An outbreak of Candida parapsilosis bloodstream infections in patients receiving parenteral nutrition. *J Infect Dis* 1984 Jan;149(1):98–102.

19. Dugleux G, Le Coutour X, Hecquard C, et al. Septicemia caused by contaminated parenteral nutrition pouches: the refrigerator as an unusual cause. *JPEN J Parenter Enteral Nutr* 1991 Jul-Aug;15(4):474–475.

20. Llop JM, Manques I, Perez JL, et al. Staphylococcus saprophyticus sepsis related to total parenteral nutrition admixtures contamination. *JPEN J Parenter Enteral Nutr* 1993 Nov-Dec;17(6):575–577.

21. Centers for Disease Control and Prevention. Postsurgical infections associated with an extrinsically contaminated intravenous anesthetic agent. *MMWR Morb Mortal Wkly Rep* 1990 Jun 29;39(25):426–427, 433.

22. Bennett SN, McNeil MM, Bland LA, et al. Postoperative infections traced to contamination of an intravenous anesthetic, propofol. *N Engl J Med* 1995 Jul 20;333(3):147–154.

23. Henry B, Plante-Jenkins C, Ostrowska K. An outbreak of Serratia marcescens associated with the anesthetic agent propofol. *Am J Infect Control* 2001 Oct;29(5):312–315.

24. Teva Pharmaceuticals. [Recall notice] Teva Pharmaceuticals USA issues a voluntary user-level nationwide recall of Propofol Injectable Emulsion 10 mg/mL 100 mL vials, lot numbers 31305429B and 31305430B. July 16, 2009. U.S. Food and Drug Administration (FDA) website. Available at: http://www.fda.gov/Safety/Recalls/ucm172474.htm.

25. Muller AE, Huisman I, Roos PJ, et al. Outbreak of severe sepsis due to contaminated propofol: lessons to learn. *J Hosp Infect* 2010 Nov;76(3):225–230.

26. Centers for Disease Control and Prevention (CDC). Enterobacter cloacae bloodstream infections associated with contaminated prefilled saline syringes—California, November 1998. *MMWR Morb Mortal Wkly Rep* 1998 Nov 13;47(44):959–690.

27. Hellinger WC, Bacalis LP, Kay RS, et al. Health care-associated hepatitis C virus infections attributed to narcotic diversion. *Ann Intern Med* 2012 Apr 3;156(7):477–482.

28. Maki DG, Botticelli MS, LeRoy ML, et al. Prospective study of replacing administration sets for intravenous therapy at 48- vs 72-hour intervals. *JAMA* 1987 Oct 2;258(13):1777–1781.

29. Trautmann M, Zauser B, Wiedeck H, et al. Bacterial colonization and endotoxin contamination of intravenous infusion fluids. *J Hosp Infect* 1997 Nov;37(3):225–236.

30. Macias AE, Ponce de Leon RS, Huertas M, et al. Endemic infusate contamination and related bacteremias. *Am J Infect Control* 2008 Feb;36(1):48–53.

31. Bach A, Motsch J, Schmidt H, et al. In-use contamination of propofol: a clinical study. *Eur J Anaesth* 1997 Mar;14(2):178–183.

32. Webb ASR, Roberts B, Breheny FX, et al. Contamination of propofol infusions in the intensive care unit: incidence and clinical significance. *Anaesth Intens Care* 1998 Apr;26(2):162–164.

33. Maki DG. Preventing infection in intravenous therapy. *Hosp Pract* 1976 Apr;11(4):95–104.

34. Goldmann DA, Martin WT, Worthington JW. Growth of bacteria and fungi in total parenteral nutrition solutions. *Am J Surg* 1973 Sep;126(3):314–318.

35. Mirtallo JM, Caryer K, Schneider PJ, et al. Growth of bacteria and fungi in parenteral nutrition solutions containing albumin. *Am J Hosp Pharm* 1981 Dec;38(12):1907–1910.

36. Melly MA, Meng HC, Schaffner W. Microbial growth in lipid emulsions used in parenteral nutrition. *Arch Surg* 1975 Dec;110(12):1479–1481.

37. Crocker KS, Noga R, Filibeck DJ, et al. Microbial growth comparisons of five commercial parenteral lipid emulsions. *JPEN J Parenter Enteral Nutr* 1984 Jul-Aug;8(4):391–395.

38. Mershon J, Nogami W, Williams JM, et al. Bacterial/fungal growth in a combined parenteral nutrition solution. *JPEN J Parenter Enteral Nutr* 1986 Sep-Oct;10(5):498–502.

39. Scheckelhoff DJ, Mirtallo JM, Ayers LW, et al. Growth of bacteria and fungi in total nutrient admixtures. *Am J Hosp Pharm* 1986 Jan;43(1):73–77.

40. Graystone S, Wells MF, Farrell DJ. Do intensive care drug infusions support microbial growth? *Anaesth Intens Care* 1997 Dec;25(6):640–642.

41. Balkhy HH, Cunningham G, Francis C, et al. A National Guard outbreak of Burkholderia cepacia infection and colonization secondary to intrinsic contamination of albuterol nebulization solution. *Am J Infect Control* 2005 Apr;33(3):182–188.

42. Hamill RJ, Houston ED, Georghiou PR, et al. An outbreak of Burkholderia (formerly Pseudomonas) cepacia respiratory tract colonization and infection associated with nebulized albuterol therapy. *Ann Intern Med* 1995 May 15;122(10):762–766.

43. Centers for Disease Control and Prevention (CDC). Nosocomial Ralstonia pickettii colonization associated with intrinsically contaminated saline solution. *MMWR Morb Mortal Wkly Rep* 1998 Apr 17;47(14):285–286.

44. McNeil MM, Solomon SL, Anderson RL, et al. Nosocomial Pseudomonas pickettii colonization associated with a contaminated respiratory therapy solution in a special care nursery. *J Clin Microbiol* 1985 Dec;22(6):903–907.

45. Templeton WC III, Eiferman RA, Snyder JW, et al. Serratia keratitis transmitted by contaminated eyedroppers. *Am J Ophthalmol* 1982 Jun;93(6):723–726.

46. Alfonso E, Kenyon KR, Ormerod D, et al. Pseudomonas corneoscleritis. *Am J Ophthalmol* 1987 Jan 15;103(1):90–98.

47. Høvding G, Sjursen H. Bacterial contamination of drops and dropper tips of in-use multidose eye drop bottles. *Acta Ophthal* 1982 Apr;60(2):213–222.

48. Tamer HR, Sweet B, Ross MB. Use and sterility of multidose ophthalmic medications. *Am J Hosp Pharm* 1994 Feb 15;51(4):500–502.

49. Talbot GH, Miller DE, Doorley M, et al. Enterobacter cloacae-contaminated cardioplegic solution. *Am J Infect Control* 1984 Aug;12(4):239–244.

50. Centers for Disease Control and Prevention (CDC). Infection with Mycobacterium abscessus associated with intramuscular injection of adrenal cortex extract—Colorado and Wyoming, 1995-1996. *MMWR Morb Mortal Wkly Rep* 1996 Aug 23;45(33):713–715.

51. Anderton A. Microbiological aspects of the preparation and administration of naso-gastric and naso-enteric tube feeds in hospitals—a review. *Hum Nutr* 1983 Dec;37(6):426–440.
52. Casewell MW, Cooper JE, Webster M. Enteral feeds contaminated with Enterobacter cloacae as a cause of septicaemia. *Br Med J (Clin Res Ed)* 1981 Mar 21;282(6268):973.
53. Bastow MD, Greaves P, Allison SP. Microbial contamination of enteral feeds. *Hum Nutr Appl Nutr* 1982 Jun;36(3):213–217.
54. Gill KJ, Gill P. Contaminated enteral feeds. *Br Med J (Clin Res Ed)* 1981 Jun 13;282(6280):1971.
55. Schuchat A, Lizano C, Broome CV, et al. Outbreak of neonatal listeriosis associated with mineral oil. *Pediatr Infect Dis J* 1991 Mar;10(3):183–189.
56. Department of Health and Human Service, Food and Drug Administration. *Pharmacovigilance review.* September 21,2011. Available at: http://media.jsonline.com/documents/FDA-final-AERS-report.pdf.
57. Paris I, Paci A, Rey JB, et al. Microbial growth tests in anti-neoplastic injectable solutions. *J Oncol Pharm Pract* 2005 Mar;11(1):7–12.
58. Rawal, BD, Nahata MC. Variation in microbial survival and growth in intravenous fluids. *Chemotherapy* 1985;31(4):318–323.
59. Karstens A, Krämer I. Viability of micro-organisms in novel anticancer drug solutions. *Eur J Hosp Pharm Sci Pract* 2007;13(2):27–32.
60. Krämer I. Viability of microorganisms in novel antineoplastic and antiviral drug solutions. *J Oncol Pharm Practice* 1998;(4):1:32–37.
61. Arduino MJ, Bland LA, McAllister SK, et al. Microbial growth and endotoxin production in the intravenous anesthetic propofol. *Infect Control Hosp Epidemiol* 1991 Sep;12(9):535–539.
62. Maki DG, Martin WT. Nationwide epidemic of septicemia caused by contaminated infusion products. IV. Growth of microbial pathogens in fluids for intravenous infusion. *J Infect Dis* 1975 Mar;131(3):267–72.
63. Vidovich MI, Peterson LR, Wong HY. The effect of lidocaine on bacterial growth in propofol. *Anesth Analg* 1999 Apr;88(4):936–938.
64. Goldmann DA, Martin WT, Worthington JW. Growth of bacteria and fungi in total parenteral nutrition solutions. *Am J Surg* 1973 Sep;126(3):314–318.
65. Kim CH, Lewis DE, Kumar A. Bacterial and fungal growth in intravenous fat emulsions. *Am J Hosp Pharm* 1983 Dec;40(12):2159–2161.
66. Scheckelhoff DJ, Mirtallo JM, Ayers LW, et al. Growth of bacteria and fungi in total nutrient admixtures. *Am J Hosp Pharm* 1986 Jan;43(1):73–77.
67. Mirtallo JM, Caryer K, Schneider PJ, et al. Growth of bacteria and fungi in parenteral nutrition solutions containing albumin. *Am J Hosp Pharm* 1981 Dec;38(12):1907–1910.
68. Kuehnert MJ, Webb RM, Jochimsen EM, et al. Staphylococcus aureus bloodstream infections among patients undergoing electroconvulsive therapy traced to breaks in infection control and possible extrinsic contamination by propofol. *Anesth Analg* 1997 Aug;85(2):420–425.
69. Koerner RJ, Morgan S, Ford M, et al. Outbreak of gram-negative septicaemia caused by contaminated continuous infusions prepared in a non-clinical area. *J Hosp Infect* 1997 Aug;36(4):285–289.
70. van Laer F, Raes D, Vandamme P, et al. An outbreak of Burkholderia cepacia with septicemia on a cardiology ward. *Infect Control Hosp Epidemiol* 1998 Feb;19(2):112–113.
71. Oren I, Hershow RC, Ben-Porath E, et al. A common-source outbreak of fulminant hepatitis B in a hospital. *Ann Intern Med* 1989 May 1;110(9):691–698.
72. Centers for Disease Control and Prevention (CDC). Acute hepatitis C virus infection attributed to unsafe injection practices at an endoscopy clinic—Nevada, 2007. *MMWR Morb Mortal Wkly Rep* 2008 May 16;57(19):513–517.
73. Patel PR, Larson AK, Castel AD, et al. Hepatitis C virus infections from a contaminated radiopharmaceutical used in myocardial perfusion studies. *JAMA* 2006 Oct 25;296(16):2005–2011.
74. Borghans JG, Stanford JL. Mycobacterium chelonei in abscesses after injection of diphtheria-pertussis-tetanus-polio vaccine. *Am Rev Respir Dis* 1973 Jan;107(1):1–8.
75. Stetler HC, Garbe PL, Dwyer DM, et al. Outbreaks of group A streptococcal abscesses following diphtheria-tetanus toxoid-pertussis vaccination. *Pediatrics* 1985 Feb;75(2):299–303.
76. Kothari T, Reyes MP, Brooks N. Pseudomonas cepacia septic arthritis due to intra-articular injections of methylprednisolone. *Can Med Assoc J* 1977 Jun 4;116(11):1230, 1232, 1235.
77. Widell A, Christenssen B, Wiebe T, et al. Epidemiologic and molecular investigation of outbreaks of hepatitis C virus infection on a pediatric oncology service. *Ann Intern Med* 1999 Jan 19;130(2):130–134.
78. Centers for Disease Control and Prevention (CDC). Exophiala infection from contaminated injectable steroids prepared by a compounding pharmacy—United States, July–November 2002. *MMWR Morb Mortal Wkly Rep* 2002 Dec 13;51(49):1109–1112.
79. Civen R, Vugia DJ, Alexander R, et al. Outbreak of Serratia marcescens infections following injection of betamethasone compounded at a community pharmacy. *Clin Infect Dis* 2006 Oct 1;43(7):831–837.
80. Food and Drug Administration, Multistate outbreak of fungal meningitis and other infections. Available at: http://www.fda.gov/drugs/drugsafety/fungalmeningitis/default.htm. Accessed on September 14, 2013.
81. Douglass K, Kastango ES, Cantor P. *The 2012 USP <797> Compliance Survey: Measuring Progress. Pharmacy Purchasing & Products* website. Available at: http://www.pppmag.com/article/1218/October_2012_Cleanrooms_Compounding/The_2012_USP_797_Compliance_Survey_Measuring_Progress/.
82. Kastango ES. The ASHP Discussion Guide for Compounding Sterile Preparations Summary of revisions to USP Chapter <797>. Bethesda, MD: American Society of Health-System Pharmacists, 2008.
83. Food and Drug Administration (FDA). *2013 Pharmacy inspections and related records.* FDA website. Available at: http://www.fda.gov/AboutFDA/CentersOffices/OfficeofGlobalRegulatoryOperationsandPolicy/ORA/ORAElectronicReadingRoom/ucm340853.htm.
84. O'Grady NP, Alexander M, Burns LA, et al. *Guidelines for the prevention of intravascular catheter-related infections, 2011.* Centers for Disease Control and Prevention website. Available at: http://www.cdc.gov/hicpac/pdf/guidelines/bsi-guidelines-2011.pdf .
85. Intravenous Nurses Society (INS). *Infusion nursing standards of practice, 2011.* INS website. Available at: http://www.ins1.org/i4a/pages/index.cfm?pageid=3310.
86. American Society of Health-System Pharmacists. ASHP guidelines on compounding sterile preparations. *Am J Health-Syst Pharm* 2014 Jan 15;71:145–166.
87. Centers for Disease Control and Prevention (CDC), National Center for Emerging and Zoonotic Infectious Diseases, Division of Healthcare Quality Promotion. *Guide to infection prevention for outpatient settings: minimum expectations for safe care.* May 2011. CDC website. Available at: http://www.cdc.gov/HAI/pdfs/guidelines/standards-of-ambulatory-care-7-2011.pdf.
88. Centers for Disease Control and Prevention (CDC), National Center for Emerging and Zoonotic Infectious Diseases (NCEZID), Division of Healthcare Quality Promotion (DHQP). *Injection safety: Questions about multiple-dose vials.* CDC website. February 9, 2011. Available at: http://www.cdc.gov/injectionsafety/providers/provider_faqs_multivials.html.
89. Antimicrobial effectiveness testing (general information chapter 51). In: *The United States Pharmacopeia*, 36th rev., and The National Formulary, 31st ed. Rockville, MD: United States Pharmacopeial Convention, 2013.
90. Felts SK, Schaffner W, Melly MA, et al. Sepsis caused by contaminated intravenous fluids. *Ann Intern Med* 1972 Dec;77(6):881–890.
91. Young JA, Collette TS, Brehm WF. Sterility of multiple dose vials after repeated use. *Am Surg* 1958 Nov;24(11):811–814.
92. Trissel LA, Ogundele AB, Ingram DS, et al. Using medium-fill simulation to establish a benchmark microbiological contamination rate for low-risk-level compounding. *Am J Health Syst Pharm* 2003 Sep 15;60(18):1853–1855.
93. U.S. Department of Health and Human Services, Food and Drug Administration (FDA), Center for Drug Evaluation and Research (CDER), Center for Biologics Evaluation and Research (CBER), Office of Regulatory Affairs (ORA). *Guidance for Industry: Sterile Drug Products Produced by Aseptic Processing—Current Good Manufacturing Practice.* September 2004. FDA website. Available at: http://www.fda.gov/downloads/Drugs/GuidanceComplianceRegulatoryInformation/Guidances/UCM070342.pdf.
94. Sehulster LM, Chinn RY, Arduino MJ, et al. Guidelines for environmental infection control in healthcare facilities: recommendations of CDC and the Healthcare Infection Control Practices Advisory Committee (HICPAC). CDC website. 2003. Available at: http://www.cdc.gov/hicpac/pdf/guidelines/eic_in_hcf_03.pdf.
95. Whyte W, Bailey PV, Tinkler J, et al. An evaluation of the routes of bacterial contamination occurring during aseptic pharmaceutical manufacturing. *J Parenter Sci Technol* 1982 May-Jun;36(3):102–107.
96. Thomas M, Sanborn MD, Couldry R. I.V. admixture contamination rates: traditional practice site versus a class 1000 cleanroom. *Am J Health Syst Pharm* 2005 Nov 15;62(22):2386–2392.
97. Sandle T. A review of cleanroom microflora: types, trends, and patterns, *PDA J Pharm Sci Technol* 2011 Jul-Aug;65(4):392–403.
98. Weissfeld AS. Microbial monitoring in the pharmacy. *Clin Microbiol Newsl* 2009;31:14.
99. Certification guide for sterile compounding facilities, Controlled Environment Testing Association, CAG-003-2006, January 2012. Available at: http://www.cetainternational.org/.
100. Agalloco J, Akers JE, Madsen R. Aseptic processing: a review of current industry practice. *Pharm Technol* 2004;28(10):126–150 (on even pages).
101. Arnold TR, Hepler CD. Bacterial contamination of intravenous fluids opened in unsterile air. *Am J Hosp Pharm* 1971 Aug;28(8):614–619.

102. Hansen JS, Hepler CD. Contamination of intravenous solutions by airborne microbes. *Am J Hosp Pharm* 1973 Apr;30(4):326–331.

103. Trissel LA, Gentempo JA, Anderson RW, et al. Using medium-fill simulation to evaluate the microbiological contamination rate for USP medium-risk-level compounding. *Am J Health Syst Pharm* 2005 Feb 1;62(3):285–288.

104. Trissel LA, Gentempo JA, Saenz LM, et al. Effect of two work practice changes on the microbiological contamination rates of pharmacy-compounded sterile preparations. *Am J Health Syst Pharm* 2007 Apr 15;64(8):837–841.

105. van Doorne H, Bakker JH, Meevis RF, et al. Influence of background air on microbial contamination during simulated I.Vs.-admixture preparation. *J Clin Pharm Ther* 1994 Jun;19(3):181–187.

106. van Grafhorst JP, Foudraine NA, Nooteboom F, et al. Unexpected high risk of contamination with staphylococci species attributable to standard preparation of syringes for continuous intravenous drug administration in a simulation model in intensive care units. *Crit Care Med* 2002 Apr;30(4):833–836.

107. Capdevila X, Jaber S, Pesonen P, et al. Acute neck cellulitis and mediastinitis complicating a continuous interscalene block. *Anesth Analg* 2008 Oct;107(4):1419–1421.

108. Pronovost P, Needham D, Berenholtz S, et al. An intervention to decrease catheter-related bloodstream infections in the ICU. *N Engl J Med* 2006 Dec 28;355(26):2725–2732.

109. Wenzel RP, Edmond RB. Team-based prevention of catheter-related infections. *N Engl J Med* 2006 Dec 28;355(26):2781–2783.

110. Head S, Enneking FK. Infusate contamination in regional anesthesia: what every anesthesiologist should know. *Anesth Analg* 2008 Oct;107(4):1412–1418.

111. Shlaes DM, Gerding DN, John JF, et al. Society for Healthcare Epidemiology of America and Infectious Diseases Society of America Committee on the Prevention of Antimicrobial Resistance: guidelines for the prevention of antimicrobial resistance in hospitals. *Clin Infect Dis* 1997 Sep;25(3):584–599.

112. ASHP statement on the pharmacist's role in antimicrobial stewardship and infection prevention and control. *Am J Health Syst Pharm*; 2010 Apr 1;67(7):575–577.

113. De Rijdt T, Willems L, Simoens S. Economic effects of clinical pharmacy interventions: a literature review. *Am J Health Syst Pharm* 2008 Jun 15;65(12):1161–1172.

114. Zabarsky TF, Sethi AK, Donskey CJ. Sustained reduction in inappropriate treatment of asymptomatic bacteriuria in a long-term care facility through an educational intervention. *Am J Infect Control* 2008 Sep;36(7):476–480.

115. Buising KL, Thursky KA, Robertson MB, et al. Electronic antibiotic stewardship—reduced consumption of broad-spectrum antibiotics using a computerized antimicrobial approval system in a hospital setting. *J Antimicrob Chemother* 2008 Sep;62(3):608–616.

116. Hermsen ED, Smith Shull S, Puumala SE, et al. Improvement in prescribing habits and economic outcomes associated with the introduction of a standardized approach for surgical antimicrobial prophylaxis. *Infect Control Hosp Epidemiol* 2008 May;29(5):457–461.

117. Patel D, Lawson W, Guglielmo BJ. Antimicrobial stewardship programs: interventions and associated outcomes. *Expert Rev Anti Infect Ther* 2008 Apr;6(2):209–222.

118. Cosgrove SE, Patel A, Song X, et al. Impact of different methods of feedback to clinicians after postprescription antimicrobial review based on the Centers For Disease Control and Prevention's 12 Steps to Prevent Antimicrobial Resistance Among Hospitalized Adults. *Infect Control Hosp Epidemiol* 2007 Jun;28(6):641–646.

119. Fishman N. Antimicrobial stewardship. *Am J Infect Control* 2006 Jun;34(5 Suppl 1):S55–S63.

120. Department of Health and Human Services, Centers for Disease Control and Prevention (CDC). *Antibiotic Resistance Threats in the United States 2013*. CDC website. Available at: http://www.cdc.gov/drugresistance/threat-report-2013/pdf/ar-threats-2013-508.pdf.

SUPPLEMENTAL RESOURCES

American Society of Health-System Pharmacists (ASHP). Available online at: www.ashp.org.

Centers for Disease Control and Prevention (CDC). Available online at: www.cdc.gov.

Food and Drug Administration (FDA). Available online at: www.fda.gov.

Infusion Nurses Society (INS). Available online at: www.ins1.org.

United States Pharmacopeial Convention, Inc. (USP). Available online at: www.usp.org.

CHAPTER 111

Laundry, Patient Linens, Textiles, and Uniforms

Carol McLay, DrPH, BSN, RN, CIC
Infection Prevention Consultant
Lexington, KY

ABSTRACT

Healthcare textiles are fabric products that touch patients and employees directly or indirectly on a daily basis. Contaminated textiles in healthcare facilities are known to be a source of substantial numbers of pathogenic microorganisms. However, adherence to the U.S. Centers for Disease Control and Prevention Guidelines for Environmental Infection Control[1] and compliance with the mandated requirements in the Occupational Safety and Health Administration Bloodborne Pathogens Standard[2] are effective in keeping the risk of actual disease transmission to patients and healthcare personnel negligible. This exemplifies the importance of the entire laundering process to render textiles safe and suitable for reuse. The key elements in the laundering process include water temperature, type of detergents, disinfectant (i.e., sodium hypochlorite [chlorine bleach]), rinsing, and finishing. The process is supplemented by common sense and hygienic approaches to collection and transport.

KEY CONCEPTS

- Hygienically clean laundry carries negligible risks to healthcare personnel and patients, provided that the clean textiles, fabric, and clothing are not inadvertently contaminated before use.

- Complying with Centers for Disease Control and Prevention environmental guidelines and Occupational Safety and Health Administration rules on bloodborne pathogens is highly effective in protecting against disease transmission through textiles.

- Efforts to reduce the occupational risk of infection associated with handling contaminated textiles should primarily focus on the appropriate use of hand hygiene, protective barriers, and removal of foreign objects from the contaminated textile product stream.

- Routine microbiological sampling of clean textiles is not recommended.

- The role of healthcare personnel attire in the transmission of bacteria and development of healthcare-associated infections is not clear. The Association of Perioperative Registered Nurses recommends that all perioperative personnel should wear disposable surgical attire or freshly laundered surgical attire that is laundered at a healthcare-accredited laundry facility.

- Healthcare laundries are an integral component of the multidisciplinary team approach necessary to improve patient outcomes.

- Linen teams with key representatives from both organizations, including infection preventionists, should be created to develop standards and polices regarding linen use and processing, and to address continuous improvement.

BACKGROUND

Although contaminated textiles and fabrics in healthcare facilities can be a source of substantial numbers of pathogenic microorganisms, the Centers for Disease Control and Prevention (CDC) states that reports of healthcare-associated diseases linked to contaminated fabrics are so few that the overall risk of disease transmission during the laundry process likely is negligible.[1] Infections thought to be occupationally acquired were frequently the result of improper handling of these textiles (i.e., the shaking of soiled linens). Efforts to reduce the occupational risk of infection associated with handling contaminated patient care and/or surgical textiles should primarily focus on the appropriate use of hand washing, protective barriers, and removal of foreign objects from the contaminated textile product stream.[3] Bacteria (*Salmonella* spp., *Bacillus cereus*), viruses (Hepatitis B virus [HBV]), fungi (*Microsporum canis*), and *Sarcoptes scabiei* (the causative agent of scabies) presumably have been transmitted from contaminated textiles and fabrics to employees by direct contact or via aerosols of contaminated lint generated from sorting and handling contaminated textiles. On further investigation, presumed occupational infections associated with textile handling were often found to be community acquired. As for the influence of contaminated textiles on patient infections, several reports in the literature have suggested that textiles may have been the source of an infection. However, because the implicated organisms were often found on a number of environmental surfaces as well as the hands of healthcare personnel (HCP), the link between the textiles and the infection has not been established.[1,4]

KEY TERMS AND DEFINITIONS

Cleaning: A process that uses a cleaning agent and physical action, such as scrubbing or wiping, to remove visible soil, organic matter, and bioburden from a surface or object, renders the surface of object safe to handle. The cleaning agent may be a wet or dry chemical. The specifics of a cleaning process are dictated by factors associated with the item to be cleaned, namely chemical compatibility, location, wetness tolerance, and surface topography and complexity.

Condition/drying area: An area where, after extraction, textiles are either conditioned (partly dried) or fully dried in a dryer or tumbler.

Contaminated: The presence of blood or other potentially infectious material (OPIM) on an item or surface.

Contaminated laundry: According to the Occupational Safety and Health Administration (OSHA), laundry that has been soiled with blood, OPIM, or that may contain sharps.

Decontamination: The use of physical or chemical means to remove, inactivate, or destroy bloodborne pathogens on a surface, or the disinfection of the item to the point where it is no longer capable of transmitting infectious particles and that the surface or item is rendered safe for handling, use, or disposal.

Extraction area: An area where excess water is removed from textiles after laundering, but before conditioning or drying.

Folding area: An area where textiles are folded.

Foreign object: Objects or items considered as nontextile items (e.g., instruments, disposable devices, sharps, personal patient property, etc.) that may potentially harm people and laundry equipment if left among the textiles.

Functional separation/barrier: An activity or structure that separates one movement, action, or space from another. Examples include structures such as walls, partitions, and carts, as well as ventilation parameters such as airflow directions and pressure. Functional separation achieved through ventilation usually employs negative air pressure to prevent potential pathogens from spreading to other areas in the facility.

Personal protective equipment (PPE): Specialized clothing or equipment worn by an employee for protection against a hazard. General work clothes (e.g., uniforms, pants, shirts, or blouses) not intended to function as protection against a hazard are not considered to be PPE. Where there is occupational exposure, the employer shall provide and maintain, at no cost to the employee, appropriate PPE such as gloves, gowns, laboratory coats, face shields or masks, and eye protection.

Hygienically clean: A clean state, free of pathogens in sufficient numbers to minimize risk of infection.

Processed: Terminology that describes items that have been laundered, cleaned, disinfected, or sterilized as appropriate for safe use in an intended activity.

Receiving area: An area where soiled textiles are sorted, usually by textile category and sometimes by degree of soiling or color.

Staging: A process for preparing the textiles for delivery and having them wrapped and ready for transport.

Other potentially infectious material (OPIM): Any biologic material, other than blood, that may provide a reservoir for infectious agents. The following human body fluids: semen, vaginal secretions, cerebrospinal fluid, synovial fluid, pleural fluid, pericardial fluid, peritoneal fluid, amniotic fluid, saliva in dental procedures, and body fluid that is visibly contaminated with blood, and all body fluids in situations where it is difficult or impossible to differentiate between body fluids; any unfixed tissue or organ (other than intact skin) from a human (living or dead); and human immunodeficiency syndrome (HIV)-containing cell or tissue cultures, organ cultures, and HIV- or HBV-containing culture medium or other solutions; and blood, organs, or other tissues from experimental animals infected with HIV and HBV.

Soiled: Describes a textile product that has been used or worn and soiled by perspiration, body oils, or one of the many other items to which it may have been exposed.

Standard Precautions: The CDC term/isolation category that incorporates universal precautions and body substance precautions and includes a group of infection prevention practices that apply to ALL patients regardless of suspected or confirmed infection status in any setting where healthcare is delivered.

Universal precautions: An approach to infection prevention that considers all textile products being sent to the laundry as being contaminated. Special Note: Under these circumstances, it is not necessary to identify the bags in which the textiles are transported in any special manner, because they will all be handled/laundered the same way.

Washing (processing) area: An area where soiled textiles are washed and in which such equipment as washers, extractors, washer-extractors, continuous-batch washers, and/or continuous processing systems is located; also known as the wash floor.

BASIC PRINCIPLES

Laundry services play a critical role in a healthcare facility's infection prevention and control program. Healthcare textiles include bed sheets, pillowcases, blankets, towels, personal clothing, patient apparel, employee uniforms, scrub suits, and gowns and drapes for surgical procedures. Contaminated textiles often contain large numbers of microorganisms from body substances such as blood, skin, stool, urine, vomitus, and other body tissues and fluids, and it is important to ensure that pathogens are not transferred to patients or HCP.

Organisms commonly found on healthcare textiles include Gram-negative bacteria, coagulase-negative staphylococci, and *Bacillus* spp. in addition to normal microbial skin flora.[4,5]

Reports on the survival of microorganisms on hospital textiles after laundering are diverse and based upon a variety of different laundry temperatures and processes. In their literature review, Fijan et al. summarized data on the persistence of pathogens on hospital textiles. Laundering conditions in the published literature were variable, with temperatures ranging from 22.2°C to 77.2°C using a variety of disinfectants. Surviving microorganisms in these studies included *Enterococcus faecium*, *Enterococcus faecalis*, *Staphylococcus aureus*, *Pseudomonas* and *Klebsiella* species, and *Clostridium difficile* spores. In addition to bacteria, molds and viruses (including rotavirus and parainfluenza virus) have been cultured from hospital textiles.[4]

Bacteria (*Salmonella* spp., *Bacillus cereus*), viruses (HBV), fungi (*M. canis*), and the scabies mite *S. scabiei* presumably have been transmitted from contaminated textiles and fabrics to employees by direct contact or via aerosols of contaminated lint generated from sorting and handling contaminated textiles. On further investigation, presumed occupational infections associated with textile handling were often found to be community acquired.[1,4,5]

Some investigators have examined the connection between healthcare textiles and infectious disease outbreaks, and their conclusions emphasize the fact that correct laundering of healthcare textiles is an important measure for preventing healthcare-associated infections (HAIs).

Several *B. cereus* HAIs in Japan were investigated, and novel multilocus sequence types were found in patients. *B. cereus* contamination was observed with reusable (dried and steamed) towels and washing machines in hospital linen rooms. The authors speculated that contamination of the towels occurred in washing machines in the hospital linen room. When towels were treated with sodium hypochlorite and then laundered by an external cleaning company, no further contamination was detected.[6]

In another investigation of a *B. cereus* bacteremia outbreak, hospital linens and the hospital washing machine were highly contaminated with *B. cereus*, which was also isolated from the intravenous fluid of symptomatic patients. All of the contaminated linens were autoclaved, the washing machine was cleaned with a detergent, and improved hand hygiene was promoted among the hospital staff. These measures successfully terminated the transmission of infection. The source of this outbreak was identified as *B. cereus* contamination of hospital linens, and the authors theorized that *B. cereus* was being transmitted from the linens to patients via catheter infection. The linens had been washed in the hospital washing machine, which reused water for washing and rinsing. Furthermore, the machine had not been cleaned for over 10 years.[7]

In 2010, the CDC presented a paper on its investigation of an outbreak of zygomycosis, a fungal-based infection that can be potentially life-threatening to patients with weakened or compromised immune systems. Hospital textiles were identified as the only common element among all the cases. Environmental

sampling performed at the hospital on the textiles and areas in contact with textiles revealed a 40 percent presence of the pathogen and only a 4 percent presence in items and areas not in contact with textiles. The facility changed its laundry provider, replaced all of its linen, and disinfected the linen storage areas. Cultures taken at the hospital 3 weeks later were all negative. The authors concluded that hospital linens likely acted as a vector bringing *Rhizopus* in contact with susceptible patients in this outbreak. *Rhizopus* might have contaminated linens at the laundry facility or during delivery to the hospital. The CDC recommends that hospital linens should be laundered, shipped, and stored in a manner that minimizes exposure to environmental contaminants.[8]

An outbreak of *Bacillus* sp. bacteremia was reported among critically ill premature infants in a neonatal intensive care unit (NICU) during a hospital expansion construction project. Cultures from several NICU workstations, the respiratory therapy workstation, and the storage room, as well as hospital linens, grew *Bacillus* sp. The outbreak task force speculated that contamination of linens could have been a factor contributing to the outbreak, as items were delivered to the loading dock adjacent to the excavation site.[9]

Through a combination of soil removal, pathogen removal, and pathogen inactivation, contaminated laundry can be rendered hygienically clean. Hygienically clean laundry carries negligible risk to HCP and patients, provided that the clean textiles, fabric, and clothing are not inadvertently contaminated before use. The laundering process consists of the proper combination of water, heat, pH, oxidation, chemical sanitizers, and drying and sanitizing. Additional factors that play a vital role in ensuring hygienically clean textiles include the physical layout of the laundry and the design of the facility infrastructure.

THE LAUNDRY SERVICE

It is estimated that 10 billion pounds of healthcare-setting textiles are processed annually.[10] Healthcare laundry is generally processed by a facility's own laundry (on-premise laundry, external hospital-owned facility, or shared laundry service) or outsourced to a commercial, retail facility with customer-owned goods or laundry facility-provided textiles. Facilities are increasingly turning to outsourcing to offset the risk and costs associated with managing textiles in-house. Laundry services are in fact the most outsourced hospital department contract.[11]

Laundry facilities that place surgical textiles (whether sterile or nonsterile) into commercial distribution come under the jurisdiction of Food and Drug Administration (FDA) regulations. In addition, laundry facilities may be subject to local and state regulations, as well as Environmental Protection Agency (EPA) and OSHA requirements.

To be eligible for reimbursement, hospitals must be compliant with the Federal Medicare Conditions of Participation (CoPs). The CoPs contain the minimum health and safety requirements that hospitals must meet. According to the CoPs, a hospital's governing body is responsible for oversight of contracted services. The governing body must ensure that a contractor furnishes services in a manner consistent with acceptable standards of practice. These conditions are driving the current movement toward using accredited healthcare laundries. Many healthcare facilities have created linen teams with key representatives from both organizations to develop standards and policies regarding linen use and processing and to address continuous improvement.

Accredited healthcare laundries are compliant with the standards promoted by the Healthcare Laundry Accreditation Council (HLAC), which is a nonprofit organization formed for the purpose of inspecting and accrediting laundries processing healthcare textiles for hospitals, nursing homes, and other healthcare facilities. HLAC's mission is to publish high standards for processing healthcare textiles in laundries and provide an inspection and accreditation process that recognizes laundries that meet these standards. The standards incorporate evidence-based, peer-reviewed best practices and recommendations for infection prevention and laundry procedures from federal agencies (e.g., the CDC) and professional entities such as the American National Standards Institute (ANSI), the Association for the Advancement of Medical Instrumentation, the Association of Perioperative Registered Nurses (AORN), the Association for Professionals in Infection Control and Epidemiology (APIC), the Facilities Guidelines Institute (FGI), and the Textile Rental Services Association of America (TRSA).

Updated HLAC standards were published in 2012. The *Accreditation Standards for Processing Reusable Textiles for use in Healthcare Facilities, 2011 Edition* covers the complete textile processing cycle, from handling and transporting soiled healthcare textiles, to in-plant processing and delivery back to the customer.[10] The standards consist of three sections.

Part I: Basic elements include such topics as laundry facilities, equipment, and personnel.

Mandatory requirements include:

- A functional barrier by negative air pressure in soiled areas.

- Warning signs about the presence of contaminated textiles and the need to follow universal precautions must be posted in work areas.

- The textile areas must be free of vermin, devoid of lint, and without obvious moisture contamination.

- Cardboard must not be used as shelf liner material.

- Hand hygiene resources must be available in or around all work areas and in personnel support areas.

- Emergency eyewash/shower equipment must be available with unobstructed access.

- Safety features (e.g., emergency lighting, signage, fire alarms, door accessibility and egress, safety perimeter for robotics, equipment guards) must be evident and operational.

- Working surfaces must be kept clean of visible soil, dust, and lint.

- Working surfaces that become contaminated with blood or OPIM must be decontaminated, cleaned, and disinfected with EPA-registered hospital disinfectants labeled tuberculocidal or registered disinfectants on the EPA Lists D and/or E.

- A written regulated medical waste management plan.

- Compliance with regulations as they pertain to air, water, and chemicals management.

- Evidence of wastewater and/or air quality permit compliance.

- Compliance with hazardous chemical regulations.

- Documentation on types of laundry equipment, equipment installation, operation, safety, preventative maintenance, and repairs.

- Descriptions of personnel qualifications and responsibilities.

- Documentation of personnel health and hygiene and use of PPE and attire.

- An occupational safety and health program based on the OSHA Bloodborne Pathogen Standard and Universal Precautions.

- An exposure control plan.

- A hepatitis B vaccination program.

- A standing process for postexposure management for blood and/or OPIM.

- A hazardous materials (e.g., nonbiological, chemical, radiological) safety plan and policy.

- Training and educational programs must include bloodborne pathogens exposure control training, hazardous substance contaminated textiles training, Department of Transportation regulations training.

Part II: Includes seven subsections on the textile processing cycle. Pertinent requirements include:

Handling, Collection, and Transportation of Soiled Healthcare Textiles

- Healthcare textiles must be handled and collected in accordance with OSHA regulations and federal guidelines, thereby minimizing potential exposure of patients, HCP, or laundry personnel to bloodborne pathogens or other infectious agents.

- Soiled healthcare textiles must be assumed to be contaminated; personnel who handle soiled textiles must follow Standard Precautions at all times.

- Soiled textiles shall be collected and handled only as necessary to complete the defined tasks, and in such a way as to minimize microbial contamination of the air and the personnel handling the textiles. Soiled textiles must not be sorted or rinsed in patient-care areas.

- The collection bags or containers must functionally contain wet or soiled textiles and prevent contamination of the environment during collection, transportation, and storage prior to processing. The containers must be leakproof, capable of being closed securely to prevent textiles from falling out, and not tear when loaded to capacity.

- The bags or other containers must be color-coded or labeled. If only soiled healthcare textiles are coming into the laundry, and all personnel are following Standard Precautions when handling these textiles, the bags do not need to be color-coded or labeled.

- The laundry provider must maintain functional separation of clean from soiled textiles in carts and/or vehicles at all times during the collection and transportation of soiled textiles.

- Standard Precautions must be observed while moving, loading, and unloading soiled textiles.

Washing, Extraction, and Drying

- The wash process shall ensure that healthcare textiles become hygienically clean.

- Three basic types of washing equipment are used in the processing of healthcare textiles: washers, washer/extractors, and continuous batch washers. Depending on the type of equipment in use, modifications in these requirements and other factors affecting the process may be necessary to ensure that quality standards are consistently met. If modifications are necessary, they shall be documented, dated, and revised as needed.

- The load size (weight) for each classification of soil shall be established by the facility and recorded for each load processed.

- The wash cycle shall comply with all applicable state and local requirements for healthcare textile processing.

- Each classification shall have established standards for the following factors:

  ○ Cycle time: prewash, wash, rinse, and final rinse times; water levels/usage (total water usage and/or water levels)

  ○ Temperature (wash cycle, bleach cycle, and rinse cycle temperatures)

  ○ Chemical usage (chemical types and usage levels for each step in the wash process)

- Clean healthcare textiles shall be extracted or dried in a manner that preserves the integrity of the textile merchandise, minimizes microbial growth after washing, and prepares the textiles for efficient ironing or folding. Damp textiles shall not be left in machines overnight.

Finishing

- The finishing process of ironing or folding textiles shall ensure that the merchandise is maintained in the same clean state as when it emerged from washing.

- The ironing or folding procedures shall meet the needs and expectations of the user. If any textiles become soiled in this process, they shall be rewashed.

- Ironing equipment shall be maintained in good operating condition so that it adequately irons, dries, and folds the textiles without excessive heat, pressure, or mechanical damage. The equipment shall maintain a temperature of at least 300 degrees on the ironer chests.

- Dry folding equipment shall be in good operating condition.

Packaging and Storing

- Packaging and storage of healthcare merchandise shall maintain the textiles in a clean state for delivery to the customer.

- The textiles may be wrapped into fluid-resistant bundles or placed bundled but unwrapped into fluid-resistant covered carts or hampers. The wrapping material may be plastic or other suitable material and shall be securely closed during transport to the customer.

- During packaging, textiles shall be handled as little as possible to prevent soiling or contamination.

- If unwrapped merchandise is placed into carts or hampers and covered, the container shall remain covered at all times until delivered to the user's textiles storage room or other designated location in the healthcare facility. If the cart does not have a solid bottom, it must be lined with heavy plastic or impervious paper before placing clean textiles inside.

- Bundled and wrapped textiles may be stored in open racks in the laundry, on the trucks, or at the user's facility, provided the integrity of bundled and wrapped textiles is not compromised.

- Unwrapped clean textiles may be stored in designated rooms.

- The laundry storage room shall only be accessible to appropriate personnel.

- Only clean linens shall be stored in this area and signage posted as "linen storage room."

- The door shall remain closed at all times.

- If any textiles become soiled during packaging and storage, they shall be reprocessed in accordance with previously stated processing guidelines.

Delivery of Cleaned Healthcare Textiles

- Maintain functional separation of clean from soiled textiles during transportation by bagging soiled textiles in fluid-resistant containers and by anchoring soiled textiles in the vehicle so that they do not spill from their containers.

- Clean and soiled textiles may be transported in the same vehicle if functional separation is maintained using physical barriers and/or space separation sufficient to protect clean textiles from contact with soiled textiles.

- Train personnel regarding proper bagging and placement of textiles in the transporting truck; ensure that all employees follow Standard Precautions at all times.

- Clean and soiled textiles shall not be stored in the same container.

- If a cart is used to transport clean textiles, the textiles shall be wrapped inside the cart; if textiles are unwrapped, the cart shall be lined with plastic or heavy paper and covered. Carts must be maintained in good working order.

- Carts, containers, covers, and liners used to collect or transport soiled textiles must be properly cleaned and disinfected after the cart is emptied and before any next use.

- The interior of the transport vehicle shall be cleaned on a regular basis or when visibly soiled.

- Vehicles must have waterless hand cleaner, PPE, and spill kits on board.

Part III: Addresses surgical pack assembly room standards, details of which will not be covered in this chapter.

The Laundering Process

The laundering process is designed to produce healthcare textiles that are free of vegetative pathogens (hygienically clean). Laundering cycles consist of flush, main wash, bleaching, rinsing, and scouring. Cleaned wet textiles are then dried, pressed, and prepared for distribution back to the healthcare facility.

According to the CDC, the antimicrobial action of the laundering process results from a combination of mechanical, thermal, and chemical factors.[1] Substantial numbers of microorganisms are removed through the process of dilution and agitation. Soaps and detergents function to suspend soil and exert microbiocidal properties. Hot water also provides an effective means of destroying organisms. A temperature of at least 160°F (71°C) for a minimum of 25 minutes is recommended for hot-water washing.[1] Alternatively, low-temperature washing at 71°F to 77°F (22°C to 25°C) plus a 125-part-per-million (ppm) chlorine bleach rinse has been found to be effective and comparable to high-temperature wash cycles.[12] The selection of hot or cold water laundry cycles may be dictated by state licensing or other standards. The cleansing action is followed by a number of cycles, such as one for the chlorine bleach, a series of rinses, and finally neutralization of any residue of the chemicals that were used. Chlorine bleach is an economical broad-spectrum germicide but may not be appropriate for all fabrics. Chlorine alternatives (e.g., activated oxygen-based detergents) may be used to ensure adequate disinfection of laundry. Dryer temperatures and cycle times are dictated by the materials in the fabrics. When textiles are laundered using proper amounts of each chemical and subjected to adequate dilution, mechanical action, and water temperatures, the patient is ensured of being provided items that are hygienically clean.

Recent improvements in technology utilized in laundry processing have been recognized by the Centers for Medicare & Medicaid Services (CMS). In January 2013, CMS[12] clarified and revised the agency's guidance for F Tag 441 on the following components of the laundry process:

Laundry detergents: Modern-day detergents are much more effective in removing soil and reducing the presence of microbes. The CMS in collaboration with the CDC has determined that facilities may use any detergents designated for laundry in laundry processing. Further, laundry detergents used within nursing homes are not required to have stated antimicrobial claims.

Water temperatures and chlorine bleach rinses: The chlorine bleach rinse is not required for all laundry items processed in low-temperature washing environments due to the availability of modern laundry detergents that are able to produce hygienically clean laundry without the presence of chlorine bleach.

Maintenance of equipment and laundry items: Facilities are not required to maintain a record of water temperatures during laundry processing cycles. The CDC recommends leaving washing machines open to air when not in use to allow the machine to dry completely and to prevent growth of microorganisms in wet, potentially warm environments. Facilities are required to follow manufacturer's instructions for washing machines, dryers, detergents, rinse aids, and other additives.

Ozone cleaning systems: The CMS in collaboration with the CDC has determined that ozone cleaning systems are acceptable methods of processing laundry.

Other Healthcare Settings

In some healthcare settings (i.e., ambulatory care, behavioral health units, rehabilitation), linens and clothing may not be routinely determined as being contaminated with blood or body fluids. These items are often washed in designated locations near patient care areas or by the patients themselves as part of their activities of daily living. In these situations, guidelines should be developed to ensure that both staff and patients are instructed on appropriate processing procedures. These should include instructions to do the following:

- Rinse all fecal matter from clothing before washing.

- Handle soiled linen as little as possible and with minimum agitation.

- Transport all items to washers in hampers or plastic bags.

- Avoid overloading the washing machine.

- Use normal laundry cycles in accordance with the washer and detergent manufacturers recommendations.

- Disinfect the washer tub and dryer.

- Perform hand hygiene after handling soiled items.

Home Laundering of Healthcare Attire

The issue of home laundering of scrubs or other surgical attire is controversial, and much attention has been recently focused on the microbial load present on these textiles. *The Guidelines for*

Environmental Infection Control in Health-Care Facilities admit that experts are divided regarding the practice of transporting clothes worn at the workplace to the HCP's home for laundering.[1] OSHA regulations prohibit home laundering of items that are considered personal protective apparel or equipment (e.g., laboratory coats); however, this regulation does not extend to uniforms and scrub suits that are not contaminated with blood or OPIM.[2]

Numerous studies have demonstrated the contamination of HCP attire including white coats, ties, and uniforms with potentially pathogenic microorganisms.[13-18] The first report of a positive correlation between bacterial contamination of HCP hands and uniforms was published by Munoz-Price et al. in 2012 after they cultured the hands and uniforms of physicians, nurses, and other HCP (e.g., therapists, technicians) from five intensive care units. Eighty-six percent of the 119 HCP in the study demonstrated bacterial growth on their hands. Eleven percent grew *S. aureus*, 6 percent grew *Acinetobacter* spp., and 2 percent grew enterococci. The presence of pathogens on the hands was associated with a greater likelihood of the presence of pathogens on white coats. This association was not observed between hands and scrubs, however. The authors postulate that this may be explained by the different laundering frequency of these garments.[16]

Several studies have raised questions about the safety and efficacy of home-laundering of surgical attire. Twomey et al. reported that the aerobic bacterial bioburden associated with surgical scrub attire was significantly greater in home-laundered attire than in scrubs laundered by the healthcare facility, scrubs sent out by the facility to a third-party company for laundering, or single-use/disposable scrubs. They concluded that home-laundering is not as effective as facility or third-party laundering in decontaminating surgical scrub attire.[19] Similar results were reported by Nordstrom et al., who conducted a comparison of bacteria on new, disposable, laundered, and unlaundered hospital scrubs and discovered that significantly higher bacteria counts were isolated from home-laundered scrubs and unwashed scrubs than from new, hospital-laundered, and disposable scrubs.[20]

Despite the mounting evidence pointing to the contamination of uniforms with organisms, there is a lack of evidence of active transmission of bacteria from uniforms to patients. Wilson et al. performed a systematic search and quality assessment of the published literature to establish current knowledge on the role of the HCP uniforms as vehicles for the transfer of pathogens. They concluded that the hypothesis that uniforms/clothing could be a vehicle for the transmission of infections is not supported by existing evidence. There is no robust evidence of a difference in efficacy of decontamination of uniforms/clothing between industrial and domestic laundry processes or evidence that the home laundering of uniforms provides inadequate decontamination.[21]

HLAC addresses this issue in its standards and explains, "it should be noted that the use of home washers of the processing of reusable surgical textiles in not recommended. Home washers are designed for retail situations, and this design does not take into account industrial environments and hazards addressed in the OSHA Bloodborne Pathogen standard."[10]

Although the CDC describes the matter as unresolved, AORN opposes the practice of permitting surgical personnel to launder soiled scrubs at home. The revised AORN "Recommended practices for surgical attire" document published in AORN's *Perioperative Standards and Recommended Practices* maintains that AORN does not support the practice of home laundering of surgical scrubs.[22]

The previous AORN recommendations[23] provided perioperative nurses with suggestions for how to home launder soiled surgical attire; however, the most current document removes these recommendations and states "Home laundering may not meet the specified measures necessary to achieve a reduction in antimicrobial levels in soiled surgical attire.[22]

The opposing policies held by these two organizations account for the differences in positions taken by some healthcare providers and the infection prevention community. Healthcare administrators and infection prevention teams must weigh the potential risk of infection transmission against the cost savings achieved through having staff launder their own scrubs. HCP should be educated on the potential for uniforms to become contaminated and steps they can take to minimize transmission of microorganisms with the healthcare setting as well as to their home environment.

Microbiological Sampling of Textiles

Adenosine triphosphate (ATP) is an enzyme that is present in all living cells, and ATP monitoring systems can detect the amount of organic matter that remains after cleaning an environmental surface, a medical device, or a surgical instrument. Many healthcare facilities are using ATP-based monitoring systems to detect and measure ATP on surfaces as a way to assess the effectiveness of their facilities' cleaning efforts. There has recently been interest in extending the use of ATP-detection technology to porous materials such as textiles. The *Guidelines for Environmental Infection Control In Health-Care Facilities* does not recommend routine microbiologic sampling of clean textiles.[1] APIC supports this recommendation and concludes that the use of ATP detection technology for determining the cleanliness of hygienically clean, reusable healthcare textiles is inappropriate and unwarranted when the HLAC standards are employed to ensure the consistent and reliable laundering of these cloth items.[24]

Microbiologic sampling during outbreak investigations is appropriate, however, if epidemiologic evidence indicates a role for healthcare textiles and clothing in disease transmission.

CONCLUSIONS

Healthcare textiles have become an important issue in infection prevention and control, and laundry services are an integral part of the multidisciplinary team approach necessary for improved patient outcomes. The use of a defined laundering process, the parameters of which are established in the industry, is essential for the production of hygienically clean textiles. The goal for healthcare laundry is achieved by consistent monitoring of the entire laundering process, coupled with best practices in infection prevention for laundry personnel and a well-designed, properly functioning laundry in accordance with accepted industry standards.

FUTURE TRENDS

Advancements in medical technology, population growth rates, changes in the demographics associated with an aging population and renewed commitment to the elimination of HAIs as well as the demand for greater transparency are all driving the healthcare textiles market.

There have been many novel developments in the composition of hospital linen products that promise to decrease the chance of carrying disease, increase a patient's ability to heal, and lessen the likelihood of the patient developing skin issues such as bed sores. Smart or "intelligent" textiles refer to textile materials or engineered structures that can potentially sense, react, and/or adapt to environmental conditions. Nano-sized particles can be used to change the surface area of fabrics used in healthcare, which increases surface tension and creates a barrier to contaminants and fluids, such as blood. The textile industry has developed different methods for obtaining fabrics and fibers with an antimicrobial action for use in hospital environments and for other purposes. Antimicrobial chemicals such as copper oxide, silver, gold, triclosan, and titanium dioxide, among others, have been impregnated into such items as linens, respiratory masks, isolation gowns, laboratory coats, and uniforms. Antimicrobial cubicle curtains and shower and window treatments are commercially available for use in patient rooms. Quality issues such as potential toxicologic and allergic side effects, potential selection for resistant microorganisms with long-term use, environmental issues, and persistence of the antimicrobial effect will require further investigation.

Over time, reducing the environmental impact in the healthcare textile industry will become increasingly important. The efficient use of natural resources will become standard by factoring pollution prevention and resource conservation into business practices.

Healthcare textiles is a dynamically expanding industry. From the accreditation process network to the creation of environmentally friendly and clean healthcare fabrics to the utilization of smart technology, the potential range of uses for medical textiles will continue to increase and offer the potential to reduce HAIs.

REFERENCES

1. Sehulster LM, Chinn RYW, Arduino MJ, et al. *Guidelines for environmental infection control in health-care facilities. Recommendations from CDC and the Healthcare Infection Control Practices Advisory Committee (HICPAC).* Chicago: American Society for Healthcare Engineering/American Hospital Association, 2004. Available at: http://www.cdc.gov/hicpac/pdf/guidelines/eic_in_hcf_03.pdf.
2. Occupational Safety & Health Administration. *Occupational exposure to bloodborne pathogens: final rule.* OSHA Standard 56 Fed Regist 1991 Dec 6;56(235);64004–64182. Available at: https://www.osha.gov/pls/oshaweb/owadisp.show_document?p_table=STANDARDS&p_id=10051.
3. American National Standard Institute (ANSI)/Association for the Advancement of Medical Instrumentation (AAMI) ST65:2008: *Processing of reusable surgical textiles for use in health care facilities.* Alexandria VA: AAMI, 2009.
4. Fijan S, Turk SS. Hospital textiles, are they a possible vehicle for healthcare-associated infections? *Int J Environ Res Public Health* 2012 Sep 14;9(9): 3330–3343.
5. Pyrek KM. *Healthcare Textiles: Laundry Science and Infection Prevention.* 2011. Available at: http://www.infectioncontroltoday.com/reports/2011/03/healthcare-textiles-laundry-science-and-infection-prevention.aspx.
6. Dohmae S, Okubo T, Higuchi W, et al. Bacillus cereus nosocomial infection from reused towels in Japan. *J Hosp Infect.* 2008 Aug;69(4):361–367.
7. Sasahara T, Hayashi S, Morisawa Y, et al. Bacillus cereus bacteremia outbreak due to contaminated hospital linens. *Eur J Clin Microbiol Infect Dis* 2011 Feb;30(2):219–226.
8. Duffy J, Harris J, Newhouse E, et al. Zygomycosis outbreak associated with hospital linens. Presented at the Fifth Decentennial International Conference on Healthcare-Associated Infections. March 19, 2010. Available at: https://shea.confex.com/shea/2010/webprogram/Paper2072.html.
9. Campbell JR., Hulten K, Baker CJ. Cluster of *Bacillus* species bacteremia cases in neonates during a hospital construction project. *Infect Control Hosp Epidemiol* 2011 Oct; 32(10):1035–1038.
10. Healthcare Laundry Accreditation Council (HLAC). *Accreditation Standards for Processing Reusable Textiles for Use in Healthcare Facilities, 2011.* Available at: http://www.hlacnet.org.
11. Kutscher B. Feeling effects of consolidation. *Modern Healthcare* [serial online]. December 15, 2012;44–50. Available at: http://www.modernhealthcare.com/article/20121215/SUPPLEMENT/312159998.
12. Director, Survey and Certification Group, to State Survey Agency Directors. *"Clarification of Interpretive Guidance at F Tag 441-Laundry and Infection Control"* Centers for Medicare & Medicaid Services, Ref S&C:13-09-NH. January 25, 2013. Available at: http://www.cms.gov/Medicare/Provider-Enrollment-and-Certification/SurveyCertificationGenInfo/Downloads/Survey-and-Cert-Letter-13-09.pdf.
13. Treakle AM, Thom KA, Furuno JP, et al. Bacterial contamination of health care workers' white coats. *Am J Infect Control* 2009;37:101–105.
14. Lopez PJ, Ron O, Parthasarathy P, et al. Bacterial counts from hospital doctors' ties are higher than those from shirts. *Am J Infect Control* 2009;37:79–80
15. Morgan DJ, Liang SY, Smith CL, et al. *Infect Control Hosp Epidemiol* 2010;31:716–721.
16. Munoz-Price LS, Arheart KL, Mills JP, et al. *Am J Infect Control* 2012 Nov;40 (9):245–248.
17. Snyder G, Thom KA, Furuno JP, et al. *Infect Control Hosp Epidemiol* 2008; 29(7):584–589.
18. Wiener-Well Y, Galuty M, Rudensky B, et al. Nursing and physician attire as possible source of nosocomial infections. *Am J Infect Control* 2011;39:555–559.
19. Twomey C, Beitz B, Johnson HB. Bacterial contamination of surgical scrubs and laundering mechanisms: infection control implications. *Infection Control Today.* October 19, 2009:10. Available at: http://www.arta1.com/cms/uploads/Bacterial%20Contamination%20of%20Surgical%20Scrubs%20and%20Laundering%20Mechanisms_%20Infection%20Control%20Implications.pdf.
20. Nordstrom JM, Reynolds KA, Gerba CP. Comparison of bacteria on new, disposable, laundered, and unlaundered hospital scrubs. *Am J Infect Control* 2012 Aug;40(6):539–543.
21. Wilson JA, Loveday HP, Hoffman PN, et al. Uniform: An evidence review of the microbiological significance of uniforms and uniform policy in the prevention and control of healthcare-associated infections. *J Hosp Infect* 2007 Aug:66(4):301–307.
22. Association of Perioperative Registered Nurses (AORN). Recommended practices for surgical attire. In: *Perioperative Standards and Recommended Practices.* Denver:AORN, Inc., 2011;57–72.
23. Association of Perioperative Registered Nurses (AORN). *Recommended Practices for Surgical Attire, 2000 Standards, Recommended Standards and Guidelines.* Denver: AORN, 2003;215.
24. Association for Professionals in Infection Control and Epidemiology (APIC). *APIC Practice Guidelines Committee (PGC) Position Statement on Adenosine Triphosphate (ATP) Testing of Reusable Textiles in Healthcare Facilities, 2012.* Available at: http://apic.org/Resource_/TinyMceFileManager/Position_Statements/APIC_position_ATP_and_reusable_textiles_082012.pdf.

SUPPLEMENTAL RESOURCES

Association for the Advancement of Medical Instrumentation (AAMI). Available at: www.aami.org.

American Society for Healthcare Engineering of the American Hospital Association (ASHE). Available at: www.ashe.org.

American National Standards Institute (ANSI). Available at: www.ansi.org.

Association for Healthcare Environment (AHE). Available at: www.ahe.org.

Facilities Guideline Institute (FGI). Available at: www.fgiguidelines.org.

Textile Rental Services Association of America (TRSA). Available at: www.trsa.org.

CHAPTER 112

Maintenance and Engineering

Stephen D. Cutter, MBA, HFDP,CHFM, SASHE
Director of Facilities
Dartmouth-Hitchcock Medical Center
Lebanon, NH

ABSTRACT

Healthcare settings vary in a number of ways, including type and physical structure of the facility, patient services, community surroundings, and geographical location. Major areas of responsibility of the maintenance and engineering staff relate to buildings, utilities, associated equipment, and property or grounds. Within these components are multiple activities ranging from preventive maintenance through major projects. A strong working relationship between the infection preventionist and maintenance and engineering staff is essential to maintain a safe environment and minimize potential risks. This chapter outlines risk elements that are common in many facilities and provides examples of interventions to address these challenges.

KEY CONCEPTS

- Settings for healthcare vary widely, both in size and scope of services.

- Maintenance and engineering responsibilities encompass many areas, including facilities/buildings, utilities, equipment, and grounds.

- Maintenance and engineering staff and infection preventionists work in partnership to provide a safe environment of care.

- Maintenance and engineering activities, facility components, and equipment have identifiable risks and interventions; therefore, recognition of the major routes of microbial spread—air, water, and surface—is fundamental to identifying risks and formulate preventative strategies.

- Preparedness through prudent and proactive maintenance is better than a reactive approach for preventing infections.

- Emergency preparedness is integrated into maintenance and engineering operations.

- Sustainable mechanical systems for energy management that include risk assessment provisions support hazard control in healthcare facilities.

- Education and training of maintenance and engineering staff and contracted workers is essential for patient, visitor, and worker safety, as well as protection of the facility and community served.

- Performance improvement activities may be used to improve maintenance and engineering processes and systems.

BACKGROUND

Healthcare facilities that provide direct patient care differ broadly in size and complexity, ranging from storefront practices to multibuilding campuses. The maintenance and engineering (MAE) staff composition also varies and may range from a part-time or as-needed "handyman" to a complex department with numerous employees and resources. Facility and utility components, as well as maintenance of buildings, support systems, equipment, and grounds, are often included in MAE responsibilities. Consideration includes compliance with applicable codes, regulations, standards, and guidelines.[1-22] (See also Chapter 4 Accrediting and Regulatory Agencies.)

Regardless of the size and scope of services, there are standard elements that must be considered to provide a safe setting for workers, patients, visitors, and others. Part of the goals and recommendations for an effective infection prevention and control program include minimizing risks of infection regardless of healthcare setting.[7-9,11,12,17,23-26] Therefore, the infection preventionist (IP) should develop a working knowledge of the challenges within the MAE arena and partner with MAE personnel to help identify risks and provide guidance for appropriate interventions. The organization's culture of safety can greatly affect worker health and patient outcomes.[12,17,18,27-32]

BASIC PRINCIPLES

Venues that offer healthcare services vary widely and include urban, suburban, and critical access hospitals; long-term acute care facilities; chronic and long-term care settings; skilled nursing facilities; ambulatory surgery sites; dialysis centers; rehabilitation centers; hospice; urgent care centers; clinics with one or more specialties; single-clinician practices in rented buildings; endoscopy centers; dentistry and oral surgery; behavioral and substance abuse centers; school clinics; infirmaries at correctional facilities; health department clinics; employee/occupational health centers; in vitro fertilization clinics; some research facilities; and other unique sites (see also chapters on specific practice settings and services; refer to index and/or table of contents).

Responsibilities of the MAE department vary in accordance with the type and size of healthcare facility but typically include the following:

1. Equipment repair and maintenance

   a. Varies broadly but would typically include patient beds, table, furniture, wheelchairs, scales, sterilizers, laboratory equipment

2. System maintenance and repair

   a. May include pneumatic tube systems, nurse call and code blue systems, duress systems, access control systems, elevators and lifts, fire alarm systems

3. Heating, ventilation, and air conditioning (HVAC) systems

   a. Critical to a safe environment, these systems include air supply, return and exhaust systems, heating, cooling, and humidification and filtration systems.

4. Utility systems management.[1,3–5,7,9,13,16,25,26,29,32–34] In addition to HVAC equipment noted above, utility systems may include:

   a. Electrical system and emergency power systems

   b. Medical gas systems including oxygen, medical air, nitrogen and medical vacuum, as well as piped anesthesia gases

   c. Potable water and wastewater systems

   d. Boiler, steam, and hot water systems

   e. Pager and communication systems

5. Facility infrastructure maintenance and repair

   a. Includes elements such as roofing, window systems, flooring, ceiling and walls, doors and hardware, etc.

6. Grounds and landscaping

7. Building renovations and alterations

   a. Responsibility for this work varies greatly but typically includes planning, design, and construction activities. Understanding the processes that frame this work is critical for the IPs so that they can provide input at the appropriate time in the process.

8. Emergency preparedness[15,16,25,34,50]

   a. An organization's emergency preparedness program is typically a collaborative effort but the MAE management and staff will have a strong role, as the systems noted above are important systems in the program.

See also Chapters 107 Environmental Services; 113 Waste Management; 114 HVAC; 115 Water Systems Issues; 116 Construction and Renovation; and 119 Emergency Management. Sustainable management of essential ventilation air and water quality requires commitment to the attention necessary to ensure consistent control of comfort and hazards associated with healthcare facilities. These hazards are identified within the environment of care, especially those associated with infection prevention systems.

Collaboration between MAE personnel, IPs, and other safety professionals will help establish appropriate measures that maximize risk reduction; such strategies should be integrated into MAE activities. Effective education and training of department and contracted employees must include infection prevention and safety components.[3,4,12,17,19,31,32,51,52] (See also Chapters 3 Education and Training; 27 Hand Hygiene; 29 Isolation Precautions; 100 Occupational Health; 101 Occupational Exposure to Bloodborne Pathogens; 103 Immunization in Healthcare Personnel; and 104 Pregnant Healthcare Personnel.)

Effective communication, measurement, documentation, analysis, and interventions are crucial steps for a successful program. Performance improvement activities may be incorporated to appraise actions or process improvement changes and to evaluate success.[7,12,13,17,23,29,30,53–56] (See also Chapters 16 Quality Concepts, and 17 Performance Indicators.)

STANDARDS FOR THE MAINTENANCE AND ENGINEERING DEPARTMENT

General Information Related to Infection Risks

Depending on the facility, the MAE department maintains, repairs, and installs various systems, such as those related to electrical power; ventilation; potable and high-purity water; waste management, including biologic and other hazardous substances; septic/sewage; thermal and humidity control; decontamination and sterilizing equipment; transportation; and systems used for research activities. The MAE may also provide support for infection prevention and control functions including sinks to facilitate hand washing; sanitary storage and transportation of supplies; HVAC systems to control airborne spread of infectious agents; effective filtration to meet a variety of air quality requirements including high-efficiency particulate air (HEPA) filtration for protective environments (PE); special filtration in operating and procedure rooms; and special exhaust systems to control fumes and infectious agents (sputum induction booths, biologic safety cabinets, plume capture, pathology dissection, and autopsy). Such activities often involve the potential for transmission of infectious agents or other hazards to the individuals (workers, patients, visitors, students, and others) in the immediate or adjacent area and to the internal and external environment.[1,2,5–8,11–14,16,19,21,23–25,28,29,33–34,36–39,42,43,45,48,51,52,57–72]

Identifying potential sources of microbes and their routes of spread—airborne, waterborne, and surface/contact—should be included in education and training for MAE employees and contracted individuals.[3,5–7,12,17–19,27–29,31,32,48,61,65,70,72] Additional educational topics should include procedures to reduce spread, use of supplies and equipment necessary to minimize contact with infectious material, and safe repair of equipment or other components. Special precautions are required when workers enter rooms where patients may be infectious (e.g., airborne infection isolation [AII] rooms or bronchoscopy suites) and include both routine maintenance and urgent/emergent activities.[6,7,62] Instruction should integrate the facility's communication procedure(s) to ensure that others are not put into harmful situations and that a potential hazard is recognized, reported, and addressed in a timely manner. (See also Chapters 3 Education and Training; 27 Hand Hygiene; 29 Isolation Precautions; 100 Occupational Health; 101 Occupational Exposure to Bloodborne Pathogens; 103 Immunization of Healthcare Personnel; and 104 Pregnant Healthcare Personnel.)

As noted above, providing appropriate education and training to MAE staff in infection risks, transmission methods, and risk mitigation strategies is a key strategy in infection prevention. Likewise, MAE staff and leadership have a responsibility to provide education and training to the facility's IPs in how facility systems operate to minimize the risks of infection transmission. Specifically, there is a great opportunity for infection prevention professionals and MAE staff to collaborate and to learn and understand how utility systems such as HVAC, water, and wastewater systems are designed and operated.

Specific Activities of the Maintenance and Engineering Department: Risks and Interventions

Maintain and repair equipment used for patient care[6–8,19,20,23,25,29,45,67,73–75]

Risks

- Equipment can become contaminated with blood, secretions, excretions, and/or drainage with potential for colonization or infection.

- Tools and components used in repair activities can become contaminated and become fomites for transmission of infectious material.

- Contamination of equipment or other surfaces during maintenance or repair activities may have potential for subsequent spread of microbes to patients or others.

- MAE staff's work activities in sensitive patient care areas may result in release of potentially infectious microbes. Examples may include accessing equipment panels in the operating room (OR) suite, working on a patient monitor in the intensive care unit, or repairing a ventilator in a room with an immunocompromised patient.

- Malfunctioning equipment may cause the release of hazardous agents.

Interventions

- When contamination (e.g., spills of medication or body fluids) of a medical device or equipment occurs, it should be removed from the patient care environment and appropriately cleaned and disinfected according to manufacturer's instructions or per facility policy/procedure. The equipment should not be returned to service until it is determined to be disinfected so that it will not become a potential hazard to patients or personnel.

- Evaluate equipment prior to purchase for ease of cleaning and disinfection or sterilization, ease of disassembly/reassembly, access to components, durability, and other features.

- Develop a policy/procedure to communicate (color-coded bag and/or biohazard label) that equipment is potentially contaminated.

- Clean and decontaminate equipment with approved germicidal detergent before and/or after maintenance, as indicated.

- Wear appropriate personal protective equipment (PPE) when in potentially hazardous areas (e.g., N95 respirator for entering an AII room).

- Wear appropriate size and type of protective gloves (cut resistant) when handling equipment that could inflict cuts or punctures or when contamination is suspected (disposable exam gloves).

- Wear appropriate attire in controlled areas in accordance with the facilities infection control protocols (e.g., jumpsuit, head and foot covers in the OR).

- Limit tools/equipment taken into controlled areas and ensure that items that are needed are clean and free of contamination. Electronics (televisions, computers, monitors, and lighting systems) accumulate dust due to electrostatic charges. Methods to safely remove dust (e.g., HEPA vacuum or specially treated cloth) are preferred over using pressurized air to blow out dust, especially in areas that could be affected by contamination (e.g., locations with immunocompromised patients, invasive procedures areas, storage of clean/sterile supplies areas, laboratories, pharmacy, or kitchens). Where cleaning methods that create dust and debris are used, the work should be completed with the patients removed and appropriate cleaning conducted before the patients are returned.

- Large-equipment removal (x-ray, laboratory instruments, whirlpools, etc.) may require special cleaning or protective wrapping to control accumulation of dust when transporting through the facility. Conversely, equipment that cannot be removed for maintenance projects should be protected.

- Perform routine cleaning with approved methods to reduce accumulation of dust and debris.

- Planned maintenance programs should be developed and implemented to minimize the risks of critical equipment failure.

- Provide and document training in decontamination procedures, PPE, and hand washing to minimize patient and worker exposure during maintenance and repair activities.

- Promptly perform first aid (rinse, wash, flush) and report injuries or exposures that occur while working with potentially contaminated equipment.

(See also Chapters 21 Risk Factors Facilitating Transmission of Infectious Agents; 27 Hand Hygiene; 29 Isolation Precautions; 55 Endoscopy; 67 Respiratory Care Services; 68 Surgical Services; 100 Occupational Health; 101 Occupational Exposure to Bloodborne Pathogens; 106 Sterile Processing Services; 107 Environmental Services; and 119 Emergency Management.)

Maintain and repair existing structures and equipment, make recommendations for appropriate materials in construction and renovation planning[1,3,5–9,12,17,23,25,33,48]

Risks

- Deterioration and damage to surfaces and finishes may result in loss of intact, cleanable surfaces, leading to potential environmental reservoirs for a variety of microbes.

- Removal of damaged building components such as stained ceiling tiles and water-damaged surfaces without taking appropriate precautions can allow for the airborne transmission of potentially infectious organisms such as fungal spores.

- Water leaks on almost any material with an organic structure such as wallboard, acoustical ceiling tiles, or insulation, may initiate growth of ubiquitous fungal spores. In addition to organic materials, soil and dirt buildup on any surface can be a food source for organisms. These can then become reservoirs for a variety of opportunistic fungal spores such as *Aspergillus fumigatus*.

- Unprotected openings in any building can provide for infiltration of unconditioned air. This may affect critical areas that require special ventilation or pressurization.

- Inappropriate materials selected during the building design, construction, or renovation can result in elevated risks of infection transmission. Flooring, wall, and ceiling materials should be selected for appropriate levels of cleaning.[1]

Interventions

- Evaluate surfaces, materials, and furnishings used for new construction and renovation projects; consider those that are nonporous and will resist deterioration and damage while maintaining durability for routine cleaning/disinfection and management of blood/body fluid spills.

- When mold (surface growth) is noted, appropriate efforts should be instituted to assure contamination control. An infection control risk assessment (ICRA)[1] should always be conducted and appropriate infection control risk mitigation recommendations (ICRMR) developed and implemented (refer to Chapter 116 Construction and Renovation). Worker protection is also a consideration. (For example, *Guidelines on Assessment and Remediation of Fungi in Indoor Environments*, by the New York City Department of Health and Mental Hygiene, is available to help determine measures to be taken for bio-aerosol management [refer to Supplemental Resources].)

- Assess the risks of routine maintenance of above-ceiling equipment and structures with infection prevention staff and develop standard operating procedures (SOPs) to minimize risks.

- Replace or repair damaged structural surfaces (e.g., countertops, sinks, floors, or tiles) as needed; use previously developed SOPs during repairs.

- Ensure maintenance of exterior surfaces to prevent air and water infiltration.

- Develop policies and procedures to be followed in the event of water intrusion, leaks, spills, or drain/sewer backups. This should be the work of a multidisciplinary committee that includes representation from risk management, safety, infection prevention, environmental services as well as MAE. Consider the *Guidelines on Assessment and Remediation of Fungi in Indoor Environments*[76] as a guidance document. Concepts include:

  ○ Use a moisture meter for objective evaluation of wet materials. Maintain water content of material below established levels for preventing microbial growth on the material (i.e., less than 20 percent water content). An infrared camera may be used to discern "hidden" (e.g., behind walls) wet areas or leaks.

  ○ Replace/repair wet ceiling tiles or other surfaces that have been wetted with clean water and that cannot be dried within 72 hours.

  ○ Replace all materials that have been wetted with unclean (gray or brown) water.

  ○ If water-damaged surfaces/areas are recognized as supporting mold/mildew, initiate necessary containment precautions before and during remediation; apply appropriate methods to clean and decontaminate prior to use or occupancy (i.e., apply an ICRA).

(See also Chapters 23 The Immunocompromised Host; 77 Environmental Gram-negative Bacilli; 78 Fungi; 95 Tuberculosis and Other Mycobacteria; 114 HVAC; 115 Water Systems Issues; and 116 Construction and Renovation.)

Maintain or repair HVAC systems; failure to do so may result in potential airborne colonization or infection for patients, visitors, and workers[1,3–8,18,25,26,33,35,37–40,42–50,56,58,59,61,64,65,68,77–80]

Risks

- Temperature and/or humidity levels that are out of the acceptable range for the room/area can result in sweating or condensation on surfaces.[1] This condensation may result in microbial growth.

- Inappropriate pressure relationships may allow for the dissemination of contaminated air, disruption of controlled airflow, or inappropriate airflow during isolation precautions or invasive procedures.[1]

- During filter changes, dissemination of dust particles may occur in the ductwork or areas surrounding the filter change; this dust may harbor opportunistic environmental microbes.

- Faulty humidification systems can cause spraying of condensate or steam on filters, leading to compromised filtration efficacy. Faulty pressure relief can cause leaking from steam debris that can create ideal conditions for mold growth.

- Inappropriately maintained cooling towers can increase the risks of waterborne pathogens such as *Legionella pneumophila* or *Pseudomonas aeruginosa*.[81]

Interventions

- Evaluate HVAC and local area exhaust systems for actual ventilation conditions when planning for new construction and renovation projects to ensure that there is adequate capacity for planned changes.

- Ensure commissioning is completed for new construction, renovation, or major changes to the HVAC system.[82]

- Schedule routine maintenance of ventilation systems to ensure that heating, cooling, humidification, and filtration subsystems are working as designed.

- Provide systems for the monitoring of critical elements related to HVAC control, including outside air/return air parameters (temperature, relative humidity, pressure relationships) in critical areas, air changes per hour for comfort and infection control, capture of hazardous gases, and fumes or other contaminants from local exhaust ventilation (e.g., laser or electrocautery plume capture, biological safety cabinets, chemical/fume hoods, stove canopies, welding activities). Validate existing conditions of special ventilation rooms where airflow direction is important as part of infection prevention (e.g., PE and AII rooms, surgical and procedure rooms, laboratories, pharmacies). This should be accomplished with calibrated equipment independent of building ventilation system controls and monitoring equipment.

- Ensure that procedures are established and followed for corrective actions when monitoring indicates unacceptable conditions per recommendations from manufacturer and/or published guidelines or standards. For example, a room monitoring device does not zero on digital readout during calibration if an alarm (sound or light) malfunctions or the enunciator for the monitored room fails.

- Schedule preventive maintenance to include regular cleaning of air intakes, supply/exhaust/return vents, ducts, and cooling towers.

- Recognize steam spraying on filters or other malfunctions that can cause mold growth; correct the condition and follow the established remediation protocols.

- Ensure that employees have appropriate PPE (e.g., dust mask or respirator) during filter changes and other maintenance activities on HVAC systems and cooling towers where the task results in anticipated risks of exposure.

- Develop and follow procedures for the inspection and replacement of air filters that minimizes the risks of transmission. Ensure that HVAC systems are shut down when these activities occur.

- Notify specific patient care areas in advance of filter changes or other scheduled maintenance that will interrupt ventilation so precautions can be taken for patients and employees affected[7] (e.g., mask patient in AII room).

- Signage and labeling of ducts and controls that service special ventilation areas (e.g., AII room, bronchoscopy suite, biological safety cabinet, areas where ethylene oxide is present) should warn of possible hazards and specific areas affected by the maintenance activity (e.g., operating room, nuclear medicine, laboratory, central processing, research); signs should provide contact information (e.g., telephone number) requesting notification or permission prior to servicing.

- Develop and follow contingency plans for ventilation outages. Contingency plans should be developed with input from clinical and infection prevention staff and should be based on risk aversion for respective outages. For example, PE rooms may have redundant or backup portable filters, especially if major fans are not on emergency power backup. Safety procedures within the unit may also include practices such as keeping doors closed whenever possible until ventilation is reestablished.

- Education and training content for IP, MAE, and clinical staff should include information on the importance of scheduling and on communication protocols to ensure minimal impact of ventilation system maintenance procedures on the safety of patients or employees. It should stress the importance of ventilation control in the OR and other specialty areas and contrast the differences between positive and negative pressure relationships.

- Include education and training for contractors who will be working with these systems; monitor to ensure compliance with expectations.

- Provide emergency ventilation service to special ventilation areas affected during planned and unplanned interruption to ensure that ventilation control for specialty areas (e.g., OR, PE, and AII rooms) is not compromised. These measures may include the appropriate type and location of portable HEPA units, how to block off or filter air supply, and/or return outlets.

- Develop policies and procedures for safe restoration of the system after planned or unplanned interruption, include communication with tenants and verification testing, as deemed necessary, based on the area.

(See also Chapters 23 The Immunocompromised Host; 29 Isolation Precautions; 84 *Legionella pneumophila*; 115 Water Systems Issues; 119 Emergency Management; and 120 Infectious Diseases Disasters.)

Maintain and repair protective hoods, biologic safety cabinets, and other local exhaust and ventilation/containment systems[1,7,15,21,36,39,45,51,65,68,72,78,79]

Risks

- Improperly maintained or nonfunctioning hood exhaust systems may result in airborne contamination of surrounding areas, staff, or area elements such as pharmaceuticals clean supplies or equipment.

- Improper function of local exhaust ventilation systems (e.g., biologic safety cabinet, portable sputum induction booth, antineoplastic preparation hood, plume capture) may result in improper airflow within the system and result in staff or patient exposure of potentially pathogenic organisms or other hazards.

Interventions

- Select appropriate systems based on design parameters, effectiveness, anticipated hazards, location, and compatibility with other equipment or systems (e.g., does not interfere with general dilution ventilation, does not block access to other equipment or controls, will not impair egress, will not exhaust near intake).

- Schedule and document routine monitoring of local exhaust ventilation systems, including measuring the capture velocity and the appropriate direct exhaust or filter mechanism (e.g., HEPA); include verification and replacement.

- Schedule, perform, and document regular preventive maintenance, including air intake, filters and blowers inspection, lubrication, and repair or replacement of parts.

- Implement corrective actions when monitoring indicates unacceptable conditions.

- Coordinate maintenance and repair activities with workers and affected areas.

- Provide certification for equipment (e.g., biologic safety cabinets and chemical flow hoods) at appropriate intervals to validate performance.

- Provide installation and maintenance of filtration systems as appropriate.

- Provide employee training for both operating and maintenance personnel to ensure that safety measures are followed.

- Follow organizational employee/occupational health protocol if exposure to hazards may have occurred.

- Label ductwork to alert workers of potential hazards, supply appropriate PPE, and include communication with the user when scheduling maintenance or shutdown.

- Provide training for personnel required to work on microbial sensitive material in the biosafety equipment to help prevent false-positive results or contamination.

(See also Chapters 67 Respiratory Care Services; 101 Occupational Exposure to Bloodborne Pathogens; 108 Laboratory Services; 110 Pharmacy Services; 113 Waste Management; 114 Heating, Ventilation and Air Conditioning; 65 Postmortem Care; 119 Emergency Management; 120 Infectious Diseases Disasters; and 121 Animal Research and Diagnostics.)

Maintain and repair plumbing supply and drainage systems[1–3,5,7–9,16,23,34,41,55,57,63,64,66,67,70,73,74,82–94]

Risks

- Nonfunctional or improperly functioning hand-washing facilities result in inadequate hand washing by patient care and support personnel.

- Leaking fluids in any area, especially critical areas (e.g., operating and delivery rooms, nursery, food preparation, serving and storage areas, or central supply) may cause fungal or microbial growth and provide an elevated risk of contamination of staff, patients, food, or patient care items.

- Leaks and spills create conditions ideal for growth of opportunistic fungi or other organisms (e.g., *Aspergillus, Pseudomonas, Acinetobacter*).

- Improperly maintained water supply components such as aerators, ice machines, or common plumbing may provide a reservoir for proliferation of microorganisms (e.g., atypical *Mycobacterium*).

- Stagnation of potable water (e.g., dead-end connections, poor design of system flow) can result in the creation of reservoirs that can exacerbate chlorine breakdown and increase the risk of microbial growth.

- Development of biofilm and sediment in pipes (e.g., aerators) may result in high levels of microbes (e.g., *Legionella, Acinetobacter, Pseudomonas*).

- Stagnant water in uncapped drains (floor drains or infrequently used fixtures) can cause obnoxious odors or become a reproductive reservoir for insects such as sewer flies.

- Interruptions of the plumbing system can cause sediment and stagnant areas in the potable water distribution system to be disturbed and cause the release of microbes (e.g., *Legionella* or atypical *Mycobacterium*) into the water supply.

- During repairs of drainage pipes (e.g., unclogging toilets and pipes), employees may be exposed to biologic, chemical (e.g., chemotherapy), and medication waste.

- Backflow, flooding, or backsplash may cause environmental contamination of surfaces, supplies, or equipment.

- An outage of the facility's water supply system may require an alternative water supply for basic sanitation, hand washing, bathing, drinking, cooking, or other needs.

- Disruption of the water supply compromises the availability of safe, plumbed emergency eye wash and shower stations.

- Failure to maintain and routinely flush emergency eye wash and shower stations increases likelihood of microbial growth.

Interventions

- Appraise potable water and sewer systems for design or redesign/improvement opportunities as appropriate when planning new construction and renovation projects and when adding new equipment connected to the system (e.g., reprocessing of endoscopes, hemodialysis).

- Conduct an assessment of the facility's water systems to see what parts of those systems are at elevated risk for contamination. Develop risk mitigation strategies for areas identified as high risk (cooling towers, water heaters, water filter systems, etc.).

- Schedule regular preventive maintenance of laboratory and sink fixtures, vacuum breakers, water supply system, ice machines, floor drains and pipes, flushing devices, special water treatment devices, hot water heaters, and storage tanks.

- Conduct a risk assessment regarding the use and maintenance of faucet aerators in the patient care environment. Consider periodic maintenance/replacement of aerators in sensitive areas.[5]

- Provide appropriate PPE for workers servicing sewer lines or toilet facilities.

- Maintain tools and equipment in a clean condition, especially those used in patient care and support environments.

- Maintain and repair steam supply system as indicated.

- Recognize and promptly correct water leaks; follow established SOPs for remediation of areas/materials that have been wetted.

- Use moisture-monitoring equipment to detect and provide objective measurement(s) of drying. Infrared cameras will allow for expedient visual analysis and determination of water damage for immediate wet material removal.

- Provide sanitation training for cleanup of sewerage backup.

- If mold is encountered after water flooding or is simply discovered, follow established organizational procedures (see "Maintain and repair existing structures and equipment, make recommendations for appropriate materials in construction and renovation planning" section above).

- Ensure that MAE employees, contracted workers, and service representatives receive education and training that is appropriate to their job; specify in the contract or service agreement.

- Maintain ongoing communication between maintenance management, operational supervisors, and the IP in order to discuss potential problems associated with plumbing and unusual infections (e.g., *Legionella* cluster).

- Develop policy and procedure for provision of services and supplies during planned and unplanned interruption of potable water and sewer service; include protocol for safe return of water/sewer once service is restored (e.g., systematic flushing from larger to smaller, need for chemical and/or heat treatment, stuck valves, cleaning of debris or sediment).

(See also Chapters 23 The Immunocompromised Host; 27 Hand Hygiene; 39 Dialysis; 55 Endoscopy; 70 Biofilms; 77 Environmental Gram-negative Bacilli; 84 *Legionella pneumophila*; 95 Tuberculosis and Other Mycobacteria; 115 Water Systems Issues and Prevention of Waterborne Infectious Diseases in Healthcare Facilities; 116 Construction and Renovation; and 119 Emergency Management.)

Maintain and repair steam supply system[1,5,7,84]

Risks

- Inadequate functioning of steam sterilizers resulting in insufficient sterilization of medical instruments and devices.

- Incomplete sanitation of cookware, dinnerware, utensils.

- Faulty humidification systems can cause spraying of condensate or steam on filters, leading to compromised filtration efficacy. Faulty pressure relief can cause leaking from steam debris that can create ideal conditions for mold growth.

Interventions

- Evaluate design and requirements when planning renovation and construction projects.

- Develop communication protocols with affected departments (central services, sterile processing, OR, etc.) to communicate steam outages.

- Schedule regular maintenance of equipment, document preventive maintenance, and document repairs.

- Monitor pressure of supplied steam; follow established policy and procedure if corrective action (e.g., valving correction) is required.

- Recognize steam spraying on filters or other malfunctions that can cause mold growth; correct the condition and follow the established remediation protocols.

- Label steam lines and incorporate potential burn hazard awareness and methods to safely work with steam in MAE education and training programs.

(See also Chapters 31 Cleaning, Disinfection, and Sterilization; 83 Food-borne Illnesses; 106 Sterile Processing; 109 Nutrition Services; and 114 Heating, Ventilation, and Air Conditioning.)

Maintain and repair refrigerators and freezers[7,8,82]

Risks

- Inadequate refrigeration of foods may permit growth of microbes, resulting in a greater likelihood of foodborne illness.

- Inadequate refrigeration of medications, biologics, vaccines, blood, and blood products may alter potency and/or chemical composition or allow proliferation of microbial contaminants.

- Condensate pans for refrigerators and/or freezers used to store food, pharmaceuticals, and blood products can create conditions for mold growth.

Interventions

- When selecting/purchasing equipment for cooling or freezing, compare features that best meet the intended use, including operating range (e.g., an automatic defrost cycle can damage temperature-sensitive items), size, location of use, cleanable surfaces, durability, and maintenance needs.

- Provide accurate temperature monitoring for refrigerators and freezers; an alarm system may be required (e.g., blood bank refrigerator) or desired.

- Establish a method to record temperature on a regular basis (e.g., visualize and document daily or observe an automated recording chart each shift); include action to take if reading is not in the acceptable range.

- Schedule routine monitoring and testing of refrigerator and freezer alarms where applicable.

- Test accuracy of thermometers; calibration may be required (e.g., blood bank, tissue freezer) by using standard regulations and/or recommendations.

- Schedule and perform regular preventive maintenance of all freezers and refrigerators; include air vents, gaskets, cooling coils, and fans.

- Walk-in refrigeration units may experience a condensation point if the building dehumidification is inadequate, resulting in mold proliferation.

- Provide training for personnel in recognizing and implementing safe maintenance of refrigerators to include appropriate cleaning methods.

(See also Chapters 23 The Immunocompromised Host; 83 Food-borne Illnesses; 109 Nutrition Services; 110 Pharmacy Services; and 119 Emergency Management.)

Maintain and repair of exhaust and vacuum systems[1,7,15,16,34,36,39,40,45,59,63,65,68,78]

Risks

- Inappropriate placement of exhaust vents in the proximity of air or gas intakes creates a potential for reintroduction of hazardous vapors, gases, aerosols, odors, particulates, and/or microbes.

- Smoke-plume control systems may be unable to remove environmental tissue smoke during surgical procedures.

- Malfunction of a medicated aerosol control booth, hood, or induction chamber can cause airborne medication (e.g., pentamidine) leakage and/or allow escape of droplet nuclei (e.g., containing *Mycobacterium tuberculosis*) during patient treatment.

- Overflow of contaminated secretions into clinical vacuum systems contaminates the vacuum controls and/or wall lines.

Interventions

- Design and install exhaust vents in appropriate locations or move them a recommended distance from air and gas intakes.[1] Label exhaust systems that may contain infectious or hazardous airflows according to local code requirements.

- Maintain overflow traps on suction apparatuses.

- Perform routine maintenance on a regular schedule (e.g., for HEPA filter capture systems using 99.97 percent efficient filters for 0.3-μm particles; conduct a filter certification periodically and when filters are changed).

- Routinely evaluate air velocity at the opening of capture devices and adjust as needed to ensure that operational specification is met; adjustable fronts on cabinets, in-cabinet equipment and supplies placement, heat-generating devices (e.g., needle/loop benchtop incinerator or gas-generated flame), and location of operator can adversely affect performance.

- Decontaminate biologic safety cabinets before maintaining or repairing them; only persons trained in decontamination of hoods/cabinets should perform maintenance or repair.

- Wash hands after manipulating or changing vacuum controls.

- Wear appropriate PPE if exposure to blood/body fluids or other hazards is anticipated.

- Notify appropriate personnel (e.g., lab, operating room, infection control) in advance of any planned maintenance or outage of vacuum or vapor capture systems.

- Plan for meeting equipment and service needs in case of unplanned loss of these utilities (e.g., portable suction machines, relocation of activities). Know the restoration procedure, including verification for return to service.

(See also Chapters 67 Respiratory Care Services; 108 Laboratory Services; 116 Construction and Renovation; and 119 Emergency Management.)

Maintain and repair of medical gas delivery systems[1,15]

Risks

- Condensation of water in medical gas system lines has the potential for transmitting microbes within the piping system directly to patients.

- Unfiltered air or other gases may expose the patient to opportunistic microbes.

- Debris may become dislodged during gas interruptions and repair and from vibrations or other disturbances.

Interventions

- Evaluate design/redesign of medical gas systems when planning renovation or construction projects.

- Install filters and air to prevent condensation in medical gas system lines. Maintain dew points within regulatory ranges.[15]

- Wash hands before and after maintenance or repair procedures.

- Install and maintain the gas distribution system according to code requirements.[15] The installation should include filtration of the product gas, especially medical air and oxygen.

- Provide filtration and/or pressure limit as appropriate to protect medical devices used for respiratory therapy.

- Anticipate and react to capture debris dislodged from interruptions, repairs, or other disturbances to the system.

(See also Chapters 67 Respiratory Care Services; 68 Surgical Services; 108 Laboratory Services; 116 Construction and Renovation; and 119 Emergency Management.)

Maintain and repair waste processing systems including incinerators, autoclaves, trash chutes, dumpsters, and compactors[1,7,9,10,13,22,51,52,65,95–99]

Risks

- Inadequate containment, transport, storage, and disposal of hazardous and/or regulated medical waste have the potential to contaminate personnel, the facility, and the external environment.

- Improper venting of chutes and compactors may spread microbes and odors to the surrounding areas.

- Riser effect from thermal currents moves particulates and odors upward through elevator shafts, etc.

- Improper containment and/or storage of waste or recyclables (e.g., soda bottles, glass jars, food cans) may result in insect or vermin infestation.

- Transport bins, carts, or vehicles may become contaminated from leakage due to poor integrity, spillage from tipping, or exterior container contamination.

- Improper sorting and containment of waste at point of creation can pose a risk for waste handlers "downstream" (e.g., sharps, laboratory cultures, radioactive treatments from nuclear medicine, pharmaceutical, and chemotherapy wastes).

Interventions

- Review design and locations of areas related to waste (e.g., soiled utility rooms, locations for sharps containers, recycling container locations, temporary storage areas, routes for transporting, chutes, ventilation in storage areas, security, etc.) when planning for renovation or construction projects.

- Provide pest control with approved methods to prevent future vermin infestation.

- Develop procedures for proper containment (e.g., bagging, boxing, container type, and labels and color-coding) of wastes as appropriate to type, composition, and volume generated. Ensure that appropriate personnel receive continuing education related to these procedures as well as require safety procedure (PPE and hand hygiene).

- Instruct personnel in the proper operation of equipment and recognition of malfunctions requiring immediate action and/or repair.

- Develop and follow procedures related to the safety and security of waste storage areas; improve as indicated (e.g., restrict access and ensure that chutes contain good seals and operational latches, appropriate sorting, correct containerization, cleanliness) in compliance with codes and regulations.

- Do not compact biologic, chemical, radioactive, or other hazardous wastes.

- Provide training that includes response to chemical, biologic, or other hazardous waste spills.

- Develop and follow procedures for recycling (e.g., beverage or food cans), including rinsing and time limits for storage; evaluate the arrangement and ensure that it is working (e.g., no complaints of odor or evidence of insects).

(See also Chapters 108 Laboratory Services; 113 Waste Management; and 119 Emergency Management.)

Maintain and repair ice makers[7,8,41,86,88]

Risks

- Condensers and ice holding bins can become contaminated, which may result in transmission of microbes to susceptible individuals.

- When ice makers are nonfunctional, tubs or basins are used to hold and carry ice, which increases probability of contamination.

- Lack of routine maintenance can increase scale/biofilm buildup in lines. This may protect or enhance microbial growth.

- Interruption or outage of potable water supply increases risk of line or ice maker contamination once water is restored.

- Improper drainage configuration may lead to back-siphon, resulting in contamination of components and subsequent contamination of ice.

- Leaks and improper drainage around ice machines can cause wall and floor damage and subsequent mold growth.

Interventions

- Select equipment that is appropriate for location, ice demand, and design and that minimizes risk of contamination (e.g., dispenser preferred over bin).

- Perform regular preventive maintenance, including cleaning condensers, flushing and descaling lines, and cleaning and disinfecting bins per manufacturer's instructions.

- Provide timely repair of nonfunctioning equipment. Consider equipment replacement if repairs cannot be made quickly.

- Educate users in obtaining ice without contaminating equipment or stored ice; consider restricting access to authorized/trained personnel.

- If patient and/or visitors are allowed to obtain ice, include instructions on procedures to minimize contamination.

- Include provisions for alternative ice source(s), including methods for safe storage, transport, and handling in case of outage.

- For anticipated or unplanned outage, include a plan to shut off equipment (e.g., turn off water supply) and ensure safe return to service once supply is restored.

- Provide integral water-resistant flooring around drains to help prevent mold growth.

(See also Chapters 23 The Immunocompromised Host; 27 Hand Hygiene; 70 Biofilm; 77 Environmental Gram-negative Bacilli; 84 *Legionella pneumophila*; 95 Tuberculosis and Other Mycobacteria; 115 Water Systems Issues and Prevention of Waterborne Infectious Diseases in Healthcare Facilities; 116 Construction and Renovation; and 119 Emergency Management.)

Maintain transport systems in the hospital[1,7,19,72]

Risks

- Blood/body fluid (e.g., from specimens due to spill or leak) may contaminate transport system pathway (e.g., pneumatic tube system), receiver station, transport cart, dumbwaiter, or elevator.

- Disruption caused by such spills can delay specimen transport and processing until the area is cleaned and disinfected.

- Workers may be exposed to bloodborne pathogens, other microbes (e.g., sputum specimen, tissue specimen), or chemicals (pharmaceuticals; preservatives such as formaldehyde).

- A specimen or medication may be lost due to a spill or leak and cause a delay in diagnosis or treatment.

Interventions

- Choose a system that best meets needs while minimizing risks (e.g., location of stations; capacity, complexity, safety of secondary containers that enclose and protect/pad; ability to access; easy to clean and disinfect).

- Train personnel in the appropriate methods and equipment to use when preparing, containing, and transporting items (e.g., specimens or medications).

- Develop and follow procedures designed to minimize risks in the advent of a spill within the pneumatic tube system.

- Consider pneumatic tube system (PTS) carrier options (leak resistant with O-rings) and packaging strategies (i.e., double-bagging) to minimize the risks of leaks within the system.

- Establish methods and communication protocols to recognize spills or leaks; include communication protocol (e.g., notification to sender, system shutdown, and alternative methods of transport), cleaning and decontamination, retrieval of "stuck" items, and restoration of system.

- Include training related to selecting and using the appropriate PPE and hand hygiene for those working on the transport system.

- If patterns of misuse are noted, consider collaboration with users to improve safe use of transport system (e.g., performance improvement activity).

(See also Chapters 27 Hand Hygiene; 100 Occupational Health; 108 Laboratory Services; 110 Pharmacy Services; and 119 Emergency Management.)

Anticipate and plan for continuation of services during outages and disasters[1,4,7,13,17,29,32,48,55,62,82]

Risks

- Loss of one or more utilities can compromise ability to safely maintain some or all services.

- Electrical outage or brownout may cause disruptions that may not be sufficiently handled by the backup emergency electrical supply or generators.

- Electrical disruption may adversely affect systems and equipment operation or the availability of emergency electrical supply to meet all needs (e.g., tripping of breakers, automatic shutoff, disruption of communications or information technology services, insufficient outlets for needs, HVAC, refrigeration, heating and cooling capacity).

- Lack of critical ventilation for AIIR, PE, and procedure areas pose a hazard to patients, workers, and visitors.

- Portable air filtration devices may be put into use without verifying appropriate type, size, operation parameters, or placement. This can create the potential for inefficient filtration, redirection of airflow, or imbalance of pressurization. Appreciably, malfunctioning units may be tampered with by patients, visitors, or staff due to noise or location within a setting.

- Water supply disruption (e.g., outage, line breakage, boil water advisory, low pressure) can affect many aspects of providing safe care, including but not limited to, hand washing, bathing, drinking, making ice, cooking and dishwashing, laundry, equipment or procedures that depend on potable water supply (e.g., making purified water for hemodialysis, cleaning and reprocessing of instruments, radiology and laboratory procedures), flushing toilets and clinical sinks, generation of steam, and humidification.

- Loss of sewer facilities may pose risks (e.g., full or overflowing toilets, no opportunity for disposal of wastes from bedpans, loss of drainage from sinks, tubs, and showers).

- Loss of one or more medical gases may cause imminent danger or interfere with provision of services (e.g., failure of life-support equipment such as ventilators may cause breathing and/or cardiovascular distress in some patients) or result in cancellation or delays in surgeries.

Interventions

- Plan for emergencies. Plans should address probability, impact (people, property, and business), preparedness, and internal/external responses.

- Perform a hazard vulnerability analysis to help identify equipment, supplies, utilities, and other resources that may be affected by various disasters (technologic events, natural or manmade disasters, human error, hazardous materials).

- Develop system failure contingency plans for essential utility systems.[13]

- Provide training and drills that include scenarios related to utility loss to test emergency preparedness and response.

- Coordinate provision of alternatives (e.g., evaluation of emergency electrical outlets, plan for negative pressure ventilation loss for AIIR, alternative supply of potable water and ice, alternatives to hand washing, obtaining portable toilets, switching to portable oxygen tanks).

- If portable air filtration units are part of the emergency filtration plan, determine the proper type, size, operation parameters, placement in rooms of anticipated use, and establish educational needs (e.g., instructions for patient and staff on proper placement and use); if the setup includes redirection of filtered air (e.g., vented out through window), ensure that emergency plan addresses how to keep venting areas sealed.

- Plan for safe restoration of utilities or equipment.

- Use an incident command or similar team structure to make decisions on limiting services, procedures, visitors, admissions, and the need for partial or full evacuation. Include infection prevention where appropriate.

- Document drills and real events. Collect information from those involved in drills or real events and analyze data to improve preparedness and response.

(See also Chapters 27 Hand Hygiene; 114 Heating, Ventilation, and Air Conditioning; 155 Water Systems Issues; 119 Emergency Management; and 120 Infectious Diseases Disasters.)

METHODS TO HELP IDENTIFY RISKS AND APPLY PERFORMANCE IMPROVEMENT

There are several tools that can be utilized to improve safety for workers and patients alike.[7,12,13,17,23,26,29,30,53-56] (See also Chapters 16 Quality Concepts, and 17 Performance Measures.)

Root Cause Analysis

A root cause analysis (RCA) can be a powerful tool when investigating an event or near miss that could result in morbidity or mortality. The goal of an RCA is to determine what happened, why it happened, and what can be done to prevent recurrence. During an RCA, basic and contributing causes are discovered by continually digging deeper, by asking "why?" at each level of cause and effect. The process is interdisciplinary and involves experts from the frontline or those most familiar with the situation. The process is impartial and helps identify changes that need to be made. A credible RCA must involve leadership, be internally consistent, and include consideration of relevant literature and resources. To be effective and thorough, it must include a determination of all factors, including human: a determination of related processes and systems with analysis of underlying cause-and-effect systems, an identification of risks and their potential contributions, and a determination of potential improvement in processes or systems.

Failure Mode and Effects Analysis

As with RCA, the failure mode and effects analysis (FMEA) is a collaborative tool or technique that helps determine which interventions or corrections may reduce the risk of an adverse event. Unlike the RCA, the FMEA is prospective; it uses a streamlined hazard analysis to identify processes and subprocesses and then determine where or in what modes they may fail. Steps in FMEA include (1) define a topic with clear definition of process to be studied; (2) assemble a team; (3) graphically describe the process; (4) conduct a hazard analysis, including listing and numbering of all potential failure modes, determine severity and probability of each, use a decision tree to analyze for further action, and list all causes for each mode; and (5) determine actions (eliminate, control, or accept) for each failure mode, describe the actions, identify outcome measures to evaluate the modified process, identify the individual(s) who will complete the recommended action, and indicate administrative concurrence.

Plan, Do, Check, Act

The four-step process of plan, do, check, act (PDCA) is easily applicable to a variety of activities. The origin of PDCA is sometimes called the Shewhart or Deming cycle, named after the inventor and subsequent prominent user, respectively. The PDCA tool may be preceded by use of the FOCUS tool. The acronym FOCUS represents finding a process to improve, organizing to improve the process, clarifying current knowledge of the process, understanding sources of process variation, and selecting the process improvement. Once a process is identified, the cycle proceeds as follows: plan the improvement and data collection process, do the improvement and data collection, check the results of the implementation, and act to hold the gain and continue or to reject and start another cycle. An example of using PDCA could be to evaluate and improve the process of education and control measures during construction activities.

Infection Control Risk Assessment, Infection Control Risk Mitigation Recommendations

The process of assessing infection control-related risks and developing risk mitigation recommendations and strategies is one that can and should be applied whenever there is a question about the most appropriate actions to be taken about any activity that has an infection risk. Critical to the process is appropriate participants, a clear understanding of the population that may be at risk, and a clear understanding of the activity being considered. After careful consideration of the activities and potential risks, a risk mitigation plan can be developed, documented, and followed. Often, control points are identified and control measures created to be measured against.

CONCLUSIONS

MAE partnership with IPs and safety personnel is essential to identifying and decreasing risks in healthcare settings. Facility and utility components, equipment, and related surroundings that are not managed appropriately may transmit infectious microbes or pose other hazards that threaten the safety of people, buildings, and the community. Regardless of setting, size, and scope of service, identifying the standard elements with collaborative risk assessment and applying appropriate interventions will reduce or eliminate these hazards. Infection prevention and MAE staff also need to work collaboratively to develop and maintain effective communication and education programs to minimize risks.

FUTURE TRENDS

Use of newer methods, such as computational fluid dynamics and other technologies to broaden our understanding of particulate and bioaerosol behavior, in addition to applying interventional strategies, will help to define and improve the design and operation parameters of mechanical systems within healthcare settings. The use of different materials in our ventilation and water distribution systems has contributed to more corrosion-resistant and more maintenance-friendly equipment. The design and construction of air handling units and cooling towers have improved dramatically in the past decade and continue to improve; this will work to minimize risks. Our understanding and implementation of risk assessment processes have also grown, and continued growth and improvement can be expected. Challenges, including budgetary constraints and environmental stewardship, will help to shape healthcare across all settings. The trending of an aging population, coupled with emerging infectious agents and globalization, will be important considerations for the future of patient and worker safety. Regulations, recommendations, and guidelines by authoritative agencies and professional organizations continue to align and refine the relationship between people and the healthcare environment. Further research that applies evidence-based weighting and consideration for each unique setting will enhance our understanding of this evolving industry we call healthcare services.

INTERNATIONAL PERSPECTIVE

Healthcare settings vary from country to country and within political boundaries. They are shaped by cultural and economic variations and can be further modified by geographical locale. Each facility has unique challenges and resources to address structure, utilities, equipment, and location parameters related to maintenance and engineering. The IP and MAE should act as a team. They should use community standards to determine the best practices but also look to international studies and best practices for evaluation and/or consideration. They must use the available resources, applicable regulations and recommendations, and available administrative support, regardless of location, to protect the health and safety of all.

REFERENCES

1. Facilities Guidelines Institute. *2010 Guidelines for Design and Construction of Healthcare Facilities.* American Society for Healthcare Engineering, 2010.
2. American National Standards Institute. *American National Standard for Emergency Eyewash and Shower Equipment.* New York: ANSI Standard Z358.1–2009.
3. Bartley JM, Olmsted RN, eds. *Construction and Renovation,* 3rd ed. Washington, DC: Association for Professionals in Infection Control and Epidemiology, Inc. Press, 2007.
4. ASHRAE. *Special Project 91—HVAC Design Manual for Hospitals and Clinics.* Atlanta, GA: American Society of Heating, Refrigerating and Air-Conditioning Engineers, Inc., 2003.
5. Bartley JM. APIC State-of-the-art-report: the role of infection control during construction in health care facilities. *Am J Infect Control* 2000 Apr;28(2):156–169.
6. Bolyard EA, Tablan OC, Williams WW, et al. Guideline for infection control in health care personnel, 1998. *Infect Control Hosp Epidemiol* 1998 Jun;19(6):407–463.
7. Sehulster LM, Chinn RY, Arduino MJ, et al. *Guidelines for environmental infection control in healthcare facilities: recommendations of CDC and the Healthcare Infection Control Practices Advisory Committee (HICPAC).* CDC website. 2003. Available at: http://www.cdc.gov/hicpac/pdf/guidelines/eic_in_hcf_03.pdf.
8. Centers for Disease Control and Prevention; Infectious Disease Society of America; American Society of Blood and Marrow Transplantation. Guidelines for preventing opportunistic infections among hematopoietic stem cell transplant recipients. *MMWR Recomm Rep* 2000 Oct;49(RR-10):1–125, CE1–7.
9. Centers for Medicare and Medicaid Services (CMS). Code of Federal Regulations. Available at: http://www.cms.gov/Medicare/Medicare-Fee-for-Service-Payment/DMEPOSFeeSched/DME_CFR.html.
10. Department of Transportation (DOT). *How to Comply with Federal Hazardous Materials Regulations.* DOT website. Available at: http://www.fmcsa.dot.gov/safety-security/hazmat/complyhmregs.htm.
11. Friedman C, Petersen KH. *Infection Control in Ambulatory Care.* Boston: Jones and Bartlett Publishers, 2004.
12. Friedman C, Barnette M, Buck AS, et al. Requirements for infrastructure and essential activities of infection control and epidemiology in out-of-hospital settings: a consensus panel report. *Infect Control Hosp Epidemiol* 1999 Oct;20(10):695–705.
13. The Joint Commission. *The 2013 Comprehensive Accreditation Manual for Hospitals.* Oakbrook Terrace, IL: The Joint Commission Publications, November 2012.
14. McCaffrey JJ, Hagg-Rickert S. Development of a Risk Management Program. In: Carroll R, ed. *Risk Management Handbook for Health Care Organizations,* 4th ed. American Society for Healthcare Risk Management. San Francisco, CA: Jossey-Bass, Inc., 2004:95–118.
15. NFPA International. *NFPA 99, Chapter 5 Gas and Vacuum Systems.* Quincy, MA: National Fire Protection Association, 2012.
16. Occupational Safety and Health Administration (OSHA). *Legionnaires' Disease.* In: OSHA Technical Manual. Washington, DC: U.S. Department of Labor, 1997:1–46. Available at: http://www.osha.gov.
17. Scheckler WE, Brimhall D, Buck AS, et al. Requirements for infrastructure and essential activities of infection control and epidemiology in hospitals: a consensus panel report. *Am J Infect Control* 1998 Feb;26(1):47–60.
18. Sutton PM, Nicas M, Harrison RJ. Tuberculosis isolation: comparison of written procedure and actual practices in three California hospitals. *Infect Control Hosp Epidemiol* 2000 Jan;21(1):28–32.
19. Occupational exposure to bloodborne pathogens; needlestick and other sharps injuries; final rule. Occupational Safety and Health Administration (OSHA), Department of Labor. Final rule; request for comment on the Information Collection (Paperwork) Requirements. *Fed Regist* 2001 Jan 18;66(12):5318–5325.
20. United States Food and Drug Administration, Center for Devices and Radiological Health. Medwatch program plus information about recalls and reporting problems with medical devices and equipment. Available at: http://www.fda.gov/forconsumers/consumerupdates/ucm290879.html.
21. United States Pharmacopeia, 27th rev., and the National Formulary 22nd ed. USP 27-N822 General Chapter <797> Pharmaceutical Compounding–Sterile Preparations. Rockville, MD: The United States Pharmacopeial Convention, 2003.
22. Wideman JM. *Points of contention in sharps injury prevention.* Infection Control Resource 2004;2(4):1,4–7. Available at: http://www.infectioncontrolresource.org/Past_Issues/IC8.pdf.
23. Boyce JM, Pittet D. Healthcare Infection Control Practices Advisory Committee, et al. Guideline for Hand Hygiene in Health-Care Settings. Recommendations of the Healthcare Infection Control Practices Advisory Committee and the HICPAC/SHEA/APIC/IDSA Hand Hygiene Task Force. Society for Healthcare Epidemiology of America/Association for Professionals in Infection Control/Infectious Diseases Society of America. *MMWR Recomm Rep* 2002 Oct 25;51(RR-16):1–45.
24. Herwaldt LA, Smith SD, Carter CD. Infection control in the outpatient setting. *Infect Control Hosp Epidemiol* 1998 Jan;19(1):41–74.
25. Rutala WA, Weber DJ. Environmental interventions to control nosocomial infections. *Infect Control Hosp Epidemiol* 1995 Aug;16(8):442–443.

26. Wideman JM. Integrating Infection Control into Projects. In: Hansen W, ed. *Infection Control During Construction Manual: Policies, Procedures, and Strategies for Compliance*. Marblehead, MA: Opus Communications, Inc., 2004.

27. American National Standards Institute (ANSI). *Criteria for Accepted Practices in Safety, Health and Environmental Training*. ANSI Standard Z490.1. New York: ANSI, 2009

28. Gershon RR, Karkashian CD, Grosch JW, et al. Hospital safety climate and its relationship with safe work practices and workplace exposure incidents. *Am J Infect Control* 2000 Jun;28(3):211–221.

29. Lundstrom T, Pugliese G, Bartley J, et al. Organizational and environmental factors that affect worker health and safety and patient outcomes. *Am J Infect Control* 2002 Apr;30(2):93–106.

30. U.S. Department of Veterans Affairs (VA). National Center for Patient Safety (NCPS). Available at: http://www.patientsafety.va.gov/.

31. Samways MC. Worker Education and Training. In: DiNardi SR, ed. *The Occupational Environment: Its Evaluation, Control, and Management*, 2nd ed. Fairfax, VA: AIHA Press, 2003:774–792.

32. Wideman JM. Education of the Project Team and Other Key Players. In: Hansen W, ed. *Infection Control During Construction Manual: Policies, Procedures, and Strategies for Compliance*. Marblehead, MA: Opus Communications, Inc., 2004.

33. Cheng SM, Streifel AJ. Infection control considerations during construction activities: land excavation and demolition. *Am J Infect Control* 2001 Oct;29(5):321–328.

34. American Society of Heating, Refrigerating, and Air-Conditioning Engineers (ASHRAE). *ASHRAE Guideline 12–2000: Minimizing the risk of legionellosis associated with building water systems*. Atlanta, GA: ASHRAE, Inc., 2000:1–16.

35. Brown S, Detzler L, Myers J, et al. The impact of environmental controls and air quality monitoring on surgical site infection rates during operating room construction. *Am J Infect Control* 1996;24:140.

36. Buchanan CR, Dunn-Rankin D. Transport of surgically produced aerosols in an operating room. *Am Indust Hyg Assoc J* 1998 Jun;59(6):393–402.

37. Fraser VJ, Johnson K, Primack J, et al. Evaluation of rooms with negative pressure ventilation used for respiratory isolation in seven midwestern hospitals. *Infect Control Hosp Epidemiol* 1993 Nov;14(11):623–628.

38. Gershey EL, Reiman J, Wood W, et al. Evaluation of a room for tuberculosis patient isolation using theatrical fog. *Infect Control Hosp Epidemiol* 1998 Oct;19(10):760–766.

39. Hermans RE, Streifel AJ. *Ventilations designs. Proceedings of the workshop on engineering controls for preventing airborne infections in workers in healthcare and related facilities*. Cincinnati, Ohio, July 14–16, 1993. Cincinnati, OH: NIOSH, 1994.

40. Kee-Chaing C, Chin-Yuan Y, Chun-Wan C. The effect of the size of openings on contaminant control between two adjacent spaces with differing air pressures. *AIHA J (Fairfax, Va)* 2003 Nov-Dec;64(6):792–798.

41. Manangan LP, Anderson RL, Arduino MJ, et al. Sanitary care and maintenance of ice-storage chests and making machines in healthcare facilities. *Am J Infect Control* 1998 Apr;26(2):111–112.

42. Mangram AJ, Horan TC, Pearson ML, et al. Guideline for prevention of surgical site infection, 1999. Centers for Disease Control and Prevention (CDC) and Hospital Infection Control Practices Advisory Committee (HICPAC). *Am J Infect Control* 1999 Apr;27(2):97–132.

43. Marshall JW, Vincent JH, Kuehn TH, et al. Studies of ventilation efficiency in a protective isolation room by the use of a scale model. *Infect Control Hosp Epidemiol* 1996 Jan;17(1):5–10.

44. Pavelchak N, DePersis RP, London M, et al. Identification of factors that disrupt negative air pressurization of respiratory isolation rooms. *Infect Control Hosp Epidemiol* 2000 Mar;21(3):191–195.

45. Pittet D, Ducel G. Infectious risk factors related to operating rooms. *Infect Control Hosp Epidemiol* 1994 Jul;15(7):456–462.

46. Rice N, Streifel A, Vesley D. An evaluation of hospital special-ventilation-room pressures. *Infect Control Hosp Epidemiol* 2001 Jan;22(1):19–23.

47. Rydock JP, Eian PK. Containment testing of isolation rooms. *J Hosp Infect* 2004 Jul;57(3):228–232.

48. Streifel AJ. Airborne infectious disease: best practice for ventilation management. *HPAC Engineering* 2003;76:97–104.

49. Thio CL, Smith D, Merz WG, et al. Refinements of environmental assessment during an outbreak investigation of invasive aspergillosis in a leukemia and bone marrow transplant unit. *Infect Control Hosp Epidemiol* 2000 Jan;21(1):18–23.

50. Wiehrdt WQ. *Smoke trail tests for negative pressure isolation rooms*. Occupational Safety and Health Administration Technical Support Memo. Washington, DC: U.S. Department of Labor, 1994.

51. National Institute for Occupational Safety and Health. *Preventing occupational exposures to antineoplastic and other hazardous drugs in health care settings* [DHHS (NIOSH)] Publication, 2004:2004–2165.

52. National Institutes for Occupational Safety and Health. *Preventing deaths and injuries while compacting or baling refuse material* DHHS (NIOSH) Publication, 2003:2003–2124.

53. Executive Learning Inc. Continual Improvement Handbook: A Quick Reference Guide for Tools and Concepts—Healthcare Version. Brentwood, TN: Executive Learning, Inc., 2003.

54. Martin PB. Risk Management's Role in Performance Improvement. In: Carroll R, ed. *Risk Management Handbook for Health Care Organizations*, 4th ed. American Society for Healthcare Risk Management. San Francisco, CA: Jossey-Bass, Inc., 2004:1257–1266.

55. Wideman JM, Bennett AM, Burns SM, et al. Emergency water disruption provides a quality improvement opportunity [Abstract]. *Am J Infect Control*, Mosby Journals on-line. 29, 2000.

56. Wideman J. Utilizing PDCA for dust control in healthcare maintenance, renovation, and construction activities [Abstract]. *Am J Infect Control* 1999;27:225.

57. Anaissie EJ, Penzak SR, Dignani C. The hospital water supply as a source of nosocomial infections. *Arch Intern Med* 2002 Jul 8;162(13):1483–1492.

58. Bartley J. Environmental control: operating room air quality. *Todays OR Nurse* 1993 Sep-Oct;15(5):11–18.

59. Benjamin GS. The Lungs. In: Plog BA, Niland J, Quinlan PJ, eds. *Fundamentals of Industrial Hygiene*, 4th ed. Itasca, IL: National Safety Council, 1996:35–51.

60. Casadevall A, Pirofski L-A. Host-pathogen interactions: redefining the basic concepts of virulence and pathogenicity. *Infect Immun* 1999 Aug;67(8):3703–3713.

61. Cole EC, Cook CE. Characterization of infectious aerosols in health care facilities: an aid to effective engineering controls and preventive strategies. *Am J Infect Control* 1998 Aug;26(4):453–464.

62. Engelhart S, Hanfland J, Glasmacher A, et al. Impact of portable air filtration units on exposure of haematology-oncology patients to airborne Aspergillus fumigatus spores under field conditions. *J Hosp Infect* 2003 Aug;54(4):300–304.

63. Fields BS, Benson RF, Besser RE. Legionella and Legionnaires' disease: 25 years of investigation. *Clin Microbiol Rev* 2002 Jul;15(3):506–526.

64. Fridkin SK, Kremer FB, Bland LA, et al. Acremonium kiliense endophthalmitis that occurred after cataract extraction in an ambulatory surgical center and as traced to an environmental reservoir. *Clin Infect Dis* 1996 Feb;22(2):222–227.

65. Siegel JD, Rhinehart E, Jackson M, et al. 2007 Guideline for isolation precautions: preventing transmission of infectious agents in healthcare settings. CDC website. Available at: http://www.cdc.gov/hicpac/pdf/isolation/Isolation2007.pdf.

66. Griffith CJ, Malik R, Cooper RA, et al. Environmental surface cleanliness and the potential for contamination during hand washing. *Am J Infect Control* 2003 Apr;31(2):93–96.

67. Halabi M, Wiesholzer-Pittl M, Schoberl J, et al. Nontouch fittings in hospitals: a possible source of Pseudomonas aeruginosa and Legionella spp. *J Hosp Infect* 2001 Oct;49(2):117–121.

68. Hansen W, ed. *A Guide to Managing Indoor Air Quality in Health Care Organizations*. Oakbrook, IL: Joint Commission on Accreditation of Healthcare Organizations Publications, 1997.

69. Noskin GA, Peterson LR. Engineering infection control through facility design. *Emerg Infect Dis* 2001 Mar-Apr;7(2):354–357.

70. Rutala WA. Water as a reservoir of nosocomial pathogens. *Infect Control Hosp Epidemiol* 1997 Sep;18(9):609–616.

71. Taylor JS. The Skin and Occupational Dermatoses. In: Plog BA, Niland J, Quinlan PJ, eds. *Fundamentals of Industrial Hygiene*, 4th ed. Itasca, IL: National Safety Council, 1996:53–82.

72. Voss A, Nulens E. Prevention and Control of Laboratory-acquired Infections. In: Murray PR, ed. *Manual of Clinical Microbiology*, 8th ed. Washington, DC: ASM Press, 2003:116–117.

73. Cox R, deBorja K, Bach MC. A pseudo-outbreak of Mycobacterium chelonae infections related to bronchoscopy. *Infect Control Hosp Epidemiol* 1997 Feb;18(2):136–137.

74. U.S. Food and Drug Administration (FDA). *FDA and CDC public health advisory: infections from endoscopes inadequately reprocessed by an automated endoscope reprocessing system*. September 10, 1999. FDA website. Available at: http://www.fda.gov/MedicalDevices/Safety/AlertsandNotices/PublicHealthNotifications/ucm062282.htm.

75. Sly RM, Josephs SH, Eby DM, et al. Dissemination of dust by central and portable vacuum cleaners. *Ann Allergy* 1985 Mar;54(3):209–212.

76. New York City Department of Health and Mental Hygiene. *Guidelines on Assessment and Remediation of Fungi in Indoor Environments*. November 2008. Available at: http://www.nyc.gov/html/doh/downloads/pdf/epi/epi-mold-guidelines.pdf.

77. Kumari DN, Haji TC, Keer V, et al. Ventilation grilles as a potential source of methicillin-resistant Staphylococcus aureus causing an outbreak in an orthopedic ward at district general hospital. *J Hosp Infect* 1998 Jun;39(2):127–133.

78. National Institutes for Occupational Safety and Health. *Control of smoke from laser/electric surgical procedures.* DHHS (NIOSH) Publication, 1996:96–128.
79. Rutala WA, Jones SM, Worthington JM, et al. Efficacy of portable filtration units in reducing aerosolized particles in the size range of mycobacterium tuberculosis. *Infect Control Hosp Epidemiol* 1995 Jul;16(7):391–398.
80. Wideman JM. Blackout of 2003: infection control implications and lessons learned for Michigan hospitals [Abstract]. *Amer J Infect Control*, Mosby Journals on-line E90;2004.
81. Bert F, Maubec E, Bruneau B, et al. Multi-resistant Pseudomonas aeruginosa outbreak associated with contaminated tap water in a neurosurgery intensive care unit. *J Hosp Infect* 1998 May;39(1):53–62.
82. U.S. Environmental Protection Agency (EPA), Office of Water, Office of Ground Water and Drinking Water. *Health Risks from Microbial Growth and Biofilms in Drinking Water Distribution Systems.* June 17, 2002. EPA website. Available at: http://www.epa.gov/ogwdw000/disinfection/tcr/pdfs/whitepaper_tcr_biofilms.pdf.
83. American Society for Healthcare Engineering: Health Facility Commissioning Guidelines, 2010.
84. Darelid J, Lofgren S, Malmvall BE. Control of nosocomial Legionnaires disease by keeping the circulating hot water temperature above 55 degrees C: experience from a 10-year surveillance programme in a district general hospital. *J Hosp Infect* 2002 Mar;50(3):213–219.
85. Ferroni A, Nguyen L, Pron B, et al. Outbreak of nosocomial urinary tract infections due to Pseudomonas aeruginosa in a paediatric surgical unit associated with tap-water contamination. *J Hosp Infect* 1998 Aug;39(4):301–307.
86. Graman PS, Quinlan GA, Rank JA. Nosocomial legionellosis traced to a contaminated ice machine. *Infect Control Hosp Epidemiol* 1997 Sep;18(9):637–640.
87. Kappstein I, Grundmann H, Hauer T, et al. Aerators as a reservoir of Acinetobacter junii: an outbreak of bacteraemia in paediatric oncology patients. *J Hosp Infect* 2000 Jan;44(1):27–30.
88. LaBombardi VJ, O'Brien AM, Kislak JW. Pseudo-outbreak of Mycobacterium fortuitum due to contaminated ice machines. *Am J Infect Control* 2002 May;30(3):184–186.
89. McDonald LC, Walker M, Carson L, et al. Outbreak of Acinetobacter spp. bloodstream infections in a nursery associated with contaminated aerosols and air conditioners. *Pediatr Infect Dis J* 1998 Aug;17(8):716–722.
90. Mermel LA, Josephson SL, Giorgio CH, et al. Association of Legionnaires' disease with construction: contamination of potable water? *Infect Control Hosp Epidemiol* 1995 Feb;16(2):76–81.
91. Baier E. *Health Hazard Information Bulletin: Potentially Hazardous Amoebae Found in Eyewash Stations.* Hazard information bulletin, United States Department of Labor and Occupational Safety and Health Administration (OSHA). December 23. 1986. Dept. of Labor, Bulletin 19861223. Available at: https://www.osha.gov/dts/hib/hib_data/hib19861223.html
92. Reingold AL. Outbreak investigations—a perspective. *Emerg Infect Dis* 1998 Jan-Mar;4(1):21–27.
93. Verweij PE, Meis JF, Christmann V, et al. Nosocomial outbreak of colonization and infection with Stenotrophomonas maltophilia in preterm infants associated with contaminated tap water. *Epidemiol Infect* 1998 Jun;120(3):251–256.
94. Wallace RJ Jr, Brown BA, Griffith DE. Nosocomial outbreaks/pseudo-outbreaks caused by nontuberculous mycobacteria. *Ann Rev Microbiol* 1998;52:453–490.
95. Almuneef M, Memish ZA. Effective medical waste management: it can be done. *Am J Infect Control* 2003 May;31(3):188–192.
96. Garcia R. Effective cost-reduction strategies in the management of regulated medical waste. *Am J Infect Control* 1999 Apr;27(2):165–175.
97. Health Care Without Harm. Non-incineration medical waste treatment technologies—a resource for hospital administrators, facility managers, health care professionals, environmental advocates, and community members. Washington, DC: Health Care Without Harm, 2001.
98. Neely AN, Maley MP, Taylor GL. Investigation of single-use versus reusable infectious waste containers as potential sources of microbial contamination. *Am J Infect Control* 2003 Feb;31(1):13–17.
99. Rutala WA. Disinfection, Sterilization and Waste Disposal—Medical Waste. In: Wenzel RP, ed. *Prevention and Control of Nosocomial Infections*, 2nd ed. Baltimore: Williams and Wilkins, 1993:483–487.

SUPPLEMENTAL RESOURCES

Allo MD, Tedesco M. Operating room management: operative suite consideration, infection control. *Surg Clin N Am* 2005;84:1291–1297.

American Industrial Hygiene Association (AIHA). Available at: http://www.aiha.org.

American Society for Healthcare Engineering (ASHE). Available at: http://www.ashe.org.

American Society of Heating, Refrigerating and Air-Conditioning Engineers, Inc. (ASHRAE). Available at: http://www.ashrae.org.

Beggs C, Kerr KG, Noakes CJ, et al. The ventilation of multi-bed hospital wards: review and analysis. *Am J Infect Control* 2008 May;36(4):250–259.

Dyck A, Exner M, Kramer A. Experimental based experiences with the introduction of a water safety plan for a multi-located university clinic and its efficacy according to WHO recommendations. *BMC Public Health* 2007 Mar 13;7:34.

EPA resources and publications on indoor air quality. Available at: http://www.epa.gov.

Exner M, Kramer A, Lajoie L, et al. Prevention and control of healthcare-associated waterborne infections in health care facilities. *Am J Infect Control* 2005 Jun;33 (5 Suppl 1):S26–S40.

Henriksen K, Isaacson S, Sadler BL, et al. The role of the physical environment in crossing the quality chasm. *Jt Comm J Qual Patient Saf* 2007 Nov;33(11 Suppl):68–80.

Krause M, Geer W, Swenson L, et al. Controlled study of mold growth and cleaning procedures on treated and untreated wet gypsum wallboard in an indoor environment. *J Occup Environ Hyg* 2006 Aug;3(8):435–441.

Leung M, Chan AHS. Control and management of hospital indoor air quality. *Med Sci Monit* 2006 Mar;12(3):SR17–23.

Li Y, Leung GM, Tang JW, et al. Role of ventilation in airborne transmission of infectious agents in the built environment—a multidisciplinary systematic review. *Indoor Air* 2007 Feb;17(1):2–18.

Memarzadeh F, Jiang J. A methodology for minimizing risk from airborne organisms in hospital isolation room. *ASHRAE Transactions* 2000;106:731–737. Available at: http://orf.od.nih.gov/PoliciesAndGuidelines/Bioenvironmental/Documents/ASHRAE_Isolation_Room_June2000_508.pdf.

Memarzadeh F, Manning A. Thermal comfort, uniformity and ventilation effectiveness in patient rooms: performance assessment using ventilation indices. *ASHRAE Transactions* 2000;106:748–761. Available at: http://orf.od.nih.gov/PoliciesAndGuidelines/Bioenvironmental/Documents/ASHRAE_transactiondoc509.pdf

Nakipoglu Y, Erturan Z, Buyukbaba-Boral O, et al. Evaluation of the contaminant organisms of humidifier reservoir water and investigation of the source of contamination in a university hospital in Turkey. *Am J Infect Control* 2005 Feb;33(1):62–63.

Department of Health and Human Services (HHS), Centers for Disease Control and Prevention (CDC), National Institute for Occupational Safety and Health (NIOSH). Guidance for filtration and air-cleaning systems to protect building environments from airborne chemical, biological, or radiological attacks. April 2003. CDC website. Available at: http://www.cdc.gov/niosh/docs/2003-136/pdfs/2003-136.pdf.

New York City Department of Health and Mental Hygiene. *Guidelines on Assessment and Remediation of Fungi in Indoor Environments.* November 2008. Available at: http://www.nyc.gov/html/doh/downloads/pdf/epi/epi-mold-guidelines.pdf.

Occupational Safety and Health Administration (OSHA). OSHA Technical Manual for Hazardous Drugs. OSHA website. Available at: http://www.osha.gov.

Perdelli F, Sartini M, Spagnolo AM, et al. A problem of hospital hygiene: the presence of aspergilli in hospital wards with different air-conditioning features. *Am J Infect Control* 2006 Jun;34(5):264–268.

Tang CS, Chung FF, Lin MC, et al. Impact of patient visiting activities on indoor climate in a medical intensive care unit: a 1-year longitudinal study. *Am J Infect Control* 2009 Apr;37(3):183–188.

University of Minnesota Department of Environmental Health and Safety. Selected topics include indoor air quality, water infiltration, and use of the wet test or moisture meter. Available at: http://www.dehs.umn.edu.

CHAPTER 113

Waste Management

William J. Pate, BS, MPH, DPH
Safety Manager, Environment of Care
University Health System
San Antonio, TX

ABSTRACT

The infection preventionist has varying levels of involvement with healthcare waste management and is often focused on regulated medical waste. An effective waste management program is complex due to numerous regulations and guidelines, evolving technologies, expanding healthcare delivery settings, emerging infectious diseases, and the potential for bioterrorism. Although responsibility for the management of healthcare waste is typically outside the area of responsibility for most infection preventionists, they may still be included in a wide range of areas related to management of healthcare wastes beyond the traditional role. This chapter provides information and resources to assist the infection preventionist with successful participation in the safe management of healthcare wastes.

KEY CONCEPTS

- Definitions of medical waste can be confusing.

- Medical waste regulations and guidance should be based on scientific analysis.

- Waste management plans should include input from the infection prevention and control program.

- The infection preventionist should be aware of new technology and emerging issues related to healthcare wastes.

- Performance improvement may be used to measure effectiveness of waste management.

- International positions for managing healthcare wastes vary considerably based on country-specific regulatory requirements and definitions.

BACKGROUND

In the late 1980s and early 1990s, medical waste caught the public's attention because of its potential for environmental contamination and disease transmission. Media sensationalism focusing on beach wash-ups and dwindling landfill space combined with fears regarding human immunodeficiency virus (HIV) transmission resulted in emotional reaction and confusion that was not based on scientific analysis.[1-4]

When asked to define the risks that healthcare wastes pose to the public and to the community, experts at the Centers for Disease Control and Prevention (CDC) stated: "There is no epidemiologic evidence to suggest that most hospital waste is any more infectious than residential waste. Moreover, there is no epidemiologic evidence that hospital waste disposal practices have caused disease in the community; therefore, identifying wastes for which special precautions are indicated is largely a matter of judgment about the relative risks of disease transmission."[5] Although this statement was originally prepared in 1985, it was restated for inclusion in the CDC's *2003 Guidelines for Environmental Infection Control in Health-Care Facilities.*[6] Although there is no documented evidence of transmission of disease to the public through healthcare waste streams, data limitations prevent firm conclusions on risk from being developed.[4]

Unfortunately, some confusion remains, compounded by inconsistent, specific, and occasionally conflicting definitions of "medical waste" or "infectious waste." This is promoted by input from individuals with little knowledge of infectious disease transmission or related microbiology. Documents have been drafted at local, state, and federal levels that lack scientific risk/benefit analysis.[1,3,6]

Hospitals and other healthcare settings have recognized the potential occupational risk of disease transmission and therefore use caution when handling and disposing of wastes.[7] Healthcare "infectious" wastes may include microbiological laboratory waste, hazardous waste, blood/body fluids, sharps, pathology wastes, pharmaceutical wastes, and certain wastes from patients who are placed in isolation.[4] Careful handling, sorting, and transportation, as well as appropriate packaging and disposal of waste from these settings may help to explain the absence of transmission in the community.

This chapter discusses healthcare waste from a practical and scientific perspective, with the majority of the chapter focusing on traditional "infectious" waste. However, the infection preventionist (IP) may be involved in other aspects related to waste management in a variety of healthcare settings. These selected issues include purchasing, design of waste disposal areas, reuse and recycling (including increasing popularity of reusable sharps disposal containers), handling and disposal of special types of waste (bacillus Calmette-Guérin [BCG], gene therapy, probiotics, piped systems waste, mixed wastes, chemotherapeutics, radioactive materials, and emerging infectious and bioterrorism agents), waste disinfection and sterilization technologies, ecological considerations, and assessment of a waste management plan using performance improvement. Accordingly, brief and pragmatic overviews of varied waste topics are included to assist the IP, and resources are provided for further consideration. Individual healthcare facilities and services must consider applicable codes, regulations, and guidelines prior to implementing or updating an effective waste management program.

BASIC PRINCIPLES

Waste-related Regulation and Guidance

On the federal level in the United States, several agencies have published regulations pertaining to "infectious," "medical," or "regulated" waste. The U.S. Environmental Protection Agency (EPA), the U.S. Occupational Safety and Health Administration (OSHA), and the U.S. Department of Transportation (DOT) have such regulations.[8-12] In addition, both the CDC and EPA have issued guidance documents pertaining to medical waste management.[5,6,12,13] At the request of the U.S. Congress, the Agency for Toxic Substances and Disease Registry prepared and published a comprehensive review of the public health implications of medical waste.[14]

The Joint Commission includes medical waste as hazardous within its Environment of Care standards through several elements of performance (EP) within EC.02.01.01 and in EP 6 under Infection Prevention and Control in standard IC.02.01.01.[9] The U.S. Postal Service has laws related to sending hazardous and biological substances through the mail.[14] The Nuclear Regulatory Commission has jurisdiction over waste that contains both biological and radiological hazards ("mixed waste").[15] The U.S. Food and Drug Administration's Center for Devices and Radiological Health has regulatory authority over selected aspects of waste management, including the designation of sharps disposal boxes as class II medical devices.[16]

Other agencies have regulations and guidelines related to wastes from healthcare settings; selected entities are identified where indicated in the chapter. (Also refer to Chapter 4 Accrediting and Regulatory Agencies.) In the United States, various state and local governments have a range of regulations related to these materials. Therefore, it is important that IPs recognize which regulations are applicable based on the authority having jurisdiction for their healthcare setting(s). IPs should remain current with applicable state and federal regulatory activity within the United States or with the authority having jurisdiction for regulatory oversight in the international community.

Waste Terminology

The primary constituent of healthcare waste that is traditionally of interest to IPs is waste capable of transmitting infectious agents. Articles on this topic offer inconsistent findings due to lack of a standardized definition of what constitutes waste capable of transmitting an infectious disease.[13] Terms such as "biomedical waste," "regulated waste," "red bag waste," "medical waste," and "infectious waste" have been used interchangeably. The same term may have a different definition depending on the resource. For example, in a background paper, the Office of Technology Assessment defined "medical waste" as "all the types of wastes produced by hospitals, clinics, doctors' offices, and other medical and research facilities. These wastes include infectious or 'red bag' hospital wastes, hazardous (including radioactive) wastes and any other general wastes."[17] In the Medical Waste Tracking Act of 1988, "medical waste" was defined as "any solid waste which is generated in the diagnosis, treatment or immunization of human beings or animals, in research pertaining thereto, or in the production or testing of biologicals."[18] Categories of waste that are included in these definitions vary from state to state and even from federal agency to federal agency.[3,6,8,10,11,13,19] To reduce confusion, the term "infectious waste" is used here to refer to "waste that is capable of producing an infectious disease."

A common misconception is to assume that the presence of a pathogen will result in infection from wastes. Pathogenic organisms are found in many different day-to-day settings. Household garbage, bed linens, soiled diapers, and unwashed hands are all examples of environments in which pathogens can routinely be found both within and outside the healthcare setting.[3,6,13] A number of studies have shown that although hospital wastes can have a greater variety of organisms than residential wastes, those from households are more heavily contaminated.[6,13] Even when generated from healthcare activities, most garbage, soiled bed linens, and diapers do not have any special handling requirements in most instances.[6] For a waste to be capable of causing infection, the following specific factors are necessary: (1) dose, (2) host susceptibility, (3) presence of a pathogen, (4) virulence of a pathogen, and (5) portal of entry. Concisely, all five of these factors must be present for infection to occur from waste.[3]

Infectious Waste Categories

Many categories of infectious waste have been proposed by a variety of associations, individuals, and agencies in the past.[3,6,13,17,19] However, if the preceding definition is strictly adhered to, developing categories of infectious waste is fairly simple and should include the following.

Contaminated Sharps

All discarded sharps (e.g., needles, scalpels) that have come into contact with potentially infectious materials should be considered infectious waste. This category of infectious waste poses the greatest risk for injuries.[3,6,8,13,20] The risk of infection is related to contamination with a sufficient dose of pathogenic organisms (such as Hepatitis B virus [HBV], Hepatitis C virus [HCV], or HIV) and the provision of a portal of entry into a susceptible host via a puncture or cut. These devices represent a significant occupational hazard to those handling and disposing of them. However, once contaminated sharps are properly placed into appropriate rigid, puncture-resistant containers, the environmental risk they pose is negligible.[1-3,6,8,13,21-24] (Also see Chapter 105 Minimizing Exposure to Blood and Body Fluids.)

Microbiologic Cultures and Stocks of Infectious Agents

Of all of the possible categories of infectious waste, untreated cultures, stocks, and amplified microbial populations pose the greatest potential for infectious disease transmission because they contain high concentrations of potentially pathogenic organisms.[6,21,22] Laboratory personnel should handle discarded cultures and stocks accordingly.[22,23] Cultures and stocks may be stored in glass containers (e.g., tubes) that, if broken, become contaminated sharps and therefore should be handled carefully. Microbiologic waste may be treated on-site prior to discarding (e.g., by autoclaving) and subsequently disposed as nonhazardous solid waste in accordance with related solid-waste disposal regulations.[6,21,22]

Animal Wastes

Discarded material originating from animals inoculated with infectious agents during research, production of biologicals, or pharmaceutical testing should be considered infectious waste.[21] These materials are similar to microbiologic cultures and stocks because they may contain high concentrations of pathogenic organisms. Therefore, animal wastes that fit into this category are handled in the same manner. Certain tissues and bodies from animal research areas may have special considerations for handling and disposal dependent on potential for zoonotic microbes; each should be addressed based on knowledge of the specific organism.[6,21]

Blood and Blood Products

Blood and blood products, as defined in the OSHA Bloodborne Pathogens standard (e.g., serum, plasma, and other components known or suspected to be contaminated with a transmissible agent) must be handled carefully. Small amounts of these materials dried on dressings or other disposable items represent an insignificant hazard once they are properly contained because of the absence of a portal of entry and a means of transmission.[8] Bulk blood, blood-tinged suctioned fluids, excretions, and secretions are considered infectious waste because they may be splashed onto mucous membranes or because the container may break and become a contaminated sharp. These fluids may be carefully poured down a drain connected to a sanitary sewer that is designed for the disposal of human waste.[6] Before disposing of these fluids in the sanitary sewer, it is important to verify that local regulations allow this practice, as there may be local prohibitions on the disposal of whole blood in the sanitary sewer. Personnel must follow Universal/Standard Precautions, including the use of personal protective equipment (PPE), due to splash and aerosolization potential.[6,8] Alternative treatment methods for inactivation or handling prior to disposal are available.

Selected Isolation Wastes

Discarded waste materials contaminated with excretions, exudates, and secretions from patients with highly communicable diseases (classification 4 by the CDC in *Classification of Etiologic Agents on the Basis of Hazard*, e.g., Ebola) treated in isolation should be classified as infectious waste.[21] Blood and sharps originating from these patients are already included in the preceding categories.

Pathology Wastes

Pathology wastes include human tissues and body parts that are collected at autopsy or during surgery. Pathology wastes do not usually fit the definition of infectious waste outlined previously. There is an absence of a portal of entry and most of these materials have been soaked in alcohol or formaldehyde and thus seldom contain pathogens. Incineration or grinding and discharging into a sanitary sewer are the common acceptable methods of treating this waste.[6,8,22]

Nonincluded Wastes

Other categories of infectious waste have been suggested even though there is no scientific justification for their inclusion.[13,17] Personnel who are responsible for developing safe handling and disposal practices for these materials must keep in mind that the waste discharged from healthcare institutions differs little from that in normal households.[6,13,17] Most persons with infectious diseases are not hospitalized. Thus, characterizing all waste as infectious increases healthcare costs and creates undue confusion and concern.[3,5,6,13,20]

WASTE MANAGEMENT PLAN

Plan Basics

The efficient waste management plan addresses every step from acquiring materials that become waste to generation of waste, discarding, collection and containment, handling, accumulation and storage, transportation, treatment, and ultimate disposal.[6,13] The key to success is a collaborative effort, including the IP's involvement.

Infectious Waste

Once a facility has a working definition of "infectious waste," the next step is to develop or update a plan for managing these materials. A management plan is addressed to some extent by regulatory, advisory, and licensing agencies such as OSHA and the CDC, various state agencies such as the Department of Natural Resources or Department of Health, as well as other bodies, such as The Joint Commission.[5,6,8,9] This written plan should include provisions for the assignment of responsibility and authority for overseeing the program to an individual, such as the IP or the facility safety officer, who is knowledgeable regarding infectious disease transmission and who is familiar with applicable federal, state, and local regulations. This will ensure that these materials are handled as required and in a scientific manner. Objectives for the plan include (1) rendering infectious waste safe for disposal; (2) ensuring that there is minimal risk to patients, personnel, visitors, and the community from exposure to pathogenic organisms associated with waste generated in the healthcare facility; (3) meeting or exceeding all federal, state, and local regulations; and (4) educating the healthcare personnel regarding the management plan and the real versus the perceived risk associated with "infectious waste." For example, the effective application of a facility-wide medical waste assessment and management plan resulted in a 58 percent reduction in volume of waste designated as medical at one facility.[25]

The other components of an "infectious waste" management plan include (1) designation, (2) segregation, (3) packaging, (4) storage, (5) transport, (6) treatment or disposal, (7) contingency planning, and (8) staff training.[8,10,26] Each component is discussed further in the following sections.

Designation

Once a facility has developed definitions for infectious and noninfectious wastes, sorting the discarded materials into the proper waste stream should align with regulatory, safety, and cost-reduction facets.[10,26] It is recommended that a list of infectious wastes generated in the facility be developed and that the generating areas be identified in the management plan. For example, blood/blood products known or suspected to be infected with transmissible agents are generated on patient floors and in surgery, the autopsy suite, clinics, emergency rooms, and ancillary departments.

Segregation

Individuals who are knowledgeable about the waste's origin and its hazard potential must segregate infectious waste at the point of origin.[13,17,19,26,27] The waste should then be placed into appropriate designated leakproof containers. Needles must never be recapped, bent, or broken by hand before being discarded. Infectious waste with multiple hazards (e.g., used sharps from patient receiving chemotherapy) must be segregated as necessary for the management and treatment of the waste characteristic with the most stringent handling requirements. For example, proper segregation of waste generated in the surgical suite can limit the volume to that which meets definitions of infectious waste if perioperative personnel can be engaged in separation at this point of use. Examples of successful segregation in this setting have been described that also offer benefits of environmental sustainability and facilitate recycling of the large quantity of materials and packaging generated during perioperative care.[28]

Packaging

Infectious waste must be packaged properly to protect patients, staff, visitors, and the public from potential exposure to infectious materials and to facilitate the proper handling, storage, treatment, or disposal of the waste.[5,6,8,10,13,29,30] Selection of the packaging must be appropriate for the type of waste being contained to maintain the integrity of the packaging during

collection, transport, storage, and disposal. States generally specify packaging requirements in their infectious waste regulations. In addition, OSHA and the CDC specify that sharps be placed in rigid puncture-proof containers.[5,6,8]

Infectious waste must be properly identified as a biohazard. Infectious waste containers should be labeled with a biohazard label or color-coded red to identify the contents. OSHA requires either red color-coding or use of the universal biohazard symbol and term "biohazard."[8,22] State regulations may require additional information on the packaging, such as the name of the generating facility, date, bilingual terminology, and so forth. Packaging used for shipment will often contain additional markings and be labeled to comply with applicable shipping regulations (e.g., orientation arrows on sharps containers).

Sharps containers must be impervious, rigid, puncture resistant, leakproof on the sides and bottom, and closable.[6,24,31] Plastic bags are appropriate for bulk solid or semisolid infectious wastes or for disposables containing residual liquids. Plastic bags should be impervious and tear resistant. Potentially infectious liquid wastes can be carefully poured down a designated sanitary sewer using appropriate engineering controls and PPE.[6,8] When this is not desirable or possible, liquid wastes should be placed in leakproof containers, such as a flask or bottle, that can be tightly capped or stoppered. Absorbent material sufficient to absorb the entire contents of the containers must be added to the outer container. Free-flowing liquids should not be poured directly into a waste container. Suction canisters must be tightly closed and placed in plastic bags. Bags may need to then be placed in a secondary container, such as a cardboard box, to preserve the integrity of the packaging during transport and storage. Semirigid or rigid secondary containers usually are required for off-site transport of infectious waste.[8,29]

Storage

Infectious waste should be treated and disposed of as soon as possible after generation.[5,6,17,19,26,29,30] Although there is no published national standard for how long infectious waste may be stored, some states may have limits on storage time at the generating facility. The proper packaging outlined here will ensure containment and exclusion of rodents and vermin. Storage areas should have limited access, and a biohazard symbol should be posted so it is readily visible to anyone with access to the area. Many states have specifications for the type of enclosure required for storage of infectious waste, and they often specify the duration of storage that is permissible. Some states have very elaborate requirements for storage areas that require the room to have floors that slope to a drain that is connected to a sanitary sewer. This provides for a safe method of cleaning up liquid spills. In any case, a system for immediate spill containment and cleanup should be available in the storage area (e.g., hose connected to steam line).

Transport

The internal and external systems used for the transportation of infectious waste must maintain the integrity of the packaging and protect handlers.[5-7,10,17-19,29,30] Mechanical waste collection devices and gravity or pneumatic-chute transport of infectious waste are discouraged due to potential damage to packaging. Leakproof carts that are readily cleanable or that can be lined with plastic are generally used for transportation of infectious waste from the generating areas to the storage area where it will be picked up for treatment. Commercial or private vehicles that are employed in the transport of infectious waste should be leakproof and identified in accordance with municipal, state, and federal regulations. IPs should be aware of regulatory requirements and provide input into relevant key operational services. For example, a facility's clinical laboratory couriers, who often pick up not only specimens but also infectious waste from affiliated physician practices and other ambulatory care facilities, commonly provide transport of infectious waste. In general, states require the registration of vehicles utilized in the transportation of infectious waste. Although some facilities will transport and treat their own infectious waste, appropriately licensed commercial companies may be contracted to transport and treat healthcare wastes.

A waste manifest documenting the shipment information must accompany transported waste. A waste manifest serves as a document that tracks the waste from the generating facility until its final disposition, and it acts as a record of the waste's movement. The waste manifest also acts as a legal document whereby the generator certifies that the waste has been correctly classified, packed, marked, and labeled according to applicable shipping regulations. Because of this, it is important that the waste manifest be reviewed and signed by a trained individual before the waste is transported off-site. The DOT considers the individual signing the waste manifest to be a hazardous materials employee, and thus the employer as required in 49 CFR must train them. Having the waste manifest signed by untrained employees can result in significant penalties. Copies of waste manifests must be retained for a minimum of 3 years under DOT regulations, although states can require longer retention time.

Treatment

Many options are available for the proper treatment of infectious waste.[2,6,10,13,14,17,21,30-35] The method selected will be determined by the amount of infectious waste generated, the capabilities of the facility, and the cost effectiveness of on-site treatment versus contracting the service to a licensed commercial vendor. The type of treatment selected will depend on municipal, state, and federal regulations. Incineration was traditionally selected by hospitals as the primary method for treating infectious waste but has decreased in application due to EPA regulations related to the Clean Air Act and control of emissions (also refer to Supplemental Resources). Depending on the type of infectious waste, acceptable methods for rendering these materials innocuous include steam sterilization, chemical disinfection, gas/vapor sterilization, and irradiation decontamination. Modern alternative technologies have broadened the scope of available treatment options. Microwave, infrared, hyperchlorination, and laser technologies are only a few of the new technologies being utilized to render infectious waste innocuous.

The treatment selected should be based on the type of waste generated and the suitability of available options. States generally require that the efficacy of the treatment methods selected be monitored. The monitoring system selected will depend on the treatment method utilized. For example, steam sterilization treatment would be monitored utilizing a biological indicator that includes *Bacillus stearothermophilus* spores.

Disposal

The direct disposal of infectious waste at a properly sited landfill does not present a threat to public health and safety, according to many experts, and is still acceptable in many areas.[6,8,13] However, perceived risk concerns and the nationwide movement away from land disposal have resulted in widespread landfill prohibitions on the disposal of untreated infectious waste in landfills. After treatment, medical wastes are usually disposed of in a sanitary landfill. Untreated liquid medical waste, such as bulk blood or the contents of suction containers, can be disposed of by carefully pouring them into the sanitary sewer when allowed by local regulations. When designing an infectious waste management plan, it may be helpful to communicate with the waste hauler contractor and local landfill representatives during the planning process. This will help ensure that the healthcare facility is in compliance with regulatory codes, and most importantly, it will help ensure education and training for those who handle and haul these materials.

Contingency Planning

Systems should be in place to address unforeseen events that may disrupt the normal treatment, transportation, and disposal of infectious waste materials.[10] Both on-site and off-site contingencies should be available. Alternate strategies should be available in case on-site treatment systems fail or if there is an unanticipated power shortage. A backup disposal contractor should be designated in case there is a disruption of the ability of the primary outside contractor to serve the facility. Emergency spill procedures should also be in place for on-site and off-site emergencies.

Training

Training of all personnel involved in the generation, handling, transporting, treatment, or disposal of infectious waste is imperative for the infectious waste management plan to be effective.[6,8,17,29,36,37] Training should include the definition of infectious waste, handling procedures, appropriate PPE, hand hygiene, labeling or coding that designates an item as infectious waste, and postexposure management. There is also specific training required by regulatory agencies such as OSHA and the DOT. For example, individuals involved in the infectious waste shipping process (which includes signing of waste manifests), must meet DOT training requirements that includes at a minimum general awareness training, function-specific training, safety training, and security awareness training. As part of this training, the employee must be tested and the employer must certify in writing that the employee has met the training requirements. Training must be completed within 90 days of hire, with refresher training completed every 3 years. The employer must maintain records associated with worker training.

Infection Prevention Implications

The IP may be involved in developing and coordinating the infectious waste management plan. The plan should be based on sound scientific information and consistent with local, state, and federal regulations and guidelines. An article by Rutala et al. contained noteworthy information related to medical waste that may be considered when developing or revising a healthcare waste management plan.[7]

- Hospitalized patients generate approximately 15 pounds of hospital waste per day, which averages to approximately 6,700 tons of daily waste by hospitals.

- About 15 percent of the total hospital waste by weight is considered "infectious waste" (1,000 tons/day).

- The cost of disposing of infectious waste is 5 to 20 times greater than that for disposal of noninfectious hospital wastes.

- With the exception of "sharps" such as needles, which have caused disease only in an occupational setting, there is no scientific evidence that medical waste has caused disease in the hospital or in the community.

- Household waste contains, on average, 100 times as many human pathogens as medical waste.

- The beach wash-ups of syringe-related materials that created nationwide concern were found to come from illegal drug use and home healthcare; hospitals were not implicated as the cause of this problem.

Other Waste Management Concerns

Purchasing

Products brought into healthcare settings and development of policies and procedures related to their use should be part of an effective infection prevention and control program.[28] Product selection should consider published recommendations and guidelines and comply with regulatory agency standards (e.g., sharps, disposal containers, or chemotherapy waste boxes).[5,6,8–13,15,16,36] Workers involved with handling of waste, such as used needles, should be included in an evaluation process.[8] (Also see Chapter 105 Minimizing Exposure to Blood and Body Fluids.) Waste minimization efforts, as part of a waste management plan, can be achieved by purchasing products that generate less waste or are substituted for existing items.

Waste Disposal Areas

Healthcare wastes of all types should be sorted at the point of creation. For example, used sharps should be immediately discarded into sharps disposal containers.[6,8,24] The design and construction of renovated or new healthcare facilities should include the IP in the process from conception through commissioning.[6,38,39] Waste handling and areas for storage and disposal should be designed and located as appropriate for the types of wastes generated by the facility.[39] (Also see Chapters 116 Construction and Renovation and 107 Environmental Services.)

Waste Reduction, Including Reuse and Recycling

The IP may be asked to help evaluate reusable items to replace single-use, disposable items in an effort to reduce waste volume. (Also see Chapter 32 Reprocessing Single-Use Devices.) Reusable containers for regulated medical waste and sharps disposal boxes are one such effort that has gained popularity with the increased emphasis on environmental stewardship. Some have raised concerns over safety of reusable sharps disposal containers in terms of adequate removal of potential contaminants after they are emptied, cleaned/disinfected, and returned to a facility.[12] Neely et al. compared recovery of surface contaminants from a disposable cardboard container with a plastic liner (note: this is not in compliance with OSHA-issued requirements for sharps containers) to a reusable plastic container.[40] The proportion and diversity of microbial contaminants on the reusable containers was higher; however, quantitative details (e.g. colony forming units) were not provided, and the majority of these contaminants were common skin commensals. Neely et al. compared the overall rate of healthcare-associated infection (HAI) before and after implementing a new policy of disinfecting the top of the reusable container and observed a statistically significant decrease; however, this study design could not account for a variety of other interventions that might account for this change. Runner cultured surfaces of reusable containers for bacteria and certain viruses delivered to a community hospital.[41] Quantitative levels of microbes recovered were not provided in the study and, as in the study by Neely et al., most of the bacteria were common skin commensals. Polymerase chain reaction (PCR) testing did identify a proportion positive for certain bloodborne viruses; however, PCR testing is very sensitive and does not always correlate with presence of viable infectious virus. The IP needs to keep the findings of both studies in perspective relative to principles of disease transmission outlined in the Waste Terminology section of this chapter. Visible soil on or inside reusable containers should prompt notification of the manufacturer and not even be placed into use. Surface contaminants, even with bloodborne infectious agents, do not represent an appreciable risk to healthcare personnel given routine hygiene for hands and the environment typical of the hospital setting. Extensive studies of risk of occupational exposure to bloodborne infectious agents have indicated that the risk strata is highest for hollow-bore devices introduced through the skin, much lower for percutaneous introduction of blood/other potentially infectious material, and likely negligible for intact skin that is in contact with a contaminated surface. By contrast there is evidence that reusable sharps containers can dramatically lower the incidence of sharps injuries to healthcare personnel during disposal of contaminated sharps.[42] As described, the IP must be involved in the evaluation, selection, and implementation of a sharps disposal system, regardless of the container design that is chosen.

A careful risk assessment should be completed to ensure that reprocessing of containers is effective and in compliance with regulations for the safety of patients and staff.[12]

Selected Special Types of Waste

Bladder Cancer Therapy with Bacillus Calmette-Guérin

Intravesical infusion of BCG to treat superficial bladder cancer was first reported in 1976 as an alternative to chemotherapy.[43] This immunotherapy was subsequently approved in 1990 by the FDA for use in the United States for carcinoma in situ, which is found in 20 to 30 percent of bladder cancer cases.[44] Intravesical administration of BCG appears to be associated with fewer adverse reactions, with influenza-like symptoms (including fever, chills and nausea) and discomfort as the most commonly reported.[44,45] However, there have been a few cases of localized and disseminated *Mycobacterium bovis* infections following infusion.[45] Treatments for bladder cancer that may be used with or without BCG include mitomycin C, thiotepa, doxorubicin, oral bropirimine, interferon alpha, keyhole limpet hemocyanin, and valrubicin.[46,47]

Little information is provided on infection prevention and the safe handling and subsequent disposal of items potentially contaminated with BCG. Although the *Mycobacterium* used for BCG is an attenuated strain, the amount of organism used for intravesical treatment is that of approximately 2,000 vaccinations.[48] Care must be taken to prevent introduction of BCG onto environmental surfaces or other items. A case of iatrogenic meningitis was reported in two immunocompromised children, presumably from contamination in the pharmacy cabinet where both chemotherapy and BCG to treat patients were prepared.[48] Control measures during BCG preparation include a combined transfer/mixing device that eliminates aerosols; the use of an applicator that connects to the catheter for infusion also prevents exposure. The entire setup should be discarded as potentially infectious waste.[49] Cleaning of potentially contaminated surfaces should be with a tuberculocidal-rated disinfectant (e.g., phenolic-based) per manufacturer's instructions. Recommendations in the United Kingdom by the Control of Substances Hazardous to Health (COSHH) regulations for worker protection include PPE (plastic apron, gloves, and face visor), disposal of materials and PPE as "clinical waste," and use of a phenolic-based disinfectant on potentially contaminated surfaces. COSHH also recommends that voided urine containing BCG be treated with a phenol-based liquid mixed in the toilet for at least 10 minutes before flushing.[49] An alternative instruction to the patient after BCG bladder instillation is to "sit down to urinate for 6 hours after treatment to avoid splashing of the urine."[50] Directions state that after each urination "during this 6-hour period, pour household bleach (about the same amount of bleach as the amount of urine) into the toilet, then wait 15 minutes before flushing" and to wash hands afterward.[50]

Gene Therapy

As of May 2000 there were 425 gene therapy protocols worldwide, with approximately 70 percent of these in the United States.[51] Although human gene transfer and treatment had originally focused on genetic deficiency diseases, more than 60 percent of trials and activities since gene therapy products approved have been aimed at cancer.[52] The vectors used in gene therapy pose a potential infectious risk; for more than 3,100 patients treated, varied protocols were used for 177 retroviruses, 65 adenoviruses, 25 poxviruses, and 3 adeno-associated viruses. The remaining 109 treatments used lipofection and other noninfectious methods. Other vectors that have been proposed or used include Epstein-Barr, baculovirus, canarypox, fowlpox, herpes simplex, vesicular stomatitis, and HIV viruses.[52]

Information related to the safety of gene therapy in healthcare settings was introduced to most IPs in a 1999 article by Evans and Lesnaw.[53] The numerous recommendations included protection of healthcare personnel, other patients, and appropriate Transmission-based Precautions. These included suggestions that waste resulting from gene therapy be handled as biohazardous material and that disposal treatment should follow medical regulated waste protocols (i.e. incineration).[52] In some localities, regulations may require inactivation on-site prior to disposal.[53]

The U.S. Food and Drug Administrations' (FDA's) Center for Biologics Evaluation and Research regulates gene therapy research and trials with the objective to ensure safety.[54,55] The National Institutes of Health Recombinant DNA Advisory Committee provides protocol development oversight.[53,56] Federal supervision at the local level is by the Institutional Review Board and the Institutional Biosafety Committee, with optional input from the Infection Control Committee.[55] The CDC has not yet developed *infection prevention* guidelines for gene therapy.[54] The major goal for IPs is to prevent transmission of the vector or any recombinant vector between persons, including those handling and preparing the vectors (i.e., pharmacy). Therefore, the existing system recommended by the National Institutes of Health and CDC for biosafety levels and disinfectants should be referenced. Another concern is vector shedding that may occur inside and outside an isolation room from the treated patient, those caring for the patient, and others entering the patient's area, including housekeeping personnel. Protocols for safe transport of the vector product and items for disposal should be established and include training based on the vector and current knowledge of the vector.[53,54] Coordination with the waste disposal company may be required. If a healthcare facility is involved in gene therapy, the IP should be consulted and involved in policy and procedure development as well as education and training. Gene therapy and vectors are evolving, and the IP should follow current guidelines as appropriate to minimize potential risks related to handling and disposal. A biological safety officer position is suggested by some as a key member of any gene therapy trial team; the role includes ensuring appropriate handling of waste materials.[56]

Probiotics

Probiotics are beneficial and endogenous microflora that include live microbial supplements; they have been studied primarily for protection of the gut (e.g., *Lactobacillus*).[57,58] The use of probiotics continues to be explored in clinical settings. Probiotics may present side effects or risks for susceptible individuals, including infection, deleterious metabolic activity, excessive immune stimulation, and gene transfer; the latter three theoretic risks have not been reported in humans. The risk of infection is low, but cases have been observed, including fungemia with *Saccharomyces boulardii* and *Lactobacillus rhamnosus*.[59] Regulation and guidelines for probiotics are limited, with concern related to inclusion as dietary/food or pharmaceutical applications.[60,61] Forms used in clinical settings may be a closed capsule or a sachet that is opened and combined with enteral nutrition or drink for ingestion.[59] Probiotic microbial supplements may be given alone or in combination with prebiotics, selected additives that may enhance survival of the probiotic strain while stimulating the body's endogenous flora.[58] Safe handling, management, and disposal of the probiotic are necessary to minimize the risk of infection. Selecting a safe place for preparation, dispensing or mixing, and disposal of associated waste materials is crucial to minimize infectious risks, especially for areas with immunocompromised patients.[59]

Piped Systems Waste

Vacuum and suction systems are part of the medical gas systems and should not be overlooked in a waste management program. The installers, inspectors, and verifiers should be certified based on codes and regulations.[62] Piped suction/vacuum systems and disposal of associated liquids are considered biohazardous. Such systems may be used for suction of body fluids in surgical and procedure areas, dentistry, laboratories, and research settings.[62–64] The waste holding tank, part of the piped vacuum system, should be installed per recommendations, with the waste tank contents discarded through a drain into the sanitary sewer system.[62]

Laser plume and surgical smoke may be evacuated into the wall suction system in some locations. Analysis of surgical smoke and aerosols has shown that viable organisms can be present, including bacteria and viruses, in addition to numerous potentially hazardous chemicals.[63–65] A case of patient-to-patient transmission of human papillomavirus has been reported during a laser procedure.[64] Use of wall suction, even with in-line filtration, is only suitable for minimal amounts of plume; a smoke evacuator system with appropriate filtration system is preferred. In both situations, the in-line filters from wall suction and plume capture equipment should be treated and discarded as potentially infectious waste.[63,64]

Plumbing systems, specifically sanitary sewers, are approved for disposal of small amounts of blood and body fluids, as mentioned, provided procedures are in place to protect the worker.[6,8] A concern over pharmaceutical wastes, specifically antibiotics entering the sewer system, has been raised.[57,66] Stewardship and potential contribution to antibiotic resistance and environmental impact warrant further study.

Mixed or Multihazardous Wastes

The most stringent regulation should be used for handling and disposal when healthcare wastes are mixed; these may include infectious wastes that also contain hazardous chemicals or radionuclides.[1,13,19,22,30,67]

Chemotherapeutics

Handling and disposal of antineoplastic and cytotoxic drugs used for chemotherapy present potential risks for patients and workers. The drugs and related supplies should be addressed in the waste management plan.[7,57] Per the National Institute for Occupational Safety and Health, workers at risk of exposure to these hazardous drugs include "shipping and receiving personnel; pharmacists and pharmacy technicians; nursing personnel; physicians; operating room personnel; environmental services personnel; and personnel involved in veterinary practices where hazardous drugs are used."[68] Because these drugs are filtered and may be concentrated by the kidneys, urine from treated patients should be handled and discarded with care.[57,68]

Radioactive Materials

Facilities using radiopharmaceutical therapy must have specific procedures in place for the handling and disposal of radioactive wastes that may also contain bloodborne pathogens (i.e., those mixed with blood, body fluids, or tissues).[67] Although radioactive patient excreta released into the sanitary sewer is typically exempted from most regulatory requirements, the collection of the same radioactive excreta into a diaper requires that this previously not-included and unregulated waste must now be managed as radioactive waste. It is important to remain cognizant of other instances when potentially infectious materials contaminated with radioactive materials can become a waste management concern for the organization. Examples include the following:

- A patient with recent dosing experienced gastrointestinal bleeding and required emergency surgery with follow-up care in the intensive care unit. Staff may be exposed to blood and tissue that is radioactive (e.g., I-sodium iodide dose for thyroid ablation) and contains potential bloodborne pathogens.[69,70] Subsequent pathology and postmortem care may also require special handling of tissues and wastes.[69]

- Brachytherapy for the treatment of prostate cancer includes implantation of radioactive seeds into the prostate. Infection prevention and waste handling for the procedure area and subsequent follow-up with the patient in the clinic or at home must be considered if this treatment is provided.[71]

- Technetium 99-m labeling is used to identify sentinel nodes for surgical excision in cancer, such as for patients with melanoma or breast cancer. Specific procedures must be developed for this radioactive material in the surgical area and laboratory where excised tissue may be processed and discarded.[72]

Most hospitals have a radiation safety officer (RSO) or health physicist that is responsible for ensuring the safe use of radioactive materials. The RSO is an invaluable resource for the IP faced with a radioactive waste management concern and can provide guidance on effective means to manage potentially infectious waste contaminated with radioactive materials.

Emerging Infectious Agents and Potential Bioterrorism Agents

Selected agents, including microbes and biologicals, have been identified based on their risk to national security or public health, and each facility must have the capacity to destroy discarded cultures and stocks on-site.[6,21] The emergence of new infectious agents may present new challenges in waste disposal, especially when knowledge about a causative agent is limited and information about transmission or infectious nature is incomplete, such as was seen with severe acute respiratory syndrome coronavirus in the early 2000s. In these cases, stringent recommendations for waste handling and disposal are often implemented.[6,73] Tissues and certain wastes from prion diseases such as Creutzfeldt-Jakob disease and the variant strain causing bovine spongiform encephalopathy, commonly called mad cow disease, require special handling and disposal.[6] (Also see Chapters 96 Viral Hemorrhagic Fevers, and 73 Creutzfeldt-Jakob Disease and Other Prion Diseases.) Incineration with a minimum secondary temperature of 1,000°C or alkaline hydrolysis using pressurized 1 N NaOH or KOH at 150°C are two possible disposal methods for animal carcasses and other tissues suspected of containing prions.[21]

Potential bioterrorism agents, such as smallpox, have prompted guidance that includes waste handling and disposal.[74,75] For example, in smallpox vaccination plans, the handling and disposal of bifurcated needles, vaccination site dressings, and discarded unused vaccine must be addressed for safe waste management.[74] (Also see Chapter 120 Infectious Diseases Disasters.)

New Technologies for Waste Treatment

Many technologies are available or under development to treat or decontaminate regulated medical wastes. Methods reduce microbial load, and the final waste product does not need to be sterile prior to disposal.[6,13,20] Processes include autoclaving, incineration, internment (anatomic wastes), chemical disinfection, grinding/shredding/disinfection methods, energy-based technology (microwave or radio waves), disinfection/encapsulation, and disposal into a sanitary sewer.[6,35] Incineration is an effective method for treating most medical wastes and is appropriate for antineoplastics; however, it should not be used for radionuclides.[13,15,64,65] Regulation at federal and state levels, due to environmental impact, has limited the availability of incinerators, so alternative methodologies—both on-site and off-site—are being utilized.[13,30,33,35,76,77] Criteria for choosing treatment include suitability for types of waste, risks related to handling, effectiveness of treatment, uniformity or quality of process, costs (capital, operating, startup, labor, materials), success of process (experience of others using same method), occupational and environmental risks, reduction in waste volume and weight, community acceptance, and applicable regulatory compliance.[13]

Performance Improvement

To help assess the effectiveness of the waste management plan, performance improvement measurements can be used. For instance, The Joint Commission standards may be referenced when identifying and documenting a performance improvement activity.[9] Examples of performance improvement related to waste include (1) monitoring exposures to body fluids and sharps injuries related to disposals of contaminated needles; (2) monitoring of the "fullness" of needle boxes to indicate if the boxes are changed at proper intervals; and (3) evaluation of sorting waste appropriately with a visual audit or evaluation of contents in waste containers (appropriate precautions are required if the latter approach is used). Periodic audits of waste generation areas and accumulation points, including questioning of staff on appropriate waste management procedures, can help an organization identify opportunities for training and process improvements. Regardless of the performance improvement monitors selected, the data should be used to ensure the program is working. Data analysis and reports of performance improvement measures provide objective measures to verify the effectiveness of any corrective actions taken and identify opportunities for improvement. Cost-reduction strategies may follow the same strategy as outlined in a report by Garcia describing interventions and related improvement measurements to reduce the volume of waste.[78]

CONCLUSIONS

This chapter provides a brief historical overview and the practical information necessary for the appropriate management of wastes generated in healthcare settings that may present an infectious risk. "The most practical approach to medical waste management is to identify waste that represent[s] a sufficient potential risk of causing infection during handling and disposal and for which some precautions likely are prudent."[5] Additional information related to waste management is provided to assist the IP with other types of waste that may be found in today's varied healthcare settings.

FUTURE TRENDS

Costs for packaging, segregation, treatment, and disposal of infectious waste will likely increase in the future. Incineration will likely continue to decline as other treatment technologies develop and regulations on incinerators become more stringent. Scientific-based studies to characterize the risks associated with healthcare wastes will assist lawmakers in updating regulations. Recycling of some items currently categorized as infectious waste is under consideration, with estimates that between 30 to 50 percent of medical waste can be recycled. As stated by Daschner, "There are no infectious risks associated with recycling hospital waste."[79] Environmental stewardship will also prompt continued interest in interventions to minimize waste volume, such as reusable disposal containers. As resources become more limited and environmental concerns intensify, innovative approaches to managing healthcare wastes will continue to evolve.

INTERNATIONAL PERSPECTIVE

A review of the permutations and combinations of waste management systems in use throughout the international community is beyond the scope of this chapter. However, the literature suggests that waste management systems vary drastically from none at all to highly regulated functioning systems.[25,79-84] Many countries have considered the regulations and guidelines promulgated in the United States to help establish their own standards. Some countries have encountered "growing pains" similar to those the U.S. healthcare community went through in the 1980s and 1990s.

For example, in Great Britain, according to one author, digging a hole, burying medical waste, and then covering successive layers with lime is a common practice when items cannot be incinerated.[80] Problems associated with infectious waste disposal practices are compounded in undeveloped countries where trash may be dumped anywhere. Trash "pickers" commonly rummage through discarded trash to find usable or salable items.[81] Children are often involved, and this practice represents another source of infectious disease exposure beyond those caused by poor sanitation, lack of safe food and water, and poor medical care. Unfortunately, in some instances, the mismanagement of healthcare waste has caused some institutions in developing countries to give up single-use syringes in favor of reusable glass syringes. While this eliminates the waste management issues, it is causing the return of infections due to the use of unsterilized syringes.[4] The following are a few examples of general infectious waste issues that have been cited in the international literature:

- Absence of professional training in how to handle these wastes[81]

- So many other medical concerns that waste management, in general, is ignored[81]

- Licensing standards are unclear, conflicting, or confusing[31,82]

- Inadequate incineration/sterilization[82]

- No plans in place for collection and storage[82]

- Some have laws/regulations, but they are not enforced[82]

- Needles and syringes are commonly thrown in the regular trash[83]

- Lack of finances/resources prohibits implementation[84]

- No availability of technologies[84]

Those in the international community looking to implement a practical, scientific, infectious waste management program can refer to the body of this chapter in addition to references cited and the supplemental resources provided.

REFERENCES

1. Hedrick E. Editorial: infectious waste management—will science prevail? *Infect Control Hosp Epidemiol* 1988 Nov;9(11):488-490.
2. Keene JH. Medical waste: a minimal hazard. *Infect Control Hosp Epidemiol* 1991 Nov;12(11):682-685.
3. Rutala WA, Mayhall CG, The Society for Hospital Epidemiology of America. SHEA position paper: medical waste. *Infect Control Hosp Epidemiol* 1992;13(1):38-48.
4. Salkin IF. *Review of Health Impacts from Microbiological Hazards in Health-Care Wastes*. World Health Organization website. 2004. Available at: http://www.who.int/water_sanitation_health/medicalwaste/en/microbhazards0306.pdf.
5. Centers for Disease Control and Prevention (CDC), Department of Health and Human Services (DHHS). Infective Waste. In: *Guideline for Handwashing and Hospital Environmental Control*, 1985. Washington, DC: U.S. Government Printing Office, 1985 (updated January 21, 1997).
6. Sehulster L, Chinn RY, CDC, et al. *Guidelines for environmental infection control in health-care facilities: recommendations of CDC and the Healthcare Infection Control Practices Advisory Committee (HICPAC)*. Chicago: American Society for Healthcare Engineering, 2004. Available at: http://www.cdc.gov/mmwr/preview/mmwrhtml/rr5210a1.htm
7. Rutala WA, Odette RI, Samsa GP. Management of infectious waste by United States hospitals. *JAMA* 1989 Sep 22-29;262(12):1635-1640.
8. Occupational Safety and Health Administration. 29 CFR Part 1910.1030. Occupational exposure to bloodborne pathogens; needlesticks and other sharps injuries; final rule. *Fed Regist* 2001 Jan 18;66(12):5318-5325.
9. The Joint Commission. *Comprehensive Accreditation Manual for Hospitals*, 2013 ed. Oakbrook Terrace, IL: Joint Commission, 2013.
10. U.S. Environmental Protection Agency, Office of Solid Waste. Standards for the tracking and management of medical waste, Preamble and Rule, 40 CFR Parts 22 and 259. *Fed Regist* 1989;54:12327-12395.
11. *Regulated Medical Waste*. Code of Federal Regulations, Title 40, section 173.197.
12. Wideman JM. Points of contention in sharps injury prevention. *Infection Control Resource* 2004;2(4):1, 4-7.
13. Gordon JG, Reinhardt PA, Denys GA. Medical Waste Management. In: Mayhall CG, ed. *Hospital Epidemiology and Infection Control*, 3rd ed. Philadelphia: Lippincott Williams & Wilkins, 2004:1773-1785.
14. U.S. Postal Service (USPS). *DMM C023: Hazardous materials*. USPS website. Available at: http://pe.usps.com/archive/pdf/dmmarchive0810/c023.pdf.
15. Nuclear Regulatory Commission (NRC). Information on waste that contains radioactive materials. NRC website. Available at: http://www.nrc.gov.
16. Food and Drug Administration (FDA), Center for Devices and Radiological Health (CDRH). Class II medical devices. Available at: http://www.fda.gov/medicaldevices/deviceregulationandguidance/guidancedocuments/ucm080198.htm
17. Agency for Toxic Substances and Disease Registry. *The Public Health Implications of Medical Waste: A Report to Congress (PB91–100271)*. Springfield, VA: National Technical Information Service, 1990.
18. Medical Waste Tracking Act of 1988: 42 U.S.C. 6992 et seq. (amending the solid Waste Disposal Act). Washington, DC, 1988, Congressional Record.
19. U.S. Environmental Protection Agency, Office of Solid Waste. *EPA Guide for Infectious Waste Management (EPA/530-SW-86-014)*. Springfield, VA: National Technical Information Service, 1986.
20. Ott J. Biohazard waste reduction strategies for success. *Am J Infect Control* 1996;24(2):115.
21. Centers for Disease Control and Prevention (CDC), National Institutes of Health (NIH), Department of Health and Human Services (DHHS). *Biosafety in Microbiological and Biomedical Laboratories*, 5th ed. Washington, DC: U.S. Government Printing Office, 2007.
22. Clinical and Laboratory Standards Institute (formerly National Committee for Clinical Laboratory Standards, NCCLS). *Clinical Laboratory Waste Management: Approved Guideline*, 3rd ed. GP05-A3. Wayne, PA: CLSI, 2011.
23. Noble MA. Prevention and Control of Laboratory-acquired Infections. In: Versalovic J, ed. *Manual of Clinical Microbiology*, 10th ed. Washington, DC: ASM Press, 2011. ASMscience website. Available at: http://www.asmscience.org/content/book/10.1128/9781555816728.
24. U.S. Department of Health and Human Services (DHHS), Public Health Service (PHS), Centers for Disease Control and Prevention (CDC), et al. *Selecting, Evaluating, and Using Sharps Disposal Containers. Department of Health and Human Services National Institute for Occupational Safety and Health (NIOSH) Publication 97–111*. Atlanta, GA: Department of Health and Human Services; 1998. Available at: http://www.cdc.gov/niosh/docs/97-111/.
25. Almuneef M, Memish ZA. Effective medical waste management: it can be done. *Am J Infect Control* 2003 May;31(3):188-192.
26. American Society for Hospital Engineering, American Hospital Association (AHA). *Hazardous Waste Management Strategies for Health Care Facilities*. Chicago, IL: AHA, 1987.
27. National Institute for Health and Clinical Excellence. *Infection: prevention and control of healthcare-associated infections in primary and community care*. National Clinical Guideline Centre; 2012:112-115.

28. Melamed A. Environmental accountability in perioperative settings. *AORN J* 2003 Jun;77(6):1157–1168.
29. Department of Transportation (DOT). *49 CFR Parts 171–179, Hazardous Materials*, 2012.
30. U.S. Environmental Protection Agency (EPA), Office of Solid Waste. *Medical Waste Management in the United States*. EPA/530-SW-90–051A. Washington, DC: U.S. Government Printing Office, 1990.
31. Occupational Safety and Health Administration (OSHA). Fact Sheet. *Protecting Yourself When Handling Contaminated Sharps*; 2011. Available at: https://www.osha.gov/OshDoc/data_BloodborneFacts/bbfact02.pdf.
32. Blumstein S, Zeller J, Sharbaugh B. APIC commentary on "Healthcare waste management: a template for action." *Am J Infect Control* 2000; 28(2):E1.
33. Karpiak BA, Pugliese G. Medical waste: declining options in the 90s. *Am J Infect Control* 1991 Feb;19(1):8–15.
34. Office of Technology Assessment (OTA), Congress of the U.S. *Finding the Rx for Managing Medical Wastes: OTA Special Report on Medical Waste Treatment Technologies*. Washington, DC: OTA, 1990.
35. Weisman E. Incinerator rule ignites interest in alternative waste methods. *Health Facil Manage* 1995 Feb;8(2):81–2, 84–85.
36. Occupational Safety and Health Administration (OSHA). *OSHA Technical manual: Section VI, Chapter 2: Controlling occupational exposure to hazardous drugs*. OSHA website. Available at: https://www.osha.gov/dts/osta/otm/otm_vi/otm_vi_2.html .
37. Department of Transportation (DOT). *Information on regulations and requirements for transport of regulated medical waste and hazardous materials*. Available at: http://www.dot.gov.
38. Scheckler WE, Brimhall D, Buck AS, et al. Requirements for infrastructure and essential activities of infection control and epidemiology in hospitals: A consensus panel report. Society for Healthcare Epidemiology of America. *Am J Infect Control* 1998 Feb;26(1):47–60.
39. American Institute of Architects, Academy of Architecture for Health, Facilities Guideline Institute. *2010 Guidelines for Design and Construction of Health Care Facilities*. Washington, DC: American Institute of Architects Press, 2010.
40. Neely AN, Maley MP, Taylor GL. Investigation of single-use versus reusable infectious waste containers as potential sources of microbial contamination. *Am J Infect Control* 2003 Feb;31(1):13–17.
41. Runner JC. Bacterial and viral contamination of reusable sharps containers in a community hospital setting. *Am J Infect Control* 2007 Oct;35(8):527–530.
42. Grimmond T, Rings T, Taylor C, et al. Sharps injury reduction using SharpsmartTM—a reusable sharps management system. *J Hosp Infect* 2003 Jul;54(3):232–238.
43. Morales A, Eidinger D, Bruce AW. Intracavitary bacillus Calmette-Guérin in the treatment of superficial bladder tumors. *J Urol* 1976 Aug;116(2):180–183.
44. Associated Press. *Government approves bacteria treatment for bladder cancer*, May 21, 1990. Available at: http://www.apnewsarchive.com/1990/Government-Approves-Bacteria-Treatment-for-Bladder-Cancer/id-d19fe8101f65bd222da339f47f4741e0.
45. Gonzalez OY, Musher DM, Brar I, et al. Spectrum of Bacille Calmette-Guérin (BCG) infection after intravesical BCG immunotherapy. *Clin Infect Dis* 2003 Jan 15;36(2):140–148.
46. Steinberg G, Bahnson R, Brosman S, et al. Efficacy and safety of valrubicin for the treatment of Bacillus Calmette-Guérin refractory carcinoma in situ of the bladder. *J Urol* 2000 Mar;163(3):761–767.
47. Smith JA Jr, Labasky RF, Cockett ATK, et al. Bladder Cancer Clinical Guidelines Panel summary report on the management of nonmuscle invasive bladder cancer (stages Ta, T1 and TIS). *J Urol* 1999 Nov;162(5):1697–1701.
48. Cumisky S. BCG immunotherapy for carcinoma of the urinary bladder. *Nurs Stand* 2000 May 31-Jun 6;14(37):45–47.
49. Stone MM, Vannier AM, Storch SK, et al. Brief report: meningitis due to iatrogenic BCG infection in two immunocompromised children. *N Engl J Med* 1995 Aug 31;333(9):561–563.
50. WebMD. BCG Vaccine—Intravesical—how to use BCG Live IVes. Available at: http://www.webmd.com/drugs.
51. Strausbaugh LJ. Gene therapy and infection control: more light on the way. *Infect Control Hosp Epidemiol* 2000 Oct;21(10):630–632.
52. Evans ME, Jordan CT, Chang SMW, et al. Clinical infection control in gene therapy: a multidisciplinary conference. *Infect Control Hosp Epidemiol* 2000 Oct;21(10):659–673.
53. Evans ME, Lesnaw JA. Infection control in gene therapy. *Infect Control Hosp Epidemiol* 1999 Aug;20(8):568–576.
54. Simpson J, Stoner NS. Implications of gene therapy for hospital pharmacists. *Pharm J* 2003;27:127–130.
55. Evans ME, Lesnaw JA. Infection control for gene therapy: a busy physician's primer. *Clin Infect Dis* 2002 Sep 1;35(5):597–605.
56. Bamford KB, Wood S, Shaw RJ. Standards for gene therapy clinical trials based on pro-active risk assessment in a London NHS Teaching Hospital Trust. *QJM.* 2005 Feb;98(2):75–86.
57. Daughton CG. Cradle-to-cradle stewardship of drugs for minimizing their environmental disposition while promoting human health. II. Drug disposal, waste reduction, and future directions. *Environ Health Perspect* 2003 May;111(5):775–785.
58. Anderson ADG, McNaught CE, Jain PK, et al. Randomised clinical trial of symbiotic therapy in elective surgical patients. *Gut* 2004 Feb;53(2):241–245.
59. Marteau P, Seksik P. Tolerance of probiotics and prebiotics. *J Clin Gastroenterol* 2004 Jul;38(6 Suppl):S67–S69.
60. Prevot MB. New regulatory trends for probiotics. *J Clin Gastroenterol* 2004 Jul;38(6 Suppl):S61–3.
61. Joint FAO/WHO Working Group Report on Drafting Guidelines for the Evaluation of Probiotics in Food. *Guidelines for the Evaluation of Probiotics in Food.* FAO/WHO 2002. Available at: ftp://ftp.fao.org/es/esn/food/wgreport2.pdf.
62. NFPA International. NFPA 99 Health Facilities Code, 2012 ed. Quincy, MA: National Fire Protection Association, 2012.
63. Association of periOperative Registered Nurses Recommended Practices Committee. Recommended practices for electrosurgery, *AORN J* 2004 Feb;79(2):432–4, 437–42, 445–50 passim.
64. Anderson K. Safe use of lasers in the operating room: what perioperative nurses should know. *AORN J* 2004 Jan;79(1):171–188.
65. National Institutes for Occupational Safety and Health. *Control of Smoke From Laser/Electric Surgical Procedures. Department of Health and Human Services (NIOSH) Publication.* Atlanta, GA: NIOSH, 1996;96–128.
66. Daughton CG. Cradle-to-cradle stewardship of drugs for minimizing their environmental disposition while promoting human health. I. Rationale for and avenues toward a green pharmacy. *Environ Health Perspect* 2003 May;111(5):757–774.
67. Nuclear Regulatory Commission (NRC). *Regulatory guide 10.8, Revision 2—guide for the preparation of applications for medical use programs.* 2008. NRC website. Available at: http://pbadupws.nrc.gov/docs/ML0819/ML081960579.pdf.
68. National Institutes for Occupational Safety and Health (NIOSH). *Preventing occupational exposures to antineoplastic and other hazardous drugs in healthcare settings.* September 2004. NIOSH website. Available at: http://www.cdc.gov/niosh/docs/2004-165/.
69. Griffiths PA, Jones GP, Marshall C, et al. Radiation protection consequences of the care of a terminally ill patient having received a thyroid ablation dose of 131I-sodium iodide. *Br J Radiol* 2000 Nov;73(875):1209–1212.
70. Denman AR, Martin S. Care of a terminally ill patient following a thyroid ablation dose of 131I-sodium iodide. *Br J Radiol* 2001 Nov;74(887):1077–1078.
71. Davis DL. Prostate cancer treatment with radioactive seed implantation. *AORN J* 1998 Jul;68(1):18, 21–23, 26–30 passim; quiz 42, 45.
72. Colgan TJ, Booth D, Hendler A, et al. Appropriate procedures for the safe handling and pathologic examination of technetium-99m-labelled specimens. *CMAJ* 2001 Jun 26;164(13):1868–1871.
73. Centers for Disease Control and Prevention (CDC). *Public Health Guidance for Community-Level Preparedness and Response to Severe Acute Respiratory Syndrome (SARS)—version 2/3.* CDC website. April 16, 2013. Available at: http://www.cdc.gov/sars/index.html.
74. Fulginiti VA, Papier A, Lane JM, et al. Smallpox vaccination: a review, part I. Background, vaccination technique, normal vaccination and revaccination, and expected normal reactions. *Clin Infect Dis* 2003 Jul 15;37(2):241–250.
75. Nolte KD, Hanzlick RL, Payne DC, et al. Medical examiners, coroners, and biologic terrorism: a guidebook for surveillance and case management. *MMWR Recomm Rep* 2004 Jun 11;53(RR-8):1–27.
76. Health Care Without Harm. *Non-incineration Medical Waste Treatment Technologies—A Resource for Hospital Administrators, Facility Managers, Health Care Professionals, Environmental Advocates, and Community Members.* Washington, DC: Health Care Without Harm, 2001.
77. State and Territorial Association on Alternate Treatment Technologies. *Technical Assistance Manual: State Regulatory Oversight of Medical Waste Treatment Technologies.* The Association, April 1994.
78. Garcia R. Effective cost-reduction strategies in the management of regulated medical waste. *Am J Infect Control* 1999 Apr;27(2):165–175.
79. Daschner F. The Hospital and Pollution: Role of the Hospital Epidemiologist in Protecting the Environment. In: Wenzel RP, ed. *Prevention and Control of Nosocomial Infections*, 3rd ed. Baltimore, MD: Williams and Wilkins, 1997:595–605.
80. Mehtar S. *Hospital Infection Control—Setting Up a Cost-effective Programme.* New York, NY: Oxford University Press, 1992:33–42.
81. Akter N, Hussain Z, Trankler J, et al. Hospital waste management and its probable health effect: a lesson learned from Bangladesh. *Indian J Environ Health* 2002 Apr;44(2):124–137.

82. Watanabe N. Present state of the medical waste disposal industry: self-regulation and trends of the industry for the future. *Rinsho Byori [Japanese Journal of Clinical Pathology]* 2000 May;Suppl 112:47–52.

83. Janjua NZ. Infection practices and sharp waste disposal by general practitioners of Murree, Pakistan. *JPMA J Pak Med Assoc* 2003 Mar;53(3):107–111.

84. Patil AD, Sherdar AV. Health-care waste management in India. *J Environ Manage* 2001 Oct;63(2):211–220.

SUPPLEMENTAL RESOURCES

American Society of Gene & Cell Therapy. Available at: http://www.asgt.org.

American Urological Association. Available at: http://www.auanet.org.

Agency for Toxic Substances and Disease Registry (ATSDR). Available at: http://www.atsdr.cdc.gov.

Association for Professionals in Infection Control and Epidemiology (APIC). Available at: http://www.apic.org.

Canadian Standards Association . Z317.10-09 Standard: Handling of Waste Materials in Health Care Facilities and Veterinary Health Care Facilities; 2009. Available at: http://www.csagroup.org.

Centers for Disease Control and Prevention (CDC). Workbook for Designing, Implementing, and Evaluating a Sharps Injury Prevention Program. Available at: http://www.cdc.gov/sharpssafety/index.html.

Centers for Disease Control and Prevention (CDC). Primary Containment of Biohazards. Selection, Installation and Use of Biological Safety Cabinets. Appendix A in BMBL 5th Edition. 2009. Available at: http://www.cdc.gov/od/ohs/.

Clinical and Laboratory Standards Institute (formerly National Committee for Clinical Laboratory Standards, NCCLS). Available at: http://www.clsi.org.

European Association of Urology. *Guidelines on Bladder Cancer.* Available at: http://www.uroweb.org/guidelines/online-guidelines/.

Friedman C, Petersen KH. *Infection Control in Ambulatory Care.* Sudbury, MA: Jones and Bartlett Publishers, 2004.

Healthcare Environmental Resource Center (HERC). Available at: http://www.hercenter.org.

International POPS Elimination Network. IPEN is a global network of public interest nongovernmental organizations united in support of a common Persistent Organic Pollutants Elimination Platform. Available at: http://www.ipen.org.

National Institutes of Health (NIH). Available at: http://www.nih.gov.

National Institutes of Health (NIH). Guide to waste disposal website. Available at: http://orf.od.nih.gov/EnvironmentalProtection/WasteDisposal/Pages/default.aspx.

Physicians for Social Responsibility (PSR) is a leading public policy organization representing the medical and public health professions and concerned citizens, working together for a healthful environment and other concerns. Available at: http://www.psr.org.

U.S. Department of Transportation (DOT). Available at: http://www.dot.gov.

U.S. Environmental Protection Agency (EPA). Available at: http://www.epa.gov.

U.S. Occupational Safety and Health Administration (OSHA). Available at: http://www.osha.gov.

U.S. Postal Service. Domestic Mail Manual (DMM) Issue 58 plus Postal Bulletin changes through PB 22125 (4–1–04) and C024—Other Restricted or Non-Mailable Matter are Available at: http://pe.usps.gov.

World Health Organization (WHO). Laboratory Biosafety Manual, 3rd ed. Revised. 2004. Available at: http://www.who.int/en.

World Health Organization (WHO). Waste From Health-Care Activities. Fact sheet no. 253. WHO; 2007. Available at: http://www.who.int/en.

World Health Organization (WHO). Health-care waste management. Fact sheet no. 281. WHO; 2011. Available at: http://www.who.int/en.

World Health Organization (WHO). Policy Paper: Safe Health-care Waste Management. 2004. Available at: http://www.who.int/water_sanitation_health/medicalwaste/hcwmpolicy/en/.

CHAPTER **114**

Heating, Ventilation, and Air Conditioning

Russell N. Olmsted, MPH, CIC
Epidemiologist, Infection Control Services
Saint Joseph Mercy Health System
Ann Arbor, MI

ABSTRACT

This chapter addresses the role of infection prevention and control in the environment with a specific focus on heating, ventilation, and air conditioning systems in healthcare facilities. Maintaining both comfort and safety of indoor air quality in healthcare facilities is essential for all occupants. Specifically, poor design and installation, system performance problems, and inadequate maintenance of heating, ventilation, and air conditioning systems have all been associated with transmission of airborne infectious agents and/or building-associated illness. Environmental containment/mitigation of airborne infectious agents (e.g., Mycobacterium tuberculosis, Aspergillus spp., varicella zoster and measles viruses, plus newly emergent pathogens such as severe acute respiratory syndrome-associated coronavirus) and preparedness for deliberate use of pathogens as bioweapons are vital areas the infection preventionist can provide expertise for their affiliated facility.

KEY CONCEPTS

- Understanding the terminology and knowing how to assess and evaluate heating, ventilation, and air conditioning systems has become part of the infection preventionist's set of skills needed to prevent and control transmission of airborne infectious agents.

- This chapter should be reviewed in conjunction with Chapter 115 Water Systems Issues and Prevention of Waterborne Infectious Diseases in Healthcare Facilities, and Chapter 116 Construction and Renovation, because many of these systems are interrelated. This chapter considers examples of ventilation-associated health hazards, regulatory agencies impacting or setting standards for ventilation specifications, and environmental monitoring.

- Details of ventilation requirements for specialty areas of healthcare facilities are included to assist with planning and design activities.

BACKGROUND

Basic Features of a Heating, Ventilation, and Air Conditioning System

The impact of ventilation on health in any setting is far-reaching and is an essential component of the infection control risk assessment (ICRA) and associated risk mitigation interventions described in Chapter 116 Construction and Renovation. Therefore, a basic understanding of key terms, concepts, and effects on the health of patients and healthcare personnel (HCP) is essential to providing appropriate input into the ICRA and assuring the heating, ventilation, and air conditioning (HVAC) system is providing as safe and comfortable an environment as possible.

HVAC describes a facility's overall air handling system: heating, ventilation, and air conditioning. Indoor air ventilation or HVAC systems supply, filter, condition (heat, cool, humidify, dehumidify), and exhaust air by a variety of design schemes. A core component of a centralized HVAC system is an air handling unit (AHU), which most often is located on a roof or in a mechanical room. Decentralized approaches in separate rooms often utilize individual fan coil units that are usually installed under windows, draw air through grills on outside walls, and mix outside air with recirculated air within the room. Both systems have infection prevention and control implications for indoor air quality (IAQ) and infection prevention and control issues related to ventilation problems. Typical components of an HVAC system are illustrated in Figure 114-1.

Additional discussion of HVAC system design are available in other resources.[1-3] Numerous studies identifying problems such as clusters or increased rates of building-associated infections attributed to HVAC systems have been described and are reviewed in this chapter.[4-11]

BASIC PRINCIPLES

Cross-transmission of Airborne Infections in Healthcare Facilities Involving Heating, Ventilation, and Air Conditioning

Although infrequent, HVAC systems can be a source of exposure and infection caused by airborne infectious agents. Specifically, airborne opportunistic pathogens or saprophytes from other reservoirs may present a hazard in general patient areas, the operating room (OR), central decontamination and

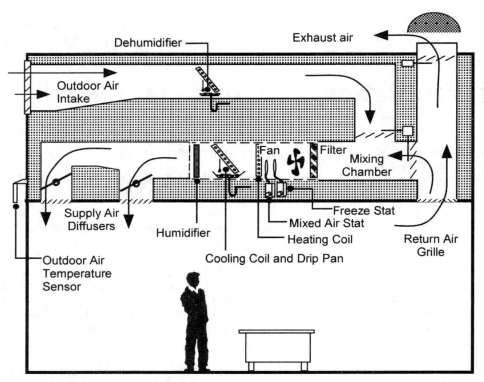

Figure 114-1. Typical HVAC system components. (From Centers for Disease Control and Prevention (CDC). Building air quality: A guide for building owners and facility managers. Appendix B: HVAC Systems and Indoor Air Quality, 1991. EPA Publication No. 400/1-91/003. CDC website. 2013. Available at: http://www.cdc.gov/niosh/baqtoc.html.)

sterilization centers, and diagnostic procedure rooms as well as in kitchens and general waiting rooms.[1-14] *Aspergillus, Rhizopus,* and *Penicillium* species, as well as fungi from other sources, may be hazardous to immunosuppressed patients.[15] Moisture-associated fungi such as *Acremonium kiliense* may contaminate an air handler and spread to patients through ventilation systems.[1,4,11,16,17] *Legionella* spp. from nearby environmental water sources may enter hospital water systems, multiply in cooling towers and evaporative condensers, and contaminate the potable water system.[1,4] The following examples of reported clusters of infections caused by various microorganisms illustrate the role HVAC systems have played in each:

- Neonatal intensive care unit (NICU) ventilation: *Rhizopus* and *Aspergillus* species were implicated in premature infants with pulmonary abscesses identified at autopsy. The outbreak was associated with fungi recovered from environmental sampling in the NICU near a construction area. Ventilation, dust above false ceilings, and ineffective barriers were all associated with the outbreak.[18]

- Cardiac surgery: An outbreak of *Aspergillus* endocarditis following open-heart surgery implicated the OR ventilation system. Investigation found the aspergilli to be ubiquitous. Critical issues included location of air intake, filtration efficiency, and number of air changes. Improving the ventilation standards to those recommended at the time appeared to prevent any new cases.[19]

- Hematology unit: An outbreak of *Aspergillus* infection among patients with leukemia or bone marrow transplantation was found to be associated with various construction-associated factors including ventilation. Interventions that appeared to control the outbreak included sealing of windows, installing nonperforated ceiling tiles, use of high-efficiency particulate air (HEPA) filter air purifiers, and other dust-reducing methods.[20]

- Surgical suite: *Cladosporium* and *Penicillium* spp. were associated with major problems in surgical suite ventilation, showing the importance of designing and maintaining HVAC systems. Important issues included the role of contaminated duct linings, need for filter replacement, and sealed windows.[13]

- Hospital: Healthcare-associated transmission of multidrug-resistant *M. tuberculosis* involved at least 13 patients in a New York hospital. Before full implementation of Centers for Disease Control and Prevention (CDC) guidelines, only 1 of 16 isolation rooms tested was under negative pressure. Many factors were identified and addressed, but installation of proper air-handling equipment and related monitoring were identified as major contributing factors in ending the outbreak.[21]

Several outbreaks representing the role of various organism and epidemiologic methods to resolve them are described in Table 114-1.[7,11-13,17,22-28] It is worth noting that association of

Table 114-1. Illustrative Studies on Impact of Microbial Contamination of Air Handling Systems and Interventions

| Year—Author (Reference) | Airborne Contaminants | | | |
	Organism	Population	Epidemiological Factors	Remedial or Preventive Measures
1986 Opal et al.[22]	*Aspergillus* spp.	BMT	Construction activity	Sealed barriers; HEPA filter; antifungal
1987 Streifel et al.[12]	*Penicillium* spp.	BMT	Moisture; rotted wood cabinet; fungal release	Replace with nonporous surfaces around sink
1987 Weems et al.[11]	*Rhizopus; Mucor* spp.	Hematological BMT	Construction activity, dust, traffic, HVAC	Construction plans: HVAC; sealed barriers to window infiltration
1990 Fox et al.[13]	*Penicillium* spp.; *Cladosporium* spp.	OR	Ventilation duct lined; contaminated fiberglass insulation	Decontamination of HVAC ductwork; filter replacement
1992 Hruszkewycz et al.[7]	*Penicillium* spp. *Aspergillus* spp.	Laboratory pseudo-outbreak	Improper airflow during renovation near lab; false ceiling in work area	Sealed ceilings; proper use of hoods and appropriate airflow controls
1994 Iwen et al.[23]	*Aspergillus* spp. Mixed fungi	BMT Unit	Improper airflow; suspected infiltration from windows	Sealed windows and balanced airflow; replaced HEPA filters
1996 Anderson et al.[24]	*Aspergillus* spp.	Pediatric oncology unit	Improper airflow from clinical waste disposal room	Sealing disposal room; HEPA filtered vacuum cleaners
1994 Pittet et al.[25]	*Aspergillus* spp.	COPD	Air filter replacement	Replace and monitor filter function
1998 Kumari et al.[26]	*Methicillin*-resistant *S. aureus*	Orthopedic patients	Ventilation grills	Cleaned, maintained pressure relationships
1997 Dearborn et al.[27]	*Stachybotrys atra*	Infants	Water damaged homes; suspected airborne toxin	Rapid/vigorous cleaning/ decontaminate with diluted bleach
1996 Fridkin et al.[17]	*Acremonium kiliensis*	Ambulatory surgery–system	Poorly designed HVAC; contaminated humidifier	Redesign; changed HEPA filters; proper HVAC maintenance
2002 Anaissie et al.[28]	*Aspergillus* spp.	BMT	Concentration of airborne fungi on shower surfaces	Clean shower floor with detergent prior to use of shower

disease with recovery of *Stachybotrys* from the environment has been re-examined in a recent review that identified flaws in the epidemiologic analysis of earlier studies of hemosiderosis in infants.[27,29] As a result, experts have not found well-substantiated supportive evidence of serious illness owing to *Stachybotrys atra* exposure in the contemporary environment. These earlier investigations now appear misleading; however, that has not deterred medicolegal claims from making it the 21st century "asbestos" problem.

VENTILATION STANDARDS, DESIGN, INTERVENTIONS, AND OUTCOMES

Regulations and Standards

Regulatory and accrediting agencies base licensing and/or certification decisions on whether facilities meet minimum construction standards. Agencies and professional groups concerned with HVAC design are similar to those involved with construction.

The broadest source of authority affecting ventilation design and implementation is the *2006 Guidelines for Design and Construction of Health Care Facilities*. This consensus document is written and published by the Facility Guidelines Institute (FGI) and the American Institute of Architects (AIA) Academy of Architecture for Health/Facility Guidelines Institute with assistance from the U.S. Department of Health and Human Services (HHS).[30] The content of this consensus document is updated every 3 to 4 years by

the FGI. Beginning with the 2010 edition, the Guidelines will be published by the American Society for Healthcare Engineering (ASHE) and FGI with assistance from HHS and should be referenced as the FGI Guidelines. In this chapter they will be referred to as the FGI/AIA Guidelines. Most states in the United States adopt these Guidelines in their entirety or with some modifications as minimum standards for design and construction of healthcare facilities in their respective states. The FGI/AIA guidelines rely heavily on input from many professional and guideline-setting organizations such The Joint Commission (TJC).[31]

Other guidelines, recommendations, and standards related to HVAC systems include:

- American Society of Heating, Refrigerating, and Air-Conditioning Engineers (ASHRAE): (1) Ventilation and filtration tables[32,33]; (2) ANSI/ASHRAE/ASHE Standard 170, Ventilation of Health Care Facilities, is a new standard that closely mirrors parameters in 2006 FGI Guidelines. FGI and ASHRAE are collaborating closely to adopt a single, unified table that describes design parameters for HVAC systems.[33]

- The CDC and its federal research agency, the National Institute for Occupational Safety and Health (NIOSH): ventilation requirements for negative air-pressure rooms, design and ventilation recommendations for positive air-pressure rooms, construction and renovation recommendations, and design of HVAC to mitigate risks from airborne chemical, biological, or radiological attacks.[1,4,5,34,35]

- National Fire Protection Association (NFPA): selected NFPA codes and standards are critical elements incorporated into the FGI/AIA Guidelines and enforced by all accreditors and regulators.[30]

- The Centers for Medicare & Medicaid Services (CMS) Conditions of Participation for Medicare and Medicaid (CoP): whereas the "physical environment" and ventilation standards include the NFPA codes, they are broadly stated. Interpretations are usually based on federal and state construction codes developed from the FGI/AIA Guidelines as noted.[36]

- State authorities having jurisdiction (AHJs): provide necessary assistance in the interpretation of federal and/or FGI/AIA Guidelines with individual state requirements. State health departments managing the plan and review function are important to the consensus review process.[3,37]

- Occupational Safety and Health Administration (OSHA): enforces aspects of air quality that may present hazards to HCP such as tuberculosis (TB) and legionellosis but also other contaminants present in the air in hospitals to include waste anesthetic gases and vapors from select chemicals.[38] Although OSHA withdrew its proposed TB standard in May 2003, it enforces aspects of air quality that may present hazards to employees, such as TB, under the auspices of the "general duty clause" using related compliance documents, or specific standards, as applicable. State regulations must be equally as effective as those required by OSHA.[39-41]

- Environmental Protection Agency (EPA): has standards related to medical waste and air contamination (e.g., incinerators and emissions) that are considered for air-intake design and placement (see Supplemental Resources). The EPA also has published or sponsored several resources related to indoor air quality and control/response to instances of mold contamination in buildings.[42]

- Voluntary accreditation agencies: for example, TJC, American Osteopathic Association (AOA), and the National Committee for Quality Assurance (NCQA).

As noted, FGI/AIA Guidelines have been adopted by TJC in its environment of care (EOC) standards, but as of 2009, TJC continues to reference the 2001 edition specifically in the Statement of Conditions that are prepared by each facility. TJC updated the EOC standards with explicit requirements for utility management that have a direct relationship with the FGI/AIA Guidelines and explicitly reference infection prevention and control issues in the intent of the EOC standards. In 2002, TJC added a requirement for performing an ICRA. They also modified the EOC standards in all accreditation manuals. TJC has stated its intent to enforce their standards in light of the 2010 Guidelines after publication in early 2010. Other agencies and managed care organizations may develop their own physical facility standards for outpatient clinics and other care sites based on CMS/CoP or indirectly on the Guidelines.[1,4,5,30,31,36] (See Chapter 4 Accrediting and Regulatory Agencies.)

Heating, Ventilation, and Air Conditioning Basic Design and Terminology

Some HVAC systems are designed to supply 100 percent outdoor (fresh) air, whereas others mix a percentage of the exhaust air (subject to code allowances) with supply air from the outdoors to save on operational costs. The air is conditioned by passing through filters and is heated/cooled, and humidified/dehumidified through the HVAC apparatus before distribution.[30,43]

Air Source

Outdoor Air

The major reason for pulling fresh, outdoor air is dilution of microbial contamination, gases, and odor control.

Recirculated Air

Given current use of nonflammable anesthesia gases, even ORs may conserve energy and use a portion of recirculated air. If any form of variable air volume (VAV) is used for energy conservation, it must not compromise the corridor-to-room pressure balancing relationships or the minimum air changes described in the 2006 Guidelines.[30] (See Table 2.1-2 of the 2006 Guidelines for specific restrictions.) Tables 114-2 and 114-3 are based on the 2006 Guidelines, Tables 2.1-2 and 2.1-3, and summarize the design specifications related to air changes and filtration. It should be noted that Table 2.1-2 describes specifications only for hospitals and ambulatory care. Chapter 3 of the 2006 Guidelines contains a similar table that is applicable to nursing homes and other long-term care facilities. Importantly, the HVAC parameters in the 2006 Guidelines, reproduced in this chapter, specify design—not operational—parameters for this utility system. The rationale is that given the wide variation in climate for various geographic regions in the United States, it would be impractical to require continuous, ongoing monitoring of air exchange, temperature, and humidity for all facilities. These latter aspects are operational—meaning, the facility-based personnel determine how often and with what mechanism these need to be monitored.

Air Changes

Air changes per hour (ACH), or the ventilation rate, are the number of times the air volume of a given space is replaced in a 1-hour period and includes sufficient changes of outside air to dilute microbial contamination and gases. Studies have shown that a minimum of two ACH of outside air is all that is needed to remove odors. However, recent work has shown that for comfort the total number in patient rooms should be six ACH. As noted in the appendix to Table 114-2 and Chapter 116 Construction and Renovation, this can be modified under certain conditions.[30,44,45] There are no standards or guidelines governing the frequency of ACH measurements for specialty areas (e.g., surgical suite or airborne infection isolation [AII] rooms). An organization should determine its own inspection and maintenance schedule based on facility-specific data. Some

Table 114-2. Ventilation Requirements for Areas Affecting Patient Care in Hospitals and Outpatient Facilities[1]*

Area Designation	Air Movement Relationship to Adjacent Area[2]	Minimum Air Changes (AC) of Outdoor Air/hr[3]	Minimum Total AC/hr[4,5]	All Air Exhausted Directly to Outdoors[6]	Recirculation by Means of Room Units[7]	Relative Humidity[8] (%)	Design Temperature[9] (°F/C)
Nursing							
Patient room	—	2	6[10]	—	—	—	70–75 (21–24)
Toilet room	In	2	10	Yes	—	—	—
Newborn nursery suite	—	2	6	—	No	30–60	72–78 (22–26)
Protective environment room[11]	Out	2	12	—	No	—	75 (24)
Airborne infection isolation room[11]	In	2	12	Yes[12]	No	—	70–75 (21–24)
Isolation alcove or anteroom	In/out	—	10	Yes	No	—	—
Patient corridor	—	—	2	—	—	—	—
Obstetrical facilities							
Delivery room[13]	Out	3	15	—	No	30–60	68–73 (20–23)
Labor/delivery/ recovery	—	2	6[10]	—	—	—	70–75 (21–24)
Labor/delivery/ recovery/ postpartum	—	2	6[10]	—	—	—	70–75 (21–24)
Emergency, surgery, and critical care							
Operating/surgical cystoscopic rooms[11,13]	Out	3	15	—	No	30–60	68–73 (20–23)[14]
Recovery rooms[13]	—	2	6	—	No	30–60	70 (21)
Critical and intensive care	—	2	6	—	No	30–60	70–75 (21–24)
Intermediate care	—	2	6[10]	—	—	—	70–75 (21–24)
Newborn intensive care	—	2	6	—	No	30–60	72–78 (22–26)
Treatment room[15]	—	—	6	—	—	—	75 (24)
Trauma room[15]	Out	3	15	—	No	30–60	70–75 (21–24)
Bronchoscopy[11]	In	2	12	Yes	No	30–60	68–73 (20–23)
Triage	In	2	12	Yes[16]	—	—	70–75 (21–24)
ER waiting rooms	In	2	12	Yes[12,16]	—	—	70–75 (21–24)
Procedure rooms	Out	3	15	—	No	30–60	70–75 (21–24)
Laser eye room	Out	3	15		No	30–60	70–75 (21–24)
X-ray (surgical/ critical care and catheterization)	Out	3	15		No	30–60	70–75 (21–24)
Anesthesia gas storage	In	—	8		—	—	—
Support areas							
Medication room	Out	—	4		—	—	
Clean workroom or clean holding	Out	—	4		—	—	
Soiled workroom or soiled holding	In	—	10		No	—	
Diagnostic and treatment							
Examination room	—	—	6		—	—	
Treatment room	—	—	6		—	—	

(continued)

Table 114-2. Ventilation Requirements for Areas Affecting Patient Care in Hospitals and Outpatient Facilities[1]* *(continued)*

Area Designation	Air Movement Relationship to Adjacent Area[2]	Minimum Air Changes (AC) of Outdoor Air/hr[3]	Minimum Total AC/hr[4,5]	All Air Exhausted Directly to Outdoors[6]	Recirculation by Means of Room Units[7]	Relative Humidity[8] (%)	Design Temperature[9] (°F/C)
Physical therapy and hydrotherapy	In	—	6	—	—	—	
Gastrointestinal endoscopy room	—	2	6	—	No	30–60	
Endoscopic instrument processing room[17]	In	—	10	Yes	No	—	
Imaging[18]							
X-ray (diagnosis and treatment)	—	—	6	—	—	—	
Darkroom	In	—	10	Yes	No	—	
Imaging waiting rooms	In	2	12	Yes[12,16]	—	—	
Laboratory[19]							
General[18]	—	—	6	—	—	—	
Biochemistry[18]	In	—	6	Yes	No	—	
Cytology	In	—	6	Yes	No	—	
Glass washing	In	—	10	Yes	—	—	
Histology	In	—	6	Yes	No	—	
Microbiology[18]	In	—	6	Yes	No	—	
Nuclear medicine	In	—	6	Yes	No	—	
Pathology	In	—	6	Yes	No	—	
Serology	In	—	6	Yes	No	—	
Sterilizing	In	—	10	Yes	—	—	
Autopsy room[11]	In	—	12	Yes	No	—	
Nonrefrigerated body—holding room	In	—	10	Yes	—	—	
Service areas							
Pharmacy	Out	—	4	—	—	—	
Food preparation center	—	—	10	—	No	—	
Warewashing	In	—	10	Yes	No	—	
Dietary day storage	In	—	2	—	—	—	
Laundry, general	—	—	10	Yes	—	—	
Soiled linen (sorting and storage)	In	—	10	Yes	No	—	
Clean linen storage	Out	—	2	—	—	—	
Soiled linen/trash chute room	In	—	10	Yes	No	—	
Bedpan room	In	—	10	Yes	—	—	
Bathroom	In	—	10	—	—	—	
Housekeeping room	In	—	10	Yes	No	—	
Sterilizing and supply							
ETO—sterilizer room	In	—	10	Yes	No	30–60	
Sterilizer equipment room	In	—	10	Yes	—	—	

(continued)

Table 114-2. Ventilation Requirements for Areas Affecting Patient Care in Hospitals and Outpatient Facilities[1]* *(continued)*

Area Designation	Air Movement Relationship to Adjacent Area[2]	Minimum Air Changes (AC) of Outdoor Air/hr[3]	Minimum Total AC/hr[4,5]	All Air Exhausted Directly to Outdoors[6]	Recirculation by Means of Room Units[7]	Relative Humidity[8] (%)	Design Temperature[9] (°F/C)
Central medical and surgical supply							
Soiled or decontamination room	In	—	6	Yes	No	—	
Clean workroom	Out	—	4	—	No	30–60	
Sterile storage	Out	—	4	—	—	70 (max)	

[1]The ventilation rates in this table cover ventilation for comfort, as well as for asepsis and odor control in areas of acute care hospitals that directly affect patient care and are determined based on healthcare facilities being predominantly "no smoking" facilities. Where smoking may be allowed, ventilation will need adjustment. Areas where specific ventilation rates are not given in the table shall be ventilated in accordance with ASHRAE Standard 62 Ventilation for Acceptable Indoor Air Quality, and ASHRAE: Handbook of Applications. Specialized patient care areas, including organ transplant units, burn units, specialty procedure rooms, etc., shall have additional ventilation provisions for air quality control as may be appropriate. Occupational Safety and Health Administration (OSHA) standards and/or National Institute for Occupational Safety and Health (NIOSH) criteria require special ventilation requirements for employee health and safety within healthcare facilities.

[2]Design of the ventilation system shall provide air movement, which is generally from clean to less clean areas. If any form of variable air volume or load shedding system is used for energy conservation, it must not compromise the corridor-to-room pressure balancing relationships or the minimum air changes required by the table.

[3]To satisfy exhaust needs, replacement air from outside is necessary. Table 2.1-230 does not attempt to describe specific amounts of outside air to be supplied to individual spaces, except for certain areas as those listed. Distribution of outside air, added to the system to balance required exhaust, shall be as required by good engineering practice. Minimum outside air quantities shall remain constant while the system is in operation. In variable volume systems, the minimum outside air setting on the air-handling unit shall be calculated using the ASHRAE 62 method.

[4]Number of air changes may be reduced when the room is unoccupied if provisions are made to ensure that the number of air changes indicated is reestablished any time the space is being utilized. Adjustments shall include provisions to ensure that the direction of air movement remains the same when the number of air changes is reduced. Areas not indicated as having continuous directional control may have ventilation systems shut down when space is unoccupied and ventilation is not otherwise needed, if the maximum infiltration or exfiltration permitted in Note 2 is not exceeded and if adjacent pressure balancing relationships are not compromised. Air quantity calculations must account for filter loading such that the indicated air change rates are provided up until the time of filter change-out. The minimum total air change requirements for the Ventilation Table shall be based on the supply air quantity in positive pressure rooms, and the exhaust air quantity in negative pressure rooms.

[5]Air change requirements indicated are minimum values. Higher values should be used when required to maintain indicated room conditions (temperature and humidity) based on the cooling load of the space (lights, equipment, people, exterior walls and windows, etc.).

[6]Air from areas with contamination and/or odor problems shall be exhausted to the outside and not recirculated to other areas. Note that individual circumstances may require special consideration for air exhaust to the outside, such as in intensive care units in which patients with pulmonary infection are treated, or rooms for burn patients.

[7]Recirculating room HVAC units refer to those local units that are used primarily for heating and cooling of air, and not disinfection of air. Because of cleaning difficulty and potential for buildup of contamination, recirculating room units shall not be used in areas marked "No." However, for airborne infection control, air may be recirculated within individual isolation rooms if HEPA filters are used. Isolation and intensive care rooms may be ventilated by reheat induction units in which only the primary air supplied from a central system passes through the reheat unit. Gravity-type heating or cooling units, such as radiators and convectors, shall not be used in operating rooms and other special-care areas. (See Footnote Appendix A7 for a description of recirculation units to be used in isolation rooms.)

[8]The ranges listed are minimum and maximum limits where control is specifically needed. The maximum and minimum limits are not intended to be independent of a spaces' associated temperature. The humidity is expected to be at the higher end of the range when the temperature is also at the higher end and vice versa. See Figure 2.1-130 for a graphic representation of the indicated changes on a psychrometric chart. Shaded area is acceptable range.

[9]Where temperature ranges are indicated, the systems shall be capable of maintaining the rooms at any point within the range during normal operation. A single figure indicates a heating or cooling capacity of at least the indicated temperature. This is usually applicable when patients may be undressed and require a warmer environment. Nothing in these guidelines shall be construed as precluding the use of temperature lower than those noted when patients' comfort and medical conditions make lower temperatures desirable. Unoccupied areas, such as storage rooms, shall have temperature appropriate for the function intended.

[10]Total air changes per room for patient rooms, intermediate care, labor/delivery/recovery rooms, and labor/delivery/recovery/postpartum rooms may be reduced to four when supplemental heating and/or cooling systems (radiant heating and cooling, baseboard heating, etc.) are used.

[11]Differential pressure shall be a minimum of 0.01-in. water gauge (2.5 Pa). If alarms are installed, allowances shall be made to prevent nuisance alarms of monitoring devices.

[12]If it is not practical to exhaust the air from airborne infection isolation rooms to the outside, the air may be returned through HEPA filters to the air-handling system exclusively serving the isolation room.

[13]National Institute for Occupational Safety and Health (NIOSH) criteria documents regarding Occupational Exposure to Waste Anesthetic Gases and Vapors, and Control of Occupational Exposure to Nitrous Oxide, indicate a need for both local exhaust (scavenging) systems and general ventilation of the areas in which the respective gases are utilized.

[14]Some surgeons may require room temperatures that are outside of the indicated range. All operating room design conditions shall be developed in consultation with surgeons, anesthesiologists, and nursing staff.

[15]The term trauma room as used here is the operating room space in the emergency department or other trauma reception area that is used for emergency surgery. The first aid room and/or "emergency room" used for initial treatment of accident victims may be ventilated as noted for the "treatment room." Treatment rooms used for bronchoscopy shall be treated as bronchoscopy rooms. Treatment rooms used for cryosurgery procedures with nitrous oxide shall contain provisions for exhausting waste gases.

[16]In a ventilation system that recirculates air, HEPA filters can be used in lieu of exhausting the air from these spaces to the outside. In this application, the return air shall be passed through the HEPA filters before it is introduced into any other spaces.

[17]The endoscopic instrument processing room is a room adjacent to the gastrointestinal endoscopy room that is utilized for cleaning of endoscopic equipment and instruments.

[18]When required, appropriate hoods and exhaust devices for the removal of noxious gases or chemical vapors shall be provided (see NFPA 99).

[19]The air movement relationships for laboratories apply between laboratory and adjacent nonlaboratory spaces. Reference DHHS publication Biosafety in Microbiological and Biomedical Laboratories (CDC and NIH) on the CDC website. Appendix footnotes for Footnotes 7 and 11 provide additional nonbinding guidance.

A7Recirculating devices with HEPA filters may have potential uses in existing facilities as interim, supplemental environmental controls to meet requirements for the control of airborne infectious agents. Limitations in design must be recognized. The design of either portable or fixed systems should prevent stagnation and short circuiting of airflow. The supply and exhaust locations should direct clean air to areas where healthcare personnel are likely to work, across the infectious source, and then to the exhaust, so that healthcare personnel are not in position between the infectious source and the exhaust location. The design of such systems should also allow for easy access for scheduled preventative maintenance and cleaning.

A11The verification of airflow direction can include a simple visual method such as smoke trail, ball-in-tube, or flutter strip. These devices will require a minimum differential air pressure to indicate airflow direction.

Adapted from American Institute of Architects/Academy of Architecture for Health, Facility Guidelines Institute. *2006 Guidelines for Design and Construction of Healthcare Facilities*. Washington, DC: The American Institute of Architects Press, 2006.

Table 114-3. Filter Efficiencies for Central Ventilation and Air Conditioning Systems in General Hospitals

Area Designation	Number of Filter Beds	Filter Efficiencies (percent)	
		Filter Bed No. 1 (MERV, %)	Filter Bed No. 2 (MERV, %)
All areas for inpatient care, treatment, and diagnosis, and those areas providing direct service or clean supplies such as sterile and clean processing, etc.	2	8 (30)	14 (90)
Protective environment	2	8 (30)	HEPA (99.97)
Laboratories	1	13 (80)	—
Administrative, bulk storage, soiled holding areas, food preparation, and laundries	1	8 (30)	—

Additional roughing or prefilters should be considered to reduce maintenance required for filters with efficiencies higher than 75 percent.

MERV, minimum efficiency rating value. MERVs are based on ASHRAE 52.2. The filtration efficiency ratings are based on average dust spot efficiency per ASHRAE 52.1-92.

American Institute of Architects/Academy of Architecture for Health, Facility Guidelines Institute. *2006 Guidelines for Design and Construction of Healthcare Facilities.* Washington, DC: The American Institute of Architects Press, 2006.

facilities set up semiannual testing for specialty areas; others schedule tests to ensure the entire facility is checked over a 5-year span. At a minimum, state licensure inspectors and/or TJC surveyors do expect to see a documented plan.

Air Pressurization and Balancing

General

Air pressure balancing describes the pressure relationships with respect to the surrounding area or corridor and can be positive (excess air supply in the room), negative (air drawn into the room), or neutral. Positive air pressure is used to keep microbial contamination out of the room and is used for immunosuppressed patients such as those undergoing bone marrow transplantation. Positive air pressure is used in ORs, special procedure rooms, and protective environment (PE), for example. Negative air pressure is used as an isolation measure to keep microbes from escaping from the room and is used for patients infected with organisms transmitted by the airborne route, such as TB, measles, and varicella. Other examples of areas requiring negative pressure include rooms such as toilet rooms, bronchoscopy room, triage, and emergency department waiting rooms.[30] (See Table 114-2 for all areas requiring positive or negative air pressure.)

Air Pressure Testing

Air pressure testing includes use of built-in pressure manometers, qualitative tests (e.g., smoke trails, electronic meters), and quantitative methods.[46] Table 114-2 (Table 2.1-2 in the 2006 Guidelines)[30] specifies that the differential pressure should be a minimum of 0.01-inch water gauge or 2.5 Pascals (Pa) for operating, bronchoscopy, and AII rooms and PEs. This quantitative measure evaluates the adequacy of the air movement relationships to adjacent areas. This is not the only important parameter, however. A published study found that detection of a pressure difference between the inside and outside of a room did not necessarily correlate with the direction of airflow.[47] It was deemed critical to employ devices that provide visual demonstration of the direction of airflow (e.g., smoke trails, flutter strips, ball-in-a-tube) in addition to continuous or built-in air monitors. The 2006 Guidelines mandate that major renovation or new construction of specialty rooms must include a "permanently installed visual means" to measure airflow direction.[30]

OSHA directives require facilities follow CDC TB Guidelines,[5,41] which specify daily verification and documentation that AII rooms remain in negative pressure with respect to the adjacent corridor when in use for care of patients with suspect or known pulmonary or laryngeal TB.[38,39] Thereafter, the CDC recommends monthly checks of AII rooms when not in use, even if electronic alarm pressurization monitors are installed.

Variations in airflow make maintaining pressure differentials difficult; the 2006 Guidelines therefore continue to strongly recommend against "reversible" room airflow.[30] The basis for this position is that point-of-use monitors may not be reliable, leakage of air from rooms is common, and personnel may not be aware if the room is in positive or negative pressurization.[48]

Filtration

HVAC systems use prefilters before fans to remove gross particulate matter (minimum efficiency 30 percent). Filters that are 85 to 90 percent efficient are placed downstream of the fans after the prefilters. This combination typically provides an overall filtration of 95 percent efficiency. HEPA filtration is defined as filtration with efficiency of 99.97 percent in removing particles 0.3 micron or more in size. Most airborne infectious microorganisms fall into a range of 0.3 to 5.0 microns. Filters that are 90 percent efficient as measured by industry standards remove sufficient particulate matter to meet minimum OR standards.[30,32,49] ASHRAE introduced a system for rating filters that is based on the size of particle or contaminant to be filtered. This measure of "minimum efficiency reporting values" (MERV) uses a scale of 1 through 16. In this system, a 30 percent efficient filter equates to MERV 8; 80 percent is equivalent to MERV 13; 90 to 95 percent equates to MERV 14; and 95 percent equals MERV 15.[33-35] Both systems can be used interchangeably. Removal and disposal of used filters requires basic care (careful handling/bagging); however, filter media, even from AII rooms, is not classified as regulated medical waste and may be disposed into the general waste stream. Studies have demonstrated the nonviability of microorganisms in used filters, such as *M. tuberculosis.*[50]

Distribution and Diffusion of Air

Airflow supply and exhaust should be controlled to ensure movement of air from "clean" to "less clean" areas, especially in critical areas. Cleaned, filtered air (supply) is typically distributed by directing airflow into the room from ceiling outlets near the center of the work area and moving to the periphery. Return air (exhaust) should be near floor level, although designs may vary. Once air enters the room, it is affected by other sources of contamination introduced by equipment and people (staff and patients) entering and leaving. Effective exhaust and removal of contaminants are basic to maintaining excellent air quality.

Laminar airflow (LAF) refers to a directional flow of air with little to no turbulence. It can be directed vertically or horizontally, and, when in place, recirculated air is usually passed through a HEPA filter. LAF is used to supply a steady stream of clean air across or down a room and is used primarily in specialty type ORs (e.g., orthopedic surgery). It is designed to move particle-free air ("ultraclean air") over the aseptic operating field at a uniform speed, removing particles from its path. The CDC *1999 Surgical Site Infection Prevention Guideline* recommended, "consider performing orthopedic implant operations in operating rooms supplied with ultraclean air," which indirectly implies a combination of LAF plus HEPA filter media.[51] Subsequent CDC Guidelines, assessing available scientific literature, reclassified this to state, "No recommendation is offered for performing orthopedic implant operations in rooms supplied with laminar airflow."[1]

Recent studies using computational fluid dynamics (CFD)-assisted modeling have examined which design optimizes removal of airborne particulates over the surgical site to attempt to resolve conflicting findings in the literature. Memarzadeh and Manning incorporated ACH, velocity, and unidirectional airflow into their CFD study with several variations in placement of personnel, equipment, and return (exhaust) air, and measured particle contamination of the surgical field. They found that ACH higher than 25 are not any more effective but that velocity and directional airflow do have greater influence on particle removal.[52,53] In addition, use of low velocity (25–35 feet/minute [fpm]) rather than traditional high velocity LAF (90–400 fpm) was also found more effective. Another key finding was that there is a thermal plume or "heat bounce" up from the incision on the patient's skin that moves particles up and away from the incision. High velocity LAF is likely negating this natural protection of the site and may be cooling the wound bed and the patient. Hypothermia contributes to risk of both infectious and noninfectious postoperative complications. FGI/AIA and ASHRAE agreed that the desired "directional" ventilation should be termed "noninduction unidirectional diffusion" to avoid the confusion with the term LAF. This term describes a unidirectional flow of air downward over the patient and the surgical team at a much lower rate of 25 to 35 fpm when compared to LAF rates of 90 fpm. The FGI/AIA 2006 Guidelines have incorporated Memarzadeh design concepts and recommend these for ventilation parameters in surgical suites as well as other invasive procedure rooms.[30]

Understanding how the latter differs from traditional LAF systems is important as Brandt et al. recently published a multihospital study that suggested an increased risk of surgical site infection associated with LAF design.[54] Details of specific HVAC design at participating hospitals are lacking from this investigation; however, it is likely that these are the older vertical, high velocity LAF which contrasts with the newer design in 2006 Guidelines.

Infection Prevention and Control Hazards, Implications, and Interventions

Air Source

The following recommendations, excerpted from the 2006 Guidelines, address many of the prevention and control interventions when used in conjunction with Tables 104-2 and 104-3. Other information that describes location and design of air intakes may be useful during outbreak investigations.[1-3] It is possible for contaminated air to be introduced into a facility because of improper location(s) and/or height of air intakes. State codes may vary somewhat from the following minimum recommendations:

- Fresh air intakes should be located at least 25 feet (7.62 meters) from exhaust outlets of ventilation systems, combustion equipment stacks, medical-surgical vacuum systems, plumbing vents, or areas that collect vehicular exhaust or other fumes.

- The bottom of outdoor air intakes serving central systems should be as high as practical but at least 6 feet (1.83 meters) above ground level or, if above the roof, 3 feet (91 cm) above the roof level.

- Exhaust outlets (also called returns) from contaminated areas should be above the roof level and arranged to minimize recirculation of exhausted air back into the building.

- In new construction and major renovation, air supply for operating and delivery rooms should be from ceiling outlets near the center of the work area. Returns (at least two, and as far apart as feasible) should be near the floor level. Supply for nurseries, labor/delivery/recovery/postpartum (LDRP) rooms, as well as rooms used for invasive procedures, should also be near the ceiling, with returns near the floor level. Exhaust grills (returns) for anesthesia evacuation or special applications may be installed in the ceiling. It should be noted that new studies are under way indicating that velocity and direction of airflow over the surgical field may be more important than location of returns as well as ACH.[52]

- State codes and building design must be checked for use of energy-conserving mechanisms, variable air volume (VAV), and systems that may be shut down or reduce ventilation of unoccupied areas as long as patient care is not compromised.

Temperature and Relative Humidity

The supply temperature, relative humidity (RH), and filtration depend on the basic design of the HVAC (100 percent outside or recirculated air) system for the building area. Airflow rates can change with variations of temperature and humidity. The current 2006 Guidelines and 2008 ASHRAE Standard 170 provide the acceptable ranges to better address temperature/humidity combinations achievable across widely variable geographic regions (see temperature and humidity standards in Table 114-2).[30,32,33]

Air Exchange and Pressure Relationships

ACH combined with differences in air pressure assist in preventing buildup and infiltration of contaminated air. Disruptions of airflow, including propped-open doors, leakage (e.g., open windows, loose door/window seals, penetrations), and blockage of air supply/return outlets, may adversely affect air quality and balance. Consider that hospital rooms are connected by doorways, corridors, stairwells, and elevator shafts. Small pressure differences, induced by natural forces such as thermal buoyancy owing to air temperature differences or mechanical fans, can generate airflows that move air from one room to another. These airflows are very sensitive to doors or windows being kept open and can change the air pressure in neighboring rooms and corridors, reducing, or even reversing, airflow directions. This highlights the importance of keeping isolation room windows and doors closed (see Table 114-2).[9,30]

Placement of Filters within Air Handling Systems

Filter efficiencies are listed in Table 114-3; see accompanying notes on proper filter placement. The 2006 Guidelines list 90 percent filters for ORs as minimal filtration efficiency, a level considered safe for clean and sterile settings. In actuality, many ORs use 95 percent or MERV 16, but use of HEPA filters is not required or recommended. It is noted that where procedures, such as organ transplantation, may call for consideration of special design, installation should meet performance needs and be reviewed on a case-by-case basis. The only room for which 99.97 percent HEPA filtration is recommended is for a PE room for highly immunosuppressed patients (e.g., bone marrow transplantation patients, as discussed in 2003 and 2004 CDC Guidelines that address environment of care and prevention of healthcare-associated pneumonia, respectively).[1,4,30,32-35,48]

Ultraviolet Germicidal Irradiation

The role of ultraviolet germicidal irradiation (UVGI) in hospitals, clinics, and nontraditional care settings still needs further delineation. Investigations into potential use of UVGI have been numerous including work by the National Institutes of Health (NIH) that shows effective cidal effects on specific airborne bacteria such as *M. tuberculosis*.[53] Although the wavelength typically used is less effective for fungi, UVGI may have a role in specific areas such as waiting rooms. Studies indicate that the addition of UVGI could substantially reduce the ACH necessary in the healthcare facility. However, there are operational realities such as maintenance of UVGI lamps and the need for all air at the point of planned use to be exposed for sufficient time to inactivate microorganisms. Therefore, UVGI may be applied as supplemental to the ventilation system design, rather than a primary mechanism to control airborne contaminants. Accordingly, NIH suggests that the ACH of the room should be set as if no UVGI system is installed.

The optimal relationship between ventilation and UVGI is not known. Because the clinical effectiveness of UVGI systems may vary, it is not recommended as a substitute for HEPA filtration, local exhaust of air to the outside, or negative pressure.[5] The use of UVGI lamps and HEPA filtration in a single unit offers little or no infection prevention or control benefits over those provided by the use of a HEPA filter alone.[55] Duct systems with UVGI are not recommended as a substitute for HEPA filters if the air from isolation rooms must be recirculated to other areas of the facility.[5] Regular maintenance of UVGI systems is crucial and usually consists of keeping the bulbs free of dust and replacing old bulbs as necessary. Recommendations from the 2003 EIC CDC guidelines only address installation:

When ultraviolet germicidal irradiation (UVGI) is used as a supplemental engineering control, install fixtures (1) on the wall near the ceiling or suspended from the ceiling as an upper air unit; (2) in the air return duct of an AII area; or (3) in designated enclosed areas or booths for sputum induction (category II).[1,5]

There is some evidence that UVGI installed inside AHUs can assist with mitigating biofouling of surfaces inside the AHU such as drip pans, cooling coils, and filter beds as well as increase operational efficiency. Definitive peer-reviewed evidence that such UVGI application is cost effective or, as claimed by some, prevents healthcare-associated infection (HAI), is not currently available.

Ventilation and Commissioning

The 2006 Guidelines[30] place new emphasis on commissioning, which is a process that verifies delivery of new construction according to contract specifications, before it is accepted by the owner. Commissioning for ventilation equipment requires identifying "acceptance criteria" permitting verification of critical ventilation specifications for air balance and filtration before the owner accepts "delivery." There must be some means to ensure that the system is delivering air quality according to specifications. The use of electronic monitors or particle counters to measure total air particulates is one means to provide this type of measure at the time the project is turned over to the owner. This method is being considered more frequently but is not considered routine testing.

No current recommendations or regulations exist regarding frequency for checking effectiveness of filters. One source suggests 6 months of checking as reasonable, and another strongly suggests certification and recertification of OR HVACs and filtration systems.[11,37] TJC, in their 2009 EOC standards, state that the [facility] "identifies in writing inspection and maintenance activities for all operating components of utility systems" and "identifies in writing the intervals for inspecting, testing, and maintaining all operating components of the utility systems on the inventory, based on criteria such as manufacturers' recommendations, risk levels, or hospital experience."[31] However, monitoring the need to change or clean filters more frequently is important during new construction or renovation (see Chapter 116 Construction and Renovation).

Infection Prevention and Control

Policies

The construction/renovation policy, as outlined in Chapter 116 Construction and Renovation, addresses issues affecting ventilation. An effective policy should do the following:

- Incorporate key design elements to ensure that departments affected by HVAC system replacement or modifications are involved in planning before new construction or major and minor renovation.

- Establish authoritative contingency plans and include processes for rapid communication when/if closures are required during construction, renovation, or power losses affecting HVAC shutdowns and startups. (See Chapter 116 Construction and Renovation, for a complete discussion of an ICRA, and Chapter 120 Infectious Disease Disasters.)

- Ensure that checklists consider some or all of the following during planning of new construction and planning during repair/renovation or other required remediation activity. Testing frequencies for new or current systems should be determined by facility-specific needs and data, but a scheduled plan of testing should be documented:

  o Location of intakes and returns

  o Use of outside or recirculated air

  o Number of air changes and proper balancing

  o Filters (number and percent efficiency for different sites)

  o Accountability for and frequency of testing of ACH and pressure

  o Specific temperature and humidity limits triggering limited use of a work area

  o Contingency plans in the event of power interruptions, contamination, and/or damage to HVAC systems. (See Chapters 112 Maintenance and Engineering, and 107 Environmental Services.)

  o Preventive maintenance and/or cleaning of ductwork, vents, and/or induction units. (See Chapter 112 Maintenance and Engineering.)

  o Disposal methods and procedures for removal of used air filters. (See Chapters 112 Maintenance and Engineering, and 113 Waste Management.)

Utility management policies, as required in TJC EOC standards, should include infection prevention and control input to prevent, detect, and reduce risk from infectious hazards. In regard to general HVAC contamination, it is critical to clean and/or replace filters if they are affected by water disruptions or flooding conditions that support fungal growth and contamination of the air supply. Recommendations for problems resulting from flooded or contaminated ventilation components (e.g., contaminated ceiling tiles) are given in Chapter 116 Construction and Renovation. When power is reestablished after a power interruption, and dampers and fans resume operation, dust released during this process may transmit infectious agents to patients and staff. Policies or protocols should address issues including: communication, operating the HVAC for some specified time to clear the ducts, followed by immediate cleaning before putting area (e.g., OR) back into service, and documentation of completion. Long-range follow-up includes surveillance of airborne infectious agents and/or HAIs.[31] (See Chapters 112 Maintenance and Engineering, and 116 Construction and Renovation.)

Environmental Monitoring

Detection and identification of certain HAIs may suggest HVAC malfunction (e.g., healthcare-associated TB, single cases of aspergillosis in severely immunosuppressed patients, healthcare-associated varicella infections). Analysis of postoperative surgical site infection rates and associated infectious agents may offer important clues to problems in the OR air system(s).[6,14,23,25,26,56-60]

- Visual monitoring: Visual monitoring of processes established for construction, renovation, or maintenance procedures is an important method for reducing the potential for infection from airborne contamination. (See Chapter 116 Construction and Renovation.)

- Specifications and commissioning: Contracts should certify to an owner's satisfaction that all specifications of HVACs have been met. Contracts should include outcome criteria that were met using specific measures.[1,2]

- Environmental air sampling and culturing: Sampling protocols and procedures in actual disease outbreaks are well substantiated.[1,2]

- Routine microbiologic surveillance: Use of routine microbiological sampling and culturing has not been recommended except as an integral part of an epidemiologic investigation. There is no clear answer for initiating environmental surveillance in the absence of actual or pending problems.[1,5,61,62]

Outbreak Investigation and Culturing

When an outbreak is identified or suspected, an environmental source may be present and confirmatory testing is appropriate. (Also see Chapter 12 Outbreak Investigations.)

A critical review of the indications for airborne particulate monitoring or cultures must be done in light of basic principles of outbreak investigation (e.g., establishing that an outbreak exists). One may also consider the following guidance:

- Purpose of culturing and appropriate methods should be identified beforehand.

- Decisions and planned actions regarding results of culturing should be anticipated before undertaking the process.

- Determination should be made whether there are existing standards to interpret results.

Air Standards

Air standards have been developed for "clean rooms" in industrial settings but do not have general applicability in healthcare settings, as outlined in ASHRAE's 1999 publication, *Clean Spaces*.[32] The final publication of the USP-797 standard on compounded sterile preparations (CSP) describes an ideal ventilation design for pharmacies. The chapter, as of June 2008, was incorporated into USP 31/NF 26 and requires minimally the use of an ISO Class 5 laminar flow workbenches for compounding. It also acknowledges the lack of standards for interpreting air quality control testing results, and refers to the CDC-EIC Guidelines on environmental sampling and testing.[1] (See Chapter 110 Pharmacy Services; see Supplemental Resources.)

Bioaerosol Standards

Absolute standards for airborne fungal spores or other bioaerosols do not exist. Many studies have measured airborne contamination, but establishing specific levels that correlate with actual disease has proved challenging given the ubiquitous nature and variety of airborne fungi.[13,63–70] Lower levels of spores have been associated with lower incidence of disease, but no one has established a "safe" level of exposure.[63] Rhame has suggested that spore counts be kept as low as possible hospitalwide, with extreme measures reserved for bone marrow transplant patients.[57,60] More recently, Falvey and Streifel were not able to demonstrate that routine monitoring of air for fungi could reliably predict cases of invasive fungal disease and instead concluded that maintenance of filtration and other methods to minimize environmental contaminants were more effective.[71]

Relative Threshold

Given the lack of absolute standards, there is general agreement that thresholds specific to a facility or area need to be established based on local, facility-specific experience. It is important that any indoor measurement also use outdoor levels for comparison as well as from other areas inside the facility that are not the focus of a particular problem investigation.[1]

Microbiological Environmental Sampling and Culturing Methods

If airborne fungal spore monitoring is necessary, a variety of sampling techniques may be considered (e.g., volumetric air sampling).[1,23] Detection of fungi such as *Aspergillus* species may require further investigation into design (air intakes), proper equipment functioning (fans and filters), or proper equipment maintenance.[22,64] One key step in interpreting results is comparing fungal spore counts from outdoor air to those levels obtained from indoor air samples. Given the filtration systems in place, elevated levels indoors might suggest amplification from a contaminated reservoir.

The type of sampling device and methodology for measuring total particulates, bioaerosols, or selective media for culturing fungi also will vary. The need for typing or "fingerprinting" specific isolates must also be considered.[1,4,23] Electronic monitors or particle counters may be useful to provide information on general levels of dust and contamination; care must be taken to distinguish between total particulates and viable bioaerosols. Measuring total airborne particulate matter (as opposed to microbiological culturing) may be used in the commissioning process for ventilation systems as addressed in the 2006 Guidelines. One current review of monitoring equipment and parameters to be considered for sampling includes a procedure often used in aspergillosis outbreaks.[24] The 2003 CDC-EIC Guidelines provides a comprehensive summary on various approaches to sampling.[1]

Planning Checklist for Environmental Surveillance Strategy

1. Determine plan and purpose of surveillance to guide prevention and interventions.

2. Review the literature for published information for values that may assist in establishing a baseline or threshold.

3. Establish your own facility-specific baseline or threshold experientially, and identify the degree of variation acceptable as a baseline (i.e., a value or range of values).

4. Determine the actions or interventions that will be taken if values are exceeded.

5. Ensure that the microbiology laboratory is involved in the plan. Most clinical microbiology laboratories are not equipped to isolate microorganisms from environmental sampling. Individuals collecting such samples should utilize a laboratory that is certified or has capabilities in environmental microbiology.

6. Determine sampling methods and culturing techniques that are appropriate for the event.

7. Ensure that collecting/sampling personnel are trained for consistency, especially with air-sampling devices. Consider budgeting for services of an outside expert consultant.

8. Conduct the sampling and quantify results (i.e., number of colonies per unit).

9. Determine if values exceed the established threshold described in item 3.

10. After analysis and communication, follow the action plan determined in item 4.

In summary, decisions regarding environmental sampling and culturing must be part of a planning process and must be laid out before undertaking the process. The methods and process used should be appropriate for the occasion. Surveillance cultures are unlikely to provide useful information to prevent or control airborne or construction-associated infections unless the standards or baseline values needed for interpretation are clearly identified. Collaboration with microbiology laboratories for sampling techniques and/or culture interpretation is essential. (See Chapter 107 Environmental Services.)

Specific Applications

Ventilation issues for each of the following areas should consider outside versus recirculated air, number of air changes, air pressure relationships, and filtration efficiencies.

Common Waiting Areas

Considerations include temporary location areas with appropriate air pressure for patients with possible airborne infections (e.g., TB) away from other occupants or protection of severely immunosuppressed patients from others. The infection preventionist should use a facility-based risk assessment when considering need and optimal location of a negative-pressure treatment room with air that is exhausted to the outside or through a HEPA filter before recirculation in common waiting areas. The 2006 Guidelines require the emergency department and radiology waiting areas be in negative pressure with respect to adjacent areas.[30]

Surgical and Critical Care Units

Provisions should be made for AII room(s) as well as rooms for managing severely immunosuppressed patients, depending on program needs.

Operating Rooms and Cardiac Catheterization Laboratories

Positive pressure, ventilation, and filtration rates are similar for all areas where invasive procedures are performed as described in the 2006 Guidelines.[30] In each, air should flow out of the room and the minimum ACH should be 15, with three of these ACH being fresh or outdoor air. The air should be filtered with an efficiency of at least 90 percent (see Table 114-3). The optimum method for managing patients with active TB requiring urgent surgical intervention has not yet been determined. However, the following principles should be followed:[1,5]

- The number of air changes provides increased dilution of potential contaminants. Charts published by NIOSH are included in the 2005 CDC TB guidelines and may assist in calculating the percentage of particles removed by time and ventilation rates. These charts can be helpful for determining the time needed before resuming use of an OR after a≈procedure on a patient with confirmed or suspected active TB disease.[5]

- Modifying the pressure relationships of the OR to neutral or negative is not recommended and could disrupt pressure balance, and has not been studied for effectiveness.

- Supplemental filtration devices, if deployed inside the OR, should be turned off during the surgical procedure.

- If a surgical suite or an OR has an anteroom, the anteroom should be either (1) positive pressure compared with both the corridor and the suite or OR (with filtered supply air); or (2) negative pressure compared with both the corridor and the suite or OR.

- Intubation and extubation location for the known/suspected TB patient should be considered. Scheduling of patient procedure (e.g., last case), masking of patient during transport and before intubation, and performing extubation in a room meeting AII ventilation requirements may be used to reduce risk of transmission.

- Extubate and allow the patient to recover in an AII room.

A recent study using submicron particles and smoke plume to mimic behavior of airborne *M. tuberculosis* if encountered in the OR found a portable anteroom-HEPA unit was much more effective in containment of airborne particles than portable HEPA devices placed inside the OR; in addition, the latter were also found to disrupt airflow patterns.[72]

Bronchoscopy/Endoscopy Treatment Rooms

Bronchoscopy procedures for persons known or suspected to have pulmonary TB should be performed in treatment rooms meeting AII room ventilation requirements. The bronchoscopic procedure often results in copious and productive coughing postprocedure; and recovery for known/suspected TB patients should be carried out in a room meeting AII ventilation requirements as well. Other measures such as having the patient wear a mask during transport, minimizing waiting times in common areas, and supplying tissues and disposal bag to patient are recommended. The 2006 Guidelines distinguish endoscopy from bronchoscopy room ventilation and recommend negative airflow and total air exhaust for bronchoscopy; negative pressure for endoscopic rooms is indicated as well. However, as indicated in the footnotes to the 2006 Guidelines Table 2.1-2, this is intended for odor control, and may vary according to need. Negative pressure is already required for the instrument decontamination/reprocessing area (see Table 114-2 and 2006 Guidelines Table 2.1-2).[30]

Protected Environments for Immunosuppressed Patients

Highly immunosuppressed patients (i.e., those with prolonged, severe granulocytopenia, most notably bone marrow recipients, possibly solid organ transplant recipients, and patients with hematologic malignancies receiving chemotherapy) require protected environments to reduce the risk of infectious complications. Such environments provide positive-pressure ventilation where the amount of HEPA-filtered air exceeds the amount of air exhausted by at least 10 percent. Effective protected environments require a "bundle" of elements—not just HEPA filtration. Other elements include highly filtered air ($\geq$95 percent efficiency for 0.3-micron particles), increased room air exchanges ($\geq$12 ACH), a sealed room, and airflow direction from the patient toward the corridor. Some facilities use LAF rooms for bone marrow transplant patients; such rooms provide directional airflow with more than 100 ACH. LAF rooms are expensive and their cost-effectiveness is somewhat controversial; therefore, many facilities use other ventilation systems for such patients.[4,15,56,73]

General Patient Care Units

These areas require minimum ventilation and filtration requirements as specified in the FGI/AIA Guidelines (see Tables 114-1 and 114-2 or FGI/AIA Guidelines Tables 7-2 and 7-3).[30]

Airborne Infection Isolation Rooms

AII rooms and PE, if needed, require, at minimum, a private room with tight sealing to prevent air infiltration to or from the room. Anterooms are not essential to maintain negative air pressure, but may be useful depending on facility design. Isolation rooms should not be designed with reversible airflow because of patient/HCP safety considerations as well as maintenance of the system. The FGI/AIA guidelines recommend 12 ACH in new facilities or those undergoing major renovation. Older facilities may only be able to achieve 6 to 12 ACH, but use of supplemental HEPA devices can increase the number to 12. As noted earlier, one study found that a balanced ventilation system does not guarantee inward airflow direction.[47] It was determined critical to employ devices that provide visual demonstration of the direction of airflow (e.g., smoke trails, flutter strips) in addition to continuous or built-in air monitors. The need for routine monitoring of AII rooms is highlighted in a recent investigation. Saravia et al. studied pressurization of 678 AII rooms in a large number of hospitals in the United States and found only 32 percent met recommended negative pressure differential; 9 percent, ironically, were found to be in positive pressure.[74] A major factor for this suboptimal performance was leakage of the AII rooms studied. Some additional recommendations on design of AII rooms are available elsewhere.[75]

Ancillary Support Areas

For food service, diagnostic imaging and treatment rooms, sterilizing and cleaning supply/distribution areas, and other service areas, see the 2006 Guidelines. Clean support areas generally require 10 ACH with airflow out of the area (positive pressure). The 2006 Guidelines recommend six ACH and minimum air filtration efficiency of 90 percent for general diagnostic and treatment rooms.[30]

General Room Design and Maintenance

Issues include identifying intakes and returns, ensuring routine cleaning, and monitoring according to type of area.[26] The use of ceiling fans in certain rooms such as LDRP or modern "birthing rooms" has been questioned but is not specifically addressed in the 2006 Guidelines. State regulators usually determine if permissible; some states do not allow ceiling fans, based on a perception of the inability to control dust.[2,37] The use of supplemental fans in patient care areas requires thoughtful consideration of many factors such as mitigating disruption of dust, cleaning of fan blades, compliance with facility electrical safety requirements, and noise. In general need for supplemental fans should be temporary, as a properly working HVAC should provide for comfortable conditions. Even with their use it is unlikely these will alter room pressurization and normal relationships between areas.

CONCLUSIONS

In summary, issues of ventilation have major impact in healthcare today as emerging pathogens and bioterrorism force new attention to ventilation and the health of building occupants. Table 114-1 illustrates a number of outbreaks associated with better-known airborne contaminants that also are serious health hazards. Even though Tables 114-2 and 114-3 are design specifications, they provide the needed guidance for measuring ventilation expectations of specialty areas for evaluation. Hopefully better understanding the ventilation systems and associated risks will reinforce the importance of early input of infection prevention into planning and prevention rather than remediation efforts resulting from poor design and maintenance.

FUTURE TRENDS

A number of issues and concerns remain and require continual research and evaluation for methods to improve patient outcomes. Some include the following:

- Surge capacity: Addressing ventilation when facilities need to increase surge capacity in response to bioterrorism or major outbreaks of airborne infectious agents.

- Fans: Concerns have been raised regarding use of fans in patient care areas. No studies or regulations have directly addressed whether fans affect health outcomes.

- Ventilation and pressure relationships: Whereas the need for negative air pressure is clear, new studies are needed to determine the ideal room pressure differential related to actual infectious agent transmission and risk for developing actual disease. This is an area beginning to be addressed.

- Ventilation duct cleaning: The efficacy of vacuuming or sanitation of ventilation ducts to enhance IAQ or prevent disease transmission is yet to be determined.

- Alternative HVAC designs:

  - Displacement ventilation. Recently there has been a renewed interest in alternatives to traditional HVAC design that aim to supply sufficient filtered air at the ceiling and return via ducts either in the ceiling or at locations in the wall around an enclosed space, such as mixing ventilation (MV). One alternative is displacement ventilation (DV). DV depends on the principle of differentials in temperature to move contaminants from an enclosed space. Cool, conditioned air is supplied at floor level and because warm air rises, the exhaust or returns are located in the ceiling. There is little in-use experience for this design relative to assessing its comparative effectiveness of DV to MV relative to containment of airborne or droplet-transmitted microorganisms, particularly in healthcare settings. One investigation did suggest this be approached cautiously in patient care areas as there was dissemination of contaminants horizontally from a patient lying in a bed in a room with DV using manikins with smoke plume for surrogate of airborne agents.[76] Others using CFD models also question efficacy of DV.[77] Those interested in more details are referred to a review by Tang et al.[9]

o Natural ventilation (NV). NV has been in place for decades. This may be all that is available in hospitals in developing countries where electrical power and utility resources severely limit mechanical systems. For United States-based facilities, other major limiting factors are extremes and variation in weather conditions. These preclude opening windows to outdoor air, for example, in Michigan hospitals in the middle of January. Also, design of mixing ventilation is optimal if the building envelope is sealed tightly, including windows. For the latter buildings, open windows can significantly alter room pressurization, energy demands on the HVAC system, and most importantly bypass existing filter media in the AHUs. Some have reported that NV is effective in removal of contaminants in settings where resources are constrained or nonexistent, such as caring for those with TB disease in Lima, Peru—but the building design is critical in even these situations.[78]

- Sustainable energy utilization and stewardship of the environment: HVAC systems require considerable energy to operate and maintain. With growing appreciation and concern over stewardship of the global environment there is considerable attention and study of alternative designs and other interventions that can support more efficient use of energy. The delicate balance is how to accomplish better efficiencies without compromising safety of patients or other occupants in healthcare facilities. At present, there are few published studies demonstrating how to maintain this balance but additional research projects and experience of providers are ongoing. Those interested in more are referred to new organizations, Practice Greenhealth and Global Health and Safety Initiatives, which are facilitating an environmentally supportive agenda. (See Supplemental Resources.)

Acknowledgement—APIC would like to acknowledge the contribution of Judene Bartley, MS, MPH, CIC to the *APIC text*.

REFERENCES

1. Centers for Disease Control and Prevention (CDC) and Healthcare Infection Control Practices Advisory Committee (HICPAC). Guidelines for environmental infection control in healthcare facilities: recommendations of CDC and the Healthcare Infection Control Practices Advisory Committee (HICPAC). *MMWR Recomm Rep* 2003;52(RR-10):1–42.
2. Bartley JM. APIC State-of-the-art-report: the role of infection control during construction in healthcare facilities. *Am J Infect Control* 2000;28:156–169.
3. Bartley JM, Olmsted RN, eds. *Construction and Renovation*, 3rd ed. Toolkit for Professionals in Infection Prevention and Control. Washington DC: Association for Professionals in Infection Control and Epidemiology, 2007.
4. Tablan OC, Anderson LJ, Besser R, et al. Guidelines for preventing health-care–associated pneumonia, 2003. Recommendations of CDC and the Healthcare Infection Control Practices Advisory Committee. *MMWR Recomm Rep* 2004;53 (RR-03):1–36.
5. Centers for Disease Control and Prevention. Guidelines for preventing the transmission of Mycobacterium tuberculosis in health-care settings, 2005. *MMWR Recomm Rep* 2005;54(RR17):1–141.
6. Li Y, Leung GM, Tang JW, et al. Role of ventilation in airborne transmission of infectious agents in the built environment—a multidisciplinary systematic review. *Indoor Air* 2007;17(1):2–18.
7. Hruszkewycz V, Ruben B, Hypes CM, et al. A cluster of pseudofungemia associated with hospital renovation adjacent to the microbiology laboratory. *Infect Control Hosp Epidemiol* 1992;13:147–150.
8. American Thoracic Society Workshop. Achieving healthy indoor air: report of the American Lung Association and American Thoracic Society Workshop. Sante Fe, NM, November 16–19, 1995. *Am J Respir Crit Care Med* 1997;156(Pt 2):S33–S64.
9. Tang JW, Li Y, Eames I, et al. Factors involved in the aerosol transmission of infection and control of ventilation in healthcare premises. *J Hosp Infect* 2006;64(2):100–114.
10. Nardell EA, Keegan J, Cheney SA, et al. Airborne infection: theoretical limits of protection achievable by building ventilation. *Am Rev Respir Dis* 1991;144:302–306.
11. Weems JJ Jr, Davis BJ, Tablan OC, et al. Construction activity: an independent risk factor for invasive aspergillosis and zygomycosis in patients with hematologic malignancy. *Infect Control* 1987;8:71–75.
12. Streifel AJ, Steven PP, Rhame FS. In-hospital source of airborne penicillium species. *J Clin Microbiol Suppl* 1987;2:1–4.
13. Fox BC, Chamberlin L, Kulich P, et al. Heavy contamination of operating room air by penicillium species: identification of the source and attempts at decontamination. *Am J Infect Control* 1990;18:300–306.
14. Bartley J. Operating room air quality. *Today's OR Nurse* 1993;15:11–18.
15. Centers for Disease Control and Prevention. Guidelines for preventing opportunistic infections among hematopoietic stem cell transplant recipients. *MMWR Recomm Rep* 2000;49(RR-10):1–125.
16. Manuel RJ, Kibbler CC. The epidemiology and prevention of invasive aspergillosis. *J Hosp Infect* 1998;39:95–109.
17. Fridkin SK, Kremer FB, Bland LA, et al. Acremonium kiliensis endophthalmitis that occurred after cataract extraction in an ambulatory surgical center and as traced to an environmental reservoir. *Clin Infect Dis* 1996;22:222–227.
18. Krasinski K, Holzman RS, Hanna B, et al. Nosocomial fungal infection during hospital renovation. *Infect Control* 1985;6:278–282.
19. Mehta G. Aspergillus endocarditis after open heart surgery: an epidemiological investigation. *J Hosp Infect* 1990;15:245–253.
20. Loo VG, Bertrand C, Dixon C, et al. Control of construction-associated nosocomial aspergillosis in an antiquated hematology unit. *Infect Control Hosp Epidemiol* 1996;17:360–364.
21. Stroud LA, Tokars JI, Grieco MH, et al. Evaluation of infection control measures in preventing the nosocomial transmission of multidrug-resistant Mycobacterium tuberculosis in a New York City hospital. *Infect Control Hosp Epidemiol* 1995;16:141–147.
22. Opal SM, Asp AA, Cannady PB Jr, et al. Efficacy of infection control measures during a nosocomial outbreak of aspergillosis associated with hospital construction. *J Infect Dis* 1986;153:634–637.
23. Iwen PC, Davis JC, Reed EC, et al. Airborne fungal spore monitoring in a protective environment during hospital construction and correlation with an outbreak of invasive aspergillosis. *Infect Control Hosp Epidemiol* 1994;15:303–306.
24. Anderson K, Morris G, Kennedy H, et al. Aspergillosis in immunocompromised paediatric patients: associations with building hygiene, design and indoor air. *Thorax* 1996;51:256–261.
25. Pittet D, Ducel G. Infectious risk factors related to operating rooms. *Infect Control Hosp Epidemiol* 1994;15:456–472.
26. Kumari DN, Haji TC, Keer V, et al. Ventilation grilles as a potential source of methicillin-resistant *Staphylococcus aureus* causing an outbreak in an orthopedic ward at district general hospital. *J Hosp Infect* 1998;39:127–133.
27. Dearborn DG, Infeld MD, Smith PG, et al. Update: pulmonary hemorrhage/hemosiderosis among infants. *MMWR Recomm Rep* 1997;46(2):33–35.
28. Anaissie EJ, Stratton SL, Dignani M, et al. Cleaning patient shower facilities: a novel approach to reducing patient exposure to aerosolized Aspergillus species and other opportunistic molds. *Clin Infect Dis* 2002;35:86–88.
29. Kuhn DM, Ghannoum MA. Indoor mold, toxigenic fungi, and Stachybotrys chartarum: infectious disease perspective. *Clin Microbiol Rev* 2003;16:144–172.
30. American Institute of Architects/Academy of Architecture for Health, Facility Guidelines Institute. *2006 Guidelines for Design and Construction of Healthcare Facilities*. Washington, DC: The American Institute of Architects Press, 2006.
31. The Joint Commission. *The 2009 Comprehensive Accreditation Manual for Hospitals*. Oakbrook Terrace, IL: The Joint Commission Publications, 2009.
32. American Society of Heating, Refrigerating, and Air-conditioning Engineers. *1999 Heating, Ventilating and Air-Conditioning (HVAC) Applications*. Atlanta: ASHRAE Press, 1999.
33. American Society of Heating, Refrigerating, and Air-conditioning Engineers. *Ventilation of Health Care Facilities ANSI/ASHRAE/ASHE Standard 170*. Atlanta: ASHRAE Press, 2008.
34. Centers for Disease Control and Prevention. Guidance for Protecting Building Environments from Airborne Chemical, Biological, or Radiological Attacks. CDC website. 2002. Available at: http://www.cdc.gov/niosh/docs/2002-139/.
35. Centers for Disease Control and Prevention. Guidance for Filtration and Air-Cleaning Systems to Protect Building Environments from Airborne Chemical, Biological, or Radiological Attacks. CDC website. 2003. Available at: http://www.cdc.gov/niosh/docs/2003-136.

36. Centers for Medicare and Medicaid Services (CMS). Code of Federal Regulations, Title 42-Public Health; CHAPTER IV—CMS, Department of Health and Human Services. Part 482—Conditions of Participation for Hospitals. GPO website. 2004. Available at: http://www.gpo.gov/fdsys/pkg/CFR-2004-title42-vol3/pdf/CFR-2004-title42-vol3-part482-toc-id1457.pdf.

37. Health Facilities Engineering Section, Division of Health Facilities and Services, Michigan Department of Community Health (MDCH). 2007 Minimum Design Standards for Health Care Facilities in Michigan. Lansing, MI: MDCH, 2007.

38. Occupational Safety and Health Administration (OSHA). Code of Federal Regulations Title 29, Part 1910.1000. Air Contaminants. GPO website. 2007. Available at: http://www.access.gpo.gov/nara/cfr/waisidx_07/29cfr1910a_07.html.

39. Occupational Safety and Health Administration. Proposed rule for occupational exposure to tuberculosis. Fed Reg 1997;62:54159–54308.

40. Occupational Safety and Health Administration. Enforcement Procedures and Scheduling for Occupational Exposure to Tuberculosis (CPL 2.106) Occupational Safety and Health Administration, 1996. OSHA website. 2013. Available at: http://www.osha.gov/pls/oshaweb/owacisp.show_document?p_table=DIRECTIVES&p_id=1586&p_text_version=FALSE.

41. Occupational Safety and Health Administration. Occupational exposure to tuberculosis. Notice of intent to withdraw proposed rule. 1827. Fed Reg 2003;68:30588–30590.

42. Environmental Protection Agency (EPA). IAQ Building Education and Assessment Model (I-BEAM). Web-based Text Modules. EPA website. 2012. Available online at: http://www.epa.gov/iaq/largebldgs/i-beam/text/index.html.

43. Beddows NA. Concerns about indoor air quality warrant review of HVAC systems. Occup Health Saf 1990;59:77–81.

44. Memarzadeh F, Manning A. Thermal comfort, uniformity and ventilation effectiveness in patient rooms: performance assessment using ventilation indices. ASHRAE Trans 2000;106:748–761.

45. Ninomura PE, Bartley J. New ventilation guidelines for healthcare facilities. ASHRAE J 2001;43:29–33.

46. Wiehrdt WQ. Smoke trail tests for negative pressure isolation rooms. Occupational Safety and Health Administration Technical Support Memo. Washington, DC: U.S. Department of Labor, 1994.

47. Pavelchak N, DePersis RP, London M, et al. Identification of factors that disrupt negative air pressurization of respiratory isolation rooms. Infect Control Hosp Epidemiol 2000;21:191–195.

48. Rice N, Streifel A, Veseley D. Room pressure. A critical parameter for special ventilation rooms. Infect Control Hosp Epidemiol 2001;22:19–23.

49. Hermans RE, Streifel AJ. Engineering controls for preventing airborne infections in workers in healthcare and related facilities: Ventilation design. National Institute for Occupational Safety Health Research Conference, July 14–16, 1993. Cincinnati, OH: Department of Health and Human Services, 1993.

50. Ko G, Burge HA, Muilenberg M, et al. Survival of mycobacteria on HEPA filter material. J Am Biol Safety Assoc 1998;3:65–78.

51. Mangram AJ, Horan TC, Pearson ML, et al. Guideline for Prevention of Surgical Site Infection, 1999. Centers for Disease Control and Prevention (CDC) Hospital Infection Control Practices Advisory Committee. Am J Infect Control 1999;27:97–132.

52. Memarzadeh F, Manning AP. Comparison of operating room ventilation systems in the protection of the surgical site. ASHRAE Trans 2002;108:3–15.

53. Memarzadeh F, Jiang J. A methodology for minimizing risk from airborne organisms in hospital isolation room. ASHRAE Trans 2002;106:731–737.

54. Brandt C, Hott E, Sohr D, et al. Operating room ventilation with laminar airflow shows no protective effect on the surgical site infection rate in orthopedic and abdominal surgery. Ann Surg 2008;248:695–700.

55. Mobile high efficiency filter air cleaners. Health Devices 1997;26:228–245.

56. Mooney BR, Reeves SA, Larsen E. Infection control and bone marrow transplantation. Am J Infect Control 1993;21:131–138.

57. Rhame FS. Prevention of nosocomial aspergillosis. J Hosp Infect 1991;18(Suppl A):466–472.

58. Fraser VF, Krista J, Primack J, et al. Evaluation of rooms with negative pressure ventilation used for respiratory isolation in seven midwestern hospitals. Infect Control Hosp Epidemiol 1993;14:623–628.

59. Weber SF, Peacock JE Jr, Do KA, et al. Interaction of granulocytopenia and construction activity as risk factors for nosocomial invasive filamentous fungal disease in patients with hematologic disorders. Infect Control Hosp Epidemiol 1990;11:235–242.

60. Overberger PA, Wadowsky RM, Schaper MM. Evaluation of airborne particulates and fungi during hospital renovation. Am Ind Hyg Assoc J 1995;56:706–712.

61. Garner JS, Favero MS. Guideline for Handwashing and Hospital Environmental Control, 1985. Washington, DC: National Technical Information Service, 1985:(PB855–923404),14.

62. Vonberg RP, Gastmeier P. Nosocomial aspergillosis in outbreak settings. J Hosp Infect 2006;63:246–254.

63. Cornet M, Levy V, Fleury L, et al. Efficacy of prevention by high-efficiency particulate air filtration or laminar airflow against Aspergillus airborne contamination during hospital renovation. Infect Control Hosp Epidemiol 1999;20:508–513.

64. Rask D, Dziekan B, Swiencicki W, et al. Air quality control during renovation in healthcare facilities. In: Healthy Buildings: Solutions to Global and Regional Concerns. Atlanta: ASHRAE Press, 1998.

65. Haberstich N. Prevention of infection during major construction and renovation in the surgery department of a large hospital. Am J Infect Control 1987;15:36–38A.

66. Turner G, Sumner R, Ornelas L, et al. Controlling construction dust in the hospital environment; a quality improvement project. Am J Infect Control 1985;23:115.

67. Brown S, Detzler L, Myers J, et al. The impact of environmental controls and air quality monitoring on surgical site infection rates during operating room construction. Am J Infect Control 1996;24:140.

68. Johnson K. Cohen M. An occupied hospital under construction: the role of environmental cultures [abstract]. Am J Infect Control 1997;25:166.

69. Gartner K, Blank M, Volosky R. Keeping the air clean—lessons from a construction project. Western Penn Hosp (PA). Am J Infect Control 1996;24:111.

70. Rath PM, Ansorg R. Value of environmental sampling and molecular typing of Aspergilli to assess nosocomial sources of aspergillosis. J Hosp Infect 1997;37:47–53.

71. Falvey DG, Streifel AJ. Ten-year air sample analysis of Aspergillus prevalence in a university hospital. J Hosp Infect 2007;67(1):35–41.

72. Olmsted RN. Pilot study of directional airflow and containment of airborne particles in the size of Mycobacterium tuberculosis in an operating room. Am J Infect Control 2008;36:260–267.

73. Philpott-Howard J. Prevention of fungal infections in hematology patients. Infect Control Hosp Epidemiol 1996;17(8):545–551.

74. Saravia SA, Raynor PC, Streifel AJ. A performance assessment of airborne infection isolation rooms. Am J Infect Control 2007;35:324–331.

75. Hayden CS. Development of an empirical model to aid in designing airborne infection isolation rooms. J Occ Env Hygiene 2007;4:198–207.

76. Qian H, Li Y, Nielsen PV, et al. Dispersion of exhaled droplet nuclei in a two-bed hospital ward with three different ventilation systems. Indoor Air 2006;16:111e128.

77. Beggs CB, Kerr KG, Noakes CJ, et al. The ventilation of multiple-bed hospital wards: Review and analysis. Am J Infect Control 2008;36:250–259.

78. Escombe AR, Oeser CC, Gilman RH, et al. Natural ventilation for the prevention of airborne contagion. PLoS Med 2007;4(2):e68.

SUPPLEMENTAL RESOURCES

ASHRAE. Special Project 91—HVAC design manual for hospitals and clinics. Atlanta: American Society of Heating, Refrigerating and Air-Conditioning Engineers, 2003.

Premier Inc. Infection Control Risk Assessment (ICRA Matrix, 14 step assessment and Permit model). Premier Inc website. 2014. Available at: http://www.premierinc.com/quality-safety/tools-services/safety/topics/construction/icra.jsp.

Centers for Disease Control and Prevention. Building air quality: A guide for building owners and facility managers. Appendix B: HVAC Systems and Indoor Air Quality, 1991. EPA Publication No. 400/1-91/003. CDC website. 2013. Available at: http://www.cdc.gov/niosh/baqtoc.html.

Environmental Protection Agency (EPA). EPA resources and publications on Indoor Air Quality. EPA website. 2013. Available at: http://www.epa.gov/iaq/pubs/index.html.

Global Health and Safety Initiatives. Available online at: http://www.healthcaredesignmagazine.com/article/global-health-and-safety-initiative.

Perdelli F, Sartini M, Spagnolo AM, et al. A problem of hospital hygiene: The presence of aspergilli in hospital wards with different air-conditioning features. Am J Infect Control 2006;34:264–268.

Practice Greenhealth. Available online at: http://www.practicegreenhealth.org.

United States Pharmacopeial Convention, Inc. (USP). Available online at: www.usp.org.

Walker JT, Hoffman P, Bennett AM, et al. Hospital and community acquired infection and the built environment design and testing of infection control rooms. J Hosp Infect 2007;65(S2):43–49.

CHAPTER 115

Water Systems Issues and Prevention of Waterborne Infectious Diseases in Healthcare Facilities

Linda Dickey, RN, MPH, CIC
Director, Epidemiology & Infection Prevention
UC Irvine Health
Orange, CA

ABSTRACT

This chapter addresses waterborne pathogen risks in healthcare settings and strategies for infection prevention and control. Waterborne pathogen risks can be significant in healthcare settings, from unexpected incidents of intrusion of water into occupied areas to mitigation of microbial contamination. As a result, water-related problems are among the most challenging infection prevention issues involving the environment of care. Prominent among these is prevention and control of Legionella *contamination of water distribution systems, which is discussed here. However,* Legionella *risks vary by geographic region, and* Legionella *is just one of many other microorganisms, including fungi, that can be present in the water distribution system. This chapter attempts to provide an overall approach to assessing risks and developing prevention strategies, including design considerations, routine preventive maintenance for operations and equipment, and remediation measures during floods or utility outages. Water disinfection/treatment options are also discussed, including considerations for use and strengths and challenges of various modalities*

KEY CONCEPTS

- Water delivery systems are an essential component of the environment of care in healthcare facilities that are dependent upon maintenance of water quality standards employed by the community public water supplier, typically a municipality in the region of the healthcare facilities. This responsibility for water quality then transitions to the facility once water enters the facility water distribution infrastructure, reflecting complementary roles for prevention.

- Waterborne bacterial and fungal contamination risks are often subtle and associated with a wide variety of sources and have potential for direct or indirect transmission. Understanding conditions that allow for waterborne pathogen growth and proliferation is critical to prevention and control. Infection preventionists need to maintain a high level of awareness for infectious agents that might be causing waterborne infectious diseases in the population they serve. This includes awareness, surveillance, and reporting of community-associated diseases to the appropriate local public health agency; diseases associated with moisture and water-distribution systems that may be facility-associated also must be reported.

- Key prevention strategies for waterborne pathogens include facility risk assessment for areas of potential growth and/or transmission, use of design strategies aimed at reducing the risk of pathogen growth or release, compliance with maintenance practices that contribute to controlling transmission risk, employment of remediation measures during emergencies, and consideration of disinfection modalities when surveillance or risk assessment indicates a need.

- *Pseudomonas* spp., atypical (or nontuberculosis) mycobacteria, and *Legionella* are the most commonly reported waterborne pathogens.

- Water-associated disease has also been reported in the community-based personal care services industry, highlighting the importance of infection prevention in nontraditional industries.

BACKGROUND

The impact of water-related contamination on health in any setting is far reaching, and consideration of water issues is an essential component of infection control risk assessment (ICRA) as described in Chapter 116 Construction and Renovation. Design engineers and architects increasingly recognize that proper planning and design have a major influence on preventing contamination of water distribution systems and reducing potential infection risks for patients, residents, and healthcare personnel (HCP). Therefore, a basic understanding of key terms, concepts, and effects on patients and HCP is essential to providing appropriate input to ICRA.

Key resources for the infection preventionists (IPs) that address water-related problems and preventive solutions include the 2003 Centers for Disease Control and Prevention (CDC) and Healthcare Infection Control Practices Advisory Committee (HICPAC) Guidelines and Recommendations for Environmental Infection Prevention in Healthcare Facilities (referred to hereafter as CDC-EIC guidelines), the 2010 Guidelines for Design and Construction of Health Care Facilities, and a resource from the Association for Professionals in Infection Control and Epidemiology, Inc. (APIC) titled *Construction and Renovation: Toolkit for Professionals in Infection Prevention and Control*.[1-3] Although planning must necessarily provide for remediation in the event of disaster—natural or manmade—the key to prevention is proactive risk assessment, thoughtful design, and routine preventive maintenance. These concepts are systematically reviewed in this chapter for water systems and fixtures and other equipment used in healthcare facilities (HCFs). At the end of this chapter are supplemental resources that may be helpful when conducting facility risk assessment or reviewing design considerations during construction.

BASIC PRINCIPLES

Terminology

The following terms may prove helpful to understanding some types of water within healthcare settings:

Black water: Waste water containing sewage contaminants

Deionized water: Purified water that has had charged ions removed. Used for various applications within healthcare, including the laboratory.

Gray water: Water (as from a sink or bath) that does not contain serious contaminants (as from toilets or diapers).

Potable water: Water suitable for drinking.

Reverse osmosis water: Water forced through a special membrane under pressure, which produces highly purified water. Typically requires remineralizing with essential trace elements before use. Used for various applications within healthcare, including in dialysis.

Basic Plumbing Design

Documented outbreaks have been associated with splashing back from sink drains containing contaminated biofilm, aerosols from shower heads, and contaminated potable (tap) water used with patient care equipment or directly with patients. IPs should understand the basic design of a water supply and waste system to provide effective input regarding plumbing system design and to understand potential factors that may contribute to suspected waterborne infections.

Water Quality

Multiple factors contribute to the quality of water in a HCF, including the methods of treatment used in the municipal water supply prior to the water coming into the facility. For example, in a 2-year, prospective environmental study in San Francisco, monochloramine was shown to reduce building *Legionella* colonization from 60 percent before treatment to 4 percent after treatment. Factors affecting increased *Legionella* colonization in San Francisco buildings included locations over 10 stories high, locations with interruptions in water service, and buildings with water heater

temperatures <50°C.[4] HCFs may obtain an annual report from the local water utility that provides updated information on water treatment and quality. This information could be helpful when performing an annual facility risk assessment for waterborne pathogens.

Drinking water quality also depends on preventive maintenance and surveillance for healthcare-associated infections (HAIs), including a high index of suspicion for infectious agents associated with moisture and water distribution systems.

WATER-ASSOCIATED INFECTIOUS AGENTS

Bacterial and fungal contamination risks are associated with potable (drinking) water. Microorganisms associated with water include *Pseudomonas, Acinetobacter, Moraxella, Aeromonas, Xanthomonas, Legionella, Aspergillus, Fusarium* spp., and atypical (nontuberculosis) mycobacteria.[5-8] All of these genera are associated with serious disease and can potentially be transmitted directly or indirectly from faucets and sinks or through inhalation of aerosols, such as those generated from construction activities or from showerheads.[5] However, based on limited quantifiable data, the risk of healthcare-associated transmission of these pathogens from water is considered relatively low.[5,9] (See Chapters 77 Environmental Gram-negative Bacilli and Chapter 84 *Legionella pneumophila*.)

When disease transmission from direct contact with waterborne microorganisms is considered, *Pseudomonas* spp., atypical mycobacteria, and *Legionella* are the most commonly reported pathogens identified. Furthermore, *Pseudomonas* and atypical mycobacteria often are related to contaminated equipment. For example, water bottles improperly filled with tap water and used for rinsing tracheal suction tubing resulted in an outbreak of *P. cepacia*.[10] Tubing that was permanently attached to showers and used for irrigating patients in a burn unit was implicated in a serious outbreak of *P. aeruginosa* bloodstream infection in five patients.[11] One letter to the editor noted an antidotal outbreak of *Chryseomonas meningosepticum* on a neonatal intensive care unit (ICU) associated with bathing infants with tap water.[12]

Contamination from atypical mycobacteria has led to many investigations of both true and pseudo-outbreaks. The frequency of nontuberculocidal mycobacteria (NTM) in potable water at a large trauma hospital was examined, showing that out of 69 water samples, 36 harbored NTM despite chlorine levels being within the range required by local guidelines.[13] A comprehensive review of both types of outbreaks caused by atypical mycobacteria has been published.[14] For example, an outbreak of postsurgical nasal cellulitis due to *Mycobacterium chelonae* resulted from inadequately sterilized surgical equipment.[15] Inadequate sterilization and rinsing of surgical instruments with contaminated potable water, the source for which was likely biofilm inside the piped water system, were factors for a cluster of cutaneous infections caused by *M. chelonae* following liposuction.[16] Others have reported on the financial burdens of pseudo-outbreaks, such as *M. gordonae* from water used during bronchoscopy, that led to unnecessary treatment

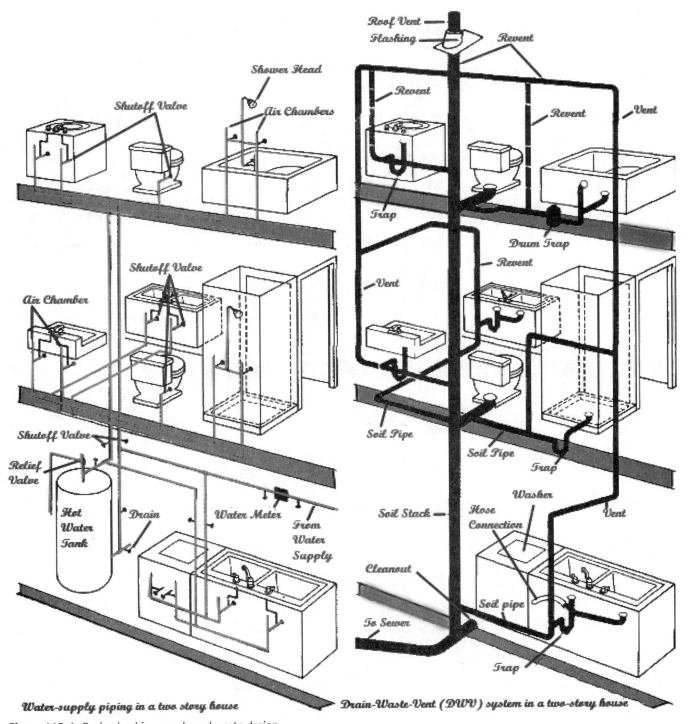

Figure 115-1. Basic plumbing supply and waste design.

Water-supply piping in a two story house

Drain-Waste-Vent (DWV) system in a two-story house

and isolation of patients suspected of having *M. tuberculosis*.[17] Water-associated disease has also been reported in the community-based personal care services industry, demonstrating that microorganisms can cause outbreaks outside of healthcare delivery settings. These reports highlight the importance

of infection prevention in nontraditional industries and in healthcare.[18] Infection prevention guidelines for this sector have been published (e.g., Health Canada's Practices for Personal Services: Tattooing, Ear/Body Piercing, and Electrolysis[19] and Infection Control Guidelines: Foot Care by Health Providers[20]).

Inhalation of aerosols of contaminated water is the primary mechanism of transmission for *Legionella*, not person-to-person transmission (also see Chapter 84 *Legionella pneumophila*). Outbreaks of *Legionella* associated with contaminated equipment often involve inhalation of contaminated aerosols. For example, two cases of healthcare-associated legionellosis in an ICU were reported to be associated with aspiration of nasogastric feedings diluted with tap water.[21] After a healthcare-associated case of *Legionella* at one Japanese hospital, an environmental investigation revealed that a steam towel warmer was contaminated with *Legionella*. Although the index case was not definitively linked to the towel warmer as the source, the authors note that the water in the apparatus may have served as a reservoir for *Legionella* and recommended draining, cleaning, and drying of the device.[22]

Other microorganisms, including fungi, have health consequences and are discussed in the consideration of environmental sources of water-associated infectious agents. See Table 115-1 for selected examples of microbial contamination of water systems and interventions in HCFs.[10,23–34] Outbreaks associated with aerosols generated from multiple sources of water in institutional settings are fully addressed. The 2004 CDC guidelines on the prevention of pneumonia and the CDC-EIC guidelines provide a comprehensive discussion of the impact of waterborne opportunistic pathogens in healthcare settings.[1,35]

ENVIRONMENTAL SOURCES OF WATER-ASSOCIATED INFECTIOUS AGENTS

As noted, various types of equipment and fixtures can promote the growth of water-associated pathogens. Important water reservoirs for these organisms include potable water systems and cooling towers, flush sinks, faucet aerators, hoppers and toilets, eyewash/drench shower stations, chests/ice machines, water baths used to thaw or warm blood products and other liquids, and whirlpool or spalike baths.[5–10,36–40] Concern has been raised about water from flower vases as a disease risk for immunosuppressed patients because potential pathogens have been isolated from such water sources. However, actual disease transmission from these sources has not been well documented and likely occurs rarely. The CDC-EIC guidelines recommend no restrictions for immunocompetent patients.

Table 115-1. Examples of Microbial Contamination of Water Systems and Interventions

Author, year (reference)	Organism	Population/Location	Epidemiologic Factors	Remedial or Preventive Measures
Crane et al., 1981[10]	*Pseudomonas paucimobilis*	ICU	Contaminated tap water	Thermal decontaminated system; revised procedures for tap water use equipment
Burns et al., 1991[23]	*Mycobacterium fortuitum*	Alcoholism rehab unit	Ward showers; tap supply	Disconnected and disinfected showers
Sniadack et al., 1993[24]	*M. xenopi*	Hospital rooms	Water supply (pseudo-outbreak)	Maintain temp >120°F (49°C; ideal 54°C)
Prodinger et al., 1994[25]	*Legionella pneumophila* serogroup 1	Renal allograft	Water distribution system	Replaced central water supply with individual room electric water heaters
Bangsborg et al., 1995[26]	*L. pneumophila* serogroups 1 and 6	Heart-lung transplant	ICU kitchen ice machine	Disinfected machine; preventive maintenance
Graman et al., 1997[27]	*L. pneumophila* serogroup 6	Patient receiving ventilation	Ice machine	Replaced supply line and treatment water system
Kool et al., 1998[28]	*L. pneumophila, Legionella* spp.	Transplant center	Water system	Hyperchlorinated supply
Biurrun et al., 1999[29]	*L. pneumophila* serogroup 6	General hospital	Water distribution system	Copper-silver ionization treatment; continuous chlorination system
Kappstein et al., 2000[30]	*Acinetobacter junii*	Pediatric oncology	Contaminated aerators	Removed, used aerators with radially/vertically arranged lamellae
Darelid et al., 2002[31]	*L. pneumophila* serogroup 1	General hospital	Water distribution system	Maintained water temperature 55°C
Anaissie et al., 2002[32]	*Aspergillus* spp.	Bone marrow transplant	Concentration of airborne fungi on shower surfaces	Cleaned shower floor with detergent prior to use of shower
Nasser et al., 2004[33]	*Burkholderia cepacia*	General hospital	Tap water used to dilute alcohol skin antiseptic	Implemented single-use alcohol swabs
Hota et al., 2009[34]	*Pseudomonas aeruginosa*	ICU and transplant unit	Biofilm inside drain and design of hand-washing stations inside patient rooms	Hand-washing stations were redesigned to prevent splashing
Lowe	Extended-spectrum B-lactamase-producing *Klebsiella oxytoca*	General hospital	Biofilm inside drain and design of hand-washing stations inside patient rooms	Change in sink cleaning regimen, sink drain modifications, antimicrobial stewardship
Kotsanas	Carbapenem-resistant Enterobacteriaceae (CRE) *K. pneumonia, S. marcescens, E. cloacae*	Intensive care unit	Sink grating and drains	Cleaning and decontamination attempts unsuccessful; plans for sink replacement
Lucero	*B. cepacia*	Outbreak among ventilated pediatric patients	Hospital tap water used during oral and tracheostomy care	Change in clinical process

However, equipment may become vehicles of pathogen transmission if it is rinsed with tap water, becomes contaminated, and comes in direct contact with mucous membranes or nonintact skin. The CDC strongly recommends eliminating water/fluid reservoirs whenever possible as an overall guiding principle.[1]

Water Distribution Systems, Cooling Towers, and Environmental Surfaces

Sources of aerosolized water, especially cooling towers, can promote the growth and dispersion of *Legionella*. Once *Legionella* is introduced into a facility's potable water system, organisms may proliferate in the heated water reservoirs, spread throughout the water distribution system (i.e., pipes), and ultimately contaminate sink faucets and showerheads.[41,42] One report also identified dysphagia as a risk for legionellosis in a postoperative patient—the source for which was contaminated ice—and appeared to involve exposure to a very high dose.[43] Facilities typically have more extensive, dedicated water treatment and delivery systems for those needing hemodialysis, which is addressed elsewhere.[1] (See Chapter 39 Dialysis.)

Other microorganisms have been reported to cause problems in the water distribution system. For example, an outbreak of group A streptococcus that spread through a maternity unit was ascribed to a handheld showerhead.[44]

Excessive moisture around pipes and insulation, condensation in drain pans, and flooding from broken pipes can lead to extensive environmental fungal contamination. Such contamination has been associated, for example, with *Penicillium* spores released from water-soaked and rotted cabinets around sinks.[45,46] Other moisture-prone surfaces that can cause problems include air-handling units and ventilation ducts. For example, a report of fungal endophthalmitis from *Acremonium kiliense* demonstrated that contaminated water in a humidifier served as a reservoir, with subsequent spread of the fungi through the air handler.[47]

Static (stagnant) water systems can serve as reservoirs of organisms in the healthcare environment by supporting bacterial growth.[48–51] When water is not moving in recirculation loops, it becomes stagnant, and the residual chlorine or other water treatments can dissipate and lose antimicrobial activity. This in turn leads to corrosion (scale and sediment) and development of biofilm that further amplifies the growth of microorganisms, particularly *Legionella*. Stagnation may result from poor design (dead legs or capped pipes left in place when an older system is renovated) or from a power loss causing pump failure, with resultant loss of water flow. Water in such systems can cause direct or indirect spread of microorganisms to patients. For example, one outbreak occurred after a water pump failed; when water pressure was restored, *Legionella* had multiplied in the water system to considerable levels.[52]

Anaissie and colleagues[6,8,40] investigated risks of fungal contamination of hospital water systems. *Fusarium* spp. in water have also been studied by Raad et al.,[7] who failed to find a source

within water systems in the facility and instead concluded that the majority were community associated. These conflicting reports highlight the need for careful epidemiologic investigation of potential sources by the IP.

Another investigation by Anaissie and colleagues[32] focused on the risk of secondary aerosolization of fungi from the wall and floor surfaces of shower facilities in a bone marrow transplant unit. The authors attempted to show an association between the cleaning of water-related environmental surfaces before patient use and a reduction in the airborne concentration of medically important filamentous fungi in a hospital ward housing immunocompromised patients.

Decorative Water Fountains, Water Walls

As organizations recognize the importance of care delivery sites as therapeutic environments, they may consider installation of features such as decorative water fountains, water walls, or other water features. Mounting evidence has clearly shown that open water features such as decorative fountains and water walls may aerosolize waterborne pathogens and can present an infection risk in healthcare and nonhealthcare settings. In 1992, one of the earliest published outbreaks of *Legionella* occurred at an Orlando, Florida, hotel: five persons developed legionellosis, and all five reported exposure to a decorative water fountain in the hotel lobby. *Legionella pneumophila* was recovered from the fountain and found to match one clinical isolate through pulsed field gel electrophoresis (PFGE). Poor maintenance and underwater lighting, which contributed to ideal water temperatures for *Legionella*, were noted as contributing factors.[53] Another community outbreak resulting in 18 cases of Legionnaire's disease was associated with exposure to a small restaurant fountain; of note, the fountain was without obvious aerosol-generating capability. The outbreak ceased with removal of the fountain.[54] A water fountain in a radiation oncology therapy unit resulted in transmission of *Legionella* to two patients receiving cancer care in the unit. Despite being equipped with water filtration and an ozone generator and records indicating routine maintenance, the design of the fountain allowed for areas of water stagnation, likely contributing to pathogen growth.[55] Another outbreak involving a water wall in a hospital lobby resulted in eight cases of legionellosis; all individuals were either outpatients or visitors to the facility. Routine maintenance was again noted; however, design features of the water wall likely contributed to the growth of *Legionella*.[56] The predominance of evidence for risk involves indoor, open features; however, outdoor fountains may also present a hazard. One paper describes an outbreak of *Legionella* among eleven individuals exposed to an outdoor decorative fountain while attending a local rock concert; a case control study implicated the fountain as the likely source.[57]

Sinks, Flushing Rim Sinks, Hoppers, and Toilets

Sinks and related fixtures may pose health risks because contamination of sink drains or faucet aerators is expected. However, the more important risk may be from splashing contaminated water onto patients or supplies, which can lead to exposure to patients or contamination of supplies and equipment. Reports of direct disease transmission are rare; one of the earliest published reports describes an outbreak caused by *P. aeruginosa* traced to a delivery room resuscitator.[5] Faucet aerators on sinks can enhance growth of waterborne organisms. A published review of pertinent literature reports that two patients in an ICU became colonized or infected with *Stenotrophomonas maltophilia* after exposure to contaminated faucet aerators. Aerators are not recommended, but if they must be used, especially in an area with immunocompromised patients, a systematic cleaning routine should be established (see further discussion below on aerators and laminar flow controls).[15,58] Poorly maintained sink traps might also be reservoirs for microorganisms if splashing is not controlled.[51] Proper sink design and appropriate preventive maintenance may reduce or eliminate these concerns. Indeed, a recent outbreak of infections caused by *P. aeruginosa* in an ICU and transplant unit identified a reservoir of the strains that matched those from patients in a biofilm in hand-washing sinks inside the patient room.[34] However, the mechanism of transmission had more to do with a hand-washing sink design that included a shallow basin, close proximity to point of care, and water that splashed from the sink to surfaces around the sink as much as 1 meter away. Several other reports have also associated sinks with waterborne pathogen transmission, including one paper noting 15 ventilated pediatric patients who became colonized with *Burkholderia* due to the use of contaminated tap water for oral and tracheostomy care. New cases stopped once use of tap water for oral and tracheostomy care was stopped.[59] Another report includes 66 patients in Toronto who acquired an extended-spectrum β-lactamase-producing *K. oxytoca*; multiple hand-washing sinks were found to be positive with the outbreak strain. After a change in sink drain design, revised strainers to reduce backsplash, and replacement of sink traps, cases were no longer noted.[60] Of particular concern is a recent report from Australia of a carbapenem-resistant Enterobacteriaceae (CRE) outbreak associated with contaminated sinks. Ten ICU patients were found positive for Enterobacteriaceae; of these, four were *S. marcescens* isolates that matched isolates from environmental sink cultures. Again, as with the Hota report,[34] sink design contributed to environmental contamination. Sinks were small and shallow, with a tap that directed water over the drain.[61] These ongoing reports illustrate the value IPs bring during the ICRA process to ensure that hand hygiene is convenient and accessible but that the fixture does not contaminate the surrounding environment with water droplets.

Faucets in "clinical" or flush ("flushing rim") sinks located in utility rooms in which aerators have been removed may benefit from installation of splashguards. These provide protection to staff and nearby equipment and environmental surfaces. Toilets have been studied for aerosol production but have not been implicated in direct disease transmission.[36] However, although toilets have not been implicated in direct disease transmission, vacuum toilet designs may contribute to less environmental contamination from mist and splash created during flushing rather than gravity toilet designs.

Stationary and Portable Eyewash/Drench Shower Stations

Eyewash/shower stations may go unused for months and pose a possibility of contamination; water-associated microorganisms (e.g., *Acanthamoeba*) have been reported to contaminate these stations.[1] Rutala and Weber[5] surveyed 40 eyewash stations and found contamination primarily with *Pseudomonas*,[62] *Legionella* spp., amoebae, and fungi. Following the report of *Acanthamoeba* contamination, the Occupational Safety and Health Administration (OSHA) issued a bulletin recommending cleaning and disinfection methods.[48] OSHA recommended a schedule for flushing that follows American National Standards Institute (ANSI) recommendations for flushing the system for a 3-minute period each week.[63]

Ice Storage Chests and Ice Machines

Contaminated ice and ice machines have been implicated as sources of infection, though such reports are not common. In one instance, a cryptosporidiosis outbreak was traced to an ice machine, and the source of contamination was an incontinent individual who was handling the ice.[64] True and pseudo-outbreaks from atypical mycobacteria contamination (e.g., *M. gordonae*) have been linked to ice machines.[65,66] One report also implicated aspiration of ice contaminated with *Legionella* spp. in a patient with a swallowing disorder.[43]

Water Baths and Related Devices

Water baths and related devices are used to warm blood or blood products (e.g., cryoprecipitate, fresh frozen plasma) and other liquids, such as intravenous solutions or peritoneal dialysate. Such baths can become contaminated with pathogenic organisms, such as *P. aeruginosa* and *Acinetobacter*, and several outbreaks or case reports possibly associated with these types of reservoirs have been identified.[1,67] To avoid contamination, manufacturer recommendations should be followed (e.g., perform leak tests), and policies for routine cleaning and disinfection should be considered. The use of impermeable plastic overwraps to keep surfaces of blood products dry and free of potential contamination is another protective measure. New warming technologies that avoid water baths (i.e., waterless systems) have been developed, and such products eliminate a potential water source for contamination.

Whirlpool/Spalike Baths

Pools, whirlpools, hot tubs, and physiotherapy tanks are used in both inpatient and outpatient settings. Specific types of spalike tubs are used in labor and delivery as "birthing tanks." Microbial contamination may involve the drains and agitators and result in cross-contamination between patients if there is inadequate cleaning and disinfection of the plumbing and drains. Skin infections related to water immersion have been recognized for many years and have been reviewed extensively by Rutala and Weber.[5] *P. aeruginosa* has been associated with hot tubs and whirlpools; burn patients are uniquely susceptible to infection, and prevention of contamination in this type of equipment has been studied extensively.[68,69]

Patient Care Equipment

Equipment that is rinsed in tap water can serve as sources of infection. For example, medication nebulizers rinsed in tap water were suspected as the source of an outbreak of legionellosis in a community hospital.[70] Gram-negative organisms can multiply to substantial concentrations under the right conditions, as noted in numerous outbreaks related to endoscopes and automatic endoscope reprocessors (AERs). For a full discussion of AER see Chapter 55 Endoscopy and the CDC-EIC recommendations on water quality for miscellaneous medical equipment connected to water systems (e.g., AER and dental equipment).[1] Meyers and colleagues[16] also describe an outbreak of infections following liposuction that was associated with rinsing of instruments with tap water.

Toxic anterior segment syndrome (TASS) has also focused attention on reprocessing and sterilization of surgical instruments used for cataract surgery. Waterborne microorganisms likely resulted in intrinsic contamination of a balanced salt solution used for this procedure and resulted in a multistate outbreak of TASS.[71] These investigations and others have stimulated publication of new recommendations to prevent TASS.[72]

PREVENTION STRATEGIES

Strategies to prevent infections associated with water depend on optimal design, appropriate preventive maintenance, risk assessment, and surveillance for HAIs that includes a high index of suspicion for infectious agents associated with moisture and water distribution systems. Importantly, identification of cases of legionellosis among the population served may reveal that the source of the pathogen is completely external to the facility where cases are identified.[73] For details on surveillance of HAIs, see Chapter 11 Surveillance.

Risk Assessment

IPs routinely perform risk assessments to identify vulnerabilities, determine actions to take if indicated, and develop a plan to monitor and plan for emergencies. An example of this is ICRA process used during design and construction (see Chapter 116 Construction and Renovation) that looks at the population to be served (or the type of service to be performed, such as a laboratory or pharmacy) in an area to be constructed and considers optimal design features and construction recommendations aimed to prevent infections.

An emerging model under proposal for assessing water risk is to develop a hazard analysis and critical control point (HACCP) plan. The HACCP process has been in use since the 1960s within the food industry to evaluate risks associated with food processing and is now being considered as an approach to evaluate water safety in multioccupant buildings such as hospitals. This process includes characterizing the waterborne pathogen infection risk associated with a building and its occupants. For buildings that meet established risk criteria, it is necessary to assemble a team to do the following:

1. Describe how water is processed for the building and used within the building, and schematically represent in a flow diagram.

2. Identify potential hazards for each step in the process.

3. Determine if the hazard is significant for each step of the process (yes/no).

4. If YES, determine the hazard control being applied or that could be applied at that step. Each step at which hazard control is applied is a "critical control point."

5. For every critical control point, determine:

    a. The critical control limit

    b. The monitoring method

    c. The frequency of monitoring

    d. Corrective actions if limit is violated

6. Verify that the overall HACCP plan is being implemented.

7. Validate plan effectiveness by providing evidence.

IPs and facility managers must work together to establish a process for assessing the risk for waterborne pathogen transmission within the HCF; surveillance data is an essential component of this assessment. Risk assessment will help guide design decisions during construction and help determine the effectiveness of maintenance activities within the facility.

Water Distribution System Design

Standards and Recommendations

Prevention and interventions rely primarily on good design and maintenance. As noted, the guiding principle to prevention is removal and elimination of water reservoirs.

Decorative Water Fountains, Water Walls

If features such as decorative water fountains or water walls are currently installed anywhere within or outside of HCFs, organizations must ensure systematic disinfection and preventive maintenance.[1] Legionellosis has been associated with decorative water features in numerous settings, including both indoor and outdoor features,[53-57] supporting the need for effective design and routine disinfection and maintenance.[5]

Potable Water Supply System

As noted in Chapter 114 Heating, Ventilation, and Air Conditioning; Chapter 116 Construction and Renovation; and the 2010 Facility Guidelines Institute (FGI) Guidelines for Design and Construction of Health Care Facilities[2] are sources of design guidance for infection prevention. Examples of important design specifications are highlighted below. For example, water delivery systems should be designed to supply water at sufficient pressure to operate all fixtures and equipment during maximum demand. Provision of two separate water lines from a looped municipal water supply system to a facility would minimize interruption of water service. General guidelines include:

- Water-service mains, branch mains, and other main waterlines should have stop (isolation) valves for each fixture. Valves isolate a portion of the water system from the remainder of the system when repair is required.

- Vacuum breakers should be installed on faucets. Approved backflow preventers (i.e., antisiphon devices) protect water supply systems from contamination in high-risk areas such as dialysis units. (See Chapter 39 Dialysis for microbiologic monitoring, as recommended by the Association for the Advancement of Medical Instrumentation [AAMI].)

- Floor drains should be avoided as much as possible and specifically should not be in operating or delivery rooms, with the exception of dedicated cystoscopic rooms.

- Drainage piping should not be installed in ceilings or exposed in operating and delivery rooms, nurseries, or other sensitive areas. If overhead drain piping is unavoidable, provisions must be made to protect the space below from leaks, condensation, and dust particles.

- Water supply pipes with dead ends should be avoided or, if found, should be minimized.

Temperature Specifications

A water heating system should have sufficient supply capacity at the temperatures and amounts specified in Table 115-2 for hospitals (see equivalent Table 2.1-5, 2010 Guidelines[2]). The

Table 115-2. Hot Water Use—General Hospital

	Hot Water Use		
	Clinical	Dietary	Laundry
Liters per sec per bed[1]	11.9	7.2	7.6
Gallons per hour per bed[1]	3	2	2
Temperature (°C)	41–49[2]	49[3]	71[4]
Temperature (°F)	105–120[2]	120[3]	160[4]

[1]Quantities indicated for design demand of hot water are for general reference minimums and shall not substitute for accepted engineering design procedures using actual number and types of fixtures to be installed. Design will also be affected by temperature of cold water used for mixing, length of run, and insulation relative to heat loss, etc. As an example, total quantity of hot water needed will be less when temperature available at the outlet is very nearly that of the source tank, and the cold water used for tempering is relatively warm.

[2]The range represents the maximum and minimum allowable temperature.

[3]Provisions shall be made to provide 180°F (82°C) rinse water at ware-washer (may be by separate booster).

[4]Provision shall be made to provide 160°F (71°C) hot water at the laundry equipment when needed. (This may be steam jet or separate booster heater.) However, it is emphasized that this does not imply that all water used would be at this temperature. Water temperatures required for acceptable laundry results vary according to type of cycle, time of operation, formula of soap and bleach, and type and degree of soil. Lower temperatures may be adequate for most procedures in many facilities but the higher temperature 160°F (71°C) should be available when needed for special conditions.

From Facility Guidelines Institute. 2010 Guidelines for Design and Construction of Health Care Facilities. Chicago: The American Society for Healthcare Engineering (ASHE), 2010: Table 2.1–5, pp 87.

temperature is measured at the point of use or inlet to the equipment. Hot water tank temperatures may be set higher. Hot water distribution systems serving patient care areas should use constant recirculation to provide continuous hot water at each outlet. In nursing facilities, the water system should be designed appropriately to supply hot water to meet the demands of resident care. The water temperature for showers and bathing should be appropriate for comfortable use, and the 2010 Guidelines permit a temperature range between 105°F (41°C) and 120°F (49°C). The guidelines seek to balance potential risks of scalding against the risks of exposure to *Legionella*, because the older standard (110°F [43°C]) is near the temperature supporting growth of *Legionella* (77°F to 108°F [25°C to 42.2°C]).[58,74,75] The CDC recommends maintaining water temperatures at 124°F (51°C) or higher and cold water temperatures at 68°F (20°C) to control *Legionella*; again, however, concerns with scalding move many building codes to limit hot water temperature to 120°F (as with the FGI Guidelines). Mixing pressure valves must then be used to control water temperature at the use outlet so that the water system can be maintained at the higher temperature without risk of scalding.[1,58] Such decisions are important safety and cost/benefit issues and are determined state by state.[76] (See Chapter 84 *Legionella pneumophila*.)

Other factors (dynamic versus static flow, type of water heating system, and water treatment) have varying effects on the system's ability to control microbial growth at the design temperatures. For example, preliminary reports suggest that use of chloramines, rather than chlorine, may reduce the risk of *Legionella* in the distribution systems of municipal water supplies.[1,28] Multiple reports support the reduced risk of hospital-associated Legionnaire's disease when municipal water treatment plants used monochloramine.[77,78] Monochloramine applications for facility use are under development but are not yet available as practical options. Chlorine dioxide, another application useful in cold water and able to penetrate pipe biofilms, has been evaluated in some institutions and used for infection prevention with some success in other countries.[79-82] A 17-month evaluation in a U.S. hospital using chlorine dioxide demonstrated its efficacy and safety in maintaining appropriate levels of chlorine dioxide and chlorites.[82,83] Other treatments with the potential to prevent or eradicate *Legionella* have been reported, such as copper-silver ion treatment, which also penetrates the biofilm and avoids pipe corrosion associated with hyperchlorination.[41,42,51,52,84,85] A published review summarizes the experiences of the first 16 hospitals to install copper-silver ionization systems for *Legionella* disinfection, covering use periods of 5 to 11 years, with a high degree of success.[86] Ultraviolet light is another modality that is successful with in vitro bactericidal effects but cannot effectively penetrate the biofilm of a contaminated water system. However, it can prevent contamination and may be used with other disinfection modalities.[87,88]

If a risk assessment is performed and it is determined that a supplemental disinfection method is indicated, Table 115-3 can provide information that may help guide appropriate selection of a water disinfection method by comparing different methods.

Table 115-3. Comparison of Water Disinfection Methods in a Hospital Environment

ITEM	DISINFECTION SYSTEM						
	SUPER HEATING & FLUSH	AUTO – CHLORINATING/ INHIBITOR SYSTEM	AUTO– CHLORAMINE SYSTEM (MONO-CHLORAMINE)	CHLORINE DIOXIDE	COPPER – SILVER IONIZATION SYSTEM	OZONATION	ULTRAVIOLET
USED ON DOMESTIC COLD WATER SYSTEM	NO	YES	YES	YES	YES	YES	YES
USED ON DOMESTIC HOT WATER SYSTEM	YES	YES	YES	YES	YES	YES	YES
CHEMICAL UTILIZED	NONE	SODIUM HYPOCHLORITE	CHLORAMINE (CHLORINE & AMMONIA)	CHLORINE DIOXIDE (SODIUM CHLORITE)	COPPER & SILVER (METALS)	NONE	NONE
BY-PRODUCT	NONE	TRIHALOMETHANES (THM'S)	TRIHALOMETHANES (THM'S) (FAR LESS THAN CHLORINE)	SOME CHEMICAL DECOMPOSITION IN FORM OF CHLORITE AND CHLORATE	NONE	SOME BROMATE & FORMALDEHYDE	OZONE
EFFECTIVE MAX. pH	NONE	7.8 pH	9 pH	10 pH	8 pH	NA	NA
ASTHETIC QUALITY (TASTE, ODOR & CLARITY)	NONE	YES – TASTE AND ODOR PROBLEMS	YES – TASTE AND ODOR PROBLEMS	NONE (BELOW .8 PPM) – REMOVES MOST TASTE AND ODORS PROBLEMS	YES – SOME CLARITY PROBLEMS (BLACK WATER)	YES – ODOR PROBLEMS	NONE – PROVIDED HIGH INTENSITY OZONE LAMPS ARE NOT USED
IMPACT ON EQUIPMENT AND SYSTEM	POTENTIAL	POTENTIAL CORROSION PROBLEMS	MINIMAL POTENTIAL CORROSION PROBLEMS	MINIMAL POTENTIAL CORROSION PROBLEMS	MINIMAL POTENTIAL DEPOSITION OF COPPER ON MILD STEEL / LOCALIZED CORROSION	POTENTIAL CORROSION PROBLEMS	POTENTIAL – CORROSION PROBLEMS IF HIGH INTENSITY OZONE LAMPS ARE USED
IMPACT ON DIALYSIS EQUIPMENT	NONE	NONE (BELOW 4 PPM) – CARBON FILTERS AND RO EQUIPMENT EFFECTIVELY REMOVES CHLORINE AND BY-PRODUCTS	SIGNIFICANTLY DIFFICULT TO REMOVE CHLORAMINES (MONOCHLORAMINES) AND BY-PRODUCTS AT 4 PPM AND BELOW - CARBON FILTERS EFFECTIVE, MEMBRANE DAMAGE	NONE (BELOW .8 PPM) – CARBON FILTERS AND RO EQUIPMENT EFFECTIVELY REMOVES CHLORINE DIOXIDE AND BY-PRODUCTS	INFORMATION CURRENTLY NOT AVAILABLE	INFORMATION CURRENTLY NOT AVAILABLE	NONE
ENVIRONMENTAL & HEALTH EFFECTS	WATER IS AT SCALDING TEMPERATURE	PRODUCES CARCINOGENIC THM'S.	PRODUCES CARCINOGENIC THM'S (less than chlorine).	NONE – DOES NOT PRODUCE THM'S AND CAN DESTROY SOME THM'S.	COPPER IS ACUTELY TOXIC TO MANY AQUATIC SPECIES AT LEVELS LOW AS 50 PPB. SYSTEM OPERATES BETWEEN 200 – 600 PPB COPPER, 10 TO 60 PPB SILVER.	NONE – BROMITE IDENTIFIED AS AN ANIMAL CARCINOGEN – EFFECTS ON HUMANS UNKNOWN	NONE
EPA APPROVED PRIMARY DRINKING WATER DISINFECTANT	NO	YES (below 4 ppm)	YES (below 4 ppm)	YES (below 8 ppm)	NO	NO	NO
BREAKS DOWN BIOFILM (AT NOMINAL OPERATING CONDITIONS)	YES	NO @ BELOW 50 PPM – MINIMAL ABOVE 50 PPM (SYSTEM OPERATES BETWEEN 2 AND 3 PPM)	NO – (SYSTEM OPERATES AT 2-3 PPM)	YES	YES / NO – DEPENDING ON PPB	NO	NO

continued

Table 115-3. Comparison of Water Disinfection Methods in a Hospital Environment (cont'd)

ITEM	SUPER HEATING & FLUSH	AUTO – CHLORINATING/ INHIBITOR SYSTEM	AUTO – CHLORAMINE SYSTEM (MONO-CHLORAMINE)	CHLORINE DIOXIDE	COPPER – SILVER IONIZATION SYSTEM	OZONATION	ULTRAVIOLET
			DISINFECTION SYSTEM				
INHIBITS BIOFILM (AT NOMINAL OPERATING CONDITIONS)	NO	MINIMAL	MINIMAL	YES	YES / NO – DEPENDING ON PPB	NO	NO
SHORT-TERM (1–2 DAYS) RESIDUAL EFFECTIVENESS AGAINST *LEGIONELLA* (DISINFECTION SYSTEM NOT OPERATING)	YES	YES	YES – FAR LESS EFFECTIVE THAN CHLORINE	YES	YES	NO	NO
LONG-TERM (1–2 WEEKS) RESIDUAL EFFECTIVENESS AGAINST *LEGIONELLA* (DISINFECTION SYSTEM NOT OPERATING)	NONE	NONE	INFORMATION CURRENTLY NOT AVAILABLE	YES	YES – FOR HOT WATER SYSTEMS ONLY	NONE	NONE
FLUSHING REQUIRED AT ALL FIXTURES AT START UP AND ON PERIODIC BASES	YES	YES	YES	YES	YES	YES	YES
CHLORINE SHOCKING OF WATER SYSTEM REQUIRED PRIOR TO SYSTEM OPERATING (SHOCKING EFFECTS BULK WATER ONLY – NO EFFECT ON BIOFILM)	NA	YES	YES	NOT REQUIRED	NOT REQUIRED	YES	YES

Used with permission from: Greg Bova, The Johns Hopkins Hospital, 2013.

APIC Text of Infection Control and Epidemiology

Any intervention that reduces the corrosion or potential for dislodgment and aerosolization of contaminants to patients or building occupants is key to overall prevention. To routinely prevent waterborne microbial contamination, the CDC currently recommends that organizations unable to attain the recommended temperatures or install thermostatic mixing valves follow a protocol to periodically increase the water temperature up to 150°F (up to 66°C) or chlorinate the water and flush it through the system.[1]

Other temperature specifications from the 2010 Guidelines concern provisions to supply 160°F (71°C) water for laundry purposes when a facility supports an onsite laundry service. Footnotes for Table 115-2 (2010 FGI Guidelines, Table 2.1-5) state that water temperature needs for laundry services will vary according to wash cycle, time of operation, formula of soap and bleach, and type and degree of soil. Significant reductions of microbial contamination can be achieved at lower temperatures, with concomitant major savings (see Chapter 111 Laundry, Patient Linens, Textiles, and Uniforms).

Equipment Design Issues

Hand-washing Stations

The major engineering and infection prevention method for reducing infection transmission is adequate and proper placement of hand-washing stations. The 2010 Guidelines define a hand-washing station as "an area providing a sink with hot and cold water supply and a faucet that facilitates easy on/off mixing capabilities. The station includes provision of cleansing agents and drying capability."[2] The guidelines require a hand-washing station in each patient room, outside the patient's cubicle curtain, and in the toilet room. Access for use is essential to prevent the spread of infection, and improper placement and maintenance can add to the environmental reservoir of contaminants. As discussed, design of the hand-washing sink and assessment after installation for unwanted dissemination of water droplets are important aspects to address.[34] If existing space (in major renovation) does not permit a sink in the patient room, state health authorities may provide a waiver and permit instead a "hand sanitation station" that is "a dispensing location for a waterless, antiseptic hand rub product that is applied to reduce the number of microorganism present on the hands."[2]

Functional consideration and placement of dispensers of waterless alcohol-based hand rub (ABHR) is strongly encouraged and endorsed by both CDC Guidelines and patient safety goals from accreditation agencies.[89,90] However, the 2014 Guidelines do not consider dispensers of ABHR as equivalent to hand-washing sinks, as CDC Guidelines prescribe the need to use soap and water for washing hands contaminated with visible proteinaceous material.[2,89]

ABHR use is a centerpiece of strategies to improve hand hygiene by HCP, and placement of ABHR in patient care areas should include input from direct care providers. Following a national stakeholder meeting regarding ABHRs and fire safety in HCFs held in July 2003, and cohosted by the CDC and the American Hospital Association (AHA), a major campaign was initiated by these organizations to encourage the installation of dispensers just inside patient rooms, treatment rooms, suites, and other acceptable areas. Results of a fire modeling risk study indicated that 1.2 L dispensers of ABHR solution could be installed safely in corridors under certain conditions, but the then existing (2003) fire codes prohibited such placement. Key codes have been modified, but design considerations remain important for ease of access as well as maintenance for functionality and safety.[91] Fire code issues continue to be a challenge and can be monitored from several sources. (In Supplemental Resources, see American Society for Healthcare Engineering and Premier Safety Institute.)

The use of automated hand-washing machines has not yet clearly improved long-term compliance with hand washing, though design efforts continue.[89,92,93]

Design Considerations for Hand-washing Facilities

- Faucets: Careful investigation into hand-washing equipment design (types of faucets) may further reduce hand contamination. Nontouch faucet fittings have increased in usage and may require extra attention to maintain temperature and pressure and may require frequent usage to avoid water contamination. Electronic-eye faucets have been the focus of study for increased correlation with *Legionella* contamination; a risk assessment is recommended to determine if their use is optimal in various settings.[94–98]

- Location: Sinks need to be placed in convenient and accessible areas but should be positioned to prevent splashing of nearby equipment and supplies.[34,99] Surfaces adjacent to water fixtures should be nonporous to resist fungal growth.[47] Areas beneath sinks should not be used for storage because of proximity to sanitary sewer connections and risks of condensation, leaks, or water damage. Accrediting and regulatory agencies discourage or cite this practice under general sanitation standards to ensure that clean materials are not at risk of contamination. Splashguards for clinical or flushing rim sinks should be considered for protection of HCP, as already noted.

- Soap: Built-in refillable soap dispensers should be avoided to reduce the need for cleaning and to prevent contamination problems.[1,89] Washable dispensers with disposable cassettes are effective in reducing contamination risks, and maintenance is far less labor intensive.

- Drying: Sufficient space should be provided for paper towel dispensers, soap, and waste disposal. Paper towel dispensers should be designed to protect against soil or dust and to provide for single-unit dispensing. Ideal designs dispense the towel without direct hand contact with the dispenser. If hot-air dryers are used, installation should preclude possible contamination by recirculation of air. Research on hand contamination during drying suggests the importance of evaluating different methods and designs, as well as the site and placement of towel dispensers.[100–103]

- Aerators: As noted, aerator usage is not recommended, though CDC guidelines indicate that removal is an unresolved issue for immunocompetent patients.[1] Proper sink design (i.e., depth of the sink, length of the spout, distance between the spout and sink drain) may reduce or eliminate the hazard. Regular cleaning also will reduce risks if aerators are used.[30,58] Some building codes do not allow aerators but will allow nonaerating, laminar flow control devices, which slow down the flow of water. Many manufacturers locate this type of control device at the base of the faucet, so it will not be visible at the outlet.

- Sink controls: Depending on local codes, faucets can be operated by hand; by elbow-, knee-, or foot-operated controls; or automatically by electronic or other sensor-driven controls (example: California code only allows "no touch" or wrist-blade controls on any acute healthcare fixture intended for hand washing). Other hand-washing machines being tested may have merit, but efficacy is not yet well described. Foot- and knee-operated and infrared sensor controls may be more expensive but are required in areas where the risk of touch contamination should be eliminated (e.g., scrub sinks for invasive procedure rooms). Blade handles on clinical sinks should be at least 6 inches long for operation without hands (i.e., elbow operated). In general patient care areas, hand-operated fixtures for routine hand washing may use single-lever or wrist-blade devices.[2] Electronic controls offer the advantages of no-touch operation and save water. Some disadvantages include the inability to adjust water temperature; most use mixing valves that deliver tepid or warm water only; most will be on emergency power but, if battery-powered, most are designed to have a visual indicator (e.g., flashing light) long before battery expiration. Some studies have found that the concentration of microorganisms is higher in fixtures with electronic control; however, there is no definitive evidence this increases infection risk for patients in areas where these are installed.[94-98] Fixture design and location may therefore be of more importance.

Newer designs are also offering automatic flushing capability to reduce stagnation of water in locations where sinks may not be used frequently; this may help reduce risk of biofilm formation, but this is not definitively known, nor is there any published evidence of clinical reduction in infection associated with these designs.

Whirlpool/Spa Bathing Facilities

Whirlpools, tubs, and spalike bathing facilities all require attention to design and maintenance to reduce risks of cross-contamination. Physical therapy tubs or Hubbard tanks commonly are used in facilities that need to provide a range of treatments. As noted, various types of bathing facilities have become available for mothers in birthing rooms, and though these facilities are similar to physical therapy units, they are somewhat different in design (see Chapter 41 Neonates and Chapter 66 Rehabilitation Services.) Procedures for use and disinfection should be consistent with the American Physical Therapy Association recommendations for tanks and equipment. The CDC-EIC guidelines provide a full description of the issues.[1]

Plumbing for spa baths or spalike tubs has longer piping than that for typical whirlpools. Thus, contaminated water may become trapped after apparent draining and could be flushed into the tub during the next use. Another example of a design problem contributing to contamination is the location of the whirlpool drain. During an outbreak investigation, it was determined that the drain of the whirlpool bathtub, contaminated with the epidemic strain, closed approximately 2.54 cm below the drain's strainer. Water from the faucet, which was not contaminated, was contaminated with P. aeruginosa from the drain when the tub was filled. The design of the drain allowed the epidemic strain to be transmitted to immunocompromised patients using the whirlpool bathtub. The authors suggest that use of whirlpool bathtubs with drains that seal at the top could eliminate this potential source of infection.[68] When considering installation of such tubs, it is essential to communicate with state regulators and others with design expertise. Cleaning and disinfecting the tub and jets with specific spa cleaning products and proper draining and flushing sequences are essential when considering their use.[104] Pipeless spa baths are now available commercially for use in HCFs as well as homes and may reduce these concerns considerably (see Supplemental Resources).

Two reported outbreaks of dermatitis and other infections associated with P. aeruginosa in swimming pools and hot tubs prompted the CDC to issue disinfection recommendations in late 2000 for facility operators.[105] Although these outbreaks occurred in hotels, the guidelines fit other institutional settings. The report noted that the use of cyanurate reduces chlorine loss from ultraviolet light exposure but also reduces the antimicrobial activity of chlorine.

To reduce the risk of Pseudomonas dermatitis and other infections from waterborne organisms, the CDC recommends that pool and hot tub operators adhere to the following[105]:

- Follow pool and hot tub recommendations and regulatory requirements for pH and disinfectant levels.

- Have a thorough knowledge of pool and hot tub operation.

- Provide training for staff members on the capabilities, maintenance, and emergency-alert procedures of remote monitoring systems.

- Closely monitor pool and hot tub chlorine levels during periods of heavy use.

- Recognize that hot tub temperatures cause chlorine to dissipate rapidly.

- Understand the appropriate use and effects of cyanurates on disinfection and testing.

Cooling Tower Design

The 2004 CDC guidelines for preventing healthcare-associated pneumonia briefly address design issues related to new cooling towers for preventing the spread of Legionella.

The 2003 CDC-EIC guidelines reinforce older recommendations that new cooling towers should be designed to direct tower drift away from the hospital air-intake system, minimizing aerosol drift; drift eliminators should be installed, and effective EPA-approved biocides should be used regularly for operational cooling towers.[1,35] Practical recommendations for design and maintenance of cooling towers may be located from engineering resources.[106,107] (See Supplemental Resources.)

Design Issues for Disposal of Human Waste

There is no safe, aesthetic management of stool and other human waste in bedpans; system design should provide for emptying bedpans without leaving the patient room or for minimal travel distance to clinical/flushing rim sinks in treatment areas. Management of fecal waste during disasters that involve extensive power loss and subsequent loss of water or sewer is critical (see Chapter 119 Emergency Management). This process is especially challenging when caring for critically ill patients. One option is to equip all patient rooms with attached bathrooms; another is installing utility rooms with clinical or flushing rim sinks between patient rooms. In ICUs this consumes precious square footage that could be dedicated to other uses, because most patients needing this care are not ambulatory. Barker and Jones,[108] using an in vitro study of dispersal of *Serratia marcescens* and a bacteriophage during flushing of a toilet fixture, demonstrated significant release of these microorganisms over short ranges and consequent contamination of the fixture. Their observations indicate that careful attention is needed regarding proximity of any toilet fixture to the immediate area around the patient. Swivette toilets that can be recessed back under a cabinet have been used in some ICUs. However, in-use experience with these has been mixed, and they are no longer included within the FGI Guidelines. The plumbing connections may leak, the low height of the fixture may make it hard to use by personnel and impractical for patients, and contamination of adjacent surfaces is possible. Patients who need critical care but have less intense acuity levels may be able to ambulate. FGI 2010 Guidelines support at minimum a toilet room or a clinical sink between two patient rooms, whether medical, coronary, or pediatric ICUs.

Preventive Maintenance

Potable Water Distribution Systems, Cooling Towers, and Environmental Surfaces

Preventive maintenance for potable water systems includes a number of issues (e.g., cleaning and disinfection of cooling towers and water fountains).

Among the most critical prevention methods is maintenance of appropriate water temperatures. The American Society of Heating, Refrigerating and Air-Conditioning Engineers (ASHRAE) recommends that cold water be stored below 68°F (20°C) and hot water above 140°F (60°C), circulating with a minimum return temperature of 124°F (51°C) or the highest allowable temperature specified in state regulations and building codes.[106] If the temperature setting of 124°F (51°C) is permitted, installation of preset thermostatic mixing valves reduces risk of scalding (as previously discussed) and is recommended by the CDC.[1] To address safety concerns, the 2006 Guidelines have defined a temperature range rather than a maximum for hot water temperatures for clinical use; that is, 105°F to 120°F (41°C to 49°C).[2]

Dead legs (capped piping with no flow) should be removed or avoided. Biocides should be applied at label dosages to control growth of other bacteria, algae, and protozoa. Removal or prevention of sediment accumulation also may reduce other niches that may amplify microbial growth. Plumbing that includes self-draining shower lines, antiscald valves, and pipe insulation may reduce contamination risks. Routine sampling is not encouraged except for tracing studies or outbreak investigations.[1] More emphasis is placed on clean equipment in excellent state of repair.[94] Hot and cold water systems should be inspected and cleaned as defined by the facility's operational and preventive maintenance schedule. Finally, filters for outside air must be kept dry because wet filters are ineffective; filters must be cleaned and replaced with a frequency directed by the manufacturer.

Dead legs caused by normally closed valves on equipment bypasses or infrequently used lines should be provided with drain valves.

Eyewash/Shower Stations

ANSI recommends flushing eyewash stations weekly for 3 minutes.[63]

Water Baths and Related Devices

If water baths and related devices are used to warm fluids, such as blood products or peritoneal dialysate, policies for routine cleaning, disinfection, and changing of the water should be in place. After cleaning, the bath/device should be filled with water to which a germicide has been added. Manufacturer recommendations should be followed (e.g., perform leak tests); wrapping blood products in impermeable plastic would also keep them dry and free of contamination.[5,67]

Ice Storage Chests and Ice-Making Machines

The CDC developed an advisory in reference to sanitary care and maintenance of ice storage chests in 1968 in response to a hospital outbreak traced to the use of contaminated ice. This advisory was published again in 1998 because of continuing requests and inquiries related to this subject.[1,66] The 2003 CDC-EIC guidelines support this advisory and recommend first checking for available instructions from the manufacturer and determining whether EPA-approved disinfectants are suitable for the equipment. If none is available, a general regimen is suggested, based on the advisory. The following procedures should be followed to reduce the likelihood of contamination of ice storage chests and ice-making machines in HCFs[1,66]:

Weekly–Monthly

- Clean ice storage chests on a preset schedule. Weekly to monthly cleaning of open chests is suggested; less frequent cleaning may be possible with ice-making machines.

- Cleaning should be done with fresh soap or detergent solution after disconnecting the unit, removing and discarding all ice, and allowing the ice storage chest to warm to room temperature. Use clean materials to scrub all surfaces, paying particular attention to door tracks, guides, and gaskets.

- After cleaning, rinse all surfaces of the chest with fresh tap water, wipe dry with clean materials, rinse again with a 10- to 100-ppm chlorine solution (1 to 8 mL of sodium hypochlorite [household bleach] per gallon of water), and allow all surfaces to dry before returning the unit to service.

Monthly–Quarterly

- On a regular schedule, perhaps monthly to quarterly, disconnect ice-making machines, discard all ice, and disassemble removable parts of the machine that come in contact with the water used to make ice. Thoroughly clean the machine and its parts with detergent and water.

- Check for the need of possible repair of any portion of the machine, replacing feeder lines as needed. Ensure the presence of an air space in the tubing that leads from the potable water inlet into the water distribution system of the ice making machine. Inspect for insect or rodent infestation under the unit and treat if necessary. Check the gasket around the door of the ice storage chest (open-compartment models) for cleanliness and evidence of possible leakage or dripping of contaminants into the chest. Clean the chest as described with detergent and water.

- Circulate a 50- to 100-ppm chlorine solution throughout the entire storage and ice making system of the machine according to the manufacturer's recommended cleaning and sanitizing procedures. Let the 50-ppm chlorine solution remain in the ice-making and storage system of the machine for 4 hours (or at least 2 hours for a 100-ppm chlorine solution).

- Remove the chlorine solution, flush the system with fresh tap water, allow the ice storage chest to dry, and then return the unit to service.

Whirlpools, Spas, and Tanks

Hydrotherapy pools and immersion tanks present unique disinfection problems. Facilities with large hydrotherapy pools containing thousands of gallons of water cannot drain the pools after each patient use; such pools are generally drained and cleaned every 1 to 2 weeks. CDC guidelines recommend installation of a water filter of sufficient size to filter all the water at least three times per day and to chlorinate the water so that a free chlorine residual of approximately 0.5 mg/L is maintained at a pH of 7.2 to 7.6. Local public health authorities can provide consultation

regarding chlorination, alternate halogen disinfectants, and hydrotherapy pool sanitation. Hubbard and immersion tanks are drained after each patient use. The CDC recommends cleaning inside surfaces with a disinfectant-detergent, then rinsing with tap water. After the last patient each day, an additional disinfection step should be performed; this involves circulating a chlorine solution (200 to 300 mg/L) through the agitator of the tank for 15 minutes and then rinsing. It also is recommended that the tank be thoroughly cleaned with a disinfectant-detergent, rinsed, wiped dry with clean cloths, and not filled until ready for use.[1]

An alternative approach to control of contamination in hydrotherapy tanks frequently used in burn units is the use of plastic liners to create a "whirlpool effect" without agitators. Such liners make it possible to minimize contact of contaminated water with the interior surface of the tank and obviate the need for agitators that may be difficult to clean and decontaminate.

If piped spa-style tubs are used, the tub and jets should be cleaned and disinfected with specific spa-cleaning products, and proper draining and flushing sequences should be used. Equipment may be stainless steel, plexiglass, or tile, but it remains critical to consult with manufacturers to identify appropriate cleaning products for their surfaces. Spa baths were originally designed for residential use, but as noted, there are better designs now available for healthcare with improved surfaces and cleanability.

Patient Care Equipment

Concerns for contamination of respiratory therapy equipment (e.g., humidifiers, nebulizers), bronchoscopes, and other patient care equipment involving water and moisture require constant vigilance. Gram-negative organisms can multiply to substantial concentrations under the right conditions. Sterile water should be used, instead of tap water, for rinsing semicritical equipment and devices used on the respiratory tract after they have been chemically disinfected.[35] Reported outbreaks have once again drawn attention to both design and disinfection issues of automatic endoscopic machines, as well as endoscope design.[109,110] Recommendations for complete air drying or rinsing with alcohol before storage were discussed in a joint bulletin issued by the CDC and the U.S. Food and Drug Administration (FDA).[111] (See Chapter 55 Endoscopy.)

Remediation Strategies

Planning hazard prevention through system and equipment design as well as preventive maintenance remain the strongest approaches to strategies. However, given the best of intentions, disruptions do occur whether during construction, natural disasters, or technical or manmade disasters. Remediation approaches are discussed in terms of utilities, water leaks/flooding, and controlling *Legionella* contamination if problems occur.

Utility Disruptions

Emergency preparedness requires a number of strategies, including sufficient storage of supplies and follow-up response protocols for planned or unplanned power loss affecting water flow. Without planning and rapid response, power outages and water service interruptions can lead to major problems. IPs should participate in planning and response to prevent, detect, and/or reduce infectious hazards, in accordance with TJC utility management and emergency management standards.[112]

Facility policies should include contingency planning for supplying water for drinking, cleaning, bathing, and toilet flushing. In addition, an unplanned disruption may affect the water distribution lines and require heating or chlorination, flushing, and water testing before resumption of use. CDC guidelines offer specific guidance on remediation strategies for the water distribution system, including conditions involving a "boiled water advisory" (BWA).[1,2,42] IPs should be aware and have access to their facility's water-quality analysis report, which must be provided to local water control authority under the auspices of the EPA. The report includes elements measured against standards such as turbidity (1 unit), microbiologic contaminants (0 coliform bacterium/100 mL), and residual disinfectant levels, such as chlorine (less than 4 mg/L chlorine).[113] A major component of contingency planning is identifying the preferred method of decontaminating the hot water system after a disruption. If there is a separate water storage and treatment system for dialysis, this should be included in the plan, including filter changes and disinfection.[1] (See Chapter 31 Cleaning, Disinfection, and Sterilization; Chapter 39 Dialysis; and Chapter 119 Emergency Management.)

Other practical considerations in planning for an infection prevention policy for water service disruptions involving a BWA are listed below; communication plans for each are critical:

- Operational: Pre-established agreement and rapid delivery in an emergency with commercial suppliers of bottled water should be in place and should consider at least a 24-hour supply. Risk assessments should include whether or not the facility has a facility-based reservoir such as a water tower or well as a backup resource, or water treatment systems to generate water for dialysis.

- Water for consumption (ice, oral hygiene, food sanitation): Boil water to rolling boil for at least 5 minutes and allow to cool for 10 to 15 minutes, or use bottled water. Posting of warning signs should include water fountains and ice machines. After the BWA is lifted, specific protocols for flushing and cleaning water fountains and ice machines are included in CDC guidelines, as noted.[1]

- Hand hygiene: Identify waterless products (gels, alcohol, packets, or wipes) to have on hand for hand washing; identify specific products that are safe and easy to use (i.e., distinguish hand-washing products from environmental cleaning products).

- Skin and wound care: Surgical incisions reseal within 24 to 48 hours after closure, and water available under a BWA including bottled water would be acceptable. However, sterile water should be used for irrigation of wounds or incision.

- Bathing and showering: Identify products (such as bottled water and no-rinse cleansing cloths) to have on hand for patient use (infants/adults); consider requesting personnel to bring bottled water for themselves to conserve supplies for patient use.

- Cleaning, disinfection, and sterilization: Because surgical instruments are sterilized after cleaning and packaging for reprocessing, any microbes present in water under a BWA will be inactivated. No additional precautions are therefore necessary for these instruments after they have undergone a proper sterilization process. Routine practices for reprocessing endoscopes with narrow internal channels, such as forced air drying and flushing internal lumens with alcohol, will mitigate any contamination from rinse water even during a BWA.

- Environmental cleaning: Identify products for environmental cleaning and wiping during the water disruption. The facility should carry out a risk assessment for water used to dilute surface disinfectants if premixed, ready-to-use disinfectant or impregnated disposable cloths are not available.

- Waste: Determine whether toilets can be flushed; if flushing is possible but water is shut off, identify locations where water may be stored and locate buckets that may be used for flushing.

- Determine the communication process to implement before use of taps and other equipment can resume.

- During the water restoration process, expect dislodging of scale with potential to adversely affect valves (e.g., toilet) that may malfunction and require disassembly with cleaning or replacement; spare parts should be on hand.

- Be prepared to clean up particulates that may be sprayed into sinks, tubs, and showers as water is restored and air pressure is purged from the pipes.

- Consider keeping restroom doors closed in high-risk patient areas until water restoration processes and cleaning of the fixtures are complete.

Flooding and Water Leakage

Water seepage and retained moisture may lead to serious bacterial and fungal contamination in the air-handling systems.[46,47] Practical suggestions for cleanup and treatment of wet surfaces, whether ceilings, walls, or flooring, are available.[1,114] Cleanup protocols affecting various surfaces and furnishings are discussed in Chapter 107 Environmental Services. The key to preventing infection problems consists of removal of the moisture source, cleanup within 24 to 48 hours, disinfecting with diluted bleach solutions, and thorough drying.[1,114,115]

Controlling Legionella

One of the major concerns for potable water contamination in HCFs is the prevention of *Legionella*, particularly following water disruptions. However, the mere presence of *Legionella* organisms in a water system does not predict the occurrence of disease outcomes. Determination of a dose-response relationship has been sought in several studies but has not yet been identified.[50] Likewise, studies of the efficacy of routine microbiologic sampling of potable water in HCFs has provided mixed results, so the 2003 CDC-EIC Guidelines remain a logical guide to a facility-based prevention program.[116,117]

Several documents outline control strategies for legionellosis. These include the 2003 CDC-EIC and 2004 Pneumonia guidelines, OSHA's technical manual, the ASHRAE Guideline, and the Cooling Technology Institute Guidelines.[1,35,74,106,107] At this writing there are also recommendations open for public comment from ASHRAE for *Legionella* risk assessment using the HACCP approach. The CDC-EIC guidelines recommend control measures for all facilities and add additional recommendations for facilities with immunosuppressed patients or transplant units (e.g., for hematopoietic stem cell transplants [HSCT] and solid organs). CDC guidelines and OSHA's technical manual provide recommendations for follow-up procedures when problems have been identified.[1,74] The CDC-EIC guidelines provide an extensive review of multiple approaches.[1]

CDC Guidelines: Legionellosis Prevention and Response

There are similar steps that should be undertaken when either a single case of laboratory-confirmed nosocomial Legionnaire's disease is identified or two or more cases of laboratory-confirmed disease, which might be healthcare-associated, occur within 6 months of each other (see the CDC-EIC guidelines for further discussion). A brief summary of steps follows[1,35]:

- Inform and consult with local public health authorities.

- Conduct an epidemiologic investigation via retrospective reviews of microbiologic, serologic, and postmortem data to identify previous cases. In addition, intensive prospective surveillance should be established to identify additional cases. Surveillance should be continued for at least 2 months, even if no further cases are identified.

- If there is evidence of ongoing transmission, an environmental investigation (culturing water samples) should be conducted to help determine the source.

- If a source is identified, decontamination measures should be instituted.

- If *Legionella* is detected in one culture (e.g., conducted at 2-week intervals during 3 months), control measures should be reassessed, modified as needed, and decontamination repeated.

- The CDC makes no recommendation for routine culturing of the water system in hospitals without HSCT or solid-organ transplant programs.

- If a case is identified in a severely immunocompromised patient or if the hospital houses severely immunocompromised patients in HSCT or solid-organ transplant programs, an environmental investigation should be initiated in addition to the epidemiologic investigation. Hospitals that do not house severely immunocompromised patients do not need to conduct an environmental investigation initially. However, if transmission is shown to be ongoing in such facilities, an environmental investigation is warranted.

- Environmental investigations involve collecting water samples from potential sources of aerosolized water, as outlined in CDC Guidelines appendices. If a source is identified, it should be immediately decontaminated. If a source is not identified, surveillance should be continued for at least 2 months and, depending on the scope of the outbreak, decontamination of the hospital's water distribution system should be undertaken or deferred pending identification of the source of *Legionella* organisms.

- If the source is a heated water system, the following decontamination steps are suggested:

  ○ Superheat (flush each distal outlet of the system for at least 5 minutes with water 160°F to 170°F [71°C–77°C]) or hyperchlorinate (flush all outlets of the system for at least 5 minutes with water containing 2 mg/L [2 ppm] free residual chlorine). Post warning signs at each outlet that is being flushed to prevent scald injury or excessive chlorine exposure to patients, staff, or visitors.

  ○ Depending on local and state regulations regarding potable water temperature in public buildings, maintain potable water at or above the temperatures recommended earlier (less than 124°F [less than 51°C]); cold water (less than 68°F [less than 20°C]) or chlorinate heated water to achieve 1 to 2 mg/L free residual chlorine at the tap. Clean hot water storage tanks and water heaters to remove accumulated scale and sediment.

  ○ Restrict immunosuppressed patients from taking showers and use only sterile water for oral consumption until *Legionella* is undetectable in hospital water.

- If cooling towers or evaporative condensers are implicated, the protocol outlined in CDC-EIC Guidelines appendices provides recommendations for further action, as well as recommendations from ASHRAE and others.[106] (See Supplemental Resources.)

- The efficacy of measures taken to reduce or eliminate *Legionella* should be assessed and modified as needed. Accurate records of control measures and environmental test results for cooling towers and potable water systems should be maintained.

Treatments

As noted, other approaches that have been recommended to prevent or control *Legionella* include ozone, ultraviolet light, chlorine dioxide, or heavy metal ions (i.e., copper/silver ions).[77-79,82-88] The CDC makes recommendations only for thermal eradication and hyperchlorination as described, but these are effective for eradication of *Legionella* for very brief periods. Analyses of the protective effects of monochloramine are encouraging, and positive results have also been achieved with copper-silver ion treatment.[42,51,52,84-86] Chlorine dioxide has been used extensively as a disinfectant in other industries as well as in HCFs in other countries with documented effectiveness. Chlorine dioxide does not produce trihalomethanes (THMs) like chlorine, has been found highly useful in controlling biofilm, and is EPA approved.[79-83]

Some recommendations related to eradication remain controversial and unresolved.[42,58,106] At this point, there is no one method that works consistently to eradicate *Legionella* permanently from water systems, and the 2003 CDC-EIC guidelines make no recommendations beyond heating and chlorination methods.[1]

OSHA Technical Manual

Several algorithms for approaching *Legionella* problems have been published.[58] (See also Chapter 84 *Legionella pneumophila*.) The OSHA online technical manual offers an algorithm for investigation of reported legionellosis cases.[74] The algorithm is geared more to a nonhealthcare setting and is focused on employees, rather than patients; however, it may be of interest to IPs in HCFs. The manual recommends that a "level 1" investigation be initiated when there is a probable basis for suspecting that the workplace water sources are contaminated with *Legionella* or when there is information that one case of Legionnaire's disease may exist. A "level 2" investigation is warranted when more than one case has been reported at the facility. If an ongoing outbreak is occurring, control measures should be initiated immediately.

Steps for a level 1 investigation are discussed in detail in the manual but are summarized here:

- Obtain an overview of all water systems at the facility.
- Conduct a walk-through investigation of the facility.
- Assess the results of the walk-through investigation to determine the course of action.
- Recommend control actions.

Steps for a level 2 investigation can be summarized as follows:

- Assess water systems as described for a level 1 investigation.
- Conduct a second walk-through survey of the facility and collect water samples.
- Initiate an employee awareness program and monitor current sick leave for new cases.
- Review worker absences to detect other cases.
- Assess results of the worker-absence survey and analysis of water systems.
- Recommend control actions.

CONCLUSIONS

The role of infection prevention in evaluating water-associated problems related to construction and routine operational functions in HCFs remains a challenging and exciting one. It is hoped that this overview of issues related to water distribution systems and equipment will assist in risk assessment, plan review and design, and preventive maintenance policies and procedures. As always, infection prevention and control programs are most successful when they facilitate multidisciplinary approaches in planning. Architectural and engineering professionals increasingly recognize

the need for collaboration with IPs, especially when they must resolve moisture and water-related fungal problems affecting ventilation. Prevention through planning can save the enormous cost of "rework" while reducing the risks of HAI from the environment. Interaction and integration of efforts with other disciplines by way of the ICRA process or similar collaborative efforts should assist in keeping infection prevention the driving force during routine maintenance and construction/renovation processes.

FUTURE TRENDS

A number of issues and concerns remain and will require continual research and evaluation of methods to further improve patient outcomes, as noted in the APIC state-of-the-art report on construction and renovation (see Supplemental Resources). Some include the following:

- Hand-washing sink and faucet designs: The degree of risk associated with various faucet and sink designs has not yet been determined and may be resolved by examining other methods of water purification and/or sink design.

- Plumbing and preventive maintenance systems: Better or alternative methods (e.g., ozone to reduce or eliminate *Legionella* contamination in potable water systems) continue to be sought. In the setting of continued low-level contamination, determination of the dose response relationship from potable water exposures resulting in disease remains elusive. This remains key to preventive water system treatments. The value of environmental cultures for *Legionella* spp. remains elusive, in part reflecting the hypervariability of levels of contamination between locations.

- Water quality: Questions also remain regarding treatment of water used to disinfect medical equipment. A controversial and unresolved question remains regarding routine sampling of rinse water used in automatic endoscopic reprocessors. The need and/or feasibility of using sterile water for direct patient care also must be further investigated.

- Filtration: Some have suggested that additional interventions such as filters at point of delivery of water can assist in prevention of transmission of waterborne pathogens such as *Legionella* spp.[118,119] However, questions remain over whether this intervention is cost effective. In addition, point-of-use filtration requires maintenance and change of filters that increase both of these variable cost elements. Advocates of these devices also point to installation into fixtures of rooms of patients who are immunocompromised. The ability to precisely predict admission of these populations to certain rooms is unlikely because there is a trend toward a universal room that could accommodate any patient. More study is warranted before widespread adoption of this approach.

- Efficacy of remediation protocols: Controlled studies on the efficacy and safety of current or newer antifungal treatments after severe water damage are needed. Clearer determinations regarding the safety of damaged drywall left in place, versus its removal, needs further elaboration. Other studies are needed to determine the efficacy and safety of other types of materials for remediation (e.g., fiberglass-reinforced drywall).

- Surfaces: Identification of better materials and surfaces that resist moisture and resultant contamination from microorganisms warrants further study.

- Environmental sustainability: There is growing emphasis on the need for stewardship of the global environment well beyond the HCF campus. This includes conservation of potable water use, recovery of "gray water," and the use of low-flow showerheads and toilets, water-free urinals, and electronic sensors for faucet control. Conservation of water is especially important for facilities located in arid climates, and this conservation also saves the energy and volume of chemicals needed to treat wastewater. The challenge is maintaining the balance between environmental sustainability without compromising safety of patients or other occupants in HCFs. Practice Greenhealth and Global Health and Safety Initiatives are organizations that are facilitating an environmentally supportive agenda, and those interested are encouraged to visit the websites for these and other similar organizations to learn more. (See Supplemental Resources.)

INTERNATIONAL PERSPECTIVE

The ability to provide and sustain the availability of clean water is a global challenge. When considering the multitude of water uses in healthcare settings, the ability to meet the needs of the patients and the HCP providing care is one of great importance. IPs should be knowledgeable regarding the many opportunities for transmission of waterborne illness and work to identify and consider viable options as part of a patient safety program, regardless of the setting or available resources.

REFERENCES

1. Sehulster L, Chinn RY. Guidelines for environmental infection control in health-care facilities. Recommendations of CDC and the Healthcare Infection Control Practices Advisory Committee (HICPAC). *MMWR Recomm Rep* 2003 Jun 6;52(RR-10):1–42.
2. The Facility Guidelines Institute. *Guidelines for the Design and Construction of Health Care Facilities.* 2010 Edition. Chicago, IL: American Society for Healthcare Engineering, January 2010.
3. Bartley JM, Olmsted RN. *Construction and Renovation: Toolkit for Professionals in Infection Prevention and Control,* 4th ed. Washington, DC: Association for Professionals in Infection Control and Epidemiology, Inc., 2010.
4. Flannary B, Gelling LB, Bugia DJ, et al. Reducing Legionella colonization of water systems with monochloramine. *Emerg Infect Dis* 2006 Apr;12(4):588–596.
5. Rutala WA, Weber DJ. Water as a reservoir of nosocomial pathogens. *Infect Control Hosp Epidemiol* 1997 Sep;18(9):609–616.
6. Anaissie EJ, Stratton SL, Dignani MC, et al. Pathogenic Aspergillus species recovered from a hospital water system: a 3-year prospective study. *Clin Infect Dis* 2002 Mar 15;34(6):780–789.
7. Raad I, Tarrand J, Hanna H, et al. Epidemiology, molecular mycology, and environmental sources of Fusarium infection in patients with cancer. *Infect Control Hosp Epidemiol* 2002 Sep;23(9):532–537.
8. Anaissie EJ, Kuchar RT, Rex JH, et al. Fusariosis associated with pathogenic fusarium species colonization of a hospital water system: a new paradigm for the epidemiology of opportunistic mold infections. *Clin Infect Dis* 2001 Dec;33(11):1871–1878.
9. Rusin PA, Rose JB, Haas CN, et al. Risk assessment of opportunistic bacterial pathogens in drinking water. *Rev Environ Contam Toxicol* 1997;152:57–83.
10. Crane LC, Tagle LC, Palutke WA. Outbreak of Pseudomonas paucimobilis in an intensive care facility. *JAMA* 1981 Aug;246(9):985–987.
11. Kolmos HJ, Thuesen B, Nielsen SV, et al. Outbreak of infection in a burns unit due to Pseudomonas aeruginosa originating from contaminated tubing used for irrigation of patients. *J Hosp Infect* 1993 May;24(1):11–21.
12. Cherian B. Price E. Water-borne infections and warming the sterile water for washing high-risk infants on neonatal intensive care units. *J Hosp Infect* 2012 Dec;82(4):303–304.
13. Fernandez-Rendon E, Cerna-Cortes JF, Ramirez-Medina MA, et al. Mycobacterium mucogenicum and other non-tuberculosis mycobacteria in potable water of a trauma hospital: a potential source for human infection. *J Hosp Infect* 2012 Jan;80(1):74–76.
14. Wallace RJ Jr, Brown BA, Griffith DE. Nosocomial outbreaks/pseudo-outbreaks caused by nontuberculous mycobacteria. *Ann Rev Microbiol* 1998;52:453–490.
15. Soto LE, Bobadilla M, Villalobos Y, et al. Post-surgical nasal cellulitis outbreak due to Mycobacterium chelonae. *J Hosp Infect* 1991 Oct;19(2):99–106.
16. Meyers H, Brown-Elliott BA, Moore D, et al. An outbreak of Mycobacterium chelonae infection following liposuction. *Clin Infect Dis* 2002 Jun 1; 34(11):1500–1507.
17. Cox R, deBorja K, Bach MC. A pseudo-outbreak of Mycobacterium chelonae infections related to bronchoscopy. *Infect Control Hosp Epidemiol* 1997 Feb;18(2):136–137.
18. Winthrop KL, Abrams M, Yakrus M, et al. An outbreak of mycobacterial furunculosis associated with footbaths at a nail salon. *N Engl J Med* 2002 May 2;346(18):1366–1371.
19. Health Canada, Laboratory Centre for Disease Control, Division of Nosocomial and Occupational Infections. Infection prevention and control practices for personal services: tattooing, ear/body piercing, and electrolysis. *Can Commun Dis Rep* 1999 Jul;25 Suppl 3:1–73.
20. Division of Nosocomial and Occupational Infectious Diseases, Bureau of Infectious Diseases, Laboratory Centre for Disease Control, Health Canada. Foot care by health care providers. *Can Commun Dis Rep* 1997 Dec;23 Suppl 8:1–7.
21. Venezia RA, Agresta MD, Hanley EM, et al. Nosocomial legionellosis associated with aspiration of nasogastric feedings diluted in tap water. *Infect Control Hosp Epidemiol* 1994 Aug;15(8):529–533.
22. Higa F, Koide M, Haroon A, et al. Legionella pneumophila contamination in a steam towel warmer in a hospital setting. *J Hosp Infect* 2012 Mar; 80(3):259–261.
23. Burns DN, Wallace RJ Jr, Schultz ME, et al. Nosocomial outbreak of respiratory tract colonization with Mycobacterium fortuitum: demonstration of the usefulness of pulsed-field gel electrophoresis in an epidemiologic investigation. *Am Rev Respir Dis* 1991 Nov;144(5):1153–1159.
24. Sniadack DH, Ostroff SM, Karlix MA, et al. A nosocomial pseudo-outbreak of Mycobacterium xenopi due to contaminated potable water supply: lessons in prevention. *Infect Control Hosp Epidemiol* 1993 Nov;14(11):636–641.
25. Prodinger WM, Bonatti H, Allerberger F, et al. Legionella pneumonia in transplant recipients: a cluster of cases of eight years' duration. *J Hosp Infect* 1994 Mar;26(3):191–202.
26. Bangsborg JM, Uldum S, Jensen JS, et al. Nosocomial legionellosis in three heart-lung transplant patients: case reports and environmental observations. *Eur J Clin Microbiol Infect Dis* 1995 Feb;14(2):99–104.
27. Graman PS, Quinlan GA, Rank JA. Nosocomial legionellosis traced to a contaminated ice machine. *Infect Control Hosp Epidemiol* 1997 Sep;18(9):637–640.
28. Kool JL, Fiore AE, Kioski CM, et al. More than 10 years of unrecognized nosocomial transmission of legionnaires' disease among transplant patients. *Infect Control Hosp Epidemiol* 1998 Dec;19(12):898–904.
29. Biurrun A, Caballero L, Pelaz C, et al. Treatment of a Legionella pneumophila-colonized water distribution system using copper-silver ionization and continuous chlorination. *Infect Control Hosp Epidemiol* 1999 Jun;20(6):426–428.
30. Kappstein I, Grundmann H, Hauer T, et al. Aerators as a reservoir of Acinetobacter junii: an outbreak of bacteraemia in paediatric oncology patients. *J Hosp Infect* 2000 Jan;44(1):27–30.
31. Darelid J, Löfgren S, Malmvall BE. Control of nosocomial Legionnaires' disease by keeping the circulating hot water temperature above 55 degrees C: experience from a 10-year surveillance programme in a district general hospital. *J Hosp Infect* 2002 Mar;50(3):213–219.
32. Anaissie EJ, Stratton SL, Dignani MC, et al. Cleaning patient shower facilities: a novel approach to reducing patient exposure to aerosolized Aspergillus species and other opportunistic molds. *Clin Infect Dis* 2002 Oct 15;35(8):E86–8.
33. Nasser RM, Rahi AC, Haddad MF, et al. Outbreak of Burkholderia cepacia bacteremia traced to contaminated hospital water used for dilution of an alcohol skin antiseptic. *Infect Control Hosp Epidemiol* 2004 Mar;25(3):231–239.
34. Hota S, Hirji Z, Stockton K, et al. Outbreak of multidrug-resistant Pseudomonas aeruginosa colonization and infection secondary to imperfect intensive care unit room design. *Infect Control Hosp Epidemiol* 2009 Jan;30(1):25–33.
35. Tablan OC, Anderson LJ, Besser R, et al. Guidelines for preventing health-care–associated pneumonia, 2003: recommendations of CDC and the Healthcare Infection Control Practices Advisory Committee. *MMWR Morb Mortal Wkly Rep* 2004 Mar 26;53(RR-3):1–36.
36. Noble MA, Isaac-Renton JL, Bryce EA, et al. The toilet as a transmission vector of vancomycin-resistant enterococci. *J Hosp Infect* 1998 Nov;40(3):237–241.

37. Ferroni A, Nguyen L, Pron B, et al. Outbreak of nosocomial urinary tract infections due to Pseudomonas aeruginosa in a pediatric surgical unit associated with tap-water contamination. *J Hosp Infect* 1998 Aug;39(4):301–307.

38. McDonald LC, Walker M, Carson L, et al. Outbreak of Acinetobacter spp. bloodstream infections in a nursery associated with contaminated aerosols and air conditioners. *Pediatr Infect Dis J* 1998 Aug;17(8):716–722.

39. Verweij PE, Meis JF, Christmann V, et al. Nosocomial outbreak of colonization and infection with Stenotrophomonas maltophilia in preterm infants associated with contaminated tap water. *Epidemiol Infect* 1998 Jun;120(3):251–258.

40. Anaissie EJ, Penzak SR, Dignani C. The hospital water supply as a source of nosocomial infections: a plea for action. *Arch Intern Med* 2002 Jul 8;162(13):1483–1492.

41. Fields BS, Benson RF, Besser RE. Legionella and Legionnaires' disease: 25 years of investigation. *Clin Microbiol Rev* 2002 Jul;15(3):506–526.

42. Butler JC, Fields BS, Breiman RF. Prevention and control of Legionella. *Infect Dis Clin Pract* 1997;6:458–464.

43. Bencini MA, Yzerman EP, Koornstra RH, et al. A case of Legionnaires' disease caused by aspiration of ice water. *Arch Environ Occup Health* 2005 Nov-Dec;60(6):302–306.

44. Claesson BE, Claesson UL. An outbreak of endometritis in a maternity unit caused by spread of group A streptococci from a showerhead. *J Hosp Infect* 1985 Sep;6(3):304–311.

45. Streifel AJ. Aspergillosis and Construction. In: Kundsin RB, ed. *Architectural Design and Indoor Microbial Pollution.* New York: Oxford University Press, 1988.

46. Streifel AJ, Steven PP, Rhame FS. In-hospital source of airborne Penicillium species spores. *J Clin Microbiol* 1987 Jan;25(1):1–4.

47. Fridkin SK, Kremer FB, Bland LA, et al. Acremonium kiliense endophthalmitis that occurred after cataract extraction in an ambulatory surgical center and as traced to an environmental reservoir. *Clin Infect Dis* 1996 Feb;22(2):222–227.

48. Miles J. *Potentially hazardous amoebae found in eyewash stations. Hazard Information bulletin, United States Department of Labor and Occupational Safety and Health Administration (OSHA).* December 1986, Department of Labor, Bulletin 19861223. OSHA website. Available at: http://www.osha.gov/dts/hib/hib_data/hib19861223.html.

49. Yu VL, Liu Z, Stout JE, Goetz A. Legionella disinfection of water distribution systems: principles, problems, and practice. *Infect Control Hosp Epidemiol* 1993 Oct;14(10):567–570.

50. Muraca P, Yu VL, Goetz A. Disinfection of water distribution systems for legionella: a review of application procedures and methodologies. *Infect Control Hosp Epidemiol* 1990 Feb;11(2):79–88.

51. Wright JB, Ruseska I, Athar MA, et al. Legionella pneumophila grows adherent to surfaces in vitro and in situ. *Infect Control Hosp Epidemiol* 1989 Sep;10(9):408–415.

52. Mermel LA, Josephson SL, Giorgio CH, et al. Association of Legionnaires' disease with construction: contamination of potable water? *Infect Control Hosp Epidemiol* 1995 Feb;16(2):76–81.

53. Hlady W, Mullen RC, Mintz CS, et al. Outbreak of Legionnaire's disease linked to a decorative fountain by molecular epidemiology. *Am J Epidemiol* 1993 Oct 15;138(8):555–562.

54. O'Loughlin RE, Kightlinger L, Werpy MC, et al. Restaurant outbreak of Legionnaires' disease associated with a decorative water fountain: an environmental and case-control study. *BMC Infect Dis* 2007 Aug 9;7:93.

55. Palmore TN, Stock F, White M, et al. A cluster of cases of nosocomial legionnaires disease linked to a contaminated hospital decorative water fountain. *Infect Control and Hosp Epidemiol* 2009 Aug;30(8):764–768.

56. Haupt TE, Heffernan RT, Kazmierczak JJ, et al. An outbreak of Legionnaires disease associated with a decorative water wall fountain in a hospital. *Infect Control Hosp Epidemiol* 2012 Feb;33(2):185–191.

57. Correia AM, Goncalves G, Reis J, et al. An outbreak of legionnaires disease in a municipality in northern Portugal. *Euro Surveill* 2001 Jul;6(7):121–124.

58. Freije MA, Barbaree JM. *Legionellae Control in Healthcare Facilities: A Guide for Minimizing Risk.* Indianapolis: HC Information Resources, 1996.

59. Lucero CA, Cohen AL, Trevino I, et al. Outbreak of Burkholderia cepacia complex among ventilated pediatric patients linked to hospital sinks. *Am J Infect Control* 2011 Nov;39(9):775–778.

60. Lowe C, Willey B, O'Shaughnessy A, et al. Outbreak of extended-spectrum B-lactamase-producing Klebsiella oxytoca infections associated with contaminated handwashing sinks(1). *Emerg Infect Dis* 2012 Aug;18(8):1242–1247.

61. Kotsanas D, Wijesooriya WR, Korman TM, et al. "Down the drain": carbapenem-resistant bacteria in intensive care unit patients and handwashing sinks. *Med J Aust* 2013 Mar 18;198(5):267–269.

62. Bert F, Maubec E, Bruneau B, et al. Multi-resistant Pseudomonas aeruginosa outbreak associated with contaminated tap water in a neurosurgery intensive care unit. *J Hosp Infect* 1998 May;39(1):53–62.

63. American National Standard for Emergency Eyewash and Shower Equipment. ANSI Z358.11990 Revision of ANSI Z358.1-198. October 5, 1989. New York: American National Standards Institute, 1989.

64. Ravn P, Lundgren JD, Kjaeldgaard P, et al. Nosocomial outbreak of cryptosporidiosis in AIDS patients. *BMJ* 1991 Feb 2;302(6771):277–280.

65. LaBombardi VJ, O'Brien AM, Kislak JW. Pseudo-outbreak of Mycobacterium fortuitum due to contaminated ice machines. *Am J Infect Control* 2002 May;30(3):184–186.

66. Manangan LP, Anderson RL, Arduino MJ, et al. Sanitary care and maintenance of ice-storage chests and ice-making machines in healthcare facilities. *Am J Infect Control* 1998 Apr;26(2):111–112.

67. Burns S. An investigation of surgical infections reveals a fluid warmer as a reservoir for bacteria. *Am J Infect Control* 1999;27(2):216.

68. Berrouane YF, McNutt LA, Buschelman BJ, et al. Outbreak of severe Pseudomonas aeruginosa infections caused by a contaminated drain in a whirlpool bathtub. *Clin Infect Dis* 2000 Dec;31(6):1331–1337.

69. Shankowsky HA, Callioux LS, Tredget EE. North American survey of hydrotherapy in modern burn care. *J Burn Care Rehabil* 1994 Mar-Apr;15(2):143–146.

70. Mastro TD, Fields BS, Breiman RF, et al. Nosocomial Legionnaires' disease and use of medication nebulizers. *J Infect Dis* 1991 Mar;163(3):667–671.

71. Kutty PK, Forster TS, Wood-Koob D, et al. Multistate outbreak of toxic anterior segment syndrome. *J Cataract Refract Surg* 2008 Apr;34(4):585–590.

72. American Society of Cataract and Refractive Surgery, American Society of Ophthalmic Registered Nurses. Recommended practices for cleaning and sterilizing intraocular surgical instruments. *Insight* 2007 Apr-Jun;32(2):22–28.

73. Phares CR, Russell E, Thigpen MC, et al. Legionnaires' disease among residents of a long-term care facility: the sentinel event in a community outbreak. *Am J Infect Control* 2007 Jun;35(5):319–323.

74. Occupational Safety and Health Administration. Legionnaires' disease. Directive Number TED 1–0.15A. In: OSHA Technical Manual Section II:7:1–46, 1999. Available at: http://www.osha.gov/dts/osta/otm/otm_iii/otm_iii_7.html.

75. Lin YS, Stout JE, Yu VL, et al. Disinfection of water distribution systems for Legionella. *Semin Respir Infect* 1998 Jun;13(2):147–159.

76. Mandel AS, Sprauer MA, Sniadack DH, et al. State regulation of hospital water temperature. *Infect Control Hosp Epidemiol* 1993 Nov;14(11):642–645.

77. Heffelfinger JD, Kool JL, Fridkin S, et al. Risk of hospital-acquired legionnaires' disease in cities using monochloramine versus other water disinfectants. *Infect Control Hosp Epidemiol* 2003 Aug;24(8):569–574.

78. Flannery B, Gelling LB, Vugia DJ, et al. Reducing Legionella colonization in water systems with monochloramine. *Emerg Infect Dis* 2006 Apr;12(4):588–596.

79. Walker JT, Mackerness CW, Mallon D, et al. Control of Legionella pneumophila in a hospital water system by chlorine dioxide. *J Ind Microbiol* 1995 Oct;15(4):384–390.

80. Hood J, Cheape G, Mead A, et al. Six Years' Experience With Chlorine Dioxide in Control of Legionella pneumophila in the Potable Water Supply of Glasgow Royal Infirmary. *Am J Infect Control* 2000;28(1):86.

81. Mackie K, Bova G, Perl T. Eradicating Legionella from the Water in a Cancer Center (CC). Poster no. 204. Abstracts, Association for Professionals in Infection Control & Epidemiology, Educational Conference & International Meeting, Nashville, Tennessee, May 21–23, 2002.

82. Bova G, Sharpe P, Keane T. Evaluation of chlorine dioxide in potable water systems for Legionella control in an acute care hospital environment. 65th Annual Water Conference, October 17-21, 2004, Pittsburg, PA.

83. Srinivasan A, Bova G, Ross T, et al. A 17-month evaluation of a chlorine dioxide water treatment system to control Legionella species in a hospital water supply. *Infect Control Hosp Epidemiol* 2003 Aug;24(8):575–579.

84. Miuetzner S, Schwille RC, Farley A, et al. Efficacy of thermal treatment and copper-silver ionization for controlling Legionella pneumophila in high-volume hot water plumbing systems in hospitals. *Am J Infect Control* 1997 Dec;25(6):452–457.

85. Goetz A, Yu VL. Copper-silver ionization: cautious optimism for Legionella disinfection and implications for environmental culturing. *Am J Infect Control* 1997 Dec;25(6):449–451.

86. Stout JE, Yu VL. Experiences of the first 16 hospitals using copper-silver ionization for Legionella control: implications for the evaluation of other disinfection modalities. *Infect Control Hosp Epidemiol* 2003 Aug;24(8):563–568.

87. Hall KK, Giannetta ET, Getchell-White SI, et al. Ultraviolet light disinfection of hospital water for preventing nosocomial Legionella infection: a 13-year follow-up. *Infect Control Hosp Epidemiol* 2003 Aug;24(8):580–583.

88. Franzin L, Cabodi D, Fantino C. Evaluation of the efficacy of ultraviolet irradiation for disinfection of hospital water contaminated by Legionella. *J Hosp Infect* 2002 Aug;51(4):269.

89. Boyce JM, Pittet D. Guideline for Hand Hygiene in Health-Care Settings. Recommendations of the Healthcare Infection Control Practices Advisory Committee and the HICPAC/SHEA/APIC/IDSA Hand Hygiene Task Force. Society for Healthcare Epidemiology of America/Association for Professionals in Infection Control/Infectious Diseases Society of America. *MMWR Recomm Rep* 2002 Oct 25;51(RR-16):1–45.

90. The Joint Commission (TJC). *2013 National Patient Safety Goals. NPSG.07.01.01 Hand Hygiene.* TJC website. Available at: http://www.jointcommission.org/standards_information/npsgs.aspx.

91. AHA/ASHE Advisory. A National Stakeholder Meeting on Alcohol-based Hand Rubs and Fire Safety in Healthcare Facilities in July, 2003.

92. Larson E, McGeer A, Quraishi ZA, et al. Effect of an automated sink on handwashing practices and attitudes in high risk units. *Infect Control Hosp Epidemiol* 1991 Jul;12(7):422–428.

93. Wurtz R, Moye G, Jovanovic B. Handwashing machines, handwashing compliance and potential for cross-contamination. *Am J Infect Control* 1994 Aug;228–230.

94. Assadian O, El-Madani N, Seper E, et al. Sensor-operated faucets: a possible source of nosocomial infection? *Infect Control Hosp Epidemiol* 2002 Jan;23(1):44–46.

95. Hargreaves J, Shireley L, Hansen S, et al. Bacterial contamination associated with electronic faucets: a new risk for healthcare facilities. *Infect Control Hosp Epidemiol* 2001 Apr;22(4):202–205.

96. Halabi M, Wiesholzer-Pittl M, Schöberl J, et al. Non-touch fittings in hospitals: a possible source of Pseudomonas aeruginosa and Legionella spp. *J Hosp Infect* 2001 Oct;49(2):117–121.

97. Merrer J, Girou E, Ducellier D, et al. Should electronic faucets be used in intensive care and hematology units? *Intensive Care Med* 2005 Dec;31(12):1715–1718.

98. Sydnor ER, Bova G, Gimburg A, et al. Electronic –eye faucets: Legionella species contamination in healthcare settings. *Infect Control Hosp Epidemiol* 2012 March;33(3):235–240.

99. Cholley P, Thouverez M, Floret N, et al. The role of water fittings in intensive care rooms as reservoirs for the colonization of patients with Pseudomonas aeruginosa. *Intensive Care Med* 2008 Aug;34(8):1428–1433.

100. Harrison WA, Griffith CJ, Michaels B, et al. Technique to determine contamination exposure routes and the economic efficiency of folded paper-towel dispensing. *Am J Infect Control* 2003 Apr;31(2):104–108.

101. Griffith CJ, Malik R, Cooper RA, et al. Environmental surface cleanliness and the potential for contamination during handwashing. *Am J Infect Control* 2003 Apr;31(2):93–96.

102. Merry AF, Miller TE, Findon G, et al. Touch contamination levels during anaesthetic procedures and their relationship to hand hygiene procedures: a clinical audit. *Br J Anaesth* 2001 Aug;87(2):291–294.

103. Gustafson DR, Vetter EA, Larson DR, et al. Effects of 4 hand–drying methods for removing bacteria from washed hands: a randomized trial. *Mayo Clin Proc* 2000 Jul;75(7):705–708.

104. Dadswell JV. Managing swimming, spa and other pools to prevent infection. *Commun Dis Rep CDR Rev* 1996 Feb 2;6(2):R37–40.

105. Centers for Disease Control and Prevention (CDC). Pseudomonas dermatitis/folliculitis associated with pools and hot tubs—Colorado and Maine, 1999–2000. *MMWR Morb Mortal Wkly Rep* 2000 Dec 8;49(48):1087–1091.

106. American Society of Heating, Refrigerating, and Air-Conditioning Engineers. ASHRAE Guideline 12–2000: Minimizing the Risk of Legionellosis Associated With Building Water Systems. Atlanta, GA: ASHRAE; 2000:1–16.

107. Cooling Technology Institute (CTI). *Legionellosis Guideline: Best Practices for Control of Legionella.* CTI Guidelines WTB-148 (08). Houston, TX: CTI; 2008. CTI website. Available at: http://www.cti.org/downloads/WTP-148.pdf.

108. Barker J, Jones MV. The potential spread of infection caused by aerosol contamination of surfaces after flushing a domestic toilet. *J Appl Microbiol* 2005;99(2):339–347.

109. Srinivasan A, Wolfenden LL, Song X, et al. An outbreak of Pseudomonas aeruginosa infections associated with flexible bronchoscopes. *N Engl J Med* 2003 Jan 16;348(3):221–227.

110. Kirschke DL, Jones TF, Craig AS, et al. Pseudomonas aeruginosa and Serratia marcescens contamination associated with a manufacturing defect in bronchoscopes. *N Engl J Med* 2003 Jan 16;348(3):214–220.

111. Food and Drug Administration (FDA) Center for Devices and Radiological Health. *FDA and CDC Public Health Advisory. Bulletin September 10, 1999. Infections From Endoscopes Inadequately Reprocessed by an Automated Endoscope Reprocessing System.* Public health advisory September 10, 1999. FDA website. Available at: http://www.fda.gov/MedicalDevices/Safety/AlertsandNotices/PublicHealthNotifications/ucm062282.htm.

112. The Joint Commission. *The 2012 Comprehensive Accreditation Manual for Hospitals.* Oakbrook Terrace, IL: Joint Commission Resources. 2012.

113. Environmental Protection Agency (EPA). *Drinking Water Contaminants.* EPA website. Available at: http://water.epa.gov/drink/contaminants/index.cfm.

114. New York City Department of Health and Mental Hygiene. Guidelines on Assessment and Remediation of Fungi in Indoor Environments. November 2008. Available at: http://www.nyc.gov/html/doh/downloads/pdf/epi/epi-mold-guidelines.pdf.

115. Brace SE. Infection control during construction: planning is key. In: Healthcare Facilities Management Series (no. 094300). Chicago: ASHE of the American Hospital Association, 1993.

116. Leoni E, Sacchetti R, Aporti M, et al. Active surveillance of legionnaires disease during a prospective observational study of community- and hospital-acquired pneumonia. *Infect Control Hosp Epidemiol* 2007 Sep;28(9):1085–1088.

117. Stout JE, Muder RR, Mietzner S, et al. Role of environmental surveillance in determining the risk of hospital-acquired legionellosis: a national surveillance study with clinical correlations. *Infect Control Hosp Epidemiol* 2007 Jul;28(7):818–824.

118. Trautmann M, Halder S, Hoegel J, et al. Point-of-use water filtration reduces endemic Pseudomonas aeruginosa infections on a surgical intensive care unit. *Am J Infect Control* 2008 Aug;36(6):421–429.

119. Sheffer PJ, Stout JE, Wagener MM, et al. Efficacy of new point-of-use water filter for preventing exposure to Legionella and waterborne bacteria. *Am J Infect Control* 2005 Jun;33(5 Suppl 1):S20–S25.

SUPPLEMENTAL RESOURCES

Bartley JM. APIC state-of-the-art-report: the role of infection control during construction in healthcare facilities. *Am J Infect Control* 2000 Apr;28(2):156–169.

American Society for Healthcare Engineering (ASHE). Codes and Standards Related to ABHR. Available at: http://www.ashe.org/advocacy/organizations/NFPA/

Association of Water Technologies (AWT). *Guideline Legionella 2003: an update and statement by the Association of Water Technologies (AWT).* June 2003. Available at: http://www.awt.org/IndustryResources/Legionella03.pdf.

Bartley J, et al. Infection control risk assessment (ICRA) matrix, 14 step assessment and permit model. Available at: http://www.premierinc.com/quality-safety/tools-services/safety/topics/construction/icra.jsp.

Canada Communicable Disease Report. Construction-related nosocomial infections in patients in health care facilities: decreasing the risk of Aspergillus, Legionella and other infections. *Can Commun Dis Rep* [serial online]. 2001;27(Suppl 2):i–x, 1–42, i–x, 1–46. Available at: http://www.phac-aspc.gc.ca/publicat/ccdr-rmtc/01pdf/27s2e.pdf.

Centers for Disease Control and Prevention (CDC), Infectious Disease Society of America, and the American Society of Blood and Marrow Transplantation. Guidelines for preventing opportunistic infections among hematopoietic stem cell transplant recipients. *MMWR Recomm Rep* [serial online] 2000;49(RR-10):1–125. Available at: http://www.cdc.gov/mmwr/PDF/rr/rr4910.pdf.

CHICA. *Canada position statement: Healthcare facility design position statement.* Available at: http://www.chica.org/pdf/HFDposition.pdf.

Global Health and Safety Initiatives. Available at: http://www.globalhealthsafety.org.

Green Guide to HealthCare. Available at: http://www.gghc.org.

Livni G, Yaniv I, Samra Z, et al. Outbreak of Mycobacterium mucogenicum bacteraemia due to contaminated water supply in a paediatric haematology–oncology department. *J Hosp Infect* 2008;70(3):253–258.

Pipeless whirlpool baths. Example of available information. Available at: http://www.sanijet.com.

Premier Safety Institute. Hand Hygiene–ABHR. Available at: http://www.premierinc.com/quality-safety/tools-services/safety/topics/hand_hygiene/#hand-rubs.

Storey E, Dangman KH, Schenck P. Guidance for clinicians on the recognition and management of health effects related to mold exposure and moisture indoors. Center for Indoor Environments and Health at University of Connecticut Health Center (UCHC) 2004. UCHC website. Available at: http://oehc.uchc.edu/CIEH.asp.

Triassi M, Di Popolo A, Ribera D'Alcalà G, et al. Clinical and environmental distribution of Legionella pneumophila in a university hospital in Italy: efficacy of ultraviolet disinfection. *J Hosp Infect* 2006;62:494–501.

U.S. Department of Health and Human Services, Public Health Service, Food and Drug Administration (FDA). *2005 food code.* FDA website. Available at: http://www.cfsan.fda.gov/~dms/fc05-toc.html.

CHAPTER 116

Construction and Renovation

Brian Cotten, PE, CHFM, FASHE
Executive Director of Design & Construction
University of Arkansas for Medical Sciences
Little Rock, AR

ABSTRACT

This chapter addresses the role of infection prevention programs in the healthcare facility environment with specific attention to construction and renovation. It also describes the background and regulatory aspects leading to the development of the infection control risk assessment. The infection control risk assessment has become an important springboard for infection prevention and control programs to provide input during design and construction project phases, whether on a small or large scale, in order to prevent hazardous risks to patients, healthcare personnel, and visitors. This chapter also discusses organizational planning and smaller ongoing renovation projects, along with details to consider for construction policy, procedures affecting external and internal projects for each phase, some aspects of emergency remediation, and infection prevention and control program issues to address before moving into a newly constructed or renovated space. This chapter addresses isolation room design, surfaces, and health issues for construction personnel. In addition, it discusses specific interventions following the infection control risk assessment, or infection control risk mitigation recommendations, whose aims are to prevent and mitigate transmission of airborne and waterborne biological contaminants during the construction or renovation project.

KEY CONCEPTS

- The infection control risk assessment is an important element in an infection prevention and control program and should be an integral part of all planning that involves renovation or construction at a healthcare facility.

- Infection preventionists should have access to and be knowledgeable about the Facility Guidelines Institute construction guidelines established by the American Society for Healthcare Engineering.

- A key element that infection preventionists bring to the construction/renovation process is creating an environment of care that supports infection prevention and promotes safety of patients and personnel.

- Infection preventionist leadership extends to planning programmatic needs and operational construction projects. Involvement with facility management staff during the beginning design phase is key to identifying necessary support structures required to prevent and control airborne and waterborne contamination.

BACKGROUND

A dramatic focus on patient safety was initiated in healthcare after publication of the Institute of Medicine's first report on patient safety in 1999; among the issues highlighted was the importance of the healthcare environment's effect on patient outcomes.[1] Care delivery processes occur in physical structures intended to be healing environments, enhancing patients' health outcomes. Along with the emphasis on patient safety, accreditation agencies such as The Joint Commission (TJC) and DNV, and government agencies such as Centers for Medicare & Medicaid Services (CMS) and Centers for Disease Control and Prevention (CDC) also encourage facilities to ensure the environment of care (EOC) in facilities does not serve as a reservoir for pathogens. Implicit in this emphasis on the EOC is preventive maintenance for critical utility systems that deliver ventilation and water to patient care areas. These changes have had a major impact since 2001 in the accrediting and regulatory arena and have intensified the need for involving infection prevention and control programs in construction and renovation projects. Infection preventionists (IPs) are expected to be aware of these requirements, providing direction and applying infection prevention principles to the process.

Planning for new construction or major renovation requires early collaboration among IPs, epidemiologists, architects, engineers, and other stakeholders to ensure that design of specific structures facilitates desired infection prevention and control program practices. An essential first step in the planning process is an infection control risk assessment (ICRA), followed by interventions, monitoring, and continuous assessment and improvement at a broad, organizational level and during operational projects. Basic information is required for planning and designing new facilities and construction and renovation in existing structures. Key issues are addressed in this chapter; more detail on processes may be found in the state-of-the-art report (SOAR) on construction in healthcare facilities by the Association for Professionals in Infection Control and Epidemiology, Inc. (APIC). Additional education and practical tools for infection prevention during construction and renovation are also available through APIC.[2,3]

BASIC PRINCIPLES

Planning and Design

Preventing transmission of infectious agents to vulnerable patient populations, healthcare personnel (HCP), and visitors within healthcare facilities is an increasingly important element in infection prevention and control programs. A key element that IPs bring to the construction/renovation process is creating an EOC that supports prevention of infection and promotes safety of patients and personnel. The physical environment in a healthcare facility may also pose risks to occupants (patients, personnel, and visitors) if enhancements to the environment are carried out without a basic understanding of the potential for creating microbial hazards and the associated morbidity and mortality that may result. Unintended exposure of occupants to microorganisms or other physical hazards is possible if contingencies for these are not included before the start of projects. For example, IPs may need to provide perspective to a request for architectural elements such as water features (e.g., an internal or external water fountain), highlighting potential risks of disease from waterborne opportunistic infectious agents, such as *Legionella* spp. By contrast, the IP can point to a substantial body of evidence that spatial separation of patients—that is, building single occupancy rooms—can mitigate the risk of cross-transmission of potential pathogens. Some of these design features that promote prevention of infection will be addressed. (See also Facility Guidelines Institute single room studies and Infection Prevention and Control Canada [IPAC] Facility Design in the Supplemental Resources for this chapter.)

Construction/Renovation/Remediation Hazards and Risk Mitigation

IPs increasingly recognize that risks may also occur during construction, renovation, preventive maintenance, and remediation of damage to indoor spaces or building infrastructure after natural or manmade disasters. Knowledge gained from published outbreaks and remediation of episodes of water intrusion have been summarized in *Guidelines for Environmental Infection Control in Health-Care Facilities (EIC)* from the Centers for Disease Control and Prevention (CDC) and the Healthcare Infection Control Practices Advisory Committee (HICPAC).[4] This resource provides a wealth of literature and recommendations that draw on lessons learned that align with initiatives from the architectural and engineering communities. Therefore, maintenance and engineering projects and routine preventive programs should be incorporated into development and implementation of a facility's ICRA program. (See Chapter 114 Heating, Ventilation, and Air Conditioning.)

Environmental dispersal of microorganisms during construction resulting in healthcare-associated infections (HAIs) has been described. Examples of airborne microbial contamination associated with construction care are given in Table 114-1 (see Chapter 114 Heating, Ventilation, and Air Conditioning); examples of water-related contamination associated with construction are given in Table 115-1 (see Chapter 115 Water

Systems Issues and Prevention of Waterborne Infectious Diseases in Healthcare Facilities). These outbreaks are reminders that there is a solid, evidence-based body of literature supporting these concerns. Environmental airborne contaminants and infectious agents are closely related to water and moisture considerations, and both figure prominently in construction activity. Additional details are available in APIC's Construction SOAR.[2]

INFECTION PREVENTION: DESIGN, HAZARDS, IMPLICATIONS, AND INTERVENTIONS

Major Hazards Resulting from Designs Lacking Infection Prevention and Control Program Input

Design

Insufficient planning can lead to compromise of air quality and potential for continued environmental contamination from fungi (e.g., *Aspergillus* spp.) or water contaminated with water-associated microorganisms (e.g., *Legionella* spp.) during construction or renovation. Patients with active tuberculosis or chickenpox are potential reservoirs of airborne infectious agents and may transmit disease to other susceptible patients or staff if airborne infection isolation (AII) rooms are improperly designed or poorly maintained. Selection of smooth, water-resistant materials during planning and design systematically prevent bacterial and fungal contamination. For example, seamless or coved backsplashes for sinks using nonporous materials prevent water from seeping into cellulosic materials that support growth of fungi. Properly designed and placed sinks reduce risk of outbreaks from water organisms.[5] One study suggested that architecture design (air handler systems and overall space considerations) may have had a role in an outbreak of influenza A in a multifacility nursing home. To prevent cases such as these, the process requires thoughtful input from IPs.[6]

Mitigation

A systematic approach to construction and renovation activity is crucial to improve safety; to reduce risk of exposure to chemicals, dust, and allergens; and to prevent transmission of infectious agents to susceptible hosts.[2,3,5-11] Construction activity as an independent risk factor for infectious diseases requires infection prevention and control program input on an ongoing basis.[12-15] One of the most difficult issues during new construction or renovation is erection of proper barriers to protect patients' movement around construction areas, though patient movement should be minimized if the patient is infected or highly immunosuppressed. At least one study found that transporting critically ill, ventilator-dependent patients from the intensive care unit for diagnostic or therapeutic procedures was an independent risk factor for ventilator-associated pneumonia (VAP); transportation needs should be considered in new design as well as during renovation.[16] (See Table 114-1 for examples of airborne microbial contamination and Table 115-1 for examples of water-related contamination associated with construction.)

Guidelines for Use in Strategic Planning

Guidelines published by the Facility Guidelines Institute (FGI) provide guidance on requirements, best practices, and trends in facility design and construction. The 2014 edition of the FGI guidelines split recommendations into two separate documents—one for hospitals and outpatient facilities and one for residential healthcare and support facilities (formerly Part 4 of the 2010 edition).[17] As consensus documents, they rely heavily on input from groups such as the American Society for Healthcare Engineering (ASHE) and the American Society of Heating, Refrigerating, and Air-Conditioning Engineers, Inc. as well as from clinicians and organizations such as APIC. The guidelines are consistent with published guidelines from the CDC and include ventilation requirements for negative air pressure rooms as specified in the CDC *Guidelines for Preventing the Transmission of Mycobacterium tuberculosis*[18] and the design and ventilation recommendations in the *Guidelines for Preventing Health-Care-Associated Pneumonia, 2003.*[19] The guidelines from FGI and CDC have set in motion an increased opportunity for long-range and ongoing involvement of infection prevention personnel in planning for construction and major renovation. The 2014 FGI guidelines continue to stress the scope and importance of the ICRA. The role of IPs in developing the ICRA is multifaceted and needed for long-range strategic planning, operational project initiatives, and ongoing maintenance activities.

Infection Prevention Risk Assessment Definition and Purpose

An ICRA must guide a strategic, proactive design to mitigate environmental sources of microbes and to prevent infectious hazards through architectural design (e.g., hand-washing and hand hygiene stations, isolation rooms, materials selection for surfaces and furnishings) and control measures to mitigate potential contamination during actual construction or renovation (e.g., dust barriers, pressure differentials, protection of air handlers). The FGI guidelines refer to activities associated with *design planning, construction planning,* and actual *preparation for the construction* project as infection control risk mitigation recommendations (ICRMR). These recommendations address specific infection control measures during a construction project. The ICRA is summarized as follows[17]:

> [T]he ICRA shall be conducted by a committee with expertise in infection control, direct patient care, risk management, facility design, construction, ventilation, safety, and epidemiology. *The committee shall provide documentation* of the risk assessment together with updated mitigation recommendations throughout planning, design, and construction and commissioning. The owner shall also provide monitoring of the effectiveness of the applied ICRMR during the course of the project. The owner shall ensure that construction-related ICRMR and ICRA-generated design recommendations are incorporated into project requirements.

More than 40 states have adopted the FGI guidelines in their entirety or with modifications as minimum standards for design and construction in healthcare facilities. The guidelines list the elements for consideration after assessing the facility's patient population and programs:

ICRA elements related to *building design features* include the following:

- Numbers, location, and types of AII and protective environment (PE) rooms

- Location of special ventilation and filtration of heating, ventilation, and air conditioning (HVAC) systems serving such areas as emergency department waiting and intake areas

- Air handling and ventilation needs in surgical services, AII and PE rooms, laboratories, local exhaust systems for hazardous agents/chemicals, and other areas with special needs

- Water systems to limit *Legionella* spp. and other waterborne opportunistic pathogens

- Finishes and surfaces

ICRA elements related to *building site areas affected by construction* include the following:

- Impact of disrupting essential services to patients and employees

- Determination of the specific hazards and protection levels for each

- Location of patients based on susceptibility to infection and definition of risks to each

- Impact of potential outages or emergencies and protection of patients during planned or unplanned outages, movement of debris, traffic flow, cleanup, and testing and certification

- Assessment of external and internal construction activities

- Location of known hazards

ICRMR preparation for *actual construction* include the following:

- Patient placement and relocation

- Standards for barriers and other protective measures required to protect adjacent areas and susceptible patients from airborne contaminants

- Temporary provisions or phasing for construction or modification of HVAC and water supply systems

- Protection of occupied patient areas from demolition

- Measures to be taken to train healthcare facility staff, visitors, and construction personnel on maintenance of interim life safety and ICRMR

Finally, the guidelines specifically require not only "installation of infection control measures" but also "continuous monitoring for effectives throughout the project." This may be done by "in-house infection control and safety staff" or "independent outside consultants." This major issue must be determined in the initial stages by the ICRA panel. In any case, "provisions for monitoring shall include written procedures for emergency suspension of work and protective measures indicating the responsibilities and limitations of each party (owner, designer, constructor, and monitor)."

There is no one best way for carrying out an ICRA or documenting the outcome that must be communicated to the architects and construction companies.

Construction and Renovation Policy, Purpose, and Policy Elements

A comprehensive construction and renovation policy (CRP) is the foundation for educating the healthcare facility's leadership on the importance of the ICRA and specifies roles and responsibilities of key stakeholders. A well-designed policy ensures timely notification to the IP and designated committee(s) for early program planning efforts. It also provides for an ICRA evaluation of the project from concept through completion and supports a systematic approach to project management. The policy should be submitted for approval by the facility's board of trustees and reviewed, updated as needed, and approved periodically.

Elements of the CRP should include key issues, beginning with ensuring at least annual review and approval by infection control committee(s) and the governing board of trustees.[2,17,20] There also should be a plan for systematic and ongoing communication of planned and current projects provided by the facility manager/construction coordinator to the IP to ensure awareness and incorporation of infection prevention and control program requirements. Organizational CRP elements should include coordination during the phases of construction including (1) construction preparation and demolition, (2) intraconstruction operations and maintenance, (3) project completion including postconstruction cleanup, (4) monitoring, and (5) commissioning.

Broadly applicable CRP elements should also include the following as appropriate:

- Authority and responsibilities for establishing orientation, training, coordination, and accountability for general contractors and subcontractors

- Strategic planning for air and water quality for each building, including types of barriers and monitors

- Authority for determining unit closure issues

- Specific expectations for contractor accountability in the event of breaches in infection prevention and control program practices and related written agreements

- Communication linkages, including documentation responsibilities

- Criteria for emergency work stoppages and processes to stop and start

- Educational needs for whom and by whom

- Occupational health expectations for contractors and subcontractors before start, as appropriate

- General traffic patterns for construction personnel patients, visitors, and HCP

- Transport and manifest approval, if required, of waste materials and supplies

- Noise and vibration issues related to the project

- Emergency preparedness plans for major utility failures— location and responsibilities

- Phasing and commissioning

Infection Preventionist Role at Organizational Level

IP leadership extends to planning programmatic needs and operational construction projects. Involvement with facility management staff during the beginning design phase is key to identifying necessary support structures required to prevent and control airborne and waterborne contamination. Early interaction prevents rework and costly redesign. Particular areas of input provided by infection prevention and control program include the following, with emphasis on ICRA planning and ICRMR elements as noted above:

- Facilitation and communication among health agencies and facility administration regarding essentials for safe practice and infection control guidelines, in the absence of clear-cut regulations

- Consultation related to current and future patient populations and care delivery systems; this includes need and number of AII and necessity of PE, scope of services, and so forth

- Evaluation of plans with consideration of system policies related to structural design and needs for patients and HCP

- Determination of impact on infection prevention and control program aspects based on scope of project

- Review of proposed construction in light of infection prevention and control program-related standards and regulations that will need to interface with federal, state, and local codes issued by the appropriate authorities having jurisdiction (AHJs)

- Review of proposed construction and making recommendations for optimal use of space and design, while ensuring positive infection prevention and control program outcomes, particularly for air and water quality

- Determination of environmental monitoring needs and budgeting for appropriate consultants

- Determination of type and methods of educational provisions for internal and external contractors

- Development of infection prevention and control program expectations into initial agreements and project checklists and contractor accountability in the event of breaches in infection control practices

Infection Prevention Role at Project Level

Project teams provide ongoing planning and monitoring during area preparation and throughout the demolition, construction, cleanup, preparation for return to service, and final project review. Projects vary in complexity with time, numbers of personnel, whether or not contractors work continuous shifts, scope and degree of activity (high or low dust generation), and proximity to patients with varying degrees of risk for infection. In every case, the focus should be on isolating the construction/renovation area, maintaining the area under negative pressure with respect to adjacent areas, and perceived breaches of agreements and monitoring responsibilities of each party. Project teams require IP participation to ensure continuous, ongoing input into desired infection prevention and control program practices. Membership varies depending on purpose and may also include architects, engineers, key subcontractors, safety, physical plant, risk, administrative, and clinical managers of the current or future space.[17] Input includes design and operational phases. Specific issues are itemized in the following text.

Design Phase

Issues frequently addressed in the design phase include budget, space constraints, appropriate finishes, specific products with infectious implications, and applicable regulations. IPs should be prepared to support their position and recommendations with published citations whenever feasible, but particularly if a recommendation is not budget neutral.[17] At a minimum, design issues to address should include the following:

- Air and water quality (e.g., HVAC and plumbing systems)

- Fixtures: sink numbers, types, placement, and operational controls (e.g., touchless electronic/infrared or manual faucet handles); sink types include hand-washing stations, instrument cleaning, and clinical/flushing rim; other considerations include dispensers for hand hygiene products and associated materials (soap, paper towels, lotion, and similar items; and placement and type of waterless alcohol-based handrubs [ABHRs]); placement of ABHRs should be included in functional programming for the construction/renovation project; an ABHR dispenser is not a substitute for a hand-washing station

- Sharps and waste disposal placement

- Surfaces: ceiling tiles, walls, counters, floor coverings, and furnishings

- Utility rooms: soiled, clean, instrument processing, holding, or workrooms

- Storage areas, including patient care supplies and personal protective equipment (PPE)

- Adjacency and flow of people, patient care-related items (e.g., food, medications, linens, supplies, equipment), laundry, and waste

Maintenance and Operational Phase

Oversight of the project team during the maintenance and operational phase includes area preparation and area review, excavation or demolition, construction, cleanup, preparation for return to service, and final project review. Project checklists for infection prevention and control program practices and interim life safety management should be used at the beginning of the project and before return of the area to full service, and include some of the following in the approved time frames[3,21–23]:

- Patient location or placement; unit closures; relocation of services

- Owner responsibilities before project start (e.g., removal of medical waste/sharps disposal containers, movable equipment and supply storage, protection of fixed equipment, relocation of hazardous chemicals)

- Consideration of tools and equipment management, including minimization of noise/vibration and minimal fumes (e.g., gas powered versus electric or hand operated); using wet methods (e.g., wet sanding, core drilling); responsibilities for PPE (e.g., disposable cover suits, head/foot covers, masks or respirators); use, location, and changing of tacky mats; cleaning supplies and equipment (mops, cloths, bucket and designated sink for discharging mop water—may consider fitting with plaster trap, high-efficiency particulate air [HEPA] vacuum)

- Construction containment barriers—type and seal (e.g., negative pressure for specific areas) plus separation of HVAC to and from the construction site, as well as use of supplemental HEPA filtration devices; protection of air intakes from entrainment of contaminants and prevention of infiltration (e.g., intact window seals, plugging penetrations) during any external projects (e.g., excavation, backfilling, landscaping)

- Construction materials; transfer and storage including protection from contamination and/or water damage

- Waste/debris management and disposal, including removal of medical waste; placement of dumpsters and/or location of temporary waste chutes

- Traffic patterns or rerouting for staff, patients, and contractors, including way finding and applicable internal and external signage and notifications (e.g., code teams, ambulance, emergency medical services); restrictions for contractors (e.g., restroom, eating, elevator)

- Compliance with federal, state, county, and local codes, standards, and regulations; phasing and inspections

- Education and training; documentation, communication—including training for routine and urgent/emergency situations for workers, staff, patients, visitors; contractor identification/badges; necessity for enhanced security; authority to stop work; protection of smoke detectors and sprinkler heads; need for hot work permits and fire watches; facility emergency codes; minimization of nuisance or false alarms; contractor parking; facility rules (e.g., smoking); consideration of employee health/communicable disease testing and immunizations

- Commissioning in phases throughout project; periodic site visits; punch lists

Codes, Standards, and Regulations

Regulatory and accrediting agencies at all levels base licensing and certification decisions on whether or not facilities meet minimum construction standards. In most cases, the federal requirements relate to the federal conditions of participation (CoP) required of providers to beneficiaries of the CMS.[24] AHJ includes a hierarchy of federal, state, and local regulations and may not always be in evidence. County and local jurisdictions for fire and plumbing safety codes may supersede some regulations and become the AHJ. National Fire Protection Association (NFPA) codes for life safety form the basis of one of the most important set of codes referenced by TJC.[17,20]

Federal Agencies

Key agencies include the Occupational Safety and Health Administration (OSHA) and CDC, including the National Institute for Occupational Safety and Health (NIOSH). CMS CoPs apply to hospitals, nursing homes, long-term care, and home care for reimbursement.[24] CMS and the Health Resources Services Administration follow the current FGI guidelines. The AIA/FGI in conjunction with HHS developed and published the guidelines for use in licensed and nonlicensed facilities. Although termed "guidelines," the FGI guidelines have the force of regulation in many states and are enforced by the TJC and CMS surveyors administering the Medicare program.[17-20] The 2014 edition has been published by the ASHE and FGI with assistance from the HHS.

OSHA, the regulatory enforcement agency for employee health and safety, has authority for all industries, including hospitals and healthcare facilities. Although a proposed tuberculosis standard was withdrawn by OSHA in May 2003, OSHA enforces some aspects of air quality that may present hazards to employees (e.g., tuberculosis, legionellosis), under the auspices of the "general duty clause," based on CDC guidelines or specific standards such as the bloodborne pathogen standard or respiratory protection standards, as applicable.[18,19,25-29]

Although the CDC is not a regulatory authority, CDC guidelines influence other recommendations or regulations that adopt CDC guidelines as standards. For example, CDC's *Guideline for Isolation Precautions: Preventing Transmission of Infectious Agents in Healthcare Settings 2007* continued the use of the term "AII rooms" (AIIRs) for patients infected with airborne infectious agents, including *Mycobaterium tuberculosis* and varicella-zoster virus; the term was adopted by the AIA guidelines for consistency.[17-19,28,29] The 2003 CDC guidelines for environmental infection control include recommendations consistent with the current FGI guidelines and TJC standards for the EOC because both the guidelines and the CDC seek to ensure that revisions are based on solid evidence.[4,20]

NIOSH, as the research arm for healthcare worker safety within the CDC, similarly influences enforcement agencies. The Environmental Protection Agency (EPA) has jurisdiction related to medical waste and standards related to water and air contamination levels and becomes indirectly crucial to certain design aspects.

State Authorities Having Jurisdiction

State AHJs are responsible for plan review and approval of certificate of need applications for construction and major renovation. They enforce federal CMS/CoP for facilities receiving Medicare or Medicaid funds and enforce state public health codes directly based on adoption of 2014 guidelines, as a whole or approved modifications, as specified in state laws and regulations. New healthcare facility construction after 2010 is based on adoption of guidelines as a whole or on codes adapted from the guidelines. The guidelines do not require "retrofitting" to earlier editions. More than half the states have adopted the guidelines in their entirety. Inquiry within each specific state's public health agency clarifies specifics for enforcement, interpretations, and code applicability for licensed and nonlicensed facilities. OSHA "state-plan states" must enforce their compliance with standards to be at least as effective as federal OSHA.[25-27]

County and Local Agencies

Construction standards for some ambulatory patient clinics or physician offices may not be under specific state licensing and construction codes but are under local building ordinances. Clarification of issues may be required to meet local fire, plumbing, and food ordinances in which the city or county or both take precedence. Enforcement is driven by the AHJ. Local health departments and water departments become crucial in enforcement of EPA standards for air and water contaminants. Local jurisdictions have a particular interest in cleaners/disinfectants because of their final discharge into local sanitary sewer systems. State and local ordinances require permits for backflow preventers when installing premixing valves for diluting cleaners/disinfectants with potable water; they also are concerned with plumbing for flush or clinical sinks related to medical waste discharge.[17]

Voluntary Standards

The guidelines have been adopted by TJC in the EOC standards, and TJC modified its EOC standards in all of its accreditation manuals to reference the current edition of NFPA 101, *Life Safety Code*. Other agencies and managed care organizations may develop their own physical facility standards for outpatient clinics and other care sites based on CMS CoP or indirectly with the guidelines.[17,20] (See Chapter 4 Accrediting and Regulatory Agencies, for a more detailed description.)

Traffic as a Contributor to Air Contamination

Infection risks and hazards may arise from patients and visitors as sources of infectious agents (e.g., varicella-zoster virus, measles virus, or other airborne infectious agents). Waste and contaminated linen, supplies, and equipment may also contribute to environmental hazards and associated odors. Prevention interventions include the following:

- Patient movement should cause minimal exposure of patients to others.

- Patients who are in AII should be transported using precautions defined by infection prevention and control program policy.

- Visitor traffic routes should minimize contact with patients, and visitors should be assessed for communicable disease (e.g., rashes, respiratory infection).

- Routes for transporting clean and sterile supplies from storage should not allow contact or permit temporary storage near contaminated materials.

- Laundry/trash chutes are contaminated, and bags can rupture during use. If chutes are operational, their design must be closely analyzed and use monitored for potential transmission of infectious agents.

- Waste transport should be designed for maximum containment, especially during construction or renovation, to reduce any risk of contributing contamination to the environment.

Specific Infection Prevention Design and Environmental Contamination

IPs must assess population needs and risks and make recommendations in new construction, renovation, remediation/repair, and preventive maintenance activities. Design issues of particular importance to infection prevention and control program, such as isolation rooms and surfaces (ceilings, floor coverings), not covered elsewhere are discussed here in greater detail, including their relationship with environmental contamination. (See Chapters 112 Maintenance and Engineering; 114 Heating, Ventilation, and Air Conditioning; and 115 Water Systems Issues and Prevention of Waterborne Infectious Diseases in Healthcare Facilities.)

Isolation Room Design: General Issues

When determining the number, types, and design of isolation rooms, it is important to consider several issues as part of an organizational needs assessment, including the patient population, mission and program goals of the facility, past experience with communicable diseases (either in the community or in the facility), and available resources within the community. Isolation rooms can serve two purposes. The first is to provide appropriate isolation for patients infected with pathogens that are transmitted by the airborne route (e.g., *M. tuberculosis,* varicella-zoster virus, rubeola [measles] virus). The major goal in this situation is to prevent transmission of pathogens from an infected patient to other patients, staff, or visitors. This is

generally achieved by maintaining AIIRs. The second purpose is to provide a PE for severely immunosuppressed patients. These two types of isolation rooms differ in several important ways. AIIRs have negative air pressure, and PE rooms have positive air pressure with respect to adjacent areas. Correct direction of airflow and properly balanced air pressure in AII or PE areas are essential elements to consider during construction and renovation. The 2010 guidelines require quantitative specifications for pressure relationships (minimum pressure differentials of 0.01-inch water gauge) for new construction and major renovation and mandate that specialty rooms must include a "permanently installed visual means" to measure airflow direction. In addition, the 2010 guidelines do not support "reversible" airflow rooms; design suggestions are included in the appendices in the AIA guidelines.[17] This position is based on the complexity of pressure relationships, concerns for serious patient and HCP outcomes if errors are made, and labor intensity needed for preventive maintenance. Saravia et al.[30] studied pressurization of 678 AIIRs in a large number of hospitals in the United States and found only 32 percent met recommended negative pressure differential; 9 percent, ironically, were found to be in positive pressure. A major factor for this suboptimal performance was leakage of the AIIRs studied. The complexities of *maintaining* air balances have been investigated, and the findings reinforce the importance of tightly sealed rooms.[31] (See Chapter 114 Heating, Ventilation, and Air Conditioning.)

Airborne Infection Isolation Rooms

AIIRs may or may not be in a designated unit. Although isolation wards have been dismantled over the past decades, specialized units may be reconsidered depending on the hospital's need. The AIIR design must include the ability to monitor directional airflow (i.e., with a visual method such as release of smoke plume) on a daily basis when in use for a patient on Airborne Precautions to ensure that the HVAC and the electronic monitor are functioning properly. AIIRs can be used for patients needing general care (e.g., no evidence of presence of an airborne infection) by simply turning off such monitor or alarms. Point-of-care monitors do not control the HVAC for the AIIRs but rather only indicate that the room is or is not in negative pressure. The filtered room air is changed more frequently than standard rooms and is safe for all patients. There is no evidence that placement of patients in AIIRs places them at increased risk of exposure to any airborne microorganisms.

Numbers of Airborne Infection Isolation Rooms

Sufficient AIIRs should be provided in newly designed or major renovated facilities; *at least one* AII room should be provided in acute care facilities. Program assessment must consider patient population, services, and programs (e.g., tuberculosis, pediatric patients). Numbers of isolation rooms no longer are based on bed ratios, but some specialties require at least one more (critical care, neonatal and newborn nurseries, and pediatric/adolescent care areas). In contrast, the 2006 FGI guidelines do not recommend a minimal required number for long-term-care facilities unless so determined by the facility during the program assessment.

The 2005 CDC tuberculosis (TB) guidelines and the 2007 CDC/HICPAC guideline for Isolation Precautions reinforce that long-term care facilities should plan to transfer patients with a potential airborne disease such as TB to an acute care facility.[18,28] and Chapter 114 Heating, Ventilation, and Air Conditioning.)

Design of AIIRs

AIIRs should have airflow from the corridor into the patient room, whereas air inside the AIIR is either directly exhausted to the outdoors or passed through HEPA filters before recirculation. Additional issues to consider include the following:

1. *Anterooms:* AIIRs are not required to have anterooms; however, if they are present, air should flow from the corridor into the anteroom.[4,17,18,30–32] To establish negative pressure, supply and exhaust flow need to be balanced first to achieve an exhaust flow of either 10 percent or greater than 50 cubic feet per minute (cfm) more than supply.[4]

2. *Ventilation:* Isolation rooms should be properly sealed and maintain a ventilation rate of equal to or greater than 12 air changes per hour. There is evidence that leakage from AIIRs is common—approximately one-third of AIIRs assessed in a recent study failed to meet CDC criteria.[30] Rooms permanently designed as AII should have the room air exhausted directly to the outside. However, there may be some situations that require the air be recirculated. If so, it must be filtered through a HEPA filter. If possible, the recirculated air should be confined to the AII room(s).[17]

3. *Supplemental Devices:* Older ventilation systems unable to meet the 2005 CDC guidelines for preventing the transmission of *M. tuberculosis* recommendations for patient isolation may require retrofitting of rooms used for isolation to ensure proper pressure relationships and minimum numbers of air changes. Supplementary controls, such as ventilation-filtration units or ultraviolet germicidal irradiation, may be useful but do not fulfill outside air requirements.[31–37] Given the variability in the design of recirculating room units (e.g., air movement capacity, dependence on room configuration, placement within the room, unit design, and noise issues leading to shutoff), such units must be assessed with great care, and adherence to strict cleaning and preventive maintenance is essential. The process and measurement of airflow in well-functioning AIIRs are described in visual and written materials published by the Frances Curry National TB Center in San Francisco.[3,36] Maintaining design specifications in isolation rooms with the wrong pressurization (i.e., room air was positive instead of negative with respect to the corridor) reinforces the need for routine maintenence.[38]

4. *Summary of Basic Requirements:*

   • Ventilation: 12 air changes per hour (ACH) (minimum 2 ACH outside air); airflow into the room; exhausted to the outside

   • An area for hand washing, gowning, and storing clean and soiled materials located directly outside or immediately inside the entry door to the room

• Perimeter walls, ceilings, floors, including penetrations, tightly sealed

• Self-closing devices on room exit doors

• Permanently installed visual mechanism to constantly measure the pressure status of the room when occupied by patients with an airborne infectious disease. The mechanism must continuously monitor the direction of the airflow.

• Separate toilet, bathtub (or shower), and hand-washing facilities are required for each AIIR.[17]

Protective Environment

CDC guidelines outline the ideal environment for populations of highly immunosuppressed individuals, though many facilities do not need such units.[19,29] Specialized care PE units are intended for severely immunosuppressed patients who have prolonged granulocytopenia, most notably bone marrow transplant recipients or solid-organ transplant recipients with hematological malignancies who are receiving chemotherapy and are severely granulocytopenic.

Properly designed and maintained PEs can prevent aspergillosis, the ultimate test of protective capabilities. PE rooms should include a "design bundle," because all elements must be in place, not just HEPA-filtered air. That is, just having HEPA filtration of supply air to an area is not adequate. The PE "bundle" requires:

1. Positive-pressure ventilation, whereby the amount of HEPA-filtered air supplied exceeds the amount of air exhausted

2. Airflow direction from the patient room toward the corridor

3. Pressure differential measuring minimally as 0.01-inch water gauge

4. HEPA-filtered air (99.97 percent efficiency for particles 0.3 μ)

5. Increased room air exchanges (12 air changes per hour)

6. Tight wall/ceiling, sealed penetrations, and intact window seals

7. Self-closing devices on corridor doors assist in maintenance of proper airflow

Some facilities may use laminar airflow rooms for bone marrow transplant recipients; these rooms provide unidirectional airflow with more than 100 air changes per hour. Laminar airflow rooms are expensive and their cost-effectiveness is controversial; many facilities use other ventilation systems for such patients.[17,19,29,39–41] Recent evidence indicates that even for severely immunocompromised populations, the types of HAIs encountered are those typical of other hospitalized patients (i.e., from invasive devices) and that extraordinary filtration of air does not necessarily offer significant disease prevention benefit.[42]

At least one PE room must be constructed that has an anteroom for highly immunosuppressed patients who have concurrent infection transmitted by the airborne route. The preferred design allows clean air to flow from the anteroom into the patient room *and* into the corridor (positive pressure), maintaining a clean anteroom for staff to don masks before entering the patient room.[4,36]

Intent of Specialized Care Room Design Issues

As noted earlier, rooms should not be designed to switch airflow from positive to negative and back. Self-closing devices on corridor doors assist in maintenance of proper airflow whether AII or PE. Rooms negative with respect to adjacent areas must be tightly sealed so that air does not infiltrate the environment from the outside or other spaces.[4,17,39-43]

In addition, air pressurization relationships should be governed by policies and procedures describing how pressure monitoring is accomplished on a routine basis, along with assigned responsibility.[17,18,25] In-wall manometers may be designed for local and remote monitoring and alarm for inappropriate pressure relationships.[38,44] Most important, new facilities built or renovated after 2001 must have a device that provides a continuous and visible means (not just audible alarms) to detect and monitor the direction of airflow.[4,17]

Maintenance must be included in infection prevention and control program policies. Assigned responsibilities for maintenance and cleaning of AII or PE rooms should include cleaning of surfaces and air-duct grates or vents, filter changes, and a check for adequate window seals to prevent infiltration. (See Chapter 112 Maintenance and Engineering.)[4,10,17,23] Data do not support routine "duct-cleaning." Tight duct sealing and use of filtration for incoming air minimize the need for cleaning. On the other hand, exhaust grilles require regular cleaning.[3,4]

Each AII and PE room should have an area for hand washing, gowning, and storing clean and soiled materials located directly outside or immediately inside the entry door of the room. Cabinets may protect materials inside the room; CMS and state-based enforcement agencies emphasize clear, unobstructed corridors in healthcare facilities. If "door caddies"—devices that hang over a door and store PPE—are used, they must meet local fire marshal codes for flammability. Negative air rooms for other specialty areas (e.g., waiting rooms in emergency departments, clinic areas, psychiatry, and postanesthetic care units) should focus on specific patient populations and determine need and feasibility of one or more rooms that could function as AIIRs for patients with suspected infections transmitted by the airborne route. (See Chapter 114 Heating, Ventilation, and Air Conditioning.)

Surfaces and Furnishings: Design, Sustainability, and Contribution to Environmental Contamination

At a time of increased use of environmentally friendly materials, there has been an increased awareness of the synergy of infection prevention and healthy outcomes for patient, workers, and the environment. Ideal features of surfaces that satisfy sustainability, infection prevention, and safe patient outcomes include cleanability and resistance to moisture, reducing the risk of fungal contamination.[4,17] Several studies reveal that the persistence of microorganisms in the environment after patient room cleaning is often found to be related to the thoroughness of cleaning protocols.[45-47] Recent studies that use tracer dyes to track and measure the thoroughness of cleaning processes are now taking on added importance.[45,46]

Work published in 2006 by Carling and colleagues[45] addressed the transmission and persistence of microorganisms in the environment. Carling et al.[46] studied the quality of cleaning of the EOC at a number of hospitals by using a solution that fluoresces when exposed to ultraviolet light to identify areas in the environment that might not have been cleaned as thoroughly as desired. These studies evaluated the methods to determine the thoroughness of routine and terminal room cleaning and disinfection. The importance of complete cleaning was demonstrated in a study by Drees and colleagues using vancomycin-resistant enterococci (VRE) as a marker of room contamination. Findings indicated that prior VRE room contamination was highly predictive of VRE acquisition, and the authors urged increased attention to environmental cleaning and disinfection. The enforcement of environmental cleaning measures and cleaner healthcare personnel hands was significantly associated with less surface contamination of VRE and a reduction in cross-transmission of VRE in an environment with a high level of endemic VRE. These collective findings put new emphasis on the need to select easily cleanable surfaces.[47]

Wall Surfaces

Smooth painted surfaces are easier to clean than textured, porous vinyl wall coverings.[4] Vinyl wall coverings have potential for fungal growth on the underside if moisture from condensation occurs, especially when located on exterior walls. Operating and delivery rooms, isolation rooms, and sterile processing areas also need a smooth finish free of fissures, open joints, and crevices that retain or permit passage of dirt particles. Epoxy-based grout permits use of smooth tile in operating rooms. Problems can be avoided if surfaces near water or water fixtures are smooth, nonporous, and water resistant (e.g., avoid laminate wood vanities).[17,21]

SURFACES AND ANTIMICROBIALS

Carpeting and Other Floor Coverings

When selecting floor coverings, facilities must consider materials that may be easily cleaned but also enhance patient comfort, particularly if acoustics is considered. For instance, although carpeting can control noise and reduce impact in the event of patient falls, it can be difficult to clean in a manner that ensures removal of microorganisms that survive in the environment (e.g., *Clostridium difficile* spores). In addition, removing stains from body fluids or chemicals that are typical in healthcare facilities can be challenging. The patient population assessment is a crucial component to factor into the final decision. Although studies have found that bacterial contamination per unit of carpet may be higher than for hard surface floors, they have failed to implicate carpeting as a source of HAIs.[48–51] One study assessed the impact of carpeting in patient rooms on environmental contamination with *C. difficile* but failed to establish environmental acquisition of pseudomembranous colitis under nonepidemic conditions.[52]

However, recent studies on retention of microorganisms and methods for assessing cleaning processes have highlighted the importance of selecting cleanable surfaces, including floor coverings.[45–47] Carpeting remains a potential reservoir of contaminants and allergens and may cause problems for cleaning and odor control. This issue is especially significant if vacuuming is infrequent or unfiltered. Additional noise from vacuum cleaners may also be problematic in some settings.[51–54] Upkeep and maintenance of any flooring selected should follow manufacturers' directions for proper cleaning materials, dilution (to avoid discoloration), and frequency of cleaning techniques. (See Supplemental Resources for resilient floor coverings.)

Surface Materials and Impregnated Antimicrobials

Given the notable increase in either replacement or extensive renovation of healthcare facilities in the United States, there has been interest in designing an environment that promotes safety but also prevents cross-transmission of infectious agents. Studies of the addition or incorporation of antimicrobials (e.g., silver) to medical devices, such as vascular and urinary catheters, has met with some success in preventing HAIs—primarily because of direct contact with the patient's mucous membrane or sterile tissue. (See Chapters 34 Intravascular Device Infections, and 33 Urinary Tract Infection.) These observations have stimulated interest in extending this to treat or incorporate antimicrobials into surfaces around the patient.

Textiles

Current evidence demonstrating the efficacy of antimicrobials when applied to or incorporated into or onto inanimate surfaces of devices, patient care equipment, fixtures, or finishes—including carpeting in patient rooms—specifically for prevention of HAIs is lacking. These treatments may act as a preservative of the treated substrate; any claims of disease prevention that have come under scrutiny by the EPA lack supportive scientific evidence. Specifically, textiles such as carpeting or cubicle curtains with antimicrobial features including textiles developed to absorb sound have never been demonstrated to reduce infectious outcomes.

Metal Surfaces—Copper

Copper has recently been the focus of investigation as one possible solution to reducing reservoirs of environmental pathogens; one study compared the use of copper versus the more commonly used stainless steel for high-touch surfaces.[55] For the first time, because of its intrinsic antimicrobial properties, the EPA has approved a new label claim for copper,

but with some important caveats because it addresses only reduction of microbes (taking 2 hours for a 3-log reduction on surfaces and fixtures)—not a health claim to reduce infection transmission or *reduction in infection rates*. Specifically, the EPA has required manufacturers to state:

> The use of a copper alloy surface is a supplement to and not a substitute for standard infection control practices; users must continue to follow all current infection control practices, including those practices related to cleaning and disinfection of environmental surfaces. The copper alloy surface material has been shown to reduce microbial contamination, but it does not necessarily prevent cross-transmission.[56]

Additional research is needed to provide evidence that a change to copper surfaces would decrease HAI rates, because it is far different than just proving that copper kills bacteria. As is often the case, what appears promising in the laboratory may be difficult to apply in natural settings. Airey and Verran[57] compared copper with other alloys using a model to simulate clinical care environments where disinfectants such as dilute sodium hypochlorite (bleach solution) are common. In addition to corrosion, there was notable buildup of cells and soil on copper, but stainless steel remained clean over the course of the 5-day study when deployed in a natural patient care setting.

No Standards Requiring Antimicrobials

In summary, manufacturers that add fungicides or antimicrobials to their products are not permitted to make health claims, and such additives should not be a criterion when selecting floor coverings. The EPA's bulletin *Consumer Products Treated with Pesticides, August 2003,* states that claims for treated articles or substances are limited to language such as, "This product contains a preservative (e.g., fungicide or insecticide) built in or applied as a coating only to protect the product."[58] Any pesticide-treated product that is not registered by the EPA cannot make public health claims. The EPA's policy is predicated on the fact that no scientific evidence exists that these products prevent the spread of germs and harmful microorganisms in humans. In conclusion, no standard or guideline from the CDC, CMS, FDA, EPA, or TJC supports use of antimicrobial impregnated fabrics in healthcare.[58,59]

Carpet/Textile Damage

Contamination of carpeting after saturation with water or during demolition has been reported as a reservoir for healthcare-associated fungal infection. *Aspergillus* spp. and other fungi may contaminate carpets.[4,51]

Carpets require regular vacuuming, shampooing, or extraction, depending on use, material, and degree of soiling. Use of HEPA filter vacuum machines is recommended during construction activity. (See Chapter 112 Maintenance and Engineering.)[4,21–23,50]

If carpeting is installed, some additional prevention interventions may be recommended to reduce risks from wet carpeting. Aesthetic considerations related to stains and odor control support recommendations to avoid carpeting in areas of frequent spillage or heavy soil, such as operating rooms, obstetrics units, bone marrow transplant units, burn units, intensive care units, chemotherapy units, kitchens, laboratories, and toilet or utility rooms. If surfaces are subject to frequent wet-cleaning methods, they should not be physically affected by germicidal disinfectants. If they also are subject to traffic when wet (e.g., kitchens), they should have a nonslip surface, and the perimeters should be sealed tightly.[4,26] Carpet cleaning should follow manufacturer's directions for proper cleaning materials, dilution, and frequency of cleaning techniques.[4]

Investigation of clustered cases of fungal infection should include examination of potential for contaminated carpeting after events such as fires or building demolition activity.[51,54,60] If major flooding has occurred, damage should be assessed for removal; if carpeting has been exposed to sewage, it should be discarded and the area disinfected with diluted bleach, cleaned, and dried. If carpet is wet from steam or potable water leaks and wet for less than 24 to 48 hours, one practical protocol includes the following (although manufacturer's directions should be consulted whenever possible to ensure that use of even diluted bleach would not decolorize the carpet)[4,21,23]:

1. Remove furniture and extract carpet with water.

2. Shampoo with diluted surfactant/detergent.

3. Soak with diluted bleach (1:10); rinse and extract with clean water to remove bleach; commercial steam cleaning is an alternative to bleach.

4. Dry within 12 to 24 hours of treatment using floor or exhaust fans to aid in drying.

5. Consider consultation with companies that provide inspection services for adjacent areas and equipment for rapid drying.

Ceiling Tile or Similar Porous Material Surfaces

Sources that may harbor infectious agents include acoustical ceiling tiles and fireproofing; filter materials may become wet after water breaks or floods and become a reservoir for fungal spores.[4,21,22,61-64] Preventive and control interventions include the following:

1. Tiles should be assessed for damage. If tiles are composed of nonporous materials, they can be cleaned with dilute hypochlorite and dried before replacement.

2. If tiles are nonporous, or if moisture is due to small steam leak, they can be cleaned with dilute hypochlorite and air dried before replacement.

3. If major water damage has occurred and porous tiles were not removed and dried within 24 to 48 hours, tiles should be discarded and replaced.

Hand Washing: Hand Sanitation Stations and Fixtures

Although ABHRs add an important new dimension to hand hygiene strategies, it is crucial that the IP conduct careful investigations into hand-washing equipment (e.g., types of faucets and methods of drying) to reduce hand contamination. Nontouch faucet fittings have increased in use and may require extra attention to maintain water temperature and pressure and require frequent use to avoid water contamination.[5,65-67] Sustainability experts recommend tap electronic devices as one method to reduce water use. This may also reduce recontamination of hands but also requires attention to frequency of usage or periodic flushing to minimize risks from tap and drain biofilm overgrowth.[5] Research on hand contamination during drying also suggests the importance of evaluating different methods and designs for drying and placement of nontouch towel dispensers.[68-71] (See Chapter 115 Water Systems Issues and Prevention of Waterborne Infectious Diseases in Healthcare Facilities; see Supplemental Resources for sink design.)

Personnel Issues and Contractor Expectations

Crucial preplanning issues that must be addressed include contract companies and the "owner" (healthcare facility) of the new or renovated building under consideration. Documentation that describes steps to take to protect patients also must consider management of contractor employees for security and infection prevention purposes. Requirements for contract personnel must be spelled out in project manual specifications documents; this includes control methods such as badges and point or portals of entrance or access to the construction site or to the healthcare facility. Check-in and checkout procedures; specific areas for donning and removing protective garb; eating facilities and toilet facilities; and facility-specific emergency procedures should be identified well before the project begins. The contractor should be involved with the review of the ICRA and should sign the ICRA document. Health requirements and education issues vary by project, especially if contractors have little to no contact with patients or personnel but should be included in principle as items that must be determined by mutual agreement between the owner and the construction company, including subcontractors.

Obtaining the cooperation of contractors is key to ensuring that the hired work crew observes appropriate behavior when entering a healthcare site. Provision of training and education by IPs and healthcare professionals to contractors and subcontractors is the first step in creating a stronger sense of partnership. Training should include information on hygiene, traffic patterns, availability of protective wear, and other dust-containment recommendations, and the training should accommodate language needs. Documents should include all expected necessary containment recommendations. These recommendations may include dust removal from clothing and shoes before entering the healthcare facility; avoidance of entry to high-risk patient and staff traffic areas; availability of cover gowns or other protective coverings for personnel; and provisions for portable toilets for the construction workers' use only, with soap and water to wash, preferably outside of the occupied healthcare facility. These precautions help limit the amount of dust being introduced into the healthcare facility. Partnership with contractors helps ensure greater respect for IP concerns among construction workers and raises the level of infection prevention program awareness regarding the different phases of the project, particularly for high dust-generating activities (e.g., demolition of a targeted building).[72] Select aspects that should be in place for contractors and subcontractors include the following:

- Proof of liability and worker's compensation insurance

- Appropriate documentation and communication agreements

- Training on owner (facility) safety and infection prevention and control program policies and any other federal/state/local authority having jurisdictional requirements

- Identification of hazardous chemicals planned for use and material safety data sheets provided to owner

- Spill response plans outlined for hazardous chemicals

- PPE availability and notice of anticipated generation of hazardous waste

- Location and access to owner emergency care services

- Assessment and documentation of interim life safety measures

- Evacuation and fire safety response plan confirmation; location of water shutoff valves as appropriate

- Plans for worksite dust containment reinforcement and attention to wall or floor penetrations

- Planned response for unusual conditions (e.g., water intrusion)

- Advance communication/notification of personnel in areas likely affected by noise or disruption of utilities

Preparation for Demolition and Construction

As the actual project begins, the project teams provide ongoing planning and monitoring during area preparation and throughout the demolition, construction, cleanup, preparation for return to service, commissioning, and final project review.[2,4,17-20] Before construction begins, the focus of preparations should be on isolation of the construction/renovation area. Some sources categorize projects in terms of minor or major risk based on the level of needed barriers; checklists and permits are developed accordingly.[2-4,21]

External Excavation Precautions

External excavation ideally is conducted during off-hours so that air handlers can be adjusted; the goal is to protect the intake as much as possible.[4] Excavation can produce an enormous amount of dust as noted in numerous outbreaks. Working during off-hours reduces traffic and opening of doors, which reduce

the volume of unfiltered air that flows into the building during excavation activity. Small projects require similar planning and vary by degree, but preparation still requires early communication with facility management. Specific educational needs (e.g., OSHA), regulations, and health issues for patients and personnel need to be addressed. A final customized checklist should be appended to the construction and renovation policy.[2]

Daily inspections should be made, particularly at the start of a project. Recording inspections and observations is recommended. The inspection should look at major areas, including the following:

- Dust containment barriers at the source are appropriate.

- The frequency in wetting excavated soil or demolished building materials, is adequate but not so wet that new hazards are created.

- Doors, windows, and other ports of entry located near the project are sealed or barred from use. This may involve coordination with local fire marshal for interim life safety measures.

- Construction worker behavior, such as removing dust and observing good hygiene before entering into healthcare grounds, is acceptable.

- Waste is kept to a minimum.

- Materials delivered and stored outside for later installation are properly protected (e.g., shrink-wrapped covering).

It is recommended that an inspection worksheet or checklist be created, with daily inspections and observations recorded and copies given to the designated individuals who can correct the situation when necessary. The worksheet should include key precautions to observe and a follow-up segment. These worksheets act as a means of communication; if a problem arises, the worksheets become evidence that due diligence was exercised by IPs and other healthcare professionals.[2,3,73]

INTERNAL CONSTRUCTION OR RENOVATION ACTIVITY

Infection Prevention Hazards, Implications, and Risks

Plans are needed to protect patient care areas if they cannot be closed or are adjacent to a major renovation (adjacent can be directly above or below a renovation area). The most important risks of internal construction or renovation include the following:

- Dust and debris may carry microorganisms (e.g., *Aspergillus* spp.).

- Ventilation systems may malfunction from accumulation of dust and debris on filters, resulting in decreased airflow and filtration.

- Patient rooms, supplies, equipment, and areas where patients may be treated may be contaminated (e.g., radiology).

Prevention Interventions

Ensuring infection prevention and control program staff membership on the project team is crucial; the team must consider all elements described earlier. A key strategy is to minimize patient, HCP, and visitor movement around major construction activity as much as possible. When admission of highly immunosuppressed patients is anticipated, patients should be educated regarding the access to the facility identified in the ICRA, and patients should be located in units as remote as possible from the construction area. Many items should be considered as follows:

1. *Barrier placement:* The goal of barrier placement in construction/renovation areas is isolation of the area from occupied areas during construction using sealed, airtight barriers. Checklists should consider signage directing pedestrian traffic away from construction area and materials and isolation of the area using airtight fire-rated barriers (drywall; plywood, with caulked seams for a tight seal; gasketed doorframes).[2,11,21–23,27,62–64]

2. *Air filtering:* It should be determined if construction area uses fresh/outside or recirculated air; filters should be added or return vents covered as needed with filter material or plastic.

3. *Noise and vibration:* The potential for vibration or disturbances to dislodge dust collected above suspended or false ceilings should be recognized and the effect of vibration on contamination of plumbing. Noise and vibration also may be disturbing or harmful to certain patient populations (e.g., premature neonates, cardiac or stroke patients, pediatric or psychiatric patients).

4. *Ventilation:* Ventilation should be monitored to ensure that exhaust maintains negative airflow in the construction zone. Other ventilation issues include verification that adjacent areas have sealed penetrations and intact ceilings; verification that facility systems can continue to provide proper air exchange rates and pressure relationships in crucial areas near construction activity, and that air is not being recirculated from the construction area into other patient care areas; accountability for and frequency of testing air pressure throughout the project; and specification of temperature and humidity limits affecting ventilation that could lead to limiting use of the work area (e.g., operating room).

5. *Debris removal:* If possible, use of a chute with HEPA-filtered negative air machines is preferred for debris removal over use of elevators; however, the chute opening should be sealed when not in use. Debris should be removed at least daily in carts with tightly fitted covers. Cart exteriors should be cleaned, and transport should occur during the lowest activity period and using the route agreed on as part of traffic flow planning.[13,23]

6. *Environmental air sampling:* Indications for taking environmental cultures should be critically reviewed because cultures are unlikely to provide useful information for prevention of possible construction-related infections. Pressure gauges can be installed in solid barriers that continuously demonstrate

proper pressure relationships, eliminating the need for other air sampling. Air sampling and testing should only be undertaken within an ICRA with input from the infection prevention and control program to ensure that testing is conducted by experienced trained staff as well as proper interpretation. Indicators for visible monitoring should be identified, and patient care staff should be educated on implications if they notice clues to potential contamination. For example, they may look for visible dust, footprints, opened doors and flies, and wet ceiling tiles, and be alert to other risks.[3] (See Chapter 114 Heating, Ventilation, and Air Conditioning.)

7. *System balancing:* After completion of construction, the ventilation systems should be balanced to design specifications. Filters should be visually examined for plugging or leakage. Preventive maintenance or cleaning of ductwork, vents, or induction units should have been agreed on beforehand.

8. *Water issues:* Water lines should be flushed thoroughly in newly renovated and adjacent areas before occupation because of increased risk of loosened internal corrosion and scale during vibration of water pipes and increased potential for water contamination.[10,11,27]

9. *Contractor cleanup:* Contractors should complete removal of partitions and clean and disinfect according to specific agreements.[21,22]

10. *Facility cleanup:* Ensure that healthcare facility staff perform routine cleaning before returning to the area to service. Recleaning and disinfection of surfaces and equipment may be necessary if punch-list items are still being addressed.

EXTERNAL CONSTRUCTION OR MAJOR RENOVATION

Infection Risks in Addition to Internal Issues

Increased potential for contaminating dust and debris on air intake filters may result in decreased airflow, allowing airborne spread of microorganisms via the ventilation system. HVAC units may be disrupted and nonfunctional during certain periods of construction. Medical vacuum systems and water supply may be affected similarly.

Prevention Interventions in Addition to Internal Construction Recommendations

Many interventions can decrease the risk during external excavation or construction. The steps begin with identifying location of air intakes with respect to location of high-risk patients. The team may consider the following:

1. *Filter changes:* The frequency of changing the prefilters should be increased. When admission is necessary, high-risk patients should be located in areas as remote from the construction area as possible.

2. *Cleaning:* Areas adjacent to construction activity should be cleaned with increased frequency.

3. *Air handler changes:* Beyond the barrier checklist outlined earlier, the team may have to consider closing down dampers temporarily in areas adjacent to construction to reduce circulation of contaminated air or fumes.

4. *Power disruptions:* When power is reestablished after a power interruption, and dampers and fans resume operation, dust released during this process may contain and transmit infectious agents to patients and staff. Policies or protocols should address issues such as communication, operating the HVAC for a specified time to run air out of the ducts, and immediate cleaning, before putting the area (e.g., operating room) back into service. Long-range follow-up includes preventive maintenance and cleaning of ducts near dampers to reduce the dust load; it also includes surveillance of airborne infectious agents or HAIs. (See Chapters 112 Maintenance and Engineering; 114 Heating, Ventilation, and Air Conditioning; and 119 Emergency Management.)[23]

5. *Verification of air handler status:* It must be ensured that the facility's systems can provide the proper air exchange rates and pressure relationships in crucial areas near construction activity; it must be ensured that air is not being circulated from the construction site into other areas of the healthcare facility.

6. *Cleaning of air handler:* Facility engineers should be contacted about special maintenance and cleaning of the ventilation system likely to be affected by construction. After completion of construction, it must be ensured that the ventilation systems are balanced to design specifications and that scheduled maintenance is determined.

7. *Final cleaning:* The new area must be thoroughly cleaned before installing furnishings, privacy curtains, and clean supplies, and permitting patient admission.

Interruptions of Normal Water Service

Special infection risks and hazards are associated with disruption of normal water service utility during construction or renovation, requiring long-range planning. (See Chapters 115 Water Systems Issues and Prevention of Waterborne Infectious Diseases in Healthcare Facilities, and 119 Emergency Management.) These hazards include (1) lack of potable water for drinking, food preparation, and ice; (2) lack of water for hand washing and bathing; and (3) lack of water for flushing toilets, clinical sinks, decontamination, sterilization, food service needs, and support services (e.g., laboratory). Anticipating and planning preventive and control interventions can minimize risks; the following should be considered:

- Schedule interruptions for low-activity times when feasible.

- Plan and arrange for volume of potable water for drinking and food preparation; include water for washing pots, pans, and nondisposables.

- Plan and arrange for supplies for patient care and cleaning.

- Provide disposable towelettes or waterless alternatives for hand washing for patients and personnel.

- Develop a plan for toilets.

Water Damage during Construction or after Floods and Other Disasters

Flooding or power interruptions during construction may lead to damage requiring special cleaning and remediation. Major water damage affecting walls, related furnishings, ceiling, or carpeting is addressed in terms of short-term and long-term solutions. Infectious risks are increased greatly for fungal contamination after major flooding that may affect all types of surfaces, particularly walls, but also ceilings, flooring, and furnishings. Moisture not visible to the eye can continue to support bacterial and fungal growth and requires rapid remedial action.[4,14,23,62-64]

The degree of decontamination needed depends on location and risks affecting ventilation systems (e.g., operating room), and additional resources may be needed. A systematic, general approach to remediation after water damage due to floods, sewage backup, steam leaks, and groundwater infiltration is suggested, based on limited but practical experiences after major flooding[4,21,23]:

1. An inventory of water-damaged areas, building materials, and furnishings should be taken, paying particular attention to carpeting under cabinets and other furnishings.

2. A moisture meter (electronic wet test meter) or infrared camera should be used to identify extent of water damage to drywall and other surfaces; environmental air sampling may be considered to monitor stages of cleanup and remediation as noted above. (See Chapter 115 Water Systems Issues and Prevention of Waterborne Infectious Diseases in Healthcare Facilities.)

3. Materials should be removed within 24 to 48 hours of water damage.

4. Decontamination is done by spraying with a chlorine-based mist, or diluted bleach, and drying. Ensure that staff are properly protected and provide good ventilation during the process.

5. Balanced ventilation should be instituted to reduce supply air volume to effect a negative air pressure area; sealing off area with tape, airflow should be checked with a smoke stick; mobile HEPA filtering machines or "air scrubbers" should be placed in areas being remediated.

6. Wall areas are identified for removal, cove base is removed, and areas are opened for drying (see later discussion).

7. Decontamination of opened wall areas and cavities is done with 1:9 dilution of copper-8-quinolinolate compound, using a pressurized spray pump.[21,23,61,62]

8. Cleanup of surface soil and removal is done with a detergent (1:200 dilution trisodium phosphate) and disposable cleaning materials followed by final cleaning with 1:10 dilution of bleach.

9. Ceilings are vacuumed with a HEPA-filtered vacuum cleaner. When area is completely dry, the wall and ceiling may be closed and covered with standard wall finishing materials; locating moisture and thorough drying are key.[21,23]

10. Specific recommendations are available if water leaks affect drywall laths, plaster, or sheetrock within 24 hours.[21,23]

11. Wall vinyl should be stripped.

12. Portions of the drywall and insulation may need to be removed (e.g., remove 12-inch section at the bottom to examine and determine the extent of damage with a moisture meter) or use an infrared camera to visualize hidden damage.

13. If needed, drywall and insulation is removed and replaced; only minimal cleaning may be required, however.

14. If major flooding has occurred and material has not been removed within 24 to 48 hours, there is increasing probability that damage already has led to microbial growth, and more extensive effort may be required.

15. Removal should be done under controlled conditions (sealed off, negative air pressure, and transported in sealed containers/cleaned carts), as noted earlier.

16. Water-soaked areas should be removed at least 12 inches above watermark and discarded, while allowing opened areas to dry.

17. Hard surfaces may be cleaned with diluted bleach without rinsing off the bleach.

18. Area is sprayed from top to bottom with antimicrobial or dilution of copper-8-quinolinolate compound.[21,23,61,62]

19. After installing replacement, the wall is sealed and finished with standard materials.[21,23]

20. Upholstered furniture cleaning after contamination requires considerations similar to carpet cleaning, including disposal in the event of major soaking due to floods, leaks, or sewage. If furniture is affected only by steam moisture, it can be dried. Hardwood with intact laminate can be cleaned and disinfected with dilute bleach. However, if laminated furniture with exposed particleboard beneath or other furniture composed of pressed wood or chip board becomes soaked, it should be disposed of because of absorption of water.[4,21,62]

REVIEW PREPARATIONS BEFORE OCCUPANCY OF NEW CONSTRUCTION

The following processes usually are done as part of an operational project team and verified by the commissioning agent. The facility's punch list is invaluable to assess and ensure that items are completed before occupancy.

The following steps are taken 1 week before moving into the new facility:

General Checks	1. Airflow, pressures, filters, location of air intakes and vents 2. Drains to the sanitary sewer system connected and functioning
Steps 2 Weeks before Moving into New Facility	1. Use processing packs to check steam, gas sterilizers. 2. Verify correct water temperatures. 3. Complete written schedules and procedures for routine maintenance of equipment, cooling towers, and suction machines (central and portable); establish documentation. 4. Determine transportation systems. 5. Walk through the facility with local health department representative and facility management personnel to ensure compliance with local and state codes.[25] 6. Perform point to point testing of all fire alarm devices.
Steps 1 Week before Moving into New Facility	1. Evaluate HVAC supplying special areas, such as operating rooms and interventional cardiology rooms. Objective evidence (air balance report) should be requested from contractor and reviewed by the commissioning agent to ensure that HVAC is providing air exchanges and filtration as designed, before owner acceptance. Assess methods for determining effectiveness of particulate matter removal. (See Chapters 114 Heating, Ventilation, and Air Conditioning, and 112 Maintenance and Engineering.) 2. Evaluate laminar air hoods for effective operation; ensure functioning according to manufacturer specifications. Ensure that a maintenance contract has been arranged and testing accomplished. 3. Open all faucets simultaneously to test drain effectiveness. 4. Check that aerators are not on designated faucets. 5. Check floor drains, and ensure that traps have water seals to prevent sewer gases from entering rooms. 6. Ensure that contractors have completed their own cleaning and disinfecting; ensure that housekeeping department has completed facility follow-up cleaning. 7. Ensure that hand hygiene products are in dispensers and that dispensers function properly and are convenient to users.[64] 8. Ensure that registered pest control and management are functioning and checked. 9. Be prepared to intensify surveillance for HAIs and monitoring of infection control practice. 10. Ensure that owner training has been completed and that all operational manuals have been turned over to the owner.

CONCLUSIONS

The role of infection preventionist in construction and renovation is a challenging and exciting one and is the ultimate demonstration of the multidisciplinary nature of the infection prevention and control program. Architectural, engineering, and environmental professionals have increasingly recognized the need for infection prevention and control program input. An improved understanding of the relationship between the environment and infection by all stakeholders has added new impetus to involving the IP to develop more sustainable yet safer environments for patients and HCP. Interaction and integration of efforts with other disciplines enable disease prevention for patients and HCP to remain the focus and are a driving force during construction and renovation.

FUTURE TRENDS

Many issues and concerns remain and require continual research and evaluation of methods to improve patient outcomes further, as follows:

1. *AIIRs and surge capacity:* Investigation continues into more flexible designs that permit facilities to increase rapidly their capacity for negative pressure in spaces or units in the event of sudden demand.

2. *Surgical suite:* Designs of operating rooms have improved in terms of airflow to optimize environmental conditions for the patient. However, sources of environmental contamination continue to prompt postoccupancy studies in current building research.

3. *Specialized areas:* Humidification effects in different climates may present challenges, not only for the surgical suite but also for other areas such as neonatal nurseries and cardiac catheterization laboratories. Studies are needed to identify the optimal temperature and humidity ranges necessary for providing staff comfort, minimizing risk of infection, and minimizing potential damage to sensitive equipment.

4. *Emergency departments and ambulatory care sites:* National Institutes of Health (NIH) studies are seeking to identify optimal engineering controls for current ambulatory care surgery settings to improve outcomes; there is also need for further delineation of the role of mobile HEPA units and ultraviolet germicidal irradiation in clinics and nontraditional care settings.

5. *Efficacy of remediation protocols:* Controlled studies on the efficacy and safety of current or newer antifungal treatments after severe water damage are needed. Clearer determinations regarding the safety of damaged drywall left in place versus its removal are needed. Other studies are needed to determine the efficacy and safety of other types of materials for remediation.

6. *Environmental surfaces:* More research is needed on the efficacy of treatments or incorporation of antimicrobials into environmental surfaces (e.g., countertops, ventilation ducts, drywall, floor coverings) relative to the prevention of transmission of microorganisms from the environment. Study of materials such as copper surfaces or devices need evaluation in natural settings. Related to surface cleaning, there is a great need for identifying new disinfectants that are effective in healthcare but environmentally friendly or "green."

REFERENCES

1. Kohn LT, Corrigan JM, Donaldson MS, eds. *To err is human: building a safer health system.* Washington, DC: Institute of Medicine, National Academy Press, 1999.
2. Bartley JM. APIC state-of-the-art report: the role of infection control during construction in health care facilities. *Am J Infect Control* 2000 Apr;28(2):156–169.
3. Bartley JM, Olmsted RN, eds. *Construction and renovation, 3rd ed: toolkit for professionals in infection prevention and control.* Washington DC: Association for Professionals in Infection Control and Epidemiology, Inc., 2007.
4. Sehulster L, Chinn RY; CDC, et al. Guidelines for environmental infection control in healthcare facilities: recommendations of CDC and the Healthcare Infection Control Practices Advisory Committee (HICPAC). *MMWR Morb Mortal Wkly Rep* 2003 Jun 6;52(RR-10):1–42.
5. Hota S, Hirji Z, Stockton K. Outbreak of multidrug-resistant *Pseudomonas aeruginosa* colonization and infection secondary to imperfect intensive care unit room design. *Infect Control Hosp Epidemiol* 2009 Jan;30(1):25–33.
6. Drinka PJ, Krause P, Schilling M, et al. Report of an outbreak: nursing home architecture and influenza-A attack rates. *J Am Geriatr Soc* 1996 Aug;44(8):910–913.
7. American Thoracic Society Workshop Achieving Healthy Indoor Air. Report of the American Lung Association and American Thoracic Society Workshop 1995, November 16–19, Santa Fe, NM. *Am J Respir Crit Care Med* 1997;156(Pt 2):S33–S64.
8. American Lung Association, U.S. EPA, Consumer Product Safety Commission, American Medical Association. *Indoor air pollution: an introduction for health professionals.* Washington, DC: EPA, U.S. Government Printing Office, 1994.
9. Rautiala S, Reponen T, Hyvarinen A, et al. Exposure to airborne microbes during the repair of moldy buildings. *Am Ind Hyg Assoc J* 1996 Mar;57(3):279–284.
10. Rutala WA, Weber DJ. Environmental interventions to control nosocomial infections. *Infect Control Hosp Epidemiol* 1995 Aug;16(8):442–443.
11. Rutala WA. Water as a reservoir of nosocomial pathogens. *Infect Control Hosp Epidemiol* 1997 Sep;18(9):609–616.
12. Tang JW, Li Y, Eames I, et al. Factors involved in the aerosol transmission of infection and control of ventilation in healthcare premises. *J Hosp Infect* 2006 Oct;64(2):100–114.
13. Weems JJ, Davis BJ, Tablan OC, et al. Construction activity: an independent risk factor for invasive aspergillosis and zygomycosis in patients with hematologic malignancy. *Infect Control* 1987 Feb;8(2):71–75.
14. Centers for Disease Control and Prevention (CDC). Sustained transmission of nosocomial Legionnaires disease—Arizona and Ohio. *MMWR Morb Mortal Wkly Rep* 1997 May 16;46(19):416–421.
15. Yu VL. Prevention and control of *Legionella*: an idea whose time has come. *Infect Dis Clin Pract* 1997;6:420–421.
16. Kollef MI, Von Harz B, Prentice D, et al. Patient transport from intensive care increases the risk of developing ventilator-associated pneumonia. *Chest* 1997 Sep;112(3):765–773.
17. Facilities Guidelines Institute. 2014 Guidelines for Design and Construction of Hospitals and Outpatient Facilities. Washington, DC, The American Institute of Architects Press, 2014.
18. Jensen PA, Lambert LA, Iademarco MF, et al., Centers for Disease Control. Guidelines for preventing the transmission of *Mycobacterium tuberculosis* in health-care settings, 2005. *MMWR Recomm Rep* 2005 Dec 30;54(RR-17):1–141.
19. Tablan OC, Anderson LJ, Besser R, et al. Guidelines for preventing health-care-associated pneumonia, 2003. Recommendations of CDC and the Healthcare Infection Control Practices Advisory Committee. *MMWR* 2004 Mar 26;53(RR-3):1–36.
20. The Joint Commission. *The 2009 comprehensive accreditation manual for hospitals.* Oakbrook Terrace, IL: The Joint Commission Publications, 2014.
21. Carter CD, Barr BA. Infection control issues in construction and renovation. *Infect Control Hosp Epidemiol* 1997 Aug;18(8):587–596.
22. University of Minnesota Extension Service, University of Minnesota Building Research Consortium IAQ Project, Department. Environmental Health and Safety: *Health care construction and IAQ*, Minneapolis, September 15–16 1997.
23. Brace SE. Infection Control During Construction: Planning Is Key. In: *Healthcare Facilities Management Series* (#094300). Chicago, IL: ASHE of American Hospital Association, 1993.
24. Centers for Medicare and Medicaid Services (CMS). *Code of Federal Regulations, Title 42-Public Health; Chapter IV—CMS, Department of Health and Human Services. Part 482—Conditions of Participation for Hospitals.* Revised October 1, 2004. Government Printing Office website, Available at: http://www.access.gpo.gov/nara/cfr/waisidx_04/42cfr482_04.html.
25. Occupational exposure to tuberculosis—OSHA. Proposed rule and notice of public hearing. *Fed Reg* 1997 Oct 17;62(201):54160–54308.
26. Health Facilities Engineering Section, Division of Health Facilities and Services, Michigan Department of Community Health. *2007 Minimum design standards for health care facilities in Michigan.* Michigan.gov website. Available at: http://michigan.gov/documents/mdch/bhs_2007_Minimum_Design_Standards_Final_PDF_Doc._198958_7.pdf.

27. Occupational Safety and Health Administration (OSHA). *OSHA Technical Manual (OTM) Section III: Chapter 7 Legionnaires' disease.* OSHA website. Available at: http://www.osha.gov/dts/osta/otm/otm_iii/otm_iii_7.html.

28. Siegel JD, Rhinehart E, Jackson M, et al. 2007 Guideline for isolation precautions: preventing transmission of infectious agents in healthcare settings. June 2007. CDC website. Available at: http://www.cdc.gov/niosh/docket/archive/pdfs/NIOSH-219/0219-010107-siegel.pdf.

29. Centers for Disease Control and Prevention (CDC). Guidelines for preventing opportunistic infections among hematopoietic stem cell transplant recipients. *MMWR Morb Mortal Wkly Rep* 2000 Oct;49(RR-10):1–125, CE1–7.

30. Saravia SA, Raynor PC, Streifel AJ. A performance assessment of airborne infection isolation rooms. *Am J Infect Control* 2007 Jun;35(5):324–331.

31. Rice N, Streifel A, Vesley D. An evaluation of hospital special-ventilation-room pressures. *Infect Control Hosp Epidemiol* 2001 Jan;22(1):19–23.

32. Fraser VJ, Johnson K, Primack J, et al. Evaluation of rooms with negative pressure ventilation used for respiratory isolation in seven Midwestern hospitals. *Infect Control Hosp Epidemiol* 1994;14:623–668.

33. Nardell EA. Fans, filters, or rays: pros and cons of the current environmental tuberculosis technologies. *Infect Control Hosp Epidemiol* 1993 Nov;14(11):623–628.

34. Marier RL, Nelson T. A ventilation-filtration unit for respiratory isolation. *Infect Control Hosp Epidemiol* 1993 Dec;14(12):700–705.

35. Macher J. The use of germicidal lamps to control tuberculosis in healthcare facilities. *Infect Control Hosp Epidemiol* 1993 Dec;14(12):723–729.

36. Frances J. TB control in institutions, 2003, Curry International Tuberculosis Center website. Available at: http://www.currytbcenter.ucsf.edu/

37. Hermans RE, Streifel AJ. Ventilations designs. Proceedings of the workshop on engineering controls for preventing airborne infections in workers in healthcare and related facilities, NIOSH, Cincinnati, July 14–16, 1994.

38. Pavelchak N, DePersis RP, London M, et al. Identification of factors that disrupt negative air pressurization of respiratory isolation rooms. *Infect Control Hosp Epidemiol* 2000 Mar;21(3):191–195.

39. Cornet M, Levy V, Fleury L, et al. Efficacy of prevention by high-efficiency particulate air filtration or laminar airflow against *Aspergillus* airborne contamination during hospital renovation. *Infect Control Hosp Epidemiol* 1999 Jul;20(7):508–513.

40. Mooney BR, Reeves SA, Larsen E. Infection control and bone marrow transplantation. *Am J Infect Control* 1993 Jun;21(3):131–138.

41. Rhame FS. Prevention of nosocomial aspergillosis. *J Hosp Infect* 1991 Jun;18 Suppl A:466–472.

42. Nusair A, Jourdan D, Medcalf S, et al. Infection control experience in a cooperative care center for transplant patients. *Infect Control Hosp Epidemiol* 2008 May;29(5):424–429.

43. Manuel RJ, Kibbler CC. The epidemiology and prevention of invasive aspergillosis. *J Hosp Infect* 1998 Jun;39(2):95–109.

44. Wiehrdt WQ. Smoke trail tests for negative pressure isolation rooms. Occupational Safety and Health Administration Technical Support Memo, U.S. Department of Labor, January 26, 1994.

45. Carling PC, Briggs J, Hylander, et al. An evaluation of patient area cleaning in 3 hospitals using a novel targeting methodology. *Am J Infect Control* 2006 Oct;34(8):513–519.

46. Carling, PC, Perry MF, Von Beheren SM. Identifying opportunities to enhance environmental cleaning in 23 acute care hospitals. *Infect Control Hosp Epidemiol* 2008 Jan;29(1):1–7.

47. Drees M, Snydman DR, Schmid CH, et al. Prior environmental contamination increases the risk of acquisition of vancomycin-resistant Enterococci. *Clin Infect Dis* 2008 Mar 1;46(5):678–685.

48. Health Facilities Forum on Carpet in Health Care Facilities Series. *Health Facil Manage* 1993 Dec;6(12):22–24, 26, 28–31 passim.

49. Anderson RL, Mackel DC, Stoler BS, et al. Carpeting in hospitals: an epidemiological evaluation. *J Clin Microbiol* 1982 Mar;15(3):408–415.

50. Lumish RM. Carpeting in hospitals: an infection control problem? *JAMA* 1989;261:2422.

51. Gerson SL, Parker P, Jacobs MR, et al. Aspergillosis due to carpet contamination. *Infect Control Hosp Epidemiol* 1994 Apr;15(4 Pt 1):221–223.

52. Skoutelis AT, Westenfelder GO, Berkerdite M, et al. Hospital carpeting and epidemiology of *Clostridium difficile. Am J Infect Control* 1994 Aug;22(4):212–217.

53. Custovic A, Simpson BM, Simpson A, et al. Domestic allergens in public places: III. house dust mite, cat, dog, and cockroach allergens in British hospitals. *Clin Exp Allergy* 1998 Jan;28(1):53–59.

54. Sly RM, Josephs SH, Eby DM, et al. Dissemination of dust by central and portable vacuum cleaners. *Ann Allergy* 1985 Mar;54(3):209–212.

55. Noyce JO, Michels H, Keevil CW. Potential use of copper surfaces to reduce survival of epidemic methicillin-resistant *S. aureus* in the healthcare environment. *J Hosp Infect* 2006 Jul;63(3):289–297.

56. Environmental Protection Agency (EPA). EPA registers copper-containing alloy products. May 2008. EPA website. Available at: http://www.epa.gov/pesticides/factsheets/copper-alloy-products.htm.

57. Airey P, Verran J. Potential use of copper as a hygienic surface; problems associated with cumulative soiling and cleaning. *J Hosp Infect* 2007 Nov;67(3):271–277.

58. Environmental Protection Agency (EPA). Consumer products treated with pesticides, August 2003, 735-F-03-006. EPA website. August 2003. Available at: http://www.epa.gov/pesticides/factsheets/treatart.htm.

59. Center for Medicare & Medicaid Services (CMS), Center for Medicaid and State Operations, Survet and Certification Group. *Revision to the hospital interpretive guidelines for infection control.* November 21, 2007. CMS website. Available at: http://www.cms.gov/Medicare/Provider-Enrollment-and-Certification/SurveyCertificationGenInfo/downloads/SCLetter08-04.pdf

60. Iwen PC, Davis JC, Reed EC, et al. Airborne fungal spore monitoring in a protective environment during hospital construction, and correlation with an outbreak of invasive aspergillosis. *Infect Control Hosp Epidemiol* 1994 May;15(5):303–306.

61. Opal SM, Asp AA, Cannady Jr PB, et al. Efficacy of infection control measures during a nosocomial outbreak of aspergillosis associated with hospital construction. *J Infect Dis* 1986 Mar;153(3):634–637.

62. Streifel AJ, Steven PP, Rhame FS. In-hospital source of airborne penicillium species. *J Clin Microbiol* 1987 Jan;25(1):1–4.

63. Fox BC, Chamberlin L, Kulich P, et al. Heavy contamination of operating room air by penicillium species: identification of the source and attempts at decontamination. *Am J Infect Control* 1990 Oct;18(5):300–306.

64. Bartley J. Environmental control: operating room air quality. *Today's OR Nurse* 1993 Sep-Oct;15(5):11–18.

65. Assadian O, El-Madani N, Seper E, et al. Sensor-operated faucets: a possible source of nosocomial infection? *Infect Control Hosp Epidemiol* 2002 Jan;23(1):44–46.

66. Hargreaves J, Shireley L, Hansen S, et al. Bacterial contamination associated with electronic faucets: a new risk for healthcare facilities. *Infect Control Hosp Epidemiol* 2001 Apr;22(4):202–205.

67. Halabi M, Wiesholzer-Pittl M, Schoberl J, et al. Non-touch fittings in hospitals: a possible source of *Pseudomonas aeruginosa* and *Legionella* spp. *J Hosp Infect* 2001 Oct;49(2):117–121.

68. Harrison WA, Griffith CJ, Michaels B, et al. Technique to determine contamination exposure routes and the economic efficiency of folded paper-towel dispensing. *Am J Infect Control* 2003 Apr;31(2):104–108.

69. Griffith CJ, Malik R, Cooper RA, et al. Environmental surface cleanliness and the potential for contamination during handwashing. *Am J Infect Control* 2003 Apr;31(2):93–96.

70. Merry AF, Miller TE, Findon G, et al. Touch contamination levels during anaesthetic procedures and their relationship to hand hygiene procedures: a clinical audit. *Br J Anaesth* 2001 Aug;87(2):291–294.

71. Gustafson DR, Vetter EA, Larson DR, et al. Effects of 4 hand-drying methods for removing bacteria from washed hands: a randomized trial. *Mayo Clin Proc* 2000 Jul;75(7):705–708.

72. Weber SF, Peacock JE, Do KA, et al. Interaction of granulocytopenia and construction activity as risk factors for nosocomial invasive filamentous fungal disease in patients with hematologic disorders. *Infect Control Hosp Epidemiol* 1990 May;11(5):235–242.

73. Cheng SM, Streifel AJ. Infection control considerations during construction activities: land excavation and demolition. *Am J Infect Control* 2001 Oct;29(5):321–328.

SUPPLEMENTAL RESOURCES

American Institute of Architects (AIA). Available at: http://www.aia.org.

American Society of Heating, Refrigerating, and Air-conditioning Engineers. *Ventilation of health care facilities ANSI/ASHRAE/ASHE Standard 170.* Atlanta, GA: ASHRAE Press, 2008.

Bartley JM; The 1997, 1998, and 1999 APIC Guidelines Committees. *APIC State-of-the-Art Report: The role of infection control during construction in health care facilities.* APIC website. Available at: http://www.apic.org/Resource_/TinyMceFileManager/Practice_Guidance/IC-During-Construction-HC-Fac.pdf.

Construction-related nosocomial infections in patients in health care facilities: decreasing the risk of Aspergillus, Legionella and other infections. *Can Commun Dis Rep* [serial online]. 2001 Jul;27 Suppl 2:i–x, 1–42, i–x, 1–46. Available at: http://www.collectionscanada.gc.ca/webarchives/20071124025823/http://www.phac-aspc.gc.ca/publicat/ccdr-rmtc/01vol27/27s2/index.html.

IPAC Canada. *Healthcare Facility Design Position Statement.* December 2008. Available at: http://www.chica.org/pdf/HFDposition.pdf.

Copper Development Association, Inc. Available at: http://www.copper.org.

Department of Health and Human Services (DHHS), Centers for Disease Control and Prevention (CDC), National Institute for Occupational Safety and Health (NIOSH). Guidance for protecting building environments from airborne chemical, biological, or radiological attacks. Publication No. 139, May 2002. CDC website. Available at: http://www.cdc.gov/niosh/docs/2002-139/.

Department of Health and Human Services (DHHS), Centers for Disease Control and Prevention (CDC), National Institute for Occupational Safety and Health (NIOSH). Guidance for filtration and air-cleaning systems to protect building environments from airborne chemical, biological, or radiological attacks. Publication No. 2003-136, April 2003. Available at: http://www.cdc.gov/niosh/docs/2003-136/pdfs/2003-136.pdf.

Facility Guidelines Institute (FGI). *Single room occupancy as a minimum*. FGI website. Available at: http://www.premierinc.com/quality-safety/tools-services/safety/topics/construction/single-room.jsp.

Grant PS, Kim AT. Infection control consultation in a 150-bed acute care hospital: making this unobserved and unmeasured critical job function visible. *Am J Infect Control* 2007 Aug;35(6):401–406.

Green Guide to HealthCare. Available at: http://www.gghc.org/.

Haiduven D. Nosocomial aspergillosis and building construction. *Med Mycol* 2009;47 Suppl 1:S210–S216.

Healthy Building Networks. *HBN PVC free resilient floor chart*. Available at: http://www.healthybuilding.net/pvc/PVCFreeResilient.html.

Kidd F, Buttner C, Kressel AB. Construction: a model program for infection control compliance. *Am J Infect Control* 2007 Jun;35(5):347–350.

Memarzadeh F, Manning AP. Comparison of operating room ventilation systems in the protection of the surgical site. *ASHRAE Transactions* [serial online]. 108:3–15, 2002. Available at: http://orf.od.nih.gov/PoliciesAndGuidelines/Bioenvironmental/Documents/ASHRAE_Final_Operating_Room_508.pdf.

Memarzadeh F, Jiang J. A methodology for minimizing risk from airborne organisms in hospital isolation room, *ASHRAE Transactions* [serial online]. 106:731–7, 2002. Available at: http://orf.od.nih.gov/PoliciesAndGuidelines/Bioenvironmental/Documents/ASHRAE_Isolation_Room_June2000_508.pdf.

Practice Greenhealth. Available at: http://www.practicegreenhealth.org.

Stockley JM, Constantine CE, Orr KE. Association of medical microbiologists' new hospital developments project group. Building new hospitals: a UK infection control perspective. *J Hosp Infect* 2006 Mar;62(3):285–299.

Storey E, Dangman KH, Schenck P. Guidance for clinicians on the recognition and management of health effects related to mold exposure and moisture indoors. *Center for Indoor Environments and Health at University of Connecticut Health Center* 2004. Available at: http://oehc.uchc.edu/CIEH.asp.

Walker JT, Hoffman P, Bennett AM. Hospital and community acquired infection and the built environment—design and testing of infection control rooms. *J Hosp Infect* 2007 Jun;65 Suppl 2:43–49.

Worley DJ, Hohler SE. OR construction project: from planning to execution. *AORN J* 2008 Dec;88(6):917–919, 923–934, 937–941.

CHAPTER 117

Public Health

Robin Roach, BSN, MS, CIC
Director, Infection Prevention and Control
Oregon Health and Science University
Portland, OR

ABSTRACT

This chapter provides an overview of the intersecting roles of infection prevention and public health within the healthcare system and the community as a whole. Public health is often considered synonymous with disease prevention. Its goal is to promote the health of the entire human population.[1] Medicine focuses on treating the illness of individuals and public health focuses on preventing morbidity and mortality within communities. To this end, public health provides coordinated leadership and guidance on both infectious and noninfectious conditions to the healthcare community and the general public. More recently, the Centers for Disease Control and Prevention's National Healthcare Safety Network plays a dominant role as a conduit for reporting healthcare-associated infections to Centers for Medicare & Medicaid Services. This chapter discusses public health's primary functions: public health basic principles, public health and infection prevention trends, and, lastly, the global perspective and highlights of collaborative efforts.

KEY CONCEPTS

- Interaction between infection prevention and public health.

- Regulatory and reporting structures at local, state, and federal levels.

- Essential public health services: monitoring the health status of the community, diagnosing and investigating health problems in the community, mobilization of community partnerships, development of public policies, enforcement of laws and regulations that protect health, linking people to health resources, assuring a competent health workforce, and researching new insights and innovations to health problems.[2]

- Other public health services: bioterrorism and emergency preparedness, primary care and personal health services delivered or funded by governmental agencies, education, training, and research.

BACKGROUND

Infection prevention and public health share a common emphasis on disease prevention. Both aim interventions at the environment, human behavior, and medical care. They benefit from ongoing collaborative relationships at local, state, federal, and global levels. Working together, they can provide at the local level a seamless, protective web for patients with communicable diseases, such as pulmonary tuberculosis, as they move across the care continuum. Regulations related to the reporting of notifiable diseases exist to protect the general public from health threats. Infection preventionists (IPs) play a vital role in the notifiable-disease reporting system, often handling the reporting for their organization.[3] Frequent interaction between IPs and public health professionals helps to foster a shared mission and interdependence—detection of a notifiable disease in a hospitalized patient often results in protection of the community's health.

For over 125 years the mission of public health has been to prevent disease and promote health.[4] The United States Public Health Service, established by President John Adams in 1798 and led by the Surgeon General, is a uniformed branch of the federal government. In 1812, the threat of yellow fever, smallpox, and cholera caused Congress to enact the National Quarantine Act.[5] In the late 19th and early 20th centuries following the scientific discoveries in bacteriology and immunology, public health became regarded as the integration of sanitation and medicine. Public health brings together many disciplines and branches of scientists to collaborate in solving complex health issues.[6]

Since those early days, new and emerging issues of public health importance dominated the national landscape. Issues such as food safety, acute and chronic disease prevention, oral health, and access to healthcare were recognized as important disease control and prevention activities. In the 21st century, interest in quarantine and community-based disease control measures reemerged. Severe acute respiratory syndrome (SARS), potentially infectious bioterrorism threats, and the growing possibility of an influenza pandemic would all require communitywide prevention and control measures.[6]

Public health functions at the global, federal, state, and local levels. The World Health Organization (WHO) functions under the United Nation's umbrella and collects information on a number of infectious diseases from countries. At the federal level, the executive order of the president provides the secretary of health and the surgeon general with the authority to isolate and quarantine individuals suspected of having cholera, diphtheria, infectious tuberculosis, plague, smallpox, yellow fever, viral hemorrhagic fevers, SARS, influenza viruses causing or potentially causing a pandemic, and emerging multidrug-resistant microorganism.[7,8]

Each state's statutes provide authority to require the reporting of certain diseases, and allow official investigations and implementation of control measures. Local health departments generally derive their authority from the state health department. The public health authority at the state, county, or city level is assigned to an individual, usually a physician, who has been appointed by a jurisdiction and taken an oath to enforce laws intended to protect the public's health. Diseases reported at the local level are compiled by the states and submitted to the Centers for Disease Control and Prevention (CDC). Notifiable disease summaries and trends are published weekly in the *Morbidity and Mortality Weekly Report* (MMWR).[9]

Ongoing public health disease surveillance and epidemiological support provide necessary information to identify outbreaks or urgent infectious situations of concern for health facilities and the community. Public health disease surveillance is gathered through systematic collection, consolidation, and evaluation of morbidity and mortality reports, providing key information on the patterns of disease occurrences. Finally, public health offers accessible educational and training materials critical to prevention and control of infectious and emergent diseases to the community and healthcare providers. The CDC's National Healthcare Safety Network (NHSN) is the most widely utilized healthcare infection tracking system. A secure, Internet-based surveillance system, the NHSN houses three former CDC surveillance systems: National Nosocomial Infections Surveillance System, National Surveillance System for Healthcare Workers, and the Dialysis Surveillance Network.[10] The NHSN permits healthcare facilities to collect, analyze, and trend healthcare-associated infections (HAI), multidrug-resistant organisms (MDRO), and healthcare personnel vaccination and blood and blood product transfusion adverse event data. Presently, more than 11,000 healthcare facilities participate in the NHSN. Participating facilities include acute care hospitals, ambulatory surgery centers, long-term care hospitals, dialysis centers, and nursing homes. The NHSN functions as an intermediary for facilities to comply with Centers for Medicare & Medicaid Services (CMS) infection reporting requirements.[11]

In 2009, the American Recovery and Reinvestment Act was signed into law. The Act's purpose was to stimulate the economic recovery and contained provisions to provide funds to state health departments to strengthen their healthcare infrastructure to address HAIs. Each state plan addresses the goal of HAI reduction including MDROs with the ultimate goal of healthcare cost reduction. Prevention partnerships have evolved from state plan implementation.[11]

BASIC PRINCIPLES

Public health has a primary focus on populations with an emphasis on disease prevention.[12] It provides a network of support services and leadership particularly related to infectious and communicable disease control. Key to understanding public health's role is a set of core public health concepts and practices, including basic public health prevention services, definitions, notifiable (reportable) disease reporting, public health surveillance and investigations, and emerging infectious disease threat oversight and leadership.

Public Health Activities and Services

The common themes describing public health encompass organized efforts to: (1) protect and promote human and environmental health, (2) prevent communicable and chronic diseases, and (3) improve health and access to health services for persons with limited resources.[4,5] Public health is defined as "the practice of preventing disease and promoting good health within groups of people, from small communities to entire countries."[6] Public health services include vaccination programs, human immunodeficiency virus/acquired immunodeficiency virus (HIV/AIDS) counseling and testing, public health community education, outbreak investigations and case follow-up, tuberculosis and sexually transmitted infection treatment, and, more recently, bioterrorism, emergency, and pandemic preparedness leadership and response. State public health laboratories provide testing when a new or unusual pathogen is suspected.[11] Nonmedical public health services may include environmental testing of surface and well water, inspection and monitoring of restaurants, and population-based statistics of community health status. In some states and communities, clinic health services are available to uninsured and underinsured residents. Public health nurse and school nurse services may be available as well.

Prevention

Many public health efforts in disease prevention are targeted at populations or at subpopulations; for example, specific age groups, at-risk or behavior-associated groups, groups of persons with the same chronic disease such as diabetics, and those sustaining hazardous exposures. Public health prevention is global and works in partnership with other countries to prevent the transmission, introduction, and spread of communicable disease into the United States and its territories.[6] These efforts may utilize primary, secondary, or tertiary prevention. Primary prevention activities are directed at avoiding disease and disability before it starts. Promoting universal vaccinations serves as primary prevention. Secondary prevention efforts focus on identifying or detecting existing health problems or conditions before they cause serious or long-term problems. Tertiary prevention activities aim to limit or reduce the condition's negative effects. IPs utilize interventions aimed at primary, secondary, and tertiary prevention regularly for both patients and healthcare personnel. Optimizing hand hygiene is primary prevention in action. Tuberculosis skin testing following an unprotected occupational exposure to a patient with active pulmonary tuberculosis exemplifies secondary prevention. Lastly, IPs conduct tertiary prevention when conducting an outbreak investigation.

Notifiable Diseases and Reporting

IPs must be familiar with public health requirements.[9] Notifiable (reportable) infectious diseases are recommended to the CDC by the Council of State and Territorial Epidemiologists (CSTE). CSTE establishes case definitions of diseases and conditions under surveillance. The list of notifiable conditions varies by state.[9] Reportable or notifiable diseases are those of public interest by reason of their contagiousness, severity, or frequency.[9] Each state determines the reportable diseases and conditions for that state and specifies the time frame for reporting and the information to be included in content of the reports. Additional diseases may become reportable as a result of a current outbreak (e.g., influenza cases), a newly emerging condition (e.g., SARS), or to track statewide (e.g., methicillin-resistant *Staphylococcus aureus* [MRSA]).[9] The list of notifiable diseases is updated periodically. Reporting is presently mandatory only at the state level.[9] Outbreaks and suspected outbreaks are also reportable in most jurisdictions. Reports are confidential and usually include basic demographic information, date of onset, city or county of residence, and laboratory testing results, when applicable.[11] This systematic reporting permits public health to investigate individual cases, as well as to develop a baseline of expected cases of diseases or conditions of concern. The most recent update to the nationally notifiable diseases was in 2011.[9] Currently, 91 conditions are nationally notifiable. New diseases or syndromes may be added to the list as they appear. Since notifiable diseases change periodically and vary state-to-state, IPs are advised to remain up-to-date with state notifiable diseases and reporting requirements.

Electronic reporting of the nationally notifiable diseases enhances reporting frequency and timeliness. The CDC receives reports from 50 state health departments, New York City, the District of Columbia, and five U.S. territories through the National Electronic Telecommunications System for Surveillance (NETSS). The CDC released NEDSS, a component of the Public Health Information System, to foster integrated and interoperable surveillance systems at local, state, and federal levels in 2001.[9] Most states and local public health jurisdictions have similar electronic reporting. IPs should request access to their state's electronic reporting system. Names, addresses, and other personal identifiers are not transmitted to the CDC in the case reports of notifiable disease but are retained at the state and local level. The CDC's MMWR publishes provisional weekly reports of notifiable diseases. The final, corrected reports are published annually in the *MMWR Summary of Notifiable Diseases, United States* and are available in electronic and paper form.

Public Health Surveillance and Investigation

Regulations related to the reporting of notifiable diseases create the framework for public health's surveillance system. For the IP, knowing local and state infectious disease rates and trends

is necessary for ongoing comparisons during review of microbiologic and other laboratory reports. Public health typically offers consultation on cluster and outbreak investigation. Any outbreak of disease that is a potential and serious threat to the general public should be reported, even if the specific disease is not listed as a notifiable disease. Particularly when outbreaks persist or overwhelm a facility's infection prevention resources, public health at the local or state level may provide needed assistance or support including laboratory services.[13] State public heath laws permit access to patient records and other personal health information related to communicable disease and outbreak investigations. The IP must be familiar with state regulations.

Emerging Infectious Disease Threat Oversight and Leadership

The ability to detect and contain new diseases was tested several times in the new millennium. SARS, monkeypox, low-level contamination of food, potential novel influenza strains, and emerging MDROs challenge our healthcare and public health infrastructure. The potential need to contain infectious individuals and quarantine persons exposed to infectious diseases triggered a renewed interest in public health laws and authority to protect communities. Emerging infectious diseases and biological threats led to a return of public health's leadership role in our country and communities.[14] The new all-hazards approach to emergency preparedness led to building alliances with traditional emergency preparedness services, healthcare facilities, and community businesses. Whether providing guidance or antibiotic prophylaxis, public health offers the infrastructure healthcare facilities can rely on for the legal authority to gain cooperation of the general public to halt the transmission of disease in the community at large.

PUBLIC HEALTH AND INFECTION PREVENTION TRENDS

Since the early 1990s, public health has voiced growing concerns about newly emerging and reemerging infectious diseases.[15] The National Center for Infectious Diseases' Emerging or Re-emerging Infectious Disease program has identified more than 50 infectious diseases and conditions. Emerging infectious diseases include newly discovered infections (SARS Co-V); old infectious diseases, thought to be conquered, which reemerged (multidrug-resistant tuberculosis); known diseases gaining a foothold on a new continent (West Nile virus infection and novel influenza); and established infectious diseases that are becoming increasingly drug resistant (MRSA, vancomycin-resistant S. *aureus*, or carbapenem-resistant Enterobacteriaceae). With varying modes of transmission, these infections represent a threat to the general public often resulting in high mortality. In 2013, the CDC released a report to increase awareness and response to the growing threat of antibiotic resistance. More than two million people become ill with antibiotic-resistant infections each year and an estimated 23,000 die annually from these infections. Every major class of bacterial pathogen has shown the ability to develop resistance to one or more of the commonly used antibiotics, and the global crisis of resistance is serious. The CDC's updated report on antibiotic resistance identifies four core actions to combat these deadly infections: preventing infections and preventing the spread of resistance; tracking resistant bacteria; improving the use of today's antibiotics; and promoting the development of new antibiotics and developing new diagnostic tests for resistant bacteria.[14] IPs are on the front lines of emerging infectious disease. With the changing epidemiology of MRSA, *Clostridium difficile*, and potential pandemic influenza issues, traditional public health measures such as prevention, surveillance, control, and containment are relied upon.

An organized system of surveillance is essential to define disease prevalence for known and new diseases.[15] Public health surveillance is the systematic and routine collection, analysis, and distribution of data. Passive surveillance relies on healthcare providers to submit required reports. Active surveillance is initiated when a new or unexpected health threat occurs and case finding is critical to determine the scope or contain and control disease spread. Syndromic surveillance has been implemented in many large communities and uses nonidentifying information about symptoms of individuals seeking care. Other public health surveillance systems are used to track trends and interventions, identify emerging issues, define public health problems, and monitor the effectiveness of interventions.[16]

When surveillance activities identify concerns, public health investigations provide necessary and timely information regarding the nature and the extent of the illness, as well as guidance on effective prevention and control measures.[17] Generally, state laws and regulations provide public health organizations with the authority to investigate and review medical records for communicable diseases and conditions of concern. IPs may be investigating a hospital-based outbreak and, at the same time, local public health workers may be following up on community contacts and exposed persons, conducting case findings, and determining the extent of the outbreaks in the community. Infectious disease outbreaks that occur in the community or overwhelm a healthcare system require assistance from knowledgeable and experienced public health epidemiologists and public health nurses. Timely distribution of information of public health importance is provided via the Health Alert Network. The Health Alert Network provides disease outbreak and other infectious disease information as well as national disaster information and updates. National, state, and local Health Alert Networks are used by public health to communicate critical health information to healthcare providers. IPs may request to receive health alerts from their local, state, and national public health agencies.

IPs often mirror in their organizations what public health does within communities. The mutual roles in prevention and preparedness and reliance on the science of epidemiology help maintain strong linkages.

CONCLUSIONS

The intersecting roles of public health and infection prevention are examined in this chapter. Infection prevention and public health have common interests of preventing and controlling disease. Public health relies on IPs for notifiable disease reporting and identification of potential community outbreaks. Public health provides infectious disease trending, epidemiological support and expertise, coordinated leadership, and guidance, as well as education and training for IPs. Recent worldwide outbreaks of SARS tested their interdependence and strengthened their collaboration, coordination, and communication. The looming threat of pandemic influenza reinforces our common goals of preventing disease and protecting our respective communities.

FUTURE TRENDS

During the events of the past several years, infection prevention and public health epidemiology and interventions became visible on the world stage. Examples of collaboration between infection prevention and public health include HCP response to the H1N1 novel strain influenza pandemic and newly emerging MDROs. Current prevention-related public health trends include preventing and controlling emergent infectious diseases collaboration, emergency preparedness and response, including syndromic surveillance, electronic notifiable disease reporting, infection prevention interventions for disasters, and coordination between acute care and public health agencies. The potential for bioterrorist-associated events today requires public health and health facilities to develop response plans, participate in community response readiness activities, develop skills and expertise in decontamination and incident command, and create methods of identifying possible bioterrorist-associated illness.[18] For more information, see Chapter 119 Emergency Management.

INTERNATIONAL PERSPECTIVE

Because infectious disease knows no borders and prevention strategies require global awareness and strategies, the CDC developed a worldwide plan in consultation with global public health partners, Protecting the Nation's Health in an Era of Globalization: CDC's Global Strategy for Addressing Infectious Diseases.[19] The six priority areas include: (1) international outbreak assistance, (2) global disease surveillance, (3) applied research on diseases of global importance, (4) application of proven public health tools, (5) global initiatives for disease control, and (6) public health training and capacity building.[19] Experience with SARS and other infectious outbreaks underscores the need to engage global partners in the prevention and control of emergent infectious diseases.[20,21] More recently, the National Center for Emerging and Zoonotic Infectious Diseases developed a strategic roadmap to address a wide range of infectious diseases globally and nationally, including rare deadly diseases such as Ebola hemorrhagic fever as well foodborne illness and HAIs.[22]

REFERENCES

1. Schneider MJ. Public health: Science, politics, and prevention. In: *Introduction to Public Health*, 3rd ed. Sudbury, MA: Jones and Bartlett Publishers, 2011:3–15.
2. Centers for Disease Control and Prevention (CDC). Office of the Director, Office of the Chief of Public Health Practice. 10 Essential Public Health Services. CDC website. 2008. Available at: http://www.cdc.gov/od/ocphp/nphpsp/EssentialPHServices.htm.
3. Scheckler WE, Brimhall D, Buck AS, et al. Requirements for infrastructure and essential activities of infection control and epidemiology in hospitals: A consensus panel report. *Infect Control Epidemiol* 1998;19:114–124.
4. Schneider MJ. Why is public health controversial? In: *Introduction to Public Health*, 3rd ed. Sudbury, MA: Jones and Bartlett Publishers, 2011:17–28.
5. U.S. Department of Health and Human Services (DHHS). U.S. Public Health Service Commissioned Corps. History. DHHS website. 2011. Available at: http://usphs.gov/aboutus/history.aspx.
6. Centers for Disease Control and Prevention (CDC). Division of Global Migration and Quarantine (DGMQ). CDC website. 2013. Available at: http://www.cdc.gov/ncezid/dgmq/.
7. U.S. Food and Drug Administration (FDA). United States Code Title 42 Chapter 6A Public Health Service Act. FDA website. 2009. Available at: http://www.fda.gov/RegulatoryInformation/Legislation/ucm148717.htm.
8. Centers for Disease Control and Prevention (CDC). Legal Authorities for Isolation and Quarantine. CDC website. 2013. Available at: http://www.cdc.gov/quarantine/AboutLawsRegulationsQuarantineIsolation.html.
9. Centers for Disease Control and Prevention. Summary of notifiable diseases: Notifiable diseases, United States, 2011. *MMWR Recomm Rep* 2013;60(53):1–111.
10. Allen-Bridson K, Morrell GC, Horan TC. Surveillance of healthcare-associated infections. In: Mayhall CG, ed. *Hospital epidemiology and infection control*, 4th ed. Philadelphia: Lippincott Williams & Wilkins, 2012:1329–1343.
11. Centers for Disease Control and Prevention (CDC). National Healthcare Safety Network. About NHSN. CDC website. 2013. Available at: http://www.cdc.gov/nhsn/about.html.
12. Harvard School of Public Health (HSPH). Public health medicine. HSPH website. 2008. Available at: www.hsph.Harvard.edu/about/public-health-medicine.
13. Association of Public Health Laboratories (APHL). Analysis, action and answers. APHL website. 2013. Available at: http://www.aphl.org/AboutAPHL/aboutphls/Pages/default.aspx.
14. Centers for Disease Control and Prevention (CDC). *Antibiotic Resistance Threats in the United States, 2013*. CDC website. 2013. Available at: http://www.cdc.gov/drugresistance/threat-report-2013/.
15. Heymann DL, ed. Reporting of communicable diseases. In: *Control of Communicable Disease Manual*, 19th ed. Washington, DC: American Public Health Association, Unit Book Press, 2008:A8–A10.
16. Centers for Disease Control and Prevention (CDC). National Notifiable Disease Surveillance System (NNDSS): Case definitions. CDC website. 2013. Available at: http://www.cdc.gov/nndss/script/casedefDefault.aspx.
17. Thacker SB. Historical development. In: Teutsch SM, Churchill RE, eds. *Principles and Practice of Public Health Surveillance*. New York: Oxford University Press, 1994.
18. Centers for Disease Control and Prevention (CDC). Emergency preparedness and response. CDC website. 2014. Available at: http://www.bt.cdc.gov/HAN/.
19. Centers for Disease Control and Prevention (CDC). Protecting the Nation's Health in an Era of Globalization: CDC's Global Infectious Disease Strategy, 2002. CDC website. 2002. Available at: http://www.cdc.gov/globalidplan/global_id_plan.pdf.
20. Linggappa JR, McDonald LC, Simone P, et al. Wrestling SARS from uncertainty. *Emerg Infect Dis* 2004;10(2):167–170.
21. Peck AJ, Newbern EC, Feikin DR, et al. Lack of SARS transmission and U.S. SARS case-patient. *Emerg Infect Dis* 2004;10(2):167–170.
22. National Center for Emerging and Zoonotic Infectious Diseases. Strategic Plan 2012-2017. Centers for Disease Control and Prevention website. 2012. Available at: http://www.cdc.gov/ncezid/pdf/strategicplan_NCEZID.pdf.

SUPPLEMENTAL RESOURCES

American Public Health Association: Available at: www.apha.org

Publishes *American Journal of Public Health*, a monthly peer-reviewed professional publication and newsletters; hosts national conferences.

Centers for Disease Control and Prevention: Available at: www.cdc.gov

Reference for guidelines, alerts, educational materials, and publications.

Centers for Disease Control and Prevention (CDC). Emerging Infectious Diseases. CDC website. 2014. Available at: www.cdc.gov/eid.

Centers for Disease Control and Prevention (CDC). Hand Hygiene in Healthcare Settings. CDC website. 2013. Available at: www.cdc.gov/handhygiene.

Centers for Disease Control and Prevention (CDC). Healthcare-associated infections. CDC website. 2013. Available at: www.cdc.gov/hai.

Centers for Disease Control and Prevention (CDC). Vaccines and Immunizations. CDC website. 2013. Available at: www.cdc.gov/vaccines/pubs/default.htm.

Heymann DL, ed. *Control of Communicable Disease Manual*, 19th ed. Washington, DC: APHA, 2008. The most widely recognized easy-to-read sourcebook on infectious diseases and control measures. Known as "the communicable disease bible" to those in the field.

Morbidity and Mortality Weekly Report (MMWR): Available at: www.cdc.gov/mmwr Prepared weekly summary of public health alerts, investigation summaries, recommendations, and reports, based on weekly reports to CDC by state health departments.

CHAPTER 118

Travel Health

Mandy Bodily-Bartrum, RN, BSN, MPH, CIC
Director of Quality and Risk Management
Vibra Hospital & Vista View Care Center
Thornton, CO

ABSTRACT

Increasing numbers of international travelers are selecting exotic destinations in the developing world. Recommendations should be individualized for each traveler and the journey and should account for personal health, health risks of specific destinations, style of travel, and activities anticipated. Immunizations are the cornerstone of protection for the traveler, but medications can be employed to prevent or treat a diverse array of other problems, such as malaria, traveler's diarrhea, motion sickness, and altitude sickness. Contingency plans should also be made for where to turn in the event of a medical emergency. Given the rapidity of change in the global health situation, those providing information need to be certain that their recommendations contain the latest and most accurate information possible.

KEY CONCEPTS

Critical steps in providing advice to travelers include:

- Reviewing medical and vaccination history

- Confirming itinerary (i.e., the names of countries and the order in which they will be visited)

- Determining required immunizations

- Determining other recommended immunizations, based on the risk of the itinerary

- Reviewing contraindications

- Certifying and recording immunizations on an international certificate of vaccination

- Providing needed prescriptions

- Providing written educational materials whenever possible

BACKGROUND

The number of people traveling abroad on an annual basis has increased dramatically during the past 25 years. Travel to the developing world presents a unique set of challenges for travelers and the physicians providing advice to them. Recommendations should be personalized for each traveler and journey, accounting for personal health, health risks of specific destinations, style of travel, and activities anticipated.[1]

A variety of sources of up-to-date information exist to assist the primary care physician in counseling the prospective traveler. The most authoritative single source is *Health Information for International Travel 2014,* a publication of the Centers for Disease Control and Prevention (CDC).[2] This source, often called the Yellow Book, is updated on a regular basis and available for a fee from the Government Printing Office. It can also be viewed online and printed through the CDC's website. (The CDC website and a variety of others providing important information regarding international travel together with their uniform resource locators [URLs] are listed in Supplemental Resources at the end of this chapter.)

BASIC PRINCIPLES

Concerns of the international travel medicine clinic beyond those for vaccine-preventable diseases can range from the intricacies of chemoprophylaxis against malaria to the more mundane advice for avoidance of illness associated with swimming. Although many of these concerns are associated with geography, climate, and environment and do not often change rapidly, they are nonetheless critical for maintaining good health while abroad.

Motion Sickness

Motion sickness may be a problem for those aboard cruise ships or other boats, airplanes, and even cars. Most individuals who face such problems while traveling may have encountered them before and know in advance what works for them under most circumstances. Dimenhydrinate and meclizine are two over-the-counter (OTC) medications that have withstood the test of time, work well for a variety of persons, and can be taken in anticipation of need. They are short acting and must be taken periodically. The transdermal scopolamine patch can be applied only once every 72 hours and still maintain effective delivery of medication. It may be especially useful if long periods of motion-induced nausea, such as might occur aboard ship, will be encountered.

Insect Bites

Recommendations to prevent insect bites include wearing appropriate clothing, using bed nets, and using appropriate insecticides. Appropriate clothing may include permethrin-sprayed clothing, long-sleeved tops, and closed-toe shoes. The U.S. Environmental Protection Agency (EPA) has approved four formulations of insecticide as being protective. These include DEET, picaridin, oil of lemon eucalyptus, and IR3535. Travelers should be sure to apply insecticide after applying any sunscreen to ensure that they are well protected.

Food and Water Risks

"Don't drink the water" is an often-heard warning for persons traveling to developing countries. Although it is a good start for protection, the warning needs to be extended for maximum effect. In some areas, milk is not pasteurized, and ice can never be assumed to be safe because freezing does not kill most pathogenic bacteria. The safest beverages are wine and beer, which are universally pasteurized, and carbonated drinks. For maximum safety, travelers should only consume food that has been thoroughly cooked and is served hot or fruit that can be peeled by the traveler. In addition, it is important to remind travelers to not use the water for brushing their teeth. A safe reminder is to have travelers leave a bottle of water in their bathroom. Travelers should also be advised to check the seals of purchased water bottles and not to drink any water from a bottle that appears to have been tampered with.

There are occasions when travelers will not have easy access to bottled water, so it is important that they have recommendations for water sterilization. Methods for water disinfection include heat, filtration, chlorine or iodine, and ultraviolet light. More information about each type of disinfection methods and advantages and disadvantages to each are available in the CDC Yellow Book.[2]

Malaria

Malaria prevention is one of the most important functions of travel medicine. It rests on appropriate use of insect repellents and barriers, such as window screens and mosquito nets, as well as the use of medication in the form of chloroquine, mefloquine, atovaquone/proguanil, and doxycycline that suppress the red blood cell stage of the disease but cannot completely eradicate all types of malaria. For that reason, persons returning from the tropics who develop any symptoms such as fever, chills, or sweats after completing prophylaxis should be evaluated for malaria.

Malaria medication may vary widely in cost, side effects, and how often the medication is to be taken before, during, and after travel. This information should be taken into account when determining what medication to prescribe for a traveler.

Traveler's Diarrhea

Although referred to by the informal name of "Montezuma's revenge" in some regions, traveler's diarrhea known by any of its other terms in different regions of the world can be serious. Prophylactic treatment with antibiotics is no longer considered appropriate or advisable because it is likely to lead to the development of resistant organisms. Moreover, the immediate use of medications such as ciprofloxacin usually dramatically limits the duration of the illness. In some countries and areas, there are ciprofloxacin-resistant bacteria and azithromycin may be provided to the traveler. Loperamide may also be added for more acute or distressing symptoms.

Cruise Ship Travel

Travelers boarding a cruise ship are by no means insulated from travel-related illness. Those affected by motion sickness may wish to take medication for prevention or control of symptoms. If the ship will be docking at ports in countries with special risks for infectious diseases, the appropriate vaccines should be administered. If travelling in the spring or summer, individuals should consider getting an influenza vaccine if they did not receive it during the prior winter season. This is important because influenza outbreaks have occurred during the off season on ships that bring together persons from around the world, including the southern hemisphere, where the flu season occurs during the months considered summer in the northern hemisphere. Finally, traveler's diarrhea, especially due to norovirus, has become more common in recent years. Because norovirus can spread quickly, attention to sanitation/hygiene aboard a cruise ship is especially important. When choosing a cruise ship, individuals may wish to review its most recent sanitation report at the CDC website.

Altitude Sickness

Persons who usually live at lower altitudes may encounter serious problems when venturing to mountainous areas or other higher elevations, especially if periods of long walking or other exertion may be required. Such problems range from a mild or moderate headache and difficulty sleeping to acute pulmonary or even cerebral edema. Whenever possible, it is best to try to acclimate to the higher altitude slowly over a period of several days through gradual ascent. When this is not possible or practical, use of prophylactic agents such as acetazolamide may be considered. These medications may be started 1 to 2 days before the ascent and are usually maintained for 24 to 48 hours after arrival at the final altitude. Although they may be extremely helpful, descent to lower altitude or the use of oxygen and emergency medical care should be considered if a major problem develops. More recently, nifedipine in a dose of 10 to 20 mg every 8 hours or sildenafil may be helpful in preventing high-altitude pulmonary edema in susceptible persons or in treating it once it occurs. Moreover, dexamethasone in doses of 4 mg every 6 hours is helpful in treating high-altitude pulmonary edema.[2]

Injuries

Overall, injuries are a more common cause of medical consultation than illnesses when traveling in a foreign country. Traffic accidents are a particular risk. Travelers may be unfamiliar with different rules of the road, driving conditions, congestion, or traffic flow. Moreover, they may be driving cars with no seat belts or with less-than-optimal maintenance. It is always advisable to limit nighttime driving to urban areas. Risks of road travel apply to those on motorcycles, bicycles, and mopeds, so pedestrians should maintain special alertness when crossing streets. The other particular concern for travelers is the risk of fires. Anyone checking into a hotel should locate primary and secondary escape routes.

Animals

Although direct contact with wild animals generally should be avoided even in developed nations, feeding or petting dogs and cats not known to be immunized against rabies is not advised when traveling in countries where rabies is present. Any animal bite from a mammal should receive prompt evaluation by a medical practitioner, including consideration of the need for rabies treatment. In addition, persons bitten by a snake should seek medical attention and determine the need for antivenom.

Swimming

Unfortunately, swimming in almost any body of unchlorinated water can pose a health risk for travelers because contaminated water may cause skin, eye, ear, or systemic infections ranging from schistosomiasis to leptospirosis. If there is any uncertainty about the safety of any given freshwater or saltwater area, travelers should not swim or wade in it.

Immunization

The CDC's *MMWR Recommendations and Reports,* a series that documents the recommendations of the Advisory Committee on Immunization Practices (ACIP), focuses on travel-specific immunizations. Because of space limitations, it does not detail routine immunizations that should be updated regardless of plans for international travel, but on the following vaccines: Hepatitis A, Japanese encephalitis (JE), meningococcal disease, rabies, typhoid fever, and yellow fever.

General Considerations for International Travel

Vaccinations are often recommended or required for the traveler; however, it is important to remember that no vaccine is 100 percent effective in protecting against illness. Vaccination is no substitute for taking precautions to reduce exposure to pathogenic agents. Specifically, for the prevention of enteric diseases, general food and water safety precautions should be employed:

- Avoid all potentially contaminated food and water, including ice.

- Avoid foods that are not adequately cooked and served hot, especially fish/shellfish.

- Eat only cooked vegetables or fruit that can be peeled by the traveler.

- Consume carbonated beverages or those made with boiled water, such as coffee and tea. Because beer and wine are

universally pasteurized, they may also be considered safe. Milk is not universally pasteurized and so may be suspect in certain locations.[2]

For protection against mosquitoes and other insect vectors of disease, travelers should sleep in well-screened quarters or use mosquito nets and wear clothing that covers most of the skin surface when outdoors during feeding periods for the insects. Permethrin may be sprayed on clothing or bed nets for additional protection. Insect repellents, preferably those containing 30 to 35 percent DEET, should be applied to exposed skin surfaces. A pyrethroid-containing flying insect spray should be used in living and sleeping areas during evening and nighttime hours. Regular inspection of the skin for attachment of ticks is appropriate where tickborne infections are a concern.[2]

TRAVEL HEALTH

U.S. Public Health Service Recommendations

Review of Routine Immunizations

Individuals should review of their immunization records with their physician or other medical provider as the first agenda item in t travel preparation. Routine immunizations should be evaluated, including tetanus, diphtheria, and pertussis/tetanus and diphtheria (Tdap/Td); measles, mumps, and rubella (MMR); polio; varicella; *Haemophilus influenzae* type b (Hib); Hepatitis A and Hepatitis B.

Polio

Poliomyelitis remains an important risk for travelers to many of the countries of Africa, southern and southeast Asia, and the Middle East. All travelers to these destinations should ensure that they are immune to polio. There have been no cases of polio in the western hemisphere due to wild-type polio virus since 1991. However, a recent outbreak of poliomyelitis was noted in May 2013 in Somalia and a cluster of cases found in Syria in October 2013.[3,4] All persons traveling to countries where polio has not been eradicated should receive a primary series (at least three doses) of either inactivated polio vaccine (IPV) or oral polio vaccine.

Because IPV contains streptomycin, neomycin, and polymyxin B, persons with a history of an anaphylactic reaction to one of these antimicrobials should not receive the vaccine. In general, it is advisable to avoid polio vaccination in pregnant women unless immediate protection is required.[5] Breastfeeding is not a contraindication to vaccination in either mother or child.

Varicella

Because the varicella-zoster virus circulates worldwide and routine use of varicella vaccine is low outside the United States, the risk to travelers may be significant. In tropical regions, chickenpox occurs later in childhood or in adolescence; therefore, the lack of interaction with small children while traveling does not eliminate the exposure risk for adults in these areas. Adults at risk should be immunized regardless of travel plans.

All persons traveling abroad should have evidence that they are immune to varicella, given one of the following:

- A personal history of varicella or shingles, based upon a healthcare provider's diagnosis

- Laboratory evidence of immunity; because more than 90 percent of adults—including 70 to 90 percent of those with no reliable history of chickenpox—are immune to varicella, serologic testing before vaccination may be cost-effective.

- Proof of receiving one (if less than school age) or two doses (if school aged or older) of varicella vaccine, each given no earlier than 12 months of age and no sooner than 28 days apart

- Birth in the United States before 1980

Persons with severe allergy to gelatin or neomycin, women known to be pregnant, and persons with immunosuppressive disorders should not be vaccinated.[2]

Immunizations That May Be Required Under International Health Regulations

Yellow Fever

Yellow fever is a viral disease transmitted by a variety of mosquito vectors to humans in South America and Africa. It causes a severe form of hepatitis with jaundice, from which the name is derived. There are three epidemiologically distinct forms of yellow fever: (1) urban, (2) intermediate, and (3) sylvatic or jungle.[6] It was estimated in 2013 that in Africa between 29,000 and 60,000 deaths would occur due to yellow fever.[6] It is estimated that travelers visiting Africa during the endemic season have a 1 in 267 risk of illness and a 1 in 1,333 risk of death from yellow fever.[6]

All yellow fever vaccines currently available contain live-attenuated virus. Because of this, it is important to note that inactivated vaccines can be administered simultaneously or at any time before or after infection; however, other live-attenuated vaccines should either be given simultaneously, or after a waiting period of 30 days, because the efficacy of live-attenuated vaccines may be affected if given sooner.[2] The vaccine must be stored at temperatures of between 5°C (41°F) and -30°C (-22°F) and preferably frozen below 0°C (32°F) until reconstituted with sterile saline. Multiple-dose vials must be held to temperatures of 5°C to 10°C (41°F to 50°F) after reconstitution; all doses must be administered within 1 hour after reconstitution or discarded.[6]

Persons Living in or Traveling to Endemic Areas, Sites of Outbreaks, and Countries with Mandatory Requirements

Any person at least 9 months of age traveling to parts of South America or Africa where yellow fever transmission is a risk should be vaccinated. In general, the CDC also recommends vaccination for persons going outside of urban areas in countries that reside in the yellow fever endemic zone. It is essential to consult the CDC Yellow Book and the accompa-

nying list of affected countries and endemic zones to obtain a current and fully informed recommendation. Infants between 4 and 9 months of age may be considered for vaccination if their destination includes countries where yellow fever is prevalent and when protection without vaccination cannot be guaranteed. Under no circumstances should infants under 4 months receive yellow fever vaccine because of the risk of encephalitis.

Vaccine Certificate Requirements

Under the current International Health Regulations adopted by the World Health Organization (WHO), countries may require an international certificate of vaccination (ICV) only against yellow fever from travelers. Smallpox was deleted from the list in 1982, and no country officially requires cholera vaccination at this time. The ICV (or yellow card) must be filled out in all details or it is not considered valid.

Yellow fever immunization must be certified by affixing a uniform stamp on the appropriate line of the ICV and must be signed by a licensed physician or his/her designate. Signature stamps are not acceptable.

In the United States, yellow fever vaccine can be administered only at an approved yellow fever vaccination center, as designated by state or territorial health departments. Vaccine recipients should receive an ICV, which is then completed, signed, and validated with an official certification stamp.

Vaccine Dosage

The dosage is the same for all ages: a single subcutaneous injection of 0.5 mL of reconstituted vaccine. See Table 118-5.

Booster Doses

International health regulations stipulate revaccination at intervals of 10 years; however, immunologic evidence suggests that immunity lasts for significantly longer and perhaps for life.

Reactions

Generally, reactions to yellow fever vaccine are mild, with 2 to 5 percent of recipients reporting headaches, myalgia, low-grade fevers, or minor symptoms for less than 10 days. Fewer than 2 of 1,000 recipients have to modify their regular activities as a result. Immediate hypersensitivity reactions, including rash, urticaria, or asthma, are uncommon, with an incidence of less than 1 per million, and occur primarily among persons with a history of egg allergy. (Persons with a history of egg anaphylaxis should not receive yellow fever vaccine.) More recently, there have been reports of more severe reactions occurring in elderly individuals, resulting in cautionary advice from the CDC to administer the vaccine only to persons truly considered at risk for the disease.[2]

Precautions and Contraindications

A. Age. As noted, infants younger than 4 months should not be vaccinated due to the risk of encephalitis. Travelers over the age of 60 should be advised that side effects and risks are often increased as compared to younger populations.

B. Pregnancy. If an international travel requirement exists without a corresponding real risk of viral infection, a waiver letter should be obtained for pregnant women. Pregnant women who must travel to areas at high risk for transmission should be vaccinated because the theoretical risk from vaccination is far outweighed by the real risk of yellow fever infections (Table 118-6).

C. Altered immunity. Because of the theoretical risk of encephalitis, persons with suppressed immune systems, including those with acquired immunodeficiency syndrome, human immunodeficiency virus (HIV), leukemia, lymphoma, generalized malignancy, or those with immune suppression due to corticosteroids, alkylating agents, antimetabolites, or radiation, should not be vaccinated. In such events, patients should be instructed in appropriate methods of avoiding mosquito bites and given the vaccination waiver by their physicians. Those with asymptomatic HIV infection who cannot avoid yellow fever exposure should be given the choice of vaccination. If necessary, measurement of the neutralizing antibody response to immunization may be requested from the state health department or the CDC.

D. Hypersensitivity. Persons with anaphylactic reactions to eggs should not be given the vaccine. Those able to eat eggs or eggs products are not considered at risk. If a hypersensitivity to eggs does exist, a letter of waiver should be written on stationery with an official health department stamp. It is also possible to do an intradermal skin test for hypersensitivity under close supervision using directions supplied in the package insert.

Letters of Waiver

If international travel requirements are the only reason to vaccinate a pregnant woman, a person with reduced immunity, or a person with hypersensitivity to eggs, a letter of waiver should be written by the physician on letterhead stationery and affixed with the uniform stamp used to validate the ICV.[2]

Vaccines That May Be Recommended for Use Specifically by International Travelers

Hepatitis A

Disease

Transmission is by the fecal-oral route, involving a variety of vehicles, including contaminated food (e.g., fruits, vegetables, other foods that are handled extensively but not cooked) or water (including ice), shellfish harvested from sewage-contaminated waters, or by direct person-to-person contact.

Epidemiology

Hepatitis A is highly prevalent throughout the developing world. Consequently, Hepatitis A vaccine is recommended for all persons traveling to or residing in countries with intermediate to high risk for transmission, which includes most areas outside the United States, Western Europe, Australia, New Zealand, Japan, and Korea.[7] (Visit the CDC website and refer to the map on the National Center for Infectious Diseases Travelers' Health page for Hepatitis A.)

Vaccine

There are three vaccines licensed by the U.S. Food and Drug Administration for use in the United States. They are formulated with inactivated vaccine adsorbed to the adjuvant aluminum hydroxide and should be given by intramuscular (IM) injection in the deltoid. Each vaccine has a corresponding pediatric formulation containing half the amount of antigen for use in children and adolescents. Vaccine efficacy is shown to be about 94 percent.[7,8]

Scheduling and Administration

Two doses of vaccine, given at time 0 and 6 to 12 months later, are recommended to assure long-term persistence of antibodies (see Table 118-1). Persistence of protective levels of antibody is predicted for a duration of at least 20 years. All inactivated vaccinations are interchangeable, including combination vaccinations containing Hepatitis A.[7]

Table 118-1. Recommended Doses of Hepatitis A Vaccine[2]

Group	Age (y)	Dose (EL U)	Volume	Number of Doses	Schedule Months
Havrix					
Children and adolescents	1–18	720	0.5 mL	2	0, 6–12
Adults	≥ 19	1,440	1.0 mL	2	0, 6–12
Vaqta					
Children and adolescents	1–18	25 units	0.5 mL	2	0, 6–18
Adults	≥ 19	50 units	1.0 mL	2	0, 6–18
Twinrix					
Adults standard regimen	≥ 18	720 EL U/20 μg	1.0 mL	3	0, 1, 6
Adults accelerated regimen	≥ 18	720 EL U/20 μg	1.0 mL	4	0, 7, 21 days + 1 year

From Centers for Disease Control and Prevention. *Health Information for International Travel*, 2014. Washington, DC: U.S. Government Printing Office, 2014 (known as the Yellow Book).

Reactions

Side effects among users of the Havrix preparation include soreness at the injection site, headache, and malaise. Among children, the most common side effects were injection site soreness, feeding difficulty, headache, and injection site induration.

The most common side effects among adult recipients of Vaqta were tenderness, pain, and warmth at the injection site and headache. Among children receiving this vaccine, the most common symptoms were pain, tenderness, and warmth at the injection site.[2]

Contraindications

Neither vaccine preparation should be given to persons with a history of an allergic reaction to alum. Havrix should not be given to those who have hypersensitivity to the preservative 2-phenoxyethanol.

The risks and benefits of disease and vaccination should be weighed when considering vaccination of a pregnant woman.

Hepatitis A Antibody Screening

Screening for antibodies to Hepatitis A may be reasonable in persons with a likely clinical history or high probability of prior infection (based on age or long-term residence in an endemic area) if the cost of screening is meaningfully lower than that of immunization and if screening will not significantly delay subsequent immunization.[8]

Japanese Encephalitis

Disease

JE is a mosquito-transmitted viral infection occurring in many parts of Asia that causes inflammation of the central nervous system. Although most cases occur with no recognizable symptoms, the case-fatality rate is about 30 percent, and neuropsychiatric sequelae occur in as many as 50 percent of survivors of clinically evident cases.

Epidemiology

Risk of infection correlates with a number of factors, including age, occupation, recreational exposure, and gender. In en-

demic regions of the world, children have the highest rates of infection. For specific information about individual countries, a detailed list can be found at the CDC website.

Fortunately, the risk for short-term travelers, especially those who visit only urban areas, is low. Consequently, JE vaccine is not recommended for all travelers to Asia. Travelers at highest risk include persons planning an extended stay of a month or longer in rural, agricultural, or other endemic areas. Vaccination should be considered for short-term travelers who will have extensive exposure due to outdoor activities during evening and nighttime hours, such as camping, bicycling, or agricultural fieldwork. A more detailed consideration of the vaccine may be found in the review by Wilder-Smith and Halstead.[9]

In high-risk areas, travelers should try to use bed nets if air-conditioned or well-screened rooms are not available. Insecticidal sprays, insect repellent (preparations with 30 percent DEET are preferred), and protective clothing to help prevent mosquito bites are also important.

Vaccine

In 2009 Ixiaro became an approved vaccination for JE and was originally approved for travelers 17 years of age and older. In May 2013, the approval for JE vaccine was expanded to children aged 2 months to 16 years. See Table 118-2 for more information.

Reactions

Local and mild systemic reactions, such as fever, headache, myalgia, and malaise, occur in approximately 10 to 20 percent of vaccine recipients. More severe allergic reactions, such as urticaria, angioedema, respiratory distress, and anaphylaxis, may occur within minutes or as long as 2 weeks after vaccination. Vaccine recipients should be observed for 30 minutes after injection and should be advised to report any significant symptoms promptly. It is advised that the last dose of vaccine not be given less than 10 days before initiation of travel so that prompt care may be rendered for adverse reactions, if necessary.

Contraindications

Persons with a history of multiple allergies, especially urticaria or angioedema, are at higher risk for reactions to JE vaccine.

Table 118-2 Japanese Encephalitis Vaccine Recommendations

Vaccine	Trade Name (Manufacturer)	Age	Dose	Route	Schedule	Booster[1]
JE vaccine, inactivated	Ixiaro (Intercell)	≥ 17 years	0.5 mL	IM	0, 28 days	≥ 1 year after primary series
		3 years through 16 years	0.5 mL	IM	0, 28 days	Data not yet available
		2 months through 2 years	0.25 mL	IM	0, 28 days	Data not yet available

From Centers for Disease Control and Prevention. *Health Information for International Travel, 2014*. Washington, DC: U.S. Government Printing Office, 2014 (known as the Yellow Book).

Anyone with a history of an allergic reaction to a mouse-derived vaccine or to JE vaccine specifically should not be vaccinated. Vaccine administration during pregnancy generally should be avoided, except in situations of high, unavoidable risk of exposure.[2]

Meningococcal Disease

Disease

Infection with *Neisseria meningitidis* causes septicemia with or without disseminated intravascular coagulation or acute meningitis. With early diagnosis and rapid antibiotic treatment, the case fatality rate has dropped from 50 percent to around 10 percent.

Epidemiology

In the sub-Saharan (Sahel) region of Africa, local outbreaks or epidemics of group A meningococcal meningitis occur frequently during the dry season, which typically extends from December to June. This is particularly true in the savannah areas extending from Mali to Ethiopia, an area of meningococcal meningitis prevalence.

The risk for most travelers to this region of Africa is low. Nonetheless, due to limited active surveillance in the area and the severe consequences of infection, travelers to this region during the dry season should be vaccinated, especially if significant contact with the local population is planned.[2]

Vaccine may be required for pilgrims to Mecca, Saudi Arabia, during the Hajj and Umrah. Vaccination is recommended for travel to any country experiencing an epidemic due to a vaccine-preventable strain (A, C, Y, W-135), as generally recognized by issuance of a CDC and or WHO travel advisory. Recently, outbreaks of meningococcal meningitis have occurred in Benin, Burkina Faso, Chad, Central African Republic, Côte d'Ivoire, Gambia, Ghana, Mali, Nigeria, and Sudan.[10]

Vaccine

Beginning in 2005, the vaccine preferred for persons 11 to 55 years of age is a conjugated tetravalent formulation of A, C, Y, and W-135 capsular antigens. Its preferred status relates to its ability to provide long-term immunity and to confer herd immunity by reducing nasopharyngeal carriage. The duration of immunity is unknown but appears to be at least 5 years. The polysaccharide vaccine is the only one recommended for use in travelers over the age of 55.[2] See Table 118-3.

Reactions

Although severe reactions are uncommon, mild local reactions such as erythema at the injection have been reported.

Contraindications

Persons with acute illness should defer vaccinations until their condition improves. The vaccine is contraindicated for those who have a severe allergic reaction to any of the components of the vaccines. Menactra is contraindicated in those with an allergy to dry natural rubber latex; however, the polysaccharide vaccine is an acceptable alternative for those individuals.[2]

Rabies

Disease

Rabies infection causes an acute and almost uniformly fatal encephalomyelitis. Presenting as vague symptoms such as dysesthesias, the disease progresses to cause weakness, paralysis, spasm of swallowing muscles, altered mental status, and convulsions.

Epidemiology

The most common means of transmission is through animal bite wounds, though contamination of open cuts or mucous membranes by infected saliva without bite exposures is possible. In many areas of the world, canine rabies is highly endemic. In foreign countries where rabies is endemic, bites of any mammalian species should be evaluated for the consideration of rabies prophylaxis.

Most of the countries of the world harbor a rabies risk. Notable exceptions are those listed in Table 118-4, which shows countries for which no rabies cases were reported during 2012. The decision to administer vaccine before international travel should be based on (1) the incidence of rabies in the countries visited,

Table 118-3. Meningococcal vaccine recommendations

Vaccine	Trade Name (Manufacturer)	Age	Dose	Route	Schedule	Booster
Meningococcal polysaccharide diphtheria toxoid conjugate vaccine	Menactra (Sanofi Pasteur)	9–23 mo 2–55 y	0.5 mL 0.5 mL	IM IM	0, 3 mo 1 dose	If at continued risk[1]
Meningococcal oligosaccharide diphtheria CRM$_{197}$ conjugate vaccine	Menveo (Novartis)	2–55 y	0.5 mL	IM	1 dose	If at continued risk[1]
Meningococcal polysaccharide vaccine	Menomune (Sanofi Pasteur)	≥ 2 y	0.5 mL	SC	1 dose	If at continued risk[2]

From Centers for Disease Control and Prevention. *Health Information for International Travel, 2014.* Washington, DC: U.S. Government Printing Office, 2014 (known as the Yellow Book).

Table 118-4. Countries Reporting No Cases of Rabies During 2012[2]

Region[1]	Countries/Localities
Africa	Cape Verde, Mauritius, Réunion, São Tomé and Príncipe, and Seychelles
Americas	North: Bermuda, Saint Pierre and Miquelon Caribbean: Antigua and Barbuda, Aruba, The Bahamas, Barbados, Cayman Islands, Dominica, Guadeloupe, Jamaica, Martinique, Montserrat, Netherlands Antilles, Saint Kitts (Saint Christopher) and Nevis, Saint Lucia, Saint Martin, Saint Vincent and Grenadines, Turks and Caicos, and Virgin Islands (UK and U.S.)
Asia and the Middle East	Hong Kong, Japan, Kuwait, Malaysia (Sabah), Qatar, Singapore, Taiwan, United Arab Emirates
Europe[2]	Albania, Austria, Belgium, Corsica, Cyprus, Czech Republic, Denmark, Finland, France, Germany, Gibraltar, Greece, Hungary, Iceland, Ireland, Isle of Man, Liechtenstein, Luxembourg, Monaco, Netherlands, Norway (except Svalbard), Portugal, Slovakia, Slovenia, Spain(except Ceuta and Melilla), Sweden, Switzerland, and United Kingdom
Oceania[3]	Australia,[3] Cook Islands, Fiji, French Polynesia, Guam, Hawaii, Kiribati, Micronesia, New Caledonia, New Zealand, Northern Mariana Islands, Palau, Papua New Guinea, Samoa, and Vanuatu

[1]Global surveillance efforts and reporting standards differ dramatically, conditions may change rapidly because of animal translocation, and bat rabies may exist in some areas that are reportedly "free" of rabies in other mammals.

[2]Bat lyssaviruses have been reported throughout Europe, including areas that are reportedly free of rabies in other wild mammals.

[3]Most of Pacific Oceania is reportedly "rabies-free," with the exception of Australia, where lyssaviruses in bats have been reported, as well as fatal human rabies cases.

From Centers for Disease Control and Prevention. *Health Information for International Travel*, 2014. Washington, DC: U.S. Government Printing Office, 2014 (known as the Yellow Book).

(2) the length of stay, (3) the types of activities planned, and (4) the availability and types of vaccine locally.[11]

Vaccine

Pre-exposure prophylaxis may be completed with a three-series injection of either human diploid cell rabies vaccine (HDCV) or purified chick embryo cell (PCEC) vaccine. Travelers should receive all three pre-exposure immunizations before travel. If three doses of rabies vaccine cannot be completed before travel, the traveler should not start the series.

Travelers who complete pre-exposure prophylaxis and are potentially exposed to the rabies virus should still seek additional medical care, as the pre-exposure prophylaxis does not eliminate the need for post-exposure prophylaxis. However, the pre-exposure vaccination may provide some amount of protection, especially if post-exposure prophylaxis must be delayed.[2]

Evaluation and Management of Bite Wounds

Post-exposure prophylaxis is needed only for bite wounds sustained in the countries listed in Table 118-4. Recommendations for post-exposure prophylaxis have been updated and provided by the ACIP.[12]

Scheduling and Administration

In the pre-exposure setting, a 1.0-mL injection of HDCV or PCEC vaccine should be given intramuscularly (IM) in the deltoid on days 0, 7, and 21 or 28.

Reactions

Local reactions, including pain, erythema, swelling, or itching at the site of injection and mild systemic reactions, such as headache, myalgias, and nausea, are not uncommon. After booster injections with HDCV, about 6 percent of recipients develop urticaria, pruritus, and malaise.

Contraindications

Pregnancy is not a contraindication to use of rabies vaccine in the post-exposure setting. If pre-exposure immunization of persons who are immunocompromised is deemed essential, post-vaccination antibody titers should be checked.

Typhoid Fever

Disease

Typhoid fever is a severe, potentially life-threatening illness due to infection with *Salmonella typhi*.

Epidemiology

Approximately 22 million cases of typhoid fever occur worldwide each year, resulting in 200,000 deaths. About 400 cases of typhoid, primarily among travelers, occur annually in the United States.

The risk to travelers exists in the developing countries of Asia, Africa, and Latin America who have exposure to contaminated food or beverages. Persons visiting friends and relatives and who are less likely to consume safe food and beverages may be particularly vulnerable.

Vaccine

Two vaccines are currently available in the United States:

* Oral live-attenuated vaccine (from the Ty21a strain of *S. entericaserotype Typhi*)

* Vi capsular polysaccharide vaccine (ViCPS) for IM use

The reported efficacy for these vaccines ranges from 50 to 80 percent. Travelers should be advised that the vaccine is not 100 percent effective and that they must use proper food and water precautions in addition to the vaccine to help prevent illness.[2]

Contraindications and Adverse Reactions

On a theoretical basis, vaccination during pregnancy should be avoided.

Table 118-5. Dosage and Schedule for Typhoid fever Vaccination

Vaccination	Age (Y)	Dose, Mode Of Administration	Number Of Doses	Dosing Interval	Boosting Interval
Oral, Live, Attenuated Ty21a Vaccine (Vivotif)[1]					
Live, Oral Vaccine (Ty21a)					
Primary series	≥ 6	1 capsule,[2] oral	4	48 hours	Not applicable
Booster	≥ 6	1 capsule,[2] oral	4	48 hours	Every 5 years
Vi Capsular Polysaccharide Vaccine					
Primary series	≥ 2	0.50 mL, intramuscular	1	Not applicable	Not applicable
Booster	≥ 2	0.50 mL, intramuscular	1	Not applicable	Every 2 years

[1]The vaccine must be kept refrigerated (35.6°F–46.4°F, 2°C–8°C).
[2]Administer with cool liquid no warmer than 98.6°F (37°C).
From Centers for Disease Control and Prevention. *Health Information for International Travel,* 2014. Washington, DC: U.S. Government Printing Office, 2014 (known as the Yellow Book).

Adverse reactions to Ty21a vaccine are rare and mainly consist of abdominal discomfort, nausea, vomiting, and rash. ViCPS vaccine is most often associated with headache and injection site reactions.[2]

Immunocompromised States

Avoid use of live, oral Ty21a vaccine in persons who are immunocompromised; instead, capsular polysaccharide vaccine should be used.

Special Considerations

Travelers who choose to vaccinate themselves via the live oral vaccine must be able to keep the tablets refrigerated during the duration of therapy. It is important to note that inactivated vaccines van be administered simultaneously or any time before or after the oral typhoid; however, other live-attenuated vaccines should either be given simultaneously, or a waiting period of 30 days is required, as the efficacy of live-attenuated vaccines may be affected if given sooner.[2]

The live, attenuated Ty21a vaccine should not be given to persons within 24 hours of taking antibiotics that can inhibit growth of the vaccine bacteria, thus reducing immunity. Immunoglobulin does not appear to cause such interference.

Vaccines Also Indicated for High-risk Populations within the United States

Hepatitis B

Hepatitis B is of low risk to most international travelers, except to persons engaging in higher-risk activities who will be visiting countries with moderate to high endemic rates of infection, which include countries in Asia, northern Canada, Greenland, and parts of South America. (See the CDC website and refer to the map on the National Center for Infectious Diseases Travelers' Health page for Hepatitis B for a graphical representation of these zones.) Persons visiting areas with intermediate to high prevalence of infection (> 2 percent) should receive a primary series of vaccine.[2]

Influenza

The risk of influenza infection to the international traveler depends on the time of year and the countries visited. In tropical regions, influenza occurs throughout the year. In temperate regions of the southern hemisphere, the main period of risk is from April through September. Even during "off season" periods for influenza, travelers may be exposed if touring with large groups of visitors from other areas of the world where influenza is actively circulating.

Persons at high risk for influenza should be advised to receive the vaccine before travel if they did not receive the vaccine from the preceding fall-winter season and if they will travel:

- To the tropics at any time during the year

- With tourist groups from other areas of the world where influenza may be occurring

- To the southern hemisphere between April and September[2]

Because influenza vaccine may be difficult to locate during the summer in North America, persons at highest risk should speak with their physicians before travel. Three types of influenza vaccine are now available: inactivated vaccine given by IM injection, inactivated injection given by intradermal injection, and live-attenuated vaccine given by nasal spray. Vaccination is recommended for all individuals over 6 months of age; however, the live-attenuated vaccine is approved only for healthy, nonpregnant persons 2 to 49 years of age.

Pneumococcal Disease

Physicians and other healthcare providers who provide pre-travel counseling for persons at high risk for pneumococcal infection[13] who have not yet received vaccine should take the opportunity to advise immunization prior to travel.

Other Vaccines

Cholera

Cholera risk is very low for travelers following standard tourist routes who observe basic recommendations regarding food and water safety. Moreover, at present, no country officially requires cholera vaccine prior to entry. However, local authorities in certain areas may nonetheless require documentation of vaccination against cholera. Where such circumstances are known to exist, it is advisable to write a letter of exemption from local requirements for cholera vaccination to avoid possible detainment at the border or the requirement for immediate vaccination.[2]

Production of the only cholera vaccine licensed in the United States has been discontinued by the manufacturer. New oral cholera vaccines are being developed that may provide a higher level of protection, but none has yet been approved by the U.S. Food and Drug Administration.[14]

Plague

The risk posed by plague to international travelers is exceedingly small, and special protection is rarely indicated for persons staying in standard tourist accommodations. Generally, vaccination has been considered for persons likely to have exposure to wild rodents or similar animals in plague-epizootic areas and for persons who will reside or work in plague-endemic areas where it may be difficult to avoid either rodents or fleas. In enzootic regions, the risk of plague is highest in semiarid grassland or mountainous areas. Factors increasing the population size or migration of wild rodents increase the likelihood of human contact with plague. Rodent-infested areas should be avoided, and sick or dead rodents should not be handled. In enzootic areas, travelers may apply insect repellants to skin and repellants and insecticides to clothing and bedding.

Production of plague vaccine has been discontinued by the manufacturer. Consequently, travelers deemed to be at high risk for plague currently should be advised to consider short-term prophylaxis with tetracycline or doxycycline during periods of exposure. In place of tetracyclines, trimethoprim-sulfamethoxazole may be considered for use in children.[15]

Smallpox

Since the global eradication of smallpox was certified by WHO in 1980 and the disease was deleted from the International Health Regulations in 1982, smallpox vaccination should no longer be administered to international travelers unless a travel advisory is issued by the CDC. The last reported endemic case of smallpox occurred in Somalia in 1977, and the last reported laboratory-associated case was acquired in the United Kingdom in 1978.

Pregnancy and Vaccinations

Table 118-6 provides a comprehensive list of vaccinations and considerations of use during pregnancy.

Seeking Medical Care Abroad

Before taking any major journey to a foreign country, travelers should always be certain to know what expenses their health

Table 118-6. Considerations for Vaccination During Pregnancy

	Vaccine	Use During Pregnancy
Diphtheria-tetanus	Toxoid	If indicated, such as lack of primary series, or no booster within past 10 years
Diphtheria-tetanus-pertussis	Toxoid-acellular	Not contraindicated, but data on safety, immunogenicity, and outcomes of pregnancy are not available. Second or third trimester is preferred, if vaccine is indicated.
Hepatitis A	Inactivated virus	Data on safety in pregnancy are not available. Should weigh the theoretical risk of vaccination against the risk of disease. Consider immunoglobulin rather than vaccine.
Hepatitis B	Recombinant or plasma-derived	Recommended for women at risk of infection.
Immunoglobulins, pooled or hyperimmune	Immunoglobulin or specific globulin preparations	Administer if indicated for pre- or post-exposure. No known risk to fetus.
Influenza	Inactivated whole virus or subunit	All women who are pregnant during the flu season; women at high risk for pulmonary complications. Vaccination may occur in any trimester.
Japanese encephalitis	Inactivated virus	Data on safety in pregnancy are not available. Should weigh the theoretical risk of vaccination against the risk of disease.
Measles	Live-attenuated virus	Contraindicated; vaccination of susceptible women should be part of postpartum care.
Meningococcal meningitis	Conjugated	Data on safety in pregnancy are not available. Weigh theoretical vaccination risk against that of disease.
Mumps	Live-attenuated virus	Contraindicated; vaccination of susceptible women should be part of postpartum care.
Pneumococcal	Polysaccharide	Administer if indicated.
Polio, inactivated	Inactivated virus	Indicated for susceptible pregnant women traveling in endemic areas or in other high-risk situations.
Rabies	Inactivated virus	Administer if indicated.
Rubella	Live-attenuated virus	Contraindicated; vaccination of susceptible women should be part of postpartum care.
Typhoid (ViCPS)	Polysaccharide	If indicated for travel to endemic areas
Typhoid (Ty21a)	Live bacterial	Data on safety in pregnancy are not available.
Varicella	Live-attenuated virus	Contraindicated; vaccination of susceptible women should be considered postpartum.
Yellow fever	Live-attenuated virus	Postponement of travel preferred. May be used if exposure unavoidable.

insurance will cover in the event of a medical emergency abroad. They should bring a copy of their health insurance ID card and a claim form, and they should be aware that even the most comprehensive standard policy will not cover evacuation to the United States in case of medical emergency. Travelers looking for additional peace of mind should consider joining the nonprofit International Association for Medical Assistance to Travelers (IAMAT) (see Supplemental Resources). It can provide a reference source containing the names of Western-trained physicians who are located in most countries of the world and who may be called on in the event of a medical emergency for a preset fee. If further assistance is needed in finding emergency care, travelers can contact the American consulate in the host country. It is advisable for travelers to have these numbers, available through the U.S. Department of State's website, before departure (see Supplemental Resources).

CONCLUSIONS

Given the complexity of recommendations for immunizations, chemoprophylaxis, and other protective measures, travel medicine has evolved to become an area of specialized interest for many practitioners. It is essential that general information be individualized to account for the itinerary, medical history of the traveler, and the type of activities anticipated.

Although immunizations remain the central element of routine protection, a variety of medications and other strategies can be used to reduce the risk or ameliorate the effects of numerous disorders, including malaria, travelers' diarrhea, motion sickness, and altitude sickness. Those providing advice to travelers should be thoroughly grounded in the basics of the field by consulting comprehensive reviews such as the most recent edition of *Health Information for International Travel*. Because travel advisories are often issued rapidly in response to an evolving health threat abroad, practitioners need to be certain that they are aware of all updates provided through the CDC and employ the most current recommendations available to protect those they serve.

FUTURE TRENDS

International travel medicine is increasingly looked on as an area of specialized practice. Those providing services to travelers need to be familiar with the full array of interventions available to ensure the health of persons traveling abroad. Certification in travel medicine is now available.

REFERENCES

1. Noble L, Wilcox A, Behrens R. Travel health consultation and risk assessment. *Infect Dis Clin North Am* 2012 Sep;26(3):575–593.
2. Brunette GW, ed. *CDC Health Information for International Travel 2014*. New York: Oxford University Press, 2013.
3. Centers for Disease Control and Prevention (CDC). Notes from the field: outbreak of poliomyelitis - Somalia and Kenya, May 2013. *MMWR Morb Mortal Wkly Rep* 2013 Jun 14;62(23):484.
4. The Global Polio Eradication Initiative. *Polio cases confirmed in Syria Arab republic.* October 29, 2013. Available at: http://www.polioeradication.org/tabid/488/iid/328/Default.aspx.
5. Prevots DR, Burr RK, Sutter RW, et al. Poliomyelitis prevention in the United States. Updated recommendations of the Advisory Committee on Immunization Practices (ACIP). *MMWR Recomm Rep* 2000 May 9;49(RR-5):1–22.
6. Vaccines and vaccination against yellow fever: WHO position paper -- June 2013. *Wkly Epidemiol Rec* 2013 Jul 5;88(27):269–283.
7. WHO position paper on hepatitis A – June 2012. *Wkly Epidemiol Rec* 2012 Jul 13;87(28/29):261–276.
8. Advisory Committee on Immunization Practices (ACIP), Fiore AE, Wasley A, et al. Prevention of hepatitis A through active or passive immunization: recommendations of the Advisory Committee on Immunization Practices (ACIP). *MMWR Recomm Rep* 2006 May 19;55(RR-7):1–23.
9. Wilder-Smith A, Halstead S. Japanese encephalitis: Update on vaccines and vaccine recommendations. *Curr Opin Infect Dis* 2010 Oct;23(5):426–431.
10. World Health Organization (WHO). *Meningococcal disease: situation in the African meningitis belt.* WHO website. May 24, 2012. Available at: http://www.who.int/csr/don/2012_05_24/en/index.html.
11. Meslin F. Rabies as a travelers risk, especially in high-endemicity areas. *J Travel Med* 2005 Apr;12 Suppl 1:S30–S40.
12. Rupprecht CE, Briggs D, Brown CM, et al. Use of a reduced (4-dose) vaccine schedule for post-exposure prophylaxis to prevent human rabies. Recommendations of the Advisory Committee of Immunization Practices (ACIP). *MMWR Reccom Rep* 2010 Mar 19;59(RR-2):1–9.
13. Centers for Disease Control and Prevention (CDC); Advisory Committee on Immunization Practices. Updated recommendations for prevention of invasive pneumococcal disease among adults using the 23-valent pneumococcal polysaccharide vaccine (PPSV23). *MMWR Recomm Rep* 2010 Sep 3;59(34):1102–1106.
14. World Health Organization. Cholera, 2005. *Wkly Epidemiol Rec* 2006;81:297–308.
15. Centers for Disease Control and Prevention (CDC), National Center for Emerging and Zoonotic Infectious Diseases (NCEZID), Division of Vector-Borne Diseases (DVBD). *Resources for clinicians: plague.* CDC website. August 3, 2012 Available at: http://www.cdc.gov/plague/healthcare/clinicians.html.

SUPPLEMENTAL RESOURCES

American Society of Tropical Medicine and Hygiene. Available at: http://www.astmh.org.

Centers for Disease Control and Prevention (CDC). Available at: http://www.cdc.gov.

Central Intelligence Agency World Factbook. Available at: http://www.odci.gov/cia/publications/pubs.html.

Fiore AE, Shay DK, Broder K, et al. Prevention and control of influenza: recommendations of the Advisory Committee on Immunization Practices (ACIP), 2008. *MMWR Recomm Rep* 2008 Aug 8;57(RR-7):1–60.

International Association for Medical Assistance to Travelers (IAMAT). Available at: http://www.iamat.org.

International Society of Travel Medicine. Available at: http://www.istm.org.

Kroger AT, Atkinson WL, Marcuse EK, et al. General recommendations on immunization: recommendations of the Advisory Committee on Immunization Practices (ACIP). *MMWR Recomm Rep* 2006 Dec 1;55(RR-15):1–48.

Pan American Health Organization (PAHO). Available at: http://www.paho.org.

Recommendations of the Advisory Committee on Immunization Practices (ACIP): use of vaccines and immune globulins in persons with altered immunocompetence. *MMWR Recomm Rep* 1993 Apr 9;42(RR-4):1–18.

United States Department of State. Available at: http://www.state.gov.

World Health Organization (WHO). Available at: http://www.who.org.

CHAPTER 119

Emergency Management

Terri Rebmann, PhD, RN, CIC
Associate Professor
Saint Louis University, School of Public Health - Institute for Biosecurity
St. Louis, MO

ABSTRACT

Many types of disasters may potentially affect healthcare, ranging from natural disasters to man-made events. Emergency management is the process by which an individual, facility, and/or community uses mitigation strategies to better prepare for, respond to, and recover from all types of disasters/ emergencies and mass casualty events. To accomplish this, an all-hazards approach must be utilized. Emergency management is a multidepartmental, multiagency endeavor that requires coordination and communication among many groups to be most effective. It is essential that infection preventionists participate in all phases of the emergency management process to decrease the mental health impact, costs, morbidity, and mortality related to mass casualty incidents.

KEY CONCEPTS

- Disasters and mass casualty incidents may be the result of nature, emerging infections, or man-made events.

- Disasters and mass casualty incidents differ from other emergencies in their large scale and potential to result in mass casualties.

- Advance planning and practicing of emergency management plans are essential to an effective response.

- Preparing for and responding to mass casualty incidents requires communication and coordination among many organizations and individuals.

- Infection preventionists have a unique skill set that enables them to better prepare for and respond to mass casualty events.

- The basic principles of emergency management remain the same for all types of disasters. Only the response interventions vary to address the specific needs of the situation.

- Preparedness includes (1) development of an emergency management plan, (2) education of responding individuals/ agencies on the plan, (3) practicing the plan, and (4) evaluating the facility or community's level of preparedness.

BACKGROUND

Globally, the number of disasters and people affected by such events has increased in the recent past. The Haitian earthquake in January 2010 and the summer heat wave later that year in Russia resulted in over 278,500 deaths, a higher disaster-related mortality toll than any year in the last two decades.[1] In 2011, the earthquake, tsunami, and subsequent radiological event in Japan resulted in almost 30,000 deaths and costs of more than $366 billion.[1] Outbreaks of emerging infectious diseases and pandemics, such as the 2009 H1N1 influenza A pandemic, have sickened and killed hundreds of thousands of people around the world. The 2009 H1N1 pandemic alone resulted in between 151,700 and 575,400 deaths worldwide, and the mortality rate was more than 1 percent.[2] Recent disasters have illustrated the need for healthcare personnel (HCP), public health officials, and healthcare institutions to become better prepared to effectively respond to these events. Disasters and mass casualty incidents may be the result of nature, emerging infections, or man-made events. Regardless of the source, disasters pose potentially devastating threats to the health and well-being of the population.

Infection preventionists (IPs) have a vital role in maintaining the health of patients, visitors, and employees in their facility and the community. The unique skill set of IPs enables them to better prepare for and respond to different types of mass casualty incidents. As experts in the fields of surveillance and epidemiology, IPs are responsible for investigating outbreaks and initiating interventions to prevent the transmission of infections that occur within healthcare. Because the infectious disease impact of a mass casualty incident will vary depending on the nature of the event, IPs must be familiar with the potential consequences of different types of disasters and mass casualty incidents. However, though interventions will vary with different types of disasters, the general principles of surveillance and epidemiology remain the same.

Historically, the role of the IP in emergency management has centered more on disaster response than on mitigation, planning, or disaster recovery. This is primarily because most disasters, such as famine and earthquakes, do not involve a communicable disease component or have a large infectious disease impact.[3,4] Therefore, emergency management planning has long been considered a role of security, facilities management, and administration rather than infection prevention.[4] As a result of the increased threat of a biological event (bioterrorism, outbreak of an emerging infectious disease, or pandemic), a shift has occurred in emergency management.

Infectious disease prevention, control, and epidemiology are being seen as a more critical component of emergency management. The role of IPs has broadened to include mass casualty event preparedness responsibilities in addition to response duties. It has become imperative for IPs to take a lead role in better preparing themselves, their facilities, and their communities for all types of mass casualty incidents. The role of IPs in emergency management has been outlined and IPs should become familiar with this role.[4]

BASIC PRINCIPLES

Disasters are one type of emergency. Disasters differ from other emergencies by the scope of the event; unlike most emergencies, disasters have the potential to result in mass casualties. Newer emergency management terminology sometimes uses the terms "mass casualty incident" and "mass casualty event" as a substitute for the term "disaster." These terms will be used interchangeably throughout the chapter. Large-scale events pose unique challenges to healthcare and public health. Although small emergencies may be managed by a handful of individuals or a single facility, a mass casualty event requires communication and coordination among many responding departments and agencies. This makes disaster preparedness more difficult. Advance planning and practicing emergency management plans are essential to an effective response.

There are many types of disasters that may potentially affect healthcare, and they can be divided into two categories by source: (1) those caused by natural forces, such as floods, earthquakes, hurricanes, and emerging infectious diseases; and (2) those resulting from intentional or unintentional man-made events, such as traditional, biological, chemical, nuclear, or radiological emergencies. Another way of categorizing mass casualty incidents is by the nature of the event in terms of whether or not it involves an infectious disease. Noninfectious disease disasters include all natural and man-made events that do not have an infectious agent as the source of the incident. Examples include hurricanes, floods, earthquakes, and all forms of terrorism except bioterrorism. Infectious disease disasters include all events that involve a biological agent/disease, such as a bioterrorism attack, a pandemic, or outbreak of an emerging infectious disease (see Chapter 120 Infectious Disease Disasters). The response will vary from incident to incident, because each mass casualty incident poses unique risks to communities and therefore requires situation-specific interventions. This is true even among disasters caused by the same force; no two earthquakes are alike, and the response to each will vary. However, the basic principles of emergency management remain the same for all types of mass casualty incidents. All disasters have potential infectious disease implications, but infectious disease disasters pose the greatest risk to communities in terms of disease transmission. IPs will be needed for planning for all types of disasters, but their involvement will be most critical for infectious disease disasters.

The potential consequences of a mass casualty event depend on many factors, including the community's social, economic, and baseline health status; the type and scope of incident; and the community's level of advance preparedness. Potential consequences of disasters are best mitigated and decreased by engaging in preparedness initiatives. These include the following: (1) developing an emergency management plan, (2) educating responding individuals/agencies about the plan, (3) practicing the plan, and (4) evaluating the facility or community's level of preparedness.

EMERGENCY MANAGEMENT

Disasters should be planned for and responded to using the principles of emergency management. Emergency management is composed of four principles: mitigation, preparedness, response, and recovery.[5]

Mitigation

Mitigation describes actions taken to decrease the potential impact of a situation. These include interventions to either prevent or reduce morbidity and mortality and ease the economic and social impact of the event on the affected community. Mitigation strategies vary depending on the type of mass casualty incident. Mitigation interventions can range from new policies or laws related to mass casualty incident assistance funding for floods or hurricanes to new laws related to the use of smallpox vaccine for a potential bioterrorism attack. Mitigation is affected by national and international policies and the infrastructure of the public health system. A stronger public health infrastructure will ensure a more rapid and effective response, which in turn will decrease the negative impact of a disaster. Putting shutters on houses in areas at risk for hurricanes and elevating houses and appliances in flood plains are examples of mitigation interventions that can decrease the impact of a potential mass casualty incident.

Preparedness

Preparedness is both a phase and the measures taken during this time. As a phase, preparedness refers to the time before an emergency occurs (see the section on Phases of a Disaster). Preparedness measures are those taken before an event that better prepare an individual, facility, or community to respond to an emergency. These include such interventions as developing a facility emergency management plan and educating the workforce to implement such a plan. In addition, practicing and evaluating the emergency management plan helps ensure the best response to a true mass casualty incident.

Response

Like preparedness, response refers to both a phase and the activities implemented during this time. As a phase, response refers to the time immediately after an emergency is detected. Response activities include interventions undertaken in response to a known or suspected event. During the response phase, personal and facility emergency management plans are implemented. In large disasters, community, regional, and federal emergency management plans may also be implemented. The response will depend on a number of factors, including the type and scope of the mass casualty incident and how rapidly the event is identified. Each mass casualty event poses unique challenges and requires individualized interventions. However, basic infection prevention and epidemiological principles remain the same, regardless of the type and scope of the disaster.

Recovery

Recovery refers to both a phase and interventions implemented during this time period. As a phase, recovery refers to the period after the emergency has been declared over. During the recovery period, the facility or community implements interventions necessary to return to its predisaster baseline (i.e., recovery interventions). Recovery activities will include the following: (1) establish short- and long-term goals to return facility or community to pre-event baseline, (2) evaluate emergency management plan implementation and gaps identified during response, (3) determine potential solutions to identified gaps in emergency management plan, (4) update emergency management plan to reflect lessons learned, (5) educate staff on changes in emergency management plan, and (6) practice new emergency management plan. This will include replenishing stocks of medical equipment and supplies and returning to daily activities and routine reporting structures. Another important component of the recovery phase is responding to the mental health impact on the community, including dealing with patients with posttraumatic stress disorder (PTSD).

Although emergency management terminology is new for many IPs, these principles can be compared and applied to infection prevention nomenclature. Mitigation strategies are synonymous with control measures that affect morbidity and mortality. Preparedness is synonymous with primary prevention. Secondary prevention interventions occur during the response phase. Lastly, the disaster recovery phase involves the implementation of tertiary prevention strategies.

It is vital that healthcare facilities and communities use an all-hazards approach to emergency management. This means that a facility or community emergency management plan must be able to accommodate all types of potential mass casualty incidents, from natural to man-made. In addition, the emergency management plan must address disasters that involve a communicable disease, such as an outbreak of an emerging infection or a bioterrorism attack using an infectious agent.

Emergency management is a multidepartmental, multiagency endeavor that requires coordination and communication among many groups to be most effective. It is essential that IPs participate in all aspects and phases of the emergency management process to decrease the mental health impact, costs, morbidity, and mortality related to mass casualty incidents.

Phases of a Disaster

All disasters consist of four phases: (1) preparedness, (2) impact, (3) response, and (4) recovery (see Figure 119-1). The first phase, preparedness, refers to the time before a mass casualty incident occurs. During this phase, there is no immediate anticipation of disaster in the near future; the length of this phase is indefinite. In some mass casualty incidents, the preparedness phase may include a warning period, during which a disaster is anticipated. Warning phases vary in length, depending on the type of mass casualty event. This may mean a day or two warning for hurricanes, hours for floods, minutes for tornadoes, or no immediate warning for earthquakes or acts of terrorism.

The second, or impact, phase includes the time while the actual mass casualty incident is occurring. This time period can vary from seconds for an earthquake to weeks for a flood. Activities undertaken during the impact phase vary, depending on the duration of this phase (seconds to weeks) and whether or not the event is immediately detected. In a covert bioterrorism attack, for instance, the release is likely to be detected only when patients become ill days to weeks after the event, making it impossible to implement interventions during the impact period. The third phase, response, begins at varying times, depending on the type of disaster and when the event is detected. In some disasters, such as a flood or hurricane, the response will most likely begin in conjunction with the impact phase. In other mass casualty incidents, such as a bombing or earthquake, the response phase will begin immediately after the impact. It is also possible for the response phase to begin long after the impact is over. Again, an example is a covert bioterrorism attack using an agent with a prolonged incubation period, such as smallpox. In this situation, the impact phase of the event (the release of aerosolized *Variola* virus) would end almost 2 weeks (i.e., the incubation period of smallpox) before the event is likely to be detected.

Regardless of when the response phase begins, it consists of interventions necessary to cope with the immediate effects of the disaster. In most mass casualty incidents, more injuries occur in the response phase, during rescue and cleanup efforts, than in the impact phase.[6]

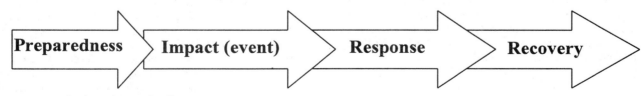

Figure 119-1. The four phases of a disaster.

The fourth and final phase of a disaster is the recovery period, which begins after the mass casualty incident has been officially declared over and no additional victims are likely to be rescued. In some disasters, the switch from response to recovery may be clearly delineated. For example, for most collapsed structure disasters, recovery efforts begin around 72 hours after the impact because it is rare for victims to survive and be rescued after that point. In other disasters, recovery activities may begin during the response phase, without a clearly defined message that the facility or community has completed the response.

Recovery period interventions include those necessary for rebuilding the facility and community in terms of physical, psychological, and economic needs. The recovery period ends when life has "gotten back to normal," even if life is not the same as before.

Infectious Disease Implications of Disasters and Mass Casualty Events

Communicable disease outbreaks are widely feared after disasters. Studies that examine the epidemiological impact of communicable diseases following mass casualty incidents find that the impact varies, depending on the situation. Studies examining acute-onset natural disasters, such as earthquakes or hurricanes, indicate that the risk of an infectious disease outbreak related to this type of event is small.[7-9] Outbreaks that occur after natural disasters often result from population displacement, such as overcrowding in community shelters, and lack of clean water or sanitation.[8] In developed countries, infectious disease outbreaks following a disaster are unusual; if they do occur, they usually involve skin, gastrointestinal, or respiratory infections.[7] Examples of this include the norovirus outbreak in a community shelter during Hurricane Katrina[7] and the doubling of infectious diseases (namely pneumonia and skin infections, including tetanus) among hospitalized patients following the 2011 Great East Japan Earthquake and tsunami.[10] In underdeveloped countries, infectious disease outbreaks following disasters are more common and are usually related to endemic pathogens, zoonotic diseases, and foodborne illness.[9] Zoonotic illnesses and vectorborne diseases increase after natural disasters due to wild and domesticated animal displacement that occurs in conjunction with human displacement, and because vector control measures may be temporarily halted.[9] Outbreaks of Hepatitis A, cholera, typhoid fever, and diarrheal illness have all been reported after natural disasters and are largely due to poor sanitation, improper food handling, and lack of healthcare access,[7] though rainfall and other environmental factors may also play a role.[11] One of the largest infectious disease outbreaks ever associated with a natural disaster occurred after the 2010 Haitian earthquake. Almost 1 year after the earthquake, an outbreak of cholera occurred in Haiti, with devastating outcomes. That outbreak accounted for over half of all cholera deaths in 2010 and was associated with more than 600,000 cases of cholera and over 7,000 deaths.[12]

Although there is a pervasive fear about potential infectious disease outbreaks caused by exposure to disaster victims' dead bodies, there is no evidence that this results in epidemics.[8] Exceptions to this would be outbreaks of cholera, viral hemorrhagic fevers, or smallpox, any of which could put people at risk from disease from exposure to victims' dead bodies if precautions are not taken.[8] Following any type of mass casualty incident, bodies of dead humans or animals should be handled using appropriate infection prevention precautions and personal protective equipment (PPE) to prevent infection transmission.[8]

Infectious disease disasters, such as a bioterrorism attack, outbreak of an emerging infectious disease, or pandemic, have the greatest potential for causing infection-related morbidity and mortality of any type of mass casualty event (see Chapter 120 Infectious Disease Disasters).

Emergency Management Preparedness

Preparedness is not a state of being perfectly prepared to respond to any type of mass casualty incident because this can never be achieved.[13] The goal is to become incrementally better prepared to respond to a disaster. Preparedness is the process of becoming better prepared to effectively recognize and respond to a mass casualty incident. This process consists of pursuing emergency management education, gaining knowledge on emergency management, planning and practicing response behaviors, and evaluating your level of preparedness.

The first step in the preparedness process is gaining knowledge through pursuit of education on emergency management. Educational topics include the following: (1) how to develop an emergency management plan, (2) what to include in an emergency management plan, (3) individuals/groups to include in the planning process, (4) how to conduct a facility assessment, (5) resource assessment, (6) designing and implementing an exercise or practice program, and (7) how to evaluate the level of preparedness of an individual, facility, or community. In addition, some disaster-specific information is required, such as information on floods, hurricanes, earthquakes, chemical and biological terrorism attacks, emerging infectious diseases, and pandemics.

Emergency Management Plans

One of the most critical elements of emergency management is the development of a comprehensive emergency management plan. There are three types of emergency management plans: (1) personal plan, (2) facility plan, and (3) community plan.[14]

Personal/Family Emergency Management Plan

A personal/family emergency management plan is designed for an individual's personal use. It should include provisions for backup care for children or adults for which you are responsible in the event that you are called in to work for an emergency during traditional nonwork hours. Your personal plan should also include a supply of food and water in case you and/or your family are trapped in your home, such as after an earthquake. Other components of a personal plan include having pet care, an out-of-state contact for your family, stores of medical equipment/supplies and PPE, and transportation during nontraditional working hours.[15]

Review your family emergency management plan with every member of your family, with special emphasis on what is to be done if the family is separated. This is an infection prevention issue because IPs will not be able to work effectively if they are worried about their family and unable to communicate with them. Recent studies indicate that many healthcare providers, including IPs, do not have a personal emergency management plan.[16,17] A 2007 study reported that only half of all IPs have a personal emergency management plan.[16] This can hinder emergency management if staff is unable to work during a mass casualty incident. It is the responsibility of all healthcare staff to have a personal plan that will allow them to work during a disaster.

Healthcare Facility Emergency Management Plan

A facility emergency management plan is a plan a healthcare facility would implement during or after a mass casualty event. Facility emergency management plan development is a multidiscipline and multiagency collaborative process; an individual working alone should not undertake it. It is best if a planning committee develops the facility emergency management plan. This committee should consist of the following members: (1) IPs, (2) hospital epidemiologist or infectious disease physician/representative, (3) nursing administration, (4) security, (5) housekeeping, (6) central supply, (7) food and nutrition, (8) hospital administration, (9) occupational health, (10) environmental health, (11) legal counsel/risk management, (12) public relations/public information officer, (13) medical staff, (14) human resources, (15) physical therapy, (16) emergency department, (17) respiratory therapy, (18) local law enforcement, (19) local FBI, (20) local emergency management services, and (21) public health representative.[18] In larger facilities, there may be many additional members and in smaller facilities there may be fewer.

In the event of a mass casualty incident, these responding groups and agencies will need to work together; it is best to have these partnerships developed before such an event occurs to ensure a better outcome. A facility emergency management plan must be a written plan that addresses issues including the following: (1) resource management (both staff and supplies), (2) communication systems/methods, (3) reporting structure, and (4) patient management. Tools are available to assist in the development of a written healthcare facility emergency management plan.[3,18–20] Although these planning tools are specific to infectious disease disaster preparedness, they can serve as the foundation for an all-hazards emergency management plan. IPs should use these tools to get involved with emergency management at the facility (i.e., hospital or healthcare facility) level.

Community Emergency Management Plan

A community emergency management plan is a plan a community would implement during or after a mass casualty incident. Community emergency management plans are a collaborative effort among traditional first responders (law enforcement, fire protection, and emergency medical services), healthcare facilities, public health officials, and other response agencies within a community. Although it was previously thought that IPs would not be needed to assist in emergency management at the community level, new evidence indicates that it is vital that IPs be involved in this activity.[4] IPs' input will be required for setting up and running alternate care sites,[21] points of dispensing (POD),[22] and community evacuation shelters,[23] and for communicating infection prevention messages to the general public.

Healthcare Facility Assessment

Facility assessment is the first step in developing a healthcare facility emergency management plan. A hazard and vulnerability assessment (HVA) should be conducted in conjunction with facility assessment. HVA tools examine region-specific hazards (flooding in floodplain areas, earthquakes in southern California, etc.). In addition, these tools assess a facility's or community's vulnerability to certain types of mass casualty events. One example is identifying hospitals that are located on a fault line and may be at an increased risk from an earthquake. An example of an HVA is one developed by Kaiser Foundation Health Plan, Inc.[24] HVA tools use a systematic approach to conducting an HVA (see Figure 119-2). The user scores the facility on such factors as the probability of a specific mass casualty incident occurring, as well as the severity or potential impact of the event if such a disaster occurred. Combined, these quantitative measures provide the facility with a relative threat/risk score. The risk score aids facilities in determining which potential disasters are highest priority for emergency management planning. An all-hazards approach must be used in emergency management so that facilities are prepared for all types of mass casualty incidents, but facilities should focus their efforts on the highest priority threats.

Performing a facility assessment related to infection prevention issues is a time-consuming, multidepartmental endeavor and should not be undertaken alone.[18] It is also important to note that The Joint Commission (TJC) has standards that address hospital emergency management, including standards that address infection prevention during disasters. TJC standards are updated fairly regularly; IPs should verify existing standards when assessing hospital emergency management plans or developing new protocols. Hospitals must address TJC standards in their emergency management plan if they wish to be accredited.

After a disaster strikes, additional healthcare facility assessments will be necessary. The evaluation of the building for structural safety is not an infection prevention issue, but evaluation for function is. Assessing the availability of a functional sewer system is an urgent priority (see the Sewage and Sanitation section), as is checking for water infiltration that can lead to mold. Dust may also pose a risk after a mass casualty incident. Because this dust may contain *Aspergillus*, the emergency management plan should specify what kind of protection is available for patients at risk for aspergillosis, procedures for reducing dust inside the facility, and policies for minimizing patient exposure to dust in and around the healthcare complex. After a natural disaster, facilities should assess that the plumbing and water systems are intact and that clean water is available

HAZARD AND VULNERABILITY ASSESSMENT TOOL
NATURALLY OCCURRING EVENTS

EVENT	PROBABILITY	SEVERITY = (MAGNITUDE - MITIGATION)						RISK
		HUMAN IMPACT	PROPERTY IMPACT	BUSINESS IMPACT	PREPARED-NESS	INTERNAL RESPONSE	EXTERNAL RESPONSE	
	Likelihood this will occur	Possibility of death or injury	Physical losses and damages	Interuption of services	Preplanning	Time, effectivness, resouces	Community/ Mutual Aid staff and supplies	Relative threat*
SCORE	0 = N/A 1 = Low 2 = Moderate 3 = High	0 = N/A 1 = Low 2 = Moderate 3 = High	0 = N/A 1 = Low 2 = Moderate 3 = High	0 = N/A 1 = Low 2 = Moderate 3 = High	0 = N/A 1 = High 2 = Moderate 3 = Low or none	0 = N/A 1 = High 2 = Moderate 3 = Low or none	0 = N/A 1 = High 2 = Moderate 3 = Low or none	0 - 100%
Hurricane	0	0	0	0	0	0	0	0%
Tornado	0	0	0	0	0	0	0	0%
Severe Thunderstorm	3	2	1	3	1	1	1	50%
Snow Fall	3	2	2	3	1	1	1	56%
Blizzard								0%
Ice Storm								0%
Earthquake								0%
Tidal Wave								0%
Temperature Extremes								0%
Drought								0%
Flood, External								0%
Wild Fire								0%
Landslide								0%
Dam Inundation								
Volcano								0%
Epidemic								0%
AVERAGE SCORE	0.38	0.25	0.19	0.38	0.13	0.13	0.13	1%

*Threat increases with percentage.

RISK = PROBABILITY * SEVERITY		
0.01	**0.13**	0.07

ASJH
3/3/2004

Figure 119-2. HVA tool for naturally occurring events.

before using the water for ingestion, cooking, cleaning, or disinfection of instruments.

During recovery, the facility will need to assess needs to return the facility to normal or baseline. This includes an assessment of the facility's emergency management plan to determine gaps that need to be addressed before another mass casualty event occurs. Facility resource assessment will remain critical; replacement of lost resources is a central component of the recovery phase. A facility may have to restock PPE, medications, and other medical supplies. They may also need to deal with a loss of staff members who fell victim to the mass casualty incident, as HCP often make up a large portion of a community's population.

Community Assessment

It is important for communities to determine their risks and vulnerabilities. Predisaster community assessments are generally broad vulnerability and risk assessments of the community.

After disaster strikes, a more focused assessment must be performed to determine who in the community is at risk. For instance, predisaster, it may be determined that floods are a risk in certain subsets of the community; however, once a flood occurs, it is imperative to rapidly assess exactly which areas of the community are affected. The information gathered during the response is usually "quick and dirty" and is utilized to identify immediate interventions required to handle the response. Data collected often include logistical data and information specific to the mass casualty incident, such as a list of people or families that live or work in a flooded area so that tetanus vaccination needs can be determined.

Assessments performed during recovery include those needed to assess the community's needs to return to normal or baseline. This includes an assessment of the community's resources and emergency management plan. In addition to replacing lost resources, the community will have to address the mental health and spiritual consequences of a large mass casualty event.

Surge Capacity

The ability of a healthcare facility to handle an influx of patients requiring medical care is known as surge capacity. Most hospitals and healthcare facilities function at maximum capacity on a routine basis and have very little surge capacity. Despite this, TJC requires hospitals to establish and improve surge capacity to meet the community's needs during a mass casualty incident. There are currently no quantitative standards in the United States regarding how much surge capacity a hospital must have. In Israel, hospitals are required to have the ability to expand to accommodate a surge of at least 20 percent over standard operating procedure.[25,26]

Surge capacity is more than simply increasing the number of patient beds. In addition to beds, surge capability resources must be available to staff those beds and manage the increased patient loads. This involves having the personnel, facilities (i.e., negative pressure rooms/areas, morgue space, laboratory processing, etc.), medical equipment/supplies (ventilators, PPE, hand hygiene products, etc.), and pharmaceuticals to care for the patients. Facilities need to factor in all surge capacity components as part of emergency management.

Researchers have examined a variety of aspects of U.S. hospital surge capacity preparedness. Although methods have been identified to simply increase bed availability by 10 to 20 percent,[25] this does not allow for a surge of patients requiring intensive care. Infectious disease disasters and terrorist events will likely result in an increased need for highly specialized treatment in intensive care beds. This can include the need for more burn and trauma intensive care beds during an incendiary event, such as a terrorist bombing, or intensive care areas that can accommodate patients needing mechanical ventilation for biological events. Even natural disasters require more resources than simply having additional beds available within the facility.

Studies indicate that most facilities fall short on having the resources and infrastructure needed to manage all aspects of patient care, especially for events that last longer than a few days.[16,27] Examples include an identified lack of ventilators, antibiotics or antiviral medications, respiratory protection (N95 respirators), negative pressure rooms/areas, laboratory support/supplies, and linens.[16,27,28] In addition, the national nursing shortage and failure to cross-train HCP limits hospitals' ability to care for an influx of severely ill patients, such as those requiring ventilatory support.[16] Some hospitals even lack 24/7 infection prevention coverage, which would make responding to an infectious disease disaster very challenging.[16]

Recent research indicates that U.S. hospitals,[16,26] home health agencies,[29] businesses,[30] and schools[31] are not as prepared as possible for mass casualty incidents of any type, especially those involving mass casualties or an infectious disease. Intensive care beds, HCP, PPE, and medical supplies are not available in sufficient numbers to address the unique needs of many mass casualty events. Even after basic surge capacity issues are better addressed, research is needed to determine how to maintain surge care for longer periods of time. Although natural disasters may be short-term events, mass casualty incidents involving a biological agent could last weeks to months. Even natural disasters can require long-term surge capacity, as was evidenced by Hurricane Katrina in 2005, the Haiti earthquake in 2010, and the Great East Japan Earthquake in 2011.

Assessing for Surge Capacity

The availability and backup supplies of both staff and equipment should be assessed. Most healthcare facilities keep less than 3 days' stock of commonly used medical supplies. In the event of a mass casualty event with an accompanying large influx of patients, daily stocks of supplies will quickly be depleted. This may include PPE such as gloves, masks, ventilators, and linens. It is best to plan for this increased need for equipment prior to an event. Memoranda of agreement between local and regional facilities and companies help ensure that equipment is available rapidly when needed. Healthcare facilities should consider forming or joining a hospital disaster alliance.

Staffing will be a major issue following a mass casualty event. More staff will be needed to address the patient management issues, such as triage, patient care, and dealing with the "worried well." It is best to have written plans for obtaining backup staff for extra shifts during a mass casualty incident. A recent study indicated that U.S. hospitals do not have sufficient staff to handle a surge of patients.[16] A 2007 study reported that only half of all U.S. hospitals have a plan for obtaining additional staff during disasters.[16] Staff will require frequent rest breaks, which will also need to be addressed in the plan. Whenever possible, it is best to have memoranda of agreement with healthcare facilities and staffing agencies or groups to ensure more rapid deployment of backup staff when needed. Another option for increasing staff surge capacity is to offer incentives to encourage employees to report to work during a mass casualty incident. Although staff indicate that incentives are one way to entice them to work during a mass casualty event, less than half of all hospitals in a 2007 study reported that they plan to offer incentives to employees.[16] Of the hospitals that did report including employee incentives in their emergency management plan, the most frequent incentives included free child or adult family member care, temporary housing and subsistence, and priority access to anti-infective therapy or vaccination.[16]

The facility emergency management plan should identify the cost of disaster-related supplies and services as completely as possible. This will facilitate requests for emergency assistance from the Federal Emergency Management Agency (FEMA). Costs of preparation should also be tracked and documented.

Alternate Care Sites

Alternate care sites are temporary locations for providing medical services during a mass casualty incident. An alternate care site may consist of a hotel, closed hospital, mobile field hospital, nursing home, converted warehouse, school, stadium/sports arena, convention center, fairground, meeting hall, gymnasium, health club, or any building or space that is adapted for providing medical care.[21,32] Alternate care sites can even include the use of large tented areas, such as those used during past smallpox outbreaks.[21] Alternate care sites are used to decrease patient flow and congestion problems at hospitals during the busiest times of the mass casualty event, allowing the hospital to manage only the most severely ill patients. The level of medical treatment provided at alternate care sites will vary by the community and the size/scope of the event. Because medical care will be administered at these sites, the risk of infection transmission exists. Therefore, it is essential that IPs be involved in developing or implementing an infection prevention program for alternate care sites, regardless of whether the site is under the umbrella of the healthcare facility or is part of the community.[21] This will necessitate IP involvement in emergency management at the community level.

Evacuation

Some mass casualty incidents will require building and/or area evacuation. This is most likely to be necessary during disasters that cause building structural damage, such as earthquakes, tornados, bombings, or explosions. For example, 11 hospitals had to be evacuated because they were floodbound, had electrical failures, or loss of water after Hurricane Katrina hit,[33] and one hospital was completely destroyed during the 2011 tornado that hit Joplin, Missouri.[34] In addition, the majority of the hospitals and healthcare facilities in New Orleans were destroyed or unable to function after Hurricane Katrina, necessitating the evacuation of tens of thousands of individuals from their homes and hospitals.[35] Safe relocation of patients, worried well, family, and visitors must be planned in advance, including transfer and patient placement protocols for potentially contagious patients.

Community Evacuation Shelters

Some disasters may require the displacement of individuals from their homes into community evacuation shelters. These shelters can house hundreds or thousands of individuals in overcrowded conditions, often with limited access to traditional sanitation, food, and water control.[23] A lack of resources for cleaning and hand hygiene supplies can contribute to disease spread in shelters. In addition, it is likely that individuals requiring community sheltering may be at increased risk for infection due to underlying illness that prevented their evacuation from the affected area.[23] All of these conditions can contribute to disease spread and infectious disease outbreaks among sheltered individuals.[23] Past experience with natural mass casualty incidents indicates that the most likely infectious diseases/conditions to occur in community evacuation shelters include skin/dermatological, gastrointestinal, and respiratory infections.[7] IP involvement is needed at the community level to assist in setting up an infection prevention program for evacuation shelters. Guidelines for preventing infectious disease transmission in shelters during disasters have been developed by the Association for Professionals in Infection Control and Epidemiology (APIC).[23]

Reporting Disasters

Healthcare facilities need procedures for reporting mass casualty incidents both internally and externally. Internally, all hospital departments will require notification of a disaster. If the mass casualty event involves an infectious disease, rapid notification of the infection prevention and/or hospital epidemiology department is vital. Externally, local and regional responding agencies must be notified of disasters. Examples of responding agencies include public health, emergency medical services, law enforcement, and emergency managers. Procedures for internal and external notification/reporting should be incorporated into the healthcare facility's emergency management plan.

Communicable Disease Reporting

Routine communicable disease reporting will need to continue during a mass casualty incident. In addition, certain communicable diseases may need to be reported in a timely manner during a disaster because of the risk of secondary spread. For example, chickenpox or measles that occurs in a disaster-affected population should be reported to the public health department right away, as these diseases can result in rapid spread in crowded surroundings such as community evacuation shelters.

Resource Management

Resource management must be well planned to ensure the best allocation of resources during a mass casualty incident. This means planning for obtaining, allocating, and distributing resources during a mass casualty event. Resources include both staff and supplies necessary to effectively recognize and respond to all types of mass casualty incidents. Does the facility have enough beds to accommodate a large surge in patients? Is there a large enough qualified staff to care for these patients? Are there adequate stocks of medical supplies, equipment, and pharmaceuticals to care for a large increase of patients? These questions must be addressed during facility emergency management planning to ensure the best response.

Resource assessment should take place as part of facility assessment. The following are items that must be assessed: (1) on-hand functional equipment, (2) sources and quantities of backup equipment, (3) on-hand pharmaceutical supplies, (4) sources and quantities of backup pharmaceutical supplies, (5) amount of available staff, (6) source and size of backup staff, and (7) surge capacity of the facility. Each event will pose unique challenges in terms of resources required. Some disasters, such as an earthquake or flood, will require physical plant resource needs, such as safe shelter, food, and water. Other mass casualty incidents may require different or additional resource needs, such as PPE, medications, and vaccines after a bioterrorism attack or pandemic (see Chapter 120 Infectious Diseases Disasters for detailed information on infectious disease emergency management).

It is best to take an all-hazards approach to emergency management. The type of disaster that will occur cannot be predicted; therefore, a broad approach will help ensure a better response to any mass casualty incident. The emergency management plan should address the possibility of prolonged loss of electricity, potable water, or another essential utility. How available resources will be assessed and maintained on an ongoing basis should be specified.

During the response phase of a mass casualty event, resources will quickly become depleted. Utilizing prearranged memoranda of agreement between healthcare facilities and vendors should help alleviate scrambling for resources during the mass casualty incident. As the disaster response progresses, constant evaluation of resource stocks must be performed so that gaps may be quickly identified and backup stocks may be obtained. IPs may have to assess available antibiotic prophylaxis or vaccination doses or amounts of PPE for isolation. They will also have to assess the amount of available drinking water and clean water for handwashing, hand hygiene products, bathing, linen management, equipment sterilization, dietary maintenance, dialysis, and toilet facilities. Another critical aspect of resource assessment during a mass casualty incident response is the assessing availability of sewage facilities to safely dispose of human waste.

Crisis Standards of Care

Despite the best planning efforts, resources may become completely depleted following a mass casualty incident. If this occurs, supplies may need to be rationed based on priority. Making prioritization decisions in advance of a mass casualty event is known as developing crisis standards of care. These prioritization algorithms are only to be used in times of crisis or disaster when routine standards of care cannot be met. For instance, decisions will need to be made about which patients will receive limited numbers of ventilators or other medical equipment. Protective equipment for staff may also need to be rationed. For example, staff who perform aerosolizing procedures that put them at high risk from airborne-spread diseases should be a top priority for respiratory protection in the form of N95 respirators or their equivalent. Lower-risk areas may need to reuse respirators, cohort infected patients, and/or use a lower level of respiratory protection. If sterilization of reusable equipment is limited, consider high-level disinfection when acceptable. Other supplies may need to be rationed or prioritized as well. Department managers should be involved in determining what amounts of supplies essential to their operation should be kept on hand. Keep in mind that operations may be heavier than usual, and that a supply adequate for three normal days may not be adequate during a mass casualty event.

Developing crisis standards of care for allocating scarce resources is an important component of emergency management and it has infectious disease implications. Deciding who receives limited doses of anti-infective therapy or vaccination can contribute to disease transmission or control. This is also true for PPE. Priorities must be determined before a mass casualty incident strikes, and procedures for safely reusing or allocating scarce PPE must be written into the facility emergency management plan. An example of existing guidance on allocating scarce resources is the APIC position paper, *Extending the Use and/or Reusing Respiratory Protection in Healthcare Settings during Disasters.*[36]

Patient Management

Patient management is the largest component of disaster response and as such is an essential facet of emergency management. Mass casualty events pose unique challenges to healthcare facilities. How will the facility juggle a large number of acutely ill patients and deal with an influx of the worried well? It will not be business as usual. Rapid triage and health assessment will be critical to decreasing morbidity and mortality. In addition, infection prevention precautions may need to be implemented in the event of a mass casualty incident involving an infectious agent. Healthcare facility emergency management plans must address patient surge, including having procedures for managing potentially contagious patients.

Triage will be an essential component of patient management. One potential danger is that the hospital emergency department can be overrun following a mass casualty incident, causing chaos that complicates patient care. One option is to set up off-site triage areas, such as alternate care sites.[32] Severely ill patients can then be transported to the hospital and less critical patients can remain at the off-site center to receive minimal care until hospital beds become available or when the patient's status becomes more critical. Off-site triage areas are recommended for handling and housing the worried well. This allows the hospital to maintain beds, staff, and supplies for the most critically ill patients. It also keeps transportation routes open both within and to the hospital to allow better flow of critically ill patients, medical supplies, and staff.

Another concern will be where to physically locate family members while patients are being triaged and treated. If the event involves an infectious disease scenario (such as a bioterrorism attack, outbreak of an emerging infectious disease, or a pandemic), arrangements will need to be made to identify potentially contagious individuals and separate them from others. These questions are best addressed during facility emergency management planning.

Two of the first steps in increasing bed surge capacity to handle the influx of patients is to empty the emergency department and discharge as many inpatients as possible to make way for incoming patients.[29] Patients' health status will need to be assessed to determine who can safely be discharged to home and who will require ongoing care at an alternate care site, long-term care, or home care. Patient discharge decision-making must take the patient's need for isolation into account. Some healthcare settings cannot accommodate a potentially contagious patient; this may limit patient discharge options and slow mass casualty incident response. During mass casualty events, such as a pandemic, all healthcare service providers will be swamped, which will make patient discharge a challenge. Hospitals should work with nonacute care agencies as part of disaster preparedness to ensure that rapid and effective patient discharge can occur during a mass casualty incident. Protocols and procedures for rapid discharge need to be arranged in advance.

Nonessential services will likely be temporarily ceased to divert resources to mass casualty incident patient management. This will include the cessation of nonemergency surgeries and other nonessential services. Facility emergency management plans should outline procedures for how essential services, such as obstetrical, emergency, dialysis, and outpatient services will be maintained. Patient transfer to other facilities may be needed; however, in mass casualty events, all local facilities may be overwhelmed. Transfer to more distant facilities may be necessary, though this may not be an option during a pandemic when all areas of the United States may be affected.

Infection Prevention Priorities Common to Various Disasters

Early Detection and Surveillance

Rapid detection of a disaster is crucial to a successful response. For all mass casualty incidents, the sooner the incident and at-risk patients are identified, the lower the likely morbidity, mortality, and cost. Planning for early detection of most mass casualty events is not necessary. For all natural disasters and even traditional or chemical terrorism, there are immediate, obvious signs that something unusual has happened, ranging from damaged buildings in an earthquake to a huge influx of patients immediately after a chemical attack. Early detection strategies are necessary for infectious disease disasters, on the other hand, because these events may be more difficult to detect, such as a covert release of an aerosolized agent. For information on syndromic surveillance and early detection of infectious disease disasters, see Chapter 120 Infectious Disease Disasters.

Surveillance

Surveillance after a mass casualty incident will likely be critical to decreasing costs, morbidity, and mortality associated with a disaster, depending on the type of event that occurred. This is especially true in the case of an infectious disease disaster, after which identification of new cases will be essential to save lives.

Infection prevention surveillance during mass casualty events must be maintained in a practical, feasible manner, even though the IP will probably be assigned to disaster-related duties.[4] Problems specific to the disaster must be detected, assessed, and acted on in a timely manner. Problems existing before the mass casualty incident must continue to be monitored—for example, an outbreak of methicillin-resistant *Staphylococcus aureus* (MRSA) that began before the disaster.

Disaster surveillance is based on the same principles as traditional surveillance but may require a more "quick and dirty" approach due to the urgency of the situation. Active surveillance initiated as part of mass casualty incident response is considered sentinel surveillance, and the primary goal is to quickly identify

new cases. Surveillance programs implemented in response to a disaster are generally short term and end when the crisis ends or shortly thereafter. This is in contrast to ongoing public health and hospital-based surveillance programs such as bloodstream infection surveillance or tuberculosis (TB) monitoring. It will also be important to conduct community-based surveillance for infections following a mass casualty event. This will include having surveillance systems in place in alternate care sites and community evacuation shelters.[21,23]

Collecting and communicating credible surveillance data during a mass casualty incident provides the best methods for stopping rumors and for focusing attention on real health problems. It must be decided who is to collect, analyze, and report the data; what is to be collected; and for how long. This information should be outlined in the facility emergency management plan (see Chapter 11 Surveillance for more information).

Surveillance during the recovery period will most likely consist of a return to routine surveillance activities. In some cases, facilities may choose to continue surveillance for indicators begun as part of sentinel surveillance. For instance, during recovery from a bioterrorism attack, facilities may choose to continue active surveillance for the causative agent disease (such as pneumonic plague or inhalational anthrax) until they are certain the outbreak is over. Ongoing active surveillance will most likely be needed after infectious disease disasters in order to continue to identify new cases.

In addition, facilities also need to decide if new surveillance indicators are necessary. After recovering from a bioterrorism attack using anthrax, some facilities may choose to initiate a new syndromic surveillance program to quickly identify a potential future infectious disease disaster using any of a number of potential agents/diseases. Obviously, this would be resource intensive and would require a joint decision between administration and infection prevention.

Some facilities may use the findings of the epidemiological investigation to determine which aspects of surveillance should be maintained or initiated. Epidemiology during the response period focuses only on the immediate needs related to the mass casualty event. Once the crisis is over, a more in-depth investigation can be performed, focusing on risk factors, groups most affected, route of transmission, interventions that worked or did not work, and so on. The results of the epidemiological investigation must be disseminated throughout the facility and public. Publication in a peer-reviewed scientific journal should also be considered to share the results and lessons learned with a wider audience.

Epidemiological Outbreak Investigation During Disaster Response and Recovery

Few mass casualty incidents require a large-scale infectious disease epidemiological investigation, but almost every disaster requires some form of investigation to identify those affected and track patient follow-up. Each mass casualty event is unique and will pose distinct differences in the investigation. Floods, hurricanes, and earthquakes will usually not require an infectious disease epidemiological investigation, though they may if respiratory, foodborne, or waterborne illnesses occur. An example of this was the extensive epidemiological investigation of the cholera outbreak following the 2010 earthquake in Haiti.[12] Infectious disease disasters, on the other hand, will likely require an extensive epidemiological investigation. In this situation, rapid identification of exposed individuals and initiation of prophylactic therapy or vaccination is essential to decreasing morbidity and mortality.

An outbreak investigation would be warranted for any mass casualty incident that involves a communicable disease or one in which epidemiological information needs to be collected and analyzed, such as risk factor and outcome data. Typically, the epidemiology performed during disaster response is limited. The response phase is generally relatively short, and there is not sufficient time to establish and implement an epidemiological investigation (this occurs more frequently during the recovery phase). This is not true for all mass casualty events; infectious disease disasters are exceptions. For infectious disease disasters, the epidemiological investigation will be crucial to halting the outbreak.

Infection Prevention and Control Coverage

It is vital to maintain around-the-clock infection prevention coverage during a mass casualty incident, even if the facility's IPs will also have disaster-related duties to perform. Research indicates that some U.S. hospitals currently lack around-the-clock infection prevention coverage; this gap needs to be addressed before a mass casualty event occurs.[16] Infection prevention coverage in nonhospital settings (such as alternate care sites and community evacuation shelters) may need to be assigned to an infection prevention designee. If this is to occur, these designees require education and training on how to implement and evaluate an infection prevention program in these settings. Infection prevention coverage in community-based nonhospital settings needs to be coordinated with community emergency managers/planners and/or public health officials.

Hand Hygiene

Hand hygiene remains one of the most essential infection prevention procedures following a mass casualty incident. Hand hygiene must be available even if tap water supplies are disrupted and/or hand hygiene products become depleted.

Healthcare facilities should maintain a stockpile of hand hygiene products, including soap and alcohol-based hand rub (ABHR) products, or have a memorandum of agreement for obtaining additional supplies during a mass casualty event. In addition, access to clean water for hand washing should be a priority (see Chapter 27 Hand Hygiene).

Patient Placement and Isolation

Patient placement and isolation procedures are generally covered in a healthcare facility's routine policies. However, mass casualty incidents may prevent facilities from implementing routine standards such as placement in a private room for isolation. Healthcare facilities should outline protocols for cohorting potentially contagious patients as part of disaster planning. In addition, healthcare facilities need protocols to ensure that airborne infection isolation precautions can still be implemented during mass casualty events. Airborne infection isolation for patients with TB or other diseases spread by airborne droplet nuclei must be maintained. The emergency management plan should state how this would be done, including having a plan for short-term and long-term negative pressure surge capacity.[18,37] Temporary negative pressure for a room or area can be established during a mass casualty incident or patients can be transported to another facility to increase negative pressure surge capacity.[37] Ventilation systems can be evaluated while on emergency power. HCP should watch for an increase in cases of TB or other airborne spread diseases in the subsequent months, as these may be related to the mass casualty event (crowding in community evacuation shelters). Treatment of TB patients in ambulatory care or directly observed therapy programs must be maintained.

Quarantine

Quarantine is another potential component of emergency management. It involves restricting individuals' movement as a means of preventing infection spread. Quarantine differs from isolation is that it restricts the movement of individuals who have a known or suspected exposure to an infectious disease or contagious individual but who are not yet showing signs of infection. Quarantine will likely only be needed during infectious disease disasters. Additional information on quarantine is provided in Chapter 120 Infectious Disease Disasters.

Occupational Health Issues

Most employee health decisions fall under the occupational health department. However, some employee health issues that arise during mass casualty incidents have infectious disease implications and must therefore have IP involvement. Examples include staff assignment to potentially contagious patients; cohorting of patients or staff; allocation of limited doses of anti-infective therapy, prophylaxis, or vaccination; and distribution of limited protective equipment. Protocols must be developed that outline procedures for following up on staff work exposures; delineating prioritization plans for limited doses of anti-infective therapy, prophylaxis, or vaccination; and allocating PPE when supplies become insufficient or depleted. Staff at high risk from infection (i.e., pregnant or immunocompromised individuals) and high-risk procedures (such as aerosolizing procedures during an outbreak of a droplet or airborne spread disease) should be identified as part of emergency management planning. Protocols should be developed that address how to decrease risk to these individuals, such as reassignment or furlough.[18]

Food and Water Safety

The most serious health hazard after most types of mass casualty incidents is the deterioration in environmental conditions, particularly in water supply and disposal of human wastes.[8,9]

Water is essential for numerous healthcare facility functions. Drinking water must be available immediately. A minimum of 2 liters per person per day must be provided for both patients and workers. Water will also be needed for hand washing, bathing, washing dishes, washing linen, sterilizing, cooking, dialysis, processing of scopes, hydrotherapy, flushing toilets, and other purposes. Waterborne diarrheal illness is a major concern after natural disasters in camps among displaced individuals and can have a high mortality rate.[38] It is vital that water safety practices be implemented after natural disasters.

During emergency management planning, estimate the amount of water that would be needed to maintain patients, HCP, and necessary healthcare facility functions for a minimum of 3 to 5 days. Backup water supplies should provide 25 gallons/day per patient. Federal agencies may be able to provide portable water purification systems and power generators. Determine how much water should be stored on-site, how much could be stored off-site, and how much could be obtained from outside resources at the time of the mass casualty event. Methods for gaining access to water resources should be described in the emergency management plan. Contracts or memoranda of agreement should be developed as part of the emergency management planning process.

If water quality is uncertain, it may be purified by (1) boiling for 1 minute, or (2) adding 1/8 teaspoon of bleach per gallon. Mix thoroughly and allow to stand for 30 minutes before using.[39]

During the response phase, tap water should be tested immediately. The role of the individual authorized to assess the water quality should be specified in the emergency management plan. Whenever water quality is questionable, clearance should be obtained from public health officials before resuming use. If its appearance or pressure is different from usual, use should be restricted. Communication regarding water safety will be essential to protect staff, visitors, and patients. New technologies now exist for treating existing water on-site rather than continuously transporting in bottled water, a practice that is more sustainable and affordable.[40]

Sources should be prominently labeled or hooded to restrict use. The plan should specify how this would be done. Assess inside or outside water resources, and plan for distribution. Water is an important resource that must remain available. On-hand quantities must be tracked as part of ongoing resource assessments taking place during the disaster response.

Food must be provided for all individuals who will remain on the premises, including quarantined individuals. Balanced meals are necessary to both physical and psychological health. During emergency management planning, food requirements needed for a mass casualty incident should be determined. Patients and staff must be included, and other groups (e.g., visitors who are present, clinic patients, and family members of the staff) should be considered. This decision should be included in the emergency management plan, and an estimate should be provided of the number of people needing to be fed.

As part of emergency management planning, the power supply to the dietary department should be assessed to ensure that food safety would be possible following a mass casualty event. At least one refrigerator and freezer should be on emergency power. Assess the adequacy of temporary lighting, if emergency power should be unavailable for an interval. Review the emergency management plan for the dietary department. It should specify the order in which food will be used to ensure food safety: (1) refrigerated food on hand, (2) food from unpowered freezers, and, lastly, (3) disaster reserve supplies. The tendency is generally to rush into reserve supplies too fast, while food in an unpowered refrigerator becomes unusable. Plan to provide food for staff (and others as you choose) as soon as the response phase begins. Available food provides both a psychological reassurance that the situation is under control and a physiologic calming effect from the stimulation of the parasympathetic nervous system, with resulting inhibition of the sympathetic nervous system.

During the mass casualty event response, food service practices must be monitored for basic sanitation. Monitor holding temperatures and the length of time food is held in the danger zone (45°F to 140°F).[21] Food that requires refrigeration that has been kept at room temperature for 2 or more hours or any food that has been kept for an hour or more in a room above 90°F should be discarded.[21] Contaminated food, most often associated with poor water safety, can result in high mortality (up to 40 percent) if diarrheal illness occurs.[38]

Sewage and Sanitation

Trash pickup may not occur as scheduled following a mass casualty incident. The emergency management plan should identify areas for sanitary storage of solid waste as well as regulated medical waste until routine sanitation practices can be resumed. In addition, toilet facilities must be available with minimal delay during a disaster. The emergency management plan should specify both short-term and long-term plans for meeting this need.

The most critical information needed will be the function of the sewer system. Earthquakes may break sewer lines; floods or hurricanes may overwhelm them. A fire or tornado would probably leave them intact. If sewer disruption is a possibility, define in the emergency management plan who will assess their function and how the results will be communicated. It is an urgent priority that toilets not be flushed if the sewers are broken, as this will result in a flood of heavily contaminated water at some unspecified location. Negotiate service contracts with a reliable chemical toilet company. Clarify whether the company can assist with disposal of wastes collected before their arrival. Decide how many units will be needed and where they will be placed, remembering that they must be accessible to the servicing trucks (a location near an outside drain is ideal).

Plan for temporary toilet facilities for the hours before the chemical toilets can be delivered. There is no aesthetic solution to this problem, and all solutions have advantages and disadvantages. A few solutions include (1) three plastic bags in a bucket,

(2) one small bag for one use only, and (3) commercial disposable urinals. The military solution of a trench is not suitable for urban environments.

Advantages to the three plastic bags in a bucket include using readily available materials and a quick setup. Tie each bag separately, and store used bags in a leak-proof container, such as a garbage can, until the chemical toilet company can collect them. Disadvantages are that they must be monitored to prevent overfilling and that this method is not pleasant. Addition of a gel powder could be considered.

Single-use small bags also use materials on hand and are a cleaner option. Disadvantages include requiring a large supply of bags, the danger of leakage, and storage of used bags.

Commercial disposable urinals can be used either individually or to fit commodes. These are relatively aesthetic, but involve added expense. One disadvantage is that they must be pre-planned and on-site before the disaster strikes.

If sewer disruption is likely, the emergency management plan should address whether the healthcare organization should remain in a building without this function. This is a factor to consider in making a decision on building evacuation. If sewers are intact, better alternatives are available, even if the water supply is interrupted.

Pouring a bucket of water down a toilet may allow temporary flushing when water service is not available, and the water used need not be clean. A crew could make rounds with a large can of water on a cart. This method works well, but is labor intensive. One flush may be available in the system. The disadvantage with this is that it is often wasted early, and then is no longer available. Use toilets without flushing until better arrangements can be made. This is not aesthetic, but it is safe if the sewers are intact.

Bedpans may be emptied into whatever container is in use for ambulatory people. Consider discarding heavily soiled bedpans, if supplies permit. An alternative is to place the pan inside a large plastic bag before use, molding the bag inside the pan to form a liner that can be discarded after use.

Anti-Infective Therapy and Vaccination

Some mass casualty events, especially biological events, may require the use of anti-infective therapy or mass vaccination interventions. Vaccine-preventable diseases that are endemic to the area hit by disaster pose the biggest risk postdisaster. For example, areas with endemic measles have experienced measles outbreaks in camps and shelters following natural disasters.[38] It is important to consider mass immunization during a measles outbreak that occurs in a disaster-affected community (such as in a community evacuation shelter) or during an infectious disease disaster.

Programs designed to distribute mass treatment, prophylaxis, or vaccination in a short period of time require unique interventions. Sites used for mass distribution of anti-infective therapy or vaccination are known as PODs. Their success will be dependent on advance planning, coordination, and communication among many groups and agencies. PODs are most effective when located off hospital property to keep noncritically ill individuals away from hospitals and treatment centers. An exception to this is facility-based occupational health programs that may distribute treatment, prophylaxis, or vaccination to employees. Information on how to implement infection prevention practices in PODs have been published.[22] Additional information on anti-infective therapy is provided in Chapter 120 Infectious Disease Disasters.

Decontamination

Decontamination is the reduction or removal of chemical or biological hazardous agents.[23] There are two means of decontamination: physical and chemical. Physical decontamination includes removing the hazardous agent through physical means, such as washing, scrubbing, or rinsing. Chemical decontamination is the use of chemical agents to remove hazardous agents.

Decontamination may or may not be necessary after a mass casualty incident, depending on the following factors: (1) type of mass casualty event, (2) how soon the event is identified, and (3) source of concern (environment or patient). For most mass casualty incidents, patient decontamination will not be necessary. One exception to this is a chemical terrorism attack, following which rapid, appropriate patient decontamination will be necessary to decrease morbidity and mortality. Patient decontamination may also be necessary after a bioterrorism attack (see Chapter 120 Infectious Disease Disasters). For many mass casualty incidents, patient decontamination will occur either at the site of the event or another off-site location designated for decontamination procedures.[23] Despite this, hospitals and healthcare facilities should be prepared to perform patient decontamination as part of having an all-hazards emergency management plan.

Patient Decontamination

Patient decontamination begins with the removal of contaminated clothing. If removal is indicated, patient clothing should be handled only by personnel wearing appropriate PPE and placed in an impervious bag to prevent further environmental contamination.

Patient decontamination recommendations for biological terrorism are different from those for certain chemicals, such as blister agents, which may respond better to dry powder decontamination compounds.[41] However, these powder agents are not widely available in the civilian population. For that reason, some hospitals or communities may choose to use traditional soap and water decontamination, regardless of the chemical agent to which the patient was exposed. After removal of contaminated clothing, patients should be instructed (or assisted, if necessary) to immediately shower with soap and water, to include the shampooing of hair. Potentially harmful practices, such as bathing patients with bleach solutions, are unnecessary and should be avoided. Clean water, saline solution, or commercial ophthalmic solutions are recommended for rinsing eyes. Another option is to use baby shampoo because it does not sting the eyes during rinsing. Special consideration must be made for children and elderly persons during patient decontamination. Children are at higher risk from hypothermia than adults, especially following decontamination. Warming blankets, heat lamps, warmers, and other such equipment must be on hand to accommodate children during patient decontamination procedures.[41] Whenever possible, warm water and decontamination facilities that can accommodate families should be made available.

Environmental Decontamination

Environmental decontamination is the removal of chemical or biological hazards from inanimate objects. Although environmental decontamination will not be necessary for most types of mass casualty incidents, it may be required in some circumstances.[41] Indoor environmental sources may require decontamination strategies following any type of mass casualty incident that results in flooding, overcrowded living conditions, or lack of clean water. An example of this is the cleaning/disinfection of alternate care sites and community evacuation shelters that is necessary following a mass casualty event.[21,23] An environmental inspection and cleaning/disinfection will be needed before reopening a room, floor, or building after it has been closed for a length of time.

Environmental decontamination will also be necessary after any mass casualty incident that involves a hazardous or infectious agent that is spread by hand-to-hand contact or contact with fomites. Some examples include a chemical terrorism event or bioterrorism attack using smallpox, anthrax, or a viral hemorrhagic fever agent. Environmental decontamination in these circumstances includes the disinfection of all horizontal surfaces using a healthcare facility-approved EPA-registered product (see Chapter 120 Infectious Disease Disasters). The use of more stringent PPE may be needed for decontamination of surfaces contaminated by chemicals. The Department of Defense website (http://www.defenselink.mil/) provides more information on decontamination strategies following a chemical terrorism attack.

Postmortem Care and Morgue Surge Capacity

In any disaster, some level of mortality is expected. Provisions must be made in advance for storage and/or transport of corpses. Most morgues can house no more than a dozen bodies. How will the facility or community morgue handle a greater number of victims (i.e., have morgue surge capacity)? Consider planning an off-site location to be used as a temporary morgue, and arrange for the services of a local mortician to handle transport of fatalities. Be sure that adequate supplies of body bags can be obtained. For most disasters, individual burial is preferred over cremation or mass burial.[8] The risk of disease transmission from corpses to the living is very low after most disasters; exceptions would include victims who had cholera, smallpox, or viral hemorrhagic fever.[8]

Pet Management

Disasters that require displacement of individuals, such as floods, hurricanes, or earthquakes, may result in patients, visitors, or staff bringing pets to hospitals or healthcare facilities. Management of service animals for disabled individuals or those that are used for healthcare-related procedures are covered in Chapter 122 Animals Visiting in Healthcare Facilities. Pets differ from service animals; hospitals cannot accept pets because of health and safety regulations. Because pets may be brought to the hospital during a mass casualty incident, healthcare facilities should coordinate with community emergency managers to arrange for pet placement in the event of a mass casualty event. During a disaster, hospitals should communicate with staff regarding where they can take their pets for temporary placement/housing in the community if displacement is necessary.

Pest Management

Natural disasters, especially hurricanes and floods, are likely to result in an increase in insects and other pests in or around the affected community due to rain and high water levels. Healthcare facilities may become infested with insects and/or vermin seeking warmth, moisture, and food. Some insects and animals may be bothersome only, but others can spread disease. Examples include the link between mice and hantavirus, or mosquitos and West Nile virus. Rodents, such as rats and mice, can spread disease by contaminating food and the environment or by biting/scratching humans. Pests can also invade medical supplies.

The following environmental controls should be implemented to minimize pests after disasters: (1) store garbage and medical waste in closed containers located away from the facility, (2) do not have open boxes or pipes within the facility as these can become nests or breeding grounds for pests, and (3) obtain pest control services as needed, including spraying for mosquitos or setting traps for mice. In addition, the facility's physical structure should be evaluated for any possible entrances for pests, and if found, should be eliminated. Examples include windows with torn or missing screens, unclosed doors that lead to the outside of the building, or sources of standing water.

Natural disasters may prevent routine garbage collection from occurring; delayed waste removal increases the risk for rodent infestation. To minimize this, food and water safety protocols should be implemented, including storing food and water in rodentproof lidded containers consisting of glass, thick plastic, or metal.

Healthcare agencies should develop protocols for safely capturing, killing, or eliminating rodents that get into the facility. Guidelines for developing these procedures are available from the Centers for Disease Control and Prevention (CDC).[42]

Vulnerable and Special Needs Populations

Although disasters can strike any community and affect people of all ages and races, regardless of health status, certain groups of individuals are more at risk from morbidity and mortality during mass casualty incidents. These individuals with special needs are known as special needs or vulnerable populations. Children, elderly persons, those who are immunocompromised, and pregnant women are examples of such groups.[43] Meeting the needs of vulnerable groups must be addressed as part of disaster planning and included in the emergency management plan at the facility and community level.

Special needs individuals are those who may need additional assistance before, during, and after a mass casualty incident in terms of maintaining their independence, communication, transportation, supervision, and access to medical care. This includes individuals who are disabled, live in institutionalized settings, or who lack transportation. Special needs individuals also include those who speak limited or no English and may have difficulty communicating with response agencies and those who are very young (pediatrics) or elderly who may be at an increased risk from morbidity or mortality from the mass casualty event.[43]

Disabled Individuals

The term "disabled" describes a broad range of afflictions that affect individuals, including conditions that impair hearing, sight, speech, and mobility. The type of disability affects how the individual can respond to a mass casualty incident. For instance, individuals with limited mobility may need extra assistance during disasters that require evacuation and require special accommodations for transportation. In addition, disabled individuals may need specialized medical equipment/supplies, such as service dogs/animals, hearing aids, translators/interpreters, walkers, wheelchairs, etc.[44] Historically, emergency management plans have lacked sufficient accommodations for disabled individuals, which has placed these individuals at risk during mass casualty events.[44] It is important to address disabled individuals in all facility and community emergency management plans.

Pediatrics

Children are at increased risk from disasters because of physiological, psychological, sociological, and developmental reasons. Young children, especially those under the age of 5, have a significantly higher mortality rate during mass casualty incidents than adults.[45] Children have a higher respiratory rate than adults and disproportionate body surface area-to-weight ratio, which puts them at risk from inhaling aerosolized biological or chemical contaminates or absorbing environmental toxins through the skin.[41] Children are also at higher risk than adults from head and chest injuries, musculoskeletal, and spinal injuries during mass casualty incidents due to a variety of physiological reasons.[46] Hypothermic and hyperthermic injuries and thermal regulatory problems are more common in children than adults after mass casualty events because of children's

body surface to body mass ratio. Volume depletion also occurs more rapidly in children than adults, making hydration an important consideration when caring for children after a mass casualty incident. More information can be found in Chapter 42 Pediatrics.

Young children have limited mobility, cognitive, and communication skills/abilities, which put them at risk during mass casualty events. Children may not be able to get away from the disaster or let others know that they need assistance. Newborns and children with immunodeficiencies are at an increased risk from infection, especially during an infectious disease disaster.

Healthcare facilities should consider that they may receive pediatric patients during mass casualty events, even if the facility is not a traditional pediatric hospital. Past mass casualty incidents indicate that most children receive medical care in general hospitals rather than pediatric facilities during mass casualty events.[45] Hospitals need to be prepared to address pediatric concerns during disasters, including the need for special medical equipment/supplies that are specific to children. Examples of such equipment include different doses of medications (sometimes based on the child's weight), smaller endotracheal tubes, needles, intravenous kits, linens, warming supplies for patient decontamination, etc. Community resource sharing would be appropriate and should be coordinated through the community emergency management reporting structure. Healthcare facilities also need to address pediatric concerns during disaster drills, something that has historically been neglected.[45]

Geriatrics

Elderly individuals are at an increased risk of morbidity and mortality following mass casualty incidents due to normal physiological changes, such as decreased mobility, impaired sight and hearing, and declining response to immunizations and medications. Most elderly individuals have a pulse/temperature dissociation that masks the signs of infection, making diagnosis much more difficult than in adults or children.[47] In addition, cognitive impairment and/or altered mental status changes common in elderly persons put this group at risk during disaster response. Frail elderly persons and those who live in institutionalized settings such as long-term care or nursing homes, assisted living, mobile home parks, and subsidized housing are especially vulnerable to mass casualty events due to limited mobility and multiple underlying medical illnesses.[47] Individuals with comorbidities, such as diabetes, cardiovascular disease, and hematological alterations, are at an increased risk because they may have limited access to medical care or pharmaceuticals during disaster response or may have adverse reactions to medications due to drug interactions. More information on elderly persons can be found in Chapter 40 Geriatrics.

Healthcare facilities, including hospitals and long-term care centers, must include accommodations for elderly persons in their emergency management plan. Extra time will be needed to evacuate areas that house frail elderly persons, and staff must be trained on how to perform these procedures. Communication between facilities is essential to providing seamless continuity of care if elderly persons are to be transferred during a mass casualty incident. Coordination will be required between the hospital and other healthcare agencies, such as home care, if elderly persons are discharged during disaster response to provide hospital surge capacity for victims from the event.

Immunocompromised Persons

Immunosuppression results in an increased risk for disease, and mass casualty events can heighten this risk due to the inherent stress involved in the event. Immunocompromised individuals can be expected to have increased complications and mortality rates following a mass casualty incident compared to healthy adults; this is especially true during infectious disease disasters such as bioterrorism, an outbreak of emerging infection, or a pandemic.[48] Very little is known about disease presentation in immunocompromised hosts, but it is believed that these individuals will likely have unusual disease presentation, which will complicate and possibly delay diagnosis.[48] Immunocompromised individuals with comorbidities are at an increased risk because they may have limited access to medical care or pharmaceuticals during disaster response or may have adverse reactions to medications due to drug interactions. More information can be found in Chapter 23 The Immunocompromised Host.

Pregnancy

Normal physiological changes during pregnancy, such as a somewhat compromised immune system, decreased ventilatory capacity, and increased respiratory tract bacterial growth, put women at an increased risk for infectious diseases. Research indicates that pregnant women are at increased risk for influenza, malaria, hepatitis, measles, and smallpox compared to nonpregnant individuals.[49] Stress of any kind, especially during mass casualty incidents, enhances this risk and has been linked to preterm labor and low birth weight.[50] Pregnant women are most at risk during an infectious disease disaster. Mortality rates were higher for pregnant women than for nonpregnant individuals during the severe acute respiratory syndrome (SARS) outbreak of 2003, the 1918 influenza pandemic, and during past smallpox outbreaks.[51] Risks exist for the fetus as well. Infectious diseases that develop in pregnant women during mass casualty events, such as past outbreaks of SARS or smallpox, can lead to spontaneous abortion or preterm birth.[51] In addition, many medications or vaccinations that might be needed during a mass casualty incident to treat or prevent disease in pregnant women could harm the fetus.[50] Examples include smallpox vaccination and live attenuated vaccines.[50] More information on pregnancy can be found in Chapter 104 Pregnant Healthcare Personnel.

Procedures for continuing to provide prenatal care, labor and delivery services, and newborn care during mass casualty incidents must be included as part of emergency management.[51,52] Healthcare facilities may choose to limit or eliminate labor and delivery services provided by their facility during a mass casualty

event as a means of increasing surge capacity for disaster victims.[52] If this is done, hospitals must develop algorithms for determining who would receive limited beds and designate which groups of pregnant women would be triaged to an alternate care site set up in the community or possibly referred for home birth.[50] During an infectious disease disaster, hospitals may elect to only provide labor and delivery services off-site as a way of physically separating pregnant women from potentially contagious patients. This procedure was effective at decreasing disease transmission during the 2003 SARS outbreak in Canada.[52]

Transportation

Transportation problems may affect a healthcare facility's ability to respond effectively to a mass casualty incident. Transportation routes need to be predetermined to allow patients, visitors, staff, and supplies to get where they need to be in a safe, rapid manner. A mass casualty event may bring large influxes of patients and the worried well, which can result in chaos if transportation routes are not predetermined. In addition, it is critical to predetermine alternative transportation routes for supplies. Temporary triage centers, ambulance entrances, and loading areas may be needed to accommodate the increased traffic. Transportation during a mass casualty incident can have infectious disease implications, so it is important to make sure that patient flow is constructed in a manner that decreases disease spread. An example is to set up separate triage areas for assessing potentially contagious people during an infectious disease disaster.

Communication and Reporting Systems

Communication refers to both the physical means of communicating information (radios, telephones, etc.) and the messages that are being communicated (risk communication). Healthcare facilities must maintain the ability to communicate between departments (internal communication) and with outside agencies (external communication) during a mass casualty incident. A backup communication system should be available in case the standard system becomes inoperable or overwhelmed. In addition, auxiliary power and secondary sites need to be established prior to an incident, and individuals need to be trained to use the communication system. Consider keeping two-way radios where they will be needed, such as in security and the emergency department. Also consider the use of "disaster first response script cards" to describe first critical steps, such as location of all staff and patients, prevention of fire, and turning off of oxygen and nonessential electrical equipment to avoid the need to locate cumbersome manuals during the stress of first response. Posters are also an effective means to communicate disaster triage and patient management strategies and algorithms.

In the event of a mass casualty event, a facility's emergency management plan will be implemented in tandem with other local, state, and federal emergency management plans. A coordinated effort is essential, regardless of the number of casualties or agencies involved. Such coordination depends on effective internal and external communication. Governmental emergency management plans are based on the National Response Framework (NRF), National Incident Management System (NIMS), and the Incident Command System (ICS), a series of principles designed to be implemented during an emergency.[53] ICS is an appropriate and effective framework for an emergency management response system, and it is both a communication and a reporting system.

ICS builds a framework for working and reporting during the response effort that is based on the need for workers to be flexible and to realize it will not be "business as usual." This means that employees may not be working in their typical roles or departments nor will they be reporting to their usual supervisors. This can be unsettling for many people. Being familiar with ICS helps people know what to expect and what their responsibilities and accountability will be during the mass casualty event.

Under ICS, individuals are assigned specific roles and a distinct chain of command comes into effect. Specific job responsibilities and parameters are defined in job action sheets and the organizational structure is outlined. It is best to practice ICS as part of emergency management planning exercises to ensure that participants understand its principles.

An excellent model for ICS in healthcare agencies is the Hospital Incident Command System (HICS).[53] In essence, HICS is an ICS modified to meet the specific needs of hospitals. Detailed information on HICS can be obtained online.[53]

The use of HICS as an emergency management system ensures that the hospital or healthcare facility will be able to quickly and effectively communicate with outside agencies, including law enforcement, emergency medical services, and fire and governmental agencies. The faster an effective communications network and emergency management plan is in place, the sooner the hospital can recover from the emergency incident and return to day-to-day functioning. This is advantageous to both the healthcare facility and the community it serves. HICS needs to be incorporated into the facility's emergency management plan as part of the organizational hierarchy and communication network specific to the management of the incident. Use of HICS also helps hospitals conform with NIMS requirements.

In HICS, new organizational charts are developed for use during the disaster response effort (Figure 119-3). Each position has a specific mission, and a job action sheet describes the responsibilities assigned to each. Two advantages of having written job action sheets are that they prevent clashes between individuals based on normal lines of authority in the workplace and they prevent duplication or confusion over job responsibilities.

The U.S. Department of Health and Human Services recommends instituting HICS in its original form.[53] Once the system is in place and the facility exercises its emergency management plan, however, minor modifications may be made. Some aspects of HICS should remain unchanged, in order to maintain continuity and avoid confusion within the facility and between the facility and outside agencies. For example, the mission statement or position title on the job action sheets should not be changed, but the checklists on the job action sheets can be modified. See Figure 119-4 for an example of a section of the HICS Operations Section Chief Job Action Sheet that covers the first 2 hours of a mass casualty incident. Always refer to the HICS training manual to determine which facets may be altered without compromising the integrity and effectiveness of the emergency management plan.

Another consideration when assessing and planning communication systems is to prearrange congregation areas for media and transportation routes. Following a mass casualty event, media coverage will be 24 hours a day, 7 days a week. Media groups will flock to the healthcare facility to obtain information and updates. Advance planning can help reduce traffic congestion and disruptions to patient and visitor flow.

During disaster response, communication is one of the most critical components of the response. Experience with emergency management plan exercises and real disasters has shown that one of the largest gaps has been in establishing and maintaining effective communication.[54] Facilities must be able to communicate both internally between departments and externally with outside agencies. In addition, communication with the general public in the community will be critical. During a crisis, accurate consistent messages must be provided to the public, as well as information regarding who is at risk and how those groups can quickly obtain treatment. IPs are unlikely to be the primary means of communication during disaster response but will play a role in overall coordination of the response and in development of media messages for the general public. Risk communication strategies should be utilized when communicating with the public after disaster strikes. See the section on risk communication in this chapter.

Communication needs will include education that takes place within the organization, in outside agencies, and with the general public. In addition, communication will involve the sharing of patient-related information with the public health departments, both local and state. Due to new confidentiality regulations, such as the Health Insurance Portability and Accountability Act (HIPAA), patient information cannot be shared between hospitals or healthcare institutions, but certain information can and should be provided to the health department performing the epidemiology investigation or while conducting syndromic surveillance.[55]

Another important component of communication during the response phase is assisting in criminal investigations. Some mass casualty incidents, such as biological or chemical terrorism, are crimes and will be extensively investigated by the FBI. As part of the investigation, the FBI will be gathering evidence, requiring participation from both healthcare and

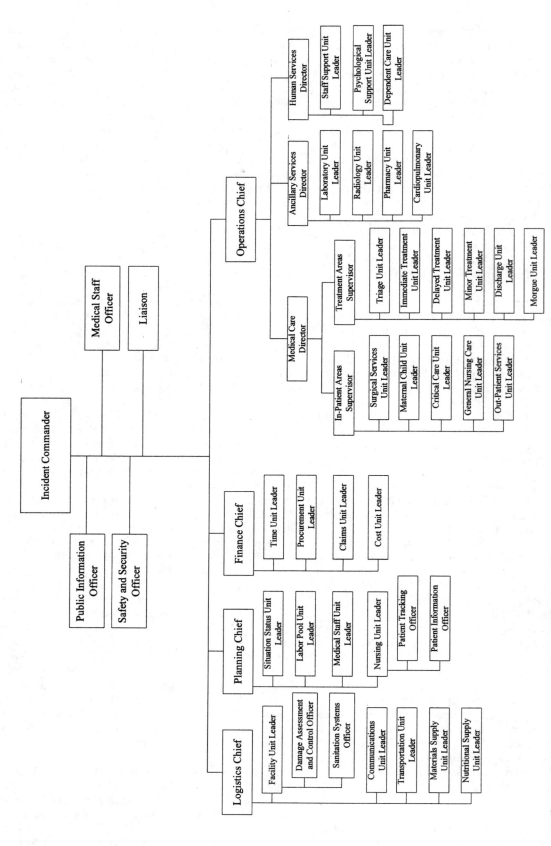

Figure 119-3. Hospital emergency incident command system organization chart.

public health agencies. These procedures are new to most healthcare professionals; forming partnerships with federal agencies in advance will make working together easier in the time of crisis. IPs do not need to know how to gather evidence correctly, but they do need to know how to communicate a potential event to the correct agencies so that the investigation can be initiated.

Information is scarce and valuable in the community disrupted by mass casualty event and can be used to help convince the

HOSPITAL EMERGENCY INCIDENT COMMAND SYSTEM—OPERATIONS SECTION

Job Action Sheet—Operations Section Chief

Revised: 5-93 Reviewed 6-98

OPERATIONS SECTION CHIEF

Position Assigned To:

You Report To: _____ (Emergency Incident Commander)

Operations Command Center: _____ Telephone:

Mission: Organize and direct aspects relating to the Operations Section. Carry out

directives of the Emergency Incident Commander. Coordinate and supervise the

Medical Services Subsection, Ancillary Services Subsection and Human Services

Subsection of the Operations Section.

Immediate: _____ Receive appointment from Emergency Incident Commander. Obtain

packet containing Section's Job Action Sheets.

_____ Read this entire Job Action Sheet and review organizational chart on back.

_____ Put on position identification vest.

_____ Obtain briefing from Emergency Incident Commander.

Figure 119-4. Example of a HICS job action sheet (operations section chief).

_____ Appoint Medical Staff Director, Medical Care Director, Ancillary Services

Director, and Human Services Director and transfer the corresponding Job

Action Sheets. (May be preestablished).

_____ Brief all Operations Section Directors on current situation and develop the

section's initial action plan. Designate time for next briefing.

_____ Establish Operations Section Center in proximity to E.O.C.

_____ Meet with the Medical Staff Director, Medical Care Director, and Nursing

Unit Leader to plan and project patient care needs.

Intermediate: _____ Designate times for briefings and updates with all Operations Section

Directors to develop/update section's action plans.

_____ Ensure that the Medical Services Subsection, Ancillary Services

Subsection and Human Services Subsection are adequately staffed and

supplied.

_____ Brief the Emergency Incident Commander routinely on the status of the

Operations Section.

Extended: _____ Ensure that all communications are copied to the Communications Unit

Leader; document all actions and decisions.

_____ Observe all staff, volunteers, and patients for signs of stress and

inappropriate behavior. Report concerns to Psychological Support Unit

Leader. Provide for staff rest periods and relief.

_____ Other concerns:

Figure 119-4. (Continued)

general public to act in the best interests of the community as a whole. If there is a need to control where the public collects (e.g., away from the emergency room entrance), place a source of reliable information (a TV set or frequently updated bulletin board) where you want the crowd. People will need to discuss their experiences as they work to comprehend them, and this can take place around the information source. This has good potential for rumor control. Information can also be shared as part of staff debriefing, which should decrease employees' stress and anxiety.[56]

During the recovery period, communication will be less stressful and intense than during the disaster response. Recovery communication will involve (1) dissemination of the epidemiological investigation findings, (2) sharing lessons learned between departments and with outside agencies, (3) evaluation of communications that took place during the disaster response, and (4) gap analysis for future mass casualty incidents. Interventions may need to be planned to fill gaps identified during the response before a future event occurs. For instance, a lack of radios may be identified as a barrier to effective disaster communication; the purchase of additional radios would then be a priority.

Risk Communication and Pre-event Messaging

Mass casualty events cause both physical and psychological stress. Communication of needed information before, during, and after a mass casualty incident is essential for preparing individuals and groups for disasters before an event occurs, as well as controlling rumors, maintaining calm, and disseminating response information to those affected during and after an event.

Risk communication is an evidence-based approach to communicating information to professionals and lay people during times of disaster or other high-stress events. It involves communication designed to motivate individuals into action or preventing them from taking an inappropriate action, depending on the situation. For example, media messages from a hospital could explain the following: (1) why, how, and where community residents should obtain vaccination following a flood; (2) the potential consequences of not obtaining vaccination during a bioterrorism attack or pandemic; (3) which groups require and do not require vaccination; and (4) which interventions cause harm or are not helpful. It is also important to note that clinical information can change rapidly during a mass casualty incident and changes in practice must be communicated quickly to staff, such as during the 2009 H1N1 pandemic.[27] The need to communicate changes in practice will be most important during an outbreak of an emerging infectious disease in which little is known about the disease or during an unusual scenario such as a bioterrorism attack.[27] Past research indicates that fear and mistrust are common among HCP and first responders during events necessitating new or changed practice standards; these changes must be effectively communicated to staff to prevent disease transmission and encourage employees to continue working during the mass casualty event. Failing to communicate effectively during a mass casualty incident can have long-lasting implications and can negatively affect citizens' trust in healthcare and public health during future events.[57] The 2001 anthrax incident taught healthcare and public health important lessons about the need to communicate more effectively with the general public. If confusing and contradictory information is communicated during a mass casualty event, people may refuse to follow recommended treatment regimens that can lead to secondary disease transmission and higher morbidity and mortality.[57] Research with the general public indicates that citizens are likely to comply with recommendations if the information source is deemed credible.[58]

Whenever possible, it is best to develop messages in advance; doing so allows a rapid, organized, objective response. This is called pre-event messaging; it means that messages are determined prior to an event. These messages serve a number of functions, including: (1) imparting information, (2) updating citizens on the progress of the event, (3) instructing the public how to obtain medical care and which measures to take to protect themselves, (4) dispelling rumors, and (5) instilling or maintaining calm. The CDC and the Association of Schools of Public Health (ASPH) have collaborated on a multidisciplinary and multistate research project to determine the content and effectiveness of pre-event messages related to biological, chemical, and radiological/nuclear terrorism. This research not only identified citizens' primary concerns about mass casualty incidents that must be addressed in pre-event messages but also identified terms that needed to be revised and/or clarified to have the strongest impact.[58] Pre-event messages were created and tested for a number of different scenarios, including infectious disease disasters, and in a variety of formats for dissemination, including radio live reads, narrated television clips, and fact sheets.[58] Findings from this research indicate that pre-event radio and television messages are less effective than written information because the general public interpret them as not credible.[58] Therefore, it is recommended that healthcare and public health agencies develop written educational materials for use during a mass casualty event. They should also be included in the agency's emergency management plan. If televised media messages are to be used during an event, it is best to use public health officials as spokespeople, because research indicates that televised media messages pertaining to emerging infectious diseases that used a public health official as the spokesperson were 15.2 times more likely to contain accurate, high-quality information.[59]

Documentation

During a mass casualty event, sensory overload sets in within minutes, making it very difficult to take in and process information. Every individual responsible for emergency management should maintain a detailed log, beginning as soon as possible after the mass casualty incident and noting first the time of the disaster and what is immediately known. This log will be a priceless resource for sequencing events, tracking accountability for decisions, and writing reports. Some experienced professions consider keeping of the disaster log the single most useful piece of advice. Documentation is also vital for the facility to receive reimbursement for the event from federal funding.

Education and Training

Staff education and training is part of healthcare facility emergency management planning to ensure that the staff understands the basics about emergency management. Topics include (1) types and consequences of mass casualty events, (2) the facility's emergency management plan, (3) staff's role in the emergency management plan, (4) how to recognize and respond to a mass casualty incident, (5) appropriate reporting and communication systems in place during disaster response, and (6) how and when to practice disaster response strategies.

A full list of educational topics that IPs need to cover for staff, patients, and visitors has been outlined in the literature.[4] Education should be provided to all staff, both medical and support services employees, and should be specific to each worker group. Infection prevention competencies for hospital-based HCP have been identified, including competencies related to emergency management, and should be used as the basis for education and training.[60]

During a mass casualty event, it may be necessary to create and disseminate educational materials. Ideally, such disaster-related educational materials should be created during emergency management planning. If not, they must be created during or after the mass casualty incident to aid in response efforts.

The materials should be event specific. For example, in the event of a mass casualty event involving a contagious agent, such as a smallpox bioterrorism attack, they will need to address control and isolation measures, treatment requirements, and prophylaxis or vaccination recommendations. Educational materials should also address how staff, patients, and visitors can protect themselves and their community during the response. Some of the information provided will concern (1) water safety, (2) sanitation control, (3) proper food preparation (temperature control, etc.), (4) agent-specific information (route of transmission, treatment, etc.), (5) isolation precautions, (6) prophylaxis, (7) vaccination, and (8) control measures.

Some staff members may not be able to get into the hospital, and inexperienced staff members who have not received infection prevention orientation may be at the bedside. Determine what information is necessary for patient and staff safety, such as Standard Precautions and the use of PPE. This information should be communicated as simply as possible, using as little time commitment as possible because the IPs will most likely be tied up with other disaster-related duties. These quick educational messages may be accomplished through posters, pocket cards, or other written methods.

Public health agencies are a valuable resource for educational materials, though their staffs will be strained by events as much as the rest of the community. They may be able to provide educational resources for the following: (1) supplying safe water, (2) coordinating requests for help from outside, and (3) managing outbreaks of communicable diseases, especially childhood rash illnesses.

Education and training during the recovery period should focus on (1) dissemination of information on the effectiveness of the disaster response, (2) areas for improvement related to disaster response, (3) changes/updates to the emergency management plan, (4) ongoing infection prevention strategies, and (5) results from data gathered during the epidemiological investigation when applicable.

Evaluating Preparedness

Evaluating preparedness is accomplished by evaluating the written emergency management plan and practicing the plan either through drills and exercises or from response to actual mass

casualty incidents. Planning checklists have been created to aid in evaluation of the infection prevention components of written emergency management plans.[18,19,22] Some regulatory agencies, including TJC, require regular execution of hospital emergency management plans, either through response to an actual disaster or by holding an exercise at least twice a year.

Emergency Management Plan Evaluation Following a Disaster

Emergency management plans should be evaluated following response to any mass casualty event. This should be done after the crisis has dissipated from the event. How effective was the emergency management plan? Was staff familiar enough with the plan to implement it effectively? Were there facets of the plan that did not work as effectively as possible? Are there areas that can be improved before the next mass casualty incident strikes?

It is critical for the facility to hold a debriefing session in which all of the responding departments and agencies discuss what was learned from the situation. Furthermore, this information should be used to generate an after-action report. This will be greatly facilitated by the availability of any disaster logs that individuals or departments maintained during the mass casualty event. Once the lessons learned from the event have been discussed and documented, the emergency management plan must be updated. If a facility discovers during response to a mass casualty incident that more decontamination gear is needed and more staff should be educated in its use, this information should be incorporated into the after-action report. Thus, a facility might institute a mandatory quarterly drill for decontamination staff to practice donning protective gear and simulating the decontamination process.

Disaster Drills and Exercises

Because most mass casualty events cannot be anticipated and TJC requires twice yearly emergency management plan execution, most healthcare facilities and communities will need to conduct drills and exercises to evaluate their emergency management plan. It is important to note that TJC requires full execution of the emergency management plan during the two exercises and that one exercise must be a community-wide drill; tabletop exercises that only involve discussion of emergency management protocols do not meet this standard.[18]

Disaster exercises/drills provide many benefits, including an opportunity to (1) identify and correct gaps in planning, (2) clarify participants' roles and responsibilities, (3) enhance coordination with internal and external agencies, (4) demonstrate how to implement the plan, and (5) introduce participants to the new reporting and communication structure. Exercise programs can make the difference between a poor and an effective response, which translates into lives and resources saved.

To conduct a healthcare facility disaster drill/exercise, the following steps are involved: (1) develop objectives for an exercise (i.e., the components of the emergency management plan that are to be evaluated); (2) conduct an exercise, during which the emergency management plan is practiced; (3) discuss the findings of the exercise in relation to the identified objectives; (4) identify gaps in preparedness as illustrated by the exercise; (5) determine solutions to the gaps identified in the disaster exercise; (6) update the emergency management plan based on the solutions delineated from the exercise; and (7) educate the staff on the updates made to the emergency management plan. This process is then repeated, with the new emergency management plan and individuals' response behaviors being evaluated. This process must be well documented for TJC and other regulatory agencies.

Responses to all types of mass casualty events require practice, whether they are natural disasters, bombings, response to victims of chemical terrorism, or mass vaccination programs in the face of a bioterrorism attack. By exercising different aspects of the emergency management plan, staff readiness for responding to any type of mass casualty incident can be assessed. The drills should address situations involving lack of electricity, water, or normal communications. Backup systems for each of these should be tested. Various scenarios should be used during disaster drills, including traditional, biological, and chemical terrorism scenarios as well as pandemics and natural disasters. It is also important to incorporate pediatric and other vulnerable population concerns during disaster exercises. These issues have historically been excluded from disaster drills but serve an important role in preparing a hospital for all types of mass casualty events.

The drills should also include decontamination strategies to help staff learn how to perform them more rapidly and correctly during an actual event. In addition, practicing decontamination procedure ensures that the facility has the equipment it will need.

CONCLUSIONS

Disasters and mass casualty events—whether caused by nature or man-made events—can have devastating consequences for public health and safety. IPs have a vital role in preparing for and responding to different types of mass casualty incidents. As experts in the fields of surveillance and epidemiology, they are responsible for investigating outbreaks and initiating interventions to prevent the transmission of infections before, during, and after mass casualty incidents. IPs must be familiar with the potential consequences of different types of mass casualty events, though they will follow the general principles of surveillance and epidemiology for each investigation and intervention. Advance planning and practicing of emergency management plans are essential to an effective response.

INTERNATIONAL PERSPECTIVE

As the frequency of disasters and the number of people affected by such events has increased, disasters have become an international concern. This is especially true for mass casualty events resulting in an increase in infectious disease, such as a bioterrorism attack or pandemic. With the ease and frequency of international travel, it is conceivable for infectious diseases to have a major global impact. SARS and the 2009 H1N1 pandemic are good examples of this phenomenon. Many countries are working to improve emergency management strategies.

Due to the frequency of terrorist activity, Israel has developed many effective measures to rapidly and effectively handle mass casualty events. Israel credits frequent events and simulation exercises to their high level of preparedness and effective response.[25,26] Israeli hospitals practice all aspects of their emergency management plans through up to 20 exercises or actual events per year.[26] Other effective interventions implemented by Israeli hospitals include (1) the use of written algorithms on cards and posters, (2) placing a staff member on the roof of the building to help direct patient flow, and (3) emphasizing disaster preparedness in all healthcare professionals.

REFERENCES

1. Guha-Sapir D VF, Below R, Ponserre S. *Annual Disaster Statistical Review 2011: The numbers and trends.* Brussels: Centre for Research on the Epidemiology of Disasters (CRED), 2012:1–49.
2. Dawood FS, Iuliano AD, Reed C, et al. Estimated global mortality associated with the first 12 months of 2009 pandemic influenza A H1N1 virus circulation: a modelling study. *Lancet Infect Dis* 2012 Dec;12(9):687–695.
3. Volkman JC, Rebmann T, Hilley S, et al. Infection prevention disaster preparedness planning for long-term care facilities. *Am J Infect Control* 2012 Apr;40(3):206–210.
4. Rebmann T. APIC State-of-the-Art Report: the role of the infection preventionist in emergency management. *Am J Infect Control* 2009 May;37(4):271–281.
5. Emergency Management Institute. *IS-230.c Fundamentals of Emergency Management.* Federal Emergency Management Agency website. 2013. Available at: http://www.training.fema.gov/EMIWeb/IS/courseOverview.aspx?code=IS-230.c.
6. Dimaggio C. A Brief Introduction to Disaster Epidemiology. In: *Introduction to Epidemiology.* New York: New York University, 2011.
7. Centers for Disease Control and Prevention (CDC). Infectious disease and dermatologic conditions in evacuees and rescue workers after Hurricane Katrina—multiple states, August-September, 2005. *MMWR Morb Mortal Wkly Rep* 2005 Sep 30;54(38):961–964.
8. Watson JT, Gayer M, Connolly MA. Epidemics after natural disasters. *Emerg Infect Dis* 2007 Jan;13(1):1–5.
9. Schneider MC, Tirado MC, Rereddy S, et al. Natural disasters and communicable diseases in the Americas: contribution of veterinary public health. *Vet Ital* 2012 Apr-Jun;48(2):193–218.
10. Aoyagi T, Yamada M, Kunishima H, et al. Characteristics of infectious diseases in hospitalized patients during the early phase after the 2011 great East Japan earthquake: pneumonia as a significant reason for hospital care. *Chest* 2013 Feb 1;143(2):349–356.
11. Jutla A, Whitcombe E, Hasan N, et al. Environmental factors influencing epidemic cholera. *Am J Trop Med Hygiene* 2013 Sep;89(3):597–607.
12. Barzilay EJ, Schaad N, Magloire R, et al. Cholera surveillance during the Haiti epidemic—the first 2 years. *New Engl J Med,* 2013 Feb 14;368(7):599–609.
13. Biddinger PD, Baggish A, Harrington L, et al. Be prepared—the Boston Marathon and mass-casualty events. *New Engl J Med* 2013 May 23;368(21):1958–1960.
14. Rebmann T. Defining bioterrorism preparedness for nurses: concept analysis. *J Adv Nurs* 2006 Jun;54(5):623–632.
15. Rebmann T, Strawn A, Swick Z, et al. Personal disaster and pandemic preparedness of U.S. human resource professionals. *Journal of Biosafety and Health Education* 2013;1(1):1–7.
16. Rebmann T, Wilson R, LaPointe S, et al. Hospital infectious disease emergency preparedness: a 2007 survey of infection control professionals. *Am J Infect Control* 2009 Feb;37(1):1–8.
17. Rebmann T, Mohr LB. Missouri nurses' bioterrorism preparedness. *Biosecur Bioterror* 2008 Sep;6(3):243–251.
18. Rebmann T. Assessing hospital emergency management plans: a guide for infection preventionists. *Am J Infect Control* 2009 Nov;37(9):708–714 e704.
19. Rebmann T, Citarella B, Subramaniam DP, Subramaniam DS. Assessing the infection prevention components of home health emergency management plans. *Am J Infect Control* 2011 Dec;39(10):849–857.

20. Rebmann T, Hilley S, McCaulley M, et al., *Infection Prevention for Ambulatory Care Centers During Disasters*. Association for Professionals in Infection Control and Epidemiology (APIC). APIC website. 2013. Available at: http://apic.org/Resource_/TinyMceFileManager/Emergency_Prep/2013_Ambulatory_Care_during_Disasters_FINAL.pdf.

21. Rebmann T, Russell J, Alexander S, et al. *Infection prevention for alternate care sites*. Association for Professionals in Infection Control and Epidemiology, 2013.

22. Rebmann T, Coll B. Infection prevention in points of dispensing. *Am J Infect Control* 2009 Nov;37(9):695–702.

23. Rebmann T, Wilson R, Alexander S, et al. *Infection prevention and control for shelters during disasters*. Association for Professionals in Infection Control and Epidemiology (APIC). APIC website. Available at: http://www.apic.org/Resource_/TinyMceFileManager/Practice_Guidance/Emergency_Preparedness/Shelters_Disasters.pdf.

24. Kaiser Foundation Health Plan I. *Medical central hazard and vulnerability analysis tool*. Kaiser Foundation Health Plan, Inc website. 2013. Available at: http://www.mcnhealthcare.com/policy/22222/Kaiser-Permanente-Medical-Center-Hazard-and-Vulnerability-Analysis-Tool.

25. Downey E, Hebert A. Best practices of hospital security planning for patient surge—a comparative analysis of three national systems. *J Health Prot Manage* 2010;26(2):55–74.

26. Kosashvili Y, Aharonson-Daniel L, Peleg K, et al. Israeli hospital preparedness for terrorism-related multiple casualty incidents: can the surge capacity and injury severity distribution be better predicted? *Injury* 2009 Jul;40(7):727–731.

27. Rebmann T, Wagner W. Infection preventionists' experience during the first months of the 2009 novel H1N1 influenza A pandemic. *Am J Infect Control* 2009 Dec;37(10):e5–e16.

28. Lautenbach E, Saint S, Henderson DK, et al. Initial response of health care institutions to emergence of H1N1 influenza: experiences, obstacles, and perceived future needs. *Clin Infect Dis,* 2010 Feb;50(4):523–527.

29. Rebmann T, Citarella B, Subramaniam DS, et al. A home health agency's pandemic preparedness and experience with the 2009 H1N1 pandemic. *Am J Infect Control* 2011 Nov;39(9):725–731.

30. Rebmann T, Wang J, Swick Z, et al. Business continuity and pandemic preparedness: US health care versus non-health care agencies. *Am J Infect Control* 2013 Apr;41(4):e27–33.

31. Rebmann T, Elliott MB, Reddick D, et al. US school/academic institution disaster and pandemic preparedness and seasonal influenza vaccination among school nurses. *Am J Infect Control* 2012 Sep;40(7):584–589.

32. Chung S, Monteiro S, Hogencamp T, et al. Pediatric alternate site of care during the 2009 H1N1 pandemic. *Ped Emerg Care* 2011 Jun;27(6):519–526.

33. Jenkins JL, McCarthy M, Kelen G, et al. Changes needed in the care for sheltered persons: a multistate analysis from Hurricane Katrina. *Am J Disaster Med* 2009 Mar-Apr;4(2):101–106.

34. Carlton PK, Bringle D. Business continuity after catastrophic medical events: the Joplin medical business continuity report. *Am J Disaster Med* 2012;7(4):321–331.

35. Klein KR, Nagel NE. Mass medical evacuation: Hurricane Katrina and nursing experiences at the New Orleans airport. *Dis Manag Resp* 2007;5(2):56–61.

36. Rebmann T, Alexander S, Bartley J, et al. *APIC position paper: Extending the use and/or reusing respiratory protection in healthcare settings during disasters*. Association for Professionals in Infection Control and Epidemiology (APIC) website. 2009. Available at: http://www.apic.org/Resource_/TinyMceFileManager/Advocacy-PDFs/APIC_Position_Ext_the_Use_and_or_Reus_Resp_Prot_in_Hlthcare_Settings1209l.pdf.

37. Rebmann T. Management of patients infected with airborne-spread diseases: an algorithm for infection control professionals. *Am J Infect Control* 2005 Dec;33(10):571–579.

38. Kouadio IK, Aljunid S, Kamigaki T, et al. Infectious diseases following natural disasters: prevention and control measures. *Expert Rev Anti Infect Ther* 2012 Jan;10(1):95–104.

39. Centers for Disease Control and Prevention (CDC). *Personal preparation and storage of safe water*. CDC wbsite. 2013. Available at: http://www.cdc.gov/healthywater/emergency/safe_water/personal.html.

40. Loo SL, Fane AG, Krantz WB, et al. Emergency water supply: a review of potential technologies and selection criteria. *Water Res* 2012 Jun;46(10):3125–3151.

41. United States Army Medical Research Institute of Infectious Diseases (USAMRIID). *The Medical Management of Biological Casualties Handbook*, 7th ed. Fort Detrick, MD: USAMRIID, 2011.

42. Centers for Disease Control and Prevention (CDC). *Rodent control after a disaster*. CDC website. 2012. Available at: http://emergency.cdc.gov/disasters/rodents.asp.

43. Baker MD, Baker LR, Flagg LA. Preparing families of children with special health care needs for disasters: an education intervention. *Social Work Health Care,* 2012;51(5):417–429.

44. Gershon RR, Kraus LE, Raveis VH, et al. Emergency preparedness in a sample of persons with disabilities. *Am J Disaster Med* 2013;8(1):35–47.

45. Allen GM, Parrillo SJ, Will J, et al. Principles of disaster planning for the pediatric population. *Prehosp Disaster Med* 2007 Nov-Dec;22(6):537–540.

46. Gausche-Hill M. Pediatric disaster preparedness: are we really prepared? *J Trauma* 2009 Aug;67(2 Suppl):S73–76.

47. Johnson A, Howe JL, McBride MR, et al. Bioterrorism and Emergency Preparedness in Aging (BTEPA): HRSA-funded GEC collaboration for curricula and training. *Geront Ger Educ* 2006;26(4):63–86.

48. Richard JL, Grimes DE. Bioterrorism: class A agents and their potential presentations in immunocompromised patients. *Clin J Oncol Nurs* 2008 Apr;12(2):295–302.

49. Sappenfield E, Jamieson DJ, Kourtis AP. Pregnancy and susceptibility to infectious diseases. *Infect Dis Obstet Gynecol* 2013;2013:752852.

50. Pfeiffer J, Avery MD, Benbenek M, et al. Maternal and newborn care during disasters: thinking outside the hospital paradigm. *Nurs Clin North Am* 2008 Sep;43(3):449–467.

51. Rebmann T. Severe acute respiratory syndrome: Implications for perinatal and neonatal nurses. *J Perinatal Neonatal Nurs* 2005 Oct-Dec;19(4):332–345.

52. Rebmann T. Preparing for pandemic influenza. *J Perinatal Neonatal Nurs* 2008 Jul-Sep;22(3):191–202.

53. U.S. Department of Health & Human Services, Radiation Emergency Medical Management (REMM). *Incident Command System and Hospital Incident Command System*. REMM website. 2013. Available at: http://www.remm.nlm.gov/ics_hics.htm.

54. Biddinger PD, Savoia E, Massin-Short SB, et al. Public health emergency preparedness exercises: Lessons learned. *Public Health Rep* 2010 Nov-Dec;125 Suppl 5:100–106.

55. Nordin JD, Kasimow S, Levitt MJ, et al. Bioterrorism surveillance and privacy: Intersection of HIPAA, the Common Rule, and public health law. *Am J Public Health* 2008 May;98(5):802–807.

56. DiBenedetto DV. Managing employee health and productivity after mass disasters: Preparing, recognizing, and responding to posttraumatic stress and other health issues—Part II. *Lippincotts Case Manag* 2006 Jan-Feb;11(1):47–51.

57. Meredith LS, Eisenman DP, Rhodes H, et al. Trust influences response to public health messages during a bioterrorist event. *J Health Comm* 2007 Apr-May;12(3):217–232.

58. Glik DC, Drury A, Cavanaugh C, et al. What not to say: Risk communication for botulism. *Biosecur Bioterror* 2008 Mar;6(1):93–107.

59. Pribble JM, Fowler EF, Kamat SV, et al. Communicating emerging infectious disease outbreaks to the public through local television news: public health officials as potential spokespeople. *Disaster Med Public Health Prep* 2010 Oct;4(3):220–225.

60. Carrico RM, Rebmann T, English JF, et al. Infection prevention and control competencies for hospital-based health care personnel. *Am J Infect Control* 2008 Dec;36(10):691–701.

SUPPLEMENTAL RESOURCES

Many resources are available on emergency management. Please see the APIC website for disaster training opportunities: http://www.apic.org/.

Other website sources include the following:

USAMRIID. Available at: http://usamriid.army.mil/.

CDC. Available at: http://www.cdc.gov/.

Johns Hopkins Center for Biodefense. Available at: http://hopkins-biodefense.org.

Saint Louis University offers distance-based graduate degrees and certificates in biosecurity and disaster preparedness, including a specialized track in infection prevention. Information on these programs can be accessed at the following website: http://www.biosecurity.slu.edu.

In addition, many public health departments offer disaster educational opportunities; check with your local and state public health department(s) for further information.

CHAPTER 120

Infectious Disease Disasters: Bioterrorism, Emerging Infections, and Pandemics

Terri Rebmann, PhD, RN, CIC
Associate Professor
Saint Louis University, School of Public Health—Institute for
   Biosecurity
St. Louis, MO

ABSTRACT

Infectious disease disasters are events that involve a biological agent/disease and that result in mass casualties, such as a bioterrorism attack, a pandemic, or an outbreak of an emerging infectious disease. Infectious disease disasters are different from other types of disasters because they increase the risk of communicable disease spread during and after the incident. Subsequently, they involve the need for specialized mitigation, planning, and response interventions to prevent and control the spread of disease. As experts in the fields of surveillance, epidemiology, and prevention of communicable disease spread, infection preventionists play a critical role in emergency management of infectious disease disasters at the personal, hospital/healthcare facility, and community level. Emergency management of infectious disease disasters is a multidepartmental and multiagency endeavor that encompasses the four principles of emergency management: mitigation, preparedness, response, and recovery.[1]

KEY CONCEPTS

- Infectious disease disasters consist of biological terrorism, emerging infectious disease outbreaks, and pandemics.

- Infectious disease disasters pose unique challenges to infection preventionists and disaster planners.

- There are a broad range of potential bioterrorism agents, including bacteria, viruses, and toxins (of microbial, plant, or animal origin). Common characteristics of this diverse group of agents include:

  o The ability to be dispersed in aerosols of 1 to 5 micron-sized particles, which can penetrate the distal bronchioles

  o The ability to deliver these aerosols with simple technology

  o The feasibility of these agents, if delivered from a line source (e.g., an airplane) upwind from the target, to infect large numbers of the population

  o The ability to spread infection, disease, panic, and fear.

- Infectious diseases continuously emerge and/or reemerge, resulting in epidemics of varying sizes and scope.

- Pandemics pose the biggest potential threat to the public's health in terms of morbidity and mortality, and there is a high likelihood of a pandemic occurring in the future.

- Infection preventionists must undertake preparedness activities to ensure that they and their healthcare facilities and communities are better prepared to effectively recognize and respond to an infectious disease disaster.

- Infectious disease disaster preparedness is an ever-evolving process that addresses the four principles of emergency management: mitigation, preparedness, response, and recovery.

BACKGROUND

Definitions of Bioterrorism, Emerging Infections, and Pandemics

Bioterrorism (also known as biological terrorism) is the intentional use of a biological agent or derivative of such an agent to inflict harm or death onto a civilian population. Biological warfare differs from bioterrorism in that the target of the attack is military personnel. For the purposes of this chapter, the term *bioterrorism* will encompass both attacks on military and civilians using a biological agent/weapon.

Emerging infections are those that are new to a population or geographical region, or have increased rapidly. Many emerging infections, such as methicillin-resistant *Staphylococcus aureus* (MRSA) and human immunodeficiency virus (HIV), routinely occur throughout the world and are not covered in this chapter. Information on MRSA and HIV can be found in Chapters 26 Antimicrobials and Resistance, and 81 HIV/AIDS. Only newly emerging (infections that are new in humans) or reemerging infections (infections that occurred in the past but are now increasing in number or changing geographical area) are addressed in this chapter. For the purposes of this chapter, the term *emerging infection* is used in lieu of the terms *newly emerging* and *reemerging infections*.

Pandemics are global outbreaks of disease in humans that exceed expected rates or morbidity and mortality.

Historical Perspective of Infectious Disease Disasters and Future Potential Impact

Bioterrorism

The use of biological agents on populations to cause harm or death is not a new concept; countries have been conducting bioterrorism for hundreds of years. Bioterrorism dates back to the 14th century, when cadavers were dropped into enemy wells to poison the drinking water.[2] Another example of bioterrorism occurred during the French and Indian War, when Native Americans were given smallpox-laden blankets. This action is believed to have initiated smallpox in this previously unexposed population and resulted in a 40 percent mortality rate. More recent examples of bioterrorism include the intentional contamination of salad bars in The Dalles, Oregon, using *Salmonella*[2] and the 2001 attack using anthrax-laden letters mailed to media organizations and politicians.

Bioterrorism has the potential to result in high morbidity and mortality, because aerosolized biological agents can infect or kill many people in a short period of time. Even nonaerosolized attacks, such as the anthrax bioterrorism attack in the United States in fall 2001, can result in morbidity, mortality, and the need to formulate a significant healthcare, public health, and emergency management response. It is not known when or if another bioterrorism attack will occur. However, bioterrorism preparedness helps mitigate potential negative outcomes, and is required by healthcare and public health regulating agencies as part of a comprehensive emergency management program.[3] The future potential impact of bioterrorism depends on the agent used, the amount disseminated, the dispersal method, the weather/release conditions, the preexisting immunity of the exposed population, and how quickly the attack is identified. The 2001 bioterrorism attack caused 22 cases of anthrax and five deaths, required over 10,000 doses of postexposure prophylaxis to be distributed, and cost more than $2.5 billion, yet was, essentially, a small event involving only the use of 2 to 3 ounces of anthrax spores.[4,5] Researchers estimating the potential morbidity, mortality, and cost associated with a bioterrorism attack indicate that an aerosolized release of *Francisella tularensis* over London could result in 2.4 million exposures, 130,000 infections, and 24,000 deaths, with an overall case fatality rate of ~18 percent.[6]

Emerging Infections

Emerging infectious disease outbreaks have occurred throughout recorded history. Examples include the Black Death in Europe, severe acute respiratory syndrome coronavirus (SARS CoV), West Nile Virus, 2009 H1N1 influenza A, Middle East respiratory syndrome coronavirus (MERS CoV), and many others. Many factors affect the emergence of infectious diseases, including social (war, human migration, and urbanization), microbial (genetic mutation, recombination, and assortment), and environmental (earthquakes, floods, deforestation, changes in animal/insect populations) determinants.[7,8]

The impact of emerging infections depends on the agent involved and the size of the event. For example, the 2012 multi-state outbreak of *Escherichia coli* 0145 was a relatively small event; 18 individuals were infected, with only a single death.[9] In contrast, the 2009 H1N1 influenza A virus developed into a pandemic, resulting in ~575,000 deaths.[10] The future potential impact of emerging infections is unknown, but it is expected that infectious diseases will continue to emerge or reemerge, resulting in epidemics of varying sizes and scope.

Pandemics

Of all types of infectious disease disasters, pandemics pose the biggest potential threat to the public's health in terms of morbidity and mortality. Historically, influenza pandemics occur on a semiregular basis. During the 20th century, three influenza pandemics (in 1918/1919, 1957/1958, and 1968/1969) resulted in more than 779,000 deaths in the United States and approximately 53 million deaths worldwide.[11] In 2009, a new strain of influenza A (H1N1) emerged and quickly became a pandemic, resulting in 151,700 to 575,400 deaths worldwide.[10] In addition, there have been several incidents in the last 40 years in which an influenza strain had the potential of causing a pandemic, including scares or pandemic "threats" with swine, Russian, and avian influenza.[11]

The potential impact of a future pandemic is staggering. It has been estimated that an influenza pandemic could infect approximately 30 percent of U.S. citizens (~90 million individuals), require the need for 45 million additional outpatient visits to healthcare agencies and 865,000 to 9,900,000 hospitalizations, result in 89,000 to 207,000 deaths, and cost between $71 and $166 billion in the United States alone.[12-14]

As experts in the fields of communicable diseases, infection prevention, and epidemiology, infection preventionists (IPs) are poised to be at the forefront during an infectious disease disaster. As such, IPs must embrace their role as experts in infectious disease emergency management and assist their healthcare facility or community in becoming better prepared to rapidly, appropriately, and effectively respond to an infectious disease disaster.

BASIC PRINCIPLES

Bioterrorism

Bioterrorism refers to the use of biological agents on civilian or military populations, animals, or crops. A combination of factors have all raised concerns about the actual use of bioterrorism agents, including the breakup of the former Soviet Union and the concomitant dispersal of scientists and agents involved in bioterrorism research, the rise of radical groups focused on destroying what they believe to be evil forces, and the discovery of Iraq's stockpiled anthrax, botulinum toxin, and other biological warfare agents.

There are a broad range of potential bioterrorism agents, including bacteria, viruses, and toxins (of microbial, plant, or animal origin). Common characteristics of this diverse group of agents include (1) the ability to be dispersed in aerosols of 1 to 5 μm particles, which can penetrate the distal bronchioles; (2) the ability to deliver these aerosols with simple technology; (3) the feasibility of these agents, if delivered from a line source (e.g., an airplane) upwind from the target, to infect large numbers of the population; and (4) the ability to spread infection, disease, panic, and fear.[15]

The most likely route of dissemination is an aerosolized release of 1- to 5-μm particles. Other methods of dissemination include oral (intentional contamination of food/water supply), percutaneous, infected animal vector (e.g., release of infected fleas), and human-to-human spread (individual infected with communicable disease walking among a crowd of healthy people). As the anthrax attacks of 2001 proved, even physical objects, such as letters, can be used to help spread biological agents.

Pandemics

Unlike a bioterrorism attack or outbreak of an emerging infection, a pandemic is usually not an event that occurs suddenly. The World Health Organization (WHO) describes six phases of a pandemic, starting with the period in which there are few to no human cases from the organism/disease to the period in which there is efficient and sustained disease spread from person to person. The six WHO pandemic phases are outlined in Table 120-1. It is expected that a pandemic will hit communities in multiple waves. Each wave will last approximately 6 to 8 weeks, making response a more prolonged event than with other types of disasters.[12] During an influenza pandemic, attack rates will likely be about 30 percent across all populations; young children are expected to be disproportionately affected and have attack rates close to 40 percent.[12] It should be noted that not all pandemics will have a slow onset. The 2009 H1N1 pandemic illustrated that a pandemic can occur suddenly and without warning.

Table 120-1. The Six Phases of a Pandemic

Phase	Description of the Phase
1	Low risk of human cases
2	Higher risk of human cases
3	No or very limited human-to-human transmission
4	Evidence of increased human-to-human transmission
5	Evidence of significant human-to-human transmission
6	Efficient and sustained human-to-human transmission

Adapted from World Health Organization (WHO). Current WHO phase of pandemic alert. WHO website. 2013. Available at: http://www.who.int/influenza/preparedness/pandemic/h5n1phase/en/index.html.

There are a number of agents that could cause a pandemic, including MERS CoV, SARS, and plague. Historically, influenza has caused the most pandemics and is expected to cause others in the future.[11] Recent pandemic threats include H5N1 and H7N9, both avian strains of influenza A.

Nature of the Pandemic Threat

As of September 6, 2013, WHO indicates that we are in pandemic phase 3: There is an agent with the capacity to cause a pandemic (influenza A/H5N1), but there is currently no or very limited human-to-human transmission. As of August 2013, there have been 637 human cases of H5N1 avian influenza, 378 of whom have died.[16] As of August 22, 2013, there have been 135 cases of H7N9, 44 of whom died.[17] It is not known whether H5N1 and/or H7N9 will continue to mutate and adapt to become more easily spread from person to person, resulting in a pandemic. It is also possible that another strain or organism could emerge and cause a pandemic. A future influenza pandemic is considered inevitable, but it is not known what strain will be involved or when the event will occur.[12]

PREPAREDNESS FOR INFECTIOUS DISEASE DISASTERS

Many of the interventions needed to detect, prevent, and control infectious disease disasters are identical to those for other types of mass casualty events (see Chapter 119 Emergency Management, for more information). However, infectious disease disasters pose unique challenges to IPs, healthcare and public health agencies, response organizations, and businesses. These differences are discussed in this chapter.

Preparedness for infectious disease disasters begins at the personal level. This means that it is the responsibility of all IPs to have a personal/family emergency management plan that will enable him/her to continue working during the infectious disease disaster. For infectious disease disasters, this includes the need to have personal protective equipment (PPE) stored at home in case the need arises for its use in community settings.[18] The United States Department of Health and Human Services (DHHS) recommends that all families stockpile respiratory protection as part of their personal pandemic plan.[19] See Chapter 119 Emergency Management, for more information on personal emergency management plans.

It is critical for healthcare facilities to become better prepared for infectious disease disasters. Infectious disease disasters will result in a large number of patients requiring hospitalization for mechanical ventilation, isolation, or highly specialized treatment in intensive care beds. Studies indicate that most healthcare facilities do not have adequate resources or the infrastructure needed to manage all aspects of patient care during an event that lasts longer than a few days, let alone the 6 to 8 weeks that may be necessary during a pandemic.[3] Deficiencies in hospital preparedness for infectious disease disasters include a lack of ventilators, antibiotics or antiviral medications, respiratory protection (N95 respirators and masks), negative pressure rooms/areas, laboratory support/supplies, and linens.[3,20] Two studies conducted during the early part of the 2009 H1N1 pandemic found that many U.S. hospitals lacked infection prevention supplies, including respirators and anti-infective therapy.[20,21] Another study reported that almost a quarter of all U.S. hospitals lack 24/7 infection prevention coverage, which would make responding to an infectious disease disaster very challenging.[3]

At the community level, it is vital that healthcare agencies become better prepared for infectious disease disasters. Hospital surges during an infectious disease disaster will trickle down into community healthcare services and cause response challenges for these agencies. Potentially contagious patients will likely be discharged to alternate care sites, long-term care, and home care during an infectious disease disaster, requiring the need for surge capacity and infection prevention strategies/ programs in these settings. Despite this, a 2010 study conducted during the H1N1 pandemic found that almost a third of all home health agencies lack any surge capacity, which would not allow hospitals to discharge patients to home health as planned.[22] Infection prevention strategies described in this chapter apply to all settings that administer healthcare services.

IPs play an important role in becoming prepared for infectious disease disasters at the personal, facility, and community levels. Preparedness activities must be undertaken by IPs to ensure that they and their healthcare facilities and communities are better prepared to effectively recognize and respond to an infectious disease disaster. As experts in infectious diseases, infection prevention, and epidemiology, IPs play a critical role in helping healthcare facilities/agencies and communities become better prepared to recognize and respond to an infectious disease disaster.

Infectious disease disaster preparedness is an ever-evolving process that addresses the four principles of emergency management: mitigation, preparedness, response, and recovery.[23] In addition, preparedness means that individuals and facilities develop an emergency management plan, practice the plan, and evaluate their level of preparedness. IPs must become better prepared not only to personally recognize and respond to an event but also to aid their healthcare facilities/agencies and communities in doing the same.

Assessment

Assessment is the first step in preparing a healthcare facility, healthcare agency, or community for an infectious disease disaster. Facility, agency, and community assessments are multidepartmental, multi agency endeavors that should not be undertaken alone. Information on emergency management plan assessment may be found in Chapter 119 Emergency Management.

Planning for Infectious Disease Disasters

Emergency management plans must address all hazards, including infectious disease disasters. For most hospitals and healthcare agencies, this will mean having an annex or section of their emergency management plan that is specific to infectious disease disasters.

Various planning guides exist to aid in preparing for infectious disease disasters, and each is aimed at a specific group/ agency. For example, the Pandemic Influenza Plan written by the DHHS is designed to be used by local and state disaster planners and public health departments.[24]

In 2009, a planning checklist was developed for hospitals to assess the infection prevention components of their emergency management plan.[25] Emergency medical services (EMS) agencies can obtain guidance from the DHHS in the Emergency Medical Services and Non-Emergency (Medical) Transport Organizations Pandemic Influenza Planning Checklist.[26] In 2012, Volkman et al.[27] published a guidance document for long-term care facilities to use when developing emergency management plans, including addressing planning for bioterrorism and pandemics. A planning checklist was published in 2011 that describes the infection prevention components needed in a home health agency emergency management plan.[28] In addition, DHHS has published a number of pandemic planning checklists for businesses, schools, and faith-based organizations.[29]

The above are just a few examples of planning guides for infectious disease disasters. Other documents are available through state health departments and healthcare agencies.

Identification of an Infectious Disease Disaster

Morbidity and mortality related to many agents that could be involved in an infectious disease disaster can be decreased if treatment, isolation, and prophylaxis are provided as soon as possible. A rapid response depends on the foundation of the plan that is in place before the event occurs and the participants' familiarity with the emergency management plan.

When even a single case of an unusual disease is suspected or identified, bioterrorism or an emerging infectious disease should be considered. Groups of nonspecific illnesses clustered in time or place should also be strongly considered for bioterrorism or an outbreak of an emerging infectious disease. This includes the clustering of flulike syndrome in patients. All cases of unusual disease, including even a single case of any of the diseases mentioned in this chapter, should be reported immediately to local public health officials; if cases are recognized during evenings or weekends, after-hours or emergency numbers should be used.

Specific diagnosis of the agents discussed in this chapter has historically relied heavily on the presence of appropriate epidemiologic exposure (e.g., exposure to infected animals during meat rendering for anthrax, ingestion of home-canned foods for botulism, or travel to an area where an emerging infectious disease is endemic). Dissemination of biological agents via an aerosol route will require diagnosis of these generally uncommon diseases without the aid of usual exposure history. Furthermore, many of these syndromes can only be diagnosed on the basis of clinical knowledge of presenting symptoms and expected disease progression. Maintaining a high level of suspicion and clinical knowledge about these diseases is essential to timely diagnosis. Assays/tests for bioterrorism agents and emerging infectious diseases are often only available in specific research laboratories (state public health laboratories, Centers for Disease Control and Prevention [CDC], or United States Army Medical Research Institute of Infectious Diseases [USAMRIID]); consult your local/state health department to arrange for appropriate testing or for consultation.

Early Recognition of an Infectious Disease Disaster

IPs may be the first to detect an infectious disease disaster, and early detection decreases morbidity and mortality. The sooner the incident and at-risk patients are identified, the higher the likelihood of decreasing morbidity, mortality, and cost associated with the event. The difference between infectious disease disasters and other mass casualty events is that infectious disease disasters are more difficult to detect. With natural disasters, and even traditional or chemical terrorism, there is an obvious sign that something unusual has happened. This can range from damaged buildings in an earthquake to a huge influx of patients immediately after a chemical attack.

In a bioterrorism event, however, an explosion is unlikely, and we may not know that there has been an attack unless the perpetrators announce it (i.e., it is an overt event), because aerosolized biological particles are odorless, colorless, and tasteless. In the case of a covert bioterrorism attack, a few days or weeks after the release, patients will begin to show symptoms and will access the medical system at that point. These patients will probably go to an emergency department or some other primary care facility. Detection will be difficult because it is unlikely that all the patients will go to the same facility or primary care provider. In this scenario, surveillance is essential to early detection of the event.

Like a bioterrorism attack, an outbreak of an emerging infectious disease may be difficult to detect. Clinicians rarely see these diseases, and the outbreak could even involve a novel strain or organism, making diagnosis very difficult. If the outbreak involves a new organism, such as the appearance of the coronavirus that causes MERS (MERS Co-V) in 2012, there may not be a laboratory test readily available for confirmation testing. Surveillance will be essential to detect a new outbreak and identify new cases once an outbreak is underway.

Early identification of a pandemic will be easier than that for bioterrorism or an outbreak of an emerging infectious disease. This is because pandemics tend to occur gradually over time, following the phases identified by WHO (see Table 120-1 for a list of the six WHO pandemic phases).[12] However, even pandemics can occur quite suddenly, as was the case with the 2009 H1N1 influenza A pandemic.[21] As the threat of a pandemic rises, IPs should continue to communicate with public health officials regarding the current status of the event.

Early recognition of an infectious disease disaster can occur by one of two methods: passive or active surveillance. See Chapter 11 Surveillance, for more information on surveillance.

Passive surveillance for infectious disease disasters refers to clinicians maintaining a high index of suspicion for potential diseases caused by bioterrorism or unusual disease presentation that may signal an emerging infectious disease. Clinicians who suspect bioterrorism may have occurred or an emerging infectious disease must report this incident to the infection prevention/infectious disease department and local health department immediately.

Active surveillance refers to surveillance activities implemented to detect bioterrorism incidents or other infectious disease disasters. However, emerging infectious diseases and most of the potential bioterrorism agents cause uncommon illnesses, such as inhalational anthrax, tularemia, monkeypox, and MERS CoV, and most facilities do not have the laboratory capability to test for these agents. This makes case finding very difficult.

An example of an active surveillance program would be one in which the data collector would contact specified people or groups in the community and ask for predetermined information or collect such information from hospitalized patients. Traditional active surveillance involves the collection of clinical information, usually in the form of laboratory tests, but can include other relevant clinical data such as chest radiograph results and patient symptoms. It is not feasible to conduct active surveillance using laboratory tests to detect an infectious disease disaster because there are too many possible causative agents. A study by Kaplan[30] examined the feasibility of conducting surveillance for bioterrorism using blood donation samples tested for a series of bioterrorism-related agents (e.g., anthrax, plague), just as donated blood is routinely tested for HIV and hepatitis. This study found that not only would detection of the event be delayed using this type of surveillance methodology, but it would also be prohibitively expensive. To screen all blood donations for bioterrorism-related agents would cost approximately $10/donor, totaling $139 million per year.[30]

BioWatch

BioWatch is an environmental monitoring program that is managed in coordination by the CDC, Environmental Protection Agency (EPA), and the United States. Department of Homeland Security. This program uses air samplers to test for aerosolized biological agents around the United States, with the goal of rapidly identifying biological events. Rapid detection of an infectious disease disaster would help minimize morbidity, mortality, and costs. The BioWatch air samplers are located in undisclosed cities and monitor the air 24 hours a day, 7 days a week. The specimens collected by BioWatch are sent to the Laboratory Response Network (LRN) and tested for various agents. When biological particles are detected in the air, a report is sent to emergency managers and public health professionals in the communities in which the agents were detected. These reports are termed "BioWatch Actionable Results" (BARs).

Communities must decide how to respond to these BARs in terms of the extent to which an investigation is conducted or interventions are implemented.

Although BioWatch has not detected a single bioterrorism attack (because no aerosolized attacks have occurred since the start of the program), BioWatch has been credited with strengthening the United States' existing biosurveillance program and enhancing coordination between public health agencies and healthcare systems as a means of increasing community resilience.[31] BioWatch is currently considered a complementary system to existing biosurveillance programs established in communities.

Syndromic Surveillance

Instead of conducting traditional active surveillance to detect an infectious disease disaster, a different approach must be used. Active surveillance for infectious disease disasters involves the use of syndromic surveillance. Historically, syndromic surveillance referred to the collection and analysis of syndrome-related data. A few examples of traditional syndromic surveillance indicators include (1) severe flulike illness indicating a new emerging pathogen (e.g., MERS CoV), pandemic influenza, or a bioterrorism attack involving the release of *Bacillus anthracis* (inhalational anthrax), *Yersinia pestis* (pneumonic plague), variola (smallpox), or other agents; (2) flaccid muscle paralysis indicating that a neurotoxin, such as botulism toxin, may have been released; (3) bleeding disorders indicating the use of a viral hemorrhagic fever agent; (4) rash indicating the release of variola virus (the cause of smallpox); or (5) gastrointestinal (GI) symptoms that present similarly to food- and waterborne illnesses, possibly indicating an intentional release on a water or food source or vendor.

The concept of syndromic surveillance has evolved over time to encompass more than simply syndrome-related data. It now consists of collecting and analyzing any nontraditional data for early detection of an infectious disease disaster. Syndromic surveillance now includes any indicator that might signal an increase in illness in the community. Some examples of data that could be collected and analyzed as part of a syndromic surveillance program include (1) number of patients seen in an emergency department; (2) number of patients presenting to the emergency department with flulike illness as their chief symptom; (3) number of patients admitted to a hospital; (4) number of EMS or ambulance runs performed each day, week, month, or other time period; (5) number of purchases of over-the-counter flu remedies; (6) number of purchases of over-the-counter diarrhea medications; or (7) other data available from healthcare facilities or agencies that may indicate a change or trend in the community. In studies, International Classification of Diseases Ninth Revision (ICD-9) codes and GI syndromes have high sensitivity and specificity in syndromic surveillance, whereas respiratory syndromes, chief symptom as an indicator, and fever alone were less sensitive measures. A 2011 study by Bellazzini and Minor[32] found that emergency department syndromic surveillance indicators, such as chief complaint or ICD-9 diagnostic codes are significantly faster at identifying an upward trend compared to laboratory-based data. Medication sales have been found to be useful indicators when used in conjunction with clinical syndrome indicators.[33] Combining multiple indicators has been found to yield the most accurate and sensitive information during syndromic surveillance, but can be expensive and resource intensive.[34,35]

Some communities are now collaborating with veterinarians and incorporating animal and insect surveillance data in the community syndromic surveillance program. Animal syndromic surveillance is important because more than 60 percent of human emerging infectious diseases are zoonotic;[36] an infectious disease outbreak among animals may be the precursor to human illness in a community. Animal syndromic surveillance began with cattle and livestock surveillance, but has expanded over time into also collecting data on companion animals. Examples of animal syndromic surveillance indicators include cattle mortality rates at farms and rendering plants, the number of visits at animal hospitals, and the number of laboratory tests requested by veterinary clinics, regardless of the results.[37] An innovative approach to public health syndromic surveillance is to combine animal and human data indicators. By doing this, it increases the sensitivity and specificity of the syndromic surveillance data being analyzed. Examples of parallel syndromic surveillance data indicators that have been collected include the following: (1) rate of influenza-like illness (ILI) in humans and in domestic cats, and (2) number of emergency room visits per day or per week at human and animal hospitals.[37]

Syndromic surveillance indicators must be evaluated in relation to facility and community illness baselines and current trends. Any upward trend or sharp increase must be evaluated as soon as possible to determine if an infectious disease disaster has occurred.

Syndromic surveillance data collection and analysis must be a component of facility and community emergency management. It should be a multiagency endeavor, including coordination and communication between hospitals, healthcare agencies (long-term care, home health), and public health.

Table 120-2 outlines syndromic surveillance indicators that healthcare facilities, schools, businesses, and veterinary clinics may consider collecting as part of their syndromic surveillance program for infectious disease disasters. All healthcare agencies, including long-term care and home health, should consider conducting syndromic surveillance. In addition, public health officials should consider partnering with schools and businesses to collect syndromic surveillance data, such as absenteeism rates related to ILI. Many syndromic surveillance programs exist (a 2004 study identified 115 such systems).[38] Facilities and agencies will need to decide which program or indicators work best for them. The CDC indicates that all hospitals should implement, at the least, a syndromic surveillance system that identifies patients with ILI; recommended sites for implementing this surveillance program include the emergency department, hospital clinics, and occupational health.[39] Syndromic surveillance programs should be coordinated with local public

Table 120-2. Syndromic Surveillance Indicators

Indicator
Flu like illness*
Flaccid muscle paralysis
Severe bleeding disorder with no discernable source
Rash
Gastrointestinal symptoms
Number of patients seen in an emergency department
Chief symptom (i.e., number of patients presenting with flulike illness as their chief symptom)
Number of patients admitted to a hospital
Number of EMS or ambulance runs
Number of calls to nurse or physician help lines triage centers
Over-the-counter pharmaceuticals sales (i.e., nonprescription medications to treat flu or gastrointestinal symptoms)
Number of individuals who use an Internet search engine (e.g., Google or Yahoo!) to look up information about flulike symptoms
Cattle or livestock morbidity or mortality rates
Domestic animal morbidity or mortality rates
Number of laboratory tests conducted at veterinary clinics
School absenteeism rates
Staff absenteeism rates at local businesses

*The CDC indicates that all hospitals should implement, at the least, a syndromic surveillance system that identifies patients and staff with influenza-like illness.[39]

health agencies to provide consistency in data collection and ensure adequate coverage across regions.

BioSense

BioSense is a national syndromic surveillance program for the United States that is run by the CDC. BioSense allows healthcare and public health agencies to quickly access and share data across regions or the nation. It was originally designed to assist with rapid identification of a bioterrorism attack but also has the opportunity to recognize an outbreak of an emerging infectious disease or pandemic, allowing for a more rapid response to the event. Data for BioSense derives from at least hundreds of hospitals, multiple state syndromic surveillance programs, and thousands of pharmacies and laboratories across the United States.[40] Most data submitted to BioSense are sent in real time, but a few sources have delayed reporting. BioSense tracks data by categorizing it into syndromes, such as ILI. Similar to other surveillance programs, spikes in BioSense data necessitate an investigation to determine whether it is a false alarm or a true infectious disease outbreak/anomaly. Most spikes in indicator rates result from predicable variation, inaccurate information provided to BioSense, misclassification of data, short-term anomalies, or a change in the community that is unrelated to an outbreak (e.g., a sale on over-the-counter pharmaceuticals that prompts increased sales). If the data spike is determined to be a potential legitimate threat, the CDC contacts the community from which the data derived to do an in-depth analysis. This may necessitate the involvement of hospitals, healthcare agencies, and local public health authorities to determine the

source of the data anomaly. Although BioSense did not help in identifying the 2009 H1N1 pandemic, BioSense data was used by the CDC Emergency Operations Center and CDC's Influenza Division to determine H1N1 vaccine prioritization schedules, inform decisions related to school and public building closures, and aid in assessing the overall severity of the pandemic in the United States.[40] Between 2010 and 2012, BioSense data was used to monitor the impact of the 2010 Gulf of Mexico oil spill, enhance surveillance for dengue, and assess the health impacts related to the 2011 Japanese tsunami and subsequent nuclear incident as well as the 2011 U.S. heat wave.[40] BioSense data has also been used to enhance hospital epidemiology studies, including studies examining healthcare-associated pneumonia and *Clostridium difficile*.[41,42]

Vulnerable Populations

Certain groups of individuals are more at risk from morbidity and mortality during an infectious disease disaster. These individuals are known as vulnerable populations. Meeting the needs of vulnerable groups must be addressed as part of infectious disease disaster planning and included in the emergency management plan at the facility and community level. General disaster planning for vulnerable populations is covered in Chapter 119 Emergency Management. Only issues that are specific to infectious disease disasters are covered in this chapter.

Pediatrics

Children, especially newborns and young children are at an increased risk for infection during most types of infectious disease disasters. Neonates may be at risk from infection during an infectious disease disaster in two ways: vertical transmission from the mother during pregnancy and healthcare-associated transmission after birth.[43] Although newborns may be provided some protection by passive immunity (receipt of antibodies from the mother while in utero), they may be susceptible to certain diseases if the mother develops an infection during pregnancy. Neonates are also more at risk from infection than adults and even older children because of their relative state of immunosuppression, which predisposes them to many types of infections. Babies who are born prematurely are also at high risk from a variety of infections.

During a bioterrorism attack involving the release of an aerosolized agent, children are at higher risk from exposure than adults because of children's increased respiratory rate, which would result in their inhalation of more infectious particles.[44] In addition, newborns and young children have more permeable skin than adults, increasing the risk of toxin absorption through the skin.[44] Children are also at higher risk during a smallpox bioterrorism incident because they have never been immunized against variola. Although most adults do not have active immunity against smallpox because their initial immunization was more than 30 years ago, individuals who receive a booster of smallpox vaccines (i.e., most adults born before 1972) are much more likely to have a sustained immune response compared with primary vaccinees (i.e., children). In addition, children infected with smallpox are more likely than adults to be misdiagnosed with chickenpox because of the increased incidence of this disease in children. Children are also expected to be at higher risk of infection and fatality during an influenza pandemic.[12]

Attending school or a childcare agency also puts infants and children at increased risk for infection during biological events. Research indicates that schools and childcare agencies are often associated with communicable disease spread among children.[45,46] Epidemiological studies indicate that school openings have been associated with spikes in cases during outbreaks and pandemics, including the 2009 H1N1 pandemic, and school closure (whether intentional event-specific closure or natural closure due to breaks/holidays) is associated with sudden drops in cases.[47,48] Close interaction at school or childcare puts children at risk from disease spread unless control measures are implemented.

Elderly

The number of elderly individuals in the United States is growing, and the fastest growing group among the elderly are those who are 85 years or older. Normal declines in physiological function that occur with aging put the elderly at higher risk for infection. In addition, many older adults have comorbidities, which put them at higher risk for infection at all times, and this risk can be magnified during an infectious disease disaster. Infectious diseases currently account for 40 percent of deaths among the elderly, and rates are expected to be even higher during a pandemic or bioterrorism attack.[49]

Diagnosing infectious diseases among the elderly can be complicated. Most elderly individuals have a pulse/temperature dissociation that masks the signs of infection, making diagnosis much more difficult in the elderly than in adults or children.[49] Therefore, triaging algorithms need to take this pulse/temperature dissociation into account and use a lower temperature as a potential indicator of infection among the elderly (see "Triage" section of this chapter). In addition to having a pulse/temperature dissociation, the elderly commonly have atypical disease presentation because of normal organ system changes and comorbidities. These factors can make diagnosis of infectious diseases very difficult among the elderly, especially during an infectious disease disaster.

Immunocompromised

Immunosuppression results in an increased risk for infectious disease, even during nondisaster times. Immunocompromised individuals can be expected to have increased complications and mortality rates after an infectious disease disaster compared with healthy adults.[50] Immunocompromised individuals with comorbidities are at an increased risk.

Very little is known about bioterrorism-related disease presentation in immunocompromised hosts, but it is believed that these individuals will likely have unusual disease presentation, which will complicate and possibly delay diagnosis.[50] In addition, disease is expected to be more severe for immunocompromised patients during an infectious disease disaster compared with healthy adults, especially among patients with HIV and cancer.

Pregnancy

Normal physiological changes during pregnancy, such as a somewhat compromised immune system, decreased ventilatory capacity, and increased respiratory tract bacterial growth, put women at an increased risk for disease.[43] Influenza infection during pregnancy may cause poor outcomes, such as longer hospital stays, more frequent hospitalization not related to delivery, and maternal death.[43] These risks were amplified in past pandemics and are expected to hold true during future influenza pandemics.[12] Mortality rates were higher for pregnant women than for nonpregnant individuals during the 1918 influenza pandemic, and influenza was the leading cause of maternal death in the 1957 pandemic.[43] Pregnant women are also at higher risk for fatality during outbreaks of emerging infectious diseases and bioterrorism; mortality rates were higher for pregnant women than for nonpregnant individuals during the SARS outbreak in 2003 and during past smallpox outbreaks.[51]

Fetuses are at risk from infection and death while the mother is pregnant. Infections women develop during pregnancy, such as SARS or smallpox, can lead to spontaneous abortion or preterm birth.[43] In addition, many medications or vaccinations that might be needed during an infectious disease disaster to treat or prevent disease in pregnant women could cause potential harm to the fetus.[52] Examples include smallpox vaccination and live attenuated vaccines.[52]

Some women with high-risk pregnancies will require specialized care/treatment while in labor and delivery, even during an infectious disease disaster. However, most women with normal pregnancies may be better served by giving birth in an alternate care site or the home to prevent exposure to communicable diseases during an infectious disease disaster.[52] Communities will need to make arrangements for continuing to provide prenatal care, labor and delivery services, and newborn care in the community during infectious disease disasters as part of emergency management.[52] Hospitals and healthcare facilities need to develop triaging algorithms for determining which women require hospitalization and which can be managed in another setting.[52] During the 2003 SARS outbreak in Canada, pregnant women delivered their babies in nonhospital settings as a way of physically separating pregnant women from potentially contagious patients; this was effective at decreasing disease transmission during labor and delivery.[43]

Reporting Infectious Disease Disasters

All cases of unusual disease or syndrome clusters should be reported immediately to local public health officials, including even a single case of any of the diseases mentioned in this chapter. If cases are recognized during evenings or weekends, after-hours or emergency numbers should be used. Phone trees should be developed as part of emergency management planning to ensure that reporting can take place around the clock. Staff should be educated to report any known or suspected patients with bioterrorism-related diseases or an emerging infectious disease to the infection prevention, infectious disease, and/or hospital epidemiology department(s). During an infectious disease disaster, reporting should occur through the facility incident command system (see Chapter 119 Emergency Management, for information on the hospital incident command system).

Epidemiology of Bioterrorism or Outbreak of an Emerging Infectious Disease

It is difficult to predict and delineate the epidemiology of a bioterrorism attack or emerging infectious disease outbreak before it occurs, but the general principles of epidemiology, infection prevention, and outbreak investigation apply. An outbreak investigation may be warranted if a communicable disease is involved or epidemiological information, such as risk factor data, needs to be collected and analyzed.

In the event of an unannounced bioterrorism attack, the epidemiological investigation will be critical to mounting an effective response. If terrorists covertly release an aerosolized biological weapon, the event will not be detected until days to weeks after the incident, when patients become ill and begin infiltrating the medical system. When this occurs, a rapid and focused epidemiological investigation will be needed to identify the possible date and location of the release. Victims' histories will be taken and examined for shared activities, such as attendance at a mutual event. It is essential that the release date and location be identified to determine other people/groups who are potentially at risk. This information can guide distribution of treatment, prophylaxis, and vaccination.

If a contagious agent is used in a bioterrorism attack, the epidemiological investigation will be even more critical. Not only will the date and location of release need to be identified, but a list of contacts (i.e., people who came into contact with infected patients since the onset of infectiousness) must be identified as well. For instance, if smallpox is released as a biological weapon, there are two distinct groups at risk of exposure: (1) those exposed to the initial release (which will be identified when the date and location of the release is determined) and (2) those exposed to infected individuals during periods of contagiousness (which will be identified in a thorough epidemiological investigation of potential contacts). These same principles will apply if the infectious disease disaster is an outbreak of a contagious emerging pathogen, although the source or potential vector may need to be identified rather than a release point.

As with any outbreak or epidemiological investigation, the three primary factors of contextual concern are person, place, and time. The basic information that will need to be determined as soon as possible after a bioterrorism attack or outbreak of an emerging infectious disease is detected includes the following: (1) identification of the causative agent, (2) establishment of the case definition, (3) determination of date of release, (4) location of release, (5) assessment of the approximate length of exposure time, and (6) determination of the potentially exposed groups. The response to an infectious disease disaster will depend on the answers to these questions. If a contagious agent (e.g., aerosolized plague or smallpox) was involved, the epidemiological investigation will be quite different from an investigation if a noncontagious agent (e.g., anthrax) was involved. In addition, the date, location, and approximate length of exposure time will affect the response needed. The epidemiological investigation and necessary response will be different for a small release in a contained area versus a large release in an open area or if the outbreak involves an insect or animal vector.

Causative Agent Identification

Regardless of whether the infectious disease disaster is a bioterrorism attack or outbreak of an emerging pathogen, it will be imperative to establish the causative agent as quickly as possible. Treatment, prophylaxis, and control measures all depend on the causative agent. Time is of the essence because patients with diseases caused by some of these agents can progress to death very rapidly without appropriate treatment. For example, untreated pneumonic plague usually progresses to death within 36 to 72 hours.[53] Although diagnosis will not be a direct responsibility of the IP, it is likely that the IP's infectious disease expertise will be consulted in the evaluation process and in deciding which, if any, isolation precautions should be implemented while awaiting confirmatory diagnosis.

Agent identification and patient diagnosis will depend a great deal on the effectiveness of the passive surveillance system used by the facility or agency. If clinicians have maintained a high index of suspicion and have a good knowledge foundation regarding the potential diseases that could be involved in an infectious disease disaster, it is more likely that the event/outbreak will be rapidly identified.

Identification of the Date and Location of Agent Release or Potential Source of Pathogen

An IP's epidemiological skills will be necessary to identify when and where the release of the biological agent(s) occurred, or the source/vector of an emerging pathogen. The date and location of release or potential source are critical to determine at-risk groups, control measures, and, depending on the agent, may determine who needs to be vaccinated and/or receive prophylaxis. To determine when and where the exposure took place, a thorough patient history of any and all victims of the bioterrorism attack must be taken. This history should focus on (1) past and current symptoms, (2) date of symptom onset, (3) severity of illness, (4) possible source of exposure, (5) route of exposure (body site affected), and (6) date and location of exposure. For example, a new painless necrotic lesion on the arm might indicate cutaneous anthrax, whereas respiratory symptoms with an accompanying widened mediastinum on chest radiograph would suggest inhalational anthrax. Both diseases result from exposure to the same agent, but the route of exposure is different.

Determining the source of exposure may be the most challenging component of the epidemiological investigation. However, it will also be one of the most critical components because it will help determine at-risk groups that might benefit from prophylaxis or vaccination. Determining the date and location of the exposure will be aided by listing all the places the patient had been during the incubation period of their illness; a travel history will be an essential component. The time period for which a history needs to be collected (i.e., the incubation period) will depend on the agent used; this time period can range from 1 day to weeks before symptom onset. If the date and location of release can be quickly determined and at-risk persons identified, a targeted prophylaxis or vaccination program can be initiated. If the date and location cannot be rapidly determined, consider mass prophylaxis or immunization to protect the community at large. Occupational risk exposures should also be assessed, especially if the person is a laboratory, healthcare, or sanitation professional, or if the person works with animals (e.g., in a veterinary clinic, meat rendering plant, or poultry or swine farm).

Potential Bioterrorism Agents

The CDC provides a list of the most likely agents to be used in a bioterrorism attack. These agents are divided into three categories (A, B, and C) with category A agents being the most likely to be used.[15] Table 120-3 reviews the most likely agents of bioterrorism.

Table 120-3. Centers for Disease Control and Prevention Bioterrorism Agents

Category A
Anthrax (*Bacillus anthracis*)
Botulism (*Clostridium botulinum* toxin)
Plague (*Yersinia pestis*)
Smallpox (variola major)
Tularemia (*Francisella tularensis*)
Viral hemorrhagic fevers (filoviruses [e.g., Ebola, Marburg] and arenaviruses [e.g., Lassa, Machupo])
Category B
Brucellosis (*Brucella species*)
Epsilon toxin of *Clostridium perfringens*
Food safety threats (e.g., *Salmonella species*, *Escherichia coli* 0157:H7, *Shigella*)
Glanders (*Burkholderia mallei*)
Melioidosis (*Burkholderia pseudomallei*)
Psittacosis (*Chlamydia psittaci*)
Q fever (*Coxiella burnetii*)
Ricin toxin from *Ricinus communis* (castor beans)
Staphylococcal enterotoxin B
Typhus fever (*Rickettsia prowazekii*)
Viral encephalitis (alphaviruses [e.g., Venezuelan equine encephalitis, eastern equine encephalitis, western equine encephalitis])
Water safety threats (e.g., *Vibrio cholerae*, *Cryptosporidium parvum*)
Category C
Emerging infectious diseases such as Nipah virus and hantavirus

Adapted from Centers for Disease Control and Prevention (CDC). CDC bioterrorism agents. CDC website. 2013. Available at: http://emergency.cdc.gov/agent/agentlist-category.asp

Clinical Manifestations of Bioterrorism-related Diseases or Emerging Pathogens

The diseases produced by bioterrorism agents could be incapacitating or lethal. Because these agents would most likely be released via an aerosol route, resulting in pulmonary infection, many of the clinical syndromes include a febrile syndrome with accompanying respiratory symptoms. Agents causing GI symptoms (e.g., nausea, vomiting, and diarrhea) are also likely to be used, and have been used in past bioterrorism attacks.[2] Other possible clinical syndromes related to bioterrorism include fever with a centrifugal rash (smallpox), a rapidly descending flaccid muscle paralysis (botulism), or a severe bleeding disorder (viral hemorrhagic fever virus).[53]

Emerging infectious diseases can demonstrate a variety of clinical manifestations, from ILI to GI disorders. Many emerging infectious diseases can be expected to be zoonotic in nature.[36] The exact clinical picture of an emerging infectious disease will be specific to the pathogen.

Triage and Screening

Triage is an important component of emergency management to quickly identify those individuals who need medical treatment first. Severely ill or injured patients need to be transferred to a medical facility as soon as possible. During an infectious disease disaster, triage involves assessment for not only disease/injury severity, but also screening for potential contagiousness. Patients and visitors may need to be screened before they are allowed entry into healthcare facilities, points of dispensing or distribution (PODs), or alternate care sites (ACS). Healthcare personnel may need to be screened before each shift, depending on the event and the associated morbidity and mortality. Table 120-4 is a generic assessment/screening form that can be used to identify potentially contagious individuals during an infectious disease disaster. This table/tool would need to be modified to be event-specific during an infectious disease disaster; screening items should be based on the case definition for the disease/condition involved in the incident. For example, a screening tool for MERS CoV might include a question related to a recent travel history to an area in which cases of MERS CoV have occurred.

Healthcare facilities, PODs, and ACS should encourage informal screening of patients, visitors, and staff for potentially contagious conditions/diseases. Posters describing signs and symptoms that should be reported to healthcare personnel should be strategically located around the facility.

Screening Area

If formal screening is to be conducted during a biological disaster, a screening area will need to be set up. Research indicates that it is most effective to limit the number of formal screening areas (to maximize available resources) by locking off extra entrances during the infectious disease disaster, provided that fire and safety codes are not violated by doing so.[21] The screening area should be set up either outside or immediately inside the entrance to the healthcare facility, and it should be manned by a

Table 120-4. Sample Generic Screening Form for Infectious Disease Disasters

Screening/Triage Form*

Name _____

Temperature: _____ (in degrees Fahrenheit)

Do you currently have any of the following symptoms?

Yes	No	
☐	☐	Cough
☐	☐	If you have a cough, is your sputum bloody?
☐	☐	Runny nose
☐	☐	Loose or unformed stools
☐	☐	Watery or explosive diarrhea stools
☐	☐	Bloody stools
☐	☐	Rash
☐	☐	If you have a rash, is it itchy?
☐	☐	Stiff/sore neck
☐	☐	Red eye or drainage from eye(s)
☐	☐	Wound or lesion
☐	☐	Have you been hospitalized within the past 3 months?
☐	☐	Have you been told that you have a multidrug-resistant organism (MRSA, VRE, etc.)?
☐	☐	Are you currently on any antibiotics/treatment? If Yes, list.

Name of person completing the form	Date

*Adapted from: Rebmann T, Hilley S, McCaulley M, et al. Infection prevention for ambulatory care centers during disasters. Association of Professionals in Infection Control and Epidemiology website. 2013. Available at: http://apic.org/Resource_/TinyMceFileManager/Emergency_Prep/2013_Ambulatory_Care_during_Disasters_FINAL.pdf.

trained screener. The screening area should have hand hygiene and PPE available for the screener(s) and visitors.

Potentially contagious individuals identified through screening should be moved immediately to an isolation room/area. A temperature of 100°F should be used as the identifier for potential infection to identify the elderly or immunocompromised individuals whose physiological changes tend to mask normal signs of infection.[49]

Anti-infective Therapy, Prophylaxis, and Vaccination

Several of the potential bioterrorism agents and emerging infectious diseases have effective treatment regimens, when such therapy is initiated early in the disease process. Immediate recognition of the disease process and rapid administration of appropriate treatment modalities are essential to decreasing the morbidity and mortality of an infectious disease disaster.

In most situations, chemoprophylaxis will be important during an infectious disease disaster. Several of the bacterial and viral agents of bioterrorism have effective postexposure prophylaxis (PEP) available in the form of either medical treatment or vaccination. Some emerging infectious diseases, such as pandemic

influenza, also have identified PEP regimens. Exceptions to the need for PEP would be diseases for which there is no known effective prophylaxis available, such as viral hemorrhagic fever, SARS, or MERS CoV. PEP should be offered to all those with a known exposure to a potentially contagious patient/person. This includes patients, visitors, staff, and volunteers. Immediate recognition of the disease involved in the infectious disease disaster and clearly defining the population exposed will be crucial for dispensing appropriate PEP to those most at risk. Information on what constitutes an exposure and contact tracing are part of the epidemiological investigation and should be coordinated with local public health officials. PEP should be offered as soon as an exposure is suspected. Delayed PEP can decrease effectiveness of the medication or vaccine and result in increased morbidity and mortality.

The DHHS currently recommends that communities and healthcare facilities consider offering preexposure prophylaxis to high-risk healthcare personnel (those with direct high-risk exposures) and front-line workers (emergency department workers, first responders, EMS personnel) during a pandemic.[55] Preexposure prophylaxis would consist of taking antiviral medications for the duration of the outbreak in the community. This strategy is expected to decrease disease transmission among the highest risk individuals and allow these groups to continue working during a pandemic by preventing illness associated with the event. Preexposure prophylaxis will require large numbers of doses of medication (a 6- to 12-week regimen/provider); the decision to allocate medication to preexposure prophylaxis needs to be examined in light of the facility's ability to provide ongoing PEP and treatment. Treatment and PEP are higher priority than preexposure prophylaxis, and this needs to be incorporated into healthcare facility/agency prioritization plans.[55] If a healthcare facility/agency's supplies of antiviral medications start to dwindle, even if supplemented from the CDC's Strategic National Stockpile (SNS), medications need to be reserved for treating cases and providing PEP.

Vaccination can be an important component of responding to an infectious disease disaster, depending on the agent/disease involved in the event. For some diseases/agents (e.g., viral hemorrhagic fever viruses, SARS, MERS CoV, and others), there is no available vaccine. Others have a vaccine, but it is only available to laboratory workers (i.e., tularemia), not approved by the U.S. Food and Drug Administration (FDA) for PEP use (i.e., anthrax), or not feasible for use as PEP because it takes months to develop immunity (i.e., botulism). Vaccination during a pandemic may be possible, but will likely be delayed. It could take weeks to months to identify the causative strain and develop an effective vaccine against it. Even after the strain is identified, it may take months to ramp up vaccine production to create enough vaccine for the entire United States or world. As of fall 2013, there were multiple FDA-approved vaccines against the current circulating strain of avian influenza A (H5N1).[56] Other vaccines against H5N1 avian influenza and other strains of influenza (H7N9 and H3N2 to name just two) are also under development. These vaccines may provide limited protection during a pandemic but would likely not be completely effective. This is because the current H5N1 avian influenza vaccines are effective against the current circulating strain. However, the influenza strain must mutate to become more easily transmissible from person to person and thus able to cause a pandemic. This mutation may render the current avian influenza vaccine less effective or ineffective. It is anticipated that vaccine distribution during a pandemic may be delayed by 9 months or more because of the time needed to develop and produce a new vaccine.[12]

In the event of a large-scale infectious disease disaster, mass distribution of medical countermeasures may be required in the form of antimicrobial therapy/prophylaxis distribution or vaccination administration. Mass distribution of medical countermeasures requires extensive upfront planning to accommodate large numbers of exposed individuals in a short period of time. Mass distribution is generally accomplished through PODs. There are two types of PODs: open and closed. Open PODs are distribution sites that dispense medical countermeasures to all community members; these sites are coordinated by local public health officials. Closed PODs are distribution sites that are located within a workplace or other private employer setting and only dispense medical countermeasures to employees and/ or employees' family members. Open POD development and implementation is a multiagency endeavor, as it will need to be a communitywide effort. Healthcare agencies should consider becoming closed PODs, so as to be able to quickly distribute medical countermeasures to their own employees, patients, visitors, and volunteers. This may ensure faster service and enable healthcare employees to continue working throughout the infectious disease disaster. If healthcare facilities or agencies want to be a closed POD site, they should work with public health officials prior to an event, as formal arrangements need to be in place in order for an agency to become a closed POD.

During an infectious disease disaster, medical countermeasures may be limited. The CDC's SNS is a national repository of medications and supplies needed for a disaster. The SNS is intended as a supplement for situations in which local resources are exceeded by need. Medications and supplies in the SNS are located throughout the United States and can be delivered to any state within 12 hours. Healthcare facilities/agencies and communities need to remember that the SNS is supplemental only. In the event of a large-scale infectious disease disaster, especially a pandemic, the current SNS supplies will not be sufficient to cover all communities. The United States experienced this during the 2009 H1N1 pandemic when many hospitals reported running out of N95 respirators early on in the pandemic, and the supplies they received from the SNS were inadequate in number or size/type.[21] Healthcare facilities/agencies and communities need to be as proactive as possible in preparing for infectious disease disasters to ensure the best response. One way to do this is to stockpile or make arrangements to obtain additional supplies during a disaster. Although this is widely regarded as an essential component of emergency management, a recent study of U.S. hospitals found that only 63 percent of hospitals are stockpiling or have arrangements to obtain additional medications (e.g., antibiotics, antivirals) during an infectious disease disaster.[3] Healthcare

facilities and communities need to prioritize who will receive limited supplies. This should be done as part of emergency management planning and not wait until supplies are insufficient or depleted. Guidance on allocating scarce resources ethically can be obtained from the Institute of Medicine.[57]

Anti-infective Therapy, Prophylaxis, and Vaccination for Elderly and Immunocompromised Individuals

Anti-infective therapy, chemoprophylaxis, and vaccination will be the same for the elderly and immunocompromised as it is for healthy adults for most diseases, but there may be more adverse effects in the elderly and immunocompromised. The elderly will be at high risk from drug-to-drug interactions and adverse events from anti-infective therapy and chemoprophylaxis during an infectious disease disaster because of their likelihood of having comorbidities.[49] Immunocompromised individuals are at increased risk from adverse events related to administration of live vaccines, such as the smallpox vaccine.

Anti-infective Therapy, Prophylaxis, and Vaccination for Pediatrics

Anti-infective therapy for children will differ from adults for most diseases. These differences range from smaller doses that are based on weight to elimination of certain medications because of adverse effects in children (e.g., teeth stain due to tetracycline in children younger than 8 years).[58] One example is that infants younger than 6 months may not be vaccinated against influenza, which would put them at risk from infection during an influenza pandemic.[43] However, infants may receive some passive immunity protection up to 6 months after birth from the mother's vaccination during pregnancy. There are identified therapies and pediatric-specific doses for most bioterrorism-related bacterial infections; antiviral therapy for pandemic influenza, SARS, and other viral illnesses; antitoxin for botulism; and vaccines for some diseases that could cause an infectious disease disaster.[58] However, there are not a lot of data available on the efficacy and safety of these medical therapies in children; further research is needed in this area.

Infection Prevention Procedures

The amount of IP involvement in disaster response depends on the agent involved. In an infectious disease disaster, IP involvement will be critical, especially if the agent is communicable. Many agents of bioterrorism are not transmitted from person to person, but some are. Most emerging infectious diseases are communicable, but a few are not. Bioterrorism agents and emerging infectious diseases that are communicable pose the greatest risk to society and will require the most involvement from an IP. Examples of potential infectious disease disasters that involve communicable diseases include pneumonic plague, smallpox, viral hemorrhagic fever viruses, SARS CoV, MERS CoV, and pandemic influenza. In these instances, infection prevention will be essential to control the outbreak, prevent future cases, and decrease morbidity and mortality associated with the event.

Isolation and Personal Protective Equipment Use

In addition to pharmacological interventions (anti-infective therapy, chemoprophylaxis, and vaccination), nonpharmacological interventions should be implemented to prevent and control disease spread during an infectious disease disaster. The primary nonpharmacological intervention involves isolation and PPE use. Standard Precautions should always be used when caring for patients, patient care equipment, and environmental controls. Respiratory etiquette (also known as respiratory or cough hygiene) should be implemented as part of routine infection prevention activities, but are especially important during infectious disease disasters. Information on Standard Precautions, isolation, and respiratory etiquette are outlined in Chapter 29 Isolation Precautions. These simple measures are very important during an infectious disease disaster, but research indicates that many healthcare personnel do not follow them correctly during biological events. An epidemiological study found that 40 percent of healthcare personnel who developed SARS after exposures to coughing patients had not been wearing a mask when exposed; many, if not all of these infections may have been prevented if the healthcare personnel had been wearing respiratory protection.[59] A study conducted in New York City during the 2009 H1N1 pandemic examined unprotected staff exposures to H1N1 patients and found that there were 277 unprotected staff exposures from 26 H1N1 patients, 65 percent (179) of which were preventable if staff had correctly followed Transmission-based Isolation Precautions.[60] Hand hygiene is also an important component of respiratory etiquette and response to an infectious disease disaster. See Chapter 27 Hand Hygiene, for more information. The final component of respiratory hygiene is spatial separation. Spatial separation for infectious disease disasters involves physically separating potentially contagious patients from noncontagious people. Approximately 3 feet is needed to prevent the spread of respiratory diseases, including those involved in infectious disease disasters, such as SARS and pneumonic plague.

The exact necessary infection prevention procedures needed for a bioterrorism attack cannot be estimated before an attack occurs. It depends on many factors, including (1) how soon the release is detected (i.e., whether decontamination and prophylaxis are necessary), (2) how soon the diagnosis is made, (3) how soon appropriate isolation was initiated (i.e., the number of potential contacts of an infected case), (4) the size of the release (i.e., the number of affected individuals), and (5) the agent used (i.e., whether the agent is contagious). However, the basic principles of infection prevention still apply. Infection prevention principles and recommendations are not altered for bioterrorism; they are the same whether the event is intentionally inflicted (bioterrorism) or a naturally occurring incident (emerging infectious disease outbreak or pandemic).

Any time a bioterrorism-related or emerging infectious disease is suspected, infection prevention guidelines for that specific agent/disease should be followed. During the beginning of an infectious disease disaster when the agent may not have been identified or when there is not enough evidence regarding the disease transmission route, IPs need to base infection prevention decisions on syndromes and symptomatology. This is referred to as syndrome-based isolation/control measures. This will be especially important during an infectious disease disaster involving a newly emerging infection because there may be limited or no information available on the causative agent. MERS CoV was an example of this situation. When MERS CoV first emerged in 2012, the transmission route and control measures needed to prevent disease spread were unknown. Infection prevention decisions were made on the basis of patients' symptoms, epidemiological information as it became available, and basic infection prevention principles.

Some general guidelines to follow when the causative agent is unknown include the following: (1) if the patient has respiratory-type symptoms (e.g., cough, sneezing, fever), Droplet Isolation Precautions should be used; (2) if the patient is severely ill with rapidly progressing respiratory symptoms and an airborne spread disease is suspected (i.e., SARS or avian influenza), Airborne Precautions should be considered; (3) if the patient has GI symptoms (e.g., nausea, vomiting, diarrhea), Contact Precautions should be used; (4) if the patient has an unusual rash (especially if it is centrifugal in pattern), smallpox should be considered and Contact and Airborne Isolation Precautions should be used; (5) if the patient is bleeding profusely from multiple orifices for no logical reason (i.e., no history of recent trauma, surgery), viral hemorrhagic fever should be considered and Contact and Airborne Isolation Precautions should be used; (6) if the patient has any type of unusual or severe lesion or wound for no logical reason (i.e., no recent history of surgery, injury), Contact Precautions should be implemented; (7) if the patient has an enlarged and very painful lymph node, bubonic plague should be suspected and Contact Precautions should be used if the skin is broken or there is draining fluid; and (8) if the patient has descending flaccid paralysis and botulism is suspected, no isolation is necessary. Table 120-5 provides an outline of syndrome-based isolation precautions that can be used during an infectious disease disaster until the causative agent is identified and/or event-specific isolation guidelines are provided by the CDC. PPE use should follow standard healthcare facility procedures, including recommendations provided as part of respiratory hygiene/cough etiquette. In the event of an outbreak of an emerging infectious disease in which the causative agent is not known, healthcare personnel should be told to follow official recommendations from their infection prevention/hospital epidemiology department, their local public health authorities, or the CDC. Healthcare personnel should be encouraged to wear PPE that is appropriate to the situation and the task that they are performing.

During routine activities, isolation is generally only implemented in hospitals. However, during an infectious disease disaster in which hospitals will be full and potentially contagious patients may be triaged to alternate care sites or home health, communities should consider educating the public regarding how to implement basic infection prevention strategies in nonhospital settings. This may include isolation and PPE use in long-term care, alternate care sites, home health, medical clinics,

Table 120-5. Syndrome-Based Isolation Categories/Control Measures for Infectious Disease Disasters in Which the Causative Agent is Unknown

Symptoms/Syndrome	Isolation Precaution Category*†
Respiratory	
Cough, runny nose, watery eyes	Droplet
Fever (>101.1°F) and cough in adults**	Droplet
Fever (>101.1°F) and cough in children	Droplet and Contact
Fever (>101.1°F), cough with bloody sputum, and weight loss or with upper lobe pulmonary infiltrate in an HIV-negative patient or any lobe of an HIV-positive patient	Airborne and Contact, plus eye protection when performing aerosol-generating procedure
Fever (>101.1°F), cough, and pulmonary infiltrate in any lobe in patient with a travel history to country with active cases of SARS or avian influenza within past 10 to 21 days**	Airborne and Contact, plus eye protection
Diarrhea or vomiting	
Vomiting	Standard
Acute diarrhea with a likely infectious cause in an incontinent or diapered patient	Contact
Watery or explosive stools, with or without blood	Contact
Skin	
Fever (>101.1°F) and rash	Airborne
Fever (>101.1°F), upper chest rash, and stiff/sore neck	Droplet
Eye infections (drainage from eye)	Standard
Draining wound/lesion that cannot be covered	Contact
Rash	
—Itchy rash without fever	Contact
—Petechial/ecchymotic with fever	Droplet for 24 hours of antimicrobial therapy
—Rash and positive history of travel to an area with a current outbreak of very high frequency in the 10 days before fever onset	Droplet and Contact, plus eye protection (goggles or face shield). Add N95 or equivalent when performing aerosol-generating procedures
—Maculopapular with cough, coryza, and fever	Airborne
—Vesicular, especially if centrifugal in pattern	Airborne and Contact

*Always use Standard Precautions.

†If the causative agent is known, the appropriate isolation precautions for that disease should be used.

**A temperature of 100°F should be used as the identifier for potential infection to identify the elderly or immunocompromised individuals whose physiological changes tend to mask normal signs of infection.[49] In addition, clinical judgment should always be used.

Adapted from Rebmann et al.[61] and Siegel et al.[64]

community-based evacuation shelters, and any other site that administers healthcare services or houses potentially contagious patients.[61] Home isolation may also be recommended for individuals who are ill and contagious but do not require inpatient treatment.

PPE and other medical supplies are expected to be insufficient or depleted during an infectious disease disaster. Guidelines for stockpiling PPE for biological events have been proposed,[62] and are summarized in Table 120-6. If supplies of respirators become insufficient during disasters, despite local and regional stockpiling efforts, healthcare agencies should implement crisis standards of care related to extending the use or reuse of respirators. Guidance for developing a respirator crisis standard-of-care policy should be based on existing guidelines.[63] See Chapter 119 Emergency Management, for more information on how to manage a shortage of PPE and other medical equipment.

Social distancing practices may also be implemented during an infectious disease disaster as a nonpharmacological intervention. Social distancing refers to a set of practices that aim to reduce disease transmission through physical separation of individuals in community settings. These practices have been outlined in DHHS' document *Community Strategy for Pandemic Influenza Mitigation*.[65] Examples of social distancing include (1) home quarantine (staying at home after exposure to a potentially contagious person); (2) closing schools and childcare programs; (3) keeping children and teenagers out of public places, such as malls, movie theaters, and other common gathering areas; (4) canceling large public gatherings of any kind; (5) encouraging people to work from home when their jobs allow or adjusting schedules to decrease the number of workers in the same place at the same time; (6) arranging for community-based medical services that keep noncontagious individuals away from potentially contagious people (e.g., setting up prenatal classes in community sites rather than at hospitals, encouraging home birth); and (7) implementing other interventions that decrease interaction between individuals in communities as a way of decreasing the risk of disease transmission.[52,65]

Quarantine

Quarantine is the separation of individuals who are not yet symptomatic but have been exposed to a contagious person and are believed to be at risk of developing an infection. These exposed individuals are quarantined or separated from others

Table 120-6. Estimated Numbers of Postexposure Prophylaxis Needed for an Infectious Disease Disaster*

Category of Staff	Respirator	Gown (disposable)	Gloves (disposable)	Goggles/Eye Protection
Little to no exposure	1 disposable per contact/exposure	1 per exposure	1 pair per contact	None
Prolonged exposure	1 **reusable** per outbreak (plus 2 cartridges/month**)	1 per exposure	1 pair per contact	1 per outbreak
Infrequent exposure(s)	1 **reusable** per outbreak (plus 2 cartridges/month**)	1 per shift	1 pair per contact	1 per outbreak

Estimates are based on staff's expected exposure risk during the event.

*Adapted from: Radonovich LJ, Magalian PD, Hollingsworth MK, et al. Stockpiling supplies for the next influenza pandemic. *Emerg Infect Dis* 2009;15(6):e1.

**Disposable respiratory cartridges are needed for reusable respirators.

as a way to rapidly identify onset of illness if it occurs and keep them away from susceptible people. Once a person in quarantine develops signs or symptoms of disease, it would be assumed that they are infected and they would need to be isolated. Quarantine also implies exclusion of healthy individuals from areas that are known or suspected of being contaminated or housing infected patients. Time periods for quarantine depend on the disease to which the person was exposed. Generally, the quarantine time is equal to the length of the incubation period for the disease to which the person was exposed. Quarantines can be voluntary or enforced.

Quarantine is only to be considered in drastic circumstances, such as the emergence of a new highly pathogenic infectious disease or the use of smallpox as a biological weapon. Quarantine can be implemented in a variety of places, including community settings (e.g., a hotel or convention center), the home, or even in hospitals (i.e., work quarantine).[43] Interventions used as part of home and work quarantine are outlined in Table 120-7. Monitoring (either self-monitoring or external) must be in place for all quarantined individuals, regardless of where they are quarantined, to identify rapidly potentially infected or contagious individuals and institute appropriate therapy. It is generally recommended that quarantined individuals be housed in separate rooms; however, a study conducted in China during the 2009 H1N1 pandemic found that there was

Table 120-7. Interventions for Implementing Home or Work Quarantine as Used during the Severe Acute Respiratory Syndrome Outbreak

Home Quarantine

Individual is instructed to:
—Wear mask when in contact with household members.
—Monitor and record temperature twice daily.
—Report any elevated temperature or other symptoms to public health.
—Stay physically separated from others in the home whenever possible, including having a separate sleeping area/room and bathroom when feasible.
—Keep separate linens (towels, sheets, pillowcases) and eating utensils (i.e., dishes, silverware) that are not shared with other household members.
—Do not have visitors.
—Do not go to any public gatherings or community activities, including shopping.
—Stay in the house at all times. If the individual must leave the house (e.g., to get the mail), he/she should take a mask to put on if someone comes into the yard.
—Walk dogs or other pets in the backyard only.

Work Quarantine (used after an individual had been exposed to illness during an occupational exposure)

Individual is instructed to:
—Work at only the healthcare facility at which the worker was exposed, and then only if symptoms are not present.
—See only essential patients in community-based clinics (if the healthcare personnel has a community practice in addition to hospital duties) and refer nonessential patients to other medical facilities. Wear a mask and have office staff wear a mask at all times.
—Monitor and record temperature and symptoms before beginning work; elevated temperatures or other symptoms should be reported to the health department.
—Drive to work alone in a private vehicle (i.e., do not use public transportation).
—Wear mask at all times when at work.
—Adhere to hand hygiene practices meticulously.
—Eat in a room that is physically separated from others if possible; if not feasible, individual should stay at least 6 feet away from others.
—Do not go to other medical centers, clinics, or hospitals unless authorized by the health department before visit.
—When not at work, the individual must follow home quarantine guidelines.

Adapted from Reynolds et al.[67]

no increased risk of infection for quarantined students housed two to a room compared to those in single-person rooms.[66] Therefore, double-occupancy quarantine housing may be considered if space is limited.

Home quarantine can be considered a means of social distancing and it was used as one such intervention in Canada during the SARS outbreak,[67] and in China,[68] Australia,[69] and Japan[70] during the 2009 H1N1 pandemic. A study conducted in Japan during the 2009 H1N1 pandemic aimed to assess the effectiveness of voluntary home quarantine among car production company personnel. This study found that voluntary home quarantine with paid time off was effective at lowering the overall incidence of infection among workers (reduced risk of infection by 20 percent); however, those who stayed home and obeyed the quarantine were two times more likely to get infected themselves compared to those who went to work.[70] This is believed to be because the workers who followed the quarantine probably had more close contact with their sick family member while they were at home. Another study conducted during the H1N1 pandemic had different findings; that study found that home quarantine may have been effective at decreasing the transmission rate early on during the pandemic, but it became significantly less effective as the rate of community transmission increased.[68]

Home quarantine should be considered if a young child requires quarantine so that the child can stay with the parent/primary caregiver. Multiple studies have found that U.S. citizens strongly prefer home quarantine over quarantine in a separate facility.[71,72] In contrast, research indicates that citizens from Hong Kong, Singapore, and Taiwan (who had experienced home quarantine during the SARS outbreak or had known individuals who had) reported that they strongly prefer quarantine in a separate facility.[72] The reasons for this difference are not known, but it is believed to be associated with the reality of home quarantine (i.e., fear of infecting household members, protective measures that needed to be implemented in the home, such as wearing a mask when around others, not sleeping in the same room). Research also indicates that U.S. citizens are more willing to comply with quarantine when it is voluntary versus when the government requests or orders it.[71]

Individuals in home quarantine may develop signs of infection and become too ill to stay at home, which would require transfer to a healthcare facility. Communication must be provided to quarantined individuals regarding: (1) why they are being quarantined, (2) how long their quarantine will last, (3) protective measures they must take while being quarantined, (4) how to monitor themselves for illness or how they will be monitored, (5) symptoms that need to be reported, (6) to whom they report symptoms or changes in health status, (7) how psychological support will be provided, (8) how compliance will be monitored, and (9) consequences for noncompliance.

Work quarantine was implemented during the SARS outbreak in Canada; results regarding its effectiveness as a means of controlling disease spread are conflicting.[73,74] In addition, hospital/work quarantines implemented during the SARS outbreak were found to be expensive and had a negative psychological effect on healthcare personnel.[67] Future use of work quarantine as a nonpharmacological intervention needs to be evaluated. If a hospital-based work quarantine is to be implemented, provisions must be made to provide sleeping arrangements, food, water, and other essential services to those quarantined.

Regardless of the setting used for quarantine, one major potential obstacle to quarantine effectiveness is a lack of compliance. Research from the SARS outbreak indicates that only about half of all quarantined individuals were compliant with all community protective measures while on home quarantine;[67] these measures included such things as not going out of the house to socialize, not attending public events, not going on vacation, not running errands, and not allowing visitors into the home. Compliance with household protective measures was even lower: Only 38.4 percent complied with household protective measures, such as using separate towels and utensils, sleeping in a separate room, and using a mask when around others in the home.[67] A study conducted in Australia during the 2009 H1N1 pandemic had similar findings; compliance with home quarantine was only 53 percent.[69] A 2010 study[71] found that those who have a higher perceived susceptibility to avian influenza are more likely to report willingness to comply with home quarantine; education campaigns could be used to increase home quarantine compliance by focusing on the risk of disease development.

When considering the implementation of quarantine, one factor that needs to be considered is the potential for psychological stress associated with being quarantined. Two studies conducted with individuals who had been quarantined during the 2003 SARS outbreak found that quarantine causes a lot of psychological stress.[67,75] Quarantined individuals report feeling frightened, lonely, bored, frustrated, angry, and fearful of becoming infected, infecting their family or friends, and losing income while being quarantined.[67,75] Research indicates that there was also a certain level of stigma associated with being quarantined during the SARS outbreak, and this contributed to psychological distress among the quarantined.[67] However, the same level of psychological distress associated with quarantine was not found during the 2009 H1N1 pandemic. A study conducted with college students who had been quarantined for 7 to 10 days found that there were no negative psychological consequences from the quarantine.[76] The researchers postulated that the higher psychological impact during the SARS outbreak may have been related to the high mortality rate seen during the SARS outbreak, which could have caused more stress among those who were quarantined compared to those who were quarantined during the H1N1 flu pandemic that had a much lower mortality rate (10 percent mortality during the SARS outbreak versus <1 percent during the H1N1 pandemic).[76] If this is true, then a future event that involves an infectious disease with a fairly high mortality rate would be expected to result in higher rates of negative psychological stress while individuals are quarantined, and this should be factored into the decision-making process

and/or addressed in mental health interventions among the quarantined.

Discussions regarding quarantine policies and procedures should include all of the following groups: (1) local law enforcement, (2) public health agencies, (3) facility administration, (4) security, (5) facility law representatives, (6) infection prevention, and (7) hospital epidemiologist or infectious disease physician/department. Other groups may need to be included, depending on the community and the agency/group that intends to implement quarantine. Current quarantine policies and procedures for healthcare facilities or agencies should be evaluated. In addition, healthcare facilities should partner with local public health officials to evaluate and update existing quarantine laws as needed.

Food Safety

For most infectious disease disasters, food safety will not be a primary concern. Pandemics, for example, will not pose a huge risk of foodborne illness, unless staffing shortages lead to poor food handling or inadequate environmental decontamination in food service industries. However, food safety will be critical if the infectious disease disaster involves a foodborne illness outbreak. Examples might include a bioterrorism attack using a foodborne illness agent, such as botulism, *Salmonella*, or *Shigella*, an agroterrorism attack that involves the infection of livestock or poultry, or if the event involves an emerging infectious disease that is linked to food sources, such as livestock.

An important aspect of biosecurity is ensuring that military and civilian food sources do not become compromised. This is one reason why veterinarians have started collaborating with public health officials to conduct surveillance of livestock: to monitor for potential bioterrorism attacks or emerging infectious zoonotic diseases. If food supplies do become compromised or contaminated, an investigation would need to be conducted. One possible intervention would include conducting environmental sampling; samples would be needed from the food involved, the processing or rendering plant or factory where the animals or food was processed, food preparation areas (if it's a restaurant), and utensils or other equipment that may be involved in the outbreak. Any facility that might be involved in the outbreak may need to be closed down temporarily. Examples include restaurants, rendering plants, dairy or animal farms, or food processing factories. Food safety education and training will be essential during foodborne outbreaks to ensure that workers understand how to safely handle food and decontaminate food preparation areas and equipment.

Water Safety

Water safety will not pose a major challenge for most infectious disease disasters. However, if terrorists were able to infiltrate and contaminate military or civilian water supplies, then water safety would be critical. In the past, military forces have deliberately contaminated wells and reservoirs as a means of poisoning civilians.[2,77] In addition, in the 1970s, two terrorist groups attempted to use biological weapons to poison water supplies.[2] Intentional contamination of a municipal water system could lead to serious medical, public health, and economic consequences. Early recognition, timely outbreak investigations, accurate diagnosis, and rapid reporting by the medical and public health community of suspected waterborne terrorism disease cases will be essential to maintaining water security and safety.

An important aspect of biosecurity is ensuring that military and civilian sources of drinking water do not become compromised. Researchers have identified multiple ways in which our water systems could become contaminated during a bioterrorism attack, including before, during, or after water treatment at water treatment plants.[77] Some have argued that contaminating water before or at the water treatment plant would be ineffective because our current water treatment mechanisms would eliminate any infectious disease risk. However, water could easily be contaminated after it leaves water treatment facilities, such as at water bottling facilities, water supply connections at buildings or in communities, or deliberate contamination of recreational water, such as swimming pools.[77]

If water supplies do become contaminated, an investigation would need to be conducted. One possible intervention would include conducting environmental sampling; samples would be needed from the area or building known to be involved, plus moving backward through the water supply chain to determine the point at which the water first became contaminated. Sampling would identify if the water was only contaminated in a single facility/building or if it became contaminated at a water bottling factory that supplies drinking water to the facility/agency. Waterborne outbreaks can be very challenging to investigate because both animals and humans need water to survive, and animals and humans can get sick from waterborne diseases and then spread them animal to animal, animal to human, or human to human. It might be very complicated to determine that a bioterrorism attack was actually an attack on a water source, if the event involves sick animals and humans. It might look like an aerosol attack on animals, or a foodborne attack on animals that then spread to humans. Any facility that might be involved in a waterborne illness outbreak may need to be closed down temporarily, including healthcare facilities. Public health officials should be notified immediately if waterborne illness is suspected within a healthcare agency.

Healthcare Personnel Surge Capacity

Agencies, organizations, and businesses, including healthcare, should expect high absenteeism rates during an infectious disease disaster. Absenteeism is expected to be higher during an infectious disease disaster than other types of mass casualty events. Up to 20 percent of the workforce may be affected by illness at the same time during a pandemic, and others will be unable or unwilling to work due to family obligations or fear.[12] WHO recommends that emergency managers plan for a 40 percent absenteeism rate during the peak of a pandemic.[12] Healthcare personnel are expected to be infected at the same rate as the general population during an infectious disease

disaster, which will further reduce healthcare facilities' and agencies' abilities to respond to such an event.[78] Healthcare facilities and agencies, including long-term care, home health, and community-based medical clinics, need to plan for this increase in healthcare personnel absenteeism. Some recommended ways for increasing healthcare personnel surge capacity include (1) having back-up contracts for obtaining extra staff; (2) providing incentives to get and keep staff; (3) prioritizing healthcare personnel for anti-infective therapy, prophylaxis, and vaccination; (4) offering anti-infective therapy, prophylaxis, and vaccination to healthcare personnel family members; (5) cohorting patients to decrease staff workload; (6) cohorting staff (dedicating healthcare personnel to provide care for potentially contagious individuals and restrict these staff from working with noninfectious individuals); and (7) cross-training staff to provide patient care outside their routine area/specialty to allow for staff resource distribution. One example of effectively using cross-trained staff to help with patient surge during an infectious disease disaster was the Children's Hospital of Philadelphia's use of nonboard-certified pediatric emergency medicine physicians and medical unit nurses in an emergency department during the 2009 H1N1 pandemic; this increased the emergency department's surge capacity when it was most needed.[79]

A variety of incentives should be considered to encourage employees to work during an infectious disease disaster. Examples include monetary bonuses, transportation, housing and subsistence, child/adult family member care, and pet care.[3] Many of the available interventions for increasing worker surge capacity are not currently being implemented in U.S. hospitals. For example, a recent study of U.S. hospitals found that less than a quarter have cross-trained their employees, less than 40 percent have plans to cohort staff, and less than half currently offer incentives to encourage staff to work during an infectious disease disaster.[3] Of U.S. hospitals that do offer incentives, the three most common incentives offered are free child or adult family member care, temporary housing and subsistence, and healthcare personnel prioritization for anti-infective therapy, prophylaxis, and vaccination.[3] There is no evidence regarding the status of healthcare personnel surge capacity during infectious disease disasters for long-term care, medical clinics, or home health, although it is assumed that surge capacity is no better for these healthcare agencies/groups than for hospitals.

One important incentive to provide healthcare personnel to encourage them to work during infectious disease disasters is to provide them safety measures. This includes prioritizing healthcare personnel for pharmaceutical interventions, such as vaccine and pre- and postexposure prophylaxis, when they are available. Research indicates that providing pharmaceutical interventions to healthcare and public health professionals and their family members significantly increases providers' willingness to work during infectious disease disasters.[80] Despite this, although approximately 80 percent of U.S. hospitals prioritize healthcare personnel to receive anti-infective therapy, prophylaxis, and vaccination during an infectious disease disaster, less than half include healthcare personnel family members in the prioritization plan for pharmacological benefits.[3]

Research indicates that providing adequate supplies of PPE for providers so they can reduce their risk of occupational exposure to infectious diseases also increases the likelihood of healthcare professionals' being willing to work during a biological event.[80] Having adequate supplies of hygiene products and negative pressure rooms for infected patients will also help in limiting the risk of exposure to healthcare personnel and maximize the chances that they will be willing and able to work during a biological event. These issues need to be addressed in healthcare facility disaster planning for infectious disease disasters, so that healthcare personnel surge capacity can be maximized.

There is a caveat to encouraging healthcare personnel to work during an infectious disease disaster: It is imperative that healthcare agencies use a liberal sick leave policy during biological events. Sick healthcare personnel can contribute to the spread of disease during infectious disease disasters, as was seen during the SARS outbreak in which one staff member who worked a single shift while ill was linked to 137 cases of SARS, 45 of whom were other healthcare personnel.[43] Sick healthcare personnel should be furloughed until they are no longer contagious, and the policy should not be punitive.

Decontamination

Decontamination may or may not be an issue after an infectious disease disaster, depending on the following factors: (1) type of event (bioterrorism vs. emerging infectious disease outbreak or pandemic), (2) causative agent, (3) how soon the event is identified, and (4) source of concern (environment or patient). Most infectious disease disasters, including bioterrorism attacks, will likely not require patient or animal decontamination. Pandemics and outbreaks of emerging infectious diseases will not require patient or animal decontamination. In the event of a covert release of a biological agent, patients will not become symptomatic and present to healthcare institutions until days to weeks after the exposure; in this instance, they will most likely have bathed and changed their clothes, thus decontaminating themselves. Only in the event of an announced bioterrorism attack (within 12 to 24 hours after the release) will exposed individuals need to be decontaminated. Patient decontamination consists of bathing, including shampooing of hair, with plain soap and water, and changing their clothing.

Given existing knowledge, environmental decontamination is not considered necessary for outside sources, such as streets, cars, or the outside of buildings after a bioterrorism attack. This is because weather plays a key role in rapidly disseminating biological agents in outside air.

Indoor environmental sources may require extensive decontamination strategies after an infectious disease disaster, but the interventions vary according to the agent involved and the nature

of the event. For example, more stringent decontamination methods are necessary for a bioterrorism attack using anthrax (because of the hardy nature of spores). As the 2001 bioterrorism attacks illustrated, equipment or areas may require specialized decontamination strategies, such as contained buildings, ventilation systems, or machinery with small parts. The costs of decontamination following the 2001 anthrax bioterrorism attack are estimated at $320 million.[4]

Other agents, such as smallpox, require diligent environmental decontamination as well. Smallpox can be spread through direct hand-to-hand contact or indirect contact with fomites, making decontamination of environmental surfaces imperative to prevent secondary transmission. Only EPA-registered, healthcare facility-approved germicides are required for environmental decontamination of smallpox, although a 0.5 percent hypochlorite solution may be used (this solution is made by mixing one part household bleach with nine parts water). In the event of a single smallpox case, scrupulous attention to contact precautions, including good housekeeping with EPA-approved germicides, would be critical to prevent secondary spread. Other potential bioterrorism agents and emerging infections that can be spread by hand-to-hand contact, such as viral hemorrhagic fevers and SARS, would require stringent environmental decontamination as well. Additional information on decontamination can be found in Chapter 119 Emergency Management.

Animal Control

Animal control may be an important nonpharmacological intervention during an infectious disease disaster, depending on the event. Contact with animals, both domesticated and nondomesticated, can lead to the spread of zoonotic illness. Management of service animals for disabled individuals or those that are used for healthcare-related procedures are covered in Chapter 122 Animals Visiting Healthcare Facilities.

Management of animals is less likely to be needed during an infectious disease disaster compared to a natural disaster that results in the displacement of individuals from their homes, but animal control may be essential during biological events that involve an animal vector, such as a West Nile virus, swine flu, or avian flu outbreak. Animal control interventions necessary for infectious disease disasters will primarily be a public health concern. Examples include surveillance of swine and poultry during avian or swine influenza pandemics, education of employees at meat rendering plants or poultry farms, and education of the general public about safe handling of animals while hunting. Animal control should not be an issue for healthcare agencies during infectious disease disasters, unless the animals are vermin.

Pest Control

Natural disasters, especially hurricanes and floods, are likely to result in an increase in insects and other pests in or around the affected community due to rain and high water levels. Healthcare facilities may become infested with insects and/or vermin seeking warmth, moisture, and food. This is less of a concern for infectious disease disasters because there most likely will not be a significant environmental disruption that will cause pests to seek out medical facilities. However, if the biological event involves a vectorborne disease, then pest control will be vital. An example would be a bioterrorism attack involving the release of fleas carrying *Yersinia pestis*, the bacteria that causes plague. If carrier fleas were released, they could easily move throughout the community on animals, such as rats, cats, or dogs, and lead to human illness. If such an event occurs, vector control interventions will be vital to stop the outbreak.

The pest control interventions needed will depend on the disease involved. In the example of a bioterrorism attack involving the release of fleas carrying *Yersinia pestis*, pest control might involve spraying the facility for fleas, or trapping and killing rats if the plague-carrying fleas get into the rat population and rats invade medical facilities. Other pest control interventions would be needed if the vector was mosquitos. Mosquito control measures would include spraying the community for mosquitos, eliminating sources of standing water, and educating the public about mosquito prevention, such as using DEET and wearing long sleeves and pants.

Pest control services should be obtained as needed during an infectious disease disaster, including spraying for mosquitos or setting traps for mice. In addition, the facility's physical structure should be evaluated for any possible entrances for pests, and if found, should be eliminated. Examples include windows with torn or missing screens, unclosed doors that lead to the outside of the building, or sources of standing water.

Postmortem Care

There is a pervasive fear about potential infectious disease outbreaks caused by exposure to disaster victims' dead bodies. However, epidemiological data indicate that there is very little risk of an epidemic related to managing the dead bodies of disaster victims—even infectious disease disasters.[81] However, some infectious disease disasters do pose a threat of disease spread from managing the dead bodies of disaster victims. Examples include outbreaks of cholera, viral hemorrhagic fevers, or smallpox, any of which could put people at risk from disease from exposure to victims' dead bodies if precautions are not taken.[81]

Most of the risk related to handling the bodies of dead victims would be to medical examiners and those involved in conducting an autopsy, because this is an aerosol-generating procedure that could expose those in the room to infectious particles. All of the CDC category A bioterrorism agents could potentially be transmitted during autopsy; in practice, tularemia, viral hemorrhagic fevers, smallpox, glanders, and Q fever have been transmitted to medical examiners while performing autopsy.[82] Therefore, it is essential that pathology departments, medical examiners, coroners, funeral directors, and morgues be informed when the hospital or community is experiencing an infectious disease disaster. This communication should be done before submission

of specimens or delivery of bodies. However, past outbreaks of anthrax and smallpox have been first identified from medical examiner autopsy findings.[82] Therefore, infection prevention is essential for all autopsies and pathology procedures.

All autopsies should be performed using Standard Precautions and following routine departmental practices for infection prevention. Standard Precautions for autopsies includes the use of scrubs, a hair bonnet/cap, impervious gown that covers arms, eye protection (face shield or goggles), shoe covers, double gloves, and respiratory protection.[82] Standard respiratory protection for autopsies consists of an N95 respirator or powered air-purifying respirators (PAPR) because of the aerosols routinely generated during the autopsy procedure (e.g., the use of an oscillating saw).[82] Autopsies should also be performed in a negative pressure room/area.[82] Additional biosafety recommendations for medical examiners and autopsy personnel can be found in "Medical Examiners, Coroners, and Biological Terrorism."[82]

Cremation is recommended for handling the bodies of smallpox and viral hemorrhagic fever victims, but mass cremation or mass burial should not be necessary.[81]

Exercises and Drills

Chapter 119 Emergency Management, outlines the need to perform exercises/drills to assess emergency management plans and how to conduct such exercises. As part of infectious disease disaster preparedness, it is vital that IPs ensure that emergency management drills regularly include a biological agent scenario. These exercises need to involve healthcare facilities, healthcare agencies (including long-term care and home health), and community response agencies to obtain a true sense of the community's preparedness for this type of event. It is also helpful to involve local businesses and schools to fully assess community preparedness for a biological event. A recent study found that although most U.S. hospitals had participated in a disaster drill involving a biological agent scenario in the previous year, approximately 15 percent had not.[3] Many of the hospitals had included community involvement in the exercise and compiled lessons learned from the exercise, but approximately 35 percent had not communicated emergency management plan changes to staff after the exercise.[3] A study conducted after the 2009 H1N1 pandemic found that less than half of all home health agencies engage in regular disaster drills of any kind.[22] A 2011 study[83] found that only 13.6 percent of U.S. businesses overall and 31.3 percent of healthcare agencies have used an infectious disease scenario in a drill or exercise during the past 2 years. Another study found that only 4 percent of schools have incorporated an infectious disease scenario into a disaster drill in the last 2 years.[84]

CONCLUSIONS

After the bioterrorism attack using anthrax-laden letters in the United States in 2001 and the numerous outbreaks of emerging infectious diseases that have occurred, including the 2009 H1N1 pandemic, preparedness for biological events has become a necessity for healthcare, public health, businesses, and schools. The world remains always poised for the next pandemic or large-scale infectious disease outbreak. Infectious disease disaster management encompasses the four principles of emergency management—mitigation, preparedness, response, and recovery—and is a multidepartmental and multiagency endeavor. As experts in the fields of surveillance and epidemiology, IPs play a critical role in hospital/healthcare facility and community preparedness, and are responsible for becoming better prepared to effectively recognize and respond to an infectious disease disaster.

Infectious disease disaster preparedness is an ever-evolving process in which facilities and IPs become better prepared to effectively recognize and respond to a mass casualty event involving a biological agent. This is accomplished through facility assessment, development of a response plan, exercise of the response plan, evaluation of the exercise and the facility's and community's level of preparedness, and incorporation of lessons learned from the evaluation into the plan (i.e., emergency management process).

FUTURE TRENDS

Many issues related to infectious disease disaster preparedness are still being debated, and response strategies are being continuously planned and updated. A few such issues include (1) status of quarantine laws, (2) reimbursement issues related to adverse events associated with the smallpox vaccine, and (3) plan for mass prophylaxis or vaccination distribution. In addition, new guidelines related to avian influenza, smallpox, and other potential infectious disease disaster agents are being evaluated and updated. It is critical for IPs to stay abreast of the ever-changing knowledge base related to infectious disease disaster preparedness and the etiological agents of concern.

INTERNATIONAL PERSPECTIVE

Infectious disease disaster preparedness is an international concern. With the ease and frequency of international travel, it is conceivable for infectious diseases to have a major global impact. SARS is a good example of this phenomenon. Whether intentionally inflicted or a natural event, an outbreak involving an infectious disease is a global issue of concern. Few countries currently have the resources to respond to an infectious disease disaster involving mass casualties.[85] Many countries are working on infectious disease disaster management strategies, both alone and in conjunction with the United States.

REFERENCES

1. Rebmann T. APIC State-of-the-Art Report: the role of the infection preventionist in emergency management. *Am J Infect Control* 2009;37(4):271–281.
2. Texas Department of State Health Services (DSHS). History of bioterrorism. Texas DSHS. 2011. Available at: http://www.dshs.state.tx.us/preparedness/bt_public_history.shtm
3. Rebmann T, Wilson R, LaPointe S, et al. Hospital infectious disease emergency preparedness: A 2007 survey of infection control professionals. *Am J Infect Control* 2009;37(1):1–8.
4. Schmitt K, Zacchia NA. Total decontamination cost of the anthrax letter attacks. *Biosecur Bioterror* 2012;10(1):98–107.
5. Learner M, Fabian GT, Drociuk D. South Carolina preparing for the threat of bioterrorism. *J S C Med Assoc* 2009;105(3):101–103.
6. Egan JR, Hall IM, Leach S. Modeling inhalational tularemia: deliberate release and public health response. *Biosecur Bioterror* 2011;9(4):331–343.
7. Kuehn BM. Human, animal, ecosystem health all key to curbing emerging infectious diseases. *JAMA* 2010;303(2):117–118, 124.
8. McMichael AJ. Globalization, climate change, and human health. *N Engl J Med* 2013;369(1):96.
9. Centers for Disease Control and Prevention (CDC). Multistate outbreak of shiga toxin-producing Escherichia coli O145 infections. CDC website. 2012. Available at: http://www.cdc.gov/ecoli/2012/O145-06-12/index.html.
10. Dawood FS, Iuliano AD, Reed C, et al. Estimated global mortality associated with the first 12 months of 2009 pandemic influenza A H1N1 virus circulation: a modelling study. *Lancet Infect Dis* 2012;12(9):655.
11. U.S. Department of Health and Human Services (DHHS). Pandemic flu history. DHHS website. 2013. Available at: http://www.flu.gov/andemic/history/index.html.
12. World health Organization (WHO). Pandemic influenza preparedness and response: A WHO guidance document. WHO website. 2009. Available at: http://www.ncbi.nlm.nih.gov/books/NBK143060/.
13. Matheny J, Toner E, Waldhorn R. Financial effects of an influenza pandemic on US hospitals. *J Health Care Finance* 2007;34(1):58–63.
14. Meltzer MI, Cox NJ, Fukuda K. The economic impact of pandemic influenza in the United States: priorities for intervention. *Emerg Infect Dis* 1999;5(5):659–671.
15. Centers for Disease Control and Prevention (CDC). Bioterrorism agents/diseases. CDC website. 2013. Available at: http://emergency.cdc.gov/agent/agentlist-category.asp.
16. World Health Organization (WHO). Cumulative number of confirmed human cases for avian influenza A(H5N1) reported to WHO. WHO website. 2013. Available at: http://www.who.int/influenza/human_animal_interface/H5N1_cumulative_table_archives/en/.
17. World Health Organization (WHO). Number of confirmed human cases of avian influenza A(H7N9) reported to WHO. WHO website. 2013. Available at: http://www.who.int/influenza/human_animal_interface/H5N1_cumulative_table_archives/en/.
18. Rebmann T, Mohr LB. Missouri nurses' bioterrorism preparedness. *Biosecur Bioterror* 2008;6(3):243–251.
19. U.S. Department of Health and Human Services (DHHS). Interim guidance on the use and purchase of facemasks and respirators by individuals and families for pandemic influenza preparedness. 2007.
20. Lautenbach E, Saint S, Henderson DK, et al. Initial response of health care institutions to emergence of H1N1 influenza: experiences, obstacles, and perceived future needs. *Clin Infect Dis* 2010;50(4):523–527.
21. Rebmann T, Wagner W. Infection preventionists' experience during the first months of the 2009 novel H1N1 influenza A pandemic. *Am J Infect Control* 2009;37(10):e5–e16.
22. Rebmann T, Citarella B, Subramaniam DS, et al. A home health agency's pandemic preparedness and experience with the 2009 H1N1 pandemic. *Am J Infect Control* 2011;39(9):725–731.
23. Federal Emergency Management Agency (FEMA). *IS-230.c Fundamentals of Emergency Management.* FEMA website. 2013. Available at: http://www.training.fema.gov/EMIWeb/IS/courseOverview.aspx?code=IS-230.c.
24. U.S. Department of Health and Human Services (DHHS). Pandemic influenza plan. DHHS website. 2005. Available at: http://www.flu.gov/planning-preparedness/federal/
25. Rebmann T. Assessing hospital emergency management plans: A guide for infection preventionists. *Am J Infect Control* 2009;37(9):708–714 e704.
26. U.S. Department of Health and Human Services (DHHS). Emergency medical services and non-emergent (medical) transport organizations pandemic influenza planning checklist. 2006.
27. Volkman JC, Rebmann T, Hilley S, et al. Infection prevention disaster preparedness planning for long-term care facilities. *Am J Infect Control* 2012;40(3):206–210.
28. Rebmann T, Citarella B, Subramaniam DP, et al. Assessing the infection prevention components of home health emergency management plans. *Am J Infect Control* 2011;39(9):849–857.
29. U.S. Department of Health and Human Services (DHHS). Pandemic planning. DHHS website. 2006. Available at: http://www.flu.gov/planning-preparedness/federal/
30. Kaplan EH. Detecting bioterror attacks by screening blood donors: a best-case analysis. *Emerg Infect Dis* 2003;9(8):909–914.
31. Goldstein DB. *BioWatch and public health surveillance: Evaluating systems for the early detection of biological threats.* Washington, DC: Institute of Medicine, 2010.
32. Bellazzini MA, Minor KD. ED syndromic surveillance for novel H1N1 spring 2009. *Am J Emerg Med* 2011;29(1):70–74.

33. Vergu E, Grais RF, Sarter H, et al. Medication sales and syndromic surveillance, France. *Emerg Infect Dis* 2006;12(3):416–421.
34. May L, Chretien JP, Pavlin JA. Beyond traditional surveillance: applying syndromic surveillance to developing settings—opportunities and challenges. *BMC Public Health* 2009;9:242.
35. Elkin PL, Froehling DA, Wahner-Roedler DL, et al. Comparison of natural language processing biosurveillance methods for identifying influenza from encounter notes. *Ann Intern Med* 2012;156(1):11–18.
36. World Health Organization (WHO). Zoonosis and food safety. WHO website. 2013. Available at: http://www.who.int/foodsafety/zoonoses/en/.
37. Dorea FC, Sanchez J, Revie CW. Veterinary syndromic surveillance: Current initiatives and potential for development. *Prev Vet Med* 2011;101(1-2):1–17.
38. Bravata DM, McDonald KM, Smith WM, et al. Systematic review: surveillance systems for early detection of bioterrorism-related diseases. *Ann Intern Med* 2004;140(11):910–922.
39. U.S. Department of Health and Human Services (DHHS). Hospital pandemic influenza planning checklist. DHHS website. 2007. Available at: http://www.flu.gov/planning-preparedness/federal/
40. Centers for Disease Control and Prevention (CDC). BioSense Fact Sheet. CDC website. 2013. Available at: http://www.cdc.gov/osels/phsipo/docs/pdf/factsheets/DNDHI_BioSense_12_232372_K_remediated_10_26_2012.pdf.
41. Benoit SR, Burkom H, McIntyre AF, et al. Pneumonia in US hospitalized patients with influenza-like illness: BioSense, 2007-2010. *Epidemiol Infect* 2013;141(4):805–815.
42. Benoit SR, McDonald LC, English R, et al. Automated surveillance of Clostridium difficile infections using BioSense. *Infect Control Hosp Epidemiol* 2011;32(1):26–33.
43. Rebmann T. Preparing for pandemic influenza. *J Perinat Neonatal Nurs* 2008;22(3):191–202.
44. Stankovic C, Mahajan P, Ye H, et al. Bioterrorism: Evaluating the preparedness of pediatricians in Michigan. *Pediatr Emerg Care* 2009;25(2):88–92.
45. Desai M, Crawley-Boevey E, Verlander NQ, et al. Factors associated with prolonged Escherichia coli O157 infection in a school outbreak. *Public Health* 2013;127(6):582–585.
46. Mellou K, Sideroglou T, Potamiti-Komi M, et al. Epidemiological investigation of two parallel gastroenteritis outbreaks in school settings. *BMC Public Health* 2013;13:241.
47. Copeland DL, Basurto-Davila R, Chung W, et al. Effectiveness of a school district closure for pandemic influenza A (H1N1) on acute respiratory illnesses in the community: a natural experiment. *Clin Infect Dis* 2013;56(4):509–516.
48. Garza RC, Basurto-Davila R, Ortega-Sanchez IR, et al. Effect of winter school breaks on influenza-like illness, Argentina, 2005-2008. *Emerg Infect Dis* 2013;19(6):938–44.
49. Johnson A, Howe JL, McBride MR, et al. Bioterrorism and Emergency Preparedness in Aging (BTEPA): HRSA-funded GEC collaboration for curricula and training. *Gerontol Geriatr Educ* 2006;26(4):63–86.
50. Richard JL, Grimes DE. Bioterrorism: class A agents and their potential presentations in immunocompromised patients. *Clin J Oncol Nurs* 2008;12(2):295–302.
51. Sappenfield E, Jamieson DJ, Kourtis AP. Pregnancy and susceptibility to infectious diseases. *Infect Dis Obstet Gynecol* 2013;2013:752852.
52. Pfeiffer J, Avery MD, Benbenek M, et al. Maternal and newborn care during disasters: thinking outside the hospital paradigm. *Nurs Clin North Am* 2008;43(3):449–467.
53. Christian MD. Biowarfare and bioterrorism. *Crit Care Clin* 2013;29(3):717–56.
54. Rebmann T, Hilley S, McCaulley M, et al. Infection prevention for ambulatory care centers during disasters. Association for Professionals in Infection Control and Epidemiology website. 2013. Available at: http://apic.org/Professional-Practice/Emergency-Preparedness
55. U.S. Department of Health and Human Services (DHHS). Considerations for antiviral drug stockpiling by employers in preparation for an influenza pandemic. DHHS website. 2013. Available at: http://www.flu.gov/planning-preparedness/business/antiviral_employer.pdf.
56. World Health Organization (WHO). Summary of status of development and availability of A(H5N1) candidate vaccine viruses and potency testing reagents. WHO website. 2013. Available at: http://www.who.int/influenza/vaccines/virus/candidates_reagents/summary_a_h5n1_cvv_20130813.pdf.
57. Institute of Medicine (IOM). Crisis standards of care: A systems framework for catastrophic disaster response. IOM website. 2012. Available at: http://www.iom.edu/Reports/2012/Crisis-Standards-of-Care-A-Systems-Framework-for-Catastrophic-Disaster-Response.aspx.
58. Gausche-Hill M. Pediatric disaster preparedness: Are we really prepared? *J Trauma* 2009;67(2 Suppl):S73–76.
59. Yassi A, Moore D, Fitzgerald JM, et al. Research gaps in protecting healthcare workers from SARS and other respiratory pathogens: an interdisciplinary, multi-stakeholder, evidence-based approach. *J Occup Environ Med* 2005;47(1):41–50.
60. Banach DB, Bielang R, Calfee DP. Factors associated with unprotected exposure to 2009 H1N1 influenza A among healthcare workers during the first wave of the pandemic. *Infect Control Hosp Epidemiol* 2011;32(3):293–295.
61. Rebmann T, Wilson R, Alexander S, et al. Infection prevention and control for shelters during disasters. Association for Professionals in Infection Control and Epidemiology website. 2013. Available at: http://www.apic.org/Resource_/TinyMceFileManager/Practice_Guidance/Emergency_Preparedness/Shelters_Disasters.pdf.
62. Radonovich LJ, Magalian PD, Hollingsworth MK, et al. Stockpiling supplies for the next influenza pandemic. *Emerg Infect Dis* 2009;15(6):e1.
63. Rebmann T, Alexander S, Bartley J, et al. APIC position paper: Extending the use and/or reusing respiratory protection in healthcare settings during disasters. Association for Professionals in Infection Control and Epidemiology website. 2009. Available at: http://apic.org/Resource_/TinyMceFileManager/Position_Statements/APIC_Position_Ext_the_Use_and_or_Reus_Resp_Prot_in_Hlthcare_Settings1209l.pdf.
64. Siegel JD, Rhinehart E, Jackson M, et al. 2007 Guideline for isolation precautions: Preventing transmission of infectious agents in health care settings. *Am J Infect Control* 2007;35(10 Suppl 2):S65–164.
65. U.S. Department of Health and Human Services (DHHS). Interim pre-pandemic planning guidance: Community strategy for pandemic influenza mitigation in the United States—Early, targeted, layered use of nonpharmaceutical interventions. DHHS website. 2007. Available at: http://www.flu.gov/planning-preparedness/community/community_mitigation.pdf.
66. Chu CY, Li CY, Zhang H, et al. Quarantine methods and prevention of secondary outbreak of pandemic (H1N1) 2009. *Emerg Infect Dis* 2010;16(8):1300–1302.
67. Reynolds DL, Garay JR, Deamond SL, et al. Understanding, compliance and psychological impact of the SARS quarantine experience. *Epidemiol Infect* 2008 July;136(7):997–1007.
68. Pang X, Yang P, Li S, et al. Pandemic (H1N1) 2009 among quarantined close contacts, Beijing, People's Republic of China. *Emerg Infect Dis* 2011;17(10):1824–1830.
69. Kavanagh AM, Bentley RJ, Mason KE, et al. Sources, perceived usefulness and understanding of information disseminated to families who entered home quarantine during the H1N1 pandemic in Victoria, Australia: a cross-sectional study. *BMC Infect Dis* 2011;11:2.
70. Miyaki K, Sakurazawa H, Mikurube H, et al. An effective quarantine measure reduced the total incidence of influenza A H1N1 in the workplace: another way to control the H1N1 flu pandemic. *J Occup Health* 2011;53(4):287–292.
71. Bauerle Bass S, Burt Ruzek S, Ward L, et al. If you ask them, will they come? Predictors of quarantine compliance during a hypothetical avian influenza pandemic: results from a statewide survey. *Disaster Med Public Health Prep* 2010;4(2):135–144.
72. Blendon RJ, DesRoches CM, Cetron MS, et al. Attitudes toward the use of quarantine in a public health emergency in four countries. *Health Aff (Millwood)* 2006;25(2):w15–25.
73. Owolabi T, Kwolek S. Managing obstetrical patients during severe acute respiratory syndrome outbreak. *J Obstet Gynaecol Can* 2004;26(1):35–41.
74. Gupta AG, Moyer CA, Stern DT. The economic impact of quarantine: SARS in Toronto as a case study. *J Infect* 2005;50(5):386–393.
75. Johal SS. Psychosocial impacts of quarantine during disease outbreaks and interventions that may help to relieve strain. *N Z Med J* 2009;122(1296):47–52.
76. Wang Y, Xu B, Zhao G, et al. Is quarantine related to immediate negative psychological consequences during the 2009 H1N1 epidemic? *Gen Hosp Psychiatry* 2011;33(1):75–77.
77. Meinhardt PL. Water and bioterrorism: preparing for the potential threat to U.S. water supplies and public health. *Annu Rev Public Health* 2005;26:213–237.
78. Nap RE, Andriessen MP, Meessen NE, et al. Pandemic influenza and pediatric intensive care. *Pediatr Crit Care Med* 2010;11(2):185–198.
79. Scarfone RJ, Coffin S, Fieldston ES, et al. Hospital-based pandemic influenza preparedness and response: strategies to increase surge capacity. *Pediatr Emerg Care* 2011;27(6):565–572.
80. Garrett AL, Park YS, Redlener I. Mitigating absenteeism in hospital workers during a pandemic. *Disaster Med Public Health Prep* 2009;3 Suppl 2:S141–147.
81. Watson JT, Gayer M, Connolly MA. Epidemics after natural disasters. *Emerg Infect Dis* 2007;13(1):1–5.
82. Nolte KD, Hanzlick RL, Payne DC, et al. Medical examiners, coroners, and biologic terrorism: a guidebook for surveillance and case management. *MMWR Recomm Rep* 2004;53(RR-8):1–27.

83. Rebmann T, Wang J, Swick Z, et al. Business continuity and pandemic preparedness: US health care versus non-health care agencies. *Am J Infect Control* 2013;41(4):e27–33.
84. Rebmann T, Elliott MB, Reddick D, et al. US school/academic institution disaster and pandemic preparedness and seasonal influenza vaccination among school nurses. *Am J Infect Control* 2012;40(7):584–589.
85. Goldrick BA, Goetz AM. Pandemic influenza: what infection control professionals should know. *Am J Infect Control* 2007;35(1):7–13.

SUPPLEMENTAL RESOURCES

Many resources are available for education and training on infectious disease disasters preparedness and the clinical description of potential infectious disease disaster agents. APIC offers many educational opportunities for infectious disease disaster related education. A few examples include multiple webinars provided through the APIC website: http://webinars.apic.org/; the APIC Position Paper, *Extending the Use and/or Reusing Respiratory Protection in Healthcare Settings During Disasters*[63]; and numerous other educational initiatives. Please see the APIC Emergency Preparedness website for additional infectious disease disaster training opportunities: http://www.apic.org /Professional-Practice/Emergency-Preparedness .

Other website sources include the following:

Centers for Disease Control and Prevention: http://www.bt.cdc.gov/

U.S. Army Medical Department. Available at: http://www.usamriid.army.mil/.

Johns Hopkins Center for Biodefense: http://www.jhsph.edu/news/news -releases/2003/preparedness-tips.html/

In addition, many public health departments offer infectious disease disaster educational opportunities; check with your local and state public health department(s) for further information.

CHAPTER 121

Animal Research and Diagnostics

Howard Rush, DVM
Associate Professor and Director
Unit for Laboratory Animal Medicine
University of Michigan Medical School
Ann Arbor, MI

Melissa Dyson, DVM, MS, DACLAM
Clinical Assistant Professor
Unit for Laboratory Animal Medicine
University of Michigan Medical School
Ann Arbor, MI

ABSTRACT

The use of animals in biomedical research is common practice. Although such occurrences are uncommon, personnel working with research animals can be exposed to pathogenic organisms that are carried by animals or that have been given to animals as part of an experiment. The most significant pathogenic agents are discussed in this chapter, along with methods to reduce risk and minimize exposure.

KEY CONCEPTS

- Experimentation on animals is an essential and common component of biomedical research.

- Within the animal research setting, most infection risks have been eliminated through improvement in the health and quality of the animals used.

- Two mechanisms to reduce the risk of infection in animal research are providing training in proper animal research methods and techniques and providing an occupational health program for people working with animals.

- A variety of policies and regulations apply to the use of animals in biomedical research. Some of these specifically address infection risks and employee health and safety.

BACKGROUND

Experimentation on animals is an essential and common component of biomedical research. Animals are used as models in identifying the cause, treatment, and prevention of human disease.[1] Estimates of the numbers of animals used in research vary; however, mice and rats account for more than 90 percent of the mammals used.[2] The remaining mammalian species utilized include hamsters, guinea pigs, rabbits, cats, dogs, pigs, sheep, and various species of nonhuman primates. In addition to mammals, many species of birds, fish, amphibians, and reptiles are used. This variety in species utilization affects the potential for exposure to naturally occurring pathogens. Individuals coming in contact with laboratory animals include scientists, research technicians, veterinarians, veterinary technicians, laboratory animal technicians, and students. Each individual engages in a variety of activities that increase the risk of infection. The purpose of this chapter is to review the factors that affect exposure to naturally occurring and induced infections in laboratory animals and some of the more significant zoonotic diseases that can be encountered.

BASIC PRINCIPLES
Animal Quality and Infection Risks

Animals used in research may be purpose-bred or acquired from the wild or from animal control facilities and shelters.[3] Purpose-bred animals, such as common laboratory rodents (rats, mice, guinea pigs, hamsters, and gerbils), are bred specifically for use in research. Some species may be rederived by cesarean section or embryo transfer and raised in a disease-free barrier to eliminate, not just control, all naturally occurring pathogens.[4] In the course of eliminating all animal pathogens, most or all human pathogens are also eliminated. Rederivation by cesarean section or embryo transfer is commonly used for rodents, whereas larger species such as dogs and cats are rarely rederived; however, extensive efforts are taken to eliminate naturally occurring pathogens by vaccination and strict isolation. Although animal pathogens are eliminated, some human pathogens may remain because rederivation is not undertaken. That is, although animal pathogens have been eliminated, some organisms that are not pathogenic for the animal but are pathogenic for humans may remain. This is because no attempt to rederive the species has occurred.[3]

Conventional animals are those that have varying and uncontrolled health backgrounds. They are generally healthy, and most have been subjected to measures to control the incidence of disease (e.g., vaccination, treatment of specific diseases). No attempt has been made to eliminate human pathogens.[3] Wild or feral animals are acquired from their natural habitat. Examples include many nonhuman primates, nontraditional rodent species (voles, squirrels, groundhogs), armadillos, and marsupials (opossum).

Wild or feral animals pose the greatest risk to humans because the indigenous microbial flora is unknown. They may harbor known and unknown human pathogens.[3] Currently, some nonhuman primates are produced in domestic colonies, but these are more like conventional animals. Most dogs and cats used in research are purpose-bred, but some are acquired from animal dealers or animal control facilities and shelters.[5] The latter animals often have been exposed to and are incubating many diseases common to that species. Even if purpose-bred, dogs and cats may still harbor naturally occurring agents that are transmissible to humans.[3] Farm animals (cow, sheep, pig, horse) are most often acquired from local farms and are conventional.[3]

Infections Caused by Naturally Occurring Pathogens Carried by Animals

Zoonoses are diseases transmitted from animals to humans. Literally hundreds of zoonoses have been reported.[6,7] Zoonotic diseases that occur within biomedical and animal research settings have been reviewed elsewhere.[8-13] Considerable progress has been made in eliminating and limiting the occurrence of these diseases, but some continue to pose threats to humans. Within the animal research setting, many of the zoonoses have been eliminated as a risk through improvement in the health and quality of the animals that are used; however, a few agents remain a concern to personnel engaged in animal research.[8,9,13,14] Several disease agents of concern are discussed here.

Conventional and wild animals pose the greatest risk to personnel working in animal research because it generally is not known at the time of acquisition whether a pathogen is present. In addition, prevalence rates of any given pathogen in the population may be low, or the organism may be carried latently or even be undetectable. For these reasons, persons working with these types of animals should assume that the animals are infected with potential pathogens and take appropriate precautions.

Through the use of preventive measures within animal facilities, including hazard containment equipment, personal protective equipment (PPE), work practices, and educational awareness, considerable progress has been made in reducing, if not eliminating, the occurrence of certain zoonotic diseases. Most contemporary laboratory animal species are acquired from quality sources (purpose-bred) that maintain animals under specific-pathogen-free conditions, thereby further reducing the risks of zoonotic pathogen infection and transmission. However, certain known zoonoses remain of concern to animal facility personnel, and emerging zoonotic pathogens also must be considered by individuals engaged in animal research.[8,9,13,14]

Pathogens Being Used in Experimentally Induced Infections in Animal Models

There are two areas in animal research in which the potential pathogen is known and prevention and treatment can be addressed in advance, namely, infectious disease research and recombinant DNA research (i.e., genetic engineering). In the former, animals serve as hosts for the study of the pathogenesis of infectious disease using known agents that are pathogenic for humans. Animals are inoculated with these pathogens under controlled conditions to permit the study of various facets of the disease process for a better understanding of pathogenesis, treatment, and prevention. In the latter, animals are administered viral agents that have been genetically engineered to be incapable of replication in the host and that contain one or more genes that are to be inserted into the host's cells. This technique allows both insertion of new genes or deletion of specific genes. The animal's genome is thus modified to create new animal models (transgenic animals).

Activities Performed by Personnel Engaged in Animal Research and Activities That Increase the Risk of Infection

Husbandry procedures are performed by support personnel who provide daily care to animals. Common husbandry procedures performed include feeding, watering, removal of soiled bedding containing urine and feces, handling and restraint of animals, and sanitizing and disinfecting cages, equipment, and facilities.[14-16] These activities expose the worker to traumatic injury from animal bites and scratches and from handling and operation of equipment.[14-16] Chemical injuries from disinfectants and sterilants also may occur.[14-16] Animal allergy is a common biologic hazard that is encountered.[14,16,17] Naturally occurring animal disease is another biological hazard. Animals undergoing experimental manipulations may have been given radioactive, chemical, or infectious agents, which may further expose the husbandry staff.[14-16] Of these activities, risk of infection is associated with animal bites and scratches, injury from soiled equipment, aerosol and contact exposure to pathogens in animal waste, and naturally occurring disease.[14-16] Individuals may be exposed by urine splashing into eyes or mucous membranes.

Biomedical procedures are performed by research personnel conducting scientific experiments using animals. In addition, veterinary medical care staff members perform many of the same procedures in providing adequate veterinary care to laboratory animals. Common procedures performed include handling and restraint of animals; injections; collection of blood, urine, feces, and other bodily fluids; surgery; necropsy; and laboratory (bench) activities, such as pipetting, preparing infectious agents and hazardous compounds, and handling animal tissue and fluids.[14-16,18] These activities expose the worker to traumatic injury from animal bites and scratches, needlesticks, lacerations from laboratory glassware and surgical and necropsy instruments, animal allergy, and naturally occurring pathogens.[14-16,18] Of these activities, infection risks are associated with animal bites and scratches, lacerations and aerosol exposure to infected tissues during surgery and necropsy, and needlesticks. Animals given radioactive, chemical, or infectious agents may pose further risk to staff.[14-16,18]

Infection Prevention Techniques That Reduce the Risk of Infection

One important mechanism for reducing the risk of infection in animal research is providing training in proper animal research methods and techniques. Handling and restraint of animals are nearly unavoidable procedures that must be performed by most individuals engaged in animal research. Proper training of personnel in handling and restraint of animals is essential to reduce injuries from animal bites and scratches.[14,16] An adjunct to proper handling and restraint is the use of anesthetics and tranquilizers to manage wild animals and fractious animals that resist handling.[14,19] It is essential that staff receive proper training in the use of these agents for chemical restraint to ensure that proper dosages are used and that animals are adequately anesthetized or tranquilized to prevent loss of animal life due to overdosage.[19] Anesthetized animals must be monitored for respiratory rate, heart rate, and temperature to maintain an appropriate level of sedation.

Another effective means to reduce the risk of employee infections in the animal research setting is to implement an occupational health program for personnel working with animals. Such programs are required under current standards.[14–16,20] The principal concern of such a health program is to protect personnel from and to monitor exposure to hazards emanating from the animals themselves, such as animal infectious agents that are transmissible to humans (zoonoses), animal bites, and allergies to animals. An effective health program for animal handlers also will take into account secondary hazards associated with working with animals, such as radiation exposure when animals are given radioactive materials during the course of an experiment and exposure to toxic chemicals that may be given to animals as part of an experimental protocol.

Health programs should include an educational program to provide staff members with information about zoonoses, personal hygiene, animal bites, allergies, and precautions to be taken by pregnant women. Under some circumstances, periodic physical examinations may be necessary. In some programs, pre-employment and postemployment serum samples may be banked for reference.[14–16,20]

A health program also includes immunization against selected diseases. Minimally, tetanus immunization should be provided. In addition, pre-exposure immunization against rabies and Hepatitis B virus should be considered if personnel will be in contact with animals that may be infected with these agents. If biohazardous agents for which vaccines are available are being used experimentally, consideration should be given to prophylactic immunization.[14–16,20]

Employees should receive instruction regarding the occupational hazards associated with animal research.[14–16,20] Many healthcare providers are unfamiliar with infectious hazards that may be encountered in the animal research setting; therefore, it is incumbent on the employee to be well informed about possible infectious hazards to assist the physician in identifying possible causes of presenting signs and symptoms and establishing a diagnosis when the employee becomes ill.

Most species of nonhuman primates are susceptible to tuberculosis; therefore, nonhuman primate colonies are routinely screened for this disease. If nonhuman primates are being used, personnel should be screened regularly for tuberculosis.[14–16,20]

Employee training should include instruction on the use of protective clothing and personal protective devices.[14–16,20] Specifically, laboratory coats or surgical gowns, gloves, surgical masks or respirators, and eye protection should be used. The type of protective clothing and devices required is determined by the risk of infection. For example, all the preceding items would be required when handling nonhuman primates of the genus *Macaca*, but only gloves and a laboratory coat when handling pathogen-free rats or mice. Personnel should wash their hands as often as necessary to maintain personal hygiene. Employees should not eat, drink, or apply cosmetics in animal rooms.

Individuals operating animal facilities should have strict policies regarding visitation. Access to animal housing areas and laboratories should be limited to authorized personnel. With prior arrangement, visits by other employees or the public may be permitted, but entry should be limited to low-risk areas.

ANIMAL RESEARCH AND DIAGNOSTICS

Applicable Regulations and Standards from Federal Agencies and Accrediting Organizations

Animal Welfare Act

The Animal Welfare Act was enacted in 1966 and has been amended multiple times.[21] The act was initially intended to prevent theft and sale of pet dogs and cats and to ensure the humane care and treatment of animals used in research. The latter objective has been expanded greatly through the amendments and currently accounts for the primary focus of the regulations.[22] The act and regulations are administered by the U.S. Department of Agriculture (USDA). Within the USDA, the responsibility rests with the Animal Care program office of the Animal and Plant Health Inspection Service.[22]

The act and regulations mandate standards for the humane handling, care, treatment, and transportation of dogs, cats, guinea pigs, hamsters, rabbits, nonhuman primates, marine mammals, and other regulated warm-blooded animals. At present, rats, mice, birds, horses, and farm animals are not regulated species.[22] The regulations require that each research facility appoint an institutional animal care and use committee (IACUC) to ensure compliance with the act. The IACUC inspects all animal facilities and reviews the institution's animal care and use program at least once every 6 months. The IACUC reviews all research activities involving animals and must approve those activities before the work can be conducted.[22] The regulations also require that each facility establish a program of adequate veterinary care for animals used in research.[22]

Public Health Service Policy on Humane Care and Use of Laboratory Animals

The *Public Health Service (PHS) Policy on Humane Care and Use of Laboratory Animals*[23] was originally published in 1971. It was revised following passage of the Health Research Extension Act of 1985 (Pub Law No. 99–158). That act required the secretary of the Department of Health and Human Services, acting through the Director of the National Institutes of Health (NIH), to establish guidelines for the proper care and treatment of animals used in research, including the appropriate use of tranquilizers, analgesics, anesthetics, paralytics, and euthanasia; appropriate presurgical and postsurgical veterinary medical and nursing care; and the organization and operation of animal-care committees. The policy is intended to implement general government recommendations on animal care and use contained in the federal publication *U.S. Government Principles for the Utilization and Care of Vertebrate Animals Used in Testing, Research, and Training*.[23] The Office of Laboratory Animal Welfare (OLAW) at the NIH is charged with ensuring compliance with the policy.[23] The policy applies to all PHS-conducted or PHS-supported activities involving animals, regardless of where they are conducted. An animal is defined as any live, vertebrate animal used or intended for use in research, training, or testing.[23]

Each institution must submit a document termed an Animal Welfare Assurance to OLAW. The assurance must describe three components: the institutional animal care and use program, whether the institutional animal care and use program is accredited, and the IACUC. The institutional official must sign the assurance. OLAW evaluates assurances to determine the adequacy of the institution's animal care program. Without an assurance, PHS-supported animal research is not permitted. Assurances are valid for as long as 4 years.[23]

The PHS policy requires each institution to appoint an IACUC, as does the Animal Welfare Act. The functions of the IACUC are as follows:

- Review the program every 6 months for humane care and use of animals using the *Guide for the Care and Use of Laboratory Animals* as the standard.[20]

- Inspect the animal facilities every 6 months using the guide as the standard.

- Prepare reports on findings and submit these to the designated institutional official.

- Review concerns involving animal care and use at the institution.

- Make recommendations to the institutional official regarding any aspect of the animal program, facilities, or training.

- Review and approve, and require modifications in or withhold approval of, proposed or ongoing activities related to the use and care of animals.

- Review and approve, and require modifications in or withhold approval of, proposed significant changes regarding the use of animals in ongoing activities.

- Be authorized to suspend activities involving animals that are not conducted in accordance with the institutional assurance, policy, guide, or Animal Welfare Act.[23]

The IACUC must conduct a review of those components of research projects related to the care and use of animals and determine that the proposed research projects are in accordance with the policy, the Animal Welfare Act, the guide, and the institutional assurance.[23] The review must confirm the following:

- Procedures are conducted to minimize pain, distress, and discomfort to the animals.

- Procedures that may cause more than momentary pain or distress are conducted using appropriate anesthetics, analgesics, and tranquilizers unless the procedure is justified for scientific reasons in writing by the investigator.

- Animals are euthanized if pain or distress cannot be relieved.

- The living conditions of animals will be appropriate for the species and contribute to their health and comfort. The housing, feeding, and nonmedical care of animals will be directed by a veterinarian or other scientist trained and experienced in the proper care, handling, and use of the animal being maintained.

- Medical care must be available and provided as needed by a veterinarian.

- Research personnel must be appropriately qualified and trained to perform the procedures described in the protocol.

- Euthanasia methods must conform to the standards in the *American Veterinary Medical Association Guidelines for the Euthanasia of Animals: 2013 Edition* unless a deviation is justified for scientific reasons in writing by the investigator.[24]

Guide for the Care and Use of Laboratory Animals

The *Guide for the Care and Use of Laboratory Animals*[20] was first published in 1963 and has gone through several revisions that mirror the changes that have occurred in the use and care of animals in research. The guide provides recommendations on the humane care and use of laboratory animals in biomedical research. The guide calls upon published reports, scientific principles, expert opinion, and professional experience in advising on the design and operation of humane animal care and use programs. Subjects covered include recommendations for institutional policies (regarding veterinary care, personnel qualifications, occupational health programs, use of hazardous agents, and animal restraint), laboratory animal husbandry (caging and housing systems, space recommendations, microenvironments and macroenvironments, food, bedding, water, sanitation, identification), veterinary medical care programs (preventive medicine, animal procurement, quarantine, diagnosis and treatment of animal disease, anesthesia and analgesia, surgery and postsurgical care, and euthanasia), and construction guidelines for animal facilities.[21]

Association for Assessment and Accreditation of Laboratory Animal Care International

The Association for Assessment and Accreditation of Laboratory Animal Care (AAALAC) International was founded in 1965 to accredit institutional animal care and use programs and facilities. AAALAC International uses the standards in the guide[20] as the benchmark for evaluating programs and facilities. Site visitors to an institution inspect the facilities and collect information on animal care and use policies and procedures. The site visit report is presented to the AAALAC Council on Accreditation, which evaluates the program and makes recommendations on accreditation. Programs that meet the standards in the guide are given the status of accredited. In addition, recommendations are made on how to improve the program in order to achieve or retain accreditation.[22]

Biosafety in Microbiological and Biomedical Laboratories

Biosafety in Microbiological and Biomedical Laboratories[25] is a joint publication of the Centers for Disease Control and Prevention (CDC) and the NIH. It contains guidelines for handling infectious agents in the laboratory and for working with animals that harbor infectious agents. Infectious agents are classified into four risk groups. Characteristics of agents, laboratory practices, safety equipment, and facility design criteria are described for each biosafety level (BSL). Corresponding animal facility practices, safety equipment, and facility design criteria are given for each animal biosafety level (ABSL).[25] There is a distinction between risk group and biosafety level. Risk groups are based on the ability of an infectious agent to cause disease in humans and the severity of that disease. The selection of BSL is based on a risk assessment that takes risk group into consideration along with mode of transmission, procedures to be performed, personnel experience, and other factors.

Biosafety Level 1 and Animal Biosafety Level 1

Agents in BSL-1 are known not to cause disease in healthy humans. Standard animal care practices and routine microbiologic practices are used. Gloves and laboratory coats would typically be worn in animal rooms. Eyewear might be recommended if there was a potential for splash or aerosol. Special safety equipment is not required in the laboratory or animal facility. Standard animal facility design and laboratory facilities can be used. A hand-washing sink should be available in the animal facility. Exhaust air is discharged to the outside without being recirculated. Rooms should be under negative pressure with respect to the hallway, if possible.

Biosafety Level 2 and Animal Biosafety Level 2

Agents in BSL-2 are known to cause disease of varying severity in humans. Such agents are considered moderate in risk. Exposure can occur by autoinoculation, ingestion, percutaneously, or via the mucous membranes. Laboratory and animal facility practices incorporate BSL-1 practices for the laboratory and ABSL-1 practices for the animal facility with additional requirements reflective of increased risk, such as restricted access, posting of biohazard warning signs, implementation of sharps precautions, appropriate decontamination (preferably by autoclaving) of all infectious wastes and animal cages prior to washing, and delineation of any medical surveillance policies.

In the laboratory, safety equipment consists of Class II biologic safety cabinets (BSCs) when a risk of aerosol or splashes exists during manipulation of the agent and laboratory coats, gloves, and face protection as needed. Similarly, in the animal facility, safety equipment consists of containment equipment specific for the animal species and PPE such as laboratory coats or gowns, gloves, face and respiratory protection (surgical masks, dust or mist masks, or respirator as appropriate for the activity being performed and the hazardous agent being used), and eye protection. When infectious materials are being manipulated, or if aerosols or splashes might be created, a BSC or other physical containment equipment should be used. For the animal facility, the availability of an autoclave is recommended. In addition, a hand-washing sink in the animal room is required. Animal rooms should be maintained under negative pressure relative to adjacent hallways.

Biosafety Level 3 and Animal Biosafety Level 3

BSL-3 facilities and practices are intended for work with indigenous or exotic agents, agents that present a potential for aerosol transmission, and agents causing serious or potentially lethal disease. ABSL-3 facilities and practices are for working with animals infected with these agents. BSL-3 and ABSL-3 build upon the standard practices, procedures, containment equipment, and facility requirements of BSL-2 and ABSL-2.

The standard and special safety practices, safety equipment, and facility requirements are similar for BSL-3 and ABSL-3. Highlights of these are provided below.

A medical surveillance program, based on an appropriately conducted risk assessment, must be available for personnel working with infected animals. Immunizations should be provided if available. Consideration should be given to the need for collection and storage of serum samples. Information should be provided on the impact of immune status on susceptibility to infection. Individuals with immune dysfunctions should be encouraged to self-identify so that appropriate counseling can be provided.

Policies for the safe handling of sharps, such as needles, scalpels, pipettes, and broken glassware must be developed and implemented.

PPE must be utilized to reduce exposure to infectious agents, animals, and contaminated equipment. A risk assessment should determine the appropriate type of PPE to be utilized. Examples of PPEs that might be used include coverall suits; wraparound or solid-front gowns; gloves; eye, face, and respiratory protection; and boots, shoe covers, or other protective footwear.

A method for decontaminating all infectious materials (including animal tissues, carcasses, contaminated bedding, unused feed, sharps, and other refuse) must be available within the facility. Several types of decontaminating systems are available (e.g., autoclave or chemical disinfection).

Whenever possible, the manipulation of infectious materials, handling of infected animals, or procedures that generate aerosols must be conducted in Class II or Class III BSCs or other physical containment devices. When a procedure cannot be performed within a BSC, a combination of PPE and other containment devices must be used.

The use of containment caging systems to reduce exposure to aerosols from infected animals and bedding should be considered.

BSL-3 and ABSL-3 facilities have special engineering and design features, including:

- Restricted access
- Double-door entry comprising an anteroom/airlock and a change room
- Showers
- Inward directional airflow, which draws air from "clean" areas and toward "contaminated" areas
- Ducted exhaust air ventilation system with discharge of exhaust air to the outside
- No recirculation of exhaust air
- Availability of an autoclave convenient to the animal rooms

Biosafety Level 4 and Animal Biosafety Level 4

BSL-4 and ABSL-4 practices and facilities are used when working with dangerous and exotic agents where there is a high risk of life-threatening disease or aerosol transmission. Agents that are related to known pathogens in this group but have an unknown level of risk or transmission also should be placed in this category. Often there is no vaccine and possibly no therapy available for these agents. There are only a few facilities in the United States equipped to handle agents in this risk group.

The standard and special safety practices, safety equipment, and facility requirements are similar for BSL-4 and ABSL-4. Highlights of these are provided here.

There are two models for BSL-4 and ABSL-4 facilities:

- A cabinet laboratory, where agents are handled in Class III BSCs
- A suit laboratory, where personnel wear a positive-pressure protective suit

BSL-4 and ABSL-4 cabinet and suit laboratories have special engineering and design features to prevent microorganisms from escaping containment:

- Rooms in the facility must be arranged to ensure sequential passage through an inner (dirty) changing area, a personal shower, and an outer (clean) change room prior to exiting.

- An automatically activated emergency power source must be provided for the exhaust system, life support systems, alarms, lighting, entry and exit controls, BSCs, and door gaskets.
- A dedicated nonrecirculating ventilation system is required. The supply and exhaust components of the ventilation system must be designed to maintain the laboratory at negative pressure.
- Redundant supply fans are recommended. Redundant exhaust fans are required. Supply and exhaust fans must be interlocked to prevent positive pressurization of the laboratory.
- The ventilation system must be monitored and alarmed to indicate malfunction or deviation from design parameters.
- Class III BSCs must be directly and independently exhausted through two high-efficiency particulate absorption filters in series. Supply air must be provided in a manner that prevents positive pressurization of the cabinet.

Entry and exit to the facility are through clothing change and shower rooms. A complete clothing change (undergarments, pants, shirts, jumpsuits, shoes, and gloves) is required to enter the facility. All persons leaving the laboratory must take a personal body shower.

In suit laboratories, all procedures must be conducted by personnel wearing a one-piece positive-pressure suit ventilated with a life support system.

An occupational medical program must be provided. The program includes medical surveillance and immunizations for agents being used; collection and storage of serum samples from at-risk personnel; and a system for reporting and documenting laboratory accidents, exposures, and employee absenteeism.

Transfer of supplies and materials into the facility is generally through a double-door autoclave, fumigation chamber, or airlock.

All equipment and supplies taken inside the laboratory must be decontaminated before removal. Decontamination of equipment that cannot be autoclaved is by gaseous or vapor methods (e.g., vaporized hydrogen peroxide or gaseous chlorine dioxide).

Protocols for emergency situations (e.g., medical emergencies, facility malfunctions, fires, escape of animals within the laboratory) must be established.

All manipulations of infectious materials within the facility must be conducted in Class III BSCs. Decontamination of materials passing out of the Class III BSC(s) is through an interlocked double-door, pass-through autoclave, dunk tank, fumigation chamber, or equivalent decontamination method.

Centers for Disease Control and Prevention Guidelines

The CDC has published infection prevention guidelines for healthcare facilities that include recommendations regarding animals brought into such facilities.[26] Guidelines for animal-assisted activities and resident animal programs include precautions against nonhuman primates and reptiles for use in healthcare facilities. Animals should be healthy, well groomed, fully vaccinated, and well trained. Immunocompromised animal care personnel should avoid contact with animal feces, saliva, urine, or litter box material. Increasingly, animals are being brought into healthcare facilities as patients or research subjects to access imaging and oncology equipment. Under such conditions, the healthcare facility should develop specific policies to address this type of usage. Human healthcare facilities should be used only if veterinary facilities are unavailable. Animal care should be under the supervision of a licensed veterinarian. Patient care areas where invasive procedures are performed should be avoided for the treatment of animal patients. Animal procedures should be scheduled late in the day when human patients are not likely to come in contact with animals. Environmental surfaces should be disinfected after animals have been removed. Likewise, equipment should be disinfected or sterilized after animal contact, or disposable equipment and supplies should be used. Reusable medical and surgical instruments should be restricted for use only in animals.

Occupational Health and Safety in the Care and Use of Nonhuman Primates

Occupational Health and Safety in the Care and Use of Nonhuman Primates[27] specifically addresses the risks associated with exposure to nonhuman primates in biomedical research. It draws on the principles and practices in Occupational Health and Safety in the Care and Use of Research Animals.[14] Infectious and noninfectious hazards are discussed, and information on risk management is provided. Recommendations on medical treatment following exposure to nonhuman primate hazards are provided.[27]

Viral Agents

Macacine herpesvirus 1 (formerly Cercopithecine herpesvirus 1 [CHV-1]) (also known as B Virus)

B virus is the most significant infectious occupational health hazard in nonhuman primate research. B virus, an alpha herpesvirus closely related to herpes simplex virus, is carried by Asian and African monkeys in the genus Macaca. The agent has been found principally in rhesus (M. mulatta) and cynomolgus (M. fascicularis), but also has been isolated from bonnet (M. radiata), Japanese (M. fuscata), Taiwan (M. cyclopis), and stump-tailed (M. arctoides) macaques.[28-30]

Initial infections in macaques are usually asymptomatic; however, lesions may occur in the oral, ocular, and genital regions. Lesions consist of fluid-filled vesicles on the dorsum of the tongue, the mucocutaneous border of the lips, the inside of the cheeks, or the genitalia. These blisters rupture, scab over, and eventually heal in 7 to 14 days. The virus is shed from active lesions. In addition, conjunctivitis may be observed. Once infection is established, B virus remains latent in the trigeminal or lumbosacral sensory ganglia. Systemic disease is rare in macaques.[28]

Transmission to humans occurs through exposure to contaminated animals (e.g., scratches, bites, splashes to mucosal membranes, contact with infected animal tissues) or contaminated equipment (e.g., needlesticks, sharp cage parts). Direct correlation cannot be made between the extent of animal-associated injury and the likelihood of infection.[28] The incubation period from exposure to symptomatic disease ranges from weeks to years (due to reactivation of latent infection). In most cases, death has occurred from 2 days to 6 months after infection. The virus propagates within the peripheral nervous tissue (ganglia) and spreads to the spinal cord and eventually the brain.[28]

Human cases of B virus are considered rare, despite its prevalence in the host species and the large numbers of macaques used in research.[31] Early-stage symptoms include influenza-like illness and headaches. On some occasions, vesicles have formed near skin wounds exposed to contaminated animals or equipment. Progression of the disease involves symptoms attributed to central nervous system infection, including alterations in vision, seizures, and respiratory failure.[29] Without treatment, mortality in infected humans is estimated to be approximately 80 percent.[28]

Detection of the virus in nonhuman primates and humans is performed by serologic testing and virus isolation at the B Virus Research and Resource Laboratory (Georgia State University, Atlanta, GA) or at the Central Public Health Laboratory (London, United Kingdom). The presence of serum antibodies indicates infection with the virus but not necessarily shedding of virus. Viral culture is often unreliable because of intermittent shedding of the virus by infected monkeys and the difficulty in recovering virus in tissue culture. Polymerase chain reaction (PCR) and reverse-transcriptase (RT)-PCR also can be used for detection of virus.[28,32]

Postexposure prophylaxis with antiviral therapy has been efficacious when instituted within 72 hours after exposure; however, studies of antiviral dosing and time courses primarily have been performed in rabbits.[28]

Guidelines for prevention of herpes B virus infection in monkey handlers have been published.[28] Because overt clinical disease is rarely observed in macaques infected with B virus, viral shedding occurs in the absence of observable indicators. All macaque monkeys should be treated as though infected, and their bodily fluids and soiled cages should be handled as if they were contaminated. Macaque monkeys should be used for research purposes only when clearly indicated. Activities involving the use of tissue, cells, blood, or serum from macaques should be performed using ABSL-2 practices. BSL-2 practices are recommended for B virus culture activities, and BSL-3 facilities are recommended for propagation of virus or work with animal models of B virus infection. B virus is classified as a select agent by the federal government and requires CDC registration for use in research.[25]

Access to areas where macaques are housed or used should be limited to those who are trained in procedures to avoid risk of infection. Personnel who might contact macaque monkeys or their bodily fluids must wear protective clothing, including long-sleeved gowns or laboratory coats, latex gloves, eye goggles or face shields, and surgical masks. Monkey handlers must be trained in the proper methods of restraint and in the use of protective clothing. Restraining or handling fully awake macaques is not recommended unless required by the approved scientific protocol. Fully awake macaques should be handled only with arm-length leather gloves, and animals should be removed from cages by the use of pole and collar restraint.

The most critical period for the prevention of B virus infection is during the first minutes after the exposure occurs.[28] Bites or scratches from macaques should be immediately and thoroughly scrubbed with antiseptic soap and water. Any exposure should be reported immediately to the appropriate supervisory personnel. The placement of monkey bite, scratch, and needlestick first aid kits in primate housing facilities has been recommended. Employees working with macaques should receive training in first aid procedures for treatment of wounds potentially contaminated with B virus.[28] Wounds sustained from working with monkeys or equipment contaminated with monkey saliva or urine should be scrubbed vigorously for 15 minutes with gauze sponges soaked in antiseptic soap. If eye splashes occur, rinse the eyes immediately with water at an eye wash station or sink for 15 minutes. If water is not available, use ocular irrigating solution. Prompt medical attention should then be sought.

Any wounds sustained from macaque exposure should be cultured for B virus, and blood should be drawn for B virus serologic testing. The patient should be educated about the clinical signs of herpes B virus infection.[28] The wound should be examined every other day for the first week and then weekly through the end of the fourth week. The wound should be assessed for vesicle formation, itching, pain, and numbness. After an observation period of 2 to 3 weeks, a second serum sample should be drawn to determine whether serum antibodies have developed.

Laboratory evaluation of the monkey associated with the human injury is an important component in treatment of the patient. At the time of exposure, the monkey should be examined for the presence of lesions; serum samples should be drawn; and viral cultures should be collected from bilateral conjunctiva, buccal mucosa, and genitalia. A convalescent serum sample should be collected 3 weeks after injury. A rise in B virus-specific antibody suggests active infection at the time of the employee's injury. The monkey colony personnel, veterinary and husbandry staff, and involved physicians should receive the results of the veterinary evaluation.[28]

If clinical signs develop, the patient should be referred to a physician who is knowledgeable about evaluation and management of B virus infections.

Hantavirus

Hantaviruses comprise a genus in the family Bunyaviridae. Each type of hantavirus, of the approximately 21 that have been identified, is associated with rodent hosts, including rats, mice, and other wild rodents. As hantaviruses continue to be isolated from the estimated 2,000 species of murid rodents, there may be greater numbers of zoonoses characterized in laboratory animal rodents.[33] Hantaviruses have not been reported in personnel working in contemporary animal facilities with commonly used laboratory rats (Rattus norvegicus) and mice (Mus musculus).

Hantaviruses cause asymptomatic infections in rodent hosts. The virus is shed in the saliva, urine, and feces of persistently infected rodents for months.[34] Transmission occurs through inhalation of infective aerosols, wound contamination, conjunctival exposure, and ingestion.[13] Infectious virus also may be present in the blood and organs of infected mice.[35] Rat cell lines have been demonstrated to be a source of infective virus.[36]

Two syndromes has been associated with hantaviral infection of humans: hemorrhagic fever with renal syndrome (HFRS) and hantavirus cardiopulmonary syndrome (HCPS). HFRS has been documented in numerous animal facility personnel, particularly in Japan, France, the United Kingdom, Singapore, and Belgium.[13] The severity of HFRS is related to the strain of virus involved. Clinical symptoms include acute onset of fever with lower back pain. HCPS, caused by the Sin Nombre virus (reservoir: deer mice Peromyscus maniculatus), is characterized by fever, myalgia, and gastrointestinal distress.[37] HCPS has not been associated with rats of the genus Rattus or mice of the genus Mus. The incubation period in humans averages from 2 to 4 weeks.[38]

Recommendations for management of hantaviruses in laboratory animal facilities have been published elsewhere.[25,33] In general, potentially infected tissue samples should be handled in BSL-2 facilities in accordance with BSL-3 practices. Experimentally infected rodents that do not excrete the virus can be housed in ABSL-2 facilities and handled using ABSL-2 practices. BSCs and other containment devices should be used whenever there is a high potential for generating aerosols. Studies in which virus is inoculated into Peromyscus maniculatus or other permissive species should be conducted at ABSL-4.

Exposure to rodents and their tissues should be prevented by using proper PPE. Treatment of symptoms in humans involves supportive care.

Lymphocytic Choriomeningitis Virus

Lymphocytic choriomeningitis virus (LCMV) is an arenavirus. It exists in the wild mouse population in all areas of the world. Infection has been reported in many potential laboratory animal species, including mice, rats, hamsters, guinea pigs, chinchillas, rabbits, dogs, nonhuman primates, swine, and chickens. Wild mice are the principal reservoir of infection for susceptible species. Laboratory mice, hamsters, marmosets, and tamarins have been implicated in transmission of disease to humans.[8,9,39,40]

Disease in infected animals is dependent on age, strain and dose of virus, and route of inoculation.[41] In adult mice, the disease is self-limiting. However, neonatally infected mice develop persistent, lifelong infections. These animals act as carriers and shed virus particles throughout their lives.[8,9,39,42] Athymic and severe-combined immunodeficient mice can harbor silent, chronic infections.[43]

Infection may be transmitted by several routes: direct skin or mucous membrane contact with the infective secretions (urine, feces, saliva), ingestion or inhalation of aerosolized virus particles from the animal room or cage, parenteral exposure, and contact with contaminated bedding material or infected ectoparasites.[14,42] In addition, tissue culture cell lines and transmissible tumors can become contaminated and harbor the virus. These can serve as either a means for transmission of the agent into mouse colonies or for infection of laboratory workers. Transmission by aerosolization is a particular hazard for pregnant women; LCMV has been shown to induce abortion in early stages of gestation and is a teratogen when a fetus is exposed in later stages of pregnancy.[42,44]

Influenza-like illness (ILI) due to LCMV infection has occurred in animal technicians, research personnel, and veterinarians. Headache, fever, and myalgia are often noted, and clinical symptoms may progress to aseptic meningitis. In immunocompetent individuals, ILI is most common clinical syndrome, but there have been reports of neurologic symptoms or more serious systemic illnesses. Immunocompromised patients are at a higher risk of illness and including reports of hemorrhagic fevers.[42] The incubation period ranges from 1 to 3 weeks.[13]

Infection can be detected in mice by virus isolation assays and PCR analysis of target tissues. Contamination of cell and tumor lines can be determined by inoculation of susceptible mice with the tumor or cell line and subsequent detection of antibodies to the virus in infected mice, or with PCR analysis of cell or tumor lines. In humans, serologic detection of rising antibody titers in paired sera is considered diagnostic.[38]

Prevention of the disease in humans is fostered by proper hygiene, including the use of latex or other medical gloves and subsequent hand washing after rodent handling.[8] ABSL-3 practices and facilities are recommended for activities with a high potential for production of aerosols, for manipulation of quantities of infectious material, or for work with infected animals.[25] Surveillance is performed by testing rodent serum for viral contaminants endemic in the colony; infected colonies may be freed of the virus by depopulation and cesarean rederivation.[38]

Orf (Contagious Ecthyma; Contagious Pustular Dermatitis)

Orf disease is caused by a parapoxvirus and occurs worldwide in sheep and goats. Typical lesions in these animal species consist of proliferative pustules around the lips, gums, nostrils, teats and udders, and urogenital openings.[14] Interdigital and coronet lesions may be associated with laminitis. The disease in goats tends to be more severe than that in sheep.[45] The virus is transmitted, from animal to animal and animal to human, most commonly by direct contact with exudates from lesions and

sometimes through fomites.[14] The virus is highly resistant to desiccation and can persist in clinically apparent lesions.

In humans, the disease begins as a solitary maculopapular or pustular lesion on the hands, arm, or face that progresses to a weeping, proliferative, umbilicated nodule.[14] The incubation period ranges from 3 to 6 days. Treatment is typically not undertaken because the disease is self-limiting over 3 to 6 weeks.

Personnel working with sheep should wear gloves and possibly other protective clothing that covers exposed skin. Laboratory sheep and goats may be given preemptive vaccinations with live attenuated virus or scarification with a suspension of infective scab material.[14,46] In addition, it is recommended to disallow entry of clinically affected animals into established research herds.

Rabies

Rabies is caused by a rhabdovirus and can infect most mammalian species, including laboratory dogs, cats, ferrets, livestock, and nonhuman primates. Initial signs of disease in animals vary considerably from agitation and confusion to ataxia and paralysis. Death can occur in animals within 2 to 7 days of illness.[45]

Suspect animals should be quarantined for 10 days after any bite injury to humans to observe for behavioral signs suggestive of infection that would warrant euthanasia.[47] Animals that meet criteria for true rabies virus infection should be necropsied, and the brain tissues should be analyzed for viral antigen.[45]

Transmission is sustained by the bite of a rabid animal or inoculation of infective saliva into mucous membranes or fresh wounds. Although no cases of rabies have been reported in animal facility personnel, it is important to monitor for this zoonotic pathogen in facilities that use random-source or conventional animals of unknown health background. In humans, rabies can cause headaches, fever, and malaise that can progress to encephalomyelitis and death due to respiratory paralysis. The incubation period can be as short as 10 days, but averages 3 to 8 weeks in length. Detection of viral antibody and viral isolation from affected tissues is necessary for diagnosis. Treatment is usually unrewarding.

Rabies in high-risk animal personnel is often prevented by pre-exposure immunization. Immediate and thorough wound disinfection is recommended. Postexposure administration of human rabies immunoglobulin at the wound site may be beneficial. National standards address prevention of rabies virus for persons in the United States.[48,49] Verification of current rabies vaccination should be mandatory for dogs, cats, and ferrets that enter the existing animal colony.

Rickettsial Agents

Cat Scratch Fever

Bartonella henselae is the etiologic agent of cat scratch fever. Cats, and occasionally dogs, are the reservoir of this agent. Infection is usually asymptomatic, though reproductive failure in female cats and peliosis hepatitis in dogs have been reported.

The cat flea is the principal vector that spreads infection within the animal population; however, flea-to-human transmission is unlikely. Infection typically occurs in humans following bites or scratches from healthy young cats and occasionally dogs. This agent is an emerging pathogen among immunosuppressed individuals and warrants appropriate precautions in animal facilities.[50,51]

Most human infections occur between September and February and follow a cat bite or scratch, usually from pet animals.[14] No cases within a laboratory animal setting have been documented. After traumatic inoculation, an erythematous papular lesion develops, followed by a vesicle and scab. Although the local lesion resolves within a week, regional lymphadenopathy develops several weeks later. The lymph node may rupture, and the patient may exhibit fever, malaise, anorexia, headache, and splenomegaly. More serious complications, though less common, include periocular lymphadenopathy, conjunctivitis, central nervous system involvement, osteolysis, hepatitis, and pneumonia. If the patient is immunocompromised, severe systemic or recurrent infection, including bacillary angiomatosis, can develop.[14] The incubation period ranges from 3 to 14 days for development of the primary lesion and as long as 50 days for development of lymphadenopathy.

Definitive diagnosis requires culture of the organism from a lesion. However, it is common to accept a combination of clinical signs, history of contact with cats, histopathological examination of biopsy tissue, and failure to isolate other causative agents from cultures as evidence of infection.[14] Systemic cat scratch disease should be included in the differential list for patients presenting with fever of unknown origin and abdominal pain, especially if there is a history of contact with a cat or kitten.[52]

Personnel handling cats should be instructed in proper restraint techniques and should use protective clothing to prevent scratches and bites. Wounds sustained from cats in particular should be thoroughly disinfected.

Q Fever

Coxiella burnetii is the etiologic agent of Q fever. Both wild and domestic species act as hosts. Within the animal facility, sheep, goats, and cattle are the most important reservoir hosts.[8,53] Dogs and cats also have been reported to serve as reservoir hosts. Infected animals are generally asymptomatic; however, in cases of severe infection, abortion and reproductive failure may occur.

Due to concerns of Coxiella burnetii as a bioterrorism agent, it has been added to the list of reportable diseases.[54]

The organism is shed in the urine, feces, milk, and birth products of domestic sheep, goats, and cattle. Transmission to humans often follows exposure to fetal membranes, birth fluids, and stillborn animals. Inhalation of infective tissues may occur during parturition. Ixodid and argasid ticks can serve as reservoirs and vectors of the organism.[45] The incubation period ranges from 2 to 3 weeks. Acute infection in humans results in

ILI, with headaches, fever, and myalgia. Pneumonia is one of the primary manifestations of acute Q fever.[55,56] Infection in pregnant women can lead to spontaneous abortion. Additionally, women who contract Q fever during pregnancy are at a higher risk of developing chronic infections than the general population.[55] Chronic infection may result in granulomatous hepatitis or endocarditis. In patients with underlying valvular disease, chronic infection may manifest as culture-negative endocarditis. Chronic infection can occur within a few months or even years after an acute infection.[55,56] Diagnosis can be made through detection of increasing antibody titers between acute and convalescent samples or by identifying the organism in infected tissues or body fluids via PCR or culture.[54,55] Doxycycline is the recommended treatment for Q fever and is most effective when given early in the course of diease.[55]

To prevent exposure to the organism, obtain only male sheep or nonpregnant female sheep for experimental purposes. Sheep also may be purchased from known Q fever-negative flocks. Employees should wear protective clothing, such as surgical masks, disposable gloves, shoe covers, and gowns or laboratory coats, when handling sheep and goats. Due to the risk of aerosol transmission, it is helpful to ensure adequate ventilation in ruminant housing areas and to keep these animals physically separated from humans. If pregnant ewes must be used for research purposes, an N95 respirator and eye protection are recommended when working with the animals during parturition and lactation or when performing surgery.[55]

Bacterial Agents

Campylobacteriosis

Multiple strains of Campylobacter have been isolated from animal species used in biomedical research, including pigs, chickens, sheep, dogs,[57] cats, ferrets,[58] hamsters,[59] and nonhuman primates.[60] Clinical disease in animals may be absent; however, young animals may exhibit more severe clinical manifestations.[45] Symptoms of overt watery to mucohemorrhagic diarrhea, fever, reduced appetite, and vomiting may occur. Abortions and stillbirths have been linked to C. fetus. Prevalence of Campylobacter in contemporary laboratory nonhuman primate colonies may be low.[61] One report of transmission from asymptomatic laboratory-housed coyotes has been documented.[62]

The organism is shed in feces. Transmission is through fecal-oral routes. Enteritis in humans has been associated with exposure to domestic animals, sheep, and pigs. Infection often is asymptomatic, but clinical syndromes can include abdominal pain, fever, lethargy, vomiting, and diarrhea. Signs typically resolve in 2 to 5 days but may extend up to several weeks.[63] In rare cases, more severe outcomes, including reactive arthritis, febrile convulsions, Guillain-Barré syndrome, and meningitis, may occur. The incubation period ranges from 1 to 10 days.

Diagnosis is made through detection of the organisms in stool samples. Supportive care, including hydration and electrolyte replacement, is recommended for treatment of symptomatic cases.

There is a low to moderate risk of transmission if proper sanitation measures are followed by animal care staff and laboratory personnel.[64] Laboratory animals that are suspected as carriers of infection should be identified and may be treated with antibiotics.

Capnocytophagosis and Pasteurellosis

Bite and scratch injuries sustained from laboratory animal species represent an important occupational hazard for animal facility personnel and research workers. The diverse bacterial flora that inhabits the oral cavities of animals, dogs and cats in particular, may be pathogenic to humans. Two agents of zoonotic importance are *Capnocytophaga canimorsus* (formerly DF-2) and *Pasteurella multocida*.

Multiple reports of *C. canimorsus* transmission to humans from their pet dogs and cats exist; however, no cases have been reported in animal facilities. If humans are exposed to this bacterium, clinical case reports indicate that splenectomy and alcoholism may be strong predisposing factors for overt disease.[65]

Clinical symptoms of *C. canimorsus* infection include cellulitis, fever, and septicemia, which may progress to endocarditis, arthritis, meningitis, and death. The incubation period ranges from 1 to 5 days after exposure. The bacteria can be cultured or identified within neutrophils. Treatment includes administration of penicillin G.[38]

Animal reservoirs for *P. multocida* include rabbits, cats, dogs, and pigs. Rabbits often show signs of rhinitis and otitis, but many may be healthy carriers. Cats and dogs have a subclinical infection that is asymptomatic. Pigs can develop atrophic rhinitis if coinfected with other bacterial strains.

Humans are commonly exposed to *Pasteurella* by bite wounds and potentially by aerosolization. Cellulitis, erythema, and swelling have been reported. Humans also may experience pneumonia, meningitis, and fatal congenital complications.[66] Bite and scratch lesions can be cultured for isolation of the bacteria. The incubation period is as long as 24 hours. Wound cleansing, debridement, and treatment with antibiotics is recommended.[67] Rabies and tetanus vaccination should also be considered for patients with animal bite wounds.

Prevention of bites and scratches from multiple species requires appropriate training for handling diverse animals with care and confidence. Gloves and other means of protective equipment should always be worn when handling animals.

Chlamydiosis

Many laboratory animal species can serve as hosts for Gram-negative *Chlamydia* and *Chlamydophila* species, including sheep, goats, dogs, cats, guinea pigs, frogs, and poultry. These animal hosts can be asymptomatic carriers or may exhibit symptoms that are species specific.[13] Sheep and goats may have pneumonia, enteritis, and reproductive complications;

dogs may have pneumonia and endocarditis; cats and guinea pigs may experience conjunctivitis and keratitis; frogs may exhibit lethargy, edema, petechiation, and disequilibrium.

Transmission to humans is through direct contact with animals or their tissues, particularly birth products of ruminants and other mammals. Inhalation of contaminated aerosols is a hazard for those working with poultry.

Disease occurs sporadically in animal facility personnel. ILI with conjunctivitis, pneumonia, and septicemia has been reported. Pregnant women are susceptible to febrile illness, congenital infection, and abortion. Following exposure, the incubation period is 1 to 4 weeks. The agents can be detected by analysis of paired sera with increasing antibody titers.

Treatment with tetracycline or doxycycline may be beneficial. Direct contact and inhalation of aerosols should be prevented through the use of appropriate PPE.

Helicobacteriosis

Multiple strains of *Helicobacter* have been isolated from a variety of animal species, including humans. Many of the same strains of *Helicobacter* have been found in the gastrointestinal tracts of both animals and humans. Fecal-oral transmission is suspected; however, further studies are necessary to determine whether animals truly serve as a source of the bacteria for zoonotic transmission to humans. *Helicobacter pylori* can infect humans and cause gastritis, but animal contact has not been implicated as a cause of the infection.[8,68] *H. suis* and *H. pullorum* have both been implicated in human disease.[69,70]

Leptospirosis

Infection is caused by spirochete bacteria of the genus *Leptospira*, including *L. canicola*, *L. hardjo*, *L. icterohaemorrhagiae*, *L. interrogans* serovar *ballum*, *L. pomona*, and *L. sejroe*. Multiple animal species can serve as reservoir hosts, including mice, rats, gerbils, hamsters, dogs, cats, ruminants, swine, and nonhuman primates. Different diseases are seen in the different animal species following infection. In mice, infection is asymptomatic. Dogs may succumb to hepatic and renal disease, with hematuria.[71,72] Ruminants may have reproductive failure, whereas nonhuman primates may experience abortions and icterohemorrhagic disease.[73,74] To detect the organisms in host species, serology can be performed to assess rising antibody titers. In addition, culture and PCR of infective urine can be performed.

Transmission to humans occurs through oral and aerosol exposure to contaminated urine, reproductive tissues, and fetal tissues. Organisms also can infect humans through abrasions in the skin and mucosal membranes.

Disease in humans is variable. Mild ILI symptoms may progress to severe infection with renal, hepatic, and pulmonary, or meningeal involvement. Weil's disease (jaundice) has been documented in animal facility personnel. The incubation period ranges from 4 to 19 days. Infection is diagnosed through serology or isolation of leptospires from blood, urine, or cerebrospinal fluid.

Treatment involves antimicrobial therapy with penicillin, cephalosporins, tetracyclines, or erythromycin.[38] Exposure to contaminated animals is prevented through the use of PPE that covers skin and mucosal surfaces. Animal vaccines are available but may not prevent transmission to humans.

Rat Bite Fever

The most common etiologic agent of rat bite fever is *Streptobacillus moniliformis*, a pleomorphic, Gram-negative rod. *Spirillum minus*, a spiral-shaped, Gram-negative rod, also has been associated with infections following rat bites but much less frequently.[8,75]

Wild and laboratory rats are the principal reservoirs, though the organisms also have been isolated from mice, gerbils, squirrels, weasels, dogs, cats, and nonhuman primates. These agents are considered part of the normal nasopharyngeal flora of rats. Clinical disease in rats and other hosts is rare but has been reported.[75,76] Detection involves isolation of the agents from the oral cavity, nares, or conjunctival sacs and identification by culture or PCR. Animal inoculation may be used for isolation of *S. minus*.[38]

In the research setting, human infections are most often associated with rat bites. Transmission also can occur after exposure to infective urine or secretions from the mouth, nares, or conjunctival sacs. Although clinical disease occurs infrequently, it must be considered in the treatment of rat bite injuries sustained by animal care and research personnel. Infection with *S. moniliformis* can lead to flulike symptoms, regional lymphadenopathy, and arthritis. Infection with *S. minus* can result in a distinctive rash with red to purple plaques.

The incubation period for *S. moniliformis* is less than 10 days; however, *S. minus* has an incubation period of 2 weeks to 3 months. Diagnosis requires isolation and culture of the organism from the primary lesion, lymph node, blood, or synovial fluid.

Treatment begins with thorough cleansing of the wound. Penicillin or tetracyclines can be administered for 7 to 10 days.[38] Tetanus prophylaxis also should be considered after bites from rodents.[12] Transmission of the agents from rodent bites can be prevented through the use of PPE, such as gloves, and by thorough disinfection of sustained wounds. In addition, personnel should be trained in proper restraint techniques when handling rodents.

Shigellosis

Shigella spp., including *flexneri, dysenteriae*, and *sonnei*, are Gram-negative anaerobes. These organisms infect nonhuman and human primates and cause diarrhea, dehydration, and

weight loss. Severe infections in monkeys also may lead to gingivitis, air sacculitis, and abortions.[77] The organisms can be cultured from fecal material placed on appropriate microbiological media.

Transmission of the agent to monkeys initially is from humans, with secondary spread to other monkeys and back to humans by the fecal-oral route. Humans infected with the bacteria also develop varying degrees of diarrhea, with fever, nausea, and potential autoimmune complications.[78] The incubation period lasts from 1 to 4 days. Antimicrobials can be administered based on culture and sensitivity results. Appropriate PPE should be worn at all times when working with nonhuman primates (see *M. herpesvirus* 1 discussion).

Tuberculosis

In animals, tuberculosis is caused by acid-fast rods of the genus *Mycobacterium*, including *M. tuberculosis, M. bovis, M. avium-intracellulare, M. avium* subsp. *paratuberculosis, M. kansasii, M. simiae, M. chelonae*, and *M. marinum*. Many species of animals are susceptible to tuberculosis, including nonhuman primates, dogs, cats, pigs, ruminants, chickens, and pigeons. Within the animal research setting, nonhuman primates, fish, and amphibians are the animals most likely to be infected with mycobacteria.[14]

Aquatic species commonly carry mycobacteria. These infections are usually subclinical in fish unless environmental stress or other diseases cause clinical symptoms. Humans can acquire cutaneous infections from handling animals or aquaria or soiled water. Lesions are usually nodules or granulomas on the skin or arms that can be diagnosed by PCR. It is recommended that personnel that work with aquatic species wear gloves that prevent skin contact with animals and water and that they wash hands after working with animals or aquaria.[79]

Monkeys do not carry usually acquire tuberculosis from other sources including humans, other animals, or environmental sources. However, once infected, transmission readily occurs between monkeys with secondary spread back to humans.[13]

Susceptibility to tuberculosis varies among all species of nonhuman primates. Macaques are the most susceptible, whereas New World primates are the least susceptible. Nonhuman primates usually become infected in their country of origin through contact with infected humans.[14,80]

The disease in nonhuman primates can be asymptomatic, but animals may succumb to acute death. Pulmonary disease is a common presentation, though intestinal and cutaneous tuberculosis with draining tracts have been reported. Nodular lesions may form in multiple organs, including vertebrae, brain, and spinal cord.

Laboratory nonhuman primates are routinely tested on arrival to the facility and thereafter for exposure to mycobacterial species. In quarantine, monkeys are usually tested every 2 weeks; however, in established colonies, quarterly testing is recommended. Intradermal skin testing (Mantoux testing), using tuberculin, is performed in captive monkeys. Positive test reactors are retested for confirmation and may undergo pulmonary radiography. Animals suspected of having tuberculosis are generally euthanized and necropsied to establish a definitive diagnosis. Mycobacterial culture is difficult and may take 4 to 8 weeks for confirmation. Serology and PCR also may be used for detection. False-negative skin testing may occur due to concurrent disease or immunosuppression. Rarely, animals with positive test results may be treated to control the disease.[14,80]

Transmission of tuberculosis is primarily by infective aerosols, but fecal-oral routes of transmission have been documented. Individuals working with nonhuman primates have an increased risk for development of a positive tuberculin skin test. In addition, personnel with tuberculosis pose a substantial risk for nonhuman primates. In humans, pulmonary, meningeal, and visceral organs and other body systems may be infected by disease agents. Progressive pulmonary disease may be fatal. Crohn's disease has been linked to M. avium subsp. paratuberculosis infection.[81] The incubation period ranges from 2 to 10 weeks for development of primary lesions or skin test positivity.[38] Diagnosis can be assisted by skin testing of personnel, PCR, RT-PCR, and pulmonary radiography. Treatment of disease is based on established antimicrobial protocols, including combination treatment with isoniazid, rifampin, and pyrazinamide.[38] Increasingly, drug-resistant mycobacterial strains are being recognized.

Occupational health programs for personnel working with nonhuman primates should include regular intradermal skin testing of at-risk facility personnel (usually annually or semiannually), training in the use of PPE, and education on tuberculosis. Individuals who develop a positive skin test should be referred to a physician for follow-up. They should be reassigned to work tasks other than nonhuman primate areas until it has been determined that they are free of tuberculosis.[14,80]

Mycotic Agents

Zoonotic fungal infections are uncommon in animal research. The most significant are dermatomycoses caused by Microsporum canis, Trichophyton mentagrophytes, and Trichophyton verrucosum. Potentially, animals obtained from random source dealers may serve as a source for infection, which presents with crusts and ulcerative skin lesions. Transmission to humans is through direct contact with infected animals. Humans develop self-limiting skin lesions, often referred to as "ringworm," that spread outward circumferentially. Treatment of the disease is accomplished by thorough cleansing with soap and water; fungicides may be applied topically. Prevent transmission through the use of appropriate PPE, particularly disposable gloves.

Protozoal Agents

Toxoplasmosis

Cats are the reservoir host for this parasite, Toxoplasma gondii.[8] Cats are infected after ingestion of infected prey animals and begin to shed oocysts within 3 weeks. Oocysts take more than 24 hours to become infective after shedding. Transmission to humans occurs through ingestion of infective oocysts. Although most human infections are subclinical, infected pregnant women are particularly at risk for congenital infections, which may result in severe neurological damage to the fetus.[8]

Immunosuppressed individuals are more likely to exhibit clinical symptoms, including lymphadenopathy, fever, and pneumonia. Transmission of this pathogen can be greatly diminished, if not eliminated, through management techniques within the facility. Litter boxes should be emptied completely on a daily basis, which eradicates fecal exposure to infective oocysts. Prevent wild rodent entry into the facility so that infection is not introduced to the laboratory cat population.[8]

Cryptosporidiosis

Many animal species can serve as reservoirs for Cryptosporidium spp.[8] Although infection may be asymptomatic in animal hosts, cats, dogs, ruminants, monkeys, and other species may develop intractable diarrhea. The disease can be severe in immunosuppressed animals. Transmission to humans is likely fecal-oral. Humans predominately exposed to livestock have contracted this infection. Disease may be asymptomatic or result in profuse watery diarrhea. The incubation period averages 1 week. Treatment with antimicrobials is often unrewarding; therefore, supportive fluid therapy should be administered. Prevent direct contact with contaminated excreta through the use of PPE.

Parasitic Agents

The risk of infection with helminth parasites originating from laboratory animals is insignificant. However, infestations with ectoparasites (e.g., mites, fleas, and ticks) derived from laboratory animals have been reported. Facility personnel may have moderate to severe, yet transient, dermatitis, eczema, pyoderma, or painful bites. More substantial consequences may result if personnel are bitten by ectoparasites harboring bacterial, rickettsial, or viral agents of human disease.[13] To control for parasitic infections within laboratory animal colonies, prompt treatment and elimination of infestation of animals and their habitats are warranted. Personnel should treat affected lesions with topical or systemic parasiticides and control exposure through the use of PPE.

CONCLUSIONS

The use of animals in biomedical research carries with it some risk of infection with zoonotic agents carried by the animals themselves or infectious agents administered to animals as part of the experimental protocol. Several significant disease-causing agents still exist in some species of animals. Herpes B virus is a cause of fatal encephalitis and is carried by macaque monkeys. Other nonfatal infectious agents that might be encountered include lymphocytic choriomeningitis, orf, cat scratch fever, Q fever, tuberculosis, and rat bite fever.

Exposure of personnel is most likely to occur in association with laboratory procedures involving the pathogen, vector, or animal-handling procedures such as necropsy, injections, handling, and restraint. When working with live animals, it is important to assess whether the pathogen or vector is shed from the infected animal and by what route, if known. In the case of handling killed animals, tissues, or fluids, personnel must be appropriately trained in methods to prevent exposure and infection.

Regulations regarding animal use require that research studies address prevention and treatment issues with infectious pathogens prior to initiation of the experimental work. Risk reduction and control are accomplished through the use of well-documented techniques and equipment such as PPE, BSCs, the use of disease-free animals, and the implementation of an occupational health program for personnel handling animals.

FUTURE TRENDS

Several areas of infectious disease research will increase in prominence in the future.

Recent outbreaks of emerging infectious diseases such as West Nile virus, severe acute respiratory syndrome, monkey-pox, and avian influenza all point to a trend for new disease agents to arise in animal populations and make the transition to the human population.[82] Research into emerging diseases is increasing worldwide and will pose new challenges with regard to development of animal models and methods of containment and management.

Another area of increasing emphasis in infectious disease research is that of bioterrorism involving infectious agents such as smallpox virus and anthrax bacteria. It should be noted that the majority of infectious agents identified as potential terrorist weapons are zoonotic agents. The use of these agents in research will undoubtedly increase in biomedical research institutions in the future as studies on pathogenesis and prevention are pursued.

Finally, increased use of infectious agents as vectors for the delivery of foreign genes to animals for the study of genetic diseases and their treatment through gene therapy can be expected. These agents, which have been genetically altered to render them nonpathogenic and replication defective (e.g., adenovirus and vaccinia virus), are used to transfect animals with the genes being studied. Although these agents are presumed to be noninfectious, until they have been used in humans and demonstrated to be safe, they must be assumed to be potentially infectious. In addition, the genes being transferred pose a potential risk to personnel, and their effects must be considered in risk assessment. In general, ABSL-2 facilities and ABSL-3 conditions should be followed.

REFERENCES

1. Paul EF. Introduction. In: Paul EF and Paul J, eds. *Why Animal Experimentation Matters: The Use of Animals in Medical Research*. New Brunswick: Transaction Publishers, 2001:1–22.
2. Bishop LJ, Nolen AL. Animals in research and education: ethical issues. *Kennedy Inst Ethics J* 2001 Mar;11(1):91–112.
3. Frost WW, Hamm TE Jr. Prevention and Control of Animal Disease. In: Rollin BE, Kesel ML, eds. *The Experimental Animal in Biomedical Research*. Volume 1, Boca Raton: CRC Press, 1990:133–149.
4. Hansen AK, Health Status and Health Monitoring. In: Hau J and Schapiro SJ, eds. *Handbook of Laboratory Animal Science*, Volume 1, Essential Principles and Practices, 3rd ed. Boca Raton: CRC Press, 2011:251–305.
5. National Research Council. *Scientific and Humane Issues in the Use of Random Source Dogs and Cats in Research*. Washington, DC: The National Academies Press, 2009.
6. Krauss H, Weber A, Appel M, et al, eds. *Zoonosis: Infectious Diseases Transmissible from Animals to Humans*, 3rd ed. Washington, DC: ASM Press, 2003.
7. Acha PN, Szyfres B, eds. *Zoonoses and Communicable Diseases Common to Man and Animals*, 3rd ed. Washington, DC: Pan American Health Organization, 2003.
8. Fox JG, Newcomer CE, Rozmiarek H. Selected Zoonoses. In: Fox JG, Anderson LC, Loew FM, Quimby FW, eds. *Laboratory Animal Medicine*. San Diego: Academic Press, 2002:1060–1105.
9. Baker DG. *Natural Pathogens of Laboratory Animals*. Washington DC: ASM Press, 2003.
10. Weigler BJ, Di Giacomo RF, Alexander S. A national survey of laboratory animal workers concerning occupational risks for zoonotic diseases. *Comp Med* 2005 Apr;55(2):183–191.
11. Hankenson C. The 3 R's for laboratory animal zoonoses. *Contemp Top Lab Anim Sci* 2003 Mar;42(2):66,68,70.
12. Weber DJ, Rutala WA. Zoonotic infections. *Occup Med* 1999 Apr-Jun;14(2):247–284.
13. Hankenson FC, Johnston NA, Weigler BJ, et al. Zoonoses of occupational health importance in contemporary laboratory animal research. *Comp Med* 2003 Dec;53(6):579–601.
14. Committee on Occupational Safety and Health in Research Animal Facilities, NRC. *Occupational Health and Safety in the Care and Use of Research Animals*. Washington, DC: National Academy Press, 1997. Available at: http://books.nap.edu/openbook/0309052998/html/index.html/.
15. Wald PH, Stave GM. Occupational medicine programs for animal research facilities. *ILAR J* 2003;44(1):57–71.
16. Trundy RL, Cook SS, Occupational Health and Safety. In: Silverman J, Suckow MA, Murthy S, eds. *The IACUC Handbook*, 2nd ed. Boca Raton: CRC Press, 2007:359–377.
17. Folletti I, Forcina A, Marabini A, et al. Have the prevalence and incidence of occupational asthma and rhinitis because of laboratory animals declined in the last 25 years? *Allergy* 2008 Jul; 63(7):834–841.
18. Foundation for Biomedical Research. Biological Hazards in the Laboratories: Protecting Yourself, Your Team, Your Work. In: *The Biomedical Investigator's Handbook for Researchers Using Animal Models*. Washington, DC: Foundation for Biomedical Research, 1987:37–43.
19. Swindle MM, Vogler GA, Fulton LK, et al. Preanesthesia, Anesthesia, Analgesia, and Euthanasia. In: Fox JG, Anderson LC, Loew FM, Quimby FW, eds. *Laboratory Animal Medicine*. San Diego: Academic Press, 2002:955–1003.
20. National Research Council. *Guide for the Care and Use of Laboratory Animals*. Washington, DC: National Academies Press, 2011. Available at: http://www.nap.edu/openbook.php?record_id=5140.
21. Animal Welfare Act, Title 9, Subchapter A, Animal Welfare, Pub Law No. 99–198, 1985. Available at: http://awic.nal.usda.gov/government-and -professional-resources/federal-laws/animal-welfare-act.
22. Anderson LC. Laws, Regulations and Policies Affecting the Use of Laboratory Animals. In: Fox JG, Anderson LC, Loew FM, Quimby FW, eds. *Laboratory Animal Medicine*. San Diego: Academic Press, 2002:19–33.
23. Office of Laboratory Animal Welfare. *Public Health Service Policy on Humane Care and Use of Laboratory Animals*. Bethesda: National Institutes of Health, 2002. Available at: http://grants.nih.gov/grants/olaw /references/phspol.htm.
24. American Veterinary Medical Association. *AVMA Guidelines for the Euthanasia of Animals: 2013 Edition*. Available at: https://www.avma .org/KB/Policies/Documents/euthanasia.pdf.
25. Chosewood LC, Wilson DE, eds. *Biosafety in Microbiological and Biomedical Laboratories (BMBL)*, 5th ed. Washington, DC: US Department of Health and Human Services, CDC, National Institutes of Health, 2009. Available at: http://www.cdc.gov/biosafety/publications/bmbl5/.
26. Sehulster L, Chinn RY. Guidelines for environmental infection control in health-care facilities. Healthcare Infection Control Practices Advisory Committee (HICPAC). *MMWR Recomm Rep* 2003 Jun 6;52(RR-10):1–42.
27. Committee on Occupational Health and Safety in the Care and Use of Nonhuman Primates, NRC. *Occupational Health and Safety in the Care and Use of Nonhuman Primates*. Washington, DC: National Academy Press, 2003. Available at: http://books.nap.edu/openbook/030908914X/html/.
28. Cohen JI, Davenport DS, Stewart JA, et al. Recommendations for prevention of and therapy for exposure to B virus (cercopithecine herpesvirus 1). *Clin Infect Dis* 2002 Nov;35(10):1191–1203.

29. Weigler BJ. Biology of B virus in macaque and human hosts: a review. *Clin Infect Dis* 1992 Feb;14(2):555–567.
30. Centers for Disease Control and Prevention (CDC). *B Virus (herpes B, monkey B virus, herpesvirus simiae, and herpesvirus B)*. CDC website. 2010. Available at: http://www.cdc.gov/herpesbvirus/index.html.
31. Huff JL, Barry PA. B-virus (Cercopithecine herpesvirus 1) infection in humans and macaques: potential for zoonotic disease. *Emerg Infect Dis* 2003 Feb;9(2):246–250.
32. Perelygina L, Patrusheva I, Manes N, et al. Quantitative real-time PCR for detection of monkey B virus (Cercopithecine herpesvirus 1) in clinical samples. *J Virol Methods* 2003 May;109(2):245–251.
33. Simmons JH, Riley LK. Hantaviruses: an overview. *Comp Med* 2002 Apr; 52(2):97–110.
34. LeDuc JW. Epidemiology of Hantaan and related viruses. *Lab Anim Sci* 1987 Aug;37(4):413–418.
35. Centers for Disease Control and Prevention. Laboratory management of agents associated with hantavirus pulmonary syndrome: interim biosafety guidelines. *MMWR Recomm Rep* 1994 May 13;43(RR-7):1–7.
36. Southee T. Hantavirus infection in rodents: a laboratory hazard. *Anim Technol* 1988;39:17–19.
37. Hartline J, Mierek C, Knutson T, et al. Hantavirus infection in North America: a clinical review. *Am J Emerg Med* 2013 Jun;31(6):978–982.
38. Chin J. *Control of Communicable Diseases Manual*, 17th ed. Washington, DC: American Public Health Association, 2000.
39. Childs JE, Wilson LJ. Lymphocytic Choriomeningitis. In: Beran GW, ed. *Handbook of Zoonoses. Section B: Viral*. 2nd ed. Boca Raton, FL: CRC Press, Inc, 1994:463–471.
40. Montali RJ, Ramsay EC, Stephensen CB, et al. A new transmissible viral hepatitis of marmosets and tamarins. *J Infect Dis* 1989 Nov;160(5):759–765.
41. Percy DH, Barthold SW. *Pathology of Laboratory Rodents and Rabbits*, 3rd ed. Ames, IA: Iowa State University Press, 2007.
42. Lapošová K, Pastoreková S, Tomášková J. Lymphocytic choriomeningitis virus: invisible but not innocent. *Acta Virol* 2013;57(2):160–170.
43. Dykewicz CA, Dato VM, Fisher-Hoch SP, et al. Lymphocytic choriomeningitis outbreak associated with nude mice in a research institute. *JAMA* 1992 Mar;267(10):1349–1353.
44. Barton LL, Mets MB. Congenital lymphocytic choriomeningitis virus infection: decade of rediscovery. *Clin Infect Dis* 2001 Aug 1;33(3):370–374.
45. Kahn CM, Line S, eds. *The Merck Veterinary Manual*, 9th ed. Whitehouse Station, NJ: Merck & Co., Merial Ltd., 2005.
46. Nettleton PF, Brebner J, Pow I, et al. Tissue culture-propagated orf virus vaccine protects lambs from orf virus challenge. *Vet Rec* 1996 Feb 24;138(8):184–186.
47. Jenkins SR, Auslander M, Conti L, et al. Compendium of animal rabies prevention and control, 2003. *J Am Vet Med Assoc* 2003 Jan 15;222(2):156–161.
48. Centers for Disease Control and Prevention. Human rabies prevention—United States, 1999. Recommendations of the Advisory Committee on Immunization Practices (ACIP). *MMWR Recomm Rep* 1999 Jan 8;48(RR-1):1–21.
49. Hanlon CA, Olson JG, Clark CJ. Article I: Prevention and education regarding rabies in human beings. National Working Group on Rabies Prevention and Control. *J Am Vet Med Assoc* 1999 Nov;215(9):1276–1280.
50. Karem KL, Paddock CD, Regnery RL. Bartonella henselae, B. quintana, and B. bacilliformis: historical pathogens of emerging significance. *Microbes Infect* 2000 Aug;2(10):1193–1205.
51. Pennisi MG, Marsilio F, Hartmann K, et al. Bartonella species infection in cats: ABCD guidelines on prevention and management. *J Feline Med Surg* 2013 Jul;15(7):563–569.
52. Liao HM, Huang FY, Wang NL, et al. Systemic cat scratch disease. *J Formos Med Assoc* 2006 Aug;105(8):674–679.
53. Williams JC, Sanchez V. Q Fever and Coxiellosis. In: Beran GW, *Handbook of Zoonoses. Section A. Bacterial, Rickettsial, Chlamydial and Mycotic*, 2nd ed. Boca Raton: CRC Press, Inc., 1994:429–446.
54. McQuiston JH, Holman RC, McCall CL, et al. National surveillance and the epidemiology of human Q fever in the United States, 1978–2004. *Am J Trop Med Hyg* 2006 Jul;75(1):36–40.
55. Anderson A, Bijlmer H, Fournier PE, et al. Diagnosis and Management of Q fever— United States, 2013: recommendations from CDC and the Q Fever Working Group. *MMWR Recomm Rep* 2013 Mar 29;62(RR-03):1–30.
56. Karakousis PC, Trucksis M, Dumler JS. Chronic Q fever in the United States. *J Clin Microbiol* 2006 Jun;44(6):2283–2287.
57. Newton CM, Newell DG, Wood M, et al. Campylobacter infection in a closed dog breeding colony. *Vet Rec* 1988 Aug 6;123(6):152–154.
58. Marini RP, Adkins JA, Fox JG. Proven or potential zoonotic diseases of ferrets. *J Am Vet Med Assoc* 1989 Oct 1;195(7):990–994.
59. Gebhart CJ, Fennell CL, Murtaugh MP, et al. Campylobacter cinaedi is normal intestinal flora in hamsters. *J Clin Microbiol* 1989 Jul;27(7):1692–1694.
60. Tribe GW, Frank A. Campylobacter in monkeys. *Vet Rec* 1980 Apr 19;106(16):365–366.
61. Vore SJ, Peele PD, Barrow PA, et al. A prevalence survey for zoonotic enteric bacteria in a research monkey colony with specific emphasis on the occurrence of enteric Yersinia. *J Med Primatol* 2001 Feb;30(1):20–25.
62. Fox JG, Taylor NS, Penner JL, et al. Investigation of zoonotically acquired Campylobacter jejuni enteritis with serotyping and restriction endonuclease DNA analysis. *J Clin Microbiol* 1989 Nov;27(11):2423–2425.
63. Galanis E. Campylobacter and bacterial gastroenteritis. *CMAJ* 2007 Sep 11;177(6):570–571.
64. Enriquez C, Nwachuku M, Gerba CP. Direct exposure to animal enteric pathogens. *Rev Environ Health* 2001 Apr-Jun;16(2):117–131.
65. Brenner DJ, Hollis DG, Fanning GR, et al. Capnocytophaga canimorsus sp. nov. (formerly CDC group DF-2), a cause of septicemia following dog bite, and C. cynodegmi sp. nov., a cause of localized wound infection following dog bite. *J Clin Microbiol* 1989 Feb;27(2):231–235.
66. Andersson S, Larinkari U, Vartia T, et al. Fatal congenital pneumonia caused by cat-derived Pasteurella multocida. *Pediatr Infect Dis J* 1994 Jan;13(1):74–75.
67. Esposto S, Picciolli I, Semino M, et al. Dog and cat bite-associated infections in children. *Eur J Clin Microbiol Infect Dis* 2013 Aug;32(8):971–976.
68. Webb PM, Knight T, Elder JB, et al. Is Helicobacter pylori transmitted from cats to humans? *Helicobacter* 1996 Jun;1(2):79–81.
69. Joosten M, Flahou B, Meyns T, et al. Case report: Helicobacter suis infection in a pig veterinarian. *Helicobacter*. 2013 Oct;18(5):392–396.
70. Skovgaard N. New trends in emerging pathogens. *Int J Food Microbiol* 2007 Dec 15;120(3):217–224.
71. Ruhl-Fehlert CI, Brem S, Feller W, et al. Clinical, microbiological and pathological observations in laboratory beagle dogs infected with leptospires of the serogroup Sejroe. *Exp Toxicol Pathol* 2000 Jun;52(3):201–207.
72. Scanziani E, Crippa L, Giusti AM, et al. Leptospira interrogans serovar sejroe infection in a group of laboratory dogs. *Lab Anim* 1995 Jul;29(3):300–306.
73. Ellis WA. Leptospirosis as a cause of reproductive failure. *Vet Clin North Am Food Anim Pract* 1994 Nov;10(3):463–478.
74. Perolat P, Poingt JP, Vie JC, et al. Occurrence of severe leptospirosis in a breeding colony of squirrel monkeys. *Am J Trop Med Hyg* 1992 May;46(5):538–545.
75. Will LA. Rat-bite Fever. In: Beran GW ed. *Handbook of Zoonoses. Section A. Bacterial, Rickettsial, Chlamydial and Mycotic*, 2nd ed. Boca Raton: CRC Press, Inc., 1994:231–242.
76. Valverde CR, Lowenstine LJ, Young CE, et al. Spontaneous rat bite fever in non-human primates: a review of two cases. *J Med Primatol* 2002 Dec; 31(6):345–349.
77. Bernacky BJ, Gibson SV, Keeling ME, et al. Nonhuman Primates. In: Fox JG, Anderson LC, Loew FM, Quimby FW, eds. *Laboratory Animal Medicine*. San Diego: Academic Press, 2002:675–791.
78. Hughes RA, Keat AC. Reiter's syndrome and reactive arthritis: a current view. *Semin Arthritis Rheum* 1994 Dec;24(3):190–210.
79. Westerfield, M. *The zebrafish book. A guide for the laboratory use of zebrafish (Danio rerio)*, 5th ed. Eugene: Univ. of Oregon Press, 2007.
80. Adams SR, Muchmore E, Richardson JH. Biosafety. In: Bennett BT, Abee CR, Henrickson R, eds. *Nonhuman Primates in Biomedical Research. Biology and Management*. San Diego: Academic Press, 1995:375–420.
81. Hermon-Taylor J, Bull T. Crohn's disease caused by Mycobacterium avium subspecies paratuberculosis: a public health tragedy whose resolution is long overdue. *J Med Microbiol* 2002 Jan;51(1):3–6.
82. Jones KE, Patel NG, Levy MA, et al. Global trends in emerging infectious diseases. *Nature* 2008 Feb 21;451(7181):990–993.

SUPPLEMENTAL RESOURCES

American Veterinary Medical Association. Available at: http://www.avma.org.

Centers for Disease Control and Prevention. Available at: http://www.cdc.gov.

World Health Organization, Zoonoses. Available at: http://www.who.int/topics/zoonoses/en/.

CHAPTER 122

Animals Visiting Healthcare Facilities

Kathleen (Kit) Darling, MS, MT, M(ASCP), CIC
Veterinary Medical Teaching Hospital
Texas A & M University
College Station, TX

ABSTRACT

People benefit from human–animal interaction socially, psychologically, and physiologically. In healthcare-related situations, programs for animal visitation, animal-assisted activities, animal-assisted therapy, and service animals are intended to assist in returning patients to wellness and independence. Healthcare facilities must establish animal and handler guidelines and program-specific infection prevention policies to provide a safe environment for animals, handlers, and patients. Healthcare providers need to understand and abide by the laws for service animals and persons with disabilities.

KEY CONCEPTS

- Animal-assisted activities, animal-assisted therapy, and visitation in healthcare facilities benefit patients socially, psychologically, and physiologically.

- The potential risks of animals in healthcare facilities include patient allergies, phobias, animal-caused injuries, and zoonoses.

- Healthcare facilities can provide a safe environment for both humans and animals by establishing guidelines and policies for the animal, handler/volunteer, patient, and infection prevention.

- Animals must meet defined health and temperament requirements to be accepted into animal-assisted therapy programs.

- When a personal pet visit is a necessary treatment intervention for the health and well-being of the patient, policies and guidelines should be established to ensure the safety of the pet, the patient, and others in the healthcare facility.

- Service animals differ from therapy animals and personal pets in their health-related roles.

- Healthcare providers must understand and abide by the rights of persons with disabilities accompanied by service animals.

BACKGROUND

Animals serve in numerous aspects of human life, providing companionship, many kinds of assistance, and livelihood.[1] Research shows that people benefit from the human–animal interaction socially (increasing interaction with others), psychologically (reducing stress and anxiety and increasing motivation and sense of well-being), and physiologically (decreasing blood pressure and possibly decreasing cardiovascular risks).[2,3] One of the main objectives of healthcare is to return patients to wellness and independence.[4] Today, animals may be used to accomplish this objective through visitation, animal-assisted activities (AAA), animal-assisted therapy (AAT), and service functions. This chapter addresses the challenges of animals in healthcare facilities and offers help to those facilities in developing guidelines and policies to provide a safe environment for both humans and animals. Areas covered include animals certified for AAA/AAT, personal pets, service animals, infection prevention and safety measures, patient suitability, and animal suitability.

BASIC PRINCIPLES

Animal-assisted interventions (AAIs) intentionally incorporate animals as part of a therapeutic or wellness improvement process. This includes AAAs in which the same animal does not necessarily visit the same person every time, and the effect of the animal visits on the participant is not formally measured or documented. It also includes AAT, a treatment modality in which the same animal visits the same patient each time, and the patient's progress as a result of the specific therapy is documented and measured.

The importance of unconditional love, the value of touch, the energy derived from acts of unselfish kindness, and the security of companionship all enhance and improve people's quality of life and health.[5,6] Animals providing visitation, AAA, and AAT, and those that are personal pets and service animals, may fulfill these conditions. Understanding the definition of each type of animal and its function is helpful in establishing policies and guidelines for animals in healthcare facilities.

AAAs are "meet and greet" activities that provide opportunities for recreation, motivation, and education. AAAs are not directed at specific therapeutic goals.[7,8] An example of AAA is animal visitation. The animal initiates contact with the patient, and the direction of the visit is determined by the patient's needs at that particular time. Animal visitation may be effective in increasing the patient's responsiveness, providing a pleasurable experience, enhancing treatment such as decreasing the need for pain medication, and helping to keep the patient in touch with reality.[5,6] Visitation may help with short-term goals. The animal visit may help foster rapport and initiate communication.[5] Visitation may take place one on one or in a group setting with a single animal or group of animals. Animal visitation may decrease loneliness and improves a patient's well-being.

AAT is directed toward specific goals in which the animal meets specific criteria as an integral part in the treatment process. A certified therapist or healthcare professional facilitates the interaction between the patient and the animal to improve physical, cognitive, emotional, and social functions.[7,8] An example of AAT is a patient brushing a dog to improve physical movement of the hand and arm.

AAT can provide multiple benefits, including fine and gross motor skills; verbal, tactile, and auditory stimulation; verbalization skills; ambulation and equilibrium; instruction-following and decision-making; memory recall; and concentrated and extended attention span. Physical, occupational, recreational, and speech therapy programs may use AAA/AAT and animal visitation.

"Service animal" is a legal term defined by the Americans with Disabilities Act (ADA). In March 2011, the ADA defined service animals as dogs that are individually trained to do work or perform tasks for a person with a disability.

Webster's II Dictionary defines pet as "an animal kept for pleasure or companionship" and a "handler" as "a person who trains or controls an animal."[9] The handler may be the animal's owner or a person who has trained the animal to obey him or her. The person who brings an animal for AAA/AAT or animal visitation may be referred to as "handler/volunteer" in this chapter. Animals that provide AAA/AAT and visitation are usually pets. A service animal is not considered a pet because it is specially trained to help a person overcome the limitations caused by the disability.[10] The term "handler" is also used when referring to the person with disabilities who has a service animal.

ANIMAL-ASSISTED ACTIVITY/ANIMAL-ASSISTED THERAPY

AAA/AAT is used in many healthcare facilities, including outpatient, acute care, rehabilitation, and extended-care facilities. AAT uses specially trained therapy animals. These animals are not a patient's pets. Dogs are the most frequently used. Other animals used include cats, birds, guinea pigs, and rabbits. In a guideline from a Working Group sponsored by the Public Health Agency of Canada and the Centre for Public Health and Zoonosis, University of Guelph, on animals visiting healthcare facilities, it was recommended that suitable animal species for AAA and AAT programs should be limited to domestic companion animals that are household pets.[11]

Animals participating in AAA/AAT and animal visitation programs must be screened and trained to ensure that they have the temperament to tolerate the equipment and environment in a healthcare facility. Abnormal behavior of an animal can easily dislodge tubes and wires or injure patients.[4]

A number of national and local animal-assisted organizations certify animals for AAA/AAT. These organizations require the animal to undergo a health screening for parasites, skin and dental problems, and necessary immunizations (per individual state law) by a veterinarian. The organization does a temperament evaluation to test the animal's aptitude for basic obedience and response to stress. Dogs must respond to the commands "heel," "sit," "down," and "stay." The temperament test is designed to evaluate the animal's behavior under conditions that they may experience when in healthcare facilities. They include reactions toward strangers, loud or startling noises, crowding, restraining hugs, and being patted or handled in a clumsy manner.[11] Cats, rabbits, and guinea pigs must be willing to remain in a basket or on a blanket when held. Certified animals commonly carry liability insurance through the certifying organization.[1] Animals that participate in AAT programs attend additional training with equipment used in the therapy activities and the environment where the therapy is done. These animals may also participate in AAA or animal visitation programs. Physical, occupational, recreation, and speech therapy may use certified animals. States may have regulations on animals visiting healthcare facilities. The facility must check on state regulations when deciding to adopt the recommendations in this chapter.

Animal Guidelines[1,4,11]

1. Animal must be a domestic companion animal. Exclude the following species, which may pose a higher risk of causing human injury or infection:

   a. Nonhuman primates

   b. Reptiles and amphibians

   c. Hamsters, gerbils, mice, and rats

   d. Prairie dogs, hedgehogs

   e. Animals that have not been litter trained or for which measures cannot be taken to prevent exposure of patients to the animal's excrement

2. Animal must not be a current resident of an animal shelter, pound, or similar facility and must be in a permanent home for at least 6 months.

3. Animal must be at least 1 year old.

4. Animal must be registered or certified for AAA/AAT.

5. Animal must pass health, skills, aptitude, and temperament tests.

6. Records of the animal's health must be up to date.

7. Animal must be appropriately restrained or on a short leash. Identification badges, bandanas, vests, and such may be required.

8. Animal must never be left alone with a patient.

9. Animals should be restricted from food preparation, service areas, and other high-risk areas identified by the healthcare facility.

10. Animals must not have been fed raw foods of animal origins within the previous 90 days.

Visit Guidelines: Infection Prevention and Safety

Most of the literature published about animals in the healthcare setting has focused on the benefits, and little has been published about the actual risks the animals pose. Some studies have examined the potential risk of animals in healthcare facilities such as allergies, phobias, zoonosis, and animal-caused injuries.[12,13]

Zoonosis (the transmission of disease between animals and humans), infection prevention, and safety are the major challenges that the healthcare facility will have to address when allowing animals to interact with patients and staff.[6] Animals can transmit infectious diseases to humans, and likewise, humans can transmit infectious diseases to animals. Animals can become transient vectors or carriers of potential human pathogens and could be responsible for cross-infection.[4]

More than 200 zoonotic diseases have been documented, but only around 35 are thought to be potential risks from animals used in AAA or AAT.[12] See Table 122-1 for the most common zoonotic diseases, compiled by the National Association of State Public Health Veterinarians. The focus of infection prevention policies for animal programs must be on good hand hygiene and the use of healthy, clean, and well-behaved animals, and designate appropriate patient populations to minimize the risks for transmission of infectious agents. After the introduction of AAT in Huntington Memorial Hospital, Pasadena, California, there was no zoonotic infections reported during 3,281 dog visits to 1,690 patients in a 5-year period.[5] In studies at two children's hospitals, neither has found increased rates of infection.[12,13]

Although many healthcare facilities have adopted AAI programs, there has been inconsistent application of infection prevention standards.[11,14] It is essential that more attention be given to the infection prevention components of AAI programs. Animals participating in AAI programs may act as carriers or reservoirs for infectious agents, thus spreading pathogens between patients and healthcare personnel. These animals may be more likely to acquire multidrug-resistant organisms than most pets. Currently, the literature review does not indicate that hospital infection rates have increased in facilities that have AAI programs.[15] Even though this is encouraging, there may be a lack of sufficient reporting or assessment of surveillance methods.[14] A report in the United Kingdom implicated a resident cat colonized with methicillin-resistant *Staphylococcus aureus* (MRSA) as a reservoir for an outbreak in a rehabilitation geriatric ward.[16] A prospective study monitored two groups of dogs participating in AAI in healthcare settings versus other settings. The results suggested that dogs visiting healthcare facilities had a greater risk of acquiring MRSA and *Clostridium difficile* than dogs visiting in other settings. The risk was greater for the dogs that licked patients or received treats from patients in healthcare facilities.[17] Proper infection prevention procedures are warranted at all times to minimize the risk of transmission between humans and animals and animals and humans.

In addition to the risk of infection, other concerns about animals in healthcare facilities include phobias, allergies, cleanliness, and animal-induced injuries (bites and scratches). Patients must be asked if they would like to visit or interact with the animal. Measures should be taken to control the animal's dander, which may be the source of some allergies. Measures include bathing the animal with allergen-reducing shampoo, wiping the animal with a pet wipe prior to the visit, and having the animal wear a T-shirt, vest, or other protective clothing. However, animal visits should not be allowed for patients with phobias or known allergies to the type of animal visiting in the facility.

If the animal has an elimination accident, gloves should be worn to remove the debris and clean up the area and hand hygiene performed after glove removal. Any organic debris and paper towels should be placed in a plastic bag in a trash container, similar to the disposal of diapers. After the area is cleaned, it must be disinfected with the facility's approved product, following the label instructions for appropriate concentration and contact time.

Bites and scratches are the major concern for animal-induced injuries. To minimize the risk of these injuries, it is important that the animals used for AAA and AAT undergo temperament testing by a person or group who is experienced in assessing animal behavior. The healthcare facility AAA/AAT program coordinator must obtain verification that the animals have had temperament evaluation.[11,14]

Healthcare facilities should develop and implement infection prevention guidelines and develop policies to minimize the potential risks associated with having animals in healthcare facilities. These should require that animals be of good temperament, well-groomed, and healthy and that that their handlers be educated on infection prevention practices, including hand hygiene. The following infection prevention and safety guidelines should be in place:

1. The healthcare facility develops policies and guidelines for the safety of the patients and animals involved in visitation, AAA, and AAT. The healthcare facility should designate a person or persons to the implementation of the policies and coordinate animal–human interactions and act as a liaison to the animal handlers visiting the facility.

2. Animals participating must have a temperament test (behavioral assessment) by an experienced person or recognized group.

3. Animals are required to be bathed within 24 hours before the visit.

4. Animals may wear a shirt, vest, or other protective clothing to control allergies. Wiping the animal with a baby or pet wipe will help control dandruff.

5. Animals must have clean ears.

6. Animals must have nails that are short with no rough edges. Animals must be trained not to scratch the patient. For additional protection, animals may wear protective foot coverings.

7. Animals must be healthy and current with immunizations, including rabies vaccination and others required in the state in which the healthcare facility is located. An annual physical examination by a licensed veterinarian should include dental and dermatological evaluation. Animals should be free of communicable diseases and parasites and be on a flea control program.

8. Animals must be free of any skin condition or wounds.

9. Handlers must ensure that animals do not lick or come in contact with a patient's open wound or devices.

10. If an animal is allowed in a patient's bed, a barrier such as a disposable cloth, towel, or sheet can be placed between the animal's coat and the patient's linen.[1] The barrier is removed and discarded when the animal leaves.

11. Animals are kept on a short leash or in a carrier or basket. The use of retractable leashes is discouraged.

12. The animal's handler/volunteer must be healthy and free of communicable diseases. The facility is strongly encouraged to consider a recommendation to handlers that they receive annual influenza shots and may be able to offer the vaccine to handlers for free as part of the annual flu vaccination program.[11]

13. When the visit or interaction is finished, the patient must wash his/her hands or use an alcohol hand sanitizer.

Patient Suitability Guidelines

Care must be taken to evaluate whether a patient is suitable for AAA/AAT or animal visitation. Special care is needed for patients with allergies, open wounds, or immunosuppression, and visitation should not be allowed in these circumstances unless the facility has developed approved criteria that must be met, including a requirement for physician evaluation, approval, and order for the visitation.

The following are patient suitability considerations.

1. Ask the patient if he/she wants to interact with the animal or has allergies or phobias to animals.

2. Exclude patients with allergies to animals; open wounds or burns; open tracheotomy; immunosuppression (as defined in the facility AAA/AAT program); agitation or aggression; or transmission precautions or isolation of any kind; or exclude others for reasons as defined by facility-specific patient populations or infection risks.[18]

3. Exclude patients who are infected with tuberculosis, *Salmonella, Campylobacter, Shigella, Streptococcus A,* MRSA, ringworm, *Giardia,* and amebiasis.[4]

4. Special requirements:

   a. An altered level of consciousness or coma may require verbal consent from a family member.

   b. Pediatric patient interactions necessitate verbal consent from parent or guardian and written consent for therapy.

   c. Wounds (not open) or healed burns must be covered during the visit, and the animal must not come in contact with these areas.

   d. If visitation is allowed for a patient with tracheotomy, the area must be completely covered.

   e. If visitation is allowed in the intensive care environment, the patient's nurse must provide guidance and assistance regarding the best way for the animal to approach the patient and avoid the equipment.[6]

5. Hand hygiene must be practiced before and after animal contact, including handler, patient, staff, and visitors.[11] It is considered most efficient to provide handlers with a portable bottle of hand sanitizer that they can offer to all who pet the animal.

Handler/Volunteer Guidelines

The animal's handler/volunteer is important in making the animal's interaction with the patient safe and beneficial. The following are handler/volunteer guidelines:

1. Work with the staff to determine how the animal's interaction will benefit the patient.

2. Neither the handler nor the animal may visit if either is ill. The program should give guidance regarding when visitations can be restarted after an illness.[11]

3. The handler/volunteer must make sure that the animal has a chance to eliminate before entering the facility.[19] The handler must pick up the elimination in a plastic bag and deposit it in the trash and wash hands.

4. The handler/volunteer must focus on the animal and remove the animal from any situation where the animal is too stressed. Be sure the animal has breaks for water and elimination needs.

5. A bite or scratch incident must be reported and investigated and, upon review, may be grounds for dismissal from the visitation program per program policy.

Personal Pets

Personal pets are a source of comfort to patients. A personal pet visit may be the best treatment intervention for the health and well-being of a patient in special situations. Personal pet visits are usually used for long-term or terminally ill patients. Personal pet visits require just as stringent a policy as visitation by certified animals. *Personal pets are allowed to interact only with their owners, handlers, and healthcare staff assisting with the visit.* These animals may not have undergone an evaluation of their temperament and obedience; thus, their behavior with others may be unpredictable. The following guidelines are recommended:[1]

1. The pet must be bathed within 24 hours before the visit.

2. A record of current vaccination should be provided prior to approval of the visit.

3. The pet must be on a short leash or in a carrier. Use of a retractable leash is not allowed.

4. The pet must be escorted into and out of the facility by designated staff.

5. The pet must not be allowed to interact with other patients or visitors.

6. Visits are limited per facility policy based on predetermined factors (facility specific).

7. The handler and patient must be informed prior to the visit that they may be asked to remove the animal from the facility at any time.

Service Animals

Service animals differ in their roles from animals that provide AAA or AAT. In September 2010, the Department of Justice revised the final regulations for the ADA for title II (state and local government) and title III (public accommodations and commercial facilities). The ADA defines a service animal as a dog that is trained to do work or perform tasks for a person with a disability. Some examples of the tasks or work may include guiding people who are visually impaired, alerting people who are hearing impaired, alerting or protecting a person who is having a seizure, pulling a wheelchair for a person who is unable to do so, calming a person with posttraumatic stress disorder, reminding a person with mental illness to take prescribed medication, or performing other duties. The ADA does not consider dogs whose sole function is to provide comfort or emotional support to be service animals. Service animals are not pets. Only dogs are recognized under titles II and III, which allow them to accompany people with disabilities in areas where the public is allowed. In a hospital, a service animal would be allowed in patient rooms, clinics, examination rooms, or cafeterias. Hospitals may exclude service animals from operating rooms or burn units where the animal's presence could compromise a sterile environment.

Some additional rules from the ADA related to service animals include:

• Service animals must be harnessed, leashed or tethered unless these devices interfere with the animal's work or the person's disability prevents using these devices.

• If it is not obvious what service an animal provides, the staff may ask only the following questions:

  o Is a service animal required because of a disability?

  o What work or task is the dog trained to perform?

The staff cannot ask the person with a disability for medical documentation, special identification card for the dog, or documentation of the dog's training, nor can staff require the dog to demonstrate its ability to perform the work or task.

• Access cannot be denied to a person with a service animal because of allergies or fear of dogs. If a person has allergies to dog dander or is afraid of a dog, accommodations should be made by assigning them to different locations in the room or different rooms in the facility.

• A person with disabilities can be asked to remove the service dog only if the dog is out of control and the handler is unable to bring it under control or if the dog is not housebroken.

• Service animals are allowed in the public area of a business that sells and prepares food even if state and local health codes prohibit animals on the premises.

• Staff is not required to provide care or food for a service animal.

The ADA has added a new and separate provision for miniature horses that have been individually trained to do work or perform tasks for people with disabilities. Miniature horses usually range in height from 24 to 34 inches (measured at the shoulder) and weigh between 70 and 100 pounds. When reasonable, entities covered by the ADA must modify their policies to permit miniature horses. The following assessment factors are to assist entities in determining whether miniature horses can be accommodated in their facility:

• Is the miniature horse housebroken?

• Is the miniature horse under the handler's control?

• Can the facility accommodate the miniature horse's type, size, and weight?

• Does the miniature horse's presence compromise legitimate safety requirements for the safe operation of the facility?[20]

Additional information concerning the ADA and service animals is on the ADA Website.

CONCLUSIONS

The human–animal bond has existed since humans began domesticating animals. Numerous studies have shown that people who value the human–animal bond can benefit physiologically, psychologically, and socially. Increasingly, animals are being used to treat acutely and chronically ill patients. Animal visitation, AAA, AAT, and service animals can provide better health and well-being to many. Although rare, the potential risks and legal liability for accidents and injuries to patients, staff, or handlers with animals in healthcare facilities exist. Healthcare providers must address the risk and liability issues by establishing guidelines and policies for animals in healthcare facilities. Guidelines and policies for animals, patient suitability, infection prevention, safety, and handlers/volunteers can provide for a safe environment for both humans and animals. After completing a study of programs involving canine visitation to hospitals

Table 122-1. Zoonotic diseases of importance in the United States, 2010

Disease	Agent	Means of transmission to humans	Most common species associated with transmission to humans[165,166]	Nationally notifiable human (H) or animal (A) cases	Severe or prolonged infection usually associated with immunosuppression	Deaths in humans reported
Acariasis (mange)	*Sarcoptes scabiei, Notoedres cati,* and other species of mites	Contact	Dogs, cats, horses, goats, sheep, swine, birds	No	No	No
Anthrax	*Bacillus anthracis*	Contact, aerosol, vector	Cattle, sheep, goats, horses	H, A	No	Yes
Avian influenza	Highly pathogenic avian influenza viruses	Contact, aerosol	Poultry, pet birds	H, A	No	Yes
Babesiosis	*Babesia microti* and other species	Vector	Cattle, rodents	A	Yes	Yes
Baylisascariasis	*Baylisascaris procyonis*	Contact	Raccoons	No	No	Yes
Bordetella bronchiseptica infection	*Bordetella bronchiseptica*	Aerosol	Dogs, pigs, rabbits, guinea pigs	No	Yes	No
Brucellosis	*Brucella melitensis, Brucella abortus, Brucella suis, Brucella canis*	Contact, aerosol	Goats, cattle, swine, dogs, horses	H, A	No	Yes
Campylobacteriosis	*Campylobacter jejuni, Campylobacter fetus, Campylobacter coli*	Contact	Cattle, sheep, goats, pigs, dogs, cats, birds, mink, ferrets, hamsters	No	No	Rare
Capnocytophaga canimorsus infection	*Capnocytophaga canimorsus, Capnocytophaga cynodegmi*	Contact	Dogs, cats	No	Yes	Yes
Cat scratch disease	*Bartonella henselae*	Contact	Cats	No	Yes	Rare
Chlamydiosis (mammalian)	*Chlamydophila abortus, Chlamydophila felis*	Aerosol, contact	Sheep, goats, llamas, cats, cattle	No	No	Yes
Contagious pustular dermatitis (orf or contagious ecthyma)	Parapoxvirus	Contact	Sheep, goats	No	No	No
Cryptococcosis	*Cryptococcus neoforms*	Aerosol	Pigeons, other birds	No	Yes	Yes
Cryptosporidiosis	*Cryptosporidium parvum*	Contact	Cattle (typically calves)	H	Yes	Yes
Dermatophilosis	*Dermatophilus congolensis*	Contact, vector	Goats, sheep, cattle, horses	No	No	No
Dermatophytosis (ringworm)	*Microsporum* spp, *Trichophyton* spp, *Epidermophyton* spp	Contact	Cats, dogs, cattle, goats, sheep, horses, rabbits, rodents	No	Yes	No
Dipylidium infection (tapeworm)	*Dipylidium caninum*	Vector	Dogs, cats	No	No	No
Escherichia coli O157:H7 infection	*Escherichia coli* O157:H7	Contact	Cattle, goats, sheep, deer	No	No	Yes
Echinococcosis	*Echinococcus granulosus, Echinococcus multilocularis*	Contact	Dogs, cats, wild canids	A	No	Yes
Ehrlichiosis or anaplasmosis	*Ehrlichia* and *Anaplasma* spp	Vector	Deer, rodents, horses, dogs	H	Yes	Yes
Equine encephalomyelitis	Togaviridae (eastern, western, and Venezuelan equine encephalomyelitis viruses)	Vector	Birds, horses	H, A	No	Yes
Erysipeloid	Erysipelothrix rhusiopathiae	Contact	Pigs, fish, crustaceans, mollusks	No	No	Yes
Giardiasis	*Giardia intestinalis* (Giardia lamblia)	Contact	Thought to be highly species specific and rarely transmitted from animals to humans	H	Yes	No
Hantaviral diseases	Hantaviruses	Aerosol	Rodents	H	No	Yes
Herpes B virus infection	Cercopithecine herpesvirus 1	Contact	Macaque monkeys	No	No	Yes
Influenza A	Influenza A virus	Contact, aerosol	Poultry, swine, ferrets	H, A	No	Yes
Larval migrans: cutaneous (hookworm)	*Ancylostoma* spp	Contact	Dogs, cats	No	No	Rare
Larval migrans: visceral, ocular, neurologic (roundworm)	*Toxocara canis, Toxocara cati*	Contact	Dogs, cats	No	No	Rare

Table 122-1. Zoonotic diseases of importance in the United States, 2010 (cont'd)

Disease	Agent	Means of transmission to humans	Most common species associated with transmission to humans[165,166]	Nationally notifiable human (H) or animal (A) cases	Severe or prolonged infection usually associated with immunosuppression	Deaths in humans reported
Leishmaniasis	*Leishmania* spp	Vector	Dogs, wild canids	A	No	Yes
Leptospirosis	*Leptospira* spp	Contact, aerosol	Rodents, pigs, cattle, sheep, goats, horses, dogs	A	No	Yes
Listeriosis	*Listeria monocytogenes*	Contact	Cattle, sheep, goats, pigs, birds, dogs, cats	H	Yes	Yes
Lyme disease	*Borrelia burgdorferi*	Vector	Small rodents, wild mammals	H	No	No
Lymphocytic choriomeningitis	Arenavirus (lymphocytic choriomeningitis virus)	Contact, aerosol	Mice, hamsters, guinea pigs	No	Yes	Yes
Monkeypox	Orthopoxvirus	Contact, aerosol	Nonhuman primates, rodents	A	No	Yes
Mycobacteriosis (nontuberculous)	*Mycobacterium avium* complex, *Mycobacterium marinum*	Aerosol, contact	Poultry, birds, aquarium fish, reptiles	No	Yes	Yes
Pasteurellosis	*Pasteurella multocida* and other species	Contact	Dogs, cats, rabbits, rodents	No	Yes	No
Plague	*Yersinia pestis*	Vector, contact, aerosol	Rodents, cats, rabbits	H, A	No	Yes
Psittacosis (human) or avian chlamydiosis (birds)	*Chlamydophila psittaci*	Aerosol, contact	Pet birds, poultry	H, A	Yes	Yes
Q fever	*Coxiella burnetii*	Contact, aerosol, vector	Goats, sheep, cattle, rodents, rabbits, dogs, cats	H, A	No	Yes
Rabies	Lyssavirus	Contact	Cats, dogs, cattle and other domestic animals; wild carnivores; raccoons; bats; skunks; foxes	H, A	No	Yes
Rat bite fever	*Streptobacillus moniliformis, Spirillum minus*	Contact	Rodents	No	Yes	Yes
Rhodococcus equi infection	*Rhodococcus equi*	Aerosol, contact	Horses	No	Yes	Yes
Rocky Mountain spotted fever	*Rickettsia rickettsii*	Vector	Dogs, rabbits, rodents	H	No	Yes
Salmonellosis	*Salmonella* spp	Contact	Reptiles, amphibians, poultry, horses, swine, cattle, pocket pets, many species of mammals and birds	H	Yes	Yes
Sporotrichosis	*Sporothirix schenckii*	Contact	Cats, dogs, horses	No	Yes	Rare
Staphylococcosis	*Staphylococcus* spp	Contact	Dogs, cats, horses	H (vancomycin-resistant *Staphlococcus aureus*)	Yes	Yes (some forms)
Streptococcosis	*Streptococcus* spp	Contact, aerosol	Swine, fish, other mammals	H (some forms)	No	Yes (some forms)
Toxoplasmosis	*Toxoplasma gondii*	Contact	Cats	No	Yes	Yes
Trichuriasis (whipworm infection)	*Trichuris suis, Trichuris trichiura, Trichuris vulpis*	Contact	Dogs, swine	No	No	Rare
Tuberculosis, bovine	*Mycobacterium bovis*	Aerosol, contact	Cattle, swine, sheep, goats	H, A	No	Yes
Tularemia	*Francisella tularensis*	Vector, contact, aerosol	Rabbits, pocket pets, wild aquatic rodents, sheep, cats, horses, dogs	H, A	No	Yes
Vesicular stomatitis	Vesicular stomatitis virus	Vector, contact, aerosol	Horses, cattle, swine, sheep, goats	A	No	No
West Nile fever	West Nile virus	Vector	Wild birds	H, A	No	Yes
Yersiniosis	*Yersinia enterocolitica*	Contact	Swine, many species of mammals and birds	No	No	No

Data regarding nationally reportable diseases were obtained from the CDC's nationally notifiable infectious diseases list, the World Organization for Animal Health (OIE) notifiable animal diseases list, and the USDA APHIS reportable diseases list.[167–169] Cases may also be notifiable at the state level; state veterinarians or state public health veterinarians should be consulted for current listings of reportable diseases in specific areas.

From Journal of the American Veterinary Medical Assn., December 15, 2010, 237, 12, Compendium of Veterinary Standard Precautions for Zoonotic Disease Prevention in Veterinary Personnel: National Association of State Public Health Veterinarians Veterinary Infection Control Committee 2010, Scheftel, 1403–1422. Used with permission.

in Ontario, Lefebvre and colleagues[21] recommend closer involvement of healthcare personnel with AAA and AAT programs to ensure that protocols are properly developed and implemented. Healthy, immunized, even-tempered, well-trained animals and maintenance of good hygiene practices help provide a safe environment. Each facility should establish written guidelines and polices for animal visitation, AAA, and AAT. Healthcare providers must understand their rights and obligations to persons with disabilities who are accompanied by service animals. Not only is welcoming a person with a service animal into a healthcare facility required by law, it is also good for public relations.

FUTURE TRENDS

Innovating and redefining the way we think about our healthcare treatments, policies, and guidelines are cornerstones to our success in healthcare. More research is needed on the human–animal bond; physiological, psychological, and social benefits of interactions with animals; and the potential and actual risks of zoonotic disease transmission. This, combined with improved infection prevention practices, will help healthcare providers establish better policies and guidelines for animals in healthcare facilities. Additional research is needed to determine whether animals are an important source of transmission of pathogens such as MRSA for humans or if most animals are colonized after contact with human carriers.[11] Does a clean, healthy, well-behaved animal pose a greater risk for the transmission of infectious agents than healthcare personnel or visitors to healthcare facilities? A study by Cole and Gawlinski[22] demonstrated that as a result of an animal visitation program, patients and staff reported feeling happier, calmer, more loved, and less anxious. Miller and Ingram[23] reported that AAT may be beneficial to individuals in the surgical waiting room by relieving stress. Enhanced guidelines and policies can be established as more research is published on the benefits and risks of animals in healthcare facilities.

INTERNATIONAL PERSPECTIVE

Because the benefits of AAA/AAT can cross cultural and political borders, the elements regarding safety and patient benefit should be considered. However, one should also take into account any cultural and religious issues that may pose challenges when animals are involved in patient care areas.

REFERENCES

1. Connor K, Miller J. Animal-assisted therapy: an in-depth look. *Dimens Crit Care Nurs* 2000 May-Jun;19(3):20–26.
2. Cole KM, Gawlinski A. Animal-assisted therapy in the intensive care unit. *Nurs Clin North Am* 1995 Sep;30(3):529–537.
3. Wells DL. The effects of animals on human health and well-being. *J Soc Issues* 2009;65(3): 523–543.
4. Khan MA, Farrag N. Animal-assisted activity and infection control implications in a healthcare setting. *J Hosp Infect* 2000 Sep;46(1):4–11.
5. Jorgenson J. Therapeutic use of companion animals in health care. *Image J Nurs Sch* 1997;29(3):249–254.
6. Barba BE. The positive influence of animals: animal-assisted therapy in acute care. *Clin Nurse Spec* 1995 Jul;9(4):199–202.
7. Pet Partners. *What are animal-assisted activities/therapy?* Pet Partners Website. Available at: http://www.petpartners.org/document. doc?id=1102.
8. American Veterinary Medical Association (AVMA). *Guidelines for animal assisted activity, animal-assisted therapy and resident animal programs.* AVMA Website. Available at: https://www.avma.org/KB/Policies/Pages/Guidelines-for-Animal-Assisted-Activity-Animal-Assisted-Therapy-and-Resident-Animal-Programs.aspx.
9. Merriam-Webster Dictionary. "pet" and "handler" Available at: http://www.merriam-webster.com/dictionary.
10. Duncan SL. APIC state-of-the-art report: the implications of service animals in health care settings. *Am J Infect Control* 2000 Apr;28(2):170–180.
11. Writing Panel of Working Group, Lefebvre SL, Golab GC, et al. Guidelines for animal-assisted interventions in health care facilities. *Am J Infect Control* 2008 Mar;36(2):78–85.
12. Guay DRP. Pet-assisted therapy in the nursing home setting: potential for zoonosis. *Am J Infect Control* 2001 Jun;29(3):178–186.
13. Brodie SJ, Biley FC, Shewring M. An exploration of the potential risks associated with using pet therapy in healthcare settings. *J Clin Nurs* 2002 Jul;11(4):444–456.
14. Lefebvre SL, Peregrine AS, Golab GC, et al. A veterinary perspective on the recently published guidelines for animal-assisted interventions in health-care facilities. *J Am Vet Med Assoc* 2008 Aug 1;233(3):394–402.
15. Lerner-DurJava L. Pet visitation: is it an infection control issue? *Am J Infect Control* 1994;22:112.
16. Scott GM, Thomson R, Malone-Lee J, et al. Cross-infection between animals and man: possible feline transmission of Staphylococcus aureus infection in humans? *J Hosp Infect* 1988 Jul;12(1):29–34.
17. Lefebvre SL, Reid-Smith RJ, Waltner-Toews DW, Weese JS. *J Am Vet Med Assoc* 2009 Jun 1;234(11):1404–1417.
18. Stanley-Hermanns M, Miller J. Animal-assisted therapy. *Am J Nurs* 2002 Oct;102(10):69–76.
19. Lerner-DurJava L. The truth about cats and dogs. *Nursing* 1999 Jul;29(7):73.
20. U.S. Department of Justice, Civil Rights Division. ADA 2010 revised requirements: service animals. July 12, 2011. Americans with Disabilities Act Website. Available at http://www.ada.gov/service_animals_2010.htm.
21. Lefebvre SL, Walther-Toews D, Peregrine A, et al. Characteristics of programs involving canine visitation of hospitalized people in Ontario. *Infect Control Hosp Epidemiol* 2006 Jul;27(7):754–758.
22. Cole KM, Gawlinski A. Animal-assisted therapy: the human-animal bond. *AACN Clinical Issues* 2000 Feb;11(1):139–149.
23. Miller J, Ingram L. Perioperative nursing and animal-assisted therapy. *AORN J* 2000 Sep;72(3):477–483.

SUPPLEMENTAL RESOURCES

Americans with Disabilities Act (ADA). Available at: http://www.ada.gov.

Coakley AB, Mahoney EK. Creating a therapeutic and healing environment with a pet therapy program. *Complement Ther Clin Pract* 2009 Aug;15(3):141–146.

Horowitz S. The human-animal bond. *Mary Ann Libert, INC* 2008;14(5):251–256.

Lefebvre SL, Reid-Smith RJ, Waltner-Toews D, et al. Incidence of acquisition of methicillin-resistant *Staphylococcus aureus, Clostridium difficile*, and other health-care-associated pathogens by dogs that participated in animal-assisted interventions. *J Am Vet Med Assoc* 2009 Jun 1;234(11):1404–1417.

Morrison ML. Health benefits of animal-assisted interventions. *Complementary Health Practice Review* 2007;12(1):51–62.

Urbanski BL, Lazenby M. Distress among hospitalized pediatric cancer patients modified by pet-therapy intervention to improve quality of life. *J Pediatr Oncol Nurs* 2012 Sep-Oct;29(5):272–282.

CHAPTER **123**

Body Piercing, Tattoos, and Electrolysis

Amanda (Robinson) Valyko, MPH, CIC
Infection Control Practitioner
Infection Control & Epidemiology
University of Michigan Health System
Ann Arbor, MI

ABSTRACT

Body piercing, tattoos, and electrolysis are becoming more common. As these practices become more prevalent in society, healthcare facilities see patients with complications from these procedures, particularly in family practice and pediatrics. In some ways, body piercing, tattoos, and electrolysis carry some of the same risks as operative procedures. There is a risk of infection to both the client and the operator. Proper infection prevention practices are important to mitigate the risk of infection; however, little regulation exists in the United States and varies by state.

KEY CONCEPTS

- Identification of the processes involved in body piercing, tattoos, and electrolysis.
- Infectious risks related to body piercing, tattoos, and electrolysis.
- Medical considerations for patients with body jewelry.
- Infection prevention techniques for skin piercing procedures.
- Occupational exposure.

BACKGROUND

Throughout history, people have adorned their bodies with art and jewelry to distinguish themselves. Such body decoration may indicate membership in various religious groups or tribes, but often tattoos or skin piercings are used to express individuality. Skin may be used as a canvas to display unique artwork. There is currently an increased interest in body piercing and tattooing, predominantly among adolescents and young adults. Designs may run the gamut of possibilities—from elaborate creations that cover the entire skin surface, to simple well-hidden designs, to those created with crude nonsterile instruments as part of gang rituals or during incarceration. Facial tattooing is also performed to create permanent cosmetic makeup for women. Tattoos and piercings may represent attributes such as individualism, risk, sexual fantasies, and uniqueness, which are important for adolescents attempting to prove their individuality.[1]

As with other medical procedures, there are risks associated with skin and mucous membrane disruption that may or may not be immediately apparent. A certain proportion of complications are due to inadequate aseptic technique performed in the studio setting, but many are due to the client's individual health considerations and personal hygiene. It is important that a person considering a tattoo or body piercing investigate the studio and the person who will perform the procedure. All professional studios should provide the client with an aftercare information sheet, identifying appropriate disinfection practices and site care to reduce the chances of infection.

Many cities and states require that studios be licensed, which generally indicates that minimum requirements have been met and an inspection has been performed by a public health department. Unfortunately, at this time there are no standardized guidelines or requirements in the United States for practices or licensure. Although there is no way to effectively estimate the percentage of people that have adverse outcomes after tattooing, body piercing, or electrolysis, they are considered to be safe procedures when performed by trained professionals.

BASIC PRINCIPLES

Body Piercing

Two techniques may be used for skin piercing: utilizing a needle or using an ear-piercing (stud) gun. It is the official position of the Association of Professional Piercers (APP) that only sterile disposable equipment is suitable for safe body piercing.[2]

Studios that use the needle technique may purchase piercing needles from a specialty supply outlet or may use hypodermic needles with the hub removed for the skin piercing procedure. All needles must be sterilized before use. The diameter of the hollow-bore needles generally varies from 6 to 18 gauge, but smaller or larger needles may be used.[3]

Most piercings are done in a sequential fashion: The tissue is secured using tools such as special forceps or a needle-receiving tube or special hand positioning, and the needle is pushed through the tissue. A cork is often held on the exit site to support the tissue and to prevent injury to the client and piercer.

Then, the jewelry is inserted, essentially pushing out the piercing needle. The needle is passed through the tissue and out the other side and is often pushed into a cork.

Ear-piercing guns (also called stud guns) hold the earring studs and use a trigger motion to force the stud into and through the earlobe. Ear-piercing guns cannot be effectively sterilized, and aerosolized blood from a previous client can contaminate the gun. If any part of the stud touches the contaminated gun, there is the possibility of transmitting bloodborne pathogens. The APP feels that most of the ear studs are not as sharp as needles, and therefore the force generated by stud guns causes more tissue damage to the earlobe.[2] If an ear-piercing gun is to be used, one with a disposable sterile cartridge that holds the stud is highly recommended.[3] The disposable cartridge is removed after piercing the ears of a client, and the remainder of the gun should be wiped with 70 percent alcohol between clients. Shops that use ear-piercing guns with a solid head (no disposable cartridge) must use high-level disinfection practices on their equipment between clients, as indicated in the manufacturer's instructions. If a glutaraldehyde product is used, the shop should be monitoring the process with indicator strips and ensuring that adequate ventilation is available. Ear-piercing guns should only be used on the fleshy part of earlobes.

Jewelry used during skin piercing should be smoothly polished and designed to permit easy cleaning. Gold (14 to 18 karat), titanium, surgical steel, or niobium jewelry is most commonly purchased because these pieces can be effectively sterilized and are less likely to cause allergic reactions. The amount of time needed for tissue healing varies. The type of jewelry used, the movement of the body site, the quality of the procedure, and site care performed by the client all affect the healing process. Healing time for piercings generally ranges from a few months to a year, depending on the site, health of the client, and aftercare. Vascularity of the area and likelihood of trauma during healing also affect healing time. The APP believes that in some instances it may be inappropriate to perform even the most standard piercing.[2] The organization recommends that their members should refuse to perform a piercing that could be dangerous, ill suited, unsuccessful, or for which they are not trained.

Tattooing

Although most of us are familiar with the concept of tattooing, a review of basic techniques may be helpful to understand the complications and risks of the procedure. Tattooing permanently deposits pigments into the skin at a depth of 1 to 2 mm to create a design. The tattoo artist may draw the design by hand or use a stenciled design that is copied onto the skin before tattooing. Fine needles held within an electric-powered tattoo machine puncture the skin several hundred times per minute. To create the colors of the design, the needles are dipped into tattoo pigments that are poured into individual cups or caps for each client. These pigments may be purchased in liquid form or may be prepared on-site from a purified powder. Because the needles puncture both the epidermis and the dermis, blood and excess pigment should be wiped away with

tissue or paper towels during the procedure.[3] Immediately after tattooing, the skin swells slightly and a small amount of bloody to colorless body fluid comes to the surface. The swelling lasts for a few hours, but it generally takes about 2 weeks for the skin to heal completely.

An electric tattoo machine is a relatively simple device, consisting of a rotating motor in a handle, a stainless steel tube that the tattoo artist holds, and a needle bar that runs through the tube and contains 1 to 14 needles that protrude from the end of the tube by approximately 2 to 3 mm. The solid-bore tattoo needles are soldered onto the needle bar, and various needle configurations are used to produce different line thicknesses and to add shading. The needles used for tattooing present the highest risk for infection. It is difficult to sterilize needles for reuse due to difficulty in adequately cleaning them before sterilization. Sterile needles must be used for only one tattooing session, on only one client.[3] When performed by a skilled, conscientious professional, procedures for skin preparation, image transferring, skin lubrication, tattoo dye preparation, and skin preparation during tattooing use good infection prevention techniques similar to those used during minor surgical procedures. Recommended instrumentation, disinfection, sterilization, and safe sharps disposal protocols are identical to standard healthcare industry practices.

Electrolysis

Electrolysis is a method for permanently removing hair by inserting a needle into a hair follicle and applying an electric current. There are several different methods currently in use: galvanic, thermolysis, and a combination of galvanic and thermolysis referred to as the blend method. Galvanic electrolysis utilizes a direct current that is sent down the hair follicle on the needle that has been inserted. This destroys the root of the hair because sodium hydroxide is produced when the electrical current interacts with the saline in the tissue. Thermolysis utilizes a high-frequency alternating current that is also sent down a needle inserted into the hair follicle. This method works by producing heat that destroys the root of the hair. This method is more rapid than galvanic electrolysis, but it may not be suitable for thick hairs. The blend method combines the previous methods and many experts consider it to be more effective.[4]

Electrolysis needles are not intended to penetrate the tissue, but in some instances they may become contaminated with blood or body fluids. The American Electrology Association's Infection Control Committee has published Infection Control Standards for the Practice of Electrology that make recommendations regarding standard precautions, hand hygiene, cleaning and disinfection of equipment, and bloodborne pathogens.

INFECTIOUS RISKS RELATED TO BODY PIERCING, TATTOOS, AND ELECTROLYSIS

It has become well recognized that tattooing and body piercing activities can transmit infectious diseases. There has also been evidence of infection transmission during electrolysis.

The primary source of information comes from case reports. Although tattooing was not uncommon in the past, there has been a significant increase in its popularity in the last few decades. The peak age range for acquiring tattoos is between 14 and 22 years old, and the incidence among females has quadrupled in the past 20 years.[5] Among 12 to 18 year olds, it is estimated that 10 to 16 percent have tattoos and 33 to 50 percent have at least one piercing other than the earlobe.

Tattoos

If proper infection prevention protocols are not followed, there is a significant risk of the spread of infection. People receiving tattoos in suboptimal environments are at greater risk of infection. The incidence of tattoos among incarcerated persons and gang members is generally high, as is the prevalence of infections with one or more bloodborne pathogens. One cannot assume that the skin piercing procedures transmitted all bloodborne infections, although some of these tattoos may have been applied using less-than-optimal techniques in a population with a high prevalence of viral hepatitis and human immunodeficiency virus (HIV). Prison tattoos have been created using ballpoint pen shafts, paper clips, sharpened guitar strings, or other pieces of metal. Lack of sterilization and skin disinfection also increases the likelihood of transmitting bacterial infections in the corrections system. The incidence of tattoos is noted to be higher among women who engage in prostitution, a significant source of infectious disease transmission both in Western cultures and in Africa.[6]

Although researchers have tried to evaluate the prevalence of Hepatitis C virus (HCV) infection in persons with body art, this has been more difficult to evaluate than other similarly transmitted diseases. Testing methods have improved; however, due to the incubation and manifestation of HCV, it can be difficult to determine when someone was infected. Hepatitis B virus (HBV) transmission has been much easier to identify. Long and Rickman reviewed 17 case studies found in the literature from 1950 to 1980.[6] Clusters of new infections were almost universally due to the lack of effective sterilization of tattoo needles between clients. As a historical note, tattooists would dip the needles into alcohol and flame them for disinfection purposes. With the current availability of small autoclaves and disposable products, the risk of infectious disease transmission has been reduced in reputable businesses.

Although we now know that HBV is more easily transmissible than HIV, there is still the possibility that tattooing may transmit HIV.[6] A case report in *Clinical Infectious Disease* discussed the possibility of HIV transmission through body piercing.[7] Other potential risk factors were denied by the patient, but could not be excluded. Needlestick simulations have shown that solid-bore needles transmit as much or more blood than hollow-bore needles used for phlebotomy; 1.2 to 2.0 μL of blood was transmitted by 23- to 27-gauge suture needles passed to a depth of 0.5 cm.[8] The issue of needle sterilization is still the key to preventing transmission of disease.

Other infectious complications of tattoos found in the literature include both bacterial and viral infections. With the rise in community-associated methicillin-resistant *Staphylococcus aureus* (CA-MRSA), it is becoming more common to see skin and soft tissue infections caused by MRSA. There have been reports of MRSA skin and soft tissue infections related to unlicensed tattoo parlors in Ohio, Kentucky, and Vermont. The severity of infection ranged from cellulitis to bacteremia requiring hospitalization and intravenous antibiotics. The infections were linked to suboptimal infection prevention practices such as appropriate hand hygiene, skin antisepsis, and appropriate disinfection and cleaning of equipment and surfaces.[9] The risk of localized infection is easily understood, as the skin contains many normal commensal bacteria that may be carried into the punctured area, even if the site is well cleaned before the procedure, similar to surgical site infections. After the procedure, appropriate aftercare techniques should be discussed with each client; distributing printed copies of instructions are highly recommended. Not all skin infections can be blamed on the tattoo artist—appropriate site care in the home is equally important. Infection is more commonly seen in nonprofessional tattoos, but serious complications may occur after any skin puncturing procedure. Transmission of warts (papilloma virus) has also been reported after tattooing procedures.[6]

There is a possibility that dyes from tattoos may cause skin irritation during magnetic resonance imaging (MRI).[10] Case reports of people with tattoos that underwent MRI indicate minor reactions such as burns, swelling, and erythema. The reaction is usually temporary and sometimes a pressure dressing can be used to prevent tissue distortion.[11] Recommendations include asking patients if they have any tattoos, informing them of the risks, and monitoring them throughout their MRI. As a precaution, a cold compress can be used on the tattoo during the MRI.[12]

Body Piercing

Body piercing has also been associated with the transmission of infections. Although tattooing and body piercing differ in the amount of exposure to needles and in procedure times, many of the infections reported occur in the weeks and months after the procedure, similar to surgical site infections. In order to prevent infections, the jewelry and needles must be sterilized before skin penetration. Needles are always single-use. Piercing guns have been recognized as being potential vehicles for infection transmission. The guns are difficult to clean and sterilize and the motion causes more trauma to the client than a regular needle.[13] Aftercare is different for piercings, as various sites may take up to 6 months or longer to heal. One of the differences in procedures is that piercings may pass through mucous membranes and that the metal left in place may cause an allergic reaction.

Piercings Not Involving Mucous Membranes

Although a wide range of infectious complications from body piercing has been reported, most of the data involves ear piercing.[14] Bacterial infections may result from improper initial piercing technique or from poor hygiene. The organisms involved in most earlobe-piercing infections are often considered normal skin flora, including *Staphylococcus* and *Streptococcus* species. Higher ear piercings in the ear cartilage have been associated with more pathogenic organisms, including *Pseudomonas* species.[14] Many of the infections that occur after earlobe piercing do not result in a physician visit, as local site care or removal of the earrings often solves the problem. Eyebrow piercings have approximately the same risk factors for infection as earlobe piercing, but there is little information available on the incidence of infection. Navel and nipple piercings are also similar in tissue characteristics. Wearing tight or textured clothing may irritate the site, potentially increasing the risk of site infection. Multiple cases of atypical mycobacterium infections after piercing have been reported. Mastitis due to *Mycobacterium abscessus* has been reported after a nipple piercing,[15] *Mycobacterium flavescens* has been reported after an eyebrow piercing, and *Mycobacterium chelonae* has been reported after a navel piercing.[16] There are case reports of infective endocarditis that required treatment with intravenous antibiotics, and in some cases surgical intervention to replace heart valves; the infections resulting from navel, earlobe, and nipple piercings.[17] There has also been a case report of tetanus after a naval piercing.[7]

Facial and Oral Piercings

Piercings that involve mucous membranes are considered to have a higher risk for infectious complications, due to their dark, warm, moist environment, which generally contains more bacterial flora, including anaerobes and yeast. A variety of facial and oral piercings are becoming more common. Barbells are placed through the lower lip in the oral cavity, exiting through the skin above the chin. Tongue piercing is also increasingly popular with adolescents and younger adults. Pierced tongues are sometimes considered easier to conceal than facial piercings, which may not be permitted in some workplaces. These piercings may result in more serious infections even after the piercing site has healed. There are multiple reports of endocarditis related to tongue and lip piercings.[17] These infections occurred from weeks after the piercing to several months after the piercing. The dental literature contains many reports of traumatic injury due to the placement of metal barbells in the mouth. Some wearers tend to "play" with the studs, moving them around in their mouths and increasing the risks of periodontal injury (gingival recession, and mucogingival defects), chipped, cracked, and broken teeth. There are also reports of aspiration of oral jewelry.[18]

Tongue piercings may be particularly painful, and the tongue may remain swollen well after the piercing procedure. Even after healing, the stud may rub the roof of the mouth, causing hard palate erosion. Martinello and Cooney reported a brain abscess linked to a tongue piercing.[19] The young woman developed severe swelling of the tongue and a foul-tasting discharge. After 2 to 3 days, she removed the barbell stud, and the symptoms resolved. One month later the woman experienced headaches, fever, nausea, vomiting, and vertigo. A computed tomography (CT) scan of the head revealed a cerebellar abscess that required drainage and 6 weeks of antibiotic therapy.[19] In general, if a piercing becomes infected, the jewelry should not be removed until the area is healed. Removing the piece while the area is still infected can result in abscess formation.[20]

Aside from the noninfectious complications, the long-term effect of oral piercings is an increased risk for transient bacteremia, hematogenous spread of bacteria to other sites, and endocarditis. It is critical that patients with oral piercings routinely undergo comprehensive periodontal assessment; however, many of those with oral piercings do not see them as health hazards and are very reluctant to remove them.[21]

Nasal piercings, usually involving a ring through a nostril or through the nasal septum, carry an increased risk of localized infection. Wearers should be careful not to touch their noses or handle the jewelry with unwashed hands, as the nares can become colonized with staphylococcal species, particularly *S. aureus*. If the wearer has a cold, the nasal drainage and nose blowing irritates the site and may lead to bacterial superinfection.

Genital Piercings

Healthcare personnel probably have the least experience with genital piercings, and little information is available in medical literature. The APP tells us that the average genital piercing customer is a more informed consumer than the usual navel, ear, or tongue piercing client. Those who elect to get them usually have already received and healed at least one other piercing and are often more informed about the piercing process and aftercare.[2] There are several clinically unaddressed issues associated with genital piercings. Potential risks of infection may be increased if tissue trauma occurs during sexual activity or if a condom is ripped by jewelry. Of course, there is the possibility for transmission of sexually transmitted diseases if condoms are not used; however, this risk is not increased simply by the presence of piercings. The professional piercer should ideally provide information on personal hygiene issues to all clients.

Medical Considerations Related to Piercing

It is becoming more common for healthcare personnel to provide care for patients with body jewelry, and it is sometimes unclear whether removal of the jewelry is necessary. Removal of these items is sometimes required for radiological purposes, and removal is not usually difficult if the patient is able to assist with the opening mechanism. In an emergency situation, attempts at removal may cause unnecessary trauma to the site and distress to the patient. In a survey of 28 accident and emergency doctors, only six were able to accurately describe the opening mechanisms of all three commonly used types of jewelry.[22] Descriptions of the types of jewelry currently used are not generally available in the medical literature, but are provided in this chapter. As the number of people getting pierced or tattooed increases in any locality, it is likely that the healthcare community will need to become more familiar with these practices and their complications.

Oral and dental complications have been reported as a result of oral piercings such as tooth fractures, gingivitis, bleeding, and gingival recessions as well as aspiration of oral piercing jewelry.[18]

Persons with immune-compromising conditions are at a higher risk of infectious complications from a piercing. The APP recognizes that some potential clients may be at higher risk for infections and other complications if they obtain a piercing, and it recommends the following guidelines for their members to discuss with a client:[3]

- An individual with heart valve disease (e.g., mitral valve prolapse) should consult their physician for prophylactic antibiotics.

- If an individual has a heart murmur, diabetes, hemophilia, autoimmune disorder, or other medical condition(s) that may negatively influence the piercing procedure or the healing process, he or she should consult a physician before deciding to have a piercing placed.

- If there is an obvious skin or tissue abnormality that may include but is not limited to rashes, lumps, bumps, scars, lesions, moles, freckles, and/or abrasions, piercings should not be performed in the area.

- If the client wants to pierce irregular or surgically altered anatomy or if the client is unsuited due to occupational, recreational, or environmental factors, it is recommended that the piercing not be performed.

- Surface-to-surface or other frequently unsuccessful (i.e., commonly rejected by the body) piercings should not be performed.

- If the client is pregnant or has impending plans to become pregnant and wishes to get a nipple, navel, or other piercing, it is advisable to refrain from piercing.

Edema and hematomas may occur after piercing procedures, due to tissue trauma. Improperly sized jewelry may irritate adjacent tissue, particularly larger, heavier pieces. Heavy jewelry or accidental pulling may lead to torn tissue, which may require surgical repair.[23] Sarcoid-like granulomas may form at a pierce site, usually in association with gold jewelry.[14] Site-specific complications reported include aspiration of oral/facial jewelry with airway obstruction; prolonged bleeding from areas with high vascularity; cellulitis of the submandibular, sublingual, and submental facial spaces; speech impairment; increased salivary flow; and obstruction of radiographs in the odontoid view on a cervical spine series in the evaluation of trauma.[14]

Noninfectious complications such as allergic reactions and tissue trauma are also associated with tattooing and body piercing procedures. Contact dermatitis from metal allergy associated with ear piercing has been widely reported. Nickel allergy has been the most common problem and usually presents as an eczematous rash.[23] Contact sensitivity to gold and silver has also been reported. Metals used in body piercing jewelry are usually surgical-grade stainless steel, solid 14 or 18 karat gold, niobium, titanium, or platinum.[14]

It is difficult to estimate the percentage of the population that has nontraditional (other than earlobe) piercings, and there is probably a wide variation in local rates. Some of the common

hospital practices, such as urinary tract catheterization, intubation, and MRI, may be affected by the presence of body jewelry, and it is essential for healthcare providers to be able to identify that their patients may have metal devices in their bodies. With an increase in nontraditional sites, it is sometimes difficult for healthcare personnel to identify potential sources for some complications or infections, particularly if the patient does not report "intimate area" piercings. This can be a sensitive issue in minors when they are being interviewed with their parents present and may result in the patient neglecting to report a nontraditional piercing.

Anderson et al. state, "Urologists should perhaps be particularly aware of the seemingly bizarre practice of genital piercing, as their specialist knowledge may sometimes be required to manage the inevitable complications."[24] There are at least eight variations on genital piercing sites for men and five for women.[14,23] It is quite common for people to have multiple genital piercings as well as piercings at other body sites. Unique and significant complications can result from genital piercing, including endocarditis, paraphimosis, and urethral puncture.[14] It should be noted that urethral puncture is not a complication from the Prince Albert piercing, one of the most common male genital piercings. For this procedure, jewelry will be placed through the urethra—it enters the urethral meatus and exits where the piercing is made on the underside of the penis at the juncture of the head and shaft. It is one of the quickest to heal, with the fewest complications.

Potential complications in pregnant women are not well defined in the literature at this time. Although nipple, navel, and genital piercing sites would obviously be affected by body changes, delivery, and nursing, the APP offers these helpful suggestions on body piercings during pregnancy:[2]

- Navel jewelry may be left in place. Some women leave jewelry in during their entire pregnancy and delivery. If during the pregnancy the piercing becomes uncomfortable, the jewelry can be replaced with Tygon or fluoropolymers such as PTFE, which are inert plastics, similar to thick fishing line. These will bend and flex with the changing body, be more comfortable, and are safer to wear. Once the pregnancy is over, jewelry may be replaced.

- Most women who have had a nipple piercing remove their jewelry for breastfeeding, which is appropriate. Some milk may come from the site of the piercing during nursing, which should not be harmful or problematic from a healed site. There is no special care recommended during pregnancy for healed piercings.

Jewelry Removal

Nurses and physicians often have to determine whether to remove body jewelry in the healthcare setting, and these decisions can be difficult. There is a misconception that all body jewelry should be removed. Consideration should be given, however, to the fact that once jewelry is removed, it may be impossible to place it back into the same site after the patient is discharged. The pierced patient may protest that jewelry should not be removed, particularly if they are aware of the common difficulty of reinserting jewelry that has been removed even for a short period of time and even from a well-healed piercing.

Body jewelry does not need to be removed in the majority of cases, but there are times when it is necessary in order to properly care for a patient. The most common scenario in which body jewelry must be removed is to obtain radiological studies. Metal jewelry can obstruct accurate readings of radiographs and CT scans and should be removed from the area being studied.[25] Patients should be questioned about piercings prior to obtaining radiological tests, as the presence of metal jewelry may not be obvious. Because of the magnetic field, all jewelry must be removed when a patient must undergo MRI. Jewelry needs to be removed for CT scans only if it is in the area being studied. Traditionally, all jewelry should be removed when a patient is having surgery.

In some cases, jewelry in genital piercings may need to be removed to perform urethral catheterization of the bladder. Nipple piercings and surface piercings of the chest may cause additional injury to the patient or caregiver if defibrillation is necessary and the paddles are placed directly over the jewelry.[26] Defibrillation should not be delayed for any reason,[27] but if the need is anticipated, jewelry should be removed to prevent burning and arcing. The jewelry may also be wrapped in cloth tape to help decrease any contact with an electrical current.

If it has been determined that body jewelry should be removed, healthcare providers should be made aware of the techniques necessary to accomplish this task. There are three basic types of body jewelry: the captive bead ring, the barbell stud, and plugs. Patients can sometimes be a valuable resource for how to remove jewelry, but in many instances they remain unaware of the procedure because they never anticipated the need for removal.

Removal of the Captive Bead Ring

Step 1: Lubricate the piercing with a small amount of saline and insert a hemostat into the ring.

Step 2: Apply generous, outward pressure on the ring while holding the bead. The bead will pull out, and the ring can be slid out of the piercing (see Figure 123-1).

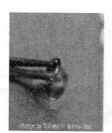

Figure 123-1. Removal of captive bead ring.

Removing this type of ring can also be accomplished using scissors (see Figure 123-2).

Step 1: Lubricate the piercing with a small amount of saline and grasp the ring with scissors where the bead and the ring meet.

Step 2: Squeeze firmly to release the bead. The bead should pop out quickly, and the ring can be removed.

These tools work for smaller rings, but larger gauge jewelry may require circlip pliers or larger clamps.

Removal of the Barbells

Step 1: Lubricate the piercing with a small amount of saline and grasp each end of the barbell with a hemostat or gloved fingers.

Step 2: Unscrew in a counterclockwise motion. The bar can then be removed from the piercing once one end is removed (see Figure 123-3).

To remove a barbell from oral piercings (see Figure 123-4), dry the area with gauze and grasp the barbell underneath the tongue. The top ball can then be unscrewed and the bar removed. Hemostats may be used to hold the barbell steady if necessary. On some jewelry, only the bottom ball will unscrew.

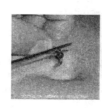

Figure 123-2. Removal of captive bead ring using scissors.

Figure 123-3. Removal of barbells.

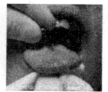

Figure 123-4. Removal of barbells from oral piercing.

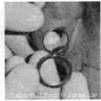

Figure 123-5. Removal of plugs.

Figure 123-6. Flared plug.

Figure 123-7. Plug with rubber O-ring.

Removal of Plugs

There are three types of plugs that are worn almost exclusively in the earlobe where the skin has been stretched. The threaded plug is held in place by a threaded ring, usually found on the back of jewelry. The ring should be unscrewed in a counter-clockwise motion, and the plug removed (see Figure 123-5).

Flared plugs (Figure 123-6) are removed by simply pulling them out. Plugs with rubber O-rings (Figure 123-7) are removed by pulling one of the O-rings off and removing the plug.

Electrolysis

Electrolysis has the potential to spread infections. While the needle is inserted into the hair follicle and should not pierce the skin, this can occur during the procedure, contaminating the needle and introducing bacteria. This has the potential to cause skin and soft tissue infections. There have been case reports of human papilloma viruses being spread through electrolysis.[28] Additionally, electrolysis has been reported to spread *Molluscum contagiosum* virus locally in an individual.[29]

Infection Prevention Interventions

It is difficult to describe the epidemiology of disease transmission after tattooing and body piercing procedures. There have not been uniform licensure requirements for body art studios or for individuals performing the procedures, and so the reporting of infections to a public health agency is generally limited

to bloodborne diseases identified by the healthcare system. The licensure varies greatly by state. Regulations may address the age of the client, client histories, sterilization processes, single-use items, apprenticeships/training, and bloodborne pathogens training. Some states leave the regulations up to local ordinances and some have no regulations whatsoever. The enforcement of the various regulations is dependent on funding of the programs, which is also variable.[30] Many local health departments may inspect the business sites, but it is questionable whether inspectors receive adequate training about the appropriate infection prevention practices they should monitor in these nontraditional settings. Also, the frequency by which the sites are inspected is variable. Sometimes it takes an adverse event for a site to be inspected. There are many opportunities for contamination, particularly for tattooing. Many of the practices being adopted by piercing studios worldwide are based on a common sense approach, as well as guidelines offered by professional organizations such as the APP or the Piercing Association of the United Kingdom.[30]

It is much easier to identify breaks in technique that could lead to the transmission of bloodborne pathogens and other infectious diseases. The recent events of reusing single-use items in healthcare clinics are a reminder that constant education and follow-up is necessary to reinforce good practices. Modern tattoo parlors are fully aware of the bad publicity that sometimes surrounds the tattoo industry, and they are trying to build reputable businesses through the following practices:

- Sterile needles must be used for only one tattoo session, on only one client.

- The studios should use separate small containers of dye that are used on only one customer and are discarded after use.

- Needles and the tips and tubes that hold them in the machine should be sterilized in an autoclave following each use. The machine itself cannot withstand autoclaving, and so it should be placed in a plastic bag during use and disinfected between customers.

- The tattoo site should be disinfected before the procedure and dressed with an antiseptic ointment and a sterile bandage.

- The artists should wear latex or nitrile gloves to protect the clients from resident and transient flora on their hands and to protect themselves from the blood of their clients.[6] If latex is used, it is important to educate staff on petroleum-based products that react with latex, making it less effective as a barrier.

- Unsafe practices used in the past should be replaced by those identified in the Occupational Safety and Health Administration (OSHA) Bloodborne Pathogens Standard and other disease prevention guidelines.

- Education and reeducation is important to keep employees updated on current safe practices.

The licensing requirements for electrolysis vary by state. According to the American Electrology Association (AEA), there are currently 33 states with state regulation of electrology. The training requirements vary. Some states require students to do a specified number of hours training. This range of required hours is 300 to 1,100 hours. Some states will accept apprenticeships for a specified amount of time. The length of apprenticeship can be a short as 600 hours and as long as 1,600 hours. Most states require an examination. Some states pair with cosmetology licensing, and continuing education can also be a requirement for recertification. Most states also require that applicants be at least 18 years of age with a high school diploma or equivalent.[31]

The AEA has also published Infection Control Standards for the practice of electrology that explains potential risks and make recommendations regarding controls. Some of their recommendations are summarized here:

- Use appropriate hand hygiene (follow Centers for Disease Control and Prevention guidelines).

- Wear gloves during activities that might contaminate hands with blood or body fluids.

- Use single-use, sterile, disposable needles and store them in a manner that will maintain sterility.

- Properly dispose of needles to avoid sharps injuries.

- Thoroughly clean and sterilize items that are reprocessed such as forceps, phoresis rollers, and tips.

- Keep the work environment clean, well lit, and ventilated.

The infection preventionist may serve as a resource for safe practices in the community. The Health Canada guidelines are an excellent reference, detailing all the safe practices that should be part of tattoo, body piercing, and electrolysis studios.[3] The following summaries have been created from this information to provide a review of the basic infection prevention practices that should be observed in these establishments.

Worksite Design: The Shop

- Work areas should be organized to prevent cross contamination of clean, disinfected, or sterile equipment with dirty equipment.

  ○ Clean zone: procedure area, hand-washing sink, sterilized packages, disinfected and clean equipment storage

  ○ Dirty zone: contaminated equipment, utility sink, holding basins for equipment that will be disinfected/sterilized

- General requirements

  ○ All surfaces should be constructed of materials that are smooth, nonporous, and easily cleaned

  ○ Good lighting and ventilation

  ○ Hot and cold running water, two sinks are highly recommended: one for hand hygiene and one for cleaning contaminated items

  ○ Cabinets or storage space (preferably enclosed) to protect supplies from dust and moisture

  ○ Public washroom access

- Instruments and equipment

  ○ Needles used for tattooing, piercing, or electrolysis must be sterile and used once per client

  ○ Reusable instruments should be smooth, noncorrosive, and constructed of materials that can be easily cleaned and sterilized (e.g., stainless steel)

  ○ Machine controls should be foot operated

  ○ An ultrasonic cleaning device with a lid may be used to preclean instruments

  ○ An autoclave should be used for sterilization

  ○ Office equipment (e.g., telephones) should not be touched during a procedure. If such equipment is considered part of the procedural equipment (e.g., magnifying glass arm, treatment table), it should be covered with a disposable plastic sheath or cleaned after each client service

- Necessary supplies

  ○ Medical-grade gloves

  ○ Single-use wooden tongue depressors or cotton swabs for removing creams, gels, or ointments from a bulk container into a smaller package for use on a single client

  ○ Clean linen or disposable towels for patient protection or cover for a work surface

  ○ Wrapping material and suitable containers to contain instruments for sterilization

  ○ Metal basins or other suitable containers for dirty equipment

  ○ Chemical time/temperature and/or humidity sensitive tape, strips, or pellets for monitoring each sterilization cycle

  ○ Spore strips or vials for testing the sterilization process weekly or monthly, as required

  ○ Liquid hand-washing soap that is provided in nonrefillable cartridges or containers

  ○ Detergent for cleaning

  ○ Commercial sharps containers

  ○ Hospital-grade disinfectants

- Disinfection and sterilization practices should be in accordance with the Spaulding classification system.

- Aseptic technique, hand-washing, and barrier procedures should be in accordance with standard hospital practices.

- Skin should be inspected for signs of infection or abnormalities, then prepped with an appropriate antiseptic solution.

- Waste should be segregated and disposed of according to regulations.

- Client records should be kept for all procedures for at least the minimum time period specified by law.

- Bloodborne pathogens precautions (Standard Precautions) should be observed.
- Material Safety Data Sheets (MSDS) should be kept for all chemicals on the premises.
- All practitioners and shop employees should be trained on infection prevention and control practices to ensure a safe environment for clients and workers.

If you should need additional information on the specific infection prevention procedures for performing tattooing, body piercing, or electrolysis, details are available in the Health Canada guidelines.[3]

Occupational Exposures

In body piercing, tattoo, and electrolysis establishments, the potential exists for occupational exposure to bloodborne pathogens. Employees should be trained to follow Standard Precautions and OSHA Bloodborne Pathogen Standards. To prevent HBV, vaccines may be offered to employees to prevent infection. A study by Hellard et al. looked at the training and knowledge among body piercing practitioners in Australia.[32] They found that there was a lack of training and knowledge regarding HCV and inconsistent cleaning and skin antisepsis protocols. These knowledge deficits have the potential to put both the practitioner and the client at risk. There should be established protocols for the procedures as well as protocols to alert practitioners on what they need to do in the event of an exposure to mitigate the risk of infection. Oberdorfer et al. reported on a trial conducted in Sydney, Australia, in 2002 in which educational intervention activities were provided to half of the tattooing/body piercing premises involved in their study.[33] No effects were found in terms of improved knowledge, but the group that received educational intervention showed a significantly greater perception of the risks of being detected and penalized for noncompliance with infection prevention guidelines.[33] This stresses the importance of standardization of certification and licensing requirements as well as site inspections.

CONCLUSIONS

Body piercing and tattooing are increasing in popularity and are considered expressions of a person's individuality. When performed by a trained professional, using established infection prevention practices, these procedures are considered relatively safe. It is important for potential clients to ask questions of the artists that will perform the procedures and to evaluate the cleanliness of the studio. There have been various reports of infectious and noninfectious complications following both procedures, but many of the risks can be minimized by the use of appropriate sterilization and disinfection practices. By providing detailed instructions on appropriate aftercare to the client, tattoo artists and body piercing professionals can further ensure a better outcome for their clients.

FUTURE TRENDS

In this era of patient safety, there will be more focus on standardizing and regulating these industries and ensuring that their practitioners are well trained in infection prevention. As tracking methods for capturing adverse events related to tattoos, piercings, or electrolysis improve, the data should drive policy and regulation.

INTERNATIONAL PERSPECTIVE

Although body piercing and tattooing are generally considered to be safe procedures when performed by a trained professional using good infection prevention methodology, there are concerns that these techniques may not be universally practiced in all parts of the world. Obviously, the body decoration that is being performed as ethnic identification may not be using optimal aseptic technique, but there is still a lack of training on safe practices in many countries. Even in the United States, there is no mandated training or certification process for body piercing and tattooing artists. Much of the training is performed in existing studios, so that less-than-optimal practices may be passed on to new practitioners unintentionally. Although it is believed that each studio has the best of intentions and does not recognize that their practices may not be as safe as they could be, it is concerning that there is not a better mechanism for practice standardization throughout the world.

Access to sterilization equipment and disinfection products also varies throughout the world, and the costs associated with providing optimal care may not be appreciated by the person responsible for making a profit with the business venture. Although site infections are obvious to the client, the potential transmission of bloodborne disease would not be immediately identified, and clusters of infection may escape detection. Travelers should be warned against obtaining tattoos in countries where the knowledge of aseptic technique is not optimal. In any country, it is important for the client to evaluate the studio setup and the artist's explanation of their safe practices.

REFERENCES

1. Barnett J. Health implications of body piercing and tattooing: a literature review. *Nurs Times* 2003;99(37):62–63.
2. The Association of Professional Piercers (APP). Frequently Asked Questions. APP website. 2013. Available at: http://www.safepiercing.org/piercing/faq/.
3. Public Health Agency of Canada (PHAC). Canada Communicable Disease Report. Infection prevention and control practices for personal services: Tattooing, ear/body piercing, and electrolysis. PHAC website. 1999. Available at: http://www.collectionscanada.gc.ca/webarchives/20071120043721/http://www.phac-aspc.gc.ca/publicat/ccdr-rmtc/99vol25/25s3/index.html.
4. Richards RN, Meharg GE. Electrolysis: Observations from 13 years and 140,000 hours of experience. *Am Acad Dermatol* 1995;33(4):662–666.
5. Ferguson H. Body piercing. *Br Med J* 1999;319:1627.
6. Long GE, Rickman LS. Infectious complications of tattoos. *Clin Infect Dis* 1994;18:610–619.
7. Pugatch D, Mileno M, Rich JD. Possible transmission of human immunodeficiency virus type 1 from body piercing. *Clin Infect Dis* 1998;26:767–768.
8. Gaughwin MD, Gowans E, Ali R, et al. Bloody needles: the volumes of blood transferred in simulations of needlestick injuries and shared use of syringes for injection of intravenous drugs. *AIDS* 1991;5:1025–1027.
9. Centers for Disease Control and Prevention. Methicillin-Resistant Staphylococcus aureus Skin Infections Among Tattoo Recipients—Ohio, Kentucky, and Vermont, 2004–2005. *Morb Mortal Wkly Rep* 2006;55(24):677–679.

10. U.S. Food and Drug Administration (FDA). Tattoos & Permanent Make Up, 2009. FDA website. 2012. Available at: http://www.fda.gov/Cosmetics/ProductandIngredientSafety/ProductInformation/ucm108530.htm.

11. Tope WD, Shellock FG. Magnetic resonance imaging and permanent cosmetics (tattoos): survey of complications and adverse events. *J Magn Reson Imaging* 2002;15:180–184.

12. MRIsafety.com. Tattoos, Permanent Cosmetics, and Eye Makeup. MRISafety.com website. 2012. Available at: http://www.mrisafety.com/safety_article.asp?subject=145.

13. Tweeten SSM, Rickman LS. Infectious complications of body piercing. *Clin Infect Dis* 1998;26:735–740.

14. Koenig LM, Carnes M. Body piercing—medical concerns with cutting-edge fashion. *J Gen Intern Med* 1999;14:379–385.

15. Bengualid V, Singh V, Singh H, et al. Mycobacterium fortuitum and anaerobic breast abscess following nipple piercing: Case presentation and review of the literature. *J Adolesc Health* 2008;42:530–532.

16. Ferringer T, Pride H, Tyler W. Body piercing complicated by atypical mycobacterial infections. *Pediatr Dermatol* 2008;25(2):219–222.

17. Armstrong ML, DeBoer S, Cetta F. Infective endocarditis after body art: A review of the literature and concerns. *J Adolesc Health* 2008;43:217–225.

18. Larzo MR, Poe MG. Adverse consequences of tattoos and body piercings. *Pediatr Ann* 2006;35(3):187–192.

19. Martinello RA, Cooney EL. Cerebellar brain abscess associated with tongue piercing. *Clin Infect Dis* 2006;36(2):e32–34.

20. Armstrong M. A clinical look at body piercing. *RN* 1998;61(9):26–29.

21. Dibart S, De Feo P, Surabian G, et al. Oral piercing and gingival recession: review of the literature and a case report. *Quintessence Int* 2002;33(2):110–112.

22. Khanna R, Kumar SS, Raju BS, et al. Body piercing in the accident and emergency department. *J Accid Emerg Med* 1999;16(6):418–421.

23. Hendricks WM. Complications of ear piercing: Treatment and prevention. *Cutis* 1991;48:386–394.

24. Anderson WR, Summerton DJ, Sharma DM, et al. The urologist's guide to genital piercing. *BJU Int* 2003;91:245–251.

25. Tweeten SS, Rickman LS. Infectious complications of body piercing. *Clin Infect Dis* 1998;26:737.

26. Meyer D. Body piercing: Old traditions creating new challenges. *J Emerg Nurs* 2000;26(6):613.

27. Hazinski MF, Cummins RO, Field JM. *2000 Handbook of Emergency Cardiovascular Care for Healthcare Providers*. Dallas, TX: American Heart Association, 2000.

28. Petrozzi JW. Verrucae planae spread by electrolysis. *Cutis* 1981;26:85.

29. Rich JD, Dickinson BP, Flaxman AB, et al. Local spread of moluscum contagiosum by electrolysis. *Clin Infect Dis* 1999;28:1171.

30. Armstrong M. Tattooing, body piercing, and permanent cosmetics: A historical and current view of state regulations, with continuing concerns. *J Environ Health* 2005;67(8):38–43.

31. The American Electrology Association (AEA). AEA website. Available at: http://www.electrology.com/.

32. Hellard M, Aitken C, Mackintosh A, et al. Investigation of infection control practices and knowledge of hepatitis C among body-piercing practitioners. *Am J Infect Control* 2003;31(4):215–220.

33. Oberdorfer A, Wiggers JH, Bowman J, et al. Monitoring and educational feedback to improve the compliance of tattooists and body piercers with infection control standards: a randomized control trial. *Am J Infect Control* 2004;32:147–154.

SUPPLEMENTAL RESOURCES

The following resources may be accessed electronically and provide an in-depth discussion of the issues associated with body piercing and tattooing. The Association of Professional Piercers site lists their current leadership under the "Contact Us" section, and you will find that the members listed there are tremendously helpful in answering any questions you may not find on the site.

The Association of Professional Piercers. Available at: http://www.safepiercing.org.

Special thanks to Elayne Angel, Bethra Szumski, and Steve Joyner from APP for their help in learning about the art of body piercing and to Joe Clark, Master Piercer and proprietor of Tattoos by Boney Joe, Zelienople, Pennsylvania, for providing technical expertise and the photographs used in this chapter.

Index

Page numbers in **boldface** type refer to tables or figures.

acute retroviral syndrome, 81:5
acyclovir, 26:6–7, 46:4–5, 80:9, 91:11, 91:13
ADA. *See* American Dental Association
adamantines, 40:5
adefovir, 97:7
adeno-associated virus (AAV), 88:2
adenosine triphosphate (ATP), 31:5, 107:16, 111:7
Adenoviridae, 79A:8
adenovirus, 46:5, 61:4, 79A:8, 91:4
adenylate cyclase (AC), 71:1
ADLs. *See* activities of daily living
admission, discharge, and transfer (ADT), 2:4, 6:3
Advisory Committee on Immunization Practices (ACIP), 4:8
    immunization and, 23:5, 51:8, 103:2, 103:5
    influenza and, 82:1, 82:4
    LTCFs and, 61:4
    Neisseria meningitidis and, 87:4
    occupational health and, 100:2
    PCV and, 74:4–5
    pertussis and, 42:12, 71:4, 71:5, 71:6
    Use of a Reduced (4-Dose) Vaccine Schedule for Postexposure
      Prophylaxis to Prevent Human Rabies of, 89:4
AEA. *See* American Electrology Association
Aeromonas, 79B:12–13
AERs. *See* automated endoscope reprocessors
AEWDs. *See* automated endoscope washer disinfectors
AFB. *See* acid-fast bacillus
affinity diagrams, 16:6
Affordable Care Act, 4:2
African sleeping sickness, 99:7
AGA. *See* American Gastroenterological Association
Agency for Health Care Policy and Research (AHCPR), 8:4
Agency for Healthcare Research and Quality (AHRQ), 4:2, 4:9, 7:6,
    9:5, 18:2, 18:3, 18:10
    best practices standard and, 8:4
    Hospital Survey on Patient Safety Culture by, 18:4
    Medical Office Survey on Patient Safety by, 18:4
    PSIs of, 18:2
Agency for Toxic Substances and Disease Registry (ATSDR), 4:3, 4:8
agglutination tests, 25:2
    HAI, 86:4
    IHA, 25:3
    latex agglutination, 94:4, 94:6
    particle agglutination, **25:3**
    RHA, 88:67
    TPHA, 25:1
    TP-PA, 91:16
Agrobacterium tumefaciens, 77:4
AHA. *See* American Hospital Association
AHC. *See* acute hemorrhagic conjunctivitis
AHCPR. *See* Agency for Health Care Policy and Research
AHRQ. *See* Agency for Healthcare Research and Quality
AHU. *See* air handling unit
AHXR. *See* acute humoral xenograft rejection
AIA. *See* American Institute of Architects
AIDS. *See* acquired immunodeficiency syndrome
AIIR. *See* airborne infection isolation room
air. *See also* heating, ventilation, and air conditioning; high-efficiency
      particulate air
    filtration of, 44:6–7
    quality of, in surgical services, 68:2–3
    standards, for HVAC, 114:12
airborne diseases, 10:7–8
    from *Aspergillus*, 78:7
    burns and, 38:3
    HVAC and, 114:1–3
airborne infection isolation room (AIIR), 29:3, 112:2–3, 114:14,
    116:2, 116:7–8
Airborne Precautions, 29:3–4
    at ambulatory care centers, 48:5, 48:9

for HSCT, 46:9–10
for influenza, 82:6
with neonates, 41:12
radiation oncology and, 58:2–3
for SOT, 45:7
in surgical services, 68:9
for VHF, 96:8
air changes per hour (ACH), 114:4, 114:8
air embolism, 18:3
air handling unit (AHU), 114:1, 116:14
air pressure testing, 114:8
alanine aminotransferase (ALT), 95:7, 97:6, 97:9, 97:11, 97:12
alarm fatigue, 18:7
albuterol, 110:3
alcohol-based hand rub (ABHR), 27:2, 107:10, 116:5
alemtuzumab, 23:8
alkaline phosphatase (ALP), 25:5
allergic bronchopulmonary aspergillosis, 78:8
allergic contact dermatitis (ACD), 53:8
ALP. *See* alkaline phosphatase
ALT. *See* alanine aminotransferase; antibiotic lock therapy
alternative medicine, 48:9
altitude sickness, 118:2
AMA. *See* American Medical Association
amantadine, 40:5
AMAP. *See* American Medical Accreditation Programs
AmB. *See* amphotericin B
ambulance, 54:10
ambulatory care centers, 48:1–12, 64:9
    Airborne Precautions and, 29:4
    Contact Precautions with, 29:3
    Droplet Precautions and, 29:3
    emergency planning at, 48:8–9
    hand hygiene and, 48:2
    laundry at, 48:7
    MDROs and, 48:5–6
    reprocessing at, 48:6
    safe injection practices at, 48:2–3
    specialties in, 48:9–12
    triage at, 48:4, **48:5**
ambulatory surgical centers (ASCs), 64:1–11
    cleaning of, 107:15–16
    CMS and, 4:9
    emergency planning for, 64:10
    safe injection practices in, 64:7–8
    SSIs and, 37:5–6
    Standard Precautions in, 64:4
    surveillance in, 64:3–4
    Transmission-based Precautions in, 64:4–5
American Academy of Family Physicians, 103:5
American Academy of Ophthalmology (AAO), 63:7
American Academy of Pediatrics (AAP), 41:3, 41:16, 109:8
American Association of Blood Banks (AABB), 108:1
American Association of Diabetes Educators (AADE), 64:8
American Association of Study of Liver Disease (AASLD), 97:10
American Association of Tissue Banks (AATB), 35:10
American College of Gastroenterology (ACG), 55:2
American College of Obstetricians and Gynecologists (ACOG), 41:16
American College of Physicians (ACP), 4:12, 4:13
American College of Surgeons (ACS), 4:12, 37:3
American Dental Association (ADA), 4:12, 8:14, 53:8, 81:10
American Dietetic Association, 109:8
American Electrology Association (AEA), 123:7–8
American Gastroenterological Association (AGA), 55:2
American Heart Association, 35:7, 74:13
American Hospital Association (AHA), 1:1, 4:2, 4:12, 4:20
American Institute of Architects (AIA), 4:20, 27:2, 50:4, 68:1,
    114:3
American Journal of Infection Control, 4:8
American Lyme Disease Foundation, 85:7

American Medical Accreditation Programs (AMAP), 4:13
American Medical Association (AMA), 8:4, 8:13, 8:15
American Osteopathic Association (AOA), 4:12, 114:4
American Public Health Association (APHA), 51:2, 53:15
American Recovery and Reinvestment Act, 117:2
American Red Cross, 68:7
American Society for Blood and Marrow Transplantation (ASBMT), 46:6
American Society for Gastrointestinal Endoscopy (ASGE), 55:2
American Society for Healthcare Engineering (ASHE), 114:3, 116:3, 116:6
American Society for Microbiology (ASM), 108:1, 108:5
American Society of Anesthesiologists (ASA), 42:6, 42:7, 68:1
American Society of Clinical Oncology (ASCO), 23:6
American Society of Colon and Rectal Surgeons (SAGES), 55:2
American Society of Healthcare Engineering, 4:20
American Society of Health-System Pharmacists (ASHP), 4:14, 110:5, 110:7
American Society of Heating, Refrigerating and Air-Conditioning (ASHRAE), 68:3, 114:12
American Society of Transplantation (AST), 45:3
American Standard Code for Information Interchange (ASCII), 6:11
   comma delimited text files, 6:3
American Standards Institute (ANSI), 6:11, 68:1, 68:6, 111:4, 115:6
American Thoracic Society (ATS), 23:8, 95:6
American Water Works Association (AWWA), 53:15
amikacin, 26:5, 75:2
aminoglycosides, 26:2, 26:5, 41:6, 41:13, 76:3, 91:22, 93:12
Amnesty International, 51:13
amniocentesis, 43:2
amoxicillin, 76:3
amoxicillin-clavulanate, 78:8
amphotericin B (AmB), 26:7, 34:18, 38:7, 78:5–6, 78:8
ampicillin, 38:7, 41:6, 41:13, 76:3, 79B:4, 79B:6
anal warts, 91:1, 91:7–10
analytic studies, 12:5, 20:1, **20:2**
Anaplasma phagocytophilum, 85:9
ANC. *See* absolute neutrophil count
Ancylostoma duodenale, 99:7
anesthesia
   for animals, 121:3
   in endoscopy, 55:5
   in perinatal care, 43:13
   in surgical services, 68:6
angiography, 60:5
Angiostrongylus cantonensis, 99:7
animal-assisted activity/animal-assisted therapy (AAA/AAT), 122:2–4
animal-assisted interventions (AAI), 42:11, 122:1–2
animals, 122:1–8. *See also* pets; viral hemorrhagic fever; zoonoses
   bacteria and, 121:10–13
   in CCCs, 52:3
   disaster management and, 120:18
   fungi and, 121:13
   hantavirus and, 121:8
   immunocompromised patients and, 44:6
   LCMV and, 121:8–9
   occupational exposure by, 121:3
   orf disease and, 121:9
   parasites and, 121:13
   protozoa from, 99:7, 121:13
   rabies and, 89:1–6
   research and diagnostics on, 121:1–14
   skin and, 92:5
   TB and, 121:3, 121:12–13
   travel health and, 118:3
   waste management and, 113:3
Animal Welfare Act, 121:3
ANSI. *See* American Standards Institute
antacid therapy, immunocompromised host and, 23:8

ante area, 110:10
anthrax, 4:3, 6:4, 72:2, **103:6**, **104:2**, 119:10
antibacterials, 26:3–6, **26:4**, **70:6**
antibiogram, 26:9, **26:10**
antibiotic lock therapy (ALT), 34:16–17, **34:17**, 92:7
antibiotic prophylaxis
   for group B *Streptococcus*, 94:6
   for hysterectomies, 91:25
   for Lyme disease, 85:9
   for *Streptococcus viridans*, 94:9
antibiotic resistance, **24:12**, 24:13–14, 33:12, 93:2–5, 94:8–9
   CDC on, 110:11
   of CoNS, 93:15
   in correctional facilities, 51:10–11
   in ophthalmology services, 63:12
   pediatrics and, 42:14–15
   Streptococcus pneumoniae and, 94:7
antibiotics, 35:2–3, 68:10. *See also specific antibiotics*
   Candida and, 78:5
   cardiac catheterization and, 50:6
   in cath lab, 50:7
   CIED and, 35:8
   for CoNS, 93:17–18
   for *Enterobacteriaceae*, 75:16
   for *Enterococcus*, 41:6
   HSCT and, 46:10
   in immunization, 103:5
   legal issues with, 8:9–10
   for *Legionella pneumophila*, 84:5
   in LTACHs, 62:4
   for LVADs, 35:9
   for Lyme disease, 85:5
   for meningitis, 74:3–4
   for meningococcal meningitis, 74:6
   for MRSA, 93:12
   for *Neisseria meningitidis*, 87:5
   neonates and, 41:13
   pediatrics and, 42:2
   PJI and, 35:6
   psychiatric patients and, 49:6
   for rotavirus, 79A:5
   for *Salmonella*, 79B:6
   for spinal implants, 35:11
   for SSIs, 37:8, 37:11–12
   for UTIs, 33:12
antibodies
   detection of
      with laboratory testing, **25:3**, 25:3–4
      for PVB19, 88:5
   Lyme disease and, 85:2
   pertussis and, 71:3
   xenotransplantation and, 69:4
antibody molecules, 22:4, **22:4**
anticapsular antibody, 94:7
anticoagulants, 34:13
antifungals, 23:8, **26:4**, 26:7, 34:18
antigen detection, 25:2–3, **25:3**
antimetabolites, **45:4**
antimicrobial lock solutions, 34:15
antimicrobial resistance, 26:10–12. *See also* antibiotic resistance
   Candida and, 78:5–6
   Enterobacteriaceae and, 75:15–16
   Enterococcus and, 76:3–4, **76:4**
   geriatrics and, 40:4–5
   infection transmission and, 26:11–12
   mechanisms of, 26:11, **26:11**
   PJI and, 35:5
   Streptococcus pneumoniae and, 94:7
Antimicrobial Resistance Prevention and Control study (ARPAC), 9:6–7

antimicrobials. *See also specific types*
    administration of, 26:1
    biofilm and, 35:2–3
    for burns, 38:6
    cellular sites of action by, **26:2**
    CIED and, 35:8
    classification of, 26:3–7
    in CVC, 34:14
    IMD and, 35:12
    indications for, 26:7–8
    for IVDA BSIs, 34:12, 34:17–18
    in LTCFs, 61:6
    for LVADs, 35:9–10
    management team, 26:12–13
    mechanisms of action of, 26:2
    optimal dosing for, **26:3**
    outcomes with, 26:8–9
    pharmacy services and, 110:10
    for PJI, 35:5
    prophylaxis with, 26:8
    for PVE, 35:7
    for spinal implants, 35:11
    for SSIs, 37:11–12
    stewardship with, 26:12–13
    surveillance for, 26:12
    vertebroplasty and, 60:10
antimicrobial soap, 27:2
antimicrobial susceptibility testing (AST), 24:8, 24:11–14, 26:10–11
antiparasitics, 26:7
antiretroviral therapy (ART), 26:7, 78:6, 81:5, 81:7–8
    HAART, 81:7, 97:11
antiseptic hand wash, 27:2
antiseptics, 34:12, 34:14, 41:2, 41:17, 107:4
antistaphylococcal penicillins, 93:3
antivirals, **26:4**, 26:6–7, 40:5–6, 80:7–8, 96:7, 97:12
    DAAs, 97:10
AOA. *See* American Osteopathic Association
AORN. *See* Association of Perioperative Registered Nurses
AOS. *See* acridine orange staining
APACHE. *See* acute physiology and chronic health evaluation
APHA. *See* American Public Health Association
APIC. *See* Association for Professionals in Infection Control and
    Epidemiology
APP. *See* Association of Professional Piercers
arbovirus, 74:1, 74:9, 98:1
ARDS. *See* acute respiratory distress syndrome
area map, 10:11
Arenaviridae, 96:2, 96:3, 96:6
Argentine hemorrhagic fever, 96:7
arginine catabolic mobile element (ACME), 93:9
ARPAC. *See* Antimicrobial Resistance Prevention and Control study
ART. *See* antiretroviral therapy
arterial blood gas (ABG), 25:5
arthritis
    from Lyme disease, 85:5
    PVB19 and, 88:3–4
    pyogenic, 94:4
arthropods, 98:1
artificial airways, 67:4
ASA. *See* American Society of Anesthesiologists
ASBMT. *See* American Society for Blood and Marrow Transplanta-
    tion
Ascaris lumbricoides, 99:7
ASCII. *See* American Standard Code for Information Interchange
ASCO. *See* American Society of Clinical Oncology
ascorbic acid. *See* vitamin C
ASCs. *See* ambulatory surgical centers
aseptic meningitis, 74:7, **74:7**
aseptic technique, 30:1–5, **30:2**
    in ambulatory care centers, 48:5

    in dental services, 53:3–5, 53:16–18
    in pharmacy services, 110:10
    in surgical services, 68:8
ASGE. *See* American Society for Gastrointestinal Endoscopy
ASHE. *See* American Society for Healthcare Engineering
ASHP. *See* American Society of Health-System Pharmacists
ASHRAE. *See* American Society of Heating, Refrigerating and
    Air-Conditioning
ASM. *See* American Society for Microbiology
aspartate aminotransferase (AST), 95:7, 96:4, 97:6
aspergillomas, 78:8
Aspergillus, 78:6–10, 119:5
    antifungals for, 26:7
    HSCT and, 46:4
    HVAC and, 114:2
    immunocompromised host and, 23:4
    from methylprednisolone, 110:7
    pediatrics and, 42:3
    SOT and, 45:4, 45:5
Aspergillus fumigatus, 44:6, 78:7
Aspergillus terreus, 78:7
aspiration pneumonia, 36:4–5, 40:2, 47:12
Association for Assessment and Accreditation of Laboratory Animal
    Care International (AAALAC), 121:4–5
Association for Professionals in Infection Control and Epidemiology
    (APIC), 18:17, 115:2
    advocacy rule of, 4:11
    behavioral health and, 49:3
    competency model of, 2:2–5, **2:3**
    construction and renovation and, 115:1
    Emergency Preparedness Committee of, 4:14
    endoscopy and, 55:2
    Guide for Adult Immunization by, 103:30
    Guide for Clostridium difficile in Healthcare Settings by, 21:8
    IG by, 4:2
    IMD and, 35:3
    IT and, 11:10
    laundry and, 111:7
    legal issues and, 8:1
    LTC and, 61:1
    MRSA Elimination Guide by, 21:8
    performance measures and, 17:2, 17:4
    publishing guidelines by, 4:14
    SEA and, 18:11
    *State of the Art Report: Use of Scrubs and Related Apparel in
        Health Care Facilities* by, 68:4
    surgical services and, 68:1
    surveillance and, 57:4
Association for the Advancement of Medical Instrumentation (AAMI),
    31:5, 39:1, 39:5, 39:7, 39:10, 68:6, 106:1, 106:9
Association of Perioperative Registered Nurses (AORN), 7:6, 55:2,
    68:1, 68:6, 106:1, 107:12, 111:4
    ASCs and, 64:9
    HCIR and, 102:4
    IUSS and, 106:14–15
    PEC and, 7:6
Association of Professional Piercers (APP), 123:1–2
assumption-of-risk defense, 8:3
AST. *See* active surveillance testing; American Society of Trans-
    plantation; antimicrobial susceptibility testing; aspartate
    aminotransferase
astrovirus, 79A:7–8
asymptomatic HIV infection, 81:5
ATP. *See* adenosine triphosphate
atracurium besylate, 110:3
ATS. *See* American Thoracic Society
ATSDR. *See* Agency for Toxic Substances and Disease Registry
automated endoscope reprocessors (AERs), 55:1, 106:8, 115:7
automated endoscope washer disinfectors (AEWDs), 55:1, 55:3–4
automated surveillance programs, 11:10

BL-4. *See* Biosafety Level 4
bladder cancer, 113:7
bladder management, 66:9–11
Blastocystis hominis, 79C:3–4, 99:7
Blastoschizomyces capitatus, 78:12
bleach, 111:6
blepharitis, 63:3
blood
  cultures
    for IVDA BSIs, 34:6
    for PVE, 35:6
  disinfectants for, 107:4–5
  minimizing exposure to, 105:1–7
  PPE and, 106:1
  safety of, by FDA, 4:8
  transfusions, 41:19, 88:6, 97:11, 97:12
  waste management and, 113:3
blood assay for *M. tuberculosis* (BAMT), 95:10, 102:2
bloodborne pathogens (BBP)
  electrolysis and, 123:7
  HBV as, 101:2–4, **101:3**
  HCP and, 101:1–2
  HCV as, 101:4–5
  HIV as, 101:5–8
  occupational exposure to, 101:1–9
Bloodborne Pathogen Standard, of OSHA, 7:6, 8:11, 28:1, 28:2,
    29:2, 39:15, 52:4, 64:10, 105:1–2, 123:7
  occupational health and, 100:7
  RSPA and, 4:11
blood-drawing procedures, 105:3–4
blood glucose monitoring, 64:8, 68:10
bloodstream infections (BSIs), **34:5**, 52:3. *See also* central line-asso-
    ciated bloodstream infections; intravenous device-associated
    BSIs
  with burns, 38:8–9
  Candida, 78:2
  CIED and, 35:8
  CTS and, 42:6
  with dialysis, 39:14–15
  Enterobacteriaceae, 75:8
  Enterococcus and, 76:6–7
  ICU and, 59:2
  IVDA and, 34:1–18, **34:2**
  LVADs and, 35:9
  with neonates, 41:12–14
  neonates and, 41:5
  patient safety and, 18:11
  pediatrics and, 42:3, 42:8–9
  pharmacy services and, 110:2, 110:4
Bloom's taxonomy, 3:3–4, **3:4**
BMT. *See* bone marrow transplant
boceprevir, 97:10
body fluids, 25:4, 51:4, 105:1–7, 106:1, 107:4–5
body piercing, 123:1–9, **123:6**, **123:7**
  occupational exposure from, 123:9
bone marrow transplant (BMT), 46:5, 78:2, 94:8
borderline-resistant *Staphylococcus aureus* (BORSA), 93:3
Bordetella pertussis. *See* pertussis
boric acid, 78:6
Borrelia burgdorferi. *See* Lyme disease
borreliacidal antibody assay, 85:6
BORSA. *See* borderline-resistant *Staphylococcus aureus*
botulinum toxin, 22:3
bovine spongiform encephalopathy (BSE), 68:7, 73:1, 73:3–4, 74:2,
    74:11–12
bowel management, 66:11–12
brachytherapy, 58:5
brain abscess, 74:2, 74:10, **74:10**
breast abscess, 43:17–18
breastfeeding/milk, 41:17–18, 43:14–16, 103:5, 104:7–8

Brief Symptom Inventory, 19:7
British Dental Society for Disability and Oral Health, 70:9
bronchoscopy, 55:5, 67:3, 114:13
Brucella, 22:7
Brugia, 99:7
BSC. *See* biological safety cabinet
BSE. *See* bovine spongiform encephalopathy
BSIs. *See* bloodstream infections
bubonic plague, 75:12–13
Bunyaviridae, 96:2, 96:3, 96:5–6
bupivacaine HCl, 110:3
Bureau of Justice Statistics, 51:2
Burgdorfer, Willy, 85:1
Burkholderia cepacia, 77:3, 110:5
Burkitt lymphoma, 80:8
burns, 38:1–11
  BSIs with, 38:8–9
  CAUTIs and, 38:9
  endocarditis and, 38:7–8
  immunocompromised hosts and, 23:3–4, **23:4**
  intravascular catheters and, 38:7–8
  laboratory testing for, 38:6
  pediatrics and, 42:7–8
  pneumonia and, 38:9
  reservoir for, 38:2
  surveillance for, 38:3–5
  TBSA and, 38:2, 38:3
  thrombophlebitis and, 38:7–8
  treatment for, 38:7
  UTIs and, 38:9
  wound infection with, 38:5–7
busulfan, 110:4
butoconazole, 91:19
BV. *See* bacterial vaginosis
B virus, 121:7–8

CABG. *See* coronary artery bypass graft
calcineurin inhibitors, **45:4**
Caliciviridae, 79A:1
calicivirus, 79A:1–4
calories, 47:4
Campylobacter, 79B:10–11, 83:1, 109:2, 121:10–11
Campylobacter fetus, 41:14
Campylobacter jejuni, 41:14
CaMRSA. *See* community-acquired MRSA
CA-MRSA. *See* community-associated MRSA
Canadian Medical Association (CMA), 4:12
canaliculitis, 63:3
Candida, 77:1, 78:2–6
  antimicrobial resistance and, 78:5–6
  CVC and, 60:5
  extrinsic contamination of, 110:3
  fluconazole and, 34:18
  HSCT and, 46:4
  ICU and, 59:6
  immunocompromised host and, 23:8
  IVDA BSIs and, 34:16
  neonates and, 41:5, 41:9, 41:13, 41:16
  perinatal care and, 43:5
  for PVE, 35:7
  SOT and, 45:4
Candida albicans, 70:5, 91:19–20, 92:5, 110:3
Candida glabrata, 78:4
Candida parapsilosis, 78:3–4, 110:3
CAP. *See* College of American Pathologists; community-acquired
    pneumonia
CAPD. *See* continuous ambulatory peritoneal dialysis
Capillaria philippinensis, 99:7
capillariasis, 99:7
Capnocytophaga, 121:11

Capnocytophaga canimorsus, 44:6
CAPTIA syphilis-G, 25:1
carbapenemase, 75:1, **75:13**
carbapenem-resistant *Enterobacteriaceae* (CRE), 26:12, 59:6, 75:15–16, 107:6, 115:6
carbuncles, 92:4
cardiac catheterization, 50:1–9, **50:4**
  HVAC and, 114:13
  in pediatrics, 50:2
  vascular procedures and, 50:2–3
cardiopulmonary resuscitation (CPR), 48:4, 54:12
cardiothoracic surgery (CTS), 42:3, 42:6
cardiovascular implantable electronic device (CIED), 35:7–9, 50:2, 50:6
CARF. See Commission on Accreditation of Rehabilitation Facilities
cart and utensil washers/disinfectors, 106:7
case-control studies, 10:9, 12:9, **12:9**, **20:2**, 20:2–3
case studies, 3:10, 12:7–10
caspofungin, 34:18, 38:7
catheter-associated bacteriuria, 33:2, 39:12–14
catheter-associated urinary tract infections (CAUTIs), 6:2, 11:5, 13:11, **13:12**, 17:4, 17:5, 33:7–11, 59:2, 59:4, 66:2, 75:7
  burns and, 38:9
  CDA for, 6:3
  DA and, 15:2
  Deficit Reduction Act and, 9:2
  as HAC, 18:3
  IP workflow for, 6:9
  legal issues and, 8:1
  LTACHs and, 62:3
  in LTC, 33:9
  pediatrics and, 42:8–9
  risk-adjusted comparisons and, 15:1
  SPC for, 14:2
catheter hubs, 34:15
catheter-related infections (CRIs), 60:4–5
catheters, 50:3, 50:8, 95:17, 105:4–5. See also specific types
  biofilm and, 70:12
  for dialysis, 39:2
  HSCT and, 46:2
cath lab, 50:3–4, **50:4**, 50:6–8
cath lab suites, 50:4
cat scratch fever, 121:9–10
causal associations, 10:3
causation, 10:6
cause of action, 8:2
CAUTIs. See catheter-associated urinary tract infections
CBC. See complete blood count
CBIC. See Certification Board of Infection and Epidemiology
CBSPD. See Certification Board for Sterile Processing and Distribution
CBT. See computer-based test
CCCs. See child care centers
CCHF. See Congo-Crimean hemorrhagic fever
CCPs. See critical control points
CCR5, 81:8
CCRT. See concurrent chemoradiation
CD. See concentration-dependent
CDA. See clinical document architecture
CDAD. See Clostridium difficile-associated diarrhea
CDC. See Centers for Disease Control and Prevention
CDI. See Clostridium difficile infection
cefazolin, 35:8, 60:10
cefdinir, 26:4
cefditoren, 26:4
cefepime, 26:4–5
cefixime, 79B:8, 91:6
cefotaxime, 26:4, 87:3–4
ceftaroline, 26:5

ceftriaxone, 26:4, 35:7, 79B:8, 87:3–4, 87:5, 91:6
CEHRT. See certified electronic health record technology
cell cytotoxicity assay, 72:3
cell-mediated immune system (CMI), 22:3–4, 40:5, 78:5
cell membrane inhibitors, 26:2, **26:2**
cells, in tables, graphs, and charts, 10:10
cellulitis, 63:3, 92:4, 92:5
  with burns, 38:6
  GAS and, 94:2, 94:3
  SSTIs and, 92:2
Center for International Blood and Marrow Transplant Research (CIBMTR), 46:6
Centers for Disease Control and Prevention (CDC), 4:3–4:8. See also Advisory Committee on Immunization Practices; Healthcare Infection Control Practices Advisory Committee; National Healthcare Safety Network; National Nosocomial Infections Surveillance
  AIDS and, 81:2
  AIIR and, 116:8
  ambulatory care centers and, 9:5
  on antibiotic resistance, 110:11
  antiparasitics and, 26:7
  APIC competency model and, 2:5
  ASCs and, 64:2, 64:11
  ATSDR of, 4:8
  behavioral health and, 49:3, 49:7
  biofilm and, 70:6
  Biosafety in Microbiological and Biomedical Laboratories by, 121:5
  BioSense and, 120:7
  bioterrorism and, 120:10, **120:10**
  BioWatch and, 120:5–6
  BSIs and, **34:5**
  C. difficile and, 47:9
  CAP and, 36:2
  CDI and, 72:4
  CJD and, 73:4
  Classification of Etiologic Agents on the Basis of Hazard by, 24:16
  conjunctivitis and, 63:5
  construction and renovation and, 115:1, 116:3, 116:6
  contact time and, 31:10–11
  correctional facilities and, 51:3–4
  CRE and, 59:6
  CSPs and, 110:7
  customer satisfaction and, 16:8
  CVC and, 60:5
  demonstration carts and, 3:11
  dental services and, 53:1, 53:8
  DHCP and, 53:6
  DHQP of, 4:3, 4:7–4:8
  dialysis and, 39:14
  Division of Tuberculosis Elimination of, 4:3
  emerging infectious diseases and, 11:12
  employee surveillance and, 8:10
  EMS and, 54:1, 54:9
  endoscopy and, 55:2–3
  Enterobacteriaceae and, 75:2
  Enterococcus and, 76:2, 76:8
  environmental monitoring and, 110:9–10
  FNS and, 109:2
  food and, 23:9
  foodborne illness and, 83:1
  GAS and, 94:4
  gene therapy, 113:7
  group B *Streptococcus* and, 94:4
  Guideline for Disinfection and Sterilization in Healthcare Facilities by, 7:6, 48:6, 66:6, 68:6
  Guideline for Environmental Infection Control in Healthcare Facilities by, 7:6

Centers for Disease Control and Prevention (CDC) *(cont.)*
   Guideline for Hand Hygiene in Healthcare Settings by, 68:8
   Guideline for Isolation Precautions: Preventing Transmission of Infectious Agents in Healthcare Settings by, 28:2, 29:1, 44:7, 64:5, 116:6
   Guideline for Prevention of Intravascular Catheter-Related Infections by, 41:13
   Guideline for Prevention of Surgical Site Infections by, 7:6
   Guideline for the Prevention of Intravascular Catheter0related Infections by, 50:7
   Guidelines for Control of CRE in Acute Care and Long-term Care Facilities by, 75:15
   Guidelines for Environmental Infection Control in Healthcare Facilities—2003 by, 110:9, 113:1, 116:2
   Guidelines for Preventing Opportunistic Infections Among Hematopoietic Stem Cell Transplant Recipients by, 44:7, 44:8
   HAIs and, 1:2–3
   hand hygiene and, 23:7, 27:1, 27:2, 27:4
   HAP and, 67:2
   HCP and, 103:1
     immunization for, 103:30
   HCV and, 97:8
   HHC and, 56:2
   HIPAA and, 6:2
   HIV and, 8:11, 81:2, 81:9
   HPS and, 96:1
   HSCT and, 46:6
   HVAC and, 114:2, 114:3
   IMD and, 35:3
   immunocompromised patients and, 44:3, 44:7
   influenza and, 40:3, 82:1
     immunization for, 40:5
   interventional radiology and, 60:2
   Isolation Precautions and, 23:7, 29:2, 29:6
   IT and, 11:10
   IVDA BSIs and, 34:2, **34:9–11**
   IV fluids and, 110:9
   laundry and, 111:1, 111:4
   legal issues and, 8:1
   Legionella pneumophila and, 84:1
   liability and, 8:3
   Lyme disease and, 85:1, 85:7
   Mantoux test and, 95:6
   MDVs and, 110:9
   measles and, 86:2
   MRSA and, 93:10
   National Center for Immunization and Respiratory Diseases of, 4:8
   National STD/HIV Hotline of, 91:9, 91:12
   Neisseria gonorrhoeae and, 91:6
   Neisseria meningitidis and, 87:2, 87:4
   neonates and, 41:2, 41:24
   occupational health and, 100:2
   parasites and, 99:6
   patient safety and, 18:2, 18:10
   PCV and, 74:4–5
   PEC and, 7:6
   pediatrics and, 42:2
   performance measures and, 17:4
   perinatal care and, 43:3
   pertussis and, 71:1, 71:3–4, **71:4**
   pharmacy services and, 110:2
   PPS and, 4:2
   pregnant HCP and, 104:1
   process measures of, 17:5
   public health and, 117:2, 117:3
   PVB19 and, 88:6
   rabies and, 89:4
   radiation oncology and, 58:3
   rehabilitation services and, 66:2, 66:6–7

   risk-adjusted comparisons and, 15:1
   rotavirus and, 79A:5–6
   RSV and, 90:
   rubella and, 86:14
   SDVs and, 110:8
   SENIC by, 9:3
   SNS of, 120:11
   SOT and, 2:5
   SP and, 106:1
   SSIs and, 37:3, 37:8, 92:4
   SSTIs and, 92:7
   STIs and, 91:3
   surgical services and, 68:1
   surveillance and, 11:1
   suture needles and, 105:5
   TB and, **95:9**, 95:9–10
   tissue allografts and, 35:10
   VAE and, 42:9
   VAP and, 67:4
   VHF and, 96:6, 96:8
   VISA and, 93:7
   VVC and, 91:19
   waste management and, 113:1, 113:2
   water and, 115:1
   WNV and, 98:3
Centers for Medicare & Medicaid Services (CMS), 1:3, 4:9–10
   ASCs and, 64:1, 64:2, 64:11
   biofilm and, 70:6
   CAP and, 36:3
   CLIA and, 4:10
   Clostridium difficile and, 4:2
   construction and renovation and, 115:1
   construction codes by, 4:9–10
   CoP for the Physical Plant by, 4:20
   customer satisfaction and, 16:8
   deemed status by, 4:10
   dialysis and, 39:2, 39:3
   emerging infectious diseases and, 11:12
   FNS and, 109:4
   HAC and, 18:3
   HAIs and, 4:2, 6:2, 6:4
   HHC and, 56:1–2
   Hospital Inpatient Reporting Program of, 59:1
   HVAC and, 114:4
   ICU and, 59:1
   Infection Control Surveyor Worksheet by, 64:2
   IPPS and, 8:16
   laundry and, 111:6
   LTCFs and, 61:2
   Medicare Quality Improvement Organizations of, 4:10
   MRSA and, 4:2
   Nursing Home Compare by, 17:10
   OASIS by, 56:5
   patient safety and, 18:10
   performance measures and, 17:1, 17:3
   PPS and, 4:2
   practice parameters and, 8:4
   professional testing program and, 25:1–2
   public health and, 117:2
   rehabilitation services and, 66:2
   SoW by, 68:11
   SSIs and, 37:7, 37:8
   state exemptions by, 4:10
   surgical services and, 68:1
central line-associated bloodstream infections (CLABSI), 4:2, 6:2, 6:9, 17:4, 17:5
   burns and, 38:8
   CDA for, 6:3
   dialysis and, 39:5
   Enterobacteriaceae and, 75:7

cleaning *(cont.)*
  improvements for, 31:9
  local reprocessing areas and, 31:6
  in MAE, 112:3
  neonates and, 41:22–23
  patient safety and, 8:7
  pediatrics and, 42:9–10
  in perinatal care, 43:3
  in radiation oncology, 58:4
  SOT and, 45:7
  in SP, 106:6–8
  TASS and, 31:6
clean room, 107:15
clean technique, 30:2
CL-EIA. *See* chemiluminescent immunoassay
CLIA. *See* Clinical Laboratory Improvement Act
clindamycin, 24:12–13, **24:13**, 26:5, 91:21, 92:7, 94:3
  for *Bacillus cereus*, 79B:15
  for MRSA, 93:13
  Staphylococcus aureus and, 93:5, **93:5**
clinical document architecture (CDA), 6:3
clinical information system (CIS), 6:7
Clinical Laboratory Improvement Act (CLIA), 4:10, 24:11–12, 25:1,
    91:4, 91:6
Clinical Laboratory Standards Institute (CLSI), 26:9, 26:10, 26:11,
    93:6, 108:1
Clinical Practice Guidelines for Antimicrobial Prophylaxis in
    Surgery, 4:14
CLIP. *See* central line insertion practices
Clonorchis sinensis, 99:8
closed-space infections, 76:7–8
Clostridium, 24:1, 24:2
Clostridium botulinum, 22:3
Clostridium difficile, 4:2, 22:2, 23:8, 31:11, 44:4, 47:910, 50:6,
    52:2, 59:2
  antifungals for, 26:8
  geriatrics and, 40:2
  HSCT and, 46:5–6
  in LTACHs, 62:4
  neonates and, 41:7
  pediatrics and, 42:2, 42:14
Clostridium difficile-associated diarrhea (CDAD), 61:6
Clostridium difficile infection (CDI), 4:3, 9:2, 15:1, 15:3–4, 17:4,
    18:11, 21:4, 72:2–5, 107:5, 110:15:3
  Contact Precautions with, 29:2
  geriatrics and, 40:2
  HO, 15:3, **15:4**
  ICU and, 59:6
  legal issues and, 8:1
  NAAT for, 15:3
  nutrition and, 47:9
  PMC and, 72:1–6
  rehabilitation services and, 66:8
Clostridium perfringens, 22:2, 83:1, 91:7, 109:2
Clostridium sordellii, 35:10
Clostridium tetani, 22:3, 25:6
CLSI. *See* Clinical Laboratory Standards Institute
CMA. *See* Canadian Medical Association
CMI. *See* cell-mediated immune system
CMS. *See* Centers for Medicare & Medicaid Services
CMV. *See* cytomegalovirus
CMV-IP. *See* cytomegalovirus-interstitial pneumonia
CNS. *See* central nervous system
coagulase-negative *Staphylococcus* (CoNS), 93:2, **93:2**, 93:15–18
  neonates and, 41:2, 41:5, 41:6, 41:13, 41:14
  SSTIs and, 92:2
  virulence of, 93:8
Coccidioides immitis, 22:5, 24:4
Code of Federal Regulations (CFR), 32:1–2
coefficient of variation (CV), 13:5

cognitive learning, 3:3
cohorting, 21:5–6, 41:2, 41:21
cohort studies, 10:9, **10:9**, **20:2**, 20:3
cold agglutinins, 25:5
colistin, 75:2
colitis, 58:5
collagen, 92:1
College of American Pathologists (CAP), 4:13, 108:1
colony-forming units (CFUs), 110:4, 110:9
colony-stimulating factors (CSFs), 23:6
colostrum, 47:10
colposcopy, 91:25
Commission on Accreditation of Rehabilitation Facilities (CARF),
    4:13, 66:2
Commission on Office Laboratory Accreditation, 4:13
common cause, 14:2, 16:5–6
common source, 12:6–7, **12:7**
common vehicle, 41:2
community-acquired MRSA (CA-MRSA), 92:2–3, **93:3**, 93:4,
    93:18
  ACME and, 93:9
  necrotizing fasciitis and, 92:5
  tattoos and, 123:3
community-acquired pneumonia (CAP), 36:1, 36:2, 36:3. *See also*
    Streptococcus pneumoniae
  Legionella pneumophila and, 84:2
community-associated MRSA (CaMRSA), 37:2, 37:11, 41:5–6,
    51:2–3
Community Strategy for Pandemic Influenza Migration (HHS),
    120:14
Compendium of Animal Rabies Prevention and Control, 89:3
A Compendium of Strategies to Prevent Healthcare-Associated
    Infections in Acute Care Hospitals, 4:14, 17:4, 68:11
complement system, 22:6, **22:7**
complete blood count (CBC), 25:5–6, 86:14
compounded sterile preparations (CSPs), 110:4, 110:7–10, **110:8**
Compounding Quality Act, 24:16
computational fluid dynamics (CFD), 114:9
computed tomography (CT), 58:2, 74:3, 74:11, 78:8
computer-based test (CBT), 2:6
computer-based training, 3:10
computerized physician order entry (CPOE), 6:6
computers. *See* information technology
concentration-dependent (CD), 70:12
concurrent chemoradiation (CCRT), 59:4
Conditions of Participation (CoP), 1:3, 111:3–4
condyloma acuminatum, 91:7–10
condyloma latum, 91:7
confidence intervals (CI), 13:16, **13:16**, 15:4–5, **15:5**
confidentiality, 8:14–15
confocal microscopy, 24:9
congenital disorders, 42:3, **42:5**
congenital heart disease (CHD), 90:1
congenital infection, 43:2
congenital rubella syndrome, 86:14, 86:15
congestive heart failure (CHF), 22:6
Congo-Crimean hemorrhagic fever (CCHF), 96:2, 96:5, 96:7
conjunctivitis, 41:16, 63:3, **63:4**, 63:4–5
  LTCFs and, 61:6
  Lyme disease and, 85:4
  in neonates, 41:17
CoNS. *See* coagulase-negative *Staphylococcus*
Consolidated Standards of Reporting Trials (CONSORT), 20:3
CONSORT. *See* Consolidated Standards of Reporting Trials
construction and renovation policy (CRP), 116:4
construction/renovation, 116:1–16
  AIIR and, 116:2, 116:7–8
  at ambulatory care centers, 48:8
  CMS codes for, 4:9–10
  codes, standards, and regulations for, 116:6

codes for, by HHS, 4:20
contamination and, 116:7
contractor expectations in, 116:11–12
demolition in, 116:12
design for, 116:2
excavation precautions in, 116:12
exterior, 116:13–15
flooding and, 116:14–15
hand washing and, 116:11
HEPA and, 116:8
interior, 116:12–13
personnel issues in, 116:11–12
PPE and, 116:5, 116:8–9
pre-occupancy review for, 116:15, **116:15**
traffic control and, 116:7
VAP and, 116:2
water and, 116:14–15
Consumer Price Inflator, 9:1
Contact Precautions, 29:2–3
  for adenovirus, 79A:8
  at ambulatory care centers, 48:5
  for *Enterococcus*, 76:8
  for genital herpes, 91:13
  for HAV, 97:3
  for MRSA, 93:14
  for neonates, 41:10
  in pediatrics, 42:14
  in radiation oncology, 58:3
  in rehabilitation services, 66:2, 66:11
  for rubella, 86:17
  for scabies, 91:15–16
  for TB, 51:7
contamination, 109:8
  construction and renovation and, 116:7
  definition of, 41:2
  of HVAC, 114:1–3, **114:3**
  laundry and, 111:2
  in pharmacy services, 110:3–11
continuous ambulatory peritoneal dialysis (CAPD), 39:13
continuous cycling peritoneal dialysis, 39:13
continuous data, 10:10, 13:17
continuous insulin infusion (CII), 68:10
continuous renal replacement therapy, 39:2
contributory negligence, 8:3
control measures, 12:4, 12:10
cooling towers, 115:5, 115:13
CoP. *See* Conditions of Participation
COPD. *See* chronic obstructive pulmonary disease
CoP for the Physical Plant (CMS), 4:20
copper, 39:8
Core Performance Measures and Associated Evaluation Criteria (TJC), 17:7, **17:8**
corneal transplant, 63:6, 69:5
coronary artery bypass graft (CABG), 17:4, 17:6, 18:4
coronaviruses, 79A:8
correctional facilities, 49:2, 51:1–13
  admissions to, 51:11–12
  EMS and, 54:15
  immunizations in, 51:8
  meningitis in, 51:10
  MRSA in, 51:10–11
  norovirus in, 51:9
  STIs in, 51:7–8
  surveillance in, 51:6, 51:12
  TB in, 51:5–7
  VZV in, 51:8
  women's health in, 51:12
correlation, 13:10–11, **13:11**, **13:12**
corticosteroids, **45:4**, 78:6, 78:8, 84:2, 99:6
Corynebacterium, 34:17

Corynebacterium diphtheriae, 22:3, 23:2, 25:6, 63:3
Cost and Benefit of Needlestick Prevention (GAO), 4:12
cough etiquette, 28:2, 29:2, 48:4
Council of State and Territorial Epidemiologists (CSTE), 71:3, 117:3
Council on Ethical and Judicial Affairs, 8:15
Cowdry type A inclusion bodies, 24:5
coxsackievirus B virus, 41:11
CPOE. *See* computerized physician order entry
CPR. *See* cardiopulmonary resuscitation
CRE. *See* carbapenem-resistant *Enterobacteriaceae*
C-reactive protein (CRP), 25:5, 35:4, 38:5–6
Creutzfeldt-Jakob disease (CJD), 73:1–13
  disinfection and sterilization for, 31:6–7, 73:6–12, **73:8–11**
  electrophysiological catheters and, 50:8
  inactivation of, 73:5–12
  nvCJD, 68:7, 73:3, 74:2, 74:11–12
  ophthalmology services and, 63:1
  postmortem care and, 65:4
  SP and, 106:16
  surgical services and, 68:7
  tissue allografts and, 35:10
  vCJD, 83:9, 107:6
CRIs. *See* catheter-related infections
critical control points (CCPs), 109:12
critical items, 31:1
Cronobacter sakazakii, 41:4
Crossing the Quality Chasm: A New Health System for the 21st Century (IOM), 18:10
CRP. *See* construction and renovation policy; C-reactive protein
cruise ships, 118:2
crusted scabies, 99:2
cryoglobulinemia, 97:10
cryotherapy, 91:8
Cryptococcus, 45:4
Cryptosporidium, 52:2, 121:13
Cryptosporidium parvum, 79C:6–7, 99:7
CSF. *See* cerebrospinal fluid
CSFs. *See* colony-stimulating factors
CSPs. *See* compounded sterile preparations
CSTE. *See* Council of State and Territorial Epidemiologists
CT. *See* computed tomography
CTL. *See* cytotoxic T-lymphocyte
CTLA4-Ig, 69:4
CTS. *See* cardiothoracic surgery
culture filtrate protein 10 (CFP-10), 95:6, 95:8
CV. *See* coefficient of variation
CVC. *See* central venous catheters
CXR. *See* chest radiograph
Cyclospora cayetanensis, 79C:7, 99:7
cystic fibrosis (CF), 70:8
cystitis, 33:2
  dacryocystitis, 63:3
  hemorrhagic, 46:5
  IC, 33:1
cytokines, 22:4, 38:3, 47:3
cytology, 25:2
cytomegalic inclusion disease, 80:6
cytomegalovirus (CMV), 23:2, 45:4, 45:5–6, 80:2, 80:6–8, 100:11
  antivirals for, 26:6–7, 80:7–8
  GVHD and, 46:2
  HSCT and, 46:5
  neonates and, 41:4, 41:12, 41:21
  perinatal care and, 43:6–7
  pregnant HCP and, 104:3–6
  rubella and, 86:14
  xenotransplantation and, 69:7
cytomegalovirus-interstitial pneumonia (CMV-IP), 80:7
cytotoxic T-lymphocyte (CTL), 80:7

DA. *See* device-associated infections

DAAs. *See* direct antiviral agents
daclatasvir, 97:10
dacryoadenitis, 63:3
dacryocystitis, 63:3
DAF. *See* decay accelerating factor
dalfopristin, 26:5
daptomycin, 26:6, 76:2, 76:6, 92:7, 93:5, 93:12–13
dark-field microscopy, 24:9
data
    analysis of
        for HHC, 56:5
        with IT, 6:14
        performance measures for, 17:6–7
        in qualitative research methods, 19:6
        in surveillance program design, 11:7
    collection of
        for HHC, 56:4–5
        with IT, 6:12–13
        performance measures and, 17:9–10, **17:10**
        in qualitative research methods, 19:4
        in surveillance program design, 11:7–8
    definition of, 13:1
    management of, with IT, 6:13–14
    for performance improvement, 17:10
    presentation of
        for epidemiology studies, 10:9–12
        in statistics, 13:17–18, **13:18**, **13:19**
    for product evaluation, 7:3
    reporting of
        for HHC, 56:5
        with IT, 6:14
        in statistics, 13:1
data points, 14:2, 14:5, 14:8
data sets, 13:1, **13:2**
decay accelerating factor (DAF), 69:4
decontamination, 106:1, 111:2, 119:13–14, 120:18
    "no touch" methods for, 31:9–10, **31:10**
decorative water fountains, 115:5, 115:7
deep vein thrombosis (DVT), 18:4, 18:18
DEET. *See* N,N-Diethyl-meta-toluamide
defibrillators, 35:7–9
Deficit Reduction Act of 2005, 8:16, 9:2, 18:3
define, measure, analyze, improve, control (DMAIC), 16:6–7
deionizers
    for dialysis, 39:6
    for water, 115:2
Delphi project, 1:6, **9:3**
dementia, 66:9
dengue hemorrhagic fever (DHF), 96:2, 96:3, 96:5
dengue shock syndrome (DSS), 96:5
density gradient gel electrophoresis (DGGE), 70:11
Densovirinae, 88:1
dental healthcare personnel (DHCP), 53:1–19
dental services, 53:1–19, **53:10**
    aseptic technique in, 53:3–5, 53:16–18
    cleaning and, 53:9–16, 107:15
    disinfection and sterilization in, 53:9–16, **53:11**, **53:12**, 53:17
    hand hygiene in, 53:3–5
    immunizations and, 53:6
    incident reporting in, 53:7, **53:7**
    laboratory asepsis in, 53:16–18
    patient screening in, 53:5–6
    post-exposure management in, 53:6–7
    radiography in, 53:16
    representative infectious diseases in, **53:4**
    reprocessing in, 53:1–2, 53:9–16
    Standard Precautions in, 53:2
    water and, 53:14–15
dental unit water systems (DUWS), 53:14–15
deoxyribonucleic acid (DNA)

antimicrobial resistance and, 26:11–12
bacteria and, 24:2
Candida and, 78:2
CMV and, 80:7
HIV and, 81:3
PCR for, 24:5, 24:8
PVB19 and, 88:2
RFLPs for, 24:8
TB and, 95:4
virulence and, 22:2
viruses, cidofovir for, 26:7
Department of Health, Education, and Welfare, 86:2
Department of Health and Human Services (HHS), 1:1, 1:3, 4:2,
        4:3, 18:2, 23:9
    ASCs and, 64:1, 64:11
    Community Strategy for Pandemic Influenza Migration by,
        120:14
    construction and renovation and, 116:6
    construction codes by, 4:20
    emergency management and, 120:3
    HHC and, 56:2
    HVAC and, 114:3
    National Action Plan to Prevent Health Care-Associated Infec-
        tions: Road Map to Elimination by, 4:2, 6:2, 64:1
    National Action Plan to Prevent Healthcare-associated Infec-
        tions: Road Map to Elimination by, 64:1
    PEP and, 120:11
    Privacy Rule by, 8:14
Department of Homeland Security, 4:2
Department of Justice, 49:2
Department of Labor, 4:10–11, 7:7, 65:1
Department of Transportation (DOT), 4:3, 113:2
Department of Veteran Affairs (VA), 4:12
dermatitis, 58:4, **58:5**
dermis, 92:1
descriptive statistics, 13:2–12
designated infection control officer (DICO), 54:1, 54:6–7
Det Norske Veritas Healthcare Inc. (DNV), 4:10, 115:1
device-associated infections (DA), 15:2, 44:3, **59:3**, 59:3–5
device utilization ratio, 11:3
dexamethasone, 74:4
DFA. *See* direct fluorescent antibody
DFUs. *See* drug-free units
DGGE. *See* density gradient gel electrophoresis
DHCP. *See* dental healthcare personnel
DHEC. *See* diarrhea-associated hemolytic *E. coli*
DHF. *See* dengue hemorrhagic fever
DHQP. *See* Division of Healthcare Quality Promotion
diabetes, 35:12, 37:10, 69:5, 94:2, 95:2
    cath lab and, 50:6
    group B *Streptococcus* and, 94:4
    PJI and, 35:5
    Streptococcus pneumoniae and, 94:7
    UTIs and, 33:7
diabetic foot infections, 92:5–6
diagnosis-related group (DRG), 9:2, 18:3
dialysate, 24:16
dialysis, 39:1–17
    BSIs with, 39:14–15
    chemical contamination levels for, **39:8**
    cleaning and, 107:15
    DHQP and, 4:7
    dialysate components and delivery system for, 39:9–10
    education for, 39:15
    HBV and, 39:14–15
    HCV and, 39:14–15, 39:16
    HDV and, 49:15
    HIV and, 39:14, 39:15
    NTM and, 95:17
    reprocessing with, 39:11–12

vascular access for, 39:1–2
water for, 39:2, 39:5–9
Dialysis Surveillance Network (DNS), 4:7, 21:1
diarrhea
    from adenovirus, 79A:8
    from *Aeromonas*, 79B:12–13
    from astroviruses, 79A:7–8
    from *Bacillus cereus*, 79B:13–15
    from *Campylobacter*, 79B:10–11
    with CDI, 72:2–3
    from cholera toxin, 22:3
    from coronaviruses, 79A:8
    disinfectants for, 107:5–6
    from *Edwardsiella tarda*, 79B:11–12
    from *Escherichia coli*, 79B:1–4
    HPS and, 96:5
    in LTCFs, 61:5–6
    from noroviruses, 79A:1–4
    from parasites, 79C:1–9, **79C:2**
    from picobirnaviruses, 79A:9
    from *Plesiomonas shigelloides*, 79B:13
    radiation oncology and, 58:5
    from rotavirus, 79A:4–7, **79A:6**
    from *Salmonella*, 79B:4–6
    from *Shigella*, 79B:6–9
    from toroviruses, 79A:8
    travel health and, 118:2
    from viruses, 79A:1–9
    from *Yersinia enterocolitica*, 79B:9–10
diarrhea-associated hemolytic *E. coli* (DHEC), 75:11
DIC. *See* disseminated intravascular coagulation
dicloxacillin, 26:4
DICO. *See* designated infection control officer
Dientamoeba fragilis, 79C:4–5, 99:7
diet. *See* food and foodborne diseases; nutrition
N,N-Diethyl-meta-toluamide (DEET), 85:8–9, 118:3
differential time to positivity (DTP), 34:7–8
diloxanide furoate, 79C:3
dimorphic fungi, 24:4
diphenoxylate, 79B:8
diphtheria-pertussis-tetanus-polio (DPTP), 110:4
diphtheria, tetanus, and pertussis vaccine (DTP), 71:2, 71:7
diphtheria, tetanus toxoids, and acellular pertussis vaccination (DTaP), 71:4, 71:7
diphtheria toxin, 22:3
Diphyllobothrium latum, 47:3, 99:7
direct antiviral agents (DAAs), 97:10
direct fluorescent antibody (DFA), 24:9, 41:10, 71:2, 79C:7, 90:3
    for *Legionella pneumophila*, 84:4
    for ophthalmia neonatorum, 91:4
    for rabies, 89:3
directly observed therapy (DOT), 51:6, 95:6–7
Dirofilaria immitis, 99:7
disaster management. *See also* bioterrorism; emerging infectious diseases; pandemics
    at ambulatory care centers, 48:8–9
    animals and, 120:18
    for ASCs, 64:10
    BioSense and, 120:7
    BioWatch and, 120:5–6
    decontamination in, 120:18
    drills and exercises, 119:22–23, 120:19
    food and, 120:16
    geriatrics and, 120:8, 120:12
    immunocompromised host and, 120:8
    isolation in, 120:13–14, **120:14**
    MAE and, 112:10–11
    pediatrics and, 120:7–8, 120:12
    PEP in, 120:11–12, **120:14**
    pest control in, 120:18–19

phases of, 119:2–4, **119:3**
    postmortem care in, 120:19
    PPE, 120:13–14
    pregnancy and, 120:8
    public reporting in, 120:8–9
    quarantine in, 120:14–16, **120:15**
    screening in, 120:10–11
    surge capacity and, 120:17–18
    syndromic surveillance for, 120:6–7, **120:7**
    triage in, 120:10–11
    water and, 120:16–17
Disaster Mortuary Operational Response Team (DMORTs), 65:2, 65:5
disinfection and sterilization, 31:1–4, **31:11**. *See also* sterile processing
    at ambulatory care centers, 48:3–4
    in ASCs, 64:6–7
    burns and, 38:5
    in CCCs, 52:3–4
    chemical agents for, **31:3**
    for CJD, 73:6–12, **73:8–11**
    CJD and, 31:6–7
    contact time for, 31:10–11
    critical items for, 31:1
    in dental services, **53:11**, **53:12**, 53:17
    dental services and, 53:9–16
    DHQP and, 4:7
    of endoscopes, 31:7–8
    in FNS, 109:4–5, **109:15**
    with germicides, 31:8
    human papilloma virus and, 31:6
    hydrogen peroxide for, 31:7
    IMD and, 35:13
    improvements for, 31:9
    in MAE, 112:3
    of medical devices, **31:1**
    neonates and, 41:19–20, 41:22–23
    noncritical items for, 31:3–4
    in ophthalmology services, 62:9, 63:12
    patient safety and, 8:7
    pediatrics and, 42:9–10
    in perinatal care, 43:3
    in radiation oncology, 58:4
    in rehabilitation services, 66:5–7
    semicritical items for, 31:2–4
    in surgical services, 68:6–7
    technologies for, **31:4**
    of water, **115:9–10**
disk approximation test, 24:12–13
disk diffusion, 24:11–12, **24:12**, **24:13**, 26:10
disseminated disease, 95:15–16
disseminated intravascular coagulation (DIC), 75:6, 96:5
Division of Healthcare Quality Promotion (DHQP), 1:2, 1:3, 4:3, 4:7–8
Division of Tuberculosis Elimination, 4:3
DMAIC. *See* define, measure, analyze, improve, control
DMORTs. *See* Disaster Mortuary Operational Response Team
DNA. *See* deoxyribonucleic acid
DNS. *See* Dialysis Surveillance Network
DNV. *See* Det Norske Veritas Healthcare Inc.
dobutamine, 110:3
donovanosis, 91:2, 91:22
dopamine, 110:3
DOT. *See* Department of Transportation; directly observed therapy
doxycycline, 26:7, 84:5, 91:4, 91:22
DPTP. *See* diphtheria-pertussis-tetanus-polio
DRG. *See* diagnosis-related group
Droplet Precautions, 29:3
    for adenovirus, 79A:8
    at ambulatory care centers, 48:5

Droplet Precautions (cont.)
    for influenza, 82:6
    for neonates, 41:10
    for rubella, 86:16
    for *Streptococcus pneumoniae*, 94:8
    for VHF, 96:8
drug-free units (DFUs), 51:5
DSS. *See* dengue shock syndrome
DTaP. *See* diphtheria, tetanus toxoids, and acellular pertussis vaccination
D-test, 26:5, 93:5, **93:5**
DTP. *See* differential time to positivity; diphtheria, tetanus, and pertussis vaccine
duty to provide care, 8:3–4
DUWS. *See* dental unit water systems
DVT. *See* deep vein thrombosis

EAEC. *See* enteroaggregative *E. coli*
EAF. *See* EPEC adherence factor
EAggEC. *See* enteroaggressive *E. coli*
Early Notification of Community-Based Epidemics (ESSENCE), 6:4, 82:7
EARS-Net. *See* European Antimicrobial Resistance Surveillance Network
EBE. *See* evidence-based education
Ebola hemorrhagic fever, 96:1, 96:3, 96:6, 96:7
EBP. *See* evidence-based practice
EBV. *See* Epstein-Barr virus
echinocandins, for *Aspergillus*, 78:9
Echinococcus, 99:7
ECM. *See* extracellular matrix
ECMO. *See* extracorporeal membrane oxygenation
ectoparasites, in correctional facilities, 51:10
ED. *See* emergency departments
education, 3:1–12
    active learning and, 3:3–5, **3:4**
    for adult learners, 3:3, **3:3**
    at ambulatory care centers, 48:5
    in ASCs, 64:10
    on bioterrorism, 3:2
    Bloom's taxonomy and, 3:3–4, **3:4**
    classroom settings for, 3:6
    in correctional facilities, 51:5
    for dialysis, 39:15
    in emergency management, 119:21–22
    evaluation of, 3:8
    in EVS, 107:20–21
    goals in, 3:2, 3:6
    on HAIs, 3:2
    on hand hygiene, 27:4
    HCP and, 3:1, 3:5
        immunization of, 103:33
    in HHC, 56:7
    for hospice, 57:3
    for immunocompromised patients, 44:8–9
    innovative instructional methods, 3:8–11
    IP and, 3:1
    learning assessment for, 3:7
    learning environment for, 3:6
    lectures in, 3:9
    for *Legionella pneumophila*, 84:9
    in LTACHs, 62:5
    in LTCFs, 61:2
    needs assessment for, 3:5–6
    patient, 21:6–7
    PD in, 3:8–9
    on pneumonia prevention, 36:4
    program development for, 3:5–7
    for SOT, 45:8
    about Standard Precautions, 28:1–2

    about TB, 51:7
    teaching styles in, **3:7**, 3:7–8
    in waste management, 113:5–6
    on zoonoses, 121:3
Edwardsiella tarda, 79B:11–12
EHEC. *See* enterohemorrhagic *E. coli*
EHR. *See* electronic health record
EIA. *See* enzyme immunoassay
EIC, water and, 115:1
EIEC. *See* enteroinvasive *E. coli*
Eikenella corrodens, 92:5
Eisenberg, John, 18:8
EK. *See* electrophoretic karyotyping
EKC. *See* epidemic keratoconjunctivitis
elderly. *See* geriatrics
electrolysis, 123:1–9
electronic health record (EHR), 6:3, 6:7–8, 6:11, 6:12–13, 8:6
electronic medical record (EMR), 6:11, 48:12
electron microscopy (EM), 24:5, 24:9–10, 79A:7
electrophoresis, 24:8
electrophoretic karyotyping (EK), 78:2
electrophysiology catheters, 50:8
elements of performance (EP), 113:2
elephantiasis, 99:7
eligible professionals (EPs), 6:5
ELISA. *See* enzyme-linked immunosorbent assay
EM. *See* electron microscopy
EMB. *See* ethambutol
embalming, 65:4
embolization, 60:6–8
emergency departments (ED), 6:4
emergency management, 119:1–20. *See also* disaster management
    alternate care sites and, 119:7–8
    community assessment for, 119:6
    decontamination and, 119:13–14
    disabilities and, 119:15
    education in, 119:21–22
    evacuation and, 119:8
    for FNS, 109:13–14
    food and, 119:11–12
    geriatrics and, 119:15–16
    hand hygiene in, 119:11
    in HHC, 56:6
    human waste and, 119:12–13
    immunization and, 119:13
    immunocompromised host and, 119:16
    isolation in, 119:11
    for mass casualty events, 119:4
    mitigation in, 119:2
    occupational health in, 119:11
    patient management in, 119:9–10
    pediatrics and, 119:15
    pest control in, 119:14
    pets and, 119:14
    plans for, 119:4–5
    postmortem care in, 119:14
    pregnancy and, 119:16
    preparedness in, 119:2, 119:4, 119:22
    public reporting and, 119:8, 119:16–21
    quarantine in, 119:11
    recovery in, 119:7
    resource management and, 119:8–9
    response in, 119:2–3
    sewage and, 119:12–13
    special needs populations and, 119:15
    standard of care in, 119:9
    surge capacity and, 119:7
    surveillance in, 119:10
    transport systems and, 119:16
    triage in, 119:9–10

Environmental Protection Agency (EPA) *(cont.)*
    germicides and, 4:10
    LTCFs and, 61:5–6
    RCS and, 67:2
    SP and, 106:1
    VHF and, 96:8
environmental sampling
    HVAC and, 114:12–14
    in surveillance, 11:12
environmental services (EVS), 107:1–22
    biohazardous waste and, 107:17
    cleaning and, 107:2–7
    disinfectants and, 107:3–7
    education in, 107:20–21
    hand hygiene and, 107:10–11, **107:20**
    laundry and, 107:12
    linens and, 107:12
    medical devices and, 107:12–13
    operating budget for, 107:19
    patient zone and, 107:2–3
    performance improvement for, 107:21
    pest control and, 107:18
    PPE and, 107:7–8
    regulatory requirements and guidelines for, 107:2
    waste management and, 107:17–18
environmental testing, 24:15–16
environment of care (EOC), 114:4, 115:1, 116:6
enzyme immunoassay (EIA), 25:1, **25:3**, 25:6, 78:7–8, 79C:7,
        81:6, 86:4
    for CDI, 72:3
    for HCV, 97:10
    for *Legionella pneumophila*, 84:4
enzyme-linked immunosorbent assay (ELISA), 24:5, 25:2, **25:3**,
        39:7, 71:3, 79A:1, 79A:5, 79A:8, 85:2, 85:6, 86:14,
        91:3–4, 97:13
    for astroviruses, 79A:7
    for CMV, 80:7
    for *E. coli*, 79B:3
    for HHV-6, 80:10
EOC. *See* environment of care
eosinophilia, 78:8
eosinophils, 22:7
EP. *See* elements of performance
EPA. *See* Environmental Protection Agency
EPEC. *See* enteropathogenic
EPEC adherence factor (EAF), 79B:3
epidemic
    definition of, 12:1
    IVDA and, 34:3–4, **34:4**
    of rubella, 86:13
    for scabies, 91:15
    in surveillance, 11:3
epidemic curve, 12:3, 12:6, **12:6**, **12:8**
epidemic keratoconjunctivitis (EKC), 63:5
epidemiological studies, 20:1–5, **20:2**
epidemiology
    association in, 10:2–10:4
    causation in, 10:2–10:4
    chain of infection and, 10:6–8, **10:7**, **10:8**
    data presentation for, 10:9–12
    with neonates, 41:3–12
    principles of, 10:1–12
    statistics in, 10:1, 13:1–2
    study design for, 10:8–12
    in surveillance, 11:3
    triangle model of disease causation in, 10:2, **10:2**
    useful terms in, 10:5–6
    uses in healthcare, 10:4–12
    web of causation in, 10:2, **10:2**
    wheel model of disease causation and, 10:2, **10:2**

epidermis, 92:1
epinephrine, 110:3
episiotomy, 43:2, 43:17
EPs. *See* eligible professionals
Epstein-Barr virus (EBV), 26:7, 39:14, 45:4, 80:2, 80:8–9, 86:3,
        86:14, 86:15
    HSCT and, 46:5
    immunocompromised host and, 23:2
    neoplasms from, 80:9
    xenotransplantation and, 69:7
error types, 18:5, **18:6**
erysipelas, 92:4, 94:2–3
erythema, 35:9, 37:11–12, 39:13
erythema infectiosum, 86:14, 88:2, 88:6
erythema migrans, 85:3–4, 85:6
erythrocyte sedimentation rate (ESR), 25:6
erythromycin, 79B:11, 91:22, 92:7, 94:3
    for *Chlamydia trachomatis*, 91:4
    for *Legionella pneumophila*, 84:5
    for *Neisseria gonorrhoeae*, 91:7
    Staphylococcus aureus and, 93:5
ESBL. *See* extended spectrum β-lactamase
ESBLs. *See* expanded-spectrum β-lactamases
Escherichia coli, 22:2, 26:4, 31:11, 33:12, 42:14, 43:5, 47:3,
        52:2, 70:7, 75:10–11, 91:24, 110:3
    cardiac catheterization and, 50:5
    diarrhea from, 79B:1–4
    neonates and, 41:5, 41:14, 41:15
    spinal implants and, 35:11
    SSIs, 92:5
    USDA and, 4:11
    UTIs and, 33:3
ESR. *See* erythrocyte sedimentation rate
ESRD. *See* end-stage renal disease
ESSENCE. *See* Early Notification of Community-Based Epidemics
ETEC. *See* enterotoxigenic *E. coli*
E-test, 24:12, **24:13**, 26:10
ethambutol (EMB), 95:6
ethical issues, 8:12–17
    with AIDS, 8:14–15
    confidentiality and, 8:14–15
    with HIV, 8:14–15, 81:9–10
    informed consent and, 8:13
    with IPC, 8:15
    obligation to provide care to all and, 8:13–14
    with risk management, 8:15–16
ethnography, 19:3
ethylene oxide (ETO), 31:1, **31:4**, 53:11, 106:1
ETO. *See* ethylene oxide
ETs. *See* exfoliative toxins
ETT. *See* endotracheal tube
EUD. *See* external urinary devices
eukaryotic parasites, 24:5
European Antimicrobial Resistance Surveillance Network (EARS-Net),
        93:10–11
European Pressure Ulcer Advisory Panel, 47:8
European Society of Clinical Microbiology and Infectious Diseases,
        9:7, 33:2
European Study Group on Nosocomial Infections, 9:6–7
evacuation, 119:8
EVD. *See* external ventricular drain
event-related sterility, 106:1, 106:16
evidence-based education (EBE), 3:5
evidence-based practice (EBP), 1:1, 3:5, 67:4
EVS. *See* environmental services
exanthem, 86:3
exfoliative toxins (ETs), 93:7, 93:10
Exophiala, 78:11–12
Exophiala dermatitidis, 110:5
expanded-spectrum β-lactamases (ESBLs), 26:12

food and nutrition services (FNS) *(cont.)*
    pest control in, 109:4–5
    purchasing in, 109:5–6
    receiving in, 109:6
    safe handling in, 109:8–9
    storage in, 109:6–7
    vending machines and, 109:15–16
    waste management in, 109:4–5
foodborne-disease outbreak (FBDO), 109:2
food diary, **47:5**
Food Safety Inspection Service (FSIS), 4:11, 109:7
forceps, 43:12
foreign objects
    cardiac catheterization and, 50:5
    laundry and, 111:2
    SSIs and, 37:11
    after surgery, as HAC, 18:3
formula feeding, 43:14–16
Forssmann, Werner, 50:1
foscarnet, 80:7–8, 80:10, 91:11
fosfomycin, 93:12
Fournier gangrene, 92:6–7
freezers, 112:7–8
frequency polygon, 13:18, **13:18**
Fresenius Medical Care, 39:3
FSIS. *See* Food Safety Inspection Service
FTA-ABS. *See* fluorescent treponemal antibody absorption
FTE. *See* full-time equivalent
FTP. *See* file transfer protocol
full-time equivalent (FTE), 9:3, 9:5, 9:7
fulminant HEV, 97:13
functional separation/barrier, 111:2
fungi, 24:4–5, 42:8, 45:5, **45:5**, 51:10, 74:1, 78:1–12, 91:22.
      See also specific fungi
    animals and, 121:13
    CTS and, 42:6
    HSCT and, 46:3–4
    neonates and, 41:9–10
furuncles, 92:4
Fusarium, 78:11, 115:5
Fusarium incarnatum-equiseti, 110:7
fusidic acid, 26:6, 92:7, 93:12
fusion inhibitors, 81:8
Fusobacterium nucleatum, 70:7

galactose-α1,3-galactose (Gal), 69:4, 69:5
α1,3-galactosyltransfens gene-knockout (GTKO), 69:4, 69:5
Gambro Health Care, 39:3
gamma benzene hexachloride, 99:3
gamma glutamyl transferase (GGT), 25:5
ganciclovir, 26:6–7, 80:7–8, 80:10
GAO. *See* Government Accounting Office
gap analysis, 16:2, **16:3**
Gardnerella, 41:16
Gardnerella vaginalis, 91:3, 91:24
Garvin, David, 18:5
GAS. *See* group A *Streptococcus*
gastroenteritis. *See also* diarrhea
    from astroviruses, 79A:7
    from *Campylobacter*, 79B:10–11
    from *Escherichia coli*, 79B:1–4
    food and, 23:9
    in LTCFs, 61:5–6
    neonates and, 41:15
    from *Salmonella*, 79B:4–6
    from *Shigella*, 79B:6–9
    from *Shigella sonnei*, 10:3–4
    from *Yersinia enterocolitica*, 79B:9–10
gastrointestinal tract (GI)
    Enterobacteriaceae, 75:9–10

foodborne illness and, 83:1
immunocompromised hosts and, 23:4
nutrition and, 47:10
pediatrics and, 42:14
TB of, 95:4
Gaussian distribution, 13:6
GBS. *See* group B *Streptococcus*; Guillain-Barré syndrome
GDH. *See* glutamate dehydrogenase
General Duty Clause, 1:4
Genesys Regional Medical Center (GRMC), 16:5
gene therapy, 113:7
genetic engineering, 69:4
genital herpes, 91:10–13
genital warts, 91:1, 91:7–10
genitourinary system (GU), 95:4
gentamicin, 26:5, 35:7, 41:13, 79B:15
geographical coordinate charts, 10:11
geriatrics, 40:1–6
    aging body system effects and, **40:3**
    disaster management and, 120:8, 120:12
    emergency management and, 119:15–16
    nutrition and, 47:11
    rehabilitation services and, 66:9
    UTIs in, 33:6
German measles. *See* rubella
germicides, 4:8, 4:10, 31:8, 44:4
germ theory, 70:2–3
Gerstmann-Sträussler-Scheinker syndrome, 73:1, 73:3, 74:2, 74:12
GGT. *See* gamma glutamyl transferase
Ghon complex, 95:3
GI. *See* gastrointestinal tract
Giardia lamblia, 47:3, 79C:5–6, 99:7
GISA. *See* glycopeptide-intermediate *S. aureus*
GISP. *See* Gonococcal Isolate Surveillance System
Global Measles & Rubella Strategic Plan, 86:2
Global Outbreak Alert and Response Network, 11:14
Global Patient Safety Challenge: Clean Care Is Safer Care, 21:9
Global Programme of Vaccines, 90:5
gloves and socks syndrome, 88:2
glucans, 94:8
glucose intolerance, 38:5
glutamate dehydrogenase (GDH), 72:3
glutamine, 47:9
glycemic control, 18:3
glycopeptide-intermediate *S. aureus* (GISA), 26:5
glycopeptides, 26:5, 93:12
glycoprotein (GP), 22:2
GMCSF. *See* granulocyte macrophage colony-stimulating factor
GNR. *See* Gram-negative rod
goal-directed checklists, 16:5
Gonococcal Isolate Surveillance System (GISP), 91:6
gonorrhea. *See* Neisseria gonorrhoeae
Good Samaritan statutes, 8:3
Government Accounting Office (GAO), 4:3, 4:12
gowns, 41:19, 50:6, 91:16
GP. *See* glycoprotein
GP41, 22:2
GPOs. *See* group purchasing organizations
graft-versus-host disease (GVHD), 23:6, 46:1, 46:2
Gram, Hans Christian, 24:10
gramicidin, 39:5
gram-negative bacilli, 23:3, 24:2, 25:6, 26:4, 26:5, 42:6, 60:5, 77:1–5, 87:3, 91:5
    burns and, 38:2, 38:5, 38:7
    cardiac catheterization and, 50:5
    CIED and, 35:8
    Contact Precautions with, 29:3
    dialysis and, 39:8, 39:10, 39:16
    geriatrics and, 40:4
    HSCT and, 46:3

hantavirus cardiopulmonary syndrome (HCPS), 121:8
hantavirus pulmonary syndrome (HPS), 96:1–2, 96:3, 96:5
HAP. *See* hospital-acquired pneumonia
HAR. *See* hyperacute rejection
hardware, for IT, 6:12
Harvard Medical Practice Study, 18:17
HAV. *See* Hepatitis A virus
Hazard Analysis Critical Control Point (HACCP), 4:11, 109:2, 109:5, 109:12–13
    water and, 115:7
hazard and vulnerability assessment (HVA), 119:5, **119:6**
HBM. *See* health belief model
HBsAg. *See* Hepatitis B surface antigen
HBV. *See* Hepatitis B virus
HCAP. *See* healthcare-associated pneumonia
HCC. *See* hepatocellular carcinoma
HCFA. *See* Health Care Financing Administration
HCIR. *See* healthcare industry representative
HCP. *See* healthcare professionals
HCPS. *See* hantavirus cardiopulmonary syndrome
HCV. *See* Hepatitis C virus
HDCV. *See* human diploid cell rabies vaccine
HDV. *See* Hepatitis D virus
HE. *See* hospital epidemiologist
head and neck cancer, 58:5
head and neck surgery, 42:7
head lice, 99:4
health belief model (HBM), **5:3**, 5:3–4
healthcare-associated infections (HAIs), 1:1. *See also specific infections*
    ambulatory care centers and, 48:2
    aseptic technique and, 30:1
    behavioral health and, 49:5
    CDC and, 1:2–3
    chain of infection and, 10:7
    CMS and, 4:2
    contact time for, 31:11
    in correctional facilities, 49:2
    cost-benefit analysis with, 1:6
    cost-effectiveness with, 1:6
    data collection on, 6:13
    in developing countries, 9:7
    DHQP and, 1:3
    documentation about, 8:6
    education on, 3:2
    effectiveness with, 1:6
    EMS and, 54:3
    Enterobacteriaceae, **75:8**
    EVS and, 107:1
    GAO and, 4:12
    HBM for, 5:3–4
    HHC and, 56:2
    HHS and, 4:2
    HICPAC and, 4:8
    hospice and, 57:4
    ICU and, 59:1, 59:2
    IMD and, 35:3
    immunocompromised patients and, 44:1
    legal issues and, 8:1
    liability and, 8:3
    LTACHs and, 62:2
    neonates and, 41:1, 41:22
    NNIS and, 4:7
    NPSG and, 4:1
    NTM and, 95:16
    ophthalmology services and, 63:1, **63:4**, **63:7**
    outcome measures for, 17:5
    Partnership for Patients Hospital Engagement Networks and, 1:2
    patient safety and, 18:2, 18:10
    performance measures and, 17:1, 17:2

perinatal care and, 43:1, 43:16–18
    pharmacy services and, 110:2
    PPS and, 4:2
    product evaluation and, 7:2
    Pseudomonas and, 77:3
    public reporting of, 8:5
    PVE and, 35:6
    QI and, 16:2, 17:10
    rehabilitation services, 66:3
    reporting of, 6:2
    risk-adjusted comparisons and, 15:1–2, 15:6
    RSV and, 90:1
    SENIC and, 9:3, 11:1
    SOT and, 2:5, 45:6
    SSIs and, 37:1
    standard of care for, 8:4–5
    Staphylococcus aureus and, 93:10
    surgical services and, 68:2
    surveillance for, 1:7, 11:1
healthcare-associated pneumonia (HCAP), 36:1, 36:2–3, 36:4, **36:5**, 45:2, **45:2**
healthcare-associated *Staphylococcus aureus* (HA-MRSA), **93:3**, 93:4
healthcare facility emergency management plan, 119:5
healthcare facility-onset (HO), 15:3, **15:4**
Healthcare Failure Mode Effect Analysis (HFMEA), 8:7
Health Care Financing Administration (HCFA), 39:3
healthcare industry representative (HCIR), 102:3–4
Healthcare Infection Control Practices Advisory Committee (HICPAC), 1:3, 4:7–4:8, 4:14, 8:5, 21:3, 29:2, 57:4, 76:8–9, 106:1
    ASCs and, 64:8
    behavioral health and, 49:7
    Guideline for Disinfection and Sterilization Practices by, 21:8
    Guideline for Isolation Precautions: Preventing Transmission of Infectious Agents in Healthcare Settings by, 28:2, 29:1
    Guidelines for the Prevention of Intravascular Catheter-Related Infections by, 70:6
    MDROs and, **93:14**
    water and, 115:1
healthcare informatics, 6:1–10, **6:7**
Healthcare Laundry Accreditation Council (HLAC), 111:4, 111:7
Healthcare Performance Improvement (HPI), 18:9
healthcare professionals (HCP). *See also* pregnant HCP
    ambulatory care centers and, 48:1
    ASCs and, 64:2, 64:9–10
    bloodborne pathogens and, 101:1–2
    Candida and, 78:3
    catheter hubs and, 34:15
    chain of infection and, 10:7
    CNS and, 74:2
    in correctional facilities, 51:4
    education and, 3:1, 3:5
    emergency management and, 119:1
    Enterococcus and, 76:2
    GAS and, 94:4
    HAIs and, 1:1
    hand hygiene and, 27:1
    HHC and, 56:3
    HIV and, 81:7
    hospice and, 57:3
    IGRA for, 95:13
    immunization of, **100:3**, 103:1–34, **103:3**
        for HAV, 103:5–9, **103:8**
        for HBV, 103:9–12
        for influenza, 82:5–6, 103:12–14
        for meningococcal disease, 103:29–30
        for polio, 103:18–19
        program establishment for, 103:30–34
        schedule for, **103:28**

Hepatitis B virus (cont.)
    PEP for, **103:10**, 104:6
    perinatal care and, 43:8
    pharmacy services and, 110:2
    PPE for, 101:3–4, **104:4**
    pregnant HCP and, 104:6
    sharps and, 113:2
    SOT and, 45:2, **45:2**
    tattoos and, 123:3
    travel health and, 118:9
    virulence of, 22:2
    xenotransplantation and, 69:7
Hepatitis C virus (HCV), 97:8–11, **97:9**
    ambulatory care centers and, 48:4
    as bloodborne pathogens, 101:4–5
    in CCCs, 52:3
    in correctional facilities, 51:2, 51:3–4
    dental services and, 53:7
    dialysis and, 39:14, 39:16
    employee surveillance for, 8:10
    EMS and, 54:9
    endoscopy and, 55:2
    fentanyl and, 110:3
    IFNs for, 26:7
    immunocompromised host and, 23:1, 23:5
    from MDVs, 110:4
    neonates and, 41:4, 41:12
    occupational health and, 100:8
    ophthalmology services and, 63:1
    PEP for, 101:5
    perinatal care and, 43:8
    pregnant HCP and, 104:7
    ribavirin for, 26:7
    sharps and, 113:2
    SOT and, 45:4
    tattoos and, 123:3
    tissue allografts and, 35:10
    virulence of, 22:2
    xenotransplantation and, 69:7
Hepatitis D virus (HDV), 49:15, 97:11–12
Hepatitis E virus (HEV), 97:12–13
hepatocellular carcinoma (HCC), 97:8
herd immunity, 10:6, 23:5, 61:5
Herellea, 110:3
herpes simplex virus (HSV)
    chancroid and, 91:2
    Cowdry type A inclusion bodies and, 24:5
    encephalitis and, 74:8
    HSCT and, 46:2, 46:4–5
    meningitis and, 74:1
    neonates and, 41:5, 41:12, 41:13
    NGU and, 91:4
    occupational health and, 100:11
    perinatal care and, 43:2, 43:8–9
    pregnant HCP and, 104:7
herpes simplex virus-1 (HSV-1), 74:9, 80:2, 80:3–4, 91:1–2, 91:10–13
herpes simplex virus-2 (HSV-2), 80:3–4, 91:1–2, 91:10–13
herpes virus, 80:1–12
    classification of, **80:2**, 80:2–3
    CNS and, 22:6
    immune system and, 80:11–12
    immunizations for, 80:11
    neonates and, 41:4
herpes zoster, 40:3, 40:6, 80:5, 100:11
HFE. *See* human factors engineering
HFMEA. *See* Healthcare Failure Mode Effect Analysis
HFRS. *See* hemorrhagic fever with renal syndrome
HHC. *See* home healthcare
HHS. *See* Department of Health and Human Services

HHV-6. *See* human herpesvirus 6
HHV-7. *See* human herpesvirus 7
HHV-8. *See* human herpesvirus 8
Hib-MenCY-TT, 87:4
HICPAC. *See* Healthcare Infection Control Practices Advisory Committee
HICS. *See* Hospital Incident Command System
high-efficiency particulate air (HEPA), 23:7
    behavioral health and, 48:7–8
    construction and renovation and, 116:5, 116:8
    in correctional facilities, 51:7
    EVS and, 107:2–3
    for HSCT, 46:4, 46:9–10
    HVAC and, 114:2, 114:8
    IMD and, 35:13
    immunocompromised patients and, 44:4, 44:7
    in laboratory services, 108:7–8
    MAE and, 112:2
    protective environment and, 29:4–5
    in surgical services, 68:2, 68:9
    TB and, 95:12
high-level disinfection (HLD), 67:2
highly active antiretroviral therapy (HAART), 81:7, 97:11
high-performance liquid chromatography (HPLC), 25:6
Hill, Bradford, 10:3
Hill's criteria, **10:3**, 10:3–4
HIPAA. *See* Health Insurance Portability and Accountability Act of 1996
histamine, 22:7
histogram, 10:11, **10:12**, 13:18, **13:19**
Histoplasma capsulatum, 23:4
HITECH. *See* Health Information Technology for Economic and Clinical Health Act
HIV. *See* human immunodeficiency virus
HL7. *See* health level seven
HLA-B27, 79B:9, 85:5
HLAC. *See* Healthcare Laundry Accreditation Council
HLA-DR4, 85:5
HLD. *See* high-level disinfection
HME. *See* heat/moisture exchangers
HMOs. *See* health maintenance organizations
hMPV. *See* human metapneumovirus
HO. *See* healthcare facility-onset
Home Access HIV-1 Test System, 81:7
home healthcare (HHC), 56:1–8
    CMS and, 4:9
    emergency management in, 56:6
    hand hygiene in, 56:2–3
    hospice and, 57:2
    providers of care for, 56:2
    Transmission-based Precautions in, 56:3
Home Health Prospective Payment System, 4:9
hookworms, 99:7
hospice, 57:1–5
hospital-acquired conditions (HAC), 1:3, 9:2, 18:3–4
hospital-acquired pneumonia (HAP), 23:8–9, 36:1, 36:2–3, 36:4, 67:2, 70:9, 84:2–4
hospital epidemiologist (HE), 9:5
Hospital Incident Command System (HICS), 54:18, 119:17, **119:18, 119:19–20**
Hospital Inpatient Reporting Program, 59:1
Hospitals in Pursuit of Excellence (HPOE), 1:2
Hospital Survey on Patient Safety Culture, by AHRQ, 18:4
HPI. *See* Healthcare Performance Improvement
HPLC. *See* high-performance liquid chromatography
HPOE. *See* Hospitals in Pursuit of Excellence
HPS. *See* hantavirus pulmonary syndrome
HPV. *See* human papilloma virus; hydrogen peroxide vapor
HQA. *See* Healthcare Quality Alliance
HRSA. *See* Health Resources and Service Administration

HSCT. *See* hematopoietic stem cell transplant
HSV. *See* herpes simplex virus
HSV-1. *See* herpes simplex virus-1
HSV-2. *See* herpes simplex virus-2
HTLV, neonates and, 41:4, 41:21
HTLV-I. *See* human T-lymphotrophic virus type I
HTML. *See* hypertext markup language
human diploid cell rabies vaccine (HDCV), 118:8
human factors engineering (HFE), 18:5
human herpesvirus 6 (HHV-6), 23:2, 26:7, 80:9–10, 86:14
human herpesvirus 7 (HHV-7), 80:9–10, 86:14
human herpesvirus 8 (HHV-8), 80:10–11
human immunodeficiency virus (HIV), 4:1–2, 8:12, 22:2, 35:10,
    81:1–11, **81:3**, **81:6**, 100:8, 105:5. *See also* acquired
    immunodeficiency syndrome
  acute retroviral syndrome and, 81:5
  ADA and, 8:14
  ART for, 26:7
  astroviruses and, 79A:7
  as bloodborne pathogens, 101:5–8
  breast milk and, 43:16
  Candida and, 78:3
  CDC and, 8:11
  chancroid and, 91:13, 91:14
  in correctional facilities, 49:2, 51:2, 51:3–4
  dental services and, 53:7
  dialysis and, 39:14, 39:15
  disinfectants for, 107:4
  as emerging infectious disease, 120:1
  employee surveillance for, 8:10
  EMS and, 54:7–8
  ethical issues with, 8:14–15, 81:9–10
  group B *Streptococcus* and, 94:4
  HBV and, 97:6
  HCV and, 97:9
  HIPAA and, 8:14
  history of, 81:1–2
  HSV and, 91:11
  human papilloma virus and, 91:8
  in immunocompromised host, 23:1, 23:2
  laboratory testing for, 81:6–7
  legal issues with, 81:9–10
  LGV and, 91:22
  meningitis and, 74:8
  mental illness and, 49:1
  Neisseria gonorrhoeae and, 91:6
  neonates and, 41:4, 41:12
  nutrition and, 47:10
  ophthalmology services and, 63:1
  OPIM and, 111:2
  PEP for, 101:6–8, **101:7**, 104:8
  perinatal care and, 43:9
  pregnancy and, 81:8
  pregnant HCP and, 104:7–8
  public health and, 81:11
  qualitative research methods with, 19:7
  rapid test for, 81:7
  rotavirus and, 79A:4
  scabies and, 91:15, 99:2
  sharps and, 113:2
  SOT and, 45:2, **45:2**, 45:6
  STIs and, 91:23–24
  syphilis and, 91:17
  T. vaginalis and, 91:18
  tattoos and, 123:3
  TB and, 95:1, 95:3
  viral load for, **81:4**, 81:4–5, 81:7
  VVC and, 91:19–20
  waste management and, 113:1

xenotransplantation and, 69:7
human metapneumovirus (hMPV), 41:10, 42:13
The Human Microbiome Project (NIH), 70:6
Human Oral Microbiome Database (NIH), 70:6
human papilloma virus (HPV), 91:7–10
  disinfection and sterilization and, 31:6
  immunization for, 45:3, 46:10, 91:1, 91:9
  Neisseria gonorrhoeae and, 91:7–8
  pregnant HCP and, 104:1, 104:8
human parvovirus B19 (PVB19), 88:1–7
  occupational health and, 100:11
  perinatal care and, 43:9–10
  pregnant HCP and, 104:9
human plague, 75:12
Human Rights Watch, correctional facilities and, 51:13
human T-lymphotrophic virus type I (HTLV-I), 41:4
human waste, 115:13, 119:12–13
humidifiers, 67:2
humoral immune system, 22:4–5
HUS. *See* hemolytic-uremic syndrome
HVA. *See* hazard and vulnerability assessment
HVAC. *See* heating, ventilation, and air conditioning
hybrid cath labs, 50:3
hydrogen peroxide, 31:7, **31:10**, 106:1, 107:14
hydrogen peroxide gas plasma, **31:4**
hydrogen peroxide vapor (HPV), 31:9–10
hydrotherapy, for burns, 38:3, 38:6
Hymenolepis nana, 99:7
hyperacute rejection (HAR), 69:2–4, **69:3**
hyperglycemia, 37:10, 38:5
hypersensitivity, 53:8, 95:15, 99:2, 103:4–5, 118:5
hypertext markup language (HTML), 6:11
hyperthermia, 38:5
hypodermic needles, 105:5
hypopyon, 63:3
hypothermia, 35:12, 37:10, 38:5, 59:4
hypothesis testing, **13:13**, 13:13–14, **13:14**
hysterectomies, 91:2–3, 91:25, **91:26**

IACUC. *See* institutional animal care and use committee
IAHCSMM. *See* International Association for Healthcare Central
    Service and Material Management
IAMAT. *See* International Association for Medical Assistance to
    Travelers
IAQ. *See* indoor air quality
IBMIR. *See* instant blood-mediated inflammatory reaction
IC. *See* interstitial cystitis
ICC. *See* infection control committee
ICD. *See* implantable cardioverter-defibrillator
ice
  FNS and, 109:11
  machines, 115:6, 115:13–14
  MAE and, 112:9
  storage, 115:6, 115:13–14
ICRA. *See* infection control risk assessment; infection risk assessment
    plan
ICRMR. *See* infection control risk mitigation recommendations
ICS. *See* Incident Command System
ICU. *See* intensive care unit
ID. *See* immunodiffusion
idiopathic thrombocytopenia, 88:5
IDSA. *See* Infectious Disease Society of America
IE. *See* infectious endocarditis
IFA. *See* immunofluorescent antibody; indirect fluorescent antibody
IFIC. *See* International Federation of Infection Control
IFNs. *See* interferons
IG. *See* Interpretive Guidelines
IgA. *See* immunoglobulin A
IgD. *See* immunoglobulin D
IgE. *See* immunoglobulin E

IgG. *See* immunoglobulin G
IgG anti-HAV. *See* immunoglobulin G anti-HAV
IgM. *See* immunoglobulin M
IGRA. *See* interferon gamma release assays
IHA. *See* indirect hemagglutination
IHI. *See* Institute for Healthcare Improvement
IHPS. *See* infantile hypertrophic pyloric stenosis
IIV. *See* inactivated influenza vaccine
IL. *See* interleukins
ILI. *See* influenza-like illness
IM. *See* infectious mononucleosis
IMD. *See* indwelling medical devices
imipenem, 75:2
immediate use steam sterilization (IUSS), 68:6–7, 106:1, 106:14–15
immune system, **22:5**
   geriatrics and, 40:5
   herpes virus and, 80:11–12
   human papilloma virus and, 91:9
   malnutrition and, 47:2–3
   mumps and, 86:8
   nutrition and, 47:1–13
   obesity and, 47:2–3, **47:3**
   overnutrition and, 47:2–3
   pediatrics and, 42:2, **42:2**
   undernutrition and, 47:2
   xenotransplantation and, 69:2–6, **69:3**
immunization, 103:32. *See also specific vaccines*
   antibiotics in, 103:5
   breastfeeding and, 103:5
   in CCCs, 52:4–5
   for cholera, 118:9–10
   in correctional facilities, 51:8
   dental services and, 53:6
   efficacy and cost analysis for, 103:2–3, **103:3**
   emergency management and, 119:13
   EMS and, 54:16
   for *Haemophilus influenzae*, 23:6, 42:12, 46:10
   for HAV, 46:10, 54:16, 97:4, 103:5–109, **103:8**, **118:5**, 118:5–6
   for HBV, 45:3, 46:10, 53:6, 97:7–8, 103:9–12, 118:9
   for HCP, **100:3**, 103:1–34, **103:3**, **103:28**
   for herpes virus, 80:11
   for herpes zoster, geriatrics and, 40:6
   HSCT and, 46:10
   for human papilloma virus, 45:3, 46:10, 91:1, 91:9, 96:7
   hypersensitivity with, 103:4–5
   ICU and, 59:7
   immunocompromised host and, 23:5–6, 23:12
   immunocompromised patients and, 44:3
   for influenza, 110:2
   for JE, **118:6**, 118:6–7
   for Lyme disease, 85:6, 85:9
   meaningful use and, 6:6
   for measles, 42:13, 86:2, 86:4–6, **86:5**, **86:6**
   for meningococcal disease, 46:10, 54:16, 103:29–30, 118:7, **118:7**
   misconceptions with, **103:4**, 103:4–5
   for mumps, 86:8, 86:10–11
   for *Neisseria meningitidis*, 87:4
   for neonates, 41:23
   patient safety and, 8:7
   pediatrics and, 42:1, 42:12–13
   perinatal care and, 43:4–5
   for pertussis, 71:4–5
   for plague, 118:10
   for pneumococcal disease, geriatrics and, 40:6
   for pneumonia, 36:3–4
   for polio, 46:10, 103:18–19
   precautions with, 103:5
   pregnancy and, 103:5, **118:10**

   for pregnant HCP, 104:2–3, **104:3**
   for PVB19, 88:7
   for rabies, 89:2, 118:7–8, **118:8**
   for rotavirus, SOT and, 45:3
   for RSV, 90:4–5
   for rubella, 86:15–16
   for smallpox, 100:12, 103:21–24, 118:10
   SOT and, 45:3, 45:8
   storage of vaccines for, **103:29**
   for *Streptococcus pneumoniae*, 94:6, 94:7–8
   for TB, 46:10, 95:8
   terms for, **103:2**
   transplantation and, 23:5–6
   travel health and, 118:3–10
   for typhoid fever, 54:16, 118:8–9, **118:9**
   for *Vaccinia*, 4:2
   for VHF, 96:7
   for VZV, 45:3, 46:10, **103:24**, 103:24–27
immunobiologics, 103:2
immunocompromised host, 23:1–12, **23:2**
   burns and, 23:3–4, **23:4**
   disaster management and, 120:8
   emergency management and, 119:16
   flowers and, 23:9–10
   food and, 23:9
   GI tract and, 23:4
   hand hygiene and, 23:7
   HAP and, 23:8–9
   immunizations and, 23:5–6, 23:12
   lungs and, 23:4
   measles and, 86:4
   opportunistic organisms and, 23:2, **23:3**
   oropharynx and, 23:4
   pathogen exposure reduction for, 23:6–11
   pets and, 23:10–11
   plants and, 23:9–10
   probiotics for, 23:11
   prophylaxis for, 23:7–8, 23:11
   PVB19 and, 88:4
   SSTIs in, 23:3–4, 92:7
   statins for, 23:12
   travel health and, 118:5
   water and, 23:9
immunocompromised patients, 44:1–10
   education for, 44:8–9
   human papilloma virus and, 91:8
   HVAC and, 114:13
   meningococcal meningitis and, 74:5
   surveillance and, 44:8
   xenotransplantation and, 69:7
immunodeficiencies, pediatrics and, 42:2–3, **42:3**, **42:4**
immunodiffusion (ID), **25:3**
immunofluorescence, 25:2
immunofluorescent antibody (IFA), 25:3, **25:3**
immunofluorescent stains, 24:11
immunoglobulin A (IgA), 22:5, **25:3**, 79A:4–5
immunoglobulin D (IgD), 22:5, **25:3**
immunoglobulin E (IgE), 22:5, **25:3**, 78:8
immunoglobulin G (IgG), 22:4, **25:3**, 86:3, 86:14–15, 97:12
   CAPTIA syphilis-G and, 25:1
   HBV and, 97:6
   Lyme disease and, 85:2
   pediatrics and, 42:2
   PVB19 and, 88:3, 88:5
   VHF and, 96:6
   WNV and, 98:3
immunoglobulin G anti-HAV (IgG anti-HAV), 97:3
immunoglobulin M (IgM), **25:3**, 79A:4, 86:4, 86:14, 91:10, 97:6
   CMV and, 104:5
   HAV and, 97:3

Influenza *(cont.)*
    geriatrics and, 40:3, 40:5–6
    HSCT and, 46:5
    immunization for, 42:13, 43:4, 82:4–5, 110:2, 118:9
        ASCs and, 64:10
        in correctional facilities, 51:8
        geriatrics and, 40:5
        for HCP, 82:5–6, 103:12–14
        HSCT and, 46:10
        infection transmission and, 21:7
        performance measures for, 17:3–4
        side effects of, 82:5
        SOT and, 45:3
    light microscopy for, 24:5
    LTCFs and, 61:4
    neonates and, 41:10
    occupational health and, 100:10–11
    pandemics of, 19:7, 120:3
    pharmacy services and, 110:2
    pregnancy and, 82:7, **82:7**
    pregnant HCP and, 104:8
    surveillance for, 11:12, 82:7–8
    travel health and, 118:9
influenza-like illness (ILI), 82:3, 85:4, 121:9
informatics, 6:1–10, **6:7**
information technology (IT), 6:1–10, **6:7**
    APIC competency model and, 2:4–5
    for bioterrorism, 6:4
    data analysis with, 6:14
    data collection with, 6:12–13
    data management with, 6:13–14
    data reporting with, 6:14
    hardware for, 6:12
    QI and, 6:4, **6:4**
    software for, 6:7–6:9, 6:12
    for surveillance, 11:10
    for syndromic surveillance, 6:4–5
informed consent, 8:13
infusate, 34:8, 110:3
Infusion Nurses Society (INS), 110:7
infusion therapy, 48:9
INH. *See* isoniazid
INICC. *See* International Nosocomial Infection Control Consortium
inpatient prospective payment system (IPPS), 8:16
inpatient rehabilitation facilities (IRFs), 66:2
INS. *See* Infusion Nurses Society
insects, 10:8, 21:2, 98:1, 99:7, 118:1–2
instant blood-mediated inflammatory reaction (IBMIR), 69:5
INSTI. *See* integrase strand transfer inhibitors
Institute for Healthcare Improvement (IHI), 1:3, 9:2, 16:5, 18:5,
        29:2, 33:11
    5 Million Lives Campaign of, 17:3, 68:10
Institute for Safe Medication Practices (ISMP), 18:9
Institute of Medicine (IOM), 4:2, 8:4, 16:1–2
    *Crossing the Quality Chasm: A New Health System for the 21st
        Century* by, 18:10
    To Err Is Human: Building a Safer Health System by, 4:9, 8:12,
        16:2, 18:1, 59:1
institutional animal care and use committee (IACUC), 121:3–4
Institutional Review Board (IRB), 1:5
integrase strand transfer inhibitors (INSTI), 81:8
integrated pest management (IPM), 109:5
integrated service digital network (ISDN), 6:11
integration, architecture, and security (IT&S), 6:8
intensive care unit (ICU), 16:5, 18:7, 59:1–7, **59:2**, 70:6, 77:2
    burns and, 42:7
    CAUTIs in, 33:8–9
    DA and, 15:2, **59:3**, 59:3–5
    in developing countries, 9:7
    Enterobacteriaceae and, 75:7

Enterococcus and, 76:2
    immunizations and, 59:7
    immunocompromised host and, 23:8–9
    NICU, 41:2, 41:3, 41:4, 111:2, 114:2
    performance measures and, 17:4
    VAP and, 9:6, 67:4
interferon gamma release assays (IGRA), 95:6, 95:13
interferon plus ribavirin (PR), 97:10
interferons (IFNs), 22:4, 22:6, 26:7, 97:10
interleukins (IL), 22:3, 22:4, 22:6
intermittent peritoneal dialysis (IPD), 39:13
International AIDS Society, 81:2
International Association for Healthcare Central Service and Material
        Management (IAHCSMM), 106:1
International Association for Medical Assistance to Travelers (IAMAT),
        118:11
International Federation of Infection Control (IFIC), 1:8, 4:14
International Nosocomial Infection Control Consortium (INICC), 9:7
International Organization for Standardization (ISO), 110:4, 110:8,
        110:10
International Society for Peritoneal Dialysis (ISPD), 39:12–13
International Transplant Nurses Society (ITNS), 45:8
Interpretive Guidelines (IG), 4:2
interpretive surveillance report, 11:8
interstitial cystitis (IC), 33:1
interventional radiology, 60:1–10
    angiography in, 60:5
    CVC and, 60:3–5
    embolization in, 60:6–8
    percutaneous endoluminal stenting in, 60:5–6
    ultrasound in, 60:8
    vertebroplasty in, 60:9–10
intracranial epidural abscess, 74:2, 74:11
intravascular catheters, 38:7–8
intravenous device-associated (IVDA) BSIs, 34:1–18, **34:2**, **34:5**,
        34:9–11
    analysis of implanted long-term devices, 34:7–8
    analysis of remote devices, 34:6–7
    anticoagulants for, 34:13
    antimicrobials for, 34:12, 34:17–18
    antiseptics for, 34:12
    barrier precautions for, 34:11
    blood cultures for, 34:6
    device replacement and, 34:12–13
    epidemic and, 34:3–4, **34:4**
    features of, **34:6**
    infection sources for, **34:3**
    infusate in, 34:8
    intravenous teams for, 34:12
    novel technology for, **34:14**, 34:14–15
    sepsis, 34:3–4
    septicemia, 34:6–8
    thrombolytics for, 34:13
    treatment of, 34:16–18
intravenous immunoglobulin (IVIG), 23:6, 41:11, 86:6, **86:6**
    for GAS, 94:3
    for PVB19, 88:2, 88:4, 88:6
    for RSV, 90:4
intravitreal, 63:3
invasive procedures, with neonates, 41:5, 41:18
investigational new drug (IND), 104:12
iodophor, 107:10
iodoquinol, 79C:3
IOM. *See* Institute of Medicine
IPAC Canada. *See* Infection Prevention and Control Canada (IPAC
        Canada)
IPC. *See* infection prevention committee
IPCC. *See* infection prevention and control committee
IPD. *See* intermittent peritoneal dialysis
IPM. *See* integrated pest management

IPPS. *See* inpatient prospective payment system
IPV. *See* inactivated polio vaccine
IRB. *See* Institutional Review Board
IRFs. *See* inpatient rehabilitation facilities
ISDN. *See* integrated service digital network
Ishikawa diagram, 16:4, **16:4**
ISMP. *See* Institute for Safe Medication Practices
ISO. *See* International Organization for Standardization
isolation, 41:2
    CNS and, 74:13–14
    in disaster management, 120:13–14, **120:14**
    in emergency management, 119:11
    waste management and, 113:3
Isolation Precautions, 29:1–8
    Airborne Precautions, 29:3–4
    behavioral health and, 49:7–9
    Contact Precautions, 29:2–3
    Droplet Precautions, 29:3
    for MDROs, 29:5–6, **29:7–8**
    for MRSA, 29:5–6
    for PE, 29:4–5
    for rubella, 86:16–17
    for TB, 51:651:6–7
isoniazid (INH), 95:7, 95:8
Isospora belli, 79C:8
ISPD. *See* International Society for Peritoneal Dialysis
IT. *See* information technology
ITCI. *See* inductive tongue-computer interface
ITNS. *See* International Transplant Nurses Society
itraconazole, 26:7, 38:7, 78:8, 78:9
IT&S. *See* integration, architecture, and security
IUSS. *See* immediate use steam sterilization
IVC. *See* inferior vena cava
IVDA. *See* intravenous device-associated BSIs
ivermectin, 91:14, 99:3, 99:5
IV fluids, 110:3, 110:9
IVIG. *See* intravenous immunoglobulin

Japanese encephalitis (JE), 74:9, 118:3, **118:6**, 118:6–7
Jarisch-Herxheimer reaction, 91:17
JCAH. *See* Joint Commission on Accreditation of Hospitals
JE. *See* Japanese encephalitis
The Joint Commission (TJC), 1:1, 1:3–4, 4:1, 4:12, 8:4, 16:8,
    18:9, 27:2, 116:6
    CAP and, 36:3
    construction and renovation and, 115:1
    Core Performance Measures and Associated Evaluation Criteria
        by, 17:7, **17:8**
    emergency management and, 119:5
    endoscopy and, 55:2
    FNS and, 109:4
    in HHC, 56:7
    HVAC and, 114:3
    Infection Control and Prevention Standards of, 16:7
    influenza immunizations and, 17:3
    IPC and, 1:5, 8:15
    Isolation Precautions and, 29:2
    LTCFs and, 61:2
    NPSG and, 8:7
    NPSG by, 17:4, 68:10
    ORYX of, 17:3
    patient safety and, 8:7, 18:2, 18:10
    PDSA and, 16:7
    performance measures and, 17:1, 17:2, 17:3, 17:4, 17:9
    prions and, 73:12
    product evaluation and, 7:1
    professional testing program and, 25:2
    PSET by, 18:3
    QI and, 16:2, 17:10
    Quality Check website of, 17:3

    RCA and, 18:2, **18:14–17**
    rehabilitation services and, 66:2
    SEA and, 18:7, 18:11
    Sentinel Event Alert by, 106:16
    SP and, 106:1
    SPC and, 14:1–2
    SUD and, 7:7
    surveillance and, 11:1, 21:5
    VAP and, 67:4
    waste management and, 113:2, 113:3
Joint Commission on Accreditation of Hospitals (JCAH), 4:12
Journal of Emergency Medical Services, 54:3
jumping genes, 26:11–12

Kaplan criteria, 79A:3–4
Kaposi's sarcoma (KS), 80:3, 80:11, 81:1
Kaposi's sarcoma-associated herpesvirus (KSHV), 80:10–11
Kashin-Beck disease, 47:8
Kawasaki disease, 86:3
KDOQI. *See* Kidney Dialysis Outcomes Quality Initiative
keratitis, 63:3, 63:5–6, **63:6**
keratoconjunctivitis, 63:3, 63:5
KFD. *See* Kyasanur Forest disease
Kidney Dialysis Outcomes Quality Initiative (KDOQI), 39:4–5
Kinyoun non fluorescent staining, 24:10–11
Kirby-Bauer method, 24:11–12, **24:12**
Klebsiella, 23:3, 41:5, 42:14, 55:2, 75:10, 110:3
Klebsiella granulomatis, 91:2
Klebsiella pneumoniae, 26:4, 26:12, 59:5, 61:8
knowledge based errors, 18:5, **18:6**
Koch, Robert, 10:3
KOH. *See* potassium hydroxide
Kolb learning style inventory, 3:7
KS. *See* Kaposi's sarcoma
KSHV. *See* Kaposi's sarcoma-associated herpesvirus
kurtosis, 13:6, **13:6**
kuru, 74:2
Kyasanur Forest disease (KFD), 96:2, 96:3, 96:5

LabID, **14:4**, 15:3–4
laboratory confirmed bloodstream infection (LCBI), 38:8
Laboratory Response Network (LRN), 108:4–5
laboratory services, 108:1–11
    accreditation for, 108:2
    barrier precautions in, 108:6–7
    biohazardous waste and, 108:9–10
    biosafety in, 24:16, 108:2–3
    biosecurity in, 108:4
    BSC in, 108:7–8, **108:8**, **108:9**
    hand hygiene in, 108:9
    HEPA in, 108:7–8
    inspection and certification for, 4:13
    LRN and, 108:4–5
    occupational exposure in, 108:10–11
    phlebotomy in, 108:8–9
    PPE in, 108:6–7
    safety equipment in, 108:6–7
    waste management and, 108:9–10
    work practice controls in, 108:5–6
laboratory testing, 25:1–7
    antibody detection with, **25:3**, 25:3–4
    antigen detection with, 25:2–3, **25:3**
    for biofilm, 70:11–12
    for burns, 38:6
    for *Enterobacteriaceae*, 75:14
    for *Enterococcus*, 76:4–5
    for genital herpes, 91:10
    for gram-negative bacilli, 77:4
    for HIV/AIDS, 81:6–7
    for human papilloma virus, 91:8

laboratory testing *(cont.)*
    for measles, 86:3–4
    for *Neisseria gonorrhoeae*, 91:5–6
    for rabies, 89:3
    for RSV, 90:3
    for rubella, 86:14–15
    for *Staphylococcus aureus*, 93:5–7
    for WNV, 98:3
labor/delivery/recovery/postpartum room (LDRP), 43:2
labor/delivery/recovery room (LDR), 43:2
β-lactam antibiotics, 26:2, **26:2**, 35:8, 37:11–12, 94:7
β-lactamase test, 24:12
Lactobacillus, 41:24–25, 70:12, 72:5
LAF. *See* laminar airflow
LAIV. *See* live-attenuated influenza vaccine
LAL. *See* limulus amebocyte lysate
laminar airflow (LAF), 68:2–3, 114:9
lamivudine, 97:7, 97:12, 101:7
LA-MRSA. *See* livestock-associated methicillin-resistant *Staphylococcus aureus*
Lancefield group D antigen, 76:1
Langerhans cells, 22:6–7
LANs. *See* local area networks
LASA. *See* look-alike/sound-alike
laser in situ keratomileusis (LASIK), 63:1, 63:6
Lassa fever, 96:2
latent tuberculosis infection (LTBI), 40:3–4, 95:5, 95:7–8
latex agglutination, 94:4, 94:6
latex allergies, 68:9
laundry services, 111:1–8
    at ambulatory care centers, 48:7
    in ASCs, 64:9
    in CCCs, 52:5
    in correctional facilities, 51:12–13
    detergents in, 111:6
    EVS and, 107:12
    in LTCFs, 61:8–9
    pediculosis and, 91:15
LBW. *See* low birth weight
LCBI. *See* laboratory confirmed bloodstream infection
LCL. *See* lower control limit
LCMV. *See* lymphocytic choriomeningitis virus
LDR. *See* labor/delivery/recovery room
LDRP. *See* labor/delivery/recovery/postpartum room
LE. *See* leukocyte esterase
LEA29Y, 69:5
Lean methods, 16:6–7
The Leapfrog Group, 17:3
Leavell's levels, 10:4
left ventricular assist devices (LVADs), 35:9–10, 59:3–4
legal issues, 8:1–17
    with antibiotics, 8:9–10
    burden of proof in, 8:2
    cause of action and, 8:2
    with EHR, 8:6
    ethical issues and, 8:12–17
    with fear of disease claims, 8:12
    with HIV, 81:9–10
    with informed consent, 8:13
    with liability, 8:5–8
    with nonpatients, 8:12–13
    obligation to provide care to all and, 8:13–14
    with patient safety, 8:6–7
    strengthening practices to reduce liability, 8:5–8
Legionella, 24:16, 26:5, 41:4, 44:5–6
    SOT and, 45:8
    water and, 115:1, 115:2, 115:4, 115:15–17
Legionella pneumophila, 53:15, 84:1–9, **84:4**
    PFGA for, 115:5
    water and, 84:2, 84:5–8, **84:7**

Legionnaire's disease, 84:3, 96:5
Leishmania, 99:7
leprosy, 96:16
Leptospira, 44:6, 121:11–12
leukemia, 78:6
leukocyte esterase (LE), 25:7, 91:23
leukocytes, 22:6, 25:6
leukocytosis, 35:4
levofloxacin, 26:5, 79B:8, 84:5, 91:4, 93:13
LFTs. *See* liver function tests
LGV. *See* lymphogranuloma venereum
liability, 8:3, 8:5–8
lice, **99:3**, 99:3–5, **99:4**
Life Safety Code (NFPA), 64:9, 116:6
light microscopy, 24:5, 24:9
limulus amebocyte lysate (LAL), 25:6
lincosamides, 26:5
lindane, 91:15, 99:4
linens, 44:4–5, 64:9, 91:15, 111:1–8
    EVS and, 107:12
    in LTCFs, 61:8–9
    VHF and, 96:8
linezolid, 26:6, 76:2, 76:6, 92:7, 93:5, 93:13
lipid A, 75:2
lipoteichoic acid (LTA), 93:8
Listeria, 41:4, 41:14
Listeria monocytogenes, 41:7, 43:6, 63:3, 74:3, 109:2
live-attenuated influenza vaccine (LAIV), 82:4, 100:10
liver function tests (LFTs), 25:5
liver transplantation, 97:3, 97:7, 97:12
livestock-associated methicillin-resistant *Staphylococcus aureus* (LA-MRSA), **93:3**, 93:4, 93:18
LLD. *See* low-level disinfection
Loa loa, 99:7
loaner instruments, 106:15
local area networks (LANs), 6:11
locality rule, 8:4
Logical Observations Identifiers Names and Codes (LOINC), 6:11
long-term acute care hospitals (LTACHs), 62:1–6
    antibiotics in, 62:4
    CMS and, 4:9
    rehabilitation services, 66:1
    sepsis in, 62:4–5
    surveillance in, 62:3
long-term care (LTC), 4:9, 61:1–10, **61:3**, 66:2
    CAUTIs in, 33:9
    Droplet Precautions and, 29:3
    in HHC, 56:2
    HSCT and, 46:10
    with IVDA, 34:16–17
    surveillance and, 11:1
long-term care facilities (LTCFs), 61:1–10
    antimicrobials in, 61:6
    cleaning of, 107:16
    GAS and, 94:2
    TB and, 95:14
look-alike/sound-alike (LASA), 18:8
loop mediated isothermal amplification, 72:3–4
lopinavir, 101:7
low birth weight (LBW), 41:6, 41:13
lower control limit (LCL), 14:5, 14:8
low-level disinfection (LLD), 67:2
LP. *See* lumbar puncture
LRN. *See* Laboratory Response Network
LTA. *See* lipoteichoic acid
LTACHs. *See* long-term acute care hospitals
LTBI. *See* latent tuberculosis infection
LTC. *See* long-term care
LTCFs. *See* long-term care facilities
lumbar puncture (LP), 29:2, 64:8, 74:3, 95:4

methicillin-resistant *Staphylococcus aureus (cont.)*
  burns and, 38:2, 38:7
  CAP and, 36:2
  cefepime and, 26:5
  clindamycin and, 26:5
  CMS and, 4:2
  in correctional facilities, 49:2, 51:10–11
  Deficit Reduction Act and, 9:2
  EVS and, 107:1
  geriatrics and, 40:2, 40:4
  HCP and, 10:7
  hydrogen peroxide for, 31:7
  ICU and, 59:5
  IHI and, 9:2
  immunocompromised hosts and, 23:4
  immunocompromised patients and, 44:7
  Isolation Precautions with, 29:5–6
  β-lactams and, 26:5
  LASIK and, 63:6
  legal issues and, 8:1
  LTACHs and, 62:5
  in LTCFs, 61:7
  molecular genetic methods of identification of, 93:6–7
  neonates and, 41:2, 41:5–6, 41:13
  ophthalmology services and, 63:12
  Panton-Valentine leukocidin of, 22:3
  p charts and, 14:7
  pediatrics and, 42:2, 42:14
  perinatal care and, 43:5
  rehabilitation services and, 66:8
  risk-adjusted comparisons and, 15:3
  Ryan White Comprehensive AIDS Resource Emergency Act of
    1990 and, 54:7
  SOT and, 45:5
  SSIs and, 37:9–10
  SSTIs and, 92:2
  surveillance for, 11:13
  tattoos and, 123:3
  TSS and, 93:7
  typing methods for, 93:7–8
  UV for, 31:9
  vancomycin for, 26:5
methicillin-susceptible *Staphylococcus aureus* (MSSA), 93:2, 93:12
Methylobacterium mesophilicum, 55:2
methylprednisolone, 110:5, 110:7
metronidazole, 26:6, 72:4, 91:18, 91:21
MHAQIP. *See* Maryland Hospital Association Quality Indicator
  Project
MHC. *See* major histocompatibility complex
mhGAP. *See* Mental Health Gap Action Programme
MIC. *See* minimal inhibitory concentration
microbial pathogenicity, **24:15**
  bacterial toxins and, 22:2–3
  CMI and, 22:3–4
  complement system and, 22:6, **22:7**
  host response and, 22:1–8
  humoral immune system and, 22:4–5
  nonspecific host defenses and, 22:5–6
  phagocytic innate cell system and, 22:6–7
microbials
  growth of, USP and, 110:10
  IMD and, 35:3
  in water, **115:4**
microbiological safety index (MSI), 68:8
microscopy. *See also specific types*
  staining for, **24:10**, 24:10–11
Microsporum canis, 78:10
midazolam HCl, 110:3
Middle East respiratory syndrome coronavirus (MERS-CoV), 3:2, 6:4,
  11:12, 120:2

minimal bacterial concentration (MBC), 24:13, 70:7
minimal effective concentration (MEC), 55:4, 106:8
minimal inhibitory concentration (MIC), 24:12, 26:2, 26:10, 70:7
  Candida and, 78:5
  Enterococcus and, 76:3
  for MRSA, 92:2
  for *Neisseria gonorrhoeae*, 91:6
Minimum Data Set (MDS), 4:9
minimum efficiency reporting values (MERV), 114:8
Minimum Standard for Hospitals (ACS), 4:12
minocycline, 75:16
MLST. *See* multilocus sequence typing
MMR. *See* measles, mumps, and rubella vaccine
MMWR. See Morbidity and Mortality Weekly Report
molds, 24:4, 44:6, 45:8, 112:4
molecular diagnostic testing, 25:4
monkeypox, 3:2, 6:4
mononuclear phagocytes, 22:6, 22:7
Montezuma's revenge, 118:2
Moraten, 86:4
Moraxella catarrhalis, 36:2
Morbidity and Mortality Weekly Report (MMWR), 4:8, 117:2
Morbillivirus, 86:1
morphine sulfate, 110:3
motion sickness, 118:1
moxifloxacin, 26:5
MPSV4. *See* polysaccharide meningococcal vaccine
MPV. *See* meningococcal polysaccharide vaccine
MRI. *See* magnetic resonance imaging
MRSA. *See* methicillin-resistant *Staphylococcus aureus*
MRSA Elimination Guide (APIC), 21:8
MS. *See* mass spectrometry
MSDS. *See* Material Safety and Data Sheets
MSI. *See* microbiological safety index
MSSA. *See* methicillin-susceptible *Staphylococcus aureus*
MTB. *See Mycobacterium tuberculosis*
mTOR. *See* mammalian target of rapamycin inhibitor
Muerto Canyon virus, 96:1
multidose vials (MDVs), 110:4, 110:8, 110:9
multidrug-resistant organisms (MDROs), 8:7–8, 17:4, 107:6, 117:3
  ambulatory care centers and, 48:5–6
  in ASCs, 64:5
  burns and, 38:5, 38:7
  Contact Precautions with, 29:3
  geriatrics and, 40:4
  HHC and, 56:2, 56:3
  hospice and, 57:4
  ICU and, 59:2, 59:5–6
  immunocompromised patients and, 44:7–8
  IP and, 110:11
  Isolation Precautions for, 29:5–6, **29:7–8**
  LTACHs and, 62:2
  in LTCFs, 61:7
  occupational health and, 100:12
  oncology and, 44:9
  pediatrics and, 42:2, 42:14–15
  perinatal care and, 43:5
  rehabilitation services and, 66:2, 66:8
  SSTIs and, 92:3
  surveillance for, 11:13, 11:14
multidrug-resistant tuberculosis (MDR-TB), 51:5, 95:2, 95:8
multilocus sequence typing (MLST), 93:8
multiple myeloma, 23:8
multistate fungal meningitis, 110:7
mumps, 86:7–12, **86:9**
  immunizations for, 86:10–11
  occupational health and, 100:9
  pharmacy services and, 110:2
  pregnant HCP and, 104:8–9
  treatment for, 86:9

mupirocin, 26:6
mycobacteria, 24:8–9, 39:8, 91:22
  NTM, 95:15–18, 115:2
Mycobacterium, 121:12–13, 123:4
Mycobacterium chelonae, 115:2
Mycobacterium gordonae, 115:2
Mycobacterium leprae, 96:16
Mycobacterium marinum, 96:16
Mycobacterium tuberculosis (MTB), 4:11, 95:2–15
  dental services and, 53:14
  disinfectants for, 107:6
  EMS and, 54:8
  endoscopy and, 31:8, 55:2
  geriatrics and, 40:5
  immunocompromised host and, 23:4
  postmortem care and, 65:3
  radiation oncology and, 58:2
  SOT and, 45:5
  in surgical services, 68:9
  water and, 115:3
Mycoplasma, 24:3–4, 24:9, 26:5
Mycoplasma genitalium, 91:4
Mycoplasma hominis, 41:16, 43:5, 91:24
Mycoplasma pneumoniae, 25:5, 86:3
mycotic aneurysm, 74:12–13
myiasis, 99:5–6
myocarditis, 82:2

NAAT. *See* nucleic acid amplification test
NADCA. *See* National Air Duct Cleaners Association
Naegleria fowler, 99:7
nafcillin, 26:4, 35:8, 37:11–12
NAP1. *See* North American pulsed-field Type 1
NASA. *See* National Aeronautics and Space Administration
NASBA. *See* nucleic acid sequence-based amplification assay
NaSH. *See* National Surveillance System for Healthcare Workers
Natick Research Laboratories, 109:12
National Accreditation for Healthcare Organizations (NIAHO), 4:10
National Action Plan to Prevent Healthcare-associated Infections: Road Map to Elimination (HHS), 4:2, 6:2, 64:1
National Aeronautics and Space Administration (NASA), 109:12
National Air Duct Cleaners Association (NADCA), 68:2
National Bioterrorism Hospital Preparedness Program, 4:9
National Center for Immunization and Respiratory Diseases, 4:8
National Childhood Immunization Initiative, 86:2, 86:13
National Childhood Vaccine Injury Act (NCVIA), 103:31–32
National Clinicians' Postexposure Prophylaxis Hotline (PEPline), 81:9
National Commission on Correctional Health Care (NCCHC), 51:2
National Committee for Clinical Laboratory Standards (NCCLS), 108:1
National Committee on Quality Assurance (NCQA), 4:13, 114:4
National Electronic Injury Surveillance System (NEISS), 105:1
National Electronic Telecommunications System for Surveillance (NETSS), 117:3
National Fire Protection Association (NFPA), 54:3, 64:9, 114:4, 116:6
National Health and Nutrition Examination Survey (NHANES), 97:8
National Healthcare Safety Network (NHSN), 1:2, 4:7, 6:13, 11:3, 11:11–12, 39:3, 41:3, 68:2
  ASCs and, 64:11
  burns and, 38:1, 42:7
  CAUTIs and, 33:11
  CDI and, 72:4
  CTS and, 42:6
  Enterobacteriaceae and, 75:7
  Enterococcus and, 76:2
  HAI reporting and, 6:24
  healthcare informatics and, 6:2–4
  ICU and, 59:1, **59:2**
  immunocompromised patients and, 44:1

influenza immunizations and, 17:4
  LTACHs and, 62:3
  pediatric SSIs and, 42:3
  performance measures and, 17:2, 17:4, 17:10
  perinatal care and, 43:16
  public health and, 117:2
  rehabilitation services and, 66:2, 66:8
  SIR and, 13:9, 21:2
  SOT and, 45:6
  SSIs and, 37:3, **37:4**, 37:6, 92:4
  VAP and, 36:3, 67:4
National Incident Management System (NIMS), 119:17
National Institute for Occupational Safety and Health (NIOSH), 1:4, 4:3, 4:8, 29:4, 54:3, 114:3, 116:6
National Institutes of Health (NIH), 4:9, 9:5, 70:6, 121:4
National Kidney Foundation, 39:4–5
National Nosocomial Infections Surveillance (NNIS), 1:2, 6:13, 8:5–6, 9:3, 17:2, 18:8
  HAIs and, 4:7
  hysterectomies and, 91:25
  public health and, 117:2
  SSIs and, 37:3
  surgical services and, 68:2
National Notifiable Disease Surveillance System (NNDSS), 84:1
National Patient Safety Foundation (NPSF), 8:12, 18:5, 18:10, 35:3
National Patient Safety Goals (NPSG), 4:1, 8:7, 17:4, 27:2, 68:10
  legal issues and, 8:1
  standard of care and, 8:4
  surveillance and, 21:5
National Practitioner Data Bank, 4:9
National Pressure Ulcer Advisory Panel, 47:8
National Quality Forum (NQF), 4:2, 8:4, 18:3, 18:9, **18:12–13**
  performance measures and, 17:3, 17:7, **17:7**
  Safe Practices for Better Health Care by, 18:10
National Response Framework (NRF), 119:17
National Sanitation Foundation (NSF), 109:15
National STD/HIV Hotline, 91:9, 91:12
National Surveillance System for Healthcare Workers (NaSH), 21:2
natural killer cells (NK), 22:4
natural ventilation (NV), 114:15
NCCHC. *See* National Commission on Correctional Health Care
NCCLS. *See* National Committee for Clinical Laboratory Standards
NCQA. *See* National Committee on Quality Assurance
NCVIA. *See* National Childhood Vaccine Injury Act
necrotizing enterocolitis (NEC), 41:6, 41:7, 41:15
necrotizing fasciitis (NF), 92:5, 92:6–7, 94:3
needlestick injury, 7:7, 8:10, 105:5–6
Needlestick Safety and Prevention Act (NSPA), 7:7, 68:8–9, 105:2
negative predictive value (NPV), 13:19
NEISS. *See* National Electronic Injury Surveillance System
Neisseria gonorrhoeae, 43:4, 91:1, 91:5–7, 91:22–23
  NGU and, 91:4
  ophthalmology services and, 63:3
  QRNG, 91:6
Neisseria meningitidis, 74:3, 74:5, 87:1–5
  Droplet Precautions and, 29:3
  head and neck surgery and, 42:7
  immunization for, 42:12
  pediatrics and, 42:2
nelfinavir, 101:7
neomycin, 26:6, 38:6
neonatal *Chlamydia trachomatis*, 91:4
neonatal intensive care unit (NICU), 41:2, 41:3, 41:4, 111:2, 114:2
neonates, 41:1–25
  BSIs with, 41:12–14
  CNS and, 41:14
  immunization for, 41:23
  immunotherapeutic agents for, 41:23–24
  invasive procedures with, 41:5, 41:18
  prophylaxis for, 41:23

Neonates *(cont.)*
    skin care for, 41:17
    surveillance for, 41:20–21, 41:24
    umbilical cord care for, 41:17
neoplasms, from EBV, 80:9
nephrotic syndrome, 92:2
NETSS. *See* National Electronic Telecommunications System for
        Surveillance
network maps, 3:9
NeuGc. *See* N-glycolylneuraminic acid
neural tube defects, 41:14
neuraminidase inhibitors, 40:5–6, 82:3
neuronal cell xenotransplantation, 69:5
neurosurgery, pediatrics and, 42:6–7
neutropenia, 23:2, 46:2, 78:6
neutrophils, 22:7, 78:5, 78:8
    ANC, 25:6, **25:6**, 29:4
newborn nursery, 41:2
New England Journal of Medicine, 74:13
new variant Creutzfeldt-Jakob disease (nvCJD), 68:7, 73:3, 74:2,
        74:11–12
NFB. *See* necrotizing fasciitis; nonfermentative bacilli
NFPA. *See* National Fire Protection Association
N-glycolylneuraminic acid (NeuGc), 69:4, 69:5
NGU. *See* nongonococcal urethritis
NHANES. *See* National Health and Nutrition Examination Survey
NHs. *See* nursing homes
NHSN. *See* National Healthcare Safety Network
niacin, 47:3
NIAHO. *See* National Accreditation for Healthcare Organizations
NICU. *See* neonatal intensive care unit
Nightingale, Florence, 17:1
NIH. *See* National Institutes of Health
NIMS. *See* National Incident Management System
95 percent CIs, 15:4–5, **15:5**
NIOSH. *See* National Institute for Occupational Safety and Health
nitrate, 39:8
nitroimidazoles, 26:6
NK. *See* natural killer cells
NNDSS. *See* National Notifiable Disease Surveillance System
NNIS. *See* National Nosocomial Infections Surveillance
NNRTIs. *See* non-nucleoside reverse transcriptase inhibitors
Nocardia, 24:10, 45:4
nominal group technique, 16:5
noncritical items, 31:3–4
nonemployees, 102:1–4
nonenterococcal group D *Streptococcus*, 94:10
nonfermentative bacilli (NFB), 77:2
nongonococcal urethritis (NGU), 91:4, 91:18
non-Hodgkin lymphoma, 80:8
non-nucleoside reverse transcriptase inhibitors (NNRTIs), 26:7, 81:8
nontuberculosis mycobacteria (NTM), 95:15–18, 115:2
norepinephrine, 110:3
norfloxacin, 79B:8
normal distribution, **13:5**, 13:5–6
normal flora, 41:2
norovirus, 51:9, 61:5–6, 79A:1–4
North American pulsed-field Type 1 (NAP1), 62:5
North American Society of Packing and Electrophysiology, 50:8
"no touch" methods, for room decontamination, 31:9–10, **31:10**
NPSF. *See* National Patient Safety Foundation
NPSG. *See* National Patient Safety Goals
NPV. *See* negative predictive value
NQF. *See* National Quality Forum
NRF. *See* National Response Framework
NRTIs. *See* nucleoside/nucleotide reverse transcriptase inhibitors
NSF. *See* National Sanitation Foundation
NSPA. *See* Needlestick Safety and Prevention Act
NTM. *See* nontuberculosis mycobacteria
nucleic acid amplification test (NAAT), 26:8, 91:3, 91:5–6, 91:22

    for CDI, 15:3, 72:3–4
    for ophthalmia neonatorum, 91:4
    for WNV, 98:3
nucleic acid hybridization, 88:5, 91:3–4, 91:23
nucleic acid sequence-based amplification assay (NASBA), 80:7
nucleoside/nucleotide reverse transcriptase inhibitors (NRTIs), 81:8,
        101:7
Nursing Home Compare, 17:10
nursing homes (NHs), 9:5
nutrition. *See also* food and nutrition services; malnutrition
    EN, 47:11–12
    geriatrics and, 47:11
    GI tract and, 47:10
    immune system and, 47:1–13
    for infants, 47:10–11
    PJI and, 35:5
    PN, 47:12
        Candida albicans from, 110:3
    wound healing and, 47:8–10
nutritional solution microbe viability, **110:6**
NV. *See* natural ventilation
nvCJD. *See* new variant Creutzfeldt-Jakob disease

OASIS. *See* Outcome and Assessment Information Set
obesity, 47:1–3, **47:3**, 68:10
obligation to provide care to all, 8:13–14
OBRA. *See* Omnibus Budget Reconciliation Act
OBU. *See* opened-but-unused
occupational exposure
    to AIDS, 8:11
    by animals, 121:3
    from blood and body fluids, 105:1–7
    to bloodborne pathogens, 101:1–9
    from catheters, 105:4–5
    in laboratory services, 108:10–11
    management algorithm for, **100:6**
    from needles, 105:5–6
    from percutaneous injuries, 105:1–7, **105:2**, **105:3**
    by pharmacy services, 110:2
    for pregnant HCP, **104:4–5**
    from tattoos, body piercing, and electrolysis, 123:9
Occupational Exposure to Bloodborne Pathogens: Needlestick and
        Other Sharps Injuries (Department of Labor), 7:7
occupational health, 100:1–15
    at ambulatory care centers, 48:7–8
    avian influenza and, 100:13
    BBP and, 100:7
    in emergency management, 119:11
    HBV and, 100:7–8
    HCV and, 100:8
    herpes zoster and, 100:11
    HHC, 56:6–7
    HIV and, 100:8
    influenza and, 100:10–11
    MDROs and, 100:12
    measles and, 100:9
    meningococcal disease and, 100:9
    mumps and, 100:9
    parvovirus and, 100:11
    pediculosis and, 100:9
    pertussis and, 100:9–10
    PPE for, 100:11–12
    RSV and, 100:11–12
    rubella and, 100:9
    SARS and, 100:12–13
    scabies and, 100:9
    smallpox and, 100:12
    Staphylococcus and, 100:12
    TB and, 100:3–7
    VZV and, 100:8

parasites, 99:1–9, 109:2, 121:13
  in correctional facilities, 51:10
  diarrhea from, 79C:1–9, **79C:2**
  eukaryotic, 24:5
  foodborne illnesses and, **83:6–7**
parenteral nutrition (PN), 47:12, 110:3
Pareto charts, 16:6
Parkinson disease, 69:5
paromomycin, 79C:3
paronychia, 92:4
participant observation, 19:4
particle agglutination, **25:3**
Partnership for Patients Hospital Engagement Networks, 1:2
Parvoviridae, 88:1
parvovirus. *See* human parvovirus B19
passive surveillance, 120:5
Pasteur, Louis, 106:1
Pasteurella, 121:11
pasteurizer, 106:4
Path Alliance Registry, 78:7
pathogen-directed therapy, 26:7–8
pathology wastes, 113:3
patient care equipment. *See* medical devices
patient education, 21:6–7
patient management, in emergency management, 119:9–10
Patient Protection and Affordable Care Act (PPACA), 6:5
patient safety, 1:7, 18:1–18
  HAC and, 18:3–4
  human factors and, 18:5–8
  incident reporting and, 18:8–9
  legal issues with, 8:6–7
  measuring, 18:4–185
  medical mistakes and, 18:1–2, **18:2**
  with medical residents, 18:7
  public reporting of, 18:3
  surveillance and, 11:11
Patient Safety and Quality Improvement Act of 2005, 18:3
Patient Safety Event Taxonomy (PSET), 18:3
Patient Safety Indicators (PSIs), 18:2
patient safety organizations (PSOs), 18:3
Patient Safety Rule, 18:3
pay-for-performance, 1:1
PBPs. *See* pharmacy bulk packages
PBS. *See* painful bladder syndrome
PCD. *See* process challenge device
PCEC. *See* purified chick embryo cell vaccine
p charts, 14:7
PCI. *See* percutaneous coronary interventions
PCMX. *See* chloroxylenol
PCP. *See* Pneumocystis jiroveci pneumonia
PCR. *See* polymerase chain reaction
PCV. *See* pneumococcal conjugate vaccine
PD. *See* positive deviance
PDCA. *See* plan-do-check-act
PDSA. *See* Plan, Do, Study, Act
PDSN. *See* public switched data network
PE. *See* protective environment; pulmonary embolism
PEC. *See* product evaluation committee
pediatrics, 42:1–15
  antibiotic resistance and, 42:14–15
  behavioral health and, 49:4–5
  bioterrorism and, 120:7–8
  burns and, 42:7–8
  cardiac catheterization in, 50:2
  congenital disorders and, 42:3, **42:5**
  CTS and, 42:3, 42:6
  disaster management and, 120:7–8, 120:12
  emergency management and, 119:15
  immune system and, 42:2, **42:2**
  immunizations and, 42:12–13

  immunodeficiencies and, 42:2–3, **42:3**, **42:4**
  influenza and, 82:7
  Lyme disease and, 85:5
  pets and, 42:11, **42:11**
  PVB19 and, 88:2
  SSIs and, 42:3–7
  surveillance in, 42:11–14
  toys and, 42:10, **42:10**
  UTIs and, 42:9
  VAE and, 42:9
  VAP and, 42:9
pediculosis, 91:14–15, **99:3**, 99:3–5, 100:9
Pediculosis capitis, 51:10, 99:3–5
Pediculosis corporis, 99:4
Pediculus pubis, 99:4
PEL. *See* primary effusion lymphoma
pelvic inflammatory disease (PID), 91:3
pelvic pain syndrome, 91:1
pelvic radiation therapy, 58:5
penicillin, 26:3–4
  Aspergillus and, 78:7
  for *Bacillus cereus*, 79B:15
  for burns, 38:7
  Campylobacter and, 79B:11
  Enterococcus and, 76:3
  for GAS, 94:3
  for group B *Streptococcus*, 94:4
  Staphylococcus aureus and, 93:2–3
penicillin G, 87:3–4, 91:17, 94:7, 94:8
penicillin-susceptible *Staphylococcus aureus* (PSSA), 26:4, 93:2, 93:12
Penicillium, 114:2
Penicillium marneffei, 23:4
pentostatin, 23:8, 110:4
PEP. *See* post-exposure prophylaxis
PEPline. *See* National Clinicians' Postexposure Prophylaxis Hotline
PEPS. *See* Price Productivity Environmental Preference Survey
peracetic acid, 106:4
percentiles, 11:5, 13:3–4
percutaneous biliary drainage, 60:9
percutaneous coronary interventions (PCI), 50:2
percutaneous endoluminal stenting, 60:5–6
percutaneous injuries, 105:1–7, **105:2**, **105:3**
percutaneous nephrostomy, 60:8–9
performance improvement, 17:10
  in ASCs, 64:2–4
  for EVS, 107:21
  in waste management, 113:9
performance improvement teams, 16:2–3, 17:3–4
Performance Measurement Coordinating Council (PMCC), 4:13, 4:14
performance measures, 17:1–11
  for data analysis, 17:6–7
  data collection and, 17:9–10, **17:10**
  evaluation of existing measures, 17:7–8, **17:8**
  NQF and, 17:7, **17:7**
  population for, 17:5–6, 17:8–9
  for QI, 17:10
  risk-adjusted comparisons and, 17:5–6, 17:7
  sample size and, 17:6
  selection of, 17:4–10
  stratification and, 17:7
  types of, 17:5
pericarditis, 82:2
perinatal care, 43:1–18, **43:5**
  cleaning in, 43:3
  disinfection and sterilization in, 43:3
  HDV and, 97:11
  immunizations and, 43:4–5
  intrapartum period, 43:11–14

polyarthritis, 88:3–4
polygalactin, 37:10
polymerase chain reaction (PCR), 22:3, 24:5, 24:8, 25:4, 26:7, 70:11, 72:3–4, 75:14, 79A:5, 79B:3, 80:7, 80:10, 84:5, 88:4, 88:5, 91:5, 95:4, 97:10, 99:2. *See also* reverse transcription polymerase chain reaction
   for adenovirus, 79A:8
   for astroviruses, 79A:7
   for *Candida*, 78:2, 78:4
   for chancroid, 91:13–14
   for *Cyclospora cayetanensis*, 79C:7
   for EBV, 80:9
   for genital herpes, 91:11
   for HDV, 97:12
   for influenza, 82:6
   for LGV, 91:22
   for pertussis, 71:3
   for rubella, 86:15
   for *Staphylococcus aureus*, 93:6
polymerase inhibitors, 97:10
polymethylmethacrylate (PMMA), 60:9–10
polymorphonuclear (PMN), 22:6, 25:6, 93:9
polymyxin, 26:6, 39:5, 75:2
polysaccharide meningococcal vaccine (MPSV4), 87:4
Pontiac fever, 84:3–4
population
   gram-negative bacilli and, 77:4
   for HHC, 56:4
   in inferential statistics, 13:12
   for mumps, 86:11
   performance measures and, 17:5–6, 17:8–9
   research study design and, 20:1
   in surveillance, 11:3, 11:5
porcine endogenous retroviruses (PERVs), 69:7
Porphyromonas gingivalis, 70:7
portable dialysis, 39:9–10
portal of entry/exit, 10:7, **10:7**, 10:8, **10:8**, 21:3–5
posaconazole, 23:8, 26:7, 38:7, 78:6, 78:9
positive deviance (PD), 3:8–9, 5:5, **5:5**
positive predictive value (PPV), 13:19
positivism, 19:2
postacute care (PAC), 66:1
post-exposure prophylaxis (PEP), 101:1, 120:11–12, **120:14**
   for HAV, 97:4
   for HBV, **103:10**, 104:6
   for HCV, 97:11, 101:5
   for HIV, 81:9, 101:6–8, **101:7**, 104:8
   for rabies, 89:1, 89:2, 89:3, 89:4, **89:4**
   for rubella, 86:17
   for VZV, 104:12
postmortem care, 57:5, 65:1–5, 65:2, 65:4, 119:14, 120:19
postpartum infection, 43:2, 43:16–18, **43:17**
postpartum period, 43:11–14
posttransplant lymphoproliferative disorder (PTLD), 45:4, 46:5, 80:8, 80:9
posttraumatic stress disorder (PTSD), 119:7
potassium hydroxide (KOH), 25:2
Pott disease, 95:4
povidone-iodine ointment, 39:5
powered air-purifying respirators (PAPR), 51:7, 100:7
PPACA. *See* Patient Protection and Affordable Care Act
PPD. *See* purified protein derivative
PPE. *See* personal protective equipment
PPM. *See* permanent pacemakers
PPS. *See* prospective payment system
PPSV. *See* pneumococcal polysaccharide vaccine
PPV. *See* positive predictive value
PR. *See* interferon plus ribavirin
PRECEDE/PROCEED, 5:2
preconception care, 43:4

predisposing factors, 5:2, **5:3**
pre-event messaging, 119:21
Preferred Reporting Items for Systematic Reviews and Meta-Analyses (PRISMA), 20:3
pregnancy. *See also* perinatal care
   BV and, 91:20–21
   Chlamydia trachomatis and, 91:4
   in correctional facilities, 51:12
   disaster management and, 120:8
   donovanosis and, 91:22
   emergency management and, 119:16
   genital herpes and, 91:12–13
   genital warts and, 91:8–9
   group B *Streptococcus* and, 94:4
   HBV immunization and, 97:7
   HEV and, 97:12, 97:13
   HIV and, 81:8
   human papilloma virus and, 91:6–7
   immunization and, 43:5, 103:5, **118:10**
   influenza and, 82:7, **82:7**
   measles and, 86:3
   pediculosis and, 91:14
   pertussis and, 71:5
   PVB19 and, 88:3, 88:4
   rubella in, 86:14, 86:15–16
   SARS and, 120:8
   syphilis and, 91:16, 91:17
   T. vaginalis and, 91:18
   travel health and, 118:5
   UTIs in, 33:5–6
pregnant HCP, 100:12, 104:1–13, **104:2**
   Airborne Precautions and, 29:4
   chickenpox and, 104:12
   CMV and, 104:3–6
   HAV and, 104:6
   HBV and, 104:6
   HCV and, 104:7
   HIV and, 104:7–8
   HSV and, 104:7
   human papilloma virus and, 104:8
   immunization for, 104:2–3, **104:3**
   influenza and, 104:8
   measles and, 104:8–9
   mumps and, 104:8–9
   occupational exposure for, **104:4–5**
   pertussis and, 104:9–10
   rubella and, 104:8–9
   smallpox and, 104:10
   syphilis and, 104:11
   TB and, 104:11
   Tdap and, 104:10
   VZV and, 104:11–12
   wound management for, 104:10
pre-market approval (PMA), 7:6
premature rupture of membranes (PROM), 43:12
prenatal care, 43:4
preseptal cellulitis, 63:3
pressure ulcers, 18:3, 47:8, **47:8**, 92:5
Prevention of Nosocomial Infections and Cost Effectiveness (PNICE), 9:3–5, **9:4**
Prevotella, 92:5
Prevotella intermedia, 70:7
Price Productivity Environmental Preference Survey (PEPS), 3:7
primaquine, 26:7
primary effusion lymphoma (PEL), 80:10
Principles of Epidemiology in Public Health Practice: An Introduction to Applied Epidemiology and Biostatistics, 11:2
prion protein scrapie (PrPsc), 73:2
prions, 68:7, 73:1–13, 74:12. *See also specific infections*
   foodborne diseases and, 83:9

quality assurance (QA), 43:15
quality assurance performance improvement (QAPI), 64:2
Quality Check website, 17:3
quality improvement (QI), 1:5, 16:1–8
    FMEA and, 16:1, 16:4
    gap analysis and, 16:2, **16:3**
    goal-directed checklists and, 16:5
    IT and, 6:4, **6:4**
    PDSA and, 16:1, **16:7**, 16:7–8
    performance improvement teams and, 16:2–3
    performance measures for, 17:10
    process control charts and, 16:5–6
    RCA and, 16:2–3
    SPC and, 14:1–2, 16:5–6
    strategic plan for, 16:2
    SWOT and, **16:4**, 16:4–7
quality indicator, 8:4, 36:3
Quality Interagency Coordination Task Force, 4:9
QualityNet, 37:9, **37:9**
quality waste, 16:1
Quantiferon-TB test, 51:6y, 100:5, **100:6**
quantiles, 13:3–4
quantitative fit test (QNFT), 100:7
quarantine, 119:11, 120:14–16, **120:15**
quinine, 26:7
quinolones, 76:3, 79B:8, 84:5, 93:13
quinupristin, 26:5
quinupristin/dalfopristin, 76:6

rabies, 89:1–6, 118:3, 121:9
    immunization for, 118:7–8, **118:8**
    management in animals, 89:3
    management in humans, 89:4
    Negri bodies for, 24:5
    testing animals for, 89:3
    travel health and, 118:7–8, **118:8**
rabies immunoglobulin (RIG), 89:2
radiation-induced colitis, 58:5
radiation oncology, 58:1–5
radioactive materials, 113:8–9
radiography, in dental services, 53:16
radioimmunoassay (RIA), 25:3, 79A:3
RADT. *See* rapid antigen detection test
Ralstonia picketti, 12:7–8, 77:4
RAM. *See* random-access memory
random-access memory (RAM), 6:11, 6:12
random error, 10:2–3
randomized clinical trials (RCTs), 20:3
range, in descriptive statistics, 13:4
rapid antigen detection test (RADT), 94:2
rapid fluorescent focus inhibition test (RFFIT), 89:4
rapid influenza diagnostic tests (RIDTs), 82:3
rapid plasma reagin (RPR), 91:16
rapid protein reagin (RPR), 25:1
rapid test, 81:7, 91:18, 96:6, 97:13
rate bite fever, 121:12
rates
    in descriptive statistics, 13:6–7
    in surveillance, 11:3, 11:4
ratio, 11:34, 13:6–7
RBC. *See* red blood cells
RCA. *See* root cause analysis
RCRA. *See* Resource Conservation and Recovery Act
RCS. *See* respiratory care services
RCTs. *See* randomized clinical trials
RDBMS. *See* relational database management system
rDNA. *See* ribosomal DNA
read-only memory (ROM), 6:11, 6:12
Real-time Outbreak Surveillance (RODS), 82:7
reasonable care standard, 8:3–4

receptor-mediated hemagglutination (RHA), 88:67
recombinant influenza vaccine (RIV), 82:4
recycling, 113:6–7
red blood cells (RBC), 25:5–6, 25:7, 88:2
    transfusion of, from pig, 69:6
refrigerators, 110:9, 112:7–8
regulated medical waste (RMW), 4:11
rehabilitation impairment group codes (RIC), 66:8
rehabilitation services, 66:1–13
    bladder management and, 66:9–11
    bowel management and, 66:11–12
    discharge planning in, 66:13
    geriatrics and, 66:9
    hand hygiene in, 66:5
    PPE in, 66:5
    respiratory therapy in, 66:12
    skin and, 66:12
    spinal cord injuries and, 66:9
    surveillance in, 66:7–9
Reiter syndrome, 91:1
relational database management system (RDBMS), 6:11
relative humidity (RH), 114:9–10
relative risk (RR), **13:9**, 13:9–10, **13:10**
reliability
    in qualitative research methods, 19:5
    science, 18:5
    testing, 13:19
REMATCH trial, 35:10
renal failure, 82:2
REPLACE, 50:4
reprocessing
    in ambulatory care centers, 48:6
    cleaning and, 31:6
    in dental services, 53:1–2, 53:9–16
    with dialysis, 39:11–12
    endoscopy and, 55:2–4
    postmortem care and, 65:2
    of SUD, 32:1–3
Research and Special Programs Administration (RSPA), 4:11–12
research study design, 20:1–5
    for analytic studies, 20:1
    for case-control studies, **20:2**, 20:2–3
    for cohort studies, **20:2**, 20:3
    for cross-sectional studies, 20:1–2
    evaluating published studies, 20:4–5
    for experimental clinical studies, **20:2**, 20:3
    population and, 20:1
    for RCTs, 20:3
    for systematic reviews, 20:3, **20:4**
resistance factors (R factors), 26:11–12
Resource Conservation and Recovery Act (RCRA), 4:10
respiratory care services (RCS), 67:1–5
    in rehabilitation services, 66:12
    VAP and, 67:1, 67:4–6
respiratory distress syndrome, 38:5, 96:5
    ARDS, 38:9
respiratory hygiene, 28:2, 29:2, 48:4
respiratory syncytial virus (RSV), 90:1–5
    Contact Precautions with, 29:2
    ELISA for, 24:5
    HSCT and, 46:2, 46:5, 46:10
    IFNs for, 26:7
    immunization for, 42:13
    LTCFs and, 61:4
    neonates and, 41:10, 41:23–24
    occupational health and, 100:11–12
    pediatrics and, 42:2
    pregnant HCP and, 104:2
    surveillance for, 11:12
    virulence of, 22:2

respiratory tract infections (RTIs), 52:2–3, 61:4–5, 75:8–9. *See also specific diseases*
restriction fragment length polymorphisms (RFLPs), 24:8
retinitis, 63:4, 80:2, 80:7
reverse osmosis (RO), 39:6, 39:10, 115:2
reverse transcription polymerase chain reaction (RT-PCR), 41:10, 79A:1, 97:10
   for B virus, 121:7–8
   for influenza, 82:3, 82:6
   for RSV, 90:3
Reye's syndrome, 82:2
R factors. *See resistance factors*
RFFIT. *See rapid fluorescent focus inhibition test*
RFLPs. *See restriction fragment length polymorphisms*
RH. *See relative humidity*
RHA. *See receptor-mediated hemagglutination*
rhadinovirus, 80:10
rheumatic fever, 94:2–3
rhinosinusitis, 70:8, **70:8**
Rhizopus, 111:2, 114:2
Rhodotorula, 78:12
RIA. *See radioimmunoassay*
ribavirin, 26:7, 41:10, 86:4, 90:3, 96:7, **96:7**, 97:10
ribonucleic acid (RNA), 22:2, 24:2, 81:3, 86:8, 86:12
   CMV and, 80:7
   measles and, 86:1
   RFLPs for, 24:8
   TB and, 95:5
ribosomal DNA (rDNA), 70:11, 76:1
RIC. *See rehabilitation impairment group codes*
Rickettsia, 24:4, 24:9, 121:9–10
Rickettsia rickettsiae, 22:2
RIDTs. *See rapid influenza diagnostic tests*
rifampin (RIF), 26:6, 35:11, 87:5, 92:7, 93:12, 95:6, 95:7–8
rifapentine, 95:8
rifaximin, 79B:4
Rift Valley fever (RVF), 96:2, 96:3, 96:5–6
RIG. *See rabies immunoglobulin*
rimantadine, 40:5
ringworm, 78:10
rinse-sampling, 24:16
risk-adjusted comparisons, 15:1–6
   CDI and, 15:3–4, **15:4**
   MRSA and, 15:3
   performance measures and, 17:5–6, 17:7
   SSIs and, 15:2–3, **15:3**
risk management, ethical issues with, 8:15–16
risk ratio, **13:9**, 13:9–10, **13:10**
ritonavir, 101:7
RIV. *See recombinant influenza vaccine*
RMW. *See regulated medical waste*
RNA. *See ribonucleic acid*
RNA interference (RNAi), 69:7
RO. *See reverse osmosis*
Rocky Mountain spotted fever, 22:2, 25:7
RODS. *See Real-time Outbreak Surveillance*
ROM. *See read-only memory; rupture of membranes*
root cause analysis (RCA), 16:2–3, 18:2, 18:11–13, **18:14–17**, 112:11
Rotarix, 79A:5
RotaTeq, 79A:5
rotavirus, 41:11, 41:15, 42:12, 42:13, 45:3, 79A:4–7, **79A:6**
RPR. *See rapid plasma reagin; rapid protein reagin*
RR. *See relative risk*
RSPA. *See Research and Special Programs Administration*
RSV. *See respiratory syncytial virus*
RTIs. *See respiratory tract infections*
RT-PCR. *See reverse transcription polymerase chain reaction*
rubella
   clinical manifestations of, 86:13–14

   immunization for, 43:5
   laboratory testing for, 86:14–15
   neonates and, 41:4
   occupational health and, 100:9
   pharmacy services and, 110:2
   pregnant HCP and, 104:8–9
   treatment for, 86:15
rubeola. *See measles*
Rubivirus, 86:12
rule based errors, 18:5, **18:6**
run charts, **14:3**, 14:3–5, **14:4**, 16:6
rupture of membranes (ROM), 43:2, 43:12
RVF. *See Rift Valley fever*
Ryan White Comprehensive AIDS Resource Emergency Act of 1990, 54:1, 54:2, **54:2**, 54:6–7, **54:8**, 54:8–9

Saccharomyces, 70:12
Saccharomyces boulardii, 72:5
safe injection practices, 28:3, 29:2, 48:2–3, 50:8, 64:7–8
Safe Medical Device Act of 1990 (SMDA), 4:9
Safe Practices for Better Health Care (NQF), 18:10
Safety Attitudes Questionnaire (SAQ), 18:4
Safety Checklist for Surgical Teams, 68:10
SAGES. *See American Society of Colon and Rectal Surgeons*
Saksenaea vasiformis, 78:10–11
SAL. *See sterility assurance level*
salicylic acid, 99:3
Salmonella, 10:8, 61:8, 75:11–12, 83:1
   for bioterrorism, 75:14, 120:2
   dental services and, 53:14
   diarrhea from, 79B:4–6
   in FNS, 109:2
   in laundry, 111:2
   neonates and, 41:4, 41:15
Salmonella typhi, 10:7, 10:8, 23:2
sample, 13:12–13
   distribution, 13:13
   in qualitative research methods, 19:3–4
   size, 13:13, 17:6
   for special environmental testing, 24:16
Sapporo-like viruses (SLVs), 79A:1
SAQ. *See Safety Attitudes Questionnaire*
saquinavir, 101:7
Sarcoptes scabiei, 91:2, 91:15–16, 99:1–3, **99:2**
SARE. *See self-achievement recertification examination*
SARS. *See severe acute respiratory syndrome*
Saunders, Cicely, 57:1
SBA. *See serum bactericidal antibody*
scabies, 91:2, 91:15–16, 99:1–3, **99:2**, 100:9
scalpels, 105:6
scanning electron microscopy (SEM), 24:9
scarlet fever, 94:2
Scedosporium, 78:10
Scedosporium apiospermum, 26:7
Schistosoma, 99:8
Scientific Registry of Transplant Recipients (SRTR), 2:5
SCIP. *See Surgical Care Improvement Project*
scleritis, 63:4
SCN. *See special care nursery*
SCOPE. *See Surveillance and Control of Pathogens of Epidemiological Importance*
scope-of-work (SoW), 68:11
SCT. *See social cognitive theory*
SCV. *See small colony variant Staphylococcus aureus*
SDVs. *See single-dose vials*
SEA. *See sentinel event alert*
selenium, 47:8
self-achievement recertification examination (SARE), 2:6
SEM. *See scanning electron microscopy; standard error of the mean*
   semicritical items, 31:2–4

Semmelweiss, Ignaz, 43:1
SENIC. *See* Study on the Efficacy of Nosocomial Infection Control
sentinel event alert (SEA), 18:7, 18:11–13, 106:16
sepsis, 34:3–4, 41:14, 62:4–5, 87:2, 94:4
septicemia, 34:6–8, 75:8, 75:12, 110:3
serious reportable events (SREs), 18:9
serious safety events (SSEs), 18:9
Serratia, 33:3, 41:4, 110:3
Serratia marcescens, 55:2, 110:4, 110:5–7, 110:7
serum bactericidal antibody (SBA), 87:4
SEs. *See* staphylococcal enterotoxins
severe acute respiratory syndrome (SARS), 3:2, 4:2, 9:2, 28:4, 29:3,
    54:3, 79A:8, 100:12–13, 120:8
  disinfectants for, 107:6
  Isolation Precautions and, 29:6
  IT for, 6:4
  public health and, 117:1–2
  surveillance for, 11:12
sexually transmitted infections (STIs), 91:1–26, **91:24**. *See also*
    specific infections
  in correctional facilities, 51:2, 51:3, 51:7–8
  Entamoeba histolytica as, 79C:3
  gynecology and, 91:3–25
  HIV and, 91:23–24
  mental illness and, 49:1
  NAAT for, 26:8
  patient safety and, 8:7
  perinatal care and, 43:4
  from protozoa, 99:7
  trends for, 91:17–18
SGNA. *See* Society of Gastroenterology Nurses and Associates
sharps, 48:3, 56:3–4, 58:3–4, 65:3, 105:1–7
  in correctional facilities, 51:4
  off-label use and, 7:7
  waste management and, 113:2–3
SHEA. *See* Society for Healthcare Epidemiology of America
Shewhart, Walter, 14:1
shiga toxin-producing *Escherichia coli* (STEC), 109:2
Shigella, 47:3, 52:2, 75:11, 79B:6–9, 121:12
Shigella sonnei, 10:3–4
shingles. *See* herpes zoster
shock, 94:2, 96:5
  DSS, 96:5
  TSS, 10:4, 86:3, 92:2, 93:7, 94:3
short-chain fatty acids, 22:5
Sigal, Leonard, 85:5
single-dose vials (SDVs), 110:4, 110:8
single-use devices (SUD), 7:7, 50:8, 55:5, 64:7, 68:6
  aseptic technique and, 30:3
  in dental services, 53:2
  reprocessing of, 32:1–3
Sin Nombre virus (SNV), 96:1
sinusitis, 70:8, **70:8**, 74:10
SIR. *See* standardized infection ratio
SIRS. *See* systemic inflammatory response syndrome
Six Sigma, 16:6–7
skewness, 13:6, **13:6**
skill based errors, 18:5, **18:6**
skilled nursing facility (SNF), 66:2
skin and soft tissue infections (SSTIs), 92:1–8
  animals and, 92:5
  antisepsis for, aseptic technique and, 30:3
  cardiac catheterization and, 50:5
  group B *Streptococcus* and, 94:4
  IMD and, 35:12
  in immunocompromised host, 23:3–4, 92:7
  LTCFs and, 61:5
  Lyme disease and, 85:4
  necrotizing fasciitis and, 92:6–7
  NTM and, 96:16

radiation oncology and, 58:4–5
  rehabilitation services and, 66:12
  SSIs and, 92:4–5
  Staphylococcus aureus and, 93:9
  surgical services and, 68:5
  trauma and, 92:5
  treatment for, 92:7
SLVs. *See* Sapporo-like viruses
Small, Bonnie, 14:1
small colony variant (SCV) *Staphylococcus aureus*, 93:2
smallpox, 29:3, 118:10
  immunization for, 103:21–24, 118:10
  occupational health and, 100:12
  pregnant HCP and, 104:10
smart networks, 3:9
SMDA. *See* Safe Medical Device Act of 1990
smoke inhalation injury, 38:3
smoking, 23:2, 35:5, 36:3–4, 45:8
SMR. *See* standardized mortality rate
SNF. *See* skilled nursing facility
SNOMED. *See* Systematized Nomenclature of Medicine
SNS. *See* Strategic National Stockpile
SNV. *See* Sin Nombre virus
SOAR. *See* state-of-the-art report
social cognitive theory (SCT), 5:4, **5:4**
Social Security Act, dialysis and, 39:3
Society for Healthcare Epidemiology of America (SHEA), 1:4, 1:6,
    9:5, 17:2, 49:3, 49:7, 55:2, 70:9, 76:8–9
  A Compendium of Strategies to Prevent Healthcare-Associated
    Infections in Acute Care Hospitals by, 4:14
  Enterobacteriaceae and, 75:2
  HIV and, 81:9
  VAP and, 67:4
Society of Gastroenterology Nurses and Associates (SGNA), 55:2
soft tissue. *See* skin and soft tissue infections
software, 6:7–6:9, 6:12
solid organ transplantation (SOT), 45:1–9
  Aspergillus and, 78:7
  BSE and, 73:3–4
  Candida and, 78:3
  candidate screening for, 45:2, **45:2**, **45:3**
  CMV and, 80:6
  donor screening for, 45:2, **45:2**
  EBV and, 80:8
  education for, 45:8
  fungi and, 45:5, **45:5**
  herpes virus and, 80:3
  immunizations and, 45:3
  immunocompromised patients and, 44:2
  immunosuppressive agents for, **45:4**
  storage of organs and tissues, 45:8
  viruses and, **45:5**, 45:5–6
  water and, 44:5
  WNV and, 98:3
SOPs. *See* standard operating procedures
SOT. *See* solid organ transplantation
Southern blot analysis, 24:8
SoW. *See* scope-of-work
SP. *See* sterile processing
Spaulding, Earle H., 31:1
Spaulding classification, 67:2
SPC. *See* statistical process control
special care nursery (SCN), 41:2
special environmental testing, 24:16
special needs populations, emergency management and, 119:15
specificity, 10:3, 11:3, 13:19, **13:19**
specimen collection, 24:14, **24:14**, 33:4
spinal cord injuries, 33:9–10, 66:9
spinal epidural abscess, 74:2, 74:10–11, **74:11**
spinal fusion, 42:7

Steam *(cont.)*
    IUSS, 68:6–7, 106:1, 106:14–15
    supply system, 112:7
STEC. *See* shiga toxin-producing *Escherichia coli*
Steere, Allen, 85:1
steering committee, 7:4
Stenotrophomonas, 33:3, 34:17, 41:4, 46:3
Stenotrophomonas maltophilia, 26:6, 77:2, 77:3, 77:4, 115:6
sterile endophthalmitis, 63:4
sterile processing (SP), 106:1–17, **106:3–4**
    CJD and, 106:16
    decontamination area for, **106:5**, 106:5–7
    inventory tracking in, 106:10
    loaner instruments and, 106:15
    point of use and, 106:5
    PPE and, 106:5–6, **106:6**
    preparation and packing in, 106:8–10
    prions and, 106:16
    product identification and traceability in, 106:10
    quality control in, 106:11
    storage and shelf life in, 106:16
    transportation and, 106:5
    TSEs and, 106:16
sterile technique, 30:3
sterility assurance level (SAL), 68:6, 106:4
sterilization. *See* disinfection and sterilization
sterilizer, 106:11
    steam, gravity-displacement, 106:4
STIs. *See* sexually transmitted infections
Strategic National Stockpile (SNS), 120:11
Strengthening the Reporting of Observational Studies in Epidemiology (STROBE), 20:1
Strengths, Weaknesses, Opportunities, Threats (SWOT), **16:4**, 16:4–7
Streptococcus, 24:2, 94:1–10, **94:4**, 110:7
    body piercing and, 123:4
    Enterococcus and, 76:1
    LTCFs and, 61:4
    vancomycin for, 26:5
Streptococcus pneumoniae, 22:2, 23:5, 26:4, 26:9, 41:7, 94:6–8
    CAP and, 36:2
    geriatrics and, 40:4
    head and neck surgery and, 42:7
    immunization for, 23:6, 42:12
    influenza and, 82:2
    meningitis and, 74:3, 74:4
    ophthalmology services and, 63:3
    pediatrics and, 42:2
Streptococcus pyogenes, 22:2, 82:2
Streptococcus viridans, 46:3, 94:8–9
streptogramins, 26:5
streptomycin, 79B:6
streptozocin, 110:4
stress incontinence, 33:3
STROBE. *See* Strengthening the Reporting of Observational Studies in Epidemiology
Strongyloides, 46:5
Strongyloides stercoralis, 99:7
structured query language (SQL), 6:11
Study on the Efficacy of Nosocomial Infection Control (SENIC), 1:2, 1:6, 4:2, 9:1, 9:3, 9:7, 11:1, 17:2, 21:5, 37:3
subacute sclerosing panencephalitis (SSPE), 86:3
suctioning, 67:3–4
SUD. *See* single-use devices
sulfate, 39:8
sulfonamides, 79B:6, 87:3
surge capacity, 119:7, 120:17–18
Surgical Care Improvement Project (SCIP), 17:3, 17:5, 35:11, 35:13, 37:8–9, 37:10, 68:3
surgical services, 68:1–12

air quality in, 68:2–3
anesthesia in, 68:6
aseptic technique in, 68:8
attire in, 68:4–5
disinfection and sterilization in, 68:6–7
environmental cleaning in, 68:5–6
HVAC and, 114:2, 114:13
interdisciplinary collaboration in, 68:11
SSIs and, 68:10–11
traffic control in, 68:3–4
TSEs and, 68:7–8
UTIs and, 33:9, **33:10**
ventilation in, 68:2–3
surgical site infections (SSIs), 4:2, 6:2, 6:9, 37:1–12, **37:3**, **37:4**, **37:6**
    in ASCs, 64:5
    CDA for, 6:3
    with cesarean section, **43:16**
    Deficit Reduction Act and, 9:2
    delayed closure for, 37:10
    Enterobacteriaceae, 75:9
    Enterococcus, 76:8
    gynecology and, 91:25
    as HAC, 18:4
    ICU and, 59:1, 59:5
    IMD and, 35:3, 35:11–12
    neonates and, 41:15–16
    NTM and, 95:16
    patient safety and, 18:2, 18:11
    pediatrics and, 42:3–7
    performance measures for, 17:4
    PJI and, 35:5
    process measures for, 17:5
    risk-adjusted comparisons and, 15:2–3, **15:3**
    SIR for, **13:9**, 37:6
    skin and, 92:4–5
    surgical services and, 68:2, 68:10–11
    surveillance for, **37:4**, 37:4–7, **37:5**
    total house surveillance for, 11:5
    wound management for, 37:12
surveillance, 11:1–14
    for antimicrobials, 26:12
    in ASCs, 64:3–4
    behavioral health and, 49:9
    benchmarks for, 11:10–11
    for bioterrorism, 11:12, 120:5
    for burns, 38:3–5
    for CAUTIs, 33:11
    in correctional facilities, 51:6y, 51:12
    in emergency management, 119:10
    for emerging infectious diseases, 11:12
    in EMS, 54:16
    environmental sampling in, 11:12
    for HAIs, 1:7, 11:1
    for HHC, 56:4
    for hospice, 57:4–5
    in ICU, 59:2
    immunocompromised patients and, 44:8
    for influenza, 82:7–8
    interpretive surveillance report and, 11:8
    IT for, 11:10
    in LTACHs, 62:3
    in LTCFs, 61:7
    mandatory and public reporting and, 11:13
    for MDROs, 11:13
    methodologies in, 11:5
    for MRSA, 93:14
    for *Neisseria gonorrhoeae*, 91:6
    for neonates, 41:20–21, 41:24
    new developments in, 11:13

NHSN and, 11:11–12
in nonhospital healthcare settings, 11:10
patient safety and, 8:7, 11:11
in pediatrics, 42:11–14
perinatal care and, 43:16–18
for pneumonia, 36:3, 36:4
postmortem care and, 65:4
program design for, 11:5–9
program evaluation for, 11:9
psychiatric patients and, 49:6
public health and, 11:12, 117:3
purposes for, 11:2
in rehabilitation services, 66:7–9
for SSIs, **37:4**, 37:4–7, **37:5**
syndromic, 6:4–5, 120:6–7, **120:7**
for TB, 51:6y
for VAE, 67:5
for VAP, 67:5
Surveillance and Control of Pathogens of Epidemiological Importance
    (SCOPE), 76:3
sustained viral response (SVR), 97:10
SV. *See* stated value
SVR. *See* sustained viral response
swine influenza, 3:2, 6:4, 82:3
switch therapy, 26:9
SWOT. *See* Strengths, Weaknesses, Opportunities, Threats
syndromic surveillance, 6:4–5, 120:6–7, **120:7**
synergy testing, 24:13, 26:9
syphilis, 25:1, 43:4, 85:6, 91:2, 91:16–17, 104:11
Systematized Nomenclature of Medicine (SNOMED), 6:11
systemic inflammatory response syndrome (SIRS), 62:4–5
systemic vasculitis, 88:5

TA. *See* teichoic acid
TAC. *See* transient aplastic crisis
TACE. *See* transarterial chemoembolization
Taenia, 99:7
tapeworms, 99:7
TASS. *See* toxic anterior segment syndrome
tattoos, 123:1–9
    occupational exposure from, 123:9
TAVR. *See* transcatheter aortic valve replacement
TB. *See* tuberculosis
TBSA. *See* total body surface area
TCA. *See* trichloacetic acid
T-cell depleting agents, **45:4**
TCT. *See* tracheal cytotoxin
Tdap. *See* tetanus-diphtheria-pertussis vaccination
team style classroom setting, 3:6
TEE. *See* total energy expenditure; transesophageal echocardiogra-
    phy
teichoic acid (TA), 93:8
teicoplanin, 76:3, 93:12
telapravir, 97:10
telavancin, 76:6
telbivudine, 97:7
TEM. *See* transmission electron microscopy
tenofovir, 97:12, 101:7
testicular torsion, 91:23
tetanospasmin, 22:3
tetanus-diphtheria-pertussis vaccination (Tdap), 40:6, 43:5, 45:3,
    46:10, 103:19–21, 104:10
tetracyclines, 79B:4, 79B:6, 91:23, 92:7, 93:13
Textile Rental Service Association of America (TRSA), 111:4
TFPI. *See* tissue factor pathway inhibitor
therapeutic hypothermia, 59:4
thiamin, 47:3, 47:8
thimerosal, 103:5, **103:6**
thrombocytopenia, with burns, 38:6
thrombolytics, for IVDA BSIs, 34:13

thrombomodulin, 69:5
thrombophlebitis, 38:7–8
thrombotic microangiopathy (TM), **69:3**, 69:4–5, 69:6
TI. *See* transanal irrigation
ticks, 85:2–3, **85:3**, **85:4**, **85:6**
tigecycline, 75:2, 75:16, 76:6, 93:5
tinidazole, 91:18, 91:21
TIPS. *See* transjugular intrahepatic portosystemic shunting
tissue factor pathway inhibitor (TFPI), 69:5
TJC. *See* The Joint Commission
T-lymphocytes, 22:3–4, **22:5**, 86:8
    CTL, 80:7
TM. *See* thrombotic microangiopathy
TMP/SMX. *See* trimethoprim-sulfamethoxazole
TNAs. *See* total nutrient admixtures
TNF. *See* tumor necrosis factor
tobramycin, 26:5, 41:13
To Err Is Human: Building a Safer Health System (IOM), 4:9,
    8:12, 16:2, 18:1, 59:1
topical antibacterials, 26:6
toroviruses, 79A:8
total body surface area (TBSA), 38:2, 38:3
total energy expenditure (TEE), 47:4
total house surveillance, 11:5
total nutrient admixtures (TNAs), 110:3
total PN, 110:7
toxic anterior segment syndrome (TASS), 31:6, 63:4, 115:7
toxic megacolon, 72:2–3
toxic shock syndrome (TSS), 10:4, 86:3, 92:2, 93:7, 94:3
toxin production testing, 25:6–7
Toxoplasma, 22:7, 41:4
Toxoplasma gondii, 23:5, 45:4, 45:6, 46:5, 99:7, 109:2, 121:13
toxoplasmosis, 46:2
toys, 42:10, **42:10**, 52:6
TPHA. *See* Treponema pallidum hemagglutination assay
TP-PA. *See* Treponema pallidum particle agglutination
tracheal cytotoxin (TCT), 71:1
tracheostomies, 67:3
traffic control, 68:3–4, 116:7
transanal irrigation (TI), 66:11
transarterial chemoembolization (TACE), 60:6–7
transcatheter aortic valve replacement (TAVR), 50:2, 50:6
transesophageal echocardiography (TEE), 34:18
transfusions, 41:19, 88:6, 97:11, 97:12
    of RBC, from pig, 69:6
transient aplastic crisis (TAC), 88:2, 88:4–5
transient elastography, 97:10
transjugular intrahepatic portosystemic shunting (TIPS), 60:7–8
transmissible spongiform encephalopathies (TSEs), 31:7, 73:1,
    73:5, 74:11–12
    SP and, 106:16
    in surgical services, 68:7–8, 68:9
transmission. *See* infection transmission
Transmission-based Precautions
    in ambulatory care centers, 48:5
    in ASCs, 64:4–5
    for aseptic meningitis, 74:7
    in HHC, 56:3
    in ICU, 59:6
    in LTCFs, 61:7–8
    for PVB19, 88:6
    in rehabilitation services, 66:4
    for *Streptococcus*, **94:4**
transmission electron microscopy (TEM), 24:9
transplantation. *See also* hematopoietic stem cell transplant; solid
    organ transplantation; xenotransplantation
    BMT, 46:5, 78:2, 94:8
    immunization and, 23:5–6
    liver, 97:3, 97:7, 97:12
transposon, 26:11

transtheoretical model (TTM), 5:5, **5:5**
transverse myelitis, 82:2
trauma, 18:3, 19:7, 92:5
travel health, 118:1–11
   altitude sickness and, 118:2
   animals and, 118:3
   cholera and, 118:9–10
   cruise ships and, 118:2
   diarrhea and, 118:2
   food and, 118:2
   HAV and, **118:5**, 118:5–6
   HBV and, 118:9
   hypersensitivity and, 118:5
   immunization and, 118:3–10
   immunocompromised host and, 118:5
   influenza and, 118:9
   insects and, 118:1–2
   malaria and, 118:2
   meningococcal disease and, 118:7, **118:7**
   motion sickness and, 118:1
   PHS and, 118:3–4
   plague and, 118:10
   pneumococcal disease and, 118:9
   polio and, 118:3
   pregnancy and, 118:5
   rabies and, 118:7–8, **118:8**
   seeking medical care abroad, 118:10–11
   smallpox and, 118:10
   swimming and, 118:3
   typhoid fever and, 118:8–9, **118:9**
   VZV and, 118:3–4
   water and, 118:2
treosulfan, 110:4
Treponema pallidum, 25:1, 91:2, 91:16–17
Treponema pallidum hemagglutination assay (TPHA), 25:1
Treponema pallidum particle agglutination (TP-PA), 91:16
triage, 48:4, **48:5**, 119:9–10, 120:10–11
triazoles, 26:7
Trichinella spiralis, 99:7
trichloacetic acid (TCA), 91:8
Trichomonas vaginalis, 91:4, 91:18–19, 99:7
trichomoniasis, 91:18–19
Trichophyton rubrum, 78:12
Trichosporon, 78:11
trichrome stain, 24:11
triclosan, 37:10, 107:10
trimethoprim-sulfamethoxazole (TMP/SMX), 26:6, 33:12, 37:11–12, 79B:4, 79B:10, 93:13, 94:4
   for *Cyclospora cayetanensis*, 79C:7
   Enterococcus and, 76:3
   for immunocompromised host, 23:7
   for pertussis, 71:3
   for SSTIs, 92:7
TRSA. *See* Textile Rental Service Association of America
Trypanosoma, 99:7
Trypanosoma cruzi, 22:7
TSEs. *See* transmissible spongiform encephalopathies
TSS. *See* toxic shock syndrome
TST. *See* tuberculin skin testing
TTM. *See* transtheoretical model
tuberculin skin testing (TST), 45:3, 49:4, 95:1–2, 95:5, 95:13, **100:6**, 102:2
   ASCs and, 64:10
   in CCCs, 52:4–5
   for mumps, 86:10
   PPD and, 100:5
tuberculosis (TB), 29:3, **36:2**, 51:7, 95:1–14, **95:3, 95:11**
   animals and, 121:3, 121:12–13
   ASCs and, 64:10
   behavioral health and, 49:4

CAP and, 36:2
in correctional facilities, 51:5–7
geriatrics and, 40:3–4
HBM for, 5:3
immunization for, HSCT and, 46:10
Isolation Precautions for, 51:651:6–7
in LTCFs, 61:2
LTCFs and, 95:14
Mantoux test for, 95:5–6, **95:6**
MDR-TB, 51:5, 95:2, 95:8
mental illness and, 49:1
neonates and, 41:9, 41:21
occupational health and, 100:3–7
OSHA and, 4:11
pediatrics and, 42:9, 42:14
postmortem care and, 65:3
PPE and, 51:7
pregnant HCP and, 104:11
radiation oncology for, 58:1
screening for, 95:5
SOT and, 45:3, 45:5
in surgical services, 68:9
surveillance for, 51:6y
treatment for, 95:6–8
tumor necrosis factor (TNF), 22:6, 93:8
typhoid fever, 54:16, 118:3, 118:8–9, **118:9**
"Typhoid" Mary Malone, 10:7
typus, 25:7

U-chart, 10:12, 14:7
UCL. *See* upper control limit
UFE. *See* uterine fibroid embolization
ultra-low penetrating air (ULPA), 68:2
ultrasonic cleaners, 106:7
ultrasound, 58:2, 60:8
ultraviolet-C (UVC), 68:3, 88:7, 107:5
ultraviolet germicidal irradiation (UVG), 95:12, 114:10
ultraviolet irradiation (UV), 31:9–10, **31:10**, 107:13
   for dialysis, 39:6
   for peritoneal dialysis, 39:13
   in surgical services, 68:3
undernutrition, 47:1, 47:2, 47:3
United Network for Organ Sharing (UNOS), 45:2
United States Department of Agriculture (USDA), 4:3, 4:11, 23:9, 83:1, 121:3
   FNS and, 109:4, 109:7
   immunocompromised patients and, 44:5
United States Pharmacopeia (USP), 18:9, 110:2, 110:8, 110:9–10
United States Preventive Services Task Force (USPSTF), 91:3, 91:5
universal precautions, 29:2
UNOS. *See* United Network for Organ Sharing
Updated U.S. Public Health Service Guidelines for the Management of Occupational Exposures to Human Immunodeficiency Virus and Recommendations for Post-exposure Prophylaxis, 81:9
Update on Cardiovascular Implantable Electronic Device Infections and Their Management (American Heart Association), 35:7
upper control limit (UCL), 14:5, 14:8
Ureaplasma urealyticum, 43:5, 91:4
urethritis, 91:5, 91:23
urge incontinence, 33:3
urinalysis, 25:7, 33:4
urinary antigen, 84:4, **84:4**
urinary tract infections (UTIs), 33:1–11, **33:4**. *See also* catheter-associated urinary tract infections
   biofilm and, 70:9
   burns and, 38:9, 42:7
   Candida and, 78:4, 78:5
   diagnosis of, 33:4